CW00802623

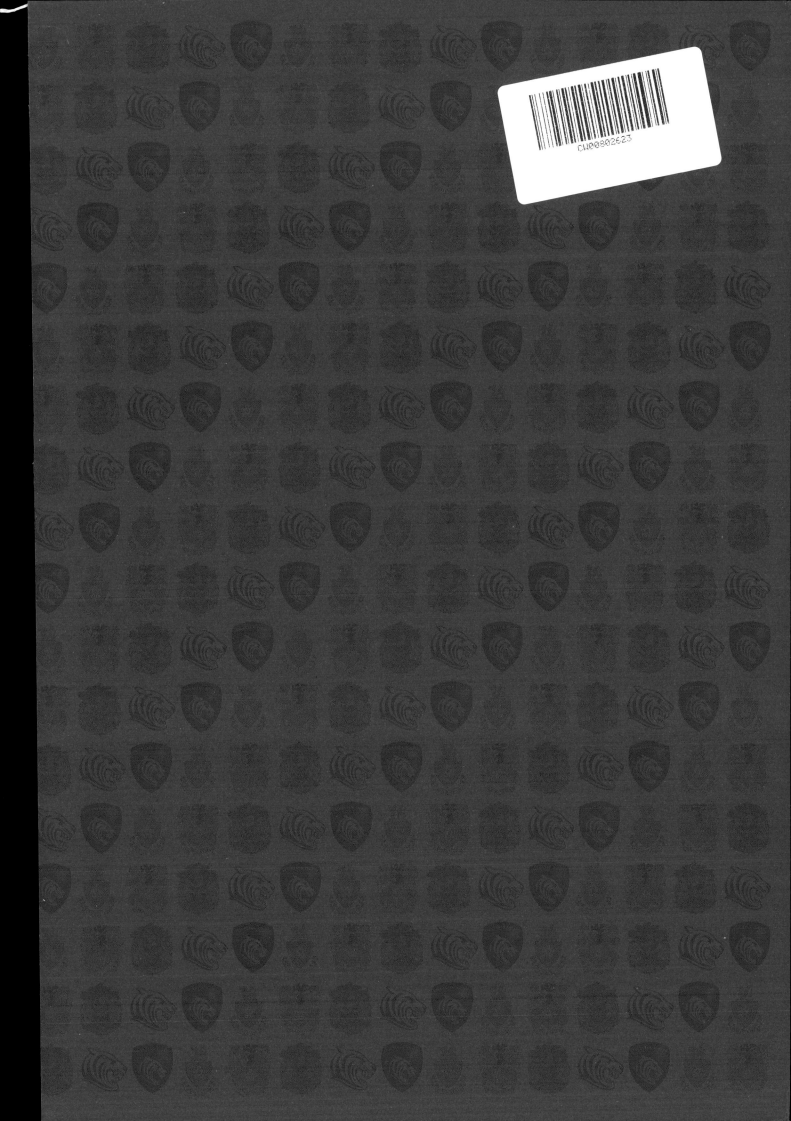

Official History of
Leicester Football Club

TIGERS

1880 - 2014

by Stuart Farmer and David Hands

PUBLISHED BY

TIGERS

Official History of Leicester Football Club

By Stuart Farmer & David Hands

First published 1993 by Polar Publishing (Leicester) Limited.

Revised and updated edition published 2014 by The Rugby Development (Trading) Limited, Marston Trussell Hall, Marston Trussell, Market Harborough, Leicestershire LE16 9TY.

A Catalogue record for this book is available from the British Library.

ISBN 978-0-9930213-0-5

Edited by Robert Hands and Gary Sherrard.

Designed by Ignition Publications Limited, 144 Long Street, Easingwold, York YO61 3JA

Printed by Greenshires Group, 160-164 Barkby Road, Leicester LE4 9LF

Original cover artwork by Bryan Organ

Digital cover artwork by Steve Boot

Interior design by Stuart Farmer and Steve Boot

Photographs and illustrations are courtesy of:
Leicester Football Club, Leicester Mercury, Andrew Maw, Leicester Mercury Archive at the University of Leicester, Richard Mobbs, Leicestershire Rugby Union Ltd archive, Leicestershire County Cricket Club, Getty Images, George Herringshaw/ASP, Simon Hoare, Action Images, Cheltenham College Archive.
Many of the photographs reproduced are from original material in the files at Leicester Football Club who retain the rights to all official photocall pictures taken by the appointed club photographer. Most of the remaining photographs are from the private collections of the authors or from albums owned by various Tigers players and supporters. We have been unable to trace the sources of all these illustrations, but any photographer involved is cordially invited to contact the publishers in writing providing proof of copyright.

Foreword

When The Tigers Tale, the last official history of the Leicester Football Club, drew to a close in 1993, the rugby world was a different place. The game was still amateur, the World Cup was still a novelty (there had been only two such tournaments), meaningful European competition was nil, there was no such competition in England as a 'premiership'.

Now the game at elite level is professional and a generation of Leicester supporters has grown up knowing no other format. Some of them may have paused to wonder why, on the shirts of the players during the 2013/14 season, there was a letter of the alphabet; the letter O, for example, for the number 15 jersey worn by the full-back and harking back to the days when players were identified by letter rather than number. Others will be unaware that, for the best part of the 20th century, the highlight of the season was the club's annual Christmas encounter with the Barbarians.

There is a rich history that was recounted, initially, in the club's centenary book published in 1980. That work, suitably updated and revised, provided most of the editorial content thirteen years later of *The Tigers Tale* but complemented by the wealth of statistical detail kept by Stuart Farmer who has since turned his hobby into a career.

At that time we stated baldly that, between 1980 and 1993, the face of the game had changed and that, in consequence, the club history needed to be brought up to date. Little did we know. Two years later the game went open, players became commodities, rugby's new businessmen started to talk about brands, the Heineken Cup became a new and incredibly welcome staple of the seasonal diet. The media discovered genuine superstars from the game - Jonah Lomu, the New Zealand wing, Jonny Wilkinson, England's fly-half, and, arguably, Martin Johnson, the Leicester lock who led England to their 2003 World Cup triumph.

Throughout it all, Leicester retained the position of England's leading club. There is no argument about that. Leicester has always been among the leaders of the domestic game, less so when power was based among the top London clubs at the start of the 20th century and in the years that followed, Midland rivals in Northampton and Coventry enjoyed periods of greater playing success, as did Bath in the 1980s.

But administrative changes at Welford Road begun during the 1970s gave Leicester a far more secure working structure than any of their peers when professionalism came along. Since then, no club can match a record of two European titles and nine league titles; between 2005-13, Leicester appeared in nine successive premiership finals. They did not win them all but they were and are invariably the team to beat. Their support base is the envy of the country, their modus operandi frequently cited by rival clubs seeking greater sustainability on and off the field.

Since the end of the 1993 season, 31 players have been capped by England out of the club, in an overall total of 82 since Jack Miles became Leicester's first home-grown international in 1903. Five of those 31 have captained their country, equalling the number of Leicester players who led England during the previous 113 years. Throw in the fact that Leicester had a defining influence on Sir Clive Woodward, England's World Cup-winning coach, and that five other individuals with links to the club have been involved with England's coaching staff, then the contribution to the national cause in the modern era has been outstanding.

There is, therefore, every reason to recalibrate Leicester's history even if, at 134 years old, there is no distinctive historical landmark to celebrate. In 2015 the professional era will be twenty years old, a long enough period from which to take stock of where rugby stands and of Leicester's role in that context. There has also been further research of times past which has thrown new light on various episodes in the club's history. We hope that, in between reminding readers of the ups and downs of recent seasons, we can give some idea of how Leicester came to occupy the prominence in the English game that it now enjoys.

The book is published by the Rugby Development Foundation, whose aim is to encourage and motivate players to develop their rugby union education to the highest level possible, irrespective of their social or financial background. The foundation supports with grants and bursaries the progression of players aged between 13-21. All profits from the sales of the book will be used to support grass-roots rugby, including the development of young players through the Leicester Academy.

Stuart Farmer and David Hands (August 2014)

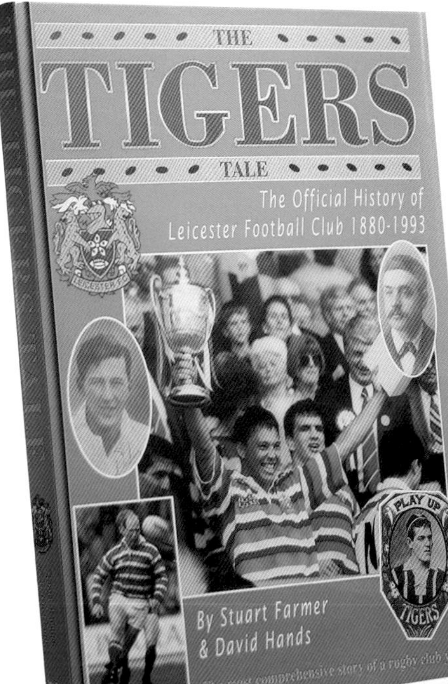

Two earlier editions of the history of the club, *Leicester Football Club* (the Centenary book) in 1980 and *The Tigers Tale* in 1993, are now both collectors' items.

The Rugby Development Foundation
A charitable company limited by guarantee registered in England and Wales.

Billy Foreman played for the Tigers between 1893-1906 and was the first individual to make 300 appearances for the first team. He captained the club from 1899-1901.

Contents

TIGERS HISTORY 1880-2014

TIGERS ILLUSTRATED HISTORY

TIGERS WHO'S WHO

TIGERS ENCYCLOPÆDIA

1880

1905

1952

1997

2006

CHAPTER 1

The Rise and Rise

Geographically, the city of Leicester lies as near as makes no matter to the centre of England. A settlement has lain there on the banks of the River Soar since the Iron Age, fortunes rising and falling with the ebb and flow of history but connected increasingly with the development of trade - a commercial centre at the crossroads of the country which makes the site of its rugby club, on one of England's bigger traffic islands, entirely apposite.

Since its very inception, the Leicester Football Club - the formal name of the Leicester Tigers before professionalism suggested a different brand name for publicity purposes - has been intimately linked with Leicester business. On the other hand, the founding fathers never anticipated that the club's shirt would one day be seen on the Great Wall of China, carried there by supporters proud to wear the colours of the European champions. Indeed the club itself, always looking for new markets, sent a delegation to China in 2006 to discover whether that country's burgeoning economy lent itself to rugby's growing worldwide profile.

Rugby has been a significant tool in spreading the city's reputation. Sport has always been an important part of Leicester life with the establishment of first-class clubs in football, cricket and rugby during the 19th century but there is a far greater diversity beyond those mainstream sports: in 1976 the *Leicester Mercury*, the local newspaper, ran a series on men and women from the city and county who were involved in that year's Olympic Games in Montreal - the series covered a runner, a walker, a gymnast, a diver, canoeists and, perhaps most unlikely of all in the becalmed Midlands, a yachtsman.

↑ The Club's first logo in 1880 was based on the town's crest.

But over the last twenty years, the rugby club has enjoyed an unprecedented prosperity both on and off the field at a time when sport's place in the national psyche, since the 2012 Olympic Games held in London, has never been higher. In 2001 and 2002, Leicester were champions of Europe and on three other occasions they have contested the final of the Heineken Cup; they have been England's premier club nine times and runners-up (since the introduction of the premiership final in 2003) on a further five occasions.

None of this is coincidence. As 'Chalkie' White, who coached Leicester for nearly 15 years, wrote in 1979: "Our game is part of society. We cannot operate our game in a vacuum. The standards of society, morality, all the bits we like and don't like, must be part of our game. [At Leicester] we work harder, we think more and some of us care." His remarks are as true today as they were 35 years ago. That work ethic has carried Leicester to the top of the national tree and, twice, to the top of the European tree. It has earned them admiration, respect, envy, criticism, a remodelled stadium which is the biggest purpose-built rugby union ground in the country outside Twickenham and membership of more than 14,000.

"We're a cross between a freemason's lodge and a Welsh working men's club," Peter Tom, the former lock who became Leicester's chairman in 1993, said. "We are not easy bedfellows, we have made plenty of mistakes but we have tried to set the same standards off the field as well as on it. There is a recognition of what a privilege it is to wear the Tigers shirt." More than a century ago, when the game was totally amateur, Leicester were so cutting edge that their officials were arraigned before a Rugby Football Union (RFU) tribunal to answer charges of professionalism; almost certainly those charges arose in part because of the desire of club administrators to apply business principles to sport.

↓ Premiership champions in 2013.

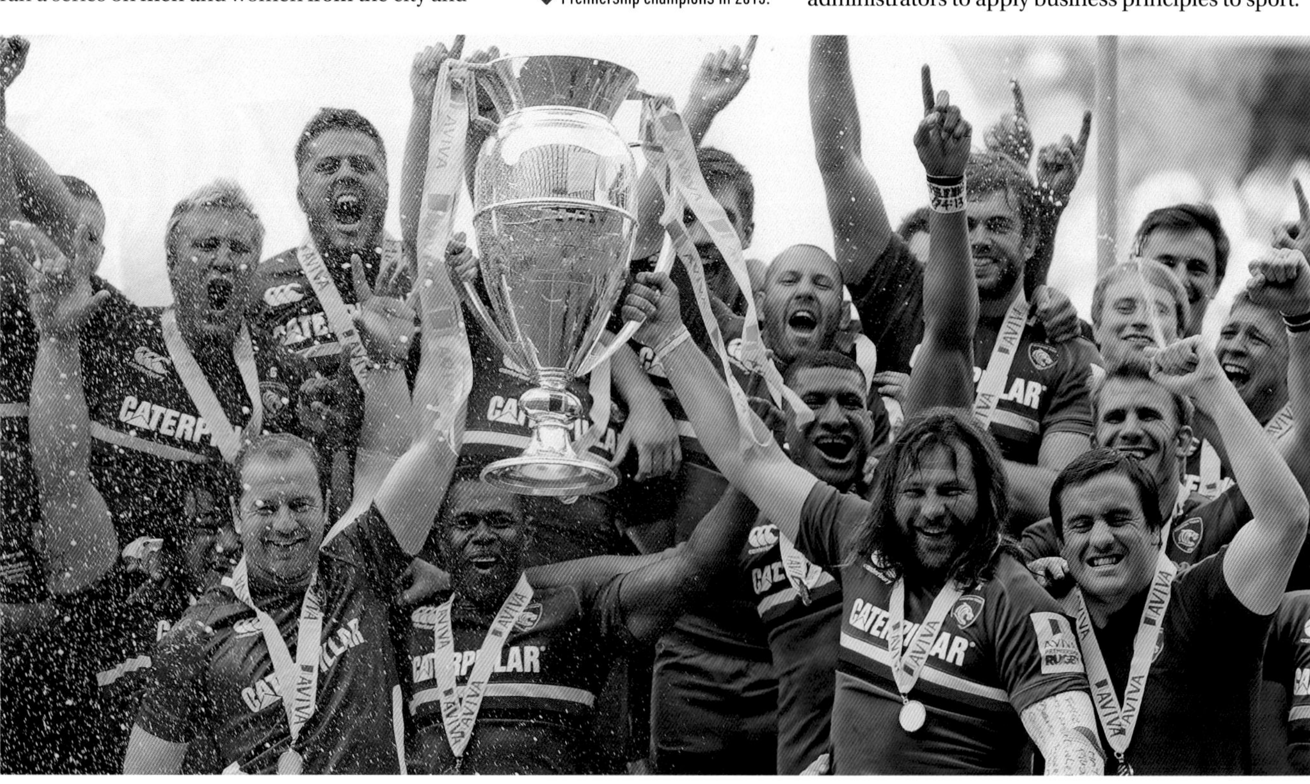

HOW THEY FINISHED

	P	W	D	L	F	A	Pts
TIGERS	**18**	**15**	**1**	**2**	**400**	**269**	**31**
Bath	18	12	3	3	373	245	27
Wasps	18	13	0	5	469	313	26
Sale	18	7	2	9	327	343	16
Orrell	18	6	3	9	256	325	15
Bristol	18	7	0	11	301	353	14
Gloucester	18	6	1	11	269	336	13
Harlequins	18	6	1	11	275	348	13
W Hartlepool	18	6	1	11	312	412	13
Northampton	18	6	0	12	267	335	12

← Division One league table at the end of the 1994/95 season.

→ Leicester's Martin Johnson holds the Webb Ellis Trophy aloft in 2003.

When the game went open in 1995, there were only five clubs in what was then the premier division of the Courage Clubs Championship with their own natural rugby hinterland. Of those, Northampton were about to be relegated though they were undergoing the restructuring which has allowed them to become once more a power in the land. Bristol were struggling, ultimately in vain, to sustain their status. Bath and Gloucester, the two big provincial clubs with no competing local football team, have had times of stress.

The fifth, Leicester, had so much more in place when planning for the new era: a ground with adequate capacity, five minutes' walk from the city centre and the railway station and capable of expansion. A reputation based both on achievements as a club and of individuals from the club who had gained fame playing for England and the British and Irish Lions - think of Dean Richards, Rory Underwood and Martin Johnson, though they were by no means the only ones. An administrative staff drawn from many individuals who were immersed in the ethos and history of the club and who were utterly determined to ensure Leicester would not sink into the uncertainty with which rugby entered the professional age.

This is not to discount the other five clubs who then constituted national division one, Harlequins, Wasps, Sale, Orrell and West Hartlepool. But every London club lacks the identity of a provincial city; Harlequins and Wasps also lacked a ground of decent size and had to establish who their core supporters were against a host of competition. The three northern clubs represented only a limited area of their own locale and Sale, the one top-flight survivor, have struggled continuously to attract the necessary support, even when they themselves became champions in 2006.

There was no guidance from the RFU over the steps to be taken. The union, unprepared for and in many cases unwilling to see the game going professional, had its own crises to navigate. For some clubs, the answer was to find a generous benefactor and several English clubs owe a huge debt, literally, to such individuals. Leicester did not wish to and, happily, did not need to go down that road. Peter Wheeler, who as well as playing hooker for Leicester and England (captaining both teams), had coached the club and was president at the time, became Leicester's first chief executive and also chaired the newly-formed clubs' association in what came to be an interminable battle with the RFU. The debt Leicester owes to Wheeler is considerable.

The extent of Leicester's ambition was illustrated by their appointment as head coach of Bob Dwyer, Australia's coach when the Wallabies won the 1991 World Cup. Though Dwyer saw them to their first European final, in 1997, he had gone before Leicester entered a unique four-year period in which they won successive league titles and back-to-back Heineken Cups, against Stade Français in 2001 and Munster in 2002. In addition they provided the Lions with their captain, Martin Johnson, in 1997 and 2001 (he remains the only player ever to lead the touring side twice) and seven players, all forwards, to the England squad that won the 2003 World Cup, of whom Johnson became the first (and still the only) northern-hemisphere captain to lift the Webb Ellis Cup.

At this stage it is worth considering Martin Osborne Johnson's place in the pantheon of rugby greatness. Every now and again, once in every one or two generations, comes along a player of quite outstanding ability: at club level, they can be divided into two kinds - one, typified at Leicester by such as Sid Penny, David Matthews and John Allen, are the stalwarts, seldom capped but by their consistency and longevity, each the backbone of the Tigers for nearly two decades.

The other is the player of outstanding international calibre. If you discount the fact that, for many years during the amateur era, Leicester attracted players such as Wavell Wakefield or Tony O'Reilly who appeared very intermittently, their number would include Bernard Gadney, the England scrum-half of the 1930s, George Beamish, the Ireland lock during the same period, and Wheeler, who made two Lions tours and arguably should have led a third.

Johnson's playing achievements outweigh all those of his predecessors and, though ten years of his career were played as a professional when loyalty can come a distant second to financial reward, he was a one-club man. Of course Leicester recognised his quality and ensured it was amply rewarded but, as sound businessmen, the club directors have never made a habit of paying what they believe to be over the odds. Here was a case of player suiting club and vice versa.

Though he spent the first seven years of his life in Birmingham, Johnson's family moved to Market Harborough and he learned his rugby with Wigston. He joined Leicester, aged 17, but spent a formative 18 months with King Country in New Zealand's North Island and reached the heights of that country's national colts team. He made his senior Leicester debut (against the RAF in February 1989) before leaving for the southern hemisphere and, by the time of his final appearance in 2005, he had become one of the greatest players ever to wear England colours.

↑ Peter Wheeler, the club's first Chief Executive.

↑ Wells, Johnson and Richards celebrate with the Allied Dunbar Premiership trophy on 16.5.1999.

Johnson crossed a lot of borders, notably that of amateur to professional. To use an old-fashioned description, he was an enforcer with something of an Old Testament, eye-for-an-eye, tooth-for-a-tooth approach which did not always endear him to opponents or their supporters. He was a grappler and mauler in the old English tradition but also possessed the new-age skills for handling and passing. What lifted him above the norm was his rugby instinct, his ability to read a game, to perceive with a clarity which seems to come naturally to a New Zealander what is required to change the pattern of play. The same gift could be seen in Dean Richards, his predecessor as Leicester captain, but down the years it has not been a distinctive attribute of leading English players.

Johnson played 84 games for England, 39 of them as captain (a figure exceeded only by Will Carling, the Harlequins centre, captain in 59 of his 72 internationals). In addition, Johnson played eight internationals during three tours with the Lions, six of them as captain. By the time of his final bow, in the Zurich Premiership final of 2005 against London Wasps, Johnson had played 362 games for Leicester whom he led on a club record 202 occasions, of which 146 were won and only 45 lost.

Probably the best tribute to him came from those Lions from the other home countries, who believed him to be the best captain under whom they had played. The fact that, between 2008-11, he was manager of England in what turned out to be a period of distinctly mixed fortunes for the national side, even though they won their only Six Nations title since 2003, should not diminish Johnson's reputation one iota; as ever he was prepared to lift his head above the parapet when invited to do so by the RFU, because he believed he had something to offer at a time when England appeared to need it.

Not that Leicester, or most leading clubs for that matter, have ever considered the individual to be above the collective. Nor, indeed, did Johnson whose commitment to the team ethic was wholehearted (not least when bargaining for an appropriate rate of pay with the RFU in 2000 on behalf of the England squad). As the professional age settled down, Leicester's recruitment policy was based firmly on attracting players who would conform to the club's approach to the game, whoever happened to be at the helm as head coach or director of rugby.

The greatest rewards came when they selected their coaches from within. The golden era of 1999-2002 came under the management of Richards and John Wells, the uncapped flanker who became not only a quality club coach but England coach too; the league titles of 2010 and 2013 were won under the guidance of Richard Cockerill, the former Leicester and England hooker who came to embody all the earthy qualities of the boot room.

Not that the club found themselves in a straitjacket over such appointments. After the departure of Wells, they turned to Pat Howard, the Australian centre who made such an impact as a player around the turn of the century. Less successful were the choices of Marcelo Loffreda, Argentina's coach, and Heyneke Meyer, from South Africa's leading Super Rugby team, the Blue Bulls; the intensity of premiership rugby led to Loffreda's departure after only eight months in 2008 and Meyer, his successor, did not last that long because family illnesses forced his premature return to South Africa (whose coach he became in 2012).

But whenever Leicester fortunes looked to have suffered a setback, the club always bounced back. It became a truism of the playing side of the game that, even when they lost league matches, Leicester almost always collected a losing bonus point; similarly, off the field, their administrators possessed the confidence to shrug off disappointment and concentrate on the next objective. Towards the end of the first decade of the 21st century, that was the development of the ground.

At one stage, some kind of amalgamation with Leicester City was a possibility. For many years, rugby and football had nestled side by side since Leicester City's ground at Filbert Street was no more than a stone's throw from Welford Road. Then they moved all of 500 yards down the road to the new Walkers [King Power] Stadium where the Tigers chose to take a handful of European matches and whose 30,000-plus capacity was an obvious attraction; less so, though, to their supporters who agitated to stay at Welford Road and who now have a stadium at their ancestral home which currently holds 24,000 and still has scope for expansion.

They should remember, of course, that they are only heading back towards the sort of crowds drawn in between the two world wars, when Welford Road could hold more than 30,000, if not in quite the same degree of comfort as today's supporter enjoys. But it is a mark of the success and the stability of the club that they could embark on a rebuilding programme in the knowledge that, even on a poor day, they would attract a greater crowd than any of their premiership peers.

Inevitably the economic recession which set in during 2008 and whose impact six years later is still being felt has forced a readjustment of priorities. But, remarkably, during that period season-ticket sales have gone up, confirming the strong relationship Leicester has with, as Tom puts it, "the citizens of the East Midlands". Plans for further ground development may be on the back burner but they remain real, as real as the achievements of the latest generation of players as they follow in the footprints of those who have gone before.

CHAPTER 2

Champions of Europe

From time immemorial, the victors in a battle have taken trophies from their beaten enemy. Roman generals were granted a triumph, parading through the streets of the capital followed by a string of captives; down the ages the capture of the enemy flag has been a badge of honour. The sporting equivalent nowadays is the open-top bus tour, victorious players brandishing aloft the winner's cup.

So it would have been a shame had there been no cup to brandish after Leicester became champions of Europe in 2001. The Heineken Cup was only six years old when it was raised aloft in the Parc des Princes Stadium in Paris by Martin Johnson and his Tigers colleagues, 34-30 victors against Stade Français in one of the most pulsating European rugby finals.

What followed was laid bare by Lewis Moody, the flanker who was a replacement that day but went on to emulate Johnson by leading his country into a World Cup campaign. There was an official reception to attend after the match was over, then the Leicester contingent embarked on a scheduled trip down the River Seine in central Paris, accompanied by a certain amount of alcohol.

Moody, writing in his autobiography *Mad Dog - an Englishman*, told how on the riverboat he was handed the cup and then used its lid to protect himself from 'assault' by Austin Healey, the England utility back who played scrum-half for Leicester that day and is now a TV analyst. One of the lid's decorations was knocked off in the scuffle but worse was to come when Ben Kay, the international lock now pursuing the same pundit's path as Healey, dropped the cup over the side of the boat.

Happily it lodged on the edge of the deck below and rolled back, otherwise there would have been no trophy to show their followers after returning to Welford Road. It had been, though, a magical day for Leicester. The English clubs had embraced the concept of European rugby far more readily than their French counterparts (with the notable exception of Toulouse), for whom success in the domestic league and the winning of the Bouclier de Brennus was far more significant.

Four years earlier Leicester had become the first English club to reach a European final (there were no English representatives in the inaugural season of 1995/96), only to be ruthlessly dispatched in Cardiff by Brive. In the intervening years Bath had won the Heineken Cup, by beating Brive (in France) in 1998, and Northampton had triumphed too, with success over Munster in 2000 at Twickenham.

Dean Richards, Leicester's manager, made no bones about the club's ambition: "Europe is something in which, if we are to move forward as a club, we have to achieve success," he said before the 2001 semi-final against Gloucester. There had been a hiccup in the pool matches against Pontypridd at Sardis Road, a venue enjoyed then by very few visitors, but an admirable quarter-final win over Swansea, even without Johnson who was undergoing a five-week suspension.

The game with Gloucester, in the lacklustre surroundings of Watford's Vicarage Road, was a nervy affair won 19-15 by Leicester who went into the final as underdogs, not least because there was nothing neutral about the venue. Parc des Princes, where France played international matches for 26 years, is next door to the Stade Jean Bouin, home of Stade Français. Against that, Leicester entered the final having pocketed two trophies - the Zurich Premiership and Championship - which had already made 2000/01 the most successful season in the club's history.

They took with them to Paris the entire club staff, from directors down to cleaners, as a thank-you for the efforts of those whose work is not always appreciated. The teams that played in the final showed how the professional game was changing the make-up of clubs across Europe: Stade Français, coached by an Australian in John Connolly, drew their players from nine different countries, from New

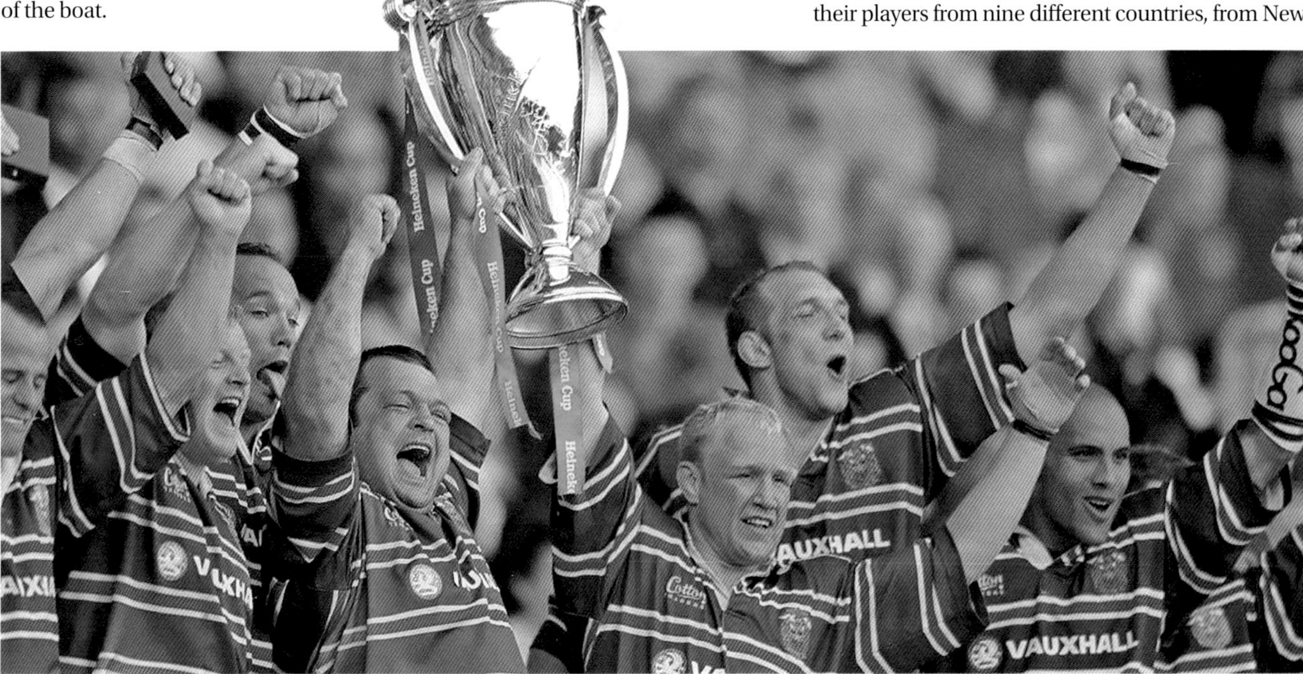

↓ 19 May 2001 Tigers become European champions for the first time.

Zealand to Uruguay. Leicester, though operating somewhat closer to home, fielded an Australian at centre, a Canadian on one wing and an Irishman on the other.

19 May 2001, was a bright, sunny day though there was nothing sunny about the French club's front row, intent on eye-balling their Leicester counterparts as the teams took the field. Within the first quarter the respective kickers, Diego Dominguez and Tim Stimpson, had landed two penalties apiece, Christophe Juillet, the home captain, had been forced off for running repairs and Fabrice Landreau, the Stade hooker, had spent time in the sin bin.

The two open-side flankers, Richard Pool-Jones and Neil Back, both England internationals (Back rather more frequently than Pool-Jones) were at each other for much of the first half and by the interval, Dominguez had kicked five penalties (two of them from more than fifty metres) to three from Stimpson. It was a tour de force by Dominguez, the diminutive Argentinian who played for Italy, since he ended the day with nine penalties and a dropped goal but it was not enough.

↑ Match programme from the 2001 Heineken Cup final.

"We said the first ten minutes of the second half were very important," Leon Lloyd, Leicester's lanky wing-turned-centre, said. "Dean told us to hold on to the ball and to be patient." In the opening minute of the second period, Pat Howard lofted a cross-kick for Geordan Murphy, the wing pushed his own grub-kick through and Lloyd toed the ball ahead to beat the covering Morgan Williams for the touchdown. Still Stade retained the lead and six minutes later, Johnson was given a yellow card for punching Juillet after a bout of jersey-tugging; in his absence, Dominguez kicked his side out to a seven-point lead.

Within three minutes of Johnson's return, Leicester were level. Lloyd escaped on a fifty-metre run but was taken out by Christophe Dominici as he pursued his own kick through. Healey tapped the penalty and Back dummied his way over for a try converted by Stimpson, who then chipped over a close-range penalty for the lead.

Back came the Parisians, Dominguez keeping the scoreboard turning over and, with two minutes remaining, the fly-half dropped a 35-metre goal which gave Stade a 30-27 lead. Now came Healey's hour: he had spent 73 minutes of the match at scrum-half but moved to fly-half when Andy Goode was taken off and Healey's break through midfield, drawing the defence to him, provided the defining moment of the final.

↓ Leon Lloyd goes over for the decisive try in Paris 2001.

He threw a long ball to Lloyd and the young centre pinned back his ears and made it to the right-hand corner for the game's third try. Stimpson, moreover, nailed the difficult conversion which meant that even another Dominguez penalty or dropped goal would not be enough. "It has to be the greatest day in the club's history," Peter Wheeler said. "This team has achieved consistently over 22 games for the last three seasons. Now they've won the European cup. It has to be the best team in recent history."

Or even a longer period. Only one member of Leicester's starting XV failed to achieve international honours: Will Johnson, younger brother of the captain. As so many other clubs have found before and since, it is hard to secure one title in a season, even harder to secure two, never mind three. London Wasps went close to emulating Leicester four years later by putting together a run of three domestic league titles and the European crown of 2004, while Leinster won a remarkable three Heineken Cups in four years between 2009-12 but no-one has surpassed Leicester's glorious four-year record of English and European success between 1999-2002.

Six weeks later, Howard was back home in Australia, playing for the ACT Brumbies against a midweek Lions XV including Leicester's Healey, Martin Corry and Dorian West. Sporting life can change very swiftly but, in one respect, everything stayed the same for the next 12 months in that Leicester retained both the Zurich Premiership and the Heineken Cup. "It's tough to stay where Leicester are at the moment but it's possible," Howard said with some prescience before his departure (he was to return in a coaching capacity four years later).

The club finished the league season 14 points clear of the second-placed club, Sale. In Europe, there was a banana-skin waiting in Wales just like the previous season, only this time it was placed at Llanelli rather than Pontypridd. The Welshmen won the last of the pool matches and then gave Leicester an almighty scare in the semi-finals at Nottingham Forest's City Ground. It took a penalty goal kicked by Stimpson from fully sixty metres, which hit first the crossbar then an upright, to win the match 13-12.

But there Leicester were, in the final again and this time against Munster at Cardiff's Millennium Stadium. The starting XV had changed: only three of the back division that won in Paris remained and they did not include Lloyd, the two-try hero of Parc des Princes. However seven of the forwards were still in place, the addition being Moody, who had held off the challenge presented by the signing of the multi-capped All Black, Josh Kronfeld, to play in the back row.

"What we achieved last season has gone," Richards said on the eve of the final. "One or two of our players have changed and many of them are coming to the end of an exceptionally concentrated period of rugby [including, in the summer of 2001, the Lions tour to Australia which involved five of the club's players]. We need to produce a special performance if we are to win."

So they did, even if there was massive controversy by the end caused by Neil Back. When a leading cleric weighs in with commentary about sporting morals, you know that rugby has crossed the sporting border. Back's crime, with the score standing at 15-9 to Leicester and the game in time added on, was to steal Munster's ball at a scrum five metres from the Leicester line by flicking it out of the hands of Peter Stringer, the Munster scrum-half, and back through his own pack; remarkably, not one of the match officials saw it and the 'hand of Back' became part of rugby lore, just like the 'hand of God' from football's Diego Maradona when Argentina beat England in the 1986 World Cup.

It was a philosophical argument with which Munster, significantly, had little truck. "If one of our boys had done it, we would have made him Lord Mayor," one of their officials said. More pertinently to the outcome, Leicester scored the two tries of the match and laid waste the Munster lineout to give themselves the platform for victory despite going into the final on the back of some inconsistent performances.

Fereti Tuilagi, the first member of the Samoan clan which has meant so much to Leicester over the past 13 years, crossed Munster's line in the first minute only to be brought back for obstruction. Thereafter the Irish province had the better of the opening quarter, Ronan O'Gara kicking two penalties, but Ireland's fly-half was upstaged by Healey, starting for Leicester this time in the number-ten shirt.

Healey's tactical vision was at its sharpest, both in his running game and his kicking. He created space for Geordan Murphy, only to see his wing turned over, but the first try came after Rod Kafer, the Australian replacement for Howard, sent Tuilagi barrelling through the middle of the field; Stimpson provided the link and Murphy scored unchallenged to leave Leicester only a point down at half-time.

O'Gara added a third penalty soon after the interval and Leicester lost their scrum-half when Jamie Hamilton was carried off with medial ligament damage. That allowed Harry Ellis, the youngster who had scored a vital try in the semi-final against Llanelli, to take the field and play his part in the second try. Leicester sent successive penalties to the corner, Kay won a messy lineout which Ellis tidied up admirably and, after a couple of rucks, Healey blasted a path past O'Gara for the score.

The conversion and a subsequent penalty by Stimpson gave Leicester a degree of breathing space and it was notable that, in the final quarter, O'Gara's normally dependable game had disappeared. Two penalty attempts flew wide, a clearance was badly sliced and though John O'Neill looked as though he had scored a Munster try, the video referee ruled that Healey's covering tackle had pushed the wing into the cornerflag.

↑ Geordan Murphy grabs a vital try in the final against Munster in 2002.

So 15-9 is how it stayed. "It has been a difficult year, everyone has tried to knock us off our perch," Richards said. "But there is a certain amount of resilience in our side that no other side has got." Within a 12-month period, Leicester won two European titles both played outside England when, for all the enthusiasm of more than 15,000 travelling Leicester fans, the majority of the crowd supported their opponents. They did so with a side more than two-thirds of which qualified to play for England and of whom six represented England in the World Cup-winning squad of 2003.

The bandwagon began to roll in 1998. True, Leicester brought silverware home in 1995 (the league title) and 1997 (the Pilkington Cup) but a playing generation had passed with the departure of Richards and John Wells (both promptly joining the management) and Rory Underwood, the flying wing. There was no obvious reason why Leicester should have carried off the premiership title at the end of the 1998/99 season; new players were being integrated, a new and inexperienced management

↓ Tigers are back-to back European champions 25.5.2002.

team was finding its feet after the departure early in 1998 of Bob Dwyer as director of rugby and there were the usual representative calls on the club's most experienced forwards.

Yet every club was in the same situation: Newcastle had bought in a very expensive team which won the league title in 1998, Saracens had chosen to buy outstanding individuals in Michael Lynagh, Philippe Sella, Kyran Bracken and François Pienaar to add star quality to the most homely of London clubs, all were seeking the appropriate formula to discover success as professional entities. Two famous names, Richmond and London Scottish, had gone to the wall (though their amateur sections kept those names very much alive).

For Leicester the truly testing year was 1999, when the fourth World Cup was hosted by Wales and the club's playing resources were stretched to the limit. This was the year in which Howard showed what an important acquisition he was: playing at inside centre he was able to mentor two teenaged half backs, Andy Goode and James Grindal, through a demanding series of games and also bring to bear an analytical mind which made him, effectively, a player-coach and in prime position to take over the direction of the backs when the South African World Cup winner, Joel Stransky, returned home.

So Leicester were able to turn themselves into the leading example in England of a successful professional rugby club. If they were unable to match, after 2002, the sustained achievements of that era, it comes as no surprise. Their rivals were not standing still, great players retire or move on, law changes force coaches to tweak how the game is played but the principles by which Leicester abide have not changed.

On the field they have based everything on primary possession from the set pieces, effective back-row forwards and a goalkicker. Without these fundamentals, you may have a back line of all the talents but in an English winter they will not thrive. Their critics have called them boring without recognising Leicester's ability to expand their game when they believe it is right to do so; Gloucester's faithful supporters in the Kingsholm Shed love to sing "Same old Leicester, always cheating" but they respect, because they are knowledgeable folk, what Leicester have done while grieving that their own team has not been able to do the same.

Grieving, in particular, after the 2006/07 season when they finished the regular league season joint top (with Leicester) but were crushed 44-16 by the Tigers in the grand final at Twickenham. That was Leicester's first league success since the halcyon days of 2002 and they repeated the dose with back-to-back wins over London Irish (2009) and Saracens (2010). A further title followed in 2013, made all the sweeter by the fact that this time it was their neighbours from Northampton who were the losers in a final which many will remember for the red card awarded to Dylan Hartley, the Northampton and England hooker.

That Leicester also beat Northampton to win the 2012 LV= Cup was an extra fillip. The cup, now with an Anglo-Welsh flavour, is a pale shadow of the competition that Leicester won in three successive years between 1979-81 and is regarded largely as a development tool. But it serves a purpose and certainly the youngsters who appeared in that final at Worcester's Sixways ground, among them Billy Twelvetrees and George Ford, have gone on to bigger and better things, even if not in Leicester colours. Indeed, a glance around the Aviva Premiership at the end of the 2013/14 season indicates the influence Leicester have had on players who are now either captains or senior figures at their current clubs.

↓ Goode, Vesty, Rabeni and Brett Deacon celebrate after beating Gloucester to win the Premiership final for the first time 12.5.2007.

CHAPTER 3

The Business of Rugby

The playing success of the club over the professional era is testimony to the ability of Leicester administrators to make fundamental change quickly. On new year's day, 1995, the year the game went open, the salaried staff cost Leicester just over £66,000, a sum accounted for by the director of rugby, Tony Russ, the groundsman, Derek Limmage, and a couple of part-time secretaries. The pre-tax profit over that financial year was not far short of £400,000.

Two years later Leicester's rugby costs leapt from £401,000 for the year ending April 1996 to £1,832,000 for the year ending April 1997 and the club was on the verge of converting from an industrial and provident society to a public limited company. The valuation of the ground in the share prospectus published in 1997 was just short of £4m but the club was running at a loss and would continue to do so for another three years.

In 2001, the first profit by an English club in the professional era was declared at £56,000, modest but significant nonetheless. At that time the full-time staff had risen to eighty (with 200 part-timers on duty on match days) and the wage bill totalled £2.5m, including expenditure on an academy system which catered for 150 young players from under-14 to under-21. On new year's day, 2015, there will be over 140 people employed by the club and if the playing squad are the public face, those who work unseen are just as important to sustaining that success.

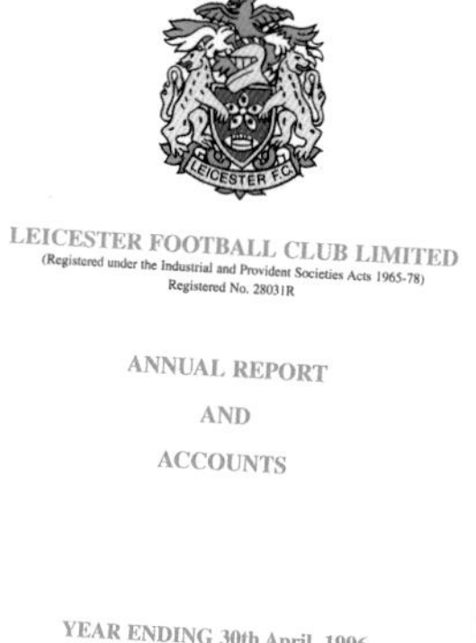

LEICESTER FOOTBALL CLUB LIMITED
(Registered under the Industrial and Provident Societies Acts 1965-78)
Registered No. 28031R

ANNUAL REPORT
AND
ACCOUNTS

YEAR ENDING 30th April, 1996
Admission to the Annual General Meeting by Production of this notice.

↑ The cover of the club's Annual Report and Accounts in 1996.

The secretary's report for 1995/96 gives a snapshot of the upheaval. Tudor Thomas, the former headmaster who was such a willing servant of the club (in any capacity), had taken over as secretary after the resignation of John Allen, the former scrum-half. Allen, a chartered accountant, did not wish to be an administrator for a professional sporting body though he returned two years later as a non-executive director to help Leicester convert to a plc. "No-one could have anticipated the speed of the changes which have already taken place," Thomas wrote.

"So be it. The game is now professional and there is no turning back. We must be positive and accept the various and varied challenges which now face us and go forward with determination, enthusiasm and enlightened thinking. I have always made it known that I have been proud to be a member of an honest amateur club. I now look forward to being part of an honest professional club. Every day there are changes and new challenges to be faced and it is obvious that we at Leicester have accepted the challenges and changes. We are determined to face the reality, implications and costs of the new game and be one of the leading clubs both in this country and in Europe. We have always been successful and we will do everything to remain so."

If there seems a certain reluctance in the report, it was shared by many. Martin Johnson painted a picture of what the first year of open rugby was like, a year in which the RFU had declared a moratorium while they tried to sort out the implications of the International Rugby Board's decision in August 1995 for which no northern-hemisphere union was prepared. "We had won the league in 1994/95 but we didn't really recruit players," Johnson, then in the early stages of his international career, said.

"We were the biggest club in terms of support but we couldn't support professionalism. The next year was horrible. As amateurs we played Saturday, midweek, Saturday. We played five games in 15 days towards the end of the '95/96 season and were beaten to the league title when we lost to Harlequins in the last minute. Bath, who we were always trying to knock off their perch, took the title and a week later we lost to them in the cup final. As a team we had never been so determined, we smashed them up front, got ahead and then lost to a penalty try. I have never felt anything like that, it was the most desolate feeling. It was the last amateur game Leicester played."

But crucially, Leicester had funds at their disposal and the biggest purpose-built club ground in the country. "The key part for me was that we were solvent, we had money in the bank," Peter Wheeler, Leicester's president in 1995 who then became the first chief executive, said. "Almost every other club was overdrawn then found themselves having to put professional staff together, plus players and coaches. It was a very frightening time but we asked ourselves one question: did we want to remain an amateur club or be the best club side in Europe? Once we made that decision, the rest followed."

Easier said than done. The XV that beat Bath in mid-April 1995 contained nine players who were, or would become, full internationals and the remainder had all played for senior England representative sides. Leicester had to make guarantees to these players that their long-term future lay at Welford Road, even while clubs up and down the land were deciding what the going rate would be in the professional game. The market was muddied by the entry at Newcastle Gosforth of Sir John Hall and at Saracens of Nigel Wray, successful businessmen with a vision for how rugby union would, or could, be and the cash to make it happen.

In the event, only one player, Tony Underwood, the England and Lions wing, left for pastures new, at Newcastle. Leicester budgeted for a wage bill of £1.5m in the first full season of open rugby and new revenue had to be generated without any central organisation to assist. The RFU controlled broadcasting contracts and much of the available sponsorship, and Leicester's first port of call was clearly their large membership, at a time when a top-rate season ticket cost £48.

The De Montfort Hall was hired for an extraordinary general meeting to accommodate every member who wanted to know in which direction their club was going. "We didn't have all the answers, no-one did," Wheeler said, "but the money in the bank bought us time. We had no idea how we would do from a share issue but we went for £3m to provide working capital. Everyone found themselves doing two or three jobs but we had the opportunity to make our own decisions."

The players, of course, were invited to give up jobs and pensions to become professional sportsmen, a short career loaded with potential for an abrupt conclusion. Which way would such senior players as Dean Richards and John Wells, both policemen, or Rory Underwood, an RAF officer, go, for their decisions could influence younger men? Richards and Underwood were both aware of the southern-hemisphere based Rugby World Championship, the short-lived organisation that planned a professional international tournament and had contacted the world's leading players (or their representatives) during the 1995 World Cup in South Africa.

"Whatever we tried, we had to ensure the ultimate survival of Leicester," Peter Tom said. "Peter Wheeler and I wanted to ensure we were financially robust enough to deal with a changing game." Leicester were fortunate that two such characters were at the helm at this time. Tom, a Cornishman who had moved to Leicester as a ten-year-old, had played lock for the club in the 1960s and proved very successful in business. He is now executive chairman of Breedon Aggregates and chairman of Channel Islands Property Funds Ltd.

His success in changing a national quarrying business into an international company meant Tom pulled no punches. "I never needed too many excuses to get into a fight," he said. "I wasn't intimidated by what was going on and we never backed off the tough decisions, those that we felt had to be made in the best interests of the club." Yet at the same time Tom articulates, in emotional terms, what the club means to him: "It manages to get into you, it becomes a labour of love. All we are is custodians, we try to pass the club on in a better state than when we started." It exercised a similar grip on Wheeler, a Londoner who arrived at Leicester as a young man to work in insurance and became integral to the club's wellbeing and reputation.

Both of them knew that, if push came to shove, Tom could help the club financially but he had no desire to become an owner and the club itself wanted to stand on its own feet. During the first season of open rugby, players with jobs trained early in the morning - Darren Garforth, the prop and scaffolder who was famously described as a 'tubular executive', would come in at 6am - while the club's administrators began to take hard decisions: the first came early in 1996 with the dismissal of Tony Russ as director of rugby and the arrival as director of coaching of Bob Dwyer.

↑ The share prospectus booket of 1997.

"We stumbled through that first year," Wheeler said. "We told the players that being professional was about more than doing the same thing and getting paid for it. That's why we wanted Bob, he did a very good job professionalising that side of the club. He was only with us for a couple of years but he did so much for us before we decided not to extend his contract."

The 1997 share issue did not raise the hoped-for £3m at a time when improved facilities were needed for supporters and players, at Welford Road and the Oval Park training ground at Oadby. The net result was a 10 per cent share in the club passing for a time to the Hong Kong and Shanghai Banking Corporation (HSBC), the multi-national financial services company who then had the right to two directors on the club board. Nor did Leicester own Welford Road, their greatest asset; true, they leased it from the city council for £10,500 a year, a small enough sum, but another decade passed before they finally gained ownership.

In the club's 1999 annual statement, Tom acknowledged a loss after tax of £1.56m (over a 14-month period in which English clubs had withdrawn from European competition) and HSBC's shares had been sold on, mainly to existing club members. But sponsorship was growing, Welford Road was working harder for its living as a conference and banqueting centre, and merchandising was on the up. There was regret that, despite winning the first of four back-to-back premiership titles, Leicester had not met its financial targets, a failure laid in part at the door of ongoing squabbles with the RFU as well as a season without the Heineken Cup.

By that time Dwyer had come and gone, and Joel Stransky, the fly-half who dropped the extra-time goal that won South Africa the World Cup in 1995, was about to leave his role as backs coach. Both had brought invaluable southern-hemisphere experience on which Richards and Wells could build but just as important was the corporate programme in which Vauxhall Motors had joined Next, Alliance and Leicester, Tetley Bitter, Bardon Aggregates, Hewlett Packard and Cotton Traders, an enviable list of sponsors.

↓ Peter Tom, the club chairman, addresses a Premier Rugby meeting.

All these changes coincided with a new generation of players. The old guard, represented by Richards and Rory Underwood, had gone even if their links with the club remained strong. "New people, like Austin Healey, Will Greenwood, Craig Joiner, gave us a breath of fresh air," Johnson, who had worked for the Midland Bank, later subsumed into HSBC, said. "We began to train full time, the camaraderie was far better because everyone lived in or around Leicester. There was no friends network outside the team, we just hung out with each other. We were mid-twenties, few of us were married and it was just great fun. Everything was new.

"As an amateur, I trained two nights a week at the club. I bought a house in Leicester at that point but if training was at 7pm, I would stay after work at the club and lift some weights before training between seven and nine-thirty. I'd be home after 10pm. The other nights, I'd be in a gym. After the game went open, we could do strength training during the day

The old Members stand was replaced by the impressive Caterpillar stand in 2009.

and be home by 6pm, you felt you had all the time in the world."

But there was far more to be organised with every passing season of professional rugby. Leicester had to take on a duty of care, for the wider welfare of their playing staff, in particular the youngsters involved with the academy. "If you are 21, 22, in the Leicester club and earning, say, £30,000 a year with your own sponsored car, getting into every nightclub you want, life's pretty good," Tom said. "Reel that on to 30, you're an average player earning £70-80,000, you have a wife, two children, a mortgage, what will you do after rugby?"

Mike Harrison, the former centre who subsequently became club president, occupies a pastoral role at Welford Road in helping provide guidance to players seeking post-rugby careers. But there is a far greater outreach represented by the club's community programme and, working in conjunction with the local authority, Tigers have dipped deep into the ethnic mix of which the city consists, including the Indian, Asian and African communities with few natural affinities to rugby.

"We advocate sport for health so we don't want people to just play rugby, we want to encourage people to play as many sports as possible, with the social and health benefits attached," Scott Clarke, Leicester's community manager, said. The programme he administers has taken 14 years to develop with rugby as the catalyst for initiatives in numeracy, literacy and increasing attainment. "We have three or four of the lowest educational wards in the country here so we have tried to develop programmes to inspire youngsters to learn."

It helps, of course, that players whose names feature every day in the local media share the workload and learn, on the way, about public speaking and relating to individuals and groups. Clarke can offer children visits to a stadium which, in Leicestershire terms, has iconic status: "Going into a sports ground is a totally different environment to school and youngsters coming to Welford Road have told us they feel privileged to be allowed in," he said. "That translates into enthusiasm to do something. We offer a brand and an ethos: hard work gets results, nothing else.

"We are a Leicester company, a high-profile company, we have a duty to put back into the community. The Junior Tigers Club has grown exponentially over the last five years and, in ten years' time, they will be the players, the season-ticket holders, the supporters of the club. All these things meet in the middle - you hope the youngsters and their parents will come along and have a good time."

Players during the amateur era undertook community initiatives - Clarke himself, as a pupil at Leicester Grammar School, heard Wheeler conduct an assembly during the 1980s and became one of the school's rugby players to acquire a free season's pass to Welford Road. Now the number of rugby camps organised by the club has grown not only regionally but internationally; Leicester have run camps in Holland for four years, they have links with Denmark and Italy, a camp took place in 2014 for the first time in Kuala Lumpur and discussions have taken place with rugby bodies in North and South America. Through the Tigers Cup for under-10s, sponsored by the Loughborough firm, Prima Solutions, Leicester are in touch with more than seventy schools in the region.

While local grants are available to assist these activities, Leicester must fund the remainder themselves while not losing sight of their core activity, the development of elite rugby. In the World Cup year of 2003, they became the first premiership club to record a turnover of more than £10 million; seven years later, when the completion of the Caterpillar Stand had raised capacity to 24,000, turnover had risen to £18.5 million and a loss of nearly £1m in 2009 had been turned into a £284,000 profit.

In that same year, such quality companies as Holland and Barrett, the health foods business, and the jewellers, Goldsmiths, joined the sponsors roster, helping Leicester invest further in training facilities and the development of a strong sports science programme. Tigers Events, the club's hospitality arm which offers packages not only at prime rugby occasions but in horse racing, tennis and Formula One motor racing, returned to profit and continues to thrive.

When Leicester won the league title for the tenth time, in 2013, they also recorded a turnover of £19m which placed them commercially in the top three rugby clubs in Europe. In so doing they turned a £1m loss on the previous season into a £396,000 profit and season-ticket sales reached a record high of 14,732. "Where," Wheeler asked, "is professional rugby going? The French have wealthy people spending twice as much as we are. At home, wealthy people are investing in Bath and Saracens, do we need someone like that?

"Is just running a business at a profit enough? What's going to happen to the salary cap? We want to see it move on but we don't want it to go silly. Where are significant new revenues coming from? Is the pond we fish in going to become a sea?" After nearly twenty years of professional rugby, Leicester are as well placed as any club in the northern hemisphere to predict the future but, as in 1995, still do not have all the answers. What they have done is created a model for the organisation of a successful rugby team and a successful rugby business, studied by most of their peers in the Aviva Premiership and by aspiring rugby bodies overseas.

"It's not about buying a team, or building a crowd, it's about establishing a character," Wheeler said. "It's getting like-minded people together, you have to live it all the time, there are no short cuts. We're not the most popular club around the place, people like to see us lose. But, just as you would test the laws of the game as a player, you search out every nook and cranny to find out what helps the club to success."

CHAPTER 4

In The Beginning

You wonder what the founding fathers would have made of it all. The chances are they would have recognised the need for change, for a sound business structure on and off the field. Success comes from hard work and Leicester has a strong commercial history - the Industrial Revolution of the 18th century and the development of trade in the 19th century, both at home and abroad, created in the city a network of small firms which, as the population grew, were able to stand tall within the county.

With the growth of the railways, the mobility of the population changed too. During the 19th century, Leicester's population leapt from 17,000 to more than 211,000 with newcomers seeking work in the hosiery, footwear and light engineering industries which brought the city so much wealth. New housing sprang up to the north and west of the centre and though leisure was not then what it is now, the multitudes of new Leicestrians wanted something else for their entertainment.

Village cricket had long been a staple for framework knitters, whose working hours allowed them time, and a new cricket ground was opened at Grace Road in 1878, the county cricket club being founded a year later. The rugby game, having been invented little more than twenty miles away in 1823 when William Webb Ellis decided to catch the ball on Big Side at Rugby School and run with it, had crossed the border from Warwickshire by 1869 at least, since in that year Leicester Athletic Society and St Margaret's were formed in the city. Neither exist now, having either merged or foundered, and though records exist at Twickenham of a Leicester club formed in 1872, it would seem this was a team representative of several junior clubs.

There was a club at Lutterworth, founded in 1873, and Oadby Wyggestonians to the east of Leicester while Moseley, Nuneaton and Coventry were formed in the same decade. Therefore the ground was ripe in 1880 for the formation of a new club. The first international match had been played between Scotland and England in 1871, the same year as the foundation of the Rugby Football Union itself; to the north Nottingham already boasted a club and it is tempting to think that rumours from the south that Northampton was about to form a club of its own could have been a motivating factor.

Whatever the spark, Leicester Societies AFC, Leicester Amateur FC and Leicester Alert decided to amalgamate to form a club that would represent the whole city. Their representatives met on 3 August 1880, at the George Hotel in the Haymarket and formed the first committee of the Leicester Football Club headed by William Alfred Wheeler as president. Wheeler, whose home was in Lancaster Street, was an enthusiastic player who would make 26 sporadic appearances for the new club during the 1880s.

The club's first captain, by 14 votes to two, was Alexander Brice, who lived in Mill Hill Lane off the London Road. His rival, John Symington, was

↓ LEICESTER FOOTBALL CLUB 1880/81
Back: Foster, Wale, Lakin, W.Wheeler (President), Sheen, Parsons, Watts, Nutt, Walker.
Middle: Salmon, Young, Brice (capt), W.Porter.
Front: A.Porter, Symington, Coleman, Sheffield.

named vice-captain; joint secretaries were appointed in John Lakin and John Parsons, and 50 players were written onto the club's books. In due course James Walker agreed to become treasurer and other committee members were Newman Haddon, Arthur Turner, Arthur Porter, Hedley Salmon and Robert Warner; this gave the new body five representatives from Leicester Societies, three from the Amateurs and three from the Alert and you might have thought that their first tasks were to establish where to play and who to play. But, 24 days later, their first act was to appoint the treasurer, their second to agree a date (24 September) for an inaugural dinner at the George, whose proprietor may have believed he was on to a good thing.

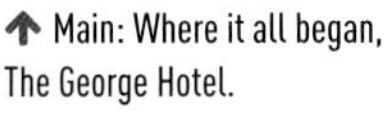

🡅 Main: Where it all began, The George Hotel.

Inset: W A Wheeler, the club's first President.

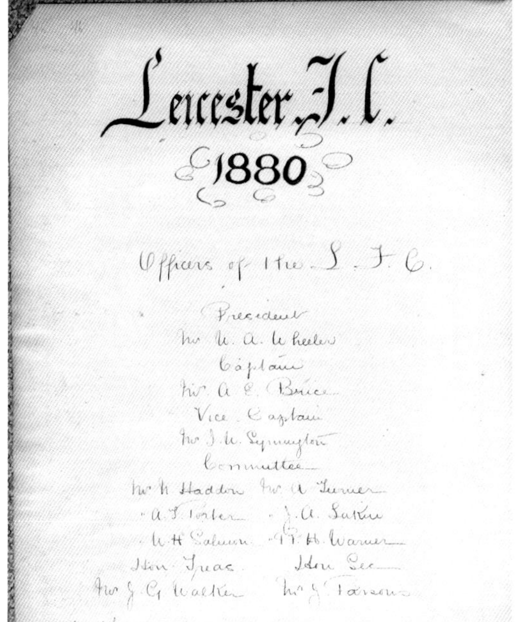

Leicester F. C.
1880

Officers of the L. F. C.

President
Mr W. A. Wheeler
Captain
Mr A. E. Bruce
Vice Captain
Mr J. W. Symington
Committee
Mr N Haddon Mr A Turner
" A. T. Porter " J. A. Lakin
" W H Salmon " R. H. Warner
Hon Treas Hon Sec
Mr J. G. Walker Mr J Parsons

DE6126/1

🡄 Title page of the original club minute book showing the first elected officers.

The colours of the new club were black and the annual subscription was set at five shillings (50p in modern currency, though the equivalent now would be nearer £50). That first meeting also laid down the bye-laws: 1) the club was to be called the Leicester Football Club; 2) the club was to play under Rugby Union rules (the laws came later); 3) colours to be black; 4) officers and committee to be chosen at an annual meeting in April; 5) the club to be managed by a committee comprising the president, captain, vice-captain, treasurer, secretary(ies) and six other members; 6) two general meetings to be held each year, in April and September; 7) all elections to be by ballot; 8) teams to be chosen weekly by the committee; 9) anyone wishing to become a member to be proposed, seconded and voted for by a majority at a general committee meeting; 10) subscriptions to be paid by 31 October each year; 11) anyone wishing to resign to give written notice to the secretary before September 1 each season.

At a subsequent meeting, a month later, the committee decided on a fine of sixpence for anyone carded to play who failed to reply (selection was notified by a postcard in those days). Anyone promising to play and failing to do so would be fined two shillings and sixpence. Small though they may sound now, these were not insignificant sums at a time when, for example, a solicitor's clerk may have earned £1 a week; two shillings and sixpence represented an eighth of that income. On the plus side, the committee decided for the inaugural season to give a prize to the player with the highest try total at the season's end. History records no such award so it may have been quietly shelved as contrary to the game's ethics.

At all events, a playing schedule of 17 matches between October and March was drawn up, the first of them against Moseley to be played at the

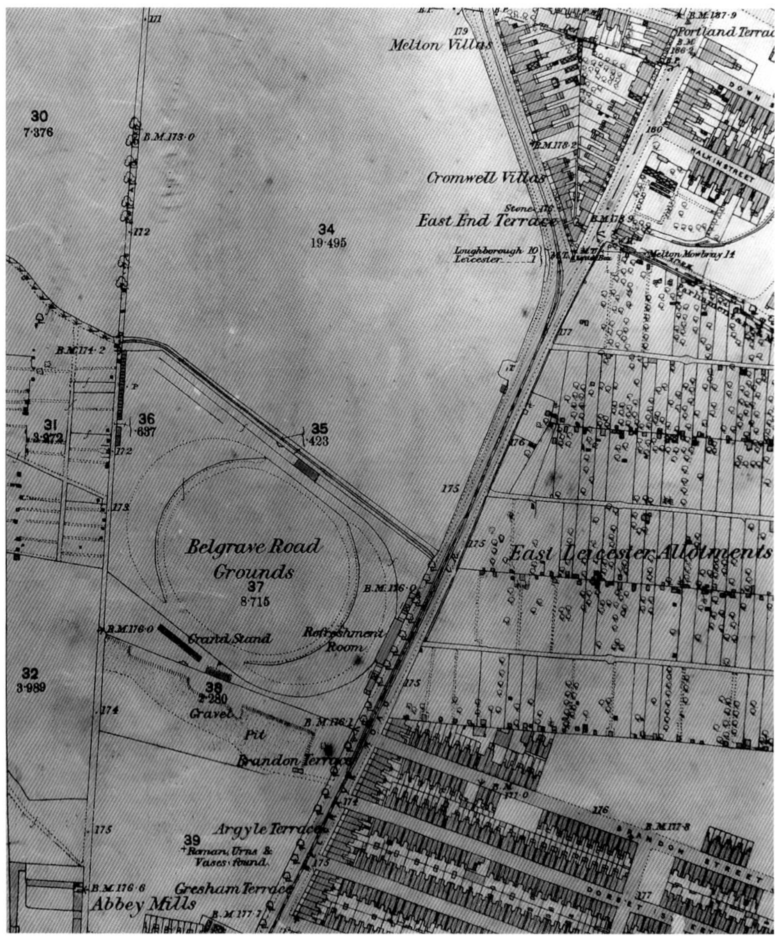

↑ Location of the Tigers' first ground on the Belgrave Road.

Belgrave Cricket and Cycle Ground. This ground, a mile north from the city centre, opened in the same year and was designed as a general sports stadium encircled by a running and cycle track. An admission charge of two pence could be made but as the season wore on, it became clear that the ground was too far out of the centre and in January 1881 Leicester relocated to Victoria Park, then a horse-racing course. They were to return to the Belgrave Road twice more, on the second occasion outbidding Leicester Fosse, the football club founded in 1884 and which was to become Leicester City.

A practice was held on the Welford Road Recreation Ground (how appropriate as things turned out) on 2 October and, ten days later, two squads were selected against Moseley. The senior team that took the field, made up of six backs and nine forwards, was: HL Foster, WA Wheeler, TD Hart, AT Porter, AE Brice, L Young, HS Biggs, AI Burford, JH Gilbert, JT Lovett, TR Pickering, WR Porter, F Sheen, A Turner, CE Worthington. This, though, was nothing like the fifteen-a-side game we recognise today. Only three years earlier, teams had been reduced from twenty-a-side, there were no specialist forwards and the backs were made up of two full-backs, two three-quarter backs and two half-backs. The mauling work of the forwards was the key to success in a game which, fewer than ten years earlier, had seen fit to ban the 'art' of hacking, largely because even Victorian England had come to the conclusion that it was barbaric and caused too many serious injuries.

The outcome of Leicester's first match was a scoreless draw which, given that Moseley had been playing for seven years, was cause for congratulation though there was some dissent from the visitors afterwards which set the tone for considerable acrimony between the two clubs over the next thirty years. Dissent, though, must have been a regular feature of matches considering that there were no touch judges and the umpires were appointed by the respective teams; if there were no umpires, the captains of the two sides had to agree whether an infringement had taken place.

After the first match a tender-hearted reader of the *Leicester Mercury* wrote to the paper: "Football [rugby] is a most exhilarating game but is it absolutely necessary that it should be played in such a manner as to endanger life and limb? In the scrimmage it is almost impossible to avoid a stray kick, meant doubtless for the ball but falling instead upon someone's shins. Surely it is not essential that these kicks should be delivered with boots which cannot fail to leave decided impressions behind."

The first victory came in the next game, against Leicester Victoria, and a further draw (also scoreless) followed against the newly-formed Northampton club - that, too, was the start of a long and largely

THE PIONEERS

A glance at the 15 Leicester players for the Club's first ever game on 23 October 1880 against Moseley makes interesting reading:

POS	NAME	AGE	BIRTHPLACE	ADDRESS	OCCUPATION
FB	William Alfred WHEELER	26	Smethwick, Staffs	28 Lancaster Street, St Mary's	Hosier's assistant
FB	Herbert L. FOSTER	18	Ealing, Middlesex	Manor House, Kibworth Harcourt	Solicitor's articled clerk
3Q	Arthur Thomas PORTER	22	Leicester	5 Turner Street, St Mary's	Leather merchant
3Q	Tom Dickenson HART	19	Nottingham	Stag Pheasant Hotel, Ashby-de-la-Zouch	Auctioneer
HB	Alexander Edward BRICE (capt)	29	Kilmersdon, Somerset	10 Mill Hill Lane, St Margaret's	Schoolmaster
HB	Lawrence YOUNG	26	Knaresborough, Yorks	99 Humberstone Rd, St Margaret's	Elementary schoolteacher
F	C.Edward WORTHINGTON	29	Barkisland, Yorks	Royal Hotel, Market Place	Art teacher at Wyggeston School
F	Frederick SHEEN	29	Leicester	13 Victoria Rd, St Margaret's	Ironmonger
F	Henry Sylvanus BIGGS	26	Ampthill, Beds	74 Noble Street, St Mary's	Wyggeston Schoolmaster
F	Arthur TURNER	26	Ipswich, Suffolk	4 Stoughton Street, St Margaret's	Leather merchant's clerk
F	John Thomas LOVETT	22	Barrow-upon-Soar	North Street, Barrow-upon-Soar	Schoolmaster
F	William Robert PORTER	23	Rockingham, Northants	142 Highcross Street, All Saints	Hosiery clerk
F	Thomas Rowland PICKERING	27	Leicester	Melton Rd, St Margaret's	Land agent
F	Arthur Ingram BURFORD	23	Leicester	6 Pocklington's Walk, Knighton	Director Burford & Co (hosiery)
F	John Harry GILBERT	22	Northampton	25 High Street, St Martin's	Hosier's assistant

Just five were born in the county. The oldest was aged only 29, whilst the youngest was 18 years of age. Just three lived outside the city. There were five school teachers, two leather merchants, a director of a hosiery company, three others employed in the hosiery trade, a legal clerk, an auctioneer, a land agent and an ironmonger.

respectful relationship. These first three games were played at home; when Leicester travelled to Market Harborough on 18 December they would have been one man short but, while enjoying a kickabout on the road outside Campbell Street Station, were joined by a passing youth called Hudson. He was asked to come on the train to make up the numbers and, when he declared he had never played rugby, was told he would be a forward and to put his head down and shove in a scrum. During the game, Hudson found the ball at his feet and dribbled it towards the try line. "Pick the ball up," came a shout, he did so and crossed the line. "Fall over," he was advised and he had scored a try in his first (possibly only) game.

However, within three months dissatisfaction with the Belgrave ground grew and an application was made to Leicestershire County Cricket Club to play on their Aylestone Road ground, with gate money to be divided between the two bodies. However the cricket ground company, possibly thinking more of the state of their turf than the income, declined so Victoria Park became home for the rest of the season.

↑ Postcard of Victoria Park in the 1880s, where Leicester played many home games.

Early in 1881, Leicester applied for membership of the Midland Counties Football Association and, a fortnight later, issued a challenge to a Midland Counties XV to play them at Coventry. The move appears to have come to nothing which may have been just as well since in March, Leicester had to pay £1 to Northampton in compensation for the Saints advertising a game for which Leicester failed to raise a side.

Still, it was a satisfactory start-up season. The senior side won nine of their games, five were drawn and only three lost, two of those defeats coming against Kettering and Moseley in the last two fixtures of the season. There were 13 other fixtures played by the second XV and the club even fielded an association football side which won seven of its eleven games. Income was recorded as £36 19s 10d but little notice had been taken in the public prints of the new club; most of the sporting space in the newspapers was occupied by horse racing, walking and cycling.

The committee had to weigh up the pros and cons of settling in at Victoria Park, far closer to the city centre and where it was hoped a stronger following could be built up. But no admission charge could be made and the secretary was forced to ask the city's estates committee for a reduction in the charge for playing at the park. The fixture list was lengthened to 20 senior-team games (12 of them away from home), though that list did not include Northampton, feathers still ruffled from the events of the first season.

↓ Hedley Salmon's 44-year association with the club included spells as player, honorary secretary, and president

Hedley Salmon, a forward who made ten appearances for the first XV during the season, became the new secretary and, when Brice resigned the captaincy through illness, that role passed to Arthur Porter. He lasted no more than five months before resigning because he felt "unable to play and fulfil the duties of captain" and the leadership went to Lawrence Young. A game at Kettering illustrates what the duties of the captain included in the early 1880s: Kettering threw the ball in and Porter called "not straight". Kettering ignored the call and, while the Leicester players stood still, the home side claimed the winning try. After much dispute, Leicester left the field with five minutes still remaining and viewed the result as a scoreless draw. "Kettering played a very rough game, scragging and kicking which made it unpleasant for us, who are not used to playing that kind of game," lamented a local report. Four months later the tables turned when Lakin "scored" a Leicester try after the Rushden umpire cried "handed on" [forward pass?]. Rushden, the home side, left the field and did not return until Young had agreed to lay the matter before the president of the Midland Counties and abide by his decision.

With so much administrative change it may not be surprising that the playing record for the season showed nine wins and nine defeats (nowadays we would call it second-season syndrome), those losses including Leicester's first entry into the Midland Counties Senior Cup. "Although knocked out by a second-rate club [Edgbaston Crusaders] in the first round of the cup ties...I think it will take the premier club [Moseley] all its time to knock us out in the final (if we do not meet before) in the forthcoming season," Salmon wrote in his report for 1881/82. The secretary was putting a positive spin on the competition: in fact, Leicester did not win the cup until a further 16 years had passed, when they did, indeed, beat Moseley.

But the club was finding its feet; the appearance of Bedford School in the 1882/83 fixtures may lift some eyebrows but they were certainly no pushovers. Leicester dropped their association football side in 1883, upon the formation of the Leicester Association Football Club which developed a year later into Leicester Fosse, and opted to try to run a third XV instead.

But the establishment of a new winter-sports club presented a different challenge since both rugby and football would be angling for support from within the city. The next five years proved an anxious time as gate receipts dwindled when Leicester returned to the Belgrave ground. Sometimes the paying attendance numbered a mere couple of hundred or fewer, start times depended on when the opposition turned up and, on one occasion, Coventry failed to appear at all. Then again, Loughborough arrived to fulfil a fixture and Leicester themselves did not turn up. The match at Stamford in December 1882 saw Leicester win with only 11 players and in February 1884 there was another set-to with Kettering, "the crowd being so disgusted at the blackguard language used by the away team [Kettering] to their own umpire on giving honest decisions against them that, after two further disputes, the teams left the ground and the match was abandoned." The Midland Cup proved something of a saving grace since the competitive element helped boost interest; in the 1883/84 season there were four cup ties (though only one at home).

During this first decade, too, Leicester could not decide which shirt colours to adopt. Clearly black did not suit, even if it did give them an initial nickname of 'the death or glory boys,' and this gave way to a chocolate and yellow confection which is, almost certainly, the origin of their famous nickname, Tigers. It is hard to be certain because of the connection that had been established with officers of the Leicestershire Regiment whose own soubriquet was Tigers. The earliest reference to the name appears to confirm the first theory: the *Leicester Daily Post* states "the Tigers stripes were keeping well together" in the match report of the game against Bedford School in February 1885.

A report in *The Leicester Post* of 28 December 1887 refers to the legendary race horse, Ormonde, which ran in the Duke of Westminster's yellow and black colours: "The chocolate and orange, which so closely resembles the yellow and black that one is justified in terming the Tigers the Ormondes of the rugby field." Maybe proximity to the hosiery trade encouraged experimentation. Leicester tried out chocolate and French grey and then claret and French grey and then the scarlet, green and white stripes with which they have become identified. Early team photographs show vertical stripes then, in 1894, a translation to horizontal stripes. There was a hiatus in the early 1900s when they wore white but scarlet, green and white became the preferred colours and remain so today, even if the commercialisation of the shirt has produced an away and European strip which are regularly changed.

When Leicester returned for the third and last time to Belgrave Road, in 1888, they took their Victoria Park supporters with them. Maybe there had been the occasional grumble from the players too: "It was bitterly cold on Saturday," *The Saturday Herald* complained after the March 1887 game with Moseley Woodstock at Victoria Park, "hence it was just a bit too bad for the players to have to strip in a large room without a fire. Surely the amount of business this match brought to the hostelry [across the road from the park where both teams changed] ought to run to half a bag of coal." Back at Belgrave, they charged five shillings (25p) for a season ticket while non-members paid three pence for entry and a further three pence if they sought the comfort of the stand. Ladies were not charged admission, though whether that was a cunning marketing ploy or acknowledgement that very few ladies wanted to watch rugby is not disclosed.

Leicester's horizons were extending: on 10 March 1888 they left the Midlands to play Manningham, the leading Yorkshire club who, in the next decade, were to become the first champions of the Northern Union before changing codes, taking up association football and becoming Bradford City. The game was played at Valley Parade in Bradford and, though Leicester went down 10-4, they were offered home and away fixtures for the next two seasons.

The 1888/89 season was the longest yet, starting on 29 September and ending on 13 April. The 35 fixtures included more northern opponents in Swinton and Oldham while Cardiff Harlequins became the first Welsh opposition in Leicester's history. When Swinton Lions visited, the Lord Mayor of Leicester took the kick-off but the club went down 11-1 (tries were worth one point in those days) in front of a crowd of 2,000. Nearly five months later, when Leicester visited Oldham, a local paper described them as "mild, gentle and lamblike exponents of the game" - in other words, southern softies.

Moreover the club reached the final of the Midland Counties Cup for the first time, though not without incident. After a first-round win over Moseley Harlequins, they went to Rugby and won, only to have the victory struck out because Leicester fielded an ineligible player, A Chettle, at full-back. The match was replayed four days later and Leicester sneaked home 4-3, the locals giving the referee, a Mr Holmes, a hard time after the final whistle. When Tommy Nutt, the Leicester back, ran to the official's assistance he "sustained a nasty cut on the head from the stick of a dastardly rough." In the semi-final, Leicester beat Stamford but, in the final played at Coventry on March 23, they lost 6-0 to Moseley in front of 4,000, of whom 1,200 had travelled from Leicester.

The next season ended with games on successive days against Cardiff and Newport - the first Easter tour - but yet again there was trouble after a match with Moseley. Leicester's home crowd was so vociferous in its criticism of the referee, a Mr McGawley from Rugby, that the matter was reported to the Midland Counties union. At a meeting on March 1, the union agreed a resolution "That an apology by the Leicester club be forwarded to Mr McGawley for the treatment of him by spectators; and that the Leicester club is prohibited from admitting any spectators, except members of the club, to any more matches this season." Nowadays, of course, it is directors of rugby who bear the brunt of official displeasure if they voice concerns about referees.

Clearly crowd problems occurred with far more frequency than they do today. In February 1891, *The Daily Mercury's* reporter was an unhappy man after the game against Old Edwardians from Birmingham: "We regret being unable to furnish our readers with a report of the latter part of the match," he wrote. "It was with difficulty that the first half of play was obtainable but, during the interval, the crowd surrounded the Press table while a little later on, some individual took possession of the table for standing room. The action of the Leicester club towards the Press leads us to suppose that, as regards to local football, success breeds contempt. We believe the match ended thus: Old Edwardians 1 goal, Leicester 1 try, spectators 10,000."

Given that this was Leicester's first loss for over four months, there may have been extra heat in the crowd's actions. Nevertheless, Leicester reached another Midland Counties Cup final, losing 8-0 to Coventry at Rugby. Defeat did not prevent a large gathering that evening at the Clarendon Restaurant, opposite where the Grand Hotel now stands in Granby Street, a restaurant which, in the souvenir programme of the match, advertised "large

⬇ Future captain and committe man Arthur McKecknie's (SIC) 1888/89 membership card.

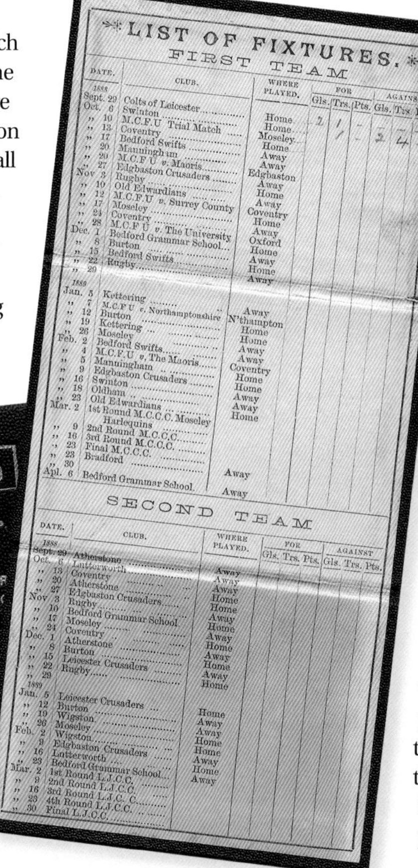

LIST OF FIXTURES.

FIRST TEAM

DATE.	CLUB.	WHERE PLAYED.
1888		
Sept. 29	Colts of Leicester	
Oct. 6	Swinton	Home
,, 10	M.C.F.U Trial Match	Home
,, 13	Coventry	Moseley
,, 17	Bedford Swifts	Home
,, 20	Manningham	Away
,, 20	M.C.F.U v. Maoris	Away
,, 27	Edgbaston Crusaders	Edgbaston
Nov 3	Rugby	Away
,, 10	Old Edwardians	Home
,, 12	M.C.F.U v. Surrey County	Away
,, 17	Moseley	Coventry
,, 24	Coventry	Home
,, 28	M.C.F.U v. The University	Away
Dec. 1	Bedford Grammar School	Oxford
,, 8	Burton	Home
,, 15	Bedford Swifts	Away
,, 22	Rugby	Home
,, 29		Away
1889		
Jan. 5	Kettering	Away
,, 7	M.C.F.U v. Northamptonshire	N'thampton
,, 12	Burton	Home
,, 19	Kettering	Home
,, 26	Moseley	Away
Feb. 2	Bedford Swifts	Away
,, 4	M.C.F.U v. The Maoris	Coventry
,, 5	Manningham	Home
,, 9	Edgbaston Crusaders	Home
,, 16	Swinton	Away
,, 18	Oldham	Away
,, 23	Old Edwardians	Home
Mar. 2	1st Round M.C.C.C. Moseley Harlequins	
,, 9	2nd Round M.C.C.C.	
,, 16	3rd Round M.C.C.C.	
,, 23	Final M.C.C.C.	
,, 23	Bradford	
,, 30		Away
Apl. 6	Bedford Grammar School	Away

SECOND TEAM

DATE.	CLUB.	WHERE PLAYED.
1888		
Sept. 29	Atherstone	Away
Oct. 6	Lutterworth	Away
,, 13	Coventry	Away
,, 20	Atherstone	Home
,, 27	Edgbaston Crusaders	Home
Nov 3	Rugby	Away
,, 10	Bedford Grammar School	Home
,, 17	Moseley	Away
,, 24	Coventry	Home
Dec. 1	Atherstone	Away
,, 8	Burton	Home
,, 15	Leicester Crusaders	Away
,, 22	Rugby	Home
,, 29		
1889		
Jan. 5	Leicester Crusaders	Home
,, 12	Burton	Away
,, 19	Wigston	Away
,, 26	Moseley	Home
Feb. 2	Wigston	Home
,, 9	Edgbaston Crusaders	Away
,, 16	Lutterworth	Home
,, 23	Bedford Grammar School	Away
Mar. 2	1st Round L.J.C.C.	
,, 9	2nd Round L.J.C.C.	
,, 16	3rd Round L.J.C.C.	
,, 23	4th Round L.J.C.C.	
,, 30	Final L.J.C.C.	

LEICESTER FOOTBALL CLUB.—SEASON, 1888-1889

PRESIDENT: T. WRIGHT, ESQ., J.P.

REV. H. J. FORTESCUE, DR. MACAULAY, GEORGE OLIVER, ESQ., J.P., J. COLLIER, ESQ. — VICE-PRESIDENTS

CAPTAIN, 1ST TEAM: J. PARSONS.

VICE-CAPTAIN, 1ST TEAM, AND ASSISTANT SECRETARY: W. R. PORTER

CAPT., 2ND TEAM: P. G. SALMON | VICE-CAPT., 2ND TEAM: H. STANY(

HONORARY TREASURER: F. J. BRETT, ST. STEPHEN'S RD.

HONORARY SECRETARY: H. W. SALMON, WEST ST., SOUTHFI

COMMITTEE: DR. H. MASON. R. S. SNOWDEN K. MCALPIN. E. MORL BROCKBANK. A. MCKECKNIE. C. B. KNIGHT.

GROUND: BELGRAVE ROAD GROUNDS.

HEADQUARTERS: WELLINGTON HOTE

COLOURS: CHOCOLATE AND FRENCH GREY.

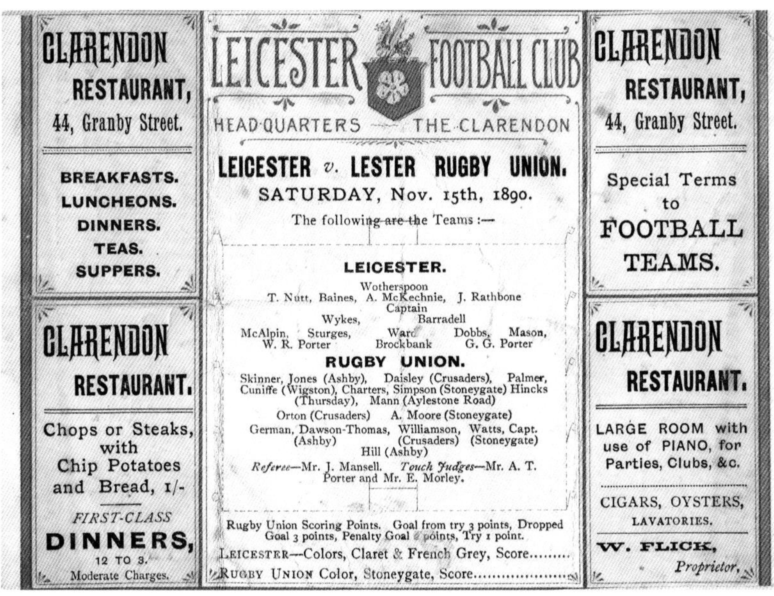

CLARENDON
RESTAURANT,
44, Granby Street.

BREAKFASTS.
LUNCHEONS.
DINNERS.
TEAS.
SUPPERS.

CLARENDON
RESTAURANT.

Chops or Steaks, with Chip Potatoes and Bread, 1/-

FIRST-CLASS
DINNERS,
12 TO 3.
Moderate Charges.

LEICESTER FOOTBALL CLUB
HEAD-QUARTERS — THE CLARENDON

LEICESTER *v.* LESTER RUGBY UNION.
SATURDAY, Nov. 15th, 1890.
The following are the Teams :—

LEICESTER.
Wotherspoon
T. Nutt, Baines, A. McKechnie, J. Rathbone
Captain
Wykes, Barradell
McAlpin, Sturges, Ward Dobbs, Mason,
W. R. Porter Brockbank G. G. Porter

RUGBY UNION.
Skinner, Jones (Ashby), Daisley (Crusaders), Palmer,
Cuniffe (Wigston), Charters, Simpson (Stoneygate) Hincks
(Thursday), Mann (Aylestone Road)
Orton (Crusaders) A. Moore (Stoneygate)
German, Dawson-Thomas, Williamson, Watts, Capt.
(Ashby) (Crusaders) (Stoneygate)
Hill (Ashby)
Referee—Mr. J. Mansell. *Touch Judges*—Mr. A. T. Porter and Mr. E. Morley.

Rugby Union Scoring Points. Goal from try 3 points, Dropped Goal 3 points, Penalty Goal [illegible] points, Try 1 point.
LEICESTER—Colors, Claret & French Grey, Score.........
RUGBY UNION Color, Stoneygate, Score.....................

CLARENDON
RESTAURANT,
44, Granby Street.

Special Terms to
FOOTBALL TEAMS.

CLARENDON
RESTAURANT.

LARGE ROOM with use of PIANO, for Parties, Clubs, &c.

CIGARS, OYSTERS,
LAVATORIES.

W. FLICK,
Proprietor.

↑ Teamsheet from the first ever game against Leicestershire at the Belgrave Road Ground in 1890.

room with use of piano for parties, clubs etc. Cigars, oysters, lavatories."

That 1890/91 season was the best so far in the club's short history. They went unbeaten from 4 October until the meeting with Old Edwardians, helped admittedly by the cancellation of eight games around Christmas because of the severity of the winter. Overall they won 18 games and lost five and, with the season over, Leicester applied for a renewal of the lease on the Belgrave Road ground. But they found the terms laid down by the Belgrave Road Ground Company to be unacceptable and members of the ground committee were instructed to look for alternative sites, including the ground at Evington Lane that they used for training.

During the final season at Belgrave, indications of Leicester's growing status were evident. For the 1891/92 season they adopted for the first time scarlet, green and white shirts though it was put to the committee that "only one jersey be given to each player each season and, if the player needs a new one during that season, he must buy it at his own expense." Such clubs as Gloucester, St Helens and Blackheath, one of the RFU's founder clubs, were added to the fixtures. The visit to Blackheath was Leicester's first to London, their travelling costs defrayed by a guarantee from their hosts. Ironically the Midland Counties Cup final came to Leicester but as a neutral venue for the clash of Coventry and Moseley, Leicester having lost in the third round to Old Edwardians.

Meanwhile ground committee meetings were held at the Clarendon Restaurant, Wyggeston School and the offices of Parsons and Co but the problem was not resolved until December 1891. With their financial situation relatively healthy, Leicester accepted the offer of a ten-year lease from the city corporation on land between the Welford and Aylestone Roads, scarcely a five-minute walk from the city centre and not much farther from the railway station. The residential area on the one side, including Chestnut, Walnut, Filbert and Hazel Streets, was offset on the other by the recreation ground which made the whole area open and spacious.

The lease was signed in March 1892 and permission obtained for the land to be artificially levelled and drained at a maximum cost of £200. In all, £1,100 was spent in preparing an entirely new playing area, a considerable sum at the time but, as history shows, money well spent. Leicester advertised in *Athletic News* the change in arrangements for the 1892/93 season, emphasising their desire to play any team of a good standard and bolstered by gate takings of £50 a match.

They were sufficiently solvent to offer Old Edwardians a guarantee of £50 to fulfil a fixture in March 1891 (though ready to double admission from sixpence to a shilling as a consequence). The usual guarantee was £10 or half the gate though the treasurer clearly worked to a sliding scale, depending on the quality of the opposition. Meanwhile the stand that had seen good service at Belgrave Road was transferred to Welford Road, tiered seating was installed and, after a practice match in the preceding week, the new ground was opened on 10 September 1892 with a game against a Leicestershire XV.

The referee was Leicester's first president, William Wheeler, and the opposition included future Tigers in Jack Broadhurst and Rupert Cooke. There were also three former Tigers, Arthur Moore, Thomas Wilks and TH 'Tom' Crumbie, who was to write his name into the club's history in no uncertain way. Although it was agreed that railings were needed to keep the playing arena clear, the new facilities were much admired and, in keeping with the occasion, 'Jack' Sturges led Leicester to a 17-0 win. In 1992, the same teams met to celebrate Welford Road's centenary, Leicester winning 40-20.

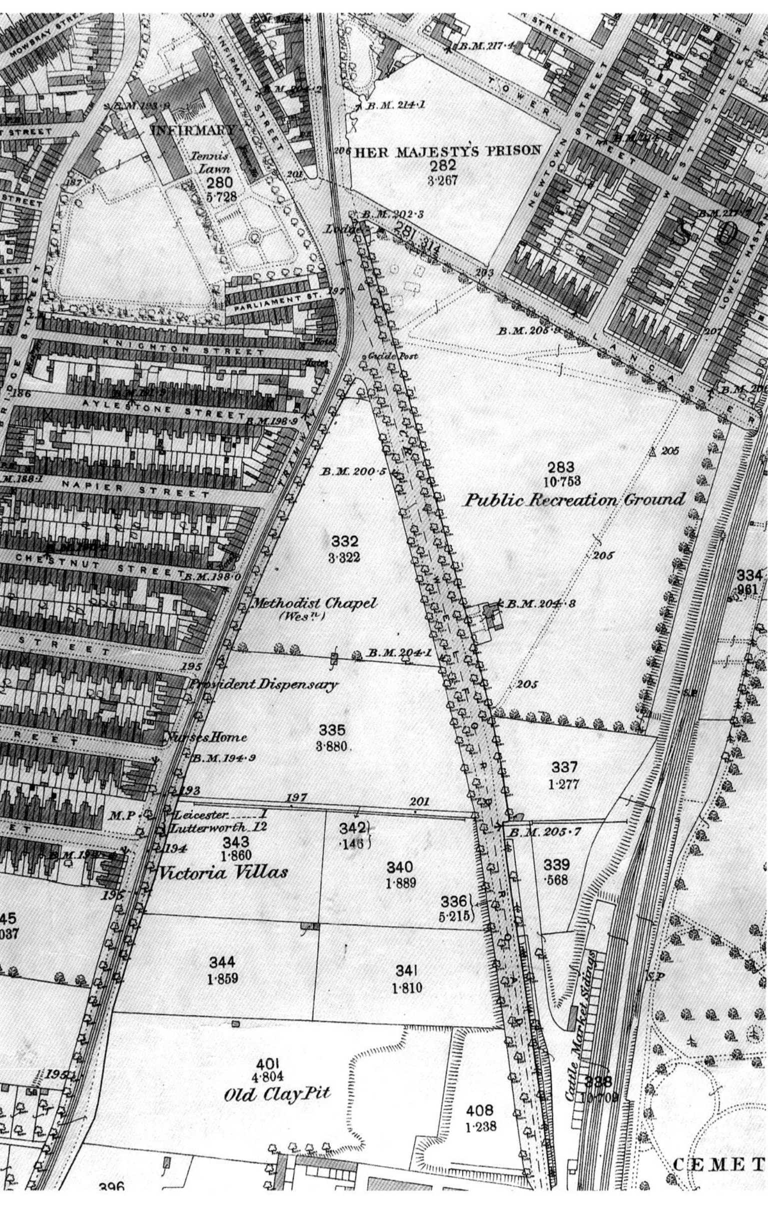

↓ Site of the new Welford Road Ground in 1891.

← LEICESTER FOOTBALL CLUB 1886/87
Back: Morley, Wheeler, Line, Collier (Umpire), B.Wilkinson, Mason, Sheffield.
Middle: McAlpin, Salmon (Vice-capt), Parsons (capt), Porter, Snowden.
Front: Apperley, McKechnie, Lovett, Coleman.

← LEICESTER FOOTBALL CLUB 'A' TEAM 1887/88
Back: Oxlade, Bonner, Nutt, Abell, Knight, Symington (Referee), Hoyle, Howard, Coltman, Massey.
Middle: Ford, Stanyon (Vice-capt), Bell (capt), Burton.
Front: Salmon, Kaye.

← TIGERS v BLACKHEATH
13 February1892
Back: Collier (Touch Judge), Ward, Whitehurst, McKechnie, Barham, Joyce, German, W.Jackson, Edmonds, Wynne, McAlpin (Hon.Sec).
Front: Meek, Ley, W.Watts (Vice-capt), Sturges (capt), Ball, Yorke.

1880/81

1880/81	
Home Ground: Belgrave Cricket and Cycle Ground then Victoria Park in January	
Captain: Alexander Brice	
Vice-captain: John Symington	

OVERALL RECORD:					T	C	PG	DG
PLD	W	D	L	Tigers scored:	21	8	0	2
17	9	5	3	Opponents scored:	15	6	0	1

GM	DATE		VEN	OPPONENTS	RESULT	TRIES	KICKS	ATT
CLUB MATCHES								
1	Oct	**23**	**H**	**Moseley**	D 0-0	-	-	400
2		**30**	**H**	**Leicester Victoria**	W 2g 4t-0	Unknown(6)	Unknown 2c	-
3	Nov	**6**	**H**	**Northampton**	D 0-0	-	-	-
4		13	a	Rushden	L 0-2g 4t	-	-	-
5		**20**	**H**	**Coventry**	W 2t-0	A.Porter, Young	-	-
6		**27**	**H**	**Burton**	D 0-0	-	-	-
7	Dec	4	a	Bedford Rovers	W 1g-1t	Hart	Foster c	-
8		11	a	Moseley	W 1g 1t-0	Unknown(2)	Unknown c	-
9		18	a	Market Harborough	W 1g 3t-0	Hudson, Lovett, Sheen, Young	W.Wheeler c	-
10	Jan	1	a	Rugby Rovers	D 0-0	-	-	-
11		**8**	**H**	**Rushden**	W 1g 1t-0	Coleman, A.Porter	W.Wheeler c	-
12	Feb	**5**	**H**	**Burton Anglesey Rovers**	W 1g 1t-0	Lovett, Watts	W.Wheeler c	-
13		**19**	**H**	**Nuneaton**	W 1g 1t-1t	Brice	Coleman d	-
14		26	a	Kettering	D 1g-1g	Lovett	W.Wheeler c	-
15	Mar	**5**	**H**	**Rugby Rovers**	W 1g-0	-	Parsons d	-
16		**12**	**H**	**Kettering**	L 0-1t	-	-	-
17		26	a	Moseley	L 0-4g 2t	-	-	-

INDIVIDUAL APPEARANCES 1880/81

Name / Game #	1	2	3	4	5	6	7	8	9	10	11	12	13	14	15	16	17	Apps	T	Gls
HJ (Henry) Barwick	-	>F	-	F	-	-	-	-	-	F	-	-	-	-	-	-	-	3	-	-
HS (Henry) Biggs	>F	-	-	-	-	-	-	-	-	-	-	-	FB	-	-	-	<FB	3	-	-
AE (Alexander) Brice	>HB*	-	F*	HB*	F*	F*	F*	-	F*	-	-	-	HB*	HB*	-	HB*	HB*	11	1	-
AI (Arthur) Burford	>F	-	-	-	F	-	-	-	F	F	-	-	-	-	-	F	-	5	-	-
JGS (Sherrard) Coleman	-	>FB	FB	3Q	-	-	3Q	-	-	-	3Q	-	3Q	3Q	3Q	3Q	3Q	10	1	1
WT (William) Coltman	-	-	-	-	-	-	-	-	-	>F	-	F	-	F	-	-	F	4	-	-
D (David) Corby	-	>FB	-	-	-	-	-	-	-	FB	-	FB	-	F	FB	F	-	6	-	-
C (Charles) Duckering	-	-	>HB	-	-	HB	-	-	<HB	-	-	-	-	-	-	-	-	3	-	-
H (Henry) Foreman	-	-	-	-	-	-	-	-	>FB	-	-	<3Q	-	-	-	-	-	2	-	-
HL (Herbert) Foster	>FB	-	FB	FB	FB	FB	FB	-	-	-	-	-	FB	FB	FB	FB	FB	11	-	1
A (Alfred) Gibbons	-	>F	-	-	-	-	-	-	-	-	-	<FB	-	-	-	-	-	2	-	-
JH (John) Gilbert	>F	-	F	-	-	F	-	-	-	-	-	-	F	-	-	-	-	4	-	-
N (Newman) Haddon	-	-	>F	-	F	-	F	-	F	-	<F	-	-	-	-	-	-	5	-	-
TD (Tom) Hart	>3Q	3Q	-	-	-	3Q	HB	-	-	-	<HB	-	-	-	-	-	-	5	1	-
J Hodgson	-	>F	-	-	-	-	-	-	-	-	-	-	-	-	-	<F	-	2	-	-
JA (John) Lakin	-	-	>3Q	-	3Q	-	3Q	-	-	-	-	-	3Q	3Q	HB	-	3Q	7	-	-
JT (Jack) Lovett	>F	-	-	F	F	-	-	-	F	-	-	F	-	F	-	-	F	7	3	-
J (Jack) Parsons	-	-	-	-	-	>F	F	-	-	-	F	-	F	F	F	-	F	7	-	1
Lt. TR (Thomas) Pickering	>F	-	-	F	-	-	-	-	-	-	-	-	-	-	-	-	<F	3	-	-
AT (Arthur) Porter	>3Q	-	-	-	3Q	3Q	3Q	-	-	3Q	3Q	-	-	-	-	-	-	6	2	-
WR (Willie) Porter	>F	-	-	-	-	-	F	-	-	F	-	-	-	-	F	F	-	5	-	-
TH (Thomas) Prentice	-	-	-	-	-	>3Q	-	-	3Q	-	-	3Q	-	-	-	3Q	-	4	-	-
JG (Joseph) Rhodes	-	>F	-	-	-	-	-	-	-	-	-	F	-	-	-	-	-	2	-	-
HW (Hedley) Salmon	-	>F	F	F	-	F	F	-	-	F	F	-	F	F	F	F	-	11	-	-
F (Fred) Sheen	>F	-	F	F	-	F	F	-	F	F	F	-	-	-	-	-	-	8	1	-
WA (William) Sheffield	-	-	>F	F	F	-	-	-	F	-	F	-	F	F	F	F	F	10	-	-
JL (James) Symington	-	-	>F	F	F	F	F	-	-	-	F*	-	F	F	-	-	F	9	-	-
WG (Guy) Taylor	-	-	-	-	>F	-	-	-	-	3Q	-	-	HB	-	-	-	3Q	4	-	-
A (Arthur) Turner	>F	-	F	F	-	F	F	-	-	-	F	-	F	F	F	F	F	11	-	-
CY (Charles) Wainwright	-	-	-	-	-	-	-	-	-	-	-	>F	-	-	-	F	-	2	-	-
A (Arthur) Wale	-	-	-	-	>3Q	-	-	-	3Q	HB	3Q	-	3Q	-	3Q	3Q	-	7	-	-
GJ (George) Walker	-	-	>3Q	-	HB	-	-	-	-	FB	-	HB	-	-	-	-	-	4	-	-
RH (Robert) Warner	-	-	-	>FB	-	-	-	-	-	-	FB	-	F	-	-	-	-	3	-	-
WFK (William) Watts	-	>F	-	>F	-	-	-	-	-	-	-	F	-	-	F	-	-	4	1	-
WA (William) Wheeler	>FB	3Q*	-	3Q	FB	FB	FB	-	FB	-	FB	3Q*	F	HB	HB*	HB	HB	14	-	4
AD (Arthur) Whitehead	-	-	>F	-	F	-	-	-	-	-	F	-	-	F	F	-	-	5	-	-
CE (Edward) Worthington	>F	-	-	-	-	F	-	-	-	-	-	-	-	-	-	-	F	3	-	-
L (Lawrence) Young	>HB	HB	HB	HB	HB	HB	HB	-	HB	-	HB	-	-	-	-	-	-	9	2	-

1 GAME: JR (Joseph) Abell >F(2), WM (William) Barwick =HB(12), TR (Tom) Bosworth =F(12), E (Edwin) Hill >F(12), EA (Edmond) Hudson =Ft(9), JH (James) Langham =F(10), Mason =HB(10), C Nemo =F(15), A (Ally) Nutt >F(2), J (John) Read =F(15), R Reading =F(9), T (Thomas) Robinson >HB(2), B (Benjamin) Shelton =F(2), L Staines >F(10), J Trebley =F(14), FE (Frank) Wheeler =F(12)

1881/82

1881/82	
Home Ground: Victoria Park	
Captain: Alexander Brice then Arthur Porter in September	

OVERALL RECORD:					T	C	PG	DG
PLD	W	D	L	Tigers scored:	19	4	0	2
20	9	2	9	Opponents scored:	34	14	0	1

INDIVIDUAL APPEARANCES 1881/82

Name / Game #	1	2	3	4	5	6	7	8	9	10	11	12	13	14	15	16	17	18	19	20	Apps	T	Gls
JR (Joseph) Abell	FB	-	-	-	-	3Q	-	-	-	-	-	-	-	-	-	-	-	-	-	-	2	-	-
HJ (Henry) Barwick	-	-	F	-	-	F	-	-	-	-	-	-	-	-	-	-	-	-	-	-	2	-	-
AE (Alexander) Brice	-	-	-	-	-	-	-	-	-	-	F	-	-	-	-	-	-	-	-	F	2	1	-
AI (Arthur) Burford	F	F	F	F	F	F	F	F	F	F	-	-	F	F	-	F	-	F	-	-	14	-	-
JGS (Sherrard) Coleman	-	-	-	3Q	-	-	-	-	-	-	-	-	3Q	3Q	-	3Q	-	3Q	3Q	3Q	7	-	-
WT (William) Coltman	-	-	F	F	-	-	-	-	-	-	-	-	-	-	-	-	-	-	-	-	2	-	-
JT (Joshua) Cressey	>F	-	F	F	F	-	-	F	-	-	-	-	-	F	-	F	-	F	F	F	10	1	-
RA (Richard) Edgell	-	-	-	-	-	-	-	-	>F	-	-	-	-	-	-	-	-	-	<F	-	2	1	-
HL (Herbert) Foster	-	-	FB	FB	FB	FB	-	-	3Q	3Q	-	-	3Q	FB	-	3Q	-	3Q	-	-	10	-	1
JH (John) Gilbert	-	-	-	-	3Q	-	FB	FB	FB	FB	-	-	FB	-	-	F	-	-	FB	FB	9	-	-
JA (John) Lakin	HB	HB	HB	HB	HB	HB	HB	HB	HB	HB	-	-	HB	HB	-	HB	-	HB	HB	HB	16	5	-
JT (Jack) Lovett	-	-	-	-	-	-	-	-	-	-	-	-	-	F	-	F	-	-	-	-	2	-	-
KA (Kenneth) Macauley	-	-	>3Q	3Q	3Q	<3Q	-	-	-	-	-	-	-	-	-	-	-	-	-	-	4	-	-
A (Ally) Nutt	-	-	-	-	F	-	-	-	-	F	-	-	-	F	-	-	-	-	-	-	3	-	-
JH (James) Parry	>F	-	-	-	-	-	-	-	-	-	<F	-	-	-	-	-	-	-	-	-	2	-	-
J (Jack) Parsons	FB	-	F	F	-	-	F	3Q	F	HB	-	-	F	F	-	F	-	F	3Q	3Q	13	1	3
AT (Arthur) Porter	-	-	3Q*	-	3Q*	>F	-	-	-	-	-	-	-	-	-	-	-	-	-	-	3	-	-
WR (Willie) Porter	F	-	F	F	-	-	F	F	F	F	-	-	F	-	-	F	-	F	-	F	11	-	-
TH (Thomas) Prentice	-	3Q	-	3Q	-	-	3Q	3Q	-	-	<FB	-	-	-	-	-	-	-	-	-	5	-	-
HW (Hedley) Salmon	F	F	-	-	-	-	-	-	F	F	F	-	F	-	-	F	-	F	F	F	10	-	-
WA (William) Sheffield	-	-	F	F	F	F	F	F	F	F	F	-	F	F	F	F	-	F	F	F	16	4	-
WM Smith	-	-	-	-	>F	-	F	F	-	-	-	-	-	-	-	-	-	-	-	-	3	1	-
L Staines	-	-	F	-	-	F	F	-	-	-	<F	-	-	-	-	-	-	-	-	-	4	-	-
W (William) Sully	>3Q	-	-	-	-	-	-	-	-	<3Q	-	-	-	-	-	-	-	-	-	-	2	-	-
JL (James) Symington	-	-	F	F	-	F*	F*	F*	F	-	-	-	F	F	-	F	-	F	F	F	12	2	1
WG (Guy) Taylor	-	-	-	-	HB	-	-	-	-	-	<HB	-	-	-	-	-	-	-	-	-	2	-	-
A (Arthur) Turner	-	-	-	-	-	-	-	-	-	-	F	-	F	-	-	-	-	-	-	F	3	-	-
CY (Charles) Wainwright	-	-	-	F	F	F	F	F	F	F	-	-	-	-	-	-	-	F	F	F	10	-	-
A (Arthur) Wale	-	-	-	-	-	-	3Q	3Q	3Q	3Q	3Q	-	3Q	3Q	3Q	3Q	-	3Q	3Q	3Q	12	1	1
WFK (William) Watts	F	-	-	-	<F	-	-	-	-	-	-	-	-	-	-	-	-	-	-	-	2	-	-
WA (William) Wheeler	-	-	-	-	-	-	-	-	-	-	-	-	-	-	-	FB	-	FB	-	-	2	-	-
AD (Arthur) Whitehead	F	-	-	F	-	F	-	F	-	-	-	-	F	F	-	-	-	F	F	-	8	1	-
CE (Edward) Worthington	F*	F	F	-	F	-	-	-	F	-	-	-	-	F	-	-	-	-	-	F	7	-	-
L (Lawrence) Young	-	-	HB	HB*	-	HB	HB	HB	HB*	-	-	-	HB*	HB*	-	HB*	-	HB*	HB*	HB*	12	1	-

1 GAME: Bodycote =HB(11), W (William) Colver >F(10), D (David) Corby <F(5), Crane =3Q(11), FWT (Fred) Dance =3Q(6), T Gray =F(11), Gurney >F(11), Holyoak =F(11), H (Henry) James =F(1), J Lang =F(7), H (Hugh) Lawson =F(19), FG (Frederick) McMurray =3Q(9), W (William) Massey >F(19), JG (Joseph) Rhodes <F(6), Seale =F(10), F (Fred) Sheen <3Q(14), EM (Ted) Smith =3Q(1), GJ (George) Walker <HB(1), RH (Robert) Warner FB(11)

GM	DATE		VEN	OPPONENTS	RESULT	TRIES	KICKS	ATT
MIDLAND COUNTIES CUP						**CUP WINNERS: MOSELEY**		
3	Oct	22	a	Edgbaston Crusaders (1)	L 0-1g 2t	-	-	-
CLUB MATCHES								
1	Oct	8	a	Moseley	L 0-3g 4t	-	-	-
2		**15**	**H**	**Burton**	L 0-3g 2t	-	-	-
4		**29**	**H**	**Rugby**	L 0-1g	-	-	-
5	Nov	5	a	Kettering	D 0-0 (Abandoned)	-	-	-
6		**12**	**H**	**Coventry**	W 1g-0	Lakin	Foster c	-
7		19	a	Nuneaton	W 1g 1t-0	W.Smith, Young	Parsons c	-
8		**26**	**H**	**Leamington Rovers**	W 1g 1t-0	Lakin, Sheffield	Parsons c	-
	Dec	3	a	Handsworth	PP			
9		**10**	**H**	**Edgbaston Crusaders**	W 2t-0	Edgell, Sheffield	-	-
10		17	a	Rugby Rovers	W 1t-0	Parsons	-	-
		24	**H**	**Narborough**	PP			
11	Jan	7	a	Rugby	L 0-3g 5t	-	-	-
12		14	a	Hinckley	L 0-1g 2t	-	-	-
13		21	a	Rugby Rovers	L 1t-1g	Lakin	-	200
14		**28**	**H**	**Kettering**	W 1g 1t-0	Whitehead	Symington d	-
15	Feb	4	a	Coventry	L 1g 1t-1g 2t	Sheffield	Wale d	-
16		11	a	Edgbaston Crusaders	W 2t-0	Cressey, Lakin	-	-
17		**18**	**H**	**Rushden**	D 0-0	-	-	-
18		**25**	**H**	**Moseley**	L 0-3t	-	-	-
19	Mar	4	a	Burton	W 4t-0	Symington(2), Sheffield, Wale	-	-
20		18	a	Rushden	W 1g 1t-1g	Brice, Lakin	Parsons c	-

The key for how to read the stats is on the last page

18 82/83	Home Ground: Belgrave Cricket and Cycle Ground	OVERALL RECORD:					T	C	PG	DG
	Captain: Lawrence Young	PLD	W	D	L	Tigers scored:	24	6	0	3
	Vice-captain: Jack Parsons	14	8	2	4	Opponents scored:	12	5	0	1

GM	DATE		VEN	OPPONENTS	RESULT	TRIES	KICKS	ATT
MIDLAND COUNTIES CUP						**CUP WINNERS: BURTON**		
3	Oct	28	a	Moseley (2)	L 0-2g 1t	-	-	-
CLUB MATCHES								
1	Oct	**7**	**H**	**Kettering**	W 1g 1t-0	Lakin, Young	Parsons c	-
2		**21**	**H**	**Bedford School**	W 2t-0	Sheffield, Wale	-	-
4	Nov	**4**	**H**	**Edgbaston Crusaders**	W 2g 1t-0	Unknown, Warner	Unknown c, Parsons d	-
5		11	a	Coventry	D 0-0	-	-	-
6		**18**	**H**	**Rugby**	L 0-2g	-	-	-
7		**25**	**H**	**Leicester Victoria**	W 4t-0	Unknown(3), Craven	-	-
8	Dec	**2**	**H**	**Burton**	W 1g 3t-1g 1t	Unknown(2), Nutt	Parsons d	-
9		9	a	Stamford	W 5g 2t-1t	Parsons, Cressey, Sheffield, Symington, Turner, Young	Parsons 4c, Cressey d	-
		16	**H**	**Rushden**	PP			
10	Jan	**13**	**H**	**Northampton**	L 0-1g 2t	-	-	-
11		**20**	**H**	**Coventry**	W 3t-0	Cressey, Sheffield, Smith	-	-
12		**27**	**H**	**Rushden**	D 1t-1t	Unknown	-	-
	Feb	**3**	**H**	**Edgbaston Crusaders**	PP			
13		10	a	Bedford School	W 1t-0	Young	-	-
14		24	a	Rushden	L 0-1t	-	-	-
	Mar	3	a	Northampton	PP			
		17	**H**	**Moseley**	PP			

INDIVIDUAL APPEARANCES 1882/83

Name / Game #	1	2	3	4	5	6	7	8	9	10	11	12	13	14	Apps	T	Gls
JR (Joseph) Abell	-	-	-	FB	-	-	3Q	-	-	FB	-	-	-	F	4	-	-
HJ (Henry) Barwick	-	-	-	-	-	-	-	-	-	<3Q	-	-	-	-	1	-	-
WM (William) Barwick	-	-	-	-	-	F	HB	-	-	<3Q	-	-	-	-	3	-	-
BC Bloxham	-	-	-	-	-	-	-	-	=FB	-	-	-	-	-	1	-	-
AI (Arthur) Burford	F	F	F	F	-	F	-	F	-	F	F	-	F	-	9	-	-
AP (Alfred) Carryer	=3Q	-	-	-	-	-	-	-	-	-	-	-	-	-	1	-	-
JGS (Sherrard) Coleman	-	-	FB	-	-	-	-	-	-	-	FB	-	-	3Q	3	-	-
WT (William) Coltman	-	-	-	-	-	-	<F	-	-	-	-	-	-	-	1	-	-
W (William) Colver	-	-	-	-	-	-	<F	-	-	-	-	-	-	-	1	-	-
TW (Thomas) Craven	-	-	-	-	-	-	=F	-	-	-	-	-	-	-	1	1	-
JT (Joshua) Cressey	F	F	F	F	F	-	-	F	F	-	F	-	F	F	10	2	1
AGJ (Alfred) Crofts	-	-	-	-	-	-	=F	-	-	-	-	-	-	-	1	-	-
FG (Frederick) Cross	-	-	-	-	-	-	-	-	-	>F	-	-	-	-	1	-	-
HL (Herbert) Foster	FB	3Q	3Q	3Q	-	3Q	-	FB	-	HB	3Q	-	FB	-	9	-	-
F (Fred) Geeson	-	-	-	-	-	-	=F	-	-	-	-	-	-	-	1	-	-
J (John) Gibson	-	-	-	-	-	-	=F	-	-	-	-	-	-	-	1	-	-
JH (John) Gilbert	F	-	-	-	-	-	-	-	-	-	-	-	-	-	1	-	-
Gurney	-	-	-	-	-	-	<F	-	-	-	-	-	-	-	1	-	-
Hayes	-	-	-	-	-	-	>3Q	-	-	<F	-	-	-	-	2	-	-
E (Edwin) Hill	-	-	-	-	-	-	<HB	-	-	-	-	-	-	-	1	-	-
JW (James) Horner	-	-	-	-	-	-	>3Q	-	-	<HB	-	-	-	-	2	-	-
FJ (Francis) Hudson	-	-	-	-	-	-	-	-	-	-	>F	-	F	<F	3	-	-
J Jelly	-	-	-	-	-	-	-	-	-	=F	-	-	-	-	1	-	-
Kenny	-	-	-	-	-	-	-	-	-	=F	-	-	-	-	1	-	-
JA (John) Lakin	HB	HB	HB	-	-	-	-	<3Q	-	-	-	-	-	-	4	1	-
JT (Jack) Lovett	-	F	-	-	-	-	-	-	-	-	-	-	-	-	1	-	-
A (Arthur) McKechnie	-	-	-	-	>FB	-	FB	-	-	F	-	-	-	-	2	-	-
JR (Jack) Marston	-	-	-	-	-	-	=F	-	-	-	-	-	-	-	1	-	-
W (William) Massey	-	-	-	-	-	-	-	-	-	F	-	-	-	-	1	-	-
A (Ally) Nutt	F	F	F	HB	HB	HB	-	HB	-	-	HB	-	HB	HB	10	1	-
J (Jack) Parsons	3Q	3Q	3Q	3Q	3Q	3Q	-	3Q	3Q	-	3Q*	-	3Q	3Q	11	1	7
WR (Willie) Porter	-	F	F	F	F	F	F	F	F	-	-	-	F	F	10	-	-
HW (Hedley) Salmon	F	F	F	F	F	F	-	F	F	-	F	-	F	F	11	-	-
JW (John) Sellers	-	-	-	-	-	-	-	=F	-	-	-	-	-	-	1	-	-
WA (William) Sheffield	F	F	F	F	F	F	-	F	HB	-	F	-	HB	HB	11	3	-
Sheppard	-	-	-	-	-	-	-	-	-	-	=HB	-	-	-	1	-	-
WM Smith	-	-	-	-	-	F	-	-	-	F	F	-	F	F	5	1	-
JL (James) Symington	F	F	F	F	F	F	-	F	F	-	F	-	-	F	10	1	-
A (Arthur) Turner	F	F	F	F	F	F	-	-	F	-	F	-	F	F	10	1	-
E Tyler	-	-	-	-	>3Q	F	-	F	HB	-	-	-	F	F	6	-	-
CY (Charles) Wainwright	-	-	-	F	F	F	-	F	-	-	F	-	F	-	6	-	-
A (Arthur) Wale	3Q	3Q	3Q	3Q	3Q	-	-	3Q	-	-	3Q	-	3Q	FB	9	1	-
RH (Robert) Warner	-	FB	-	F	-	FB	-	-	-	-	-	-	-	-	3	1	-
W Warren	=F	-	-	-	-	-	-	-	-	-	-	-	-	-	1	-	-
CE (Edward) Worthington	-	-	F	-	-	-	-	-	F	-	-	-	-	-	2	-	-
L (Lawrence) Young	HB*	HB*	HB*	HB*	HB*	HB*	-	HB*	3Q*	-	-	-	3Q*	3Q*	10	3	-

18 83/84	Home Ground: Victoria Park	OVERALL RECORD:					T	C	PG	DG
	Captain: Sherrard Coleman	PLD	W	D	L	Tigers scored:	35	12	0	5
	Vice-captain: Joshua Cressey	22	14	3	5	Opponents scored:	22	9	0	0

INDIVIDUAL APPEARANCES 1883/84

Name / Game #	1	2	3	4	5	6	7	8	9	10	11	12	13	14	15	16	17	18	19	20	21	22	Apps	T	Gls
JR (Joseph) Abell	F	F	F	-	-	F	F	F	F	F	F	-	-	F	-	-	-	-	-	-	-	F	11	-	-
WJ (Walter) Anson	-	>F	F	F	F	F	F	F	F	F	F	F	-	-	F	F	F	F	-	F	-	-	16	1	-
AE (Alexander) Brice	-	-	-	-	-	-	-	-	-	-	-	-	F	-	-	-	-	-	-	-	-	F	2	-	-
AI (Arthur) Burford	-	-	-	-	F	F	-	-	-	F	-	F	F	F	F	F	F	-	-	F	-	-	10	-	-
JGS (Sherrard) Coleman	3Q*	3Q*	3Q*	3Q*	3Q*	3Q*	3Q*	3Q*	3Q*	-	3Q*	3Q*	3Q*	3Q*	3Q*	-	3Q*	3Q*	-	3Q*	3Q*	3Q*	19	5	2
TA Cook	=3Q	-	-	-	-	-	-	-	-	-	-	-	-	-	-	-	-	-	-	-	-	-	1	-	-
JT (Joshua) Cressey	F	F	F	F	F	F	F	-	F	F*	-	F	F	F	F	F*	F	F	-	F	F	F	19	1	-
FG (Frederick) Cross	F	-	-	-	-	-	-	F	-	-	-	-	F	3Q	-	-	-	-	-	-	F	F	6	-	-
C Dickinson	-	-	-	-	-	-	-	-	-	>HB	F	-	-	-	F	F	3Q	-	-	F	-	-	6	-	-
HL (Herbert) Foster	-	-	-	-	-	-	3Q	HB	HB	-	-	-	HB	HB	HB	HB	HB	HB	-	HB	HB	HB	12	2	3
WW (William) Judd	-	-	-	>F	-	F	-	-	F	-	FB	-	F	F	-	-	F	F	-	-	F	F	10	-	-
JT (Jack) Lovett	F	F	F	F	F	F	F	F	F	F	-	F	F	F	F	F	F	F	-	F	F	F	20	6	-
A (Arthur) McKechnie	-	-	-	-	-	-	FB	FB	FB	FB	-	FB	FB	FB	FB	FB	FB	FB	-	FB	FB	FB	14	-	3
A (Ally) Nutt	HB	HB	HB	3Q	3Q	3Q	HB	-	3Q	3Q	3Q	HB	-	-	-	-	-	-	-	-	-	-	11	8	-
J (Jack) Parsons	3Q	3Q	3Q	3Q	3Q	-	-	3Q	-	3Q	3Q	3Q	-	-	3Q	3Q	-	-	-	3Q	3Q	-	13	1	9
AT (Arthur) Porter	-	-	-	-	-	-	-	-	-	-	-	-	-	-	3Q	3Q	-	3Q	-	3Q	-	3Q	5	-	-
SG (Samuel) Porter	-	-	-	-	-	-	-	-	-	-	>F	-	F	F	-	-	-	F	-	-	-	F	5	-	-
WR (Willie) Porter	F	F	F	F	F	F	F	F	F	F	F	F	F	F	F	F	F	-	-	F	F	-	19	-	-
Rev. TG (Thomas) Ridley	-	-	-	-	-	-	-	-	-	-	-	-	=3Q	-	-	-	-	-	-	-	-	-	1	-	-
HW (Hedley) Salmon	F	F	F	F	F	-	F	F	-	F	F	F	F	F	F	F	F	-	-	-	F	F	17	-	-
WA (William) Sheffield	F	HB	HB	HB	HB	HB	HB	HB	HB	HB	HB	HB	HB	HB	HB	HB	HB	HB	-	HB	HB	HB	21	5	-
JL (James) Symington	-	F	F	F	HB	HB	F	F	F	F	F	F	-	-	F	F	F	F	-	F	F	<F	18	2	-
CY (Charles) Wainwright	F	F	F	F	F	F	F	F	F	F	F	<F	-	-	-	-	-	-	-	-	-	-	12	1	-
A (Arthur) Wale	-	FB	FB	FB	FB	3Q	3Q	3Q	3Q	3Q	3Q	3Q	3Q	3Q	3Q	3Q	-	3Q	-	3Q	3Q	3Q	19	1	-
RH (Robert) Warner	FB	-	-	-	F	<FB	-	-	-	-	-	-	-	-	-	-	-	-	-	-	-	-	3	-	-
AD (Arthur) Whitehead	F	F	F	F	F	F	F	F	F	-	-	F	-	F	-	F	F	F	-	F	-	-	15	1	-
L (Lawrence) Young	HB	3Q	3Q	HB	-	-	-	-	-	-	HB	-	-	-	-	-	-	-	-	-	-	-	5	-	-

GM	DATE		VEN	OPPONENTS	RESULT	TRIES	KICKS	ATT
MIDLAND COUNTIES CUP						**CUP WINNERS: MOSELEY**		
3	Oct	20	a	Stafford (1)	W 2g 6t-0	Nutt(5), Anson, Cressey, Symington	Parsons 2c	-
4		27	a	Rushden (2)	D 0-0	-	-	-
12	Jan	**12**	**H**	**Rushden (2-replay)**	D 1t-1t	Wale	-	2000
16	Feb	16	a	Rushden (2-2nd replay)	W 1t-0	Lovett	-	2000
20	Mar	15	a	Moseley (3)	L 1t-1g	Foster	-	-
CLUB MATCHES								
1	Oct	6	a	Moseley	L 0-3g 2t	-	-	-
2		**13**	**H**	**Rugby**	W 1g 2t-0	Lovett, Nutt, Sheffield	Parsons c	-
		22	a	South Warwickshire Rovers	PP (did not turn up)			
5	Nov	**3**	**H**	**Burton**	W 3g 1t-0	Nutt, Sheffield	Parsons c/d, Coleman d	-
6		10	a	Kettering	L 1t-1g 1t	Lovett	-	-
		17	**H**	**Bedford Rovers**	PP (rain)			
7		24	a	Bedford School	W 1g-1t	Wainwright	Foster c	-
8	Dec	**1**	**H**	**Coventry**	W 1t-0	Parsons	-	1000
9		**8**	**H**	**Derby Wanderers**	W 1g 2t-1t	Coleman, Nutt, Sheffield	Foster c	-
10		15	a	Rugby	W 1g-1t	Lovett	Parsons c	-
		22	**H**	**Bedford Rovers**	PP			
11		**29**	**H**	**South Warwickshire Rovers**	W 2g-1g	Coleman	Parsons c/d	-
13	Jan	19	a	Coventry	L 0-2g 3t	-	-	-
14		26	a	Bedford Rovers	W 1t-0	Sheffield	-	-
	Feb	2	a	Coventry	PP			
15		**9**	**H**	**Kettering**	W 1g-0 (Abandoned)	Coleman	Parsons c	-
17		23	a	Burton	D 1t-1t	Symington	-	-
18	Mar	**1**	**H**	**Bedford School**	L 1g-1g 1t	Whitehead	McKechnie c	-
19		**8**	**H**	**Rushden**	W 1t-0	Unknown	-	-
21		22	a	South Warwickshire Rovers	W 1g 1t-0	Lovett	Foster d	-
22		29	a	Derby Wanderers	W 3g 3t-1t	Coleman(2), Foster, Lovett, Sheffield	Coleman d, McKechnie 2c	-

The key for how to read the stats is on the last page

1884/85

1884/85		OVERALL RECORD:					T	C	PG	DG
Home Ground: Victoria Park										
Captain: Sherrard Coleman		PLD	W	D	L	Tigers scored:	14	6	0	6
Vice-captain: Joshua Cressey		18	8	1	9	Opponents scored:	19	6	0	1

GM	DATE		VEN	OPPONENTS	RESULT	TRIES	KICKS	ATT
MIDLAND COUNTIES CUP						**CUP WINNERS: MOSELEY**		
2	Oct	18	a	Moseley Woodstock (1)	W 1g-1t	Coleman	Parsons c	-
3		**25**	**H**	**Burton (2)**	W 2g-1t	-	Coleman d, Parsons d	3000
18	Mar	21	a	Moseley (3)	L 0-2g 2t	-	-	-
CLUB MATCHES								
1	Oct	**11**	**H**	**Moseley**	W 3g 1t-0	McAlpin(2), Coleman	Coleman d, Parsons 2c	-
4	Nov	1	a	Derby County	L 1t-2t	Wale	-	-
5		**8**	**H**	**Nottingham**	W 1g 2t-0	Coleman, W.Sheffield, Wale	Parsons c	2000
6		**15**	**H**	**Rushden**	L 1t-1g	W.Sheffield	-	-
7		22	a	Bedford School	W 2g-0	-	Coleman d, Parsons d	-
8		29	a	Coventry	L 1t-1g 1t	W.Sheffield	-	-
	Dec	**6**	**H**	**Burton**	PP			
9		13	a	Rugby	L 0-1t	-	-	-
10		20	a	Nottingham	L 0-1t	-	-	-
11		**27**	**H**	**Bedford Swifts**	W 1g-0	Wale	Parsons c	1500
	Jan	**10**	**H**	**Derby County**	PP			
12		**17**	**H**	**Rugby**	W 1g 1t-0	A.Porter	Coleman d	2000
13	Feb	14	a	Burton	W 1g-1t	W.Sheffield	McKechnie c	-
14		**21**	**H**	**Bedford School**	L 0-1g	-	-	-
15		28	a	Rushden	D 0-0	-	-	-
16	Mar	7	a	Moseley	L 0-3t	-	-	-
17		**14**	**H**	**Leicester Past XV**	L 1t-2g	Unknown	-	-

INDIVIDUAL APPEARANCES 1884/85

Name / Game #	1	2	3	4	5	6	7	8	9	10	11	12	13	14	15	16	17	18	Apps	T	Gls
JR (Joseph) Abell	F	-	-	F	F	F	F	F	F	-	-	-	-	-	F	-	-	-	8	-	-
Addison	-	-	-	-	-	-	-	=3Q	-	-	-	-	-	-	-	-	-	-	1	-	-
WJ (Walter) Anson	-	-	-	-	-	-	-	-	-	-	-	-	-	<F	-	-	-	-	1	-	-
E (Dickie) Bell	-	-	-	-	-	-	-	-	-	-	-	-	-	-	>F	-	-	-	1	-	-
AE (Alexander) Brice	F	-	-	-	-	F	-	-	-	F	-	-	-	-	-	-	-	-	3	-	-
S (Stanley) Broadbent	-	-	-	-	>F	F	-	-	F	-	F	F	F	F	F	F	-	F	10	-	-
AI (Arthur) Burford	F	F	F	F	F	F	F	<F	-	-	-	-	-	-	-	-	-	-	8	-	-
C Clarke	-	-	-	-	-	-	-	-	-	-	-	-	-	-	-	>FB	-	-	1	-	-
JGS (Sherrard) Coleman	3Q*	3Q*	3Q*	-	3Q*	3Q*	3Q*	3Q*	3Q*	3Q*	3Q*	HB*	3Q*	3Q*	-	-	-	3Q*	14	3	4
JT (Joshua) Cressey	F	-	F	F	F	F	F	F	F	F	-	F	-	-	F	F	-	F	13	-	-
FG (Frederick) Cross	-	F	-	-	-	F	<F	-	-	-	-	-	-	-	-	-	-	-	3	-	-
C Dickinson	3Q	3Q	<F	-	-	-	-	-	-	-	-	-	-	-	-	-	-	-	3	-	-
HL (Herbert) Foster	HB	HB	HB	-	-	-	3Q	HB	HB	-	-	-	HB	-	-	-	-	<HB	8	-	-
JH Gibbs	-	-	-	-	-	-	-	-	-	=F	-	-	-	-	-	-	-	-	1	-	-
JH (John) Gilbert	-	-	-	-	-	-	-	-	-	-	<F	-	-	-	-	-	-	-	1	-	-
R Harvey	-	-	-	-	=F	-	-	-	-	-	-	-	-	-	-	-	-	-	1	-	-
WW (William) Judd	-	F	-	3Q	-	-	<F	-	-	-	-	-	-	-	-	-	-	-	3	-	-
A (Arthur) Loveday	-	-	-	=F	-	-	-	-	-	-	-	-	-	-	-	-	-	-	1	-	-
JT (Jack) Lovett	F	F	F	F	F	F	F	F	F	F	F	F	F	F	F	F	-	F	17	-	-
K (Kenneth) McAlpin	>F	F	F	F	F	F	HB	-	F	F	F	F	F	F	F	F	-	F	16	2	-
A (Arthur) McKechnie	FB	FB	FB	FB	FB	FB	FB	FB	FB	FB	-	FB	FB	FB	3Q	HB	-	FB	16	-	1
J Meekin	-	-	-	-	-	-	-	-	>F	-	<HB	-	-	-	-	-	-	-	2	-	-
E Neild	-	-	-	-	-	-	-	>F	-	-	-	-	-	-	-	-	-	-	1	-	-
A (Ally) Nutt	-	-	-	-	-	-	-	-	-	HB	F	-	-	-	-	-	-	-	2	-	-
J (Jack) Parsons	3Q	3Q	3Q	-	3Q	3Q	3Q	3Q	3Q	3Q	3Q	3Q	-	3Q	-	-	-	3Q	13	-	7
CJ Pearce	-	-	-	-	-	-	>F	<F	-	-	-	-	-	-	-	-	-	-	2	-	-
AT (Arthur) Porter	-	-	3Q	-	-	-	-	-	-	-	-	3Q	3Q	3Q	3Q	3Q	-	3Q	7	1	-
SG (Samuel) Porter	-	-	-	F	F	-	F	-	-	F	F	F	F	F	F	F	-	-	10	-	-
WR (Willie) Porter	F	F	F	-	F	F	-	F	F	F	F	F	F	F	-	F	-	F	14	-	-
HW (Hedley) Salmon	F	F	F	F*	HB	HB	F	F	F	F	F	F	F	F	F	F	-	F	17	-	-
JE (Edward) Sheffield	-	-	-	-	-	-	-	-	-	-	>FB	-	-	-	FB	3Q	-	-	3	-	-
WA (William) Sheffield	HB	HB	HB	HB	HB	HB	HB	HB	HB	HB	HB	HB	HB	HB	HB*	HB*	-	HB	17	4	-
WM Smith	-	-	-	-	-	-	-	-	F	F	F	F	F	F	F	F	-	F	9	-	-
E Tyler	-	-	-	-	-	-	-	-	-	-	-	-	-	-	<HB	-	-	-	1	-	-
A (Arthur) Wale	3Q	3Q	3Q	3Q	3Q	3Q	-	3Q	3Q	3Q	3Q	3Q	3Q	HB	3Q	3Q	-	3Q	16	3	-
WH (William) Watson	-	-	-	=3Q	-	-	-	-	-	-	-	-	-	-	-	-	-	-	1	-	-
WA (William) Wheeler	-	-	-	3Q	-	-	-	-	-	-	-	-	-	-	-	-	-	-	1	-	-
AD (Arthur) Whitehead	-	-	F	-	-	-	-	-	-	-	-	F	-	F	-	F	-	<F	5	-	-
L (Lawrence) Young	-	-	-	<HB	-	-	-	-	-	-	-	-	-	-	-	-	-	-	1	-	-

1885/86

1885/86	OVERALL RECORD:					T	C	PG	DG	MK
Home Ground: Victoria Park										
Captain: William Sheffield	PLD	W	D	L	Tigers scored:	17	5	0	1	0
	15	8	2	5	Opponents scored:	14	8	0	2	1

INDIVIDUAL APPEARANCES 1885/86

Name / Game #	1	2	3	4	5	6	7	8	9	10	11	12	13	14	15	Apps	T	Gls
JR (Joseph) Abell	F	-	-	-	-	-	-	-	F	-	-	-	F	F	F	5	-	-
Allinson	-	-	-	-	=F	-	-	-	-	-	-	-	-	-	-	1	-	-
E (Dickie) Bell	-	-	-	-	-	-	HB	HB	HB	F	HB	HB	HB	HB	-	8	-	-
Benson	-	-	-	-	-	>3Q	<3Q	-	-	-	-	-	-	-	-	2	-	-
Dr. T (Tom) Birkett	-	-	-	-	-	-	-	-	>F	-	F	F	-	-	<F	4	1	-
FR (Frederick) Bonner	-	-	-	-	-	-	-	-	-	-	>F	-	-	-	-	1	-	-
AE (Alexander) Brice	-	-	-	-	HB	F	-	-	-	-	-	-	-	-	-	2	-	-
S (Stanley) Broadbent	F	-	F	-	-	F	F	F	-	-	-	-	<F	-	-	6	-	-
JGS (Sherrard) Coleman	-	-	-	-	-	-	-	-	-	-	-	3Q	3Q	3Q	3Q	4	1	-
Flinn	-	-	-	-	-	-	-	-	-	-	-	-	-	-	=3Q	1	-	-
G Friend	>3Q	-	3Q	3Q	-	-	3Q	3Q	3Q	-	-	-	<3Q	-	-	7	1	-
C (Charles) Fuller	-	-	>F	-	-	-	-	-	-	-	-	-	-	-	-	1	-	-
TS (Tom) Gordon	>F	-	-	-	-	-	-	-	F	-	F	F	-	F	-	5	-	-
King	-	-	-	-	-	-	-	-	-	-	>F	-	-	<F	-	2	-	-
W Leakey	-	-	-	-	-	>3Q	3Q	-	-	3Q	3Q	3Q	-	-	<3Q	6	2	-
le Manco	-	-	-	-	-	-	-	-	-	-	=3Q	-	-	-	-	1	-	1
E Line	-	-	>F	F	F	F	F	F	F	-	F	F	F	F	F	12	-	-
JT (Jack) Lovett	F	-	F	F	F	F	F	F	F	F	F	F	F	F	F	14	-	-
K (Kenneth) McAlpin	F	-	F	-	-	-	-	-	-	F	F	F	F	F	F	8	1	-
A (Arthur) McKechnie	FB	-	FB	FB	3Q	FB	FB	FB	-	FB	-	-	FB	FB	FB	11	-	1
ER (Joey) Morley	-	-	-	-	>F	-	-	-	F	-	F	F	-	-	F	5	-	-
Myrtle	-	-	-	-	-	-	-	-	-	-	=FB	-	-	-	-	1	-	-
FS (Frank) Noon	>3Q	-	<3Q	-	-	-	-	-	-	-	-	-	-	-	-	2	2	-
A (Ally) Nutt	HB	-	HB	HB	-	F	F	F	-	F	-	-	-	-	-	7	-	-
J (Jack) Parsons	3Q	-	-	3Q	3Q	3Q	3Q	3Q	3Q	3Q	-	3Q	3Q	3Q	3Q	12	2	3
SG (Samuel) Porter	F	-	-	F	F	-	-	-	-	-	-	-	-	-	-	3	-	-
WR (Willie) Porter	F	-	F	F	F	F	F	F	F	F	-	F	-	F	F	12	-	-
H (Hugh) Rotherham	-	-	-	-	-	-	-	-	-	=HB	-	-	-	-	-	1	-	-
HW (Hedley) Salmon	F	-	F	F	F	F	F	F	-	F	-	-	F	F	-	10	-	-
PG (Percy) Salmon	-	-	-	-	>FB	-	-	-	-	-	-	-	-	-	-	1	-	-
JE (Edward) Sheffield	-	-	-	-	3Q	-	-	-	<3Q	-	-	-	-	-	-	2	-	-
WA (William) Sheffield	HB*	-	HB*	HB*	HB*	HB*	HB*	HB*	HB*	HB*	HB*	HB*	HB*	HB*	HB*	14	1	-
J Smith	-	-	-	-	-	-	-	-	-	=3Q	-	-	-	-	-	1	-	-
WM Smith	F	-	F	F	F	F	F	F	F	F	-	F	F	-	-	11	-	-
HG (Harry) Topham	-	-	-	>F	-	HB	-	-	-	-	-	-	-	-	<HB	3	-	-
A (Arthur) Wale	-	-	3Q	3Q	-	3Q	-	3Q	<3Q	-	-	-	-	-	-	5	-	-
WA (William) Wheeler	-	-	-	-	-	-	-	3Q	FB	-	3Q	FB	-	3Q	-	5	-	-
B Wilkinson	-	-	>F	F	F	-	F	F	-	F	F	F	F	F	F	11	1	-
CE (Edward) Worthington	-	-	-	-	-	-	-	-	-	F	-	-	<F	-	-	2	-	-

GM	DATE		VEN	OPPONENTS	RESULT	TRIES	KICKS	ATT
MIDLAND COUNTIES CUP						**CUP WINNERS: MOSELEY**		
	Mar	13	a	Coventry (2)	PP (snow)			
15		20	a	Coventry (2)	L 0-1g	-	-	-
CLUB MATCHES								
1	Oct	**10**	**H**	**Moseley Woodstock**	W 2g 1t-0	Noon(2), McAlpin	Parsons 2c	-
2		**17**	**H**	**Lutterworth**	L 0-2g	-	-	-
3		**24**	**H**	**Rushden**	W 1g 1t-1t	Unknown(2)	Unknown c	-
4		**31**	**H**	**Burton**	W 1g 2t-0	Parsons, Wilkinson	Parsons d	-
5	Nov	7	a	Rugby	L 0-3g 1t	-	-	-
6		**14**	**H**	**Coventry**	W 1t-0	Leakey	-	-
7		21	a	Bedford School	W 1t-0	Leakey	-	-
8		**28**	**H**	**Nottingham**	W 1g-0	Parsons	McKechnie c	2000
	Dec	**12**	**H**	**Bedford School**	PP (frost)			
9		**26**	**H**	**Moseley**	L 0-2g 1t	-	-	4000
10	Jan	16	a	Nottingham	D 0-0	-	-	-
		23	**H**	**Kettering**	PP (frost)			
11		30	a	Burton	L 1g-2g 2t	Birkett	le Manco c	-
12	Feb	**6**	**H**	**Bedford Swifts**	W 4t-0	Unknown(3), W.Sheffield	-	2000
13		**20**	**H**	**Rugby**	W 1t-0	Friend	-	-
14		27	a	Rushden	D 1t-1t	Coleman	-	-
	Mar	**6**	**H**	**Leicester Past XV**	PP (frost)			

The key for how to read the stats is on the last page

18	86/87	Home Ground: Victoria Park	OVERALL RECORD:					T	C	PG	DG	PTS
		Captain: Jack Parsons	PLD	W	D	L	Tigers scored:	39	19	0	4	89
		Vice-captain: Hedley Salmon	17	8	5	4	Opponents scored:	17	9	0	0	35

GM	DATE		VEN	OPPONENTS	RESULT	TRIES	KICKS	ATT
MIDLAND COUNTIES CUP						**CUP WINNERS: MOSELEY**		
15	Mar	12	a	Rugby (sf)	L 0-3 (aet)	-	-	-
CLUB MATCHES								
1	Oct	**9**	**H**	**Town & District XX**	W 11-0	Coleman(2), Morley, Smith	McKechnie 2c, Parsons d	-
2		16	a	Moseley Woodstock	W 17-0	Mason(2), Snowden(2), Apperley, Bonner, Coleman	Parsons 5c	-
3		**23**	**H**	**Moseley**	L 0-4	-	-	-
4		30	a	Rushden	W 15-3	Coleman(2), Apperley, Voce	Parsons 4c, McKechnie d	-
5	Nov	**6**	**H**	**Kettering**	W 4-0	Apperley, McKechnie	Parsons c	-
6		20	a	Coventry	D 0-0	-	-	3000
7		**27**	**H**	**Bedford**	W 10-0	Apperley(2), B.Wilkinson(2), Cressey, Porter	McKechnie c, Parsons c	-
	Dec	**4**	**H**	**Rugby**	PP (frost)			
8		**11**	**H**	**Rushden**	W 2-1	Coleman, Sheffield	-	-
		28tu	**H**	**Rushden**	PP (frost)			
	Jan	1	a	Old Edwardians	PP (fog)			
		8	**H**	**Burton**	PP (snow)			
9		**22**	**H**	**Coventry**	D 3-3	McAlpin	Parsons c	-
10		29	a	Kettering	D 0-0	-	-	-
	Feb	**5**	**H**	**Old Edwardians**	PP			
11		12	a	Bedford	D 0-0	-	-	-
12		19	a	Moseley	L 0-15	-	-	-
13		26	a	Rugby	D 0-0	-	-	-
14	Mar	**5**	**H**	**Moseley Woodstock**	W 11-0	Snowden(3), Parsons, Coleman, J.Wilkinson	Parsons c/d	3000
		19	**H**	**Bedford School**	PP			
16		**26**	**H**	**Nottingham**	W 15-0	Parsons, Coleman, Mason, Morley, Porter, Snowden	Parsons d, McKechnie 3c	-
17	Apr	2	a	Nottingham	L 1-6 (Abandoned)	Apperley	-	-

INDIVIDUAL APPEARANCES 1886/87

Name / Game #	1	2	3	4	5	6	7	8	9	10	11	12	13	14	15	16	17	Apps	T	Pts
JR (Joseph) Abell	-	-	-	-	-	F	F	-	<F	-	-	-	-	-	-	-	-	3	-	-
F (Fred) Apperley	-	>3Q	3Q	3Q	3Q	3Q	3Q	3Q	3Q	3Q	-	3Q	-	3Q	3Q	3Q	<3Q	14	6	6
E (Dickie) Bell	-	-	-	-	-	-	-	-	-	-	FB	-	-	-	-	-	-	1	-	-
FR (Frederick) Bonner	F	F	F	-	-	-	-	-	-	-	-	-	-	-	-	-	-	3	1	1
AE (Alexander) Brice	-	-	-	-	<F	-	-	-	-	-	-	-	-	-	-	-	-	1	-	-
JGS (Sherrard) Coleman	3Q	3Q	3Q	3Q	-	3Q	3Q	3Q	3Q	3Q	-	3Q	3Q	3Q	3Q	3Q	-	14	8	8
JS (Joseph) Collier	-	-	-	-	-	-	-	-	-	-	-	-	=FB	-	-	-	-	1	-	-
JT (Joshua) Cressey	F	F	F	F	F	F	F	F	F	<F	-	-	-	-	-	-	-	10	1	1
TS (Tom) Gordon	-	-	-	F	F	-	-	-	-	-	-	F	<F	-	-	-	-	4	-	-
TF (Thomas) Hoyle	-	-	-	-	>FB	FB	-	FB	FB	FB	-	FB	-	-	-	-	-	6	-	-
E Line	F	-	-	F	F	F	F	F	F	F	-	F	F	-	F	-	-	11	-	-
JT (Jack) Lovett	F	F	F	-	F	-	-	-	F	-	-	-	F	-	F	F	-	8	-	-
K (Kenneth) McAlpin	-	F	F	F	-	F	HB	F	HB	F	-	F	HB	-	F	-	-	11	1	1
A (Arthur) McKechnie	FB	FB	FB	FB	3Q	HB	FB	3Q	-	F	-	-	3Q	FB	3Q	FB	FB	14	1	16
Dr. H (Henry) Mason	>F	F	F	F	F	F	F	F	F	F	F	-	F	F	F	F	-	15	3	3
W (William) Massey	-	-	-	-	-	-	-	-	-	-	-	<F	-	-	-	-	-	1	-	-
ER (Joey) Morley	F	F	F	F	F	F	F	F	F	F	-	F	F	-	F	F	-	14	2	2
HJW (Henry) Oxlade	>3Q	-	-	-	-	-	-	-	-	HB	3Q	HB	-	HB	-	-	-	5	-	-
J (Jack) Parsons	3Q*	3Q*	3Q*	3Q*	3Q*	3Q*	3Q*	3Q*	3Q*	3Q*	3Q*	3Q*	3Q*	3Q*	3Q*	3Q*	-	16	2	37
WR (Willie) Porter	F	F	F	-	F	F	F	-	-	F	-	F	F	-	F	F	-	11	2	2
HW (Hedley) Salmon	-	-	-	-	-	-	F	F	F	F	-	F	F	F	F	-	-	8	-	-
WA (William) Sheffield	HB	HB	HB	HB	-	-	-	HB	-	-	HB	-	-	-	HB	-	-	7	1	1
WM Smith	F	F	F	F	-	-	-	-	-	-	-	-	-	-	-	-	-	4	1	1
RS (Dickie) Snowden	>HB	HB	HB	HB	HB	HB	HB	HB	HB	HB	HB	HB	HB	HB	HB	HB	-	16	6	6
J Voce	-	-	-	>F	HB	F	F	<F	-	-	-	-	-	-	-	-	-	5	1	1
WA (William) Wheeler	-	-	-	-	-	-	-	-	-	-	-	-	3Q	-	FB	-	-	2	-	-
B Wilkinson	F	F	F	-	F	F	F	F	F	-	-	F	F	-	F	-	-	11	2	2
JS Wilkinson	-	-	-	>F	-	-	-	-	-	F	3Q	-	-	F	-	-	-	4	1	1

18	87/88	Home Ground: Victoria Park	OVERALL RECORD:					T	C	PG	DG	PTS
		Captain: Jack Parsons	PLD	W	D	L	Tigers scored:	45	19	0	3	92
		Vice-captain: Hedley Salmon	21	11	3	7	Opponents scored:	20	9	1	2	47

INDIVIDUAL APPEARANCES 1887/88

Name / Game #	1	2	3	4	5	6	7	8	9	10	11	12	13	14	15	16	17	18	19	20	21	Apps	T	Pts
Atkins	-	-	-	-	-	>F	-	-	-	-	-	-	-	-	-	-	-	-	-	-	-	1	-	-
HM (Henry) Barradell	-	-	-	-	-	-	-	-	-	-	>F	F	F	F	F	-	-	<F	-	-	-	6	-	-
JE (Jack) Barradell	-	-	-	-	-	-	-	-	-	-	-	>FB	-	-	-	-	3Q	-	-	-	-	2	-	-
JW (John) Billson	-	-	-	-	-	-	-	-	-	-	-	-	-	-	-	-	-	-	-	-	=F	1	-	-
HH (Harry) Brockbank	>F	-	F	F	F	F	-	F	F	F	F	F	F	3Q	-	F	F	F	F	F	-	17	3	5
BC (Bramwell) Burton	-	-	-	>F	-	-	-	-	-	-	-	-	-	-	-	-	-	-	-	-	-	1	-	-
JGS (Sherrard) Coleman	3Q	3Q	3Q	3Q	3Q	3Q	3Q	3Q	3Q	3Q	3Q	3Q	3Q	-	-	-	-	3Q	3Q	3Q	-	16	7	7
CW (Charles) Ford	-	-	-	-	>3Q	-	-	-	-	-	-	-	-	-	-	-	-	-	-	-	-	1	-	-
C (Charles) Fuller	-	-	-	-	-	-	-	-	-	-	-	-	F	F	F	F	<F	-	-	-	-	5	-	-
RR (Bob) Golding	-	-	-	-	-	-	-	-	-	-	-	>3Q	-	-	3Q	-	-	-	-	-	-	2	-	-
AE (Amos) Greenwell	>3Q	-	-	-	-	-	-	-	-	-	-	-	-	-	-	-	-	-	-	-	-	1	-	-
Griffin	-	-	-	-	-	-	=3Q	-	-	-	-	-	-	-	-	-	-	-	-	-	-	1	-	-
TF (Thomas) Hoyle	-	-	3Q	FB	FB	<FB	-	-	-	-	-	-	-	-	-	-	-	-	-	-	-	4	-	-
CB (Charles) Knight	-	-	-	-	-	-	-	-	-	-	-	>HB	-	-	-	-	-	-	-	-	-	1	-	-
E Line	F	F	F	F	-	-	-	-	-	-	-	-	-	-	-	-	-	-	-	-	-	4	-	-
JT (Jack) Lovett	-	F	F	F	F	F	-	F	F	F	F	F	F	F	F	F	F	F	F	F	-	18	-	-
K (Kenneth) McAlpin	F	F	F	3Q	F	F	-	F	F	F	F	F	F	F	HB	F	F	F	F	F	-	19	1	1
A (Arthur) McKechnie	FB	FB	-	3Q	3Q	3Q	-	FB	FB	FB	-	-	FB	FB	FB	FB	FB	FB	FB	FB	-	16	-	2
J (James) Mansell	-	-	-	-	-	-	-	-	-	-	-	-	-	-	-	>3Q	-	3Q	-	-	-	2	-	-
Dr. H (Henry) Mason	F	F	F	F	F	F	F	F	F	F	F	F	F	F	-	F	F	F	F	F	-	19	1	1
GDM (George) Moore	>F	F	F	F	<F	-	-	-	-	-	-	-	-	-	-	-	-	-	-	-	-	5	-	-
ER (Joey) Morley	F	F	F	F	F	F	-	F	F	F	F	F	F	F	F	F	F	F	F	F	-	19	1	1
HJW (Henry) Oxlade	HB	HB	HB	HB	HB	HB	HB	HB	HB	HB	-	-	HB	HB	HB	HB	HB	HB	HB	HB	-	18	5	14
J (Jack) Parsons	3Q*	3Q*	3Q*	3Q*	3Q*	3Q*	3Q*	3Q*	3Q*	3Q*	HB*	3Q*	3Q*	3Q*	3Q*	3Q*	3Q*	HB*	3Q*	3Q*	3Q*	21	8	36
EV (Edgar) Phillips	-	-	-	-	-	>3Q	3Q	3Q	3Q	3Q	3Q	-	-	3Q	3Q	3Q	3Q	3Q	<3Q	-	-	12	10	10
EH (Ernest) Pilsbury	>3Q	3Q	-	-	-	-	-	-	-	-	HB	HB	3Q	-	-	-	-	-	-	3Q	-	6	1	1
WR (Willie) Porter	-	F	F	-	F	F	-	F	F	F	F	-	F	F	F	F	F	F	F	F	-	16	1	1
HW (Hedley) Salmon	F	F	-	-	-	-	-	F	-	-	F	<F	-	-	-	-	-	-	-	-	-	5	1	1
WA (William) Sheffield	-	-	-	-	-	-	-	-	F	<F	-	-	-	-	-	-	-	-	-	-	-	2	-	-
WM Smith	-	-	-	F	F	-	-	F	F	F	F	F	F	F	F	F	F	F	F	F	-	15	2	2
RS (Dickie) Snowden	HB	HB	HB	HB	HB	HB	HB	HB	HB	HB	-	-	HB	HB	-	HB	HB	-	HB	HB	-	16	1	1
H (Bert) Stanyon	-	-	=FB	-	-	-	-	-	-	-	-	-	-	-	-	-	-	-	-	-	-	1	-	-
A (Arthur) Sulley	-	-	-	-	-	-	-	-	-	-	>3Q	-	-	-	-	-	-	-	-	-	-	1	1	5
WA (William) Wheeler	-	-	-	-	-	-	-	-	-	-	FB	-	-	-	-	-	-	-	-	-	-	1	-	-
B Wilkinson	-	-	-	-	-	-	F	-	-	-	-	-	-	F	-	-	F	-	F	F	-	5	2	2
JS Wilkinson	-	-	-	-	-	F	-	F	F	F	-	-	-	-	F	F	-	F	F	F	-	9	-	-
AE (Mamma) Wright	>F	F	F	-	-	-	-	-	-	-	-	3Q	-	-	<F	-	-	-	-	-	-	5	-	-

GM	DATE		VEN	OPPONENTS	RESULT	TRIES	KICKS	ATT
MIDLAND COUNTIES CUP						**CUP WINNERS: BURTON**		
	Mar	**17**	**H**	**Stoke-on-Trent (3)**	PP			
20		**24**	**H**	**Burton (sf)**	D 0-0	-	-	-
Note: *#20 Burton progressed to the final 7-3 on minors*								
CLUB MATCHES								
1	Oct	1	a	Coventry	D 0-0	-	-	5000
2		**8**	**H**	**Kettering**	W 3-0	-	Oxlade d	3000
3		15	a	Bedford	L 0-8	-	-	-
4		22	a	Moseley	L 0-7	-	-	-
5		**29**	**H**	**Bedford School**	W 7-0	Coleman(2), Oxlade	Unknown c, Parsons c	-
6	Nov	12	a	Kettering	W 10-3	Parsons, Coleman, Snowden	Parsons 2c/d	-
		19	**H**	**Coventry**	PP (frost)			
7		26	a	Peterborough & District	W 13-0	Coleman(2), Phillips(2), Oxlade, Mason, B.Wilkinson	Oxlade 3c	-
8	Dec	**3**	**H**	**Rugby**	W 6-0	Parsons, Oxlade	Parsons 2c	4000
9		**10**	**H**	**Northampton Unity**	W 17-0	Parsons(3), Phillips(2), Coleman, McAlpin, Oxlade	Parsons 3c/d	-
10		**17**	**H**	**Burton**	L 0-5	-	-	-
11		**24**	**H**	**Rushden**	W 9-1	Sulley, Brockbank, Phillips, Pilsbury, Salmon	Sulley 2c	-
12		**31**	**H**	**Nottingham**	W 4-0	Brockbank(2)	Parsons c	-
13	Jan	7	a	Burton	L 0-1	-	-	3000
14		**14**	**H**	**Nottingham**	W 8-0	Parsons(2), Phillips(2), Smith, B.Wilkinson	Brockbank c	-
15		21	a	Rugby	L 0-5	-	-	-
		28	a	Burton	PP (frost)			
16	Feb	**4**	**H**	**Moseley**	D 0-0	-	-	3000
17		11	a	Bedford School	W 7-3	Phillips, Porter, Smith	Parsons 2c	-
		18	a	Bedford	PP (snow)			
		25	a	Northampton Unity	PP (snow)			
18	Mar	**3**	**H**	**Northampton**	W 4-0	Phillips(2), Coleman, Morley	-	-
19		10	a	Manningham	L 4-10	Oxlade, Parsons	McKechnie c	-
21		31	a	Northampton	L 0-4	-	-	-

The key for how to read the stats is on the last page

18	88/89										
Home Ground: Belgrave Cricket and Cycle Ground		OVERALL RECORD:					T	C	PG	DG	PTS
Captain: Jack Parsons then Dickie Snowden in December		PLD	W	D	L	Tigers scored:	55	14	1	4	98
		34	12	7	15	Opponents scored:	61	18	1	5	115

GM	DATE		VEN	OPPONENTS	RESULT	TRIES	KICKS	ATT
MIDLAND COUNTIES CUP						**CUP WINNERS: MOSELEY**		
27	Mar	**2**	**H**	**Moseley Harlequins (1)**	W 2-0	Brockbank, McKechnie	-	-
29		9	a	Rugby (2)	W 6-5	A.Porter	McKechnie d, Brockbank c	3000
30		13w	a	Rugby (2-replay)	W 4-3	McKechnie, A.Porter	Brockbank c	-
31		**16**	**H**	**Stratford-upon-Avon (sf)**	W 4-3	B.Wilkinson	A.Porter d	5000
32		23		Moseley (f)	L 0-6	-	-	4000
Note: *#29 Match replayed due to an ineligible player*								
CLUB MATCHES								
1	Sep	**29**	**H**	**Town & County Colts**	W 7-0	Brockbank, McAlpin, Mason	Parsons 2c	-
2	Oct	**6**	**H**	**Swinton**	L 1-11	Brockbank	-	2000
3		**13**	**H**	**Coventry**	D 1-1	Snowden	-	2000
4		17w	a	Bedford	D 1-1	McAlpin	-	-
5		20	a	Manningham	L 0-9	-	-	3000
6		27	a	Edgbaston Crusaders	D 2-2	Coleman, Mansell	-	-
7	Nov	**3**	**H**	**Rugby**	D 0-0	-	-	-
8		10	a	Old Edwardians	L 1-4	B.Wilkinson	-	-
9		**17**	**H**	**Moseley**	L 4-5	Gilbey, Morley	Brockbank c	1500
10		24	a	Coventry	D 0-0	-	-	-
11	Dec	**1**	**H**	**Bedford School**	L 1-4	Beasley	-	-
12		8	a	Burton	L 0-5	-	-	-
13		**15**	**H**	**Bedford**	D 3-3	Willey(2), Brockbank	-	-
14		22	a	Rugby	L 1-4	Wilcock	-	-
15		**26w**	**H**	**Rushden**	W 10-0	Mason(2), Beasley, Coleman, Gilbey, Wilcock	Brockbank 2c	-
16		**29**	**H**	**Nottingham**	W 13-0	A.Nutt(2), Coleman, McKechnie	Brockbank 3c/d	1000
	Jan	5	a	Kettering	PP (frost)			
17		**12**	**H**	**Burton**	W 7-0	Coleman(2)	McKechnie d, Brockbank c	-
18		**19**	**H**	**Kettering**	D 4-4	Willey	Brockbank p	-
19		26	a	Moseley	L 0-10	-	-	-
20	Feb	2	a	Bedford	L 1-3	Bell	-	-
21		**5tu**	**H**	**Manningham**	L 0-4	-	-	1000
22		**9**	**H**	**Edgbaston Crusaders**	W 3-1	Bell, Ley, McKechnie	-	-
23		16	a	Swinton	L 0-10	-	-	200
24		18m	a	Oldham	L 0-3	-	-	-
25		**23**	**H**	**Old Edwardians**	W 5-4	McAlpin, Mason, Snowden	Brockbank c	-
26		**28th**	**H**	**Leicester Swifts**	W 13-0	McAlpin(3), McKechnie(2), Chettle, Mansell, A.Nutt, W.Porter	McKechnie 2c	-
28	Mar	**6w**	**H**	**Bedford**	W 4-3	Knott(3), McAlpin	-	-
		23	a	Bradford	PP (cup)			
33		**30**	**H**	**Cardiff Harlequins**	L 0-5	-	-	-
	Apr	6	a	Bedford School	PP			
34		**13**	**H**	**Town & District XVIII**	L 0-2	-	-	-
Neutral Venue: *#32 at the Butts - Coventry*								

INDIVIDUAL APPEARANCES 1888/89

Name / Game #	1	2	3	4	5	6	7	8	9	10	11	12	13	14	15	16	17	18	19	20	21	22	23	24	25	26	27	28	29	30	31	32	33	34	Apps	T	Pts
EE (Edward) Beasley	-	-	-	-	-	-	>F	F	F	F	F	-	F	F	F	F	F	<F	-	-	-	-	-	-	-	-	-	-	-	-	-	-	-	-	11	2	2
E (Dickie) Bell	-	-	-	-	-	-	-	-	-	-	-	-	-	F	F	HB	-	-	F	F	F	F	F	F	F	-	F	-	F	F	F	F	F	-	16	2	2
H (Herbert) Bostock	-	-	-	-	-	-	-	-	-	>F	<F	-	-	-	-	-	-	-	-	-	-	-	-	-	-	-	-	-	-	-	-	-	-	-	2	-	-
HH (Harry) Brockbank	F	F	F	-	F	F	F	F	F	F	F	F	F	-	F	F	F	F	F	F	-	F	F	F	F	-	F	FB	F	F	F	F	F	FB	30	4	30
BC (Bramwell) Burton	F	F	F	-	-	<F	-	-	-	-	-	-	-	-	-	-	-	-	-	-	-	-	-	-	-	-	-	-	-	-	-	-	-	-	4	-	-
A Chettle	-	-	-	-	-	-	-	-	-	-	-	-	-	-	-	-	-	-	-	-	-	-	>FB	FB	-	FB	-	3Q	FB	-	-	-	FB	-	6	1	1
JGS (Sherrard) Coleman	3Q	-	3Q	FB	3Q	3Q	-	3Q	-	F	F	3Q	-	-	F	F	F	F	F	F	F	F	-	-	F	-	F	F	F	F	F	3Q	F	F	26	5	5
J Fernie	-	>3Q	-	3Q	-	-	-	-	-	-	3Q	-	-	-	-	-	-	-	-	-	-	-	-	-	-	-	-	-	-	-	-	-	-	<3Q	4	-	-
WJ Gilbey	-	-	-	-	-	-	-	-	>HB	HB	-	HB	3Q	F	HB	HB	F	F	F	F	F	F	HB	HB	HB	F	HB	-	HB	HB	HB	HB	HB	-	23	2	2
AE (Amos) Greenwell	F	-	-	<F	-	-	-	-	-	-	-	-	-	-	-	-	-	-	-	-	-	-	-	-	-	-	-	-	-	-	-	-	-	-	2	-	-
J Hall	-	-	-	-	-	-	-	-	-	-	-	-	-	-	-	-	-	-	-	-	-	-	>F	<F	-	-	-	-	-	-	-	-	-	-	2	-	-
Sgt. TJ (Tom) Jacombs	-	-	-	-	-	-	-	-	-	-	-	-	-	>F	-	FB	FB	-	-	F	FB	-	-	F	-	-	FB	F	-	-	-	-	-	F	9	-	-
Rev. RG (Robert) Ley	-	-	-	>HB	HB	-	HB	-	HB	HB	HB	-	HB	HB	-	-	HB	HB	-	HB	HB	HB	-	-	HB	HB	-	-	HB	HB	HB	HB	HB	HB	21	1	1
JT (Jack) Lovett	F	-	-	-	-	-	-	-	-	-	-	F	F	F	F	F	-	-	F	-	-	-	F	-	-	-	-	-	-	-	-	-	F	-	9	-	-
K (Kenneth) McAlpin	F	F	F	F	F	F	3Q	HB	3Q	3Q	HB	F	F	F	-	F	F	F	F	F	F	F	F	F	F	F	F	F	F	F	F	F	F	F	33	7	7
A (Arthur) McKechnie	FB	FB	FB	-	FB	FB	FB	FB	FB	FB	-	3Q	3Q	3Q	3Q	3Q	3Q	3Q	3Q	3Q	3Q	3Q	3Q	3Q	-	3Q	3Q	3Q	3Q	3Q	3Q	3Q	3Q	3Q	31	6	16
J (James) Mansell	-	-	3Q	-	3Q	3Q	3Q	3Q	3Q	F	FB	FB	FB	-	-	-	-	-	FB	FB	F	FB	-	-	-	F	F	F	-	-	-	-	-	3Q	18	2	2
Dr. H (Henry) Mason	F	F	-	-	-	F	F	F	F	3Q	3Q	F	F	-	F	F	F	F	-	-	F	F	-	-	F	-	F	F	-	F	F	F	F	F	24	4	4
ER (Joey) Morley	F	F	F	F	F	F	F	F	F	F	F	F	F	-	F	F	F	F	F	F	F	F	F	F	F	-	F	-	F	F	F	F	F	F	31	1	1
A (Ally) Nutt	-	F	F	-	-	-	-	-	F	-	-	3Q	-	-	HB	3Q	3Q	3Q	3Q	3Q	-	3Q	-	-	3Q	3Q	3Q	-	3Q	3Q	3Q	3Q	<3Q	-	19	3	3
F (Tommy) Nutt	-	-	-	-	-	-	-	-	-	-	-	-	-	-	-	-	-	-	-	-	-	-	-	-	>FB	-	-	-	F	FB	FB	-	-	F	5	-	-
HJW (Henry) Oxlade	HB	HB	HB	-	3Q	HB	HB	HB	-	-	-	-	-	-	-	-	-	-	HB	-	-	-	-	-	-	-	-	-	-	-	-	-	-	-	8	-	-
J (Jack) Parsons	3Q*	3Q*	3Q*	3Q*	3Q*	3Q*	-	-	-	-	-	-	-	-	-	-	-	-	-	-	-	-	-	-	-	-	-	-	-	-	-	<FB	-	-	7	-	4
E Peddie	-	-	-	-	-	-	-	-	-	-	-	-	-	-	-	-	-	-	-	-	-	-	-	-	-	-	-	>HB	-	-	-	-	-	<HB	2	-	-
EH (Ernest) Pilsbury	3Q	<3Q	-	-	-	-	-	-	-	-	-	-	-	-	-	-	-	-	-	-	-	-	-	-	-	-	-	-	-	-	-	-	-	-	2	-	-
AT (Arthur) Porter	-	-	-	-	-	-	-	-	-	-	-	-	3Q	3Q	3Q	3Q	3Q	3Q	3Q	3Q	3Q	3Q	3Q	3Q	3Q	3Q	3Q	-	3Q	3Q	3Q	<3Q	-	-	19	2	5
SG (Samuel) Porter	-	-	-	F	-	-	F	-	-	-	-	-	-	-	-	<F	-	-	-	-	-	-	-	-	-	-	-	-	-	-	-	-	-	-	3	-	-
WR (Willie) Porter	F	F	F	F	F	F	F	F	-	-	F	F*	F*	-	F*	F*	F	F	F	-	F	F	F	F*	F	F	F	F	F	F	F*	F*	F*	F*	30	1	1
J Robertson	-	-	-	-	-	-	-	-	-	-	-	-	-	-	-	-	-	-	-	-	-	-	>3Q	<3Q	-	-	-	-	-	-	-	-	-	-	2	-	-
PG (Percy) Salmon	-	-	-	-	-	-	-	-	F	<F	-	-	-	-	-	-	-	-	-	-	-	-	-	-	-	-	-	-	-	-	-	-	-	-	2	-	-
F (Fred) Simpson	-	-	-	>F	-	-	-	F	F	-	-	-	-	-	-	-	-	-	-	-	-	-	-	-	-	-	-	-	-	-	-	-	-	-	3	-	-
GPD (Darnell) Smith	>F	F	F	F	F	F	F	F	F	-	<F	-	-	-	-	-	-	-	-	-	-	-	-	-	-	-	-	-	-	-	-	-	-	-	10	-	-
WM Smith	-	F	F	-	F	F	F	F	-	-	-	F	F	<F	-	-	-	-	-	-	-	-	-	-	-	-	-	-	-	-	-	-	-	-	9	-	-
RS (Dickie) Snowden	HB	HB	HB	HB	HB	HB	3Q*	3Q*	3Q*	3Q*	3Q*	HB	HB	HB*	-	-	HB*	HB*	HB*	HB*	HB*	HB*	HB*	-	3Q*	HB*	HB*	HB*	F*	-	-	-	-	-	26	2	2
H Stannard	-	-	-	-	-	-	-	-	-	-	-	-	-	-	-	-	-	-	-	-	-	-	>F	<F	-	-	-	-	-	-	-	-	-	-	2	-	-
JH Wilcock	-	-	-	-	-	-	-	-	-	-	-	-	-	>3Q	3Q	-	-	-	-	-	-	-	-	-	-	-	-	-	-	-	-	-	-	-	2	2	2
B Wilkinson	-	-	F	F	F	F	F	F	F	F	F	-	-	-	-	-	-	-	-	-	-	-	-	-	-	-	-	-	-	F	F	F	F	F	14	2	2
JS Wilkinson	-	-	-	F	F	-	-	-	-	-	-	-	-	-	-	-	-	-	-	-	-	-	-	-	-	-	-	-	-	F*	F	F	-	<F	6	-	-
WJ (William) Willey	-	-	-	-	-	-	-	-	-	-	-	-	>F	F	F	-	F	F	F	-	-	F	F	F	F	-	F	-	<F	-	-	-	-	-	12	3	3

1 GAME: Atkins <F(12), J Buckle >F(28), Burbridge =F(25), W Cowley =F(10), AB (Arthur) Fforde =3Q(4), W (Bill) Hadfield =F(21), CB (Charles) Knight <FB(15), "Knott" =3Qt(28), FH (Frank) Lea =FB(14), WH (William) McMurray >F(14), Mosby =FB(18), E Neild 3Q(33), HR (Herbert) Orr =3Q(21), GG (George) Porter >F(20), WH (Jack) Sturges >F(28), J Walsh =HB(24), White =F(11)

The key for how to read the stats is on the last page

18 89/90	Home Ground: Belgrave Cricket and Cycle Ground
	Captain: Willie Porter

OVERALL RECORD:					T	C	PG	DG	PTS
PLD	W	D	L	Tigers scored:	25	8	1	1	46
27	5	2	20	Opponents scored:	81	29	1	1	144

GM	DATE		VEN	OPPONENTS	RESULT	TRIES	KICKS	ATT
MIDLAND COUNTIES CUP					**CUP WINNERS: OLD EDWARDIANS**			
23	Mar	1	a	Stratford-upon-Avon (1)	L 0-13	-	-	-
CLUB MATCHES								
1	Sep	28	a	Stratford-upon-Avon	L 0-7	-	-	-
2	Oct	**5**	**H**	**Old Edwardians**	L 2-7	-	Brockbank p	-
3		**12**	**H**	**Rugby**	W 4-0	Sturges	McKechnie d	-
4		19	a	Oldham	L 0-10	-	-	-
5		**26**	**H**	**Bedford School**	L 3-4	W.Porter	McKechnie c	-
6	Nov	**2**	**H**	**Mossley**	L 3-4	Mason	McKechnie c	2000
7		9	a	Moseley	L 0-7	-	-	-
8		**16**	**H**	**Oldham**	L 0-6	-	-	2000
9		23	a	Swinton	L 0-12	-	-	-
10		**30**	**H**	**Northampton**	W 3-0	Neild	McKechnie c	-
	Dec	7	a	Rugby	PP			
11		**14**	**H**	**Coventry**	D 3-3	Ball	McKechnie c	-
12		**21**	**H**	**Stratford-upon-Avon**	L 0-2	-	-	-
13		**26th**	**H**	**Manchester Free Wanderers**	W 15-0	Sulley(4), McKechnie, Mason, H.German, Gilbey, Sturges	Sulley c, McKechnie c, Ball c	4000
14		28	a	Coventry	L 0-3	-	-	-
	Jan	**4**	**H**	**Swinton**	PP (frost)			
		11	a	Mossley	PP			
15		**18**	**H**	**Leamington Town**	W 3-0	McKechnie(2), W.Porter	-	-
16		**20m**	**H**	**Swinton**	L 0-6	-	-	-
17		25	a	Manningham	L 0-6	-	-	-
18	Feb	**1**	**H**	**Burton**	L 1-8	Neild	-	-
19		5w	a	Rugby	L 0-15	-	-	-
		6th	a	Bedford School	PP			
20		**8**	**H**	**Moseley**	L 1-5	McKechnie	-	6000
21		**15**	**H**	**Manningham**	L 2-5	Ball, McKechnie	-	-
22		22	a	Old Edwardians	L 0-9	-	-	-
24	Mar	**5w**	**H**	**Ashby-de-la-Zouch**	W 5-1	McKechnie(2), Coleman	Wallace c	-
25		29	a	Burton	D 0-0	-	-	-
26	Apr	7m	a	Cardiff	L 0-2	-	-	6000
27		8tu	a	Newport	L 1-9	H.German	-	-

INDIVIDUAL APPEARANCES 1889/90

Name / Game #	1	2	3	4	5	6	7	8	9	10	11	12	13	14	15	16	17	18	19	20	21	22	23	24	25	26	27	Apps	T	Pts
A (Abel) Ashworth E+	-	-	-	-	-	-	-	-	-	-	-	-	-	-	-	-	-	-	-	-	-	-	-	-	-	>C	<C	2	-	-
J (Jesse) Ball	>W	-	-	C	-	-	-	-	-	W	W	C	FB	W	-	-	W	C	W	W	W	W	W	-	-	-	-	14	2	4
JE (Jack) Barradell	-	-	-	-	-	-	-	-	-	-	-	-	-	-	HB	-	-	-	-	-	-	HB	-	HB	HB	-	-	4	-	-
CO (Charles) Barrow	-	-	>F	F	<F	-	-	-	-	-	-	-	-	-	-	-	-	-	-	-	-	-	-	-	-	-	-	3	-	-
E (Dickie) Bell	HB	HB	-	HB	HB	HB	HB	F	F	F	F	F	-	HB	-	-	F	F	-	F	-	F	<F	-	-	-	-	17	-	-
HH (Harry) Brockbank	-	F	-	F	-	-	-	-	-	-	-	-	-	-	-	-	-	-	-	-	-	-	-	-	-	-	-	2	-	2
EJ (Edmund) Byrne	-	-	-	-	-	-	-	-	-	-	-	-	-	-	-	-	-	-	-	-	-	-	-	-	>W	<W	-	2	-	-
GT (George) Cattell	-	-	-	-	-	-	-	-	-	-	-	-	-	-	-	-	-	-	-	-	-	-	-	-	-	>W	<C	2	-	-
Rev. RHB (Dick) Cattell E+	-	-	-	-	-	-	-	-	-	-	-	-	-	-	-	-	-	-	-	-	-	-	-	-	-	>HB	<HB	2	-	-
EW Chamberlain	-	-	-	-	-	-	-	-	-	-	-	-	-	-	-	-	>HB	HB	HB	HB	HB	HB	HB	-	-	-	-	7	-	-
A Chettle	W	FB	FB	FB	-	W	W	FB	<FB	-	-	-	-	-	-	-	-	-	-	-	-	-	-	-	-	-	-	8	-	-
JGS (Sherrard) Coleman	F	F	F	F	F	W	C	-	F*	C	C	W	C	C	W	F	W	F	W	F	F	W	F	HB	F	F	F	26	1	1
EM (Edward) Dawson-Thomas	-	-	-	-	-	-	-	>C	W	-	FB	-	-	-	-	-	-	-	-	-	-	-	-	-	-	-	-	3	-	-
JH (John) Dunmore	-	-	-	-	-	-	-	-	-	-	-	-	-	-	-	-	-	-	>HB	-	-	-	-	-	<F	-	-	2	-	-
H (Harry) German	-	-	-	-	-	-	-	-	>W	-	-	-	F	-	-	-	-	-	C	-	-	-	-	-	F	F	F	6	2	2
WJ Gilbey	-	-	HB	-	HB	-	HB	HB	-	F	F	F	HB	HB	-	-	-	-	-	HB	HB	-	HB	-	-	-	-	12	1	1
Sgt. TJ (Tom) Jacombs	F	F	-	-	-	-	-	-	F	-	-	-	-	-	-	-	-	-	F	-	-	-	-	F	-	-	-	5	-	-
TW (Thomas) Lawrence	-	>F	-	-	F	-	-	-	F	F	-	-	-	-	-	-	-	-	-	-	-	F	<F	-	-	-	-	6	-	-
Rev. RG (Robert) Ley	-	-	HB	-	-	-	-	-	-	-	-	-	HB	-	-	-	-	-	-	-	-	-	-	-	-	-	-	2	-	-
JT (Jack) Lovett	-	-	-	-	-	F	F	F	F	-	-	-	-	-	F	-	F	F	-	-	<F	-	-	-	-	-	-	8	-	-
WD (William) Ludlow	-	-	-	-	-	-	-	-	-	-	-	-	-	-	-	-	-	-	-	-	-	-	-	-	-	>F	<F	2	-	-
D (Donal) McAlpin	-	-	-	-	-	-	-	-	-	-	-	-	-	-	>FB	FB	FB	FB	FB	FB	FB	FB	<FB	-	-	-	-	9	-	-
K (Kenneth) McAlpin	F	F	-	F	F	F	F	F	F	F	F	F	F	F	F	F	F	F	-	F	F	F	F	F	F	F	F	25	-	-
A (Arthur) McKechnie	-	-	C	C	C	C	C	W	C	W	W	FB	W	W	C	C	C	W	-	W	C	C	W	W	-	FB	W	23	7	20
WH (William) McMurray	-	-	-	-	-	-	-	-	-	-	-	-	-	F	F	-	<F	-	-	-	-	-	-	-	-	-	-	3	-	-
O (Owen) McSally	-	-	-	-	-	-	-	-	-	-	-	-	-	-	>F	-	-	-	-	-	-	-	-	-	HB	-	-	2	-	-
Dr. H (Henry) Mason	-	-	F	-	-	F	F	F	-	>F	F	F	F	F	-	F	-	-	-	F	-	F	-	F	-	-	-	13	2	2
ER (Joey) Morley	F	F	F	F	F	F	F	F	-	F	F	F	F	F	-	-	-	F	-	F	F	F	F	-	-	-	-	18	-	-
E Neild	-	-	F	-	-	-	-	HB	HB	HB	HB	HB	-	-	HB	HB	HB	HB	-	-	-	-	-	-	-	HB	HB	12	2	2
F (Tommy) Nutt	-	-	-	-	W	-	-	-	-	-	-	-	-	-	W	F	-	-	-	C	W	-	C	C	C	-	FB	9	-	-
GA Ogden	-	-	-	-	-	-	>W	-	HB	HB	HB	HB	-	<FB	-	-	-	-	-	-	-	-	-	-	-	-	-	6	-	-
HJW (Henry) Oxlade	-	W	W	-	-	<HB	-	-	-	-	-	-	-	-	-	-	-	-	-	-	-	-	-	-	-	-	-	3	-	-
GG (George) Porter	-	-	-	-	-	-	-	-	F	-	-	F	F	F	F	-	-	-	-	-	-	-	-	-	F	-	-	6	-	-
WR (Willie) Porter	F*	F*	F*	F*	F*	F*	F*	F*	-	F*	F*	F*	F*	F*	F*	F*	F*	F*	F*	F*	F*	F*	F*	F*	F*	F*	F*	26	2	2
J (John) Powers	-	-	>F	-	F	F	F	-	-	-	-	-	F	<F	-	-	-	-	-	-	-	-	-	-	-	-	-	6	-	-
T (Thomas) Robinson	-	-	-	-	-	-	-	-	-	-	-	-	-	-	-	-	-	-	F	-	-	-	-	<F	-	-	-	2	-	-
FA Rogers	-	-	-	-	-	-	-	-	-	-	-	-	-	-	-	-	-	-	-	-	-	-	-	-	>W	C	<W	3	-	-
WS Sheppard	-	-	-	>W	-	F	-	-	-	-	-	-	-	-	-	-	-	-	-	F	<F	-	-	-	-	-	-	4	-	-
WH (Jack) Sturges	F	-	F	F	F	F	F	F	F	F	F	F	F	F	F	F	F	F	F	F	F	F	F	F	F	F	F	26	2	2
A (Arthur) Sulley	-	-	-	-	-	-	-	-	-	-	-	-	W	-	-	W	-	-	-	-	-	-	-	-	-	-	-	2	4	6
Rev. LF (Leonard) Ward	-	>F	F	F	F	F	F	F	F	F	F	-	F	-	F	F	-	F	F	F	F	F	-	-	F	F	F	21	-	-
JH Wilcock	-	C	-	-	-	-	-	-	-	-	-	W	-	-	-	-	-	<W	-	-	-	-	-	-	-	-	-	3	-	-
B Wilkinson	-	-	-	-	-	-	-	-	-	-	-	-	-	-	-	-	-	-	-	-	-	-	-	-	-	F	<F	2	-	-
TR (Thomas) Wilks	-	-	-	-	-	-	-	-	-	-	-	-	-	-	-	-	>F	-	-	-	F	-	F	<F	-	-	-	4	-	-
WA Williamson	>C	W	W	W	<W	-	-	-	-	-	-	-	-	-	-	-	-	-	-	-	-	-	-	-	-	-	-	5	-	-
WL (William) Wotherspoon	>FB	-	-	-	FB	-	FB	-	-	FB	-	-	-	-	-	-	-	-	-	-	-	-	-	-	FB	-	-	5	-	-
Dr. SR (Sam) Wright	-	-	-	-	-	-	-	-	-	-	-	>F	-	F	-	-	<F	-	-	-	-	-	-	-	-	-	-	3	-	-
JW (Jack) Yorke	-	-	-	-	-	-	-	-	-	-	-	-	-	-	>F	-	-	-	-	-	-	-	F	-	-	-	-	2	-	-

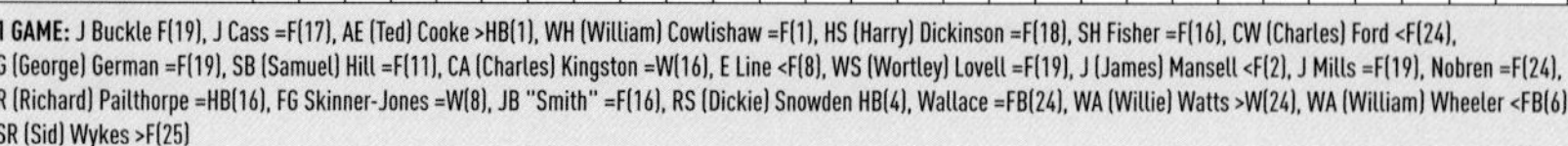
1 GAME: J Buckle F(19), J Cass =F(17), AE (Ted) Cooke >HB(1), WH (William) Cowlishaw =F(1), HS (Harry) Dickinson =F(18), SH Fisher =F(16), CW (Charles) Ford <F(24), G (George) German =F(19), SB (Samuel) Hill =F(11), CA (Charles) Kingston =W(16), E Line <F(8), WS (Wortley) Lovell =F(19), J (James) Mansell <F(2), J Mills =F(19), Nobren =F(24), R (Richard) Pailthorpe =HB(16), FG Skinner-Jones =W(8), JB "Smith" =F(16), RS (Dickie) Snowden HB(4), Wallace =FB(24), WA (Willie) Watts >W(24), WA (William) Wheeler <FB(6), SR (Sid) Wykes >F(25)

Ted Cooke made his Tigers debut against Stratford in 1889 and went on to make 158 appearances for the first team over the next nine seasons.

The key for how to read the stats is on the last page

18	90/91	OVERALL RECORD:					T	C	PG	DG	MK	PTS
Home Ground: Belgrave Cricket and Cycle Ground												
Captain: Arthur McKechnie		PLD	W	D	L	Tigers scored:	60	28	3	4	1	137
Vice-captain: Jack Sturges		25	18	2	5	Opponents scored:	30	15	0	4	0	72

GM	DATE		VEN	OPPONENTS	RESULT	TRIES	KICKS	ATT
MIDLAND COUNTIES CUP						**CUP WINNERS: COVENTRY**		
18	Mar	**7**	**H**	**Bromsgrove (1)**	W 14-0	Dobbs(4), Yorke(2)	Ward 4c	-
19		**14**	**H**	**Handsworth (2)**	W 2-1	-	Ward p	-
21		**21**	**H**	**Old Edwardians (sf)**	W 7-4 (aet)	Rathbone, Ward	Wynne d, Brockbank c	10000
25	Apr	4		Coventry (f)	L 0-8	-	-	-
CLUB MATCHES								
1	Oct	**4**	**H**	**Moseley**	W 9-6	Nutt, Pilsbury, Ward	Brockbank 2c/p	4000
2		**8w**	**H**	**Ashby-de-la-Zouch**	W 8-0	McAlpin, Rathbone, Sturges	Barradell d, McKechnie c	-
3		11	a	Old Edwardians	D 1-1	Ward	-	-
4		**18**	**H**	**Leicester Crusaders**	W 10-1	Sturges(3), McKechnie	Brockbank 2c/p	-
5		**25**	**H**	**Edgbaston Crusaders**	W 11-0	Nutt(2), Dobbs, Sturges	Brockbank 2c, McKechnie d	-
6	Nov	**1**	**H**	**Bedford School**	W 6-3	Dobbs	Ward c/m	4000
7		8	a	Bedford	W 7-6	Dobbs(2), Ward	Brockbank 2c	-
8		**15**	**H**	**Leicestershire XV**	W 8-1	McKechnie, Nutt, Wykes	Barradell d, Brockbank c	-
9		**22**	**H**	**Sale**	W 3-1	McKechnie	Brockbank c	-
		29	**H**	**Leamington Town**	PP			
10	Dec	6	a	Rugby	W 8-0	Ward(3), McKechnie, Dawson-Thomas, Sturges	McKechnie c	-
		13	a	Coventry	PP (frost)			
		20	**H**	**Northampton**	PP (frost)			
		26f	**H**	**Old Denstonians**	PP (frost)			
		27	**H**	**Rugby**	PP (frost)			
	Jan	**3**	**H**	**Coventry**	PP (frost)			
		10	a	Northampton	PP (frost)			
		17	a	Edgbaston Crusaders	PP			
11		**24**	**H**	**Bedford**	W 6-0	Dobbs(3), Sturges	Brockbank c	-
12		**31**	**H**	**Handsworth**	W 5-1	Mason(2), Sturges	Brockbank c	4000
13	Feb	**7**	**H**	**Wolverton**	W 8-0	Baines, Barradell, Dobbs, McKechnie	Brockbank 2c	-
14		**9m**	**H**	**Rugby**	W 2-0	Brockbank, Yorke	-	2000
15		14	a	Bedford School	W 12-4	Dobbs, Ley, W.Porter, Sturges	Brockbank 4c	-
16		**21**	**H**	**Old Edwardians**	L 1-3	W.Porter	-	10000
17		28	a	Moseley	L 0-11	-	-	-
	Mar	**9m**	**H**	**Swinton**	PP			
		11w	a	Ashby-de-la-Zouch	PP (no team)			
20		**16m**	**H**	**Swinton**	L 0-10	-	-	-
22		**28**	**H**	**Mossley**	W 5-3	Ward, Sturges, Watts	Ward c	-
23		**30m**	**H**	**Kirkstall**	D 0-0	-	-	-
24		**31tu**	**H**	**Penygraig**	L 4-8	W.Porter, Rathbone	Brockbank c	6000

***Neutral Venue:** #25 at Cricket Club - Rugby*

INDIVIDUAL APPEARANCES 1890/91

Name / Game #	1	2	3	4	5	6	7	8	9	10	11	12	13	14	15	16	17	18	19	20	21	22	23	24	25	Apps	T	Pts
SM (Seth) Baines	-	>FB	-	-	-	-	-	W	-	-	-	-	C	W	W	-	-	-	-	-	-	C	W	C	-	8	1	1
Rev. CM (Charles) Barham	-	-	-	-	-	-	-	-	-	-	-	-	-	-	-	-	-	-	-	-	-	-	>W	-	-	1	-	-
JE (Jack) Barradell	HB	HB	HB	HB	FB	HB	FB	HB	F	-	-	-	HB	-	-	-	-	-	-	-	-	-	F	F	-	12	1	7
FR (Frederick) Bonner	-	<F	-	-	-	-	-	-	-	-	-	-	-	-	-	-	-	-	-	-	-	-	-	-	-	1	-	-
HH (Harry) Brockbank	F	-	F	F	F	-	F	F	F	F	F	F	F	F	F	F	F	-	F	F	F	F	F	F	F	22	1	45
J Buckle	-	-	-	-	-	<F	-	-	-	-	-	-	-	-	-	-	-	-	-	-	-	-	-	-	-	1	-	-
BD (Bissill) Carlisle	-	-	-	-	-	-	-	-	-	-	-	-	-	>FB	-	-	-	FB	-	-	-	-	-	-	-	2	-	-
AE (Ted) Cooke	-	-	-	-	-	-	-	-	-	-	-	-	-	-	-	-	-	-	-	-	-	-	-	W	-	1	-	-
EM (Edward) Dawson-Thomas	-	-	-	-	-	-	-	-	-	W	-	-	-	<C	-	-	-	-	-	-	-	-	-	-	-	2	1	1
GC (George) Dobbs	>F	F	F	-	F	F	F	F	F	F	F	F	F	-	F	-	F	F	C	F	F	F	-	F	<F	21	13	13
Rev. EE (Ernest) Farmer	-	-	-	-	-	-	-	-	>W	C	C	C	-	-	-	W	W	C	W	W	W	W	-	-	C	12	-	-
WJ Gilbey	-	-	HB	HB	HB	HB	HB	-	HB	HB	HB	HB	-	-	HB	HB	-	F	F	-	F	HB	-	-	F	16	-	-
C (Charles) Grimmett	-	-	-	=C	-	-	-	-	-	-	-	-	-	-	-	-	-	-	-	-	-	-	-	-	-	1	-	-
J (Joseph) Hale	-	-	-	-	-	-	-	-	-	-	-	-	-	=F	-	-	-	-	-	-	-	-	-	-	-	1	-	-
RH (Richard) Hincks	-	-	-	-	-	-	-	-	-	-	>F	F	F	F	F	F	F	F	<F	-	-	-	-	-	-	9	-	-
AL (Arthur) Jackson	-	-	-	>F	-	-	-	F	-	-	-	-	-	-	-	-	-	-	-	-	-	-	-	-	-	2	-	-
Sgt. TJ (Tom) Jacombs	-	<F	-	-	-	-	-	-	-	-	-	-	-	-	-	-	-	-	-	-	-	-	-	-	-	1	-	-
A Johnson	-	-	-	-	-	-	=W	-	-	-	-	-	-	-	-	-	-	-	-	-	-	-	-	-	-	1	-	-
Rev. RG (Robert) Ley	-	-	-	-	-	-	-	-	-	-	HB	HB	-	HB	HB	HB	HB	HB	HB	HB	HB	-	-	-	HB	11	1	1
K (Kenneth) McAlpin	F	F	F	F	F	F	F	F	F	F	F	F	F	F	F	F	F	F	F	F	F	-	-	-	F	22	1	1
A (Arthur) McKechnie	C*	W*	W*	FB*	W*	W*	C*	W*	W*	C*	W*	W*	W*	W*	C*	W*	W*	W*	FB*	FB*	FB*	FB*	FB*	FB*	FB*	25	5	12
O (Owen) McSally	-	HB	-	-	-	-	-	-	-	-	-	-	-	-	-	-	-	-	-	-	-	HB	HB	HB	-	4	-	-
Dr. H (Henry) Mason	F	F	F	F	F	F	F	F	F	F	F	F	F	-	F	F	-	F	F	F	F	F	F	-	<F	22	2	2
G (George) Metcalf	-	-	-	-	-	-	-	-	-	-	-	-	-	-	-	-	-	-	-	-	-	-	>F	<F	-	2	-	-
E Neild	-	W	-	-	-	-	-	-	-	-	-	-	-	-	-	-	-	-	-	-	-	-	-	-	-	1	-	-
F (Tommy) Nutt	W	-	C	-	W	C	W	C	C	W	W	W	W	-	W	C	C	C	C	-	C	C	C	W	W	21	4	4
HC (Harry) Pilsbury	>W	C	C	W	C	C	-	-	-	-	-	-	-	-	-	-	-	-	-	-	-	-	-	-	-	6	1	1
GG (George) Porter	-	-	-	-	-	-	<F	-	-	-	-	-	-	-	-	-	-	-	-	-	-	-	-	-	-	1	-	-
WR (Willie) Porter	-	F	F	F	F	F	F	F	F	-	F	-	-	-	F	F	F	-	-	-	-	F	F	F	-	15	3	3
J Rathbone	>C	C	W	W	C	W	-	C	-	-	-	-	-	-	-	-	-	W	W	C	W	-	-	C	W	13	3	3
RS (Dickie) Snowden	-	-	-	-	-	-	-	-	-	-	-	-	-	-	-	-	-	-	-	-	-	-	HB	-	-	1	-	-
WH (Jack) Sturges	F	F	F	F	F	F	F	F	F	F	F	F	F	F	F	F	F	F	F	F	F	F	F	-	F	24	10	10
A (Arthur) Sulley	-	-	-	-	-	-	-	-	-	-	-	-	-	-	-	-	-	-	-	C	-	-	-	-	-	1	-	-
A (Arthur) Turner	<HB	-	-	-	-	-	-	-	-	-	-	-	-	-	-	-	-	-	-	-	-	-	-	-	-	1	-	-
Rev. LF (Leonard) Ward	F	-	F	F	F	F	F	F	F	F	-	F	F	F	F	F	F	F	F	F	F	F	-	F	F	22	8	25
WA (Willie) Watts	-	-	-	-	-	-	-	-	-	-	-	-	-	-	-	-	-	-	-	W	C	W	C	-	C	5	1	1
WL (William) Wotherspoon	FB	-	FB	-	-	FB	-	FB	FB	FB	FB	FB	FB	C	FB	FB	<FB	-	-	-	-	-	-	-	-	13	-	-
SR (Sid) Wykes	F	F	-	F	-	-	F	HB	F	F	F	F	F	F	-	F	F	-	-	F	-	F	F	F	-	17	1	1
Rev. O (Owen) Wynne	-	-	-	-	>HB	-	HB	-	HB	HB	-	-	HB	HB	-	-	HB	HB	HB	HB	HB	-	-	HB	HB	13	-	3
JW (Jack) Yorke	F	-	F	F	F	F	-	-	-	F	F	F	F	F	F	F	F	F	F	F	F	F	F	F	F	21	3	3

➜ Leicester began playing for the Midland Counties Cup in 1882, but did not win it until 1898, and then held onto it for eight successive seasons.

18	91/92	Home Ground: Belgrave Cricket and Cycle Ground
		Captain: Jack Sturges
		Vice-captain: Willie Watts

OVERALL RECORD:					T	C	PG	DG	MK	PTS
PLD	W	D	L	Tigers scored:	58	29	0	0	0	203
31	15	2	14	Opponents scored:	49	17	0	2	0	157

GM	DATE		VEN	OPPONENTS	RESULT	TRIES	KICKS	ATT
MIDLAND COUNTIES CUP						**CUP WINNERS: COVENTRY**		
24	Mar	**12**	**H**	**Leicester Swifts (2)**	W 12-0	Rathbone(2), Ward	Ward 2c	5000
26		19	a	Old Edwardians (3)	L 0-21	-	-	1500
CLUB MATCHES								
1	Oct	**3**	**H**	**Wolverton**	W 41-0	Edmonds(2), Nutt(2), Sturges(2), Ward, Barham, Stewart, W.Watts	Ward 7c	-
2		10	a	Old Edwardians	W 4-0	Brockbank, Sturges	-	-
3		14w	a	Bedford School	L 7-12	Sturges, Sulley	Ward c	-
4		**17**	**H**	**Edgbaston Crusaders**	W 28-0	Brockbank(2), Barham(2), Ball, Sturges, Ward, W.Watts	Brockbank 4c	-
5		**24**	**H**	**Moseley**	L 0-2	-	-	-
		28w	a	Ashby-de-la-Zouch	PP (no team)			
6		**31**	**H**	**Gloucester**	L 0-15	-	-	-
7	Nov	**7**	**H**	**Burton**	L 0-2	-	-	5000
8		**14**	**H**	**Coventry**	W 5-0	Ward	Brockbank c	-
9		21	a	Bedford	D 0-0	-	-	-
10		28	a	Ashby-de-la-Zouch	W 5-0	Barham	Ward c	-
11	Dec	**5**	**H**	**Rugby**	W 15-0	Ball(2), Edmonds, Morrison, W.Watts, Yorke	McKechnie c	-
12		12	a	Burton	L 0-2	-	-	-
		19	**H**	**Leicestershire XV**	PP (frost)			
		21m	**H**	**West Hartlepool**	PP (frost)			
13		**26**	**H**	**Leicester Swifts**	W 4-0	Daniells, Memory	-	2000
		28m	**H**	**Penygraig**	PP			
14	Jan	2	a	Gloucester	L 0-6	-	-	-
15		9	a	Coventry	L 0-7	-	-	-
		16	**H**	**Bedford**	PP (frost)			
16		23	a	Rugby	D 0-0	-	-	-
17		**30**	**H**	**Bedford School**	L 0-5	-	-	-
18	Feb	**6**	**H**	**Old Edwardians**	L 0-2	-	-	7000
19		13	a	Blackheath	L 0-37	-	-	-
20		**20**	**H**	**Handsworth**	W 2-0	Rathbone	-	2000
21		**27**	**H**	**Stourbridge**	W 17-0	German(2), Ward, W.Watts	Ward 3c	-
22	Mar	**2w**	**H**	**Ashby-de-la-Zouch**	W 21-0	Rathbone(4), Snowden, Sturges	Ward 3c	-
23		**5**	**H**	**Stratford-upon-Avon**	W 12-7	Ward, Joyce, Sturges	Ward 2c	3000
25		**14m**	**H**	**Swinton**	L 0-13	-	-	-
27		**26**	**H**	**Edgbaston Crusaders**	W 13-0	Rathbone(2), McKechnie, McSalley, Simpson	W.Watts c	-
	Apr	2	a	Moseley	PP (cup)			
28		9	a	Handsworth	W 12-4	Ward, Edmonds, Porter	Ward 2c	-
29		15f	a	Dukinfield	W 5-4	German	McKechnie c	-
30		16	a	St Helens	L 0-6	-	-	-
31		18m	a	Walkden	L 0-12	-	-	-

INDIVIDUAL APPEARANCES 1891/92

Name / Game #	1	2	3	4	5	6	7	8	9	10	11	12	13	14	15	16	17	18	19	20	21	22	23	24	25	26	27	28	29	30	31	Apps	T	Pts
SM (Seth) Baines	C	C	C	C	-	C	C	C	C	-	C	W	-	-	W	-	-	-	-	-	-	-	-	W	-	-	-	-	-	-	-	12	-	-
J (Jesse) Ball	-	-	-	W	W	C	C	W	C	W	C	W	-	-	C	C	C	C	C	-	W	-	C	C	W	W	W	-	-	-	-	20	3	6
Rev. CM (Charles) Barham	C	W	W	W	W	W	W	C	W	W	W	C	-	W	W	W	W	C	<W	-	-	-	-	-	-	-	-	-	-	-	-	18	4	8
HH (Harry) Brockbank	F	F	-	F	F	F	-	F	F	-	-	-	F	F	-	F	F	F	-	<F	-	-	-	-	-	-	-	-	-	-	-	13	3	21
BD (Bissill) Carlisle	-	-	-	-	-	-	-	-	-	-	-	-	-	-	-	-	-	-	-	-	-	FB	-	-	FB	-	-	-	-	-	-	2	-	-
FR (Frank) Charters	-	-	-	-	-	-	-	-	-	-	-	-	-	-	-	-	-	-	-	>W	-	-	-	-	-	-	-	W	W	-	W	4	-	-
JGS (Sherrard) Coleman	-	-	-	-	-	-	-	-	-	-	-	-	W	<C	-	-	-	-	-	-	-	-	-	-	-	-	-	-	-	-	-	2	-	-
JT (John) Edmonds	>F	F	F	F	F	F	F	F	F	F	F	F	-	F	F	F	F	F	F	F	F	-	F	F	-	F	F	F	-	-	-	25	4	8
Rev. EE (Ernest) Farmer	-	-	-	-	C	W	-	-	-	-	F	<F	-	-	-	-	-	-	-	-	-	-	-	-	-	-	-	-	-	-	-	4	-	-
JW (John) Gall	>F	F	F	F	F	<F	-	-	-	-	-	-	-	-	-	-	-	-	-	-	-	-	-	-	-	-	-	-	-	-	-	6	-	-
H (Harry) German	-	-	-	-	-	-	-	-	-	-	-	-	-	W	-	-	-	W	C	-	C	-	-	F	W	C	-	-	F	F	C	10	3	6
AL (Arthur) Jackson	-	-	F	-	-	-	-	-	-	-	-	-	F	-	F	-	-	-	-	F	-	F	-	-	F	-	-	-	F	-	F	8	-	-
W (Walter) Jackson	-	-	-	-	-	-	-	-	-	-	>F	-	-	-	-	-	-	-	F	F	F	-	F	F	F	F	F	F	F	F	F	13	-	-
HWA (Harry) Joyce	-	-	-	-	-	-	-	-	-	-	-	-	-	>F	-	F	-	-	F	-	F	-	F	-	-	F	-	-	F	F	F	9	1	2
R (Robert) Lakin	-	-	-	-	-	-	-	-	-	-	-	-	-	-	-	-	-	-	-	-	-	-	-	-	>F	-	-	-	F	F	F	4	-	-
Rev. RG (Robert) Ley	HB	HB	-	HB	HB	HB	HB	-	HB	-	-	-	-	-	HB	-	HB	HB	HB	HB	HB	-	HB	HB	-	HB	-	-	-	-	-	16	-	-
J Lucas	-	-	-	-	-	-	>F	-	-	F	F	-	F	-	<F	-	-	-	-	-	-	-	-	-	-	-	-	-	-	-	-	5	-	-
A (Arthur) McKechnie	FB	FB	-	FB	FB	FB	FB	FB	FB	FB	FB	FB	-	FB	FB	FB	FB	FB	FB	FB	FB	-	FB	FB	-	FB	FB	FB	FB	FB	FB	27	1	8
O (Owen) McSally	-	-	HB	-	-	-	-	-	-	C	-	HB	-	HB	-	HB	-	-	-	-	HB	-	HB	HB	HB	HB	HB	HB	HB	HB	<HB	15	1	2
JWM (John) Meek	>F	F	F	F	F	F	-	F	F	F	F	F	F	F	F	F	F	F	F	-	-	-	-	-	-	-	-	F	F	F	-	21	-	-
JC (Joseph) Memory	-	-	-	-	-	-	-	-	-	-	-	-	>HB	-	-	-	-	-	-	HB	-	HB	-	-	-	-	-	HB	-	-	-	4	1	2
ER (Joey) Morley	-	-	-	-	-	-	F	F	F	F	F	F	F	F	F	F	<F	-	-	-	-	-	-	-	-	-	-	-	-	-	-	11	-	-
J Morrison	-	-	-	-	-	-	-	>HB	HB	HB	HB	-	-	HB	-	<HB	-	-	-	-	-	-	-	-	-	-	-	-	-	-	-	6	1	2
F (Tommy) Nutt	W	-	-	-	-	-	-	-	-	-	-	-	-	-	-	W	C	-	-	-	-	-	-	-	-	-	-	-	-	<W	-	4	2	4
J (John) Patchett	-	-	-	-	-	-	>F	-	-	-	-	-	-	-	-	-	-	-	-	-	-	-	-	-	F	-	F	F	-	-	-	4	-	-
J Rathbone	-	-	-	-	-	-	-	-	-	-	-	-	-	C	-	-	-	-	-	C	-	C	W	W	C	-	W	-	W	W	W	10	9	18
HJ (Harry) Simpson	-	-	-	-	-	-	-	-	-	-	-	-	>F	-	-	-	-	-	-	-	-	F	-	-	-	-	F	-	-	-	-	3	1	2
RS (Dickie) Snowden	-	-	-	-	-	-	-	-	-	-	-	-	-	-	-	-	-	-	-	-	-	HB	-	-	-	-	-	-	-	-	HB	2	1	2
W Stewart	>F	F	-	F	F	F	F	F	F	F	F	-	F	F	F	F	F	F	-	F	F	-	F	F	F	F	F	-	-	-	-	23	1	2
WH (Jack) Sturges	F*	F*	F*	F*	F*	F*	F*	F*	F*	F*	-	F*	F*	F*	F*	F*	F*	F*	F*	F*	F*	F*	F*	F*	F*	F*	F*	F*	F*	F*	F*	30	7	14
W (Bill) Sykes	-	-	-	-	-	-	-	-	-	-	-	-	-	-	-	-	-	-	-	-	>F	F	F	F	<F	-	-	-	-	-	-	5	-	-
Rev. LF (Leonard) Ward	F	F	F	F	F	F	F	F	F	F	-	F	-	F	F	F	F	F	F	F	F	F	F	F	-	F	F	F	-	F	<F	27	7	77
WA (Willie) Watts	W	C	C	C	C	-	W	W	W	C	W*	C	W	-	C	C	W	W	W	W	W	W	W	-	-	W	C	C	C	C	C	27	4	11
Rev. JBH (John) Whitehurst	-	-	-	-	-	-	-	-	-	-	-	-	-	-	-	-	>F	F	F	F	F	-	F	F	-	<F	-	-	-	-	-	8	-	-
W Wilby	-	-	-	-	-	-	-	-	-	-	-	-	-	-	-	-	-	-	-	-	-	>F	-	-	<F	-	-	-	-	-	-	2	-	-
SR (Sid) Wykes	-	-	-	-	-	-	-	-	-	-	-	-	HB	-	-	-	-	-	-	-	-	-	-	-	-	F	F	F	F	F	<F	7	-	-
Rev. O (Owen) Wynne	HB	HB	HB	-	-	HB	HB	HB	-	-	HB	HB	-	-	HB	-	HB	HB	HB	-	-	-	-	-	HB	-	-	-	-	-	-	13	-	-
JW (Jack) Yorke	F	F	F	F	F	F	F	F	F	F	F	F	-	-	-	-	-	F	F	F	F	F	F	F	F	F	F	F	F	F	F	26	1	2

1 GAME: TH (Tom) Crumbie >W(28), AE (Alfred) Daniells =Ft(13), WJ Gilbey <HB(5), AS (Arthur) Hancock =FB(13), R (Reuben) Hargreaves =F(22), J Henson >C(22), K (Kenneth) McAlpin F(12), A (Arthur) Moore >HB(27), C (Charley) Moore =W(2), E Neild <HB(30), A Nicholson =F(3), EA (Snooks) Nuttall =W(22), FG (Fred) Orton >HB(10), HC (Harry) Pilsbury <FB(3), WR (Willie) Porter <Ft(28), A (Arthur) Sulley Wt(3), FC (Freddy) Toone >HB(29), F (Frank) Tyler =HB(4), CE (Charlie) Watts >C(13)

The key for how to read the stats is on the last page

CHAPTER 5

Grounds for Celebration

1892/1893

The acquisition of a new ground, of course, brought attendant administrative problems. The regular monthly committee meeting became a weekly one as autumn of 1892 turned to winter and the workload on individuals grew. The ground committee ordered the installation of fencing at Welford Road and then discovered their new commercial role: applications for perimeter advertising came flooding in and, in some trepidation, the club turned to the city estates committee, expecting to be accused of making money by illegal means. However, they were assured that advertising was entirely legitimate and, confidence growing, received an offer from Messrs Scott and Pearson to distribute an advertisement sheet including the names of the contending teams on match day.

Leicester being the thriving commercial centre it was and is, the committee advertised matches in the local newspapers on Fridays and Saturdays and, for 15 shillings a week, posted slips on the cars and buses of the Tramways Company. Few in the city could not be aware of the young sporting body and various requests to hire the new ground were received: the YMCA applied successfully for Easter Monday, the county rugby union played there and the Press and Panto Company as well, though what the latter body got up to, history does not record.

To sustain their boast of a ground protected against frost the ground committee spent their Octobers in search of straw. At 37 shillings a ton they were authorised to spend no more than £50 while they also lashed out on a 30-foot flagpole at sevenpence a foot with a flag costing 35 shillings. Consideration was even given to floodlighting, for training purposes, but the committee baulked at the cost of 12 naphtha lamps and turned the idea down.

On the field, however, all was not entirely well. The local press complained of "reprehensible" tactics by the Lancashire club Pendleton in a 9-2 defeat ("such brutality was never intended to be introduced to our sports") while already Tigers were drawing on students from Cambridge University and occasionally faced problems when the youngsters were not available. For the home game with Moseley that season for instance, three-quarter Hugh Bryan, it was reported, "in company with his fellow collegians, had been gated for a week and so could not leave the Alma Mater." Moseley won that match by three goals and six tries to nil and in the Gloucester game "the Westerners pushed the scrum in the easiest manner possible" and won by two goals and three tries to nil. Against Coventry, however, Leicester introduced the Reverend Henry C Wilkinson, late of the Leeds Parish Church Club, and resorted to the four three-quarter system. With two more reverends, Ley and Wynne, at half-back, perhaps God was on their side and they forced a draw. The reverend Robert George Ley was reported by the *Wyvern* newspaper to be "the People's Idol never known to be out of form and when he wears the scarlet, green and white jersey it adds 25% to the gate receipts!"

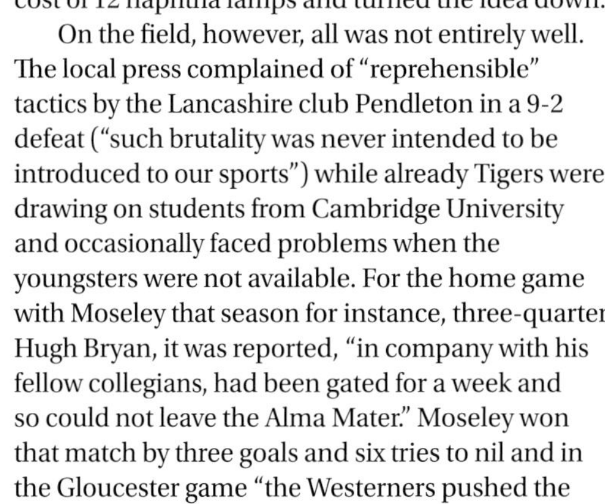

⬇ Frederick Brett was the club's honorary treasurer from 1890-95.

In the new year came the first visitors from London, Guy's Hospital, playing the Tigers on 21 January 1893. The Tigers' initial visit to London had been the preceding year when they came away from Blackheath a thoroughly chastened side, beaten 37-0. Guy's were the first of four London sides in a season dominated by home games, although most opposition came from the Midlands and the north. The derby matches produced attendances up to 7,000 and club membership tickets rose to six shillings; by the end of the season Frederick John Brett, the treasurer, was not entirely unhappy with a deficit of £476 and five shillings considering the costs of preparing the new ground.

There were rumours that this might be the last year of Midland Counties Cup competition, that there might soon be a Midland Counties league, but they came to nothing. The game of the season was the second-round Midland Counties Cup match with Coventry: the Leicester committee speculated by doubling admission charges and accumulated £220, 17 shillings and elevenpence from a gate of more than 10,000 which, unhappily, saw Leicester beaten 12-0. Extra seating was required and even so the accommodation was not sufficient. Leicester ended their longest season yet with 16 wins from their 36 games.

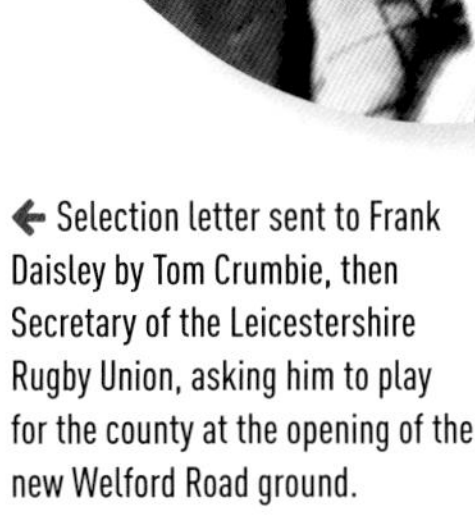

Leicestershire Rugby Football Union
20 Clubs Affiliated
The Senior Challenge Cup
The Junior Challenge Cup
Hon Sec. T.H. Crumbie.

34, Highcross St.
Leicester 1st Sept 1892

Leicester v L. R. U.
Sept 10th 1892

Dear Sir,
I have pleasure in informing you that you have been chosen to play in the above match.
Shall be pleased to hear that you will be able to meet me at 3-30 pm at the dressing room "The Bedford" on that date.
Trusting to having an enjoyable game I remain Faithfully yours
T. Crumbie

Mr Daisley.

🡐 Selection letter sent to Frank Daisley by Tom Crumbie, then Secretary of the Leicestershire Rugby Union, asking him to play for the county at the opening of the new Welford Road ground.

1893/1894

The workload on the club officials had increased hugely and the annual meeting in 1893 pondered whether to appoint a paid secretary at an annual salary between £20-£25 with bonuses for increased membership! At the subsequent half-yearly general meeting on 15 September (held in the Temperance Hall) members heard that John Henry Hancock had taken over as secretary and 250 new members had already been "elected"; there is no record of the new official's bonus. Seating accommodation was being expanded as the club pushed forward its ambitious plans, which included hosting some kind of forerunner of the old divisional championship, a match between the Midlands and the Western Counties.

This season the club moved from the Bedford Hotel to the George Hotel for their headquarters - there was no clubhouse at the ground then - though they continued to change at the Bedford and trot across to the ground pursued by small boys and admiring female glances! A professional trainer was appointed to alleviate their aches and pains and he seems to have worked wonders, for they made an excellent start to the 1893/94 season. Shrewdly the season opened against a Leicestershire XV and Leicester Crusaders, a recognition of local talent and useful training matches for the club before the first visit to Welford Road of Kent Wanderers; seven London teams were included on the fixture list as well as Penygraig from Wales and Bective Rangers from Dublin, the first Irish opponents.

↑ The Bedford Hotel on the corner of Knighton Street and Aylestone Road was the club's headquarters and changing rooms from 1892 until the clubhouse was built in 1909.

↑ Beer mat from the Bedford Hotel featuring captain Edward Redman.

↓ Midland Counties Cup final action, Tigers (in vertical stripes) v Coventry at Rugby, 31.3.1894.

A favourite of the crowd was the centre, Bob Hesmondhalgh, known for reasons which must remain obscure as 'Clasher'; whether he was as well favoured by Mrs Hesmondhalgh is not revealed, for a few hours after their marriage at St Andrew's church on 14 April 1894, Clasher was playing against Manchester Free Wanderers, helping his club to a 9-0 win rather than being locked in nuptial bliss. Such sacrifice doubtless contributed to the testimonial match which was contemplated on his behalf.

Again Tigers reached the Midland Counties Cup final but lost to Coventry at the Rugby Cricket Club ground in Bilton Road, and there were complaints from members that none of the cup ties had been at home, which had hit finances.

The Evening Mail reported: "The town of Rugby was taken by storm. Everything in the shape of a conveyance had been pressed into service, from the lordly four-in-hand and palatial saloon to the farmer's wagon and the 'cattle truck' third. All types of cycle extant might have been observed on the road or piled up in their hundreds near the enclosure, from the latest pattern of high-frame pneumatics irreverently called the 'buck jumper,' down to the worn out jigger of a decade ago, whose tyre was fastened on apparently by miles of string.

"A bevy of fair cyclists in their charming tailor-made costumes held a prominent position in the enclosure next to the Press Stand. Indeed all Coventry seemed to be there, and had secured the best positions before the Leicester excursions got in."

There were also letters to the local press complaining that Tigers players had been overlooked for representative honours by the Midland Counties while the president pointed out to members how they should "keep their feelings in bound and not be led to make uncharitable remarks during the game." One committee minute unlikely to recur these days is the one which agreed to "consult Mr Field as to the probable cost of repairing Mr Akers' teeth." 'Tough' Akers was also a boxer of some repute and there is no indication of which sport he was engaged in when the damage was suffered.

1894/1895

The annual meeting was told that there were now 920 members of the club, which was growing weekly, amid warnings through circulars regarding professionalism from the Rugby Football Union.

Some outstanding players were filtering in and out of Leicester's sides now and Edward Redman captained in 1895 a first XV which included scrum-half Billy Foreman, who came to Leicester with the Kent Wanderers, was found a public house to manage and promptly stayed. The Nottinghamshire cricketer AO (Arthur) Jones made his debut in the last game of the 1894/95 season, at full back, just in time to see Leicester pass 500 points, having conceded less than 100. The second game of that season, indeed, had been quite an occasion for it was against Burfield Rangers, holders of the Leicestershire Senior Cup. It was intended as a warm-up for more serious affairs and at the end of it Tigers ran out winners by 71-0, for many years their record score, though equalled against a Bedford XV during the 1918/19 season. To be fair, the local press could only make it 69-0, a conversion having gone astray somewhere in a match when 17 tries were scored. The referee made it 71 though and his word was law - as that official pointed out afterwards, there wasn't really any doubt who had won!

It had been a tremendous season, tempered only by the failure to win the Midland Counties Cup, Tigers going down to Moseley 0-11 at the Reddings in the semi-finals on 23 March – a game in which passions ran so high that the Birmingham club refused to arrange any fixtures against the Tigers for the following eight seasons. For a change the acrimony between the two sides was off the field as a series of letters were sent and received claiming extra expenses and unprofessional attitudes levelled at each other.

Off the field Leicester had grown in stature too, helping to form the Leicester Schools League and establishing a midweek team, the Leicester Thursday, for players unavailable at the weekend. The schools league arose as the result of a letter published locally from an enthusiastic member, Frederick St Clair Pain, of Forest House in Clarendon Park, who called for an annual dinner and the presentation of "a cup to be presented among the public elementary schools, the final to be played at the ground." After appropriate debate Leicester agreed to guarantee £25 towards the cost of forming a schools league and two club members and former players, William Wheeler and Arthur Jackson, were appointed to the organising committee. It was the first of several significant alliances with the youth of the city and the club.

The organisation for the team and supporters to away games was remarkable: the club booked trains with the Midland Rail Company, the North-Western, the Great North Railway and the South and HW line to games at Rugby, Coventry, Northampton and Nuneaton respectively, though kick-off times tended to fluctuate depending on arrival of the trains. The club even issued free rail passes to away games for the local rugby writers - well, it is never a bad thing to have the press on your side. Moreover the welfare of the players was looked after by an insurance policy against injury while training or playing. The policy permitted the payment of twenty shillings a week to an injured player but no more than £10 for any one accident. In due course the (inaptly named for Leicester) Ocean Insurance Company insured the club's three teams for an annual premium of £25, though since it was raised by 50 per cent the following year there would seem to have been rather too many claims.

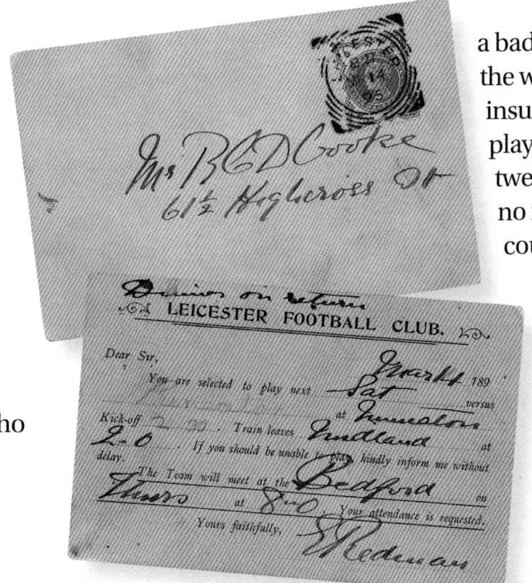
LEICESTER FOOTBALL CLUB.
Dear Sir,
You are selected to play next Sat March 189 versus
Kick-off ... Train leaves Midland at
If you should be unable to play, kindly inform me without delay.
The Team will meet at the Bedford on Thurs at 8-0. Your attendance is requested.
Yours faithfully,
E Redman

Selection card posted to Rupert Cooke for his 41st and final first-team game for Tigers, 16 March 1895, signed by skipper Edward Redman

Bobby Lewis was a one-season wonder, scoring 24 tries during his only Tigers campaign in 1894/95.

Public relations were uppermost in the committee's mind too: various local associations were allowed to hire the ground while the Friar Lane Sunday School's annual children's treat went ahead free of charge. All these activities served to reduce the debt on the ground, if only by £64, but since spending amounted to a further £1,600 the bank clearly had faith in the club as a going concern.

A newcomer to the team, from Richmond, had been Frank Jackson, reputedly one of the fastest wings in the Midlands. Looking back on those days 60 years later, Jackson said: "There was a lot more scrummaging and to my way of thinking it was a more skilful part of the game than it is now. Scrums lasted longer but although this made play rather dull for the spectators it was far more interesting for the players.

"I remember how Leicester were the first club to spread sand on the pitch during frosty weather. The sand was used so that a match against Coventry should not be cancelled because a large gate was expected. One of the Tigers' officials, Tom Pettifor, promised me a new hat if I scored a try. I scored the try alright but I never got the hat!"

It was all change off the pitch - the treasurer, Frederick Brett, tendered his resignation after five years in the post in May but it is unclear whether this was due to criticism of his performance because almost immediately St Clair Pain tabled a proposal at the AGM "that a sub-committee is appointed whose duties shall be to deal generally with the finances of the club." The proposal was carried but there was still "a hearty vote of thanks" given to Brett in the committee meeting minutes, and the September general meeting went further with a toast: "to mark the club's deep sense of the admirable way in which he carried out the onerous duties of the office during a time when such assistance was vital to the wellbeing of the club." William Swingler was appointed to look after the purse strings.

Tom Pettifor had succeeded John Hancock as secretary, after Salmon had resigned through pressure of business, but then Pettifor too resigned in early August 1895 because he was due to be frequently engaged in business away from the city. His successor was hugely significant: Thomas Henry Crumbie had played for and captained Leicester Swifts and for Tigers' A side, and had also been the A team secretary before he became Leicester's secretary on 2 August 1895, at the age of 27. He also turned out three times for the first XV between 1892-97 and had been secretary of the Leicestershire Rugby Union since 1892. Crumbie was to occupy his new role for the next 33 years and his influence on the club's fortunes went far beyond that.

Agenda for the 1894/95 AGM.

← TIGERS v COVENTRY EXCELSIOR 4 March 1893
Back: Collier (Touch Judge), Touhey, Wilkinson, Sewell, R.Cooke, Hesmondhalgh, McAlpin (Hon.Sec).
Middle: Yorke, W.Jackson, Patchett, Sturges (capt), T.Cooke, Edmonds.
Front: Bryan, Toone, McKechnie, Ley.

← LEICESTER FOOTBALL CLUB 1893/94
Back: Collier (Touch Judge), Day, Touhey, Wilkinson (Vice-capt), Rendle, Hesmondhalgh, Cave (Team attendant), Parsons (President).
Middle: W.Jackson, Vity, T.Cooke (capt), Foreman, Akers, Simpson.
Front: Carey, C.Watts, Hitchcock, Banks.

← LEICESTER FOOTBALL CLUB 1894/95
Back: Collier (Touch Judge), Pettifor (Hon.Sec), Swain, Vity, Banks, Jones, Akers, Salmon (Committee Member), Snowden (Committee Member).
Middle: Parsons (President), Hitchcock, W.Jackson, Redman (capt), Hesmondhalgh, Dann, T.Cooke.
Front: Brown, F.Jackson, Simpson, Foreman (Vice-capt), Lewis.

18	92/93	Home Ground: Welford Road
		Captain: Jack Sturges
		Vice-captain: Willie Watts

OVERALL RECORD:					T	C	PG	DG	MK	PTS
PLD	W	D	L	Tigers scored:	63	17	4	10	2	237
36	16	5	15	Opponents scored:	66	30	1	4	0	241

GM	DATE		VEN	OPPONENTS	RESULT	TRIES	KICKS	ATT
MIDLAND COUNTIES CUP						**CUP WINNERS: COVENTRY**		
29	Mar	**4**	**H**	**Coventry Excelsior (1)**	W 18-0	Bryan(2), Wilkinson(2), T.Cooke, Hesmondhalgh	Bryan p, T.Cooke c	-
30		**11**	**H**	**Coventry (2)**	L 0-12	-	-	10000
CLUB MATCHES								
1	Sep	**10**	**H**	**Leicestershire XV**	W 17-0	T.Cooke, Rathbone, Sewell, Toone, W.Watts	T.Cooke c, McKechnie d	-
2		**17**	**H**	**Manchester Free Wanderers**	L 0-5	-	-	-
3		**24**	**H**	**South Northamptonshire**	W 39-0	Ley(2), Toone(2), W.Watts(2), Bryan, Sturges, Yorke	T.Cooke 3c/p, R.Cooke 3c	2000
4	Oct	1	a	Rugby	W 18-0	Ball(2), Bryan, W.Watts, T.Cooke	Bryan d, W.Watts d	-
5		**8**	**H**	**Old Edwardians**	D 2-2	W.Watts	-	-
6		**15**	**H**	**Pendleton**	L 2-9	Edmonds	-	3000
7		22	a	Moseley	L 0-27	-	-	-
8		29	a	Burton	D 2-2	Edmonds	-	-
9	Nov	**5**	**H**	**Bedford School**	L 2-26	Ley	-	-
10		12	a	Coventry	L 2-12	W.Watts	-	-
11		**14m**	**H**	**Salford**	L 0-6	-	-	-
12		**16w**	**H**	**Ashby-de-la-Zouch**	W 8-0	Williams(4)	-	-
13		**19**	**H**	**Gloucester**	L 0-16	-	-	-
14		**26**	**H**	**Bedford**	W 8-0	Greenwood, Hesmondhalgh	Bryan d	-
15	Dec	**3**	**H**	**Kirkstall**	W 12-5	Hesmondhalgh, S.Page, Sewell	Bown c, McKechnie c	-
		10	a	Bedford	PP (frost)			
16		**17**	**H**	**Sale**	W 7-0	Bryan, Greenwood	Bryan c	-
17		**24**	**H**	**Coventry**	D 5-5	King	Bryan c	-
18		**26m**	**H**	**Swinton**	L 0-10	-	-	-
		31		Stourbridge	PP (frost)			
	Jan	7	a	Old Edwardians	PP (frost)			
19		**14**	**H**	**Burton**	D 2-2	King	-	-
20		**21**	**H**	**Guy's Hospital**	D 11-11	Sturges(2)	Hesmondhalgh d, Bryan c	-
21		**28**	**H**	**Rugby**	L 6-20	Toone	Hesmondhalgh d	6000
22	Feb	**4**	**H**	**St Thomas' Hospital**	L 4-7	-	T.Cooke m	-
23		8w	a	Bedford School	L 4-7	Bryan, Hitchcock	-	-
24		**11**	**H**	**Old Merchant Taylors**	L 0-2	-	-	-
25		18	a	Gloucester	L 0-12	-	-	-
26		**23th**	**H**	**St Bartholomew's Hospital**	W 9-4	Edmonds, Moore, Touhey	T.Cooke c	-
27		**25**	**H**	**Moseley**	W 6-4	Toone	Bryan d	7000
28	Mar	1w	a	Ashby-de-la-Zouch	W 4-0	Hitchcock, C.Watts	-	-
31		**18**	**H**	**Handsworth**	W 16-0	H.Simpson	Bryan c/2d, T.Cooke p	-
32	Apr	**3m**	**H**	**Broughton Rangers**	W 5-0	Hitchcock	T.Cooke c	-
33		**4tu**	**H**	**York**	W 6-4	H.Simpson	McKechnie d	-
34		**15**	**H**	**Kent Wanderers**	W 9-5	C.Watts(2), Touhey	Day p	-
35		**22**	**H**	**Manningham**	L 2-19	T.Cooke	-	-
36		**29**	**H**	**Cardiff Harlequins**	W 11-7	Broadhurst, C.Watts	T.Cooke c/m	-

INDIVIDUAL APPEARANCES 1892/93

Name / Game #	1	2	3	4	5	6	7	8	9	10	11	12	13	14	15	16	17	18	19	20	21	22	23	24	25	26	27	28	29	30	31	32	33	34	35	36	Apps	T	Pts
J (Jesse) Ball	C	FB	C	C	C	C	W	W	-	-	-	W	-	-	-	-	-	-	-	-	-	-	-	-	-	-	-	-	-	-	-	-	-	-	-	-	9	2	4
JE (Jack) Barradell	-	-	-	-	-	-	-	-	-	-	-	-	-	-	-	-	-	-	HB	-	-	-	-	HB	-	-	-	<HB	-	-	-	-	-	-	-	-	3	-	-
H (Henry) Bown	>F	-	-	-	-	-	-	-	-	-	W	-	-	C	C	C	F	C	F	-	-	-	<HB	-	-	-	-	-	-	-	-	-	-	-	-	-	9	-	3
F (Frank) Brown	-	-	-	-	-	-	-	-	-	-	-	-	-	-	-	-	-	-	-	-	-	-	>FB	-	-	FB	-	-	-	-	-	-	-	-	-	-	2	-	-
H (Hugh) Bryan	-	-	>W	W	W	W	-	C	-	-	-	-	C	W	-	W	W	W	-	W	W	-	W	W	-	-	W	-	W	W	W	-	-	-	-	-	18	6	47
RCD (Rupert) Cooke	-	>F	F	F	F	F	F	F	F	F	F	F	F	F	F	F	F	F	F	F	F	F	-	F	F	F	F	F	F	F	F	F	F	F	F	F	34	-	9
AE (Ted) Cooke	F	F*	F	F	F	F	F	F	F	F	F	F*	F	F	F	F	F	F	F	F	F	F	-	F	F	F	F	F	F	F	F	F	F	F	F	F	35	4	46
E (Edward) Dann	-	-	-	-	-	-	-	-	-	-	-	-	-	-	-	-	-	-	>F	F	F	-	F	F	-	-	-	-	-	-	-	-	-	F	-	-	6	-	-
GF (George) Day	-	-	-	-	-	-	-	-	-	-	-	-	-	-	-	-	-	-	-	-	-	-	-	>W	-	-	-	-	-	-	-	C	C	FB	FB	-	5	-	3
JT (John) Edmonds	-	F	-	F	F	F	F	F	F	F	F	F	F	F	F	F	F	-	F	F	F	F	-	F	-	F	F	-	F	F	F	-	-	-	-	-	25	3	6
J (John) Greenwood	-	-	-	-	-	-	-	-	-	-	-	-	-	>F	F	F	F	F	-	F	F	-	-	-	-	-	-	-	-	-	-	F	F	-	-	F	10	2	4
WR (Bob) Hesmondhalgh	-	-	-	-	-	-	-	-	-	-	-	-	-	>W	W	W	C	C	C	C	C	C	C	C	W	C	C	C*	C	C	-	C	W	W	W	W	22	3	14
AE (Alfred) Hitchcock	-	-	-	-	-	-	-	-	>F	-	-	F	-	-	-	-	-	-	-	-	-	-	W	-	C	W	-	W	-	-	-	W	W	W	W	W	11	3	6
AL (Arthur) Jackson	-	-	-	-	-	-	-	-	-	-	-	-	-	-	-	-	-	-	-	-	-	-	-	F	-	-	-	-	-	-	-	-	F	F	F	-	4	-	-
W (Walter) Jackson	-	-	F	-	-	-	F	F	F	F	F	F	F	F	F	F	-	-	-	-	F	F	F	F	F	F	F	F	F	F	F	F	-	F	F	F	26	-	-
HWA (Harry) Joyce	F	<F	-	-	-	-	-	-	-	-	-	-	-	-	-	-	-	-	-	-	-	-	-	-	-	-	-	-	-	-	-	-	-	-	-	-	2	-	-
J (Jabez) King	-	-	-	-	-	-	-	-	-	-	-	-	-	-	-	-	>F	F	W	W	-	-	-	-	-	-	-	-	-	-	-	-	-	-	F	-	5	2	4
Rev. RG (Robert) Ley	HB	-	HB	-	HB	-	HB	HB	W	-	HB	-	-	-	-	HB	HB	-	-	-	-	-	-	-	-	-	HB	-	HB	HB	HB	-	-	HB	-	-	14	3	6
A (Arthur) McKechnie	FB	-	FB	FB	FB	FB	C	FB	FB	FB	-	-	FB	FB	FB	FB	FB	FB	FB	FB	FB	FB	-	FB	-	-	FB	-	FB	FB	FB	FB	FB	-	-	FB	27	-	11
CJ Mason	-	-	-	-	-	-	-	-	-	>C	<C	-	-	-	-	-	-	-	-	-	-	-	-	-	-	-	-	-	-	-	-	-	-	-	-	-	2	-	-
JWM (John) Meek	-	-	-	-	-	-	-	-	-	-	-	-	-	-	-	-	-	-	F	-	-	-	-	-	-	-	-	F	-	-	-	-	-	-	-	-	2	-	-
JC (Joseph) Memory	-	HB	-	HB	-	-	-	-	HB	-	-	-	-	-	-	-	-	-	-	-	-	-	-	-	-	-	-	-	-	-	-	-	-	-	-	-	3	-	-
A (Arthur) Moore	-	-	-	-	-	-	-	-	-	-	-	-	-	-	HB	-	-	-	-	-	-	-	-	-	-	HB	-	-	-	-	-	-	-	-	-	-	2	1	2
CA Page	>W	W	-	-	-	-	-	-	-	-	-	-	-	-	-	-	-	-	-	-	-	-	-	-	-	-	-	-	-	-	-	-	-	-	-	-	2	-	-
SE Page	-	-	-	-	-	-	-	-	>C	W	-	-	W	-	<W	-	-	-	-	-	-	-	-	-	-	-	-	-	-	-	-	-	-	-	-	-	4	1	2
Rev. AW (Albert) Parkes	-	>F	F	F	F	F	F	F	-	F	F	F	F	F	-	-	-	-	-	-	-	-	-	-	-	-	-	<F	-	-	-	-	-	-	-	-	13	-	-
J (John) Patchett	F	F	F	F	F	F	F	F	F	F	F	-	F	F	F	F	-	F	F	F	F	F	-	-	W	F	F	-	F	F	F	-	F	F	F	F	30	-	-
J Rathbone	C	<C	-	-	-	-	-	-	-	-	-	-	-	-	-	-	-	-	-	-	-	-	-	-	-	-	-	-	-	-	-	-	-	-	-	-	2	1	2
A (Arthur) Sewell	>F	F	F	F	F	F	F	F	F	F	F	-	F	F	F	F	F	F	F	F	-	F	F	F	F	F	F	F	F	<F	-	-	-	-	-	-	28	2	4
F (Fred) Simpson	-	-	-	-	-	-	-	-	-	-	-	F	-	-	-	-	-	-	-	-	-	-	F	-	-	-	-	F	-	-	-	-	<F	-	-	-	4	-	-
HJ (Harry) Simpson	-	-	-	-	-	-	-	-	-	-	-	F	-	-	-	-	-	-	-	-	-	-	-	-	-	-	-	F	-	-	F	F	HB	HB	HB	HB	8	2	4
RS (Dickie) Snowden	-	-	-	-	-	-	-	-	-	-	-	-	-	-	-	-	-	-	HB	HB	-	-	-	-	HB	HB	-	-	-	-	-	<HB	-	-	-	-	5	-	-
W Stewart	F	<F	-	-	-	-	-	-	-	-	-	-	-	-	-	-	-	-	-	-	-	-	-	-	-	-	-	-	-	-	-	-	-	-	-	-	2	-	-
WH (Jack) Sturges	F*	-	F*	F*	F*	F*	F*	F*	F*	F*	F*	-	F*	F*	F*	F*	F*	F*	F*	F*	F*	F*	F*	F*	F*	F*	F*	-	F*	F*	F*	F*	F*	F*	F*	<F*	33	3	6
FC (Freddy) Toone	HB	HB	HB	HB	HB	HB	HB	HB	HB	HB	-	-	HB	HB	-	-	-	HB	-	HB	HB	HB	-	HB	HB	-	HB	-	HB	<HB	-	-	-	-	-	-	21	5	10
J (James) Touhey	-	-	-	-	-	-	-	-	-	-	-	-	-	-	-	-	-	-	-	-	-	-	-	-	>F	F	F	F	-	F	F	F	F	F	F	F	11	2	4
CE (Charlie) Watts	-	-	-	-	-	-	-	-	-	-	-	-	-	-	-	-	-	-	-	-	-	-	F	-	-	-	-	W	-	-	HB	HB	HB	C	HB	HB	8	4	8
WA (Willie) Watts	W	W	W	W	W	W	-	-	W	W	W	-	W	HB	HB	HB	-	-	W	-	-	W	-	-	-	W	-	-	-	-	-	-	-	-	-	-	16	6	16
Rev. HC (Henry) Wilkinson	-	-	-	-	-	-	-	-	-	-	-	-	-	-	-	-	>W	W	-	-	W	W	-	-	-	-	W	-	W	W	W	-	-	-	C	C	10	2	4
D Williams	-	-	>F	F	F	F	F	F	F	F	F	F	F	-	F	F	F	F	-	F	F	F	-	-	<F	-	-	-	-	-	-	-	-	-	-	-	19	4	8
Rev. O (Owen) Wynne	-	-	-	-	-	HB	-	-	-	HB	HB	-	HB	-	-	-	HB	HB	-	-	HB	<HB	-	-	-	-	-	-	-	-	-	-	-	-	-	-	8	-	-
JW (Jack) Yorke	F	F	F	F	F	F	-	-	-	-	-	-	-	-	-	-	-	-	-	-	-	F	F	F	F	F	F	F	F	F	F	F	F	F	F	<F	21	1	2

1 GAME: SM (Seth) Baines <FB(11), JTL (Jack) Broadhurst =Ct(36), BD (Bissill) Carlisle <FB(25), EW Chamberlain <FB(12), FR (Frank) Charters <C(31), TH (Tom) Crumbie W(12), H (Harry) German W(8), J Henson <C(12), EC (Ellis) Johnson =HB(12), K (Kenneth) McAlpin <HB(12), AH (Arthur) Mann =W(7), FG (Fred) Orton <HB(28), GW (George) Orton >FB(28), A (Arthur) Sulley <W(32), Swift =FB(7), DW Thomas =C(25), CF Thompson =HB(23), HC (Charles) Thorpe =F(23), AJ Young =F(23)

The key for how to read the stats is on the last page

18	93/94	
		Home Ground: Welford Road
		Captain: Ted Cooke
		Vice-captain: Rev Henry Wilkinson

OVERALL RECORD:					T	C	PG	DG	MK	PTS
PLD	W	D	L	Tigers scored:	68	29	3	2	1	283
37	23	3	11	Opponents scored:	32	16	1	4	1	151

GM	DATE		VEN	OPPONENTS	RESULT	TRIES	KICKS	ATT
MIDLAND COUNTIES CUP						**CUP WINNERS: COVENTRY**		
31	Mar	**17**	**H**	**Stoneygate (3)**	W 26-0	Hesmondhalgh(3), Hitchcock(2), W.Jackson, Touhey, Wilkinson	W.Jackson c	-
32		24	a	Rugby (sf)	W 6-5	Banks, Vity	-	-
35		31		Coventry (f)	L 0-11	-	-	-
CLUB MATCHES								
1	Sep	**16**	**H**	**Leicestershire XV**	W 26-6	Hitchcock(2), T.Cooke, Memory, Redman, C.Watts	T.Cooke c, R.Cooke 3c	-
2		**23**	**H**	**Leicester Crusaders**	W 23-0	Hitchcock(2), T.Cooke, Hesmondhalgh, W.Jackson	T.Cooke 4c	-
3		**30**	**H**	**Kent Wanderers**	L 6-14	C.Watts	T.Cooke p	-
4	Oct	**2m**	**H**	**Swinton**	D 0-0	-	-	-
5		**7**	**H**	**Gloucester**	L 3-8	C.Watts	-	-
6		**14**	**H**	**Coventry**	L 0-3	-	-	-
7		**21**	**H**	**Moseley**	W 6-5	Hesmondhalgh, C.Watts	-	-
8		25w	a	Bedford School	W 11-4	Hesmondhalgh, Hitchcock, Touhey	Hesmondhalgh c	-
9		**28**	**H**	**Burton**	W 7-5	Simpson	T.Cooke m	-
10	Nov	**4**	**H**	**Edgbaston Crusaders**	W 11-4	Foreman, Hitchcock, Touhey	Banks c	-
11		11	a	Coventry	L 0-8	-	-	-
12		**18**	**H**	**Rugby**	W 3-0	Hitchcock	-	-
13		25	a	Rugby	W 8-7	C.Watts	T.Cooke p, McKechnie c	-
	Dec	2	a	Old Edwardians	PP (frost)			
14		9	a	Moseley	D 0-0	-	-	-
15		**16**	**H**	**Sale**	W 10-0	C.Watts, Hesmondhalgh	C.Watts d	-
16		23	a	Bedford	L 6-8	T.Cooke, Foreman	-	-
17		**26tu**	**H**	**Penygraig**	W 13-3	Bryan, Hesmondhalgh, Wilkinson	Bryan 2c	-
18		**27w**	**H**	**Pontefract**	W 21-3	Bryan, Banks, T.Cooke, C.Watts, Wilkinson	Bryan 3c	-
19		**30**	**H**	**Bedford**	L 3-7	-	Bryan p	7000
20	Jan	**1m**	**H**	**Bective Rangers**	W 5-0	Touhey	Bryan c	-
		6	a	Gloucester	PP (frost)			
21		13	a	Burton	W 5-3	Bryan	Bryan c	-
22		**20**	**H**	**St Thomas' Hospital**	D 0-0	-	-	-
23		**27**	**H**	**Old Leysians**	L 0-3	-	-	-
24	Feb	**3**	**H**	**Handsworth**	W 19-0	Foreman(2), Hesmondhalgh, Carey, Harlow	Foreman c, Hesmondhalgh c	-
25		**10**	**H**	**Guy's Hospital**	L 0-15	-	-	-
26		**12m**	**H**	**St Bartholomew's Hospital**	W 18-0	Foreman(2), Hesmondhalgh, T.Cooke	Foreman c, Hesmondhalgh 2c	-
27		**17**	**H**	**Old Edwardians**	W 5-0	Hitchcock	Hesmondhalgh c	-
28		**24**	**H**	**Bedford School**	W 3-0	Akers	-	-
29	Mar	**3**	**H**	**Croydon**	W 3-0	Foreman	-	8000
30		**10**	**H**	**Ambleside**	W 16-5	Hesmondhalgh, T.Cooke, Touhey, Wilkinson	Hesmondhalgh c, Foreman c	-
33		**26m**	**H**	**Broughton Rangers**	L 3-16	Hesmondhalgh	-	-
34		**27tu**	**H**	**East Sheen**	L 3-5	Barth	-	-
36	Apr	**7**	**H**	**Old Merchant Taylors**	W 5-3	T.Cooke	T.Cooke c	-
37		**14**	**H**	**Manchester Free Wanderers**	W 9-0	T.Cooke	T.Cooke c, Brown d	-

Neutral Venue: *#35 at Cricket Club - Rugby*

INDIVIDUAL APPEARANCES 1893/94

Name / Game #	1	2	3	4	5	6	7	8	9	10	11	12	13	14	15	16	17	18	19	20	21	22	23	24	25	26	27	28	29	30	31	32	33	34	35	36	37	Apps	T	Pts
A (Arthur) Akers	-	-	-	-	-	-	-	-	-	-	-	-	>F	F	-	F	F	F	F	F	F	F	F	F	F	F	F	F	F	F	F	F	-	-	F	-	-	20	1	3
G (George) Banks	>F	F	F	F	-	F	F	F	F	F	F	F	F	F	F	F	F	F	F	F	F	F	F	F	-	-	-	-	-	-	F	F	F	-	F	F	F	29	2	8
W (William) Barth	-	-	-	-	-	-	-	-	-	-	-	-	-	-	-	-	-	-	-	-	-	-	-	-	-	-	>C	C	C	-	-	-	W	W	-	<C	-	6	1	3
GE (George) Blunt	-	-	-	-	-	-	-	-	-	-	-	-	-	-	-	-	-	=FB	-	-	-	-	-	-	-	-	-	-	-	-	-	-	-	-	-	-	-	1	-	-
F (Frank) Brown	FB	-	-	FB	FB	FB	FB	FB	FB	FB	FB	FB	-	-	-	FB	FB	-	-	-	FB	-	-	FB	-	FB	-	-	FB	-	-	-	-	FB	-	FB	FB	19	-	4
H (Hugh) Bryan	-	-	-	-	-	-	-	-	-	-	-	-	-	-	-	W	W	W	W	W	C	-	-	-	-	-	-	-	-	-	-	W	-	-	W	-	-	8	3	26
W Burton	-	-	-	-	-	-	-	-	-	-	-	-	-	-	-	-	-	-	-	-	-	-	-	-	>F	-	-	-	-	-	-	-	-	-	-	-	-	1	-	-
E Butler	-	-	-	-	-	-	-	-	-	-	-	-	-	-	-	-	-	-	-	-	-	-	-	-	-	-	-	-	-	-	-	-	-	-	-	-	=C	1	-	-
WH (William) Carey	-	-	>F	F	F	F	F	F	F	F	F	F	-	-	F	F	F	F	F	-	-	F	F	F	F	-	F	F	F	F	F	-	F	-	F	F	<F	28	1	3
RCD (Rupert) Cooke	F	F	F	F	F	-	-	-	-	-	-	-	-	-	-	-	-	-	-	-	-	-	-	-	-	-	-	-	-	-	-	-	-	-	-	-	-	5	-	6
AE (Ted) Cooke	F*	F*	F*	F*	F*	F*	F*	-	F*	F*	F*	F*	F*	F*	F*	F*	F*	F*	F*	F*	F*	F*	F*	F*	F*	F*	F*	F*	F*	F*	F*	F*	F*	-	F*	F*	F*	35	8	48
E (Edward) Dann	-	-	-	-	-	-	-	F	-	-	-	-	-	-	-	-	-	-	-	F	F	F	-	F	-	-	-	-	-	-	-	-	F	-	-	-	-	6	-	-
GF (George) Day	-	W	W	-	-	-	-	-	-	-	-	-	-	-	-	-	-	-	-	-	-	-	-	-	FB	-	FB	FB	-	FB	FB	FB	FB	-	<FB	-	-	10	-	-
JT (John) Edmonds	-	<F	-	-	-	-	-	-	-	-	-	-	-	-	-	-	-	-	-	-	-	-	-	-	-	-	-	-	-	-	-	-	-	-	-	-	-	1	-	-
WJ (Billy) Foreman	-	-	-	-	>HB	HB	HB	HB	HB	HB	HB	HB	HB	HB	HB	HB	-	-	HB	HB	HB	HB	HB	HB	HB	HB	HB	HB	HB	HB	HB	HB	-	HB	HB	HB	HB	30	7	27
H (Harry) German	-	-	-	-	-	-	-	-	-	-	F	F	-	F	F	F	F	F	F	-	F	HB	<F	-	-	-	-	-	-	-	-	-	-	-	-	-	-	11	-	-
RR (Bob) Golding	-	-	-	-	-	-	-	-	-	-	-	-	-	-	-	-	-	-	-	-	-	-	-	-	-	-	-	-	-	F	-	-	-	F	-	-	-	2	-	-
J (John) Greenwood	F	-	<F	-	-	-	-	-	-	-	-	-	-	-	-	-	-	-	-	-	-	-	-	-	-	-	-	-	-	-	-	-	-	-	-	-	-	2	-	-
A (Arthur) Harlow	-	-	-	-	-	-	-	-	-	-	-	-	-	-	-	-	-	-	-	-	-	-	-	>F	<F	-	-	-	-	-	-	-	-	-	-	-	-	2	1	3
WR (Bob) Hesmondhalgh	C	W	C	C	W	C	C	C	C	C	C	C	C	W	C	-	C	C	C	-	-	-	W	W	C	C	C	W	W	C	C	C	C	C	C	W	C	33	12	48
G (George) Hicken	-	-	-	-	-	-	-	-	-	-	-	-	-	-	-	-	-	-	-	-	-	-	-	-	-	-	-	>HB	-	-	-	-	-	-	-	-	-	1	-	-
AE (Alfred) Hitchcock	W	C	W	W	W	C	C	C	C	C	C	C	C	C	W	W	-	-	-	-	W	W	C	C	W	W	W	C	C	W	W	C	-	-	-	C	W	30	10	30
AL (Arthur) Jackson	-	-	-	-	F	-	-	-	-	-	-	-	-	F	-	-	-	-	-	F	F	-	-	-	-	F	-	-	-	-	-	F	-	-	-	-	-	6	-	-
W (Walter) Jackson	F	F	F	F	F	F	F	F	F	F	F	F	F	F	F	F	F	F	F	F	F	-	F	F	F	F	F	F	F	F	F	F	F	F	F	F	F	36	2	8
G (George) Jones	-	-	-	-	-	-	-	-	-	-	-	-	-	-	-	-	-	-	-	-	-	-	-	-	-	>F	-	-	-	-	-	-	-	-	-	-	-	1	-	-
J (Jabez) King	F	F	-	-	-	W	-	-	-	-	-	-	-	<F	-	-	-	-	-	-	-	-	-	-	-	-	-	-	-	-	-	-	-	-	-	-	-	4	-	-
R (Robert) Lakin	-	-	-	-	-	-	-	-	-	-	-	-	-	-	-	-	-	-	-	-	-	F	-	-	-	-	-	-	-	-	-	-	-	<F	-	-	-	2	-	-
Rev. RG (Robert) Ley	-	-	-	HB	-	-	-	-	-	-	-	-	-	-	-	-	-	HB	-	-	-	-	-	-	-	-	-	-	-	-	-	-	HB	<HB	-	-	-	4	-	-
A (Arthur) McKechnie	-	FB	FB	-	-	-	-	-	-	-	-	-	FB	FB	FB	-	-	-	FB	FB	W	FB	<FB	-	-	-	-	-	-	-	-	-	-	-	-	-	-	10	-	2
JWM (John) Meek	-	-	-	-	-	-	-	F	F	F	-	-	F	-	-	-	-	-	-	-	-	-	-	-	-	F	-	-	-	-	-	-	-	-	-	-	-	5	-	-
JC (Joseph) Memory	HB	<HB	-	-	-	-	-	-	-	-	-	-	-	-	-	-	-	-	-	-	-	-	-	-	-	-	-	-	-	-	-	-	-	-	-	-	-	2	1	3
A (Arthur) Moore	-	-	-	-	-	-	-	-	-	-	-	-	-	-	-	-	<HB	-	-	-	-	-	-	-	-	-	-	-	-	-	-	-	-	-	-	-	-	1	-	-
J (John) Patchett	-	-	-	-	-	-	-	-	-	-	F	-	-	-	-	-	-	-	-	-	-	-	-	-	-	-	-	-	-	-	-	-	-	<F	-	-	-	2	-	-
BR (Bertie) Philbrick	-	-	-	-	-	-	-	-	-	-	-	-	-	-	-	-	-	-	-	-	-	-	-	-	-	-	-	-	-	-	-	-	-	=F	-	-	-	1	-	-
Dr. J (Jack) Pole-Kitson	-	-	-	-	-	-	-	-	-	-	-	-	-	-	-	-	-	-	-	-	-	=F	-	-	-	-	-	-	-	-	-	-	-	-	-	-	-	1	-	-
E (Eddie) Redman	>F	F	F	F	F	F	F	F	F	F	-	F	F	HB	F	-	-	-	-	-	-	-	-	-	-	-	-	-	-	-	-	-	-	-	-	-	-	14	1	3
Dr. AR (Arthur) Rendle	>F	F	F	F	F	F	F	F	F	F	F	F	F	F	F	F	F	F	F	F	-	F	-	-	-	-	F	F	F	F	F	F	F	F	F	F	<F	32	-	-
WK Roberts	-	-	-	-	-	-	-	-	-	-	-	-	-	-	-	-	-	-	-	=HB	-	-	-	-	-	-	-	-	-	-	-	-	-	-	-	-	-	1	-	-
HJ (Harry) Simpson	HB	-	HB	HB	HB	HB	HB	HB	HB	HB	HB	HB	HB	-	HB	HB	HB	HB	HB	F	HB	-	HB	HB	HB	HB	HB	-	HB	HB	HB	HB	HB	-	HB	HB	HB	32	1	3
RP (Paddy) Swain	-	-	-	-	-	-	-	-	-	-	-	-	-	-	-	-	-	-	-	-	-	-	-	-	>F	F	F	F	F	-	-	-	-	F	-	F	F	8	-	-
J (James) Touhey	F	F	F	F	F	F	F	F	F	F	F	F	F	F	F	F	F	F	F	F	F	F	F	F	F	F	F	F	F	F	F	F	F	F	F	F	<F	37	5	15
E (Edward) Vity	-	-	-	-	-	-	-	-	-	-	-	-	-	-	-	-	-	-	-	-	-	-	>F	F	F	F	F	F	F	F	F	F	F	-	F	F	F	14	1	3
GE (George) Ward	-	-	-	-	-	-	=F	-	-	-	-	-	-	-	-	-	-	-	-	-	-	-	-	-	-	-	-	-	-	-	-	-	-	-	-	-	-	1	-	-
CE (Charlie) Watts	W	HB	HB	W	C	F	W	W	W	W	W	W	W	W	C	C	C	C	C	C	C	C	C	W	-	-	-	-	-	C	C	W	C	C	C	-	-	30	7	25
WA (Willie) Watts	-	-	-	C	C	-	-	-	-	-	-	-	-	-	-	<C	-	-	-	-	-	-	-	-	-	-	-	-	-	-	-	-	-	-	-	-	-	3	-	-
Rev. HC (Henry) Wilkinson	-	-	-	-	-	W	W	W*	W	W	W	W	W	-	W	-	W	W	W	W	-	W	W	-	W	W	W	W	W	W	W	-	W	W*	W	W	<W	27	4	12

The key for how to read the stats is on the last page

1894/95		OVERALL RECORD:					T	C	PG	DG	MK	PTS
Home Ground: Welford Road		PLD	W	D	L	Tigers scored:	130	59	3	7	0	545
Captain: Eddie Redman		38	27	2	9	Opponents scored:	20	8	1	2	2	95
Vice-captain: Billy Foreman												

GM	DATE		VEN	OPPONENTS	RESULT	TRIES	KICKS	ATT
MIDLAND COUNTIES CUP						CUP WINNERS: MOSELEY		
29	Mar	2	H	Worcester (1)	W 53-0	Lewis(6), Rice(2), Fox, Hesmondhalgh, F.Jackson	Fox 6c, Hesmondhalgh d, F.Jackson 2c	-
30		9	H	Leicester Crusaders (2)	W 33-0	Lewis(3), Hesmondhalgh(2), Fox, R.Cooke	Hesmondhalgh d, Fox 4c	-
31		16	a	Nuneaton (3)	W 19-0	F.Jackson(2), Fox, Hesmondhalgh, Lewis	Fox 2c	-
32		23	a	Moseley (sf)	L 0-11	-	-	4000
Note: #22 Agreed at kick-off that the result was a draw!								
CLUB MATCHES								
1	Sep	1	a	Huddersfield	L 3-7	Vity	-	6000
2		8	H	Burfield Rangers	W 71-0	Lewis(3), G.Jones(3), Foreman(2), Fox(2), T.Cooke, Hitchcock, W.Jackson, Redman, Simpson, Steinitz, Vity	Lewis 6c, T.Cooke 3c, Bryan c	-
3		15	H	Leicestershire XV	W 31-5	Fox(2), Hesmondhalgh(2), Lewis, Bryan	Lewis 5c	-
4		22	a	Northampton	W 11-0	Hesmondhalgh(2), Foreman	Lewis c	5000
5		29	H	Manchester Free Wanderers	W 38-0	Lewis(4), Hesmondhalgh(2), Hitchcock(2), Banks, Simpson	Lewis c, Fox 3c	-
6	Oct	6	H	Old Edwardians	W 0-3	-	-	-
7		13	H	Burton	W 27-0	Fox(2), T.Cooke, Foreman, Hesmondhalgh, W.Jackson, Simpson	Fox 3c	-
8		20	a	Coventry	L 0-3	-	-	6000
9		27	a	Rugby	L 0-5	-	-	-
10	Nov	3	H	Guy's Hospital	W 6-0	T.Cooke, Swain	-	-
11		10	H	Bedford School	W 6-5	F.Jackson, Simpson	-	-
12		17	H	Moseley	W 10-0	Lewis, Simpson	Fox 2c	8000
13		24	H	Swinton	W 15-3	T.Cooke, G.Jones, Lewis	Fox 3c	-
14		27tu	H	Halifax	L 0-8	-	-	-
15	Dec	1	H	St Thomas' Hospital	W 21-0	T.Cooke, F.Jackson, Lewis, Swain, Vity	Fox 3c	-
16		8	H	St Bartholomew's Hospital	W 6-3	T.Cooke, Foreman	-	-
17		15	a	Gloucester	D 0-0	-	-	-
18		22	H	Bedford	W 14-3	Fox(2), G.Jones, Lewis	Fox c	-
19		26w	H	Pontypridd	W 24-0	Fox, Bryan, Butler, Hesmondhalgh, Vity	Fox c/p, Lewis d	-
20		27th	H	Middlesex Wanderers	W 10-0	Banks, G.Jones	Bryan d	-
21		29	H	Edgbaston Crusaders	W 11-0	Fox, Redman, Rice	Bryan c	-
22	Jan	3th	H	Bective Rangers	D 4-0	-	Lewis d	-
		5	H	Handsworth	PP (frost)			
		12	a	Bedford	PP (frost)			
23		19	a	Moseley	W 9-0	T.Cooke(2), Fox	-	-
24		26	H	Coventry	W 5-0	F.Jackson	Fox c	-
25	Feb	2	H	Old Edwardians	L 16-0	Fox, T.Cooke, Hesmondhalgh, F.Jackson	Fox 2c	-
		9	H	Rugby	PP			
		13w	a	Bedford School	PP (frost)			
26		16	H	Gloucester	W 9-0	Nicholson	Lewis d, Fox c	-
27		23	a	Burton	L 6-8	Whitehead	Fox p	-
28		26tu	H	Huddersfield	D 0-0	-	-	-
33	Mar	30	H	Leeds	L 0-8	-	-	-
34	Apr	6	H	Sale	W 14-0	F.Jackson(3), Swain	Lewis c	-
35		13	H	Northampton	W 21-7	Bryan(2), Lewis, T.Cooke, G.Jones, Swain	Bryan c, Lewis d	-
36		15m	H	Penarth	L 0-13	-	-	-
37		16tu	H	Kirkstall	W 47-0	Hesmondhalgh(2), Butler(2), G.Jones(2), Rice(2), Lewis, T.Cooke, Foreman, Swain	Hesmondhalgh c/p, Lewis 3c	-
38		20	a	Bedford	W 5-3	Whitehead	F.Jackson c	3000

INDIVIDUAL APPEARANCES 1894/95

Name / Game #	1	2	3	4	5	6	7	8	9	10	11	12	13	14	15	16	17	18	19	20	21	22	23	24	25	26	27	28	29	30	31	32	33	34	35	36	37	38	Apps	T	Pts
A (Arthur) Akers	F	-	-	F	F	F	-	-	F	F	F	F	F	F	F	F	F	F	F	F	F	-	F	F	F	F	F	F	-	F	F	F	-	-	-	F	F	-	28	-	-
G (George) Banks	F	-	F	F	F	F	F	F	F	F	-	F	F	F	F	F	F	-	F	F	F	F	F	F	F	F	F	-	-	F	F	F	-	-	-	-	-	-	27	2	6
WH (William) Bradford	-	-	-	-	-	-	-	-	-	-	-	-	-	-	-	-	-	-	-	-	-	-	-	-	-	-	-	-	-	-	-	-	-	>F	F	-	F	F	4	-	-
F (Frank) Brown	FB	FB	FB	-	-	-	FB	FB	FB	FB	FB	FB	FB	FB	FB	FB	FB	FB	-	-	-	<FB	-	-	-	-	-	-	-	-	-	-	-	-	-	-	-	-	16	-	-
H (Hugh) Bryan	W	W	W	-	-	-	-	-	-	-	-	-	-	-	-	-	-	-	W	W	W	W	-	-	-	-	-	-	-	-	-	-	-	-	W	W	-	-	9	4	22
W Burton	-	-	-	-	-	-	-	-	-	-	-	-	-	-	-	-	-	-	-	-	-	-	-	-	-	F	-	F	-	-	-	-	-	-	-	-	-	-	2	-	-
FGA (Fred) Butler	-	-	-	-	>FB	-	-	-	-	-	-	-	-	-	-	-	-	-	FB	-	FB	-	-	-	-	-	-	-	-	-	-	C	W	-	C	C	W	<W	9	3	9
RCD (Rupert) Cooke	-	-	-	-	-	-	-	-	-	-	-	-	-	-	-	-	-	-	-	-	-	-	-	-	-	-	-	-	-	F	<F	-	-	-	-	-	-	-	2	1	3
AE (Ted) Cooke	-	F	F	F	F	F	F	F	F	F	F	F	F	F	F	F	F	F	F	F	F	F	F	F	F	-	-	-	-	F	F	F	F	F	F	F	F	F	33	11	39
E (Edward) Dann	-	-	-	-	-	-	F	F	-	F	F	-	-	-	-	-	-	-	-	F	-	-	-	-	-	-	-	F	-	-	-	-	F	F	F	F	-	-	10	-	-
T (Thomas) Elkington	-	-	-	-	-	-	-	-	-	-	-	-	-	-	-	-	-	-	-	-	-	-	-	>FB	FB	FB	FB	FB	FB	FB	FB	FB	FB	FB	FB	<FB	-	-	13	-	-
WJ (Billy) Foreman	HB	HB	HB	HB	HB	HB	HB	HB	HB	HB	HB	HB	HB	HB	HB	HB*	HB*	HB	HB	HB	HB	HB	HB	HB	HB	HB	HB	HB	HB	-	HB	HB	HB	HB	HB	HB	HB	HB	37	6	18
F Fox	>W	W	W	W	W	W	W	W	-	-	-	W	W	W	W	-	W	W	W	W	W	W	W	W	W	W	W	-	W	W	<C	-	-	-	-	-	-	-	26	15	115
S (Shirley) Harrison	-	-	-	-	-	-	-	-	-	-	-	-	-	-	-	-	-	-	-	-	-	-	-	-	-	-	>C	-	-	-	-	-	-	-	-	-	-	F	2	-	-
WR (Bob) Hesmondhalgh	C	C	C	C	C	FB	C	C	C	C	C	C	C	C	-	-	C	C	C	C	C	C	C	C	C	C	C	-	C	C	W	W	C	C	C	W	C	C	35	15	58
AE (Alfred) Hitchcock	-	F	F	W	W	W	-	-	W	W	W	-	-	-	-	W	-	-	-	-	-	-	-	-	-	-	-	-	-	-	-	-	<C	-	-	-	-	-	10	3	9
AL (Arthur) Jackson	F	-	-	-	-	-	-	-	-	-	-	-	-	-	-	-	-	-	-	-	-	F	-	-	-	-	-	-	-	-	-	F	-	-	-	-	-	-	3	-	-
FA (Frank) Jackson	-	-	-	-	-	>C	W	W	W	W	W	W	-	W	W	C	W	W	-	-	-	-	W	W	W	-	-	W	W	W	W	W	W	W	-	-	-	C	23	10	36
W (Walter) Jackson	F	F	F	F	F	F	F	F	-	F	F	F	F	F	F	F	F	F	F	F	F	F	F	F	F	-	F	F	F	F	F	F	-	-	-	-	-	-	30	2	6
G (George) Jones	F	F	F	F	F	F	F	F	-	F	F	F	F	F	F	F	F	F	-	F	F	F	F	F	F	F	F	-	-	-	-	-	F	F	F	F	F	F	31	9	27
R (Bobby) Lewis	>C	C	C	C	C	C	C	C	C	C	C	C	C	C	C	C	C	C	C	-	C	C	C	C	C	W	-	C	C	C	C	C	-	C	W	C	C	<W	35	24	122
Dr. CH (Charles) Nicholson	-	-	-	-	-	-	-	-	-	-	-	-	-	-	-	-	-	-	-	-	-	-	-	-	-	>F	F	F	-	-	-	-	F	F	F	F	-	-	7	1	3
RE (Rowland) Page	-	-	-	-	-	-	-	-	>F	-	-	-	-	-	-	-	-	-	-	-	-	-	-	-	-	-	-	F	-	-	-	-	F	-	-	-	F	-	4	-	-
E (Eddie) Redman	F*	F*	F*	F*	F*	F*	F*	F*	F*	F*	F*	F*	F*	F*	C*	-	-	F*	F*	C*	F*	F*	F*	F*	F*	F*	W*	F*	F*	F*	F*	F*	F*	W*	F*	F*	F*	F*	36	2	6
WR (Tuffie) Rice	-	-	-	-	-	-	-	-	-	-	-	-	-	>F	F	F	F	F	F	F	F	F	F	F	F	F	F	F	F	F	F	F	F	F	F	F	F	<F	25	5	15
HJ (Harry) Simpson	HB	HB	HB	HB	HB	HB	HB	HB	HB	HB	HB	HB	HB	HB	HB	HB	HB	HB	HB	-	HB	HB	HB	HB	-	HB	-	-	HB	HB	HB	HB	-	HB	HB	-	-	HB	31	5	15
JJ (John) Steinitz	-	>F	<F	-	-	-	-	-	-	-	-	-	-	-	-	-	-	-	-	-	-	-	-	-	-	-	-	-	-	-	-	-	-	-	-	-	-	-	2	1	3
RP (Paddy) Swain	F	F	F	F	F	F	F	F	F	F	F	F	F	-	F	F	F	F	F	F	-	F	F	F	F	F	F	W	F	HB	F	F	F	F	F	F	W	F	36	5	15
E (Edward) Vity	F	F	-	F	F	F	F	F	F	-	F	F	F	F	F	F	F	F	F	-	<F	-	-	-	-	-	-	-	-	-	-	-	-	-	-	-	-	-	18	4	12
ME (Monty) Whitehead	-	-	-	-	-	-	-	-	-	-	-	-	-	-	-	-	-	-	-	-	-	-	-	-	-	-	>F	-	-	-	-	-	-	-	-	-	-	F	2	2	6
AW (Archie) Woodyatt	-	-	-	-	-	-	-	-	-	-	-	-	>W	-	-	W	-	-	-	-	-	-	-	-	-	C	-	C	-	-	-	-	-	-	-	-	-	-	4	-	-
EC (Ernest) Wykes	-	-	-	-	-	-	-	-	-	-	-	-	-	-	-	-	-	-	-	-	-	-	-	-	>HB	-	HB	-	-	-	-	-	-	-	-	HB	HB	-	4	-	-

1 GAME: T (Tom) Betts =F(30), English =HB(28), HB (Harry) Freeman =F(29), W (William) Gale >FB(37), JW (Josh) Garner >F(34), H Greenway =HB(20), SW (Septimus) Harper-Smith =F(9), W Haynes =FB(20), G (George) Hicken HB(33), AB (Abraham) Inchley =FB(4), AO (Arthur) Jones >FB(38), C (Charles) Kinton >F(29), JWM (John) Meek F(37), GW (George) Orton <F(29), FW (Francis) Stocks =FB(23), JE (Joseph) Walker =F(29)

The key for how to read the stats is on the last page

CHAPTER 6

Crumbie Takes the Reins

1895/1896

It would be difficult to overstate Tom Crumbie's contribution to rugby in the city and county. He had his own printing and stationery business in Leicester's Halford Street and much of the money he made there - as well as the duties of the staff - must have been directed at Welford Road. He was a man whose sole purpose in life would appear to have been the welfare and prestige of the Leicester Football Club; many criticisms could be, and were, levelled at him, that he was dictatorial, that he ignored local talent, but nobody could ever doubt the impact he made.

He regarded the players as part of his family - "my boys", he called them - and nothing was too much for them. In return he expected certain standards and he inspired immense loyalty in those who worked for him and played for him. It was his practice to call individual players into his reserved compartment on the train to away games to have a little talk to them before the game. But his demands for discipline had to be met: travelling to play in the West Country he ordered a bottle of beer for every player but when he heard that one player had asked for a second he found out who it was, gave him the return half of his ticket to Leicester, and put him off the train at Birmingham (having ensured initially that he had a reserve travelling).

↑ Tom Crumbie, whose vision shaped the club for years to come.

A teetotaller himself, he was also a diabetic but he seldom let ill-health get on top of him. He was accustomed to running the line for his club and continued to do so well into the 1920s, even when his eyes were beginning to fail. His kindness and entertainment of his own players, referees and guests of the club, combined with his flair for organisation, made him in many ways the perfect secretary-manager, a title which betrayed his professional approach to his job, even if it was never bestowed on him during his life.

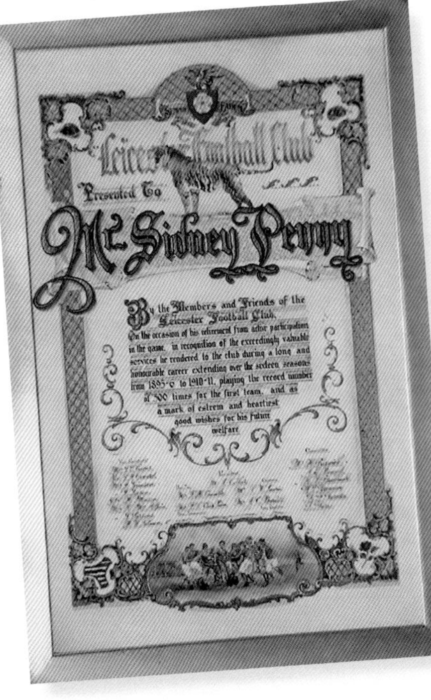

↓ Sid Penny's inscribed picture celebrating '500' first-team games.

It was Crumbie who dragged Tigers into national prominence, by discontinuing the B team during the 1890s and the A team in 1905, making Leicester an invitation club and introducing players into the side from all over the country. It was a policy which did not make for consistency since frequently teams playing away went without the "stars" who only made the trip to Welford Road for home games. But it ensured that the Leicester public saw, as near as possible, the best rugby on offer in the country and explained why the club had gates of anything from 6,000 upwards every Saturday. During the Crumbie era, 26 players from the club were capped and Leicester came to dominate the Midland scene.

Crumbie inherited an unenviable position as these were very difficult days for rugby because the Northern Union, later to become the Rugby League, had been formed on 29 August 1895. Numerous fixtures were lost: in 1894/95 the list included Swinton, Huddersfield, Manchester Free Wanderers, Leeds, Halifax and Kirkstall. Over the next two years they all went and Leicester looked largely to Wales for replacements. The 1895/96 season began not against Warrington and Stockport but with a hurriedly arranged fixture against Nuneaton at Welford Road. On 31 August it was minuted in committee that "the committee be empowered to arrange matches for dates broken by the Northern League and that the production of fixture cards be postponed for a week for the purpose of announcing new matches failing which cards to be issued showing blank dates."

There were also several important ground alterations for the forthcoming season: part of the Members' Stand was to be reserved for those who wished to pay an extra subscription of 10s 6d. The current occupiers of those seats being members of the Press, this necessitated the building of a Press Box on the opposite side of the ground near the touchline, according a much better view of the game. Turnstiles were to be provided at the Aylestone Road entrance, and the Welford Road gates would be closed except on special occasions. It was decided to use only one price of season ticket, set at 4s 6d, and books of admission tickets were issued to members for the first time.

In his initial season Crumbie had fertile ground in which to work and his elevation happened to coincide with the beginning of the senior career of Sid Penny, whose name occupies an honoured place in the club's history. Penny had played for the local club, St Peter's, and for Leicester A before making his debut early in 1896: his first-class career did not end until 14 years later, after 491 first-team appearances for Tigers and caps for the Midland Counties and England. His number of games for Leicester has been passed by only one other player, David Matthews, who recorded his 502nd game in 1974.

Penny was also the first in a long and distinguished line of Leicester hookers. Whatever else the club may have lacked at any time, it has seldom lacked a first-class hooker; George Ward, Doug Norman, Edward Nicholson, Peter Wheeler, Richard Cockerill, Dorian West, George Chuter and most recently, Tom Youngs, have all followed Penny into England's national side.

After reaching what was thought at the time to be 500 games for the first-team, Leicester gave Penny a special dinner in honour of his achievement, at the Leicester Constitutional Club, on

29 December 1910. It was the evening following the Barbarians game, so there was a notable gathering to see the club's president, Joseph Collier, present the player with a magnificent inscribed picture and describe how invaluable Penny had been to the club: "He seems good enough for another quarter of a century," said the president, to which the modest Sidney replied that, pleased though he was to be there, he would rather have been pushing in the scrum.

Penny was asked to go to Australia and New Zealand with the Anglo-Welsh party of 1908 but he was playing in the days when touring overseas was the good fortune of the moneyed gentry. An employee in the shoe trade, there was never any prospect of him being able to accept the invitation, and there were doubts in his family at one time that he would be able to play for England against Australia in 1909 - his best suit was not fit for travel. He made the game, which England lost 9-3 at Blackheath, and though he won no more caps, there can have been few honours so genuinely earned.

In his first full season, injuries and unavailability militated against Leicester and even the climate came in for blame: against Gloucester it struck a local reporter as more like the tropics with a quoted temperature of 112 degrees - which made it pretty hot. "In spite of the great heat and the consequent terrible perspiration it caused players, the game was fast and vigorously fought from start to finish", the story ran. Two months later heavy showers on the day before the game with Northampton meant Leicester did not have to call upon the Fire Brigade to water the ground!

In their first seven matches Tigers scored 103 points and conceded only eight. It was not untypical of the customs of the time, however, that William Yiend, who had been capped for England while with Hartlepool Rovers, played for the club this season when he was available, once at least to the exclusion of Arthur Akers who had been pencilled in against Coventry because Yiend had said that he would not be available but turned up at the last moment looking for a game.

There was huge local mirth at the demise of Rugby (who, the season before, had declined to play on what they described as sand). Some 7,000 spectators saw Rugby collapse in the second half to a 33-0 defeat, though the return in the new year was far harder, a 3-0 win to Leicester. There were a couple of notable wins, by 44 points in successive matches, over Bridgwater & Albion and St Bartholomew's Hospital, Frank Jackson scoring three tries in the first game and six in the second. As the Midlands Cup approached there was a sardonic reference in the *Leicester Mercury*: "So far as we have been able to ascertain the cup is, at the time, really in existence, having escaped the perils which appear to surround trophies of this kind when they are lodged for a brief period in the city of Birmingham" (an obvious allusion to the loss of soccer's FA Cup). The relationship declined between the club and the Midland Counties committee, who had hinted at professionalism on Leicester's part over the transfer of the full-back, Alfred Butlin, from Rugby to Leicester, though a Rugby Football Union hearing completely cleared Leicester and laid any blame for mismanagement at the Midlands' door (a subsequent letter to the

↑ Billy Foreman's wedding with virtually all his Tigers team-mates as guests.

Mercury suggested it was high time Leicester seceded from the Midland Counties Rugby Union and "threw in their lot with the Northern Union, which would furnish a greater attraction and better football for their supporters"). This debate would return to haunt Leicester.

Ironically enough, it was Moseley who dispatched Leicester from the cup competition in the third round, by a penalty to nil at The Reddings. It was a grave disappointment but there was still the end-of-season tour to the West Country to come.

In the meantime club fly-half Billy Foreman just about found time for his wedding to Lydia Alice Veasey at St Matthew's Church on Wednesday 8 April 1896 – a day earlier he turned out and was the only scorer for the Tigers in their 3-0 defeat of Cheltenham at Welford Road, the *Chronicle* recording: "During the morning the happy couple left for Plymouth, amid the hearty congratulations of numerous friends and admirers, for their honeymoon. This arrangement will enable Mr Foreman to re-join his colleagues and assist them in their forthcoming tour through the west." And assist he did, playing in both fixtures at Devonport Albion and Bridgwater.

The *Mercury* waxed lyrical about the train journey from Leicester to Devonport: "The attractive scenery en route, the passing glimpses of the Malverns, the picturesque heights and bosky slopes of Devon all aroused admiration - as also did the appetising luncheon baskets provided for the team by the kindly forethought of the committee." Devonport Albion spoiled the Sunday School atmosphere by beating them 11-3 but there was little time to speculate on what might have been; trips had been organised for the players, visits to the dockyards, tours of warships, steamboat trips up the Tamar among a fleet of ironclads and torpedo boats. Buoyed up by this martial spirit, the lads gallantly beat Bridgwater the next day, by 3-0.

↑ Frank Jackson was the top try scorer in season 1895/96, with 22.

At the end of the season, for the first time in their history, the Tigers held two pieces of silverware with the A team claiming the Leicestershire Senior Cup and the B team winning the Leicestershire Junior Cup.

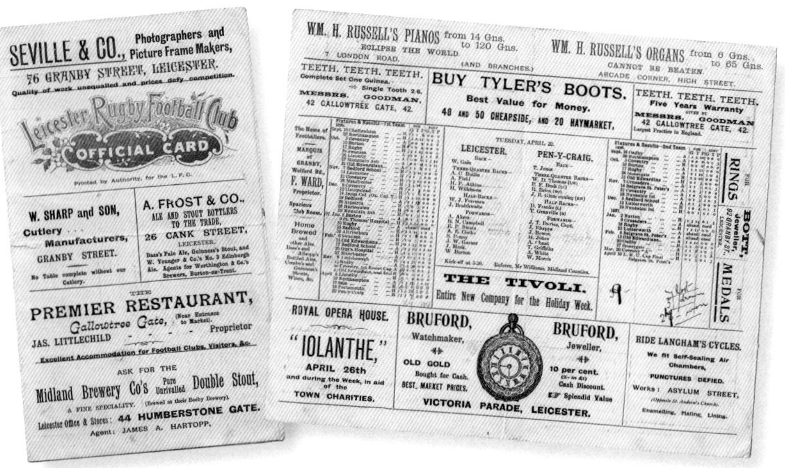

↑ Match card from the final game of the 1896/97 season against Penygraig.

1896/1897

The new season dawned with much speculation in the press as to whether the elusive Midland Counties Cup would be won. Leicester's love affair with the trophy was growing with each passing year. It was all systems go up to the semi-finals, the Tigers having easily accounted for Rugby in the second round and Coventry 6-3 after extra time in round three, both matches being played away from Welford Road. When it was learned that the semi would be at home against Old Edwardians there was much optimism. But it turned into another false dawn as the Birmingham based club scored the only try in front of 4,285 partisan Leicester supporters.

On the club fixtures front the team lost only once - at Burton - between the end of October and mid-April, the sequence starting with an 8-3 victory at Old Edwardians' Wake Green Road ground, which was abandoned four minutes early due to failing light. The six defeats in the season were all away from home, and three of those were during the tour to Wales in October.

1897/1898

Things were moving in the right direction, though. In 1897, after strictures from the Midland Counties, who said Leicester's pitch would not be used for cup ties unless the surface was re-laid, the ground was returfed; not, one imagines, without regret, for the sandy surface had permitted Leicester to play when other clubs were forced by frost to cancel.

The intense rivalry which had been building between Leicester and Northampton since the two began regular hostilities in 1894/95 was perfectly illustrated with their meetings this season: 12,000 people showed up at Welford Road on 6 November to see Tigers triumph 10-0 and led to the production of a mock mourning card which read:

In Memory of the Northampton FC.
Who perished after a 'Severe Mauling'
By The 'Leicester Tigers,'
Saturday, Oct 6th, 1897.
Game to the last.

Somehow the fans got so carried away with the victory that they even managed to put the wrong date, 6 October instead of 6 November, on the card.

Revenge was quick in coming – just two weeks later the Saints won the return at Franklin's Gardens 18-6, and such was the confidence in winning that retaliatory mourning cards were prepared in advance and sold to fans even as they left the ground.

Death of Leicester Tigers,
Franklin's Gardens, Northampton,
November 20th 1897 (Jubilee).
The resurrection of the Saints.
The "Tigers" came over from Leicester Town
Assured that the "Saints" they were going to down;
But the "Saints" on the grass were a little too tough,
And the funeral cards are giving them snuff,
R.I.P.

The Northampton Independent newspaper said: "Never has such a scene been witnessed at St. James' End as that which was witnessed at the conclusion of the game. Right from Franklin's Gardens to the clubhouse, the Green Man [now the Thomas á Becket pub], there was a dense crowd of enthusiasts, who cheered heartily the Northampton men as they proceeded to the dressing room, and a section of whom gave a childish exhibition by hooting the Leicester players. Outside the clubhouse there was a struggling mass of humanity, swaying to and fro, and vehicular traffic was carried on with only the greatest difficulty. On all hands congratulations to the Northampton men on their achievements."

The following year the B team was discontinued but by then Tigers had ensured their best playing season to date, culminating in their triumph in the Midland Counties Cup for the first time. The captain in 1897/98 was AO Jones, who distinguished himself by playing centre, full-back and scrum-half before new year and then leading his team to wins over Rugby (31-0), Burton (17-0), Coventry (12-5) and, in the cup final, Moseley, whom they beat 5-3 at the Butts in Coventry. There was a change of date to a Wednesday afternoon (6 April 1898) because, after lengthy correspondence, the two sides and the Midland Counties Union could not agree when to play the game. The

→ The Reverend Albert Carey-Elwes was a try scorer in the game at home to Rugby in the Midland Counties Cup.

Tigers gave an ultimatum that they would not contest the final at all unless it was played before their tour of Wales and in the end that is what transpired. Jones was forced to miss the final on medical advice, the team being: Alf Butlin; Harry Wilkinson, Percy Oscroft, Percy Atkins, Frank Jones; Billy Foreman (capt), Jacky Braithwaite; Edward Redman, Bob Campbell, Arthur Akers, John Garner, Sid Penny, George Keeton, Monty Whitehead, Walter Jackson.

The only try of the final came from the centre, Oscroft after just three minutes, with Frank Jones, younger brother of AO, converting. Fred Byrne kicked a penalty for Moseley but after three near misses Tigers had brought home the bacon. Thousands lined the streets between Leicester station and the George Hotel as the Highfields Brass Band led the team from the station playing *See the conquering heroes come*. The team made their way "down a Granby Street choked with cheering people, holding the cup aloft."

In the George Hotel by the Clock Tower the cup was filled with champagne time after time. While the team were celebrating inside, the crowd outside were clamouring for a further view of the team. One by one they came to the windows, and the ovation was equally hearty for Tom Crumbie, the secretary, and John Parsons, the president.

Leicester Fosse Football Club even got into the act by sending a telegram to the Tigers, stating: "The shareholders of the Fosse Football Club Limited, now assembled at the Clarendon Restaurant, heartily congratulate you on your brilliant victory today."

There were speeches and receptions before the inevitable comeuppance, when they toured in Wales and lost to Swansea and Llanelly (before the days when the "y" became an "i"). Nevertheless it was the start of a marvellous run in the Midland Counties Cup, which Leicester retained for the next eight years.

1898/1899

It is surprising how frequently the club undertook short tours in those days, to South Wales, the West Country and the North. The 1898/99 season saw them start with eight home games - always good for morale - and the playing surface "under the influence of scythe and roller was in first-class condition and looked not unlike a cricket pitch. All vestiges of sand had disappeared and the ground lost its erstwhile seaside appearance." The first tour that season was to Wales in November, the team and a few supporters leaving Leicester at 5.28 on a Friday evening and reaching Swansea soon after midnight. Despite what was described as "a strict training lunch" they lost 20-0 at St Helen's, but took comfort in a 5-3 win over Treherbert the next day.

This was the Tigers' first victory in Wales and reporters for Leicester's two evening newspapers, the *Mercury* and the *Post*, each wanted to be "first with the news". The representative of newspaper A had the presence of mind to order the town's only cab to be awaiting him outside the ground after the match. The reporter for newspaper B, realising his own predicament when the whistle went for a 5-3 win, mingled with the crowd as they left the exit, and, on seeing A safely housed in his cab, himself mounted the rear axle and rode into town unobserved. On reaching the Post Office, B jumped off and commandeered the only phone while A was paying the cabman!

↑ Tigers retain the Midland Counties Cup beating Nuneaton in the final on 1 April 1899 at Coventry.

After the usual heavy Christmas programme (never less than three games in four days and soon to become four in five) which now included a Scottish opponent for the first time in the guise of Edinburgh Royal High School - the second tour was to Devonport Albion (lost 10-7) and Exeter (won 3-0) before retaining the Midland Counties Cup with a 20-3 win over Nuneaton.

1899/1900

Tigers made a terrific start to the new season and remained unbeaten until November, when Cambridge University lowered the Leicester colours at Grange Road. The team won 25 of their 36 matches and successfully defended the Midland Counties Cup title for a third successive season, overcoming Moseley 13-4 in the final at Coventry, after disposing of Five Ways Old Edwardians, Coventry and Rugby in the earlier rounds.

↑ Commemorative souvenir celebrating Tigers winning the Midland Counties Cup three times in succession.

1900/1901

The turn of the century brought new honours as Leicester's name, and their facilities after the expenditure of a further £1,300, drew national attention. An estimated 12,000 watched the 4-0 win over Northampton, "inspired by the Highfields Band", as one report put it, and there was a successful campaign for the Midland Counties Cup: the game against Old Edwardians was remembered with little affection after injuries to 12 players, including a twisted knee for Frank Jackson which ended his season. The final (at Coventry) brought a 13-4 win over Moseley and the Highfields Band met the team's train when it returned and played them back to the George Hotel in triumph.

1901/1902

There must have been a disappointed response from the crowd which arrived to watch the November match with Swansea in 1901 when, after Mr. Ashton the referee had declared the ground playable, the Swansea captain refused to play because it was too hard. But compensation was at hand: Leicester went to Kingsholm and beat Gloucester 3-0, the first team to win there for three seasons, while on 8 February 1902, the Welford Road ground was honoured with an international, England beating Ireland 6-3. There were no Leicester players involved but a crowd of around 14,000 watched - among them the correspondent of *The Athletic News*, who complained; "I don't know what kind of thin people write for the Press in Leicester but if the authorities had measured a local scribe and found he measured only 13 inches across the bust, it is time that journalist took a course of Mellin's food." If Mellin's food was to journalists what spinach was to Popeye, then the result must have been noted for it was not long before the Press box at the ground became a degree more commodious.

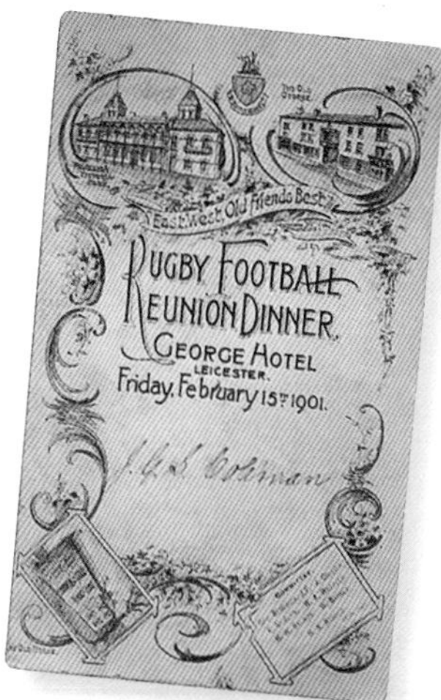

↑ Invitation card to old player, Sherrard Coleman, for the Tigers' 21st anniversary dinner.

↓ Action from the Tigers' visit to Newport on 5.4.1902.

1902/1903

Membership by now had reached 1,200 and the experiment of granting season tickets to the cheap sides of the ground at a nominal cost of three shillings increased receipts from £15 to £60. Relationships with Moseley improved to the extent that, in the 1902/03 season, "friendly" fixtures were resumed after a gap of eight years though there may have been subtle irony in the granting of the proceeds (over £194) from the second match to the Leicester Infirmary! Nor was friendly the word used to describe the match with Llanelly (before a crowd of 11,000 with gate receipts of £122): "Certain of Llanelly's players included foul and off-side play...and the Welshmen can consider themselves lucky that penalty goals are not added to Tigers' score of 15-3," wrote the local scribe censoriously.

Jack Miles became the first home-produced international from the club when he played on the wing against Wales in 1903 (he went to Medway Street School and played for Medway Athletic and Stoneygate before joining Leicester). It was his only cap and England lost 21-5 at St Helen's in Swansea.

↑ Jack Miles was the first player to be capped directly from the Leicester club in 1903.

1903/1904

However, there were complaints at the start of the following season when four of the first five games were lost: "The heavy fixture list of the club will not permit neglect of training and without training, proficiency cannot be attained," stormed *The Leicester Daily Post*.

Injuries and absentees did not help the cause though things were not quite as bad as they seemed the day a full-back, William Gale, played twice for the club. Having distinguished himself for Leicester A on Victoria Park one Saturday morning, he turned out against Treherbert in the afternoon when AO Jones missed his rail connection over the Christmas period. He can't have done too badly because Leicester won 18-3, assisted also by the Cardiff international centre 'Pussy' Jones who happened to be on holiday in Leicester at the time. So taken was Jones with the Leicester organisation that he even toured with them to Hartlepool a few days later.

The local press made a pertinent point, too, after the match with Bristol when the timekeeping of the referee became an issue. During the first half no more than 31 minutes were played, according to unofficial clock watchers who were expecting two 35-minute halves. However the second half lasted 42 minutes the assumption being that, allowing for an injury to Miles, the referee was making up for the earlier deficiency. A voice from the stand cried out: "It will be morning soon," and the reporter observed how strange it was that people who paid to see a game so often wanted the end to be signalled. The club retained the Midland Counties Cup for the seventh consecutive year, beating Moseley 13-3 but their overall record in 1904 was indifferent. It was, though, illuminated by George Keeton, who played in England's pack in all three internationals that season.

1904/1905

Somebody should have realised that a trip to Swansea on 19 November 1904 was like no ordinary day when Mr Games, the nominated referee from Abercarn, missed his train and was late in arriving. A substitute was found in Billy Bancroft, the former Wales full-back and a veteran of 33 consecutive internationals, who officiated until well into the first half, when Games eventually ran onto the field.

At half-time Swansea led 8-0, through tries by WH Hunt and Danny Rees, the second being converted by George Davis (it was three points for a try in those days). That score stood until 15 minutes from time when the Tigers succeeded in pushing their opponents over the line, and carried the ball with them. Jacky Braithwaite dived into the scrummage and claimed a try. Mr Games shook his head and ordered another scrum and again Braithwaite took a dive after the ball - this time between the legs of colleagues. However Alf Goodrich was there before him, dropping on the ball and the try was allowed, George Yeld kicking the conversion.

The game ended with an 8-5 victory to Swansea, but the intrigue was only just beginning. Leicester appealed to the Welsh Union for the try

Tigers take on Nottingham in the Midland Counties Cup final at Coventry in 1906.

by Braithwaite and on 30 December the RFU took up their case. It was considered, after discussion, that the referee had erred on a point of law, and the try claimed be awarded to Leicester, making the result of the match a draw. By 9 January the Welsh Union had agreed and the result was officially changed though how such a conclusion was reached is hard to understand. There was even talk about a special arrangement being made for a Leicester player to travel to Swansea to attempt the conversion to see if they could win the game. In the end commonsense prevailed, but Swansea went on to remain unbeaten for the entire season and earn the accolade "invincibles" with a won 24, drawn 4, lost 0 record.

1905/1906

The following year came one of those defining moments for rugby union, the tour of Dave Gallaher's New Zealanders. The first All Blacks, whose only defeat came against Wales (and that by a disputed try), set new standards for preparation, skills and tactics, and when they reached Leicester for the fifth game of their tour, they had scored 55, 41, 41 and 32 points against their first four opponents.

They had taken a rather complacent country by storm and they did the same to Leicester, winning 28-0 on 30 September before 20,000 people - a gate which produced £392, of which 70 per cent was said to have gone to the visitors. Leicester's team, the first time they had met a

Leicester Member's book 1905/06.

THE LEICESTER
Football Club.
SEASON 1905-6.

LEICESTER FOOTBALL CLUB.

OFFICERS: SEASON 1905-1906.

President: J Collier, Esq.

Vice-Presidents:

J. C. Cooper, Esq. J Parsons, Esq.
J. Gimson, Esq. H. W Salmon, Esq.
Dr. H. Mason. Alderman A. E. Sawday.
K. McAlpin, Esq. H. N Stroud, Esq.

Captain First Team Mr. S. Matthews.

Vice-Captain First Team: Mr. A. E. Hind.

Hon. Sec.: Mr T H. Crumbie, Free Lane, Halford Street.

Telegrams—"Crumbie, Leicester." Nat. Tel. 480.

Hon. Treasurer

Mr. F St. Clair Pain, 255 Clarendon Park Rd.

Captain "A" Team: Mr M. Barrowcliffe.

Vice-Captain "A" Team: Mr R. Hives.

Hon. Secretary "A" Team: Mr B. L. Atkinson.

Committee Messrs. H. H. Brockbank, W. J Foreman, S. C. Packer, C. A. Page, T Thorpe, and F K. Ward.

Auditors:

Messrs. J Wheelwright & W H. Tarratt.

touring side, was: AO Jones; Alfred Parsons, Dr. N McFarlane, James Bainbridge, Alfred Hind; Bertie Hills, Jacky Braithwaite; Sammy Matthews (captain), Sid Penny, Tom Goodrich, Alf Goodrich, Richard Russell, Fred Jackson, Dudley Atkins, Percy Atkins. The Tigers, unbeaten before the game, held the tourists for half an hour before George Smith scored the first of six tries. 'Carbine' Wallace, 'Bunny' Abbott, 'Bubs' Tyler, 'Simon' Mynott and George Nicholson scored the others, Wallace converting five times. The club XV was clearly outclassed and there was some objection - as there was all through the tour - of Gallaher's role as a "rover". But at the reception after the match Gallaher paid tribute to Leicester: "When we were down south we were told that when we got to Leicester we should know about it. Well, we do know about it. You gave us one of the hardest games I have ever played in."

He may have been in a generous mood but the remark was at least indicative of Leicester's standing in England and that season four Tigers were capped by England: half-back Jacky Braithwaite, three-quarter Ernest Hind, full-back John Jackett and forward Richard Russell played against New Zealand (for Braithwaite and Russell it was their only cap) and forward Alfred Kewney (then with Rockcliff) won the first of 16 caps against Scotland. A month after playing the club, the All Blacks returned to Welford Road to play a Midland Counties XV containing seven Tigers. At that stage the tourists had scored 429 points and conceded 10, so the Midlands did well to hold them to 21-5, Russell scoring the Midlands try.

It was not the last the club were to see of some of the New Zealanders (the international apart). On 13 January they lost 20-0 at Gloucester who fielded three New Zealanders (two of them, Mynott and McGregor, were responsible for all the Gloucester tries). Apparently the touring side had offered to help Leicester out but, even though they had only five regulars, the offer was not taken up. In 1906, Jackett was in the England side beaten 16-6 by Ireland at Leicester and as the season neared its end there was dissent in the camp, as Hind, then vice-captain and scorer of 37 tries in 1902/03, left to play for Nottingham and there was criticism of the club's failure to raise strong sides for away fixtures. In addition, the proud Midland Counties Cup run ended after eight successive victories because the Tigers had opted out of the

Tigers entertain the All Blacks for the first time, 1.10.1905.

competition in a dispute with the Midland Counties Union, arguing that senior clubs should be exempt from playing in the earlier rounds.

During the season various clubs, among them Leicester, had experimented with the New Zealand style of play, packing seven forwards, but without conspicuous success. Against Devonport Albion, in a 3-3 draw, Leicester packed down with a 2-3-2 scrum formation (which New Zealand retained for another twenty years) and Percy Atkins at wing forward.

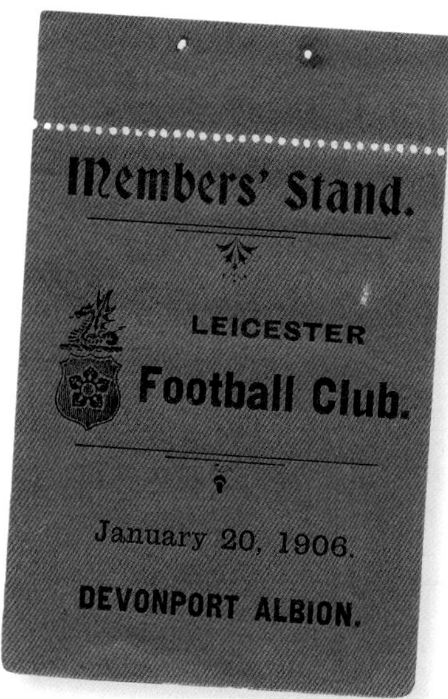

↑ Match ticket from the 1905/06 season ticket booklet.

1906/1907

The start of the season signalled a change in the club colours, *The Leicester Guardian* describing "white jersey, blue knickers and black stockings with white and gold tops. In addition the players will wear a badge depicting a most ferocious looking tiger." The badge was to be hand-embroidered onto each jersey at a cost of three shillings each. Tigers wore the new colours for the first time for the second game of the new campaign against West Hartlepool, as the first opponents the previous week were Hartlepool Rovers, who also wore white as their main kit, so Tigers reverted to blue.

Both clubs imitated the New Zealanders, playing three three-quarters, two five-eighths, a scrum-half and a rover. It was not a happy experiment and in October Tigers reverted to four three-quarters, two half-backs and eight forwards against Richmond. They won 11-0 and it was, according to the *Leicester Mercury*, "a triumph for the old style of play."

Meanwhile another touring side was in Britain, the first South African visitors, captained by Paul Roos. They visited Welford Road on 29 September and beat a Midland Counties XV containing seven Tigers by 29-0, not so much because of any innovative style of play but by sheer athleticism. The Leicester players in that match were Bainbridge, Braithwaite, Russell, Penny, Matthews, Alf Goodrich and Percy Atkins, a crowd of between 13 and 14,000 producing a gate of £500. Russell was captain of Leicester that season and, in an age when specialisation had reached only a short distance into rugby, he left his usual place in the pack to play on the wing for a few games, such was the injury situation around Christmas.

It was not a vintage season, with bad weather forcing seven cancellations including the Christmas tour of the north, but a promising scrum-half emerged in George Wood, known as 'Pedlar', in succession to Braithwaite. An interesting statistic from the season was the number of penalties kicked, which aggregated seven. This was not untypical. Given the number of penalties kicked in just one match in modern times, it must be remembered that, over 100 years ago, fewer penalties would have been awarded and there were few specialist kickers of the heavy leather ball. Moreover, the drop kick may still have been regarded as more worthy of attention, as it was worth four points.

↓ Scrum-half Pedlar Wood made his Tigers debut at home to Newport on 10 November 1906. He went on to play 388 games.

During the season the A team had been disbanded after briefly competing in the new county competition known as the Leicester Football Club Alliance. Crumbie had decided that the A team served little purpose any more because Leicester would be in future an invitation club. No subscriptions or entry fee would be payable with the travel expenses of bringing "guest" players to the Tigers falling on the treasurer, St Clair Pain, through increased gate receipts.

1907/1908

At the start of the season another young player emerged from that rugby nursery in Leicester, Medway Street School. Then 19, Frederick 'Tim' Taylor formed a long and profitable half-back combination with Pedlar Wood which culminated in their both winning caps in 1914, against Wales. It was the second outstanding half-back pairing the club had produced, following Braithwaite and Foreman, and it was by no means the last. Neither player was very big - Taylor in particular was very slight while Wood was short but stocky - but they soon became favourites with the Leicester crowd.

These were hard times, though. "Leicester on the down grade" said one newspaper headline which was as near to screaming blue murder as newspapers allowed then. Against Oxford University "too many of the men...showed the white feather and absolutely refused to go down to a ball to stop the rushes of the opposition." Tigers lost 27-6, suffered a poor tour to the West Country and were then drubbed on their own pitch by London Scottish 39-0. The tide turned over Christmas with a win over Coventry - always good for a celebration - and at the season's end, John Jackett, Fred Jackson and Tom Smith were invited to tour New Zealand and Australia with the Anglo-Welsh party, the first Leicester players to go abroad with a major touring side, although Hind had been to South Africa with Mark Morrison's team in 1903 while he was still at Cambridge University. The troubles of one season, however, were as nothing when compared with the troubles of 1908/09.

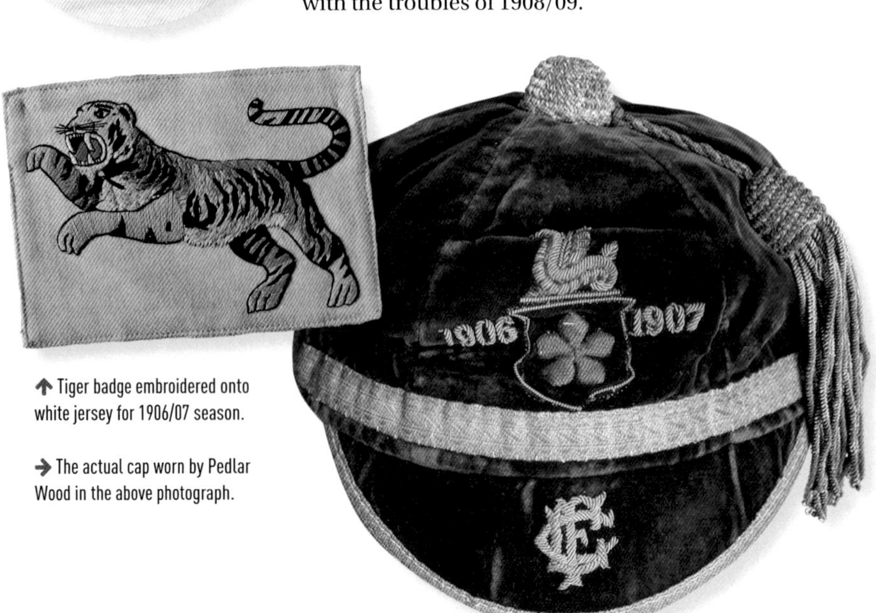

↑ Tiger badge embroidered onto white jersey for 1906/07 season.

→ The actual cap worn by Pedlar Wood in the above photograph.

↑ LEICESTER FOOTBALL CLUB 1895/96
Back: Wheeler, P.Swain, Cooke, G.Jones, Yiend, Nicholson, Woodyatt, Snowden (Committee Member), Swingler (Hon.Tres), Crumbie (Hon.Sec).
Middle: Salmon, W.Jackson, Redman (capt), Campbell, Hesmondhalgh, A.Jones, Parsons (President).
Front: Whitehead, Simpson, Foreman (Vice-capt), F.Jackson, Field.

↑ LEICESTER FOOTBALL CLUB 1898/99
Back: Collier (Touch Judge), Parsons (President), Crumbie (Hon.Sec), Stroud (Hon.Tres).
Middle: Wilkinson, F.Jones, Thompson, Lincoln, Woodyatt.
Seated: Akers, Penny, A.Jones (capt), Foreman (Vice-capt), Matthews, Garner.
Front: Campbell, Scott, Butlin, Braithwaite.

↑ LEICESTER FOOTBALL CLUB 1901/02
Back: Crumbie (Hon.Sec), D.Atkins, P.Atkins, H.Wilkinson, Keeton, Andrews, Crowson, Stroud (Hon.Tres).
Middle: Collier (President), Miles, Penny, A.Hind (Vice-capt), Garner (capt), Matthews, Foreman, Goodrich.
Front: Robinson, Butlin, Hawley, Braithwaite.

↑ LEICESTER FOOTBALL CLUB 1902/03
Back: Crumbie (Hon.Sec), H.Hind, P.Atkins, Watchorn, Bennett, D.Atkins, F.Jones, Stroud (Hon.Tres).
Middle: Collier (President), Miles, Penny, Foreman, Ar.Jones (capt), A.Hind (Vice-capt), Matthews, T.Goodrich.
Front: Robinson, Braithwaite, Dakin, Blackburn.

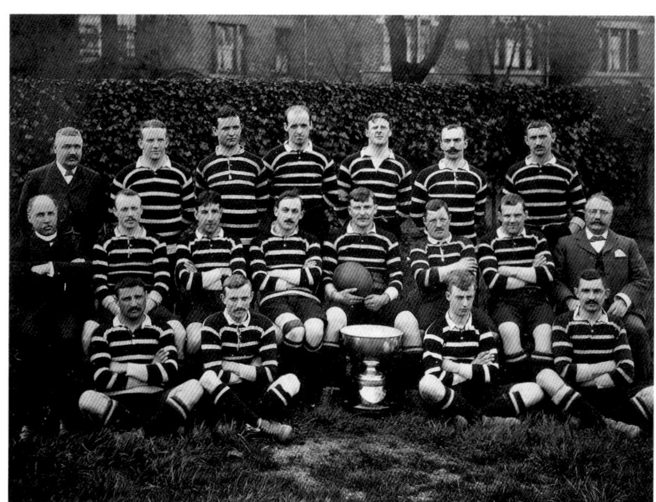

↑ LEICESTER FOOTBALL CLUB 1904/05
Back: Crumbie (Hon.Sec), D.Atkins, Bennett, Parsons, Russell, P.Atkins, T.Goodrich.
Middle: Collier (President), Hills, J.Jackett, A.Hind (Vice-capt), Matthews (capt), Braithwaite, Penny, Pain (Hon.Tres).
Front: A.Goodrich, Lockman, Bainbridge, Dann.

↑ LEICESTER FOOTBALL CLUB 1906/07
Back: Pain (Hon.Tres), Braithwaite (Vice-capt), A.Goodrich, Bourns, Stafford, Atkins, Hives, Crumbie (Hon.Sec).
Middle: Collier (President), Penny, Watson, F.Jackson, Hobbs, Smith, Hardyman.
Front: P.Wood, T.Jackson, J.Jackett, K.Wood, Scott.
Inset: Matthews (capt), Russell (capt).

18	95/96	
		Home Ground: Welford Road
		Captain: Eddie Redman
		Vice-captain: Billy Foreman

OVERALL RECORD:					T	C	PG	DG	MK	PTS
PLD	W	D	L	Tigers scored:	106	47	3	4	1	441
39	23	6	10	Opponents scored:	27	6	4	2	0	113

GM	DATE		VEN	OPPONENTS	RESULT	TRIES	KICKS	ATT
MIDLAND COUNTIES CUP						**CUP WINNERS: COVENTRY**		
30	Mar	**7**	**H**	**Wolverhampton (1)**	W 38-0	F.Jackson(2), Field, Akers, Butlin, Cooke, Foreman, Whitehead	Field 7c	-
31		**14**	**H**	**Leicester Crusaders (2)**	W 18-0	F.Jackson, Field, Butlin, G.Jones	F.Jackson d, Field c	-
32		21	a	Moseley (3)	L 0-3	-	-	-
CLUB MATCHES								
	Sep	7	a	Warrington	PP (Northern union)			
		14	a	Stockport	PP (Northern union)			
1		**21**	**H**	**Nuneaton**	W 24-0	F.Jackson(4), Campbell, Thomson	F.Jackson c, Field 2c	-
2		**28**	**H**	**Gloucester**	W 6-0	Hesmondhalgh, Nicholson	-	-
3	Oct	**5**	**H**	**Northampton**	W 3-0	-	Cooke p	-
4		12	a	Bedford	L 3-8	Nicholson	-	-
5		**19**	**H**	**Guy's Hospital**	W 19-0	Foreman(2), Cooke, F.Jackson, Woodyatt	Field 2c	-
6		26	a	Burton	W 15-0	Cooke, Hesmondhalgh, G.Jones, Woodyatt	Cooke p	-
7	Nov	**2**	**H**	**Rugby**	W 33-0	F.Jackson(3), Field, Cooke, Dann, Foreman, Hesmondhalgh, F.Jones	F.Jackson 2c, Field c	-
8		**9**	**H**	**Coventry**	L 0-3	-	-	-
9		16	a	Old Edwardians	D 0-0	-	-	-
10		23	a	Swinton	L 0-13	-	-	-
11		**30**	**H**	**Bedford**	W 13-0	Field(2), Whitehead	Field 2c	-
12	Dec	**7**	**H**	**Bedford School**	W 9-3	A.Jones, F.Jones, G.Jones	-	-
13		**14**	**H**	**Swinton**	L 0-6	-	-	-
14		21	a	Northampton	L 8-11	Butlin, Whitehead	Field c	7000
15		**26th**	**H**	**Salford**	D 0-0	-	-	-
16		**27f**	**H**	**Leicestershire XV**	W 40-3	A.Jones(5), Bryan, Foreman, Cooke, G.Jones, Pickard	A.Jones c, Bryan 3c, Foreman c	-
17		**28**	**H**	**Harlequins**	L 0-6	-	-	-
18	Jan	**1w**	**H**	**Bective Rangers**	D 0-0	-	-	-
19		4	a	Gloucester	L 12-20	Field	Field c/m, Redman p	-
20		**11**	**H**	**St Thomas' Hospital**	W 16-0	Akers(2), Field, F.Jackson	Field c, F.Jones c	-
21		**18**	**H**	**Bridgwater**	W 44-3	Butlin(3), F.Jackson(3), G.Jones(3), Redman	Field 5c, A.Jones d	-
22		**20m**	**H**	**St Bartholomew's Hospital**	W 44-0	F.Jackson(6), Butlin, Pickard, Whitehead, Yiend	Field 7c	-
23		25	a	Coventry	D 0-0	-	-	-
24	Feb	**1**	**H**	**Sale**	W 5-0	Foreman	Field c	-
25		8	a	Rugby	W 3-0	Yiend	-	-
26		12w	a	Bedford School	W 15-0	Foreman(2), Burton, F.Jones, Wilkinson	-	-
27		**15**	**H**	**Old Edwardians**	D 3-3	Whitehead	-	-
28		**22**	**H**	**Burton**	W 18-0	Pickard(3), Foreman	Field 3c	-
29		**29**	**H**	**Croydon**	W 9-0	Akers	Butlin d, Field c	-
33	Mar	28	a	Northampton	L 4-5	-	Butlin d	5000
34	Apr	**4**	**H**	**Wortley**	W 16-5	Campbell(2), Ball, Pickard	Field 2c	-
35		**6m**	**H**	**Hartlepool Rovers**	W 8-4	Butlin, Wilkinson	Field c	-
36		**7tu**	**H**	**Cheltenham**	W 3-0	Foreman	-	-
37		11	a	Devonport Albion	L 3-11	F.Jackson	-	-
38		13m	a	Bridgwater	W 3-0	Butlin	-	-
39		18	a	Hartlepool Rovers	D 6-6	Brownson, Wilkinson	-	-

INDIVIDUAL APPEARANCES 1895/96

Name / Game #	1	2	3	4	5	6	7	8	9	10	11	12	13	14	15	16	17	18	19	20	21	22	23	24	25	26	27	28	29	30	31	32	33	34	35	36	37	38	39	Apps	T	Pts
A (Arthur) Akers	-	-	-	F	-	F	F	-	F	F	F	F	F	F	F	-	F	F	F	F	F	F	F	F	F	-	F	F	F	F	F	F	F	F	F	F	F	F	-	31	4	12
AS (Shirley) Atkins	-	-	-	-	-	-	-	-	-	-	>W	-	W	W	-	W	-	-	-	-	-	-	-	-	-	-	-	-	-	-	-	-	-	-	-	-	-	-	-	4	-	-
J (Jesse) Ball	-	-	-	C	-	-	-	-	-	-	-	-	-	-	-	-	-	-	-	-	-	-	-	-	-	-	-	-	-	-	-	-	-	W	-	-	-	-	-	2	1	3
G (George) Banks	-	-	-	-	-	-	-	-	-	-	-	-	-	-	-	-	-	-	-	-	-	-	-	-	-	-	-	-	F	-	F	-	-	-	-	-	-	-	-	2	-	-
WH (William) Bradford	F	F	F	F	-	-	-	-	-	-	-	-	-	F	-	-	-	-	F	-	-	-	F	-	-	<F	-	-	-	-	-	-	-	-	-	-	-	-	-	8	-	-
J (Jacky) Braithwaite E+	-	-	-	>SH	-	-	-	-	-	-	-	-	-	-	-	-	-	-	SH	SH	SH	-	-	-	-	SH	-	-	-	-	-	-	-	-	-	-	-	SH	SH	7	-	-
H (Hugh) Bryan	-	-	-	-	-	-	-	-	-	-	-	-	-	-	-	C	W	-	-	-	-	-	-	-	-	-	-	-	-	-	-	-	-	-	-	-	-	-	-	2	1	9
W Burton	-	-	-	-	-	-	-	-	-	-	-	-	-	-	-	-	-	F	-	-	-	-	-	-	-	F	-	-	-	-	-	-	-	-	-	-	-	-	-	2	1	3
AC (Alf) Butlin	-	-	-	-	-	-	-	-	-	>W	-	-	-	C	W	-	FB	FB	W	-	W	W	W	W	FB	W	W	FB	W	W	W	W	W	FB	FB	W	W	W	-	24	9	35
RN (Bob) Campbell	>F	F	F	F	F	F	F	F	F	F	F	F	F	F	F	F	F	F	-	F	F	F	F	F	F	-	F	F	F	F	F	F	F	F	F	F	F	F	F	37	3	9
C Clarke	-	-	-	-	-	-	-	-	-	-	-	-	-	-	-	-	-	-	-	-	-	-	-	-	-	-	-	-	-	-	-	-	-	SH	SH	SH	<SH	-	-	4	-	-
TE Coates	-	-	-	-	-	>F	-	-	F	-	F	F	F	-	-	-	-	-	-	-	-	-	-	F	F	-	F	F	<F	-	-	-	-	-	-	-	-	-	-	10	-	-
AE (Ted) Cooke	F	F	F	F	F	F	F	F	F	-	F	-	F	-	F	F	F	F	F	F	F	F	F	F	F	-	F	F	F	F	F	F	F	F	F	F	F	F	F	35	5	21
E (Edward) Dann	-	-	-	-	-	-	F	-	-	<F	-	-	-	-	-	-	-	-	-	-	-	-	-	-	-	-	-	-	-	-	-	-	-	-	-	-	-	-	-	2	1	3
A (Archie) Field	>W	W	W	W	W	W	W	W	W	C	C	C	C	C	-	-	-	C	C	C	C	C	C	C	W	C	C	W	C	C	C	C	C	C	C	C	C	C	W	36	7	101
WJ (Billy) Foreman	FH	FH*	FH*	W*	FH*	FH	FH	FH	FH	FH	FH	FH	FH	FH	FH	FB	-	-	-	FH	FH	FH	FH	FH	FH	FH	FH	SH	FH	FH	-	FH	-	FH	FH	FH	FH	FH	FH	34	10	32
W (William) Gale	-	-	-	FB	-	-	-	-	-	FB	-	-	-	-	-	-	-	-	-	-	-	-	-	-	-	-	-	-	-	-	-	-	-	-	-	FB	-	FB	-	4	-	-
JW (Josh) Garner	-	-	-	-	-	FB	-	-	-	F	-	-	F	F	-	F	-	-	F	-	-	-	-	-	-	-	-	-	-	-	-	-	-	-	-	-	F	F	-	8	-	-
WR (Bob) Hesmondhalgh	C	C	C	C	C	C	C	C	C	-	-	W	-	-	-	-	-	-	-	-	-	-	-	-	-	-	-	-	-	-	-	-	-	-	-	-	-	-	-	10	3	9
FA (Frank) Jackson	W	W	W	-	C	W	W	W	W	-	W	W	W	-	-	-	-	-	-	W	W	W	W	W	W	-	W	-	-	W	W	W	-	-	-	-	W	-	-	22	22	76
W (Walter) Jackson	F	F	F	F	F	F	F	F	F	F	F	F	F	F	F	F	-	F	F	F	F	F	F	F	F	F	F	F	F	F	F	F	F	F	F	-	F	F	F	37	-	-
Dr. Jamieson	-	-	-	-	-	-	-	-	-	-	-	-	-	-	>C	F	<F	-	-	-	-	-	-	-	-	-	-	-	-	-	-	-	-	-	-	-	-	-	-	3	-	-
AO (Arthur) Jones	FB	FB	FB	-	FB	-	FB	FB	FB	W	FB	FB	FB	FB	FB*	W*	C*	W	FB	FB	FB	FB	FB	FB	-	FB	FB	-	FB	FB	FB	FB	FB	-	-	-	FB	-	-	30	6	24
Rev. FH (Frank) Jones	-	-	-	-	-	-	>C	C	C	-	C	C	C	SH	W	-	-	-	-	C	C	-	C	C	-	C	C	C	C	C	C	C	C	-	W	-	-	-	-	21	3	11
G (George) Jones	F	F	F	F	F	F	F	F	F	F	F	F	F	F	F	F	F	F	F	F	F	F	-	-	-	-	-	-	-	F	F	F	F	F	F	F	-	F	<F	31	7	21
Dr. CH (Charles) Nicholson	-	F	F	F	F	-	-	-	-	-	-	-	-	-	SH	-	C	FH	FH	-	-	-	-	-	-	-	-	-	-	-	-	-	-	-	-	-	-	-	-	8	2	6
SH (Sid) Penny E+	-	-	-	-	-	-	-	-	-	-	-	-	-	-	-	-	-	-	>F	F	F	-	F	F	F	F	F	-	-	-	-	-	-	-	-	F	F	F	-	11	-	-
EH (Ezra) Pickard	-	-	-	-	-	-	-	-	-	-	-	-	-	-	-	>C	-	-	-	-	-	C	-	-	-	-	-	C	-	-	-	-	W	C	-	C	C	C	-	8	6	18
E (Eddie) Redman	F*	-	-	-	-	F*	F*	F*	F*	F*	F*	F*	F*	F*	F	SH	F	F*	F*	F*	F*	F*	F*	F*	C*	F*	F*	F*	F*	F*	FH*	F*	F*	F*	F*	F*	F*	F*	F*	35	1	6
HJ (Harry) Simpson	SH	SH	SH	-	SH	-	-	SH	-	-	SH	SH	SH	-	-	-	-	-	-	-	-	-	SH	SH	SH	-	SH	FH	SH	SH	SH	<SH	-	-	-	-	-	-	-	17	-	-
RP (Paddy) Swain	F	F	F	FH	F	SH	SH	F	SH	SH	-	-	-	-	-	-	FH	-	-	-	-	SH	-	-	-	-	-	-	-	-	-	-	-	-	-	-	-	-	-	12	-	-
GF (George) Walker	-	-	-	-	-	-	-	-	-	-	-	-	-	-	-	-	-	-	-	-	-	-	-	-	-	-	-	-	-	>F	F	-	-	-	-	-	-	-	-	2	-	-
CE (Charlie) Watts	-	-	-	-	-	-	-	-	-	-	-	-	-	-	-	FH	-	-	-	-	-	-	-	-	-	-	-	W	-	-	-	-	SH	-	-	-	-	-	-	3	-	-
ME (Monty) Whitehead	F	F	F	-	F	F	F	F	F	F	F	F	-	F	F	-	F	F	-	F	F	F	F	F	F	F	F	F	F	F	F	F	F	F	F	F	F	-	-	33	5	15
H (Harry) Wilkinson	-	>C	-	-	-	-	-	-	-	-	-	-	-	-	C	-	W	W	W	W	-	-	-	-	C	W	-	-	-	-	-	-	-	W	C	W	-	W	W	13	3	9
AW (Archie) Woodyatt	-	-	-	-	W	C	-	-	-	C	-	-	-	-	-	-	-	-	-	-	-	-	-	-	-	-	-	-	-	-	-	-	-	-	-	-	-	-	C	4	2	6
SW Wright	-	-	-	-	-	-	-	-	-	-	-	-	-	-	-	-	-	>C	<C	-	-	-	-	-	-	-	-	-	-	-	-	-	-	-	-	-	-	-	-	2	-	-
W (William) Yiend E6	-	-	-	-	-	>F	-	-	F	-	-	-	F	-	-	-	F	-	-	-	-	F	-	-	F	-	-	-	-	-	-	F	F	F	<F	-	-	-	-	10	2	6

1 GAME: E (Edward) Bolus >F(28), W Bottomley =F(36), JM (Monty) Brownson =Ct(39), H (Harry) Collins =F(26), WJ (Walter) Collis =FB(39), WJN (William) Davis I9 =F(15), AO (Aubrey) Dowson E+ =W(29), W Everson =W(14), RR (Bob) Golding <F(39), S (Shirley) Harrison F(16), J Hart =F(4), G (George) Hicken <FH(33), AL (Arthur) Jackson <F(16), WS (Willie) Jagger >W(35), GH (George) Keeton E+ >F(26), P Kenyon =F(39), WF (William) Lincoln >F(39), A Mason =C(3), M (Martinus) Swain >SH(17), Lt. AC (Arthur) Thompson =Ct(1), EC (Ernest) Wykes SH(18)

The key for how to read the stats is on the last page

18 96/97

Home Ground: Welford Road	OVERALL RECORD:					T	C	PG	DG	MK	PTS
Captain: Arthur Jones	PLD	W	D	L	Tigers scored:	95	36	1	4	0	376
Vice-captain: Billy Foreman	39	27	5	7	Opponents scored:	26	9	1	1	0	103

GM	DATE		VEN	OPPONENTS	RESULT	TRIES	KICKS	ATT
MIDLAND COUNTIES CUP						**CUP WINNERS: MOSELEY**		
31	Mar	13	a	Rugby (2)	W 30-0	F.Jones(3), Wilkinson(2), Butlin, Foreman, Redman	Field 2c, A.Jones c	-
32		20	a	Coventry (3)	W 6-3 (aet)	Butlin, Wilkinson	-	-
33		**27**	**H**	**Old Edwardians (sf)**	L 0-3	-	-	4285
CLUB MATCHES								
1	Sep	**19**	**H**	**Cheltenham**	W 8-0	Field, Foreman	Field c	2772
2		**26**	**H**	**Northampton**	W 11-3	Field, Foreman, Wilkinson	Field c	3833
3	Oct	3	a	Coventry	L 0-6	-	-	4000
4		**10**	**H**	**Burton**	D 0-0	-	-	2701
5		**17**	**H**	**Rugby**	W 23-0	Redman(2), Field, Cooke, Foreman	Field 4c	2099
6		24	a	Swansea	L 5-8	Field	Field c	-
7		26m	a	Llanelly	L 0-14	-	-	-
8		27tu	a	Mountain Ash	L 0-11	-	-	-
9		31	a	Old Edwardians	W 8-3 (Abandoned 66')	Akers, Wilkinson	Field c	-
10	Nov	**7**	**H**	**Bedford School**	W 14-0	Field, Butlin, F.Jones, Wilkinson	Field c	1182
11		**14**	**H**	**Lancaster**	W 3-0	Foreman	-	2040
12		**21**	**H**	**Coventry**	W 19-0	Wilkinson(2), Braithwaite, Field, Foreman	A.Jones 2c	5993
13		**28**	**H**	**Manchester**	W 24-3	Foreman(2), Wilkinson(2), Braithwaite, Lincoln	Field 2c, A.Jones c	1685
	Dec	3th	a	Nuneaton	PP (frost)			
14		**5**	**H**	**Coventry**	W 3-0	Wilkinson	-	4377
15		**12**	**H**	**Hampstead**	W 8-0	A.Jones, Mosby	A.Jones c	667
16		**14m**	**H**	**Jesus College, Oxford**	W 16-0	Lincoln, Penny, Walker, Wilkinson	A.Jones d	511
17		19	a	Bedford	W 13-0	Field(2), Wilkinson	A.Jones 2c	2000
18		**26**	**H**	**Aspatria**	D 3-3	-	A.Jones p	3195
19		**28m**	**H**	**Harlequins**	D 0-0	-	-	2285
20		**29tu**	**H**	**Mountain Ash**	W 3-0	A.Jones	-	3225
21	Jan	2	a	Burton	L 3-4	Braithwaite	-	-
22		**9**	**H**	**St Thomas' Hospital**	W 21-0	Wilkinson(2), Field, Butlin, Foreman	Field 3c	660
		16	**H**	**Rugby**	PP (snow)			
23		**23**	**H**	**Bedford**	W 11-5	Foreman	A.Jones 2d	1308
24		**30**	**H**	**Altrincham**	W 6-0	F.Jackson, F.Jones	-	1703
25	Feb	**6**	**H**	**Swansea**	W 5-0	Whitehead	A.Jones c	3716
26		**13**	**H**	**Old Edwardians**	W 13-0	Whitehead(2), Swain	A.Jones 2c	1593
27		17w	a	Bedford School	W 19-9	Butlin(2), Foreman(2), F.Jones	Field c, A.Jones c	-
28		**20**	**H**	**Guy's Hospital**	W 17-3	Redman(2), Braithwaite, Field, Swain	F.Jones c	2020
29		27	a	Manchester	D 5-5	F.Jones	Field c	-
30	Mar	**6**	**H**	**Littleborough**	W 32-0	Field(2), Swain(2), Wilkinson(2), Cooke, Foreman	F.Jones 4c	2470
34	Apr	**3**	**H**	**Nuneaton**	W 9-0	Wilkinson(2), F.Jones	-	551
35		**5m**	**H**	**Llanelly**	D 0-0	-	-	1682
36		10	a	Northampton	L 11-15	Atkins, Foreman, Wilkinson	F.Jones c	10000
37		**17**	**H**	**Sale**	W 6-0	Akers, Swain	-	350
38		**19m**	**H**	**Portsmouth**	W 14-5	Atkins(2), Field, Wilkinson	F.Jones c	2063
39		**20tu**	**H**	**Penygraig**	W 7-0	Butlin	Braithwaite d	2074

INDIVIDUAL APPEARANCES 1896/97

Name / Game #	1	2	3	4	5	6	7	8	9	10	11	12	13	14	15	16	17	18	19	20	21	22	23	24	25	26	27	28	29	30	31	32	33	34	35	36	37	38	39	Apps	T	Pts
A (Arthur) Akers	-	F	F	F	-	F	F	F	F	F	F	F	-	F	F	F	-	F	F	-	-	F	F	F	F	F	-	F	F	F	-	-	-	F	F	F	F	F	F	29	2	6
HP (Percy) Atkins	-	-	-	-	-	-	-	-	-	-	-	-	-	-	-	-	-	-	-	-	-	-	-	-	-	-	-	-	-	-	-	-	-	-	>W	W	W	W	W	5	3	9
E (Edward) Bolus	-	-	-	-	-	-	-	-	-	-	-	-	-	-	-	-	-	-	-	-	-	-	-	-	-	-	-	-	-	-	-	-	-	-	-	F	-	F	F	3	-	-
J (Jacky) Braithwaite E+	-	-	-	-	SH	SH	-	-	-	SH	SH	SH	SH	SH	SH	SH	SH	SH	SH	SH	SH	SH	SH	SH	SH	SH	SH	SH	SH	SH	SH	SH	SH	SH	SH	SH	SH	SH	SH	32	4	16
H (Hugh) Bryan	-	-	-	-	-	-	-	-	-	-	-	-	-	-	-	-	-	-	-	W	<W	-	-	-	-	-	-	-	-	-	-	-	-	-	-	-	-	-	-	2	-	-
W Burton	-	-	-	-	-	-	-	-	-	-	-	-	-	-	-	-	-	-	-	-	-	-	-	-	-	-	-	-	-	-	-	-	-	-	F	-	F	-	-	2	-	-
AC (Alf) Butlin	W	W	FB	FB	W	FB	FB	FB	W	W	W	W	W	W	W	W	W	-	FB	W	FB	W	W	-	W	W	W	FB*	FB*	FB	W	W	W	FB	FB	FB	FB	FB	C	37	7	21
RN (Bob) Campbell	F	F	-	F	F	-	-	-	F	F	F	F	F	F	F	F	F	F	F	F	F	F	F	F	F	F	F	F	F	F	F	F	F	F	F	F	F	F	F	35	-	-
C Chapman	-	-	-	-	-	-	-	-	-	-	-	-	-	-	-	>W	-	<W	-	-	-	-	-	-	-	-	-	-	-	-	-	-	-	-	-	-	-	-	-	2	-	-
AE (Ted) Cooke	F	F	F	F	F	F	F	F	-	-	-	-	-	-	-	-	-	-	-	-	-	-	-	-	-	-	F	F	F	F	F	F	F	-	F	-	-	-	-	16	2	6
TH (Tom) Crumbie	-	-	-	-	-	-	-	-	-	-	-	-	-	-	-	-	-	-	-	-	<F	-	-	-	-	-	-	-	-	-	-	-	-	-	-	-	-	-	-	1	-	-
A (Archie) Field	C	C	C	C	C	W	C	W	C	C	C	C	C	C	-	-	C	-	-	C	C	C	C	C	C	C	W	C	C	C	C	C	C	C	C	C	C	C	<C	35	13	75
WJ (Billy) Foreman	FH	FH	FH*	FH*	FH	FH*	FH*	FH*	FH	FH	FH	FH	FH	FH	FH	FH	-	FH	FH	FH	FH	FH	FH	FH	FH	FH	FH	FH	-	FH*	FH	FH	FH	FH*	FH*	FH*	FH*	FH*	FH*	37	14	42
W (William) Gale	-	-	-	-	-	-	-	-	-	-	-	-	-	-	-	-	-	-	-	FB	-	-	-	-	-	-	-	-	-	-	-	-	-	-	-	-	-	-	FB	2	-	-
JW (Josh) Garner	-	-	F	-	-	F	F	-	-	F	F	F	F	F	F	F	F	F	F	F	F	F	F	F	F	F	F	F	F	F	F	F	F	F	F	F	F	F	F	33	-	-
R Gilbert	-	-	-	-	-	-	-	-	-	-	-	-	-	-	-	-	>F	-	-	F	F	-	-	-	-	-	<F	-	-	-	-	-	-	-	-	-	-	-	-	4	-	-
E Goddard	-	-	-	-	-	-	-	>C	-	-	-	-	-	-	-	-	-	-	-	-	-	-	-	-	-	-	-	-	-	-	-	-	-	-	-	-	-	-	-	1	-	-
S (Shirley) Harrison	-	-	-	-	-	-	-	-	-	-	-	-	-	-	-	-	-	-	-	-	-	-	-	-	-	-	-	-	-	-	-	-	-	-	-	<F	-	-	-	1	-	-
FA (Frank) Jackson	-	-	W	W	W	-	-	-	-	-	-	-	-	-	-	-	-	-	-	-	-	-	-	W	-	-	-	-	-	-	-	-	-	-	-	-	-	-	-	4	1	3
W (Walter) Jackson	F	F	F	F	F	F	F	F	F	F	F	F	F	F	-	-	F	F	F	F	F	F	F	F	F	F	-	F	F	F	F	F	F	-	-	-	-	-	-	30	-	-
WS (Willie) Jagger	-	-	-	-	-	W	W	<W	-	-	-	-	-	-	-	-	-	-	-	-	-	-	-	-	-	-	-	-	-	-	-	-	-	-	-	-	-	-	-	3	-	-
Jenkins	-	-	-	-	-	-	-	=SH	-	-	-	-	-	-	-	-	-	-	-	-	-	-	-	-	-	-	-	-	-	-	-	-	-	-	-	-	-	-	-	1	-	-
AO (Arthur) Jones	FB*	FB*	-	-	FB*	-	-	-	FB*	FB*	FB*	FB*	FB*	FB*	FB*	FB*	FB*	FB*	W*	C*	C*	FB*	FB*	FB*	FB*	FB*	FB*	-	-	-	FB*	FB*	FB*	-	-	-	-	-	-	25	2	43
Rev. FH (Frank) Jones	C	C	C	C	C	-	-	-	C	C	W	C	W	C	C	-	C	C	-	-	-	C	C	C	C	C	C	C	W	C	C	C	C	W	C	C	C	C	-	31	8	38
GH (George) Keeton E+	-	-	-	-	-	-	-	-	-	-	-	-	-	-	-	-	-	-	F	-	-	-	-	-	-	-	-	-	-	-	-	-	-	-	-	-	-	-	-	1	-	-
WF (William) Lincoln	F	-	F	-	-	F	F	F	F	-	-	-	F	-	F	F	F	F	-	F	F	-	-	-	-	-	F	-	-	-	-	-	-	F	-	-	-	-	-	15	2	6
JWM (John) Meek	-	-	-	-	-	-	-	-	-	-	-	-	-	-	-	-	-	-	-	-	-	-	-	-	-	-	-	-	-	-	-	-	-	-	-	-	F	F	<F	3	-	-
EP (Ervine) Mosby	-	-	-	-	-	-	-	-	-	-	-	-	-	-	-	>C	-	-	-	-	-	-	-	-	-	-	-	-	W	-	-	-	-	-	-	-	-	-	-	2	1	3
Dr. CH (Charles) Nicholson	F	F	-	F	-	-	-	-	SH	-	-	-	F	-	-	-	-	-	-	-	-	-	-	-	-	-	-	-	-	<F	-	-	-	-	-	-	-	-	-	6	-	-
RE (Rowland) Page	-	-	F	-	-	-	-	F	F	F	-	-	F	-	F	-	-	F	F	F	F	F	-	-	-	-	-	-	-	-	-	-	-	F	-	-	F	-	-	13	-	-
SH (Sid) Penny E+	F	F	F	F	F	F	F	F	F	F	F	F	F	F	-	F	F	-	-	F	F	F	F	F	F	F	F	F	F	F	F	F	F	-	F	F	F	F	F	35	1	3
FH (Fzra) Pickard	-	-	-	-	-	-	-	-	-	-	-	-	-	-	-	-	-	-	<C	-	-	-	-	-	-	-	-	-	-	-	-	-	-	-	-	-	-	-	-	1	-	-
E (Eddie) Redman	F	F	-	F	F	F	F	F	F	F	F	F	-	F	F	F	F	F	F	F	-	-	F	F	F	F	F	F	F	-	F	F	F	C	F	-	-	-	-	30	5	15
F Sarson	-	-	-	-	-	-	-	-	-	-	-	-	-	-	-	-	-	-	-	-	-	-	-	-	-	-	-	-	-	-	-	-	-	=F	-	-	-	-	-	1	-	-
JT (John) Simcoe	-	-	-	-	-	-	-	-	-	-	-	-	-	-	-	-	=FH	-	-	-	-	-	-	-	-	-	-	-	-	-	-	-	-	-	-	-	-	-	-	1	-	-
RP (Paddy) Swain	SH	SH	SH	SH	F	-	-	-	F	F	F	F	F	F	F	-	-	F	W	-	-	F	F	F	F	F	-	W	FH	W	F	F	F	F	-	F	F	F	F	30	5	15
Thomas	-	-	-	-	-	-	=SH	-	-	-	-	-	-	-	-	-	-	-	-	-	-	-	-	-	-	-	-	-	-	-	-	-	-	-	-	-	-	-	-	1	-	-
GF (George) Walker	-	-	-	-	-	-	-	-	-	-	-	-	-	-	-	C	-	<C	-	-	-	-	-	-	-	-	-	-	-	-	-	-	-	-	-	-	-	-	-	2	1	3
CE (Charlie) Watts	-	-	-	-	-	C	<C	-	-	-	-	-	-	-	-	-	-	-	-	-	-	-	-	-	-	-	-	-	-	-	-	-	-	-	-	-	-	-	-	2	-	-
ED (David) Whetstone	-	-	-	-	-	-	-	-	-	-	-	-	-	-	-	>F	-	-	-	-	-	-	-	-	-	-	-	-	-	-	-	-	-	-	-	-	F	F	-	3	-	-
ME (Monty) Whitehead	F	F	F	F	F	F	F	F	-	-	F	F	-	F	F	F	F	-	-	-	-	F	F	F	F	F	F	F	F	F	F	F	F	-	F	F	-	-	-	28	3	9
H (Harry) Wilkinson	W	W	W	W	-	C	W	C	W	W	C	W	C	W	W	C	W	W	C	-	W	W	W	W	W	W	C	W	C	W	W	W	W	W	W	W	W	W	W	37	21	63
F (Frederick) Woodford	-	-	-	-	-	-	-	-	-	-	-	-	-	-	-	-	-	-	=F	-	-	-	-	-	-	-	-	-	-	-	-	-	-	-	-	-	-	-	-	1	-	-

The key for how to read the stats is on the last page

18	97/98	Home Ground: Welford Road	Trophy Cabinet: Midland Counties Cup(1)
		Captain: Arthur Jones	
		Vice-captain: Billy Foreman	

OVERALL RECORD:					T	C	PG	DG	MK	PTS
PLD	W	D	L	Tigers scored:	116	48	3	8	1	489
38	31	0	7	Opponents scored:	24	11	4	1	0	110

GM	DATE		VEN	OPPONENTS	RESULT	TRIES	KICKS	ATT
MIDLAND COUNTIES CUP						**CUP WINNERS: LEICESTER TIGERS**		
31	Mar	**5**	**H**	**Rugby (1)**	W 31-0	Wilkinson(3), F.Jackson(2), A.Jones, Atkins, Carey-Elwes, Keeton	A.Jones 2c	4497
32		**12**	**H**	**Burton (2)**	W 17-0	F.Jackson(3), A.Jones	A.Jones c/p	6203
33		19	a	Coventry (sf)	W 12-5	Wilkinson	A.Jones c/p/d	9000
34	Apr	6w		Moseley (f)	W 5-3	Oscroft	F.Jones c	-
CLUB MATCHES								
1	Sep	**4**	**H**	**Leicestershire XV**	W 31-0	Wilkinson(3), Joyce, Cooke, Foreman, Lincoln	Joyce 2c/d, F.Jones c	2000
2		**11**	**H**	**Nuneaton**	W 22-8	F.Jones(2), Foreman(2), Braithwaite, Oscroft	F.Jones c, Braithwaite c	5000
3		**18**	**H**	**Cheltenham**	W 29-0	Oscroft(2), Redman(2), Atkins, Braithwaite, Foreman	Oscroft c, A.Jones 2c, F.Jones c	-
4		**25**	**H**	**Handsworth**	W 17-4	Foreman(2), F.Jones, Swain	A.Jones p, Butlin c	-
5	Oct	**2**	**H**	**Llanelly**	W 13-0	A.Jones(2), F.Jackson	A.Jones 2c	10000
6		**4m**	**H**	**Bristol**	W 9-5	Atkins, Foreman, F.Jackson	-	-
7		**9**	**H**	**Burton**	W 22-3	Wilkinson(2), Foreman, Penny, Swain, Whitehead	A.Jones 2c	6000
8		**16**	**H**	**Rugby**	W 23-0	A.Jones, Braithwaite, Lincoln, Mosby, Whitehead	A.Jones 4c	4000
9		**23**	**H**	**Coventry**	W 7-3	Akers	A.Jones d	10000
10		**30**	**H**	**Old Edwardians**	W 19-0	Atkins(2), Wilkinson(2), Mosby	F.Jones 2c	5000
11	Nov	**6**	**H**	**Northampton**	W 10-0	A.Jones, Foreman	A.Jones 2c	12000
12		**13**	**H**	**Bedford School**	W 29-0	A.Jones(3), Wilkinson(3), Braithwaite, Redman, Swain	F.Jones c	-
13		20	a	Northampton	L 8-16	Atkins, Foreman	A.Jones c	13000
14		**27**	**H**	**Swansea**	L 0-3	-	-	-
15	Dec	4	a	Rugby	W 12-0	Wilkinson(2), Butlin, Lincoln	-	-
16		11	a	Manchester	W 3-0	F.Jones	-	-
17		**18**	**H**	**Bedford**	W 14-0	Wilkinson(2), Mosby, Keeton	Mosby c	-
18		**24f**	**H**	**Olney**	W 20-3	F.Jones(2), A.Jones, Oscroft	A.Jones 4c	1746
19		**27m**	**H**	**Mountain Ash**	W 14-5	Braithwaite, F.Jackson	A.Jones 2c, Oscroft d	4736
20		**28tu**	**H**	**Harlequins**	W 7-3	Braithwaite	A.Jones d	3468
21	Jan	1	a	Bedford	L 0-3	-	-	-
22		8	a	Coventry	W 9-0	Mosby	A.Jones c/d	-
23		**15**	**H**	**Sale**	W 20-0	Akers(2), Wilkinson(2), A.Jones, Penny	A.Jones c	2675
24		**22**	**H**	**Coventry**	W 9-0	Mosby	Mosby c, A.Jones d	4291
25		**29**	**H**	**Manchester**	W 16-3	Wilkinson(2), Campbell, Hills	A.Jones 2c	2906
26	Feb	**5**	**H**	**Guy's Hospital**	W 10-0	Banks, F.Jones	A.Jones 2c	2010
27		8tu	a	Bedford School	W 11-0	Cave(2), Whitehead	Butlin c	-
28		12	a	Old Edwardians	W 7-0	Lincoln	A.Jones m	-
29		**19**	**H**	**St Bartholomew's Hospital**	W 16-0	Carey-Elwes(2), Atkins, Keeton	Braithwaite 2c	2511
30		26	a	Burton	L 0-3	-	-	-
	Mar	26	a	Burton	PP			
35	Apr	9	a	Swansea	L 0-17	-	-	-
36		11m	a	Llanelly	L 0-5	-	-	-
37		12tu	a	Bristol	W 14-10	Foreman, Wilkinson	Oscroft 2c/d	-
38		16	a	Northampton	L 3-8	Wilkinson	-	12000

***Neutral Venue:** #34 at the Butts - Coventry*

INDIVIDUAL APPEARANCES 1897/98

Name / Game #	1	2	3	4	5	6	7	8	9	10	11	12	13	14	15	16	17	18	19	20	21	22	23	24	25	26	27	28	29	30	31	32	33	34	35	36	37	38	Apps	T	Pts
A (Arthur) Akers	-	-	-	F	F	F	F	F	F	F	-	-	-	-	F	F	-	-	-	-	-	F	F	-	F	F	F	F	F	F	-	F	F	F	F	F	F	F	24	3	9
HP (Percy) Atkins	W	C	C	C	C	W	W	W	W	C	W	-	W	W	C	-	C	W	-	-	-	C	C	C	-	-	-	-	W	C	C	-	-	C	-	W	W	W	26	7	21
G (George) Banks	-	-	-	-	-	-	-	-	-	-	-	-	-	-	-	-	-	-	-	-	-	-	-	-	-	<F	-	-	-	-	-	-	-	-	-	-	-	-	1	1	3
J (Jacky) Braithwaite E+	SH	SH	SH	SH	SH	SH	SH	SH	SH	SH	SH	SH	SH	SH	SH	SH	SH	-	SH	SH	SH	SH	SH	SH	-	SH	SH	SH	SH	SH	-	SH	SH	SH	SH	-	SH	SH	34	6	24
W Burton	-	-	<F	-	-	-	-	-	-	-	-	-	-	-	-	-	-	-	-	-	-	-	-	-	-	-	-	-	-	-	-	-	-	-	-	-	-	-	1	-	-
AC (Alf) Butlin	FB	-	W	W	FB	FB	FB	FB	FB	FB	FB	FB	FB	FB	W	C	FB	FB	-	FB	FB	FB	FB	FB	FB	FB	FB	FB	FB	FB	FB	FB	FB	FB	FB	FB	FB	FB	36	1	7
RN (Bob) Campbell	F	F	F	F	F	F	F	F	F	F	F	F	F	F	F	F	F	-	F	F	-	-	-	F	F	F	F	F	F	F	F	F	F	F	F	F	F	F	34	1	3
Rev. A (Albert) Carey-Elwes	>F	F	F	F	F	F	-	-	F	F	F	F	F	F	F	F	F	F	-	F	F	F	-	F	F	F	F	F	F	F	F	-	-	-	-	-	-	-	27	3	9
CF (Charles) Cave	-	-	-	-	-	-	-	-	-	-	-	-	-	-	-	-	-	-	-	-	-	-	-	-	-	-	=W	-	-	-	-	-	-	-	-	-	-	-	1	2	6
C (Charles) Cheshire	-	-	-	-	-	-	-	=W	-	-	-	-	-	-	-	-	-	-	-	-	-	-	-	-	-	-	-	-	-	-	-	-	-	-	-	-	-	-	1	-	-
AE (Ted) Cooke	F	<F	-	-	-	-	-	-	-	-	-	-	-	-	-	-	-	-	-	-	-	-	-	-	-	-	-	-	-	-	-	-	-	-	-	-	-	-	2	1	3
WJ (Billy) Foreman	FH*	FH*	FH	FH	FH	FH*	FH	FH	FH	FH*	FH	FH	FH	FH	-	FH*	FH	FH	FH	FH	FH	FH	FH	FH	FH	FH	-	-	-	FH*	SH	FH	FH	FH*	FH*	FH*	FH*	FH*	34	11	33
W (William) Gale	-	-	-	-	-	-	-	-	-	-	-	-	-	-	FB	FB	-	-	-	-	-	-	-	-	-	-	-	-	-	-	-	-	-	-	-	-	-	-	2	-	-
JW (Josh) Garner	F	F	F	-	F	F	F	F	F	F	F	F	F	F	F	F	F	F	F	F	F	F	F	F	F	F	F	F	F	F	F	F	F	F	F	F	F	F	37	-	-
D (David) Gilbert	-	-	-	-	-	-	-	-	-	-	-	-	-	-	-	-	-	-	-	-	>F	-	F	-	-	-	F	-	-	-	-	-	-	-	-	-	-	-	3	-	-
WR (Bob) Hesmondhalgh	-	-	-	-	-	-	-	-	-	-	-	-	-	-	-	-	-	-	-	-	-	-	-	-	-	-	-	-	-	<W	-	-	-	-	-	-	-	-	1	-	-
B (Bertie) Hills	-	-	-	-	-	-	-	-	-	-	-	-	-	-	>FH	-	-	-	-	-	-	-	-	-	SH	-	-	FH	-	-	-	-	-	-	-	SH	-	-	4	1	3
FA (Frank) Jackson	-	-	-	-	W	W	-	-	-	-	-	-	-	-	-	-	-	-	W	C	W	-	-	-	-	-	-	W	-	-	W	W	-	-	-	-	-	-	8	8	24
W (Walter) Jackson	F	F	-	F	-	F	F	F	F	F	F	F	F	F	F	F	F	F	F	F	F	F	F	F	F	-	-	-	F	F	-	-	-	F	F	-	F	F	29	-	-
AO (Arthur) Jones	-	-	FB*	FB*	C*	-	C*	C*	C*	-	C*	C*	C*	C*	-	-	C*	SH*	FB*	C*	C*	C*	C*	C*	C*	C*	-	C*	-	-	FH*	C*	C*	-	-	-	-	-	24	11	124
Rev. FH (Frank) Jones	C	C	C	C	W	-	-	-	C	W	-	C	-	C	-	C	-	C	C	W	C	-	-	-	-	C	C	-	-	-	-	C	C	W	W	-	-	-	20	7	35
R (Ralph) Joyce	=W	-	-	-	-	-	-	-	-	-	-	-	-	-	-	-	-	-	-	-	-	-	-	-	-	-	-	-	-	-	-	-	-	-	-	-	-	-	1	1	11
GH (George) Keeton E+	-	-	-	-	-	F	-	-	-	-	-	-	-	-	-	-	F	F	-	-	F	F	-	-	-	-	F	-	F	-	F	-	F	F	F	F	F	F	14	3	9
WF (William) Lincoln	F	-	-	-	-	-	-	F	F	F	-	-	F	-	F	F	-	F	-	F	F	F	F	F	-	-	FH	F	-	-	F	F	-	-	F	F	-	-	19	4	12
S (Sammy) Matthews	-	-	-	-	-	-	-	-	-	-	-	-	-	-	-	-	-	-	-	-	-	>W	-	-	W	W	W	C	C	C	-	-	-	-	-	-	-	-	7	-	-
EP (Ervine) Mosby	-	-	-	-	-	-	C	C	-	C	-	W	W	-	W	W	W	-	-	W	-	W	W	W	W	-	-	-	-	-	-	-	-	-	-	C	C	C	16	5	19
PW (Percy) Oscroft	-	>W	W	-	-	-	-	-	-	-	C	-	-	-	-	-	-	C	C	-	-	-	-	-	-	-	-	-	-	-	C	-	W	C	C	-	C	C	11	5	29
RE (Rowland) Page	<F	-	-	-	-	-	-	-	-	-	-	-	-	-	-	-	-	-	-	-	-	-	-	-	-	-	-	-	-	-	-	-	-	-	-	-	-	-	1	-	-
SH (Sid) Penny E+	F	F	F	F	F	F	F	F	F	F	F	F	F	F	-	F	F	F	F	F	-	F	F	-	F	F	-	F	F	F	F	F	F	F	F	F	F	F	34	2	6
E (Eddie) Redman	-	-	F	F	F	-	F	-	-	-	F	F	F	F	F	-	F	F	F	-	F	F	F	F	F	F	-	-	F	F	F	F	F	F	-	F	-	F	26	3	9
Skelton	-	-	-	-	-	-	-	-	-	-	-	-	-	-	-	-	-	-	-	=F	-	-	-	-	-	-	-	-	-	-	-	-	-	-	-	-	-	-	1	-	-
RP (Paddy) Swain	-	F	F	W	F	C	F	F	-	-	F	F	C	<F	-	-	-	-	-	-	-	-	-	-	-	-	-	-	-	-	-	-	-	-	-	-	-	-	11	3	9
A Thomas	-	=FB	-	-	-	-	-	-	-	-	-	-	-	-	-	-	-	-	-	-	-	-	-	-	-	-	-	-	-	-	-	-	-	-	-	-	-	-	1	-	-
ED (David) Whetstone	-	-	-	-	-	-	-	-	-	-	-	-	-	-	-	-	-	-	F	-	-	-	F	F	-	-	F	F	-	-	F	F	F	-	-	-	F	-	9	-	-
ME (Monty) Whitehead	-	F	F	F	F	F	F	F	F	-	F	F	F	F	F	F	F	-	F	F	F	-	-	F	F	F	F	F	-	F	-	F	F	F	F	F	F	F	31	3	9
H (Harry) Wilkinson	C	W	-	-	-	C	W	-	W	W	W	W	-	W	C	W	W	W	W	-	W	-	W	W	C	W	C	W	C	W	W	W	W	W	W	W	W	W	31	24	72
AW (Archie) Woodyatt	-	-	-	-	-	-	-	-	-	-	-	-	-	-	-	-	-	-	-	-	-	-	-	-	-	-	-	-	W	-	-	-	-	-	C	C	-	-	3	-	-
EC (Ernest) Wykes	-	-	-	-	-	-	-	-	-	-	-	-	-	-	-	-	-	-	-	-	-	-	-	-	-	-	-	-	FH	-	-	-	-	-	-	-	-	-	1	-	-
SC (Samuel) Yeomans	-	-	-	-	-	-	-	-	-	>F	-	-	-	-	-	-	-	F	F	-	-	-	-	-	-	-	-	-	-	-	-	-	-	-	-	-	-	-	3	-	-

The key for how to read the stats is on the last page

18	98/99	Home Ground: Welford Road	Trophy Cabinet: Midland Counties Cup(2)	OVERALL RECORD:					T	C	PG	DG	MK	PTS
		Captain: Arthur Jones		PLD	W	D	L	Tigers scored:	124	53	6	14	2	560
		Vice-captain: Billy Foreman		44	28	4	12	Opponents scored:	43	17	2	7	0	197

GM	DATE		VEN	OPPONENTS	RESULT	TRIES	KICKS	ATT
MIDLAND COUNTIES CUP						**CUP WINNERS: LEICESTER TIGERS**		
36	Mar	**11**	**H**	**Belgrave St Peter's (2)**	W 68-3	Wilkinson(4), F.Jackson(2), A.Jones(2), Oscroft(2), Brackenbury, Lincoln, Campbell, Scott	Wilkinson c, F.Jackson d, A.Jones d, Oscroft c, Brackenbury c, Lincoln c, Akers c, Ball c, Garner c, F.Jones c, Lloyd-Evans c	-
37		**18**	**H**	**Five Ways Old Edwardians (3)**	W 41-7	Wilkinson(4), F.Jackson(3), Scott, Thompson	A.Jones 4c, F.Jones 3c	-
38		**25**	**H**	**Moseley (sf)**	D 0-0	-	-	10000
39		29w	a	Moseley (sf-replay)	W 8-3	F.Jones, Woodyatt	A.Jones c	-
40	Apr	1		Nuneaton (f)	W 20-3	F.Jones(3), Wilkinson(2), Woodyatt	F.Jones c	8000
CLUB MATCHES								
1	Sep	**3**	**H**	**Nuneaton**	W 17-3	F.Jones, Foreman, Oscroft	F.Jones 2c, Braithwaite m	-
2		**10**	**H**	**Treherbert**	W 6-3	A.Jones, Oscroft	-	-
3		**17**	**H**	**Handsworth**	W 35-3	Wilkinson(2), A.Jones, P.Atkins, F.Jones, Keeton, Penny	A.Jones 3c/2d	-
4		**24**	**H**	**Devonport Albion**	W 10-4	F.Jones(2)	F.Jones 2c	-
5	Oct	**1**	**H**	**Llanelly**	L 4-10	-	A.Jones d	10000
6		**8**	**H**	**Manchester**	W 38-0	F.Jones(2), Whitehead(2), A.Jones, Wilkinson, Foreman, Keeton	F.Jones c, A.Jones d, Wilkinson d, Braithwaite 2c	-
7		**12w**	**H**	**Bedford School**	W 25-3	Wilkinson(3), Braithwaite(2), Carey-Elwes, Penny	Goddard d	-
8		**15**	**H**	**Rugby**	W 44-0	Wilkinson(2), P.Atkins(2), A.Jones, Braithwaite, Foreman, Goddard, Whitehead	Wilkinson d, A.Jones 5c/p	-
9		22	a	Richmond	L 3-5	Wilkinson	-	-
10		**29**	**H**	**Old Edwardians**	W 18-5	A.Jones, Lincoln	A.Jones 2c/2d	-
11	Nov	**5**	**H**	**Northampton**	W 6-3	Wilkinson	A.Jones p	15000
12		12	a	Coventry	L 3-5	Braithwaite	-	8000
13		19	a	Swansea	L 0-20	-	-	-
14		21m	a	Treherbert	W 5-3	Braithwaite	A.Jones c	-
15		**26**	**H**	**Lansdowne**	D 5-5	Mosby	A.Jones c	-
16	Dec	3	a	Northampton	W 4-0	-	A.Jones d	12000
17		10	a	Burton	W 27-3	Braithwaite(3), Wilkinson(2), Foreman, F.Jackson	Mosby 3c	1000
18		17	a	Manchester	L 0-4	-	-	-
19		**24**	**H**	**Sale**	W 20-3	F.Jackson(2), A.Jones(2), F.Jones, Wilkinson	F.Jones c	-
20		**26m**	**H**	**Llwynypia**	D 0-0	-	-	10000
21		**27tu**	**H**	**Harlequins**	W 9-3	Wilkinson(2), Penny	-	3000
22		**31**	**H**	**Cardiff**	L 3-8	-	F.Jones p	-
23	Jan	**2m**	**H**	**Edinburgh Royal High School**	L 5-6	Foreman	F.Jones c	-
24		7	a	Devonport Albion	L 7-10	Foreman	A.Jones m	-
25		9m	a	Exeter	W 3-0	F.Jones	-	-
26		**14**	**H**	**Richmond**	W 20-3	Wilkinson(3), Page(2), F.Jones	F.Jones c	8000
27		**21**	**H**	**Exeter**	D 0-0	-	-	-
28		**28**	**H**	**Coventry**	W 9-8	Woodyatt(2), Braithwaite	-	-
29	Feb	**4**	**H**	**Burton**	W 21-4	A.Jones, Mosby, Whitehead, Wilkinson	A.Jones p, Woodyatt 3c	-
30		8w	a	Bedford School	W 17-0	Wilkinson(2), Woodyatt	A.Jones 2c/d	-
31		11	a	Old Edwardians	W 6-3	Whitehead, Wilkinson	-	-
32		14tu	a	Nuneaton	W 8-3	Foreman, F.Jackson	A.Jones c	-
33		**18**	**H**	**Swansea**	L 6-14	-	A.Jones 2p	12000
34		**25**	**H**	**Northampton**	W 24-5	F.Jackson, Lincoln, Matthews, Wilkinson	Mosby 4c/d	8000
35	Mar	4	a	Gloucester	L 3-6	Wilkinson	-	3000
41	Apr	**3m**	**H**	**Pontypridd**	L 0-3	-	-	-
42		**4tu**	**H**	**Carlisle**	W 6-0	Wilkinson(2)	-	-
43		8	a	Cardiff	L 0-19	-	-	4000
44		**15**	**H**	**Gloucester**	W 6-4	Mosby, Wilkinson	-	-

***Neutral Venue:** #40 at the Butts - Coventry*

INDIVIDUAL APPEARANCES 1898/99

Name / Game #	1	2	3	4	5	6	7	8	9	10	11	12	13	14	15	16	17	18	19	20	21	22	23	24	25	26	27	28	29	30	31	32	33	34	35	36	37	38	39	40	41	42	43	44	Apps	T	Pts
A (Arthur) Akers	-	F	-	-	F	-	-	-	-	-	F	-	F	F	F	F	F	F	-	F	F	F	F	F	F	-	F	-	-	-	-	-	F	F	F	F	F	F	F	F	F	F	F	<F	28	-	2
M (Maxwell) Aldred	-	-	-	-	-	-	-	-	-	-	-	-	-	-	-	-	-	-	>F	-	-	-	F	F	F	F	F	F	-	-	-	-	-	-	-	-	-	-	-	-	-	-	-	-	7	-	-
HP (Percy) Atkins	W	W	W	-	W	-	C	C	C	-	-	-	-	-	C	-	C	-	-	-	-	-	-	-	-	-	-	-	-	-	-	-	-	-	-	-	-	-	-	-	-	-	C	-	10	3	9
AS (Shirley) Atkins	-	-	-	-	-	-	F	F	F	F	-	-	-	-	-	-	-	-	-	-	-	-	-	-	-	-	-	-	-	-	-	-	-	-	-	-	-	-	-	-	-	-	-	-	4	-	-
HE (Harold) Brackenbury	-	-	-	-	-	-	-	-	-	>F	F	F	F	F	F	F	F	F	-	-	-	-	-	-	-	-	-	-	-	F	F	-	-	-	-	<F	-	-	-	-	-	-	-	-	12	1	5
J (Jacky) Braithwaite E+	SH	SH	SH	SH	SH	SH	SH	SH	SH	SH	SH	SH	SH	SH	SH	SH	SH	SH	SH	SH	SH	SH	-	SH	SH	SH	SH	SH	-	SH	SH	SH	SH	SH	SH	-	FH	SH	SH	SH	SH	SH	SH	SH	41	9	35
AC (Alf) Butlin	FB	W	FB	FB	FB	FB	FB	FB	FB	FB	FB	FB	FB	FB	FB	FB	FB	FB	FB	W	W	FB	FB	FB	FB	FB	FB	FB	FB	FB	FB	FB	FB	FB	FB	FB	FB	FB	FB	FB	FB	FB	FB	FB	44	-	-
RN (Bob) Campbell	F	F	F	F	F	F	F	F	F	F	F	F	F	F	F	F	F	F	F	F	F	F	-	-	-	F	F	F	F	F	F	F	F	F	F	F	F	F	F	F	F	F	F	F	41	1	3
Rev. A (Albert) Carey-Elwes	-	-	-	-	-	F	F	F	F	-	-	F	-	-	-	-	-	-	-	-	-	-	-	-	-	-	-	-	-	-	-	-	-	-	-	-	-	-	-	-	-	-	-	-	5	1	3
WJ (Billy) Foreman	FH*	FH	FH	FH	FH	FH	-	FH	FH	FH	FH	FH	FH	FH	FH	FH	FH*	-	-	FH	FH	FH	FH	FH	FH*	FH	-	FH	FH	FH	FH	FH	FH	FH*	FH*	-	-	FH	FH	FH	FH*	FH*	-	FH*	37	7	21
AH (Arthur) Frith	-	-	-	-	-	-	-	-	-	-	-	-	-	>W	-	-	-	-	-	-	-	-	-	-	-	-	-	-	-	-	-	-	-	-	-	-	-	-	-	-	-	-	W	-	2	-	-
W (William) Gale	W	-	-	-	-	-	-	-	-	-	-	-	-	-	-	-	-	-	-	-	-	-	-	-	-	-	-	-	-	-	W	-	-	-	-	-	-	-	-	-	-	-	-	-	2	-	-
JW (Josh) Garner	-	-	-	-	-	-	-	-	F	F	F	F	F	F	F	F	F	F	F	F	F	F	F	F	F	F	F	F	F	F	F	-	F	F	F	F	F	F	F	F	F	F	F	F	35	-	2
D (David) Gilbert	F	-	-	-	-	-	-	-	-	-	-	-	-	-	-	-	-	-	-	-	-	-	-	-	-	-	-	F	F	-	-	F	-	-	-	-	-	-	-	-	-	-	-	F	5	-	-
E Goddard	-	-	-	-	-	W	W	W	W	W	-	W	-	-	-	-	-	-	-	-	-	-	-	-	-	-	-	-	-	-	-	-	-	-	-	-	-	-	-	-	-	W	-	-	7	1	7
FA (Frank) Jackson	-	-	-	-	-	-	-	-	-	-	-	-	-	-	-	-	W	-	W	-	-	-	-	-	-	-	-	-	-	-	-	C	-	W	W	W	W	-	-	-	-	-	-	-	7	10	34
W (Walter) Jackson	-	F	F	F	F	F	F	<F	-	-	-	-	-	-	-	-	-	-	-	-	-	-	-	-	-	-	-	-	-	-	-	-	-	-	-	-	-	-	-	-	-	-	-	-	7	-	-
AO (Arthur) Jones	-	FB*	C*	C*	C*	C*	C*	C*	C*	C*	C*	C*	C*	C*	W*	C*	-	C*	FH*	FB*	FB*	C*	C*	C*	-	C*	C*	C*	C*	C*	C*	W*	C*	-	-	FH*	C*	C*	C*	C*	-	-	-	-	35	10	125
Rev. FH (Frank) Jones	C	C	C	C	C	C	-	-	-	-	-	-	-	-	-	-	-	-	C	C	C	C	C	C	C	C	-	-	-	-	-	-	-	-	-	C	C	C	C	C	C	C	-	C	22	13	68
GH (George) Keeton E+	-	F	F	F	F	F	-	-	-	-	-	-	-	-	-	-	-	-	F	F	F	F	F	-	-	F	-	-	-	-	-	-	-	-	-	-	F	-	-	-	F	-	-	-	13	2	6
C (Charles) Kinton	-	-	-	-	-	-	-	-	-	-	-	-	-	-	F	F	-	F	-	-	-	-	-	-	-	-	-	-	-	-	-	-	-	-	-	-	-	-	-	-	-	F	-	F	5	-	-
J (John) Langdon	-	-	-	-	-	-	-	-	-	-	-	-	-	-	-	-	-	-	-	-	-	-	-	-	-	-	-	-	-	>F	-	<F	-	-	-	-	-	-	-	-	-	-	-	-	2	-	-
WF (William) Lincoln	F	F	F	F	F	F	F	F	F	F	F	F	F	F	W	F	F	F	F	F	F	W	F	F	F	F	F	F	F	F	F	F	F	F	F	F	F	F	F	F	W	F	F	F	44	3	11
O (Owen) Lloyd-Evans	-	-	-	-	-	-	>FH	-	-	-	-	-	-	-	-	-	-	FH	-	-	-	-	SH	-	-	-	-	-	-	-	-	-	-	-	-	SH	<SH	-	-	-	-	-	-	-	5	-	2
S (Sammy) Matthews	F	-	F	F	F	F	F	F	F	F	F	F	F	-	-	-	F	-	F	F	F	F	F	F	F	F	F	F	F	-	F	-	F	F	F	F	F	F	F	F	F	-	-	F	35	1	3
EP (Ervine) Mosby	-	-	-	-	-	-	-	-	-	C	C	C	C	C	C	W	C	C	-	-	-	-	-	W	C	-	C	-	W	-	C	-	-	C	C	-	-	-	-	-	C	C	-	C	19	3	27
T Orme	-	-	-	-	-	-	-	-	-	-	-	-	-	-	-	-	-	-	-	-	-	-	-	-	-	-	-	-	-	>F	-	<F	-	-	-	-	-	-	-	-	-	-	-	-	2	-	-
PW (Percy) Oscroft	C	C	-	W	-	-	-	-	-	-	W	-	-	-	-	C	-	-	C	C	C	-	-	-	-	-	-	-	-	-	-	-	C	C	C	C	-	-	-	-	-	-	-	W	13	4	14
CA Page	-	-	-	-	-	-	-	-	-	-	-	-	-	-	-	-	-	-	-	-	-	-	W	-	W	W	W	W	-	-	-	W	-	-	-	-	-	-	-	-	-	-	-	-	6	2	6
SH (Sid) Penny E+	F	F	F	F	F	F	F	F	F	F	F	-	F	F	F	F	F	F	F	F	F	F	F	F	F	F	F	F	F	-	F	F	F	F	F	-	-	F	F	F	F	F	F	F	40	3	9
S Ramsey	-	-	-	-	-	-	-	-	-	-	-	-	-	-	-	-	-	-	-	-	-	-	-	>F	F	-	-	-	-	-	-	-	-	-	-	-	-	-	-	-	-	-	-	-	2	-	-
Lt. MS Scott	-	-	-	-	-	-	-	-	-	-	-	-	-	-	-	-	-	-	-	-	-	-	-	-	-	-	-	-	-	-	>F	F	F	F	F	F	F	F	F	F	F	F	F	-	13	2	6
WE Thompson	-	-	-	-	-	-	>F	-	-	-	-	-	-	-	-	-	-	-	F	-	F	F	F	F	F	F	-	-	-	-	-	-	-	-	-	-	F	-	-	F	F	-	F	-	12	1	3
ED (David) Whetstone	-	F	F	F	-	-	-	-	-	-	-	-	-	-	-	-	-	-	-	-	-	-	-	-	-	-	-	-	F	-	-	-	-	-	-	-	-	-	-	-	-	F	-	-	5	-	-
ME (Monty) Whitehead	-	-	F	F	F	F	-	F	F	F	F	F	F	F	F	F	-	F	-	-	-	-	-	-	-	-	F	F	F	F	F	-	F	F	F	-	-	F	F	-	-	-	-	-	24	5	15
H (Harry) Wilkinson	-	-	W	W	W	W	W	W	W	-	W	W	W	W	-	W	W	W	W	W	W	W	W	W	W	W	W	W	W	W	W	C	W	W	W	W	W	W	W	W	W	W	C	W	40	37	121
AW (Archie) Woodyatt	-	-	-	-	-	-	-	-	-	W	-	-	W	-	-	-	-	W	-	-	-	-	-	-	-	-	-	C	C	W	-	-	W	-	-	-	-	W	W	W	-	-	<W	-	11	5	21
SC (Samuel) Yeomans	-	-	-	-	-	-	-	-	-	-	-	-	-	F	F	-	F	-	-	<F	-	-	-	-	-	-	-	-	-	-	-	-	-	-	-	-	-	-	-	-	-	-	-	-	4	-	-

1 GAME: AC (Arthur) Andrews >FH(43), J (Jesse) Ball <F(36), E (Edward) Bolus <F(2), AJ (Arthur) Currington =F(43), RC (Richard) Garratt =F(30), B (Bertie) Hills FH(27), AG (Arthur) Keywood =F(32), MC (Mark) Morrison S10 GB+ >F(22), T Patrick =F(1), E (Eddie) Redman F(1), C (Charles) Timlock >F(12), WJ (William) Voakes >SH(29), CWS (Charles) Wetherell =C(30)

The key for how to read the stats is on the last page

18 99/00	Home Ground: Welford Road	Trophy Cabinet: Midland Counties Cup(3)
	Captain: Billy Foreman	
	Vice-captain: Arthur Jones	

OVERALL RECORD:					T	C	PG	DG	MK	PTS
PLD	W	D	L	Tigers scored:	98	41	3	13	1	441
36	25	3	8	Opponents scored:	38	15	2	4	1	170

#	Month	Date	Venue	Opponent	Result	Tries	Kicks	Att
MIDLAND COUNTIES CUP						**CUP WINNERS: LEICESTER TIGERS**		
29	Mar	10	a	Five Ways Old Edwardians (2)	W 28-0	Wilkinson(2), Oscroft, Braithwaite, Goddard, Lincoln	Oscroft d, Scott 2c, A.Jones c	-
30		17	a	Coventry (3)	W 8-3	Braithwaite, Wilkinson	A.Jones c	5000
31		**24**	**H**	**Rugby (sf)**	W 19-0	Foreman, Oscroft, Scott, Wilkinson	A.Jones c/p, F.Jones c	2000
32		31		Moseley (f)	W 13-4	F.Jones(2), Foreman	A.Jones c, F.Jones c	10000
CLUB MATCHES								
1	Sep	**2**	**H**	**Nuneaton**	W 17-3	Oscroft, Campbell, Kinton	Oscroft 2c/d	4000
2		**9**	**H**	**Handsworth**	W 27-0	Miles(3), Wilkinson(2), Braithwaite, P.Atkins	Wilkinson c, Braithwaite c, Gale c	-
3		**16**	**H**	**Percy Park**	W 13-0	Wilkinson(2), Lincoln	Mosby 2c	6000
4		**23**	**H**	**Aberavon**	W 20-6	Aldred, Penny, Wilkinson	Mosby 2c/p, A.Jones d	8000
5		**30**	**H**	**Devonport Albion**	D 0-0	-	-	8000
6	Oct	**7**	**H**	**Exeter**	W 11-0	F.Jones, Wilkinson	A.Jones c/p	8000
7		**14**	**H**	**Coventry**	W 21-0	Foreman(2), Oscroft, F.Jones, Wilkinson	Oscroft c, Braithwaite 2c	-
8		**21**	**H**	**Richmond**	W 15-0	Wilkinson(2), Oscroft	A.Jones c/d	-
9		**25w**	**H**	**Bedford School**	W 29-3	Miles(2), Swain(2), Gale, Goodrich, Lee, Penny, Voakes	Mosby c	-
10		**28**	**H**	**Old Edwardians**	W 30-0	Oscroft(2), Butlin(2), Mosby, Wilkinson	Oscroft d, Mosby 3c, A.Jones c	-
11	Nov	**4**	**H**	**Northampton**	W 4-0	-	Oscroft d	12000
12		8w	a	Cambridge University	L 0-19	-	-	-
13		**11**	**H**	**Keighley**	W 12-9	Hind, Wilkinson	A.Jones m, Mosby c	-
		18	**H**	**Llanelly**	PP (fog)			
14		**25**	**H**	**Swansea**	L 0-5	-	-	8000
15	Dec	2	a	Northampton	D 3-3	Foreman	-	8000
16		9	a	Coventry	W 8-5	Oscroft(2)	Mosby c	-
		16	**H**	**Burton**	PP (frost)			
17		23	a	Cardiff	L 0-26	-	-	-
18		**26tu**	**H**	**Llwynypia**	W 9-3	Wilkinson(2), Lincoln	-	-
19		**27w**	**H**	**Harlequins**	W 25-8	Wilkinson(2), Braithwaite, Hind, F.Jones	Braithwaite d, A.Jones c/d	-
20		30	a	Exeter	W 11-3	Foreman(2), Wilkinson	Mosby c	2000
21	Jan	1m	a	Devonport Albion	L 0-22	-	-	5000
22		**6**	**H**	**Bristol**	W 9-0	Braithwaite	Butlin d, Mosby c	-
23		13	a	Richmond	W 9-3	Wilkinson(2), Miles	-	-
24		20	a	Burton	W 23-0	Miles(3), Wilkinson(2)	Wilkinson d, Mosby 2c	-
25		**27**	**H**	**Gloucester**	L 3-10	Wilkinson	-	6000
	Feb	**3**	**H**	**Cardiff**	PP (snow)			
		10	a	Old Edwardians	PP			
26		**17**	**H**	**Treherbert**	W 8-0	-	A.Jones 2d	-
27		24	a	Gloucester	D 0-0	-	-	2000
		27tu	a	Nuneaton	PP			
28	Mar	**3**	**H**	**Manchester**	W 31-5	Oscroft, Foreman, Goddard, Lincoln, Whetstone, Whitehead, Wilkinson	Oscroft d, Scott 2c, Butlin c	-
33	Apr	**7**	**H**	**Nuneaton**	W 30-4	Braithwaite(2), Lincoln(2), P.Atkins, Voakes, Whitehead, Wilkinson	Gale 3c	-
34		14	a	Swansea	L 5-15	Wilkinson	Mosby c	10000
35		16m	a	Llanelly	L 0-8	-	-	3000
36		17tu	a	Cheltenham	L 0-3	-	-	-

Neutral Venue: *#32 at the Butts - Coventry*

INDIVIDUAL APPEARANCES 1899/00

Name / Game #	1	2	3	4	5	6	7	8	9	10	11	12	13	14	15	16	17	18	19	20	21	22	23	24	25	26	27	28	29	30	31	32	33	34	35	36	Apps	T	Pts
M (Maxwell) Aldred	F	F	F	F	F	F	-	-	-	F	-	F	-	F	F	-	F	-	-	F	F	-	-	-	-	-	-	-	-	-	-	-	-	F	F	-	15	1	3
HP (Percy) Atkins	C	F	F	F	-	F	F	F	-	F	F	F	F	F	F	F	-	F	F	F	F	F	-	F	F	F	-	-	-	-	-	-	C	-	F	F	25	2	6
AS (Shirley) Atkins	-	-	-	-	-	-	-	-	-	-	-	-	-	-	-	-	-	-	<F	-	-	-	-	-	-	-	-	-	-	-	-	-	-	-	-	-	1	-	-
JL Baker	-	-	-	-	-	-	-	-	-	-	-	-	-	-	-	-	>F	-	F	-	-	-	<F	-	-	-	-	-	-	-	-	-	-	-	-	-	3	-	-
J (Jacky) Braithwaite E+	SH	SH	SH	SH	SH	SH	SH	SH	-	SH	SH	SH	-	SH	SH	SH	SH	SH	SH	SH	SH	SH	SH	SH	SH	SH	SH	SH	SH	SH	SH	SH	FH	SH	SH	SH	34	7	31
AC (Alf) Butlin	W	FB	W	W	W	-	F	W	W	W	W	-	F	F	F	F	F	F	FB	FB	W	FB	FB	FB	FB	FB	FB	FB	FB	FB	FB	FB	FB	FB	-	FB	33	2	12
RN (Bob) Campbell	F	F	F	F	F	-	F	F	-	F	F	F	F	F	F	-	F	F	F	F	F	F	F	F	F	F	F	-	F	F	F	F	F*	-	-	-	29	1	3
Rev. A (Albert) Carey-Elwes	-	-	-	-	-	-	-	-	<F	-	-	-	-	-	-	-	-	-	-	-	-	-	-	-	-	-	-	-	-	-	-	-	-	-	-	-	1	-	-
WJ (Billy) Foreman	FH*	FH*	FH*	FH*	FH*	FH*	FH*	FH*	-	-	FH*	FH*	FH*	FH*	FH*	FH*	FH*	FH*	FH*	FH*	FH*	FH*	FH*	FH*	FH*	FH*	FH*	FH*	FH*	FH*	FH*	FH*	-	FH*	FH*	FH*	33	8	24
AH (Arthur) Frith	-	-	-	-	-	-	-	-	-	-	-	<C	-	-	-	-	-	-	-	-	-	-	-	-	-	-	-	-	-	-	-	-	-	-	-	-	1	-	-
W (William) Gale	FB	C	C	C	-	-	-	-	C	-	-	C	-	-	-	-	-	C	-	-	-	-	-	-	-	-	-	-	-	-	-	-	C	-	-	-	8	1	11
JW (Josh) Garner	F	F	F	F	F	F	F	F	-	F	F	F	-	-	-	-	-	-	-	-	-	-	-	-	-	F	F	F	F	F	F	F	F	F	F	F	22	-	-
D (David) Gilbert	F	F	-	-	-	-	-	-	F	<F	-	-	-	-	-	-	-	-	-	-	-	-	-	-	-	-	-	-	-	-	-	-	-	-	-	-	4	-	-
E Goddard	-	-	-	-	-	-	-	-	-	-	-	-	-	-	-	-	-	-	-	-	-	-	-	-	-	-	W	W	W	-	-	-	-	-	-	-	3	2	6
TW (Tom) Goodrich	-	-	-	-	-	-	-	-	>F	-	-	-	-	-	-	F	F	-	F	-	-	F	F	F	F	F	F	F	-	-	-	-	-	-	-	-	11	1	3
AE (Alfred) Hind E+	-	-	-	-	-	>W	W	-	-	-	-	W	W	-	-	W	W	W	W	W	-	-	-	-	-	-	-	-	-	-	-	-	-	-	-	-	9	2	6
AE Hodder	-	-	-	-	-	-	-	-	=F	-	-	-	-	-	-	-	-	-	-	-	-	-	-	-	-	-	-	-	-	-	-	-	-	-	-	-	1	-	-
FA (Frank) Jackson	-	-	-	-	-	-	-	-	-	-	-	-	-	W	-	-	-	-	-	-	-	-	-	-	-	W	-	-	-	-	-	-	-	-	-	-	2	-	-
AO (Arthur) Jones	-	-	FB	FB	FB	FB	FB	FB	FB*	FB*	FB	FB	FB	FB	FB	FB	FB	FB	C	-	FB	-	C	C	C	C	C	C	C	W	W	W	-	-	-	-	28	1	43
Rev. FH (Frank) Jones	-	-	-	-	C	C	C	-	-	-	-	-	-	-	-	-	C	-	C	C	C	C	C	-	-	-	-	-	-	C	C	C	-	-	-	-	12	4	22
GH (George) Keeton E+	-	-	-	-	-	-	F	-	-	-	-	-	-	-	-	-	-	-	-	-	-	-	-	-	-	-	-	-	-	-	-	-	-	-	-	-	1	-	-
C (Charles) Kinton	<F	-	-	-	-	-	-	-	-	-	-	-	-	-	-	-	-	-	-	-	-	-	-	-	-	-	-	-	-	-	-	-	-	-	-	-	1	1	3
JF (John) Lee	-	-	-	-	-	-	-	-	=F	-	-	-	-	-	-	-	-	-	-	-	-	-	-	-	-	-	-	-	-	-	-	-	-	-	-	-	1	1	3
WF (William) Lincoln	-	F	F	F	-	F	F	F	F	-	F	F	F	F	F	F	F	F	-	F	F	F	F	F	F	-	F	F	F	F	F	F	W	F	FB	<F	31	6	18
S (Sammy) Matthews	F	F	F	F	F	F	F	F	-	F	F	F	F	F	F	F	-	F	F	F	F	F	-	F	F	F	-	F	F	F	F	F	F	F	F	F	32	-	-
JH (Jack) Miles E+	-	>W	-	-	-	-	-	-	W	-	-	-	-	-	W	-	-	-	-	-	-	W	W	W	W	-	C	-	-	-	-	-	-	-	-	-	8	9	27
EP (Ervine) Mosby	-	C	C	C	-	-	-	C	C	C	C	-	C	C	C	C	-	-	-	C	C	C	-	C	-	-	-	-	-	-	-	-	-	C	C	C	18	1	36
SCT (Sydney) Neumann	-	-	-	-	-	-	-	-	-	-	-	-	-	-	-	-	-	-	-	-	-	-	-	-	-	-	-	-	-	-	-	-	-	>W	W	W	3	-	-
HSJ (Herbert) Nicol	-	-	-	-	-	-	-	-	-	-	-	-	-	-	-	-	-	-	-	-	-	-	-	-	-	-	-	-	-	-	-	-	-	-	=C	-	1	-	-
PW (Percy) Oscroft	C	-	-	-	C	C	C	C	-	C	C	-	C	C	C	C	C	C	-	-	-	-	-	-	C	C	-	C	C	C	C	C	-	-	-	C	21	10	56
SH (Sid) Penny E+	F	F	F	F	F	-	-	F	F	F	F	-	F	-	F	F	F	F	F	F	F	F	F	F	F	F	F	F	F	F	F	F	F	-	-	-	29	2	6
S Ramsey	-	-	-	-	-	-	-	-	-	-	-	-	-	-	-	-	<F	-	-	-	-	-	-	-	-	-	-	-	-	-	-	-	-	-	-	-	1	-	-
Lt. MS Scott	-	-	-	-	F	F	F	F	-	F	F	F	F	F	-	F	-	F	F	F	F	F	F	F	F	F	F	F	F	F	F	F	F	F	F	F	29	1	11
H Straker	-	-	-	-	-	-	-	-	-	-	-	-	-	-	-	-	-	-	-	-	-	-	-	-	-	-	-	-	-	-	-	-	>F	F	F	<F	4	-	-
M (Martinus) Swain	-	-	-	-	-	-	-	-	FH	-	-	-	-	-	-	-	-	-	-	-	-	-	-	-	-	-	-	-	-	-	-	-	-	-	-	-	1	2	6
WE Thompson	-	-	F	F	F	F	-	-	-	-	-	-	-	-	-	-	-	-	-	-	-	-	-	-	-	-	-	-	-	-	-	-	-	-	-	-	4	-	-
C (Charles) Timlock	F	-	-	-	-	-	-	-	F	-	-	-	-	-	-	-	-	-	-	-	-	-	-	-	-	-	-	-	-	-	-	-	-	-	-	-	2	-	-
WJ (William) Voakes	-	-	-	-	-	-	-	-	SH	FH	-	-	SH	-	-	-	-	-	-	-	-	-	-	-	-	-	-	-	-	-	-	-	SH	C	-	-	5	2	6
AO (Dickie) Watson	-	-	-	-	-	-	-	-	-	-	-	-	-	-	-	-	-	-	-	-	-	-	-	-	-	-	-	-	-	-	-	-	-	>F	F	<F	3	-	-
ED (David) Whetstone	-	-	-	-	-	-	-	-	-	-	-	-	-	-	-	-	-	-	-	-	-	F	F	-	-	-	F	F	F	F	F	F	F	F	F	F	12	1	3
ME (Monty) Whitehead	-	-	-	-	F	F	-	F	-	-	F	F	■F	F	F	F	-	F	-	F	F	-	F	F	F	F	F	F	F	F	F	F	F	-	-	-	23	2	6
H (Harry) Wilkinson	W	W	W	W	W	W	W	W	-	W	W	W	W	W	W	W	W	W	W	W	W	W	W	W	W	W	W	W	W	W	W	W	W	W	W	W	35	28	90

The key for how to read the stats is on the last page

19 00/01

Home Ground: Welford Road	Trophy Cabinet: Midland Counties Cup(4)	OVERALL RECORD:					T	C	PG	DG	MK	PTS
Captain: Billy Foreman		PLD	W	D	L	Tigers scored:	96	38	5	13	0	431
Vice-captain: Josh Garner		37	24	2	11	Opponents scored:	37	10	1	3	1	150

GM	DATE		VEN	OPPONENTS	RESULT	TRIES	KICKS	ATT
MIDLAND COUNTIES CUP						**CUP WINNERS: LEICESTER TIGERS**		
30	Mar	**9**	**H**	**Burton (2)**	W 21-0	H.Wilkinson(4), Neumann	A.Jones 3c	2000
31		**16**	**H**	**Stoneygate (3)**	W 41-0	H.Wilkinson(4), Neumann(2), Aldred, Atkins, Braithwaite, Whetstone, Yeld	A.Jones 2c/d	2000
32		**23**	**H**	**Nuneaton (sf)**	W 30-9	Braithwaite(2), A.Jones, Atkins, H.Wilkinson	A.Jones 2c/p/d, Butlin d	4000
33		30		Moseley (f)	W 8-3 (aet)	Foreman, H.Wilkinson	A.Jones c	-
CLUB MATCHES								
1	Sep	**1**	**H**	**Nuneaton**	W 20-0	Neumann(2), Foreman, H.Wilkinson	Campbell d, Gale 2c	4000
2		**8**	**H**	**Portsmouth**	W 16-3	H.Wilkinson(2), Atkins, Hind	Gale 2c	-
3		**15**	**H**	**Handsworth**	W 61-0	Hind(4), Foreman(3), Atkins(2), Braithwaite(2), H.Wilkinson, T.Goodrich, Mee, Neumann	H.Wilkinson c, Garner 4c, Butlin c/d	3000
4		**22**	**H**	**Plymouth**	W 5-0	H.Wilkinson	Garner c	10500
5		**29**	**H**	**Exeter**	W 23-0	H.Wilkinson(4), Braithwaite, Foreman, Neumann	F.Jones c	-
6	Oct	**6**	**H**	**Devonport Albion**	L 0-6	-	-	8000
7		**13**	**H**	**Northampton**	D 0-0	-	-	10000
8		**20**	**H**	**Llanelly**	W 4-3	-	Butlin d	10000
9		**27**	**H**	**Old Edwardians**	W 10-0	Foreman, Whetstone	Mosby 2c	4000
10	Nov	3	a	Cardiff	L 0-8	-	-	10000
11		5m	a	Llanelly	W 12-6	Mosby, T.Goodrich	Mosby c, A.Jones d	-
12		**10**	**H**	**Manchester**	W 18-3	Braithwaite, Garner, Jackson, H.Wilkinson	A.Jones d, Mosby c	4000
13		17	a	Swansea	L 4-16	-	Mosby d	-
14		24	a	Coventry	L 8-10	Goddard, Matthews	Mosby c	-
15	Dec	**1**	**H**	**Cambridge University**	W 8-0	Foreman(2)	Mosby c	-
16		8	a	Northampton	W 4-0	-	Braithwaite d	12000
17		**15**	**H**	**Burton**	W 20-8	H.Wilkinson(3), Neumann	Braithwaite d, Mosby 2c	-
18		22	a	Newport	L 0-11	-	-	4000
19		**24m**	**H**	**Lennox**	W 7-0	Foreman	Braithwaite d	-
20		**26w**	**H**	**Llwynypia**	W 22-0	Atkins, Braithwaite, Foreman, Matthews, Whetstone, H.Wilkinson	Oscroft 2c	7000
21		**27th**	**H**	**Edinburgh Royal High School**	W 9-3	Hind(2)	Butlin p	-
22		29	a	Devonport Albion	L 0-8	-	-	7000
23		31m	a	Exeter	W 21-0	Campbell, Hind, Peard	A.Jones 3c/2p	-
24	Jan	**5**	**H**	**Cheltenham**	W 23-11	A.Jones(2), Hind(2), H.Wilkinson	A.Jones 4c	3000
		12	a	Richmond	PP (fog)			
25		**19**	**H**	**Gloucester**	L 0-5	-	-	3000
26	Feb	**9**	**H**	**Cardiff**	W 4-3	-	H.Wilkinson d	-
27		**16**	**H**	**Coventry**	W 12-0	H.Wilkinson(2), Mosby, E.Wilkinson	-	10000
		20w	a	Bedford School	PP			
28		**23**	**H**	**Swansea**	D 0-0	-	-	12000
29	Mar	2	a	Burton	W 11-0	Foreman(2), H.Wilkinson	A.Jones c	-
34	Apr	6	a	Gloucester	L 0-6	-	-	-
35		8m	a	Bristol	L 3-10	Atkins	-	-
36		9tu	a	Plymouth	L 3-11	A.Jones	-	5000
37		**13**	**H**	**Newport**	L 3-7	-	Oscroft p	-

Neutral Venue: *#33 at Cricket Club - Rugby*

INDIVIDUAL APPEARANCES 1900/01

Name / Game #	1	2	3	4	5	6	7	8	9	10	11	12	13	14	15	16	17	18	19	20	21	22	23	24	25	26	27	28	29	30	31	32	33	34	35	36	37	Apps	T	Pts
M (Maxwell) Aldred	F	F	F	F	-	F	F	F	-	F	F	-	F	F	F	F	F	-	-	-	-	F	F	F	F	F	F	F	-	F	F	F	F	F	F	F	F	29	1	3
HP (Percy) Atkins	F	F	F	-	F	C	F	F	F	-	-	-	-	-	-	-	-	C	-	F	F	-	-	F	F	F	F	F	F	C	C	F	-	-	C	C	F	23	7	21
J (John) Barnes	-	-	-	-	-	-	-	-	-	-	-	-	-	-	-	-	-	-	-	-	-	-	-	-	-	-	-	-	-	-	-	-	-	=W	-	-	-	1	-	-
J (Jacky) Braithwaite E+	SH	SH	SH	SH	SH	SH	SH	SH	-	SH	SH	SH	SH	SH	SH	SH	SH	SH	SH	SH	SH	SH	SH	SH	SH	SH	SH	SH	SH	SH	SH	SH	SH	SH	SH	SH	SH	36	8	36
AC (Alf) Butlin	FB	FB	FB	FB	FB	FB	FB	FB	FB	FB	FB	FB	FB	FB	FB	FB	FB	FB	FB	FB	FB	FB	FB	FB	FB	FB	FB	FB	FB	FB	FB	FB	FB	FB	FB	FB	FB	37	-	17
RN (Bob) Campbell	F	F	F	F	F	-	F	F	F	F	F	F	F	F	F	F	F	-	F	-	F	F	F	F	-	F	F	F	F	F	F	F	F	-	-	-	-	29	1	7
WI (Isaiah) Dann	-	-	-	-	-	-	-	-	-	-	-	-	-	-	-	-	-	-	>F	-	-	-	-	-	-	-	-	-	-	-	-	-	-	-	-	-	-	1	-	-
WJ (Billy) Foreman	FH*	FH*	FH*	FH*	FH*	FH*	FH*	FH*	FH*	FH*	FH*	-	FH*	FH*	FH*	FH*	-	FH*	FH*	FH*	FH*	FH*	FH*	FH*	FH*	FH*	FH*	FH*	FH*	FH*	FH*	FH*	FH*	FH*	FH*	FH*	FH*	35	13	39
W (William) Gale	C	C	-	-	-	-	-	-	-	-	-	-	-	-	-	-	-	-	-	-	-	-	-	-	-	-	-	-	-	-	-	-	-	-	-	-	-	2	-	8
JW (Josh) Garner	F	F	F	F	F	F	F	F	F	F	F	F*	F	F	F	F	F*	F	F	F	F	F	F	F	F	F	F	F	F	F	F	F	F	F	F	F	F	37	1	13
E Goddard	-	-	-	-	-	-	-	-	-	-	-	-	W	W	-	-	-	W	-	-	C	-	-	-	<W	-	-	-	-	-	-	-	-	-	-	-	-	5	1	3
A (Alf) Goodrich	-	-	-	-	-	-	-	-	-	-	-	>F	-	-	-	-	-	F	F	-	-	-	-	-	-	-	-	-	-	-	-	-	-	-	-	-	-	3	-	-
TW (Tom) Goodrich	F	F	F	F	F	F	-	F	F	F	W	F	F	F	F	F	F	F	-	F	-	F	F	F	F	F	F	F	F	F	F	F	F	F	F	F	F	34	2	6
G Green	-	-	-	-	-	-	-	-	-	-	-	-	-	-	-	-	-	-	-	-	-	-	-	-	-	-	-	-	-	-	=F	-	-	-	-	-	-	1	-	-
B (Bertie) Hills	-	-	-	-	-	-	-	-	-	-	-	-	-	-	-	-	-	-	-	-	-	-	-	-	-	-	-	-	-	-	-	-	-	-	-	W	-	1	-	-
AE (Alfred) Hind E+	-	W	W	W	W	W	W	-	-	-	-	-	-	-	-	-	-	-	W	W	W	W	W	W	-	-	-	-	-	-	-	-	W	-	-	-	W	14	10	30
FA (Frank) Jackson	-	-	-	-	-	-	-	-	W	W	-	W	-	-	-	-	W	-	-	-	-	-	-	-	-	-	-	-	-	-	-	-	-	-	-	-	-	4	1	3
AO (Arthur) Jones	-	-	-	-	-	-	-	-	-	C	C	C	C	C	C	C	-	-	-	-	-	-	C	C	-	C	C	C	C	C	C	C	C	-	-	C	-	18	4	69
Rev. FH (Frank) Jones	-	-	-	-	C	C	C	-	-	-	-	-	-	-	-	-	-	-	-	C	C	-	-	-	-	-	-	-	-	-	-	-	-	-	-	-	-	5	-	2
S (Samuel) Lines	-	-	-	-	-	-	-	-	-	-	>F	F	-	-	F	-	-	F	F	F	F	-	F	-	F	-	-	-	-	-	-	-	-	-	-	F	-	10	-	-
Maj. B (Bernard) McCraith	-	-	-	-	-	-	-	-	-	-	-	-	-	-	-	-	-	>F	F	-	F	F	F	F	-	-	-	-	-	-	-	-	-	F	F	F	-	9	-	-
S (Sammy) Matthews	F	F	F	F	F	F	F	F	F	F	F	F	F	F	F	F	F	F	F	F	F	F	F	-	F	F	F	-	F	F	-	-	F	-	-	-	F	30	2	6
GC (Garnet) Mee	-	-	>C	-	-	-	-	-	-	-	-	-	-	-	-	-	-	-	-	-	-	-	-	-	-	-	-	-	-	-	-	-	-	-	-	-	-	1	1	3
JH (Jack) Miles E+	W	-	-	-	-	-	-	-	-	-	-	-	-	-	-	-	-	-	-	-	-	-	-	-	-	-	-	-	-	-	-	-	-	-	-	-	-	1	-	-
EP (Ervine) Mosby	-	-	-	C	-	-	-	C	C	C	C	C	C	C	C	C	C	C	-	-	-	C	-	-	C	C	C	C	-	-	-	<C	-	-	-	-	-	18	2	26
SCT (Sydney) Neumann	C	C	C	C	C	-	C	C	C	-	-	-	-	-	W	W	C	-	-	-	W	C	-	C	C	-	-	-	W	W	W	W	-	C	W	-	C	22	8	24
PW (Percy) Oscroft	-	-	-	-	-	-	-	-	-	-	-	-	-	-	-	-	-	-	C	C	-	-	-	-	-	-	-	-	-	-	-	-	C	-	-	-	<C	4	-	7
EJ (Ernest) Peard	-	-	-	-	-	-	-	-	-	-	-	-	-	-	-	-	-	-	-	-	-	-	=C	-	-	-	-	-	-	-	-	-	-	-	-	-	-	1	1	3
SH (Sid) Penny E+	F	F	F	F	F	F	F	F	F	F	F	F	F	F	F	F	F	F	F	F	F	F	-	F	F	F	F	F	F	F	F	F	F	F	F	F	F	36	-	-
H (Howard) Poole	-	-	-	-	-	-	-	-	-	-	=F	-	-	-	-	-	-	-	-	-	-	-	-	-	-	-	-	-	-	-	-	-	-	-	-	-	-	1	-	-
Powell-John	-	-	-	-	-	-	-	-	-	-	-	-	-	-	-	-	-	-	-	-	-	-	=W	-	-	-	-	-	-	-	-	-	-	-	-	-	-	1	-	-
E (Eddie) Redman	-	-	-	-	-	-	-	-	-	-	<F	-	-	-	-	-	-	-	-	-	-	-	-	-	-	-	-	-	-	-	-	-	-	-	-	-	-	1	-	-
WE Thompson	-	-	-	-	-	<F	-	-	-	-	-	-	-	-	-	-	-	-	-	-	-	-	-	-	-	-	-	-	-	-	-	-	-	-	-	-	-	1	-	-
CR (Charles) Watchorn	-	-	-	-	-	-	-	-	-	-	-	-	-	-	-	-	-	-	-	-	-	-	-	-	-	-	-	-	-	-	-	-	-	>F	F	-	-	2	-	-
ED (David) Whetstone	F	F	F	F	F	F	F	-	F	F	-	-	F	F	F	F	F	F	-	F	F	F	F	F	-	F	F	F	F	F	F	F	F	F	-	F	-	30	3	9
ME (Monty) Whitehead	-	-	-	-	-	-	-	-	-	-	-	-	-	-	-	-	-	-	-	-	-	-	-	-	-	-	-	F	-	-	-	-	-	F	F	-	F	4	-	-
E (Edwin) Wilkinson	-	-	-	-	-	-	-	-	>W	-	-	-	-	-	-	-	-	-	C	-	-	-	-	-	-	W	W	W	C	-	-	-	-	-	C	W	-	8	1	3
H (Harry) Wilkinson	W	W	W	W	W	W	W	W	-	W	W	W	W	W	W	W	W	W	W	W	-	W	-	W	W	W	W	W	W	W	W	W	W	C	W	-	W	33	28	90
EC (Ernest) Wykes	-	-	-	-	-	-	-	W	SH	-	-	FH	-	-	-	-	FH	-	-	-	-	-	-	-	-	-	-	-	-	-	-	-	-	-	-	-	-	4	-	-
GG (George) Yeld	-	-	-	>F	F	F	F	F	F	F	-	F	F	F	-	F	F	-	-	-	-	-	-	-	F	-	-	-	F	F	F	F	F	W	F	F	F	22	1	3

1901/02												
Home Ground: Welford Road	Trophy Cabinet: Midland Counties Cup(5)	OVERALL RECORD:					T	C	PG	DG	MK	PTS
Captain: Josh Garner		PLD	W	D	L	Tigers scored:	79	23	3	10	0	332
Vice-captain: Alfred Hind		35	21	3	11	Opponents scored:	35	13	4	2	0	151

GM	DATE		VEN	OPPONENTS	RESULT	TRIES	KICKS	ATT
MIDLAND COUNTIES CUP						**CUP WINNERS: LEICESTER TIGERS**		
26	Mar	8	a	Nuneaton (2)	W 14-0	Miles(2)	Butlin 2c, H.Wilkinson d	5000
27		**15**	**H**	**Camp Hill Old Edwardians (3)**	W 25-0	P.Atkins(2), Braithwaite, Crowson, Foreman, A.Hind, Miles	Butlin c, Hawley c	4000
28		**22**	**H**	**Burton (sf)**	W 18-3	Miles(2), Braithwaite, P.Atkins	Braithwaite d, Butlin c	-
29		29		Moseley (f)	W 5-0	A.Hind	Butlin c	8000

GM	DATE		VEN	OPPONENTS	RESULT	TRIES	KICKS	ATT
CLUB MATCHES								
1	Sep	**7**	**H**	**Nuneaton**	W 27-3	Miles(3), P.Atkins, Braithwaite, Matthews, Whetstone	Garner 3c	3000
2		**14**	**H**	**Castleford**	W 10-3	Miles(2)	Braithwaite d	4000
3		**21**	**H**	**Bristol**	L 3-6	Miles	-	5000
4		**28**	**H**	**Devonport Albion**	L 3-13	-	Braithwaite p	10000
5	Oct	**5**	**H**	**Exeter**	W 13-0	Foreman, Penny, H.Wilkinson	Braithwaite d	-
6		**12**	**H**	**Coventry**	W 21-0	Braithwaite, Dakin, Watchorn, E.Wilkinson, H.Wilkinson	Yeld 3c	6000
7		**19**	**H**	**Llanelly**	W 7-3	H.Wilkinson	Braithwaite d	-
8		**26**	**H**	**Plymouth**	D 3-3	A.Hind	-	12000
9	Nov	**2**	**H**	**Burton**	W 23-0	Foxon(2), Goodrich, Matthews, Neumann	Braithwaite d, Yeld 2c	-
10		**9**	**H**	**Old Edwardians**	W 30-5	A.Hind(2), Braithwaite, Gale, Miles, Penny, Watchorn, H.Wilkinson	Braithwaite d, Gale c	4000
		16	**H**	**Swansea**	PP (frost)			
11		23	a	Northampton	W 11-6	A.Hind(2), H.Wilkinson	Yeld c	10000
12		30	a	Cambridge University	L 3-21	-	Yeld p	-
13	Dec	**7**	**H**	**Rugby**	W 24-3	Hills(2), Miles(2), Dakin, Mee	Yeld 3c	4000
		14	a	Old Edwardians	PP (snow)			
		21	**H**	**Newport**	PP (frost)			
14		**26th**	**H**	**Llwynypia**	W 8-0	Dakin, A.Hind	Gale c	7000
15		**27f**	**H**	**West Hartlepool**	L 0-12	-	-	-
16		**28**	**H**	**Old Merchant Taylors**	L 0-3	-	-	2000
17	Jan	4	a	Swansea	L 0-11	-	-	3000
18		6m	a	Llanelly	D 0-0	-	-	-
		11	a	Richmond	PP			
19		18	a	Devonport Albion	L 0-13	-	-	7000
20		20m	a	Plymouth	L 3-5	Smith	-	-
21		21tu	a	Exeter	D 0-0	-	-	-
22		25	a	Gloucester	W 3-0	-	Yeld p	-
23	Feb	**1**	**H**	**Percy Park**	W 14-5	A.Hind, Garner	A.Hind d, Braithwaite d	-
		15	a	Coventry	PP			
24		**22**	**H**	**Northampton**	W 14-0	Miles(2), P.Atkins, H.Wilkinson	Butlin c	8000
25	Mar	**1**	**H**	**Gloucester**	W 6-0	Braithwaite, Miles	-	8000
30		31m	a	Cardiff	L 3-8	Miles	-	15000
31	Apr	1tu	a	Bristol	L 0-8	-	-	-
32		5	a	Newport	L 9-11	Keeton(2), Hawley	-	3000
33		**12**	**H**	**Cardiff**	W 4-3	-	H.Wilkinson d	9000
34		**17th**	**H**	**Midlands XV**	W 14-3	Miles(2), P.Atkins, H.Wilkinson	Braithwaite c	-
35		19	a	Nuneaton	W 14-0	Matthews(2), Garner, Robinson	Butlin c	400

Neutral Venue: *#29 at the Butts - Coventry*

INDIVIDUAL APPEARANCES 1901/02

Name / Game #	1	2	3	4	5	6	7	8	9	10	11	12
A Andrews	-	-	-	-	-	-	-	-	-	-	-	-
WR (Willie) Arnold W+	-	-	-	-	-	-	-	-	-	-	-	-
DB (Dudley) Atkins	>F	F	F	-	F	F	F	F	F	F	F	F
HP (Percy) Atkins	C	F	-	-	-	-	F	W	-	-	F	F
AG (Artie) Bowman	-	>C	-	-	-	-	-	FB	-	-	-	-
J (Jacky) Braithwaite E+	FH	FH	FH	SH	SH	SH	SH	SH	FH	FH	SH	SH
G (George) Brownless	-	-	-	-	-	-	-	-	>SH	<SH	-	-
AC (Alf) Butlin	FB	FB	FB	FB	FB	FB	FB	-	FB	FB	FB	FB
RN (Bob) Campbell	F	-	<F	-	-	-	-	-	-	-	-	-
G (George) Crowson	-	-	-	-	-	-	-	-	-	-	-	-
WR (Reid) Dakin	-	-	-	>W	-	C	-	C	C	C	C	C
WJ (Billy) Foreman	-	-	-	-	FH	FH	FH	FH	-	-	FH	FH
AH (Arthur) Foxon	-	-	-	-	-	-	-	-	>F	-	-	-
W (William) Gale	-	-	C	-	-	-	-	-	-	F	-	-
JW (Josh) Garner	F*	F*	-	F*	F*	F*	F*	F*	F*	F*	F*	F*
TW (Tom) Goodrich	F	-	-	F	F	F	F	F	F	F	F	F
WE (William) Hawley	-	-	-	-	-	-	-	-	-	-	-	-
B (Bertie) Hills	-	-	-	-	-	-	-	-	-	-	-	-
AE (Alfred) Hind E+	-	-	-	-	-	-	W	C	W	W	W	W
HA (Harold) Hind	-	-	-	-	-	-	-	-	-	-	-	-
A (Alewyn) Jones	-	-	-	-	-	-	-	-	-	-	-	-
GH (George) Keeton E+	-	-	-	-	-	-	-	-	-	-	-	-
HE (Tim) Kingston	-	-	-	-	-	-	-	-	-	-	-	-
S (Samuel) Lines	F	-	-	F	F	F	-	F	-	-	-	-
S (Sammy) Matthews	F	F	F	F	F	F	F	F	F	F	F	F
EW (Bill) Merry	-	-	-	-	-	-	-	-	-	-	-	-
JH (Jack) Miles E+	W	W	C	C	C	-	C	-	-	C	C	C
SCT (Sydney) Neumann	-	-	-	-	W	W	C	-	<C	-	-	-
CA Page	W	-	W	-	-	-	-	-	-	-	-	-
SH (Sid) Penny E+	F	F	F	F	F	F	F	F	F	F	F	F
W Robinson	-	-	-	-	-	-	-	-	>F	-	-	-
H Smalley	-	>SH	SH	-	-	-	-	-	-	-	-	-
Cpt. JWD (Dixie) Smith	-	-	-	-	-	-	-	-	-	-	-	-
WJ (William) Voakes	-	-	-	-	-	-	-	-	-	-	-	-
CR (Charles) Watchorn	-	F	F	F	F	F	F	F	-	F	F	-
ED (David) Whetstone	F	F	<F	-	-	-	-	-	-	-	-	-
E (Edwin) Wilkinson	-	W	-	-	-	C	-	-	-	-	-	-
H (Harry) Wilkinson	C	C	W	W	W	W	W	W	W	W	W	W
A Woodward	-	-	-	-	-	-	-	-	-	-	-	-
GG (George) Yeld	-	-	F	F	F	F	F	F	F	F	F	F

Name / Game #	13	14	15	16	17	18	19	20	21	22	23	24
A Andrews	-	-	-	-	-	-	-	-	-	-	>F	-
WR (Willie) Arnold W+	-	-	-	-	-	-	-	>C	<C	-	-	-
DB (Dudley) Atkins	-	F	-	F	F	F	-	-	-	F	F	F
HP (Percy) Atkins	F	F	-	-	-	-	-	-	-	F	-	F
AG (Artie) Bowman	FB	-	-	-	-	-	W	-	-	-	-	-
J (Jacky) Braithwaite E+	SH	SH	SH	SH	SH	SH	FH	SH	SH	FH	SH	SH
G (George) Brownless	-	-	-	-	-	-	-	-	-	-	-	-
AC (Alf) Butlin	-	FB	FB	FB	FB	FB	FB	FB	FB	FB	FB	FB
RN (Bob) Campbell	-	-	-	-	-	-	-	-	-	-	-	-
G (George) Crowson	-	-	>F	-	-	-	F	F	-	-	-	-
WR (Reid) Dakin	C	C	C	-	-	C	-	-	-	-	-	C
WJ (Billy) Foreman	-	FH	-	-	-	-	-	-	-	-	FH	FH
AH (Arthur) Foxon	F	-	-	-	-	-	-	-	-	-	-	-
W (William) Gale	F	F	-	-	-	-	C	F	-	-	-	-
JW (Josh) Garner	F*	F*	F*	F*	F*	F*	F*	F*	F*	F*	F*	F*
TW (Tom) Goodrich	F	-	F	F	F	-	F	F	F	F	-	F
WE (William) Hawley	-	>C	C	C	C	C	C	W	W	C	-	-
B (Bertie) Hills	FH	-	FH	FH	-	-	-	-	-	SH	-	-
AE (Alfred) Hind E+	-	W	W	W	W	W	-	-	-	W	W	W
HA (Harold) Hind	-	>F	F	-	F	F	-	-	-	F	F	-
A (Alewyn) Jones	-	-	-	-	-	-	-	>C	C	-	C	-
GH (George) Keeton E+	-	F	-	F	F	F	-	-	-	-	-	-
HE (Tim) Kingston	-	-	-	-	>FH	<FH	-	-	-	-	-	-
S (Samuel) Lines	-	-	-	-	-	-	F	-	F	-	-	-
S (Sammy) Matthews	F	F	F	F	F	F	F	F	F	F	F	F
EW (Bill) Merry	-	-	-	-	-	-	>F	F	<F	-	-	-
JH (Jack) Miles E+	C	-	W	C	W	W	-	-	-	W	W	W
SCT (Sydney) Neumann	-	-	-	-	-	-	-	-	-	-	-	-
CA Page	-	-	-	-	-	-	-	-	-	-	-	-
SH (Sid) Penny E+	F	F	F	F	F	F	F	F	F	F	F	F
W Robinson	-	-	F	F	-	F	F	-	F	-	-	F
H Smalley	-	-	-	-	-	-	-	-	-	-	-	-
Cpt. JWD (Dixie) Smith	-	-	-	-	-	-	-	>W	W	-	-	-
WJ (William) Voakes	-	-	-	-	-	-	SH	FH	-	-	-	-
CR (Charles) Watchorn	-	-	-	-	-	-	-	-	-	-	F	-
ED (David) Whetstone	-	-	-	-	-	-	-	-	-	-	-	-
E (Edwin) Wilkinson	-	-	-	-	-	-	-	-	-	-	-	-
H (Harry) Wilkinson	W	W	-	W	C	-	-	-	-	C	C	C
A Woodward	-	-	-	-	-	-	>W	F	<F	-	-	-
GG (George) Yeld	F	-	F	F	F	F	-	-	-	F	F	-

Name / Game #	25	26	27	28	29	30	31	32	33	34	35	Apps	T	Pts
A Andrews	F	-	F	F	-	-	F	F	-	F	F	8	-	-
WR (Willie) Arnold W+	-	-	-	-	-	-	-	-	-	-	-	2	-	-
DB (Dudley) Atkins	F	F	F	F	F	F	F	F	F	F	F	29	-	-
HP (Percy) Atkins	F	F	F	W	F	F	F	-	F	F	-	19	6	18
AG (Artie) Bowman	-	-	-	-	-	-	-	-	FB	-	-	5	-	-
J (Jacky) Braithwaite E+	SH	SH	SH	SH	SH	SH	SH	SH	SH	SH	SH	35	6	51
G (George) Brownless	-	-	-	-	-	-	-	-	-	-	-	2	-	-
AC (Alf) Butlin	FB	FB	FB	FB	FB	FB	FB	FB	-	FB	FB	32	-	14
RN (Bob) Campbell	-	-	-	-	-	-	-	-	-	-	-	2	-	-
G (George) Crowson	-	F	F	F	F	-	F	-	-	F	<F	10	1	3
WR (Reid) Dakin	C	-	-	-	-	-	-	-	-	C	C	15	3	9
WJ (Billy) Foreman	FH	FH	FH	FH	FH	FH	FH	FH	FH	FH	FH	20	2	6
AH (Arthur) Foxon	-	-	-	-	-	-	-	-	-	-	-	2	2	6
W (William) Gale	-	-	-	-	-	-	-	-	-	-	-	6	1	7
JW (Josh) Garner	F*	F*	F*	F*	F*	F*	F*	F*	F*	F*	F*	34	2	12
TW (Tom) Goodrich	F	F	F	F	F	F	F	F	F	F	F	30	1	3
WE (William) Hawley	-	C	C	C	C	C	-	C	<C	-	-	16	1	5
B (Bertie) Hills	-	-	-	-	-	-	-	-	-	-	-	4	2	6
AE (Alfred) Hind E+	W	W	W	-	W	W	W	-	W	W	-	22	9	31
HA (Harold) Hind	-	-	-	-	-	-	-	-	-	-	-	6	-	-
A (Alewyn) Jones	-	-	-	-	-	C	C	C	-	-	-	6	-	-
GH (George) Keeton E+	-	-	-	-	F	F	-	F	F	-	-	8	2	6
HE (Tim) Kingston	-	-	-	-	-	-	-	-	-	-	-	2	-	-
S (Samuel) Lines	F	-	-	-	-	-	-	-	-	-	-	8	-	-
S (Sammy) Matthews	-	F	F	F	F	F	F	F	F	-	F	33	4	12
EW (Bill) Merry	-	-	-	-	-	-	-	-	-	-	-	3	-	-
JH (Jack) Miles E+	W	W	W	W	W	W	W	-	W	W	-	26	20	60
SCT (Sydney) Neumann	-	-	-	-	-	-	-	-	-	-	-	4	1	3
CA Page	-	-	-	-	-	-	-	-	-	-	W	3	-	-
SH (Sid) Penny E+	F	F	F	F	F	F	F	F	F	F	F	35	2	6
W Robinson	F	-	-	F	-	F	-	F	F	F	F	14	1	3
H Smalley	-	-	-	-	-	-	-	-	-	-	-	2	-	-
Cpt. JWD (Dixie) Smith	-	-	-	-	-	-	-	-	-	-	-	2	1	3
WJ (William) Voakes	-	-	-	-	-	-	-	-	-	-	-	2	-	-
CR (Charles) Watchorn	-	-	-	-	-	-	-	-	-	-	-	10	2	6
ED (David) Whetstone	-	-	-	-	-	-	-	-	-	-	-	3	1	3
E (Edwin) Wilkinson	-	-	-	-	-	-	-	-	-	-	W	3	1	3
H (Harry) Wilkinson	C	C	C	C	C	-	C	W	C	C	C	29	7	29
A Woodward	-	-	-	-	-	-	-	-	-	-	-	3	-	-
GG (George) Yeld	-	F	-	-	-	-	-	-	-	-	-	18	-	24

1 GAME: G Ackroyd =C(5), M (Maxwell) Aldred <F(2), Chapman =W(32), W (William) Duffin =FH(21), G Gimson =F(24), FA (Frank) Jackson C(4), E (Edward) Lines =F(4), Maj. B (Bernard) McCraith <F(3), GC (Garnet) Mee <Wt(13), AC (Arthur) Oldershaw =SH(1), EJ (Katie) Walton E4 =FH(4), ME (Monty) Whitehead <F(12)

The key for how to read the stats is on the last page

19 02/03	Home Ground: Welford Road	Trophy Cabinet: Midland Counties Cup(6)	OVERALL RECORD:					T	C	PG	DG	MK	PTS
	Captain: Arthur Jones		PLD	W	D	L	Tigers scored:	117	42	4	10	0	487
	Vice-captain: Alfred Hind		36	26	1	9	Opponents scored:	43	10	2	4	0	171

GM	DATE		VEN	OPPONENTS	RESULT	TRIES	KICKS	ATT
MIDLAND COUNTIES CUP						**CUP WINNERS: LEICESTER TIGERS**		
29	Mar	**14**	**H**	**Stratford-upon-Avon (1)**	W 39-0	A.Hind(5), Braithwaite(2), P.Atkins(2), Miles	A.Hind c, Braithwaite c, Ar.Jones c/p	-
30		**21**	**H**	**Belgrave (2)**	W 54-0	A.Hind(6), Dakin(3), Braithwaite, Ar.Jones, P.Atkins	Braithwaite 4c, Ar.Jones 2c/d, Matthews c	4000
31		**28**	**H**	**Nuneaton (sf)**	W 49-11	A.Hind(5), Miles(4), Braithwaite, Dakin, Ar.Jones	Braithwaite 5c/p	-
32	Apr	4		Rugby (f)	W 18-0	A.Hind(2), Dakin, Miles	Ar.Jones 3c	6000
CLUB MATCHES								
1	Sep	**13**	**H**	**Exeter**	W 21-0	A.Hind(2), D.Atkins, Dakin, Miles	Butlin d, Braithwaite c	-
2		**20**	**H**	**Bristol**	W 7-0	Braithwaite	Butlin d	6000
3		**27**	**H**	**Plymouth**	W 12-0	Miles(2), A.Hind, Matthews	-	11000
4	Oct	**4**	**H**	**Devonport Albion**	W 10-7	Ar.Jones	Ar.Jones p/d	10000
5		**11**	**H**	**Richmond**	W 18-3	A.Hind(2), Miles(2)	Matthews 3c	10000
6		**18**	**H**	**London Welsh**	W 13-0	A.Hind, Scott	Ar.Jones p/d	8000
7		**25**	**H**	**Llanelly**	W 15-3	Dakin, A.Hind, Miles	Reynolds d, Matthews c	11000
8	Nov	1	a	Newport	L 0-6	-	-	10000
9		3m	a	Llanelly	L 3-16	A.Hind	-	1500
10		8	a	Moseley	W 17-10	Miles(2), D.Atkins, Foreman, A.Hind	Ar.Jones c	-
11		**15**	**H**	**Northampton**	W 13-0	Barrowcliffe, A.Hind, Matthews	Ar.Jones 2c	7000
12		**22**	**H**	**Castleford**	W 19-0	A.Hind, Miles, Watchorn	Ar.Jones 3c/d	8000
13		**29**	**H**	**Cambridge University**	W 6-0	Matthews, Miles	-	7000
14	Dec	**6**	**H**	**Coventry**	W 11-0	Foxon, Miles, Page	T.Goodrich c	5000
15		13	a	Northampton	W 12-6	D.Atkins, Watchorn	Butlin d, Matthews c	7000
16		20	a	Cardiff	L 0-6	-	-	8000
17		**26f**	**H**	**Edinburgh Royal High School**	W 10-0	Braithwaite, Miles	Gale 2c	-
18		**27**	**H**	**Bective Rangers**	W 37-0	Braithwaite(2), Dakin(2), Foreman(2), Miles(2), A.Hind	Braithwaite c, Gale 4c	10000
19	Jan	3	a	Devonport Albion	L 3-9	Dakin	-	10500
20		5m	a	London Welsh	W 15-5	Braithwaite, Dakin, Page	A.Goodrich d, Gale c	-
21		**10**	**H**	**Gloucester**	W 6-3	A.Hind, Page	-	9000
		17	**H**	**Newport**	PP (frost)			
22		**24**	**H**	**Cardiff**	L 5-14	Matthews	Braithwaite c	8000
23		31	a	Swansea	L 5-24	Reynolds	Matthews c	5000
24	Feb	**7**	**H**	**Old Edwardians**	W 25-0	A.Hind(2), Foreman(2), D.Atkins, Braithwaite, Miles	A.Hind d	4000
25		**14**	**H**	**Moseley**	W 17-0	A.Hind(3), T.Goodrich, Miles	Matthews c	10000
26		21	a	Coventry	W 9-3	Miles(2), Ar.Jones	-	5000
27		**28**	**H**	**Swansea**	L 3-8	Dakin	-	15000
28	Mar	7	a	Gloucester	W 9-5	Braithwaite, Dakin, A.Hind	-	2000
33	Apr	11	a	Exeter	D 0-0	-	-	2000
34		13m	a	Plymouth	L 0-15	-	-	8000
35		14tu	a	Bristol	W 6-0	Miles, Rapsey	-	4000
36		**18**	**H**	**Newport**	L 0-17	-	-	10000

Neutral Venue: *#32 at the Butts - Coventry*

INDIVIDUAL APPEARANCES 1902/03

Name / Game #	1	2	3	4	5	6	7	8	9	10	11	12	13	14	15	16	17	18	19	20	21	22	23	24	25	26	27	28	29	30	31	32	33	34	35	36	Apps	T	Pts
AC (Arthur) Andrews	-	-	-	-	-	-	-	-	-	-	-	-	-	-	-	-	-	-	-	-	-	-	-	-	-	-	-	-	-	-	-	-	<FH	-	-	-	1	-	-
A Andrews	F	F	-	-	F	-	-	F	F	-	-	-	-	-	-	-	-	-	F	F	-	-	-	-	-	-	-	-	-	-	-	-	-	-	-	-	7	-	-
DB (Dudley) Atkins	F	F	F	F	F	F	F	F	F	F	F	-	F	F	F	F	F	F	F	F	-	F	F	F	F	F	F	F	F	F	F	F	F	F	-	F	33	4	12
HP (Percy) Atkins	F	F	F	F	F	F	F	F	-	-	-	-	-	-	-	-	-	-	-	-	-	-	-	F	F	F	F	F	F	F	F	F	F	-	F	-	19	3	9
FN Barker	-	-	-	-	-	-	-	-	-	-	-	-	-	-	-	-	=C	-	-	-	-	-	-	-	-	-	-	-	-	-	-	-	-	-	-	-	1	-	-
MH (Matt) Barrowcliffe	-	-	-	-	-	-	-	-	-	-	>C	-	-	-	-	-	-	-	-	-	-	-	-	-	-	-	-	-	-	-	-	-	-	-	-	-	1	1	3
L (Leonard) Bennett	-	-	-	-	-	-	-	-	-	-	-	-	-	-	-	-	-	-	-	-	-	-	-	-	-	-	-	-	-	-	-	-	-	>F	F	F	3	-	-
W (William) Blackburn	-	-	-	-	-	-	-	-	-	-	-	-	-	-	-	-	-	-	-	-	-	-	-	>FB	-	-	FB	FB	-	FB	FB	FB	FB	FB	FB	FB	10	-	-
AG (Artie) Bowman	-	-	-	-	-	-	FB	-	FB	FB	-	-	-	-	-	W	-	-	-	-	-	-	<FB	-	-	-	-	-	-	-	-	-	-	-	-	-	5	-	-
J (Jacky) Braithwaite E+	SH	SH	SH	SH	SH	-	-	SH	SH	SH	SH	SH	SH	SH	SH	SH	SH	SH	SH	SH	SH	SH	-	SH	SH	SH	SH	SH	SH	SH	SH	SH	SH	SH	SH	SH	33	11	62
AC (Alf) Butlin	FB	FB	FB	FB	FB	FB	-	-	-	-	-	FB	FB	-	<FB	-	-	-	-	-	-	-	-	-	-	-	-	-	-	-	-	-	-	-	-	-	9	-	12
WR (Reid) Dakin	C	-	C	C	C	SH	SH	C	-	-	-	-	-	C	C	C	C	C	C	C	C	C	C	C	C	C	C	C	C	W	C	C	C	C	C	C	30	13	39
WI (Isaiah) Dann	-	-	-	-	-	-	-	-	-	F	F	F	-	F	F	-	F	-	-	-	-	-	-	-	-	-	-	-	-	-	-	-	-	-	-	-	6	-	-
WJ (Billy) Foreman	FH	FH	FH	FH	FH	FH	FH	FH	FH	FH	FH	FH	FH	FH*	FH*	-	FH	FH	FH	FH	FH	FH	FH	FH	FH	FH	FH	FH	FH	FH	FH	FH	-	FH	FH	FH	34	5	15
AH (Arthur) Foxon	-	-	-	-	-	-	-	-	-	-	-	-	-	F	F	F	F	F	F	-	F	-	<F	-	-	-	-	-	-	-	-	-	-	-	-	-	8	1	3
AE (Arthur) Freear I3	-	-	-	-	-	-	-	-	-	-	-	-	-	-	-	-	-	-	-	-	-	-	-	-	-	-	-	-	-	-	-	-	-	-	>W	-	1	-	-
W (William) Gale	-	-	-	-	-	-	-	-	-	-	FB	-	-	FB	C	FB	FB	FB	FB	FB	FB	-	-	-	F	-	-	-	-	-	-	-	-	F	-	-	11	-	14
JW (Josh) Garner	-	-	F	<F	-	-	-	-	-	-	-	-	-	-	-	-	-	-	-	-	-	-	-	-	-	-	-	-	-	-	-	-	-	-	-	-	2	-	-
A (Alf) Goodrich	-	-	-	-	-	-	-	-	-	-	-	-	-	-	F	-	-	-	-	F	-	-	-	-	-	-	-	-	-	-	-	-	-	-	-	-	2	-	4
TW (Tom) Goodrich	F	F	F	F	F	F	F	F	F	F	F	F	F	F	F	F	-	-	F	F	F	F	F	F	F	F	F	F	F	F	F	F	F	F	F	F	34	1	5
AE (Alfred) Hind E+	W	W	W	W	W	W	W	W	W	W	W	W	W	-	-	-	W	W	W*	W*	W*	W*	W*	W*	W	W	W	W	W	W	W	W	-	-	-	W*	30	37	117
HA (Harold) Hind	F	F	F	F	F	F	F	F	F	F	F	F	F	F	-	F	F	F	F	F	F	F	-	F	F	F	F	F	F	F	F	F	F	F	F	F	34	-	-
A (Alewyn) Jones	-	-	-	-	-	-	-	-	-	-	-	-	-	-	-	<C	-	-	-	-	-	-	-	-	-	-	-	-	-	-	-	-	-	-	-	-	1	-	-
AO (Arthur) Jones	C*	C*	C*	C*	C*	C*	C*	C*	C*	C*	C*	C*	C*	-	-	-	-	-	-	-	-	-	-	-	C*	C*	C*	C*	C*	C*	C*	C*	-	-	-	-	21	4	61
Rev. FH (Frank) Jones	-	-	-	-	-	-	-	-	-	-	-	-	-	-	-	-	-	-	-	-	-	-	-	-	-	-	-	-	-	-	-	-	-	-	-	C	1	-	-
GH (George) Keeton E+	-	-	-	-	-	-	-	-	-	-	-	-	-	-	-	F	-	-	-	-	-	-	-	-	-	-	-	-	-	-	-	-	-	-	-	-	1	-	-
S (Samuel) Lines	-	-	-	-	-	F	-	-	F	-	-	-	-	-	-	-	-	-	-	-	-	-	-	-	-	-	-	-	-	-	-	-	-	-	-	-	2	-	-
S (Sammy) Matthews	F	F	F	F	F	F	F	F	F	F	F	F	F	F	F	F*	F*	F*	F	F	F	F	F	F	F	F	F	F	F	F	F	F	F*	F*	F*	F	36	4	28
JH (Jack) Miles E1	W	W	W	W	W	W	W	W	W	W	W	W	W	W	-	-	W	W	W	-	-	W	-	W	W	W	-	-	W	-	W	W	W	W	W	W	28	25	75
MC (Mark) Morrison S20 GB+	-	-	-	-	-	-	-	-	-	-	-	-	-	-	-	-	-	<F	-	-	-	-	-	-	-	-	-	-	-	-	-	-	-	-	-	-	1	-	-
CA Page	-	-	-	-	-	-	-	-	-	-	-	-	-	C	W	-	-	-	-	W	W	-	-	-	-	-	-	-	-	-	-	-	-	-	-	-	4	3	9
AJ (Arthur) Palfreyman	-	-	-	-	-	-	-	-	-	-	-	-	-	-	-	-	-	>C	C	C	C	C	-	-	-	-	-	-	-	-	-	-	C	C	-	-	7	-	-
AO (Alfred) Parsons	-	-	-	-	-	-	-	-	-	-	-	-	-	-	-	-	-	-	-	-	-	-	-	-	-	-	-	-	-	-	-	-	>W	W	-	-	2	-	-
SH (Sid) Penny E+	F	F	F	F	F	F	F	F	F	F	F	F	F	F	-	-	F	F	F	F	F	F	F	F	-	F	F	F	F	F	F	F	F	F	F	F	33	-	-
WG Rapsey	-	-	-	-	-	-	-	-	-	-	-	-	-	-	-	-	-	-	-	-	-	-	-	-	-	-	-	-	-	-	-	-	-	-	>C	-	1	1	3
HP (Harry) Reynolds	-	-	-	-	-	>C	C	FB	C	C	-	C	C	-	-	-	-	-	-	-	-	-	C	C	FB	FB	W	-	FB	-	-	-	-	-	-	-	13	1	7
W Robinson	F	F	-	-	-	-	F	F	F	-	-	F	F	F	F	F	F	F	F	F	F	F	F	F	F	F	F	F	F	F	F	F	F	F	F	F	30	-	-
Lt. MS Scott	-	-	F	F	F	F	F	-	-	F	F	-	F	-	-	-	-	-	-	-	F	F	F	F	-	-	F	-	-	-	-	-	-	-	-	-	13	1	3
WJ (William) Voakes	-	-	-	-	-	-	-	-	-	-	-	-	-	-	-	<FH	-	-	-	-	-	-	-	-	-	-	-	-	-	-	-	-	-	-	-	-	1	-	-
J Voss	-	-	-	-	-	-	-	-	-	-	-	-	-	-	-	>W	-	-	-	-	-	-	-	-	-	-	-	-	-	-	-	-	-	-	-	-	1	-	-
G (George) Ward	-	-	-	-	-	-	-	-	-	-	-	=F	-	-	-	-	-	-	-	-	-	-	-	-	-	-	-	-	-	-	-	-	-	-	-	-	1	-	-
CR (Charles) Watchorn	-		-	-	-	-	-	-	-	F	F	F	F	-	F	F	F	F	-	-	F	F	F	-	F	F	-	F	F	F	F	F	F	-	F	F	21	2	6
E (Edwin) Wilkinson	-	-	-	-	-	-	-	-	-	-	-	-	-	-	-	-	-	-	-	-	-	-	-	-	-	-	-	-	-	<C	-	-	-	-	-	-	1	-	-
H (Harry) Wilkinson	-	C	-	-	-	-	-	-	-	-	-	-	-	W	W	-	-	-	-	-	-	FB	W	-	-	-	-	-	-	-	-	-	-	-	-	-	5	-	-
EC (Ernest) Wykes	-	-	-	-	-	-	-	-	-	-	-	-	-	-	-	-	-	-	-	-	-	-	SH	-	-	-	-	W	-	-	-	-	-	-	-	-	2	-	-

The key for how to read the stats is on the last page

19 03 04	Home Ground: Welford Road	Trophy Cabinet: Midland Counties Cup(7)
	Captain: Arthur Jones	
	Vice-captain: Sammy Matthews	

OVERALL RECORD:					T	C	PG	DG	MK	PTS
PLD	W	D	L	Tigers scored:	81	25	3	9	0	338
39	19	3	17	Opponents scored:	69	25	3	3	1	282

GM	DATE		VEN	OPPONENTS	RESULT	TRIES	KICKS	ATT
MIDLAND COUNTIES CUP						**CUP WINNERS: LEICESTER TIGERS**		
33	Mar	12	H	**Nottingham (1)**	W 30-3	Miles(3), Braithwaite(2), D.Atkins, Hills, Sutton	Braithwaite c, A.Jones d	3000
34		19	H	**Five Ways Old Edwardians (2)**	W 29-3	Dakin(2), Sutton, A.Goodrich, Hills	Sutton d, Braithwaite c/d, A.Jones d	1500
35		26	H	**Nuneaton (sf)**	W 25-0	Dakin(3), Miles(3), Hills	A.Jones d	2000
36	Apr	2		Moseley (f)	W 13-3	D.Atkins, Russell, Sutton	A.Jones 2c	5000
CLUB MATCHES								
1	Sep	12	H	**Hartlepool Rovers**	W 11-4	Braithwaite, Freear, Miles	T.Goodrich c	7000
2		19	a	Devonport Albion	L 0-5	-	-	8500
3		21m	a	Plymouth	L 8-12	Dakin, Freear	T.Goodrich c	4500
4		22tu	a	Exeter	L 3-6	Russell	-	-
5		26	H	**West Hartlepool**	L 7-8	Miles	Blackburn d	8000
6	Oct	3	H	**Plymouth**	D 8-8	Miles, Russell	A.Jones c	9500
7		10	H	**Old Edwardians**	W 22-6	Miles(3), Dakin, Matthews	Braithwaite 2c, Russell p	4000
8		17	H	**Bristol**	W 13-9	P.Atkins, Foreman, Miles	Braithwaite c, Russell c	7000
9		24	H	**Moseley**	W 12-0	Sutton	A.Jones c/p/d	8000
10		31	H	**Cardiff**	L 0-24	-	-	10000
11	Nov	7	H	**London Welsh**	L 0-11	-	-	4000
12		14	H	**Northampton**	W 14-3	A.Hind, D.Smith	A.Hind d, A.Jones c, Russell c	10000
13		21	H	**Swansea**	L 0-11	-	-	8000
14		28	a	Cambridge University	L 0-6	-	-	1000
15	Dec	5	H	**Coventry**	W 14-5	Foreman, Miles, D.Smith, Sutton	A.Jones c	2000
16		12	H	**Exeter**	W 3-0	Miles	-	4000
17		17th	H	**Oxford University**	L 0-6	-	-	2000
18		19	H	**Newport**	L 0-7	-	-	5000
19		26	H	**Treherbert**	W 18-3	A.Hind, D.Atkins, P.Atkins, P.Jones	A.Hind d, Russell c	9000
20		28m	H	**Cheltenham**	W 21-0	Miles(3), A.Hind(2)	A.Jones 2c, Russell c	5000
21		29tu	a	Northampton	W 14-5	A.Hind(2), Sutton(2)	A.Jones c	7000
22	Jan	1f	a	West Hartlepool	D 0-0	-	-	5000
23		2	a	Hartlepool Rovers	L 3-14	Keeton	-	5000
24		4m	a	Castleford	W 16-5	Andrews(2), Russell, P.Jones	Russell 2c	-
25		16	a	Gloucester	L 0-21	-	-	2000
26		23	H	**Devonport Albion**	L 0-13	-	-	7000
27		30	a	Swansea	L 0-17	-	-	-
28	Feb	6	H	**Harlequins**	W 8-0	Russell, A.Hind	Russell c	1000
29		13	a	Moseley	W 6-5	Miles, Sutton	-	-
30		20	H	**Castleford**	W 28-5	A.Hind(3), Miles(2), Sutton(2)	Russell 2c/p	2000
31		27	a	Richmond	L 0-8	-	-	-
32	Mar	5	H	**Gloucester**	W 3-0	Braithwaite	-	4000
37	Apr	4m	a	Newport	L 3-22	A.Swain	-	7000
38		5tu	a	Bristol	D 0-0	-	-	2000
39		9	a	Cardiff	L 6-24	Blackburn, T.Goodrich	-	6000

Neutral Venue: *#36 at Burton-on-Trent*

INDIVIDUAL APPEARANCES 1903/04

Name / Game #	1	2	3	4	5	6	7	8	9	10	11	12	13	14	15	16	17	18	19	20	21	22	23	24	25	26	27	28	29	30	31	32	33	34	35	36	37	38	39	Apps	T	Pts
A Andrews	-	-	-	-	-	-	-	-	-	-	-	-	-	-	-	-	-	-	-	-	-	F	F	F	-	F	F	-	-	-	-	-	-	F	-	-	-	F	<F	8	2	6
DB (Dudley) Atkins	F	F	F	F	F	F	F	-	F	-	F	F	F	F	F	F	F	F	F	F	F	-	-	-	F	F	F	F	-	F	F	F	F	F	F	F	F	F	-	32	3	9
HP (Percy) Atkins	F	-	F	F	F	F	F	F	F	F	F	F	F	-	-	F	F	F	F	F	-	-	-	-	-	-	-	-	-	-	-	-	-	-	-	-	-	-	-	17	2	6
MH (Matt) Barrowcliffe	-	-	-	-	-	-	-	W	-	-	-	-	-	-	-	-	-	-	-	-	-	-	-	-	-	-	-	-	-	-	-	-	-	-	-	-	-	-	-	1	-	-
CT (Christopher) Bassett	-	-	-	-	-	-	-	-	-	-	-	-	-	-	-	-	-	-	-	-	-	-	-	=F	-	-	-	-	-	-	-	-	-	-	-	-	-	-	-	1	-	-
L (Leonard) Bennett	-	-	-	-	-	-	-	-	-	-	-	-	-	-	-	-	-	-	-	-	-	-	-	-	-	-	-	-	F	-	-	-	-	-	-	-	F	C	-	3	-	-
W (William) Blackburn	FB	FB	FB	FB	FB	-	-	-	-	-	-	-	-	-	-	-	-	-	-	-	-	-	-	-	-	-	-	-	-	-	-	-	FB	FB	FB	FB	-	-	C	10	1	7
J (Jacky) Braithwaite E+	SH	SH	SH	-	SH	SH	SH	SH	SH	SH	SH	SH	-	-	-	SH	-	-	-	-	-	SH	SH	SH	SH	SH	SH	SH	SH	SH	SH	SH	SH	SH	SH	SH	SH	SH	SH	30	4	26
Lt-Col. JC (Jimmy) Burdett	-	-	-	-	-	-	-	-	-	-	-	-	-	-	>F	-	-	-	-	-	-	-	-	-	-	-	-	-	-	-	-	-	-	-	-	-	-	-	-	1	-	-
E Cameron	-	-	-	-	-	=FB	-	-	-	-	-	-	-	-	-	-	-	-	-	-	-	-	-	-	-	-	-	-	-	-	-	-	-	-	-	-	-	-	-	1	-	-
WR (Reid) Dakin	C	C	C	C	C	W	C	-	-	-	-	C	C	W	-	-	-	-	-	-	-	-	-	C	-	C	C	-	-	-	-	-	W	W	W	-	-	-	W	17	7	21
WJ (Billy) Foreman	FH	FH	FH	FH	-	-	-	FH	FH	FH*	-	FH	-	-	FH	FH	FH	FH	FH	FH	FH	FH	FH	FH	-	FH	FH*	FH	FH	FH	FH	-	-	-	-	-	FH	-	-	25	2	6
AE (Arthur) Freear I3	W	W	W	W	W	-	-	-	-	-	-	-	-	-	-	-	<C	-	-	-	-	-	-	-	-	-	-	-	-	-	-	-	-	-	-	-	-	-	-	6	2	6
W (William) Gale	-	-	F	F	-	-	-	-	-	-	-	-	-	-	-	-	-	-	<FB	-	-	-	-	-	-	-	-	-	-	-	-	-	-	-	-	-	-	-	-	3	-	-
CM (Chauncey) Gillespie	-	-	-	-	-	-	=W	-	-	-	-	-	-	-	-	-	-	-	-	-	-	-	-	-	-	-	-	-	-	-	-	-	-	-	-	-	-	-	-	1	-	-
A (Alf) Goodrich	-	-	-	-	-	-	F	F	F	F	F	-	-	F	F	-	F	F	-	-	-	F	F	F	F	F	F	F	F	F	F	F	F	F	F	F	F	F	F	27	1	3
TW (Tom) Goodrich	F	F	F	F	F	F	F	F	-	F	FB	F	F	F	F	F	F	-	F	F	F	-	-	-	F	-	F	F	F	F	F	F	F	F	F	F	F	F	F	33	1	7
B (Bertie) Hills	-	-	-	-	-	-	-	-	-	-	-	-	-	-	-	-	-	-	-	-	-	-	-	-	-	-	-	-	-	-	-	FH	FH	FH	FH	FH	C	FH	FH	8	3	9
AE (Alfred) Hind E+	-	-	-	-	-	-	-	-	W	-	-	W	W	-	-	W	W	W	W	W	W	W	W	W	W	W	W	W	W	W	W	-	-	-	-	W	-	-	-	20	10	38
HA (Harold) Hind	F	F	-	-	F	F	-	F	F	F	F	F	F	F	-	F	-	F	F	F	F	F	F	F	F	F	F	F	F	F	F	F	F	-	F	F	F	F	F	33	-	-
AO (Arthur) Jones	-	-	-	-	C*	C*	-	-	C*	-	C*	FB*	FB*	-	FB*	FB*	FB*	FB*	-	FB*	FB*	-	-	-	-	-	-	C*	C*	C*	C*	-	C*	C*	C*	C*	-	-	-	20	-	37
W (Pussy) Jones W2	-	-	-	-	-	-	-	-	-	-	-	-	-	-	-	-	-	-	>C	C	C	C	C	C	-	-	-	-	-	-	-	-	-	-	-	-	-	-	<C	7	2	6
GH (George) Keeton E3	-	-	-	-	-	-	-	-	-	-	-	-	-	-	-	-	-	-	-	-	-	F	F	-	F	-	-	-	-	-	-	-	-	-	-	-	-	-	-	3	1	3
HSB (Harry) Lawrie	-	-	-	-	-	-	-	-	-	-	-	-	-	-	-	-	-	-	-	-	-	-	-	-	-	-	>FB	FB	FB	FB	FB	FB	-	-	-	-	FB	-	-	7	-	-
JP (Peter) Lockman	-	-	-	-	-	-	-	-	-	-	-	-	-	-	-	-	-	-	-	-	-	-	-	-	-	-	-	-	-	-	-	-	-	-	-	-	-	>FB	FB	2	-	-
S (Sammy) Matthews	F*	F*	F*	F*	F	F	F*	F*	F	F	F	F	F	F*	F	F	F	F	F*	F	F	F*	F*	F*	F*	F*	-	F	F	F	F	F*	F	F	F	F	F*	F*	F*	38	1	3
JH (Jack) Miles E1	W	W	W	W	W	W	W	W	-	W	-	-	W	-	W	W	W	W	W	W	W	-	-	-	W	W	-	W	W	W	W	W	W	W	W	W	W	<W	-	30	21	63
CA Page	-	-	-	-	-	-	-	-	-	-	<W	-	-	-	-	-	-	-	-	-	-	-	-	-	-	-	-	-	-	-	-	-	-	-	-	-	-	-	-	1	-	-
AJ (Arthur) Palfreyman	-	-	-	-	-	-	FB	FB	FB	FB	-	-	-	C	C	C	-	C	C	-	-	-	-	-	C	<C	-	-	-	-	-	-	-	-	-	-	-	-	-	11	-	-
AO (Alfred) Parsons	-	-	-	-	-	-	-	-	-	-	-	-	-	-	-	-	-	-	-	-	-	-	-	-	-	-	-	-	-	-	-	-	-	-	-	-	-	-	W	1	-	-
SH (Sid) Penny E+	F	-	-	-	F	-	-	F	-	-	-	-	-	F	F	F	F	F	F	F	F	F	F	F	F	F	F	F	F	F	F	F	F	F	F	F	F	F	F	29	-	-
HP (Harry) Reynolds	-	-	C	<C	-	-	-	-	-	-	-	-	-	-	-	-	-	-	-	-	-	-	-	-	-	-	-	-	-	-	-	-	-	-	-	-	-	-	-	2	-	-
W Robinson	-	F	-	<F	-	-	-	-	-	-	-	-	-	-	-	-	-	-	-	-	-	-	-	-	-	-	-	-	-	-	-	-	-	-	-	-	-	-	-	2	-	-
RF (Richard) Russell E+	-	>F	F	F	F	F	F	F	F	F	-	F	F	-	-	F	-	F	F	F	F	F	F	F	F	F	-	F	-	F	F	F	F	F	F	F	-	-	-	29	5	39
Lt. MS Scott	-	-	-	-	-	-	F	F	F	F	F	F	F	-	-	-	-	-	-	-	-	-	-	-	-	-	F	-	F	-	-	-	-	-	-	-	-	-	-	9	-	-
AJ Smith	-	-	-	-	-	-	-	-	-	-	-	-	-	-	-	-	-	-	-	-	-	-	-	-	-	-	-	-	-	-	-	-	-	-	-	-	-	-	>F	1	-	-
Cpt. JWD (Dixie) Smith	-	-	-	SH	FH	FH	FH	-	-	C	FH	W	FH	W	W	-	-	-	-	-	-	W	W	W	FB	-	W	-	-	-	-	W	-	-	-	-	W	W	-	18	2	6
N (Norman) Sutton	>C	C	-	-	-	C	C	C	C	C	C	C	C	C	C	C	C	C	-	C	C	C	C	-	C	-	-	C	C	C	C	C	C	C	C	C	C	C	-	31	10	34
AE (Albert) Swain	>F	F	F	F	F	F	-	-	F	F	F	F	F	F	F	F	F	F	F	F	F	-	-	-	-	F	F	F	F	F	F	F	F	F	F	F	F	F	-	32	1	3
M (Martinus) Swain	-	-	-	-	-	-	-	-	-	-	-	-	-	-	-	-	-	-	-	SH	SH	-	-	-	<FH	-	-	-	-	-	-	-	-	-	-	-	-	-	-	3	-	-
C (Charles) Timlock	-	-	-	-	-	-	-	-	-	-	-	-	-	-	-	-	<F	-	-	-	-	-	-	-	-	-	-	-	-	-	-	-	-	-	-	-	-	-	-	1	-	-
H Toone	-	-	-	-	-	-	-	>C	W	W	W	-	-	-	-	-	-	-	-	-	-	-	-	-	-	-	-	-	-	-	-	<C	-	-	-	-	-	-	-	5	-	-
CR (Charles) Watchorn	F	F	F	-	-	F	F	-	-	-	F	-	-	F	F	-	-	-	-	-	F	F	F	F	-	-	-	-	-	-	-	-	-	-	-	-	-	-	F	13	-	-
JR (Jamie) Watson	-	-	-	-	-	-	-	-	-	-	-	-	-	>FH	-	-	-	-	-	-	-	-	-	-	-	-	-	-	-	-	-	-	-	-	-	-	-	-	-	1	-	-
H (Harry) Wilkinson	-	-	-	-	-	-	-	-	-	-	-	-	-	-	-	-	-	-	-	-	-	-	-	-	-	-	C	-	-	-	-	-	-	-	-	-	-	-	-	1	-	-
GH (Danny) Woodford	-	-	-	-	-	-	-	-	-	-	-	-	-	>FB	-	-	-	-	-	-	-	-	-	-	-	<FB	-	-	-	-	-	-	-	-	-	-	-	-	-	2	-	-
EC (Ernest) Wykes	-	-	-	-	-	-	-	-	-	-	-	-	SH	SH	SH	-	SH	SH	SH	-	-	FB	FB	<FB	-	-	-	-	-	-	-	-	-	-	-	-	-	-	-	9	-	-

The key for how to read the stats is on the last page

1904/05					T	C	PG	DG	MK	PTS
Home Ground: Welford Road	**Trophy Cabinet:** Midland Counties Cup(8)	OVERALL RECORD:								
Captain: Sammy Matthews	PLD	W	D	L	Tigers scored: 94	34	3	1	0	363
Vice-captain: Alfred Hind	37	21	6	10	Opponents scored: 46	17	2	5	0	198

GM	DATE		VEN	OPPONENTS	RESULT	TRIES	KICKS	ATT
MIDLAND COUNTIES CUP						**CUP WINNERS: LEICESTER TIGERS**		
28	Mar	11	a	Coventry (2)	W 17-0	Bainbridge(3), Braithwaite, J.Jackett	Matthews c	4000
29		**18**	**H**	**Five Ways Old Edwardians (3)**	W 26-6	Bainbridge(2), Russell, A.Hind, J.Jackett	Russell 4c/p	4000
30		**25**	**H**	**Rugby (sf)**	W 23-0	Hills(2), Braithwaite, A.Hind, T.Jackson, Parsons, Russell	Hills c	3000
31	Apr	1		Nottingham (f)	W 31-0	A.Hind(3), Parsons(3), Hills	Braithwaite d, J.Jackett c, Jones c, Matthews c	10000
CLUB MATCHES								
1	Sep	**10**	**H**	**Hartlepool Rovers**	W 8-3	Hills, D.Smith	Yeld c	5000
2		**17**	**H**	**Plymouth**	W 9-0	Braithwaite, Parsons, A.Swain	-	8000
3		**24**	**H**	**West Hartlepool**	W 11-4	McFarlane, Matthews, Russell	Braithwaite c	-
4	Oct	**1**	**H**	**Devonport Albion**	L 3-11	T.Jackson	-	11000
5		**8**	**H**	**Birkenhead Park**	W 16-8	P.Atkins, Hills, McFarlane, Parsons	Braithwaite 2c	-
6		**15**	**H**	**Bristol**	W 11-5	P.Atkins, Braithwaite, Parsons	Yeld c	6000
7		22	a	Moseley	W 3-0	D.Smith	-	2000
8		**29**	**H**	**Richmond**	W 13-6	P.Atkins(2), Parsons	Yeld 2c	5000
9	Nov	5	a	Oxford University	L 3-4	-	Yeld p	400
10		**12**	**H**	**Coventry**	W 18-0	D.Smith(2), H.Hind, McFarlane	Russell 3c	6000
11		19	a	Swansea	D 8-8	Braithwaite, A.Goodrich	Yeld c	5000
		26	**H**	**Cambridge University**	PP (frost)			
12	Dec	3	a	Northampton	D 0-0	-	-	10000
13		**10**	**H**	**London Scottish**	W 8-3	H.Hind, Parsons	Russell c	3000
14		**17**	**H**	**Northampton**	W 8-0	A.Hind, Parsons	Russell c	10000
		24	**H**	**Old Merchant Taylors**	PP (frost)			
15		**26m**	**H**	**Edinburgh Royal High School**	D 6-6	Braithwaite	Russell p	3000
16		**27tu**	**H**	**Rugby**	W 35-15	Russell(2), Keeton(2), Simpson(2), Wilkinson(2), Braithwaite, A.Goodrich, A.Hind	Russell c	3000
17		**29th**	**H**	**Fettes-Lorettonians**	L 0-16	-	-	8000
18		31	a	West Hartlepool	L 3-6	Parsons	-	2000
19	Jan	2m	a	Hartlepool Rovers	W 13-3	Russell(2), Wilkinson	Braithwaite 2c	3000
20		**7**	**H**	**Cardiff**	L 8-16	Russell, Wilkinson	Braithwaite c	9000
21		14	a	Coventry	W 19-11	Bainbridge(2), Parsons(2), Hills	Braithwaite c, Matthews c	3000
		21	**H**	**Newport**	PP (frost)			
22		**28**	**H**	**Gloucester**	W 6-3	A.Goodrich, Parsons	-	6000
23	Feb	4	a	Harlequins	W 9-0	Bainbridge, Braithwaite, Wilkinson	-	2000
24		**11**	**H**	**Moseley**	D 8-8	Matthews, Parsons	Jones c	4000
25		**18**	**H**	**Swansea**	D 0-0	-	-	12000
26		25	a	Newport	L 5-9	Braithwaite	Matthews c	5000
27	Mar	4	a	Devonport Albion	L 0-13	-	-	9000
32	Apr	8	a	Cardiff	L 0-6	-	-	10000
33		**15**	**H**	**Old Edwardians**	W 17-5	Bainbridge, Hills, A.Hind, T.Jackson, Matthews	Braithwaite c	2000
34		22	a	Gloucester	L 0-9	-	-	4000
35		24m	a	Plymouth	D 5-5	Parsons	Matthews c	6000
36		25tu	a	Bristol	L 0-5	-	-	3000
37		**29**	**H**	**Newport**	W 13-4	Russell, Dann, Parsons	Russell 2c	8000

Neutral Venue: *#31 at the Butts - Coventry*

INDIVIDUAL APPEARANCES 1904/05

Name / Game #	1	2	3	4	5	6	7	8	9	10	11	12	13	14	15	16	17	18	19	20	21	22	23	24	25	26	27	28	29	30	31	32	33	34	35	36	37	Apps	T	Pts
DB (Dudley) Atkins	-	-	-	-	-	-	-	-	-	F	-	-	F	-	-	-	-	-	-	-	-	F	F	F	F	F	F	F	F	F	F	-	F	F	F	-	F	16	-	-
HP (Percy) Atkins	-	-	-	-	C	F	F	F	-	C	-	F	-	F	F	-	F	-	-	F	-	-	-	F	F	-	-	F	-	-	F	-	F	-	-	-	-	15	4	12
JW (James) Bainbridge	-	-	-	-	-	-	-	-	-	-	-	-	-	-	-	-	-	-	-	-	>C	C	C	C	C	C	C	C	C	C	C	C	C	C	C	C	C	17	9	27
L (Leonard) Beaver	-	-	-	-	-	-	-	-	-	-	-	-	-	-	-	-	-	-	-	-	-	-	>F	-	-	-	-	F	-	<F	-	-	-	-	-	-	-	3	-	-
L (Leonard) Bennett	-	-	-	-	-	-	-	-	-	-	-	-	-	-	-	-	-	-	-	-	-	-	-	-	-	-	-	-	-	-	-	F	-	F	-	F	<F	4	-	-
W (William) Blackburn	FB	FB	FB	FB	FB	FB	FB	FB	FB	FB	-	FB	FB	FB	-	-	FB	FB	-	FB	FB	<FB	-	-	-	-	-	-	-	-	-	-	-	-	-	-	-	18	-	-
J (Jacky) Braithwaite E+	SH	SH	SH	SH	SH	SH	SH	SH	SH	-	SH	SH	-	SH	SH	SH	SH	SH	SH	SH	SH	SH	SH	SH	SH	SH	SH	SH	SH	SH	SH	SH	SH	SH	SH	SH	SH	35	9	47
Lt-Col. JC (Jimmy) Burdett	F	-	-	-	-	-	-	-	-	-	-	-	-	-	-	-	-	-	-	-	-	-	-	-	-	-	F	-	-				-	-	-	-	-	2	-	-
WR (Reid) Dakin	-	C	C	C	C	C	C	C	C	-	C	W	C	-	C	C	C	C	-	FH	F	W	-	-	-	-	-	-	-	-	-	-	-	-	-	-	-	18	-	-
WI (Isaiah) Dann	F	-	-	-	-	-	-	-	-	-	F	-	-	-	-	F	-	F	F	-	-	F	-	F	-	F	-	-	-	-	-	-	F	F	-	F	F	12	1	3
L Elliott	-	-	-	-	-	-	-	-	-	-	-	-	-	-	>FB	FB	-	-	-	-	-	-	-	-	-	-	-	-	-	-	-	-	-	-	-	-	-	2	-	-
A (Alf) Goodrich	F	F	F	F	-	F	F	F	F	F	F	F	F	F	F	F	F	F	F	F	F	F	F	F	F	F	F	F	F	F	F	F	F	F	F	F	F	36	3	9
TW (Tom) Goodrich	-	F	-	F	F	F	F	F	F	-	F	F	F	-	F	F	F	F	F	F	F	F	F	F	F	F	F	F	F	F	F	F	F	-	F	F	F	32	-	-
B (Bertie) Hills	FH	FH	FH	FH	FH	FH	FH	FH	FH	FH	FH	FH	FH	FH	-	-	-	-	-	-	FH	-	-	-	FH	FH	-	FH	FH	FH	FH	-	FH	FH	-	-	FH	24	7	23
AE (Alfred) Hind E+	-	-	-	-	-	-	-	-	-	-	-	-	W	W	W	W	-	-	-	-	-	C	W	C	W	W	-	W	W	W	W	-	W	W	-	W	W	17	8	24
HA (Harold) Hind	F	F	F	F	F	-	F	-	F	F	F	F	F	F	-	-	-	F	F	<F	-	-	-	-	-	-	-	-	-	-	-	-	-	-	-	-	-	15	2	6
R (Dick) Jackett	-	-	-	-	-	-	-	-	-	-	-	-	-	-	-	-	-	-	-	-	-	-	-	-	-	-	-	-	-	-	-	-	-	-	>F	F	-	2	-	-
EJ (John) Jackett E+ AW+	-	-	-	-	-	-	-	-	-	-	-	-	-	-	-	-	>FH	FH	FH	-	-	FH	FH	FH	C	C	-	C	C	C	C	C	-	C	C	C	C	17	2	8
T (Tom) Jackson	-	-	>F	F	F	-	-	-	-	-	-	-	-	-	-	-	-	-	-	-	-	-	-	-	-	-	-	-	F	F	F	F	F	F	F	F	-	11	3	9
AO (Arthur) Jones	-	-	-	-	-	-	-	-	-	-	-	-	-	-	-	-	-	-	-	-	-	-	FB	FB	FB	-	-	FB	-	FB	FB	-	-	-	-	-	-	6	-	4
GH (George) Keeton E3	-	-	-	-	-	-	-	-	-	-	-	-	-	-	-	F	F	<F	-	-	-	-	-	-	-	-	-	-	-	-	-	-	-	-	-	-	-	3	2	6
JP (Peter) Lockman	-	-	-	-	-	-	-	-	-	-	-	-	-	-	-	-	-	-	-	-	-	-	-	-	-	-	-	-	-	-	-	FB	-	FB	FB	FB	<FB	5	-	-
Dr. N McFarlane	>W	W	W	W	W	W	W	-	W	W	W	-	C	C	C	-	-	W	W	W	-	-	-	-	-	-	W	-	-	-	-	-	-	-	-	-	-	17	3	9
RW (Robert) Marris	-	-	-	-	-	-	-	-	-	-	-	-	-	-	-	-	-	-	-	-	-	-	-	-	-	-	-	-	-	-	-	>W	<W	-	-	-	-	2	-	-
S (Sammy) Matthews	F*	F*	F*	F*	F*	F*	F*	F*	F*	F*	F*	F*	F*	F*	F*	F*	F*	F*	F*	F*	F*	F*	F*	F*	F*	F*	F*	F*	F*	F*	F*	F*	F*	F*	F*	F*	F*	37	3	19
AO (Alfred) Parsons	-	W	W	W	W	W	W	W	W	W	W	C	W	W	W	-	W	W	W	W	W	W	W	W	W	W	W	W	W	W	W	W	-	W	W	W	W	34	17	51
SH (Sid) Penny E+	-	F	F	F	F	F	-	F	F	F	F	-	F	F	F	F	F	-	-	-	F	F	F	F	F	F	F	F	F	F	F	F	F	F	F	-	F	30	-	-
Ridsdale	-	-	-	-	-	-	-	-	-	-	-	-	-	-	-	-	-	-	-	-	-	-	-	-	-	-	-	-	-	-	-	-	-	-	>FH	<FH	-	2	-	-
RF (Richard) Russell E+	F	F	F	F	F	F	F	F	F	F	-	F	F	F	F	F	F	F	F	F	F	-	-	-	F	-	F	-	F	F	F	-	-	F	F	F	F	29	9	57
FR (Frank) Simpson	-	-	-	-	-	-	-	-	-	-	-	>W	-	-	-	-	<W	-	-	-	-	-	-	-	-	-	-	-	-	-	-	-	-	-	-	-	-	2	-	-
Cpt. JWD (Dixie) Smith	W	C	C	-	-	C	C	C	C	C	C	C	SH	C	-	-	-	-	-	C	-	-	-	-	-	-	-	-	FB	-	-	-	FB	-	W	-	-	16	4	12
AE (Albert) Swain	F	F	F	F	F	F	F	F	F	F	F	F	F	F	F	-	-	-	-	F	F	F	F	F	F	F	F	F	F	-	-	-	-	-	-	-	-	25	1	3
JR (Jamie) Watson	-	-	-	-	-	-	-	-	-	SH	-	-	-	-	-	-	-	-	-	-	-	-	-	-	-	-	FH	-	-	-	-	FH	-	-	-	-	-	3	-	-
H (Harry) Wilkinson	-	-	-	-	-	-	-	-	-	-	-	-	-	-	-	C	C	C	C	C	W	-	C	W	-	<FB	-	-	-	-	-	-	-	-	-	-	-	9	5	15
GG (George) Yeld	F	F	F	-	F	F	F	F	F	-	F	F	-	F	F	F	F	F	F	F	F	-	F	-	-	-	-	-	-	-	-	-	-	-	-	-	-	19	-	13

1 GAME: BL (Bert) Atkinson >FB(11), W Dale >FB(27), WJ (Billy) Foreman FH(16), T Hall >C(33), RE (Ralph) Hemingway =F(22), FA (Frank) Jackson <W(8), S (Samuel) Lines <F(26), D (Dan) Rees W5 =C(1), GA (George) Sanderson S+ =F(19), J (Jerry) Sanderson =FB(19), Lt. MS Scott F(10), FH (Frank) Shaw >C(21), J Simpson =Wt(16), H Smalley <FH(15), AJ Smith <F(32), W Smith =F(32), T Sturrock =C(19), N (Norman) Sutton <C(1), P (Percy) Swain >C(27), Dr. CHB Thompson =C(4)

The key for how to read the stats is on the last page

19 05/06	
Home Ground: Welford Road	
Captain: Sammy Matthews	
Vice-captain: Alfred Hind	

OVERALL RECORD:					T	C	PG	DG	MK	PTS
PLD	W	D	L	Tigers scored:	49	16	4	5	0	211
37	17	6	14	Opponents scored:	60	25	4	5	1	266

GM	DATE		VEN	OPPONENTS	RESULT	TRIES	KICKS	ATT
CLUB MATCHES								
1	Sep	**9**	**H**	**Hartlepool Rovers**	W 8-3	Bainbridge(2)	Braithwaite c	4000
2		**16**	**H**	**West Hartlepool**	W 16-3	D.Atkins, P.Atkins, Bainbridge, Matthews	Braithwaite c, Yeld c	7000
3		**23**	**H**	**Plymouth**	D 0-0	-	-	10000
4		**30**	**H**	**New Zealand**	L 0-28	-	-	20000
5	Oct	7	a	Devonport Albion	D 3-3	P.Atkins	-	6000
6		9m	a	Plymouth	D 0-0	-	-	1500
7		10tu	a	United Services	L 3-6	Hardyman	-	1000
8		**14**	**H**	**Bristol**	D 11-11	Russell, Bainbridge	Russell p, Braithwaite c	5000
9		**21**	**H**	**Moseley**	W 16-8	Braithwaite, Bainbridge, A.Goodrich, Hind	Braithwaite 2c	5000
10	Nov	**4**	**H**	**Oxford University**	W 10-8	P.Atkins, Hind	A.Jones d	6000
11		**11**	**H**	**Swansea**	L 0-3	-	-	-
12		**18**	**H**	**Northampton**	L 3-10	D.Atkins	-	-
13		**25**	**H**	**Llanelly**	W 6-0	Hind(2)	-	-
14	Dec	2	a	Northampton	L 0-8	-	-	-
15		9	a	London Scottish	L 7-17	Braithwaite	Underwood d	-
16		16	a	Richmond	W 5-3	Bainbridge	A.Jones c	-
17		**23**	**H**	**Coventry**	W 6-5	P.Atkins, A.Jones	-	-
18		**26tu**	**H**	**Birkenhead Park**	W 12-5	D.Atkins, Hind, Russell	A.Jones p	-
19		**27w**	**H**	**United Services**	W 25-4	Russell(2), Watson(2), Gimson	A.Jones 3c/d	-
20		**28th**	**H**	**Fettes-Lorettonians**	L 0-3	-	-	-
21		30	a	West Hartlepool	W 11-3	Matthews, Worsley	Russell p, Braithwaite c	-
22	Jan	1m	a	Hartlepool Rovers	L 0-8	-	-	-
23		6	a	Rugby	W 12-8	P.Atkins, Bainbridge	A.Jones c/d	-
24		13	a	Gloucester	L 0-20	-	-	-
25		**20**	**H**	**Devonport Albion**	W 11-9	Braithwaite, Tarr, Underwood	Matthews c	-
26		27	a	Moseley	W 3-0	Underwood	-	-
27	Feb	3	a	Coventry	L 3-12	-	J.Jackett p	5000
		10	**H**	**Harlequins**	PP			
28		17	a	Swansea	L 0-20	-	-	-
29		**24**	**H**	**Newport**	L 0-8	-	-	-
30	Mar	**3**	**H**	**Cardiff**	D 3-3	Bainbridge	-	-
31		**10**	**H**	**Headingley**	W 7-4	Underwood	Braithwaite d	-
32		17	a	Birkenhead Park	W 3-0	Russell	-	-
33		**24**	**H**	**Bedford**	W 13-5	Bainbridge, Penny, Underwood	Braithwaite 2c	-
34	Apr	**7**	**H**	**Old Edwardians**	W 14-0	McFarlane(2), Bainbridge, Underwood	Braithwaite c	3000
35		14	a	Newport	L 0-25	-	-	-
36		16m	a	Cardiff	L 0-13	-	-	-
37		17tu	a	Bristol	D 0-0	-	-	-

INDIVIDUAL APPEARANCES 1905/06

Name / Game #	1	2	3	4	5	6	7	8	9	10	11	12	13	14	15	16	17	18	19	20	21	22	23	24	25	26	27	28	29	30	31	32	33	34	35	36	37	Apps	T	Pts
DB (Dudley) Atkins	FB	F	F	F	F	F	F	F	F	F	F	F	F	-	F	F	F	F	F	F	-	-	-	-	-	-	-	-	-	-	-	-	-	-	-	-	-	19	3	9
HP (Percy) Atkins	F	F	F	WF	WF	WF	WF	WF	WF	WF	F	F	F	-	F	-	F	F	SH	-	-	-	SH	-	F	FH	-	-	F	F	F	-	-	-	-	-	-	23	5	15
JW (James) Bainbridge	C	C	C	C	C	C	C	C	C	C	C	-	C	C	C	C	C	C	-	-	-	-	W	-	C	C	C	-	C	C	C	C	C	C	-	-	-	27	10	30
J (Jacky) Braithwaite E1	SH	SH	SH	SH	SH	SH	SH	SH	SH	SH	SH	SH	SH	-	SH	SH	SH	SH	-	SH	SH	SH	-	SH	SH	SH	-	SH	SH	SH	SH	SH	SH	SH	SH	SH	SH	33	3	31
WR (Reid) Dakin	-	-	-	-	-	-	-	-	-	-	-	-	-	-	-	-	-	-	-	C	C	C	<C	-	-	-	-	-	-	-	-	-	-	-	-	-	-	4	-	-
W Dale	-	-	-	-	FB	FB	FB	FB	-	-	FB	-	-	-	-	-	-	-	-	-	-	-	-	-	-	-	-	-	-	-	-	-	-	-	-	-	-	5	-	-
WI (Isaiah) Dann	-	-	-	-	F	-	-	-	-	-	-	-	-	F	-	-	-	-	F	-	F	F	-	-	-	-	-	-	-	-	-	-	-	-	-	-	-	5	-	-
L Elliott	-	-	-	-	-	-	-	-	-	-	-	-	-	-	-	-	-	-	-	-	FB	FB	FB	FB	-	-	-	-	<FB	-	-	-	-	-	-	-	-	5	-	-
HB (Horace) Freer	-	-	-	-	-	-	-	-	-	-	-	-	-	-	-	>F	-	-	-	-	-	-	-	F	F	F	F	<F	-	-	-	-	-	-	-	-	-	6	-	-
WG George	-	-	-	-	-	-	-	-	-	-	-	-	-	-	-	-	-	-	-	-	-	-	>F	F	F	F	F	F	F	F	F	-	-	<F	-	-	-	10	-	-
C (Christopher) Gimson	-	-	-	-	-	-	-	-	-	-	-	-	-	-	-	-	-	-	>F	F	-	F	F	-	-	-	-	-	-	-	-	-	-	-	-	-	-	4	1	3
A (Alf) Goodrich	F	F	F	F	F	F	-	F	F	-	F	F	F	F	F	F	F	F	F	F	F	F	F	F	F	F	F	F	F	F	F	F	F	F	F	F	F	35	1	3
TW (Tom) Goodrich	F	F	F	F	F	F	F	F	F	F	F	F	F	F	F	F	-	-	-	-	-	-	-	-	-	-	F	-	-	F	F	F	-	-	-	-	-	20	-	-
G (George) Greasley	-	-	-	-	-	-	-	-	-	-	-	-	-	-	-	-	-	-	-	-	-	-	-	-	-	-	>F	-	-	-	-	F	F	F	-	-	-	4	-	-
FW (Fred) Hardyman	-	-	-	-	-	>W	W	-	-	-	-	-	-	W	W	W	-	-	W	-	-	-	-	-	-	-	-	-	-	-	-	-	-	-	W	W	W	9	1	3
GH (George) Hayward	-	-	-	-	-	-	-	-	-	-	-	-	-	-	-	-	-	-	-	-	-	-	-	-	-	-	-	-	-	-	-	>FB	FB	FB	FB	FB	FB	6	-	-
B (Bertie) Hills	FH	FH	FH	<FH	-	-	-	-	-	-	-	-	-	-	-	-	-	-	-	-	-	-	-	-	-	-	-	-	-	-	-	-	-	-	-	-	-	4	-	-
AE (Alfred) Hind E2	W	W	W	W	-	-	-	W	W	W	W	W	W	-	-	-	W	W	-	W	-	-	-	-	W	<W	-	-	-	-	-	-	-	-	-	-	-	15	5	15
R (Richard) Hives	-	-	-	-	-	-	-	-	-	-	-	-	-	>F	-	F	F	F	F	F	F	-	F	F	F	F	F	F	F	FH	-	-	F	F	-	F	-	18	-	-
TB (Thomas) Hogarth E1	-	-	-	-	-	-	-	-	-	-	-	-	-	-	-	-	-	-	-	-	-	-	-	-	-	-	-	-	-	-	-	-	-	-	>F	F	F	3	-	-
R Ireland	-	-	-	-	-	-	-	-	-	-	-	-	-	>F	F	<F	-	-	-	-	-	-	-	-	-	-	-	-	-	-	-	-	-	-	-	-	-	3	-	-
R (Dick) Jackett	-	-	-	-	-	F	F	-	-	-	-	-	-	-	-	-	-	-	-	-	-	-	-	-	-	-	-	F	-	-	-	-	-	-	-	-	-	3	-	-
EJ (John) Jackett E5 AW+	-	-	-	-	C	C	C	-	C	FB	-	FB	FB	-	-	C	FB	FB	FB	FB	FH	FH	-	-	FB	FB	FB	FB	W	FB	FB	-	FH	FH	FH	W	C	26	-	3
FS (Fred) Jackson AW+	-	-	-	>F	F	F	F	F	F	F	F	F	F	F	F	-	-	-	-	-	-	-	F	F	F	F	F	-	F	F	F	F	F	F	F	F	F	26	-	-
T (Tom) Jackson	-	-	-	-	-	-	-	-	-	-	-	-	-	-	-	-	-	-	-	F	F	F	-	W	-	-	-	-	-	-	-	-	-	-	-	-	-	4	-	-
HJF (Harold) Jeffries	-	-	-	-	-	-	-	-	-	-	-	-	-	>SH	FH	FH	<FH	-	-	-	-	-	-	-	-	-	-	-	-	-	-	-	-	-	-	-	-	4	-	-
AO (Arthur) Jones	-	FB	FB	FB	-	-	-	-	FB	C	C	C	C	-	-	FB*	C	FH	FH	-	-	-	FH	-	-	-	-	-	-	-	-	-	-	-	-	-	-	13	1	28
Rev. FH (Frank) Jones	-	-	-	-	-	-	-	-	-	-	-	-	-	-	-	-	W	C	<C	-	-	-	-	-	-	-	-	-	-	-	-	-	-	-	-	-	-	3	-	-
AL (Alf) Kewney E4	-	-	-	-	-	-	-	-	-	-	-	-	-	-	-	-	-	-	-	-	-	-	-	-	-	-	-	-	-	-	-	-	-	-	>F	F	F	3	-	-
Dr. N McFarlane	C	C	C	C	W	W	W	C	W	W	W	C	W	C	W	-	-	-	-	-	-	-	-	-	-	-	-	C	W	-	W	W	W	W	-	-	-	21	2	6
S (Sammy) Matthews	F*	F*	F*	F*	F*	F*	F*	F*	F*	F*	F*	F*	F*	F*	F*	-	F*	F*	F*	F*	F*	F*	F*	-	F*	F*	-	F*	F*	F*	F*	F*	F*	F*	F*	F*	F*	34	2	8
AO (Alfred) Parsons	W	W	W	W	-	-	-	W	-	-	-	W	-	-	-	-	-	-	-	-	-	-	-	-	-	-	-	-	-	-	-	-	-	-	-	-	-	6	-	-
SH (Sid) Penny E+	F	F	F	F	F	F	F	F	F	F	F	F	F	F	F	F	F	F	F	F	F	F	F	F	F	F	-	F	F	F	F	F	F	F	F	F	F	36	1	3
RF (Richard) Russell E1	F	F	F	F	-	-	-	F	F	F	F	F	F	-	-	-	F	F	F	F	F	F	F	F*	-	F	-	-	F	F	F	F	F	-	F	F	F	27	5	21
Lt. MS Scott	-	-	-	-	-	-	-	-	-	-	-	-	-	-	-	-	-	-	-	-	F	F	-	-	-	-	-	-	-	-	-	-	-	-	-	-	-	2	-	-
TW (Tom) Smith AW+	-	-	-	-	-	-	-	-	-	-	-	-	-	-	-	-	-	-	-	-	-	-	-	-	-	-	-	-	-	-	-	>F	F	F	F	-	F	5	-	-
C (Christopher) Stafford	>F	-	-	-	-	-	F	-	-	-	-	-	-	-	-	-	-	-	-	-	-	-	-	-	-	-	-	-	-	-	-	-	-	-	-	-	-	2	-	-
Lt. FN (Frank) Tarr E+	-	-	-	-	-	-	-	-	-	-	-	-	-	-	-	-	-	-	-	-	-	-	-	>C	C	-	-	-	-	-	-	-	-	-	W	C	-	4	1	3
DE (Daniel) Underwood	-	-	-	-	>W	-	-	-	-	-	-	-	-	W	C	W	-	W	W	W	W	W	W	W	W	W	W	-	-	W	W	W	W	W	C	-	<W	21	5	19
CR (Charles) Watchorn	-	-	-	-	-	-	-	-	-	-	-	-	-	-	-	F	F	F	-	-	-	-	-	-	-	-	-	-	-	-	-	-	-	-	-	-	-	3	-	-
JR (Jamie) Watson	-	-	-	-	FE	FE	FE	FE	FE	FE	FH	FH	FH	-	-	-	-	-	C	FH	W	W	C	C	FH	C	C	C	C	C	C	C	C	C	C	C	C	28	2	6
Lt. CFA (Christopher) Worsley-Worswick	-	-	-	-	-	-	-	-	-	-	-	-	-	-	-	-	-	-	-	-	>C	<C	-	-	-	-	-	-	-	-	-	-	-	-	-	-	-	2	1	3
A Wright	-	-	-	-	-	-	-	-	-	-	-	-	-	-	-	-	-	-	-	-	-	-	-	-	-	-	-	>FH	FH	-	FH	-	-	-	-	FH	<FH	5	-	-
GG (George) Yeld	F	F	F	-	-	-	-	-	-	-	-	-	-	-	-	-	-	-	-	-	-	-	-	-	-	-	-	-	-	-	-	-	-	-	-	-	-	3	-	2

1 GAME: AW (Albert) Adcock =FB(15), BL (Bert) Atkinson <FB(14), MH (Matt) Barrowcliffe <FH(27), G (Gerald) Bolus =F(27), L Charles =W(27), GP (George) Chitham =W(28), Cpt. WR (Walter) Evans =F(10), WJ (Billy) Foreman <SH(27), JR Hart-Davis =C(20), JT (Jimmy) Jose =W(28), FW Payne =FH(14), F (Fred) Pyart =F(24), E Raven =F(28), HR (Hugh) Somerville =FH(32), P (Percy) Swain <FH(24), E Ward =W(30)

The key for how to read the stats is on the last page

1906/07

Home Ground: Welford Road
Captain: Richard Russell
Vice-captain: Jacky Braithwaite

OVERALL RECORD:					T	C	PG	DG	MK	PTS
PLD	W	D	L	Tigers scored:	68	22	7	0	0	269
33	16	5	12	Opponents scored:	38	8	4	1	0	146

GM	DATE		VEN	OPPONENTS	RESULT	TRIES	KICKS	ATT
CLUB MATCHES								
1	Sep	**8**	**H**	**Hartlepool Rovers**	W 8-0	Bainbridge, Russell	Coles c	-
2		**15**	**H**	**West Hartlepool**	W 9-3	Hardyman, Russell	Coles p	-
3		**22**	**H**	**Plymouth**	W 14-0	Bainbridge, A.Goodrich, Hardyman	Jones c/p	8500
4	Oct	**6**	**H**	**Devonport Albion**	L 0-8	-	-	5000
5		**13**	**H**	**Bristol**	D 0-0	-	-	-
6		20	a	Moseley	W 3-0	Watson	-	-
7		**27**	**H**	**Richmond**	W 11-0	Greasley, Smith, Watson	Braithwaite c	-
8	Nov	3	a	Oxford University	L 6-11	Hardyman, Russell	-	-
9		**10**	**H**	**Newport**	D 3-3	Hardyman	-	-
10		17	a	Swansea	L 0-8	-	-	-
11		**24**	**H**	**Llanelly**	L 3-5	-	Matthews p	-
12	Dec	1	a	Northampton	D 3-3	Watson	-	-
13		**8**	**H**	**London Scottish**	L 3-8	K.Wood	-	-
14		**15**	**H**	**Headingley**	W 12-3	Hall, Hardyman, Hives, F.Jackson	-	-
15		22	a	Coventry	D 0-0	-	-	-
16		**24m**	**H**	**Edinburgh Royal High School**	W 26-0	Matthews(2), P.Wood(2), D.Jackett, T.Jackson	Hives 4c	-
		26w	**H**	**Birkenhead Park**	PP (snow)			
17		**27th**	**H**	**Fettes-Lorettonians**	D 3-3	Russell	-	-
		29	a	West Hartlepool	PP (snow)			
		31m	a	Hartlepool Rovers	PP (snow)			
	Jan	1tu	a	Headingley	PP (snow)			
18		**5**	**H**	**Harlequins**	W 9-0	Hardyman, F.Jackson, T.Jackson	-	-
19		**12**	**H**	**Percy Park**	W 37-6	Hardyman(4), F.Jackson(2), T.Jackson, Russell, K.Wood	Hives 5c	-
20		**19**	**H**	**Coventry**	W 9-3	Scott, Watson, K.Wood	-	-
		26	**H**	**Moseley**	PP (frost)			
	Feb	2	a	Bedford	PP (frost)			
		9	**H**	**Cardiff**	PP (frost)			
21		**16**	**H**	**Swansea**	W 12-3	Hobbs, F.Jackson	J.Jackett 2p	-
22		23	a	Newport	L 0-14	-	-	-
23	Mar	**2**	**H**	**Gloucester**	W 17-5	Scott(2), K.Wood(2), P.Wood	Russell c	-
24		**9**	**H**	**Northampton**	W 11-0	Scott(2), K.Wood	P.Wood c	9000
25		16	a	Birkenhead Park	W 13-3	Smith(2), Hobbs	P.Wood 2c	-
26		**23**	**H**	**London Welsh**	L 3-5	P.Wood	-	-
27		30	a	Llanelly	L 3-6	Kirk	-	-
28	Apr	1m	a	Cardiff	L 0-9	-	-	20000
29		2tu	a	Bristol	L 5-13	Tarr	F.Jackson c	-
30		6	a	Devonport Albion	L 0-9	-	-	-
31		8m	a	Plymouth	L 8-9	K.Wood	F.Jackson c/p	4000
32		**13**	**H**	**Old Edwardians**	W 19-0	K.Wood(2), J.Jackett, T.Jackson	F.Jackson 2c, Kirk p	-
33		**20**	**H**	**London**	W 19-6	Russell(2), F.Jackson, Smith, Wilson	Russell c, F.Jackson c	-

INDIVIDUAL APPEARANCES 1906/07

Name / Game #	1	2	3	4	5	6	7	8	9	10	11	12	13	14	15	16	17	18	19	20	21	22	23	24	25	26	27	28	29	30	31	32	33	Apps	T	Pts
HP (Percy) Atkins	WF	WF	WF	<SH	-	-	-	-	-	-	-	-	-	-	-	-	-	-	-	-	-	-	-	-	-	-	-	-	-	-	-	-	-	4	-	-
JW (James) Bainbridge	FE	FE	FE	FE	FE	FE	<FH	-	-	-	-	-	-	-	-	-	-	-	-	-	-	-	-	-	-	-	-	-	-	-	-	-	-	7	2	6
Bateman	-	-	-	-	-	-	-	-	-	-	-	-	-	-	-	-	-	-	-	-	-	-	-	-	-	-	-	-	-	-	=SH	-	-	1	-	-
C (Charles) Bourns	-	>F	-	F	F	F	-	F	F	-	-	F	F	F	-	-	-	-	-	-	-	-	-	-	F	F	-	-	-	-	F	-	-	12	-	-
J (Jacky) Braithwaite E1	SH	SH	SH*	-	SH	SH	SH	-	-	-	-	-	FH	SH	<SH*	-	-	-	-	-	-	-	-	-	-	-	-	-	-	-	-	-	-	9	-	2
F Coles	>C	<C	-	-	-	-	-	-	-	-	-	-	-	-	-	-	-	-	-	-	-	-	-	-	-	-	-	-	-	-	-	-	-	2	-	5
W Dale	-	-	-	-	-	-	-	-	-	-	-	-	-	-	-	-	-	-	-	-	-	-	-	-	-	-	-	-	-	FB	FB	-	FB	3	-	-
HO East	-	-	-	-	-	-	-	=FB	-	-	-	-	-	-	-	-	-	-	-	-	-	-	-	-	-	-	-	-	-	-	-	-	-	1	-	-
GR (Gerald) Ellis-Danvers	-	-	=W	-	-	-	-	-	-	-	-	-	-	-	-	-	-	-	-	-	-	-	-	-	-	-	-	-	-	-	-	-	-	1	-	-
C (Christopher) Gimson	-	-	-	-	-	-	F	-	-	-	-	-	-	-	-	-	-	-	-	-	-	-	-	-	-	-	F	F	F	-	-	F	F	6	-	-
A (Alf) Goodrich	-	F	F	F	F	F	F	F	F	F	F	F	F	F	-	-	F	F	F	F	F	F	F	F	F	F	F	F	-	F	-	-	F	27	1	3
TW (Tom) Goodrich	-	-	-	-	-	-	-	-	-	-	-	-	-	-	-	-	-	-	-	-	-	-	-	-	-	-	-	-	-	-	F	F	-	2	-	-
G (George) Greasley	-	-	-	-	-	F	F	F	-	F	F	-	-	-	F	-	-	-	F	-	-	-	-	-	-	-	-	F	F	-	-	-	-	9	1	3
T Hall	-	-	-	-	-	-	-	-	-	-	-	-	-	W	W	W	-	-	-	-	-	W	-	-	-	-	-	-	-	-	-	-	-	4	1	3
FW (Fred) Hardyman	W	W	W	W	W	W	W	W	W	W	W	-	W	W	W	W	W	W	W	W	W	W	-	W	W	W	W	W	W	W	W	-	<W	30	10	30
GH (George) Hayward	-	-	-	FB	W	W	-	-	-	-	-	FB	FB	FB	FB	-	-	FB	FB	FB	-	-	FB	-	FB	-	FB	<FB	-	-	-	-	-	14	-	-
R (Richard) Hives	F	-	F	F	F	-	-	-	-	-	-	-	-	F	F	F	F	-	F	-	-	F	-	-	-	-	-	-	F	-	-	-	-	11	1	21
AJ (Arthur) Hobbs	>F	F	F	F	F	F	F	F	F	F	F	F	F	-	-	-	-	F	F	F	F	F	F	F	F	F	F	F	F	F	F	F	F	29	2	6
R (Dick) Jackett	-	-	-	-	-	-	-	-	-	-	-	-	-	-	-	F	F	-	-	-	-	-	-	-	-	-	-	-	-	-	F	-	-	3	1	3
EJ (John) Jackett E9 AW+	FB	FB	FB	C	FB	FB	FB	-	FB	FB	-	-	-	-	-	FB	FB	-	-	-	FB	FB	W	FB	-	FB	W	W	W	W	W	W	C	23	1	9
FS (Fred) Jackson AW+	F	F	F	F	-	-	-	-	-	-	-	-	-	F	F	F	-	F	F	F	F	F	F	F	F	F	F	F	F	F	F	F	F	23	6	31
T (Tom) Jackson	-	-	-	-	-	-	W	C	C	C	FB	C	C	-	-	C	C	C	C	C	C	C	C	-	C	C	-	-	FB	C	C	<C	-	21	4	12
AO (Arthur) Jones	-	-	C	-	-	-	-	-	-	-	-	-	-	-	-	-	-	-	-	-	-	-	-	C	-	-	-	-	-	-	-	-	-	2	-	5
L (Lionel) Kirk	-	-	-	-	-	-	-	-	-	-	-	-	-	-	-	-	-	-	-	-	-	-	-	-	-	-	>FH	SH	FH	-	-	SH	SH	5	1	6
Dr. N McFarlane	W	<W	-	-	-	-	-	-	-	-	-	-	-	-	-	-	-	-	-	-	-	-	-	-	-	-	-	-	-	-	-	-	-	2	-	-
S (Sammy) Matthews	F	F	F	-	F	F	F	F	F	F*	F	F	F	-	F	F*	F	F	F	F	F	F	F	F	F*	F*	F*	F*	F*	F	-	F*	F	30	2	9
AO (Alfred) Parsons	-	-	-	<W	-	-	-	-	-	-	-	-	-	-	-	-	-	-	-	-	-	-	-	-	-	-	-	-	-	-	-	-	-	1	-	-
SH (Sid) Penny E+	F	F	F	F	F	F	-	F	F	F	F	F	F	F	F	F	F	F	-	F	F	F	F	F	F	F	-	-	-	F	F*	F	F	28	-	-
RF (Richard) Russell E1	F*	F*	-	F*	F*	F*	F*	W*	W*	-	W*	W*	F*	F*	-	-	F*	F*	F*	F*	F*	F*	F*	F*	-	-	-	-	-	F*	-	-	F*	22	7	25
AF (Algernon) Scott	-	-	-	-	-	-	-	-	-	-	-	-	-	-	-	-	>W	W	W	W	W	-	W	W	W	W	-	-	-	-	-	-	W	10	5	15
FH (Frank) Shaw	-	-	-	-	-	-	-	-	-	-	C	-	-	-	-	-	-	-	-	-	-	-	-	-	-	-	-	-	-	-	-	<FB	-	2	-	-
G (George) Shingler	-	-	-	-	-	-	-	-	-	-	-	-	-	-	-	-	-	-	-	-	-	-	-	-	-	-	-	-	-	-	-	>W	-	1	-	-
TW (Tom) Smith AW+	F	-	F	F	F	F	F	F	F	F	F	F	-	F	F	F	F	F	-	F	F	F	F	F	F	F	F	F	F	F	F	F	F	30	4	12
C (Christopher) Stafford	-	-	-	-	-	-	F	F	F	F	F	F	F	-	F	F	-	F	F	F	F	-	F	F	F	F	F	F	F	F	F	<F	-	23	-	-
AE (Albert) Swain	-	-	-	-	-	-	-	-	F	F	F	F	F	F	F	F	<F	-	-	-	-	-	-	-	-	-	-	-	-	-	-	-	-	9	-	-
Lt. FN (Frank) Tarr E+	-	-	-	-	-	-	-	SH	-	-	-	-	-	-	-	-	-	-	-	-	-	-	-	-	-	-	C	C	C	-	-	-	-	4	1	3
J Voss	-	-	-	-	-	-	-	-	-	W	-	<W	-	-	-	-	-	-	-	-	-	-	-	-	-	-	-	-	-	-	-	-	-	2	-	-
JR (Jamie) Watson	FH	FH	FH	FH	FH	FH	C	FH	FH	FH	FH	FH	W	C	C	FH	FH	FH	FH	FH	FH	FH	FH	FH	FH	FH	-	FH	-	FH	-	-	-	28	4	12
TA (Tom) Weston	-	-	-	-	-	-	-	-	-	-	-	-	-	-	-	-	-	-	-	-	-	-	-	-	-	-	=F	-	-	-	-	-	-	1	-	-
TW (Thomas) Wilson	-	-	-	-	-	-	-	-	-	-	-	-	-	-	-	-	-	-	-	-	-	-	-	-	-	-	-	-	-	-	>FH	FH	FH	3	1	3
KB (Kenneth) Wood GB+	-	-	-	-	>C	C	C	C	C	C	C	C	C	C	C	C	C	C	C	C	C	C	C	C	C	C	C	C	C	C	C	C	C	29	9	27
GW (Pedlar) Wood E+	-	-	-	-	-	-	-	-	>SH	SH	SH	SH	SH	FH	FH	SH	SH	SH	SH	SH	SH	SH	SH	SH	SH	SH	SH	-	SH	SH	-	-	-	21	4	18

The key for how to read the stats is on the last page

1907/08	
Home Ground: Welford Road	
Captain: Richard Russell	
Vice-captain: Sammy Matthews	

OVERALL RECORD:					T	C	PG	DG	MK	PTS
PLD	W	D	L	Tigers scored:	87	32	4	3	0	349
36	18	4	14	Opponents scored:	56	26	6	5	0	258

GM	DATE		VEN	OPPONENTS	RESULT	TRIES	KICKS	ATT
CLUB MATCHES								
1	Sep	**14**	**H**	**Hartlepool Rovers**	W 19-5	Tarr(2), Hobbs, Wilson	Jackson 2c/p	-
2		**21**	**H**	**West Hartlepool**	W 48-5	Jackson(3), Watson(3), K.Wood(2), P.Wood, Faussett, Gimson, Russell	Jackson 2c, P.Wood 2c, J.Jackett d	7000
3		**28**	**H**	**Plymouth**	L 0-3	-	-	-
4	Oct	**5**	**H**	**Manchester**	W 32-6	Gimson(2), Jackson, A.Goodrich, Hobbs, Taylor, Watson, K.Wood	Jackson 2c, Russell 2c	-
5		**12**	**H**	**Bristol**	W 11-10	Jackson, P.Wood	Jackson c, Russell p	-
6		**19**	**H**	**Moseley**	W 17-0	Jackson, Hobbs, Russell, Watson, K.Wood	Jackson c	-
7		26	a	Richmond	L 6-10	A.Goodrich	J.Jackett p	-
8	Nov	**2**	**H**	**Oxford University**	L 6-27	Mann, Watson	-	-
9		**9**	**H**	**Swansea**	L 0-5	-	-	-
10		16	a	Devonport Albion	L 0-5	-	-	4000
11		18m	a	Plymouth	L 0-12	-	-	3500
12		**23**	**H**	**Llanelly**	D 5-5	K.Wood	Jackson c	-
13		**30**	**H**	**Penarth**	D 3-3	Penny	-	-
14	Dec	7	a	London Scottish	L 0-39	-	-	-
15		14	a	Gloucester	L 6-8	P.Wood(2)	-	-
16		**21**	**H**	**Coventry**	W 6-0	P.Lawrie, P.Wood	-	8000
17		**26th**	**H**	**Fettes-Lorettonians**	W 21-8	Hobbs(2), Gimson, H.Lawrie, Watson	Jackson 3c	-
18		**27f**	**H**	**Bective Rangers**	W 9-0	T.Hall, Penny, P.Wood	-	-
19		**28**	**H**	**Birkenhead Park**	W 11-5	Jackson(3)	Gimson c	-
20	Jan	1w	a	West Hartlepool	W 14-7	Dyke(2), Goodman, J.Jackett	Jackson c	-
21		2th	a	Hartlepool Rovers	L 3-4	Dyke	-	-
		4	a	Harlequins	PP			
		11	**H**	**Cardiff**	PP (snow)			
22		**18**	**H**	**Bedford**	W 40-0	Jackson(3), Watson(2), Hobbs, J.Jackett, P.Lawrie, D.Smith, P.Wood	Jackson 2c, Watson c, K.Wood d	-
23		25	a	Moseley	L 0-3	-	-	-
24	Feb	**1**	**H**	**Northampton**	W 13-3	Hobbs, P.Lawrie, D.Smith	Jackson 2c	-
25		**8**	**H**	**Gloucester**	W 11-0	D.Smith(2), Jackson	Jackson c	-
26		15	a	Swansea	L 0-11	-	-	-
27		**22**	**H**	**Newport**	D 5-5	Jackson	Jackson c	-
28		29	a	Coventry	W 5-3	Hobbs	Jackson c	6000
29	Mar	**7**	**H**	**Devonport Albion**	W 16-0	Edwards, D.Smith, P.Wood	Jackson 2c/p	-
30		14	a	Birkenhead Park	W 13-4	Edwards(2), K.Wood	Jackson 2c	-
31		**21**	**H**	**London Welsh**	W 8-5	Kirk, D.Smith	Jackson c	-
32		28	a	Northampton	L 3-11	Edwards	-	8000
	Apr	4	a	Headingley	PP			
33		11	a	Newport	L 4-22	-	K.Wood d	7000
34		18	a	Llanelly	D 0-0	-	-	-
35		20m	a	Cardiff	L 11-24	Kirk, P.Lawrie, Mills	Gimson c	-
36		21tu	a	Bristol	W 3-0	Kirk	-	-

INDIVIDUAL APPEARANCES 1907/08

Name / Game #	1	2	3	4	5	6	7	8	9	10	11	12	13	14	15	16	17	18	19	20	21	22	23	24	25	26	27	28	29	30	31	32	33	34	35	36	Apps	T	Pts
DB (Dudley) Atkins	F	-	-	-	-	-	F	F	F	F	F	-	-	F	F	F	F	F	-	-	-	-	-	-	-	-	-	F	F	F	F	F	-	-	-	-	16	-	-
WH (William) Bingham	-	-	-	-	-	-	-	-	-	-	-	-	-	-	-	-	-	-	-	-	-	-	-	-	>F	F	F	-	-	-	F	-	F	-	-	-	5	-	-
C (Charles) Birch	-	-	-	-	-	-	-	-	-	-	-	-	-	-	-	-	-	-	-	-	-	-	-	-	-	-	-	-	-	-	-	-	>FB	FB	-	-	2	-	-
C (Charles) Bourns	-	-	-	F	F	<F	-	-	-	-	-	-	-	-	-	-	-	-	-	-	-	-	-	-	-	-	-	-	-	-	-	-	-	-	-	-	3	-	-
S Brittain	-	-	-	-	-	-	-	-	-	-	-	-	-	-	-	-	-	-	-	-	-	-	-	-	-	-	-	-	-	-	-	-	-	-	>F	<F	2	-	-
D Campbell	-	-	-	-	-	-	-	-	-	-	-	-	-	-	-	-	-	-	-	-	-	-	-	-	-	-	-	-	-	-	-	-	>W	F	-	<F	3	-	-
J (Maffer) Davey E1 AW+	-	-	-	-	-	-	-	-	-	-	-	-	-	-	-	-	-	-	-	>FH	<FH	-	-	-	-	-	-	-	-	-	-	-	-	-	-	-	2	-	-
JCM (John) Dyke W1	-	-	-	-	-	-	-	-	-	-	-	-	-	-	-	-	-	-	-	>W	<W	-	-	-	-	-	-	-	-	-	-	-	-	-	-	-	2	3	9
R Eathorne	-	-	-	-	-	-	-	-	-	-	-	-	-	-	-	-	-	-	-	>FB	FB	-	-	-	-	FB	FB	FB	-	-	-	<FB	-	-	-	-	6	-	-
TL Edwards	-	-	-	-	-	-	-	-	>W	-	-	W	W	W	-	-	-	-	W	-	-	-	-	-	W	W	W	W	W	W	-	<W	-	-	-	-	12	4	12
DE (Dan) Ellwood	-	-	-	-	-	-	-	-	-	-	-	-	-	-	-	-	-	-	-	-	-	-	-	-	-	-	-	-	-	-	-	-	-	-	>FB	FB	2	-	-
2Lt CR (Charles) Fausset	-	>W	W	<W	-	-	-	-	-	-	-	-	-	-	-	-	-	-	-	-	-	-	-	-	-	-	-	-	-	-	-	-	-	-	-	-	3	1	3
JW (John) Freer	-	-	-	-	-	-	-	-	-	-	-	>F	F	-	F	-	-	-	-	-	-	-	-	-	-	-	-	-	-	-	-	-	<F	-	-	-	4	-	-
C (Christopher) Gimson	-	F	F	F	F	-	-	-	-	-	-	-	-	-	-	F	F	F	F	F	F	-	-	-	-	-	-	-	-	-	-	F	F	F	F	F	15	4	16
EW (Ernest) Goodall	-	-	-	-	-	>FH	-	<FH	-	-	-	-	-	-	-	-	-	-	-	-	-	-	-	-	-	-	-	-	-	-	-	-	-	-	-	-	2	-	-
EL (Ernest) Goodman	-	-	-	-	-	-	-	-	-	-	-	-	-	-	-	-	-	-	-	>C	C	-	-	-	-	-	-	-	-	-	-	-	-	C	-	-	3	1	3
A (Alf) Goodrich	F	F	F	F	F	F	F	F	-	-	-	F	-	-	-	-	-	-	-	-	-	F	-	F	F	F	F	F	F	F	F	F	-	F	-	F	21	2	6
WJ (Worthy) Gulliver	-	-	-	-	>W	W	W	-	-	-	-	-	W	<W	-	-	-	-	-	-	-	-	-	-	-	-	-	-	-	-	-	-	-	-	-	-	5	-	-
T Hall	-	-	-	-	-	-	-	-	-	-	-	-	-	-	-	-	-	W	W	-	-	W	<W	-	-	-	-	-	-	-	-	-	-	-	-	-	4	1	3
W Hall	>F	F	F	F	F	F	F	F	F	F	F	F	-	F	-	-	-	F	-	F	F	-	F	-	-	-	-	-	-	-	-	-	F	-	-	-	18	-	-
AJ (Arthur) Hobbs	F	F	F	F	F	F	-	F	F	F	F	F	F	-	F	-	F	-	F	F	F	F	F	F	F	F	-	F	F	F	-	F	F	F	F	F	30	8	24
TB (Thomas) Hogarth E1	-	-	-	-	-	-	-	-	-	-	-	-	-	-	-	-	-	-	-	-	-	-	-	-	-	F	-	-	-	-	-	-	-	F	F	F	4	-	-
J Hubbard	-	-	-	-	-	-	-	-	-	-	-	-	>F	F	-	-	-	-	-	-	-	F	F	F	-	-	F	-	F	-	-	-	-	-	-	-	7	-	-
R (Dick) Jackett	-	-	-	-	-	-	-	-	-	F	F	-	-	-	-	-	F	F	F	F	F	-	-	-	-	F	-	-	-	-	-	-	-	-	-	-	8	-	-
EJ (John) Jackett E9 AW+	-	FB	FB	FB	FB	W	C	-	FB	FB	FB	FB	FB	-	FB	FB	FB	FB	FB	W	W	FB	-	FB	FB	C	C	C	FB	FB	FB	-	-	-	-	-	27	2	13
FS (Fred) Jackson AW+	F	F	F	F	F	F	F	F	F	F	F	F	F	-	F	F	F	F	F	F	F	F	-	F	F	-	F	F	F	F	<F	-	-	-	-	-	28	14	98
AL (Alf) Kewney E4	-	-	-	-	-	-	-	-	-	-	-	-	-	-	-	-	-	-	-	-	-	-	-	-	-	-	-	-	-	-	-	-	-	F	F	F	3	-	-
L (Lionel) Kirk	-	-	-	-	-	-	-	-	-	-	-	-	-	-	-	-	-	-	-	-	-	-	-	-	-	-	-	-	-	-	SH	W	-	SH	SH	W	5	3	9
HSB (Harry) Lawrie	-	-	-	-	-	-	-	-	-	-	-	-	-	-	-	-	W	W	-	-	-	-	-	-	-	-	-	-	-	-	-	-	-	-	-	-	2	1	3
PW (Percy) Lawrie E+	-	-	-	-	-	-	-	-	-	>C	C	C	C	C	W	W	-	-	-	-	-	W	W	C	W	W	W	W	W	-	-	-	W	W	W	W	19	4	12
MM (Maurice) Mann	-	-	-	-	-	-	-	>W	W	W	W	W	-	-	W	W	W	-	-	-	-	-	C	-	-	-	-	-	-	-	-	-	-	-	-	-	9	1	3
S (Sammy) Matthews	-	-	-	-	-	-	F*	F	F	F	F*	F	F	F*	F*	F*	F*	F*	-	F*	F*	F*	F*	F*	F*	F*	F*	F*	F*	F*	F*	F*	F*	F*	<F*	-	28	-	-
A Mills	-	-	-	-	-	>F	-	-	-	-	-	-	-	-	F	F	-	F	F	-	-	F	F	F	F	-	F	F	F	F	F	-	-	-	F	-	15	1	3
SH (Sid) Penny E+	F	F	F	F	F	F	F	F	F	F	F	F	F	F	F	F	F	F	F	F	F	F	F	F	F	F	F	F	-	F	F	F	F	F	F	F	35	2	6
RF (Richard) Russell E1	F*	F*	F*	F*	F*	F*	-	F*	F*	W*	-	F*	F*	-	-	-	-	-	-	-	-	-	-	-	-	-	-	-	-	-	-	-	-	-	-	-	11	2	13
Cpt. JWD (Dixie) Smith	-	-	-	-	-	FB	FB	FB	C	FH	FH	FH	C	FB	C	C	C	C	C	-	-	C	FB	C	C	C	C	C	C	C	W	-	C	W	W	-	27	6	18
TW (Tom) Smith AW+	F	F	F	W	-	-	-	-	-	-	-	-	F	F	F	F	F	-	F	F	F	F	F	F	F	F	F	F	F	F	F	<F	-	-	-	-	23	-	-
Lt. FN (Frank) Tarr E+	W	W	W	-	-	-	-	-	-	-	-	-	-	-	-	-	-	-	-	C	C	-	-	-	-	-	-	-	-	-	C	C	-	-	-	-	7	2	6
FM (Tim) Taylor E+	-	-	-	>FH	FH	-	-	-	-	-	-	-	-	-	-	-	-	-	-	-	-	-	-	-	-	-	-	-	-	-	-	-	-	-	-	-	2	1	3
J Thompson	-	-	-	-	-	-	-	-	-	-	-	-	-	-	-	-	-	-	-	-	-	-	-	-	-	-	-	-	-	-	-	-	-	-	>FH	<FH	2	-	-
CR (Charles) Watchorn	-	-	-	-	-	-	-	-	-	-	-	-	-	F	-	F	-	-	F	-	-	-	-	-	-	-	-	-	-	W	-	F	-	-	-	-	5	-	-
JR (Jamie) Watson	C	C	C	C	C	C	W	C	FH	-	-	-	FH	FH	FH	FH	FH	FH	FH*	-	-	FH	FH	FH	FH	FH	FH	FH	FH	FH	W	FH	FH	-	C	C*	30	9	29
TW (Thomas) Wilson	FH	<FH	-	-	-	-	-	-	-	-	-	-	-	-	-	-	-	-	-	-	-	-	-	-	-	-	-	-	-	-	-	-	-	-	-	-	2	1	3
KB (Kenneth) Wood GB+	C	C	C	C	C	C	C	C	C	C	C	C	-	C	C	C	C	C	C	-	-	C	C	W	C	-	-	-	C	C	C	C	C	C	C	C	30	6	26
GW (Pedlar) Wood E+	SH	SH	SH	SH	SH	SH	SH	SH	SH	SH	SH	SH	SH	SH	SH	SH	SH	SH	SH	SH	SH	SH	SH	SH	SH	SH	SH	SH	SH	SH	FH	SH	SH	FH	-	SH	35	8	28
L Wright	-	-	-	-	-	-	>F	-	F	-	-	-	-	-	-	-	-	-	-	-	-	-	<F	-	-	-	-	-	-	-	-	-	-	-	-	-	3	-	-

1 GAME: A (Arthur) Armstrong =F(14), BB (Barrie) Bennetts E+ >W(11), G (George) Bond =FH(7), Rev. RJP (Jackson) Burbery =W(5), W Dale <FB(1), DD (Denys) Dobson E6 GB4 =F(11), TW (Tom) Goodrich F(10), R (Richard) Hives <W(1), W Lawrence =W(24), D Lewis =W(8), G (George) Middleton >F(33), Timson =F(7), H Wale =FH(3)

The key for how to read the stats is on the last page

CHAPTER 7

Club in the Dock

1908/1909

Celebrations in the Midlands were muted at the selection of John Jackett, Fred Jackson and Tom Smith to tour down under. Leicester may have been pleased enough at such signal recognition of their status as, arguably, the pre-eminent club in England (thanks largely to their run of success in the Midlands Cup) though Harlequins, among others, would have contested such a claim.

But some perceived their methods as belonging outside the amateur ethos and their old rivals from Moseley were scratching away at that particular itch. It was, after all, only 13 years since the great schism and the formation of the Northern Union; the guardians of amateurism on the RFU, notably the president, Arnold Crane, who himself represented the Midlands, were eager for their game to appear whiter than white.

A fascinating book was published in 2012, written by Tom Mather and entitled *Rugby's Greatest Mystery - who really was F S Jackson?* Not the catchiest title, perhaps, but as a work of research, Mather has proved a human bloodhound. Much of what he writes has to be conjecture because, at this remove, many of the trails have gone cold but there is reason for the suppositions he does make and, if he is correct, Tom Crumbie does not emerge too well from the whole episode when Leicester were charged with professionalism.

Crumbie's ambition for Leicester was transparent, his enthusiasm for attracting the best players in England to Welford Road obvious. The question is: how did he set about attracting such players? Location was one advantage, Leicester being so central to the whole country and with longstanding links to northern clubs, even if those links had been fractured by the Northern Union's breakaway to play rugby league. Then there was the ground, capable of staging international rugby at a time when Twickenham had yet to be built.

As we have seen, there is no doubt that the players were well looked after and, if one notable player suddenly became available, he would be hoicked into the team at the expense of someone else. Jackett, an outstanding full-back from Cornwall who won 13 caps for England between 1905-09, made his Leicester debut in 1904; Jackson, a forward who was also apparently from Cornwall, first appeared a year later in the XV that played New Zealand; Smith, another forward, was born in Rearsby and was a thorough-going local boy whose debut came in 1906.

Both Jackett and Smith eventually signed for rugby league clubs but Jackson would appear to have played rugby league already for Swinton, albeit under another name, before joining Leicester. He seems a chameleon-like character, and Mather's research confirms reports that he played in Wales under the name of Ivor Gabe. But whatever alias he adopted, one thing was clear: he was a fine player, a strong, try-scoring forward and a good goalkicker.

Having spent time in South Africa during the Boer War, he returned to play his rugby in Wales and is then traced to Swinton, now a Northern Union club, under the name of John Jones. In 1902 he appears playing for Camborne (as Jackson), was linked with Plymouth and made a guest appearance for London Welsh. Leicester recognised his quality when playing for Cornwall and, though he intimated he would spend time in Leicester on business, it is difficult to conceive the club not assisting him with, shall we say, generous travel expenses.

How much he told Crumbie of his playing career is impossible to know but Jackson seems an intensely secretive man with a notable ability to cover his tracks. He was seldom photographed though he sits in the captain's place in Leicester's 1906/07 team picture. It may be that Crumbie chose not to ask, for the sake of including such a distinguished player in Leicester ranks. The long and the short of it is that, if he had played rugby league, he was ineligible to play for a union club and risked professionalising those who associated with him.

Matters came to a head in 1908. There had already been accusations of veiled professionalism made against Leicester, alleging that the club enticed players away from other clubs; a RFU sub-committee on professionalism investigated the club's books and, specifically, Jackson's background and came to no adverse conclusion. But while Jackson and the Anglo-Welsh party set sail for New Zealand, the RFU's annual meeting agenda included a complaint from Moseley expressing its belief that veiled professionalism existed within the union game.

Moreover their representative at the annual meeting, Mr Godfrey, speaking on behalf of his unwell colleague, Mr Byrne, gave plenty of examples justifying the Moseley motion. Percy Adams, from Old Edwardians, seconded the motion and though Crumbie was able to speak in defence of Leicester, when it came to a vote plenty of mud stuck, some of

↑ Tom Smith's cap from the Anglo-Welsh tour to New Zealand in 1908.

↓ The club's first 'Lions', Tom Smith, Fred Jackson and John Jackett, set sail for New Zealand.

it to Sammy Matthews, Leicester's captain between 1904-06 and again 1907-08, who had signed professional forms for Hull in 1899 but had received no money and had never played for the northern club; he had broken none of the regulations as they then existed.

The clincher was an affidavit from Swinton saying they were convinced that the Jackson who had played for Cornwall was the same man who had played for them as Jones in 1901. The motion was defeated, but only by ten votes and, with the story now in the public domain, the RFU decided Jackson should be suspended from playing until he could answer the charges. That decision was communicated to the Anglo-Welsh party, for whom Jackson had just made his international debut in the first of three games against New Zealand, a 32-5 defeat in Dunedin.

↑ Sammy Matthews retired from playing in 1908 after a glorious 10-year career for the Tigers during which he crammed in 340 games.

Rather than playing in the second international, Jackson left the party and sailed for Australia. He never returned to England but did return to New Zealand where he raised a family, one of whom, Everard Jackson, played for New Zealand just before the Second World War. But Leicester had still to cope with the fall-out of the RFU meeting since Jackson, Smith (who was approached by Northern Union representatives in Queenstown) and Matthews were all alleged to have either signed for, or received money from, a Northern Union club; it was also claimed that Jackson, Jackett, Alf Kewney and Tom Hogarth had joined Leicester in violation of the regulations relating to professionalism.

At an RFU meeting on 5 October 1908, Jackson, Smith, Matthews and Fred Hardyman, a wing, were declared professionals and an inquiry was ordered into Leicester's affairs. T C Pring, A Hartley and F Hugh Fox, all of whom had either been or would become president of the RFU, were appointed to conduct the inquiry and, when required to give evidence, it was Leicester's contention that all four players had been in touch with Northern Union clubs without telling anyone at Leicester (save Matthews, of whom Crumbie had already said that his offence had occurred years before and was not contrary to the rules).

↓ Itinerary for the 1909 Easter Tour.

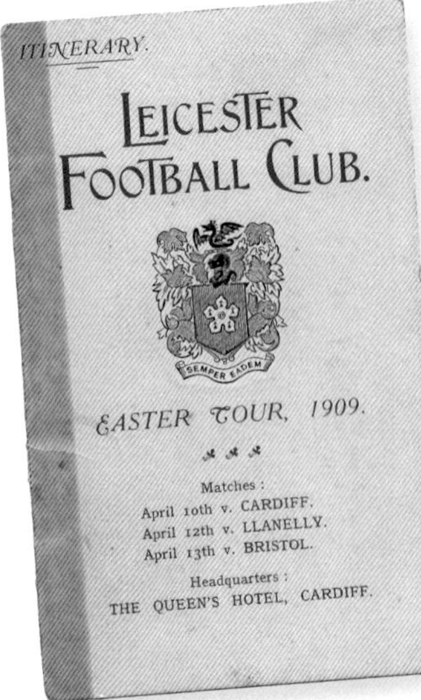

ITINERARY.

LEICESTER FOOTBALL CLUB.

EASTER TOUR, 1909.

Matches :
April 10th v. CARDIFF.
April 12th v. LLANELLY.
April 13th v. BRISTOL.

Headquarters :
THE QUEEN'S HOTEL, CARDIFF.

At a distance it sounds, at best, incredibly naive. But Mather's contention in his book is that the RFU simply could not afford to lose Leicester to the Northern Union, which could have resulted had the RFU expelled the club. Leicester formed, as it were, a bulwark on the eastern side of the country against the possible depredations of the professional game and when the inquiry reached its climax, at Leicester's Grand Hotel on 14-15 January 1909, the RFU cleared Leicester of any wrongdoing in what would nowadays be described as a total whitewash.

"With regard to the first charge [against Smith, Matthews and Jackson], your committee could obtain no evidence of this [professionalism] and consequently dismissed the charge," the RFU statement said a fortnight later. "With regard to the second charge [against Kewney and the other three players], after hearing the evidence of Kewney, Hogarth, Jackett and others, your committee was quite satisfied that there had been no breach of the professional laws. They were much struck with the way evidence was given, especially that by Kewney and Hogarth whose sincerity it was impossible to doubt and whose presence in the ranks of the Leicester club was quite satisfactorily accounted for.

"Various doubtful items on the accounts, especially relating to travelling expenses, were satisfactorily explained and your committee endorses the findings of the previous committee on this head.

"Your committee is strongly of the opinion that the allegations against the Leicester club are largely due to the fact that the club, having a strong team with a good match list, attracts players who are unable to get such good football in other localities but that, however undesirable this may be, the players have not benefitted pecuniarily thereby."

Arnold Crane had already resigned as RFU president, unhappy with the turn of events, and the statement was a slap in the face for, specifically, Moseley and any club who considered their players to have been poached by Leicester. The other side of the coin was that Leicester were vindicated and Crumbie's approach justified; he must have been a happy (and relieved) man as he sat in the Welford Road stand that same afternoon and watched an England team including three of his players (Jackett, Kewney and Frank Tarr) beat France 22-0.

On the playing front, the season as a whole went well despite defeats against Welsh opposition and to local rivals Northampton and Coventry. Gil Hopkins, a young prop who had joined in 1908, had taken the opportunity created by the absence of the banned players and at much the same time a player who would become his brother-in-law was making a name for himself. Percy Lawrie, a wing from Wyggeston School and the local Stoneygate club, was to win two England caps and become one of Leicester's most enduring players.

"Percy was one of the finest wingers I've ever seen," Hopkins said seventy years later, comparing Lawrie with Bryan Williams, the outstanding New Zealand wing of the 1970s who later coached Samoa and became president of the NZRFU. "Percy was almost the spitting image of Williams, build and everything. Frank Tarr was a lovely player and as for the forwards, well, it will give you an idea what they were like when you think that, in 1913, when the Midland Counties won the championship, there were ten Leicester players in the side and five of the club's forwards went for an England trial."

It says something about the whole confused circumstances of the rival rugby codes that, at the end of the season, a dozen members of the touring Australian side were banned from union for having appeared for the rival-code Kangaroos, who were touring the Northern Union clubs at the same time. It was at precisely this time that rugby league was growing rapidly in Australia and claiming a grip on the population that union has never been able to loosen.

When the Wallabies came to Welford Road, they were beaten 16-5 by a Midlands team including Kenneth Wood, the Leicester centre who came close to England honours and scored the game's first try. With him were Sid Penny and Arthur Hobbs, a forward who Northampton alleged was poached from them by Leicester; it was against Australia that the faithful Penny won his only cap in

Action from the 8-all draw in Cardiff on 10 April 1909 (Tigers in white)

1909. As if to refute the notion that Leicester teams consisted entirely of imported talent, there were 12 local players in the XV that beat Coventry in the Midlands Cup final, the club having re-entered the competition after a four-year absence. The outsiders were Jackett, Hobbs and Hogarth, who had travelled down from Hartlepool at the start of the season to play for Leicester.

1909/1910

As if putting to bed the row over professionalism, George Rowland Hill, one of the most distinguished holders of the RFU presidency, performed the opening ceremony on 4 September 1909 for Leicester's new clubhouse. The club had decided, the previous April, to spend £1,150 on a new building and the work was completed in the summer, prior to the first game of the new season against Stratford. It gave Leicester their own changing rooms, committee room and a gymnasium, allowing them to move from the Bedford Hotel across the Aylestone Road where they had been accustomed to preparing for games. At the same time they reverted to the scarlet, green and white colours they had worn before and which would now become their standard strip.

Hopkins, in a far-reaching interview in 1979, painted in vivid colours how rugby was in those pre-First World War days and the larks - some might describe them as vandalism - so commonplace in the amateur game throughout the twentieth century: "Tim Taylor and Pedlar Wood, I reckon, were the best pair of halves in the country...and, compared with some of today's teams, our three-quarters seemed to go more smoothly. There's too much kicking today. When I was playing the club always played 15-man rugby although I still remember one game down at Swansea when Wood, who had an enormous swing, went to pass the ball one way, the whole of the Swansea back division went the same way and he went round the other side and scored under the posts. I've never seen a lot of fellows look so silly.

"He was a crafty devil. But then, in my day, there was none of this tapping at a lineout, you had to catch the ball and there was old Pedlar waiting for it. And we had a lot of fun among ourselves, on the train when we went on tour. One time when we were in Swansea - you know how popular lava bread is down there - well, we got some of this black stuff and put it in some of the beds.

Original sketch of the clubhouse when opened in 1909.

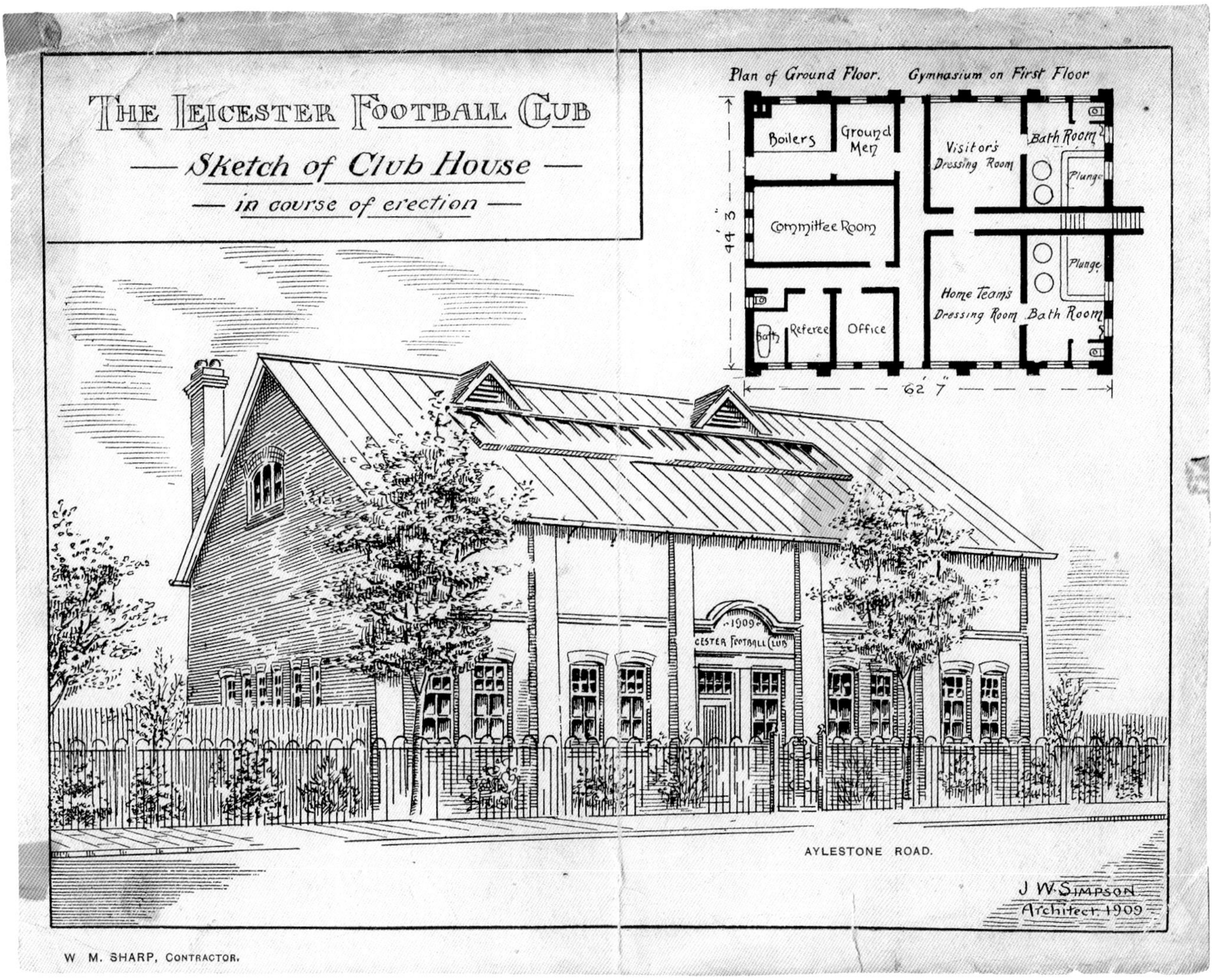

"There was one hotel in Plymouth where we were barred. It had one of these open staircases and Coventry had been there before us, chucking a lot of bedding down the stairs, so we had to go to the Albion instead. It was in the West Country and Wales that we had our hardest games - we always used to get the ball when we played London sides. Once [in March 1912] against the Harlequins we were getting loads of ball and the referee, from London, kept penalising us so Adrian Stoop, the Harlequins captain, went up to his player who was taking the free kicks and told him to put it directly into touch, not to gain any advantage.

"At half-time, Stoop went across to Mr Crumbie who was standing on the touchline and told him that if he wanted to take the whistle, there would be no objection from Harlequins. Stoop, of course, was an exceptionally fine player and a gentleman. I think it was this same match that the referee sent off Harry Lawrie [Percy's brother, who played in the pack] and no-one knew what it was for so Stoop sent off one of his own men, J V Rees, to level things up [moreover Stoop afterwards explained to the press exactly what had occurred and why].

"In Wales we expected the referees to be against us. At Neath we slammed in a couple of tries in a very few minutes and the crowd came storming on to the ground, shaking their fists at the referee and, of course, he was intimidated. We seldom came away from Wales with the spoils, though we drew with Cardiff on two occasions.

"In my time Leicester was a fairly local side. We trained Tuesdays and Thursdays, and during the four years before the war we were about the best English side, without a doubt. When we played Moseley it was a certain win, and it was much the same against Coventry and Northampton. We won three of the five games I played against the Barbarians, one was drawn and we lost the other by a conversion. I always admired the Baa-baas' style of play because they played the open game but it is team spirit that wins matches and that's what we had.

"There was very little dirty play and I remember Tom Crumbie saying once to Sid Penny after he'd seen him hit someone on the field: 'As many games as you've played for Leicester, if you do that again you'll never play another one.' We played clean football. If you play dirty football, you're not playing football at all. There was a marvellous atmosphere at the club.

"There was one occasion when we'd lost unexpectedly to Headingley and the next time we played them, we were determined to win. On the train north I was talking to Pedlar Wood and I said we should throw the ball around. We won that game 32-6. I've seen so many international games when the players kicked so much you couldn't have called it a handling code."

Hopkins was only 20 when he played in that first match in what would become an annual fixture with the Barbarians, the invitation side founded in 1890, until the encounter lapsed after the coming of the professional era in 1995. It became the highlight of the Christmas holiday period, if not the entire season so strong were the sides brought by the Barbarians who, not infrequently, fielded players chasing an international place and who needed an extra trial, in the view of the national selectors.

↑ Honorary secretary Tom Crumbie also ran the line for many years.

↓ Pedlar Wood's 15 tries in season 1910/11 included his 50th during his Tigers' career, against Plymouth on 6.3.1911.

The starting point was the withdrawal in 1908 of the Scottish side, Fettes-Lorettonians, from what had been a regular Christmas meeting. The Baa-baas were asked to come instead to be part of the Welford Road holiday festival which included games against Cinderford, Birkenhead Park and Penarth - four games in six days. The two sides produced a 9-9 draw, two late tries by Pedlar Wood and George Greasley going with an earlier effort by Jimmy Burdett, and a wonderful series was born.

The match was refereed by AO Jones, with no complaints to be heard about the ref being a 'homer', and both sides overcame poor conditions well. The Barbarians were led by Lieutenant Walter Caradini Wilson, an ex-Richmond player and at that time an officer in the Leicestershire Regiment though he had also played for Leicester against Northampton the previous April. Wilson, capped twice by England in 1907, joined the Baa-baas committee in 1909 and, two days after the inaugural game, played for Leicester against Headingley and scored a try. Leicester's XV against the Barbarians was: Dan Ellwood; Jack Dickens, Kenneth Wood, Dixie Smith, John Jackett; Jamie Watson (captain), Pedlar Wood; Tom Hogarth, Jimmy Burdett, Sid Penny, George Greasley, Gil Hopkins, Jimmy Allen, Christopher Gimson, Wilfred Ellis.

Three months later, Percy Lawrie won the first of his two England caps in a 14-5 win over Scotland at Inverleith. He was selected only once more, a year later, and again against the Scots but at Twickenham where he scored one of England's three tries in a 13-8 win. In between those two matches, Kenneth Wood toured South Africa with the British team led by Tom Smyth; he played in the first and third internationals against the Springboks so joins the ranks of those capped by the Lions but never by their home country. Indeed, Wood liked South Africa so much that he later emigrated but not before he had made his 121st appearance for Leicester in 1919.

1910/1911

The second encounter with the Barbarians, in 1910, went rather better with a 29-3 win, helping Leicester to an aggregate of 106 points against 16 in their four Christmas games. Those included the 25-5 win over Birkenhead Park at the end of which Sid Penny was chaired off, in the belief that it was his 500th appearance though subsequent research has brought him up short of that mark.

Two days after the Christmas programme they toured in the north and played Headingley, Hartlepool Rovers and Manchester, a grand total of seven matches in ten days. Pedlar Wood ended the 1910/11 season with 15 tries, the same as his tally for the previous season, but the Midland Cup campaign ended with defeat by Coventry in the fourth round.

1911/1912

The following season, though, the cup returned to Welford Road when Leicester beat Coventry 16-0. As noteworthy as that result was, Newbold-on-Avon were beaten 65-0 in the semi-final, a scoreline made up entirely of tries and conversions; four of the 17 tries went to Percy Lawrie and three each to Tim Taylor, James Hargrave and Harry Lawrie.

↓ Illustrated scroll awarded to Joseph Collier in 1912 in recognition of his 32 years of continuous service to the club.

1912/1913

The winning form was carried over into the 1912/13 season which began with eight wins (seven at home), the scalps including Bridgend, Neath, Aberavon, Newport and Llanelly, though another Welsh club, Swansea, brought the unbeaten run to an end. Another touring side from the southern hemisphere was on the horizon too: Billy Millar's second South Africans played a Midland Counties XV at Welford Road on 9 November with 11 Tigers appearing on their home ground - Percy and Harry Lawrie, Frank Tarr, Samuel Hunter, Pedlar Wood, Tim Taylor, Jimmy Allen, Gil Hopkins, George Greasley, William Dalby and George Ward.

Dalby scored the solitary try in a 25-3 defeat, the Midlands struggling to match the Springbok forwards. At half-time the crowd was entertained with fireworks and the match was filmed by four "cinematograph" operators (one from the Granby Street picture house). Leicester's unbeaten home record finally fell to Gloucester on 4 January, 1913, in what was the club's sixth game in ten days.

Still, there was little doubt that Leicester's fame was spreading, notably among the fair sex. "There is one most striking characteristic of the Leicester club," a local writer opined without indicating the depths of his, or her, research. "More ladies attend the Leicester matches than is the case in any other centre - either rugby or association - in the kingdom. The presence of the ladies tends to maintain a high tone and not only in the club itself but amongst the spectators generally."

England called on the services of George Ward (three times) and Frank Tarr (once) in what turned out to be a grand-slam season. Indeed Ward, the former Belgrave forward, cried off the trip to Dublin to play Ireland, presumably because of the travel though there was also a suggestion that international rugby did not appeal to him. Whatever the cause, he was back for the clincher against Scotland at Twickenham and won three more caps the following season; he was still playing rugby after the First World War, when he was past forty.

The Midlands Cup also reached a rare conclusion when two teams from the same city contested the final: Belgrave Premier Works had worked wonders to beat Syston Street Old Boys, Rugby and Newbold on their way to the final but it was a step too far and, predictably, they went down to Leicester 39-8, the result constituting Leicester's twelfth win in 16 years.

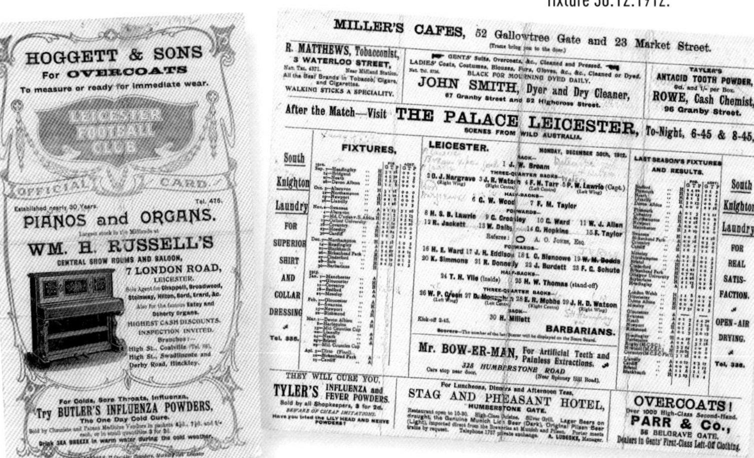
HOGGETT & SONS
For OVERCOATS
To measure or ready for immediate wear.

LEICESTER FOOTBALL CLUB

OFFICIAL CARD.

Established nearly 30 Years. Tel. 476.
PIANOS and ORGANS.
WM. H. RUSSELL'S
CENTRAL SHOW ROOMS AND SALOON,
7 LONDON ROAD, LEICESTER.
Sole Agent for Chappell, Broadwood, Steinway, Hilton, Bord, Erard, &c.
HIGHEST CASH DISCOUNTS. INSPECTION INVITED.
Branches:— High St., Coalville. High St., Swadlincote and Derby Road, Hinckley.

For Colds, Sore Throats, Influenza,
Try BUTLER'S INFLUENZA POWDERS.
The One Day Cold Cure.
Drink SEA BREEZE in warm water during the cold weather.

MILLER'S CAFES, 52 Gallowtree Gate and 23 Market Street.

R. MATTHEWS, Tobacconist, 3 WATERLOO STREET, Near Midland Station. All the Best Brands in Tobacco, Cigars, and Cigarettes. WALKING STICKS A SPECIALITY.

GENTS' Suits, Overcoats, &c., Cleaned and Pressed. LADIES' Coats, Costumes, Blouses, Furs, Gloves, &c., &c., Cleaned or Dyed. BLACK FOR MOURNING DYED DAILY. JOHN SMITH, Dyer and Dry Cleaner, 67 Granby Street and 52 Highcross Street.

TAYLER'S ANTACID TOOTH POWDER, 6d. and 1/- per Box. ROWE, Cash Chemist, 96 Granby Street.

After the Match—Visit THE PALACE LEICESTER, To-Night, 6-45 & 8-45, SCENES FROM WILD AUSTRALIA.

South Knighton Laundry FOR SUPERIOR SHIRT AND COLLAR DRESSING. Tel. 386.

FIXTURES.

LEICESTER. MONDAY, DECEMBER 30th, 1912.
BACK— 1 J. W. Bream
THREE-QUARTER BACKS— 2 G. J. Hargrave (Right Wing) 3 J. R. Watson (Right Centre) 4 F. N. Tarr (Left Centre) 5 P. W. Lawrie (Capt.) (Left Wing)
HALF-BACKS— 6 G. W. Wood 7 F. M. Taylor
FORWARDS— 8 H. S. B. Lawrie 9 G. Greasley 10 G. Ward 11 W. J. Allen 12 R. Jackett 13 W. Dalby 14 G. Hopkins 15 F. Taylor
Referee: A. O. Jones, Esq.
FORWARDS— 16 H. E. Ward 17 J. H. Eddison 18 L. G. Blencowe 19 W. M. Dodds 20 K. Simmons 21 R. Donnelly 22 J. Burdett 23 F. C. Schute
HALF-BACKS— 24 T. H. Vile (inside) 25 H. W. Thomas (stand-off)
THREE-QUARTER BACKS— 26 W. P. Geen (Left Wing) 27 (Left Centre) 28 E. R. Mobbs (Right Centre) 29 J. H. D. Watson (Right Wing)
BACK— 30 H. Millett
Kick-off 2.45. BARBARIANS.

LAST SEASON'S FIXTURES AND RESULTS.

South Knighton Laundry FOR REAL SATIS-FACTION. OPEN-AIR DRYING. Tel. 336.

Mr. BOW-ER-MAN, For Artificial Teeth and Painless Extractions. 328 HUMBERSTONE ROAD (Near Spinney Hill Road). Cars stop near door.

THEY WILL CURE YOU. TYLER'S INFLUENZA and FEVER POWDERS. Sold by all Shopkeepers, 3 for 2d. BEWARE OF CHEAP IMITATIONS. Have you tried the LILY HEAD AND NERVE POWDERS?

For Luncheons, Dinners and Afternoon Teas, STAG AND PHEASANT HOTEL, HUMBERSTONE GATE.

OVERCOATS! Over 1000 High-Class Second-Hand. PARR & Co., 56 BELGRAVE GATE. Dealers in Gents' First-Class Left-Off Clothing.

↓ Programme for the Barbarians fixture 30.12.1912.

1913/1914

The club's high standing was reflected in the number of players required for representative matches in the 1913/14 season which - and this is a familiar lament - had an impact on their playing record. The first visit by Pontypool ensured no long unbeaten run (Leicester lost 8-3) but they only went down 3-0 to Gloucester with ten regulars absent. Seven of those ten played in the England v the Rest trial and Ward, Tim Taylor and Pedlar Wood all appeared against Wales, the only time the two half-backs were capped.

Bad weather forced the postponement of the Barbarians game until February and, when it was played, Leicester went down 5-3. Yet it was almost a moral victory, since they provided the Baa-baas with two late replacements in Harry Lawrie and Steve Farmer, and it was Farmer, formerly of Aylestone St James, who scored the winners' try. It was a surprise when Leicester went out of the Midland Cup, beaten in the second round by Coventry, and the season ended in disgrace when Pedlar Wood was sent off in the final game, a first-time loss to Birkenhead Park; Wood, it was alleged, used "wrong scrum tactics" which might equate to persistent infringement.

During that final, glorious summer before the outbreak of war, the Members' Stand underwent reconstruction (which continued even after war was declared, with the groundsman's services being retained). When it was first built, in 1899, the ground could hold 19,800, of whom 3,000 were seated; it would have been interesting to see how full the ground would have been had plans to bring Toulouse to Welford Road gone ahead but the French club wanted too large a guarantee. Even so, Dublin County were scheduled to play the Tigers in November until the outbreak of war with Germany on 4 August sent sport scurrying to the sidelines.

Leicester's committee met on 31 August to consider whether they could continue the match programme and agreed with the RFU's resolution to proceed as far as was possible while donating 25 per cent of the gross gates to the Prince of Wales War Relief Fund. Three days later, a second committee meeting accepted that all rugby might be discontinued and the secretary was told to offer the clubhouse and ground for whatever use the military authorities might require.

← LEICESTER FOOTBALL CLUB 1908/09
Back: Russell, Burdett, Wilson, K.Wood, H.Lawrie, Goodrich, Middleton, Mills.
Middle: Crumbie (Hon.Sec), T.Hogarth, Hobbs, Penny, Watson (capt), Hopkins, Goodman, Pain (Hon.Tres), Collier (President).
Front: P.Lawrie, J.Jackett, Greasley, P.Wood, Kewney, Ellwood.
Inset: Smith, McIntyre.

← LEICESTER FOOTBALL CLUB 1911/12
Back: Crumbie (Hon.Sec), Hopkins, Hogarth, Ward, Bream, H.Lawrie, Collier (President).
Middle: Pain (Hon.Tres), Dalby, Hobbs, J.Watson, P.Lawrie (capt), Burdett (Vice-capt), Tarr, Allen.
Front: Hunter, S.Taylor, T.Taylor, Wood, J.Hargrave, Greasley.

← LEICESTER FOOTBALL CLUB 1913/14
Back: Crumbie (Hon.Sec), S.Taylor, Burton, E.Wynne, Wilson, H.Lawrie (Vice-capt), Hargrave.
Middle: Pain (Hon.Tres), Allen, Dalby, Hopkins, P.Lawrie (capt), G.Ward, Hunter, Salmon (President).
Front: Bream, Farmer, Wood, C.Wynne, Mellor, T.Taylor, Tarr.

19	08/09	Home Ground: Welford Road	Trophy Cabinet: Midland Counties Cup(9)	OVERALL RECORD:					T	C	PG	DG	MK	PTS
		Captain: Sammy Matthews		PLD	W	D	L	Tigers scored:	112	45	3	7	3	472
		Vice-captain: Jamie Watson		41	27	1	13	Opponents scored:	55	20	8	7	1	260

GM	DATE		VEN	OPPONENTS	RESULT	TRIES	KICKS	ATT
MIDLAND COUNTIES CUP						**CUP WINNERS: LEICESTER TIGERS**		
34	Mar	**20**	**H**	**Stoneygate (4)**	W 24-3	Watson(3), P.Lawrie(2), Gimson	Gimson c, H.Lawrie 2c	-
35		**27**	**H**	**Stratford-upon-Avon (sf)**	W 17-8	Greasley, Penny, Watson, K.Wood, P.Wood	Gimson c	2000
36	Apr	3		Coventry (f)	W 8-3	P.Lawrie(2)	Gimson c	4000
CLUB MATCHES								
1	Sep	**5**	**H**	**Stratford-upon-Avon**	W 19-3	P.Lawrie(3), Kirk	Kirk c/m, P.Wood c	-
2		**12**	**H**	**Hartlepool Rovers**	W 17-0	Kirk, P.Lawrie, Smith, K.Wood	Kirk c/p	-
3		**19**	**H**	**Neath**	L 5-8	P.Wood	P.Wood c	-
4		**26**	**H**	**Headingley**	W 20-6	P.Lawrie(2), K.Wood, P.Wood	K.Wood d, P.Wood 2c	-
5	Oct	**1th**	**H**	**1st Leicestershire Regiment**	W 38-0	Smith(3), P.Lawrie(2), K.Wood(2), P.Wood, Taylor, Watson	P.Lawrie c, P.Wood 3c	-
6		**3**	**H**	**Devonport Albion**	W 6-3	P.Lawrie, Taylor	-	7000
7		**10**	**H**	**Bristol**	W 13-0	Hobbs, Mills, Smith	Yeld 2c	-
8		14w	a	Birkenhead Park	W 9-6	P.Lawrie(2), K.Wood	-	-
9		17	a	Northampton	L 3-11	P.Lawrie	-	8000
10		**24**	**H**	**Richmond**	W 30-11	Ferguson(2), Hopkins(2), H.Lawrie(2), Hobbs, Watson	Yeld 3c	-
11		**31**	**H**	**Cardiff**	W 7-0	H.Lawrie	J.Jackett d	-
12	Nov	**7**	**H**	**Newport**	W 10-5	Hubbard, P.Lawrie	H.Lawrie d	-
13		14	a	Swansea	L 0-14	-	-	-
14		16m	a	Neath	L 0-13	-	-	-
15		**21**	**H**	**Llanelly**	W 10-3	P.Wood	J.Jackett p/d	-
16		**28**	**H**	**London Scottish**	W 39-4	H.Lawrie(3), Watson(2), P.Wood, Hopkins, P.Lawrie, Smith	H.Lawrie 2c, P.Wood 2c, K.Wood d	-
17	Dec	5	a	Manchester	W 17-12	P.Wood(2), Hobbs, Mann, Roberts	P.Lawrie c	-
18		12	a	Gloucester	L 3-13	P.Wood	-	-
19		19	a	Coventry	L 0-12	-	-	-
20		**26**	**H**	**Birkenhead Park**	W 18-6	P.Lawrie(2), Smith, K.Wood	H.Lawrie 3c	-
21		**28m**	**H**	**Penarth**	W 8-6	Hobbs, P.Lawrie	H.Lawrie c	-
		31th	**H**	**Fettes-Lorettonians**	PP			
22	Jan	1f	a	Headingley	L 0-6	-	-	-
23		2	a	Hartlepool Rovers	L 8-10	P.Lawrie, Smith	J.Jackett c	-
24		9	a	Bedford	W 8-5	Hubbard, Lewis	H.Lawrie c	4000
25		**16**	**H**	**Moseley**	W 25-5	P.Lawrie(2), H.Lawrie, Goodrich, Greasley, Lewis	H.Lawrie 2c/m	5000
26		23	a	Moseley	W 13-6	Flude, Greasley, P.Wood	H.Lawrie 2c	-
27	Feb	4th	a	Richmond	W 13-0	Heard, P.Lawrie, K.Wood	H.Lawrie 2c	-
28		**6**	**H**	**Coventry**	L 0-7	-	-	-
29		**13**	**H**	**Swansea**	W 3-0	P.Wood	-	-
30		20	a	Newport	L 5-9	K.Wood	H.Lawrie c	-
31		**27**	**H**	**Gloucester**	W 23-11	T.Hogarth, Hopkins, McIntyre, Middleton, Penny	J.Jackett 2c, P.Lawrie d	-
32	Mar	6	a	Devonport Albion	L 0-12	-	-	6000
33		**13**	**H**	**Harlequins**	L 13-20	H.Lawrie	H.Lawrie p/m, J.Jackett d	8000
37	Apr	10	a	Cardiff	D 8-8	Gimson, P.Lawrie	Gimson c	10000
38		12m	a	Llanelly	L 3-11	Smith	-	7000
39		13tu	a	Bristol	W 3-0	P.Lawrie	-	-
40		**17**	**H**	**London Welsh**	W 10-0	Greasley, P.Wood	Gimson 2c	-
41		**24**	**H**	**Northampton**	W 16-0	Greasley, Hobbs, P.Lawrie, P.Wood	J.Jackett c, Russell c	-

Neutral Venue: *#36 at Beeston - Nottingham*

INDIVIDUAL APPEARANCES 1908/09

Name / Game #	1	2	3	4	5	6	7	8	9	10	11	12	13	14	15	16	17	18	19	20	21	22	23	24	25	26	27	28	29	30	31	32	33	34	35	36	37	38	39	40	41	Apps	T	Pts
DB (Dudley) Atkins	-	-	-	-	-	-	-	-	-	F	<F	-	-	-	-	-	-	-	-	-	-	-	-	-	-	-	-	-	-	-	-	-	-	-	-	-	-	-	-	-	-	2	-	-
WH (William) Bingham	-	-	F	-	F	-	-	-	-	-	-	-	-	-	-	-	<F	-	-	-	-	-	-	-	-	-	-	-	-	-	-	-	-	-	-	-	-	-	-	-	-	3	-	-
C (Charles) Birch	FB	FB	FB	-	FB	FB	-	-	-	-	-	FB	-	-	-	-	FB	<FB	-	-	-	-	-	-	-	-	-	-	-	-	-	-	-	-	-	-	-	-	-	-	-	8	-	-
EE (Ernest) Booth NZ3	-	-	-	-	-	-	-	-	-	-	-	-	-	-	-	-	-	-	-	-	-	-	-	-	-	-	>C	-	C	-	W	C	<C	-	-	-	-	-	-	-	-	5	-	-
A (Alfred) Brice W18	-	-	-	-	-	-	-	-	-	-	-	-	-	-	-	-	-	-	-	-	-	>FH	<FH	-	-	-	-	-	-	-	-	-	-	-	-	-	-	-	-	-	-	2	-	-
Lt-Col. JC (Jimmy) Burdett	-	-	-	-	-	-	-	-	-	-	-	-	-	-	-	-	-	-	-	-	-	-	-	F	-	-	-	-	-	-	F	F	F	-	-	-	-	F	F	F	F	8	-	-
J (James) Duthie E1	-	-	-	-	-	-	-	-	-	-	-	-	-	-	-	-	-	-	-	-	-	>F	F	-	-	-	-	-	-	-	-	-	-	-	-	-	F	<F	-	-	-	4	-	-
DE (Dan) Ellwood	-	-	-	-	-	-	-	-	-	-	-	-	-	-	-	-	-	-	-	-	-	-	-	-	-	-	-	-	-	-	-	-	-	-	-	-	FB	FB	FB	FB	FB	5	-	-
MW (Matthias) Flude	-	-	-	-	-	-	-	-	-	-	-	-	-	-	-	-	-	-	-	-	-	-	-	-	-	>C	-	-	-	-	-	-	-	-	-	-	-	-	-	W	-	2	1	3
C (Christopher) Gimson	F	-	F	-	-	-	-	-	-	-	-	-	-	-	-	-	-	-	F	F	F	-	-	-	-	-	-	-	F	-	-	-	-	F	F	W	F	F	-	F	-	12	2	18
A (Alf) Goodrich	F	F	F	-	F	F	F	F	F	F	F	F	F	F	F	F	F	-	-	-	-	-	-	-	F	F	F	F	F	F	-	F	F	F	F	F	-	<F	-	-	-	28	1	3
G (George) Greasley	-	F	F	F	F	F	F	-	-	-	-	-	-	-	-	-	F	F	F	F	F	-	F	F	F	F	F	F	F	F	F	F	F	F	F	F	F	-	F	F	F	29	5	15
W Hall	F	-	-	F	<F	-	-	-	-	-	-	-	-	-	-	-	-	-	-	-	-	-	-	-	-	-	-	-	-	-	-	-	-	-	-	-	-	-	-	-	-	3	-	-
AD (Arthur) Heard	-	-	-	-	-	-	-	-	-	-	-	-	-	-	-	-	-	-	-	-	-	-	-	-	-	-	>W	-	-	-	-	-	-	-	-	-	W	W	W	-	-	4	1	3
AJ (Arthur) Hobbs	F	F	F	F	F	F	F	F	F	F	F	F	F	F	F	F	F	F	-	F	F	F	F	F	F	F	-	-	-	-	-	-	-	F	F	F	F	F	F	F	F	33	5	15
A (Anthony) Hogarth	-	-	-	-	-	-	-	-	-	-	-	-	-	-	-	-	-	-	-	-	-	>F	F	-	-	-	-	-	-	-	-	-	-	-	-	-	-	-	-	-	-	2	-	-
TB (Thomas) Hogarth E1	-	F	-	-	-	F	-	F	F	-	-	-	F	F	F	F	-	F	F	F	F	F	F	-	F	F	F	F	F	F	F	-	-	-	F	F	F	F	F	F	F	28	1	3
WG (Gil) Hopkins	>F	F	-	F	-	-	-	-	-	F	F	F	-	-	-	F	F	-	F	-	F	-	-	F	F	F	-	-	F	F	F	F	F	F	F	F	F	-	F	F	F	25	4	12
J Hubbard	-	-	F	F	F	F	F	F	F	F	-	F	F	F	F	F	-	-	-	-	-	-	-	<F	-	-	-	-	-	-	-	-	-	-	-	-	-	-	-	-	-	14	2	6
R (Dick) Jackett	-	-	-	-	-	-	-	-	-	-	-	-	F	F	F	-	-	-	-	-	-	-	-	-	-	-	F	F	-	-	-	-	-	-	-	-	-	-	-	-	-	5	-	-
EJ (John) Jackett E13 AW3	-	-	-	-	-	-	FB	FB	FB	-	FB	-	FB	FB	FB	FB	-	-	FB*	FH*	FB*	C*	W*	-	-	FB	-	FB	-	FB*	FB	FB	FB	-	-	FB	C	-	C	C*	C	24	-	23
AL (Alf) Kewney E9	-	-	-	-	-	F	F	-	F	-	F	-	-	-	F	-	-	F	-	F	-	-	-	-	-	-	-	F	-	-	-	-	-	-	-	-	-	F	F	-	F	11	-	-
L (Lionel) Kirk	W	<FH	-	-	-	-	-	-	-	-	-	-	-	-	-	-	-	-	-	-	-	-	-	-	-	-	-	-	-	-	-	-	-	-	-	-	-	-	-	-	-	2	2	16
WH (William) Kitchen	-	-	-	-	-	-	-	-	-	-	-	-	-	-	-	-	-	-	-	-	-	>FB	FB	FB	FB	-	-	-	-	-	-	-	-	-	FB	-	-	-	-	-	-	5	-	-
HSB (Harry) Lawrie	-	-	-	-	-	-	-	W	W	W	W	W	W	W	W	W	-	FH	-	FB	FH	-	-	C	C	W	FH	W	FB	FH	-	W	C	FB	-	-	-	-	-	-	-	22	8	69
PW (Percy) Lawrie E+	W	W	W	W	W	W	W	W	W	W	W	W	W	W	W	W	W	W	C	W	W	W	W	W	W	-	W	W	W	W	C	W	W	W	-	W	W	W	W	W	W	39	28	92
L-Cpl. JE (Joseph) Lewis	-	-	-	-	-	-	-	-	-	-	-	-	-	-	-	-	-	-	>W	W	-	W	-	W	W	W	-	-	-	-	-	-	-	-	-	-	-	-	-	-	-	6	2	6
Lt. AS (Arthur) McIntyre	-	-	-	-	-	-	-	-	-	-	-	-	-	-	-	-	-	>W	W	-	-	-	-	F	-	-	F	F	F	F	F	F	F	W	W	F	F	-	F	F	-	16	1	3
MM (Maurice) Mann	-	-	-	-	-	-	W	-	-	-	-	-	-	-	-	-	<C	-	-	-	-	-	-	-	-	-	-	-	-	-	-	-	-	-	-	-	-	-	-	-	-	2	1	3
G (George) Middleton	-	-	-	-	-	-	-	-	-	-	-	F	-	F	-	F	F	F	F	-	F	F	F	F	F	-	F	-	F	F	F	F	F	F	-	-	-	-	-	-	-	18	1	3
A Mills	F	F	F	F	-	F	F	-	F	F	F	F	F	-	F	F	F	F	F	F	F	F	F	F	F	F	F	F	-	F	F	F	F	F	F	F	-	-	<F	-	-	33	1	3
HK (Herbert) Pearce	-	-	-	-	-	-	-	-	-	-	-	-	-	-	-	-	-	-	-	-	-	-	-	-	-	-	-	-	-	>W	W	-	-	-	-	-	-	C	-	-	-	3	-	-
SH (Sid) Penny E1	F	F	F	F	F	F	F	F	F	F	F	F	F	F	F	F	-	F	F	F	F	F	F	-	F	F	F	F	F	F	F	F	F	F	F	F	F	-	F	F	F	38	2	6
RF (Richard) Russell E1	-	-	-	-	-	-	-	-	-	-	-	-	-	-	-	-	-	-	-	F	W	-	-	-	-	-	-	-	-	-	-	-	-	-	-	-	-	-	-	-	F	3	-	2
A Simpson	-	-	-	-	-	-	-	-	-	-	-	-	-	-	-	-	>F	<F	-	-	-	-	-	-	-	-	-	-	-	-	-	-	-	-	-	-	-	-	-	-	-	2	-	-
Cpt. JWD (Dixie) Smith	-	W	W	FB	W	C	C	C	C	FB	C	C	C	C	C	C	C	C*	FH	C	C	-	C	C*	C	C	FB*	C	W	C	-	C	W	C	C	C	C	C	C	-	-	36	9	27
FM (Tim) Taylor E+	-	-	FH	FH	FH	W	-	-	-	-	-	-	-	-	-	-	-	-	-	-	-	-	-	-	-	-	-	-	-	-	-	-	-	-	-	-	-	-	-	-	-	4	2	6
CR (Charles) Watchorn	F	F	-	F	F	-	-	F	-	-	-	-	-	-	-	-	-	-	-	-	-	-	-	-	-	-	-	-	-	-	-	-	-	-	-	-	-	-	-	-	-	5	-	-
JR (Jamie) Watson	C*	C*	C*	C*	C*	FH*	FH*	FH*	FH*	FH*	FH*	FH*	FH*	FH*	FH*	FH*	FH*	-	-	-	-	-	-	-	FH*	FH*	-	FH*	FH*	-	FH*	FH*	FH*	FH*	FH*	FH*	FH*	FH*	FH*	-	FH*	31	8	24
KB (Kenneth) Wood GB+	C	C	C	C	C	C	C	C	C	C	C	C	C	C	C	C	-	C	C	C	C	C	C	-	-	-	C	C	C	C	C	-	-	C	C	C	-	-	-	-	-	30	9	35
GW (Pedlar) Wood E+	SH	SH	SH	SH	SH	SH	SH	SH	SH	SH	SH	SH	SH	SH	SH	SH	SH	SH	SH	SH	SH	SH	SH	SH	SH	SH	SH	SH	SH	SH	SH	SH	SH	SH	SH	SH	SH	SH	SH	SH	SH	41	13	57
GG (George) Yeld	-	-	-	-	-	-	F	F	F	F	F	F	<F	-	-	-	-	-	-	-	-	-	-	-	-	-	-	-	-	-	-	-	-	-	-	-	-	-	-	-	-	7	-	10

1 GAME: Cpl. WA (Bill) Dalby >F(19), WI (Isaiah) Dann <F(22), Cpl RJC (Robert) Ferguson =Ct(10), J Fitzgerald =FH(1), EL (Ernest) Goodman W(41), C Green =F(8), OJ (James) Hargrave >FH(40), E (Edgar) Morgan W+ AW2 =F(14), JW Morton =W(4), SC (Sydney) Roberts =Wt(17), G (George) Shingler <W(35), Sgt. JA (John) Thomas =F(26), J Wilkinson >C(40), Lt. WC (Walter) Wilson E2 >C(41), J (Jim) Woollerton =FH(24)

19 09/10

Home Ground: Welford Road	Trophy Cabinet: Midland Counties Cup(10)	OVERALL RECORD:					T	C	PG	DG	MK	PTS
Captain: Jamie Watson		PLD	W	D	L	Tigers scored:	109	45	6	0	2	441
Vice-captain: John Jackett		39	24	5	10	Opponents scored:	52	21	4	1	0	214

GM	DATE		VEN	OPPONENTS	RESULT	TRIES	KICKS	ATT
MIDLAND COUNTIES CUP						**CUP WINNERS: LEICESTER TIGERS**		
33	Mar	19	H	Nuneaton (4)	W 35-5	Dickens(3), Taylor(3), P.Wood(2), Scott	J.Jackett 2c, H.Lawrie 2c	4000
34		26	a	Burton (sf)	W 34-8	P.Wood(2), Burdett, Hobbs, Hogarth, P.Lawrie, Taylor, K.Wood	H.Lawrie 5c	2000
37	Apr	2		Coventry (f)	W 8-6	P.Wood	J.Jackett c/m	10000
CLUB MATCHES								
1	Sep	4	H	Stratford-upon-Avon	W 43-0	K.Wood(3), P.Lawrie(2), Heard, Hobbs, Hopkins, Smith, Watson, P.Wood	H.Lawrie 5c	-
2		11	H	Hartlepool Rovers	W 29-3	P.Lawrie(3), Heard(2), P.Wood	Gimson 4c/p	-
3		18	H	Neath	W 13-5	Heard, Tarr, K.Wood	H.Lawrie 2c	-
4		25	H	Manchester	W 22-5	Heard(2), Hobbs, P.Lawrie, P.Wood	H.Lawrie 2c/p	-
5	Oct	2	H	Headingley	W 32-6	P.Lawrie(4), H.Lawrie, Hobbs, Watson, P.Wood	H.Lawrie 4c	-
6		9	H	Bristol	W 12-8	P.Lawrie(3)	H.Lawrie p	-
7		16	H	Northampton	L 3-11	-	H.Lawrie p	-
8		23	a	Richmond	L 0-3	-	-	-
9		30	a	Devonport Albion	L 3-5	P.Lawrie	-	4000
10	Nov	6	H	Cardiff	D 3-3	Flude	-	8000
11		13	H	Swansea	D 0-0	-	-	-
12		20	a	Newport	L 3-23	P.Lawrie	-	-
13		27	a	Birkenhead Park	W 3-0	Smith	-	-
14	Dec	4	a	Stratford-upon-Avon	W 5-0	Taylor	H.Lawrie c	-
15		11	a	Northampton	W 8-3	K.Wood	H.Lawrie c/m	7000
16		18	H	Coventry	W 11-0	Dickens, Heard, K.Wood	H.Lawrie c	5000
17		24f	H	Cinderford	W 17-6	Heard(3), Dickens, P.Wood	Gimson c	-
18		27m	H	Birkenhead Park	W 14-6	Watson(2), Greasley, Smith	H.Lawrie c	-
19		28tu	H	Penarth	W 12-6	P.Wood(2), Allen, J.Jackett	-	8000
20		29w	H	Barbarians	D 9-9	Burdett, Greasley, P.Wood	-	-
21		31f	a	Headingley	W 17-3	Greasley(2), Dickens, Wilson, P.Wood	Gimson c	-
22	Jan	1	a	Hartlepool Rovers	W 13-8	Barrow, Hargrave	J.Jackett 2c/p	-
23		8	a	London Welsh	W 16-6	Dickens, Hargrave, Watson, P.Wood	H.Lawrie 2c	-
24		15	H	Gloucester	D 0-0	-	-	-
		22	a	Moseley	PP (frost)			
		29	H	Bedford	PP (frost)			
25	Feb	5	a	Coventry	W 3-0	P.Lawrie	-	-
26		12	a	Swansea	L 0-9	-	-	-
27		14m	a	Neath	L 0-11	-	-	-
28		19	H	Newport	L 5-6	Dickens	H.Lawrie c	10000
29		26	H	Moseley	W 16-0	P.Lawrie(2), Taylor, Watson	J.Jackett 2c	4000
30	Mar	5	H	Devonport Albion	L 3-8	-	H.Lawrie p	7000
31		9w	a	Moseley	W 20-0	Watson(2), Heard, Hobbs, P.Lawrie, Penny	J.Jackett c	-
32		12	a	Harlequins	W 3-0	P.Lawrie	-	-
35		28m	a	Cardiff	D 10-10	K.Wood(2)	J.Jackett 2c	-
36		29tu	a	Bristol	L 5-15	P.Lawrie	J.Jackett c	-
38	Apr	9	H	London Welsh	W 11-3	Cross, Smith, Watson	J.Jackett c	-
39		16	a	Gloucester	L 0-14	-	-	-

***Neutral Venue:** #37 at Newdigate Ground - Nuneaton*

INDIVIDUAL APPEARANCES 1909/10 Name / Game #	1	2	3	4	5	6	7	8	9	10	11	12	13	14	15	16	17	18	19	20	21	22	23	24	25	26	27	28	29	30	31	32	33	34	35	36	37	38	39	Apps	T	Pts
WJ (Jimmy) Allen	-	-	-	-	-	-	-	-	-	-	-	>F	-	-	F	-	F	-	F	F	F	F	F	F	F	-	-	F	F	F	-	-	F	F	F	-	F	F	-	18	1	3
JV (James) Barrow	-	-	-	-	-	-	-	-	-	-	-	-	-	-	-	-	-	-	-	-	>C	C	-	-	-	C	C	-	-	-	F	F	-	-	-	-	-	-	-	6	1	3
Lt-Col. JC (Jimmy) Burdett	F	F	F	F	F	F	F	F	-	F	F	F	F	F	F	F	-	F	F	F	-	-	F	F	F	-	-	F	F	F	-	F	F	F	F	F	F	F	F	32	2	6
CW (Charlie) Cross	-	-	-	-	-	-	-	-	-	-	-	-	-	-	-	-	-	-	-	-	-	-	-	-	-	-	-	-	-	-	-	-	-	-	-	-	-	>F	-	1	1	3
Cpl. WA (Bill) Dalby	-	-	-	-	-	-	-	-	-	-	-	-	-	-	-	-	F	-	F	-	-	-	-	-	-	-	-	-	-	-	-	-	-	-	-	-	-	-	-	2	-	-
JT (Jack) Dickens	-	-	-	-	-	-	-	-	-	-	-	>C	-	-	-	W	W	C	W	W	W	W	C	-	W	-	C	C	C	W	-	-	<W	-	-	-	-	-	-	15	8	24
Dunkley	-	-	-	-	-	-	-	-	-	-	-	-	-	=FB	-	-	-	-	-	-	-	-	-	-	-	-	-	-	-	-	-	-	-	-	-	-	-	-	-	1	-	-
WS (Wilfrid) Ellis	-	-	-	-	-	-	-	-	>F	F	F	F	F	F	F	F	F	F	-	F	F	F	F	F	F	-	-	F	F	-	-	-	F	F	-	F	<F	-	-	22	-	-
DE (Dan) Ellwood	-	-	-	-	-	-	-	FB	-	-	-	FB	-	-	-	FB	-	FB	FB	FB	-	FB	-	FB	-	-	-	-	-	-	-	-	-	-	FB	FB	-	-	-	10	-	-
MW (Matthias) Flude	-	-	-	-	-	-	-	W	W	W	W	W	-	-	-	-	-	-	-	-	-	-	W	-	-	-	-	-	-	-	-	-	-	-	-	-	-	-	-	6	1	3
C (Christopher) Gimson	-	F	F	C	-	-	-	-	-	-	-	-	-	-	-	-	F	F	F	F	F	-	-	-	-	F	-	-	-	-	-	-	-	-	-	-	-	-	-	9	-	15
TW (Tom) Goodrich	-	-	-	-	-	-	-	-	F	-	-	-	-	F	-	-	F	-	F	-	F	-	-	-	-	F	F	-	-	-	<F	-	-	-	-	-	-	-	-	8	-	-
G (George) Greasley	F	F	F	F	F	F	F	F	F	F	F	-	-	-	-	F	-	F	F	F	F	F	F	-	F	F	F	F	F	F	F	F	F	-	F	F	F	F	F	32	4	12
WH Grier	-	-	-	-	-	-	-	-	-	-	-	-	-	-	-	-	-	-	-	-	-	-	-	-	-	-	=F	-	-	-	-	-	-	-	-	-	-	-	-	1	-	-
OJ (James) Hargrave	-	-	-	-	-	-	-	-	-	-	-	-	-	-	-	-	-	-	-	-	-	FH	FH	FH	-	-	-	-	-	-	-	-	-	-	-	-	-	-	-	3	2	6
AD (Arthur) Heard	W	W	W	W	W	W	W	-	-	-	-	-	W	W	W	W	W	W	-	-	-	-	-	-	-	-	-	W	W	-	W	<W	-	-	-	-	-	-	-	17	11	33
AJ (Arthur) Hobbs	F	F	F	F	F	F	F	F	-	F	F	F	F	F	F	-	-	F	-	-	F	F	-	-	-	F	F	-	F	F	F	F	F	F	F	-	F	F	F	29	5	15
TB (Thomas) Hogarth E1	F	F	F	F	-	F	F	F	-	F	-	F	F	F	F	-	-	-	-	F	-	F	-	F	-	-	-	-	F	-	-	F	-	F	F	-	F	-	-	20	1	3
WG (Gil) Hopkins	F	F	F	-	F	F	F	F	F	F	F	F	F	F	F	F	F	F	-	F	F	F	F	F	F	F	F	F	F	F	F	F	F	F	-	F	F	F	F	36	1	3
R (Dick) Jackett	-	-	-	-	-	-	-	-	-	-	-	-	-	-	-	-	-	-	-	-	-	-	-	-	-	-	-	-	-	-	-	-	-	-	F	F	-	-	F	3	-	-
EJ (John) Jackett E13 AW3	FB	FB	FB	FB	FB	FB	FB	SH	-	-	FB	-	FB*	-	-	-	FB	W	W	W	FB*	W*	FB	W	FB	FB*	FB*	FB	FB	FB	FB	FB	FB	FB	W	W	FB	FB	FB	33	1	33
HSB (Harry) Lawrie	F	-	F	F	F	F	F	F	F	FB	F	F	-	SH	FB	F	-	F	F	-	-	-	F	F	F	F	F	F	-	F	-	-	F	F	-	-	-	-	-	25	1	72
PW (Percy) Lawrie E1	W	W	W	W	W	W	W	W	W	W	W	W	W	W	W	-	-	-	-	-	-	-	-	-	W	W	W	W	W	W	W	W	-	W	W	W	W	W	W	29	22	66
WM (Will) Leather	-	-	-	-	-	-	-	-	-	-	-	-	-	-	-	-	-	-	>FH	-	W	-	-	-	-	-	W	-	-	-	C	-	-	-	-	<FH	-	-	-	5	-	-
Lt. AS (Arthur) McIntyre	-	F	-	F	F	F	F	F	F	-	-	-	F	F	F	F	-	-	-	-	F	F	F	F	F	F	F	F	-	F	-	F	-	-	F	F	-	-	-	23	-	-
G (George) Middleton	F	-	-	F	F	-	-	-	-	-	-	-	-	-	-	-	-	-	-	-	-	-	-	-	-	-	-	-	-	-	-	-	-	-	-	-	-	-	-	3	-	-
F Morris	-	-	-	-	-	-	-	-	-	-	-	-	-	-	-	-	-	-	-	-	-	-	-	-	-	-	-	-	-	-	=F	-	-	-	-	-	-	-	-	1	-	-
W (William) Oldham E2 AW1	-	-	-	-	-	-	-	-	-	-	-	-	-	-	-	-	-	-	-	-	-	-	-	-	-	-	-	-	-	-	-	-	-	-	-	-	-	-	=F	1	-	-
HW (Harry) Palfreyman	-	-	-	-	-	-	-	-	>FB	-	-	-	-	-	-	-	-	-	-	-	-	-	-	-	-	-	-	-	-	-	-	-	-	-	-	-	-	-	-	1	-	-
SH (Sid) Penny E1	F	F	F	F	F	F	F	F	F	F	F	F	F	F	F	F	F	F	F	F	-	F	F	F	F	F	F	F	F	F	F	F	F	F	-	F	F	F	F	37	1	3
AF (Algernon) Scott	-	-	-	-	-	-	-	-	-	-	-	-	-	-	-	-	-	-	-	-	-	-	-	-	-	-	-	-	-	-	-	-	<W	-	-	-	-	-	-	1	1	3
Cpt. JWD (Dixie) Smith	C	C	-	-	-	C	C	C	C	C	C	-	C	C	C	C	C	C	C	C	-	-	-	C	C	W	-	C	-	C	-	-	C	W	-	-	W	W	W	26	4	12
Lt. FN (Frank) Tarr E3	-	-	C	-	C	-	-	-	-	-	-	-	-	-	-	-	-	-	-	-	-	-	-	-	-	-	-	-	-	-	-	-	-	-	-	-	-	-	-	2	1	3
FM (Tim) Taylor E+	-	-	-	-	-	-	-	-	-	-	-	-	FH	FH	-	FH	-	-	-	-	-	-	-	-	-	FH	FH	-	FH	FH	FH	FH	FH	FH	FH	-	FH	-	FH	14	6	18
JAG (George) Ward E+	-	-	-	-	-	-	-	-	-	-	-	-	-	-	-	-	-	-	-	-	-	-	-	-	-	-	-	-	-	-	>F	-	-	-	F	F	-	F	F	5	-	-
CR (Charles) Watchorn	-	-	-	-	-	-	-	-	F	F	F	-	F	-	-	F	<F	-	-	-	-	-	-	-	-	-	-	-	-	-	-	-	-	-	-	-	-	-	-	6	-	-
JR (Jamie) Watson	FH*	FH*	FH*	FH*	FH*	FH*	FH*	FH*	FH*	FH*	FH*	FH*	-	-	FH*	-	FH*	FH*	C*	FH*	-	-	C*	W*	FH*	-	-	FH*	C*	C*	C*	C*	C*	C*	C*	C*	C*	FH*	C*	32	9	27
Lt. WC (Walter) Wilson E2	-	-	-	-	-	-	-	-	-	-	-	-	-	-	-	-	-	-	-	-	FH	-	-	-	-	-	-	-	-	-	-	C	-	-	-	-	-	C	-	3	1	3
KB (Kenneth) Wood GB+	C	C	C	C	C	C	C	C	C	C	C	C	C	C	C	C	C	-	-	C	C	C	W	C	C	C	-	-	-	-	-	-	-	C	C	C	C	C	C	30	9	27
GW (Pedlar) Wood E+	SH	SH	SH	SH	SH	SH	SH	-	SH	SH	SH	SH	SH	-	SH	SH	SH	SH	SH	SH	SH	SH	SH	SH	SH	SH	SH	SH	SH	SH	SH	SH	SH	SH	SH	SH	SH	SH	SH	37	15	45

The key for how to read the stats is on the last page

1910/11

Home Ground: Welford Road
Captain: Jamie Watson
Vice-captain: John Jackett

OVERALL RECORD:					T	C	PG	DG	MK	PTS
PLD	W	D	L	Tigers scored:	134	37	15	3	2	539
42	23	6	13	Opponents scored:	59	21	6	4	1	256

GM	DATE		VEN	OPPONENTS	RESULT	TRIES	KICKS	ATT
MIDLAND COUNTIES CUP						**CUP WINNERS: COVENTRY**		
37	Mar	18	a	Coventry (4)	L 6-21	Pearce	H.Lawrie p	4500
CLUB MATCHES								
1	Sep	**3**	**H**	**Hartlepool Rovers**	W 25-0	P.Lawrie(3), Allen, Smith, Wood	H.Lawrie 2c/m	-
2		**10**	**H**	**Plymouth**	W 8-4	P.Lawrie(2)	H.Lawrie c	9500
3		**17**	**H**	**Neath**	W 3-0	-	H.Lawrie m	-
4		**24**	**H**	**Llanelly**	L 12-16	Allen, Wood	T.Taylor d, H.Lawrie c	11000
5	Oct	**1**	**H**	**Devonport Albion**	W 9-6	H.Lawrie, P.Lawrie, Watson	-	10000
6		6th	a	Birkenhead Park	W 34-6	P.Lawrie(2), Wood(2), Barrow(2), D.Jackett(2), Watson	P.Lawrie c/p, Wood c	-
7		**8**	**H**	**Bristol**	W 20-8	Hargrave(2), P.Lawrie, T.Taylor	H.Lawrie c/2p	-
8		15	a	Northampton	W 14-3	Hargrave, T.Hogarth, P.Lawrie	J.Jackett c/p	-
9		**22**	**H**	**Newport**	L 6-8	-	J.Jackett 2p	13000
10		**29**	**H**	**Cardiff**	L 0-6	-	-	-
11	Nov	**5**	**H**	**Cinderford**	D 3-3	P.Lawrie	-	10000
12		12	a	Swansea	L 5-6	Burdett	J.Jackett c	4000
13		14m	a	Neath	L 3-18	Kilby	-	-
14		**19**	**H**	**Coventry**	W 25-3	Burdett, P.Lawrie, T.Taylor, Watson, Wood	H.Lawrie 2c/2p	9000
15		**26**	**H**	**London Welsh**	W 29-7	Allen(2), P.Lawrie, Hargrave, T.Taylor, Watson, Wood	P.Lawrie c/p, H.Lawrie p	-
16	Dec	3	a	Bedford	W 6-3	Burdett, P.Lawrie	-	-
17		**10**	**H**	**Northampton**	D 0-0	-	-	9000
18		17	a	Coventry	D 3-3	P.Lawrie	-	-
19		**24**	**H**	**Headingley**	W 19-8	P.Lawrie, T.Taylor, Watson, Wilkinson, Wood	Gimson 2c	-
20		**26m**	**H**	**Birkenhead Park**	W 25-5	P.Lawrie(3), Atterbury, Hopkins, Watson	P.Lawrie c/p, Gimson c	-
21		**27tu**	**H**	**Kendal**	W 33-0	P.Lawrie, Cross, Hobbs, T.Hogarth, Middleton, Pearce, Tarr, T.Taylor	P.Lawrie c, Wilkinson 2c/p	-
22		**28w**	**H**	**Barbarians**	W 29-3	P.Lawrie(3), Greasley, D.Jackett, Tarr, Wood	P.Lawrie c, Gimson 3c	9000
23		30f	a	Headingley	L 4-7	-	P.Lawrie d	-
24		31	a	Hartlepool Rovers	L 7-9	-	Pearce d, P.Lawrie p	4000
25	Jan	2m	a	Manchester	W 12-6	T.Taylor(2), P.Lawrie, Wood	-	-
26		7	a	London Welsh	W 9-8	Gimson, Pearce, Watson	-	500
27		**14**	**H**	**Gloucester**	W 3-0	Greasley	-	-
28		21	a	Moseley	W 21-3	Ansell(2), T.Taylor(2), Hargrave, Hobbs, Wood	-	-
29		**28**	**H**	**Moseley**	W 21-5	J.Jackett(2), Fisher, Greasley, Hargrave, H.Lawrie	Bream p	5000
30	Feb	4	a	Blackheath	D 9-9	Allen, Hargrave, Hopkins	-	-
31		**11**	**H**	**Swansea**	L 0-3	-	-	-
32		18	a	Newport	L 3-14	Gimson	-	6000
33		**25**	**H**	**Richmond**	W 33-0	Allen(2), P.Lawrie(2), Burdett, Hargrave, H.Lawrie, T.Taylor, Watson	Gimson 3c	-
34	Mar	4	a	Devonport Albion	L 0-9	-	-	-
35		6m	a	Plymouth	D 6-6	Allen, H.Lawrie	-	-
36		**11**	**H**	**Harlequins**	W 11-8	Hobbs, T.Taylor, Wood	Gimson c	-
38		**25**	**H**	**Nottingham**	W 49-0	P.Lawrie(3), Wood(3), Hargrave(2), Bream, Burdett, Hobbs, T.Taylor, Watson	Gimson 5c	-
39	Apr	8	a	Cardiff	L 3-16	T.Taylor	-	12000
40		15	a	Gloucester	D 5-5	P.Lawrie	H.Lawrie c	3000
41		17m	a	Llanelly	L 3-6	Wood	-	-
42		18tu	a	Bristol	W 23-5	Thomas(2), Gimson, P.Lawrie, T.Taylor	Gimson c, P.Lawrie c, H.Lawrie 2c	-

INDIVIDUAL APPEARANCES 1910/11

Name / Game #	1	2	3	4	5	6	7	8	9	10	11	12	13	14	15	16	17	18	19	20	21	22	23	24	25	26	27	28	29	30	31	32	33	34	35	36	37	38	39	40	41	42	Apps	T	Pts
WJ (Jimmy) Allen	F	F	F	F	F	F	F	F	F	F	F	F	F	F	F	F	-	-	F	-	-	-	-	-	-	-	F	F	-	F	F	F	F	F	F	-	F	F	F	F	F	F	31	8	24
JR (James) Ansell	-	-	-	-	-	-	-	-	-	-	-	-	-	-	-	-	-	-	-	-	-	-	-	-	-	-	-	>C	-	-	<W	-	-	-	-	-	-	-	-	-	-	-	2	2	6
J (Joseph) Atterbury	-	-	-	-	-	-	-	-	-	-	-	-	-	-	-	-	-	-	-	>F	-	-	F	F	-	<F	-	-	-	-	-	-	-	-	-	-	-	-	-	-	-	-	4	1	3
JW (Billy) Bream	-	-	-	-	-	-	-	-	-	-	-	-	-	-	-	-	-	-	-	-	-	-	-	-	-	-	-	-	>C	-	C	-	C	C	C	C	C	C	-	-	C	-	9	1	6
Lt-Col. JC (Jimmy) Burdett	F	F	F	F	F	-	F	F	F	F	F	F	-	F	F	F	-	F	F	F	-	F	-	-	-	-	-	F	-	F	F	-	F	F	F	F	F	F	-	F	F	F	30	5	15
DE (Dan) Ellwood	FB	-	-	-	-	-	-	-	-	-	-	-	FB	FB	-	-	FB	-	FB	-	-	FB	-	FB	FB	-	-	-	FB	-	-	FB	-	-	-	-	-	-	-	-	FB	-	11	-	-
MW (Walter) Fisher	-	-	-	-	-	-	-	-	-	-	-	-	-	-	-	-	-	-	-	-	-	-	-	>FH	C	-	-	-	SH	-	-	-	-	-	-	-	-	-	-	-	-	-	3	1	3
C (Christopher) Gimson	-	-	F	-	-	F	-	-	-	-	-	-	-	F	-	-	-	F	F	F	-	F	F	-	F	F	F	F	-	F	F	F	F	-	-	F	-	F	F	-	F	F	21	3	41
EL (Ernest) Goodman	-	-	-	-	-	-	-	-	-	-	-	-	-	-	-	-	-	-	-	-	-	-	-	-	-	-	-	-	-	-	-	-	-	W	<W	-	-	-	-	-	-	-	2	-	-
G (George) Greasley	F	-	F	F	F	F	F	F	F	-	F	F	-	-	-	F	F	F	-	F	F	F	F	-	F	F	F	F	F	F	F	F	F	F	F	F	F	F	F	-	-	-	32	3	9
OJ (James) Hargrave	-	-	W	-	-	-	W	W	-	-	W	W	W	W	W	W	W	W	-	W	-	W	-	-	-	W	W	W	W	W	W	W	W	-	-	W	W	W	W	W	-	W	27	10	30
AJ (Arthur) Hobbs	F	F	F	F	F	F	F	F	F	F	-	F	F	F	F	F	F	F	F	-	F	F	F	F	F	F	F	F	-	F	F	F	F	-	F	F	F	F	F	F	F	F	38	4	12
A (Anthony) Hogarth	-	-	-	-	-	-	-	-	-	-	-	-	-	-	-	-	-	-	-	-	-	-	-	F	<F	-	-	-	-	-	-	-	-	-	-	-	-	-	-	-	-	-	2	-	-
TB (Thomas) Hogarth E1	-	-	-	-	-	-	-	F	F	-	F	-	-	F	F	F	F	F	-	-	F	F	-	-	r	-	-	F	F	F	F	-	-	F	-	F	F	-	F	F	F	F	21+1	2	6
WG (Gil) Hopkins	F	F	F	F	F	F	F	F	F	F	-	F	F	F	F	F	F	F	F	F	-	F	F	F	F	F	F	-	-	F	F	F	F	F	F	F	F	F	F	F	F	F	38	2	6
R (Dick) Jackett	-	-	-	-	F	F	F	-	-	-	-	F	-	-	-	-	-	-	-	-	-	F	F	-	-	-	-	-	-	-	-	F	-	F	F	-	-	-	F	-	-	-	10	3	9
EJ (John) Jackett E13 AW3	-	FB	FB*	FB	FB	FB	FB	FB	FB	FB	FB*	FB	C*	-	FB	-	W	-	-	FB	-	-	-	-	-	FB	FB	FB	W	FB	FB	W	FB	FB	FB	FB	FB	FB	FB	FB	-	FB	31	2	19
AL (Alf) Kewney E13	-	-	-	-	-	-	-	-	-	-	-	-	-	-	-	-	-	-	-	F	F	-	-	F	F	-	-	-	-	-	-	-	-	-	-	-	-	-	-	F	F	-	6	-	-
GE (George) Kilby	-	-	-	-	-	-	-	-	-	-	-	-	>F	-	-	-	-	-	<F	-	-	-	-	-	-	-	-	-	-	-	-	-	-	-	-	-	-	-	-	-	-	-	2	1	3
HSB (Harry) Lawrie	F	F	F	F	F	-	F	F	-	F	F	F	F	F	F	FB	F	FB	-	-	-	-	-	-	-	F	F	F	F	-	-	-	F	F	F	F	F	F	F	F	-	F	29	4	56
PW (Percy) Lawrie E2	W	W	W	W	W	W	W	W	W	W	W	W	W	W	W	W	-	W	W	W	W	W*	W*	W*	W*	-	W	-	-	W	-	-	W	W	W	W	-	W	W	W	W*	W	35	31	121
G (George) Middleton	-	F	-	-	-	-	-	-	F	F	F	-	-	-	-	-	-	-	-	-	F	-	-	-	-	-	-	-	F	-	-	-	-	-	-	-	-	<F	-	-	-	-	7	1	3
HW (Harry) Palfreyman	-	-	-	-	-	-	-	-	-	-	-	-	-	-	-	-	-	-	-	-	SH	-	FH	-	-	-	-	-	-	-	-	-	-	-	-	-	-	-	-	-	-	-	2	-	-
HK (Herbert) Pearce	-	-	-	-	-	-	-	-	-	W	-	-	-	-	-	-	-	-	W	-	W	-	W	C	W	W	-	-	-	-	-	-	-	-	-	-	W	-	-	-	W	-	9	3	13
SH (Sid) Penny E1	F	F	-	F	-	F	-	-	-	-	-	-	-	-	-	-	-	-	-	<F	-	-	-	-	-	-	-	-	-	-	-	-	-	-	-	-	-	-	-	-	-	-	5	-	-
HH (Harry) Robinson	-	-	-	-	-	-	-	-	-	>F	F	-	-	F	F	F	F	F	F	F	F	-	F	F	-	F	F	-	F	-	-	F	-	-	F	-	-	-	-	-	<F	-	18	-	-
Cpt. JWD (Dixie) Smith	C	W	C	W	-	-	-	-	-	-	C	C	-	-	-	-	-	-	-	-	-	-	-	-	-	-	-	-	-	-	-	-	-	-	-	-	-	-	-	-	-	-	6	1	3
Lt. FN (Frank) Tarr E3	C	C	C	C	C	C	C	C	C	C	C	-	-	C	-	-	-	C	-	C	C	C	-	-	C	-	-	-	-	-	-	-	-	-	-	-	-	-	C	-	-	-	18	2	6
F (Sos) Taylor E+	-	-	-	-	-	-	-	-	-	-	-	-	-	-	-	-	-	-	-	-	-	-	-	-	-	-	-	-	>F	-	-	F	-	-	-	-	-	-	-	-	-	-	2	-	-
FM (Tim) Taylor E+	-	FH	FH	FH	FH	FH	FH	FH	FH	FH	FH	FH	FH	FH	FH	FH	FH	FH	FH	-	FH	FH	-	-	FH	FH	FH	FH	-	FH	FH	FH	FH	FH	FH	FH	FH	FH	FH	FH	FH	FH	37	14	46
AL (Alf) Thomas	-	-	-	-	-	-	-	-	-	-	-	-	-	-	-	-	-	-	-	-	-	-	-	-	-	-	-	-	-	-	-	-	-	-	-	-	-	-	-	>C	-	C	2	2	6
JAG (George) Ward E+	F	F	F	F	F	F	F	F	F	F	F	F	F	-	F	F	F	F	F	-	F	F	F	F	F	F	F	F	-	F	F	-	F	F	-	F	F	-	-	F	-	F	34	-	-
JR (Jamie) Watson	FH*	C*	-	C*	C*	C*	C*	C*	C*	C*	-	C*	-	C*	C*	C*	C*	C*	C*	FH*	C*	-	-	-	-	C*	C*	C*	FH*	C*	C*	C*	C*	C*	C*	C*	C*	C*	C*	C*	-	C*	34	9	27
A White	-	-	-	-	-	-	-	-	-	-	-	-	-	-	-	-	-	-	-	-	-	-	-	>F	<F	-	-	-	-	-	-	-	-	-	-	-	-	-	-	-	-	-	2	-	-
J Wilkinson	-	-	-	-	-	-	-	-	-	-	-	-	-	-	C	C	C	-	C	-	FB	C	C	C	-	C	C	W	C	C	-	C	-	-	-	-	-	-	-	-	-	-	14	1	10
GW (Pedlar) Wood E+	SH	SH	SH	SH	SH	SH	SH	SH	SH	SH	SH	SH	SH	SH	SH	SH	SH	SH	SH	SH	-	SH	SH	SH	SH	SH	SH	SH	-	SH	SH	SH	SH	SH	SH	SH	SH	SH	SH	SH	SH	SH	40	15	47

1 GAME: JV (James) Barrow <Wt(6), BB (Barrie) Bennetts E2 <C(23), H (Harry) Britten =W(9), Sgt. LS (Leo) Burton >F(29), CW (Charlie) Cross Ft(21), MW (Matthias) Flude <W(5), AO (Arthur) Jones <C(20), WH (William) Kitchen <FB(23), R Leggitt =F(13), L-Cpl. JE (Joseph) Lewis <W(24), Lt. AS (Arthur) McIntyre F(17), TE (Thomas) Maddocks >C(41), WG Rapsey <C(13), FC (Fred) Robinson =F(13), I (Ike) Spicer >F(29), Lt. WC (Walter) Wilson E2 <W(1)

19	11/12	Home Ground: Welford Road	Trophy Cabinet: Midland Counties Cup(11)
		Captain: Percy Lawrie	
		Vice-captain: Jimmy Burdett	

OVERALL RECORD:					T	C	PG	DG	MK	PTS
PLD	W	D	L	Tigers scored:	117	43	7	2	1	469
39	21	2	16	Opponents scored:	65	24	5	3	0	270

GM	DATE		VEN	OPPONENTS	RESULT	TRIES	KICKS	ATT
MIDLAND COUNTIES CUP						**CUP WINNERS: LEICESTER TIGERS**		
33	Mar	16	a	Rugby (4)	W 24-5	J.Hargrave(2), P.Lawrie(2), Burdett, T.Taylor	Bream 3c	3000
34		**23**	**H**	**Newbold (sf)**	W 65-0	P.Lawrie(4), J.Hargrave(3), H.Lawrie(3), T.Taylor(3), McIntyre(2), Tarr, S.Taylor	Bream 7c	2145
35		30		Coventry (f)	W 16-0	Greasley, Hogarth, P.Lawrie	Bream 2c/p	3000
CLUB MATCHES								
1	Sep	**2**	**H**	**Bedford**	W 22-3	J.Hargrave(2), P.Lawrie, T.Taylor, J.Watson, Wood	Bream 2c	-
2		**9**	**H**	**Plymouth**	W 13-4	Allen, Wood	Bream 2c/p	7000
3		**16**	**H**	**Neath**	D 3-3	J.Hargrave	-	8000
4		**23**	**H**	**Llanelly**	W 13-0	P.Lawrie, J.Watson	H.Lawrie 2c/m	9000
5		30	a	Devonport Albion	L 0-16	-	-	3000
6	Oct	2m	a	Plymouth	L 3-11	T.Taylor	-	-
7		**7**	**H**	**Coventry**	W 22-0	T.Taylor(2), J.Hargrave, H.Lawrie, P.Lawrie, J.Watson	Bream 2c	3249
8		**14**	**H**	**Northampton**	W 16-3	T.Taylor(2), Greasley, P.Lawrie	H.Lawrie 2c	7068
9		21	a	Newport	L 0-5	-	-	5000
10		**28**	**H**	**Manchester**	W 19-0	Burdett, Hogarth, Hopkins, P.Lawrie	Bream 2c/p	3194
11	Nov	**4**	**H**	**Swansea**	L 8-16	Hopkins	Bream c/p	5165
12		11	a	Birkenhead Park	W 16-9	J.Hargrave(2), L.Hargrave, T.Taylor	Bream 2c	-
13		18	a	Coventry	W 4-0	-	Ellwood d	4000
14		**25**	**H**	**Cardiff**	L 5-6	Hobbs	Bream c	5339
15	Dec	2	a	Moseley	W 9-3	Broadley(2), J.Hargrave	-	-
16		9	a	Northampton	W 8-3	Greasley, J.Hargrave	Bream c	5000
17		**16**	**H**	**Bristol**	W 8-3	Burdett, J.Hargrave	Bream c	2144
18		**23**	**H**	**Cinderford**	W 21-5	P.Lawrie(3), Hobbs, Hopkins	Smitten d, Bream c	2562
19		**26tu**	**H**	**Birkenhead Park**	W 21-5	P.Lawrie(2), Ward(2), Bream, S.Taylor, Wood	-	4230
20		**27w**	**H**	**Glasgow University**	W 26-3	Broadley(3), Allen, Greasley, J.Hargrave	Allen 4c	5064
21		**28th**	**H**	**Barbarians**	W 13-6	Burdett, Hopkins, D.Jackett	Allen 2c	5897
22		30	a	Headingley	D 6-6	Greasley	Bream p	-
23	Jan	**6**	**H**	**London Welsh**	W 8-0	J.Hargrave, P.Lawrie	Bream c	803
24		**13**	**H**	**Gloucester**	L 0-7	-	-	3486
25		**20**	**H**	**Devonport Albion**	L 0-6	-	-	3938
26		**27**	**H**	**Moseley**	W 31-3	P.Lawrie(3), J.Hargrave(2), Tarr(2), Hopkins, J.Watson	Allen c, Bream c	2416
	Feb	3	a	Gloucester	PP (frost)			
27		10	a	Swansea	L 3-32	P.Lawrie	-	6000
28		12m	a	Neath	L 3-14	J.Hargrave	-	-
29		**17**	**H**	**Newport**	L 3-8	Greasley	-	3534
30		24	a	Richmond	L 3-13	Greasley	-	-
31	Mar	**2**	**H**	**Headingley**	L 12-14	Wood(2), J.Hargrave, H.Lawrie	-	1499
32		9	a	Harlequins	L 6-18	Greasley, P.Lawrie	-	-
36	Apr	6	a	Llanelly	L 10-17	Hogarth, H.Lawrie	Bream 2c	10000
37		8m	a	Cardiff	L 0-11	-	-	-
38		9tu	a	Bristol	L 6-8	Burdett	Bream p	-
39		**13**	**H**	**Blackheath**	W 23-4	Tarr(2), Dalby, Greasley, J.Hargrave, P.Lawrie	Bream c/p	4223

Neutral Venue: *#35 at Cricket Club - Rugby*

INDIVIDUAL APPEARANCES 1911/12

Name / Game #	1	2	3	4	5	6	7	8	9	10	11	12	13	14	15	16	17	18	19	20	21	22	23	24	25	26	27	28	29	30	31	32	33	34	35	36	37	38	39	Apps	T	Pts
WJ (Jimmy) Allen	F	F	F	F	F	F	F	F	F	F	F	F	F	F	-	F	F	F	-	F	F	F	F	F	F	F	F	F	F	F	F	F	F	F	F	F	F	F	-	36	2	20
PA (Percy) Baker	-	-	-	-	-	-	-	-	-	-	-	-	-	-	-	-	-	-	-	-	-	-	-	-	-	-	-	-	-	-	-	=FB	-	-	-	-	-	-	-	1	-	-
JW (Billy) Bream	C	C	C	-	-	C	C	-	-	C	W	C	W	FB	C	C	C	C	C	-	-	C	FB	-	FB	FB	FB	C	FB	FB	-	-	FB	FB	FB	FB	FB	FB	FB	30	1	88
FRC (Frank) Broadley	-	-	-	-	-	-	-	-	-	-	-	-	-	>W	W	W	W	-	-	W	-	W	-	-	W	-	-	-	-	-	-	-	-	-	-	-	W	-	-	8	5	15
Lt-Col. JC (Jimmy) Burdett	F	F	F	F	F	-	F	F	F	F	F*	F*	F*	F*	-	F*	F*	F	F	-	F	-	F	F	F*	F	F	-	F	F*	F*	-	F	F	F	F	F	F	F	33	5	15
AW Carr	-	-	-	-	-	-	-	-	-	-	-	-	-	-	-	-	-	-	>W	C	-	-	C	<C	-	-	-	-	-	-	-	-	-	-	-	-	-	-	-	4	-	-
Cpl. WA (Bill) Dalby	-	-	-	-	-	-	-	-	-	-	-	-	-	-	-	-	-	-	-	-	-	-	-	-	-	-	-	-	-	-	-	-	-	-	-	F	F	F	F	4	1	3
C Dodson	-	-	-	-	-	-	-	-	-	-	-	-	-	-	-	-	-	-	-	=F	-	-	-	-	-	-	-	-	-	-	-	-	-	-	-	-	-	-	-	1	-	-
W Elliott	-	-	-	-	-	-	-	-	-	-	-	-	-	-	-	-	-	-	-	-	-	-	-	-	-	>F	F	-	-	-	-	-	-	-	-	-	-	-	-	2	-	-
DE (Dan) Ellwood	FB	FB	FB	FB	-	FB	FB	FB	FB	FB	-	FB	FB	-	-	FB	FB	FB	FB	FB	FB	FB	-	FB	-	-	-	-	-	-	-	-	-	-	-	-	-	-	-	19	-	4
MW (Walter) Fisher	-	-	-	-	-	-	-	-	-	-	-	-	-	-	SH	-	-	SH	-	SH	-	SH	SH	-	-	-	-	-	-	-	-	-	-	-	-	SH	-	-	-	6	-	-
TH (Tommy) Fitchett	-	>F	F	-	-	-	-	-	-	-	-	-	-	-	-	-	-	-	-	F	-	<F	-	-	-	-	-	-	-	-	-	-	-	-	-	-	-	-	-	4	-	-
C (Christopher) Gimson	-	-	-	F	F	F	-	-	F	<F	-	-	-	-	-	-	-	-	-	-	-	-	-	-	-	-	-	-	-	-	-	-	-	-	-	-	-	-	-	5	-	-
G (George) Greasley	F	F	F	F	F	F	F	F	-	-	F	-	-	F	F	F	F	-	F	F	F	F	F	F	F	F	-	-	F	F	F	F	F	F	F	-	-	F	F	30	9	27
OJ (James) Hargrave	W	W	W	W	W	-	W	W	W	W	W	W	W	W	W	W	W	W	-	W	W	-	W	W	W	W	C	W	W	W	W	W	W	W	W	W	-	-	W	34	21	63
LO (Leonard) Hargrave	-	-	-	-	-	-	-	-	-	-	-	=W	-	-	-	-	-	-	-	-	-	-	-	-	-	-	-	-	-	-	-	-	-	-	-	-	-	-	-	1	1	3
SG (Samuel) Harvey	-	-	-	-	-	=W	-	-	-	-	-	-	-	-	-	-	-	-	-	-	-	-	-	-	-	-	-	-	-	-	-	-	-	-	-	-	-	-	-	1	-	-
AJ (Arthur) Hobbs	-	-	-	-	-	-	-	-	-	-	F	F	F	F	F	F	-	F	F	-	F	F	F	F	F	-	F	F	F	F	F	F	F	F	F	-	F	F	F	25	2	6
TB (Thomas) Hogarth E1	-	-	-	-	-	-	-	F	-	F	F	-	F	F	F	-	-	F	F	-	F	F	-	-	F	-	F	F	-	F	-	F	F	-	F	F	F	-	F	20	3	9
WG (Gil) Hopkins	F	F	F	F	F	F	F	F	F	F	F	F	F	F	F	-	F	F	F	-	F	W	F	F	F	F	F	F	F	F	F	F	F	F	F	-	F	F	F	36	5	15
SA (Sam) Hunter	-	-	-	-	-	-	-	-	-	-	-	-	-	-	-	-	-	-	-	-	-	-	-	-	-	-	-	-	-	-	-	-	-	-	-	-	-	-	>C	1	-	-
R (Dick) Jackett	-	-	-	-	F	F	-	-	F	-	-	-	-	-	-	-	-	-	-	-	F	F	-	-	-	-	-	-	F	-	-	-	-	-	-	-	-	-	-	6	1	3
EJ (John) Jackett E13 AW3	-	-	-	-	FB	-	-	-	-	-	-	-	-	-	<FB	-	-	-	-	-	-	-	-	-	-	-	-	-	-	-	-	-	-	-	-	-	-	-	-	2	-	-
AL (Alf) Kewney E15	-	-	-	-	-	-	-	-	-	-	-	-	-	-	-	-	-	F	F	-	-	-	-	-	-	-	-	-	-	-	-	-	-	-	-	-	-	-	-	2	-	-
HSB (Harry) Lawrie	F	F	F	F	F	F	F	F	F	F	FB	F	F	-	F	F	F	-	-	F*	-	-	F	-	-	-	-	-	F	C	F	■F	C	C	C	F	C	C	-	28	6	29
PW (Percy) Lawrie E2	W*	W*	W*	W*	W*	W*	W*	W*	W*	W*	-	-	-	-	-	-	-	W*	W*	-	W*	C*	W*	W*	-	W*	W*	W*	W*	-	-	W*	W*	W*	W*	W*	W*	W*	W*	28	24	72
Lt. AS (Arthur) McIntyre	-	-	-	-	-	-	-	-	-	-	-	-	-	-	-	-	F	-	-	-	-	-	F	F	-	-	-	-	W	W	-	-	-	<F	-	-	-	-	-	6	2	6
TE (Thomas) Maddocks	-	-	-	-	-	-	-	-	-	-	-	-	-	-	-	-	-	-	-	-	-	-	-	-	-	-	<W	-	-	-	-	-	-	-	-	-	-	-	-	1	-	-
A Redding	-	-	-	-	-	-	-	-	-	-	-	-	-	-	-	-	-	-	-	-	-	-	-	-	-	-	-	>F	-	-	-	-	-	-	-	-	-	-	-	1	-	-
F (Fred) Rees	-	-	-	-	-	-	-	-	-	-	-	-	-	-	-	-	-	-	-	-	-	-	-	-	-	-	-	=FB	-	-	-	-	-	-	-	-	-	-	-	1	-	-
Lt. MS Scott	<F	-	-	-	-	-	-	-	-	-	-	-	-	-	-	-	-	-	-	-	-	-	-	-	-	-	-	-	-	-	-	-	-	-	-	-	-	-	-	1	-	-
G Sharpe	-	-	-	-	-	-	-	-	-	-	-	>F	F	F	F	F	-	F	-	F	-	-	F	F	-	F	-	-	-	-	-	-	-	-	-	F	-	<F	-	12	-	-
Cpt. JWD (Dixie) Smith	-	-	-	-	-	-	-	-	-	-	-	-	-	-	-	-	-	-	-	-	-	-	-	-	-	-	-	-	-	-	<FB	-	-	-	-	-	-	-	-	1	-	-
P (Percy) Smitten	-	-	-	-	-	-	-	-	-	-	-	-	-	-	-	-	-	>FH	-	FH	-	FH	FH	FH	-	-	C	-	-	-	-	-	-	-	-	FH	FH	W	-	9	-	4
Lt. FN (Frank) Tarr E3	-	-	-	C	C	-	-	C	C	C	C	C	C	C	-	C	-	-	C	C	C	-	-	C	C	C	-	C	C	C	C	C	C	C	C	-	-	-	C	25	5	15
F (Sos) Taylor E+	F	F	F	F	-	F	F	F	F	F	F	F	-	-	F	F	F	-	F	F	-	F	-	-	F	F	F	F	F	-	F	F	F	F	F	F	F	-	F	30	2	6
FM (Tim) Taylor E+	FH	FH	FH	FH	FH	FH	FH	FH	FH	FH	FH	FH	FH	FH	FH	-	-	-	-	-	-	-	-	-	FH	FH	FH	FH	FH	FH	FH	FH	FH	FH	FH	-	-	-	FH	27	11	33
AL (Alf) Thomas	-	-	-	-	-	-	-	-	-	-	-	-	-	-	-	-	-	-	-	-	C	-	-	-	-	-	-	-	-	-	-	-	-	-	-	C	C	<FH	-	4	-	-
JD (James) Thomson	-	-	-	-	-	-	>F	-	-	-	-	-	-	-	-	-	-	-	-	F	-	-	-	-	-	-	-	-	-	-	-	-	-	-	-	-	-	-	-	2	-	-
JAG (George) Ward E+	F	F	F	F	F	F	F	F	F	F	F	F	F	F	F	F	F	F	F	-	F	F	-	F	F	F	F	F	F	F	F	F	F	F	F	F	F	F	F	37	2	6
SL (Sidney) Waterman	-	-	-	-	-	-	-	-	-	-	-	-	-	-	-	-	=C	-	-	-	-	-	-	-	-	-	-	-	-	-	-	-	-	-	-	-	-	-	-	1	-	-
J Watkins	-	-	-	-	-	-	-	-	-	-	-	-	-	-	-	-	-	-	-	-	-	-	-	-	-	-	-	=F	-	-	-	-	-	-	-	-	-	-	-	1	-	-
JR (Jamie) Watson	C	C	C	C	C	C	C	C	C	-	C	-	C	C	C*	FH	FH	C	FH	-	FH	-	C	-	C	C	-	-	C	-	-	-	-	-	-	-	-	-	-	22	4	12
W Watson	-	-	-	-	-	-	-	-	-	-	-	-	-	-	-	-	-	-	-	-	-	-	-	-	-	-	-	-	-	-	=C	-	-	-	-	-	-	-	-	1	-	-
J Wilkinson	-	-	-	-	-	-	-	-	-	-	-	-	-	-	-	-	-	-	-	-	-	-	-	-	-	-	-	-	-	-	-	C	-	-	-	C	-	C	-	3	-	-
GW (Pedlar) Wood E+	SH	SH	SH	SH	SH	SH	SH	SH	SH	SH	SH	SH	SH	SH	-	SH	SH	-	SH	-	SH	-	-	SH	SH	SH	SH	SH	SH	SH	SH	SH	SH	SH	SH	-	SH	SH	SH	33	5	15

The key for how to read the stats is on the last page

1912/13

Home Ground: Welford Road	**Trophy Cabinet:** Midland Counties Cup(12)	OVERALL RECORD:					T	C	PG	DG	MK	PTS
Captain: Percy Lawrie		PLD	W	D	L	Tigers scored:	154	65	8	5	0	636
Vice-captain: Jimmy Burdett		41	29	3	9	Opponents scored:	69	25	8	2	0	289

GM	DATE		VEN	OPPONENTS	RESULT	TRIES	KICKS	ATT
MIDLAND COUNTIES CUP						**CUP WINNERS: LEICESTER TIGERS**		
33	Mar	15	a	Stratford-upon-Avon (4)	W 36-11	Hunter(3), Dalby(2), Hargrave(2), Burton, Farmer, T.Taylor	Bream 3c	1000
37		29	a	Coventry (sf)	W 9-0	P.Lawrie(3)	-	2000
38	Apr	**5**	**H**	**Belgrave Premier Works (f)**	W 39-8	Dalby(3), Hunter(2), P.Lawrie(2), Farmer(2), Greasley, T.Taylor	Hunter c, P.Lawrie c, Bream c	2853
CLUB MATCHES								
1	Sep	**7**	**H**	**Headingley**	W 18-0	P.Lawrie, S.Taylor, T.Taylor, Wood	Bream 3c	2897
2		**14**	**H**	**Bridgend**	W 32-3	Allen(2), Hunter(2), P.Lawrie, Dalby, H.Lawrie	P.Lawrie d, Bream 2c/p	4099
3		**21**	**H**	**Neath**	W 13-6	P.Lawrie(2), Dalby	Hunter d	5485
4		**28**	**H**	**Devonport Albion**	W 6-0	P.Lawrie	Bream p	7195
5	Oct	**5**	**H**	**Aberavon**	W 18-0	Allen(2), Greasley, P.Lawrie	Bream 3c	4275
6		12	a	Northampton	W 12-5	Hargrave, Hunter	P.Lawrie d, Bream c	-
7		**19**	**H**	**Newport**	W 6-0	Hargrave, T.Taylor	-	6975
8		**26**	**H**	**Llanelly**	W 26-3	Greasley(2), P.Lawrie, Tarr, T.Taylor	Bream 4c/p	2697
9	Nov	2	a	Swansea	L 13-26	H.Lawrie, T.Taylor, Wood	Hunter 2c	15000
10		4m	a	Aberavon	L 3-13	-	Hunter p	-
11		13w	a	Oxford University	L 14-26	Dalby(2), H.Lawrie, Wood	P.Lawrie c	-
12		16	a	Coventry	W 16-0	Hunter(2), P.Lawrie, T.Taylor	Hunter c, H.Lawrie c	3000
13		**23**	**H**	**Moseley**	W 24-0	Waddell(2), Hunter, Tarr, Ward	Bream 3c/p	2512
14		**30**	**H**	**Cardiff**	D 3-3	-	Bream p	3844
15	Dec	**7**	**H**	**Northampton**	W 18-5	Allen, Dalby, Farmer, H.Lawrie	Bream 3c	3736
16		14	a	Headingley	W 41-0	Dalby(2), Tarr(2), Farmer, Hargrave, Hunter, T.Taylor, Ward	Bream 7c	-
17		21	a	Blackheath	W 27-14	Farmer(2), Allen, Jackett, Tarr, T.Taylor, Watson	Bream 3c	-
18		**26th**	**H**	**Birkenhead Park**	W 26-6	Tarr(2), Greasley, Kewney, P.Lawrie, Wood	Bream 4c	2115
19		**27f**	**H**	**Cinderford**	W 12-3	Jackett, P.Lawrie, Tarr, Ward	-	4062
20		**28**	**H**	**Sale**	W 15-3	P.Lawrie(2), Allen	P.Lawrie d, Bream c	3868
21		**30m**	**H**	**Barbarians**	W 15-11	P.Lawrie(2), Hargrave, Wood	Bream p	3880
22	Jan	2th	a	Manchester	W 24-11	P.Lawrie(2), Burton, Dalby, Pemberton, Wood	P.Lawrie d, Bream c	-
23		**4**	**H**	**Gloucester**	L 8-13	Allen	Bream c/p	1412
24		**11**	**H**	**Coventry**	W 6-3	Farmer, P.Lawrie	-	652
25		18	a	Bedford	W 26-9	Broadley(2), Burton, Farmer, S.Taylor, T.Taylor	Bream 4c	-
26		25	a	Moseley	W 23-3	Wood(2), Farmer, H.Lawrie, P.Lawrie	Bream 4c	-
27	Feb	1	a	Gloucester	L 3-11	P.Lawrie	-	-
28		**8**	**H**	**Swansea**	D 0-0	-	-	10513
29		15	a	Newport	L 5-16	T.Taylor	Bream c	-
30		**22**	**H**	**Richmond**	W 25-8	P.Lawrie(2), Greasley, Hargrave, Hunter, Tarr, S.Taylor	Bream 2c	3555
31	Mar	1	a	Devonport Albion	D 3-3	P.Lawrie	-	4000
32		**8**	**H**	**Harlequins**	W 17-3	Allen, Dalby, H.Lawrie, S.Taylor, Wood	Bream c	8908
34		22	a	Llanelly	L 0-8	-	-	-
35		24m	a	Neath	L 0-31	-	-	-
36		25tu	a	Bristol	W 6-0	F.Atkins, Hargrave	-	-
39	Apr	12	a	Birkenhead Park	W 13-0	P.Lawrie, MacMillan, Wood	Bream 2c	-
40		19	a	Cardiff	L 10-14	MacMillan, Timms	Bream 2c	8000
41		**26**	**H**	**London**	W 25-10	Dalby(2), Wood(2), Allen, Tarr, Twigg	Bream 2c	3607

INDIVIDUAL APPEARANCES 1912/13

Name / Game #	1	2	3	4	5	6	7	8	9	10	11	12	13	14	15	16	17	18	19	20	21	22	23	24	25	26	27	28	29	30	31	32	33	34	35	36	37	38	39	40	41	Apps	T	Pts
WJ (Jimmy) Allen	F	F	F	F	F	F	-	-	-	-	F	F	F	F	F	F	F	F	-	F	F	F	F	F	F	F	F	F	F	F	F	F	F	F	-	F	F	F	-	F	F	34	10	30
FA (Fred) Atkins	-	-	-	-	-	-	-	-	-	-	-	-	-	-	-	-	-	-	-	-	-	-	-	-	-	-	-	-	-	-	-	-	-	-	>SH	<SH	-	-	-	-	-	2	1	3
GE (George) Atkins	-	-	-	-	-	-	-	-	-	-	-	-	-	-	>FH	-	-	-	-	-	-	-	-	-	-	-	-	-	-	-	-	-	-	-	FH	FH	-	-	-	FH	-	4	-	-
JW (Billy) Bream	FB	FB	FB	FB	FB	FB	FB	FB	-	-	-	-	FB	FB	FB	FB	FB	FB	-	FB	FB	FB	FB	FB	FB	FB	FB	FB	FB	FB	FB	FB	FB	-	-	FB	FB	FB	FB	FB	FB	34	-	137
J (Joseph) Brewin	-	-	-	-	-	-	-	-	-	-	-	-	-	-	-	-	-	-	-	-	-	-	-	-	-	-	-	-	-	-	-	-	-	-	-	-	-	-	=F	-	-	1	-	-
FRC (Frank) Broadley	-	-	-	-	-	-	-	-	-	-	-	-	W	-	-	-	-	-	-	-	-	-	-	-	W	-	-	-	-	-	-	-	-	-	-	-	-	-	-	-	-	2	2	6
WR (Walter) Buckler	-	-	-	-	-	-	-	-	-	-	-	-	-	-	-	-	-	-	-	-	-	-	>F	-	F	F	F	-	F	-	-	-	F	-	-	F	-	-	-	-	-	7	-	-
Lt-Col. JC (Jimmy) Burdett	-	-	F	-	<F	-	-	-	-	-	-	-	-	-	-	-	-	-	-	-	-	-	-	-	-	-	-	-	-	-	-	-	-	-	-	-	-	-	-	-	-	2	-	-
Sgt. LS (Leo) Burton	-	-	-	-	F	-	F	F	-	F	-	F	F	-	F	F	F	-	F	F	-	F	F	F	F	F	F	-	-	F	F	F	F	-	-	F	F	F	F	-	F	26	3	9
Cpl. WA (Bill) Dalby	F	F	F	F	F	F	F	F	F	F	F	F	-	F	F	F	F	F	-	F	F	F	F	F	F	F	F	F	W	F	F	F	F	-	F	-	F	F	W	F	F	37	16	48
Lt. SE (Sydney) Dove	-	-	-	-	-	-	-	-	-	-	-	-	-	-	-	-	-	-	-	-	-	-	-	-	-	-	-	-	-	-	-	-	-	-	>C	-	-	-	-	-	-	1	-	-
JH (John) Eddison E4	-	-	-	-	-	-	-	-	-	-	-	-	-	-	-	-	-	-	-	=F	-	-	-	-	-	-	-	-	-	-	-	-	-	-	-	-	-	-	-	-	-	1	-	-
DE (Dan) Ellwood	-	-	-	-	-	-	-	-	-	-	-	FB	-	-	-	-	-	-	FB	-	-	-	-	-	-	-	-	-	-	-	-	-	-	FB	FB	-	-	-	-	-	-	4	-	-
Lt. S (Steve) Farmer	>C	C	-	C	-	-	-	-	FB	-	-	-	W	W	W	W	W	-	W	-	-	-	W	W	C	W	-	W	C	-	C	-	W	-	W	C	-	W	-	-	-	21	10	30
MW (Walter) Fisher	-	-	-	-	-	-	-	-	-	-	-	-	-	-	-	-	-	-	SH	-	-	-	-	-	-	-	-	-	-	-	-	-	-	-	-	-	-	-	-	-	-	1	-	-
G (George) Greasley	F	F	-	F	F	F	F	F	F	F	F	F	F	F	F	F	-	F	-	F	F	-	-	F	F	F	F	F	F	F	-	F	F	-	F	F	F	F	F	-	-	32	6	18
OJ (James) Hargrave	-	-	-	-	C	W	W	W	W	-	-	W	FH	W	W	W	W	W	-	W	W	W	-	-	-	-	W	-	-	W	W	W	W	W	-	W	W	-	-	-	FH	24	8	24
AJ (Arthur) Hobbs	F	F	F	F	-	F	F	F	F	F	F	-	<F	-	-	-	-	-	-	-	-	-	-	-	-	-	-	-	-	-	-	-	-	-	-	-	-	-	-	-	-	11	-	-
TB (Thomas) Hogarth E1	-	-	-	-	-	-	-	-	F	F	-	-	-	-	-	-	-	F	-	-	-	F	-	-	-	-	-	-	-	-	-	-	F	F	F	-	-	-	-	-	-	7	-	-
WG (Gil) Hopkins	F	F	F	F	-	F	F	F	F	F	F	F	F	F	F	F	F	F	F	-	F	F	F	F	F	F	-	F	F	F	F	F	F	F	-	-	F	F	F	F	F	36	-	-
SA (Sam) Hunter	C	C	C	C	C	C	C	C	C	C	-	C	C	C	C	C	-	C	-	-	-	-	-	-	-	C	C	C	C	C	-	C	C	C	-	-	C	C	-	-	-	26	13	54
R (Dick) Jackett	-	-	-	-	-	-	-	-	-	-	-	-	-	F	-	-	F	-	F	F	F	-	-	-	-	-	-	F	F	-	F	-	-	F	F	F	-	-	-	F	-	12	2	6
DJ Jones	-	-	-	>W	<W	-	-	-	-	-	-	-	-	-	-	-	-	-	-	-	-	-	-	-	-	-	-	-	-	-	-	-	-	-	-	-	-	-	-	-	-	2	-	-
WH Jones	-	-	-	-	-	-	-	-	-	-	-	-	-	-	-	-	-	-	-	-	-	-	-	-	-	-	-	-	-	-	-	-	-	-	-	>F	-	-	-	-	-	1	-	-
WJ Jones	-	-	-	-	-	-	-	-	-	-	=W	-	-	-	-	-	-	-	-	-	-	-	-	-	-	-	-	-	-	-	-	-	-	-	-	-	-	-	-	-	-	1	-	-
AL (Alf) Kewney E16	-	-	-	-	-	-	-	-	-	-	-	-	-	-	-	-	-	F	-	-	-	<F	-	-	-	-	-	-	-	-	-	-	-	-	-	-	-	-	-	-	-	2	1	3
A (Arthur) King	-	-	-	-	-	-	-	-	-	-	-	-	-	-	-	-	-	-	=FH	-	-	-	-	-	-	-	-	-	-	-	-	-	-	-	-	-	-	-	-	-	-	1	-	-
HSB (Harry) Lawrie	F	F	F	F	F	F	F	F	F	FB	F	F	-	F	F*	F	F	F	F	-	F	-	F	F	F	F	-	F	-	-	-	F	-	F	F	-	F	F	F	F	F	32	6	20
PW (Percy) Lawrie E2	W*	W*	W*	W*	W*	W*	W*	W*	W*	W*	W*	W*	-	-	-	-	-	W*	W*	W*	W*	W*	W*	W*	W*	W*	W*	W*	W*	W*	W*	W*	-	W*	W*	W*	W*	W*	C*	W*	W*	35	28	104
JMC (Clem) Lewis W4	-	-	=C	-	-	-	-	-	-	-	-	-	-	-	-	-	-	-	-	-	-	-	-	-	-	-	-	-	-	-	-	-	-	-	-	-	-	-	-	-	-	1	-	-
D MacMillan	-	-	-	-	-	-	-	-	-	-	-	-	-	-	-	-	-	-	-	-	-	-	-	-	-	-	-	-	-	-	-	-	-	-	-	-	-	-	>W	W	W	3	2	6
HJ (Herbert) Pemberton	-	-	-	-	-	-	-	-	-	-	-	-	-	-	-	-	-	-	-	-	-	=C	-	-	-	-	-	-	-	-	-	-	-	-	-	-	-	-	-	-	-	1	1	3
F (Frank) Read	-	-	-	-		-	-	-	-	-	>FB	-	-	-	-	-	-	-	-	-	-	-	-	-	-	-	-	-	-	-	-	-	-	-	-	-	-	-	-	-	-	1	-	-
A Redding	-	-	-	-	-	-	-	-	-	-	-	-	-	-	-	-	-	-	-	-	-	-	-	-	-	-	F	-	F	-	-	-	-	F	F	F	-	-	-	-	-	5	-	-
Lt. FN (Frank) Tarr E4	-	-	-	-	-	-	-	C	C	C	-	C	C*	C*	-	C*	C*	C	C	C	C	C	C	C	-	-	C	C	-	C	-	C	-	-	-	-	C	-	C	C	C	23	10	30
F (Sos) Taylor E+	F	F	F	F	F	F	F	F	F	F	F	F	F	F	F	F	F	-	F	F	F	F	F	F	F	F	F	F	F	F	F	F	F	F	-	-	F	F	F	F	F	38	4	12
FM (Tim) Taylor E+	FH	FH	FH	FH	FH	FH	FH	FH	FH	-	FH	FH	-	FH	-	FH	FH	FH	-	FH	FH	FH	FH	FH	FH	FH	FH	FH	FH	FH	FH	FH	FH	FH	-	-	FH	FH	FH	-	-	33	11	33
JD (James) Thomson	-	-	-	-	-	-	-	-	-	-	-	-	-	-	-	-	-	-	<F	-	-	-	-	-	-	-	-	-	-	-	-	-	-	-	-	-	-	-	-	-	-	1	-	-
Dr. GE Timms	-	-	-	-	-	-	-	-	-	-	-	-	-	-	-	-	-	-	-	-	-	-	-	-	-	-	-	-	-	-	-	-	-	-	-	-	-	-	-	>C	C	2	1	3
Sgt. JE (John) Twigg	-	-	-	-	-	-	-	-	-	-	-	-	-	-	-	-	-	-	-	-	-	-	-	-	-	-	-	-	-	>F	F	-	-	F	F	F	-	-	F	F	F	8	1	3
DA (David) Waddell	>W	W	W	-	-	C	-	-	-	W	C	-	F	-	F	-	F	-	F	-	-	-	<F	-	-	-	-	-	-	-	-	-	-	-	-	-	-	-	-	-	-	11	2	6
JAG (George) Ward E3	F	F	F	F	F	F	F	F	F	F	F	F	F	F	-	F	-	F	F	F	F	F	-	F	-	-	F	F	F	F	F	F	-	-	F	-	F	F	F	F	F	33	3	9
JR (Jamie) Watson	-	-	-	-	-	-	C	-	-	FH	C	-	-	-	C	-	C	-	C	C	C	-	C	C	C	C	-	-	-	-	C	-	C	C	C	C	-	C	-	-	-	18	1	3
GW (Pedlar) Wood E+	SH	SH	SH	SH	SH	SH	SH	SH	SH	SH	SH	SH	SH	SH	SH	SH	SH	SH	-	SH	SH	SH	SH	SH	SH	SH	SH	SH	SH	SH	SH	SH	SH	SH	-	-	SH	SH	SH	SH	SH	38	12	36

The key for how to read the stats is on the last page

1913/14

19 13/14	
Home Ground: Welford Road	
Captain: Percy Lawrie	
Vice-captain: Harry Lawrie	

OVERALL RECORD:					T	C	PG	DG	MK	PTS
PLD	W	D	L	Tigers scored:	98	40	8	3	0	410
39	21	3	15	Opponents scored:	73	18	5	3	0	282

GM	DATE		VEN	OPPONENTS	RESULT	TRIES	KICKS	ATT
MIDLAND COUNTIES CUP						**CUP WINNERS: VOID - COVENTRY USED INELIGIBLE PLAYERS**		
33	Mar	21	a	Newbold (4)	W 27-0	Dalby, Hunter, H.Lawrie, P.Lawrie, E.Wynne	Bream 3c/2p	-
34	Apr	**4**	**H**	**Coventry (sf)**	L 0-8	-	-	5466
CLUB MATCHES								
Gm	*Date*		*Ven*	*Opponents*	*Result*	*Tries*	*Kicks*	*Att*
1	Sep	**6**	**H**	**Bedford**	W 17-8	Burton(2), Bream, Hargrave, T.Taylor	Bream c	3256
2		**13**	**H**	**Bath**	W 19-5	Allen, Hargrave, Hunter, S.Taylor, Timms	Bream 2c	3498
3		**20**	**H**	**Pontypool**	L 3-8	Hargrave	-	5161
4		27	a	Devonport Albion	D 8-8	Farmer, Wood	Bream c	5000
5	Oct	**4**	**H**	**Headingley**	W 17-6	P.Lawrie(2), Dalby, Tarr, T.Taylor	Bream c	4405
6		**11**	**H**	**Northampton**	W 21-3	G.Ward(2), Dalby, Hopkins, Timms	Bream 3c	4829
7		**18**	**H**	**Coventry**	W 14-6	Timms(2), S.Taylor	Bream c/p	5666
8		25	a	Newport	L 8-11	Hopkins, H.Lawrie	Bream c	-
9	Nov	**1**	**H**	**Llanelly**	W 23-0	Dalby, T.Taylor, Timms, Wood	Bream 4c/p	7233
10		**8**	**H**	**Swansea**	W 6-3	Hargrave, P.Lawrie	-	5960
11		**13th**	**H**	**Oxford University**	W 12-9	T.Taylor, Wood	Bream 2p	2636
12		15	a	Northampton	W 27-3	P.Lawrie(2), T.Taylor(2), Timms	Bream 4c, Hargrave d	4000
13		**22**	**H**	**Aberavon**	D 3-3	Dove	-	6389
14		29	a	Moseley	W 10-0	T.Taylor, Timms	Bream 2c	-
15	Dec	**6**	**H**	**Cardiff**	W 10-3	Dalby, P.Lawrie	Dove d	5445
16		13	a	Headingley	W 21-6	Hargrave(3), P.Lawrie(2), Tarr	Bream p	-
17		**20**	**H**	**Blackheath**	L 8-10	T.Taylor, Timms	Ellwood c	4909
18		**26f**	**H**	**Birkenhead Park**	W 26-8	Hargrave(2), Bream, Dalby, T.Taylor, C.Wynne	Bream 4c	8272
19		**27**	**H**	**Jed-Forest**	W 25-5	C.Wynne(3), Allen, Broadley	Bream 3c/d	5472
		29m	**H**	**Barbarians**	PP (snow)			
	Jan	1	a	Sale	PP (snow)			
20		3	a	Gloucester	L 0-3	-	-	-
21		**10**	**H**	**Manchester**	W 21-6	Hargrave(2), Fisher, P.Lawrie, C.Wynne	Allen c, H.Lawrie c, Mellor c	1827
22		17	a	Coventry	W 3-0	Dalby	-	4000
23		**24**	**H**	**Devonport Albion**	W 9-3	Hargrave, H.Lawrie, P.Lawrie	-	5458
24		31	a	Swansea	L 0-13	-	-	8000
25	Feb	2m	a	Pontypool	L 3-24	Allen	-	-
26		**7**	**H**	**Moseley**	W 16-3	P.Lawrie, Mellor, Timms, Twigg	Bream 2c	1874
27		**14**	**H**	**Newport**	W 13-8	Dalby, P.Lawrie, T.Taylor	Bream 2c	9520
28		21	a	Richmond	D 0-0	-	-	-
29		**23m**	**H**	**Barbarians**	L 3-5	Dalby	-	4000
30		**28**	**H**	**Bristol**	W 8-3	P.Lawrie(2)	Bream c	4635
31	Mar	7	a	Harlequins	L 3-15	Wood	-	3000
32		**14**	**H**	**Gloucester**	L 3-6	-	P.Lawrie p	4026
35	Apr	11	a	Llanelly	L 5-15	T.Taylor	Mellor c	-
36		13m	a	Penarth	L 9-20	Dove, Jackett, S.Taylor	-	-
37		14tu	a	Bath	L 3-14	Allen	-	-
38		15w	a	Cardiff	L 6-8	C.Wynne(2)	-	8000
39		18	a	Birkenhead Park	L 0-23	-	-	-

INDIVIDUAL APPEARANCES 1913/14

Name / Game #	1	2	3	4	5	6	7	8	9	10	11	12	13	14	15	16	17	18	19	20	21	22	23	24	25	26	27	28	29	30	31	32	33	34	35	36	37	38	39	Apps	T	Pts
WJ (Jimmy) Allen	F	F	F	-	-	-	F	F	F	F	F	F	F	F	-	F	F*	-	F	-	F	F	F	F	F	F	F	F	F	F	F	F	F	F	F	-	F	F	-	31	4	14
AW (Alf) Bates	-	-	-	-	-	-	-	-	-	-	-	-	-	-	-	-	-	-	-	-	-	-	-	-	-	-	-	-	-	-	-	-	-	-	>C	-	SH	-	-	2	-	-
JW (Billy) Bream	FB	FB	FB	FB	FB	FB	FB	FB	FB	FB	FB	FB	FB	FB	FB	FB	-	FB	FB	C	-	-	FB	C	C	FB	FB	FB	FB	FB	-	-	<FB	-	-	-	-	-	-	28	2	101
FRC (Frank) Broadley	-	-	-	-	-	-	-	-	-	-	-	-	-	-	-	-	W	-	W	-	-	-	-	-	-	-	-	-	-	-	-	-	-	-	-	-	-	-	-	2	1	3
Sgt. LS (Leo) Burton	F	F	F	-	F	-	-	F	F	-	F	-	F	F	-	F	-	F	F	F	F	F	F	F	F	F	F	F	F	-	F	F	F	F	-	F	F	-	<F	29	2	6
Cpl. WA (Bill) Dalby	F	F	F	F	F	F	F	W	F	F	F	-	F	F	F	F	F	F	-	C	W	F	F	W	W	F	F	F	F	F	F	C	F	W	F	F	-	F	<F	36	9	27
Lt. SE (Sydney) Dove	-	-	-	C	-	-	-	-	-	-	-	C	C	-	C	-	C	C	-	-	-	C	C	-	-	-	-	-	-	-	W	-	-	-	-	C	<C	-	-	11	2	10
Lt. S (Steve) Farmer	C	-	-	W	-	C	-	-	-	-	-	-	-	C	W	-	-	-	-	-	-	-	-	-	-	-	-	-	-	C	C	-	-	-	-	-	-	-	-	7	1	3
MW (Walter) Fisher	-	-	-	-	-	-	-	-	-	-	-	-	-	-	-	-	-	-	-	SH	SH	<SH	-	-	-	-	-	-	-	-	-	-	-	-	-	-	-	-	-	3	1	3
W Hall	-	-	-	>F	F	F	F	F	-	F	-	F	F	-	F	-	F	-	F	F	-	F	F	-	<F	-	-	-	-	-	-	-	-	-	-	-	-	-	-	15	-	-
L Hamblin	-	-	-	-	-	-	-	-	-	-	-	-	-	-	-	-	-	-	-	-	-	-	-	-	-	-	-	-	-	-	-	-	-	-	-	-	>W	C	-	2	-	-
OJ (James) Hargrave	C	W	W	W	W	W	W	C	-	W	W	W	W	W	-	W	W	W	-	-	FH	FH	W	C	<C	-	-	-	-	-	-	-	-	-	-	-	-	-	-	21	12	40
HW (Herbert) Hill	-	-	-	-	-	-	-	-	-	-	-	-	-	-	-	-	-	-	-	-	-	-	-	-	-	-	-	-	-	-	-	-	-	-	>F	F	-	F	-	3	-	-
TB (Thomas) Hogarth E1	-	-	-	-	-	-	-	-	-	-	-	-	-	-	F	-	-	F	F	F	-	-	-	-	-	-	-	-	-	-	-	-	F	F	-	F	<F	-	-	8	-	-
WG (Gil) Hopkins	-	F	F	F	F	F	F	F	F	F	F	F	F	F	F	F	F	F	F	-	F	F	F	F	F	F	F	F	F	F	F	F	F	F	-	F	F	F	F	36	2	6
PJ (Percy) Hougham	-	-	-	-	-	-	-	-	-	-	-	-	-	-	-	-	-	-	-	-	-	-	-	-	-	-	-	-	-	-	>FB	FB	-	<FB	-	-	-	-	-	3	-	-
SA (Sam) Hunter	-	W	W	-	-	-	-	-	-	-	-	-	-	-	-	-	-	-	-	-	-	-	-	-	-	C	W	C	-	C	-	-	C	C	-	-	-	-	-	8	2	6
R (Dick) Jackett	-	-	-	F	-	-	-	-	-	-	-	-	-	-	-	-	-	-	F	F	-	-	-	-	-	-	F	-	-	-	-	-	-	-	F	F	-	<F	-	7	1	3
WH Jones	-	F	-	-	-	-	-	-	-	-	-	-	-	-	-	-	-	-	-	-	-	-	-	-	-	-	-	-	-	-	-	-	-	-	-	-	-	-	<F	2	-	-
HSB (Harry) Lawrie	F*	-	F*	F*	F	F	F	F	F	F	F	F	-	F	-	F	-	F*	-	-	F	-	F	F	-	-	-	-	-	F	F	F	F	F*	-	-	-	-	-	22	3	11
PW (Percy) Lawrie E2	-	-	-	-	W*	W*	W*	W*	W*	W*	W*	W*	W*	W*	W*	W*	-	-	-	-	C*	W*	W*	W*	W*	W*	W*	W*	W*	W*	W*	W*	W*	-	-	-	W*	-	W*	27	15	48
JB (Jimmy) Leather	-	-	-	-	-	-	-	-	-	-	-	-	-	-	-	-	-	-	-	-	-	-	-	-	-	-	-	-	>F	-	-	-	-	-	F	<F	-	-	-	3	-	-
D MacMillan	W	-	-	-	-	-	-	-	<W	-	-	-	-	-	-	-	-	-	-	-	-	-	-	-	-	-	-	-	-	-	-	-	-	-	-	-	-	-	-	2	-	-
F (Fred) Mellor	-	-	-	-	-	-	-	-	-	-	-	-	-	-	-	-	-	-	-	>FB	FB	FB	-	FB	FB	W	-	W	W	W	-	W	W	W	FB	FB	-	FB	FB	16	1	7
A Redding	-	-	-	-	-	-	-	-	-	-	-	-	-	-	F	-	-	-	F	F	-	F	-	F	F	-	-	-	-	-	-	-	-	-	F	-	-	F	<F	9	-	-
RO (Robert) Ringrose	-	-	-	-	-	-	-	-	-	-	-	-	-	-	-	-	-	-	-	-	-	-	-	-	-	-	-	-	-	-	-	-	-	-	>W	W	C	W	-	4	-	-
GH (Gordon) Salmon	-	-	-	-	-	-	-	-	-	-	-	-	-	-	-	-	-	-	-	-	-	-	-	-	-	-	-	-	-	-	-	-	-	-	-	>C	FH	-	<C	3	-	-
J Sutcliffe	-	-	-	-	-	-	-	-	-	-	-	-	-	-	-	-	-	-	-	-	-	-	-	-	-	-	-	-	-	-	-	-	-	-	>W	W	FB	-	<F	4	-	-
Lt. FN (Frank) Tarr E4	-	C*	C	-	C	-	C	C	C	C	C	-	-	-	-	C	-	C	<C*	-	-	-	-	-	-	-	-	-	-	-	-	-	-	-	-	-	-	-	-	11	2	6
F (Sos) Taylor E+	F	F	F	F	F	F	F	F	-	F	F	F	F	F	F	F	F	F	-	F	F	-	-	-	-	-	-	-	-	-	-	F	F	F	-	F	F	-	F	25	3	9
FM (Tim) Taylor E1	FH	FH	FH	FH	FH	FH	FH	FH	FH	FH	FH	FH	FH	FH	FH	FH	FH	FH	-	-	-	-	FH	FH	FH	FH	FH	FH	FH	FH	FH	FH	FH	FH	FH	FH	-	FH	FH	34	11	33
Dr. GE Timms	W	C	C	C	C	C	C	-	C	C	C	C	C	C	C	C	C	-	C	-	-	-	-	-	-	C	C	C	C	-	C	<C	-	-	-	-	-	-	-	23	9	27
Sgt. JE (John) Twigg	-	F	F	F	F	F	-	F	F	F	F	F	F	F	F	F	F	-	F	F	F	F	F	F	F	F	F	F	F	F	F	<F	-	-	-	-	-	-	-	29	1	3
JAG (George) Ward E6	F	F	F	F	F	F	F	F	F	-	-	F	F	F	-	F	F	F	-	-	F	-	-	F	F	F	-	F	F	F	-	-	-	F	F	-	-	F	-	25	2	6
JR (Jamie) Watson	-	-	-	-	-	-	-	-	-	-	-	-	-	-	-	-	-	-	FH	<FH*	-	-	-	-	-	-	-	-	-	-	-	-	-	-	-	-	-	-	-	2	-	-
Dr. G Wilson	-	-	-	-	-	>F	F	-	F	F	F	F	-	-	F	-	F	F	-	F	F	F	F	F	F	F	F	F	F	F	F	F	F	F	-	-	<F	-	-	25	-	-
SG (Sydney) Wolfe	-	-	-	-	-	-	-	-	-	-	-	-	-	-	-	-	-	-	-	-	-	-	-	-	-	>F	F	F	-	F	F	F	-	-	F	-	F	F	<F	10	-	-
GW (Pedlar) Wood E1	SH	SH	SH	SH	SH	SH	SH	SH	SH	SH	SH	SH	SH	SH	SH	SH	SH	SH	-	-	-	-	SH	SH	SH	SH	SH	SH	SH	SH	SH	SH	SH	SH	SH	SH	-	SH	■SH	34	4	12
CHL (Charles) Wynne	-	-	-	-	-	-	-	-	-	-	-	-	-	-	-	-	-	>W	W	-	W	W	-	-	-	-	-	-	-	-	-	-	-	-	-	-	-	W	W	6	7	21
EE (Ernest) Wynne	-	-	-	-	-	-	-	-	-	-	-	-	-	-	-	-	-	-	-	-	>C	C	C	-	-	-	C	-	-	-	-	-	C	C	-	-	-	-	<C	7	1	3

1 GAME: GE (George) Atkins <SH(19), DE (Dan) Ellwood FB(17), G (George) Greasley F(1), J Leader =F(37), FCW (Fred) Newman =C(29), RF (Richard) Russell E1 <F(1), K Storey =C(35), W Ward >W(20), WJ (William) Watts W1 >C(38), J Wilkinson <W(20)

The key for how to read the stats is on the last page

CHAPTER 8

Aiming High

1914/1915

Britain's declaration of war against Germany on 4 August 1914, brought another upsurge of activity at Welford Road, whose objective was purely military. Rugby activities ceased, many of the players joined up, and Tom Crumbie turned his attention to raising as many men as possible for active service. The club premises were loaned for army and auxiliary purposes and formed the headquarters for two artillery units and a pioneer corps. It is not difficult to imagine Crumbie overseeing recruitment in much the same way he oversaw the rugby club - and conceivably exercising similar authority - and all told 3,500 officers and men joined the colours.

Just two charity games were eventually played in the 1914/15 season, both at Welford Road against the Barbarians. The first on 2 January 1915, was staged "for encouragement of recruiting and in aid of patriotic funds", with each side playing a man short. The game on 27 March was again played "for the encouragement of local recruiting", and the total proceeds of the match were donated to the Leicester Royal Infirmary. There was a paid attendance of 3,662 and 4,255 for the matches, which took place largely because of the patriotic drive of Barbarians committeeman and player Edgar Mobbs, the Northampton and England centre who was killed at Zillebeke in Belgium two years later, aged 35, and Crumbie. Three other Barbarians players in these games would not return from the war, along with the Tigers forward, Archibald Bowell, who played in the first game.

↑ Lieutenant Frank Tarr of the Leicestershire Regiment, one of the Tigers players who did not return from the war.

1918/1919

When the Armistice was signed on 11 November 1918, at least seventeen Tigers had lost their lives, including that outstanding centre, Frank Tarr, killed at Ypres in 1915. Several more had been injured but recovered to help Leicester to an outstanding decade. It seems incredible but only six weeks after the guns had finally ceased on the Continent, a Leicester XV - and a good Leicester XV - was in action again at Welford Road.

The reconstructed Members' Stand, completed before war broke out, was officially opened over Christmas 1918, and on Boxing Day Percy Lawrie led out Tigers for their first game in three and a half years, against the 4th battalion of the Leicestershire Regiment. George Ward, Arthur Bull and Pedlar Wood, all of whom had made their names before the war, were there to help Leicester to a 6-5 win over the service unit, Lawrie scoring two tries before a crowd of 3,317. Also on call at that time were two men destined to make lasting names for themselves, Harold Day and Frank 'Sos' Taylor.

↑ On Boxing Day 1918 Percy Lawrie became the club's leading try-scorer of all time, a record he still holds, passing Harry Wilkinson's previous mark set 20 years before.

Of necessity most of Leicester's 19 fixtures in what remained of the 1918/19 season were against service sides, all at Welford Road, but the rugby-starved Leicester public got the best of what was available. Apart from attracting sides like the South African and New Zealand Armed Forces to play the club, Leicester helped host the services tournament which played a notable part that season, in a variety of venues up and down the country, in putting rugby back on its feet.

Against the New Zealand Forces, captained by 'Ranji' Wilson, Tigers lost 19-0 with the following team: Frank Read; Harold Day, CD Carter, Myley Abraham, Percy Lawrie (capt); Edward Myers, Pedlar Wood; CD Ferris, Gordon Vears, William Collopy, Arthur Bull, J Woolley, Sos Taylor, Jimmy Allen, George Ward. Of that side Lawrie, Wood, Bull and Ward had already been capped by England, and Collopy by Ireland. Day, Myers and Taylor were to join them as England caps within a couple of years, which indicated the strength of Leicester's line-up and also a possible reason why, on 15 February 1919, they equalled the club's then record of points scored in one match when they beat a Bedford XV 71-0.

It is perhaps a little hard on Bedford that they should have entered Tigers' record book this way, since they were represented largely by players from service depots in the area and boys from the school. There, however, it stood for more than sixty years as Leicester ran in 19 tries, seven of them converted. Teddy Haselmere collected five tries on one wing, Harold Day four on the other, while centre Norman Coates and fly-half Alf Bates each scored three. Since the game was played for just over an hour there was fractionally over a point a minute in which the crowd could revel.

The following week the Llanelly and Wales centre, Willy Watts, made his debut against the Australian Armed Forces (lost 6-8) and twice before the season ended, Wavell Wakefield played at Welford Road, for the RAF against the club and against the Canadian Armed Forces. In another four years he was to captain Leicester, so at the time allowing the club to claim him as their most capped player - a distinction they shared with Harlequins, Wakefield's original club, until his feat was overtaken by Peter Wheeler in 1982.

The season ended with 12 wins and seven defeats but during the summer Leicester lost the services of one of their most enthusiastic supporters, their treasurer of the past 15 years, Frederick St Clair Pain. His active connection with the club had begun 25 years earlier when he initiated, by his lively correspondence in the local press, the formation of the Schools League whose administration must have contributed to the foundation by Leicester schoolmaster Joseph Cooper in 1904 of the English Schools Rugby Union. The club recognised new talent and Mr St Clair Pain served them long and well before his death in 1919, doubtless happy to see that a £3,000 debt on the Members' Stand had been cleared by a public appeal coupled with gate receipts.

1919/1920

The first full season after the war opened against Bath when each club fielded three survivors from pre-war days. For Leicester it became a record-breaker in many ways. The club scored more points, 756, than they had ever scored before or were to do again for 50 years, and the minute, nine-stone wing Teddy Haselmere scored the staggering total of 59 tries - no-one else before or since has even reached 40.

Haselmere (born Hasselmeier), from Rugby, had been introduced to the club by Jimmy 'Jumbo' Allen, one of their leading forwards, when the game resumed after the war and he was the first to pay tribute to his centres in helping him to his record number of tries. Inside him he had the dependable Norman Coates who joined Leicester from Bath, Willy Watts and more of a similar ilk, while he also benefited from Tigers' new style of play. For this was the season they began to play with seven forwards and eight backs, largely due to the return from service of the pre-war fly-half, Tim Taylor.

Leicester had acquired the services of another outstanding fly-half, Alf Bates, who could turn on a sixpence and whose individual running captivated the crowds - even if he not infrequently lost his own players in the intricacies of his side-stepping. Crumbie therefore decided that he could afford to play a man short in the forwards, in order to accommodate Taylor and Bates, the one at fly-half, the other at five-eighth. It was a novelty that must have taken a lot of clubs by surprise and, provided the midfield players always ran straight, it meant the wings inevitably had an overlap.

Haselmere was the first to benefit from this, his exceptional speed bringing him tries in 27 of the 41 games. Twice he scored five times, against Burton and Headingley, and against Burton he aggregated 31 points in a 58-0 win, since he also kicked six conversions and a dropped goal; this remained the individual record in a game until beaten by Dusty Hare in 1981. Curiously enough, however, the club had an even better all-round player on the other wing in Alastair Smallwood, one of the outstanding players of his time.

Smallwood was born in Scotland but educated at Newcastle Royal Grammar School and went on to Gonville and Caius College, Cambridge, on an organ scholarship. A man of many parts, he won his Blue in 1919, dropping a goal in Cambridge's 7-5 win over Oxford - the first Varsity Match to feature a penalty goal - and he then took up a teaching appointment at Uppingham. The first of his 14 caps came in 1920, when he was picked at centre in the 8-3 win over France, and he was never in a losing England team until his last game, when Scotland won 14-11 at Murrayfield in 1925.

A man who placed considerable emphasis on the running game, it is slightly ironic that two of Smallwood's high spots in his career revolved around drop goals. The first won the only Varsity Match in which he played; the second won the 1923 international against Wales 7-3 when Leonard Corbett flicked a pass between his legs to Smallwood who overcame his surprise sufficiently well to drop a goal from 45 yards.

That was the match in which Leo Price scored a famous try straight from Wakefield's kick-off at the start of the game. Price caught the ball from the kick-off, dropped for goal, followed up his own kick and touched down for a try. Since Price was also playing for Leicester at the time, the club's players were responsible for all the points.

A TIGER'S SUCCESS.

E. Haselmere.

The Tigers flying wing three-quarter again showing his best form on the rack." Last Saturday at Desborough won the furlong race in clever style 23½ secs. There are more "pots" iting for him.

↑ Teddy Haselmere ran in an incredible 59 tries in the 1919/20 season.

↑ Tigers' prolific try-scoring back, Alastair Smallwood.

It is Smallwood too who holds Leicester's record for the number of tries scored by an individual in one match. In the last match of the Christmas holiday in 1922, against Manchester at Welford Road, he scored seven tries in a 36-0 win, his hand-off and swerve baffling the opposition on a day when Tigers were fielding a severely weakened team. In the book which many players of a past generation regarded as something of a bible, *Rugger* by Wavell Wakefield and Howard Marshall, Smallwood was described thus:

"He...was always experimenting and attempting new methods of attack. Certainly he was one of the most enterprising, as well as one of the cleverest, post-War backs. It was he who started the wings throwing in from touch instead of the scrum-half, with a view to getting a swift return pass from a short throw-in and thus having a clear run along the line before the defence was in position.

"He also had a useful habit of bluffing the opposition and I shall never forget once when he had raced back, apparently to touch down, but picked up the ball instead and quietly walked right up to the opposition players who were following up instead of trying to dodge them. When he nearly reached them he handed out the ball as if he were giving it to them and so taken aback were they that he was able suddenly to slip round them and go all out to start an attack.

"Of course it was risky but it came off for Smallwood could always size up the possibilities of the situation accurately...He always insisted that his centre should let him have the ball early to give him plenty of time and room in which to manoeuvre and he had the invaluable knack of keeping in touch with his centre so that real combination between the two was possible."

Also capped in 1920 was Sos Taylor, the former Medway Street Old Boys forward who had received

→ Harold Day gained his first England cap against Wales in 1920 after only six first-team games for the Tigers.

such serious wounds on active service with the Leicestershire Regiment that he had been told he would never play rugby again. His sterling efforts brought him international honours, at the age of 29, against France and Ireland, while during that season the Leicester pack also had the services of JE 'Jenny' Greenwood, captain of England that year and later an outstanding president of the RFU. Greenwood distinguished himself by kicking 10 conversions in the 62-3 win over Richmond, and another debutant that season was a schoolboy international full-back of pre-war days, Doug Norman, now a forward and 11 years later to win his cap for England as a hooker.

If the club's playing members should seem to take the limelight it is not entirely surprising, considering the personnel Tom Crumbie called on. Yet much good work was going on off the field, with the erection of a new stand - appropriately enough, called the New Stand and later to be renamed the Crumbie Stand following the death in 1928 of the secretary. It was part of Crumbie's aim to make the club's facilities the best in the country and attract regular internationals to the Midlands, blithely ignoring the development of the Twickenham ground.

In that respect it could be said that the Welford Road playing arena became one huge white elephant, for England (for whom it was primarily designed) played only one international there following the completion of the New Stand. Yet again, later generations can only admire Mr Crumbie's ambitions on Leicester's behalf, for his efforts gave the city a stadium second only to four national playing arenas in the British Isles and a foundation on which the club's administrators have built over the last twenty years.

↑ Doug Norman was a schoolboy international in 1911.

↓ Easter tour card of 1921.

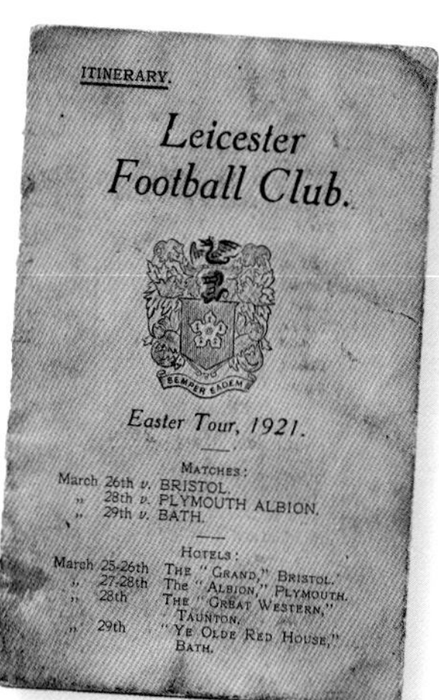

ITINERARY.

Leicester Football Club.

SEMPER EADEM

Easter Tour, 1921.

MATCHES:
March 26th v. BRISTOL.
" 28th v. PLYMOUTH ALBION.
" 29th v. BATH.

HOTELS:
March 25-26th THE "GRAND," BRISTOL.
" 27-28th THE "ALBION," PLYMOUTH.
" 28th THE "GREAT WESTERN," TAUNTON.
" 29th "YE OLDE RED HOUSE," BATH.

1920/1921

It had been hoped that the stand would be ready for the start of the 1920/21 season but the official opening was made on October 2 by the President of the RFU, Ernest Prescott, before the game against Headingley. The stand, and additional improvements, cost over £21,000 and saddled the club with a debt that was to plague them for years. But that was all in the future - the wife of the club president, Mrs Hedley Salmon, presented a new flag and the players obliged with a 33-3 win, featuring a line-up at three-quarter of Haselmere, Smallwood, Tim Taylor, Percy Lawrie and Day, a back division to match any in the country. Of that quintet Lawrie, who started to play for Leicester in 1907 as an 18-year-old, went on until 1924 and accumulated the staggering total of 206 tries - far and away the club record. Since he captained the club before and after the war (during which he served a lieutenant in the Royal Artillery) his influence was far-reaching.

It was to be another outstanding season. Newport, with a 22-3 win, deprived the club of their unbeaten record in the ninth game and there was a degree of criticism of the eight-backs formation - not surprising since, no matter how good a collection of forwards could be recruited, there had to be occasions when seven men were thoroughly outplayed by eight. Interestingly enough, Leicester reverted to eight forwards for the game with the Barbarians, which they won 8-6 thanks to two tries from Tim Taylor.

Leicester was the venue for the England v The South game, during which there were trials for Haselmere, Smallwood, Sos Taylor and Day, while the club helped Leicestershire to the final of the County Championship. The Midland Counties Union had been disbanded after the war and this was the first season of the new county groupings, the fourth system tried for the County Championship. Yorkshire were beaten 8-5 in the semi-final at Welford Road and it was an all-Leicester team that represented the county in the final against Gloucestershire at Kingsholm. The XV was: J Wilkinson; Fred Mellor, Percy Lawrie, JR Markham, Teddy Haselmere, Tim Taylor, Pedlar Wood, Sos Taylor, George Ward, Charlie Cross, Doug Norman, Jimmy Allen, Wal Buckler, John Wickson, Ernest Ward. Unfortunately the dream faded as Percy Lawrie scored Leicestershire's only points with a dropped goal in a 31-4 defeat.

One of the forwards, Charlie Cross, who had made his debut the season before, was to distinguish himself in another way before the season ended. On the way from Chester for the game in which the Tigers took Birkenhead Park's ground record, he leapt from the leading car and pulled up a runaway horse and cart - a feat which no doubt inspired his team-mates in the game that day. Times, of course, had changed, and the team no longer travelled in style by train. Motor cars were now so common that they had taken over from the train for away games - just as well, since that day a coal strike had prevented many of the trains from running.

It had long been decided to make the last game of the season a charity match, in aid of the Royal Infirmary in Leicester, a laudable habit which was maintained up to the Second World War. To begin with this match was against a London XV - subsequently it was generally the match with Blackheath and it was in the 1921 Infirmary Match that Wavell Wakefield made his debut for Leicester, scoring two tries in a 20-5 win which gave the Tigers the admirable record of 31 wins, eight defeats and two draws for the season. The same match the following season meant that £950 of the required £1,000 had been raised, allowing the consecration of a memorial bed at the Infirmary commemorating players killed during the Great War.

↓ The change in the Tigers' formation for this match is clearly shown duly amended in this programme.

TELEPHONE 325.
W. & L. STAFFORD,
Old Established High Class
FAMILY BUTCHERS.
Hotels and Business Establishments Catered for on best possible terms.
Victoria Parade, Leicester.

SINGERS,
120 BELGRAVE ROAD,
FOR
Drop-Head Machines with 3 or 5 Drawers, Also Boot and Tailoring Machines.
Any make of Machines taken in part exchange. Immediate attention given to Repairs. All kinds of parts kept in stock. A. GASK, Sales Manager.

For Artistic Furniture and Carpets
Estimates free
GOODLYS Ltd
Moderate prices
27 Market Street, Leicester

J. Lumbers & Son,
JEWELLERS.
28 GRANBY STREET (Opposite the Post Office).
Fine Selection of Goods suitable for Christmas Presents at moderate prices.
REPAIRS IN ALL BRANCHES. Christmas Pudding and Cake Charms.
'PHONE, 2057.

The Albion Dining Rooms,
GALLOWTREE GATE,
Proprietor W. C. H. COLLINS.
Breakfast, Dinners and Teas.
Hot Joints from 11 a.m. to 10.30 p.m.
WORTHINGTON'S BOTTLED ALES.
Wines, Cigars, Tea and Coffee at all hours.

Phone 174x.
WYVERN LAUNDRY Ltd.,
CLEANING & DYEING SAVE BUYING.
Send your Suits, Raincoats, Overcoats, Costumes, Curtains, Etc. Etc. TO-DAY
Carpets Beaten or Cleaned. Returned Quickly.

GRIFFITHS,
The Leading Cash Tailor,
23 BELVOIR STREET,
Phone 3389.
FOR SMART TAILORING AT REASONABLE PRICES.

LEICESTER — Wednesday, Dec. 29th, 1920.

BACK—
1 J. Wilkinson.

THREE-QUARTER BACKS—
2 A. M. Smallwood (Right Wing), 3 P. W. Lawrie (Capt). (Right Centre), 4 W. Watts, 5 G. M. Thomas (Left Centre), 6 E. Haselmere (Left Wing)

HALF-BACKS—
7 G. W. Wood, 8 F. M. Taylor

FORWARDS—
9 G. Ward, 10 F. Taylor, 11 W. C. Hicks, 12 C. W. Cross, 13 N. Coates, 14 D. J. Norman, 15 W. Buckler

O

FORWARDS—
16 W. D. Doherty, 17 V. H. Neser, 18 A. W. L. Row, 19 V. Grenning, 20 A. F. Blakiston, 21 P. H. Lawless, 22 A. H. Shelswell, 23 F. Spriggs

HALF-BACKS—
24 A. T. Young, 25 W. H. Udy

THREE-QUARTER BACKS—
26 Q. E. M. A. King (Left Wing), 27 E. F. van der Riet (Left Centre), 28 S. Cook (Right Centre), 29 G. N. Lowe (Right Wing)

BACK—
30 T. A. Shaw

BARBARIANS

Referee: Mr. D. HELLEWELL (Yorkshire.)

CARR'S
FEVER . .
POWDERS
For Colds, Influenza, etc.

Semper Eadem
LEICESTER'S HEALTH CENTRE
SOLARIUM BATHS (Better than Turkish Baths) CURE
Rheumatism, Lumbago, Neuritis, Sciatica and Kindred Ailments.
THE SANITARIUM, 19 LONDON ROAD, LEICESTER.

Xmas Presents.
PERFUMES by Du Barry, Atkinson, Yardley, Piver, Grossmith, etc., 6d. to 63/-
MANICURE SETS 3/- to 80/-
VACUUM FLASKS 4/11 to 40/-
Safety Razors, Gillette, Autostrop, etc.
KODAKS, 12/6 to £25.
Photo Albums, Hair Brushes, Fountain Pens
YOUNG AND SONS 16 Gallowtree Gate, LEICESTER.

H. MORGAN,
THE KEY SHOP,
21 HIGH CROSS STREET
Large Stock of Padlocks
WHOLESALE OR RETAIL.
IMMEDIATE ATTENTION GIVEN TO REPAIRS.

THE FLU FLEW. Established 1840
BUTLER'S
Fever and Influenza Powders.
THE ONE DAY COLD CURE.
Suitable alike for Young and Old.
Sold by all Stores, 3 Powders for 2d.
Beware of Imitations. See Photo on each Powder.

Page's Cycle Depot.
CLEARANCE SALE.
GREAT REDUCTIONS.
Guaranteed Cycles from £8 10s.
Accessories at Keenest Prices.
250 CHARNWOOD STREET.

TYLER'S
FASHIONABLE
FOOTWEAR . .
2 LONDON ROAD (Opposite Y.M.C.A)

FOR SHIRTS
that are GUARANTEED TO FIT and Wear Well
T. E. SNOWDEN
42½ & 44a HUMBERSTONE GATE and 6 GALLOWTREE GATE.
We have always Specialised in Extra Large sizes and fittings in Shirts and Underwear.
A full range of all the Leading Brands Always in Stock.

1921/1922

More ground improvements were carried out during the summer of 1921, terracing being built up in front of the New Stand and the extension to the Members' Stand giving a seating capacity of 10,250. Subscriptions for the stand seats were now 25 shillings (15 shillings for ladies and boys) and the unemployed were allowed in free at each end of the ground (on production of their out-of-work cards). But the new season began on an unhappy note with the death in the R38 airship disaster over Hull of Flt-Lt Godfrey Main Thomas, DFC, who had played three-quarter off and on during the previous two seasons.

Scrum-half Alfred Godfrey makes a break against Swansea on 5.11.1921.

Nevertheless there were 12,000 for the opening match against Bath, there were caps for Day and Smallwood, and Leicester became the first English club to win at Swansea for 26 years. It was the last season for scrum-half Pedlar Wood, however. Having made his debut in 1906 and played 388 games for Leicester, he was to join Nuneaton the following season where he concluded his career.

Harold Day's first cap had come against Wales in 1920 and two years later he played against Wales and France, a fourth cap coming his way in 1926 when he was called into the side at a late hour against Scotland. Fondly remembered by some of his contemporaries as one of the slowest wings to represent his country, Day made up for this by his phenomenal place-kicking and it was not uncommon to see him landing goals from his own half at Welford Road.

In the course of eight seasons he scored over 1,000 points for the club, regularly topping 100 points in a season, and if that does not sound much by contemporary standards, it should be remembered that the old leather balls were far heavier than today's flighty affairs, that there were far fewer opportunities for penalty kicks and that Day, a schoolmaster at Felsted, Essex, missed quite a lot of games either because of representative calls or because he was unable to travel away on any regular basis.

Recalling his days as a Tiger 30 years later, Day commented on the team's formation of eight backs: "I have preserved four foolscap pages from EHD Sewell [the noted rugby critic], addressed to me as captain, proving that it could never work. We won our next game by 40-odd points against Moseley. I received a postcard from him suggesting we took on stronger opponents.

"Our success was due to a supply of great half-backs. At scrum-half, following that fearless box of tricks Pedlar Wood we had John Russell, whose neglect by Scotland was a mystery, Guy German and Edward Massey. For fly-halves there were PG Scott, Ralph Buckingham and Harry Greenlees."

1922/1923

Of course this was after the retirement of Tim Taylor and the loss, in 1922, of Alf Bates who joined the professional ranks with Oldham. But little, it seemed, could halt the Leicester points machine. In the 33-5 win over Nuneaton, Day scored 15 points and in the following match, a 46-5 success over Headingley, he registered 20 points from two tries, four conversions and two penalties. He may have lacked a degree of pace at international level but there was no doubting his worth at club level. There was an interesting addition to the three-quarter line in the shape of Andrew Roxburgh, a former Leicester City player who did well enough with the oval ball to win a regular place over the next two seasons.

Over the Christmas period Leicester entertained their first guests from France, Racing Club de France, and won 4-0 with a Haselmere dropped goal on an occasion graced by the presence of the French consul and attaché, both representing their country's embassy in London. But there was nothing like the high jinks that occurred in the game against London Irish, when an aghast the *Leicester Evening Mail* reporter recorded: "An incident which convulsed the crowd followed. Wright [the Leicester wing] had received the ball but was grasped by Stanley. The two players struggled for a time and then the Tiger broke away but left his knickers in the hands of the Irishman. Wright commenced to run, unaware of the disaster which had overtaken him. He quickly realised his position and collapsed to the ground where he was quickly surrounded by the rest of the players until he was supplied with a new garment." Tigers won 22-3 and Wright got his try - would players today collapse in the same modest heap?

HLV Day runs with the ball against London Welsh with Frank Wood on his outside.

There were caps this season for Smallwood and Price while Scotland capped the Melrose forward, JR 'Jock' Lawrie, who was to join Leicester the next year. The club's two England players were in the XV which beat Ireland 23-5 in the last home international to be played at Welford Road, on 10 February 1923. A crowd of around 20,000 saw both men score a try in a game dominated by the half-back expertise of Cecil Kershaw and WJA 'Dave' Davies.

Four days later the club made their first trip to foreign parts, returning the visit of Racing Club de France. It was quite a tour, for after the game in Paris they were due to return to play United Services Portsmouth and Plymouth Albion. Perhaps the best way to describe the trip is through the eyes of one of the club's forwards, Henry Grierson, who was not only a useful player but a man of words who, in 1924, published an entertaining anecdotal book, called *The Ramblings of a Rabbit.*

The party left Leicester for London on the Sunday and crossed the Channel the following day, via Folkestone-Boulogne, and so to the Hotel St James and Albany in Paris. The game was on the Tuesday and, according to Grierson, "was a real bad show. They were a fine side and just about good enough to beat us without any outside assistance, but they were packed with it in the form of a French referee. He was mustard and nearly blew us off the field."

Tigers, with some of their leading players unable to travel, lost 19-9 but it seems reasonable to assume that their evening at the Folies Bergères the night before may not have helped form. The post-match dinner was held at Maxims and it must have been a bleary-eyed bunch of rugby players who assembled for departure on Wednesday. Indeed, some of them may have been fortunate to depart at all, for the practical joker, Norman Coates, and little Tim Taylor had an altercation with a French taxi driver during the night and wound up in the police cells. It is not known whether Coates' allegation to the gendarmerie that Taylor was a "gendarme anglais" was the main reason for their release or not.

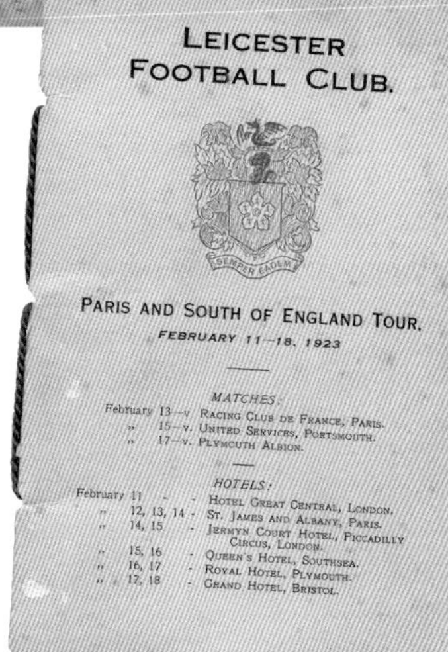
ITINERARY

LEICESTER FOOTBALL CLUB.

SEMPER EADEM

PARIS AND SOUTH OF ENGLAND TOUR.
FEBRUARY 11—18, 1923

MATCHES:
February 13—v. Racing Club de France, Paris.
" 15—v. United Services, Portsmouth.
" 17—v. Plymouth Albion.

HOTELS:
February 11 - - Hotel Great Central, London.
" 12, 13, 14 - St. James and Albany, Paris.
" 14, 15 - Jermyn Court Hotel, Piccadilly Circus, London.
" 15, 16 - Queen's Hotel, Southsea.
" 16, 17 - Royal Hotel, Plymouth.
" 17, 18 - Grand Hotel, Bristol.

↑ Main: Tigers gather outside the Stade Colombes prior to their first game in France, 13 February 1923. Seager, Sambrook, Lawrence, Coates, Wallace, Sharratt, Roxburgh, Ward (capt), Wright, T Taylor, Haselmere, Cross, Jones, S Taylor, Thorneloe.

Inset: Itinerary for Tigers' tour to Paris and the south of England, February 1923.

Little, it seemed, could keep Coates down and as the tour party passed through customs at Dover the *Leicester Mercury* reporter, who had omitted to declare some scent, became the butt of his humour. Coates knew nothing of the perfume residing in the reporter's bag but happily informed officials: "Don't you believe him, he's a prevaricator. His grip is packed with contraband, search him!" The scent was discovered and the extra duty made it an expensive present at 25 shillings. Maybe the *Mercury's* expense account footed the bill. When his playing days were over the irrepressible Coates ran the line for many seasons and became one of the well-known characters at Welford Road, along with the pre-war forward, Tom Goodrich, who became groundsman in 1922.

That particular tour continued at Portsmouth on the Thursday with a game against the services side (drawn 3-3) and then to Plymouth for the match with the Albion on the Saturday (lost 5-15). The next day they returned, via Bristol, to Leicester.

In the same season 13 Tigers played in the Leicestershire side beaten 8-6 at Bridgwater by Somerset in the County Championship final and only a couple of points prevented Tigers from beating Newport in the Welsh club's invincible season. Day kicked two penalties but Leicester lost 7-6 before a crowd of 16,000 people - they were to make up for that later in the year.

↑ LEICESTER FOOTBALL CLUB 1919/20
Back: Thorpe (Hon.Tres), S.Taylor, G.Ward, Hicks, Vears, Coates, Watts, Lawrie.
Middle: Salmon (President), Barrett, Francis, Wilkinson, Allen (capt), Cross, Thomas, Crumbie (Hon.Sec).
Front: D.Norman, Haselmere, Bates, Wood, T.Taylor.

↑ LEICESTER FOOTBALL CLUB 1921/22
Back: Crumbie (Hon.Sec), Godfrey, German, Thorneloe, H.Usher, Hicks, Sharratt, Lawrence, Wilkinson, Smallwood.
Middle: Thorpe (Hon.Tres), S.Taylor, Norman, Ward (Vice-capt), Lawrie (capt), Day, Coates, Cross, B.Usher.
Front: Russell, Wilkins, T.Taylor, Haselmere, Sambrook, Buckler.

19 14/15	Home Ground: Welford Road	OVERALL RECORD:					T	C	PG	DG	MK	PTS
	Captain: Percy Lawrie	PLD	W	D	L	Tigers scored:	6	3	0	0	0	24
	Vice-captain: Frank Tarr	2	1	1	0	Opponents scored:	3	0	0	0	0	9

GM	DATE		VEN	OPPONENTS	RESULT	TRIES	KICKS	ATT
CLUB MATCHES								
1	Jan	**2**	**H**	**Barbarians**	W 21-6	Pearce(2), P.Wood(2), Allen	P.Lawrie 2c, H.Lawrie c	3662
2	Mar	**27**	**H**	**Barbarians**	D 3-3	Manton	-	4255

INDIVIDUAL APPEARANCES 1914/15					
Name / Game #	1	2	Apps	T	Pts
WJ (Jimmy) Allen	F	-	1	1	3
GP (George) Baines	>F	<F	2	-	-
2Lt AGE (Archibald) Bowell	=F	-	1	-	-
FRC (Frank) Broadley	-	<W	1	-	-
CW (Charlie) Cross	F	-	1	-	-
CL (Cyril) Curle	>W	<C	2	-	-
C Freer	>FB	-	1	-	-
H Hirst	-	=W	1	-	-
WG (Gil) Hopkins	F	F	2	-	-
A Kitchener	-	=F	1	-	-
HSB (Harry) Lawrie	<F	-	1	-	2
PW (Percy) Lawrie E2	C*	C*	2	-	4
S Livingstone	-	=F	1	-	-
AV (Albert) Manton	-	>F	1	1	3
F (Fred) Mellor	-	FB	1	-	-
J Morris	-	=F	1	-	-
AJ Osbourne	-	>F	1	-	-
HK (Herbert) Pearce	<W	-	1	2	6
FM (Tim) Taylor E1	FH	FH	2	-	-
JAG (George) Ward E6	F	F	2	-	-
KB (Kenneth) Wood GB2	C	-	1	-	-
GW (Pedlar) Wood E1	SH	SH	2	2	6

← Blazer badge worn by Tigers players prior to the First World War.

19 18/19	Home Ground: Welford Road	OVERALL RECORD:					T	C	PG	DG	MK	PTS
	Captain: Percy Lawrie	PLD	W	D	L	Tigers scored:	77	35	2	3	0	319
	Vice-captain: Jimmy Allen	19	12	0	7	Opponents scored:	28	8	2	3	1	121

GM	DATE		VEN	OPPONENTS	RESULT	TRIES	KICKS	ATT
CLUB MATCHES								
1	Dec	**26th**	**H**	**4th Leicestershire Regiment**	W 6-5	Lawrie(2)	-	3317
2		**27f**	**H**	**3rd Leicestershire Regiment**	W 8-3	Lawrie, Manton	Bull c	3393
	Jan	**4**	**H**	**New Zealand Services**	PP (snow)			
3		**11**	**H**	**New Zealand Services**	L 0-19	-	-	8123
4		**18**	**H**	**Machine Gun Corps**	W 27-5	Day(2), P.Wood(2), Allen, Farmer, Murmann	Day 3c	1490
5		**25**	**H**	**New Zealand M.G.C.**	W 16-5	Allen(2), Bull	Allen 2c/p	1769
6	Feb	**1**	**H**	**Coventry**	W 21-3	Day(3), Allen, Vears	Day 3c	2017
7		**8**	**H**	**Gloucester XV**	W 15-0	Bull, Taylor	Day c/p/d	1921
8		**15**	**H**	**Bedford & District**	W 71-0	Haselmere(5), Day(4), Bates(3), Coates(3), Roberts(2), Hegarty, P.Wood	Day 3c, Allen 4c	2853
9		**22**	**H**	**Australian Forces**	L 6-8	Smitten, Watts	-	4228
10	Mar	**1**	**H**	**Yorkshire**	W 19-0	Haselmere(3), Bates, Lawrie	Haselmere 2c	5065
11		**22**	**H**	**Coventry**	W 27-0	Bates(3), Blower, Lawrie, Taylor, Watts	Allen 2c, Haselmere c	2776
12		**29**	**H**	**Moseley**	W 21-6	Bates(2), Lawrie, Watts, P.Wood	Haselmere 3c	3483
13	Apr	**3th**	**H**	**South African Forces**	L 4-6	-	Bates d	4036
14		**5**	**H**	**Cardiff**	L 3-10	Lawrie	-	6052
15		**10th**	**H**	**Canadian Forces**	W 19-3	Lawrie(2), Bates, Watts, Wilkins	Haselmere c, Page c	2927
16		**19**	**H**	**Royal Air Force**	L 8-22	Allen, Haselmere	Allen c	5541
17		**21m**	**H**	**British Army**	L 5-8	Ward	Haselmere c	5958
18		**22tu**	**H**	**England M.G.C.**	W 39-11	Haselmere(3), Bates(2), Buckler, Smitten, Vears, Watts	Haselmere 3c, Allen 3c	4660
19		**26**	**H**	**Royal Naval Division**	L 4-7	-	Bates d	3203

INDIVIDUAL APPEARANCES 1918/19																						
Name / Game #	1	2	3	4	5	6	7	8	9	10	11	12	13	14	15	16	17	18	19	Apps	T	Pts
M (Myley) Abraham I5	-	-	>C	-	-	-	<C	-	-	-	-	-	-	-	-	-	-	-	-	2	-	-
WJ (Jimmy) Allen	-	F	F	F*	F*	F*	F*	F*	-	F	F	F	F	F	F	F	F	F*	F*	17	5	42
SR (Stanley) Bassett	-	>F	-	F	C	-	-	<F	-	-	-	-	-	-	-	-	-	-	-	4	-	-
AW (Alf) Bates	-	FH	-	-	-	-	-	FH	FH	FH	SH	FH	FH	FH	FH	FH	FH	FH	FH	13	12	44
WL (William) Blower	-	-	-	-	-	-	-	-	>F	-	F	-	-	-	F	-	-	<F	-	4	1	3
WR (Walter) Buckler	-	-	-	-	-	-	-	-	-	-	-	-	-	-	-	F	-	F	-	2	1	3
AG (Arthur) Bull E1	>F	F	F	F	F	F	F	F	F	F	F	-	F	F	F	F	-	-	F	16	2	8
CL Burton	>W	-	-	W	-	-	-	-	-	-	-	-	-	-	-	-	-	-	-	2	-	-
N (Norman) Coates	-	-	-	-	-	-	>C	C	C	C	C	-	-	-	-	-	-	-	-	5	3	9
WP (William) Collopy I4	-	-	>F	-	<C	-	-	-	-	-	-	-	-	-	-	-	-	-	-	2	-	-
HLV (Harold) Day E+	-	-	>W	W	-	W	W	W	-	-	-	-	-	-	-	-	-	-	-	5	9	54
SH (Samuel) Dennis	-	-	-	-	-	-	-	-	-	-	-	-	-	-	-	-	>F	F	F	3	-	-
DJ Ferguson	-	-	-	>F	F	F	F	-	F	F	F	F	F	F	-	F	F	-	F	13	-	-
G (George) Greasley	-	-	-	-	F	F	F	-	-	-	-	-	-	-	F	-	<F	-	-	5	-	-
FHX (Frederick) Gwynne	-	-	-	-	-	-	-	-	-	-	-	-	-	-	-	-	>C	<C	-	2	-	-
EE (Teddy) Haselmere	>FH	W	-	-	-	C	W	W	W	W	FH	W	W	W	W	W	W	W	W	16	12	58
C Hegarty	-	-	-	-	-	-	-	>F	F	F	-	F	F	F	-	<F	-	-	-	7	1	3
WG (Gil) Hopkins	-	-	-	-	-	-	-	-	-	-	F	F	F	F	F	F	<F	-	-	7	-	-
EM (Edward) Knight	>F	F	-	-	-	-	-	-	-	-	F	<F	-	-	-	-	-	-	-	4	-	-
PW (Percy) Lawrie E2	W*	W*	W*	-	-	-	-	-	-	W*	W*	W*	W*	W*	C*	W*	W*	-	-	11	9	27
AV (Albert) Manton	C	C	-	-	-	-	-	F	-	-	-	-	-	-	-	-	<F	-	-	4	1	3
WL (William) Murmann	-	>C	-	C	SH	<C	-	-	-	-	-	-	-	-	-	-	-	-	-	4	1	3
AL Neale	-	-	-	-	-	-	-	-	-	-	>W	<C	-	-	-	-	-	-	-	2	-	-
FH (Fred) Norman	>F	<F	-	-	-	-	-	-	-	-	-	-	-	-	-	-	-	-	-	2	-	-
AJ Osbourne	-	-	-	-	-	-	-	-	-	F	-	-	-	-	-	-	-	-	<F	2	-	-
H Page	-	-	-	-	-	-	-	-	-	-	-	-	>FB	FB	FB	<FB	-	-	-	4	-	2
F (Frank) Read	-	FB	FB	FB	FB	FB	FB	FB	FB	FB	-	-	-	-	-	-	FB	-	<FB	11	-	-
H Scott	-	-	-	-	>W	<W	-	-	-	-	-	-	-	-	-	-	-	-	-	2	-	-
P (Percy) Smitten	-	-	-	FH	FH	FH	FH	-	W	-	-	-	-	-	-	-	-	F	-	6	2	6
I (Ike) Spicer	-	-	-	-	-	-	-	-	-	-	-	-	F	F	F	-	-	F	F	5	-	-
F (Sos) Taylor E+	-	F	F	F	F	F	F	F	F	F	F	F	-	-	-	-	-	-	-	11	2	6
G (Gordon) Vears	-	-	>F	F	F	F	F	F	F	F	-	-	F	F	F	F	F	F	F	15	2	6
JAG (George) Ward E6	F	F	F	F	F	F	F	F	F	-	F	-	-	F	F	F	F	F	F	16	1	3
WJ (William) Watts W1	-	-	-	-	-	-	-	-	C	C	C	C	C	C	C	C	C	C	C	11	5	15
Lt-Col. GM (Gilbert) Wilkins	-	-	-	-	-	-	-	-	-	-	-	-	-	-	>W	-	-	W	-	2	1	3
GW (Pedlar) Wood E1	SH	SH	SH	SH	-	SH	SH	SH	SH	SH	-	SH	SH	SH	SH	SH	SH	SH	SH	17	4	12
Cpt. J Woolley	>F	F	F	-	-	F	F	-	<F	-	-	-	-	-	-	-	-	-	-	6	-	-

1 GAME: JN (Joe) Beasley =C(14), AJ Bloor =F(12), W Booth =F(4), JW (John) Burdett =C(16), CD Carter =C(3), R Cartwright =F(12), GE (George) Davie =F(1), AJ Davies =FB(18), WH (William) Earles =FB(11), Lt. S (Steve) Farmer <Ct(4), CD Ferris =F(3), C Freer <C(1), JG (George) Halford E+ =F(13), L Hamblin <C(13), A Higgins =FB(12), NL Higginson =F(1), E (Edward) Myers E+ >FH(3), HW (Harry) Palfreyman <FB(1), F Richards =F(5), RO (Robert) Ringrose W(19), HS Roberts =Ct(8), FS Scholes =F(1), SA (Stuart) Smith >F(10), J Willcox =W(5), KB (Kenneth) Wood GB2 <C(19)

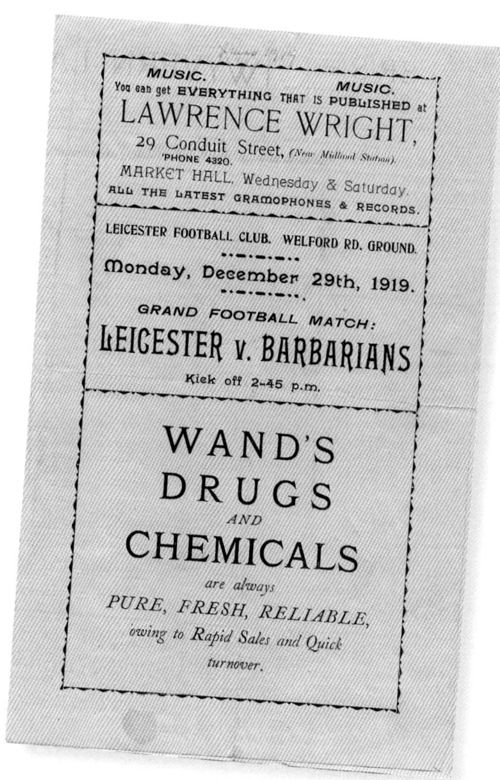

The key for how to read the stats is on the last page

1919/20

Home Ground: Welford Road
Captain: Jimmy Allen

OVERALL RECORD:					T	C	PG	DG	MK	PTS
PLD	W	D	L	Tigers scored:	192	71	10	2	0	756
41	27	1	13	Opponents scored:	68	26	6	5	0	294

GM	DATE		VEN	OPPONENTS	RESULT	TRIES	KICKS	ATT
CLUB MATCHES								
1	Sep	6	H	**Bath**	L 3-16	Haselmere(Penalty)	-	4882
2		13	H	**Royal Naval Depot**	W 32-0	Haselmere(2), Allen, Bates, Hicks, Wood	Haselmere 3c/p, Allen c/p	2924
3		20	H	**Coventry**	W 39-3	Haselmere(2), Bates(2), Coates, Hicks, Parker, Watts, Wood	Haselmere 6c	4433
4		27	H	**Plymouth Albion**	W 11-5	Haselmere, S.Taylor	Haselmere p, Allen c	3675
5	Oct	4	H	**Burton**	W 58-0	Haselmere(5), Coates(2), Bates, Brown, Spicer, G.Ward, Watts	Haselmere 6c/d, Ferguson 3c	4540
6		11	H	**Llanelly**	L 6-9	Clarke, Watts	-	5477
7		18	H	**Bristol**	W 24-16	Haselmere(2), Brown, Clarke, Coates	Haselmere 2p, Allen p	5969
8		25	H	**Newport**	L 0-11	-	-	5196
9	Nov	1	H	**Royal Navy**	W 9-3	Haselmere(2), Coates	-	4583
10		8	a	Swansea	L 6-10	Bates, Coates	-	-
11		10m	a	Llanelly	L 5-8	Haselmere	Haselmere c	-
12		12w	a	Oxford University	L 8-16	Haselmere	Haselmere c/p	-
13		15	a	Northampton	D 6-6	Bates, Haselmere	-	8000
14		22	H	**British Army**	W 19-8	Haselmere(3), S.Taylor, Vears	Haselmere 2c	3535
15		29	H	**Cardiff**	L 0-3	-	-	2430
16	Dec	6	a	Moseley	W 23-5	Haselmere(2), Watts(2), Allen, Ringrose, T.Taylor	Haselmere c	-
17		13	a	Blackheath	L 0-5	-	-	3000
18		20	H	**Bedford**	W 43-0	Haselmere(3), Watts(3), Crookes(2), Coates, T.Taylor, Vears	Haselmere d, Coates 2c, Bates c	2475
19		26f	H	**Birkenhead Park**	W 23-0	Haselmere(3), T.Taylor(2), Crookes, Ringrose	Wilkinson c	9743
20		27	H	**Royal Air Force**	W 22-5	Bates(2), Ringrose(2), Haselmere, Wood	Butcher 2c	8226
21		29m	H	**Barbarians**	W 17-6	Bates, Crookes, Haselmere, Hicks, Wood	Butcher c	10000
22	Jan	1th	a	Manchester	W 30-8	Haselmere(4), Bates, Coates, T.Taylor, Watts	Bates 3c	-
23		3	H	**Gloucester**	W 14-9	T.Taylor(2), Bates, Wood	Hicks c	5619
24		10	a	Coventry	W 12-0	Coates(2), Crookes, T.Taylor	-	2000
25		17	H	**Headingley**	W 54-11	Haselmere(5), Coates(2), Bates, Hicks, Ringrose, T.Taylor, G.Ward, Wood	Haselmere c, D.Norman 3c, W.Norman 2c, Wilkinson p	3569
26		24	a	British Army	W 22-3	Bates(3), Rowlands(2), Allen	W.Norman 2c	2000
27		31	H	**Swansea**	L 9-11	Haselmere, Rowlands, Watts	-	6075
28	Feb	7	H	**Moseley**	W 22-6	Bates(2), Barrett, Rowlands, S.Taylor, Wood	J.Greenwood 2c	3459
29		14	a	Newport	L 5-37	Bates	W.Norman c	-
30		21	H	**Richmond**	W 62-3	Haselmere(4), Coates(3), T.Taylor(2), Watts(2), Bates, Hicks, Wood	J.Greenwood 10c	4982
31		28	a	Cardiff	W 16-3	Bates, D.Norman, T.Taylor, Wood	Wilkinson 2c	-
32	Mar	6	H	**Harlequins**	W 20-0	G.Ward(3), Haselmere, Read, T.Taylor	J.Greenwood c	4678
33		13	a	Gloucester	W 3-0	D.Norman	-	2000
34		20	H	**Northampton**	W 18-0	Haselmere(2), Coates, T.Taylor	Allen 3c	13001
35		27	H	**London**	W 15-6	Coates, Cross, S.Taylor, Wood	D.Norman p	7213
36	Apr	3	a	Bristol	L 9-13	Watts(2), Haselmere	-	-
37		5m	a	Plymouth Albion	L 8-13	Barrett	Wilkinson c/p	-
38		6tu	a	Bath	L 8-16	Coates, Haselmere	Wilkinson c	-
39		10	H	**Old Merchant Taylors**	W 29-8	Haselmere(4), Barrett, Coates, T.Taylor	Wilkinson 4c	2933
40		17	a	Birkenhead Park	W 21-6	Thomas(2), Allen, Bates, Coates, Haselmere, Hicks	-	-
41		24	a	Northampton	W 25-6	Haselmere(4), Vears, Watts, Wood	Wilkinson 2c	12000

INDIVIDUAL APPEARANCES 1919/20

Name / Game #	1	2	3	4	5	6	7	8	9	10	11	12	13	14	15	16	17	18	19	20	21	22	23	24	25	26	27	28	29	30	31	32	33	34	35	36	37	38	39	40	41	Apps	T	Pts
WJ (Jimmy) Allen	-	F*	F*	F*	F*	F*	F*	F*	F*	F*	F*	F*	F*	F*	F*	F*	F*	F*	F*	-	F*	F*	F*	F*	-	F*	F*	-	F*	F*	-	F*	F*	F*	F*	F*	-	F*	F*	F*	F*	35	4	28
AE (Alfred) Barrett	-	-	-	-	-	-	-	-	-	-	-	-	-	-	-	-	-	-	-	-	-	-	-	-	-	-	-	>W	-	-	W	W	W	W	W	-	W	-	<W	-	-	8	3	9
AW (Alf) Bates	FH	FH	FH	C	FH	FH	FH	FH	FH	FH	FH	FH	FH	FH	FH	FH	FH	FH	FH	FH	FH	FH	FH	FH	SH	FH	FH	FH	FH	FH	SH	FH	FH	FH	FH	FH	-	FH	FH	FH	FH	40	21	71
A Brown	-	-	-	>W	F	F	F	<F	-	-	-	-	-	-	-	-	-	-	-	-	-	-	-	-	-	-	-	-	-	-	-	-	-	-	-	-	-	-	-	-	-	5	2	6
EG (Edward) Butcher	-	-	-	-	-	-	-	-	-	>W	C	C	-	-	-	-	-	-	-	W	<C	-	-	-	-	-	-	-	-	-	-	-	-	-	-	-	-	-	-	-	-	5	-	6
RA Clarke	-	-	-	-	>W	W	C	W	W	-	-	<C	-	-	-	-	-	-	-	-	-	-	-	-	-	-	-	-	-	-	-	-	-	-	-	-	-	-	-	-	-	6	2	6
N (Norman) Coates	-	C	C	C	C	C	C	C	C	C	-	-	-	-	W	W	C	C	-	-	-	W	C	C	C	-	-	-	-	C	C	C	C	C	C	C	C	C	C	C	C	29	20	64
A Crookes	-	-	-	-	-	-	-	-	-	-	-	-	-	-	-	-	>W	W	W	-	W	SH	W	W	-	<W	-	-	-	-	-	-	-	-	-	-	-	-	-	-	-	8	5	15
CW (Charlie) Cross	-	-	-	-	-	-	-	-	-	-	-	-	-	-	-	-	-	-	-	-	-	F	F	F	F	F	F	F	F	F	F	F	F	F	F	F	F	F	F	F	F	20	1	3
A Drew	-	>F	F	-	<F	-	-	-	-	-	-	-	-	-	-	-	-	-	-	-	-	-	-	-	-	-	-	-	-	-	-	-	-	-	-	-	-	-	-	-	-	3	-	-
W Elliott	-	-	-	-	-	-	-	-	-	-	-	-	-	-	-	F	F	-	-	<F	-	-	-	-	-	-	-	-	-	-	-	-	-	-	-	-	-	-	-	-	-	3	-	-
DJ Ferguson	F	F	F	F	F	F	F	F	F	F	F	-	-	F	F	F	F	F	F	-	F	F	F	<F	-	-	-	-	-	-	-	-	-	-	-	-	-	-	-	-	-	21	-	6
DG (Gwyn) Francis W1	-	-	-	-	-	-	-	-	-	-	-	-	>F	-	-	-	-	-	-	-	-	-	-	-	-	-	F	F	F	-	F	-	F	F	-	F	-	F	-	F	F	11	-	-
JE (John) Greenwood E13	-	-	-	-	-	-	-	-	-	-	-	-	-	-	-	-	-	-	-	-	-	-	-	-	-	-	-	>F	-	F	-	<F	-	-	-	-	-	-	-	-	-	3	-	26
EE (Teddy) Haselmere	W	W	W	W	W	W	W	W	W	W	W	W	W	W	W	W	W	W	W	W	W	W	-	W	W	W	W	W	W	W	W	W	W	W	W	W	W	W	W	W	W	40	59	242
WT (Bill) Havard W1	-	-	-	-	-	-	-	-	>F	-	-	<F	-	-	-	-	-	-	-	-	-	-	-	-	-	-	-	-	-	-	-	-	-	-	-	-	-	-	-	-	-	2	-	-
Lt-Col. WC Hicks	>F	F	F	F	F	F	F	F	F	F	F	F	F	F	F	-	-	F	F	F	F	F	F	-	F	F	-	-	F	F	F	-	F	-	F	F	F	F	F	F	F	34	6	20
PCH (Percy) Homer	-	-	-	-	-	-	-	-	-	-	-	-	-	-	-	-	-	-	-	-	-	-	-	>F	F	F	<F	-	-	-	-	-	-	-	-	-	-	-	-	-	-	4	-	-
PP (Philip) Hope	-	-	-	-	-	-	-	-	-	-	>W	<W	-	-	-	-	-	-	-	-	-	-	-	-	-	-	-	-	-	-	-	-	-	-	-	-	-	-	-	-	-	2	-	-
DJ (Doug) Norman E+	-	-	-	-	-	-	-	-	-	-	-	-	-	-	-	-	-	-	-	-	-	-	-	-	>F	-	-	-	-	-	F	F	F	F	F	F	F	-	F	-	-	9	2	15
Cpt. W Norman	-	-	-	-	-	-	-	-	-	-	-	-	-	-	-	-	-	-	-	-	-	-	-	-	>F	F	F	-	<F	-	-	-	-	-	-	-	-	-	-	-	-	4	-	10
B Parker	-	>F	F	F	-	-	-	-	-	F	F	-	F	-	F	-	-	F	-	-	F	F	F	-	-	-	-	-	-	-	-	F	-	-	-	-	<F	-	-	-	-	13	1	3
RO (Robert) Ringrose	-	-	-	-	-	-	-	-	-	-	-	-	-	-	-	C	-	-	C	C	-	-	C	-	C	-	-	C	<W	-	-	-	-	-	-	-	-	-	-	-	-	7	5	15
A Rowlands	-	-	-	-	-	-	-	-	-	-	-	-	-	>C	C	-	C	-	-	-	-	-	-	-	-	C	C	<C	-	-	-	-	-	-	-	-	-	-	-	-	-	6	4	12
RBY (Robert) Simpson	-	-	-	-	-	-	-	-	-	-	-	-	>C	-	-	-	-	-	-	-	-	C	-	-	-	-	-	-	-	-	-	-	-	-	-	-	-	-	-	-	-	2	-	-
I (Ike) Spicer	-	F	F	F	F	F	F	F	-	-	-	F	-	-	<F	-	-	-	-	-	-	-	-	-	-	-	-	-	-	-	-	-	-	-	-	-	-	-	-	-	-	9	1	3
F (Sos) Taylor E2	-	-	F	F	-	F	F	F	F	F	F	F	F	F	F	F	F	F	F	F	F	F	-	F	-	-	-	F	-	F	F	-	-	-	F	F	F	F	F	F	F	30	4	12
FM (Tim) Taylor E1	-	-	-	-	-	-	-	-	-	-	-	-	-	-	-	C	C	C	C	C	C	C	C	C	C	C	C	C	C	W	C	C	C	C	C	C	FH	C	C	C	C	26	15	45
Flt-Lt. GM (Godfrey) Thomas	-	-	-	-	-	-	-	-	-	-	-	-	-	-	-	-	-	-	-	-	-	-	-	-	-	-	-	-	-	-	-	-	-	-	-	>C	C	C	-	C	W	5	2	6
JE (Eric) Thorneloe	-	>W	W	FB	FB	FB	FB	-	-	-	-	-	<W	-	-	-	-	-	-	-	-	-	-	-	-	-	-	-	-	-	-	-	-	-	-	-	-	-	-	-	-	7	-	-
NT (Trevor) Thorneloe	-	-	-	-	-	-	-	-	>F	F	F	-	F	F	F	F	F	F	F	F	F	-	F	-	-	-	-	F	F	-	-	-	-	F	-	-	F	-	-	-	-	17	-	-
G (Gordon) Vears	F	F	-	F	F	F	F	F	F	F	F	F	F	F	F	F	F	F	F	F	-	-	-	F	F	F	F	F	F	F	F	F	F	F	F	-	F	F	F	F	F	36	3	9
JAG (George) Ward E6	F*	F	F	F	F	F	F	F	F	F	F	F	F	F	-	-	F	-	F	F*	F	F	F	F	F*	F	F	F*	F	F	F*	F	F	F	F	-	F*	F	F	F	F	37	5	15
WJ (William) Watts W1	C	C	C	-	C	C	-	C	C	C	C	-	C	C	C	C	-	C	C	C	-	C	-	C	-	C	C	-	C	C	-	-	C	C	C	W	-	W	C	W	C	30	15	45
J Wilkinson	-	-	-	-	-	-	-	>FB	FB	FB	FB	FB	FB	FB	FB	FB	FB	FB	FB	-	FB	FB	FB	FB	FB	FB	FB	FB	FB	FB	FB	FB	FB	FB	FB	FB	FB	FB	FB	FB	FB	33	-	28
GW (Pedlar) Wood E1	SH	SH	SH	SH	SH	SH	SH	SH	SH	SH	SH	SH	SH	SH	SH	SH	SH	-	SH	SH	SH	-	SH	SH	FH	SH	SH	SH	SH	SH	FH	SH	SH	SH	SH	SH	SH	SH	SH	SH	SH	39	11	33

1 GAME: AG (Arthur) Bull E1 <F(12), ER Butler =F(36), WG (William) Coltman =W(7), HLV (Harold) Day E1 W(27), SH (Samuel) Dennis <F(1), SG (Stanley) Ellis =F(1), DE (Dan) Ellwood <FB(2), AD (Alfred) Godfrey >FH(4), SC (Sidney) Greenwood >F(16), HM (Henry) Horsley =W(14), SA (Sam) Hunter <FB(3), WH Hynd =F(20), O (Oswald) Jenkins =C(31), OEH (Oswald) Leslie =C(21), GG Marshall =FB(21), F (Fred) Mellor FB(1), CP (Cecil) Oscroft >SH(18), W Pollard >W(23), C Read >Ct(32), E Rice =F(1), CJ (John) Seager >C(1), SA (Stuart) Smith F(14), H (Henry) Sturgess =F(1), JAC (John) Thornton >W(25), W Ward <W(1)

The key for how to read the stats is on the last page

1920/21

Home Ground: Welford Road
Captain: Percy Lawrie
Vice-captain: George Ward

OVERALL RECORD:					T	C	PG	DG	MK	PTS
PLD	W	D	L	Tigers scored:	151	69	9	4	2	640
41	31	2	8	Opponents scored:	77	24	6	7	0	325

GM	DATE		VEN	OPPONENTS	RESULT	TRIES	KICKS	ATT
CLUB MATCHES								
1	Sep	4	H	Bath	W 37-6	Coates, Haselmere, Hicks, S.Taylor, Thomas, Watts, P.Wood	Wilkinson 6c, Bates d	4652
2		11	H	Plymouth Albion	W 9-3	Lawrie(2), Cross	-	4689
3		18	H	United Services	W 32-7	Wa.Buckler(2), Haselmere(2), Ward(2), Lawrie, Thomas	Wilkinson 4c	5791
4		22w	a	Rugby	W 22-6	Haselmere(2), Bates, Coates, Watts, P.Wood	Wilkinson 2c	4500
5		25	H	Bradford	W 33-10	Day(2), Lawrie(2), Coates, Cross, Thomas	Wilkinson 4c, Haselmere d	3849
6	Oct	2	H	Headingley	W 33-3	Bates(3), Haselmere(2), Day, Hicks, Smallwood	Haselmere c/p, Wilkinson 2c	5733
7		9	H	Llanelly	W 23-3	Haselmere(3), S.Taylor, T.Taylor	Thomas m, Wilkinson p, Day c	7395
8		16	H	Bristol	W 23-12	Lawrie, Smallwood, T.Taylor, Thornton, Ward	Wilkinson 4c	6773
9		23	a	Newport	L 3-22	-	Wilkinson p	14000
10		30	H	Aberavon	W 11-6	Day, S.Taylor	Day m, Wilkinson c	7481
11	Nov	6	H	Oxford University	W 11-9	Haselmere(2), Lawrie	Wilkinson c	5150
12		13	H	Cambridge University	L 11-14	Lawrie, Smallwood, P.Wood	Day c	8608
13		20	H	British Army	W 19-12	Watts(2), Haselmere, Lawrie, Vears	Wilkinson 2c	3829
14		27	a	Cardiff	L 8-11	Day, P.Wood	Day c	12000
15	Dec	4	H	Moseley	W 33-5	Day(3), Coates(3), Cross, Lawrie, F.Wood	Day 3c	2451
16		11	H	Blackheath	W 6-5	Coates	Day p	5147
17		24f	a	Coventry	W 6-0	Haselmere, Watts	-	-
18		27m	H	Birkenhead Park	W 21-14	Haselmere(3), Lawrie, Norman	Wilkinson 3c	10530
19		28tu	H	Royal Air Force	W 28-16	Lawrie(2), Wa.Buckler, Haselmere, Norman, Wickson	Wilkinson 5c	8203
20		29w	H	Barbarians	W 8-6	T.Taylor(2)	Wilkinson c	4346
21	Jan	1	H	Manchester	W 38-9	Haselmere(3), Coates, Lawrie, Simpson, Watts, Wickson, P.Wood	Wilkinson 4c/p	1888
22		8	a	Gloucester	L 3-12	Coates	-	6000
23		15	a	Bradford	W 24-20	Lawrie(2), Day, Coates, T.Taylor, P.Wood	Day 3c	-
24		17m	a	Headingley	W 14-0	Smallwood(2), Haselmere, Simpson	Day c	-
25		22	H	Coventry	W 3-0	Norman	-	2959
26		29	a	Llanelly	L 3-13	Lawrie	-	8000
27	Feb	5	a	Richmond	W 13-3	Haselmere(2), Coates	Lawrie 2c	2000
28		12	H	Newport	D 3-3	-	Day p	9909
29		23w	a	Moseley	D 11-11	Haselmere(2)	Lawrie p, Wilkinson c	-
30		26	H	Cardiff	W 14-9	Coates, Haselmere, Smallwood, S.Taylor	Day c	6271
31	Mar	5	a	Harlequins	L 3-11	Watts	-	-
32		12	H	London Welsh	W 24-8	Day(2), Lawrie(2), Allen, Haselmere	Day 2c, Wilkinson c	3666
33		19	a	Northampton	L 0-12	-	-	8000
34		26	a	Bristol	W 10-7	Norman, P.Wood	Day 2c	8000
35		28m	a	Plymouth Albion	L 5-15	Day	Day c	-
36		29tu	a	Bath	W 20-14	Allen, Haselmere, Lawrie	Day 2c/p/d	-
37	Apr	2	H	Gloucester	W 3-0	S.Taylor	-	5373
38		9	H	Northampton	W 30-0	Lawrie(2), Ward(2), Haselmere, Souster	Lawrie d, Wilkinson 4c	3920
39		12tu	a	Nuneaton	W 19-3	Lawrie(2), Gibbs, Greenwood, S.Taylor	Wilkinson 2c	-
40		16	a	Birkenhead Park	W 3-0	Lawrie	-	10000
41		23	H	London	W 20-5	Day(2), Wakefield(2), Haselmere	Day c/p	7101

INDIVIDUAL APPEARANCES 1920/21

Name / Game #	1	2	3	4	5	6	7	8	9	10	11	12	13	14	15	16	17	18	19	20	21	22	23	24	25	26	27	28	29	30	31	32	33	34	35	36	37	38	39	40	41	Apps	T	Pts
WJ (Jimmy) Allen	-	-	-	F	-	-	-	-	-	-	-	-	-	-	-	-	-	-	F	-	F	-	-	-	-	-	-	-	-	-	-	F	-	-	-	F	-	-	<F	-	-	6	2	6
AW (Alf) Bates	SH	SH	SH	SH	SH	<SH	-	-	-	-	-	-	-	-	-	-	-	-	-	-	-	-	-	-	-	-	-	-	-	-	-	-	-	-	-	-	-	-	-	-	-	6	4	16
WR (Billy) Beaver	-	-	-	-	-	-	-	-	-	-	-	-	-	-	-	-	-	-	-	-	-	-	-	-	-	-	>C	W	<C	-	-	-	-	-	-	-	-	-	-	-	-	3	-	-
WR (Walter) Buckler	F	F	F	-	F	F	-	F	-	F	F	F	F	F	F	-	F	F	F	F	F	F	F	F	F	F	F	F	-	F	F	F	F	F	F	-	F	F	-	F	F	34	3	9
WE (Will) Buckler	-	-	-	-	-	-	-	-	-	-	-	-	-	-	-	-	-	-	-	-	-	-	-	-	-	-	>F	-	<F	-	-	-	-	-	-	-	-	-	-	-	-	2	-	-
AH Burgess	-	-	-	-	-	-	-	-	-	-	-	-	-	-	>C	-	<C	-	-	-	-	-	-	-	-	-	-	-	-	-	-	-	-	-	-	-	-	-	-	-	-	2	-	-
CL Burton	-	-	-	-	-	-	-	-	-	-	W	-	-	-	-	-	-	-	-	-	-	-	-	-	-	-	-	-	-	-	-	-	-	-	-	-	-	-	-	-	-	1	-	-
N (Norman) Coates	C	-	C	C	C	F	F	C	F	F	F	F	F	F	F	F	-	-	F	F	F	F	F	F	F	F	C	F	F	F	F	-	-	C	F	C	C	C	C	F	C	36	12	36
AJ Coulter	-	-	-	-	-	-	-	-	-	-	-	-	-	-	-	-	-	-	=F	-	-	-	-	-	-	-	-	-	-	-	-	-	-	-	-	-	-	-	-	-	-	1	-	-
CW (Charlie) Cross	F	F	F	F	F	F	F	F	F	F	F	F	-	F	F	F	F	F	-	F	F	F	F	F	F	F	F	F	-	F	F	F	F	F	F	F	F	F	F	F	F	38	3	9
HLV (Harold) Day E1	-	-	-	-	W	W	W	-	-	W	-	W	-	C	W	W	-	-	-	-	-	W	W	C	-	-	-	C	-	C	C	C	-	C	C	C	-	-	-	-	C	19	14	99
WJ Gibbs	-	-	-	-	-	-	-	-	-	-	-	-	-	-	-	-	-	-	-	-	-	-	-	-	-	-	-	-	-	-	-	-	-	>W	W	-	W	W	W	W	W	7	1	3
AD (Alfred) Godfrey	-	-	-	-	-	-	-	-	-	-	-	-	-	-	-	-	-	-	-	-	-	-	-	-	-	-	-	-	C	-	-	-	SH	-	-	SH	-	-	C	-	-	4	-	-
SC (Sidney) Greenwood	-	-	-	-	-	-	-	-	-	-	-	-	-	-	-	-	-	-	-	-	-	-	-	-	-	F	-	-	-	-	-	-	-	-	-	-	-	-	<F	-	-	2	1	3
EE (Teddy) Haselmere	W	W	W	W	W	W	W	W	W	W	W	W	W	-	-	-	W	W	W	W	W	W	W	W	W	W	W	W	W	W	W	W	W	W	W	W	W	C	W	C	W	38	31	102
Lt-Col. WC Hicks	F	F	F	-	F	F	F	F	F	F	F	-	F	F	F	F	F	-	-	F	F	-	F	F	-	-	-	F	-	F	-	F	F	F	F	-	F	F	-	-	F	28	2	6
HW (Herbert) Hill	-	-	-	-	-	-	-	-	-	-	-	-	-	-	-	-	-	-	<F	-	-	-	-	-	-	-	-	-	-	-	-	-	-	-	-	-	-	-	-	-	-	1	-	-
AE (Arthur) Inchley	-	-	-	-	-	-	-	-	-	-	-	-	-	-	-	-	-	-	-	-	-	-	-	-	-	-	-	-	-	>W	-	W	<W	-	-	-	-	-	-	-	-	3	-	-
RC Jones	-	-	-	-	-	-	-	-	-	-	-	-	-	-	-	-	-	-	-	-	-	-	-	-	-	-	-	-	-	-	-	-	-	-	=C	-	-	-	-	-	-	1	-	-
PW (Percy) Lawrie E2	-	C*	W*	-	C*	C*	C*	C*	C*	C*	C*	C*	C*	C*	C*	W*	C*	C*	C*	C*	C*	C*	C*	-	C*	W*	C*	C*	C*	C*	C*	C*	C*	C*	C*	W*	C*	C*	C*	C*	C*	38	25	86
F (Fred) Mellor	-	-	-	-	-	-	-	-	-	-	-	-	-	-	-	-	-	-	-	-	-	-	-	-	-	-	FB	-	-	-	<W	-	-	-	-	-	-	-	-	-	-	2	-	-
DJ (Doug) Norman E+	F	F	F	F	F	F	F	F	F	-	F	F	F	-	F	F	F	F	F	F	F	F	F	-	F	F	F	F	F	F	F	F	F	F	-	-	-	-	-	-	-	31	4	12
CP (Cecil) Oscroft	-	-	-	-	-	-	-	-	-	-	-	-	-	-	-	-	-	-	<SH	-	-	-	-	-	-	-	-	-	-	-	-	-	-	-	-	-	-	-	-	-	-	1	-	-
GA (Arthur) Palmer	-	-	-	-	-	-	-	-	-	-	-	-	-	-	-	-	-	-	-	-	-	-	-	-	-	-	-	-	>F	-	-	-	-	-	-	-	-	-	-	-	-	1	-	-
C Read	-	-	-	C	-	-	-	-	-	-	-	-	-	-	-	-	-	-	-	-	-	-	-	-	-	-	-	-	-	-	-	-	<C	-	-	-	-	-	-	-	-	2	-	-
H (Herb) Sharratt	-	-	-	-	-	-	-	-	-	-	-	-	-	-	-	-	-	-	-	-	-	-	-	-	-	-	-	-	>F	-	-	-	-	-	-	F	F	F	F	F	F	7	-	-
RBY (Robert) Simpson	-	-	-	-	-	-	-	-	-	-	-	-	-	-	-	-	-	-	C	-	C	C	C	C	C	C	-	-	-	-	-	-	-	-	-	-	-	-	-	-	-	7	2	6
DG (Donald) Slack	-	-	-	-	-	-	-	-	-	-	-	-	-	-	-	-	-	-	-	-	-	-	-	-	-	-	=W	-	-	-	-	-	-	-	-	-	-	-	-	-	-	1	-	-
AM (Alastair) Smallwood E6	-	-	-	-	-	>C	-	C	-	-	-	C	-	-	-	C	-	C	W	W	-	-	-	W	C	-	-	-	-	C	-	-	-	-	-	-	C	-	-	C	-	12	6	18
FC (Frederick) Souster	-	-	-	-	-	-	-	-	-	-	-	-	-	-	-	-	-	-	-	-	-	-	-	-	-	-	-	-	>W	-	-	-	-	-	-	C	-	W	-	W	-	4	1	3
F (Sos) Taylor E2	F	F	F	F	F	F	F	F	F	F	F	F	F	F	-	F	F	F	-	F	-	F	F	F	F	F	F	F	F	F	F	-	-	-	-	F	F	F	F	F	-	33	6	18
FM (Tim) Taylor E1	C	C	C	C	-	C	FH	FH	FH	FH	FH	FH	FH	FH	FH	FH	FH	FH	FH	FH	-	FH	FH	FH	FH	FH	FH	-	FH	FH	FH	FH	-	FH	FH	-	FH	FH	FH	FH	FH	36	5	15
Flt-Lt. GM (Godfrey) Thomas	C	C	C	-	C	-	C	-	C	C	C	C	C	C	-	C	-	-	-	C	-	-	-	<C	-	-	-	-	-	-	-	-	-	-	-	-	-	-	-	-	-	14	3	12
JAC (John) Thornton	-	-	-	-	-	-	-	<W	-	-	-	-	-	-	-	-	-	-	-	-	-	-	-	-	-	-	-	-	-	-	-	-	-	-	-	-	-	-	-	-	-	1	1	3
G (Gordon) Vears	F	F	F	F	F	-	F	F	F	F	-	F	F	F	F	F	F	F	-	-	-	F	F	-	F	-	F	F	-	-	F	F	F	F	F	F	F	F	F	F	F	32	1	3
WW (Wavell) Wakefield E8	-	-	-	-	-	-	-	-	-	-	-	-	-	-	-	-	-	-	-	-	-	-	-	-	-	-	-	-	-	-	-	-	-	-	-	-	-	-	-	-	>F	1	2	6
EW (Ernest) Ward	-	-	-	-	-	-	-	-	-	-	-	-	-	-	-	-	-	-	-	-	-	-	-	-	-	-	-	-	-	-	-	>F	F	F	F	<F	-	-	-	-	-	5	-	-
JAG (George) Ward E6	F*	F	F	F*	F	F	F	F	F	F	F	F	F	F	-	F	F	F	-	F	F	F	F	F*	F	F	-	F	-	F	F	-	F	F	F	-	F	F	F	F	F	35	5	15
WJ (William) Watts W1	W	W	-	W	-	-	C	-	C	-	-	-	C	W	C	C	C	C	C	-	FH	C	-	-	-	C	-	FH	-	-	C	-	-	-	-	-	-	-	-	-	-	17	7	21
J (John) Wickson	-	-	-	>F	-	-	-	-	-	-	-	-	-	-	F	-	-	F	F	F	F	-	-	F	-	F	F	-	F	-	-	F	F	-	-	F	-	-	-	-	-	13	2	6
J Wilkinson	FB	FB	FB	FB	FB	FB	FB	FB	FB	FB	FB	FB	FB	FB	FB	FB	FB	FB	FB	FB	FB	FB	FB	FB	FB	FB	-	FB	FB	FB	FB	FB	FB	FB	FB	FB	FB	FB	FB	FB	FB	40	-	103
FE (Frank) Wood	-	-	-	-	-	-	-	-	>W	C	-	-	W	W	W	-	W	W	-	-	W	-	-	-	W	-	-	-	-	-	-	-	-	-	-	-	-	-	-	-	-	9	1	3
GW (Pedlar) Wood E1	FH	FH	FH	FH	FH	FH	SH	SH	SH	SH	SH	SH	SH	SH	SH	SH	SH	SH	-	SH	SH	SH	SH	SH	SH	SH	SH	SH	SH	SH	SH	SH	FH	SH	SH	FH	SH	SH	SH	SH	SH	40	7	21
L Woodhead	-	-	-	-	-	-	-	-	-	-	=C	-	-	-	-	-	-	-	-	-	-	-	-	-	-	-	-	-	-	-	-	-	-	-	-	-	-	-	-	-	-	1	-	-

1921/22

Home Ground:	Welford Road
Captain:	Percy Lawrie
Vice-captain:	George Ward

OVERALL RECORD:					T	C	PG	DG	MK	PTS
PLD	W	D	L	Tigers scored:	140	50	8	4	0	560
44	29	4	11	Opponents scored:	61	25	8	6	0	281

GM	DATE		VEN	OPPONENTS	RESULT	TRIES	KICKS	ATT
CLUB MATCHES								
1	Sep	3	H	**Bath**	W 13-6	Day, Coates, Watts	Day d	12000
2		10	H	**Plymouth Albion**	L 4-5	-	Haselmere d	13000
3		12m	a	Burton	W 22-3	Haselmere(4), Day, Souster	Day 2c	-
4		17	H	**United Services**	W 6-5	Lawrie	Wilkinson p	18000
5		24	H	**Bradford**	W 16-15	Lawrie(2), Sharratt, Smallwood	Day 2c	13000
6		28w	a	Sheffield	W 17-6	Gibbs(2), Coates, Godfrey, Lawrie	Wilkinson c	-
7	Oct	1	H	**Headingley**	W 14-5	Lawrie(2), Gibbs, Godfrey	Wilkinson c	14000
8		8	H	**Llanelly**	W 6-3	Lawrie	Day p	16000
9		15	H	**Aberavon**	W 19-6	Craigmile(2), Day, Haselmere	Day 2c/p	16000
10		22	H	**Northampton**	W 29-4	Day(2), Coates, Godfrey, Lawrie, Norman, Sharratt	Day 2c, Wilkinson 2c	12000
11		27th	a	Cambridge University	W 13-11	Coates, Lawrie, Smallwood	Day 2c	-
12		29	H	**Newport**	L 6-10	Norman	Day p	20000
13	Nov	5	H	**Swansea**	L 3-5	-	Day p	14000
		12	H	**Lansdowne**	PP (fog)			
14		16w	a	Oxford University	L 5-12	German	Day c	-
15		19	H	**Coventry**	W 28-0	Haselmere(2), S.Taylor(2), Day, Godfrey, T.Taylor, Wilkins	Coates c, Wilkinson c	12000
16		26	H	**Cardiff**	W 9-3	Coates(2)	Day p	14000
17	Dec	3	a	Moseley	W 12-0	Godfrey(2), T.Taylor, Wilkins	-	-
18		10	a	Blackheath	D 6-6	Norman, Wilkins	-	8000
19		17	H	**Bristol**	L 11-14	Coates, Sharratt, T.Taylor	Sambrook c	12000
20		24	H	**Royal Air Force**	W 6-5	Wilkins	Wilkinson p	-
21		26m	H	**Birkenhead Park**	W 11-6	Buckler, Haselmere, Watts	Sambrook c	14000
22		27tu	H	**Barbarians**	W 28-10	Day, Coates, Cross, Hicks, B.Usher, Wilkins	Day 3c, Wilkinson d	16000
23		31	H	**Wakefield**	W 30-0	Smallwood(3), Cross, Haselmere, Wilkins	Wilkinson 4c/d	10000
24	Jan	2m	a	Manchester	W 21-5	Cross, Haselmere, Lawrence, Smallwood, B.Usher	Wilkinson 3c	-
25		7	H	**Gloucester**	L 9-10	Cross, Pollard, Wilkins	-	10000
26		14	a	Swansea	W 13-9	Day(2), S.Taylor	Day 2c	5000
27		16m	a	Llanelly	L 3-13	Wilkins	-	-
28		21	H	**Pill Harriers**	W 24-0	Craigmile(3), Godfrey, Lawrence	Sambrook 3c/p	-
29		28	a	Coventry	W 23-5	Day, Coates, Craigmile, Haselmere, Norman	Day 4c	-
30	Feb	4	H	**Richmond**	W 6-5	Coates, Lawrence	-	8000
31		11	a	Newport	L 9-24	Coates, Haselmere, Norman	-	-
32		15w	H	**British Army**	W 8-3	Bradbury, Wilkins	Sambrook c	3000
33		18	H	**Moseley**	W 26-3	Haselmere(3), Cross, Godfrey, S.Taylor, T.Taylor, Wood	Coates c	9000
34		25	a	Cardiff	D 3-3	Morgan	-	10000
35	Mar	4	H	**Harlequins**	W 8-0	Haselmere, Smallwood	Hicks c	14000
36		11	H	**London Welsh**	W 24-5	Godfrey, Hett, Lawrence, T.Taylor, Wilkins, Wood	Haselmere 2c, Thorneloe c	-
37		18	a	Northampton	W 11-7	Coates, Cross, Haselmere	Sambrook c	8000
38		25	a	Gloucester	L 3-17	T.Taylor	-	-
39		27m	a	Bradford	W 17-6	Coates, Cross, Haselmere, T.Taylor, Wilkins	Day c	-
40	Apr	1	H	**London**	W 33-3	Day(2), Cross(2), Hicks(2), Smallwood, Haselmere, Wilkins	Day 2c, Smallwood c	10000
41		8	a	Birkenhead Park	L 5-15	T.Taylor	Hicks c	6000
42		15	a	Bristol	D 0-0	-	-	-
43		17m	a	Plymouth Albion	D 0-0	-	-	-
44		18tu	a	Bath	L 0-8	-	-	-

INDIVIDUAL APPEARANCES 1921/22

Name / Game #	1	2	3	4	5	6	7	8	9	10	11	12	13	14	15	16	17	18	19	20	21	22	23	24	25	26	27	28	29	30	31	32	33	34	35	36	37	38	39	40	41	42	43	44	Apps	T	Pts
F/O. CD (Cyril) Adams	-	-	-	-	-	-	-	-	-	-	-	-	-	-	-	-	-	-	-	-	-	-	-	-	-	-	-	-	-	-	-	-	-	-	-	-	-	>F	-	-	-	-	F	-	2	-	-
WR (Walter) Buckler	F	F	-	F	-	-	-	-	-	-	-	-	F	F	F	F	F	F	F	F	F	-	F	F	F	F	F	F	F	F	F	F	F	F	F	F	F	F	F	F	F	F	-	<F	33	1	3
N (Norman) Coates	F	F	F	F	F	F	F	F	F	F	F	F	C	-	C	C	C	C	C	-	F	F	F	-	C	C	C	C	F	F	C	C	C	C	C	C	C	W	C	C	C	W	-	C	40	13	43
HWC (Hugh) Craigmile	-	-	-	-	>W	-	C	W	W	W	-	W	-	-	-	-	-	-	-	-	-	-	-	-	-	-	-	C	<C	-	-	-	-	-	-	-	-	-	-	-	-	-	-	-	8	6	18
CW (Charlie) Cross	F	F	F	F	F	F	F	F	F	F	-	F	F	-	-	F	F	F	-	F	F	F	F	F	F	■F	F	F	F	F	F	-	F	-	-	F	F	F	F	F	F	F	F	F	37	9	27
HLV (Harold) Day E3	C	C	C	-	C	-	-	C	C	C	C	C	C	C	C	C	-	-	-	-	-	C	-	-	-	C	C	-	C	C	-	-	-	-	-	-	-	C	C	C	-	C	-	-	22	12	101
GJ (Guy) German	-	-	-	-	-	-	-	>SH	SH	SH	SH	SH	-	SH	SH	-	-	-	SH	SH	SH	SH	SH	-	SH	SH	SH	-	-	-	-	-	-	-	-	-	SH	-	-	-	SH	-	-	-	17	1	3
WJ Gibbs	-	-	-	W	-	W	W	-	-	-	-	-	-	W	-	-	-	-	-	-	-	-	-	-	-	-	-	-	-	-	-	-	-	-	-	-	-	-	-	-	-	-	-	-	4	3	9
AD (Alfred) Godfrey	-	FH	FH	-	SH	SH	C	C	C	C	C	C	SH	C	C	C	SH	C	C	C	C	C	C	C	-	-	-	SH	SH	SH	C	-	C	C	C	C	C	C	C	-	C	-	W	FH	36	9	27
EE (Teddy) Haselmere	W	W	W	C	W	-	-	-	W	W	W	W	W	C	W	W	W	W	W	W	W	W	W	W	W	-	-	W	W	W	W	C	W	W	W	W	W	W	W	W	W	W	W	W	39	19	65
Lt-Col. WC Hicks	F	F	F	F	F	F	F	F	F	F	F	F	F	F	F	F	F	F	-	-	-	F	F	-	-	F	-	-	-	-	F	F	-	F	F	-	-	F	F	F	F	<F	-	-	30	3	13
RW Holmes	-	-	-	-	-	-	-	-	-	-	-	-	-	-	-	-	-	-	-	-	-	-	-	-	-	-	-	>W	-	-	-	-	W	<W	-	-	-	-	-	-	-	-	-	-	3	-	-
G Hoyle	-	-	-	-	-	-	-	-	-	-	-	-	>C	-	-	-	C	C	<C	-	-	-	-	-	-	-	-	-	-	-	-	-	-	-	-	-	-	-	-	-	-	-	-	-	4	-	-
SF (Frank) Lawrence	-	-	-	-	-	-	>F	F	F	F	F	F	F	F	F	F	F	F	F	F	-	-	-	F	F	F	F	F	F	F	F	F	F	F	F	F	F	F	-	-	-	-	F	F	31	4	12
PW (Percy) Lawrie E2	C*	C*	-	C*	C*	C*	C*	C*	-	C*	C*	C*	-	-	-	-	-	-	-	-	-	-	-	-	-	-	-	-	-	-	-	-	-	-	-	-	-	-	-	-	-	-	-	-	10	9	27
DJ (Doug) Norman E+	-	F	F	F	F	F	F	F	F	F	F	F	F	F	F	F	-	F	F	F	F	F	F	F	F	-	F	F	F	F	F	F	F	F	F	-	-	-	F	F	F	-	F	F	37	5	15
W Pollard	-	-	-	-	-	-	-	-	-	-	-	-	-	-	-	-	-	-	-	-	-	-	-	-	C	W	-	-	-	-	-	-	-	-	-	-	-	-	-	-	-	-	-	-	2	1	3
JC (John) Russell	-	-	-	-	-	-	-	-	-	-	-	-	-	-	-	-	-	-	-	-	-	-	-	-	-	-	-	-	-	-	-	>SH	-	SH	SH	-	-	SH	SH	SH	C	SH	SH	SH	10	-	-
LC (Claude) Sambrook	-	-	>C	-	FB	-	-	-	-	-	-	-	-	-	-	-	-	-	FB	-	FB	-	-	-	-	-	-	FB	FB	FB	FB	FB	FB	FB	FB	FB	FB	FB	FB	FB	FB	FB	FB	FB	21	-	17
H (Herb) Sharratt	F	-	F	F	F	F	F	F	F	F	F	F	F	F	F	-	F	-	F	F	-	-	-	-	-	-	-	F	-	-	-	F	F	-	-	F	F	-	-	-	-	-	-	-	22	3	9
AM (Alastair) Smallwood E8	-	-	-	-	C	-	-	-	-	-	W	-	-	-	-	-	-	-	-	C	C	C	C	C	-	-	-	-	-	C	-	-	-	-	C	-	-	-	-	C	-	C	C	C	13	8	26
FC (Frederick) Souster	W	W	W	W	-	W	W	W	C	-	-	-	<W	-	-	-	-	-	-	-	-	-	-	-	-	-	-	-	-	-	-	-	-	-	-	-	-	-	-	-	-	-	-	-	9	1	3
HJ (Harold) Storrs	-	-	-	-	-	-	-	-	-	-	-	-	-	-	-	-	-	-	-	-	-	-	-	-	-	-	-	-	-	-	-	-	-	-	-	-	-	-	-	-	-	>C	C	W	3	-	-
F (Sos) Taylor E2	F	F	-	-	-	-	-	-	-	-	-	-	-	F	F	F	F	F	F	F	F	F	F*	F	F	F	F	F	F	F	F*	F*	F	F	F	F	F*	F	F	F	F	F	F	F	33	4	12
FM (Tim) Taylor E1	FH	-	-	FH	FH	FH	FH	FH	FH	FH	FH	FH	FH	FH	FH	FH	FH	FH	FH	FH	FH	FH	FH	FH	FH	FH	FH	FH	FH	FH	FH	FH	FH	FH	FH	FH	FH	FH	FH	FH	FH	FH	FH	-	41	8	24
NT (Trevor) Thorneloe	-	-	-	-	-	-	-	-	-	-	-	-	-	-	-	-	-	-	F	-	-	-	-	-	F	-	-	-	-	-	-	F	-	-	-	F	F	-	-	-	-	-	-	-	5	-	2
Flt-Lt. RHC (Bob) Usher	-	-	-	-	-	-	-	-	-	-	-	-	-	-	-	-	-	-	-	-	-	>F	F	F	-	F	F	-	-	-	F	-	-	F	F	-	F	F	F	F	F	F	F	F	16	2	6
HN (Herbert) Usher	-	-	-	-	-	-	-	-	-	-	-	-	-	-	-	-	-	-	-	-	-	-	>C	C	C	-	C	C	C	C	-	C	C	-	-	-	<C	-	-	-	-	-	-	-	10	-	-
G (Gordon) Vears	-	-	F	-	<F	-	-	-	-	-	-	-	-	-	-	-	-	-	-	-	-	-	-	-	-	-	-	-	-	-	-	-	-	-	-	-	-	-	-	-	-	-	-	-	2	-	-
JAG (George) Ward E6	F	F	F*	F	-	-	F	F	F*	F	F	F	F*	F*	F*	F*	F*	F*	F*	F*	F*	F*	-	F*	F*	F*	F*	F*	F*	F*	-	-	F*	F*	F*	F*	-	F*	F*	F*	F*	F*	F*	F*	38	-	-
WJ (William) Watts W1	C	C	C	C	-	-	-	-	-	-	-	-	-	-	-	-	W	-	-	-	C	-	-	-	-	C	W	-	-	-	-	-	-	-	-	-	-	-	-	-	-	-	C	C	10	2	6
J (John) Wickson	-	-	-	-	F	F	-	-	-	-	-	-	-	-	-	-	-	-	-	-	-	-	-	-	-	-	-	-	-	-	-	-	-	-	-	-	-	-	-	-	-	-	-	-	2	-	-
WC Wilkins	-	-	-	-	-	-	-	-	-	-	-	-	-	>W	W	W	C	W	W	W	W	W	W	W	W	W	W	-	W	W	W	W	-	-	W	W	W	-	W	W	W	-	-	-	24	12	36
J Wilkinson	FB	FB	FB	FB	-	FB	FB	FB	FB	FB	FB	FB	FB	FB	FB	FB	FB	FB	-	FB	-	FB	FB	FB	FB	FB	<FB	-	-	-	-	-	-	-	-	-	-	-	-	-	-	-	-	-	24	-	38
GW (Pedlar) Wood E1	SH	SH	SH	SH	-	-	SH	-	-	-	-	-	-	-	-	-	-	SH	-	-	-	-	-	SH	-	-	-	-	-	-	SH	-	SH	-	-	SH	-	-	-	-	-	-	-	-	10	2	6

1 GAME: A Bradbury =Wt(32), EG (Ernie) Coleman >F(11), DG (Gwyn) Francis W1 <F(31), TW (Thomas) Gabriel >C(20), AW Harris =F(21), AS (Alan) Hett >Ct(36), Col. Hitch =F(6), CL Lowe >F(42), A (Arthur) Morgan =Ct(34), P (Percy) Smitten <C(6), A Tearle =F(6), F Turnbull =SH(16)

The key for how to read the stats is on the last page

1922/23	
Home Ground: Welford Road	
Captain: Percy Lawrie	
Vice-captain: George Ward	

OVERALL RECORD:					T	C	PG	DG	MK	PTS
PLD	W	D	L	Tigers scored:	129	55	18	7	1	582
45	30	5	10	Opponents scored:	62	19	6	9	0	278

GM	DATE		VEN	OPPONENTS	RESULT	TRIES	KICKS	ATT
CLUB MATCHES								
1	Sep	**2**	**H**	**Bath**	W 16-8	Day, Storrs	Day c/d, Norman d	11000
2		**9**	**H**	**Plymouth Albion**	L 6-11	-	Sambrook 2p	10000
3		**16**	**H**	**Neath**	W 6-3	Storrs	Day p	-
4		20w	a	Rugby B.T.H.	W 19-0	Lawrie, Buchanan, Coates, Haselmere, T.Taylor	Lawrie 2c	1500
5		**23**	**H**	**Nuneaton**	W 33-5	Day, Buchanan, Coates, Cross, Storrs, F.Wright	Day 4c/p, Haselmere d	10000
6		**30**	**H**	**Headingley**	W 46-5	Day(2), Smallwood(2), Coates, Grierson, Russell, Storrs, S.Taylor, F.Wright	Day 4c/2p, Sambrook c	10000
7	Oct	**7**	**H**	**Llanelly**	L 3-4	T.Taylor	-	14000
8		11w	a	Moseley	W 19-6	Haselmere(2), German, Marques, Norman	Lawrie 2c	-
9		**14**	**H**	**Aberavon**	W 3-0	F.Wright	-	12000
10		21	a	Newport	L 3-17	-	Day p	7000
11		**28**	**H**	**Oxford University**	W 28-0	S.Taylor(2), T.Taylor(2), Coates, F.Wright	Day 5c	14000
12	Nov	**4**	**H**	**Swansea**	W 8-0	Haselmere, F.Wright	Day c	12000
13		**11**	**H**	**Cambridge University**	W 15-6	Day(2), T.Taylor	Day c, Haselmere d	17000
14		18	a	Northampton	W 21-3	Bryson(2), Day, T.Taylor	Day 3c, Sambrook m	-
15		**25**	**H**	**Cardiff**	L 3-7	-	Day p	15000
16	Dec	2	a	Harlequins	W 10-6	Sharratt, F.Wright	Sambrook 2c	2000
17		**9**	**H**	**Blackheath**	W 9-3	Day(2)	Day p	12000
18		**16**	**H**	**Bristol**	D 0-0	-	-	11000
19		23	a	Coventry	W 14-0	Coates(2), Haselmere, T.Taylor	Sambrook c	-
20		**26tu**	**H**	**Birkenhead Park**	W 11-5	Smallwood, Russell, Sharratt	Smallwood c	-
21		**27w**	**H**	**Barbarians**	D 3-3	S.Taylor	-	-
22		**28th**	**H**	**Racing Club de France**	W 4-0	-	Haselmere d	-
23		**30**	**H**	**Manchester**	W 36-0	Smallwood(7), Haselmere(2), Sharratt	Smallwood c, Sambrook 2c	-
24	Jan	1m	a	Headingley	W 35-0	Francis(3), G.Jones(2), Baker, Cross, Sharratt, F.Wright	Thorneloe 3c, Sambrook c	-
25		**6**	**H**	**Royal Air Force**	W 14-3	C.Jones, T.Taylor	Haselmere d, Sambrook 2c	10000
26		13	a	Swansea	W 6-4	Haselmere, Usher	-	-
27		**20**	**H**	**London Irish**	W 22-3	J.Davis, Roxburgh, S.Taylor, Wardrop, F.Wright	Sambrook 2c/p	10000
28		**27**	**H**	**Coventry**	W 22-5	F.Wright(2), Sharratt, S.Taylor	Day 2c/2p	10000
29	Feb	3	a	Richmond	W 13-5	Coates, Haselmere, Sharratt	Thorneloe 2c	3000
30		13tu	a	Racing Club de France	L 9-19	Cross, T.Taylor, Wallace	-	-
31		15th	a	United Services	D 3-3	-	Thorneloe p	-
32		17	a	Plymouth Albion	L 5-15	T.Taylor	Sambrook c	7000
33		24	a	Cardiff	L 0-24	-	-	5000
34	Mar	**3**	**H**	**Harlequins**	W 11-4	Smallwood, T.Taylor, Ward	Smallwood c	-
35		**10**	**H**	**Northampton**	W 14-11	Day, Haselmere, S.Taylor, F.Wright	Day c	-
36		**17**	**H**	**London Welsh**	W 33-8	Pollard(2), S.Taylor(2), Day, Grierson	Day 4c/p, Sambrook d	9000
37		31	a	Bristol	W 3-0	Haselmere	-	-
38	Apr	2m	a	Llanelly	L 0-19	-	-	-
39		3tu	a	Aberavon	D 8-8	Haselmere(2)	Sambrook c	-
40		4w	a	Bath	L 3-17	-	Day p	-
41		**7**	**H**	**London Scottish**	W 30-12	Thorneloe(2), Day, Burton, Cross, Price, T.Taylor	Day 3c/p	10000
42		9m	a	Nuneaton	W 12-3	Haselmere(2), Lawrie, Pollard	-	-
43		18w	a	Birkenhead Park	D 6-6	Coates, Ward	-	-
44		**21**	**H**	**London**	W 11-10	Bryson, Burton, T.Taylor	Lawrie c	10000
45		**28**	**H**	**Newport**	L 6-7	-	Day 2p	16000

INDIVIDUAL APPEARANCES 1922/23

Name / Game #	1	2	3	4	5	6	7	8	9	10	11	12	13	14	15	16	17	18	19	20	21	22	23	24	25	26	27	28	29	30	31	32	33	34	35	36	37	38	39	40	41	42	43	44	45	Apps	T	Pts
S (Stan) Brown	-	-	-	-	-	-	-	-	-	-	-	-	-	-	-	-	-	-	-	-	-	-	-	-	-	-	>SH	SH	-	-	-	-	-	-	-	-	-	-	-	-	-	-	-	-	-	2	-	-
Flt-Lt. OC (Oliver) Bryson	-	-	-	-	-	-	>C	-	-	W	C	C	C	C	C	C	C	C	C	-	-	-	-	-	-	C	C	C	-	-	C	-	-	C	-	-	-	-	-	-	-	-	-	C	-	17	3	9
JCR (Rankin) Buchanan S10	>F	F	F	F	F	-	-	-	-	-	-	-	-	-	-	-	-	-	-	-	-	-	-	-	-	-	-	-	-	-	-	-	-	-	-	-	-	-	-	F	-	-	-	-	F	7	2	6
CL Burton	-	-	-	-	-	-	-	-	-	-	-	-	-	-	-	-	-	-	-	-	-	-	-	-	-	-	-	-	-	-	-	-	-	-	-	-	-	-	-	W	W	-	W	W	W	5	2	6
N (Norman) Coates	C	C	F	C	F	F	F	C	C	C	C	C	-	C	F	C	F	-	F	C	-	C	-	-	-	-	-	F	C	C	-	C	C	-	-	C	C	C	C	C	-	C	C	C	C	33	8	24
EJ Crisp	-	-	-	>FB	-	-	-	-	FB	<FB	-	-	-	-	-	-	-	-	-	-	-	-	-	-	-	-	-	-	-	-	-	-	-	-	-	-	-	-	-	-	-	-	-	-	-	3	-	-
CW (Charlie) Cross	-	-	F	-	F	F	F	F	F	F	F	F	F	F	F	F	F	-	F	F	-	F	F	F	F	-	F	F	F	F	-	-	F	F	F	-	F	F	F	-	F	-	-	F	-	32	4	12
HS Davis	-	-	-	-	-	-	-	-	-	-	-	-	-	-	-	-	-	-	-	-	-	-	>W	-	<W	-	-	-	-	-	-	-	-	-	-	-	-	-	-	-	-	-	-	-	-	2	-	-
JE (John) Davis	-	-	-	-	-	-	-	-	-	-	-	-	-	-	-	-	-	-	-	-	-	-	>F	-	-	-	F	-	-	-	-	-	-	-	-	-	-	-	-	-	-	F	F	-	-	4	1	3
HLV (Harold) Day E3	C	-	C	-	C	C	C	-	C	C	C	C	C	C	C	-	C	-	-	-	-	-	-	-	-	-	-	FB	-	-	-	-	-	-	C	C	C	-	-	C	C	-	-	-	C	20	12	140
T Fletcher	-	-	-	-	-	-	-	-	-	-	-	-	-	-	-	-	-	-	-	-	-	-	-	-	-	-	-	-	-	-	-	-	-	-	-	-	-	>C	<C	-	-	-	-	-	-	2	-	-
GJ (Guy) German	-	F	SH	SH	-	-	-	SH	-	-	-	-	-	-	-	-	-	-	-	-	-	-	-	-	-	-	-	-	SH	-	-	-	SH	SH	SH	-	-	SH	SH	-	-	-	SH	-	-	11	1	3
AD (Alfred) Godfrey	FH	C	-	-	-	-	C	C	-	-	-	-	-	-	-	-	-	-	-	-	-	-	-	-	-	-	-	-	-	-	-	-	-	-	-	-	-	-	-	-	-	-	-	-	-	4	-	-
H (Henry) Grierson	-	-	>F	F	-	F	F	F	F	F	F	-	F	F	-	F	-	F	F	-	F	-	F	-	-	-	-	F	F	-	F	-	-	-	-	F	-	F	F	-	<F	-	-	-	-	22	2	6
EE (Teddy) Haselmere	W	W	C	C	C	C	W	W	W	C	W	W	C	W	W	C	C	C	W	C	C	W	C	W	C	W	W	W	W	C	W	C	W	W	W	W	W	W	W	W	W	W	C	W	W	45	15	61
L (Lew) Jenkins W2	-	-	-	-	-	-	-	-	-	-	-	-	-	-	-	-	-	-	-	-	-	-	-	-	-	-	-	-	-	-	-	-	-	-	-	-	-	>F	-	<F	-	-	-	-	-	2	-	-
CW (Charles) Jones W3	-	-	-	-	-	-	-	-	-	-	-	-	-	-	-	-	-	>F	-	F	F	F	-	F	F	F	-	-	-	F	F	F	F	F	-	F	F	F	F	-	-	F	F	F	F	20	1	3
SF (Frank) Lawrence	F	F	-	F	-	-	F	F	F	F	F	F	-	F	F	F	F	F	-	F	-	-	F	F	F	F	-	-	-	F	-	F	-	F	F	F	F	-	F	-	F	F	-	-	-	28	-	-
PW (Percy) Lawrie E2	-	-	-	C*	C*	-	-	FB*	-	-	-	-	-	-	-	-	-	C*	-	-	-	-	-	-	-	-	-	-	-	-	-	-	-	-	-	-	-	-	-	C*	C*	C*	-	C*	C*	9	2	16
CL Lowe	-	-	-	-	-	-	-	-	-	-	-	-	-	-	-	-	-	-	-	F	-	-	<F	-	-	-	-	-	-	-	-	-	-	-	-	-	-	-	-	-	-	-	-	-	-	2	-	-
EJ (Edward) Massey E+	-	-	-	-	-	-	-	-	-	-	-	-	-	-	-	-	-	-	-	-	-	-	-	>SH	-	-	-	-	-	-	-	-	-	-	-	-	-	-	-	-	-	-	-	SH	SH	3	-	-
DJ (Doug) Norman E+	F	F	F	F	-	F	F	F	F	F	F	F	F	-	-	F	-	F	F	F	F	F	-	-	F	F	F	F	F	-	F	F	F	F	F	F	F	F	F	-	-	F	F	F	-	35	1	7
W Pollard	-	-	-	-	-	-	-	-	-	-	-	-	-	-	-	-	-	-	-	-	-	-	-	-	-	-	-	-	-	-	-	-	-	-	-	W	-	-	-	-	-	C	-	-	-	2	3	9
HL (Leo) Price E4	-	-	-	-	>F	F	-	-	-	-	F	-	F	-	-	-	F	-	-	-	F	FH	-	-	-	-	-	-	-	-	-	-	-	-	-	-	-	-	-	-	C	-	-	-	-	8	1	3
A (Andy) Roxburgh	-	-	-	-	-	-	-	-	-	-	-	-	-	-	-	-	-	-	>C	C	C	C	C	-	C	C	C	C	C	C	C	C	-	C	C	C	C	-	-	-	SH	SH	FH	-	-	20	1	3
JC (John) Russell	SH	-	-	-	SH	SH	SH	-	SH	SH	SH	SH	SH	SH	SH	SH	SH	SH	SH	SH	SH	SH	-	-	-	SH	-	-	-	-	-	SH	-	-	-	SH	SH	-	C	SH	-	-	-	-	-	24	2	6
LC (Claude) Sambrook	FB	FB	FB	-	FB	FB	FB	-	-	-	FB	FB	FB	FB	FB	FB	FB	FB	FB	FB	FB	FB	FB	FB	FB	FB	FB	-	FB	FB	FB	FB	FB	FB	FB	FB	FB	FB	FB	FB	FB	FB	-	FB	FB	39	-	42
CJ (John) Seager	-	-	-	-	-	-	-	-	-	-	-	-	-	-	-	-	-	-	-	-	-	-	-	-	-	-	-	-	-	SH	<SH	-	-	-	-	-	-	-	-	-	-	-	-	-	-	2	-	-
H (Herb) Sharratt	-	-	-	-	-	F	-	F	F	F	-	F	-	F	F	F	-	F	-	F	F	F	F	F	F	F	F	F	F	F	F	F	F	F	F	F	F	F	F	F	-	F	F	F	F	34	6	18
AM (Alastair) Smallwood E12	-	-	C	-	-	C	-	-	C	-	-	-	W	-	C	-	-	-	-	W	C	C	C	-	-	-	-	C	-	-	-	-	-	C	C	-	-	-	-	-	-	-	-	-	-	12	11	39
HJ (Harold) Storrs	C	-	W	-	W	W	-	-	-	-	-	-	-	-	-	-	-	-	-	-	-	-	-	-	-	-	-	-	-	-	-	-	-	-	-	-	-	-	-	-	-	-	-	-	-	4	4	12
F (Sos) Taylor E2	F	F	F	F	F	F	F	F	F	F	F	F	F	F	F	F	F	-	F	-	F	F	F	F	F	F	F	F	F	F	F	F	F	F	F	F	F	F*	-	F	F	-	F	F	F	41	9	27
FM (Tim) Taylor E1	-	-	FH	FH	FH	FH*	FH*	FH	FH*	FH*	FH*	FH	FH	FH	FH	FH	FH	FH	FH	FH	FH*	-	FH*	FH*	FH*	FH	FH	FH*	FH	FH	FH*	FH	FH	FH	FH	FH*	FH*	-	-	-	FH	FH	-	FH	<FH	38	13	39
NT (Trevor) Thorneloe	-	-	-	-	-	-	-	F	-	-	-	-	-	-	-	-	-	-	-	-	-	-	-	F	F	-	-	-	F	F	F	F	F	-	F	F	F	-	F	F	F	F	-	-	F	16	2	19
Flt-Lt. RHC (Bob) Usher	F	F	-	-	F	-	F	-	F	F	F	F	F	F	F	-	F	F	F	-	F	F	-	-	-	F	-	F	-	-	F	-	-	-	-	-	-	-	-	F	F	-	F	F	F	24	1	3
CB (Charles) Wales	-	-	-	-	-	-	-	-	-	-	-	-	-	-	-	-	-	-	-	-	-	-	-	-	-	-	-	-	-	-	-	-	-	-	-	-	-	>FH	FH	-	-	-	-	-	-	2	-	-
JAG (George) Ward E6	F*	F*	F*	F	F	-	-	-	-	-	-	F*	F*	F*	F*	F*	F*	F	F*	F*	-	F*	-	-	-	F*	F*	-	F*	F*	-	F*	F*	F*	F*	-	-	-	-	-	F	F	F*	F	F	28	2	6
D Wardrop	-	-	-	-	-	-	-	-	-	-	-	-	-	-	-	-	-	-	-	-	-	-	-	-	-	>C	<C	-	-	-	-	-	-	-	-	-	-	-	-	-	-	-	-	-	-	2	1	3
WC Wilkins	-	-	-	-	-	-	-	-	-	-	-	-	-	-	-	W	W	W	W	W	W	-	-	-	-	-	-	-	-	-	-	-	-	-	-	-	-	-	-	-	-	-	-	-	-	6	-	-
FC (Frederick) Wright	>W	W	W	W	W	W	W	W	W	W	W	W	W	W	W	W	W	W	C	-	W	W	W	W	W	W	W	W	W	W	-	W	W	W	W	-	W	W	W	-	-	W	<W	-	-	38	11	33

1 GAME: F/O. CD (Cyril) Adams F(40), GG (George) Aitken S2 =FH(40), A (Ambrose) Baker W5 >Ft(24), HS (Harry) Carter =SH(23), AM (Tarzan) David =C(33), C Dudley =W(32), A Francis =Ct(24), A (Arthur) Frowen =FH(2), TW (Thomas) Gabriel <C(2), AS (Alan) Hett <C(24), G Jones =Ct(24), A King >C(29), CJ (Charles) King-Turner =C(33), MA Macdonald =W(4), AC Marques =Ct(8), J (John) Morton =FB(43), Paisley =C(38), RS (Ron) Palmer >C(43), DJ Reeves =F(1), Flt-Lt. CB Riddle =W(31), Sgt. Snaith =C(31), S Stenson =SH(25), GC Taylor >C(25), W (Billy) Wallace GB+ >Wt(30), HB (Henry) Watney =F(4), GW (Pedlar) Wood E1 <SH(2), GWS (George) Wright =F(27)

The key for how to read the stats is on the last page

CHAPTER 9

Service Station

1923/1924

This season has to be known as Wakefield's season, even though it was very far from the most successful one in terms of mere statistics. One of the most distinguished players to represent his country, Wavell Wakefield had made a name for himself as an all-round athlete at school at Sedbergh, and later in the RAF, with Harlequins and at Cambridge University. First capped in 1920, he came to the Midlands to work for Boots in Nottingham, and made his home in Leicester.

He was, naturally, a notable capture for Tom Crumbie and made his first appearance of the season in the third game, scoring a try in an 8-3 win over Neath. He won fame as a back row player but Tigers happily used him at centre in his next game, when he again scored a try in the 24-9 away win over Headingley. He took over the captaincy of the side from George Ward and it was under his leadership that Leicester finally stopped Newport's unbeaten run, when they came to Welford Road and lost 7-5, Percy Lawrie scoring the winning try.

← WAVELL WAKEFIELD
Between 1920 and 1970, Wavell Wakefield's was the most famous name in English rugby. Captain of the England side that won a grand slam in 1924, the last of his three years with Leicester, he was among the foremost thinkers and innovators in the country, both as a player and subsequently as a referee and administrator (he was president of the RFU in 1950/51). A back-row forward who could adapt to playing centre to great effect, he was unavailable to lead the 1930 Lions to Australasia, a role that fell to Leicester's Doug Prentice. He became a Conservative MP and was knighted for public services in 1944, becoming Baron Wakefield of Kendal in 1963.

Picture caption: Wavell Wakefield in conversation with the Neath captain after Tigers' 8-3 victory, 15.9.1923.

It must have been a frustrating experience for him, however, to play in a seven-man pack. As the architect of a style of back row play which helped England to dominate the 1920s and always one of the game's leading tacticians, he found himself in a side which not infrequently did not possess a back row. Sometimes the Leicester scrum packed three-four, sometimes three-two-two; sometimes, indeed, they played four-three before the laws laid down the exact number of players to constitute a front row. He was unhappy, too, with the eight backs, feeling that too frequently players were crowded out on the wings but, as a man of considerable tact, refrained from offending Crumbie, who originated the pattern of play. His feelings must have been reflected elsewhere though, for the former scrum-half Billy Foreman suggested a return to the conventional style of play in committee without achieving anything.

During his one season with Leicester, Wakefield also captained England and, 45 years later as Lord Wakefield of Kendal, he had fond memories of Leicester. He recalled vividly that success against Newport: "They were a well-drilled and disciplined side captained by Jack Wetter, the Welsh international half-back, who was not only a fine player but an excellent tactician. I am pleased to say we took away their unbeaten record and we deserved to win, but in my view Wetter and his side had the moral victory.

"When Newport were in the lead and I wanted to open up the game, and he wanted to close it up and keep it tight, then the game became closed up. When we got into the lead and I wanted to close the game and he wanted to open it up, then in spite of all we could do the game became open.

"In another match I remember that we started an attack from our own goal-line. Eventually the ball was passed to me and, as I was rounding the opposition full-back on the half way line, in a despairing clutch my shorts were torn off and I had to run the length of the field with no shorts and no jock strap. I sat on the ball behind the goal posts until another pair of shorts arrived. Tom Crumbie later observed that on the next Saturday he had never had such a good gate!

"Another character was our hooker, George Ward. There was not much he did not know about front row play in general and hooking in particular. Before I joined Leicester, when I was captain of Cambridge in 1922, after Leicester had played the university I arranged for him to give the university some coaching and it was most valuable.

"The season I played with Leicester was most enjoyable. England won all her matches and the Tigers, with the strongest fixture list in the UK, had a good and balanced side of talented players... it was a happy side, with a wonderful team spirit inspired by dear old Tom Crumbie, who insisted on taking the touchline although he was nearly blind and could hardly walk, let alone run.

"Except when there was a quick throw-in, there was a gentlemen's agreement by both sides that we would line up where we reckoned the ball went into touch and the side entitled to throw in the ball would get ready to throw it in so that when dear old Tom arrived to put up his flag there was no problem, although if the ball happened to go into touch somewhere near where Tom happened to be, then the home side invariably had the advantage of a yard or two.

"He was exceedingly kind to me when I came as a stranger to Leicester and he dispensed his genial hospitality to everyone connected with the game. He looked after the members of the team as if they were his children; nothing was too much trouble for him and he kept an open house for all players who wished to take advantage of his friendliness."

Tigers in action against Racing Club de France in Paris, 4.3.1924

Again there were international honours for the club: apart from Wakefield, Price and Day were capped by England and Jock Lawrie by Scotland, while Leicester's consistent full-back, Claude Sambrook, was an England reserve. The club renewed their acquaintance with the Racing Club de France, winning 24-5 but going down at the Stade Bergeyre by 22-3.

Off the field, however, there were intimations of mortality from Crumbie. His efforts on the club's behalf had taken their toll and he was, anyway, suffering from diabetes. In March 1924, he notified the committee of his impending resignation but other counsels prevailed.

Grierson's *Ramblings of a Rabbit* gives another snapshot of life at the Tigers: "The ground is situated in the angle formed by two wide thoroughfares - Welford Road and Aylestone Road - both of which contain double tracks of tram lines.

"The ground therefore is easily accessible and, what is far more important, can be emptied in five minutes. You walk straight in and you walk straight out. There is an enormous cement motor park at the back of the reserved stand, and as all cars are made to enter from the Aylestone entrance they can, after the match, drive off at once into Welford Road.

"To see the crowd leave the ground at the conclusion of a game - the gates are invariably ten thousand - is a revelation to those whose only experience of this kind of thing is Twickenham.

"Adjoining the ground is a large building - the Junior Training Hall - where dances and exhibitions are held, and, being equipped with up-to-date kitchens, hot luncheons and six course dinners can be, and are, provided for visiting teams.

"The ground itself is a fine one - perhaps a trifle short from goal line to dead ball line - but that's only a detail.

"The stands can accommodate about eight thousand and the ground thirty thousand.

"The players' dressing-rooms are first rate and the referee has a properly furnished room with a private bath complete.

"The secretary's job is a very big one at Leicester - there are some six thousand members - and the raising of teams and arrangement of tours all need a vast amount of attention. But Tom Crumbie is fortunate in being the possessor of a very large and successful stationery business, which means that he has a full and competent staff available to do the donkey work for him.

"Leicester adopt the seven forward formation, with an extra outside labelled 'dead' centre. The forwards pack 3-2-2 (sometimes 3-4), and the only point to be noted about the former method is this, and it affects the back row pair: one goes in the middle, and the other packs on that flank into which the ball will most probably be put, thereby affording adequate support to the front row where it is most needed.

"This gives you an extra back to play about with, and mighty useful he is if everyone runs straight.

"As I have already indicated, we have big gates at Leicester, ten to fourteen thousand generally, with a large proportion of the fair sex."

1924/1925

Tom Crumbie was still at the helm when the new season, and the New Zealanders, arrived. This was the year of Cliff Porter's "Invincible" All Blacks and Leicester had lost the services of Wakefield, who had resumed his club career with Harlequins, and Bob Usher, unfortunately killed in a flying accident.

The ground was packed to the seams with 35,000 people for the game between Leicester and the tourists on 4 October, but they were in for a disappointment. Leicester lost 27-0 with the following XV: Claude Sambrook; Oliver Bryson, Morton Holden, PG Scott, Alastair Smallwood, Leo Price, Edward Massey, John Russell; Jock Lawrie, Rankin Buchanan, George Ward, Doug Prentice, William Roderick, Herb Sharratt, John Davis. The oddity of the Leicester formation was that it aped New Zealand's, including as it did seven forwards and eight backs - one of whom, Leo Price, was a forward. They adopted a similar formation two years later against another team from down under, the touring New Zealand Maori.

Price and Alastair Smallwood played as five-eighths with two genuine half-backs, Edward Massey and John Russell, inside them. Contemporary reports suggest that Price's distribution skills were strictly limited, not that

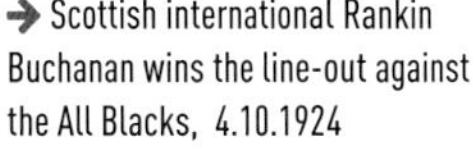

Scottish international Rankin Buchanan wins the line-out against the All Blacks, 4.10.1924

↑ Mad scramble for the ball during the County Championship final in 1925.

the All Blacks granted much room for manoeuvre. The hallmark of the New Zealanders' win was their cover in defence, support for the man with the ball and the way they hustled the Leicester halves into error. Aided by some poor Leicester tackling they ran in tries through Les Cupples, Jock Richardson, John Steel, Frederick Lucas, 'Son' White and 'Snowy' Svenson, Mark Nicholls kicking three conversions and a penalty.

The best to be said of the game, from the local viewpoint, was the profit of £1,000 but there was some consolation that season. For Leicestershire, represented entirely by Leicester players, won the County Championship, for the first, and so far the only, time. The XV included two more players who were to become great favourites with the Welford Road crowd, George Beamish and Ralph Buckingham, and was: Claude Sambrook, Alastair Smallwood, Harold Day, Oliver Bryson, Harold Sambrook, Morton Holden, Ralph Buckingham, Guy German, George Ward, Jock Lawrie, George Beamish, Herb Sharratt, Doug Prentice, Doug Norman, Trevor Thorneloe.

Beamish, Bryson and Holden scored tries, Day landing a conversion and a penalty, in the 14-6 win over Gloucestershire at Bristol and, coupled with the caps awarded to Massey and Smallwood (England) and Beamish (Ireland) helped turn a disappointing start into a proud finish. The season was rounded off, as usual in those days, with the Easter tour to Wales and a sample itinerary was: April 10 - leave Leicester in cars, dinner at the Grand Hotel, Bristol; April 11 - visit zoological gardens (a.m.), game v Bristol, leave for Monmouth and dinner at the Beaufort Arms. April 12 - motor through the Wye Valley to Chepstow and back; April 13 - leave for Llanelly, lunch at the Stepney Hotel, game v Llanelly, back to Monmouth in time for an 8.15 p.m. dinner; April 14 - leave for Bath, lunch at Ye Olde Red House, game v Bath, leave for dinner at the Swan's Nest Hotel, Stratford; leave for Leicester.

How strictly the timetable was adhered to remains an unknown factor and the fact that only 45 minutes was allowed for dinner on the final day means the tour party should undoubtedly have arrived back in Leicester with a severe bout of indigestion.

LAMBERT & BUTLER'S CIGARETTES
G. R. BEAMISH
(R.A.F. & IRELAND)

Another fine crop of players had now taken root in the Leicester side. There was the RAF connection, when players posted to Cranwell and Midland stations generally tended to head for Leicester. Charles Medhurst, Oliver Bryson, Bob Usher, John Russell, all were servicemen but the best known of the RAF players to come to Leicester at that time has to be George Beamish, the Ireland forward whose three brothers also played for the Tigers at one time or another.

Outside the service ranks came Edward Massey, capped three times in 1925, a pupil at Ampleforth College who, in the days before substitutes, played the last hour of his first international, against Scotland, with a broken collarbone and a partially dislocated shoulder. There were some notable local products too, in Doug Prentice and Ralph Buckingham, the first a pupil of Wyggeston School who joined Westleigh before coming as a back row forward to the Tigers in 1923; the second born in Blaby and educated at Stoneygate School and Rossall, before returning to the Stoneygate club and playing for Leicester first in 1925.

1925/1926

It was, however, a time of transition. No club can go through a decade without the graph indicating their success ratio taking a downward curve now and then, and Leicester were no exception. The very fact that they could call on so many servicemen told against them when duty demanded these same players should be elsewhere - during the 1925/26 season John Russell was not regularly available, George Beamish played only 10 games and Massey had gone abroad. Several youngsters had to be introduced and there was increasing criticism of the seven-man pack.

No doubt the service presence accounted for an increase in the social side of the club's doings: the Tigers Ball at the Junior Training Hall (later the Granby Hall) over Christmas 1925 attracted 450 revellers, who were entertained by the La Veeda orchestra and the songs of the visiting Barbarians. In strict contrast a fortnight later, the 500 visiting Swansea supporters provided entertainment before, during and doubtless after the game by

↓ Guy German makes a break with Doug Norman in support against Harlequins at Twickenham, 5.12.1925.

their hymn singing (they brought their own conductor), climbing the goalposts and a would-be George Formby who played the ukulele in the committee box.

The new year saw Tigers make their first trip to Scotland when they lost 5-8 to Heriot's Former Pupils at Inverleith, in what was to be their only visit north of the border until 1996.

The Welford Road crowd had the novelty, too, of a couple of New Zealanders introduced into the side around the turn of the year, two straight-running, forthright backs in Jeff FitzGerald and CB Tate, and a newcomer at fly-half who was to make a considerable impact, Harry Greenlees.

1926/1927

Later that year, in November 1926, came more New Zealanders, the Maori party captained by Wattie Barclay. This particular touring team had created something of a storm by refusing to play under Welsh referees in Wales earlier in the tour, but they had an enjoyable game at Welford Road when they beat the Tigers 15-13 before a crowd of 20,000. It was not an entirely typical Leicester performance, for their speedy wings, Ewart Farndon and Ted Flewitt, got few opportunities and Day inside them at five-eighth was suffering from a leg injury and should not have played.

The team was: Claude Sambrook; Ewart Farndon, Oliver Bryson, Ted Flewitt, Harold Day, Ralph Buckingham, Harry Greenlees, John Russell; Doug Prentice, Doug Norman, Ernie Coleman, Henry Greenwood, 'Mog' Christie, Victor Beamish, Guy German. The club XV led 8-3 at the interval, Farndon scoring a try which Prentice, who also kicked a penalty, converted. Pat Potaka scored the Maori try but in the second half Alby Falwasser got an interception try and a dropped goal by W Wilson put the tourists ahead. Prentice scored a try, which he converted himself, to restore Leicester's lead but a try by Samuel Gemmell, converted by ETW Love, tipped the balance.

Farndon, who scored 13 tries in 1925/26, said of the sides he played in: "We were a great team together, wonderfully friendly and on tours we stuck together. We used to play tricks on Tom Crumbie of course, in spite of his general insistence on strict discipline. He wouldn't allow a Tigers player to turn out for the Barbarians - he felt that playing for the club and county was enough football for anyone. On one occasion Trevor Thorneloe did defy his injunction and turned out for the Barbarians, and Tom promptly dropped him."

1927/1928

But the days of the great administrator were drawing to a close. Prematurely aged and nearly blind, Crumbie recovered from illness in time for the 1927/28 season and it doubtless warmed his heart to see Leicester score exactly 100 points in their first four games, aided now by George and Victor Beamish. He also saw an all-Leicester XV represent the county against

ITINERARY.

Leicester Football Club.

New Year Tour, 1926.

Matches

Jan 1st v. MANCHESTER.
" 2nd v. HERIOTONIANS (Edinburgh).
" 4th v. NORTHERN (Newcastle).

Headquarters
North British Hotel, Edinburgh.

↑ Jeff FitzGerald's tour card for the New Year Tour of 1926.

the touring side from New South Wales, the Waratahs of AC 'Johnnie' Wallace who left such a lasting impression in this country. The XV was Claude Sambrook; Ewart Farndon, Ralph Buckingham, Harold Day (capt), Frank Wood; Harry Greenlees, John Russell; Doug Prentice, Doug Norman, Ernie Coleman, George Beamish, Douglas Ryley, Mog Christie, Frank Lawrence, Harry Briers.

The Australian side led 9-3 at half-time and won 20-8, Day scoring a first-half try for the County XV and converting a later try by Farndon. That made it 9-8 but then Russell left the field with a broken collarbone and the Waratahs took full advantage to score three more tries. There were further honours for the club when Buckingham and Farndon played in the first England trial, held at Welford Road, while Greenlees received a Scottish trial and went on to win caps against the Waratahs, Wales and France that season.

Buckingham had already been capped the season before, against France. It was, in fact, his only cap and he was unlucky that it came on a day when England were hard pressed (they lost 3-0) and the backs were on the defensive. A dependable and versatile player, he was travelling reserve for his country 10 times and recalled what the club was like shortly before the death, in March 1928, of Tom Crumbie:

↑ Harold Day scores for the county with Frank Wood in support against the touring Waratahs, 29.10.1927.

"It was different from any club I had known. Normally you were proposed, seconded and worked your way up from the lower sides. It was rather like playing for the Barbarians when you were invited to play for Leicester. And after the match we used to go to the "Big Window", a room at the Prince Leopold on the corner of Welford Road. We had Tom Goodrich to look after our kit and he was the kindest man possible. Nothing was too much for him, he polished the boots, soles and all.

"I think football today is probably better but in the mid-20s we produced play almost as good. But the wing forward was the man who ruined open rugby: it started with [Tom] Voyce and [Arthur] Blakiston in 1924 and gradually developed from the days when, basically, there were two scrums whose only job was to get the ball for the backs."

Buckingham it was who was involved in a light-hearted incident with his great friend, Ted Flewitt, after a sailing excursion on the Norfolk Broads. Flewitt was the man who "took the rap" to the glee of the local press when he was fined £5, with four shillings and sixpence costs, for holding up a motorist and playing football in the highway at Purgh St Margaret's. A group of men, in yachting clothing, threatened to put a car driven by a journalist from Attleborough in the river, after the overbearing scribe broke up their impromptu game on the road. It was said in court that "the young man who kicked the ball was not present...he had played against France". The chairman of the bench delivered himself of the opinion that he was sorry to see young men making fools of themselves. Three years later the unfortunate Flewitt was killed in an aeroplane crash at Castle Bromwich.

With the club well on the way to another successful season, the man who made so much of it possible, Tom Crumbie, died. Although his health had been deteriorating for several years, he still maintained his record of never missing a club match - even when serving on Rugby Football Union committees in London - until November 1927. Then the strain of travelling told and, though he passed his 60th birthday in February 1928, a few weeks later, on 13 March, he died.

It is not too much to say that, for Leicester, it was the end of an era, for in many ways Crumbie had been the club for 33 years. Particularly this was true when Leicester became an invitation side, for then the club was, in essence, the 15 players who happened to turn out each Saturday. Crumbie was the cog around which it all revolved.

The *Leicester Mercury's* rugby critic, AC Tole, who wrote under the pseudonym Cyrus, wrote: "He was more than a mere secretary-manager of the club; in a sense he epitomised the Tigers in his own genial personality...His house at Smeeton Westerby was 'Liberty Hall' and seldom a Sunday went by without a group of Tigers foregathering there to talk over tactics and prospects...He had a knack of getting people to do what he wanted."

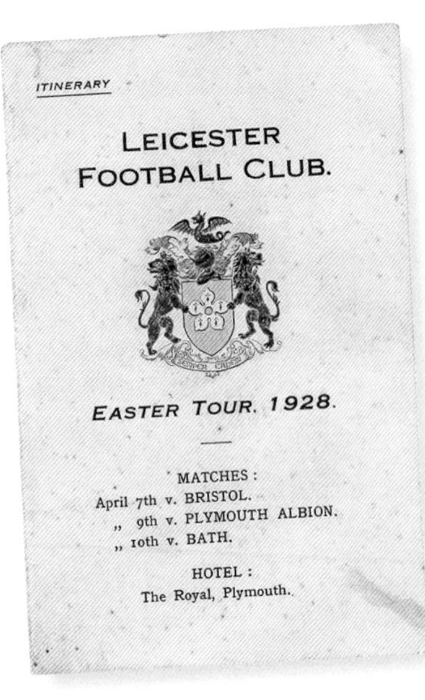

ITINERARY

LEICESTER FOOTBALL CLUB.

EASTER TOUR. 1928.

MATCHES:
April 7th v. BRISTOL.
„ 9th v. PLYMOUTH ALBION.
„ 10th v. BATH.

HOTEL:
The Royal, Plymouth.

↑ Tour card for the trip to face Bristol, Plymouth and Bath at Easter 1928.

↓ Doug Prentice captained the Lions on their tour to Australia and New Zealand in 1930.

← Tom Crumbie died in March 1928 after a long and very significant association with his beloved Tigers.

St Peter's Church was packed for the funeral service, not only by friends he had made in the rugby world but by trade acquaintances, for he had been at one time a vice-president of the Leicester Master Printers' Association. One of the original Leicester players and administrators, Joseph Collier, attended the funeral and the following Saturday the Tigers paid their own special tribute. Crumbie's usual seat in the committee box was left vacant and the Imperial Band played *Solemn Melody* as Leicester and Penarth took the field wearing black armbands.

Day kicked the penalty which gave Leicester a 3-0 win though they were without Prentice, who was playing for England against Scotland that day, for this was the season when he won his three caps. Prentice recalled in 1947, "during Crumbie's last few seasons he was a very sick man. I used to motor out to his home in the country on Monday evenings to help him pick the Leicester team for the following Saturday. One Monday morning my name appeared in the papers in the selected England team. Dear old Tom greeted me that evening by saying, 'I'm very glad, Doug, the cap has come at last, but mind you don't get hurt. We play Coventry the following week!'"

It would doubtless have pleased the late secretary to know that Doug Prentice was to captain the British touring team to Australasia in 1930, to manage a British tour to Argentina in 1936 and to become secretary of the Rugby Football Union between 1947 and 1962.

Day and Prentice shared the scoring honours at the end of the season. Although Frank Wood, younger brother of Pedlar, headed the try-scorers with 19, Day totalled 123 points and Prentice 105, while the indefatigable Doug Norman only missed the last game of the season.

Leicester concluded their playing season with a win in the inaugural Leicestershire seven-a-side competition. Organised in aid of the Infirmary, the Tigers beat Aylestone Athletic 30-3 in the final and not unnaturally were to dominate the tournament for the next few years. They also concluded the season with a new secretary, JE Thorneloe, who was appointed on 4 April.

Eric Thorneloe was to do as much for Leicester in his own quiet way as his predecessor. Stocky and tough, with a resonant voice, Thorneloe had emerged from the First World War with a distinguished record and the Military Cross. He resumed playing with Westleigh but had one season, 1920/21, when he played on seven occasions for Leicester as a wing or full-back. A knee injury forced him to retire in 1925, by which time he had become secretary to Westleigh (1920) and to Leicestershire (1923).

Among his first duties was to help decide on a fitting memorial to Crumbie. The club set up a committee to debate the problem and six months later recommended that the New Stand be renamed the Crumbie Stand and that a Memorial Fund be established to help pay off the debt on the stand. But inevitably there were problems as the new administration felt its way. Crumbie, after all, had been very much a one-man band and had done his printing firm no good at all by subverting much of its time and effort to rugby matters.

1928/1929

The transitional period began to be reflected on the field and the 1928/29 season was the worst since the war. Day played only five matches and was one of a maddening crop of injuries. Tigers had the services of the Old Laurentians forward, Philip 'Pop' Dunkley who was to win six England caps in the 1930s and a new name appeared ten times at full-back, the 21-year-old Westleigh player, Bobby Barr.

There was a rift too in Tigers' longstanding link with Cardiff. Early in the season Leicester beat the Welsh club 8-5 at Welford Road, when two Cardiff forwards were sent off for arguing with the referee. But in the return Tigers lost by a similar score in what was to prove to be the last match between the clubs for several years. Cardiff had been in the habit of playing two "1st XVs" on occasions and Leicester felt they were getting the second best of the two teams. Their objections were not met and the fixture was dropped - it was a disheartening note to end with.

→ Doug Norman, here shown in action against Blackheath, 14 April 1928, missed only the last game of the 1927/28 season.

↑ LEICESTER FOOTBALL CLUB 1924/25
Back: Crumbie (Hon.Sec), Dynes, Russell, Davis, Coates, A.Palmer, Scott, Lawrence, Massey, S.Smith, Sinclair.
Middle: Thorpe (Hon.Tres), Beamish, Norman, Sharratt, Ward, Day (capt), Lawrie, Prentice, Thorneloe, Bryson, McAlpin (President).
Front: Buckingham, H.Sambrook, German, R.Palmer, Smallwood, C.Sambrook, Holden.

↑ LEICESTER FOOTBALL CLUB 1926/27
Back: Buckingham, Sambrook, Coates, Greenwood, Briers, Christie, Ryley, Lawrence, Barlow, Burton.
Middle: Crumbie (Hon.Sec), Thorpe (Hon.Tres), Farndon, Prentice, Day (capt), Norman, Wood, Coleman, Faire (President).
Front: Russell, Greenlees, Thompson, Flewitt, Edmiston, V.Beamish.

↑ LEICESTER FOOTBALL CLUB SEVENS TEAM 1927/28
Back: Thorneloe (Hon.Sec), Wood, Hall, Coleman.
Front: Norman, Prentice (capt), Greenlees, Farndon.

↑ LEICESTER FOOTBALL CLUB 1928/29
Back: Greenwood, Briers, Manson, Dunkley, Graves, F.Wood, J.Cramphorn, Barlow, Edmiston, Thorneloe (Hon.Sec).
Middle: Coleman, G.Beamish, Norman, Prentice (capt), Buckingham, Greenlees, Farndon.
Front: Saunders, Barr, Flewitt, Hall, Burton.

1923/24													
Home Ground: Welford Road	OVERALL RECORD:						T	C	PG	DG	MK	PTS
Captain: Wavell Wakefield	PLD	W	D	L	Tigers scored:		102	51	24	4	0	496
Vice-captain: George Ward	46	24	3	19	Opponents scored:		106	39	5	6	1	438

GM	DATE		VEN	OPPONENTS	RESULT	TRIES	KICKS	ATT
CLUB MATCHES								
1	Sep	1	H	Bath	W 6-3	-	P.Lawrie 2p	7000
2		8	H	Plymouth Albion	W 14-5	P.Lawrie, Bryson	P.Lawrie 2c/d	7000
3		15	H	Neath	W 8-3	Wakefield	Day c/p	10000
4		17m	a	Headingley	W 24-9	Bryson(3), Bemrose, Wakefield, Wallace	Day 3c	-
5		22	H	Cross Keys	L 6-8	Price, Storrs	-	8000
6		29	H	Aberavon	L 0-8	-	-	10000
7	Oct	6	H	Llanelly	L 8-9	G.Taylor	P.Lawrie c/p	9000
8		13	H	Moseley	W 9-8	Wakefield	Day 2p	9000
9		20	H	Newport	W 7-5	P.Lawrie	Price d	10000
10		27	H	Nuneaton	D 0-0	-	-	8000
11		31w	a	Oxford University	L 11-23	Bryson(2), Godfrey	P.Lawrie c	-
12	Nov	3	a	Swansea	D 5-5	Day	Day c	4000
13		5m	a	Llanelly	L 0-23	-	-	-
14		10	a	Cambridge University	W 14-11	Smallwood(2), Russell	Sambrook c/p	-
15		17	H	Northampton	W 13-3	Day(2), J.Lawrie	Day 2c	12000
16		24	a	Cardiff	L 3-9	-	Day p	-
17		26m	a	Neath	L 6-37	Prentice, Wickson	-	-
18	Dec	1	a	Harlequins	L 8-10	Norman	Day c/p	-
19		8	a	Blackheath	W 14-7	Bryson, Holden	Day 2c, Medhurst d	-
20		15	H	Bristol	W 11-0	W.Wilkins	Day c/2p	9000
21		22	a	Coventry	D 0-0	-	-	-
22		26w	H	Birkenhead Park	W 17-3	Simpson(2), Day, Prentice, Wakefield	Day c	-
23		27th	H	Barbarians	L 3-5	-	Day p	-
24		29	H	Racing Club de France	W 24-5	Day, German, Wakefield	Day 3c/3p	12000
25	Jan	1tu	a	Manchester	W 22-8	Day(2), Coates, German, Prentice, S.Taylor	Day 2c	-
26		5	H	United Services	W 22-5	J.Lawrie, P.Lawrie, Prentice, Simpson, Usher	Day 2c/p	8000
27		12	H	Swansea	L 0-9	-	-	-
28		19	H	Royal Air Force	L 6-9	Day, Thorneloe	-	9000
29		26	H	British Army	L 13-15	P.Lawrie(2), W.Wilkins	Day 2c	9000
30	Feb	2	H	Richmond	W 29-11	Day(2), Parker, Prentice, Smallwood, S.Taylor	Day 4c/p	9000
31		9	a	Newport	L 8-22	Prentice	Thorneloe c/p	-
32		16	H	Cardiff	W 13-0	Smallwood, Usher, W.Wilkins	Day 2c	-
33		23	H	Coventry	W 14-6	P.Lawrie, Sharratt, W.Wilkins	Day c/p	-
34	Mar	1	H	Harlequins	W 14-5	Bryson, Prentice, W.Wilkins	Day c/p	-
35		4tu	a	Racing Club de France	L 3-22	-	Day p	-
36		8	a	Northampton	L 16-19	Coates, Smallwood	Day 2c/2p	-
37		15	H	London Welsh	W 12-5	Day, Kenney, P.Lawrie, W.Wilkins	-	-
38		22	H	Old Blues	L 12-18	Smallwood(3), W.Wilkins	-	8000
39		29	H	Royal Air Force	W 10-6	Wakefield(2)	Day 2c	7000
40		31m	a	Nuneaton	W 21-5	Coates(2), Bryson, P.Lawrie, Russell	Day 3c	-
41	Apr	5	H	Richmond	L 14-17	Smallwood, Wakefield, W.Wilkins	Day c/p	10000
42		12	a	Birkenhead Park	W 14-6	Day, P.Lawrie	Day 2c, P.Lawrie d	-
43		19	a	Bristol	L 0-11	-	-	10000
44		21m	a	Plymouth Albion	W 34-12	Wallace(4), J.Lawrie(2), Day, Coates	Day 5c	-
45		22tu	a	Bath	L 3-28	Sharratt	-	-
46		26	a	Bedford	W 5-0	C.Burton	Day c	3000

INDIVIDUAL APPEARANCES 1923/24

Name / Game #	1	2	3	4	5	6	7	8	9	10	11	12	13	14	15	16	17	18	19	20	21	22	23	24	25	26	27	28	29	30	31	32	33	34	35	36	37	38	39	40	41	42	43	44	45	46	Apps	T	Pts
JMA (John) Bemrose	-	-	-	>F	-	F	-	-	-	-	-	-	-	-	-	-	-	-	-	-	-	-	-	-	-	-	-	-	-	-	-	-	-	-	-	-	-	<F	-	-	-	-	-	-	-	-	3	1	3
JS (John) Boswell	-	-	-	-	-	-	-	-	-	-	-	-	-	-	>SH	SH	<SH	-	-	-	-	-	-	-	-	-	-	-	-	-	-	-	-	-	-	-	-	-	-	-	-	-	-	-	-	-	3	-	-
Flt-Lt. OC (Oliver) Bryson	C	C	C	C	C	C	-	W	W	-	W	-	-	W	-	-	-	W	W	-	W	-	-	-	-	-	C	-	-	-	-	-	-	W	-	-	-	-	-	W	W	-	-	-	-	-	17	9	27
CL Burton	W	W	W	-	-	-	-	-	-	-	W	-	-	-	-	-	-	-	-	-	-	-	-	-	-	-	-	-	-	-	-	-	-	-	W	-	-	-	-	-	-	-	-	-	-	<W	6	1	3
N (Norman) Coates	-	C	FH	FH	FH	FH	C	FH	C	C	C*	C	-	C	-	-	-	C	C	C*	-	FH	-	-	C	C*	C	C	C	C	C	C	C	C	SH	C	-	-	C	C	-	C	C	C	-	-	33	5	15
HW Cox	-	-	-	-	-	-	-	-	-	-	-	-	-	-	-	-	-	-	-	-	-	-	-	-	-	-	-	-	-	-	-	-	-	-	-	-	-	-	-	-	-	-	>FH	FH	SH	FH	4	-	-
JE (John) Davis	-	F	-	F	F	F	F	-	-	F	-	F	F	F	F	-	-	F	F	F	F	-	F	F	-	-	-	F	-	-	-	-	-	-	-	-	-	-	-	-	-	-	-	-	-	-	17	-	-
HLV (Harold) Day E3	-	-	C	W	-	-	-	C	C	C	-	C	-	-	C	C	-	C	C	C	C	C	W	C	C	C	C	C	C	C	-	C	C	C	C	C	C	C	C	C	C	C	C	C	-	C	35	13	186
GJ (Guy) German	SH	SH	SH	SH	-	SH	-	F	F	-	-	-	-	-	-	-	-	SH	SH	SH	F	-	-	SH	F	F	F	-	SH	SH	SH	SH	-	SH	F	SH	F	-	FH	F	SH	SH	SH	SH	-	F	30	2	6
AD (Alfred) Godfrey	-	-	-	-	-	-	-	-	-	-	C	FH	FH	C	C	-	-	-	-	-	-	-	-	-	FH	-	-	-	-	-	-	-	FH	-	C	C	C	-	-	-	-	-	-	-	-	-	10	1	3
MS (Morton) Holden	-	-	-	-	-	-	-	-	-	-	-	-	-	-	-	>W	C	FB	W	FB	-	W	-	-	-	W	W	-	-	-	-	-	-	-	-	-	-	-	-	-	-	-	-	-	-	-	8	1	3
CW (Charles) Jones W3	F	F	-	F	F	F	-	F	-	-	F	C	<C	-	-	-	-	-	-	-	-	-	-	-	-	-	-	-	-	-	-	-	-	-	-	-	-	-	-	-	-	-	-	-	-	-	9	-	-
WL (Bill) Kenney	-	-	-	-	-	-	-	-	-	-	-	-	-	-	-	-	-	-	-	-	-	-	-	-	-	-	-	-	-	-	-	-	-	-	-	-	>W	W	W	-	-	W	-	-	W	-	5	1	3
SF (Frank) Lawrence	-	-	-	-	-	-	-	-	-	W	F	-	-	-	-	-	-	-	-	-	-	-	-	-	-	-	-	-	-	F	W	-	F	-	-	-	F	-	-	F	-	-	-	-	-	-	7	-	-
JR (Jock) Lawrie S11	>F	F	F	-	-	F	F	F	F	F	-	F	-	F	F	F	-	F	-	F	F	F	F	F	-	F	F	-	F	-	F	F	-	F	-	F	-	-	F	F	F	F	F	F	-	F	32	4	12
PW (Percy) Lawrie E2	C	C	C	C	C	-	C	C	C	C	C	-	-	C	C	C	-	C	C	C	FH	C	C	C	W	C	-	C	W	C	C	C	C	C	-	W	C	-	C	C	C	C	-	-	<C	-	36	9	52
EJ (Edward) Massey E+	-	-	-	-	-	-	-	-	-	-	SH	-	-	-	-	-	-	-	-	-	-	-	SH	-	-	-	-	-	-	-	-	-	-	-	-	-	-	-	-	-	-	-	-	-	-	SH	3	-	-
Flt-Lt. CEH (Charles) Medhurst	-	-	-	-	-	-	-	-	-	-	-	-	-	-	>W	W	FH	FH	FH	FH	-	-	-	FH	-	FH	FH	FH	-	-	-	-	-	-	-	-	FH	FH	-	-	FH	FH	-	-	C	C	16	-	4
DJ (Doug) Norman E+	F	-	F	F	F	-	-	F	F	F	F	F	F	F	-	F	F	F	F	F	-	F	F	-	-	-	-	F	F	F	F	-	F	-	F	F	-	-	F	-	-	-	-	-	-	-	26	1	3
RVM (Reginald) Odbert I+	-	-	-	-	-	-	-	-	-	-	-	-	-	-	>FH	FH	W	-	-	-	-	-	-	-	-	-	-	-	-	-	-	-	-	-	-	-	-	-	-	-	-	-	-	-	-	-	3	-	-
HMG Parker	-	-	-	-	-	-	-	-	-	-	-	-	-	-	-	-	-	-	-	-	-	-	-	-	-	-	-	>W	W	W	<C	-	-	-	-	-	-	-	-	-	-	-	-	-	-	-	4	1	3
FD (Doug) Prentice E+ GB+	-	-	-	-	-	-	-	-	-	-	-	-	-	-	-	-	>F	F	-	F	-	F	-	-	F	F	-	F	F	F	F	F	F	F	F	F	F	-	F	F	F	F	F	F	F	F	24	7	21
HL (Leo) Price E4	-	-	-	-	W	-	-	C	FH	-	-	-	-	FH	-	-	-	-	-	-	-	-	-	-	-	-	-	-	FH	-	-	-	-	-	-	-	-	-	-	-	-	-	-	-	-	-	5	1	7
A (Andy) Roxburgh	FH	FH	-	-	-	-	-	-	-	<FH	-	-	-	-	-	-	-	-	-	-	-	-	-	-	-	-	-	-	-	-	-	-	-	-	-	-	-	-	-	-	-	-	-	-	-	-	3	-	-
JC (John) Russell	-	-	-	-	SH	C	SH	SH	SH	-	-	SH	-	SH	-	-	-	-	-	-	SH	SH	-	-	SH	SH	SH	-	-	-	-	-	-	-	-	-	-	-	-	SH	-	-	-	-	-	-	13	2	6
LC (Claude) Sambrook	FB	FB	FB	FB	FB	FB	FB	FB	FB	FB	FB	FB	-	FB	FB	FB	FB	-	FB	-	FB	FB	FB	FB	FB	FB	FB	FB	FB	FB	FB	FB	FB	FB	FB	FB	-	-	FB	FB	FB	FB	FB	FB	FB	FB	41	-	5
H (Herb) Sharratt	F	F	-	F	F	F	-	-	-	-	F	F	F	F	F	F	F	F	F	-	F	F	-	F	F	F	F	-	F	F	F	F	F	F	F	F	F	-	F	F	F	F	F	F	F	F	37	2	6
RBY (Robert) Simpson	-	-	-	-	-	-	-	-	-	-	-	-	-	-	-	-	-	-	-	W	C	C	C	C	C	<W	-	-	-	-	-	-	-	-	-	-	-	-	-	-	-	-	-	-	-	-	7	3	9
AM (Alastair) Smallwood E12	-	-	W	-	-	-	-	-	W	-	-	-	-	W	-	-	-	-	-	-	-	-	W	W	-	-	-	-	-	FH	-	FH	-	FH	-	FH	-	C	-	-	C	W	W	W	-	-	14	9	27
SA (Stuart) Smith	-	-	-	-	-	-	-	-	-	-	-	-	-	-	-	-	-	-	-	-	-	-	-	-	-	-	-	SH	-	-	FH	W	SH	-	-	-	SH	SH	SH	-	-	-	-	-	-	-	7	-	-
WJ (Wilfred) Streather	-	-	-	-	-	-	-	-	-	-	-	-	-	-	-	-	-	-	-	-	-	-	-	-	-	-	-	-	-	-	-	-	-	-	-	-	-	-	-	-	-	>F	-	F	F	-	3	-	-
F (Sos) Taylor E2	F	F	F	-	-	-	F	F	F	F	F	-	-	-	F	F	F	-	F	F	-	-	F	F	F	F	-	F	F	F	F	F	F	F	-	F	F	-	F	F	F	F	F	-	F	<F	33	2	6
DJ Thomas	-	-	-	-	-	-	>W	-	-	-	-	-	-	-	-	-	-	-	-	-	W	W	-	-	W	-	W	-	-	-	-	-	-	-	-	-	-	-	-	-	-	-	-	-	-	-	5	-	-
NT (Trevor) Thorneloe	-	-	F	F	-	F	F	-	-	-	-	-	-	-	-	-	-	-	-	F	F	-	F	-	F	F	F	F	-	F	F	-	F	-	F	-	-	-	-	-	-	-	-	-	-	-	15	1	8
Flt-Lt. RHC (Bob) Usher	-	F	F	-	F	-	F	-	F	F	F	F	-	F	F	F	-	F	F	F	F	F	F	F	F	F	F	-	-	-	-	F	-	F	-	-	-	F	-	-	F	F	F	F	<F	-	29	2	6
WW (Wavell) Wakefield E20	-	-	F*	C*	F*	C*	F*	F*	F*	F*	-	-	-	F*	F*	F*	-	-	F*	-	-	F*	F*	F*	-	-	F*	-	F*	F*	-	F*	-	F*	-	F*	-	F*	F*	-	F*	F*	F*	C*	-	<C*	28	8	24
W (Billy) Wallace GB+	-	-	-	W	-	-	-	-	-	-	-	-	-	-	-	-	-	-	-	-	-	-	-	-	-	-	-	-	-	-	-	-	-	-	-	-	-	-	-	-	-	-	W	W	W	-	4	5	15
JAG (George) Ward E6	F*	F*	F	F	F	F	F	F	F	F	-	F*	F*	F	F	F	F*	F*	F	-	F*	-	F	F	F*	-	F	F*	F	-	F*	F	F*	F	F*	F	F*	-	F	F*	F	-	F	F	-	-	37	-	-
WC Wilkins	-	-	-	-	-	-	-	-	-	-	-	-	W	-	W	C	W	W	-	W	C	-	-	W	-	-	-	-	C	W	W	W	W	W	C	-	W	W	W	W	<W	-	-	-	-	-	20	8	24

1 GAME: F/O. CD (Cyril) Adams <F(45), JS (John) Atkins =F(28), A (Ambrose) Baker W5 <F(13), BA (Bernard) Batchelor =F(1), AF (Freddie) Blakiston E12 GB+ =F(46), FK (Francis) Boston =F(38), AFB (Arthur) Brodbeck >FH(40), HC (Hyde) Burton E+ =W(35), RA (Roland) Castle =W(8), AS Cohen =F(35), CW (Charlie) Cross <F(22), R Evans =C(17), WJ Gibbs W(46), D Hunt-Davies =C(13), I (Ivor) Jones =FB(13), FE (Fred) Oliver =SH(10), GA (Arthur) Palmer F(17), RS (Ron) Palmer C(17), W Pollard <W(7), R Randall =F(13), R Robinson =FH(23), H Smith =C(13), E Stagg =F(45), JT Stephens =F(11), S Thomas =SH(13), FHR (Fleckney) Turney >C(1), F/O. EC Wackett =F(38), CHM (Charles) Waldock >FH(45), WJ (William) Watts W1 <C(7), AP (Al) Wayte =FH(35), J (John) Wickson <Ft(17), CHL (Charles) Wynne <W(28)

2 GAMES: CNS (Norman) Boston >F(37)<F(38), LAC. SG Collins >F(38)<F(46), FA (Frederick) Crowhurst >F(12)<F(13), LC (Leslie) Gamble >FB(37)FB(38), EE (Teddy) Haselmere W(1)<W(2), E Hopkins >W(12)<W(13), ADT Roberts >F(44)<F(45), Flt-Lt. PG Scott >C(38)C(43), HJ (Harold) Storrs Wt(5)<W(6), GC Taylor FHt(7)<FH(11), FS Wells >W(10)W(12), RH (Reginald) Wetton >W(33)<W(36), Lt-Col. GM (Gilbert) Wilkins C(5)<W(6)

The key for how to read the stats is on the last page

19	24/25	Home Ground: Welford Road	OVERALL RECORD:					T	C	PG	DG	MK	PTS
		Captain: Harold Day	PLD	W	D	L	Tigers scored:	107	47	14	4	2	479
			40	27	3	10	Opponents scored:	77	28	6	3	1	320

GM	DATE		VEN	OPPONENTS	RESULT	TRIES	KICKS	ATT
CLUB MATCHES								
1	Sep	**6**	**H**	**Bath**	W 14-11	Smallwood(2), Norman	Day c/p	6000
2		10w	a	Rugby B.T.H.	W 24-0	Day(3), Lawrence, Lawrie, Roxburgh	Day 3c	-
3		**13**	**H**	**Nuneaton**	W 14-9	Bryson, Kenney	Massey 2p, Smallwood c	3000
4		**20**	**H**	**Plymouth Albion**	L 9-11	Bryson	Massey 2p	4000
5		**27**	**H**	**Cross Keys**	W 8-0	Holden, Lawrie	C.Sambrook c	7000
6	Oct	**4**	**H**	**New Zealand**	L 0-27	-	-	35000
7		**11**	**H**	**Llanelly**	W 6-3	Day, Holden	-	7000
8		18	a	Newport	L 9-33	Norman	Massey p, C.Sambrook p	7000
9		**25**	**H**	**Oxford University**	L 10-11	-	Day p/m, Dynes d	-
10		29w	a	Moseley	W 15-5	Buckingham(2), R.Palmer, H.Sambrook, Thorneloe	-	-
11	Nov	**1**	**H**	**United Services**	W 9-0	Day, Massey	Russell m	4000
12		**8**	**H**	**Cambridge University**	W 39-3	Smallwood(4), Day, Holden, Kenney, Prentice, Scott	Day 6c	8000
13		**15**	**H**	**Swansea**	L 3-18	-	Day p	7000
14		22	a	Northampton	W 6-3	H.Sambrook, Scott	-	6000
15		**29**	**H**	**Cardiff**	D 3-3	-	Day p	7000
16	Dec	6	a	Harlequins	W 17-11	Day, Bryson, Coates, Scott, Sharratt	Day c	2000
17		13	a	Blackheath	W 9-0	Day(2), Buckingham	-	3000
18		**20**	**H**	**Bristol**	W 23-6	Smallwood(3), Bryson, Buckingham, Prentice	Lawton p, C.Sambrook c	7000
19		**26f**	**H**	**Birkenhead Park**	W 13-11	Day, Buckingham, Holden	Day 2c	-
20		**27**	**H**	**Heriot's FP**	W 22-0	Day, Holden, Prentice, Smallwood	Day 3c, Dynes d	-
21		**29m**	**H**	**Barbarians**	W 16-6	Prentice(2), Lawrie, Smallwood	Day 2c	6000
22	Jan	**3**	**H**	**Manchester**	W 13-5	Buckingham, Holden, Lawrie	Day 2c	5000
23		10	a	Swansea	L 8-14	Day	Day c/p	-
24		17	a	Coventry	W 9-3	Buckingham, Holden, Scott	-	-
25		**24**	**H**	**British Army**	W 23-0	Prentice(2), Holden, Sharratt, Smallwood	Day 4c	4000
26		31	a	Richmond	W 13-4	Day, Dynes, Holden	Day 2c	-
27	Feb	7	a	Plymouth Albion	W 11-3	Holden, Sharratt, Wells	Thorneloe c	5000
28		**14**	**H**	**Newport**	D 6-6	Buckingham, Wells	-	8000
29		21	a	Cardiff	L 6-14	Holden, Lawrie	-	-
30		**28**	**H**	**Coventry**	W 3-0	Day	-	4000
31	Mar	**7**	**H**	**Harlequins**	W 25-11	Sharratt(2), Day, Beamish, Smallwood	Day 5c	5000
32		**14**	**H**	**Northampton**	W 8-3	Sharratt	Day c/p	7000
33		**21**	**H**	**Old Blues**	W 16-14	Buckingham, R.Palmer, S.Smith, Waldock	Day 2c	3000
34		23m	a	United Services	L 0-3	-	-	-
35	Apr	**4**	**H**	**Blackheath**	W 16-13	Bryson(2), Buckingham, H.Sambrook	Day 2c	5000
36		7tu	a	Nuneaton	W 19-13	Scott(2), Prentice	Day 3c, Sharratt d	-
37		11	a	Bristol	L 10-14	Beamish, Buckingham	Day 2c	8000
38		13m	a	Llanelly	L 3-14	Beamish	-	-
39		14tu	a	Bath	D 10-10	Atkins, Bryson	Buckingham d	4000
40		18	a	Birkenhead Park	W 11-5	Day(2)	Day c/p	5000

INDIVIDUAL APPEARANCES 1924/25

Name / Game #	1	2	3	4	5	6	7	8	9	10	11	12	13	14	15	16	17	18	19	20	21	22	23	24	25	26	27	28	29	30	31	32	33	34	35	36	37	38	39	40	Apps	T	Pts
AP (Alfred) Atkins I1	-	-	-	-	-	-	-	-	-	-	-	-	-	-	-	-	-	-	-	-	-	-	-	-	-	-	-	-	-	-	-	-	-	-	-	-	>W	-	<W	-	2	1	3
GR (George) Beamish I3 GB+	-	-	-	-	-	-	-	-	-	-	-	-	-	-	-	-	-	-	-	>F	F	-	F	-	-	-	-	-	-	-	F	-	F	-	F	F	F	F	-	F	10	3	9
TH (Harry) Briers	-	-	-	-	-	-	-	-	-	-	-	-	-	-	-	-	-	-	-	-	-	-	-	>F	F	-	-	-	-	-	-	-	F	-	-	-	-	F	-	-	4	-	-
Flt-Lt. OC (Oliver) Bryson	W	-	W	W	W	W	-	-	W	FE	W	-	W	-	C	W	-	W	-	-	-	-	-	-	-	-	-	-	-	W	W	-	W	-	W	-	W	W	C	W	20	7	21
RA (Ralph) Buckingham E+	-	>C	-	-	-	-	-	-	-	C	-	-	-	-	-	-	W	W	FE	FE	FE	FE	FH	FH	FH	FH	FH	C	FE	FE	FE	FH	FH	FH	FH	FH	FH	FH	FH	FH	26	11	37
N (Norman) Coates	-	-	-	FH	-	-	-	-	-	F	F	F	SH	-	-	F	F	F	F	F	F	F	F	F	-	-	-	-	-	-	-	-	-	-	-	-	-	-	-	-	14	1	3
RJ (Dick) Collopy I13	-	-	-	-	-	-	-	-	-	-	-	-	-	-	-	-	-	-	-	-	-	-	-	-	-	-	-	-	-	-	-	-	-	-	-	-	>F	F	F	-	3	-	-
JE (John) Davis	F	F	F	-	F	F	-	-	-	-	-	-	-	-	-	-	-	-	-	-	-	-	-	-	-	-	-	-	-	-	-	-	-	-	-	-	-	-	-	-	5	-	-
HLV (Harold) Day E3	C*	C*	-	-	-	-	W*	-	FB*	-	C*	FB*	FB*	C*	FB*	C*	C*	-	C*	C*	C*	C*	C*	C*	C*	C*	-	-	C*	C*	C*	C*	C*	-	C*	C*	C*	C*	-	C*	29	17	161
ED (Ernie) Dynes	-	-	-	-	>FE	-	FE	C	FE	FE	FE	FE	FE	FE	FH	FE	FE	FE	FH	FH	FH	FH	-	-	FE	FE	-	FE	-	-	-	FE	-	-	-	-	-	FE	FE	FE	24	1	11
WJ Gibbs	-	-	-	-	-	-	-	-	-	-	-	-	-	-	-	-	-	-	W	-	<W	-	-	-	-	-	-	-	-	-	-	-	-	-	-	-	-	-	-	-	2	-	-
MS (Morton) Holden	-	-	-	-	C	C	C	-	C	-	-	C	W	W	W	-	-	-	W	W	-	W	W	W	W	W	W	W	W	-	FE	-	-	-	FE	-	-	-	FE	FE	22	11	33
WL (Bill) Kenney	W	-	W	W	W	-	FB	W	W	W	W	<W	-	-	-	-	-	-	-	-	-	-	-	-	-	-	-	-	-	-	-	-	-	-	-	-	-	-	-	-	10	2	6
SF (Frank) Lawrence	-	F	F	F	-	-	F	F	F	F	F	F	-	F	-	F	-	-	-	F	-	-	F	F	F	F	F	F	-	-	-	F	-	F	-	-	-	-	F	-	21	1	3
JR (Jock) Lawrie S11	F	F	F	F	F	F	F	-	F	-	-	F	F	F	F	F	F	F	-	-	F	F	-	-	-	F	F	F	F	F	F	W	F	-	F	F	F	-	-	-	28	5	15
EJ (Edward) Massey E3	SH	-	FH	SH	FH	FH	FH	FH	FH	SH	FH	FH	FH	FH	SH	-	SH	-	-	SH	SH	-	SH	-	SH	SH	SH	-	SH	FH	SH	<SH	-	-	-	-	-	-	-	-	25	1	18
CB (Christopher) Moller	-	-	-	-	-	-	-	-	-	-	-	-	-	-	-	-	-	-	-	-	-	-	-	-	-	-	-	-	-	-	-	-	-	-	-	>W	-	-	<W	-	2	-	-
DJ (Doug) Norman E+	F	F	F	F	F	-	F	F	F	F	F	-	F	F	F	F	F	F	-	F	F	F	F	F	F	F	F	F	F	F	F	F	F	F	F	-	F	F	F	F	36	2	6
GA (Arthur) Palmer	-	-	-	-	-	-	-	-	-	-	-	-	-	-	-	-	-	-	-	-	-	-	-	-	-	-	-	-	F	F	-	F	F	F	-	F	-	F	F	F	9	-	-
RS (Ron) Palmer	-	-	-	-	-	-	-	-	-	FH	-	-	-	-	-	-	-	-	FE	-	-	-	FE	FE	-	-	-	FH	-	-	-	-	FE	FE	-	FE	-	-	-	-	8	2	6
MGS (Malcolm) Parker	-	>F	<F	-	-	-	-	-	-	-	-	-	-	-	-	-	-	-	-	-	-	-	-	-	-	-	-	-	-	-	-	-	-	-	-	-	-	-	-	-	2	-	-
FD (Doug) Prentice E+ GB+	F	-	-	F	F	F	F	F	F	F	F	F	F	F	F	-	F	F	F	F	F	F	F	-	F	F	F	F	F	F	F	F	-	F	F	F	-	-	-	-	31	8	24
HL (Leo) Price E4	-	-	-	FE	-	FE	-	-	F	-	-	-	-	-	<F	-	-	-	-	-	-	-	-	-	-	-	-	-	-	-	-	-	-	-	-	-	-	-	-	-	4	-	-
Maj. WBN (William) Roderick	-	-	-	-	>F	F	F	F	F	F	-	F	F	F	F	F	F	F	F	-	F	F	<F	-	-	-	-	-	-	-	-	-	-	-	-	-	-	-	-	-	17	-	-
W Roxburgh	-	>FH	FE	<FE	-	-	-	-	-	-	-	-	-	-	-	-	-	-	-	-	-	-	-	-	-	-	-	-	-	-	-	-	-	-	-	-	-	-	-	-	3	1	3
JC (John) Russell	-	-	SH	-	SH	SH	SH	SH	SH	-	SH	SH	-	-	-	-	-	SH	SH	-	-	SH	-	SH	-	-	-	SH	-	SH	-	-	-	-	-	-	SH	SH	-	SH	17	-	3
LC (Claude) Sambrook	FB	FB	FB	FB	FB	FB	-	FB	-	FB	FB	-	-	FB	-	FB	FB	FB	FB	FB	FB	FB	FB	FB	FB	FB	FB	FB	FB	FB	FB	FB	FB	FB	FB	FB	FB	FB	FB	FB	35	-	7
HA (Harold) Sambrook	>C	-	FE	-	-	-	FE	-	FE	W	FE	-	FE	FE	FE	FE	FE	FE	-	-	-	FE	FE	FE	FE	FE	FE	FE	FE	FE	-	FE	-	-	FE	-	FE	FE	-	-	25	3	9
Flt-Lt. PG Scott	-	-	-	C	FE	W	W	C	-	-	-	FE	C	W	FE	W	W	-	-	FE	FE	-	-	W	-	-	-	-	-	-	-	-	W	W	-	FE	FE	W	-	-	19	6	18
H (Herb) Sharratt	F	-	F	F	F	F	F	F	F	F	F	F	F	F	F	F	F	F	F	F	F	F	F	F	F	F	F	F	F	F	F	F	-	F	F	F	F	F	F	F	38	6	22
FO Sinclair	-	-	-	-	-	-	-	-	-	-	-	-	-	-	-	-	-	-	-	-	-	-	-	-	-	-	-	-	-	-	-	-	>F	F	-	F	F	<F	-	-	5	-	-
AM (Alastair) Smallwood E14	C	-	C	-	-	FE	-	-	-	-	-	W	-	-	W	-	-	C	-	W	W	-	-	-	W	-	-	-	-	W	W	-	-	-	W	-	-	-	-	-	12	13	41
SA (Stuart) Smith	-	-	-	-	-	-	-	-	-	-	-	-	-	-	-	FH	FH	-	-	-	-	-	-	-	-	-	-	-	FH	-	-	-	SH	SH	-	SH	-	-	SH	-	7	1	3
WJ (Wilfred) Streather	F	F	F	-	-	-	-	-	-	-	-	-	-	-	-	-	-	-	F	<F	-	-	-	-	-	-	-	-	-	-	-	-	-	-	-	-	-	-	-	-	5	-	-
NT (Trevor) Thorneloe	-	-	-	F	F	-	F	-	-	F	F	F	F	F	F	F	F	F	F	-	-	F	-	F	F	F	F	F	F	F	F	F	F	-	F	-	-	-	F	F	27	1	5
CHM (Charles) Waldock	-	-	-	-	-	-	-	-	-	-	-	-	-	SH	-	SH	-	-	-	-	-	-	-	-	-	-	-	-	-	-	-	-	FE	FE	-	-	-	-	-	-	4	1	3
JAG (George) Ward E6	F	F	-	F	-	F	-	F	-	-	F	-	F	-	-	-	-	-	F	-	-	-	-	F	F	F	F	F	F	F	F	F	-	F	F	F	F	-	F	F	23	-	-
FS Wells	-	-	-	-	-	-	-	-	-	-	-	-	-	-	-	-	-	-	-	-	-	W	W	-	-	W	W	W	W	-	-	W	-	-	-	-	-	-	-	-	7	2	6

1 GAME: AC Bennett =C(34), AFB (Arthur) Brodbeck SH(2), JCR (Rankin) Buchanan S16 <F(6), EG (Ernie) Coleman F(40), RR Colquhoun =W(8), HW Cox <W(2), WE (Ewart) Farndon >W(40), GJ (Guy) German SH(35), AD (Alfred) Godfrey <C(2), A King <W(36), T (Tommy) Lawton A2 =FH(18), Flt-Lt. CEH (Charles) Medhurst <FH(1), E (Edward) Myers E18 <FH(31), J (John) Shentall =W(34), A Smith =C(27), WE (Wilfrid) Squirrell >FE(27), DJ Thomas <W(2), I (Ivor) Williams =F(8), GDI (George) Younger =F(8)

The key for how to read the stats is on the last page

1925/26

Home Ground: Welford Road
Captain: Harold Day

OVERALL RECORD:					T	C	PG	DG	MK	PTS
PLD	W	D	L	Tigers scored:	96	49	17	4	1	456
41	22	4	15	Opponents scored:	85	29	15	2	1	369

GM	DATE		VEN	OPPONENTS	RESULT	TRIES	KICKS	ATT
CLUB MATCHES								
1	Sep	5	H	**Bath**	W 23-8	Smith(2), Holden, Farndon	Holden d, Thorneloe 2c/p	-
2		12	H	**Nuneaton**	W 18-0	Holden, Thorneloe, Farndon, Norman	Holden d, Thorneloe c	-
3		19	H	**Plymouth Albion**	D 6-6	-	Day p, H.Sambrook m	-
4		23w	a	Percy Park	D 5-5	Scott	Thorneloe c	3000
5		26	H	**Bridgwater & Albion**	W 19-6	Wells(2), Coleman, Ward	Day 2c/p	-
6	Oct	1th	a	Nuneaton	L 5-13	Farndon	Thorneloe c	-
7		3	H	**Northern**	W 20-3	Bryson(2), Coleman, Thorneloe	Day 2c, Holden d	8000
8		10	H	**Coventry**	W 8-6	Coleman	Day c/p	-
9		17	H	**Newport**	W 6-5	Prentice	Day p	12000
10		24	a	Moseley	L 8-11	Smith	Day c/p	-
11		31	H	**Northampton**	W 11-5	Bryson, Moore	Day c/p	12000
12	Nov	7	H	**Cambridge University**	D 3-3	Scott	-	8000
13		12th	a	Oxford University	L 3-27	Coleman	-	-
14		14	a	Swansea	L 3-17	-	Day p	5000
15		21	H	**United Services**	W 6-0	Moore	Day p	8000
16		28	a	Cardiff	L 3-9	Prentice	-	12000
17	Dec	5	a	Harlequins	W 11-9	Lawrie, Scott	Day c/p	-
18		12	a	Blackheath	W 10-7	Buckingham(2)	Day 2c	-
19		19	H	**Bristol**	W 12-5	Day, Lawrie, Tate	Day p	-
20		26	H	**Birkenhead Park**	W 16-3	Flewitt(2), Bryson, Buckingham	Day 2c	9000
21		28m	H	**Barbarians**	W 14-9	Farndon(2), Day, Flewitt	Day c	11000
22	Jan	1f	a	Manchester	L 10-12	Day, Buckingham	Day 2c	-
23		2	a	Heriot's FP	L 5-8	Buckingham	Day c	6000
24		4m	a	Northern	L 6-8	Buckingham, Farndon	-	-
25		9	H	**Swansea**	D 8-8	Buckingham	Day c/p	9000
26		16	H	**Royal Air Force**	W 21-3	Buckingham(2), Day, Farndon, Thorneloe	Day 3c	5000
27		23	H	**British Army**	W 8-5	Moore(2)	Day c	9000
28		30	H	**Richmond**	W 18-0	Farndon(2), Day, Whitley	Day 3c	9000
29	Feb	6	H	**London Scottish**	W 22-11	Day(2), Burton, Coleman, Cramphorn, Flewitt	Day 2c	8000
30		13	a	Newport	L 11-14	Buckingham, Flewitt	Day c/p	7000
31		20	H	**Cardiff**	W 8-3	Buckingham	Day c/p	10000
32		27	a	Coventry	L 8-21	Buckingham, Farndon	Day c	6000
33	Mar	6	H	**Harlequins**	L 10-11	Day, Cramphorn	Day 2c	9000
		13	a	Northampton	PP			
34		20	H	**Old Blues**	W 21-5	Thorneloe, Buckingham, Cramphorn, Farndon, Lawrie	Thorneloe 3c	7000
35		27	a	United Services	W 28-21	Day, Cramphorn, Greenlees, Prentice	Day 3c/2p, Frisby d	-
36	Apr	3	a	Bristol	L 6-13	Bernard, Day	-	12000
37		5m	a	Plymouth Albion	L 13-14	Cramphorn, Lawrie	Day 2c/p	5000
38		6tu	a	Bath	W 13-6	Bryson, Flewitt, Hopkins	Day 2c	-
39		10	a	Birkenhead Park	L 16-28	Farndon(2), Flewitt(2)	Prentice c, Thorneloe c	8000
40		15th	a	Northampton	L 0-18	-	-	12000
41		17	H	**Blackheath**	W 14-3	Bryson, Buckingham, Christie, Norman	Day c	5000

INDIVIDUAL APPEARANCES 1925/26

Name / Game #	1	2	3	4	5	6	7	8	9	10	11	12	13	14	15	16	17	18	19	20	21	22	23	24	25	26	27	28	29	30	31	32	33	34	35	36	37	38	39	40	41	Apps	T	Pts
GR (George) Beamish I3 GB+	F	-	F	F	F	-	F	F	-	-	F	F	-	F	F	-	-	-	-	-	-	-	-	-	-	-	-	-	-	-	-	-	-	-	-	-	-	-	-	-	-	10	-	-
AE (William) Beith	-	-	-	-	-	-	-	-	-	-	-	-	-	-	-	-	-	-	-	>F	F	F	-	-	-	-	-	-	-	-	-	-	-	-	-	-	-	-	-	-	-	3	-	-
TH (Harry) Briers	-	-	-	-	-	-	-	-	-	-	-	-	F	F	-	F	F	F	F	F	-	F	F	F	F	F	F	F	F	-	F	F	-	-	-	-	F	-	F	-	-	19	-	-
Flt-Lt. OC (Oliver) Bryson	W	W	-	-	-	-	W	W	W	-	FE	FE	FE	-	FE	FE	W	-	C	FE	FE	W	FE	FE	W	-	-	-	-	-	FE	FE	-	FE	-	-	-	FE	-	FE	W	24	6	18
RA (Ralph) Buckingham E+	FH	-	-	FH	FH	FH	FH	FH	-	-	FH	FH	FH	FH	FH	FH	FH	FH	-	FH	FH	FH	FH	C	FH	FH	FH	FH	FH	FH	FH	FH	FH	FH	FE	FH	FH	FH	FH	FH	FH	36	14	42
LW (Langley) Burton	-	-	-	-	-	-	-	-	-	-	-	-	-	-	-	-	-	-	-	>SH	-	-	-	SH	SH	SH	-	-	SH	SH	-	SH	SH	-	-	-	-	-	SH	-	-	9	1	3
Cpl. MG (Mog) Christie	-	-	-	-	-	-	-	-	-	-	-	-	-	-	-	-	-	-	-	-	-	-	-	-	-	-	-	-	-	-	-	-	-	-	-	-	-	-	-	>F	F	2	1	3
N (Norman) Coates	-	-	-	-	-	-	-	-	-	-	-	-	-	-	-	-	-	-	-	-	-	-	-	-	-	-	-	-	-	F	F	-	-	F	-	F	-	F	-	C	-	6	-	-
EG (Ernie) Coleman	F	F	F	F	F	F	F	F	F	F	F	F	F	F	F	F	F	F	F	-	F	F	F	F	F	F	F	F	F	F	F	F	F	-	F	F	F	F	F	F	F	39	5	15
RJ (Dick) Collopy I13	-	-	F	F	-	C	F	F	-	<F	-	-	-	-	-	-	-	-	-	-	-	-	-	-	-	-	-	-	-	-	-	-	-	-	-	-	-	-	-	-	-	6	-	-
CT (Charlie) Cramphorn	-	-	-	-	-	-	-	-	-	-	-	-	-	-	-	-	-	-	-	-	-	-	-	-	-	-	-	>C	C	C	-	C	C	C	C	-	C	-	-	-	-	8	5	15
JE (John) Davis	-	F	-	F	-	F	-	-	-	-	-	-	-	-	-	-	-	-	-	-	-	-	-	-	-	-	-	-	-	-	-	-	<F	-	-	-	-	-	-	-	-	4	-	-
HLV (Harold) Day E4	-	-	C*	-	C*	-	C*	C*	C*	C*	C*	C*	-	C*	C*	C*	C*	C*	FH*	C*	C*	C*	C*	-	FE*	FE*	FE*	FE*	FE*	FE*	FE*	FE*	FE*	-	FE*	FE*	FE*	FE*	-	-	FE*	32	10	156
ED (Ernie) Dynes	FE	FH	-	-	-	<FE	-	-	-	-	-	-	-	-	-	-	-	-	-	-	-	-	-	-	-	-	-	-	-	-	-	-	-	-	-	-	-	-	-	-	-	3	-	-
JHF (Harry) Edmiston	-	-	-	-	-	-	-	-	-	-	-	-	-	-	-	-	-	-	-	-	-	-	-	-	-	-	-	-	-	-	-	-	-	>F	F	F	F	F	F	F	F	8	-	-
WE (Ewart) Farndon	W	W	-	W	W	FE	-	W	W	W	W	W	W	W	W	W	-	W	W	W	W	W	W	W	W	W	W	W	-	W	W	W	W	W	W	-	W	W	W	W	-	35	13	39
JE (Jeff) FitzGerald	-	-	-	-	-	-	-	-	-	-	-	-	-	-	-	-	-	>FE	FE	-	-	<FE	-	-	-	-	-	-	-	-	-	-	-	-	-	-	-	-	-	-	-	3	-	-
ECA (Ted) Flewitt	-	-	-	-	-	-	-	-	-	-	-	-	-	-	-	-	-	-	-	>W	W	-	W	FE	FE	FE	FE	FE	W	W	W	W	FE	W	W	W	W	W	W	W	W	21	8	24
WLE (Wally) Frisby	-	-	-	-	-	-	-	-	-	-	-	-	-	-	-	-	-	-	-	-	-	-	-	>FB	-	-	-	-	-	-	-	-	-	-	FB	-	-	-	<FB	-	-	3	-	4
LC (Leslie) Gamble	-	-	-	-	-	-	-	-	-	-	-	-	-	-	-	-	-	-	-	-	-	-	-	-	-	-	-	-	-	-	-	-	-	-	-	FB	FB	FB	-	FB	-	4	-	-
GJ (Guy) German	-	-	-	-	-	-	-	-	-	-	-	-	F	-	-	-	F	-	-	-	-	F	-	-	-	-	-	-	-	-	-	-	-	-	-	-	-	-	-	-	-	3	-	-
HD (Harry) Greenlees S+	-	-	-	-	-	-	-	-	-	-	-	-	-	-	-	-	-	-	-	-	-	-	-	-	-	-	-	-	-	-	-	-	-	>SH	SH	-	SH	-	-	SH	SH	5	1	3
MS (Morton) Holden	C	FE	-	-	-	-	FE	FE	FE	FE	-	-	-	W	-	-	-	-	-	-	-	-	-	-	-	C	C	-	-	-	-	-	-	-	-	-	-	-	-	-	-	9	2	18
ECR (Edward) Hopkins	-	-	-	-	-	-	-	-	-	-	-	-	-	-	-	-	-	-	-	-	-	-	-	-	>C	-	-	-	-	-	-	-	-	-	-	C	-	C	FE	-	C	5	1	3
S Jones	-	-	-	-	-	>W	-	-	-	-	-	-	-	-	-	<W	-	-	-	-	-	-	-	-	-	-	-	-	-	-	-	-	-	-	-	-	-	-	-	-	-	2	-	-
SF (Frank) Lawrence	-	-	-	-	-	-	-	-	-	-	-	-	-	-	-	-	-	-	-	-	-	-	FB	F	-	-	-	F	-	-	-	-	-	-	-	-	-	-	-	-	F	4	-	-
JR (Jock) Lawrie S11	F	F	F	-	F	-	-	-	F	F	F	F	-	F	F	F	F	F	F	F	F	-	F	-	F	F	F	F	F	F	F	F	F	F	F	F	F	-	F	<F	-	32	4	12
Dr. JH (Joseph) Moore	-	-	-	-	-	-	>W	-	-	-	W	W	W	C	W	-	C	W	W	-	-	-	-	-	-	-	W	W	-	-	-	-	<W	-	-	-	-	-	-	-	-	12	4	12
DJ (Doug) Norman E+	F	F	F	F	F	F	F	-	F	F	F	F	F	F	F	F	F	F	F	F	F	F	F	F	F	F	F	F	F	F	F	F	F	F	F	F	F	F	F	F	F	40	2	6
GWC (George) Parker	-	-	-	-	-	-	-	-	>F	F	F	F	F	-	F	-	F	-	F	F	F	-	-	-	F	F	F	-	F	F	F	F	F	F	F	F	F	F	-	-	-	23	-	-
FD (Doug) Prentice E+ GB+	-	-	-	-	-	-	-	F	F	F	F	F	F	F	F	F	F	F	F	F	F	F	F	F	F	F	F	F	F	F	-	F	F	F	F	F	F	F	F	F	F	33	3	11
J (John) Raven	-	-	-	-	-	-	-	-	-	-	-	-	-	-	-	>SH	-	-	-	-	-	-	-	-	-	-	<SH	-	-	-	-	-	-	-	-	-	-	-	-	-	-	2	-	-
JC (John) Russell	-	-	-	-	-	-	-	-	-	-	-	-	-	-	SH	-	SH	SH	SH	-	SH	SH	SH	FH	-	-	-	-	-	-	SH	-	-	-	-	SH	-	SH	-	-	-	11	-	-
LC (Claude) Sambrook	FB	FB	FB	FB	FB	FB	FB	FB	FB	FB	FB	FB	FB	FB	FB	FB	FB	FB	FB	FB	FB	FB	-	-	FB	FB	FB	FB	FB	FB	FB	FB	-	-	-	-	-	-	-	-	FB	31	-	-
HA (Harold) Sambrook	FE	FE	C	FE	FE	-	-	-	FH	FH	-	-	-	-	-	-	-	-	-	-	-	-	-	-	-	-	-	-	FE	<FE	-	-	-	-	-	-	-	-	-	-	-	9	-	3
Flt-Lt. PG Scott	-	-	W	C	FE	-	FE	FE	FE	FE	FE	FE	FE	-	FE	FE	W	-	-	-	-	-	-	-	-	-	-	-	-	-	-	-	-	FE	-	FE	FE	-	FE	FE	FE	19	3	9
H (Herb) Sharratt	F	F	F	-	F	F	F	F	F	F	F	F	-	-	-	<F	-	-	-	-	-	-	-	-	-	-	-	-	-	-	-	-	-	-	-	-	-	-	-	-	-	12	-	-
SA (Stuart) Smith	SH	SH	SH	SH	SH	SH	SH	SH	SH	SH	SH	SH	SH	SH	-	-	-	-	-	-	-	-	-	-	-	-	-	-	-	-	-	-	-	-	-	-	-	-	-	-	-	14	3	9
CB (Cyril) Tate	-	-	-	-	-	-	-	-	-	-	-	-	-	-	-	-	-	>FE	FE	FE	FE	FE	FE	<W	-	-	-	-	-	-	-	-	-	-	-	-	-	-	-	-	-	7	1	3
NT (Trevor) Thorneloe	F	F	F	F	F	F	F	F	F	-	-	-	F	F	F	F	F	F	F	F	F	F	-	F	F	F	F	F	F	F	F	F	F	F	F	-	-	F	F	F	F	35	4	33
CHM (Charles) Waldock	-	-	FH	<FE	-	-	-	-	-	-	-	-	-	-	-	-	-	-	-	-	-	-	-	-	-	-	-	-	-	-	-	-	-	-	-	-	-	-	-	-	-	2	-	-
JAG (George) Ward E6	F	F	F	F	F	F	F	F	-	-	-	-	-	-	-	-	-	F	-	-	-	-	F	<F	-	-	-	-	-	-	-	-	-	-	-	-	-	-	-	-	-	11	1	3
FS Wells	-	-	W	W	W	<W	-	-	-	-	-	-	-	-	-	-	-	-	-	-	-	-	-	-	-	-	-	-	-	-	-	-	-	-	-	-	-	-	-	-	-	4	2	6

1 GAME: P/O. PRG (Paddy) Bernard =Wt(36), GE (Eddie) Beynon W2 =W(29), L (Len) Boulter =W(10), TE Burrows >C(31), DC Clarke =FH(35), A Curry =FB(33), A (Arthur) Derry =W(26), JH Moon =F(14), GA (Arthur) Palmer <F(6), N (Noel) Rees =C(39), DN (Nathan) Rocyn-Jones W1 =FB(34), AM (Alastair) Smallwood E14 <C(2), CB (Charles) Wales <C(13), A (Jock) Wemyss S7 =F(23), H (Herbert) Whitley E+ GB3 =SHt(28)

The key for how to read the stats is on the last page

1926/27

Home Ground: Welford Road
Captain: Harold Day

OVERALL RECORD:					T	C	PG	DG	MK	PTS
PLD	W	D	L	Tigers scored:	123	56	15	0	0	526
41	23	1	17	Opponents scored:	73	37	4	12	0	353

GM	DATE		VEN	OPPONENTS	RESULT	TRIES	KICKS	ATT
CLUB MATCHES								
1	Sep	4	H	Bath	W 14-0	Farndon, Flewitt, Russell	Day c/p	7000
2		11	H	Coventry	L 9-11	Flewitt(2), Buckingham	-	11000
3		15w	a	Rugby B.T.H.	W 27-5	Buckingham(3), Shipton, Barlow, Christie, Flewitt	Shipton c, Greenwood 2c	-
4		18	H	Plymouth Albion	W 31-7	Day(2), Buckingham(2), Flewitt, Prentice	Day 5c/p	9000
5		25	H	London Welsh	W 8-0	Day	Day c/p	-
6	Oct	2	H	Northern	W 41-7	Flewitt(3), Day(2), Buckingham, Burton, Coleman, C.Cramphorn, Farndon, Greenlees	Day c, Prentice 3c	8000
7		9	H	Bective Rangers	W 24-3	Buckingham(2), Flewitt(2), Day, C.Cramphorn	Day 3c	7000
8		16	a	Newport	W 19-17	Day, Farndon, Flewitt, Greenlees	Day 2c/p	4000
9		23	H	Moseley	W 42-0	Dykes(4), C.Cramphorn(2), Greenlees(2), Buckingham, Russell	Day 5c, Flewitt c	8000
10		27w	a	Cambridge University	L 0-18	-	-	-
11		30	a	Northampton	L 9-18	Farndon, Flewitt, Prentice	-	12000
12	Nov	6	H	United Services	W 15-5	Buckingham(3)	Day 3c	4000
13		13	H	Oxford University	W 6-3	Farndon, Prentice	-	4000
14		20	H	Swansea	L 11-16	Farndon, Greenlees	Prentice c/p	7000
15		27	H	NZ Maori	L 13-15	Prentice, Farndon	Prentice 2c/p	20000
16		29m	H	Cardiff	W 8-7	Dykes	Prentice c/p	-
17	Dec	4	a	Harlequins	L 3-5	Farndon	-	-
18		11	a	Blackheath	L 6-18	Dykes	Prentice p	-
19		18	H	Bristol	W 11-3	C.Cramphorn(2), Flewitt	Day c	5000
20		24f	a	Coventry	L 3-11	Prentice	-	5000
21		27m	H	Birkenhead Park	W 19-11	Buckingham(3), C.Cramphorn, Hopkins	Prentice 2c	-
22		28tu	H	Barbarians	W 13-8	Farndon, Flewitt, Greenlees	Prentice 2c	9000
23	Jan	1	H	Manchester	W 11-8	C.Cramphorn, Farndon, Sweatman	Prentice c	5000
24		8	a	Swansea	L 3-8	Buckingham	-	-
25		15	H	Gloucester	W 11-3	Russell, Sweatman	Prentice c/p	7000
26		22	H	Percy Park	W 21-4	Buckingham(2), Farndon, Wood	Prentice 3c/p	-
27		26w	H	Royal Air Force	W 11-3	Barlow, Flewitt	Prentice c/p	-
28		29	a	Richmond	L 6-13	Buckingham, Nelson	-	3000
29	Feb	5	a	London Scottish	L 5-18	Glover	Yarnall c	1000
30		12	H	Newport	L 8-12	Buckingham, Edmiston	Day c	7000
31		19	a	Bath	L 8-18	Flewitt	Day c/p	5000
32		26	a	Cardiff	L 3-8	Glover	-	2000
33	Mar	5	H	Harlequins	W 11-3	Day(2), Edmiston	Day c	7000
34		19	a	Birkenhead Park	L 6-9	Flewitt	Day p	-
35		26	H	Old Merchant Taylors	W 17-0	Flewitt(2), Greenlees	Day c/2p	-
36	Apr	2	a	Gloucester	L 3-12	Barlow	-	8000
37		9	H	Blackheath	W 13-3	Farndon(2), Wood	Day 2c	6000
38		16	a	Bristol	L 6-26	Edmiston, Wood	-	7000
39		18m	a	Plymouth Albion	W 18-3	Flewitt(3), Greenlees	Day 3c	-
40		19tu	a	Bridgwater & Albion	W 28-9	Wallace(3), Day, Barlow, Coleman, Greenwood, Wood	Day 2c	-
41		30	H	Northampton	D 5-5	Edmiston	Day c	9000

INDIVIDUAL APPEARANCES 1926/27

Name / Game #	1	2	3	4	5	6	7	8	9	10	11	12	13	14	15	16	17	18	19	20	21	22	23	24	25	26	27	28	29	30	31	32	33	34	35	36	37	38	39	40	41	Apps	T	Pts
Maj. EM (Morgan) Barlow	-	-	>W	-	-	-	-	-	-	-	-	W	W	W	-	-	-	-	-	-	W	-	-	W	-	-	W	-	W	-	-	-	-	-	-	W	-	-	W	W	-	11	4	12
FV (Victor) Beamish	>F	F	-	-	-	-	-	-	F	F	-	F	F	F	F	F	F	-	F	F	F	-	-	F	-	-	-	-	-	-	-	F	F	F	-	F	F	F	-	-	F	21	-	-
TH (Harry) Briers	-	-	-	-	-	-	-	-	-	-	-	-	-	-	-	-	-	F	F	-	-	-	-	-	F	-	F	F	-	-	F	F	F	F	F	-	-	-	-	-	-	10	-	-
Flt-Lt. OC (Oliver) Bryson	FE	FE	-	FE	-	-	-	-	-	-	-	-	-	-	C	-	-	-	-	-	-	-	-	-	-	-	-	-	-	W	-	-	<W	-	-	-	-	-	-	-	-	6	-	-
RA (Ralph) Buckingham E1	FE	FE	FH	FE	FE	FE	FE	FE	FE	FE	FE	FE	FE	FE	FE	FH	FH	-	-	FE	FH	FE	-	FE	-	FH	FE	FE	-	FE	FE	FE	FE	-	FE	-	FE	FE	-	-	FE	32	21	63
LW (Langley) Burton	-	-	-	-	-	SH	-	-	-	-	SH	SH	SH	-	-	-	SH	SH	-	-	-	-	-	-	-	SH	-	-	-	-	SH	-	-	-	SH	-	SH	SH	-	-	-	11	1	3
Cpl. MG (Mog) Christie	F	F	F	-	F	-	F	-	F	F	F	F	-	F	F	-	F	-	F	F	-	F	F	F	F	-	-	-	-	F	-	F	-	F	-	F	-	F	F	-	F	25	1	3
N (Norman) Coates	-	-	-	-	-	-	-	-	-	-	-	-	-	-	-	-	-	-	F	F	F	-	-	-	-	-	-	-	-	-	F	-	-	-	-	F*	F	<F	-	-	-	7	-	-
EG (Ernie) Coleman	F	F	F	F	F	F	-	F	F	F	F	F	F	F	F	F	F	F	F	F	F	F	F	F	F	F	F	F	-	F	F	-	F	F	F	F	F	F	F	F	F	38	2	6
CT (Charlie) Cramphorn	-	-	FE	-	C	C	C	C	C	C	C	C	C	C	-	C	C	C	C	FB	FE	-	C	FE	-	FE	FE	C	-	-	<C	-	-	-	-	-	-	-	-	-	-	23	8	24
HLV (Harold) Day E4	C*	-	-	C*	FE*	FE*	FE*	FE*	FE*	-	-	FE*	FE*	FE*	FE*	-	-	-	FE*	-	-	-	-	-	-	-	-	FE*	-	FE*	FE*	-	FE*	FE*	FE*	-	FE*	FE*	FE*	FE*	FE*	23	10	122
JM Dykes	-	-	-	-	-	>F	F	F	F	F	F	F	F	-	-	F	F	F	-	-	F	F	W	F	F	F	-	-	-	F	F	-	-	-	<F	-	-	-	-	-	-	20	6	18
JHF (Harry) Edmiston	F	F	F	F	F	F	F	F	-	-	-	-	-	-	-	-	-	-	-	F	-	F	F	F	F	F	F	-	-	F	-	-	F	C	F	-	-	F	-	F	F	22	4	12
WE (Ewart) Farndon	W	W	W	W	W	W	W	W	W	W	W	W	W	W	W	W	W	W	W	W	W	W	W	W	W	W	-	W	-	W	W	W	W	W	W	W	W	W	-	-	W	37	13	39
ECA (Ted) Flewitt	W	W	FE	W	W	W	W	W	W	W	W	-	-	-	W	W	W	W	W	W	C	W	FE	-	W	W	W	W	C	-	W	W	-	W	W	FE	W	W	FE	FE	W	35	22	68
GJ (Guy) German	-	-	-	-	-	-	-	-	-	-	-	-	-	-	F	F	-	-	-	-	-	F	<F	-	-	-	-	-	-	-	-	-	-	-	-	-	-	-	-	-	-	4	-	-
DB Glover	-	-	>F	-	-	-	-	-	-	-	-	-	-	-	-	-	-	-	-	-	-	-	-	-	-	-	-	-	F	-	-	F	-	-	-	-	-	-	-	-	-	3	2	6
HD (Harry) Greenlees S+	FH	FH	-	FH	FH	FH	FH	FH	FH	FH	FH	FH	FH	FH	FH	-	-	FH	-	FH	-	FH	FH	FH	FH	-	FH	FH	-	FH	FH	FH	FH	FH	FH	FH	FH	FH	FH	FH	FH	34	8	24
AH (Henry) Greenwood	-	>F	F	F	F	F	F	F	F	F	F	F	F	F	F	-	F	F	F	F	F	F	F	F	-	F	F	F	-	F	F	F	F	F	-	-	-	-	F	F	-	32	1	7
JD Hodgkinson	-	-	-	-	-	-	-	-	-	>FE	-	-	-	-	-	-	-	-	-	-	-	-	-	-	-	-	-	-	FH	-	-	-	-	-	-	-	-	-	-	-	-	2	-	-
MS (Morton) Holden	-	-	-	-	-	-	-	-	-	-	-	-	-	-	-	-	-	-	-	-	-	-	-	-	-	-	C	-	-	-	-	<FE	-	-	-	-	-	-	-	-	-	2	-	-
ECR (Edward) Hopkins	-	-	-	-	-	-	-	-	-	-	-	-	-	-	-	-	-	-	-	-	FE	C	-	-	FE	-	-	-	-	C	-	-	-	-	-	-	-	-	-	-	-	4	1	3
SF (Frank) Lawrence	F	F	-	F	-	-	F	F	F	-	F	-	F	F	-	F	-	-	-	-	-	-	-	-	-	F	F	F	F	-	-	-	-	-	F	F	F	-	F	F	-	19	-	-
JB (Jimmy) Nelson S12	-	-	-	-	-	-	-	-	-	-	-	-	-	-	-	-	-	-	-	-	-	-	-	-	-	-	>SH	<SH	-	-	-	-	-	-	-	-	-	-	-	-	-	2	1	3
DJ (Doug) Norman E+	F	F	F	F	F	F	F	F	F	F	F	F	F	F	F	F	F	F	-	-	-	-	F	-	F	F	F	F	-	F	F	F	F	F	F	F	F	F	F	F	F	35	-	-
GWC (George) Parker	-	-	F	F	F	<F	-	-	-	-	-	-	-	-	-	-	-	-	-	-	-	-	-	-	-	-	-	-	-	-	-	-	-	-	-	-	-	-	-	-	-	4	-	-
FD (Doug) Prentice E+ GB+	-	-	-	F	F	F	F	F	-	F	F	F	F	F	F	F	F	F	F	F	F	F	F	F	F	F	F	F	-	F	F	F	F	F	F	-	F	F	F	F	F	35	5	70
JC (John) Russell	SH	SH	-	SH	SH	-	SH	SH	SH	SH	-	-	-	SH	SH	SH	-	-	SH	SH	SH	SH	SH	SH	SH	-	-	-	-	SH	-	SH	SH	-	-	SH	-	-	SH	SH	SH	25	3	9
DWR (Douglas) Ryley	-	-	-	-	-	-	-	-	-	-	-	-	-	-	-	-	-	-	-	-	-	-	-	-	-	-	-	-	-	-	-	-	-	-	-	>F	F	-	F	F	F	5	-	-
LC (Claude) Sambrook	FB	FB	FB	FB	FB	FB	FB	FB	FB	FB	FB	FB	FB	FB	FB	FB	FB	FB	-	-	-	FB	FB	FB	FB	FB	FB	FB	-	FB	FB	FB	FB	FB	FB	-	-	-	-	-	-	31	-	-
GL (Len) Shipton	-	>C	C	-	-	-	-	-	-	-	-	-	-	-	-	-	-	-	-	-	-	-	-	-	-	-	-	-	-	-	-	-	-	-	-	-	-	-	-	-	-	2	1	5
SA (Stuart) Smith	-	-	-	-	-	-	-	-	-	-	-	-	-	-	-	-	-	-	-	-	-	-	-	-	FE	-	-	-	FE	-	-	-	-	SH	-	-	-	-	-	-	-	3	-	-
EA (Eric) Sweatman	-	-	-	-	-	-	-	-	-	-	-	-	-	-	-	-	>FE	FE	FE	FE	-	-	FE	C	C	C	-	-	-	-	-	-	-	-	-	-	-	-	-	-	-	8	2	6
WS (William) Thompson	-	-	-	-	-	-	-	-	-	-	-	-	-	-	-	-	-	-	-	-	>FB	-	-	-	-	-	-	-	-	-	-	-	-	-	-	FB	FB	FB	FB	FB	FB	7	-	-
NT (Trevor) Thorneloe	-	-	-	-	-	-	-	-	-	-	-	-	-	-	-	-	-	-	-	-	F	-	-	-	-	-	-	F	-	-	-	-	-	-	-	-	-	-	-	-	-	2	-	-
W (Billy) Wallace GB1	-	-	-	-	-	-	-	-	-	-	-	-	-	-	-	-	-	-	-	-	-	-	-	-	-	-	-	-	-	-	-	-	-	-	-	-	-	-	W	W	-	2	3	9
FE (Frank) Wood	-	-	-	-	-	-	-	-	-	-	-	-	-	-	-	-	FE	-	FH	C	-	FE	-	-	-	FE	-	-	-	-	-	C	C	FE	C	C	C	C	C	C	C	15	4	12
AL (Arthur) Yarnell	-	-	-	-	-	-	-	-	-	-	-	-	-	-	-	>FE	-	-	-	-	-	-	-	-	-	-	-	-	<FE	-	-	-	-	-	-	-	-	-	-	-	-	2	-	2

1 GAME: JL Baxter =F(29), CESJ (Charles) Beamish I+ >F(18), AE (William) Beith <F(1), TB (Thomas) Bovell-Jones =F(29), TE Burrows FE(16), JW Colquhoun =SH(29), JF (John) Cramphorn >SH(3), LC (Leslie) Gamble <FB(19), G Hudson =F(29), A Murray >FB(29), PG (Philip) Price =FE(18), A Purt =W(29), Flt-Lt. PG Scott <FE(11), RP Stephens =F(29), JL Tebbutt =F(29), FHR (Fleckney) Turney FE(36)

The key for how to read the stats is on the last page

1927/28

Home Ground: Welford Road
Captain: Harold Day

OVERALL RECORD:					T	C	PG	DG	MK	PTS
PLD	W	D	L	Tigers scored:	123	63	13	3	0	546
39	21	4	14	Opponents scored:	75	23	4	4	1	302

GM	DATE		VEN	OPPONENTS	RESULT	TRIES	KICKS	ATT
CLUB MATCHES								
1	Sep	3	H	**Bath**	W 33-0	Farndon(2), Wood(2), Day, Buckingham, Flewitt	Day 6c	7000
2		10	H	**Hartlepool Rovers**	W 40-8	Farndon(3), Buckingham(2), Christie(2), Day, Flewitt, Prentice	Day 5c	7000
3		17	H	**Nuneaton**	W 13-5	G.Beamish, Ryley	Day 2c/p	7000
4		24	H	**Plymouth Albion**	W 14-8	Christie(2), Farndon, Flewitt	Day c	7000
5	Oct	1	a	United Services	W 3-0	-	Day p	-
6		8	H	**Old Blues**	W 18-11	Day, G.Beamish, Flewitt, Prentice	Day 3c	6000
7		15	H	**Newport**	L 5-8	Farndon	Day c	10000
8		22	a	Moseley	W 27-0	Day(2), Wood(2), Farndon, Flewitt, Greenlees	Day 2c, Prentice c	-
9	Nov	5	H	**Cambridge University**	D 14-14	Prentice, Buckingham	Prentice 2c, Greenlees d	7000
10		10th	H	**Oxford University**	W 14-3	Prentice, Buckingham, Farndon, Greenlees	Prentice c	-
11		12	H	**Northampton**	D 3-3	-	Day p	7000
12		19	a	Swansea	L 3-6	G.Beamish	-	-
13		26	H	**Cardiff**	W 15-7	Wood(2), Buckingham	Wood d, Day c	5000
14	Dec	3	a	Harlequins	L 0-3	-	-	-
15		10	a	Blackheath	L 3-21	G.Beamish	-	4000
		17	H	**Bristol**	PP (frost)			
16		24	H	**Bridgwater & Albion**	W 29-0	Farndon(3), V.Beamish, Christie, Lawrence	Day 4c/p	5000
17		26m	H	**Birkenhead Park**	W 32-0	Farndon(2), Wood(2), Day, Briers, Hall, Smith	Day 4c	-
18		27tu	H	**Barbarians**	W 16-13	Day(2), Prentice, Sweatman	Day 2c	10000
		31	a	Coventry	PP (frost)			
	Jan	2m	a	Manchester	PP (frost)			
19		3tu	a	Hartlepool Rovers	W 20-0	Prentice, Christie, Smith, Wood	Prentice c/2p	-
20		7	H	**Swansea**	W 11-0	Christie, Lawrence	Prentice c/p	7000
21		14	a	Gloucester	L 3-6	-	Day p	4000
22		21	H	**London Welsh**	W 22-0	Dunkley(2), Lawrence, Prentice, Smith, Wood	Day 2c	-
23		25w	H	**Royal Air Force**	W 16-11	Barlow(3), Wood	Prentice 2c	2000
		28	H	**Richmond**	PP (did not turn up)			
24	Feb	4	H	**London Scottish**	W 32-3	Prentice(2), Buckingham, Coleman, Dunkley, Tyler, Wood	Prentice 4c/p	3000
25		11	a	Newport	L 3-11	Barlow	-	3000
26		18	H	**Coventry**	W 25-16	Barlow, Buckingham, Coleman, Dunkley, Lawrence, Smith	Prentice 2c/p	9000
27		25	a	Cardiff	L 8-25	Coleman, Lawrence	Sambrook c	3000
28	Mar	3	H	**Harlequins**	D 18-18	Wood(2), Christie	Prentice 3c/p	6000
29		10	a	Northampton	L 3-6	Coleman	-	6000
30		17	H	**Penarth**	W 3-0	-	Day p	6000
31		24	H	**Old Merchant Taylors**	W 25-0	Barlow(2), Buckingham(2), Wood(2), Tyler	Norman c, Prentice c	6000
32		31	H	**Gloucester**	W 18-6	Prentice(2), Day	Day c/p, Franklin d	6000
33	Apr	7	a	Bristol	L 11-14	Wallace(2), Wood	Prentice c	8000
34		9m	a	Plymouth Albion	D 15-15	Prentice, Greenlees, Wood	Prentice 3c	4000
35		10tu	a	Bath	L 3-11	Prentice	-	2000
36		14	H	**Blackheath**	L 8-10	Farndon, Lawrence	Prentice c	3000
37		19th	H	**Richmond**	L 5-9	Wood	Thorneloe c	2000
38		21	a	Birkenhead Park	L 10-16	Day, Edmiston	Day 2c	3000
39		25w	a	Coventry	L 5-15	Greenlees	Prentice c	-

INDIVIDUAL APPEARANCES 1927/28

Name / Game #	1	2	3	4	5	6	7	8	9	10	11	12	13	14	15	16	17	18	19	20	21	22	23	24	25	26	27	28	29	30	31	32	33	34	35	36	37	38	39	Apps	T	Pts
LJ (Lewis) Adcock	-	-	-	-	-	-	-	-	-	-	-	-	-	-	-	-	-	-	-	-	-	>W	W	-	-	-	-	W	-	W	-	-	-	-	-	-	W	-	-	5	-	-
Maj. EM (Morgan) Barlow	-	-	-	-	-	-	-	-	-	-	-	-	-	-	-	-	W	-	W	W	-	W	C	W	W	W	W	W	W	W	W	-	-	W	W	W	W	W	-	18	7	21
GR (George) Beamish I7 GB+	P	P	P	P	P	P	P	P	-	-	-	L	L	P	P	P	P	P	L	P	-	-	-	-	-	L	-	-	-	L	-	L	L	L	P	L	-	-	-	24	4	12
FV (Victor) Beamish	BR	BR	BR	BR	BR	BR	BR	BR	BR	BR	BR	BR	L	L	L	L	BR	BR	-	L	-	-	-	BR	L	L	-	-	L	P	-	L	BR	BR	-	-	-	-	-	27	1	3
E Braithwaite	-	-	-	-	-	-	-	-	-	-	-	-	-	-	-	-	-	-	-	-	-	-	>BR	BR	BR	-	-	-	-	-	-	-	-	-	-	-	-	-	-	3	-	-
TH (Harry) Briers	-	-	-	-	-	-	BR	BR	BR	BR	BR	BR	BR	-	-	BR	BR	-	BR	-	BR	BR	BR	L	L	BR	L	BR	BR	-	BR	-	-	-	BR	-	L	BR	BR	24	1	3
AFB (Arthur) Brodbeck	-	-	-	-	-	-	-	-	-	-	-	-	-	-	-	-	-	-	-	-	-	-	-	-	-	-	-	-	-	-	-	-	-	-	-	-	<SH	-	-	1	-	-
RA (Ralph) Buckingham E1	FH	FH	C	C	C	FH	-	FH	C	C	C	C	C	-	-	FH	FH	C	FH	-	C	-	C	FH	-	C	-	FH	FH	-	C	C	C	C	-	C	-	-	-	27	10	30
TE Burrows	-	-	-	-	-	-	-	-	-	-	-	-	-	W	<W	-	-	-	-	-	-	-	-	-	-	-	-	-	-	-	-	-	-	-	-	-	-	-	-	2	-	-
JS (John) Cambridge	-	-	-	-	-	-	-	-	-	-	-	-	-	-	-	-	-	-	-	-	-	-	-	-	-	-	-	-	-	-	-	-	-	-	-	-	-	>BR	<BR	2	-	-
Cpl. MG (Mog) Christie	BR	BR	BR	BR	BR	BR	BR	-	L	L	-	L	W	BR	BR	BR	-	BR	W	L	L	-	-	-	-	-	-	L	-	-	-	BR	L	L	L	L	-	-	-	24	8	24
EG (Ernie) Coleman	L	L	L	L	L	L	L	L	P	P	P	P	P	L	L	L	L	L	P	-	P	P	P	P	H	P	H	P	P	H	P	P	P	P	-	P	H	H	H	37	4	12
HLV (Harold) Day E4	C*	C*	C*	C*	C*	C*	C*	C*	-	-	C*	C*	C*	C*	C*	C*	C*	C*	-	-	C*	FH	-	-	-	-	-	-	-	C*	-	C*	-	-	-	-	-	C*	-	21	10	123
PE (Pop) Dunkley E+	-	-	-	-	-	-	-	-	-	-	-	-	-	-	-	-	-	-	-	-	-	>BR	-	BR	-	BR	-	BR	BR	-	BR	BR	-	-	-	BR	-	P	-	9	4	12
JHF (Harry) Edmiston	BR	BR	BR	BR	BR	BR	-	-	-	-	-	-	-	-	-	-	-	L	L	BR	L	L	-	-	-	-	-	-	-	BR	L	BR	-	BR	L	-	P	L	L	19	1	3
WE (Ewart) Farndon	W	W	-	W	W	W	W	W	W	W	W	W	-	-	W	W	W	W	-	W	W	-	-	-	-	-	-	-	-	-	-	-	-	-	W	W	-	W	-	20	15	45
ECA (Ted) Flewitt	W	W	W	W	-	W	W	W	-	-	-	-	-	-	-	-	-	-	-	-	-	-	-	-	-	-	-	-	-	-	-	-	-	-	-	-	C	-	W	9	5	15
HWF (Herbert) Franklin	-	-	-	-	-	-	-	-	>FB	-	-	-	FB	FB	-	FB	-	FB	FB	FB	FB	-	-	-	-	FB	-	-	FB	FB	FB	FB	FB	FB	FB	FB	FB	FB	FB	20	-	4
WH (William) Graves	-	-	-	-	-	-	-	-	-	-	-	-	-	-	-	-	-	-	-	-	-	-	-	-	-	-	>BR	-	-	-	BR	-	-	-	-	-	BR	-	BR	4	-	-
HD (Harry) Greenlees S3	SH	SH	FH	FH	FH	-	FH	SH	FH	FH	FH	FH	FH	FH	-	-	-	FH	-	FH	FH	-	-	-	-	FH	FH	-	-	-	FH	FH	FH	FH	FH	FH	-	FH	FH	26	4	16
AC Hall	-	-	-	-	-	-	-	-	-	-	>L	-	BR	BR	BR	-	L	-	BR	BR	BR	-	-	-	-	-	L	-	-	-	-	-	BR	BR	BR	-	L	L	P	15	1	3
JD Hodgkinson	-	-	-	-	-	-	-	-	-	-	-	-	-	-	<FH	-	-	-	-	-	-	-	-	-	-	-	-	-	-	-	-	-	-	-	-	-	-	-	-	1	-	-
HN (Henry) Knox	-	-	-	-	-	-	-	-	-	-	-	-	-	-	-	-	-	-	-	-	-	-	-	-	-	-	-	>BR	BR	BR	-	-	BR	-	BR	BR	-	-	L	7	-	-
GF (George) Lashmore	-	-	-	-	-	-	-	-	-	-	-	-	-	-	-	-	-	-	-	-	-	-	-	-	>BR	-	BR	-	-	-	-	-	-	-	-	-	-	-	-	2	-	-
SF (Frank) Lawrence	-	-	-	-	-	-	-	BR	BR	BR	BR	BR	BR	BR	BR	BR	BR	BR	BR	BR	BR	L	L	L	P	BR	P	L	L	BR	L	-	-	-	-	<BR	-	-	-	25	6	18
NWR (Norman) Mawle	-	-	-	-	-	-	-	-	-	-	-	-	-	-	-	-	-	-	-	-	-	-	-	-	-	-	-	-	-	-	-	-	-	-	-	-	=BR	-	-	1	-	-
Dr. ML (Maurice) Millard	-	-	-	-	-	-	-	-	-	-	-	-	-	-	-	-	-	-	-	-	-	>BR	BR	-	BR	-	-	-	-	L	-	-	-	-	-	-	-	-	-	4	-	-
SH (Shirley) Moore	-	-	-	-	-	-	-	-	>W	-	-	-	-	-	-	-	-	-	-	-	-	-	-	-	-	-	-	-	-	-	-	-	-	-	-	-	-	-	W	2	-	-
DJ (Doug) Norman E+	H	H	H	H	H	H	H	H	H	H	H	H	H	H	H	H	H	H	H	H	H	H	H	H	P	H	P	H	H	P	H	H	H	H	H	H	P	P	-	38	-	2
Lt. AL (Tony) Novis E+ GB+	-	-	-	-	-	-	-	-	-	-	-	-	-	-	-	-	-	-	-	-	-	-	-	-	-	-	-	-	-	-	-	-	-	-	>C	-	-	-	-	1	-	-
RS (Ron) Palmer	-	-	-	-	-	-	-	-	-	-	-	-	-	-	-	-	-	-	-	-	-	-	-	-	-	-	-	-	-	-	-	-	-	-	-	-	FH	-	C	2	-	-
CH (Peter) Pearse	-	-	-	-	-	-	-	-	-	-	-	-	-	-	-	-	-	-	-	-	-	-	-	-	-	-	-	-	-	-	-	-	-	-	-	-	-	>BR	-	1	-	-
FD (Doug) Prentice E3 GB+	P	P	P	P	P	P	P	P	P	P	P	P	P	P	P	P	P	P	P	P	P	P	P	P	-	P	-	P	P	-	P	P	P	P	P	P	-	-	P	34	13	105
JC (John) Russell	-	-	SH	SH	SH	SH	SH	-	-	-	-	-	-	-	-	-	-	SH	-	SH	SH	-	-	SH	-	-	SH	-	SH	-	-	SH	SH	SH	-	-	-	-	-	14	-	-
DWR (Douglas) Ryley	L	L	L	L	L	L	L	L	L	L	<L	-	-	-	-	-	-	-	-	-	-	-	-	-	-	-	-	-	-	-	-	-	-	-	-	-	-	-	-	11	1	3
LC (Claude) Sambrook	FB	FB	FB	FB	FB	FB	FB	-	-	-	FB	FB	-	-	FB	-	FB	-	-	-	-	FB	FB	FB	FB	-	FB	<FB	-	-	-	-	-	-	-	-	-	-	-	17	-	2
L (Len) Shipton	-	-	-	-	-	-	-	-	-	-	-	-	-	C	-	-	-	-	-	-	-	-	-	-	W	-	W	-	-	-	-	-	-	-	-	-	-	-	-	3	-	-
SA (Stuart) Smith	-	-	-	-	-	-	-	-	SH	SH	SH	SH	SH	SH	SH	SH	SH	-	SH	-	-	SH	SH	-	SH	SH	-	SH	C	SH	SH	-	-	-	SH	SH	-	-	SH	21	4	12
WE (Wilfrid) Squirrell	-	-	-	-	-	-	-	-	-	-	-	-	-	-	-	-	-	-	-	-	-	-	FH	-	-	-	-	-	-	FH	-	-	-	-	-	-	-	SH	-	3	-	-
EA (Eric) Sweatman	-	-	-	-	-	-	-	-	-	W	-	-	-	-	-	W	-	W	-	C	-	-	-	W	-	-	-	-	C	-	-	-	-	-	-	-	-	-	-	6	1	3
WS (William) Thompson	-	-	-	-	-	-	-	FB	-	FB	-	-	-	-	-	-	-	-	-	-	-	-	-	-	-	-	-	-	-	-	-	-	-	-	-	-	-	-	-	2	-	-
NT (Trevor) Thorneloe	-	-	-	-	-	-	-	-	-	-	-	-	-	-	-	-	-	-	-	-	-	-	-	-	-	-	-	-	-	-	-	-	-	-	-	-	BR	-	-	1	-	2
FHR (Fleckney) Turney	-	-	-	-	-	-	-	-	-	-	-	-	-	-	-	-	-	-	-	-	-	-	-	-	<C	-	-	-	-	-	-	-	-	-	-	-	-	-	-	1	-	-
HP (Henry) Tyler	-	-	-	-	-	-	-	-	-	-	-	-	-	-	-	-	-	-	>C	-	-	C	-	C	C	C	C	C	-	-	W	W	C	-	-	-	-	-	-	10	2	6
W (Billy) Wallace GB1	-	-	-	-	-	-	-	-	-	-	-	-	-	-	-	-	-	-	-	-	-	-	-	-	-	-	-	-	-	-	-	-	W	W	-	-	-	-	-	2	2	6
L Watts	-	-	-	-	-	-	-	-	-	-	-	-	-	-	-	-	-	-	-	-	-	-	>L	-	-	-	<BR	-	-	-	-	-	-	-	-	-	-	-	-	2	-	-
FE (Frank) Wood	C	C	W	-	W	C	C	C	C	C	W	W	W	W	C	C	C	-	C	C	W	C	W	C	FH	W	C	C	W	C	C	W	W	C	C	C	C	C	C	37	19	61

The key for how to read the stats is on the last page

19 28/29

Home Ground: Welford Road
Captain: Doug Prentice

OVERALL RECORD:					T	C	PG	DG	MK	PTS
PLD	W	D	L	Tigers scored:	94	41	11	1	0	401
38	16	1	21	Opponents scored:	83	38	13	4	0	380

GM	DATE		VEN	OPPONENTS	RESULT	TRIES	KICKS	ATT
CLUB MATCHES								
1	Sep	**1**	**H**	**Bath**	W 17-5	Flewitt(3), Prentice, F.Wood	Norman c	5000
2		**8**	**H**	**Old Blues**	W 27-15	Buckingham(2), Edmiston, Farndon, Greenlees, Hall, F.Wood	Prentice 3c	5000
3		**15**	**H**	**Plymouth Albion**	L 3-5	-	Prentice p	5000
4		**22**	**H**	**Nuneaton**	W 10-3	Farndon, Flewitt	Prentice 2c	6000
5		**29**	**H**	**Moseley**	W 16-0	Flewitt(3), Greenlees	Prentice 2c	5000
6	Oct	**6**	**H**	**Rosslyn Park**	W 25-9	Flewitt(3), Prentice(2), Buckingham(2)	Prentice 2c	5000
7		**13**	**H**	**Coventry**	D 9-9	Jones	Prentice 2p	10000
8		20	a	Newport	L 5-9	Flewitt	Prentice c	6000
9		27	a	Northampton	L 8-11	Flewitt	Prentice c/p	-
10	Nov	3	a	Cambridge University	L 3-20	-	Prentice p	-
11		**10**	**H**	**Cardiff**	W 8-5	Prentice, Farndon	Prentice c	-
12		**17**	**H**	**Swansea**	W 9-5	Prentice, Jones	Prentice p	7000
13		**24**	**H**	**Bedford**	W 27-9	Flewitt(2), Day, Buckingham, Burton, Farndon, Symington	Day c, Prentice 2c	5000
14		29th	a	Oxford University	L 3-10	Barlow	-	-
15	Dec	1	a	Harlequins	L 5-17	Jones	Dunkley c	-
16		8	a	Blackheath	L 8-29	Dunkley, Greenwood	Prentice c	-
17		**15**	**H**	**Bristol**	L 3-8	Prentice	-	-
18		22	a	Nuneaton	W 22-0	Barlow(2), Farndon(2), J.Cramphorn, Flewitt	Prentice 2c	-
19		**26w**	**H**	**Birkenhead Park**	L 13-27	Prentice, Greenwood	Prentice 2c/p	-
20		**27th**	**H**	**Barbarians**	L 8-24	Edmiston, Odbert	Prentice c	10000
21		**29**	**H**	**Manchester**	L 12-16	J.Cramphorn(2)	Barlow d, Edmiston c	5000
	Jan	5	a	Swansea	PP (frost)			
22		12	a	Gloucester	L 3-11	J.Cramphorn	-	-
23		**19**	**H**	**London Welsh**	W 13-3	J.Cramphorn, Greenwood, Greenlees	Day 2c	5000
24		**24th**	**H**	**Royal Air Force**	L 6-8	J.Cramphorn, G.Wood	-	1000
25		26	a	Richmond	L 3-12	Flewitt	-	-
26	Feb	2	a	London Scottish	W 28-3	Greenlees(2), Prentice, Coleman, Farndon, Russell	Prentice 5c	-
27		**9**	**H**	**Newport**	W 3-0	Buckingham	-	5000
		16	a	Coventry	PP (frost)			
28		**23**	**H**	**Northampton**	L 8-10	Buckingham, Russell	R.Palmer c	8000
	Mar	**2**	**H**	**Harlequins**	PP (frost)			
29		9	a	Bridgwater & Albion	L 5-6	Farndon	Prentice c	-
30		16	a	Cardiff	L 5-8	Buckingham	Prentice c	5000
31		18m	a	Swansea	L 16-24	Prentice, J.Cramphorn	Prentice 2c/2p	-
32		**23**	**H**	**Gloucester**	W 12-3	Buckingham, Russell	Prentice 2p	6000
33		30	a	Bristol	L 8-14	Farndon, Stephens	Prentice c	6000
34	Apr	1m	a	Plymouth Albion	W 16-5	Prentice, J.Cramphorn, Dunkley, Flewitt	Prentice 2c	5000
35		2tu	a	Bath	W 16-9	Farndon(2), Prentice, Greenlees	Prentice 2c	3000
36		6	a	Birkenhead Park	L 0-3	-	-	4000
37		**13**	**H**	**Blackheath**	W 18-13	Barlow, Burton, Dunkley, Farndon, Greenwood, Hall	-	3000
38		15m	a	Coventry	L 0-12	-	-	5000

INDIVIDUAL APPEARANCES 1928/29

Name / Game #	1	2	3	4	5	6	7	8	9	10	11	12	13	14	15	16	17	18	19	20	21	22	23	24	25	26	27	28	29	30	31	32	33	34	35	36	37	38	Apps	T	Pts
Maj. EM (Morgan) Barlow	-	-	-	-	-	-	-	-	-	-	-	-	-	W	-	-	-	W	W	W	W	W	-	-	-	-	-	-	-	-	-	-	-	-	-	-	W	-	7	4	16
RJ (Bobby) Barr E+	-	-	-	-	-	-	-	-	-	>FB	-	-	-	-	-	-	-	-	-	-	-	-	-	-	-	FB	-	-	-	FB	FB	-	FB	FB	FB	FB	FB	FB	10	-	-
GR (George) Beamish I11 GB+	L	-	L	-	P	-	L	-	L	-	L	L	-	P	H	L	-	-	-	-	-	P	L	-	-	L	-	-	-	-	-	-	P	L	P	P	H	-	18	-	-
FV (Victor) Beamish	L	L	L	L	L	L	L	L	L	-	L	-	L	L	P	-	L	-	-	L	P	-	L	-	L	L	-	<L	-	-	-	-	-	-	-	-	-	-	20	-	-
E Braithwaite	-	-	-	-	-	-	-	-	-	-	-	L	BR	BR	BR	-	-	-	-	-	-	-	-	-	<BR	-	-	-	-	-	-	-	-	-	-	-	-	-	5	-	-
TH (Harry) Briers	-	-	-	-	-	-	-	-	-	BR	-	-	-	-	-	-	-	L	-	-	-	BR	-	-	-	-	BR	BR	-	-	BR	-	-	-	-	BR	-	-	7	-	-
S (Stan) Brown	-	-	-	-	-	-	-	-	-	-	-	-	-	-	-	-	-	-	-	-	-	-	-	-	-	-	-	-	-	SH	<SH	-	-	-	-	-	-	-	2	-	-
RA (Ralph) Buckingham E1	C	C	C	FH	C	C	C	FH	C	C	C	C	FH	-	-	C	-	FH	FH	C	-	C	-	C	C	C	C	C	C	C	FH	C	-	-	-	C	C	FH	30	9	27
FML (Fred) Bunney	-	-	-	-	-	-	-	-	-	-	-	-	-	-	-	-	-	-	-	>SH	-	-	-	<SH	-	-	-	-	-	-	-	-	-	-	-	-	-	-	2	-	-
LW (Langley) Burton	-	-	-	-	SH	SH	SH	C	-	-	-	-	SH	-	-	-	-	-	-	-	-	-	-	-	-	-	-	-	-	-	-	-	-	-	-	-	SH	-	6	2	6
EG (Ernie) Coleman	P	P	P	P	-	P	P	P	P	P	P	P	P	H	-	P	P	P	P	P	H	H	P	-	P	P	P	-	P	P	H	P	-	H	L	L	P	P	33	1	3
JF (John) Cramphorn	-	-	-	C	C	C	-	C	-	-	-	-	-	-	W	C	C	C	-	-	C	C	C	W	-	C	C	W	W	C	C	C	-	W	<C	-	-	-	21	8	24
HLV (Harold) Day E4	-	-	-	-	-	-	-	-	C	-	-	C	C	-	-	-	-	-	-	-	-	-	C	-	<C	-	-	-	-	-	-	-	-	-	-	-	-	-	5	1	9
PE (Pop) Dunkley E+	-	-	-	-	-	BR	BR	L	BR	L	-	BR	-	-	L	L	-	-	BR	L	-	L	-	-	L	-	BR	-	L	L	-	L	L	P	-	-	BR	L	20	3	11
JHF (Harry) Edmiston	BR	L	BR	L	L	BR	-	-	-	-	-	-	-	-	-	-	BR	-	C	BR	BR	BR	-	L	-	BR	-	-	-	-	-	-	-	BR	-	BR	BR	L	17	2	8
WE (Ewart) Farndon	W	W	W	W	W	W	W	W	W	W	W	W	W	W	W	W	W	W	W	W	W	-	-	-	W	W	W	W	W	W	W	W	W	-	W	W	W	W	34	12	36
ECA (Ted) Flewitt	W	W	W	W	W	W	W	W	W	-	W	W	W	-	-	W	-	C	-	-	-	-	-	-	W	-	-	-	-	W	C	W	C	W	W	C	C	W	24	17	51
HWF (Herbert) Franklin	-	-	FB	-	FB	FB	FB	-	FB	-	-	-	FB	FB	-	-	-	-	<FB	-	-	-	-	-	-	-	-	-	-	-	-	-	-	-	-	-	-	-	8	-	-
WH (William) Graves	-	BR	-	-	-	-	-	BR	-	BR	-	-	-	-	-	-	-	L	BR	-	BR	-	-	-	-	-	-	BR	BR	BR	-	BR	-	-	BR	-	-	<BR	12	-	-
HD (Harry) Greenlees S5	FH	FH	FH	SH	FH	FH	FH	-	FH	FH	FH	FH	-	-	-	-	-	-	-	-	-	-	W	FH	FH	FH	FH	-	FH	-	-	FH	-	FH	FH	FH	FH	-	22	6	18
AH (Henry) Greenwood	BR	BR	BR	BR	BR	-	-	-	BR	-	BR	BR	BR	BR	BR	BR	BR	BR	L	BR	-	-	BR	-	BR	BR	L	H	L	L	L	BR	BR	BR	L	-	L	P	30	4	12
AC Hall	BR	BR	BR	BR	BR	BR	BR	BR	-	-	-	-	BR	-	BR	BR	BR	BR	L	BR	L	L	BR	-	BR	BR	BR	P	BR	-	-	L	L	BR	-	L	L	-	28	2	6
Sgt. DR (Dai) Jones	-	-	-	>BR	BR	L	BR	BR	BR	L	BR	BR	L	L	L	BR	L	-	-	-	-	-	-	-	-	-	L	L	-	BR	<P	-	-	-	-	-	-	-	18	3	9
JG (John) Llewelyn	-	-	-	-	-	-	-	-	-	-	-	-	-	-	-	-	-	-	-	-	-	-	-	-	-	-	-	-	-	-	-	-	>FH	C	C	-	-	C	4	-	-
CS (Charlie) Manson	>FB	FB	-	FB	-	-	-	FB	-	W	-	FB	-	-	FB	FB	FB	FB	-	FB	FB	FB	FB	FB	FB	-	FB	FB	FB	-	-	FB	-	-	-	-	-	-	20	-	-
Dr. ML (Maurice) Millard	-	-	-	-	-	-	-	-	-	-	BR	-	-	-	-	-	-	-	-	-	L	-	<BR	-	-	-	-	-	-	-	-	-	-	-	-	-	-	-	3	-	-
DJ (Doug) Norman E+	H	H	H	H	H	H	H	H	H	H	H	H	H	P	P	H	H	H	H	H	P	-	H	H	H	H	H	P	H	H	-	H	H	L	H	H	P	H	36	-	2
RVM (Reginald) Odbert I1	-	-	-	-	-	-	-	-	-	-	-	-	-	-	-	-	-	-	-	FH	FH	-	FH	-	-	-	-	FH	C	-	-	-	C	C	-	-	-	-	7	1	3
AP (Phil) Palmer	-	-	-	-	-	-	-	-	-	-	-	-	-	-	-	-	-	-	-	-	-	>BR	-	BR	-	-	-	<BR	-	-	-	-	-	-	-	-	-	-	3	-	-
RS (Ron) Palmer	-	-	-	-	-	-	-	-	-	-	-	-	-	-	-	-	-	-	-	-	-	-	-	-	-	-	-	C	-	-	-	-	-	-	-	-	-	<C	2	-	2
FD (Doug) Prentice E3 GB+	P*	P*	P*	P*	P*	P*	P*	P*	P*	P*	P*	P*	P*	-	-	P*	P*	P*	P*	P*	-	P*	P*	P*	P*	P*	P*	-	P*	P*	P*	P*	P*	P*	P*	P*	-	-	32	11	134
JC (John) Russell	SH	SH	SH	-	-	-	-	SH	SH	SH	SH	SH	-	-	SH	SH	SH	-	SH	-	-	-	-	-	SH	SH	SH	SH	SH	-	-	SH	SH	SH	SH	SH	-	SH	23	3	9
SH (Stan) Saunders	-	-	-	-	-	-	-	-	-	-	-	-	-	-	-	-	-	-	-	-	-	-	-	-	-	-	-	-	>BR	BR	L	BR	BR	-	BR	BR	BR	BR	9	-	-
SA (Stuart) Smith	-	-	-	-	-	-	-	-	-	-	-	-	-	C	C	-	C	SH	-	-	SH	SH	SH	-	-	-	-	-	-	-	-	-	-	-	-	-	-	-	7	-	-
WE (Wilfrid) Squirrell	-	-	-	-	-	-	-	-	-	-	-	-	-	-	FH	-	FH	-	C	-	-	<FH	-	-	-	-	-	-	-	-	-	-	-	-	-	-	-	-	4	-	-
RJ Stephens	-	-	-	-	-	-	-	-	-	-	-	-	-	-	-	-	-	-	-	-	-	-	-	-	-	-	-	-	-	-	-	-	>BR	-	BR	-	-	<BR	3	1	3
Maj. KW (Kenneth) Symington	-	-	-	-	-	-	-	-	-	>C	C	-	C	-	-	-	<W	-	-	-	-	-	-	-	-	-	-	-	-	-	-	-	-	-	-	-	-	-	4	1	3
NT (Trevor) Thorneloe	-	-	-	-	-	-	-	-	-	-	-	-	-	BR	-	-	-	-	BR	-	-	-	-	L	-	-	-	-	-	-	-	-	-	-	-	-	-	-	3	-	-
W Waterfield	-	-	-	-	-	-	-	-	-	-	-	-	-	-	-	-	-	-	-	-	-	-	-	-	-	-	-	-	-	>FH	<W	-	-	-	-	-	-	-	2	-	-
FE (Frank) Wood	C	C	C	C	-	-	C	-	-	-	-	-	-	-	-	-	-	-	-	-	-	-	-	-	-	-	-	-	-	-	-	-	-	-	-	-	-	-	5	2	6
GH Wood	-	-	-	-	-	-	-	-	-	-	-	-	-	-	-	-	-	-	-	-	-	>W	W	W	-	W	-	-	-	-	-	-	-	-	-	-	-	-	4	1	3

1 GAME: LJ (Lewis) Adcock W(27), PC (Paul) Alexander =C(14), NJ (Norman) Bacon >C(21), FL (Frank) Cramphorn =C(15), TGP (Tom) Crick =BR(21), HCW (Harold) Eking =P(24), JWG (Jo) Hume S1 =C(24), HN (Henry) Knox <SH(14), WE (William) Lole =FH(14), D McArthur =BR(31), A Murray <FB(11), Lt. AL (Tony) Novis E2 GB+ C(20), G Phillpotts =FH(16), Dr. Strang =BR(10), DI (Daniel) Todman =BR(24), FB Traders =BR(31), W Turnbull =BR(18), W (Billy) Wallace GB1 <W(33), PE (Puggy) Ward >BR(24), Lt-Col. REH (Richard) Ward =W(36)

The key for how to read the stats is on the last page

CHAPTER 10

Life After Crumbie

1929/1930

A new decade was at hand. Some of the great names of the 1920s had gone, like Day and Russell, others, like Prentice, were approaching the end of their careers. Leicester were anxious to resume their pre-eminent position of the early 20s and new stars were beginning to adorn the firmament, perhaps the foremost of them being Bernard Gadney.

Gadney, born in Oxford and educated at Stowe where he captained the school XV, played for English Public Schools in 1929 before joining Richmond. But the London club had Fred Bunney as their scrum-half and, upon taking a teaching appointment in Brackley, Gadney joined Leicester and made his debut in November 1929, in a 4-3 win over Nuneaton.

He was one of a reserve pair of halves, the Scottish cap Greenlees suffering from a wrist injury and the first choice scrum-half, Langley Burton, also on the casualty list. Gadney, it was said, "started well but fell away in the second half... He should be a useful substitute when Burton, as so often happens, is unable to accompany the team away." It was a hasty judgement by the local rugby reporter, but not more hasty than that made by no less a personage than *The Times* rugby correspondent, who took it upon himself to inform others that Gadney was too big and too slow and would never make a first class footballer. It is hoped that both these gentlemen made due apology as Gadney became one of the brightest lights in the England teams of the 1930s.

As ever a touch of humour remained, even when the team was struggling for form: one (unnamed) Tiger took the field in an away game without removing his false teeth and dashed hastily back to the changing room to thrust them into his coat pocket. The match over, bath taken, equilibrium restored, the player looked for his teeth and found that, since they were not in his own pocket, he must have placed them in the wrong coat. Eric Thorneloe was forced to circulate the other 14 players the next day before the errant molars were restored to an embarrassed owner.

Another debutant in the second half of the season was DA Kendrew, an Uppingham School pupil destined to become Major-General Sir Douglas Kendrew, enjoy an outstanding service career and to become the Governor of Western Australia. He was only 21 when he was posted to the Leicestershire Regiment's South Wigston Regimental Headquarters but England had already capped him in their pack - it was Leicester's misfortune that his Army duties prevented him from playing with any great regularity and England's that he was available to win only 10 caps.

↑ The local newspaper wish the Tigers tourists well for their Lions tour.

There were more international honours for Greenlees and George Beamish with their respective countries and Doug Norman and the promising ex-Aylestone St James forward Stan Saunders were given trials. Gadney, now noted for his breaks from the scrum, was voted the most improved player of the season and three of the club's members, Prentice, Beamish and Kendrew, went to Australasia with the 1930 British Isles party, Prentice as captain after Wavell Wakefield had been unable to accept the invitation. Beamish played in all five internationals of the tour but Prentice took the unusual step of standing down for three of them, conceding his place to players in better form.

Leicester's season ended with three wins from three games on tour, and with 26 wins against 10 defeats, the future looked rosy. But off the field financial matters were causing the committee a headache. A meeting in June decided on a series of economies, to help with the running of the club and to reduce the debt on the stand. The band was to be discontinued at a saving of £90 p.a., grants to the referees' society and the Leicester Alliance were to be decreased, season ticket prices were increased, against a background of falling gate receipts and declining members' subscriptions.

Significantly too, there had been a suggestion during the season that the A team should be revived. It was perhaps the first sign of a definite change from the policies instituted by Crumbie, although the local clubs were still comparatively happy to supply Leicester at short notice. Bill Parker, from South Leicester, was one such. A back row player, he represented the Tigers off and on for four years and not infrequently turned up for a game, only to find a full complement of players already present. "We accepted being turned away," he said, "because it was an honour to be considered by the Tigers - although we didn't like missing a game." But the smooth organisation on away trips remained - typical may have been the

↓ Tigers' long trip to London to face Blackheath in December 1929 ended in a 6-13 defeat.

DOUGLAS KENDREW
Douglas 'Joe' Kendrew was, by a distance, Leicester's most-decorated player during a military career which included service in both the Second World War and the Korean War. Major-General Sir Douglas Kendrew was awarded three bars to his DSO, appointed CBE in 1944 and KCMG in 1963, and when he retired from the Army, became Governor of Western Australia for ten years. A formidable prop who would have won more than ten England caps but for his military commitments, he retained a lasting affection for Leicester and, when settling into retirement in Northamptonshire, said: "I don't want to live too far away from the family and I need to be within striking distance to watch the Tigers."

game at Blackheath when the team took the train to London, the bus to Blackheath and returned for dinner at Simpson's-in-The-Strand. Afterwards there was a ticket each for the Palladium, coffee and sandwiches on the train home and a free taxi from the station at Leicester to each player's home.

Major-General Kendrew, affectionately known at the club as 'Joe', also recalled with fondness his playing days with Leicester as a Second Lieutenant with the Royal Leicestershires: "There were many outstanding players but the real personality and the man that mattered was Eric Thorneloe. He stamped his mark on the side. He ran the club and nothing was too much trouble for him and he set a very high standard.

"We were welcomed when we turned up to play. We had our rugger clothes laid out in the changing rooms, the equipment provided was of the very highest standard. I retain a very vivid impression of the tremendous enjoyment which everyone seemed to get out of taking part in a game. It was always hard and vigorous yet there was a certain 'joie de vivre' feeling and not the desperate sense of earnestness which seems to possess players these days.

"Eric was a clever secretary. One day when I was playing AL Novis and CD Aarvold [both leading England players] were with me and were travelling down south and decided to watch the Tigers play. I introduced them both to Eric. He was delighted to see them and immediately pressed them to take part in the game! They both accepted and a placard was paraded around the ground for everyone to see, saying that Novis and Aarvold were playing instead of so-and-so and so-and-so. I felt a bit sorry for those who had stood down but the club and spectators enjoyed Eric's new recruits. He was a great secretary for collecting players. If he could include anyone who was in the Leicester area who had a reputation he would prevail upon him to wear the Tigers jersey.

"Another enjoyment was the way we played. We were a good side with few weak links. We played attractive rugger, giving the ball plenty of air and the leadership on the field was well-directed and well-planned. I cannot remember a dirty game or any unpleasant moments. We played for the love of the game and the great enjoyment we got out of it all and the quality of the team members who understood the basic skills. With men like George Beamish, Harry Greenlees and Doug Norman you knew that we could hold our own in any company."

1930/1931

Harry Greenlees, the former Rossall and West of Scotland player, took over the captaincy of the club in 1930/31, but it was not a very happy season for him since injury caused him to miss the second half. For the second year running Tigers featured a New Zealander in their backs; the previous season it had been Ian McNicol, a fly-half, now it was to be a powerful wing, GR White, a serviceman in the RAF.

The side was affected, however, by injury to Farndon, leading try scorer the previous season with 23, and Gadney, who underwent an operation for appendicitis. Kendrew, Prentice and Beamish were all late starters after returning from New Zealand where Prentice had contracted an irritating ear infection. But the presence of such luminaries at the club no doubt assisted the BBC in their decision to broadcast the match against Waterloo on 29 November 1930, the first radio commentary on a Leicester match which, happily, was won 21-5. Less happily, in the new year the club President, Sir Samuel Faire, died and the team honoured his memory by wearing black armbands in the game with Richmond on 24 January. Ralph Buckingham was having another injury-plagued season and the club was forced to sound a rallying call to their waning support.

Ralph Buckingham (with the ball but without the stripes) takes on Nuneaton 26.9.1931.

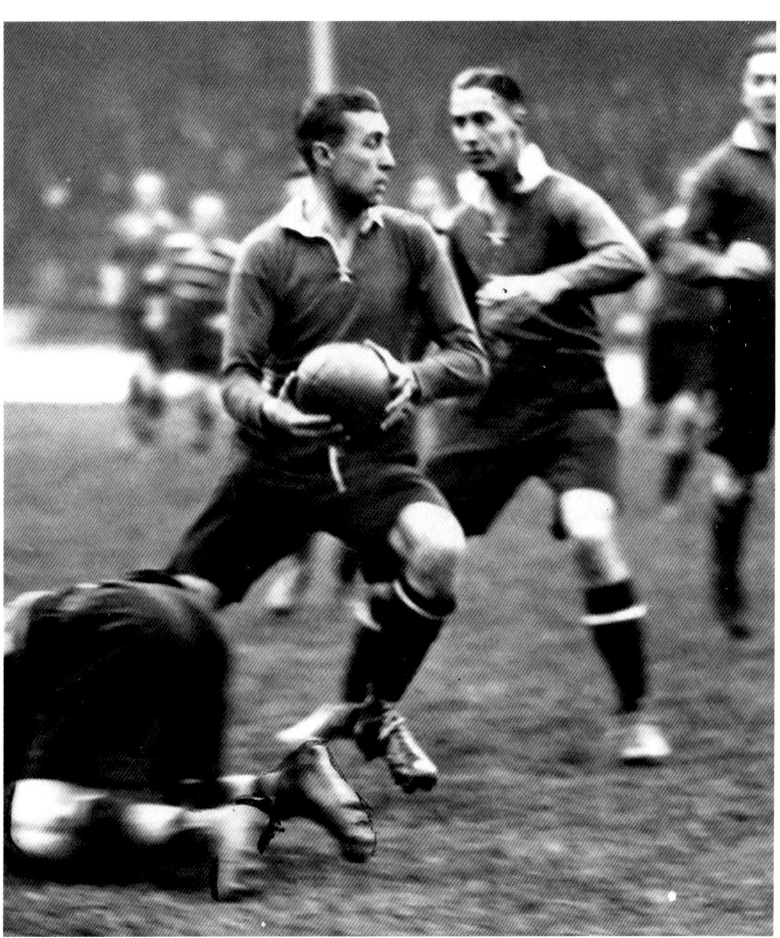

Despite these upsets the record was a good one, 23 wins against 12 defeats and, in an attempt to raise extra money, Prentice brought an English Touring XV to Welford Road in April 1931, to play Leicester. It was not a very good game but the club were better off by £286 and it was as good a way as any for Prentice to retire from the game, having recorded 575 points for Tigers - not bad for a man who began life as a soccer player before picking up rugby during service with the ANZACs during the war, when he was wounded sufficiently badly for doubts to be cast on his ability to play again. His final match was that against Blackheath when he took over the captaincy from Doug Norman (himself a replacement for Greenlees) and, under the refereeing eye of Wavell Wakefield, kicked three conversions and a penalty.

1931/1932

Greenlees led the side again in 1931/32 and the first five games were won without conceding a point. But the popular Scotsman could not escape the injury hoodoo which followed him around and he was out of action again in October, Leicester calling on the Nuneaton fly-half Reginald Odbert who had been capped by Ireland against France three years earlier. Another Irishman to come into the side on a more permanent basis was PB Coote, inevitably known as 'Paddy,' an RAF serviceman who was to prove himself a superb centre before his career was cruelly cut short by injury.

Money problems were still evident, judging by the club's appeal in August to the public trying to raise £5,000 to reduce debts. An application to run greyhounds at the ground had been refused that year but gates were still poor and members' subscriptions had gone down by £7,600 over the last 10 years. Since 1914, £40,000 had been spent on the ground but the strength of support had changed radically. Eric Thorneloe complained that "no other club caters for its supporters in the way of members' subscriptions and season tickets at such a cheap rate as is offered by the Leicester club." Members were permitted to take guests into the Crumbie Stand for the normal admission charge, a facility extended to the reserved section of the Members Stand. It should be remembered, though, that this was a time of abnormal recession and Leicestrians, like any other, were short of cash. The most notable contribution to the appeal was the £250 presented by the Leicestershire Rugby Union.

The club began to sell team sheets at one penny each and, for the first time, pondered the possibility of a supporters' club. To help identification backs, as well as forwards, were lettered. But whatever the trials being endured by the treasurer, William Newby 'Billy' Bradshaw, there is no doubting that everything else this season paled beside the achievement of the Leicestershire and East Midlands XV which became the only side to beat Bennie Osler's touring South African party.

It was one of the greatest games to have been played at Welford Road and seven Leicester players took part, one of them, George Beamish, captaining the combined side. It was possibly Beamish's finest hour, even though the big lock had already collected 18 of his 25 Irish caps and was well known as not only a rumbustious forward but a talented captain.

↑ Scotland international Harry Greenlees skippered the Tigers in his final season.

The Springboks arrived in Leicester on the morning of the match, 14 November 1931, and in the afternoon cars stretched all the way up Welford Road and spilled into the sidestreets as 25,000 people made their way to the ground. It was, said the *Leicester Mercury's* Cyrus, "one of those games we dream about but very seldom see."

The combined side was: Bobby Barr (Leicester); Jeff Hardwicke (Leicester), Ralph Buckingham (Leicester), Charlie Brumwell (Bedford), Len Ashwell (Bedford); Charlie Slow (Northampton), Bernard Gadney (Leicester); Henry Greenwood (Leicester), Doug Norman (Leicester), Ray Longland (Northampton), Thomas Harris (Northampton), Anthony Roncoroni (West Herts), William Weston (Northampton), George Beamish (Leicester, captain), Eric Coley (Northampton).

Osler rested himself for the game, which must have helped the counties' cause since so much of the Springboks' play revolved around his kicking, and the tourists fielded: Jackie Tindall; Floors Venter, JC van der Westhuizen, Geoff Gray, Morris Zimerman; MG 'Tiny' Francis, Danie Craven; Fanie Louw, Phil Mostert, Schalk du Toit, Flip Nel, Lucas Strachan, Nic Bierman, Jack Dold, George Daneel.

Barr, brave and solid as a rock, had now established himself as Leicester's last line of defence while Hardwicke had impressed as a clever wing since joining from Stoneygate two years before. Buckingham's quality was well known and Gadney was on the threshold of a brilliant international career. Beamish and Norman were established players while Henry Greenwood had earned his position with his hard, no-nonsense play.

In the game itself the counties went into an early lead thanks to a dropped goal by Charles Slow, and they never lost it. To many people this

↓ Morris Zimerman (4th from left) poses with his Springbok teammates at the Honourable Artillery Company before their game against London.

has always remained Slow's match and after the Springbok wing Zimerman had crossed for the first of his four tries, the Northampton fly-half went through for a try which was converted. Louw left the field for treatment to a knee injury, returning just before half-time, but by then the counties led 19-6.

A dribble and pick-up by Buckingham had laid on a second try for Slow, Weston converting and though Zimerman scored again, a punt ahead by Slow enabled Hardwicke to cross for the counties' third try, to which Weston again added the goal points. Zimerman opened the second half scoring but then Weston broke away and sent Beamish off on a run to the line for a try greeted with tremendous enthusiasm and converted by the faithful Weston.

Down by 24-9 the Springboks responded but Barr survived all the pressure placed on him. Nevertheless the tourists scored through Gray, following a dribble, and then Francis dropped a goal to narrow the gap to eight points. Gray made the break for Zimerman's fourth try and a conversion by Francis made it 24-21. It is not difficult to imagine how tense a moment it must have been, for the players and the crowd, willing their team on. The counties shook off their lethargy, with Buckingham in exceptional form, and Weston kicked the only penalty of the game. Then Slow dribbled through and Buckingham crossed in the corner to put his side out of reach, the counties winning 30-21.

Beamish had to make a speech before the crowd dispersed and four days later the counties

🡅 The victorious skipper, Doug Norman, with the Springbok head.

🡇 Programme from the famous Leicestershire and East Midlands victory over the touring South Africans in 1931.

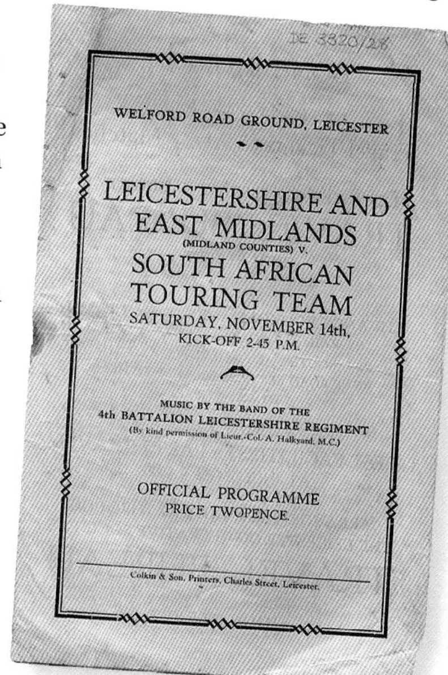

WELFORD ROAD GROUND, LEICESTER

LEICESTERSHIRE AND EAST MIDLANDS
(MIDLAND COUNTIES) V.
SOUTH AFRICAN TOURING TEAM

SATURDAY, NOVEMBER 14th, KICK-OFF 2-45 P.M.

MUSIC BY THE BAND OF THE 4th BATTALION LEICESTERSHIRE REGIMENT
(By kind permission of Lieut.-Col. A. Halkyard, M.C.)

OFFICIAL PROGRAMME
PRICE TWOPENCE.

Colkin & Son, Printers, Charles Street, Leicester.

received due tribute from the South Africans in the shape of the Springbok head, a trophy awarded to the first team to beat South Africa on a tour. For the Tigers' players a more tangible reward came in the form of trials for Barr, Gadney, Greenwood and Norman and subsequently caps for all of them save Greenwood. The 30 points scored by the counties was a record for a British team against any major touring side.

Although Slow - a late addition to the original XV after Greenlees and Coote dropped out because of injury - was the man of the match, the plan of the match was Beamish's. He had played for the Combined Services against the Springboks the week before (and was to captain Ireland against them) and Bernard Gadney recalled vividly the build-up to the game: "I had watched the Springboks play against London and I thought they were unbeatable. But Beamish said our forwards would have to shake them up, and when the ball came out it never got beyond the centre, but was always played back inside.

"And our forwards were colossal. Mind you, Osler didn't play in this game and the Springboks may have been a little more open than usual. Before the game Beamish said to me: 'Understand one thing - no loose play, because if there is, they'll score.' I remember, quite early in the game I threw out a bad pass which they seized on and almost got away and I thought George was going to kick me off the field!

"The Springboks were superb coverers and we thought we wouldn't have much chance if we tried to play it out to the wings. So we kept the ball coming back to the pack and they kept going extraordinarily well all through the game, men like Ray Longland, Bill Weston, they were superb."

Buckingham, too, remembered his pre-match instructions: "Beamish said to Brumwell and me: 'I don't mind if they have the ball but I want you two centres to hit them so hard they won't know what's going on.' As soon as they got the ball, we did just that. I've never known anything like the atmosphere of that match. It was so close and after I had scored the last try I could hardly get off the ground I was so tired."

On the strength of the tumultuous game played by the East Midlands, Bobby Barr and Doug Norman won their first caps for England, in the side beaten 12-5 by Wales at Swansea. They played sufficiently well to go through to the next game, against the Springboks, which the tourists won 7-0 and Barr, though he played well in most respects, had the misfortune to be concerned in both the Springbok scores. In fielding a kick ahead on his own line the ball went loose and he slipped in turning to touch down, the referee awarding a try to Ferdie Bergh. And it was from a clearance kick of his that Brand collected near touch in front of the West Stand and fired over a huge dropped goal which made the match safe.

Barr won a third cap that season, against Ireland, but Norman was dropped following the Springbok game. It was, nevertheless, a major achievement for the hooker. Having been capped at schoolboy level as a full-back before the First World War, he had served in Mesopotamia and made his debut for Leicester in 1919. His first

↑ Line-out action from the Tigers' 13-10 victory over Northampton 24.10.1931.

trial came in 1921 but he had to wait until he was 34 for his cap and few begrudged him the honour.

On the domestic front Leicester's unbeaten home record survived until the last day of October when Cambridge University won 26-6 and Gadney, unlucky with injuries this season, ignored offers to play rugby league from the two Hull clubs. Leicester encountered a particularly butter-fingered referee in the January game with Rosslyn Park, since twice the official dropped his whistle in the mud and, despite all the assistance of Norman Coates from touch, it was so clogged up that he had to finish the game by waving his hands wildly to indicate no-side. The giant George Beamish played in the final game against Blackheath before taking up an RAF posting in the Middle East.

1932/1933

Doug Norman captained the club in his twelfth season but was unlucky enough to be injured in the second game, against Old Blues. Ernie Coleman was recalled to the colours in his absence and Kendrew tried his hand at hooking before Norman resumed, in a 6-3 win over Gloucester. The permutations in the front row were particularly interesting in view of an International Board circular then going the rounds, which urged clubs to "return to honest scrummaging" and cut out specialisation in the forwards. In other words, back to the old, first up, first down days of before the war.

The spirit of the game as it was then may have been captured by a booklet which the Leicestershire Schools Union had compiled, with articles by Norman, Buckingham, Barr and Greenlees, called *Hints on Rugger for Schools and Clubs.* Among the technicalities dealt with appeared this passage: "The essence of rugby football is that it is played by those who believe that a game should be played for the love of the game itself, and not for what they can make out of it; that is, by true amateurs. As soon as money matters become involved in a game, there is always a loophole for all sorts of abuses to creep in. Players commence to consider their own immediate value, and very soon the aim of true sportsmanship is apt to become lost.

"Never descend to such tricks as holding a player in a tackle long after he has parted with the ball, or tackling a player deliberately after he has kicked a ball to prevent him from following up, knowing that the referee will be following the flight of the ball. These actions and the practice of stealing up off-side behind the referee's back are tricks which no gentleman would consider for a moment. In other words, always play the game in such a spirit that at any time afterwards you will never be able to recall any incident of which you might be ashamed. There is much more abiding value in an honourable defeat than in a victory gained by shady means."

Such tenets are worth remembering today but Leicester in 1932 had other problems, besides upholding the traditions of the game. The financial position was still shaky, despite an increase of £900 in gate receipts and season tickets and another economy was introduced when after-match tea was switched from the nearby Granby Halls to the upstairs room of the clubhouse. It seems curious that the committee had not thought of it before! Gallant as ever, the committee were considering the needs of their lady guests, but estimates for a new ladies' lavatory were too high and the matter was deferred.

New talent was still becoming available and in October 1932, Leicester played an all-Irish centre pairing against Coventry, Paddy Coote and Morgan Crowe, who helped in a 16-4 win. Dr Crowe had come to work at Leicester's Royal Infirmary, following the footsteps of medical men like Kilgour Wiener, John Buchanan, Henry Knox and Joseph Moore, all of whom had helped Leicester since the war. A Dubliner, he was to prove one of the most popular players at Welford Road during his three-year stay, famed for his practical jokes as well as his abstention from tobacco and alcohol.

When he joined Leicester he had already been capped 10 times by Ireland and he was joined, not quite so regularly, in the side by another cap, SSC Meikle, from Waterloo. Stephen Meikle won his only England cap at fly-half in 1929 but he turned in some exceptional performances for Leicester on the wing.

The 1932/33 season, at club level, held great promise early on when Leicester went 12 games without defeat. Number 13 proved their undoing when they lost at Cambridge University, a day when the Leicester scrum packed in the 3-4-1 formation and there were local complains that, if Albert Freethy, the referee, had applied the advantage law correctly Leicester would have won. 'Twas ever thus. Their ground record fell to Old Merchant Taylors in the next game and, with players called away for trials and Gadney unavailable through injury for most of the first half of the season, form slumped. Representative honours continued to come the club's way, however, among them an invitation to play for England to the hard-working lock, George Vallance, who had joined Leicester from Nottingham in 1930.

Vallance, Kendrew, Cyril Lewis and Gadney had all been picked for trials, although Gadney could not play and when everyone was expecting Kendrew to be picked against Wales, he was omitted and

↑ Doug Norman and Ralph Buckingham, here in action against Coventry, passed on their expertise to the Leicestershire Schools Union.

Vallance was called up. Unfortunately for him influenza put him out of action for a time and, though he played in a game for Richmond so that the selectors could see whether he was fit, Vallance asked them not to consider him because he felt he could not give 100 per cent. He never had another chance of representing his country, Tony Roncoroni of Richmond coming in and holding his place all season.

When England played Ireland, though, Gadney was in for his first cap, and Kendrew was restored to the front row. With George Beamish on the Irish side, Leicester were well represented and Gadney scored a try, Kendrew kicked a conversion and England won 17-6. For their game with Scotland, Ireland called up Crowe and gave Coote his first cap. And in March, there was another significant recruit to the club in the form of Charles Slow, whom so many at Welford Road remembered fondly. He had lost his place in Northampton's side, missing the 21-3 defeat they gave Leicester, and switched allegiance, making his debut in a 31-12 win over London Welsh.

1933/1934

During this season Slow's partnership with Gadney really began to blossom though not at Swansea, since Slow missed the Cardiff connecting train. But Leicester lost Coote in much unhappier circumstances: in that same game at St Helen's, Coote, a fearless tackler, collided with one of the Welsh three-quarters, who had to leave the field. Coote carried on but collapsed in the train on the way home and was rushed to the RAF hospital at Uxbridge with a severely damaged neck. He was on the dangerously ill list for a long time and, though he finally recovered, he never played rugby again.

For the 1933 game against the Barbarians, GWC Meikle joined his brother Stephen in Leicester's line up and became only the second Tigers player to score three tries against the Baa-baas. Usually a centre, Graham Meikle was on the wing for his first appearance in Leicester colours and he had inside him the fine Bath centre, Ron Gerrard, whom the selectors wanted to see prove his fitness before picking him for England.

LEICESTERSHIRE RUGBY UNION.

SEVEN-A-SIDE COMPETITION

(By kind permission of the Rugby Football Union)

LEICESTER FOOTBALL CLUB GROUND WELFORD ROAD

(By kind permission of the Committee)

SATURDAY, APRIL 28th, 1934

Commencing at 2-30 p.m.

IN AID OF THE LEICESTER ROYAL INFIRMARY

PROGRAMME

PRICE ONE PENNY

After helping Leicester to a 21-10 win, the next day Graham Meikle was playing for Waterloo against Tigers, who included in their ranks five of the beaten Barbarian XV. It may have been nice for the spectators but there can be little doubt that it must have rankled with those players whom the club dropped and there is little question that Tigers' somewhat cavalier treatment of the local men did them little good in the long term.

At least it was Gadney, a Leicester regular, who really dominated the headlines this season. He and Kendrew were both picked against Wales, with Kendrew expected to get the captaincy, but when he pulled out it was Gadney who was given the leadership of his country, and his half-back partner Slow was named a reserve for the match. It was a singular honour for the club, for though Jenny Greenwood and Wavell Wakefield had captained England while playing for Leicester, Gadney was the first home-produced player to captain his country.

His first outing as skipper - only his fifth cap - was crowned with success, for Wales were beaten (though it was suggested that a representative Leicester XV could have beaten Wales that day). He then led England to the Triple Crown, being joined in the Calcutta Cup-winning XV by Kendrew and Slow. For the fly-half it was his only England cap but for Leicester it was the second time they had provided England's halves, Wood and Taylor having done the job once before the war. In addition to captaining England successfully, Gadney captained the East Midlands - again with Slow as his partner - to the County Championship.

The 1933/34 season ended with a successful tour of the West Country, on which they were joined by the Northern back row forward, Jack 'Mac' Hodgson, who had toured with the 1930 Lions and was capped by England in 1932 and 1934. It was on this tour, under the guidance of Hodgson (Northern's youngest captain at the age of 19), that Leicester changed their scrum formation very successfully from 3-2-3 to 3-4-1. The eight forwards had been restored shortly after Crumbie's death but this latest change, despite earlier experimentation, had been picked up from Guy's Hospital and Leicester found that their scrummaging greatly improved. The club had been invited to play in the Middlesex Sevens but they decided to stay loyal to the Leicestershire event.

↓ Tigers, with letters on their backs, take on Blackheath at the Rectory Field 9.12.1933.

← LEICESTER FOOTBALL CLUB 1929/30
Back: Coates (Touch Judge), Hall, Wiener, Manson, C.Williams, Cotton, Gadney, Bradshaw (Hon.Tres), Thorneloe (Hon.Sec).
Middle: Greenwood, Beamish, Greenlees, Prentice (capt), Norman, Buckingham, Coleman.
Front: Saunders, Farndon, Kendrew, Clarke, Flewitt.

← LEICESTER FOOTBALL CLUB 1930/31
Back: Coates (Touch Judge), Gadney, Manson, Constantine, Greenwood, P.Clarke, Bolus, Smith, Barlow, Bradshaw (Hon.Tres), Thorneloe (Hon.Sec).
Middle: Wiener, Coleman, Norman, Greenlees (capt), Prentice, Buckingham, Beamish.
Front: Llewelyn, Morris, Barr, Vallance, McNichol, Hardwicke, Saunders.

← LEICESTER FOOTBALL CLUB 1932/33
Back: Bradshaw (Hon.Tres), Saunders, Morris, Oscroft, Pearse, Lewis, Wormleighton, Bates, Thorneloe (Hon.Sec).
Middle: Hughes, Gadney, Buckingham, D.Norman (capt), Beamish, Coote, H.Edmiston.
Front: Jackson, Harris, Berry, Hardwicke, Slow, Greaves.
Inset: Crowe, Vallance.

← LEICESTER FOOTBALL CLUB 1933/34
Back: Bradshaw (Hon.Tres), Llewelyn, Greaves, Parker, Adams, Jackson, G.Harris, Thorneloe (Hon.Sec).
Middle: Slow, Berry, Gadney, Buckingham (capt), Crowe, Edmiston, Hughes.
Front: Wormleighton, Loxton, Robinson, Hewitt.

1929/30

Home Ground: Welford Road
Captain: Doug Prentice

OVERALL RECORD:					T	C	PG	DG	MK	PTS
PLD	W	D	L	Tigers scored:	119	42	14	7	0	511
39	26	3	10	Opponents scored:	71	29	13	3	0	322

GM	DATE		VEN	OPPONENTS	RESULT	TRIES	KICKS	ATT
CLUB MATCHES								
1	Sep	**7**	**H**	**Bath**	W 19-6	Llewellyn(2), Greenwood, Hall	Prentice 2c/p	4000
2		**14**	**H**	**Plymouth Albion**	W 12-6	Greenlees, Flewitt	Greenlees d, Prentice c	10000
3		**21**	**H**	**Old Blues**	W 28-5	Babington(2), Farndon(2), Prentice, Burton, Greenlees	Prentice p, Norman 2c	5000
4		**28**	**H**	**Nuneaton**	W 24-8	Farndon(2), Babington, Burton, Flewitt	Prentice 3c/p	5000
5	Oct	**5**	**H**	**Coventry**	L 6-11	-	Prentice 2p	5000
6		12	a	Gloucester	L 11-20	Burton, Farndon	Prentice c/p	3000
7		**19**	**H**	**Newport**	W 12-6	Babington	Prentice c/p, Llewellyn d	8000
8		**26**	**H**	**Northampton**	W 10-3	Beamish(2)	Prentice 2c	7000
9	Nov	**2**	**H**	**Cambridge University**	D 14-14	Farndon(2), Babington, Greenlees	Prentice c	7000
10		9	a	Nuneaton	W 4-3	-	Llewelyn d	-
11		16	a	Swansea	L 8-12	Beamish(2)	Prentice c	5000
12		23	a	Moseley	W 20-3	Flewitt(2), Llewellyn, Coleman	Llewellyn d, Prentice 2c	-
13		**30**	**H**	**Oxford University**	W 6-3	Prentice, G.Williams	-	10000
14	Dec	7	a	Harlequins	D 8-8	Farndon, Gadney	Prentice c	-
15		14	a	Blackheath	L 6-13	Prentice	Prentice p	4000
16		**21**	**H**	**Bristol**	W 9-5	Flewitt, Pott	Prentice p	5000
17		**26th**	**H**	**Barbarians**	L 14-21	Llewellyn, Pott, C.Williams	Prentice c/p	20000
18		**27f**	**H**	**Waterloo**	W 21-13	Beamish(2), Pott	Prentice c/2p, Llewellyn d	6000
19		**28**	**H**	**Birkenhead Park**	W 16-8	Flewitt(2), Prentice, Lashmore	Prentice 2c	5000
20	Jan	1w	a	Manchester	W 9-8	J.Ewin(3)	-	-
21		**4**	**H**	**Swansea**	L 6-11	Flewitt	Wood p	6000
22		**11**	**H**	**Rosslyn Park**	W 17-11	Llewellyn(3), Flewitt, Gadney	Prentice c	5000
23		**18**	**H**	**London Welsh**	L 6-9	Flewitt	Prentice p	6000
24		**25**	**H**	**Richmond**	L 5-6	Flewitt	Norman c	4000
25		**30th**	**H**	**Royal Air Force**	W 23-11	Farndon(3), Flewitt(3), Beamish	Beamish c	-
26	Feb	**1**	**H**	**London Scottish**	W 10-6	Norman, Flewitt	Norman 2c	4000
27		8	a	Newport	L 5-22	C.Williams	Norman c	4000
28		**15**	**H**	**Bridgwater & Albion**	W 17-3	Farndon(2), Drummond, Flewitt, Gadney	Norman c	5000
29		22	a	Northampton	W 18-3	Beaty-Pownall, Farndon, Flewitt, Gadney	Prentice 3c	6000
30	Mar	**1**	**H**	**Harlequins**	L 13-15	Gadney(2), Farndon	Prentice 2c	8000
31		**8**	**H**	**Bedford**	W 20-3	Coleman, Gadney, Kendrew, C.Williams	Manson d, Norman 2c	6000
32		**15**	**H**	**Percy Park**	W 31-3	Farndon(3), Buckingham(2), Clarke, Cotton, Gadney, Wiener	Coleman c, Norman c	4000
33		22	a	Coventry	W 11-6	Prentice, Buckingham, Carryer	Prentice c	6000
34		**29**	**H**	**Gloucester**	W 16-5	Flewitt, Gadney, Greenlees, Saunders	Cotton d	7000
35	Apr	5	a	Birkenhead Park	D 8-8	Buckingham, Greenlees	Norman c	5000
36		**12**	**H**	**Blackheath**	W 22-9	Farndon(2), Flewitt, Gadney, Hall, Saunders	Greenlees c, Norman c	6000
37		19	a	Bristol	W 9-3	Buckingham, Farndon, Flewitt	-	7000
38		21m	a	Plymouth Albion	W 11-9	Farndon, Flewitt, Greenwood	Thorneloe c	5000
39		22tu	a	Bath	W 6-3	Farndon, Kerby	-	-

INDIVIDUAL APPEARANCES 1929/30

Name / Game #	1	2	3	4	5	6	7	8	9	10	11	12	13	14	15	16	17	18	19	20	21	22	23	24	25	26	27	28	29	30	31	32	33	34	35	36	37	38	39	Apps	T	Pts
JL (John) Anstee	-	-	-	-	-	-	-	-	-	-	-	-	-	-	-	-	-	-	-	-	-	-	-	-	-	>BR	-	-	-	-	-	-	-	-	<H	-	-	-	-	2	-	-
T Babington	-	>C	C	C	C	-	C	-	C	-	C	C	C	C	C	C	-	-	-	-	-	-	C	FH	-	FH	<C	-	-	-	-	-	-	-	-	-	-	-	-	16	5	15
GR (George) Beamish I14 GB+	-	L	L	P	-	P	P	P	-	P	P	BR	P	P	-	-	P	P	P	-	-	-	-	-	H	-	-	-	-	P	-	-	-	P	-	-	-	-	-	17	7	23
Lt. CC (Christopher) Beaty-Pownall	-	-	-	-	-	-	-	-	-	-	-	-	-	-	-	-	-	-	-	>W	-	-	-	-	C	C	-	-	C	-	-	-	-	-	-	C	-	-	-	5	1	3
TH (Harry) Briers	-	-	-	-	-	-	L	-	<BR	-	-	-	-	-	-	-	-	-	-	-	-	-	-	-	-	-	-	-	-	-	-	-	-	-	-	-	-	-	-	2	-	-
RA (Ralph) Buckingham E1	C	C	C	C	FH	C	-	C	-	-	-	-	C	-	-	-	C	-	-	-	-	-	-	-	-	-	-	-	-	-	-	FH	C	C	C	C	C	C	C	17	5	15
LW (Langley) Burton	SH	SH	SH	SH	SH	SH	SH	SH	SH	-	-	-	-	-	-	-	-	-	-	-	-	-	-	-	-	-	-	-	-	-	C	-	-	-	-	-	-	-	-	10	3	9
R (Rupert) Carryer	-	-	-	-	-	-	-	-	-	-	-	-	-	-	-	-	-	-	-	-	-	-	-	-	-	-	-	-	-	-	-	>C	C	-	-	-	-	-	FB	3	1	3
PS (Percy) Clarke	-	-	-	-	-	-	-	-	-	-	-	-	-	-	-	-	-	-	-	-	-	-	-	>BR	BR	BR	BR	BR	BR	BR	BR	BR	-	BR	BR	BR	BR	L	L	15	1	3
EG (Ernie) Coleman	P	P	P	BR	BR	BR	BR	BR	L	BR	BR	P	BR	BR	L	P	BR	BR	L	L	P	L	BR	L	BR	L	L	L	L	BR	L	L	BR	BR	L	L	L	P	P	39	2	8
RD (Ralph) Cotton	-	-	-	-	-	-	-	-	-	>C	-	-	-	C	-	-	-	-	C	C	-	W	-	-	-	-	-	C	C	C	-	C	-	C	<C	-	-	-	-	11	1	7
FC (Fred) Drummond	-	-	-	-	-	-	-	-	-	-	-	-	-	-	-	-	-	-	-	-	>BR	-	BR	BR	-	-	BR	BR	-	-	-	-	-	-	-	-	-	-	-	5	1	3
JHF (Harry) Edmiston	BR	BR	-	-	-	-	-	-	-	-	-	-	-	-	-	-	-	-	-	-	-	-	-	-	-	-	-	-	-	-	-	-	-	-	-	-	-	-	-	2	-	-
JJM (John) Ewin	-	-	-	-	-	-	-	-	-	-	-	-	-	-	-	-	-	-	-	>W	-	-	-	-	-	-	-	-	-	-	<W	-	-	-	-	-	-	-	-	2	3	9
WE (Ewart) Farndon	W	W	W	W	W	W	-	-	W	W	W	W	W	W	W	W	W	W	W	-	W	-	W	W	W	W	W	W	W	W	W	W	W	W	-	W	W	W	C	34	23	69
ECA (Ted) Flewitt	-	W	W	W	W	W	W	W	C	C	W	W	W	W	W	W	W	W	W	-	W	W	W	W	W	W	W	W	W	W	-	-	W	W	W	W	C	C	W	35	21	63
BC (Bernard) Gadney E+	-	-	-	-	-	-	-	-	-	>SH	SH	SH	SH	SH	SH	SH	SH	-	SH	C	SH	SH	C	SH	-	SH	SH	SH	SH	SH	SH	SH	SH	SH	SH	SH	SH	SH	SH	28	10	30
HD (Harry) Greenlees S6	FH*	FH	FH	FH	-	-	FH	FH	FH	-	FH	-	-	-	-	-	-	-	-	-	-	FH	-	-	-	-	-	-	-	C	FH*	-	FH	FH	FH*	FH*	FH*	FH*	FH*	18	5	21
AH (Henry) Greenwood	L	BR	BR	BR	L	BR	BR	BR	BR	-	-	H	L	BR	BR	L	L	BR	BR	-	L	BR	BR	L	-	L	L	BR	BR	BR	BR	L	BR	-	-	L	L	L	L	33	2	6
AC Hall	L	L	L	L	P	L	-	L	L	L	L	P	-	L	BR	BR	-	L	-	L	-	BR	-	-	-	-	-	-	-	-	-	BR	-	-	BR	BR	BR	BR	BR	23	2	6
JT (Jeff) Hardwicke	-	-	-	-	-	-	>W	-	W	W	-	-	-	-	-	-	-	-	-	-	-	-	-	-	-	-	-	-	-	-	-	W	-	-	W	-	-	-	-	5	-	-
RB Harvey	-	-	-	-	-	-	-	-	-	-	-	-	-	-	-	-	-	-	-	-	>BR	-	<P	-	-	-	-	-	-	-	-	-	-	-	-	-	-	-	-	2	-	-
DA (Joe) Kendrew E2	-	-	-	-	-	-	-	-	-	-	-	-	-	-	-	-	-	-	-	-	-	-	-	-	-	-	-	>P	-	-	H	-	P	L	-	-	-	-	-	4	1	3
Sgt. WIG (William) Kerby	-	-	-	-	-	-	-	-	-	-	-	-	-	-	-	-	-	-	-	-	-	-	-	-	-	-	-	-	-	-	-	-	-	-	-	-	-	>BR	BR	2	1	3
GF (George) Lashmore	-	-	-	-	-	-	-	-	-	-	-	-	-	-	-	-	-	-	BR	<BR	-	-	-	-	-	-	-	-	-	-	-	-	-	-	-	-	-	-	-	2	1	3
JG (John) Llewelyn	C	-	-	-	-	-	C	C	-	FH	C	FH	FH	FH	FH	FH	FH	FH	FH	-	-	C	-	-	-	-	-	-	-	-	-	-	-	-	-	-	-	-	-	14	7	37
CS (Charlie) Manson	FB	FB	-	FB	FB	FB	FB	FB	FB	FB	FB	FB	FB	FB	FB	FB	FB	FB	-	-	FB	FB	FB	FB	FB	FB	FB	FB	FB	FB	FB	FB	FB	FB	FB	FB	FB	FB	-	35	-	4
DJ (Doug) Norman E+	H	H	H	H	H	H	H	H	H	H	H	BR	H	H	H	-	H	H	H	P	-	H	H	P	P	P	P	H	H	H	P	P	H	H	P	P	P	P	P	37	1	27
DS (Donald) Oscroft	-	-	-	-	-	-	-	-	-	-	-	-	-	-	-	-	-	>C	-	-	-	-	-	C	-	-	-	-	-	-	-	-	-	-	-	-	-	-	-	2	-	-
JRH (Johnny) Pott	-	-	-	-	-	>FH	-	W	-	-	-	C	-	-	C	C	C	C	C	FH	-	C	-	-	-	-	-	-	FH	FH	-	-	-	-	-	-	-	-	-	12	3	9
FD (Doug) Prentice E3 GB+	P	P*	P*	P*	P*	P*	P*	P*	P*	P*	P*	L*	P*	P*	P*	P*	P*	P*	P*	-	-	P*	P*	-	-	-	-	P*	P*	P*	-	-	P*	P*	-	-	-	-	-	26	5	106
JC (John) Russell	-	-	-	-	-	-	-	-	-	-	-	-	-	-	-	-	-	SH	-	SH	-	-	SH	-	<SH	-	-	-	-	-	-	-	-	-	-	-	-	-	-	4	-	-
SH (Stan) Saunders	BR	BR	BR	L	L	L	L	L	P	L	L	BR	L	-	P	H	L	-	BR	H	H	P	L	H	P	H	H	-	P	L	L	P	L	BR	L	P	P	H	H	36	2	6
GL (Len) Shipton	-	-	-	-	-	-	-	-	-	-	-	-	-	-	-	-	-	-	-	FB	-	-	-	-	-	-	FH	<FH	-	-	-	-	-	-	-	-	-	-	-	3	-	-
WS (William) Thompson	-	-	-	-	-	-	-	-	-	-	-	-	-	-	-	-	-	-	FB	-	-	-	-	C	-	-	C	-	-	-	-	-	-	-	-	-	-	-	-	3	-	-
NT (Trevor) Thorneloe	-	-	-	-	-	-	-	-	-	-	-	-	-	-	-	BR	-	-	-	-	L	-	-	-	L	-	-	-	-	-	-	-	-	-	-	-	-	<BR	-	4	-	2
JW Townsend	>BR	-	-	-	BR	-	-	-	-	-	-	-	-	-	-	-	-	-	-	-	<BR	-	-	-	-	-	-	-	-	-	-	-	-	-	-	-	-	-	-	3	-	-
HP (Henry) Tyler	-	-	-	-	-	-	-	-	-	-	-	-	-	-	-	-	-	-	-	-	-	-	-	-	C	<C	-	-	-	-	-	-	-	-	-	-	-	-	-	2	-	-
GR White	-	-	-	-	-	-	-	-	-	-	-	-	-	-	-	-	-	-	-	-	-	-	-	-	-	-	-	-	-	-	-	-	-	-	-	-	>W	W	W	3	-	-
Dr. RAK (Kilgour) Wiener	-	-	-	-	-	>BR	BR	BR	BR	BR	BR	L	BR	L	L	L	BR	L	L	P	P	L	L	P	L	P	P	L	L	L	P	H	L	L	P	H	H	-	-	32	1	3
CH Williams	-	-	>BR	BR	BR	-	-	-	-	-	-	-	-	-	-	BR	BR	-	-	BR	-	BR	-	BR	BR	BR	BR	-	BR	-	BR	BR	BR	-	BR	BR	BR	-	-	18	3	9
GES (George) Williams	-	-	-	-	-	-	-	-	-	>BR	BR	-	BR	BR	BR	-	-	-	-	-	-	-	-	-	-	-	-	-	-	-	-	-	-	-	-	-	-	-	-	5	1	3
FE (Frank) Wood	-	-	-	-	C	C	-	-	-	-	-	-	-	-	-	-	-	-	-	-	<C	-	-	-	-	-	-	-	-	-	-	-	-	-	-	-	-	-	-	3	-	3

1 GAME: JR (Dick) Auty E+ >FH(25), RJ (Bobby) Barr E+ FB(3), GA (George) Cornell =C(21), PE (Pop) Dunkley E+ BR(18), BHL (Bert) Ewin =C(31), JD Jenkins =FH(23), GT Kemp =BR(39), I (Ian) McNichol >FH(21), SA (Stuart) Smith C(28), RW (Richard) Toach =W(1), GPC (George) Vallance >BR(20)

The key for how to read the stats is on the last page

19	30/31	Home Ground: Welford Road	OVERALL RECORD:					T	C	PG	DG	MK	PTS
		Captain: Harry Greenlees	PLD	W	D	L	Tigers scored:	118	45	10	9	0	510
			39	23	4	12	Opponents scored:	72	36	6	3	0	318

GM	DATE		VEN	OPPONENTS	RESULT	TRIES	KICKS	ATT
CLUB MATCHES								
1	Sep	**6**	**H**	**Bath**	D 3-3	Llewellyn	-	4000
2		**13**	**H**	**Old Blues**	W 20-0	Llewellyn(2), Buckingham, Farndon, Kerby	Greenlees p, Norman c	-
3		**20**	**H**	**Plymouth Albion**	W 20-9	Greenlees, Farndon, Saunders, White	Greenlees 2c/d	5000
4		**27**	**H**	**Nuneaton**	W 20-0	White(2), Buckingham, P.Clarke, Saunders	Greenlees p, Greenwood c	6000
5	Oct	4	a	Coventry	L 8-21	Farndon(2)	Greenlees c	8000
6		**11**	**H**	**Gloucester**	W 27-8	Buckingham(3), Farndon(2), Gadney, White	Manson 3c	7000
7		18	a	Newport	L 4-20	-	Greenlees d	6500
8		25	a	Northampton	W 6-3	Farndon	Greenlees p	5500
9	Nov	**1**	**H**	**Old Merchant Taylors**	L 3-8	Greenlees	-	5000
10		5w	a	Oxford University	W 16-9	Auty(2), Buckingham, Smith	Constantine c, Manson c	-
11		8	a	Cambridge University	L 6-28	Beamish, Farndon	-	3000
12		**15**	**H**	**Swansea**	D 0-0	-	-	5000
13		**22**	**H**	**Moseley**	W 12-6	Buckingham, Greenlees, Saunders, White	-	4000
14		**29**	**H**	**Waterloo**	W 21-5	Greenlees(2), Buckingham, Constantine, Saunders	Prentice 3c	3000
15	Dec	6	a	Harlequins	L 11-13	Buckingham, Saunders, White	Prentice c	-
16		13	a	Blackheath	W 4-3	-	Llewellyn d	5000
17		**20**	**H**	**Bristol**	W 11-0	Prentice, Farndon	Prentice c/p	5000
18		**26f**	**H**	**Barbarians**	L 6-13	Buckingham	Prentice p	8000
19		**27**	**H**	**Birkenhead Park**	W 25-9	Farndon, Hopkins, Smith, Wiener	Prentice 2c/p, Llewellyn c/d	5000
20		**29m**	**H**	**Manchester**	W 16-3	Norman, Saunders, Wood	Llewellyn d, Prentice p	3000
21	Jan	3	a	Swansea	L 0-17	-	-	6000
		10	**H**	**Rosslyn Park**	PP (frost)			
22		**17**	**H**	**London Welsh**	W 14-8	Buckingham, Gadney, Norman, Vallance	Prentice c	5000
23		24	a	Richmond	W 11-6	Buckingham, Ungoed-Thomas, White	Prentice c	3000
24		**29th**	**H**	**Royal Air Force**	W 25-6	Moore(2), Saunders(2), P.Clarke, Hardwicke, Llewellyn	Prentice 2c	2000
25		31	a	Percy Park	W 6-5	Gadney, Hardwicke	-	2000
26	Feb	7	a	London Scottish	D 8-8	Prentice, Llewellyn	Prentice c	-
27		**14**	**H**	**Newport**	L 5-9	Saunders	Norman c	7500
28		21	a	Bath	L 9-19	Coleman, Hardwicke	Prentice p	-
29		**28**	**H**	**Northampton**	D 10-10	Gadney, Hardwicke	Hart d	6000
30	Mar	**7**	**H**	**Harlequins**	W 32-3	Buckingham(2), Prentice, Greenlees, Vallance, Wiener	Prentice 5c, Greenlees d	6000
31		**14**	**H**	**Bedford**	W 23-0	Prentice(2), Gadney, Hardwicke, Ungoed-Thomas	Prentice 4c	5000
32		**21**	**H**	**Coventry**	W 13-0	Constantine, Gadney	Greenlees p/d	7000
33		28	a	Gloucester	L 8-16	Coleman, Vallance	Prentice c	4000
34	Apr	4	a	Bristol	W 13-8	Prentice, Auty, Hardwicke	Prentice 2c	10000
35		6m	a	Plymouth Albion	W 21-13	Prentice, Barlow, Gadney, Hardwicke, Saunders	Prentice 3c	4000
36		7tu	a	Bridgwater & Albion	W 37-0	Bolus(3), Gadney(3), Buckingham, Barlow, Cleaver, Hardwicke, Llewellyn	Buckingham c, Norman c	-
37		11	a	Birkenhead Park	L 8-9	Prentice, Gadney	Prentice c	5500
38		**16th**	**H**	**British Touring Team**	L 3-15	Meikle	-	6000
39		**18**	**H**	**Blackheath**	W 25-5	Constantine, Gadney, McNichol, Morris	Prentice 3c/p, Llewellyn d	4000

INDIVIDUAL APPEARANCES 1930/31

Name / Game #	1	2	3	4	5	6	7	8	9	10	11	12	13	14	15	16	17	18	19	20	21	22	23	24	25	26	27	28	29	30	31	32	33	34	35	36	37	38	39	Apps	T	Pts
JR (Dick) Auty E+	-	-	-	-	-	-	-	-	-	FH	-	-	-	FH	-	-	-	-	-	-	-	-	-	-	-	-	-	-	-	-	-	-	-	FH	-	-	-	-	-	3	3	9
Maj. EM (Morgan) Barlow	-	-	-	-	-	-	-	-	-	-	-	-	-	-	-	-	-	-	-	W	W	W	-	-	-	-	-	-	-	-	-	-	-	-	W	W	W	-	-	6	2	6
RJ (Bobby) Barr E+	-	-	-	-	-	-	-	-	-	-	-	-	-	-	-	-	-	-	-	-	-	-	-	FB	-	FB	FB	-	FB	FB	FB	FB	FB	FB	-	FB	FB	FB	FB	13	-	-
BR (Brian) Baxter	>BR	-	-	-	-	-	-	-	-	-	-	-	-	-	-	-	-	-	-	-	-	-	-	-	-	-	-	-	-	-	-	-	-	-	-	-	BR	-	-	2	-	-
GR (George) Beamish I18 GB5	-	-	-	-	-	-	-	-	-	-	H	H	P	-	P	-	-	-	-	-	-	-	-	-	P	-	-	-	-	-	-	-	-	-	-	-	P	-	P	7	1	3
Lt. CC (Christopher) Beaty-Pownall	W	W	C	C	C	-	-	-	-	-	-	-	-	-	-	-	-	-	-	-	-	-	-	-	-	-	-	-	-	-	-	-	-	-	-	-	-	-	-	5	-	-
A Bolus	-	-	-	-	-	-	-	-	-	-	-	-	-	-	-	-	-	-	-	-	-	-	-	-	-	-	-	>FH	-	W	-	FH	FH	-	C	C	FH	C	-	8	3	9
RA (Ralph) Buckingham E1	C	C	C	C	C	C	-	C	C	C	FH	C	C	C	C	C	FH	C	C	C	FH	C	FH	-	-	-	-	C	C	C	C	C	C	C	C	C	-	C	C	33	15	47
R (Rupert) Carryer	-	-	-	-	-	-	-	-	-	-	C	-	-	-	C	-	C	-	-	-	C	C	-	-	C	-	-	-	-	-	-	-	-	-	-	-	-	-	-	6	-	-
PS (Percy) Clarke	BR	L	L	BR	BR	BR	BR	L	P	BR	-	BR	BR	-	-	BR	BR	-	-	BR	BR	-	-	BR	BR	-	-	BR	-	BR	BR	BR	<BR	-	-	-	-	-	-	23	2	6
LH (Leonard) Cleaver	-	-	-	-	-	-	-	-	-	-	-	-	-	-	-	-	-	-	-	-	-	-	-	-	-	-	-	-	-	-	-	-	-	-	>BR	BR	-	-	-	2	1	3
EG (Ernie) Coleman	L	L	L	L	L	H	H	H	H	P	L	L	-	L	L	P	P	L	P	L	L	P	P	L	L	P	H	P	P	L	P	H	P	P	P	P	L	H	L	38	2	6
HA (Hugh) Constantine	-	-	-	-	-	>BR	-	BR	BR	BR	BR	-	-	BR	BR	-	BR	BR	BR	BR	-	-	-	-	-	-	-	-	BR	-	-	BR	-	BR	BR	BR	-	L	BR	18	3	11
WE (Ewart) Farndon	W	W	W	W	W	W	W	W	-	-	W	-	-	-	-	W	W	W	W	-	C	W	W	-	W	W	W	-	-	-	-	-	-	-	-	-	-	-	-	19	10	30
ECA (Ted) Flewitt	-	-	-	-	-	C	C	C	W	<W	-	-	-	-	-	-	-	-	-	-	-	-	-	-	-	-	-	-	-	-	-	-	-	-	-	-	-	-	-	5	-	-
BC (Bernard) Gadney E+	SH	SH	SH	SH	SH	SH	SH	SH	-	-	-	-	-	-	-	-	-	-	-	-	-	SH	SH	SH	SH	SH	SH	SH	SH	SH	SH	SH	SH	SH	SH	SH	SH	SH	SH	26	12	36
HD (Harry) Greenlees S6	FH*	FH*	FH*	FH*	FH*	FH*	FH*	FH*	FH*	-	-	FH*	FH*	C	FH*	FH*	-	FH*	-	FH*	-	-	-	-	-	-	-	C*	FH*	FH*	FH*	C*	-	C*	-	-	-	-	-	22	6	52
AH (Henry) Greenwood	L	BR	-	BR	L	-	-	-	L	-	-	BR	-	L	BR	BR	BR	-	BR	-	BR	-	-	-	-	-	BR	-	-	-	BR	BR	BR	BR	BR	BR	-	BR	-	20	-	2
AC Hall	-	-	BR	L	BR	L	L	BR	BR	L	BR	-	BR	-	-	-	-	BR	-	BR	-	BR	-	BR	BR	BR	-	-	-	-	-	-	-	-	-	-	-	-	-	16	-	-
JT (Jeff) Hardwicke	-	-	-	-	-	-	-	-	-	-	-	-	-	-	-	-	-	-	-	-	-	-	-	W	W	W	W	W	W	-	W	W	-	W	W	W	W	W	W	14	8	24
TM (Thomas) Hart S2	-	-	-	-	-	-	-	-	-	-	-	-	-	-	-	-	-	-	-	-	-	-	-	-	-	-	>C	-	<C	-	-	-	-	-	-	-	-	-	-	2	-	4
DH (Don) Herbert	-	-	-	-	-	-	>C	-	-	-	-	-	-	-	-	-	-	-	-	-	-	FH	C	-	-	-	C	-	-	-	-	-	-	-	-	-	-	-	-	4	-	-
Sgt. WIG (William) Kerby	-	BR	BR	-	BR	-	BR	-	BR	BR	-	-	-	-	-	-	-	-	-	-	-	-	-	-	-	-	-	-	-	-	-	-	-	-	-	-	-	-	-	6	1	3
JG (John) Llewelyn	C	C	-	-	-	-	-	-	-	-	-	-	-	-	-	C	-	C	FH	C	-	-	-	FH	FH	FH	-	-	W	C	C	-	-	W	FH	FH	-	-	FH	16	6	36
I (Ian) McNichol	-	-	-	-	-	-	-	-	-	-	-	-	-	-	-	-	-	-	-	-	-	-	-	-	-	-	-	-	-	-	-	-	-	-	-	-	C	-	C	2	1	3
CS (Charlie) Manson	FB	FB	FB	FB	FB	FB	FB	FB	FB	FB	FB	FB	FB	FB	FB	FB	FB	FB	FB	FB	FB	FB	FB	-	FB	-	-	FB	-	-	-	-	-	-	FB	-	-	-	-	26	-	8
CL (Clarence) Millar	-	-	-	-	-	-	-	-	-	-	-	-	-	-	-	-	-	-	-	-	-	-	-	-	-	-	-	>BR	-	-	-	-	-	-	-	-	BR	-	-	2	-	-
DE (Denis) Morris	-	-	-	-	-	-	-	-	-	-	-	>W	W	W	W	W	-	-	-	-	-	-	-	-	-	-	-	-	-	-	-	W	-	-	-	-	-	W	W	8	1	3
DJ (Doug) Norman E+	P	P	P	P	P	P	P	P	P	P*	P*	P	P	P*	P	P	P*	P	P*	P	P*	P*	P*	P*	P*	P*	P*	P	P	P	P	P	P*	P	P*	P*	P*	P*	P	39	2	12
AP (Pat) Pattinson	-	-	-	-	-	-	-	-	-	-	-	-	-	-	-	-	-	-	-	-	-	>BR	<BR	-	-	-	-	-	-	-	-	-	-	-	-	-	-	-	-	2	-	-
FD (Doug) Prentice E3 GB2	-	-	-	-	-	-	-	-	-	-	-	-	H	H	H	H	H	H	H	H	H	H	H	H	H	H	-	H	H	H	H	-	H	H	H	H	H	-	<H*	24	8	104
SH (Stan) Saunders	P	P	P	P	P	P	L	P	-	H	P	P	L	P	L	L	L	P	L	P	P	L	L	P	-	L	P	L	L	P	-	L	L	L	L	L	L	P	BR	36	10	30
SA (Stuart) Smith	-	-	-	-	-	-	-	-	SH	SH	SH	SH	SH	SH	SH	SH	-	SH	SH	SH	SH	-	-	-	-	C	-	-	-	-	-	-	C	-	-	-	C	-	-	15	2	6
EA (Eric) Sweatman	-	-	-	-	-	-	-	-	C	C	C	C	-	-	-	-	<C	-	-	-	-	-	-	-	-	-	-	-	-	-	-	-	-	-	-	-	-	-	-	5	-	-
AL (Lynn) Ungoed-Thomas	-	-	-	-	-	-	-	-	-	-	-	-	-	-	-	-	-	-	-	-	-	-	>C	-	C	C	FH	W	-	W	W	<W	-	-	-	-	-	-	-	8	2	6
GPC (George) Vallance	BR	BR	BR	BR	-	BR	BR	BR	L	-	BR	BR	BR	BR	BR	L	-	BR	L	L	L	L	L	BR	BR	L	L	L	BR	BR	L	P	L	-	-	-	-	L	L	32	3	9
Dr. PFR (Percy) Venables	-	-	-	-	-	-	-	-	-	-	-	-	-	-	-	-	-	-	-	-	-	-	>BR	-	-	BR	BR	BR	BR	BR	<BR	-	-	-	-	-	-	-	-	7	-	-
GR White	-	-	W	W	W	W	W	W	W	W	-	W	W	W	W	-	W	W	-	-	W	-	<W	-	-	-	-	-	-	-	-	-	-	-	-	-	-	-	-	16	7	21
Dr. RAK (Kilgour) Wiener	H	H	H	H	H	L	P	L	-	L	L	L	L	BR	-	BR	L	L	BR	-	BR	BR	BR	-	L	BR	L	-	L	L	L	L	BR	L	L	L	BR	-	BR	33	2	6
GH Wood	-	-	-	-	-	-	-	-	-	-	W	-	-	-	-	-	-	-	-	<W	-	-	-	-	-	-	-	-	-	-	-	-	-	-	-	-	-	-	-	2	1	3

1 GAME: CD (Carl) Aarvold E11 GB5 =C(24), N (Norman) Bowen =C(13), SH (Sid) Bowers >SH(17), TW (Tom) Clarke =BR(27), JL (Jimmy) Farrell I25 GB5 =L(24), SF (Frank) Herbert >W(33), ECR (Edward) Hopkins Ct(19), BJ (Bernard) Hurren =BR(34), SSC (Stephen) Meikle E1 >FHt(38), SH (Shirley) Moore Wt(24), Lt. AL (Tony) Novis E5 GB3 <C(24), JSR (Jim) Reeve E8 GB4 =W(19), F West =BR(38), GES (George) Williams BR(38)

The key for how to read the stats is on the last page

1931/32

Home Ground: Welford Road
Captain: Harry Greenlees

OVERALL RECORD:					T	C	PG	DG	MK	PTS
PLD	W	D	L	Tigers scored:	89	30	10	5	0	377
38	18	6	14	Opponents scored:	74	42	8	4	0	346

GM	DATE		VEN	OPPONENTS	RESULT	TRIES	KICKS	ATT
CLUB MATCHES								
1	Sep	**5**	**H**	**Bath**	W 6-0	Gadney(2)	-	3000
2		**12**	**H**	**Old Blues**	W 16-0	Gadney(2), Barlow, Hardwicke	Barr 2c	2000
3		**19**	**H**	**Plymouth Albion**	W 8-0	Buckingham, Gadney	Norman c	6000
4		**26**	**H**	**Nuneaton**	W 25-0	Barlow, Constantine, Gadney, Hardwicke, Vallance	D.Herbert d, Norman 2c, Barr c	3000
5	Oct	**3**	**H**	**Coventry**	W 9-0	Barlow(2), Hardwicke	-	10000
6		10	a	Gloucester	L 6-12	Gadney, Hardwicke	-	4000
7		**17**	**H**	**Newport**	D 8-8	Beamish, Buckingham	Barr c	7000
8		**24**	**H**	**Northampton**	W 13-10	Beamish, Coote, Vallance	Greenlees d	6000
9		**31**	**H**	**Cambridge University**	L 6-26	Hardwicke	Greenlees p	7000
10	Nov	**5th**	**H**	**Oxford University**	L 5-10	Morris	Greenlees c	3000
11		**7**	**H**	**Old Merchant Taylors**	W 20-8	Hardwicke(2), Morris(2), Coleman, Greenwood	Norman c	5000
12		21	a	Swansea	L 0-11	-	-	2000
13		**28**	**H**	**Moseley**	W 17-5	Barlow, Coleman, Hardwicke, Morris	Norman c/p	5000
14	Dec	**5**	**H**	**Harlequins**	W 11-0	Coote(2), Hardwicke	Greenlees c	5000
15		12	a	Blackheath	W 14-8	Greenlees, Buckingham, Coote	Greenlees c, Barr p	2000
		19	**H**	**Bristol**	PP (fog)			
16		**26**	**H**	**Birkenhead Park**	D 10-10	Coote, Vallance	Greenlees 2c	6000
17		**28m**	**H**	**Barbarians**	L 13-14	Greenlees, Constantine, Gadney	Greenlees 2c	10000
18		**29tu**	**H**	**Waterloo**	D 11-11	Greenwood(2), Williams	Greenlees c	-
	Jan	1f	a	Manchester	PP (frost)			
19		**2**	**H**	**Swansea**	D 3-3	Greenwood	-	3000
20		**9**	**H**	**Rosslyn Park**	W 14-5	Gadney(2), Hardwicke(2)	Greenlees c	-
21		**16**	**H**	**London Welsh**	L 3-9	-	Greenlees p	3000
22		**23**	**H**	**Richmond**	L 0-13	-	-	4000
23		**28th**	**H**	**Royal Air Force**	W 14-3	Auty, F.Herbert, Vallance	Barr c/p	1000
24		30	a	Moseley	W 9-0	Beamish, Greenwood, F.Herbert	-	-
25	Feb	**6**	**H**	**London Scottish**	L 6-24	Vallance	Barr p	4000
26		13	a	Newport	L 0-21	-	-	2000
27		**20**	**H**	**Gloucester**	W 7-5	Hardwicke	Greenlees d	4000
28		27	a	Northampton	L 0-18	-	-	4000
29	Mar	**5**	**H**	**Harlequins**	W 13-11	Berry, Moore, Saunders	Greenlees d	5000
30		**12**	**H**	**Bedford**	W 18-10	Hardwicke, Moore, Norman	Vallance c/p, Greenlees d	5000
31		19	a	Coventry	L 10-33	Berry, Moore	Greenlees c, Kendrew c	3000
32		26	a	Bristol	L 6-13	-	Coote 2p	-
33		28m	a	Plymouth Albion	W 18-8	Beamish, Beaty-Pownall, Hodder	Greenlees 3c, Coote p	-
34		29tu	a	Bath	L 9-11	Beamish(2), Hardwicke	-	-
35	Apr	**2**	**H**	**Bridgwater & Albion**	W 30-5	Morris(2), Bates, Buckingham, Gadney, Hardwicke, Pearse, Saunders	Barr c, Greenwood c, Vallance c	4000
36		**4m**	**H**	**Nuneaton**	D 3-3	Palmer	-	-
37		9	a	Birkenhead Park	D 13-13	Buckingham, Constantine, Vallance	Greenlees 2c	3000
38		**16**	**H**	**Blackheath**	L 3-5	Gadney	-	3000

INDIVIDUAL APPEARANCES 1931/32

Name / Game #	1	2	3	4	5	6	7	8	9	10	11	12	13	14	15	16	17	18	19	20	21	22	23	24	25	26	27	28	29	30	31	32	33	34	35	36	37	38	Apps	T	Pts
JR (Dick) Auty E+	-	-	-	-	-	-	-	-	-	J	-	-	-	-	-	-	-	-	-	-	-	-	J	-	-	-	-	-	-	-	-	-	-	-	-	-	-	-	2	1	3
Maj. EM (Morgan) Barlow	-	K	K	K	K	K	K	-	-	-	-	-	K	-	-	-	-	-	<N	-	-	-	-	-	-	-	-	-	-	-	-	-	-	-	-	-	-	-	8	5	15
RJ (Bobby) Barr E3	0	0	0	0	0	0	0	0	0	0	0	0	-	-	0	0	-	-	-	-	-	0	0	-	0	-	0	-	0	0	-	0	-	0	0	0	0	0	26	-	21
EE (Edward) Bates	-	-	-	-	-	-	-	-	-	-	-	-	-	-	-	-	-	-	-	-	-	-	-	-	-	-	-	-	>M	J	J	-	-	-	J	J	J	J	7	1	3
GR (George) Beamish I22 GB5	B	B	B	B	B	B	B	B	-	-	-	B	-	A	-	-	G	G	-	-	-	-	-	G	-	-	-	-	-	-	-	G	G	H	-	-	-	G	17	6	18
Lt. CC (Christopher) Beaty-Pownall	-	-	-	-	-	-	-	-	-	-	-	-	-	-	-	-	-	-	-	-	-	-	-	-	-	-	-	-	-	M	M	-	M	<M	-	-	-	-	4	1	3
JTW (Tom) Berry E+	-	-	-	-	-	-	-	-	-	-	-	-	-	-	-	-	-	-	-	-	-	-	-	-	-	-	-	-	>G	G	E	-	-	F	F	G	H	H	8	2	6
RA (Ralph) Buckingham E1	M	M	M	M	M	-	M	M	M	M	J	J	J	J	M	M	M	0	J	M	M	-	M	J	J	-	-	-	-	-	-	-	-	-	M	M	M	M	27	5	15
Cpl. MG (Mog) Christie	-	-	-	-	H	H	H	H	G	F	G	H	G	-	-	-	-	-	-	-	-	-	-	<F	-	-	-	-	-	-	-	-	-	-	-	-	-	-	10	-	-
EG (Ernie) Coleman	C	-	-	-	-	-	-	F	F	E	E	F	F	B	C	B	B	B	A	B	A	A	G	-	G	F	F	-	-	-	-	-	-	-	H	-	-	-	21	2	6
DW (Dennis) Colston	-	-	-	-	-	-	-	-	-	-	-	-	-	-	-	-	-	-	-	-	-	-	-	-	-	>I	-	<I	-	-	-	-	-	-	-	-	-	-	2	-	-
HA (Hugh) Constantine	-	-	G	G	-	F	F	-	-	G	-	-	H	G	G	-	E	-	-	-	-	-	-	-	-	-	-	G	-	-	-	F	F	-	-	E	F	F	15	3	9
PB (Paddy) Coote I+	-	-	-	-	-	>M	-	K	-	-	-	-	-	L	L	L	L	-	M	-	-	-	-	-	-	-	-	-	-	-	-	M	J	-	-	-	-	-	9	5	24
WE (Ewart) Farndon	K	-	-	-	-	-	-	-	-	-	K	<K	-	-	-	-	-	-	-	-	-	-	-	-	-	-	-	-	-	-	-	-	-	-	-	-	-	-	3	-	-
BC (Bernard) Gadney E2	I	I	I	I	I	I	-	-	I	-	I	I	-	-	I	I	I	I	-	I	-	I	I	I	I	-	I	-	I	-	-	-	-	-	I	-	-	I	22	12	36
A (Alistair) Graham	-	-	-	-	-	-	-	-	-	-	-	-	-	-	>H	H	H	-	G	G	F	F	-	H	H	<H	-	-	-	-	-	-	-	-	-	-	-	-	10	-	-
HD (Harry) Greenlees S6	J*	J*	J*	-	J*	-	-	J*	J*	L*	-	-	-	I*	J*	J*	J*	J*	-	J*	J*	J*	-	-	-	-	J*	J*	J*	L*	I*	J*	I*	I*	L*	-	I*	<L*	26	2	58
AH (Henry) Greenwood	-	F	F	F	F	E	E	G	E	-	F	E	C	-	E	A	A	A	B	-	C	C	C	A	C	C	C	D	C	C	C	A	A	D	A	-	C	A	33	5	17
AC Hall	H	G	-	-	-	-	-	-	-	-	-	-	-	-	-	-	-	-	-	-	-	-	A	-	A	A	A	A	A	A	A	C	C	C	-	-	-	-	13	-	-
JT (Jeff) Hardwicke	N	N	N	N	N	N	N	N	N	N	N	N	N	N	N	N	N	N	-	N	N	N	N	N	N	N	N	N	N	N	N	N	N	N	N	-	-	N	35	15	45
DH (Don) Herbert	-	L	L	L	L	L	-	L	L	-	L	M	L	-	-	-	-	-	-	-	-	<M	-	-	-	-	-	-	-	-	-	-	-	-	-	-	-	-	11	-	4
SF (Frank) Herbert	-	-	-	-	-	-	-	-	-	-	-	-	-	K	-	-	-	K	K	-	K	K	K	K	K	-	-	-	-	-	-	-	-	-	-	K	N	-	10	2	6
FS (Francis) Hodder	-	-	-	-	-	-	-	-	-	-	-	-	-	-	-	-	-	-	-	-	-	-	-	>M	-	-	-	M	-	-	-	L	L	L	-	-	-	-	5	1	3
ECR (Edward) Hopkins	-	-	-	-	-	-	L	-	-	-	-	-	-	-	-	-	-	<M	-	-	-	-	-	-	-	-	-	-	-	-	-	-	-	-	-	-	-	-	2	-	-
DH (Douglas) Howson	-	-	-	-	-	-	-	-	-	-	-	-	-	-	-	-	-	-	>I	-	I	-	-	-	-	-	-	-	-	-	-	-	-	-	-	-	-	-	2	-	-
AP (Alan) Hughes	>F	H	H	H	G	G	G	-	H	-	H	-	-	H	-	C	-	-	C	C	H	-	-	C	E	G	G	F	E	E	G	-	E	-	-	-	A	C	25	-	-
WA (Wilf) Jackson	-	-	-	-	-	-	-	-	-	-	-	-	-	-	-	-	-	-	-	-	-	-	-	-	-	-	-	-	-	-	>L	-	-	-	-	-	L	-	2	-	-
Sgt. WIG (William) Kerby	-	-	-	-	-	-	-	-	-	H	-	-	-	-	-	-	-	-	-	-	-	H	F	-	<F	-	-	-	-	-	-	-	-	-	-	-	-	-	4	-	-
Sgt. CGR (Cyril) Lewis	-	-	-	-	-	-	-	-	-	-	-	-	-	-	-	-	-	-	-	-	-	-	-	-	-	-	-	-	-	-	-	>E	D	-	-	-	-	-	2	-	-
I (Ian) McNichol	-	-	-	-	-	-	-	-	-	-	-	-	-	-	-	K	-	L	<L	-	-	-	-	-	-	-	-	-	-	-	-	-	-	-	-	-	-	-	3	-	-
CS (Charlie) Manson	-	-	-	-	-	-	-	-	-	-	-	-	0	0	-	-	0	-	0	0	0	-	-	0	-	0	-	0	-	-	0	-	0	-	-	-	-	-	11	-	-
CL (Clarence) Millar	-	-	-	-	-	-	-	-	-	-	-	-	-	-	-	-	-	-	-	A	B	-	-	-	-	-	-	-	-	-	-	-	-	-	-	-	-	-	2	-	-
SH (Shirley) Moore	-	-	-	-	-	-	-	-	-	-	-	-	-	-	-	-	-	-	-	-	-	-	-	-	-	K	K	K	K	K	K	K	K	-	-	N	<K	-	10	3	9
DE (Denis) Morris	-	-	-	-	-	-	-	-	K	K	M	L	M	M	K	-	K	-	-	L	L	L	L	L	L	L	L	L	L	-	-	-	-	K	K	-	-	K	21	6	18
DJ (Doug) Norman E2	A	A	A	A*	A	A*	A*	A	A	A	A*	A*	A*	-	A	-	-	-	-	-	-	B	B*	B*	B*	B*	B	B	B	B	-	B	B	B	B	B*	B	B	30	1	16
RVM (Reginald) Odbert I1	-	-	-	J	-	J	<J	-	-	-	-	-	-	-	-	-	-	-	-	-	-	-	-	-	-	-	-	-	-	-	-	-	-	-	-	-	-	-	3	-	-
WE (Bill) Parker	-	-	-	-	-	-	-	-	-	-	-	-	-	>F	-	G	-	H	H	H	G	G	-	-	-	-	-	-	-	-	-	-	-	-	-	-	-	-	7	-	-
CH (Peter) Pearse	-	-	-	-	-	-	-	-	-	-	-	-	-	-	-	-	-	-	-	-	-	-	H	-	-	-	H	H	F	H	D	H	-	E	E	F	-	-	10	1	3
SH (Stan) Saunders	E	D	D	D	D	-	-	D	C	C	C	D	D	E	F	F	F	-	F	F	E	-	-	-	-	-	-	-	H	F	F	-	H	G	G	D	G	-	26	2	6
SA (Stuart) Smith	-	-	-	-	-	-	I	I	-	<I	-	-	-	-	-	-	-	-	-	-	-	-	-	-	-	-	-	-	-	-	-	-	-	-	-	-	-	-	3	-	-
GPC (George) Vallance	D	C	C	C	C	C	C	C	B	B	B	C	B	C	B	D	D	E	E	E	-	D	D	D	D	E	E	-	D	D	-	-	-	-	C	C	D	E	32	6	25
Dr. RAK (Kilgour) Wiener	G	E	E	E	E	D	D	E	D	D	D	G	E	D	D	E	C	D	D	D	D	E	E	E	-	D	D	E	-	-	-	D	-	A	D	A	E	D	33	-	-

1 GAME: NJ (Norman) Bacon <M(27), BR (Brian) Baxter <H(31), A Bolus <L(1), SH (Sid) Bowers I(13), LW (Langley) Burton M(25), GCM (Guy) Falla =C(18), KC (Kenneth) George >H(36), AK (Arthur) Halliday =I(36), WG (Bill) Jeffery =I(30), DA (Joe) Kendrew E2 B(31), DPC (Denis) Manley =K(20), RF Nobleston =I(32), DS (Donald) Oscroft M(26), RA Palmer >Lt(36), F/O. BV Reynolds =C(28), WA (Arnold) Sime >J(34), LA Smith =J(26), GES (George) Williams <Ft(18)

The key for how to read the stats is on the last page

19 32/33

Home Ground: Welford Road	OVERALL RECORD:					T	C	PG	DG	MK	PTS
Captain: Doug Norman	PLD	W	D	L	Tigers scored:	93	38	10	8	1	420
	37	23	0	14	Opponents scored:	69	38	8	6	0	331

GM	DATE		VEN	OPPONENTS	RESULT	TRIES	KICKS	ATT
CLUB MATCHES								
1	Sep	3	H	**Bedford**	W 10-5	Buckingham, Hardwicke	Morris d	5000
2		10	H	**Old Blues**	W 11-5	Vallance, Bates, Buckingham	Vallance c	5000
3		17	H	**Plymouth Albion**	W 13-8	Coote, Hardwicke, Lewis	Coote d	6000
4		24	H	**Bristol**	W 3-0	-	Payne p	6000
5	Oct	1	H	**Coventry**	W 16-4	Coote(2), Gadney, Morris	Coote 2c	6000
6		8	a	Bridgwater & Albion	W 11-6	Crowe, Jackson	Vallance p, Manson c	-
7		15	a	Newport	W 10-6	Hardwicke(2)	Coote 2c	-
8		17m	H	**Bective Rangers**	W 26-0	Meikle(2), Vallance(2), Hardwicke	Coote 3c, Crowe m, Kendrew c	-
9		22	a	Northampton	W 9-6	Bates	Coote c/d	7000
10		29	H	**Gloucester**	W 6-3	Buckingham	Coote p	4000
11	Nov	5	H	**Moseley**	W 37-7	Kendrew(2), Coote, H.Edmiston, Meikle, Bradley, Constantine, Crowe	Coote c/d, H.Edmiston p, Meikle c, Manson c	-
12		9w	a	Oxford University	W 21-5	Meikle(4), Auty	Coote 3c	-
13		12	a	Cambridge University	L 3-8	H.Edmiston	-	-
14		19	H	**Old Merchant Taylors**	L 5-27	Hardwicke	Vallance c	4000
15		26	H	**Nuneaton**	W 12-0	Bradley, Constantine	Vallance 2p	-
16	Dec	3	a	Harlequins	W 22-13	Hardwicke(2), Crowe, Beamish, Buckingham, Tindall	Crowe 2c	-
17		10	a	Blackheath	L 11-14	Constantine, Hughes, Tindall	H.Edmiston c	-
18		17	H	**Waterloo**	L 3-13	Saunders	-	4000
19		24	a	Bedford	L 10-13	Saunders, Stanyon-Jacques	H.Edmiston 2c	2000
20		26m	H	**Birkenhead Park**	W 14-5	Coote, Buckingham, Crowe, Hardwicke	Coote c	12000
21		27tu	H	**Barbarians**	L 10-22	Burton, Dunkley	H.Edmiston d	10000
22		28w	H	**Manchester**	W 9-8	Berry, Greaves	H.Edmiston p	4000
23		31	a	Swansea	L 0-11	-	-	-
24	Jan	7	H	**Rosslyn Park**	W 3-0	Buckingham	-	5000
25		21	H	**Bath**	W 11-0	Crowe, Buckingham	Crowe c/p	-
		26th	H	**Royal Air Force**	PP (frost)			
		28	a	Richmond	PP (frost)			
26	Feb	4	a	London Scottish	L 11-13	Hardwicke(2), Bates	H.Edmiston c	-
27		11	H	**Newport**	L 7-10	-	Bates d, Crowe p	4000
28		18	a	Gloucester	W 11-9	Buckingham, Hardwicke, Oscroft	Crowe c	3000
		25	H	**Swansea**	PP (snow)			
29	Mar	4	H	**Harlequins**	L 11-18	Buckingham, Crowe, Saunders	H.Edmiston c	6000
30		11	H	**Northampton**	L 3-21	Oscroft	-	5000
31		18	a	Coventry	L 0-5	-	-	4000
32		25	H	**London Welsh**	W 31-12	Saunders(3), Buckingham(2), Adams, Vallance	Crowe 5c	5000
33	Apr	1	a	Birkenhead Park	W 18-11	Buckingham(2), Berry, Saunders	Slow d, D.Norman c	3000
34		8	H	**Blackheath**	L 11-18	Buckingham(2), Slow	D.Norman c	5000
35		15	a	Bristol	W 12-4	Beamish, Crowe	Slow d, D.Norman c	5000
36		17m	a	Plymouth Albion	W 11-6	Beamish, Crowe, Jackson	D.Norman c	-
37		18tu	a	Bath	L 8-15	Buckingham	Harris c/p	3000

INDIVIDUAL APPEARANCES 1932/33

Name / Game #	1	2	3	4	5	6	7	8	9	10	11	12	13	14	15	16	17	18	19	20	21	22	23	24	25	26	27	28	29	30	31	32	33	34	35	36	37	Apps	T	Pts
N (Newton) Adams	-	-	-	-	-	-	-	-	-	-	-	-	-	-	-	-	-	-	-	-	-	-	-	-	-	-	-	-	-	>H	-	G	G	-	-	-	G	4	1	3
LJ (Lewis) Adcock	-	-	-	-	-	-	-	-	-	-	N	-	-	-	-	-	-	-	-	-	-	-	<K	-	-	-	-	-	-	-	-	-	-	-	-	-	-	2	-	-
JR (Dick) Auty E+	-	-	-	-	-	-	-	-	-	-	-	J	-	-	-	-	-	-	-	-	J	-	-	-	-	-	-	-	-	-	-	-	-	-	-	-	-	2	1	3
RJ (Bobby) Barr E3	0	0	0	0	0	-	-	0	0	0	-	0	0	-	-	-	0	0	0	-	-	-	-	-	-	-	-	-	-	-	-	-	-	-	-	-	-	13	-	-
EE (Edward) Bates	J	J	J	J	J	-	-	J	J	J	-	N	-	J	-	J	J	J	J	J	-	J	J	J	J	J	J	J	J	J	J	0	0	-	-	N	<J	29	3	13
GR (George) Beamish I25 GB5	-	-	G	G	G*	-	G	G*	G	-	-	G	G	G	-	G	-	-	-	-	G	-	-	-	-	-	-	-	-	-	G	-	-	G	G	<G	-	15	3	9
HJ (Harold) Bennett	-	-	-	-	-	>B	B	-	-	-	B	-	-	-	B	-	-	-	-	-	-	B	-	-	-	-	B	B	B	-	-	-	-	-	-	-	A	9	-	-
JTW (Tom) Berry E+	H	H	H	-	F	-	H	F	H	-	-	-	H	-	-	-	-	H	H	G	-	F	E	D	E	E	G	E	E	E	F	E	H	H	H	H	H	27	2	6
SH (Sid) Bowers	-	-	-	-	-	-	-	-	-	-	-	-	-	-	-	-	-	-	-	-	-	-	I	-	-	-	-	I	-	-	I	-	-	-	-	-	-	3	-	-
EG Bradley	-	-	-	-	-	>K	-	-	-	-	K	-	-	-	K	-	-	-	<N	-	-	-	-	-	-	-	-	-	-	-	-	-	-	-	-	-	-	4	2	6
RA (Ralph) Buckingham E1	M	M	M*	N*	-	-	J*	-	K*	K	-	-	K	M	-	M	M	M	L	K	K	M*	L	K	K	L	K*	K*	K*	L	K	K	N	K	K	K	K	31	16	48
LW (Langley) Burton	-	-	-	-	-	-	-	-	-	-	I	-	-	I	-	-	-	-	-	I	<I	-	-	-	-	-	-	-	-	-	-	-	-	-	-	-	-	4	1	3
LH (Leonard) Cleaver	-	-	-	-	-	-	-	-	-	-	-	-	-	-	-	-	-	-	-	-	-	-	-	-	-	-	-	-	-	-	-	-	-	-	-	A	<D	2	-	-
EG (Ernie) Coleman	-	-	-	-	B	-	-	-	-	D	E	-	D	E	-	D	E	E	D	E	-	-	D	E	-	-	-	-	-	<D	-	-	-	-	-	-	-	13	-	-
HA (Hugh) Constantine	-	-	-	-	-	F	-	-	-	-	G	-	-	-	G	-	G	-	-	-	-	-	-	-	-	-	-	-	-	-	-	-	-	-	-	-	-	4	3	9
PB (Paddy) Coote I1	-	-	K	M	M	-	M	M	M	M	M	M	M	-	-	-	-	-	-	M	M	-	-	-	-	-	-	-	-	-	-	-	-	M	-	-	-	13	5	56
MP (Morgan) Crowe I12	-	-	-	-	>L	M	L	L	L	L	L	L	L	L	J	L	L	-	M	L	L	-	-	M	L	-	L	L	L	-	L	L	-	-	M	M	-	25	8	51
JHF (Harry) Edmiston	G	G	F	H	H	E	F	-	F	F	F	F	F	F	-	-	F	F	G	F	F	H	F	F	F	F	F	F	F	F	-	F	-	F	-	F	-	30	2	26
JG (John) Edmiston	-	-	-	-	-	-	-	-	-	-	-	-	-	-	-	-	-	-	-	-	-	-	-	-	>I	-	<I	-	-	-	-	-	-	-	-	-	-	2	-	-
BC (Bernard) Gadney E4	I	I	I	I	I	-	-	-	I	I	-	I	-	-	-	-	-	-	-	-	-	-	-	I	-	I	-	-	I	I	-	I	I	I	I	I	I	18	1	3
G (George) Greaves	-	-	-	>A	C	-	D	E	E	E	-	E	-	A	-	C	-	C	A	-	-	C	C	C	-	C	C	C	C	A	-	-	-	C	C	C	C	23	1	3
AH (Henry) Greenwood	A	B	A	C	-	-	C	C	C	C	-	-	-	-	<A	-	-	-	-	-	-	-	-	-	-	-	-	-	-	-	-	-	-	-	-	-	-	9	-	-
JT (Jeff) Hardwicke	N	N	N	-	N	-	N	N	N	-	-	-	-	N	-	N	N	N	-	N	N	N	-	N	N	N	N	N	N	N	N	N	-	N	N	-	N	26	12	36
RA Harris	-	-	-	-	-	-	-	-	-	-	-	-	-	-	-	-	-	-	-	-	-	>0	-	0	0	0	0	0	0	0	0	-	-	0	0	0	<0	13	-	5
CD Henderson	-	-	-	-	-	-	-	-	-	-	-	-	-	-	-	-	-	-	>F	-	-	<E	-	-	-	-	-	-	-	-	-	-	-	-	-	-	-	2	-	-
SF (Frank) Herbert	-	-	-	-	-	N	-	-	-	-	-	-	-	-	-	-	-	-	K	-	-	K	-	-	-	K	-	-	-	-	-	-	K	-	-	-	-	5	-	-
L Holden	-	-	-	-	-	-	-	-	-	-	-	-	-	-	-	>0	-	-	-	<0	-	-	-	-	-	-	-	-	-	-	-	-	-	-	-	-	-	2	-	-
DH (Douglas) Howson	-	-	-	-	-	I	I	I	-	-	-	-	I	-	I	I	I	<I	-	-	-	-	-	-	-	-	-	-	-	-	-	-	-	-	-	-	-	8	-	-
AP (Alan) Hughes	E	E	C	B	A	-	A	A	A	-	-	A	A	C	-	A	A	A	-	A	A	-	A	A	A	A	A	A	A	-	A	A	A	A	A	-	-	28	1	3
WA (Wilf) Jackson	-	-	-	-	-	L	-	-	-	-	-	-	-	-	-	-	-	-	-	-	-	-	M	-	-	-	-	-	-	K	-	M	L	L	L	L	M	9	2	6
DA (Joe) Kendrew E4	-	-	-	-	-	-	-	B	B	A	C	C	C	-	C	-	-	-	-	-	-	-	-	-	-	-	-	-	-	-	-	-	-	-	-	-	-	7	2	8
Sgt. CGR (Cyril) Lewis	-	-	E	D	D	-	E	-	-	G	D	D	-	-	E	-	-	-	-	-	E	-	-	-	-	-	E	-	-	-	E	-	E	E	E	E	E	16	1	3
CS (Charlie) Manson	-	-	-	-	-	0	-	-	-	-	0	-	-	0	-	-	-	-	-	-	-	-	-	-	-	-	-	-	-	-	-	-	-	-	-	-	-	3	-	4
SSC (Stephen) Meikle E1	-	-	-	-	-	-	-	K	-	-	J	K	J	-	-	-	-	-	-	-	-	-	-	-	-	-	-	-	-	-	-	-	-	-	-	-	-	4	7	23
DE (Denis) Morris	K	K	-	K	K	-	K	-	-	N	-	-	N	K	-	-	-	-	-	-	-	-	-	-	-	-	-	-	-	-	-	-	-	-	-	-	-	8	1	7
EG (Ernest) Nixon	-	-	-	-	-	-	-	-	-	-	-	-	-	-	-	-	-	-	-	>D	D	<D	-	-	-	-	-	-	-	-	-	-	-	-	-	-	-	3	-	-
DJ (Doug) Norman E2	B*	A*	-	-	-	-	-	-	-	B*	-	B*	B*	B*	-	B*	B*	B*	B*	B*	B*	-	B*	B*	B*	B*	-	-	-	B*	B*	B*	B*	B*	B*	B*	<B*	24	-	8
FJ Norman	-	-	-	-	-	-	-	-	-	-	-	-	-	-	>H	-	-	-	-	-	-	-	-	H	<H	-	-	-	-	-	-	-	-	-	-	-	-	3	-	-
DS (Donald) Oscroft	-	-	-	-	-	-	-	-	-	-	-	-	-	-	-	-	-	L	-	-	-	L	N	L	M	M	M	M	M	M	M	-	M	-	-	-	L	13	2	6
WE (Bill) Parker	-	-	-	-	-	-	-	-	-	-	-	-	-	-	-	-	-	-	-	-	-	-	-	-	G	G	-	-	-	-	-	-	-	-	-	-	-	2	-	-
JF Payne	-	>L	L	<L	-	-	-	-	-	-	-	-	-	-	-	-	-	-	-	-	-	-	-	-	-	-	-	-	-	-	-	-	-	-	-	-	-	3	-	3
CH (Peter) Pearse	F	F	-	F	-	-	-	H	-	H	-	H	-	H	F	-	-	-	-	-	-	-	G	G	-	-	H	G	G	-	-	-	-	-	-	-	-	13	-	-
SH (Stan) Saunders	C	C	-	-	-	-	-	-	-	-	H	-	-	-	-	F	H	G	E	H	-	G	H	-	-	H	-	H	H	G	H	H	F	-	-	-	-	17	7	21
CF (Charles) Slow E+	-	-	-	-	-	-	-	-	-	-	-	-	-	-	-	-	-	-	-	-	-	-	-	-	-	-	-	-	-	-	-	>J	J	J	J	J	-	5	1	11
NJ Tindall	-	-	-	-	-	-	-	-	-	-	-	-	-	-	>N	K	K	K	-	-	-	-	-	-	-	-	-	-	-	-	-	-	-	-	-	-	-	4	2	6
GPC (George) Vallance	D	D	D	E	E	D*	-	D	D	-	-	-	E	D	D*	-	-	-	-	-	-	-	-	-	D	D	D	D	D	-	D	D	D	D	D	D	-	22	4	25
Dr. RAK (Kilgour) Wiener	-	-	-	-	-	-	-	-	-	-	-	-	-	-	-	E	D	<D	-	-	-	-	-	-	-	-	-	-	-	-	-	-	-	-	-	-	-	3	-	-
JL (Jack) Wormleighton	-	-	-	-	-	>C	-	-	-	-	A	-	-	-	-	-	C	-	C	C	-	A	-	-	C	-	-	-	-	C	C	C	C	-	-	-	-	11	-	-

1 GAME: SN (Spencer) Bevan >0(7), TGF (Thomas) Cleaver =H(16), WHV Cotton =0(23), PE (Pop) Dunkley E2 Ht(21), KC (Kenneth) George <G(6), AC Hall <A(6), FS (Francis) Hodder <M(15), JIT Jones =J(6), TPK (Keith) Oakley =F(37), HE Packer =L(1), RJ (Reg) Pemberton =B(3), STA (Stephen) Radcliffe =0(21), AH (Henry) Rew =C(21), AF (Arthur) Sibson >L(15), WA (Arnold) Sime I(22), CGJ (Charles) Stanley >F(35), KA (Kenneth) Stanyon-Jacques >It(19), WS (William) Thompson <0(15), DL Thornton =H(6)

The key for how to read the stats is on the last page

1933/34	Home Ground: Welford Road	OVERALL RECORD:					T	C	PG	DG	MK	PTS
	Captain: Ralph Buckingham	PLD	W	D	L	Tigers scored:	100	36	15	16	0	481
		43	25	1	17	Opponents scored:	79	40	6	9	1	374

GM	DATE		VEN	OPPONENTS	RESULT	TRIES	KICKS	ATT
CLUB MATCHES								
1	Sep	**2**	**H**	**Bedford**	W 26-13	Slow, Buckingham, Gadney, Hardwicke, Jackson	Slow d, Crowe 2c/p	1338
2		**9**	**H**	**Old Blues**	W 33-0	Gadney(4), Hardwicke(2), Adams, Jackson	Manson 2c, Vallance p, Crowe c	1088
3		**16**	**H**	**Plymouth Albion**	W 15-4	Bennett, Darnill, Drummond, Gadney, Jackson	-	2292
4		**23**	**H**	**Gloucester**	L 4-18	-	Slow d	1560
5		**30**	**H**	**London Welsh**	W 25-9	Crowe(2), Darnill, Jackson, Vallance	Crowe 3c, Slow d	1630
6	Oct	7	a	Coventry	D 5-5	Slow	Crowe c	-
7		**14**	**H**	**Bridgwater & Albion**	W 22-5	Slow, Lloyd, Shepherd, Vallance	Slow d, Constantine 2c, Edmiston c	346
8		**19th**	**H**	**Bective Rangers**	L 3-14	-	Edmiston p	889
9		**21**	**H**	**Newport**	L 3-9	-	Edmiston p	1857
10		**28**	**H**	**Northampton**	W 10-3	Gadney, Slow	Crowe 2c	1745
11	Nov	4	a	Moseley	L 3-16	-	Edmiston p	-
12		**9th**	**H**	**Oxford University**	W 12-8	Buckingham, Slow	Coote d, Crowe c	1501
13		**11**	**H**	**Cambridge University**	W 13-10	Coote(2)	Coote p, Crowe 2c	2048
14		18	a	Swansea	L 6-8	Hewitt	Coote p	1500
15		25	a	Nuneaton	L 13-19	Lloyd(2)	Constantine p, Llewellyn c, Manson c	-
16	Dec	2	a	Harlequins	W 4-0	-	Crowe d	-
17		9	a	Blackheath	L 14-17	Gadney, G.Harris, Hewitt, Lloyd	Constantine c	-
18		**16**	**H**	**Bristol**	W 10-6	Buckingham	Barr d, Crowe p	1419
19		23	a	Bedford	L 10-20	Buckingham, Darnill	Crowe 2c	-
20		**26tu**	**H**	**Birkenhead Park**	W 5-3	Slow	Crowe c	2622
21		**27w**	**H**	**Barbarians**	W 21-10	G.Meikle(3), Crowe, Gerrard	G.Meikle d, Crowe c	10000
22		**28th**	**H**	**Waterloo**	W 7-6	Jackson	Fyfe d	765
23		**30**	**H**	**Rosslyn Park**	W 11-5	Drummond, Gray, Jackson	Constantine c	931
24	Jan	1m	a	Manchester	W 12-3	Gray(3), Drummond	-	-
25		**6**	**H**	**Swansea**	L 0-3	-	-	1132
26		**13**	**H**	**Rugby**	W 12-0	Darnill(3), Hewitt	-	955
27		**20**	**H**	**Bath**	W 12-8	Hewitt(2), Adams, Reed	-	1025
28		**27**	**H**	**Richmond**	W 26-3	Adams, Buckingham, Gadney, C.Harris, G.Harris	Constantine 2c/p, Slow d	1439
29	Feb	**1th**	**H**	**Royal Air Force**	W 21-11	Slow(2), Berry, G.Harris, Jackson, Sime, Tindall	-	292
30		**3**	**H**	**London Scottish**	L 5-6	Robinson	Crowe c	693
31		10	a	Newport	L 3-15	Parker	-	-
32		17	a	Gloucester	L 7-35	-	Slow d, Crowe p	6000
33		24	a	Northampton	L 8-14	Adams	Crowe c/p	-
34	Mar	**3**	**H**	**Harlequins**	W 15-0	Crowe, Buckingham	Crowe c/p, Slow d	1611
35		**10**	**H**	**Guy's Hospital**	W 19-0	Hewitt(3), Robinson, Wormleighton	McLean 2c	828
36		17	a	Bath	L 0-8	-	-	2000
37		**24**	**H**	**Coventry**	L 3-14	-	Crowe p	1580
38		31	a	Bristol	W 5-3	Crowe	Crowe c	7000
39	Apr	2m	a	Plymouth Albion	L 10-11	McLean, G.Harris	McLean d	3500
40		3tu	a	Exeter	W 15-10	Jackson	Slow 2d, Barr d	-
41		7	a	Birkenhead Park	W 13-5	Crowe, Gray, Hughes	Crowe c, Edmiston c	2500
42		**14**	**H**	**Blackheath**	L 11-14	Adams, Gadney, Jackson	Crowe c	1605
43		**21**	**H**	**Old Merchant Taylors**	W 9-3	Gadney, Hewitt	Crowe p	2262

INDIVIDUAL APPEARANCES 1933/34

Name / Game #	1	2	3	4	5	6	7	8	9	10	11	12	13	14	15	16	17	18	19	20	21	22	23	24	25	26	27	28	29	30	31	32	33	34	35	36	37	38	39	40	41	42	43	Apps	T	Pts
N (Newton) Adams	-	H	-	F	F	F	-	-	G	-	-	-	-	-	-	D	-	-	-	-	-	-	G	-	D	E	E	E	-	-	-	H	H	H	H	-	E	-	-	H	-	G	G	19	5	15
LB (Louis) Baillon	-	-	-	-	-	-	-	-	-	-	-	-	-	-	-	>I	-	I	I	I	-	I	-	I	-	-	-	-	-	-	-	-	-	-	-	-	-	-	-	-	-	-	-	6	-	-
RJ (Bobby) Barr E3	-	-	-	-	-	-	-	-	-	-	-	0	0	0	-	0	0	0	0	0	0	-	0	-	0	0	0	0	0	0	0*	-	0	0	0	0	0	0	0	0	-	-	-	25	-	8
CESJ (Charles) Beamish I4	-	-	-	-	-	-	-	-	-	-	-	-	-	-	-	-	-	-	C	C	D	-	-	-	-	-	-	-	-	-	-	E	-	-	-	-	-	-	-	-	-	-	-	4	-	-
HJ (Harold) Bennett	B	B	B	B	B	B	-	-	-	-	-	-	-	-	-	-	-	-	-	-	-	-	-	B	-	-	-	-	-	-	-	-	-	-	-	-	-	-	-	-	-	-	-	7	1	3
JTW (Tom) Berry E+	G	E	E	E	E	E	-	E	E	E	-	-	-	-	-	-	E	E	E	E	-	-	-	-	-	-	-	-	D	D	D	D	D	D	D	E	D	D	D	D	D	D	D	28	1	3
RA (Ralph) Buckingham E1	N*	N*	N*	N*	N*	N*	-	N*	N*	N*	-	N*	N*	K*	-	N*	J*	N*	J*	-	-	-	-	-	-	-	N*	N*	N*	-	-	-	N*	N*	N*	N*	N*	N*	N*	N*	-	K*	K*	29	6	18
HA (Hugh) Constantine	-	-	-	-	-	-	E	G	-	G	-	G	G	G	G	H	G	G	-	-	E	D	E	-	-	-	-	<G	-	-	-	-	-	-	-	-	-	-	-	-	-	-	-	14	-	18
PB (Paddy) Coote I1	-	-	-	-	-	K	-	-	M	-	-	L	L	<M	-	-	-	-	-	-	-	-	-	-	-	-	-	-	-	-	-	-	-	-	-	-	-	-	-	-	-	-	-	5	2	16
MP (Morgan) Crowe I13	M	M	M	M	M	M	-	-	-	M	-	M	M	J	-	M	-	M	M	M*	M*	-	-	-	-	L*	M	-	M	M*	-	M*	M	M	-	M	M	M	M	M	M*	L	L	30	6	87
EW (Edgar) Darnill	-	-	>K	K	K	-	-	-	K	K	N	-	-	-	-	-	-	-	K	K	-	K	N	-	K	N	-	-	-	K	K	K	-	-	-	-	-	-	-	-	-	-	-	15	6	18
FC (Fred) Drummond	H	-	D	H	G	-	H	-	-	-	F	-	-	-	-	-	-	-	-	-	-	H	H	F	F	-	-	-	-	-	-	-	-	-	-	-	-	-	-	-	-	-	-	10	3	9
JHF (Harry) Edmiston	-	-	H	-	H	G	F	H	H	F	H	F	-	-	-	-	-	-	-	-	-	-	-	-	-	-	-	-	-	-	H	-	-	-	-	-	-	-	-	-	H	H	H	13	-	13
BC (Bernard) Gadney E7	I	I	I	I	I	I	-	-	-	I	-	I	I	-	-	-	I	-	-	-	I	-	I*	-	-	-	-	I	-	-	-	-	-	I	-	-	-	I	-	-	-	I	I	17	11	33
TE (Thomas) Goodman	-	-	-	-	-	-	-	-	-	-	-	-	-	-	-	-	-	-	-	-	-	-	-	-	>I	I	I	-	-	I	I	I	<I	-	-	-	-	-	-	-	-	-	-	7	-	-
GB (Brian) Gray	-	-	-	-	-	-	-	-	-	-	-	-	-	-	-	-	-	-	-	>N	-	-	K	K	-	-	-	-	-	-	-	-	-	-	-	-	-	-	K	-	N	<N	-	6	5	15
G (George) Greaves	-	-	-	-	-	-	C	-	-	-	C	-	-	-	C	C	-	C	A	-	C	-	C	C	A	C	C	C	C	C	B	B	C	B	B	B	B	C	-	C	C	C	C	27	-	-
HG (Harold) Griffin	-	-	-	-	-	-	-	-	-	-	>E	-	-	-	<E	-	-	-	-	-	-	-	-	-	-	-	-	-	-	-	-	-	-	-	-	-	-	-	-	-	-	-	-	2	-	-
JT (Jeff) Hardwicke	K	K	-	-	-	-	-	-	-	-	-	-	-	-	-	-	N	-	-	-	-	-	-	-	-	-	-	-	-	-	-	-	-	-	-	-	-	-	-	-	-	-	-	3	3	9
CS Harris	-	-	-	-	-	-	-	-	-	-	-	-	-	-	-	-	-	-	-	-	-	-	>F	-	E	G	H	H	H	H	-	-	-	-	-	-	H	-	<H	-	-	-	-	9	1	3
GN Harris	-	-	-	-	-	>H	-	F	F	H	-	H	H	F	-	F	F	F	-	F	F	F	-	-	-	F	F	F	F	F	F	F	F	F	F	F	F	F	F	G	F	F	<F	31	4	12
SF (Frank) Herbert	-	-	-	-	-	-	K	-	-	-	K	-	-	-	N	-	-	-	-	-	-	-	-	-	N	-	-	-	-	-	-	-	-	-	-	-	-	-	-	-	-	-	-	4	-	-
EPA Hewitt	-	-	-	-	-	-	-	-	-	-	-	>K	K	N	K	K	K	K	-	-	-	-	-	-	-	K	K	K	-	N	N	N	K	K	K	K	K	K	-	K	-	-	<N	21	9	27
JM (John) Hodgson E6 GB2	-	-	-	-	-	-	-	-	-	-	-	-	-	-	-	-	-	-	-	-	-	>G	-	-	-	-	-	-	-	-	-	-	-	-	-	-	-	H	G	E	-	-	-	4	-	-
AP (Alan) Hughes	-	-	-	-	A	A	-	C	C	C	-	A	A	A	-	A	A	A	-	A	A	B	A	A	-	A	A	A	A	A	A	A	A	A	A	A	A	A	A	-	A	A	A	33	1	3
WA (Wilf) Jackson	L	L	L	L	L	L	-	M	L	L	-	-	-	L	-	L	M	L	L	L	-	N	M	M	L	-	L	L	L	-	L	L	L	L	L	L	L	-	L	L	L	M	M	34	9	27
DA (Joe) Kendrew E5	-	-	-	-	-	-	-	-	-	-	B*	D	D	D	-	-	D	B	-	-	-	-	-	-	-	-	-	-	-	-	-	-	-	-	-	-	-	-	-	-	-	-	-	6	-	-
Sgt. CGR (Cyril) Lewis	E	G	G	G	-	-	G	-	-	-	D	-	-	E	D	-	-	-	-	-	-	-	-	-	-	-	-	-	-	-	-	-	-	-	-	G	-	G	E	F	-	-	-	12	-	-
JG (John) Llewelyn	-	-	-	-	-	-	L	L	-	-	-	-	-	-	J	-	-	-	-	-	-	-	-	-	-	-	-	-	-	-	-	-	-	-	-	-	-	-	-	-	0	<0	-	5	-	2
I Lloyd	-	-	-	-	-	-	>M	K	-	-	-	-	-	-	L	-	L	-	-	-	-	L	L	M	-	-	-	-	L	M	-	-	-	<M	-	-	-	-	-	-	-	-	-	10	4	12
SA (Sydney Arthur) Loxton	-	-	-	-	-	-	>B	B	B	B	-	B	B	B	-	B	B	-	B	B	B	-	B	-	B	B	B	B	B	B	-	-	B	-	-	-	-	B	B	B	B	B	B	26	-	-
JR (John) McLean	-	-	-	-	-	-	-	-	-	-	-	-	-	-	-	-	-	-	>N	-	-	-	-	-	-	-	-	-	-	-	-	-	J	-	J	J	-	L	J	-	-	-	-	6	1	11
CS (Charlie) Manson	0	0	0	0	0	0	0	-	0	0	0	-	-	-	0	-	-	-	-	-	-	<0	-	-	-	-	-	-	-	-	-	-	-	-	-	-	-	-	-	-	-	-	-	12	-	6
NC (Norman) Page	-	-	-	-	-	-	-	-	-	-	-	-	-	-	-	-	-	-	-	-	-	-	-	>0	-	-	-	-	-	-	-	0	-	-	-	-	-	-	-	<0	-	-	-	3	-	-
WE (Bill) Parker	-	-	-	-	-	-	-	-	-	-	G	-	F	H	-	G	H	H	G	G	G	-	-	-	G	-	G	-	G	G	G	G	G	G	G	H	G	-	-	-	-	-	-	20	1	3
NF Reed	-	-	-	-	-	-	-	-	-	-	-	-	-	-	-	-	-	-	-	-	-	-	-	-	>J	M	J	M	-	J	<J	-	-	-	-	-	-	-	-	-	-	-	-	6	1	3
MA (Moggie) Robinson	-	-	-	-	-	-	-	-	-	-	-	-	>E	C	-	E	C	D	D	D	-	A	D	D	C	D	D	D	E	E	C	C	E	E	E	D	C	E	-	-	E	E	E	27	2	6
SH (Stan) Saunders	F	F	-	-	-	-	-	-	-	-	-	-	-	-	-	-	-	-	H	H	-	-	-	H	H	<H	-	-	-	-	-	-	-	-	-	-	-	-	-	-	-	-	-	7	-	-
WA (Arnold) Sime	-	-	-	-	-	-	-	I	-	-	-	-	-	-	-	-	-	-	-	-	-	-	-	-	-	-	-	-	I	-	-	-	-	-	-	-	-	-	-	-	-	-	-	2	1	3
CF (Charles) Slow E1	J	J	J	J	J	J	J	J	J	J	J	J	J	-	-	J	-	J	-	J	J	-	J	-	-	J	-	J	J	-	-	J	-	J	-	-	J	J	-	J	J	J	J	29	8	60
CGJ (Charles) Stanley	A	A	A	A	-	-	<A	-	-	-	-	-	-	-	-	-	-	-	-	-	-	-	-	-	-	-	-	-	-	-	-	-	-	-	-	-	-	-	-	-	-	-	-	5	-	-
FM Tomlin	-	-	-	-	-	-	-	-	-	-	-	-	-	-	-	-	-	-	-	-	-	-	-	-	-	-	-	-	-	-	-	-	-	>I	I	I	-	I	<I	-	-	-	-	5	-	-
GPC (George) Vallance	D	D	-	D	D	D	D	D	D	D	-	-	-	-	-	-	-	-	-	-	-	-	-	-	-	-	-	-	-	-	-	-	-	-	-	-	-	-	-	-	-	-	-	9	2	9
DF (David) Walker	-	-	-	-	-	-	-	-	>I	-	I	-	-	I	<I	-	-	-	-	-	-	-	-	-	-	-	-	-	-	-	-	-	-	-	-	-	-	-	-	-	-	-	-	4	-	-
JL (Jack) Wormleighton	C	C	C	C	C	C	-	A	A	A	-	C	C	-	-	-	-	-	-	-	-	-	-	-	-	-	-	-	-	-	-	-	C	C	C	-	-	C	A	-	-	-	-	16	1	3
NA (Norman) York	-	-	-	-	-	-	-	-	-	-	-	>E	-	-	-	-	-	-	-	-	-	-	-	E	-	-	-	-	-	-	-	-	-	-	-	-	-	-	-	-	-	-	-	2	-	-

1 GAME: JL (John) Barker >I(41), JA (Jock) Beattie S16 =E(22), CT (Charles) Bloxham =F(19), CJ (Cyril) Byrne =A(11), RWK (Raymond) Clark >J(24), F/O. TI (Thomas) Davies =M(11), RW (Bob) Fallowell >H(21), R Flint =B(15), KC (Ken) Fyfe S3 =L(22), RA (Ronald) Gerrard E10 =Lt(21), HG (Harry) Greasley >G(24), Cpt. JN (John) Harrison =N(24), RE (Robert) Lauder =J(22), GWC (Graham) Meikle E3 >Kt(21), SSC (Stephen) Meikle E1 <N(21), DE (Denis) Morris K(41), 0 (Oliver) Neal >A(15), RD (Roger) Orchard >L(11), HGO (Tuppy) Owen-Smith E3 =M(22), CH (Peter) Pearse F(3), WH Preston =E(31), FC Scott =H(15), P Sharpe =F(15), WV (William) Sheppard >Nt(7), AF (Arthur) Sibson <M(15), KA (Kenneth) Stanyon-Jacques I(7), NJ Tindall <Kt(29), N (Noel) Townsend >G(41), JA (Jack) Waters S6 GB+ =C(22), RE Wright =0(8)

The key for how to read the stats is on the last page

CHAPTER 11

Paupers and the Prince

1934/1935

Debt still hung heavily over the club. Support had not picked up as much as Leicester needed and those who came regularly seldom, if ever, saw the same XV do service from one week to the next. Leicester were using between 60 and 80 players a season which could hardly make for continuity and besides, there was a growing amount of alternative attractions. At the club's annual meeting, the joint treasurer, Mr Bradshaw, declared: "It is up to the supporters if they want to save the club."

The supporters responded. The Leicester Rugby Supporters' Club was formed, under the presidency of the former forward, Charlie Cross. Grants to the Leicester Alliance were ended and the ladies of the club took over serving the teas. It is not very surprising at this traumatic stage in the club's life that the committee turned down an invitation from Amatori Club, Milan, to make a tour in Italy - they had to concentrate on the home front. (The same Milan club helped Leicester celebrate their ground centenary in 1992.)

The idea of the supporters' club had come from the other joint treasurer, Mr James G Grahame, whose three daughters had taken out a permanent loan on the rugby world by marrying Harry Greenlees and the brothers Stephen and Graham Meikle. The club's function, it was stressed, was to support rugby throughout the city and county but their primary fundraising efforts, dances, socials, fetes and funfairs, were directed towards Leicester's coffers and in the five seasons before the Second World War they raised £2,225 for the Tigers. Over 300 people attended the inaugural meeting, at the Granby Halls, while another source of income was developed in the letting of Welford Road for professional boxing shows.

The 1934/35 season began with the decision of the former Coalville forward, GN Harris, who had improved spectacularly during 1934, to join Salford Rugby League Club (he was to be followed North a year later by another ex-Coalville player, centre I Lloyd, who joined Barrow). But on the credit side Leicester had the services of Lancashire's Roy Leyland at centre, Hodgson in the back row, and a useful Scottish fly-half, John McLean. When asked why he preferred to play for Leicester when his work was in London, Hodgson is reputed to have replied: "I haven't got a bowler hat and an umbrella so I can't join 'Quins and I certainly haven't got a sports car to admit me to Blackheath so I'm happy to have a couple of hours on the train and play for Leicester."

Leicester's first ever souvenir programme was devised and sold by the Supporters' Club for the 1934 Barbarians game.

Hodgson, whose business interests subsequently took him to Johannesburg and then Turkey, later became the brother-in-law of another player then on the fringe of Leicester's regular side, JTW Berry, a back row forward from the Market Harborough area who played his first game in Tigers' colours in 1932. In the early 30s Tom Berry played a lot of his rugby for Market Harborough, near his farm, but he was to win a reputation as an immensely hard-working forward which brought him three England caps before the outbreak of the Second World War. His administrative qualities were to take him further than that, for he became manager to the first England side to go on a short tour in 1963 to New Zealand and subsequently the first Leicester member to become President of the Rugby Football Union over the 1968/69 season.

At this stage, however, Berry was still hoping for a regular spot with the club, in what was to be the consistent Ralph Buckingham's last season. It was a memorable swansong, however. Buckingham formed part of a back division that would have done any England side proud: in the game against Harlequins it was hoped to field an all-international back division when Barr, Graham Meikle, Leyland, Crowe, Buckingham, Slow and Gadney were named, but Slow dropped out.

In addition Buckingham, along with Barr, got his first game for the Barbarians, against the East Midlands, and he became the club's first choice goal-kicker after 10 years when he had never place-kicked at all. "Anyone ought to be able to kick goals, Bernard," said Buckingham to his captain, Gadney, one day when the kicks were not going over at all. "You have a shot then," said Gadney and Buckingham did so well that for the first time in his career he became the club's leading scorer.

In his last home match, against Blackheath, he scored 15 points in a 39-8 win and in his last match for Tigers, on tour against Exeter, he passed 100 points. His attitude to the game can perhaps be encapsulated in the remark he once made: "We all like to win but to lose well if we can't." He got a good send off from the Press too, for Dai Gent, writing in *The Sunday Times,* said: "Quite one of the best club players any side in the country has ever had. Versatile, skilful and always cheerful, Buckingham has rendered his club grand service."

During the 1934/35 international season Gadney found himself for once on the sidelines, as his old rival Jimmy Giles of Coventry was given a chance by the selectors. Perhaps a selector

Miss M Martin's lady's season tickets for 1934/35 and 1935/36

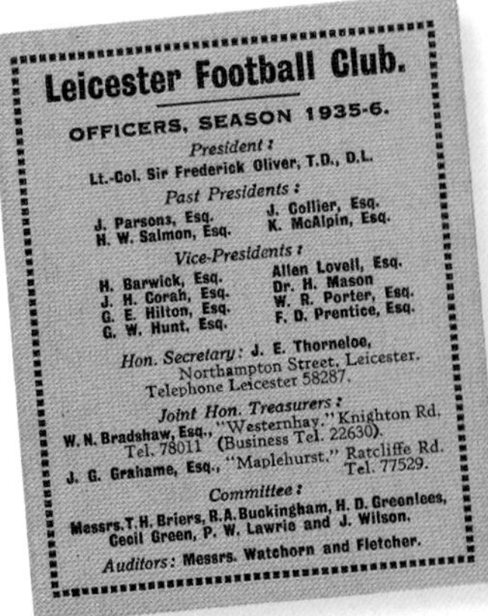

Leicester Football Club.

OFFICERS, SEASON 1935-6.

President:
Lt.-Col. Sir Frederick Oliver, T.D., D.L.

Past Presidents:
J. Parsons, Esq. J. Collier, Esq.
H. W. Salmon, Esq. K. McAlpin, Esq.

Vice-Presidents:
H. Barwick, Esq. Allen Lovell, Esq.
J. H. Corah, Esq. Dr. H. Mason
G. E. Hilton, Esq. W. R. Porter, Esq.
G. W. Hunt, Esq. F. D. Prentice, Esq.

Hon. Secretary: J. E. Thorneloe, Northampton Street, Leicester. Telephone Leicester 58287.

Joint Hon. Treasurers:
W. N. Bradshaw, Esq., "Westernhay," Knighton Rd. Tel. 78011 (Business Tel. 22630).
J. G. Grahame, Esq., "Maplehurst," Ratcliffe Rd. Tel. 77529.

Committee:
Messrs. T. H. Briers, R. A. Buckingham, H. D. Greenlees, Cecil Green, P. W. Lawrie and J. Wilson.

Auditors: Messrs. Watchorn and Fletcher.

No. 234

Leicester Football Club.
WELFORD ROAD GROUND.

LADY'S TICKET 18/-
INCLUDING TAX 2/10.
SEASON 1934-5.

ADMITS TO
Members' Stand
(CENTRE)

Not Transferable.

Hon. Sec.

ADMIT
Miss M

SEMPER EADEM

THIS RECEIPT MUST BE AFFIXED ON THE SPACE PROVIDED ON BACK OF TICKET.

Leicester Football Club.
93 1/7/ 1934
Received the sum of
For Season Ticket No. 234
18/-
M iss M. Martin

W. N. BRADSHAW
J. G. GRAHAME
Joint Hon. Treasurers.

attended the club game against London Welsh in December when, firstly, the opposition were delayed on their journey by train and had to be ferried to the ground by a fleet of taxis then, secondly, Gadney sent a telegram to say he was held up at Banbury; at 2.45 pm a second telegram arrived from the hapless scrum-half (expense no object): "Engine broken down - fill my place." But 35 minutes later, the player arrived, Buckingham moved to the wing and Newton Adams back to the pack and the two clubs played 25 minutes each way with no interval. Enough to confuse any selector! But Gadney returned for England in the Calcutta Cup game, with Headingley's Dick Auty as his half-back partner. Auty had played several games for Leicester and was well known as a brilliant attacker, even if his defensive qualities were not quite so marked. Kendrew had taken over from Gadney as England's captain and the 22-year-old Leyland played in all three games, the only caps of a distinguished career, though he was to go with the British Lions to South Africa in 1938.

Another youngster made his bow for Tigers this season too, an 18-year old product of Trent College, Prince Alexander Obolensky. Playing on the wing over the Christmas period, he scored two tries in a 12-8 defeat against Birkenhead Park. It was remarkable then that a Russian prince, born in St Petersburg, should have been playing first class rugby but Obolensky's subsequent career for Oxford University and England showed just what a talented performer he was.

← ALEXANDER OBOLENSKY
Prince Alexander Obolensky claimed the melancholy distinction of being the first England international to lose his life in the Second World War, when his Hawker Hurricane fighter aeroplane crashed during a training exercise at Martlesham Heath in Suffolk. Obolensky came to England as a child after the Russian Revolution and was educated at Trent College and Brasenose College, Oxford. His rugby immortality rests firmly on the second of two tries he scored in England's 13-0 win over New Zealand in 1936, when he dummied his way diagonally, from the right wing to score in the left corner. He became a naturalised Briton later that year and was commissioned into the RAF Volunteer Reserve in 1938.

1935/1936

In 1935 Crowe returned to Ireland and Leyland left to join Richmond, which left something of a hole in the centre, but on the credit side was the acquisition of the Oxford University and England hooker, Edward Nicholson. He joined a club the best part of £6,000 in debt but still to the forefront as far as the England selectors were concerned. For this was the season of Jack Manchester's All Blacks and Obolensky's match against them.

The Russian prince, the RAF centre SG 'Ranji' Walker and Charles Beamish had all played for the Midlands XV beaten 9-3 by the All Blacks at Coventry and seven more Leicester players appeared in the Leicestershire and East Midlands XV beaten 16-3 by the tourists before a 27,000 crowd at Welford Road. In the backs were Barr, Slow, Gadney, John Charles and John Fox - the latter two both products of Stoneygate, the one a wing, the other a hard-tackling centre - while the pack included Nicholson and MA 'Moggie' Robinson. Also in the side was Morgan Crowe but this time there was no repeat of the famous win of four years previously.

Slow, the hero against the Springboks, pulled a leg muscle in the first quarter and left the field, Bill Weston coming out of the pack to cover for him. Reduced to 14 men for most of the match, the combined side had to concede the game although Gadney and Charles both went close, and Longland scored the counties' try.

On the club scene there were rumbles that Leicester rugby was on the way down, with six defeats in nine games. There was a 0-0 draw with the Barbarians and a rash of honours tended to gloss over some indifferent results. Gadney, Kendrew, Nicholson and Obolensky were picked for England against the All Blacks, with Gadney captaining the side, and although years later that match is remembered for Obolensky's spectacular

↑↓ Team lineups and programme from the touring New Zealanders' game at Welford Road 16.11.1935.

brace of tries in a 13-0 win, Gadney was more inclined to recall the contribution of England's pack early in the game: "We had a very heavy pack - just like Leicestershire did against the Springboks - and we decided to shove very hard in the first two or three scrums, to make the New Zealanders feel worried. After the match Jack Manchester told me: 'That first scrum, I knew we were up against it.' When we got the ball I tended to break, as I did with Leicester, which made them think we were trying to go through that way."

However, most people remember the game for Obolensky's second try, when he turned up on the wrong side of the field - a not infrequent occurrence - and took advantage of a slight hesitation by Peter Cranmer to run diagonally through the All Blacks' defence. For Kendrew it was his fifth appearance against these particular tourists, having done duty against them for Combined Services, London Counties (twice), Ulster (where he was stationed) and England. Later in the season, against Ireland, he was picked at hooker when Nicholson was dropped and Hodgson was picked against an Irish XV including

Gadney and Obolensky on their way to Wales for the visit of England in January 1936.

Charles Beamish. But only Gadney and Obolensky survived through the season to play against Scotland.

The season ended with only 15 wins and 20 defeats and the club established a special committee to look for talent in Leicester. Of the 84 players used that season, 41 were local and a game against a Rest of Leicester XV in April left Tigers with an unimpressive 13-3 win. There were calls for the revival of the A team as a stepping stone for local talent, and it was obvious that change was in the air.

Three Leicester members spent the summer with a British team in Argentina, Gadney (as captain), Charles Beamish and Obolensky, with a fourth Leicester man, Doug Prentice, acting as manager.

Charles Beamish, one of four brothers to play for Tigers, toured Argentina with the Lions in the summer of 1936.

1936/1937

The club's talent scouts came up with a list of names of local players worth consideration by Leicester, 70 of them being invited to pre-season training at Welford Road. Among other things Tigers were short of a hooker, having lost Nicholson to Guy's Hospital the previous season, and the consistent Melton Mowbray farmer Sydney Loxton having retired.

But it was not an auspicious opening to the 1936/37 season. Bedford won the first game 18-12, the first time since the war they had won at Leicester and the first time since 1919 that Tigers had lost their initial game. The experiment of playing a back row forward, Rodney Willcox, at centre, was discontinued fairly rapidly and form picked up. Gadney returned to action to help in a fine 18-18 draw at Newport and Leicester became the first club to beat Oxford University - including Obolensky - and they then beat a full-strength Gloucester 7-3.

The Hinckley hooker George Ridgway, despite being sent off in a county match for persistent foot-up, was picked for Major R V Stanley's XV against Oxford and then won a reserve place for England's first trial. Another newcomer to make a distinct impression - as much for his youth as anything else - was the Wyggeston School captain, JR Preston, who played centre against Birkenhead Park over the Christmas holidays. All but one of the six December fixtures were lost, including that against the Barbarians which began with a minute's silence in memory of their founder, Percy Carpmael, who died that year.

Once more the club had hit a low spot: there was a run of 12 defeats in the space of 13 matches and though Berry and Barr were called on as reserves for England against Wales, Tigers could make no excuses about losing a large number of players to trial and international games. To add to their depression, their leading player, Gadney, accepted a post at a school in Leeds and this was to be his seventh and last season with Leicester. Another, the former Aylestone St James and RAF prop George Greaves, joined the rugby league club Castleford and for the first time in 17 years, Leicester lost all three games on their West Country tour at Easter.

No longer were they cock of the Midlands roost. After the defeat at Coventry there were numerous complaints about the tactics of the Coventry wing forwards, who allegedly spent much of the match virtually offside. A fortnight later the Rugby Football Union approved an experiment in the game with Northampton at Welford Road, law 17(b) being tampered with so that players were prohibited from advancing at a set scrum in front of their own forwards until the ball had gone. The result was, according to the *Leicester Mercury*, "a gloriously open game", won by the Saints 11-4.

But overall the results were the worst since 1888/89, with 14 wins and 23 defeats, even if a very young Leicester XV beat Bristol and Blackheath in the last two games. The crowning insult was defeat in the first round of the Leicestershire Sevens, against Aylestone Athletic, a competition in which Leicester had been in the final every year since its inception.

Confusion in stripes, Leicester beat Bath 11-0 at Welford Road 28.11.1936.

1937/1938

Obviously the policy of picking players who would be regularly available - which meant in practice more home-based players - was going to take time to come good. But the 1937/38 season brought another useful crop of promising youngsters, among them the Hinckley forward Denis Bolesworth, a former Uppingham School pupil Bill Bainbridge who had played a couple of games the previous season as a schoolboy and whose father had appeared for the club before the war, and the Aylestone St James full-back, Ernest Watkin.

Slightly better known, at the time, was the Welsh trials centre Gwyn Thomas, who joined from Burton, but sadly he spent most of the season out of action through injury. Honours were comparatively few, Berry and Ridgway becoming non-travelling England reserves against Wales and Berry being forced to turn down a place in the Barbarians XV against the East Midlands because of injury. The Baa-baas, incidentally, had done Leicester no favours by picking Gadney and Auty at half-back against them over Christmas. The two were now in harness for Headingley and assisted the guest side to a record 34-0 win, Auty scoring three tries.

Bainbridge distinguished himself by playing every game during the season and travelling some 10,000 miles to do so since he lived in Warrington. Curiously, having played 41 consecutive games for the club, the following season he joined Birkenhead Park since Leicester were better off for locks and could afford to ignore his qualities. Another son of a famous father found his way into the side this season, in the shape of Gordon Lawrie, son of Percy, who made his debut against Blackheath.

It was a 16-0 win for Leicester but the limelight undoubtedly went to former Newbold back row player, Fred Doe, who scored four tries. In 13 games he scored nine tries and played regularly the next season, sufficiently well to get an England trial, though Warwickshire never picked him for their county side. Cecil Beamish played on tour, following in the well-trodden footprints of brothers George, Charles and Victor, and the season ended on a hopeful note with a 27-0 win over Bath, the best win of the season.

It had also been a good year for the Stoneygate wing Frank Herbert, who topped Leicester's points chart with 77. Herbert scored 12 tries during 1937/38 in a comeback which must have caused some blushes at Welford Road. He made his Leicester debut as far back as 1931 but he never won a regular place until the two seasons which preceded the Second World War - certainly a case of better late than never.

↑ Sir Frederick Oliver was president of the club between 1931-1939.

↑ Programme from Tom Berry's England debut.

1938/1939

The storm clouds were gathering over Europe as Leicester went into the 1938/39 season, which was unfortunate because prospects for a fairly young side looked bright. Tom Berry captained a team which included the Scottish cap from Dunfermline, Maurice Henderson, who had become a PE instructor at Loughborough Colleges, and the England trials centre Francis Edwards, who joined from Birkenhead Park. But for the Second World War, Francis would surely have become a senior cap as he was a very fine player but he had to make do with a wartime international selection. Another centre, Reginald Squibbs, who had spent much of the previous year injured, joined from Loughborough and did enough to win a Welsh trial while the Leicester pack included Peter Jerwood, who had played against them the previous season while he had been a student at Cambridge University.

In fact Tigers had a strong link with the Light Blues this season, and when the two clubs met in a game refereed by Wavell Wakefield, Leicester had Ronnie Knapp - then a student at Cambridge - at fly-half while the University had Jim Parsons at scrum-half. Parsons had first played for Leicester four years earlier while still at Rydal School and he fought a protracted battle with the Old Wyggestonians scrum-half Eric Bevins for the right to succeed Gadney. On the day the students had the edge, winning 28-22.

For the first time since 1934 Leicester beat Coventry 6-0, despite an injury to Bevins which reduced them to 14 men, and they did remarkably well to beat Northampton 5-3 on the last day of the old year: snow prevented the Hinckley men, Bolesworth and Ridgway, reaching Northampton and Leicester started with a six-man pack, to be reinforced during the game by York and Lees, both of whom were spectating. Berry, Edwards, Ridgway, Doe and Tony Anthony, another back row forward, played in England's first trial and there were Scottish trials for Henderson and the former Loughborough Colleges centre Wilfred Young, while Squibbs had to turn down a Welsh trial because he had influenza. Another newcomer, Keith Downes, a centre from Cambridge who joined Leicester over Christmas, was named in a Welsh trial despite the fact that he had been born to Scottish parents at Birkenhead and lived most of his life in England. His Welsh "qualification" was that he had gone to Rydal School in North Wales, but, probably confused by it all, he withdrew from the trial.

Edwards scored two tries from the wing to help the Tigers to an 8-6 win over the Barbarians and the club were delighted to see their skipper, Berry, picked at last for England in the back row, even though he spent much of the season in the second row. Kept out for so long by Northampton's consistent Bill Weston, Berry played in all England's games while Edwards and Downes were reserves for their respective countries - Downes had opted for Scotland. Obolensky, now with Rosslyn Park, made a final appearance in Leicester colours against Richmond at the request of the England selectors and Gadney was available to tour at the season's end. Tragically his old Leicester and East Midlands partner, Charles Slow, missing from the first-class game for two seasons, was killed in a motoring accident returning from playing the last game of the season with Stony Stratford.

Nevertheless, in all respects it had been a much improved year. The Supporters' Club, working away in the background, had played an immense part in bolstering the club's finances and the players responded by winning 20 of their 36 games. In a year when Loughborough reached the Universities Athletic Union final, Leicester had received a lot of help from Colleges members and a curious statistic from that season was that Tigers used ten fly-halves.

1939/1940

There was every reason to suppose that the new decade would be a bright one. Fixtures were due to be renewed with Cardiff and Gadney was hoping to be available again. The Australians were to tour but no sooner had they set foot in this country than war was declared against Germany - it was a long way to come to play no rugby. The first game of the 1939/40 season should have been against Bedford but only one member of the opposition, the Irish international wing Victor Lyttle, appeared so a hurriedly organised Rest XV played Leicester and lost 20-6. The Territorial Army had called up its members and, for the second time in 25 years, rugby closed down.

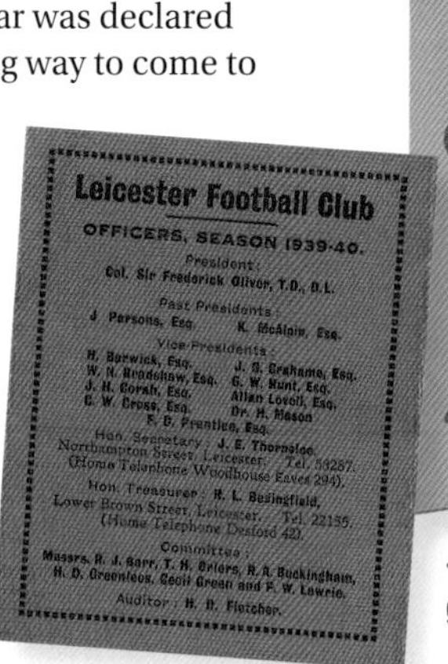

Leicester Football Club

OFFICERS, SEASON 1939-40.

President:
Col. Sir Frederick Oliver, T.D., D.L.

Past Presidents:
J. Parsons, Esq. K. McAlpin, Esq.

Vice-Presidents:
H. Barwick, Esq. J. S. Grahame, Esq.
W. N. Bradshaw, Esq. G. W. Hunt, Esq.
J. H. Corah, Esq. Allan Lovell, Esq.
C. W. Cross, Esq. Dr. H. Mason
F. B. Prentice, Esq.

Hon. Secretary: J. E. Thorneloe,
Northampton Street, Leicester. Tel. 58287.
(Home Telephone Woodhouse Eaves 294).

Hon. Treasurer: R. L. Bedingfield,
Lower Brown Street, Leicester. Tel. 22135.
(Home Telephone Desford 42).

Committee:
Messrs. R. J. Barr, T. H. Briers, R. A. Buckingham,
H. D. Greenlees, Cecil Green and F. W. Lawrie.

Auditor: H. B. Fletcher.

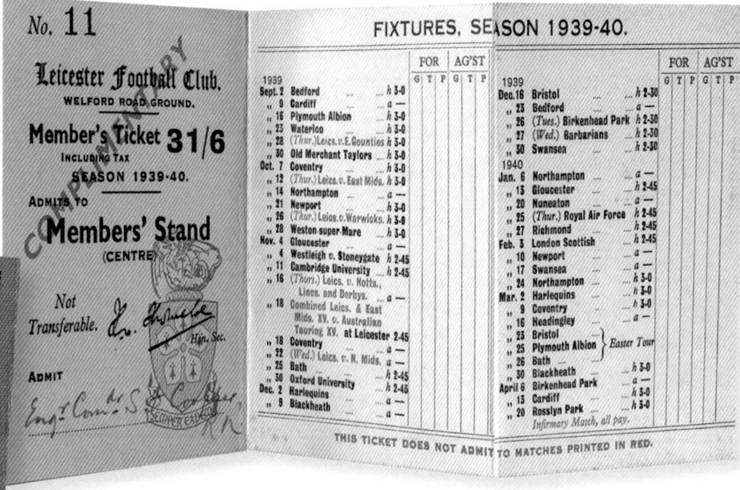

No. 11

Leicester Football Club.
WELFORD ROAD GROUND.

Member's Ticket 31/6
INCLUDING TAX
SEASON 1939-40.

ADMITS TO
Members' Stand
(CENTRE)

COMPLIMENTARY

Not Transferable. J. E. Thorneloe Hon. Sec.

ADMIT Engr. Comdr. S. G. Cooper R.N.

SEMPER EADEM

FIXTURES, SEASON 1939-40.

Date	Fixture		FOR G	FOR T	FOR P	AG'ST G	AG'ST T	AG'ST P
1939								
Sept. 2	Bedford	h 3-0						
„ 9	Cardiff	a —						
„ 16	Plymouth Albion	h 3-0						
„ 23	Waterloo	h 3-0						
„ 28	(Thur.) Leics. v. E. Counties	h 3-0						
„ 30	Old Merchant Taylors	h 3-0						
Oct. 7	Coventry	h 3-0						
„ 12	(Thur.) Leics. v. East Mids.	h 3-0						
„ 14	Northampton	a —						
„ 21	Newport	h 3-0						
„ 26	(Thur.) Leics. v. Warwicks.	h 3-0						
„ 28	Weston-super-Mare	h 3-0						
Nov. 4	Gloucester	a —						
„ 4	Westleigh v. Stoneygate	h 2-45						
„ 11	Cambridge University	h 2-45						
„ 16	(Thurs.) Leics. v. Notts., Lincs. and Derbys.	a —						
„ 18	Combined Leics. & East Mids. XV. v. Australian Touring XV.	at Leicester 2-45						
„ 18	Coventry	a —						
„ 22	(Wed.) Leics. v. N. Mids.	a —						
„ 25	Bath	h 2-45						
„ 30	Oxford University	h 2-45						
Dec. 2	Harlequins	a —						
„ 9	Blackheath	a —						

Date	Fixture		FOR G	FOR T	FOR P	AG'ST G	AG'ST T	AG'ST P
1939								
Dec. 16	Bristol	h 2-30						
„ 23	Bedford	a —						
„ 26	(Tues.) Birkenhead Park	h 2-30						
„ 27	(Wed.) Barbarians	h 2-30						
„ 30	Swansea	h 2-30						
1940								
Jan. 6	Northampton	a —						
„ 13	Gloucester	h 2-45						
„ 20	Nuneaton	a —						
„ 25	(Thur.) Royal Air Force	h 2-45						
„ 27	Richmond	h 2-45						
Feb. 3	London Scottish	h 2-45						
„ 10	Newport	a —						
„ 17	Swansea	a —						
„ 24	Northampton	h 3-0						
Mar. 2	Harlequins	h 3-0						
„ 9	Coventry	h 3-0						
„ 16	Headingley	a —						
„ 23	Bristol	Easter Tour						
„ 25	Plymouth Albion	Easter Tour						
„ 26	Bath	Easter Tour						
„ 30	Blackheath	h 3-0						
April 6	Birkenhead Park	a —						
„ 13	Cardiff	h 3-0						
„ 20	Rosslyn Park (Infirmary Match, all pay.)	h 3-0						

THIS TICKET DOES NOT ADMIT TO MATCHES PRINTED IN RED.

↑ Member's ticket for the aborted 1939/40 season given to ex-England international Sydney Coopper RN.

↑ LEICESTER FOOTBALL CLUB 1935/36
Back: Tolton (Referee), Barr, York, T.Bevan, Goode, Hopkin, Willcox, Bradshaw (Hon.Tres).
Middle: Rogers, Adams, Robinson, Berry, Gadney (capt), Hodgson, Vallance, Charles, Fox.
Front: Bottrill, Parsons.

↑ LEICESTER FOOTBALL CLUB 1936/37
Back: Thorneloe (Hon.Sec), Bottrill, Preston, Crick, Obolensky, Bainbridge, Willcox, Ridgway, Grahame (Jt Hon.Tres), Bradshaw (Jt Hon.Tres).
Middle: Rogers, Wormleighton, Adams, Barr (capt), Berry, Vallance, Parsons.
Front: Squibbs, Moseby, Sharp, Cooke.

↑ LEICESTER FOOTBALL CLUB 1937/38
Back: Watkin, Taylor, Vallance, Bainbridge, Bolesworth, G.Herbert, Doe, Glover, Stapleton, Thorneloe (Hon.Sec).
Middle: Fowler, Fox, Berry, Barr (capt), Ridgway, F.Herbert, Anthony.
Front: Clark, Preston, Bevins, Lawrie.

↑ LEICESTER FOOTBALL CLUB 1938/39
Back: Thorneloe (Hon.Sec), Squibbs, Ridgway, Stapleton, Doe, Jerwood, Richards, Bottrill, Bedingfield (Hon.Tres), Buckingham (Touch Judge).
Middle: Henderson, G.Herbert, Anthony, F.Herbert, Berry (capt), Barr, Vallance, Parsons, Bolesworth.
Front: Treharne, Fox, Bevins, Taylor.
Inset: Young, Edwards.

1934/35	Home Ground: Welford Road											
	Captain: Bernard Gadney											

OVERALL RECORD:					T	C	PG	DG	MK	PTS
PLD	W	D	L	Tigers scored:	109	50	6	9	1	484
44	26	4	14	Opponents scored:	64	26	7	6	0	289

GM	DATE		VEN	OPPONENTS	RESULT	TRIES	KICKS	ATT
CLUB MATCHES								
1	Sep	1	H	**Bedford**	W 10-8	Jackson	Slow d/m	2216
2		8	H	**Penarth**	W 41-0	Shepherd(4), Adams(3), Drummond, Hughes, McLean, Slow	Shepherd c, Buckingham 2c, C.Lewis c	1431
3		10m	H	**Bridgend**	W 8-3	Berry, Shepherd	Giles c	1320
4		15	H	**Plymouth Albion**	W 20-0	Drummond(2), Buckingham, Loxton	M.Crowe 2c, McLean d	1841
5		22	a	Bedford	W 9-5	Gadney, Jackson, Leyland	-	-
6		27th	H	**Llanelly**	W 6-3	Hardwicke, Palmer	-	1421
7		29	H	**Waterloo**	W 29-5	Shepherd(3), Adams, M.Crowe, Drummond, Hardwicke	Buckingham 2c, McLean d	787
8	Oct	6	H	**Coventry**	W 10-3	M.Crowe, McLean	M.Crowe c, Meikle c	3426
9		8m	H	**Bective Rangers**	W 11-6	Gadney, Shepherd	McLean p, M.Crowe c	852
10		13	a	Bridgwater & Albion	D 0-0	-	-	1000
11		20	a	Newport	L 13-24	Adams, Fallowell, Shepherd	Buckingham c, McLean c	4000
12		27	a	Northampton	L 3-11	Buckingham	-	5000
13	Nov	3	H	**Moseley**	W 9-8	Morris, Oakes	C.Lewis p	678
14		7w	a	Oxford University	W 11-0	Jackson, Leyland	Buckingham c/p	1000
15		10	a	Cambridge University	L 4-24	-	Slow d	-
16		17	a	Rugby	W 8-6	Meikle, Slow	Kendrew c	3000
17		24	H	**Nuneaton**	L 9-10	C.Barker, Meikle, Pearse	-	460
18	Dec	1	a	Harlequins	L 4-10	-	J.Barker d	-
19		8	a	Blackheath	W 13-6	Adams(2)	Buckingham 2c/p	-
20		15	H	**Bristol**	W 12-8	Shepherd	Buckingham c/p, Slow d	1349
21		22	H	**London Welsh**	W 8-0	-	C.Barker d, Fox d	640
22		26w	H	**Birkenhead Park**	L 8-12	Obolensky(2)	Buckingham c	5247
23		27th	H	**Barbarians**	L 5-6	Berry	Buckingham c	8500
24		28f	H	**Manchester**	W 3-0	Drummond	-	409
25		29	H	**Gloucester**	W 27-0	Gadney(2), Jackson(2), Kaye, Shepherd, Vallance	Buckingham 3c	1733
26	Jan	5	H	**Swansea**	L 3-5	Adams	-	1247
27		12	H	**Old Merchant Taylors**	W 17-0	Buckingham, Adams, Fox, McLean, Vallance	Buckingham c	892
28		19	a	Bath	L 0-12	-	-	1500
29		24th	H	**Royal Air Force**	L 0-4	-	-	754
30		26	a	Richmond	W 11-4	Fox, Greasley, Morris	Buckingham c	-
31	Feb	2	a	London Scottish	W 9-3	Adams	Slow d, Buckingham c	-
32		9	H	**Newport**	D 0-0	-	-	1495
33		16	a	Swansea	L 0-3	-	-	-
34		23	H	**Northampton**	W 13-8	Shepherd(2), Auty	Buckingham 2c	3152
35	Mar	2	H	**Harlequins**	D 5-5	Vallance	Buckingham c	2536
36		9	a	Coventry	L 0-11	-	-	3000
37		16	H	**Rosslyn Park**	W 20-10	L.Baillon, Charles, Greasley, M.Robinson	Buckingham 4c	729
38		23	a	Gloucester	L 0-32	-	-	-
39		30	H	**Bath**	W 11-6	Charles(2), Vallance	Buckingham c	804
40	Apr	6	a	Birkenhead Park	W 24-6	Charles(3), Buckingham, Gadney	Buckingham 3c/p	2000
41		13	H	**Blackheath**	W 39-8	Slow(2), Buckingham, Charles, M.Crowe, Delgado, Gadney, Loxton, Wormleighton	Buckingham 6c	2471
42		20	a	Bristol	L 6-11	P.Crowe, Obolensky	-	5000
43		22m	a	Plymouth Albion	D 3-3	Obolensky	-	-
44		23tu	a	Exeter	W 42-0	Gadney(3), Walker(3), Delgado(2), M.Crowe, Slow	M.Crowe c, Slow c, Buckingham 3c, Hodgson c	-

INDIVIDUAL APPEARANCES 1934/35

Name / Game #	1	2	3	4	5	6	7	8	9	10	11	12	13	14	15	16	17	18	19	20	21	22	23	24	25	26	27	28	29	30	31	32	33	34	35	36	37	38	39	40	41	42	43	44	Apps	T	Pts
N (Newton) Adams	-	F	H	H	F	G	G	E	F	-	G	H	-	F	F	-	-	H	G	H	H	-	H	-	G	F	F	F	-	-	F	F	F	F	F	F	F	F	F	F	F	G	-	F	34	10	30
WT (William) Alldridge	-	-	-	-	-	-	-	-	-	-	-	-	>L	-	-	L	-	-	-	-	-	-	-	-	-	-	-	K	-	-	-	-	N	-	-	-	-	-	-	-	-	-	-	-	4	-	-
Dr. CC (Clifford) Barker	-	-	-	-	-	-	-	-	-	-	-	-	-	-	-	-	>M	M	M	-	M	<M	-	-	-	-	-	-	-	-	-	-	-	-	-	-	-	-	-	-	-	-	-	-	5	1	7
JL (John) Barker	-	-	-	-	-	-	-	-	-	I	I	I	I	-	-	-	-	I	I	I	-	I	-	I	-	<I	-	-	-	-	-	-	-	-	-	-	-	-	-	-	-	-	-	-	10	-	4
RJ (Bobby) Barr E3	0	0	0	0	0	0	0	0	0	-	0	0	-	-	-	-	-	0	0	0	0	0	0	-	0	-	0	0	0	0	0	-	0	0	0	0	-	0	0	0	0	0	0	0	34	-	-
CESJ (Charles) Beamish I7	-	-	-	-	-	-	-	-	-	-	-	-	-	-	-	-	-	F	-	F	-	-	-	-	F	-	-	-	-	-	-	-	-	-	-	-	-	-	-	-	-	-	-	-	3	-	-
HJ (Harold) Bennett	-	-	-	-	B	-	-	-	-	B	-	-	B	B	-	B	B	-	-	-	-	B	-	B	-	-	-	-	-	-	-	-	-	-	-	-	-	B	-	-	-	-	-	A	10	-	-
JTW (Tom) Berry E+	D	D	D	D	D	E	D	D	E	-	D	D	-	D	D	-	-	G	E	G	G	-	F	H	-	G	G	G	G	F	G	G	G	G	G	D	G	G	-	G	G	F	G	E	37	2	6
JSW (James) Bignal	-	-	-	-	-	-	-	-	-	>A	-	-	A	-	-	<A	-	-	-	-	-	-	-	-	-	-	-	-	-	-	-	-	-	-	-	-	-	-	-	-	-	-	-	-	3	-	-
RA (Ralph) Buckingham E1	K	N	N*	N	N	N*	L	-	N	-	K*	N*	-	N	-	-	-	N*	N*	K*	N	N*	N	0*	N	K*	K	J*	-	L	N	L*	L	M	J	J	N*	N	L	L	M	N	N	<N	37	5	101
R (Rupert) Carryer	-	-	-	-	-	-	-	-	-	-	-	-	-	-	0	0	0	-	-	-	-	-	-	-	-	0	-	-	-	-	-	<0	-	-	-	-	-	-	-	-	-	-	-	-	5	-	-
JB (John) Charles	-	-	-	-	-	-	-	-	-	-	-	-	-	-	-	-	-	-	-	-	-	-	-	-	-	-	-	-	-	-	-	>N	-	N	K	N	K	-	K	K	K	-	-	-	8	7	21
MP (Morgan) Crowe I13	-	-	-	M	M	M	M	M	M	-	L	M	-	M	-	-	-	-	-	-	-	-	-	-	-	-	-	-	-	-	-	-	-	-	L	M	M	-	M	-	L	M	L	<M	17	4	22
PM (Philip) Crowe I1	-	-	-	-	-	-	-	-	-	-	-	-	-	-	-	-	-	-	-	-	-	-	-	-	-	-	-	-	-	-	-	-	-	-	-	-	-	-	-	>M	-	L	M	-	3	1	3
AG (George) Delgado	-	-	-	-	-	-	-	-	-	-	-	-	-	-	-	-	-	-	-	-	-	-	-	-	-	-	-	-	-	>N	K	K	K	K	-	K	-	K	-	-	N	-	-	<K	9	3	9
FC (Fred) Drummond	H	H	G	F	G	F	H	F	G	-	-	G	-	H	H	-	-	-	H	-	-	-	-	F	-	-	-	-	-	-	-	-	-	-	-	-	-	-	-	-	-	-	-	-	14	5	15
RW (Bob) Fallowell	G	-	-	-	-	-	F	G	-	-	H	-	D	-	-	-	-	-	-	-	-	-	-	-	-	-	-	-	-	-	-	-	-	-	-	<G	-	-	-	-	-	-	-	-	6	1	3
JBS (John) Fox	-	-	-	-	-	-	-	-	-	-	-	-	-	-	-	-	-	>L	K	N	K	L	-	-	-	N	N	-	M	-	-	-	-	-	-	-	-	-	-	-	-	-	-	-	8	2	10
BC (Bernard) Gadney E8	I*	I*	-	I*	I*	-	I*	I*	I*	-	-	-	-	I*	I*	I*	-	-	-	-	I*	-	I*	-	I*	-	I*	-	I*	I*	I*	-	I*	I*	I*	I*	-	I*	I*	I*	I*	I*	I*	I*	28	9	27
HG (Harry) Greasley	-	-	-	-	-	-	-	-	-	-	-	-	-	-	G	-	-	-	F	-	F	F	-	-	-	H	H	H	F	H	H	H	H	H	H	H	H	H	G	H	-	-	-	G	20	2	6
G (George) Greaves	-	-	-	-	-	D	-	-	-	C	-	-	-	-	-	-	-	-	-	-	-	-	-	A	-	-	-	-	-	-	-	-	A	A	-	B	A	A	-	-	-	-	-	-	8	-	-
JM (John) Hodgson E6 GB2	E	G	F	-	-	-	-	-	-	-	-	-	-	-	-	-	-	-	-	-	-	-	-	-	H	-	-	-	-	-	-	-	-	-	-	-	-	-	H	-	H	H	H	H	9	-	2
AP (Alan) Hughes	A	A	A	A	A	A	A	A	A	-	A	A	-	A	A	-	-	-	C	A	A	A	-	C	A	A	A	A	A	A	A	A	-	-	-	<A	-	-	-	-	-	-	-	-	27	1	3
WA (Wilf) Jackson	M	L	L	L	L	-	-	-	L	-	M	-	-	K	L	-	L	-	-	-	-	-	-	M	L	M	M	M	M	-	L	-	M	-	-	-	-	L	-	-	-	-	-	-	19	5	15
DA (Joe) Kendrew E7	-	-	-	-	-	-	-	-	-	-	-	-	C*	C	B	C	-	-	-	-	-	-	A	-	-	-	-	-	-	-	-	-	-	-	-	-	-	-	-	-	-	-	-	-	5	-	2
F/O. HJF (Hugh) le Good	-	-	-	-	-	-	-	-	-	>L	-	-	M	-	<N	-	-	-	-	-	-	-	-	-	-	-	-	-	-	-	-	-	-	-	-	-	-	-	-	-	-	-	-	-	3	-	-
Sgt. CGR (Cyril) Lewis	F	E	-	-	E	-	-	-	-	E	F	-	E	-	-	-	E	E	-	-	-	-	-	-	D	-	-	-	-	G	D	D	-	D	D	-	-	-	-	D	E	E	E	D	19	-	5
R (Roy) Leyland E3	-	-	>M	-	K	-	-	L	-	-	-	K	-	L	-	-	-	-	-	-	-	-	L	-	-	-	-	-	-	-	-	-	-	-	M	-	-	-	-	-	-	-	-	-	7	2	6
SA (Sydney Arthur) Loxton	B	B	B	B	-	B	B	B	-	-	B	B	-	-	-	-	-	B	B	B	B	-	B	-	B	B	B	B	-	B	B	B	B	B	B	-	B	-	B	-	B	B	B	B	30	2	6
JR (John) McLean	L	M	-	J	J	J	J	J	J	-	J	L	-	J	M	-	-	J	J	L	J	J	J	J	J	J	J	-	J	-	-	-	-	-	-	-	-	-	-	-	-	-	-	-	23	3	22
GWC (Graham) Meikle E3	-	-	-	-	-	-	-	K	-	-	-	-	-	-	-	K	K	-	-	-	-	-	K	N	-	-	-	-	N	-	-	-	-	-	N	-	-	-	-	-	-	-	-	-	7	2	8
DE (Denis) Morris	-	-	-	-	-	-	-	-	-	-	-	-	N	-	K	N	-	-	-	-	-	-	-	-	-	-	-	-	-	<K	-	-	-	-	-	-	-	-	-	-	-	-	-	-	4	2	6
CSCR (Colin) Oakes	-	-	-	-	-	-	-	-	-	-	-	-	>H	-	-	F	<D	-	-	-	-	-	-	-	-	-	-	-	-	-	-	-	-	-	-	-	-	-	-	-	-	-	-	-	3	1	3
AS (Alexander) Obolensky E+	-	-	-	-	-	-	-	-	-	-	-	-	-	-	-	-	-	-	-	-	-	>K	-	K	-	-	-	-	-	-	-	-	-	-	-	-	-	-	-	-	-	K	K	-	4	4	12
DS (Donald) Oscroft	-	-	-	-	-	-	-	-	-	J	-	-	J	-	-	M	<J	-	-	-	-	-	-	-	-	-	-	-	-	-	-	-	-	-	-	-	-	-	-	-	-	-	-	-	4	-	-
CH (Peter) Pearse	-	-	-	E	-	-	-	-	-	-	-	-	-	-	-	H	F	-	-	-	-	-	-	-	-	-	-	-	-	-	-	-	-	-	-	-	-	-	-	-	-	-	-	-	3	1	3
MA (Moggie) Robinson	-	-	E	G	H	H	E	H	H	-	-	F	-	-	E	-	-	A	D	E	D	E	E	D	-	E	E	E	E	E	E	E	E	E	A	-	E	E	A	A	A	A	A	-	33	1	3
WV (William) Sheppard	N	K	K	K	-	-	N	N	K	N	N	-	K	-	-	-	N	K	L	M	L	-	M	L	M	L	L	L	K	-	M	M	-	L	-	L	L	M	N	-	-	-	-	-	29	14	44
CF (Charles) Slow E1	J	J	J	-	-	-	-	-	-	-	-	J	-	-	J	J	-	-	-	J	-	-	-	-	-	-	-	-	-	-	J	J	J	-	-	-	-	-	J	J	J	J	J	J	16	5	36
NE Starkey	-	-	-	-	-	-	-	-	-	>H	-	-	F	-	-	-	<H	-	-	-	-	-	-	-	-	-	-	-	-	-	-	-	-	-	-	-	-	-	-	-	-	-	-	-	3	-	-
N (Noel) Townsend	-	-	-	-	-	-	-	-	-	G	-	-	G	-	-	G	G	-	-	-	-	-	-	-	-	-	-	-	-	-	-	-	-	-	-	-	-	-	-	-	-	-	-	-	4	-	-
GPC (George) Vallance	-	-	-	-	-	-	-	-	D	D	E	E	-	E	-	-	-	D	-	D	E	D	D	E	E	D	D	D	D	D	-	-	-	-	E	-	D	D	D	E	D	D	D	-	25	4	12
JL (Jack) Wormleighton	C	C	-	C	C	C	C	C	C	-	C	C	-	-	C	-	-	C	A	C	C	C	C	-	C	C	C	C	C	C	C	C	C	C	C	C	C	C	C	C	C	C	C	C	37	1	3

1 GAME: WN (William) Ash =C(17), RO (Richard) Baillon >O(14), J (Jack) Ball >I(17), SN (Spencer) Bevan <O(10), TW (Tom) Bevan >O(13), JD (James) Burrows =O(37), ER (Edward) Coutts-Deacon =F(43), K (Kenneth) Cummings =N(26), PE (Pop) Dunkley E2 <H(22), JHF (Harry) Edmiston <F(10), RDM (Denis) Evers =I(28), RL (Robert) Francks >M(10), JL (Jimmy) Giles E2 GB+ >I(3), FE Harris =E(39), J Kaye =Kt(25), JTE (John) Kenney =A(17), DW Lewis >I(6), ADG (Austin) Matthews =G(14), CL (Clarence) Millar <B(40), O (Oliver) Neal <D(16), RA Palmer <Lt(6), GE (George) Pollard >N(40), JRH (Johnny) Pott <L(29), BV (Basil) Robinson =K(10), H (Herbert) Toft E+ =B(29), P/O. SG (Ranji) Walker >Lt(44), PA Warner =E(16), AA (Alfred) Wyman =B(9), NA (Norman) York C(3)

2 GAMES: JR (Dick) Auty E1 J(30)Jt(34), LB (Louis) Baillon Jt(37)J(38), DE (Eric) Bevins >I(32)I(37), GE (Eric) Fowler >G(24)H(29), JT (Jeff) Hardwicke Kt(6)<Kt(7), W Phillips >D(33)<E(36), JP Reidy >G(22)<G(23)

The key for how to read the stats is on the last page

19	35/36	Home Ground: Welford Road	OVERALL RECORD:					T	C	PG	DG	MK	PTS
		Captain: Bernard Gadney	PLD	W	D	L	Tigers scored:	59	29	16	10	1	326
			38	15	3	20	Opponents scored:	82	27	7	7	0	349

GM	DATE		VEN	OPPONENTS	RESULT	TRIES	KICKS	ATT
CLUB MATCHES								
1	Sep	**7**	**H**	**Bedford**	W 30-11	Charles(2), Gadney, Obolensky, Vallance	Smith 4c/p, Slow d	2101
2		**14**	**H**	**Penarth**	W 38-0	Beamish(2), Vallance(2), Adams, Charles, Fox, Obolensky, Slow	Smith 4c/p	1941
3		**21**	**H**	**Plymouth Albion**	W 13-3	Shepherd(3)	Slow d	1669
4		**28**	**H**	**Waterloo**	W 26-9	Obolensky, Shepherd, Slow	Hodgson 2c/3p, Barr d	1828
5	Oct	5	a	Coventry	L 11-12	Obolensky	Hodgson c/2p	-
6		**12**	**H**	**Bridgwater & Albion**	L 10-17	Shepherd, Townsend	Hodgson 2c	1104
7		**19**	**H**	**Newport**	L 3-7	Charles	-	1918
8		**26**	**H**	**Northampton**	W 14-0	Berry, Shepherd	Fox d, Slow d	2195
9	Nov	2	a	Moseley	W 15-3	Morgan, Shepherd, Willcox	Slow 3c	-
10		**9**	**H**	**Cambridge University**	L 9-21	Shepherd, Charles	Shepherd p	2061
11		14th	a	Oxford University	L 4-16	-	Fox d	-
12		23	a	Nuneaton	W 5-3	Shepherd	Hodgson c	2000
13		**30**	**H**	**Bristol**	L 3-13	Gadney	-	1314
14	Dec	7	a	Harlequins	L 5-11	Willcox	Hodgson c	200
15		14	a	Blackheath	L 5-6	Shepherd	Kendrew c	3000
		21	a	Bedford	PP (frost)			
16		**26th**	**H**	**Birkenhead Park**	W 10-7	Adams	Slow d, Barr p	2088
17		**27f**	**H**	**Barbarians**	D 0-0	-	-	7000
18		**28**	**H**	**Rosslyn Park**	D 0-0	-	-	918
19	Jan	1w	a	Manchester	L 5-6	Auty	Hodgson c	-
20		**4**	**H**	**Swansea**	W 6-5	Morgan	Hodgson p	970
21		**11**	**H**	**Gloucester**	L 6-16	Hopkin	Hodgson p	1763
22		18	a	Bath	L 0-14	-	-	1500
		25	**H**	**Richmond**	PP (King died)			
23		**30th**	**H**	**Royal Air Force**	W 5-3	Fox	Hodgson c	443
24	Feb	**1**	**H**	**London Scottish**	D 3-3	Gadney	-	610
25		8	a	Newport	L 0-20	-	-	3000
26		15	a	Swansea	L 0-24	-	-	3500
27		22	a	Northampton	L 0-6	-	-	1500
28		**29**	**H**	**Old Merchant Taylors**	W 6-3	Bottrill	York p	307
29	Mar	**7**	**H**	**Harlequins**	L 11-14	Bottrill(2), Meikle	Hodgson c	1039
30		14	a	Gloucester	L 7-21	-	L.Baillon d, York p	5000
31		**21**	**H**	**Bath**	W 5-0	Willcox	Hodgson c	486
32		**28**	**H**	**Coventry**	L 8-19	Slow	York c/p	1863
33	Apr	2th	a	Bedford	W 7-6	-	Slow d, Hodgson p	-
34		4	a	Birkenhead Park	L 3-10	Charles	-	2000
35		11	a	Bristol	L 6-13	Willcox	York m	4000
36		13m	a	Plymouth Albion	L 8-9	Gadney, Vallance	Hodgson c	-
37		14tu	a	Exeter	W 24-12	Charles(3), Adams, Bottrill, Slow	G.Herbert 2c, Hodgson c	500
38		**18**	**H**	**Blackheath**	W 15-6	Slow, Willcox	Slow d, York c/p	1504

INDIVIDUAL APPEARANCES 1935/36

Name / Game #	1	2	3	4	5	6	7	8	9	10	11	12	13	14	15	16	17	18	19	20	21	22	23	24	25	26	27	28	29	30	31	32	33	34	35	36	37	38	Apps	T	Pts
N (Newton) Adams	H	F	G	F	F	-	F	F	-	-	-	F	F	-	F	F	E	E	-	D	F	H	F	H	F	E	F	F	G	-	-	H	-	E	G	H	G	-	28	3	9
WT (William) Alldridge	-	-	-	-	-	-	-	-	-	-	-	-	-	-	-	-	-	-	N	-	-	-	-	-	-	-	-	-	-	K	-	-	-	M	-	-	-	-	3	-	-
JD (John) Anderson	-	-	-	-	-	-	-	-	-	-	-	>J	-	-	-	-	-	M	<K	-	-	-	-	-	-	-	-	-	-	-	-	-	-	-	-	-	-	-	3	-	-
JR (Dick) Auty E1	-	-	-	-	-	-	-	-	-	-	-	-	-	-	-	-	J	-	J	-	-	-	J	-	-	-	-	-	-	-	-	-	-	-	-	-	-	-	3	1	3
LB (Louis) Baillon	-	-	-	-	-	-	-	-	-	-	-	-	-	M	-	-	-	-	-	-	-	-	-	-	-	-	-	-	-	<L	-	-	-	-	-	-	-	-	2	-	4
J (Jack) Ball	-	-	-	-	-	-	-	-	I	-	-	I	-	-	-	-	-	-	-	-	-	-	-	-	-	-	-	-	-	-	-	-	-	-	-	-	-	-	2	-	-
RJ (Bobby) Barr E3	0	0	0	0	0	-	0	0	0*	0	-	-	0	0*	0*	0*	0	0*	0*	-	0*	0*	0*	0	0*	0*	0	0*	0	0*	0*	0	0*	0	0	0	-	-	32	-	7
CESJ (Charles) Beamish I11	F	H	-	G	H	-	-	-	-	H	-	D	-	-	-	H	-	-	-	-	D	-	-	<G	-	-	-	-	-	-	-	-	-	-	-	-	-	-	9	2	6
JTW (Tom) Berry E+	-	-	D	E	D	-	G	G	G	G	G	G	E	G	G	G	G	G	F	G	G	-	E	D	D	D	E	E	E	G	E	E	G	-	E	E	E	G	33	1	3
TW (Tom) Bevan	-	-	-	-	-	-	-	-	-	-	-	0	-	-	-	-	-	-	-	-	-	-	-	-	-	-	-	-	-	-	-	-	-	-	-	-	-	<0	2	-	-
WJH (Bill) Bottrill	-	-	-	-	-	-	-	-	-	-	-	-	-	-	-	-	-	-	-	-	-	-	-	-	-	>K	N	K	K	-	K	K	-	K	K	K	K	-	10	4	12
JB (John) Charles	N	N	N	-	-	-	N	N	N	N	-	-	J	-	K	-	-	-	-	-	-	-	-	N	M	-	M	N	N	-	N	N	-	N	-	N	N	-	19	9	27
PM (Philip) Crowe I1	-	-	-	-	-	-	-	-	-	-	-	-	-	-	-	-	-	-	-	-	-	-	-	-	-	-	-	-	-	-	-	-	-	-	-	L	<L	-	2	-	-
JBS (John) Fox	M	M	M	-	-	-	M	M	M	M	M	-	L	-	-	N	-	-	-	M	-	K	K	M	-	-	-	M	-	-	-	-	-	-	N	-	M	-	17	2	14
RL (Robert) Francks	-	-	-	-	-	M	-	-	-	-	-	-	-	-	-	-	-	-	-	-	-	-	-	-	-	-	-	-	-	-	-	-	-	-	-	-	-	<K	2	-	-
BC (Bernard) Gadney E12	I*	I*	I*	I*	I*	-	I*	I*	-	I*	-	-	I*	-	-	-	I*	-	-	-	-	-	-	I*	-	-	I*	-	I*	-	-	I*	-	I*	I*	M*	-	-	17	4	12
RE (Ronnie) Gerrard	-	-	-	>L	M	-	L	L	-	-	-	-	-	-	-	-	-	-	-	-	-	L	-	L	L	M	-	-	-	-	-	-	-	-	-	-	-	-	8	-	-
GE (George) Goode	-	-	-	-	-	-	-	-	-	-	-	-	-	-	-	-	-	-	-	-	-	-	-	-	-	-	-	>L	M	M	L	L	-	L	L	-	-	<M	8	-	-
G (George) Greaves	-	-	-	-	-	A	-	C	A	A	-	-	A	A	-	C	C	-	A	-	-	-	-	-	-	-	-	-	-	C	-	-	-	A	-	A	C	A	14	-	-
HC (Cyril) Harrison	-	-	-	-	-	>L	-	-	-	-	-	-	-	-	-	-	-	-	-	-	<M	-	-	-	-	-	-	-	-	-	-	-	-	-	-	-	-	-	2	-	-
GB (Geoff) Herbert	-	-	-	-	-	>C	-	-	-	-	-	-	-	-	-	-	-	-	C	-	-	D	-	E	E	A	D	D	D	-	-	-	-	-	-	-	D	-	10	-	4
JM (John) Hodgson E7 GB2	G	G	H	H	G	G*	H	-	-	-	F	H	-	H	-	-	F	F	G	F*	H	-	H	-	-	H	-	-	F	-	F	-	H	H	F	F	<F*	-	24	-	50
J (John) Hopkin	-	-	-	-	-	-	-	-	>H	-	-	-	-	-	-	-	-	-	-	E	A	G	-	F	G	G	G	G	-	H	G	-	-	F	-	-	-	<F	13	1	3
Dr. EA (Ewen) Jack	-	>E	<E	-	-	-	-	-	-	-	-	-	-	-	-	-	-	-	-	-	-	-	-	-	-	-	-	-	-	-	-	-	-	-	-	-	-	-	2	-	-
WA (Wilf) Jackson	-	-	-	-	-	-	-	-	-	-	-	-	-	-	-	-	-	-	-	-	-	-	M	-	-	-	-	-	-	-	-	-	N	-	-	-	-	-	2	-	-
DA (Joe) Kendrew E10	-	-	-	-	-	-	-	-	-	-	-	A*	-	-	A	-	-	A	-	-	-	-	-	-	-	-	-	-	-	-	-	-	-	-	B	B	B	<B	7	-	2
Sgt. CGR (Cyril) Lewis	E	-	-	-	-	-	-	E	-	-	-	-	-	E	<D	-	-	-	-	-	-	-	-	-	-	-	-	-	-	-	-	-	-	-	-	-	-	-	4	-	-
SA (Sydney Arthur) Loxton	B	B	B	B	A	-	A	-	-	C	-	B	B	B	B	D	-	B	-	<B	-	-	-	-	-	-	-	-	-	-	-	-	-	-	-	-	-	-	14	-	-
GWC (Graham) Meikle E3	-	-	-	-	K	-	-	-	-	-	-	-	-	-	-	-	-	L	-	-	-	-	-	-	-	-	-	-	L	-	-	-	-	-	-	-	-	-	3	1	3
WR Morgan	-	-	-	-	-	-	-	-	>K	K	-	N	N	N	-	-	-	-	-	N	-	-	N	K	<K	-	-	-	-	-	-	-	-	-	-	-	-	-	9	2	6
ES (Ernie) Nicholson E5	-	-	-	-	>B	B	B	B	B	B	-	-	-	-	-	-	B	-	-	-	<B	-	-	-	-	-	-	-	-	-	-	-	-	-	-	-	-	-	8	-	-
AS (Alexander) Obolensky E4	K	K	-	N	N	-	-	-	-	-	-	-	-	-	-	-	K	-	-	-	-	-	-	-	-	-	-	-	-	-	-	-	-	-	-	-	-	-	5	4	12
RD (Roger) Orchard	-	-	-	-	-	-	-	-	-	-	-	-	-	-	-	M	-	-	<M	-	-	-	-	-	-	-	-	-	-	-	-	-	-	-	-	-	-	-	2	-	-
J (Jim) Parsons	-	-	-	-	-	-	-	-	-	-	-	-	-	-	-	>I	-	-	-	I	-	I	-	-	I	I	-	I	-	I	I	-	I	-	-	I	I	I	12	-	-
TG (George) Ridgway	-	-	-	-	-	-	-	-	-	-	-	-	-	-	-	>B	-	-	-	-	-	-	B	-	-	-	-	-	-	-	-	-	B	-	-	-	-	-	3	-	-
MA (Moggie) Robinson	A	A	A	A	E	-	D	A	D	E	-	E	D	C	E	E	D	D	D	C	-	B	C	B	B	B	B	B	B	B	B	B	C	B	A	-	A	D	34	-	-
AV (Alan) Rogers	-	-	-	-	-	-	-	-	-	-	-	-	-	-	>J	L	-	-	-	L	L	-	-	-	-	L	L	J	J	-	M	J	J	J	J	J	0	-	15	-	-
I (Ian) Shaw	-	-	-	-	-	>0	-	-	-	-	-	-	-	-	-	-	-	-	-	<0	-	-	-	-	-	-	-	-	-	-	-	-	-	-	-	-	-	-	2	-	-
WV (William) Sheppard	-	-	K	K	-	K	K	K	L	L	N	M	K	K	N	K	N	N	-	K	N	N	-	-	-	-	<K	-	-	-	-	-	-	-	-	-	-	-	19	10	33
WA (Arnold) Sime	-	-	-	-	-	-	-	-	-	-	I	-	-	-	I	-	-	-	-	-	-	-	-	-	-	-	-	-	-	-	-	-	-	-	-	-	-	-	2	-	-
CF (Charles) Slow E1	J	J	J	J	J	J	J	J	J	J	-	-	-	-	-	J	M	J	L	J	-	J	-	J	J	J	J	-	-	-	J	M	L	-	M	-	J	J	26	5	45
WA (Walter) Smith	>L	L	L	-	-	-	-	-	-	-	-	-	-	-	<M	-	-	-	-	-	-	-	-	-	-	-	-	-	-	-	-	-	-	-	-	-	-	-	4	-	22
WG (Guy) Toone	-	-	-	-	-	-	-	-	-	-	-	-	-	-	-	-	-	-	-	-	-	-	-	-	>N	N	-	-	-	N	-	-	<K	-	-	-	-	-	4	-	-
GPC (George) Vallance	D	D	-	D	-	D	E	D	-	-	D	-	-	D	-	-	-	-	-	-	E	E	D	-	-	-	-	-	-	E	D	D	D	D	D	D	-	E	19	4	12
P/O. SG (Ranji) Walker	-	-	-	M	L	-	-	-	-	-	-	L	M	J	-	-	-	-	-	-	-	M	-	-	-	-	-	-	-	<J	-	-	-	-	-	-	-	-	7	-	-
RJ (Rodney) Willcox	-	-	-	-	-	-	-	-	>F	F	H	-	G	F	-	-	-	H	H	H	-	F	G	-	H	F	H	H	H	F	H	F	F	G	H	G	H	H	24	5	15
E Williams	-	-	-	-	-	-	-	-	-	-	-	-	-	-	-	-	-	>I	I	-	-	-	<I	-	-	-	-	-	-	-	-	-	-	-	-	-	-	-	3	-	-
JL (Jack) Wormleighton	C	C	C	C	C	-	C	-	C	D	A	C	C	-	C	A	A	C	-	A	C	A	A	A	C	-	A	A	A	A	A	A	-	-	-	-	-	-	27	-	-
NA (Norman) York	-	-	-	-	-	-	-	-	-	-	-	-	-	-	-	-	-	-	-	-	-	C	-	C	A	C	C	C	C	D	C	C	A	C	C	C	-	C	15	-	19

1 GAME: T (Thomas) Arundel =J(21), RO (Richard) Baillon <O(11), HJ (Harold) Bennett <B(19), OV (Owen) Bevan =C(11), WJ Bird =B(11), RB Black =E(6), SH (Sid) Bowers <I(6), MJ (Maurice) Bullus >H(17), MA (Maxwell) Crosbie =K(11), EW (Edgar) Darnill <K(12), FC (Fred) Drummond <F(3), EW (Ewan) Evans-Evans =E(11), JE (James) Forrest S3 =K(18), JL (Jimmy) Giles E2 GB+ <I(21), HG (Harry) Greasley H(8), DL (David) Grieves =L(38), Rev. ER (Edwin) Haddon =E(19), GA (George) Harris =K(21), SF (Frank) Herbert N(6), TF (Thomas) Huskisson E+ =E(33), HJ (Harry) Kenyon >L(11), WE (Walter) Kyle =N(38), DW Lewis <I(14), R (Roy) Leyland E3 L(17), DA Lindsay =E(9), MD (Malcolm) Milman =L(23), WE (Bill) Parker <F(6), CH (Peter) Pearse <H(13), JS Peebles =L(14), AC Potter =M(33), JG Rogers =L(15), N (Noel) Townsend <Ht(6), ER (Reg) Vine =G(32), CH Williams <H(15), GF Williams =J(11)

The key for how to read the stats is on the last page

1936/37

Home Ground: Welford Road	OVERALL RECORD:					T	C	PG	DG	MK	PTS
Captain: Bobby Barr	PLD	W	D	L	Tigers scored:	70	28	12	9	0	338
	39	14	2	23	Opponents scored:	95	37	11	10	0	432

GM	DATE		VEN	OPPONENTS	RESULT	TRIES	KICKS	ATT
CLUB MATCHES								
1	Sep	**5**	**H**	**Bedford**	L 12-18	Charles, Gerrard, Willcox	York p	1420
2		**12**	**H**	**Waterloo**	W 13-6	Adams, Vallance	York 2c/p	397
3		**19**	**H**	**Plymouth Albion**	W 20-5	Gerrard(2), Bottrill, Parsons	York 4c	1315
4		**26**	**H**	**Northampton**	W 22-3	Slow(2), Adams, Bottrill, Parsons	York c/p, Barr c	2572
5	Oct	3	a	Coventry	L 3-17	-	York p	4000
6		**10**	**H**	**Headingley**	D 8-8	York	York c/p	1461
7		17	a	Newport	D 18-18	Adams, Bottrill, Meikle, Parsons	York 3c	4000
8		24	a	Northampton	L 3-12	Parsons	-	2500
9		**31**	**H**	**Old Merchant Taylors**	W 22-3	Meikle(2), York, Mackay, Wormleighton	York p, Taylor d	825
10	Nov	4w	a	Oxford University	W 16-13	Gadney(2), Bottrill	York 2c/p	1500
11		**7**	**H**	**Gloucester**	W 7-3	Parsons	Barr d	1919
12		14	a	Cambridge University	L 6-8	Meikle(2)	-	2000
13		**21**	**H**	**Nuneaton**	W 27-3	Meikle(3), Bottrill(2), Gadney, Taylor	York 3c	1015
14		**28**	**H**	**Bath**	W 11-0	Allen	Barr d, Meikle d	873
15	Dec	5	a	Harlequins	L 5-24	MacLeod	York c	-
16		12	a	Blackheath	L 12-13	Slow, Vallance	Slow d, York c	3000
17		19	a	Bedford	L 3-8	-	York p	2500
18		**26**	**H**	**Birkenhead Park**	L 0-8	-	-	3979
19		**28m**	**H**	**Barbarians**	L 5-20	Adams	York c	11000
20		**29tu**	**H**	**Manchester**	W 9-6	Leyland	York 2p	711
21	Jan	2	a	Swansea	L 3-10	Preston	-	1000
22		9	a	Gloucester	L 12-14	Taylor, Preston	Taylor d, York c	7000
23		**16**	**H**	**Moseley**	W 3-0	Preston	-	616
24		23	a	Richmond	W 12-11	Slow, Berry	Slow d, Taylor c	-
25		**28th**	**H**	**Royal Air Force**	L 4-16	-	Taylor d	104
26		**30**	**H**	**Coventry**	L 3-12	Taylor	-	563
27	Feb	6	a	London Scottish	L 0-16	-	-	2000
28		**13**	**H**	**Newport**	L 0-22	-	-	614
29		**20**	**H**	**Swansea**	L 5-23	Sturtridge	Meikle c	1341
30		**27**	**H**	**Northampton**	L 4-11	-	Slow d	975
31	Mar	**6**	**H**	**Harlequins**	L 3-11	Mackay	-	1364
32		**13**	**H**	**London Welsh**	W 9-0	Allen, Bottrill, Obolensky	-	4000
33		20	a	Coventry	L 11-24	Gerrard, Mackay	York c/p	4000
34		27	a	Bristol	L 0-11	-	-	5000
35		29m	a	Plymouth Albion	L 3-10	Auty	-	-
36		30tu	a	Bath	L 13-17	Bruce-Lockhart, Obolensky, Squibbs	York 2c	3000
37	Apr	3	a	Birkenhead Park	L 11-21	Cooke, Squibbs	York c/p	3000
38		**10**	**H**	**Bristol**	W 11-3	Preston(2), Rogers	Barr c	3000
39		**17**	**H**	**Blackheath**	W 9-4	Cooke, Moseby, Obolensky	-	2000

INDIVIDUAL APPEARANCES 1936/37

Name / Game #	1	2	3	4	5	6	7	8	9	10	11	12	13	14	15	16	17	18	19	20	21	22	23	24	25	26	27	28	29	30	31	32	33	34	35	36	37	38	39	Apps	T	Pts
N (Newton) Adams	F	F	F	G	F	F	F	G	F	G	F	F	H	-	-	H	-	H	H	-	-	F	G	G	F	-	-	-	-	-	-	H	H	F	H	G	G	F	F	28	4	12
WT (William) Alldridge	-	-	L	-	-	-	-	M	-	-	-	-	-	-	-	-	-	-	-	-	-	-	L	N	K	-	-	L	-	-	-	-	-	-	-	-	-	-	-	6	-	-
WM Allen	>G	G	-	E	-	G	-	E	G	-	G	G	G	G	G	-	G	G	G	G	E	E	E	E	D	G	F	D	D	D	-	G	E	E	<D	-	-	-	-	29	2	6
JR (Dick) Auty E1	-	-	-	-	-	-	-	-	-	J	-	-	-	-	-	J	-	-	-	-	-	-	-	-	-	-	-	-	-	-	-	-	-	K	K	N	-	-	-	5	1	3
W (Bill) Bainbridge	-	-	-	-	-	-	-	-	-	-	-	-	-	-	-	-	-	-	-	-	-	-	-	-	-	-	-	-	-	-	-	-	-	-	-	-	>E	E	E	3	-	-
RJ (Bobby) Barr E3	0*	0*	0*	0*	0*	0*	-	0*	0*	0*	0*	0*	0*	0*	-	0*	0*	0*	0*	0*	0*	0*	0*	0*	0*	0*	0*	0*	0*	0*	0*	0*	0*	0*	0*	0*	0*	0*	0*	37	-	12
JTW (Tom) Berry E+	C	H	G	F	-	-	G	F	-	-	H	H	F	F	F*	F	F	F	F	-	-	G	F	F	G	H	-	F	F	F	F	F	F	G	G	E	F	G	G	32	1	3
WJH (Bill) Bottrill	K	N	K	K	K	K	K	N	K	K	K	K	K	K	K	-	K	K	K	K	-	N	K	K	-	K	K	K	K	K	K	N	K	-	-	-	-	-	-	30	7	21
RB (Rab) Bruce-Lockhart S1	-	-	-	-	-	-	-	-	-	-	-	-	-	-	-	-	-	-	-	-	-	-	-	-	-	-	-	-	-	-	-	-	-	>J	J	<J	-	-	-	3	1	3
MJ (Maurice) Bullus	-	-	-	-	-	-	-	-	-	H	-	-	-	-	-	-	-	-	-	-	-	-	-	-	-	-	-	-	-	-	-	-	-	H	F	H	-	-	-	4	-	-
KH (Ken) Cooke	-	-	-	-	-	-	-	-	-	-	-	-	-	-	-	-	-	>N	-	-	-	-	-	-	-	-	-	-	-	-	-	-	-	-	-	-	K	N	N	4	2	6
PC (Peter) Crick	-	-	-	-	-	-	-	-	-	-	-	-	-	-	-	-	-	-	-	>H	H	-	H	H	H	F	G	G	G	H	H	-	G	-	-	F	H	H	<H	16	-	-
HV (Viv) Crosby	-	-	-	-	-	>B	-	-	-	-	-	-	-	-	-	-	-	-	-	-	-	-	-	-	<B	-	-	-	-	-	-	-	-	-	-	-	-	-	-	2	-	-
MS Douglas	-	-	-	-	-	-	-	-	-	-	-	-	-	-	-	-	-	-	-	-	-	-	-	-	-	-	-	-	-	-	-	-	>J	-	-	-	<J	-	-	2	-	-
JBS (John) Fox	-	K	N	N	N	N	-	-	-	-	-	-	-	-	-	-	-	-	-	-	-	-	-	-	-	-	-	-	-	-	-	-	-	-	-	-	-	-	-	5	-	-
BC (Bernard) Gadney E13	-	-	-	-	-	-	I*	-	I	I	-	I	I	I	-	I	-	I	-	-	-	I	-	-	-	-	-	-	-	-	I	I	-	-	-	-	-	-	-	11	3	9
RE (Ronnie) Gerrard	M	L	M	L	L	L	L	K	M	L	-	-	-	-	0	N	N	-	-	-	-	-	-	-	N	-	-	N	-	-	-	-	L	-	-	-	L	-	-	17	4	12
G (George) Greaves	-	C	A	A	A	A	A	A	A	A	A	-	A	-	-	A	-	A	A	-	-	-	-	-	-	-	-	<A	-	-	-	-	-	-	-	-	-	-	-	15	-	-
HJ (Harry) Kenyon	-	-	-	-	-	-	-	-	-	M	-	-	-	-	-	-	-	-	-	-	-	-	-	-	M	-	-	-	-	-	-	-	-	-	-	-	-	-	-	2	-	-
R (Roy) Leyland E3	-	-	-	-	-	-	-	-	-	-	-	-	-	-	-	-	-	-	M	<M	-	-	-	-	-	-	-	-	-	-	-	-	-	-	-	-	-	-	-	2	1	3
RB Mackay	-	-	-	-	-	-	-	-	>N	N	N	N	N	-	-	-	-	-	-	-	-	-	-	-	-	N	N	-	N	N	N	-	N	-	-	-	-	-	-	11	3	9
JN MacLeod	-	-	-	-	-	-	-	-	-	-	-	-	-	>N	<N	-	-	-	-	-	-	-	-	-	-	-	-	-	-	-	-	-	-	-	-	-	-	-	-	2	1	3
AO Mann	-	-	-	-	-	-	-	-	-	-	-	-	-	-	-	-	-	-	-	-	-	-	-	>I	-	-	I	<I	-	-	-	-	-	-	-	-	-	-	-	3	-	-
GWC (Graham) Meikle E3	-	-	-	M	M	M	M	L	L	-	M	M	M	M	-	-	M	-	-	-	-	-	-	-	-	-	-	M	M	M	<J	-	-	-	-	-	-	-	-	15	8	30
WG (William) Moseby	-	-	-	-	-	-	-	-	-	-	-	-	-	-	-	-	-	-	-	-	-	-	-	-	-	-	-	-	-	-	-	-	-	-	>L	-	-	J	J	3	1	3
AS (Alexander) Obolensky E4	-	-	-	-	-	-	-	-	-	-	-	-	-	-	-	-	-	-	-	-	-	K	-	-	-	-	-	-	-	-	-	K	-	-	-	K	-	-	K	4	3	9
J (Jim) Parsons	I	I	I	I	I	I	N	I	-	-	I	-	-	-	-	I	K	I	-	I	I	I	-	-	I	I	-	-	-	-	-	-	I	I	I	I	I	I	I	24	5	15
GE (George) Pollard	-	-	-	-	-	-	-	-	-	-	-	-	-	-	-	-	-	-	-	N	N	-	N	-	-	-	-	-	-	-	-	-	-	-	-	-	-	-	-	3	-	-
JR Preston	-	-	-	-	-	-	-	-	-	-	-	-	-	-	-	-	-	>M	-	-	K	M	M	M	-	M	M	-	-	-	-	M	M	N	N	-	N	K	-	13	5	15
WH (Harry) Richards	-	-	-	-	>G	-	-	-	-	-	-	-	-	-	-	-	-	-	-	-	G	-	-	-	-	-	H	-	-	G	-	-	-	-	-	-	-	-	-	4	-	-
TG (George) Ridgway	B	-	B	B	B	-	B	B	B	B	B	B	B	B	B	B	B	B	B	B	B	B	-	B	-	B	B	B	B	B	B	B	B	B	B	B	B	B	B	35	-	-
MA (Moggie) Robinson	-	-	-	-	-	-	-	-	-	-	-	-	-	-	-	-	-	-	-	-	-	-	B	-	-	-	-	-	-	-	<D	-	-	-	-	-	-	-	-	2	-	-
AV (Alan) Rogers	-	-	-	-	-	-	-	-	-	-	-	-	-	-	-	-	-	-	-	-	-	-	-	-	-	-	-	-	-	-	-	-	-	-	-	-	-	L	L	2	1	3
JR Sharp	-	-	-	-	-	-	-	-	-	-	-	-	-	-	-	-	-	-	-	-	>A	C	D	D	-	E	E	E	-	-	E	C	C	C	A	D	C	C	C	16	-	-
CF (Charles) Slow E1	J	J	J	J	J	-	-	-	-	-	J	J	J	J	J	M	J	J	J	J	J	-	J	J	-	J	J	-	-	J	-	<J	-	-	-	-	-	-	-	22	4	24
RA (Reginald) Squibbs	-	-	-	-	-	-	-	-	-	-	-	-	-	-	-	-	-	-	-	-	-	-	-	-	-	-	-	-	-	>L	L	L	-	-	M	M	M	M	M	8	2	6
JAS (Sandy) Taylor	-	-	-	-	-	>J	J	J	J	-	L	L	L	L	L	L	L	L	L	L	M	L	-	L	J	L	L	J	L	-	-	-	-	-	-	-	-	-	-	22	3	23
G (Gwyn) Thomas	-	-	-	-	-	-	-	-	-	-	-	-	-	-	-	-	-	-	-	-	>L	-	-	-	-	-	-	-	-	-	-	-	-	M	-	L	-	-	-	3	-	-
GPC (George) Vallance	E	E	E	-	-	E	E	-	D	D	D	D	E	E	E	E	E	E	E	E	D	-	-	-	E	D	D	-	E	E	-	E	D	D	E	-	D	D	D	30	2	6
PE (Puggy) Ward	-	B	-	-	D	-	C	C	-	-	-	A	-	A	A	-	A	-	-	C	-	A	A	A	A	A	A	C	C	C	C	-	-	-	-	-	-	-	-	19	-	-
RJ (Rodney) Willcox	L	M	H	H	H	H	H	H	H	F	-	-	-	H	H	G	H	-	-	F	F	-	-	-	-	-	-	<H	-	-	-	-	-	-	-	-	-	-	-	17	1	3
G (Gordon) Wooller	-	-	-	-	-	-	-	-	-	-	-	-	-	-	>M	-	-	-	-	-	-	-	-	-	<L	-	-	-	-	-	-	-	-	-	-	-	-	-	-	2	-	-
JL (Jack) Wormleighton	A	A	C	C	C	C	-	-	C	-	C	C	C	C	C	C	C	C	C	A	-	-	C	C	C	C	C	-	A	A	A	A	-	-	C	A	-	A	<A	30	1	3
NA (Norman) York	D	D	D	D	E	D	D	D	E	E	E	E	D	D	D	D	D	D	D	D	C	D	-	-	-	-	-	-	-	-	-	D	A	A	-	C	A	-	-	27	2	90

1 GAME: J (Jack) Ball I(23), JG Baxter =G(31), AD (Denis) Bolesworth >C(10), DA (David) Campbell E2 =H(22), JB (John) Charles <Nt(1), KD (Keith) Downes >M(31), HG (Harry) Greasley <H(1), TA (Tommy) Kemp E2 =J(22), VJ (Victor) Lyttle I+ =N(19), RL Moore =H(29), CH (Claude) Quarry =I(29), KA (Kenneth) Stanyon-Jacques I(30), LW Stevenson =0(7), GS (Gordon) Sturtridge A9 =Jt(29), FL (Frank) Williams =L(34)

The key for how to read the stats is on the last page

1937/38

Home Ground: Welford Road	OVERALL RECORD:					T	C	PG	DG	MK	PTS
Captain: Bobby Barr	PLD	W	D	L	Tigers scored:	67	25	28	4	0	351
	38	16	2	20	Opponents scored:	97	41	10	1	0	407

GM	DATE		VEN	OPPONENTS	RESULT	TRIES	KICKS	ATT
CLUB MATCHES								
1	Sep	**4**	**H**	**Bedford**	L 12-18	Fowler(2)	Bainbridge 2p	3000
2		**11**	**H**	**Sale**	W 11-8	Parsons, Thomas	Bainbridge c/p	2000
3		**18**	**H**	**Plymouth Albion**	W 16-6	Thomas(2), Moseby	Bainbridge 2c/p	4000
4		**25**	**H**	**Waterloo**	L 6-18	Adams(2)	-	3000
5	Oct	**2**	**H**	**Coventry**	L 4-23	-	Taylor d	5500
6		9	a	Northampton	L 6-16	Fox, Squibbs	-	3000
7		**16**	**H**	**Newport**	W 12-3	Fox	Barr c/p/d	5000
8		**21th**	**H**	**Oxford University**	L 11-14	Anthony, Squibbs	Barr c/p	-
9		**23**	**H**	**Northampton**	W 10-3	Moseby, Taylor	Barr 2c	5000
10		**30**	**H**	**Rosslyn Park**	L 9-10	Rogers	Bainbridge p, G.Herbert p	-
11	Nov	6	a	Gloucester	L 9-14	Moseby, Ward	G.Herbert p	5000
12		**13**	**H**	**Cambridge University**	W 19-17	F.Herbert, Bolesworth, Fox, Gerrard	F.Herbert 2c, G.Herbert p	4000
13		20	a	Nuneaton	W 8-0	Fox	G.Herbert p, F.Herbert c	1000
14		**27**	**H**	**Bristol**	D 3-3	-	F.Herbert p	-
15	Dec	4	a	Harlequins	W 11-8	Bevins, F.Herbert	G.Herbert c/p	1000
16		11	a	Blackheath	W 11-9	Bevins, Clark, F.Herbert	G.Herbert c	2000
17		18	a	Bedford	L 0-3	-	-	2500
18		**27m**	**H**	**Birkenhead Park**	W 16-11	F.Herbert, Berry	F.Herbert p, Taylor d, Bainbridge p	7000
19		**28tu**	**H**	**Barbarians**	L 0-34	-	-	12000
20	Jan	**1**	**H**	**Swansea**	W 8-5	F.Herbert, Preston	F.Herbert c	4000
21		**8**	**H**	**Gloucester**	D 6-6	Clark, F.Herbert	-	-
22		15	a	Headingley	L 5-11	F.Herbert	G.Herbert c	200
23		**22**	**H**	**Richmond**	W 9-3	Bainbridge, Obolensky, Young	-	3000
24		**27th**	**H**	**Royal Air Force**	L 3-5	Young	-	1000
25		29	a	Coventry	L 9-28	-	Bevins 3p	3000
26	Feb	**5**	**H**	**London Scottish**	W 11-3	Doe, Rogers	Bevins c/p	3000
27		12	a	Newport	L 0-14	-	-	3000
28		19	a	Swansea	L 8-21	Doe	Bevins c/p	4000
29		26	a	Northampton	L 3-12	-	Bevins p	2500
30	Mar	**5**	**H**	**Harlequins**	L 6-11	Doe	Bevins p	4000
31		**12**	**H**	**London Welsh**	W 13-5	Anthony, Young	Bevins 2c/p	4000
32		**19**	**H**	**Bath**	W 20-3	Young(2), Anthony, Glover, F.Herbert, Preston	Bevins c	3000
33		**26**	**H**	**Coventry**	L 6-21	-	F.Herbert 2p	4000
34	Apr	2	a	Birkenhead Park	L 6-14	F.Herbert, Stanyon-Jacques	-	2000
35		**9**	**H**	**Blackheath**	W 16-0	Doe(4)	F.Herbert 2c	2000
36		16	a	Bristol	L 11-14	F.Herbert, Stapleton	F.Herbert c/p	4000
37		18m	a	Plymouth Albion	L 10-13	Doe, F.Herbert	Fox d	-
38		19tu	a	Bath	W 27-0	F.Herbert, Doe, Fox, G.Herbert, Young	F.Herbert 3c/2p	-

INDIVIDUAL APPEARANCES 1937/38

Name / Game #	1	2	3	4	5	6	7	8	9	10	11	12	13	14	15	16	17	18	19	20	21	22	23	24	25	26	27	28	29	30	31	32	33	34	35	36	37	38	Apps	T	Pts
N (Newton) Adams	G	G	H	G	-	G	-	-	-	-	G	-	-	-	-	-	H	-	-	-	-	-	-	-	-	-	-	-	-	G	-	-	-	F	-	-	-	-	9	2	6
WT (William) Alldridge	-	-	-	-	-	-	-	-	-	-	-	-	-	-	-	-	-	-	-	M	M	M	M	-	M	-	-	<J	-	-	-	-	-	-	-	-	-	-	6	-	-
SEA (Tony) Anthony	>F	F	F	F	F	F	G	H	H	F	-	F	F	F	F	F	G	-	-	G	G	-	G	-	G	G	-	G	G	-	G*	G*	G	G	G	F	F	F	31	3	9
W (Bill) Bainbridge	D	D	G	D	D	D	F	G	G	G	D	E	G	E	E	D	D	D	E	D	D	D	D	E	D	D	D	D	D	D	D	D	D	D	D	D	D	<G	38	1	27
RJ (Bobby) Barr E3	O*	O*	O*	O*	O*	O*	O*	O*	O*	O*	O*	O*	O*	O*	O*	O*	O*	O*	O*	O*	O*	O*	-	-	-	O*	O*	O*	O*	-	-	-	-	-	-	-	-	-	26	-	18
EPR (Eric) Bates	-	-	-	-	-	-	-	-	-	-	-	-	-	-	-	-	-	-	-	-	-	-	-	-	-	-	-	-	-	-	-	-	-	-	-	>E	E	D	3	-	-
CH (Cecil) Beamish	-	-	-	-	-	-	-	-	-	-	-	-	-	-	-	-	-	-	-	-	-	-	-	-	-	-	-	-	-	-	-	-	-	-	-	>G	G	-	2	-	-
JTW (Tom) Berry E+	H	H	-	-	H	H	H	F	F	H	F	G	-	G	H	H	-	F	F	-	H	G	F*	H*	F*	F	F	F	F	-	-	-	-	-	-	-	-	-	24	1	3
DE (Eric) Bevins	-	-	-	-	-	-	-	-	-	I	I	-	I	I	I	I	I	I	I	I	I	I	I	-	I	I	I	I	I	I	I	I	-	-	I	I	-	I	24	2	40
AD (Denis) Bolesworth	-	A	A	A	A	A	-	A	A	D	C	C	C	C	C	C	-	A	A	A	A	A	C	C	A	A	-	-	A	A	A	A	A	A	-	-	-	-	29	1	3
WJH (Bill) Bottrill	-	K	-	-	-	-	K	K	-	-	-	-	-	-	-	-	-	-	-	-	-	-	-	-	-	-	-	-	-	-	-	-	-	-	-	-	-	-	3	-	-
J Brooks	-	-	-	-	-	-	-	-	-	-	-	-	-	-	-	-	-	-	-	-	-	-	-	-	-	-	>K	N	<K	-	-	-	-	-	-	-	-	-	3	-	-
RWK (Raymond) Clark	-	-	-	-	-	M	J	J	J	L	L	J	M	J	J	J	J	J	-	-	J	J	J	J	J	M	-	L	M	-	K	-	-	-	J	J	J	<J	26	2	6
FC (Fred) Doe	-	-	-	-	-	-	-	-	-	-	-	-	-	-	-	-	-	-	-	-	-	-	-	>G	-	H	-	H	H	H	H	H	H	H	H	H	H	H	13	9	27
GE (Eric) Fowler	E	E	E	E	E	-	D	-	E	E	-	D	D	D	D	-	-	G	D	F	F	F	E	-	E	E	-	E	E	E*	-	-	F	-	<F	-	-	-	25	2	6
JBS (John) Fox	K	-	K	-	K	N	N	N	K	K	K	K	K	K	K	K	K	-	-	-	-	-	-	-	-	-	-	-	L	M	L	M	M	M	M	K	M	N	25	5	19
RE (Ronnie) Gerrard	-	-	N	N	-	K	-	-	-	-	-	M	L	-	L	L	L	M	<L	-	-	-	-	-	-	-	-	-	-	-	-	-	-	-	-	-	-	-	10	1	3
DB Glover	-	-	-	-	G	-	-	-	-	-	-	-	-	-	-	-	-	-	-	-	-	-	-	-	-	-	-	-	-	-	E	E	E	E	E	-	-	-	6	1	3
SF (Frank) Herbert	-	-	-	-	-	-	-	-	-	-	-	N	N	N	N	N	N	N	N	N	N	N	N	-	N	N	-	-	-	-	-	N	N*	N*	N*	N*	N*	K*	21	12	77
GB (Geoff) Herbert	-	-	-	-	-	-	E	E	D	A	A	A	A	A	A	A	A	C	C	C	C	C	A	A	-	C	C	-	-	-	-	C	C	C	C	C	C	E	27	1	24
G (Gordon) Lawrie	-	-	-	-	-	-	-	-	-	-	-	-	-	-	-	-	-	-	-	-	-	-	-	-	-	-	-	-	-	-	-	-	-	-	>L	-	-	L	2	-	-
WG (William) Moseby	J	-	J	J	-	-	I	L	L	J	J	-	J	-	-	-	-	-	-	-	K	-	-	K	K	J	J	-	-	-	-	-	-	-	-	-	-	-	14	3	9
AS (Alexander) Obolensky E4	-	-	-	-	-	-	-	-	-	-	-	-	-	-	-	-	-	-	-	-	-	-	K	-	-	-	-	-	N	K	-	-	-	-	-	-	-	-	3	1	3
J (Jim) Parsons	I	I	I	I	I	-	-	-	I	-	-	I	-	-	-	-	-	-	-	-	-	-	-	-	-	-	-	-	-	-	-	-	-	-	-	-	-	-	7	1	3
GE (George) Pollard	N	N	-	-	-	-	-	-	N	N	N	-	-	-	-	-	-	-	-	-	-	-	-	-	-	K	N	K	-	-	<N	-	-	-	-	-	-	-	9	-	-
JR Preston	-	-	-	-	-	-	-	-	-	-	-	-	-	-	-	-	-	-	-	K	-	-	-	-	-	-	-	-	-	N	-	K	K	K	K	-	K	-	7	2	6
TG (George) Ridgway	B	B	B	B	B	B	B	B	B	B	-	B	B	B	B	-	-	B	B	B	B	B	B	B	B	B	-	B	B	B	B	B	B	B	B	B	B	B	34	-	-
AV (Alan) Rogers	-	L	L	L	L	-	-	-	-	M	-	-	-	-	-	-	-	-	-	L	-	-	-	-	L	L	M	-	J	J	J	J	J	<J	-	-	-	-	15	2	6
JR Sharp	C	C	C	C	C	C	C	C	C	C	E	-	E	-	-	-	C	-	-	-	-	-	-	-	-	-	A	<A	-	-	-	-	-	-	-	-	-	-	15	-	-
RA (Reginald) Squibbs	M	M	-	K	M	L	M	M	-	-	M	L	-	L	-	-	-	-	-	-	-	-	-	-	-	-	-	-	-	-	-	-	-	-	-	-	-	-	10	2	6
KA (Kenneth) Stanyon-Jacques	-	-	-	-	-	-	-	-	-	-	-	-	-	-	-	-	-	-	-	-	-	-	-	-	-	-	-	-	-	-	-	-	-	I	-	-	<I	-	2	1	3
JA (Jim) Stapleton	-	-	-	-	-	-	-	-	-	-	-	-	-	-	-	>B	B	-	-	-	-	-	-	-	C	-	-	B	-	C	C	-	-	-	A	A	-	A	9	1	3
JAS (Sandy) Taylor	-	-	-	-	J	J	-	-	M	-	-	-	-	-	-	-	-	L	J	J	L	-	-	-	-	-	-	-	-	-	-	-	-	-	-	-	-	-	7	1	11
G (Gwyn) Thomas	L	J	M	M	-	-	<L	-	-	-	-	-	-	-	-	-	-	-	-	-	-	-	-	-	-	-	-	-	-	-	-	-	-	-	-	-	-	-	5	3	9
GPC (George) Vallance	-	-	D	H	-	E	A	D	-	-	-	-	-	-	G	E	E	E	G	E	E	E	-	D	-	-	E	-	-	-	-	-	-	-	-	-	-	-	15	-	-
SC (Sidney) Wade	-	-	-	-	-	-	-	-	-	-	-	-	-	-	-	-	-	>K	K	-	-	-	-	N	-	-	-	-	-	-	-	-	-	-	-	-	-	-	3	-	-
PE (Puggy) Ward	A	-	-	-	-	-	-	-	-	-	H	H	H	H	-	G	F	H	H	H	-	H	H	F	H	-	H	C	C	F	F	F	-	-	-	-	-	-	20	1	3
CE (Ernie) Watkin	-	-	-	-	-	-	-	-	-	-	-	-	-	-	-	-	-	-	-	-	-	-	>O	O	O	-	-	-	-	O	O	O	O	O	O	O	O	O	12	-	-
WG (Wilfred) Young	-	-	-	-	-	-	-	-	-	-	-	-	-	>M	M	M	M	-	M	-	-	L	L	M	-	-	L	-	-	-	M	L	L	L	-	L	L	M	16	6	18

1 GAME: D (Don) Black =G(27), CP (Charles) Cromar =B(11), RA (Richard) Crowhurst =L(30), M (Michael) Forrester =M(36), NFF (Norman) Giddings =L(24), CK Jolliffe =I(33), P Lane =I(6), RB Mackay <N(5), JH McKee =A(37), AJ Rowe >M(28), WA (Arnold) Sime <I(8), GJ (Glynmor) Treharne >K(22), HL (Harold) Varnish =C(38), KA (Ken) Wait =I(24)

The key for how to read the stats is on the last page

19 38/39	Home Ground: Welford Road	OVERALL RECORD:					T	C	PG	DG	MK	PTS
	Captain: Tom Berry	PLD	W	D	L	Tigers scored:	83	31	20	6	0	395
		36	20	3	13	Opponents scored:	74	36	16	3	0	354

GM	DATE		VEN	OPPONENTS	RESULT	TRIES	KICKS	ATT
CLUB MATCHES								
1	Sep	**3**	**H**	**Bedford**	L 0-18	-	-	4000
2		**10**	**H**	**Headingley**	D 3-3	-	Jerwood p	3500
3		**17**	**H**	**Plymouth Albion**	W 10-6	Bottrill, Preston	Watkin 2c	4000
4		**24**	**H**	**Waterloo**	L 3-18	Doe	-	4000
5	Oct	1	a	Coventry	L 3-5	-	F.Herbert p	2000
6		**8**	**H**	**Northampton**	W 8-3	Bevins, Bottrill	Jerwood c	5000
7		15	a	Newport	L 8-11	Anthony, Bottrill	F.Herbert c	5000
8		**22**	**H**	**Neath**	W 20-13	Henderson(2), Squibbs, F.Herbert	Squibbs c, Jerwood 2p	5000
9		**29**	**H**	**Old Merchant Taylors**	W 15-5	Young(2), F.Herbert, McLean, Squibbs	-	3000
10	Nov	**5**	**H**	**Gloucester**	L 13-17	Adams, Bolesworth	F.Herbert 2c, Jerwood p	5000
11		9w	a	Oxford University	W 17-3	McLean(2)	F.Herbert 2c, Kenyon d, Bullus p	-
12		12	a	Cambridge University	L 22-28	F.Herbert, Berry, Doe, Young	F.Herbert 2c/p, Watkin p	4000
13		**19**	**H**	**Coventry**	W 6-0	Vallance	Squibbs p	6000
14		**26**	**H**	**Bristol**	W 14-6	Young(2), Berry, Edwards	F.Herbert c	4000
15	Dec	3	a	Harlequins	L 11-20	Knapp	F.Herbert c/p, Jerwood p	1000
16		10	a	Blackheath	L 8-22	Doe, Ridgway	F.Herbert c	-
17		**17**	**H**	**Rosslyn Park**	W 14-5	Fox, Parsons, Squibbs	Jerwood p, F.Herbert c	3000
		24	a	Bedford	PP (frost)			
18		**26m**	**H**	**Birkenhead Park**	W 6-3	Downes, Edwards	-	3000
19		**27tu**	**H**	**Barbarians**	W 8-6	Edwards(2)	F.Herbert c	10000
20		31	a	Northampton	W 5-3	Bottrill	F.Herbert c	2000
	Jan	7	a	Swansea	PP			
21		14	a	Gloucester	L 3-8	-	Jerwood p	5000
22		**21**	**H**	**Nuneaton**	W 14-3	Downes(2), F.Herbert, Squibbs	Jerwood c	-
		26th	**H**	**Royal Air Force**	PP			
23		28	a	Richmond	W 21-13	Edwards(2), Anthony, Berry, Doe	White 3c	4000
24	Feb	4	a	London Scottish	L 8-17	Bottrill, Edwards	Jerwood c	2000
25		**11**	**H**	**Newport**	L 9-23	Henderson	Taylor d, Jerwood c	4000
26		**18**	**H**	**Swansea**	W 9-5	Doe	Squibbs 2p	5000
27		**25**	**H**	**Northampton**	D 14-14	Bottrill, Henderson, Parsons, Treharne	Squibbs c	4000
28	Mar	**4**	**H**	**Harlequins**	W 13-3	Doe, Parsons, Squibbs	Young d	3000
29		**11**	**H**	**Bath**	W 17-3	Edwards, Roderick, Treharne, Vallance	Jerwood p, Squibbs c	3000
30		**18**	**H**	**London Welsh**	W 12-6	Bottrill, Treharne	Downes 2p	2500
31		25	a	Coventry	W 20-14	Downes, Bottrill, Edwards, Treharne, Young	Downes c/p	2500
32	Apr	1	a	Birkenhead Park	D 3-3	G.Herbert	-	2000
33		8	a	Bristol	L 10-18	Henderson, Treharne	Jerwood c, Squibbs c	5000
34		10m	a	Plymouth Albion	W 10-3	Young, Bottrill	Young d	-
35		11tu	a	Bath	W 28-3	Downes, Anthony, Bolesworth, Gadney, G.Herbert, Treharne	Downes 3c, Squibbs d	-
36		**15**	**H**	**Blackheath**	L 10-23	Fox	Taylor d, Jerwood p	3000

INDIVIDUAL APPEARANCES 1938/39

Game #	1	2	3	4	5	6	7	8	9	10	11	12	13	14	15	16	17	18	19	20	21	22	23	24	25	26	27	28	29	30	31	32	33	34	35	36	Apps	T	Pts
N (Newton) Adams	E	E	-	-	-	-	-	-	-	E	-	-	-	-	-	-	<G	-	-	-	-	-	-	-	-	-	-	-	-	-	-	-	-	-	-	-	4	1	3
SEA (Tony) Anthony	-	G	H	H	F	F	F	G	F	-	G	H	F	H	-	-	-	G	G	G	H	F	G	F	G	G	G	-	-	G	G	G	G	F	F	<F	29	3	9
H Barker	-	-	-	-	-	-	-	-	-	-	-	-	-	-	-	-	-	-	-	-	-	-	-	-	-	-	-	-	-	-	-	-	-	>G	<G	-	2	-	-
RJ (Bobby) Barr E3	-	-	-	-	-	-	-	-	-	-	-	-	0	0	0	0	0	0	0	0	0	0	0	0	0	0	0	0	0*	0*	0	0	0	0	0	<0*	24	-	-
EPR (Eric) Bates	-	-	-	-	-	-	-	-	-	-	-	-	-	-	-	-	-	-	-	-	-	-	-	-	-	-	-	-	-	-	-	-	D	D	<D	-	3	-	-
JTW (Tom) Berry E3	H*	-	E*	E*	E*	E*	E*	F*	-	H*	E*	E*	H*	F*	-	H*	-	F*	F*	F*	-	-	H*	-	-	F*	F*	F*	-	-	D*	E*	-	-	-	-	22	3	9
DE (Eric) Bevins	I	I	I	I	I	I	I	I	I	I	-	I	I	I	I	I	-	-	-	-	-	-	-	-	-	-	-	-	-	-	-	-	-	-	-	-	15	1	3
AD (Denis) Bolesworth	A	A	A	A	C	A	A	A	A	A	A	A	A	A	A	A	A	-	-	-	A	A	A	A	A	A	A	A	A	A	A	A	A	A	A	A	33	2	6
WJH (Bill) Bottrill	-	-	K	K	K	N	K	N	N	K	-	K	-	-	-	-	-	K	K	K	K	K	-	K	K	K	N	N	N	N	N	N	N	N	N	<N	27	9	27
AE (Albert) Brown	-	-	-	-	-	-	-	-	-	-	-	-	-	-	>E	E	-	-	-	-	-	-	-	-	-	-	-	-	-	-	-	-	-	-	-	-	2	-	-
FC (Fred) Doe	G	H	G	G	G	G	G	-	G	G	F	G	G	G	-	G	F	E	E	H	G	G	F	G	E	E	E	G	-	E	E	-	F	E	E	H	32	6	18
KD (Keith) Downes	-	-	-	-	-	-	-	-	-	-	-	-	-	-	-	-	-	M	M	M	M	M	M	-	M	N	-	-	-	L	M	M	L	L	<M	-	14	5	32
FG (Francis) Edwards	-	-	-	-	-	-	-	-	-	-	-	-	>N	K	-	-	-	L	L	-	L	-	K	L	-	L	L	L	L	-	L	L	-	-	-	-	13	9	27
JBS (John) Fox	-	-	-	-	-	-	-	-	-	-	-	-	-	-	-	K	K	-	-	-	-	-	-	-	-	-	-	-	-	-	-	-	-	-	-	<L	3	2	6
BC (Bernard) Gadney E14	-	-	-	-	-	-	-	-	-	-	-	-	-	-	-	-	-	-	-	-	-	-	-	-	-	-	-	-	-	-	-	-	I*	I*	<I*	-	3	1	3
W (Bill) Garner	-	-	-	-	-	-	-	-	-	-	-	-	-	-	>F	-	<H	-	-	-	-	-	-	-	-	-	-	-	-	-	-	-	-	-	-	-	2	-	-
MM (Maurice) Henderson S3	>F	L*	F	F	H	H	H	H	H	-	-	F	-	-	-	-	-	H	H	-	F	H	-	H	H	H	H	H	H	F	F	F	H	-	-	-	24	5	15
SF (Frank) Herbert	N	-	-	N	N	K	N	K	K*	N	N	N	K	N	N*	N	N*	N	N	N	N*	N*	-	N*	<N*	-	-	-	-	-	-	-	-	-	-	-	22	4	47
GB (Geoff) Herbert	-	-	-	C	A	C	C	C	C	C	C	C	C	C	C	C	C	C	C	C	C	C	C	C	C	-	-	-	-	C	C	C	C	C	C	<C	29	2	6
HP (Peter) Jerwood	>D	D	D	D	D	D	D	D	D	D	D	D	D	D	G	D	D	D	D	D	D	D	E	D	D	D	D	D	D	-	-	D	E	-	-	D	32	-	37
ER (Ronnie) Knapp	-	-	-	-	-	-	-	>J	-	J	-	J	-	-	L	<L	-	-	-	-	-	-	-	-	-	-	-	-	-	-	-	-	-	-	-	-	5	1	3
JP (Peter) Lambert	-	-	-	-	-	-	-	-	-	-	-	-	-	>J	J	J	-	-	-	-	-	-	-	-	-	-	-	-	-	-	-	-	-	-	-	-	3	-	-
G (Gordon) Lawrie	M	<M	-	-	-	-	-	-	-	-	-	-	-	-	-	-	-	-	-	-	-	-	-	-	-	-	-	-	-	-	-	-	-	-	-	-	2	-	-
JR (John) McLean	J	J	L	L	J	J	J	-	J	M	<M	-	-	-	-	-	-	-	-	-	-	-	-	-	-	-	-	-	-	-	-	-	-	-	-	-	10	3	9
J (Jim) Parsons	-	-	-	-	-	-	-	-	-	-	-	-	-	-	-	-	I	I	I	I	I	I	I	I	I	I	I	I	I	I	I	I	-	-	-	<I	17	3	9
JR Preston	-	K	N	-	-	-	-	-	-	-	-	-	-	-	-	-	-	-	-	-	-	-	-	-	-	-	-	-	-	-	-	-	-	-	-	-	2	1	3
TG (George) Ridgway	B	B	B	B	B	B	B	B	B	B	B	-	-	B	-	B	B	B	B	-	B	-	-	-	B	B	B	B	B	-	-	-	-	-	-	-	22	1	3
J (John) Roderick	-	-	-	-	-	-	-	-	-	-	-	-	-	-	-	-	-	-	-	-	-	-	-	-	-	-	-	-	>F	H	H	H	-	H	<H	-	6	1	3
R (Ron) Smith	-	-	>M	M	-	-	-	-	-	-	-	-	-	-	-	-	-	-	-	-	-	-	-	-	-	-	-	-	-	-	-	-	-	-	-	-	2	-	-
RA (Reginald) Squibbs	L	-	-	-	L	L	M	L	L	-	-	M	L	L	-	-	M	-	-	-	-	L	-	-	-	M	M	M	M	M	-	-	M	M	L	<M	20	5	36
JA (Jim) Stapleton	C	C	C	-	-	-	-	-	-	-	-	B	B	-	B	-	-	A	A	-	-	B	B	B	-	C	C	C	C	B	B	B	B	B	B	B	22	-	-
JAS (Sandy) Taylor	-	-	-	-	-	-	-	-	-	-	-	-	-	-	-	-	-	-	-	L	-	J	-	J	J	-	-	-	-	-	-	J	-	-	J	J	7	-	8
GJ (Glynmor) Treharne	-	-	-	-	-	-	-	-	-	-	-	-	-	-	K	-	-	-	-	-	-	-	-	-	-	-	K	K	K	K	K	K	K	K	K	<K	11	6	18
GPC (George) Vallance	-	-	-	-	-	-	-	E	E	-	-	-	E	E	D	-	E	-	-	E	E	E	D	E	-	-	-	E	E	D	-	-	-	-	-	<E	15	2	6
PE (Puggy) Ward	-	-	-	-	-	-	-	-	-	F	-	-	-	-	H	<F	-	-	-	-	-	-	-	-	-	-	-	-	-	-	-	-	-	-	-	-	3	-	-
CE (Ernie) Watkin	0	0	0	0	0	0	0	0	0	0	0	0	-	-	-	-	-	-	-	-	-	-	-	-	-	-	-	-	-	-	-	-	-	-	-	-	12	-	7
GA White	-	-	-	-	-	-	-	-	-	-	-	-	-	-	-	-	-	>J	J	-	-	-	<J	-	-	-	-	-	-	-	-	-	-	-	-	-	3	-	6
A (Aneurin) Williams	-	-	>J	<J	-	-	-	-	-	-	-	-	-	-	-	-	-	-	-	-	-	-	-	-	-	-	-	-	-	-	-	-	-	-	-	-	2	-	-
KB (Ken) Willis	-	-	-	-	-	-	-	-	-	-	-	-	-	-	-	-	>J	-	-	J	<J	-	-	-	-	-	-	-	-	-	-	-	-	-	-	-	3	-	-
WG (Wilfred) Young	-	-	-	-	M	M	L	M	M	L	-	L	M	M	M	M	-	-	-	-	-	-	L	M	L	J	J	J	J	J	J	-	J	<J	-	-	22	7	29

1 GAME: JR (Dick) Auty E1 <J(11), R (Ron) Ball =J(13), MJ (Maurice) Bullus <H(11), AC (Alan) Deere =L(17), DB Glover <F(2), KV (Keith) Hassall =G(29), HJ (Harry) Kenyon <L(11), H (Harry) Lees =A(20), AS (Alexander) Obolensky E4 <N(23), EJ (Ted) Parfitt >I(11), WH (Harry) Richards G(36), TA Riley =K(1), AJ Rowe <F(25), J Sargeant =N(2), SC (Sidney) Wade <K(11), NA (Norman) York <B(20)

19 39/40	Home Ground: Welford Road	OVERALL RECORD:					T	C	PG	DG	MK	PTS
	Captain: Tom Berry	PLD	W	D	L	Tigers scored:	3	2	1	1	0	20
		1	1	0	0	Opponents scored:	1	0	1	0	0	6

GM	DATE		VEN	OPPONENTS	RESULT	TRIES	KICKS	ATT
CLUB MATCH								
1	Sep	**2**	**H**	**The Rest**	W 20-6	Watkin, Cooke, Doe	Watkin c, Taylor c/d, Jerwood p	-

INDIVIDUAL APPEARANCES 1939/40

Name / Game #	1	Apps	T	Pts
JTW (Tom) Berry E3	F*	1	-	-
DE (Eric) Bevins	I	1	-	-
AD (Denis) Bolesworth	A	1	-	-
KH (Ken) Cooke	<N	1	1	3
FC (Fred) Doe	<E	1	1	3
HP (Peter) Jerwood	D	1	-	3
GA (George) Lebens	=G	1	-	-
SD Pearce	=K	1	-	-
JR Preston	<L	1	-	-
TG (George) Ridgway	<B	1	-	-
JA (Jim) Stapleton	<C	1	-	-
JAS (Sandy) Taylor	<J	1	-	6
CE (Ernie) Watkin	0	1	1	5

The key for how to read the stats is on the last page

CHAPTER 12

Post War Recovery

1940-45

"We Never Close" may have been the motto of London's famous Windmill Theatre during the war but it could very well have been true for rugby in Leicestershire. Obviously regular fixtures had gone by the board but Eric Thorneloe spared no efforts to keep the game going by raising a side to play other Midlands teams and bringing Barbarian XVs to Leicester to raise money for charity.

RED CROSS AND ST. JOHN
PRISONERS OF WAR FUND
Leicester Football Club Ground
AYLESTONE AND WELFORD ROADS
SATURDAY, MARCH 17, 1945
LEICESTERSHIRE
HARLEQUINS
versus
COVENTRY
Kick-off 3-15 p.m.
Official Programme
GIVE GENEROUSLY
INSTRUMENTAL BANDS OF THE A.T.C.
(By kind permission of the Officers Commanding)

His endeavours were boosted by a new organisation, the Leicestershire Harlequins, formed to give a game to servicemen passing through the county, local players home on leave and anyone still in the area who wanted to play. Four enthusiasts, Doug Norman, RC Nunn, CG Smith and CA Davis, ran the Harlequins who played their first game on 4 October 1941. Several times they were able to field as many as three XVs and when the war ended, 34 members of the Harlequins figured in Tigers' teams.

Under normal circumstances 1940 would have been a gala occasion for Leicester, since it was the year of their diamond jubilee. In fact it was the year the club suffered one of the first of its war

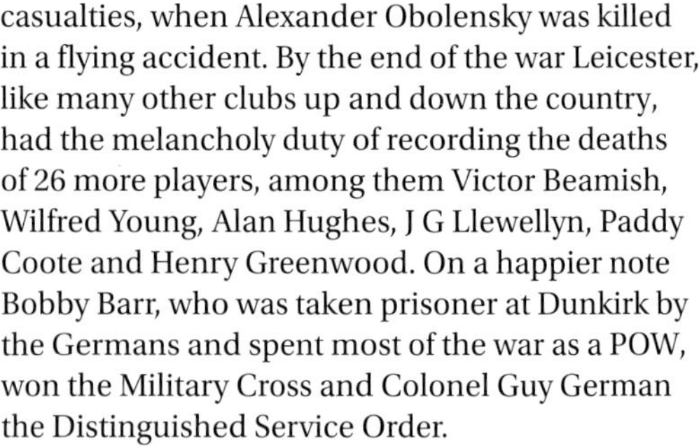

casualties, when Alexander Obolensky was killed in a flying accident. By the end of the war Leicester, like many other clubs up and down the country, had the melancholy duty of recording the deaths of 26 more players, among them Victor Beamish, Wilfred Young, Alan Hughes, J G Llewellyn, Paddy Coote and Henry Greenwood. On a happier note Bobby Barr, who was taken prisoner at Dunkirk by the Germans and spent most of the war as a POW, won the Military Cross and Colonel Guy German the Distinguished Service Order.

It is conceivable that there was more rugby in Leicester during the war than in any other centre in the country and when hostilities ended, a grateful letter arrived from the Army Rugby Union thanking the Leicestershire officials for their work in raising over £10,700 for service charities.

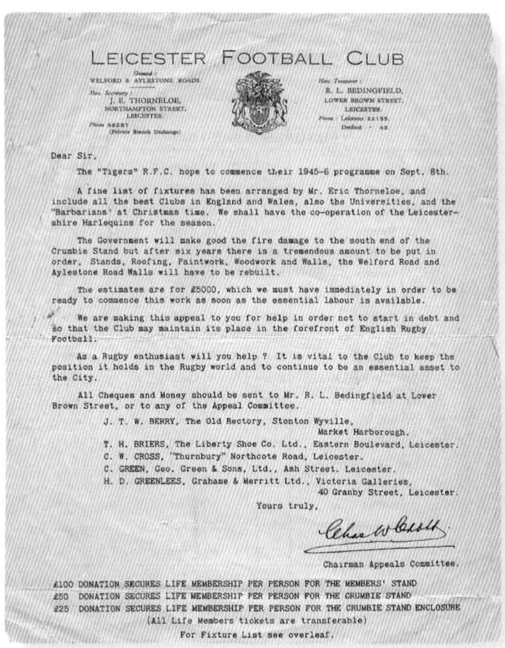

LEICESTER FOOTBALL CLUB

Ground: WELFORD & AYLESTONE ROADS.

Hon. Secretary: J. E. THORNELOE, NORTHAMPTON STREET, LEICESTER. Phone 58287 (Private Branch Exchange)

Hon. Treasurer: R. L. BEDINGFIELD, LOWER BROWN STREET, LEICESTER. Phone: Leicester 22155. Desford - 42

Dear Sir,

The "Tigers" R.F.C. hope to commence their 1945-6 programme on Sept. 8th.

A fine list of fixtures has been arranged by Mr. Eric Thorneloe, and include all the best Clubs in England and Wales, also the Universities, and the "Barbarians' at Christmas time. We shall have the co-operation of the Leicestershire Harlequins for the season.

The Government will make good the fire damage to the south end of the Crumbie Stand but after six years there is a tremendous amount to be put in order, Stands, Roofing, Paintwork, Woodwork and Walls, the Welford Road and Aylestone Road Walls will have to be rebuilt.

The estimates are for £5000, which we must have immediately in order to be ready to commence this work as soon as the essential labour is available.

We are making this appeal to you for help in order not to start in debt and so that the Club may maintain its place in the forefront of English Rugby Football.

As a Rugby enthusiast will you help ? It is vital to the Club to keep the position it holds in the Rugby world and to continue to be an essential asset to the City.

All Cheques and Money should be sent to Mr. R. L. Bedingfield at Lower Brown Street, or to any of the Appeal Committee.

J. T. W. BERRY, The Old Rectory, Stonton Wyville, Market Harborough.
T. H. BRIERS, The Liberty Shoe Co. Ltd., Eastern Boulevard, Leicester.
C. W. CROSS, "Thurnbury" Northcote Road, Leicester.
C. GREEN, Geo. Green & Sons, Ltd., Ash Street. Leicester.
H. D. GREENLEES, Grahame & Merritt Ltd., Victoria Galleries, 40 Granby Street, Leicester.

Yours truly,

Chas W Cross

Chairman Appeals Committee.

£100 DONATION SECURES LIFE MEMBERSHIP PER PERSON FOR THE MEMBERS' STAND
£50 DONATION SECURES LIFE MEMBERSHIP PER PERSON FOR THE CRUMBIE STAND
£25 DONATION SECURES LIFE MEMBERSHIP PER PERSON FOR THE CRUMBIE STAND ENCLOSURE
(All Life Members tickets are transferable)
For Fixture List see overleaf.

➔ Letter from Charlie Cross, chairman of the Appeals Committee, requesting donations to help with post-war renovations.

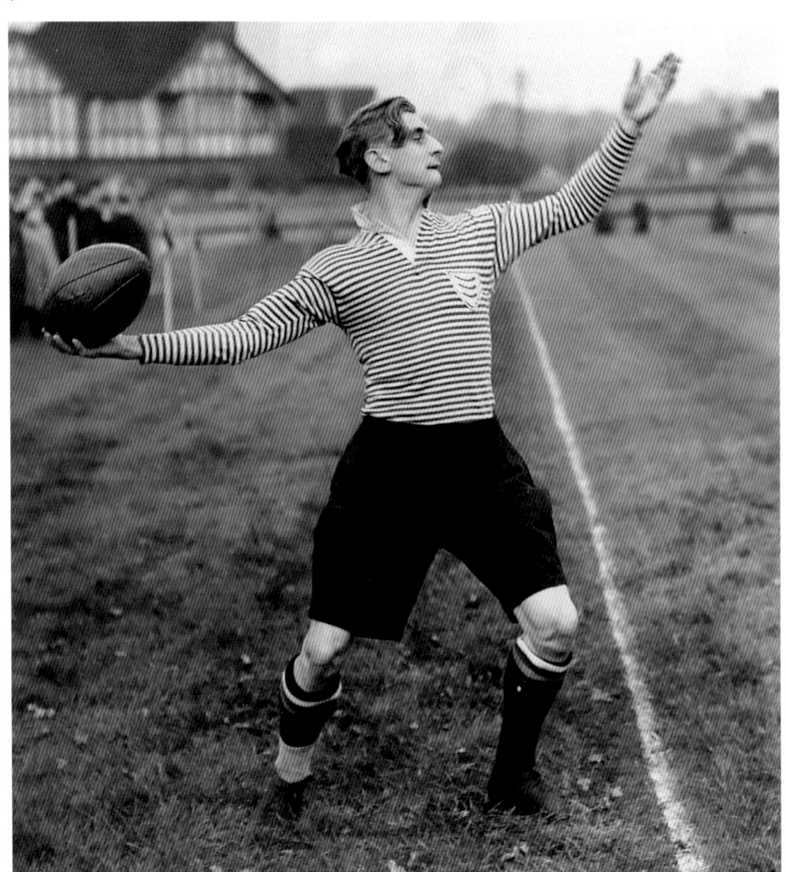

➔ Prince Obolensky was tragically an early casualty of the war.

1945/1946

The end of the war in Europe was celebrated with VE Day on 8 May 1945, and 15 days later the Tigers committee held their first meeting to contemplate the future. They had a lot to think about - they were still some £1,800 in debt and likely to be more so in view of the work to be done to the ground which had been damaged during the war; the roof of the Crumbie Stand had been hit during air raids, there was a collapsed wall at the Welford Road end and renovation was needed to the stands.

A select committee was formed to launch a public appeal for funds while the affairs of the club were in the capable hands of Billy Bradshaw, the president, and Rodney Bedingfield, the treasurer, with Thorneloe remaining as secretary and Ralph Buckingham becoming team secretary. During the summer there were several meetings between the secretary and Doug Norman, since it was envisaged that the Leicestershire Harlequins would form the basis for the post-war Tigers.

And so it turned out. During the 1945/46 season it was decided to run two teams, the first to be called the Leicester Football Club, the second to be called the Leicestershire Harlequins. The selection committee comprised three Leicester members and three Harlequins members and

← Francis Edwards played in both of the uncapped Red Cross wartime internationals for England v Wales.

the arrangement, after some initial teething problems, settled down well enough. There were only four defeats after Christmas and in January 1946, a Leicestershire and East Midlands XV played Charles Saxton's Kiwis, the New Zealand Army touring side which did so much to put rugby back on its feet after the war.

There was an excellent nucleus of experienced players to build round. Tom Berry, now considerably nearer 40 than 30, captained the side and with him he had Watkin, Bolesworth, Harry Richards and Cecil Beamish. In due course Francis Edwards, who had played in service internationals during the war, returned from Burma while a former Wyggestonian schoolboy who was still serving in the Royal Navy, Bill Moore, did so well at scrum-half that England picked him in two Victory internationals.

Ironically enough, Moore, the grandson of the former Leicester half-back Billy Foreman, played only eight games for Tigers that season, none of them at scrum-half. Seven of his appearances were at centre, the eighth at fly-half, but he played at scrum-half for Devonport Services, for the Navy and Leicestershire and the East Midlands. But much of the credit for a successful resumption had to go to the two "old hands", Berry and Edwards, even though they knew few of their playing colleagues at the start of the season.

Berry, in a reserved occupation during the war, had played no rugby for five years: "It was quite amazing when I turned up for pre-season training how few of the players I recognised," he said. "I felt almost as if I were starting playing for the Tigers all over again. Soon we all got to know each other and I was asked to lead the side for the next two years which, on reflection, I think were the most enjoyable rugger-playing days of my life."

The first game of the newly-constructed club, played on 8 September 1945, could hardly have been harder; it was against Cardiff, the first between the clubs since the rift some 15 years earlier. Leicester lost 12-6 at the Arms Park and in the pack was a 22-year-old back-row forward from Alderman Newton's School in Leicester, Jerry Day, who thus began a period of service to the club maintained for the next 37 years.

While the players did their utmost to recapture the lustre of pre-war days, the committee had to iron out more damage to the clubhouse which had been used by the Army during the war. The occupying military had the delightful habit of boring holes in the floor, so extensive repairs had to be made. No doubt the treasurer welcomed the funds brought by another group of servicemen, the Kiwis, when they played Leicestershire and the East Midlands at Welford Road on 31 January 1946, before an enthusiastic crowd.

ITINERARY

LEICESTER FOOTBALL CLUB

EASTER TOUR, 1946.

MATCHES:
April 20th v. BRISTOL.
April 22nd v. EXETER.
April 23rd v. BATH.

HOTEL:
Rougemont Hotel, Exeter.
Telephone: 3433.

↑ Easter tour card 1946.

Leicester had eight players in the combined XV, with a claim on Maurice Henderson, who joined Bedford after the war. The team was: Ernie Watkin (Leicester); Arthur Butler (Harlequins), Francis Edwards, Haydn Thomas (both Leicester), Bob Pell; JM Pell (both Northampton), Bill Moore; Denis Bolesworth (both Leicester), Geoffrey Kelly (Bedford), Ray Longland (Northampton), Nick Hughes (Leicester), Rex Willsher (Bedford), Tom Berry, Cecil Beamish (both Leicester), Maurice Henderson (Bedford). Berry captained the side in the only game he ever played against a touring party, having been kept out of all the regional games before the war by Northampton's consistent Bill Weston. But the Kiwis took the honours 14-0, tries coming from J Sherratt, Pat Rhind and Eric Boggs, with a penalty and a conversion from HE Cook, and the locals were left with the memory of some good runs from Edwards, Haydn Thomas and Pell, with some outstanding work in the loose from Henderson.

The 1945/46 season ended with the very precise record of 16 wins, two draws and 16 defeats, and at the annual meeting that year it was decided that the Harlequins XV should be replaced by an A XV, a decision which was to have lasting consequences. It was 40 years since Leicester had fielded a second string and it was a move that met with considerable hostility from clubs on whom Tigers had previously relied, like Stoneygate, Westleigh and Old Wyggestonians.

Junior clubs such as these had supported Leicester staunchly when called upon for players but they felt disinclined, not unnaturally, to see their players go to Leicester's second team when Tigers were still, in essence, an invitation club. There was hot division too, among the Leicester committee, some of whom looked back fondly to the Crumbie era of one team, and those who looked forward and saw that sooner or later Leicester would have to conform and become a proper members' club running two or three XVs. The arguments began to rumble back and forth, and were to do so, with increasing vehemence, for another 10 years - the long-term consequences were still being felt in the 1970s.

↑ Bill Moore played in two Victory internationals for England.

On a happier note, in June 1946, Leicester began their old players' membership. The qualification for this, which has not altered, was a minimum of 20 games for the senior side which earned the individual his player's tie.

1946/1947

The controversial A XV made its bow on 21 September, against Rolls Royce, while the senior side had already got off the ground with a 12-0 win over Bedford. It was virtually a brand new three-quarter line and Tigers scored four tries, three of them coming from a 22-year-old South African, Mel Channer, then serving in the RAF at Cosford. Channer had played a handful of games the previous season, first in the centre and then at fly-half. His brilliance was to be of considerable importance to the club's playing record during the next eight years.

A useful start to the season was spoiled somewhat when Waterloo, with John Heaton and his cousin Dickie Guest in their three-quarter line, won 34-19 at Welford Road, the highest aggregate score at the ground since Richmond were beaten 62-3 in 1919 and equalling the highest total ever scored at that point against Leicester, by the Barbarians in 1937. In those days club games were played over two 35-minute halves, although when Leicester played Cambridge University, the referee agreed to two 40-minute halves (to help Cambridge's preparation for the university match) which allowed Leicester to kick the winning penalty in the 36th minute of the second half.

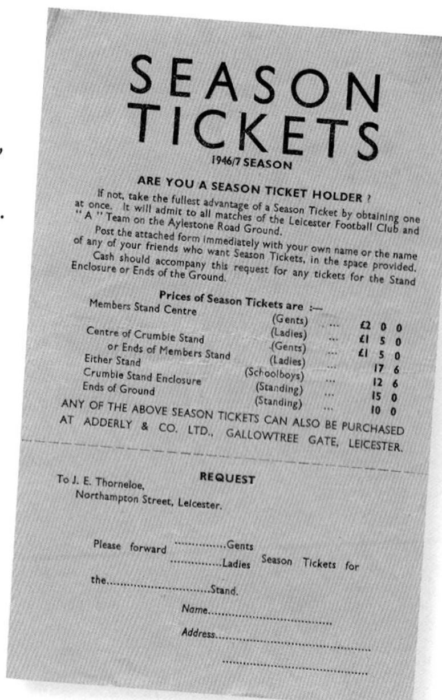

SEASON TICKETS
1946/7 SEASON

ARE YOU A SEASON TICKET HOLDER ?

If not, take the fullest advantage of a Season Ticket by obtaining one at once. It will admit to all matches of the Leicester Football Club and "A" Team on the Aylestone Road Ground.

Post the attached form immediately with your own name or the name of any of your friends who want Season Tickets, in the space provided.

Cash should accompany this request for any tickets for the Stand Enclosure or Ends of the Ground.

Prices of Season Tickets are :—

Members Stand Centre	(Gents) ...	£2 0 0
	(Ladies) ...	£1 5 0
Centre of Crumbie Stand or Ends of Members Stand	(Gents) ...	£1 5 0
Either Stand	(Ladies) ...	17 6
	(Schoolboys) ...	12 6
Crumbie Stand Enclosure	(Standing) ...	15 0
Ends of Ground	(Standing) ...	10 0

ANY OF THE ABOVE SEASON TICKETS CAN ALSO BE PURCHASED AT ADDERLY & CO. LTD., GALLOWTREE GATE, LEICESTER.

REQUEST

To J. E. Thorneloe,
Northampton Street, Leicester.

Please forward ....Gents / ....Ladies Season Tickets for the..............................Stand.

Name..............................

Address..............................

....

Season ticket prices for the 1946/47 campaign.

The long-standing connection of the Goodrich family with the club ended when Albert Goodrich, who had succeeded his uncle Tom as groundsman, left. A proposed Christmas fixture with the Racing Club de France fell through when the French club decided not to travel, so Leicester played Rugby instead and enjoyed a comfortable 24-3 win.

Then winter took a hand. Bill Moore just had time to play his first game of the season, and earn his first full England cap, when the weather brought all sport in the country to a standstill. Snow and ice halted proceedings for two months and there were nine cancellations before the season was finally completed and Tom Berry announced his intention to retire from the first-class game. Happily he retained an active connection with the club by agreeing to lead and coach the A team, who had won 14 of their 21 games in their first season back.

1947/1948

The captaincy passed to another pre-war player, Peter Jerwood, who was able to welcome two newcomers into his three-quarter line. They were AC Towell and DEB Rees, both of whom made an immediate impact. Allan Towell had won an England trial with Middlesbrough and was coming to study at Loughborough Colleges, while Danny Rees, from Bridgend, came to the club from Colleges. In the first match of the new season, against Bedford, Towell scored a try from centre in a 22-3 win, but was outshone by his captain who registered two tries. In the next match, a 31-11 win over Bath, Rees made his debut, also at centre, and was twice among the try-scorers in a match during which Channer dropped three goals.

Another newcomer that season was a hefty lock from Leicester Thursday and the club's A side, Eric Lacey, who made his bow in a 6-5 defeat against Neath. But there was much activity off the field too as Leicester found themselves forced to organise a meeting with five junior clubs, Oadby, Old Newtonians, South Leicester, Stoneygate and Westleigh, over the A team controversy. That their discussions were inconclusive is indicated by the deathly silence which followed the meeting.

In the meantime the Australians, having missed out badly in their 1939/40 tour, were back in the country under the leadership of Bill McLean. It was not the happiest of tours and the Wallabies found themselves involved in several incidents, particularly in Wales, but nothing marred their 17-11 win over Leicestershire and the East Midlands at Welford Road on 15 November 1947.

The worst aspect of the day, from a local point of view, was that Berry took a weakened club XV to Cardiff where they received a 50-5 battering (when Cardiff visited Leicester a fortnight later the Welshmen won 8-4). Meanwhile there were 25,000 at Welford Road to watch Jerwood captain the combined side, which was: Ernie Watkin (Leicester); R Jones, Lewis Cannell, Thomas Gray, Niall Bailey; Ronnie Knapp, Eddie O'Mullane (all Northampton); Denis Bolesworth, Eddie Neal (both Leicester), Geoffrey Kelly (Bedford), Nick Hughes (Leicester), Bob Hamp, Don White (both Northampton), Peter Jerwood (Leicester), Dick Furbank (Bedford). Danny Rees had been picked on the wing but injury prevented him from playing, while Moore too was unavailable.

The Australians, an extremely fit combination, eased their way into a commanding lead. By half-time they had run up an 11-0 lead, their acting captain, Colin Windon, having scored two tries, a third coming from Thomas Bourke with Alan Walker converting the first of Windon's tries. Jim Stenmark had run in a fourth try before Ernie Watkin kicked a penalty and then Knapp dropped a goal. Windon's third try made it 17-7 but a dropped goal from over 40 yards by Watkin ensured the counties were not disgraced.

Selection card sent to Tom Berry inviting him to play in his final first-team match.

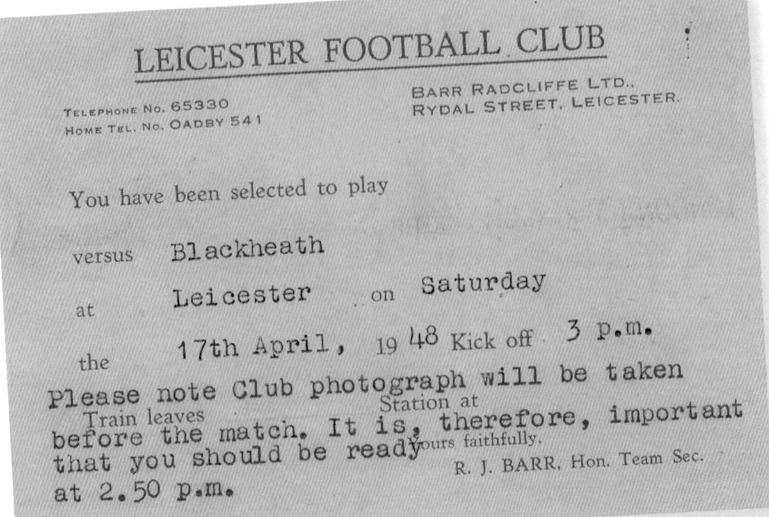

LEICESTER FOOTBALL CLUB

TELEPHONE No. 65330
HOME TEL. No. OADBY 541

BARR RADCLIFFE LTD.,
RYDAL STREET, LEICESTER.

You have been selected to play

versus Blackheath

at Leicester on Saturday

the 17th April, 1948 Kick off 3 p.m.

Train leaves Station at

Please note Club photograph will be taken before the match. It is, therefore, important that you should be ready at 2.50 p.m.

Yours faithfully,
R. J. BARR, Hon. Team Sec.

The club side, however, was struggling, with Channer on leave in South Africa, Moore out of action with a septic leg, Rees also injured and Towell on call for Yorkshire. The victory over Harlequins on 6 December was the first since 20 September but there were better things against the Barbarians, who won by only 15-10. Towell, who had moved to fly-half, was outstanding. He had made the switch from centre in October and his impressive play over the season as a whole won him first a reserve place for England in the Calcutta Cup match and, on Easter Monday, his first cap at centre against France. He partnered another debutant, Northampton's Lew Cannell, but on the day France were much the better side and won 15-0 in Paris.

On the club front it was unfortunate that the grand gathering of old players on 16 April, 1948, had to discuss a season ruined by injuries and outside calls. But at least they were all there the following day when Berry finally called it a day as a player by leading the senior side against Blackheath, being chaired off after a 6-5 win. Watkin became the first club player to pass 100 points in a season since 1935 (his aggregate was 102).

Another who had come to the end of his playing career was the RAF Squadron Leader, HP 'Nick' Hughes, who had played for Waterloo before moving to Leicestershire during the war. He was to become president of the club in 1969 but on his first encounter with Leicester he found life quite different from that he had known in the north-west: "At Waterloo I remember standing next to Jack Heaton in the bar and if I spoke to him I felt chuffed. They ran several sides of course. There was none of that at Leicester.

"Eric Thorneloe was very opposed to a bar. The upstairs clubroom at Welford Road was a tea room and hardly anyone came. There were no teas for members or spectators while being a member of the supporters' club meant nothing more than paying half a crown for a badge." The social side of life at Leicester consisted of a couple of barrels of beer - not conspicuous for its quality - for the two first XVs upstairs before they adjourned to the 'Big Window'. Ladies, by common consent, were strictly forbidden before the magic hour of 8pm when they might join their husbands or boyfriends, assuming by then that they wanted to.

It was not for another ten years, after Bobby Barr had become secretary, that the club were decadent enough to run a bar, following some strong lobbying by Francis Edwards. And it was nearly another 10 years later before the club really began to utilise the assets at its disposal and hold regular functions in the clubhouse - but by then the essential nature of the Leicester Football Club had undergone a dramatic change.

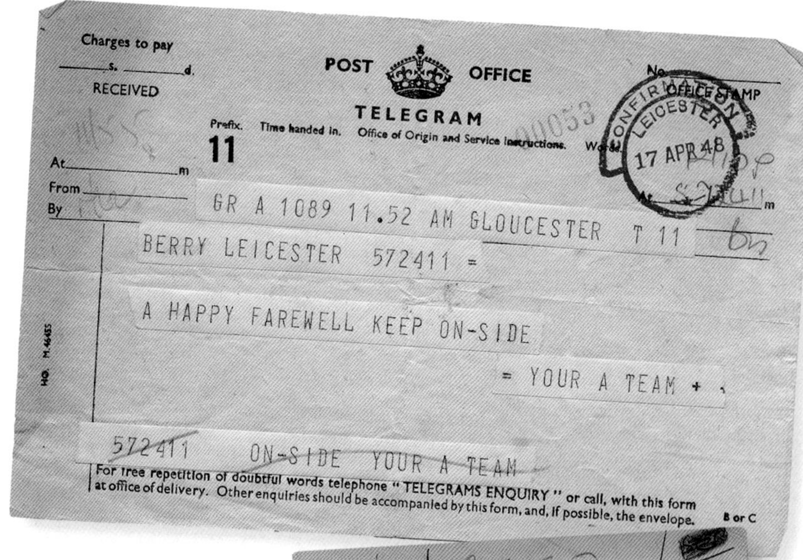
Charges to pay s. d.
RECEIVED
POST OFFICE
TELEGRAM
Prefix. Time handed in. Office of Origin and Service Instructions. Words.
11
At m
From
By
17 APR 48
GR A 1089 11.52 AM GLOUCESTER T 11
BERRY LEICESTER 572411 =
A HAPPY FAREWELL KEEP ON-SIDE
= YOUR A TEAM +
572411 ON-SIDE YOUR A TEAM
For free repetition of doubtful words telephone "TELEGRAMS ENQUIRY" or call, with this form at office of delivery. Other enquiries should be accompanied by this form, and, if possible, the envelope.

Telegram wishing Tom Berry well for his 277th and last first-team game.

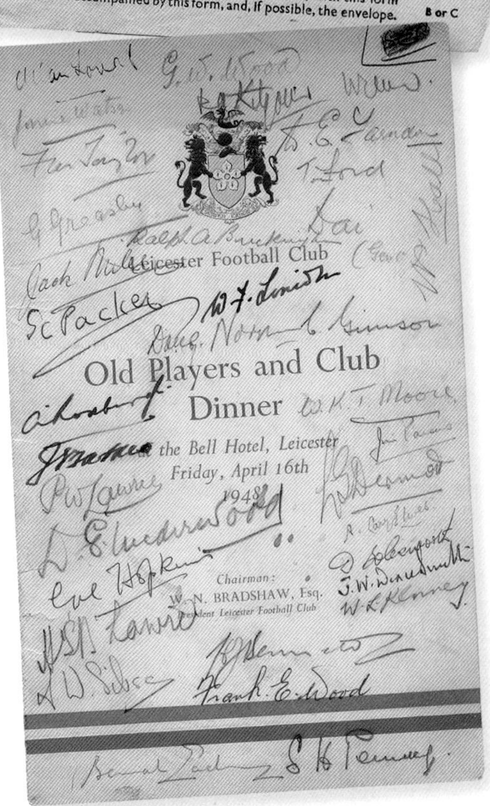

Autographed menu card for the Old Players and Club Dinner at the Bell Hotel in 1948.

Tom Berry poses with the Leicestershire Sevens trophy.

← Membership card number 1 for the Tigers' Rugby Supporters' Club in season 1948/49.

1948/1949

Peter Jerwood was absent through illness early in the 1948/49 season and that consistent hooker, Eddie Neal, retired, to be succeeded by the diminutive (five feet two inches tall) Ronnie Tudor. The Welsh influence in the back division from Rees, Ken Nicholas from Newbridge and Gwynne Lawrence, a native of Swansea but educated at Alderman Newton's School in Leicester, failed to have the desired effect and, for the second season running, victories were outweighed by defeats.

Jerwood announced his retirement from first-class rugby, having achieved an England trial and a Barbarians tie after the war, but the following season he was persuaded back into harness for several games, which enabled him to watch the progress of two new forwards, Peter Thorneloe (nephew of the secretary) and the thickset, former Aylestone St James player, RV Stirling.

Bob Stirling, a regular RAF officer, had spent most of the war in India where he met his wife, a cousin of Tom Berry's. He returned to this country late in 1947, was posted to Cranwell and, on Berry's recommendation, joined the "Jimmies" before progressing into Leicester's A side. Although his experience was confined to station rugby he quickly made an impact and, though only five feet ten inches tall, Leicester played him in the second row as much for his line-out ability as anything else.

↑ Eric Thorneloe completed 20 years as honorary secretary of the club.

It was the former Leicester player and Ireland cap, George Beamish, who suggested to Stirling that he should play prop for the RAF and in that position he won all his 18 England caps, though when he became a regular for Leicester in 1948 he was only a year short of his 30th birthday. The last year of the decade, however, gave no indication that the clouds over the club's playing record were lifting. The committee decided against electric floodlighting at the ground (too expensive) and the division over the A team continued.

1949/1950

On the field the record at the end of the 1949/50 season, 15 wins against 23 defeats, was the worst winning percentage for over a decade. For all that, the season was by no means featureless. It began with rumours that Clem Windsor, one of the 1947/48 Australian party who had played at Welford Road, was to join the club after coming to work at Leicester General Hospital. In fact he did not play and so missed the first post-war victory over Newport, only the twelfth win over the Gwent club since fixtures between them began. Towell was leading the side and for the last two months of 1949, he experimented by playing himself at wing forward, by no means unsuccessfully.

A new recruit joined over Christmas, from Loughborough Colleges, the centre George Cullen, and immediately lifted club morale. He distinguished himself against Nuneaton by scoring in every possible way in a 16-8 win and enjoyed a very successful Easter tour. Bill Moore was capped three times by England and, on the odd occasion, Tigers enjoyed the services of the RAF and Scotland forward, Stephen Wright.

The seeds of rapid improvement were there, with players of the quality of Stirling, Moore and Cullen available, while there was the strength and consistency of the pre-war forward Denis Bolesworth and the promise of back row men like Harry Sibson and Leicester University College student Tom Bleasdale to look forward to. Even though Towell moved to Bedford during the close season, under the captaincy of Moore the 1950s opened well.

↓ George Cullen became the first Leicester player in almost 50 years to claim a 'full house' doing so against Nuneaton 15.4.1950.

1950/1951

The 33-9 win over Plymouth was Leicester's biggest for years, the back row was reinforced by England international Bob Weighill - later to be secretary to the Rugby Football Union; Cullen was in fine form both in general play and as a kicker, while in Stan Pratt Leicester had unearthed yet another talented hooker. There were trials for Moore, Cullen and Stirling while Bleasdale and Sibson were in reserve, though only Stirling was capped, playing all four internationals that England played that year.

By now Leicester had formulated a policy to try to make their A team acceptable to junior clubs in the county. They circulated a statement of intent, that their aim was to encourage local players, and that local clubs should release players for up to six games. A nucleus would be retained as A team regulars while, in return, Leicester would make their facilities and playing experience available. Seven clubs, Leicester Thursday, Belgrave, Lutterworth, Aylestonians, Loughborough, South Wigston Old Boys and Melton Mowbray, went along with the policy but the five who had originally stood out against the A team did not. Yet again there was stalemate.

Better news for the backroom boys was that Berry was asked to act as an England selector while the club received an invitation to guest in the Middlesex Sevens. It was the Tigers' first appearance in the tournament and they put out the following VII: Gwynne Lawrence, Ken Nicholas, Haydn Thomas, Bill Moore, Tom Bleasdale, Stan Pratt, Denis Bolesworth. Unfortunately the abbreviated game was not their forte and they went out in the first round, beaten 8-5 by Harlequins 2nds, Moore scoring a try which Nicholas converted.

But 23 wins against 13 defeats was a distinct improvement on the past few years so nobody grumbled too much. And, for the first time, Leicester were televised in action, against London Scottish at Richmond. Ironically enough, that same season, the club had refused to allow the BBC to film the Baa-baas match, fearing that the gate would be down.

↑ Programme from Tigers' first appearance in the Middlesex Sevens, 1951.

↓ Tigers were televised for the first time in this game against London Scottish at Richmond Athletic Ground.

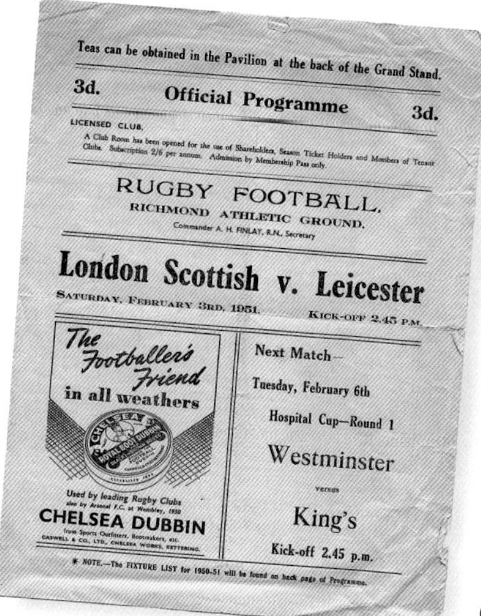

1951/1952

At the other end of 1951, Leicester welcomed back the mercurial Channer from South Africa and were delighted to acquire the services of the international wing, Ian Botting, capped by England against Ireland and Wales in 1950 having toured South Africa with New Zealand the previous year though he was not selected for any of the tests. Channer, of course, was not the only rugby-playing South African in the country that season, for Basil Kenyon's Fourth Springboks were sweeping all before them (save the London Counties).

Stirling played against them three times - for the Combined Services, England and the Barbarians - but not at Leicester when they played a Midland Counties XV drawn from Leicestershire, East Midlands and Oxfordshire. On 29 December, on a glutinous Welford Road playing surface, the following Midlands XV put up a brave display before going down 3-0: A Smailes (Richmond); Niall Bailey, Lew Cannell (both Northampton), Allan Towell (Bedford), Gwynne Lawrence (Leicester); 'Tich' Haynes, Murray Fletcher (both Bedford); Michael Berridge, Trevor Smith, JH Whiting (all Northampton), Eric Lacey (Leicester), John Bance (Bedford), Harry Sibson, Tom Bleasdale (both Leicester), Don White (Northampton, captain).

It was the only time on tour that the Springboks failed to cross their opponents' goal-line, a tribute in itself to the admirable work of the Midlands team. Gwynne Lawrence, who was enjoying such a notable season for Leicester, took the eye in the early stages but inevitably the main battle was fought up front, Lacey losing his jersey in the struggle. At half-time there was no score but a penalty by Basie Viviers was enough to see the tourists through.

Lawrence and Moore were Leicester's ever-presents that season, Moore's final season as he retired following the 25-3 win over Sale, chaired off the field. Cullen once again scored over a century of points, despite going through a slightly sticky patch at the end of 1951, and retains fond memories of the Easter tour to the West Country which formed the regular end-of-season climax:

"At this time we were still on friendly terms with the management of the Rougemont Hotel in Exeter, though how they survived the weekend mystified us all. Their stirrup pump fire extinguishers, left over from the war and placed strategically at various levels on a wide spiral staircase and landings surrounding the main lounge, disappeared quickly after one tour when they had been used freely by one player, clad in a jock strap only, to keep Tigers players, guests and management at bay for fully 30 minutes."

Cullen, of course, had joined the club at a time when they were still able to preserve some of the pre-war features and were eagerly watched by crowds starved by the war of live sport. Gradually counter-attractions were eroding the numbers of supporters and it was clear as 1952 developed that a crisis was looming. Early in the year the president, Billy Bradshaw, had tendered his resignation but had been persuaded to stay on. At an emergency committee meeting in June Bradshaw warned that considerable economies were necessary, in view of falling gates and the way county rugby on Saturdays was hitting the club. The best way out, he suggested, was to disband the A XV. The majority of the committee disagreed: they decided the club should pay for no drinks, cheaper travel should be investigated and the A XV retained by an 8-5 vote. The following month Bradshaw resigned in protest and Charlie Cross was elected president.

← A montage of the three programmes from the 1952 Easter Tour.

LEICESTER FOOTBALL CLUB 1945/46
Back: Bradshaw (President), Norman (A Team Hon.Sec), T.Adams, Matts, A.Brown, B.Brown, Hughes, Bedingfield (Hon.Tres), Thorneloe (Hon.Sec).
Middle: Cole, Richards, F.Edwards, Berry (capt), Dermott, Day, Neal.
Front: Stimpson, Harris, Stokes, Davies.
Inset: Moore, Beamish, Bolesworth, Watkin, Thomas, Channer.

LEICESTER FOOTBALL CLUB 1947/48
Back: Thorneloe (Hon.Sec), Bedingfield (Hon.Tres), Sibson, Quine, Ellis, Hughes, Lacey, P.Herbert, Brown, Rees, Towell, Nicholas, Bradshaw (President), Barr (Team Hon.Sec).
Front: Tudor, B.Moore, Dermott, Berry, Jerwood (capt), Watkin, Bolesworth, Channer, Neal.

LEICESTER FOOTBALL CLUB 1948/49
Back: Bradshaw (President), Bedingfield (Hon.Tres), Brown, Stirling, Rees, Thorneloe, Bennett, Sibson, Barr (Team Hon.Sec), Thorneloe (Hon.Sec), Read (Touch Judge).
Middle: Tudor, Bolesworth, Lacey, Towell, Jerwood (capt), B.Moore, Ellis, Nicholas, Matts.
Front: Tucker, Lawrence, Barrow, Harvey, Selkirk.
Inset: P.Herbert, Norton.

LEICESTER FOOTBALL CLUB 1949/50
Back: Bedingfield (Hon.Tres), Bradshaw (President), Thomas, Norton, Bleasdale, Smith, Thompson, Marshall, Deacon, Barr (Team Hon.Sec), Read (Touch Judge).
Middle: Nicholas, Jerwood, Moore, Towell (capt), Bolesworth, Sibson, Thorneloe.
Front: Terrington, Cullen, Tudor, Pratt.
Inset: Lacey.

LEICESTER FOOTBALL CLUB 1950/51
Back: Thorneloe (Hon.Sec), Barr (Team Hon.Sec), Jerwood, Kail, Cullen, Hacker, Lewis, F.Chawner, Lawrence, Bradshaw (President), Bedingfield (Hon.Tres).
Middle: Bleasdale, Nicholas, Lacey, Bolesworth, Moore (capt), Stirling, Sibson, Thomas, Pratt.
Front: Matthews, Marshall.

LEICESTER FOOTBALL CLUB 1951/52
Back: E.Thorneloe (Hon.Sec), Bradshaw (President), Fisk, Marshall, P.Thorneloe, Smith, Botting, Lawrence, Nicholas, Bedingfield (Hon.Tres), Barr (Team Hon.Sec).
Middle: Sibson, Cullen, Channer, Bolesworth, Moore (capt), Bleasdale, Lacey, Pratt, Barrow.
Front: Gee, Redfern.
Inset: Thomas, Stirling.

1945/46

Home Ground: Welford Road
Captain: Tom Berry

OVERALL RECORD:					T	C	PG	DG	MK	PTS
PLD	W	D	L	Tigers scored:	49	16	17	3	0	242
34	16	2	16	Opponents scored:	58	23	13	2	0	278

GM	DATE		VEN	OPPONENTS	RESULT	TRIES	KICKS	ATT
CLUB MATCHES								
1	Sep	8	a	Cardiff	L 6-12	T.Adams	Richards p	6000
		15	**H**	**Plymouth Albion**	PP			
2		**22**	**H**	**Waterloo**	L 6-11	-	Watkin 2p	2000
		29	**H**	**Old Merchant Taylors**	PP			
3	Oct	**6**	**H**	**Coventry**	L 3-13	Gornall	-	3000
4		**13**	**H**	**Nuneaton**	W 8-3	T.Adams, B.Edwards	Richards c	1000
5		**20**	**H**	**Newport**	L 6-8	Bolesworth	Watkin p	-
6		27	a	Northampton	L 0-5	-	-	-
7	Nov	3	a	Gloucester	L 0-27	-	-	-
8		**10**	**H**	**Cambridge University**	W 6-3	A.Brown, Parfitt	-	2000
9		**17**	**H**	**Rugby**	W 9-3	Harris, Rees, Thomas	-	-
10		**24**	**H**	**Bath**	W 9-3	A.Brown, Thomas	Watkin p	-
11	Dec	1	a	Harlequins	L 4-15	-	Davies d	-
12		8	a	Guy's Hospital	L 5-6	Harris	Richards c	-
13		**15**	**H**	**Bristol**	L 0-8	-	-	1500
14		22	a	Bedford	L 3-6	B.Brown	-	-
15		**26w**	**H**	**Barbarians**	L 0-3	-	-	7000
16		**27th**	**H**	**New Zealand Services**	L 3-19	-	Tahany p	3000
17		**29**	**H**	**Swansea**	D 6-6	-	Davies p, Watkin p	2000
18	Jan	**5**	**H**	**Cardiff**	W 12-8	T.Adams, F.Edwards	Davies c/d	3000
19		**12**	**H**	**Gloucester**	L 11-12	T.Adams, F.Edwards	Watkin p, Davies c	2000
		19	a	Nuneaton	PP			
20		**26**	**H**	**Richmond & Blackheath**	W 14-6	T.Adams, Berry, Dermott, F.Edwards	Davies c	1000
21	Feb	**2**	**H**	**London Scottish**	W 14-5	F.Edwards(2), Thomas	Davies c/p	-
22		9	a	Newport	L 5-15	Stimpson	Davies c	-
23		16	a	Swansea	L 6-19	Harris	Davies p	3000
24		**23**	**H**	**Northampton**	W 6-0	Cole, Harris	-	2000
25	Mar	**2**	**H**	**Harlequins**	D 8-8	Day	Davies c/p	-
26		9	a	Coventry	W 5-3	Thomas	Davies c	-
27		**16**	**H**	**Bedford**	W 10-9	Channer, F.Edwards	Richards c, Watkin c	-
28		**23**	**H**	**Rosslyn Park**	W 10-0	-	Matts 2p/d	-
29		30	a	Rugby	W 8-6	Stimpson, Watkin	Matts c	-
30	Apr	**6**	**H**	**Middlesex Hospital**	W 20-11	F.Edwards(2), T.Adams, Berry, Stimpson	Davies p, Matts c	-
31		13	a	Waterloo	W 8-6	Channer, Day	Matts c	-
32		20	a	Bristol	W 9-6	F.Edwards, Thomas	Watkin p	3000
33		22m	a	Exeter	L 5-8	T.Adams	Watkin c	-
34		23tu	a	Bath	W 17-5	Channer(3), A.Brown	Channer c, Watkin p	-

INDIVIDUAL APPEARANCES 1945/46

Name / Game #	1	2	3	4	5	6	7	8	9	10	11	12	13	14	15	16	17	18	19	20	21	22	23	24	25	26	27	28	29	30	31	32	33	34	Apps	T	Pts
JA (John) Adams	-	-	-	-	-	-	-	-	-	-	-	-	-	>N	-	-	N	<K	-	-	-	-	-	-	-	-	-	-	-	-	-	-	-	-	3	-	-
AM (Tony) Adams	>J	J	-	J	J	J	J	-	J	J	-	J	J	-	N	N	L	M	M	N	N	-	-	M	N	N	-	-	-	M	M	N	N	K	25	7	21
CH (Cecil) Beamish	-	-	-	-	-	D	D	-	-	G	G	-	G	-	G	G	-	-	-	-	G	G	-	G	-	-	<G	-	-	-	-	-	-	-	11	-	-
JTW (Tom) Berry E3	H*	H*	F*	F*	F*	F*	-	F*	F*	F*	F*	H*	F*	G*	H*	H*	F*	F*	F*	F*	F*	F*	F*	F*	F*	F*	F*	F*	F*	F*	F*	F*	G*	H*	33	2	6
Flt-Sgt. AC (Anthony) Blandy	-	-	>J	<M	-	-	-	-	-	-	-	-	-	-	-	-	-	-	-	-	-	-	-	-	-	-	-	-	-	-	-	-	-	-	2	-	-
AD (Denis) Bolesworth	-	C	C	C	C	C	-	-	-	-	-	-	C	C	A	A	-	A	A	-	A	A	-	A	-	-	A	-	A	-	A	-	-	-	17	1	3
JG (John) Brennand	-	-	-	-	-	-	-	-	-	-	>N	N	<N	-	-	-	-	-	-	-	-	-	-	-	-	-	-	-	-	-	-	-	-	-	3	-	-
BCM (Basil) Brierley	>K	K	<K	-	-	-	-	-	-	-	-	-	-	-	-	-	-	-	-	-	-	-	-	-	-	-	-	-	-	-	-	-	-	-	3	-	-
AE (Albert) Brown	E	E	D	A	-	-	C	C	C	C	C	C	A	D	-	D	D	-	-	D	-	-	-	-	C	C	-	C	-	C	-	A	A	C	22	3	9
WA (Bill) Brown	-	-	-	>E	E	E	E	G	E	D	-	E	D	E	-	E	E	E	E	-	D	-	E	-	E	E	E	E	E	E	E	D	E	-	25	1	3
MR (Mel) Channer	-	-	-	-	-	-	-	-	-	-	-	-	-	-	-	-	-	-	-	-	-	-	-	-	-	-	>M	-	J	-	J	J	J	M	6	5	17
SA (Sammy) Cole	-	-	-	-	-	-	-	-	-	-	-	>I	-	I	I	I	I	I	I	-	I	I	-	I	I	-	I	I	-	I	I	I	I	-	17	1	3
RJ (Roy) Cramb	-	-	>N	N	N	N	-	-	-	-	-	-	-	-	-	-	-	-	-	-	-	-	-	-	-	-	N	<N	-	-	-	-	-	-	6	-	-
JF Davies	-	-	-	-	-	-	-	-	-	-	>M	-	M	J	J	J	J	J	J	J	J	J	J	J	J	J	-	-	-	J	L	-	-	<J	18	-	37
JD (Jerry) Day	>F	F	H	H	H	H	H	H	H	H	H	F	H	H	-	-	-	-	-	H	H	H	H	-	H	H	H	H	H	H	H	H	H	F	28	2	6
LG (Digger) Dermott	>A	A	A	D	A	A	A	A	A	A	A	A	-	A	C	-	C	C	C	A	C	C	A	C	A	A	C	A	C	A	C	C	C	A	32	1	3
JR Dunn	>N	<N	-	-	-	-	-	-	-	-	-	-	-	-	-	-	-	-	-	-	-	-	-	-	-	-	-	-	-	-	-	-	-	-	2	-	-
B (Bryn) Edwards	-	-	-	>K	K	<K	-	-	-	-	-	-	-	-	-	-	-	-	-	-	-	-	-	-	-	-	-	-	-	-	-	-	-	-	3	1	3
FG (Francis) Edwards	-	-	-	-	-	-	-	-	-	-	-	L	L	L	L	L	-	L	L	L	L	L	M	-	L	-	L	L	-	L	-	L	L	L	18	9	27
RF (Dickie) Harris	-	-	-	-	-	-	>K	K	K	K	K	K	K	K	K	K	K	-	K	K	K	K	N	K	K	K	K	K	K	K	K	K	K	-	26	4	12
J (John) Harrison	-	-	-	-	-	-	-	-	-	-	-	-	-	-	-	-	-	-	-	-	-	-	-	-	-	>I	-	-	I	-	-	-	-	I	3	-	-
Dr. HP (Nick) Hughes	>G	D	E	-	D	-	-	D	D	-	D	-	E	-	D	-	-	D	-	-	-	D	-	D	D	-	-	-	-	-	D	-	D	D	16	-	-
WA (Wilf) Jackson	-	M	-	-	M	M	-	0	M	<M	-	-	-	-	-	-	-	-	-	-	-	-	-	-	-	-	-	-	-	-	-	-	-	-	6	-	-
RA Laing	-	-	-	-	-	-	-	>M	-	-	-	-	-	-	-	-	-	-	<N	-	-	-	-	-	-	-	-	-	-	-	-	-	-	-	2	-	-
GA (George) Matts	-	-	-	-	-	-	-	-	-	-	-	-	-	-	-	-	-	-	-	-	-	-	-	-	-	-	-	>0	0	0	0	-	-	-	4	-	16
WKT (Bill) Moore E+	>M	-	-	-	-	-	-	-	-	-	-	-	-	M	M	M	M	-	-	-	-	-	-	L	-	L	-	J	-	-	-	-	-	-	8	-	-
AE (Eddie) Neal	>B	B	B	B	B	B	B	B	B	B	B	B	B	B	B	B	-	-	-	B	B	B	B	-	-	-	-	-	B	B	B	B	B	B	26	-	-
LA (Laurie) Norman	-	-	-	-	-	-	-	-	-	-	-	-	-	-	-	-	-	-	-	-	-	-	>0	0	0	<0	-	-	-	-	-	-	-	-	4	-	-
EJ (Ted) Parfitt	-	-	-	-	-	-	I	<I	-	-	-	-	-	-	-	-	-	-	-	-	-	-	-	-	-	-	-	-	-	-	-	-	-	-	2	1	3
ER Pierce	>I	I	-	-	I	I	-	-	I	I	I	-	<I	-	-	-	-	-	-	-	-	-	-	-	-	-	-	-	-	-	-	-	-	-	8	-	-
LAC. G Rees	-	-	-	-	-	-	-	>N	N	N	-	-	-	-	-	-	-	<N	-	-	-	-	-	-	-	-	-	-	-	-	-	-	-	-	4	1	3
WH (Harry) Richards	D	G	G	G	G	G	G	E	G	E	E	D	-	F	E	F	G	G	G	E	E	E	C	E	G	D	D	D	D	D	G	E	F	E	33	-	9
HW Smith	-	-	-	-	-	-	-	>J	-	-	-	<M	-	-	-	-	-	-	-	-	-	-	-	-	-	-	-	-	-	-	-	-	-	-	2	-	-
K (Ken) Stimpson	-	-	-	-	-	-	-	-	-	-	-	-	-	-	-	-	-	-	-	-	-	>N	K	N	-	-	-	-	N	N	-	-	-	<N	6	3	9
LJ (Lew) Stokes	-	-	-	-	-	-	>F	-	-	-	-	G	-	-	-	-	H	H	H	G	-	-	G	H	-	G	-	G	G	G	-	G	-	G	14	-	-
MP (Peter) Tahany	>C	-	-	-	-	-	-	-	-	-	-	-	-	-	-	C	B	B	-	-	-	-	-	-	-	-	-	-	-	-	-	-	-	-	4	-	3
HG (Haydn) Thomas	-	-	-	>L	L	L	L	L	L	L	J	-	-	-	-	-	-	-	-	M	M	M	L	-	M	M	J	M	M	-	-	M	M	-	19	5	15
PBL (Peter) Thorneloe	-	-	-	-	-	-	-	-	-	-	-	-	-	-	-	-	>A	-	D	C	-	-	-	-	-	-	-	-	-	-	-	-	-	-	3	-	-
RE (Ronnie) Tudor	-	-	-	-	-	-	-	-	-	-	-	-	-	-	-	-	-	-	>B	-	-	-	-	B	B	B	B	B	-	-	-	-	-	-	6	-	-
EJ Warner	-	-	>I	<I	-	-	-	-	-	-	-	-	-	-	-	-	-	-	-	-	-	-	-	-	-	-	-	-	-	-	-	-	-	-	2	-	-
CE (Ernie) Watkin	0	0	0	0	0	0	0	-	0	0	0	0	0	0	0	0	0	0	0	0	0	0	-	-	-	-	0	-	L	-	-	0	0	0	26	1	31

1 GAME: J (Jack) Ball <I(20), TH Barker =D(23), L (Lawrence) Bithell =I(23), Cpl. W (Bill) Gornall =Mt(3), DA (Daniel) Griffiths =L(3), MM (Maurice) Henderson S3 <F(15), RJA (Robert) Hutt =L(11), Flt-Lt. Kemp =L(1), D Langley =N(31), WG (William) Moseby <L(2), L (Leonard) Price-Stephens =N(7), G Rogers =M(7)

19 46/47		OVERALL RECORD:					T	C	PG	DG	MK	PTS
Home Ground: Welford Road		PLD	W	D	L	Tigers scored:	72	31	13	6	0	341
Captain: Tom Berry		32	18	1	13	Opponents scored:	50	20	15	5	1	258

GM	DATE		VEN	OPPONENTS	RESULT	TRIES	KICKS	ATT
CLUB MATCHES								
1	Sep	**7**	**H**	**Bedford**	W 12-0	Channer(3), Phipps	-	3000
2		**14**	**H**	**Bath**	W 6-3	Adams	Watkin p	2000
3		**21**	**H**	**Plymouth Albion**	W 12-4	Channer(2), Adams, Rhodes	-	3000
4		25w	a	Nuneaton	W 11-0	Freer	Watkin c/2p	-
5		**28**	**H**	**Waterloo**	L 19-34	Cole, Edwards, Ellis	Watkin 2c/2p	3000
6	Oct	3th	a	Rugby	W 10-6	Edwards, Lambert	Doyle d	-
7		5	a	Coventry	L 3-17	-	Watkin p	4000
8		**12**	**H**	**Neath**	D 6-6	Lambert	Watkin p	3000
9		19	a	Newport	L 6-14	Neal	Watkin p	3500
10		**26**	**H**	**Northampton**	L 5-7	Freer	Watkin c	2000
11		30w	a	Oxford University	L 3-15	-	Rhodes p	-
12	Nov	**2**	**H**	**Gloucester**	W 16-3	Ryley(2), Channer, Edwards	Watkin 2c	3000
13		9	a	Cambridge University	W 3-0	-	Watkin p	1500
14		**16**	**H**	**Cardiff**	L 8-19	P.Herbert, Jerwood	Rhodes c	3500
15		**23**	**H**	**Guy's Hospital**	W 26-5	Dermott, Edwards, Freer, P.Herbert, Rhodes, Ryley	Watkin 4c	2000
16		**30**	**H**	**Swansea**	W 11-6	Channer, Ryley	Rhodes p, Watkin c	2000
17	Dec	7	a	Harlequins	W 7-0	Jerwood	Channer d	-
18		14	a	Blackheath	W 10-6	Channer, Thomas	Channer d	-
		21	**H**	**Bristol**	PP (frost)			
19		**26th**	**H**	**Birkenhead Park**	W 32-5	Freer(3), Channer(2), Ryley	Channer d, Watkin 5c	-
20		**27f**	**H**	**Barbarians**	L 3-8	Edwards	-	7000
21		**28**	**H**	**Rugby**	W 24-3	Thomas(4), Edwards	Watkin 3c/p	3000
22	Jan	**4**	**H**	**Headingley**	W 20-13	Stapleford(2), Channer, Edwards, Jerwood, Lynch	Rhodes c	3000
23		11	a	Gloucester	L 5-10	Edwards	Watkin c	6000
24		**18**	**H**	**Nuneaton**	W 22-0	Bolesworth, Freer, Lynch, Ryley	Watkin 3c, Rhodes d	2000
		25	a	Richmond	PP (frost/snow)			
		30th	**H**	**Royal Air Force**	PP (frost/snow)			
	Feb	1	a	London Scottish	PP (frost/snow)			
		8	**H**	**Newport**	PP (frost/snow)			
		15	a	Swansea	PP (frost/snow)			
		22	a	Northampton	PP (frost/snow)			
	Mar	**1**	**H**	**Harlequins**	PP (frost/snow)			
		8	**H**	**Coventry**	PP (frost/snow)			
25		15	a	Cardiff	L 5-17	Rhodes	Watkin c	-
26		22	a	Bedford	W 9-0	Freer, Hacker, Ryley	-	3000
27		**29**	**H**	**Rosslyn Park**	W 18-9	Edwards(3), Freer	Watkin 3c	1500
28	Apr	5	a	Bristol	L 0-6 (Abandoned 64')	-	-	2000
29		7m	a	Plymouth Albion	L 3-8	-	Watkin p	-
30		8tu	a	Bath	L 8-12	Channer, Thomas	Watkin c	-
31		12	a	Birkenhead Park	L 6-13	Freer, Ryley	-	2000
32		**19**	**H**	**Blackheath**	W 12-9	Ryley, Edwards	Ryley d, Watkin c	2500

INDIVIDUAL APPEARANCES 1946/47																																			
Name / Game #	1	2	3	4	5	6	7	8	9	10	11	12	13	14	15	16	17	18	19	20	21	22	23	24	25	26	27	28	29	30	31	32	Apps	T	Pts
AM (Tony) Adams	J	J	J	J	J	-	-	-	-	-	-	-	-	-	-	-	-	-	-	-	-	-	-	-	-	-	-	-	-	N	-	-	6	2	6
P (Paul) Ash	-	-	-	-	-	-	-	-	-	-	>J	-	-	-	-	-	-	-	-	-	-	-	-	-	-	-	-	-	J	-	-	-	2	-	-
JTW (Tom) Berry E3	F*	F*	F*	F*	F*	F*	F*	F*	F*	F*	F*	F*	F*	-	-	F*	F*	F*	F*	F*	F*	F*	F*	F*	F*	F*	F*	F*	F*	F*	F*	F*	30	-	-
DE (Eric) Bevins	-	-	-	-	-	-	I	-	-	-	-	-	-	-	-	-	-	-	-	-	-	-	-	-	<I	-	-	-	-	-	-	-	2	-	-
AD (Denis) Bolesworth	-	-	-	A	A	C	A	A	A	A	A	A	A	A	A	A	A	A	A	A	A	A	A	A	A	A	A	A	A	A	A	A	29	1	3
AE (Albert) Brown	C	C	C	D	C	A	D	D	-	D	<E	-	-	-	-	-	-	-	-	-	-	-	-	-	-	-	-	-	-	-	-	-	10	-	-
WA (Bill) Brown	D	D	D	E	D	D	E	-	D	-	-	D	D	D	D	D	D	D	-	D	D	D	D	D	D	D	D	E	D	D	-	D	27	-	-
JCK (John) Campbell	-	-	-	-	-	-	-	-	-	-	-	-	-	-	-	-	-	=M	-	-	-	-	-	-	-	-	-	-	-	-	-	-	1	-	-
MR (Mel) Channer	L	L	M	-	-	-	M	J	J	J	L	J	J	J	J	J	J	J	J	J	J	J	-	-	-	-	-	-	L	J	J	-	22	12	48
WV Clarke	-	-	-	-	-	=K	-	-	-	-	-	-	-	-	-	-	-	-	-	-	-	-	-	-	-	-	-	-	-	-	-	-	1	-	-
SA (Sammy) Cole	I	I	I	-	I	-	-	I	I	I	-	I	I	I	I	I	I	I	-	I	I	I	-	-	-	-	-	-	-	<I	-	-	18	1	3
LG (Digger) Dermott	A	A	A	C	-	-	C	C	C	C	C	C	C	C	C	C	-	C	C	C	-	-	C	C	C	C	C	C	C	C	C	C	27	1	3
LT (Laurie) Doyle	-	-	-	-	-	>J	J	-	-	-	-	-	-	N	-	-	-	-	M	-	-	-	-	-	-	-	J	-	-	-	-	-	5	-	4
FG (Francis) Edwards	-	-	L	L	L	L	L	-	L	L	M	L	L	M*	L*	L	L	L	L	L	L	L	L	L	L	L	L	L	M	M	-	L	28	12	36
DR (Roger) Ellis	>K	K	-	M	N	-	K	-	-	-	-	-	K	-	-	-	-	-	-	-	-	-	-	J	-	-	-	-	-	-	-	-	7	1	3
AT (Tom) Ford	-	-	-	-	-	-	-	-	-	-	-	-	-	-	-	-	-	-	-	-	-	-	-	-	-	>E	<E	-	-	-	-	-	2	-	-
WR (Bill) Freer	-	-	-	>K	K	N	-	K	K	K	N	K	-	-	K	-	N	N	N	N	-	K	K	N	N	N	N	K	K	-	N	M	23	10	30
F (Frank) Gough	-	-	-	>I	-	I	-	-	-	-	<I	-	-	-	-	-	-	-	-	-	-	-	-	-	-	-	-	-	-	-	-	-	3	-	-
JH (John) Hacker	-	-	-	-	-	-	-	-	-	-	-	-	-	-	-	-	-	-	-	-	-	-	-	-	-	>G	-	-	-	G	-	-	2	1	3
RF (Dickie) Harris	-	-	-	-	-	-	<N	-	-	-	-	-	-	-	-	-	-	-	-	-	-	-	-	-	-	-	-	-	-	-	-	-	1	-	-
VJ (Viv) Harrison	-	-	-	-	-	-	-	-	-	-	-	-	-	-	-	-	-	-	-	-	-	-	-	-	>J	<J	-	-	-	-	-	-	2	-	-
WC (Bill) Herbert	-	-	-	-	-	-	-	-	-	-	-	-	-	-	-	-	-	-	-	-	-	-	-	-	-	-	-	-	-	-	-	>I	1	-	-
PAH (Peter) Herbert	-	-	-	-	-	-	-	-	-	-	>H	-	H	H	H	H	H	-	H	-	H	-	-	-	-	-	-	-	-	-	-	-	8	2	6
Dr. HP (Nick) Hughes	-	-	-	-	-	-	-	-	-	-	-	-	-	-	-	-	-	-	E	E	-	E	E	E	E	-	G	D	E	-	D	-	10	-	-
HP (Peter) Jerwood	E	E	E	G	E	E	G	E	E	E	D	E	E	E	E	E	E	E	D	G	-	G	G	G	G	-	-	G	-	E	E	G	28	3	9
TM (Trevor) Jones	-	-	-	-	-	-	-	-	-	-	-	-	-	-	-	-	-	-	-	-	-	-	-	-	-	-	-	-	-	-	>M	-	1	-	-
JP (Peter) Lambert	-	-	-	-	-	M	-	<L	-	-	-	-	-	-	-	-	-	-	-	-	-	-	-	-	-	-	-	-	-	-	-	-	2	2	6
M (Martin) Lynch	-	-	-	-	-	>H	-	-	-	-	-	-	-	-	-	-	G	H	-	H	G	H	H	H	H	H	H	H	H	H	H	<H	16	2	6
GA (George) Matts	-	-	-	-	-	-	-	-	-	-	-	-	-	-	-	-	-	-	-	-	-	-	-	-	-	-	-	-	-	-	0	-	1	-	-
J Milton	-	-	-	-	-	-	-	-	-	-	-	-	-	-	-	-	-	-	-	-	=E	-	-	-	-	-	-	-	-	-	-	-	1	-	-
WKT (Bill) Moore E2	-	-	-	-	-	-	-	-	-	-	-	-	-	-	-	-	-	-	I	-	-	-	I	-	-	I	I	I	I	-	I	-	7	-	-
AE (Eddie) Neal	B	B	B	B	-	-	B	B	B	B	B	B	B	B	B	B	B	B	B	B	B	B	B	B	B	B	B	B	B	B	B	B	30	1	3
G (Gordon) Phipps	>N	N	<N	-	-	-	-	-	-	-	-	-	-	-	-	-	-	-	-	-	-	-	-	-	-	-	-	-	-	-	-	-	3	1	3
PEF (Peter) Rhodes	>M	M	K	-	M	-	-	M	M	M	0	M	M	L	M	M	M	-	-	M	N	M	M	M	M	M	M	M	-	K	L	N	26	3	23
WH (Harry) Richards	G	G	G	H	G	G	-	G	G	<G	-	-	-	-	-	-	-	-	-	-	-	-	-	-	-	-	-	-	-	-	-	-	9	-	-
RJ (Bob) Ryley	-	-	-	-	-	-	-	-	-	-	>K	N	N	K	N	N	K	K	K	K	-	-	-	K	K	K	K	N	N	-	K	J	18	9	31
HW (Harry) Sibson	-	-	-	-	-	-	-	-	-	-	-	-	-	-	-	-	-	-	-	-	-	-	-	-	-	-	-	-	-	-	-	>E	1	-	-
JR (Rodney) Stapleford	-	-	-	-	-	-	-	>N	N	N	-	-	-	-	-	K	-	-	-	-	K	N	N	-	-	-	-	-	-	-	-	-	7	2	6
LJ (Lew) Stokes	H	H	H	N	H	-	H	H	H	H	-	H	-	F	<F	-	-	-	-	-	-	-	-	-	-	-	-	-	-	-	-	-	12	-	-
MP (Peter) Tahany	-	-	-	-	-	-	-	-	-	-	G	G	G	G	G	G	C	G	G	-	-	C	-	-	-	-	-	-	G	-	G	-	12	-	-
HG (Haydn) Thomas	-	-	-	-	-	-	-	-	-	-	-	-	-	-	-	-	-	r	-	-	M	-	J	-	-	-	-	J	-	L	-	-	4+1	6	18
WE (Bill) Thompson	-	-	-	-	-	-	-	-	-	-	-	-	-	-	-	-	-	-	-	-	>C	-	-	-	-	-	-	-	-	-	-	-	1	-	-
RE (Ronnie) Tudor	-	-	-	-	B	B	-	-	-	-	-	-	-	-	-	-	-	-	-	-	-	-	-	-	-	-	-	-	-	-	-	-	2	-	-
AB (Bernard) Vesty	-	-	-	-	-	-	-	-	-	-	-	-	-	-	-	-	-	-	-	-	-	-	-	-	-	-	-	-	-	-	-	=K	1	-	-
CE (Ernie) Watkin	0	0	0	0	0	0	0	0	0	0	-	0	0	0	0	0	0	0	0	0	0	0	0	0	0	0	0	0	0	0	-	0	30	-	91
CJ (Chris) Weston	-	-	-	-	-	-	-	-	-	-	-	-	-	-	-	-	-	-	-	-	-	-	-	=I	-	-	-	-	-	-	-	-	1	-	-

The key for how to read the stats is on the last page

19 47/48

Home Ground: Welford Road

Captain: Peter Jerwood

OVERALL RECORD:					T	C	PG	DG	PTS
PLD	W	D	L	Tigers scored:	83	37	20	8	415
38	17	1	20	Opponents scored:	77	40	18	11	409

GM	DATE		VEN	OPPONENTS	RESULT	TRIES	KICKS	ATT
CLUB MATCHES								
1	Sep	6	H	Bedford	W 22-3	Jerwood(2), Adams, Dermott, Ryley, Towell	Watkin 2c	3000
2		13	H	Bath	W 31-11	Rees(2), Adams, Dermott, Tahany	Channer c/3d, Jerwood c	2000
3		20	H	Plymouth Albion	W 12-3	Adams, Freer, Rees, Ryley	-	2500
4		27	a	Waterloo	L 6-23	Ryley	Watkin p	-
5	Oct	4	H	Coventry	L 14-19	Adams(2), Jerwood	Channer c/p	5000
6		11	a	Neath	L 5-6	Thomas	Watkin c	-
7		18	H	Newport	L 10-21	-	Watkin 2p, Gaunt d	6000
8		25	a	Northampton	L 0-11	-	-	7000
9		29w	H	Oxford University	L 10-16	-	Watkin 2p, B.Herbert d	1000
10	Nov	1	a	Gloucester	L 6-20	Ellis(2)	-	7000
11		8	H	Cambridge University	L 10-11	Ash, Ashley	Watkin 2c	-
12		15	a	Cardiff	L 5-50	P.Herbert	Bowen c	7000
13		22	a	Swansea	D 3-3	Sibson	-	2500
14		29	H	Cardiff	L 4-8	-	Towell d	3000
15	Dec	6	a	Harlequins	W 11-5	Rees(2), Ashley	Watkin c	500
16		13	H	Middlesex Hospital	W 14-3	Towell(2), Freer, B.Moore	Watkin c	2000
17		20	H	Bristol	L 13-16	Towell(2)	Jerwood c/p, Watkin c	1000
18		26f	H	Barbarians	L 10-15	Jerwood, Towell	Watkin 2c	12000
19		27	H	Birkenhead Park	W 19-8	Gaunt(2), Jerwood, Quine	Jerwood c/p, Norman c	1500
20	Jan	3	a	Headingley	L 3-7	-	Jerwood p	200
21		10	H	Gloucester	L 6-13	Towell	Jerwood p	-
22		17	a	Nuneaton	W 14-0	Quine, Ryley	Watkin c/2p	-
23		24	H	Richmond	W 24-8	Quine(2), Ryley(2), Jerwood, Jones	Watkin 3c	2000
24		29th	H	Royal Air Force	W 11-0	Bolesworth, Dermott, Ryley	Watkin c	1500
25		31	a	Blackheath	W 22-11	Lacey, Jerwood, B.Moore	Lacey d, Watkin 3c/p	-
26	Feb	7	H	London Scottish	L 5-14 (Abandoned)	Bolesworth	Watkin c	4000
27		14	a	Newport	L 6-32	Tahany	Watkin p	4000
28		21	H	Swansea	L 3-5	Tahany	-	-
29		28	H	Northampton	W 14-7	Rees(2), Ellis	Watkin c/p	5000
30	Mar	6	H	Harlequins	W 32-3	Jerwood, Ellis, B.Moore, Rees, Sibson	Jerwood p, Watkin 4c/2p	4000
31		13	a	Coventry	W 5-0	P.Herbert	Watkin c	7000
32		20	a	Rugby	W 5-0	Terrington	Watkin c	1000
33		27	a	Bristol	L 14-20	Hunter(2), Channer, Rees	Watkin c	5000
34		29m	a	Plymouth Albion	L 10-14	Hunter	Channer d, Watkin p	5000
35		30tu	a	Bath	W 16-3	Bolesworth, Channer, Ellis, Nicholas	Watkin 2c	3000
36	Apr	3	a	Bedford	L 0-6	-	-	3000
37		10	a	Birkenhead Park	W 14-9	Ellis(2), Bolesworth	Watkin c/p	-
38		17	H	Blackheath	W 6-5	Rees(2)	-	2000

INDIVIDUAL APPEARANCES 1947/48

Name / Game #	1	2	3	4	5	6	7	8	9	10	11	12	13	14	15	16	17	18	19	20	21	22	23	24	25	26	27	28	29	30	31	32	33	34	35	36	37	38	Apps	T	Pts
AM (Tony) Adams	N	M	M	L	N	-	-	-	-	-	-	-	-	-	-	L	K	K	K	M	L	<L	-	-	-	-	-	-	-	-	-	-	-	-	-	-	-	-	12	5	15
P (Paul) Ash	-	-	-	-	-	-	-	-	-	-	J	J	J	-	-	-	<L	-	-	-	-	-	-	-	-	-	-	-	-	-	-	-	-	-	-	-	-	-	4	1	3
FMT (Fred) Ashley	-	-	-	-	-	-	-	-	-	-	>M	-	-	M	L	M	M	M	-	-	-	-	-	-	-	-	-	-	-	-	-	-	-	-	-	-	-	-	6	2	6
TH (Tom) Barratt	-	-	-	-	-	-	-	-	-	>K	-	<K	-	-	-	-	-	-	-	-	-	-	-	-	-	-	-	-	-	-	-	-	-	-	-	-	-	-	2	-	-
JTW (Tom) Berry E3	-	-	-	-	-	-	-	-	-	-	-	F*	-	-	-	-	-	-	-	-	-	-	-	-	-	-	-	-	-	-	-	-	-	-	-	-	-	<H*	2	-	-
AD (Denis) Bolesworth	A	A	A	A	-	A	A	A	A	A	A	-	A	A	A	A	A	A	A	A	A	A	A	A	A	A	A	A	A	A	A	A	A	A	A	A	A	A	36	4	12
HJR (Harry) Bowen	-	-	-	-	-	-	-	-	-	-	-	=0	-	-	-	-	-	-	-	-	-	-	-	-	-	-	-	-	-	-	-	-	-	-	-	-	-	-	1	-	2
WA (Bill) Brown	D	D	D	D	D	D	-	-	-	D	D	D	D	D	D	D	D	D	D	D	D	-	D	-	D	D	D	D	D	D	D	-	D	-	D	D	E	D	31	-	-
MR (Mel) Channer	J	J	J	J	J	-	-	-	-	-	-	-	-	-	-	-	-	-	-	-	-	-	-	-	-	-	L	-	-	-	-	-	J	J	J	L	-	M	11	2	29
JD (Jerry) Day	-	-	-	-	-	-	-	-	-	-	-	-	-	-	-	-	-	-	-	-	-	G	-	-	-	F	-	-	-	-	-	D	-	-	-	-	-	-	3	-	-
LG (Digger) Dermott	C	C	C	C	C	C	C	C	C	C	C	A	C	C	C	C	C	C	-	C	C	C	C	C	C	C	C	C	C	C	-	-	C	C	-	C	C	<C	34	3	9
FG (Francis) Edwards	-	-	-	-	-	-	-	-	-	-	-	-	-	-	-	-	-	-	-	-	-	-	-	-	-	-	-	M	-	-	-	M	-	-	-	-	<M	-	3	-	-
DR (Roger) Ellis	-	-	-	-	-	-	N	L	N	L	K	-	-	-	-	-	-	-	-	-	-	-	-	N	K	K	K	L	K	K	N	-	K	K	K	K	N	K	19	7	21
IP (Ian) Farmer-Wright	-	-	-	-	-	-	-	-	-	-	-	-	-	-	-	-	-	-	-	-	-	-	-	=M	-	-	-	-	-	-	-	-	-	-	-	-	-	-	1	-	-
WR (Bill) Freer	-	N	N	N	-	K	-	K	-	N	-	N	K	K	-	K	N	N	N	N	-	-	-	-	-	-	-	-	-	-	-	-	-	-	-	-	-	-	14	2	6
JL Gaunt	-	-	-	-	-	>J	J	-	J	J	-	-	-	-	-	-	-	-	<L	-	-	-	-	-	-	-	-	-	-	-	-	-	-	-	-	-	-	-	5	2	10
WC (Bill) Herbert	-	-	-	I	-	-	-	-	I	I	I	I	I	I	I	-	-	-	-	I	-	-	-	-	-	-	-	-	-	-	-	-	-	-	-	-	-	-	9	-	4
PAH (Peter) Herbert	-	-	-	-	-	-	-	-	-	-	F	H	H	H	H	H	H	H	H	H	H	H	H	H	H	-	F	F	F	F	F	F	-	-	F	F	F	F	25	2	6
Dr. HP (Nick) Hughes	E	E	E	E	E	-	D	D	D	-	E	-	-	E	E	E	E	E	-	-	-	-	-	E	-	G	-	-	-	-	-	-	-	<D	-	-	-	-	17	-	-
IW (Ian) Hunter	-	-	-	-	-	-	-	-	-	-	-	-	-	-	-	-	-	-	-	-	-	-	-	-	-	-	-	>N	N	N	K	N	N	N	N	-	-	-	8	3	9
HP (Peter) Jerwood	G*	G*	G*	G*	G*	G*	G*	G*	G*	G*	G*	-	G*	G*	-	G*	G*	G*	G*	G*	G*	D*	G*	G*	G*	H*	G*	G*	G*	G*	G*	G*	-	G*	G*	G*	G*	G	35	8	45
TM (Trevor) Jones	-	-	-	-	-	-	-	-	L	M	N	L	N	N	K	N	-	-	-	K	K	N	N	-	-	-	N	-	-	-	-	-	-	-	-	-	-	-	13	1	3
EC (Eric) Lacey	-	-	-	-	-	>E	E	E	E	E	-	E	E	-	-	-	-	-	E	-	E	E	E	D	E	E	-	E	E	E	E	E	E	E	E	-	D	E	24	1	7
GA (George) Matts	-	-	-	-	-	-	-	-	-	-	-	-	-	-	-	-	-	-	-	-	-	-	-	-	-	-	-	K	-	-	-	-	-	-	-	-	-	-	1	-	-
WKT (Bill) Moore E2	I	I	I	-	I	I	I	I	-	-	-	-	-	-	-	I	I	I	I	-	I	I	I	I	I	I	I	I	I	I	I	I	I	I	I	I	I	I	29	3	9
Maj. PJDA (Peter) Moore	-	-	-	-	-	-	-	-	-	-	-	-	-	-	-	-	-	-	=C	-	-	-	-	-	-	-	-	-	-	-	-	-	-	-	-	-	-	-	1	-	-
AE (Eddie) Neal	B	B	B	B	B	B	B	-	-	-	-	-	-	-	-	B	B	B	-	B	B	B	B	B	B	B	B	B	-	B	-	-	-	B	-	-	-	-	21	-	-
WK (Ken) Nicholas	-	-	-	-	-	-	-	-	-	-	-	-	-	-	-	-	-	-	-	-	-	-	-	-	-	-	-	-	-	>M	M	K	M	M	M	N	-	L	8	1	3
RA (Roland) Norman	-	-	-	-	-	-	-	-	-	-	-	-	-	-	-	-	-	-	>0	0	-	-	-	-	-	-	-	-	-	-	-	-	-	-	-	-	-	-	2	-	2
E Pell	-	-	-	-	-	-	-	=N	-	-	-	-	-	-	-	-	-	-	-	-	-	-	-	-	-	-	-	-	-	-	-	-	-	-	-	-	-	-	1	-	-
DA (David) Quine	-	-	-	-	-	-	-	-	-	-	-	-	-	-	-	-	-	-	>M	L	M	M	M	-	L	L	-	-	M	-	-	-	-	-	-	-	-	-	8	4	12
DER (Danny) Rees	-	>L	L	-	L	L	L	-	-	-	-	-	L	L	M	-	-	-	-	-	-	-	-	-	-	-	-	-	L	L	L	L	L	L	L	M	K	N	18	11	33
PEF (Peter) Rhodes	M	-	-	-	-	-	-	-	-	-	-	-	-	-	-	-	-	-	-	-	-	-	L	-	M	M	M	-	-	-	-	-	-	-	-	-	-	-	5	-	-
RJ (Bob) Ryley	K	K	K	K	K	N	K	M	K	-	-	-	-	-	-	-	-	-	-	-	N	K	K	K	N	<N	-	-	-	-	-	-	-	-	-	-	-	-	15	7	21
JR (John) Scott	-	-	-	-	-	-	-	-	-	-	-	>G	-	-	G	-	-	-	-	-	-	-	-	-	F	-	H	-	-	-	<H	-	-	-	-	-	-	-	5	-	-
HW (Harry) Sibson	H	H	H	H	H	H	H	H	H	H	H	-	F	F	F	F	F	F	F	F	F	F	F	F	-	-	-	-	-	H	-	-	H	H	H	H	H	-	29	2	6
SC Simmonds	-	-	-	-	-	-	-	-	-	-	-	-	-	-	-	-	-	=L	-	-	-	-	-	-	-	-	-	-	-	-	-	-	-	-	-	-	-	-	1	-	-
TM Simpson	-	-	-	-	-	-	-	-	-	-	-	-	-	-	-	-	-	-	-	-	-	-	-	-	-	-	-	-	-	-	-	-	-	-	-	=E	-	-	1	-	-
LW Smith	-	-	-	-	-	-	-	-	-	-	-	-	-	-	-	-	-	-	-	=E	-	-	-	-	-	-	-	-	-	-	-	-	-	-	-	-	-	-	1	-	-
R (Ron) Smith	-	-	-	-	-	-	-	-	-	-	-	-	-	-	-	-	-	-	-	-	-	-	-	-	-	-	-	-	-	-	-	-	-	-	-	-	L	-	1	-	-
JR (Rodney) Stapleford	-	-	-	-	-	-	-	-	-	-	-	-	-	-	<N	-	-	-	-	-	-	-	-	-	-	-	-	-	-	-	-	-	-	-	-	-	-	-	1	-	-
MP (Peter) Tahany	F	F	F	F	F	F	F	F	F	F	-	-	-	-	-	-	-	-	-	-	-	-	-	-	-	-	E	H	H	-	C	H	F	<F	-	-	-	-	17	3	9
HL (Harry) Terrington	-	-	-	-	-	-	-	-	-	-	>L	M	-	-	-	-	-	-	-	-	-	-	-	L	-	-	-	-	-	-	-	J	-	-	-	-	-	-	4	1	3
HG (Haydn) Thomas	-	-	-	-	-	M	M	-	-	-	-	-	-	-	-	-	-	-	-	-	-	-	-	-	-	-	-	-	-	-	-	-	-	-	-	-	-	-	2	1	3
WE (Bill) Thompson	-	-	-	-	A	-	-	-	-	-	-	C	-	-	-	-	-	-	-	-	-	-	-	-	-	-	-	-	-	-	-	-	-	-	-	-	-	-	2	-	-
PBL (Peter) Thorneloe	-	-	-	-	-	-	-	-	-	-	-	-	-	-	-	-	-	-	-	-	-	-	-	-	-	-	-	-	-	-	-	C	G	-	C	-	-	-	3	-	-
AC (Allan) Towell E1	>L	-	-	M	M	-	-	J	M	-	-	-	M	J	J	J	J	J	J	J	J	J	J	J	J	J	J	J	J	J	J	-	-	-	-	J	J	J	27	7	25
RE (Ronnie) Tudor	-	-	-	-	-	-	-	B	B	B	B	B	B	B	B	-	-	-	B	-	-	-	-	-	-	-	-	-	B	-	B	B	B	-	B	B	B	B	17	-	-
CE (Ernie) Watkin	0	0	0	0	0	0	0	0	0	0	0	-	0	0	0*	0	0	0	-	-	0	0	0	0	0	0	0	0	0	0	0	0	0*	0	0	0	0	0	35	-	102

The key for how to read the stats is on the last page

19 48/49	Home Ground: Welford Road	OVERALL RECORD:					T	C	PG	DG	PTS
	Captain: Peter Jerwood	PLD	W	D	L	Tigers scored:	57	18	27	10	318
		37	16	1	20	Opponents scored:	75	30	19	8	366

GM	DATE		VEN	OPPONENTS	RESULT	TRIES	KICKS	ATT
CLUB MATCHES								
1	Sep	**4**	**H**	**Bedford**	L 3-21	-	Rhodes p	3000
2		**11**	**H**	**Bath**	W 15-3	Ellis(2), Rees(2)	Rhodes p	3500
3		**18**	**H**	**Plymouth Albion**	W 19-0	Nicholas, Quine, Sibson, Towell	Matts 2c/p	2500
4		**25**	**H**	**Waterloo**	W 17-8	Ellis, Quine, Rees, Towell	Matts c/p	4000
5	Oct	2	a	Coventry	L 9-15	Ellis, Rees, Towell	-	4000
6		**9**	**H**	**Richmond**	W 14-6	Ashley, Rees	Matts c/d, Nicholas p	3500
7		16	a	Newport	L 3-22	Rees	-	6000
8		**23**	**H**	**Northampton**	L 6-8	-	Matts p, Towell d	6000
9		27w	a	Oxford University	L 3-15	Nicholas	-	-
10		**30**	**H**	**St Mary's Hospital**	L 3-8	-	Nicholas p	3000
11	Nov	6	a	Gloucester	L 16-18	Bolesworth, P.Herbert, Hunter	Matts 2c, Norman d	6000
12		13	a	Cambridge University	L 5-26	Ellis	Matts c	3500
13		**20**	**H**	**Cardiff**	L 0-6	-	-	8500
14		**27**	**H**	**Middlesex Hospital**	W 20-6	Bolesworth, Sibson, Stirling	Nicholas c/p, Rees d, Terrington d	2000
15	Dec	4	a	Harlequins	L 3-5	Rees	-	400
16		11	a	Blackheath	W 10-3	Ellis, Rees	Harvey 2c	1500
17		**18**	**H**	**Bristol**	L 6-21	Lacey	Harvey p	4000
18		**27m**	**H**	**Birkenhead Park**	L 9-16	Ellis	Jerwood 2p	5500
19		**28tu**	**H**	**Barbarians**	W 9-8	Jerwood, Lacey	Jerwood p	15000
20	Jan	**1**	**H**	**Headingley**	W 6-3	Nicholas	Jerwood p	2000
21		**8**	**H**	**Gloucester**	W 6-3	Bennett	Jerwood p	3000
22		15	a	Bedford	L 0-3	-	-	2500
23		22	a	Cardiff	L 6-22	-	Harvey 2p	20000
24		**27th**	**H**	**Royal Air Force**	W 12-5	Rees, Towell	Harvey 2p	2000
25		**29**	**H**	**Rosslyn Park**	L 6-9	Barrow	Towell d	3000
	Feb	5	a	London Scottish	PP (frost)			
26		**12**	**H**	**Newport**	L 3-22	-	Jerwood p	3500
27		**19**	**H**	**Swansea**	W 14-3	P.Herbert, Norton, Rees	Matts p, Jerwood c	3500
28		26	a	Northampton	D 9-9	-	Matts 2p, Towell d	4000
29	Mar	**5**	**H**	**Harlequins**	W 6-0	Towell	Matts p	2500
30		**12**	**H**	**Coventry**	L 0-6	-	-	3500
31		**19**	**H**	**Nuneaton**	W 9-3	Rees	Jerwood 2p	2500
32		26	a	Swansea	L 12-15	Thomas	B.Moore 2d, Towell d	-
33	Apr	2	a	Birkenhead Park	L 6-11	Lawrence, Norton	-	2000
34		**9**	**H**	**Blackheath**	W 23-6	Ellis, Lacey, Lawrence, Nicholas, Tucker	Matts 4c	3500
35		16	a	Bristol	L 9-17	Nicholas	Jerwood p, Matts p	3000
36		18m	a	Plymouth Albion	W 13-11	Lacey, B.Moore, Rees	Matts 2c	3000
37		19tu	a	Bath	W 8-3	Bennett, Brown	Matts c	-

INDIVIDUAL APPEARANCES 1948/49

Name / Game #	1	2	3	4	5	6	7	8	9	10	11	12	13	14	15	16	17	18	19	20	21	22	23	24	25	26	27	28	29	30	31	32	33	34	35	36	37	Apps	T	Pts
FMT (Fred) Ashley	-	-	-	-	-	M	<M	-	-	-	-	-	-	-	-	-	-	-	-	-	-	-	-	-	-	-	-	-	-	-	-	-	-	-	-	-	-	2	1	3
EA (Eric) Barrow	-	-	-	-	-	-	-	>F	-	-	-	-	-	-	-	F	-	-	-	-	-	-	-	F	F	H	H	H	H	H	F	F	F	H	G	H	H	16	1	3
ER (Peter) Bennett	-	-	-	-	-	-	-	-	-	-	-	-	>N	M	M	L	M	L	K	-	L	L	L	M	-	L	M	M	M	M	K	K	K	-	-	M	L	21	2	6
AD (Denis) Bolesworth	A	A	A	A	A	A	C	A	A	A	A	A	A	A	A	A	A	A	A	A	A	A	A	A	A	A	A	A	A	A	A	A	A	A	A	A	A	37	2	6
WA (Bill) Brown	E	E	E	E	D	E	D	D	D	D	D	D	D	-	D	D	E	-	D	D	-	D	D	D	D	-	-	-	-	-	-	-	-	-	-	-	<E	23	1	3
JD (Jerry) Day	-	-	-	-	-	-	-	-	-	-	G	G	G	D	-	H	F	H	H	H	H	-	G	H	-	-	-	-	-	-	-	H	-	-	-	-	-	13	-	-
HB (Howard) Deacon	-	-	-	-	-	-	-	-	-	-	-	-	>O	O	O	-	-	O	-	-	-	-	-	-	-	-	-	-	-	-	O	O	O	-	-	-	-	7	-	-
DR (Roger) Ellis	N	N	N	N	N	-	-	-	-	-	-	N	-	-	N	N	-	N	-	-	N	N	N	-	-	-	-	-	-	-	-	-	-	N	N	K	K	16	8	24
JH (John) Hacker	-	-	-	-	-	-	-	-	-	-	-	-	-	-	-	-	-	-	-	C	C	H	C	-	C	-	-	-	-	-	-	-	-	-	-	-	-	5	-	-
J (John) Harrison	-	-	-	-	-	-	-	-	-	-	I	I	I	I	J	J	-	-	-	I	J	I	-	-	-	I	-	I	-	-	-	-	-	-	-	-	-	11	-	-
Dr. JJM (Paddy) Harvey	-	-	-	-	-	-	-	-	-	-	-	-	-	-	-	>O	O	-	O	O	O	O	O	O	O	O	-	-	-	-	-	-	-	-	-	-	-	10	-	19
WC (Bill) Herbert	-	-	-	-	-	-	-	I	-	I	-	-	-	-	-	-	-	-	-	-	-	-	-	-	-	-	-	-	-	-	I	-	I	-	-	-	-	4	-	-
PAH (Peter) Herbert	F	H	H	H	F	H	F	-	F	F	F	F	F	F	F	-	-	F	F	F	F	F	F	-	-	F	F	F	F	F	-	-	-	-	-	F	F	27	2	6
IW (Ian) Hunter	-	-	-	-	-	-	-	K	-	-	<N	-	-	-	-	-	-	-	-	-	-	-	-	-	-	-	-	-	-	-	-	-	-	-	-	-	-	2	1	3
HP (Peter) Jerwood	-	-	G*	G*	G*	G*	G*	G*	G*	G*	-	-	-	G*	G*	G*	H*	G*	G*	E*	D*	G*	-	-	G*	G*	G*	G*	G*	G*	G*	G*	G*	G*	F*	G*	G*	30	1	32
TM (Trevor) Jones	-	-	-	-	-	N	N	N	K	<N	-	-	-	-	-	-	-	-	-	-	-	-	-	-	-	-	-	-	-	-	-	-	-	-	-	-	-	5	-	-
EC (Eric) Lacey	D	D	D	D	E	-	-	-	-	-	-	-	-	-	-	-	D	E	E	-	E	E	E	E	E	D	D	D	D	D	D	D	D	D	D	D	-	24	4	12
CGS (Gwynne) Lawrence	-	-	-	-	-	-	-	-	-	-	-	-	-	-	-	-	-	-	-	-	-	-	-	-	-	-	-	-	-	-	>M	M	M	M	M	-	-	5	2	6
RD (Bob) Matthews	-	-	-	-	-	-	-	-	-	-	-	-	-	-	-	-	-	-	-	>K	-	-	-	N	N	-	-	-	-	-	-	-	-	-	-	-	-	3	-	-
GA (George) Matts	-	-	O	O	O	O	O	O	O	O	O	O	-	-	-	-	-	-	-	-	-	-	-	-	-	-	O	O	O	O	-	-	-	O	O	O	O	18	-	55
WKT (Bill) Moore E4	I	I	I	I	I	-	I	-	-	-	-	-	-	-	I	I	I	I	I	-	I	-	I	I	I	-	I	-	I	I	-	I	-	I	I	I	I	23	1	9
JA (Jeff) Moore	-	-	-	-	-	>I	-	-	<I	-	-	-	-	-	-	-	-	-	-	-	-	-	-	-	-	-	-	-	-	-	-	-	-	-	-	-	-	2	-	-
AE (Eddie) Neal	B	B	B	B	<B	-	-	-	-	-	-	-	-	-	-	-	-	-	-	-	-	-	-	-	-	-	-	-	-	-	-	-	-	-	-	-	-	5	-	-
WK (Ken) Nicholas	-	L	L	L	L	L	L	L	L	L	M	M	L	L	L	-	-	-	L	L	M	J	J	J	M	J	L	-	L	L	L	L	L	K	K	-	-	30	5	26
RA (Roland) Norman	-	-	-	-	-	-	-	-	-	-	J	<J	-	-	-	-	-	-	-	-	-	-	-	-	-	-	-	-	-	-	-	-	-	-	-	-	-	2	-	3
D (David) Norton	-	-	-	-	-	-	-	-	-	-	-	-	-	-	-	-	-	-	-	-	-	-	-	-	-	-	>C	E	E	E	E	E	E	-	-	E	-	8	2	6
JRD (David) Palmer	>L	-	-	-	-	-	-	-	M	-	-	-	-	-	-	-	-	-	N	<M	-	-	-	-	-	-	-	-	-	-	-	-	-	-	-	-	-	4	-	-
S (Stan) Pratt	-	-	-	-	-	-	-	-	-	-	-	-	-	-	-	-	-	-	-	-	-	-	-	-	-	-	-	>B	B	B	B	B	-	-	-	-	-	5	-	-
DA (David) Quine	K	M	M	M	M	-	-	-	-	-	-	-	-	-	-	-	-	-	-	-	-	-	-	-	-	-	-	-	-	-	-	-	-	-	-	-	-	5	2	6
GDO (Geoffrey) Randle	-	-	-	-	-	-	-	-	-	-	-	-	-	-	-	-	-	>J	J	-	-	-	-	-	-	-	-	-	-	-	-	-	-	-	-	-	-	2	-	-
DER (Danny) Rees	-	K	K	K	K	K	K	M	-	K	K	K	K	K	K	K	K	K	-	-	K	K	K	K	K	N	N	N	N	N	N	-	-	-	-	N	N	29	12	39
PEF (Peter) Rhodes	M	<O	-	-	-	-	-	-	-	-	-	-	-	-	-	-	-	-	-	-	-	-	-	-	-	-	-	-	-	-	-	-	-	-	-	-	-	2	-	6
JG (Iain) Selkirk	-	-	-	-	-	-	-	-	-	-	-	-	-	-	-	-	-	-	-	-	-	-	-	-	-	-	-	-	-	-	>H	-	H	F	<H	-	-	4	-	-
HW (Harry) Sibson	H	F	F	F	H	F	H	H	H	H	H	H	H	H	H	-	-	-	-	-	-	-	-	-	-	-	-	-	-	-	-	-	-	-	-	-	-	15	2	6
RV (Bob) Stirling E+	>G	G	-	-	-	D	E	E	E	E	E	E	E	E	E	E	G	D	-	-	-	-	-	-	-	-	-	-	-	-	-	-	-	E	E	-	D	18	1	3
HL (Harry) Terrington	-	-	-	-	-	-	-	-	-	-	-	-	J	J	-	-	J	-	-	-	-	-	-	-	-	-	-	-	-	-	-	-	-	-	-	-	-	3	-	3
HG (Haydn) Thomas	-	-	-	-	-	-	-	-	N	M	-	-	-	-	-	-	N	-	-	-	-	-	-	-	-	-	J	-	-	-	-	N	-	-	-	-	-	5	1	3
PBL (Peter) Thorneloe	C	C	C	C	C	C	A	C	C	C	C	C	C	C	C	C	C	C	C	G	G	C	H	G	H	C	-	C	C	C	C	C	C	C	C	C	C	36	-	-
RC (Bob) Timson	-	-	-	-	-	-	-	-	-	-	-	-	-	-	-	-	-	-	-	-	-	-	-	-	-	>K	K	K	K	<K	-	-	-	-	-	-	-	5	-	-
AC (Allan) Towell E1	J*	J*	J	J	J	J	J	J	J	J	L*	L*	M*	-	-	M	L	M	M	-	-	M	M*	L*	L	M	J	L	J	J	J	J	J	L	L	L	M	33	5	27
GR (Geoff) Tucker	-	-	-	-	-	-	-	-	-	-	-	-	-	-	-	-	-	-	-	-	-	-	-	-	-	-	-	-	-	-	-	-	-	>J	J	J	J	4	1	3
RE (Ronnie) Tudor	-	-	-	-	-	B	B	B	B	B	B	B	B	B	B	B	B	B	B	B	B	B	B	B	B	B	B	-	-	-	-	-	B	B	B	B	B	27	-	-
1 GAME: F (Frank) Chawner >E(27), LT (Laurie) Doyle J(20), J Fletcher =E(26), WR (Bill) Freer <N(33), KJ (Ken) Jones W13 L+ =N(14), JP (Jim) Morris >J(25), R (Ron) Smith <N(20), WE (Bill) Thompson C(24), CE (Ernie) Watkin <O(1)																																								

The key for how to read the stats is on the last page

1949/50

Home Ground: Welford Road
Captain: Allan Towell

OVERALL RECORD:					T	C	PG	DG	PTS
PLD	W	D	L	Tigers scored:	47	18	24	7	270
39	15	1	23	Opponents scored:	77	36	18	6	375

GM	DATE		VEN	OPPONENTS	RESULT	TRIES	KICKS	ATT
CLUB MATCHES								
1	Sep	**3**	**H**	**Bedford**	L 6-16	-	Matts p/d	3000
2		**10**	**H**	**Bath**	W 9-0	Nicholas, P.Herbert	Nicholas d	2000
3		**17**	**H**	**Plymouth Albion**	L 3-5	-	Matts p	-
4		24	a	Waterloo	L 13-16	P.Herbert, Nicholas	Moore 2c, Matts p	1000
5		**26m**	**H**	**Cardiff**	L 6-11	Rees	Bennett d	7000
6	Oct	**1**	**H**	**Coventry**	L 3-6	-	Harvey p	2500
7		8	a	Richmond	W 12-8	Lacey, Lawrence, Nicholas, Rees	-	-
8		**15**	**H**	**Newport**	W 13-8	Barrow, Rees, Thomas	Harvey 2c	-
9		22	a	Northampton	L 3-14	-	Harvey p	-
10		**27th**	**H**	**Oxford University**	L 0-22	-	-	-
11		29	a	Swansea	L 6-14	Thorneloe	Nicholas d	10000
12	Nov	5	a	Gloucester	L 6-18	-	Harvey 2p	5000
13		**12**	**H**	**Cambridge University**	W 11-3	Lawrence, Rees, Sibson	Harvey c	-
14		**19**	**H**	**Neath**	L 3-8	-	Harvey p	-
15		**26**	**H**	**Middlesex Hospital**	W 6-3	-	Harvey p, Terrington d	-
16	Dec	3	a	Harlequins	L 3-14	Sibson	-	-
17		10	a	Blackheath	W 11-6	Nicholas, Terrington	Morris c/p	-
18		**17**	**H**	**Bristol**	W 5-3	Thomas	Morris c	-
19		24	a	Rugby	L 3-16	-	Morris p	-
20		**26m**	**H**	**Birkenhead Park**	L 0-5	-	-	-
21		**27tu**	**H**	**Barbarians**	L 0-29	-	-	15000
22		31	a	Bath	W 11-5	Cullen, Sibson	Quine c/p	-
23	Jan	**7**	**H**	**Cardiff**	D 3-3	-	Quine p	7000
24		**14**	**H**	**Gloucester**	W 6-3	Rees	Terrington d	-
25		21	a	Headingley	L 3-5	-	Terrington p	-
		26th	**H**	**Royal Air Force**	PP (frost)			
		28	a	Rosslyn Park	PP (frost)			
26	Feb	**4**	**H**	**London Scottish**	W 16-3	Morris, Lacey, Rees, Thorneloe	Morris 2c	-
27		11	a	Newport	L 3-13	-	Morris p	-
28		**18**	**H**	**Rugby**	W 9-6	Rees(2)	Morris p	-
29		**25**	**H**	**Northampton**	L 3-9	Bolesworth	-	-
30	Mar	**4**	**H**	**Harlequins**	L 9-11	Guffick	Matts 2p	-
31		11	a	Coventry	L 3-9	-	Matts p	-
32		18	a	Nuneaton	L 3-5	Rees	-	-
33		**25**	**H**	**Swansea**	L 8-25	Nicholas	Quine c/p	-
34	Apr	1	a	Birkenhead Park	L 6-13	Thomas	Quine p	-
35		8	a	Bristol	L 3-20	Thomas	-	-
36		10m	a	Plymouth Albion	W 24-3	Cullen(2), Thomas(2), Bleasdale	Cullen 2c/p, Terrington c	-
37		11tu	a	Exeter	W 8-6	Bleasdale, Thompson	Cullen c	-
38		**15**	**H**	**Nuneaton**	W 16-8	Cullen(2)	Cullen c/p/d, Terrington c	4000
39		**22**	**H**	**Blackheath**	W 14-3	Jerwood, Quine, Smith	Cullen c/p	-

INDIVIDUAL APPEARANCES 1949/50

Name / Game #	1	2	3	4	5	6	7	8	9	10	11	12	13	14	15	16	17	18	19	20	21	22	23	24	25	26	27	28	29	30	31	32	33	34	35	36	37	38	39	Apps	T	Pts
EA (Eric) Barrow	-	-	-	-	-	F	H	F	H	H	H	H	-	-	-	-	-	-	-	-	-	-	-	-	-	-	-	-	-	-	-	-	-	F	-	-	-	-	-	8	1	3
ER (Peter) Bennett	L	L	M	M	L	M	-	-	-	-	-	-	L	-	-	-	-	-	-	-	-	-	-	-	L	-	-	-	-	-	-	-	-	-	-	-	-	-	-	8	-	3
T (Tom) Bleasdale	-	-	-	-	-	-	-	-	-	-	-	>E	G	-	-	-	-	-	-	-	-	-	-	-	-	-	-	-	-	E	-	-	G	G	G	H	F	G	G	10	2	6
AD (Denis) Bolesworth	A	A	-	-	A	A	A	-	A	A	A	A	A	A	A	A	A	A	A	A	-	A	A	A	A	A	A	A	A	A	A	A	A	A	A	-	A	A	A	34	1	3
F (Frank) Chawner	E	E	E	-	-	-	-	-	-	-	-	-	-	-	D	D	E	-	E	H	-	-	-	-	-	-	-	-	-	-	-	-	-	-	-	-	-	-	-	8	-	-
L (Len) Chawner	-	-	-	-	-	-	-	-	-	-	-	-	-	-	-	-	-	-	-	-	-	-	-	-	-	>B	B	B	-	-	-	-	-	-	-	-	-	-	-	3	-	-
GH (George) Cullen	-	-	-	-	-	-	-	-	-	-	-	-	-	-	-	-	-	-	-	>M	M	L	L	L	-	-	L	-	-	-	M	-	-	M	-	M	L	L	L	12	5	37
JD (Jerry) Day	-	-	-	-	-	-	-	G	-	-	-	-	H	H	H	G	G	-	G	G	G	G	G	G	-	-	-	-	-	-	-	-	-	-	-	-	-	-	-	12	-	-
HB (Howard) Deacon	-	-	-	-	-	-	-	-	-	-	-	-	-	-	-	-	0	0	0	0	0	0	0	0	0	0	0	0	0	-	-	-	-	-	-	-	-	-	-	13	-	-
DR (Roger) Ellis	N	N	<N	-	-	-	-	-	-	-	-	-	-	-	-	-	-	-	-	-	-	-	-	-	-	-	-	-	-	-	-	-	-	-	-	-	-	-	-	3	-	-
JM (Dave) Guffick	-	-	-	-	-	-	-	-	-	-	-	-	-	-	-	-	-	-	-	-	-	-	-	-	-	-	-	-	-	>J	-	-	-	-	-	-	-	-	-	1	1	3
JH (John) Hacker	-	-	A	C	-	-	-	-	-	-	-	-	-	-	-	-	-	-	-	-	-	-	-	-	-	-	-	-	-	-	-	-	-	-	-	-	-	-	-	2	-	-
J (John) Harrison	-	-	-	-	-	-	-	-	-	-	-	-	-	-	-	-	-	-	-	-	-	-	-	-	I	-	<I	-	-	-	-	-	-	-	-	-	-	-	-	2	-	-
Dr. JJM (Paddy) Harvey	-	-	-	-	-	0	0	0	0	0	0	0	0	0	0	<0	-	-	-	-	-	-	-	-	-	-	-	-	-	-	-	-	-	-	-	-	-	-	-	11	-	24
WC (Bill) Herbert	-	-	-	-	-	-	-	I	I	-	-	-	-	I	-	I	-	I	I	-	-	-	<I	-	-	-	-	-	-	-	-	-	-	-	-	-	-	-	-	7	-	-
PAH (Peter) Herbert	H	H	H	F	F	-	-	-	-	-	-	-	-	-	-	-	-	-	-	-	-	-	-	-	-	-	-	-	-	-	-	-	-	-	-	-	-	-	-	5	2	6
NP (Noel) Huntley	>B	B	B	B	-	-	-	-	-	-	-	-	-	-	-	-	-	-	B	-	-	-	-	-	<B	-	-	-	-	-	-	-	-	-	-	-	-	-	-	6	-	-
HP (Peter) Jerwood	-	-	-	-	-	-	-	-	-	-	-	-	E	E	G	-	-	G	H	-	-	-	-	-	-	-	-	-	-	-	-	-	-	-	H	E	-	D	<E	9	1	3
EC (Eric) Lacey	D	D	D	D	D	D	D	D	-	D	D	D	D	D	-	-	-	-	-	-	-	-	E	D	D	D	D	D	D	D	D	D	D	D	D	C	-	-	-	27	2	6
DA (David) Lammiman	-	-	-	-	-	-	-	-	-	-	-	-	-	-	-	-	-	-	-	-	-	-	-	-	-	-	-	-	-	-	-	>K	K	-	-	-	-	-	-	2	-	-
CGS (Gwynne) Lawrence	-	-	-	-	K	-	M	M	M	M	M	M	M	M	M	-	-	-	K	K	-	-	-	-	-	-	-	K	-	-	-	-	-	-	-	-	-	-	-	13	2	6
R (Roy) McConnell	-	-	-	-	-	-	-	-	-	-	-	-	-	-	-	-	-	-	-	-	-	-	-	-	-	-	-	-	-	-	-	-	-	=N	-	-	-	-	-	1	-	-
R (Rae) Marshall	-	-	-	-	-	-	-	-	-	-	-	-	-	-	-	-	-	-	-	-	-	-	-	-	-	-	-	-	-	-	-	>0	0	0	0	0	0	0	0	8	-	-
RD (Bob) Matthews	-	-	-	-	-	-	-	-	-	-	-	N	-	-	-	-	-	-	-	-	-	-	-	-	-	-	-	-	-	-	-	-	-	-	-	-	-	-	-	1	-	-
GA (George) Matts	0	0	0	0	0	-	-	-	-	-	-	-	-	-	-	-	-	-	-	-	-	-	-	-	-	-	-	-	-	0	<0	-	-	-	-	-	-	-	-	7	-	21
WKT (Bill) Moore E7	I	I	I	I	I	I	I	-	-	I	I*	I*	I*	-	I	-	I	-	-	I*	I	I	-	I*	-	I	-	I	-	I	I	-	I	I	I	I	M	I	-	27	-	4
JP (Jim) Morris	-	-	-	-	-	-	-	-	-	-	-	-	-	-	-	J	J	M	M	-	J	-	-	-	-	L	M	M	M	M	L	M	-	-	L	-	-	-	-	13	1	23
RW (Roy) Murgatroyd	-	-	-	-	-	-	-	-	-	-	-	-	-	-	-	-	-	-	-	-	-	-	-	-	-	-	-	-	>I	-	-	I	-	-	-	-	-	-	-	2	-	-
WK (Ken) Nicholas	-	K	L	L	K	L	L	L	L	L	L	L	K	K	K	K	K	K	-	-	K	K	K	K	M	K	N	L	K	K	-	L	L	-	N	N	K	K	-	33	5	21
D (David) Norton	-	-	-	E	E	E	E	C	C	C	C	C	C	C	-	-	-	-	-	-	E	-	-	C	C	C	C	C	-	-	-	-	-	-	-	D	<E	-	-	19	-	-
J (John) Noton	-	-	-	-	-	-	-	-	-	-	-	-	-	-	-	-	-	-	-	-	-	-	-	-	-	-	-	-	-	-	-	-	-	-	-	-	>I	-	I	2	-	-
S (Stan) Pratt	-	-	-	-	-	-	-	-	-	-	-	-	-	B	-	-	-	-	-	-	-	-	-	-	-	-	-	-	B	B	-	-	B	B	B	-	B	B	B	9	-	-
DA (David) Quine	-	-	-	-	-	-	-	-	-	-	-	-	-	-	-	-	-	-	L	L	L	M	M	M	-	-	-	-	-	-	-	-	M	L	-	-	-	-	N	9	1	19
GDO (Geoffrey) Randle	-	-	-	-	-	-	-	-	-	-	-	-	-	-	-	-	-	-	J	J	-	-	-	-	-	-	-	-	-	-	-	-	-	-	-	-	-	-	-	2	-	-
DER (Danny) Rees	K	-	-	N	N	N	N	N	N	N	N	-	N	N	N	N	N	N	N	N	N	N	N	N	K	N	-	N	N	N	N	N	<N	-	-	-	-	-	-	29	9	27
CL (Calvin) Round	>J	J	J	<J	-	-	-	-	-	-	-	-	-	-	-	-	-	-	-	-	-	-	-	-	-	-	-	-	-	-	-	-	-	-	-	-	-	-	-	4	-	-
HW (Harry) Sibson	F	F	F	H	H	H	F	H	F	F	F	F	F	F	F	F	F	F	F	F	F	F	F	F	F	F	F	F	F	F	F	H	-	-	F	F	-	H	H	36	3	9
RH (Ron) Smith	-	-	-	-	-	-	-	-	-	-	-	-	-	-	>E	E	D	D	D	D	D	D	D	E	E	E	E	E	E	-	E	E	E	E	E	-	D	E	D	23	1	3
RV (Bob) Stirling E+	G	G	G	G	G	G	-	E	E	E	E	-	-	-	-	-	-	-	-	-	-	-	-	-	-	-	-	-	-	-	-	-	-	-	-	-	-	-	-	10	-	-
HL (Harry) Terrington	-	-	-	-	-	-	-	-	-	-	J	J	J	J	J	L	M	-	-	-	-	J	J	J	J	J	J	J	J	-	J	J	J	J	J	J	J	J	<J	24	1	16
HG (Haydn) Thomas	-	-	-	-	-	K	K	K	K	K	K	K	-	-	-	M	L	L	-	-	-	-	-	-	N	M	K	-	L	L	K	-	-	K	K	K	N	N	K	22	6	18
WE (Bill) Thompson	-	-	-	-	-	-	G	-	-	-	-	-	-	-	-	-	-	-	-	-	-	-	-	-	-	-	-	-	C	C	C	C	C	C	C	A	C	C	<C	12	1	3
PBL (Peter) Thorneloe	C	C	C	A	C	C	C	A	G	G	G	G	-	G	C	C	C	C	C	C	C	C	C	H	G	G	G	G	G	G	G	G	F	-	-	G	G	F	F	36	2	6
AC (Allan) Towell E1	M*	M*	K*	K*	J*	J*	J*	J*	J*	J*	-	-	-	L*	L*	H*	H*	H*	-	-	H*	H*	H*	-	H*	H*	H*	H*	H*	H*	H*	F*	H*	H*	M*	L*	H*	M*	<M*	33	-	-
GR (Geoff) Tucker	-	-	-	-	-	-	-	-	-	-	-	-	-	-	-	-	-	<J	-	-	-	-	-	-	-	-	-	-	-	-	-	-	-	-	-	-	-	-	-	1	-	-
RE (Ronnie) Tudor	-	-	-	-	B	B	B	B	B	B	B	B	B	-	B	B	B	B	-	B	B	B	B	B	-	-	-	-	-	-	B	B	-	-	-	<B	-	-	-	21	-	-
STH (Steven) Wright S1	-	-	-	-	-	-	-	-	>D	-	-	-	-	-	-	-	-	E	-	E	A	<E	-	-	-	-	-	-	-	-	-	-	-	-	-	-	-	-	-	5	-	-

The key for how to read the stats is on the last page

19 50/51	Home Ground: Welford Road	OVERALL RECORD:					T	C	PG	DG	PTS
	Captain: Bill Moore	PLD	W	D	L	Tigers scored:	85	41	22	13	442
		38	23	2	13	Opponents scored:	55	23	24	6	301

GM	DATE		VEN	OPPONENTS	RESULT	TRIES	KICKS	ATT
CLUB MATCHES								
1	Sep	**2**	**H**	**Bedford**	L 11-14	Cullen, Hacker	Brookman c/d	-
2		**9**	**H**	**Bath**	W 8-6	Cullen, Quine	Cullen c	-
3		**16**	**H**	**Plymouth Albion**	W 33-9	Cullen, Bolesworth, Lacey, Lawrence, Nicholas, Sibson	Cullen 2d, Brookman 3c/d	-
4		**23**	**H**	**Waterloo**	W 14-0	Cullen, Lawrence	Brookman c/2d	-
5		**30**	**H**	**Cardiff**	L 0-3	-	-	-
6	Oct	7	a	Coventry	L 0-9	-	-	-
7		**14**	**H**	**Richmond**	W 34-11	Lacey(2), Cullen, Hacker, Sibson	Cullen 2c/4p, Nicholas d	-
8		21	a	Newport	L 6-19	-	Cullen p/d	15000
9		25w	a	Oxford University	D 6-6	-	Brookman 2p	-
10		**28**	**H**	**Northampton**	W 26-8	Lawrence(2), Bolesworth, Nicholas, Sibson, Thomas	Cullen 2c, Morris 2c	-
11	Nov	**4**	**H**	**Gloucester**	W 19-14	Cullen(2), Lacey, Sibson	Cullen p, Morris 2c	-
12		11	a	Cambridge University	W 8-6	Thomas	Cullen d, Morris c	-
13		18	a	Cardiff	L 6-17	-	Morris 2p	-
14		**25**	**H**	**Middlesex Hospital**	W 22-5	Lawrence(3), Thomas(2), Nicholas	Morris 2c	-
15	Dec	2	a	Harlequins	L 10-16	Matthews, Thomas	Morris 2c	-
16		9	a	Blackheath	W 20-9	Lawrence, Moore, Pratt, Sibson, Thomas	Morris c/p	-
		16	**H**	**Bristol**	PP (frost)			
		23	**H**	**Rugby**	PP (frost)			
17		**26tu**	**H**	**Birkenhead Park**	W 14-11	Cullen(2), Lacey, Sibson	Morris c	5000
18		**27w**	**H**	**Barbarians**	D 13-13	Lawrence, Sibson, Thomas	Morris 2c	15000
19		**30**	**H**	**Headingley**	W 26-11	Cullen, Bolesworth, Nicholas, Thomas	Cullen 2p, Morris 4c	-
20	Jan	6	a	Nuneaton	W 3-0	Kail	-	-
21		13	a	Gloucester	W 8-3	Thomas	Morris c/p	-
22		20	a	Bedford	W 15-11	Lawrence, Thomas	Morris 2p/d	-
23		**25th**	**H**	**Royal Air Force**	W 21-3	Cullen, Lawrence, Sibson	Cullen d, Morris 3c/d	-
24		**27**	**H**	**Rosslyn Park**	L 8-12	Thomas	Morris c/p	-
25	Feb	3	a	London Scottish	W 14-0	Lawrence(2), Thomas	Morris c/p	-
26		**10**	**H**	**Newport**	L 0-16	-	-	20000
27		17	a	Bath	W 15-3	Thomas(2), Cullen, Nicholas, Sibson	-	-
28		24	a	Northampton	W 14-5	Cullen(2), Thomas(2)	Cullen c	-
29	Mar	**3**	**H**	**Harlequins**	W 8-3	Kail	Cullen c/p	-
30		**10**	**H**	**Coventry**	L 5-13	Kail	Cullen c	-
31		**17**	**H**	**Swansea**	L 3-8	Sibson	-	-
32		24	a	Bristol	W 11-3	Kail, Morris	Cullen c/p	-
33		26m	a	Plymouth Albion	L 3-6	Barrow	-	-
34		27tu	a	Exeter	W 5-0	Cullen	Cullen c	-
35		31	a	Bedford	L 0-3	-	-	-
36	Apr	7	a	Birkenhead Park	W 13-3	Cullen, Matthews, Sibson	Cullen 2c	-
37		14	a	Swansea	L 6-19	-	Cullen 2p	-
38		**21**	**H**	**Blackheath**	W 14-3	Bleasdale, Nicholas, Pratt	Cullen c/d	-

INDIVIDUAL APPEARANCES 1950/51

Name / Game #	1	2	3	4	5	6	7	8	9	10	11	12	13	14	15	16	17	18	19	20	21	22	23	24	25	26	27	28	29	30	31	32	33	34	35	36	37	38	Apps	T	Pts
EA (Eric) Barrow	-	-	-	-	-	-	-	-	G	-	G	G	F	-	-	-	-	-	-	G	-	E	E	E	-	-	-	-	-	-	-	-	G	G	G	-	-	-	11	1	3
T (Tom) Bleasdale	-	-	-	-	-	F	F	H	H	F	F	F	H	G	G	G	G	G	G	D	G	G	G	G	G	G	G	G	G	G	G	G	-	-	-	G	G	G	30	1	3
AD (Denis) Bolesworth	A	A	A	A	A	A	A	A	A	A	A	A	A	A	A*	A	A	A	A	A	A*	A*	A*	A*	A	A	A	A	A	A	A	A	A	A*	A*	A*	A	A	38	3	9
F (Franklyn) Brookman	>J	J	J	J	J	J	J	J	<N	-	-	-	-	-	-	-	-	-	-	-	-	-	-	-	-	-	-	-	-	-	-	-	-	-	-	-	-	-	9	-	28
F (Frank) Chawner	-	-	-	-	-	-	-	-	D	-	E	E	-	-	E	-	-	-	-	E	E	-	-	-	-	E	E	E	E	E	E	E	E	E	E	E	E	E	19	-	-
L (Len) Chawner	-	-	-	-	-	-	-	-	-	B	-	-	-	B	-	-	-	-	-	-	-	-	-	-	-	-	-	-	B	B	B	-	-	B	-	-	-	-	6	-	-
GH (George) Cullen	L	L	L	L	L	L	L	M	L	L	L	L	-	L	-	M	L	L	L	M	M	L	L	L	L	L	K	N	M	L	M	L	L	L	M	J	J	J	36	16	128
JD (Jerry) Day	G	F	F	F	F	-	-	-	-	-	-	-	-	-	-	-	-	-	-	-	-	-	-	-	-	-	-	-	-	-	-	-	-	-	-	-	-	-	5	-	-
HB (Howard) Deacon	-	-	-	-	-	-	-	-	-	-	-	-	-	-	-	-	-	-	-	-	-	-	-	-	-	-	0	0	0	0	0	0	0	0	<0	-	-	-	9	-	-
JM (Dave) Guffick	-	-	-	-	-	-	-	-	J	-	-	-	-	-	-	-	-	-	-	-	-	-	-	-	-	-	-	-	-	-	-	-	-	-	-	-	-	-	1	-	-
JH (John) Hacker	C	C	C	C	C	C	C	C	C	C	C	C	C	C	C	C	C	C	C	C	C	C	C	C	C	C	C	C	C	C	C	-	C	C	C	-	C	-	35	2	6
JC (Colin) Kail	>F	-	-	-	-	-	-	-	-	-	-	-	-	H	H	H	H	H	H	H	H	H	H	H	H	H	H	H	H	H	H	H	H	H	H	H	H	<H	26	4	12
EC (Eric) Lacey	D	D	D	D	D	D	D	D	-	D	D	D	D	D	D	D	D	D	D	-	D	D	D	D	D	D	D	D	D	D	D	D	-	D	-	D	D	D	34	5	15
DA (David) Lammiman	<N	-	-	-	-	-	-	-	-	-	-	-	-	-	-	-	-	-	-	-	-	-	-	-	-	-	-	-	-	-	-	-	-	-	-	-	-	-	1	-	-
CGS (Gwynne) Lawrence	-	N	N	N	N	N	N	K	-	N	N	N	K	N	L	K	N	N	N	K	K	N	N	N	N	N	L	M	L	N	-	-	-	-	N	M	M	M	32	13	39
RA Lewis	-	-	-	>0	0	0	0	0	0	0	0	0	0	-	-	-	-	-	-	0	0	0	0	0	0	<0	-	-	-	-	-	-	-	-	-	-	-	-	17	-	-
BJ (John) McTigue	-	-	-	-	-	-	-	-	-	-	-	-	-	-	>I	-	-	-	-	-	<I	-	-	-	-	-	-	-	-	-	-	-	-	-	-	-	-	-	2	-	-
R (Rae) Marshall	0	0	0	-	-	-	-	-	-	-	-	-	-	0	0	0	0	0	0	-	-	-	-	-	-	-	-	-	-	-	-	-	-	-	-	0	0	0	12	-	-
RD (Bob) Matthews	-	-	-	-	-	-	-	-	-	-	-	-	-	-	K	-	-	-	-	-	-	-	-	-	-	-	-	-	N	-	N	-	K	K	-	N	N	N	8	2	6
WKT (Bill) Moore E7	-	-	-	I*	I*	I*	I*	I*	I*	I*	I*	I*	I*	I*	-	I*	I*	I*	I*	I*	-	-	-	-	I*	I*	I*	I*	I*	I*	I*	I*	I*	-	-	-	I*	I*	27	1	3
JP (Jim) Morris	-	-	-	-	-	-	-	-	-	J	J	J	L	J	J	J	J	J	J	J	J	J	J	J	J	J	J	J	J	J	J	J	J	J	J	-	-	-	26	1	79
RW (Roy) Murgatroyd	I	-	-	-	-	-	-	-	-	-	-	-	-	-	-	-	-	-	-	-	-	I	<I	-	-	-	-	-	-	-	-	-	-	-	-	-	-	-	3	-	-
WK (Ken) Nicholas	K	K	K	K	K	K	K	N	K	K	K	K	N	K	-	N	K	K	K	N	N	K	K	K	K	K	N	K	K	K	K	N	N	N	K	K	K	K	37	6	21
J (John) Noton	-	I	I	-	-	-	-	-	-	-	-	-	-	-	-	-	-	-	-	-	-	-	-	-	-	-	-	-	-	-	-	-	-	I	I	I	-	-	5	-	-
S (Stan) Pratt	B	B	B	B	B	B	B	B	B	-	B	B	B	-	B	B	B	B	B	B	B	B	B	B	B	B	B	B	-	-	-	B	B	-	B	B	B	B	32	2	6
DA (David) Quine	M	M	M	M	-	-	-	-	-	-	-	-	-	-	-	-	-	-	-	-	-	-	-	-	-	-	-	-	-	-	-	<K	-	-	-	-	-	-	5	1	3
WH Redfern	-	-	-	-	-	-	-	-	-	-	-	-	-	-	>N	-	-	-	-	-	-	-	-	-	-	-	-	-	-	-	-	-	-	-	-	-	-	-	1	-	-
JK (John) Shepherd	-	-	-	-	-	-	-	-	-	-	-	-	-	-	-	-	-	-	-	-	-	-	-	=I	-	-	-	-	-	-	-	-	-	-	-	-	-	-	1	-	-
HW (Harry) Sibson	H	H	H	H	H	H	H	F	F	H	H	H	G	F	F	F	F	F	F	F	F	F	F	F	F	F	F	F	F	F	F	F	F	F	F	F	F	F	38	11	33
RH (Ron) Smith	-	-	-	-	-	-	-	-	E	-	-	-	-	-	-	-	-	-	-	-	-	-	-	-	-	-	-	-	-	-	-	-	-	-	D	-	-	-	2	-	-
RV (Bob) Stirling E4	E*	E	E	E	E	E	E	E	-	E	-	-	E	E	-	E	E	E	E	-	-	-	-	-	E	-	-	-	-	-	-	C	D	-	-	C	-	C	20	-	-
HG (Haydn) Thomas	-	-	-	-	M	M	M	L	M	M	M	M	M	M	M	L	M	M	M	L	L	M	M	M	M	M	M	L	-	M	L	M	M	M	L	L	L	L	33	16	48
RHG (Bob) Weighill E4	-	>G*	G*	G	G	G	G	G	-	<G	-	-	-	-	-	-	-	-	-	-	-	-	-	-	-	-	-	-	-	-	-	-	-	-	-	-	-	-	8	-	-
JR Williams	-	-	-	-	-	-	-	-	-	-	-	-	=J	-	-	-	-	-	-	-	-	-	-	-	-	-	-	-	-	-	-	-	-	-	-	-	-	-	1	-	-

The key for how to read the stats is on the last page

19 51/52

Home Ground: Welford Road				OVERALL RECORD:		T	C	PG	DG	PTS
Captain: Bill Moore										
PLD	W	D	L		Tigers scored:	66	29	21	9	346
35	16	2	17		Opponents scored:	53	30	20	4	291

GM	DATE		VEN	OPPONENTS	RESULT	TRIES	KICKS	ATT
CLUB MATCHES								
1	Sep	**1**	**H**	**Bedford**	L 3-6	-	Morris p	-
2		**8**	**H**	**Bath**	W 6-3	-	Morris 2p	-
3		**15**	**H**	**Plymouth Albion**	W 14-9	Bleasdale, Bolesworth, Lacey, Nicholas	Morris c	-
4		22	a	Waterloo	W 6-5	Bleasdale, F.Chawner	-	-
5		**29**	**H**	**Moseley**	W 17-3	Bolesworth, Cullen, Lawrence	Morris c/p/d	1508
6	Oct	**6**	**H**	**Coventry**	L 13-20	Bleasdale, Sibson	Morris 2c/d	2758
7		13	a	Richmond	W 23-5	Bleasdale(3), Thomas	Cullen 4c/p	-
8		**20**	**H**	**Newport**	L 3-16	Doyle	-	3053
9		**25th**	**H**	**Oxford University**	L 16-20	Bleasdale(2), Lawrence	Cullen 2c/p	960
10		27	a	Northampton	L 11-13	Cullen, Nicholas	Cullen c/p	-
11	Nov	3	a	Gloucester	L 8-16	Cullen	Cullen c/p	-
12		**10**	**H**	**Cambridge University**	L 6-8	Lawrence	Cullen p	2504
13		**17**	**H**	**Middlesex Hospital**	W 28-8	Ashurst(2), Cullen, Bleasdale, Channer, Pratt	Cullen 2c/2p	1134
		24	a	Neath	PP (rain)			
14	Dec	1	a	Harlequins	L 3-9	-	Fisk p	-
15		**8**	**H**	**Blackheath**	L 3-6	Bleasdale	-	957
16		**15**	**H**	**Bristol**	W 8-5	Ashurst	Channer d, Fisk c	947
17		22	a	Rugby	D 6-6	Bleasdale	Channer d	-
18		**26w**	**H**	**Birkenhead Park**	L 3-6	-	Cullen p	3003
19		**27th**	**H**	**Barbarians**	W 13-8	Sibson, Smith, Thomas	Cullen 2c	12000
20	Jan	5	a	Bath	W 6-0	Cullen, Lawrence	-	-
21		**12**	**H**	**Gloucester**	W 9-5	Lawrence	Cullen p, Fisk d	1331
22		19	a	Bedford	L 3-5	Bolesworth	-	-
23		**24th**	**H**	**Royal Air Force**	D 8-8	Bleasdale	Thomas d, Barrow c	439
		26	a	Headingley	PP (snow)			
	Feb	**2**	**H**	**London Scottish**	PP (frost)			
		9	a	Newport	PP (King died)			
24		16	a	Moseley	W 8-0	Bolesworth, Moore	Cullen c	-
25		**23**	**H**	**Northampton**	L 3-5	Cullen	-	2936
26	Mar	**1**	**H**	**Harlequins**	L 12-22	Beaver	Cullen 2p, Barrow p	1323
27		8	a	Coventry	L 6-13	-	Cullen p/d	-
28		**15**	**H**	**Swansea**	W 8-0	Botting	Barrow p, Cullen c	1372
29		**22**	**H**	**Nuneaton**	W 22-11	Cullen, Botting, Doyle, Lawrence	Cullen 2c/2p	1068
30		29	a	Cardiff	L 8-14	Cullen	Cullen c, Channer d	500
31	Apr	5	a	Birkenhead Park	L 0-10	-	-	-
32		12	a	Bristol	W 19-12	Channer, Bleasdale, Matthews, Thomas	Channer d, Cullen 2c	-
33		14m	a	Plymouth Albion	W 19-0	Botting(2), Lawrence(2), Gee	Cullen 2c	-
34		15tu	a	Exeter	L 0-11	-	-	-
35		**19**	**H**	**Sale**	W 25-3	Botting(2), Lawrence(2), Cullen, Gee, Sibson	Cullen 2c	916

INDIVIDUAL APPEARANCES 1951/52

Name / Game #	1	2	3	4	5	6	7	8	9	10	11	12	13	14	15	16	17	18	19	20	21	22	23	24	25	26	27	28	29	30	31	32	33	34	35	Apps	T	Pts
ADB (Derek) Ashurst	-	-	-	-	-	-	-	-	-	>H	H	H	H	H	H	H	H	H	-	F	-	-	-	-	-	-	-	-	-	-	-	-	-	-	-	10	3	9
EA (Eric) Barrow	-	-	-	-	-	-	-	-	-	-	-	-	-	G	-	F	F	G	F	G	F	F	F	F	F	F	H	H	F	F	F	H	H	H	H	21	-	8
K Beaver	-	-	-	-	-	-	-	-	-	-	-	-	-	-	-	-	-	-	-	-	-	-	-	-	-	>A	C	<C	-	-	-	-	-	-	-	3	1	3
T (Tom) Bleasdale	G	G	G	G	G	G	G	G	G	G	G	G	G	-	G	G	G	-	G	-	G	-	G	G	G	G	G	G	G	G	G	G	G	G	G	31	13	39
AD (Denis) Bolesworth	C	C	C	A	C	C	A	C	A	A	A	A	A	A	-	A	A	A	A	A	A	A	A	A	A	-	-	-	A	A	A	A	A	C	A	31	4	12
IJ (Ian) Botting E2	-	-	-	-	-	-	-	-	-	-	-	-	-	>K	K	-	-	-	-	-	-	N	K	-	K	K	N	N	N	-	-	-	K	K	K	12	6	18
MR (Mel) Channer	-	-	-	-	-	-	-	-	-	-	-	J	J	J	J	J	J	J	J	-	-	-	-	-	-	-	-	J	-	J	J	J	J	-	J	14	2	18
F (Frank) Chawner	E	E	E	D	E	E	C	A	C	C	C	C	C	C	-	-	-	-	-	-	-	-	-	-	-	-	-	-	-	-	-	-	D	A	-	16	1	3
L (Len) Chawner	-	-	-	-	-	-	-	B	B	B	-	-	-	-	-	-	-	-	-	-	-	-	-	-	-	-	-	-	-	-	-	-	B	B	-	5	-	-
RF Church	>H	H	H	H	H	H	H	H	<H	-	-	-	-	-	-	-	-	-	-	-	-	-	-	-	-	-	-	-	-	-	-	-	-	-	-	9	-	-
GH (George) Cullen	M	M	M	M	L	L	L	M	M	M	M	M	M	L	M	-	-	M	M	L	L	L	-	M	M	M	K	L	L	M	M	L	M	M	M	32	9	118
JD (Jerry) Day	-	-	F	-	-	-	-	F	F	F	F	F	F	F	F	-	-	-	-	-	-	G	-	-	-	-	-	-	-	-	-	-	-	-	-	10	-	-
LT (Laurie) Doyle	-	-	-	-	-	-	J	J	J	J	J	-	-	-	-	-	-	-	-	-	-	-	-	-	-	-	-	-	<J	-	-	-	-	-	-	6	2	6
JW (Jim) Fisk	-	-	-	-	-	-	-	-	-	-	-	-	-	>O	O	O	O	O	O	O	O	O	O	O	O	O	O	O	O	O	O	O	O	-	O	21	-	8
GE (Gordon) Gee	-	-	-	-	-	-	-	-	-	-	-	-	-	-	-	-	-	-	-	-	-	-	-	-	-	-	-	-	>M	L	L	-	L	L	L	6	2	6
JH (John) Hacker	-	-	<A	-	-	-	-	-	-	-	-	-	-	-	-	-	-	-	-	-	-	-	-	-	-	-	-	-	-	-	-	-	-	-	-	1	-	-
JKL (Joe) Hughes	-	-	-	-	-	-	-	-	-	-	-	-	-	-	-	>M	L	N	-	-	-	-	-	-	-	-	-	-	-	K	<K	-	-	-	-	5	-	-
JG (John) Kennewell	-	-	-	-	-	-	-	-	-	-	-	-	-	-	-	-	-	>E	-	-	-	-	-	-	-	-	-	-	-	-	-	-	-	-	-	1	-	-
PH (Peter) Konig	-	-	-	-	-	-	-	-	-	-	-	-	-	-	-	-	-	-	-	-	-	-	-	-	-	-	-	-	-	-	-	-	>F	-	-	1	-	-
EC (Eric) Lacey	D	D	D	E	D	D	D	D	D	D	D	D	D	D	D	D	-	-	D	D	D	D	D	D	D	D	D	D	D	D	D	D	-	D	D	32	1	3
CGS (Gwynne) Lawrence	N	N	N	L	M	M	K	N	N	N	K	K	K	N	L	L	M	L	N	K	K	K	N	N	N	L	M	M	K	N	N	K	N	N	N	35	10	30
R (Rae) Marshall	O	O	O	O	O	O	O	O	O	O	O	O	O	-	-	-	-	-	-	-	-	-	-	-	-	-	-	-	-	-	-	-	-	O	-	14	-	-
RD (Bob) Matthews	-	-	-	-	N	-	-	-	-	-	-	-	-	-	-	K	N	K	-	-	N	-	-	-	-	-	-	K	-	-	-	N	-	-	-	7	1	3
WKT (Bill) Moore E7	I*	I*	I*	I*	I*	I*	I*	I*	I*	I*	I*	I*	I*	I*	I*	I*	I*	I*	I*	I*	I*	I*	I*	I*	I*	I*	I*	I*	I*	I*	I*	I*	I*	I*	I*	35	1	3
JP (Jim) Morris	J	J	J	J	J	J	-	-	-	-	-	-	-	-	-	-	-	-	-	-	-	-	-	-	-	-	-	-	-	-	-	-	-	<J	-	7	-	26
WK (Ken) Nicholas	K	K	K	N	K	K	N	K	K	K	-	-	-	-	-	-	-	-	K	J	J	J	J	J	J	J	J	-	-	-	-	-	-	-	-	19	2	6
S (Stan) Pratt	B	B	B	B	B	B	B	-	-	-	B	B	B	B	B	B	B	B	B	B	B	B	B	B	B	B	B	B	B	B	B	B	-	-	B	30	1	3
WH Redfern	-	-	-	-	-	N	-	-	-	L	N	N	N	-	N	N	K	-	-	N	-	-	-	K	-	<N	-	-	-	-	-	-	-	-	-	11	-	-
HW (Harry) Sibson	F	F	-	F	F	F	F	-	-	-	-	-	-	-	-	-	-	F	H	H	H	H	H	H	H	H	F	F	H	H	H	F	-	F	F	23	3	9
RH (Ron) Smith	-	-	-	-	-	-	-	-	E	-	E	-	-	E	E	E	E	D	E	E	E	E	E	E	E	E	E	E	E	E	E	E	E	E	E	24	1	3
RV (Bob) Stirling E9	A	A	-	C	A	A	E	E	-	E	-	E	E	-	A	-	D	-	C	-	-	-	-	-	-	-	-	-	-	-	-	-	-	-	-	13	-	-
JR (Ray) Tate	-	-	-	-	-	-	-	-	-	-	-	-	-	-	-	-	-	-	-	-	>M	-	M	-	-	-	L	-	-	-	-	-	-	-	-	3	-	-
HG (Haydn) Thomas	L	L	L	K	-	-	M	L	L	-	L	L	L	M	-	-	-	-	L	M	-	M	L	L	L	-	-	-	-	-	-	M	-	-	-	18	3	12
PBL (Peter) Thorneloe	-	-	-	-	-	-	-	-	-	-	-	-	-	-	C	C	C	C	-	C	C	C	C	C	C	C	A	A	C	C	C	C	C	-	C	19	-	-

The key for how to read the stats is on the last page

CHAPTER 13

At a Stand Still

1952/1953

Perhaps it was not surprising that the next season should have proved mediocre, though it was a pity for the veteran prop Denis Bolesworth, who had been elected captain. Anyone looking for signs of optimism might have noticed the emergence of two very promising back row forwards, the Cambridge Blue John Jenkins and Peter Konig from Moat Old Boys. The season started well enough and included the first win at Coventry for four years following five successive home games: "A good indication of the ferocity of the game was the number of times play was stopped to replace players' shorts," commented the local scribe - a case of post-war shortages?

But then the rot set in and even the recall of the officially retired Moore could not stop it. Leicester lost at Blackheath for the first time since the war and Stirling's commitments allowed him to play only infrequently though England still benefited from his remarkable consistency - he was to captain the national side in 1954, after he had left Leicester for Wasps. The consequences of having too many services players were heavily rubbed in when the RAF beat Tigers for the first time since the war, Channer collecting eight points for the airmen who won 12-11. This was one of the major reasons for the poor showing during the season though the club were very unlucky with injuries: Lacey broke an ankle in pre-season training and was not able to play once, Sibson and Bleasdale both sustained nagging injuries which kept them out. Compared with the previous season's total of 34, the club used 45 players in the senior side and it was obvious that a new-look Leicester was in the making.

It was with considerable reluctance that Stirling left the Tigers, a direct consequence of his posting to the Air Ministry in London where he was involved in Saturday morning work. "There was an excellent spirit at the club," he said of his days at Welford Road, "and to get into the Tigers first XV was a great thing. We always tried to play open, aggressive rugby."

Not so aggressive though as the story Stirling told against himself of an Easter tour game at Bristol might indicate. He had been on an RAF ground defence course before joining the tour party and, up to the eyebrows in supposed corpses, could not prevent himself from attracting the referee's attention during the game to an injured player by calling out: "Referee, man wounded." There was also the problem of representing two sides, the club and the force, so that when he found himself playing for the RAF against Leicester, it may not have been entirely inexcusable that, at the first scrum, Stirling was seen to pack down in the Leicester second row.

↑ A new club crest was introduced and worn on the blazers of the players who had played in 20 matches.

↓ Doug Norman's old players' season ticket for 1953/54.

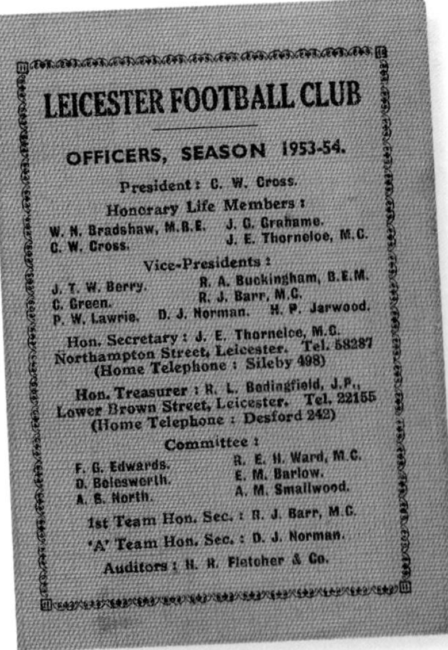

LEICESTER FOOTBALL CLUB

OFFICERS, SEASON 1953-54.

President: C. W. Cross.

Honorary Life Members:
W. N. Bradshaw, M.B.E. J. G. Grahame.
C. W. Cross. J. E. Thorneloe, M.C.

Vice-Presidents:
J. T. W. Berry. R. A. Buckingham, B.E.M.
C. Green. R. J. Barr, M.C.
P. W. Lawrie. D. J. Norman. H. P. Jarwood.

Hon. Secretary: J. E. Thorneloe, M.C.
Northampton Street, Leicester. Tel. 58287
(Home Telephone: Sileby 498)

Hon. Treasurer: R. L. Bedingfield, J.P.,
Lower Brown Street, Leicester. Tel. 22155
(Home Telephone: Desford 242)

Committee:
F. G. Edwards. R. E. H. Ward, M.C.
D. Bolesworth. E. M. Barlow.
A. S. North. A. M. Smallwood.

1st Team Hon. Sec.: R. J. Barr, M.C.
'A' Team Hon. Sec.: D. J. Norman.
Auditors: H. R. Fletcher & Co.

1953/1954

The improvement during the 1953/54 season was radical, 22 wins against 13 defeats, and speaks much for the qualities of John Jenkins who was the new captain. There was evidence of the new broom at work in the first game, when the former Moseley centre SM Duff, the Loughborough Colleges centre John Elders and the West Countryman David Hazell, all made their debuts against Bedford at full-back, centre and prop respectively.

Lacey was back in action and Channer had a new partner at scrum-half in AW Black. 'Gus' Black, capped six times between 1947-50 for Scotland and a Lion in New Zealand in 1950, was on the same RAF station as Channer and had played a couple of games the previous season but now he was to prove a tower of strength before being posted during the 1954/55 season to the West Country, when he joined Bristol.

Elders had played for Leicestershire in 1952 before going to teach in South Wigston and he gave Tigers magnificent service, joining that band of players who, in other circumstances, might well have been capped for their country but who in the end missed out. He was unlucky to coincide with the likes of Lew Cannell, Jeff Butterfield and Phil Davies, but on his day he was as good a centre as most in the country. Hazell, another Loughborough Colleges product, was more lucky for he was capped four times in 1955. He had broken a Colleges points-scoring record in 1951/52 by registering 162 points - including 54 conversions as against 12 penalties which must be considered typical of Colleges rugby.

The team began well, early victories including the first win over Coventry at Welford Road since the war, by 14-3. The escutcheon was promptly blotted when Moseley were allowed their first win in Leicester since 1895/96 (fixtures, it should be remembered, had not been continuous) but honour was partially restored by handing Northampton their first defeat of the season, again at Welford Road.

As the year neared its end, two displays at Welford Road, completely contrasting in nature, stood out. The first was the performance of the Midland Counties against Bob Stuart's All Blacks, when the combined side held the tourists to a 3-0 margin, a penalty kicked by Ron Jarden being sufficient to win the game. Five Leicester players were in the side, Cullen (playing on the wing), Elders, Hazell, Bleasdale and Jenkins who was also captain.

Shortly before the game three of Northampton's internationals, Don White, Lew Cannell and John Hyde were forced to drop out and the side which represented the Midlands was: John Hodgkins; Don MacNally (both Northampton), Roger Hosen (Loughborough Colleges), John Elders, George Cullen (both Leicester); Allan Towell (Bedford), JW Hobbs (Gloucester); Ron Jacobs, Trevor Smith (both Northampton), David Hazell (Leicester), Dick Hawkes (Northampton),

John Jenkins, Tom Bleasdale (both Leicester), Vic Leadbetter (Northampton), Peter Collingridge (Bedford).

There were 20,000 in the ground to watch Jarden put his side in front after only six minutes but, with the Midlands pack working hard, the All Blacks found themselves pressurised and owed much to the steadiness of that outstanding full-back, Bob Scott. Allan Towell had a splendid game, in defence and attack, and only an outburst of spleen by the crowd when Scott was aiming for goal after a controversial penalty marred the occasion.

A letter from the tour manager, JN Millard, to Eric Thorneloe, illustrated what the tourists thought of Leicester: "I am very glad indeed that we altered our programme to allow us to have a longer stay in your city. I wish to congratulate all those who had any part in staging the match on Saturday. The crowd was handled very efficiently and I realise the demonstration made when Scott was kicking a goal was no fault of yours. Your team played a very fine game and they made a magnificent attempt during the last few minutes to pull the match out of the fire."

Three weeks later anyone in that crowd who regretted the lack of scoring received compensation as the Barbarians hammered Leicester 39-11, the chief architects of what was then the Baa-baas' highest points tally against the club (it was passed in 1974) being Ken Jones with three tries, Butterfield and Davies with two each. Black and Hazell worked hard for Leicester with the prop scoring a try, penalty and a conversion.

January and February of 1954 were bleak months, however. For the first time in seven seasons Leicester failed to achieve the double over Bath and the first win since Boxing Day came on 20 February as service calls took their toll. But spring brought doubles over Coventry and Harlequins, a 6-6 draw with Swansea whose try was scored, ironically, by ex-Tigers star Gwynne Lawrence, and the retirement after the final game, with Sale, of that consistent prop Bolesworth, after 18 years in the game. Hazell scored 102 points, easily leading the scoring charts, and Leicester looked ahead to the season when they would celebrate their 75th birthday.

1954/1955

Leicester were no nearer to a solution regarding the A team and the leading local junior clubs but, on the administrative side, there was a major change with the appointment of a paid official in the shape of Major Albert Chilton, to work as general secretary at £250 a year. It had long been obvious that the burden of detail in running the club put such a strain on the honorary secretary and his business affairs that a full-time official was required and Major Chilton fitted the bill. A regular officer who had been serving at South Wigston, his appointment signified an end to the near monopoly of power which had been invested in the secretary ever since Tom Crumbie occupied that post.

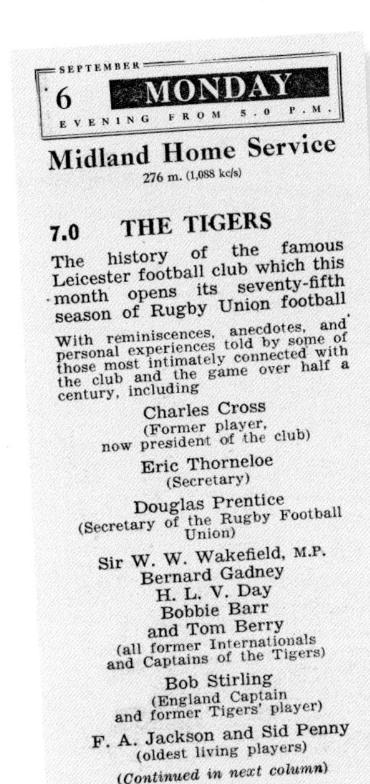

SEPTEMBER
6 MONDAY
EVENING FROM 5.0 P.M.

Midland Home Service
276 m. (1,088 kc/s)

7.0 THE TIGERS

The history of the famous Leicester football club which this month opens its seventy-fifth season of Rugby Union football

With reminiscences, anecdotes, and personal experiences told by some of those most intimately connected with the club and the game over half a century, including

Charles Cross
(Former player, now president of the club)

Eric Thorneloe
(Secretary)

Douglas Prentice
(Secretary of the Rugby Football Union)

Sir W. W. Wakefield, M.P.
Bernard Gadney
H. L. V. Day
Bobbie Barr
and Tom Berry
(all former Internationals and Captains of the Tigers)

Bob Stirling
(England Captain and former Tigers' player)

F. A. Jackson and Sid Penny
(oldest living players)

(Continued in next column)

Peter Cranmer
(former International)

John Jenkins
(present captain)

Story written by Roland Orton
Narrator, Ronald Baddiley
Production by H. Saunders-Jacobs

Denis Morris writes on page 8

↑ Radio Times listing of the broadcast celebrating the 75th anniversary of the club.

↓ Souvenir brochure from the 75th Anniversary Dinner at the Bell Hotel.

LEICESTER FOOTBALL CLUB
1880
1955
CELEBRATION DINNER
FOR 75th ANNIVERSARY
APRIL 29th, 1955
BELL HOTEL, LEICESTER

Among his first duties would have been to assist in organising the club's 75th anniversary dinner, fixed for the Bell Hotel the following April, and check the last details of the programme that went out on BBC Radio on 6 September, commemorating Leicester's distinguished past. A host of famous names took part in the programme, among them Wavell Wakefield, Bernard Gadney, Tom Berry and Bob Stirling, and it probably pained them slightly to see how the current pack was struggling.

There were frequent changes among the forwards, including the introduction of the 1950 British Lions and Ireland captain, Karl Mullen, who hooked against Moseley. Mullen was a doctor at Derby Hospital and it was hoped that he would become regularly available, but it was not to be. At the same time, ironically, as the Tigers were in the toils, Leicestershire had found a winning combination. An 8-0 win over Notts, Lincs and Derby made them Midlands champions for the first time since 1927 and later in the year a single penalty prevented them from progressing to the county championship final, Lancashire - with Tom Bleasdale in their ranks - winning 3-0 at Blundellsands.

Elders captained the county XV and gradually several of the successful Leicestershire players found their way into the Leicester ranks, though not the young MJK Smith - to become better known as the Warwickshire and England cricket captain - who helped Oxford University to an 18-0 win over the club. It was one of those "chicken and egg" situations: was the club making hay out of the county's victorious run or were the individual players imbued with the desire to play a higher standard of rugby week after week, which meant leaving their junior clubs and joining Tigers? In any event, Stoneygate lock John Ford, who had been asked as a reserve for an England trial after his county displays, made his debut against Blackheath. Two more December debutants, against Birkenhead Park, were the Westleigh full-back Brian Small (then studying at Cambridge University) and the Hinckley hooker John Stevens.

Stevens, in particular, showed immense promise, as did another newcomer, John Thompson, who made his debut at lock against London Scottish after service with Aylestone Athletic and Leicester A. Confirmation of the promise shown by this new material came when Tigers beat Swansea at St Helen's for the first time in 31 years, Elders and Peter Thorneloe scoring the tries which helped the club to an 8-5 win. At the end of the 1954/55 season, Hazell, Channer and Irish scrum-half Tom O'Connor were invited to play for the Midland Counties against a Dublin combination at Lansdowne Road, which was doubtless a pleasant way for Hazell to end the season.

The Nottingham schoolmaster had played in all England's games, kicking two penalties against France and one against Scotland. He had been the club's only cap, although back row man Ron Smith had won a trial place. The points total for the season of 454 was a post-war record, very satisfying for the skipper, John Jenkins, who had played in every game.

1955/1956

Three months later the club had cause to wonder just what the future had in store. At the July annual meeting in 1955, the A team was discontinued. According to the club president, Charlie Cross, it had "served its purpose but had now become an expensive luxury." There would be no problems filling positions, said Mr Cross, because Leicester had the support of all the local teams. But the committee remained divided on the appropriate way to guide the club; the older members saw the move as a return to the great days of the Crumbie era. A younger member of the committee, more prophetically, said: "Within three years you will form yourselves into a club with three or four sides."

In the meantime it was apparent that a certain number of players would be leaving the club - if it is possible to "leave" an invitation club - since there was only one XV to play for. Lacey, in any event, had retired from first-team football after 175 games and as one stalwart made his way out, another made his way in. For although the first game of the 1955/56 season, against Bedford, was lost 11-20 there was a newcomer to the back row who was to leave a distinct mark on the club, the 18-year-old David Matthews who, the previous year, had been captaining Oakham School. It was to be 19 years and more than 500 games later that Matthews ended his first-class career, though by no means his connection with Leicester.

In another respect it was to be quite a season for youth, for Leicestershire chose to overlook the talents of Cullen and named a Wyggeston schoolboy, Michael Wade, against Warwickshire - the start of a distinguished career for the 18-year-old Wade which was to bring him three England caps. The younger generation must have been watched with approval by two distinguished visitors and ex-players to the game with Coventry, George Beamish - now knighted, an Air Vice Marshal and serving with Transport Command - and Denis Morris, ex-Conservative councillor and now director of BBC Midlands. Nevertheless Cullen, who had scored a try in Leicester's notable 6-3 win over Cardiff (the first against a Welsh club since 1946) reached a landmark when he passed 500 points for the club in a game against Old Blues. He was subsequently recalled by the county who won the Midlands group with a 17-0 success over East Midlands.

In general, however, Leicester's backs were not playing well, though Bleasdale from the forwards got an England trial. Maybe it added more point to the new training lights which came into operation in December 1955, while in the same month Wade made his debut for Tigers. He took part in a 0-0 draw at Bedford, playing opposite one of his masters from school, Ken Nicholas, who had moved to Bedford two years earlier.

Wade kept his place for the Christmas game against the Barbarians because the club captain, Elders, was injured and played against Birkenhead Park to complete the four-day Christmas programme. The Barbarians match was to be Mel Channer's last game for Leicester before returning to South Africa and, as if in his honour, the Tigers played superbly against a guest XV composed - with one exception - of 1955 British Lions. Tries by Tony O'Reilly (two) and Robin Roe helped push Leicester to a 12-3 defeat but it was a memorable moment for Channer who was playing on the wing. He scored 327 points for the club during his years with them but the nearest he came to a cap was a Scottish trial in 1954.

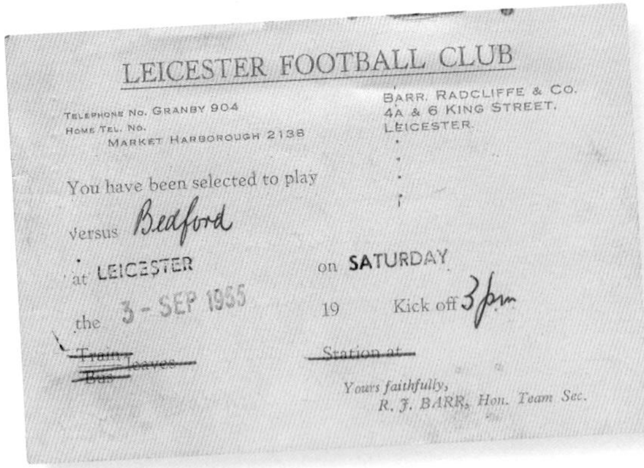

LEICESTER FOOTBALL CLUB

TELEPHONE No. GRANBY 904
HOME TEL. No.
MARKET HARBOROUGH 2138

BARR, RADCLIFFE & CO.
4A & 6 KING STREET,
LEICESTER.

You have been selected to play
versus *Bedford*
at LEICESTER on SATURDAY
the 3 - SEP 1955 19 Kick off *3pm*
~~Train~~ ~~leaves~~ ~~Bus~~ ~~Station at~~

Yours faithfully,
R. J. BARR, Hon. Team Sec.

↑↓ Selection postcard and programme from David Matthews's debut (note the wrong date on cover!)

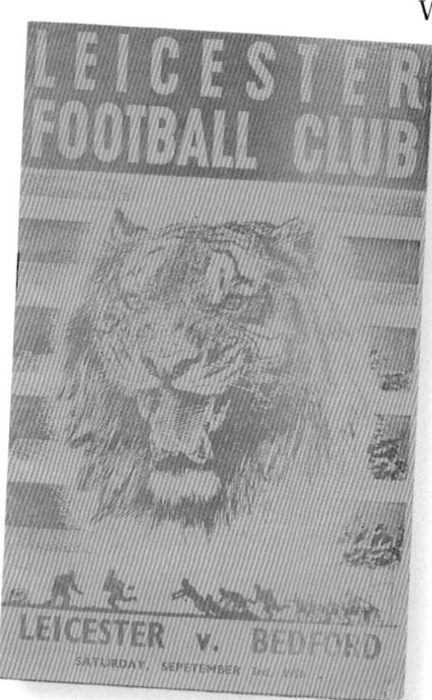

All the more regrettable, therefore, was the subsequent 3-0 defeat by Rugby, their first win at Welford Road of the century. It marked something of a decline in form and the first three months of 1956 went by with only two wins. Leicester were never able to field the same XV in successive matches but at least they could hold their heads high after a remarkable game at Llanelly, when they were beaten 24-20, three goals and three tries against a goal, four tries and a penalty. Better goal-kicking might have won them the game, which made the departure of Hazell for Somerset at the season's end the more poignant.

There had been some credits from the season, though. Elders had led Leicestershire, including ten Tigers, to the county championship semi-final when they were beaten 9-3 by Devon at Welford Road, while for both county and club, Wade had been the man of the moment. A useful fly-half, Mike Freer from Kibworth, had come into the club side late on and there was every reason to suppose that the 1955 Lions captain, Robin Thompson of Ireland, would join during the summer. He trained with the club as they prepared for the 1956/57 season but then spoiled it all by joining Warrington as a rugby league player.

↓ David Hazell stands guard over team mate Jim Ford during the match with Loughborough College 5.10.1955.

1956/1957

Further blows came when Wade and the new captain, Bleasdale, were injured in pre-season training and the scrum-half, Tom O'Connor, who had been given a trial by Ireland the previous season, joined Northampton because of the lack of opportunity in a club running only one side. It did not help when Nicholas, their former wing, scored the winning points for Bedford in the first match of the new season.

If supporters wanted something fresh to take their minds off this melancholy news, they got it in the shape of a Romanian touring side which played at Welford Road on 8 September. Bleasdale had visited Romania at the end of the previous season, guesting with Harlequins, though the visit had been arranged in 1955. It was a XV representing the combined clubs of Bucharest and they met the following Leicester side: Brian Small; Peter Baker, John Elders (captain), Brian Smith, Bob Matthews; Mike Freer, Mike Lubbock; Frank Chawner, John Stevens, John Thompson, Ron Smith, Jim Ford, Derek Ashurst, John McCormack, Peter Konig.

The visitors proved tough customers. After presenting scarves to the Leicester players and throwing flowers into the crowd, they gave nothing away in terms of tackling, cover defence and man-to-man marking. Their main weakness was the failure to exploit openings but they scored in each half, Ion Dobre and Anastasia Marinache each dropping a goal. In reply, back row forward Derek Ashurst kicked two penalties (though he had no previous reputation as a goalkicker) and the match ended as a 6-6 draw. Peter Thorneloe gave each of the Romanians a model tiger with a cub and they also went away with a club tie each and an official history of the club, which had been written by Brian Thompson, formerly rugby correspondent of the *Leicester Mercury* and later the newspaper's board chairman.

The first two months of the year brought little reward, however. Two wins from eleven games was hardly what the Leicester public were accustomed to, even if there was an interesting newcomer from Westleigh in the shape of a New Zealand-born back row man, Colin Martin, who made his debut against Newport in September and also solved something of a goal-kicking problem, since Ashurst was unable to maintain the performance he had shown against the Romanians.

Off the field though, things were starting to hum. During the summer the club had appointed a sub-committee to investigate the constitution of the club, following suggestions at the annual meeting that the A XV should be reformed. The committee, chaired by Doug Norman, consisted of Tom Berry, Tom Bleasdale, Francis Edwards, Alastair Smallwood and Harry Richards, all of them men with immense experience both in the playing side of the game and its administration.

↑ The two teams pose for a commemorative photograph before Romania's first match at Welford Road, 8.9.1956.

→ Doug Norman characterised by artist 'Samson' in 1956.

↓ The official club history given to each Romanian player.

↑ Action from the 3-3 draw with Cambridge University on 10 November1956 featuring Frank Chawner, Rex Skelton, John Thompson and Freddy Doore.

The result of their endeavours was a report with nine suggestions which, since it was adopted by the main committee by an overwhelming majority, helped establish the direction the club was to take in the foreseeable future. It is therefore worth giving their findings in some detail: the main recommendation was that the Tigers should be a club in the real sense of the word, running three XVs and leaving behind any idea of being an invitation club which, the committee pointed out, had alienated many local players. The second XV was to be known as the Extra Firsts and the third as the Colts.

The Colts XV was regarded as a "must", for herein, said the committee, lay the future of the club. In view of this it is somewhat ironic that later developments modified the Colts XV into a Swifts XV (with an intended emphasis upon youth) and the Leicester club had to wait another 16 years for a genuine youth side.

↓ Programme for Leicester's first game in Ireland against Lansdowne at Lansdowne Road 17.11.1956

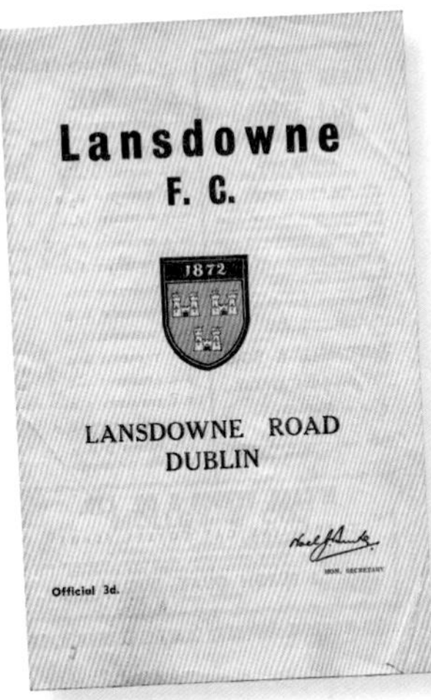

It was hoped that neither of the proposed new sides would become a financial burden, therefore a finance sub-committee was recommended in order to investigate new ways of raising extra cash. Taking note of the attitude of several local clubs while the A XV had been in existence, the sub-committee stressed that "under the new arrangements, the club, being based on three XVs, and the likelihood of players being attracted from outside districts, in due course, the new working should not handicap local clubs or players, any of whom can play for the premier XV."

Perhaps the most essential recommendation was that every member of the general committee had to be 100 per cent behind the new arrangements, as distinct from the divided loyalties during the running of the A XV. The report was outlined, as well, to a meeting of the old players whose help was to be vital. To give further point to the sub-committee's endeavours Ron Smith (after seven years with the club) and Ashurst (five years) joined Northampton and Coventry respectively after losing their places. It was obvious that Tigers had to reshape their entire way of life, for they could not afford to have players of this quality leaving the club. The upshot was the adoption, virtually in its entirety, of the report with the Extra First XV to begin in 1957/58 and the Colts the following season.

ITINERY.

Leicester F.C. v Lansdowne 17th. November 1956

and Old Belvedere 18th. November 1956.

Friday, 16th. November. 9.45 p.m. Arrive Dublin Airport. Met by Lansdowne Members in cars and conveyed to Hotels, Moira and Jury's.

Saturday, 17th. Nov. Morning free. Lunch at Hotels.

1.30 pm. Assemble in Hotels.

1.45 pm. Leave in cars for Lansdowne Road.

2.45 pm. Kick Off v Lansdowne.

6.15 p.m. Dinner in clubhouse Lansdowne Rd.

8.30 pm. Dance in clubhouse, Lansdowne Rd.

Sunday, 18th. Nov. Morning free. Lunch in hotels.

1.30 p.m. assemble in hotels.

~~1.[illegible] p.m. Leave in cars for Anglesea Rd.~~

2.45 pm. Kick Off v Old Belvedere.

4.30 pm. Tea after match.

5 p.m. leave in cars for Dublin Airport.

5.40 p.m. Check in Dublin Airport.

↑ Tour itinerary for the Tigers' first trip to Ireland in November 1956.

The last season under the old regime wound its way to a close, and even if it was far from memorable, it was by no means uneventful. Having entertained Romanians at its beginning, Leicester paid their first visit to Ireland in November 1956, where they lost 17-16 to Lansdowne at the famous Lansdowne Road ground, and 23-3 just round the corner at Anglesea Road, to an Old Belvedere XV which included Tony O'Reilly. They impressed Irish observers with their open style of play and the heavy defeat in the second match was at least partially due to open-handed Irish hospitality the night before.

Elders was given an England trial, where he had the big Wasps wing Ted Woodward as a co-centre, and was regrettably dropped for the second trial. Eight Tigers helped Leicestershire to become Midlands champions again though once more they were to go down to Devon in the semi-final at Torquay, beaten 11-6. The public were getting more for their money as Leicester began to play 40 minutes each way, when the opposition agreed, rather than 35 - though the club's comparative lack of success may not have made this seem a progressive step.

England wing Peter Thompson scored five tries against the club for the Barbarians, who won 23-6 and on the same day, as if to emphasise the passing of the old order, Percy Lawrie died, having retired from committee work only two years earlier. One of his contemporaries, 'Sos' Taylor, had died only a couple of months earlier and in March 1957, Eric Thorneloe informed the committee of his decision to resign as secretary. He had not been well for some time but it meant the end of a term of office which lasted 28 years and had seen two dozen internationals pass through the club. Bobby Barr, the first-team secretary, succeeded him and two months later, Thorneloe became the club's president when Charlie Cross died in office.

At least the players were able to give Thorneloe something of a "going away" present as the season drew to a close. They beat Newport for the first time in eight years at Welford Road and achieved the not inconsiderable triumph of fielding the same side in successive games for the first time in two years when the team that did duty against Newport went in en bloc against the British Police. Home matches ended with a 19-3 win over Llanelly and lock forward John Thompson became the only ever-present for the season. But tempering this successful conclusion was the news that Elders (later to coach England) was to leave the club after four years, for an appointment in Newcastle. With Cullen, who had been plagued by an ankle injury all season, also nearing the end of his career with Leicester, it was, in so many ways, the end of an era.

LEICESTER FOOTBALL CLUB 1952/53
Back: E.Thorneloe (Hon.Sec), Cross (President), Pratt, L.Chawner, Botting, Jenkins, Bleasdale, R.Smith, Konig, Sibson, Bedingfield (Hon.Tres), Jerwood, Barr (Team Hon.Sec).
Middle: Nicholas, Barrow, Moore, Bolesworth (capt), Lawrence, P.Thorneloe, Cullen.
Front: Clarke, Fisk.

LEICESTER FOOTBALL CLUB 1953/54
Back: E.Thorneloe (Hon.Sec), Walker (Referee), Barr (Team Hon.Sec), Haines, Shuttlewood, Konig, Elders, Ashurst, Matthews, Cross (President), Bedingfield (Hon.Tres).
Front: Sibson, Smith, Bolesworth, Channer, Jenkins (capt), Lacey, Pratt, Marshall, Hazell.
Inset: Baker, Black, P.Thorneloe, Bleasdale, Cullen.

LEICESTER FOOTBALL CLUB 1954/55
Back: E.Thorneloe (Hon.Sec), Barr (Team Hon.Sec), Stevens, Ashurst, Konig, Ford, Small, Taylor, Brook, Cross (President), Bedingfield (Hon.Tres).
Middle: Marshall, F.Chawner, R.Smith, Jenkins (capt), Elders, Bleasdale, P.Thorneloe.
Front: Doore, Lee.

LEICESTER FOOTBALL CLUB 1955/56
Back: Barr (Team Hon.Sec), Stevens, McCormack, Lubbock, Ford, Small, Brook, E.Thorneloe (Hon.Sec).
Middle: Bedingfield (Hon.Tres), Chawner, Hazell, Bleasdale, Elders (capt), R.Smith, P.Thorneloe, Konig, Cross (President).
Front: Freer, Thompson, Wade, B.Matthews.

LEICESTER FOOTBALL CLUB 1956/57
Back: E.Thorneloe (Hon.Sec), Barr (Team Hon.Sec), Freer, Skelton, Marshall, Rawson, B.Smith, Wade, Cullen, Cross (President), Bedingfield (Hon.Tres).
Middle: Lubbock, Ford, Chawner, Elders, Bleasdale (capt), P.Thorneloe, Thompson, Konig, Small.
Front: Walker, McCormack.
Inset: Baker.

19 52/53	Home Ground: Welford Road	OVERALL RECORD:					T	C	PG	DG	PTS
	Captain: Denis Bolesworth	PLD	W	D	L	Tigers scored:	65	19	23	5	317
		35	15	3	17	Opponents scored:	62	31	22	4	326

GM	DATE		VEN	OPPONENTS	RESULT	TRIES	KICKS	ATT
CLUB MATCHES								
1	Sep	**6**	**H**	**Bedford**	W 16-10	Bleasdale, F.Chawner, Matthews	Cullen 2c/p	1624
2		**13**	**H**	**Bath**	W 9-3	Botting, Konig	Channer p	1946
3		**20**	**H**	**Plymouth Albion**	W 27-6	Konig(2), Cullen, Bolesworth, F.Chawner, Jones	Cullen c, Barrow 2c, Channer d	1235
4		**22m**	**H**	**Cardiff**	L 6-9	-	Barrow p, Channer p	2917
5		**27**	**H**	**Waterloo**	W 15-14	Jenkins, Lawrence	Cullen 2p, Channer p	1267
6	Oct	4	a	Coventry	W 20-8	Barrow, Lawrence, R.Smith	Cullen c/2p, Channer p	-
7		18	a	Nuneaton	L 6-9	-	Barrow p, Fisk p	-
8		22w	a	Oxford University	D 6-6	Botting, Konig	-	-
9		25	a	Northampton	L 0-11	-	-	-
10	Nov	**1**	**H**	**Gloucester**	L 3-6	Jenkins	-	1080
11		8	a	Cambridge University	L 0-8	-	-	-
12		**15**	**H**	**Rugby**	W 8-6	Sibson	Channer c/p	818
13		**22**	**H**	**Nuneaton**	D 3-3	Shuttlewood	-	564
		29	a	Rugby	PP (frost)			
	Dec	6	a	Harlequins	PP (frost)			
14		13	a	Blackheath	L 8-15	Barrow, R.Smith	Cullen c	-
15		**20**	**H**	**Bristol**	W 6-5	-	Channer p/d	361
16		**26f**	**H**	**Barbarians**	L 9-22	Lawrence	Channer p/d	15000
		27	**H**	**Birkenhead Park**	PP (fog)			
17	Jan	3	a	Bath	W 8-5	Konig, Lawrence	Cullen c	-
18		10	a	Gloucester	L 6-10	Jenkins, R.Smith	-	-
19		**17**	**H**	**Middlesex Hospital**	W 9-3	Botting, Shuttlewood	Cullen p	744
20		24	a	Bedford	W 18-3	Botting, Jones, Lawrence	Cullen 3c/p	-
21		**29th**	**H**	**Royal Air Force**	L 11-12	Bolesworth	Fisk c/2p	620
22		**31**	**H**	**Rosslyn Park**	W 9-6	Lawrence(2), Bleasdale	-	473
23	Feb	7	a	London Scottish	L 9-13	Cullen	Cullen d, Channer d	-
24		**14**	**H**	**Newport**	L 3-14	-	Cullen p	1322
25		21	a	Moseley	L 9-14	Botting, Lawrence	Cullen p	-
26		**28**	**H**	**Northampton**	L 9-10	Botting, Cullen, Lawrence	-	1892
27	Mar	**7**	**H**	**Harlequins**	D 6-6	Botting, Nicholas	-	1540
28		**14**	**H**	**Coventry**	L 10-16	Cullen, Jenkins	Barrow 2c	1371
29		21	a	Swansea	L 3-8	Lawrence	-	-
30		**28**	**H**	**Headingley**	W 12-8	Botting, Cullen, Jenkins	Barrow p	526
31	Apr	4	a	Bristol	L 0-6	-	-	-
32		6m	a	Plymouth Albion	W 8-5	Botting, Jenkins	Barrow c	-
33		7tu	a	Exeter	W 13-5	Cullen(2), F.Chawner	Cullen 2c	-
34		11	a	Birkenhead Park	L 8-22	Lawrence, R.Smith	Fisk c	-
35		18	a	Sale	W 24-19	Cullen(3), Lawrence(2), Konig, Nicholas	Barrow p	-

INDIVIDUAL APPEARANCES 1952/53

Name / Game #	1	2	3	4	5	6	7	8	9	10	11	12	13	14	15	16	17	18	19	20	21	22	23	24	25	26	27	28	29	30	31	32	33	34	35	Apps	T	Pts
A (Alan) Baker	-	-	-	-	-	-	-	-	-	-	-	-	>D	-	-	-	-	-	-	-	-	-	-	-	-	-	-	-	-	-	-	-	-	-	-	1	-	-
EA (Eric) Barrow	F	F	F	F	F	F	F	F	F	F	F	-	-	F	G	F	G	G	G	-	-	-	-	F	F	F	F	F	F	F	F	F	F	F	F	29	2	28
DG (David) Belasco	-	-	-	-	-	-	-	-	-	>K	-	-	-	N	-	-	-	-	-	-	-	-	-	-	-	-	-	-	-	-	-	-	N	K	K	5	-	-
AW (Gus) Black S6 L2	-	-	-	-	-	-	-	-	-	-	-	-	-	-	-	-	-	-	-	-	-	-	-	-	-	-	-	-	>I	-	I	I	-	-	-	3	-	-
T (Tom) Bleasdale	G	G	-	-	-	-	G	-	G	-	-	-	-	-	-	-	-	-	-	E	E	E	E	H	G	H	H	H	H	G	G	H	H	H	G	20	2	6
AD (Denis) Bolesworth	A*	A*	A*	A*	A*	A*	A*	A*	A*	A*	A*	-	-	A*	A*	A*	A*	A*	A*	A*	A*	A*	A*	A*	A*	A*	A*	A*	A*	A*	A*	A*	A*	A*	A*	33	2	6
IJ (Ian) Botting E2	-	K	K	K	-	K	-	K	K	-	K	N	N	-	K	K	K	K	K	K	K	K	K	K	K	K	K	K	-	K	-	K	<K	-	-	26	9	27
K (Keith) Branston	-	-	-	-	-	-	=J	-	-	-	-	-	-	-	-	-	-	-	-	-	-	-	-	-	-	-	-	-	-	-	-	-	-	-	-	1	-	-
MR (Mel) Channer	J	J	J	J	J	J	-	J	J	-	-	J	-	-	L	J	-	-	O	-	-	L	L	-	-	-	-	-	-	-	J	M	-	-	-	16	-	35
F (Frank) Chawner	E	E	E	E	E	E	C	E	-	E	E	-	-	E	-	-	-	-	E	-	-	-	-	E	-	E	E	-	E	E	E	E	D	C	C	22	3	9
L (Len) Chawner	-	-	-	-	-	-	-	-	B	-	-	B	B	-	-	-	-	-	B	B	B	-	-	-	-	-	-	-	-	-	-	-	B	-	-	7	-	-
WJ Clarke	-	-	-	-	-	-	-	-	-	-	-	-	-	-	>J	-	J	J	J	J	J	J	J	J	-	J	J	J	J	J	-	J	-	J	J	17	-	-
GH (George) Cullen	M	M	M	-	M	M	-	-	M	M	J	-	-	M	M	M	M	M	M	M	-	M	M	M	M	M	M	M	M	M	M	L	M	-	L	28	10	82
JD (Jerry) Day	-	-	-	-	-	-	-	-	-	-	-	E	A	-	-	-	-	-	-	-	-	-	-	-	-	-	-	-	-	-	-	-	-	-	-	2	-	-
JW (Jim) Fisk	O	O	O	O	O	O	O	O	O	O	O	O	-	O	-	-	-	-	-	O	O	O	O	O	O	O	O	O	-	O	O	O	O	<O	-	27	-	13
GE (Gordon) Gee	-	L	L	L	L	-	<M	-	-	-	-	-	-	-	-	-	-	-	-	-	-	-	-	-	-	-	-	-	-	-	-	-	-	-	-	5	-	-
JM (Dave) Guffick	-	-	-	-	-	-	-	-	L	J	-	-	-	-	-	-	-	-	-	-	-	-	-	-	-	-	-	-	-	-	-	-	-	-	-	2	-	-
PAH (Peter) Herbert	-	-	-	-	-	-	-	-	-	-	-	<H	-	-	-	-	-	-	-	-	-	-	-	-	-	-	-	-	-	-	-	-	-	-	-	1	-	-
PE (Peter) Hudson	-	-	-	-	-	-	-	-	-	-	-	>A	<C	-	-	-	-	-	-	-	-	-	-	-	-	-	-	-	-	-	-	-	-	-	-	2	-	-
JM (John) Jenkins	-	-	>G	G	G	G	E	G	-	G	G	G	G*	G	E	G	E	E	-	G	G	G	G	G	E	G	-	E	G	D	D	G	G	G	E	30	6	18
KD Jones	>I	I	I	I	I	-	I	-	I	I	I	-	-	I	I	-	I	-	-	I	I	I	<I	-	-	-	-	-	-	-	-	-	-	-	-	16	2	6
JG (John) Kennewell	-	-	-	-	-	-	-	-	-	-	-	D	E	-	-	-	-	-	-	-	<D	-	-	-	-	-	-	-	-	-	-	-	-	-	-	3	-	-
PH (Peter) Konig	H	H	H	H	H	H	H	H	H	H	H	-	-	H	H	H	H	H	H	H	H	H	H	-	H	-	G	G	-	H	H	-	-	-	H	27	6	18
CGS (Gwynne) Lawrence	L	N	N	N	N	N	N	N	N	N	N	-	-	K	N	N	N	N	N	N	N	N	N	N	N	N	N	N	N	N	N	N	L	N	<N	33	13	39
RE (Bob) Leslie	-	-	-	-	-	-	-	=L	-	-	-	-	-	-	-	-	-	-	-	-	-	-	-	-	-	-	-	-	-	-	-	-	-	-	-	1	-	-
KR (Keith) Macdonald S+	-	-	-	>M	-	L	-	-	-	L	L	<L	-	-	-	-	-	-	-	-	-	-	-	-	-	-	-	-	-	-	-	-	-	-	-	5	-	-
R (Rae) Marshall	-	-	-	-	-	-	-	-	-	-	-	-	O	-	O	O	O	O	-	-	-	-	-	-	-	-	-	-	O	-	-	-	-	-	O	7	-	-
RD (Bob) Matthews	N	-	-	-	K	-	K	-	-	-	-	-	-	-	-	-	-	-	-	-	-	-	-	-	-	-	-	-	-	-	-	-	-	-	-	3	1	3
JW Milne	-	-	-	-	-	-	-	-	-	-	-	-	=H	-	-	-	-	-	-	-	-	-	-	-	-	-	-	-	-	-	-	-	-	-	-	1	-	-
WKT (Bill) Moore E7	-	-	-	-	-	-	-	-	-	-	-	I	I	-	-	I	-	I	I	-	-	-	-	I	I	I	I	I	-	I	-	-	I	I	<I	14	-	-
WK (Ken) Nicholas	K	-	-	-	-	-	-	-	-	-	-	-	-	-	-	-	-	-	-	-	-	-	-	L	L	L	L	L	K	L	K	-	J	L	M	12	2	6
J (John) Noton	-	-	-	-	-	I	-	I	-	-	-	-	-	-	-	-	-	-	-	-	-	-	-	-	-	-	-	-	-	-	-	-	-	-	-	2	-	-
S (Stan) Pratt	B	B	B	B	B	B	B	B	-	B	B	-	-	B	B	B	B	B	-	-	-	B	B	B	B	B	B	B	B	B	B	B	-	B	B	28	-	-
G (George) Pym	-	-	-	-	-	-	-	-	-	-	-	-	>J	J	-	-	-	-	-	-	-	-	-	-	J	-	-	-	-	-	-	-	-	-	-	3	-	-
GDO (Geoffrey) Randle	-	-	-	-	-	-	-	-	-	-	-	-	-	-	-	<L	-	-	-	-	-	-	-	-	-	-	-	-	-	-	-	-	-	-	-	1	-	-
J (John) Shuttlewood	-	-	-	-	-	-	-	-	-	-	-	>M	L	L	-	-	L	L	L	L	L	-	-	-	-	-	-	-	L	-	L	-	-	M	-	11	2	6
HW (Harry) Sibson	-	-	-	-	-	-	-	-	-	-	-	F	F	-	F	-	F	F	F	F	F	F	F	-	-	-	-	-	-	-	-	-	-	-	-	10	1	3
DH (Derek) Smith	-	-	-	-	-	-	-	-	-	-	>M	-	<M	-	-	-	-	-	-	-	-	-	-	-	-	-	-	-	-	-	-	-	-	-	-	2	-	-
RH (Ron) Smith	D	D	D	D	D	D	D	D	E	D	-	-	-	D	D	E	D	D	D	D	-	D	D	D	D	D	D	D	D	-	-	D	E	D	D	29	4	12
DL (Don) Sproul	-	-	-	-	-	-	-	=M	-	-	-	-	-	-	-	-	-	-	-	-	-	-	-	-	-	-	-	-	-	-	-	-	-	-	-	1	-	-
RV (Bob) Stirling E13	C	C	C	-	-	C	-	C	D	-	D	C*	-	-	-	D	-	-	-	C	C	C	C	-	-	-	-	-	-	-	<C	-	-	-	-	14	-	-
JR (Ray) Tate	-	-	-	-	-	-	<L	-	-	-	-	-	-	-	-	-	-	-	-	-	-	-	-	-	-	-	-	-	-	-	-	-	-	-	-	1	-	-
HG (Haydn) Thomas	-	-	-	-	-	-	-	-	-	-	-	-	-	-	-	-	-	-	-	-	<M	-	-	-	-	-	-	-	-	-	-	-	-	-	-	1	-	-
PBL (Peter) Thorneloe	-	-	-	C	C	-	-	-	C	C	C	-	-	C	C	C	C	C	C	-	-	-	-	C	C	C	C	C	C	C	-	C	C	E	-	21	-	-
A (Anthony) Ward	-	-	-	-	-	-	-	-	-	-	-	>K	<K	-	-	-	-	-	-	-	-	-	-	-	-	-	-	-	-	-	-	-	-	-	-	2	-	-

The key for how to read the stats is on the last page

1953/54

Home Ground: Welford Road
Captain: John Jenkins

OVERALL RECORD:					T	C	PG	DG	PTS
PLD	W	D	L	Tigers scored:	83	34	20	10	407
37	22	2	13	Opponents scored:	74	24	25	6	363

GM	DATE		VEN	OPPONENTS	RESULT	TRIES	KICKS	ATT
CLUB MATCHES								
1	Sep	5	H	Bedford	W 12-6	Shuttlewood(2), Channer	Channer d	1762
2		12	H	Bath	W 24-6	Cullen, Channer, Elders, Jenkins, Konig	Cullen 2c/p, Hazell c	1080
3		19	H	Plymouth Albion	W 25-3	Sibson(2), Hazell, Elders, Shuttlewood	Hazell 2c, Channer d, Duff p	1150
4		21m	H	Cardiff	L 3-12	-	Channer d	2670
5		26	a	Harlequins	W 9-6	Bleasdale, Shuttlewood	Cullen p	-
6	Oct	3	H	Coventry	W 14-3	Channer	Channer d, Cullen c/p, Baker p	2258
7		10	a	Cheltenham	L 0-5	-	-	-
8		15th	H	Loughborough College	W 15-9	Bleasdale, Pratt, Pym	Black d, Nicholas d	1022
9		17	H	Moseley	L 3-6	Bleasdale	-	1360
10		21w	H	Oxford University	W 13-9	Grove(2), Nicholas	Duff 2c	481
11		24	H	Northampton	W 12-8	Black	Belasco d, Channer d, Cullen p	2241
12		31	H	Rugby	W 15-6	Lacey, Sibson, Smith	Channer 2p	549
13	Nov	7	H	Gloucester	W 13-8	Bleasdale, Clarke, Elders	Hazell 2c	877
14		14	H	Cambridge University	W 17-14	Elders(2), Black	Hazell c/2p	1604
15		21	a	Nuneaton	L 11-17	Lee	Channer 2p, Marshall c	-
16	Dec	5	a	Waterloo	L 9-12	Nicholas(2), Bolesworth	-	-
17		12	H	Blackheath	W 19-9	Shuttlewood(2), Hazell	Hazell 2c/2p	923
18		19	H	Bristol	W 8-6	Hazell(2)	Channer c	382
19		26	H	Birkenhead Park	W 13-8	Hazell, Ashurst, Bleasdale	Hazell 2c	2750
20		28m	H	Barbarians	L 11-39	Hazell, Ashurst	Hazell c/p	15000
21	Jan	2	a	Bath	D 3-3	-	Baker p	-
22		9	a	Gloucester	L 0-19	-	-	-
23		16	a	Headingley	L 3-12	Thorneloe	-	-
24		23	a	Bedford	L 5-22	Elders	Hazell c	-
		30	a	Rosslyn Park	PP (frost)			
	Feb	4th	H	Royal Air Force	PP (frost)			
		6	H	London Scottish	PP (frost)			
25		13	a	Newport	L 3-20	Jenkins	-	-
26		20	H	Middlesex Hospital	W 12-3	Lee(2), Sibson	Marshall p	726
27		27	a	Northampton	L 5-19	Thorneloe	Hazell c	-
28	Mar	6	H	Harlequins	W 12-3	Doore, Jenkins, Marshall, Thorneloe	-	767
29		13	a	Coventry	W 10-8	Konig, Richards	Hazell 2c	-
30		20	H	Swansea	D 6-6	-	Hazell 2p	1667
31		27	H	Loughborough College	W 22-0	Haines, Konig, Lacey, Lee, Matthews	Hazell 2c, Clarke d	798
32	Apr	3	a	Birkenhead Park	W 14-9	Elders, Konig, Matthews	Hazell c/p	-
33		10	H	Nuneaton	W 13-3	Hazell, Shuttlewood, Smith	Hazell 2c	711
34		17	a	Bristol	L 3-18	Richards	-	-
35		19m	a	Plymouth Albion	W 18-3	Konig(3), Bolesworth	Hazell 3c	-
36		20tu	a	Exeter	L 5-9	Konig	Hazell c	-
37		24	H	Sale	W 27-14	Channer(2), Hazell, Elders, Matthews, Smith	Channer d, Hazell 3c	524

INDIVIDUAL APPEARANCES 1953/54

Name / Game #	1	2	3	4	5	6	7	8	9	10	11	12	13	14	15	16	17	18	19	20	21	22	23	24	25	26	27	28	29	30	31	32	33	34	35	36	37	Apps	T	Pts
ADB (Derek) Ashurst	-	-	-	-	-	-	H	-	-	-	-	H	-	-	-	-	-	H	H	H	H	K	H	H	-	-	F	F	H	F	F	F	F	F	F	H	F	20	2	6
A (Alan) Baker	-	-	D	D	E	E	-	D	E	E	E	-	E	E	-	E	E	E	E	D	D	D	D	D	-	-	E	E	-	-	-	-	-	-	E	E	-	23	-	6
EA (Eric) Barrow	G	G	G	F	-	-	<G	-	-	-	-	-	-	-	-	-	-	-	-	-	-	-	-	-	-	-	-	-	-	-	-	-	-	-	-	-	-	5	-	-
DG (David) Belasco	-	-	-	-	K	K	-	-	N	N	K	-	-	N	-	-	-	-	-	-	-	-	-	-	N	-	-	-	-	-	-	-	-	-	-	<N	-	8	-	3
ER (Peter) Bennett	-	-	-	-	-	-	-	-	-	-	-	-	-	-	-	-	-	-	-	-	-	-	-	-	-	-	-	-	-	-	-	-	-	-	-	<L	-	1	-	-
DE (Derek) Bircumshaw	-	-	-	-	-	-	-	-	-	-	-	-	-	-	-	-	-	-	-	-	-	-	-	-	-	-	-	-	-	>G	G	-	-	-	-	-	-	2	-	-
AW (Gus) Black S6 L2	I	I	I	I	I	I	I	I	-	-	I	I	-	I	-	-	-	I	-	<I	-	-	-	-	-	-	-	-	-	-	-	-	-	-	-	-	-	13	2	9
T (Tom) Bleasdale	F	F	-	-	G	-	-	G	H	H	H	-	H	H	-	-	G	G	G	G	-	-	-	-	-	-	-	-	-	-	-	-	-	-	-	-	-	13	5	15
AD (Denis) Bolesworth	-	-	-	C	A	A	-	-	-	C	-	C	-	A	A	C	-	-	-	-	-	-	-	-	-	-	-	-	-	-	-	-	-	-	A	-	C	10	2	6
MR (Mel) Channer	J	J	J*	J	J	J	J*	J	J	-	J	J*	-	J	J*	J*	-	J	-	J	-	-	-	N	-	-	-	-	L	-	-	-	-	-	-	-	L	19	5	47
F (Frank) Chawner	-	-	-	-	-	-	C	-	-	-	-	A	-	-	C	A	-	-	-	-	A	-	C	-	E	C	-	-	-	-	-	-	-	-	-	-	-	8	-	-
L (Len) Chawner	-	-	-	-	-	-	-	-	-	-	-	-	-	B	-	B	-	-	-	-	-	-	-	-	B	-	-	-	-	-	-	-	B	-	-	-	-	4	-	-
WJ Clarke	-	-	-	-	-	-	-	-	-	J	-	-	J	-	-	-	-	-	J	-	J	I	J	J	-	-	-	-	-	-	M	L	L	M	M	<M	-	13	1	6
IDF (Ian) Coutts S2	-	-	-	-	-	-	-	-	-	=M	-	-	-	-	-	-	-	-	-	-	-	-	-	-	-	-	-	-	-	-	-	-	-	-	-	-	-	1	-	-
GH (George) Cullen	L	L	L	L	L	L	-	-	M	-	L	-	M	-	-	-	M	-	-	-	-	-	-	-	-	-	-	-	-	-	-	-	-	-	-	-	-	10	1	21
JD (Jerry) Day	-	-	-	-	-	-	D	-	-	-	-	G	-	-	<G	-	-	-	-	-	-	-	-	-	-	-	-	-	-	-	-	-	-	-	-	-	-	3	-	-
FR (Freddy) Doore	-	-	-	-	-	-	-	-	-	-	-	-	-	-	-	-	-	-	-	-	-	-	-	-	>I	I	I	I	I	I	I	I	-	I	I	-	-	10	1	3
SM Duff	>O	O	O	O	-	O	O	O	O	O	O	O	O	O	-	-	-	-	-	-	-	<M	-	-	-	-	-	-	-	-	-	-	-	-	-	-	-	14	-	7
J (John) Elders	>M	M	M	M	M	M	-	M	L	L	M	-	L	L	-	-	L	L	L	M	M	L	L	L	M	L	L	L	M	M*	L*	M	M	-	L	-	M	31	8	24
NJ (Norman) Grove	-	-	-	-	-	-	-	-	>I	I	-	-	I	-	-	-	I	-	I	-	-	-	-	<I	-	-	-	-	-	-	-	-	-	-	-	-	-	6	2	6
JM (Dave) Guffick	-	-	-	-	-	-	-	-	-	-	-	-	-	-	-	-	-	-	-	-	-	-	-	-	-	<J	-	-	-	-	-	-	-	-	-	-	-	1	-	-
D (Dennis) Haines	-	-	-	-	-	-	>M	-	-	-	-	L	-	M	L	L	J	M	M	L	L	J	M	-	L	-	J	J	J	J	J	J	J	J	J	J	J	24	1	3
DSG (David) Hazell E+	>A	A	A	A	C	C	-	C	C	-	C	-	C	C	-	-	C	C	C	A	C	C	-	C	A	-	A	A	A	C	C	A	C	C	C	C	A	30	8	102
DJ (David) Hytch	-	-	-	-	-	-	-	-	-	-	-	-	-	-	-	-	-	-	-	-	-	-	>I	-	-	-	-	-	-	-	-	-	<I	-	-	-	-	2	-	-
JM (John) Jenkins	D*	D*	-	G*	D*	G*	-	E*	G*	G*	G*	-	G*	G*	-	-	D*	D*	D*	E*	G*	G*	G*	G*	G*	G*	D*	D*	D*	-	-	D*	D*	D*	G*	D*	D*	30	3	9
PH (Peter) Konig	H	H	H	H	H	H	-	H	-	-	-	-	-	-	H	H	H	-	-	-	-	-	-	-	H	H	H	H	F	H	H	H	H	H	H	I	I	23	8	24
EC (Eric) Lacey	E	E	E	E	-	-	E	-	-	-	-	E	-	-	E	D	-	-	-	-	-	-	-	-	-	E	-	-	E	D	E	E	E	E	D	-	E	17	2	6
G (Geoffrey) Lee	-	-	-	-	-	-	-	-	-	-	-	-	-	-	>N	-	-	N	N	N	N	-	N	K	-	K	-	N	N	N	N	N	-	-	-	-	-	13	4	12
JT (John) McCormack	-	-	-	-	-	-	-	-	-	-	-	-	-	-	-	-	-	-	-	-	-	>H	-	-	-	-	-	-	-	-	-	-	-	-	-	-	-	1	-	-
R (Rae) Marshall	-	-	-	-	O	-	-	-	-	-	-	-	-	-	O	O	O	O	O	O	O	O	O	O	O	O	O	O	O	O	O	O	O	O	O	O	O	24	1	8
RD (Bob) Matthews	-	-	-	-	-	-	-	-	-	-	-	-	-	-	-	-	N	-	-	-	-	-	-	-	K	N	-	-	-	-	K	K	N	N	N	-	N	9	3	9
WK (Ken) Nicholas	N	K	K	K	-	-	N	K	K	K	N	N	N	-	-	<N	-	-	-	-	-	-	-	-	-	-	-	-	-	-	-	-	-	-	-	-	-	12	3	12
J (John) Noton	-	-	-	-	-	-	-	-	-	-	-	-	-	-	I	I	-	-	-	-	<I	-	-	-	-	-	-	-	-	-	-	-	-	-	-	-	-	3	-	-
S (Stan) Pratt	B	B	B	B	B	B	-	B	B	B	B	-	B	-	-	-	B	B	B	B	B	B	B	B	-	B	B	B	B	B	B	B	-	B	B	B	<B	30	1	3
N Pugh	-	-	-	-	-	-	>B	-	-	-	-	B	-	-	<B	-	-	-	-	-	-	-	-	-	-	-	-	-	-	-	-	-	-	-	-	-	-	3	-	-
G (George) Pym	-	-	-	-	-	-	L	L	-	-	-	M	-	-	M	M	-	-	-	-	-	-	-	M	J	M	M	M	-	<L	-	-	-	-	-	-	-	11	1	3
K (Ken) Richards	-	-	-	-	-	-	-	-	-	-	-	-	-	-	-	-	-	-	-	-	-	-	-	-	-	-	>K	K	K	K	-	-	-	K	-	<K	-	6	2	6
J (John) Shuttlewood	K	N	N	N	N	N	K	N	-	-	-	K	K	K	K	K	K	K	K	K	K	N	K	-	-	-	N	-	-	-	-	-	K	L	K	-	<K	25	7	21
HW (Harry) Sibson	-	-	F	-	F	F	F	F	F	F	F	F	F	F	F	F	F	F	F	F	F	F	F	F	F	F	-	-	-	-	-	-	-	-	-	F	H	25	4	12
RH (Ron) Smith	-	-	-	-	-	D	-	-	D	D	D	D	D	D	D	G	-	-	-	-	E	E	E	E	D	D	G	G	G	E	D	G	G	G	-	G	G	25	3	9
PBL (Peter) Thorneloe	C	C	C	-	-	-	A	A	A	A	A	-	A	-	-	-	A	A	A	C	-	A	A	A	C	A	C	C	C	A	A	C	A	A	-	A	-	27	3	9

The key for how to read the stats is on the last page

19 54/55	Home Ground: Welford Road	OVERALL RECORD:					T	C	PG	DG	PTS
	Captain: John Jenkins	PLD	W	D	L	Tigers scored:	86	41	36	2	454
		40	21	2	17	Opponents scored:	89	36	29	4	438

GM	DATE		VEN	OPPONENTS	RESULT	TRIES	KICKS	ATT
CLUB MATCHES								
1	Sep	**4**	**H**	**Bedford**	W 17-8	Brook, Konig, Lee, Taylor	Hazell c/p	1200
2		**11**	**H**	**Bath**	W 5-3	Konig	Hazell c	738
3		**18**	**H**	**Plymouth Albion**	W 19-11	Taylor(2), Cullen	Channer c/2p, Hazell c	905
4		**20m**	**H**	**Cardiff**	L 11-14	Baker	Channer c/2p	2603
5		25	a	Harlequins	L 16-28	Channer, Bleasdale	Channer 2c/2p	-
6	Oct	2	a	Coventry	L 14-29	Smith	Channer c/3p	-
7		**6w**	**H**	**Loughborough College**	W 19-3	Konig, Taylor	Channer 2c/3p	451
8		9	a	Cheltenham	W 11-9	Channer, Cullen, Darlington	Channer c	-
9		**16**	**H**	**Northampton**	L 5-9	Doore	Hazell c	2037
10		20w	a	Oxford University	L 0-18	-	-	-
11		**23**	**H**	**Moseley**	W 9-8	Doore, Matthews	Channer p	758
12		30	a	Rugby	W 10-3	Brook, Elders	Hazell 2c	-
13	Nov	**6**	**H**	**Gloucester**	W 12-6	McCormack(2), Thorneloe	Hazell p	605
14		13	a	Cambridge University	L 6-12	-	Channer d, Hazell p	-
15		**20**	**H**	**Nuneaton**	W 11-3	Matthews, O'Connor	Channer c/p	522
16		**27**	**H**	**Old Blues**	W 13-6	Symonds(2), Bircumshaw	Cullen 2c	570
17	Dec	**4**	**H**	**Waterloo**	W 11-8	Cullen(Penalty)(2), F.Chawner	Channer c	855
18		11	a	Blackheath	L 9-11	Symonds, Taylor	Channer p	-
19		**18**	**H**	**Bristol**	L 11-17	Brook, Elders, Konig	Marshall c	682
20		**27m**	**H**	**Birkenhead Park**	L 11-13	Channer, Lee	Hazell c/p	2195
21		**28tu**	**H**	**Barbarians**	L 13-22	Channer, Elders	Hazell 2c/p	20000
22	Jan	1	a	Bath	W 12-6	Cullen(3), Bircumshaw	-	-
23		8	a	Gloucester	L 9-11	Cullen, Konig, Lee	-	-
		15	**H**	**Headingley**	PP (snow)			
24		22	a	Bedford	W 9-0	Bircumshaw, Cullen	Small p	-
25		**27th**	**H**	**Royal Air Force**	W 9-8	Brook(2)	Channer p	495
26		**29**	**H**	**Rosslyn Park**	W 19-12	F.Chawner, Elders, Taylor	Hazell 2c/2p	625
27	Feb	5	a	London Scottish	W 11-9	Lee, Taylor	Channer c/p	-
28		**12**	**H**	**Newport**	L 3-9	-	Channer p	1188
		19	**H**	**British Police**	PP (snow)			
		26	a	Northampton	PP (snow)			
29	Mar	**5**	**H**	**Harlequins**	L 8-14	Brook	Hazell c/p	1582
30		**12**	**H**	**Coventry**	D 11-11	Brook, O'Connor, Stevens	Small c	1083
31		19	a	Swansea	W 8-5	Elders, Thorneloe	Marshall c	-
32		26	a	Cardiff	L 9-32	Hazell, Cullen	Hazell p	-
33	Apr	2	a	Birkenhead Park	D 0-0	-	-	-
34		9	a	Bristol	W 19-12	Brook, Cullen, Elders	Hazell 2c/2p	-
35		11m	a	Plymouth Albion	L 13-15	Hazell(2)	Hazell 2c/p	-
36		12tu	a	Exeter	W 31-0	Elders(3), Brook(2), Bleasdale, Taylor	Hazell 5c	-
37		**16**	**H**	**Llanelly**	L 15-18	Ashurst(2), Cullen	Elders d, Hazell p	1046
38		18m	a	Northampton	W 8-6	Cullen, Taylor	Hazell c	-
39		23	a	Moseley	L 10-14	Brook, Taylor	Hazell 2c	-
40		**30**	**H**	**Sale**	W 17-15	Konig	Cullen 4p, Small c	1164

INDIVIDUAL APPEARANCES 1954/55

Name / Game #	1	2	3	4	5	6	7	8	9	10	11	12	13	14	15	16	17	18	19	20	21	22	23	24	25	26	27	28	29	30	31	32	33	34	35	36	37	38	39	40	Apps	T	Pts
ADB (Derek) Ashurst	F	F	F	F	F	F	F	-	-	-	-	-	-	-	-	-	-	-	F	-	-	-	-	-	-	-	-	-	-	-	F	F	F	F	-	-	F	F	-	-	14	2	6
A (Alan) Baker	E	E	E	E	E	-	-	-	-	-	-	-	-	-	<E	-	-	-	-	-	-	-	-	-	-	-	-	-	-	-	-	-	-	-	-	-	-	-	-	-	6	1	3
PT (Peter) Baker	-	-	-	-	-	-	-	-	-	-	-	-	-	-	-	-	-	-	-	-	-	>L	L	M	M	-	-	-	-	-	M	L	L	L	L	L	M	M	-	-	12	-	-
MD Barratt	-	-	-	-	-	-	-	-	-	-	=H	-	-	-	-	-	-	-	-	-	-	-	-	-	-	-	-	-	-	-	-	-	-	-	-	-	-	-	-	-	1	-	-
DE (Derek) Bircumshaw	-	-	-	-	-	-	A	-	-	-	-	-	-	-	-	F	-	F	-	-	-	F	H	H	H	H	H	H	H	-	-	-	-	-	-	-	-	-	-	-	11	3	9
T (Tom) Bleasdale	G	G	G	G	G	G	G	G	G	G	G	-	-	-	-	-	F	-	-	F	F	-	-	-	-	-	-	-	-	-	-	-	-	-	F	F	-	-	F	F	18	2	6
AD (Denis) Bolesworth	-	-	-	-	-	-	-	-	-	-	-	-	-	-	-	-	-	-	-	-	-	-	-	-	-	-	-	-	-	<A	-	-	-	-	-	-	-	-	-	-	1	-	-
D (David) Brook	>K	K	K	K	K	K	-	L	L	N	M	K	N	N	-	-	N	-	N	L	M	J	J	J	K	M	M	M	L	L	J	J	J	J	J	J	J	J	J	J	36	11	33
RD (Dave) Brookhouse	-	-	-	-	-	-	>B	B	B	B	-	-	-	-	B	B	B	B	B	-	-	-	-	-	-	-	B	-	-	-	-	-	-	-	-	-	-	-	-	-	10	-	-
MR (Mel) Channer	J	J	J	J	J	J	J	J	J	-	J	-	-	J	J	-	J	J	-	J	J	-	-	-	J	J	J	J	J	J	-	-	-	-	-	-	-	-	-	-	22	4	91
F (Frank) Chawner	-	C	-	-	-	-	C	C	C	C	C	D	C	C	A	C	C	C	C	C	-	A	C	C	C	C	C	C	-	C	C	C	C	C	-	-	C	C	C	C	31	2	6
L (Len) Chawner	-	-	B	B	B	<B	-	-	-	-	-	-	-	-	-	-	-	-	-	-	-	-	-	-	-	-	-	-	-	-	-	-	-	-	-	-	-	-	-	-	4	-	-
GH (George) Cullen	L	L	L	L	-	-	-	K	K	K	M	N	K	K	K	K	K	K	K	K	K	K	K	K	-	K	L	-	-	K	K	K	-	K	K	-	K	K	M	K	32	13	55
B (Bryan) Darlington	-	>N	N	N	N	N	-	N	<N	-	-	-	-	-	-	-	-	-	-	-	-	-	-	-	-	-	-	-	-	-	-	-	-	-	-	-	-	-	-	-	7	1	3
FR (Freddy) Doore	I	I	I	I	I	I	I	I	I	I	I	I	I	I	-	I	-	I	-	-	-	-	-	I	-	-	I	-	-	-	-	-	-	I	I	-	-	-	I	I	22	2	6
J (John) Elders	O	O	O	O	O	O	M	M	O	L	L	M	L	L	-	L	-	L	L	-	L	M	-	L	L	L	-	L	M	M	L	-	M	M	M	M	L	L	L	L	34	9	30
JG (Jim) Ford	-	-	-	-	-	-	-	-	-	-	-	-	-	-	-	-	-	>E	E	E	-	D	-	E	E	-	-	E	E	E	D	D	E	D	D	-	E	E	E	E	18	-	-
BR (Bernard) Golder	-	-	-	-	>L	L	L	-	-	<M	-	-	-	-	-	-	-	-	-	-	-	-	-	-	-	-	-	-	-	-	-	-	-	-	-	-	-	-	-	-	4	-	-
D (Dennis) Haines	-	-	-	-	-	-	-	-	-	J	-	J	J	-	-	J	-	-	J	-	-	-	-	-	-	-	-	-	-	-	-	-	-	-	-	-	-	-	-	-	5	-	-
DSG (David) Hazell E4	A	A	A	A	A	A	-	A	A	-	A	A	A	A	-	-	-	A	-	A	A	-	-	-	A	-	-	A	-	-	-	A	A	A	C	C	A	A	A	-	25	3	96
JM (John) Jenkins	D*	D*	D*	D*	D*	D*	D*	D*	D*	D*	D*	G*	G*	G*	G*	G*	G*	G*	G*	G*	G*	G*	G*	F*	F*	G*	G*	F*	F*	F*	G*	G*	G*	G*	G*	G*	G*	G*	G*	G*	40	-	-
PH (Peter) Konig	H	H	H	H	H	H	H	H	H	H	-	H	-	-	H	-	-	H	H	-	H	H	F	-	-	-	F	-	K	H	H	H	H	H	H	H	H	H	H	H	30	6	18
EC (Eric) Lacey	-	-	-	-	-	-	-	-	-	-	-	-	E	E	D	E	E	-	D	-	E	-	E	D	D	E	D	D	D	D	-	-	-	-	-	D	-	-	-	-	16	-	-
G (Geoffrey) Lee	N	-	-	-	-	-	K	-	-	-	-	-	-	-	-	-	-	-	-	N	-	-	N	-	-	-	K	K	-	N	N	N	N	-	N	N	-	-	-	<N	13	4	12
JT (John) McCormack	-	-	-	-	-	-	-	-	-	-	-	-	H	H	-	H	H	-	-	H	-	-	-	-	-	-	-	-	-	-	-	-	-	-	-	-	-	-	-	-	5	2	6
R (Rae) Marshall	-	-	-	-	-	-	-	O	O	-	O	O	O	O	O	O	O	O	O	O	-	O	-	-	-	-	O	-	-	-	O	-	-	-	O	-	-	-	O	-	17	-	4
RD (Bob) Matthews	-	-	-	-	-	-	-	-	-	-	K	-	-	-	N	-	-	-	-	-	-	-	-	-	-	-	-	-	-	-	-	-	-	-	-	-	-	-	N	-	3	2	6
KD (Karl) Mullen I25 L3	-	-	-	-	-	-	-	-	-	-	=B	-	-	-	-	-	-	-	-	-	-	-	-	-	-	-	-	-	-	-	-	-	-	-	-	-	-	-	-	-	1	-	-
T (Tom) O'Connor	-	-	-	-	-	-	-	-	-	-	-	-	-	-	>I	-	I	-	I	I	I	I	I	-	I	I	-	I	I	I	I	I	I	-	-	I	I	I	-	-	18	2	6
HW (Harry) Sibson	-	-	-	-	-	-	-	F	F	F	F	F	-	-	<F	-	-	-	-	-	-	-	-	-	-	-	-	-	-	-	-	-	-	-	-	-	-	-	-	-	6	-	-
BTC (Brian) Small	-	-	-	-	-	-	-	-	-	-	-	-	-	-	-	-	-	-	-	>O	-	O	O	O	O	O	-	O	O	O	-	O	O	O	-	O	O	O	-	O	16	-	7
BAF (Brian) Smith	-	-	-	-	-	-	-	-	-	-	-	-	-	>M	-	-	-	-	-	-	-	-	-	-	-	-	-	-	-	-	-	-	-	-	-	-	-	-	-	-	1	-	-
RH (Ron) Smith	-	-	-	-	-	E	E	E	E	E	E	E	D	D	-	D	D	D	-	D	D	E	D	G	G	D	-	G	G	G	E	E	D	E	E	E	D	D	D	D	32	1	3
J (John) Stevens	-	-	-	-	-	-	-	-	-	-	-	-	-	-	-	-	-	-	-	>B	B	B	B	B	B	B	-	B	B	B	B	B	B	B	B	B	B	B	B	B	20	1	3
IGH Stewart	>B	B	-	-	-	-	-	-	-	-	-	-	-	<B	-	-	-	-	-	-	-	-	-	-	-	-	-	-	-	-	-	-	-	-	-	-	-	-	-	-	3	-	-
LW (Len) Swanwick	-	-	-	-	-	-	-	-	-	-	-	>B	<B	-	-	-	-	-	-	-	-	-	-	-	-	-	-	-	-	-	-	-	-	-	-	-	-	-	-	-	2	-	-
FB (Brian) Symons	-	-	-	-	-	-	-	-	-	-	-	-	-	-	>L	M	L	M	-	M	-	-	-	-	-	-	-	-	-	-	-	-	-	-	-	-	-	-	-	-	5	3	9
JE (John) Taylor	>M	M	M	M	M	M	N	-	M	-	-	L	M	-	M	N	M	N	M	-	N	N	M	N	N	N	N	N	N	-	-	M	K	N	-	K	N	N	K	M	32	10	30
JS (John) Thompson	-	-	-	-	-	-	-	-	-	-	-	-	-	-	-	-	-	-	-	-	-	-	-	-	-	-	>E	-	-	-	-	-	-	-	-	-	-	-	-	-	1	-	-
PBL (Peter) Thorneloe	C	-	C	C	C	C	-	-	-	A	-	C	F	F	C	A	A	-	A	-	C	C	A	A	A	F	A	A	C	-	A	-	-	-	A	A	-	-	-	A	26	2	6

The key for how to read the stats is on the last page

1955/56

Home Ground: Welford Road	OVERALL RECORD:					T	C	PG	DG	PTS
Captain: John Elders	PLD	W	D	L	Tigers scored:	68	31	30	7	377
	41	17	2	22	Opponents scored:	82	28	23	9	398

GM	DATE		VEN	OPPONENTS	RESULT	TRIES	KICKS	ATT
CLUB MATCHES								
1	Sep	**3**	**H**	**Bedford**	L 11-20	T.O'Connor	Cullen c/p, Channer p	1250
2		**10**	**H**	**Bath**	W 24-11	Channer(2), Cullen, Ashurst, Elders	Channer c/d, Cullen 2c	690
3		**17**	**H**	**Plymouth Albion**	W 23-6	Cullen, Ashurst, Elders, Hazell, Taylor	Cullen 4c	876
4		**19m**	**H**	**Cardiff**	W 6-3	Cullen	Channer p	2798
5		24	a	Harlequins	L 6-10	Cullen	Cullen p	-
6	Oct	**1**	**H**	**Coventry**	L 8-11	Chawner	Hazell p, Channer c	1979
7		**5w**	**H**	**Loughborough College**	W 11-6	Ashurst, Hunt	Hazell c/p	197
8		**8**	**H**	**Cheltenham**	W 25-3	Channer, Bleasdale, Jenkins, McCormack	Channer d, Cullen 2c/2p	859
9		**15**	**H**	**Moseley**	W 16-3	Cullen(2), Elders	Cullen 2c/p	782
10		**19w**	**H**	**Oxford University**	L 3-6	-	Shephard p	318
11		22	a	Northampton	L 10-19	J.O'Connor, Thorneloe	Hazell 2c	-
12		**29**	**H**	**Old Blues**	W 8-0	Elders(2)	Cullen c	605
13		**31m**	**H**	**Bective Rangers**	L 6-9	-	Channer d, Cullen p	389
14	Nov	5	a	Gloucester	L 11-22	Bleasdale, Elders	Cullen c/p	-
15		**12**	**H**	**Cambridge University**	L 14-21	Elders, McCormack	Cullen c/2p	1426
16		19	a	Nuneaton	L 6-9	Lewis	Channer p	-
17		26	a	Moseley	W 13-9	Cullen, Marshall	Cullen 2c/p	-
18	Dec	3	a	Waterloo	L 6-13	Matthews	Channer p	-
19		**10**	**H**	**Blackheath**	W 6-3	Cullen	Channer d	626
20		**17**	**H**	**Bristol**	L 8-16	Ford	Channer c/p	404
21		24	a	Bedford	D 0-0	-	-	-
22		**26m**	**H**	**Birkenhead Park**	W 17-5	Hazell, Bleasdale, Brook, Matthews, Wade	Hazell c	1235
23		**27tu**	**H**	**Barbarians**	L 3-12	Konig	-	15000
24		31	a	Headingley	W 8-5	Cullen, Ashurst	Cullen c	-
25	Jan	2m	a	Northern	W 11-8	Cullen, Chawner, McCormack	Cullen c	-
26		7	a	Bath	L 0-11	-	-	-
27		**14**	**H**	**Gloucester**	W 9-5	-	Hazell 2p, Small d	607
28		**21**	**H**	**Rugby**	L 0-3	-	-	347
29		28	a	Rosslyn Park	L 0-6	-	-	-
	Feb	**2th**	**H**	**Royal Air Force**	PP			
		4	**H**	**London Scottish**	PP (frost)			
30		11	a	Newport	L 3-10	-	Hazell d	-
		18	**H**	**Wasps**	PP (frost)			
		25	**H**	**Northampton**	PP (frost)			
31	Mar	**3**	**H**	**Harlequins**	L 14-15	Lubbock	Hazell c/3p	908
32		10	a	Coventry	L 0-3	-	-	-
33		**17**	**H**	**Swansea**	D 9-9	Lubbock, Thorneloe	Hazell p	650
34		**24**	**H**	**Loughborough College**	W 6-5	Chawner, Matthews	-	391
35		31	a	Bristol	L 0-14	-	-	-
36	Apr	2m	a	Plymouth Albion	W 11-9	Hazell, Brook	Hazell c/p	-
37		3tu	a	Exeter	W 23-12	Cullen, Hazell, Bleasdale, Elders, Konig	Cullen p, Hazell p, Small c	-
38		7	a	Birkenhead Park	W 8-6	Elders	Wade d, Hazell c	-
39		14	a	Llanelly	L 20-24	Brook, Chawner, T.O'Connor, Thorneloe, Wade	Small c/p	-
40		21	a	Cardiff	L 5-20	Matthews	Hazell c	-
41		**23m**	**H**	**Northampton**	L 9-16	Thompson	Hazell 2p	1628

INDIVIDUAL APPEARANCES 1955/56

Name / Game #	1	2	3	4	5	6	7	8	9	10	11	12	13	14	15	16	17	18	19	20	21	22	23	24	25	26	27	28	29	30	31	32	33	34	35	36	37	38	39	40	41	Apps	T	Pts
ADB (Derek) Ashurst	F	F	F	F	F	H	F	-	-	F	-	-	-	-	F	F	F	F	F	F	F	F	F	F	F	F	-	-	-	F	F	H	H	H	H	-	-	F	H	-	-	28	4	12
G Bates	-	-	-	-	-	-	-	-	-	-	-	-	-	-	-	-	-	-	-	-	-	-	-	-	-	-	-	-	=B	-	-	-	-	-	-	-	-	-	-	-	-	1	-	-
DE (Derek) Bircumshaw	-	-	-	-	-	-	-	-	-	-	-	-	-	-	-	G	-	-	-	-	-	-	-	-	-	-	-	-	G	-	-	-	-	-	-	-	-	-	-	-	-	2	-	-
T (Tom) Bleasdale	G	G	-	G	G	-	-	G	F	-	G	-	F	F	G	-	-	-	G	G	G	G	G	-	-	-	-	F	-	G	-	-	-	-	-	-	G	-	-	G	H	20	4	12
D (David) Brook	N	N	M	M	M	M	J	L	K	J	J	J	N	M	N	M	N	N	M	N	-	N	-	N	N	N	N	N	N	J	J	L	N	N	N	M	N	N	N	L	N	39	3	9
MR (Mel) Channer	J	J	J	J	J	J	-	J	J	-	-	-	J	-	J	J*	J	J	J*	J	J	-	<N*	-	-	-	-	-	-	-	-	-	-	-	-	-	-	-	-	-	-	17	3	42
F (Frank) Chawner	C	C	-	C	C	C	C	C	C	C	C	C	C	C	C	-	C	C	C	C	C	-	C	C	C	C	C	C	-	C	C	C	C	C	C	C	C	C	C	C	C	37	4	12
WR (Roger) Coley	-	-	-	-	-	-	-	-	-	=K	-	-	-	-	-	-	-	-	-	-	-	-	-	-	-	-	-	-	-	-	-	-	-	-	-	-	-	-	-	-	-	1	-	-
GH (George) Cullen	K	K	K	K	K	-	-	K	L	-	-	K	K	K	K	-	K	-	K	-	N	-	K	K	L	-	-	K	-	K	K	-	-	-	K	K	K	K	-	-	-	24	11	102
HD (Hugh) Doherty	-	>B	B	-	-	B	-	-	-	-	-	-	-	-	-	<B	-	-	-	-	-	-	-	-	-	-	-	-	-	-	-	-	-	-	-	-	-	-	-	-	-	4	-	-
FR (Freddy) Doore	-	-	-	-	-	-	-	-	-	-	-	-	-	-	-	-	-	-	-	-	-	I	I	-	-	-	-	-	-	-	-	-	-	-	-	-	-	-	-	-	-	2	-	-
J (John) Elders	M*	M*	L*	L*	L*	L*	M*	M*	M*	M*	M*	L*	L*	L*	L*	-	L*	L*	-	M*	L*	-	-	L*	-	-	M*	M*	-	M*	M*	M*	M*	M*	M*	L*	M*	M*	M*	M*	M*	34	9	27
CA (Tony) Flower	-	-	-	-	-	-	-	-	-	-	-	-	-	-	-	>D	-	-	-	-	-	-	-	-	-	-	-	-	<E	-	-	-	-	-	-	-	-	-	-	-	-	2	-	-
JG (Jim) Ford	-	-	E	-	-	-	D	E	E	E	E	E	E	E	E	-	E	E	E	E	E	-	E	E	E	E	-	E	-	E	E	E	E	E	E	E	-	-	-	-	-	27	1	3
ME (Mike) Freer	-	-	-	-	-	-	-	-	-	-	-	-	-	-	-	-	-	-	-	-	-	-	-	-	-	-	-	>J	-	-	-	-	-	J	J	J	J	J	J	-	J	8	-	-
D (Dennis) Haines	-	-	-	-	-	-	-	-	-	-	-	-	-	-	-	-	-	-	-	-	-	J	J	J	J	J	J	-	J	-	-	J	J	-	L	-	-	-	-	J	-	11	-	-
I (Ivor) Harris	-	-	-	-	-	-	-	-	-	-	-	-	-	-	-	-	-	-	-	-	-	-	-	-	-	-	-	-	>K	-	N	<K	-	-	-	-	-	-	-	-	-	3	-	-
DSG (David) Hazell E4	-	-	A	A	A	A	A	A	A	-	A	A	A	-	-	-	-	A	A	-	A	A	A	-	-	-	A	-	-	A	A	A	A	A	-	A	A	A	-	A	<A	26	4	67
J (John) Horn	-	-	-	-	-	-	-	-	-	-	-	-	-	-	-	-	-	-	-	>L	K	L	M	M	M	-	L	L	L	-	-	-	-	-	-	-	-	-	-	-	-	9	-	-
PB (Pat) Hunt	-	-	-	-	-	-	>K	-	-	N	-	-	-	-	-	-	-	-	-	-	-	-	-	-	-	-	-	-	-	-	-	-	-	-	-	-	-	-	-	-	-	2	1	3
JM (John) Jenkins	E	E	G	E	E	E	G	F	G	G	-	D	<D	-	-	-	-	-	-	-	-	-	-	-	-	-	-	-	-	-	-	-	-	-	-	-	-	-	-	-	-	12	1	3
PH (Peter) Konig	-	-	H	H	-	-	-	-	-	-	-	-	-	-	-	-	-	H	H	H	H	H	H	H	-	H	F	H	-	H	H	F	G	F	F	F	F	H	F	H	F	24	2	6
BA (Brian) Lewis	-	-	-	-	-	-	-	-	-	-	-	-	-	-	-	>L	M	M	-	-	-	-	-	-	-	-	-	-	M	N	L	N	-	L	-	-	-	-	-	-	-	8	1	3
MGS (Mike) Lubbock	-	-	-	-	-	-	-	>I	-	I	I	I	-	I	I	I	I	I	I	I	I	-	-	I	-	I	I	I	-	I	I	I	I	-	I	-	-	-	-	I	I	23	2	6
JT (John) McCormack	-	-	-	-	-	-	H	H	H	H	H	H	H	H	H	H	H	-	-	-	-	-	-	-	H	-	H	-	F	-	-	-	-	-	-	H	H	G	G	F	-	19	3	9
R (Rae) Marshall	-	-	-	-	-	-	-	-	-	-	-	-	-	-	-	O	O	-	-	-	-	-	-	-	-	-	-	-	O	-	-	-	-	-	-	-	-	-	-	-	-	3	1	3
RD (Bob) Matthews	-	-	-	-	-	-	-	-	-	-	K	N	-	N	-	K	-	K	N	K	-	K	-	-	K	K	K	-	-	-	-	-	K	K	-	N	-	-	K	K	K	17	4	12
DJ (David) Matthews	>H	H	-	-	H	F	-	-	-	-	-	-	-	-	-	-	-	-	-	-	-	-	-	-	-	-	-	-	-	-	-	-	-	-	-	-	-	-	-	-	-	4	-	-
J (John) O'Connor	-	-	-	-	>N	N	N	-	-	-	<N	-	-	-	-	-	-	-	-	-	-	-	-	-	-	-	-	-	-	-	-	-	-	-	-	-	-	-	-	-	-	4	1	3
T (Tom) O'Connor	I	I	I	I	I	I	I	-	I	-	-	-	I	-	-	-	-	-	-	-	-	-	-	-	I	-	-	-	I	-	-	-	-	I	-	I	I	I	<I	-	-	16	2	6
HG (Harry) Powley	-	-	-	-	-	-	-	-	-	-	-	-	-	-	-	-	-	-	-	-	-	-	-	-	-	-	-	-	>H	-	-	-	-	-	-	-	-	-	-	-	-	1	-	-
CD (Cliff) Shephard	-	-	-	-	-	>K	L	N	N	L	L	M	M	J	M	N	-	-	L	-	-	-	-	-	-	M	-	-	-	-	-	-	-	-	-	-	-	-	-	N	-	14	-	3
RP (Rex) Skelton	-	-	-	-	-	-	-	-	-	-	-	-	-	-	-	-	-	-	-	-	-	-	-	-	-	-	-	-	>A	-	-	-	-	-	-	-	-	-	-	-	-	1	-	-
BTC (Brian) Small	O	O	O	O	O	O	O	O	O	O	O	O	O	O	O	-	-	O	O	O	O	O	O	O	O	O	O	O	-	O	O	O	O	O	O	O	O	O	O	O	O	38	-	10
BAF (Brian) Smith	L	L	-	-	-	-	-	-	-	-	-	-	-	-	-	-	-	-	-	-	-	-	-	-	-	L	-	-	-	-	-	-	-	-	-	-	-	-	-	-	-	3	-	-
RH (Ron) Smith	D	D	D	D	D	D	E	D	D	D	D	-	-	D	D	-	D	D	D	D	D	D	D	D	D	D	D	D	-	D	D	D	D	D	D	D	D	D	D	D	D	37	-	-
J (John) Stevens	B	-	-	B	B	-	B	B	B	B	B	B	B	B	B	-	B	B	B	B	B	B	B	B	B	B	B	B	-	B	B	B	B	B	B	B	B	B	B	B	B	36	-	-
JE (John) Taylor	-	-	N	N	-	-	-	-	-	-	-	-	-	-	-	-	-	-	-	-	-	-	-	-	-	-	-	-	-	-	-	-	-	-	-	-	-	-	-	-	-	2	1	3
JS (John) Thompson	-	-	-	-	-	-	-	-	-	-	-	G	G	G	-	E	G	G	-	-	-	E	-	G	G	G	E	G	D	-	-	-	-	-	A	-	E	E	E	E	E	19	1	3
PBL (Peter) Thorneloe	A	A	C	-	-	G	-	-	-	A	F	F	-	A	A	C	A	-	-	A	-	C	-	A	A	A	G	A	C	-	G	G	G	G	G	G	-	-	A	-	G	27	3	9
A Toone	-	-	-	-	-	-	-	-	-	-	-	-	-	-	-	=A	-	-	-	-	-	-	-	-	-	-	-	-	-	-	-	-	-	-	-	-	-	-	-	-	-	1	-	-
MR (Mike) Wade E+	-	-	-	-	-	-	-	-	-	-	-	-	-	-	-	-	-	-	-	-	>M	M	L	-	-	-	-	-	-	L	-	-	L	-	-	-	L	L	L	-	L	9	2	9

The key for how to read the stats is on the last page

1956/57

Home Ground: Welford Road	OVERALL RECORD:					T	C	PG	DG	MK	PTS
Captain: Tom Bleasdale	PLD	W	D	L	Tigers scored:	77	38	25	1	0	385
	43	18	6	19	Opponents scored:	79	31	34	5	1	419

GM	DATE		VEN	OPPONENTS	RESULT	TRIES	KICKS	ATT
CLUB MATCHES								
1	Sep	1	H	**Bedford**	L 8-11	B.Smith(2)	Small c	714
2		8	H	**Romania**	D 6-6	-	Ashurst 2p	3165
3		15	H	**Plymouth Albion**	W 18-0	Chawner, B.Matthews, B.Smith	Ashurst 3c, Baker d	587
4		17m	H	**Cardiff**	L 9-18	Brook, Elders	Ashurst p	1885
5		22	a	Harlequins	L 11-34	B.Smith(3)	Small c	-
6		29	a	Newport	L 3-22	-	Martin p	-
7	Oct	6	a	Coventry	L 13-17	Brook, Skelton	Martin 2c/p	-
8		13	H	**Richmond**	W 19-8	Baker(2), Thorneloe	Martin 2c/2p	980
9		20	a	Cheltenham	L 0-3	-	-	-
10		24w	a	Oxford University	L 0-9	-	-	-
11		27	H	**Northampton**	D 9-9	Baker, Rawson	Martin p	1452
12	Nov	3	H	**Gloucester**	W 14-8	Baker, Konig, Rawson, Skelton	Martin c	708
13		10	H	**Cambridge University**	D 3-3	-	Martin p	1273
14		17	a	Lansdowne	L 16-17	Elders, Wade, Walker	Martin 2c/p	-
15		18s	a	Old Belvedere	L 3-23	-	Martin p	-
16		24	H	**Old Blues**	W 11-8	Elders, Konig, Wade	Martin c	-
17	Dec	1	H	**Waterloo**	L 3-11	Baker	-	-
18		8	a	Blackheath	W 8-6	Baker, Konig	Martin c	-
19		15	H	**Bristol**	L 6-11	-	Elders p, Martin p	-
20		22	a	Rugby	D 11-11	Rawson, Bleasdale, Lewis	Rawson c	-
21		26w	H	**Birkenhead Park**	W 3-0	Rawson	-	1158
22		27th	H	**Barbarians**	L 6-23	-	Martin 2p	10000
23		29	H	**Headingley**	L 0-3	-	-	887
24	Jan	5	a	Bath	D 3-3	Ford	-	-
25		12	a	Gloucester	W 6-0	Horn, Rawson	-	-
26		19	a	Bedford	D 3-3	-	Martin p	-
27		26	H	**Rosslyn Park**	W 8-0	Baker, Chawner	Martin c	500
28		31th	H	**Royal Air Force**	L 8-18	Shephard	Martin c/p	219
29	Feb	2	a	London Scottish	L 5-23	Baker	Gavins c	-
30		9	H	**Newport**	W 13-3	Bleasdale, Elders, Konig	Martin 2c	1259
31		16	H	**British Police**	W 16-8	Konig(2), Bleasdale, Rawson	Martin 2c	858
32		23	a	Northampton	W 13-6	Rawson(2), Thompson	Martin 2c	-
33	Mar	2	H	**Harlequins**	W 8-3	Bleasdale(2)	Martin c	1980
34		9	H	**Coventry**	W 10-3	Rawson, Wade	Martin 2c	1150
35		14th	H	**Loughborough College**	W 8-6	Bircumshaw	Elders p, Small c	193
36		16	a	Swansea	L 6-11	Chawner	Martin p	-
37		23	H	**Nuneaton**	W 12-8	Elders	Martin 3p	587
38		30	H	**Sale**	W 25-11	Martin, Elders, Rawson, B.Smith, Wade	Martin 2c/2p	877
39	Apr	6	a	Birkenhead Park	L 8-13	Gavins, Konig	Gavins c	-
40		13	H	**Llanelly**	W 19-3	Rawson(2), Bleasdale, Chawner	Cullen 2c, Elders p	1382
41		20	a	Bristol	L 8-11	Lubbock, B.Smith	Martin c	-
42		22m	a	Plymouth Albion	W 16-11	Bleasdale, Cullen, Elders, B.Smith	Gavins 2c	-
43		23tu	a	Exeter	L 10-14	Elders, Shephard	Martin 2c	-

INDIVIDUAL APPEARANCES 1956/57

Name / Game #	1	2	3	4	5	6	7	8	9	10	11	12	13	14	15	16	17	18	19	20	21	22	23	24	25	26	27	28	29	30	31	32	33	34	35	36	37	38	39	40	41	42	43	Apps	T	Pts
ADB (Derek) Ashurst	-	H	H	H	F	F	-	-	-	-	-	-	-	-	-	-	-	-	-	-	-	-	-	-	-	-	-	-	-	-	-	-	-	-	-	-	-	-	-	-	-	-	-	5	-	15
PT (Peter) Baker	-	N	N	-	N	M	-	N	N	-	N	N	N	N	N	N	N	N	-	-	-	N	N	N	N	N	N	-	K	N	N	N	-	N	-	-	<N	-	-	-	-	-	-	26	8	27
DE (Derek) Bircumshaw	-	-	-	-	-	-	-	-	G	-	-	-	-	-	-	-	-	-	-	-	-	-	-	-	-	-	-	C	C	-	-	-	-	-	C	-	D	-	<C	-	-	-	-	6	1	3
T (Tom) Bleasdale	-	-	-	-	-	-	-	-	-	-	-	G*	G*	G*	G*	G*	G*	G*	G*	G*	G*	G*	G*	G*	G*	G*	G*	G*	G*	G*	G*	G*	G*	G*	G*	G*	G*	G*	G*	G*	G*	G*	D*	32	7	21
D (David) Brook	N	-	-	N	-	N	K	-	-	K	-	-	-	-	K	-	-	-	-	-	N	-	<L	-	-	-	-	-	-	-	-	-	-	-	-	-	-	-	-	-	-	-	-	8	2	6
RD (Dave) Brookhouse	-	-	-	-	-	-	-	-	-	-	-	-	-	-	-	-	-	-	-	-	-	-	-	-	-	-	-	-	<B	-	-	-	-	-	-	-	-	-	-	-	-	-	-	1	-	-
F (Frank) Chawner	C	C	C	C	A	C	C	C	-	A	C	C	C	A	A	C	C	A	C	A	C	C	C	A	A	-	C	-	-	C	C	A	C	C	A	C	C	C	A	C	A	C	C	39	4	12
M (Mike) Crane	-	-	-	-	-	>I	-	-	-	-	-	-	-	-	-	-	-	-	-	-	-	-	-	-	-	-	-	-	-	-	-	<I	-	-	-	-	-	-	-	-	-	-	-	2	-	-
GH (George) Cullen	-	-	-	-	-	-	-	-	-	-	-	-	-	-	-	-	-	-	-	-	-	-	-	-	-	-	-	-	-	-	-	-	L	-	-	N	-	-	-	L	L	L	<L	6	1	7
FR (Freddy) Doore	-	-	I	I	I	-	I	I	I	I	I	I	I	I	I	I	I	I	I	I	-	-	-	-	-	-	-	-	I	-	-	-	-	I	-	-	-	-	-	-	-	-	<I	20	-	-
J (John) Elders	M*	M*	M*	M*	M*	L*	M*	M*	-	M*	M*	M	M	M	L	M	-	M	M	M	M	M	-	M	L	-	M	-	-	M	M	M	M	M	M	M	M	M	M	M	M	M	M	37	8	33
JG (Jim) Ford	E	E	E	E	E	D	E	D	-	-	D	D	D	D	D	D	D	D	D	D	D	D	D	D	D	D	D	-	-	D	D	D	D	D	D	D	-	D	D	D	D	D	-	37	1	3
ME (Mike) Freer	J	J	J	J	J	J	-	-	J	-	J	J	J	J	J	J	J	J	J	J	J	J	J	J	J	J	J	J	J	J	J	J	J	J	J	J	J	J	J	J	J	J	J	40	-	-
MN (Mike) Gavins E+	-	-	-	-	-	-	-	-	-	-	-	-	-	-	-	-	-	-	-	-	-	-	-	-	-	-	-	>O	O	-	-	-	-	-	-	-	-	O	O	-	O	O	-	6	1	11
BI (Bryan) Hailes	-	-	-	-	-	-	-	-	-	-	-	-	-	-	-	-	-	-	-	-	-	-	-	-	-	-	-	>D	<D	-	-	-	-	-	-	-	-	-	-	-	-	-	-	2	-	-
D (Dennis) Haines	-	-	-	-	-	-	J	J	-	-	-	-	-	-	-	-	-	-	-	-	-	-	-	-	-	-	-	-	-	-	-	-	-	-	-	-	-	-	-	-	-	-	-	2	-	-
J (John) Horn	-	-	-	-	-	-	-	-	-	-	-	-	-	-	-	-	-	-	-	-	-	-	-	-	M	L	L	M	<M	-	-	-	-	-	-	-	-	-	-	-	-	-	-	5	1	3
TW (Tom) Hoskins	-	-	-	-	-	-	-	-	-	-	-	-	-	-	-	-	-	-	-	-	-	-	-	-	-	-	-	-	-	-	-	-	-	-	-	-	-	-	-	-	-	-	=B	1	-	-
PB (Pat) Hunt	-	-	-	-	-	-	-	-	K	-	-	-	-	-	-	-	-	-	-	-	-	-	-	-	-	-	-	-	-	-	-	-	-	-	-	-	-	-	-	-	-	-	-	1	-	-
HG (Harry) Jessop	-	-	-	-	-	-	-	-	-	-	-	-	-	-	-	-	-	-	-	-	-	-	-	-	-	-	-	-	-	-	-	-	-	-	-	-	-	-	-	-	-	-	>K	1	-	-
PH (Peter) Konig	F	F	F	F	H	-	F	F	F	H	F	F	F	H	H	F	F	H	F	H	F	F	F	H	H	H	F	F	F	F	F	H	F	F	H	H	F	F	H	F	H	-	-	40	7	21
BA (Brian) Lewis	-	-	-	-	-	-	-	-	-	-	-	-	-	-	-	-	M	-	N	N	L	-	M	-	-	-	-	K	-	-	-	-	-	-	<L	-	-	-	-	-	-	-	-	7	1	3
MGS (Mike) Lubbock	I	I	-	-	-	-	-	-	-	-	-	-	-	-	-	-	-	-	-	-	I	I	I	I	I	I	I	I	-	I	I	-	I	-	I	I	I	I	I	I	I	I	-	21	1	3
JT (John) McCormack	G	G	G	G	G	-	-	-	-	-	-	-	-	-	-	-	-	-	-	F	-	-	-	-	-	-	-	-	H	-	-	-	-	-	F	-	-	-	F	H	-	H	<F	12	-	-
R (Rae) Marshall	-	-	-	-	-	-	-	-	O	-	-	-	-	-	-	-	-	-	-	-	-	-	-	-	-	-	-	-	-	-	-	-	-	-	-	-	-	-	-	<O	-	-	-	2	-	-
CG (Colin) Martin	-	-	-	-	-	>G	G	G	-	G	G	H	H	F	F	H	-	F	H	-	H	H	H	-	F	F	H	H	-	H	H	F	H	H	-	F	H	H	-	-	F	-	H	29	1	110
RD (Bob) Matthews	K	K	K	K	K	<K	-	-	-	-	-	-	-	-	-	-	-	-	-	-	-	-	-	-	-	-	-	-	-	-	-	-	-	-	-	-	-	-	-	-	-	-	-	6	1	3
DJ (David) Matthews	H	-	-	-	-	H	-	-	H	-	-	-	-	-	-	-	-	-	-	-	-	-	-	-	-	-	-	-	-	-	-	-	-	-	-	-	-	-	-	-	-	F	G	5	-	-
K (Ken) Milne	-	-	-	-	-	-	-	-	-	-	=A	-	-	-	-	-	-	-	-	-	-	-	-	-	-	-	-	-	-	-	-	-	-	-	-	-	-	-	-	-	-	-	-	1	-	-
HG (Harry) Powley	-	-	-	-	-	-	-	-	D	<D	-	-	-	-	-	-	-	-	-	-	-	-	-	-	-	-	-	-	-	-	-	-	-	-	-	-	-	-	-	-	-	-	-	2	-	-
RO (Dick) Rawson	-	-	-	-	-	-	-	>K	-	N	K	K	K	K	-	K	K	K	K	K	K	K	K	K	K	K	K	-	-	K	K	K	K	K	K	K	K	K	K	K	K	-	-	30	12	38
GT (George) Reay	-	-	-	-	-	-	-	-	>M	<J	-	-	-	-	-	-	-	-	-	-	-	-	-	-	-	-	-	-	-	-	-	-	-	-	-	-	-	-	-	-	-	-	-	2	-	-
CD (Cliff) Shephard	-	-	-	-	-	-	-	-	-	-	-	-	-	-	-	-	-	-	-	-	-	-	-	-	-	-	-	N	N	-	-	L	N	-	N	-	-	-	-	-	-	K	N	7	2	6
RP (Rex) Skelton	A	-	-	-	-	A	A	A	A	C	-	A	A	C	-	A	A	C	A	C	A	A	A	C	C	C	A	A	-	-	-	-	-	-	-	-	-	-	-	-	-	-	-	22	2	6
BTC (Brian) Small	O	O	O	O	O	O	O	O	-	O	O	O	O	O	O	O	O	O	O	O	O	O	O	O	O	O	O	-	-	O	O	O	O	O	O	O	O	-	-	-	-	-	O	35	-	6
BAF (Brian) Smith	L	L	L	L	L	-	N	-	-	-	-	-	L	-	-	-	-	-	-	-	-	-	-	-	-	-	-	-	-	-	-	-	-	-	-	-	-	N	N	N	N	N	-	12	9	27
RH (Ron) Smith	-	D	D	D	D	-	-	-	-	-	-	-	-	-	-	-	-	-	-	-	-	-	-	-	-	-	-	-	-	-	-	-	-	-	-	-	-	-	-	-	-	-	-	4	-	-
J (John) Stevens	B	B	B	B	B	B	B	B	-	-	-	-	-	-	B	-	-	-	-	-	-	-	-	-	-	-	-	<B	-	-	-	-	-	-	-	-	-	-	-	-	-	-	-	10	-	-
JS (John) Thompson	D	A	A	A	C	E	D	E	E	E	E	E	E	E	E	E	E	E	E	E	E	E	E	E	E	E	E	E	E	E	E	E	E	E	E	E	E	E	E	E	E	E	E	43	1	3
PBL (Peter) Thorneloe	-	-	-	-	-	-	H	H	C*	F	H	-	-	-	C	-	H	-	-	-	-	-	-	F	-	A	-	-	A	A	A	C	A	A	-	A	A	A	-	A	C	A	A	22	1	3
MR (Mike) Wade E+	-	-	-	-	-	-	L	L	L	L	L	L	-	L	M	L	L	L	L	L	-	L	-	L	-	M	-	L	L	L	L	-	-	L	-	L	L	L	L	-	-	-	-	25	4	12
MR (Mike) Walker	-	-	-	-	-	-	-	-	>B	B	B	B	B	B	-	B	B	B	B	B	B	B	B	B	B	B	B	-	-	B	B	B	B	B	B	B	B	B	B	B	B	B	-	31	1	3

The key for how to read the stats is on the last page

CHAPTER 14

Looking to the Future

1957/1958

The effect of the steps taken in 1957 was to change Leicester from a club hanging on grimly to memories of the years between the two world wars to an organisation with a bright future and new traditions to establish. If any one man could be said to have moulded that future in a very definite way it was probably the 24-year-old New Zealander, Colin Martin, whose influence on the club in the 1960s was of paramount importance.

A graduate in engineering, he played in A grade rugby in Auckland and for the New Zealand Universities. But it looked as though a promising career was to be nipped in the bud when he suffered severe back injuries following an accident when the car in which he was travelling was hit by a train on a level crossing. He recovered to join the Shell Oil Company, who promptly dispatched him to Holland where he watched sufficient rugby to encourage him to take up the game once more.

With no ill effects and deciding that drilling for oil in Indonesia or Kuwait was unlikely to provide a boost to his rugby career, he came to England to seek a job, on a temporary basis, arriving in Leicester to work with English Electric at Whetstone. "My first visit to Tigers was on a summery Thursday evening in July," recalled Martin. "I remember being overawed by the size of the ground and the stands, reminiscent of provincial grounds in New Zealand.

"Training commenced with a wild game of soccer and was dominated by a strapping 17-stone speedster, later to be identified as Tom Bleasdale. After a few beers in the bar I started to understand the organisation and realised I may well be out of my depth, having not played serious rugby for nearly two years." Martin was advised to join Westleigh and played several games for that club before receiving an invitation to play for Leicester, whose organisation and fixture list, he found, closely resembled that of a New Zealand provincial side.

"My first impression of playing with Leicester was that, in spite of vigorous individual training, we had little team training, simply because less than half the team turned up for practice. My first game, against Newport, soon demonstrated that the Welsh clubs did not suffer from this weakness. We seemed to have many talented individuals to call on but frequently they were unable to play and often lived miles from Leicester. It was apparent, talking to many of the senior players, that this approach, while extremely successful in the past, was increasingly inadequate for the needs of the day."

↓ Ian Swan, the Scotland wing, made his debut in 1957 and became skipper in 1958/59.

The times, of course, were changing. Reviewing the situation before the 1957/58 season, the club found itself in debt by £1,766 and decided to imitate the county cricket club and raise funds via a football competition, guided by a well-known Leicester entertainer and sports enthusiast, Billy Butler, who had done so much for the cricket club. Ken Kinder, president of the club 20 years later, worked hard with him to get the scheme off the ground and it proved very successful.

Also successful was a meeting with local clubs in September to explain Leicester's plans on a revised team structure. At the same time it was agreed that the proposed Colts XV should be called the Swifts, enabling older players to be picked although the accent was to be on youth. With Barr now in office as club secretary, Jerry Day and Rodney Willcox became the new team secretaries. It was obvious there were going to be some rough edges to be smoothed over: accusations of poaching from junior clubs were made but this is hardly an uncommon feature in any day or age. There was the integration of the three teams and the worry about how much money would be needed. There was also the very real counter-attraction just across the road, for Leicester City were in the First Division of the Football League.

With this in mind Tigers welcomed with open arms a new recruit, Scottish international wing 'Ian' Swan, who joined from Coventry. John Spence Swan, then 26, had already won 16 of his 17 caps and had been with Coventry for two years before moving. With him came Derek Ashurst while Ron Smith returned from Northampton and a new scrum-half, Herbert Victor White, who had captained Camborne in 1957/58, took up a teaching appointment in Nottingham and joined Leicester. 'Chalkie' White was to have a certain amount of influence on his new club, too.

Swan made his debut in the 1957/58 season's first game, against Bedford, and a month later must have been highly delighted to run in two tries against Coventry, but it was sad that no place could be found for Cullen who, not surprisingly since he had lived and worked there for some time, gave his last season to Bedford. Players nowadays may complain of too much rugby but it was reported that Wade looked exhausted against Cheltenham: the youngster, then on national service, played against Richmond the previous Saturday, for his unit on the Wednesday, for the county the next day and then Tigers.

↓ Rex Skelton, supported by Cliff Shephard and Tom Bleasdale, takes on Harlequins 1.3.1958.

↑ Gordon Almey (on the left) in the thick of the action when Loughborough College visited Welford Road 13.3.1958.

The Extras, captained by John Taylor, won their first five games and scored over 100 points in the process but the senior XV found it difficult to field a settled back division. They were trying to play an open game but lacked cohesion, and their first away win did not come until the end of November, at Moseley. In the meantime the local press speculated during the November match against Old Blues, in the light of Leicester City's brand new floodlights, that maybe it was time for Tigers to make a similar investment. The Scottish lock and 1955 British Lion, Ernie Michie, found a place in the side in December - reminiscent of the good old, bad old days - but there was a depressing showing on 21 December when the touring Australians beat Leicestershire and East Midlands at Welford Road by 18-3.

The combined XV was Jim Hetherington (Northampton); Ian Swan, Mike Wade (both Leicester), Bob Leslie (Sale), John Hyde (Northampton); RG Smith (Northampton), LG Karseras (Loughborough Colleges); Ron Jacobs (Northampton), G Franklin (Bedford), Jon Fellows-Smith, CP Daniels (both Northampton), Tom Bleasdale (Leicester), David Hayward (Cardiff), Mal Tansey (Hinckley), Don White (Northampton, captain). Of the forwards, Bleasdale, Hayward and White distinguished themselves but the backs lacked punch and the game proved a triumph for the Australian full-back Jim Lenehan who scored two tries and three conversions. A further try came from Alan Morton while Ron Harvey kicked a penalty, the Midlanders' only reply coming from a penalty by White.

Over Christmas John Elders, on holiday in Leicester, played three games in three days for the club and back row forward Bob Small joined brother Brian in the team against Birkenhead Park. Also back in the side was David Matthews, following a two-year break with Stoneygate, but seven wins from 20 games in the first half of the season was hardly the stuff dreams are made of. To add to the depression as 1958 opened was the knowledge that the RAF were to claim Wade and wing Richard Rawson, while Scotland claimed Swan for his last cap, against France.

There was speculation in the new year that Ireland's Tony O'Reilly might join the club, since it was rumoured that he had been given a business appointment in the Midlands, but for the present, life for the senior side was decidedly hard. The halves and back row were unsettled, though the introduction of the dynamic Kibworth flanker, Gordon Almey, proved a successful step.

Loughborough Colleges gained their first win over the club by 6-3 in March, which had the effect on Leicester of bringing out their best the next day, against Swansea. The Welsh club went down 20-8, their first defeat in England of the season, and the hero was a Yorkshireman studying at Loughborough, Lyn Tatham, who scored a try and a dropped goal even though he was reduced to a passenger on the wing by injury.

The 1957/58 season ended on a high note, with the first hat-trick of victories on the Easter tour since the war. That included a 5-3 win over Bristol, then noted as one of the best sides in the country. Maurice Key, a full-back from East Anglia, gained plaudits for his general play while Elders was also back in circulation. For the second season in succession Thompson played every game, giving him 87 consecutive appearances.

Wade, who never played as many games for Leicester as the club might have liked because of national service, studies at Cambridge University, business commitments and injury, has vivid memories of Easter tours and all that led up to them. When working in the USA, he recalled his career with Leicester thus: "There was the tradition and pageant of the Barbarians game, starting with lunch at the Bell Hotel. The nervousness and awe of meeting the rugby legends in the Baa-baas party, the bus journey to Welford Road now totally consumed by nerves, the astonishment at the size and mood of the holiday crowd milling around outside the ground.

"The uplift from the crowd cheering the home team. Too busy now for nerves - trying like hell to get a few quick points on the board in order to be still in the game when the inevitable deluge of Barbarian attacks began in the second half. The utter exhaustion of the last 15 minutes, trying to stay on one's feet and trying to make one's legs move fast enough to make just one more tackle.

↓ Basketball was played at Welford Road with the Harlem Globetrotters' visit in the summer of 1958.

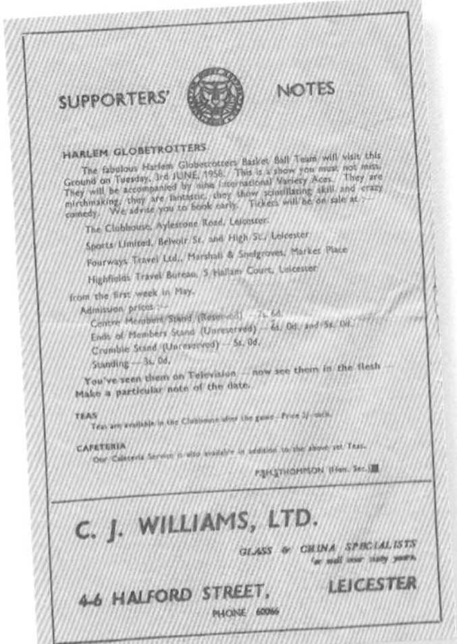

SUPPORTERS' NOTES

HARLEM GLOBETROTTERS

The fabulous Harlem Globetrotters Basket Ball Team will visit this Ground on Tuesday, 3rd JUNE, 1958. This is a show you must not miss. They will be accompanied by nine International Variety Aces. They are mirthmaking, they are fantastic, they show scintillating skill and crazy comedy. We advise you to book early. Tickets will be on sale at :—

The Clubhouse, Aylestone Road, Leicester.

Sports Limited, Belvoir St. and High St., Leicester

Fourways Travel Ltd., Marshall & Snelgroves, Market Place

Highfields Travel Bureau, 5 Hallam Court, Leicester

from the first week in May.

Admission prices :—

Centre Members Stand (Reserved) — 7s. 6d.

Ends of Members Stand (Unreserved) — 6s. 0d. and 5s. 0d.

Crumbie Stand (Unreserved) — 5s. 0d.

Standing — 3s. 0d.

You've seen them on Television — now see them in the flesh — Make a particular note of the date.

TEAS

CAFETERIA

C. J. WILLIAMS, LTD.

GLASS & CHINA SPECIALISTS

4-6 HALFORD STREET, LEICESTER

"The post-game celebrations...the reluctant move to the Sportsmen's Club or other institutions naive enough to agree to put on a rugby dinner...a prolonged dinner guaranteed to produce irate wives and girlfriends waiting impatiently to be summoned to the dance...the agony of the next day, not so bad as a student but horrendous later in one's career when it meant a return to work.

"The post Baa-baas let-down...enthusiasm picking up again rapidly after a few unexpected losses, especially if accompanied by a few demotions to the Extra Firsts...the slow build-up to the Easter Tour, zenith of the season...the relatively serious beginnings of the tour with the game against Bristol...the warm-up for the tour starting after the game in the Bristol clubhouse.

"Easter Sunday, determined to have a good time despite the seemingly serious efforts of the local populace to put a damper on proceedings by daring to observe a religious holiday. The Easter Monday morning trip to Plymouth...the almost equal mix of white and green faces on the bus...the dread of having to play before noon...the first half of the game taking place as if being played by bodies other than our own...the mocking exhortations of those team members lucky enough not to have to play.

"Half-time...suddenly compos mentis again, looking up at the scoreboard and finding that we are only 20 points down...the mad scramble in the second half to win the game despite the deficit...the realisation that we would have to do it playing up a slope which now seemed as steep as Everest...did we really win the toss and choose ends? Who the hell is captain today anyway?

"The festivities continue...a trip to the races, a few wins, many, many losses... Tuesday morning, the most disorganised muster ever for the trip to Exeter...a mountain of hotel guests' shoes in the foyer of the hotel, inextricably interlaced... the fear/panic on the faces of some of the guests, the utter contempt of the remainder, the obvious relief of the hotel staff at the prospect of our final departure. The trip to Exeter...a few half-hearted water-pistol battles and games of liar dice.

"Rejuvenated at lunch...a vague recollection of being pressed into service as a pro tem cleric to bless the food...a repeat performance of the contempt of the other hotel guests. The game over against Exeter and a hurried departure followed by the long trip home to Leicester. The bus disgorging its zombie-like passengers, complete with crumpled blazers and flannels into the Welford Road car park. Finally creeping into bed in the early morning. Is it still Easter? The end of the season arriving mercifully before the body is totally destroyed."

Many players of that era will have the same recollections of their Easter Tour, even if the venue was different. Certainly the West Country visit has a hallowed place in the memories of those players lucky enough to make it - possibly an equally hallowed place in the memories of those hotel managers unlucky enough to host it. But, many would say sadly, the Easter tour for a first-class club is over, another casualty of the competitive structure introduced during the 1980s and confirmed by the arrival of professionalism.

↑ England international Phil Horrocks-Taylor joined Tigers in 1958 and was selected for the Lions a year later.

1958/1959

Ian Swan was elected captain for the 1958/59 season, the first season for the Swifts XV. Leicester were making their intentions plain by running a three-week coaching course for promising schoolboys and local club players, under the guidance of Alastair Smallwood who had put so many Uppingham schoolboys on the right road and who was now president of the Leicestershire Schools Rugby Union. Doug Norman was president of the County RU so it could hardly be said that the club did not have friends in the right places, though obviously local clubs were able to benefit from the use of Leicester's experience and facilities.

There were several interesting newcomers, among them Leighton Jenkins who was capped five times by Wales in 1954 and 1956 as a number eight. He had played for Leicestershire in 1955 while at Loughborough and was now taking up a teaching appointment at Oakham. Another ex-Loughborough Colleges and Leicestershire debutant was the wing Harry Jessop, who could generally be distinguished on the field because he played in a scrum cap. Michael Gavins, a product of Leeds University and Loughborough, came into the side on a regular basis at full-back and among the younger elements to join were the former Wyggeston School prop John Bailey and the Lutterworth Grammar School centre Trevor Allen.

The first week of the season brought even better news when the rumour spread that Philip Horrocks-Taylor, capped by England twice the season before, was to join the club and that Tony O'Reilly would become a member in October. It is always nice to have internationals coming to a club, though the appearance of Horrocks-Taylor put even more pressure on the fly-half spot where Leicester already had Lyn Tatham, Mick Freer and another newcomer, Gordon Blackett from Newcastle.

In the event Tatham opted to play for Loughborough Colleges and, since Horrocks-Taylor was a Yorkshireman from Halifax, it was obvious that Leicester would not have his services during the county championship season. With Wade going up to Cambridge, there was also a gap in the centre, which offered a partial solution to the problem of too many fly-halves.

There was a new, and rather special, game at the season's start. It had been agreed the previous season that Leicester should play a XV raised by the former Welsh international Watcyn Thomas, in order to raise funds for the English Schools Rugby Union - the union had, after all, been founded in Leicester at the start of the century. The money was aimed at boosting 15 group rugby and the result of the first game, apart from bringing Leicester an 18-3 win, was £250 into the union's coffers. The fixture was to be maintained for 11 years, Leicester losing just twice to sides which frequently resembled Barbarian XVs in strength.

For the first time since the 1935/36 season, Leicester went through September undefeated, even if Coventry provided their comeuppance in Horrocks-Taylor's debut game. Later in October came O'Reilly's first game in Leicester's colours, against Northampton, and it is a matter of

↓ Chalkie White demonstrates the perfect dive pass against Cambridge University 8.11.1958.

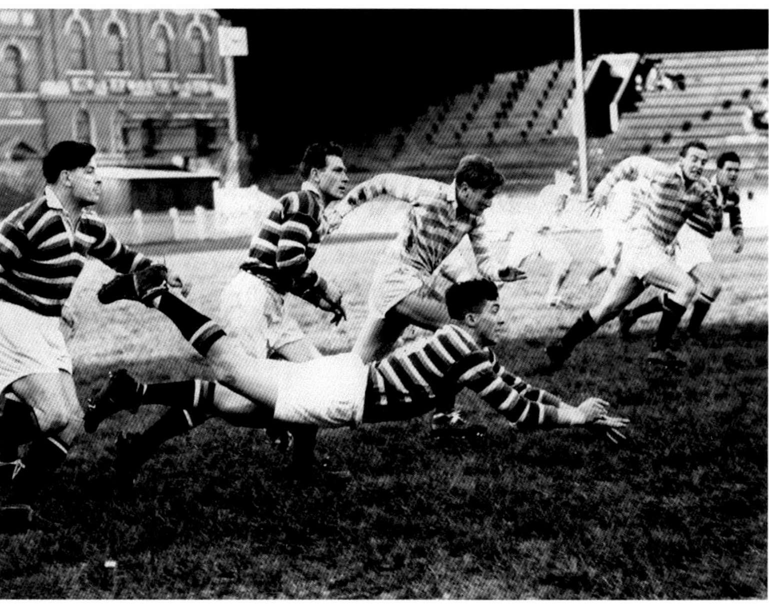

↑ TIGERS v BECTIVE RANGERS
15 November 1958
Back: Kelleher (referee), White, O'Reilly, Horrocks-Taylor, Thompson, Constable, Skelton, Matthews, Gavins, Bolesworth (Team Hon.Sec).
Middle: Freer, Walker, Swan (capt), Bleasdale, Chawner.
Front: Almey, Shephard.

record that that game too was lost, the Irishman conceding a penalty try. At that time O'Reilly, who first played at centre for Leicester, had made 17 appearances for Ireland as well as collecting rave reviews for his 1955 tour of South Africa with the Lions - and he was still only 22. His displays for the 1959 Lions in Australia and New Zealand confirmed his place in rugby legend, even had he not gone on to make a huge impact on the business world.

Certainly the club was not short of colour, even if they lost O'Reilly's services temporarily when touring in Ireland again, for in the second game the Irishman swapped sides to represent his former club, Old Belvedere. Not surprisingly gates were going up and there was talk that another international, Irish scrum-half Andy Mulligan, might be joining, though this was one rumour that proved groundless. That willing lock John Thompson established a club record for consecutive games of 103 and, away from Welford Road, Wade won his Blue for Cambridge on the wing and scored two tries in the Light Blues' 17-6 win over Oxford University.

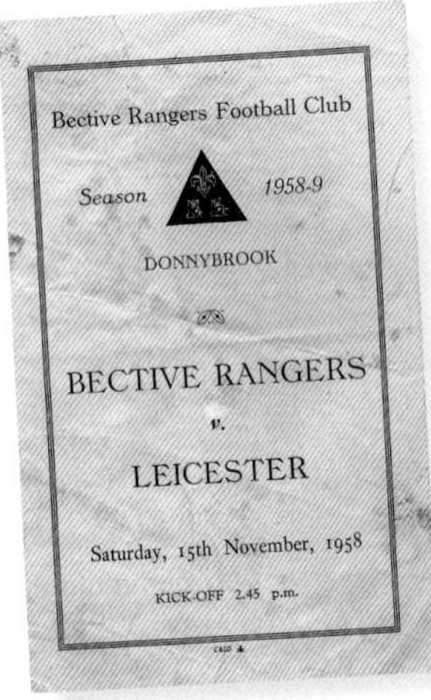
Bective Rangers Football Club
Season 1958-9
DONNYBROOK
BECTIVE RANGERS
v.
LEICESTER
Saturday, 15th November, 1958
KICK-OFF 2.45 p.m.

The 19-year-old former schools international Gordon Blackett made his debut in December against Bristol and though he was to appear comparatively few times for Leicester, he left an indelible impression on many of his contemporaries. Martin described him as one of the most talented uncapped players he had ever played with: "His touchline punting was almost unbelievable in accuracy and it is difficult to recall him dropping a pass. In fact it was Gordon who brought it home to me the positive influence of schoolboy soccer on English rugby players, particularly backs." Chalkie White was another immensely impressed with the ability of the young northerner.

Unfortunately several of the leading players were unavailable for the Barbarians game, played for a change on Boxing Day. O'Reilly had a broken shoulder bone, Horrocks-Taylor had influenza and Swan was absent but this did not prevent the Tigers collecting their first win since 1951. Matthews, wing Cliff Shephard and Jenkins scored the tries in a 9-3 win and Blackett was superb while the pack boasted an exceptionally mobile back five, with Martin and Bleasdale in the second row, Matthews, Jenkins and Almey in the back row.

Although he was injured, O'Reilly impressed many Leicester regulars with the work he was prepared to put in off the field, helping to bring fresh approaches in training and new attitudes towards the game in general. Lower down the line Ron Smith was doing an exceptionally valuable job in bringing on the Swifts. O'Reilly returned to score his first try for the club against London Scottish before the internationals claimed him and another comeback man was the retired Eric Lacey. Horrocks-Taylor failed to appear after being best man at a wedding in the morning when Wasps paid their first visit to Leicester so Almey moved out to the three-quarters and Lacey was called from his shop to play in the pack. Leicester won 22-0 against a side containing five caps.

It had not been an entirely successful season, one of the problems having been the availability - or otherwise - of leading players. The internationals from the four home countries, for instance, Swan, Horrocks-Taylor, O'Reilly and Jenkins, never played in a side together.

Another invitation to play in the Middlesex Sevens resulted in an entry to the Oxford Sevens, in order to prepare a reasonable squad. Leicester reached the semi-finals of the Oxford tournament, where they lost to Wasps, but at the Middlesex it was defeat in the second round, again at the hands of Wasps. In the first round White scored a try in the 3-0 win over Old Colfeians and repeated the effort in the 6-3 defeat by Wasps. The Leicester VII was: Ian Swan, Mike Wade, Phil Horrocks-Taylor, Chalkie White, David Matthews, Arthur Jones, Leighton Jenkins (Bleasdale played in the first round but was injured).

On the credit side Gavins established a post-war points record of 145, passing Cullen's 128 (1950/51) with 14 points from the 23-9 home win over Llanelly. It was eleven points short of Harold Day's haul in 1925/26 and nearly 100 short of Teddy Haselmere's club record.

And for the first time since the war, a current Leicester player was picked by the British Lions, even if Tigers could hardly claim too much of the credit for Tony O'Reilly, who was selected from Dublin's Old Belvedere club. He was to be joined midway through the tour by Horrocks-Taylor, who replaced the injured Irishman Mick English. O'Reilly played in all six tests, two in

↓ Tony O'Reilly on duty for the Lions against the Junior All Blacks in September 1959.

↑ Action from Tigers' victory over Llanelly at Welford Road 18.4.1959.

Australia and four in New Zealand where he scored a record 17 tries in 17 appearances.

There was satisfaction, too, from the records of the Extras and the Swifts. The Extras won 24 games, losing five times, and scored 432 points. The Swifts won 14, drew four and lost eight, which was a very respectable tally for an entirely new side finding its way to the right strength of fixture. The first team had 19 wins against 14 losses and three ever-presents in Bleasdale, Almey and the former Old Wyggs prop, Rex Skelton, while Freer missed only one game, which made it a pity that a change in his job during the summer meant he would not be regularly available.

That same summer saw the resignation of Eric Thorneloe as president, Rodney Bedingfield succeeding him and Ron Gerrard taking over as treasurer. Thorneloe had not been well and his death in August 1959, was as much the passing of an era as Tom Crumbie's had been. His attitude to the club had been very similar to Crumbie's and of course he had been a direct link to the halcyon days of the 1920s. He was, in the words of the club's first historian, Brian Thompson, "a scrupulously fair man. He probably did as much for Tigers, in a different way, as Crumbie did. He gave them the sort of consolidation they needed and he was a man of unfailing wisdom."

A sub-committee was appointed to consider a permanent memorial to him and their recommendation was for a framed picture of Thorneloe to hang in the clubhouse, honours boards commemorating officers, captains and internationals, and clocks for the stands.

1959/1960

There was a minute's silence before the first game of the new season, against Bedford, but the club were unable to give their former secretary the kind of memorial they would have preferred, since they lost 11-20. The game marked the debut of the burly Headingley and England trials wing David Senior, who had moved to work in Nottingham and had joined Leicester, while another debutant was Brian Wigley from Lutterworth.

Change was in the air, for though Leighton Jenkins had been elected club captain he was taking a commission in the RAF and was away on a refresher course in the Isle of Man. He subsequently resigned the post and Bleasdale took over once more. Neither O'Reilly nor Horrocks-Taylor were available before Christmas and Swan's firm were moving him to the south of England. Wade was still at Cambridge (he had toured with a combined Oxford and Cambridge party to the Far East during the summer) and the promising Hartlepool Rovers centre John Dee, later capped by England, failed to get a place at Loughborough and did not join. One significant newcomer, however, was the 1950 British Lion and Wales prop, John Robins, who had received a lecturing appointment at Loughborough.

↑ Graham Willars made his debut in 1959/60.

Robins' stay with Leicester, as a player, was comparatively short and much of his rugby was played in the Extras but he proved one of the most consistent place-kickers since the days of Harold Day besides retaining much of his old ability and added one of the foremost intellects in the game to the club's strength. His name was held in high esteem at Loughborough and, though he had an unhappy tour as assistant manager to the 1966 British Lions, his service to the game went on in his work for student rugby in England.

Another newcomer was the Moat Old Boys flanker, Graham Willars, who made his debut against Cheltenham in October and then distinguished himself in his next game, against Oxford University, by falling offside and giving the Dark Blues the penalty which won the match 6-3. With competition for back row places always fierce it was some time before Willars became a regular but it was his vision for the game which helped the club develop so well in the late 60s and early 70s.

Spectators at the Nuneaton game included Joe Erskine, the Welsh boxer then training in Leicester for his British and Empire title fight against Henry Cooper, though it was not hard men that Leicester sought. Their problems were at half-back, for though White was settled at scrum-half after battling it out with Mike Lubbock for some seasons, he had a succession of different partners including Blackett, Freer, Tatham, Horrocks-Taylor and John Berry, eldest of Tom Berry's four rugby-playing sons.

There was great joy though at the 8-3 win over Llanelly at Stradey Park, tempered slightly by the

↓ Chalkie White, supported by Colin Martin and Arthur Jones, take on Watcyn Thomas XV, 16.9.1959.

sending-off of Almey for fighting. It was the first away win over the Welsh club since the 1900/01 season and Peter Konig, recalled to the back row, got a try, Gavins converting it and dropping a goal. A proposed trip to play Lourdes in France was called off because the French wanted more than just the one game and, as 1960 dawned, Leicester had their first experience of playing under floodlights, losing 9-19 at Newport who were inspired by two will o'the wisp half-backs, Brian Jones and Billy Watkins. On the credit side was the 6-3 defeat of Gloucester, who arrived at Welford Road with a club record of 13 consecutive victories behind them.

↑ Welford Road as it was in October 1959.

O'Reilly, who damaged a shoulder in the Golden Jubilee match with the Barbarians, was back in the side until Ireland called on him as a late replacement for the unfit Michael Flynn against England in February. The telegram which arrived on the Friday from the Irish RFU was alleged to have read: "Situation desperate, you are needed." O'Reilly's reply ran: "Arriving 11.45, De Gaulle," which, even allowing for the famed O'Reilly sense of humour, must have made the selectors ponder.

42 GTG 10.45 AM POPESGROVE HL 59
BARR RUGBY GROUND AYLESTONE ROAD LEICESTER
PLEASE CONVEY TO PRESIDENTS OF BARBARIANS AND LEICESTER THE CONGRATULATIONS OF THE PRESIDENT AND COMMITTEE OF THE RUGBY FOOTBALL UNION ON YOUR JUBILEE MATCH WITH ALL GOOD WISHES FOR MANY MORE YEARS OF ENJOYABLE GAMES MAY I ADD MY PERSONAL CONGRATULATIONS AND EXPRESS MY REGRET BEING UNABLE TO BE WITH YOU =DOUGLAS PRENTICE+ +

↓ A congratulatory telegram from Doug Prentice, now of the RFU, on the occasion of the Tigers v Barbarians Golden Jubilee match, Christmas 1959.

Records fell with a rush as the 1959/60 season neared its end, success after Christmas being much assisted by the regular presence of Horrocks-Taylor. Gavins became the club's second highest points scorer with 153 while Senior shattered the post-war record for tries, held jointly by George Cullen and Haydn Thomas at 16, by running in 23. Newport were beaten 17-11 at Welford Road, Robins kicking four penalties and a conversion, but that marked one of O'Reilly's last performances, for his firm were moving him to southern Ireland. It also occasioned the admirable *Daily Mail* headline "Man bites Tiger" when two teeth had to be removed from Almey's head, left there after a collision between him and Geoff Whitson, the Newport forward.

O'Reilly made 16 appearances in two seasons but was able to play in the Leicester VII which qualified for the Middlesex Tournament. The club seemed determined to wipe out the memory of their two previous visits and fielded the following team: David Senior, Tony O'Reilly, Phil Horrocks-Taylor, Chalkie White, George Cherry, Arthur Jones, Tom Bleasdale. In the first round Senior scored three tries as Leicester dispatched the holders Loughborough Colleges, 19-0. O'Reilly and George Cherry also scored tries, Horrocks-Taylor converting twice, but their second round game with St Luke's College, Exeter, was drawn 10-10 at full time and they lost to a sudden death try. Senior and O'Reilly had scored tries which Horrocks-Taylor had converted, but unhappily the fly-half missed a penalty at the end of proper time which might have won the match.

← LEICESTER FOOTBALL CLUB 1957/58
Back: Barr (Hon.Sec), Shephard, Skelton, Martin, B.Smith, Michie, Almey, White, Key, Bedingfield (Hon.Tres).
Front: Lubbock, Walker, Swan, B.Small, Bleasdale (capt), Chawner, Thompson, Matthews, Freer.

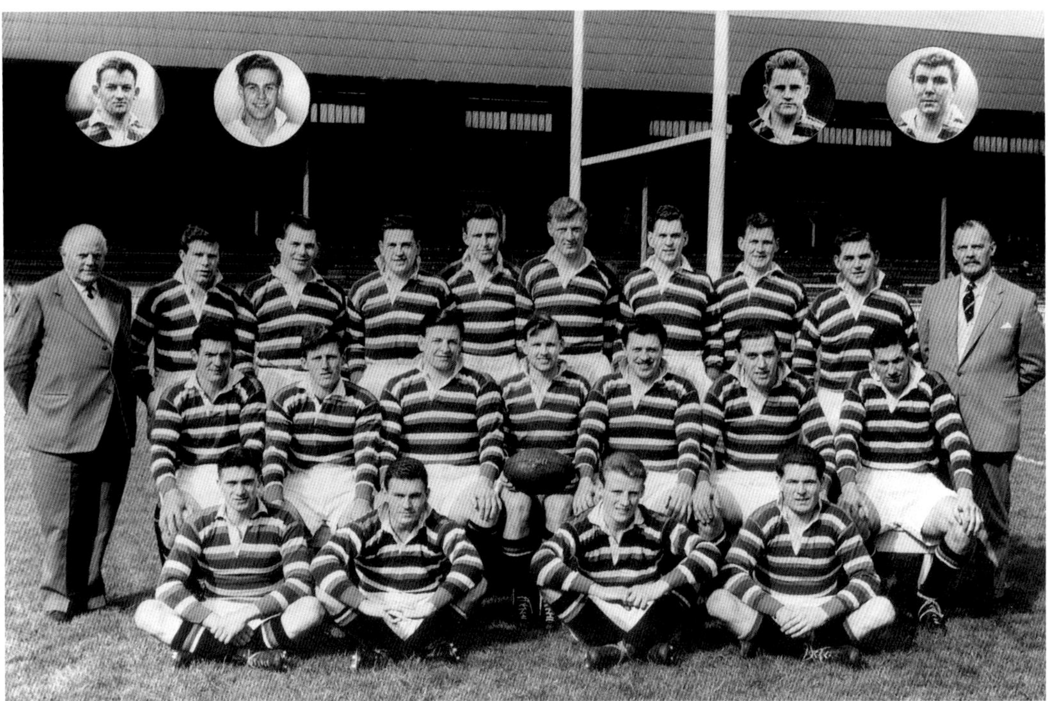

← LEICESTER FOOTBALL CLUB 1958/59
Back: Bedingfield (Hon.Tres), Almey, Skelton, Allen, Horrocks-Taylor, Jenkins, Jessop, Gavins, Lubbock, Barr (Hon.Sec).
Middle: Matthews, Freer, Bleasdale, Swan (capt), Chawner, Thompson, Martin.
Front: White, Shephard, Walker, Key.
Inset: Blackett, Rawson, Jones, O'Reilly.

← LEICESTER FOOTBALL CLUB 1959/60
Back: Gerrard (Hon.Tres), Almey, Konig, Willars, Perry, Cherry, Addison, Bolesworth (Team Hon. Sec), Bedingfield (President).
Middle: Senior, O'Reilly, Martin, Bleasdale (capt), Gavins, Horrocks-Taylor, Robins.
Front: Freer, C.White, Jones.

19 57/58	Home Ground: Welford Road	OVERALL RECORD:					T	C	PG	DG	PTS
	Captain: Tom Bleasdale	PLD	W	D	L	Tigers scored:	60	29	29	3	334
		39	14	6	19	Opponents scored:	85	34	24	4	407

GM	DATE		VEN	OPPONENTS	RESULT	TRIES	KICKS	ATT
CLUB MATCHES								
1	Sep	**7**	**H**	**Bedford**	W 11-5	Skelton, B.Smith	Martin c/p	1092
2		**14**	**H**	**Bath**	W 26-3	Wade(2), Bleasdale, B.Smith	Martin 4c/2p	981
3		**21**	**H**	**Plymouth Albion**	W 19-14	Rawson, B.Smith, Swan, Walker	Martin 2c/p	907
4		28	a	Harlequins	L 6-19	Swan	Martin p	-
5	Oct	**5**	**H**	**Coventry**	W 16-3	Wade, Swan(2)	Martin 2c/p	1500
6		12	a	Richmond	L 3-28	-	Key d	-
7		**19**	**H**	**Cheltenham**	D 3-3	-	Martin p	818
8		**23w**	**H**	**Oxford University**	L 3-16	-	Martin p	461
9		26	a	Northampton	D 3-3	-	Martin p	-
10	Nov	2	a	Gloucester	L 8-12	Swan(2)	Martin c	-
11		9	a	Cambridge University	L 3-30	Swan	-	-
12		**16**	**H**	**Old Blues**	W 8-3	Rawson, White	Martin c	413
13		23	a	Moseley	W 16-8	Bleasdale, R.Smith, Swan	Martin 2c/p	-
14		**30**	**H**	**Newport**	L 8-9	B.Smith	Martin c/p	1419
15	Dec	7	a	Waterloo	D 3-3	-	Martin p	-
16		**14**	**H**	**Blackheath**	L 6-13	Wade	Martin p	527
17		21	a	Bristol	L 6-12	-	Gavins 2p	-
18		**26th**	**H**	**Birkenhead Park**	L 8-15	Matthews, Moseley	Leete c	982
19		**27f**	**H**	**Barbarians**	L 6-25	-	Martin 2p	14500
20		28	a	Rugby	W 6-3	Elders, Wade	-	-
21	Jan	4	a	Bath	D 8-8	Almey, Elders	Martin c	-
22		**11**	**H**	**Gloucester**	L 0-11	-	-	638
23		18	a	Bedford	D 6-6	Shephard	Br.Small p	-
		25	**H**	**Rosslyn Park**	PP (frost)			
24		**30th**	**H**	**Royal Air Force**	W 11-9	Br.Small, Williams	Key c/p	111
25	Feb	**1**	**H**	**London Scottish**	D 6-6	Shephard	Key p	465
		8	a	Newport	PP (snow)			
26		15	a	Wasps	L 3-9	Matthews	-	-
27		**22**	**H**	**Northampton**	L 8-11	Lubbock	Key c/p	742
28	Mar	**1**	**H**	**Harlequins**	W 9-0	Bleasdale, B.Smith, Williams	-	921
29		**8**	**H**	**Leicestershire XV**	W 6-0	Swan	Tatham p	323
30		**13th**	**H**	**Loughborough College**	L 3-6	-	Tatham p	135
31		**15**	**H**	**Swansea**	W 20-8	Tatham, Swan, Williams	Tatham d, Key c/2p	531
32		22	a	Nuneaton	L 5-13	Bleasdale	Key c	-
33		**29**	**H**	**Headingley**	L 6-13	Shephard	Key p	557
34	Apr	5	a	Bristol	W 5-3	Swan	Key c	-
35		7m	a	Plymouth Albion	W 16-9	Gavins, Lubbock, Neil	Gavins 2c/p	-
36		8tu	a	Exeter	W 21-6	Freer, Bleasdale, Chawner, Elders	Freer d, Gavins 3c	-
37		12	a	Birkenhead Park	L 11-13	Bleasdale, Swan, Wade	Matthews c	-
38		19	a	Llanelly	L 11-33	Bleasdale, Shephard, Taylor	Key c	-
39		23w	a	Coventry	L 11-16	Swan	Gavins c/2p	-

INDIVIDUAL APPEARANCES 1957/58

Name / Game #	1	2	3	4	5	6	7	8	9	10	11	12	13	14	15	16	17	18	19	20	21	22	23	24	25	26	27	28	29	30	31	32	33	34	35	36	37	38	39	Apps	T	Pts
GA (Gordon) Almey	-	-	-	-	-	-	-	-	-	-	-	-	-	-	-	-	>F	-	-	-	F	-	H	H	H	H	H	H	H	H	H	H	H	H	H	H	F	F	H	19	1	3
T (Tom) Bleasdale	G*	G*	G*	-	-	G*	G*	G*	G*	G*	G*	G*	G*	G*	G*	G*	-	G*	G*	G*	D*	G*	G*	G*	G*	G*	G*	G*	G*	-	G*	G*	G*	G*	G*	G*	G*	G*	G*	35	7	21
F (Frank) Chawner	C	C	C	C	C	A	C	-	C	A	A	-	C	-	A	-	-	A	A	-	-	-	-	-	-	-	-	C	C	C*	C	C	C	C	-	C	A	A	C	25	1	3
G (George) Cherry	-	-	-	-	-	-	-	-	-	-	-	-	-	-	-	-	-	>C	-	A	A	C	C	-	C	-	-	-	-	-	-	-	-	-	-	-	-	-	-	6	-	-
J (John) Elders	-	-	-	-	-	-	-	-	-	-	-	-	-	-	-	-	-	L	L	L	L	-	-	-	-	-	-	-	-	-	-	-	-	L	L	M	-	-	-	7	3	9
DB (David) Fletcher	-	-	-	>J	-	-	-	-	-	-	-	-	-	-	-	-	-	-	-	-	-	-	-	<J	-	-	-	-	-	-	-	-	-	-	-	-	-	-	-	2	-	-
JG (Jim) Ford	-	-	-	E	E	D	-	-	-	-	-	-	-	-	-	-	-	E	-	<E	-	-	-	-	-	-	-	-	-	-	-	-	-	-	-	-	-	-	-	5	-	-
ME (Mike) Freer	J	J	J	-	-	J	J	J	J	J	J	J	J	J	J	J	J	-	J	J	-	J	J	-	L	J	-	-	-	-	-	J	J	J	J	J	J	J	J	29	1	6
MN (Mike) Gavins E+	-	-	-	-	-	-	-	-	-	-	-	-	-	-	-	-	0	-	-	-	-	-	-	-	-	-	-	-	-	-	-	-	L	-	M	K	-	-	L	5	1	30
Cpl. J (John) Gordon	-	-	-	-	-	-	-	-	-	-	-	-	-	-	-	-	-	-	-	-	-	-	-	-	-	-	-	-	-	=L	-	-	-	-	-	-	-	-	-	1	-	-
D (Dennis) Haines	-	-	-	-	-	-	-	-	-	-	-	-	-	-	-	-	-	-	-	-	-	-	-	-	-	-	-	-	-	<M	-	-	-	-	-	-	-	-	-	1	-	-
MR (Maurice) Key	-	-	-	-	-	>0	-	-	-	-	-	0	-	-	-	-	-	-	-	-	-	-	-	0	0	0	0	0	0	0	0	0	0	0	-	0	-	0	0	16	-	33
PH (Peter) Konig	F	F	-	H	F	-	F	F	F	H	H	-	-	-	-	-	-	-	-	-	-	-	-	-	-	-	-	-	-	F	-	-	-	-	-	-	-	-	-	10	-	-
SF (Stan) Leete	-	-	-	-	-	-	-	-	-	-	>M	M	-	M	N	K	K	K	K	-	N	-	-	-	-	-	-	-	-	K	-	-	-	-	-	-	-	-	-	10	-	2
MGS (Mike) Lubbock	I	I	I	I	I	I	-	-	-	-	I	-	-	-	-	-	-	I	-	-	-	-	I	I	I	I	I	I	I	I	I	I	-	-	I	-	-	-	-	19	2	6
CG (Colin) Martin	H	H	H	F	H	F	H	H	H	F	F	H	H	H	F	H	G	-	H	-	G	H	-	-	-	-	-	-	-	-	-	-	-	-	-	E	-	-	-	21	-	75
DJ (David) Matthews	-	-	F	G	G	H	-	-	-	-	-	F	F	F	H	F	H	F	F	F	H	F	F	F	F	F	F	F	F	G	F	F	F	F	F	F	H	H	F	32	2	8
EJS (Ernie) Michie S15	-	-	-	-	-	-	-	-	-	-	-	-	-	-	>D	D	E	-	-	-	-	D	D	-	D	E	E	E	-	-	<D	-	-	-	-	-	-	-	-	10	-	-
LG (Len) Moseley	-	-	-	-	-	-	>B	-	B	-	-	-	-	-	-	-	-	B	-	-	-	B	-	-	-	-	-	-	B	B	-	-	-	-	-	B	-	-	-	7	1	3
2Lt. RM (Bob) Muddimer	-	-	-	-	-	-	>E	E	E	-	-	-	-	-	-	-	-	-	-	-	-	-	-	-	-	-	-	-	-	-	-	-	E	E	E	-	-	E	<E	8	-	-
MJ (Mike) Neil	-	-	-	-	-	-	-	-	-	-	-	-	-	-	-	-	-	-	-	-	-	>K	-	-	-	-	-	-	-	-	N	N	-	-	<K	-	-	-	-	4	1	3
RO (Dick) Rawson	K	K	K	K	K	K	K	-	-	N	-	N	K	-	-	-	-	-	-	-	-	-	-	-	-	-	-	-	-	-	-	-	-	-	-	-	-	K	-	11	2	6
DL (David) Sellicks	-	-	-	-	>J	-	-	-	-	-	-	-	-	-	-	-	-	J	-	-	<J	-	-	-	-	-	-	-	-	-	-	-	-	-	-	-	-	-	-	3	-	-
CD (Cliff) Shephard	-	-	-	-	-	N	-	N	-	-	-	-	-	-	-	N	N	N	-	-	-	-	K	N	N	N	N	N	N	N	M	L	K	N	N	N	N	M	K	22	4	12
GB Siggins	-	-	-	-	-	-	-	-	-	-	-	-	-	-	-	-	-	-	-	-	-	=M	-	-	-	-	-	-	-	-	-	-	-	-	-	-	-	-	-	1	-	-
RP (Rex) Skelton	A	A	A	A	A	C	-	A	A	C	C	A	A	A	C	A	C	-	C	C	C	A	A	A	A	A	A	A	A	A	A	A	A	A	C	A	C	C	A	37	1	3
RW (Bob) Small	-	-	-	-	-	-	-	-	-	-	-	-	-	-	-	-	-	>H	-	-	-	-	-	-	-	-	-	-	-	-	-	-	-	-	-	-	0	-	-	2	-	-
BTC (Brian) Small	0	0	0	0*	0*	-	0	0	0	0	0	-	0	0	0	0	L*	0	0	0	0	0	0	L	J	M	-	-	-	-	-	-	-	-	0	-	-	-	-	25	1	6
BAF (Brian) Smith	M	M	M	M	-	-	-	M	M	L	N	L	M	N	M	L	M	M	N	K	M	L	L	M	K	L	L	L	L	-	-	-	-	-	-	-	-	-	-	26	5	15
RH (Ron) Smith	E	E	E	-	-	-	-	-	-	D	E	E	D	E	-	-	-	-	D	-	-	-	-	D	-	-	-	-	E	D	-	E	-	-	-	-	<E	-	-	14	1	3
D (Dennis) Storer	-	-	-	-	-	-	-	-	>K	-	-	-	-	-	-	-	-	-	-	N	-	<N	-	-	-	-	-	-	-	-	-	-	-	-	-	-	-	-	-	3	-	-
JS (Ian) Swan S17	>N	N	N	N	N	-	N	K	N	K	K	K	N	K	K	-	-	-	-	-	K	-	N	-	-	K	M	M	M	-	L	M	N	K	-	-	L	L	M	27	13	39
L (Lyn) Tatham	-	-	-	-	-	-	-	-	-	-	-	-	-	-	-	-	-	-	-	-	-	-	-	-	-	-	>J	J	J	J	J	-	-	-	-	-	-	-	-	5	1	12
JE (John) Taylor	-	-	-	-	M	M	M	L	-	-	-	-	-	-	-	-	-	-	-	-	-	-	-	-	-	-	-	-	-	-	-	-	-	-	-	-	K	N	-	6	1	3
JS (John) Thompson	D	D	D	D	D	E	D	D	D	E	D	D	E	D	E	E	D	D	E	D	E	E	E	E	E	D	D	D	D	E	E	D	D	D	D	D	D	D	D	39	-	-
PBL (Peter) Thorneloe	-	-	-	-	-	-	-	-	-	-	-	-	-	-	-	<C	-	-	-	-	-	-	-	-	-	-	-	-	-	-	-	-	-	-	-	-	-	-	-	1	-	-
JA (Jim) Turner	-	-	-	-	-	-	>A	C	-	-	-	C	-	C	-	-	<A	-	-	-	-	-	-	-	-	-	-	-	-	-	-	-	-	-	-	-	-	-	-	5	-	-
MR (Mike) Wade E+	L	L	L	L	L	L	L	-	L	M	L	-	L	L	L	M	-	-	M	M	-	-	M	-	M	-	-	-	-	-	-	-	M	M	-	L	M	-	-	22	6	18
MR (Mike) Walker	B	B	B	B	B	B	-	B	-	B	B	B	B	B	B	B	B	-	B	B	B	-	B	B	B	B	B	B	-	-	B	B	B	B	B	-	B	B	B	32	1	3
HV (Chalkie) White	-	-	-	-	-	-	>I	I	I	I	-	I	I	I	I	I	I	-	I	I	I	I	-	-	-	-	-	-	-	-	-	-	I	I	-	I	I	I	I	20	1	3
SH (Stephen) Wilcock	-	-	-	-	-	-	-	-	-	-	-	-	-	-	-	-	-	-	-	=H	-	-	-	-	-	-	-	-	-	-	-	-	-	-	-	-	-	-	-	1	-	-
G (Glyn) Williams	-	-	-	-	-	-	-	-	-	-	-	-	-	-	-	-	-	-	-	-	-	-	-	>K	-	-	K	K	K	-	K	K	-	-	-	-	-	-	<N	7	3	9
J (John) Woolley	-	-	-	-	-	-	-	-	-	-	-	-	-	-	-	-	-	-	-	-	-	-	-	>C	-	C	C	-	-	-	-	-	-	-	A	-	-	-	-	4	-	-

The key for how to read the stats is on the last page

1958/59

Home Ground: Welford Road except #22 at Welford Road Rec

Captain: Ian Swan

OVERALL RECORD:					T	C	PG	DG	PTS
PLD	W	D	L	Tigers scored:	73	32	31	5	391
38	19	5	14	Opponents scored:	62	27	27	4	333

GM	DATE		VEN	OPPONENTS	RESULT	TRIES	KICKS	ATT
CLUB MATCHES								
1	Sep	**6**	**H**	**Bedford**	W 20-11	Bleasdale, Jenkins, Jessop	Gavins c/3p	-
2		**13**	**H**	**Bath**	W 25-6	Shephard(2), Bleasdale, Jenkins, Matthews	Gavins 2c/2p	-
3		**15m**	**H**	**Watcyn Thomas XV**	W 18-3	Bleasdale, Freer, Jenkins, Walker	Gavins 3c	-
4		**20**	**H**	**Plymouth Albion**	W 18-5	Almey, Bleasdale, White	Gavins 3c/p	-
5		27	a	Harlequins	D 11-11	Jessop(Penalty)	Gavins c/2p	-
6	Oct	4	a	Coventry	L 9-14	Jenkins	Gavins 2p	-
7		**11**	**H**	**Richmond**	W 6-3	Swan	Gavins p	-
8		18	a	Cheltenham	L 3-5	Almey	-	-
9		22w	a	Oxford University	L 8-11	Constable, Horrocks-Taylor	Gavins c	-
10		**25**	**H**	**Northampton**	L 3-10	-	Gavins p	-
11	Nov	**1**	**H**	**Gloucester**	L 6-12	Chawner	Gavins p	-
12		**8**	**H**	**Cambridge University**	W 8-3	Gavins, Swan	Gavins c	-
13		15	a	Bective Rangers	L 11-16	Swan, White	Gavins c/p	-
14		16s	a	Old Belvedere	L 3-14	Horrocks-Taylor	-	-
15		22	a	Moseley	D 6-6	-	Freer d, Gavins p	-
16		29	a	Newport	L 0-29	-	-	5000
17	Dec	**6**	**H**	**Waterloo**	W 13-11	Almey, Martin, Rawson	Gavins 2c	-
18		13	a	Blackheath	L 0-3	-	-	-
19		**20**	**H**	**Bristol**	W 17-6	Swan(2), Jenkins, Lubbock, Rawson	Gavins c	-
20		**26f**	**H**	**Barbarians**	W 9-3	Jenkins, Matthews, Shephard	-	12000
21		**27**	**H**	**Birkenhead Park**	D 8-8	Elders, Jones	Gavins c	-
	Jan	3	a	Bath	PP (frost)			
		10	a	Gloucester	PP (frost)			
		17	a	Bedford	PP (frost)			
22		**24**	**H**	**Rosslyn Park**	W 8-6	Almey, Swan	Gavins c	-
23		31	a	Headingley	W 6-3	Swan	Gavins p	-
24	Feb	7	a	London Scottish	W 21-3	Bleasdale, O'Reilly, Shephard, Tatham	Gavins 3c/p	-
25		**14**	**H**	**Newport**	L 3-19	-	Blackett d	-
26		**21**	**H**	**Wasps**	W 22-0	O'Reilly(2), Blackett, Lubbock	Blackett d, Gavins 2c/p	-
27		28	a	Northampton	L 13-22	Almey, Martin	Gavins 2c/p	-
28	Mar	**7**	**H**	**Harlequins**	W 9-6	Horrocks-Taylor	Gavins 2p	-
29		**12th**	**H**	**Loughborough College**	W 9-6	Almey(2)	Gavins p	-
30		**14**	**H**	**Coventry**	W 13-11	Almey, Horrocks-Taylor, Wade	Gavins 2c	-
31		21	a	Bradford	D 8-8	Wade	Gavins c/p	-
32		28	a	Bristol	L 9-17	Allen, Shephard	Freer d	-
33		30m	a	Plymouth Albion	W 11-6	Allen, Almey, Shephard	Martin c	-
34		31tu	a	Exeter	D 3-3	-	Martin p	-
35	Apr	4	a	Birkenhead Park	L 6-10	-	Horrocks-Taylor d, Key p	-
36		**11**	**H**	**Nuneaton**	W 16-3	Allen, Bleasdale, Horrocks-Taylor	Key 2c/p	-
37		**18**	**H**	**Llanelly**	W 23-9	Allen, Almey, Shephard	Gavins c/4p	-
38		22w	a	Bedford	L 9-11	Horrocks-Taylor, Shephard	Gavins p	-

INDIVIDUAL APPEARANCES 1958/59

Name / Game #	1	2	3	4	5	6	7	8	9	10	11	12	13	14	15	16	17	18	19	20	21	22	23	24	25	26	27	28	29	30	31	32	33	34	35	36	37	38	Apps	T	Pts
T (Trevor) Allen	-	-	-	-	-	-	-	-	-	-	-	-	-	-	-	-	-	-	-	-	-	-	-	-	-	-	>M	-	-	-	L	L	L	M	L	L	L	-	8	4	12
GA (Gordon) Almey	H	H	H	H	F	F	F	F	H	F	H	H	H	H	H	F	H	H	F	H	H	H	F	F	H	N	H	H	H	H	F	F	K	K	H	H	H	F	38	10	30
ADB (Derek) Ashurst	-	-	-	-	-	-	-	-	-	-	-	-	-	G	-	-	-	-	-	-	-	-	-	-	-	-	-	-	-	-	-	-	O	O	-	-	-	-	3	-	-
G (Gordon) Blackett	-	-	-	-	-	-	-	-	-	-	-	-	-	-	-	-	-	-	>J	J	-	-	-	-	J	J	-	-	-	J	-	-	-	-	-	-	-	-	5	1	9
T (Tom) Bleasdale	D*	D	D*	D*	D	D	E	D	D	E	D	D	G	E	D	E	D*	D*	D	D*	D*	D	G	D	D*	F*	D	D	D*	G	E*	E*	F*	H*	D	G	D	D	38	6	18
F (Frank) Chawner	A	A	A	A	C	C	C	C	C	A	C	C	C	-	A	C	C	C	A	C	C	C	C	C	C	C	C	C	A	C	A	C	C	C	C	C	C	C	37	1	3
HE (Harry) Constable	-	-	-	-	-	-	-	-	>G	-	-	-	E	-	-	-	-	-	-	-	-	-	-	-	-	-	-	-	-	-	-	-	-	-	G	-	-	-	3	1	3
J (John) Elders	-	-	-	-	-	-	-	-	-	-	-	-	-	-	-	-	-	-	-	-	<M	-	-	-	-	-	-	-	-	-	-	-	-	-	-	-	-	-	1	1	3
ME (Mike) Freer	J	J	J	J	J	-	M	M	M	J	J	J	M	M	J	J	J	L	L	L	J	M	M	L	M	L	L	M	M	L	M	J	J	J	M	M	M	L	37	1	9
MN (Mike) Gavins E+	O	O	O	O	O	O	O	O	O	M	M	M	O	L	M	M	O	-	O	O	O	O	O	O	L	O	O	O	O	O	O	O	-	-	-	-	O	O	33	1	145
MW (Mick) Hanney	-	-	-	-	-	-	-	-	-	-	-	-	-	-	-	-	-	>J	-	-	-	-	-	-	-	-	-	-	-	-	J	-	-	-	-	-	-	-	2	-	-
JP (Phil) Horrocks-Taylor E2 L+	-	-	-	-	-	>J	J	J	J	-	-	-	J	J	-	-	-	-	-	-	-	J	J	-	-	-	J	J	J	M	-	-	-	-	J	J	J	J	16	6	21
PB (Pat) Hunt	-	-	-	N	-	K	-	N	<N	-	-	-	-	-	-	-	-	-	-	-	-	-	-	-	-	-	-	-	-	-	-	-	-	-	-	-	-	-	4	-	-
LH (Leighton) Jenkins W5	>G	G	G	G	G	G	G	G	-	G	G	G	-	-	G	G	G	G	G	G	G	G	-	G	G	G	G	G	G	-	G	G	G	G	-	-	G	G	31	6	18
HG (Harry) Jessop	L	N	M	M	N	M	K	K	-	N	-	N	-	N	-	-	K	M	-	-	-	-	-	-	K	-	-	L	-	-	-	-	-	-	-	-	-	-	15	2	6
A (Arthur) Jones	-	-	-	-	-	-	-	-	-	-	-	-	-	-	-	-	>B	B	B	B	B	B	B	B	B	B	B	-	-	B	B	B	-	B	B	B	-	-	17	1	3
MR (Maurice) Key	-	-	-	-	-	-	-	-	-	O	O	O	-	-	O	O	-	O	-	-	-	-	-	-	O	-	-	-	-	-	-	-	-	-	O	O	-	-	9	-	10
PH (Peter) Konig	-	-	-	-	-	-	-	-	-	-	-	-	-	-	-	-	F	F	-	-	-	-	-	-	-	-	-	-	-	-	-	-	-	-	-	-	-	-	2	-	-
EC (Eric) Lacey	-	-	-	-	-	-	-	-	-	-	-	-	-	-	-	-	-	-	-	-	-	-	-	-	-	<D	-	-	-	-	-	-	-	-	-	-	-	-	1	-	-
SF (Stan) Leete	-	-	-	-	-	-	-	-	<K	-	-	-	-	-	-	-	-	-	-	-	-	-	-	-	-	-	-	-	-	-	-	-	-	-	-	-	-	-	1	-	-
MGS (Mike) Lubbock	-	-	-	-	-	-	-	-	-	-	-	-	-	I	-	I	I	-	I	I	-	I	I	I	I	I	I	I	I	I	I	I	-	-	I	I	I	I	20	2	6
CG (Colin) Martin	-	-	-	-	-	-	-	-	-	-	-	-	-	-	-	-	E	E	E	E	E	E	E	E	E	E	E	E	E	E	D	D	E	D	-	D	E	E	21	2	11
DJ (David) Matthews	F	F	F	F	H	H	H	H	F	H	F	F	F	F	F	H	-	-	H	F	F	F	H	H	F	H	F	F	F	F	H	H	H	F	F	F	F	H	36	2	6
LG (Len) Moseley	-	-	-	-	-	-	-	-	-	-	B	B	-	-	B	<B	-	-	-	-	-	-	-	-	-	-	-	-	-	-	-	-	-	-	-	-	-	-	4	-	-
AJF (Tony) O'Reilly I21 L4	-	-	-	-	-	-	-	-	-	>L	L	L	L	-	-	-	L	-	-	-	-	-	-	M	-	M	-	-	-	-	-	-	-	-	-	-	-	-	7	3	9
RO (Dick) Rawson	K	-	N	-	-	-	-	-	-	-	-	-	-	-	K	K	N	K	K	K	K	-	-	-	-	-	-	-	-	-	-	-	-	-	K	-	-	-	10	2	6
B (Brian) Rigney	-	-	-	-	-	-	-	-	-	-	-	-	-	>B	-	-	-	-	-	-	-	-	-	-	-	-	-	-	-	-	-	-	-	-	-	-	-	-	1	-	-
CD (Cliff) Shephard	N	K	K	K	K	N	N	-	-	-	-	-	N	-	N	-	-	-	-	N	N	K	N	N	-	K	K	N	K	-	N	N	M	L	N	-	K	N	25	8	24
RP (Rex) Skelton	C	C	C	C	A	A	A	A	A	C	A	A	A	A	C	A	A	A	C	A	A	A	A	A	A	A	A	A	C	A	C	A	A	A	A	A	A	A	38	-	-
BTC (Brian) Small	-	-	-	-	-	-	-	-	-	-	-	-	-	O	-	-	-	-	-	-	-	-	-	-	-	-	-	-	-	-	-	-	-	-	-	-	-	-	1	-	-
JS (Ian) Swan S17	-	M*	-	-	M*	L*	L*	L*	L*	K*	K*	K*	K*	K*	L*	L*	-	-	N*	-	-	N*	K*	K*	-	-	N*	K*	-	N*	-	-	-	-	K*	N*	N*	<K*	24	7	21
FB (Brian) Symons	-	-	-	-	-	-	-	-	-	-	-	-	-	-	-	-	<M	-	-	-	-	-	-	-	-	-	-	-	-	-	-	-	-	-	-	-	-	-	1	-	-
L (Lyn) Tatham	-	-	-	-	-	-	-	-	-	-	-	-	-	-	-	-	-	-	-	-	-	L	L	J	-	-	-	-	-	-	-	-	-	-	-	-	-	-	3	1	3
JE (John) Taylor	-	-	-	-	-	-	-	-	-	-	N	-	-	-	-	N	-	N	M	-	-	-	-	-	K	-	-	-	N	-	-	K	N	<N	-	-	-	-	9	-	-
JS (John) Thompson	E	E	E	E	E	E	D	E	E	D	E	E	D	D	E	D	-	-	-	-	-	-	D	-	-	-	-	-	-	D	-	-	D	E	E	E	-	-	22	-	-
MR (Mike) Wade E+	M	L	L	L	L	-	-	-	-	-	-	-	-	-	-	-	-	-	M	L	-	-	-	-	-	-	-	-	L	K	K	M	-	-	-	-	-	M	12	2	6
MR (Mike) Walker	B	B	B	B	B	B	B	B	B	B	-	-	B	-	-	-	-	-	-	-	-	-	-	-	-	-	-	B	B	-	-	-	B	-	-	-	B	B	16	1	3
HV (Chalkie) White	I	I	I	I	I	I	I	I	I	I	I	I	I	-	I	-	-	I	-	-	I	-	-	-	-	-	-	-	-	-	-	-	I	I	-	-	-	-	18	2	6
J (John) Woolley	-	-	-	-	-	-	-	-	-	-	-	-	-	<C	-	-	-	-	-	-	-	-	-	-	-	-	-	-	-	-	-	-	-	-	-	-	-	-	1	-	-

The key for how to read the stats is on the last page

1959/60

	Home Ground: Welford Road	OVERALL RECORD:					T	C	PG	DG	PTS
	Captain: John Jenkins then Tom Bleasdale	PLD	W	D	L	Tigers scored:	74	29	48	8	448
		40	22	4	14	Opponents scored:	68	27	33	6	375

GM	DATE		VEN	OPPONENTS	RESULT	TRIES	KICKS	ATT
CLUB MATCHES								
1	Sep	**5**	**H**	**Bedford**	L 11-20	Shephard, Wigley	Gavins c/p	872
2		**12**	**H**	**Bath**	W 12-11	Rawson	Gavins 2p, Tatham d	661
3		**16w**	**H**	**Watcyn Thomas XV**	W 23-16	Ashurst, Smith	Gavins c/4p, Blackett d	993
4		**19**	**H**	**Plymouth Albion**	W 25-11	Shephard(2), Blackett	Gavins 2c/4p	696
5		26	a	Harlequins	L 11-18	Bleasdale, Wigley	Gavins c/p	-
6	Oct	**3**	**H**	**Coventry**	W 21-13	Almey, Senior, Smith, C.White	Gavins 3c/p	1672
7		10	a	Richmond	L 3-11	-	Gavins p	-
8		**17**	**H**	**Cheltenham**	W 23-3	Smith(2), Jessop, Matthews, Senior	Gavins c/2p	511
9		**21w**	**H**	**Oxford University**	L 3-6	Senior	-	551
10		24	a	Northampton	L 14-17	Smith, Gavins, Senior	Smith d, Gavins c	-
11		**31**	**H**	**Nuneaton**	W 29-6	Senior(3), Jessop, Wigley	Gavins c/4p	810
12	Nov	7	a	Gloucester	L 13-18	Jones, Senior, Wigley	Gavins 2c	-
13		14	a	Cambridge University	L 0-17	-	-	-
14		21	a	Llanelly	W 8-3	Konig	Gavins c/d	-
15		**28**	**H**	**Moseley**	D 6-6	-	Gavins 2p	716
16	Dec	5	a	Waterloo	W 8-0	Senior(2)	Gavins c	-
17		**12**	**H**	**Blackheath**	W 8-5	O'Reilly	Gavins c/p	840
18		**19**	**H**	**Bristol**	L 3-11	-	Blackett d	524
19		**26**	**H**	**Birkenhead Park**	L 3-36	-	Robins p	1390
20		**28m**	**H**	**Barbarians**	L 9-17	Martin	Gavins 2p	15000
21	Jan	2	a	Bath	D 0-0	-	-	-
22		**9**	**H**	**Gloucester**	W 6-3	Senior	Gavins p	566
		16	a	Bedford	PP			
23		23	a	Rosslyn Park	D 0-0	-	-	-
24		**28th**	**H**	**Royal Air Force**	L 6-11	-	Gavins 2p	92
25		**30**	**H**	**Headingley**	W 9-6	Horrocks-Taylor, Senior	Gavins p	367
26	Feb	**6**	**H**	**London Scottish**	W 15-3	Senior(2), Freer, Ring	Gavins p	382
27		13	a	Newport	L 9-19	-	Freer 2d, Gavins p	6000
28		20	a	Wasps	W 3-0	-	Gavins p	-
29		**27**	**H**	**Northampton**	D 6-6	Tatham	Gavins p	1981
30	Mar	**5**	**H**	**Harlequins**	W 16-6	Almey(2), Rawson	Gavins c/d, Robins c	1096
31		**12**	**H**	**Leicestershire XV**	W 11-3	Konig, Ring	Robins c/p	249
32		**19**	**H**	**Bradford**	W 30-6	Senior(2), Almey, Freer, Martin, O'Reilly	Robins 2c/p, Gavins c/p	411
33		**26**	**H**	**Loughborough Colleges**	W 18-0	Almey, Gavins, Martin	Robins 3c/p	403
34	Apr	2	a	Birkenhead Park	W 16-3	Senior(2)	Robins 2c/2p	-
35		**9**	**H**	**Newport**	W 17-11	Konig	Robins c/4p	1836
36		16	a	Bristol	L 6-21	Senior	Gavins p	-
37		18m	a	Plymouth Albion	W 20-9	Senior(3), O'Reilly(2), Rawson	Rawson c	-
38		19tu	a	Exeter	W 9-0	Horrocks-Taylor, O'Reilly, Rawson	-	-
39		**23**	**H**	**Rugby**	W 9-6	Allen, Jessop	Martin p	413
40		27w	a	Bedford	L 9-17	Senior	Robins 2p	-

INDIVIDUAL APPEARANCES 1959/60

Name / Game #	1	2	3	4	5	6	7	8	9	10	11	12	13	14	15	16	17	18	19	20	21	22	23	24	25	26	27	28	29	30	31	32	33	34	35	36	37	38	39	40	Apps	T	Pts
JH (Jeff) Addison	-	-	-	-	-	-	-	-	-	-	>E	E	E	E	D	-	D	E	E	E	E	E	E	D	E	D	E	E	E	-	D	E	E	E	-	-	-	-	-	-	22	-	-
T (Trevor) Allen	-	-	-	-	-	-	-	-	-	-	-	-	-	-	-	-	-	-	-	-	-	-	-	-	-	-	-	-	-	-	-	-	-	-	-	-	-	-	N	-	1	1	3
GA (Gordon) Almey	H	-	-	-	-	G	K	-	-	-	-	-	F	■F	F	-	H	-	H	H	-	-	-	-	-	-	H	F	H	H	H	H	H	F	F	H	D	E	F	-	22	5	15
ADB (Derek) Ashurst	-	G	G	G	-	-	-	-	-	-	-	-	-	G	G	-	-	-	-	-	-	-	-	-	-	-	-	-	G	-	-	-	-	-	-	-	F	H	G	F	10	1	3
JH (John) Berry	-	-	-	-	-	-	-	-	-	-	-	-	>J	-	-	-	-	-	J	-	-	-	-	-	-	-	-	-	-	-	-	-	-	-	-	-	-	-	-	-	2	-	-
MJ (Martin) Birkett	-	-	-	-	-	-	-	-	-	-	-	-	-	-	-	-	-	-	>K	-	-	-	-	-	-	-	-	-	-	-	-	-	-	-	-	-	-	-	-	-	1	-	-
G (Gordon) Blackett	-	-	J	J	-	J	J	-	-	-	-	-	-	-	-	-	-	J	-	J	-	-	-	-	<J	-	-	-	-	-	-	-	-	-	-	-	-	-	-	-	7	1	9
T (Tom) Bleasdale	D*	-	D*	D*	G*	-	G*	D*	G*	G*	G*	G*	G*	-	-	G*	G*	H*	G*	G*	G*	G*	G*	G*	G*	G*	G*	G*	-	G*	G*	G*	G*	G*	G*	G*	G*	G*	-	G*	34	1	3
F (Frank) Chawner	-	-	-	-	-	-	-	-	-	-	-	-	-	-	-	-	-	-	-	-	-	-	-	-	-	-	-	-	-	-	-	-	-	-	-	C	A	C	A	-	4	-	-
G (George) Cherry	-	A	A	C	C	C	C	A	A	A	C	C	C	C	C	C	C	-	C	C	C	C	A	A	A	A	A	A	A	A	A	A	A	A	C	-	-	-	-	C	34	-	-
HE (Harry) Constable	A	D	-	-	D	D	D	-	D	<D	-	-	-	-	-	-	-	-	-	-	-	-	-	-	-	-	-	-	-	-	-	-	-	-	-	-	-	-	-	-	7	-	-
ME (Mike) Freer	L	L	L	M	-	-	-	J	-	J	L	J	-	J	J	J	J	-	L	N	L	L	L	M	N	N	L	N	N	N	-	N	N	N	N	N	-	-	-	-	29	2	12
MN (Mike) Gavins E+	O	O	O	O	O	O	O	O	O	O	O	O	-	O	O	O	O	O	-	O	O	O	O	O	O	O	O	O	O	O	-	O	O	O	O	O	-	O	-	O	35	2	153
HB Griffiths	-	-	-	-	-	-	-	-	-	-	-	-	-	-	=M	-	-	-	-	-	-	-	-	-	-	-	-	-	-	-	-	-	-	-	-	-	-	-	-	-	1	-	-
MW (Mick) Hanney	-	-	-	-	J	-	-	-	-	-	-	-	-	-	-	-	-	-	-	-	-	-	-	-	-	-	-	-	-	-	-	-	-	-	-	-	-	-	<J	-	2	-	-
MJ (Mike) Hemphrey	-	-	-	-	-	-	-	-	-	-	-	-	-	-	-	-	-	-	-	-	>A	-	C	C	-	-	-	C	-	-	-	-	-	-	-	-	C	A	C	-	7	-	-
AS (Alan) Hopkins	-	-	-	-	-	-	-	-	-	-	-	-	-	-	-	-	-	-	=N	-	-	-	-	-	-	-	-	-	-	-	-	-	-	-	-	-	-	-	-	-	1	-	-
JP (Phil) Horrocks-Taylor E2 L1	-	-	-	-	-	-	-	-	-	-	J	-	-	-	-	-	-	L	-	L	J	J	-	-	L	J	-	J	J	J	J	J	J	-	J	J	J	J	-	-	17	2	6
LH (Leighton) Jenkins W5	-	-	-	-	-	-	-	-	-	-	-	-	-	-	-	-	-	<G	-	-	-	-	-	-	-	-	-	-	-	-	-	-	-	-	-	-	-	-	-	-	1	-	-
HG (Harry) Jessop	-	-	-	-	-	-	-	L	L	M	M	L	M	M	-	M	-	-	-	-	-	-	-	-	-	-	-	-	-	-	-	-	-	-	-	-	-	-	K	<M	10	3	9
A (Arthur) Jones	B	B	B	B	B	B	B	-	-	B	B	B	B	B	B	B	B	B	-	B	B	B	-	B	-	B	B	B	B	B	B	B	B	B	B	B	B	<B	-	-	33	1	3
MR (Maurice) Key	-	-	-	-	-	-	-	-	-	-	-	-	O	-	-	-	-	-	O	-	-	-	-	-	-	-	-	-	-	-	-	-	-	-	-	-	-	-	-	-	2	-	-
PH (Peter) Konig	F	H	H	H	H	H	H	F	F	F	F	H	H	H	H	H	F	F	-	-	H	F	F	F	F	F	-	-	-	-	F	F	-	-	H	-	-	-	<I	-	28	3	9
MGS (Mike) Lubbock	I	I*	-	-	-	-	-	-	-	-	-	-	-	-	-	I	I	I	-	-	-	-	-	-	I	-	-	-	-	-	-	-	-	-	-	-	-	-	-	-	6	-	-
CG (Colin) Martin	E	E	E	E	E	E*	E	E	-	E	D	D	D	D*	E*	D	E	D	-	D	-	D	D	-	D	E	D	D	D*	D	E	D	D	D	D	E	E	-	E*	D	35	3	12
DJ (David) Matthews	G	F	F	F	F	F	-	G	-	-	-	-	-	-	-	F	-	-	F	F	-	H	-	-	-	-	-	-	-	-	-	-	-	-	-	-	-	-	-	-	11	1	3
AJF (Tony) O'Reilly I22 L10	-	-	-	-	-	-	-	-	-	-	-	-	-	-	-	-	L	-	-	M	-	-	-	-	-	M	-	-	-	-	-	M	M	-	L	L	L	L	-	-	9	5	15
DG (David) Perry E+	-	-	-	-	-	-	-	-	-	-	-	-	-	-	-	-	-	-	-	-	-	-	-	-	-	-	-	-	-	-	-	-	-	-	>E	D	-	D	-	<E	4	-	-
RO (Dick) Rawson	-	K	-	-	-	-	-	-	-	-	-	-	-	-	-	-	-	-	-	-	-	-	-	-	-	-	-	K	K	K	N	-	-	-	-	-	N	N	-	N	8	4	14
A (Alan) Rees	-	-	-	-	-	-	-	-	-	-	-	-	-	-	-	-	-	-	-	-	-	-	-	-	-	-	-	-	-	-	-	-	-	=J	-	-	-	-	-	-	1	-	-
B (Brian) Rigney	-	-	-	-	-	-	-	-	-	-	-	-	-	-	-	-	-	-	-	-	-	-	B	-	<B	-	-	-	-	-	-	-	-	-	-	-	-	-	-	-	2	-	-
BD (Brian) Ring	-	-	-	-	-	-	-	-	-	-	-	-	-	>L	L	L	M	-	-	-	M	M	M	L	M	L	M	L	L	L	L	-	-	L	-	M	M	M	M	L	21	2	6
JD (John) Robins W11 L5	-	-	-	-	-	-	-	-	-	-	-	-	-	-	-	-	>A	A	A	A	-	A	-	-	C	C	C	-	C	C	C	C	C	C	A	-	-	-	-	A	16	-	56
D (David) Senior	>K	-	-	-	K	K	-	K	K	K	K	K	L	K	K	K	K	K	-	K	K	K	K	-	K	K	K	-	-	-	K	K	K	K	K	K	K	K	-	K	30	23	69
CD (Cliff) Shephard	N	N	N	N	N	N	N	-	-	-	-	-	-	-	-	-	-	-	M	-	N	N	N	N	-	-	N	-	-	-	-	-	-	-	-	-	-	-	-	-	13	3	9
RP (Rex) Skelton	C	C	C	A	A	A	A	C	C	C	A	A	A	A	A	A	-	C	-	-	-	-	-	-	-	-	-	-	-	-	-	-	-	-	-	A	-	-	-	-	18	-	-
BTC (Brian) Small	-	-	-	-	-	L	M	-	-	-	-	-	-	-	-	-	-	-	-	-	-	-	-	-	-	-	-	-	-	-	O	-	-	-	-	-	O	-	O	-	5	-	-
BAF (Brian) Smith	-	-	K	K	L	M	L	M	M	L	-	M	K	-	-	-	-	-	-	-	-	-	-	<K	-	-	-	-	-	-	-	-	-	-	-	-	-	-	-	-	11	5	18
DG (Derek) Standerwick	-	-	-	-	-	-	-	-	-	-	-	-	-	-	-	-	-	-	-	-	-	-	-	-	-	-	-	-	-	-	-	-	-	-	-	-	-	-	=L	-	1	-	-
L (Lyn) Tatham	J	J	M	L	-	-	-	-	J	-	-	-	-	-	-	-	-	-	-	-	-	-	J	J	-	-	J	M	M	M	-	L	L	M	M	-	-	-	-	J	16	1	6
JS (John) Thompson	-	-	-	-	-	-	-	-	E	-	-	-	-	-	-	E	-	-	D	-	D	-	-	E	-	-	-	-	-	E	-	-	-	-	-	-	-	-	D	-	7	-	-
MR (Mike) Wade E+	-	-	-	-	-	-	-	-	-	-	-	-	-	-	-	-	-	M	-	-	-	-	-	-	-	-	-	-	-	-	-	-	-	-	-	-	-	-	-	-	1	-	-
MR (Mike) Walker	-	-	-	-	-	-	-	B	B	-	-	-	-	-	-	-	-	-	B	-	-	-	-	-	-	-	-	-	-	-	-	-	-	-	-	-	-	-	B	B	5	-	-
TN (Trevor) Watkiss	-	-	-	-	-	-	-	-	-	-	-	-	-	-	-	-	-	-	-	-	-	-	-	-	-	-	-	-	-	-	=M	-	-	-	-	-	-	-	-	-	1	-	-
HV (Chalkie) White	-	-	I	I	I	I	I	I	I	I	I	I	I	I	I	-	-	-	I	I	I	I	I	I	-	I	I	I	I	I	I	I	I	I	I	I	I	I	-	I	33	1	3
JH (John) White	-	-	-	-	-	-	=F	-	-	-	-	-	-	-	-	-	-	-	-	-	-	-	-	-	-	-	-	-	-	-	-	-	-	-	-	-	-	-	-	-	1	-	-
BT (Brian) Wigley	>M	M	-	-	M	-	-	N	N	N	N	N	N	N	N	N	N	<N	-	-	-	-	-	-	-	-	-	-	-	-	-	-	-	-	-	-	-	-	-	-	14	4	12
GG (Graham) Willars	-	-	-	-	-	-	-	>H	H	H	H	F	-	-	-	-	-	-	-	-	F	-	H	H	H	H	F	H	F	F	-	-	F	H	-	F	H	F	H	H	21	-	-

The key for how to read the stats is on the last page

CHAPTER 15

Martin Takes the Helm

1960/1961

Colin Martin was elected captain for 1960/61, a position he had never dreamed of occupying but an indication of his standing within the club. The pressure on back row places was eased with the decision of David Perry (later capped by England from Bedford), who had come into the side just prior to the 1960 Easter tour, to rejoin Harlequins and there were more additions from Lutterworth Grammar School, where Lyn Tatham was a master. John Allen, a scrum-half of whom more later, joined his brother Trevor, the Cooper brothers, Dick and John (better known as a 400 metres hurdles silver medallist at the Tokyo Olympics before his death in the 1974 Paris air disaster) came straight from school to join Brian Wigley and David Bird at the club.

On 22 October, before the game with Northampton, Tom Voyce, President of the RFU, "unveiled" the clocks on each stand which were to be the main memorials to Eric Thorneloe. Northampton rather spoiled the occasion by winning 9-0 though there may have been one or two Tigers with sore heads since the club's 80th birthday dinner had been held the night before.

Then, a fortnight later, Avril Malan's Fifth Springboks were in town. It was to be another historic match at Welford Road, for though the Midland Counties XV could not beat the tourists as did their predecessors of 1931, their 3-3 draw was the best result of any British side until the Barbarians beat South Africa 6-0 in the last match of the tour.

"What a little concerted team practice did for that XV who, with a simple and single-minded approach...played the Springboks at their own game and produced a result and a game few of those present will forget," said Martin, who captained the combined side. It was the fifth game of the tour and the Midlands XV was: Mike Gavins (Leicester); Keith Chilton (London Welsh), Barry Williams (Bedford), Jeff Butterfield (Northampton), Bob Leslie (Northampton); Ian Laughland (London Scottish), David Stevens (Blackheath); Ron Jacobs, Andy Johnson, R Wilkins, CP Daniels (all Northampton), John Thompson (Leicester), 'Budge' Rogers (Bedford), Colin Martin (Leicester, captain), Don White (Northampton).

LEICESTERSHIRE
and
EAST MIDLANDS
versus
SOUTH AFRICA
(The Springboks)
Saturday, 5th November, 1960

➔ Colin Martin (letter D) leads from the front against Llanelly 25.3.1961.

It was a major achievement for Don White, who had played against every touring side since the war, but unluckily it was his fumbling of a loose ball near the Midlands line which gave the Springbok lock, 'Stompie' van der Merwe, the chance to seize a try early on. Before half-time, however, the South African centre, Bennie van Niekerk, pulled a leg muscle and though he played on after treatment, Doug Hopwood was withdrawn from the pack to cover for him. The Midlands proceeded to set about the Springbok seven, giving their halves the chance to progress up the touchline.

But it was from their own 25-yard line that the counties equalised. Budge Rogers gathered a missed place kick and opened up play, the centres putting Keith Chilton away down the right wing. Just over halfway he kicked ahead but the bouncing ball eluded him and the Springbok cover as White, whose run must have started 100 yards away, arrived for the try. It was not a difficult conversion but Gavins, who had played a magnificent game, missed his kick and the match was drawn.

"We had four kickers in the team," said Martin. "Don White, Keith Chilton, Mike and myself, but I was in no doubt who should take it at such a late stage in the game - the full-back." At the post-match reception the Springboks manager, Ferdie Bergh, described the Midlands pack as the most rugged they had encountered and he had little cause to change his mind as the tour progressed. Even though it was a Midland Counties XV in name, it was in fact the old Leicestershire and East Midlands combination and both bodies received a memento in the shape of a shield and a plaque.

Although it had been an indifferent first half of the season for Leicester, the results of Martin's captaincy were beginning to show. "I set out to build on what Tom Bleasdale had already achieved," said the New Zealander. "More particularly I endeavoured to combine the spearhead-style of New Zealand forward play with the swift flanking attacks characteristic of English rugby. My task was made much less difficult by the presence of one of the game's great generals, Phil Horrocks-Taylor, at fly-half."

There were signs of this when Leicester went down 14-5 to the Barbarians, O'Reilly making a guest appearance for Leicester. In the opposing XV was another international, Ken Scotland, whose name had already been linked with Leicester when he had completed his course at Cambridge. Not that Leicester had any lack of faith in their current full-back, Gavins, who received the reward his consistency merited when picked by England against Wales at Cardiff.

Unfortunately he became one of the many players to have been capped once, against Wales, when England lost, in a season when England

obviously did not know who was the best full-back in the country, having played Don Rutherford, Gavins and John Willcox in succession. Gavins was Leicester's first new England cap since Hazell six years before, though it had been whispered in previous seasons that Ireland might have played him since a great-grandparent had been Irish.

At much the same time Leicester decided to try out their promising half-backs, Richard Cooper and John Allen, against the RAF on the Welford Road Recreation Ground. In an atmosphere seldom conducive to good rugby, the youngsters came up against the wily rugby league fly-half Alex Murphy and the nuggety Gloucester scrum-half Micky Booth, and the servicemen won 11-6.

Before the season's end there were two landmarks. Bleasdale, who made his debut in 1949, played his 300th game for the club against Newport and Horrocks-Taylor was recalled by England for the Calcutta Cup match. His tactical kicking put considerable pressure on the Scots and he placed a penalty in England's 6-0 win. In the 22 matches he played for Leicester that season, they won 17. Without him they won 7 out of 20, an impressive statistic.

The 24 wins that season were a post-war record and the 14 tries by David Matthews was the best by a forward since Bill Dalby in 1912/13. Off the field there was, though, an element of sorrow at the disbanding of the supporters' club. It had performed prodigies in its early days but of late it had been rather less meaningful, and the Leicester committee took over its main functions of organising programmes, teas and the like. Perhaps not surprisingly the committee turned down the idea of floodlighting (the cheapest estimate was £6,000) since the rent for the ground was going up, from £225 to £1,000, although the city council had always borne in mind the part played by Leicester in attracting people to the city.

↑ Action from the loss to Harlequins at Twickenham 24.9.1960.

← **Tony O'Reilly**
With his film-star looks, ready wit and voracious try-scoring ability on tour with the Lions in 1955 and 1959, Tony O'Reilly was destined for success in more than one field. It duly came in the international business world, most notably with the H J Heinz Company of Pittsburgh, Pennsylvania whose chairman he became, and as newspaper magnate of the Independent News & Media group. He toured South Africa with the Lions as an 18-year-old wing (though several of his 29 Ireland appearances came at centre) and, four years later, set a tour record of 17 tries in New Zealand and Australia. His final international appearance came after a seven-year hiatus, when he played against England in 1970 as a late replacement and arrived for training in a chauffeur-driven limousine.

1961/1962

It was also, as it happens, an unhappy decision when Tigers agreed to play the first match of the 1961/62 season away. It had always been their custom to open the season at home but Bedford were opening their new clubhouse and marked the occasion by winning 21-13, a match whose second half was screened live by BBC Television cameras.

Malcolm Greenhow, the former Bedford and RAF centre, made his debut in that game and two games later, against Bath, Ken Scotland made his first appearance, having moved to work at Tamworth. At this time Scotland had won 18 of his 27 Scottish caps and had proved himself a player of quite outstanding ability. A pupil from the famous George Heriot School, he had captained Cambridge University - as did Wade a year later - and toured with the Lions in 1959. During his career he showed himself capable of playing anywhere behind the scrum but, regretfully, his debut game marked Bath's first win at Welford Road for 42 years.

Leicester were badly in need of some inspiration. They had lost Gavins to Moseley (which was nearer the full-back's Wolverhampton home) and the pre-Christmas period bought them little success. Several changes were made in the pack and John Allen and the RAF's Mike Dymond were challenging White for the scrum-half position. The Yorkshire contingent, Horrocks-Taylor, former Northampton centre Ian Gibson and Senior were missing for long periods. Interestingly, in the light of recent law changes, Leicester and Bristol played an experimental lineout variation which obliged the forwards to stand a yard apart but clearly the refereeing was not strict enough. The contemporary report said there was no obvious difference and certainly no clear tunnel between the players.

Wade was leading an unbeaten Cambridge to success in the Varsity Match and, upon his return to the club at Christmas, he brought with him the Light Blues' promising prop, Nick Drake-Lee. Nevertheless it was just as well the Barbarians game was postponed until March because of frost, despite the efforts of some spaceship-like heaters hired by the secretary from the Syston firm of En-Tout-Cas. Drake-Lee made his debut in the first month of the new year, on the occasion when Bath performed the double over Tigers, and in the same month Wade won the first of his three caps for England, playing in an incredibly dull 0-0 draw against Wales.

It should be added that his next game, a 16-0 win over Ireland, was very much better, Wade scoring a try. The big centre was the first Leicestershire-born player to be capped from Tigers since Bill Moore and the 16th international to have played for the club since the war.

Wade, however, was dropped for the Calcutta Cup game, in which Horrocks-Taylor made his fourth England appearance. In the opposing ranks was Scotland who had played in all his country's internationals, severely limiting his club appearances (in addition he missed the encounter with Rosslyn Park to ensure that his wife gave birth in Scotland and that the child would thus be eligible for his native country). Nevertheless, the full-back topped the points scorers' list, with 138 from 24 games in what had been a remarkably inconsistent season.

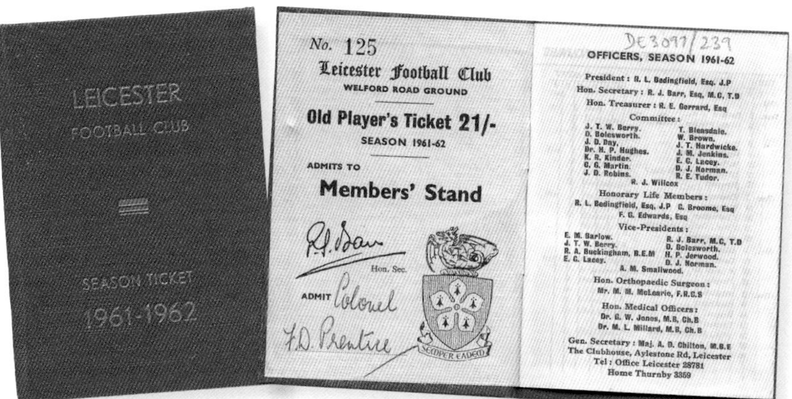

Old Player's ticket for season 1961/62 in the name of Colonel FD (Doug) Prentice.

There had been some interesting newcomers after Christmas, the former Wyggeston School and Loughborough Colleges product Michael Harrison playing centre in the side that lost to Bath and also when they beat Northampton for the first time in five years. A new lock forward from Hull University and Loughborough, Robert Errington Rowell, had scored a try in his debut against the Colleges and, at 22 had a long future in the game. The veteran prop Frank Chawner had made a remarkable comeback while David Bird, on the wing, was confirming the good impression he had already made. Behind the scenes Tom Berry had been named chairman of the England selectors, at much the same time that Doug Prentice was being forced by ill health to retire as secretary to the Rugby Football Union; he died in October 1962.

The points total for the 1961/62 season beat the previous year by six, so 496 was the target now for would-be record breakers. But before play resumed for a season changes were being made. Bobby Barr succeeded Rodney Bedingfield as club president and the secretary's post was filled by Ron Gerrard, the new treasurer being the quiet but efficient Stan Thorpe. There was considerable debate over the development of the clubhouse, particularly in view of the city council's scheme to widen the Aylestone Road which would have led to an arterial highway running through the existing changing rooms.

It came to nothing, fortunately, and the same fate met the suggestion that the club should purchase underground electric heating for the pitch (perhaps no-one wanted a repetition of the re-arranged Barbarians game of 1961/62, a dull game won by the Baa-baas 5-3).

1962/1963

The 1962/63 season began with four Berrys on the club's books, though not even father Tom could have hoped to see them all appear in the same senior XV. It was, still, a proud moment for the senior Berry who was preparing to go as manager on England's first short tour overseas, to New Zealand in 1963.

After a storming climax to the opening game with Bedford - trailing 13-6 with five minutes to go, Wade scored one try and was knocked unconscious in the process, then Bob Small crossed for the decisive score - the club went on to win its first five games before going down to Harlequins at Twickenham, a match in which England wing John Young (later a national selector) proved chivalry was not dead by refusing to run in a try after the referee had failed to spot a Harlequin knock-on.

Fixtures resumed with Swansea after a gap of five years and Leicester celebrated with a brilliant 29-6 win at St Helen's. The forward play was exceptional, the backs incisive, and Horrocks-Taylor went over for two tries while Scotland registered 17 points. The following week the club received a letter from Swansea secretary David Price which ran: "I have been asked by my committee to write to you concerning the very fine game at St Helen's. It was a great pleasure to see Leicester back...and the quality of your football pleased our members greatly. I believe our spectators expressed their evident satisfaction as the teams left the field. Well done." One illustration of the high regard that Welsh clubs in general held for Leicester.

For the second year running bad weather forced the postponement of the Barbarians game although Scotland travelled 600 miles and the lock Mike Jones 400 miles for a game which was not played. Scotland returned the next day for a national game and was subsequently asked to captain his country. At the same time he moved back to Edinburgh to work and joined Heriot's FP (Former Pupils) in January 1963. It was a surprise blow for Leicester who thereby lost a great entertainer, who scored 240 points in the 40 matches he played.

Not that Leicester had to rush around for a replacement, for Graham Pulfrey from Newark was

David Matthews scores one of Tigers' two tries in their first loss of the season to Harlequins at Twickenham 22.9.1962.

playing well at full-back after making his debut in September 1962, and the weather had taken a grip on sport up and down the country. It was the big freeze-up which hit the club's hopes of a record number of wins (before the break they had won 14 from 19 games). Twelve weeks went by without a game although there was satisfaction when England gave Drake-Lee the first of his eight caps - against Wales at Cardiff in England's last win in the Principality for 28 years.

Play resumed on 2 March against Harlequins in the somewhat surreal surrounds of Teddington where some 300 watched two of England's most successful clubs free of charge. The Baa-baas came on 28 March with, among others, Gordon Blackett in their ranks. Blackett was now with Gosforth and was later to turn professional. The Leicester back row of Martin, Matthews and Bob Small was in tremendous form and the club won 16-9. But April brought disappointment: with Horrocks-Taylor, Gibson, Senior and Dymond unavailable, Leicester scratched from the Middlesex Sevens, lost every match on the Easter tour and came home to lose to Rugby at Welford Road. Having lost only five games before that, they emerged from the abbreviated season with 21 wins and nine defeats. For the second successive season, David Matthews had played in every game.

While their seniors were crumbling, the Swifts had been carving their own niche in the club's record book. Well marshalled by the experienced Peter Konig, they had gone through the season unbeaten, with 21 victories, 626 points for and 85

↑ The Tiger skin that hung in the Tiger Bar for many years.

against. No-one could have complained if they had taken receipt of the tiger skin which was presented to the club at the 1963 annual meeting by a former player of the 1920s, Charlie Cramphorn, whose brother, also a former Tiger, had brought it specially from India.

1963/1964

Martin's three years as captain came to an end when Wade was elected to the post for the 1963/64 season. He had lost the services of Senior and Jones who had moved away but Cambridge Blue Malcolm Bussey had come to teach at Uppingham and was available on the wing, while London Welshman Keith Chilton, who had been working for two years just outside Leicester, at Whetstone, also joined.

It was to be another significant season, for where Martin had concentrated on honing the forwards into a force to be feared, Wade began to work on the backs. He introduced new ideas at training, in pre-match preparation and, off the field, gave the lead to the move for Saturday dances in the largely neglected upstairs clubroom. The players became increasingly involved in the running of club functions although the state of the clubroom was not impressive. It had metal rafters in the roof, a wooden floor, and if you fell down the chances of splinters in an uncomfortable part of the anatomy were very good.

For all that, it had atmosphere - a bit too much on occasions, though at least in a rugby club there is seldom a shortage of bouncers. And it helped to make players and members feel that it was really their club, rather than the preserve of two or three individuals.

Initially, on the field, there were experiments. Horrocks-Taylor, who had played in four of England's six tour games, including the three tests against New Zealand (twice) and Australia, returned to his native Yorkshire in September, so a fly-half was required. Richard Cooper was tried there before his return to Hull University, then Harrison, before Wade decided to play there himself. The move was a distinct success but at the same time David Matthews' long run of successive games ended. He passed John Thompson's record 103 and finally wound up with 109 before being rested.

It was also the season of Wilson Whineray's Fifth All Blacks, who came to Welford Road three days after Christmas, giving local enthusiasts a surfeit of good rugby, since they had been able to watch the Barbarians beat Leicester 13-6 on Boxing Day. It was to be another epic Midlands performance against a touring side with Leicestershire and the East Midlands fielding the following XV: Jack Smith (Bedford); David Bird (Leicester), Bob Leslie (Northampton), LR Drury (Bedford), Mike Wade (Leicester); Freddie Hawkins, Clive Ashby (both Wasps); Ron Jacobs (Northampton, captain), Andy Johnson (Northampton), Nick Drake-Lee (Leicester), Bob Rowell (Leicester), CP Daniels (Northampton), David Coley (Bedford), Colin Martin (Leicester), Budge Rogers (Bedford).

For Bird - known inevitably as Dickie - it was to be the outstanding game of his career. A fast, elusive runner who ended the season as the club's leading try-scorer with 14, he was robbed of a try in the second half when the referee failed to allow the combined side advantage after an All Blacks knock-on. Another Leicester player, Bob Rowell, had a significant match, trading blow for blow - sometimes literally - with his opposite number as the Midlands forwards showed no inclination to knuckle under to Whineray's pack.

Kevin Briscoe kicked two first-half penalties to put the tourists six points up at half-time but offside against Earle Kirton gave Coley a successful penalty. A try from Malcolm Dick made it 9-3 but a magnificent solo try by Wasps fly-half Fred Hawkins put the Midlands XV right back into contention. It was not until injury time that the All Blacks made the game safe with a try by Alan Stewart, converted by Briscoe, but the Midlands forwards had shown the All Blacks could be held and Colin Martin must have been delighted with their performance against his fellow countrymen.

Drake-Lee had already been picked for England against New Zealand but Rowell had not. The selectors, impressed with his showing at Leicester, rectified that by capping him against Wales which meant that the lock had reached international status in the rare circumstances in those days of being capped without ever playing in a trial game. England achieved a 6-6 draw and Rowell was unfortunately dropped for the next game, although he did achieve a second cap the following season, again against Wales.

↓ Ex-player Bobby Barr was president of the Tigers between 1962-65.

With Wade and John Allen combining well at half-back the season for Leicester proved the best for 30 years. Chilton chalked up 135 points and there were 26 wins, including an unbeaten Easter tour. The club had proved they were capable of more expansive football, with Harrison and Gibson combining well in the centre. During the summer, work finally began on the erection of floodlights at Welford Road, despite criticism at the annual meeting that they were merely an attempt to increase club prestige. No, said the committee, they were an amenity for club, for members and for Leicestershire - and they organised a game against a Midlands XV on 8 October to mark the official "lighting-up" time.

The annual meeting also threw up the subject of rats. There were, a member claimed, too many rat holes and too many rats at the ground and was told by Bobby Barr that the efforts of the local pest exterminator had proved in vain; the president endeavoured to lighten the proceedings by describing the appearance of a dead rat in one scrum during a Barbarians match though discussion of the sewer running beneath the ground from the cattle market must have kept subsequent questions to a minimum.

↑ LEICESTER FOOTBALL CLUB 1960/61
Back: Barr (Hon.Sec), T.Allen, Matthews, Thompson, Beason, Skelton, Tatham, Bolesworth (Team Hon.Sec), Bedingfield (President).
Middle: Gibson, Almey, Horrocks-Taylor, Martin (capt), Walker, Bleasdale, Gavins.
Front: Shephard, White.

↑ LEICESTER FOOTBALL CLUB 1961/62
Back: Barr (Hon.Sec), Bolesworth (Team Hon.Sec), Allen, Hopkins, Shephard, Jones, Rowell, Riley, B.Small, Bird, Cherry, Bedingfield (President).
Middle: Walker, Wade, Horrocks-Taylor, Martin (capt), Scotland, Chawner, Almey, Senior.
Front: Matthews, Tatham, Gibson, C.White, Drake-Lee.

↑ LEICESTER FOOTBALL CLUB 1962/63
Back: Barr (President), Evans, Cooper, Skelton, Gibson, Rowell, Beason, R.Small, Bolesworth (Team Hon.Sec).
Middle: Wade, Almey, Matthews, Martin (capt), Walker, Chawner, Horrocks-Taylor.
Front: Shephard, Bird, Dymond.
Inset: Riley, White.

↑ LEICESTER FOOTBALL CLUB 1963/64
Back: Barr (President), Freer, Walker, Sayer, Beason, Raine, Rowell, Willars, Almey, Harrison, Bussey, Bolesworth (Team Hon.Sec), Gerrard (Hon.Sec).
Middle: Gibson, Chawner, Skelton, Martin, Wade (capt), Matthews, Chilton, Bird.
Front: Allen, P.Edwards.

19 60/61

Home Ground: Welford Road except #25 at Welford Road Rec	OVERALL RECORD:					T	C	PG	DG	PTS
Captain: Colin Martin	PLD	W	D	L	Tigers scored:	86	50	38	6	490
	42	24	2	16	Opponents scored:	65	20	29	3	331

GM	DATE		VEN	OPPONENTS	RESULT	TRIES	KICKS	ATT
CLUB MATCHES								
1	Sep	**3**	**H**	**Bedford**	D 9-9	Bird	Gavins 2p	581
2		**7w**	**H**	**Watcyn Thomas XV**	L 12-19	Ashurst	Gavins 3p	1819
3		10	a	Bath	W 19-11	Senior(3), Horrocks-Taylor, Tatham	Gavins 2c	-
4		**17**	**H**	**Plymouth Albion**	W 30-3	Senior(3), Bleasdale, Horrocks-Taylor, Matthews, Ring	Gavins 3c/p	578
5		24	a	Harlequins	L 0-6	-	-	-
6	Oct	1	a	Coventry	L 3-16	-	Key p	-
7		**8**	**H**	**Richmond**	W 6-3	-	Gavins 2p	387
8		15	a	Cheltenham	L 8-11	Senior, Small	Key c	-
9		19w	a	Oxford University	W 24-3	Ashurst, Bird, Matthews, Tatham, White	Martin 3c, Ring d	-
10		**22**	**H**	**Northampton**	L 0-9	-	-	1028
		29	a	Nuneaton	PP (rain)			
11	Nov	5	a	Gloucester	L 8-11	Freer, Ring	Small c	-
12		**12**	**H**	**Cambridge University**	L 6-20	-	Martin 2p	1122
13		19	a	Newport	L 8-12	Matthews, Skelton	Martin c	-
14		26	a	Moseley	W 18-13	Tatham, Freer, Matthews	Tatham d, Martin 2c, Gavins c	-
15	Dec	**3**	**H**	**Waterloo**	W 5-0	Shephard	Martin c	69
16		10	a	Blackheath	L 0-5	-	-	-
17		**17**	**H**	**Bristol**	W 12-9	Haddon	Martin 2p, Wade d	567
18		24	a	Rugby	W 31-3	Shephard(2), Almey, Martin, Senior, Wade, Willars	Gavins 5c	-
19		**26m**	**H**	**Birkenhead Park**	D 3-3	Shephard	-	778
20		**27tu**	**H**	**Barbarians**	L 5-14	Freer	Gavins c	6944
21		31	a	Headingley	L 6-11	-	Gavins 2p	-
22	Jan	**7**	**H**	**Bath**	W 16-3	Senior(2)	Gavins 2c/2p	109
23		**14**	**H**	**Gloucester**	W 21-3	Freer, Horrocks-Taylor, Martin, Senior	Robins 3c/p	527
24		21	a	Bedford	W 6-0	Almey, Freer	-	-
25		**26th**	**H**	**Royal Air Force**	L 6-11	Almey	Cooper p	-
26		**28**	**H**	**Rosslyn Park**	W 13-0	Allen, Freer, Shephard	Gavins 2c	214
27	Feb	4	a	London Scottish	L 3-17	Martin	-	-
28		**11**	**H**	**Newport**	W 20-8	Matthews(2), Shephard	Robins c/3p	639
29		**18**	**H**	**Wasps**	W 14-8	Allen	Robins c/3p	852
30		25	a	Northampton	L 3-8	-	Tatham d	-
31	Mar	**4**	**H**	**Harlequins**	W 29-6	Shephard(2), Almey, Bleasdale, Freer, Matthews, Senior	Robins 4c	915
32		**9th**	**H**	**Loughborough Colleges**	W 14-8	Bleasdale, Small	Gavins c/2p	230
33		**11**	**H**	**Coventry**	L 3-12	-	Small d	1479
34		18	a	Bradford	W 14-6	Matthews	Gavins c/3p	-
35		**25**	**H**	**Llanelly**	W 26-6	Matthews(2), Freer, Senior	Robins 4c/p, Horrocks-Taylor d	823
36	Apr	1	a	Bristol	L 5-14	White	Martin c	-
37		3m	a	Plymouth Albion	W 3-0	Matthews	-	-
38		4tu	a	Exeter	W 11-6	Senior(2), Matthews	Gavins c	-
39		**8**	**H**	**Birkenhead Park**	W 26-6	Shephard(3), Matthews	Gavins 4c/2p	690
40		**15**	**H**	**Liverpool**	W 11-9	Freer, Matthews	Gavins c/p	455
41		19w	a	Nuneaton	W 11-0	Allen(2)	Gavins c/p	-
42		**22**	**H**	**Northern**	W 22-9	Shephard(3)	Gavins 2c/3p	408

INDIVIDUAL APPEARANCES 1960/61

Name / Game #	1	2	3	4	5	6	7	8	9	10	11	12	13	14	15	16	17	18	19	20	21	22	23	24	25	26	27	28	29	30	31	32	33	34	35	36	37	38	39	40	41	42	Apps	T	Pts
JH (Jeff) Addison	-	-	-	-	-	-	-	-	-	-	E	-	D	D	D	D	E	G	E	E	E	<E	-	-	-	-	-	-	-	-	-	-	-	-	-	-	-	-	-	-	-	-	11	-	-
JA (John) Allen	-	-	-	-	-	-	-	-	-	-	-	-	-	-	-	-	-	-	-	-	-	-	-	-	>I	-	-	-	-	-	-	-	-	-	-	-	-	I	-	-	-	-	2	-	-
T (Trevor) Allen	-	-	-	-	-	-	K	-	K	-	M	K	N	K	L	L	K	-	K	-	K	-	-	K	-	K	L	M	N	M	-	M	-	-	-	-	M	L	-	-	L	<K	22	4	12
GA (Gordon) Almey	-	-	-	-	F	H	F	-	-	-	-	-	-	-	-	H	H	F	F	F	F	F	F	F	F	F	F	F	F	F	F	F	F	-	F	-	-	-	F	F	F	F	26	4	12
ADB (Derek) Ashurst	H	H	F	H	G	G	G	F	F	H	H	H	F	H	F	G	-	-	-	-	-	-	-	-	-	-	-	-	-	-	-	-	-	-	-	-	-	-	-	-	-	-	16	2	6
R (Bob) Beason	>E	E	-	-	-	-	-	-	-	-	-	-	-	-	-	-	-	-	-	-	-	-	-	-	-	-	-	C	C	C	A	C	C	A	C	C	C	C	C	C	A	C	17	-	-
DW (David) Bird	>K	K	N	-	-	K	M	L	N	K	K	N	K	N	K	K	-	-	-	-	-	-	-	-	-	-	-	-	-	-	-	-	-	-	-	-	L	-	-	-	-	-	15	2	6
T (Tom) Bleasdale	G	G	G	G	-	-	-	G	G	G	-	G	-	-	-	-	G	-	G	G	G	G	G	G	G	G	G	G	G	G	G	G	G	G	G	G	G	-	G	G	G	G	32	3	9
AE (Arthur) Chapman	-	-	-	-	-	-	-	-	-	-	-	-	-	-	-	-	-	-	-	-	-	-	-	-	-	-	-	-	-	-	-	-	-	>J	-	-	-	-	-	-	-	-	1	-	-
F (Frank) Chawner	-	-	-	-	-	-	-	-	-	-	-	-	-	-	-	-	-	-	A	-	-	-	-	-	A	-	-	-	-	-	-	-	-	-	-	-	-	-	-	-	-	-	2	-	-
G (George) Cherry	-	-	-	A	A	A	C	C	-	-	D	-	-	-	-	-	-	-	-	-	-	-	-	-	-	-	-	-	-	-	-	-	-	-	-	-	-	-	-	-	-	-	6	-	-
RC (Dick) Cooper	-	-	-	-	-	-	-	-	-	-	-	-	-	-	-	-	-	-	>J	-	-	-	-	-	J	-	-	-	-	-	-	-	-	-	-	-	-	-	-	-	-	-	2	-	3
ME (Mike) Freer	N	N	-	N	N	N	N	N	-	N	N	-	M	M	J	J	M	-	M	M	M	M	M	M	M	M	J	L	L	L	L	-	L	-	L	L	-	-	M	M	-	-	32	9	27
MN (Mike) Gavins E1	0	0	0	0	0	-	0	-	-	0	-	0	-	0	-	-	-	0	-	0	0	0	-	-	-	0	0	0	0	0	-	0	-	0	-	-	0	0	0	0	0	0	26	-	126
IM (Ian) Gibson	-	-	-	-	-	-	-	-	-	-	-	-	-	-	-	-	-	-	-	-	-	-	-	-	-	-	-	-	-	-	-	-	-	-	-	-	-	-	-	-	-	>L	1	-	-
AL (Alastair) Graham-Bryce	-	-	-	-	-	-	-	-	-	-	-	-	-	-	-	-	-	-	-	-	-	-	-	-	=E	-	-	-	-	-	-	-	-	-	-	-	-	-	-	-	-	-	1	-	-
PA (Peter) Haddon	-	-	-	-	-	-	-	-	>A	A	C	C	C	C	C	C	C	C	-	C	C	C	C	A	C	C	C	-	-	-	-	<A	-	-	-	-	-	-	-	-	-	-	19	1	3
RA (Roderick) Harris	-	-	-	-	-	-	-	-	-	-	-	-	-	-	-	-	-	>B	-	-	-	B	-	-	-	-	-	-	<B	-	-	-	-	-	-	-	-	-	-	-	-	-	3	-	-
MJ (Mike) Hemphrey	A	A	C	-	-	-	-	-	-	-	-	-	-	-	-	-	-	-	C	-	-	-	-	-	-	-	-	-	-	-	-	-	-	-	-	-	B	F	-	-	-	-	6	-	-
JP (Phil) Horrocks-Taylor E3 L1	-	-	J	J	J	J	-	-	J	-	-	-	-	-	-	-	-	J	-	J	-	J	J	J	-	J	-	-	J	-	J	-	J	-	J	J	J	J	J	J	J	J	22	3	12
MR (Maurice) Key	-	-	-	-	-	0	-	<0	-	-	-	-	-	-	-	-	-	-	-	-	-	-	-	-	-	-	-	-	-	-	-	-	-	-	-	-	-	-	-	-	-	-	2	-	5
Cpl. RV (Redvers) King	-	-	>E	<D	-	-	-	-	-	-	-	-	-	-	-	-	-	-	-	-	-	-	-	-	-	-	-	-	-	-	-	-	-	-	-	-	-	-	-	-	-	-	2	-	-
CJ (Colin) Littlewood	-	-	-	-	-	-	-	>J	-	J	<J	-	-	-	-	-	-	-	-	-	-	-	-	-	-	-	-	-	-	-	-	-	-	-	-	-	-	-	-	-	-	-	3	-	-
MGS (Mike) Lubbock	-	-	-	-	-	-	I	-	-	I	I	-	I	I	-	-	-	-	<I	-	-	-	-	-	-	-	-	-	-	-	-	-	-	-	-	-	-	-	-	-	-	-	6	-	-
CG (Colin) Martin	D*	D*	D*	E*	D*	D*	D*	D*	E*	E*	-	D*	G*	G*	G*	E*	D*	D*	D*	D*	D*	D*	D*	D*	-	D*	D*	D*	D*	D*	E*	D*	D*	D*	D*	D*	D*	D*	E*	D*	E*	D*	40	3	37
DJ (David) Matthews	F	F	H	F	H	F	H	H	H	F	G	F	H	F	H	F	F	-	H	-	-	-	H	H	H	H	H	H	H	H	H	H	H	H	H	H	H	H	H	H	H	H	38	14	42
AJF (Tony) O'Reilly I24 L10	-	-	-	-	-	-	-	-	-	-	-	-	-	-	-	-	-	-	-	<N	-	-	-	-	-	-	-	-	-	-	-	-	-	-	-	-	-	-	-	-	-	-	1	-	-
RO (Dick) Rawson	-	-	-	-	-	-	-	-	-	-	-	-	-	-	-	-	-	-	-	-	-	-	-	-	-	-	K	K	-	-	-	-	N	<N	-	-	-	-	-	-	-	-	4	-	-
BD (Brian) Ring	L	L	L	M	-	-	L	-	L	M	L	M	L	L	M	M	-	-	-	-	<L	-	-	-	-	-	-	-	-	-	-	-	-	-	-	-	-	-	-	-	-	-	14	2	9
JD (John) Robins W11 L5	-	-	-	-	-	-	-	-	-	-	-	-	-	-	-	-	-	-	-	-	-	-	A	C	-	A	-	A	A	A	C	-	A	-	A	-	-	-	-	-	-	-	9	-	50
D (David) Senior	-	-	K	K	K	-	-	K	-	-	-	-	-	-	-	-	-	K	-	K	-	K	K	-	N	-	-	-	-	K	K	K	K	K	K	K	K	K	K	K	K	-	21	15	45
CD (Cliff) Shephard	-	-	-	-	-	-	-	-	-	-	-	L	-	-	N	N	N	N	N	-	N	-	-	N	K	N	N	N	K	N	N	N	M	-	-	N	N	N	N	N	N	N	24	14	42
RP (Rex) Skelton	C	C	A	C	C	C	A	A	C	C	A	A	A	A	A	A	A	A	-	A	A	A	-	-	-	-	A	-	-	-	-	-	-	C	-	A	A	A	A	A	C	A	30	1	3
RW (Bob) Small	-	-	-	-	-	-	-	-	-	-	F	-	-	-	-	-	-	-	-	-	-	-	-	-	-	-	-	-	-	-	-	-	-	F	-	-	F	G	-	-	-	-	4	-	-
BTC (Brian) Small	-	-	-	-	-	-	-	M	0	-	0	-	0	-	0	0	0	-	0	-	-	-	0	0	0	-	-	-	-	-	0	L	0	L	0	0	-	-	-	-	-	-	17	2	11
L (Lyn) Tatham	J	J	M	L	L	L	J	-	M	L	-	J	J	J	-	-	J	L	-	-	J	L	L	L	L	L	M	J	M	J	M	J	-	M	M	M	-	-	L	-	M	M	32	3	15
JS (John) Thompson	-	-	-	-	E	E	E	E	D	D	-	E	E	E	E	-	-	E	-	-	-	-	E	E	D	E	E	E	E	E	D	E	E	E	E	E	E	E	D	E	D	E	31	-	-
MR (Mike) Wade E+	M	M	-	-	M	M	-	-	-	-	-	-	-	-	-	-	L	M	L	L	-	N	N	-	-	-	-	-	-	-	-	-	-	-	N	-	-	M	-	L	-	-	13	1	6
MR (Mike) Walker	B	B	B	B	B	B	B	B	B	B	B	B	B	B	B	B	B	-	B	B	B	-	B	B	B	B	B	B	-	B	B	B	B	B	B	B	-	B	B	B	B	B	38	-	-
HV (Chalkie) White	I	I	I	I	I	I	-	I	I	-	-	I	-	-	I	I	I	I	-	I	I	I	I	I	-	I	I	I	I	I	I	I	I	I	I	I	I	-	I	I	I	I	34	2	6
GG (Graham) Willars	-	-	-	-	-	-	-	-	-	-	-	-	-	-	-	-	-	H	-	H	H	H	-	-	-	-	-	-	-	-	-	-	-	-	-	F	-	-	-	-	-	-	5	1	3

The key for how to read the stats is on the last page

19 61/62

Home Ground: Welford Road										
Captain: Colin Martin										

OVERALL RECORD:					T	C	PG	DG	MK	PTS
PLD	W	D	L	Tigers scored:	84	53	42	4	0	496
41	22	2	17	Opponents scored:	69	36	25	9	1	384

GM	DATE		VEN	OPPONENTS	RESULT	TRIES	KICKS	ATT
CLUB MATCHES								
1	Sep	2	a	Bedford	L 13-21	Freer, Tatham	Gavins 2c/p	-
2		6w	H	Watcyn Thomas XV	W 17-10	Senior(2), Matthews, Shephard	Gavins c/p	1742
3		9	H	Bath	L 11-12	Almey, Senior	Scotland c/p	731
4		16	H	Plymouth Albion	L 9-11	Shephard	Scotland 2p	429
5		23	a	Harlequins	W 13-6	Allen, Shephard	Scotland 2c/p	-
6		27w	H	Rugby	W 25-6	Edwards, Shephard, Tatham	Scotland 2c/3p/d	274
7		30	H	Newport	L 3-9	-	Scotland p	1142
8	Oct	7	H	Coventry	L 6-19	-	Scotland 2p	2274
9		14	a	Richmond	L 3-24	-	Scotland p	-
10		21	H	Cheltenham	W 12-3	Bird, Horrocks-Taylor	Scotland 2p	461
11		25w	H	Oxford University	W 14-11	Mainwaring	Scotland c/3p	395
12		28	a	Northampton	L 13-29	Bird, Matthews	Martin 2c/p	-
13	Nov	4	a	Gloucester	L 11-26	Bird	Scotland c/2p	-
14		11	a	Cambridge University	L 3-11	Mainwaring	-	-
15		18	H	Leicestershire XV	W 10-6	Almey, Mainwaring	Scotland 2c	279
16		25	H	Moseley	W 23-9	Matthews(2), Greenhow, Skelton	Scotland 4c/p	498
17	Dec	2	a	Waterloo	L 3-5	Matthews	-	-
18		9	a	Blackheath	L 6-11	Greenhow	Scotland p	-
19		16	H	Bristol	W 8-6	Bird, Dymond	Hopkins c	497
20		23	a	London Irish	W 6-3	Matthews	Martin p	-
		26tu	H	Birkenhead Park	PP (frost)			
		27w	H	Barbarians	PP (frost)			
		30	H	Headingley	PP (frost)			
21	Jan	6	a	Bath	L 5-8	Tatham	Martin c	-
22		13	H	Gloucester	W 16-3	Chawner, Senior, Wade	Martin 2c/p	635
23		20	H	Bedford	W 19-0	Senior(2), Bird, Tatham	Martin 2c, Scotland p	461
24		27	a	Rosslyn Park	L 8-14	Tatham(2)	Martin c	-
25	Feb	3	H	London Scottish	W 20-0	Almey, Bird, Jones, Wade	Robins c/p, Tatham d	328
26		10	a	Newport	L 10-22	Greenhow, Matthews	Robins 2c	-
27		17	a	Wasps	D 6-6	Greenhow	Scotland p	-
28		24	H	Northampton	W 5-0	Shephard	Martin c	654
	Mar	3	H	Harlequins	PP (snow)			
29		8th	H	Loughborough Colleges	W 16-0	Martin, Freer, Rowell	Martin 2c, Freer d	133
30		13tu	a	Coventry	L 5-10	Almey	Martin c	-
31		17	H	Royal Air Force	W 14-10	Matthews, Senior	Martin c/2p	354
32		24	H	Bradford	W 32-5	Bird(3), Senior(3), Gibson	Martin 3c/p, Scotland c	509
33		29th	H	Barbarians	L 3-5	-	Scotland p	11000
34		31	a	Llanelly	L 3-12	Scotland	-	-
35	Apr	5th	H	Nuneaton	W 19-3	Senior(3)	Senior d, Martin c/p, Scotland c	268
36		7	a	Birkenhead Park	W 34-3	Tatham(2), Drake-Lee, Matthews, Wade	Scotland 5c/3p	-
37		9m	H	Maesteg	W 13-11	Scotland, Senior	Scotland c/p, Martin c	407
38		14	a	Liverpool	W 6-3	-	Scotland 2p	-
39		21	a	Bristol	D 11-11	Matthews	Martin c/2p	-
40		23m	a	Plymouth Albion	W 11-6	Bird, Senior, Bo.Small	Martin c	-
41		24tu	a	Exeter	W 31-14	Wade(3), Bird, Matthews, Senior	Martin 5c/p	-

INDIVIDUAL APPEARANCES 1961/62

Name / Game #	1	2	3	4	5	6	7	8	9	10	11	12	13	14	15	16	17	18	19	20	21	22	23	24	25	26	27	28	29	30	31	32	33	34	35	36	37	38	39	40	41	Apps	T	Pts
JA (John) Allen	-	-	-	I	I	I	I	I	I	I	I	I	I	I	-	-	I	-	-	-	-	-	-	-	-	-	-	-	-	-	-	-	-	-	-	-	-	-	-	I	-	13	1	3
GA (Gordon) Almey	F	F	F	F	-	-	-	-	-	-	-	-	-	F	F	F	F	F	F	-	F	-	-	F	F	-	F	F	F	H	-	F	F	-	F	-	F	-	F	-	-	22	4	12
ADB (Derek) Ashurst	-	-	-	-	-	-	-	-	-	-	-	-	-	-	-	-	-	-	-	F	-	F	-	-	-	F	-	-	-	-	-	-	-	F	-	-	-	-	-	-	-	4	-	-
R (Bob) Beason	A	A	C	C	-	-	-	-	-	-	-	-	-	-	-	-	-	-	-	-	-	-	-	-	-	-	-	-	-	-	-	-	-	-	-	-	-	-	-	-	-	4	-	-
DW (David) Bird	-	-	-	-	-	-	-	K	N	L	L	K	K	M	-	K	L	K	K	K	K	N	N	N	N	K	K	N	K	N	N	N	N	N	N	K	-	N	N	N	N	32	11	33
T (Tom) Bleasdale	G	G	G	G	G	G	G	G	G	G	G	G	G	G	G	G	G	G	G	G	G	G	-	-	-	-	-	-	-	-	-	-	-	-	-	-	-	-	-	-	-	22	-	-
WA (Tony) Cavender	-	-	-	-	>F	F	F	F	F	F	F	F	<F	-	-	-	-	-	-	-	-	-	-	-	-	-	-	-	-	-	-	-	-	-	-	-	-	-	-	-	-	9	-	-
F (Frank) Chawner	-	-	-	-	-	-	-	-	-	C	C	C	C	A	C	A	A	A	C	A	A	A	A	A	C	A	C	C	A	A	A	A	C	A	A	A	A	A	A	A	A	32	1	3
G (George) Cherry	C	C	A	A	C	A	A	A	A	-	-	-	-	-	-	-	-	-	-	-	-	-	-	-	-	-	-	A	C	C	C	-	-	-	-	-	-	-	-	C	-	14	-	-
RJ (Roger) Clarke	-	-	-	-	-	-	-	-	-	-	-	-	-	-	-	-	>K	-	-	-	-	-	-	-	-	-	-	-	-	-	-	-	-	<K	-	-	-	-	-	-	-	2	-	-
BJ (Brian) Collins	-	-	-	-	-	-	-	-	-	-	-	-	-	-	-	-	-	-	-	-	-	-	-	-	-	-	-	-	-	-	-	-	-	-	=B	-	-	-	-	-	-	1	-	-
RC (Dick) Cooper	-	-	-	-	-	-	-	-	-	-	-	-	-	-	-	-	-	-	-	J	-	-	-	-	-	-	-	-	-	-	-	-	-	L	-	-	-	-	-	-	J	3	-	-
NJ (Nick) Drake-Lee E+	-	-	-	-	-	-	-	-	-	-	-	-	-	-	-	-	-	-	-	-	>C	C	-	-	-	-	-	-	-	-	-	C	A	C	C	C	C	C	C	-	-	10	1	3
MJ (Mike) Dymond	-	-	-	-	-	-	-	-	-	-	-	-	-	-	>I	I	-	I	I	-	-	-	-	-	-	-	-	-	-	-	I	-	-	-	-	-	-	-	-	-	-	5	1	3
PG (Peter) Edwards	-	-	-	>B	B	B	B	B	B	B	B	B	B	B	B	B	B	B	B	B	B	B	-	B	-	-	-	B	-	-	-	-	-	-	-	-	-	-	-	B	-	22	1	3
ME (Mike) Freer	L	-	-	L	-	-	-	M	M	-	-	L	M	-	-	-	-	-	N	L	-	L	M	-	-	-	-	-	M	-	-	-	-	-	-	-	-	M	-	-	-	12	2	9
MN (Mike) Gavins E1	O	O	-	-	-	-	-	-	-	-	-	-	-	-	-	-	-	-	-	-	-	-	-	-	-	-	-	-	-	-	-	-	-	-	-	-	-	-	-	-	-	2	-	12
IM (Ian) Gibson	-	-	M	-	L	-	-	-	-	-	M	M	-	-	M	M	M	M	L	-	L	-	-	-	-	-	-	-	-	-	L	L	-	-	L	L	M	-	L	-	M	17	1	3
M (Malcolm) Greenhow	>M	-	-	-	-	-	-	-	-	-	-	-	-	-	L	L	-	L	-	-	-	-	-	-	-	M	M	-	L	-	-	-	-	-	-	-	-	-	-	M	-	8	4	12
MJ (Mike) Harrison	-	-	-	-	-	-	-	-	-	-	-	-	-	-	-	-	-	-	-	-	>M	-	-	-	-	-	-	M	-	-	-	-	-	-	-	-	-	L	-	-	-	3	-	-
MJ (Mike) Hemphrey	-	-	-	-	-	-	-	-	-	-	-	-	-	-	-	-	-	-	-	O	-	-	-	-	-	-	-	-	-	-	-	-	-	-	-	-	-	-	-	-	C	2	-	-
DK Hill	-	-	-	-	-	-	-	-	-	-	-	-	-	-	-	-	-	-	-	-	-	-	-	-	-	-	-	-	-	-	=J	-	-	-	-	-	-	-	-	-	-	1	-	-
G (Gareth) Hopkins	-	-	-	-	-	-	-	-	-	-	-	-	-	-	>O	-	O	-	O	-	-	-	O	-	O	O	-	-	-	O	O	-	-	-	-	-	-	-	O	O	O	11	-	2
JP (Phil) Horrocks-Taylor E4 L1	-	J	J	J	J	J	J	-	-	J	-	-	-	-	-	-	-	-	-	-	-	-	-	J	J	-	-	-	J	J	-	J	J	J	-	-	J	J	J	J	-	18	1	3
JM (Mike) Jones	-	-	-	-	>E	E	-	E	D	E	-	E	E	E	E	E	E	D	E	E	E	E	E	D	E	E	D	D	-	E	-	D	E	E	D	D	D	-	D	D	-	31	1	3
R (Dick) Mainwaring	-	-	-	-	-	-	-	-	-	>N	N	-	-	K	K	N	<N	-	-	-	-	-	-	-	-	-	-	-	-	-	-	-	-	-	-	-	-	-	-	-	-	6	3	9
CG (Colin) Martin	D*	D*	D*	D*	D*	D*	D*	D*	E*	D*	D*	D*	D*	D*	D*	D*	D*	E*	D*	D*	D*	D*	G*	G*	G*	G*	G*	G*	G*	G*	G*	G*	G*	G*	G*	G*	G*	G*	G*	G*	G*	41	1	83
DJ (David) Matthews	H	H	H	H	H	H	H	H	L	H	H	H	H	H	H	H	H	H	H	H	H	H	H	H	H	H	H	H	H	F	H	H	H	H	H	H	H	H	H	H	H	41	11	33
D (David) Moeller	-	-	-	-	-	-	-	-	=H	-	-	-	-	-	-	-	-	-	-	-	-	-	-	-	-	-	-	-	-	-	-	-	-	-	-	-	-	-	-	-	-	1	-	-
DT (David) Noble	-	-	-	-	-	-	=E	-	-	-	-	-	-	-	-	-	-	-	-	-	-	-	-	-	-	-	-	-	-	-	-	-	-	-	-	-	-	-	-	-	-	1	-	-
PW (Peter) Riley	-	-	-	-	-	-	-	-	-	-	>E	-	-	-	-	-	-	-	-	-	-	-	D	E	D	D	E	E	D	D	D	-	-	-	-	-	-	E	-	-	D	12	-	-
JD (John) Robins W11 L5	-	-	-	-	-	-	-	-	-	-	-	-	-	-	-	-	-	-	-	-	-	-	-	-	A	<C	-	-	-	-	-	-	-	-	-	-	-	-	-	-	-	2	-	9
RE (Bob) Rowell E+	-	-	-	-	-	-	-	-	-	-	-	-	-	-	-	-	-	-	-	-	-	-	-	-	-	-	-	-	>E	-	E	E	D	D	E	E	E	D	E	E	E	12	1	3
KJF (Ken) Scotland S22 L5	-	-	>O	O	O	O	O	O	O	O	J	-	J	J	J	O	J	O	-	-	-	-	J	-	-	-	O	-	-	-	-	O	O	O	O	O	O	O	-	-	-	24	2	138
D (David) Senior	K	K	K	K	K	K	K	-	-	-	-	-	-	-	-	-	-	-	-	-	-	K	K	K	K	-	-	-	-	-	K	K	K	-	K	-	K	-	K	K	K	19	16	51
CD (Cliff) Shephard	N	N	-	N	N	N	N	N	K	K	K	N	N	N	N	-	-	N	-	N	N	-	-	-	-	N	N	K	N	K	-	-	-	-	-	N	-	K	-	-	-	24	5	15
RP (Rex) Skelton	-	-	-	-	-	-	-	-	-	A	A	A	A	C	A	C	C	C	A	C	-	-	C	C	-	-	A	-	-	-	-	-	-	-	-	-	-	-	-	-	-	14	1	3
RW (Bob) Small	-	-	-	-	-	-	-	-	-	-	-	-	-	-	-	-	-	-	-	-	-	-	F	-	-	-	-	-	-	-	F	-	-	-	-	F	-	F	-	F	F	6	1	3
BTC (Brian) Small	-	-	-	-	-	-	-	-	-	-	O	O	O	O	-	-	-	-	M	-	O	O	-	O	-	-	-	-	O	-	-	-	-	-	-	-	-	-	-	-	-	9	-	-
KT (Ken) Smith	-	-	-	-	-	-	-	-	-	-	-	-	-	-	-	-	-	-	-	-	-	-	-	-	-	>L	L	L	-	-	-	-	-	-	-	-	-	-	-	-	-	3	-	-
L (Lyn) Tatham	J	M	L	M	-	M	M	J	J	M	-	J	L	L	-	J	-	J	J	-	J	J	L	L	L	J	J	J	-	L	-	-	L	M	J	J	L	-	-	-	-	29	8	27
JS (John) Thompson	E	E	E	<E	-	-	-	-	-	-	-	-	-	-	-	-	-	-	-	-	-	-	-	-	-	-	-	-	-	-	-	-	-	-	-	-	-	-	-	-	-	4	-	-
MR (Mike) Wade E3	-	L	N	-	M	L	L	L	-	-	-	-	-	-	-	-	-	-	-	M	-	M	-	M	M	-	-	-	-	M	M	M	M	-	M	M	N	-	M	L	L	20	6	18
MR (Mike) Walker	B	B	B	-	-	-	-	-	-	-	-	-	-	-	-	-	-	-	-	-	-	-	B	-	B	B	B	-	B	B	B	B	B	B	-	B	B	B	B	-	B	18	-	-
HV (Chalkie) White	I	I	I	-	-	-	-	-	-	-	-	-	-	-	-	-	-	-	-	I	I	I	I	I	I	I	I	I	I	I	-	I	I	I	I	I	I	I	I	-	I	23	-	-
JC (John) White	-	-	-	-	-	-	-	-	-	-	-	-	-	-	-	-	-	-	-	-	-	-	-	-	-	-	-	>O	-	-	-	-	-	-	-	-	-	-	-	-	-	1	-	-
MJB (Mark) Wrench	-	-	-	-	>A	C	C	C	<C	-	-	-	-	-	-	-	-	-	-	-	-	-	-	-	-	-	-	-	-	-	-	-	-	-	-	-	-	-	-	-	-	5	-	-

The key for how to read the stats is on the last page

19	**62**/**63**	Home Ground: Welford Road	OVERALL RECORD:					T	C	PG	DG	PTS
		Captain: Colin Martin	PLD	W	D	L	Tigers scored:	66	35	23	2	343
			31	21	1	9	Opponents scored:	49	12	18	6	243

GM	DATE		VEN	OPPONENTS	RESULT	TRIES	KICKS	ATT
CLUB MATCHES								
1	Sep	**1**	**H**	**Bedford**	W 18-13	Bird, Dymond, Bo.Small, Wade	Scotland 3c	574
2		**5w**	**H**	**Watcyn Thomas XV**	W 21-3	Bird(2), Gibson	Scotland 3c/2p	1481
3		8	a	Bath	W 21-5	Scotland, Chawner, Gibson, Matthews, Senior	Scotland 3c	-
4		12w	a	Sheffield	W 19-0	Riley(2), Matthews	Scotland 2c/2p	-
5		**15**	**H**	**Plymouth Albion**	W 11-6	Bird, Chawner, Harrison	Tatham c	496
6		22	a	Harlequins	L 8-12	Drake-Lee, Matthews	Scotland c	-
7		29	a	Swansea	W 29-6	Horrocks-Taylor(2), Drake-Lee, Gibson	Scotland 4c/3p	5000
8	Oct	6	a	Coventry	L 9-16	Drake-Lee	Scotland 2p	-
9		**13**	**H**	**Richmond**	W 21-3	Smith(2), Scotland, Matthews, Bo.Small	Scotland 3c	597
10		20	a	Cheltenham	D 0-0	-	-	-
11		24w	a	Oxford University	L 0-12	-	-	-
12		**27**	**H**	**Northampton**	W 12-9	Jones, Smith	Scotland 2p	1130
13	Nov	3	a	Gloucester	W 8-6	Bird, Chawner	Scotland c	-
14		**10**	**H**	**Cambridge University**	W 6-0	-	Scotland p/d	845
15		17	a	Newport	L 3-12	Dymond	-	-
16		24	a	Moseley	W 11-9	Martin, Matthews	Scotland c/p	-
17	Dec	**1**	**H**	**Waterloo**	W 22-3	Chawner, Gibson, Matthews, Senior, Bo.Small	Scotland 2c/p	592
18		**8**	**H**	**Blackheath**	W 8-6	Bo.Small	Scotland c/d	197
19		**15**	**H**	**Bristol**	W 8-6	Matthews	Martin c/p	330
		22	**H**	**London Irish**	PP (fog)			
		26w	**H**	**Birkenhead Park**	PP (frost)			
		27th	**H**	**Barbarians**	PP (frost)			
		29	a	Headingley	PP (frost)			
	Jan	**5**	**H**	**Bath**	PP (frost)			
		12	**H**	**Gloucester**	PP (frost)			
		19	a	Bedford	PP (frost)			
		26	**H**	**Rosslyn Park**	PP (frost)			
	Feb	2	a	London Scottish	PP (frost)			
		9	**H**	**Newport**	PP (frost)			
		16	**H**	**Wasps**	PP (frost)			
		23	a	Nottingham	PP (frost)			
20	Mar	2	a	Harlequins	W 15-8	Bird, Gibson, Rowell	Martin 3c	300
		7th	**H**	**Loughborough Colleges**	PP (frost)			
21		**9**	**H**	**Coventry**	L 3-21	-	Martin p	491
22		**16**	**H**	**Royal Air Force**	W 9-0	Bo.Small	Martin 2p	200
23		23	a	Saracens	W 25-6	Bird, Gibson, Matthews, Senior, Bo.Small	Martin 2c/2p	-
24		**28th**	**H**	**Barbarians**	W 16-9	Bird, Dymond, Matthews, Wade	Martin 2c	2401
25		**30**	**H**	**Llanelly**	W 6-3	Senior	Cooper p	276
26	Apr	3w	a	Nuneaton	W 8-3	Chawner, Riley	Martin c	-
27		6	a	Birkenhead Park	W 6-3	Matthews	Martin p	-
28		13	a	Bristol	L 8-31	Sayer	Martin c/p	-
29		15m	a	Plymouth Albion	L 0-14	-	-	-
30		16tu	a	Exeter	L 9-12	Bird, Gibson, Matthews	-	-
31		**20**	**H**	**Rugby**	L 3-6	Cowman	-	139

INDIVIDUAL APPEARANCES 1962/63

Name / Game #	1	2	3	4	5	6	7	8	9	10	11	12	13	14	15	16	17	18	19	20	21	22	23	24	25	26	27	28	29	30	31	Apps	T	Pts
JA (John) Allen	-	-	-	-	-	-	-	-	-	-	-	-	-	-	-	-	-	-	-	-	I	-	-	-	-	-	-	-	-	-	-	1	-	-
GA (Gordon) Almey	-	-	-	-	-	-	-	-	-	-	-	-	-	-	-	-	-	-	-	-	-	-	-	-	-	-	-	-	F	H	-	2	-	-
ADB (Derek) Ashurst	-	-	-	G	<G	-	-	-	-	-	-	-	-	-	-	-	-	-	-	-	-	-	-	-	-	-	-	-	-	-	-	2	-	-
R (Bob) Beason	D	D	D	D	E	-	-	-	A	A	C	A	A	C	A	C	C	C	C	A	A	A	-	-	-	-	-	-	-	-	-	19	-	-
DW (David) Bird	N	N	N	K	N	N	N	N	N	N	N	K	N	-	-	-	N	N	N	N	L	N	N	N	-	-	N	N	N	N	N	26	9	27
MJ (Martin) Birkett	-	-	-	-	-	-	-	-	-	-	-	-	-	-	-	-	-	-	-	-	<N	-	-	-	-	-	-	-	-	-	-	1	-	-
T (Tom) Bleasdale	-	-	-	-	-	-	-	-	-	-	-	-	-	-	-	-	G	-	-	E	-	-	-	-	-	-	-	-	-	-	-	2	-	-
F (Frank) Chawner	C	C	C	A	C	C	C	C	C	C	A	C	C	A	C	A	A	A	A	C	C	C	C	A	A	A	A	A	A	A	A	31	5	15
RC (Dick) Cooper	-	-	-	J	-	-	L	-	-	-	-	-	-	-	-	M	-	-	J	-	-	-	-	-	J	M	J	-	-	-	-	7	-	3
RL (Richard) Cowman	-	-	-	-	-	-	-	-	-	-	-	-	-	-	-	-	-	-	-	-	-	-	-	-	-	-	>K	-	-	-	<K	2	1	3
WA Davidson	-	-	-	-	-	-	-	-	-	-	-	-	-	-	-	-	-	-	-	-	>J	J	-	-	-	-	-	-	-	-	<J	3	-	-
NJ (Nick) Drake-Lee E4	A	A	-	-	A	A	A	A	-	-	-	-	-	-	-	-	-	-	-	-	-	-	A	C	C	C	-	-	-	-	C	11	3	9
MJ (Mike) Dymond	I	-	I	-	-	I	-	-	-	I	-	I	I	I	I	I	I	-	I	-	-	-	-	I	-	-	-	-	I	I	-	14	3	9
PG (Peter) Edwards	-	-	-	-	-	-	-	-	-	-	-	-	-	-	-	-	-	-	-	B	B	B	-	-	-	-	-	-	-	B	-	4	-	-
GW (Geoff) Evans	-	-	-	-	-	-	-	-	-	-	-	-	>L	L	L	-	-	L	L	-	-	-	-	-	-	-	M	-	-	-	-	6	-	-
IM (Ian) Gibson	L	L	M	-	-	M	M	L	-	-	-	-	-	-	-	-	M	-	-	L	-	M	L	M	L	L	-	L	L	L	-	16	7	21
M (Malcolm) Greenhow	-	-	-	-	-	-	-	-	-	<M	-	-	-	-	-	-	-	-	-	-	-	-	-	-	-	-	-	-	-	-	-	1	-	-
MJ (Mike) Harrison	-	M	-	M	M	-	-	M	L	L	M	L	M	M	M	L	-	-	-	-	-	-	-	-	-	-	-	-	-	-	-	12	1	3
MJ (Mike) Hemphrey	-	-	-	-	-	-	-	-	-	-	-	-	-	-	-	-	-	-	-	-	-	-	-	-	-	-	-	-	-	<C	-	1	-	-
G (Gareth) Hopkins	-	-	-	-	-	-	-	-	-	-	-	-	-	-	-	-	-	-	-	-	-	-	-	-	-	-	-	<0	-	-	-	1	-	-
JP (Phil) Horrocks-Taylor E4 L1	J	J	J	-	J	J	J	J	J	J	J	J	-	-	J	-	-	-	-	J	-	-	J	J	-	J	-	-	-	-	-	16	2	6
GA (Alan) John	-	-	-	-	-	-	-	-	-	-	-	-	>0	0	0	0	0	0	0	-	-	-	-	-	-	-	-	-	0	-	-	8	-	-
JM (Mike) Jones	-	-	-	-	-	E	E	D	E	D	D	D	D	E	D	D	D	-	D	-	E	D	-	D	-	-	-	-	E	<D	-	18	1	3
CG (Colin) Martin	G*	G*	G*	-	-	G*	G*	G*	G*	G*	G*	G*	G*	G*	G*	G*	-	G*	G*	G*	G*	G*	G*	G*	G*	G*	G*	G*	-	-	G*	26	1	47
DJ (David) Matthews	F	F	H	H	H	H	H	H	H	H	H	H	H	H	H	H	F	H	H	H	F	H	H	F	H	H	H	F	H	F	F	31	11	33
PGS (Graham) Pulfrey	-	-	-	-	>0	-	-	-	-	-	-	-	-	-	-	-	-	-	-	-	-	-	-	-	-	-	-	-	-	-	-	1	-	-
PW (Peter) Riley	E	E	E	E	-	-	-	-	-	-	-	-	-	-	-	-	-	E	-	-	-	-	E	-	E	E	E	E	G	G	D	13	3	9
RE (Bob) Rowell E+	-	-	-	-	D	D	D	E	D	E	E	E	E	D	E	E	E	D	E	D	D	E	D	E	D	D	D	D	D	E	E	27	1	3
MF (Malcolm) Sayer	-	-	-	-	-	-	-	-	-	-	-	-	-	-	-	-	-	-	-	-	-	-	-	-	>N	N	L	K	K	K	M	7	1	3
KJF (Ken) Scotland S26 L5	0	0	0	0	-	0	0	0	0	0	0	0	J	J	-	J	J	<J	-	-	-	-	-	-	-	-	-	-	-	-	-	16	2	102
D (David) Senior	-	K	K	N	K	-	K	K	-	-	K	-	-	-	K	-	K	-	-	-	-	K	K	K	K	<K	-	-	-	-	-	14	4	12
CD (Cliff) Shephard	-	-	-	-	-	K	-	-	-	-	-	N	K	K	-	K	-	K	K	K	K	-	-	-	-	-	-	-	-	-	-	9	-	-
RP (Rex) Skelton	-	-	A	C	-	-	-	-	-	-	-	-	-	-	-	-	-	-	-	-	-	-	-	-	-	-	C	C	C	-	-	5	-	-
RW (Bob) Small	H	H	F	F	F	F	F	F	F	F	F	F	F	F	F	F	H	F	F	F	H	F	F	H	F	F	F	H	-	0	H	30	6	18
BTC (Brian) Small	-	-	-	-	-	-	-	-	-	-	-	-	-	-	-	-	-	-	-	0	0	0	0	0	0	0	0	J	J	J	<0	12	-	-
KT (Ken) Smith	-	-	-	L	-	-	-	-	M	K	L	<M	-	-	-	-	-	-	-	-	-	-	-	-	-	-	-	-	-	-	-	5	3	9
L (Lyn) Tatham	M	-	L	-	L	<L	-	-	-	-	-	-	-	-	-	-	-	-	-	-	-	-	-	-	-	-	-	-	-	-	-	4	-	2
MR (Mike) Wade E3	K	-	-	-	-	-	-	-	K	-	-	-	-	N	N	N	L	M	M	M	M	L	M	L	M	-	-	M	M	M	L	18	2	6
MR (Mike) Walker	B	B	B	B	B	B	B	B	B	B	B	B	B	B	B	B	B	B	B	-	-	-	B	B	B	B	B	B	B	-	B	27	-	-
HV (Chalkie) White	-	I	-	I	I	-	I	I	I	-	I	-	-	-	-	-	-	I	-	I	-	I	I	-	I	I	I	I	-	-	I	16	-	-

The key for how to read the stats is on the last page

19	63/64	Home Ground: Welford Road	OVERALL RECORD:					T	C	PG	DG	PTS
		Captain: Michael Wade	PLD	W	D	L	Tigers scored:	91	44	36	2	475
			41	26	3	12	Opponents scored:	54	25	23	5	296

GM	DATE		VEN	OPPONENTS	RESULT	TRIES	KICKS	ATT
CLUB MATCHES								
1	Sep	2m	a	Torquay Athletic	W 18-5	Almey, Cooper, Matthews, Rowell	Chilton 3c	-
2		**7**	**H**	**Bedford**	W 9-0	Chawner, Gibson	Martin p	567
3		**11w**	**H**	**Watcyn Thomas XV**	W 12-5	Bird, Bussey, Matthews	Chilton p	1024
4		**14**	**H**	**Bath**	W 22-3	Matthews(2), Almey, Bussey, Gibson	Chilton 2c, Martin p	502
5		**21**	**H**	**Plymouth Albion**	W 13-9	Bussey, Gibson, Rowell	Chilton 2c	492
6		28	a	Harlequins	L 6-13	Allen, Gibson	-	-
7	Oct	**5**	**H**	**Coventry**	L 0-8	-	-	1284
8		12	a	Richmond	W 11-8	Wade	Chilton c/2p	-
9		**19**	**H**	**Headingley**	W 9-3	Almey, Harrison	Chilton p	478
10		26	a	Northampton	W 11-0	Harrison	Chilton c/2p	-
11		**30w**	**H**	**Oxford University**	L 0-16	-	-	382
12	Nov	**2**	**H**	**Gloucester**	L 3-9	Bird	-	590
13		9	a	Cambridge University	D 9-9	Matthews	Chilton 2p	-
14		16	a	Rugby	L 11-20	Harrison(2), Bird	Martin c	-
15		**23**	**H**	**Moseley**	W 17-12	Bussey(2), Wade	Chilton c/2p	288
16		**30**	**H**	**Cheltenham**	W 9-3	Bird, Sayer	Chilton p	266
17	Dec	7	a	Waterloo	W 29-10	Bussey(2), Sayer(2), Bird	Martin 4c/2p	-
18		**14**	**H**	**Blackheath**	W 8-3	Almey	Martin c/p	239
		21	**H**	**Bristol**	PP			
19		**26th**	**H**	**Barbarians**	L 6-13	-	Martin 2p	4284
20	Jan	4	a	Bath	L 0-11	-	-	-
21		11	a	Gloucester	W 11-0	Almey, Bird, Sayer	Martin c	-
		18	a	Bedford	PP (frost)			
22		25	a	Rosslyn Park	W 14-8	Allen, Almey, Chilton, Harrison	Martin c	-
23	Feb	**1**	**H**	**London Scottish**	W 5-3	Harrison	Martin c	462
24		8	a	Birkenhead Park	W 17-8	Chilton, Bird	Chilton c/2p, Pulfrey d	-
25		15	a	Wasps	W 30-3	Bussey(2), Matthews(2), Harrison, Rowell	Chilton 6c	-
26		**22**	**H**	**Northampton**	W 27-3	Chilton(2), Bird(2), Harrison	Chilton 3c/2p	549
27		29	a	Llanelly	L 6-10	-	Chilton 2p	-
28	Mar	**7**	**H**	**Harlequins**	L 0-6	-	-	351
29		**12th**	**H**	**Loughborough Colleges**	W 12-3	-	Chilton 3p, Freer d	165
30		**14**	**H**	**British Army**	W 14-3	Almey, Bussey, Wade	Chilton c/p	200
31		**21**	**H**	**Royal Air Force**	W 27-3	Harrison(2), Chilton, Bird, Gibson	Chilton 2p, Martin 3c	185
32		28	a	Bristol	W 16-9	Bird(3), Rowell	Martin 2c	-
33		30m	a	Plymouth Albion	D 5-5	Harrison	John c	-
34		31tu	a	Exeter	W 16-6	Matthews, Small	Martin 2c/2p	-
35	Apr	**4**	**H**	**Swansea**	L 6-11	Bird	Martin p	498
36		**8w**	**H**	**Nuneaton**	W 22-8	Allen, Chilton, P.Edwards, Harrison, Matthews, Willars	Martin 2c	389
37		11	a	Newport	D 8-8	Bussey, Wade	Martin c	-
38		15w	a	London Irish	W 13-11	Matthews(2), Beason	Martin 2c	-
39		**18**	**H**	**Saracens**	W 9-3	Bussey, Chilton, Gibson	-	462
40		22w	a	Coventry	L 6-14	-	Martin 2p	-
41		29w	a	Bedford	L 8-11	Chilton	Martin c/p	-

INDIVIDUAL APPEARANCES 1963/64

Name / Game #	1	2	3	4	5	6	7	8	9	10	11	12	13	14	15	16	17	18	19	20	21	22	23	24	25	26	27	28	29	30	31	32	33	34	35	36	37	38	39	40	41	Apps	T	Pts
JA (John) Allen	-	-	I	-	I	I	I	I	I	I	-	-	-	-	-	-	I	I	I	I	I	I	I	I	I	I	I	I	I	I	I	I	I	I	I	I	I	I	I	I	I	32	3	9
GA (Gordon) Almey	F	H	H	F	H	-	F	F	F	F	-	F	F	F	H	H	-	F	H	-	F	F	H	-	-	-	-	-	H	<F	-	-	-	-	-	-	-	-	-	-	-	21	7	21
R (Bob) Beason	E	E	E	E	E	E	-	-	-	-	-	-	-	-	C	C	A	C	C	A	E	-	E	E	E	D	E	-	-	-	A	-	C	E	E	D	-	D	E	E	E	27	1	3
DJ (David) Beaty	-	>C	C	C	-	C	-	A	C	C	C	C	-	-	-	-	-	-	-	-	-	-	-	-	-	-	-	-	-	-	-	-	-	-	-	-	-	-	-	-	-	9	-	-
DW (David) Bird	N	N	N	N	N	N	N	N	N	N	N	N	N	N	N	N	N	N	N	N	N	N	N	N	N	N	N	N	N	N	N	N	N	-	N	N	N	N	N	N	N	40	14	42
T (Tom) Bleasdale	-	-	-	-	-	-	-	-	-	-	-	-	-	-	-	-	C	A	-	<C	-	-	-	-	-	-	-	-	-	-	-	-	-	-	-	-	-	-	-	-	-	3	-	-
WM (Malcolm) Bussey	>K	K	K	K	K	K	K	K	-	K	K	K	K	K	K	K	K	K	K	K	-	K	K	K	K	K	K	K	K	K	-	K	-	-	K	-	K	-	K	K	-	33	12	36
F (Frank) Chawner	C	A	A	A	A	A	C	C	A	A	A	-	C	C	A	A	-	-	-	-	-	-	-	A	A	-	-	-	A	-	-	-	-	-	-	-	-	-	<A	-	-	19	1	3
G (George) Cherry	-	-	-	-	-	-	-	E	-	E	D	E	E	<E	-	-	-	-	-	-	-	-	-	-	-	-	-	-	-	-	-	-	-	-	-	-	-	-	-	-	-	6	-	-
K (Keith) Chilton	>0	0	0	0	0	0	0	0	0	0	0	0	0	0	0	0	0	0	0	0	0	0	0	M	0	0	0	0	0	0	0	0	-	0	0	0	-	-	0	0	0	38	8	135
RC (Dick) Cooper	J	-	-	J	-	J	-	-	-	-	-	-	-	-	-	-	-	-	-	-	-	-	-	-	-	-	-	-	-	-	-	-	M	M	-	-	-	-	-	-	-	5	1	3
NJ (Nick) Drake-Lee E7	A	-	-	-	C	-	A	-	-	-	-	-	-	-	-	-	-	-	A	-	A	A	A	-	-	C	C	A	-	A	-	A	A	A	A	A	A	A	-	A	A	20	-	-
MJ (Mike) Dymond	I	I	-	I	-	-	-	-	-	-	-	I	I	<I	-	-	-	-	-	-	-	-	-	-	-	-	-	-	-	-	-	-	-	-	-	-	-	-	-	-	-	6	-	-
PG (Peter) Edwards	-	-	-	-	-	-	-	-	-	-	-	-	-	B	B	-	B	B	B	B	B	B	B	B	B	B	B	B	B	B	B	B	B	B	B	B	B	B	B	B	B	27	1	3
AN (Tony) Edwards	-	-	-	-	-	-	-	-	-	-	-	-	-	-	-	-	-	-	-	-	-	-	-	-	-	-	-	-	>E	<E	-	-	-	-	-	-	-	-	-	-	-	2	-	-
GW (Geoff) Evans	-	-	L	-	-	-	-	-	-	-	-	-	-	-	-	-	-	-	-	-	-	-	-	-	-	-	-	-	-	-	-	-	-	-	-	-	-	-	-	-	-	1	-	-
ME (Mike) Freer	-	-	-	-	-	-	-	-	-	L	-	-	-	-	-	-	-	M	-	-	-	-	-	-	-	-	-	M	J	M	-	-	-	-	-	-	-	-	L	L	L	8	-	3
IM (Ian) Gibson	M	L	-	L	L	M	M	L	-	-	L	-	-	-	-	-	-	-	M	L	L	M	M	-	M	M	M	-	M	-	M	M	-	-	L	M	L	M	M	-	-	24	6	18
MJ (Mike) Harrison	-	-	-	-	-	-	J	J	J	J	J	J	M	L	L	L	M	L	L	-	K	L	L	L	L	L	L	L	L	-	L	L	L	L	M	L	M	L	-	M	M	32	12	36
JP (Phil) Horrocks-Taylor E9 L1	-	J	J	-	<J	-	-	-	-	-	-	-	-	-	-	-	-	-	-	-	-	-	-	-	-	-	-	-	-	-	-	-	-	-	-	-	-	-	-	-	-	3	-	-
GA (Alan) John	-	-	-	-	-	-	-	-	-	-	-	-	-	-	-	-	-	-	-	-	-	-	-	-	-	-	-	-	-	-	-	-	0	-	-	-	-	-	-	-	-	1	-	2
CG (Colin) Martin	-	G	G	G	G	G	G	G	-	-	-	G	G	G	G	G	G	G	G	G	G	G	G	-	-	-	-	E	-	G	G	G	-	G	G	G	G	G	G	G	G	31	-	83
DJ (David) Matthews	H	F	F	H	F	H	H	H	H	H	H	H	H	H	F	F	F	-	-	-	-	-	-	F	F	F	F	F	F	H	F	F	F	H	F	F	F	H	F	F	F	35	11	33
D (Des) Morgan	-	-	-	-	-	-	-	-	-	-	-	>A	A	<A	-	-	-	-	-	-	-	-	-	-	-	-	-	-	-	-	-	-	-	-	-	-	-	-	-	-	-	3	-	-
PGS (Graham) Pulfrey	-	-	-	-	-	-	-	-	-	-	-	-	-	-	-	-	-	-	-	-	-	-	-	0	-	-	-	-	-	-	-	-	-	-	-	-	0	0	-	-	-	3	-	3
A (Alan) Raine	-	-	-	-	-	-	-	-	-	-	-	-	-	-	>E	E	D	E	E	E	D	E	-	-	-	E	-	-	-	-	E	E	E	-	D	E	D	E	D	D	D	19	-	-
PW (Peter) Riley	-	-	-	-	-	-	E	-	E	D	E	-	-	-	-	-	-	-	-	-	-	-	-	-	-	-	-	-	-	-	-	-	-	-	-	-	-	-	-	-	-	4	-	-
RE (Bob) Rowell E1	D	D	D	D	D	D	D	D	D	-	-	D	D	D	D	D	E	D	D	D	-	D	D	D	D	-	D	D	D	D	D	D	D	D	-	-	E	-	-	-	-	31	4	12
MF (Malcolm) Sayer	L	-	-	-	-	-	-	-	L	-	M	L	L	M	M	M	L	-	-	M	M	-	-	-	-	-	-	-	-	L	K	-	K	K	-	-	-	-	-	-	K	16	4	12
CD (Cliff) Shephard	-	-	-	-	-	-	-	-	K	-	-	-	-	-	-	-	-	-	-	-	-	-	-	-	-	-	-	-	-	-	-	-	-	-	-	-	-	-	-	-	-	1	-	-
RP (Rex) Skelton	-	-	-	-	-	-	-	-	-	-	-	-	-	-	-	-	-	-	-	-	C	C	C	C	C	A	A	C	C	C	C	C	-	C	C	C	C	C	C	C	C	20	-	-
RW (Bob) Small	-	-	-	-	-	F	-	-	G	-	-	-	-	-	-	-	-	-	-	-	-	-	-	G	G	G	G	G	G	-	-	-	G	F	-	-	-	-	-	-	-	10	1	3
K (Keith) Stewart	-	-	-	-	-	-	-	-	-	-	-	-	-	-	-	-	-	-	-	-	-	-	-	-	-	-	-	-	-	-	-	-	-	>N	-	K	-	K	-	-	-	3	-	-
PWG (Peter) Tom	>G	-	-	-	-	-	-	-	-	-	-	-	-	-	-	-	-	-	-	-	-	-	-	-	-	-	-	-	-	-	-	-	-	-	-	-	-	-	-	-	-	1	-	-
MR (Mike) Wade E3	-	M*	M*	M*	M*	L*	L*	M*	M*	M*	-	M*	J*	J*	J*	J*	J*	J*	J*	J*	J*	J*	J*	J*	J*	J*	J*	J*	-	J*	J*	J*	J*	J*	J*	J*	J*	J*	J*	J*	J*	38	4	12
MR (Mike) Walker	B	B	B	B	B	B	B	B	B	B	B	B	B	-	-	B	-	-	-	-	-	-	-	-	-	-	-	-	-	-	-	-	-	-	-	-	-	-	-	-	-	14	-	-
HV (Chalkie) White	-	-	-	-	-	-	-	-	-	-	I	-	-	-	I	<I	-	-	-	-	-	-	-	-	-	-	-	-	-	-	-	-	-	-	-	-	-	-	-	-	-	3	-	-
IA (Ian) Wilkie	-	-	-	-	-	-	-	-	-	-	>F	-	-	-	-	-	-	-	-	F	-	-	-	-	-	-	-	-	-	-	-	-	-	-	-	-	-	F	-	-	-	3	-	-
GG (Graham) Willars	-	-	-	-	-	-	-	-	-	-	-	-	-	-	-	-	H	H	F	H	H	H	F	H	H	H	H	H	-	-	H	H	H	-	H	H	H	-	H	H	H	21	1	3
MJ (Mike) Willcox	-	-	-	-	-	-	-	-	-	>G	G	-	-	-	-	-	-	-	-	-	-	-	-	-	-	-	-	-	-	-	-	-	-	-	-	-	-	-	-	-	-	2	-	-

CHAPTER 16

Matthews to the Fore

1964/1965

New laws had come into operation for the 1964/65 season, restricting the activities of wing forwards and making the backs lie deeper. Obviously it was to encourage more open play after some of the dull games of the early 60s but Leicester's hopes of profiting from it took a knock when 10 regulars went on the casualty list during the first month, among them the captain, Mike Wade. Feeling his responsibilities he may have tried to return to action too early but his knee injury eventually forced him to have a cartilage operation and, effectively, ended his playing career at the time when he was proving so valuable to the club.

In the first seven weeks of the season Wade, Harrison, Martin and Drake-Lee captained the club before Harrison stepped into the breach in November, following Wade's enforced resignation. It was Harrison who had distinguished himself in the inaugural floodlit game with three tries as Leicester won 31-8 following the switching on by the Rugby Football Union's treasurer, Bill Ramsay. The Midlands XV included the exceptional Llanelly teenager, Terry Price (then at Leicester University and sadly killed in a road accident in 1993), and the Wyggeston School scrum-half, DR Elliott.

Richmond claimed their first win in 33 years in October but the following month, Leicester enhanced their reputation in Ireland in a splendid game against Old Belvedere. The Irish club won 16-14, Chilton becoming only the third Tiger to score in every possible way to claim 11 points himself, but Bussey almost won the game with a late run and their hosts were loud in their praise. There were trials for Harrison and Rowell but Tigers were having problems at fly-half again, in Wade's absence. Another Berry, David, was given an opportunity there and, with Martin increasingly unavailable because of his business commitments, another Antipodean made his bow in the back row against Headingley in December, Australian No 8 John Quick, alongside David Matthews playing his 250th match - the halfway stage for the flanker.

A few days later the Barbarians succumbed 12-11, Bird scoring a try despite difficulties when his contact lenses became steamed up. There were caps for Drake-Lee and Rowell against Wales, in both cases their last, and a new recruit to the club in the shape of Kevin Paul Andrews, a lock from Bath who had moved to Burton-on-Trent. Andrews, who had played for Hampshire in the County Championship final of 1962, made his debut in a 10-30 defeat against Newport but overall the season proved mediocre, a reflection perhaps on the difficulties over injuries and the consequent problem of being unable to field a settled side.

↑ Floodlit rugby was staged at Welford Road for the first time when a Midlands Combination XV were invited to take on the Tigers.

→ Peter Tom during the game against Richmond at the Athletic Ground 9.10.1965

← David Matthews leads the side out against Nuneaton.

1965/1966

There was, however, a significant merger of talents for 1965/66. Matthews was elected captain and Martin, his playing career now over, offered to help coach the players. "The experiment of a coach other than the captain was a relatively new concept in English rugby," said Martin. "In my view it faced up to the times. Captains were men with family and business responsibilities and needed support, competition was increasing year by year and certainly no longer could 15 brilliant individuals defeat a well-organised team.

"In addition I had always held the view that players liked to play the game well and a coach/captain combination could more readily achieve that objective, with one important rider - the captain is ultimately in charge, the coach has a supportive role."

Matthews, then 28, thought his opportunity of captaining the club had gone although he had always hoped for the chance: "I wanted Leicester to be top of the rugby world and I like to think what people may recall about my time as captain was the organisation. The club had struggled for so many years and I had to decide the best way of improving things. So I tried to play as much of the game in the opposition 25 as I could, although that was foreign to my innermost thoughts on the game."

A lot of Martin's thinking had rubbed off on Matthews and the new captain spent considerable time discussing the game with Wade, too. "I never wanted to do more on a rugby field than play running rugby," said Matthews. "But success had to come first." There can be no doubt that Matthews achieved that goal: in his first season as captain, the team won 30 games, in the second they won 33 to break the club record which had stood at 31 (1897/98 and 1920/21).

During 1965, Drake-Lee took up an appointment at Stonyhurst School and moved to Manchester but a glut of fly-halves joined the club, Bill Coutts from Loughborough Colleges, Martin Bedggood from Moseley and Rod Coady, another Australian. Both Quick and Coady were from Sydney, the back row man having played for Randwick before coming to this country to practise dentistry at Market Harborough, where he had initially joined the junior club Kibworth. Coady, an Eastern Suburbs player down under, was a master at Bushloe School, Wigston, and the two first played together in a 14-3 win over Plymouth Albion.

Quick's finest moment was to come at Christmas time against the Barbarians. On a day when the Leicester back row of Matthews, Quick and Bob Small were in commanding form, the Australian scored three tries in a 14-10 win, joining the elite group to have run in a hat-trick against the Baa-baas. It was a fitting honour for an outstanding back row and an outstanding captain when Matthews was invited to represent the Barbarians that season in the Mobbs Memorial Match.

There were trials for John Allen and Kevin Andrews, who was proving a very successful pack leader, but that was the nearest two very fine players came to being capped. Allen had the misfortune to be injured during one trial but it must have been a bitter pill to see England play three scrum-halves that season, Jeremy Spencer, Trevor Wintle and Clive Ashby, and feel that he had perhaps missed the boat.

Off the field it was Doug Norman's first year as president but the general secretary, Major Chilton, announced his resignation in November 1965, because of ill-health. For the same reason the groundsman, Bill Nash, resigned and his place went to the energetic Fred Cox. The post of general secretary was advertised at £1,100 a year, though a clerical error in the committee minutes made it £11,000 which would have had considerable appeal even to captains of industry.

The successful applicant was Air Commodore SG 'Ranji' Walker, who had played for the club 30 years before and who took over at much the same time as Jerry Day became club secretary in succession to Ron Gerrard, who had retired. Day had appeared at intervals for the senior side during the five years following the war but had not held down a regular place. He had played loyally for the A XV before ending his career with Aylestone St James. When the club was reformed he became team secretary for the Extra Firsts and subsequently for the senior XV.

↑ David Matthews's player's tickets for the three seasons he was captain.

↓ Doug Norman, Tigers' long-serving player and committeeman, was president of the club from 1965-68.

His election was revealed at the annual meeting of 1966, when the club gleefully reviewed the progress made on the field during the previous season. Quick headed the try scorers with 15 and Chilton's 181 points (22 of them came in a massive 43-3 win over London Irish) was the best since Haselmere in 1920. Oxford and Cambridge universities had been beaten in the same season for the first time in 11 years though on the debit side Bob Rowell was moving away from the area to work in Manchester. Another famous name from the past, 'Tim' Taylor, had died, not long after the death in May 1965 of another great, Sid Penny.

1966/1967

Rowell continued initially to travel from Burnley to play with Leicester as the 1966/67 season got under way, though he later joined Fylde. The club was bursting with wings in September and could afford to play two England triallists, Roy Sleigh and Mike Brownhill, in the Extras since Bird and Bussey were holding down the first-team spots. Another England triallist on the strength was the former Bristol prop, Roger Grove, but Leicester's front row man contending for honours early on was Field Walton, one of five Leicester players named in the Midland Counties (East) XV which met the Australians captained by John Thornett in the second game of their tour at Welford Road, on 22 October. That quartet included Peter Tom, who had made his debut at lock two years earlier; his primary influence was to come much later.

The combined XV was: Brian Page (Northampton); Malcolm Bussey, Keith Chilton (both Leicester), Keith Savage, Glenn Robertson; Jon Cooley, Trevor Wintle; David Powell, Andy Johnson (all Northampton), Field Walton (Leicester), Peter Larter (Northampton), Peter Tom (Leicester), Budge Rogers (Bedford, captain), John Pallant (Nottingham), David Matthews (Leicester).

It was not the most memorable display by the combined side. The Australians won 17-9 and it was only the East Midlands' back-row and full-back Brian Page who came out of the match in credit. Page collected all his side's points and began the scoring with a penalty. A try by John Brass made it 3-3 at half-time then heavyweight wing Alan Cardy got another. Page dropped a fine goal to level matters before Phil Hawthorne dropped a goal and Stewart Boyce scored the third Australian try. Page banged over another penalty but Boyce's second try, converted by Phil Gibbs, gave the tourists a comfortable margin.

Andrews also played against the Australians, for Midland Counties (West), but it was Harrison and Matthews who were given trials by England while in December 1966, a Welshman named David Lyons had one of his few first-team games at centre, against Bristol. It was Lyons who, six years later, played such an important part in establishing a Leicester Youth side. The club gained the services, at the same time, of an England triallist from Loughborough Colleges, hooker John Elliott, and

↑ Mike Harrison goes over for the Tigers' third try in their 14-3 win over the Barbarians at Christmas 1966.

a couple of months later a raw youngster from the Loughborough Town club, Garry Adey, made his debut at lock against the Colleges.

The wins continued to roll in - among them victory over Northampton in new scarlet shirts purchased for use under the new lights - and, for the second season running, the club passed 500 points. Andrews won his Barbarians tie and, on the Easter tour, was accorded the singular honour for an uncapped player of captaining the Baa-baas, against Penarth. To round matters off, Harrison and Matthews were picked for a Midlands XV against a London and Home Counties XV, as the English regions girded their loins for the coming encounter with the 1967 All Blacks.

1967/1968

Matthews was elected for a third successive year as captain, despite his personal misgivings, and the 1967/68 season started off magnificently, all three teams going through September unbeaten. During the summer there had been a slight change in the administrative style, when 'Ranji' Walker left the area and the post of general secretary was left unfilled. It had not been an entirely happy marriage of the differing functions of the secretary's job and Jerry Day, like his famous predecessors, Crumbie and Thorneloe, a man who ran his own business, gathered everything back under the one hat.

The senior XV won their first seven games before drawing with Coventry and then losing to Richmond, but, sadly, there were no Leicester players on view when the next touring side came to Welford Road. Brian Lochore's New Zealanders were the first of the International Board countries to make a shortened tour of the British Isles and a revised fixture list had to be worked out. Accordingly the Midlands joined forces with the Home Counties and played the following team on 28 October, 1967: Bob Hiller; J T Cox (both Harlequins), Danny Hearn (Bedford), Bob Lloyd (Harlequins), Rodney Webb; A James, Bill Gittings (all Coventry); Phil Judd (Coventry, captain), Bert Godwin (Coventry), Tony Horton (Blackheath), John Owen (Coventry), Peter Larter (Northampton), Budge Rogers (Bedford), George Sherriff (Saracens), Bob Taylor (Northampton).

The All Blacks won 15-3 but the match will be remembered more for the tragic injury to the England centre Danny Hearn, who broke his neck in a tackle on Ian MacRae. The combined XV played the bulk of the match with 14 men and Budge Rogers and George Sherriff performed prodigies about the field, while Bob Taylor deputised well in the centre. There was no score at half-time but the outcome was inevitable, Fergie McCormick kicking three penalties, Malcolm Dick scoring a try and Mac Herewini dropping a goal. Bob Lloyd scored a fine try for the counties.

Meanwhile the club's form was patchy although one individual, Graham Willars, was consistency itself and had at last won a regular back row spot. After two successful seasons it was not entirely surprising that the club was having difficulty living up to its own standards, and their form had made them a marked team wherever they went. The absence of a place-kicker, Chilton having left the area, may have had a lot to do with it and meant another burden for Matthews, since he took over the kicking role.

In the second half of the season, however, the hard-pressed captain had some of the weight lifted from his shoulders. Martin had returned to New Zealand in 1967 (after an intended stay of two years had turned into 11) and the task of coaching, still an unofficial job, devolved upon 'Chalkie' White and Rex Skelton. Both players had been overtaken by time and younger, more promising men in terms of first-team appearances but they stayed with the club, involved themselves in committee work and were happy to lend some new ideas in the general approach to the game at a time when Matthews was under considerable pressure.

It was some time before their influence - more particularly that of White - was felt. In the meantime Leicester made their way to a respectable aggregate of wins, helped by a new recruit from Cardiff, Michael Evans, who, as well as being a useful centre or fly-half, could kick goals too. Matthews injured a knee towards the end of the season and Quick took over the captaincy, but returned to Australia at the end of the campaign.

Plans were afoot to change the sequence of Easter tours, after years of visiting the West Country. After 1968/69, tours were to be undertaken in alternative years, in order to give Leicester fans something to look forward to in the holiday period and to try to draw bigger crowds. It was to change the emphasis of the season for Leicester, even if barmen in the West heaved a collective sigh of relief.

↓ David Matthews's new training regime during the summer on Welford Road Rec paid dividends for the club.

← LEICESTER FOOTBALL CLUB 1965/66
Back: Day (Team Hon.Sec), Martin, Quick, Beason, Bedggood, Harrison, Walker, Tom, Beaty, Sayer, Walton, Pulfrey, Norman (President), Gerrard (Hon.Sec).
Middle: Small, Chilton, Matthews (capt), Andrews, J.Allen, Willars.
Front: Bird, Bussey, Coady, Edwards.

← LEICESTER FOOTBALL CLUB 1966/67
Back: Thorpe (Hon.Tres), Norman (President), Bussey, Walker, Grove, Walton, Beason, Bedggood, Tom, Pulfrey, Brownhill, D.Berry, Day (Hon.Sec).
Middle: Sleigh, Willars, Chilton, Andrews, D.Matthews (capt), Harrison, Quick, J.Allen, Edwards.
Front: Elliott, Aldwinckle.

← LEICESTER FOOTBALL CLUB 1967/68
Back: Norman (President), Thorpe (Hon.Tres), Mawbey, Grove, Betts, Small, Bann, Cooper, Sayer, Pulfrey, White (Coach), Day (Hon.Sec).
Middle: Bird, Walton, Harrison, D.Matthews (capt), Andrews, J.Allen, Raine.
Front: D.Berry, Brownhill, Aldwinckle, Elliott.

1964/65

Home Ground: Welford Road	OVERALL RECORD:					T	C	PG	DG	PTS
Captain: Michael Wade then Mike Harrison in November	PLD	W	D	L	Tigers scored:	76	41	40	3	439
	41	20	2	19	Opponents scored:	91	40	19	7	431

GM	DATE		VEN	OPPONENTS	RESULT	TRIES	KICKS	ATT
CLUB MATCHES								
1	Sep	3th	H	**Watcyn Thomas XV**	L 11-12	Chilton, Matthews, Rowell	Martin c	1878
2		5	H	**Bedford**	W 9-6	Rowell	Martin 2p	510
3		12	a	Bath	W 31-8	Bird(2), Bussey(2), Cooper, Willars	Martin 5c/p	-
4		19	H	**Plymouth Albion**	W 13-0	Matthews, Harrison	Matthews c, Chilton c/p	448
5		26	a	Harlequins	L 3-19	Willars	-	-
6	Oct	3	a	Coventry	L 3-19	-	Pulfrey p	-
7		8th	H	**Midlands XV**	W 31-8	Harrison(3), Evans, Stewart, Willars	Martin 5c/p	1506
8		10	H	**Richmond**	L 3-27	-	Martin p	484
9		17	a	Cheltenham	W 8-0	Martin	Martin c/p	-
10		21w	a	Oxford University	L 6-16	-	Chilton 2p	-
11		24	a	Swansea	L 0-19	-	-	-
12		31	H	**Nuneaton**	W 19-5	Harrison(2), Chilton, Perkins	Martin 2c/p	409
13	Nov	1s	a	Old Belvedere	L 14-16	Chilton, J.Allen	Chilton c/p/d	-
14		7	a	Gloucester	L 9-22	Drake-Lee, Matthews	Chilton p	-
15		14	H	**Cambridge University**	W 11-0	Drake-Lee	Martin c/2p	687
16		21	a	Rugby	L 0-14	-	-	-
17		28	a	Moseley	W 6-3	-	Chilton 2p	-
18	Dec	5	H	**Waterloo**	W 22-6	J.Allen(2), Drake-Lee, Matthews, Raine	Chilton 2c/p	248
19		12	a	Headingley	W 21-6	Harrison(3), Quick	Chilton 3c/p	-
20		19	H	**Bristol**	L 9-14	Raine	Chilton 2p	503
		26	H	**Birkenhead Park**	PP			
21		28m	H	**Barbarians**	W 12-11	Bird, Matthews	Martin 2p	4978
22	Jan	2	H	**Bath**	W 11-8	Beason, Bussey, Raine	Chilton c	474
23		9	H	**Gloucester**	W 21-0	Chilton(2), J.Allen, Matthews, Quick	Chilton 3c	181
24		16	a	Bedford	W 22-3	Bussey, Harrison, Matthews, Wilkie	Chilton 2c/p/d	-
25		23	H	**Rosslyn Park**	W 13-5	Evans, Martin	Chilton 2c/p	517
		30	H	**Llanelly**	PP			
26	Feb	6	a	London Scottish	W 11-6	Bussey, Matthews, Rowell	Martin c	-
27		13	H	**Newport**	L 10-30	Bussey, Matthews	Chilton 2c	806
28		20	H	**Wasps**	L 9-12	-	Chilton 3p	470
29		27	a	Northampton	L 8-18	Harrison	Chilton c/p	-
30	Mar	6	H	**Harlequins**	L 11-13	Bussey, Willars	Bussey d, Chilton c	518
31		11th	H	**Loughborough Colleges**	L 11-24	Bussey	Chilton c/2p	947
32		13	H	**Newbridge**	L 6-15	Willars	Chilton p	197
33		19f	H	**Royal Air Force**	D 0-0	-	-	402
34		27	a	Saracens	D 3-3	-	Chilton p	-
35		31w	H	**Northampton**	W 14-3	Bird	Martin c/3p	840
36	Apr	3	a	Birkenhead Park	W 17-13	Bird(2), Glover, Willars	Pulfrey p, Martin c	-
37		10	a	Newport	L 3-15	-	Martin p	-
38		17	a	Bristol	L 3-18	-	Martin p	-
39		19m	a	Plymouth Albion	W 6-0	Bird, Willars	-	-
40		20tu	a	Exeter	L 3-11	-	Martin p	-
41		24	a	Northern	W 16-3	Bird(2), Chilton, Matthews	Martin 2c	-

INDIVIDUAL APPEARANCES 1964/65

Name / Game #	1	2	3	4	5	6	7	8	9	10	11	12	13	14	15	16	17	18	19	20	21	22	23	24	25	26	27	28	29	30	31	32	33	34	35	36	37	38	39	40	41	Apps	T	Pts
GR (George) Allen	-	-	>L	-	L	-	-	-	-	-	-	-	-	M	-	-	-	-	-	-	-	-	-	-	-	-	-	-	-	-	-	-	-	-	-	-	-	-	-	-	-	3	-	-
JA (John) Allen	I	I	I	I	I	I	I	I	I	I	I	I	I	I	I	I	I	I	I	I	I	I	I	I	I	I	I	I	I	I	-	-	-	-	I	I	I	I	-	-	I	35	4	12
KP (Kevin) Andrews	-	-	-	-	-	-	-	-	-	-	-	-	-	-	-	-	-	-	-	-	-	-	-	-	-	-	>E	D	-	D	G	G	G	G	-	-	-	-	-	-	-	7	-	-
R (Bob) Beason	E	E	D	E	E	E	E	E	-	-	-	-	-	-	-	-	-	-	-	A	-	A	-	A	-	-	A	-	-	-	-	-	-	-	-	-	A	-	C	C	A	16	1	3
DJ (David) Beaty	-	-	-	-	-	-	-	-	-	A	-	-	-	-	-	-	-	-	-	-	-	-	-	-	-	-	-	-	-	-	-	-	-	-	-	-	-	-	-	-	-	1	-	-
DMH (David) Berry	-	-	-	-	-	-	-	-	-	-	-	-	-	-	-	-	>J	J	J	J	J	J	J	J	J	J	J	-	-	-	-	-	-	J	J	J	-	-	-	-	-	14	-	-
MF (Malcolm) Billingham	-	-	-	-	-	-	-	-	-	-	=G	-	-	-	-	-	-	-	-	-	-	-	-	-	-	-	-	-	-	-	-	-	-	-	-	-	-	-	-	-	-	1	-	-
DW (David) Bird	N	-	N	N	N	N	-	-	-	-	-	-	-	-	-	-	-	-	N	N	N	N	N	N	N	-	N	N	N	-	-	N	N	N	N	N	N	N	N	N	N	25	9	27
WM (Malcolm) Bussey	K	K	K	-	-	-	-	-	-	-	-	K	K	-	-	-	-	-	-	K	K	K	K	K	K	K	K	K	K	K	K	K	-	K	K	-	K	K	K	K	K	25	8	27
K (Keith) Chilton	O	O	O	O	K	-	-	-	N	N	N	O	O	O	O	O	O	O	O	O	O	O	O	O	O	O	O	O	O	O	O	O	O	O	-	-	-	-	I	L	L	34	6	127
RC (Dick) Cooper	-	-	J	-	-	-	-	O	J	J	-	-	-	-	-	-	-	-	-	-	-	-	-	-	-	-	-	-	-	-	-	-	-	-	-	-	-	-	-	-	-	4	1	3
NJ (Nick) Drake-Lee E8	-	-	C	C	A	A*	A	-	A	-	A*	A	A	A*	C	A	C	A	C	-	A	-	A*	-	A	A	-	A	A	A	A	A*	A	A	C	A	-	A	A	A	-	31	3	9
PG (Peter) Edwards	B	B	B	B	B	B	B	B	B	B	B	B	B	B	B	B	B	B	B	B	B	B	B	B	B	B	B	B	B	B	B	B	B	B	B	B	B	B	B	B	B	41	-	-
RK (Bob) Ellis	-	-	-	-	-	-	-	-	>F	<F	-	-	-	-	-	-	-	-	-	-	-	-	-	-	-	-	-	-	-	-	-	-	-	-	-	-	-	-	-	-	-	2	-	-
GW (Geoff) Evans	-	M	-	M	M	-	L	L	L	L	L	-	-	L	L	M	M	M	L	M	-	-	M	L	L	M	-	-	L	L	L	L	M	-	L	L	L	L	-	-	-	28	2	6
ME (Mike) Freer	-	-	-	-	-	-	-	-	-	-	M	-	-	N	K	N	N	K	K	-	-	-	-	-	-	-	-	-	-	-	<I	-	-	-	-	-	-	-	-	-	-	8	-	-
A (Alan) Gardiner	-	>J	-	-	-	J	-	-	-	-	-	-	-	-	-	-	K	-	-	-	-	-	-	-	-	-	-	J	<J	-	-	-	-	-	-	-	-	-	-	-	-	5	-	-
IM (Ian) Gibson	M	-	-	-	-	L	-	N	-	-	-	L	L	-	-	-	-	L	-	L	M	M	L	-	M	L	L	L	-	-	N	M	<K	-	-	-	-	-	-	-	-	17	-	-
J (Jess) Glover	-	-	-	-	-	-	-	-	-	-	-	-	-	-	-	-	-	-	-	-	-	-	-	-	-	-	-	-	-	-	-	-	-	-	-	>K	-	-	-	-	M	2	1	3
MJ (Mike) Harrison	L	L	M	L	-	-	M	M	M	M*	-	M	M*	-	M	L*	L*	-	M*	-	L*	L*	-	M*	-	-	M*	M	M*	M*	M*	-	L*	M*	M*	M*	M*	M*	M*	M*	-	30	11	33
MA Higginson	-	-	-	-	-	-	-	-	-	-	-	-	-	-	-	=K	-	-	-	-	-	-	-	-	-	-	-	-	-	-	-	-	-	-	-	-	-	-	-	-	-	1	-	-
CA (Chris) Holroyd	-	-	-	-	-	>M	-	-	-	-	-	-	-	K	-	-	-	-	-	-	-	-	-	-	-	-	-	-	-	-	-	-	-	L	-	-	-	-	L	-	-	4	-	-
KA (Keith) Jackson	-	-	-	-	-	-	-	-	-	=K	-	-	-	-	-	-	-	-	-	-	-	-	-	-	-	-	-	-	-	-	-	-	-	-	-	-	-	-	-	-	-	1	-	-
KB Jones	-	-	-	-	-	-	>K	<K	-	-	-	-	-	-	-	-	-	-	-	-	-	-	-	-	-	-	-	-	-	-	-	-	-	-	-	-	-	-	-	-	-	2	-	-
CG (Colin) Martin	G	G*	G*	G	-	-	G	G	G*	-	-	G*	-	-	G*	G	G	G*	-	G*	G	-	-	G	G*	G*	-	G*	G	G	-	-	-	-	G	G	G	G	G	G	G*	27	2	97
DJ (David) Matthews	H	H	F	F	H	H	H	H	-	-	-	H	H	F	F	F	F	H	F	H	H	H	H	F	F	H	F	F	H	H	H	F	F	F	F	H	H	F	F	F	H	38	10	32
TD (Des) O'Regan	-	-	-	-	-	-	-	-	-	-	-	-	-	-	-	-	-	-	-	-	-	-	-	-	-	-	-	-	-	-	-	>I	I	I	-	-	-	-	-	<I	-	4	-	-
D (David) Perkins	-	-	-	-	-	-	-	-	-	-	>J	J	J	J	J	J	-	-	-	-	-	-	-	-	-	-	-	-	-	J	J	J	J	-	-	-	J	J	J	J	J	15	1	3
PGS (Graham) Pulfrey	-	-	-	-	O	O	O	-	O	O	O	-	-	-	-	-	-	-	-	-	-	-	-	-	-	-	-	-	-	-	-	-	-	-	O	O	O	O	O	O	O	13	-	6
J (John) Quick	-	-	-	-	-	-	-	-	-	-	-	-	-	-	-	-	-	-	>G	-	-	G	G	-	-	-	G	-	F	-	-	-	-	-	-	-	-	-	-	-	-	5	2	6
A (Alan) Raine	-	-	-	-	-	-	-	-	-	-	-	-	-	-	-	-	E	D	-	D	-	D	-	D	E	-	-	-	-	-	E	E	-	-	-	-	-	-	-	-	-	8	3	9
RE (Bob) Rowell E2	D	D	E	D	D	D	D	D	D	D	D	D	D	D	D	D	-	-	D	-	D	-	D	-	D	D	D	E	D	-	-	-	D	D	D	D	E	D	E	E	D	33	3	9
CD (Cliff) Shephard	-	-	-	-	-	<K	-	-	-	-	-	-	-	-	-	-	-	-	-	-	-	-	-	-	-	-	-	-	-	-	-	-	-	-	-	-	-	-	-	-	-	1	-	-
RP (Rex) Skelton	A	A	-	-	-	-	-	A	C	C	C	C	C	C	-	-	-	-	-	-	-	-	-	-	-	-	-	-	-	-	-	-	-	-	-	-	-	-	-	-	-	9	-	-
RW (Bob) Small	-	-	-	-	-	F	-	-	H	G	F	-	G	G	-	-	-	-	-	-	-	-	-	-	-	-	-	-	-	-	-	-	-	-	-	-	-	-	-	-	-	6	-	-
K (Keith) Stewart	-	N	-	K	-	-	N	-	K	-	K	N	N	-	N	-	-	N	-	-	-	-	-	-	-	N	-	-	-	<N	-	-	-	-	-	-	-	-	-	-	-	11	1	3
PWG (Peter) Tom	-	-	-	-	-	-	-	-	E	E	E	E	E	E	E	E	D	E	E	E	E	E	E	E	-	E	-	-	E	E	D	D	E	E	E	E	D	E	D	D	E	30	-	-
MR (Mike) Wade E3	J*	-	-	J*	J*	-	J*	J*	-	-	-	-	-	-	-	-	-	-	-	-	-	-	-	-	-	-	-	-	-	-	-	-	-	-	-	-	-	-	-	-	-	5	-	-
FLJ (Field) Walton	>C	C	A	A	C	C	C	C	-	-	-	-	-	-	A	C	A	C	A	C	C	C	C	C	C	C	C	C	C	C	C	C	C	C	A	C	C	C	-	-	C	33	-	-
IA (Ian) Wilkie	-	-	-	-	-	-	-	-	-	H	H	-	-	-	-	-	-	-	-	-	-	-	-	H	-	F	-	-	-	<F	-	-	-	-	-	-	-	-	-	-	-	5	1	3
GG (Graham) Willars	F	F	H	H	F	-	F	F	-	-	-	F	F	H	H	H	H	F	H	F	F	F	F	-	H	-	H	H	-	F	-	H	H	H	H	F	F	H	H	H	F	33	7	21
MJ (Mike) Willcox	-	-	-	-	G	<G	-	-	-	-	-	-	-	-	-	-	-	-	-	-	-	-	-	-	-	-	-	-	-	-	-	-	-	-	-	-	-	-	-	-	-	2	-	-

The key for how to read the stats is on the last page

19	65/66	Home Ground: Welford Road	OVERALL RECORD:					T	C	PG	DG	PTS
		Captain: David Matthews	PLD	W	D	L	Tigers scored:	102	42	35	3	504
			44	30	1	13	Opponents scored:	50	25	20	3	269

GM	DATE		VEN	OPPONENTS	RESULT	TRIES	KICKS	ATT
CLUB MATCHES								
1	Sep	4	a	Bedford	L 6-11	Bird	Chilton p	-
2		**8w**	**H**	**Watcyn Thomas XV**	W 5-0	Harrison	Chilton c	-
3		**11**	**H**	**Bath**	W 9-3	J.Allen, Harrison	Chilton p	446
4		**15w**	**H**	**Leicestershire XV**	W 35-8	Bussey(2), Harrison(2), J.Allen, Bird, Quick	White 4c/2p	371
5		**18**	**H**	**Plymouth Albion**	W 14-3	Chilton, Quick	Chilton c/2p	324
6		25	a	Harlequins	W 8-3	Quick	Chilton c/p	-
7		29w	a	Nuneaton	W 13-0	Chilton, Matthews	Chilton c/p, Pulfrey c	-
8	Oct	**2**	**H**	**Coventry**	D 5-5	Chilton	Chilton c	1181
9		9	a	Richmond	L 3-13	-	Pulfrey p	-
10		**16**	**H**	**Cheltenham**	W 33-5	Quick(2), Chilton, Bedggood, Bussey, Harrison, Matthews, Small	Chilton 3c/p	408
11		**20w**	**H**	**Oxford University**	W 14-11	Bedggood, Bussey, Pulfrey	Bedggood p, Chilton c	630
12		**23**	**H**	**Nottingham**	W 14-0	Small(2), Bird	Chilton c/p	426
13		**30**	**H**	**Swansea**	W 9-8	J.Allen	Bedggood p, Chilton p	796
14		31s	a	Old Belvedere	L 6-12	Tom	Pulfrey p	-
15	Nov	6	a	Gloucester	W 3-0	Quick	-	-
16		13	a	Cambridge University	W 19-3	J.Allen, Bussey, Harrison, Matthews, Small	Chilton 2c	-
17		**20**	**H**	**London Irish**	W 43-3	Matthews(2), Quick(2), Bird, Bussey, Small	Chilton 5c/4p	380
18		**27**	**H**	**Moseley**	W 9-6	Matthews(2), Quick	-	317
19	Dec	4	a	Waterloo	W 19-0	Rowell(2), Chilton	Chilton 2c/2p	-
20		11	a	Blackheath	W 6-3	Harrison	Pulfrey p	-
21		**18**	**H**	**Bristol**	L 9-11	Chilton, Harrison	Chilton p	523
22		**28tu**	**H**	**Barbarians**	W 14-10	Quick(3)	Chilton c/p	8256
23	Jan	1	a	Bath	W 9-3	Bedggood, Bussey, Small	-	-
24		**8**	**H**	**Gloucester**	L 0-3	-	-	535
		15	**H**	**Bedford**	PP (frost)			
		22	a	Rosslyn Park	PP (frost)			
25		29	a	Llanelly	L 3-14	Scattergood	-	-
26	Feb	**5**	**H**	**London Scottish**	W 9-3	Bussey, Harrison	Chilton p	177
		12	**H**	**Newport**	PP (frost)			
27		**16w**	**H**	**Bedford**	W 9-5	Bussey, Coady, Quick	-	665
28		19	a	Wasps	W 5-3	Chilton	Chilton c	-
29		**26**	**H**	**Northampton**	W 16-11	Bird, Bussey, Harrison, Walton	Chilton 2c	2344
30	Mar	**5**	**H**	**Harlequins**	W 14-3	Bussey, Harrison	Chilton c/2p	1001
31		**10th**	**H**	**Loughborough Colleges**	W 33-3	Bird(2), J.Allen, Bussey, Coady, Small, Penalty	Chilton 3c/2p	850
32		12	a	Coventry	L 11-13	Matthews	Chilton c/p, Coady d	-
33		15tu	a	Moseley	L 3-6	-	Chilton p	-
34		**18f**	**H**	**Royal Air Force**	W 16-10	J.Allen(2), Coutts, Willars	Coutts 2c	559
35		24th	a	Northampton	W 9-3	Brownhill, Chilton, Harrison	-	-
36		**26**	**H**	**Headingley**	L 5-10	Tom	Chilton c	284
37		**29tu**	**H**	**Fylde**	W 25-6	Quick(2), Small(2), Chilton, Bird	Chilton 2c, Pulfrey d	475
	Apr	2	a	Birkenhead Park	PP			
38		9	a	Bristol	L 0-15	-	-	-
39		11m	a	Plymouth Albion	L 0-15	-	-	-
40		12tu	a	Exeter	L 0-6	-	-	-
41		**16**	**H**	**Saracens**	W 14-8	Willars	Chilton c/3p	241
42		23	a	Newport	L 0-8	-	-	-
43		**27w**	**H**	**Rugby**	W 13-0	Bussey, Small, Willars	Chilton 2c	460
44		29f	a	Newbridge	W 14-3	Small, Willars	Chilton c/p, Coady d	-

INDIVIDUAL APPEARANCES 1965/66

Name / Game #	1	2	3	4	5	6	7	8	9	10	11	12	13	14	15	16	17	18	19	20	21	22	23	24	25	26	27	28	29	30	31	32	33	34	35	36	37	38	39	40	41	42	43	44	Apps	T	Pts
GR (George) Allen	L	M	L	-	-	-	-	-	-	-	-	-	-	-	-	-	-	-	-	-	-	-	-	-	-	-	-	-	-	-	-	-	-	-	-	-	-	-	-	-	-	-	-	-	3	-	-
JA (John) Allen	I	I	I	I	I	I	I	I	I	I	I	I	I	I	I	I	I	I	I	I	-	I	-	I	-	I	I	I	I	I	I	I	I	I	I	I	I	I	I	I	I	I	I	I	41	7	21
KP (Kevin) Andrews	E	E	E	-	D	D	D	E	E	D	D	D	D	E	D	D	D	-	-	D	-	D	-	-	D*	D	D	D	D	D	D	D	D	D*	D*	D*	D*	-	-	-	D*	D*	D*	D*	35	-	-
R (Bob) Beason	A	A	A	-	A	-	-	-	-	-	A	-	-	-	-	-	-	-	A	-	A	-	A	-	-	-	-	-	A	A	A	A	A	A	A	A	-	A	A	A	C	C	A	A	23	-	-
DJ (David) Beaty	C	C	C	C	C	A	A	A	A	A	-	A	A	A	A	A	A	A	-	A	-	C	-	C	-	C	C	C	-	-	-	-	-	-	-	-	A	-	-	-	-	-	-	-	24	-	-
BM (Bev) Bedggood	-	>J	J	L	L	-	-	-	-	J	J	J	J	J	J	J	-	-	-	L	-	-	M	-	M	-	-	-	-	-	-	-	M	-	-	-	M	-	-	L	M	L	-	-	19	3	15
DMH (David) Berry	-	-	-	J	-	-	L	-	-	-	-	-	-	-	-	-	-	-	-	-	-	-	-	-	J	-	-	-	-	-	-	-	J	-	-	-	J	-	-	-	-	-	-	-	5	-	-
RTH (Richard) Berry	-	-	-	-	-	-	-	>H	H	-	-	-	-	-	-	-	-	-	-	-	-	-	-	-	G	-	-	-	-	-	-	-	-	-	-	-	-	-	-	-	-	-	-	-	3	-	-
DW (David) Bird	K	K	N	K	N	N	K	N	N	N	N	N	N	N	N	N	N	N	N	N	N	N	N	N	N	N	N	N	N	N	N	N	N	-	-	-	N	N	N	N	N	N	N	N	41	8	24
JM (Mike) Brownhill	-	-	-	-	-	-	-	-	-	-	-	-	-	-	-	-	-	-	-	-	-	-	-	-	-	-	-	-	-	-	-	-	-	>N	N	N	-	K	-	-	-	-	-	K	5	1	3
T (Tom) Burch	-	-	-	-	-	-	-	-	-	-	-	-	-	-	-	-	-	-	-	-	-	-	-	-	=K	-	-	-	-	-	-	-	-	-	-	-	-	-	-	-	-	-	-	-	1	-	-
WM (Malcolm) Bussey	N	N	K	N	K	K	N	K	K	K	K	K	K	K	K	K	K	K	K	K	K	K	K	K	-	K	K	K	K	K	K	K	K	K	K	K	K	-	K	K	K	K	K	-	41	13	39
K (Keith) Chilton	O	O	O	-	O	L	M	M	L	L	L	L	L	L	L	L	M	M	M	-	M	L	L	L	-	M	L	L	L	L	L	L	L	L	L	L	L	L	L	-	L	M	M	M	40	9	181
RJ (Rod) Coady	-	-	-	-	>J	J	J	J	J	-	-	-	-	-	-	-	J	J	J	J	J	J	J	J	-	J	J	J	J	J	J	J	-	-	-	-	-	J	J	J	J	J	J	<J	27	2	12
RC (Dick) Cooper	J	-	-	-	-	-	-	-	-	-	-	-	-	-	-	-	-	-	-	-	-	-	-	-	-	-	-	-	-	-	-	-	-	-	-	-	-	-	-	-	-	-	-	-	1	-	-
WC (Bill) Coutts	-	-	-	-	-	-	-	-	-	-	-	-	-	-	-	-	-	-	-	-	-	-	-	-	-	-	-	-	-	-	-	-	-	>J	J	<J	-	-	-	-	-	-	-	-	3	1	7
PG (Peter) Edwards	B	B	B	B	-	-	-	-	-	-	-	-	-	-	-	-	-	-	-	-	-	-	-	-	B	B	B	B	B	B	B	B	B	B	B	B	-	B	B	B	B	B	B	B	23	-	-
GW (Geoff) Evans	-	-	-	-	-	-	-	-	-	-	-	-	-	-	M	-	-	-	-	-	-	-	-	-	<L	-	-	-	-	-	-	-	-	-	-	-	-	-	-	-	-	-	-	-	2	-	-
MJ (Mike) Harrison	M	L	M	M	M	M	-	L	M	M	M	M	M	M	-	M	L	L	L*	M	L*	M	-	M	-	L	M	M	M	M	M	M	-	M	M	M	-	M	M*	M*	-	-	-	-	34	12	36
CG (Colin) Martin	-	-	-	-	-	-	-	-	-	-	-	-	-	-	-	-	-	-	-	-	-	-	-	-	-	-	-	-	-	-	-	-	-	-	-	-	-	-	-	<E	-	-	-	-	1	-	-
DJ (David) Matthews	H*	F*	F*	F*	F*	H*	H*	F*	F*	F*	H*	F*	F*	H*	H*	F*	H*	H*	-	H*	-	F*	H*	F*	-	F*	H*	H*	H*	F*	F*	F*	F*	-	-	-	-	F*	-	-	-	-	-	-	31	8	24
GR (Guy) Millar	-	-	-	-	-	-	-	-	-	-	-	-	-	-	-	-	-	-	-	-	>I	-	I	-	I	-	-	-	-	-	-	-	-	-	-	-	-	-	-	-	-	-	-	-	3	-	-
PGS (Graham) Pulfrey	-	-	-	-	-	O	O	O	O	O	O	O	O	O	O	O	O	O	O	O	O	O	O	O	O	O	O	O	O	O	O	O	O	O	O	O	O	O	O	O	O	O	O	O	39	1	17
J (John) Quick	G	G	G	G	G	G	G	G	G	G	G	G	G	G	G	G	G	G	G	G	G	G	G	G	-	G	G	G	G	G	G	G	G	G	G	G	G	G	G	G	G	G	G	G	43	15	45
A (Alan) Raine	-	-	-	D	-	-	-	-	-	-	-	-	-	-	-	-	-	-	-	-	-	-	-	-	E	-	-	-	-	-	-	-	-	-	-	-	-	-	-	-	-	-	-	-	2	-	-
RE (Bob) Rowell E2	-	-	-	-	-	-	-	-	-	-	-	-	-	-	-	-	-	D	D	-	D	-	D	D	-	-	-	-	-	-	-	-	-	-	-	-	-	D	E	-	-	-	-	-	7	2	6
MF (Malcolm) Sayer	-	-	-	-	-	-	-	-	-	-	-	-	-	-	-	-	-	-	-	-	-	-	-	-	-	-	-	-	-	-	-	-	-	-	-	-	-	-	-	-	-	-	L	L	2	-	-
IMS (Ian) Scattergood	-	-	-	-	-	-	-	-	-	-	-	-	-	-	-	-	-	-	>H	-	F	-	-	-	<H	-	-	-	-	-	-	-	-	-	-	-	-	-	-	-	-	-	-	-	3	1	3
RP (Rex) Skelton	-	-	-	-	-	-	-	-	-	-	-	-	-	-	-	-	-	-	-	-	-	-	-	-	A	-	-	-	-	-	-	-	-	-	-	-	-	-	-	-	-	-	-	-	1	-	-
RW (Bob) Small	-	H	H	H	H	F	F	-	-	H	F	H	H	F	F	H	F	F	F	F	H	H	F	H	F	H	F	F	F	H	H	H	H	H	H	F	H	H	H	F	F	F	H	H	41	11	33
PWG (Peter) Tom	D	D	D	E	E	E	E	D	D	E	E	E	E	D	E	E	E	E	E	E	E	E	E	E	-	E	E	E	E	E	E	E	E	E	E	E	E	E	D	D	E	E	E	E	43	2	6
MR (Mike) Walker	-	-	-	-	B	B	B	B	B	B	B	B	B	B	B	B	B	B	B	B	B	B	B	B	-	-	-	-	-	-	-	-	-	-	-	-	B	-	-	-	-	-	-	-	21	-	-
FLJ (Field) Walton	-	-	-	A	-	C	C	C	C	C	C	C	C	C	C	C	C	C	C	C	C	A	C	A	C	A	A	A	C	C	C	C	C	C	C	C	C	C	C	C	A	A	C	C	40	1	3
JC (John) White	-	-	-	<O	-	-	-	-	-	-	-	-	-	-	-	-	-	-	-	-	-	-	-	-	-	-	-	-	-	-	-	-	-	-	-	-	-	-	-	-	-	-	-	-	1	-	14
GG (Graham) Willars	F	-	-	-	-	-	-	-	-	-	-	-	-	-	-	-	-	-	-	-	-	-	-	-	-	-	-	-	-	-	-	-	-	F	F	H	F	-	F	H	H	H	F	F	11	4	12

19	66/67	Home Ground: Welford Road
		Captain: David Matthews

OVERALL RECORD:					T	C	PG	DG	PTS
PLD	W	D	L	Tigers scored:	98	40	39	6	509
46	33	2	11	Opponents scored:	44	16	29	9	278

GM	DATE		VEN	OPPONENTS	RESULT	TRIES	KICKS	ATT
CLUB MATCHES								
1	Sep	1th	H	**Watcyn Thomas XV**	W 21-9	Bird(2), Chilton(2), Pulfrey	J.Allen 2c, Cooper c	-
2		3	H	**Bedford**	W 14-3	J.Allen, Bussey	J.Allen c/p, Chilton p	476
3		10	a	Bath	L 8-14	Harrison	Chilton p, J.Allen c	-
4		13tu	H	**Nuneaton**	W 22-6	Brownhill(3), Bussey, Pulfrey	Chilton c/p, J.Allen c	341
5		17	H	**Plymouth Albion**	D 6-6	-	Chilton 2p	333
6		19m	H	**Irish Wolfhounds**	L 3-15	-	J.Allen p	1892
7		24	a	Harlequins	L 5-8	Brownhill	J.Allen c	-
8	Oct	1	a	Coventry	D 8-8	Bussey, Tom	J.Allen c	-
9		8	H	**Richmond**	W 22-3	J.Allen, Bussey, D.Matthews, Sleigh	J.Allen c/p, Pulfrey d, Bedggood c	406
10		15	H	**Northampton**	W 17-9	J.Allen, Brownhill, Pulfrey	Chilton c/2p	819
11		19w	H	**Oxford University**	W 9-3	-	Bedggood 2p, Grove p	401
12		22	a	Cheltenham	W 11-0	Brownhill, Sleigh	A.Matthews c/p	-
13		28f	a	Swansea	L 0-11	-	-	-
14	Nov	5	a	Gloucester	W 3-0	-	Chilton p	-
15		12	H	**Cambridge University**	W 6-0	-	Chilton 2p	531
16		19	H	**Newport**	W 16-6	Quick(2)	Chilton 2c/p, Sleigh d	627
17		26	a	Moseley	W 13-0	Chilton, Harrison, Quick	Chilton c, J.Allen c	-
18	Dec	3	a	Waterloo	L 6-10	Willars	D.Berry d	-
19		10	H	**Blackheath**	W 3-0	-	Saunders d	419
20		17	H	**Bristol**	W 25-12	Quick(2), J.Allen, Lyons, D.Matthews, Sleigh, Tom	Chilton 2c	856
21		24	a	London Irish	W 3-0	-	Chilton p	-
22		27tu	H	**Barbarians**	W 14-3	Andrews, Bird, Brownhill, Harrison	J.Allen c	4683
23		31	a	Headingley	L 6-9	-	Chilton 2p	-
	Jan	7	H	**Bath**	PP			
24		14	H	**Gloucester**	W 9-3	J.Allen, Brownhill	Chilton p	471
25		21	a	Bedford	L 9-14	Brownhill(2)	Chilton p	-
26		28	H	**Rosslyn Park**	W 19-0	Andrews, Brownhill, D.Matthews, Quick	Chilton 2c/p	222
27	Feb	4	a	London Scottish	L 10-17	Brownhill, Millar	A.Matthews 2c	-
28		11	a	Newport	L 6-20	-	Chilton 2p	5000
29		18	H	**Wasps**	W 6-3	Quick	Chilton p	431
30		24f	a	Northampton	W 8-3	J.Allen	J.Allen p, Grove c	-
31		28tu	H	**Bath**	W 11-3	Bedggood, Raine	J.Allen c/p	308
32	Mar	4	H	**Harlequins**	W 14-0	Quick(2), Andrews, Brownhill	Chilton c	436
33		8w	H	**Loughborough Colleges**	W 14-6	Andrews, Bussey, Harrison	D.Berry d, J.Allen c	571
34		11	H	**Coventry**	L 5-6	D.Matthews	J.Allen c	1032
35		17f	H	**Royal Air Force**	W 35-9	Brownhill(2), Elliott(2), Harrison(2), Millar, Quick, Tom	Chilton 3c, Bedggood c	365
36		25	a	Bristol	L 0-17	-	-	-
37		27m	a	Plymouth Albion	W 16-3	Sleigh(2), Quick	J.Allen 2c/p	-
38		28tu	a	Exeter	W 12-8	D.Berry(2), Small	J.Allen p	-
39	Apr	1	H	**Birkenhead Park**	W 14-6	Elliott(2), Sleigh	Chilton c/p	315
40		8	H	**Llanelli**	W 17-8	Sleigh(2), Andrews	J.Allen c/p, Pulfrey p	423
41		11tu	H	**Moseley**	W 3-0	Quick	-	454
42		15	a	Saracens	W 11-3	D.Matthews, Sleigh	Chilton c/p	-
43		18tu	H	**Sale**	W 20-3	Aldwinckle, Bedggood, D.Matthews, Pulfrey	A.Matthews c/p, D.Berry d	317
44		22	H	**Aberavon**	W 9-0	Grove, Walton	Chilton p	441
45		26w	H	**Rugby**	W 11-3	Brownhill, Elliott	Bedggood c/p	580
46		29	H	**Fylde**	W 9-8	Aldwinckle, Brownhill	D.Matthews p	350

INDIVIDUAL APPEARANCES 1966/67

Name / Game #	1	2	3	4	5	6	7	8	9	10	11	12	13	14	15	16	17	18	19	20	21	22	23	24	25	26	27	28	29	30	31	32	33	34	35	36	37	38	39	40	41	42	43	44	45	46	Apps	T	Pts
GJ (Garry) Adey E+	-	-	-	-	-	-	-	-	-	-	-	-	-	-	-	-	-	-	-	-	-	-	-	-	-	-	-	-	-	-	-	-	>D	-	D	-	E	E	-	-	-	-	E	-	-	-	5	-	-
PJ (Peter) Aldwinckle	-	-	-	-	-	-	-	-	-	-	-	-	-	-	-	-	-	-	-	-	-	-	-	-	-	-	-	-	-	-	-	-	-	-	-	-	-	-	-	-	-	>I	I	I	I	I	5	2	6
GR (George) Allen	-	-	-	-	-	-	-	-	-	-	L	L	-	-	-	-	-	-	-	-	-	-	-	-	-	-	-	-	-	-	-	-	-	-	-	-	-	-	-	-	-	-	-	-	-	-	2	-	-
JA (John) Allen	I	I	I	I	I	I	I	I	I	I	I	-	I	I	I	I	I	I	I	I	I	I	I	I	I	I	-	I	I	I	I	I	I	I	-	I	I	I	I	I	I	-	-	-	-	-	38	6	74
KP (Kevin) Andrews	E	D	D	D	D	D	D	D	D	D	D*	D*	E	E	D	E	D	D*	D	D	D	D	D	-	D	E	D*	D	D	D	-	E	E	D	-	D	-	-	D	E	E	D	-	D	D	E	40	5	15
R (Bob) Beason	-	-	A	A	-	-	-	-	-	-	-	C	-	-	-	-	-	-	-	-	-	-	-	A	-	-	E	-	-	-	-	-	-	-	-	-	A	A	A	C	C	-	-	-	A	-	11	-	-
DJ (David) Beaty	A	C	C	C	C	C	C	-	A	-	C	-	-	-	A	-	A	-	-	-	-	-	A	-	-	-	-	-	-	-	C	-	A	-	-	-	-	-	-	-	-	-	-	-	-	-	14	-	-
BM (Bev) Bedggood	-	-	-	-	M	-	L	M	M	M	M	M	M	M	M	-	-	-	-	-	-	-	-	-	-	J	J	J	J	J	L	L	L	L	L	-	L	L	-	L	L	-	L	J	L	L	28	2	21
DMH (David) Berry	-	-	-	-	-	-	-	-	-	J	J	-	J	J	J	J	J	J	-	J	J	J	J	J	J	-	-	-	-	-	J	J	J	J	J	J	J	J	J	J	J	J	J	-	M	-	28	2	15
RTH (Richard) Berry	-	-	G	G	G	-	-	-	-	-	H	-	-	-	-	-	-	-	-	-	-	-	-	-	-	-	G	-	-	-	-	-	G	-	-	-	-	-	-	-	-	-	-	-	-	G	7	-	-
SE (Steve) Betts	-	-	-	-	-	-	-	-	-	-	-	-	-	-	-	-	-	-	-	-	-	-	-	-	-	-	-	-	-	-	>F	-	-	-	-	-	-	-	-	-	-	-	-	-	-	-	1	-	-
DW (David) Bird	N	N	-	-	-	-	-	-	-	-	K	-	-	-	-	-	-	-	-	-	K	K	K	K	K	K	-	-	K	K	-	-	-	-	-	-	-	-	-	-	-	-	-	-	-	-	11	3	9
JM (Mike) Brownhill	-	-	-	N	N	N	N	N	-	N	-	N	-	N	N	N	N	N	N	N	N	N	N	N	N	N	N	N	N	N	N	N	N	N	N	N	N	-	N	N	N	N	-	N	N	N	38	17	51
WM (Malcolm) Bussey	K	K	K	K	K	K	K	K	K	K	-	-	K	-	-	-	-	K	-	-	-	-	-	-	-	-	K	K	-	-	-	-	K	-	-	-	-	K	-	-	-	-	K	-	-	-	17	5	15
K (Keith) Chilton	M	L	L	L	L	L	-	L	L	L	-	-	L	L	L	L	L	L	L	L	L	L	L	L	L	L	-	L	L	-	-	K	-	K	K	L	-	-	L	-	-	L	-	<L	-	-	32	3	108
RC (Dick) Cooper	J	J	J	-	-	-	-	-	-	-	-	-	-	-	-	-	-	-	-	-	-	-	-	-	-	-	-	-	-	-	-	-	-	-	-	-	-	-	-	-	-	-	-	-	-	-	3	-	2
T (Terry) Davis	-	-	-	-	-	-	-	-	-	-	-	-	-	-	-	-	=K	-	-	-	-	-	-	-	-	-	-	-	-	-	-	-	-	-	-	-	-	-	-	-	-	-	-	-	-	-	1	-	-
PG (Peter) Edwards	-	-	-	B	B	-	-	-	-	B	B	-	-	-	-	-	-	-	B	B	B	B	B	B	B	B	B	B	-	-	-	-	-	-	-	-	-	B	-	-	-	-	B	B	-	-	17	-	-
JJ (John) Elliott	-	-	-	-	-	-	-	-	-	-	-	-	-	-	-	-	-	-	-	-	-	-	-	-	-	-	-	-	>B	B	B	B	B	B	B	B	B	-	B	B	B	B	-	-	B	B	15	5	15
J (Joe) Grindall	-	-	-	-	-	-	-	-	-	-	-	>H	-	-	-	-	-	-	-	-	-	-	-	-	-	-	<F	-	-	-	-	-	-	-	-	-	-	-	-	-	-	-	-	-	-	-	2	-	-
RV (Roger) Grove	-	-	-	-	-	-	-	>C	-	A	A	-	A	A	-	A	-	A	A	A	A	A	-	-	A	A	A	A	A	A	A	A	-	A	A	A	-	-	-	A	A	A	-	A	-	A	27	1	8
MJ (Mike) Harrison	L	M	M	M	-	M	M	-	-	-	-	-	-	-	-	M	M	-	M	-	M	M	M	M	M	M	-	-	-	-	M	M	M	M	M	M	M	M*	M	M	M	M	M	M	-	M	30	6	18
GA (Alan) John	-	-	-	-	-	-	-	-	-	-	-	-	-	-	-	-	-	-	-	-	-	-	-	-	-	-	0	0	-	-	0	-	-	-	-	-	-	-	-	-	-	-	-	-	-	-	3	-	-
D (David) Lyons	-	-	-	-	-	-	-	-	-	-	-	-	-	-	-	-	-	>M	-	M	-	-	-	-	-	-	M	M	M	<M	-	-	-	-	-	-	-	-	-	-	-	-	-	-	-	-	6	1	3
JR (John) Marriott	-	-	-	-	-	-	-	-	-	-	-	-	-	-	-	-	-	-	-	-	-	-	-	=D	-	-	-	-	-	-	-	-	-	-	-	-	-	-	-	-	-	-	-	-	-	-	1	-	-
A (Andy) Matthews	-	-	-	-	-	-	-	-	-	-	-	>A	-	-	-	-	-	-	-	-	-	-	-	-	-	-	C	-	-	-	-	-	-	-	-	-	-	-	-	-	-	-	A	-	-	-	3	-	14
DJ (David) Matthews	H*	H*	H*	H*	H*	H*	H*	H*	H*	H*	-	-	H*	H*	H*	H*	H*	-	H*	H*	H*	H*	H*	H*	H*	H*	-	H*	H*	H*	H*	H*	H*	H*	H*	H*	H*	-	H*	H*	H*	H*	H*	H*	H*	H*	41	6	21
GR (Guy) Millar	-	-	-	-	-	-	-	-	-	-	-	-	-	-	-	-	-	-	-	-	-	-	-	-	-	-	I	-	-	-	-	-	-	-	I	-	-	-	-	-	-	-	-	-	-	-	2	2	6
D (David) Perkins	-	-	-	-	-	-	-	-	-	-	-	J	-	-	-	-	-	-	-	-	-	-	-	-	-	-	-	-	-	-	-	-	-	-	-	-	-	-	-	-	-	-	-	-	J	J	3	-	-
PGS (Graham) Pulfrey	0	0	0	0	0	0	0	0	0	0	0	0	0	0	0	0	0	0	0	0	0	0	0	0	-	0	-	-	0	0	-	0	0	0	0	0	0	0	0	0	0	0	0	0	0	0	42	4	18
J (John) Quick	G	G	-	-	-	-	G	G	G	G	G	-	G	G	G	G	G	G	G	G	G	G	G	G	G	G	-	G	G	G	G	G	-	G	G	G	G	G	G	G	G	G	G	G	G	-	38	12	36
A (Alan) Raine	-	-	-	-	-	-	-	-	-	-	E	E	-	-	-	-	-	-	-	-	-	-	-	-	-	-	-	-	-	-	E	-	-	-	-	-	-	-	-	-	-	-	-	-	-	-	3	1	3
RE (Bob) Rowell E2	D	E	E	E	E	E	E	-	-	-	-	-	-	-	-	-	-	-	-	-	-	-	-	-	-	-	-	-	-	-	-	-	-	-	-	-	-	-	-	-	-	-	-	-	-	-	7	-	-
E (Eric) Saunders	-	-	-	>J	J	J	J	J	J	-	-	-	-	-	-	-	-	-	<J	-	-	-	-	-	-	-	-	-	-	-	-	-	-	-	-	-	-	-	-	-	-	-	-	-	-	-	7	-	3
R (Roy) Sleigh	-	-	>N	-	-	-	-	-	N	-	N	K	N	K	K	K	-	-	K	K	-	-	-	-	-	-	-	-	-	-	-	-	-	-	-	K	K	N	K	K	K	K	N	K	K	K	21	9	30
RW (Bob) Small	F	F	F	F	F	G	-	-	-	-	F	G	-	-	-	-	-	F	-	-	-	-	-	-	-	-	H	-	-	-	-	-	-	-	-	-	-	F	-	-	-	-	-	-	-	-	11	1	3
PWG (Peter) Tom	-	-	-	-	-	-	-	E	E	E	-	-	D	D	E	D	E	E	E	E	E	E	E	E	E	D	-	E	E	E	D	D	-	E	E	E	D	D	E	D	D	E	D	E	E	D	35	3	9
R Tucker	-	-	-	-	-	-	-	-	-	-	-	=I	-	-	-	-	-	-	-	-	-	-	-	-	-	-	-	-	-	-	-	-	-	-	-	-	-	-	-	-	-	-	-	-	-	-	1	-	-
MR (Mike) Wade E3	-	-	-	-	-	-	-	-	-	-	-	-	-	-	-	-	-	-	-	-	-	-	-	-	-	-	L	-	-	L	<K	-	-	-	-	-	-	-	-	-	-	-	-	-	-	-	3	-	-
MR (Mike) Walker	B	B	B	-	-	B	B	B	B	-	-	B	B	B	B	B	B	<B	-	-	-	-	-	-	-	-	-	-	-	-	-	-	-	-	-	-	-	-	-	-	-	-	-	-	-	-	14	-	-
FLJ (Field) Walton	C	A	-	-	A	A	A	A	C	C	-	-	C	C	C	C	C	C	C	C	C	C	C	C	C	C	-	C	C	C	-	C	C	C	C	C	C	C	C	-	-	C	C	C	C	C	38	1	3
GG (Graham) Willars	-	-	-	-	-	F	F	F	F	F	-	F	F	F	F	F	F	H	F	F	F	F	F	F	F	F	-	F	F	F	-	F	F	F	F	F	F	H	F	F	F	F	F	F	F	F	38	1	3
J (Jim) Wyness	-	-	-	-	-	-	-	-	-	-	-	-	-	-	-	-	-	-	-	-	-	-	-	-	=0	-	-	-	-	-	-	-	-	-	-	-	-	-	-	-	-	-	-	-	-	-	1	-	-

The key for how to read the stats is on the last page

1967/68

1967/68										
Home Ground: Welford Road except #12 at Stoneygate RFC, #19 #41 at Welford Road Rec	OVERALL RECORD:					T	C	PG	DG	PTS
Coach: Chalkie White	PLD	W	D	L	Tigers scored:	96	41	34	4	484
Captain: David Matthews	41	23	4	14	Opponents scored:	60	25	27	9	338

GM	DATE		VEN	OPPONENTS	RESULT	TRIES	KICKS	ATT
CLUB MATCHES								
1	Sep	2	a	Bedford	W 24-8	Quick(2), Grove	J.Allen 3c/p, D.Matthews 2p	-
2		**7th**	**H**	**Watcyn Thomas XV**	W 13-0	D.Matthews, Beason, Sleigh	D.Matthews c, J.Allen c	680
3		**9**	**H**	**Bath**	W 17-8	Harrison, Pulfrey, Willars	J.Allen c/2p	447
4		**16**	**H**	**Plymouth Albion**	W 17-5	D.Berry, Willars	J.Allen c/2p, Harrison d	260
5		23	a	Harlequins	W 8-3	J.Allen, Quick	D.Matthews c	-
6		**30**	**H**	**Saracens**	W 12-5	Brownhill, Pulfrey, Tom, Willars	-	345
7	Oct	**4w**	**H**	**Nuneaton**	W 17-8	D.Matthews, Grove, Tom	D.Matthews 2p, Grove c	457
8		**7**	**H**	**Coventry**	D 6-6	Sleigh(2)	-	1178
9		14	a	Richmond	L 0-13	-	-	-
10		21	a	Northampton	L 3-12	Brownhill	-	-
11		25w	a	Oxford University	L 0-3	-	-	-
12		**28**	**H**	**Cheltenham**	L 8-11	D.Matthews	Bedggood c/p	-
13	Nov	**4**	**H**	**Gloucester**	W 9-6	Jackson, Quick	D.Matthews p	59
14		11	a	Cambridge University	L 14-19	Quick(3), Sayer	J.Allen c	-
15		18	a	Rugby	D 3-3	-	D.Matthews p	-
16		**25**	**H**	**Moseley**	W 11-9	Bird(2), Harrison	D.Matthews c	303
17	Dec	2	a	Waterloo	W 11-3	Sleigh(2), Bird	A.Matthews c	-
		9	a	Blackheath	PP (frost)			
18		**16**	**H**	**Bristol**	W 17-12	Harrison(2), Quick	D.Matthews c/2p	500
19		**23**	**H**	**London Irish**	W 17-0	Bird(2), J.Allen, D.Berry	D.Matthews c/p	-
20		**27w**	**H**	**Barbarians**	L 6-15	Pulfrey	D.Matthews p	15000
21		30	a	Newport	L 5-10	Quick	D.Matthews c	-
22	Jan	6	a	Bath	D 11-11	D.Berry, Sayer	D.Matthews c/p	-
		13	a	Gloucester	PP (snow)			
23		**19f**	**H**	**Bedford**	D 3-3	D.Matthews	-	480
24		27	a	Rosslyn Park	L 14-16	J.Allen, Bird, Sayer	D.Matthews c/p	-
25	Feb	**3**	**H**	**London Scottish**	W 19-11	Pulfrey, Sleigh	Evans 2c/2p, D.Berry d	114
26		**10**	**H**	**Newport**	L 8-12	Bird(2)	Evans c	878
27		17	a	Wasps	W 19-9	Sleigh(2), Quick	Evans 2c/p/d	-
28		20tu	a	Moseley	W 14-8	J.Allen, Grove, Pulfrey, Sleigh	Evans c	-
29		**24**	**H**	**Northampton**	W 9-6	Harrison, Sleigh	Evans p	612
30	Mar	**2**	**H**	**Harlequins**	L 5-10	D.Matthews	Evans c	342
31		**7th**	**H**	**Loughborough Colleges**	W 32-9	Aldwinckle(3), Betts, Bird, Quick, Sayer	Evans 4c/p	441
		9	a	Coventry	PP			
32		**15f**	**H**	**Royal Air Force**	W 29-8	D.Matthews(2), Harrison(2), Sleigh(2), Bird, Elliott	D.Matthews c, Evans p	303
33		**19tu**	**H**	**Leicestershire President's XV**	W 14-8	Pulfrey, Smith	Evans c/2p	205
34		**23**	**H**	**Swansea**	W 17-8	Bird	Evans c/4p	138
35		30	a	Aberavon	L 8-13	Betts, Brownhill	D.Matthews c	-
36	Apr	**6**	**H**	**Headingley**	W 11-6	Sayer	D.Matthews c/2p	236
37		13	a	Bristol	L 0-9	-	-	-
38		15m	a	Plymouth Albion	W 27-3	Bird(2), D.Berry, Betts, Brownhill	Evans 2c/p/d, J.Allen c	-
39		16tu	a	Stroud	L 8-9	Betts, Pulfrey	Evans c	-
40		20	a	Llanelli	L 5-14	Quick	Cooper c	-
41		**27**	**H**	**Manchester**	W 13-6	Walton, Penalty	Cooper 2c/p	-

INDIVIDUAL APPEARANCES 1967/68

Name / Game #	1	2	3	4	5	6	7	8	9	10	11	12	13	14	15	16	17	18	19	20	21	22	23	24	25	26	27	28	29	30	31	32	33	34	35	36	37	38	39	40	41	Apps	T	Pts
GJ (Garry) Adey E+	-	E	-	-	-	-	-	-	-	-	-	-	-	-	-	-	E	E	E	E	E	D	E	-	-	-	-	-	-	-	-	-	-	-	-	-	D	D	E	D	-	12	-	-
PJ (Peter) Aldwinckle	-	-	-	-	-	-	-	-	-	-	-	I	-	-	-	-	I	-	-	-	-	-	-	-	-	-	-	-	-	-	I	I	I	I	I	I	I	-	I	-	-	10	3	9
GR (George) Allen	-	-	-	-	-	-	J	<J	-	-	-	-	-	-	-	-	-	-	-	-	-	-	-	-	-	-	-	-	-	-	-	-	-	-	-	-	-	-	-	-	-	2	-	-
JA (John) Allen	I	I	I	I	I	I	I	I	I	I	I	-	I	I	I	I	-	I	I	I	I	I	I	I	I	I	I	I	I	I	-	-	-	-	-	-	-	I	-	I	I	31	4	43
KP (Kevin) Andrews	D	-	D	E	E	D	D	D	D	D	-	-	E	E	E	E	D*	D	D	D	-	-	-	-	-	D	D	E	D	D	D	D	D	D	D	D	-	-	-	E	-	29	-	-
EE (Eric) Bann	-	-	-	-	-	-	-	-	-	-	-	-	-	-	-	-	-	-	-	-	-	-	-	-	-	-	-	-	-	-	-	-	-	-	-	-	-	-	-	-	>E	1	-	-
R (Bob) Beason	C	A	C	C	C	C	C	C	C	C	C	A	-	-	-	-	-	-	-	-	-	-	-	-	-	-	A	-	-	-	-	-	-	C	C	-	-	-	A	-	-	16	1	3
DJ (David) Beaty	-	-	A	-	-	-	-	-	-	-	-	-	-	-	-	-	-	-	-	-	-	-	-	-	-	-	-	-	-	-	-	-	-	-	-	-	-	-	-	-	-	1	-	-
BM (Bev) Bedggood	L	M	-	-	-	L	L	L	L	L	L	L	L	L	<M	-	-	-	-	-	-	-	-	-	-	-	-	-	-	-	-	-	-	-	-	-	-	-	-	-	-	12	-	5
DMH (David) Berry	J	J	-	J	J	J	-	-	J	J	J	J	J	J	J	J	-	J	J	J	J	J	J	J	J	-	-	-	-	-	-	-	-	M	-	J	-	M	M	-	-	25	4	15
RTH (Richard) Berry	-	-	-	-	-	-	G	G	-	G	-	-	-	-	-	-	-	-	-	-	-	-	-	-	-	-	-	-	-	-	-	-	B	-	-	-	-	-	-	-	-	4	-	-
SE (Steve) Betts	-	-	-	-	-	-	-	-	-	-	H	H	-	-	-	-	H	-	-	-	-	-	-	-	-	-	-	-	-	-	F	F	F	H	H	H	F	H	H	H	H	14	4	12
DW (David) Bird	-	-	-	-	-	-	-	-	-	-	-	-	-	-	-	N	N	N	N	N	N	N	N	N	N	N	N	N	N	N	N	N	N	K	K	N	K	K	K	K	K	26	13	39
JM (Mike) Brownhill	N	N	N	N	N	N	N	N	N	N	-	-	-	-	-	-	-	-	-	-	-	-	-	-	-	-	-	-	-	-	-	-	-	N	N	-	N	N	N	N	N	17	4	12
WM (Malcolm) Bussey	-	-	K	K	K	K	<K	-	-	-	-	-	-	-	-	-	-	-	-	-	-	-	-	-	-	-	-	-	-	-	-	-	-	-	-	-	-	-	-	-	-	5	-	-
RC (Dick) Cooper	-	-	-	-	-	-	-	-	-	-	-	-	-	-	-	-	-	-	-	-	-	-	-	-	-	-	-	-	-	-	-	-	-	-	-	-	-	-	-	J	J	2	-	9
PG (Peter) Edwards	-	-	-	-	-	B	B	-	-	-	B	-	-	-	-	-	-	-	-	-	B	B	B	B	B	-	-	-	-	-	-	-	-	-	-	-	-	B	B	<B	-	11	-	-
JJ (John) Elliott	B	B	B	B	B	-	-	B	B	B	-	B	B	B	B	B	B	B	B	B	-	-	-	-	-	B	B	B	B	B	B	B	-	B	B	B	B	-	-	-	B	29	1	3
M (Mike) Evans	-	-	-	-	-	-	-	-	-	-	-	-	-	-	-	-	-	-	-	-	>M	-	-	-	L	J	J	J	J	J	J	J	J	J	J	-	J	J	J	-	-	15	-	77
KA (Keith) Freeston	-	-	-	-	-	-	-	-	-	-	-	-	-	-	-	-	=J	-	-	-	-	-	-	-	-	-	-	-	-	-	-	-	-	-	-	-	-	-	-	-	-	1	-	-
J (Jess) Glover	-	-	-	-	-	-	-	-	-	-	N	N	-	-	-	-	-	-	-	-	-	-	-	-	-	-	-	-	-	-	-	-	-	-	-	-	-	-	-	-	-	2	-	-
RV (Roger) Grove	A	C	-	A	A	A	A	A	A	A	A	-	A	-	A	-	-	A	A	A	A	A	A	A	A	A	-	A	A	A	A	A	A	A	A	A	A	A	-	A	A	34	3	11
MJ (Mike) Harrison	M	L	M	M	M	M	M	M	M	M	M	M	-	-	L	M	M	M	M	M	-	M	M	M	M	M	M	M	M	M	M	M	M	-	-	-	-	-	-	-	-	30	7	24
CA (Chris) Holroyd	-	-	L	L	L	-	-	-	-	-	-	-	-	-	-	-	-	-	-	-	-	-	-	-	-	-	-	-	-	-	-	-	-	-	-	-	-	-	-	-	-	3	-	-
G (Graham) Jackson	-	-	-	-	-	-	-	-	-	-	-	-	>N	N	N	-	-	-	-	-	-	-	-	-	-	-	-	-	-	-	-	-	-	-	-	-	-	-	-	-	-	3	1	3
GA (Alan) John	-	-	-	<O	-	-	-	-	-	-	-	-	-	-	-	-	-	-	-	-	-	-	-	-	-	-	-	-	-	-	-	-	-	-	-	-	-	-	-	-	-	1	-	-
B (Brian) Llewellyn	-	-	-	-	-	-	-	-	-	-	-	-	-	-	-	-	-	-	-	-	-	-	-	-	-	-	-	=G	-	-	-	-	-	-	-	-	-	-	-	-	-	1	-	-
A (Andy) Matthews	-	-	-	-	-	-	-	-	-	-	-	-	-	A	-	A	A	-	-	-	-	-	-	-	-	-	-	-	-	-	-	-	-	-	-	-	-	-	-	-	-	3	-	2
DJ (David) Matthews	H*	H*	H*	H*	H*	H*	H*	H*	H*	H*	G*	G*	H*	H*	H*	H*	-	H*	H*	H*	H*	H*	H*	H*	H*	H*	H*	H*	H*	H*	H*	H*	H*	F*	F*	F*	-	-	-	-	F*	36	7	85
JW (John) Mawbey	-	-	-	-	-	-	-	-	-	-	-	-	-	-	-	-	-	-	-	-	-	-	-	-	-	-	-	-	-	-	-	>L	-	L	M	M	L	L	L	M	M	9	-	-
D (David) Perkins	-	-	J	-	-	-	-	-	-	-	-	-	-	-	-	-	-	-	-	-	-	-	-	-	-	-	-	-	-	-	-	-	-	-	-	-	-	-	-	-	-	1	-	-
PGS (Graham) Pulfrey	O	O	O	-	O	O	O	O	O	-	O	O	O	O	O	O	O	O	O	O	O	O	O	O	O	O	O	O	O	O	O	O	O	O	O	O	O	O	O	O	O	39	7	21
J (John) Quick	G	G	G	G	G	G	-	-	G	-	-	-	G	G	G	G	G	G	G	G	G	G	G	G	G	G	G	-	G	G	G	G	-	G	G	G	G*	G*	G*	<G*	-	33	12	36
A (Alan) Raine	-	-	-	-	-	-	-	-	-	-	E	D	-	-	-	-	-	-	-	-	-	-	-	E	E	E	E	D	E	E	E	E	E	E	E	E	E	E	D	-	D	19	-	-
M (Mike) Ryan	-	-	-	-	-	-	-	-	-	=O	-	-	-	-	-	-	-	-	-	-	-	-	-	-	-	-	-	-	-	-	-	-	-	-	-	-	-	-	-	-	-	1	-	-
MF (Malcolm) Sayer	-	-	-	-	-	-	-	-	-	-	-	-	M	M	-	L	L	L	L	L	L	L	L	L	-	L	L	L	L	L	L	-	L	-	L	L	-	-	-	-	L	21	5	15
R (Roy) Sleigh	K	K	-	-	-	-	-	K	K	K	K	K	K	K	K	K	K	K	K	K	K	K	K	K	K	K	K	K	K	K	K	K	K	-	-	K	-	-	-	-	-	29	12	36
RS (Bob) Smith	-	-	-	-	-	-	-	-	-	-	-	-	-	-	-	-	-	-	-	-	-	-	-	-	-	-	-	-	-	-	-	-	>G	-	-	-	H	F	-	F	G	5	1	3
T (Trevor) Spence	-	-	-	-	-	-	-	-	-	-	-	-	-	-	-	-	-	-	-	-	-	-	-	-	-	-	-	-	-	-	-	-	-	-	-	-	>M	-	-	L	-	2	-	-
PWG (Peter) Tom	E	D	E	D	D	E	E	E	E	E	D	E	D	D	D	D	-	-	-	-	D	E	D	D	<D	-	-	-	-	-	-	-	-	-	-	-	-	-	-	-	-	21	2	6
FLJ (Field) Walton	-	-	-	-	-	-	-	-	-	-	-	C	C	C	C	C	C	C	C	C	C	C	C	C	C	C	C	C	C	C	C	C	C	-	-	C	C	C	C	C	<C	28	1	3
GG (Graham) Willars	F	F	F	F	F	F	F	F	F	F	F	F	F	F	F	F	F	F	F	F	F	F	F	F	F	F	F	F	F	F	-	-	-	-	-	-	-	-	F	-	-	31	3	9

The key for how to read the stats is on the last page

CHAPTER 17

Out with the Old

1968/1969

British rugby was changing. After years of being kicked around by Springboks, All Blacks and, latterly, Frenchmen, players and administrators were taking a new, more critical look at their game. The Australians, no doubt to their amazement, found their kicking restrictions accepted by the International Board and players were no longer able to kick to touch on the full outside their own 25-yard lines. It was a major breakthrough and the statuesque variety of full-back became obsolete overnight.

↑ 1968 saw the last visit to Welford Road of the charity side run by Watcyn Thomas.

Leicester, in the person of their new captain, Graham Willars, embraced the changing atmosphere with delight. A constructive, intelligent flanker who must have been a joy to play with, and in many respects against because he was such an honest footballer, Willars wanted a game in which all 15 players could participate fully, in which they could find their own entertainment as well as providing enjoyment for spectators. Since he worked in telecommunications, Willars was also able to get his message across, as captain and, subsequently, as coach and president.

It was also to be a formative season off the field. For the first time Leicester provided the President of the RFU in the person of Tom Berry (whose service as a national selector had ended two years before) and he was able to launch an appeal to improve club facilities. The target was £30,000, the object being to turn the clubhouse into a worthwhile social centre which could be used all year.

A natural consequence of such an appeal, however, was the wish for a successful side, a side that would draw larger crowds, a money-spinning side. Not that the last few years had been unsuccessful in terms of results, far from it; but there was considerable scope for development of the club's game. "I decided we had to use our backs more," said Willars. "It didn't matter what standard they were, we had to use them.

"Once they started developing, using the ball in all situations, if you scored two tries and the opposition scored one, that to me was good. I always felt it didn't matter how many points the opposition got, if we got more then I was quite happy."

To assist Willars in his endeavours was Chalkie White, who had become the unofficial club coach - not without a degree of resentment from committeemen who thought it was vaguely unsporting and senior players who had been used to working things out for themselves - because of his close relationship with Matthews. After illness had effectively terminated his playing career by keeping him out of action for 18 months, White had been invited to join the committee, with no particular role. "My forte at the time was to associate closely with the players. I never thought about coaching but the opportunity occurred because David asked me to help," he said.

Leicester were lucky to have the right man available at the right time. Although he had been a fairly unexceptional player as a scrum-half, White had a great variety of experience, having played schools and colleges rugby (at Isleworth), service rugby, club rugby in the south-west and Midlands, and county championship rugby in the north. His job as a teacher at Nottingham High School allowed him sufficient time to devote to the task of coaching a first-class club (not to mention a captive squad of schoolboys available as a testing ground) and the tremendous encouragement of his family allowed him to develop that task.

White saw himself as a visionary. The problem for such men, of course, is always to convince others that their road is the right one, and White and Willars were lucky to have each other during that opening period of coaching, when they were of necessity working from game to game, although it did not take long before White realised there had to be long-term objectives.

"I did not mind laying down fairly tight guidelines," said White. "Some players, capable of more, did not respond, they had no sympathy with what I was doing. And in all fairness, I don't think I ever went to the trouble of making it clear - there was no avenue to do so, no need, I was creating a precedent."

Precedent or not, the Willars/White team was successful, for the 1968/69 season produced 657 points, second only to the 756 of 1919/20.

Drake-Lee rejoined the club briefly at the start of the season and so did Gavins, although as far as the full-back position was concerned there was a young Scotsman from Hawick and Jordanhill, Robin Money, who was beginning to press for a place.

Matthews, relieved of the burden of captaincy, celebrated with 21 tries, the best individual total since Senior in 1960 and the record for a forward until surpassed by Simon Povoas who scored 25 during the 1989/90 season. It rapidly became the season of the comeback men: in addition to Drake-Lee and Gavins, Harrison, having retired

↑ Chalkie White coached the Tigers between 1967-82.

↑ John Allen and David Matthews in tandem, here against the Barbarians

at the end of the previous season to concentrate on his work at Wyggeston School, rejoined the club while Rowell returned at the start of 1969. Newcomers included a promising back row man from Loughborough Colleges, Christopher Baynes, and a centre who could also play wing, Bob Barker from Stoneygate.

It was not a season for individual honours, although Elliott, the hooker from Nottingham who played a key role as selector during England's grand-slam era of 1991 and 1992, won an England trial. This was just as well since it enabled the captain and the coach to concentrate on building the side, knowing they would not lose a vital player halfway through the season. Matthews and Allen played in all 43 games and the Easter tour, the last to the West Country, was a memorable one. Doug Norman, who played in 1929/30, the first time Tigers had enjoyed an unbeaten tour, and White, who had played in the last unbeaten touring side, that of 1958, were both there to see the club go through their three games unbeaten, Matthews scoring his 100th try for the club against Bristol.

Regrettably the appeal fund's success did not match the football. Outside consultants had been brought in to suggest ways and means of raising cash, then their services were dispensed with. It seemed apparent that a lack of enthusiasm from the general public would mean a cutback in the club's ambitious plans. There were complaints from members that they did not feel part of the club and, with the season half gone, only some £7,000 had been raised. That total doubled by the end of the season but it was still less than half the projected amount.

The committee decided to hang on for the rest of the year to see whether the appeal fund was going to grow any more and, in the meantime, sanctioned the formation of a 200 club, another fundraising entity which proved immediately more successful. Other topics were in the air: leagues, a knockout competition, and the club president, Dr Nick Hughes, was on record suggesting regional competitions. He must have derived a certain ironic satisfaction when such competitions were introduced eight years later. In general, Leicester favoured competition within regional pools, the leaders from each pool going forward to a knockout competition.

↑ Dr Nick Hughes became president of the club in 1968.

1969/1970

The summer months passed quickly, for the 1969/70 season which was approaching produced a problem British rugby had never previously faced: a Springbok tour with demonstrations. The anti-apartheid forces in this country had laid their plans with considerable care to make sure that Dawie de Villiers' Sixth Springboks never settled to the task of actually playing rugby, and the game against the Midland Counties (East) at Welford Road on 8 November was the second of the tour. The Leicestershire Rugby Union laid their counter plans, in conjunction with the police, while the Leicester club privately congratulated itself on undertaking no alterations or improvements to the ground before the Springboks passed through.

Kevin Andrews, the 29-year-old lock, was captaining the club in what was his last season and there were several newcomers in the wings, notably the former Rosslyn Park fly-half or full-back, Arthur Chapman, who made an important points contribution in his 17 games. Perhaps the most obvious success of the season, however, was to be a new centre who joined from Headingley, Michael Yandle. Yandle, a Welsh schools cap, had learned to play his rugby in Llanelli before his job as a research chemist took him to "foreign" parts. His first game for the club was not auspicious: Bedford recorded their biggest win over the Tigers, by 39-5, though there was some comfort in the 33-21 win over the Irish Wolfhounds and a 48-6 defeat of Gosforth, in which Chapman scored 18 points.

There were others who were to become mainstays during the 1970s: John Duggan, a wing with Irish qualifications who, though a student at Loughborough Colleges, preferred to play his rugby with Oakham; a young Welshman from Aberamman, Bleddyn Jones, who had taken up a teaching post in Leicester; a couple of props from the Colleges, Philip Vesty and Chris Owen, and a blond hooker from Old Brockleians whose job with an insurance company had brought him to Leicester, Peter John Wheeler.

They all began their Leicester careers in the Swifts, though in October the club had the interesting situation of Elliott hooking for Notts, Lincs and Derby, Richard Berry for Leicestershire and Wheeler for Kent. So much new blood jostling for a place, however, gave the selection committee

↓ The Springboks' visit to Welford Road 8 November 1969 was disrupted by anti-apartheid demonstrators.

problems so it was not entirely surprising that only three Leicester players were included in the combined XV which met the Springboks in front of a 15,000 crowd. The side was Graham Pulfrey (Leicester); Roger Morris (Hinckley), Peter Sweet (Northampton), David Small (Bedford), Glenn Robertson (Northampton); Pat Briggs (Bedford, captain), John Allen (Leicester); Stuart Onyett (Bedford), Andy Johnson, David Powell (both Northampton), J Harrison (Boston), Peter Larter (Northampton), David Matthews (Leicester), Bryan West, Bob Taylor (both Northampton).

The tourists had begun by losing 6-3 to Oxford University and they only just got home, by 11-9, at Welford Road, in a match interrupted by abuse from demonstrators and intrusions on to the pitch. Piet Visagie opened the scoring with a penalty before Larter levelled with a huge kick from a penalty on halfway. Playing with the gusting wind, the Midlands took advantage of the tourists' uncertainty to score tries through Glenn Robertson and Peter Sweet, a dropped goal by Visagie making the score 9-6 at half-time. It was backs to the wall in the second half for the East Midlands, with the back row working overtime, but with only 10 minutes left, Visagie made the break to give Piet van Deventer a try, Visagie's conversion winning the game.

With the South Africans gone, Leicester totalled up the amount of cash they had raised and embarked on phase one of their planned redevelopment. The ground floor of the clubhouse was restructured to include an extra changing room, a foyer and an office for the secretary. Upstairs was redesigned as an all-purpose room for general functions, as well as the usual post-match imbibing, and a kitchen was added. Just outside the clubhouse, the banking at the Aylestone Road end of the ground was levelled to give car parking space, though this did cut down the amount of standing room available at big matches.

At much the same time Doug Norman resigned as fixture secretary, the task passing to Bob Beason. It was an indication of changing times that Beason, still playing well after nearly ten years with the club, should become an office holder too. It was not many years before that the idea of a player holding such a post had been virtually unthinkable.

← Bob Beason and David Matthews concentrate on a line-out against Newport 18.4.1970.

CLUBHOUSE DEVELOPMENT FUND-1968

the past

The Target-£30,000

↑ Brochure appealing for donations to the clubhouse redevelopment fund.

With the team struggling to make an impact, there was much discussion of playing policy and whether a club coaching panel should be instituted. Those who wished to see the Swifts scrapped were over-ruled, though it was agreed that a greater emphasis should be placed on young players in the Swifts. November 1969, saw Jones make his debut at fly-half instead of the injured Chapman, against Wilmslow, but his first game was overshadowed by the first appearance in a Leicester shirt of the Scotland and British Lions flanker, Rodger Arneil.

Arneil, then 25, had made his name on the 1968 Lions' visit to South Africa and had won seven of his 21 caps. He played little more than a dozen games for the club during his two seasons at Welford Road but while there he gave them what so many back rows then lacked - height, weight and speed. At six feet four inches tall and nearly 15 stone he was a considerable asset, apart from the prestige attached to an international then at the summit of his powers.

↑ Tigers wing Trevor Spence passes to Graham Willars despite the attentions of David Duckham during the Barbarians game in 1969.

In the same month Wheeler made his first appearance in the senior side, against Moseley, but it was not until the new year that Leicester managed to climb out of the doldrums in which they had settled. At that stage they had to recover from the indignity of a 35-0 defeat at the hands of the Barbarians, the highest score the guest XV had put together. It was the 50th encounter between the two sides and the Baa-baas turned in a golden display, with David Duckham scoring five tries and equalling Peter Thompson's effort of 1956. Keith Fielding scored two tries, John Jeffrey and Bob Phillips one each, and a young full-back called JPR Williams kicked four conversions.

There was some consolation for the club when they achieved the "double" against Gloucester, Barker scoring all the points in the second victory at Kingsholm. The former Stoneygate wing had become a regular member of the side, and a useful place-kicker, even though he was the only player who could, in the words of the club coach, make the ball turn three different directions before it crossed the bar. A canny footballer with the knack of turning up in the right place at the right time, he was to score 158 tries for Leicester, a post-war record until beaten by Barry Evans in 1989/90, though still well short of Percy Lawrie's 206.

For the first time since 1895, Leicester stayed home at Easter and entertained Liverpool, Fylde and Manchester over the holiday period. Even though all three games were won, however, the attendances were disappointing. Equally disappointing was the decision at the season's end of the captain, Andrews, to retire, leaving behind this epitaph on the club: "They are without doubt the best club I have played for...They have the right attitude to the game and this is why they will always be a great club."

Another leading forward, Bob Small, was retiring and though they won for the first time in 16 years at Coventry, Leicester completed a not entirely happy season, when they crashed 43-11 at Llanelli with Rowell being sent off for questioning the referee's decisions. The last Leicester player to have been sent off during a game had been Almey, also at Llanelli, 10 years before.

1970/1971

Going into the 70s, Leicester decided there had to be a fresh outlook on relations with local clubs. They had appointed a coaching panel of Chalkie White, Bob Small and David Lyons for their own purposes; now they organised another panel, headed by Kevin Andrews, to visit the junior clubs in Leicestershire and discuss moves to and from the county's senior club. It was hard to break down the accumulation of prejudices which had built up, on both sides, but the attempt had to be made and similar ventures continued, in one form or another, during the next eight years. The immediate response, in general, from the junior clubs was that they felt two sides would be sufficient for Leicester's purposes but that they would support a youth XV.

ITINERARY

LEICESTER FOOTBALL CLUB

Easter Tour 1971

MATCHES

10th April
First XV v. Liverpool F.C.
Extra First v. Liverpool 'A'

12th April
First XV v. Fylde F.C.
Extra First v. Fylde 'A'

13th April
First XV v. Manchester F.C.

HOTEL

The Queen's, Southport
Telephone 4104

↑ Easter Tour card 1971.

In the meantime there were problems restoring the image of the 1st XV. John Allen had been elected captain but the scrum-half did not always see eye to eye with the coach and ex scrum-half, White, and perhaps the element of discord in their views of the game may have been reflected in the results. The season was notable in one respect, for one of White's contemporaries as a player, the full-back Mike Gavins, returned for one more season, and returned with a bang. He played in 14 games which was enough to make him top scorer with 115 points.

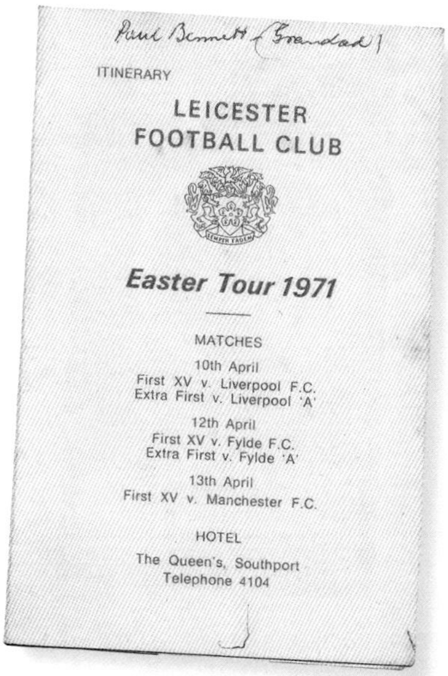

Among the newcomers was a centre from Nottingham, Brian Hall, who was to form a profitable partnership with Yandle, and a full-back from the West Country who was studying at Leicester University, David Whibley. Ten Tigers played in the Leicestershire XV which beat Durham 25-14 in the county's jubilee game and there were six in the Midland Counties (East) XV which lost to the touring Fijians at Welford Road on 7 November 1970, among them an athletic lock, Eric Bann, who had joined the club two seasons before. A player of immense potential and probably the best line-out exponent Leicester had over the two decades before the arrival of Martin Johnson, Bann never reached the heights which his talent suggested he should.

The Midland XV was: P Jenkins (Loughborough Colleges); John Duggan, Mike Yandle, Brian Hall (all Leicester), Barrie Oldham; Jon Cooley (both Northampton), Vic Lewis; Stuart Onyett (both Bedford), Andy Johnson (Northampton), David Powell (Northampton, captain), Eric Bann (Leicester), Peter Larter, Bob Taylor (both Northampton), Garry Adey, Chris Baynes (both Leicester). Replacements: Dusty Hare (Nottingham), David Matthews (Leicester).

The local side lost 24-14, after leading 11-8 at half-time. Pio Bosco Tikoisuva and Meli Kurisaru scored tries for the tourists, Cooley got one back for the Midlands and Jenkins kicked a conversion, a penalty and a dropped goal. After the break Josateki Sovau scored a try, converted by George Barley, and the game took an ugly turn, fists flying, and the Midlands lost Cooley, injured. His place at fly-half was taken by a teenager from Nottingham, WH 'Dusty' Hare, who had only recently broken through from junior football, the IRB only allowing substitutions for injured players for the first time in international games the previous season. Jenkins kicked another penalty but tries by Semesa Sikivou, Kurisaru and Sovau, one improved by Barley, put the game well out of reach.

There was some compensation in the selection of Adey for the only under-25 XV ever picked by England to play the Fijians. Wheeler was a replacement for the match which was played in miserable conditions; Adey had been suffering from influenza during the week and may not have done himself justice, since he was the only member of the side who did not to go on to get a trial.

It was, though, the start of an exceptional decade for Wheeler. He got the slice of luck everyone needs, even the good players, when Elliott dropped out through injury and missed the Barbarians game. Wheeler, not without a blush, recalls that it was he who delivered the injury during a training evening but, having got the first-team place, he kept it, to such good effect that Elliott eventually moved clubs and joined Nottingham.

As well as being a good hooker, Wheeler was a remarkably fine all-round footballer. In his first season he proved a useful addition to the place-kicking strength; fast and hard, he could

↓ John Allen tidies up poor line-out ball against Northampton 17.10.1970.

also tackle, distribute the ball and kick well out of hand. Sufficient of these qualities came through for him to be chosen, with Matthews, for the London, Midland and Home Counties XV which played the RFU President's XV at Welford Road on 7 April 1971, as part of the Rugby Football Union's centenary celebrations.

The President's men won 18-13 in a game notable for a remarkable try by the Springbok lock, Frik du Preez, but Wheeler was on his way. On tour in the north-west, he claimed 32 of 47 points scored by the club against Liverpool, Fylde and Manchester, and 29 of those came from the boot. And though there was no fairy story ending with a place in the British Lions side to Australasia that summer - Arneil was chosen from Leicester (as replacement for Mick Hipwell), the club's first Lion since 1959 - Wheeler was picked for England's tour to the Far East.

1971/1972

What had started as a thoroughly mediocre year was turning out to be quite eventful. Thinking ahead ten years, the club elected their own centenary committee (Tom Berry, Doug Norman and Bob Beason) and decided to undertake, for the first time, a pre-season training weekend. Chalkie White took his troops to Cromer in August for a valuable couple of days, although the value of the trip took some time to appear. The new season, marked by the appearance of a new-look, 16-page programme, was clouded by five successive defeats, attendance at training was poor, Arneil joined Northampton and the England wing, Keith Fielding, after joining the club from Moseley, hastily returned there after Leicester decided he was not good enough for their first XV.

The turning point came against Gloucester, previously undefeated by an English club that season, who crashed 31-9 at Welford Road. Money, the full-back, had taken the afternoon off to attend a wedding and Whibley seized his opportunity with both hands to become the goal-kicker the club desperately needed and turn in such a consistently high standard that he very nearly went from Leicester Extras to a full cap in one season. After only nine first-class games he won an area trial and in the new year there were senior trials.

Unfortunately he could not help Leicester win their first venture in the Rugby Football Union's national knockout competition. Drawn against Notts, the game was played on a Sunday at Beeston, the home side having Hare to help them to a 10-3 win. It was another 18 years before Nottingham, as they became, repeated that success. There was compensation at Christmas in a splendid 20-14 win over the Barbarians, Barker joining the ranks of the few by scoring three tries. The game was a fitting tribute, too, to Doug Norman, who died early the same day. 1971 had also seen the death of two stalwarts, Rodney Bedingfield and HLV Day, the latter after a distinguished career as a player, a referee and rugby correspondent.

In the meantime the club were planning a step which ranks as one of their most important decisions since the war. An article had appeared in the *Leicester Mercury,* written by the paper's rugby correspondent, Paul Neale, describing the activities of a schools side, the Leicester Ravens, composed of some of the best 14 and 15 year-olds in the county. It was organised by David Lyons, who had a genius for bringing the best out of young players, and the article mooted the possibility of the Ravens becoming, in effect, a Tigers youth side.

It was a gift horse which Jerry Day, for one, was not going to look in the mouth and he threw all his support behind the project. A special club sub-committee recommended Leicester seek the advice and co-operation of leading rugby-playing schools, to constitute a youth sub-committee for the side's management, to organise as many fixtures as possible outside Leicestershire, but not more than 20 in a season, to charge a subscription of £1 with full membership rights and, in particular, that the youth team should train separately and should not be used to fill gaps in the three senior sides.

In March 1972, a former Leicestershire RU president, Joe Pickup, became secretary of the junior football sub-committee and Lyons, a teacher at Roundhill School, Syston, and Michael Deathe, a Hinckley schoolmaster, were appointed youth coaches and joined the club's coaching committee. On 15 April 1972, Leicester Youth took the field for the first time and beat Nottingham Cubs 78-9. They followed this up with a 76-0 win over Derbyshire Youth and the first report on the team's activities in the club committee minutes noted, somewhat drily in the circumstances: "This was felt to be a promising start."

LEICESTER FOOTBALL CLUB

1971 - 72

↑ Tigers introduced a new programme design for season 1971/72.

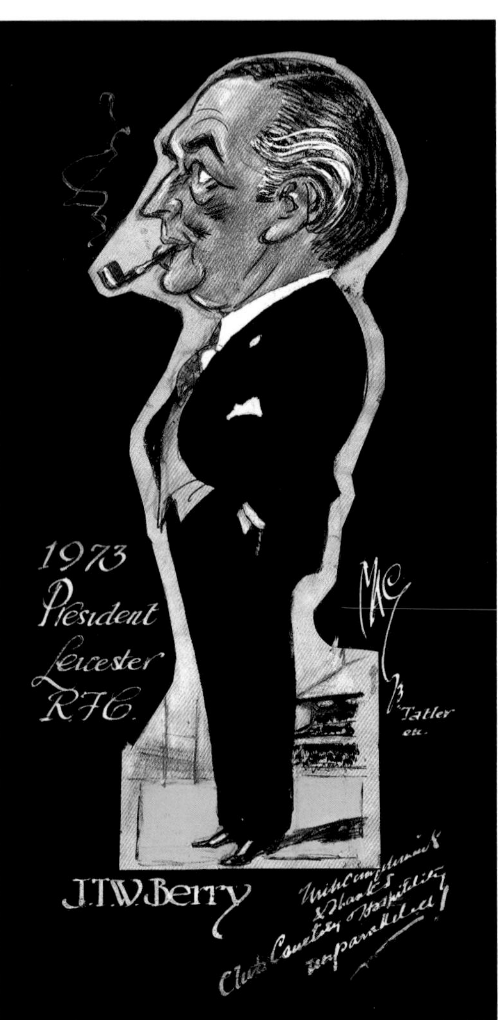

← LFC President Tom Berry was elected to the Centenary Committee.

Of the side that played the Cubs, the scrum-half, Stephen Kenney, was to make the most impact, winning England colts and under-23 caps with his exciting, running style which was worth, in the opinion of many outside observers, even higher honours. The team was: Marcus Hellyer; Richard Lett, Mark Wyatt, Stuart Dexter, Keith Smith; John Flint, Steve Kenney (captain); Phil Hemsill, Mick Briggs, Cez Siwek, John Fraser, Richard Hull, Jez Krych, Gus Collington, Paul Bennett.

The quality of the youth rugby was exceptional but the most valuable aspect of the side's creation was the insight into the future of the senior side. With a coach already keen on long-term planning, the youth team enabled Leicester to think in terms of the next decade rather than the next two or three seasons. Within six short years the youth had produced their first full international in Paul Dodge, one of the boys directly influenced by Lyons in those formative years of the early 70s.

While the youth side was coming into being, their seniors were not standing still. Casting aside the disappointments of the early part of the 1971/72 season they scored fifty points for the first time since the 1919/20 season (against the RAF) and went out in a blaze of glory, winning at Newport for the first time in 39 years and, in the same match, passing the previous highest points tally of 756, recorded in 1920. They wound up with 789 points, Whibley scored 200 points (the best since Haselmere in 1920) and Barker 26 tries (the best since Haselmere in 1921). To cap it all, Whibley was named in the England party to tour South Africa, the assistant manager of the tour being John Elders.

Alan Old made his Tigers debut in 1972 and toured with the Lions two years later.

Another tourist was the Middlesbrough fly-half, Alan Old, capped in all the home internationals and against South Africa and the scorer of a then record number of points (24) in England's 60-21 win over Griqualand West. An appointment to the teaching staff at Worksop College brought Old south and he joined Leicester, along with a New Zealander who had played in the centre for Auckland, Gary Weinberg, who was in England on business.

AGB Old, one of the best, and certainly one of the most under-rated, fly-halves capped by England during the 70s, helped bring a new confidence to the club's back division which was not exactly lacking in it anyway, with characters like Hall and Yandle playing. The pity of it was that he was available for so few games, because of his commitments to Yorkshire in the county championship and the demands made on him by England. He and Bleddyn Jones alternated for the fly-half position, and occasionally they played in the same side, with Old at centre.

LEICESTER FOOTBALL CLUB 1968/69
Back: Thorpe (Hon.Tres), Hughes (President), Bann, Beaty, Smith, Baynes, Pulfrey, Barker, Adey, Matthews, Sleigh, White (Coach), Day (Hon.Sec).
Middle: Betts, Harrison, Evans, Andrews, Willars (capt), Allen, Elliott, Grove, Mawbey, Brownhill.
Front: Bird, Money, Spence, Cooper.

LEICESTER FOOTBALL CLUB 1969/70
Back: White (Coach), Hughes (President), Bird, Spence, Jackson, Adey, Pulfrey, Arneil, Willars, Baynes, Day (Hon.Sec), Sibson (Team Hon.Sec).
Middle: Barker, Skelton, Matthews, Harrison, Andrews (capt), Allen, Elliott, Beason, Rowell.
Front: Jones, Duggan, Money, Yandle.

LEICESTER FOOTBALL CLUB 1970/71
Back: Sibson (Team Hon.Sec), Thorpe (Hon.Tres), Hughes (President), Nicholls, Baynes, Barker, Adey, Bann, Shaw, Arneil, Beason, White (Coach), Day (Hon.Sec).
Middle: Hall, Wheeler, Grove, Allen (capt), Matthews, Yandle, Willars, Duggan.
Front: Bird, Money, Elliott, Jones.

LEICESTER FOOTBALL CLUB 1971/72
Back: Day (Hon.Sec), White (Coach), Yandle, Nicholls, Hall, Watson, Adey, Matthews, Mortimer, Rowell, Barker, Horner, Berry (President), Sibson (Team Hon.Sec).
Middle: Wheeler, Willars, Grove (capt), Beason, Money.
Front: Jones, Allen.

19 68/69		OVERALL RECORD:					T	C	PG	DG	PTS
	Home Ground: Welford Road	PLD	W	D	L	Tigers scored:	122	48	56	9	657
	Coach: Chalkie White	43	27	4	12	Opponents scored:	81	40	38	7	461
	Captain: Graham Willars										

GM	DATE		VEN	OPPONENTS	RESULT	TRIES	KICKS	ATT
CLUB MATCHES								
1	Sep	**5th**	**H**	**Watcyn Thomas XV**	W 25-14	Smith(2), Andrews, Lockett, Matthews	Harris 2c/p/d	701
2		**7**	**H**	**Bedford**	W 16-15	Matthews(2), Harris, Sleigh	Harris 2c	455
3		14	a	Bath	W 12-6	Andrews	Harris 2p, Evans d	-
4		**17tu**	**H**	**Nuneaton**	L 12-19	Matthews(2), Mawbey	Evans p	320
5		**21**	**H**	**Plymouth Albion**	W 33-8	Evans(2), Bird(2), Matthews(2)	Evans 2c, Harris c/2p, Mawbey d	308
6		28	a	Harlequins	D 9-9	-	Evans 3p	-
7	Oct	5	a	Coventry	L 12-17	Sleigh(2)	Evans p/d	-
8		**8tu**	**H**	**Rugby**	W 12-11	Jackson	Evans 3p	194
9		**12**	**H**	**Richmond**	W 28-19	Mawbey(2), Jackson, Sleigh	Cooper 2c/4p	301
10		**19**	**H**	**Northampton**	D 17-17	Barker	Evans c/4p	699
11		**23w**	**H**	**Oxford University**	W 24-8	Jackson(2), Sleigh(2), Sayer	Evans 3c/p	287
12		26	a	Swansea	W 14-9	Evans, Allen	Evans c/2p	-
13	Nov	2	a	Gloucester	L 3-9	-	Evans p	-
14		**9**	**H**	**Cambridge University**	W 9-6	Sleigh(2)	Evans p	322
15		16	a	Newport	L 0-18	-	-	-
16		23	a	Moseley	L 3-16	Smith	-	-
17		**30**	**H**	**Old Belvedere**	W 18-5	Matthews(2), Mawbey, Sayer	Cooper 3c	309
18	Dec	**7**	**H**	**Waterloo**	L 8-12	Harris	Cooper c/p	171
19		**14**	**H**	**Blackheath**	W 17-0	Evans, Andrews, Mawbey, Sayer	Evans c/p	170
20		**21**	**H**	**Bristol**	W 20-3	Mawbey, Betts, Matthews, Money	Mawbey d, Evans c/p	270
		27f	**H**	**Barbarians**	PP			
21	Jan	**4**	**H**	**Bath**	W 14-13	Grove, Matthews	Evans c/2d	412
22		**11**	**H**	**Gloucester**	W 12-8	Allen	Evans 2p/d	229
		18	a	Bedford	PP			
23		**25**	**H**	**Rosslyn Park**	W 15-11	Bird, Elliott, Spence	Bann 2p	384
24	Feb	1	a	London Scottish	W 14-3	Bird, Matthews, Spence	Bann c/p	-
		8	**H**	**Newport**	PP (frost)			
		15	**H**	**Wasps**	PP (snow)			
		18tu	**H**	**Moseley**	PP (frost)			
		22	a	Northampton	PP (snow)			
25		**27th**	**H**	**Barbarians**	L 11-19	Allen, Grove, Matthews	Bann c	10000
26	Mar	**1**	**H**	**Harlequins**	L 3-11	-	Bann p	308
27		**5w**	**H**	**Loughborough Colleges**	W 24-9	Elliott, Grove, Sleigh, Spence	Evans 3p, Bann p	290
28		**8**	**H**	**Coventry**	L 6-20	Allen	Evans p	529
29		**13th**	**H**	**Royal Air Force**	W 29-0	Sleigh(2), Evans, Allen, Andrews, Matthews, Willars	Evans c, Bann 3c	166
30		**19w**	**H**	**Coventry**	W 15-6	Matthews(2), Bann, Harrison	Evans p	285
31		22	a	Headingley	L 0-22	-	-	-
33		**29**	**H**	**Bradford**	W 24-10	Spence(2), Baynes, Bird, Harrison	Evans 3c/p	199
34	Apr	5	a	Bristol	D 11-11	Bird, Matthews	Evans c/p	-
35		7m	a	Plymouth Albion	W 12-9	Bird, Brownhill	Cooper 2p	-
36		8tu	a	Stroud	W 45-6	Allen(2), Betts(2), Bann, Barker, Baynes, Brownhill, Harrison, Matthews, Spence	Cooper 6c	-
37		**12**	**H**	**Birkenhead Park**	W 25-8	Bird(3), Allen, Elliott, Matthews	Cooper 2c/p	178
39		**19**	**H**	**Llanelli**	D 9-9	-	Matthews 3p	413
40		22tu	a	Moseley	L 0-11	-	-	-
41		**26**	**H**	**Hartlepool Rovers**	W 17-8	Barker(2), Brownhill	Cooper c/2p	180
43	May	**3**	**H**	**Broughton Park**	W 8-5	Allen, Barker	Cooper c	175
FLOODLIT CUP								
32	Mar	26w	a	Gloucester	W 6-0	-	Evans 2p	-
38	Apr	**16w**	**H**	**Moseley**	L 24-26	Baynes, Brownhill, Harrison, Matthews	Cooper c/2p, Bann 2c	377
42		**30w**	**H**	**Cheltenham**	W 41-15	Adey(3), Brownhill(2), Spence(2), Baynes, Matthews	Cooper 4c/p, Pulfrey d	185

INDIVIDUAL APPEARANCES 1968/69

Name / Game #	1	2	3	4	5	6	7	8	9	10	11	12	13	14	15	16	17	18	19	20	21	22	23	24	25	26	27	28	29	30	31	32	33	34	35	36	37	38	39	40	41	42	43	Apps	T	Pts
GJ (Garry) Adey E+	-	-	-	-	-	-	-	-	-	-	-	-	-	-	D	E	-	-	-	-	-	-	-	-	-	-	-	-	-	-	-	E	E	-	E	D	E	-	E	D	-	F	F	11	3	9
JA (John) Allen	I	I	I	I	I	I	I	I	I	I	I	I	I	I	I	I	I	I	I	I	I	I	I	I	I	I	I	I	I	I	I	I	I	I	I	I	I	I	I	I	I	I	I	43	9	27
KP (Kevin) Andrews	D	D	D	D	D	E	D	D	D	D	D	D	D	D	-	-	D	D	D	D	E	D	D	D	D	D	E	E	D	D	D	D	D	D	D	-	D	E	D	-	D	D	D	39	4	12
EE (Eric) Bann	-	-	-	-	-	-	-	-	-	-	-	-	E	E	E	D	E	E	E	E	D	E	E	E	E	E	D	D	E	E	E	-	-	E	-	E	-	D	-	E	E	E	E	26	2	35
RG (Bob) Barker	-	-	-	-	-	-	-	-	-	>M	-	-	-	-	-	-	-	-	-	-	-	-	-	-	-	-	L	L	-	-	-	L	L	M	L	L	L	L	M	L	L	L	L	15	5	15
CJ (Chris) Baynes	-	-	-	-	-	-	-	-	-	-	-	-	-	-	-	-	-	-	-	-	-	-	-	-	-	-	-	-	-	>H	H	H	H	F	-	F	-	H	H	H	H	H	H	12	4	12
R (Bob) Beason	-	-	-	-	-	-	-	-	-	-	A	A	-	-	-	-	-	-	-	-	-	-	-	-	-	-	-	-	-	-	-	-	-	-	-	-	-	-	-	-	-	-	-	2	-	-
DJ (David) Beaty	C	C	C	C	C	C	C	C	C	C	-	C	C	C	A	C	C	C	A	C	C	C	C	C	C	C	C	C	C	C	C	C	C	C	-	-	C	-	C	A	C	C	<C	39	-	-
DMH (David) Berry	J	-	-	-	-	-	-	-	-	-	-	-	-	-	-	-	-	-	-	-	-	-	-	-	-	-	-	-	-	-	-	-	-	-	-	-	-	-	-	-	-	-	-	1	-	-
JH (John) Berry	-	-	-	-	-	-	-	-	<L	-	-	-	-	-	-	-	-	-	-	-	-	-	-	-	-	-	-	-	-	-	-	-	-	-	-	-	-	-	-	-	-	-	-	1	-	-
RTH (Richard) Berry	B	B	B	-	-	B	B	B	B	-	-	-	-	-	-	-	-	-	-	B	-	-	-	-	-	-	-	-	-	-	B	-	-	-	B	-	-	-	-	-	-	-	-	10	-	-
SE (Steve) Betts	-	-	-	-	-	-	-	-	-	F	H	H	H	H	H	-	F	H	H	H	H	-	-	-	-	-	H	H	H	-	-	-	-	-	H	H	H	-	-	-	-	-	-	17	3	9
DW (David) Bird	-	N	N	K	K	-	-	-	-	-	-	-	-	-	-	-	-	N	N	N	N	N	N	N	N	N	-	-	N	K	N	N	N	K	K	-	N	N	N	N	-	-	-	24	10	30
JM (Mike) Brownhill	-	-	-	-	-	-	-	-	-	-	-	-	-	-	-	-	K	K	K	K	-	-	-	-	-	-	-	-	-	-	-	K	-	-	N	N	-	K	K	K	K	K	<K	13	6	18
P (Pete) Clements	-	-	-	>G	<G	-	-	-	-	-	-	-	-	-	-	-	-	-	-	-	-	-	-	-	-	-	-	-	-	-	-	-	-	-	-	-	-	-	-	-	-	-	-	2	-	-
RC (Dick) Cooper	-	-	-	-	-	-	-	-	J	-	-	-	-	-	-	-	J	J	-	-	-	-	-	-	-	-	-	-	-	-	-	-	-	-	J	J	J	J	-	-	J	J	J	10	-	81
JH (John) Dawson	-	-	-	-	-	-	-	-	-	-	-	-	-	-	-	-	-	-	-	-	-	-	-	-	-	-	-	-	-	-	-	-	-	-	>A	C	-	C	-	C	-	-	-	4	-	-
NJ (Nick) Drake-Lee E8	-	-	-	-	-	-	-	-	-	-	-	-	-	-	-	<A	-	-	-	-	-	-	-	-	-	-	-	-	-	-	-	-	-	-	-	-	-	-	-	-	-	-	-	1	-	-
JJ (John) Elliott	-	-	-	-	-	-	-	-	-	B	B	B	B	B	B	B	B	B	B	-	B	B	B	B	B	B	B	B	B	B	-	B	B	B	-	B	B	B	B	B	B	B	B	31	3	9
M (Mike) Evans	-	J	J	J	J	J	J	J	-	J	J	J	J	J	J	J	-	-	J	J	J	J	J	J	J	J	J	J	J	J	J	J	J	J	-	-	-	-	-	-	-	-	-	30	5	150
J (Jess) Glover	-	-	-	-	-	N	<K	-	-	-	-	-	-	-	-	-	-	-	-	-	-	-	-	-	-	-	-	-	-	-	-	-	-	-	-	-	-	-	-	-	-	-	-	2	-	-
RV (Roger) Grove	-	-	-	-	-	A	A	A	A	A	C	-	A	A	C	-	A	A	C	A	A	A	A	A	A	A	A	A	A	A	A	A	A	A	C	A	A	A	A	-	A	A	A	35	3	9
N Haines	-	-	-	-	-	-	-	-	-	-	-	-	>N	-	-	-	<N	-	-	-	-	-	-	-	-	-	-	-	-	-	-	-	-	-	-	-	-	-	-	-	-	-	-	2	-	-
D (David) Harris	>L	L	L	M	M	-	-	-	-	-	-	-	-	-	-	-	-	<0	-	-	-	-	-	-	-	-	-	-	-	-	-	-	-	-	-	-	-	-	-	-	-	-	-	6	2	34
MJ (Mike) Harrison	-	-	-	-	-	-	-	-	-	-	-	-	-	-	-	-	-	-	-	-	L	L	M	L	L	L	M	-	L	M	M	-	M	L	-	M	M	M	L	M	M	-	-	18	4	12
CA (Chris) Holroyd	-	-	-	-	-	-	-	-	-	-	-	-	-	-	K	<K	-	-	-	-	-	-	-	-	-	-	-	-	-	-	-	-	-	-	-	-	-	-	-	-	-	-	-	2	-	-
G (Graham) Jackson	-	-	-	-	-	-	-	K	K	K	K	K	K	K	-	-	-	-	-	-	-	-	-	-	-	-	-	-	-	-	-	-	-	-	-	-	-	-	-	-	-	-	-	7	4	12
ME (Mike) Lockett	>N	-	-	<N	-	-	-	-	-	-	-	-	-	-	-	-	-	-	-	-	-	-	-	-	-	-	-	-	-	-	-	-	-	-	-	-	-	-	-	-	-	-	-	2	1	3
DJ (David) Matthews	H	H	H	H	H	H	H	H	H	G	G	G	F*	G	G	G	G	G	G	G	G	H	H	H	H	H	G	G	G	G	G	G	G	G	G	G*	G	G	F*	F*	F*	G*	G*	43	21	72
JW (John) Mawbey	-	-	-	L	L	L	M	M	M	L	L	L	M	M	M	M	M	M	L	M	M	M	L	M	M	M	-	M	M	L	L	-	-	-	-	-	-	-	-	-	-	M	<M	29	6	24
RS (Robin) Money	-	-	-	-	-	-	-	>0	-	0	-	0	0	0	0	0	0	-	0	0	0	0	0	-	-	-	-	-	0	0	0	0	0	0	0	0	0	0	0	0	0	-	-	26	1	3
D Morley	>A	A	A	A	A	-	-	-	-	-	-	-	-	-	-	-	-	-	-	-	-	-	-	-	-	-	-	-	-	-	-	-	-	-	-	-	-	-	-	-	-	-	-	5	-	-
D (David) Perkins	-	-	-	-	-	-	-	-	-	-	-	-	-	-	-	-	-	-	-	-	-	-	-	-	-	-	-	-	-	-	-	-	-	-	-	-	-	-	J	<J	-	-	-	2	-	-
PGS (Graham) Pulfrey	0	0	0	0	0	0	0	-	0	-	0	-	-	-	-	-	-	-	-	-	-	-	-	0	0	0	0	0	-	-	-	-	-	-	-	-	-	-	-	-	-	0	0	16	-	3
A (Alan) Raine	E	E	E	E	E	D	E	E	E	E	E	<E	-	-	-	-	-	-	-	-	-	-	-	-	-	-	-	-	-	-	-	-	-	-	-	-	-	-	-	-	-	-	-	12	-	-
MF (Malcolm) Sayer	-	-	-	-	-	-	-	-	-	-	M	M	L	L	L	L	L	L	M	<L	-	-	-	-	-	-	-	-	-	-	-	-	-	-	-	-	-	-	-	-	-	-	-	10	3	9
R (Roy) Sleigh	K	K	K	-	N	K	N	N	N	N	N	N	-	N	N	N	-	-	-	-	-	-	-	-	-	-	K	K	K	N	K	-	-	-	-	-	-	-	-	-	-	-	-	19	11	33
RS (Bob) Smith	G	G	G	-	-	G	G	G	G	-	-	-	G	-	-	H	-	-	-	-	-	G	G	G	G	G	-	-	-	-	-	-	-	-	-	-	-	-	G	G	G	-	-	17	3	9
T (Trevor) Spence	M	M	M	-	-	M	L	L	-	-	-	-	-	-	-	-	-	-	-	-	K	K	K	K	K	K	N	N	-	-	-	M	K	N	M	K	K	-	-	-	N	N	N	23	8	24
A (Alan) Whitehall	-	-	-	>B	<B	-	-	-	-	-	-	-	-	-	-	-	-	-	-	-	-	-	-	-	-	-	-	-	-	-	-	-	-	-	-	-	-	-	-	-	-	-	-	2	-	-
GG (Graham) Willars	F*	F*	F*	F*	F*	F*	F*	F*	F*	H*	F*	F*	-	F*	F*	F*	H*	F*	F*	F*	F*	F*	F*	F*	F*	F*	F*	F*	F*	F*	F*	F*	F*	H*	F*	-	F*	F*	-	-	-	-	-	36	1	3

The key for how to read the stats is on the last page

19 69/70	Home Ground: Welford Road	OVERALL RECORD:					T	C	PG	DG	PTS
	Coach: Chalkie White	PLD	W	D	L	Tigers scored:	123	57	48	8	651
	Captain: Kevin Andrews	44	26	3	15	Opponents scored:	101	49	46	8	563

GM	DATE		VEN	OPPONENTS	RESULT	TRIES	KICKS	ATT
CLUB MATCHES								
1	Sep	6	a	Bedford	L 5-39	Sleigh	Evans c	-
2		**10w**	**H**	**Leicester & District**	W 27-9	Chapman, Allen, Elliott, Small, Spence	Chapman 3c/2p	329
3		**13**	**H**	**Bath**	W 14-11	Barker, Spence	Chapman c/2p	240
4		**15m**	**H**	**Irish Wolfhounds**	W 33-21	Chapman, Betts, Jackson, Spence	Chapman 3c/4p/d	884
5		**20**	**H**	**Gosforth**	W 48-6	Jackson(2), Spence(2), Yandle(2), Chapman, Barker, Dawson, Owen, Pulfrey	Chapman 6c/p	205
6		23tu	a	Nuneaton	W 19-9	Spence(3), Betts	Evans 2c/p	-
7		27	a	Harlequins	L 11-17	Elliott	Chapman c/2p	-
8		30tu	a	Fylde	W 17-16	Adey, Barker	Cooper c/3p	-
9	Oct	**2th**	**H**	**Moseley**	W 12-3	Adey, Betts, Grove	Chapman p	482
10		**4**	**H**	**Coventry**	L 11-14	Chapman	Chapman c/2p	907
11		11	a	Richmond	L 19-22	Baynes(2), Elliott, Owen	Chapman 2c/p	-
12		18	a	Northampton	L 8-29	Chapman, Rowell	Chapman c	-
13		22w	a	Oxford University	L 0-23	-	-	-
14		**25**	**H**	**Swansea**	D 9-9	-	Chapman 3p	361
15	Nov	**1**	**H**	**Gloucester**	W 15-12	Bird, Small, Spence	Chapman p/d	312
16		8	a	Cambridge University	L 11-36	Millar, Owen, Spence	Chapman c	-
17		**15**	**H**	**Wilmslow**	L 13-23	Matthews, Arneil	Matthews c/p, Bann c	129
18		**19w**	**H**	**Combined Services**	D 6-6	Jones, Matthews	-	218
19		**22**	**H**	**Moseley**	L 14-17	Bann, Jackson, Willars	Chapman c/p	333
		29	a	Saracens	PP (snow)			
20	Dec	**6**	**H**	**Waterloo**	W 19-3	Aldwinckle, Bann, Matthews, Spence	Chapman c/p, Cooper c	128
21		13	a	Blackheath	W 21-11	Dawson, Elliott, Jackson, Matthews	Cooper 3c, Pulfrey d	-
22		20	a	Bristol	L 0-20	-	-	-
23		**27**	**H**	**Barbarians**	L 0-35	-	-	4163
24	Jan	3	a	Bath	L 9-13	Baynes, Willars	Barker p	-
25		10	a	Gloucester	W 8-6	Barker	Barker c/p	-
26		**17**	**H**	**Bedford**	W 6-5	Baynes	Barker p	266
27		24	a	Rosslyn Park	W 3-0	Bird	-	-
28		**30f**	**H**	**Headingley**	L 12-16	-	Barker 4p	208
29	Feb	4w	a	Cheltenham	D 6-6	Bird, Elliott	-	-
		6f	**H**	**London Scottish**	PP (frost)			
		14	a	Newport	PP (frost)			
		18w	a	Moseley	PP (frost)			
30		21	a	Wasps	W 11-5	Adey, Baynes	Barker c/p	-
31		**27f**	**H**	**Northampton**	W 14-9	Adey, Allen, Bird, Jones	Barker c	408
	Mar	**4w**	**H**	**Gloucester**	PP (snow)			
		7	**H**	**Harlequins**	PP (snow)			
32		**11w**	**H**	**Loughborough Colleges**	W 27-3	Barker, Adey, Allen, Duggan, Harrison, Jones	Barker 3c/p	251
33		14	a	Coventry	L 6-9	Andrews	Money d	-
34		**18w**	**H**	**Royal Navy**	W 27-6	Allen(3), Andrews(2)	Barker 3c/2p	254
35		**20f**	**H**	**Royal Air Force**	W 16-13	Duggan, Yandle	Barker 2c/p, Allen d	300
36		**28**	**H**	**Liverpool**	W 11-0	Matthews, Money	Barker c/p	267
37		**30m**	**H**	**Fylde**	W 20-12	Elliott(2), Harrison, Matthews	Barker c/p, Jones d	338
38		**31tu**	**H**	**Manchester**	W 19-0	Barker, Harrison, Jackson, Matthews	Barker 2c/p	194
39	Apr	4	a	Birkenhead Park	W 41-3	Duggan(3), Jackson(2), Barker, Arneil, Money, Riley, Yandle(Penalty)	Barker 4c/p	-
40		**11**	**H**	**Newport**	W 13-3	Harrison, Rowell	Barker 2c/p	305
41		18	a	Llanelli	L 11-43	Marshall	Barker c/p, Money d	-
42		23th	a	Coventry	W 11-6	Baynes, Jones, Yandle	Barker c	-
43		**25**	**H**	**Halifax**	W 31-8	Barker(2), Allen, Duggan, Harrison, Jones, Matthews	Barker 2c/p, Money d	224
44	May	**2**	**H**	**New Brighton**	W 17-6	Duggan, Elliott	Barker c/3p	209

INDIVIDUAL APPEARANCES 1969/70

Name / Game #	1	2	3	4	5	6	7	8	9	10	11	12	13	14	15	16	17	18	19	20	21	22	23	24	25	26	27	28	29	30	31	32	33	34	35	36	37	38	39	40	41	42	43	44	Apps	T	Pts
GJ (Garry) Adey E+	-	-	-	-	-	-	-	G	G	G	G	-	-	-	-	-	-	-	G	G	G	-	-	-	G	G	G	G	G	G	G	G	G	G	G	G	-	G	-	-	G	G	G	G	24	5	15
PJ (Peter) Aldwinckle	-	-	-	-	-	-	-	-	-	-	-	-	-	-	-	-	-	I	I	I	-	-	-	-	-	-	-	-	-	-	-	-	I	-	-	-	<I	-	-	-	-	-	-	-	5	1	3
JA (John) Allen	I	I	I	I	I	I	I	I	I	I	I	I	-	I	I	-	-	-	-	-	I	I	I	I	I	I	I	I	I	I	I	I	-	I	I	I	-	I*	I	I	I	I	I	I*	36	7	24
KP (Kevin) Andrews	D*	D*	D*	D*	D*	D*	D*	D*	D*	D*	D*	D*	D*	D*	D*	D*	-	D*	D*	D*	D*	D*	D*	D*	D*	D*	D*	D*	D*	D*	D*	D*	D*	D*	D*	D*	D*	-	D*	D*	D*	D*	<D*	-	41	3	9
RJ (Rodger) Arneil S12 L4	-	-	-	-	-	-	-	-	-	-	-	-	-	-	-	-	>H	F	-	-	H	H	-	-	-	-	H	-	-	H	-	H	H	-	-	-	-	-	H	H	-	-	-	-	10	2	6
EE (Eric) Bann	E	-	-	-	-	-	E	E	E	E	E	-	-	-	E	E	D	E	E	E	-	-	E	E	-	-	-	-	-	-	-	-	-	-	-	-	-	E	-	-	-	-	-	-	15	2	8
RG (Bob) Barker	M	M	M	M	M	L	L	L	L	L	L	L	-	L	L	L	L	-	-	-	-	-	-	L	L	L	L	N	N	N	N	N	N	N	K	N	N	N	M	N	N	N	N	M	37	9	145
CJ (Chris) Baynes	F	-	-	-	-	-	-	F	-	H	F	H	-	-	-	-	-	-	-	-	-	F	F	F	F	H	F	F	F	F	H	F	F	F	F	-	-	-	F	F	F	F	F	F	25	6	18
R (Bob) Beason	-	-	-	-	-	-	-	C	-	-	-	-	-	-	-	-	-	-	A	-	-	A	A	C	C	C	A	A	A	A	C	A	A	A	-	A	C	A	C	A	C	C	C	C	24	-	-
RTH (Richard) Berry	-	-	-	-	-	-	-	B	-	-	-	-	B	<B	-	-	-	-	-	-	-	-	-	-	-	-	-	-	-	-	-	-	-	-	-	-	-	-	-	-	-	-	-	-	3	-	-
SE (Steve) Betts	H	F	H	H	H	H	H	-	H	-	-	-	H	H	H	H	-	<H	-	-	-	-	-	-	-	-	-	-	-	-	-	-	-	-	-	-	-	-	-	-	-	-	-	-	13	3	9
DW (David) Bird	-	N	-	-	-	-	-	-	-	-	-	N	N	N	N	K	K	-	-	-	-	-	-	K	K	K	K	K	K	K	K	-	-	-	-	K	K	-	-	-	-	-	-	-	17	4	12
P (Peter) Broadbent	-	-	-	-	-	-	-	-	-	-	-	-	-	-	-	-	-	-	-	-	-	-	-	=G	-	-	-	-	-	-	-	-	-	-	-	-	-	-	-	-	-	-	-	-	1	-	-
J (John) Broome	-	-	-	-	-	-	-	=M	-	-	-	-	-	-	-	-	-	-	-	-	-	-	-	-	-	-	-	-	-	-	-	-	-	-	-	-	-	-	-	-	-	-	-	-	1	-	-
AE (Arthur) Chapman	-	J	J	J	J	-	J	-	J	J	J	J	J	J	J	J	-	-	J	J	-	J	<J	-	-	-	-	-	-	-	-	-	-	-	-	-	-	-	-	-	-	-	-	-	17	5	126
RC (Dick) Cooper	-	-	-	-	-	-	-	J	M	-	-	-	-	-	-	M	-	L	M	L	L	L	M	-	-	-	-	-	-	-	-	-	-	-	-	-	-	-	-	-	-	-	-	-	9	-	19
JH (John) Dawson	A	C	C	C	C	-	-	-	-	-	-	C	C	C	C	A	C	-	-	-	C	C	C	A	A	A	C	C	C	C	A	C	C	C	C	C	-	C	A	-	A	A	A	-	32	2	6
MJ (John) Duggan	-	-	-	-	-	-	-	-	-	-	-	-	-	-	-	-	-	-	-	-	-	-	-	>N	N	N	-	-	-	-	-	K	K	K	N	-	-	-	N	K	K	K	K	K	13	7	21
JJ (John) Elliott	B	B	B	B	B	B	B	-	B	B	B	B	-	-	B	-	B	B	-	B	B	-	B	B	B	B	B	B	B	B	-	B	B	B	B	B	B	-	B	B	B	B	B	B	36	8	24
M (Mike) Evans	J	-	-	-	-	J	-	-	-	-	-	-	<L	-	-	-	-	-	-	-	-	-	-	-	-	-	-	-	-	-	-	-	-	-	-	-	-	-	-	-	-	-	-	-	3	-	9
RV (Roger) Grove	C	-	-	-	-	A	A	-	A	A	A	A	A	-	A	-	A	A	-	A	-	-	-	-	-	-	-	-	-	-	-	-	-	-	A	-	A	-	-	-	-	-	-	-	14	1	3
DA (Dave) Hanna	-	-	-	-	-	-	-	-	-	-	-	-	-	-	-	-	-	-	-	-	-	-	-	-	-	-	-	-	-	-	-	-	-	-	-	-	-	-	-	-	-	-	-	>D	1	-	-
MJ (Mike) Harrison	-	-	-	-	-	-	-	-	-	-	-	-	-	-	-	-	-	-	-	-	-	-	-	-	-	-	N	L	M	M	M	M	M	M	L	M	M	M	-	L	L	M	M	-	16	5	15
NG (Nick) Humphries	-	-	-	-	-	-	-	=A	-	-	-	-	-	-	-	-	-	-	-	-	-	-	-	-	-	-	-	-	-	-	-	-	-	-	-	-	-	-	-	-	-	-	-	-	1	-	-
J (John) Ingleby	-	-	-	-	-	-	-	-	-	-	-	-	-	-	-	-	-	-	-	-	-	-	-	-	-	-	-	-	-	-	-	-	-	-	-	-	-	>J	-	-	J	-	-	-	2	-	-
G (Graham) Jackson	-	-	-	K	K	K	K	K	K	K	K	K	K	-	-	-	-	N	N	N	K	K	K	-	-	-	-	-	-	-	-	-	-	-	-	-	-	K	K	-	-	-	-	N	19	8	24
B (Bleddyn) Jones	-	-	-	-	-	-	-	-	-	-	-	-	-	-	-	-	>J	J	-	-	J	-	-	J	J	J	J	J	J	J	J	J	J	J	J	J	J	-	J	J	-	J	J	J	22	5	18
M (Mike) Marshall	-	-	-	-	-	-	-	-	-	-	-	-	-	-	-	-	-	-	-	-	-	-	-	-	-	-	-	-	-	-	-	-	-	-	-	-	-	-	-	-	>H	-	-	-	1	1	3
DJ (David) Matthews	-	-	-	-	-	-	-	-	-	-	-	G	-	G	-	-	G*	G	F	F	F	G	G	-	-	-	-	-	-	-	-	-	-	-	-	F	F	H	-	G	-	H	H	H	16	8	29
GR (Guy) Millar	-	-	-	-	-	-	-	-	-	-	-	-	I	-	-	I	I	-	-	-	-	-	-	-	-	-	-	-	-	-	-	-	-	-	-	-	-	-	-	-	-	-	-	-	3	1	3
RS (Robin) Money	0	-	-	-	-	-	-	-	-	-	-	-	0	-	-	0	-	-	-	-	-	-	-	0	0	0	0	0	0	0	0	0	0	0	0	0	0	0	0	0	0	0	0	0	24	2	15
C (Chris) Owen	-	>A	A	A	A	C	C	-	C	C	C	-	-	A	-	C	-	C	C	C	-	-	-	-	-	-	-	-	-	-	-	-	-	-	-	-	-	-	-	-	-	-	-	-	14	3	9
PGS (Graham) Pulfrey	-	0	0	0	0	0	0	0	0	0	0	0	-	0	0	-	0	0	0	0	0	0	<0	-	-	-	-	-	-	-	-	-	-	-	-	-	-	-	-	-	-	-	-	-	20	1	6
PW (Peter) Riley	-	-	-	-	-	-	-	-	-	-	-	-	-	-	-	-	-	-	-	-	E	E	-	-	-	-	-	-	-	-	-	-	-	-	-	-	G	-	G	-	-	-	-	-	4	1	3
RE (Bob) Rowell E2	-	E	E	E	E	E	-	-	-	-	-	E	E	E	-	-	E	-	-	-	-	-	-	-	E	E	E	E	E	E	E	E	E	E	E	E	E	D	E	E	■E	E	E	E	29	2	6
RP (Rex) Skelton	-	-	-	-	-	-	-	-	-	-	-	-	-	-	-	-	-	-	-	-	A	-	-	-	-	-	-	-	-	-	-	-	-	-	-	-	-	-	-	C	-	-	-	<A	3	-	-
R (Roy) Sleigh	K	-	<K	-	-	-	-	-	-	-	-	-	-	-	-	-	-	-	-	-	-	-	-	-	-	-	-	-	-	-	-	-	-	-	-	-	-	-	-	-	-	-	-	-	2	1	3
RW (Bob) Small	-	G	G	G	G	G	G	-	-	-	-	-	G	-	G	<G	-	-	-	-	-	-	-	-	-	-	-	-	-	-	-	-	-	-	-	-	-	-	-	-	-	-	-	-	9	2	6
RS (Bob) Smith	<G	-	-	-	-	-	-	-	-	-	-	-	-	-	-	-	-	-	-	-	-	-	-	-	-	-	-	-	-	-	-	-	-	-	-	-	-	-	-	-	-	-	-	-	1	-	-
T (Trevor) Spence	N	K	N	N	N	N	N	N	N	N	N	-	-	K	K	N	N	K	K	K	N	N	<N	-	-	-	-	-	-	-	-	-	-	-	-	-	-	-	-	-	-	-	-	-	21	11	33
PJ (Peter) Wheeler E+ L+	-	-	-	-	-	-	-	-	-	-	-	-	-	-	-	>B	-	-	B	-	-	B	-	-	-	-	-	-	-	-	B	-	-	-	-	-	-	B	-	-	-	-	-	-	5	-	-
VJ (Vic) Wigley	-	-	-	-	-	-	-	-	-	-	-	-	>M	-	-	-	-	-	-	-	-	-	-	-	-	-	-	-	-	-	-	-	-	-	-	-	-	-	-	-	-	-	-	-	1	-	-
GG (Graham) Willars	-	H	F	F	F	F	F	H	F	F	H	F	F	F	F	F	F	-	H	H	-	-	H	H	H	F	-	H	H	-	F	-	-	H	H	H	H	F	-	-	-	-	-	-	30	2	6
MJ (Mike) Yandle	>L	L	L	L	L	M	M	-	-	M	M	M	-	M	M	-	M	M	L	M	M	M	L	M	M	M	M	M	L	L	L	L	L	L	M	L	L	L	L	M	M	L	L	L	40	5	15

1970/71

19 70/71	
Home Ground:	Welford Road
Coach:	Chalkie White
Captain:	John Allen

OVERALL RECORD:						T	C	PG	DG	PTS
PLD	W	D	L		Tigers scored:	116	54	63	3	654
45	23	2	20		Opponents scored:	86	36	49	6	495

GM	DATE		VEN	OPPONENTS	RESULT	TRIES	KICKS	ATT
CLUB MATCHES								
1	Sep	2w	a	Newport	L 6-16	-	Gavins 2p	-
2		5	H	**Bedford**	W 14-5	Jones	Gavins c/3p	390
3		9w	H	**Leicester & District**	W 43-16	Baynes(3), Duggan(3), Adey, Hall, Jackson, Willars, Yandle	Gavins 5c	168
4		12	a	Bath	L 9-11	Barker, Yandle	Gavins p	-
5		15tu	a	Burton	W 22-6	Barker(2), Duggan, Owen	Cooper 2c/2p	-
6		19	H	**Harrogate**	W 39-8	Baynes(2), Duggan(2), Hall, Willars, Yandle	Gavins 6c/2p	251
7		26	a	Harlequins	W 20-17	Adey, Barker, Jones	Gavins c/3p	-
8	Oct	3	a	Coventry	L 14-18	Duggan	Gavins c/3p	-
9		10	H	**North of Ireland**	W 14-3	Elliott, Yandle	Gavins c/2p	285
10		17	H	**Northampton**	D 6-6	Hall	Gavins p	1070
11		21w	H	**Oxford University**	L 9-14	Adey, Barker	Gavins p	236
12		24	a	Swansea	L 3-21	-	Whibley p	-
13		31	H	**Saracens**	W 9-3	Elliott	Gavins 2p	247
14	Nov	7	a	Gloucester	L 15-25	-	Whibley 4p, Jones d	-
15		14	H	**Cambridge University**	W 24-11	Arneil, Barker, Elliott, Jones, Yandle	Gavins 3c/p	168
16		21	H	**Newport**	L 12-16	-	Gavins 4p	477
17		28	a	Moseley	L 13-16	Yandle(2), Bann	Gavins 2c	-
18	Dec	5	H	**Waterloo**	W 40-3	Allen(2), Duggan(2), Matthews(2), Hall, Owen	Barker 5c/2p	193
19		12	H	**Blackheath**	W 23-6	Barker(2), Jones, Yandle	Barker c/2p, Money d	170
20		19	a	Bristol	L 0-10	-	-	-
21		26	H	**Barbarians**	L 6-18	Allen, Jones	-	2518
	Jan	2	H	**Bath**	PP (frost)			
22		9	H	**Gloucester**	W 17-15	Allen, Baynes	Bann c/2p, Wheeler p	229
23		15f	a	Cardiff	L 8-12	Baynes	Wheeler c/p	-
24		23	H	**Rosslyn Park**	W 16-9	Owen(2), Wheeler	Wheeler 2c/p	334
25		30	a	Headingley	L 0-8	-	-	-
26	Feb	6	a	London Scottish	L 9-16	Barker, Nicholls, Wheeler	-	-
27		13	a	Newport	L 8-27	Hall, Matthews	Wheeler c	-
28		17w	a	Moseley	L 0-11	-	-	-
29		20	H	**Wasps**	W 17-3	Duggan(3), Yandle	Wheeler c/p	179
30		26f	a	Northampton	L 8-9	Baynes, Duggan	Bann c	-
31	Mar	2tu	H	**Loughborough Colleges**	D 12-12	Nicholls	Bann 3p	328
32		6	H	**Harlequins**	W 11-6	Adey, Baynes, Bird	Wheeler c	153
33		13	H	**Coventry**	L 11-15	Bird	Bann c/2p	464
34		19f	H	**Royal Air Force**	W 11-6	Nicholls, Yandle	Bann c/p	196
35		24w	a	Nuneaton	L 3-8	-	Wheeler p	-
36		27	H	**Llanelli**	W 12-3	Wheeler, Nicholls	Wheeler 2p	202
37		31w	H	**Rugby**	W 21-6	Barker(2), Allen, Dawson, Yandle	Wheeler 3c	206
38	Apr	3	H	**Birkenhead Park**	W 23-11	Nicholls(2), Adey, Barker, Baynes, Yandle	Wheeler p, Bann c	122
39		10	a	Liverpool	L 8-14	Willars	Wheeler c/p	-
40		12m	a	Fylde	W 22-20	Baynes, Grove, Nicholls	Wheeler 2c/3p	-
41		13tu	a	Manchester	W 17-9	Wheeler, Nicholls	Wheeler c/3p	-
42		17	H	**Richmond**	W 33-8	Baynes(2), Duggan(2), Arneil, Bann, Hall	Wheeler 3c/2p	111
43		24	H	**Sale**	W 3-0	-	Wheeler p	110
44		28w	a	Bedford	L 11-12	Money, Yandle	Wheeler c/p	-
45	May	1	a	New Brighton	W 32-6	Nicholls(3), Duggan(2), Bird, Money	Wheeler 4c, Jones d	-

INDIVIDUAL APPEARANCES 1970/71

Name / Game #	1	2	3	4	5	6	7	8	9	10	11	12	13	14	15	16	17	18	19	20	21	22	23	24	25	26	27	28	29	30	31	32	33	34	35	36	37	38	39	40	41	42	43	44	45	Apps	T	Pts
GJ (Garry) Adey E+	G	G	G	G	G	G	G	G	G	G	G	G	G	-	-	-	-	-	-	-	-	-	-	-	-	G	G	G	G	G	G	G	G	G	G	G	G	G	G	G	G	G	G	G	E	33	5	15
JA (John) Allen	I*	I*	I*	I*	I*	I*	I*	I*	I*	I*	I*	I*	I*	I*	I*	I*	I*	I*	I*	I*	I*	I*	I*	I*	I*	I*	I*	I*	I*	I*	I*	I*	I*	I*	I*	I*	I*	I*	I*	I*	-	I*	I*	I*	I*	44	5	15
RJ (Rodger) Arneil S18 L4	-	-	-	-	-	-	H	-	-	-	-	-	H	H	H	H	H	H	H	-	H	-	-	H	H	-	F	-	F	-	-	-	-	-	-	-	-	-	-	-	-	H	<H	-	-	15	2	6
EE (Eric) Bann	D	D	-	E	-	-	-	-	-	E	E	E	E	-	D	D	D	E	D	D	E	D	-	E	E	D	-	-	-	E	D	E	E	D	D	E	D	D	-	-	-	D	E	D	-	30	2	40
RG (Bob) Barker	-	-	-	N	K	K	K	K	K	K	M	K	L	M	K	K	K	K	K	N	N	-	L	L	M	L	M	N	-	-	-	-	-	N	N	N	N	N	N	-	-	-	-	-	-	30	12	60
CJ (Chris) Baynes	F	F	F	F	F	F	F	F	F	H	H	F	-	-	F	F	F	F	F	F	F	F	F	F	F	F	-	F	-	F	F	F	F	F	F	F	F	F	F	F	F	F	F	F	F	41	13	39
R (Bob) Beason	C	C	C	C	-	-	-	-	C	C	C	C	C	C	C	C	C	-	-	-	-	-	-	A	A	A	-	-	-	C	C	C	C	-	-	-	-	-	-	-	-	C	C	C	A	24	-	-
DMH (David) Berry	-	-	-	-	-	-	-	-	-	-	-	-	-	-	-	-	-	-	-	-	-	-	-	-	-	-	-	-	-	J	J	J	J	-	-	<J	-	-	-	-	-	-	-	-	-	5	-	-
DW (David) Bird	-	-	-	-	-	-	-	-	-	-	K	-	K	K	M	-	-	-	-	-	-	-	-	-	-	-	-	M	M	M	M	M	M	-	L	-	-	-	-	-	L	L	L	L	L	16	3	9
RC (Dick) Cooper	-	-	J	-	O	-	-	-	-	-	-	-	-	-	-	-	-	-	-	-	-	-	-	-	-	-	-	-	-	-	-	-	-	-	-	-	-	-	-	-	-	-	-	-	-	2	-	10
JH (John) Dawson	A	A	A	A	A	A	A	A	A	A	A	A	A	A	A	A	A	A	A	A	A	A	A	-	-	-	A	A	A	A	A	■A	A	A	A	A	C	A	C	C	C	-	-	<A	-	39	1	3
MJ (John) Duggan	N	N	N	-	N	N	N	N	N	N	N	N	N	-	-	N	N	N	N	K	K	N	N	N	-	-	N	-	N	N	N	N	N	-	-	-	-	-	-	N	N	N	N	N	N	33	17	51
JJ (John) Elliott	-	-	-	-	B	B	B	B	B	B	B	B	B	-	B	B	B	B	B	<B	-	-	-	-	-	-	-	-	-	-	-	-	-	-	-	-	-	-	-	-	-	-	-	-	-	15	3	9
DJ (Dave) Forfar	-	-	-	-	-	-	-	-	-	-	-	-	-	-	-	-	-	-	-	-	-	-	-	-	-	-	-	-	-	-	-	-	-	-	-	-	-	-	-	-	>H	-	-	-	-	1	-	-
MN (Mike) Gavins E1	O	O	O	O	-	O	O	O	O	O	O	-	O	-	O	O	<O	-	-	-	-	-	-	-	-	-	-	-	-	-	-	-	-	-	-	-	-	-	-	-	-	-	-	-	-	14	-	115
J Golding	-	-	-	-	-	-	-	-	-	-	-	-	-	-	-	-	-	>D	<E	-	-	-	-	-	-	-	-	-	-	-	-	-	-	-	-	-	-	-	-	-	-	-	-	-	-	2	-	-
RV (Roger) Grove	-	-	-	-	-	-	-	-	-	-	-	-	-	-	-	-	-	-	-	-	-	-	-	-	-	-	-	-	-	-	-	-	-	-	-	-	A	C	A	A	A	A	A	-	C	8	1	3
BP (Brian) Hall	>L	M	L	L	L	L	L	L	L	L	L	L	-	-	L	L	L	L	L	L	L	L	-	-	N	M	L	L	-	-	-	-	-	-	-	-	-	-	-	-	-	M	-	-	-	25	6	18
DA (Dave) Hanna	-	-	-	-	-	E	E	E	<E	-	-	-	-	-	-	-	-	-	-	-	-	-	-	-	-	-	-	-	-	-	-	-	-	-	-	-	-	-	-	-	-	-	-	-	-	4	-	-
MJ (Mike) Harrison	-	-	-	-	-	-	-	-	-	-	-	-	-	-	-	-	-	-	-	-	-	-	-	-	-	-	-	-	-	-	-	-	-	L	M	M	L	<M	-	-	-	-	-	-	-	5	-	-
G (Graham) Jackson	K	K	K	K	-	-	-	-	-	-	-	-	-	N	-	-	-	-	-	-	-	K	K	K	K	N	-	-	-	-	-	-	-	-	-	-	-	-	-	-	-	-	-	-	-	10	1	3
B (Bleddyn) Jones	J	J	-	J	J	J	J	J	J	J	J	J	J	J	J	J	J	J	J	J	J	J	J	J	J	J	J	J	J	-	-	-	-	J	J	-	J	J	J	J	J	J	J	J	J	39	5	21
NJ (Nick) Joyce	-	-	-	-	-	-	-	-	-	-	-	-	-	-	-	-	-	-	-	-	-	-	-	-	-	-	-	-	-	-	-	-	-	-	-	-	-	-	-	>D	-	-	-	E	D	3	-	-
DJ (David) Matthews	-	-	-	-	-	-	-	-	H	F	F	-	F	-	G	G	G	G	G	G	G	G	G	G	G	H	H	H	H	H	H	H	H	H	H	H	H	H	-	-	-	-	-	-	G	29	3	9
RS (Robin) Money	-	-	-	-	-	-	-	-	-	-	-	-	-	-	-	-	-	O	O	O	O	O	O	O	O	O	O	-	O	O	O	O	O	O	O	O	O	O	O	O	O	O	O	O	O	27	2	9
MR (Mike) Mortimer	-	-	-	-	-	-	-	-	-	-	-	-	-	-	-	-	-	-	-	-	-	-	-	-	-	-	-	-	-	-	-	-	-	>C	C	C	-	-	-	-	-	-	-	-	-	3	-	-
P (Peter) Nicholls	-	-	-	-	-	-	-	-	-	-	-	-	-	-	-	-	-	-	-	-	-	-	-	-	-	>K	K	K	K	K	K	K	K	K	K	K	K	K	K	K	K	K	K	K	K	20	11	33
C (Chris) Owen	-	-	-	-	C	C	C	C	-	-	-	-	-	G	-	-	-	C	C	C	C	C	C	C	C	C	C	C	C	-	-	-	-	-	-	-	-	-	-	-	-	-	-	-	-	17	4	12
DA (David) Pickering	-	-	-	-	-	-	-	-	-	-	-	-	-	-	-	-	-	-	-	-	-	-	-	-	-	-	-	-	-	>B	B	-	-	-	-	-	-	-	-	-	-	-	-	-	-	2	-	-
RE (Bob) Rowell E2	-	-	-	-	-	-	-	-	-	-	-	-	-	-	-	-	-	-	-	-	-	-	-	-	-	-	-	E	-	D	E	D	D	-	E	D	E	E	E	-	D	-	-	-	-	11	-	-
DM (Dave) Shaw	>E	E	E	D	D	D	D	D	D	D	D	D	D	D	E	E	E	-	-	E	D	E	D	D	D	E	D	D	D	-	-	-	-	E	-	-	-	-	D	E	E	E	D	-	-	33	-	-
D (Dave) Truman	-	-	-	-	-	-	-	-	-	-	-	-	-	-	-	-	-	-	-	-	-	-	-	-	-	-	-	-	-	-	-	-	-	-	-	-	-	-	-	-	>I	-	-	-	-	1	-	-
RJ (Bob) Watson	-	-	>D	-	E	-	-	-	-	-	-	-	-	E	-	-	-	-	-	-	-	-	E	-	-	-	E	-	E	-	-	-	-	-	-	-	-	-	-	-	-	-	-	-	-	6	-	-
PJ (Peter) Wheeler E+ L+	B	B	B	B	-	-	-	-	-	-	-	-	-	B	-	-	-	-	-	-	B	B	B	B	B	B	B	B	B	-	-	B	B	B	B	B	B	B	B	B	B	B	B	B	B	28	4	111
DF (Dave) Whibley	-	-	-	-	-	-	-	-	-	-	-	>O	-	O	-	-	-	-	-	-	-	-	-	-	-	-	-	O	-	-	-	-	-	-	-	-	-	-	-	-	-	-	-	-	-	3	-	15
VJ (Vic) Wigley	-	-	-	-	-	-	-	-	-	-	-	-	-	L	-	-	-	-	-	-	-	-	-	-	-	-	-	-	-	-	-	-	-	-	-	-	-	-	L	<L	-	-	-	-	-	3	-	-
GG (Graham) Willars	H	H	H	H	H	H	-	H	-	-	-	H	-	F	-	-	-	-	-	H	-	H	H	-	-	-	-	-	-	-	-	-	-	-	-	-	-	-	H	H	-	-	-	H	H	16	3	9
MJ (Mike) Yandle	M	L	M	M	M	M	M	M	M	M	-	M	M	-	M	M	M	M	M	M	M	M	M	M	L	-	-	-	L	L	L	L	L	M	-	L	M	L	M	M	M	-	M	M	M	38	13	39

The key for how to read the stats is on the last page

1971/72

Home Ground: Welford Road
Coach: Chalkie White
Captain: Roger Grove

OVERALL RECORD:					T	C	PG	DG	PTS
PLD	W	D	L	Tigers scored:	123	54	59	4	789
41	26	3	12	Opponents scored:	59	31	64	5	505

GM	DATE		VEN	OPPONENTS	RESULT	TRIES	KICKS	ATT
RFU CLUB COMPETITION						**CUP WINNERS: GLOUCESTER**		
16	Nov	21s	a	Nottingham (1)	L 3-10	-	Whibley p	-
CLUB MATCHES								
1	Sep	4	a	Bedford	L 16-35	Duggan(2), Matthews	Wheeler 2c	-
2		8w	H	Leicester & District	W 16-13	Money, Truman	Money d, Wheeler c/p	195
3		11	H	Bath	W 22-10	Bann, Baynes, Nicholls, Yandle	Bann 3c	202
4		15w	H	Nuneaton	W 12-6	Duggan	Bann c/2p	320
5		18	a	Liverpool	L 8-18	Allen, Nicholls	-	-
6		25	a	Harlequins	L 9-28	Nicholls	Matthews c/p	-
7	Oct	2	H	Coventry	L 10-25	Duggan	Bann 2p	552
8		9	a	Richmond	L 12-18	-	Whibley 4p	-
9		16	a	Northampton	L 4-12	Nicholls	-	-
10		20w	a	Oxford University	W 17-10	Duggan, Hall, Nicholls	Whibley c/p	-
11		23	H	Swansea	D 7-7	Duggan	Whibley p	376
12		30	a	Rugby	D 12-12	-	Whibley 4p	-
13	Nov	6	H	Gloucester	W 31-9	Barker, Baynes, Owen, Willars	Whibley 3c/3p	361
14		13	a	Cambridge University	W 24-9	Barker, Yandle	Whibley 2c/3p, Hall d	-
15		20	H	New Brighton	W 29-7	Baynes(2), Barker, Jones, Willars	Whibley 3c/p	169
17		27	H	Moseley	W 11-9	Adey, Willars	Whibley p	201
18	Dec	4	a	Waterloo	W 31-6	Barker(2), Horner(2), Yandle	Whibley 4c/p	-
19		11	a	Blackheath	W 15-13	Barker, Baynes, Money	Barker p	-
20		18	H	Bristol	W 39-13	Hall(2), Barker, Baynes, Horner, Jones, Money	Barker c/3p	287
21		28tu	H	Barbarians	W 20-14	Barker(3)	Whibley c/2p	15000
22	Jan	1	a	Bath	L 15-17	Adey, Horner, Money	Barker p	-
23		8	a	Bridgend	L 12-20	Adey, Barker, Wheeler	-	-
24		16s	H	Bedford	L 10-19	Rowell, Wheeler	Whibley c	-
25		22	a	Rosslyn Park	W 15-10	Duggan(2), Barker	Whibley p	-
26		29	H	Headingley	W 25-6	Bann(2), Duggan(2), Wheeler	Whibley c/p	122
27	Feb	3th	H	Royal Navy	W 15-7	Barker, Duggan, Wheeler	Whibley p	80
28		5	H	London Scottish	W 10-9	Duggan	Whibley 2p	59
29		12	H	Newport	W 21-9	Duggan(2), Jones	Whibley 3p	267
		16w	H	Moseley	PP (power strike)			
30		19	a	Wasps	W 25-3	Whibley, Adey, Barker, Hall	Whibley 3c/p	-
31		26	H	Northampton	L 15-24	Hall	Whibley c/3p	265
32	Mar	4	H	Harlequins	W 15-8	Barker, Duggan	Whibley 2c/p	416
		8w	H	Loughborough Colleges	PP (power strike)			
		11	a	Coventry	PP (county final)			
33		18	H	Royal Air Force	W 50-9	Duggan(3), Barker(2), Allen, Forfar, Hall, Jones, Mortimer	Whibley 2c/2p	116
		22w	a	Gloucester	PP			
34		25	a	Sale	D 13-13	Watson	Whibley 3p	-
35	Apr	1	H	Birkenhead Park	W 58-9	Barker(3), Jones(2), Bann, Hall, Money, Wheeler	Whibley 8c/2p	308
36		3m	H	Fylde	W 30-12	Barker, Jackson, Joyce, Pickering, Shaw	Barker 2c, Whibley 2p	377
37		4tu	H	Wilmslow	W 25-0	Allen, Barker, Jackson, Matthews	Wheeler 3c, Yandle d	335
38		8	a	Llanelli	L 4-15	Duggan	-	-
39		15	H	Nottingham	W 40-9	Wheeler(Penalty)(2), Barker(2), Duggan(2), Cooper, Matthews	Wheeler c, Cooper 3c	377
40		22	a	Newport	W 25-11	Barker(2), Hall	Wheeler 2c/2p, Jones d	-
41		29	a	Hartlepool Rovers	W 18-11	Duggan(2)	Wheeler 2c/2p	-

INDIVIDUAL APPEARANCES 1971/72

Name / Game #	1	2	3	4	5	6	7	8	9	10	11	12	13	14	15	16	17	18	19	20	21	22	23	24	25	26	27	28	29	30	31	32	33	34	35	36	37	38	39	40	41	Apps	T	Pts
GJ (Garry) Adey E+	-	-	-	G	G	G	G	E	G	E	G	G	G	G	G	G	G	G	-	G	G	G	G	G	G	G	G	G	G	G	G	G	G	G	-	-	-	-	G	G	G	33	4	16
JA (John) Allen	-	-	-	-	I	I	I	-	-	-	-	-	-	-	-	-	I	I	I	I	I	I	I	I	I	I	I	I	I	I	I	I	I	I	I	I	I	I	I	I	I	28	3	12
EE (Eric) Bann	D	-	E	E	E	-	E	D	-	-	-	-	-	-	-	-	-	-	-	-	-	-	-	-	E	D	E	D	D	-	-	D	D	-	D	-	D	D	D	D	D	19	4	36
RG (Bob) Barker	-	-	-	-	-	-	-	-	-	-	-	L	K	K	K	K	K	K	K	K	K	K	K	K	K	K	K	K	K	K	K	K	K	K	K	K	K	K	K	K	K	30	26	125
CJ (Chris) Baynes	F	F	F	F	F	F	-	-	-	G	-	F	F	F	F	F	F	F	F	F	F	F	-	-	-	-	-	-	-	-	-	-	-	-	-	-	-	-	-	-	-	18	6	24
R (Bob) Beason	C	-	-	-	-	-	-	-	-	A	A	A	A	C	C	C	C	C	A	C	C	C	C	C	C	C	C	-	-	-	-	-	-	-	-	-	-	-	-	-	-	19	-	-
DW (David) Bird	-	-	-	-	-	-	M	M	M	M	M	M	N	N	N	N	-	-	-	-	-	-	-	-	-	-	-	-	-	-	-	-	-	-	-	-	-	-	-	-	-	10	-	-
RC (Dick) Cooper	-	-	-	-	-	-	-	-	-	-	-	-	-	-	-	-	-	-	-	-	-	-	-	-	-	-	-	-	-	-	-	-	-	-	-	-	-	0	<0	-	-	2	1	10
MJ (John) Duggan	N	N	N	N	N	-	N	N	N	N	N	N	-	-	-	-	-	-	-	-	-	-	-	-	N	N	N	N	N	N	-	N	N	N	-	-	-	N	N	N	N	24	23	92
KJ (Keith) Fielding E10	-	-	-	-	-	=N	-	-	-	-	-	-	-	-	-	-	-	-	-	-	-	-	-	-	-	-	-	-	-	-	-	-	-	-	-	-	-	-	-	-	-	1	-	-
DJ (Dave) Forfar	-	-	H	-	-	-	H	F	F	F	F	-	-	-	-	-	-	-	-	-	-	-	F	F	F	F	F	-	F	F	F	H	F	F	F	F	F	-	-	-	-	20	1	4
RS (Roy) French	-	-	-	-	-	-	-	>B	-	-	-	-	-	-	-	-	-	-	-	-	-	-	-	-	-	-	-	-	-	-	-	-	-	-	-	-	-	-	-	-	-	1	-	-
RV (Roger) Grove	A*	A*	A*	A*	A*	A*	A*	A*	A*	-	-	-	-	A*	A*	A*	A*	A*	C*	A*	A*	A*	-	A*	A*	A*	A*	A*	A*	-	A*	A*	A*	A*	A*	A*	A*	A*	A*	A*	A*	35	-	-
BP (Brian) Hall	L	L	L	L	L	L	L	L	L	L	L	-	L	L	L	L	-	M	L	L	L	L	L	L	M	L	L	L	L	M	L	L	L	L	L	L	L	L	L	M	L	39	8	35
G (Graham) Horner	-	-	-	-	-	-	>J	J	J	-	-	-	-	-	-	-	N	N	N	N	N	N	N	N	-	-	-	-	-	-	N	-	-	-	-	-	-	-	-	-	-	12	4	16
G (Graham) Jackson	K	-	-	-	-	-	-	-	-	-	-	-	-	-	-	-	-	-	-	-	-	-	-	-	-	-	-	-	-	-	-	-	-	-	-	N	N	-	-	-	-	3	2	8
B (Bleddyn) Jones	J	J	J	J	J	J	-	-	-	-	-	J	J	J	J	J	J	J	J	J	J	J	J	J	J	J	J	J	J	J	-	J	J	J	J	J	J	J	J	J	J	35	6	27
NJ (Nick) Joyce	-	E	-	-	-	-	-	-	-	-	-	-	-	-	-	-	-	-	-	-	-	-	-	-	-	-	-	-	-	-	-	-	-	-	-	G	-	G	-	-	-	3	1	4
J (John) Lacey	-	-	-	-	-	-	-	-	=E	-	-	-	-	-	-	-	-	-	-	-	-	-	-	-	-	-	-	-	-	-	-	-	-	-	-	-	-	-	-	-	-	1	-	-
DJ (David) Matthews	G	-	G	H	H	H	F	G	-	-	-	-	-	-	-	-	-	-	G	-	-	-	-	-	-	-	-	-	-	-	-	-	-	-	G	-	G	F	H	H	H	14	3	17
GR (Guy) Millar	-	-	-	-	-	-	-	I	I	-	-	-	-	-	-	-	-	-	-	-	-	-	-	-	-	-	-	-	-	-	-	-	-	-	-	-	-	-	-	-	-	2	-	-
RS (Robin) Money	0	0	0	0	0	0	0	-	-	J	J	-	-	-	-	-	0	-	0	0	-	0	0	-	-	-	-	-	-	0	0	-	-	-	N	-	0	-	-	0	0	20	5	23
D Morley	-	-	-	-	-	-	-	-	-	-	-	-	-	-	-	-	-	-	-	-	-	-	<A	-	-	-	-	-	-	-	-	-	-	-	-	-	-	-	-	-	-	1	-	-
MR (Mike) Mortimer	-	C	C	C	C	C	-	-	-	-	-	-	-	-	-	-	-	-	-	-	-	-	-	-	-	-	-	C	C	C	C	C	C	C	C	C	C	C	C	C	C	19	1	4
P (Peter) Nicholls	-	K	K	K	K	K	K	K	K	K	K	K	-	-	-	-	-	-	-	-	-	-	-	-	-	-	-	-	-	-	-	-	-	-	-	-	-	-	-	-	-	11	5	20
C (Chris) Owen	-	-	-	-	-	-	C	C	C	C	C	C	<C	-	-	-	-	-	-	-	-	-	-	-	-	-	-	-	-	-	-	-	-	-	-	-	-	-	-	-	-	7	1	4
DA (David) Pickering	-	-	B	B	B	B	B	-	-	-	-	-	-	-	-	-	-	-	B	B	-	-	-	-	-	-	-	-	-	-	-	-	B	-	-	B	-	-	-	-	-	9	1	4
PW (Peter) Riley	-	<G	-	-	-	-	-	-	-	-	-	-	-	-	-	-	-	-	-	-	-	-	-	-	-	-	-	-	-	-	-	-	-	-	-	-	-	-	-	-	-	1	-	-
RE (Bob) Rowell E2	-	-	-	-	-	-	-	-	-	-	D	E	E	D	E	D	D	D	D	D	D	D	E	E	D	E	-	-	E	E	E	-	-	-	-	-	-	-	-	-	-	19	1	4
RJ (Dick) Royce	-	-	-	-	-	-	-	-	-	-	-	-	-	-	-	-	-	-	-	-	-	-	-	-	-	-	>H	<F	-	-	-	-	-	-	-	-	-	-	-	-	-	2	-	-
DM (Dave) Shaw	E	D	D	D	D	D	D	-	D	D	-	D	-	-	-	-	-	-	-	E	E	E	D	D	-	-	D	E	-	D	D	E	-	-	-	D	-	-	-	-	-	21	1	4
D (Dave) Truman	I	I	I	I	-	-	-	-	-	I	I	I	I	I	I	I	-	-	-	-	-	-	-	-	-	-	-	-	-	-	-	-	-	-	-	-	-	-	-	-	-	11	1	4
PN (Phil) Vesty	-	-	-	-	-	-	-	-	-	-	-	-	-	-	-	-	-	-	-	-	-	-	-	-	-	-	-	-	-	>A	-	-	-	-	-	-	-	-	-	-	-	1	-	-
GH (George) Walton	-	-	-	-	-	-	-	-	-	-	-	-	-	-	-	-	-	-	-	-	-	-	-	-	-	-	-	-	-	-	-	-	-	=D	-	-	-	-	-	-	-	1	-	-
RJ (Bob) Watson	-	-	-	-	-	E	-	-	-	-	E	-	D	E	D	E	E	E	E	-	-	-	-	-	-	-	-	-	-	-	-	-	E	E	E	E	E	E	E	E	E	18	1	4
PJ (Peter) Wheeler E+ L+	B	B	-	-	-	-	-	-	B	B	B	B	B	B	B	B	B	B	-	-	B	B	B	B	B	B	B	B	B	B	B	B	-	B	B	-	B	B	B	B	B	31	7	65
DF (Dave) Whibley	-	-	-	-	-	-	-	0	0	0	0	0	0	0	0	0	L	0	-	-	0	-	-	0	0	0	0	0	0	L	M	0	0	0	0	0	-	-	-	-	-	25	1	200
GG (Graham) Willars	H	H	-	-	-	-	-	H	H	H*	H*	H*	H*	H	H	H	H	H	H	H	H	H	H*	H	H	H	-	H	H	H*	H	F	H	H	H	H	H	H	F	F	F	35	3	12
MJ (Mike) Yandle	M	M	M	M	M	M	-	-	-	-	-	-	M	M	M	M	M	L	M	M	M	M	M	M	L	M	M	M	M	-	J	M	M	M	M	M	M	M	M	L	M	34	3	15

CHAPTER 18

White Aims High

1972/1973

From the outset of the 1972/73 season Graham Willars, the captain, and White were determined on a target of 30 wins and 1,000 points; failure was relative, in that the side finished with 29 wins and 988 points, with 683 against. It was the highest points aggregate in the club's history, yet twice Leicester conceded 40 points.

It was a season of change as long-serving prop Roger Grove retired, Whibley had to concentrate on his studies and, halfway through the season, moved to London along with the talented reserve hooker, David Pickering, the players joining Richmond and London Scottish respectively. Old was lost to the side after injuring a leg in the Barbarians match and Willars too fell by the way through injury, which provided an opportunity for a young student from Madeley College who had been playing with Nottingham, Paul Ringer, to come in on the back row. A hard, no-nonsense flanker, Ringer was subsequently troubled by a chest complaint and there were few at Leicester who anticipated that, six years later, he would be capped by Wales.

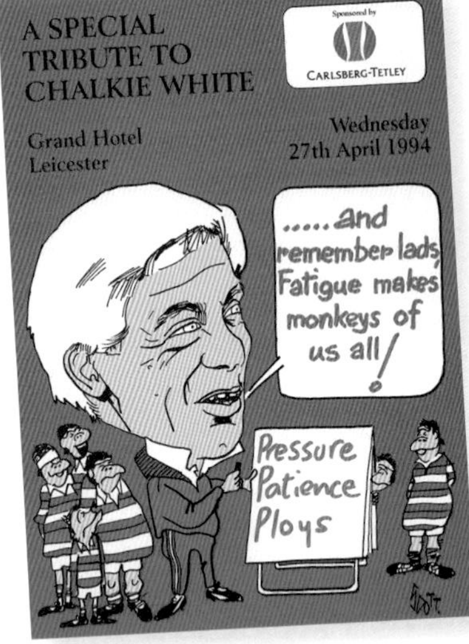

In 1994 Chalkie White was honoured by the club with a special dinner at the Grand Hotel.

A local centre, John Ingleby, played 23 games during the 1972/73 season and scored 200 points, all but 12 of them from the boot, while Barker scored 29 tries. Neither, however, was in the Midland Counties (East) side which played Ian Kirkpatrick's All Blacks at Welford Road on 13 January, 1973, for which they were duly grateful, no doubt, when the tourists ran out winners by 43-12. There were eight Leicester players in the combined XV which was coached by White and was: David Whibley; John Duggan, Mike Yandle (all Leicester), Graham Phillips, Roger Morris (both Northampton); Bleddyn Jones, John Allen (both Leicester); David Powell (Northampton, captain), Peter Wheeler (Leicester), Peter Duffy, Peter Larter (both Northampton), Bob Wilkinson (Cambridge University), Chris Baynes, Garry Adey (both Leicester), Ian Clayton (Nottingham).

Garry Adey breaks in first round cup action against Bedford at Goldington Road.

It was one of the few occasions on tour when the All Blacks cut loose, prompted by Lyn Colling at scrum-half. Duggan and Yandle sent in Allen for the counties' try which Whibley converted, besides kicking two penalties. Against that was a flood of tries from Robertson, Batty, Hurst, Burgess, Colling, Stewart, Sutherland and Kirkpatrick, Karam converting four times and landing a penalty. With Jones having to leave the match injured (he was replaced by Nottingham's Alan Davies who subsequently won greater fame as a coach, to Nottingham, England B and Wales), it was not a good day for the locals.

In the knockout cup competition it was Leicester's best season and remained so until 1977/78. They beat Bedford away (21-17) then Hinckley (16-4) before losing disappointingly in the quarter-finals at Sale (7-0).

1973/1974

Plans for bettering what had been a record season in terms of points took a knock in summer 1973 when Yandle, who had been elected club captain, moved to work in Swansea. Wheeler was elected instead, to be faced with a schedule which included two touring sides in the first eight games.

The first visitors were Fiji, invited to this country to help Swansea celebrate their centenary. They drew a crowd of 12,000 to an evening match at Welford Road on 11 September 1973, and home pride was considerable when Leicester, with the following team, beat them 22-17: Robin Money; Bob Barker, John Ingleby, Brian Hall, John Duggan; Bleddyn Jones, John Allen; Phil Vesty, Peter Wheeler (captain), Mike Mortimer, Eric Bann, Bob Watson, David Forfar, Garry Adey, Paul Ringer. Leicester stayed in the game through Ingleby kicking four penalties to go with Wheeler's try but, with 10 minutes left, the Fijians led 17-16. However a blind-side move put Barker over for a try improved by Ingleby and the 1973/74 season was off to a tremendous start.

The second touring side, nicknamed the "Galloping Greens", were Randwick from Australia, winners the previous season of the Sydney senior grade final. They began their British tour at Welford Road on 3 October and again Leicester proved triumphant with a 15-10 win in a hard encounter. Wheeler kicked two penalties, Money dropped a goal and, in injury-time, a superb try by Jones, converted by Ingleby, made sure.

If anything more were needed to make it possibly the most cosmopolitan season the club had yet enjoyed, the Japanese played the Midland Counties at Welford Road a week later. Wheeler, Adey and Ringer played for the Midlands but it was a poor game, won by the local side 10-6. It heralded a series of reverses: in the third defeat

to become the chairman of the England selectors. Matthews made two more senior appearances before calling it a day.

Before the season's end there were three more causes for celebration: Wheeler played his first game for the Barbarians, against the East Midlands, and scored three tries which created a Baa-baas record for a hooker. Allen was also chosen for the Barbarians for the first time, playing against Penarth and Newport on the Easter tour. And, at Stradey Park, Leicester played superbly to deprive Llanelli of their ground record with an 11-10 win.

That game at Llanelli when, ironically, Leicester's two tries came from Welshmen, Bleddyn Jones and Frank Jones, would have warmed the cockles of the recently-reformed Supporters' Club, which was revived that winter. Also off the field, Tom Berry handed over as president to Rodney Willcox; another Leicester member, Peter Jerwood, became president of Leicestershire, and Fred Cox resigned as groundsman, his position going to Derek Limmage.

Wheeler was due to serve his second term as captain but the club lost the services of Old during the summer. The fly-half was unlucky enough to suffer severe ligament damage after a late tackle in the seventh match of the Lions tour, against the Proteas - this when he had set a Lions record by

↑ Bob Barker in the thick of the action during the Barbarians game 1973.

↓ David Matthews beats Bedford and England flanker Budge Rogers to the ball during the annual Barbarians game.

of the season, at Northampton, Ringer was sent off and Adey carried off; seven penalties by Peter Butler helped Gloucester to a 29-6 win at Welford Road and, in the first round of the knockout competition, Leicester went down 22-6 at Northampton, Arneil rubbing salt into the wound by scoring against his old club. The only mitigating feature as 1974 approached was Old's selection for England against the touring Australians and Wheeler's elevation as deputy hooker to England's John Pullin.

Old achieved a notable treble by playing in the 20-3 win over Australia, becoming one of the few players at that time to have shared in wins over South Africa, New Zealand and Australia, all within the space of 18 months. He had been the only Leicester player on the short trip to New Zealand in August/September, which culminated in the 16-10 win over the All Blacks. He was to play in all the internationals during 1973/74 and earn selection for the 1974 British Lions who toured South Africa, captained by Willie John McBride.

After the flying start, the season tended to tail off for Leicester. There was a quirky incident at Rosslyn Park when a new centre, Ted Holley, tripped over a step emerging from the dressing room and had to be replaced before the game began; there was an unhappy moment when the club suspended one of their props, Mike Mortimer (later to become a referee), after a fracas during the home game with Bedford. Both club and player aired their views on the incident which ended with neither side entirely happy. Much more pleasure was derived by the celebration, on 23 February 1974, of David Matthews' 500th game for Leicester, against Northampton, which ended with the veteran flanker being carried from the field shoulder high after Leicester had won 15-9.

Matthews' own, wry comment on his achievement was: "You've got to have a lot of willpower and luck as well - I was very lucky with injuries." Perhaps more to the point was Matthews' belief in himself as a player; he never won a cap but this did not mean he ever considered himself second best to any rival he played against. It was entirely fitting that the man to pay tribute to Matthews at a special dinner, and present him with an engraved cigarette box, was his great back row rival from Bedford, DP 'Budge' Rogers, later

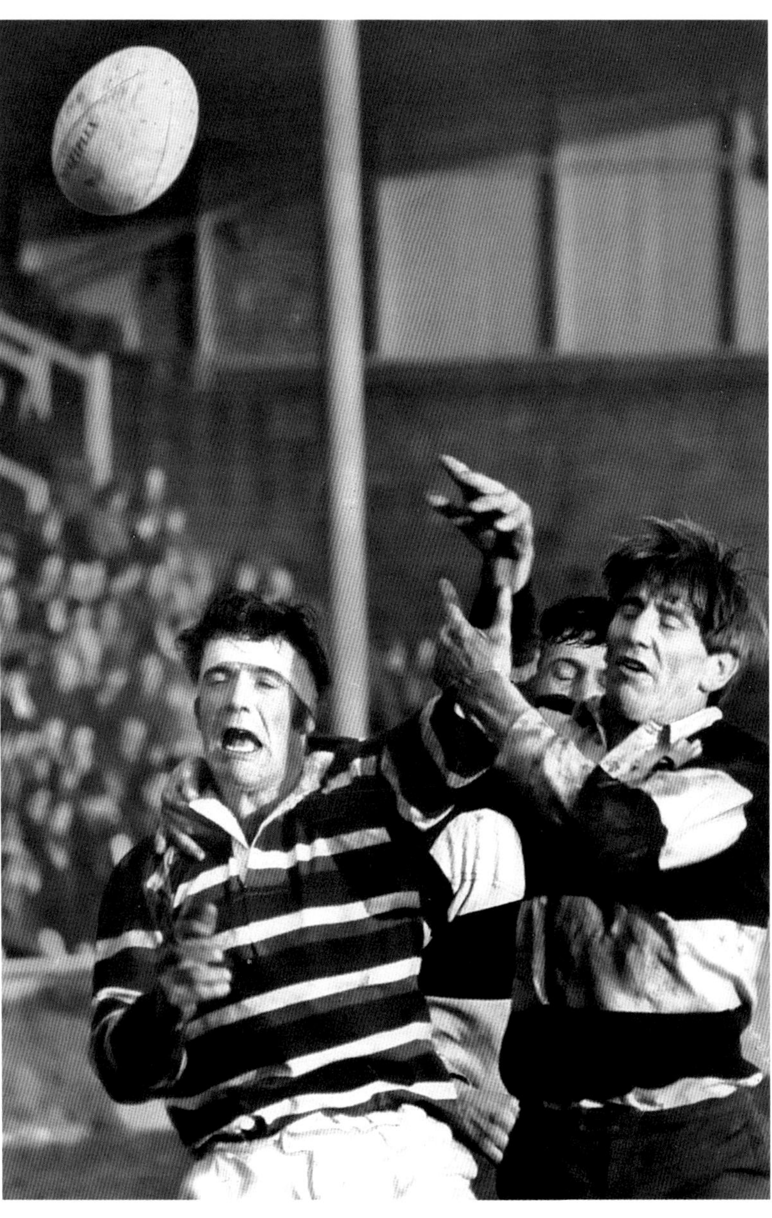

scoring 37 points in the 97-0 win over South West Districts (from a try, a penalty and 15 conversions) and looked a more likely bet for the test spot than Phil Bennett. He returned home after a spell in hospital and returned to Yorkshire, later joining the Sheffield club and continuing to oversee, in his county team, the progress of several potential internationals.

1974/1975

There was little indication at the start of 1974/75 that it was to be the worst season for 17 years, for on 1 September 1974, Leicester won the inaugural Midland seven-a-side tournament, sponsored by Carlsberg. It was held at Welford Road and on the way to the final, Leicester disposed of the Middlesex Sevens winners, Richmond. In the final they beat a brave, inexperienced Moseley VII by 18-16 with the following team: Robin Money, John Reeve, Brian Hall, Bleddyn Jones, Mike Marshall, Peter Wheeler, Graham Willars.

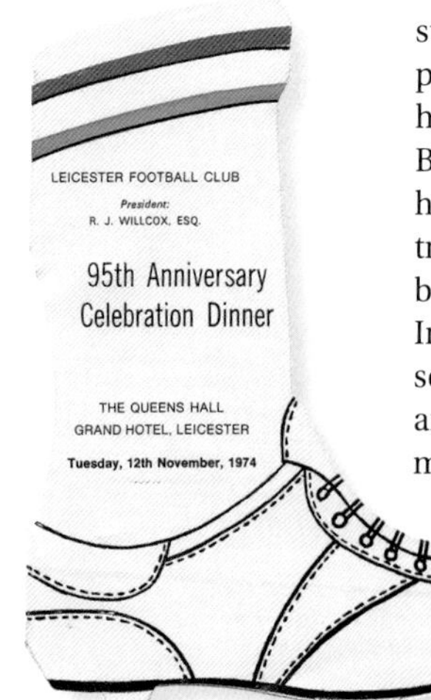

LEICESTER FOOTBALL CLUB
President:
R. J. WILLCOX, ESQ.
95th Anniversary
Celebration Dinner
THE QUEENS HALL
GRAND HOTEL, LEICESTER
Tuesday, 12th November, 1974

Souvenir menu from Tigers' 95th anniversary celebration dinner.

Ex-Tiger Dave Whibley gets on the wrong side of Bob Rowell during the Richmond game 12.10.1974.

Among the newcomers to the club was an England reserve prop, Robin James Cowling, who had been a member of the Gloucester side which won the first knockout competition (not that Leicester, this year, had an interest in the competition since they had failed to qualify the previous season). A hard, very competent player, Cowling gave added bite to the Leicester front row: as the season progressed another new face was that of 'Jock' Millican, capped by Scotland as a flanker three years previously but now seeking to re-establish himself after a badly broken leg had kept him out of action for a season.

In December the first player from the youth team to graduate to the senior XV, a flanker turned front row, 'Jez' Krych, made his debut against Blackheath and he was followed later in the season, against Moseley, by a back row forward, 'Gus' Collington. Both Krych and another player who was still in the Youth XV, Paul Dodge, were in the squad for the Barbarians match but in the event, neither played in the overwhelming 43-4 defeat. Nine tries were scored against Leicester as the Barbarian backs ran riot, though the score does no justice to the efforts of the home forwards. It was the biggest total the Baa-baas had ever recorded.

In a miserable December, Leicester lost four successive games, but took solace from the gradual progression of their captain, Wheeler, towards his first cap. He had been a replacement for the Barbarians in their 13-13 draw with New Zealand, he played for England against the Rest in the final trial (with Cowling in the opposing front row) and both he and Cowling were on the bench against Ireland. Cowling remained there for the rest of the season but Wheeler replaced Pullin against France, and won his second cap against Wales at Cardiff, a match in which he sustained a neck injury which, initially, looked as though it might wreck his career, though as it turned out, it only meant a lay-off for the rest of the season.

In the new year Willars retired from first-team rugby, though he could not be prevented from making several one-game comebacks. Changes in the centre and back row meant the side could never settle down and John Allen was nearing the end of a distinguished career at scrum-half. A black statistic against the season was the sending-off of three players: lock Nick Joyce against Northampton, and Cowling and Rowell together in the game at Fylde. In the latter game Leicester redeemed themselves by winning 21-19 despite having only 13 men for an hour. The Youth scrum-half, Kenney, won an England Colts cap against the Welsh Youth and Bleddyn Jones, apart from playing in every game, was named director of mini-rugby for Leicestershire, with Frank Jones and Duggan assisting him.

1975/1976

It had been more than a decade since the club had recorded more defeats than victories (20 against 19) and the improvement the following season was only marginal since 1975/76 brought 23 wins and 21 defeats. Yet the circumstances for the side captained by Money were much changed: for this was the season when a group of original youth team members "came of age" and qualified for senior rugby. Money outlined his requirements for success thus: "Correct attitude of the players; healthy competition for all positions; blending together the talent we have available in the club, both youth and experience." In the latter case, easier said than done: two of the youngsters, John Flint at half-back and Dodge in the centre, were picked for the first match, against Bedford, and though Bedford won 24-12 Leicester had at least discovered a kicker of talent in Flint who landed four penalties.

Kenney came into the side for the next match but the strain began to tell on the youngsters when they ran into the "heavy brigade", Coventry, Richmond and Northampton in October. Cowling broke a leg in one of England's regional training sessions and the forwards as a whole were not sufficiently on top of their game to be able to afford much protection to their young halves. It was the tragedy of the season that Flint, a footballer of genuine ability, suffered such a battering in carrying out defensive duties that his confidence drained away, he was injured, and though he played again in the club's lower sides, it was virtually the end of his first-class career, before it had even begun.

Dodge, on the contrary, went from strength to strength. Physically bigger than Flint and not in such an exposed position as fly-half, Dodge was able to show all the skills of passing, running and kicking which had caught the eye of club officials when he was in the Youth team. As well as playing centre for the club, he played full-back for Leicestershire and, still only 17, was pitched into representative rugby on 12 November when he was a member of the Midland Counties (East) XV which achieved a notable, and entirely unexpected, 11-8 win over the touring Australians, led by John Hipwell, at Welford Road under lights - the first time the Wallabies had played a floodlit game.

Wheeler captained a side containing three current Leicester players and, in Hare, Rod McMichael and Nigel Gillingham, three future ones. The combined XV was: Dusty Hare (Nottingham); Keith Parker (Northampton), Paul Dodge (Leicester), Nigel French (Wasps), Barrie Oldham (Northampton); Rod McMichael (Westleigh), Ian George (Northampton); John Pearce (Nottingham), Peter Wheeler (Leicester), Will Dickinson (Nottingham), Bob Wilkinson (Bedford), Nigel Gillingham (Loughborough Colleges), Graham Phillips (Northampton), Garry Adey (Leicester), Peter Sweet (Northampton).

Ian Clayton of Nottingham replaced Bob Wilkinson after only 20 minutes but, despite the disruption, the Midland XV played sound, effective football, Parker scoring two tries and Hare kicking a penalty against tries by Hipwell and Laurie Monaghan. Another group of touring Australians, from the Sydney club Eastern Suburbs, brought Leicester relief when Tigers were able to end a dismal run of eight successive defeats with a 22-15 win but alas for hopes of success in the knockout competition (now sponsored and renamed the John Player Cup), the following week Leicester went down 10-7 at Liverpool in the first round in a match dominated by their forwards.

It was, essentially, a season of individual achievement rather than team success, although there were three notable games, against the Barbarians, Nottingham and Northampton. All three featured the Loughborough Grammar School full-back, Marcus Rose, then 18, who had come into the side against Bristol the week before Christmas because Money had hamstring trouble which effectively wrecked his season. Rose provided a spark of inspiration sadly lacking, playing with flair and originality, kicking goals when least expected and showing all the easy poise which made many Leicester folk feel they had another international on their hands. "I had an invitation to play in London on Boxing Day but I turned it down and just intended to go and watch the Baa-baas," Rose said. Instead he found himself playing in the match which, though lost 20-11, was a distinct improvement on the season before. Two months later, in only his fifth game, Rose scored 13 points against Northampton to bring his aggregate to 52; it was as well Leicester were away from

↑ Jim Kempin and Nick Joyce, partially obscured, contest the ball in the Barbarians game in December 1975.

↓ CASG Club pennant.

home that day since, during the match between the Swifts and Norwich at Welford Road, a cavity appeared in the middle of the pitch. It turned out to be the club's old friend, the sewer, though no rats were reported this time.

Rowell took over the leadership of the side and helped tighten up the forward play which may have contributed to the two caps won by Adey that season. He and Wheeler had both played in the trials, Wheeler going through to play in all the internationals save the last, against France, when a foot injury kept him out. Adey made his England debut against Ireland and stayed to play in a poor team performance against the French.

It was an honour applauded by back-row forwards up and down the country, who recognised in Adey one of the game's grafters. Unspectacular, often unseen, Adey took an immense amount of work on his broad shoulders, appropriate for one who worked in the family construction firm in Loughborough: his reward was two caps, and selection for the Barbarians, both on their Easter tour and their 1976 summer visit to Canada when he was accompanied by Wheeler. The hooker, incidentally, had captured a unique record by playing three times against the Australians, for the Midland Counties (East), for England and the Barbarians, and each time on the winning side (scoring a try in the Barbarians game). He was the only Englishman to do so, indeed the only Englishman in the Baa-baas XV against the tourists. At a lesser level, Dodge emulated Kenney by winning an England Colts cap, scoring eight points against Wales in a 12-13 defeat.

There was a strong contingent of Leicester support for Adey in Paris, since the club had decided to accept an invitation to play a French second division club, CASG (later merged with Stade Français), whose ground at the Jean Bouin Stadium is next door to the Parc des Princes, the former international stadium and scene of Tigers' first European Cup triumph 25 years later. It was Leicester's first trip abroad (excluding Ireland) since 1923, an amazing record considering how easy travel had become. Not every first-team regular was available but Leicester still beat the French club 20-8, with the knowledgeable Willars making a brief return to duty. The weekend visit was in every sense a success, off the field as well as on: at the post-match reception the Leicester president, Rodney Willcox, made the entente even more cordiale with a speech which was not quite English and not quite French (Franglais perhaps?) but which, assisted by generous amounts of vin rouge, went down exceptionally well.

Back home Leicester had been going through the traumatic experience (for a senior club of their traditions) of playing in the Midland Cup to qualify for the following season's John Player Cup. It is the only time they have had to do so and they had to survive games with Nottingham (easily), Westleigh (by a whisker) and Kettering (uncomfortably) before making sure of a place in the last 32. Off the field there had been a flurry of action: Allen's playing career ended in December 1975, after a massive 457 appearances and he promptly took over as club treasurer from Stan Thorpe, who retired gracefully after 14 years of dedicated assistance.

↑ Rodney Willcox was president of the club between 1974-77.

↑ John Reeve scored two tries and gets the ball away against Sale 27.3.1976.

In January 1976, an ad hoc committee was established with the following brief: to examine, report and make such recommendations as they think fit on the structure and organisation of the Leicester Football Club and the Leicester FC social club with particular reference to: a) the playing structure of the club; b) the relationship of the club to other major clubs, the constituent body and local clubs; c) the administration of the club in its entirety; d) the financial objectives of the club.

Such self-examination had been in the air a long time and it proved a profitable exercise, even if no radical reorganisation of the club resulted. Functions of the officers and various committees were redefined and the post of club chairman created, while the presidential term was established at two years instead of three. The first chairman, in due course, was Bob Beason, who handed over the duties of fixture secretary in June 1976, to John Berry, eldest son of the club's former president.

There was also a recommendation that Messrs Allen, Beason and Willars should meet a delegation of local club representatives, under the chairmanship of the Leicestershire RU secretary, John Simpson. Late in the year there were several meetings which helped contrive a better atmosphere than had existed for a considerable time, although the main bone of contention, the Swifts, received another vote of confidence from the ad hoc committee.

In the meantime it was entirely fitting that, at the end of a long and incredibly hot summer, new visitors to Welford Road (which had hosted, for the first time, in April that year, a game between the England under-23 XV and the English Students) should be a Caribbean touring side which played a Leicester XV composed largely of Extras and Swifts players, the tourists going down 18-15. The new captain, in his 38th year, was Rowell and, in what turned out to be his last season, he went out with a bang. Determined to drag the side back to its position of pre-eminence, he worked hard on the forwards and by the season's end he was able to retire a happy man.

1976/1977

Early in the 1976/77 season there were fresh honours when Dodge won his England under-23 cap against Cornwall, subsequently playing against Japan, and the club celebrated with their biggest ever defeat of Northampton, by 40-13. Dodge was joined by Wheeler, Adey and the flanker, David Forfar, in the North and Midlands XV which, coached by Chalkie White, beat the touring Argentinians 24-9 at Welford Road on 9 October. It was the first defeat of their short tour and the combined XV was: Dusty Hare (Nottingham); John Carleton (Orrell), Paul Dodge (Leicester), Tony Bond (Broughton Park), Mike Slemen (Liverpool); John Horton (Bath), Steve Smith (Sale); Colin White (Gosforth), Peter Wheeler (Leicester), Fran Cotton (Sale, captain), Dick Trickey (Sale), Bill Beaumont (Fylde), David Forfar (Leicester), Garry Adey (Leicester), Tony Neary (Broughton Park).

The man of the match was undoubtedly Hare, who kicked five penalties and converted a try by Slemen, while Horton dropped a goal. Gonzalo Beccar Varela (two) and Martin Sansot kicked penalties for the Pumas but the manner of the English side's win brought criticism from a variety of quarters for White, because he had instructed his players to keep the game tight, playing to their own known strengths. The criticism seemed quite unrealistic and not entirely divorced from the reasons why English rugby struggled throughout the 70s.

The following week Hare, who had been capped by England in their win over Wales in 1974, joined Leicester amid allegations of poaching and scored 22 points in his first senior game, a 46-8 win over Oxford University. It was a significant change of allegiance, for Leicester had never possessed such a points accumulator as the Newark farmer and, considering the world record he established, may not do so again. Although a good enough full-back to be capped by his country, it was his ability as a place-kicker which gave Leicester the freedom to play expansive rugby, a style which also involved Hare (who began life as a fly-half) as a runner.

In a good December, five Leicester players went for England trials: Wheeler, Adey, Forfar, Hare and Cowling, and two of them played throughout England's season, the front row

↑ Tigers go out of the John Player Cup in the second round tie against Moseley at The Reddings.

men, Wheeler and Cowling. It was a particularly delighted Cowling who made his international debut against Scotland, for he had been only a replacement in the first trial but, at the age of 32, he had seized his opportunity, going on to win eight caps, a number which would have been increased but for injury. "I am not happy with anything I do in life unless I can be successful," the farming prop said. "To be second best is not sufficient for me. In rugby football I don't enjoy playing unless I win, but I haven't forgotten that at the grass roots of the game one can't win all the time."

The Barbarians were beaten 12-8 though there was an unhappy note when the club's promising teenage prop, Steve Redfern, was sent off with Chris Howcroft of London Welsh, on the Exiles' first visit to Welford Road for nearly forty years. Since the club put out an SOS to members of the public to come in and help clear the artificial covers spread over the pitch to ensure the match went ahead, there must have been some who wondered if it was worth it.

Nevertheless the momentum was sustained in a 17-6 win over Wakefield in a much postponed John Player Cup first round game which eventually had to be played at Clarence Fields, Headingley. Alas for high hopes, the second round of the cup brought only a 23-9 defeat at Moseley but the season was by no means done. There was a return visit by CASG, who played a night match in a torrential downpour, the game being abandoned 11 minutes from time with Leicester leading 28-4.

Rowell and Cowling made first appearances for the Barbarians, Hare and Cowling going on the Easter tour. Redfern and reserve hooker John White joined Dodge as England under-23 players when they played on their home ground against the English Students. For White, a product of Linwood Old Boys in Leicester and overshadowed by the formidable presence of Wheeler, it was a joyful moment; he had been a replacement for the England under-23s against Japan while still in Leicester's third team and now he had won an under-23 cap proper without ever having played regularly in his club's senior side.

White was in the party Leicester sent to Twickenham when they guested in the Middlesex Sevens at the season's end but, in common with their forerunners, they failed to distinguish themselves. In the first round they beat Old Reigatians 16-12, thanks to a sudden death try by Money, the earlier scores coming from Reeve and Dodge, who also converted the tries. But they crashed out 34-0 to the eventual winners, Richmond. The VII was: John Reeve, Paul Dodge, Robin Money, Steve Kenney, Kevin Steptoe, John White, Graham Willars. In a rash of end-of-term honours, two youth players, a lock, Rupert Precious, and a wing, Derek Butler, won England Schools (16 group) caps and Dodge and Redfern were named for the England under-23 tour to Canada.

The proliferation of representative sides to play for, and to play against, had already become apparent during the 70s as travel became easier. But the major honour in a senior player's career was still a British Lions place, and Wheeler achieved that when he was selected for the 1977 party to tour New Zealand and Fiji. He went as the number two hooker to Bobby Windsor (Pontypool) but he returned firmly established as first choice in one of the most competitive packs in Lions history.

Unfortunately, however, Dodge and Redfern were to enjoy their trip to Canada somewhat more than Wheeler. Dodge was an automatic choice against Canada but Redfern paid the penalty for being the cover for both tight and loose head props, playing in three of the provincial games. In New Zealand Wheeler was recognised as being one of the most consistent members of an occasionally inconsistent party and, after being passed over for the First Test, played in the next three, forming a formidable front row with Fran Cotton and Graham Price. He also became one of the most photographed players in the country when he stuffed the match ball up his jersey after the Lions had won the Second Test. Overall, however, it was not the happiest of tours and few of the players were sorry when it ended.

↓ Bob Rowell and the captain of French club CASG exchange gifts prior to kick-off 18.2.1977.

↑ LEICESTER FOOTBALL CLUB 1972/73
Back: Thorpe (Hon.Tres), Day (Hon.Sec), Duggan, Horner, Forfar, Baynes, Watson, Vesty, Mortimer, Adey, D.Matthews, Rowell, Berry (President), White (Coach), Sibson (Team Hon.Sec).
Middle: Allen, Yandle, Willars (capt), Wheeler, Money.
Front: Hall, Edwards, Jones, Barker.

↑ LEICESTER FOOTBALL CLUB 1973/74
Back: White (Coach), Sibson (Team Hon.Sec), Duggan, Watson, Adey, Mortimer, Forfar, Marshall, Allen, Berry (President), Day (Hon.Sec).
Middle: Needham, B.Jones, Money, Wheeler (capt), Barker, Rowell, T.Ringer.
Front: P.Ringer, Hall.

↑ LEICESTER FOOTBALL CLUB 1974/75
Back: Willcox (President), White (Coach), Mortimer, Willars, Roy French, Ray French, Hall, Reeve, Kempin, Allen, Cowling, Thorpe (Hon.Tres), Day (Hon.Sec), Sibson (Team Hon.Sec).
Middle: Adey, Money, Barker, Wheeler (capt), F.Jones, Joyce, Rowell.
Front: Bracewell, B.Jones, Nicholls, Holley, Forfar.

↑ LEICESTER FOOTBALL CLUB 1975/76
Back: White (Coach), Willcox (President), Mortimer, Hall, Adey, Millican, Joyce, Forfar, Cowling, Kempin, Allen (Hon.Tres), Day (Hon.Sec), Sibson (Team Hon.Sec).
Middle: Duggan, Wheeler, Barker, Money (capt), Rowell, Marshall, Dodge.
Front: Holley, Walley, Kenney, B.Jones, Ray French.

↑ LEICESTER FOOTBALL CLUB 1976/77
Back: Sibson (Team Hon.Sec), Day (Hon.Sec), Allen (Hon.Tres), Burwell, Cowling, Wheeler, Joyce, Adey, Redfern, Willcox (President), White (Coach).
Middle: Hall, Duggan, Barker, Rowell (capt), Kempin, Dodge, Forfar.
Front: Hare, Jones, Kenney, White.

19 72/73	Home Ground: Welford Road except #30 at Welford Road Rec Coach: Chalkie White Captain: Graham Willars

OVERALL RECORD:					T	C	PG	DG	PTS
PLD	W	D	L	Tigers scored:	148	87	72	2	988
46	29	2	15	Opponents scored:	99	46	59	6	683

GM	DATE		VEN	OPPONENTS	RESULT	TRIES	KICKS	ATT
RFU CLUB COMPETITION						**CUP WINNERS: COVENTRY**		
6	Sep	27w	a	Nuneaton (Prel)	W 23-22	Barker, Duggan, Money	Whibley c/3p	-
20	Dec	23	a	Bedford (1)	W 21-17	Wheeler, Barker, Duggan, Willars	Wheeler p, Barker c	-
28	Feb	3	a	Hinckley (2)	W 16-4	Adey, Wheeler	Whibley c/2p	-
34	Mar	10	a	Sale (qf)	L 0-7	-	-	-
CLUB MATCHES								
1	Sep	**2**	**H**	**Bedford**	W 25-6	Barker, Baynes, Wheeler, Willars	Whibley 3c/p	234
2		**9**	**H**	**Bath**	W 34-4	Barker(2), Baynes, Jones, Willars, Yandle	Whibley 2c/2p	139
3		**16**	**H**	**Liverpool**	W 65-3	Barker(3), Adey(2), Wheeler(2), Allen, Baynes, Duggan, Rowell, Willars	Whibley 7c/p	259
4		20w	a	Nottingham	W 26-12	Duggan(2), Churchward, Jones	Whibley 2c/2p	-
5		23	a	Harlequins	W 30-18	Bann, Baynes, Duggan, Hall, Yandle	Whibley 5c	-
7		30	a	Percy Park	W 32-18	Duggan(2), Barker, Hall, Shaw	Whibley 3c/2p	-
8	Oct	7	a	Coventry	L 6-45	-	Whibley 2p	3000
9		**14**	**H**	**Richmond**	W 44-7	Bann(2), Barker(2), Whibley, Adey, Duggan	Whibley 5c/2p	255
10		**21**	**H**	**Northampton**	L 12-22	Hall	Whibley c/2p	551
11		**25w**	**H**	**Oxford University**	W 36-3	Weinberg(2), Wheeler, Whibley, Bann, Barker, Young	Wheeler 2c, Whibley 2c	285
12		28	a	Swansea	L 25-33	Duggan(Penalty)(2), Jones	Whibley 2c/3p	-
13	Nov	4	a	Gloucester	D 13-13	Barker(2)	Whibley c/p	-
14		**11**	**H**	**Cambridge University**	W 28-10	Barker, Duggan, Forfar, Jones, Mortimer, Yandle	Whibley 2c	213
15		18	a	Newport	L 24-32	Barker, Duggan, Weinberg, Wheeler	Whibley c/2p	-
16		25	a	Moseley	L 16-19	Baynes, Mortimer	Ingleby c/2p	-
17	Dec	**2**	**H**	**Waterloo**	W 30-12	Baynes(2), Ingleby, Barker	Ingleby 4c/2p	47
18		**9**	**H**	**Blackheath**	W 35-0	Duggan(3), Barker, Money, Willars	Ingleby 4c/p	194
19		16	a	Bristol	L 7-11	Willars	Ingleby p	-
		23	**H**	**London Welsh**	PP (cup)			
21		**27w**	**H**	**Barbarians**	W 26-16	Adey, Allen, Wheeler, Willars	Barker c/2p, Old c	3890
22		**30**	**H**	**Cardiff**	L 13-29	Barker, Baynes	Barker c/p	764
23	Jan	6	a	Bath	L 0-42	-	-	-
24		**15m**	**H**	**Gloucester**	W 20-12	Barker, Horner, Mortimer, Nicholls	Ingleby 2c	197
25		21s	a	Bedford	L 9-37	Barker	Ingleby c/p	-
26		**25th**	**H**	**Royal Navy**	W 29-12	Adey, Duggan, Horner, Money, Wheeler	Bann c/p, Ingleby 2c	155
27		**27**	**H**	**Rosslyn Park**	W 13-11	Bann, D.Matthews	Whibley c/p	103
	Feb	3	a	London Scottish	PP (cup)			
29		**10**	**H**	**Newport**	W 27-3	Duggan(2), Barker	Ingleby 3c/2p, Money d	115
30		**17**	**H**	**Wasps**	L 4-10	Allen	-	-
31		**20tu**	**H**	**Moseley**	L 9-14	-	Ingleby 2p, Hilliker d	472
32		23f	a	Northampton	L 12-22	Adey, Bann	Ingleby 2c	-
33	Mar	**3**	**H**	**Harlequins**	L 21-25	Adey, Willars	Ingleby 2c/3p	360
		7w	**H**	**Loughborough Colleges**	PP			
		10	**H**	**Coventry**	PP (cup)			
35		**16f**	**H**	**Royal Air Force**	W 47-19	Yandle(2), Ingleby, Bann, Duggan, Money	Ingleby 4c/5p	130
36		**21w**	**H**	**Rugby**	W 34-21	Bann, Barker, Wheeler, Yandle	Ingleby 3c/4p	206
37		**24**	**H**	**Llanelli**	W 21-11	Duggan	Ingleby c/5p	278
38		28w	a	Headingley	W 34-10	Ingleby, Bann, Barker, Duggan, Yandle	Ingleby 4c/2p	-
39		31	a	Nuneaton	W 21-3	Jones, Wheeler	Ingleby 2c/3p	-
40	Apr	7	a	Birkenhead Park	D 10-10	Ringer	Ingleby 2p	-
41		**11w**	**H**	**Sale**	W 22-7	Jones(2), Barker, Roy French	Ingleby 3c	172
42		**14**	**H**	**Birmingham**	W 19-7	Barker, Nicholls, Ringer	Ingleby 2c/p	83
43		21	a	Broughton Park	W 10-9	Barker, Edwards	Old c	-
44		23m	a	Fylde	W 14-12	Wheeler, Yandle	Old 2p	-
45		24tu	a	Wilmslow	L 10-16	Barker	Old 2p	-
46		**28**	**H**	**Hartlepool Rovers**	W 15-7	Barker, Duggan, Watson	Wheeler p	158

INDIVIDUAL APPEARANCES 1972/73

Name / Game #	1	2	3	4	5	6	7	8	9	10	11	12	13	14	15	16	17	18	19	20	21	22	23	24	25	26	27	28	29	30	31	32	33	34	35	36	37	38	39	40	41	42	43	44	45	46	Apps	T	Pts
GJ (Garry) Adey E+	-	G	G	G	G	G	G	G	G	G	G	G	G	G	G	G	-	-	-	G	G	G	G	E	G	E	-	E	G	G	G	G	G	G	-	-	-	-	-	-	G	G	G	G	G	G	35	8	32
JA (John) Allen	I	I	I	I	I	I	I	-	I	I	I	I	I	I	I	I	I	I	I	I	I	I	I	I	I*	-	-	I	I	I	I	I	I	I	I	I*	I*	I*	I*	I*	I*	I*	-	I*	I*	I*	42	3	12
EE (Eric) Bann	D	D	D	E	D	-	-	D	D	D	D	E	D	D	D	D	D	D	D	D	D	D	-	D	D	D	D	-	-	-	-	D	D	D	D	D	D	E	D	-	D	D	E	D	E	-	37	9	41
RG (Bob) Barker	K	K	K	K	K	K	K	K	K	K	L	K	K	K	K	K	K	L	L	K	K	K	K	L	L	K	K	K	K	K	-	-	K	K	K	K	K	K	K	K	K	K	K	K	K	M	44	29	131
CJ (Chris) Baynes	G	F	F	H	F	H	-	F	-	-	-	-	-	-	-	F	G	G	G	H	F	F	H	-	F	-	H	-	-	-	-	-	-	-	-	F	-	-	-	-	-	-	-	H	<H	-	20	8	32
DW (David) Bird	-	-	-	-	-	-	-	-	-	-	-	-	-	-	-	-	-	-	-	-	-	-	-	M	-	-	-	-	-	-	-	-	-	-	-	-	-	-	-	-	-	-	<L	-	-	-	2	-	-
M (Mark) Churchward	-	-	-	>A	-	-	<A	-	-	-	-	-	-	-	-	-	-	-	-	-	-	-	-	-	-	-	-	-	-	-	-	-	-	-	-	-	-	-	-	-	-	-	-	-	-	-	2	1	4
MJ (John) Duggan	N	N	N	N	N	N	N	N	N	N	N	N	N	N	N	N	N	N	N	N	N	N	N	-	N	N	N	N	N	-	-	-	N	N	N	N	N	N	-	-	-	-	-	-	-	N	35	23	92
N (Ted) Edwards	-	-	-	-	-	-	-	-	-	-	-	-	-	-	-	-	-	-	-	-	-	-	-	-	-	-	-	-	-	-	-	-	-	-	-	-	-	-	-	-	-	-	>N	N	N	O	4	1	4
DJ (Dave) Forfar	F	-	-	-	-	-	F	-	F	F	F	F	F	H	H	-	H	H	H	-	-	-	-	G	H	H	-	H	H	H	H	H	H	H	F	H	H	H	H	H	H	F	H	-	-	H	32	1	4
RW (Ray) French	-	-	-	-	-	-	-	-	-	-	-	-	-	-	-	-	-	-	-	-	-	-	-	-	-	-	-	-	-	-	-	-	-	-	-	>C	C	C	-	-	C	C	C	C	-	-	7	-	-
RV (Roger) Grove	A	-	A	-	A	A	-	A	A	A	A	-	A	-	A	A	-	A	A	A	A	A	-	A	A	<A	-	-	-	-	-	-	-	-	-	-	-	-	-	-	-	-	-	-	-	-	19	-	-
BP (Brian) Hall	L	L	L	L	L	-	L	-	L	L	-	-	L	-	-	-	-	-	-	-	-	-	-	-	-	-	-	-	-	-	-	-	-	-	-	-	-	-	-	-	-	-	-	-	-	-	9	3	12
C (Cliff) Hilliker	-	-	-	-	-	-	-	-	-	-	-	-	-	>L	-	-	-	-	-	-	-	-	-	-	-	-	-	-	-	-	<L	-	-	-	-	-	-	-	-	-	-	-	-	-	-	-	2	-	3
G (Graham) Horner	-	-	-	-	-	-	-	-	-	-	-	-	-	-	-	-	-	-	-	-	-	-	-	K	-	J	-	-	-	-	-	-	-	-	-	-	-	-	-	N	-	-	-	-	-	K	4	2	8
J (John) Ingleby	-	-	-	-	-	-	-	-	-	-	-	-	-	-	-	L	L	M	L	-	-	-	-	J	J	L	J	L	L	L	N	L	L	L	L	L	L	L	L	M	L	L	-	-	-	-	23	3	200
B (Bleddyn) Jones	J	J	J	J	J	J	J	J	J	J	J	J	J	J	J	J	J	J	J	J	J	J	J	-	-	-	-	J	J	J	J	J	J	J	J	J	J	J	J	J	J	J	I	J	J	J	42	7	28
A (Andy) Matthews	-	-	-	-	-	-	-	-	-	-	-	-	-	-	-	-	-	-	-	-	-	-	-	-	-	-	-	-	-	-	-	-	-	-	-	-	-	-	C	<C	-	-	-	-	-	-	2	-	-
DJ (David) Matthews	-	-	-	-	-	-	-	-	-	-	-	-	-	-	-	-	-	-	-	-	-	-	-	H	-	G	G	G	-	-	-	-	-	-	G	G	G	G	G	G	-	-	F	F	F	F	14	1	4
RS (Robin) Money	-	-	-	-	-	O	-	-	-	-	-	-	-	-	-	O	O	O	O	O	O	O	O	O	O	O	O	-	O	O	O	O	O	O	O	O	O	O	O	O	O	O	O	O	O	-	30	4	19
MR (Mike) Mortimer	C	C	C	C	C	C	C	C	C	C	C	C	C	C	C	C	C	C	C	C	-	-	C	C	C	C	C	C	C	C	C	C	C	C	C	-	-	-	-	-	-	-	-	-	C	C	35	3	12
P (Peter) Nicholls	-	-	-	-	-	-	-	-	-	-	-	-	-	-	-	-	-	-	-	-	-	-	-	N	K	-	-	-	-	N	K	K	-	-	-	-	-	-	N	-	N	N	-	-	-	-	8	2	8
AGB (Alan) Old E5	-	-	-	-	-	-	-	>L	-	-	-	-	-	-	-	-	-	-	-	-	L	-	-	-	-	-	-	-	-	-	-	-	-	-	-	-	-	-	-	-	-	-	J	L	L	-	5	-	16
DA (David) Pickering	-	-	-	-	-	B	-	-	-	-	-	-	-	-	-	-	-	B	-	-	-	B	B	-	-	-	-	-	-	B	B	B	-	-	-	-	-	-	-	B	-	<B	-	-	-	-	9	-	-
P (Paul) Ringer W+	-	-	-	-	-	-	-	-	-	-	-	-	-	-	-	-	-	-	-	-	-	-	-	-	-	-	-	-	-	-	-	-	-	-	-	-	>F	F	F	F	F	H	-	-	-	-	6	2	8
RE (Bob) Rowell E2	E	E	E	D	E	E	E	-	E	E	E	D	E	E	E	E	E	E	E	E	E	E	E	-	E	-	-	D	D	E	D	E	E	E	E	E	E	D	E	D	E	E	-	E	-	E	40	1	4
DM (Dave) Shaw	-	-	-	-	-	D	D	<E	-	-	-	-	-	-	-	-	-	-	-	-	-	-	-	-	-	-	-	-	-	-	-	-	-	-	-	-	-	-	-	-	-	-	-	-	-	-	3	1	4
D (Dave) Truman	-	-	-	-	-	-	-	-	-	-	-	-	-	-	-	-	-	-	-	-	-	-	-	-	-	I	<I	-	-	-	-	-	-	-	-	-	-	-	-	-	-	-	-	-	-	-	2	-	-
PN (Phil) Vesty	-	-	-	-	-	-	-	-	-	-	-	A	-	A	-	-	A	-	-	-	C	C	-	-	-	-	A	A	A	A	A	A	A	A	A	A	A	A	A	A	A	A	A	A	A	A	25	-	-
RJ (Bob) Watson	-	-	-	-	-	-	-	-	-	-	-	-	-	-	-	-	-	-	-	-	-	-	D	-	-	-	E	-	E	D	E	-	-	-	-	-	-	-	-	E	-	-	D	-	D	D	9	1	4
GR (Gary) Weinberg	-	-	-	-	-	-	-	-	-	-	>M	L	-	-	L	-	-	-	-	L	-	L	<L	-	-	-	-	-	-	-	-	-	-	-	-	-	-	-	-	-	-	-	-	-	-	-	6	3	12
PJ (Peter) Wheeler E+ L+	B	B	B	B	B	-	B	B	B	B	B	B	B	B	B	B	B	-	B	B	B	-	A	B	B	B	B	B	B	-	-	-	B	B	B	B	B	B	B	-	-	-	B	B	B	B	37	12	58
DF (Dave) Whibley	O	O	O	O	O	L	O	O	O	O	O	O	O	O	O	-	-	-	-	-	-	-	-	-	-	-	L	<O	-	-	-	-	-	-	-	-	-	-	-	-	-	-	-	-	-	-	17	2	164
GG (Graham) Willars	H*	H*	H*	F*	H*	F*	H*	H*	H*	H*	H*	H*	H*	F*	F*	H*	F*	F*	F*	F*	H*	H*	F*	F*	-	F*	F*	F*	F*	F*	F*	F*	F*	F*	H*	-	-	-	-	-	-	-	-	-	-	-	34	8	32
MJ (Mike) Yandle	M	M	M	M	M	M	M	M	M	M	-	M	M	M	M	M	M	-	M	M	M	M	M	-	M	M	M	M	M	M	M	M	M	M	M	M	M	M	M	L	M	M	M*	M	M	<L	43	8	32

1 GAME: R (Bob) Beason <A(2), RS (Roy) French Bt(41), G (Graham) Jackson <K(18), GR (Guy) Millar <I(8), R (Bob) Williams =N(32), J (Jeff) Young =Kt(11)

The key for how to read the stats is on the last page

19	73/74	Home Ground: Welford Road	OVERALL RECORD:					T	C	PG	DG	PTS
		Coach: Chalkie White	PLD	W	D	L	Tigers scored:	104	49	71	4	739
		Captain: Mike Yandle then Peter Wheeler	43	24	3	16	Opponents scored:	80	34	69	4	607

GM	DATE		VEN	OPPONENTS	RESULT	TRIES	KICKS	ATT
RFU CLUB COMPETITION						**CUP WINNERS: COVENTRY**		
15	Nov	6tu	a	Northampton (1)	L 6-22	-	Ingleby 2p	-
CLUB MATCHES								
1	Sep	1	a	Bedford	L 15-35	Adey, Duggan	Ingleby 2c/p	-
2		**5w**	**H**	**Nottingham**	W 12-9	-	Ingleby 4p	-
3		**8**	**H**	**Bath**	W 16-3	Barker, B.Jones	Ingleby c/2p	-
4		**11tu**	**H**	**Fiji**	W 22-17	Barker, Wheeler	Ingleby c/4p	12000
5		15	a	Liverpool	W 19-3	Adey, B.Jones, Nicholls	Ingleby 2c/p	-
6		22	a	Harlequins	W 33-3	Ingleby, Adey, Forfar, B.Jones, Mortimer, Nicholls	Ingleby 3c/p	-
7		29	a	Saracens	W 16-10	Hall(2)	Ingleby c/p, Old p	-
8	Oct	**3w**	**H**	**Randwick**	W 15-10	B.Jones	Wheeler 2p, Money d, Ingleby c	-
9		**6**	**H**	**Coventry**	L 16-22	Old, Wheeler	Old d, Ingleby c/p	-
10		13	a	Richmond	W 16-0	Adey, Duggan	Ingleby c/p, Hall d	-
11		20	a	Northampton	L 7-26	Hall	Ingleby p	-
12		24w	a	Oxford University	D 16-16	Barker, Duggan, Holley, Wheeler	-	-
13		**27**	**H**	**Swansea**	D 21-21	B.Jones	Ingleby c/5p	-
14	Nov	**3**	**H**	**Gloucester**	L 6-29	-	Ingleby 2p	-
16		10	a	Cambridge University	W 24-6	Adey(2), Wheeler	Ingleby 3c/2p	-
17		**17**	**H**	**Fylde**	W 33-10	Allen, Bann, Forfar, Hall, B.Jones, Nicholls	Ingleby 3c/p	-
18		**24**	**H**	**Moseley**	L 13-24	Duggan	Ingleby 3p	-
	Dec	1	a	Waterloo	PP (frost)			
19		8	a	Blackheath	W 16-6	Bann, Wheeler	Old c/2p	-
20		**15**	**H**	**Bristol**	W 20-3	Barker(2), Allen, Duggan	Old 2c	-
21		22	a	London Welsh	W 18-12	Adey, Money	Old 2c/2p	-
22		**27th**	**H**	**Barbarians**	L 7-16	Duggan	Old p	15000
23		**29**	**H**	**Headingley**	W 22-15	Ingleby, Marshall, Money	Ingleby 2c/2p	-
24	Jan	5	a	Bath	L 3-20	-	Barker p	-
25		12	a	Gloucester	L 10-27	Marshall(2)	Wheeler c	-
26		**19**	**H**	**Bedford**	W 20-6	Bann, Needham, Reeve	Barker c/2p	-
27		26	a	Rosslyn Park	L 3-18	-	Old p	-
		30w	**H**	**Royal Navy**	PP			
28	Feb	**2**	**H**	**London Scottish**	W 15-9	-	Barker 5p	-
		9	a	Newport	PP (waterlogged)			
29		16	a	Wasps	L 0-13	-	-	-
		20w	a	Moseley	PP (power strike)			
30		**23**	**H**	**Northampton**	W 15-9	Old	Old c/3p	-
31	Mar	**2**	**H**	**Harlequins**	L 9-13	Horner	Barker c/p	-
32		9	a	Coventry	W 36-16	Barker(2), Hall(2), Old, Wheeler, Willars	Barker d, Old p, Wheeler c	-
		12tu	**H**	**Loughborough Colleges**	PP			
33		**15f**	**H**	**Royal Air Force**	L 7-12	Needham	Barker p	-
34		20w	a	Rugby	D 12-12	Hall	Old c/2p	-
35		23	a	Sale	L 17-25	Nicholls(2)	Old 3p	-
36		**26tu**	**H**	**Loughborough Colleges**	W 30-9	Allen(2), Barker, Money, P.Ringer	Barker 2c/2p	-
37		30	a	Llanelli	W 11-10	B.Jones, F.Jones	Barker p	-
38	Apr	**6**	**H**	**Birkenhead Park**	W 27-16	Adey(2), Bann(2), Reeve	Wheeler 2c/p	-
39		13	a	Middlesbrough	W 17-4	Barker(2), Hall	Old p, Wheeler c	-
40		15m	a	Gosforth	L 18-28	Barker, Joyce	Old 2c/2p	-
41		16tu	a	Harrogate	W 56-10	Duggan(3), Thomas(2), B.Jones, Joyce, Money, Mortimer, Reeve, Rowell	Wheeler 6c	-
42		20	a	Bristol	L 8-29	Hall, Reeve	-	-
43		**27**	**H**	**Nuneaton**	W 36-3	Duggan(2), Barker, Marshall, Mortimer, Penalty	Wheeler 3c/2p	-

INDIVIDUAL APPEARANCES 1973/74

Name / Game #	1	2	3	4	5	6	7	8	9	10	11	12	13	14	15	16	17	18	19	20	21	22	23	24	25	26	27	28	29	30	31	32	33	34	35	36	37	38	39	40	41	42	43	Apps	T	Pts
GJ (Garry) Adey E+	G	G	G	G	G	G	G	-	-	G	G	-	-	G	G	G	G	G	G	G	G	G	-	-	-	G	G	E	E	E	E	-	G	G	G	G	G	G	G	-	-	H	G	33	9	36
JA (John) Allen	I	I	I	I	I	I	I	-	I	-	I	I	I	I	I	I	I*	I	-	I	I	I	I*	I*	I	I*	I	-	-	I	-	I	I*	-	-	I*	I*	I	-	-	-	I*	I	32	4	16
EE (Eric) Bann	D	D	D	D	D	D	D	-	D	D	-	-	D	-	D	E	D	D	D	D	D	D	-	D	D	D	D	D	-	-	-	-	-	E	D	-	-	D	-	-	-	-	-	26	5	20
RG (Bob) Barker	K	K	K	K	K	K	K	K	K	K	K	K	K	K	K	K	K	K	-	K	K	K	K	L	K	K	K	K	K	-	K	K	K	-	N	K	K	-	K	K	-	-	K	37	12	98
MJ (John) Duggan	N	N	N	N	-	-	-	N	N	N	-	N	N	N	N	N	-	N	N	N	N	N	-	-	-	-	-	-	-	N	N	N	N	N	-	N	N	-	N	N	N	-	N	28	11	44
DJ (Dave) Forfar	F	F	F	F	F	F	F	F	F	F	F	F	F	F	F	F	F	F	F	F	F	F	F	F	-	F	F	-	F	H	F	-	-	-	-	-	-	-	-	-	-	-	-	29	2	8
RW (Ray) French	-	-	-	-	-	-	-	-	-	-	-	-	-	-	-	-	-	-	-	-	-	-	-	-	-	-	C	-	-	-	-	-	-	C	-	-	-	-	-	-	-	-	-	2	-	-
RS (Roy) French	-	-	-	-	-	-	-	-	-	-	-	-	-	-	-	-	B	-	-	-	-	-	B	B	-	B	-	B	B	-	B	-	B	-	-	B	B	-	-	-	B	B	-	12	-	-
BP (Brian) Hall	-	M	M	L	M	M	L	L	L	M	L	-	-	L	L	M	L	L	L	M	L	L	L	-	L	M	M	M	M	M	M	M	M	L	L	M	M	M	L	M	-	M	M	38	9	39
J (John) Hill	-	-	-	-	-	-	-	-	-	-	-	-	-	-	-	-	-	-	-	-	-	-	-	-	-	-	-	>L	L	-	-	-	-	-	M	L	L	-	-	-	-	-	-	5	-	-
ER (Ted) Holley	>L	-	-	-	-	-	-	-	-	-	-	L	M	-	-	-	-	-	-	-	-	-	-	M	M	L	-	-	-	-	-	-	-	-	-	-	-	-	-	-	-	-	-	6	1	4
G (Graham) Horner	-	-	-	-	-	-	-	-	-	-	-	-	-	-	-	-	-	-	-	-	-	-	-	N	-	-	-	-	J	-	J	-	J	-	-	-	-	-	-	-	-	<N	-	5	1	4
J (John) Ingleby	M	L	L	M	L	L	M	M	M	L	M	M	L	M	M	L	M	M	-	-	-	-	M	-	-	-	-	-	-	-	-	-	-	-	-	-	-	-	-	-	-	-	-	19	2	154
B (Bleddyn) Jones	J	J	J	J	J	J	-	J	-	J	J	J	J	J	J	J	J	J	J	J	J	J	J	J	J	J	J	J	-	L	L	L	L	M	-	J	J	J	J	L	J	J	J	39	8	32
F (Frank) Jones	-	-	-	-	-	-	-	-	-	-	-	-	-	-	-	-	-	-	-	-	-	-	-	-	-	-	-	-	-	-	-	-	-	-	-	>H	H	H	H	H	-	-	-	5	1	4
NJ (Nick) Joyce	-	-	-	-	-	-	-	-	-	-	-	-	-	-	-	-	-	-	-	-	-	-	-	-	-	-	-	-	-	-	-	-	-	-	-	-	-	-	-	G	G	G	-	3	2	8
DL (Danny) Kirk	-	-	-	-	-	-	-	>I	-	I	-	-	-	-	-	-	-	-	I	-	-	-	-	-	-	-	-	I	I	-	I	-	-	I	I	-	-	-	-	-	-	-	-	8	-	-
M (Mike) Marshall	-	H	-	-	-	-	-	-	-	-	-	G	G	-	-	-	-	-	-	-	-	-	G	G	G	-	-	G	-	-	-	-	-	H	H	-	-	-	-	-	-	-	H	10	4	16
DJ (David) Matthews	H	-	-	-	-	-	-	-	G	-	-	-	-	-	-	-	-	H	-	-	-	-	-	-	-	-	-	-	G*	G*	G*	<G	-	-	-	-	-	-	-	-	-	-	-	7	-	-
RS (Robin) Money	O	O	O	O	O	O	O	O	O	O	O	O	O	O	O	O	O	O	O	O	O	O	O	-	O	O	O	O	O	O	O	O	O	O	O	O	O	O	O	O	O	O	O	42	4	19
MR (Mike) Mortimer	C	C	C	C	C	C	C	C	C	C	C	C	C	C	C	C	C	C	C	C	C	C	C	C	C	C	-	C	C	C	C	C	C	A	C	C	C	C	C	C	C	C	C	42	3	12
RE (Ray) Needham	-	>A	-	-	-	-	-	-	-	-	-	-	-	-	-	-	A	A	A	A	A	A	A	A	A	A	A	A	A	A	A	A	A	-	A	A	A	A	A	A	A	A	A	27	2	8
P (Peter) Nicholls	-	-	-	-	N	N	N	-	-	-	N	-	-	-	-	-	N	-	-	-	-	-	-	-	-	-	-	-	-	-	-	-	-	K	K	-	-	-	-	-	-	-	-	7	5	20
AGB (Alan) Old E11	-	-	-	-	-	-	J	-	J	-	-	-	-	-	-	-	-	-	M	L	M	M	-	-	-	-	L	-	-	J	-	J	-	J	J	-	-	-	M	<J	-	-	-	13	3	90
J (John) Reeve	-	-	-	-	-	-	-	-	-	-	-	-	-	-	-	-	-	-	>K	-	-	-	N	K	N	N	N	-	-	-	-	-	-	-	-	-	-	K	-	-	K	K	-	9	4	16
P (Paul) Ringer W+	-	-	H	H	H	H	H	G	H	H	■H	H	H	H	H	H	H	-	H	H	H	H	H	H	H	H	H	H	H	-	H	F	F	F	F	F	F	F	F	F	F	F	F	39	1	4
T (Tim) Ringer	-	-	-	-	-	-	-	-	-	-	-	-	-	-	-	-	-	-	-	-	-	-	-	-	-	-	-	-	-	-	-	-	-	-	-	-	-	-	-	-	>L	L	L	3	-	-
RE (Bob) Rowell E2	-	-	-	-	-	-	-	-	-	-	D	D	-	E	E	D	E	E	E	E	E	E	E	E	-	E	E	-	D	D	D	D	D	-	-	D	E	E	D	E	E	E	E	28	1	4
DB (Dennis) Sobey	-	-	-	-	-	-	-	-	-	-	-	-	-	-	-	-	-	-	-	-	-	-	-	-	-	-	-	>N	N	K	-	-	-	-	-	-	-	<N	-	-	-	-	-	4	-	-
SJ (Steve) Solomons	-	-	-	-	-	-	-	-	-	-	-	-	-	-	-	-	-	-	-	-	-	-	-	>O	-	-	-	-	-	-	-	-	-	-	-	-	-	-	-	-	-	-	-	1	-	-
M (Mike) Thomas	-	-	-	-	-	-	-	-	-	-	-	-	-	-	-	-	-	-	-	-	-	-	-	-	-	-	-	-	-	-	-	-	-	-	-	-	-	>L	-	-	M	-	-	2	2	8
PN (Phil) Vesty	A	-	A	A	A	A	A	A	A	A	A	A	A	A	A	A	-	-	-	-	-	-	-	-	-	-	-	-	-	-	-	-	-	-	-	-	-	-	-	-	-	-	-	15	-	-
TA (Tim) Walley	-	-	-	-	-	-	-	-	-	-	-	-	-	-	-	-	-	-	-	-	-	-	-	-	-	-	-	-	-	-	-	-	-	-	-	-	-	-	>I	I	I	-	-	3	-	-
RJ (Bob) Watson	E	E	E	E	E	E	E	E	E	E	E	-	E	D	-	-	-	-	-	-	-	-	D	-	E	-	-	-	-	-	-	E	E	D	E	E	D	-	E	D	D	D	D	26	-	-
J (Jim) Watts	-	-	-	-	-	-	-	>D	-	-	-	<E	-	-	-	-	-	-	-	-	-	-	-	-	-	-	-	-	-	-	-	-	-	-	-	-	-	-	-	-	-	-	-	2	-	-
PJ (Peter) Wheeler E+ L+	B*	B*	B*	B*	B*	B*	B*	B*	B*	B*	B*	B*	B*	B*	B*	B*	-	B*	B*	B*	B*	B*	-	-	B*	-	B*	-	-	B	-	B*	-	B*	B*	-	-	B*	B*	B*	H*	-	B*	32	6	67
GG (Graham) Willars	-	-	-	-	-	-	-	H	-	-	-	-	-	-	-	-	-	-	-	-	-	-	-	-	F	-	-	F*	-	F	-	H	H	-	-	-	-	-	-	-	-	-	-	6	1	4

The key for how to read the stats is on the last page

19 74/75

Home Ground: Welford Road except #30 at Welford Road Rec	
Coach: Chalkie White	
Captain: Peter Wheeler	

OVERALL RECORD:					T	C	PG	DG	PTS
PLD	W	D	L	Tigers scored:	72	31	60	4	542
40	19	1	20	Opponents scored:	80	37	61	7	598

GM	DATE		VEN	OPPONENTS	RESULT	TRIES	KICKS	ATT
CLUB MATCHES								
1	Sep	**7**	**H**	**Bedford**	W 19-12	Wheeler, P.Ringer	Wheeler c/3p	-
2		14	a	Bath	L 9-15	Hall	Wheeler c/p	-
3		**21**	**H**	**Liverpool**	W 37-6	Watson(3), Wheeler(2), Adey, B.Jones	Wheeler 3c, Money d	-
4		25w	a	Nottingham	W 10-3	Duggan	Allen d, Wheeler p	-
5		28	a	Harlequins	L 10-32	Mortimer	Wheeler 2p	-
6	Oct	2w	a	Nuneaton	W 26-10	Forfar, Kirk, Marshall	Wheeler c/4p	-
7		5	a	Coventry	L 3-13	-	Wheeler p	-
8		**12**	**H**	**Richmond**	L 9-16	-	Wheeler 3p	-
9		**19**	**H**	**Northampton**	D 13-13	Adey, Willars	Wheeler c/p	-
10		**23w**	**H**	**Oxford University**	W 20-13	Duggan, Reeve, Willars	Wheeler c/2p	-
11		26	a	Swansea	L 7-9	Forfar	Allen p	-
12	Nov	2	a	Gloucester	L 7-24	Adey	Wheeler p	-
13		**9**	**H**	**Cambridge University**	W 16-10	Adey, Hill	Allen c/2p	-
14		16	a	Newport	L 9-24	Duggan	Wheeler c/p	-
15		**23**	**H**	**Moseley**	L 4-22	Reeve	-	-
16		**29f**	**H**	**Saracens**	W 10-6	Adey, Holley	Hall c	-
17	Dec	**7**	**H**	**Waterloo**	W 21-9	B.Jones(2), Reeve(2)	Wheeler c/p	-
18		**14**	**H**	**Blackheath**	L 13-25	Duggan(2)	Allen c/p	-
19		21	a	Bristol	L 10-15	Money	Barker 2p	-
20		**27f**	**H**	**Barbarians**	L 4-43	Duggan	-	17000
21		28	a	Headingley	L 3-24	-	Wheeler p	-
22	Jan	**4**	**H**	**Bath**	W 14-3	Duggan, Ray French, Reeve	Hall c	-
23		**8w**	**H**	**Royal Navy**	W 21-7	Duggan, Hall, Reeve	Wheeler 3p	-
24		**11**	**H**	**Gloucester**	W 18-4	Duggan	Wheeler c/4p	-
25		18	a	Bedford	L 19-23	Duggan(2), Barker	Barker 2c/p	-
26		**25**	**H**	**Rosslyn Park**	W 12-6	Burwell	Wheeler c/2p	-
	Feb	1	a	London Scottish	PP (waterlogged)			
27		**8**	**H**	**Newport**	L 6-10	-	Wheeler 2p	-
28		**15**	**H**	**Wasps**	L 22-25	Barker, Burwell	Barker c/4p	-
29		**19w**	**H**	**Moseley**	L 9-27	Barker	Barker c/p	-
30		22	a	Northampton	L 6-20	-	Barker 2p	-
31	Mar	**1**	**H**	**Harlequins**	L 9-15	Duggan	Barker c/p	-
32		**8**	**H**	**Neath**	W 19-6	Barker, Kempin	Barker c/3p	-
		11tu	**H**	**Loughborough Colleges**	PP (waterlogged)			
		14f	**H**	**Royal Air Force**	PP (waterlogged)			
33		**19w**	**H**	**Rugby**	W 25-0	Barker, Bracewell, Duggan, Forfar	Barker 3c/p	-
34		22	a	Sale	L 0-23	-	-	-
35		**29**	**H**	**Orrell**	W 13-9	Bracewell, F.Jones	Barker c/p	-
36		**31m**	**H**	**Gosforth**	W 18-15	Barker, Bracewell	Barker c, Money 2d, Allen c	-
37	Apr	5	a	Birkenhead Park	W 19-13	Bracewell(2), Allen	Barker 2c/p	-
38		**12**	**H**	**Bristol**	L 10-12	Nicholls	Barker p, Wheeler p	-
39		19	a	Fylde	W 21-19	Barker, Bracewell, B.Jones, Money	Wheeler c/p	-
40		**26**	**H**	**Middlesbrough**	W 21-17	Wheeler, Adey, Barker	Wheeler 3p	-

INDIVIDUAL APPEARANCES 1974/75

Name / Game #	1	2	3	4	5	6	7	8	9	10	11	12	13	14	15	16	17	18	19	20	21	22	23	24	25	26	27	28	29	30	31	32	33	34	35	36	37	38	39	40	Apps	T	Pts
GJ (Garry) Adey E+	G	G	G	G	G	-	G	G	G	G	G	G	G	G	G	G	G	-	-	E	G	G	G	G	G	G	G	G	D	G	G	G	G	G	-	G	G	G	G	G	36	6	24
JA (John) Allen	I	I	I	I	I	-	I	-	I	I	I	I	I	I	I	I*	I	I*	I*	I	-	I*	I	I	I*	I	I	I*	I*	I*	I*	I*	I*	I*	I*	I*	I	I	I	I	37	1	25
RG (Bob) Barker	-	-	-	-	-	-	-	-	-	-	-	-	-	-	-	-	-	-	N	-	-	-	-	-	K	K	K	K	K	K	K	K	K	N	N	N	N	K	K	K	17	8	112
KH (Ken) Bracewell	-	-	-	-	-	-	-	-	-	-	-	-	-	-	-	-	>M	L	L	M	L	L	L	L	-	-	-	-	-	-	-	L	L	L	L	L	L	L	L	L	17	6	24
TR (Terry) Burwell	-	-	-	-	-	-	-	-	-	-	-	-	-	-	-	-	-	-	-	-	-	-	-	-	>L	L	L	L	L	L	L	-	-	-	-	-	-	-	M	-	8	2	8
AP (Angus) Collington	-	-	-	-	-	-	-	-	-	-	-	-	-	-	-	-	-	-	-	-	-	-	-	-	-	-	-	-	>G	-	-	-	-	-	-	-	-	-	-	-	1	-	-
RJ (Robin) Cowling E+	>A	A	A	A	A	A	A	A	A	A	A	A	A	A	A	A	A	-	-	A	A	-	A	A	-	A	A	-	A	A	A	A	A	A	A	A	A	A	■A	A	35	-	-
MJ (John) Duggan	-	-	N	N	N	N	N	N	N	N	N	N	N	N	N	N	N	N	-	N	N	N	N	N	N	N	N	-	N	N	N	N	N	-	-	-	-	-	-	-	29	13	52
N (Ted) Edwards	N	N	<K	-	-	-	-	-	-	-	-	-	-	-	-	-	-	-	-	-	-	-	-	-	-	-	-	-	-	-	-	-	-	-	-	-	-	-	-	-	3	-	-
DJ (Dave) Forfar	H	H	H	H	F	H	H	H	F	-	F	F	H	H	H	H	H	H	H	F	F	H	H	H	F	H	-	H	H	H	F	H	H	H	G	H	H	H	H	H	38	3	12
RW (Ray) French	-	-	-	-	-	-	-	-	-	C	C	C	C	C	C	C	C	C	C	C	C	C	C	C	C	C	C	A	C	C	C	C	C	C	-	-	-	-	-	-	25	1	4
RS (Roy) French	-	-	-	-	-	-	-	-	-	-	-	-	-	-	-	B	-	B	B	-	-	B	-	-	B	-	-	-	B	B	B	-	B	B	B	B	-	-	-	-	12	-	-
BP (Brian) Hall	M	M	-	-	-	-	L	L	-	-	-	-	-	-	M	L	L	M	M	L	M	M	M	M	M	M	M	M	M	M	M	M	M	M	M	M	M	M	-	-	28	2	12
J (John) Hill	-	-	-	-	-	-	-	-	L	L	L	L	L	<M	-	-	-	-	-	-	-	-	-	-	-	-	-	-	-	-	-	-	-	-	-	-	-	-	-	-	6	1	4
ER (Ted) Holley	-	-	-	-	-	M	M	M	M	M	M	M	M	L	L	M	-	-	-	-	-	-	-	-	-	-	-	-	-	-	-	-	-	-	-	-	-	-	-	M	12	1	4
J (John) Ingleby	-	-	-	-	-	<O	-	-	-	-	-	-	-	-	-	-	-	-	-	-	-	-	-	-	-	-	-	-	-	-	-	-	-	-	-	-	-	-	-	-	1	-	-
B (Bleddyn) Jones	J	J	J	J	J	J	J	J	J	J	J	J	J	J	J	J	J	J	J	J	J	J	J	J	J	J	J	J	J	J	J	J	J	J	J	J	J	J	J	J	40	4	16
F (Frank) Jones	-	-	-	-	-	-	-	-	-	-	-	-	-	-	-	-	-	-	-	-	-	-	-	-	-	-	-	-	-	-	-	-	-	-	H	F	F	F	F	F	6	1	4
NJ (Nick) Joyce	-	-	-	-	-	E	-	E	E	D	D	E	D	D	D	D	D	D	D	-	D	D	-	E	-	D	D	-	-	■D	D	D	-	-	D	E	-	D	D	D	26	-	-
JS (Jim) Kempin	-	-	-	-	-	-	-	-	-	>H	-	-	-	-	-	-	-	-	-	-	-	F	F	F	-	-	H	F	F	F	H	F	F	F	F	-	-	-	-	-	13	1	4
DL (Danny) Kirk	-	-	-	-	-	I	-	<I	-	-	-	-	-	-	-	-	-	-	-	-	-	-	-	-	-	-	-	-	-	-	-	-	-	-	-	-	-	-	-	-	2	1	4
J (Joz) Krych	-	-	-	-	-	-	-	-	-	-	-	-	-	-	-	-	-	>A	-	-	-	-	-	-	-	-	-	-	-	-	-	-	-	-	-	-	-	-	-	-	1	-	-
M (Mike) Marshall	-	-	-	-	-	G	-	-	-	-	-	-	-	-	-	-	F	F	-	-	-	-	-	-	-	-	-	-	-	-	-	-	-	-	-	-	-	-	-	-	3	1	4
JG (Jock) Millican S3	-	-	-	-	-	-	-	-	-	-	-	-	-	-	-	-	-	-	-	-	-	-	-	-	>H	F	F	-	-	-	-	-	-	-	-	-	-	-	-	-	3	-	-
RS (Robin) Money	O	O	O	O	O	-	O	O	O	O	O	O	O	O	O	O	O	O	O	O	O	O	O	O	-	O	O	O	O	-	O	O	O	O	O	O	O	O	O	O	37	2	17
MR (Mike) Mortimer	C	C	C	C	C	C	C	C	C	-	-	-	-	-	-	-	-	-	-	-	-	-	-	-	-	-	-	-	-	-	-	-	-	-	C	C	C	C	C	C	15	1	4
RE (Ray) Needham	-	-	-	-	-	-	-	-	-	-	-	-	-	-	-	-	-	-	A	-	-	A	-	-	A	-	-	-	-	-	-	-	-	-	-	-	-	-	-	-	3	-	-
P (Peter) Nicholls	K	K	-	K	K	K	K	K	K	-	-	-	-	-	-	-	-	-	-	-	-	-	-	-	-	-	-	-	-	-	-	-	-	-	-	-	-	N	N	<N	11	1	4
AB (Andy) Northen	-	-	-	-	-	-	-	-	-	-	-	-	-	-	-	-	-	-	-	-	-	-	-	-	-	-	-	-	-	-	-	-	>E	E	E	-	E	-	-	-	4	-	-
J (John) Reeve	-	-	-	-	-	-	-	-	-	K	K	K	K	K	K	K	K	K	K	K	K	K	K	K	-	-	-	N	-	-	-	-	-	K	K	K	K	-	-	-	20	6	24
P (Paul) Ringer W+	F	F	F	F	H	F	F	F	-	-	-	-	F	-	-	-	-	-	F	<H	-	-	-	-	-	-	-	-	-	-	-	-	-	-	-	-	-	-	-	-	11	1	4
T (Tim) Ringer	-	-	M	M	L	<L	-	-	-	-	-	-	-	-	-	-	-	-	-	-	-	-	-	-	-	-	-	-	-	-	-	-	-	-	-	-	-	-	-	-	4	-	-
RE (Bob) Rowell E2	D	D	E	D	E	D	D	D	D	E	E	D	E	E	E	E	E	E	E	D	E	E	D	D	E	E	E	D	-	E	E	E	D	D	-	D	D	E	■E	E	38	-	-
SJ (Steve) Solomons	-	-	-	-	-	-	-	-	-	-	-	-	-	-	-	-	-	-	-	-	-	-	-	-	O	-	-	-	-	O	-	-	-	-	-	-	-	-	-	-	2	-	-
CWJ (Charlie) Tassell	-	-	-	-	-	-	-	-	-	-	-	-	-	-	-	-	-	-	-	-	-	-	-	-	-	-	-	=C	-	-	-	-	-	-	-	-	-	-	-	-	1	-	-
M (Mike) Thomas	L	L	L	L	<M	-	-	-	-	-	-	-	-	-	-	-	-	-	-	-	-	-	-	-	-	-	-	-	-	-	-	-	-	-	-	-	-	-	-	-	5	-	-
TA (Tim) Walley	-	-	-	-	-	-	-	-	-	-	-	-	-	-	-	-	-	-	-	-	I	-	-	-	-	-	-	-	-	-	-	-	-	-	-	-	-	-	-	-	1	-	-
RJ (Bob) Watson	E	E	D	E	D	-	E	-	-	-	-	-	-	-	-	-	-	-	-	-	-	-	E	-	D	-	-	E	E	-	-	-	-	-	-	-	-	-	-	-	10	3	12
PJ (Peter) Wheeler E2 L+	B*	B*	B*	B*	B*	B*	B*	B*	B*	B*	B*	B*	B*	B*	B*	-	B*	-	-	B*	B*	-	B*	B*	-	B*	B*	-	-	-	-	-	-	-	-	-	B*	B*	B*	B*	26	4	156
JR (John) White	-	-	-	-	-	-	-	-	-	-	-	-	-	-	-	-	-	-	-	-	-	-	-	-	-	-	-	>B	-	-	-	B	-	-	-	-	-	-	-	-	2	-	-
GG (Graham) Willars	-	-	-	-	-	-	-	-	H	F	H	H	-	F	F	F	-	G	G	G	H	-	-	-	-	-	-	-	-	-	-	-	-	-	-	-	-	-	-	-	11	2	8

The key for how to read the stats is on the last page

19 75/76	Home Ground: Welford Road	Trophy Cabinet: Midland Cup	OVERALL RECORD:					T	C	PG	DG	PTS
	Coach: Chalkie White		PLD	W	D	L	Tigers scored:	107	51	70	6	758
	Captain: Robin Money		45	23	1	21	Opponents scored:	101	46	73	6	733

GM	DATE		VEN	OPPONENTS	RESULT	TRIES	KICKS	ATT
RFU CLUB COMPETITION (JOHN PLAYER CUP)						**CUP WINNERS: GOSFORTH**		
14	Nov	22	a	Liverpool (1)	L 7-10	Barker 79	Dodge p	-
MIDLAND CUP (QUALIFICIATION FOR JOHN PLAYER CUP)								
29	Feb	**24tu**	**H**	**Nottingham (qual)**	W 31-9	Millican(2), Barker, Ray French, Kenney	Rose 4c/d	-
33	Mar	**9tu**	**H**	**Westleigh (qf)**	W 19-15	Cowling	Rose 4p/d	-
40	Apr	10	a	Kettering (sf)	W 14-6	Ray French, Reeve	Barker 2p	-
CLUB MATCHES								
1	Sep	6	a	Bedford	L 12-24	-	Flint 4p	-
2		**10w**	**H**	**Nuneaton**	W 46-3	Kempin(2), Kenney(2), Flint, Barker, Duggan, Mortimer	Flint 4c/p, Denner p	-
3		**13**	**H**	**Bath**	W 37-7	Duggan(2), Allen, Bann, Barker, Wheeler	Flint 5c/p	-
4		20	a	Mountain Ash	W 22-19	Bann, Bracewell, Dodge	Flint 2c/2p	-
5		27	a	Harlequins	L 17-45	Barker, Wheeler	Flint 3p	-
6	Oct	**4**	**H**	**Coventry**	L 18-31	Barker, Hall	Flint 2p, Dodge 2c	-
7		11	a	Richmond	L 14-20	Duggan, Wheeler	Flint 2p	-
8		18	a	Northampton	L 12-28	Wheeler	Flint c/2p	-
9		22w	a	Oxford University	L 17-39	Barker, Mortimer, Walley	Flint c/p	-
10		**25**	**H**	**Swansea**	L 6-25	-	Dodge 2p	-
11	Nov	**1**	**H**	**Gloucester**	L 12-22	Hall	Barker c/p, Dodge p	-
12		8	a	Cambridge University	L 3-28	-	Dodge p	-
13		**15**	**H**	**Eastern Suburbs**	W 22-15	Barker, Hall, Marshall	Barker 2c/2p	-
		22	a	Moseley	PP (cup)			
15		**29**	**H**	**Saracens**	W 40-4	Barker(3), Dodge, Duggan, Forfar, B.Jones	Barker 4c, Dodge 2c	-
16	Dec	6	a	Waterloo	L 7-13	Duggan	Barker p	-
17		**10w**	**H**	**Nottingham**	W 10-6	Dodge	Dodge p, Barker p	-
18		13	a	Blackheath	W 13-8	Duggan, Kenney	Hall d, Barker c	-
19		**20**	**H**	**Bristol**	W 17-16	Dodge, Duggan	Rose 3p	-
20		**27**	**H**	**Barbarians**	L 11-20	Dodge, Rowell	Rose p	15000
21	Jan	2f	a	Bath	W 12-3	Dodge, Forfar	Denner 2c	-
22		10	a	Gloucester	W 9-4	Joyce	Denner c/p	-
23		**16f**	**H**	**Bedford**	W 28-18	Dodge, Duggan, Kempin	Rose 2c/4p	-
24		24	a	Rosslyn Park	L 7-26	Barker	Barker p	-
		31	a	London Welsh	PP			
	Feb	**4w**	**H**	**Royal Navy**	PP			
25		**7**	**H**	**London Scottish**	W 23-4	Duggan(2), Joyce, Wheeler	Barker 2c/p	-
26		14	a	Newport	L 16-38	Kempin, Rowell	Barker c/2p	-
27		**18w**	**H**	**Headingley**	W 24-6	Dodge(2), Barker	Barker 3c/2p	-
28		21	a	Wasps	D 10-10	Marshall	Barker 2p	-
30		**28**	**H**	**Northampton**	W 24-12	Rose, Duggan, Kenney	Rose 3p, Barker d	-
31	Mar	**2tu**	**H**	**Moseley**	L 7-13	White	Barker p	-
32		**5f**	**H**	**Harlequins**	L 6-28	Collington	Barker c	-
34		13	a	Coventry	L 4-22	Barker	-	-
35		**16tu**	**H**	**Royal Air Force**	W 29-7	Barker(2), Collington, Hall, Millican, White	Barker c, Rose p	-
36		20	a	C.A.S.G. Paris	W 20-8	Holley, Reeve, Willars	Money 2d, B.Jones c	-
		23tu	**H**	**Loughborough Colleges**	PP			
37		**27**	**H**	**Sale**	L 16-18	Reeve(2), Barker, Kempin	-	189
38		30tu	a	Burton President's XV	W 30-15	Barker(2), Collington, Millican, Reeve	Barker 2c/2p	-
39	Apr	**3**	**H**	**Birkenhead Park**	W 18-14	Barker, Hall	Barker 2c/2p	114
		10	a	Bristol	PP (cup)			
41		17	a	Middlesbrough	L 9-19	Dodge	Dodge c/p	-
42		19m	a	Gosforth	L 9-27	Barker	Barker p, Dodge c	-
43		20tu	a	Harrogate	W 17-3	Duggan, Roy French, Walley	Barker c/p	-
44		**24**	**H**	**Fylde**	W 22-13	Bracewell, Kempin	Dodge 3p, Barker c/p	113
45	May	1	a	Rugby	L 11-12	Adey, Hall	Barker p	-

Note: *The final of the Midland Cup was played on 1.9.1976*

INDIVIDUAL APPEARANCES 1975/76

Name / Game #	1	2	3	4	5	6	7	8	9	10	11	12	13	14	15	16	17	18	19	20	21	22	23	24	25	26	27	28	29	30	31	32	33	34	35	36	37	38	39	40	41	42	43	44	45	Apps	T	Pts
GJ (Garry) Adey E2	G	G	G	-	G	G	G	-	-	E	G	G	G	G	G	-	-	-	-	G	G	G	G	G	G	G	G	G	G	G	-	-	G	G	-	-	-	-	-	G	-	-	-	G	G	28	1	4
JA (John) Allen	I	-	<I	-	-	-	-	-	-	-	-	-	-	-	-	-	-	-	-	-	-	-	-	-	-	-	-	-	-	-	-	-	-	-	-	-	-	-	-	-	-	-	-	-	-	1+1	1	4
EE (Eric) Bann	D	-	D	D	D	D	D	-	-	D	<D	-	-	-	-	-	-	-	-	-	-	-	-	-	-	-	-	-	-	-	-	-	-	-	-	-	-	-	-	-	-	-	-	-	-	8	2	8
RG (Bob) Barker	-	K	K	N	K	K	K	K	K	-	K	K	K	K	K	K	K	K	-	K	K	K	K	K	K	K	K	K	K	K	K	K	K	K*	K*	-	K	K	K	K	K	K	K	K	K	41	21	203
AC (Andy) Beevers	-	-	-	-	-	-	-	-	-	-	-	-	-	-	-	-	-	-	-	-	-	-	-	-	-	-	-	-	-	-	-	-	-	-	>E	E	-	-	G	-	-	-	E	-	-	4	-	-
KH (Ken) Bracewell	-	M	M	M	M	-	-	-	N	K	-	-	-	-	-	-	-	-	-	-	-	-	-	-	L	-	-	-	-	M	M	M	-	L	-	-	-	-	-	-	-	-	-	<L	-	12	2	8
AP (Angus) Collington	-	-	-	G	-	-	-	G	G	G	-	-	-	-	-	-	-	-	-	-	-	-	-	-	-	-	-	-	-	-	G	G	-	-	G	G	G	G	-	-	-	G	G	-	-	12	3	12
RJ (Robin) Cowling E+	A	A	A	A	A	-	-	-	-	-	-	-	-	-	-	-	A	A	A	A	A	A	A	A	A	A	A	A	A	A	A	A	A	A	A	-	A	A	A	A	-	-	-	-	-	28	1	4
JD (Jeff) Denner	-	>0	-	-	-	-	-	-	-	-	-	-	-	-	-	-	-	-	-	-	0	<0	-	-	-	-	-	-	-	-	-	-	-	-	-	-	-	-	-	-	-	-	-	-	-	3	-	12
PW (Paul) Dodge E+ L+	>L	L	L	L	L	L	L	L	L	L	L	L	L	L	L	L	L	L	L	L	L	L	L	L	-	-	L	L	L	-	-	-	L	-	-	-	-	-	L	L	L	L	L	J	L	35	10	82
MJ (John) Duggan	N	N	N	-	N	N	N	N	-	N	N	-	N	N	N	N	N	N	N	N	N	N	N	N	N	N	N	N	N	N	-	N	N	-	-	-	-	-	-	-	-	-	N	N	N	32	13	52
J (John) Flint	>J	J	J	J	J	J	J	J	<J	-	-	-	-	-	-	-	-	-	-	-	-	-	-	-	-	-	-	-	-	-	-	-	-	-	-	-	-	-	-	-	-	-	-	-	-	9	1	84
DJ (Dave) Forfar	-	-	-	-	-	-	-	F	H	F	F	F	H	F	F	H	G	G	G	F	H	-	F	F	H	H	-	-	-	-	-	-	-	-	-	-	-	-	-	-	-	-	-	-	-	18	2	8
RW (Ray) French	-	-	-	-	-	-	-	-	-	-	-	-	-	-	-	-	-	-	C	C	C	C	C	C	C	C	C	-	C	C	C	C	C	C	C	C	C	C	C	C	C	C	C	C	C	26	2	8
RS (Roy) French	-	-	-	B	-	-	-	-	-	-	-	-	-	-	-	B	B	B	B	-	B	B	B	B	-	-	-	-	-	-	-	-	-	-	-	-	-	-	-	-	-	B	B	B	B	13	1	4
AF (Alistair) Grocock	-	-	-	-	-	-	-	-	-	-	>C	C	C	-	-	-	-	-	-	-	-	-	-	-	-	-	-	-	-	-	-	-	-	-	-	-	-	-	-	-	-	-	-	-	-	3	-	-
BP (Brian) Hall	M	-	-	-	-	M	M	M	-	M	M	M	M	M	M	M	M	M	M	M	-	-	-	-	-	L	-	-	-	-	-	-	-	-	L	-	L	L	M	M	M	M	M	M	M	26	6	27
C (Chris) Hemsley	-	-	-	-	-	-	-	-	-	-	-	-	-	-	-	-	-	-	-	-	-	-	-	-	-	-	-	-	-	-	>N	-	-	-	N	<K	-	-	-	-	-	-	-	-	-	3	-	-
ER (Ted) Holley	-	-	-	-	-	-	-	-	-	-	-	-	-	-	-	-	-	-	-	-	M	M	M	M	M	M	M	M	M	L	L	L	M	M	M	M	M	M	-	-	-	-	-	-	-	18	1	4
B (Bleddyn) Jones	-	-	-	-	-	-	-	-	M	J	J	J	J	J	J	J	J	J	J	J	J	J	J	J	J	J	J	J	J	J	J	J	J	J	J	J	J	J	J	J	J	J	J	-	J	36	1	6
F (Frank) Jones	-	H	-	-	-	F	<F	-	-	-	-	-	-	-	-	-	-	-	-	-	-	-	-	-	-	-	-	-	-	-	-	-	-	-	-	-	-	-	-	-	-	-	-	-	-	3	-	-
NJ (Nick) Joyce	E	E	E	E	-	-	-	-	D	-	E	E	D	E	E	E	E	E	D	D	E	D	D	D	D	D	-	-	E	E	E	E	-	D	D	D	D	E	D	D	D	D	-	E	D	36	2	8
JS (Jim) Kempin	F	F	F	F	F	-	-	-	-	-	-	-	-	-	-	F	H	H	H	H	F	F	H	H	F	F	F	F	F	F	F	F	F	-	-	H	F	F	F	F	F	F	F	F	F	33	6	24
S (Steve) Kenney	-	>I	-	I	I	-	-	-	-	-	-	-	-	-	-	-	I	I	I	I	I	I	I	I	I	I	I	I	I	I	I	I	I	-	I	I	I	-	-	-	I	-	-	-	-	24	5	20
J (Jez) Krych	-	-	-	-	-	-	-	-	-	-	-	-	-	-	-	-	-	-	-	-	-	-	-	-	-	-	-	C	-	-	-	-	-	-	-	A	-	-	-	-	A	A	A	A	A	7	-	-
D (Dave) Macey	-	-	-	-	-	-	-	-	-	-	-	-	-	-	-	-	-	-	-	-	-	-	-	-	-	-	>E	E	-	-	-	-	-	<E	-	-	-	-	-	-	-	-	-	-	-	3	-	-
M (Mike) Marshall	-	-	-	-	-	H	H	H	F	H	H	H	F	H	H	G	F	F	F	-	-	H	-	-	-	-	-	H	-	-	-	-	-	F	-	-	-	-	-	-	-	-	-	-	-	17	2	8
JG (Jock) Millican S3	H	-	H	H	H	-	-	-	-	-	-	-	-	-	-	-	-	-	-	-	-	-	-	-	-	-	H	-	H	H	H	H	H	H	H	-	H	H	H	H	H	H	H	H	H	21	4	16
RS (Robin) Money	0*	-	0*	0*	0*	0*	0*	0*	0*	0*	0*	0*	0*	0*	0*	0*	0*	0*	-	-	-	-	-	0*	0*	0*	0*	0*	-	-	-	-	-	-	-	0*	0*	0*	0*	0*	0*	0*	0*	0*	0*	32	-	6
MR (Mike) Mortimer	C	C	C	C	C	C	C	C	C	C	A	A	A	C	C	C	C	<C	-	-	-	-	-	-	-	-	-	-	-	-	-	-	-	-	-	-	-	-	-	-	-	-	-	-	-	18	2	8
RE (Ray) Needham	-	-	-	-	-	-	-	-	A	A	-	-	-	-	-	-	-	-	-	-	-	-	-	-	-	-	-	-	-	-	-	-	-	-	-	-	-	-	-	-	-	-	-	-	-	2	-	-
AB (Andy) Northen	-	D	-	-	-	-	-	-	-	-	-	-	-	-	-	-	-	-	-	-	-	-	-	-	-	-	-	-	-	-	-	-	<E	-	-	-	-	-	-	-	-	-	-	-	-	2	-	-
L (Larry) Parkes	-	-	-	-	-	-	-	-	-	-	-	-	-	-	-	-	-	-	-	-	-	-	-	-	-	-	-	-	-	-	-	-	-	-	-	>L	-	-	-	-	-	-	-	-	-	1	-	-
J (John) Reeve	K	-	-	K	-	-	-	-	-	-	-	N	-	-	-	-	-	-	K	-	-	-	-	-	-	-	-	-	-	-	-	-	-	N	-	N	N	N	N	N	N	N	-	-	-	12	5	20
WMH (Marcus) Rose E+	-	-	-	-	-	-	-	-	-	-	-	-	-	-	-	-	-	-	>0	0	-	-	0	-	-	-	-	-	0	0	-	-	0	-	0	-	-	-	-	-	-	-	-	-	-	7	1	70
RE (Bob) Rowell E2	-	-	-	-	E	E	E	D	E	-	-	D	E	D	D	D	D	D	E*	E*	D*	E*	E*	E	E	E	D	D	D*	D*	D*	D*	D*	-	-	-	E	D	E	E	E	E	D	D	E	36	2	8
SJ (Steve) Solomons	-	-	-	-	-	-	-	-	-	-	-	-	-	-	-	-	-	-	-	-	-	-	-	-	-	-	-	-	-	-	0	0	-	0	-	-	-	-	-	-	-	-	-	-	-	3	-	-
PN (Phil) Vesty	-	-	-	-	-	A	A	A	-	-	-	-	-	A	A	<A	-	-	-	-	-	-	-	-	-	-	-	-	-	-	-	-	-	-	-	-	-	-	-	-	-	-	-	-	-	6	-	-
TA (Tim) Walley	-	-	-	-	-	I	I	I	I	I	I	I	I	I	I	I	-	-	-	-	-	-	-	-	-	-	-	-	-	-	-	-	-	I	-	-	-	I	I	I	-	I	I	I	I	19	2	8
RJ (Bob) Watson	-	-	-	-	-	-	-	<E	-	-	-	-	-	-	-	-	-	-	-	-	-	-	-	-	-	-	-	-	-	-	-	-	-	-	-	-	-	-	-	-	-	-	-	-	-	1	-	-
PJ (Peter) Wheeler E6 L+	B	B*	B	-	B	B	B	B	-	B	B	B	B	B	B	-	-	-	-	B	-	-	-	-	B	B	-	-	B	B	-	-	B	-	-	-	-	-	-	-	-	-	-	-	-	19	5	20
JR (John) White	-	-	-	-	-	-	-	-	B	-	-	-	-	-	-	-	-	-	-	-	-	-	-	-	-	-	B	B	-	-	B	B	-	B	B	B	B	B	B	B	B	-	-	-	-	13	2	8
GG (Graham) Willars	-	-	-	-	-	-	-	-	-	-	-	-	-	-	-	-	-	-	-	-	-	-	-	-	-	-	-	-	-	-	-	-	-	-	F	F	-	-	-	-	G	-	-	-	-	3	1	4

The key for how to read the stats is on the last page

19	76/77	Home Ground: Welford Road except #8 at Welford Road Rec
		Coach: Chalkie White
		Captain: Bob Rowell

OVERALL RECORD:					T	C	PG	DG	PTS
PLD	W	D	L	Tigers scored:	105	64	67	1	752
39	26	0	13	Opponents scored:	55	24	46	6	424

GM	DATE		VEN	OPPONENTS	RESULT	TRIES	KICKS	ATT
RFU CLUB COMPETITION (JOHN PLAYER CUP)						**CUP WINNERS: GOSFORTH**		
	Dec	4	a	Wakefield (1)	PP (snow)			
		11	a	Wakefield (1)	PP (frost)			
23	Jan	22	a	Wakefield (1)	W 17-6	Dodge 25, Duggan 32, Rowell 77	Dodge c, Hare p	-
26	Feb	12	a	Moseley (2)	L 9-23	-	Hare 3p	-
MIDLAND MERIT TABLE (2ND)						**WINNERS: MOSELEY**		
2	Sep	**4**	**H**	**Bedford**	W 34-13	Hall, Joyce, Kempin, Kenney, Rowell	Rose 4c/2p	535
5		**21tu**	**H**	**Birmingham**	W 37-15	Barker, Duggan, Joyce, Kenney, Wheeler	Rose 4c/3p	368
7	Oct	2	a	Coventry	L 15-18	Rose, Jones	Rose 2c/p	-
9		**16**	**H**	**Northampton**	W 40-13	Wheeler(2), Barker, Duggan, Ray French, Kenney, Parkes	Barker 3c/2p	819
12		30	a	Nottingham	W 19-6	Barker, Wheeler	Hare c/3p	-
16	Nov	**27**	**H**	**Moseley**	L 6-19	-	Hare 2p	1178
30	Mar	2w	a	Nuneaton	W 32-6	Hare, Duggan, Hall, Kenney, Redfern	Hare 3c/2p	-
36	Apr	**9**	**H**	**Rugby**	W 31-9	Duggan(2), Money(2), Adey	Dodge 4c/p	429
CLUB MATCHES								
1	Sep	**1w**	**H**	**Solihull (f)**	W 39-0	Hall(2), Barker, Dodge, Kempin, Reeve, Wheeler	Rose 4c/p	373
		8w	a	Saracens	PP (hard ground)			
3		11	a	Bath	L 10-19	Ray French, Kempin	Rose c	-
4		**18**	**H**	**Mountain Ash**	W 45-3	Barker(3), Rose(2), Adey(2), Reeve	Rose 5c/p	507
6		25	a	Harlequins	W 23-4	Kenney(2), Dodge	Rose c/3p	-
8	Oct	**9**	**H**	**Richmond**	W 24-12	Holley, Kenney	Barker 2c/4p	-
10		**20w**	**H**	**Oxford University**	W 46-8	Kenney(2), Barker, Beevers, Cowling, Dodge	Hare 5c/4p	598
11		23	a	Swansea	W 15-9	Forfar	Hare c/3p	-
13	Nov	6	a	Gloucester	L 12-14	Duggan	Hare c/2p	-
14		**13**	**H**	**Cambridge University**	W 33-6	Hare, Barker, Duggan, Kenney	Hare 4c/2p/d	1035
15		20	a	Wasps	W 7-0	Duggan	Hare p	-
	Dec	**4**	**H**	**Waterloo**	PP (cup)			
		11	**H**	**Blackheath**	PP (cup)			
17		**18**	**H**	**Bristol**	W 7-3	Dodge	Rose p	359
18		**28tu**	**H**	**Barbarians**	W 12-8	Dodge	Hare c/2p	21000
19	Jan	**1**	**H**	**Bath**	W 20-4	Dodge, Duggan, Hall, Kenney	Rose 2c	448
20		**8**	**H**	**Gloucester**	L 10-25	Hall, White	Hare c	646
21		14f	a	Bedford	L 0-18	-	-	-
22		**19w**	**H**	**Royal Navy**	W 25-6	Hall(2), Adey, Duggan	Hare 3c/p	317
		22	**H**	**Rosslyn Park**	PP (cup)			
24		**29**	**H**	**London Welsh**	W 19-10	Newton, Wheeler	Dodge c/3p	1689
25	Feb	5	a	London Scottish	L 0-15	-	-	-
		12	**H**	**Newport**	PP (cup)			
27		16w	a	Headingley	W 16-12	Hare, Duggan	Hare c/2p	-
28		**18f**	**H**	**C.A.S.G. Paris**	W 28-4 (Abandoned 69')	Duggan(2), White(2), Burwell, Parkes	Dodge 2c	411
29		26	a	Northampton	W 23-3	Duggan, Joyce, Kempin, Kenney	Hare 2c/p	-
31	Mar	**5**	**H**	**Harlequins**	L 16-27	Burwell, Ray French	Hare c/2p	416
32		**12**	**H**	**Coventry**	W 24-10	Dodge	Hare c/6p	957
33		**18f**	**H**	**Loughborough Colleges**	W 14-3	Burwell, Dodge	Hare 2p	450
34		26	a	Sale	W 23-14	Duggan(2), Hare, Forfar	Hare 2c/p	-
35	Apr	2	a	Birkenhead Park	L 3-9	-	Hare p	-
37		**11m**	**H**	**Gosforth**	L 6-18	-	Dodge 2p	839
38		16	a	Bristol	L 9-16	Reeve	Holley c/p	-
39		23	a	Moseley	L 3-16	-	Hare p	-
		30	**H**	**Middlesbrough**	PP (Sevens)			

Note: *#1 1975/76 Midland Cup final*

INDIVIDUAL APPEARANCES 1976/77

Name / Game #	1	2	3	4	5	6	7	8	9	10	11	12	13	14	15	16	17	18	19	20	21	22	23	24	25	26	27	28	29	30	31	32	33	34	35	36	37	38	39	Apps	T	Pts
GJ (Garry) Adey E2	G	G	G	G	G	G	G	-	G	G	G	G	G	G	G	G	-	G	-	-	G	G	G	G	G	G	G	G	G	G	G	G	G	G	G	G	G	G	G	35	4	16
RG (Bob) Barker	K	K	L	K	K	K	K	K	K	K	K	K	K	K	K	K	-	K	K	K	K	K	K	-	-	-	-	-	-	-	-	-	-	-	-	-	-	-	-	22	9	64
AC (Andy) Beevers	-	-	-	-	-	-	-	-	-	E	E	<E	-	-	-	-	-	-	-	-	-	-	-	-	-	-	-	-	-	-	-	-	-	-	-	-	-	-	-	3	1	4
TR (Terry) Burwell	-	-	-	-	-	-	-	-	-	-	-	-	-	-	-	-	-	-	-	-	-	-	r	-	-	-	L	K	K	K	K	K	K	K	K	K	K	K	-	12+1	3	12
AP (Angus) Collington	-	-	x	-	-	-	-	G	-	-	-	-	-	r	-	-	G	-	G	G	r	-	-	-	-	-	-	-	-	-	-	-	-	-	-	-	-	r	-	4+3	-	-
RJ (Robin) Cowling E4	A	A	A	A	A	A	A	A	A	A	A	A	A	A	A	A	-	A	-	-	-	A	A	A	-	A	-	-	A	-	-	A	A	A	-	-	-	A	A	27	1	4
PW (Paul) Dodge E+ L+	M	M	M	M	M	M	M	-	-	M	M	M	M	M	M	M	M	M	M	M	M	M	M	M	M	M	-	M	M	M	M	M	M	-	M	M	M	-	M	34	9	70
MJ (John) Duggan	-	-	-	-	N	N	N	N	N	N	N	-	N	N	N	N	N	N	N	N	N	N	N	N	N	N	N	N	N	N	N	N	N	N	N	N	-	-	N	32	17	68
DJ (Dave) Forfar	H	H	H	F	H	H	H	-	H	H	H	H	H	H	H	H	-	H	-	H	H	H	H	H	H	H	H	H	H	H	H	H	H	H	H	H	H	H	H	36	2	8
RW (Ray) French	C	C	C	C	C	C	C	C	C	C	C	-	-	-	-	-	-	-	-	-	-	-	-	-	-	-	-	-	-	A	A	-	-	C	A	-	-	-	C	16	3	12
RS (Roy) French	-	B	-	-	-	B	-	<B	-	-	-	-	-	-	-	-	-	-	-	-	-	-	-	-	-	-	-	-	-	-	-	-	-	-	-	-	-	-	-	3	-	-
AF (Alistair) Grocock	-	-	-	-	-	-	-	-	-	-	-	-	-	-	-	-	C	-	C	C	-	-	-	-	-	-	-	-	-	-	-	-	-	-	-	A	A	C	-	6	-	-
BP (Brian) Hall	L	L	L	N	L	L	L	L	L	L	L	L	L	L	L	L	L	L	L	L	L	L	L	L	L	-	-	-	L	L	L	-	-	-	-	L	L	L	L	32	8	32
WH (Dusty) Hare E1	-	-	-	-	-	-	-	-	-	>0	0	0	0	0	0	0	-	0	-	0	0	0	0	-	0	0	0	-	0	0	0	0	0	0	0	-	-	-	0	23	4	199
AG (Arthur) Hazlerigg	-	-	-	-	-	-	-	-	-	-	-	-	-	-	-	-	-	-	-	-	-	-	-	-	-	-	>E	E	-	-	-	-	-	-	-	D	D	E	-	5	-	-
ER (Ted) Holley	x	-	-	-	-	-	-	M	-	-	-	-	-	-	-	-	-	-	-	-	-	-	-	-	-	-	-	-	-	-	-	-	-	L	-	-	-	<M	-	3	1	9
SR (Steve) Johnson	x	-	-	-	-	-	>D	-	-	-	-	-	E	-	-	-	H	-	H	-	-	-	-	-	-	-	-	-	-	-	x	-	-	-	-	F	F	F	F	8	-	-
B (Bleddyn) Jones	J	J	J	J	J	J	J	J	J	J	J	J	J	J	J	J	J	J	J	J	J	J	J	J	J	L	-	J	J	J	J	J	J	J	J	J	J	J	J	38	1	4
NJ (Nick) Joyce	E	E	E	D	D	E	-	D	E	-	-	-	-	E	D	E	E	E	E	E	E	E	E	E	E	D	-	-	E	E	E	E	E	E	E	E	E	D	E	32	3	12
JS (Jim) Kempin	F	F	F	H	F	F	F	F	F	F	F	F	F	F	F	F	F	F	F	F	F	F	F	F	F	F	F	F	F	F	F	F	F	F	F	-	x	-	-	35	4	16
S (Steve) Kenney	I	I	I	I	I	I	I	I	I	I	I	I	I	I	I	I	I	I	I	I	I	I	I	I	I	I	-	I	I	I	I	I	I	I	I	I	I	-	I	37	12	48
J (Jez) Krych	-	-	-	-	-	-	-	-	-	-	-	-	-	-	-	C	A	C	A	A	A	-	-	-	-	-	-	-	-	-	-	-	-	-	-	-	-	-	-	6	-	-
RDJ (Rod) McMichael	-	-	-	-	-	-	-	-	-	-	-	-	-	-	-	-	-	-	-	-	-	-	-	-	-	>J	J	-	-	-	-	-	-	-	-	-	-	-	-	2	-	-
M (Mike) Marshall	-	x	-	-	-	-	-	-	-	-	-	-	-	-	-	-	-	-	-	-	-	-	-	-	-	-	-	-	-	-	-	-	-	-	<r	-	-	-	-	0+1	-	-
JG (Jock) Millican S3	-	-	-	-	x	-	-	<H	-	-	-	-	-	-	-	-	-	-	-	-	-	-	-	-	-	-	-	-	-	-	-	-	-	-	-	-	-	-	-	1	-	-
RS (Robin) Money	-	-	-	-	-	-	-	0	0	-	-	-	-	-	-	-	-	-	-	-	-	-	r	0	-	-	-	-	0	-	-	-	-	-	-	0	0	0	-	7+1	2	8
RE (Ray) Needham	-	-	-	-	-	-	-	-	-	-	-	-	-	-	-	-	-	-	-	-	-	-	-	-	A	-	A	A	-	-	-	-	-	-	-	-	-	-	-	3	-	-
MJ (Mick) Newton	-	-	-	-	-	-	-	-	-	-	-	-	-	-	-	-	>K	-	-	-	-	-	-	K	K	-	-	-	-	-	-	-	-	-	-	-	-	-	-	3	1	4
L (Larry) Parkes	-	-	-	-	-	-	-	-	M	-	-	-	-	-	-	-	-	-	-	-	-	-	-	-	-	-	M	L	-	-	-	L	L	M	L	-	-	-	-	7	2	8
JB (John) Rawes	-	-	-	-	-	-	-	-	-	-	-	-	-	-	-	-	-	-	-	-	-	-	-	-	-	-	-	-	-	-	-	-	-	-	=B	-	-	-	-	1	-	-
SP (Steve) Redfern E+	-	-	-	-	-	-	-	-	-	-	-	>C	C	C	C	-	-	-	-	-	C	C	C	■C	C	C	C	C	C	C	C	C	C	-	C	C	C	-	-	20	1	4
J (John) Reeve	N	N	N	N	-	-	-	-	-	-	-	N	-	-	-	-	-	-	-	-	-	-	-	-	-	K	K	x	-	-	-	-	-	-	-	N	N	<K	-	10	3	12
WMH (Marcus) Rose E+	0	0	0	0	0	0	0	-	-	-	-	-	-	-	-	-	0	-	0	-	-	-	-	-	-	-	-	-	-	-	-	-	-	-	-	-	-	-	-	9	3	94
RE (Bob) Rowell E2	D*	D*	D*	E*	E*	D*	E*	E*	D*	D*	D*	D*	D*	D*	E*	D*	D*	D*	D*	D*	D*	D*	D*	D*	D*	E*	D*	D*	D*	D*	D*	D*	D*	D*	D*	-	-	-	D*	36	2	8
TA (Tim) Walley	-	-	-	-	-	-	-	-	-	-	-	-	-	-	-	-	-	-	-	-	-	-	-	-	-	-	I	-	-	-	-	-	-	-	-	-	-	I	-	2	-	-
D (Dave) Webb	-	-	-	-	-	-	-	-	-	-	-	-	-	-	-	-	-	-	-	-	-	-	-	-	-	-	-	-	-	-	-	-	-	-	-	-	-	=B	-	1	-	-
PJ (Peter) Wheeler E10 L+	B	-	B	B	B	-	B	-	B	B	B	B	B	B	-	B	-	B	-	-	-	-	-	B	-	B	-	-	B	-	-	B	-	-	-	-	-	-	-	17	6	24
JR (John) White	-	-	-	-	-	-	-	-	-	-	-	-	-	-	B	-	B	-	B	B	B	B	B	-	B	-	B	B	-	B	B	-	B	B	-	B	B	-	B	17	3	12
GG (Graham) Willars	-	-	-	-	-	-	-	-	r	-	-	-	-	-	-	-	-	-	-	-	-	-	-	-	-	-	-	x	-	-	-	-	-	-	-	-	-	-	-	0+1	-	-

The key for how to read the stats is on the last page

CHAPTER 19

The Coming of the Cup

1977/1978

Peter Wheeler returned from his Lions tour to a well-earned rest from rugby as Brian Hall took up the captaincy from the now retired Rowell. Not for the first time, the season opened with defeat at Bedford but the next four years were to see the establishment of a side whose success was unparalleled in the club's history. The 1977/78 season saw Leicester to the John Player Cup final, and the following three seasons they won the trophy to confirm their standing as the leading club side in England.

Bob Barker on the way to 1,000 career points scored two tries in this game against Liverpool, 17.9.1977.

The new season opened with a new scoreboard at the Welford Road end - the gift of the Loughborough building materials firm run by the Adey family - and a new wing, 'Tim' Barnwell, who had made a reputation for himself with Coventry as a consistent try-scorer. But it was an old wing, Barker, who sealed a niche for himself in the club's history when he reached 1,000 points with the first of two tries in a 23-17 win over Harlequins. He was followed into the record books by Duggan on the opposite wing, who passed 500 points against Sale and all of them scored in tries.

A notable recruit from the youth team was the former Wyggeston schoolboy, Ian Smith, a flanker who made his senior debut when he was still 19. 'Dosser' Smith, like his predecessors, Matthews and Willars, was to become captain and later coach to the club. With more than 500 points overall going into December, the season looked like being a memorable one. Eight Leicester players were chosen for the Midlands East XV in the inter-divisional tournament, then in its inaugural year: Hare, Dodge, Barker, Hall, Cowling, Smith, Kempin and Adey, with Hall captaining the side. Barnwell, still qualified for Warwickshire, played for Midlands West, who won a dreary game 12-6 at Coventry.

The match that never was! Tigers played away to Oxford University on 19 October 1977, however Llanelli would have you believe that Leicester played at Stradey Park that night. All the way through the programme, including the cover, it should have read Leinster.

The Leicester ground record eventually succumbed to the Barbarians before a crowd numbered at 19,000 but three players were chosen for England against France: Wheeler, Cowling and Hare, who had waited four years for his second cap. Although England lost 15-6 in Paris, the game was notable for a display of exceptional courage by Cowling, who dislocated a shoulder in the second half after tearing a shoulder muscle in the first half. With both England replacements used up after injuries to Andy Maxwell and Peter Dixon (only two were allowed in those days), Cowling stayed on the field when every scrum was agony for him. It was the end of his season.

There was some solace when Dodge who, with Hare, had played in an England XV against the USA the previous October, was picked for his first cap against Wales. He joined Wheeler (Hare had been dropped) in the side beaten 9-6 at a muddy, wet Twickenham. It was the first time since the early 1930s that four Leicester players had appeared for England during the same season.

At the same time the John Player Cup run began. For the first time since the competition's inception, Leicester were drawn at home, as they were throughout the tournament until the final. Three penalties by Hare saw them through round one, 9-3 against Hartlepool Rovers. Round two saw Rosslyn Park beaten 25-16 thanks to tries by Barker, Kenney and Forfar, Hare converting twice and kicking three penalties. The quarter-final round brought a 20-11 win over Northampton, Joyce and Duggan scoring tries while Hare and Dodge shared four penalties.

During the game, however, Hall broke two ribs and was missing when Leicester beat Coventry 25-16 in the semi-final. Dodge scored the try that finally ensured victory and allowed Leicester a chuckle at the thought that now the BBC would have to televise them - something the corporation was alleged not to enjoy because Leicester's lettering made identification more difficult for commentators. Jones scored Leicester's other try, Hare kicked three penalties, a conversion and a dropped goal, and a newcomer from Sheffield, Bill Reichwald, playing instead of Hall, dropped a goal.

The final, at Twickenham on 15 April, was against Gloucester, winners of the first knockout competition. It was touch and go whether Hall would lead the side out but, with the co-operation of Stoneygate and Oadby Wyggs, who allowed him to play in their game during the week of the final, he declared himself fit. The match, though, was something of a let-down. The attendance was 24,000, double the previous highest for a cup final, but Gloucester, with a virtual monopoly of possession, closed the game down. The result perhaps justified their decision, since they won 6-3 (a try by Richard Mogg, converted by Peter Butler, against a penalty by Hare). But the feeling remained that they could have won by considerably more had they not kicked so much ball away.

Leicester's team was: Dusty Hare; John Duggan, Paul Dodge, Brian Hall (captain), Bob Barker; Bleddyn Jones, Steve Kenney; Ray Needham, Peter Wheeler, Steve Redfern, Nick

↑ Robin Money's decade with the Tigers came to an end when he moved jobs.

Joyce, Arthur Hazlerigg, Steve Johnson, Garry Adey, David Forfar.

There was a moment, late in the game, when Leicester had a faint sniff of victory: they managed to work an overlap for Barker some 40 metres out but Mogg appeared from the opposite wing to close him down just as a try looked a possibility. It was to be the last chance of cup glory for the likes of Jones, Hall and Barker; the following season Jones retired, after 333 games, easily the most by a fly-half for the club, while Hall and Barker found younger players jostling them for positions. Steve Kenney declared, in the unnaturally quiet Twickenham changing room after the final: "We wanted to win today for the blokes who won't have another chance."

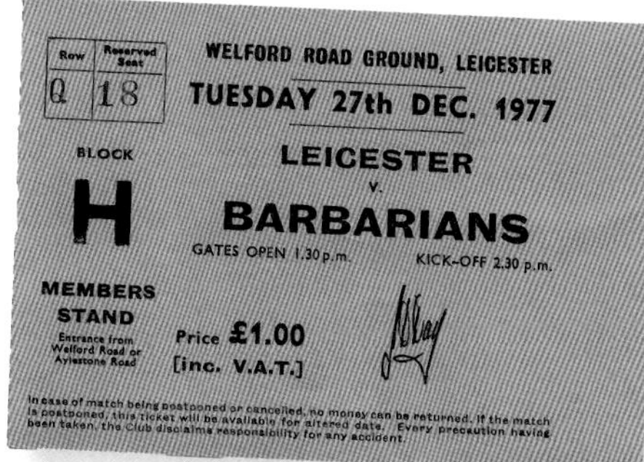

Their success in reaching the final was recognised with receptions from both the Lord Mayor of Leicester and the chairman of the county council. From a playing point of view, the form of Johnson, a recruit two seasons before from the Leicestershire Police side, and Forfar brought them selection for the first England B side, which visited Romania at the start of the close season, while Dodge, as captain, and Rose went with the under-23s to Holland. Rose had not appeared for the club since early in the season because he was a student at Durham University but he had continued to do them proud in student representative sides.

Forfar, however, who had made his first appearance for the club back in 1971 after joining from Syston and had not been far away from under-23 honours two years later, had to drop out of the B party because of a thigh injury which was to linger on and prevent him from playing at all during the 1978/79 season.

Hare ended the season with 304 points, a club record by a long way, but it was Robin Money's last season with the club after 258 appearances, since business moved the little Scot to Wilmslow. Always a popular player, one of Money's trademarks had been to head high, bouncing balls into touch on the basis that, owing to his size, it was as easy to do that as adopt a more conventional method. Rounding off the season's honours list was another colts cap, this time awarded to the young lock, Rupert Precious, who played against Wales and France.

Success in the John Player Cup, of course, meant welcome additions to the club's funds, although there was also an appeal to members to help defray the cost of re-roofing the Crumbie Stand, the work being carried out during the summer of 1978. There were also changes in hand to the main clubhouse, with a new annexe, toilets and secretarial room being built on to the ground floor, and a new President's Room upstairs. The work was completed in time for an official opening by the president of the Barbarians, Herbert Waddell, before the annual game in December that year.

1978/1979

Peter Wheeler was elected captain for the new season with the club riding the crest of a wave of popularity, reflected in the increase in membership which doubled in the space of 12 months and, at the end of 1979, was verging on 2,000, having been around 750 at the start of 1978. In the second game of the season, against Nuneaton, Dodge completed 100 games for the club while still only 20.

In the opening game the former Loughborough Colleges captain, Nigel Gillingham, had made his debut and became regularly available, save when duty for the RAF prevented it. For a player of 6ft 5in and nearly 17 stone, Gillingham was exceptionally mobile and a fine ball handler and his introduction to the second row added welcome weight and height.

The pack, even when every regular was available, was never notable for sheer physique so there was more reliance on technique, with younger players like Redfern and Smith learning from the seniors - Wheeler, Cowling and Adey.

When Jones announced his retirement, Leicester found the England B fly-half, Les Cusworth, knocking on their door. Cusworth had gained a reputation while with Wakefield as an expert at dropping goals but there was much more to his play than that. He had a creative spark which

↓ Gus Collington contesting a line-out against Cambridge University 11.11.1978.

quickly helped give the Leicester midfield more penetration, once he had decided that it was not worth continuing the battle for the number-10 shirt at Moseley with Martin Cooper. He soon settled into the Leicester side, becoming one more player to derive considerable benefit from White's coaching.

There was some consolation for the cup final defeat when Leicester came away from Kingsholm in November with a 9-7 win over Gloucester and a few days later, on 18 November, the All Blacks were at Welford Road again. Graham Mourie's side, under-rated before and after the completion of their tour despite the achievement of winning all four internationals, had a hard game against the Midlands XV which contained eight Leicester players, with three more among the replacements.

The Midlands XV was: Dusty Hare; John Duggan, Paul Dodge, Brian Hall (all Leicester), Paul Knee (Coventry); Martin Cooper, Chris Gifford (both Moseley); Robin Cowling (Leicester), Peter Wheeler (Leicester, captain), Will Dickinson (Richmond), Barry Ninnes (Coventry), Nigel Horton (Toulouse), Jon Shipsides (Coventry), Garry Adey, Ian Smith (both Leicester). Among the six replacements were Rose, Cusworth and White.

↑ The cup run begins. Tim Barnwell ploughing through the snow against Northampton 27.1.1979.

↑ Garry Adey drives over the line in the second round cup tie against Broughton Park 24.2.1979.

The tourists won 20-15, by taking the chances offered them in the way which had become their trademark. Bryan Williams, Mourie and Mark Taylor scored tries and Richard Wilson collected a penalty, a conversion and a dropped goal. Against that the Midlands put together four penalties and a dropped goal by Hare, a performance that consolidated his place in the England team the following week.

Gillingham captained the Combined Services against the New Zealanders four days later and at Twickenham the following Saturday, Hare was joined by Wheeler, Cowling and Dodge in a disappointing game which England lost 16-6, Hare dropping a goal and kicking a penalty. On the domestic side Leicester moved merrily on, not perhaps as consistent as they might have been but capable, at their best, of playing rugby unparalleled by another English club side. The Barbarians found that out on an appalling day at Welford Road when the Tigers, with Kenney in superb form, gave possibly their best display of the season to win 18-6.

The second half of the season brought the cup competition and a home draw with Northampton, who were beaten as convincingly as 29-3 might suggest. With frost and snow about there had been grave dangers of the match being postponed but members and supporters rallied round to clear snow off the pitch and Northampton duly succumbed, tries coming from Terry Burwell, Barnwell, Adey and Hare, who also converted twice and kicked two penalties. The other points came from a Burwell dropped goal. Broughton Park went much the same way in the second round, again at Welford Road, when Dodge, Adey, Cusworth and Smith scored tries and Hare kicked a conversion, three penalties and a dropped goal in a 30-7 win.

The club's achievements had been recognised already by the council but it was acknowledged further in a thoughtful leader in the *Leicester Diocesan News and Views* - not, perhaps, the most likely vehicle for sporting acclaim. Vive le sport, cried the editor, for its provision of recreation after the cares and worries of everyday life. It was time, he opined, for Leicestershire to awaken to the fact that its fine rugby team was worthy of greater support, week in and week out. Hear, hear, cried the club and, suitably inspired, went on to greater things.

After being drawn at home on six occasions, however, it had to happen sooner or later that Leicester went away and they did so to Bedford in the quarter-finals. It was an important game because they had to prove to themselves, if nobody else, that they could play well away from Welford Road when it mattered. They did, Hare turning on his own particular magic with a try, a conversion and four penalties - Burwell scored the other try - in a 22-12 win. A fortnight later they were away again, to Wasps in the semi-final, and under the beady eye of the BBC's cameras, they overwhelmed the home club 43-7.

It was a performance without equal in the competition's admittedly brief history: that so many points should have been scored in a semi-final, and coming before an audience augmented by television viewers boosted Leicester's image to new heights. Leicester cut loose, with Cusworth in brilliant form, and they ran in tries by Mick Newton (two), Barnwell (two), Redfern, Hare, Burwell and Collington, Hare converting four times and kicking a penalty.

Gus Collington puts the icing on the cake in grabbing Tigers' eighth try in the victory over Wasps.

In the meantime Moseley were beating Gosforth 6-3 to reach the final at Twickenham on 21 April. It was important to Leicester that, before the final, they played Neath and Maesteg over Easter at home; the Welsh clubs gave them two hard games, both of which were won. The next week Twickenham, it seemed, belonged to Leicester. The crowd of 18,000 was not as big as the previous year but it seemed they were nearly all from Leicester, who even managed to produce a jazz band led by Bob Beason, playing their own inimitable, and almost unidentifiable, version of *Tiger Rag*.

The unlucky Duggan, who had been in the losing final a year previously, failed to recover from a broken arm in time so the young wing, Newton, a youth team product, kept his place. Cowling, whom injury had prevented from appearing against his old club, Gloucester, was there, as was Barnwell; both had previously been on the winning side in the final, for Gloucester and Coventry respectively.

The Leicester side was: Dusty Hare; Mick Newton, Paul Dodge, Terry Burwell, Tim Barnwell; Les Cusworth, Steve Kenney; Robin Cowling, Peter Wheeler (captain), Steve Redfern, Nick Joyce, Arthur Hazlerigg, Steve Johnson, Garry Adey, Ian Smith.

It was a final unmatched for excitement if not for technical excellence. For an hour the Moseley forwards dominated the match, and if their backs had taken every chance offered, they might have established an unbeatable lead. After Hare had dropped a goal in the eighth minute, Moseley went ahead through a fine try by Rob Laird, converted by Richard Akenhead, and a dropped goal by Cooper, made it 9-3 to Moseley at half-time.

Tigers' triumphant team as they collect their first John Player Cup trophy at Twickenham.

Akenhead kicked a penalty but missed another and the match was entering the final quarter when Hare kicked his first penalty. By that time Moseley had lost Barrie Corless and Derek Nutt through injury and though they had very adequate replacements for centre and back row, their forward effort was waning. Another penalty by Hare made it 12-9 and wave upon wave of Leicester attacks surged towards the Moseley line - which held. There were just three minutes of official time left when Leicester won a scrum five metres out and Kenney broke round to dive in for the decisive try which Hare converted. The whole move was immortalised by Van Hopkins in his BBC Radio Leicester commentary, "Kenney moving through, and he's over."

It was a win as much for character as anything else. From the technical point of view Moseley had been better in several departments but Leicester, with the disappointment of 12 months previously nagging at them, would not allow victory to slip away this time. They had also picked up the important All Black habit of being a full 80-minute side. So it was back to Leicester with the spoils, a civic reception (the Lord Mayor had been at Twickenham but had been obliged to leave at half-time) and the knowledge that if anyone should ask "Where do we go from here?", the answer was: the club centenary.

The excitement of the cup win overshadowed events elsewhere; Hare had been dropped yet again after the New Zealand match, and Cowling suffered the same fate after playing against Scotland and Ireland. Dodge and Wheeler played through the five nations (the same two players had appeared for an England XV against Argentina early in the season) and both were named for England's tour to the Far East, together with Hare.

Under-23 honours went to the young flanker, Smith, to Redfern again and, at last, to Kenney, the latter pair touring France and Italy. In the Far East the senior threesome had mixed fortunes and it is fair to say that none of them came home with an enhanced reputation. Dodge was overplayed and his form in the opening games of the new season was such as to suggest that he was stale.

1979/1980

Such are the problems success brings. Another occurred when the club selectors decided not to pick the XV which won the John Player Cup for the first game of the season, at Bedford. Forfar, after a season's absence through injury, reclaimed a back row spot from Johnson and a newcomer, Clive Woodward, was paired at centre with Dodge at the expense of Burwell. There were murmurs in and around the club, even though the selected XV "scraped" home by 34-12.

The new man, Woodward, was not unknown to Leicester since he had been a student for four years at Loughborough University and had captained

↑ Steve Kenney on defence during the 12-27 loss to Swansea on 27.10.1979.

the side. Already an England colts and under-23 cap, he had played fly-half and centre with considerable success and was one of not many midfield players in the country possessed of both the eye for a break and the speed to exploit it. He swiftly added an England B cap to his honours when he played against France B at the end of September, while Forfar was also given the B cap he would have got had he been fit enough to go to Romania in 1978.

But the thoughts of the club had turned firmly towards retention of the cup and arrangements for the centenary season in 1980/81. Two years earlier the idea of a world tour had been proposed as one way of celebrating the centenary and this was adopted, though the fixture-making proved a little difficult. Originally a grandiose sweep through Australia, New Zealand, Fiji and the USA had been envisaged for August 1980, however, it proved awkward to find fixtures in New Zealand and the eventual arrangements produced three games in Australia and three in Fiji, against the Queensland state side, Randwick and Eastern Suburbs then two Fijian regional selections and a Fijian RU Chairman's XV.

Plans for celebrations nearer home were also developing while within the club the advances of the last few seasons brought members flowing in and increased revenue via a club shop, selling mementoes, jerseys, ties and more, so successfully that on one occasion during the season the "take" for the day entered four figures. It was sad that the membership secretary, the former full-back Ernie Watkin, did not live to see the club to its 100th birthday. He died a fortnight before the club's third successive appearance in the John Player Cup final.

In an increasingly professional sporting world, Leicester's amateur organisation was coping well, on all fronts. In the playing context there had been a slight hiccup when Bath won 10-9 at Welford Road in the third match of the season. More significant was the defeat, again at home, at the hands of Swansea by 27-12 who went on to prove themselves the outstanding club combination in Britain by the season's end. Nevertheless, club form was quite good enough for nine players to be picked in the Midland Counties XV against yet another New Zealand touring side, again captained by Graham Mourie.

The Midlands-All Blacks game at Welford Road was the third of the New Zealanders' short tour

↑ Match programme from the John Player Cup semi-final against Harlequins at Twickenham.

and the visitors won 33-7. The Midlands XV was: Dusty Hare (Leicester); Michael Perry (Moseley), Paul Dodge, Clive Woodward (both Leicester), Paul Knee (Coventry); Les Cusworth (Leicester), Ian Peck (Cambridge University); Robin Cowling, Peter Wheeler (captain), Steve Redfern (all Leicester), Nigel Horton (Toulouse), Russell Field (Moseley), Graham Phillips (Bedford), Garry Adey, Dave Forfar (both Leicester).

The Midlands worked well in the tight, less well in the loose, and poorly amongst the backs. Woodward made holes in the New Zealand defence but lost his support in the process and with Hare not having one of his best kicking days, the Midlands were 23-0 down before they scored. Richard Wilson kicked three penalties before half-time, Fraser, Burgoyne and Mexted scored tries, the last of them converted by Wilson. At this stage Hare kicked a penalty and Paul Knee ran in a good try, which prompted further All Black tries from Fraser and Fleming, the second converted by the faithful Wilson.

Three weeks later, on 24 November, three Leicester players faced the All Blacks again, this time for England at Twickenham. Hare was called up at full-back; Cusworth won his first cap at fly-half and Wheeler retained the hooking berth but Dodge, after eight successive games, was dropped. The All Blacks scraped home 10-9 and England did little to encourage their supporters for the coming five nations. Hare kicked England's three penalties but Cusworth, called upon to play a game like that demonstrated by Alan Old when the Northern Division had decisively beaten the All Blacks the previous week, was unable to do so with sufficient accuracy.

Meanwhile, apart from representative calls, injuries were afflicting the club side and the number of players used in the senior side moved rapidly into the thirties. The side was playing inconsistent rugby but even in the troughs they were quite capable of beating most opposition, in itself the sign of a class team. One of their most enjoyable outings was the 42-4 win at Northampton, another step along the road to the top of the Midland merit table. The Barbarians came and went over Christmas, beating the club 9-8 in a match played in a quagmire but with great intensity of spirit on both sides. Leicester scored two tries to one but could convert neither; it was a heartening performance with the cup approaching once more and immediately afterwards Duggan scored his 150th try for the club in a 55-3 romp against Headingley.

The holders had been drawn at home to Orrell, the Northern merit table leaders, and Leicester were happy enough to begin the defence of the cup with a 16-7 win, Smith scoring a try, Hare kicking two penalties and Cusworth two dropped goals. One of the most impressive aspects of Leicester's win was their scrummaging, and this feature was to be repeated in the subsequent rounds.

Before the second round, however, Woodward won his first England cap. While Dodge had begun the season indifferently, and Woodward on a high note, the two centres had swapped positions in terms of club form, for Dodge was now back at his best and Woodward seemed to have lost touch somewhat. However, England had decided to call him up as a replacement for the game with Ireland, retaining Hare and Wheeler but replacing Cusworth with John Horton of Bath. During the game, won 24-9 by England, Sale's Tony Bond broke a leg and Woodward went on for his first cap. He was retained against France and was joined by Dodge for the game against Wales, an appalling game which Hare's three penalties permitted England to win 9-8 against a Welsh team reduced to 14 men when the former Leicester flanker, Paul Ringer, now with Llanelli, was sent off.

In a far more appealing finale against Scotland, Woodward was quite outstanding in broken play as England achieved their first triple crown and grand slam for 23 years. It was another feather in the club's cap that four Leicester players should have participated in the country's triumph and that a fifth should also have represented England, reminiscent of the balmy days of the 1900s and the 1930s.

The John Player Cup second round brought together the 1979 finalists, Moseley and Leicester, at The Reddings but there was seldom much doubt of the outcome this time, Dodge excelling himself in a 17-7 win. He scored one try, Burwell another, Hare kicked two penalties and Cusworth again dropped a goal. As if in celebration, Cusworth registered 30 points against Harlequins from two tries, three penalty goals, five conversions and a dropped goal, a virtuoso performance bettered only once before by Teddy Haselmere in 1919.

It was Cusworth who stole the honours in the third-round cup tie, against London Scottish at Welford Road. The game had virtually been decided by half-time, even though only seven points had been scored, and the tries came from Smith and Cusworth, who also dropped a goal. Hare added three penalties and a conversion. He recorded another dozen in the cup semi-final three weeks later, with four penalties in the 16-9 defeat of Harlequins at Twickenham. A try by Dodge made up the tally but it was by no means an emphatic win in a game spoiled by a strong wind.

Nevertheless, Leicester were in the final for the third year running, and were everybody's favourites to beat London Irish - except, naturally enough, the Irish. Had it not been for the fact that they won the cup, April would have been a poor month for Leicester since they lost four more games, failed in their effort to score 1,000 points for the season and to establish a record number of wins.

That is looking at it coldly. Ironically, had they had taken into account the 20 points scored against an International XV in a fundraising match at Welford Road on 1 April, it would have made the round 1,000. But that game, an attractive affair designed to add cash to the tour fund and won by the star-studded guest XV 22-20, was not included in the first-class fixtures. Two hard games in Wales followed over Easter, a scrappy win over Neath distinguished only by a marvellous 90-metre try from Burwell and a 21-13 defeat at Pontypool Park where the local side kicked five penalties and two dropped goals against a goal, a try and a penalty, leaving something of a sour taste in Leicester mouths - though not quite as sour as the taste left in Steve Johnson's mouth earlier in the year when he played for the British Police against their French opposites and was raked so severely that the lacerations to his head required forty stitches.

Leicester came through Easter without Wheeler and Woodward, both of whom had been picked for the British Lions tour to South Africa in the summer of 1980. The honours were not confined to the seniors, however, for two youth players, Stuart Redfern, brother of the 1st XV prop, and Rob Tebbutt, won England colts caps at prop and flanker respectively, against Wales and France.

There was one match that Wheeler and Woodward could not miss though, the John Player Cup final at Twickenham on 19 April. Leicester were at strength but, sadly, could not include their experienced wing, Duggan, who had damaged a hamstring against Neath and, for the second year running, took a back seat through injury. The Leicester team was: Dusty Hare; Tim Barnwell, Clive Woodward, Paul Dodge, Terry Burwell; Les Cusworth, Steve Kenney; Robin Cowling, Peter Wheeler (captain), Steve Redfern, Nick Joyce, Nigel Gillingham, Steve Johnson, Garry Adey, Ian Smith.

There was a 27,000 crowd, including a vast Leicester contingent, which established a then record gate for the final. If they were expecting a classic, they were disappointed but the Leicester contingent were happy enough to see the Tigers triumph 21-9, thanks to four penalties and a dropped goal by Hare, and two dropped goals by Cusworth. There was none of the excitement of the previous year, largely because it was always obvious that Leicester would win.

London Irish, basing their game around the unflagging efforts of their back row and scrum-half, covered and disrupted to the extent that they preserved their record of keeping their line intact in all cup games, and they had the satisfaction of scoring a try themselves, through the lock, Mike

↓ Garry Adey and Steve Kenney stop a London Irish attack during the 1980 Cup final at Twickenham.

Smythe. Clive Meanwell's conversion made the interval score 12-6, Cusworth having opened matters with a neat drop goal and Hare having kicked three penalties. Hare dropped his goal and kicked another penalty before Meanwell landed an Irish penalty but Cusworth popped over another drop to conclude the scoring. It had been an efficient display, Leicester exerting control whenever they needed to, and it gave them the opportunity of going into their centenary season as cup holders.

With his 40th minute penalty in the final Hare, after only three and a half years with the club, passed HLV Day's all-time club record of 1,151 points that had stood for 55 years.

Coincidentally, the win at Twickenham was also the 33rd of the season, equalling the record established by the 1966/67 side, but the 34th eluded them in lackadaisical displays against Moseley and Rosslyn Park. Still, it was not a bad way to end the decade and to begin the next 100 years and, as an indication of how success had permeated the club's other sides, the records in 1979/80 for the four XVs were:

	W	D	L	F	A
1st XV	33	0	9	980	420
Extras	26	1	8	897	373
Swifts	25	2	3	876	214
Youth	18	3	3	614	171

Hare had raised the record for points scored in one season to 319 and, for once, there was a second player well into three figures, since Cusworth totalled 173, including 13 dropped goals. Duggan ended his 11th full season equal with Bob Barker's post-war club mark of 158 tries and, not merely a statistical quirk, Graham Willars, whose career was alleged to have ended five years previously, made his 336th senior appearance when coming on as a replacement in the last game of the 1979/80 season, giving him two complete decades of playing service to the club.

The year, however, had something more to offer before the centenary celebrations began. The British Lions, hit by injuries throughout their 18-match tour in South Africa in the summer of 1980, called upon eight replacements, among them Dodge who joined the tour party when the Welsh centre, David Richards, was injured. Dodge stepped straight into the international side when he was chosen for the third test, joining both his club colleagues. Wheeler was first choice hooker throughout the series and played in all four tests while Woodward, centre in the second Test, played on the wing in the third.

↑ For the first time, three Tigers play in a Lions test team, the third test against the Springboks in 1980: Peter Wheeler, Paul Dodge and Clive Woodward.

The prospect of seeing three Tigers playing for the Lions was too much for Chalkie White, who flew to Port Elizabeth for the third test. Sadly the Lions lost 12-10, Woodward's failure to cover a quick throw-in conceding the crucial try; thus the series was lost 3-1 but Dodge retained his place for the last Test, won by the Lions 17-13, and gave every indication in his five tour games that he should have been an original selection.

Woodward, with 53 points from four tries, five conversions, eight penalties and a dropped goal, ended the tour as second highest points scorer behind Ollie Campbell. Woodward's emergence as a place-kicker was of considerable significance to the tour results and, while not entirely a surprise, his consistency was unexpected in view of the lack of practice he had both at Leicester, where Hare and Cusworth looked after the kicking duties, and at college where he had been only an occasional kicker. Three players on a major tour was something Leicester had not achieved since the 1908 Anglo-Welsh tour to Australasia.

↑ LEICESTER FOOTBALL CLUB 1977/78
Back: Sibson (Team Hon.Sec), Day (Hon.Sec), Allen (Hon.Tres), Duggan, Redfern, Collington, Johnson, Hazlerigg, Adey, Needham, Smith, C.White (Coach), Kinder (President).
Front: Hare, Money, J.White, Walley, Jackson, Hall (capt), Barker, Joyce, Kenney, Dodge.

↑ LEICESTER FOOTBALL CLUB 1979/80
Back: White (Coach), Lacey (President), Allen (Hon.Tres), Hall, Redfern, Joyce, Adey, Collington, Cowling, I.Smith, Duggan, Day (Hon.Sec), Thomas (Team Hon.Sec).
Middle: Woodward, Hare, Wheeler (capt), Burwell, Dodge.
Front: Barnwell, Cusworth, Kenney, Duffelen.
Inset: Merriman, Johnson.

1977/78	Home Ground: Welford Road	OVERALL RECORD:					T	C	PG	DG	PTS
	Coach: Chalkie White	PLD	W	D	L	Tigers scored:	122	71	66	7	849
	Captain: Brian Hall	41	27	2	12	Opponents scored:	79	40	54	5	573

GM	DATE		VEN	OPPONENTS	RESULT	TRIES	KICKS	ATT
RFU CLUB COMPETITION (JOHN PLAYER CUP)						**CUP WINNERS: GLOUCESTER**		
27	Jan	**28**	**H**	**Hartlepool Rovers (1)**	W 9-3	-	Hare 3p	1090
29	Feb	**25**	**H**	**Rosslyn Park (2)**	W 25-16	Barker 47, Kenney 75, Forfar 78	Hare 2c/3p	1927
31	Mar	**11**	**H**	**Northampton (qf)**	W 20-11	Duggan 24, Joyce 79	Dodge 2p, Hare 2p	3778
36	Apr	**1**	**H**	**Coventry (sf)**	W 25-16	Dodge 68, Jones 76	Hare c/3p/d, Reichwald d	6472
38		15		Gloucester (f)	L 3-6	-	Hare p	25282
MIDLAND MERIT TABLE (5TH)						**WINNERS: BEDFORD**		
1	Sep	3	a	Bedford	L 19-38	Barker, Rose	Hare c/3p	-
2		**6tu**	**H**	**Nuneaton**	W 51-10	Barker(4), Rose(2), Hall, Joyce, White	Hare 6c/p	365
4		14w	a	Birmingham	W 28-9	Barnwell(2), Forfar	Hare 2c/3p/d	-
8	Oct	**1**	**H**	**Coventry**	W 20-6	Hare, Barker, Barnwell	Hare c/2p	980
10		15	a	Northampton	L 10-26	Collington, Hall	Barker c	-
16	Nov	**15tu**	**H**	**Nottingham**	W 57-6	Barker(3), Duggan(2), Hall(2), Hare, Adey, Kenney	Hare 4c/2p/d	406
39	Apr	**22**	**H**	**Moseley**	W 21-15	Duggan, Jones	Hare 2c/2p/d	1599
40		26w	a	Rugby	L 13-17	Collington, Wheeler	Hare c/p	-
CLUB MATCHES								
3	Sep	**10**	**H**	**Bath**	W 39-26	Hall(2), Rose(2), Dodge, Kenney	Hare 3c/3p	286
5		**17**	**H**	**Liverpool**	W 35-3	Barker(2), Dodge, Joyce, Kenney, Parkes	Hare 4c/p	548
6		20tu	a	Sheffield	W 47-3	Barker(4), Johnson, Kenney, Parkes, Redfern	Hare 6c/p	-
7		24	a	Harlequins	W 23-17	Barker(2), Smith	Hare c/3p	-
9	Oct	8	a	Richmond	L 6-9	-	Hare 2p	-
11		19w	a	Oxford University	W 14-9	Barker, Duggan, Jones	Dodge c	-
12		**22**	**H**	**Swansea**	W 33-16	Barker, Duggan, Hall, Johnson	Barker 3c/p, Dodge c/2p	1310
13		29	a	Saracens	D 19-19	Duggan(2), McMichael	Hare 2c/p	-
14	Nov	**5**	**H**	**Gloucester**	W 28-15	Barker, Joyce, Redfern, Smith	Hare 3c/2p	1216
15		12	a	Cambridge University	W 37-15	Duggan(2), Redfern(2), Hall, Wheeler	Hare 5c/p	-
17		**19**	**H**	**Wasps**	W 20-12	Hare, Barker	Hare 3p/d	1023
18		**26**	**H**	**Sale**	W 26-12	Barker, Duggan, Kenney, Smith, White	Hare 3c	701
19	Dec	**3**	**H**	**Waterloo**	W 14-3	Burwell, Johnson, Money	Needham c	620
20		10	a	Blackheath	L 14-19	Barker, Reichwald	Barker 2p	-
21		**17**	**H**	**Bristol**	W 19-14	Barker	Barker 5p	877
22		**27tu**	**H**	**Barbarians**	L 6-12	Hare	Hare c	19000
23		**31**	**H**	**Headingley**	W 22-10	Barker, Barnwell	Hare c/3p/d	971
24	Jan	7	a	Bath	L 16-28	Joyce, Smith, White	Needham 2c	-
25		14	a	Gloucester	L 6-39	Kempin	Hare c	-
26		**20f**	**H**	**Bedford**	W 12-6	Jones	Barker c/2p	330
		21	a	C.A.S.G.	PP			
		28	a	Rosslyn Park	PP (cup)			
28	Feb	**1w**	**H**	**Royal Navy**	D 0-0	-	-	322
		4	**H**	**London Scottish**	PP (frost)			
		11	a	Newport	PP (frost)			
		15w	**H**	**Sale**	PP (frost)			
		18	a	Fylde	PP (frost)			
		25	**H**	**Northampton**	PP (cup)			
30	Mar	**4**	**H**	**Harlequins**	L 20-22	Duggan, Hall, Joyce, Reichwald	Hare 2c	368
		11	a	Coventry	PP (cup)			
32		**14tu**	**H**	**Loughborough Colleges**	W 26-23	Adey, Duggan, Hazlerigg, Jones	Barker 2c/2p	431
33		**17f**	**H**	**Royal Air Force**	W 30-6	Barnwell(4), Barker, Parkes	Barker 3c	306
34		25	a	Neath	L 0-11	-	-	-
35		27m	a	Maesteg	W 15-6	Hare, Dodge	Hare 2c/p	-
	Apr	**1**	**H**	**Birkenhead Park**	PP (cup)			
37		8	a	Bristol	L 0-23	-	-	-
		15	a	Middlesbrough	PP (cup)			
41		**29**	**H**	**Northern**	W 21-16	Hare, Dodge	Hare 2c/3p	831

INDIVIDUAL APPEARANCES 1977/78

Name / Game #	1	2	3	4	5	6	7	8	9	10	11	12	13	14	15	16	17	18	19	20	21	22	23	24	25	26	27	28	29	30	31	32	33	34	35	36	37	38	39	40	41	Apps	T	Pts
GJ (Garry) Adey E2	-	-	-	-	-	-	D	-	-	-	G	G	G	G	G	G	G	G	-	-	-	G	G	-	G	G	G	G	G	G	G	G	G	G	-	G	G	G	G	F	-	26	2	8
RG (Bob) Barker	K	K	K	K	K	K	K	K	K	K	K	K	K	K	K	K	K	K	-	K	K*	N	N*	-	K	K	K	K	K	K	K	K*	K*	K*	-	K	K	K	K	-	K	37	27	164
RC (Tim) Barnwell	-	-	-	>N	N	N	N	N	N	N	-	-	-	-	-	-	-	-	-	-	-	K	K	K	N	N	N	-	-	-	-	-	N	r	K	-	N	-	-	K	-	17+1	8	32
TR (Terry) Burwell	x	-	-	-	-	-	-	-	-	-	0	-	-	-	-	x	-	r	K	N	-	-	-	N	-	-	-	-	-	-	-	-	-	-	-	-	M	-	-	-	-	5+1	1	4
AP (Angus) Collington	-	x	-	-	-	-	-	G	G	G	-	-	-	-	r	x	-	-	G	-	G	-	-	G	-	-	x	-	-	-	x	-	-	-	G	-	r	x	-	G	G	9+2	2	8
RJ (Robin) Cowling E5	-	-	-	-	-	-	-	-	-	-	-	-	-	-	-	A	A	A	-	-	-	A	A	-	-	-	-	-	-	-	-	-	-	-	-	-	-	-	-	-	-	5	-	-
PW (Paul) Dodge E3 L+	M	M	M	M	M	M	M	-	M	-	M	M	M	M	M	M	M	M	-	-	-	M	M	-	M	M	M	-	M	-	M	-	-	-	M	M	-	M	M	M	M	29	5	36
MJ (John) Duggan	-	-	-	-	-	-	x	-	-	-	N	N	N	N	N	N	N	N	-	-	N	-	-	-	-	-	-	N	N	N	N	N	-	N	N	N	-	N	N	N	N	21	13	52
DJ (Dave) Forfar	F	F	F	F	F	-	-	-	-	-	-	-	-	-	-	-	-	-	-	-	-	-	-	-	-	H	H	H	H	H	H	-	H	-	-	H	-	H	H	-	-	15	2	8
BP (Brian) Hall	L*	L*	L*	L*	L*	L*	L*	L*	L*	L*	L*	L*	L*	L*	L*	L*	L*	L*	-	L*	-	L*	-	L*	L*	L*	L*	L*	L*	L*	L*	-	-	-	-	-	-	L*	-	-	L*	30	9	36
WH (Dusty) Hare E2	0	0	0	0	0	0	0	0	0	-	-	-	0	0	0	0	0	0	-	-	-	0	0	-	0	-	0	0	0	0	0	-	-	-	0	0	0	0	0	0	0	30	6	304
NS (Neil) Hartley	-	-	-	-	-	-	-	>I	-	-	-	-	-	-	-	-	-	-	-	I	I	-	-	-	-	-	-	-	-	-	-	-	-	-	-	-	-	-	-	-	-	3	-	-
AG (Arthur) Hazlerigg	E	E	E	E	E	E	E	E	E	E	E	D	E	-	-	-	-	-	E	E	E	-	D	-	D	D	E	E	E	-	E	E	E	-	E	E	E	E	E	E	-	31	1	4
NA (Nick) Jackson	-	-	-	-	-	-	-	-	-	-	-	-	-	-	-	-	-	-	-	-	-	-	-	-	-	-	-	-	-	>E	-	-	-	E	D	-	-	-	-	-	D	4	-	-
SR (Steve) Johnson	G	G	G	G	G	G	G	F	F	H	H	H	H	H	-	-	-	-	F	G	H	H	H	H	H	-	F	F	F	F	F	-	F	H	H	F	-	F	F	-	-	32	3	12
B (Bleddyn) Jones	J	J	J	J	J	J	J	J	J	J	J	-	-	-	-	J	J	J	J	J	J	J	J	J	J	J	J	J	J	J	J	J	-	J	J	J	J	J	J	J	J	36	5	20
NJ (Nick) Joyce	D	D	D	D	D	-	-	D	D	D	D	E	D	D	D	D	D	D	D	D	D	D	-	D	-	-	D	D	D	D	D	D	D	D	-	D	D	D	D	D	-	34	6	24
JS (Jim) Kempin	H	H	H	H	H	F	H	-	-	-	-	-	-	-	H	H	H	F	-	H	r	-	F	-	F	-	-	-	-	-	-	H	-	-	-	-	-	-	-	-	H	16+1	1	4
S (Steve) Kenney	I	I	I	I	I	I	I	-	I	I	I	I	I	I	I	I	I	I	I	-	-	I	I	I	-	I	I	I	I	I	I	I	I	I	I	I	I	I	I	-	I	36	6	24
J (Jez) Krych	-	-	-	-	-	-	-	C	-	-	-	-	-	-	-	-	-	-	-	-	-	-	-	A	A	C	x	-	-	-	-	-	A	-	-	-	-	-	-	-	-	5	-	-
RDJ (Rod) McMichael	-	x	-	-	-	-	-	-	-	-	-	J	J	J	J	-	-	-	-	-	-	-	-	-	-	-	-	-	-	-	-	-	<J	-	-	-	-	-	-	-	-	5	1	4
RS (Robin) Money	-	-	-	-	-	-	-	-	-	0	-	0	-	-	-	-	-	-	0	0	0	-	-	0	-	0	x	-	-	-	r	0	0	0	-	-	<r	x	-	-	-	10+2	1	4
RE (Ray) Needham	A	A	A	A	A	A	A	A	A	A	A	A	A	A	A	-	-	-	A	A	A	-	-	C	C	A	A	A	A	A	A	A	-	A	A	-	A	A	A	A	A	34	-	6
JS (Steve) Newsome	-	-	-	-	-	-	-	-	-	-	-	-	-	>E	E	E	E	E	-	-	-	E	E	E	<E	-	-	-	-	-	-	-	-	-	-	-	-	-	-	-	-	9	-	-
L (Larry) Parkes	-	-	-	-	r	r	-	M	-	M	r	-	-	-	-	-	-	-	M	-	M	-	L	M	-	-	-	-	-	-	r	L	L	L	r	-	-	-	-	-	-	9+5	3	12
SP (Steve) Redfern E+	C	C	C	C	C	C	C	-	C	C	C	C	C	C	C	C	C	C	C	C	C	C	C	-	-	-	C	C	C	C	C	C	-	C	C	C	C	C	C	C	C	36	4	16
WM (Bill) Reichwald	-	-	-	-	-	-	-	-	-	-	-	-	-	-	-	-	-	-	>L	M	L	-	-	-	-	-	x	M	-	M	-	M	M	M	L	L	L	x	L	L	-	13	2	11
WMH (Marcus) Rose E+	N	N	<N	-	-	-	-	-	-	-	-	-	-	-	-	-	-	-	-	-	-	-	-	-	-	-	-	-	-	-	-	-	-	-	-	-	-	-	-	-	-	3	5	20
IR (Ian) Smith	-	-	-	-	-	>H	F	H	H	F	F	F	F	F	F	F	F	H	-	F	F	F	-	F	-	F	-	-	-	-	-	F	-	F	F	-	F	x	x	-	-	22	4	16
TA (Tim) Walley	-	-	-	-	-	-	-	-	-	-	-	-	-	-	-	-	-	-	-	-	-	-	-	-	I	-	x	-	-	-	x	-	-	-	-	-	-	x	-	I	-	2	-	-
PJ (Peter) Wheeler E14 L3	-	-	-	-	-	-	-	-	-	-	-	-	B	B	B	B	B	-	-	-	-	B	B	-	-	-	-	-	B	-	B	-	-	-	B*	B*	B*	B	B*	B*	B	16	2	8
JR (John) White	B	B	B	B	B	B	B	B	B	B	B	B	-	-	-	-	-	B	B	B	B	-	-	B	B	B	B	B	-	B	x	B	B	B	-	-	-	x	-	-	-	25	3	12
GG (Graham) Willars	-	-	-	-	-	-	-	-	-	-	-	-	-	-	-	-	-	-	H*	-	-	-	-	-	-	-	-	-	-	-	-	-	-	-	-	-	-	-	-	H	F	3	-	-

1 GAME: AF (Alistair) Grocock <A(36), N (Neil) Holloway >C(33), AI (Alistair) Meldrum =E(26), RE (Bob) Rowell E2 <E(41), KN (Kevin) Steptoe >D(6), PJ (Paul) Strickland >H(37), ID (Ian) Tomalin =N(19)

The key for how to read the stats is on the last page

19	78/79	Home Ground: Welford Road	Trophy Cabinet: John Player Cup(1)	OVERALL RECORD:					T	C	PG	DG	PTS
		Coach: Chalkie White		PLD	W	D	L	Tigers scored:	106	57	69	13	784
		Captain: Peter Wheeler		34	24	0	10	Opponents scored:	40	28	43	9	372

GM	DATE		VEN	OPPONENTS	RESULT	TRIES	KICKS	ATT
RFU CLUB COMPETITION (JOHN PLAYER CUP)						**CUP WINNERS: LEICESTER TIGERS**		
22	Jan	**27**	**H**	**Northampton (1)**	W 29-3	Burwell 19, Barnwell 40, Adey 46, Hare 50	Hare 2c/2p, Burwell d	2333
24	Feb	**24**	**H**	**Broughton Park (2)**	W 30-7	Dodge 39, Adey 50, Cusworth 60, I.Smith 70	Hare c/3p/d	2858
28	Mar	24	a	Bedford (qf)	W 22-12	Hare 30, Burwell 58	Hare c/4p	-
30	Apr	7	a	Wasps (sf)	W 43-7	Redfern 18, Barnwell 25/75, Hare 26, Newton 51/72, Burwell 70, Collington 79	Hare 4c/p	-
33		21		Moseley (f)	W 15-12	Kenney 75	Hare c/2p/d	20000
MIDLAND MERIT TABLE (2ND)						**WINNERS: COVENTRY**		
1	Sep	**2**	**H**	**Bedford**	W 37-12	Barnwell, Dodge, Duggan, Hall	Hare 3c/5p	1374
2		5tu	a	Nuneaton	W 33-6	Barnwell(2), Hare, Duggan, Kenney, Wheeler	Hare 2p/d	-
4		**13w**	**H**	**Birmingham**	W 35-15	Cowling, Johnson, Joyce, I.Smith, Wheeler	Hare 3c/3p	797
8	Oct	7	a	Coventry	L 23-27	Hare, Hall, Wheeler	Hare c/3p	-
10		**21**	**H**	**Northampton**	W 32-6	Hare, Burwell, Collington, Duggan, Wheeler	Hare 3c/2p	1898
16	Nov	**25**	**H**	**Moseley**	W 15-10	Barnwell(2)	Cusworth 2c/p	499
		28tu	a	Nottingham	PP (frost)			
29	Mar	**31**	**H**	**Rugby**	W 43-9	Barnwell(2), Adey, Cowling, Johnson, Kempin	Hare 5c/3p	1987
CLUB MATCHES								
3	Sep	9	a	Bath	W 25-6	Duggan, Joyce, I.Smith	Hare 2c/2p/d	-
5		**16**	**H**	**London Welsh**	L 12-18	-	Hare 3p/d	1924
6		23	a	Harlequins	L 9-21	-	Hare 2p/d	-
7		**30**	**H**	**Saracens**	W 34-9	Dodge(2), Duggan(2), Burwell, Johnson	Hare 2c/2p	1309
9	Oct	**14**	**H**	**Richmond**	W 12-0	Duggan	Hare c/2p	1276
11		**25w**	**H**	**Oxford University**	W 33-15	I.Smith(2), Burwell, Dodge, Joyce, White	Hare 3c/p	857
12		28	a	Swansea	L 12-21	-	Hare 3p, Cusworth d	-
13	Nov	4	a	Gloucester	W 9-7	-	Hare p/2d	-
14		**11**	**H**	**Cambridge University**	W 34-7	Burwell, Collington, Hall, Kenney, Newton	Hare 4c/2p	715
15		18	a	Wasps	L 14-36	Burwell, Parkes	Key 2p	-
	Dec	2	a	Waterloo	PP (frost)			
17		**9**	**H**	**Blackheath**	W 30-0	Kenney(2), Barnwell, Duggan, Hall	Hare 2c/p/d	805
18		15f	a	Bristol	L 15-18	Barnwell, White	Hare 2c/p	-
19		23	a	London Welsh	L 6-12	Dodge	Hare c	-
20		**27w**	**H**	**Barbarians**	W 18-6	Adey, Johnson	Hare 2c/2p	14000
		30	a	Headingley	PP (frost)			
	Jan	**6**	**H**	**Bath**	PP (frost)			
		13	**H**	**Gloucester**	PP (frost)			
21		20	a	Bedford	L 8-10	Needham, Newton	-	-
		27	**H**	**Rosslyn Park**	PP (cup)			
23	Feb	3	a	London Scottish	W 34-0	Hare(2), Barnwell, Parkes	Hare 3c/3p, Cusworth d	-
		10	**H**	**Newport**	PP (frost)			
		17	**H**	**Fylde**	PP (frost)			
		24	a	Northampton	PP (cup)			
25		**28w**	**H**	**Royal Navy**	W 21-3	Barnwell, Cusworth, Joyce, Kempin	Hare c/p	500
26	Mar	**3**	**H**	**Harlequins**	W 33-3	Barnwell, Cusworth, Kempin, Kenney, Newton	Hare 5c/p	543
27		10	a	Northampton	L 9-16	-	Dodge 3p	-
		10	**H**	**Coventry**	PP (cup)			
		13tu	**H**	**Loughborough Students**	PP (frost)			
		16f	**H**	**Royal Air Force**	PP (frost)			
		24	a	Sale	PP (cup)			
	Apr	7	a	Birkenhead Park	PP (cup)			
31		**14**	**H**	**Neath**	W 25-15	Burwell, Johnson, Kenney	Hare 2c/3p	1798
32		**16m**	**H**	**Maesteg**	W 26-9	White(2), I.Smith	Dodge c/2p, Cusworth d, Hare p	2190
		21	**H**	**Bristol**	PP (cup)			
34		28	a	Moseley	L 8-14	White(2)	-	-

INDIVIDUAL APPEARANCES 1978/79

Name / Game #	1	2	3	4	5	6	7	8	9	10	11	12	13	14	15	16	17	18	19	20	21	22	23	24	25	26	27	28	29	30	31	32	33	34	Apps	T	Pts
GJ (Garry) Adey E2	G	G	G	G	G	G	-	G	-	-	-	-	-	-	-	G	G	G	G	G	-	G	G	G	G	-	G	G	G	G	-	G	G	G	23	4	16
RG (Bob) Barker	-	x	-	-	N	N	-	-	M	M	K	-	x	-	N*	x	-	-	-	-	-	-	-	-	-	-	K	-	-	-	-	r	-	-	7+1	-	-
RC (Tim) Barnwell	K	K	K	K	K	K	K	K	K	K	-	K	K	-	K	K	K	K	K	K	K	K	K	N	K	K	-	K	K	K	-	K	K	K	30	15	60
TR (Terry) Burwell	-	-	-	-	-	-	L	r	L	L	M	L	L	L	M	M	x	M	L	L	L	L	M	M	M	M	M	L	L	M	M	M	M	M	26+1	9	39
AP (Angus) Collington	-	x	-	-	-	x	G	-	G	G	G	G	G	G	G	x	-	r	-	x	G	x	-	r	-	G	-	x	-	r	G	-	x	-	11+3	3	12
RJ (Robin) Cowling E8	A	A	A	A	A	A	A	A	A*	A	A*	A	A	A*	-	-	-	-	A	A	-	A	-	A	A*	A*	A*	A	A	A	A*	A*	A	A*	28	2	8
L (Les) Cusworth E+	-	-	-	-	-	-	-	-	-	-	-	>J	J	J	-	J	J	J	J	J	J	J	J	J	J	J	-	J	J	J	J	J	J	J	21	3	28
C (Chris) DeLuca	-	-	-	-	-	-	-	-	-	-	-	-	-	-	=B	-	-	-	-	-	-	-	-	-	-	-	-	-	-	-	-	-	-	-	1	-	-
PW (Paul) Dodge E8 L+	L	M	M	L	L	M	M	M	-	J	L	M	M	-	-	-	M	-	M	M	-	M	-	L	-	-	J	M	M	L	L	L	L	-	24	6	41
MJ (John) Duggan	N	N	N	N	-	-	N	N	N	N	N	N	N	N	-	N	N	N	N	N	-	N	-	-	-	-	-	-	-	x	K	N	-	-	20	8	32
NK (Nigel) Gillingham	>E	E	E	E	E	E	E	E	-	E	-	E	E	E	-	-	E	-	-	-	-	-	-	-	-	x	-	-	-	-	-	-	-	x	13	-	-
BP (Brian) Hall	M	L	L	M	M	L	-	L	-	-	x	-	-	M	-	L	L	L*	-	-	-	-	-	-	-	-	x	-	-	-	x	-	x	L	12	4	16
WH (Dusty) Hare E3	O	O	O	O	O	O	O	O	O	O	O	O	O	O	-	-	O	O	O	O	-	O	O	O	O	O	-	O	O	O	O	O	O	-	29	8	350
AG (Arthur) Hazlerigg	-	D	-	-	-	D	D	D	D	x	E	x	D	D	D	E	-	E	E	E	D	E	E	E	E	E	E	E	E	E	E	E	E	E	27	-	-
N (Neil) Holloway	-	-	-	-	-	-	-	-	-	-	C	-	x	-	-	-	-	-	-	-	-	-	-	-	-	-	-	-	C	-	-	-	-	<C	3	-	-
NA (Nick) Jackson	-	-	-	-	-	-	x	-	-	-	-	-	-	-	-	-	x	-	-	-	-	-	-	-	r	-	-	-	-	-	r	-	-	-	0+2	-	-
SR (Steve) Johnson	F	F	F	F	F	F	H	F	F	F	-	F	F	F	F	F	F	H	F	F	-	F	F	F	-	-	-	-	H	F	F	-	F	-	26	5	20
B (Bleddyn) Jones	J	J	J	J	J	<J	-	-	-	-	-	-	-	-	-	-	-	-	-	-	-	-	-	-	-	-	-	-	-	-	-	-	-	-	6	-	-
NJ (Nick) Joyce	D	-	D	D	D	-	-	-	E	D	D	D	-	-	E	D	D	D	D	D	E	D	D*	D	D	D	D	D	D	D	D	D	D	D	28	4	16
JS (Jim) Kempin	-	-	-	-	x	-	-	r	-	-	F	-	-	-	-	-	-	-	-	-	F	-	-	-	F	F	F	F	F	-	H	F	x	<F	10+1	3	12
S (Steve) Kenney	I	I	I	I	I	I	I	I	I	I	I	I	I	I	I	I	I	I	I	I	I	I	I	I	I	I	I	I	-	I	I	I	I	-	32	7	28
AM (Andy) Key	-	-	-	x	x	-	-	-	-	x	-	x	-	-	>O	O	-	-	-	x	O	-	-	-	x	-	O	-	-	-	-	-	-	O	5	-	6
J (Jez) Krych	-	-	-	-	-	-	-	-	-	-	-	-	-	-	A	A	A	A	-	-	A	-	A	-	-	-	x	-	-	x	-	-	x	-	6	-	-
RE (Ray) Needham	C	C	C	C	C	C	C	C	C	C	-	C	C	C	C	C	C	C	C	C	C	C	C	C	C	-	-	-	-	-	-	-	-	-	24	1	4
MJ (Mick) Newton	-	-	-	-	-	-	-	-	-	-	-	-	-	K	x	-	-	-	-	-	N	-	N	K	N	N	N	N	N	N	N	-	N	N	13	5	20
L (Larry) Parkes	x	-	-	-	-	-	-	-	-	-	-	-	-	-	L	-	-	-	-	-	M	x	L	x	L	L	L	x	-	x	-	-	-	-	6	2	8
R (Dick) Peters	-	-	-	-	-	-	-	-	-	-	-	-	-	>r	-	-	-	-	-	-	-	-	-	-	-	-	-	-	-	-	-	-	-	<r	0+2	-	-
SP (Steve) Redfern E+	-	-	-	-	-	-	-	-	-	-	-	-	-	-	-	-	-	-	-	-	-	-	-	-	-	C	C	C	-	C	C	C	C	-	7	1	4
WM (Bill) Reichwald	-	-	-	-	-	r	J	J	J	-	J	-	-	-	<J	-	-	-	-	-	-	-	-	-	-	-	-	-	-	-	-	-	-	-	5+1	-	-
GJ (Graham) Smith	-	-	-	-	-	-	-	-	-	-	-	-	-	>H	H	-	-	-	-	-	-	-	-	-	-	-	-	-	-	-	-	-	-	-	2	-	-
IR (Ian) Smith	H	H	H	H	H	H	F	H	H	H	H	H	H	-	-	H	H	F	H	H	-	H	H	H	H	H	H	H	-	H	-	H	H	H	29	6	24
PJ (Paul) Strickland	-	-	x	-	-	-	-	-	x	-	r	-	-	-	-	-	-	-	-	-	<H	-	x	-	-	-	-	-	-	-	-	-	-	-	1+1	-	-
TA (Tim) Walley	-	-	-	-	-	-	-	-	-	-	-	-	-	-	-	-	-	-	-	-	-	-	-	-	-	-	-	-	I	x	-	-	x	I	2	-	-
PJ (Peter) Wheeler E19 L3	B*	B*	B*	B*	B*	B*	B*	B*	-	B*	-	B*	B*	-	-	-	B*	-	B*	B*	-	B*	-	B*	-	-	-	B*	B*	B*	-	-	B*	-	20	4	16
JR (John) White	-	-	-	-	-	-	-	-	B	-	B	-	-	B	-	B	-	B	-	-	B	-	B	-	B	B	B	-	-	x	B	B	x	B	13	6	24
KR (Kelvin) Wilford	-	-	-	x	-	-	-	-	-	-	-	-	-	-	-	-	-	-	-	-	-	-	-	-	-	-	-	-	-	-	-	>r	-	-	0+1	-	-

The key for how to read the stats is on the last page

19 79/80	Home Ground: Welford Road	Trophy Cabinet: John Player Cup(2), Midland Merit Table	OVERALL RECORD:					T	C	PG	DG	PTS
	Coach: Chalkie White assisted by Rod Oakes		PLD	W	D	L	Tigers scored:	129	79	79	23	980
	Captain: Peter Wheeler		42	33	0	9	Opponents scored:	43	22	60	8	420

GM	DATE		VEN	OPPONENTS	RESULT	TRIES	KICKS	ATT
RFU CLUB COMPETITION (JOHN PLAYER CUP)						**CUP WINNERS: LEICESTER TIGERS**		
25	Jan	**26**	**H**	**Orrell (1)**	W 16-7	I.Smith 20	Cusworth 2d, Hare 2p	4335
29	Feb	23	a	Moseley (2)	W 17-7	Burwell 20, Dodge 70	Hare 2p, Cusworth d	-
32	Mar	**8**	**H**	**London Scottish (qf)**	W 22-0	Cusworth 30, I.Smith 71	Cusworth d, Hare c/3p	6174
36		29	a	Harlequins (sf)	W 16-9	Dodge 10	Hare 4p	-
40	Apr	19		London Irish (f)	W 21-9	-	Hare 4p/d, Cusworth 2d	27000
MIDLAND MERIT TABLE (1ST)						**WINNERS: LEICESTER TIGERS**		
1	Sep	1	a	Bedford	W 34-12	Hare(2), Needham, Woodward	Hare 3c/4p	-
2		**4tu**	**H**	**Nuneaton**	W 22-9	Barnwell(2), Wheeler	Hare 2c/2p	1048
4		**12w**	**H**	**Birmingham**	W 38-0	Woodward(4), Duggan, Forfar, Jackson, Key	Woodward 2c, Cusworth c	-
8	Oct	**6**	**H**	**Coventry**	W 25-3	Barnwell, Duggan, Hall	Hare 2c/3p	2799
10		20	a	Northampton	W 42-4	Hare(2), Barnwell(2), Woodward(2), Cusworth, Dodge	Hare 5c	-
14	Nov	13tu	a	Nottingham	W 28-8	Hare, Dodge, Redfern, K.Williams	Hare 3c/d, Cusworth d	-
16		23f	a	Moseley	L 6-13	-	Dodge 2p	-
CLUB MATCHES								
3	Sep	**8**	**H**	**Bath**	L 9-10	-	Hare 2p/d	1334
5		**15**	**H**	**London Welsh**	W 27-25	Woodward	Cusworth c/7p	1783
6		22	a	Harlequins	W 21-6	I.Smith(2), Burwell	Hare 3c/p	-
7		29	a	Saracens	W 15-13	Kenney	Hare c/2p/d	-
9	Oct	13	a	Richmond	W 28-13	Barnwell(2), Duggan, Woodward	Hare 3c/p/d	-
11		24w	a	Oxford University	W 18-15	Barnwell	Hare c/3p/d	-
12		**27**	**H**	**Swansea**	L 12-27	-	Hare 4p	3036
	Nov	**5m**	**H**	**Gloucester**	PP			
13		10	a	Cambridge University	W 34-0	Duggan(2), Hare, Cusworth, Gillingham, Wheeler	Hare 5c	-
15		**17**	**H**	**Wasps**	W 23-4	Wheeler(2), Burwell, Woodward	Hare 2c/p	1883
17	Dec	**1**	**H**	**Waterloo**	W 18-13	Cusworth, Dodge	Cusworth d, Hare 2c/p	1755
18		8	a	Blackheath	W 24-6	Hall, Woodward	Hare 2c/4p	-
19		**15**	**H**	**Bristol**	W 22-14	Gillingham, Woodward	Hare c/2p/d, Cusworth d	1725
20		22	a	London Welsh	W 12-6	-	Hare 2p/d, Cusworth d	-
21		**27th**	**H**	**Barbarians**	L 8-9	Adey, Burwell	-	10856
22		**29**	**H**	**Headingley**	W 55-3	Barnwell(2), Woodward(2), Hare, Dodge, Duggan, Kenney, I.Smith	Hare 8c, Poulson d	1454
23	Jan	5	a	Bath	W 22-12	Burwell, Cowling, I.Smith	Key 2c/2p	-
24		12	a	Gloucester	L 15-20	-	Key 4p, Poulson d	-
		18f	**H**	**Bedford**	PP (frost)			
26	Feb	**2**	**H**	**London Scottish**	W 14-9	Barnwell(2), Hall	Manship c	629
27		9	a	Newport	W 16-14	Cusworth, Woodward	Cusworth c/p/d	-
28		16	a	Hartlepool Rovers	W 25-6	Gillingham, I.Smith, K.Williams	Cusworth 2c/3p	-
		23	**H**	**Northampton**	PP (cup)			
30		**27w**	**H**	**Royal Navy**	W 54-3	Duggan(3), Johnson(2), Burwell, Collington, Cowling, Dodge, Jackson, Kenney, Wheeler	Cusworth 2c, Hare c	825
31	Mar	**1**	**H**	**Harlequins**	W 54-10	Cusworth(2), K.Williams(2), Duggan, Gillingham, Joyce, Redfern	Cusworth 5c/3p/d	1322
		8	a	Coventry	PP (cup)			
33		**11tu**	**H**	**Loughborough Students**	W 34-6	Collington(2), Kenney(2), Burwell	Cusworth 4c/p/d	795
34		**14f**	**H**	**Royal Air Force**	W 38-0	Burwell(2), Duggan(2), Collington, Redfern	Cusworth 4c/2p	822
35		**22**	**H**	**Sale**	W 24-7	Dodge(2), Duggan	Hare 3c/2p	2792
		29	**H**	**Birkenhead Park**	PP (cup)			
37	Apr	5	a	Neath	W 10-6	Burwell	Cusworth 2p	-
38		7m	a	Pontypool	L 13-21	Barnwell, Gillingham	Cusworth c/p	-
39		12	a	Bristol	L 13-16	Dodge, Johnson	Hare c/p	-
		19	**H**	**Pontypridd**	PP (cup)			
41		**26**	**H**	**Moseley**	L 20-27	Hare, Cowling, Jackson, Joyce	Hare 2c	2175
42		29tu	a	Rosslyn Park	L 15-18	Hare, Cusworth	Hare 2c/p	-

INDIVIDUAL APPEARANCES 1979/80

Name / Game #	1	2	3	4	5	6	7	8	9	10	11	12	13	14	15	16	17	18	19	20	21	22	23	24	25	26	27	28	29	30	31	32	33	34	35	36	37	38	39	40	41	42	Apps	T	Pts
GJ (Garry) Adey E2	G	G	G	-	G	G	G	G	-	G	-	G	G	G	G	G	G	G	G	G	G	G	G	G	G	-	-	-	-	-	-	G	-	-	-	x	x	G	G	G	G	-	27	1	4
RG (Bob) Barker	x	x	-	-	-	r	-	-	-	-	-	-	-	-	-	<N	-	-	-	-	-	-	-	-	-	-	-	-	-	-	-	-	-	-	-	-	-	-	-	-	-	-	1+1	-	-
RC (Tim) Barnwell	K	K	K	-	-	K	-	K	K	K	K	K	-	-	-	-	-	-	-	-	x	K	K	K	K	K	K	-	-	-	-	-	-	-	-	x	K	K	K	N	K	-	20	13	52
IM (Ian) Bridgwood	-	-	=B	-	-	-	-	-	-	-	-	-	-	-	-	-	-	-	-	-	-	-	-	-	-	-	-	-	-	-	-	-	-	-	-	-	-	-	-	-	-	-	1	-	-
TR (Terry) Burwell	-	N	-	M	M	M	L	x	-	-	L	r	-	-	N	L	K	K	K	K	K	-	L	M	x	M	N	L	K	K	L	K	K	K	K	K	M	N	N	K	M	K	32+1	10	40
AP (Angus) Collington	-	-	-	-	x	-	-	x	G	-	G	-	-	r	-	-	-	-	-	-	x	F	-	-	x	G	G	G	G	G	G	r	G	G	G	G	G	-	-	x	F	G	16+2	4	16
RJ (Robin) Cowling E8	-	-	-	-	-	-	-	-	-	-	A	A	A	A	A	A*	A	A	A	A	A	-	C*	A*	A	A*	A	A*	A	A	A*	A	A*	A*	A	A	A*	A*	A*	A	A*	A*	31	3	12
L (Les) Cusworth E1	J	J	J	J	J	J	J	J	J	J	-	J	J	J	J	-	J	-	J	J	J	-	-	-	J	J	J	J	J	J	J	J	J	J	J	J	J	J	J	J	J	J	36	8	173
PW (Paul) Dodge E10 L+	M	M	M	0	-	-	-	-	M	M	M	M	M	M	M	J	M	J	M	M	M	M	-	-	L	-	M	-	L	L	-	L	-	-	L	L	-	M	L	L	L	M	30	10	46
M (Mark) Duffelen	-	-	-	-	-	-	-	-	-	-	-	-	-	-	-	>B	-	-	-	-	-	-	B	B	-	B	-	B	-	-	B	-	B	B	-	x	B	B	B	x	B	B	13	-	-
MJ (John) Duggan	N	-	N	N	N	-	K	N	N	N	N	N	N	-	-	-	N	N	N	N	N	N	N	N	N	N	-	N	N	N	N	N	N	N	N	N	N	-	-	-	N	N	33	13	52
DJ (Dave) Forfar	F	F	F	F	F	-	-	F	F	H	-	F	-	-	F	F	H	H	-	-	-	-	-	-	-	-	-	-	-	-	-	-	-	-	H	-	-	r	H	-	-	-	15+1	1	4
MV (Malcolm) Foulkes-Arnold	-	-	-	>D	-	-	-	-	-	x	-	-	-	-	-	-	-	-	-	-	-	-	-	x	-	-	D	x	-	r	-	-	-	-	-	-	-	-	-	-	-	-	2+1	-	-
NK (Nigel) Gillingham	E	D	D	-	E	E	E	D	D	E	D	D	D	D	D	E	D	D	D	D	D	D	D	D	D	F	F	D	-	-	D	E	D	-	-	E	E	E	E	E	-	-	35	5	20
BP (Brian) Hall	-	-	x	-	0	-	M	M	-	-	-	-	-	-	-	M	-	M	-	-	-	-	M	L	-	L	-	M	x	-	M	x	M	L	-	-	L	L	-	x	-	L	15	3	12
WH (Dusty) Hare E8	0	0	0*	-	-	0	0	0	0	0	0	0	0	0	0	-	0	0	0	0	0	0	-	-	0	-	-	-	0	0	-	0	-	-	0	0	-	-	0	0	0	0	29	9	319
AG (Arthur) Hazlerigg	D	E	E	E	D	D	D	E	E	D	E	E	E	E	E	D	E	E	E	E	E	E	E	E	E	E	E	-	E	E	-	-	-	E	E	-	D	-	-	-	-	E	33	-	-
NA (Nick) Jackson	-	x	-	G	-	r	-	-	-	-	-	-	-	-	-	-	-	-	-	x	-	-	-	-	-	-	-	F	x	H	-	-	F	x	-	-	-	-	-	-	E	F	6+1	3	12
SR (Steve) Johnson	-	H	-	-	-	F	F	-	-	-	H	x	F	F	-	H	F	F	F	F	F	-	F	F	F	-	-	-	F	F	F	F	-	F	F	F	F	F	F	F	-	-	26	3	12
NJ (Nick) Joyce	-	-	-	-	-	-	-	-	-	-	x	-	-	-	-	-	-	-	-	-	-	-	-	-	-	D	-	E	D	D	E	D	E	D	D	D	-	D	D	D	D	D	15	2	8
S (Steve) Kenney	I	I	I	I	-	I	I	I	I	I	I	I	I	I	I	I	I	-	-	-	I	I	I	I	I	I	I	I	I	I	I	I	I	I	I	I	r	I	I	I	I	I	37+1	5	20
AM (Andy) Key	-	-	-	r	-	-	-	-	-	-	-	-	-	-	-	0	-	-	-	-	-	-	0	0	-	-	-	-	-	-	-	-	-	-	-	x	0	0	-	x	-	-	5+1	1	26
J (Jez) Krych	-	-	-	-	-	-	-	-	-	-	-	-	-	-	-	-	-	-	-	-	-	A	A	-	-	-	-	-	-	-	-	-	-	-	-	-	-	-	-	-	x	-	2	-	-
D (Dave) Manship	-	-	-	-	-	-	-	-	-	-	-	-	-	-	-	-	-	-	-	-	-	-	-	-	-	>0	0	0	-	-	0	-	0	0	x	-	-	-	-	-	-	-	6	-	2
MJP (Mick) Merriman	-	-	-	-	-	-	-	-	-	-	-	-	-	-	-	-	-	>I	I	I	-	-	-	-	-	-	-	-	-	-	-	-	-	-	-	x	I	-	-	x	-	-	4	-	-
RE (Ray) Needham	C	C	A	A	A	A	C	A	A	A	-	-	-	-	-	-	-	-	-	-	-	-	-	-	-	-	-	-	-	-	-	-	-	-	-	x	-	-	-	x	-	-	10	1	4
L (Larry) Parkes	x	-	-	-	r	-	x	-	-	-	-	-	-	-	-	x	-	-	x	-	-	x	-	-	-	-	x	-	-	-	-	-	L	M	-	-	-	-	-	-	-	-	2+1	-	-
MJ (Mike) Poulson	-	-	-	-	-	-	-	-	-	-	-	-	-	-	-	-	-	-	-	-	-	>J	J	J	-	-	-	-	-	-	x	-	-	-	-	-	-	-	-	-	-	-	3	-	6
SP (Steve) Redfern E+	-	-	C	C	C	C	-	C	C	C	C	C	C	C	C	C	C	C	C	C	C	C	-	C	C	C	C	C	C	C	C	C	C	C	C	C	C	C	C	C	C	C	38	3	12
IR (Ian) Smith	H	-	H	H	H	H	H	H	H	F	-	H	H	H	H	-	-	-	H	H	H	H	H	H	H	H	H	H	H	-	H	H	-	H	-	H	H	H	-	H	H	-	32	7	28
PD (Phil) Smith	-	-	-	-	-	-	-	-	-	-	=J	-	-	-	-	-	-	-	-	-	-	-	-	-	-	-	-	-	-	-	-	-	-	-	-	-	-	-	-	-	-	-	1	-	-
SJ (Steve) Solomons	-	-	-	-	-	-	-	-	-	-	r	-	-	-	-	-	-	-	-	-	-	-	-	-	-	-	x	-	-	-	-	-	H	-	-	-	-	-	x	-	-	H	2+1	-	-
PH (Paul) Stone	>A	A	-	-	-	-	A	-	-	-	-	-	-	-	-	-	-	-	-	-	-	-	-	-	-	-	-	-	-	-	-	-	-	-	-	-	-	-	-	-	-	-	3	-	-
TA (Tim) Walley	-	-	-	-	<I	-	-	-	-	-	-	-	-	-	-	-	-	-	-	-	-	-	-	-	-	-	-	-	-	-	-	-	-	-	-	-	-	-	-	-	-	-	1	-	-
PJ (Peter) Wheeler E24 L3	B*	B*	-	B*	B*	B*	B*	B*	B*	B*	B*	B*	B*	B*	B*	-	B*	B*	B*	B*	B*	B*	-	-	B*	-	B*	-	B*	B*	-	B*	-	-	B*	B*	-	-	-	B*	-	-	28	5	20
KR (Kelvin) Wilford	-	-	x	x	-	-	-	-	x	-	F	-	-	-	x	x	-	r	-	-	-	-	-	-	-	x	-	-	-	-	r	-	-	-	<r	-	-	-	-	-	-	-	1+3	-	-
GG (Graham) Willars	-	-	-	-	-	-	-	-	-	-	-	-	-	-	-	-	-	-	-	-	-	-	-	-	-	-	-	-	-	-	-	-	-	-	-	-	-	-	-	-	-	r	0+1	-	-
DJ (Dave) Williams	-	-	-	-	-	-	-	-	-	x	-	-	x	>K	-	-	-	-	-	-	-	-	-	-	-	-	-	-	-	-	-	-	-	-	-	-	-	-	-	-	x	-	1	-	-
AK (Kevin) Williams	-	-	-	>K	K	N	N	-	-	-	-	-	K	N	K	K	-	r	-	-	-	-	-	-	-	-	-	K	-	-	K	-	-	x	-	-	-	-	-	-	-	-	10+1	4	16
CR (Clive) Woodward E4 L+	>L	L	L	L	L	L	-	L	L	L	-	L	L	L	L	-	L	L	L	L	L	L	-	-	M	-	L	-	M	M	-	M	-	-	M	M	-	-	M	M	-	-	28	15	64

The key for how to read the stats is on the last page

CHAPTER 20

Centenary

1980/1981

Leicester's departure for Australia in August 1980 could hardly have found the club in better heart though even now, Peter Wheeler was thinking ahead: a convinced campaigner for more competitive rugby and improving the players' lot, Wheeler believed that a tour of this magnitude was essential to a progressive club every three years or so with lesser tours in between. It was not a view which found uniform agreement from those who felt that the money raised for tours could be better spent on the fabric of the club.

Wheeler's argument was that the players are the club and, if they are well-prepared and enthusiastic, then the club prospers anyway. Enthusiastic they were as they embarked on the three-week, six-match trip and evidently well-prepared since during the stopover in Vancouver three of the players (aptly Nick Joyce, the lock and a policeman, was one) disarmed a woman apparently intent on stabbing her husband to death with an eight-inch knife.

The high point of the Australian section of the tour was the meeting with Randwick, Sydney's champion club, which perhaps left Leicester under-prepared for the opening encounter against the might of Queensland at Ballymore: cluttered with internationals such as Paul McLean, Andrew Slack, Roger Gould and Peter Grigg the state side proved too strong for a team just off the plane and won 22-12, Garry Adey scoring both of Leicester's tries and Hare converting twice.

Eastern Suburbs, in Sydney, proved easier meat but if the backs dominated that game it was forward power which beat Randwick 31-19 at Coogee Oval in the clash of champions: Ian Smith and John White scored tries while Hare lobbed over five penalties, a dropped goal and a conversion and Cusworth threw in another dropped goal. Suitably heartened Leicester flew to Fiji and won all three games, against Lautoka 12-6, Combined Fijian Services 8-4 and a Fiji Chairman's XV 12-0 (Hare three penalties and a Cusworth dropped goal). The final game was the only one in which Wheeler played, a neck injury having limited his activities to those of tour leader rather than tour captain. But all in all it proved valuable experience and admirable preparation for the season ahead.

Those at home had not been idle either. Gate takings during the previous season had risen by £15,000 and season-ticket returns doubled, a reflection both of the club's mounting popularity and the capacity of their own voluntary workers to deal with it. When the domestic season opened Welford Road was in prime condition with over 1,000 new seats in the Members' Stand, new floodlighting and enough new paintwork to satisfy a sergeant-major, all after the expenditure of some £50,000.

↓ First day cover to celebrate the centenary of the club posted at Welford Road on 10.10.1980.

The fixture list included in the first two months visits from the Irish Wolfhounds - a guest side with whom Cusworth, for one, enjoyed many happy moments playing sevens - Romania and Queensland. Hare and Woodward scored tries against the Wolfhounds in a slim 10-6 win but the work of the tour was not immediately apparent in the early-season defeat at Bath. Worse came in October when the Romanians arrived at the end of their tour of Ireland during which they had drawn 13-13 with what was in all but name the full Irish XV: Tigers crashed 39-7 and Florica Murariu, the 24-times capped visiting flanker, scored four tries. Leicester's limited response came from Kevin Williams' try and Hare's penalty.

Spirits were briefly raised by the return match with Queensland, who found Leicester less accommodating on home soil and lost 21-9, the only defeat of their five-match tour of England and Scotland.

But when the defence crumbled against Gloucester at Kingsholm by 31-4 it was evident hard work was going to be necessary if the centenary was not going to be something of a whimper; adding point to such thoughts was the knowledge that a Rugby Football Union committee headed by John Burgess, the former England coach, was going the rounds of the country discussing the way ahead, in particular a revised competitive structure including league rugby. The Burgess Report had its critics and Jerry Day warned against their possible consequences: "If a club wanted to compete with any success in a league system it would have to become almost professional - with all the inherent risks that entails," Day said. "The pressure to win would, of course, produce more inhibited rugby." Set against that was Wheeler's opinion that "leagues are long overdue. Either we have a successful

↓ Tigers run out for the tour fixture in the searing heat of Lautoka, Fiji.

international side or we simply carry on as we are. Players would benefit by having that extra competitive edge."

Wheeler's return to action from injury assisted a revival while the captain himself, together with Woodward, represented England and Wales against Scotland and Ireland in one of the Welsh Rugby Union's centenary celebration games, Woodward scoring a try and dropping a goal in his XV's 37-33 win (for good measure Wheeler played in the WRU's final centenary game the following April). Wheeler also captained the Midlands in a somewhat dreary revival of the divisional championship, then played on a knockout basis in which the North took the trophy by virtue of their 6-0 win over a Midland XV including five Leicester backs.

The Barbarians match produced a breathless 28-24 win for the visitors and more points in the fixture than ever before; it also helped project Kevin Williams, the young PE teacher at City of Leicester School who had taken over from Duggan on the wing, into the Welsh squad though his reward did not come until the next season when he played for Wales B against the Australians.

Four Leicester players appeared on the senior side in the England trial and the same quartet - Hare, Dodge, Woodward and Wheeler - went forward to the opening international, against Wales which was a triumph for Hare in that he scored all England's 19 points but a disaster for Woodward in that his accidental offside in midfield gave Steve Fenwick the chance to kick the winning goal in Wales's 21-19 win. Unlike a year earlier Hare could not convert the late penalty which would have restored England's fortunes.

In what was to prove a disappointing England season, after the euphoria of 1980, England retained the services of their Leicester players in the 23-17 win over Scotland (in which Woodward scored a try and Hare kicked 11 points) but then dismissed Hare and called up, instead, Rose which was a bittersweet pill for the club. The young full-back responded by scoring a try against Ireland, in Dublin, and then setting up another for Dodge in a 10-6 win; but he could not prevent a French grand slam at Twickenham despite kicking four penalties.

Back at Welford Road, Leicester embarked on the cup trail in the knowledge that this would be the last season for two great stalwarts, Garry Adey and Robin Cowling. An ankle injury, increased work commitments and the demands of a young family led to Adey's announcement of impending retirement in January while Cowling's job as a farm manager took him back to his native Ipswich and subsequently to Cornwall where he remained involved in the game as a forwards coach and latterly as team manager to Exeter Chiefs.

The club opened with a 34-3 win at Roundhay and followed up with a 27-14 win over Bristol, Hare kicking seven goals from eight attempts on a slippery surface. Conditions were not much better against Sale in the quarter-final: earlier in the week Welford Road had been almost under water but it drained sufficiently well to allow Leicester their 21-7 win in which, again, Hare's place-kicking was outstanding with five goals out of five.

If Leicester had found the going hard before, they had to redouble their effort in the semi-final at London Scottish. This proved to be the first extra-time cup tie when, at the end of normal time, the score stood locked at 12-12. No-one could have been feeling the pace more than Wheeler, Woodward and Cusworth, who had returned only 24 hours earlier from Hong Kong where they had helped the Barbarians win the prestigious Sevens.

↑ Peter Wheeler, Steve Kenney and Steve Johnson during the nail-biting cup semi-final at London Scottish.

Leicester used two replacements, Woodward suffered concussion and thought he was still in Hong Kong, Johnson and Wheeler finished with various wounds after an unrelenting yet gripping struggle in which two dropped goals by Cusworth finally settled the issue. The club were through to an unprecedented fourth successive final, against Gosforth, and those Leicester supporters who made the trip (many did not as a protest against unreasonably high ticket charges at the Richmond Athletic Ground) must have thought their money well spent.

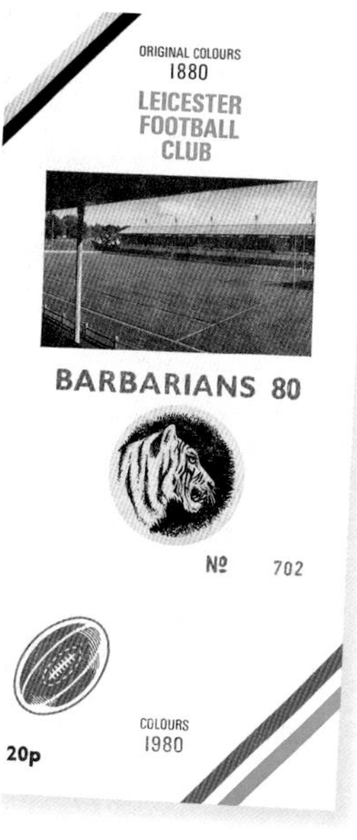

↑ Programme from the 1980 Barbarians game.

The following climactic month contained more than even the most romantic novelist could have wished for: first came the emergence from retirement of Adey as the club, anxious about the well-being of Angus Collington who damaged a shoulder against the Scottish, asked their No 8 for one more effort. Adey's best was so good that the unlucky Collington, so often a bridesmaid on the big occasion, found himself a replacement yet again for a cup final.

Then came Hare's assault on the world points-scoring record, that of 3,651 established by the late Sam Doble, of Moseley and, briefly, England, in the middle 1970s. It was to Moseley that Leicester went in mid-April: Hare, then 28, needed six points. He scored 14 to conclude the game with 3,658 of which 1,578 were scored for Nottingham, 1,532 for Leicester and the remainder from international and other representative games. "I couldn't tell anyone else how to kick," Hare said. "All you can say is, get the run-up right. It's like a fast bowler, you must have the right approach and you must keep your head down. If I'm having a poor spell it's usually because the rhythm has gone, what's happening when I get to the ball to kick it."

Everything was coming together at the right moment: centenary, world record and a cup final at Twickenham on 2 May with a team which read: Dusty Hare; Kevin Williams, Paul Dodge, Clive Woodward, Tim Barnwell; Les Cusworth, Steve

↑ Chalkie White and his team with the John Player Cup after their third successive victory in the final.

Kenney; Robin Cowling, Peter Wheeler (captain), Steve Redfern, Nick Joyce, Nick Jackson, Steve Johnson, Garry Adey, Ian Smith.

It was Wheeler's last match as captain after three magnificent years; it was the last appearance in Leicester colours for Adey and Cowling (who led the team out) before 24,000 people. Chalkie White had warned beforehand about the effect of nearly two years of continuous rugby but he need not have worried as Leicester, against a Gosforth team whose forwards, critics predicted, would take charge of the match, produced the most remarkable of three consecutive cup wins. The front row was rock-like and though Steve Bainbridge presented problems in the line-out they were not insuperable. The midfield organisation was watertight and Cusworth, as he was to do throughout the 1980s, pulled the strings like a conjurer. Even when Gosforth had pulled back to 12-9 and dominated possession in the third quarter they lacked the guile - and perhaps the big-match experience which was Leicester's - to use it effectively.

Hare, on his way to a club record of 358 points for the season, kicked two first-half penalties and converted a try by Kenney against David Johnson's two penalties. Brian Patrick's penalty from fifty yards narrowed the gap and Johnson might have levelled the scores with a penalty but he missed. Leicester threw everything into attack, Steve Johnson made the extra man and Woodward sent Barnwell speeding on his way to the try-line. Going into injury-time Hare pursued his own chip ahead to score a try which he converted; the result was secure and Johnson "limped" off, allowing Collington to leave the replacements bench and take a place in the side for which he had worked so hard during the season. It mattered little that Rob Cunningham scored late in the day for Gosforth; Leicester had equalled their record for wins in a season by their 22-15 success and the cup was at their lips.

Moreover it was theirs for keeps. John Player, the sponsors, had offered it as a permanent trophy to any side good enough to win three times in a row. "Just looking at the cup reminds you not only of the matches but the good times afterwards," Wheeler said. "It also means a lot to the people of the city and our way of thanking them for their support will be to show the cup off at pubs and clubs so there's no question of it gathering dust."

Six days later 700 gathered at the De Montfort Hall for almost the final act of a memorable centenary season (that it was not the final act was only because Leicester had agreed to send a team to the Middlesex sevens the following day; although they overcame Loughborough Students it was hardly surprising, in view of the night before, that they then succumbed to Saracens). The centenary dinner was a night of tributes, a night for sentiment for Eric Lacey, the president, and good humour from Max Boyce, the Welsh humorist and self-confessed rugby nut.

↑ LEICESTER FOOTBALL CLUB 1980/81
Back: Day (Hon.Sec), Thomas (Team Hon.Sec), Needham, Johnson, Collington, Richardson, Jackson, Joyce, Adey, Redfern, Smith, Lacey (President), White (Coach).
Middle: Key, K.Williams, Kenney, Hare, Wheeler (capt), Cowling, Woodward, Barnwell, Burwell.
Front: Merriman, Tressler. Inset: Cusworth.

1980	CENTENARY TOUR	OVERALL RECORD:					T	C	PG	DG	PTS
	Coach: Chalkie White assisted by Rod Oakes	PLD	W	D	L	Tigers scored:	10	7	10	5	99
	Captain: Nick Joyce	6	5	0	1	Opponents scored:	7	4	6	0	54

GM	DATE		VEN	OPPONENTS	RESULT	TRIES	KICKS	ATT
1	Aug	6w	a	Queensland	L 12-22	Adey(2)	Hare 2c	-
2		10s	a	Eastern Suburbs	W 24-3	Barnwell, Key, Williams	Cusworth 3c/2p	-
3		13w	a	Randwick	W 31-19	Smith, White	Hare c/5p/d, Cusworth d	6000
4		16	a	Lautoka	W 12-6	Smith	Hare c/2d	2000
5		20w	a	Fiji Combined Services	W 8-4	Barnwell, Cusworth	-	-
6		23	a	Fiji Chairman's XV	W 12-0	-	Hare 3p, Cusworth d	-

INDIVIDUAL APPEARANCES 1980 CENTENARY TOUR									
Name / Game #	1	2	3	4	5	6	Apps	T	Pts
GJ (Garry) Adey E2	G	-	G	-	E	G	4	2	8
RC (Tim) Barnwell	K	K	K	-	N	N	5	2	8
TR (Terry) Burwell	r	M	L	-	L	L	4+1	-	-
AP (Angus) Collington	-	G	-	G	-	r	2+1	-	-
L (Les) Cusworth E1	J	J	J	-	J	J	5	1	22
PW (Paul) Dodge E10 L2	M	-	M	J	-	M	4	-	-
M (Mark) Duffelen	-	B	-	B	-	-	2	-	-
MJ (John) Duggan	N	-	-	<N	-	-	2	-	-
DJ (Dave) Forfar	-	H	-	F	G	F	4	-	-
NK (Nigel) Gillingham	E	D	-	-	-	-	2	-	-
BP (Brian) Hall	L	-	-	-	-	-	1	-	-
WH (Dusty) Hare E8	O	-	O	O	-	O	4	-	41
NA (Nick) Jackson	-	E	E	E	D	E	5	-	-
SR (Steve) Johnson	F	F*	F*	-	F*	H	5	-	-
NJ (Nick) Joyce	D*	r	D	D*	r	D	4+2	-	-
S (Steve) Kenney	I	-	I	-	I	-	3	-	-
AM (Andy) Key	-	O	-	L	O	-	3	1	4
MJP (Mick) Merriman	-	I	-	I	-	I	3	-	-
RE (Ray) Needham	A	C	-	A	A	-	4	-	-
L (Larry) Parkes	-	L	-	M	<M	-	3	-	-
SP (Steve) Redfern E+	C	-	C	C	C	C	5	-	-
IR (Ian) Smith	H	-	H	H	H	-	4	2	8
PH (Paul) Stone	-	A	A	-	-	A	3	-	-
PJ (Peter) Wheeler E24 L7	-	-	-	-	-	B*	1	-	-
JR (John) White	B	-	B	-	<B	-	3	1	4
AK (Kevin) Williams	-	N	N	K	K	K	5	1	4

← LEICESTER FOOTBALL CLUB CENTENARY TOUR 1980
Back: Smith, Redfern, Collington, Johnson, Jackson, Gillingham, Joyce, Adey, Forfar, White (coach).
Middle: Duggan, Hare, Dodge, Duffelen, Wheeler (capt), Williams, Burwell, Barnwell, Needham, Stone.
Front: Hall, Key, Cusworth, Merriman, White, Kenney, Parkes.

The key for how to read the stats is on the last page

19 80/81	Home Ground: Welford Road	Trophy Cabinet: John Player Cup(3), Midland Merit Table	OVERALL RECORD:					T	C	PG	DG	PTS
	Coach: Chalkie White assisted by Rod Oakes		PLD	W	D	L	Tigers scored:	121	78	82	18	940
	Captain: Peter Wheeler		41	33	1	7	Opponents scored:	63	28	57	16	527

GM	DATE		VEN	OPPONENTS	RESULT	TRIES	KICKS	ATT
RFU CLUB COMPETITION (JOHN PLAYER CUP)						**CUP WINNERS: LEICESTER TIGERS**		
25	Jan	24	a	Roundhay (3)	W 34-3	Cusworth 20, Barnwell 45, Cowling 78	Cusworth d, Hare 2c/4p, Dodge d	3000
31	Feb	**28**	**H**	**Bristol (4)**	W 27-14	K.Williams 17, Smith 70	Hare 2c/5p	6212
33	Mar	**14**	**H**	**Sale (qf)**	W 21-7	K.Williams 74	Hare c/4p, Cusworth d	8023
36	Apr	4	a	London Scottish (sf)	W 18-12 (aet)	-	Hare 4p, Cusworth 2d	4000
41	May	2		Gosforth (f)	W 22-15	Kenney 14, Barnwell 65, Hare 80	Hare 2c/2p	24000
MIDLAND MERIT TABLE (1ST)						**WINNERS: LEICESTER TIGERS**		
1	Sep	2tu	a	Nuneaton	W 10-6	Barnwell	Hare 2p	-
2		**6**	**H**	**Bedford**	W 43-6	Barnwell(2), Adey, Gillingham, Johnson, Smith	Hare 5c/3p	1649
5		**17w**	**H**	**Birmingham**	W 36-12	Cusworth(2), Johnson, Kenney, K.Williams	Cusworth 5c/2p	1411
8	Oct	4	a	Coventry	W 22-19	Dodge, K.Williams	Hare c/4p	-
10		**18**	**H**	**Northampton**	W 25-21	Hare, Cusworth, Kenney, Woodward	Hare 3c/p	2744
15	Nov	**11tu**	**H**	**Nottingham**	W 23-10	Jackson, Joyce, Knowles, K.Williams	Hare 2c/p	1538
17		**22**	**H**	**Moseley**	D 10-10	Barnwell	Cusworth d, Hare p	3750
CLUB MATCHES								
3	Sep	**10w**	**H**	**Irish Wolfhounds**	W 10-6	Hare, Woodward	Hare c	3186
4		13	a	Bath	L 4-13	Dodge	-	-
6		**20**	**H**	**London Welsh**	W 30-15	Adey, Gillingham, Kenney, K.Williams	Hare 4c/p/d	2508
7		27	a	Harlequins	W 45-15	Hare, Barnwell, Dodge, Gillingham, Needham, Woodward	Hare 6c/3p	-
9	Oct	**11**	**H**	**Richmond**	W 38-6	Dodge(2), Hare, Barnwell, Joyce	Hare 3c/4p	2556
11		**22w**	**H**	**Romania**	L 7-39	K.Williams	Hare p	5501
12		**25**	**H**	**Queensland**	W 21-9	K.Williams	Hare c/3p/2d	3677
13	Nov	1	a	Gloucester	L 4-31	Dodge	-	-
14		**8**	**H**	**Cambridge University**	W 50-7	Hare(3), Dodge, Knowles, Redfern, K.Williams	Hare 5c/2p, Cusworth d, Woodward d	2066
16		15	a	Wasps	W 18-12	-	Hare 4p, Cusworth 2d	-
18		**29**	**H**	**Saracens**	W 22-13	Barnwell(2), Dodge	Dodge 2c/2p	1956
19	Dec	6	a	Waterloo	W 27-7	Hall, Joyce, Kenney, Key	Cusworth 2p/d, Dodge c	-
20		**13**	**H**	**Blackheath**	W 46-9	Merriman, Poulson, Johnson, Joyce, Key, K.Williams	Merriman 5c/3p, Poulson d	1741
21		20	a	Bristol	W 9-6	-	Merriman 2p, Poulson d	-
22		**29m**	**H**	**Barbarians**	L 24-28	Smith, Wheeler, K.Williams, Woodward	Hare 4c	16000
23	Jan	**3**	**H**	**Bath**	W 13-11	Jackson, Smith	Key c/p	2352
24		**10**	**H**	**Gloucester**	W 14-9	Cusworth, Barnwell, Redfern	Cusworth c	2881
		16f	a	Bedford	PP			
26		**31**	**H**	**Ballymena**	W 39-7	Smith(2), Woodward(2), Dodge, K.Williams	Hare 3c/3p	2894
27	Feb	7	a	London Scottish	W 30-7	Cusworth, Collington, Knowles, K.Williams	Cusworth 2d, Hare c/2p	-
28		**14**	**H**	**Newport**	W 37-6	Wheeler(2), Johnson, Kenney	Hare 3c/5p	3636
29		**18w**	**H**	**Royal Navy**	W 22-12	Jackson, Johnson, K.Williams	Cusworth 2c/p, Key p	1242
30		21	a	London Welsh	L 10-46	K.Williams	Key 2p	-
		28	a	Northampton	PP (cup)			
32	Mar	**7**	**H**	**Harlequins**	W 29-6	Barnwell, Burwell, Collington, Jackson, Smith	Key 3c/p	802
		14	**H**	**Coventry**	PP (cup)			
		17tu	**H**	**Loughborough Students**	PP (rain)			
34		**20f**	**H**	**Royal Air Force**	W 22-3	Johnson(2), Barnwell, Joyce, K.Williams	Manship c	1090
35		28	a	Sale	L 6-15	-	Hare 2p	-
	Apr	4	a	Birkenhead Park	PP (cup)			
37		10f	a	Pontypridd	L 6-25	Hare	Hare c	-
38		**18**	**H**	**Neath**	W 22-3	Barnwell, Johnson, Wheeler	Hare 2c/2p	2217
39		**20m**	**H**	**Pontypool**	W 18-13	Adey, Dodge, Smith	Hare 3c	3864
40		25	a	Moseley	W 26-13	Newton(2), Hare, Smith	Hare 2c/2p	-
		28tu	**H**	**Rosslyn Park**	PP			

Neutral Venue: *#41 at Twickenham*

INDIVIDUAL APPEARANCES 1980/81

Name / Game #	1	2	3	4	5	6	7	8	9	10	11	12	13	14	15	16	17	18	19	20	21	22	23	24	25	26	27	28	29	30	31	32	33	34	35	36	37	38	39	40	41	Apps	T	Pts
GJ (Garry) Adey E2	G	G	G	G	-	G	G	G	G	G	G	G	G	G	-	-	-	-	-	-	-	-	-	-	-	-	-	-	-	-	-	-	-	-	-	-	-	-	G	G	<G	16	3	12
RC (Tim) Barnwell	K	K	K	K	K	K	K	K	K	K	K	K	K	K	K	K	K	K	K	-	-	K	K	K	K	K	K	K	K	K	K	K	K	K	K	K	K	K	K	-	K	38	14	56
DS (Duncan) Black	-	-	-	-	-	-	-	-	-	-	-	-	-	-	>r	-	-	-	-	-	x	-	-	-	-	-	-	x	-	-	-	-	-	H	-	-	G	x	x	x	-	2+1	-	-
TR (Terry) Burwell	L	L	L	L	-	x	-	-	x	-	x	x	-	-	x	-	r	-	-	L	L	-	L	L	x	-	-	-	L	L	-	L	-	L	-	-	L	M	-	-	-	14+1	1	4
AP (Angus) Collington	x	-	-	x	G	-	-	x	-	-	x	x	-	F	G	G	G	G	G	G	G	G	G	G	G	G	G	G	G	G	G	G	G	-	-	G	-	G	-	-	r	23+1	2	8
JTC (Tim) Cooke	-	-	-	x	x	-	-	x	-	-	-	-	>r	-	-	-	-	-	x	M	-	-	x	-	-	-	-	-	r	-	-	-	-	x	-	-	-	-	-	-	-	1+2	-	-
RJ (Robin) Cowling E8	-	-	-	-	-	-	-	-	-	-	A	A	A	A*	A*	A*	A	A*	A	A*	A*	A	A*	A*	A	A	A	A	A*	A*	A	A*	A	A*	A*	A	A	-	A	A*	<A	30	1	4
L (Les) Cusworth E1	J	J	J	J	J	J	J	J	J	J	J	J	J	J	J	J	J	-	J	-	-	J	-	J	J	J	J	J	J	-	J	-	J	J	-	J	J	-	-	J	J	32	6	88
PW (Paul) Dodge E14 L2	-	-	-	M	-	L	L	L	L*	L	L	L	L	L	L	L	L	L	L	-	-	M	-	-	M	L	L	L	-	-	L	-	L	-	L	M	M	-	L	M	M	28	10	55
IR (Ian) Dodson	-	-	-	-	-	-	-	-	-	-	-	-	-	-	-	-	-	-	-	-	-	-	-	-	-	-	-	-	-	-	-	>J	-	-	J	-	-	-	-	-	-	2	-	-
M (Mark) Duffelen	B	B	B	B	-	B	B	B	-	B	B	B	<B	-	-	-	-	-	-	-	-	-	-	-	-	-	-	-	-	-	-	-	-	-	-	-	-	-	-	-	-	11	-	-
DJ (Dave) Forfar	H	-	-	-	H	-	-	F	F	F	H	-	F	-	-	-	-	-	-	-	-	-	-	-	-	-	-	-	-	-	-	-	-	-	-	-	-	-	-	-	-	7	-	-
MV (Malcolm) Foulkes-Arnold	-	-	-	-	D	-	-	-	E	D	-	-	D	-	-	r	-	x	-	-	-	-	-	-	-	-	-	-	-	-	-	-	-	-	-	-	-	-	-	-	-	4+1	-	-
AD (Dave) Gavins	-	-	-	-	-	-	-	-	-	-	-	-	-	-	-	-	-	-	-	-	-	-	x	-	-	-	-	-	-	-	-	-	-	-	=r	-	-	-	-	-	-	0+1	-	-
NK (Nigel) Gillingham	-	E	E	E	E	E	E	E*	-	E*	E	E	E	E	E	E	-	-	-	-	-	-	-	-	-	-	-	-	-	-	-	-	-	-	-	-	-	-	-	-	-	14	3	12
BP (Brian) Hall	-	-	-	-	L	-	x	-	-	-	x	x	-	x	-	-	-	M	M	-	-	x	M	M	-	x	-	-	M	M	x	M	x	M	M	r	-	-	-	-	x	11+1	1	4
WH (Dusty) Hare E10	O	O	O	O	-	O	O	O	O	O	O	O	O	O	O	O	O	-	-	-	-	O	-	-	O	O	O	O	-	-	O	-	O	-	O	O	O	O	O	O	O	30	10	358
NA (Nick) Jackson	E	r	x	-	r	-	r	-	-	-	-	-	-	-	F	-	E	E	E	E	E	E	E	E	E	E	E	E	E	E	E	E	E	G	G	E	D	E	E	E	E	27+3	4	16
SR (Steve) Johnson	F*	F*	F*	F*	F*	F*	F*	-	-	-	F*	F*	H*	-	-	F	F	F	F	F	F	F	F	F	F	F	-	F	F	F	F	-	F	F	F	F	-	F	-	F	F	32	8	32
NJ (Nick) Joyce	D	D	D	D	-	D	D	D	D	-	D	D	-	D	D	D	D	D	D	D	D	D	D	D	D	D	D	D	D	D	D	D	D	D	D	D	-	D	D	D	D	37	5	20
S (Steve) Kenney	I	I	I	I	I	I	I	I	I	I	I	I	I	I	I	I	I	I	I	-	-	I	I	-	I	I	I	I	I	I	I	I	I	I	I	I	I	-	I	I	I	37	6	24
AM (Andy) Key	x	-	r	-	O	-	-	-	-	-	-	-	-	-	-	-	-	O	O	O	O	-	O	O	-	-	-	-	O	J	-	O	-	-	-	x	x	L	M	L	x	13+1	2	31
MS (Mac) Knowles	-	-	-	-	-	-	-	-	-	-	-	-	-	>H	H	H	x	-	-	H	-	-	-	-	-	r	F	-	x	-	x	F	x	-	-	r	F	-	F	-	-	8+2	3	12
D (Dave) Manship	-	-	-	-	-	-	-	-	-	-	-	-	-	-	-	-	-	-	-	-	-	-	-	-	-	-	-	-	-	O	-	-	-	O	-	-	-	-	-	-	-	2	-	2
MJP (Mick) Merriman	-	-	-	-	-	-	-	-	-	-	x	x	-	-	-	-	-	-	-	I	I	-	-	I	-	-	-	-	-	-	-	-	-	-	-	x	-	I	-	-	x	4	1	29
MJ (Mike) Nangreave	-	-	-	-	-	-	-	-	-	x	-	-	-	=r	-	-	-	-	-	-	-	-	-	-	-	-	-	-	-	-	-	-	-	-	-	-	-	-	-	-	-	0+1	-	-
RE (Ray) Needham	A	A	A	A	-	-	A	A	A	A	x	x	C	-	-	-	-	-	-	C	C	x	-	-	r	-	r	-	-	-	-	-	-	-	-	-	-	-	-	-	-	11+2	1	4
MJ (Mick) Newton	-	-	-	-	-	-	-	-	-	-	-	-	-	-	-	x	-	-	N	K	K	-	-	-	-	-	-	-	-	-	-	-	-	-	x	-	-	r	r	K	-	4+2	2	8
MJ (Mike) Poulson	-	-	-	-	-	-	-	-	-	-	-	-	-	-	-	-	-	J	-	J	J	-	J	-	-	-	-	-	-	-	-	-	-	-	-	-	-	-	-	-	-	4	1	10
SP (Steve) Redfern E+	C	C	C	C	C	C	C	C	C	C	C	C	-	C	C	C	C	C	C	-	-	C	C	C	C	C	C	C	C	C	C	C	C	C	-	C	C	A	-	C	C	36	2	8
WP (Wayne) Richardson	-	-	-	-	-	-	-	-	-	-	-	-	-	-	-	-	-	-	-	-	-	-	-	-	-	-	-	-	-	x	-	-	-	-	>C	x	x	C	C	-	x	3	-	-
IR (Ian) Smith	-	H	H	H	-	H	H	H	H	H	-	H	-	-	-	-	H	H	H	-	H	H	H	H	H	H	H	H	H	H	H	H	H	-	H	H	H	H	H	H	H	32	9	36
SJ (Steve) Solomons	-	-	-	-	-	x	-	-	x	-	-	-	r	-	-	-	-	-	-	<r	-	-	-	-	-	-	-	-	-	-	-	-	-	-	-	-	-	-	-	-	-	0+2	-	-
PH (Paul) Stone	-	-	-	-	A	A	-	-	-	-	-	-	-	-	-	-	-	-	-	-	-	-	-	x	-	-	-	-	-	-	-	x	-	-	-	-	-	-	-	-	-	2	-	-
CJ (Chris) Tressler	-	-	-	-	>B	-	-	-	B	-	-	-	-	B	B	B	-	B	-	B	B	-	B	B	-	-	-	-	B	B	-	B	-	B	B	x	-	-	-	B	x	16	-	-
DP (Dean) Waddingham	-	-	-	-	-	-	-	-	-	-	-	-	-	-	-	-	-	-	>r	-	-	-	-	-	-	-	-	-	-	-	-	-	-	E	E	-	E	-	-	-	-	3+1	-	-
PJ (Peter) Wheeler E28 L7	-	-	-	-	-	-	-	-	-	-	x	-	-	-	-	-	B*	-	B*	-	-	B*	-	-	B*	B*	B*	B*	-	-	B*	-	B*	-	-	B*	B*	B*	B*	-	B*	14	4	16
DJ (Dave) Williams	-	-	-	-	-	-	-	-	-	x	-	-	-	-	-	-	-	-	-	x	-	-	N	-	-	-	x	-	-	-	-	x	-	-	-	-	-	-	-	N	-	2	-	-
AK (Kevin) Williams	N	N	N	N	N	N	N	N	N	N	N	N	N	N	N	N	N	N	-	N	N	N	-	N	N	N	N	N	N	N	N	N	N	N	N	N	N	N	N	-	N	38	16	64
CR (Clive) Woodward E8 L2	M	M	M	-	M	M	M	M	M	M	M	M	M	M	M	M	M	-	-	-	-	L	-	-	L	M	M	M	-	-	M	-	M	-	-	L	-	J	J	-	L	27	6	27

CHAPTER 21

End of the Day

1981/1982

Whatever followed such an overflowing season was bound to bring a sense of anti-climax. Peter Wheeler, to no-one's surprise, declared his unavailability for England's summer tour to Argentina although Dusty Hare, Clive Woodward and Paul Dodge all travelled, Woodward scoring two tries in the drawn first test and Hare kicking seven and eight points respectively in the two internationals.

In Leicester there was a sad start to the season with the death of Ken Kinder, president in the first cup-winning year and a committeeman since 1958. Chalkie White lamented that the club's success had not attracted more new talent - although Nick Youngs had joined the club from Bedford - but existing members quivered at the news of Wheeler's elevation to Justice of the Peace, the law bench being an arena not unknown to rugby players the worse for wear, notably on tour.

A touring team composed largely of players from the Extras and the Swifts returned in good heart from a close-season tour of Florida and Steve Johnson, the new captain, was full of optimism for the new season. He had every reason to be as Leicester brushed aside a series of opponents and Jerry Day pondered whether playing standards elsewhere in the country were declining. Following up the thought, he asked the newly-formed Senior Clubs Association whether they would care to constitute their own criteria for a "first-class" club. "We are so far in front of everyone else that we can play at half-pace and still win," Day opined, on the eve of a 49-12 demolition job of Harlequins at Twickenham.

Even that was as nothing compared with the club's then record win of 78-8 over Birmingham at the Portway, Hare scoring three of their 14 tries and converting 11 of them for another club record tally of 34 points. Pride goeth before a fall: Richmond forced a draw and Leicester lost their unbeaten record in mid-October to Northampton on a day when seven club players appeared for the Midlands against the touring Australians at Welford Road and two more were on the bench. Remarkably one of those two was Hare because Marcus Rose was preferred at full-back and kicked two penalties and a conversion in the 16-10 victory which got the touring side off to a thoroughly bad start.

The Midlands team was: Marcus Rose (Cambridge University); Steve Holdstock (Nottingham), Huw Davies (Cambridge University), Clive Woodward, Tim Barnwell; Les Cusworth (all Leicester), Steve Thomas (Coventry); Steve Redfern (Leicester), Peter Wheeler (Leicester, captain), Steve Wilkes (Coventry), Nick Joyce (Leicester), Vince Cannon (Northampton), Nick Jeavons (Moseley), Graham Robbins (Coventry), Ian Smith (Leicester).

↑ Jerry Day played for Leicester in 1945, and went on to become honorary secretary from 1966-1982.

Dodge would have played but his withdrawal with a hamstring injury on the morning of the match meant the removal of Huw Davies from fly-half to centre and Cusworth's inclusion in a match where the tries came from Steve Holdstock and Nick Jeavons. The Australians struggled in their next four games, including a 10-9 win over a Wales B side including Kevin Williams, although when Youngs played against them for London they were building up a head of steam.

They beat Ireland in the first international and returned to Leicester on 25 November to play the club, an unusual honour granted in recognition of the outstanding achievements of the past three seasons. Not that Leicester were in wonderful shape: defeats against Swansea and Gloucester and the loss of Tim Barnwell with a broken jaw had seen to that. Moreover, Steve Kenney injured a leg against Nottingham and Williams had sustained an eye injury playing for Wales B, which gave scope for a youngster from Hinckley, Barry Evans, just 20, to come into the side.

Evans's speed impressed everyone and Youngs, the squat, powerful son of a farmer, made his debut at scrum-half although by the time the Wallabies returned, Kenney had recovered. Leicester's team was: Dusty Hare; Barry Evans, Clive Woodward, Paul Dodge, Tim Barnwell; Les Cusworth, Steve Kenney; John Deacon, Peter Wheeler, Steve Redfern, Nick Joyce, Nick Jackson, Steve Johnson, David Forfar, Ian Smith.

With only a half-hour gone Leicester had already lost the experienced Forfar, who was badly trampled on the leg and had to be replaced by a youngster, Duncan Black. But the Tigers lived up to their nickname. They roared into an Australian

↓ Les Cusworth and Steve Johnson get to grips with the Wallaby, Mark Ella.

↑ Tigers dispose of Northampton at Franklin's Gardens in the fourth round cup tie 27.2.1982.

side including Paul McLean, Michael O'Connor, Mark Ella, Greg Cornelsen and Mark Loane to such an effect that they led 6-3 at the interval and 15-12 with only two minutes remaining. Hare had kicked dropped goals from 45 and 50 yards, and two penalties with Cusworth dropping another goal from a heel against the head. McLean kicked two penalties and the conversion to Mick Martin's try and the full-back levelled matters with a third penalty before Ella, to local anguish, dropped the goal that made the score 18-15 to the Australians. There was even more anguish when, in the sixth minute of injury-time, Hare's long-range penalty scraped the outside of an upright.

Not that such a brave performance influenced the England selectors unduly: as the Australians left for Wales and Scotland both Cusworth and Hare were overlooked for the December trial. Huw Davies and Rose played in the international against Australia on 2 January alongside Dodge, Woodward and Wheeler who contributed to a 15-11 victory (Dodge recalling his goal-kicking skills by converting Jeavons' try). There was a degree of comfort for Cusworth, too, since he was elevated to the replacements and remained there for the 9-9 draw against Scotland in which his three colleagues played.

Bad weather forced the postponement of the Barbarians match (and of Australia's tour finale against the Baa-baas) and sent Leicester scurrying down to Torquay in search of a match to prepare for their defence of the John Player Cup. The Devon Riviera toned them up sufficiently for a 53-19 win over Hartlepool Rovers in the opening round.

A hamstring injury removed Dodge from England's game with Ireland at Twickenham which the Irish, heading for a triple crown, won 16-15. But Dodge and Cusworth both joined Wheeler and Woodward in the side to play France in Paris, earning Cusworth only his second cap after the one-off against New Zealand in 1979. Even better from the club's point of view was the restoration of Hare, bringing to five the Leicester players who shared in the 27-15 victory over France - a tally to which Hare contributed (for the second time in his international career) 19 points from five penalties and two conversions, one of them of a try by Woodward. To general approbation the same XV did duty in a 17-7 win over Wales, Hare kicking three penalties.

Things were looking up. Leicester disposed of Northampton 23-10 in the cup and then went through a re-run of the 1981 final, though this time Gosforth subsided 18-9. Hare overtook his own club record for a season against the RAF, having passed 5,000 career points against Wales, and all seemed set fair for the semi-final against Moseley. Alas, after 18 consecutive cup wins, the dream died at The Reddings, kicked to death by Mike Perry's penalties and dropped goals against a Cusworth try in a 12-4 defeat.

White blamed poor preparation, with players away in Hong Kong and others on business courses: "It's all very well people saying what a good run we've had and it had to end some time. That's the sort of attitude that gets you beaten. You're only as good as your last game - and we were bad." Moseley's satisfaction must have been even more intense, given the long history of rivalry between the clubs, and they went on to the only drawn cup final, against Gloucester.

All of a sudden it seemed as though the wheels were being removed from the Leicester chariot: out of the cup and two leading officials resigning their posts in Jerry Day and the chairman of selectors, Bob Rowell. Both pleaded pressure of business and, in the case of Day, perhaps a slight sense of disenchantment with the game. As someone who, running his own business - like Tom Crumbie - had put his all into Leicester for so long, Leicester owed Day a debt that could never be repaid. Outspoken and opinionated, he also recognised that the game was changing and realised that he did not necessarily want to go with it.

↑ The two packs lock horns (Tigers in red) during the cup quarter-final against Gosforth 13.3.1982.

He stayed to see heavy defeats by Bristol and Moseley (again) offset by a spectacular 36-32 victory over the Barbarians and an Easter tour to Wales in which, almost unnoticed at Neath, a young No 8 called Dean Richards made his debut.

At the annual meeting that summer John Allen moved from the post of treasurer to secretary and members discovered that White, too, was soon to leave. After thirty years in teaching, the abrasive, intense, hugely influential coach had accepted a post with the Rugby Football Union, as one of the newly-created divisional technical administrators - in his case for the South and South-West Division, based in Taunton. It was a most unlikely marriage since White had at times been immensely critical of rugby's establishment but part of his motivation was the realisation that he would not be invited to

⬆ Ian Smith (centre) eyes the ball as Leicester beat Gloucester 30-20 at Welford Road 3.12.1983.

coach England, an ambition which hit the buffers in 1979 when he was passed over for Mike Davis, the Sherborne School master.

But the creation of new, professional posts within the game offered an opportunity to one who cared so deeply about rugby and White was encouraged to change roles by Don Rutherford, England's technical administrator and another deep thinker where the game's future was concerned. "I reckon," White said before he left, "that if, at the end of a season, I have given every player the opportunity to play to his potential, I'm satisfied. There's not a lot of original thought I've been capable of: I crib and I steal and I plagiarise. But I tell players that if they cheat me on the training field, they'll cheat their team-mates in the game and in all other aspects of life. Players have to be themselves - I am the catalyst for others.

"Our game is part of society, it cannot be isolated from what is happening in society. We cannot operate our game in a vacuum. The standards of society, morality, all the bits we like and don't like, must be part of our game. In our own right at Leicester, we have to be trendsetters because there is so much more going for us. We work harder, we think more and some of us care."

White's opinions brought him at times into conflict with administrators, coaches, press and players but no-one who knew him ever doubted his commitment to his view of the game. His departure from Leicester to take up his new post in January 1983 was of enormous significance, though it has always been the club's strength that when one baton is dropped, someone is always waiting to pick it up: from Day to Allen, from Allen to Bob Beason as treasurer, from White to, in this case, Graham Willars.

Meanwhile Hare, Woodward, Cusworth and Wheeler took themselves off on a fairly undemanding tour of the USA and Canada with England, Barry Evans made off to the Far East with England Students. In a crowded summer the four England men, plus Dodge, also accepted places in an invitation party to play three games in South Africa to mark the re-opening of the Ellis Park Stadium in Johannesburg - a decision with political consequences locally while the club, again under Johnson's captaincy, made a five-match visit to Zimbabwe, beating the national side 22-18 in the first "test" in Bulawayo with tries from Barnwell, Black and Smith, and drawing the second 15-15 in Harare with the only Tigers try coming from Johnson.

1982/1983

The portents for a good start to the new season were not good since several first-teamers were unavailable - some because of work, some resting from their summer labours while Woodward was trying to throw off a troublesome shoulder injury. Results were uneven, though that was scarcely reflected in selection for the Midlands against the touring Fijians at Welford Road on 6 October. The seven Tigers who played included Brian Hall, now only an occasional in the club's senior side, and Terry Roberts, that hardy lock from Gosforth who established a brief connection with Leicester.

The team was: Dusty Hare (Leicester); Steve Holdstock (Nottingham), Paul Dodge (Leicester), Huw Davies (Coventry), John Goodwin (Moseley); Les Cusworth (Leicester), Steve Thomas (Coventry); Lee Johnson (Coventry), Peter Wheeler (Leicester, captain), Gary Pearce (Northampton), Terry Roberts (Leicester), Vince Cannon (Northampton), Bob Salmon (Nottingham), Steve Johnson (Leicester), Gary Rees (Nottingham).

It was not the happiest of tours for Fiji, who lost all ten games, but this was one of their better performances, aided by the goal-kicking of Severo Koroduadua who landed four penalties added to a try from Esala Labalaba. Unfortunately for him Hare was more than equal in this department, scoring a try, kicking two conversions and three penalties to go with Lee Johnson's try and a penalty try. A week later Barry Evans scored two tries against the hapless tourists when England Students beat them 26-9 at Bristol, so there was little surprise when England ran all over them to the extent of 60-19 in a non-caps match: Hare kicked six conversions, Dodge and Cusworth were among the try-scorers.

Domestically the first was heard of a youngster from Loughborough Students, John Wells, who scored two tries on his debut against Harlequins at Twickenham and indicated a long-term successor to Johnson, now in his last season. But Leicester saved their best for the Barbarians, which marked White's final game with the club, and his players did him proud, winning 36-16 and scoring five tries before a capacity 17,000 crowd. Three of the tries fell to Evans, whose speed left as experienced a wing as Mike Slemen opposite looking very reflective and helped the Leicester player to an England trial.

Leicester saw White off with a dinner at the Grand Hotel and Willars, assistant to Leicester Youth for two years but coach for only one, quietly slotted in: "I'm prepared to put the work in if the players are," he said. "It may be an amateur game but the rewards - victory, pride and prestige - are worth working for." That attitude earned Leicester a 21-9 win over Bath despite playing the second half without Nick Jackson, the lock, who became the first club player in five years to be sent off after retaliating against Roger Spurrell, the Bath flanker.

Five Leicester players were named in the England team to play France with two more, Evans and Steve Redfern, in an extended training squad. But Woodward withdrew because of his shoulder problems, thereby missing a 19-15 defeat in which Hare (four penalties) and Cusworth (dropped goal) kicked all England's points. Wheeler's ankle ligaments, damaged in the cup win over High Wycombe, kept him out of the match with Wales when England came as close to winning in Cardiff as at any time since 1963.

A Leicester move called the "Chattanooga Choo-choo" earned John Carleton a try in a 13-13 draw and Hare's two penalties took him past Bob Hiller's England record of 138 points. Cusworth's dropped goal did the fly-half no good because he and Steve Smith, the scrum-half, were promptly dropped for the Calcutta Cup match. A sequence of injuries led to Smith's restoration but England's fortunes plummeted: Hare, Dodge and Wheeler were in the side beaten 22-12 by Scotland and, though they were joined for the Irish match at Lansdowne Road by Woodward and Nick Youngs, winning his first cap, England crashed 25-15. Hare's five penalties gave him 42 of the 55 points England scored in the championship and brought him selection for the 1983 Lions tour to New Zealand.

There had been considerable speculation, not only in Leicester, that Wheeler would captain the Lions: in the event he was not chosen at all, the captaincy going to Ciaran Fitzgerald on the back of Ireland's successful season and the other hooking place going to Colin Deans of Scotland. Nor did Dodge receive the call though Woodward, whose form and fitness had been in doubt all season, did. In view of the controversies which surrounded the tour one could only wonder at the decisions made in March by the Lions selectors: Deans was clearly the better hooker but could not oust the captain whose leadership qualities, apt enough for Ireland, could not prevent a 4-0 whitewash by New Zealand. Since three different centre pairings appeared in the tests it is reasonable to suggest that Dodge might have had a contribution to make too.

Hare's selection for the Lions caused him to miss the 1983 cup final. Leicester opened with an easy 47-18 win over a spirited High Wycombe and then saw off Cusworth's old club, Wakefield, 30-14; Youngs scored two tries in a tight 18-4 win over Harlequins but the club then showed that they had not lost their capacity for running rugby by dismissing London Scottish 30-9 in the semi-final. Cusworth scored one of five tries in a series of displays which appeared to become better and better in the wake of his England disappointment.

↑ Third round cup tie action at home to High Wycombe sees Clive Woodward tackling his opposite number.

As they rolled back to Twickenham to play Bristol in the cup final, Leicester decided to include Woodward, who felt he needed the match practice, but not Hare whose desire not to risk his Lions place met with a sympathetic view at Welford Road and gave an unexpected place at full-back to young Ian Dodson.

Steve Johnson's 207th and last appearance was a marvellous game, quite the best final in the 12 years of the competition, which Bristol won 28-22 before a then record crowd of 33,000. Yet in the midst of the back-slapping for both clubs there was concern for Tim Barnwell, the Leicester wing helped off late in the first half after a heavy collision with David Palmer, Bristol's hooker. Barnwell was taken to hospital and later underwent a five-hour operation to remove a blood clot on the brain; it was the end of his playing career, during which he proved himself one of the most elusive - if not most disciplined - runners to appear in a Leicester shirt. Happily he made a complete recovery and, apart from resuming a successful business career, also made a name for himself as a commentator on Leicester matches for local radio.

The match itself brought together the two most attractive teams in England, neither of them inhibited by the occasion. Leicester's team was: Ian Dodson; Barry Evans, Paul Dodge, Clive Woodward, Tim Barnwell; Les Cusworth, Nick Youngs; Stuart Redfern, Peter Wheeler, Steve Redfern, Nigel Gillingham, Malcolm Foulkes-Arnold, Steve Johnson (captain), Dean Richards, Ian Smith.

Cusworth took over Hare's role as goal-kicker and immediately scored two of four first-half penalties to which Stuart Barnes replied with one of his own. Evans scored the first try of the match which took Leicester past 1,000 points for the season for the first time and a second loomed for the wing had Barnwell's pass gone to hand; but it went down and John Carr, the big Bristol wing, kicked on to score his second try which Barnes converted, as he did a further penalty to leave the interval score locked at 16-16. Ian Bates had replaced Barnwell but Bristol's power was growing: Simon Hogg shredded the midfield defence and Bob Hesford smashed into the corner, Barnes converting twice and leaving Leicester only the consolation of the last word, by Ian Smith which Cusworth converted. Cusworth's, too, was the last word on the match: "This was the best final I've played in and we lost. What more is there to say about the game?"

↓ Tigers win the line-out against Neath during the 21-6 victory on 2.4.1983.

← LEICESTER FOOTBALL CLUB 1981/82
Back: Sibson (President), Day (Hon. Sec), Youngs, Collington, Dodson, Dodge, Smith, Jackson, Joyce, Gillingham, Ste.Redfern, Kenney, Richardson, Deacon, Thomas (Team Hon.Sec), White (Coach).
Middle: K.Williams, Hare, Johnson (capt), Barnwell, Cusworth.
Front: Hall, Wheeler, Tressler, Black.

← LEICESTER FOOTBALL CLUB 1982/83
Back: Beason (Hon.Tres), Sibson (President), Willars (Coach), Hare, Jackson, Gillingham, Foulkes-Arnold, Ste.Redfern, Smith, Whitcombe, Wheeler, Allen (Hon.Sec), Thomas (Team Hon.Sec).
Middle: Barnwell, Poulson, Dodge, Richards, Johnson (capt), Stu.Redfern, Evans, Tressler, Tebbutt, Woodward.
Front: K.Williams, Kenney, Cusworth, Youngs.

1982		OVERALL RECORD:					T	C	PG	DG	PTS
	ZIMBABWE TOUR										
	Coach: Chalkie White assisted by Rod Oakes	PLD	W	D	L	Tigers scored:	20	12	7	2	131
	Captain: Steve Johnson	5	3	1	1	Opponents scored:	6	5	13	0	73

GM	DATE		VEN	OPPONENTS	RESULT	TRIES	KICKS	ATT
1	Jul	24	a	Mashonaland	L 23-28	Barnwell(2), Jackson, Tressler	Poulson 2c/d	-
2		27tu	a	Matabeleland	W 25-12	Barnwell(2), Afflick	Dodson 2c/3p	-
3		31	a	Zimbabwe	W 22-18	Barnwell, Black, Smith	Dodson 2c/p, Poulson p	-
4	Aug	4w	a	Zimbabwe Midlands	W 46-0	Evans(2), Youngs(2), Dodson, Barnwell, Afflick, Foulkes-Arnold, Williams	Dodson 4c, Barnwell c	-
5		7	a	Zimbabwe	D 15-15	Johnson	Poulson c/2p/d	-

INDIVIDUAL APPEARANCES 1982 ZIMBABWE TOUR

Name / Game #	1	2	3	4	5	Apps	T	Pts
V (Vendis) Afflick	-	L	-	L	-	2	2	8
RC (Tim) Barnwell	K	K	K	K	K	5	6	26
DS (Duncan) Black	-	G	G	F	G	4	1	4
TR (Terry) Burwell	-	M	N	M	-	3	-	-
AP (Angus) Collington	G	-	-	G	-	2	-	-
J (John) Deacon	A	A	A	-	A	4	-	-
IR (Ian) Dodson	M	J	M	J	M	5	1	32
BJ (Barry) Evans E+	N	N	r	N	N	4+1	2	8
MV (Malcolm) Foulkes-Arnold	-	E	E	D	E	4	1	4
BP (Brian) Hall	L	-	L	-	L	3	-	-
NA (Nick) Jackson	E	-	-	E	r	2+1	1	4
SR (Steve) Johnson	F*	F*	F*	-	F*	4	1	4
NJ (Nick) Joyce	D	D	D	r	D	4+1	-	-
S (Steve) Kenney	-	I	I	-	r	2+1	-	-
MJ (Mike) Poulson	J	-	J	-	J	3	-	21
WP (Wayne) Richardson	-	C	-	A	-	2	-	-
IR (Ian) Smith	H	r	H	r	H	3+2	1	4
RS (Rob) Tebbutt	-	H	-	H	-	2	-	-
DG (Dave) Thomas	-	>B	-	<B	-	2	-	-
CJ (Chris) Tressler	B	-	B	-	B	3	1	4
MA (Martin) Whitcombe	C	-	C	C	C	4	-	-
AK (Kevin) Williams	O	O	O	O	O	5	1	4
NG (Nick) Youngs E+	I	-	-	I	I	3	2	8

↑ LEICESTER FOOTBALL CLUB ZIMBABWE TOUR 1982
Back: Richardson, Tebbutt, Black, Foulkes-Arnold, Jackson, Collington, Whitcombe, Deacon, Afflick.
Middle: Dodson, Burwell, Thomas, Youngs, Kenney, Tressler, Evans, Poulson, Smith.
Front: Ford (Physiotherapist), Joyce, White (Coach), Barnwell, Sibson (President), Johnson (capt), Allen (Manager), Hall, Oakes (Asst.Manager), Williams.

The key for how to read the stats is on the last page

1981/82

19 81/82	Trophy Cabinet: Midland Merit Table	OVERALL RECORD:					T	C	PG	DG	PTS
Home Ground: Welford Road		PLD	W	D	L	Tigers scored:	124	78	75	16	925
Coach: Chalkie White assisted by Rod Oakes		40	27	2	11	Opponents scored:	61	35	53	13	512
Captain: Steve Johnson											

GM	DATE		VEN	OPPONENTS	RESULT	TRIES	KICKS	ATT
RFU CLUB COMPETITION (JOHN PLAYER CUP)						**CUP WINNERS: GLOUCESTER AND MOSELEY (SHARED)**		
21	Jan	**23**	**H**	**Hartlepool Rovers (3)**	W 53-19	Evans 2, Johnson 25, Hare 30, Smith 34, Dodge 40, Deacon 50, Youngs 55/80, Barnwell 79	Hare 4c/3p	4299
26	Feb	27	a	Northampton (4)	W 23-10	Barnwell 27, Hare 40, Evans 65	Hare c/3p	5500
29	Mar	**13**	**H**	**Gosforth (qf)**	W 18-9	Smith 12	Hare c/3p, Cusworth d	8485
34	Apr	3	a	Moseley (sf)	L 4-12	Cusworth 76	-	-
MIDLAND MERIT TABLE (1ST)						**WINNERS: LEICESTER TIGERS**		
1	Sep	5	a	Bedford	W 28-4	Barnwell, Dodge, Wheeler, Woodward	Hare 3c/2p	-
2		**8tu**	**H**	**Nuneaton**	W 38-3	Barnwell(2), Black(2), K.Williams	Hare 3c/3p, Cusworth d	1876
4		16w	a	Birmingham	W 78-8	Hare(3), Cusworth(3), Barnwell(2), Woodward(2), Black, Dodge, Johnson, Smith	Hare 11c	-
7	Oct	**3**	**H**	**Coventry**	W 28-6	Barnwell(2), Woodward	Hare 2c/4p	4472
9		16f	a	Northampton	L 6-22	-	Poulson p/d	-
14	Nov	17tu	a	Nottingham	W 16-3	Evans(2)	Hare c/p/d	-
17		**28**	**H**	**Moseley**	W 22-15	Evans, Smith	Hare c/2p, Woodward 2d	2481
CLUB MATCHES								
3	Sep	**12**	**H**	**Bath**	W 44-6	Dodge, Johnson, Merriman, Wheeler, K.Williams, Woodward	Hare 4c/3p/d	2889
5		**19**	**H**	**London Welsh**	W 19-6	Dodge, Joyce, Wheeler, K.Williams	Hare p	3315
6		26	a	Harlequins	W 49-12	Barnwell(2), Black(2), Cooke(2), Dodge, Merriman	Hare 4c/2p, Cusworth d	-
8	Oct	10	a	Richmond	D 6-6	-	Hare 2p	-
10		**24**	**H**	**Swansea**	L 12-19	Whitcombe, Woodward	Hare 2c	6333
11		31	a	Saracens	W 34-14	Hare, Barnwell, Evans, Smith	Hare 3c/4p	-
12	Nov	**7**	**H**	**Gloucester**	L 9-12	-	Hare 3p	5145
13		14	a	Cambridge University	W 12-9	Hare	Hare c/p, Cusworth d	-
15		**21**	**H**	**Wasps**	W 27-18	Barnwell, Evans, Woodward	Hare 3c/2p/d	3300
16		**25w**	**H**	**Australia**	L 15-18	-	Hare 2p/2d, Cusworth d	12470
18	Dec	**5**	**H**	**Waterloo**	W 49-3	Dodge(2), Hare, Collington, Jackson, Woodward	Dodge d, Hare 5c/3p/d	2295
		12	a	Blackheath	PP			
		19	**H**	**Bristol**	PP (frost)			
		29tu	**H**	**Barbarians**	PP (frost)			
19	Jan	2	a	Bath	D 9-9	Youngs	Hare c/p	-
		9	a	Gloucester	PP (snow)			
		15f	**H**	**Bedford**	PP (snow)			
20		17s	a	Torquay Athletic	W 44-4	Youngs(2), Hare, Barnwell, Evans, Gillingham, Hall, Smith	Hare 6c	-
22		30	a	London Welsh	W 22-7	Hare, Evans	Hare c/4p	-
23	Feb	**6**	**H**	**London Scottish**	W 19-6	Barnwell, Hall, Smith	Hare 2c/p	1712
24		13	a	Newport	L 15-16	Woodward	Hare c/3p	-
25		20	a	Orrell	L 4-12	Hall	-	-
27	Mar	**3w**	**H**	**Royal Navy**	W 17-12	Barnwell, Evans	Poulson 3p	1257
28		**5f**	**H**	**Harlequins**	L 7-13	Poulson	Poulson p	1639
		13	a	Coventry	PP (cup)			
30		**16tu**	**H**	**Loughborough Students**	W 12-9	-	Hare 4p	956
31		**19f**	**H**	**Royal Air Force**	W 33-9	Barnwell, Collington, Evans, Smith	Hare 2c/3p, Cusworth 2c	1323
32		**23tu**	**H**	**Rugby**	W 28-7	Barnwell, Black, Collington, Dodson, Smith	Poulson c/2p	1057
33		**27**	**H**	**Sale**	W 14-10	Marriott, Poulson	Dodge 2p	2887
	Apr	**3**	**H**	**Birkenhead Park**	PP (cup)			
35		10	a	Neath	W 25-14	Poulson(2), Hall, Youngs	Poulson 3c/p	-
36		12m	a	Pontypool	L 16-32	Youngs(2), Woodward	Woodward c, Cusworth c	-
37		17	a	Bristol	L 4-38	Dodson	-	-
38		**20tu**	**H**	**Barbarians**	W 36-32	Smith(2), Barnwell, Cusworth, Wheeler, K.Williams	Hare 6c	15000
39		24	a	Moseley	L 9-30	Hall	Hare c/p	-
40		30f	a	Ballymena	W 21-18	Barnwell	Hare c/4p/d	-

INDIVIDUAL APPEARANCES 1981/82

Name / Game #	1	2	3	4	5	6	7	8	9	10	11	12	13	14	15	16	17	18	19	20	21	22	23	24	25	26	27	28	29	30	31	32	33	34	35	36	37	38	39	40	Apps	T	Pts
V (Vendis) Afflick	-	-	-	-	-	-	-	-	-	-	-	-	-	-	-	-	x	-	>M	L	-	-	L	-	-	-	L	M	-	-	-	r	-	-	r	-	L	-	-	-	6+2	-	-
RC (Tim) Barnwell	K	K	K	K	K	K	K	K	-	K	K	K	-	-	K	K	K	K	K	K	K	K	K	K	K	K	K	-	K	K	K	K	K	K	K	K	K	K	K	K	36	20	80
DS (Duncan) Black	r	G	G	G	G	G	G	G	-	G	-	x	-	-	-	r	E	-	-	-	r	-	-	D	-	x	G	G	x	F	x	G	-	x	-	F	-	-	-	-	15+3	6	24
AP (Angus) Collington	G	-	-	-	-	-	-	-	-	-	-	-	-	-	-	-	-	G	G	G	G	G	G	G	G	G	-	-	G	G	G	F	G	G	-	G	G	G	G	G	21	3	12
JTC (Tim) Cooke	-	-	-	-	-	r	-	-	-	-	-	<r	x	-	-	-	-	-	-	-	-	-	x	-	-	-	-	-	-	-	-	-	-	-	-	-	-	-	-	-	0+2	2	8
L (Les) Cusworth E3	J	J	J	J	J	J	J	J	-	J	J	J	J	J	J	J	-	J	-	-	J	-	-	J	-	J	-	-	J	-	J	-	-	J	-	J	J	J	-	J	26	5	41
J (John) Deacon	>A	A	A	A	A	A	A	A	A	-	A	A	A	A	A	A	A	A	A	A	A	A	A	A	A	A	A	A	A	-	-	A	A	A	A	A	-	A	A	-	35	1	4
PW (Paul) Dodge E20 L2	L	L	L	M	L	L	L	L	-	-	L	L	L	L	L	L	L	L	-	-	L	L	-	-	-	L	-	-	L	L	L	-	L	L	-	-	-	L	L	L	27	8	41
IR (Ian) Dodson	-	-	x	-	-	-	x	-	L	x	-	-	-	-	-	-	-	-	J	J	-	J	J	-	L	-	M	-	-	-	r	L	r	x	L	O	M	x	r	-	11+3	2	8
BJ (Barry) Evans E+	-	-	-	-	-	-	-	-	-	-	>N	N	N	N	N	N	N	N	N	N	N	N	N	N	N	N	N	N	N	N	N	N	-	N	-	-	N	-	-	-	24	11	44
DJ (Dave) Forfar	-	x	-	-	-	-	-	-	G	-	G	G	G	G	G	<G	-	-	-	-	-	-	-	-	-	-	-	-	-	-	-	-	-	-	-	-	-	-	-	-	7	-	-
MV (Malcolm) Foulkes-Arnold	-	-	-	-	-	-	-	-	E	E	E	E	E	-	-	-	-	-	E	E	E	E	-	-	-	-	-	E	-	-	E	-	E	-	-	-	-	-	-	E	13	-	-
NK (Nigel) Gillingham	-	-	-	-	-	-	-	-	-	-	D	D	D	-	E	-	D	D	D	D	D	D	D	-	D	D	D	-	-	-	-	E*	-	-	D	D	E	x	-	-	18	1	4
BP (Brian) Hall	-	r	-	-	x	-	-	-	M	M	-	-	-	r	x	x	-	-	L	M	x	-	M	L	M	x	-	L	x	-	-	M	M	x	M	M	-	M	M	-	14+2	5	20
WH (Dusty) Hare E14	O	O	O	O	O	O	O	O	-	O	O	O	O	O	O	O	O	O	O	O	O	O	O	O	-	O	-	-	O	O	O	-	-	O	-	-	O	O	O	O	32	10	396
AG (Arthur) Hazlerigg	-	-	-	-	-	-	-	E	<D	-	-	-	-	-	-	-	-	-	-	-	-	-	-	-	-	-	-	-	-	-	-	-	-	-	-	-	-	-	-	-	2	-	-
NA (Nick) Jackson	E	-	E	-	E	E	E	-	-	-	-	-	-	E	-	E	-	E	-	-	-	-	-	E	E	E	E	-	E	E	-	-	-	E	E	E	-	E	E	-	19	1	4
SR (Steve) Johnson	F*	F*	F*	F*	F*	F*	F*	F*	-	F*	F*	F*	F*	F*	F*	F*	G*	-	F*	F*	F*	F*	F*	F*	F*	F*	F*	F*	F*	-	F*	-	F*	F*	F*	-	F*	F*	F*	F*	35	3	12
NJ (Nick) Joyce	D	D	D	D	D	D	D	D	-	D	-	-	-	D	D	D	-	-	-	-	-	-	E	-	-	-	-	D	D	D	D	D	D	D	-	-	D	D	D	D	24	1	4
S (Steve) Kenney	I	-	-	-	-	-	-	-	I	I	I	I	I	I	-	I	I	-	-	-	-	-	-	-	-	-	-	-	-	-	-	-	-	x	-	-	-	-	-	-	9	-	-
AM (Andy) Key	-	-	-	-	-	N	-	-	O	-	-	-	-	-	-	x	-	-	-	-	-	-	-	-	-	-	-	-	-	-	-	-	-	-	-	-	-	-	-	-	2	-	-
MS (Mac) Knowles	-	-	-	-	-	-	-	x	<H	-	-	-	-	-	-	-	-	-	-	-	-	-	-	-	-	-	-	-	-	-	-	-	-	-	-	-	-	-	-	-	1	-	-
D (Dave) Manship	-	-	-	-	-	-	-	-	-	-	-	-	-	-	-	-	-	-	-	-	-	-	-	-	<O	-	-	-	-	-	-	-	-	-	-	-	-	-	-	-	1	-	-
AN (Adey) Marriott	-	-	-	-	-	-	-	-	-	-	-	-	-	-	-	-	-	-	-	-	-	-	-	-	-	-	>r	r	-	-	-	-	r	-	-	-	H	-	-	-	1+3	1	4
MJP (Mick) Merriman	-	I	I	I	I	I	I	<I	-	-	-	-	-	-	-	-	-	-	-	-	-	-	-	-	-	-	-	-	-	-	-	-	-	-	-	-	-	-	-	-	7	2	8
RE (Ray) Needham	-	-	-	-	-	-	r	-	-	-	-	-	-	-	-	-	-	x	-	-	-	-	-	-	-	-	C	C	C	C	-	-	-	x	-	-	-	-	-	<A	5+1	-	-
MJ (Mick) Newton	x	-	-	-	-	-	-	x	K	-	-	-	-	K	-	-	-	-	-	-	-	-	-	-	-	-	x	K	-	-	-	-	<N	-	-	-	-	-	-	-	4	-	-
MJ (Mike) Poulson	-	-	-	-	-	-	-	-	J*	-	-	-	-	-	-	-	J	-	-	-	-	-	-	-	J	-	J	J	-	J	-	J	J	-	J	r	-	-	J	-	10+1	4	51
SP (Steve) Redfern E+	-	C	C	C	C	C	C	C	-	C	C	C	C	-	-	C	C	C	C	-	C	C	C	C	C	C	-	-	-	-	C	C	-	-	-	-	-	-	-	-	23	-	-
SB (Stuart) Redfern	-	-	-	-	-	-	-	-	-	-	-	-	-	-	-	-	-	-	-	x	-	-	-	-	-	-	-	-	-	>A	A	-	-	-	-	-	-	-	-	-	2	-	-
D (Dean) Richards E+ L+	-	-	-	-	-	-	-	-	-	-	-	-	-	-	-	-	-	-	-	-	-	-	-	-	-	-	-	-	-	-	-	-	-	-	>G	-	-	-	-	-	1	-	-
WP (Wayne) Richardson	C	-	-	-	x	-	-	-	C	x	-	-	-	-	x	-	-	-	-	-	-	-	-	-	-	-	-	-	-	-	-	r	C	C	C	C	C	C	C	C	10+1	-	-
IR (Ian) Smith	H	H	H	H	H	H	H	H	-	H	H	H	H	H	H	H	H	H	H	H	H	H	H	H	H	H	H	H	H	H	H	H	H	H	H	H	-	H	H	H	38	11	44
PH (Paul) Stone	-	-	<r	-	-	x	-	-	-	-	-	-	-	-	-	-	-	-	-	-	-	-	-	-	-	-	-	-	-	-	-	-	-	-	-	-	-	-	-	-	0+1	-	-
RS (Rob) Tebbutt	-	-	-	-	-	-	-	-	>F	-	-	-	x	-	-	-	F	F	-	-	-	-	-	-	x	-	-	-	-	-	-	-	-	-	-	-	-	-	-	-	3	-	-
CJ (Chris) Tressler	-	-	-	-	-	B	-	-	B	-	-	-	-	-	-	x	B	-	B	B	-	-	B	-	B	-	B	B	-	-	-	B	B	x	B	-	-	-	B	-	13	-	-
DP (Dean) Waddingham	-	E	-	E	-	-	-	-	-	-	-	-	-	-	-	-	-	-	-	-	-	-	-	-	-	-	-	-	-	-	-	-	-	-	-	-	-	-	-	-	2	-	-
PJ (Peter) Wheeler E33 L7	B	B	B	B	B	-	B	B	-	B	B	B	B	B	B	B	-	B*	-	-	B	B	-	B	-	B	-	-	B	B*	B	-	-	B	-	B*	B	B	-	B	27	4	16
MA (Martin) Whitcombe	-	-	-	-	-	-	-	-	>r	A	-	-	-	C	C	x	r	-	x	C	-	-	r	-	-	-	-	-	-	-	-	-	-	-	-	-	A	-	-	-	5+3	1	4
DJ (Dave) Williams	-	-	-	-	-	-	-	-	-	-	-	-	-	-	-	-	-	x	x	-	-	-	-	-	r	-	-	-	-	-	-	-	-	-	N	-	-	-	-	-	1+1	-	-
AK (Kevin) Williams	N	N	N	N	N	-	N	N	N	N	-	-	-	K	-	-	-	-	-	r	-	-	-	-	-	-	O	O	-	-	-	O	O	-	O	N	-	N	N	N	19+1	4	16
CR (Clive) Woodward E15 L2	M	M	M	L	M	M	M	M	-	L	M	M	M	M	M	M	M	M	-	-	M	M	-	M	-	M	-	-	M	M	M	-	-	M	-	L	-	-	-	M	27	10	48
NG (Nick) Youngs E+	-	-	-	-	-	-	-	-	-	-	-	-	-	-	>I	x	-	I	I	I	I	I	I	I	I	I	I	I	I	I	I	I	I	I	I	I	I	I	I	I	24	8	32

The key for how to read the stats is on the last page

19 82/83	Home Ground: Welford Road	Trophy Cabinet: Midland Merit Table
	Coach: Chalkie White then Graham Willars in January. Assisted by Rod Oakes	
	Captain: Steve Johnson	

OVERALL RECORD:					T	C	PG	DG	PTS
PLD	W	D	L	Tigers scored:	139	87	87	7	1012
44	33	0	11	Opponents scored:	64	35	74	10	578

GM	DATE		VEN	OPPONENTS	RESULT	TRIES	KICKS	ATT
RFU CLUB COMPETITION (JOHN PLAYER CUP)						**CUP WINNERS: BRISTOL**		
26	Jan	22	H	**High Wycombe (3)**	W 47-18	Evans 5, Barnwell 19/72/75, Hare 23/68, Wheeler 34, Foulkes-Arnold 41, Kenney 78	Hare 4c/p	4928
31	Feb	26	H	**Wakefield (4)**	W 30-14	Woodward 20, Barnwell 22, Richards, Evans	Hare 4c/2p	6656
34	Mar	12	H	**Harlequins (qf)**	W 18-4	Youngs 48/77	Hare 2c/p, Cusworth d	8748
37		26	a	London Scottish (sf)	W 30-9	Evans 38, Richards 42, Barnwell, Cusworth	Cusworth d, Hare 4c/d	-
44	Apr	30		Bristol (f)	L 22-28	Evans 17, Smith 76	Cusworth c/4p	34000
MIDLAND MERIT TABLE (1ST)						**WINNERS: LEICESTER TIGERS**		
1	Sep	4	H	**Bedford**	W 28-15	Black, Foulkes-Arnold, Johnson, Smith	Cusworth 2c/2p, Dodge c	2582
2		7tu	a	Nuneaton	W 41-11	Barnwell(2), K.Williams(2), Dodge, Black, Johnson, Smith	Dodge p, Cusworth 3c	-
4		14tu	H	**Birmingham**	W 18-3	D.Williams(2), Smith	Cusworth 3c	1576
7	Oct	2	a	Coventry	W 14-12	Kenney, Whitcombe	Hare 2p	-
15	Nov	17w	H	**Nottingham**	W 22-9	Evans, Ste.Redfern	Hare c/4p	1577
17		27	H	**Moseley**	W 22-15	Cusworth, Richards	Hare c/4p	3746
38	Mar	29tu	H	**Rugby**	W 53-3	Evans(4), D.Williams(2), Dexter, Foulkes-Arnold, Marriott	Cusworth 3c/3p, Dodge c	1076
CLUB MATCHES								
3	Sep	11	a	Bath	L 15-24	Collington	Cusworth 3p, Dodge c	-
5		18	H	**London Welsh**	L 15-17	Johnson, Ste.Redfern	Hare 2c/p	3023
6		25	a	Harlequins	W 29-25	Cusworth(2), Wells(2), Kenney	Dodge c/p, Hare 2c	-
8	Oct	9	H	**Richmond**	W 21-8	Johnson, Wheeler	Hare 2c/3p	2898
9		16	H	**Northampton**	W 15-10	Barnwell(2), D.Williams	Dodson p	2236
10		20w	H	**Oxford University**	W 41-3	Evans(2), Barnwell, Black, Collington, Cusworth	Hare 4c/3p	1537
11		23	a	Swansea	L 12-29	-	Hare 3p, Cusworth d	-
		27w	H	**Randwick**	PP			
12		30	H	**Saracens**	W 51-15	Dodge(2), Barnwell, Evans, Hall, Jackson, Youngs	Hare 7c/3p	3117
13	Nov	6	a	Cardiff	L 9-32	-	Hare 3p	-
14		13	H	**Cambridge University**	W 38-6	Johnson(2), Kenney(2), Barnwell, Evans	Hare 4c/2p	2762
16		20	a	Wasps	L 7-15	Hare	Cusworth p	-
18	Dec	1w	a	Gloucester	W 21-10	Hare, Woodward	Hare 2c/3p	-
19		4	a	Waterloo	W 10-9	Barnwell	Hare 2p	-
20		11	H	**Blackheath**	W 28-21	Richards, Tebbutt, Whitcombe	Hare 2c/4p	3002
21		18	a	Bristol	L 6-21	-	Poulson p/d	-
22		29w	H	**Barbarians**	W 36-16	Evans(3), Cusworth, Kenney	Hare 2c/4p	17000
23	Jan	1	H	**Bath**	W 21-9	Hare, Evans	Hare 2c/2p, Cusworth d	4590
24		8	H	**Gloucester**	W 23-9	Barnwell, Johnson, Kenney	Poulson c/3p	3063
25		14f	a	Bedford	W 13-3	Evans, Richards	Poulson c/p	-
27		29	a	London Welsh	L 12-25	-	Hare 4p	-
28	Feb	5	a	London Scottish	W 18-12	Evans	Poulson c/4p	-
29		12	H	**Newport**	W 21-9	Cusworth(2), Youngs	Hare 3c/p	4404
30		19	H	**Orrell**	W 18-12	Johnson, Richards	Hare 2c/2p	2365
		26	a	Northampton	PP (cup)			
32	Mar	2w	H	**Royal Navy**	W 22-0	Barnwell, Evans, Joyce, Smith	Cusworth 3c	1132
33		5	H	**Harlequins**	L 3-13	-	Cusworth p	1395
		12	H	**Coventry**	PP (cup)			
35		15tu	H	**Loughborough Students**	W 46-17	Evans(2), Smith(2), Collington, Foulkes-Arnold, D.Williams	Cusworth 6c/2p	1018
36		18f	H	**Royal Air Force**	W 34-0	D.Williams(2), Barnwell, Bates, Burwell, Kenney	Poulson c/2p, Cusworth c	1169
		26	a	Sale	PP (cup)			
39	Apr	2	H	**Neath**	W 21-6	Cusworth, Stu.Redfern, Smith, Youngs	Cusworth c/p	3226
40		4m	H	**Pontypool**	L 6-20	Marriott	Cusworth c	4368
		9	H	**Bristol**	PP (cup)			
41		12tu	a	Northampton	L 9-18	Youngs	Cusworth c/p	-
42		16	a	Maesteg	W 17-13	Barnwell, Evans, Youngs	Cusworth c/d	-
43		23	a	Moseley	W 29-10	Woodward(2), Evans, Poulson, Tebbutt	Cusworth 3c/p	-
		30	a	Ballymena	PP (cup)			

Neutral Venue: *#44 at Twickenham*

INDIVIDUAL APPEARANCES 1982/83

Name / Game #	1	2	3	4	5	6	7	8	9	10	11	12	13	14	15	16	17	18	19	20	21	22	23	24	25	26	27	28	29	30	31	32	33	34	35	36	37	38	39	40	41	42	43	44	Apps	T	Pts
V (Vendis) Afflick	x	-	-	x	-	-	x	-	L	-	-	-	-	-	-	-	-	-	-	-	x	-	-	x	-	-	-	-	-	-	-	-	-	-	-	-	-	-	L	L	-	-	-	-	3	-	-
RC (Tim) Barnwell	K	K	-	-	-	K	K	K	K	K	K	K	K	K	K	K	K	K	K	K	K	K	K	K	K*	K	K	K	K	K	K	K	K	K	-	K	K	-	-	-	K	K	K	<K	37	17	68
I (Ian) Bates	-	-	-	-	-	-	-	-	x	-	-	-	-	-	-	-	-	-	-	-	-	-	-	-	-	-	-	>L	-	-	-	L	-	-	M	M	-	M	-	-	L	L	L	r	8+1	1	4
DS (Duncan) Black	E	E	E	G	-	E	-	E	x	D	E	x	-	-	-	-	-	F	r	-	-	x	-	-	-	x	-	-	-	-	-	r	-	-	-	r	x	-	-	-	-	-	-	-	9+3	3	12
TR (Terry) Burwell	-	-	x	N	-	r	-	-	-	-	-	-	-	M	-	-	-	-	-	-	M	-	-	L	L	-	-	-	-	r	-	-	-	-	L	L	<r	-	-	-	-	-	-	-	7+3	1	4
AP (Angus) Collington	G	G	G	x	-	-	-	-	-	G	G	-	r	-	-	-	-	-	-	-	x	-	-	-	-	-	-	-	-	-	x	-	-	x	G	-	-	r	G	G	-	x	-	-	8+2	3	12
L (Les) Cusworth E5	J	J	J	J	J	J*	J	J	-	J*	J	J	J	J	J	J	J	-	J	J	-	J	J	-	-	J	-	-	J	J	J	J	J	J	J	J*	J	J	J	J	J	J	J	J	37	9	166
J (John) Deacon	A	A	<A	-	-	-	-	-	-	-	-	-	-	-	-	-	-	-	-	-	-	-	-	-	-	-	-	-	-	-	-	-	-	-	-	-	-	-	-	-	-	-	-	-	3	-	-
CD (Colin) Dexter	-	-	-	-	-	-	-	x	-	-	-	x	-	-	-	-	-	-	>r	-	-	-	-	-	-	-	-	x	-	-	-	-	-	-	-	-	-	r	O	O	-	r	x	-	2+3	1	4
TR ("Thumper") Dingley	-	-	-	-	-	-	-	-	>A	A	A	A	A	-	-	-	-	-	-	-	-	-	-	-	A	-	-	-	-	-	-	-	-	-	-	-	x	<A	-	-	-	-	-	-	7	-	-
PW (Paul) Dodge E24 L2	M	M	L	M	L	L	L	M	-	L	L	M	M	-	-	-	M	M	L	-	-	M	M	-	-	M	L	-	M	M	M	-	-	M	-	-	M	L	M	M	-	-	-	M	28	3	26
IR (Ian) Dodson	L	L	M	L	M	M	M	-	J	-	-	-	-	-	-	-	-	-	-	-	L	x	-	M	M	x	-	-	-	-	-	-	-	-	-	-	-	-	-	-	x	-	O	O	13	-	3
BJ (Barry) Evans E+	-	-	-	-	-	-	-	-	-	N	N	N	N	N	N	N	N	N	N	N	-	N	N	-	N	N	N	N	N	N	N	N	N	N	N	-	N	N	N	N	N	N	N	N	32	24	96
MV (Malcolm) Foulkes-Arnold	D	D	D	D	-	-	-	-	-	-	-	-	-	-	-	-	-	-	-	-	-	-	-	E	E	E	E	E	E	E	E	D	E	E	E	E	E	E	E	E	E	E	E	E	25	4	16
CE (Claude) Gerald	-	-	-	-	-	-	-	-	-	-	-	-	-	-	-	-	-	-	-	-	-	-	-	-	-	-	-	-	-	-	-	-	-	-	-	-	-	-	x	>r	-	-	-	-	0+1	-	-
NK (Nigel) Gillingham	-	-	-	E	-	-	D	D	D	E	D	E	E	E	r	E	-	D*	D	D	D	D	D	D	-	D	D	D	D	D	D	-	D	D	-	-	-	-	-	-	D	D	D	D	29+1	-	-
BP (Brian) Hall	-	-	K	-	r	-	-	L	M	M	M	L	L	L	M	M	-	-	-	M	-	-	-	-	-	-	-	M	L	-	x	-	M	-	-	-	-	-	-	-	-	-	-	-	14+1	1	4
WH (Dusty) Hare E18	-	-	-	-	O	O	O	O	-	O	O	O	O	O	O	O	O	O	O	O	-	O	O	-	-	O	O	-	O	O	O	-	-	O	-	-	O	-	-	-	-	-	-	-	24	5	285
NA (Nick) Jackson	-	-	-	-	G	G	G	-	G	-	-	G	G	-	E	G	E	E	E	E	E	E	■E	-	-	-	-	-	-	-	-	-	-	-	-	-	D	D	D	D	-	-	-	x	19	1	4
SR (Steve) Johnson	F*	F*	F*	F*	F*	-	F*	F*	F*	-	F*	F*	F*	G*	G*	F*	F*	-	F*	F*	F*	F*	F*	F*	-	F*	F*	F*	F*	F*	F*	F*	F*	F*	F*	-	F*	H*	F*	F*	F*	F*	F*	<F*	39	8	32
NJ (Nick) Joyce	-	-	-	-	D	D	-	-	-	-	-	-	-	D	D	D	D	-	-	-	-	-	-	-	D	-	-	-	-	-	-	E	-	-	D	D	-	-	-	-	-	-	-	-	10	1	4
S (Steve) Kenney	I	I	I	I	I	I	I	I	-	-	-	-	-	I	I	I	I	I	I	I	I	I	I	I	I	I	I	-	-	-	-	I	I	-	I	I	x	-	-	I	-	-	-	x	27	8	32
J (Jez) Krych	-	-	-	-	-	-	-	-	-	-	-	-	-	<A	-	-	-	-	-	-	-	-	-	-	-	-	-	-	-	-	-	-	-	-	-	-	-	-	-	-	-	-	-	-	1	-	-
TJH (Tommy) Lawton	-	-	-	-	-	-	-	-	-	-	-	-	-	>-	>x	-	-	-	H	x	-	-	-	-	-	-	-	-	-	x	-	-	-	-	-	-	-	-	-	-	-	-	-	-	2	-	-
AN (Adey) Marriott	-	-	-	-	-	-	-	-	-	F	-	-	-	-	F	-	-	-	-	-	-	-	-	x	F	-	-	-	r	-	-	-	x	-	r	F	-	F	x	r	-	-	-	-	5+3	2	8
MJ (Mike) Poulson	O	O	O	O	-	-	-	-	-	-	-	-	-	-	-	-	x	J	-	-	J	-	-	J	J	-	J	J	-	-	-	O	O	x	-	O	x	O	-	-	O	O	r	x	16+1	1	48
SP (Steve) Redfern E+	x	-	-	C	A	C	C	C	-	C	C	C	C	C	C	C	C	C	C	C	-	C	C	-	C	C	C	C	C	C	C	-	C	C	C	C	C	C	C	C	C	-	C	C	36	2	8
SB (Stuart) Redfern	-	-	-	A	-	-	-	-	-	-	-	-	-	-	-	-	A	-	-	-	A	-	-	A	-	-	-	-	A	A	A	A	A	A	A	A	A	-	A	A	A	A	A	A	19	1	4
D (Dean) Richards E+ L+	-	-	-	-	-	-	-	G	-	-	-	-	-	-	-	-	G	G	G	G	G	G	G	G	G	G	G	G	G	G	G	G	G	G	-	G	G	G	-	-	G	G	G	G	26	6	24
WP (Wayne) Richardson	-	-	x	-	-	-	x	-	-	-	-	-	-	-	-	-	-	-	-	-	-	-	-	-	-	-	-	-	-	-	-	C	-	-	-	-	-	-	-	-	-	C	-	x	2	-	-
TC (Terry) Roberts	-	-	-	-	>E	-	E	-	E	-	-	D	<D	-	-	-	-	-	-	-	-	-	-	-	-	-	-	-	-	-	-	-	-	-	-	-	-	-	-	-	-	-	-	-	5	-	-
IR (Ian) Smith	H	H	H	H	H	H	H	H	-	-	-	-	-	H	-	-	-	-	-	-	-	H	H	H	H	H	H	H	H	-	H	H	-	H	H	H	H	-	H	H	H	H	H	H	29	8	32
RS (Rob) Tebbutt	-	-	-	-	-	-	-	-	H	H	H	H	H	-	H	H	H	H	-	H	H	-	x	-	-	-	-	x	-	H	-	-	H	-	-	-	-	-	-	-	-	-	r	-	13+1	2	8
CJ (Chris) Tressler	B	B	B	B	B	B	-	-	B	-	-	-	-	B	-	-	B	B	B	-	B	-	-	B	B	-	B	B	B	-	-	B	B	-	B	B	x	B	B	B	B	B	-	x	26	-	-
JM (John) Wells	-	-	-	-	x	>F	-	-	-	-	-	-	-	-	-	-	-	-	-	-	-	-	-	-	-	-	-	-	-	-	-	-	-	-	-	-	-	-	-	-	x	-	-	-	1	2	8
PJ (Peter) Wheeler E36 L7	-	-	-	-	-	-	B	B	-	B	B	B	B	-	B	B	-	-	-	B	-	B	B	-	-	B	-	-	-	B	B	-	-	B	-	-	B	-	-	-	-	-	B	B	18	2	8
MA (Martin) Whitcombe	C	C	C	-	C	A	A	A	C	-	-	-	-	-	A	A	-	A	A	A	C	A	A	C	-	A	A	A	-	-	-	-	-	-	-	-	-	-	-	-	-	-	-	-	20	2	8
DJ (Dave) Williams	-	-	-	K	K	-	-	-	N	-	-	-	-	-	-	-	-	-	-	r	N	-	x	N	-	-	-	-	x	-	-	r	x	-	K	r	-	K	K	<K	-	-	-	-	9+3	8	32
AK (Kevin) Williams	N	N	N	-	N	N	N	N	O	r	-	-	r	-	-	-	-	-	-	-	O	-	-	O	O	-	-	O	-	-	-	-	-	-	O	N	-	-	-	-	-	-	-	-	14+2	2	8
CR (Clive) Woodward E16 L2	-	-	-	-	-	-	-	-	-	-	-	-	-	-	L	L	L	L	M	L	-	L	L	-	-	L	M	-	-	L	L	M	L	L	-	-	L	-	-	-	M	M	M	L	20	4	16
NG (Nick) Youngs E1	-	-	-	-	-	-	-	-	I	I	I	I	I	-	-	-	-	-	-	-	-	-	-	-	-	-	-	I	I	I	I	-	-	I	-	-	I	I	I	-	I	I	I	I	17	7	28

The key for how to read the stats is on the last page

CHAPTER 22

End of Play for Wheeler

1983/1984

If anyone imagined it would be a quiet summer, the Lions tour apart, they were wrong. There was intense speculation that a professional touring circus would be established by an Australian journalist, David Lord, and since Leicester had so many members of the England squad their names were inevitably linked - on whatever tenuous grounds - with the potential party of 200 players. Large sums of money were bandied around and late in the year a fixture schedule was even published but it came to nothing - though it did serve to emphasise the degree to which the game was changing that the project was taken very seriously indeed.

Dusty Hare was selected for the Lions trip to New Zealand in 1983.

While Hare and Woodward shared the trials and tribulations of New Zealand, Wheeler, Cusworth and Youngs took themselves off to South Africa in an international squad which helped Western Province celebrate its centenary. Wheeler was, too, in the throes of writing an autobiography which duly appeared in the autumn entitled *Rugby From The Front* - a year later Hare followed him into print with *Dusty* - the proceeds from both books going to help different sporting organisations, Leicester among them.

As things turned out, Wheeler's book was premature: 1983/84, his final international season, was also the one in which he captained England. During the summer Budge Rogers, the chairman of selectors, resigned, as did Mike Davis, the coach, and two other selectors; Derek Morgan took over as chairman and Dick Greenwood (father of the future Leicester and England centre, Will) as coach and among their first actions was Wheeler's appointment to lead England against Canada, a match organised as preparation for the November international against the touring All Blacks. At 35 the honour came late but no less merited as England struggled to extract themselves from the malaise of the previous season.

Hare, Dodge and Youngs joined him in the non-cap match at Twickenham which England won in foul conditions 27-0; though the rain did not stop, Hare achieved a perfect six kicks out of six, three conversions and three penalties. Selection for the game against New Zealand, however, did not happen until after the Midlands had played the touring side in a game at Welford Road on 8 November 1983, which surely matched that of 1931 against the South Africans.

The All Blacks, captained by Stuart Wilson, were a curious team, neither fish nor fowl. Five of the tight forwards who had swept aside the Lions in the summer were unable to tour, nor did David Loveridge, the influential scrum-half. The inexperience of those who did showed throughout the visit to England and Scotland and their opponents, burning from the shame endured by the Lions, were not about to treat them lightly in consequence; indeed the England selectors co-ordinated their plans closely with the four divisional sides so that all could contribute to the style of rugby Greenwood sought when it came to the international.

Nevertheless New Zealand won their first four games and arrived in Leicester as exponents of a wonderfully proud tradition. Under the Leicester lights (New Zealand's first ever floodlit game in Britain), though, they met their match against a team including Stuart Redfern, the 22-year-old younger brother of Steve, the tight-head prop, and winner of an England under-23 cap the previous season. The Midlands team was: Dusty Hare (Leicester); Steve Holdstock (Nottingham), Paul Dodge, Clive Woodward (both Leicester), John Goodwin (Moseley); Les Cusworth, Nick Youngs; Stuart Redfern (all Leicester), Peter Wheeler (Leicester, captain), Gary Pearce (Northampton), Bob Wilkinson (Bedford), Vince Cannon (Northampton), Nick Jeavons (Moseley), Graham Robbins (Coventry), Gary Rees (Nottingham).

Wheeler, the captain, acknowledged his team faced a "mammoth task" but added that, "if Dusty bangs over all his kicks we may sneak it by a point or two." Never a truer word. Two immense kicks, one a penalty, one dropped, from his own half by Hare gave the Midlands a famous 19-13 win, only the fifth by an English team over New Zealand since they started touring in 1905. The New Zealanders were only four days away from the international with Scotland and did not field their strongest available XV (though the pack was little short of international strength) but nothing should detract from the way the Midlands hurled themselves into their task, notably Gary Rees, the Nottingham flanker whose tackling was of the highest quality.

Martin Whitcombe, Peter Wheeler and Stuart Redfern about to engage.

Robbie Deans opened the scoring for the All Blacks with the first of two early penalties, which enveloped a close-range try by Graham Robbins, Coventry's No 8 who was replaced late in the game by Dean Richards. The Midlands bombarded their opponents with high kicks from half-back but fell further behind early in the second half to Deans's third goal before Hare closed the gap with a penalty. Steve Pokere, pursuing a speculative kick through, scored a try which kept the Midlands at arm's length but when Rees made the extra man the Leicester centres were able to work space for Steve Holdstock to cross and Hare's conversion levelled matters.

Then Wheeler's team went for broke. They attacked from long range, Bob Wilkinson and Vince Cannon stayed in the line-out contest and, roared on by 17,000, they battered away at the New Zealand half. Yet it was from their own territory that they clinched matters: Hare missed his easiest penalty attempt of the night before he took aim from around 55 metres and landed a mighty kick which gave his team the lead. Then, when Murray Mexted failed to find touch with a clearance, Hare gathered on his own 10-metre line and let fly at the distant posts with the dropped goal which disbelieving New Zealanders watched descend over the bar.

It was a mighty match and it earned caps for six Leicester players - Hare, Dodge, Woodward, Cusworth, Youngs and Wheeler - 11 days later. At Twickenham they won again, by 15-9, Hare kicking three penalties and converting Maurice Colclough's try though the match cost Wheeler five weeks away from the game with a broken bone in his hand. Older Leicester supporters could happily reminisce about England's previous home win over New Zealand, in 1936, when Leicester's Bernard Gadney was the captain.

↑ Dean Richards supported by Steve Kenney during Tigers' third round cup defeat against Coventry at Coundon Road 28.1.1984.

↑ Six Tigers for England. Hare, Youngs, Wheeler, Cusworth, Dodge and Woodward take on the All Blacks at Twickenham.

Meanwhile the club itself was not doing badly. Under the captaincy of Ian Smith they established a club record of 16 successive wins from the start of a season until the massed ranks of England players at Twickenham cost them defeat against Wasps. In September they beat the touring national team from Zimbabwe 29-12 and, a month later, Rory Underwood - the Middlesbrough wing who joined the club at the start of the season after his posting to RAF Cranwell - made his first-team debut against Birmingham, and his second game in a 25-0 victory over Northampton. "I noticed the step up in class," Underwood said, "but it was a tremendous education to train and play with the Leicester back division, all of whom were internationals except Barry Evans and me. I don't think I could have had a more unblinkered, unstereotyped experience at such a young age."

Underwood, already a B international from the previous season, served notice of intent with three tries in the 61-10 win over Saracens and two more tries in the 30-26 win over the Barbarians earned him a place in England's training squad. Meanwhile calamity had struck: Smith broke a thumb and missed a month while, against Blackheath at the Rectory Field, Dodge suffered a spiral fracture of the leg. It wrecked his entire season, although he was able to tour South Africa in the summer, and to many observers it took an indefinable edge from his game, even though he recovered to play international rugby again and to give the club another seven years.

Piling on the agony Leicester, without the injured Cusworth, lost their first John Player Cup outing, to Coventry 13-9. Denied possession by their neighbours Leicester might still have won had not Woodward, after a 70-metre run, stumbled in changing direction to avoid pursuit just short of the posts. This, John Allen said, would be a test of the supporters: "Many have been attracted by our cup success but we hope we've also persuaded them that our style of rugby is worth watching every Saturday afternoon."

Perhaps not surprisingly the remainder of the season was inconsistent, with Leicester turning on the power against mediocre sides but struggling against the better ones. Even so there was some compensation from the international scene: although Dodge was absent, Leicester were able to offer a then club record of seven players to the game against Ireland at Twickenham. After defeat in Scotland, Underwood was called up for his first cap on the left wing, joining Hare, Woodward, Cusworth, Youngs, Wheeler and, in the second half, Steve Redfern who came on for what proved to be his only cap as a replacement for the injured Colin White.

But that 12-9 win was England's only success of the season: although Underwood and Hare scored tries against France, and Hare converted both as well as kicking two penalties, England

↑ Malcolm Foulkes-Arnold outjumps his Bedford counterpart 10.3.1984.

lost 32-18 and all they could offer against Wales was Hare's five penalties in a 24-15 defeat. It was a sad conclusion to Wheeler's distinguished international career of 41 caps. Not that the hooker announced his retirement, but he was not available for the summer tour to South Africa and acknowledged that, at his age, it would be surprising if England did not start to look elsewhere.

Amid much controversy the Rugby Football Union voted to go ahead with the visit to South Africa and England departed with Hare, Dodge and Youngs in their ranks, leaving behind a simmering row between Leicester and the Labour-controlled city council which wished to prevent the club using the Welford Road Recreation Ground - later renamed Nelson Mandela Park - for training and playing purposes because they opposed sporting links with South Africa.

Indeed in August that year the council banned Leicester from using the Recreation Ground for a 12-month period because their response to a council questionnaire was deemed inadequate: included in the club's considered response, which joined with the council in a condemnation of apartheid, was an emphasis that the same objective may be achieved in different ways. "Rugby union players, as amateur sportsmen, have individual choice as to when and where they play, subject only to the constraints of the RFU rules and club loyalty," their statement read. The club's appeal went all the way to the House of Lords where five law lords ruled unanimously against the council; that the ban was due to expire two months after the hearing was not the point and Lord Templeman, giving judgement, said: "The laws of this country are not like the laws of Nazi Germany. A private individual or a private organisation cannot be obliged to display zeal in the pursuit of an object sought by a public authority and cannot be obliged to publish views dictated by a public authority."

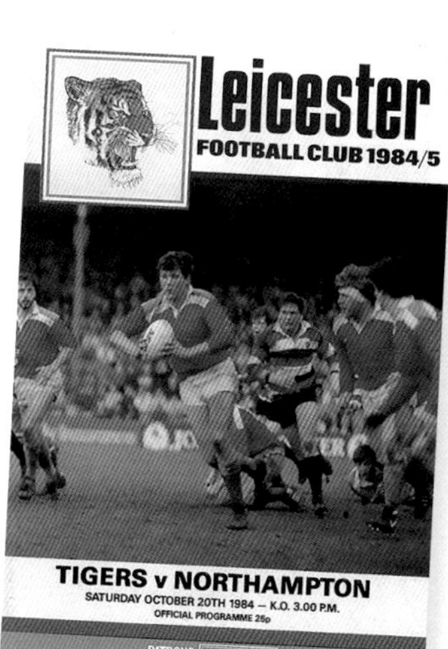

While such weighty matters were being considered, Evans, Stuart Redfern, John Wells and the young hooker, Chris Tressler, toured Spain with England under-23 while Leicester themselves departed for the United Arab Emirates where they played matches in Bahrain and Dubai and heard from afar the decline of their colleagues elsewhere: Dodge returned home early with an ankle injury, Youngs lost his international place to the ginger-headed dynamo from Bath, Richard Hill, and Hare, though he kicked four penalties in the first international and three in the second, played out his final two England appearances in undistinguished circumstances.

1984/1985

Hare announced his retirement from international rugby in September, having played more times at full-back for England (25) than any previous incumbent and having scored more points (240). Hare was always under-valued by England, who dropped and recalled him five times, and his decision, taken at 31 for "family and business reasons" was probably a case of jumping before being pushed: the following weekend England's first squad of the season included Marcus Rose, Nick Stringer and Chris Martin as full-backs. Happily Hare continued to ply his trade with Leicester and Stringer was given first shot at filling his boots in an England XV which played an RFU President's XV to celebrate 75 years of rugby at Twickenham: Underwood, unavailable for the South African tour, Woodward and the younger Redfern joined him in a low-key match lost 27-10.

It soon became apparent that Leicester's stock was declining: the early-season confrontation with Bath, new holders of the cup, ended in favour of the West Countrymen and Tigers had to scramble around for a scrum-half, Youngs having decided to play out the South African season in Durban and Kenney being injured. Ian Smith, captain once more, suffered further damage to his hand and the protracted, and potentially costly, wrangle with the council cast a gloom over proceedings. Even worse was the prospect of losing Cusworth to a Manchester-based building society, a situation relieved when he started a new career as a trainee insurance broker with the Leicester firm of P & G Bland, who later became close allies of the club.

Still, there was the prospect of the touring Australians to look forward to. Leicester had already formed valuable links down under, and a healthy respect for their achievements, though no-one was aware of quite how much Andrew Slack's Wallabies would achieve in Britain. It was significant that their England representation had declined in the space of seven months from seven to one, when only Underwood (who played against the Australians four times, for the Combined Services, the North and the Barbarians) was named in a very raw England XV beaten 19-3 on 3 November, and Leicester supporters looked forward to their Midland players proving a point three days later at Welford Road.

All seven of their heroes were there in a Midland team which read: Dusty Hare (Leicester); Steve Holdstock (Nottingham), Paul Dodge, Clive Woodward (both Leicester), John Goodwin (Moseley); Les Cusworth, Nick Youngs (both Leicester); Lee Johnson (Coventry), Peter Wheeler (Leicester, captain), Gary Pearce, Vince Cannon (both Northampton), Neil Mantell, Peter Cook (both Nottingham), Graham Robbins (Coventry), Ian Smith (Leicester). It was a stage from which Wheeler conceivably could reclaim his England place, having rebuffed the challenge at home of young Tressler, but not by the time the match had finished.

Alan Jones, the Australian coach, described the Midlands as "the other England side, if only they were selected" but by the end of a match which he was relieved his team had won 21-18, Jones was incandescent with rage at the sending-off by Winston Jones, the Welsh referee, of Mark McBain, his reserve hooker, and Wheeler. It was the turning point of a match the Midlands might have won since they led 18-9 at that stage through Hare's five penalties and a dropped goal by Simon Hodgkinson, the replacement for the injured Cusworth, with less than 12 minutes left; but in the resulting confusion Australia's Peter Grigg crossed for a try and James Black, nerve holding remarkably well under the Welford Road lights, kicked the conversion and two penalties.

At that time any English player sent off, at whatever level, was automatically barred from consideration for the national side for the remainder of the season, a ruling to which Wheeler objected - not so much on his own behalf as for younger players with their way to make - owing to its arbitrary nature. The following season it was discarded. But Wheeler, who had never been sent off in his lengthy career, was also fuming that the referee had acted on something he did not witness: he and McBain had niggled at each other throughout the game and they did so once more with arm-swinging gestures which did not connect. They were dismissed for punching and, though Wheeler subsequently produced video evidence purporting to show that no blows had landed, the then mandatory 30-day suspension stood.

There was more than a suspicion that the referee reacted to the roar of the crowd rather than any physical violence witnessed, having spoken to both players earlier in the game. "We weren't having a stand-up brawl and what went on was insignificant both in terms of the game and in terms of the two of us," Wheeler said. Sadly, though Wheeler appeared at the disciplinary hearing in Dublin, along with McBain and his management, Winston Jones submitted only a written report which could not be challenged at the time. It was an unnecessary cloud which tarnished the career of one of Leicester's most remarkable players though, to his credit, Wheeler faded with dignity from the playing scene, playing as and when he could and in whichever team Leicester chose to pick him.

But he had remained long enough to see the beginning of fundamental change to the domestic competitive structure: England and the English were beginning to tire of being cannon fodder and there was talk of a new divisional championship, of a national club merit table if not leagues, of husbanding the country's playing resources far more effectively. Leicester had long since agreed that a merit table might be beneficial and were building for the future: at the start of the season a five-year sponsorship was agreed with Ind Coope, the brewers, designed to help offset the costs of refurbishing Welford Road, at the time the most expensive ground outside Twickenham. In the new year plans were unveiled for ground improvements costing £100,000: the changing rooms and additional facilities were to be moved underneath the Crumbie Stand for the 1985/86 season and the room created in the Aylestone Road clubhouse turned into a members' bar and lounge. In the wake of the fire which destroyed the Bradford City Football Club stand, in which 56 died, later in the season a further £60,000 was set aside to comply with safety requirements.

↑ Les Cusworth scored two tries in the 1984 Barbarians fixture.

By the time Christmas came, Wheeler had regained his place in the side which gave the Barbarians their biggest drubbing in the series, by 35-11. Dodge had been recalled to the England squad and even the unwelcome news that Steve Redfern had decided to turn professional with the new Sheffield Eagles rugby league club did not cast too great a shadow. Redfern, then 26 and with 241 appearances to his credit since joining Tigers from Coalville, was the first England international to go to rugby league for eight years. The new year also brought word that Dodge had been invited to captain England against Romania. Nigel Melville, who led England in his debut international against Australia, had damaged his knee and Dodge offered experience and solidity to a team desperately in need of it. He was the fourth captain in ten months, Wheeler having been briefly succeeded by John Scott, and was given a side including five newcomers - among them Rob Andrew and Wade Dooley. Dodge had been sounded out by Derek Morgan during the South African tour but the selection came, nonetheless, as a surprise to a player whose only previous leadership experience had been an undemanding game between England under-23 and Holland.

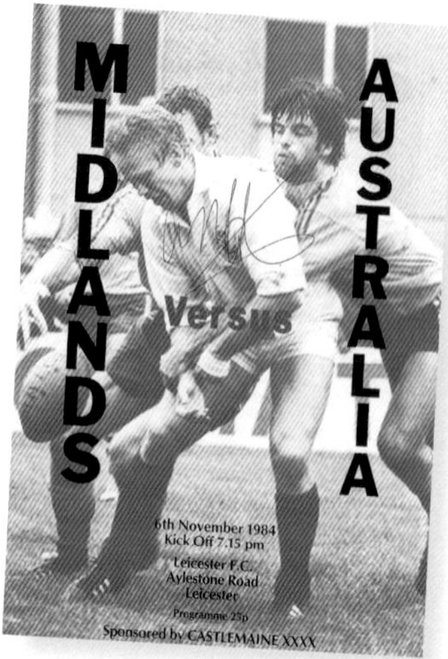

He retained the role for seven games, including the two internationals in New Zealand during the summer. 1985, though, was Dodge's international swansong: he became England's then most-capped centre with 32 games but his more subtle skills were seldom appreciated at international level. At 6ft 2in he had physical presence but far more than that, he had a footballing brain and handling skills which could have been far better used than they were; his organisational powers were always far better understood by those who played alongside him (or against him) than those who watched.

Underwood, who thought his RAF career would keep him out of top-class rugby this season, was alongside him though unable to tour in the summer. But again England made hard work of a season disrupted by bad weather: one try in the 22-15 win over Romania, a surprise draw with France, a snatched victory over Scotland, but they could not deny Ireland the triple crown. Although Dodge set up a try for Underwood with his cross-kick, a late dropped goal gave the Irish the verdict 13-10 at Lansdowne Road and Wales made off with the spoils at Cardiff as usual.

Underwood may well have thought club rugby came slightly easier, to judge from the start Leicester made to the John Player Cup. Two years earlier Bristol had taken the trophy, the previous season they were beaten finalists: but on 26 January Tigers erased them from the competition with a dazzling 43-4 victory at Welford Road. It was a quite clinical dissection of a good Bristol side, in which Underwood, with four tries, was the chief surgeon. Hare kicked four conversions and four penalties, Wheeler took three heels against the head, Woodward popped over a dropped goal and Cusworth was at his most impish.

When Liverpool were beaten 37-9 hopes rose even higher, only to be flattened when Leicester could only draw 10-10 at Coundon Road, Coventry going through to the semi-finals by virtue of scoring two tries to one. Ironically Coventry went out in the same way, by the same score, to London Welsh. The season tailed off in a welter of injuries, one of them to Wheeler who damaged elbow ligaments, and even the two matches played on a brief visit to France, at Saint Claude and Chambéry, were lost. Barry Evans played in the end-of-season B international against Italy at Twickenham but otherwise Leicester looked forward to life under Cusworth in 1985/86.

Life, that is, in the John Smith's Merit Table, division A. This was the first, tentative dabble with a structured season though the tables themselves were worked on a percentage basis since half the competing teams did not play each other: thus, in a 12-club table, Leicester played 10 matches, more than anyone else including Gloucester, the eventual winners, and in some cases 50 per cent more. Just to complicate matters new laws came into force including scrum and tackle laws, designed to keep players on their feet rather than creating pile-ups on the ground.

↑ Rory Underwood scored a Tigers cup record four tries against Bristol on 26.1.1985.

↑↓ Tigers toured south and east France in May 1985, playing against Chambéry and Saint Claude.

1985/1986

As if to emphasise change, the club bade farewell to Clive Woodward who, after some months of speculation, announced that he had accepted a business move to Australia. He had won 21 England caps and proved himself a player of immense flair: he and Dodge complemented each other perfectly, Dodge offering the security for the will o' the wisp Woodward to go where his fancy took him. Yet Woodward was also a tremendous support player because he had the vision to see what was possible - if not always what was probable. He led the side out for his final match, against Bath, who failed to acknowledge the occasion by winning 40-15.

There was no shortage of competition to partner Dodge: Ian Bates had been joined by Steve Burnhill, a tourist in South Africa with Dodge in 1984, and Tim Buttimore, a Coventry centre with some of Woodward's mercurial talent. Meanwhile Dodge himself, after captaining England to a narrow 18-13 defeat in the first international with New Zealand in the summer (six penalties

→ Clive Woodward runs out for the last time in a Tigers shirt at home to Bath 14.9.1985.

by Kieran Crowley accounted for England's loss) and an unpleasant, in every sense, 42-15 defeat in the second, found himself omitted from the first England training squad. In a party of 37 Leicester had only two: Underwood, whose flying duties affected his availability, and Richards, whose attitude to training made even the relaxed Graham Willars grumble: "One day I might turn him into a fitness freak but at the moment I can't see it," Willars said while extolling the England potential of the young No 8.

Enter the divisional championship, which was a genuine regional competition or an extended trial, depending on your viewpoint. The Midlands team was dominated by Nottingham and Coventry players, which rankled somewhat at Leicester since they had beaten both: only Dodge and Cusworth played in the team that won the title by beating the North and London at home and the South-West away, their mauling style projecting Graham Robbins, the Coventry No 8, into the England team.

Leicester meanwhile rolled forward reasonably comfortably, running up substantial wins against London Welsh, Coventry and Oxford University, and enjoying an 18-10 triumph over Swansea before Cardiff brought them to ground. But they remained not entirely convincing, the mauling by Bath taking time to work its way from the corporate system. Underwood played his first club match of the season in the 19-16 defeat by the Barbarians but clearly the club was saving itself for the cup to come in the new year.

Certainly there was little prospect on the international front: Underwood retained his place but even he missed the game with Scotland because of an ankle injury, the first time in 54 internationals and 11 years that Leicester had not been represented in an England side. It may have been a judicious one to miss: England crashed 33-6, the second time in eight months they had lost by the record margin of 27 points. The effect was to introduce Richards to international rugby: the 22-year-old policeman from Hinckley replaced Robbins against Ireland and marked the occasion by scoring two tries in a 25-20 win. Even Clive Norling, the Welsh referee, congratulated him on his debut and both he and Underwood remained for the final match, a defeat by France.

Richards was then, and subsequently remained, a mould-breaker: Wheeler, for example, was an outstanding forward in the breed of the modern hooker, who had many of the ball skills of a back-row forward but was identifiable as one of a type. Richards was entirely his own man: loose-limbed, unathletic in build but a man of immense presence even though he was not the tallest of No 8s. Socks round ankles, shirt flapping wildly, with considerable mauling power, he conformed in no way to the textbook of back row play - he just turned up wherever the ball happened to be. And, happily for Leicester, international rugby was never the be-all and end-all for him: Richards was as happy playing with his club as he was to turn out for England at Twickenham.

For some obscure reason he and Underwood were both included, at the season's end, in an England under-23 side against Spain.

A week later Underwood, leaping up the scale, was playing for the British Lions against the Rest of the World in the first of the two special matches celebrating the centenary of the International Rugby Football Board. Seven of that side in Cardiff - Underwood, Gavin Hastings, Brendan Mullin, Robert Jones, Wade Dooley, Donal Lenihan and John Jeffrey - subsequently joined forces in the 1989 Lions tour party to Australia. On this occasion they lost and Underwood was in the defeated side three days later when a Five Nations XV played the Overseas Unions at Twickenham.

Dean Richards in typical action, his try helping to knock Harlequins out of the cup at the quarter-final stage.

Richards was on hand when Leicester began their John Player Cup campaign by extracting revenge from Coventry for the disappointment of the previous season: they had to work hard for a 21-14 win at Coundon Road, losing Underwood with an ankle injury on the way, and then had to wait for the vagaries of the weather before scoring eight tries (three to Richards) in a 46-6 victory over Broughton Park in a Sunday cup tie. In fact it was hard to keep Richards out of the news: he scored again, his 18th try of the season, when Leicester beat Harlequins 15-8 in the quarter-final at the Stoop Memorial Ground, paving the way for a dramatic semi-final against Bath - the club whose ebullient young forwards had treated Tigers with such disrespect the previous September.

Everyone in Leicester, it seemed, wanted a ticket for the match but for those who obtained one there was only disappointment: the club's first cup defeat at Welford Road. Bath won 10-6 (a scoreline that was to return to haunt Leicester three years later) and deserved to, their juggernaut pack rolling back the Leicester forwards. The contest at scrum-half between Youngs and Hill failed to materialise after Youngs left the field in the first quarter and the side that scored the try (through Simon Halliday) won the match, and went forward to beat Wasps in the final. Since Leicester also finished fourth in the new merit table their standing in English club terms was confirmed: nearly but not quite.

Leicester
FOOTBALL CLUB 1985-6
TIGERS v BATH
SATURDAY APRIL 5TH 1986 — K.O. 2.30 P.M.
OFFICIAL PROGRAMME 30p
PATRONS IND COOPE

Semi-final programme for the visit of Bath.

1984	EMIRATES TOUR	OVERALL RECORD:					T	C	PG	DG	PTS
	Coach: Graham Willars assisted by Rod Oakes	PLD	W	D	L	Tigers scored:	19	11	0	0	98
	Captain: Ian Smith	2	2	0	0	Opponents scored:	0	0	2	0	6

GM	DATE		VEN	OPPONENTS	RESULT	TRIES	KICKS	ATT
1	Apr	27f	a	Arabian Gulf	W 54-3	Cusworth(2), Kenney(2), Dodge, Evans, Foulkes-Arnold, Richardson, Wells, Williams	Hare 7c	-
2		29s	a	South Gulf Select XV	W 44-3	Foulkes-Arnold(2), Dexter, Evans, I.Smith, Tressler, Wells, Whitcombe, Youngs	Dodson 3c, Hare c	-

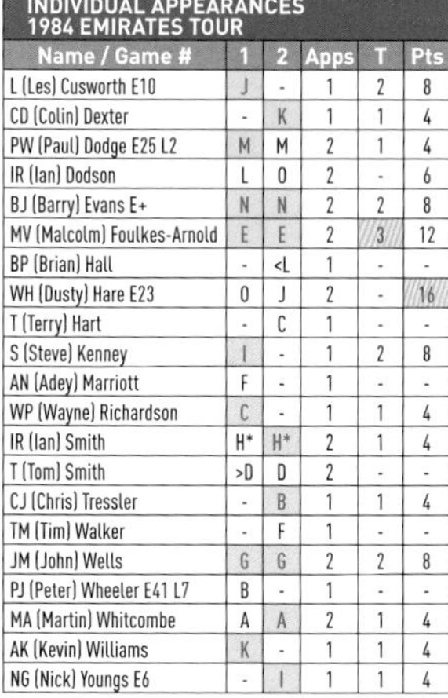

INDIVIDUAL APPEARANCES 1984 EMIRATES TOUR					
Name / Game #	1	2	Apps	T	Pts
L (Les) Cusworth E10	J	-	1	2	8
CD (Colin) Dexter	-	K	1	1	4
PW (Paul) Dodge E25 L2	M	M	2	1	4
IR (Ian) Dodson	L	O	2	-	6
BJ (Barry) Evans E+	N	N	2	2	8
MV (Malcolm) Foulkes-Arnold	E	E	2	3	12
BP (Brian) Hall	-	<L	1	-	-
WH (Dusty) Hare E23	O	J	2	-	16
T (Terry) Hart	-	C	1	-	-
S (Steve) Kenney	I	-	1	2	8
AN (Adey) Marriott	F	-	1	-	-
WP (Wayne) Richardson	C	-	1	1	4
IR (Ian) Smith	H*	H*	2	1	4
T (Tom) Smith	>D	D	2	-	-
CJ (Chris) Tressler	-	B	1	1	4
TM (Tim) Walker	-	F	1	-	-
JM (John) Wells	G	G	2	2	8
PJ (Peter) Wheeler E41 L7	B	-	1	-	-
MA (Martin) Whitcombe	A	A	2	1	4
AK (Kevin) Williams	K	-	1	1	4
NG (Nick) Youngs E6	-	I	1	1	4

← LEICESTER FOOTBALL CLUB 1983/84
Back: Willars (Coach), Beason (Hon.Tres), Allen (Hon.Sec), Wheeler, Richards, Dodge, Walker, Ste.Redfern, Foulkes-Arnold, Gillingham, Black, Whitcombe, Hare, Herbert (President), Thomas (Team Hon.Sec).
Middle: Stu.Redfern, Marriott, K.Williams, Kenney, Smith (capt), Tressler, Evans, Bates, Tebbutt, Woodward.
Front: Dodson, Pell.

← LEICESTER FOOTBALL CLUB 1984/85
Back: Willars (Coach), Thomas (Team Hon.Sec), Herbert (President), Wheeler, Dodge, Wells, Foulkes-Arnold, Richards, Richardson, Stu.Redfern, Bates, Beason (Hon.Tres), Allen (Hon.Sec).
Front: Woodward, Hare, Cusworth, Evans, I.Smith (capt), Harris, Kenney, Youngs, Tressler.

← LEICESTER FOOTBALL CLUB 1985/86
Back: Willars (Coach), Thomas (Team Hon.Sec), Wells, Richards, Foulkes-Arnold, Davidson, W.Richardson, Redfern, Beason (President), Allen (Hon.Sec), Farrands (Hon.Tres).
Middle: Williams, Kenney, Dodge, Cusworth (capt), Hare, Tressler, Evans, Tebbutt.
Front: Bates, Burnhill.

INDIVIDUAL APPEARANCES 1985 FRANCE TOUR					
Name / Game #	1	2	Apps	T	Pts
V (Vendis) Afflick	r	L	1+1	-	-
I (Ian) Bates	M	M	2	-	-
B (Bernie) Bowers	r	<B	1+1	-	-
MR (Mark) Charles	G	-	1	-	-
MJ (Mark) Cleaver	>N	N	2	-	-
CD (Colin) Dexter	K	O	2	-	-
D (Darren) Grewcock	>I	-	1	-	-
PR (Phil) Kendall	>J	<J	2	-	4
S (Steve) Kenney	-	I	1	-	-
SB (Stuart) Redfern	r	A	1+1	-	-
D (Dean) Richards E+ L+	E	G	2	1	4
WP (Wayne) Richardson	C	C	2	-	-
GC (Graham) Robb	<L	-	1	1	4
PT (Peter) Sly	>O	<r	1+1	-	-
IR (Ian) Smith	H*	H*	2	-	-
RS (Rob) Tebbutt	-	F	1	-	-
CJ (Chris) Tressler	B	r	1+1	-	-
DP (Dean) Waddingham	D	<D	2	-	-
JM (John) Wells	F	E	2	1	4
MA (Martin) Whitcombe	A	-	1	-	-
JB (Jon) Wood	-	=K	1	-	-

1985	SOUTH & EAST FRANCE TOUR	OVERALL RECORD:					T	C	PG	DG	PTS
	Coach: Graham Willars assisted by Rod Oakes	PLD	W	D	L	Tigers scored:	3	2	0	0	16
	Captain: Ian Smith	2	0	0	2	Opponents scored:	8	5	1	0	45

GM	DATE		VEN	OPPONENTS	RESULT	TRIES	KICKS	ATT
1	May	10f	a	Chambéry	L 6-32	Robb	Kendall c	-
2		12s	a	Saint Claude	L 10-13	Richards, Wells	Kendall c	-

The key for how to read the stats is on the last page

19	83/84	**Home Ground:** Welford Road	**Trophy Cabinet:** Midland Merit Table	OVERALL RECORD:					T	C	PG	DG	PTS
		Coach: Graham Willars assisted by Rod Oakes		PLD	W	D	L	Tigers scored:	144	83	83	13	1030
		Captain: Ian Smith		41	28	1	12	Opponents scored:	70	33	68	9	577

GM	DATE		VEN	OPPONENTS	RESULT	TRIES	KICKS	ATT
RFU CLUB COMPETITION (JOHN PLAYER SPECIAL CUP)						**CUP WINNERS: BATH**		
26	Jan	28	a	Coventry (3)	L 9-13	-	Hare 3p	7000
MIDLAND MERIT TABLE (1ST)						**WINNERS: LEICESTER TIGERS**		
1	Sep	3	a	Bedford	W 68-3	Evans(3), K.Williams(2), Black, Dexter, Dodge, Dodson, Marriott, Tressler, Woodward	Cusworth 10c	-
2		**6tu**	**H**	**Nuneaton**	W 59-4	Evans(4), Cusworth, Black, Dexter, Foulkes-Arnold, Stu.Redfern, K.Williams	Cusworth 5c/3p	-
6		**21w**	**H**	**Birmingham**	W 40-3	Gillingham(2), K.Williams(2), Black	Hare 4c/4p	-
8	Oct	**1**	**H**	**Coventry**	W 39-9	Dodge, Cusworth, Dexter, Dodson, Tebbutt, Youngs(Penalty)	Dodge 3c/2p, Cusworth d	-
38	Apr	**11w**	**H**	**Moseley**	W 31-22	K.Williams(2), Pell, Tressler	Hare 3c/3p	-
CLUB MATCHES								
3	Sep	**10**	**H**	**Bath**	W 18-15	-	Cusworth 6p	-
4		**14w**	**H**	**Zimbabwe**	W 29-12	Dodson, Evans, Stu.Redfern, K.Williams	Cusworth 2c/3p	-
5		**17**	**H**	**London Welsh**	W 14-9	Evans, Youngs	Cusworth d, Dodge p	-
7		24	a	Harlequins	W 20-18	Dodge(2), Poulson, Youngs	Hare 2c	-
9	Oct	8	a	Richmond	W 10-0	Evans	Hare 2p	-
10		15	a	Northampton	W 25-0	Richards(2), Evans, Tebbutt, Walker	Cusworth p, Dodson c	-
11		19w	a	Oxford University	W 36-7	Smith(2), Dodge, Cusworth, Penalty	Dodge 5c/p, Poulson d	-
12		**22**	**H**	**Swansea**	W 41-3	Hare, Evans, Marriott, Smith, K.Williams, Youngs	Hare 4c/3p	5570
13		29	a	Saracens	W 61-10	Underwood(3), Whitcombe(2), Youngs(2), Hare, Stu.Redfern	Hare 8c/2p, Cusworth d	-
14	Nov	**5**	**H**	**Cardiff**	W 29-24	Evans, Smith, Underwood, Youngs	Hare 2c/3p	8000
15		12	a	Cambridge University	W 35-16	Evans(3), Dodge(2), Black, Cave	Dodge c, Cusworth c/p	-
16		15tu	a	Nottingham	W 20-9	Bates, K.Williams	Poulson 2p/2d	-
17		**19**	**H**	**Wasps**	L 18-23	Hall, Whitcombe	Poulson 2c/2p	-
18		26	a	Moseley	W 15-6	Evans, Foulkes-Arnold	Hare 2c/p	-
19	Dec	**3**	**H**	**Gloucester**	W 30-20	Underwood(2)	Hare 2c/6p	-
20		10	a	Blackheath	L 3-21	-	Cusworth d	-
21		**17**	**H**	**Bristol**	L 12-15	Marriott	Hare c/2p	-
22		**28w**	**H**	**Barbarians**	W 30-26	Underwood(2), Evans, Youngs	Hare c/3p, Cusworth d	16800
23		31	a	London Welsh	W 16-14	Richards	Hare 3p, Cusworth d	-
24	Jan	7	a	Bath	L 0-14	-	-	-
25		14	a	Gloucester	L 21-22	Richards, Woodward	Cusworth 2c/3p	-
		21	**H**	**Bedford**	PP (frost)			
27	Feb	**4**	**H**	**London Scottish**	L 12-16	-	Dodson 4p	-
28		11	a	Newport	W 19-15	Evans, Underwood	Cusworth 2d, Hare c/p	-
29		18	a	Orrell	L 8-21	Dodson, Richardson	-	-
30		**25**	**H**	**Rosslyn Park**	W 25-16	Cusworth(2), Richards(2), Evans	Hare c/p	-
		25	**H**	**Northampton**	PP (cup)			
31	Mar	**3**	**H**	**Harlequins**	W 35-20	Pell, Evans, Foulkes-Arnold, Gillingham, Kenney, Richards	Pell 2c, Dodson 2c/p	-
32		**10**	**H**	**Bedford**	W 64-9	Underwood(3), Youngs(2), Evans, Joyce, Richards, Woodward	Hare 8c/4p	-
		10	a	Coventry	PP (cup)			
33		**13tu**	**H**	**Loughborough Students**	W 26-9	Richards(2), Bates, Foulkes-Arnold	Dodson c/2p, Pell c	-
34		**16f**	**H**	**Royal Air Force**	W 26-3	Evans(2), Black(2), Dodson, K.Williams	Evans c	-
35		**24**	**H**	**Sale**	W 25-10	Gerald(2), Foulkes-Arnold, Richardson, Wheeler	Cusworth c/p	-
36		31	a	Headingley	L 3-12	-	Dodson p	-
37	Apr	**7**	**H**	**Waterloo**	D 18-18	-	Hare 5p, Pell d	-
39		14	a	Bristol	L 16-43	K.Williams(2)	Cusworth c/d, Hare p	-
40		21	a	Neath	L 24-28	Dexter, Hall, K.Williams	Hare 3c/2p	-
41		23m	a	Pontypool	L 0-19	-	-	-

INDIVIDUAL APPEARANCES 1983/84

Name / Game #	1	2	3	4	5	6	7	8	9	10	11	12	13	14	15	16	17	18	19	20	21	22	23	24	25	26	27	28	29	30	31	32	33	34	35	36	37	38	39	40	41	Apps	T	Pts
V (Vendis) Afflick	-	-	-	-	-	-	-	-	-	-	-	-	-	x	-	-	-	x	-	-	-	x	-	-	-	-	-	-	M	-	L	-	L	L	-	-	-	-	-	-	-	4	-	-
SR (Steve) Avent	-	-	-	-	-	-	-	-	-	-	-	-	-	-	-	-	>M	-	-	-	-	-	-	-	-	-	-	-	-	-	-	-	-	-	-	-	-	-	-	r	L	2+1	-	-
I (Ian) Bates	-	L	x	x	-	L	-	L	-	M	-	-	L	M	-	M	-	M	-	-	M	M	L	-	M	M	M	M	-	M	M	M	M	M	-	L	M	M	-	-	-	23	2	8
DS (Duncan) Black	r	G	x	x	-	G	-	-	G	-	E	-	-	-	G	G	x	-	-	-	-	-	-	G	-	x	-	-	-	x	-	-	x	G	G	-	D	G	G	E	G	14+1	6	24
B (Bernie) Bowers	-	-	-	-	-	-	-	-	>B	B	B	-	-	-	B	-	-	-	-	-	-	-	-	-	-	-	-	-	-	-	-	-	B	B	-	-	-	-	-	-	-	6	-	-
P (Paul) Cave	-	-	-	-	-	-	-	-	-	-	-	-	-	-	>O	-	-	-	-	r	-	-	<r	-	-	-	-	-	-	-	x	-	-	-	-	-	-	-	-	-	-	1+2	1	4
LC (Lewis) Clifford	-	-	-	-	-	-	-	-	-	-	-	-	-	-	-	-	-	-	-	-	-	-	-	-	-	-	-	-	-	-	-	-	-	-	-	-	>r	-	-	B	-	1+1	-	-
L (Les) Cusworth E10	J	J	J	J	J	-	-	J*	J*	J*	J	J	J	J	J	-	-	J	J	J*	J*	J*	J*	-	J*	-	-	J	-	J	-	J	-	-	J	-	-	-	J	-	J	26	5	145
CD (Colin) Dexter	r	O	O	-	x	-	-	N	-	-	O	-	-	-	-	r	-	-	x	-	-	-	-	-	-	-	-	-	-	-	-	-	x	r	O	-	-	-	-	N	-	6+3	4	16
PW (Paul) Dodge E25 L2	M	M	M	M	M	M	M	M	L	-	M	M	-	-	L	-	-	L	M	M	-	-	-	-	-	-	-	-	-	-	-	-	-	-	-	M*	-	-	M	-	-	17	7	58
IR (Ian) Dodson	O	-	-	O	O	-	r	O	-	O	-	-	-	-	-	-	-	-	-	-	-	-	-	M	O	x	O	-	O	-	O	-	O	O	-	O	-	-	x	L	O	16+1	5	52
BJ (Barry) Evans E+	N	N	N	N	N	-	N	-	N	N	N	N	-	N	N	N	N	N	N	N	N	N	N	N	N	N	N	N	N	N	N	N	N	N	-	N	N	N	-	-	N	35	24	98
MV (Malcolm) Foulkes-Arnold	E	E	E	E	E	E	E	E	-	-	-	-	E	E	E	E	E	E	E	E	E	E	E	E	E	E	E	E	E	E	E	E	E	E	E	-	E	E	E	-	E	35	5	20
CE (Claude) Gerald	-	-	-	-	-	-	-	-	-	-	-	-	-	-	-	-	x	-	-	-	-	-	-	-	-	-	x	-	K	-	-	-	-	-	N	-	-	-	r	-	-	2+1	2	8
NK (Nigel) Gillingham	D	D	D	D	D	D	D	D	-	D	D	D	D	D	D	D	D	D	D	D	D	D	D	-	-	D	D	D	D	D	D	-	-	-	-	D	-	D	D	D	<D	33	3	12
BP (Brian) Hall	-	-	-	-	-	-	-	-	-	-	-	-	-	-	-	L	L	-	-	-	-	-	M	L*	-	-	L	x	L	x	-	-	-	-	M	-	L	-	-	M	M	10	2	8
WH (Dusty) Hare E23	-	-	-	-	-	O	O	-	O	-	-	O	O	O	-	-	-	O	O	O	O	O	O	-	-	O	-	O	-	O	-	O	-	-	-	-	O	O	O	O	-	20	2	239
T (Terry) Hart	-	-	-	-	-	-	-	-	>C	C	-	-	-	-	-	-	-	-	-	-	-	-	-	-	-	-	-	-	-	-	-	-	-	C	-	-	-	-	-	-	-	3	-	-
NJ (Nick) Joyce	-	-	-	-	-	-	-	-	-	-	-	-	-	-	-	-	-	-	-	-	-	-	-	D	D	-	-	-	-	-	-	D	D	-	-	-	-	-	-	-	-	4	1	4
S (Steve) Kenney	-	-	-	x	-	-	-	-	-	I	-	-	-	-	-	I	I	-	-	I	-	-	I	-	-	I	I	-	I	-	I	-	I	I*	I	-	I*	I*	I	I	I	17	1	4
TJH (Tommy) Lawton	-	-	-	-	-	-	-	-	D	-	-	<E	-	-	-	-	-	-	-	-	x	-	-	-	-	-	-	-	-	-	-	-	-	-	-	-	-	-	-	-	-	2	-	-
AN (Adey) Marriott	F	F	F	F	F	F	F	F	F	-	G	F	G	F	-	-	-	-	-	F	F	F	H	F	H	F	-	-	F	F	F	F	F	F	F	F	F	F	F	F	-	32	3	12
RT (Richard) Pell	-	-	-	-	-	-	-	-	-	-	-	-	-	-	-	-	-	-	-	-	-	-	-	>J	-	J	J	-	J	-	J	-	J	J	-	-	J	J	-	J	-	10	2	17
MJ (Mike) Poulson	-	x	-	x	-	J	J	-	-	-	r	-	-	-	-	J	<J	-	-	-	-	-	-	-	-	-	-	-	-	-	-	-	-	-	-	-	-	-	-	-	-	4+1	1	29
SP (Steve) Redfern E1	C	C	C	C	C	-	-	C	-	-	-	-	-	-	-	-	-	C	C	-	C	C	C	-	-	C	C	C	-	C	-	C	C	-	A	C	C	C	C	C	C	24	-	-
SB (Stuart) Redfern	A	A	A	A	A	A	A	A	A	-	A	A	A	A	A	A	A	-	-	-	-	-	-	-	-	-	-	-	-	A	A	A	A	A	-	A	A	A	A	A	A	27	3	12
D (Dean) Richards E+ L+	G	-	G	G	G	-	G	G	-	G	-	G	-	G	-	-	G	G	G	G	G	G	G	-	G	G	G	G	G	G	G	G	G	-	-	G	G	-	-	-	-	27	10	40
WP (Wayne) Richardson	-	-	-	x	-	C	C	-	-	-	-	-	-	-	-	-	-	-	-	C	-	-	-	C	C	-	-	-	C	-	-	-	-	-	C	-	-	-	-	-	-	7	2	8
IR (Ian) Smith	H*	H*	H*	H*	H*	H*	H*	-	-	-	H*	H*	H*	H*	H*	H*	H*	H*	H*	-	-	-	-	-	-	-	H*	H*	H*	H*	H*	H*	H*	-	H*	-	-	-	H*	H*	H*	27	4	16
RS (Rob) Tebbutt	-	-	-	-	-	-	r	H	H	H	F	-	F	-	F	F	F	F	F	H	H	H	F	H	F	H	F	F	-	-	-	-	-	H	-	H	-	-	-	-	-	21+1	2	8
CJ (Chris) Tressler	B	B	-	x	-	B	-	-	-	-	-	-	-	B	-	B	B	B	B	B	B	B	B	B	B	-	B	-	B	-	B	-	-	-	-	B	B	B	B	-	B	22	2	8
R (Rory) Underwood E3 L+	-	-	-	-	-	>K	-	-	-	K	-	-	K	K	-	K	K	-	K	K	K	K	K	K	-	-	-	K	-	K	-	K	-	-	-	K	-	-	K	-	-	17	12	48
DP (Dean) Waddingham	-	-	-	-	-	-	-	-	E	E	-	-	-	-	-	-	-	-	-	-	-	-	-	-	-	-	-	-	-	-	-	-	-	D	D	E	-	-	-	-	-	5	-	-
TM (Tim) Walker	-	-	-	-	-	-	-	>r	-	F	-	-	-	r	-	-	-	-	r	-	-	-	-	-	x	-	-	x	-	-	-	x	-	-	-	-	H	H	-	-	-	3+3	1	4
JM (John) Wells	-	x	-	-	x	-	-	-	-	-	-	-	-	-	-	-	-	-	-	-	-	-	r	-	-	-	-	-	-	-	-	-	-	-	-	r	-	-	r	G	F	2+3	-	-
PJ (Peter) Wheeler E41 L7	-	-	B	B	B	-	B	B	-	-	-	B	B	-	-	-	-	-	-	-	-	-	-	-	-	B*	-	B	-	B	-	B	-	-	B	-	-	-	-	-	-	12	1	4
MA (Martin) Whitcombe	-	-	-	-	-	-	-	-	-	A	C	C	C	C	C	C	C	A	A	A	A	A	A	A	A	A	A	A	A	-	C	-	-	-	-	-	-	x	-	-	-	21	3	12
G (Gareth) Williams	-	-	-	-	-	-	-	-	-	-	-	-	-	-	>I	-	-	-	-	-	-	-	-	<I	x	-	-	-	-	-	-	-	-	-	-	-	-	-	-	-	-	2	-	-
AK (Kevin) Williams	K	K	K	K	K	N	K	K	K	-	K	K	N	-	K	O	O	K	-	-	x	-	-	O	K	K	K	-	-	-	K	-	K	K	K	r	K	K	N	K	K	29+1	14	56
CR (Clive) Woodward E21 L2	L	-	L	L	L	-	L	-	M	L	L	L	M	L	M	-	-	-	L	L	L	L	-	-	L	L	-	L	-	L	-	L	-	-	L	J	-	-	L	-	-	24	3	12
NG (Nick) Youngs E6	I	I	I	I	I	I	I	I	I	-	I	I	I	I	-	-	-	I	I	-	I	I	-	-	I	-	-	I	-	I	-	I	-	-	-	I	-	-	-	-	-	22	10	40

The key for how to read the stats is on the last page

19 84/85

Home Ground: Welford Road
Coach: Graham Willars assisted by Rod Oakes
Captain: Ian Smith

OVERALL RECORD:					T	C	PG	DG	PTS
PLD	W	D	L	Tigers scored:	129	78	79	18	963
39	26	2	11	Opponents scored:	64	31	57	9	516

GM	DATE		VEN	OPPONENTS	RESULT	TRIES	KICKS	ATT
RFU CLUB COMPETITION (JOHN PLAYER SPECIAL CUP)						**CUP WINNERS: BATH**		
25	Jan	**26**	**H**	**Bristol (3)**	W 43-4	Underwood 8/45/56/79, Williams 54	Hare 4c/4p, Woodward d	8000
27	Feb	23	a	Liverpool (4)	W 37-9	Evans 24/65, Wells 70, Underwood 80	Hare 3c/3p, Cusworth 2d	-
29	Mar	9	a	Coventry (qf)	D 10-10	Dodge 30	Hare 2p	11200
***Note:** #29 Coventry progressed 2-1 on tries*								
MERIT TABLES						**NATIONAL WINNERS: SALE. MIDLANDS WINNERS: NOTTINGHAM**		
1	Sep	**1**	**H**	**Bedford**	W 38-12	Ste.Redfern(2), Evans, Penalty	Hare 2c/5p, Cusworth d	5000
2		4tu	a	Nuneaton	W 30-6	Black, Cusworth, Dodson, Gerald, Hartley	Hare 2c/2p	-
3		8	a	Bath	L 6-17	Underwood	Cusworth c	-
4		**12w**	**H**	**Birmingham**	W 41-4	Dexter, Hartley, Stu.Redfern, T.Smith, Tressler, Williams, Woodward	Hare 5c/p	-
6		22	a	Harlequins	W 25-15	Underwood(2), Ste.Redfern	Hare 2c/3p	-
8	Oct	6	a	Coventry	W 38-6	Wells(2), Dexter, Foulkes-Arnold, Williams, Youngs	Hare 4c/2p	-
10		**20**	**H**	**Northampton**	W 24-4	Youngs(2)	Hare 2c/4p	-
15	Nov	**13tu**	**H**	**Nottingham**	W 12-6	-	Hare 3p/d	3400
17		**24**	**H**	**Moseley**	L 19-22	Robb, Youngs	Hare c/3p	-
18	Dec	1	a	Gloucester	L 15-37	Harris, Richards	Hare 2c/p	-
20		15	a	Bristol	W 14-4	Evans(2), Hare	Hare c	-
33	Mar	23	a	Sale	L 3-9	-	Hare p	-
CLUB MATCHES								
5	Sep	**15**	**H**	**London Welsh**	W 18-9	Cusworth	Cusworth d, Hare c/3p	-
7		**29**	**H**	**Saracens**	W 22-15	Dodge, Williams	Hare c/4p	-
9	Oct	**13**	**H**	**Richmond**	W 55-21	Evans(2), Stu.Redfern(2), Wells, Williams, Youngs	Hare 6c/5p	-
11		**24w**	**H**	**Oxford University**	W 26-9	Kenney(2), I.Smith, Wells, Williams	Cusworth c, Pell c, Woodward c	-
12		27	a	Swansea	L 12-25	Roy	Hare c/p, Cusworth d	-
13	Nov	3	a	Cardiff	L 21-47	Dexter(2), Hare, Williams	Hare c/p	-
14		**10**	**H**	**Cambridge University**	W 33-9	Wells(3), Afflick, Stu.Redfern	Harris 2c/2p/d	2900
16		17	a	Wasps	D 16-16	Underwood	Pell 2p, Harris p, Woodward d	-
19	Dec	**8**	**H**	**Blackheath**	W 50-14	Evans(4), Underwood(2), Hare, Cusworth, Richards	Hare 4c/2p	-
21		22	a	London Welsh	L 17-25	Evans, Tressler, Underwood	Hare c/p	-
22		**27th**	**H**	**Barbarians**	W 35-11	Cusworth(2), Evans, Richards, I.Smith, Williams	Hare 4c/p	17000
	Jan	5	a	Ballymena	PP (frost)			
23		**12**	**H**	**Gloucester**	W 27-6	Hare, Williams	Hare 2c/4p/d	-
24		**19**	**H**	**Bedford**	W 20-0	Evans(2), Cusworth, Richards	Hare 2c	-
26	Feb	2	a	London Scottish	W 19-10	Evans(2)	Cusworth 2d, Harris c/p	-
		9	**H**	**Newport**	PP (frost)			
		16	**H**	**Orrell**	PP (frost)			
		23	a	Northampton	PP (cup)			
28	Mar	**2**	**H**	**Harlequins**	W 35-19	Hare, Cusworth, Stu.Redfern, Richards, Woodward	Hare 3c/p/d, Cusworth d	-
30		**12tu**	**H**	**Loughborough Students**	W 42-3	Youngs(3), Hare, Foulkes-Arnold, Richards, Steptoe	Hare 4c/p, Harris d	-
31		**15f**	**H**	**Royal Air Force**	W 38-3	Williams(2), Harris, Richards, Richardson, I.Smith, Steptoe, Youngs	Hare 3c	-
32		**20w**	**H**	**Royal Navy**	W 40-16	Collington(2), Afflick, Dodge, Evans, Youngs	Hare 5c/2p	1000
34		**30**	**H**	**Headingley**	L 9-13	-	Hare 2p, Harris d	-
35	Apr	**6**	**H**	**Neath**	W 24-17	Dexter, Stu.Redfern, Youngs	Hare 3c/p, Cusworth d	3200
36		**8m**	**H**	**Pontypool**	L 6-22	-	Hare 2p	5000
37		**13**	**H**	**Bristol**	L 15-21	-	Hare 5p	-
38		20	a	Gosforth	W 19-10	Wells, Youngs	Harris c/2p, Cusworth d	-
39		27	a	Moseley	L 9-10	Harris	Hare c/p	-

INDIVIDUAL APPEARANCES 1984/85

Name / Game #	1	2	3	4	5	6	7	8	9	10	11	12	13	14	15	16	17	18	19	20	21	22	23	24	25	26	27	28	29	30	31	32	33	34	35	36	37	38	39	Apps	T	Pts
V (Vendis) Afflick	-	-	-	-	x	-	-	-	-	r	-	-	-	K	-	-	K	-	-	-	-	-	L	L	-	L	-	-	-	L	M	M	L	L	-	-	-	-	-	10+1	2	8
SR (Steve) Avent	-	-	-	-	-	x	-	-	-	-	-	-	-	-	-	<M	-	-	-	-	-	-	-	-	-	-	-	-	-	-	-	-	-	x	-	-	-	-	-	1	-	-
I (Ian) Bates	-	L	-	M	M	M	L	M	L	L	-	-	L	-	-	-	M	M	-	L	-	-	-	-	-	-	-	-	-	M	-	-	-	M	L	L	L	L	M	19	-	-
DS (Duncan) Black	-	G	E	-	-	x	G	-	<G	-	-	-	-	-	-	-	-	-	-	-	-	-	-	-	-	-	-	-	-	-	-	-	-	-	-	-	-	-	-	5	1	4
MR (Mark) Charles	-	-	-	-	-	-	-	-	-	-	-	-	x	-	-	-	-	-	-	-	-	-	-	-	-	-	-	-	-	-	-	>r	G	r	-	G	x	-	G	3+2	-	-
LC (Lewis) Clifford	-	-	-	-	-	x	-	-	-	-	-	-	-	B	-	-	-	-	-	-	-	-	-	-	-	-	-	-	-	-	-	-	-	-	-	-	-	-	-	1	-	-
AP (Angus) Collington	-	-	x	-	-	-	-	r	-	-	x	r	-	-	-	-	-	-	-	-	x	-	-	-	-	G	-	x	-	-	-	G	-	-	r	-	-	x	-	2+3	2	8
L (Les) Cusworth E10	J	J	J	J	J	J*	-	J*	J	J	J	J	-	-	-	-	-	-	J	J	J	J	J	J	J	J*	J	J	J	-	J	-	-	-	J*	J*	J	J*	J	28	7	62
CD (Colin) Dexter	-	-	r	K	-	-	K	K	-	-	x	-	K	-	-	x	-	x	-	K	-	-	-	-	-	-	-	-	-	-	-	-	K	K	K	K	-	K	K	11+1	5	20
PW (Paul) Dodge E30 L2	M	M	M	-	-	-	M	L	M	M	M	L	M	M	M	-	-	-	M	M	M	M	-	-	M	-	M	M	M	-	-	L	M*	-	M	M	M	-	-	25	3	12
IR (Ian) Dodson	-	r	0	x	-	-	-	-	-	-	-	-	-	-	-	-	-	-	-	-	-	-	-	-	-	0	-	-	-	x	-	-	-	-	-	x	-	0	-	3+1	1	4
BJ (Barry) Evans E+	N	-	-	-	-	-	x	-	N	N	N	N	-	N	-	-	-	-	N	N	N	N	N	N	-	N	N	N	N	N	N	N	-	-	N	N	N	N	N	24	18	72
RW (Ray) French	-	-	-	-	-	-	-	-	-	-	-	C	-	-	-	-	-	-	-	-	-	-	-	-	-	-	-	-	-	-	-	-	-	-	-	-	-	-	-	1	-	-
MV (Malcolm) Foulkes-Arnold	E	E	D	-	E	E	D	E	E	E	E	D	E	E	E	E	E	E	E	E	E	E	E	E	E	E	E	E	E	E	E	E	E	E	-	-	E	D	E	36	2	8
CE (Claude) Gerald	r	N	-	-	-	-	-	-	-	-	-	-	-	-	-	-	-	-	-	-	x	-	-	-	-	-	-	-	-	-	-	-	-	-	-	-	-	-	-	1+1	1	4
WH (Dusty) Hare E25	0	0	-	0	0	0	0*	0	0	0	-	0	0	-	0	-	0*	0	0	0	0	0	0	0	0	-	0	0	0	0	0	0	0	0	0	0	0	-	0	33	6	386
JC (Jez) Harris	-	-	-	-	-	-	>J	-	-	-	-	-	-	J	r	0	-	J	-	x	-	x	M	-	x	M	x	-	x	J	L	J	J	J	-	-	r	M	L	13+2	3	47
T (Terry) Hart	-	-	-	-	-	-	-	-	-	-	-	-	-	<r	-	-	-	-	-	-	-	-	-	-	-	-	-	-	-	-	-	-	-	-	-	-	-	-	-	0+1	-	-
NS (Neil) Hartley	-	I	I	I	I	<I	-	-	-	-	-	-	-	-	-	-	-	-	-	-	-	-	-	-	-	-	-	-	-	-	-	-	-	-	-	-	-	-	-	5	2	8
NA (Nick) Jackson	-	-	-	-	-	-	-	-	-	-	-	-	-	-	-	-	F	-	-	-	-	-	D	-	-	-	-	-	-	-	-	-	-	-	-	-	-	-	-	2	-	-
NJ (Nick) Joyce	D	D	-	D	-	-	-	D	D	D	-	-	-	-	-	-	-	D	D	D	D	D	-	D	D	-	D	-	-	-	-	-	-	-	-	-	-	-	-	14	-	-
S (Steve) Kenney	I	-	-	-	-	-	-	-	-	-	I	-	I	-	I	-	-	I	I	I	I	I	I	I	I	I	I	I	I	-	-	-	I	I	-	I	-	-	-	19	2	8
AN (Adey) Marriott	-	x	-	x	-	H	H	H	-	-	F	F	-	F	x	-	-	-	-	-	-	x	x	-	x	H	x	F	x	x	-	-	-	-	-	x	F	-	-	9	-	-
RT (Richard) Pell	-	-	-	-	-	-	-	-	-	-	0	-	J	-	J	J	J	-	x	-	-	-	r	-	-	-	-	x	-	-	-	-	-	-	x	-	-	-	-	5+1	-	8
SP (Steve) Redfern E1	C	C	C	C	C	C	C	C	C	C	A	-	C	C	C	C	<C	-	-	-	-	-	-	-	-	-	-	-	-	-	-	-	-	-	-	-	-	-	-	16	3	12
SB (Stuart) Redfern	A	A	A	A	A	A	-	A	A	A	-	A	A	A	A	A	A	A	A	A	A	A	A	A	A	A	A	A	A	A	A	A	A	A	A	A	A	A	A	37	6	24
D (Dean) Richards E+ L+	G	-	G	G	G	-	G	G	-	G	-	E	G	-	G	G	G	G	G	G	G	G	G	G	G	-	G	G	G	G	G	-	-	G	G	-	G	G	-	29	7	28
WP (Wayne) Richardson	-	-	-	-	-	-	-	-	-	-	C	-	-	-	-	-	-	C	C	C	C	C	C	C	C	-	C	C	C	C	C	C	C	C	C	C	C	C	C	22	1	4
GC (Graham) Robb	-	-	-	-	-	-	-	-	-	-	-	-	-	-	-	-	>r	-	-	-	-	-	-	M	-	-	-	-	-	-	-	-	-	-	-	-	-	-	-	1+1	1	4
SA (Steve) Roy	-	-	-	-	-	-	-	-	>r	-	-	r	x	-	-	-	-	-	-	-	-	-	-	-	-	r	-	-	-	-	-	x	-	-	-	-	-	r	<r	0+5	1	4
IR (Ian) Smith	H*	H*	H*	H*	H*	-	-	-	H*	H*	H*	H*	H*	H*	H*	H*	-	H*	H*	H*	H*	H*	H*	H*	H*	-	H*	H*	H*	H*	H*	H*	-	H*	-	-	H*	-	H*	30	3	12
T (Tom) Smith	-	-	-	E	-	D	E	-	-	-	D	-	-	-	-	-	x	x	-	-	-	-	-	-	-	-	-	-	-	-	-	-	-	-	E	E	-	-	-	6	1	4
KN (Kevin) Steptoe	-	-	-	-	-	-	-	-	-	-	-	-	-	-	-	-	-	-	-	r	-	-	-	-	-	D	-	D	D	D	D	-	-	D	D	D	D	-	-	9+1	2	8
LJ (Lindsay) Stratton	-	-	-	-	-	-	-	-	-	x	-	-	-	-	-	x	-	-	-	-	-	-	-	-	-	-	-	-	-	-	-	-	>H	-	-	-	-	-	-	1	-	-
RS (Rob) Tebbutt	-	-	-	-	-	-	-	-	-	-	-	-	F	-	-	-	-	-	-	-	-	-	-	-	-	-	-	-	-	-	-	F	F	-	H	H	-	H	-	6	-	-
CJ (Chris) Tressler	B	B	B	B	B	B	B	-	-	-	B	-	B	-	B	B	B	B	B	B	B	-	-	B	-	-	-	-	-	B	B	-	-	B	B	B	B	B	B	25	2	8
R (Rory) Underwood E9 L+	-	-	K	-	K	K	-	-	-	-	-	-	-	-	K	K	-	K	K	-	K	-	-	-	K	-	K	K	K	-	-	-	-	-	-	-	K	-	-	13	12	48
DP (Dean) Waddingham	-	-	-	-	-	-	-	-	r	-	-	-	D	D	D	D	D	-	x	-	-	-	-	-	-	-	-	-	-	-	-	D	D	-	-	-	-	E	D	9+1	-	-
TM (Tim) Walker	x	-	-	-	-	-	x	-	-	-	-	-	-	-	-	-	-	-	-	-	-	-	-	-	-	<r	-	-	-	-	-	-	-	-	-	-	-	-	x	0+1	-	-
JM (John) Wells	F	F	F	F	F	F	F	F	F	F	G	G	-	G	F	F	H	F	F	F	F	F	F	F	F	F	F	-	F	F	F	-	-	F	F	F	-	F	F	34	9	36
PJ (Peter) Wheeler E41 L7	-	-	-	-	-	-	-	B	B	B	-	B	-	-	-	-	-	-	-	-	-	B	B	-	B	B	B	B	B	-	-	B	B	-	-	-	-	-	-	13	-	-
MA (Martin) Whitcombe	-	-	-	-	-	-	A	-	-	-	-	-	-	-	-	-	-	-	-	-	-	-	-	-	-	C	-	-	-	-	-	-	-	-	-	-	-	-	-	2	-	-
GG (Graham) Willars	-	-	-	-	-	-	-	-	-	-	-	-	-	r	-	-	-	-	-	-	-	-	-	-	-	-	-	-	-	-	-	-	-	-	-	-	-	-	-	0+1	-	-
AK (Kevin) Williams	K	K	N	N	N	N	N	N	K	K	K	K	N	0	N	N	N	N	-	-	-	K	K	K	N	K	-	-	-	K	K	K	N	N	-	-	-	-	-	28	11	44
CR (Clive) Woodward E21 L2	L	-	L	L	L	L	-	-	-	-	L	M	-	L	L	L	L	L	L	-	L	L	-	-	L	-	L	L	L	-	-	-	-	-	-	-	-	-	-	19	2	16
NG (Nick) Youngs E6	-	-	-	-	-	-	I	I	I	I	-	I	-	I	-	I	I	-	-	-	-	-	-	-	-	-	-	-	-	I	I	I	-	-	I	-	I	I	I	15	12	48

The key for how to read the stats is on the last page

19	85/86	Home Ground: Welford Road
		Coach: Graham Willars assisted by Rod Oakes
		Captain: Les Cusworth

OVERALL RECORD:					T	C	PG	DG	PTS
PLD	W	D	L	Tigers scored:	122	84	65	5	866
36	26	0	10	Opponents scored:	63	33	50	4	480

GM	DATE		VEN	OPPONENTS	RESULT	TRIES	KICKS	ATT
RFU CLUB COMPETITION (JOHN PLAYER SPECIAL CUP)						CUP WINNERS: BATH		
25	Jan	25	a	Coventry (3)	W 21-14	Evans 6	Hare c/3p, Cusworth 2d	8000
	Feb	22	a	Broughton Park (4)	PP (frost)			
28	Mar	9s	a	Broughton Park (4)	W 46-6	Richards(3), Evans, Youngs, Wells, Foulkes-Arnold, Tressler	Hare 7c	-
30		22	a	Harlequins (qf)	W 15-8	Cusworth 25, Richards 75	Hare 2c/p	-
33	Apr	**5**	**H**	**Bath (sf)**	L 6-10	-	Hare 2p	15000
JOHN SMITH'S MERIT TABLE A (4TH)						WINNERS: GLOUCESTER		
3	Sep	**14**	**H**	**Bath**	L 15-40	Evans	Hare c/3p	-
6		28	a	Harlequins	W 19-9	Youngs(2), Tebbutt	Hare 2c/p	-
14	Nov	12tu	a	Nottingham	W 15-9	Evans	Hare c/3p	3000
15		**16**	**H**	**Wasps**	W 19-6	Youngs(2)	Hare c/3p	-
16		23	a	Moseley	L 6-7	-	Hare 2p	-
18	Dec	**7**	**H**	**Gloucester**	L 9-15	-	Hare 3p	-
20		**21**	**H**	**Bristol**	W 30-25	Richards(2), Burnhill, Evans	Hare 4c/2p	3700
22	Jan	**4**	**H**	**Headingley**	W 23-7	Dodge(2), Davidson, Penalty	Hare 2c/p	2500
26	Feb	**1**	**H**	**London Scottish**	W 24-0	Tebbutt(2), Penalty	Hare 3c/p, Dodge d	2000
35	Apr	**19**	**H**	**Gosforth**	W 56-15	Evans(2), Richards(2), Hare, Burnhill, Harris, Kenney, Williams	Hare 7c/2p	-
CLUB MATCHES								
1	Sep	7	a	Bedford	W 52-6	Hare(3), Evans(3), Woodward(2), Williams	Hare 5c/2p	-
2		**10tu**	**H**	**Nuneaton**	W 30-12	Davidson, Evans, Wells, Williams, Woodward	Hare 2c/2p	-
4		18w	a	Birmingham	W 33-6 (Abandoned 70')	Williams(2), Hare, Cusworth, Redfern, Whitcombe	Hare 3c/p	-
5		21	a	London Welsh	W 38-15	Richards(2), Davidson, Redfern, Tebbutt	Hare 3c/4p	-
7	Oct	**5**	**H**	**Coventry**	W 42-16	Hare, Tebbutt, Wells, Williams, Youngs	Hare 5c/4p	-
8		12	a	Richmond	W 27-13	Evans, Foulkes-Arnold, Wells	Hare 2c/3p, Cusworth c	-
9		19	a	Northampton	W 14-6	Tebbutt, Wells	Hare 2p	-
10		23w	a	Oxford University	W 32-7	Richards(3), Burnhill, Cusworth, Kenney	Hare 4c	-
11		**26**	**H**	**Swansea**	W 18-10	Hare, Tebbutt	Hare 2c/2p	-
12	Nov	**2**	**H**	**Cardiff**	L 15-20	Davidson, Tressler	Hare 2c/p	-
13		9	a	Cambridge University	W 31-9	Richards(2), Dexter, Youngs	Hare 3c/2p/d	-
17		30	a	Saracens	W 36-12	Pell(2), Richards(2), Hare, Wells, Youngs	Hare 4c	-
19	Dec	14	a	Blackheath	W 16-12	Evans	Hare 4p	-
21		**28**	**H**	**Barbarians**	L 16-19	Youngs(2), Burnhill	Hare c, Harris c	17000
23	Jan	11	a	Gloucester	L 10-15	Evans, Richards	Hare c	-
24		**18**	**H**	**Bedford**	W 33-3	Evans(2), Richards(2), Burnhill, Youngs	Dodson 3c, Dodge p	-
27	Feb	**8**	**H**	**Northampton**	W 25-15	Cusworth, Dodge, Tebbutt	Hare 2c/3p	-
		8	a	Newport	PP (cup)			
		15	a	Orrell	PP (frost)			
		22	**H**	**Northampton**	PP (cup)			
		26w	**H**	**Royal Navy**	PP (frost)			
	Mar	**1**	**H**	**Harlequins**	PP (frost)			
		8	a	Coventry	PP (cup)			
		11tu	**H**	**Loughborough Students**	PP			
29		**14f**	**H**	**Royal Air Force**	W 52-15	Burnhill(3), Charles(2), Evans(2), Hare, Davidson, Williams	Hare 6c	-
		22	**H**	**Sale**	PP (cup)			
31		29	a	Neath	W 15-11	Charles, Evans	Hare 2c/p	-
32		31m	a	Pontypool	L 6-39	-	Dodge p, Harris d	-
	Apr	**5**	**H**	**Waterloo**	PP (cup)			
34		12	a	Bristol	L 3-29	-	Hare p	-
36		**26**	**H**	**Moseley**	L 18-19	Kenney	Hare c/4p	-

INDIVIDUAL APPEARANCES 1985/86

Name / Game #	1	2	3	4	5	6	7	8	9	10	11	12	13	14	15	16	17	18	19	20	21	22	23	24	25	26	27	28	29	30	31	32	33	34	35	36	Apps	T	Pts
I (Ian) Bates	-	-	-	M	L	L	L	L	L	-	L	L	I	L	-	-	-	M	-	M	-	-	-	-	-	L	-	-	-	L	M	N	x	-	-	-	16	-	-
N (Niall) Beazley	-	-	-	-	-	-	-	-	-	-	-	-	-	-	x	-	-	=r	-	-	-	-	-	-	-	-	-	-	-	-	-	-	-	-	-	-	0+1	-	-
SB (Steve) Burnhill	>r	-	-	-	-	-	-	-	-	L	-	-	-	-	-	-	-	-	M	L	L	L	L	L	L	-	L	L	L	-	L	-	L	L	L	L	16+1	8	32
TJ (Tim) Buttimore	-	-	x	>L	-	-	-	-	-	-	-	x	-	-	L	L	L	L	-	-	-	-	-	-	-	-	-	-	-	-	-	L	-	-	-	-	6	-	-
MR (Mark) Charles	-	G	-	-	-	-	-	G	-	-	-	-	-	-	-	G	-	-	G	x	-	-	-	-	-	-	G	-	G	-	G	G	-	G	-	-	9	3	12
LC (Lewis) Clifford	-	-	-	-	-	-	-	x	-	-	-	-	-	-	-	-	-	-	-	-	-	-	-	-	-	-	-	-	B	-	-	B	x	-	-	-	2	-	-
AP (Angus) Collington	-	-	-	-	-	-	r	-	-	-	-	-	x	-	-	-	-	-	-	-	-	-	x	-	-	-	-	-	-	-	-	<H	-	-	-	-	1+1	-	-
L (Les) Cusworth E10	J*	-	J*	J*	J*	J*	J*	J*	J*	J*	J*	J*	J*	J*	J*	J*	J*	-	-	-	J*	J*	J*	J*	J*	J*	J*	J*	J*	J*	J*	-	J*	-	-	-	28	4	24
JS (John) Davidson	-	>D	D	E	D	-	D	D	D	E	D	D	-	D	-	-	-	-	-	D	D	D	D	D	D	D	-	D	D	D	-	-	D	-	D	D	24	5	20
CD (Colin) Dexter	-	-	-	-	-	-	-	-	-	K	-	K	K	K	K	K	K	K	K	-	-	-	-	x	-	-	-	-	-	-	x	K	-	-	-	-	10	1	4
PW (Paul) Dodge E32 L2	M	M	M	-	M	M	M	M	M	M	M	M	M	M	M	M	M	-	-	-	M	M	M	M	M	M	M	M	M	M	-	M	M	M	M	M	31	3	21
IR (Ian) Dodson	-	x	-	-	-	-	-	-	x	-	-	-	-	-	-	-	-	-	-	x	-	-	-	0	-	-	-	-	x	-	-	0	-	-	-	-	2	-	6
BJ (Barry) Evans E+	N	N	N	N	N	-	-	N	N	N	N	N	N	N	N	N	-	N	N	N	N	N	N	N	N	N	N	N	N	N	N	-	N	N	N	N	32	19	76
MV (Malcolm) Foulkes-Arnold	E	E	E	-	E	E	E	E	E	-	E	E	E	E	E	E	E	E	-	-	E	E	E	E	E	E	E	E	E	E	-	E	E	E	E	E	31	2	8
RW (Ray) French	-	-	-	-	-	-	-	-	-	C	-	-	-	-	-	-	-	-	-	-	-	C	-	-	-	-	-	C	C	-	-	C	-	-	-	-	5	-	-
CE (Claude) Gerald	-	-	-	-	-	N	N	-	-	-	-	-	-	-	-	-	-	-	-	-	-	-	-	-	-	-	-	-	-	-	-	-	-	-	-	-	2	-	-
D (Darren) Grewcock	-	-	-	-	-	-	-	-	-	-	-	-	-	-	-	-	-	-	-	-	-	-	-	-	-	-	-	-	-	-	-	-	-	I	-	-	1	-	-
WH (Dusty) Hare E25	0	0	0	0	0	0	0	0	0	0	0	0	0	0	0	0	0	0*	0*	0*	0	0	0	-	0	0	0	0	0	0	0	-	0	0*	0*	0*	34	9	386
JC (Jez) Harris	-	J	-	-	-	-	-	-	-	-	x	-	-	x	-	x	-	-	L	J	r	-	-	-	r	-	r	x	-	x	-	J	x	J	J	J	7+3	1	9
NJ (Nick) Joyce	D	-	-	D	-	D	-	-	-	D	-	-	D	-	-	-	D	<D	-	-	-	-	-	-	-	-	-	-	-	-	-	-	-	-	-	-	7	-	-
S (Steve) Kenney	-	I	-	I	-	-	-	-	-	I	-	-	-	-	-	-	-	I	I	I	-	-	-	-	-	I	-	-	-	I	-	I*	r	-	I	I	11+1	3	12
KP (Kevin) MacDonald	-	-	-	-	-	>r	-	-	-	x	-	-	x	-	-	-	-	-	-	-	-	-	x	-	-	-	-	-	-	-	-	-	-	-	x	-	0+1	-	-
AN (Adey) Marriott	-	x	F	-	-	-	-	-	-	-	-	-	F	x	-	-	-	F	F	F	x	-	-	-	r	-	-	x	-	x	-	-	x	F	F	-	7+1	-	-
RT (Richard) Pell	-	-	-	-	x	-	-	r	-	-	-	-	-	-	-	-	N	J	<J	-	-	-	-	-	-	-	-	-	-	-	-	-	-	x	-	-	3+1	2	8
SB (Stuart) Redfern	A	A	A	A	A	A	A	A	A	-	A	A	A	A	A	A	A	-	-	-	A	A	A	A	A	A	A	A	A	A	-	A	A	A	A	A	31	2	8
D (Dean) Richards E2 L+	G	-	-	G	G	G	G	-	G	G	G	G	G	G	G	-	G	G	-	G	G	G	G	G	G	G	-	G	-	G	-	-	G	-	G	G	26	20	80
L (Lee) Richardson	-	-	-	-	-	-	-	-	-	-	-	-	-	-	-	-	-	-	>D	-	-	-	-	x	-	-	-	-	-	-	D	-	-	D	-	-	3	-	-
WP (Wayne) Richardson	-	-	-	-	C	C	C	C	C	x	C	C	C	C	C	C	C	C	C	C	C	-	C	C	C	C	C	-	-	C	C	-	C	C	C	C	27	-	-
GJ (Graham) Smith	-	-	r	-	-	-	-	-	-	-	-	-	<H	-	x	-	-	-	-	-	-	-	-	-	-	-	-	-	-	-	-	-	-	-	-	-	1+1	-	-
IR (Ian) Smith	-	-	-	-	-	-	-	-	-	F	-	x	-	-	-	-	-	-	-	-	-	-	-	-	-	-	-	-	r	-	-	-	-	-	-	-	1+1	-	-
T (Tom) Smith	x	-	-	-	-	-	-	-	-	-	x	-	-	-	-	-	-	-	E	E	-	-	-	-	-	-	D	-	-	-	E	D	-	-	-	-	5	-	-
KN (Kevin) Steptoe	-	-	-	-	-	-	-	-	x	-	-	-	-	-	D	D	x	r	-	-	-	<r	-	-	-	-	-	-	-	-	-	-	-	-	-	-	2+2	-	-
LJ (Lindsay) Stratton	-	-	-	-	x	-	-	-	-	-	-	-	-	-	-	-	-	-	-	-	-	-	-	-	-	r	-	-	-	-	r	<F	-	x	-	-	1+2	-	-
RS (Rob) Tebbutt	H	H	H	H	H	H	H	H	H	H	H	H	-	H	H	H	H	H	H	H	H	H	H	H	H	H	H	H	H	H	H	-	H	H	H	H	34	8	32
CJ (Chris) Tressler	-	-	-	B	B	B	B	B	B	-	B	B	B	B	B	B	B	B	B	B	B	B	B	B	B	B	B	B	-	B	B	-	B	B	B	B	30	2	8
R (Rory) Underwood E12 L+	-	-	-	-	-	-	-	-	-	-	-	-	-	-	-	-	-	-	-	-	K	K	-	-	K	-	K	K	-	-	K	-	-	K	-	-	7	-	-
JM (John) Wells	F	F	G	F	F	F	F	F	F	-	F	F	-	F	F	F	F	-	-	-	F	F	F	F	F	F	F	F	F	F	F	-	F	-	-	F	28	6	24
PJ (Peter) Wheeler E41 L7	B	B*	B	-	-	-	-	-	-	<B	-	-	-	-	-	-	-	-	-	-	-	-	-	-	-	-	-	-	-	-	-	-	-	-	-	-	4	-	-
MA (Martin) Whitcombe	C	C	C	C	-	-	-	-	-	A	-	-	-	-	-	x	-	A	A	A	-	-	-	-	-	-	-	-	-	-	A	<r	-	-	-	-	9+1	1	4
AK (Kevin) Williams	K	K	K	K	K	K	K	K	K	-	K	-	-	-	-	-	-	-	-	K	-	-	K	K	-	K	-	-	K	K	-	-	K	-	K	K	19	7	28
CR (Clive) Woodward E21 L2	L	L	<L	-	-	-	-	-	-	-	-	-	-	-	-	-	-	-	-	-	-	-	-	-	-	-	-	-	-	-	-	-	-	-	-	-	3	3	12
NG (Nick) Youngs E6	I	-	I	-	I	I	I	I	I	-	I	I	I	I	I	I	I	-	-	-	I	I	I	I	I	-	I	I	I	-	I	-	I	-	-	-	24	11	44

The key for how to read the stats is on the last page

CHAPTER 23

New World

1986/1987

English rugby braced itself for change in the second half of the 1980s: though the merit tables continued during 1986/87 all the talk was of a new league system, to be introduced the following season and involving more than 1,200 clubs - the biggest of its kind in the world. There would be, of course, an inaugural World Cup to be played in New Zealand and Australia in the summer of 1987.

Leicester was as well prepared for the future as any club in England, and better than most, thanks to changes in the club administration over the previous decade and the success which had brought a new generation of supporters into a ground already the envy of many for its ability to host big matches. Membership had risen to 4,500, a profit on the previous season was announced at over £46,000 and the club was prepared to spend a further £100,000 on ground improvements, mostly to comply with the Safety of Sports Grounds Act (a year later, as developments continued, the Welford Road bank, that mound of ash and gravel hated by players who had sweated up and down it in the pursuit of greater fitness, was levelled).

Newcomers to the club included Harry Roberts, a hooker born in Zambia, brought up in Zimbabwe and finished (in rugby terms) in the Transvaal where he had played provincial rugby. Roberts, strong and mobile, had a chequered career with the club in his restless pursuit of international honours, hindered by a recurring shoulder problem; six years later he returned to Welford Road as part of the first South African tour party to visit Britain in 23 years but even then he was doomed to miss the cap he so desperately sought.

Cusworth was captain again, hoping for a return to the expansive rugby he so enjoyed, although not even he would have anticipated a club record on 17 September in the last ever fixture against the old Birmingham club. Leicester won 95-6 and Hare established an individual record of 43 points, which carried him past 6,000 for his career. Nick Youngs led the 15-try romp with four and, though the club promptly tripped up at Harlequins, they were at it again when London Welsh visited Welford Road: this time the margin was 69-4, the worst defeat in the long and proud history of the Welsh, twelve tries of which Underwood scored four and Evans two.

Not that anyone doubted Leicester's quality behind the scrum but Willars, as coach, was keen to develop the forward strength: his degree of success was indicated by victory at Swansea and that momentum was sustained against the touring Fijian Barbarians who crashed 39-14 at Welford Road. The Fijians were making a world tour on a shoestring and their best contribution to the evening's entertainment was their singing in the clubhouse afterwards: they were also impressed by Tom Smith, the young Leicester lock, and extended an invitation - happily accepted - for him to play for them in a subsequent game against West Hartlepool (doubtless Smith would have been even happier to have played for them in Fiji).

Even so Cusworth was less than happy: "Rugby should take a hard look at itself and ask what spectators are being offered," he said. "We [and he was not referring only to Tigers] are playing a negative, stop-start game with little good second-phase ball and this leads to hardly any decent handling moves. The problem is that these days a side's initial thought is to go out and stop the other playing whereas it should be to create and make something happen. Leicester are as guilty as anyone. We used to play a high-risk game which was entertaining. Now results have become all-important."

↑ The Fijians visited Welford Road as part of their World Tour.

In other words, Leicester could play only when the opposition was of insufficient stature to stop them: against the better clubs, the Baths and Wasps, they adopted defensive mode. For what it was worth, their style gave them six representatives in the divisional championships, though the Midlands did not distinguish themselves and Dodge broke a bone in his hand during the first game. At much the same time a young prop from Reading, Paul Burnell, made his debut as a replacement against Saracens though it was not until he moved to London Scottish that Scotland decided here was a potential international - and, as it turned out in 1993, a British Lion.

One of the problems of competitive rugby, of course, was the knock-on effect from representative calls and the divisional

↓ John Wells takes on Orrell on 21.2.1987.

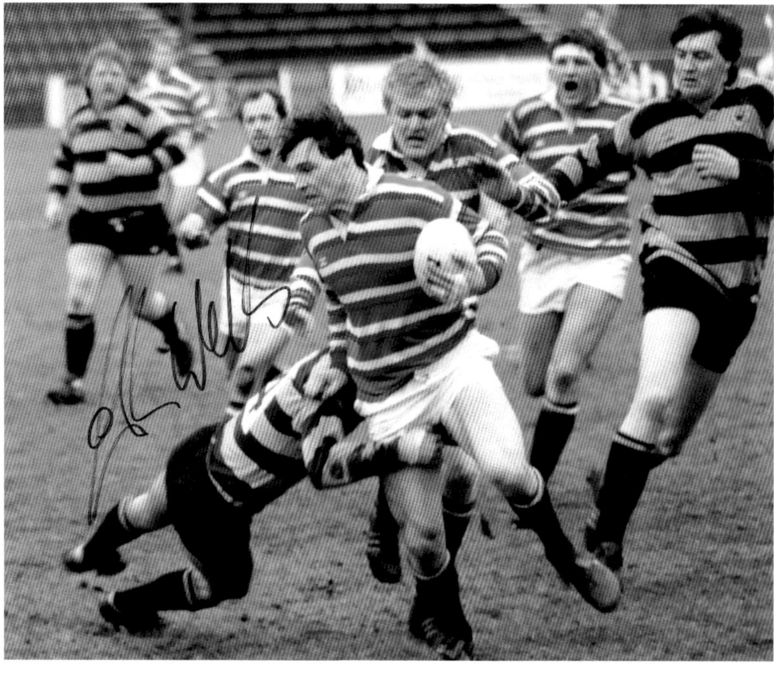

↑ Paul Dodge in National Merit Table action against Harlequins at Welford Road 7.3.1987.

championship left Leicester in no doubt that they should "de-merit" their game with Bristol in December. Bristol were aggrieved that Leicester should not have done so much earlier, knowing of the clash with the divisional game, and promptly made their feelings known by administering a 39-9 defeat; the same thing happened against Gloucester, who also won heavily at Kingsholm and added interest by winning the merit table game at Leicester 14-12.

Adding injury to insult, Dean Richards damaged medial ligaments in his knee (playing against his police colleagues when bad weather forced Leicester to re-arrange their fixtures and meet Metropolitan Police). He and Underwood had been try-scorers in an England XVs win over Japan in October and both were regarded as automatic choices for England for the five nations championship and the World Cup: but the injury kept Richards out of three of the four championship matches, leaving Underwood to battle on alone through a season of gloom unrelieved until the 21-12 victory over Scotland in the final match. Leicester could though, take vicarious pleasure from the return to international rugby of Marcus Rose, now playing his rugby with Harlequins.

They could even call upon a player of unstinting enthusiasm to fill Richards' boots: Simon Povoas, then 20, spent a career in the giant shadow of the England No 8 but his quality allowed him to surpass Richards' record for tries scored in a season by a forward and took him to the England B squad. Here he stepped up to score in a much-postponed John Player Cup game against Rosslyn Park in which Leicester were taken to the wire at 18-15. Evans, too, returned after a season adversely affected by a damaged Achilles tendon and scored in the next cup round, a 19-6 win over Gosforth. Cusworth nudged the England selectors with a try and dropped goal in the 17-7 quarter-final win at Bristol, at a time when the national number ten shirt seemed to be in limbo after the sour international against Wales in Cardiff, but again they looked elsewhere.

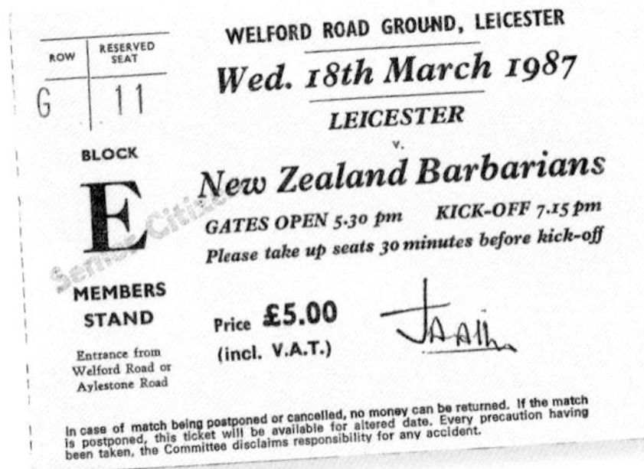
ROW G | RESERVED SEAT 11

BLOCK E

MEMBERS STAND

Entrance from Welford Road or Aylestone Road

WELFORD ROAD GROUND, LEICESTER

Wed. 18th March 1987

LEICESTER

v.

New Zealand Barbarians

GATES OPEN 5.30 pm *KICK-OFF 7.15 pm*

Please take up seats 30 minutes before kick-off

Price £5.00 (incl. V.A.T.)

In case of match being postponed or cancelled, no money can be returned. If the match is postponed, this ticket will be available for altered date. Every precaution having been taken, the Committee disclaims responsibility for any accident.

↓ Steve Kenney on the break during the defeat to the New Zealand Barbarians 18.3.1987.

Richards returned for the Calcutta Cup match but Cusworth's disappointment was mirrored by the 13-6 semi-final defeat at Wasps: again a case of so far but yet no farther. Another Barbarian side, this time from New Zealand on a world tour with something not far short of a complete All Blacks party, brought further gloom to Leicester with a comprehensive 33-3 win at Welford Road: players such as John Kirwan, David Kirk, Steve McDowell and the then uncapped Michael Jones were to win fame a few months later when New Zealand won the Webb Ellis Cup at the end of the inaugural World Cup - a tournament in which Richards and Underwood played for an England team of no great distinction and which departed at the quarter-final stage, beaten by Wales.

Leicester had the limited comfort of finishing second to Bath in the John Smith's Merit Table A but were now more concerned about their assault on the first league season proper: to which end the club set out, yet again, on a tour down under. The end of the season was a clutter of minor cameos: of Willars coming on as a replacement in the match with Waterloo and at 47 becoming the Tigers' oldest player ever, and of Hare missing his club points record for the season by three.

Meanwhile Leicester's forward planning committee was looking at recruitment: "The player market has become very competitive because there are so few talented players around," Cusworth, retiring as captain, said. "But the situation has to be very carefully monitored to make sure we get the best for the club without losing sight of what the game is all about." There was little encouragement from the Leicestershire AGM that summer, which reported that few youngsters played rugby regularly and at any standard in the city schools.

Cusworth's successor was Paul Dodge, who led Leicester off to Australia where they made a slightly lower-key entry than seven years earlier, losing to Western Australia 26-19 but then beating a Western Australian President's XV, a Manly side including Clive Woodward at fly-half, and Ponsonby in Auckland, New Zealand. They returned to Brisbane to lose 37-13 to a Queensland side fielding nine internationals and collected an easy win over Singapore Cricket Club on the way home.

1987/1988

The pre-season preparation paid dividends: Leicester's first match in the newly-formed Courage Clubs Championship was against England's acknowledged top club, Bath, merit-table winners and cup holders. Tigers had not beaten Bath since 1983 and both their England players, Richards and Underwood, were absent but Dodge denied any inferiority complex: "We know we are there or thereabouts. It's just a question of lifting our game one notch higher." Lift it they did: in a wonderful advertisement for league rugby, completely absorbing and full of skill, Leicester won 24-13, Cusworth scoring a try, dropping a goal and setting up a try for Jez Harris, the replacement wing.

In a sense that one game teed up the whole season, regardless of the fact that Tigers promptly went walkabout and lost to London Welsh in the absence of the maestros, Cusworth and Hare, both at Underwood's wedding. It gave Leicester the belief that they could compete with anyone, a belief sustained throughout a season which saw them take the inaugural league title. It was not that they were unbeatable - as the Welsh had already proved - but that they had the inner resolve which could carry them through games against apparently better-equipped clubs: only once did it let them down in the league, against Orrell who thereby began a run of success against Leicester.

That resolve had to survive various vicissitudes: Willars was unwell and had to stand back from the regular coaching duties which allowed Peter Wheeler to expand in that direction. In fact later in the year Wheeler took the "hands-on" role with Willars heading a coaching panel as Leicester appreciated the difficulties for one man of running the whole show. Dodge, too, suffered a setback with a broken kneecap which kept him out of action for three months.

Against that was the promise of a new acquisition from Nottingham, Peter Thornley, a flanker who went on to win an England B place the next season before a persistent back injury ended his first-class career prematurely. Thornley doubtless enjoyed himself in the 22-13 win over Nottingham, the early-season league leaders by virtue of having played more games than anyone else, and Leicester hit the top of the first division by beating Moseley 21-3 with a forward performance as dominant as anything they produced that season. Yet throughout it was the direction given by Cusworth and Hare that permitted Leicester to turn the screw: there were few good decision-makers in the country at the time and Leicester had two of them. "Les is the most experienced and skilled attacking fly-half in the country," Geoff Cooke, the new England team manager, said after he watched Cusworth orchestrate the win at The Reddings.

WELFORD ROAD GROUND, LEICESTER
Saturday 13th February 1988
JOHN PLAYER SPECIAL CUP
LEICESTER
v
BATH
B 17
BLOCK N
GATES OPEN 2.00 pm KICK-OFF 3.30 pm
CRUMBIE STAND
Entrance at Aylestone Road
Price £3.00 (incl. V.A.T.)

↑↓ Match programme and ticket from Bath's visit to Welford Road in the fourth round of the cup.

Remarkably the Midlands found room for only three Tigers (they added a fourth, Buttimore, for the final game) in the divisional championship but four were called up for England's trial, all on the senior side: Underwood, Cusworth, Richards and the deserving Wells. The blind-side flanker had made a name for himself in an unspectacular way but on the day the Rest XV, prepared by Alan Davies, overturned the England XV 13-7 and the selectors went for the height of Mickey Skinner. Save for an appearance for an England XV against Italy two years later, it was the nearest Wells got to a cap.

A few days earlier Leicester had rattled up nine tries in a remarkable 48-30 win over the Barbarians and Leicester's cup ran over when England picked Cusworth to play fly-half against France in Paris. It was a remarkable comeback, at 33, though fully deserved on form: the sad aspect was that Cusworth's 12 caps were won over a nine-year period. What might he have achieved with some degree of continuity? He, Richards and Underwood played in the Parc des Princes while, next door in the Jean Bouin Stadium, Wells helped England B to victory over their French counterparts. Alas, a mistake by England's captain, Mike Harrison, led to the try which gave France their 10-9 win and Cusworth could only wonder that he, a talented drop-kicker, should have missed four such goals.

In their absence another Underwood made his debut in an easy win over Bedford: Tony Underwood, nearly six years younger than Rory and a student at Leicester University, failed to score then but his time was to come. Evans and Rory Underwood held down the places in the first cup game of the season, a 15-0 win over Rosslyn Park, which earned them a fourth-round tie with none other than Bath. It was the West Countrymen's second bite at the cherry and this time they did not miss: Leicester were eased out of the cup 13-6 on their own ground.

↓ Rory Underwood helps Tigers go to the top of the Division One table following their victory over Moseley at The Reddings 28.11.1987.

February, Leicester would claim, was a wicked month: a week earlier their three representatives had been in an England side beaten 11-3 by Wales at Twickenham then came the cup exit. That was closely followed by the loss of their 100 per cent league record in a 30-6 defeat at Orrell. All they needed was what the England selectors duly provided: the dropping of Cusworth in favour of Rob Andrew for the Calcutta Cup match in Edinburgh (if Leicester felt battered that was as nothing compared to the Calcutta Cup's fate after being removed from the post-match banquet by two players who then proceeded to play rugby with it. To Leicester's embarrassment, one of the guilty men turned out to be Richards who was

duly suspended for one international by the Rugby Football Union for his part in the prank).

Northampton offered an unlikely aid to recovery when Leicester beat them 35-9 and Rory Underwood, requiring practice on the right wing after England had switched him from his normal left-wing position, scored four tries. It was a switch with which Underwood was not entirely happy but a 35-3 victory over Ireland in which he ended a try-drought by scoring twice was considerable solace.

Leicester, in need of the same, found it over Easter weekend: a fortnight earlier they had played Lansdowne after a 90-year gap and another Irish club, Ballymena, gave Cusworth the chance to become the 26th player to appear 300 times for Leicester. Two days later, after a 39-15 win over Waterloo, the league title was theirs and, happily, in front of their own supporters. Though many players contributed significantly during the season, the XV which did a lap of honour with the new trophy was: Dusty Hare; Barry Evans, Ian Bates, Tim Buttimore (replaced by Paul Dodge), Rory Underwood; Les Cusworth, Steve Kenney; Stuart Redfern, Harry Roberts, Wayne Richardson, Tom Smith, Malcolm Foulkes-Arnold, John Wells, Dean Richards, Peter Thornley.

It was a happy coincidence that Dodge was able to share in the final league match, at the end of an injury-wrecked season. Yet again Hare laid the foundations with four penalties and four conversions, alongside tries by Evans, Underwood, Thornley and a penalty try, and a dropped goal by Cusworth. After the celebrations were over Wheeler outlined the reasons for success: "We had problems in other positions but no other club in England could match the spine in our side - Harry Roberts, Dean Richards, Steve Kenney or Nick Youngs, Les Cusworth and Dusty Hare....The teams with the half-backs are the ones that did best in the Courage league."

Tigers even managed to retain their equilibrium for the final weeks of the season: they ended a record Bristol run of 21 games and passed 1,000 points for the season after dismissing Gosforth 65-0, Underwood and Richards each scoring three tries. Hare would doubtless have established a personal record had he not carelessly dropped a five-bar gate on his foot while out farming and broken his toe: the emergency sent Jez Harris haring down the road to Leicester from Hinckley and he arrived, breathless but in time to score 25 points against Gosforth and round off the season with 17 points in the 41-3 victory over Moseley which carried Leicester to a season's aggregate of 1,077 points and 32 victories.

↑ Mud glorious mud! Lansdowne make their first trip to Welford Road for 90 years and are greeted with testing conditions 18.3.1988.

Richards and Underwood departed with England on their tour of Australia and Fiji where they were joined by both Evans and Buttimore. Evans received a late call-up when Wakefield's Mike Harrison was injured and, in due course, received the caps which many in Leicester believed he should have won earlier: no-one doubted his try-scoring capacity - there were few quicker wings than the former student at Hinckley's John Cleveland College - but his handling and defensive skills occasionally let him down. However, he was called up for his international debut in the second international against Australia and won a second against Fiji at the tour's end.

Buttimore had planned to go to Australia anyway and play with Woodward at Manly but when John Buckton, the Saracens centre, was injured against Queensland, Buttimore was brought into the England party to cover. Although it was not an outstandingly successful tour, Underwood (who began the tour by playing in a World XV against Australia) continued his try-scoring feats with one in each of the internationals against the Wallabies and two against Fiji.

1988/1989

At home Leicester were not sitting back and basking in reflected glory: Kevin Andrews, the club chairman, called for hard work to maintain the club's standing and more money was committed to ground improvements - this time £150,000 to replace the old Nissen hut (erected as a "temporary" measure in 1947) alongside the clubhouse. The club had announced a profit of more than £24,000 and they were delighted to start a new season with a new sponsor - Ansells, the brewers, who were prepared to commit £100,000 to Leicester over a five-year period in what was then believed to be the most substantial agreement in English club rugby.

Nevertheless it was disappointing to lose players of potential - Buttimore in Australia, Burnhill to Sale, Rob Tebbutt to Northampton and Paul Burnell to London Scottish (later in the season he was called into Scotland's squad). Leicester knew well the value of strength in depth and, on the eve of a new season, Wheeler called for greater investment in the playing squad: regular tours and consideration of a paid director of rugby.

↓ Les Cusworth and Paul Dodge with the Courage League trophy.

It was even more disappointing to lose to Orrell so early in the league season, the Lancashire club running in three tries to none. Even the reorganisation consequent upon an injury to Nick Youngs - Cusworth went to scrum-half, Hare to fly-half and a new recruit from Wakefield, John Liley, came in at full-back - could not entirely explain Orrell's success. Another newcomer, Aadel Kardooni, a scrum-half of Iranian descent who had played for England Schools and Wasps, made his debut against Swansea.

What Leicester were suffering from, of course, was the backlash which those at the top always suffer: teams try harder against the league champions and the quality of the club's reserves was being tested. At the same time there were difficulties behind the scenes: Wheeler had discovered there were not enough hours in the day for family and sport while trying to establish a new insurance business and had to step down as coach. A month later, despite speculation that Chalkie White might return, the club had brought in an old favourite, David Matthews, the former flanker, with Allen Foster, a 37-year-old PE officer in the Prison Service, as fitness and conditioning coach; once again the long-term commitment of individuals to Leicester was paying dividends.

As the club struggled to cope with the increasing pressures placed on an amateur organisation, their leading players were doing battle once more with the Australians. Six of them, including the whole back row, played in a side captained by Cusworth for the Midlands: Simon Hodgkinson (Nottingham); Barry Evans, Paul Dodge (both Leicester), Gary Hartley, Steve Hackney (both Nottingham); Les Cusworth (Leicester), Steve Thomas (Coventry); Lee Johnson, Brian Moore, Glyn Mosses, Peter Cook (all Nottingham), Martin Bayfield (Metropolitan Police), John Wells, Dean Richards, Peter Thornley (all Leicester). It was by no means the most powerful combination the Midlands could field but, struck down by injuries as they were, they did well to hold the Australians to 25-18.

Indeed victory came as a great relief to the visitors who had lost to the other three divisions on a tour in which Underwood again played against them four times - for the North, England, the Combined Services and the Barbarians. The Midland backs were short of penetration and they lost Steve Hackney - later to join Leicester - in the first half, replacing him with Clifton Jones, the Nottingham centre. Richards wrenched himself over for a close-range try which Simon Hodgkinson converted, as well as kicking four penalties, but tries by Nick Farr-Jones, James Grant and Brad Girvan, alongside the goal-kicking of the recently-arrived Michael Lynagh (two conversions, three penalties) earned victory.

A week later, after David Campese had taken apart an England Students XV including Tony Underwood, it was a different story. England, beaten twice in the summer, turned on an exciting open style of rugby under the captaincy, for the first time, of Will Carling to win at Twickenham 28-19. It was a magnificent, fluid game in which two tries within six minutes by Rory Underwood tilted the balance: the first after deft play by Rob Andrew, the second after a forward drive sparked by Richards, both coming in the same north-west corner.

The Australians left and the divisional championship came, bringing with it places for eight Leicester players in the Midland ranks but to no great effect. Harris made one appearance at full-back while the Underwood brothers both turned out for the North, Tony for the first time. Indeed the younger Underwood was not only called into the divisional ranks but, in the new year, made the England B side against France on his home club ground.

The league title, meanwhile, was slipping inexorably away: held to a draw by Nottingham and then beaten by Harlequins on a day when neither Rory Underwood nor Richards could play, not even Hare's kicking could save Leicester. The Barbarians brought no relief: Campese, the Australian wing and by a distance one of the greatest entertainers in world rugby, did everything except a juggling act and scored one of seven tries in a 36-19 victory, the heaviest loss Leicester had suffered for 14 years.

A pick-me-up was required: it came from two directions, one the unusual direction of Buckingham Palace. The new year's honours included an MBE for William Henry Hare for his contribution to rugby and Hare celebrated in style: on the last day of the old year, at the age of 36, he

➔ Wallaby legend, David Campese, sees the funny side as a Tigers supporter finds an unusual vantage point during the Barbarians game 28.12.1988.

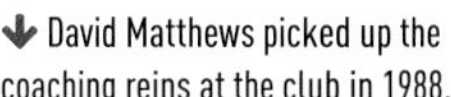

🡇 David Matthews picked up the coaching reins at the club in 1988.

🡇 Dusty Hare celebrates passing 7,000 career points following the game at Nuneaton on New Year's Eve 1988.

converted his own try to pass 7,000 career points in a 39-13 victory over Nuneaton. The stage may have been less grandiose than the achievement but he received a wonderful reception from the crowd at the Harry Cleaver Ground and champagne in the dressing room.

The wine, though, went a bit flat in the course of a 28-0 league drubbing by Gloucester and it took the cup - now the Pilkington Cup after a change of sponsorship - to lift Leicester. A 37-6 victory over Liverpool St Helens was just the tonic: three tries for Kardooni but four dropped goals by Cusworth who also scored a try for good measure. For the third successive year Rosslyn Park lay in wait but their challenge petered out in a 23-9 defeat with Richards the rock on which Leicester built.

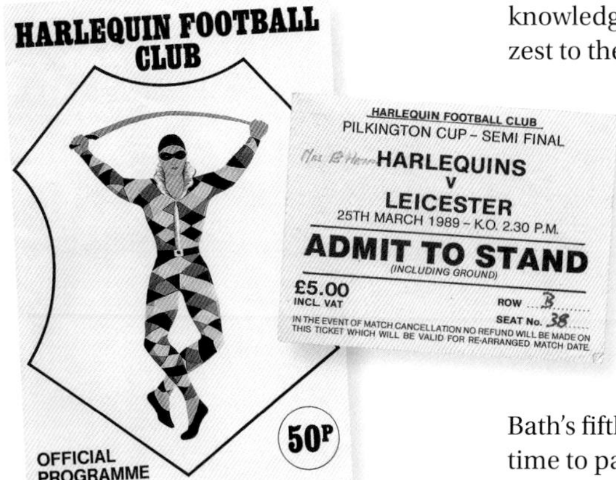

↑ Cup semi-final ticket and match programme from the 16-7 victory at Harlequins on 25.3.1989.

He and Rory Underwood had taken their by now customary places in England's championship team and, after a disappointing draw with Scotland, victories over Ireland and France left them with hope of the title. That hope foundered in the rain of Cardiff, though both had done enough to win selection in the British Lions tour party to visit Australia during the summer, under the captaincy of Finlay Calder, the Scottish flanker.

In February a young schools cap, Martin Johnson, made his senior debut at lock against the RAF before being invited to play junior rugby in New Zealand, where he developed so well that he found a place in their national under-21 side. Leicester, though, were focusing their thoughts on the cup quarter-final with Wasps and were disappointed to discover that a knee injury sustained playing against Ireland would keep Rory Underwood out of it. That, though, let in brother Tony and it was his try that made the difference in a 22-18 win, erasing the memory of the semi-final defeat two seasons earlier.

Cusworth landed two more dropped goals and Hare kicked four penalties in what looked suspiciously like a scripted conclusion to his marvellous career: it was by now common knowledge that Hare was to retire and that added zest to the semi-final against the cup holders, Harlequins, at The Stoop. Sure enough the full-back made sure of a finale at Twickenham: not only did he kick a couple of goals, he latched on to a cross-kick by Cusworth to score a try in a 16-7 win. Kardooni scored another and Cusworth dropped his 30th cup goal to ensure another meeting with Leicester's nemesis, Bath.

It was Leicester's sixth final and Bath's fifth and before they reached it Hare had time to pass 400 points in a season for the first time, scoring 17 against Ballymena. Retirement dinners were planned, and eaten, and the opportunity taken to welcome Ian Smith to the 300 club in the match with Moseley. Coincidentally, the week before the cup final, Leicester and Bath met in the league, having failed to win permission for the final to count towards both competitions. Since Bath had already won the title and Leicester were comfortably placed in mid-table the result was of little consequence and both clubs fielded second XVs, Leicester winning 15-12.

When it mattered, however, they did not and Hare's magic moment was denied him. The 1989 cup final was a titanic struggle, decided only two minutes from time when a battered and weary Tigers defence finally let Stuart Barnes over for the decisive try. Leicester's team was: Dusty Hare; Barry Evans, Paul Dodge (captain), Ian Bates, Rory Underwood; Les Cusworth, Aadel Kardooni; Stuart Redfern, Troy Thacker, Wayne Richardson, Malcolm Foulkes-Arnold, Tom Smith, John Wells, Dean Richards, Ian Smith. A then world record for a club game of 58,000 people packed Twickenham and those from Leicester cheered themselves hoarse when Hare kicked two penalties to give his club the half-time advantage.

The second half was a different story: Bath waxed stronger and stronger up front, with Damian Cronin having a storming game. Barnes kicked a penalty and Leicester, denied possession, could win no relief; a second penalty, with barely 12 minutes left, pulled Bath level and Leicester were like a boxer clinging to the ropes. Barnes's knockout punch, making the score 10-6, came too late for them to organise any kind of rally and Bath recorded English rugby's first double. Hare, with hardly a backward glance, left the scene with a club record of 438 points for the season, 4,507 for Leicester and 7,191 throughout a career which began at 17 and closed nearly twenty years later.

"We owe him a great debt," Cusworth said of his departing colleague. "Without him we would not have been able to play such attractive 15-man rugby over the years. By guaranteeing us, on average, nine points a game, he relieved the pressure, allowed us to relax and play football. There will never be another like him and his record points haul will never be broken. The best tribute I can pay him is that if my life depended on a kick, I'd give it straight to him, no question."

↓ Barry Evans outstrips Fred Sagoe during the Pilkington Cup final defeat to Bath at Twickenham.

LEICESTER FOOTBALL CLUB 1986/87
Back: Beason (President), Thomas (Team Hon.Sec), Willars (Coach), Richards, Dexter, Foulkes-Arnold, Charles, Smith, Jackson, W.Richardson, Redfern, Ray French, Allen (Hon.Sec), Farrands (Hon.Tres).
Middle: Buttimore, Evans, Dodge, Hare, Cusworth (capt), Bates, Kenney, Tebbutt, Wells.
Front: Tressler, Roberts.

LEICESTER FOOTBALL CLUB 1987/88
Back: Thomas (Team Hon.Sec), Allen (Hon.Sec), Tressler, Redfern, Povoas, T.Smith, Foulkes-Arnold, Charles, Dexter, Mann, Wells, Roberts, Andrews (President), Farrands (Hon.Tres).
Front: Harris, Buttimore, Bates, Evans, Dodge (capt), Cusworth, Kenney, Tebbutt, Burnhill

LEICESTER FOOTBALL CLUB 1988/89
Back: Allen (Hon.Sec), Farrands (Hon.Tres), Bates, Marriott, T.Smith, Grant, Foulkes-Arnold, Richards, Wells, W.Richardson, Redfern, Matthews (Coach), Foster (Coach), Thomas (Team Hon.Sec).
Front: Kardooni, Tressler, Gerald, Harris, T.Underwood, Dodge (capt), Cusworth, I.Smith, Evans, R.Underwood.

1987

1987	WORLD TOUR	OVERALL RECORD:					T	C	PG	DG	PTS
	Coach: Graham Willars	PLD	W	D	L	Tigers scored:	28	18	9	0	175
	Captain: Paul Dodge	6	4	0	2	Opponents scored:	12	7	5	2	100

GM	DATE		VEN	OPPONENTS	RESULT	TRIES	KICKS
1	Aug	2s	a	Western Australia	L 19-26	Burnhill, Dodge	Hare c/3p
2		4tu	a	Western Australia President's XV	W 28-10	Bates, Dexter, Povoas, Wells	Harris 3c/2p
3		9s	a	Manly	W 21-10	Povoas, Tressler, Youngs	Hare 3c/p
4		12w	a	Ponsonby	W 26-17	Povoas(3), Evans	Harris 2c/2p
5		16s	a	Queensland	L 13-37	Charles, Youngs	Hare p, Harris c
6		18tu	a	Singapore Cricket Club	W 68-0	Dexter(3), Evans(3), Burnhill(2), Bates, Buttimore, Foulkes-Arnold, Marriott, Roberts	Harris 8c

INDIVIDUAL APPEARANCES 1987 WORLD TOUR

Name / Game #	1	2	3	4	5	6	Apps	T	Pts
I (Ian) Bates	-	M	M	-	L	M	4	2	8
AP (Paul) Burnell S+ L+	A	-	A	-	-	-	2	-	-
SB (Steve) Burnhill	K	L	-	L	-	L	4	3	12
TJ (Tim) Buttimore	L	N	L	-	N	r	4+1	1	4
MR (Mark) Charles	G	-	-	-	G	-	2	1	4
L (Les) Cusworth E10	J	-	J*	J	J	O*	5	-	-
CD (Colin) Dexter	-	K	K	K	K	K	5	4	16
PW (Paul) Dodge E32 L2	M*	O*	-	M*	M*	-	4	1	4
BJ (Barry) Evans E+	N	-	N	N	-	N	4	4	16
MV (Malcolm) Foulkes-Arnold	E	-	E	-	E	D	4	1	4
RW (Ray) French	-	C	-	-	<C	-	2	-	-
WH (Dusty) Hare E25	O	r	O	-	O	-	3+1	-	23
JC (Jez) Harris	-	J	-	O	r	J	3+1	-	40
S (Steve) Kenney	-	I	-	I	-	I	3	-	-
PJ (PJ) Mann	D	D	-	D	D	-	4	-	-
AN (Adey) Marriott	F	-	F	-	r	F	3+1	1	4
SJ (Simon) Povoas	-	G	G	G	-	G	4	5	20
SB (Stuart) Redfern	-	A	r	A	A	A	4+1	-	-
WP (Wayne) Richardson	C	-	C	C	r	C	4+1	-	-
H (Harry) Roberts	-	B	-	B	-	B	3	1	4
IR (Ian) Smith	H	-	-	H	-	H	3	-	-
T (Tom) Smith	r	E	D	E	-	E	4+1	-	-
RS (Rob) Tebbutt	-	H	H	-	H	-	3	-	-
CJ (Chris) Tressler	B	-	B	-	B	-	3	1	4
JM (John) Wells	r	F	-	F	F	-	3+1	1	4
NG (Nick) Youngs E6	I	-	I	-	I	-	3	2	8

LEICESTER FOOTBALL CLUB WORLD TOUR 1987
Back: Willars (Coach), Lacey (Committee), Farrands (Hon.Tres), Beason (Committee), Richardson, Charles, Tebbutt, Wells, Ford (Physiotherapist), Roberts, Buttimore. Middle: Jolleys (Doctor), Kenney, Evans, Dexter, Foulkes-Arnold, T.Smith, Mann, Marriott, Burnhill, French, Jackson (Committee), I.Smith, Cusworth. Front: Harris, Tressler, Hare, Allen (Hon. Sec), Dodge (capt), Andrews (President), Bates, Povoas, Redfern.

19	86/87	Home Ground: Welford Road	OVERALL RECORD:					T	C	PG	DG	PTS
		Coach: Graham Willars	PLD	W	D	L	Tigers scored:	118	79	76	14	900
		Captain: Les Cusworth	39	26	1	12	Opponents scored:	73	29	63	10	569

GM	DATE		VEN	OPPONENTS	RESULT	TRIES	KICKS	ATT
RFU CLUB COMPETITION (John Player Special Cup)						**Cup winners: Bath**		
	Jan	31	a	Rosslyn Park (3)	PP (frost)			
27	Feb	14	a	Rosslyn Park (3)	W 18-15	Povoas 43	Hare c/3p, Cusworth d	-
29		**28**	**H**	**Gosforth (4)**	W 19-6	Evans 30, Charles 60	Hare c/2p, Cusworth d	5857
31	Mar	14	a	Bristol (qf)	W 17-7	Cusworth 35, Dexter 60	Cusworth d, Hare 2p	-
34		28	a	Wasps (sf)	L 6-13	-	Hare 2p	-
JOHN SMITH'S MERIT TABLE A (2ND)						**WINNERS: BATH**		
3	Sep	13	a	Bath	L 3-6	-	Hare p	-
7	Oct	4	a	Coventry	W 13-12	Cusworth, Richards	Hare c/p	-
14	Nov	**8**	**H**	**Nottingham**	W 9-3	-	Hare 3p	6158
16		15	a	Wasps	W 17-13	Richards, Youngs	Hare 2p, Cusworth d	-
17		**22**	**H**	**Moseley**	W 22-6	Richards(2)	Hare c/4p	4589
24	Jan	**10**	**H**	**Gloucester**	L 12-14	-	Hare 4p	4955
26	Feb	7	a	London Scottish	D 12-12	-	Hare 3p, Harris d	-
28		**21**	**H**	**Orrell**	W 30-22	Hare, Dexter, Kenney	Hare 6p	2123
30	Mar	**7**	**H**	**Harlequins**	W 18-8	Kenney, Tebbutt	Hare 2c/2p	1942
CLUB MATCHES								
1	Sep	**6**	**H**	**Bedford**	W 22-10	Evans(2), Dodge	Hare 2c/2p	3140
2		9tu	a	Nuneaton	W 49-6	Underwood(4), Richards(2), Hare, W.Richardson, Williams	Hare 5c/p	-
4		**17w**	**H**	**Birmingham**	W 95-6	Youngs(4), Tebbutt(3), Hare(2), Buttimore, Charles, Davidson, Dodge, Evans, Redfern	Hare 13c/3p	1927
5		**20**	**H**	**London Welsh**	W 69-4	Underwood(4), Evans(2), Richards(2), Redfern, W.Richardson, Tressler, Youngs	Hare 9c/p	3582
6		27	a	Harlequins	L 12-20	Penalty	Hare c/p, Cusworth d	-
8	Oct	**11**	**H**	**Richmond**	W 36-19	Cusworth, Dodge, Evans	Hare 3c/6p	3440
9		**18**	**H**	**Northampton**	W 24-15	Richards(2)	Hare 2c/4p	3583
10		**22w**	**H**	**Oxford University**	W 33-16	Richards(3), Evans, Roberts, Youngs	Hare 3c/p	1744
11		25	a	Swansea	W 13-11	Dodge, Richards	Cusworth d, Hare c	-
12	Nov	1	a	Cardiff	L 10-16	Redfern, Wells	Hare c	8000
13		**4tu**	**H**	**Fiji Barbarians**	W 39-14	Williams(2), Buttimore, Dodge, Grewcock, Lane	Hare 6c/p	5059
15		12w	a	Cambridge University	W 32-10	Buttimore, Clifford, Ray French, Lane, I.Smith, Underwood	Cusworth 4c	-
18		**29**	**H**	**Saracens**	W 19-16	Burnell	Hare 5p	3255
19	Dec	6	a	Gloucester	L 6-41	Penalty	Hare c	-
20		**13**	**H**	**Blackheath**	W 17-10	Charles, Youngs	Hare 2p, Harris d	2877
21		20	a	Bristol	L 9-39	Marriott	Hare c/p	-
22		**27**	**H**	**Barbarians**	L 18-22	Hare, Richards	Hare 2c/2p	16000
23	Jan	3	a	Headingley	W 22-19	Povoas(2), Dexter, Youngs	Hare 3c	-
		16f	a	Bedford	PP			
25		24	a	Metropolitan Police	W 39-0	Richards(2), Cusworth, Foulkes-Arnold, Redfern, Tebbutt, Underwood	Cusworth 3c/d, Dodson c	-
		31	a	Gosforth	PP (cup)			
	Feb	**14**	**H**	**Newport**	PP (cup)			
		28	a	Northampton	PP (cup)			
	Mar	**14**	**H**	**Coventry**	PP (cup)			
32		**18w**	**H**	**NZ Barbarians**	L 3-33	-	Hare p	6430
33		**20f**	**H**	**Loughborough Students**	W 44-16	Richards(3), Dexter(2), Dodge, T.Smith, Wells	Hare 6c	985
		28	a	Sale	PP (cup)			
35	Apr	4	a	Waterloo	W 15-9	Charles	Cusworth 2d, Hare c/p	-
36		**11**	**H**	**Bristol**	L 23-29	Burnhill(2), Bates	Hare c/3p	3140
37		**18**	**H**	**Neath**	L 12-17	-	Cusworth 2d, Hare 2p	3134
38		**20m**	**H**	**Pontypool**	W 37-12	Buttimore(2), Burnell, Dexter, Povoas	Hare 4c/2p/d	2849
39		25	a	Moseley	L 6-22	-	Hare 2p	-

INDIVIDUAL APPEARANCES 1986/87

Name / Game #	1	2	3	4	5	6	7	8	9	10	11	12	13	14	15	16	17	18	19	20	21	22	23	24	25	26	27	28	29	30	31	32	33	34	35	36	37	38	39	Apps	T	Pts
V (Vendis) Afflick	-	-	-	-	-	-	-	-	-	-	-	-	-	-	-	-	-	-	x	-	-	-	-	-	-	-	-	x	-	-	-	-	-	-	-	x	r	x	<r	0+2	-	-
I (Ian) Bates	-	M	-	-	-	-	-	-	-	-	-	-	-	N	M	-	-	-	-	M	M	M	M	M	-	N	N	-	-	-	-	x	L	x	-	L	L	L	L	15	1	4
PG (Paul) Brookes	-	-	-	-	-	-	-	-	-	-	-	-	-	-	>A	-	-	-	A	A	-	-	-	-	-	-	-	-	-	-	-	-	-	-	-	-	-	-	-	3	-	-
AP (Paul) Burnell S+ L+	-	-	-	-	-	-	-	-	-	-	-	-	-	-	-	-	-	>r	-	-	-	-	-	-	-	-	-	-	-	-	-	-	A	-	-	-	C	C	C	4+1	2	8
SB (Steve) Burnhill	-	-	-	-	-	-	-	-	-	-	-	-	-	-	-	-	-	-	-	-	-	-	-	-	-	-	-	-	-	-	-	-	-	-	-	K	K	-	K	3	2	8
TJ (Tim) Buttimore	L	L	L	L	L	L	L	L	L	L	L	L	L	L	L	L	L	L	M	L	L	L	L	L	L	L	L	-	L	L	L	L	-	L	L	N	N	N	N	37	5	20
MR (Mark) Charles	-	-	x	G	-	-	-	G	-	-	x	G	G	x	G	-	-	-	G	G	G	-	-	x	-	-	-	-	G	r	-	-	x	-	G	G	-	F	-	12+1	4	16
LC (Lewis) Clifford	-	-	-	-	-	-	x	-	-	-	-	-	r	-	B	-	-	-	x	-	x	-	-	-	-	-	-	-	-	-	-	-	-	x	B	r	<r	x	x	2+3	1	4
PD (Paul) Coltman	-	-	-	-	-	-	-	-	-	-	-	-	-	-	-	-	-	-	-	-	-	-	-	-	-	-	-	-	-	-	-	-	-	-	-	-	-	-	>A	1	-	-
L (Les) Cusworth E10	J*	J*	J*	-	J*	J*	J*	J*	J*	J*	J*	J*	J*	J*	J*	J*	J*	J*	-	-	-	J*	J*	J*	J*	-	J*	J*	J*	J*	J*	J*	J*	J*	J*	J*	J*	J*	J*	34	4	63
JS (John) Davidson	E	E	E	E	E	<E	-	-	-	-	-	-	-	-	-	-	-	-	-	-	-	-	-	-	-	-	-	-	-	-	-	-	-	-	-	-	-	-	-	6	1	4
CD (Colin) Dexter	x	x	-	x	-	x	-	-	-	-	-	-	-	-	-	-	-	-	K	K	K	-	K	x	-	K	-	K	-	K	K	-	K	K	K	-	-	K	-	12	6	24
PW (Paul) Dodge E32 L2	M	-	M	M	M	M	M	M	M	M	M	M	M	M	-	M	M	M	-	-	-	-	-	-	M	M	M	M	M	M	M	M	M	M	M	M	M	M	M	31	6	24
IR (Ian) Dodson	-	-	-	-	-	-	-	x	-	-	-	-	-	-	0	-	-	-	L	-	x	-	-	-	<0	-	-	-	-	-	-	-	x	-	-	-	-	-	-	3	-	2
BJ (Barry) Evans E+	N	-	N	N	N	N	N	N	-	N	-	N	-	-	-	-	-	-	-	-	-	N	-	-	-	-	-	N	N	-	N	N	-	N	N	-	-	-	-	16	8	32
MV (Malcolm) Foulkes-Arnold	D	D	D	D	D	D	D	D	D	D	D	D	D	D	E	D	D	D	D	D	D	D	D	-	D	E	E	E	E	E	E	E	D	E	-	E	E	-	-	35	1	4
RW (Ray) French	-	-	-	-	-	-	-	-	-	-	-	-	-	-	C	-	-	-	-	-	A	-	C	C	C	C	C	C	C	C	C	C	-	-	C	-	-	-	-	13	1	4
D (Darren) Grewcock	-	-	-	-	-	-	-	-	-	-	-	-	r	-	-	x	-	-	-	-	-	-	-	-	-	-	-	-	-	-	-	-	-	-	-	-	-	-	-	0+1	1	4
WH (Dusty) Hare E25	0	0	0	0	0	0	0	0	0	0	0	0	0	0	-	0	0	0	0*	0*	0*	0	0	0	-	0*	0	0	0	0	0	0	0	0	0	0	0	0	0	37	5	393
JC (Jez) Harris	-	-	-	J	-	-	-	-	-	r	-	-	-	x	-	-	-	-	J	J	J	x	x	-	x	J	x	L	r	-	x	-	-	x	-	-	-	-	-	6+2	-	6
NA (Nick) Jackson	-	-	-	-	-	-	-	-	-	-	-	-	-	-	-	-	-	-	-	-	-	-	-	D	-	D	D	D	D	D	D	D	-	D	D	-	D	D	D	13	-	-
S (Steve) Kenney	-	-	-	-	-	-	-	-	-	-	-	-	-	I	I	-	-	-	-	-	-	-	-	-	I	I	I	I	I	I	I	I	-	I	I	I	I	I	I	16	2	8
RJ (Russell) Lane	-	-	-	-	-	-	-	-	-	-	-	-	>N	-	N	-	-	x	N	-	-	-	-	-	-	x	-	-	-	-	-	-	-	-	-	-	-	-	-	3	2	8
KP (Kevin) MacDonald	-	-	-	-	x	-	-	-	-	-	-	x	-	-	r	-	-	-	-	x	-	-	-	-	-	-	-	-	-	r	-	-	-	-	-	-	-	-	-	0+2	-	-
PJ (PJ) Mann	-	-	-	-	-	-	-	-	-	-	-	x	-	-	>D	-	-	-	-	-	-	-	-	-	-	-	-	x	-	-	-	-	-	-	-	-	-	-	-	1	-	-
AN (Adey) Marriott	-	-	-	-	-	-	-	-	x	-	-	-	-	-	-	-	x	-	-	F	F	x	-	-	r	-	x	-	x	-	-	-	-	x	-	-	-	-	-	2+1	1	4
SJ (Simon) Povoas	x	>r	-	x	-	-	-	-	-	r	-	-	-	-	F	x	-	-	F	-	-	-	G	-	-	G	G	G	-	G	-	-	-	-	-	-	G	G	G	10+2	4	16
SB (Stuart) Redfern	A	A	A	A	A	A	A	A	A	A	A	A	A	A	-	A	A	A	-	-	-	A	A	A	A	A	A	A	A	A	A	A	-	A	A	A	A	A	-	33	4	16
D (Dean) Richards E3 L+	G	G	G	-	G	G	G	-	G	G	G	-	-	G	-	G	G	G	-	-	-	G	-	G	G	-	-	-	-	-	G	G	G	G	-	-	-	-	-	20	20	80
L (Lee) Richardson	-	-	-	-	r	-	-	-	-	-	-	-	-	-	-	-	-	-	-	-	-	-	-	-	-	-	-	-	-	-	-	-	-	-	-	-	-	-	-	0+1	-	-
WP (Wayne) Richardson	C	C	C	C	C	C	C	C	C	C	C	C	C	C	-	C	C	C	C	C	C	C	-	-	-	-	-	-	-	-	-	-	C	C	-	C	-	-	-	24	2	8
H (Harry) Roberts	-	-	-	-	-	-	>B	B	B	B	B	B	B	B	-	B	B	B	B	B	B	B	-	-	-	-	-	-	-	-	-	-	-	-	-	-	-	-	-	15	1	4
IR (Ian) Smith	H	H	H	-	H	H	H	H	-	-	-	-	-	-	H	-	-	H	-	-	-	-	-	-	-	-	-	-	-	-	x	x	H	-	-	-	-	H	H	12	1	4
T (Tom) Smith	-	-	-	-	-	-	E	E	E	E	E	E	E	E	-	E	E	E	E	E	E	E	E	E	E	-	-	-	-	-	-	-	E	-	E	D	-	E	E	23	1	4
RS (Rob) Tebbutt	-	-	-	H	-	-	-	-	H	H	H	H	H	H	-	H	H	-	H	H	H	H	H	H	H	H	H	H	H	H	H	H	-	H	H	H	H	-	-	27	5	20
CJ (Chris) Tressler	B	B	B	B	B	B	-	-	-	-	-	-	-	-	-	-	-	-	-	-	-	-	B	B	B	B	B	B	B	B	B	B	B	B	-	B	B	B	B	22	1	4
R (Rory) Underwood E16 L+	-	K	K	-	K	K	K	-	K	K	K	-	-	K	K	K	K	K	-	-	-	K	-	K	K	-	K	-	K	-	-	K	-	-	-	-	-	-	-	19	10	40
JM (John) Wells	F	F	F	F*	F	F	F	F	F	F	F	F	F	F	-	F	F	F	-	-	-	F	F	F	F	F	F	F	F	F	F	F	F	F	F	F	F	-	F	34	2	8
GG (Graham) Willars	-	-	-	-	-	-	-	-	-	-	-	-	-	-	-	-	-	-	-	-	-	-	-	-	-	-	-	-	-	-	-	-	-	-	<r	-	-	-	-	0+1	-	-
AK (Kevin) Williams	K	N	x	K	-	-	-	K	N	-	N	K	K	-	-	N	N	N	-	N	N	-	N	N	N	-	-	-	-	N	-	-	<N	-	-	-	-	-	-	18	3	12
NG (Nick) Youngs E6	I	I	I	I	I	I	I	I	I	I	I	I	I	-	-	I	I	I	I	I	I	I	I	I	-	-	-	-	-	-	-	-	I	x	-	-	-	-	-	23	9	36

The key for how to read the stats is on the last page

19	87/88	Home Ground: Welford Road	Trophy Cabinet: Courage League Division 1(1)	OVERALL RECORD:					T	C	PG	DG	PTS
		Coaches: Graham Willars and Peter Wheeler		PLD	W	D	L	Tigers scored:	145	100	81	18	1077
		Captain: Paul Dodge		38	32	0	6	Opponents scored:	49	32	43	11	422

GM	DATE		VEN	OPPONENTS	RESULT	POS/LGE	TRIES	KICKS	ATT
COURAGE LEAGUE DIVISION 1 (1ST)						**CHAMPIONS: LEICESTER TIGERS**			
3	Sep	**12**	**H**	**Bath**	W 24-13	3	Dexter 20, Cusworth 65, Harris 70	Cusworth d, Hare 3p	4651
5		26	a	Harlequins	W 12-9	3	Evans 16	Hare c/p/d	-
6	Oct	**3**	**H**	**Coventry**	W 32-16	2	Charles 2, W.Richardson 36, Burnhill 65, Kenney 70	Hare 2c/3p, Cusworth d	4757
14	Nov	14	a	Nottingham	W 22-13	3	Richards 60	Hare 5p, Cusworth d	-
15		**21**	**H**	**Wasps**	W 12-9	2	-	Hare 3p, Cusworth d	6003
16		28	a	Moseley	W 21-3	1	Richards 74, Evans 79	Hare 2c/3p	-
19	Dec	**19**	**H**	**Bristol**	W 15-10	1	Evans 53	Hare c/3p	4086
28	Feb	20	a	Orrell	L 6-30	1	-	Hare 2p	-
33	Mar	**26**	**H**	**Sale**	W 42-15	1	Bates 14, Charles 56/72/80, Evans 75	Hare 5c/4p	3890
35	Apr	**4m**	**H**	**Waterloo**	W 39-15	1	Penalty 5, Evans 56, Thornley 70, R.Underwood 78	Hare 4c/4p, Cusworth d	7130
			H	**Gloucester**	PP (not scheduled)	-			
RFU CLUB COMPETITION (JOHN PLAYER SPECIAL CUP)						**CUP WINNERS: HARLEQUINS**			
24	Jan	23	a	Rosslyn Park (3)	W 15-0	D2	Thornley 79	Hare c/3p	-
27	Feb	**13**	**H**	**Bath (4)**	L 6-13	D1	Youngs 62	Hare c	11755
CLUB MATCHES									
1	Sep	5	a	Bedford	W 29-9		Bates, Evans, Tebbutt, Penalty	Hare 2c/2p/d	-
2		**8tu**	**H**	**Nuneaton**	W 52-0		Dexter(2), Dodge(2), Tebbutt(2), Burnhill, Buttimore, Povoas	Harris 8c	1794
4		**19**	**H**	**London Welsh**	L 6-9		-	Dodge p, Nockles p	3427
7	Oct	10	a	Richmond	W 20-6		Cusworth, Kenney, Richards	Hare c/2p	-
8		17	a	Northampton	W 47-0		Evans(3), Cusworth, Redfern, Richards, R.Underwood	Hare 5c/3p	-
9		21w	a	Oxford University	W 17-6		Evans(2)	Harris 3p	-
10		**24**	**H**	**Swansea**	L 9-17		-	Hare 3p	5416
11		31	a	Llanelli	L 15-20		Buttimore, R.Underwood	Hare 2c, Cusworth d	-
12	Nov	**7**	**H**	**Cardiff**	W 27-19		Richards	Hare c/6p/d	4821
13		**10tu**	**H**	**Cambridge University**	W 64-6		Dexter(3), Bates(2), Buttimore, Foulkes-Arnold, Povoas, Roberts, T.Smith, Wells	Hare 7c/2p	1595
17	Dec	**5**	**H**	**Gloucester**	W 19-12		Evans, Povoas	Hare c/3p	3578
18		12	a	Blackheath	W 16-15		Harris, Kenney	Harris c/p/d	-
20		**28m**	**H**	**Barbarians**	W 48-30		Hare, Buttimore, Evans, Redfern, Richards, Thornley, R.Underwood, Wells, Youngs	Hare 6c	15920
21	Jan	**2**	**H**	**Headingley**	W 37-6		Povoas(2), Dexter, Mann, Youngs, Penalty	Hare 5c, Harris d	3512
22		9	a	Gloucester	L 16-30		Kenney	Hare 4p	5000
23		**16**	**H**	**Bedford**	W 42-9		Youngs(3), Evans(2), Bates, Povoas, Roberts	Hare 5c	2154
25		30	a	London Welsh	W 41-6		Evans(2), Cusworth, Richards, R.Underwood, Youngs, Penalty	Hare 5c/p	-
	Feb	**3w**	**H**	**Toulon**	PP				
26		**6**	**H**	**London Scottish**	W 34-15		Povoas(3), Evans, Kenney	Harris 4c/2p	2129
29		**27**	**H**	**Northampton**	W 35-9		R.Underwood(4), Dexter, Roberts	Hare 4c/p	2778
30	Mar	5	a	Saracens	W 28-8		Grewcock, Roberts, Tebbutt	Hare 2c/3p, Harris d	-
31		**8tu**	**H**	**Royal Air Force**	W 51-0		Dexter(2), Tebbutt(2), Harris, Charles, Evans, Grewcock	Harris d, Hare 8c	1314
		12	a	Coventry	PP				
		15tu	**H**	**Loughborough Students**	PP (frost)				
32		**18f**	**H**	**Lansdowne**	W 38-13		Charles(2), Bates, Evans, Grewcock, Harris, Kenney, Roberts	Hare 3c	1679
34	Apr	2	a	Ballymena	W 19-16		Gerald	Hare 5p	-
36		9	a	Bristol	W 15-12		-	Cusworth 3d, Hare 2p	4000
37		**16**	**H**	**Gosforth**	W 65-0		Richards(3), R.Underwood(3), Harris, Grewcock, Redfern, Tebbutt, Wells	Harris 9c/d	3416
38		**23**	**H**	**Moseley**	W 41-3		Thornley(3), Dexter(2), Bates	Harris 4c/2p/d	3994

INDIVIDUAL APPEARANCES 1987/88

Name / Game #	1	2	3	4	5	6	7	8	9	10	11	12	13	14	15	16	17	18	19	20	21	22	23	24	25	26	27	28	29	30	31	32	33	34	35	36	37	38	Apps	T	Pts
I (Ian) Bates	L	M	L	L	L	L	M	L	M	L	M	M	M	M	M	M	M	M	M	M	M	M	M	M	M	M	M	L	-	L	-	M	M	-	M	L	L	L	35	7	28
AP (Paul) Burnell S+ L+	-	-	-	-	-	-	-	-	C	-	-	C	C	C	-	-	-	-	-	-	-	C	<C	-	-	-	-	-	-	-	-	-	-	-	-	-	-	-	6	-	-
SB (Steve) Burnhill	-	L	-	K	-	K	-	-	L	x	-	-	N	N	-	-	L	L	L	-	L	L	L	-	-	K	K	r	M	K	-	L	K	<L	-	-	-	-	19+1	2	8
TJ (Tim) Buttimore	-	N	-	J	K	-	L	-	-	-	L	L	L	L	L	L	-	-	-	L	-	-	-	L	L	L	L	N	L	-	L	-	L	r	L	-	-	-	20+1	4	16
MR (Mark) Charles	-	x	-	-	-	G	-	x	-	-	-	-	-	-	-	-	-	-	-	-	-	-	-	-	x	-	-	-	G	G	G	G	G	<G	-	-	-	-	7	7	28
GM (Gareth) Collins	-	-	-	-	-	-	-	-	-	-	-	-	-	-	-	-	-	-	-	-	-	=r	-	-	-	-	-	-	-	-	-	-	-	-	-	-	-	-	0+1	-	-
PD (Paul) Coltman	-	-	-	-	-	-	-	-	-	-	-	-	-	-	-	-	-	-	-	-	-	-	-	-	-	-	-	-	-	-	A	-	-	-	-	-	-	-	1	-	-
L (Les) Cusworth E12	J	-	J	-	J	J	J*	J	-	J	J*	J*	J*	J*	J*	J*	-	-	-	J*	-	-	-	J*	J*	-	J*	J	J*	-	-	-	J*	J	J*	J	J	J	25	4	43
CD (Colin) Dexter	K	K	K	-	-	-	K	-	K	-	-	x	K	-	-	-	K	K	K	-	K	K	-	-	-	-	-	-	K	-	K	K	-	K	-	-	-	K	16	12	48
PW (Paul) Dodge E32 L2	M*	O*	M*	M*	M*	M*	-	M*	O*	M*	-	-	-	-	-	-	-	-	-	-	-	-	-	-	-	O*	-	M*	-	M*	M*	-	-	M*	r	M*	M*	M*	17+1	2	11
BJ (Barry) Evans E+	N	-	N	N	N	N	-	N	N	N	N	N	-	-	N	N	N	N	N	N	N	N	N	N	N	N	N	-	-	N	N	N	N	-	N	N	N	-	30	20	80
MV (Malcolm) Foulkes-Arnold	-	E	-	-	-	D	D	D	E	D	D	D	D	D	-	-	-	-	-	-	-	-	-	E	E	E	E	-	D	D	D	D	D	D	D	D	D	D	24	1	4
CE (Claude) Gerald	-	-	-	-	-	-	-	-	-	-	-	-	-	-	-	-	-	-	-	-	-	-	-	-	-	-	-	-	-	-	-	-	-	N	-	-	-	N	2	1	4
AJS (Alex) Gissing	-	-	-	-	-	-	-	-	>D	-	-	-	-	-	-	-	-	-	-	-	-	-	-	-	-	-	-	-	-	-	-	-	-	-	-	-	-	-	1	-	-
D (Darren) Grewcock	-	-	-	-	-	-	-	-	I	-	-	-	-	x	-	x	-	r	x	-	-	x	-	-	x	-	-	-	x	I	I	r	-	I	-	-	r	-	4+3	4	16
WH (Dusty) Hare E25	O	-	O	-	O	O	O	O	-	O	O	O	O	O	O	O	O*	-	O*	O	O*	O*	O*	O	O	-	O	O	O	O	O	O*	O	O	O	O	-	-	31	1	374
JC (Jez) Harris	-	J	r	-	-	-	-	-	J	-	-	-	x	-	-	-	J	J	J	x	J	J	J	x	-	J	r	-	-	J	J	J	x	-	-	-	O	O	14+2	5	114
DA (Dave) Hopper	-	-	-	-	-	-	-	-	-	-	-	-	-	-	-	-	-	-	-	-	-	-	-	-	-	-	-	-	-	-	>C	C	-	C	-	-	-	-	3	-	-
S (Steve) Kenney	I	I	I	I	I	I	I	I	-	I	I	I	I	I	I	I	I	I*	-	-	-	I	-	-	-	I	-	I	-	-	-	I	I	-	I	I	I	I	26	6	24
RJ (Russell) Lane	-	-	-	x	-	-	<N	-	-	-	x	-	-	-	-	-	-	-	-	-	-	-	-	-	-	-	-	-	-	-	-	-	-	-	-	-	-	-	1	-	-
KP (Kevin) MacDonald	x	-	-	-	-	r	-	x	-	-	-	-	-	-	-	-	-	-	-	-	-	-	-	-	-	-	-	-	-	-	-	-	-	-	-	-	-	-	0+1	-	-
PJ (PJ) Mann	D	D	D	D	D	-	-	-	-	-	-	-	-	-	D	D	D	D	D	D	D	D	D	D	D	-	D	<D	-	-	-	-	-	-	-	-	-	-	18	1	4
AN (Adey) Marriott	-	-	r	-	-	x	-	F	-	-	-	-	-	x	-	-	F	F	F	x	F	F	F	-	-	-	-	F	-	F	F	F	-	-	-	-	x	-	11+1	-	-
RJ (Rob) Nockles	-	x	-	>O	-	-	-	-	r	-	-	-	-	-	x	-	-	O	-	-	-	-	-	-	-	-	-	-	-	-	r	-	-	-	-	x	-	-	2+2	-	3
SJ (Simon) Povoas	G	G	G	G	G	-	-	-	G	-	G	-	G	-	G	-	G	G	G	-	G	G	G	x	-	G	x	-	-	-	-	-	-	-	-	-	-	-	16	9	36
SB (Stuart) Redfern	A	A	A	A	A	A	A	A	A	A	A	A	A	A	A	A	A	A	A	A	A	A	A	A	A	A	A	A	A	A	-	A	A	A	A	A	A	A	37	3	12
D (Dean) Richards E11 L+	-	-	-	-	-	E	G	G	-	G	-	G	-	G	-	G	-	-	-	G	-	-	-	G	G	-	G	G	-	-	-	-	-	-	G	G	G	G	16	10	40
L (Lee) Richardson	-	-	-	-	-	-	-	-	-	-	-	-	-	-	-	-	r	-	x	-	-	-	-	-	-	D	-	-	-	x	-	-	-	-	-	-	-	-	1+1	-	-
WP (Wayne) Richardson	C	C	C	C	C	C	C	C	-	C	C	-	-	-	C	C	C	C	C	C	C	-	-	C	C	C	C	C	C	C	-	-	C	-	C	C	C	C	29	1	4
H (Harry) Roberts	-	B	B	B	-	-	-	-	-	-	-	B	B	B	B	B	B	B	B	B	B	B	B	B	B	B	B	B	B	B	B	B	B	-	B	-	-	B	27	5	20
IR (Ian) Smith	x	-	-	-	r	-	-	-	H	r	-	-	-	-	-	r	-	-	-	-	-	-	-	-	-	-	-	-	-	-	x	-	x	F	-	x	-	-	2+3	-	-
T (Tom) Smith	E	-	E	E	E	-	E	E	-	E	E	E	E	E	E	E	E	E	E	E	E	E	E	-	-	-	-	E	E	E	E	E	E	E	E	E	E	E	31	1	4
RS (Rob) Tebbutt	H	H	H	H	H	H	-	H	F	H	H	x	-	-	-	-	H	H	H	-	-	-	-	-	-	-	-	r	H	H	H	H	H	-	x	-	H	x	19+1	7	28
TA (Troy) Thacker	-	-	-	-	-	-	-	-	-	-	-	-	-	-	-	-	-	-	-	-	x	-	-	-	-	x	-	-	-	-	-	-	-	>B	-	B	B	-	3	-	-
PT (Peter) Thornley	-	-	-	x	-	-	>H	-	-	-	x	H	H	H	H	H	-	-	-	H	H	H	H	H	H	H	H	H	-	-	-	-	-	H	H	H	-	H	19	6	24
CJ (Chris) Tressler	B	-	-	-	B	B	B	B	B	B	B	-	-	-	-	-	-	-	-	-	-	-	x	-	-	-	-	-	r	-	-	x	-	-	-	-	-	-	8+1	-	-
R (Rory) Underwood E23 L+	-	-	-	-	-	-	-	K	-	K	K	K	-	K	K	K	-	-	-	K	-	-	-	K	K	-	-	K	N	-	-	-	-	-	K	K	K	-	15	12	48
T (Tony) Underwood E+ L+	-	-	-	-	-	-	-	-	-	-	-	-	-	-	-	-	-	-	-	-	-	-	>K	-	-	-	-	-	-	-	-	-	-	-	-	-	-	-	1	-	-
JM (John) Wells	F	F	F	F	F	F	F	-	-	F	F	F	F	F	F	F	-	-	-	F	-	-	-	F	F	F	F	-	F	-	-	-	F	-	F	F	F	F	25	3	12
NG (Nick) Youngs E6	-	-	-	-	-	-	-	-	-	-	-	-	-	-	-	-	-	-	I	I	I	-	I	I	I	-	I	-	I	-	-	-	-	-	-	-	-	-	8	7	28

The key for how to read the stats is on the last page

19	88/89		OVERALL RECORD:					T	C	PG	DG	PTS
		Home Ground: Welford Road	PLD	W	D	L	Tigers scored:	110	67	98	14	910
		Coaches: David Matthews with Allen Foster	38	28	1	9	Opponents scored:	76	38	56	9	575
		Captain: Paul Dodge										

GM	DATE		VEN	OPPONENTS	RESULT	POS/LGE	TRIES	KICKS	ATT
COURAGE LEAGUE DIVISION 1 (6TH)						**CHAMPIONS: BATH**			
2	Sep	**10**	**H**	**Wasps**	W 15-6	3	-	Hare 5p	4844
4		24	a	Liverpool St Helens	W 23-12	2	Reid 5, Richards 17, Thornley 43, R.Underwood 56	Hare 2c/p	-
6	Oct	**8**	**H**	**Orrell**	L 15-27	5	-	Hare 5p	4836
9		22	a	Nottingham	D 12-12	6	Evans 26	Hare c/2p	4000
13	Nov	12	a	Waterloo	W 34-22	4	Richards 13/39, Cusworth 32, Redfern 52, Evans 57, Kardooni 76	Cusworth d, Harris 2c/p	-
14		**19**	**H**	**Rosslyn Park**	W 28-15	2	Hare 35, Warwood 74	Hare c/6p	4423
15		**26**	**H**	**Harlequins**	L 21-31	4	Hare 1, Kardooni 35, T.Underwood 65	Hare 3c/p	3989
22	Jan	14	a	Gloucester	L 0-28	7	-	-	-
31	Mar	**11**	**H**	**Bristol**	W 13-12	6	Evans 39	Hare 2p, Cusworth d	4889
35	Apr	8	a	Moseley	L 13-22	6	Grant 5	Hare 3p	-
37		**22**	**H**	**Bath**	W 15-12	6	MacDonald 35	Liley 3p, Harris c	2177
RFU CLUB COMPETITION (PILKINGTON CUP)						**CUP WINNERS: BATH**			
24	Jan	28	a	Liverpool St Helens (3)	W 37-6	D1	Kardooni 22/29, Cusworth 52, Evans 71	Cusworth 4d, Hare 3c/p	-
26	Feb	11	a	Rosslyn Park (4)	W 23-9	D1	Wells 20, Evans 54, I.Smith 72	Hare c/3p	-
29		**25**	**H**	**Wasps (qf)**	W 22-18	D1	T.Underwood 20	Hare 4p, Cusworth 2d	8644
32	Mar	25	a	Harlequins (sf)	W 16-7	D1	Hare 14, Kardooni 17	Hare c/p, Cusworth d	6000
38	Apr	29		Bath (f)	L 6-10	D1	-	Hare 2p	59300
CLUB MATCHES									
1	Sep	**3**	**H**	**Bedford**	W 40-10		Cusworth, Evans, R.Underwood, West	Cusworth d, Hare 3c/5p	3482
3		17	a	Northampton	W 30-19		Richards(3), Hare, Youngs	Hare 2c/2p	-
5	Oct	1	a	Coventry	W 45-7		Hare(2), Evans(2), Richards, R.Underwood, Youngs	Hare 7c/p	-
7		15	a	Swansea	L 16-35		Evans	Harris 3p/d	-
8		**18tu**	**H**	**Oxford University**	W 24-6		T.Smith	Hare c/5p, Harris d	1886
10		**30s**	**H**	**Llanelli**	L 15-29		-	Hare 5p	3977
11	Nov	5	a	Cardiff	L 24-26		Hare, Evans, T.Underwood	Hare 3c/2p	-
12		8tu	a	Cambridge University	W 23-21		Kenney, Thornley, Warwood	Hare c/3p	-
16	Dec	**3**	**H**	**Gloucester**	W 19-13		T.Underwood 60	Hare 4p/d	3240
17		**10**	**H**	**Blackheath**	W 22-12		MacDonald 8, Warwood 63, Penalty 75	Hare 2c/2p	2945
18		17	a	Richmond	W 16-7		Gerald(2)	Hare c/2p	-
19		**28w**	**H**	**Barbarians**	L 19-36		Kardooni 27, Evans 75	Hare c/3p	17000
20		31	a	Nuneaton	W 39-13		Grant(2), Hare, Harris, Bates, Dexter	Hare 3c/2p, Harris d	-
21	Jan	**7**	**H**	**Headingley**	W 53-7		Hare 6/12/33, Dodge 39, Grant 46, I.Smith 50, Evans 57, Wells 62, T.Underwood 74	Hare 7c/p	3973
23		20f	a	Bedford	W 16-3		Bates, T.Underwood	Hare c/2p	-
25	Feb	**4**	**H**	**Northampton**	W 42-8		Hare 4, Grant 30, I.Smith 43, Evans 51/71/78, T.Underwood 68, Poole 80	Hare 5c	2172
27		**14tu**	**H**	**Royal Air Force**	W 34-12		T.Smith 12, Gerald 21, Dexter 38, T.Underwood 48, I.Smith 66, Kenney 78	Harris 2c/2p	1502
28		**18**	**H**	**Moseley**	W 27-10		Penalty 18, Evans 51/72	Hare 3c/3p	2559
		25	a	London Welsh	PP (cup)				
30	Mar	**4**	**H**	**Saracens**	W 25-6		T.Smith 55, Grant 70, Marriott 71	Hare 2c/3p	1862
		14tu	**H**	**Loughborough Students**	PP (cup)				
		25	a	Sale	PP (cup)				
33		**27m**	**H**	**Ballymena**	W 21-17		I.Smith 31	Hare c/5p	3111
34	Apr	1	a	London Scottish	W 20-15		Gerald, Grant, Redfern, R.Underwood	Harris 2c	-
36		15	a	Gosforth	W 47-14		Bates(2), Evans(2), Dodge, Richards, Thacker	Hare 5c/3p	-

***Neutral Venue:** #38 at Twickenham*

INDIVIDUAL APPEARANCES 1988/89

Name / Game #	1	2	3	4	5	6	7	8	9	10	11	12	13	14	15	16	17	18	19	20	21	22	23	24	25	26	27	28	29	30	31	32	33	34	35	36	37	38	Apps	T	Pts
I (Ian) Bates	L	L	L	L	L	L	L	L	L	L	-	-	-	-	-	-	M	M	L	L	L	L	L	L	L	L	L	L	L	L	L	L	L	-	L	L	-	L	30	4	16
WP (Willy) Carr	-	-	-	-	>F	<F	-	x	-	-	-	-	-	-	-	-	-	-	-	-	-	-	-	-	-	-	-	-	-	-	-	-	-	-	-	-	-	-	2	-	-
PD (Paul) Coltman	-	-	-	-	-	-	-	-	x	-	<C	-	-	-	-	-	-	-	-	-	-	-	-	-	-	-	-	-	-	-	-	-	-	-	-	-	-	-	1	-	-
L (Les) Cusworth E12	J*	J	J	J	J	J	-	-	J	-	J	-	J	J	J	-	-	-	J	-	J	J	J	J	J	J*	-	J*	J	J	J	J	-	-	J	J	-	J	26	3	42
CD (Colin) Dexter	-	-	-	-	-	-	K	-	-	K	-	-	x	-	-	-	K	K	-	K	-	-	-	-	-	-	r	-	-	K	-	-	K	x	-	K	<K	-	9+1	2	8
PW (Paul) Dodge E32 L2	-	M*	M*	M*	M*	M*	M*	M*	M*	-	M*	M*	M*	M*	M*	-	-	-	M*	M*	M*	M*	M*	M*	M*	-	-	-	M*	M*	M*	M*	M*	M*	M*	M*	-	M*	29	2	8
BJ (Barry) Evans E2	N	N	N	-	N	N	N	-	N	-	N	N	N	N	N	-	-	-	N	-	N	-	N	N	N	N	-	N	N	N	N	-	-	-	N	N	-	N	25	19	76
MV (Malcolm) Foulkes-Arnold	D	D	D	D	D	D	D	-	D	D	D	-	D	D	D	D	D	D	-	D	D	D	D	D	D	D	D	D	D	D	D	D	D	D	D	D	-	D	34	-	-
CE (Claude) Gerald	-	-	K	N	-	-	-	N	-	N	-	-	-	-	-	N	N	N	-	N	-	N	-	-	-	-	N	-	-	-	-	x	N	N	-	-	N	-	13	4	16
AJS (Alex) Gissing	-	-	-	-	-	-	-	-	-	-	-	x	-	-	-	-	-	-	-	-	-	-	-	-	-	-	-	-	-	-	-	-	-	-	-	-	D	-	1	-	-
MR (Mark) Grant	-	-	-	-	-	-	-	-	-	-	-	-	-	-	>G	G	G	G	G	G	G	G	-	-	G	x	-	G	-	G	G	-	G	G	G	x	-	-	15	7	28
WH (Dusty) Hare E25	0	0	0	0	0	0	-	0	0	0*	0	0	-	0	0	0*	0*	0*	0	0	0	-	0	0	0	0	-	0	0	0	0	0	0	-	0	0	-	<0	32	12	438
JC (Jez) Harris	M	x	-	-	-	-	J	J	x	J	-	J	0	-	-	-	-	-	x	J	-	0	-	x	-	M	J	M	x	-	-	x	J	J	-	-	J	x	14	1	45
DA (Dave) Hopper	-	-	-	-	-	-	-	-	-	C	-	C	-	-	-	x	-	-	-	-	-	r	C	C	C	C	C	-	-	-	-	-	-	-	-	-	-	-	7+1	-	-
NA (Nick) Jackson	-	-	-	-	-	-	-	-	-	-	-	-	-	-	-	-	-	-	-	-	-	-	-	-	-	-	-	-	-	-	-	-	-	-	-	-	<G	-	1	-	-
MO (Martin) Johnson E+ L+	-	-	-	-	-	-	-	-	-	-	-	-	-	-	-	-	-	-	-	-	-	-	-	-	-	-	>E	-	-	-	-	-	-	-	-	-	E	-	2	-	-
A (Aadel) Kardooni	-	-	-	-	-	-	>I	I	I	I	I	-	I	I	I	I	I	I	I	I	-	I	I	I	I	I	-	I	I	I	I	I	I	I	I	I	-	I	28	6	24
S (Steve) Kenney	I	-	-	-	-	-	-	-	-	r	-	I	-	-	-	-	-	-	-	-	I	-	-	-	-	-	I*	-	-	-	-	x	-	-	-	-	I*	x	5+1	2	8
AM (Andy) Key	-	-	x	-	-	-	-	-	-	-	-	-	-	-	-	-	-	-	-	-	-	-	-	-	-	-	-	-	-	x	-	-	x	-	-	x	L	-	1	-	-
D (Dave) Kitching	-	-	-	-	-	-	-	-	-	-	-	-	-	-	-	-	-	-	-	-	-	-	-	-	-	-	>A	-	-	-	A	x	-	-	-	-	A	x	3	-	-
JG (John) Liley	-	-	-	-	-	>r	0	-	-	-	-	-	-	-	-	-	-	-	-	-	-	-	-	-	r	x	0	-	-	-	x	-	-	0	x	-	0	-	4+2	-	9
KP (Kevin) MacDonald	-	-	-	x	-	-	x	-	-	-	-	-	-	-	x	J	J	J	-	-	x	-	-	-	-	-	-	-	-	-	-	-	-	-	-	-	M	-	4	2	8
AN (Adey) Marriott	-	x	F	-	-	-	F	F	F	F	-	-	-	x	-	F	F	-	r	H	-	-	-	x	-	-	-	F	x	F	F	x	-	H	-	-	F	x	13+1	1	4
J (John) Murphy	-	-	-	-	-	-	-	-	-	-	-	-	-	-	-	-	-	-	-	-	-	-	x	-	-	-	>F	-	-	-	-	-	-	x	-	-	H	-	2	-	-
RJ (Rob) Nockles	-	-	-	-	-	-	-	r	-	-	-	<r	-	-	-	x	-	-	-	-	-	-	-	-	-	-	-	x	-	-	-	-	-	-	-	-	x	-	0+2	-	-
MD (Matt) Poole	-	-	-	-	-	-	-	>D	-	-	-	D	-	-	-	-	-	-	-	-	-	-	-	-	r	-	-	-	-	-	x	-	x	E	r	-	-	-	3+2	1	4
SJ (Simon) Povoas	G	-	-	-	-	r	G	G	-	G	G	G	-	-	-	-	-	-	-	-	-	-	-	-	-	-	-	-	-	-	-	-	-	-	-	-	-	-	6+1	-	-
SB (Stuart) Redfern	A	A	A	A	A	A	A	A	A	A	A	A	A	A	A	A	A	A	A	A	A	A	A	A	A	A	-	A	A	A	-	A	A	A	A	A	-	A	35	2	8
MT (Mark) Reid	-	>5	E	5	E	5	E	-	5	E	E	-	5	5	E	-	-	-	<D	-	-	-	-	-	-	-	-	-	-	-	-	-	-	-	-	-	-	-	13	1	4
D (Dean) Richards E19 L+	-	G	G	G	G	G	-	-	G	-	-	-	G	G	-	-	-	-	-	-	-	-	G	G	-	G	-	-	G	-	-	G	-	-	-	G	-	G	15	8	32
L (Lee) Richardson	-	-	-	-	x	-	-	-	-	x	-	-	-	-	-	-	-	-	-	-	x	-	-	-	-	-	r	-	-	-	-	-	-	-	-	-	C	-	1+1	-	-
WP (Wayne) Richardson	C	C	C	C	C	C	-	-	-	-	-	-	C	C	C	C	C	C	C	C	C	C	-	-	-	-	-	C	C	C	C	C	C	C	C	C	-	C	26	-	-
IR (Ian) Smith	-	-	-	r	H	-	-	H	H	H	-	F	H	H	x	H	H	H	H	-	H	H	H	H	H	H	H	H	H	H	H	H	H	-	H	H	-	H	27+1	5	20
T (Tom) Smith	E	-	-	-	-	-	x	E	-	-	-	E	-	-	-	E	E	E	E	E	E	E	E	E	E	E	G	E	E	E	E	E	E	-	E	E	-	E	24	3	12
W (Wayne) Steedman	-	-	-	-	-	-	-	-	-	-	-	-	-	-	-	>M	-	r	-	-	-	-	x	-	-	-	<M	-	-	-	-	-	-	-	-	-	-	-	2+1	-	-
TA (Troy) Thacker	B	-	-	-	-	-	-	-	-	-	-	B	x	-	-	-	-	-	-	-	-	-	B	B	B	B	B	B	B	B	B	B	-	B	B	B	-	B	16	1	4
PT (Peter) Thornley	H	H	H	H	-	H	H	-	-	-	H	H	-	-	<H	-	-	-	-	-	-	-	-	-	-	-	-	-	-	-	-	-	-	-	-	-	-	-	9	2	8
CJ (Chris) Tressler	-	B	B	B	B	B	B	B	B	B	B	-	B	B	B	B	B	B	B	B	B	B	-	-	-	-	-	-	-	-	-	x	B	-	-	-	B	x	22	-	-
R (Rory) Underwood E32 L+	K	K	-	K	K	K	-	-	K	-	-	-	K	K	-	-	-	-	K	-	-	-	-	K	-	K	-	-	-	-	K	K	-	K	-	-	-	K	15	4	16
T (Tony) Underwood E+ L+	-	-	-	-	-	-	-	K	-	-	K	K	-	-	K	K	-	-	-	-	K	K	K	-	K	-	K	K	K	-	-	N	-	-	K	-	-	x	14	8	32
AM (Alan) Warwood	-	-	-	-	x	-	-	-	-	>M	L	L	L	L	L	L	L	L	-	-	-	x	-	-	-	-	-	-	-	-	-	-	-	L	-	-	-	-	10	3	12
JM (John) Wells	F	F	-	F	-	-	-	-	-	-	F	-	F	F	F	-	-	-	F	F	F	F	F	F	F	F	-	-	F	-	-	F	F	F	F	F	-	F	22	2	8
DE (Dorian) West E+	>r	-	x	-	-	-	-	-	-	-	-	-	-	-	-	-	x	F	-	-	-	-	-	-	-	-	-	x	-	-	-	-	-	-	-	-	-	-	1+1	1	4
RD (Bob) White	-	-	-	-	-	-	>C	C	<C	-	-	-	-	-	-	-	-	-	-	-	-	-	-	-	-	-	-	-	-	-	-	-	-	-	-	-	-	-	3	-	-
NG (Nick) Youngs E6	-	I	I	I	I	<I	-	-	-	-	-	-	-	x	-	-	-	-	-	-	-	-	-	-	-	-	-	-	-	-	-	-	-	-	-	-	-	-	5	2	8

The key for how to read the stats is on the last page

CHAPTER 24

Seeds of Professionalism

1989/1990

During the summer Rory Underwood and Dean Richards departed for Australia with the Lions. Both players appeared in all three internationals as the Lions won the series 2-1 and Richards would have captained the team in the final match, against an ANZAC XV, but for injury; four years later, against Canterbury in New Zealand, he enjoyed that honour.

Indeed Richards's powerful, mauling play was the bedrock of the Lions success and his combination with Mike Teague, the England flanker, created a momentum that the Australians, in the second and third internationals, found hard to counter. He came home to lead Leicester into a new season: it was a brief flirtation with authority because, in the first league match (at Wasps) Richards damaged his shoulder so badly that it effectively terminated his season, Cusworth taking over the captaincy.

The club, meanwhile, had warmed up with a tour to the USA (during which they played the national team) and now watched with interest to see how Hare's successor at full-back would go. It was an unenviable position for John Liley, since invidious comparisons were bound to be made, but in the event he could not have wished for a better first full season. Liley, a swimming pool attendant in Wakefield but who turned to accountancy in Leicester, announced himself with two tries, two conversions and five penalties in an ugly 41-18 win over Pontypridd.

It was the Welsh club's first visit to Leicester since the previous century and, sadly, they lived up to a reputation for violent play which preceded them. Nigel Bezani, their prop, was sent off and Leicester subsequently dropped them from their fixture list. When defeat against Wasps followed, Leicester may have felt that life after Hare was not going to be easy, except that nothing could stop Liley. A genuinely two-footed goal-kicker, Liley's receding hairline even gave him a vague resemblance to Hare and he certainly enjoyed the chance to counter-attack, just like his predecessor.

➜ Stuart Redfern ploughs on during the victory against Moseley 31.3.1990.

There were difficulties, too, in keeping three outstanding wings happy: the Underwood brothers and Evans constituted a formidable trio but the last named felt that he was being overlooked too frequently for comfort. Even so, the trip to Orrell was a good one to miss: yet again Leicester crashed, this time 33-10, and already their league expectations were looking thin. The situation was not improved when it was discovered that Dodge required an exploratory knee operation, though the question of too many wings was (temporarily) resolved when Tony Underwood broke his jaw playing for the North in the divisional championship.

On the representative front, however, matters were far more satisfactory: Rory Underwood played in Paris when the Lions, reformed on the occasion of the bicentenary of the French Revolution, beat France and when the touring Fijians arrived in England, the wing positively blasted them out of the international with England. He scored five tries in his 34th international, equalling the record set by 'Dan' Lambert in 1907 for one match and catching up the 66-year-old record held by Cyril Lowe as England's leading try-scorer with 18. Moreover, to their great delight, the brothers appeared together for the Barbarians at Twickenham in the finale to the New Zealand tour of Wales and Ireland. Although the Baa-baas lost 21-10, Tony Underwood's flair for attack shone so brightly that confident predictions were made that he was ready to follow his brother into the national team.

Leicester as a unit, however, found it hard to put their act together. Kardooni's form had slipped which gave Steve Kenney the chance to play his 350th game against Saracens and there was local criticism when four players - Evans, Ashley Johnson, Tebbutt and Buttimore (the latter two having rejoined the club during the summer) - went to play sevens in Dubai only for three of them to find they were required for the league match with Harlequins. Evans and Buttimore made frantic efforts to return to London in time to play but, inevitably, their indifferent preparation saw Leicester slip to defeat. A fortnight later Harry Roberts left the club, for business reasons, and joined Richmond (when the two clubs met later in the season Roberts scored Richmond's only try in a 44-12 defeat).

After much debate Leicester decided to take the paid road and advertised for a director of coaching. It was a road which Northampton, their near-neighbours, had already taken when they appointed Barrie Corless, the former England centre, and other clubs, at various levels of the game, were finding it a necessary step, to relieve the amateur administrators of an increasingly onerous burden. It was a major step, partly because the club committee were aware of Leicester's long and proud tradition of self-help and partly because of the sheer economic burden imposed by a salaried official; from the beginning, though, it was made clear that the newcomer would be an adjunct to the existing (unpaid) coaches rather than a replacement.

🡐 John Liley scored a then record 439 points during the 1989/90 season.

Three months later Leicester had their man: Tony Russ, 43, a teacher from Thorpe Hall School in Southend but who came from Burton and went to school locally in Ashby-de-la-Zouch. Russ had done wonders as coach to Saracens, his success in earning them promotion to the first division helping him to posts with the London divisional side, the new England under-21 side and England Students; indeed those latter two appointments gave him a very good appreciation of the young talent available up and down the country, including a blond flanker from Barkers' Butts, Coventry, who played in England's first under-21 international, against Romania - Neil Back.

Russ's role differed from that of Corless in that there was no commercial element involved: "This is the first job which is 100 per cent rugby and there is no-one to look for as a role model," Russ said, accepting that status for himself when he took up his £20,000 position in August 1990. John Allen, stressing the duality of rugby in the nineties, said: "We involve a lot of our members in various sub-committees and we need to retain those people, the same as we need to retain the sort of people who are coaching our teams at the moment. I think it's very important we don't lose those who want to be involved, without thinking of payment. But what we do need is someone whose job it is to prepare a framework, so that when the amateurs come to the club the way has been prepared for them to make their contribution more effective."

At least the players emerged from the doldrums to make a point against the Barbarians: Rory Underwood scored two tries in a 32-16 victory, Wells and Thacker vying for the title of man of the match. Indeed it had not been a bad month for Troy Thacker, since he played through the divisional championship: had injury not hindered his career a bright future appeared to lie ahead. Moreover, a new, young second-row partnership was settling together: Matt Poole and Alex Gissing, who had won England honours at under-21 and colts level, gave promise of solidity in an area where Leicester had seldom been dominant.

Still the club could not get it right in the league so they turned to the cup: Povoas, increasingly effective as Richards's replacement, scored three tries in the 43-3 demolition of London Welsh and then it was Liley's turn to rattle the scoreboard: the full-back scored 27 points in the 43-15 win over West Hartlepool in the fourth round. But Leicester faltered at the quarter-final stage at Franklin's Gardens: the second-division leaders, Northampton, removed them from the competition with a conclusive 23-7 victory.

🡓 Tony Russ becomes the club's first salaried director of coaching.

Although the selectors rang the changes and produced an improved performance in the league against Bristol, Leicester's spirits were not lifted when they lost for only the second time to their northern neighbours, Nottingham. That match was on the eve of the grand-slam decider between Scotland and England at Murrayfield, the result of which must have completed a disastrous weekend for any fervent Leicester and England supporter.

Up to that point everything had gone so well for England, and Rory Underwood. Expansive wins against Ireland, France and Wales, with the Leicester wing scoring in each match to extend the national try-scoring record; moreover when he played against Wales he became England's most-capped back with 37 and celebrated (despite a dose of 'flu) with two tries. But in Edinburgh the wheels came off the England bus: against an implacable Scottish defence they lost 13-7, a result which had long-term consequences in terms of style and attitude.

In a different scoring key, Barry Evans scored five tries in a 70-4 club win against the RAF which erased the post-war try-scoring record of 158 held jointly by Bob Barker and John Duggan and helped carry Evans to a career total of 169 before he left to join Coventry. Liley, too, was closing on Hare's seasonal record set only 10 months earlier: 18 points in the 66-12 win over London Scottish (in which Underwood scored five tries) did him no harm and the target was further reduced in substantial wins over Ballymena and Gosforth which helped Leicester to a record points aggregate for the season of 1,109 and Povoas to a record tally for a forward of 25 tries. It is worth recording, too, that the most successful team in the club was the Extras, who lost only once and suggested strength in depth for the future.

Ironically the climax of the season was to come at Bath - Liley required 15 points to pass Hare's 438 and Cusworth bade the game farewell. Few players have been held in greater affection at Leicester

🡓 Rory Underwood scores one of the five tries he tallied against London Scottish 7.4.1990.

← Les Cusworth signs off after his 365th and last first-team game for Tigers at Bath 28.4.1990.

than the little fly-half. "Over the years he more than anyone else has persuaded people to continue supporting the game," Chalkie White said. "If you were in two minds about sitting in front of the television or going to watch Les Cusworth, you'd go to the match. The perfect player doesn't exist and Les's imperfections were conspicuous but also misunderstood. His fingertip tackling left people wondering who was doing what but his intelligence, his nous, more than compensated."

Dusty Hare, too, paid tribute to Cusworth: "Les has been so important to Leicester because he makes us tick. Apart from, perhaps, Stuart Barnes, he is the only fly-half in England who can take the game by the scruff of the neck and dictate it." In Leicester's final home game of the season, against Gosforth, Kardooni gave Cusworth the final try and he was chaired off; typically Cusworth himself recalled the player with whom he had been so long associated and who was also retiring, Steve Kenney, both of them having played 365 games for the club. They were an alliterative pair, Cusworth and Kenney, both of them with distinct gifts which, happily, were allowed to blossom at Welford Road.

Kenney, a fiery-tempered performer in his youth, was possessed of one of the quickest breaks from scrum-half most people had seen; disappointment matured him and he would surely have played well over 400 games but for the presence at the club of Nick Youngs in the middle 1980s. His unswerving loyalty to Leicester created a great well of sympathy among Leicester members, all of whom were delighted to see it sustained when he was elected to the committee.

Cusworth, meanwhile, received a warm welcome in his final match at Bath though the generosity of the applause did not extend to the result: Bath won 26-15 but Liley got his record by scoring a try (his eighteenth of the season), converting it and kicking three penalties - it carried him to 439 points for the season, a quite outstanding achievement and one which allowed Liley himself to emerge from the long shadow cast by Hare. Indeed his form carried Liley into the England touring team to Argentina in the summer, alongside Tony Underwood and Matt Poole.

Not that it was the happiest of tours for the Tigers trio. The touring party was a mixture of youth and experience since several senior players chose to take the summer off, knowing what 1991 would bring. There were caps to be won but Underwood, plagued by injury at home, could not find his best form away and had a muted trip, being overtaken by Nigel Heslop; Liley, too, found the step up in class demanding while Poole, as a youngster, was there to learn from such as Wade Dooley and Nigel Redman. The party lurched from one crisis to another, losing four of the seven games and seldom coping with the indifferent local refereeing.

→ Brian Smith in high-kicking form for Ireland during the 1991 Five Nations.

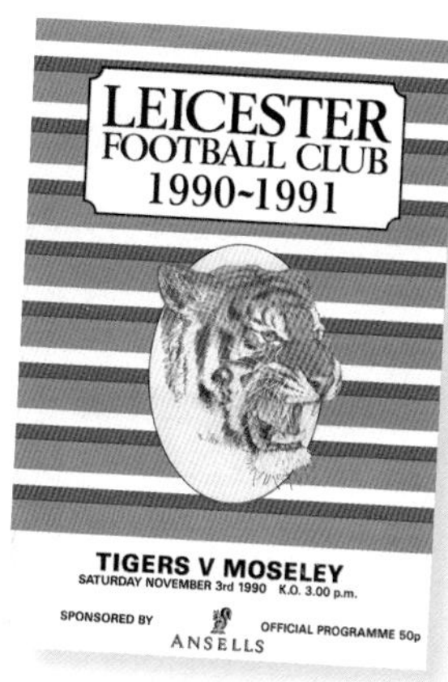

LEICESTER
FOOTBALL CLUB
1990-1991
TIGERS V MOSELEY
SATURDAY NOVEMBER 3rd 1990 K.O. 3.00 p.m.
SPONSORED BY
ANSELLS
OFFICIAL PROGRAMME 50p

1990/1991

Back in Leicester the club pondered how best to replace Cusworth, knowing that this was likely to be Paul Dodge's last season. The national divisions of the Courage league had been extended from 12 to 13 clubs and the introduction of the Heineken League in Wales meant considerable adjustment to the fixture list, including the loss of the prized game with Llanelli. At least Richards was fit again to take over the reins of captaincy and the fly-half problem appeared solved when Brian Smith, the talented Australian studying at Oxford University, joined the club: Smith, already capped by the Wallabies, played international rugby in every position behind the scrum. Not everyone approved when he was selected for Ireland and even fewer did when, near the end of the season, he chose to accept a rugby league offer with the Sydney club, Balmain Tigers (he is now head coach at London Irish).

Jez Harris had entertained reasonable hopes of replacing Cusworth but Smith's arrival altered the perspective. Amid a clutch of other newcomers one stood out: Neil Back, who arrived from Barkers' Butts via Nottingham with a reputation as one of the fittest flankers in the country. Back seemed destined for the game's top honours: with his distinctive lock

of floppy blond hair, his irrepressible energy and ball-handling skills, he seemed made for the style of play which was traditionally Leicester's.

In fact, while the Underwoods and Richards played for an England XV in a game designed to celebrate the centenary season of the Barbarians, Back emerged as a replacement for Karl Janik in the Baa-baas back row and almost stole the show in an 18-16 England win. Leicester, for their part, enjoyed a cosmopolitan start to the season with a match against the touring Romanian national side: ten years earlier they had suffered a rude shock at the hands of the Romanians but this time, though their forwards found themselves struggling, Leicester emerged with a slightly fortuitous 15-12 win thanks to four penalties and a dropped goal by Liley.

Nonetheless the league campaign opened well: Back claimed the headlines as Gloucester were beaten and then Wasps, the 1990 champions, fell 22-12 on their own patch. Victory over Nottingham made it three out of three until Leicester tripped over at the unlikely venue of Roehampton: Rosslyn Park ran up a 17-6 lead and had the strength to hold off a late rally which left Leicester 17-15 losers.

The representative honours were returning too: Argentina, having drawn their series 1-1 with England in the summer, now came for the "return" and lost to an Ireland side containing Smith only to an injury-time penalty. A week later their limitations were underscored by England, who won 51-0, Rory Underwood scoring three tries and Richards returning at No 8. It was a heavy international weekend, for Liley and Evans played in an England B XV which beat Namibia 31-16 at Welford Road (Liley kicking five penalties and two conversions) and, two days later, a different B XV drew 12-12 with an Emerging Australians team at Wasps. Tony Underwood, now at Cambridge University, played on the wing and Back at flanker: "We'd have won if it hadn't been for the little blond guy," Peter Slattery, the Australian captain, said admiringly.

But not even "the little blond guy" could stop Bath in the league: 9-3, all penalties, may not sound the most entertaining of matches as Bath's forwards took a grip on a compelling game which was never relaxed. It would have been a bold man who predicted that, a week later in the Pilkington Cup (a restructuring process of the competition had moved the entry of the first-division clubs in the third round to a pre-Christmas date) at the Bath Recreation Ground, that result would be reversed.

Yet it was, and without Back. A bizarre training accident left him with a back strain while neither of the first-choice wings nor Gissing at lock was available: yet on a filthy day Leicester had the character to put the league result to the back of their minds and remove the holders from the cup competition 12-0. Back's replacement, Rob Tebbutt, played an utterly inspired game and Martin Johnson showed how much his experience in New Zealand had advanced his play in a game which precipitated him into the divisional team; it was the first cup tie Bath had lost at home since 1982. Brian Smith scored the try from a kick-and-chase, and Liley kicked the goals, and Richards was aptly described by Stuart Barnes as not merely a mountain but an entire Himalayan range.

Four other Leicester players joined Johnson in the Midlands team but, sadly, the young lock missed the second half of the season with the recurrence of a shoulder injury. It came as no surprise that the Barbarians match was sold out well in advance, reflecting a membership now just short of 7,000; the league match with Bath had drawn over 11,000 and at Christmas, with temporary seating at the Welford Road end, 17,500 people were able to watch Leicester (led on the day by Rory Underwood in the absence through injury of Richards) lose 26-21. But there were no post-Christmas blues: when the league resumed in the new year Leicester went to resurgent Northampton and mauled them 28-18, Rory Underwood scoring three tries of which the last was an utter gem, indicative of the confidence and skill with which the England wing was now playing.

Not only Underwood: Kardooni, at scrum-half, had accepted the increased responsibility bequeathed by the retiring Cusworth and was able to carry his team forward with or without the assistance of Smith. The development of young forwards like Johnson and Gissing provoked debate over a new "golden era" for the club, which was promptly squashed when Wasps arrived at Welford Road in the cup and departed with a 15-13 victory. Although Tony Underwood scored the only try of the game, Rob Andrew kicked five penalties, the fifth after a controversial decision against the Leicester front row for dropping the scrum - and also after a delay of ten minutes while a spectator in the crowd received treatment after he had collapsed.

Coinciding with news of the death at the age of 71 of the former Leicester and England prop, Bob Stirling, it made a gloomy weekend for the club. There was some comfort in that Liley and Back were

↑ Neil Back arrived from Nottingham and made an immediate impact.

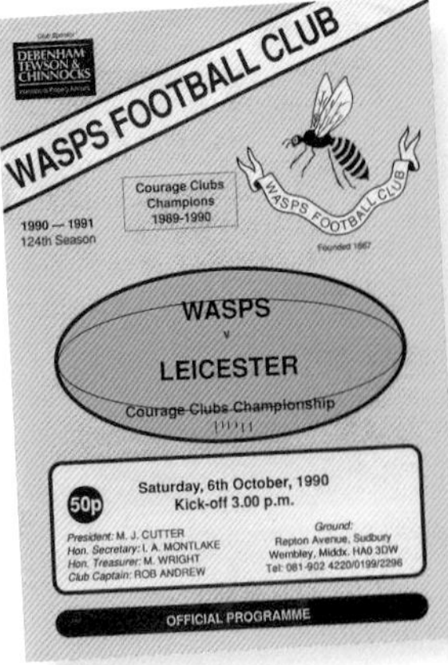

↑ Wasps were beaten 22-12 at Sudbury in the league.

regulars for England B for much of the season and that England, with Rory Underwood and Richards to the fore, should be progressing towards a grand slam. Given the rock of Simon Hodgkinson's place kicking, England disposed of Wales and Scotland but needed all the steadying influence of Richards and a quite brilliantly taken try by Underwood to beat the fighting Irish in Dublin. The outcome rested on the final match with the other unbeaten country, France, and to the unrivalled joy of players, management and supporters, England won 21-19. The French scored three tries, one of them from their own goal-line qualifying as the try of this or any other tournament, but England offered traditional qualities of organisation and determination, embellished by Hodgkinson's goal-kicking and another try by Underwood.

Leicester still hoped for an impact on the Courage league but narrow defeats against Bristol and Harlequins terminated such optimism; in between those games they also lost Smith to rugby league amid a shower of recrimination from Ireland, who had hoped to build their World Cup back division around him. Smith's time at Welford Road had been brief; quite unlike Paul Dodge who played his 436th and what was intended to be his final game for the club in a 43-19 victory at Moseley, alongside old friends in Ian Smith and Malcolm Foulkes-Arnold who were also retiring.

↑ Paul Dodge called it a day after 437 first-team games in an 18-year playing career.

At 33 Dodge had been afflicted by a variety of injuries over the previous three years, perhaps the body's way of reminding him that he had been playing first-class rugby since he was 17 and that it was time for a rest. Chalkie White called him "Colossus". Peter Wheeler, recalling his own disappointment when he was omitted from the 1983 Lions, described how he went down to training at Leicester after the fateful announcement and found Dodge - whose disappointment at his treatment must have equalled Wheeler's - there before him, as industrious as ever: "He was 25, at the peak of his career," Wheeler said. "The tour would have been just right for him. He deserved to go far more than I because he was so far ahead of the rivals for his position in terms of ability, compared with my own situation. He was training faithfully: Mr Reliable."

It is not exaggerating to say that, at his peak, Dodge could do it all: that he scored his 93rd try in his final match speaks volumes for his ability as a strike force in the centre but it was the service he gave his wings that marked him out. If he became known in representative circles for the length of his left-footed kicking, that is not how his club colleagues saw him. His timing of the pass, his tackling and midfield organisation stamped him as a player of uncommon class. But as well as being a quality player he was a thoroughly likeable man, self-effacing but always willing to go the extra mile.

↑ LEICESTER FOOTBALL CLUB 1989/90
Back: Allen (Hon.Sec), Farrands (Hon.Tres), Small (President), Bates, Tebbutt, Marriott, T.Smith, Gissing, Poole, Wells, Povoas, W.Richardson, Redfern, Matthews (Coach), Foster (Coach), Thomas (Team Hon.Sec).
Middle: Buttimore, Harris, Kardooni, Kenney, T.Underwood, Richards (capt), Cusworth, Evans, I.Smith, R.Underwood.
Front: Gerald, Liley.

↑ LEICESTER FOOTBALL CLUB 1990/91
Back: Allen (Hon.Sec), Small (President), Redfern, Richardson, Poole, T.Smith, Wells, Rowntree, Marriott, Thomas (Team Hon.Sec), Matthews (Coach), Russ (Director of coaching).
Middle: Sandford, Tressler, Harris, Wills, Richards (capt), Key, Dodge, Back, R.Underwood, Bates.
Front: Kardooni, T.Underwood.

1989	AMERICAN TOUR	OVERALL RECORD:					T	C	PG	DG	PTS
	Coaches: David Matthews with Allen Foster	PLD	W	D	L	Tigers scored:	18	11	3	1	106
	Captain: Paul Dodge	3	2	0	1	Opponents scored:	1	0	4	1	43

GM	DATE		VEN	OPPONENTS	RESULT	TRIES	KICKS
1	Aug	13s	a	Vail	W 48-3	Liley(3), Grant(3), Gerald(2), Richardson(2)	Liley 2c, Harris 2c
2		17th	a	Denver Barbarians	W 46-16	MacDonald(3), Bates, Foulkes-Arnold, Povoas, Tressler	Harris 6c/p, Cusworth d
3		20s	a	United States	L 12-24	Gerald	Liley c/2p

Leicester Football Club
American Tour 1989
Vail and Denver-Colorado-USA
11 to 22 August 1989

INDIVIDUAL APPEARANCES 1989 AMERICAN TOUR

Name / Game #	1	2	3	Apps	T	Pts
I (Ian) Bates	-	M	L	2	1	4
L (Les) Cusworth E12	-	J*	J	2	-	3
PW (Paul) Dodge E32 L2	L*	r	M*	2+1	-	-
MV (Malcolm) Foulkes-Arnold	-	E	D	2	1	4
CE (Claude) Gerald	K	-	N	2	3	12
MR (Mark) Grant	G	-	-	1	3	12
JC (Jez) Harris	J	O	K	3	-	19
A (Aadel) Kardooni	I	-	I	2	-	-
S (Steve) Kenney	-	I	-	1	-	-
AM (Andy) Key	-	K	-	1	-	-
D (Dave) Kitching	A	C	-	2	-	-
JG (John) Liley	O	-	O	2	3	24
KP (Kevin) MacDonald	N	N	-	2	3	12
AN (Adey) Marriott	-	H	r	1+1	-	-
MD (Matt) Poole	D	D	-	2	-	-
SJ (Simon) Povoas	-	G	G	2	1	4
SB (Stuart) Redfern	-	A	A	2	-	-
L (Lee) Richardson	C	-	C	2	2	8
IR (Ian) Smith	H	-	H	2	-	-
T (Tom) Smith	E	-	E	2	-	-
TA (Troy) Thacker	B	-	B	2	-	-
CJ (Chris) Tressler	-	B	-	1	1	4
AM (Alan) Warwood	M	L	-	2	-	-
JM (John) Wells	F	F	F	3	-	-

19 89/90

Home Ground: Welford Road							T	C	PG	DG	PTS
Coaches: David Matthews with Allen Foster	OVERALL RECORD:										
Captain: Dean Richards then Les Cusworth in September	PLD	W	D	L		Tigers scored:	172	101	67	6	1109
	37	28	0	9		Opponents scored:	60	33	52	6	480

GM	DATE		VEN	OPPONENTS	RESULT	POS/LGE	TRIES	KICKS	ATT
COURAGE LEAGUE DIVISION 1 (5TH)						**CHAMPIONS: WASPS**			
2	Sep	9	a	Wasps	L 12-29	10	Kardooni 71	Liley c/2p	-
4		**23**	**H**	**Bedford**	W 60-3	5	Liley 4/35/80, R.Underwood 9/50, I.Smith 12, T.Underwood 56, Povoas 61, Wells 67/75, Bates 80	Liley 5c/p, Cusworth d	4336
7	Oct	14	a	Orrell	L 10-33	8	T.Underwood 20	Harris d, Liley p	-
9		**28**	**H**	**Nottingham**	W 15-6	7	Penalty 56, Redfern 72	Liley 2c/p	6290
12	Nov	**11**	**H**	**Saracens**	W 34-6	5	T.Underwood 23, Thacker 48, Liley 55/78, Povoas 63, R.Underwood 71	Liley 2c/2p	4968
13		18	a	Rosslyn Park	W 23-9	4	Sandford 23/29, Povoas 63, Evans 67/74	Liley p	-
14		25	a	Harlequins	L 12-15	6	-	Liley 4p	-
21	Jan	**13**	**H**	**Gloucester**	L 16-26	6	R.Underwood 78	Liley 4p	8203
30	Mar	10	a	Bristol	W 13-11	6	Bates 1, Evans 34	Liley c/p	-
33		**31**	**H**	**Moseley**	W 38-20	5	Gerald 27/31/75, Liley 45, Kardooni 54/80	Liley 4c/2p	4320
37	Apr	28	a	Bath	L 15-26	5	Liley 46	Liley c/3p	-
RFU CLUB COMPETITION (PILKINGTON CUP)						**CUP WINNERS: BATH**			
23	Jan	27	a	London Welsh (3)	W 43-3	D3	Povoas 11/17/24, Cusworth 32/80, Wells 71/76	Liley 6c/p	-
24	Feb	**10**	**H**	**West Hartlepool (4)**	W 43-15	D3	R.Underwood 4, Gissing 30, Povoas 60, Thacker 68, Liley 78/80	Liley 5c/3p	5802
27		24	a	Northampton (qf)	L 7-23	D2	Evans 80	Liley p	-
CLUB MATCHES									
1	Sep	**2**	**H**	**Pontypridd**	W 41-18		Liley 37/75, T.Underwood 55, Dodge 62	Liley 2c/5p, Cusworth 2d	4431
3		**16**	**H**	**Northampton**	W 34-12		Gerald 10, Povoas 35, Sandford 58, Poole 73	Liley 3c/4p	4389
5		30	a	Llanelli	L 18-27		R.Underwood(2), Povoas	Liley 3c	-
6	Oct	**7**	**H**	**Coventry**	W 35-6		R.Underwood 34, Liley 65, Povoas 71, Bates 80	Liley 2c/5p	4566
8		24tu	a	Oxford University	W 30-15		Povoas(2), Cusworth, Evans, Tebbutt	Liley 2c/2p	-
10	Nov	**3f**	**H**	**Cardiff**	W 23-15		Evans 9, Bates 30, I.Smith 55, Kardooni 74	Liley 2c/p	4877
11		**7tu**	**H**	**Cambridge University**	W 27-9		Povoas 46, Thacker 58, Redfern 72	Harris 3c/3p	2566
15	Dec	2	a	Gloucester	L 13-19		Sandford(2)	Key c/p	-
16		9	a	Blackheath	W 22-10		Gerald(2), MacDonald, Povoas	Key 3c	-
17		**16**	**H**	**Richmond**	W 44-12		Sandford(2), MacDonald, Marriott, Poole, Povoas, Redfern, I.Smith	Liley 3c/2p	3504
18		**27w**	**H**	**Barbarians**	W 32-16		R.Underwood 6/58, I.Smith 34, Evans 46, Kenney 68	Liley 3c/2p	17200
19		**30**	**H**	**Nuneaton**	W 26-19		Liley 23, Povoas 38/74, Gerald 79	Liley 2c/2p	3222
20	Jan	6	a	Headingley	W 21-12		Povoas 24, Gissing 56	Liley 2c/2p, Cusworth d	-
22		19f	a	Bedford	W 54-0		Gerald(3), Povoas(2), Evans, Gissing, Kenney, W.Richardson	Liley 9c	-
	Feb	3	a	Northampton	PP (rain)				
25		**13tu**	**H**	**Royal Air Force**	W 70-4		Evans 1/21/29/42/45, Kardooni 10/51/78, Harris 15/25/58, Key 55/74, Gissing 62, Buttimore 70	Harris 2c, Buttimore c, Cusworth 2c	1836
26		16f	a	Moseley	W 16-6		Poole	Liley 3p, Cusworth d	-
		24	**H**	**London Welsh**	PP (cup)				
28	Mar	3	a	Rugby	W 35-4		Kardooni(2), Buttimore, Cusworth, Evans, Poole	Liley 4c/p	-
29		**6tu**	**H**	**Loughborough Students**	W 34-3		Tebbutt 10, Evans 36/74, Thacker 65, Liley 70	Liley 4c/2p	1742
31		16f	a	Nottingham	L 0-10		-	-	-
32		**24**	**H**	**Sale**	W 28-9		Kardooni 10, Buttimore 80, Povoas 80	Liley 2c/4p	3060
34	Apr	**7**	**H**	**London Scottish**	W 66-12		Hopper 14, Povoas 17/42, R.Underwood 24/49/55/70/80, Gerald 45/57/68, Liley 65, Buttimore 77	Liley 7c	3004
35		14	a	Ballymena	W 48-10		Liley(2), Kardooni(2), Sandford(2), Gerald, Key, Tebbutt	Liley 6c	-
36		**21**	**H**	**Gosforth**	W 51-7		Evans 3, Povoas 25/76, Liley 29, Gerald 38, Bates 40, Kardooni 49/61, Cusworth 78	Liley 6c/p	4417

INDIVIDUAL APPEARANCES 1989/90

Name / Game #	1	2	3	4	5	6	7	8	9	10	11	12	13	14	15	16	17	18	19	20	21	22	23	24	25	26	27	28	29	30	31	32	33	34	35	36	37	Apps	T	Pts
JM (Jason) Aldwinckle	-	-	-	-	-	-	-	>r	-	-	-	-	-	-	-	-	-	-	-	-	-	-	-	-	-	-	-	-	-	-	B	B	-	-	-	-	-	2+1	-	-
I (Ian) Bates	L	L	L	L	L	L	L	-	L	L	L	L	L	L	-	-	-	L	L	L	L	L	L	L	-	L	L	L	L	L	L	L	L	L	-	L	L	31	5	20
TJ (Tim) Buttimore	-	-	-	-	-	-	-	-	-	-	-	-	-	M	M	-	-	M	M	M	M	M	M	M	M	M	M	M	M	M	M	M	-	M	-	M	M	20	4	18
MJ (Mark) Cleaver	-	-	-	-	-	-	-	-	-	-	-	-	-	-	r	-	r	-	-	-	-	-	-	-	-	-	-	-	-	-	-	x	-	-	-	x	-	0+2	-	-
L (Les) Cusworth E12	J	J	J*	J*	J*	x	-	J*	J*	J*	J*	J*	J*	J*	J*	J*	J*	J*	-	J*	J*	J*	J*	J*	J*	J*	J*	J*	-	J*	J*	J*	J*	J*	J*	J*	<J*	33	5	39
PW (Paul) Dodge E32 L2	M	M	-	M	-	-	M	M	M	M	-	M	M	-	-	-	-	-	-	-	-	-	-	-	-	-	-	-	-	-	-	-	-	-	-	-	-	9	1	4
BJ (Barry) Evans E2	N	-	-	-	-	-	-	N	N	N	N	-	N	N	-	-	-	N	-	N	N	N	N	N	N	N	N	N	N	N	-	N	-	-	-	N	-	21	17	68
MV (Malcolm) Foulkes-Arnold	D	D	D	D	-	D	-	-	-	-	-	-	-	-	-	-	-	-	-	-	-	-	-	-	-	-	-	-	-	-	-	-	-	-	-	-	-	5	-	-
CE (Claude) Gerald	-	-	N	-	x	-	-	-	-	-	-	-	-	-	N	N	N	-	N	-	-	K	-	-	-	K	-	-	K	-	N	K	N	N	N	K	<N	15	15	60
AJS (Alex) Gissing	-	-	-	-	D	-	D	D	D	D	D	D	D	D	D	D	D	D	-	D	D	D	D	D	D	D	D	-	-	-	-	-	-	-	-	-	D	22	4	16
MR (Mark) Grant	r	-	-	-	-	-	-	-	-	-	-	-	r	-	-	-	-	-	-	-	-	-	-	-	G	-	-	-	G	-	-	D	D	D	D	D	G	8+2	-	-
PJ (Paul) Grant	-	-	-	-	-	-	-	-	-	-	-	-	-	-	-	-	-	-	-	-	-	-	-	-	-	-	-	-	-	-	-	-	-	-	-	>r	-	0+1	-	-
JC (Jez) Harris	-	x	M	-	-	J	J	-	-	-	O	x	-	-	O	-	-	-	x	-	-	-	x	x	O	-	x	-	J	-	-	-	-	-	x	-	-	7	3	34
DA (Dave) Hopper	-	-	-	-	-	-	-	-	-	-	-	-	-	-	-	-	-	-	-	-	-	-	-	-	C	-	-	C	C	C	C	-	-	C	-	-	-	6	1	4
A (Aadel) Kardooni	I	I	I	I	I	I	I	I	I	I	-	-	-	-	-	-	-	-	-	-	-	-	-	-	I	-	-	I	I	-	I	I	I	I	I	I	I	20	14	56
S (Steve) Kenney	-	-	-	-	-	-	-	-	-	-	I	I	I	I	I	I	I	I	I*	I	I	I	I	I	-	I	I	-	-	<I	-	-	-	-	-	-	-	17	2	8
AM (Andy) Key	-	-	-	-	-	-	-	-	-	-	-	-	-	-	L	O	L	r	-	x	-	-	-	-	K	-	-	-	-	-	r	-	-	x	M	-	-	5+2	3	23
D (Dave) Kitching	-	-	-	-	-	-	-	-	x	-	-	-	-	-	-	-	-	-	A	-	A	<A	-	-	-	-	-	-	-	-	-	-	-	-	-	-	-	3	-	-
JG (John) Liley	O	O	O	O	O	O	O	O	O	O	-	O	O	O	-	-	O	O	O	O	O	O	O	O	-	O	O	O	O	O	O	O	O	O	O	O	O	33	18	439
KP (Kevin) MacDonald	-	-	-	r	M	-	-	x	-	x	-	-	-	x	-	L	M	-	J	-	-	-	-	-	x	-	-	-	-	x	-	-	-	-	-	-	-	4+1	2	8
AN (Adey) Marriott	-	-	-	r	F	F	-	-	-	-	-	-	-	x	F	F	F	x	H	-	-	-	x	x	-	F	x	-	-	F	F	-	-	F	-	-	-	10+1	1	4
J (John) Murphy	-	-	-	-	-	-	-	-	-	-	-	-	-	-	-	-	x	-	-	-	x	x	-	-	x	-	-	-	F	x	-	-	-	-	-	-	-	1	-	-
MD (Matt) Poole	-	-	E	-	-	-	-	E	-	-	E	-	-	E	-	E	E	-	D	E	E	E	E	E	E	E	E	D	D	D	D	E	E	E	E	E	-	24	4	16
SJ (Simon) Povoas	-	r	G	G	G	G	G	G	G	G	G	G	G	G	G	G	G	G	G	G	G	G	G	G	-	G	G	G	-	G	G	G	G	G	G	G	F	33+1	25	100
SB (Stuart) Redfern	A	A	A	A	A	A	A	A	A	A	A	A	A	A	A	A	A	A	-	A	-	-	A	A	A	A	A	A	A	A	A	A	A	A	A	A	A	34	3	12
D (Dean) Richards E20 L3	G*	G*	-	-	-	-	-	-	-	-	-	-	-	-	-	-	-	-	-	-	-	-	-	-	-	-	-	-	-	-	-	-	-	-	-	-	-	2	-	-
L (Lee) Richardson	-	-	-	-	-	-	-	-	-	-	C	-	-	-	-	x	-	-	-	<C	-	-	-	-	-	x	-	-	-	-	-	-	-	-	-	-	-	2	-	-
WP (Wayne) Richardson	C	C	C	C	C	C	C	C	C	C	-	C	C	C	C	C	C	C	C	-	C	C	C	C	-	C	C	-	-	-	-	C	C	-	C	C	C	29	1	4
H (Harry) Roberts	B	B	B	B	B	B	B	-	-	-	-	-	-	-	-	-	-	-	-	-	-	-	-	-	-	-	-	-	-	-	-	-	-	-	-	-	-	7	-	-
P (Peter) Sandford	-	-	>K	-	-	-	-	-	-	-	x	-	K	K	K	K	K	-	K	K	-	-	-	-	-	-	-	-	-	-	-	-	K	-	K	-	-	10	9	36
IR (Ian) Smith	H	H	H	H	H	H*	H*	H	H	H	-	H	H	-	H	-	H	H	-	H	H	H	H	H	-	H	H	-	-	H	H	-	r	-	x	-	-	24+1	4	16
T (Tom) Smith	E	E	-	E	E	E	E	-	E	E	-	E	E	-	E	-	-	E	E	-	-	-	-	-	-	-	-	E	E	E	E	-	-	-	-	-	E	18	-	-
RS (Rob) Tebbutt	-	-	-	-	x	-	-	F	-	-	H	x	-	H	-	H	-	-	-	-	-	-	-	-	H	-	-	H	H	-	x	H	H	H	H	H	H	13	3	12
TA (Troy) Thacker	-	x	-	-	-	-	x	B	B	B	B	B	B	B	-	-	-	B	B	B	B	B	B	B	B	B	B	B	B*	B	-	-	-	-	-	-	-	20	4	16
CJ (Chris) Tressler	x	-	-	-	-	-	-	-	-	-	-	-	-	-	B	B	B	-	-	-	-	-	-	-	-	-	-	-	-	-	-	-	B	B	B	B	B	8	-	-
R (Rory) Underwood E38 L3	-	K	-	K	K	K	K	-	K	-	-	K	-	-	-	-	-	K	-	-	K	-	K	K	-	-	K	-	-	K	-	-	-	K	-	-	K	15	15	60
T (Tony) Underwood E+ L+	K	N	-	N	N	N	N	K	-	K	K	N	-	-	-	-	-	-	-	-	-	-	-	-	-	-	-	K	-	-	K	-	-	-	-	-	-	12	4	16
AM (Alan) Warwood	-	-	-	-	-	M	x	L	-	-	M	-	-	-	-	M	-	-	-	-	-	x	-	-	L	-	-	-	-	-	-	-	M	-	L	-	x	7	-	-
JM (John) Wells	F	F	F	F	-	-	F	-	F	F	F	F	F	F	-	-	-	F	F	F	F	F	F	F	F	-	F	F	-	-	-	F	F	-	F	F	-	25	4	16
DE (Dorian) West E+	-	-	x	-	-	-	-	-	-	-	x	-	-	-	r	-	-	-	-	r	-	-	-	-	-	-	-	-	-	-	-	x	-	-	-	-	-	0+2	-	-
SR (Steve) Wills	-	-	-	-	-	-	-	-	-	-	-	-	-	-	-	-	-	-	-	-	-	-	-	-	-	x	-	-	>r	-	-	-	x	-	-	-	-	0+1	-	-

The key for how to read the stats is on the last page

19 90/91	
Home Ground: Welford Road	
Head Coach: Tony Russ assisted by David Matthews	
Captain: Dean Richards	

OVERALL RECORD:						T	C	PG	DG	PTS
PLD	W	D	L		Tigers scored:	130	74	79	7	926
37	28	0	9		Opponents scored:	43	26	59	11	434

GM	DATE		VEN	OPPONENTS	RESULT	POS/LGE	TRIES	KICKS	ATT
COURAGE LEAGUE DIVISION 1 (4TH)						**CHAMPIONS: BATH**			
5	Sep	22	H	**Gloucester**	W 18-6	3	Richards 75	Liley c/4p	6323
6	Oct	6	a	Wasps	W 22-12	1	T.Smith 40, Gissing 80	Liley c/4p	-
7		13	H	**Nottingham**	W 25-9	1	B.Smith 23, Key 55	B.Smith d, Liley c/4p	7019
8		20	a	Rosslyn Park	L 15-17	3	Wills 35, Bates 76	Liley 2c/p	-
10		27	H	**Saracens**	W 29-6	3	R.Underwood 16, Wright 48, Dodge 59, Wells 67, Sandford 75	Liley 3c/p	5747
13	Nov	10	a	Liverpool St Helens	W 28-7	2	R.Underwood 30, Richards 35, Sandford 53, Liley 79	Liley 3c/2p	800
14		17	H	**Bath**	L 3-9	3	-	Liley p	12758
22	Jan	12	a	Northampton	W 28-18	2	Liley 2, R.Underwood 10/37/52, Bates 13	Liley c/p, B.Smith d	-
	Feb	9	H	**Orrell**	PP (snow)	-			
29	Mar	9	a	Bristol	L 6-10	3	-	Liley p, B.Smith d	-
31		23	H	**Harlequins**	L 12-15	4	-	Liley 3p, Harris d	6248
36	Apr	20	H	**Orrell**	W 15-12	5	Richards 22	Harris c/3p	5271
37		27	a	Moseley	W 43-19	4	R.Underwood 18/48/58, Wells 50, Dodge 66, T.Underwood 68/72	Liley 6c, Harris d	-
RFU CLUB COMPETITION (PILKINGTON CUP)						**CUP WINNERS: HARLEQUINS**			
15	Nov	24	a	Bath (3)	W 12-0	D1	B.Smith 38	Liley c/2p	-
24	Jan	26	H	**Wasps (4)**	L 13-15	D1	T.Underwood 47	Liley 3p	11155
CLUB MATCHES									
1	Sep	1	H	**Bedford**	W 57-6		B.Smith 10, R.Underwood 30/43, Bates 37/66, Liley 39, Richards 58, T.Underwood 71/74, Back 77	Liley 7c/p	4319
2		4tu	H	**Romania**	W 15-12		-	Liley 4p/d	4811
3		8	a	Cardiff	L 9-35		Wells	Liley c/p	-
4		15	H	**Northampton**	W 26-3		T.Smith 66, Bates 75	Liley 6p	5312
9	Oct	23tu	H	**Oxford University**	W 23-22		Cleaver(2), Sandford	Wills c/3p	2373
11	Nov	3	H	**Moseley**	L 10-16		Wright 80	Harris 2p	3182
12		6tu	a	Cambridge University	W 22-10		Dodge(Penalty), Marriott	Liley c/4p	-
16	Dec	1	a	Gloucester	L 15-18		Gissing, Sandford, T.Smith	Harris p	-
		8	H	**Blackheath**	PP (snow)				
17		15	H	**Bristol**	W 26-3		Gissing, Key, Sandford, Penalty	Harris 2c/2p	3852
18		22	a	Coventry	W 27-3		Liley(2), Buttimore, R.Underwood, T.Underwood	Liley 2c/p	-
19		27th	H	**Barbarians**	L 21-26		R.Underwood, T.Underwood	Liley 2c/3p	16877
20		29	a	Nuneaton	W 32-6		Bates, Dodge, Gissing, Sandford, T.Underwood	Liley 3c/p, Harris d	-
21	Jan	5	H	**Headingley**	W 29-6		Grant(2), B.Smith, Gissing, Wills	B.Smith 3c/p	3212
23		18f	a	Bedford	W 41-7		Harris, Bates, Gissing, Grant, Hamilton, Key, T.Smith	Harris 5c/p	-
25	Feb	2	H	**Wakefield**	W 17-8		Back, McAdam	Harris 3p	2260
		16	H	**Rugby Lions**	PP (snow)				
26		23	a	London Welsh	W 59-3		Liley(2), T.Smith(2), T.Underwood(2), Bates, Dodge, Richards, Tressler, R.Underwood	B.Smith 6c/p	-
27	Mar	2	a	Richmond	W 40-18		Povoas(2), Bates, Gissing, Key, Tebbutt, Wills	Harris 3c/2p	-
28		5tu	H	**Loughborough Students**	W 57-13		Kardooni(2), Liley, Gissing, Richards, Sandford, T.Smith, Tressler, S.Wigley, Penalty	Liley 7c/p	1641
30		16	a	Nottingham	W 13-12		Cleaver	Liley 3p	-
32		30	H	**Coventry**	W 15-12		Harris, Kardooni, Rowntree	Liley p	3309
		30	H	**Swansea**	PP (league)				
33	Apr	1m	H	**Wasps**	W 39-18		Back, Dodge, Kardooni, Wills	Harris 4c/5p	4736
34		6	a	Saracens	W 10-6		R.Underwood, T.Underwood	Liley c	-
		6	a	London Scottish	PP (league)				
35		13	H	**London Irish**	W 54-16		Sandford(2), Back, Grant, Kardooni, Rowntree, T.Underwood, Wells, Penalty	Harris 6c/2p	3974
		20	a	Newcastle Gosforth	PP (league)				

INDIVIDUAL APPEARANCES 1990/91

Name / Game #	1	2	3	4	5	6	7	8	9	10	11	12	13	14	15	16	17	18	19	20	21	22	23	24	25	26	27	28	29	30	31	32	33	34	35	36	37	Apps	T	Pts
NA (Neil) Back E+ L+	>H	H	-	H	H	H	H	H	-	H	-	-	-	H	-	-	-	H	H	H	H	H	-	H	H	H	-	-	-	-	-	-	H	H	H	H	H	22	4	16
MSJP (Matt) Barkes	-	x	-	-	-	-	-	-	-	-	-	-	-	-	-	-	-	-	-	-	-	-	-	-	>B	-	-	-	-	-	-	B	-	-	-	-	-	2	-	-
I (Ian) Bates	M	-	M	L	L	M	M	M	-	M	M	M	-	M	M	-	-	M	M	M	M	M	M	M	M	L	M	-	L	-	M	-	-	-	M	M	M	27	9	36
PG (Paul) Brookes	-	-	-	-	-	-	-	-	<A	-	-	-	-	-	-	-	-	-	-	-	-	-	-	-	-	-	-	-	-	-	-	-	-	-	-	-	-	1	-	-
TJ (Tim) Buttimore	L	L	L	-	x	L	L	-	-	-	-	-	-	-	-	-	-	L	L	x	N	-	-	-	-	-	-	<M	-	-	-	-	-	-	-	-	-	9	1	4
MJ (Mark) Cleaver	-	-	-	-	-	-	-	-	N	-	-	-	-	-	-	-	-	-	-	-	-	-	-	-	-	-	-	x	-	N	x	N	N	-	-	-	-	4	3	12
PW (Paul) Dodge E32 L2	-	M	-	M*	M	-	-	-	M*	L	L*	L	L	L	L	-	M*	-	x	L*	L*	L	L*	L	L*	M	L*	-	M	L*	L	M	M*	M*	L*	L	L	28	6	24
WM (Bill) Drake-Lee	-	-	>r	-	-	-	-	-	H	-	x	H	-	-	-	-	-	-	-	-	x	-	-	-	-	-	-	-	-	-	-	H	r	-	-	-	-	3+2	-	-
BJ (Barry) Evans E2	-	N	N	N	N	N	N	-	-	-	-	-	-	N	-	-	-	-	-	-	-	-	-	-	-	-	N	N	N	-	-	-	-	-	-	-	-	10	-	-
MV (Malcolm) Foulkes-Arnold	-	-	-	-	-	-	-	-	D	-	-	-	-	-	-	-	-	-	-	-	-	-	-	-	x	-	-	-	-	-	-	-	-	-	-	-	D	2	-	-
AJS (Alex) Gissing	-	-	-	D	D	D	D	D	-	D	-	D	-	D	-	D	D	-	D	D	D	D	D	D	-	-	D	D	D	-	-	-	D	-	-	-	-	20	8	32
MR (Mark) Grant	x	-	-	G	-	-	-	-	-	-	G	-	-	-	-	G	G	G	G	G	G	x	G	-	-	-	-	-	-	-	-	x	-	G	G	-	-	11	4	16
JG (Jamie) Hamilton	-	-	-	-	-	-	-	-	-	-	-	-	-	-	-	-	-	-	-	>I	I	-	I	-	-	-	I	-	-	-	-	x	-	-	-	-	I	5	1	4
JC (Jez) Harris	x	J	J	-	J	x	-	-	-	J	J	-	M	x	x	J	J	-	J	J	-	-	J	x	J	-	J	J	-	J	J	J	J	J	J	J	J	22	2	122
PD (Paul) Hilyer	-	-	>B	-	-	-	-	-	-	-	-	-	-	-	-	-	-	-	-	-	-	-	-	-	-	-	-	-	-	-	-	-	-	-	-	-	-	1	-	-
MO (Martin) Johnson E+ L+	-	-	-	-	-	-	-	-	-	-	-	-	-	-	D	-	-	D	-	-	-	-	-	-	D	D	-	-	-	D	-	-	-	-	-	-	-	5	-	-
A (Aadel) Kardooni	I	I	I	I	I	I	I	I	-	-	-	I	I	I	I	I*	I	I	I	-	-	I	-	I	I	I	-	I	I	I	I	I	I	I	I	I	-	29	5	20
AM (Andy) Key	-	x	-	-	-	-	r	L	-	-	N	N	x	-	N	M	L	-	-	-	-	x	N	-	N	-	K	-	x	M	N	L	L	-	-	x	-	13+1	4	16
JG (John) Liley	O	O`	O	O	O	O	O	O	-	O	-	O	O	O	O	-	-	O	O	O	-	O	-	O	-	O	-	O	O	O	O	O	-	O	x	-	O	26	8	280
A (Andy) McAdam	-	-	-	-	-	-	-	-	-	-	-	-	-	-	-	>N	O	-	-	-	-	-	O	-	O	-	-	-	-	-	-	-	-	-	-	-	-	4	1	4
KP (Kevin) MacDonald	-	-	x	-	-	-	-	x	J	-	-	r	-	-	-	L	x	-	-	-	-	-	-	-	x	-	x	-	-	-	-	-	x	<L	-	-	-	3+1	-	-
AN (Adey) Marriott	-	-	-	F	x	x	-	-	F	x	-	F	-	x	x	F	F	F	F	F	F	-	H	-	F	-	-	-	x	-	-	-	-	-	-	r	-	11+1	1	4
MD (Matt) Poole	-	-	-	-	-	-	-	-	E	-	D	E	D	-	-	-	-	-	-	E	-	-	x	-	-	-	-	-	-	-	D	D	E	D	D	D	-	11	-	-
SJ (Simon) Povoas	-	x	G	-	-	-	-	-	G	-	-	-	-	-	-	-	-	-	-	-	-	-	-	-	G	-	G	F	-	G	x	-	G	-	-	-	-	7	2	8
SB (Stuart) Redfern	A	A	A	A	A	A	A	A	-	A	A	A	A	A	A	A	A	A	A	A	A	A	A	A	A	A	A	-	A	A	A	A	A	A	A	A	A	35	-	-
D (Dean) Richards E25 L3	G*	G*	-	-	G*	G*	G*	G*	-	G*	-	G*	G*	G*	G*	-	-	-	-	-	-	G*	-	G*	-	G*	-	G*	G*	-	G*	G*	-	-	-	G*	G*	20	6	24
WP (Wayne) Richardson	C	C	C	C	C	C	C	C	-	C	-	C	C	C	C	C	C	-	C	C	C	-	C	C	C	C	C	-	C	-	-	-	-	C	-	-	-	25	-	-
H (Harry) Roberts	-	-	-	-	-	-	-	-	B	-	-	<B	-	-	-	-	-	-	-	-	-	-	-	-	-	-	-	-	-	-	-	-	-	-	-	-	-	2	-	-
CG (Graham) Rowntree E+ L+	-	-	-	-	-	-	-	-	>C	-	C	-	-	-	-	-	-	C	-	-	-	C	-	-	-	-	-	A	-	C	C	C	C	-	C	C	C	12	2	8
P (Peter) Sandford	-	-	K	-	-	-	-	-	K	N	K	K	N	-	K	K	N	-	-	K	K	-	K	-	K	x	-	K	-	K	-	K	K	x	K	-	-	18	9	36
BA (Brian) Smith A/I15	>J	-	-	J	-	J	J	J	-	-	-	J	J	J	J	-	-	J	-	-	J	J	-	J	-	J	-	-	<J	-	-	-	-	-	-	-	-	15	4	49
IR (Ian) Smith	-	-	-	-	-	-	-	x	-	-	-	r	-	-	-	-	-	-	-	-	-	-	-	-	-	-	-	-	-	-	-	-	-	-	-	-	-	0+1	-	-
T (Tom) Smith	E	E	E	E	E	E	E	E	-	E	E	-	E	E	E	E	E	E	E	-	E	E	E	E	E	E	E	E	E	E	E	E	-	E	E	E	E	33	7	28
RS (Rob) Tebbutt	-	x	H	x	-	-	x	-	x	-	H	-	H	-	H	H	H	-	x	-	-	-	-	-	-	-	H	H	H	H	<H	-	-	-	-	x	-	11	1	4
CJ (Chris) Tressler	B	B	-	B	B	B	B	B	-	B	B	-	B	B	B	B	B	B	B	B	B	B	B	B	-	B	B	B	B	B	B	-	B	B	B	B	B	32	2	8
R (Rory) Underwood E43 L3	K	K	-	-	K	K	K	K	-	K	-	-	K	K	-	-	-	K*	K*	-	-	K	-	K	-	K	-	-	K	-	K	-	-	K	-	K	K	19	14	56
T (Tony) Underwood E+ L+	N	-	-	K	-	-	-	-	-	-	-	-	-	-	-	-	K	N	N	N	-	N	-	N	-	N	-	-	-	-	-	-	-	N	N	N	N	13	12	48
MW (Mark) Upex	>D	D	<D	-	-	-	-	-	-	-	-	-	-	-	-	-	-	-	-	-	-	-	-	-	-	-	-	-	-	-	-	-	-	-	-	-	-	3	-	-
RA (Richard) Wareham	-	x	-	-	-	-	-	-	-	-	-	-	-	-	-	-	-	>r	-	-	-	-	-	-	-	-	-	C	-	x	-	-	-	-	-	-	-	1+1	-	-
JM (John) Wells	F	F	F*	-	F	F	F	F	-	F	F	-	F	F	F	-	-	-	-	-	-	F	F	F	-	F	F	-	F	F	F	F	F	F	F	F	F	26	4	16
ST (Steve) Wigley	-	-	-	-	-	-	-	-	>L	-	-	-	-	-	-	-	-	-	-	-	-	-	x	-	-	-	-	L	-	-	-	-	-	-	-	-	-	2	1	4
SR (Steve) Wills	-	-	-	-	-	-	-	N	O	x	O	-	-	-	-	O	-	-	-	-	O	-	-	-	-	-	O	-	-	-	-	-	O	-	O	O	x	9	4	27
DJ (David) Wright	-	x	-	-	-	-	-	-	>I	I	<I	-	-	-	-	-	-	-	-	-	-	-	-	-	-	-	-	-	-	-	-	-	-	-	-	-	-	3	2	8

The key for how to read the stats is on the last page

CHAPTER 25

World Comes to Leicester

1991/1992

With the retirement of Paul Dodge, the last link with the Leicester of the 1970s and those early cup finals was severed. Yet Leicester had cause to look back to the 70s and their own internal reorganisation, grateful for the foresight of those administrators of an earlier generation, as famous names such as Coventry and London Welsh failed to keep the league pace.

In 1991 Leicester dropped their third team, the Swifts, and replaced it with an under-21 team so as to bridge the gap more effectively between youth and senior rugby. Steve Solomons, a full-back with the club during the 70s, returned from a successful coaching spell with Vipers to help run the under-21s and Dodge had scarcely retired before he was coaxed back to help.

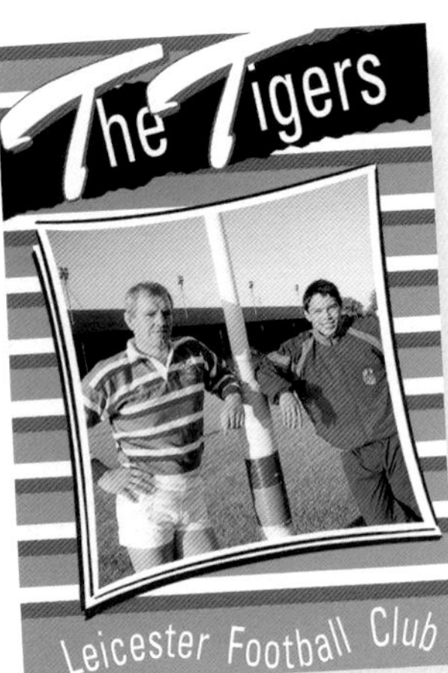

↑ Tigers produced this leaflet in 1991 to try to attract new players to the club.

Then there was the World Cup. Leicester had long known they were to host one of the tournament's pool games, the first full international played at Welford Road since 1923, but the price for clubs up and down the country during the first two months of the new season was a collapse in interest while the spectacle of the World Cup swept the country. A Leicester squad had toured Canada in search of early-season form and youngsters like Graham Rowntree - who had made his debut at prop against Oxford University the previous season - Laurence Boyle and Richard Wareham all found places in the opening match, against Bedford.

England's preparations for the global tournament involved Rory Underwood and Dean Richards, both of whom had toured Australia and Fiji during the summer with the national side. England opened the World Cup by losing to New Zealand at Twickenham and it was the All Blacks who furnished Welford Road with international flavour, playing Italy in pool one of a competition spread throughout the four home unions and France. Nor did they have matters all their own way; they won 31-21 but Italy scored three tries and there were hints that the holders of the Webb Ellis Cup were not at their best.

England progressed to the quarter-finals where, against France in Paris, they sprang a shock of seismic proportions (in Leicester anyway) by dropping Richards. The move worked and, in the semi-final against Scotland, Underwood led the side out at Murrayfield in celebration of his fiftieth cap. For the final against Australia at Twickenham, England chose so conspicuous a reversal of the tactics which had got them there that they lost 12-6. It was impossible not to wonder whether Richards might have exerted a calming influence and proved the focal point of a more direct style of play.

It left the No 8 raring for rugby with his mates and Leicester needed him. Their club form had been unimpressive, the divisional championship proved disruptive even though the Midlands, with half a dozen Leicester representatives, won the title. Five defeats in nine games was not the stuff of champions with coach Ian Smith having to emerge from retirement (not long after a bad car accident) against Sale when Neil Back missed the team bus - and the coach scored a try in the 12-9 defeat.

The Tuesday following the World Cup final, Richards was back, against Cambridge University. Underwood re-appeared in the second league game, a win over Wasps when Jez Harris dropped three goals. Back joined Rory Underwood and Richards in England's squad for the five nations, seven Leicester players were named in an England development squad and Tigers even went to the top of the league table when they beat London Irish.

It was a false dawn: Bath demolished Leicester's pretensions with a 37-6 win, a difficult debut at fly-half for the recent recruit from Orrell, Gerry Ainscough. Even though a new clubhouse addition, the Barbarians Room, was opened for the entertainment of sponsors and as a venue for the club's memorabilia, it seemed unlikely that any new trophies would find their way there. In the league Leicester were consistent only in their inconsistency while in the Pilkington Cup they foundered 15-9 against Harlequins in the semi-final at The Stoop.

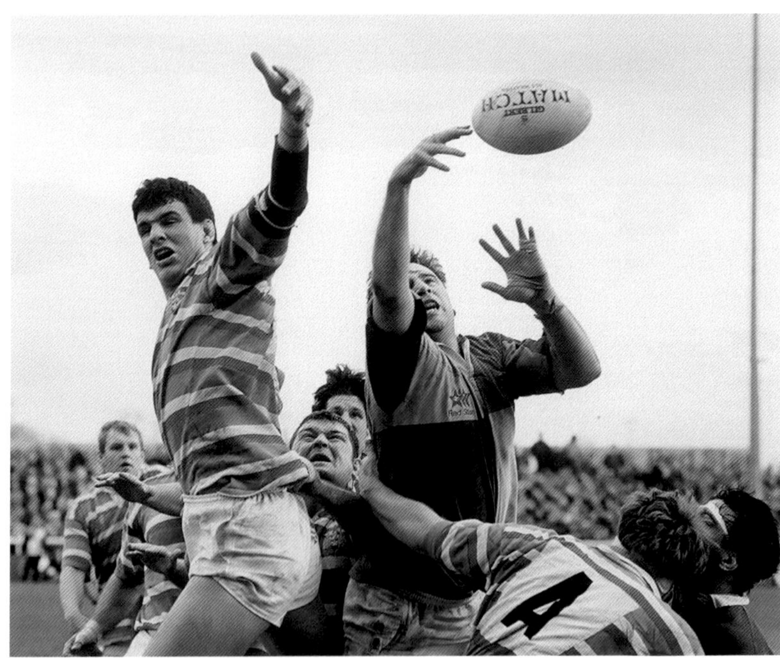

↑ Martin Johnson in aerial combat during the cup semi-final against Harlequins.

Richards had the satisfaction of reclaiming his international place, coming off the bench against Scotland to play a significant role in England's 25-7 win, an occasion marked by Underwood senior's first try against the Scots. England went on to a second successive grand slam, when Rory Underwood announced that he was to retire from international rugby at the age of 28, in the interests of his family and his flying career (a summer off proved sufficient for him to return six months later, appetite renewed).

Meanwhile Leicester sought to conclude their league campaign with a degree of style: they lost a mighty battle with Northampton 22-19 but, four days later, scored 100 points in a match for the first time. The unfortunate victims were Liverpool St Helens, who left Welford Road having conceded 19 tries (which equalled Leicester's record). Tony Underwood scored six tries, failing by one to equal Alastair Smallwood's record of 70 years earlier. But the season's end was so demanding that Wells questioned the place of a two-match Easter programme while two long-serving front-row forwards, Stuart Redfern and Chris Tressler, announced their retirement after 324 and 264 games respectively.

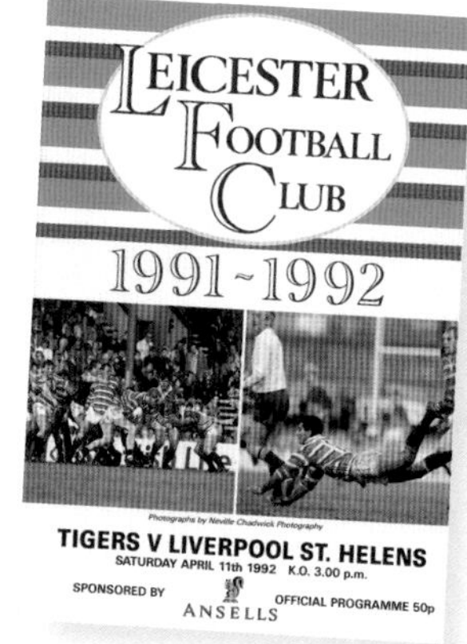

↑ Programme from the record victory over Liverpool St Helens, 11.4.1992.

Not that the season was over for all: Tony Underwood, Neil Back, Steve Hackney and Aadel Kardooni toured New Zealand with an England B squad. All four played in the two games against a New Zealand XV, Underwood junior so well that the *New Zealand Rugby Almanack* elected him one of their five players of the year, a rare honour for one from the northern hemisphere. Rowntree and Steve Wills played for England's under-21 side and Boyle in the Student World Cup in Italy for a side now coached by Les Cusworth.

So many honours for young players was encouraging, as was the form of Leicester's youth side who lost only four games and were a credit to Paul Stone, in his last season as coach before moving to Nuneaton. Despite a mid-season financial hiatus caused by the weather, the club's profit was £109,000 and membership, the biggest in England by a distance, stood at 7,400 and rising; Ansells, the brewers, were happy to renew their sponsorship for a further five years, a deal worth more than £180,000.

↑ Commercial Manager, Roy Jackson.

1992/1993

Change was in the air on a broader scale. New laws, including the introduction of the five-point try, were brought in and the Senior Clubs Association approved a switch in the 1993/94 season to a home-and-away league format. It was not a change with which John Allen, for one, concurred, Leicester having voted for eight-club national divisions as opposed to the ten clubs which was eventually agreed, thereby creating a league season of 18 rather than 14 games.

"You'll have 18 league games and with a good cup run, that becomes 24," Allen said. "Take three divisional matches, five internationals, that's 32. A couple of squad weekends leaves only one spare Saturday. There's no way some of these lads are going to go through the whole season doing that. With these extra six games, clubs are going to have to look very carefully at how they use players."

Leicester had to find a fitting way of celebrating 100 years of rugby at Welford Road. They decided to host a morning of rugby for youngsters on the same day that they played an England XV. This would be followed by a midweek meeting with Leicestershire, commemorating the match against the county in 1892, and concluded with a glamorous encounter against Mediolanum Amatori Milan, the Italian club to which those two remarkable Australian players, David Campese and Mark Ella, belonged.

It seemed that Leicester themselves stood on the edge of a fresh era: newcomers included Richard Cockerill, the England under-21 hooker, and two backs from Nottingham, Stuart Potter and Wayne Kilford. A new facility opened at Wigston Road, Oadby, where Leicester had invested over £400,000 in a training ground to relieve the main pitch at Welford Road. Oadby Wyggestonian, the well-known local club, remained there but the clubhouse was extended, floodlighting installed and the pitches regraded at what was renamed Oval Park. The official inauguration came in December with a game between the Droglites, the 'Old Tigers' club, and a Rugby Union Writers' Club XV and in return, the writers were installed on match days in the old weights room under the Crumbie Stand, which was converted into a press working area. At the far end of Welford Road, the Tiger Room was opened in the clubhouse illustrating different phases in the club's development.

With such heavy expenditure, Leicester welcomed a three-year contract with the local insurance and sports marketing firm, P & G Bland, to act as commercial advisors. Roy Jackson, who had done so well as the club's commercial manager on a part-time basis for several seasons, was overwhelmed by the volume of work and professional assistance was needed. That the new advisors had Peter Wheeler as a managing director and included Cusworth, Rowntree and Hackney among their employees kept the appointment within, as it were, the family.

England used the centenary fixture as a warm-up for the autumn internationals against Canada and South Africa but deprived the club of Back and Tony Underwood. Hackney, replacing Underwood on the wing, scored the club's try in an underwhelming 18-11 defeat. John Liley kicked a couple of penalties against two tries for the England XV by Nigel Heslop, a conversion and penalty by Jonathan Webb and a dropped goal by Rob Andrew but one of the main talking points was the display of Leicester's spritely front row of Rowntree, Cockerill and Darren Garforth - better known, later on, as the ABC Club.

Something close to a second XV accounted for Leicestershire 40-20 before the arrival of Milan, without Campese but still packed with Italy and Argentina internationals. This was by far the best game of the celebratory programme, full of vivid passages of play with Leicester winning 40-24 and showing that the new laws could be made to work given better support play. The start of the league programme was different altogether, given the restructuring which would lead to the relegation of four clubs from the first division, seven from the second and eight from the third so as to form a new fourth national division.

↑ Tony Underwood (in red) in flight against West Hartlepool 10.10.1992.

For much of the season it seemed that if you were not in the top four, you were in danger of relegation. Leicester began well enough but though Back returned from a shoulder injury sustained in the England XV game to play against Wasps, his side lost by a single point. A terrific display by Tony Underwood against West Hartlepool helped propel him towards his first England cap, against Canada at Wembley (Twickenham's East Stand was being rebuilt), which also turned out to be the only international of the season for Richards.

England preferred Bath's Ben Clarke at No 8 in a quest for greater speed and height in the back row when the mauling strength of Richards might have suited the new laws better. But the Midlands kept the faith and Richards captained their side against the South Africans at Welford Road on 4 November, the first major Springbok tour since 1981 and the first to Britain since 1969/70, when political demonstrations against apartheid created such disruption. They were short of confidence but still made short work of the Midlands, winning 32-9 against the following XV: John Liley; Steve Hackney, Ian Bates, Stuart Potter (all Leicester), Harvey Thorneycroft; John Steele (both Northampton), Aadel Kardooni (Leicester); Mark Linnett (Moseley), John Olver, Gary Pearce, Martin Bayfield (all Northampton), Martin Johnson (Leicester), Peter Shillingford (Moseley), Dean Richards (Leicester, captain), Rob Tebbutt (Northampton).

The Springboks, aided by the local knowledge of Harry Roberts, now their number-two hooker, scored tries through Faffa Knoetze (two), Danie Gerber and Deon Oosthuysen with Naas Botha, the captain, kicking three conversions and two penalties. All the Midlands could offer were two penalties by Liley (who missed five other attempts) and a dropped goal by Steele. Tony Underwood scored a try against the Springboks for England B at Bristol as the touring side won 20-16 but they received their come-uppance at Twickenham where England won 33-16.

↓ Graham Rowntree celebrates the opening try from Dean Richards in the cup semi-final against Northampton 10.4.1993.

It was the first time since 1938 that England fielded brothers, Rory Underwood on the left wing and Tony on the right, and it was Rory, acting as pivot, who sent Tony away for his first international try. But for both England and Leicester there were hardships ahead: autumnal success did not presage a good five nations and a 13-3 win at Welford Road by Bath indicated another league title for Leicester's closest rivals. Moreover England, when naming a squad for warm-weather training in Lanzarote, took the Underwood brothers and Johnson but chose to omit both Richards and Back.

The Pilkington Cup offered some comfort: on the same weekend that Leicester won their third-round game against London Scottish at Richmond, five former cup holders - among them Bath, at Waterloo - lost and Jez Harris began to make his mark. Though he had been at the club for 12 years, this was Harris's first season as a regular and the Market Harborough boat builder made every game count.

In the new year Leicester unveiled plans to take advantage of increased interest in rugby: "We have to look to the future and develop the ground which again will benefit players and members," Graham Willars, now the club president, said. That a rugby club could contemplate refurbishments costing over £1 million, increasing capacity to 25,000, spoke well for the administration and may have helped build resolve in a team settling into a formidable unit.

Welford Road hosted an A international (the letter B was discarded earlier in the season, the team remained England's second string) between England and France, in which Tony Underwood, Back and Johnson were all named. But on the morning of the match, Johnson was summoned to join the senior England side in training at Richmond - Wade Dooley, the Preston Grasshoppers lock, had a thigh strain and Johnson received his first cap. He had taken no part in any meaningful preparation but, at Twickenham the next day, he grew into the game with France which was won by the narrowest of margins, 16-15. Although Dooley returned for the subsequent championship games, Johnson was already on the Lions radar for the summer tour to New Zealand.

England struggled to maintain their standards of the previous two seasons but the return of their internationals boosted Leicester's cup campaign. Nottingham, now with Dusty Hare as director of rugby, fell 28-3 and Exeter were summarily dismissed 76-0; a league loss at Bristol was Leicester's only defeat in the second half of the season. Adding to the general sense of wellbeing was the selection by the Lions of both Underwoods and, for all the vicissitudes of the previous 18 months, Richards. Back, Garforth, Hackney, Johnson and Rowntree were chosen by England for a tour to Canada and were later joined by Potter. For those of the club's players who missed the representative trips, there was a five-match visit to South Africa in August.

🡅 Tigers skipper John Wells proudly holds aloft the Pilkington Cup.

First, though, there was the domestic season to finish. The cup semi-final with Northampton at Welford Road was televised live but the cameras had no impact on the crowd. For the first time in cup history, the game was a sell-out and, by half-time, the tie was effectively over with Leicester leading 23-3. Northampton were out-run, out-thought and out-fought, losing 28-6 in stark contrast to the nail-biting league game in January when Leicester won 13-12 at Franklin's Gardens.

The cup final was against Harlequins, the last game of a magnificent career for Peter Winterbottom, the England flanker into whose shoes Back was so desperate to step. Leicester were more concerned that Back and Matt Poole should have recovered from injury, also that no more than 14,500 tickets were available to their supporters from the RFU. They were confident they could sell 20,000 for a stadium reduced to a 56,500 capacity because of building work.

On a warm, hazy day, Leicester fielded the following team in their seventh cup final: John Liley; Tony Underwood, Ian Bates, Stuart Potter, Rory Underwood; Jez Harris, Aadel Kardooni; Graham Rowntree, Richard Cockerill, Darren Garforth, Martin Johnson, Matt Poole, John Wells (captain), Dean Richards, Neil Back.

Harlequins lost Brian Moore, the international hooker, on the morning of the game to a groin strain and though they scored first through Rob Glenister, a try converted by Paul Challinor, they lost 23-16. Both teams might have preferred a running game but neither produced one save in patches - notably when Liley veered out of his own half and, from the ruck, Harris and Back sent Potter dummying through for the best score of the afternoon.

Liley converted before Challinor kicked the first of three penalties and Harlequins led 13-10 at the interval, Harris having pegged them back with a trademark dropped goal. Liley levelled matters with a penalty and Johnson scored a rare try from a free kick but Leicester could not put clear water between the two sides and were grateful for the breathing space of Liley's final penalty.

During the summer an all-weather surface was added to the facilities at Oval Park and tributes were paid on the death of Tom Berry, aged 82. He played for his country, chaired the national selection panel, managed England overseas and presided over the RFU while still maintaining a close link, personally and through his rugby-playing sons, with Leicester.

Three teams left for summer tours: the Lions to New Zealand, England A to Canada and England under-21s to Australia, among them Chris Johnson, Leicester's hooker, who was part of the team that beat Australia 22-12 in Sydney alongside a clutch of future World Cup winners. England A had scarcely won their second international 19-14 when Martin Johnson discovered he was required by the Lions, as a replacement once again for Dooley who had to return home after the death of his father.

The lock spent some 56 hours travelling to New Zealand's South Island, watched the Lions lose the first test 20-18 and then excelled against Taranaki and Auckland to win promotion into the XV for the second test in Wellington. He joined Richards and Rory Underwood in the 20-7 victory, the Lions' biggest success in New Zealand in which Underwood scored the Lions try, outpacing John Kirwan in a 40-metre dash. All three retained their places for the decisive third test in Auckland but the All Blacks cantered away with the series 30-13.

Tigers embarked on their only tour to South Africa in the August, winning all five games played all over the Republic in Cape Town, Pietermaritzburg, Empangeni and Durban.

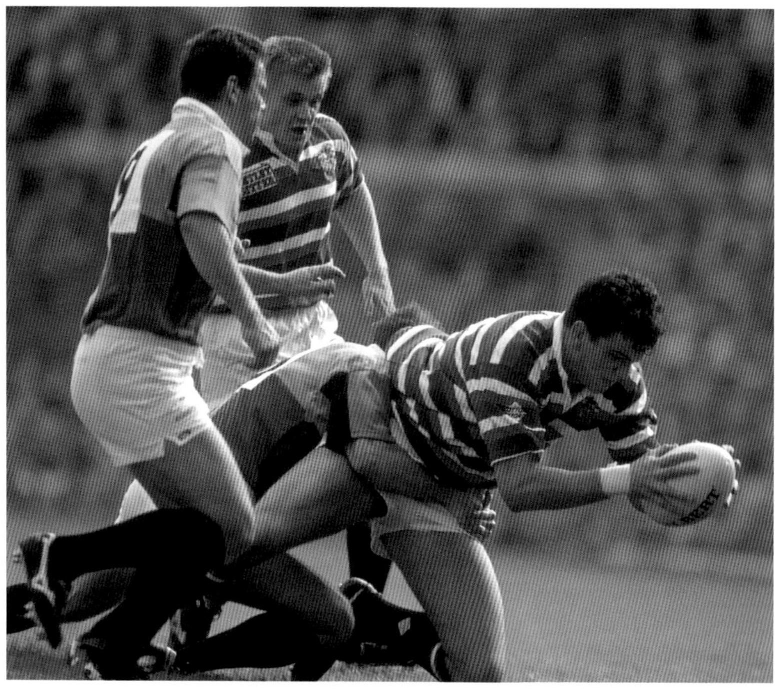

🡇 Martin Johnson scores the decisive try in the 1993 cup final against Harlequins at Twickenham.

1991 CANADA TOUR

Head Coach: Tony Russ assisted by David Matthews
Captain: John Wells

OVERALL RECORD:					T	C	PG	DG	PTS
PLD	W	D	L	Tigers scored:	9	6	12	0	84
4	3	0	1	Opponents scored:	5	4	12	0	64

GM	DATE		VEN	OPPONENTS	RESULT	TRIES	KICKS	ATT
1	Aug	14w	a	Edmonton	W 30-18	Hackney, D.Wigley, S.Wigley	Liley 3c/4p	-
2		17	a	Alberta	W 16-9	Back, Hackney	Liley c/2p	-
3		20tu	a	British Columbia	W 23-18	Grant, Hackney, D.Wigley	Wills c/3p	-
4		23f	a	British Columbia President's XV	L 15-19	Hilyer	Liley c/3p	-

INDIVIDUAL APPEARANCES 1991 CANADA TOUR							
Name / Game #	1	2	3	4	Apps	T	Pts
Name							
NA (Neil) Back E+ L+	-	H	-	H	2	1	4
MSJP (Matt) Barkes	B	-	-	-	1	-	-
I (Ian) Bates	M	M	M	-	3	-	-
LS (Laurence) Boyle	-	>L	L	L	3	-	-
MJ (Mark) Cleaver	K	r	K	<K	3+1	-	-
WM (Bill) Drake-Lee	H	-	-	-	1	-	-
DE (Darren) Eagland	>A	-	A	-	2	-	-
AJS (Alex) Gissing	D	-	D	D	3	-	-
MR (Mark) Grant	-	G	G	-	2	1	4
ST (Steve) Hackney	>N	N	N	N	4	3	12
JG (Jamie) Hamilton	r	I	-	-	1+1	-	-
JC (Jez) Harris	-	J	x	J	2	-	-
PD (Paul) Hilyer	-	B	B	B	3	1	4
MO (Martin) Johnson E+ L+	-	D	E	-	2	-	-
A (Aadel) Kardooni	I	-	I*	I	3	-	-
JG (John) Liley	O*	O	-	O	3	-	37
AN (Adey) Marriott	F	-	H	-	2	-	-
MD (Matt) Poole	E	E	x	E	3	-	-
SJ (Simon) Povoas	G	-	F	G	3	-	-
WP (Wayne) Richardson	C	-	-	-	1	-	-
CG (Graham) Rowntree E+ L+	r	A	x	A	2+1	-	-
RA (Richard) Wareham	-	C	C	C	3	-	-
JM (John) Wells	-	F*	x	F*	2	-	-
DL (Dave) Wigley HK+	>J	-	J	-	2	2	8
ST (Steve) Wigley	L	-	x	-	1	1	4
SR (Steve) Wills	-	K	O	M	3	-	11

↑ LEICESTER FOOTBALL CLUB 1991/92
Back: Allen (Hon.Sec), Willars (President), T.Underwood, Hackney, Poole, M.Johnson, Kardooni, Redfern, Garforth, I.Smith (Coach), Russ (Director of coaching), Thomas (Team Hon.Sec).
Front: Sandford, Richards, Povoas, Boyle, Wells (capt), Harris, Bates, Tressler, Liley.

↑ LEICESTER FOOTBALL CLUB 1992/93
Back: Allen (Hon.Sec), Russ (Director of coaching), Willars (President), T.Underwood, Povoas, Poole, M.Johnson, Richards, Hackney, Rowntree, Garforth, Dodge (Coach), Thomas (Team Hon.Sec), Smith (Coach).
Front: Sandford, Kilford, Potter, Bates, J.Harris, Wells (capt), Kardooni, Back, Cockerill, Liley, Boyle.

INDIVIDUAL APPEARANCES 1993 SOUTH AFRICA TOUR								
Name / Game #	1	2	3	4	5	Apps	T	Pts
Name								
NA (Neil) Back E+ L+	-	-	-	H*	H	2	-	-
I (Ian) Bates	L	-	M	M	-	3	-	-
LS (Laurence) Boyle	-	L	-	-	-	1	-	-
BS (Ben) Brier	-	F	H	F	-	3	-	-
R (Richard) Cockerill E+	B	-	B	-	B	3	-	-
WM (Bill) Drake-Lee	-	H	F	-	-	2	2	10
DJ (Darren) Garforth E+	C	-	r	C	C	3+1	1	5
AJS (Alex) Gissing	D	D	-	D	-	3	1	5
PJ (Paul) Grant	G	E	D	r	-	3+1	2	10
D (Darren) Grewcock	r	I	I	-	-	2+1	2	10
JC (Jez) Harris	J	r	J	-	M	3+1	-	3
DA (Derek) Jelley	A	-	A	-	-	2	1	5
CAP (Chris) Johnson	r	B	r	B	-	2+2	3	15
A (Aadel) Kardooni	I	-	-	I	I	3	1	5
WA (Wayne) Kilford	-	O	N	O	N	4	-	-
JG (John) Liley	O	-	O	r	O	3+1	-	54
NG (Niall) Malone I2	-	>J	-	J	J	3	-	10
MD (Matt) Poole	-	-	-	E	E	2	-	-
S (Stuart) Potter E+	M	M	L	L	L	5	3	15
TR (Tom) Reynolds	N	-	-	-	-	1	1	5
ND (Nigel) Richardson	H	-	r	-	G	2+1	1	5
WP (Wayne) Richardson	-	C	C	-	-	2	-	-
CG (Graham) Rowntree E+ L+	-	A	-	A	A	3	-	-
P (Peter) Sandford	K	N	-	K	r	3+1	2	10
T (Tom) Smith	E	-	E	G	D	4	1	5
JM (John) Wells	F*	G*	G*	-	F*	4	1	5
DL (Dave) Wigley HK+	-	K	K	N	K	4	2	10

1993 SOUTH AFRICA TOUR

Head Coach: Tony Russ assisted by Ian Smith and Paul Dodge
Captain: John Wells

OVERALL RECORD:					T	C	PG	DG	PTS
PLD	W	D	L	Tigers scored:	24	17	10	1	187
5	5	0	0	Opponents scored:	3	1	5	0	32

GM	DATE		VEN	OPPONENTS	RESULT	TRIES	KICKS	ATT
1	Aug	7	a	Western Province Defence XV	W 75-3	Johnson(3), Garforth, Gissing, Jelley, Kardooni, Potter, Reynolds, N.Richardson	Liley 8c/2p, Harris d	-
2		11w	a	Gardens Tech	W 25-0	Drake-Lee, Grewcock, Sandford, Wells	Malone c/p	-
3		14	a	Natal Development XV	W 58-8	Grant(2), Drake-Lee, Grewcock, Potter, Smith, Wigley	Liley 7c/3p	-
4		17tu	a	Zululand Regional XV	W 15-8	Sandford, Wigley	Malone c/p	-
5		20f	a	Natal Selectors' XV	W 14-13	Potter	Liley 3p	-

The key for how to read the stats is on the last page

19	91/92	Home Ground: Welford Road	OVERALL RECORD:					T	C	PG	DG	PTS
		Head Coach: Tony Russ assisted by Ian Smith and Paul Dodge	PLD	W	D	L	Tigers scored:	142	83	61	7	938
		Captain: John Wells	36	21	1	14	Opponents scored:	66	39	72	6	576

GM	DATE		VEN	OPPONENTS	RESULT	POS/LGE	TRIES	KICKS	ATT
COURAGE LEAGUE DIVISION 1 (6TH)						**CHAMPIONS: BATH**			
12	Nov	16	a	Gloucester	L 3-21	11	-	Liley p	-
13		**23**	**H**	**Wasps**	W 31-12	6	R.Underwood 16, Wells 80	Liley c/4p, Harris 3d	6961
15	Dec	7	a	Nottingham	W 27-14	5	R.Underwood 18/73	Liley 2c/4p, Harris d	-
16		21	a	Saracens	W 20-9	4	Back 63, Wells 70, Hackney 76	Liley c/2p	-
18	Jan	**4**	**H**	**London Irish**	W 36-13	1	Hackney 2/21/39, R.Underwood 15/47, Liley 62, Richards 77	Liley 4c	6743
19		11	a	Bath	L 6-37	5	-	Liley 2p	-
	Feb	**8**	**H**	**Northampton**	PP (cup)	-			
25		29	a	Orrell	L 9-21	6	-	Liley 3p	-
28	Mar	**14**	**H**	**Bristol**	W 25-9	5	T.Underwood 27, Ainscough 34, Garforth 38, Boyle 80	Liley 3p	5812
29		**21**	**H**	**Rosslyn Park**	W 51-16	5	R.Underwood 12/18/75, Liley 55/72, Ainscough 65, Kardooni 69	Liley 7c/3p	4538
30		28	a	Harlequins	L 13-20	5	Povoas 69, Wills 78	Wills c/p	-
32	Apr	**7tu**	**H**	**Northampton**	L 19-22	6	Harris 2, Grewcock 55	Liley c/3p	8915
36		**25**	**H**	**Rugby Lions**	D 22-22	6	R.Underwood 12, Bates 30, T.Underwood 47/57	Liley 3c	5255
RFU CLUB COMPETITION (PILKINGTON CUP)						**CUP WINNERS: BATH**			
14	Nov	30	a	Fylde (3)	W 34-6	D3	Back 10, Wells 15/70, Penalty 25, Kardooni 38, Richards 48/63	Liley 3c	-
	Jan	25	a	Waterloo (4)	PP (ice)	D2			
22	Feb	8	a	Waterloo (4)	W 20-12	D2	Garforth 24, Richards 37/55	Liley c/2p	-
24		22	a	Newcastle Gosforth (qf)	W 10-0	D2	Penalty 17, Kardooni 62	Liley c	2500
31	Apr	4	a	Harlequins (sf)	L 9-15	D1	Liley 67	Liley c/p	6000
CLUB MATCHES									
1	Sep	7	a	Bedford	W 25-18		Bates, Boyle, Gissing	Liley 2c/3p	-
2		**14**	**H**	**Cardiff**	W 23-18		Liley, M.Grant, Wells	Liley c/3p	5081
3		21	a	Northampton	L 17-21		Back, Hackney, Povoas	Liley c/p	-
4		**24tu**	**H**	**Northern Division**	L 3-28		-	Liley p	2022
5		28	a	Headingley	W 58-10		Povoas(4), Hackney(2), T.Smith(2), Liley, Hamilton, Harris	Liley 7c	-
6	Oct	**5**	**H**	**Coventry**	L 20-22		Povoas(2), Drake-Lee	Harris 2p, Wills c	3299
		12	a	Bristol	PP				
7		**19**	**H**	**Gloucester**	L 12-22		Sandford	Harris c/p/d	1723
8		22tu	a	Oxford University	W 13-12		Garforth, M.Grant	Liley c/p	-
9		26	a	Sale	L 9-12		I.Smith	Liley c/p	-
10	Nov	2	a	Moseley	L 15-16		-	Liley 4p, Harris d	-
11		**5tu**	**H**	**Cambridge University**	W 27-12		Back(2), B.Evans, Richards, Tressler	Liley 2c/p	1782
	Dec	**14**	**H**	**Rosslyn Park**	PP (frost)				
17		**27f**	**H**	**Barbarians**	L 21-29		R.Underwood(2)	Liley 2c/3p	16119
20	Jan	**18**	**H**	**Bedford**	W 45-24		M.Grant(2), Hackney(2), Gissing, Kardooni, Sandford	Wills 4c/3p	2015
21	Feb	**1**	**H**	**Wakefield**	W 48-20		Liley(2), Kardooni(2), Povoas(2), Hackney, Warwood	Liley 5c/2p	733
23		**15**	**H**	**Nuneaton**	W 50-6		Hackney(2), Kardooni(2), Sandford(2), Liley, Harris, Redfern, T.Smith	Liley 5c	1270
		22	**H**	**London Welsh**	PP (cup)				
26	Mar	**3tu**	**H**	**Loughborough Students**	W 39-10		Povoas(3), Wills, Key, Rowntree	Wills 3c/3p	1803
27		**7**	**H**	**Richmond**	W 50-19		Hackney(3), Bates(2), Liley, Garforth, Gissing	Liley 6c/p, Harris d	1085
		21	**H**	**Nottingham**	PP (league)				
	Apr	**4**	**H**	**London Scottish**	PP (cup)				
33		**11**	**H**	**Liverpool St Helens**	W 100-0		T.Underwood(6), Grewcock(3), Hackney(3), Wills(2), Ainscough, Boyle, Drake-Lee, Marriott, Wells	Ainscough 11c, Liley c	2948
34		**18**	**H**	**Ballymena**	W 22-9		Ainscough, Garforth, Key, Sandford	Ainscough 3c	3754
35		20m	a	Wasps	L 6-19		-	Harris 2p	-

INDIVIDUAL APPEARANCES 1991/92

Name / Game #	1	2	3	4	5	6	7	8	9	10	11	12	13	14	15	16	17	18	19	20	21	22	23	24	25	26	27	28	29	30	31	32	33	34	35	36	Apps	T	Pts
GC (Gerry) Ainscough	-	-	-	-	-	-	-	-	-	-	-	-	-	-	-	-	-	-	>J	-	J	J	-	J	J	-	-	J	J	J	J	-	J	J	-	<J	12	4	44
NA (Neil) Back E+ L+	-	H	H	-	-	-	-	-	-	-	H	H	H	H	H	H	H	H	-	-	-	-	-	H	H	-	-	H	H	H	H	H	-	-	-	-	17	5	20
MSJP (Matt) Barkes	-	-	-	x	-	-	-	B	-	-	-	-	-	-	x	-	-	-	-	-	-	-	-	-	-	B	-	-	-	-	x	-	B	-	<B	-	4	-	-
I (Ian) Bates	M	M	L	M	L	-	-	-	M	L	M	L	L	M	L	L	L	L	L	L	L	M	L	L	L	-	M	L	L	L	L	-	M	-	-	M	29	4	16
LS (Laurence) Boyle	L	L	-	L	M	M	M	M	L	M	L	M	-	-	-	-	-	-	-	-	-	-	-	M	M	-	-	M	M	M	M	M	L	-	-	L	20	3	12
WM (Bill) Drake-Lee	-	-	-	H	H	H	-	-	-	-	-	-	-	-	-	-	-	-	-	H	H	-	-	-	-	-	-	-	-	-	-	-	H	-	H	H	8	2	8
BJ (Barry) Evans E2	N	N	-	-	-	N	-	-	-	-	N	N	-	-	-	-	-	-	-	-	-	-	-	-	-	-	-	-	-	-	-	-	-	-	-	-	5	1	4
DJ (Darren) Garforth E+	-	-	>C	C	C	C	-	C	C	C	C	C	C	C	C	C	C	C	C	C	C	C	C	C	C	C	C	C	-	C	C	C	C	C	C	C	32	5	20
AJS (Alex) Gissing	D	D	D	D	-	D	-	-	-	-	-	-	-	-	-	-	-	-	D	D	-	-	-	-	E	D	D	-	-	-	-	-	-	-	-	-	10	3	12
MR (Mark) Grant	-	G	-	-	-	-	D	G	-	-	x	x	x	-	-	-	-	-	x	G	-	-	-	-	G	-	-	-	x	-	-	-	-	-	G	-	6	4	16
PJ (Paul) Grant	x	-	-	-	-	-	-	-	-	x	-	-	-	-	-	-	-	-	-	-	-	-	-	-	-	E	-	-	-	-	-	-	-	-	E	-	2	-	-
D (Darren) Grewcock	-	-	-	-	-	-	-	I	-	-	-	-	-	-	-	-	-	-	-	-	x	-	x	-	-	I	-	-	-	-	I	I	I	I	x	I	7	4	16
ST (Steve) Hackney	K	K	K	K	K	-	-	-	-	-	-	K	N	N	N	N	N	N	N	N	N	-	N	N	N	-	N	-	-	N	x	N	N	N	-	x	23	18	72
JG (Jamie) Hamilton	-	-	I	-	I	I	-	-	-	-	-	-	-	-	-	-	-	-	-	-	-	-	-	-	-	-	-	-	-	r	x	-	-	-	I	-	4+1	1	4
JC (Jez) Harris	J	J	J	J	J	J	J	-	J	J	J	J	J	J	J	J	J	J	x	J	-	-	J	x	-	J	J	x	-	-	x	J	-	O	J	-	24	3	50
PD (Paul) Hilyer	B	-	-	<B	-	-	-	-	-	-	-	-	-	-	-	-	-	-	-	-	-	-	-	-	-	-	-	-	-	-	-	-	-	-	-	-	2	-	-
MO (Martin) Johnson E+ L+	E	-	-	-	D	-	-	D	D	D	D	D	D	D	D	D	D	D	-	-	D	D	-	D	D	-	-	D	D	D	D	D	D	-	-	-	23	-	-
EM (Eddie) Jones	-	-	-	-	-	-	-	>r	-	-	-	-	-	-	-	-	-	-	-	B	-	-	<r	-	-	x	-	-	-	-	-	-	-	-	-	-	1+2	-	-
A (Aadel) Kardooni	I	I	-	I	-	-	I	-	I	I	I	I	I	I	I	I	I	I	I	I	I	I	I	I	I	-	I	I	I	I	-	-	-	-	-	-	25	8	32
AM (Andy) Key	-	-	M	-	-	L	-	-	-	x	-	-	M	L	M	M	M	M	M	-	-	-	-	-	-	M*	-	-	-	-	-	L	-	<L	-	-	12	2	8
JG (John) Liley	O	O	O	O	O	-	-	O*	O	O	O	O	O	O	O	O	O	O	O	-	O	O	O	O	O*	-	O	O	O	-	O	O	O	-	-	O*	29	10	305
AN (Adey) Marriott	H	-	-	-	-	-	F	-	-	H	-	-	-	-	-	-	-	-	-	-	-	-	-	x	F	F	-	-	-	-	-	-	r	r	-	<F	6+2	1	4
J (John) Murphy	-	-	x	-	-	-	H	H	-	-	-	-	-	-	-	-	-	-	-	-	r	H	H	-	r	H	H	x	-	x	-	x	-	H	-	x	8+2	-	-
MD (Matt) Poole	-	-	-	-	-	-	-	-	-	-	E	E	E	E	E	E	E	E	E	E	E	E	E	E	-	-	E	E	E	E	E	E	E	D	-	D	23	-	-
SJ (Simon) Povoas	G	-	G	G	G	G	G	-	G	G	-	-	G	x	G	-	G	r	F	-	G	-	G	-	-	G	G	G	-	G	r	G	G	G	-	G	22+2	13	52
SB (Stuart) Redfern	-	-	-	-	-	-	-	A	-	A	A	A	A	A	A	A	A	A	A	A	A	A	A	A	A	-	A	A	A	A	A	A	-	A	-	<A	25	1	4
D (Dean) Richards E33 L3	-	-	-	-	-	-	-	-	-	-	G	G	-	G	-	G	-	G	G	-	-	G	-	G	-	-	-	-	G	-	G	-	-	-	-	-	10	6	24
WP (Wayne) Richardson	-	C	-	-	-	-	C	-	-	-	-	-	-	-	-	-	-	-	-	-	-	-	-	-	-	-	-	-	C	-	-	-	-	-	-	-	3	-	-
CG (Graham) Rowntree E+ L+	A	A	A	A	A	A	A	-	A	-	-	-	-	-	-	-	x	-	-	-	-	-	-	-	-	A	-	-	-	-	x	-	A	-	A	x	11	1	4
DR (Damion) Ryan	-	-	-	-	-	-	>L	<L	-	-	-	-	-	-	-	-	-	-	-	-	-	-	-	-	-	-	-	-	-	-	-	-	-	-	-	-	2	-	-
P (Peter) Sandford	-	-	-	N	-	K	K	K	K	K	K	-	-	-	-	-	-	-	-	K	K	-	K	-	-	K	K	-	-	-	-	-	-	K	K	-	14	5	20
T (Tom) Smith	-	E	E	E	E	E	E*	E	E	E	-	-	-	-	-	x	-	-	-	-	-	-	D	-	-	-	-	-	-	-	-	-	-	E	D*	E	13	3	12
CJ (Chris) Tressler	-	B	B	-	B	B*	B	-	B	B	B	B	B	B	B	B	B	B	B	-	B	B	B	B	B	-	B	B	B	B	B	B	-	B	-	<B	29	1	4
R (Rory) Underwood E55 L3	-	-	-	-	-	-	-	-	-	-	-	-	K	K	K	K	K	K	K	-	-	K	-	K	-	-	-	K	K	-	K	-	-	-	-	K	13	11	44
T (Tony) Underwood E+ L+	-	-	N	-	-	-	-	-	-	-	-	-	-	-	-	-	-	-	-	-	-	N	-	-	K	-	-	N	N	K	N	K	K	-	-	N	10	9	36
AM (Alan) Warwood	-	-	x	-	-	-	-	-	-	-	-	-	x	-	-	-	-	-	-	M	M	L	M	-	-	L	L	-	-	-	-	-	-	M	<L	-	8	1	4
JM (John) Wells	F*	F*	F*	F*	F*	-	-	-	F*	F*	F*	F*	F*	F*	F*	F*	F*	F*	H*	F*	F*	F*	F*	F*	-	-	F*	F*	F*	F*	F*	F*	F*	F*	-	-	29	6	24
DL (Dave) Wigley HK+	x	-	-	-	-	-	N	N	N	N	r	x	-	-	-	x	-	-	-	-	-	x	-	-	x	N	-	-	-	-	-	-	-	r	M	-	6+2	-	-
SR (Steve) Wills	-	r	-	-	N	O	O	-	-	-	-	-	-	x	-	-	x	x	-	O	-	-	-	-	-	O	-	-	r	O	-	x	r	-	-	-	6+3	4	55

1 GAME: BS (Ben) Brier >F(6), AM (Ashley) Johnson ><J(8), A (Andy) McAdam O(35), S (Sam) Quick =F(8)x(20), TR (Tom) Reynolds >N(35), AR (Alan) Royer =r(4)x(27), IR (Ian) Smith <Ht(9), RA (Richard) Wareham C(1)x(2)x(6)

The key for how to read the stats is on the last page

1992/93

Home Ground: Welford Road	Trophy Cabinet: Pilkington Cup(4)	OVERALL RECORD:					T	C	PG	DG	PTS
Head Coach: Tony Russ assisted by Ian Smith and Paul Dodge		PLD	W	D	L	Tigers scored:	122	66	70	13	991
Captain: John Wells		37	30	0	7	Opponents scored:	52	26	47	4	465

GM	DATE		VEN	OPPONENTS	RESULT	POS/LGE	TRIES	KICKS	ATT
COURAGE LEAGUE DIVISION 1 (3RD)						**CHAMPIONS: BATH**			
5	Sep	19	a	London Irish	W 30-14	1	Liley 23, T.Underwood 27, N.Richardson 68	Liley 3c/3p	2500
6		**26**	**H**	**Gloucester**	W 22-21	2	Hackney 16, Kardooni 29, N.Richardson 52	Liley 2c/p	7476
7	Oct	3	a	Wasps	L 13-14	3	Potter 12	Liley c/2p	-
8		**10**	**H**	**West Hartlepool**	W 21-8	2	Potter 56, Liley 68	Liley c/3p	5848
11		24	a	London Scottish	W 18-11	2	Poole 57, T.Underwood 65	Liley c/2p	-
12		**31**	**H**	**Saracens**	W 30-3	1	Penalty 22, Cockerill 59, R.Underwood 79	Liley 3c/2p, J.Harris d	6162
16	Nov	**21**	**H**	**Bath**	L 3-13	4	-	Liley p	10309
20	Jan	9	a	Northampton	W 13-12	3	Back 80	Liley c/2p	7300
25	Feb	**13**	**H**	**Orrell**	W 9-0	3	-	Liley 3p	7723
29	Mar	13	a	Bristol	L 10-15	3	Kardooni 76	Liley c/p	-
31		**27**	**H**	**Harlequins**	W 23-0	3	N.Richardson 60, Povoas 74	Liley 2c/2p, J.Harris d	7962
36	Apr	24	a	Rugby Lions	W 28-5	3	R.Underwood 32, T.Underwood 37, Grewcock 77	J.Harris 2c/2d, Kilford p	-
RFU CLUB COMPETITION (PILKINGTON CUP)						**CUP WINNERS: LEICESTER TIGERS**			
17	Nov	29s	a	London Scottish (3)	W 20-11	D1	Liley 41, Hackney 45	Liley 2c/p, J.Harris d	-
22	Jan	23	a	Nottingham (4)	W 28-3	D2	R.Underwood 33, Back 42, T.Underwood 45	Liley 2c/3p	-
27	Feb	**27**	**H**	**Exeter (qf)**	W 76-0	D3	Povoas 7, T.Underwood 28/52/57, Back 30, Richards 35/40, Potter 45, Liley 67/80, R.Underwood 69, Cockerill 75, Grewcock 76	Liley 4c/p	9000
33	Apr	**10**	**H**	**Northampton (sf)**	W 28-6	D1	Richards 16, Back 33, Boyle 74	Liley 2c/2p, J.Harris d	16069
37	May	1		Harlequins (f)	W 23-16	D1	Potter 19, M.Johnson 50	Liley 2c/2p, J.Harris d	56400
CLUB MATCHES									
1	Sep	1tu	a	Sheffield	W 27-7		Poole 20, Hackney 60, Kardooni 70	Liley 3c/p, J.Harris d	-
2		**5**	**H**	**England XV**	L 11-18		Hackney 68	Liley 2p	7726
3		**9w**	**H**	**Leicestershire XV**	W 40-20		Grewcock 48, Murphy 53, Reynolds 59, I.Harris 65, Drake-Lee 73	I.Harris d, Boyle 2p, Kilford 3c	1995
4		**12**	**H**	**Mediolanum Milano**	W 40-24		N.Richardson 21, Povoas 56, Hackney 64, Garforth 74	Liley 4c/4p	4048
9	Oct	17	a	Moseley	L 14-20		Sandford 25	J.Harris 2p, Kilford p	-
10		**20tu**	**H**	**Oxford University**	W 27-15		M.Johnson, Hackney, Eagland	Kilford 3c/2p	1662
13	Nov	3tu	a	Cambridge University	L 18-23		Drake-Lee 15, Kilford 24/60	Kilford p	-
14		7	a	Orrell	W 33-18		Sandford 14, Liley 30/33, Kilford 59	Liley 2c/3p	-
15		**13f**	**H**	**Northampton**	W 28-3		Bates 48, Hackney 72, Poole 79	Liley 2c/3p	5936
18	Dec	5	a	Gloucester	L 13-36		Sandford 63/77	J.Harris d	-
		12	a	Blackheath	PP				
19		**28m**	**H**	**Barbarians**	W 41-23		Liley 3, Wells 23, R.Underwood 40, Garforth 46, Grewcock 61, T.Underwood 76	Liley 4c/p	16400
	Jan	**2**	**H**	**Leeds**	PP (frost)				
21		15f	a	Bedford	W 16-13		Liley 47	Liley c/2p, J.Harris d	-
23		30	a	Coventry	W 37-17		Kilford 40/68, Garforth 43, Boyle 58, T.Underwood 75	J.Harris 3c/2p	-
24	Feb	**6**	**H**	**Rosslyn Park**	W 52-10		Hackney 6, Povoas 20, Sandford 27, Potter 43, Liley 52/79, Rowntree 61, Kardooni 65	Liley 3c/p, J.Harris d	3508
26		20	a	Nuneaton	W 61-18		Hackney 14/30/55/75, Back 19/31, Boyle 39, Kardooni 44, Sandford 65/67/73	Liley 3c	-
		27	a	London Welsh	PP (cup)				
	Mar	**2tu**	**H**	**Loughborough Students**	PP (cup)				
28		**5f**	**H**	**Moseley**	W 25-5		Kardooni 36, Povoas 62	Liley 5p	3009
30		19f	a	Nottingham	W 27-7		Boyle 3/75, Hopper 15, Sandford 20, Kilford 27	Liley c	-
32	Apr	3	a	Richmond	W 29-15		Liley 23, Bates 39, Hackney 41	Liley c/3p, Green d	-
		10	a	Ballymena	PP (cup)				
34		**12m**	**H**	**Wasps**	W 14-13		C.Johnson 67	Green 3p	3516
35		**17**	**H**	**Sale**	W 43-8		Hackney 2, Kilford 16/65, Rowntree 42, N.Richardson 53, Evans 55, Sandford 61	Kilford 4c	3458

Neutral Venue: *#37 at Twickenham*

INDIVIDUAL APPEARANCES 1992/93

Name / Game #	1	2	3	4	5	6	7	8	9	10	11	12	13	14	15	16	17	18	19	20	21	22	23	24	25	26	27	28	29	30	31	32	33	34	35	36	37	Apps	T	Pts
NA (Neil) Back E+ L+	-	-	-	-	-	-	H	H	H*	-	H	H	-	-	H	H	H	-	H	H	-	H	-	H	H	H	H	-	H	-	-	-	H	-	-	-	H	18	6	30
I (Ian) Bates	L	L	-	M	L	L	L	L	M	-	L	L	-	-	L	L	M	L	L	L	M	M	L	L	-	-	L	-	M	-	L	L	L	-	-	L	L	27	2	10
LS (Laurence) Boyle	x	x	L	-	-	-	-	-	-	-	M	-	M	L	-	x	-	M	x	-	-	-	M	-	L	M	-	M	x	M	r	-	r	M	L	r	x	12+3	5	31
BS (Ben) Brier	-	-	-	-	-	-	-	-	x	r	-	-	-	-	-	-	-	-	-	-	-	-	-	r	-	-	-	-	-	-	-	F	-	F	x	-	-	2+2	-	-
EM (Eliot) Buckby	-	-	>D	-	-	-	-	-	-	-	-	-	-	-	-	-	-	-	-	-	<D	-	-	-	-	-	-	-	-	-	-	-	-	-	-	-	-	2	-	-
R (Richard) Cockerill E+	>B	B	-	B	B	B	B	B	B	-	B	B	-	B	B	B	B	-	B	B	-	B	-	B	B	B	B	-	B	-	B	-	B	-	-	B	B	26	2	10
WM (Bill) Drake-Lee	-	-	H	-	-	-	-	-	-	H	-	-	H	H	-	-	-	H	-	-	H	-	H	-	-	-	-	-	-	-	-	-	-	-	-	-	-	7	2	10
DE (Darren) Eagland	x	-	A	x	-	-	-	-	-	A	-	-	-	-	-	-	-	<A	-	-	-	-	-	-	-	-	-	-	-	-	-	-	-	-	-	-	-	3	1	5
JL (Jason) Evans	-	-	-	-	-	-	-	-	-	>M	-	-	L	r	-	-	-	-	-	-	-	-	-	-	-	-	-	-	-	L	-	-	-	-	M	-	-	4+1	1	5
DJ (Darren) Garforth E+	C	C	C	C	C	C	C	C	C	-	C	C	C	C	C	C	C	-	C	C	C	C	C	C	C	C	C	-	C	-	C	C	C	-	-	C	C	31	3	15
MR (Mark) Grant	G	x	G	-	-	-	-	x	-	G	-	-	-	-	-	G	x	-	-	x	-	-	-	-	-	G	r	-	-	-	-	-	-	-	-	-	-	5+1	-	-
PJ (Paul) Grant	-	-	E	-	-	-	-	-	D	E	-	-	E	-	-	-	-	D	-	-	-	-	E	-	E	E	-	D	E	D	-	-	-	E	-	-	-	12	-	-
DN (Dan) Green	-	-	-	-	-	-	-	-	-	-	-	-	-	-	-	-	-	-	-	-	-	-	-	-	-	-	-	-	-	-	-	>J	-	J	<J	-	-	3	-	12
D (Darren) Grewcock	-	x	I	x	-	-	-	x	-	I	-	-	-	-	-	-	-	I	I	-	I	-	-	r	-	-	r	-	-	I	-	I	x	I	-	I	x	9+2	4	20
A (Andy) Grimsdell	-	-	-	-	-	-	-	-	-	-	-	-	-	-	-	x	-	-	-	-	-	-	x	-	-	-	-	-	-	>H	-	-	-	-	-	r	-	1+1	-	-
ST (Steve) Hackney	N	N	-	N	-	N	N	N	-	N	-	N	-	-	N	N	N	-	-	-	N	-	-	N	N	N	-	-	N	-	-	N	-	-	N	-	-	18	14	70
JG (Jamie) Hamilton	-	-	-	-	x	-	-	-	I	-	-	-	I	-	-	-	-	-	-	-	-	-	x	-	-	-	-	x	-	-	-	-	-	x	I	-	-	3	-	-
IJ (Ian) Harris	-	-	>J	-	-	-	-	-	-	<J	-	-	-	-	-	-	-	x	-	-	-	-	-	-	-	-	-	-	-	-	-	-	-	-	-	-	-	2	1	8
JC (Jez) Harris	J	J	-	J	J	J	J	J	J	-	J	J	J*	J	J	J	J	J	J	J	J	J	J	J	J	J	J	J	J	J	J	-	J	-	-	J	J	32	-	55
DA (Dave) Hopper	-	-	-	-	-	-	-	-	-	C	-	-	-	-	-	-	-	C	-	-	-	-	-	-	-	-	-	C	-	C	-	-	-	C	C	-	x	6	1	5
CAP (Chris) Johnson	-	-	-	-	-	-	-	-	-	-	-	-	-	-	-	-	-	-	-	-	-	-	-	-	-	-	-	-	-	>r	-	B	x	B	B	-	x	3+1	1	5
MO (Martin) Johnson E1 L+	-	-	-	-	-	-	-	-	-	D	D	D	-	D	D	D	D	-	D	D	-	D	-	D	D	D	D	-	D	-	D	D	D	-	D	D	D	21	2	10
A (Aadel) Kardooni	I	I	-	I	I	I	I	I	-	-	I	I	-	I	I	I	I	-	-	I	-	I	I	I	I	I	I	I	I	-	I	-	I	-	-	-	I	25	6	30
WA (Wayne) Kilford	-	x	>O	-	-	-	x	-	O	O	x	-	O	N	K	-	x	O	-	-	-	x	O	-	x	-	-	L	-	N	N	-	-	O	O	O	-	14	8	75
JG (John) Liley	O	O	-	O	O	O	O	O	-	-	O	O	-	O	O	O	O	-	O	O	O	O	-	O	O	O	O	O	O	O	O	O	O	-	-	-	O	28	12	330
NFC (Neil) Martin	-	-	-	-	-	-	-	-	-	>F	-	-	<F	-	x	-	-	x	-	-	-	-	-	-	-	-	-	-	-	-	-	-	-	-	-	-	-	2	-	-
J (John) Murphy	-	x	F	-	x	-	x	-	F	-	-	x	-	F	-	-	-	-	-	-	-	-	-	-	-	-	-	-	-	-	x	-	-	-	-	-	-	3	1	5
MD (Matt) Poole	E	E	-	E	E	E	E	E	E	-	E	E	D	E	E	E	E	E	E	E	E	E	-	E	-	-	E	E	-	-	E	E	E	-	E	E	E	29	3	15
S (Stuart) Potter E+	>M	M	M	L	M	M	M	M	L	-	-	M	-	M	M	M	L	-	M	M	L	L	-	M	M	L	M	-	L	-	M	M	M	-	-	M	M	28	5	25
SJ (Simon) Povoas	-	G	-	G	G	G	G	G	G	-	x	F	-	-	F	F	F	G	x	-	G	x	G	G	x	-	F	G	r	G	G	-	x	G*	F	-	x	21+1	5	25
TR (Tom) Reynolds	-	-	N	-	-	-	-	-	K	-	-	-	N	-	-	-	-	N	-	-	-	-	-	-	-	-	-	N	-	-	-	-	-	N	-	-	-	6	1	5
D (Dean) Richards E34 L3	D	D	-	D	D	D	D	D	-	-	G	G*	-	G*	G*	-	G*	-	G	G	-	G	D	-	G	-	G*	-	G	E	-	-	G	-	G*	G	G	24	3	15
ND (Nigel) Richardson	>H	H	-	H	H	H	-	-	-	-	-	-	-	-	-	-	-	-	-	-	-	-	-	-	-	-	-	H	-	-	H	H	x	H	H	H	x	11	5	25
CG (Graham) Rowntree E+ L+	A	A	-	A	A	A	A	A	A	-	A	A	A	A	A	A	A	-	A	A	A	A	A	A	A	A	A	A	A	A	A	A	A	-	A	-	A	32	2	10
P (Peter) Sandford	K	-	K	-	-	-	-	-	N	-	-	-	K	K	-	-	-	K	-	-	K	-	N	K	-	K	-	K	-	K	-	-	-	K	K	-	-	14	10	50
TA (Troy) Thacker	-	-	B*	x	-	-	-	-	-	B	-	-	-	-	-	-	-	-	-	-	B	-	B	-	-	-	-	B	-	<B	-	-	-	-	-	-	-	6	-	-
R (Rory) Underwood E60 L3	-	K	-	-	K	K	-	-	-	K*	K	K	-	-	-	K*	K	-	K	K	-	K	-	-	K	-	K	-	K	-	K	-	K	-	-	K	K	18	5	25
T (Tony) Underwood E4 L+	-	-	-	K	N	-	K	K	-	-	N	-	-	-	-	-	-	-	N	N	-	N	K	-	-	-	N	-	-	-	-	K	N	-	-	N	N	14	9	45
RA (Richard) Wareham	-	x	r	-	-	-	-	-	-	-	-	-	B	-	-	-	-	<B	-	-	-	-	-	-	-	-	-	x	-	-	-	-	-	-	-	-	-	2+1	-	-
JM (John) Wells	F*	F*	-	F*	F*	F*	F*	F*	-	-	F*	-	-	-	-	-	-	F*	F*	F*	F*	F*	F*	F*	F*	F*	-	F*	F*	F*	F*	G*	F*	-	-	F*	F*	25	1	5
SR (Steve) Wills	-	-	-	r	-	x	-	-	-	L	-	x	-	-	-	-	-	-	-	-	-	-	-	-	-	-	-	-	-	-	-	-	-	-	-	-	-	1+1	-	-

1 GAME: PW (Paul) Dodge E32 L2 <r(32), MV (Malcolm) Foulkes-Arnold D(34), NR (Niall) Griffiths x(33)=A(34), S (Steve) Harris =r(26), DA (Derek) Jelley >A(36), WP (Wayne) Richardson r(14), RJ (Roy) Robson x(4)x(6)=G(13), SJ (Stuart) Towns =r(9), TO (Toby) White >r(26)x(32)x(34), ST (Steve) Wigley <L(34)

The key for how to read the stats is on the last page

CHAPTER 26

Final Demands

1993/1994

The fact that Leicester had four representatives with the Lions, their status as cup winners and their general optimism about the future had the desired impact. The average gate during 1992/93 had been around 7,000 but now membership spiralled towards 10,000 and a feasibility study on the development of the ground proposed a 3,000-seat stand at the Welford Road end costing £1.75 million. Dean Richards resumed the captaincy after a two-year break from the role but Rory Underwood opted for a two-month rest after the Lions tour and missed the first five league games.

Just to stir the pot, New Zealand made a 13-match tour of England and Scotland which brought them once more to Welford Road to play the Midlands whose XV was: John Steele (Northampton); Steve Hackney, Stuart Potter, Ian Bates (all Leicester), Harvey Thorneycroft (Northampton); Paul Challinor (Harlequins), Matt Dawson (Northampton); Graham Rowntree (Leicester), John Olver, Gary Pearce (both Northampton), Martin Johnson (Leicester), Steve Lloyd (Moseley), John Wells, Dean Richards (captain), Neil Back (all Leicester).

In a hard-fought encounter, the All Blacks prevailed 12-6, a brace of penalties each from Shane Howarth and Matt Cooper against two kicked for the Midlands by Steele. Rowntree and Back played against the All Blacks again, for England A at Gateshead, and four Leicester players - the Underwood brothers, Johnson and Richards - gained some measure of revenge for the loss of the Lions series in New Zealand when they helped England win 15-9 at Twickenham.

Rory Underwood, meanwhile, was demonstrating an unexpected versatility in his club career by playing centre against Harlequins, Will Carling and all, and Leicester enjoyed the home win over the league leaders, Bath, if only by 9-6. Injury to Liley extended Jez Harris's responsibilities to those of goalkicker and, against the Barbarians over Christmas, he showed his full range with a try, six conversions, two penalties and a dropped goal in a 51-14 win. But in the new year Leicester lost Richards for two months with a dislocated elbow against Orrell which kept him out of all but the last match of the five nations championship.

England finally grasped the nettle and selected Back for his first cap, the visit to Scotland alongside the Underwoods and Johnson. Ten Leicester players were named in three representative sides - the seniors, the A side against Italy and an Emerging England XV against Spain. Potter played centre in all three A internationals with Kardooni and Cockerill on the bench while Matt Poole and Darren Garforth were joined in the Emerging Players squad by Harris (the fly-half scored a try, nine conversions and a penalty in the 86-17 win over Spain in Elche).

Meanwhile Leicester sustained a challenge on both league and cup fronts. A run of 18 consecutive victories equalled a club record and included cup wins over Blackheath, London Irish, Moseley and, in the semi-finals, Orrell on their own ground by 31-18. But the old nemesis, Bath, awaited and this was to be their season, the last under Jack Rowell who was replacing Geoff Cooke as England manager and included in his new coaching panel Les Cusworth, to look after the England backs.

Bath beat Leicester 14-6 at a muddy Recreation Ground and that is how the league ended, Bath first and Leicester second. The two clubs met again in the Pilkington Cup final at Twickenham, before which was an important date at Leicester's Grand Hotel, the retirement dinner staged for Chalkie White, now 65 and standing down as the RFU's technical director for the south-west. White was made an honorary life member six years later.

↓ Matt Poole, Richard Cockerill and Martin Johnson in the thick of the action as Tigers go down 6-14 in a mudbath at Bath.

The final proved a damp squib. Though a world record crowd (for a club match) of 68,000 demonstrated what an occasion it had become, the match never caught fire. Bath won 21-9 to clinch a league and cup double, and were demonstrably superior in most areas of the game. Leicester's team was: Wayne Kilford; Tony Underwood, Stuart Potter, Laurence Boyle, Rory Underwood; Jez Harris, Aadel Kardooni; Graham Rowntree, Richard Cockerill, Darren Garforth, Martin Johnson, Matt Poole, John Wells, Dean Richards (captain), Neil Back.

Harris kicked three first-half penalties to finish the club season on 314 points but Tony Swift and Mike Catt scored tries for Bath, Jonathan Callard added a conversion and three penalties, while Harris was adrift with three kicking opportunities in the second half and the game slipped away from Leicester.

↓ Jez Harris was the top scorer in 1993/94 with 314 points.

Rowell chose six Leicester players to tour South Africa in the summer - the Underwood brothers, Richards, Johnson, Rowntree and Poole, later to be joined by Potter who replaced the injured Bath centre, Jeremy Guscott. Not that Johnson's tour lasted long: a punch by the Transvaal prop, Johan le Roux, sent him home with concussion and he missed the tumultuous 32-15 win over the Springboks in Pretoria in which the Underwoods and Richards shared. Seven Leicester players were named in a provisional World Cup squad a month later with Back receiving the call once more but Poole being omitted.

While their players were slugging it out in the southern hemisphere, Leicester confirmed their forward planning for Welford Road over the next ten years. The primary item was a new Welford Road stand though it took a while for planning permission to filter through; when it did, in March 1995, the estimated cost was between £2-3 million. How ironic that, at much the same time, leading RFU officials were warning that the game could tear itself apart, through money or on-field violence, tacit admission of the degree to which the amateur ethic was under threat.

1994/1995

The forthcoming World Cup overshadowed the entire season. Having reached the 1991 final, England laid down playing strictures on club appearances on the weekends prior to internationals and in the closing month of April. A powerful new medium had also entered the lists: the satellite television channel, Sky Sports, agreed a £6 million deal with the RFU to show club rugby while the BBC revamped their own *Rugby Special* programme in response. Sky's arrival raised the bar of rugby coverage significantly, though Leicester's first appearance on their programme on the second week of the Courage Clubs Championship was less than entertaining, a 6-0 win against Orrell.

On every hand the potential arrival of professional rugby was discussed: the French were said to be ready to form a paid competition, South Africa perceived it as inevitable and even the International Rugby Football Board admitted it could do little to prevent union players who had gone to league returning to the amateur enclosure, unless they wanted a string of law suits dumped in their lap. England players had tried to maximise their sporting fame in a commercial sense for several seasons and Leicester eventually formed their own player-promotion company, named A2O.

The club also became involved in talks about a European 'super cup' for the 1995/96 season, involving among others Bath, Cardiff, Swansea, Toulouse and Brive. As luck would have it, the Welsh and French clubs took part in the first season of European competition, after the game went open, but the English clubs did not participate until 1996/97. Meanwhile Leicester went eight league games without loss, including a 20-20 draw at Bath. The clash of England's Titans at the Recreation Ground brought together two clubs who had won all six of their league games, though Bath were presumed to be the more formidable having lost only twice in the league at home in the previous eight years.

But they were held here, thanks to the latest of tries by Jamie Hamilton which earned Leicester their draw. Hamilton, normally a scrum-half, would not have been playing but for the fact that Tony Underwood was held up by heavy traffic and did not reach the Recreation Ground in time. Bath could complain that they scored two tries while Harris kicked penalty after penalty, five in all, until Hamilton's telling intervention.

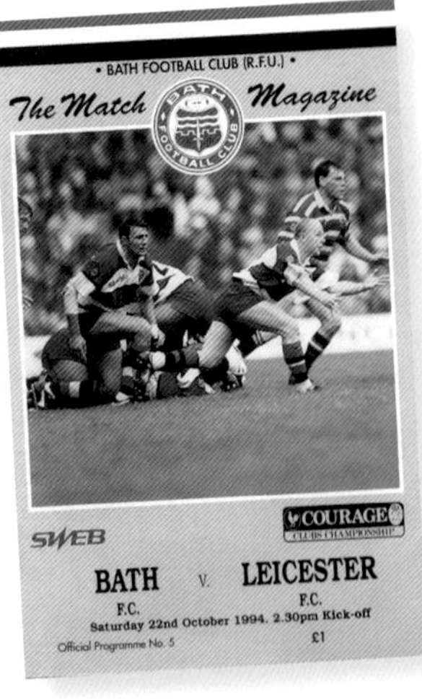

↓ Programme from the 20-20 draw at Bath 22.10.1994.

Bristol finally lowered Leicester colours with a 31-22 win at the Memorial Ground and the rumble of league competition probably evoked greater interest than England's two autumn internationals, against Romania and Canada. Leicester gave eight players to the Midlands squad that won the unloved divisional championship, among them the young Yorkshire centre, Diccon Edwards, who had joined from Wakefield at the start of the season.

↑ Neil Back takes on Northampton in their own back yard 7.1.1995.

Neil Back helped the Barbarians beat the touring South Africans 23-15 but a shadow fell across Leicester's traditional Christmas fixture with the Baa-baas. The RFU confirmed that, in 1995/96, a league programme would be scheduled for 30 December, three days after the date of the game which would force Leicester to decide which fixture took precedence. Nor did the Barbarians find it easy to raise a team of its usual strength and only seven internationals were included for the game that Leicester won 31-18, an occasion overtaken by the signal achievement of Richards scoring his 100th try for the club. He became only the second forward in the club's history to do so, David Matthews having totalled 119 between 1955 and 1974.

Leicester opened their Pilkington Cup campaign with a straightforward 56-11 win over Blackheath and they followed that up, with a measure of satisfaction, by beating Bristol 16-8 on their own ground though short of the services of Johnson who had pulled a hamstring in England's 20-8 win over Ireland. The national team went on to another grand slam during which Richards became the world's most-capped No 8, adding six Lions appearances to his 41 for England which took him past Mervyn Davies, the former Wales player. In the finale against Scotland at Twickenham, Rowntree took the field as a temporary replacement for Jason Leonard and thereby won his first cap.

Away from the international arena, Bath ground remorselessly on in the league with not a blemish on their record save three draws. Leicester headed the pursuit but seemed doomed to second place again and may have thought the cup offered a safer bet. Liley scored all their points in a tight quarter-final at Sale but the first sign of a chink in Bath's armour came when they lost by a point at third-placed Wasps; on the same day Leicester struggled to a 12-6 win at West Hartlepool and suddenly found themselves top of the pile on points difference. Over-excited by the prospect they promptly lost a home cup semi-final to Wasps 25-22.

← Skipper John Wells gets to grips with his opposite number at Wasps, Dean Ryan, in the cup semi-final at Welford Road 1.4.1995.

The mid-April meeting with Bath was seen as the league title clincher and Leicester won 31-21, thanks to the organisation of their forwards at set-pieces and re-starts. Liley kicked five penalties and Harris dropped three goals before Rory Underwood scored the interception try that settled the outcome. Once more they were top with two games remaining and a 20-10 win at Sale left them two points clear of their rivals; even without five of their England players who had to be rested, Leicester cleared the final hurdle, against Bristol, 17-3.

"This means everything to me," Richards said as his colleagues celebrated the club's second league title. "I have played for Leicester since I was 18 and when we won the league seven years ago it was a momentous occasion. But for me to be captain just about surpasses that." Leicester also won the second-team competition and the under-21 title, confirmation as their new stand rose that the club was in good health. The naming rights for the new structure had gone to the Alliance and Leicester Building Society for a five-year period which added to the club's coffers. To put the icing on the cake, Liley led Leicester to victory over the South African township side, Ithuba, in the final of the Middlesex sevens at Twickenham, their first success at the world-famous tournament.

But Leicester, and every other English club, needed the rosiest of health as professional rugby loomed ever larger. When rugby league accepted a summertime Super League, funded by Rupert Murdoch's News Limited group, it meant far greater wealth available to the other code and, therefore, greater temptation for leading union players to swap. Representatives of Leicester and Bath pressed for a European competition involving 12 clubs and to be held in November/December, with semi-finals and a final later in the season. But the RFU poured cold water on the scheme, at least until the 1996/97 season, little knowing how the calendar was about to be ripped up by events in South Africa and Paris later in the year.

Meanwhile the Underwoods, Johnson, Rowntree, Richards and Back all set off with England for the World Cup base in Durban. Rory Underwood, who scored five tries during the tournament, and Johnson played every minute of England's six games as they reached the semi-finals and then foundered against a New Zealand side inspired by Jonah Lomu, the giant wing. Rowntree made his first start, against Italy, but when push came to shove, Back made way for a back-row combination of Tim Rodber, Ben Clarke and Richards. Tony Underwood scored a critical try in the 25-22 defeat of Australia in the quarter-finals and his older brother scored two against the All Blacks but only when England were chasing a hopeless cause, trailing as they did by 30-3 just after half-time.

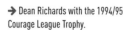

→ Dean Richards with the 1994/95 Courage League Trophy.

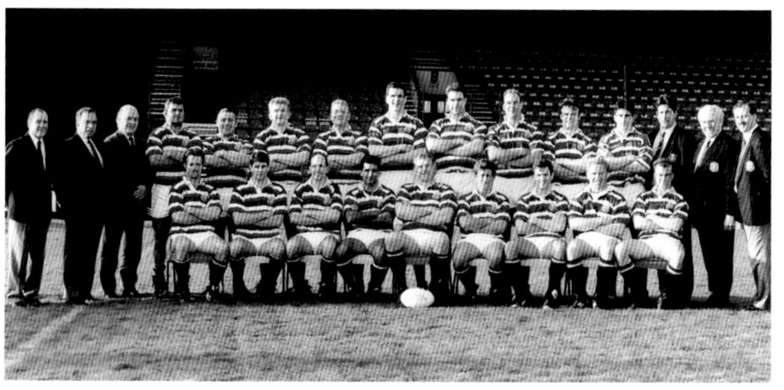

↑ LEICESTER FOOTBALL CLUB 1993/94
Back: Hill (Team Hon.Sec), Russ (Director of rugby), Allen (Hon.Sec), Garforth, Cockerill, Rowntree, Jelley, M.Johnson, Poole, Tarbuck, Drake-Lee, Malone, Dodge (Assistant coach), Thomas (President), Smith (Assistant coach).
Front: Boyle, Kilford, Liley, Kardooni, Richards (capt), Harris, Potter, Back, Hackney.

↑ LEICESTER FOOTBALL CLUB 1994/95
Back: Hill (Team Hon.sec), Russ (Director of rugby), Dowson (Fitness advisor), Garforth, Rowntree, Jelley, Wells, Poole, P.Grant, Smith, Tarbuck, Robinson, Potter, Drake-Lee, Back, Dodge (Assistant coach), Smith (Assistant coach), Allen (Hon.Sec), Thomas (President).
Front: R.Underwood, Cockerill, Liley, Hackney, Kardooni, Richards (capt), Harris, Hamilton, Kilford, Edwards.

19	93/94	Home Ground: Welford Road
		Head Coach: Tony Russ assisted by Ian Smith and Paul Dodge
		Captain: Dean Richards

OVERALL RECORD:					T	C	PG	DG	PTS
PLD	W	D	L	Tigers scored:	105	66	94	16	987
35	27	0	8	Opponents scored:	58	36	55	4	539

GM	DATE		VEN	OPPONENTS	RESULT	POS/LGE	TRIES	KICKS	ATT
COURAGE LEAGUE DIVISION 1 (2ND)						**CHAMPIONS: BATH**			
2	Sep	11	a	Northampton	L 10-19	8	T.Underwood 79	Harris c/p	-
3		**18**	**H**	**Orrell**	W 23-18	7	Back 27, Potter 63	Liley 2c/p, Harris 2d	7529
4		25	a	Gloucester	W 23-14	4	Hackney 23/30, Back 80	Liley c/p, Harris d	6000
5	Oct	**2**	**H**	**Wasps**	W 38-6	2	Back 4, Wells 37, Poole 56, Richards 79	Harris 3c/3p/d	8883
6		9	a	Newcastle Gosforth	W 22-13	2	Back 39	Harris c/4p/d	-
12	Nov	**13**	**H**	**Harlequins**	L 3-10	3	-	Liley p	9915
13		**20**	**H**	**Bath**	W 9-6	2	-	Liley 2p, Harris d	11682
14	Dec	4	a	London Irish	W 22-10	2	Kardooni 3, Harris 29	Harris 2p/2d	-
15		**11**	**H**	**Bristol**	W 21-9	2	-	Harris 7p	7575
18	Jan	**8**	**H**	**Northampton**	W 36-9	2	T.Underwood 68, Poole 70, Kilford 80	Harris 3c/3p/2d	12661
19		15	a	Orrell	W 18-0	2	Boyle 14, Kilford 23, Harris 72	Harris p	-
21		**29**	**H**	**Gloucester**	W 28-8	2	T.Underwood 51	Harris c/7p	10611
23	Feb	12	a	Wasps	W 15-13	2	-	Harris 4p/d	-
27	Mar	**12**	**H**	**Newcastle Gosforth**	W 66-5	2	Hackney 3/5, T.Underwood 15/19/49/76, Back 34/80, Rowntree 61, Robinson 66	Harris 5c/2p	8128
29		26	a	Harlequins	W 25-13	2	Back 2, Potter 28, Richards 80	Harris 2c/2p	-
31	Apr	9	a	Bath	L 6-14	2	-	Harris 2p	8000
33		**23**	**H**	**London Irish**	W 38-3	2	Boyle 42, Hackney 57, T.Underwood 59, Potter 68, Smith 76	Harris 2c/3p	7777
34		30	a	Bristol	L 22-40	2	Tarbuck 32, C.Johnson 50, Reynolds 79	Liley 2c/p	-
RFU CLUB COMPETITION (PILKINGTON CUP)						**CUP WINNERS: BATH**			
16	Dec	18	a	Blackheath (4)	W 16-10	D3	Back 10/65	Kilford 2p	-
20	Jan	**22**	**H**	**London Irish (5)**	W 43-10	D1	T.Underwood 13, R.Underwood 38, Rowntree 49, Wells 70, Garforth 77	Harris 3c/4p	10024
25	Feb	**26**	**H**	**Moseley (qf)**	W 12-6	D2	-	Harris 3p/d	10000
30	Apr	2	a	Orrell (sf)	W 31-18	D1	Potter 48/77, R.Underwood 61	Harris 2c/4p	5000
35	May	7		Bath (f)	L 9-21	D1	-	Harris 3p	68000
CLUB MATCHES									
1	Sep	**4**	**H**	**Amatori Milano**	W 53-7		Drake-Lee 29/45, M.Johnson 39, McAdam 49, Rowntree 54, Kilford 58, Kardooni 68/70	Harris 5c/d	5368
7	Oct	16	a	Swansea	L 19-45		Murphy 65, Reed 69	Eagle 3p	-
8		**21th**	**H**	**South African Barbarians**	L 18-24		-	Harris 6p	4244
9		30	a	Saracens	W 14-8		Hopper 79	Kilford 3p	-
10	Nov	**2tu**	**H**	**Cambridge University**	W 31-27		Drake-Lee 18, Tarbuck 27, Eagle 80	Liley 2c/4p	1890
11		**6**	**H**	**Loughborough Students**	W 48-32		Drake-Lee 8, Eagle 13, Gabriel 29, Evans 37/56, Jelley 45, Tarbuck 62	Liley 5c/p	2346
17	Dec	**28tu**	**H**	**Barbarians**	W 51-14		Potter 2/80, R.Underwood 31, Rowntree 42, Harris 70, T.Underwood 77	Harris 6c/2p/d	14137
22	Feb	**4f**	**H**	**Coventry**	W 63-5		Hackney 7/47, C.Johnson 12, O.Wingham 29, P.Grant 55, Tarbuck 59, Liley 66, Malone 75, Kilford 80	Liley 6c/p, Malone d	3306
24		**18f**	**H**	**Otley**	W 62-27		Penalty 22, Hackney 37/67, Gabriel 45, Malone 53, Poole 65, Kilford 75	Liley 6c/5p	3077
		18f	**H**	**Bedford**	PP (league)				
		26	**H**	**London Welsh**	PP (cup)				
26	Mar	4f	a	Moseley	W 21-15		Malone 2, Reynolds 37	Liley c/3p	-
28		**16w**	**H**	**Nottingham**	W 44-10		Liley 17/42, Kardooni 45, Aldwinckle 62, Robinson 72, Grimsdell 78	Liley 4c/2p	2528
	Apr	2	a	Ballymena	PP (cup)				
32		16	a	Sale	L 27-50		Liley 13, Tarbuck 44, Gabriel 52	Liley 3c/p, Malone d	-

***Neutral Venue:** #35 at Twickenham*

INDIVIDUAL APPEARANCES 1993/94

Name / Game #	1	2	3	4	5	6	7	8	9	10	11	12	13	14	15	16	17	18	19	20	21	22	23	24	25	26	27	28	29	30	31	32	33	34	35	Apps	T	Pts
JM (Jason) Aldwinckle	x	-	-	-	-	-	-	-	-	x	B	-	-	x	-	r	-	x	-	-	-	-	-	-	-	B	x	B	x	-	-	B	-	x	-	4+1	1	5
NA (Neil) Back E2 L+	-	H	H	H	H	H	-	-	-	-	-	H	H	-	H	H	H	H	H	H	-	-	H	-	H	-	H	-	H	-	-	-	-	-	H	18	9	45
I (Ian) Bates	M	M	M	M	M	M	-	M	-	-	-	-	-	-	-	-	-	-	-	-	-	-	-	-	-	-	-	-	-	-	-	L	-	-	-	8	-	-
LS (Laurence) Boyle	-	-	-	-	-	-	-	-	-	-	-	-	-	-	-	L	L	L	M	L	M	L	M	-	M	-	M	-	L	L	L	-	L	-	<L	15	2	10
R (Richard) Cockerill E+	B	B	B	B	B	B	-	B	-	B	-	B	B	B	B	B	B	B	x	B	B	-	B	-	B	-	B	-	B	B	B	-	B	-	B	25	-	-
WM (Bill) Drake-Lee	H	-	-	-	-	-	H	H	H	H	H	-	-	H	x	-	-	-	-	-	H	H	-	H	-	H	-	H	-	H	H	H	-	H	x	16	4	20
G (Grant) Eagle	-	-	-	-	-	-	>J	-	M	L	<L	-	x	-	-	x	-	-	x	-	-	-	-	-	-	-	-	-	-	-	-	-	-	-	-	4	2	19
JL (Jason) Evans	-	-	-	-	-	-	L	L	L	M	<M	-	-	-	-	-	-	-	-	-	-	x	-	-	-	x	-	x	-	-	-	-	-	-	-	5	2	10
BJ (Brian) Gabriel	x	-	-	-	-	-	>I	x	I	-	I	I	-	-	-	-	-	-	-	-	-	I	-	I	-	I	-	-	-	x	-	I	-	<I	-	9	3	15
DJ (Darren) Garforth E+	C	C	C	C	C	C	-	C	-	-	-	C	C	C	C	C	C	C	C	C	C	-	C	-	C	-	C	C	C	C	C	-	C	-	C	26	1	5
AJS (Alex) Gissing	-	-	-	-	-	-	-	D	D	D	<D	-	-	-	-	-	-	-	-	-	-	-	-	-	-	-	-	-	-	-	-	-	-	-	-	4	-	-
PJ (Paul) Grant	-	-	-	-	-	-	D	-	-	-	-	-	-	-	-	-	-	-	-	-	-	D	-	D	-	D	-	E	-	-	-	E	D	D	-	8	1	5
ST (Steve) Hackney	N	N	N	N	N	N	-	-	-	-	-	N	N	N	N	N	-	N	-	-	-	N	-	N	-	N	N	-	N	N	N	N	N	N	-	22	9	45
JG (Jamie) Hamilton	-	-	x	-	x	r	-	-	-	-	-	-	-	-	x	-	r	x	-	x	-	-	x	-	x	-	-	-	x	-	x	-	r	r	x	0+4	-	-
JC (Jez) Harris	J	J	J	J	J	J	-	J	-	-	-	J	J	J	J	-	J	J	J	J	J	-	J	-	J	-	J	-	J	J	J	-	J	-	J	24	3	314
DA (Dave) Hopper	-	-	-	-	-	-	-	-	C	-	<C	-	-	-	-	-	-	-	-	-	-	-	-	x	-	x	-	-	-	-	-	-	-	-	-	2	1	5
DA (Derek) Jelley	-	-	-	-	x	-	A	A	A	A	A	-	-	A	x	-	-	-	-	-	x	A	-	A	-	A	-	A	-	x	-	A	-	A	x	12	1	5
CAP (Chris) Johnson	-	x	x	x	-	x	B	x	B	-	-	x	x	-	-	-	x	-	B	x	-	B	-	-	x	-	-	-	-	x	x	-	-	B	x	5	2	10
MO (Martin) Johnson E6 L2	D	D	D	D	D	D	-	-	-	-	-	D	D	D	D	D	D	D	D	D	D	-	D	-	D	-	-	-	D	D	D	-	-	-	D	22	1	5
A (Aadel) Kardooni	I	I	I	I	I	I	-	I	-	I	-	-	I	I	I	I	I	I	I	I	I	-	I	-	I	-	I	I*	I	I	I	-	I	-	I	26	4	20
WA (Wayne) Kilford	K	O	-	-	O	O	O	O	O	-	-	x	-	K	O	O	O	O	O	O	O	K	O	K	O	-	O	-	O	O	-	-	O	-	O	24	5	40
JG (John) Liley	O	-	O	O	-	-	-	-	-	O	O	O	O	O	-	-	-	-	-	-	x	O	-	O	-	O	-	O	-	-	-	O*	-	O	-	14	4	153
NG (Niall) Malone I2	-	-	-	-	-	-	-	x	-	J	J	-	-	r	-	J	-	-	-	-	-	J	-	J	-	J	r	J	-	x	-	J	-	J	x	9+2	3	21
J (John) Murphy	r	-	-	x	-	-	r	-	-	-	-	x	-	-	-	F	-	-	-	-	-	x	-	-	-	-	-	-	-	-	-	-	-	-	-	1+2	1	5
MD (Matt) Poole	E	E	E	E	E	E	-	E	E	-	-	E	E	E	E	E	E	E	E	E	E	-	E	E*	E	-	E	-	E	E	E	-	-	-	E	26	3	15
S (Stuart) Potter E+	L	L	L	L	L	L	-	-	-	-	-	L	L	L	L	M	M	M	L	M	L	-	L	-	L	-	-	-	M	M	M	-	M	-	M	23	7	35
SJ (Simon) Povoas	-	-	r	F	x	-	G	-	-	<G	-	-	-	-	-	-	-	-	-	-	-	-	-	-	-	-	-	-	-	-	-	-	-	-	-	3+1	-	-
SD (Steve) Reed	-	-	-	-	-	-	>K	K	N	-	-	-	-	-	-	-	-	-	-	-	-	-	-	-	-	-	-	<K	-	-	-	-	-	-	-	4	1	5
TR (Tom) Reynolds	-	-	-	-	-	-	N	N	-	-	-	-	-	-	-	-	-	-	-	-	-	-	-	-	-	K	-	N	-	-	-	K	-	K	-	6	2	10
D (Dean) Richards E36 L6	G*	G*	G*	G*	G*	G*	-	G*	-	-	-	G*	G*	G*	G*	G*	G*	G*	G*	-	-	-	-	-	-	-	G*	-	G*	G*	G*	-	G*	-	G*	21	2	10
ND (Nigel) Richardson	-	-	-	-	-	-	-	-	-	-	-	-	-	-	-	-	-	x	r	-	-	-	-	-	-	-	-	-	-	-	-	-	<H	-	-	1+1	-	-
RP (Richie) Robinson	-	-	-	-	-	-	>M	-	r	x	-	-	-	-	-	-	-	-	-	-	-	M	-	L	-	L	L	M	-	-	-	M	-	M	-	8+1	2	10
SM (Stewart) Roke	-	-	-	-	-	-	-	-	-	-	-	-	-	-	-	-	-	-	-	-	-	-	-	>M	-	M	-	L	-	-	-	-	-	L	-	4	-	-
CG (Graham) Rowntree E+ L+	A	A	A	A	A	A	-	-	-	-	-	A	A	-	A	A	A	A	A	A	A	-	A	-	A	-	A	-	A	A	A	-	A	-	A	23	4	20
P (Peter) Sandford	-	-	-	-	-	K	-	-	-	K	<K	-	-	-	-	-	-	-	-	-	-	-	-	-	-	-	-	-	-	-	-	-	-	-	-	3	-	-
T (Tom) Smith	-	-	-	-	-	-	E*	-	-	E*	E*	-	-	-	-	-	-	-	-	-	-	E*	-	-	-	E*	D	-	-	-	-	-	E	E*	-	8	1	5
CR (Chris) Tarbuck	-	x	-	-	-	>r	F	x	F	F	F	-	x	-	-	-	-	-	-	r	G	G	G	F	G	F	x	F	-	-	-	G	-	G	x	13+2	5	25
R (Rory) Underwood E65 L6	-	-	-	-	-	-	-	-	K*	-	-	M	M	M	M	K	K	-	K	K	K	-	K	-	K	-	-	-	K	K	O	-	-	-	K	16	3	15
T (Tony) Underwood E8 L+	-	K	K	-	-	-	-	-	-	-	-	K	K	-	K	-	N	K	N	N	N	-	N	-	N	-	K	-	-	-	K	-	K	-	N	16	10	50
JM (John) Wells	F	F	F	-	F	F	-	F	-	-	-	F	F	F	F	-	F	F	-	G*	F*	-	F*	-	F*	-	F	-	F	F	F	-	F	-	F	22	2	10
TO (Toby) White	-	-	-	-	-	-	-	-	G	-	G	-	-	x	-	x	r	-	-	-	x	x	-	G	x	<G	-	x	x	x	-	-	-	x	-	4+1	-	-
DL (Dave) Wigley HK+	-	-	-	K	K	-	-	-	J	N	N	-	-	-	-	-	-	-	-	-	-	-	-	x	-	-	-	-	-	x	-	-	-	-	-	5	-	-
JMW (Jim) Wingham	x	-	-	-	-	-	>C	-	-	-	-	-	-	-	-	-	-	-	-	-	-	C	x	C	-	C	-	r	-	-	-	C	x	C	-	6+1	-	-
OJ (Oscar) Wingham	-	-	-	-	-	-	-	-	-	-	x	-	-	-	-	-	-	-	>F	F	-	F	x	-	-	-	-	-	-	-	-	F	r	F	-	5+1	1	5

1 GAME: BS (Ben) Brier <r(10), MV (Malcolm) Foulkes-Arnold <D(32), MR (Mark) Grant x(9)D(28), D (Darren) Grewcock x(2)r(4), A (Andy) Grimsdell <Gt(28)x(31), RTNM (Rob) Harding >B(24), WW (Will) Johnson >r(32), A (Andy) McAdam rt(1), WP (Wayne) Richardson <C(10), DA (David) Wraith =r(7)

The key for how to read the stats is on the last page

1994/95										
Home Ground: Welford Road	**Trophy Cabinet:** Courage League Division 1(2), Middlesex Sevens(1)	OVERALL RECORD:					T	C	PG	DG	PTS
Director of Coaching: Tony Russ assisted by Ian Smith and Paul Dodge		PLD	W	D	L	Tigers scored:	71	48	101	14	796
Captain: Dean Richards		32	28	1	3	Opponents scored:	32	18	68	9	427

GM	DATE		VEN	OPPONENTS	RESULT	POS/LGE	TRIES	KICKS	ATT
COURAGE LEAGUE DIVISION 1 (1ST)						**CHAMPIONS: LEICESTER TIGERS**			
2	Sep	**10**	**H**	**Northampton**	W 28-15	2	Hackney 22, T.Underwood 80	Harris 6p	10037
3		17	a	Orrell	W 6-0	3	-	Harris 2p	-
4		**24**	**H**	**Gloucester**	W 16-6	2	M.Johnson 67	Liley c/3p	9384
5	Oct	1	a	Wasps	W 23-18	2	T.Underwood 44	Harris 5p/d	-
6		**8**	**H**	**West Hartlepool**	W 33-16	2	Murphy 35/70, Liley 67, M.Johnson 73	Liley 2c/3p	9025
7		15	a	Harlequins	W 40-13	1	Hackney 44/60, Kardooni 50, Liley 70	Harris 4c/3p/d	-
8		22	a	Bath	D 20-20	1	Hamilton 71	Harris 5p	8000
9		**29**	**H**	**Sale**	W 37-20	1	Hackney 4/41, T.Underwood 17	Harris 2c/5p/d	9653
10	Nov	5	a	Bristol	L 22-31	2	Tarbuck 80	Harris c/4p/d	-
16	Jan	7	a	Northampton	W 20-18	2	Wigley 7, Penalty 37	Harris 2c/p/d	7000
17		**14**	**H**	**Orrell**	W 29-19	2	Kilford 23, Tarbuck 71	Harris 2c/5p	9523
21	Feb	11	a	Gloucester	L 3-9	2	-	Harris p	-
24	Mar	**4**	**H**	**Wasps**	W 21-6	2	R.Underwood 56/68	Liley c/3p	10075
27		25	a	West Hartlepool	W 12-6	1	-	Harris 3p/d	-
29	Apr	**8**	**H**	**Harlequins**	W 22-8	2	T.Underwood 71	Liley c/4p, Harris d	8673
30		**15**	**H**	**Bath**	W 31-21	1	R.Underwood 80	Liley c/5p, Harris 3d	12483
31		22	a	Sale	W 20-10	1	Liley 54	Liley 3p, Harris 2d	3000
32		**29**	**H**	**Bristol**	W 17-3	1	Potter 5	Liley 3p, Harris d	12196
RFU CLUB COMPETITION (PILKINGTON CUP)						**CUP WINNERS: BATH**			
14	Dec	**17**	**H**	**Blackheath (4)**	W 56-11	D3	Potter 11, Liley 26, Back 43, R.Underwood 63, Hackney 68	Liley p, Harris 5c/6p	6487
19	Jan	28	a	Bristol (5)	W 16-8	D1	Kardooni 39	Liley c/2p, Harris p	9500
23	Feb	25	a	Sale (qf)	W 14-12	D1	Liley 41	Liley 3p	3500
28	Apr	**1**	**H**	**Wasps (sf)**	L 22-25	D1	R.Underwood 46	Liley c/5p	12395
CLUB MATCHES									
1	Sep	**3**	**H**	**Saracens**	W 33-8		Kardooni 18/80, T.Underwood 41, Kilford 47	Harris 2c/2p/d	6440
11	Nov	19	a	Oxford University	W 24-19		P.Grant 4, Binns 12, McAdam 30, Grewcock 69	Liley 2c	-
12		26	a	Cambridge University	W 24-13		Robinson 25, O.Wingham 47	Kilford c/4p	-
13	Dec	**3**	**H**	**Loughborough Students**	W 37-15		Jelley 17, Wigley 21, Murphy 31, Hamilton 51, C.Johnson 56	Wigley 3c/2p	2269
		9f	**H**	**Otley**	PP				
15		**27tu**	**H**	**Barbarians**	W 31-18		Potter 8/70, Poole 31, Richards 78	Malone 4c/p	14614
18	Jan	20f	a	Old Belvedere	W 29-7		Binns 33, Hackney 76, C.Johnson, Kardooni, Robinson	Liley 2c	-
20	Feb	3f	a	Coventry	W 30-17		Robinson 5, Mansell 47, Tarbuck 69	Liley 3c/3p	-
22		17f	a	Bedford	W 26-10		McAdam 9, Evans 21, Roke 30, Hamilton 76	Malone 3c	-
25	Mar	**11**	**H**	**Moseley**	W 25-16		Hackney 30	Malone c/6p	3881
26		17f	a	Nottingham	W 29-9		McAdam 31/76, Kilford 54, Roke 60	Malone 3c/p	-

INDIVIDUAL APPEARANCES 1994/95

Name / Game #	1	2	3	4	5	6	7	8	9	10	11	12	13	14	15	16	17	18	19	20	21	22	23	24	25	26	27	28	29	30	31	32	Apps	T	Pts
JM (Jason) Aldwinckle	B	x	x	-	x	-	x	-	-	-	-	-	-	x	-	-	x	-	-	B	-	B	x	x	-	B	x	-	x	-	-	-	4	-	-
NA (Neil) Back E2 L+	-	-	H	H	H	H	-	H	H	H	-	-	-	H	H	H	H	-	H	-	H	-	H	H	-	-	-	H	H	H	-	-	18	1	5
I (Ian) Bates	M	-	-	-	-	-	-	-	-	-	-	-	-	-	-	-	-	-	-	-	-	-	-	-	-	M	-	-	-	-	-	-	2	-	-
SM (Simon) Beatham	-	-	-	-	-	-	-	-	-	-	>M	M	-	-	-	-	-	<L	-	-	-	-	-	-	-	-	-	-	-	-	-	-	3	-	-
RD (Dick) Beaty	-	-	-	-	-	-	-	-	-	-	-	-	-	-	-	-	-	=H	-	-	-	-	-	-	-	-	-	-	-	-	-	-	1	-	-
SJ (Simon) Binns	-	-	-	-	-	-	-	-	-	-	>J	J	J	-	-	-	-	J	-	-	-	-	-	-	-	-	-	-	-	-	-	-	4	2	10
R (Richard) Cockerill E+	-	B	B	x	B	x	B	B	x	B	-	-	-	B	B	B	B	-	B	-	x	-	B	B	B	-	B	B	B	B	B	B	20	-	-
PK (Phil) Delaney	-	-	-	-	-	-	-	-	-	-	-	-	-	-	-	-	-	-	-	>J	-	-	-	-	-	-	-	-	-	-	-	-	1	-	-
WM (Bill) Drake-Lee	H	H	-	-	x	-	H	-	-	-	H	H	H	-	-	-	-	-	-	H	-	H	-	-	H	H	H	-	-	-	H	H	13	-	-
D (Diccon) Edwards	>L	M	M	M	M	M	M	M	M	M	-	-	-	M	M	M	M	-	L	-	M	M	M	L	-	-	M	M	<M	-	-	-	22	-	-
MJE (Mark) Ellis	=r	-	-	-	-	-	-	-	-	-	-	-	-	-	-	-	-	-	-	-	-	-	-	-	-	-	-	-	-	-	-	-	0+1	-	-
BJ (Barry) Evans E2	-	-	-	-	-	-	-	-	-	-	N	N	N	-	-	N	-	-	-	N	-	N	-	-	-	N	-	-	-	-	-	-	7	1	5
RJ (Rob) Field	-	-	-	-	-	-	-	-	>E	-	E	-	-	-	-	-	-	-	-	-	-	-	-	-	-	-	-	-	-	-	-	-	2	-	-
CM (Carl) Fripp	-	-	-	-	-	-	-	-	-	-	-	>E	-	-	-	-	-	E	-	-	-	x	-	-	-	-	-	-	-	-	-	-	2	-	-
DJ (Darren) Garforth E+	C	C	C	C	C	C	C	C	C	C	-	-	-	C	C	C	C	-	C	-	C	-	C	C	-	-	C	C	C	C	C	△C	24	-	-
CR (Clark) Goodwin	-	-	-	-	-	-	-	-	-	-	-	=r	-	-	-	-	-	-	-	-	-	-	-	-	-	-	-	-	-	-	-	-	0+1	-	-
MR (Mark) Grant	-	-	-	-	-	-	-	-	-	-	-	-	G	-	-	-	-	-	-	-	-	-	-	-	-	-	-	-	<r	-	-	-	1+1	-	-
PJ (Paul) Grant	D	-	-	-	-	-	-	-	-	-	D	D	D	-	-	-	x	D	-	D	-	D	-	-	D	D	-	-	D	-	r	D	11+1	1	5
D (Darren) Grewcock	-	x	-	x	-	x	-	-	r	-	I	-	r	-	r	r	-	r	-	-	x	-	-	x	-	-	x	-	x	-	-	-	1+5	1	5
ST (Steve) Hackney	-	N	N	-	-	N	N	-	N	N	-	-	-	N	N	-	N	N	-	-	N	-	N	-	N	-	-	-	N	-	N	N	16	8	40
JG (Jamie) Hamilton	-	-	x	-	x	-	-	N	-	x	-	I	I	r	I	I	x	-	x	I	-	I	x	-	I	I	-	x	I	x	x	x	10+1	3	15
JC (Jez) Harris	J	J	J	-	J	-	J	J	J	J	-	-	-	J	-	J	J	-	J	-	J	-	J	J	-	-	J	J	J	J	J	J	21	-	225
DA (Derek) Jelley	A	-	-	-	-	-	-	-	A	A	A	A	A	-	x	x	-	A	-	A	-	A	-	-	A	A	-	x	A	-	-	A	13	1	5
CAP (Chris) Johnson	-	-	-	B	-	B	-	x	B	x	B	B*	B*	-	-	-	-	B	x	-	B	-	-	-	-	-	-	x	-	x	x	x	8	2	10
MO (Martin) Johnson E12 L2	-	D	D	D	D	D	D	D	D	D	-	-	-	D	-	D	D*	-	-	-	-	-	D	D	-	-	D	D	-	D	D	-	18	2	10
A (Aadel) Kardooni	I	I	I	I	I	I	I	I	I	I	-	-	-	I	-	-	I	I	I	-	I	-	I	I	-	-	I	I	-	I	I	I	22	5	25
WA (Wayne) Kilford	O	O	O	-	-	-	O	-	-	-	-	O	-	-	O	O	O	-	-	-	-	O	-	-	O	O	-	-	-	-	-	K	12	3	29
JG (John) Liley	-	-	-	O	O	O	r	O	O	O	O*	-	-	O	-	-	-	O	O	O	O	-	O	O	-	-	O	O	O	O	O	O	20+1	5	169
A (Andy) McAdam	-	-	K	-	-	-	-	-	-	-	K	K	K	-	-	-	K	K	-	K	K	K	-	-	K	K	K	-	-	-	-	-	12	4	20
NG (Niall) Malone I3	-	-	-	J	-	J	-	-	-	-	-	-	-	-	J	-	-	-	-	-	-	J	-	-	J	J	-	x	-	-	-	-	6	-	46
L (Leigh) Mansell	-	-	-	-	-	-	-	-	-	-	-	-	>C	-	-	-	-	C	-	C	-	C	-	-	C	<C	-	-	-	-	-	-	6	1	5
J (John) Murphy	-	x	-	-	-	r	-	-	x	-	G	G	F	r	x	x	-	x	-	-	-	F	-	x	F	<F	-	x	-	-	-	-	6+2	3	15
JJP (JJ) Oelofse	-	-	-	-	-	-	-	-	-	-	-	-	-	-	-	-	-	-	-	-	-	-	-	-	-	>r	-	-	-	-	-	-	0+1	-	-
MD (Matt) Poole	-	E	E	E	E	E	-	-	-	-	-	-	-	-	D	E	E	-	D	-	D	E	E	E	E	-	E	E	E	E	E	E	20	1	5
S (Stuart) Potter E+	-	L	L	L	L	L	L	L	L	L	-	-	-	L	L	-	L	-	M	-	L	-	L	-	-	-	L	L	L	L	L	L	21	4	20
D (Dean) Richards E42 L6	G*	G*	G*	G*	G*	G*	-	G*	G*	-	-	-	-	G*	G*	G*	-	-	G*	-	G*	-	G*	G*	-	-	-	-	-	G*	-	G*	17	1	5
RP (Richie) Robinson	-	-	-	-	-	-	-	-	-	-	L	L	L	-	-	L	-	M	-	L	-	-	-	M	L	-	-	-	-	M	M	M	11	3	15
SM (Stewart) Roke	-	-	-	-	-	-	-	-	-	-	-	-	M	-	-	-	-	-	-	M	-	L	-	-	M	L	-	-	-	-	-	-	5	2	10
CG (Graham) Rowntree E1 L+	-	A	A	A	A	A	A	A	-	-	-	-	-	A	A	A	△A	-	A	-	A	-	A	A	-	-	A	A	-	A	A	-	19	-	-
T (Tom) Smith	E	-	-	-	-	-	E	E	-	E	-	-	E	E	E	-	-	-	E	E*	E	-	-	-	-	<E	-	x	-	-	-	-	11	-	-
CR (Chris) Tarbuck	-	-	x	-	-	-	G	x	-	G	-	-	-	F	F	F	G	G	r	G	-	G*	x	F	G*	G*	G	G	G	x	G	x	16+1	3	15
R (Rory) Underwood E73 L6	K	-	-	K	K	K	-	K	-	K	-	-	-	K	K	-	-	-	K	-	-	-	-	K	-	-	N	K	-	K	K	-	14	5	25
T (Tony) Underwood E16 L+	N	K	-	N	N	-	K	x	K	-	-	-	-	-	-	-	-	-	N	-	-	-	K	N	-	-	-	N	K	<N	-	-	12	5	25
JM (John) Wells	F	F	F	F	F	F	F*	F	F	F*	-	-	-	-	-	-	-	F*	F	-	F	-	F	-	-	-	F*	F*	F*	F	F*	F	20	-	-
DL (Dave) Wigley HK+	-	-	-	-	-	-	-	-	-	-	-	-	O	-	-	<K	-	-	-	-	-	-	-	-	-	-	-	-	-	-	-	-	2	2	22
SR (Steve) Wills	r	-	-	-	-	-	-	-	-	-	r	-	-	-	-	-	-	-	-	<r	-	-	-	-	-	-	-	-	-	-	-	-	0+3	-	-
JMW (Jim) Wingham	-	-	-	-	-	-	-	-	-	-	C	C	-	-	-	-	-	-	-	-	-	-	-	-	-	-	-	-	-	-	-	-	2	-	-
OJ (Oscar) Wingham	-	-	-	-	-	-	r	-	-	x	F	F	-	-	-	-	F	-	-	F	x	-	-	-	-	-	x	-	-	-	-	-	4+1	1	5

The key for how to read the stats is on the last page

CHAPTER 27

Open for Business

1995/1996

Perhaps the most momentous event of the 1995 World Cup did not happen on the field of play. It took place, instead, at a press conference in Johannesburg on the eve of the final between South Africa and New Zealand, when it was announced that News Corporation was to spend £340 million on a ten-year agreement with the three southern-hemisphere giants, South Africa, New Zealand and Australia. There would be a new international competition, a new provincial competition and, inevitably, leading players would be made wealthy.

Tudor Thomas stepped in as honorary secretary of the club.

Amateurism, at the top end of rugby union, died that day after a protracted illness and the obituary was spelled out when the International Rugby Board met at a special meeting in Paris two months later. The board chairman, Wales's Vernon Pugh, had completely rewritten the regulations to provide for an "open" game: "The IRB has played no part whatsoever to protect or speak for the sport it is supposed to be governing," Pugh said in a confidential memorandum.

All this happened four days before the start of the new season. English rugby was simply not ready for such a dramatic about-turn and the RFU declared a year-long moratorium on professionalism while it worked out the way ahead. That left the clubs to decide for themselves what to do, how to handle contract negotiations, what the market rate should be and what the impact would be for their supporters. John Allen, for one, had no doubts; after 13 years as Leicester secretary and an association of more than thirty years with the club, he resigned since he chose not to be an administrator of a professional sport.

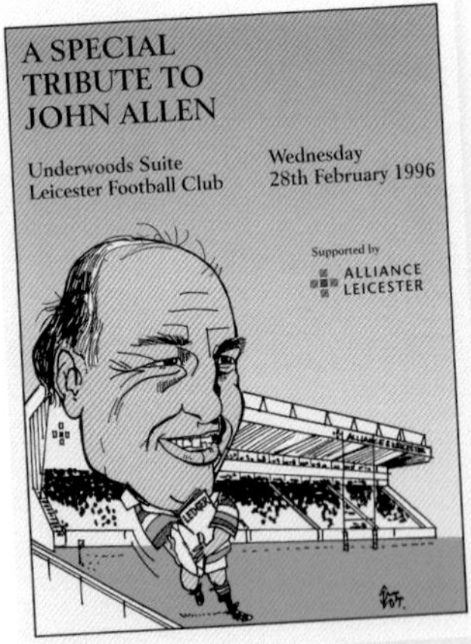

A SPECIAL
TRIBUTE TO
JOHN ALLEN
Underwoods Suite
Leicester Football Club
Wednesday
28th February 1996
Supported by
ALLIANCE
LEICESTER

When John Allen stepped down as Honorary Secretary he was accorded a special tribute dinner.

"I have always forecast that certain individuals would have to decide between staying and going and, during the summer, a professional game has become inevitable," Allen, then 53 and an accountant by profession, said. "I have enjoyed dealing with players whose loyalty to the club has been outstanding but once you start talking about contracts, that relationship is bound to change. It will create some chaos for a year or two until everyone knows what the ground rules will be and what people can afford."

Several clubs took advantage of the offers from wealthy businessmen to fund them - Sir John Hall at Newcastle Gosforth and Nigel Wray at Saracens were the earliest examples, the one seeking to build a multi-sports empire on Tyneside, the other showing a commitment to the unfashionable North London club which has lasted ever since. Peter Wheeler became chairman of a new body, English First-Division Rugby, and was therefore at the sharp end of the debate over professionalism which included the proposition that the RFU should offer central contracts to their leading players.

The ten first division clubs, plus recently-relegated Northampton, met at Leicester amid general unhappiness at the RFU's sluggish reaction, which involved the establishment of a commission to study how to manage the new era: "We want to co-operate fully with the RFU but they don't seem to want to listen to us," Wheeler, whose new organisation forecast that each club would need to find £1 million of new money to fund the professional game, said. "This is as important a commission as any set up in the past 100 years and all its aspects affect the first division totally."

The £1 million turnover in 1994 which made Leicester one of England's wealthiest clubs seemed like very small beer. Ian Smith, the coach, spoke of the need for a squad of between 30-40 players "to allow us to interchange in all positions" and Sir John Hall, described by Russ as "a threat to every club in division one" was a guest at the home game with Bath, doubtless so that Leicester could pick the brains of a newcomer to their sport as well as showing Hall how the champion club organised themselves.

Allen's position was filled, on an interim basis, by Tudor Thomas, that longstanding servant; Tony Underwood was among the first players to declare themselves a full-time professional and, a month later and after eight years at Leicester, was among a swathe of high-profile recruits by Newcastle. On 30 December Wheeler, still the club president, was named Leicester's first chief executive.

Three months later and on his fiftieth birthday, Russ was dismissed as director of rugby after six years at Welford Road. Some of his duties had been taken over by Wheeler in his new role and the club decided the need was for a director of coaching. Almost immediately links were made between Leicester and Bob Dwyer, who coached Australia to victory at the 1991 World Cup but whose tenure with the Wallabies ended four months after their departure from the 1995 tournament.

Amid such fundamental change, the playing side of the game took something of a back seat. Newcomers included Eric Miller, a young Irish back-row forward, and with the opening of the new stand, capacity at Welford Road went up to 16,900. Most of those places were sold when Bath, still the cup holders, arrived to show Leicester they remained as formidable as ever by winning 14-9, though the game was no great advert for the newly-professionalised sport. Still, a crowd of 15,500 was a handful more than Leicester City attracted for their meeting with Southend United the same day.

Richards, the captain, received a yellow card for stamping and when he earned another against Gloucester the following week, he was given a two-week suspension under new disciplinary regulations imposed by the RFU. It was going to be that sort of season, peaks and troughs, though few were surprised as Bath and Leicester dominated the league table as winter approached, Leicester's

record including victory by a record margin (43-6) over Bristol bolstered by eight John Liley penalties, a league and Tigers all-time record.

↑ John Liley broke the club record for penalties in a game, against Bristol.

But not even the prolific full-back could stop newly-enriched Saracens recording their first ever success over Leicester, a 25-21 home win. Only two Leicester players, Rory Underwood and Johnson, took part in England's 24-14 loss at Twickenham to the new world champions, South Africa, and though the club celebrated the official opening of the Alliance and Leicester Stand with a 39-14 win over touring Transvaal, it was clear a new order was rising from the composition of the Midlands XV that played Western Samoa at Welford Road, which was: James Quantrill (Rugby); Rob Subbiani (Bedford), Matt Allen (Northampton), Ben Whetstone (Bedford), Harvey Thorneycroft; Paul Grayson, Matt Dawson (all Northampton); Graham Rowntree, Richard Cockerill, Darren Garforth (all Leicester), Jon Phillips, Martin Bayfield, Tim Rodber (all Northampton, captain), Chris Tarbuck, Neil Back (both Leicester).

↑ The programme from the cup semi-final trip to London Irish.

The Midlands won 40-19, two penalty tries indicating the forward dominance of the home side, but the most notable element was the display of the two young Northampton half-backs, Grayson and Dawson, which elevated them both to the England side that beat Samoa 27-9 a fortnight later. Garforth played for the England A side that beat the tourists 55-0 at Gateshead while Rowntree joined Underwood, a try scorer, and Johnson at Twickenham.

In this disorganised season, while touring teams, the county championship and the new Heineken Cup competition involving teams from Wales, Ireland, France, Italy and Romania, held centre stage, Leicester played such old friends as Cambridge University, London Welsh and Harrogate. It was as though they were saving themselves for the next climactic meeting with Bath, at the Recreation Ground, when a 15-14 win shattered Bath's unbeaten record.

Though Bath scored eight early points, reflecting a season when their "total rugby" averaged 40 points a game at home, Leicester's forwards came to control a game played in filthy conditions and Liley kicked five penalties to bring them victory. Johnson and Rowntree were called up by England for the five nations, along with Underwood and there was a recall to the replacements for Richards against France in what was to be his international swansong, as it was for Underwood. Garforth played in the A international against France and was joined by Cockerill for the 24-22 win over New South Wales at Welford Road.

Leicester extracted revenge over Saracens, winning the fifth-round Pilkington Cup match 40-16, and in the quarter-finals Harlequins left Welford Road beaten 24-9. London Irish, coached by the former Leicester centre, Clive Woodward, fared no better in the semi-finals, losing 46-21 on their own ground and conceding six tries to a rampant Leicester.

England, meanwhile, ground out their 22nd championship win, scoring the grand total of three tries in four games, one of them against Wales to Underwood which was his fiftieth (and last) international score. Richards, who had received the MBE at a Buckingham Palace investiture in February, started the away game with Scotland, from whom England won the championship on points difference, and produced an utter tour de force, dominating the breakdown just when Scotland wanted quick ball to release an exciting back division. The finale, a 28-15 win over Ireland, was Underwood's 85th game for his country and the 48th appearance for Richards.

It left Underwood holding England's record for appearances and tries, Richards as his country's most-capped No 8. Both were then, and remain, contenders for any greatest England team in history; there have been plenty of talented wings, few with the finishing power and natural strength that Underwood brought to the role plus an enviable record for staying injury-free. Richards was unique, a force of nature; neither the fastest nor the fittest, he compensated with a formidable rugby intellect and a mauling strength sufficient to build a side around.

Six days after the semi-final cup win over London Irish, Leicester headed for new ground in every sense: Central Park, Wigan, where the local rugby league team had become one of the greatest units that code had seen. Orrell had agreed a ground-sharing scheme with Wigan and the league fixture with Leicester was the first under the new agreement. It was not a singular success; as Leicester fended off queries about the dismissal of Russ, their director of rugby, the players bumbled to a 38-10 win and fewer than 4,000 attended.

→ Martin Johnson secures line-out possession in the cup quarter-final against Harlequins.

↑ TIGERS v WEST HARTLEPOOL
17 February 1996
Back: Cockerill, Garforth, Rowntree, Wells, M.Johnson, Poole, Robinson, Delaney, Wyer-Roberts, McAdam.
Front: Aldwinckle, Liley, Harris, Hackney, Richards (capt), Kardooni, Back, Underwood, Shaw.

The month that followed was played out against a backdrop of disagreement between the leading clubs and the RFU, who also had their hands full because of their desire to negotiate television contracts for international matches separately from their Celtic colleagues. Leicester faced a fixture pile-up of five games in 15 days, including the inaugural Sanyo Cup match - at Twickenham - which paired the Courage champions with a Rest of the World XV coached by Dwyer, who was coming to the end of an ill-starred spell coaching Stade Français in Paris.

Some 32,000 watched Leicester lose 40-31 (the Underwood brothers appeared on opposite sides), and though they made £50,000 from the day it was a commitment they could have done without. Nevertheless they kept winning until the final weekend in April, when Harlequins secured a two-point victory, Liley missing six of nine kicks at goal. On the same day Bath were held at home to a 38-38 draw by Sale but found themselves champions by a single point.

A week later, Leicester and Bath met once more at Twickenham in the Pilkington Cup final, having demanded during the run-up a greater share of the gate receipts from a fixture that attracted 75,000 than the £40,000 each on offer. Ill temper was in the air, not least because of the threat of England's leading clubs to withdraw from RFU competitions in 1996/97, and overflowed into the game in which Leicester fielded the following XV: John Liley; Steve Hackney, Stuart Potter, Richie Robinson, Rory Underwood; Niall Malone, Aadel Kardooni; Graham Rowntree, Richard Cockerill, Darren Garforth, Martin Johnson, Matt Poole, John Wells, Dean Richards (captain), Neil Back.

With one minute of normal time remaining, Leicester led 15-9. At that stage Steve Lander, the referee, having already warned Leicester of the possibility of a penalty try, was as good as his word after Leicester had been penalised on three successive occasions while fending off Bath's assault on their line. Jonathan Callard's conversion gave Bath the double and left Leicester hearts broken.

Leicester had sufficient possession to have made the game safe but failed to do so. They scored a try as early as the eighth minute, when Garforth broke from the halfway line and Malone supported to score. Liley converted, though once more it was not to be his day since he missed five kicks from seven; three penalties by Callard gave Bath a slim interval lead but Liley overhauled them with his one successful penalty and, with five minutes remaining, Poole scored direct from a line-out. But Bath, outplayed up front for most of the game, raised all their combative spirit until they forced Lander to award the first penalty try seen in a domestic cup final.

But the talking point was what happened as the players made their way to the changing room. Back shoved Lander to the ground, a reaction cutting right across the game's famed regard for the authority of the match official; the flanker claimed he thought he was shoving his opposite number, Andy Robinson, out of the way. His post-match apology was in no way sufficient, an RFU investigation was staged and less than a fortnight later, the flanker was suspended for six months. Given that a lifetime ban was the steepest punishment for the offence, Back could be said to have got off lightly, particularly since the suspension included the summer months and forced him to miss little more than two months of the next season.

A club statement expressed disappointment at the severity of the sentence but the newly-formed Rugby Union Players' Association struck a sensible line: "Obviously the RFU felt that the game had been brought into disrepute and we support this attempt to uphold the good name of rugby," Richard Moon, their secretary, said. "We don't want to go down the road of other sports where the officials are abused and jostled by players. Rugby players will be reminded by this ban that they are in the shop window and watched by millions of youngsters."

At the same time Back was one of five Leicester players (with Johnson, Rowntree, Garforth and Cockerill) to agree a five-year contract, giving all of them as much security as the new oval world could offer. There was, inevitably, a changing of the guard: Jez Harris moved to Coventry, one of five to leave, while newcomers included a clutch of promising backs - Liley's younger brother, Rob, Will Greenwood, Craig Joiner, and the man with the most revs in the first division, the Orrell scrum-half/wing, Austin Healey.

The senior clubs threatened a breakaway from the RFU but, after eight hours of talks in London, a compromise was hammered out. Before May ended, Leicester were able to announce Dwyer as their new director of coaching while Ian Smith gave up his teaching post at Uppingham to become the full-time coach, to be joined later by Duncan Hall, a former Australia lock. Dwyer, on a three-year contract, brought at 55 a maturity of coaching equalled by few in the world, together with a completely different outlook on the organisation of the game. "Professionalism is a state of mind," Dwyer, who won 46 of his 72 tests as Australia's coach, said: "It's not about being paid, it's how you approach things."

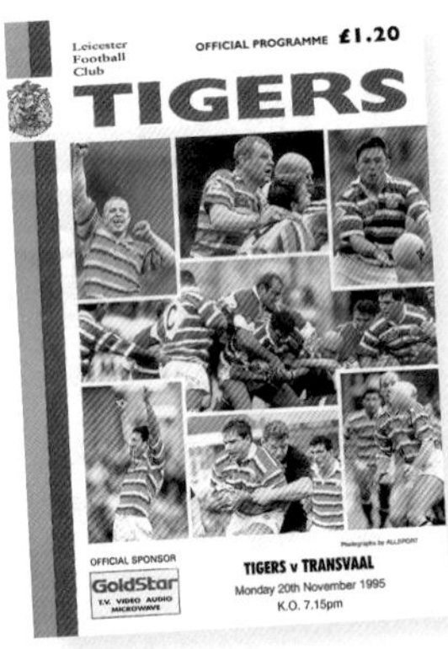

↑ Transvaal came to Welford Road to open the new Alliance and Leicester stand.

↓ Steve Lander awarding the critical penalty try to Bath in the cup final at Twickenham.

19	95/96		OVERALL RECORD:					T	C	PG	DG	PTS
	Home Ground: Welford Road		PLD	W	D	L	Tigers scored:	143	93	102	7	1228
	Director of Coaching: Tony Russ then Ian Smith and Paul Dodge in late March		37	32	0	5	Opponents scored:	52	32	76	8	576
	Captain: Dean Richards											

GM	DATE		VEN	OPPONENTS	RESULT	POS/LGE	TRIES	KICKS	ATT
COURAGE LEAGUE DIVISION 1 (2ND)						**CHAMPIONS: BATH**			
2	Sep	**9**	**H**	**Saracens**	W 31-3	2	Hackney 8, Underwood 48, Robinson 67	Liley 2c/4p	12500
3		16	a	Sale	W 16-12	1	Potter 80	Liley c/2p, Malone p	2500
4		**23**	**H**	**Bath**	L 9-14	4	-	Liley 3p	16000
5		30	a	Gloucester	W 27-14	4	Back 44, Kilford 74	Liley c/5p	6000
6	Oct	7	a	West Hartlepool	W 19-12	3	Garforth 20, Cockerill 65	Liley 3p	5000
7		**14**	**H**	**Orrell**	W 22-3	2	Hackney 69	Liley c/5p	10640
8		21	a	Wasps	W 21-11	2	Liley 31, Tarbuck 53	Liley c/2p/d	3500
9		**28**	**H**	**Bristol**	W 43-6	2	Underwood 22, Cockerill 61, Hackney 65	Liley 2c/8p	11388
10	Nov	4	a	Harlequins	W 29-25	2	Underwood 47, Penalty 55	Liley 2c/5p	4500
11		11	a	Saracens	L 21-25	2	Hackney 3, Robinson 50	Liley c/3p	3000
	Dec	**30**	**H**	**Sale**	PP (frost)	-			
20	Jan	6	a	Bath	W 15-14	2	-	Liley 5p	8500
	Feb	**10**	**H**	**Gloucester**	PP (cup)	-			
25		**17**	**H**	**West Hartlepool**	W 48-15	2	Hackney 3/78, Kardooni 32/58/76, Back 65	Liley 6c/p, Harris d	8311
	Mar	**9**	**H**	**Sale**	PP (5 Nations)	-			
		23	**H**	**Gloucester**	PP (cup)	-			
30		30	a	Orrell	W 38-10	2	Underwood 40/79, Wells 45, Liley 50	Liley 3c/4p	3637
31	Apr	**6**	**H**	**Wasps**	W 15-12	2	-	Liley 4p, Malone d	11702
32		13	a	Bristol	W 43-29	2	Underwood 30/45, Liley 42, Potter 76	Liley 4c/4p, Harris d	6000
33		**17w**	**H**	**Sale**	W 32-10	2	Back 9, Kardooni 43/65/80, Richards 77	Harris 2c/p	9149
35		**24w**	**H**	**Gloucester**	W 28-6	2	Garforth 14, Underwood 59, Liley 80	Liley 2c/3p	9777
36		**27**	**H**	**Harlequins**	L 19-21	2	Liley 30, Back 73	Liley 3p	11000
RFU CLUB COMPETITION (PILKINGTON CUP)						**CUP WINNERS: BATH**			
18	Dec	23	a	Exeter (4)	W 27-0	D4	Hamilton 25/49, Penalty 40	Liley 3c/2p	5000
	Jan	**27**	**H**	**Saracens (5)**	PP (cup)	D1			
24	Feb	**10**	**H**	**Saracens (5)**	W 40-16	D1	Penalty 43/66, Harris 77	Liley 2c/7p	12184
26		**24**	**H**	**Harlequins (qf)**	W 24-9	D1	Kardooni 61, Garforth 77	Liley c/4p	12792
29	Mar	23	a	London Irish (sf)	W 46-21	D2	Underwood 3, Wells 22, M.Johnson 26, Delaney 52, Harris 68, Poole 79	Harris d, Liley 5c/p	6750
37	May	4		Bath (f)	L 15-16	D1	Malone 8, Poole 75	Liley c/p	75000
CLUB MATCHES									
1	Sep	**2**	**H**	**Northampton**	W 23-17		Penalty 46, Becconsall 58, Potter 74	Harris c/2p	9150
12	Nov	**17f**	**H**	**Loughborough Students**	W 57-15		O.Wingham 5/40, Jelley 26/53, Miller 28, J.Wingham 45, Shaw 59, Kilford 64, West 78	Harris 6c	1910
13		**20m**	**H**	**Transvaal**	W 39-14		Back 45/63, Wells 80	Liley 3c/6p	10382
14		**25**	**H**	**Rugby Lions**	W 36-19		Delaney 18, Jelley 35, West 56, Barlow 60, Field 79	Harris c/3p	4434
15	Dec	2	a	Cambridge University	W 44-15		Kardooni 40/74, P.Grant 42, Jelley 51, Hackney 69	Liley 5c/2p, Harris d	-
16		**9**	**H**	**London Welsh**	W 62-19		P.Grant 8/16, Poole 12, Delaney 33, Drake-Lee 50, West 53/70, Hackney 64/66/77	Harris 6c	4970
17		16	a	Harrogate	W 58-22		J.Wingham 14/57, Delaney 16, Hamilton 40, West 42/51, Kilford 54, Tarbuck 66/80	Jones 5c/d	1000
19		**27w**	**H**	**Barbarians**	W 51-25		Underwood 29/63, Kardooni 43, Hackney 50/52, Richards 57, Back 72	Harris 5c/2p	15634
21	Jan	**13**	**H**	**Glasgow & District**	W 58-25		McAdam 4, Hackney 10/59, Kardooni 15, Penalty 39, Garforth 41, Back 64, Poole 71, Liley 79	Liley 5c/p	5134
22		**19f**	**H**	**Bedford**	W 38-13 (Abandoned 70')		Tarbuck 7/31, Hackney 17, J.Wingham 21, West 56, Liley 66	Liley 4c	3533
23	Feb	**2f**	**H**	**Coventry**	W 30-16		Hackney 32/67, Tarbuck 40, Kardooni 53	Liley 2c/2p	3133
		24	a	Northampton	PP (cup)				
27	Mar	**1f**	**H**	**Nottingham**	W 30-15		Hamilton 23/32, West 58, Cudmore 73	Jones 2c/2p	2997
		9	a	Moseley	PP (league)				
28		**15f**	**H**	**Old Belvedere**	W 43-17		Overend 4, Tarbuck 25, Liley 34, Cudmore 56, Hamilton 59, Jelley 79	Liley 5c/p	2506
		23	a	Cardiff	PP (league)				
	Apr	20	a	Wakefield	PP (Sanyo Cup)				
34		21s		Sanyo World XV	L 31-40		Hackney 4, Tarbuck 11/43, Richards 26, Potter 32	Liley 3c	31700

Note: *#34 at Twickenham for Sanyo Cup*

INDIVIDUAL APPEARANCES 1995/96

Name / Game #	1	2	3	4	5	6	7	8	9	10	11	12	13	14	15	16	17	18	19	20	21	22	23	24	25	26	27	28	29	30	31	32	33	34	35	36	37	Apps	T	Pts
JM (Jason) Aldwinckle	-	-	x	-	-	-	-	-	-	-	-	-	-	-	-	-	-	-	-	-	-	-	-	-	x	-	-	x	-	r	-	r	-	-	-	x	-	0+2	-	-
NA (Neil) Back E5 L+	H	H	H	H	H	H	H	H	H	H	-	-	H	-	-	-	-	-	H	H	H	-	-	H	H	H	-	H	△H	-	H	△H	H	H	-	H	H	25	8	40
I (Ian) Bates	-	-	-	-	-	-	L	-	-	<M	-	-	-	-	-	-	-	-	-	-	-	-	-	-	-	-	-	-	-	-	-	-	-	-	-	-	-	2	-	-
RT (Richard) Cheffins	-	-	-	-	-	-	-	-	-	-	-	>K	-	N	L	L	L	-	-	-	-	<r	-	-	-	-	-	-	-	-	-	-	-	-	-	-	-	5+1	-	-
R (Richard) Cockerill E+	B	B	B	B	B	B	-	B	B	B	B	-	B	-	-	-	-	B	B	B	r	-	B	B	B	B	-	-	B	B	B	B	B	B	B	B	B	27+1	2	10
A (Andy) Cudmore	-	-	-	-	-	-	-	-	-	-	-	-	-	-	-	-	-	-	-	-	-	-	-	-	-	-	>K	K	-	-	-	-	-	-	-	-	-	2	2	10
PK (Phil) Delaney	-	-	-	-	-	-	-	-	-	-	-	L	M	M	M	M	M	M	M	L	L	-	L	L	L	L	-	-	L	-	x	-	-	x	-	-	-	15	4	20
WM (Bill) Drake-Lee	-	-	-	-	-	x	x	-	-	-	H	-	-	-	H	H	H	H	-	-	-	H	H	x	-	-	H	-	-	H	-	-	-	-	H	-	x	10	1	5
RJ (Rob) Field	-	-	-	-	-	-	-	-	-	-	-	E	-	E	E	-	-	-	-	-	-	-	E	-	-	-	E	E	-	-	-	-	E	-	-	-	-	7	1	5
PT (Perry) Freshwater E+	-	-	-	-	-	-	-	-	-	-	-	-	-	-	-	-	-	-	-	-	x	-	x	-	-	-	>C	C	-	r	-	-	-	-	-	-	-	2+1	-	-
DJ (Darren) Garforth E+	C	C	C	C	C	C	C	C	C	C	C	-	C	-	-	-	-	C	C	△C	C	-	C	C	C	C	-	-	C	C	C	C	C	C	C	C	C	29	4	20
PJ (Paul) Grant	-	-	-	-	-	-	-	x	-	-	D	D	r	D	D	D	D	-	D	-	D	D	D	-	-	-	D	D	x	-	-	-	-	x	-	-	-	12+1	3	15
D (Darren) Grewcock	-	r	x	x	x	x	x	-	<r	x	x	-	x	-	-	-	-	-	-	-	-	-	-	x	-	-	-	-	-	-	-	-	-	-	-	-	-	0+2	-	-
ST (Steve) Hackney	N	N	N	N	N	N	N	N	N	N	N	-	N	-	N	N	N	N	N	-	N	N	N	N	N	N	-	N	N	N	N	N	N	N	N	N	N	33	18	90
JG (Jamie) Hamilton	I	I	I	I	I	-	-	r	-	-	-	-	-	-	-	I	I	I	x	x	-	I	-	I	-	x	I	I	x	-	r	-	x	r	I	x	x	13+3	6	30
JC (Jez) Harris	J	-	-	-	-	J	J	J	-	-	x	J*	-	L	J*	J	-	x	J	J	-	J	x	J	J	J	O	-	J	x	-	J	O	<r	x	-	x	18+1	2	88
DA (Derek) Jelley	-	-	-	-	x	-	-	-	r	-	-	A	x	A	A	A	A	-	-	x	A	A	A	-	-	-	A	A	x	-	-	-	x	r	-	-	x	10+2	5	25
MO (Martin) Johnson E24 L2	D	D	D	D	△D	D	D	D	D	D	-	-	D	-	-	-	-	D	-	D	-	-	-	D	D	D	-	-	D	D	D	D	D	D	D	D	D	25	1	5
WW (Will) Johnson	-	-	-	-	-	-	-	-	-	-	-	r	-	F	G	-	F	-	-	-	G	-	-	-	-	-	-	x	-	G	G	r	-	x	-	-	-	6+2	-	-
MB (Matt) Jones	-	-	-	-	-	-	-	-	-	-	-	>r	-	J	-	-	J	-	-	-	-	-	-	-	-	-	J	J	-	-	-	-	-	-	-	-	-	4+1	-	23
A (Aadel) Kardooni	-	-	-	-	-	I	I	I	I	I	I	-	I	-	I	-	-	x	I	I	I	-	I	-	I	I	-	-	I	I	I	I	I	I	-	I	I	22	12	60
WA (Wayne) Kilford	O	-	-	-	K	-	-	-	-	x	-	O	x	O	-	O	O	-	O	<N	-	-	-	-	-	-	-	-	-	-	-	-	-	-	-	-	-	8	3	15
JG (John) Liley	-	O	O	O	O	O	O	O	O	O	O	-	O	-	O	-	-	O	-	O	O	O*	O	O	O	O	-	O	O	O	O	O	-	O	O	O	O	29	8	446
A (Andy) McAdam	-	-	-	-	-	-	K	-	-	-	-	x	-	-	-	-	K	-	-	-	K	K	K	-	x	-	x	-	-	-	-	x	K	<r	-	x	-	6+1	1	5
NG (Niall) Malone I3	-	J	J	J	J	-	-	-	J	J	J	-	J	-	-	-	-	J	x	-	-	-	J	x	-	x	-	-	x	J	J	-	J	J	J	J	J	17	1	11
JW (James) Overend	-	-	-	-	-	-	-	-	-	-	-	>M	-	-	-	-	-	-	-	-	M	L	M	M	-	-	-	M	-	M	M	-	-	-	-	-	-	8	1	5
MD (Matt) Poole	E	E	E	E	E	E	E	E	E	E	E	-	E	-	-	E	E	E	E	E	E	E	-	E	E	E	-	-	E	E	E	E	-	E	E	E	E	30	4	20
S (Stuart) Potter E+	M	M	L	M	M	L	M	M	M	-	M	-	-	-	-	-	-	-	-	-	-	M	-	-	-	-	-	-	-	-	-	M	M	M	M	M	M	17	4	20
TR (Tom) Reynolds	-	-	-	-	-	-	-	-	-	-	-	N	-	-	K	K	-	-	-	-	-	-	-	-	-	-	<N	-	-	-	-	-	-	-	-	-	-	4	-	-
D (Dean) Richards E48 L6	G*	G*	G*	△G*	△G*	G*	-	-	G*	-	G*	-	G*	G*	-	G*	-	G*	G*	G*	-	-	-	G*	G*	G*	-	-	G*	-	-	G*	△G*	G*	G*	G*	G*	24	3	15
RP (Richie) Robinson	L	L	M	L	L	M	-	L	L	L	L	-	L	-	-	-	-	L	L	M	-	-	-	-	M	M	M	L	M	L	L	L	L	L	L	L	<L	27	2	10
CG (Graham) Rowntree E8 L+	A	A	A	A	A	A	A	A	A	A	A	-	A	-	-	-	-	A	A	A	-	-	-	A	A	A	-	-	A	A	A	A	A	A	A	A	A	27	-	-
JO (Jun) Shaw	-	-	-	-	-	-	-	-	-	-	-	>I	-	I	-	-	x	-	-	-	r	x	r	-	<r	-	-	x	-	x	-	x	-	-	-	-	-	2+3	1	5
NA (Neil) Spence	-	-	-	-	-	-	-	-	-	-	-	>H	-	<H	-	-	-	-	-	-	-	-	-	-	-	-	-	-	-	-	-	-	-	-	-	-	-	2	-	-
CR (Chris) Tarbuck	-	x	-	x	-	-	G	G	x	G	x	-	x	-	-	-	G*	x	F	x	-	G	G*	F	-	x	G*	G*	x	-	-	F	x	F	r	<F	x	13+1	9	45
R (Rory) Underwood E85 L6	-	K	K	K	-	K	-	K*	K	K*	K	-	K	-	-	-	-	K	K	K	-	-	-	K	K	K	-	-	K	K*	K*	K	-	K	K	K	K	23	11	55
JM (John) Wells	F	F	F	F	F	F	F*	-	F	F	F	-	F	-	-	F	-	F	x	F	F*	-	-	-	F	F	-	-	F	F	F	-	F	r	F	-	F	23+1	3	15
DE (Dorian) West E+	x	-	-	-	-	-	-	-	-	-	-	B	x	B	B	B	B	x	x	x	B	B	-	x	-	x	B	B	x	-	x	-	x	r	x	-	x	9+1	8	40
JMW (Jim) Wingham	-	-	-	-	-	x	x	-	-	x	-	C	-	-	C	C	C	-	-	-	-	C	-	-	-	-	-	-	-	-	-	-	-	-	-	-	-	5	4	20
OJ (Oscar) Wingham	r	-	x	-	r	-	-	F	-	r	-	F	-	-	F	-	-	-	-	-	-	F	F	-	-	-	F	F	-	-	-	-	-	-	-	-	-	7+3	2	10

1 GAME: TA (Tim) Barlow >Kt(14)x(28), GM (Garry) Becconsall >rt(1)x(27)x(35), AG (Guy) Bibby =r(17)x(27), SJ (Simon) Binns <J(21), NP (Nick) Clapinson C1 x(12)=C(14), BJ (Barry) Evans E2 <K(1), RTNM (Rob) Harding x(14)<r(22)x(27), CAP (Chris) Johnson x(2)x(4)<B(7)x(8), ERP (Eric) Miller I+ L+ >Gt(12)x(31)x(36), SM (Stewart) Roke <L(27)

The key for how to read the stats is on the last page

CHAPTER 28

Brive Encounter

1996/1997

If the clubs hoped to have resolved some of professionalism's teething problems, they had only to watch the events of the summer to understand how stony was the road ahead. The RFU negotiated a separate broadcasting deal with BSkyB, the satellite company, worth £87.5 million and were promptly threatened with expulsion from the five nations championship, a dispute which lasted two months before a face-saving resolution was found.

Prior to the season's start Leicester organised a four-team tournament involving Agen, Cardiff and Boroughmuir, though only 8,000 turned up to watch the two-day festival at Welford Road; Agen won against a Leicester side whose 22 points consisted of a converted penalty try and five penalties.

↑ The International Challenge Cup in August 1996 marked the Tigers' first games of professional rugby. Here Austin Healey makes his first-team debut in the final against Agen.

Dean Richards, already on sabbatical from the Leicestershire Police, decided to leave the force to concentrate, as club captain, on what seemed likely to be his last season as a player. Two days before the start of England's first proper professional season, the management board of English Professional Rugby Union Clubs Ltd proposed the withdrawal of the leading 24 clubs from the RFU. So frustrated were the players with the inability of the game's administrators to find a way forward that they boycotted an England squad training session at Bisham Abbey.

Leicester opened the league campaign with a 25-23 defeat to Saracens at Enfield. The game illustrated how clubs were realigning, in that Saracens fielded their recently-acquired superstars, Philippe Sella (France), Michael Lynagh (Australia) and Kyran Bracken (England). Bob Dwyer, for his first league match in charge, omitted John Wells from his back row, preferring Eric Miller, though he played both men in the next outing, a 28-25 win over Bath at Welford Road in which John Liley kicked seven penalties and, joy of joy for the home crowd who had seen the cup lost to such a score less than five months earlier, converted a penalty try.

A new agreement with Next and Cotton Traders, the leisurewear companies, brought £500,000-worth of sponsorship money on board but when Leicester lost the league encounter with Wasps, it constituted their worst start to a season in seven years. They were fifth in the league when they made their European debut. The expansion of the Heineken Cup to include England and Scotland made it a far more representative tournament and Leicester opened their campaign with a 27-10 win over Leinster in Dublin. A young wing, Leon Lloyd from Coventry, made his competition debut instead of the injured Rory Underwood.

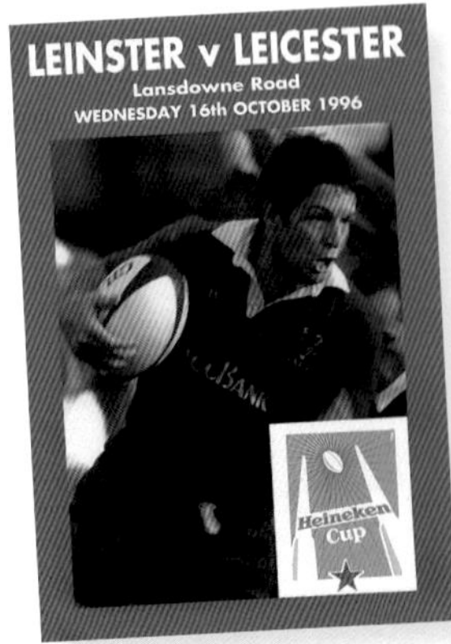

↑ The programme from Tigers' first-ever Heineken Cup match.

It was the start of Underwood's retreat from first-team rugby. He was now 33, had balanced an elite sporting career for the previous 14 years with a demanding job as an RAF pilot and had a young family. One of the reasons for the appointment of Dwyer was the hard edge he would bring to selection and though Underwood was a try-scorer in the 43-3 romp against the Scottish Borders, Lloyd, 19, was preferred for the testing trip to Pau and he scored the outstanding individual try that clinched an invaluable 19-14 win in south-west France, to hand Pau only their second home defeat of the season.

Just as the visit to Leinster had given Leicester a fresh experience, so did Pau. The Stade du Hameau proved the most intimidating of arenas, the proximity of an abusive crowd something that Dwyer too had to deal with when he escorted the injured Lloyd off the pitch near the end and three players, Wells, Richard Cockerill and Martin Johnson, received treatment to eye injuries, provoking allegations of gouging. "We talked about accepting and enjoying the environment in which the French play their rugby," Dwyer said. "It's a good test of character and we showed a fair bit of that."

Leicester's love affair with Europe was well and truly established and victory over Llanelli (no home-and-away fixtures in those early days) earned a quarter-final against Harlequins. A week before the clash of the two English clubs, Neil Back returned from his six-month ban against Neath at The Gnoll in the new Anglo-Welsh Cup, a competition seriously undermined by the quality of teams turned out by many of the Welsh clubs. At much the same time, Leicester confirmed that the Christmas game with the Barbarians would be moved to February to avoid a clash with the league programme; it was the beginning of the end for a much-loved fixture.

Back was restored to the side that beat Harlequins 23-13 at Welford Road before Rowntree and Johnson moved on to internationals with England against Italy and Argentina. Steve Hackney, Will Greenwood and Austin Healey made A appearances against Argentina at Northampton and South Africa A at Gloucester. Leicester and the other leading clubs, still at odds with the RFU, withheld players from the various divisional sides that played Argentina and a clutch of other touring teams from the southern hemisphere.

One of them, from Western Samoa, played a composite Leicester/Northampton team at Welford Road and won a low-key affair 33-20, three days before Leicester beat Northampton 23-9 in a league match, a result which carried them to the top of the table and where the spectators included Joel Stransky, whose dropped goal in extra-time had won the 1995 World Cup for South Africa. The following week, Leicester confirmed Stransky as

Joel Stransky
Joel Stransky arrived at Welford Road as the man who won the 1995 World Cup for South Africa. Not only that Stransky, the Western Province fly-half, kicked all South Africa's points in the pulsating 15-12 win over New Zealand, his winning dropped goal coming in the second half of extra- time and earning him sporting immortality. He had lost his place on tour in Britain the year before but injuries elsewhere gave him a second chance in the World Cup which he grasped with both hands. A shrewd, mature presence on the field, injury disrupted his two years with Leicester but he helped coach the backs and, on returning to South Africa, became a TV analyst.

their first significant overseas signing (a few days earlier, Saracens had signed François Pienaar, the Springbok captain).

Stransky, 29, brought with him the experience of 23 caps as his country's fly-half, during which he scored 240 points. Meanwhile Leicester kept their noses in front of Wasps in the league by beating Harlequins under the leadership of Martin Johnson and the new year brought the much-anticipated Heineken Cup semi-final against Toulouse, the inaugural winners. A spell of freezing weather forced Leicester, at a cost of £8,000, to cover the Welford Road playing surface with a hot-air balloon, the ground was passed fit to play and Leicester, showing tremendous appetite, destroyed the holders 37-11. Rob Liley produced probably his best game of the season, Greenwood showed form that interested the 1997 Lions coaching panel and Leicester scored five tries.

For the rest of January, players and supporters looked forward to the trip to Cardiff to play Brive in the European final. Stransky made his debut as a replacement in the league loss at Northampton, England called up Greenwood and Back to the five nations squad along with Rowntree, Garforth and Johnson while the A squad included Rob Liley, Healey, Cockerill and the other Leicester hooker, Dorian West. But for the cup final on 25 January, Leicester went back to experience and chose Underwood on the left wing, leaving Lloyd and Miller, capped for the first time by Ireland against Italy earlier in the month, on the bench.

Leicester: John Liley; Steve Hackney, Will Greenwood, Stuart Potter, Rory Underwood (Leon Lloyd 74); Rob Liley, Austin Healey; Graham Rowntree, Richard Cockerill, Darren Garforth (Perry Freshwater 17-22), Martin Johnson, Matt Poole, John Wells, Dean Richards (captain, Eric Miller 67), Neil Back.
Brive: Sébastien Viars; Gerald Fabre, Christophe Lamaison, David Venditti, Sébastien Carrat; Alain Penaud (captain; Romuald Paillat, 70), Philippe Carbonneau; Didier Casadei (Eric Bouti, 72), Laurent Travers, Richard Crespy, Eric Allegret, Grant Ross (Tony Rees, 67), Loic van der Linden (Yann Domi, 79), François Duboisset (Thierry Labrousse, 49), Gregori Kacala.
Referee: Derek Bevan (Wales).

Lions skipper, Martin Johnson, holds the trophy aloft after the 2-1 series victory against the Springboks.

Some 20,000 travelled from Leicester to swell the crowd beyond 41,000 but they returned home disappointed. Leicester lost 28-9, conceding four tries and beaten in nearly every aspect of play by one of France's less fashionable clubs. The line-out was a disaster area which Brive won 19-8 and two players, Gregori Kacala, the flanker, and Sébastien Viars, from full-back, created havoc wherever they went.

Viars scored the first try after a penalty from Christophe Lamaison but three penalties from John Liley edged Leicester ahead 9-8 just after the interval. It was the poorest possible reflection on the run of play, to which Brive promptly attended: Gerald Fabre nipped over on the right wing and a wonderful try made by Lamaison and scored by Sébastien Carrat on the other wing made the result certain. Just to make sure Lamaison, who kicked only one conversion, dropped a goal and Viars sent Carrat over for his second try.

There was little time for reflection: a week later Johnson and Rowntree started the 41-13 win over Scotland with the uncapped duo, Healey and Garforth, on the bench. Remarkably, two England A sides were named, to play Scotland and Otago respectively, with Greenwood captaining the first accompanied by Cockerill and Back while West played against the New Zealand province at Bristol, Rob Liley coming off the bench as a replacement.

Johnson was asked to captain the Leicester team that beat Bath 39-28, at The Recreation Ground, in the postponed sixth-round Pilkington Cup tie, with Richards confined to the bench. The team as a whole responded in the best possible way to the disappointment of Cardiff and scored five tries - they had never scored as many as four in any league or cup game against Bath. From the opening moments they played with a panache to which Bath could not respond though, in the quarter-final against Newcastle, it took six penalties by Stransky to quell the hosts 18-8.

A weakened team (including a youthful Lewis Moody) lost 38-22 to the Barbarians, the match marking Richards's 300th appearance for Leicester and there were indications that all was not well behind the scenes between Ian Smith, the coach, and the Australian duo of Dwyer and Hall. Against that Johnson was named captain of the 1997 Lions to tour South Africa with Leicester also contributing Back, Greenwood, Healey, Miller and Rowntree to the tour squad.

Johnson and Rowntree had been ever presents in the England side that won a triple crown but gave best to grand slam-winning France in the five nations. During the championship, Healey made his debut as a replacement against Ireland and started against Wales, the game in which Garforth also made a cameo appearance as a replacement to win his first cap. Johnson, who followed in the footsteps of Doug Prentice, the Leicester lock who led the 1930 Lions in New Zealand, was named ahead of five other touring players who had led their countries - Ieuan Evans (Wales), Rob Wainwright and Gregor Townsend (Scotland), Jason Leonard (England) and Keith Wood (Ireland).

John Wells attempts to evade the attentions of Sale full-back Jim Mallinder in the Pilkington Cup final.

The appointment came three days after Leicester had made their way into the Pilkington Cup final, thanks to a 26-13 win over Gloucester at Kingsholm that possessed none of the flamboyance that had beaten Bath. However, success in two cup competitions, combined with bad mid-winter weather, left league fixtures piling up for Leicester in the last month of the season: they faced a schedule of seven games in 22 days and, though they manoeuvred their way past Wasps, the league leaders, they lost at Gloucester and Bath. Remarkably they remained second in the table despite defeat at London Irish and summoned up enough energy to beat Saracens at home but Harlequins won by a point at Welford Road and a 20-20 draw at Sale left Leicester clinging on to fourth place, and Heineken Cup qualification, behind Harlequins, Bath and the champions, Wasps.

1996/97											
Home Ground: Welford Road	**Trophy Cabinet:** Pilkington Cup(5)	OVERALL RECORD:					T	C	PG	DG	PTS
Director of Coaching: Bob Dwyer assisted by Duncan Hall		PLD	W	D	L	Tigers scored:	175	112	124	3	1480
Captain: Dean Richards		46	35	1	10	Opponents scored:	85	48	84	6	791

GM	DATE		VEN	OPPONENTS	RESULT	POS/LGE	TRIES	KICKS	ATT
COURAGE LEAGUE DIVISION 1 (4TH)						**CHAMPIONS: WASPS**			
3	Aug	31	a	Saracens	L 23-25	8	J.Liley 78, Underwood 79	J.Liley 2c/3p	6231
4	Sep	**7**	**H**	**Bath**	W 28-25	8	Penalty 80	J.Liley c/7p	10368
6		14	a	Orrell	W 29-12	6	Greenwood 24, Potter 68, Hackney 80	J.Liley c/4p	2380
7		22s	a	Wasps	L 7-14	6	Penalty 10	J.Liley c	10686
8		**28**	**H**	**Gloucester**	W 32-14	6	Hackney 8, Cockerill 27, Penalty 49, Underwood 69	J.Liley 3c/2p	9597
9	Oct	5	a	West Hartlepool	W 30-19	5	Drake-Lee 30, Penalty 36, Greenwood 41	J.Liley 3c/3p	2300
14		**30w**	**H**	**London Irish**	W 46-13	3	W.Johnson 2, R.Liley 7/60, Kardooni 54, Penalty 68, Austin 76	R.Liley 5c/2p	8263
	Nov	9	a	Bristol	PP (autumn tests)	-			
20	Dec	**8s**	**H**	**Northampton**	W 23-9	4	Back 23, Potter 80	J.Liley c/2p, R.Liley c/p	11839
22		18w	a	Bristol	W 38-12	1	Hackney 51, Potter 56/67, R.Liley 70	J.Liley 3c/4p	2000
24		28	a	NEC Harlequins	W 34-18	1	Underwood 4/55, J.Liley 27, Greenwood 53	J.Liley c/4p	5772
	Jan	**4**	**H**	**Sale**	PP (European Cup)	-			
26		11	a	Northampton	L 19-22	3	Back 7/49	J.Liley 3p	7907
27		**18**	**H**	**Bristol**	W 53-19	1	Greenwood 6, Underwood 23, Healey 41, Stransky 48, Penalty 67, Lloyd 76	J.Liley 4c/5p	9122
	Feb	8	a	London Irish	PP (cup)	-			
34	Mar	**4tu**	**H**	**Sale**	W 25-9	2	Penalty 28	Stransky c/6p	7320
35		**8**	**H**	**West Hartlepool**	W 48-3	2	Garforth 23, Healey 32, Greenwood 40, Joiner 50, Stransky 62, Austin 76	Stransky 3c/4p	8709
		22	a	Gloucester	PP (HK sevens)	-			
		29	**H**	**Wasps**	PP (cup)	-			
38	Apr	**2w**	**H**	**Wasps**	W 18-12	2	-	Stransky 6p	17000
39		**5**	**H**	**Orrell**	W 36-14	2	Malone 6/65, Hackney 13, Underwood 33, Poole 38, Joiner 72	J.Liley 3c	9022
40		8tu	a	Gloucester	L 30-32	2	Joiner 14, J.Liley 23, Kardooni 68, Underwood 78	Stransky 2c/2p	6310
41		12	a	Bath	L 9-47	2	-	Stransky 3p	8500
42		16w	a	London Irish	L 18-25	2	Poole 5, Fletcher 57	R.Liley c/2p	3456
43		**19**	**H**	**Saracens**	W 22-18	2	Penalty 63	J.Liley c/5p	10791
44		**26**	**H**	**NEC Harlequins**	L 12-13	4	-	J.Liley 2p, Stransky 2p	12504
45	May	3	a	Sale	D 20-20	4	Potter 40, Penalty 63	Stransky 2c/2p	4250
HEINEKEN CUP						**EUROPEAN CHAMPIONS: BRIVE**			
11	Oct	16	a	Leinster	W 27-10	2	Rowntree 39, Kardooni 65, Wells 73	R.Liley 3c/2p	3500
12		**19**	**H**	**Scottish Borders**	W 43-3	1	Miller 33, Underwood 40, Hackney 54, Poole 70, J.Liley 77, West 80	R.Liley 5c/p	4609
13		26	a	Pau	W 19-14	1	Lloyd 51	R.Liley c/4p	9000
15	Nov	**2**	**H**	**Llanelli**	W 25-16	1	Drake-Lee 33, Lloyd 53, Healey 65, Rowntree 76	R.Liley c/p	8405
17		**16**	**H**	**NEC Harlequins (qf)**	W 23-13	-	Cockerill 45, R.Liley 80	R.Liley 2c/3p	10263
25	Jan	**4**	**H**	**Toulouse (sf)**	W 37-11	-	Hackney 7, Back 18, Garforth 48, Penalty 65, Healey 72	J.Liley 3c/2p	16000
28		25		Brive (f)	L 9-28	-	-	J.Liley 3p	40664
RFU CLUB COMPETITION (Pilkington Cup)						**CUP WINNERS: LEICESTER TIGERS**			
23	Dec	**21**	**H**	**Newbury (5)**	W 26-21	D4S	Potter 32, Hackney 41, Underwood 48	R.Liley c/2p, Austin p	4374
	Jan	25	a	Bath (6)	PP (European Cup)	D1			
30	Feb	8	a	Bath (6)	W 39-28	D1	Greenwood 18/57, Potter 32, Back 41, Hackney 65	Stransky 4c/p/d	8500
32		22	a	Newcastle Falcons (qf)	W 18-8	D2	-	Stransky 6p	5700
37	Mar	29	a	Gloucester (sf)	W 26-13	D1	Hackney 77	Stransky 5p/2d	12500
46	May	10		Sale (f)	W 9-3	D1	-	Stransky 3p	75000
ANGLO-WELSH LEAGUE									
5	Sep	11w	a	Pontypridd	W 48-10		Penalty 5, West 11, Greenwood 35, Underwood 45/80, Potter 49, Hackney 59	J.Liley 5c/p	3500
		25w	**H**	**Bridgend**	PP				
10	Oct	**8tu**	**H**	**Bridgend**	W 60-22		W.Johnson 12, Miller 27, West 34, Underwood 37/41, Jelley 52, Hackney 59, Lloyd 61, Austin 65	J.Liley 6c/p	2044
16	Nov	6w	a	Neath	W 36-19		W.Johnson 11, Read 14, Malone 40, Kardooni 53, Underwood 68	Malone 4c/p	2000
	Jan	**29w**	**H**	**Pontypridd**	PP				
	Apr	2w	a	Bridgend	PP (league)				
		16w	**H**	**Neath**	PP (league)				
INTERNATIONAL CHALLENGE CUP									
1	Aug	**25s**	**H**	**Boroughmuir (sf)**	W 72-33		Hackney 12/39/41, Pain 19/54, Moody 20/78, Kardooni 27, R.Liley 33/75, Joiner 58	R.Liley 7c/p	3000
2		**26m**	**H**	**Agen (f)**	L 22-28		Penalty 79	Jones c/3p, J.Liley 2p	4000
CLUB MATCHES									
18	Nov	**22f**	**H**	**Loughborough Students**	W 84-6		Grant 1/59, Drake-Lee 3, Lloyd 15/52, West 17/38/76, W.Johnson 43, Austin 47, Jelley 61/78, Underwood 62, Malone 79	Malone 6c, Pflugler c	2402
19		**30**	**H**	**Cambridge University**	W 84-5		Greenwood 2/12/21/52/76, Penalty 8, Hackney 15, R.Liley 19, Underwood 23/79, Jasnikowski 30, Richards 42, Healey 57, J.Liley 67	R.Liley 7c	2702
	Dec	**4w**	**H**	**Western Samoa**	PP				
21		13f	a	Bedford	W 45-22		Miller 2, Underwood 7, Malone 10/34, Lloyd 24, Austin 51/80	Malone 5c	2000
		27f	**H**	**Barbarians**	PP (league)				
29	Jan	31f	a	Coventry	W 33-8		Underwood 6/72, Penalty 53, Austin 75	Stransky c/3p, Jones c	2500
	Feb	**11tu**	**H**	**Otago**	PP				
31		14f	a	Old Belvedere	W 41-17		Becconsall 4, Stransky 22, J.Liley 39, Edwards 55, Joiner 76	Stransky 5c/2p	1000
33		**25tu**	**H**	**Barbarians**	L 22-38		Jelley 17/26, Kardooni 62	J.Liley 2c/p	11351
36	Mar	14f	a	Nottingham	W 32-20		West 11, Jelley 29, Freshwater 51, Austin 56, Read 77	R.Liley 2c/p	500

Neutral Venues: *#28 at National Stadium - Cardiff, #46 at Twickenham*

A week later Leicester and Sale met again, in the Pilkington Cup final at Twickenham, of which the least said the better. Leicester's team was: Niall Malone; Craig Joiner, Will Greenwood, Stuart Potter, Leon Lloyd; Joel Stransky, Austin Healey (Aadel Kardooni 72-76); Graham Rowntree, Richard Cockerill, Darren Garforth, Martin Johnson (captain), Matt Poole, John Wells (Dean Richards, 68), Eric Miller, Neil Back.

Leicester won 9-3, the first try-less final for 15 years, Stransky kicking three penalties from seven attempts, Simon Mannix one from four for Sale. "At the start of the year, we would not have said that, realistically, we could expect to be the second team in Europe or the most successful team in England, which we are by a long shot," Dwyer said. "The most important thing for us now is that, with this title, we are in a position to attract money to the club." Moreover, it boosted local pride since Leicester City had already won the football League Cup and, nine months earlier, Leicestershire had lifted cricket's county championship.

The fact that Leicester boasted six Lions with Garforth and Cockerill involved in England's tour to Argentina (where Cockerill made his debut) also added to the club's attraction. England had to share the series with the Pumas but, to popular acclaim, the Lions beat South Africa 2-1 under Johnson's guidance; the captain played in all three tests with Back, Healey and Miller making contributions in the second and third internationals. But a serious injury against the Free State Cheetahs ended Greenwood's tour; he had been playing as well as any of the touring party's midfield backs when he was caught in a heavy tackle, his head hit the unyielding Bloemfontein turf and only prompt intervention by James Robson, the Lions doctor, which unblocked his windpipe, saved his life.

Tigers take the Pilkington Cup crown with a 9-3 victory over Sale at Twickenham.

LEICESTER FOOTBALL CLUB 1996/97
Back: Joiner, Barlow, Pain, Freshwater, Rowntree, Wells, Jelley, Garforth.
Middle: Austin, Dwyer (Director of coaching), R.Liley, Beatham, Miller, Fripp, Fletcher, M.Johnson, Poole, Field, J.Wingham, Moody, Smith (Assistant coach), Drake-Lee.
Front: Malone, Cockerill, Healey, J.Liley, Underwood, Richards (capt), Potter, Kardooni, West, Greenwood, Hackney, Jones.

INDIVIDUAL APPEARANCES 1996/97

Game #	1	2	3	4	5	6	7	8	9	10	11	12	13	14	15	16	17	18	19	20	21	22	23	24	25	26	27	28	29	30	31	32	33	34	35	36	37	38	39	40	41	42	43	44	45	46	Apps	T	Pts
DJ (Dave) Addison	-	-	-	-	-	-	-	-	-	-	-	-	-	-	-	-	-	-	-	-	-	-	-	-	-	-	-	-	x	-	>G	-	-	-	-	-	-	-	-	-	-	G	-	-	-	-	2	-	-
JM (Jason) Aldwinckle	-	-	-	-	-	-	-	r	-	-	-	-	-	-	-	-	-	-	-	-	-	-	-	-	-	-	-	-	B	-	-	-	-	-	-	-	-	-	-	-	-	-	-	-	-	-	1+1	-	-
GM (Greg) Austin	-	>L	-	-	x	-	-	x	-	L	O	x	r	M	x	O	-	r	-	x	O	-	O	-	-	-	-	-	r	-	-	-	-	r	r	L	-	-	-	-	-	<r	-	-	-	-	8+6	8	43
NA (Neil) Back E5 L+	-	-	-	-	-	-	-	-	-	-	-	-	-	-	-	H	H	-	H	H	-	H	-	H	H	H	H	H	-	H	-	H	-	H	H	-	H	H	H*	H	H	-	H	H	H	H	23	5	25
TA (Tim) Barlow	-	-	-	-	-	-	-	-	-	-	-	-	-	-	-	-	-	-	-	-	-	-	-	-	-	-	-	-	-	-	K	-	K	-	-	N	-	-	-	-	-	-	-	-	-	-	3	-	-
GM (Garry) Becconsall	r	x	x	x	I	I	x	-	x	-	-	-	-	-	-	r	x	I	-	-	r	x	I	-	-	-	-	-	-	-	I	-	-	-	-	-	-	-	-	-	-	-	-	-	-	-	5+3	1	5
R (Richard) Cockerill E+	x	B	B	B	r	B	B	B	B	r	B	x	B	-	B	B	B	-	B	B	-	-	-	B	B	x	B	B	-	B	-	B	-	B	-	-	B	B	x	B	B	r	B	B	B	B	29+3	2	10
PK (Phil) Delaney	x	-	-	-	-	-	-	-	x	-	-	-	-	r	-	-	-	-	-	-	-	-	-	-	-	-	-	-	-	-	-	-	-	-	-	-	-	-	r	-	-	x	-	-	-	-	0+2	-	-
WM (Bill) Drake-Lee	-	H	H	-	-	-	r	H	H	-	x	r	H	H	H	r	-	H	-	-	H	x	H	-	x	x	-	-	H	-	-	x	H	r	F	-	x	x	F	r	r	H	r	-	<r	x	15+8	3	15
RA (Roland) Edwards	-	-	-	-	-	-	-	-	-	-	-	-	-	-	-	-	-	-	-	-	-	-	-	-	-	-	-	-	-	-	>r	-	-	-	-	r	-	-	-	x	r	-	-	-	-	-	0+3	1	5
NC (Nnamdi) Ezulike	-	-	-	-	-	-	-	-	-	-	-	-	-	-	-	-	-	-	-	-	-	-	-	-	-	-	-	-	-	-	>r	-	-	-	-	K	-	-	-	-	-	K	x	-	-	-	2+1	-	-
RJ (Rob) Field	E	x	-	-	E	E	-	-	-	-	-	-	-	-	-	△D	r	E	D	E	D	-	E	-	-	-	-	-	D	-	E	-	r	r	E	<E	-	-	-	-	-	-	-	-	-	-	13+3	-	-
NR (Neil) Fletcher	-	-	-	-	x	-	-	-	>D	-	-	-	x	E	-	E	-	-	-	-	E	E	D	-	x	-	E	x	E	-	r	-	D	E	x	D	E	r	D	△r	r	D	x	r	-	-	14+5	1	5
PT (Perry) Freshwater E+	r	C	-	-	-	-	-	-	-	-	-	-	-	-	-	A	-	A	A	-	A	r	A	-	-	-	A	r	A	-	B	-	A	-	A	A	-	-	-	-	-	-	-	-	-	-	12+3	1	5
GR (Greg) Fry	-	-	-	-	-	x	-	-	-	-	-	-	-	-	-	-	-	>r	-	-	-	-	-	-	-	-	-	-	-	-	-	-	r	-	-	<I	-	-	-	-	-	-	-	-	-	-	1+2	-	-
DJ (Darren) Garforth E1	-	-	C	C	C	C	△C	C	C	C	C	C	△C	x	C	x	C	-	C	C	-	C	C	C	C	C	C	C	-	C	-	C	-	C	C	-	C	C	C	C	C	r	C	C	C	C	35+1	2	10
PJ (Paul) Grant	-	-	-	-	-	-	-	-	-	-	-	-	-	-	-	-	-	D	-	-	-	-	-	-	-	-	-	-	-	-	-	-	-	-	-	<r	-	-	-	-	-	-	-	-	-	-	1+1	2	10
WJH (Will) Greenwood E+ L+	-	>M	x	L	L	L	M	L	L	-	L	-	-	-	M	-	M	-	M	M	-	L	M	L	M	M	M	M	-	M	-	M	-	M	M	-	M	M	-	-	M	-	-	-	-	M	27	13	65
ST (Steve) Hackney	N	N	N	N	N	N	N	N	N	N	N	N	N	-	N	-	N	-	N	N	-	N	N	N	N	N	-	N	N	N	-	N	N	N	N	-	N	N	N	N	N	-	N	<N	x	x	36	15	75
SM (Steve) Hart	-	-	-	-	-	-	-	-	-	-	-	-	-	-	-	-	-	>G	-	-	-	-	-	-	-	-	-	-	-	-	-	-	-	-	-	<H	-	-	-	-	-	-	-	-	-	-	2	-	-
AS (Austin) Healey E2 L+	-	>I	I	I	-	-	I	I	I	x	x	I	I	x	I	-	I	-	I	I	-	I	x	I	I	I	I	I	-	△I	-	I	-	I	I	-	I	I	r	-	I	I	x	r	I	I	28+2	5	25
MT (Mark) Jasnikowski	-	-	-	-	-	-	-	-	-	-	-	-	-	-	-	-	-	>r	L	-	M	-	-	-	-	-	-	-	x	-	L	-	-	-	-	-	-	-	-	-	-	M	x	-	-	-	4+1	1	5
DA (Derek) Jelley	-	-	-	-	-	x	-	-	-	A	x	A	x	A	x	C	x	C	x	x	C	-	-	-	x	-	-	-	C	-	A	-	C	-	x	C	-	-	A	-	-	A	-	-	-	-	12	6	30
MO (Martin) Johnson E30 L2	D	D	D	D	D	D	D	△D	-	D*	D*	D*	D	D	D	-	D	-	-	D	-	D	-	D*	D	D	D	D	-	D*	-	D*	-	D*	D*	-	D*	D	r	D	D	-	D*	D	D*	D*	34+1	-	-
WW (Will) Johnson	x	-	-	G	G	-	-	-	-	G	G	G	x	F	x	F	-	F	-	-	G	-	x	r	-	F	r	-	G	-	F	△G	r	G	-	G	-	-	-	-	-	-	-	-	-	-	15+3	4	20
CA (Craig) Joiner S17	>K	r	-	-	-	-	-	-	-	-	-	-	-	-	-	-	-	-	-	-	-	-	-	-	-	-	-	-	-	-	M	L	L	L	K	-	K	L	L	L	K	N	L	M	L	N	16+1	5	25
MB (Matt) Jones	-	J	J	-	-	-	r	-	-	-	-	-	-	-	-	-	-	-	-	-	-	-	-	x	-	-	-	-	M	-	-	-	<r	-	-	-	-	-	-	-	-	-	-	-	-	-	3+2	-	13
A (Aadel) Kardooni	I	-	-	-	-	-	-	x	-	I	I	x	x	I	r	I	-	-	-	x	I	-	-	x	x	x	r	x	I	x	-	x	I	x	r	-	x	r	I	I	-	x	I	I	x	<r	12+5	6	30
JG (John) Liley	x	O	O	O	O	O	O	O	O	O	x	O	O	O	O	x	O	-	O	O	x	O	x	O	O	O	O	O	O	O	O	O	O	O	O	-	O	-	O	O	O	-	O	<O	-	-	35	6	272
RJ (Rob) Liley	>J	-	-	x	J	J	J	J	J	x	J	J	J	J	J	x	J	-	J	J	-	J	J	-	J	J	x	J	-	-	-	r	J	x	r	J	-	x	J	x	-	J	J	<r	x	x	24+3	7	167
LD (Leon) Lloyd E+	-	-	-	-	-	-	-	-	-	>r	K	x	K	N	K	N	K	N	-	K	N	K	-	M	K	-	N	r	-	K	-	K	-	K	-	-	r	K	-	K	-	-	-	-	K	K	20+3	7	35
NG (Niall) Malone I3	L	r	L	J	-	x	-	-	-	J	r	L	L	L	L	J	x	J	x	x	J	x	-	J	x	-	-	x	-	x	-	-	M	-	-	-	x	O	M	M	r	O	M	x	O	O	20+3	6	63
ERP (Eric) Miller I4 L+	-	F	F	H	H	-	H	G	G	H	H	H	-	-	-	-	r	-	r	r	F	-	F	G	-	-	-	r	-	G	-	-	-	-	G	-	G	F	G	F	F	-	G	-	G	G	23+4	3	15
LW (Lewis) Moody E+ L+	>H	-	x	x	r	H	-	-	-	-	-	-	-	-	-	-	-	-	-	-	r	-	-	-	-	-	-	-	-	-	-	-	F	-	-	-	-	-	-	-	-	r	-	F	-	-	4+3	2	10
JW (James) Overend	-	-	-	-	-	-	-	-	-	-	-	-	-	-	-	L	-	L	-	-	-	-	-	-	-	-	-	-	-	-	-	-	-	-	-	-	-	-	-	-	-	-	-	-	-	-	2	-	-
MD (Matt) Poole	r	E	E	E	-	-	E	E	E	E	E	E	E	-	E	-	E	-	-	-	-	-	-	E	E	E	-	E	-	E	-	E	E	-	-	-	-	E	E	E	E	E	E	E	E	E	28+1	3	15
S (Stuart) Potter E+	M	-	M	M	M	M	L	M	M	M	M	M	M	-	-	-	L	-	-	L	L	M	L	-	L	L	L	L	L	L	-	-	-	-	L	-	L	-	-	-	L	L	-	L	M	L	30	8	40
MS (Mitch) Read	-	-	-	-	-	-	-	-	-	-	-	-	-	-	-	>M	-	M	-	-	-	-	-	-	-	-	-	-	-	-	N	-	-	-	-	M	-	-	-	-	-	-	-	-	-	-	4	2	10
D (Dean) Richards E48 L6	-	G*	G*	-	-	G*	G*	-	-	-	-	-	G*	G*	G*	G*	G*	-	G*	G*	-	G*	G*	-	G*	G*	G*	G*	-	r	D*	-	G*	-	r	-	r	G*	r	G*	G*	-	-	G*	r	r	23+6	1	5
CG (Graham) Rowntree E14 L+	A	A	A	A	A	△A	A	A	A	-	A	x	A	C	A	-	A	-	-	A	-	A	x	A	A	A	r	A	-	A	-	A	-	A	-	-	A	A	r	A	A	C*	A	A	A	A	32+2	2	10
JT (Joel) Stransky SA22	-	-	-	-	-	-	-	-	-	-	-	-	-	-	-	-	-	-	-	-	-	-	-	-	-	>r	J	-	J	J	J	J	-	J	J	-	J	J	-	J	J	-	-	J	J	J	14+1	3	195
R (Rory) Underwood E85 L6	O*	K	K	K*	K*	K	K	K*	K*	K	-	K	r	K	x	K	r	K	K	-	K	-	K	K	r	K	K	K	K	-	-	-	-	-	-	-	-	r	K	r	r	-	K	K	<N	-	26+6	20	100
JM (John) Wells	F	x	-	F	F	F	F	F	F	F	F	-	F	-	F	-	F	-	F	F	-	F	-	F	F	-	F	F	-	F	-	F	-	F	-	-	F	-	-	-	-	-	F	r	F	F	26+1	1	5
DE (Dorian) West E+	B	x	-	x	B	-	x	-	x	B	x	B	x	B	x	r	x	B*	x	x	B*	B	B	x	x	B	-	x	-	x	-	x	B	r	B	B*	x	x	B	x	x	B	x	r	x	x	15+3	7	35
JMW (Jim) Wingham	C	-	x	-	-	-	-	-	-	x	-	-	-	-	-	-	-	x	-	-	x	-	-	-	-	-	-	-	-	-	C	-	r	-	-	r	-	-	-	-	-	-	-	-	-	-	2+2	-	-
OJ (Oscar) Wingham	-	-	-	-	-	x	-	r	x	r	-	F	-	x	-	-	-	x	-	-	-	-	-	-	-	-	-	-	F*	-	H	-	-	-	-	F	-	-	-	-	-	F	-	-	-	-	5+2	-	-

1 GAME: TW (Tom) Butler =E(19), A (Andy) Cudmore <O(36), DJ (David) Docherty =r(36), CM (Carl) Fripp <r(29), BD (Ben) Green =r(36), BJ (Ben) Pain =Gt(1), HM (Heinz) Pflugler =O(18), NE (Nick) Webb x(29)=r(31)

The key for how to read the stats is on the last page

CHAPTER 29

Deano's First Step

1997/1998

It was a summer of revolving doors. The most significant departure was that of Rory Underwood, after 14 years, 236 games and 134 tries. "The increased demands of professional rugby have made it difficult to fulfil work, family and playing commitments," Underwood, 34, said. He moved on only after a testimonial game against a British Isles XV and joined Bedford, as did Aadel Kardooni; Steve Hackney and John Liley left for Moseley, Rob Liley for Harlequins.

Their replacements seemed exotic: Martin Corry moved from Bristol to Welford Road to boost the back row, Fritz van Heerden, the South African back-five forward, arrived, Michael Horak, the South Africa under-21 full-back, came via a spell in rugby league with Perth Western Reds academy together with two Fijian backs, Waisale Serevi and Marika Vunibaka. "They're two of the most exciting players in world rugby," Bob Dwyer said of the Fijians.

But rugby was in tumult. There was civil war among factions on the RFU; Tony Hallett, the RFU acting chief executive, resigned and Courage withdrew as sponsors of the league, to be replaced by Allied Dunbar, the insurance company. Pilkington, the glass company, also ended their sponsorship of the domestic cup and Jack Rowell resigned as England manager. Les Cusworth, England's assistant coach, became director of rugby at ambitious Worcester and in Rowell's place came Clive Woodward, the former Leicester centre who, after returning from a period of working in Australia, had coached Henley, London Irish and Bath's backs, while also spending a season with the England under-21 squad.

Woodward, on a three-year contract, became England's first fully-paid coach at the age of 41 and his first training squad included five Leicester players: Will Greenwood, Austin Healey, Graham Rowntree, Martin Johnson and Neil Back. An emerging players squad included Corry, who had made his club debut a few days earlier, against Gloucester, with Serevi - whose range of skills allowed him to play both half-back positions, though mostly at fly-half - on the wing. Johnson led the side, having been appointed club captain in succession to Richards.

While all this was going on, Leicester decided the time was right to become an unquoted public limited company.

↓ Ex-Tiger Clive Woodward took over the reins at England.

An extraordinary general meeting at the Granby Halls accepted the need for change, though not without argument from some members over the benefits of remaining an amateur organisation. Peter Tom, who played 130 games for Leicester between 1963-68, moved from being chairman of the committee to chairman of a board committed to raising the kind of money that would allow Leicester to compete with peers who had attracted a sugar daddy. Tom's involvement as a club official stemmed from a habit of standing with friends at Welford Road and moaning about the game. Challenged to do something about it, Tom joined the committee and a working party considering the future direction of the club. Season-ticket holders were offered either 250 or 350 shares each with the aim of raising some £3 million of new money though they fell short of the target.

A successful businessman, Tom developed Aggregate Industries before its sale for £1.8 billion, and became instrumental in Tigers' commercial development. His company were major sponsors, while his expertise and contacts ensured Tigers were able to receive funding for major projects including stadium development. In the next 20 years as chairman, club revenues grew 40-fold to £20 million as 14,500 season ticket holders helped to fill a 24,000 capacity stadium and the team enjoyed consistent success.

The 1997/98 season was a week old when European rugby returned, Leicester beating Milan but losing to Leinster. They also won 22-17 in Toulouse. Sadly, Graham Willars, the former flanker, coach and president, died that week from cancer aged 57. Victory over Leinster followed, but Toulouse condemned Leicester to a play-off for a quarter-final place by winning 23-22 at Welford Road.

In the Allied Dunbar Premiership, Serevi was at scrum-half for a 33-22 defeat of Bath but a work permit for Vunibaka never materialised and he played one senior game, scoring a hat-trick.

As Leicester prepared for their Heineken Cup play-off with Glasgow & District, England named six of their players in a 28-strong training squad for the toughest baptism of fire imaginable for Woodward. Garforth was elevated to join Johnson, Back, Greenwood, Healey and Rowntree for the series against Australia, New Zealand (twice) and South Africa on successive weekends.

Leicester's European play-off produced a record as Glasgow were dismissed 90-19 at Welford Road. It was the highest total by a side in the fledgling tournament, the greatest number of tries (14) and the biggest individual points tally, 35 for Stransky of which 15 came from the fly-half's three tries, though Horak scored four from full-back. A week later it was all over: there was to be no echo of that famous victory in Pau the previous season, the French club winning the quarter-final 35-18 against a Leicester side fielding Serevi at scrum-half and Richards at lock.

Remarkably, with ten weeks of the season gone, Leicester had played only three domestic league games and sat seventh in the table. Their best players departed for England duty while the club dipped a toe into a new development tournament, the Cheltenham & Gloucester Cup, and Johnson found himself in trouble. He and Greenwood, winning his first cap, started the 15-15 draw with Australia, Cockerill and Healey playing off the bench, but against New Zealand at Old Trafford, Johnson punched Justin Marshall, the All Blacks scrum-half, and was subsequently suspended for one match by his own management.

The same match was distinguished by Cockerill, laying claim to the number-two jersey, snarling defiance at Norm Hewitt, his opposite number, as New Zealand performed their traditional haka. With Garforth also starting and Back appearing as a replacement, Leicester's contribution to the national cause was growing and, a week later, Back started against the Springboks at open-side flanker as part of the back-row trio that would win worldwide renown - Back, Lawrence Dallaglio (Wasps) and Richard Hill from Saracens.

Though England lost to New Zealand and South Africa, a 26-26 draw in the second match with the All Blacks, at Twickenham, brought a measure of satisfaction. Corry came off the bench for an Emerging England XV against New Zealand at Huddersfield (alongside Healey, Rowntree, Garforth and Back) while Rowntree, supplanted in the England senior side by Jason Leonard, held his place in the England A side beaten 30-19 by the All Blacks at Welford Road, when Stuart Potter also shared in a notable defensive display.

Healey had played scrum-half at Huddersfield, the position in which the Lions had chosen him. But Woodward, recognising his creative versatility, played him on the left wing in the final international of the autumn and would go on to choose him on both wings in the future. It was confirmation of the view held by Dwyer, that Healey could play virtually anywhere in the back division bar centre, though the player was not always in tune with the coach's opinion.

Leicester, meanwhile, had given debuts to Van Heerden and a young Irishman, Geordan Murphy, in the new cup competition. They also unveiled their biggest signing - quite literally - in the 22-stone shape of Lewis Capes, son of the international shot putter, Geoff. He had been playing American football and was a good illustration of the cross-fertilisation of sporting activities that Woodward, among others, was looking for. But Capes junior was not a success, though Leicester pushed up to third in the league table before losing 25-19 at home to Newcastle, already on course to their first and so far only league title.

Johnson was awarded the OBE in the new year's honours for his leadership of the Lions though the fifth-round cup (now under the auspices of Tetley's Bitter) encounter with Saracens occupied his thoughts more. Leicester had beaten Saracens 22-21 at Watford in the league just before Christmas but the tables turned in the cup game, Lynagh kicking his side to a 14-13 win. When Leicester also lost at Gloucester in the league, it left Newcastle and Saracens neck and neck at the top with everyone else also-rans. Rumours circulated about Dwyer's future and stories emerged of a substantial training-ground spat between him and Healey.

↑ Richard Cockerill finds Martin Johnson at Stade du Hameau in Pau in the Heineken Cup quarter-final 9.11.1997.

→ Springbok Fritz van Heerden made his Tigers debut against Rotherham in the Cheltenham & Gloucester Cup 14.11.1997

↓ Richard Cockerill takes on the haka before the All Blacks test at Old Trafford 22.11.1997.

↑ Dean Richards took over as coach in February 1998.

After the loss to Gloucester, Dwyer himself hinted at a rupture: "If the coach is doing everything right but the players are not responding, there are two options - change the players or change the coach," he said. There was an option to extend his original contract which the Leicester board chose not to take up and, after canvassing the views of the players, Dwyer and the club parted company, though a single abstention meant that the board was not entirely unanimous. In his place came Richards, still at that time playing back row or lock though mainly in the second team, and John Wells, the one as coach and manager of first-team affairs, the other as forwards coach with Stransky lined up to coach the backs as well as play fly-half.

"It is for others to provide the precise reasons for this decision," Dwyer said in a statement, confirming a degree of acrimony behind the scenes. "In my opinion it has not been an unsuccessful time for Leicester." It was a gamble on Richards's intuitive rugby skills and ability to manage players, just as it was on the ability of Wells to coach at elite level with no previous experience. On their first outing under new management, Leicester beat London Irish 62-21 in the Cheltenham & Gloucester Cup quarter-finals.

England, meanwhile, launched into the five nations with five Leicester players in the XV which lost 24-17 to France in Paris: Greenwood, Healey, Garforth, Johnson and Back would have been joined by Cockerill but for injury but Leicester still had a hooker in the squad in Dorian West, who won his first cap as a replacement at France's new venue, the Stade de France. It was England's only loss of the season: Back, Healey and Greenwood were among the try-scorers in the record 60-26 defeat of Wales, Healey scored again in the 34-20 win over Scotland and Cockerill crossed the try line in the 35-17 win over Ireland.

Throughout the tournament the clubs were at odds with the RFU, concerned at the demands made on leading players, the shape of the season and control of the professional game. Woodward laid down an ultimatum to his players to choose between club or country and, not surprisingly, many players opted for their clubs. A rash of withdrawals from England's summer tour down under began, which quickly became a raging epidemic of players either injured, requiring operations or, indeed, suspended for ill-discipline.

Leicester's season showed no sign of picking up: a development XV crashed 73-19 to the Barbarians and they lost to Gloucester in the semi-finals of the Cheltenham & Gloucester Cup. They lost 27-10 to Newcastle at Gateshead, a game in which Greenwood was sent off for butting Rob Andrew and Back left the field claiming to have been bitten on the thumb. It was the club's second red card in a two-month period, Corry having been sent off against Northampton, but no further action was taken against Greenwood.

Johnson, struggling with a groin injury, pulled out of England's summer trip to the southern hemisphere which became known as the "Tour from Hell". In the end Woodward omitted, or was forced to omit, 16 front-rank players and included 17 uncapped players in his squad, among them Stuart Potter and Lewis Moody who joined other Leicester colleagues in Healey, Cockerill and Rowntree.

Another member of the touring party was Tim Stimpson, the full-back who had fallen out of favour at Newcastle but on whom Leicester had long had designs. Stimpson toured with the 1997 Lions and agreed terms with Leicester before England's departure. David Lougheed, the Canada wing, was also signed, as was a little Australian centre who became so fundamental a part of Leicester's success over the next decade, Pat Howard. A crop of England under-18 players, Adam Balding, James Grindal and Andy Goode, arrived at Welford Road over the summer in time to see the departure of Serevi, the Fijian whose attacking gifts were extraordinary but not suited to the sustained demands and poor playing conditions of an English winter, and Eric Miller, returning to Leinster.

Three Leicester players, Healey, Cockerill and Rowntree, started in what remains England's record defeat, the 76-0 loss to Australia in Brisbane where Potter won his only cap, as a replacement for eight minutes in the first half. The same trio played in the losses to New Zealand (64-22 and 40-10) and the two front-row forwards played in the 18-0 loss to South Africa, a relative triumph. Stimpson appeared in all four games but Moody had to be content with midweek defeats against a New Zealand Academy XV and New Zealand Maori, both character-building experiences for so young a player.

1998/1999

Character was needed by every player going into the third full season of professional rugby. Their employers, at the clubs and the RFU, having come to a notional understanding in May (the Mayfair Agreement, the third such effort in three years which alone told of the degree of difference), remained at loggerheads, the union itself was torn apart and threatened with disciplinary action by the International Rugby Board.

No more alphabet soup at the Memorial Ground! The wearing of letters on shirts was banned.

At a more parochial level, Leicester had to come to terms with the decision by English Rugby Partnership that the country's leading 24 clubs, those in the shop window of a sport desperate to encourage greater support and understanding, should have a uniform system of player-identification. Leicester's traditional lettering system - and that of Bristol which was the opposite to Leicester's so that where A was the loose-head prop at Welford Road, it was the full-back at the Memorial Ground - was to be no more.

English clubs had ruled themselves out of Europe nor was there was a British League to offer excitement beyond domestic competition, for which reason the size of the Allied Dunbar Premiership was increased to 14 clubs. Leicester's management team was still bedding in so a 49-15 win over Harlequins as the Premiership opened was welcome. After four games, Leicester were unbeaten but more than 17,000 watched Saracens win 22-10 at Watford to end the run. Graham Rowntree exacerbated a damaged knee but Leicester forwards remained popular with Woodward - the complete front row, plus Martin Johnson and Neil Back, appeared in his squad for the autumn internationals together with Austin Healey and Will Greenwood.

Pat Howard broke his jaw in a collision with Martin Corry during club training but there were some eye-catching displays from Geordan Murphy at full-back and Greenwood indicated a complete recovery from a shoulder operation with two tries in the 36-13 defeat of Bath. Adding to a general sense of wellbeing was the appointment of Johnson, the club captain, to lead England; it might only have been a World Cup qualifying game against Holland at Huddersfield while Lawrence Dallaglio was recovering from a twisted knee but it marked the start of a proud period for the English game.

A record seven Leicester players started against the Dutch - Greenwood and Healey in the backs, Cockerill, Garforth, Johnson and Back in the pack together with Corry, whose only two previous caps had come on tour in Argentina in 1997. Corry was one of nine try-scorers in the 110-0 rout, so was Cockerill though they could not match the appetite of Back who gobbled up four of England's 16 tries. The subsequent encounter with Italy, again under Johnson's captaincy and in which Greenwood scored a crucial try in the 23-15 win, was far harder.

Greenwood was forced to withdraw from the next international, against Australia, with the groin injury which was to take such a heavy toll on him over the next year. Nevertheless Healey, Cockerill, Garforth, Johnson and Back remained for the disappointing 12-11 loss to Australia and the more

encouraging 13-7 win which ended South Africa's hopes of a grand-slam tour and their run of 17 successive international wins. Lower down the international scale, a North and Midlands under-21 XV beat the junior world champions, South Africa, 22-16 at Welford Road with five Leicester players - Goode, Balding, Ben Smith, Scott Read and Sam Skinner - in their ranks and Moody helped England's under-21 side lower the touring team's colours again at Twickenham.

Fiji's national side beat a second-string Leicester 22-16 as they rambled through Britain and cost the club the services of Stransky, who damaged knee ligaments. He was replaced by Howard for the return of the Premiership which brought Leicester a 31-18 win over Newcastle, the champions. The restoration of the Barbarians fixture to its Christmas date proved a better occasion than the match which Leicester lost 38-24 to a far from vintage guest XV. As January wore on, Leicester and Northampton remained locked together at the top of the Premiership.

Leicester stretched away with wins over Richmond and Harlequins but during the 31-10 win over London Irish, Healey flicked a foot on the head of his opposing scrum-half, Kevin Putt. He was cited for stamping and promptly dropped by England from the squad preparing to play Scotland. Leicester suspended him for three weeks but an RFU disciplinary panel decided he should be banned for eight weeks, unavailable for all but the final game of the five nations.

So England went through the championship with their four hard-core Leicester forwards, Johnson, Back, Cockerill and Garforth, winning against Scotland, Ireland and France but losing, in the most dramatic manner possible, the grand-slam match with Wales at Wembley (Wales's 'home' ground during the completion of the Millennium Stadium in Cardiff). Johnson received a yellow card for a stamping incident involving John Leslie, the Scotland centre, but left the field with a shoulder injury as England struggled to win 24-21.

Geordan Murphy on top of his game and starting to make a real impact in the team.

A week after Johnson's misdemeanour at Twickenham, he was in the headlines against Richmond. Having disposed of Barking and Leeds very comfortably in the Tetley's Bitter Cup, Leicester were optimistic about success in the quarter-final against a club about to hit the financial buffers. But they lost Johnson to the sin bin for a professional foul in the first half, during which Richmond scored two tries and created a cushion which Leicester, losing 15-13, did not overcome. That the white card (which then denoted ten minutes in the sin bin) was subsequently quashed did not thrill Leicester and Johnson was given another in the Premiership clash with Northampton a fortnight later.

Yet so outstanding was Johnson's play in that match that the Premiership title was, in effect, decided by Leicester's 22-15 win over their nearest challengers with two months still to run. At one stage Leicester were reduced to 13 men with Howard's spell in the sin bin overlapping that of Johnson but still Northampton, on their own ground, could only kick penalties and when they, in turn, lost a forward to the sin bin, Leicester clinched the match by grinding out a penalty try.

They were able, too, to reflect on a return to Europe, the English clubs agreeing to end their boycott of the Heineken Cup and also accepting the principle of a salary cap of £1.5 million for the next season. That decision coincided with Richmond going into administration and the struggles of other clubs to make ends meet; there was a self-evident need to stabilise club finances as far as possible and to be able to offer supporters a consistent programme, hence the decision to play Premiership games throughout the 1999 World Cup, to be played in Britain, Ireland and France, despite opposition from Leicester, who wanted to delay the start of the competition.

Their third league title was made mathematically certain at Newcastle where Stimpson kicked seven penalties against his former club in a 21-12 win. With the second team winning the midweek league shield, Leicester could claim genuine strength in depth, having been without two international centres, Greenwood and Potter, and two international half-backs, Stransky and Healey, for long periods of the season. Some 13,000 turned out at Welford Road for the final game, the 72-37 win over relegated West Hartlepool.

↑ Tigers secure their first Premiership title at holders Newcastle 2.5.1999.

There was one more fixture to play, the Scottish Amicable Trophy match which paired the Premiership winners with their old friends, the Barbarians, at Twickenham. Over 40,000 people saw the Baa-baas win 55-33 but the match was overshadowed by revelations in the now-defunct Sunday tabloid newspaper, *News of the World*, that trapped Lawrence Dallaglio, the England captain, in a drugs sting.

He resigned the captaincy which was passed to Johnson. When the Leicester lock led England out against Australia in Sydney in June, there were a further 37 games as captain to come before he finally stood down, having won the 2003 World Cup against the same opponents on the same ground. Travelling with him for the centenary test was Leon Lloyd, who had played for England A during the season and was one of four uncapped players picked by Woodward; Stimpson, Healey, Rowntree, Garforth, Cockerill, Back and Corry also boarded the flight south for what was both a World Cup camp as well as a fixture with the Wallabies. Greenwood would have travelled too had he not spent the previous seven months searching for a cure for his pelvic condition. It led him, eventually, to Munich to consult the world-famous specialist, Hans-Wilhelm Müller-Wolfahrt, and ended an agonising period.

↑ LEICESTER FOOTBALL CLUB 1997/98
Back: Geeson (Physiotherapist), Freshwater, Garforth, Rowntree, Barlow, Edwards, W.Johnson, Stransky, Jones, Miller.
Middle: Duggan (Fitness coach), Shephard (Team secretary), Jelley, Corry, Greenwood, Richards, Moody, Poole, Fletcher, Gustard, Hall (Director of coaching development), Dwyer (Director of coaching).
Front: Hamilton, West, Joiner, Cockerill, M.Johnson (capt), Back, Healey, Potter, Malone, Overend.

↑ LEICESTER FOOTBALL CLUB 1998/99
Back: Stuart, Freshwater, Becconsall, Hamilton, Greenwood, Stimpson, Gustard, W.Johnson, Moody, Lougheed, Horak, Rowntree, Garforth.
Middle: Smith (Extras coach), Wells (Forwards coach), Shephard (Team secretary), Howard, Miller, Malone, Poole, Corry, Fletcher, van Heerden, Lloyd, Stransky (Player coach), Overend, Ferris, Ezulike, Duggan (Fitness advisor), Geeson (Physiotherapist), Richards (Rugby manager).
Front: Key (Extras coach), Murphy, Potter, Cockerill, Back, Joiner, M.Johnson (capt), Healey, Edwards, M.Read, Jelley, Webb, Fife (Fitness advisor).

19 97/98	Home Ground: Welford Road Director of Coaching: Bob Dwyer then Dean Richards in mid-February Captain: Martin Johnson

OVERALL RECORD:					T	C	PG	DG	PTS
PLD	W	D	L	Tigers scored:	148	105	86	5	1223
40	24	2	14	Opponents scored:	101	68	74	6	881

GM	DATE		VEN	OPPONENTS	RESULT	POS/LGE	TRIES	KICKS	ATT
ALLIED DUNBAR PREMIERSHIP 1 (4TH)						**CHAMPIONS: NEWCASTLE FALCONS**			
	Aug	23	a	Wasps	PP (carnival)	-			
1		**30**	**H**	**Gloucester**	W 33-16	2	Horak 19, Greenwood 76, Back 79	Stransky 3c/4p	11159
8	Oct	18	a	Northampton	L 6-25	7	-	Stransky 2p	8186
9		**25**	**H**	**Bath**	W 33-22	6	Healey 17, Stransky 36, Greenwood 50	Stransky 3c/4p	16000
	Nov	2s	a	Wasps	PP (European Cup)	-			
16	Dec	**13**	**H**	**Sale**	W 55-15	4	M.Johnson 8, Gustard 33, Moody 43, Penalty 55, West 57, Horak 69/75	Stransky 4c/4p	10695
17		16tu	a	Richmond	L 15-32	5	Potter 33, Greenwood 74	Horak c/p	2076
18		**20**	**H**	**NEC Harlequins**	W 27-3	3	Penalty 39, Greenwood 61, Back 76	Serevi 2c/p, Horak c/p	11606
19		26f	a	Saracens	W 22-21	3	van Heerden 54	Stransky c/4p/d	14291
20		**30tu**	**H**	**Newcastle Falcons**	L 19-25	3	Penalty 37	Stransky c/4p	16000
22	Jan	**17**	**H**	**Wasps**	W 45-21	3	Horak 19, Healey 56, Penalty 74, Stransky 75, Serevi 77	Stransky 4c/4p	15000
24	Feb	1s	a	Gloucester	L 25-32	3	Horak 35/72, Joiner 49	Stransky 2p, Serevi 2c	7963
26		**14**	**H**	**London Irish**	W 34-19	4	Greenwood 55/64, Lloyd 79	Stransky 2c/5p	10762
28		28	a	Bristol	W 27-24	4	Lloyd 13, Back 24, Potter 48	Stransky 3c/2p	3143
29	Mar	**7**	**H**	**Northampton**	D 15-15	4	Back 38, Joiner 80	Stransky c/p	14500
30		14	a	Bath	L 5-16	4	Joiner 32	-	8200
33		**28**	**H**	**Richmond**	W 42-19	4	Potter 16, Greenwood 31/34/70, Back 46, Rowntree 78	Stransky 3c/p/d	10146
34	Apr	11	a	Sale	L 21-35	4	Cockerill 8, Miller 33	Stransky c/3p	4000
35		18	a	NEC Harlequins	W 23-14	4	Stransky 11, Lloyd 80	Stransky 2c/2p/d	5362
36		**25**	**H**	**Saracens**	D 10-10	4	Hamilton 47	Stransky c/p	16900
37		29w	a	Wasps	L 13-17	4	Joiner 27/63	Stransky p	3791
38	May	4m	a	Newcastle Falcons	L 10-27	5	Back 31	Stransky c/p	7210
39		**10s**	**H**	**Bristol**	W 34-25	4	Gustard 14, Stransky 38/61, Healey 49, Joiner 58	Stransky 3c/p	8678
40		17s	a	London Irish	W 55-16	4	Back 3/16, Barlow 7, Horak 22/72, Gustard 57/75, Hamilton 69	Stransky 6c/p	2500
HEINEKEN CUP						**EUROPEAN CHAMPIONS: BATH**			
2	Sep	**7s**	**H**	**Amatori Milano**	W 26-10	1	Greenwood 22/32, Horak 75	Stransky c/3p	9782
3		12f	a	Leinster	L 9-16	2	-	Stransky 3p	7000
4		20	a	Toulouse	W 22-17	1	Miller 41	Stransky c/5p	13000
5		**27**	**H**	**Leinster**	W 47-22	2	Barlow 45, Healey 59, Malone 63, Rowntree 70, Greenwood 78	Healey d, Serevi 2c/2p, Stransky 3p	10392
6	Oct	**4**	**H**	**Toulouse**	L 22-23	2	Greenwood 24, Serevi 39, Back 45	Serevi 2c/p	12500
7		12s	a	Amatori Milano	W 37-29	2	Lloyd 3, Serevi 30, M.Johnson 50, Greenwood 80	Stransky 4c/3p	2000
10	Nov	**1**	**H**	**Glasgow & District (po)**	W 90-19	-	Horak 4/24/41/59, Corry 17, Stransky 20/39/74, Cockerill 27/50, Richards 32, Healey 34, Greenwood 61, Lloyd 65	Stransky 10c	6486
11		9s	a	Pau (qf)	L 18-35	-	Back 35, Serevi 61	Stransky c/2p	13000
RFU CLUB COMPETITION (TETLEY'S BITTER CUP)						**CUP WINNERS: SARACENS**			
	Jan	3	a	Coventry (4)	PP (waterlogged)	P2			
21		10	a	Coventry (4)	W 50-14	P2	West 20/51, Lloyd 29/79, Penalty 70	Stransky 5c/4p, G.Murphy d	4000
23		24	a	Saracens (5)	L 13-14	P	Stransky 43	Stransky c/2p	9528
CHELTENHAM & GLOUCESTER CUP						**WINNERS: GLOUCESTER**			
12	Nov	**14f**	**H**	**Rotherham**	W 60-19	P2	Hamilton 4, Stransky 25, West 31, Potter 43, Malone 49, Ezulike 70/76, Barlow 80	Stransky 7c/2p	3680
14		**28f**	**H**	**London Irish**	W 18-16	P	W.Johnson 2, Jelley 60	Stransky c/2p	3900
15	Dec	6	a	Exeter	W 50-20	P2	M.Read 2/20, Barlow 16, Boer 17, G.Murphy 27/34, Jelley 70	Stransky 6c/p	2000
25	Feb	7	a	Orrell	W 25-24	P2	Barlow 38, Serevi 40, M.Read 56	G.Murphy 2c/2p	500
27		**22s**	**H**	**London Irish (qf)**	W 62-21	P	G.Murphy 2, Stransky 5, M.Read 21, Lloyd 23/42/53, Corry 35, West 47, Hamilton 56, Poole 65	Stransky 6c	3048
32	Mar	**21**	**H**	**Gloucester (sf)**	L 15-53	P	Horak 15, Malone 56	Horak c/p	4495
CLUB MATCHES									
13	Nov	**21f**	**H**	**Loughborough Students**	W 71-7		Edwards 1/40, Boer 8, G.Murphy 8/65/80, Jelley 31, Jasnikowski 42, Vunibaka 58/67/72	G.Murphy 8c	2475
31	Mar	**17tu**	**H**	**Barbarians**	L 19-73		W.Johnson 23, S.Read 47, Barlow 65	Malone 2c	7314

INDIVIDUAL APPEARANCES 1997/98

Name / Game #	1	2	3	4	5	6	7	8	9	10	11	12	13	14	15	16	17	18	19	20	21	22	23	24	25	26	27	28	29	30	31	32	33	34	35	36	37	38	39	40	Apps	T	Pts
DJ (Dave) Addison	-	-	-	-	-	-	-	-	-	-	-	D	D	D	-	x	x	x	r	x	-	-	-	-	-	-	-	-	-	-	x	-	-	-	-	-	-	-	-	-	3+1	-	-
JM (Jason) Aldwinckle	-	-	-	-	-	-	-	-	-	-	-	-	-	-	-	-	-	-	-	-	-	-	-	-	-	-	-	-	-	-	B	B	-	-	-	r	B	x	-	-	3+1	-	-
NA (Neil) Back E12 L2	H	H	H	H	H	H	x	H	H	H	H	-	-	-	-	-	-	H	H	H	H	H	△H	-	-	H	-	H*	H	-	-	-	H	H	H	H	H	H	H	H	27	10	50
TA (Tim) Barlow	-	-	-	K	N	K	x	x	-	-	-	N	r	N	K	-	-	-	-	-	-	-	-	-	K	-	r	-	-	-	r	K	-	-	-	-	-	K	K	<K	11+3	6	30
SA (Steven) Beaufoy	-	-	-	-	-	-	-	-	-	-	-	-	-	>r	r	-	-	-	-	-	-	-	-	-	-	-	-	-	-	-	<C	-	-	-	-	-	-	-	-	-	1+2	-	-
GM (Garry) Becconsall	-	-	-	-	-	-	-	-	-	-	-	-	-	-	-	-	-	-	-	-	-	-	-	-	-	-	-	-	-	-	r	r	-	-	-	-	-	-	-	-	0+2	-	-
JF (Jake) Boer	-	-	-	-	-	-	-	-	-	-	-	>H	H	x	H	-	x	-	-	-	-	-	-	-	H	-	<H	-	-	-	-	-	-	-	-	-	-	-	-	-	5	2	10
R (Richard) Cockerill E9	B	B	B	B	B	B	B	B	△B	B	B	-	-	-	-	x	B	B	B	△B	x	B	-	-	-	B	-	B	△B	B	-	-	B	B	r	-	-	-	r	B	23+2	3	15
ME (Martin) Corry E2 L+	>F	F	F	F	F	F	G	F	F	F	F	-	-	-	-	-	-	G	F	-	-	F	F	G	-	G	D	D	■G	-	-	-	r	x	r	r	r	E	E	E	23+4	2	10
PK (Phil) Delaney	-	-	-	-	-	-	-	-	-	-	-	-	-	-	-	-	-	-	-	-	-	-	-	-	r	-	-	-	-	-	-	-	-	-	-	-	-	-	-	<M	1+1	-	-
RA (Roland) Edwards	-	-	-	-	-	-	-	-	-	-	-	r	I	-	r	-	-	x	-	-	-	-	-	r	I	<I	x	-	-	-	-	-	-	-	-	-	-	-	-	x	3+3	2	10
NC (Nnamdi) Ezulike	-	-	-	-	-	-	-	-	-	-	-	K	-	-	-	-	-	-	-	-	-	-	-	-	-	-	-	-	-	-	K	-	-	-	-	-	-	-	-	-	2	2	10
NR (Neil) Fletcher	-	-	-	x	r	-	-	-	-	-	-	-	-	-	-	-	-	-	-	-	-	x	x	-	r	-	-	x	-	-	D	D	-	-	-	-	-	-	-	-	2+2	-	-
PT (Perry) Freshwater E+	-	x	x	r	A	-	x	x	x	A	r	A	A	A	A	r	A	x	r	A	A	x	x	x	A	x	A	x	r	r	x	A	x	r	r	r	r	r	r	r	12+13	-	-
DJ (Darren) Garforth E11	C	C	C	C	C	C	C	C	C	r	C	-	-	-	-	C	r	C	C	C	C	C	C	C	-	C	C	C	C	C	-	-	C	△C	C	C	C	△C	C	C	31+2	-	-
WJH (Will) Greenwood E8 L+	M	M	M	-	r	M	M	M	M	M	M	-	-	-	-	M	M	M	-	-	-	-	M	M	-	M	-	M	M	M	-	-	M	M	-	M	M	■M	M	-	24+1	15	75
PSK (Paul) Gustard	-	-	-	-	>r	r	r	-	x	r	-	G	G	F	F	F	△F	r	-	-	G	r	-	F	F	△r	F	r	F	F	-	-	-	r	r	F	F	r	F	F	16+11	4	20
JG (Jamie) Hamilton	r	r	I	x	r	x	x	x	x	x	x	I	-	I	I	I	I	-	-	-	-	-	-	-	-	-	I	I	r	x	I	I	I	I	I	I	r	x	r	I	15+6	4	20
AS (Austin) Healey E11 L2	I	I	r	I	I	I	I	I	I	I	I	-	-	-	-	N	r	I	N	N	I	I	I	-	-	x	-	N	I	I	-	-	N	N	-	r	I	I	I	-	25+3	5	28
MJ (Michael) Horak E+	>O	O	O	O	O	O	O	O	O	O	O	-	-	O	-	O	O	K	x	O	N	N	N	N	-	-	-	x	O	O	-	N	O	O	O	O	O	O	O	N	31	14	85
MT (Mark) Jasnikowski	-	-	-	-	-	-	-	-	-	-	-	-	L	-	L	-	-	-	-	-	-	-	-	-	L	-	-	-	-	-	<r	-	-	-	-	-	-	-	-	-	3+1	1	5
DA (Derek) Jelley	x	-	-	-	-	x	-	-	-	-	-	x	C	C	C	-	-	-	-	x	r	-	x	-	-	-	-	-	-	-	-	-	-	-	-	-	-	-	-	-	3+1	3	15
MO (Martin) Johnson E37 L5	D*	D*	D*	D*	D*	D*	D*	D*	D*	D*	D*	-	-	-	-	D*	D*	D*	△D*	D*	D*	D*	D*	D*	-	D*	-	-	D*	D*	-	-	D*	△D*	D*	D*	D*	D*	D*	D*	31	2	10
WW (Will) Johnson	-	-	-	r	-	r	-	-	-	-	x	x	-	G	G	r	G	-	-	-	-	-	-	r	G	-	-	-	x	r	G	G	G	G	G	-	G	G	△G	G	13+5	2	10
CA (Craig) Joiner S20	K	K	K	M	-	-	-	-	x	r	x	-	-	L	-	x	N	N	x	K	-	x	-	L	-	-	-	-	N	N	-	M	K	K	N	N	N	N	N	-	19+1	6	30
AJS (Andrew) Leeds A14	-	-	-	-	-	-	-	-	-	-	-	-	-	-	-	-	-	>O	O	-	M	O	O	<O	-	-	-	-	-	-	-	-	-	-	-	-	-	-	-	-	6	-	-
LD (Leon) Lloyd E+	x	r	x	r	K	-	K	K	K	K	K	-	-	K	-	K	K	-	K	-	K	K	K	K	-	K	K	K	K	K	-	-	r	r	K	K	K	-	-	-	22+4	10	50
D (Darren) Mackenzie	-	-	-	-	-	-	-	-	-	-	-	-	-	-	-	-	-	-	-	-	-	-	-	-	-	-	-	-	-	-	>H	H	-	-	-	-	-	-	-	-	2	-	-
NG (Niall) Malone I3	-	-	x	x	M	x	L	x	x	r	x	M	-	-	r	r	r	-	-	-	-	-	-	-	x	x	r	x	x	x	J	L	x	x	x	-	x	x	<r	-	5+6	3	19
ERP (Eric) Miller I8 L1	G	G	G	G	G	G	F	G	G	G	G	-	-	-	-	G	-	-	G	G	-	-	G	△r	-	-	G	G	-	G	-	-	F	F	F	G	-	<F	-	-	23+1	2	10
LW (Lewis) Moody E+ L+	r	-	-	-	-	-	H	x	-	-	-	-	-	H	-	H	H	F	r	r	F	G	r	H	-	F	-	F	r	H	-	-	-	-	-	x	x	-	x	r	11+6	1	5
GEA (Geordan) Murphy I+ L+	-	-	-	-	-	-	-	-	-	-	-	>O	O	r	O	-	-	-	-	x	O	-	-	-	O	O	O	O	-	-	O	O	-	-	-	-	-	-	-	O	11+1	6	59
JJP (JJ) Oelofse	-	-	-	-	-	-	-	-	-	-	-	-	-	-	-	-	-	-	-	-	-	-	-	-	C	-	-	-	-	-	<A	x	-	-	-	-	-	-	-	-	2	-	-
JW (James) Overend	x	x	-	-	-	-	x	-	-	-	-	-	r	M	M	-	-	r	M	M	L	M	r	r	M	L	M	-	-	-	-	-	-	-	M	r	L	L	L	L	14+5	-	-
MD (Matt) Poole	E	E	E	E	E	E	E	E	E	E	-	-	-	-	-	-	-	-	-	-	-	-	-	-	D	-	r	-	E	x	E	E	r	-	-	-	-	x	x	r	14+3	1	5
S (Stuart) Potter E+	L	L	L	L	L	L	-	L	L	L	L	L	-	-	-	L	L	L	L	L	-	L	L	-	-	-	L	L	L	L	-	-	L	L	L	L	-	-	-	-	26	4	20
MS (Mitch) Read	-	-	-	-	-	N	-	-	-	-	-	-	N	x	N	-	-	-	-	x	x	-	-	-	N	N	N	-	-	-	N	-	-	-	-	-	-	-	-	-	7	4	20
SS (Scott) Read	-	-	-	-	-	-	-	-	-	-	-	-	-	-	-	-	-	-	-	-	-	-	-	-	-	-	-	-	-	-	>M	r	-	-	-	-	-	-	-	-	1+1	1	5
D (Dean) Richards E48 L6	-	x	r	-	-	-	-	-	-	r	E	-	-	-	D	-	-	-	-	<S	x	-	-	-	-	-	-	-	-	-	-	-	-	-	-	-	-	-	-	-	3+2	1	5
DJ (Duncan) Roke	-	-	-	-	-	-	-	-	-	-	-	>r	M	-	r	-	-	-	-	-	-	-	-	-	-	-	-	-	-	-	L	-	-	-	-	-	-	-	-	<r	2+3	-	-
CG (Graham) Rowntree E15 L+	A	A	A	A	r	A	A	A	A	C	A	-	-	-	-	A	C	A	△A	-	-	A	A	A	-	A	r	A	A	A	-	-	A	A	A	A	A	△A	A	A	29+2	2	10
WT (Waisale) Serevi Fi13	>N	N	N	N	r	J	N	N	N	N	N	-	J	-	-	-	-	J	I	I	x	r	x	I	<J	x	-	-	-	-	-	-	-	-	-	-	-	-	-	-	16+2	5	53
JT (Joel) Stransky SA22	J	J	J	J	J	-	J	J	J	J	J	J*	-	J*	J*	J	J	-	J	J	J	J	J	J	-	J	J*	J	J	J	-	J*	J	J	J	J	J	J	J	J	35	11	459
FJ (Fritz) van Heerden SA13	-	-	-	-	-	-	-	-	-	-	-	>E	E	E	E	E	E	E	E	E	E	E	E	E	E*	E	E	E	-	△E	-	F	E	E	E	E	E	-	-	-	24	1	5
JM (John) Wells	-	x	x	-	-	-	-	-	-	-	r	F	<F*	-	-	-	-	-	-	-	-	-	-	-	-	-	-	-	-	-	-	-	-	-	-	-	-	-	-	-	2+1	-	-
DE (Dorian) West E2	x	x	x	x	r	x	x	x	x	x	x	B	x	B	B	B	r	r	x	x	B	r	B	B	-	x	B	x	r	r	-	-	x	r	B	B	-	B	B	x	12+7	5	25
JMW (Jim) Wingham	-	-	-	-	-	-	-	-	-	-	-	C	<r	-	-	-	-	-	-	-	-	-	-	-	-	-	-	-	-	-	-	-	-	-	-	-	x	-	-	-	1+1	-	-
OJ (Oscar) Wingham	-	-	-	-	-	-	-	-	-	-	-	-	r	-	r	-	-	-	-	-	x	-	-	-	r	-	r	-	-	-	F*	r	-	-	-	-	-	-	-	-	1+5	-	-
B (Ben) Wyer-Roberts	-	-	-	-	-	-	-	-	-	-	-	x	>B	x	r	-	-	-	-	-	-	-	-	-	-	-	-	-	-	-	<r	x	-	-	-	-	-	-	-	-	1+2	-	-

1 GAME: TJ (Tim) Cornell =r(13), JT (James) Ferris >r(13)x(35), MJ (Marek) Kwisiuk >r(25)x(27), TD (Tom) Murphy x(24)=B(25), BTA (Ben) Pennington =r(31), RN (Richard) Pope =r(13), MD (Marika) Vunibaka Fi+ =Kt(13), EP (Elliot) Webb >C(32)

The key for how to read the stats is on the last page

19 98/99	Home Ground: Welford Road	Trophy Cabinet: Allied Dunbar Premiership(3)	OVERALL RECORD:					T	C	PG	DG	PTS
	Rugby Manager: Dean Richards assisted by Joel Stransky and John Wells		PLD	W	D	L	Tigers scored:	125	77	89	1	1049
	Captain: Martin Johnson		38	24	0	14	Opponents scored:	72	45	82	4	708

GM	DATE		VEN	OPPONENTS	RESULT	POS/LGE	TRIES	KICKS	ATT
ALLIED DUNBAR PREMIERSHIP 1 (1ST)						**CHAMPIONS: LEICESTER TIGERS**			
1	Sep	**5**	**H**	**NEC Harlequins**	W 49-15	1	Ezulike 4, Healey 12, Cockerill 37, Lloyd 47/55, Back 75, Stransky 80	Stransky 4c/2p	13130
2		12	a	London Scottish	W 38-3	1	Stransky 15, Ezulike 18, Stimpson 26, Gustard 63	Stransky 3c/4p	2138
3		**19**	**H**	**Northampton Saints**	W 35-25	1	Ezulike 10, Healey 20, Stimpson 22, Back 46	Stransky 3c/3p	13292
4		26	a	Bedford	W 32-23	1	Ezulike 4, Potter 11, Penalty 50, Back 80	Stransky 2c/p, Stimpson c/p	4165
6	Oct	11s	a	Saracens	L 10-22	3	Lloyd 39	Stransky c/p	17347
7		**17**	**H**	**Manchester Sale**	W 31-15	2	Back 4/74, Gustard 40	Stransky 2c/4p	9861
8		20tu	a	London Irish	L 23-24	3	Lloyd 21, Healey 71	Stransky 2c/3p	2950
9		**24**	**H**	**Richmond**	W 27-0	2	Back 16, Garforth 23, Stransky 78	Stransky 3c/2p	8443
10	Nov	1s	a	West Hartlepool	W 45-15	1	Murphy 21/42, Stransky 34, Overend 79/80	Murphy p, Stransky 4c/3p	1846
11		**7**	**H**	**Bath Rugby**	W 36-13	1	Greenwood 3/7, Overend 17, Gustard 58, Stransky 77	Stransky 4c/p	15873
12		15s	a	Wasps	L 17-45	1	Murphy 21, Gustard 53	Stransky 2c/p	6027
16	Dec	**12**	**H**	**Newcastle Falcons**	W 31-18	1	Back 6/40, Stuart 80	Murphy 2c/2p, Stimpson 2p	11226
17		19	a	Gloucester	W 23-18	1	Lougheed 11	Stimpson 6p	7222
18		**26**	**H**	**Bedford**	W 26-0	1	Back 30, Cockerill 40, Lougheed 65	Stimpson c/3p	10689
23	Jan	**16**	**H**	**London Scottish**	W 24-12	1	van Heerden 6/54, Lloyd 41	Murphy 2p, Stimpson p	9985
24		**23**	**H**	**Gloucester**	W 23-16	1	Lougheed 22/39, Stransky 61	Stimpson c/2p	11394
25		26tu	a	Richmond	W 23-11	1	Lougheed 26, M.Johnson 49, Jelley 73	Stimpson 2p, Stransky c	7981
27	Feb	6	a	NEC Harlequins	W 34-9	1	Moody 28, Back 49, Lloyd 58/74, Stransky 78	Stransky 3c/p	6212
28		**13**	**H**	**London Irish**	W 31-10	1	Lougheed 39, Lloyd 80	Stransky 7p	15132
30	Mar	13	a	Northampton Saints	W 22-15	1	Joiner 24, Corry 65, Penalty 80	Stimpson 2c/p	10000
31		**27**	**H**	**Wasps**	W 16-6	1	Back 79	Stimpson c/3p	12449
32	Apr	3	a	Bath Rugby	L 16-24	1	Penalty 80	Stimpson 3p, Howard c	8500
33		**17**	**H**	**Saracens**	W 25-18	1	Corry 21	Stimpson c/6p	13823
34		24	a	Manchester Sale	W 41-17	1	Healey 16, Lougheed 22, Corry 31, Back 49/69	Stimpson 2c/4p	4800
35	May	2s	a	Newcastle Falcons	W 21-12	1	-	Stimpson 7p	5207
37		**16s**	**H**	**West Hartlepool**	W 72-37	1	Back 4/10/59, Healey 27/42, Joiner 31, Howard 33, Lougheed 36, Corry 40, Gustard 62, Murphy 65/77	Murphy c, Stimpson 5c	12958
RFU CLUB COMPETITION (TETLEY'S BITTER CUP)						**CUP WINNERS: WASPS**			
22	Jan	**9**	**H**	**Barking (4)**	W 65-6	N2S	Lloyd 4/28/37/74, Hamilton 9/49, Lougheed 22, Stimpson 29, Moody 63, Freshwater 66, Stuart 80	Stimpson 3c, Stransky 2c	4884
26		**30**	**H**	**Leeds Tykes (5)**	W 49-0	P2	Cockerill 2, Corry 6, Back 16/50, Healey 30, Penalty 47, Jelley 77	Stransky 7c	5930
29	Feb	27	a	Richmond (qf)	L 13-15	P	Back 48, Corry 72	Stimpson p	7088
CHELTENHAM & GLOUCESTER CUP						**WINNERS: GLOUCESTER**			
14	Nov	29s	a	Rugby Lions (1 - 1st leg)	L 5-8	P2	Horak 70	-	1500
	Dec	**6s**	**H**	**Rugby Lions (1 - 2nd leg)**	PP (frost)	P2			
21	Jan	**6w**	**H**	**Rugby Lions (1 - 2nd leg)**	L 11-23	P2	Smith 5	Boden p, Horak p	1593
Note: *#14/#21: Rugby Lions won 31-16 on aggregate*									
CLUB MATCHES									
5	Oct	**2f**	**H**	**Cardiff**	L 20-35		Stransky 26, Stuart 69	Stransky c/2p, Goode c	9038
13	Nov	**20f**	**H**	**Swansea**	L 7-20		Stransky 23	Stransky c	5053
15	Dec	**3th**	**H**	**Fiji**	L 16-22		van Heerden 21	Murphy 3p, Stransky c	4761
19		**29tu**	**H**	**Barbarians**	L 24-38		Back 8, Lloyd 14, Joiner 40, Stimpson 48	Stimpson 2c	14750
20	Jan	2	a	Cardiff	L 13-29		Freshwater 26	Stimpson c/p, Goode d	9903
36	May	8	a	Swansea	L 22-34		Lougheed 27/39, Penalty 70	Murphy 2c/p	5000
38		23s		Barbarians	L 33-55		Ferris 16, Moody 40/42, West 66, Rowntree 71	Murphy 3c, Stimpson c	40000
Note: *#38 at Twickenham for Scottish Amicable Trophy*									

INDIVIDUAL APPEARANCES 1998/99

Name / Game #	1	2	3	4	5	6	7	8	9	10	11	12	13	14	15	16	17	18	19	20	21	22	23	24	25	26	27	28	29	30	31	32	33	34	35	36	37	38	Apps	T	Pts
DJ (Dave) Addison	-	-	-	-	-	-	-	-	-	x	-	5	E	<4	-	-	-	-	-	-	-	-	-	-	-	-	-	-	-	-	-	-	-	-	-	-	-	-	3	-	-
NA (Neil) Back E20 L2	7	7	7	r	-	7	7	7	7	7	7	-	-	-	-	7	7	7	H	-	-	x	7*	-	-	7	8	7	7	7	7	7	7	7	7	-	7	-	25+1	20	100
AL (Adam) Balding	-	-	-	-	-	-	-	-	-	-	-	-	-	>8	-	x	x	r	-	r	7	r	x	x	x	-	-	-	-	-	-	-	-	-	-	r	r	r	2+6	-	-
GM (Garry) Becconsall	-	-	-	-	-	-	-	-	r	x	-	-	-	-	-	-	-	-	-	-	-	-	-	-	-	-	x	-	-	-	-	-	x	x	x	13	-	<r	1+2	-	-
R (Richard) Cockerill E21	2	2	2	2	r	2	-	x	2	2	2	-	-	-	-	2	2	2	B	-	-	-	2	2	2	2	2	2	2	2	2	2	2	2	2	-	2	2	27+1	3	15
ME (Martin) Corry E6 L+	8	8	8	8	G	8	8	8	8	-	8	-	-	-	-	8	8	8	-	-	-	8	4	8	8	8	7	8	8	8	8	8	8	8	8	-	8	8	29	6	30
NC (Nnamdi) Ezulike	11	11	11	11	-	11	14	11	11	11	11	-	-	-	-	-	-	-	-	-	11	-	-	-	-	-	-	-	r	r	r	14	-	-	-	-	-	-	12+3	4	20
JT (James) Ferris	-	-	-	-	r	-	-	-	-	-	-	x	-	9	x	-	-	-	-	x	9	-	-	-	-	-	-	-	x	x	x	r	-	-	-	14	-	<14	4+2	1	5
NR (Neil) Fletcher	r	r	x	x	D	x	r	r	5	5	5	4	D	-	D	x	x	r	E	4	-	-	-	x	x	r	r	x	-	-	-	x	-	-	-	5	-	-	10+7	-	-
PT (Perry) Freshwater E+	-	-	-	-	-	-	r	r	r	r	-	r	B	1	r	-	-	-	r	1	-	2	-	-	-	-	-	-	-	-	-	-	-	-	-	1	-	-	5+7	2	10
DJ (Darren) Garforth E19	3	3	3	3	-	3	3	3	3	3	3	-	-	-	-	3	3	3	-	-	-	-	3	3	3	r	3	3	3	3	3	3	3	3	3	-	3	3	27+1	1	5
AJ (Andy) Goode E+	-	-	-	-	>r	-	-	-	r	x	-	x	r	10	-	-	-	-	r	10	-	-	-	-	-	-	-	-	-	-	x	x	-	-	-	-	-	-	2+4	-	5
WJH (Will) Greenwood E10 L+	-	-	-	-	M	r	13	13	-	-	13	-	-	-	-	-	-	-	-	-	-	-	-	-	-	-	-	-	-	-	-	-	-	-	-	-	-	-	4+1	2	10
PSK (Paul) Gustard	6	6	6	6	x	6	6	6	6	8	6	8	G	-	-	6	6	6	-	-	-	-	-	-	-	-	-	-	r	x	x	r	x	r	r	6	r	7	17+5	5	25
JG (Jamie) Hamilton	x	x	r	9	I	x	x	x	-	-	r	9	I	-	I	x	x	x	r	9	r	9	r	x	x	r	-	x	9	9	9	9	9	r	r	9	r	9	14+9	2	10
AS (Austin) Healey E18 L2	9	9	9	-	-	9	9	9	9	9	9	-	-	-	-	9	9	9	I	-	-	x	9	9	9	9	9	9	-	-	-	-	r	9	9	-	9	-	22+1	7	35
MJ (Michael) Horak E+	-	-	x	x	r	x	r	r	r	x	x	11	0	14	K	x	x	r	r	14	15	-	-	-	-	-	<r	-	-	-	-	-	-	-	-	-	-	-	6+7	1	8
PW (Pat) Howard A20	>12	12	12	12	-	12	12	12	-	-	-	-	-	-	M	10	12	12	-	-	-	-	12	12	12	12	12	12	10	10	12	12	10	10	10	-	12	10	26	1	7
R (Rob) Hurrell	-	-	-	-	-	-	-	-	-	-	-	-	-	>5	x	-	-	-	r	5	5	4	-	-	-	-	-	-	-	-	-	-	-	-	-	<r	-	-	4+2	-	-
DA (Derek) Jelley	1	x	r	1	C	1	1	1	1	1	1	1	A	x	A	1	r	r	A	r	-	1	r	1	r	1	r	r	r	1	r	r	r	r	1	r	r	1	20+15	2	10
MO (Martin) Johnson E45 L5	4*	4*	4*	4*	-	4*	4*	4*	4*	4*	4*	-	-	-	-	4*	4*	4*	D*	-	-	x	-	4*	4*	4*	4*	4*	4*	4*	4*	4*	4*	4*	4*	-	4*	4*	28	1	5
WW (Will) Johnson	-	-	-	-	F	-	-	-	r	r	-	-	-	-	-	-	-	-	G	8	8	6	8	6	6	r	r	r	x	r	x	r	x	r	x	8	-	-	9+8	-	-
CA (Craig) Joiner S21	-	-	r	-	N	-	-	-	-	-	-	x	N	-	N	-	-	-	N	13	12	-	-	r	13	13	13	13	13	13	13	13	13	13	13	-	13	13	19+2	3	15
LD (Leon) Lloyd E+	14	14	14	14	K	14	11	14	14	14	14	14	K	-	L	11	14	14	K	-	-	14	14	14	14	14	14	14	14	14	14	-	14	14	14	-	14	-	32	13	65
DC (Dave) Lougheed C25	>r	r	-	-	-	-	-	-	-	-	-	-	-	11	r	14	11	11	-	11	-	11	11	11	11	11	11	11	11	11	11	11	11	11	11	11	11	11	22+3	11	55
LW (Lewis) Moody E+ L+	x	r	r	7	H	x	r	r	r	6	r	7	H	x	-	-	-	-	r	7	-	7	6	7	7	6	6	6	6	6	6	6	6	6	6	7	6	6	23+7	4	20
GEA (Geordan) Murphy I+ L+	-	-	-	-	-	-	-	-	15	15	15	15	-	r	0	15	10	10	J	x	-	r	15	-	x	r	-	x	x	r	10	10	x	r	r	15	r	15	14+7	5	68
JW (James) Overend	r	r	-	-	-	-	-	-	13	13	12	13	M	<13	-	-	-	-	-	-	-	-	-	-	-	-	-	-	-	-	-	-	-	-	-	-	-	-	6+2	3	15
MD (Matt) Poole	-	-	-	-	r	-	-	-	-	-	<r	-	-	-	-	-	-	-	-	-	-	-	-	-	-	-	-	-	-	-	-	-	-	-	-	-	-	-	0+2	-	-
S (Stuart) Potter E1	13	13	13	13	-	13	-	-	-	-	-	-	-	-	-	13	13	13	L	-	-	13	13	13	-	-	-	-	-	-	-	-	-	-	-	-	-	-	12	1	5
CG (Graham) Rowntree E21 L+	r	1	1	-	-	r	-	-	-	-	r	-	-	-	-	r	1	1	C	3*	-	3*	1	r	1	3	1	1	1	r	1	1	1	1	r	3	1	r	19+8	1	5
BE (Ben) Smith	-	-	-	-	-	-	-	-	-	-	-	>r	x	x	F	-	-	-	-	r	<4	-	-	-	-	-	-	-	-	-	-	-	-	-	-	-	-	-	2+2	1	5
TRG (Tim) Stimpson E11 L1	>15	15	15	15	0	15	15	15	-	-	-	-	-	15	-	r	15	15	0	15	-	15	r	15	15	15	15	15	15	15	15	15	15	15	15	-	15	r	27+3	4	191
JT (Joel) Stransky SA22	10	10	10	10	J	10	10	10	10	10	10	10*	J*	-	J*	-	-	-	-	-	-	10	10	10	10	10	10	10	-	-	-	-	-	-	-	10*	<10	-	23	9	242
JH (Jono) Stuart	-	-	-	x	>L	-	r	x	12	12	r	12	L	12	r	12	x	r	M	12	-	12	r	r	x	r	r	r	12	12	-	-	12	12	12	x	r	<12	16+10	3	15
H (Harry) Toews C4	-	-	-	>r	A	-	x	-	-	-	-	3	C	3	C	-	-	-	-	x	<3	x	-	-	-	-	-	-	-	-	-	-	-	-	-	-	-	-	6+1	-	-
FJ (Fritz) van Heerden SA13	5	5	5	5	E*	5	5	5	-	-	-	-	-	-	E	5	5	5	-	-	-	5	5	5	5	5	5	5	5	5	5	5	5	5	5	-	5	5	28	3	15
DE (Dorian) West E2	-	-	-	r	B	r	2	2	r	r	r	2	r	2	B	r	x	x	r	2	-	r	r	r	r	r	r	r	r	r	r	r	r	r	r	2	r	r	8+24	1	5
OJ (Oscar) Wingham	-	-	-	-	-	-	-	-	-	-	-	6	F	6*	G	-	-	-	F	6	<6*	-	x	-	-	-	-	-	-	-	-	-	-	-	-	-	-	-	7	-	-

1 GAME: JM (Jason) Aldwinckle <r(1)x(2)x(3), JI (Jon) Boden x(14)=10(21), G (Gareth) Bowen =r(21), MJ (Matt) Cornish =H(15), PJ (Phil) Greenbury >r(36), AR (Angus) Innes =4(36), S (Sam) Joy =r(21), MJ (Marek) Kwisiuk <2(21), D (Darren) Mackenzie x(12)x(13)<7(14)x(15), MWJ (Mark) Meenan x(36)=r(38), MS (Mitch) Read <12(36), SS (Scott) Read x(13)x(20)13(21), S (Sam) Skinner =1(21), EP (Elliot) Webb <r(5), P (Pete) Williams =14(21)

The key for how to read the stats is on the last page

CHAPTER 30

Captain Fantastic

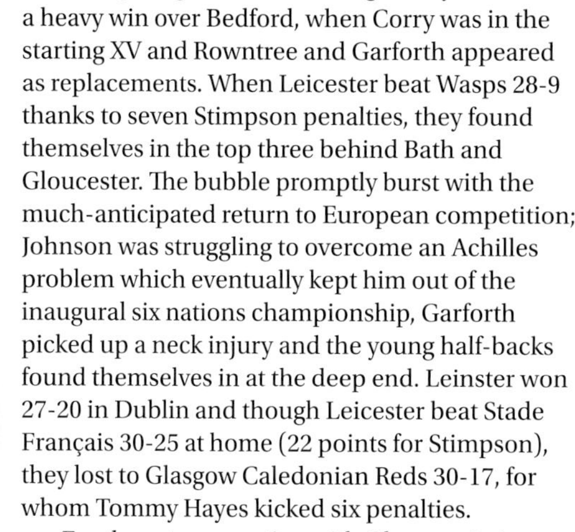

→ Neil Back and Pat Howard stop Stade Français in their tracks on 27.11.1999.

1999/2000

Leicester, more concerned with managing the start of the season when the World Cup would remove a clutch of players, recruited Ben Kay, the Waterloo lock, and Peter Short, a back-five forward from Moseley, but the new season did not start well. Joel Stransky announced his retirement, the knee he damaged against Fiji eight months earlier having failed to recover though the South African remained as backs coach. Moreover players found their salaries being adjusted, and not necessarily upwards, after the imposition of the salary cap and the £1.5 million loss sustained by Leicester in the financial year, which was not entirely offset by a new £1 million agreement with Vauxhall, the car manufacturers.

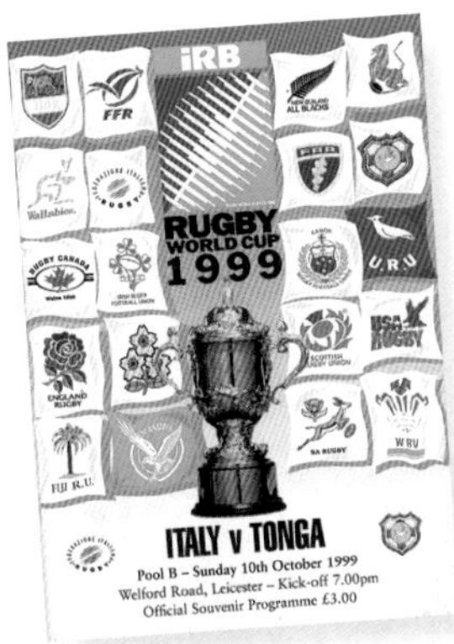

Austin Healey and Will Greenwood were named in England's World Cup squad along with their forward colleagues, Martin Johnson, the captain, Graham Rowntree, Darren Garforth, Richard Cockerill, Neil Back and Martin Corry. Tim Stimpson missed the cut which left him free to play in Leicester's first defence of their Premiership title - at Northampton where the home side cut Leicester to shreds, scoring six tries in a 46-24 win. The only consolation was that the league organisers had agreed that, during the World Cup period, wins would be worth two points whereas they would be worth three after the tournament was over.

South Africa called up Fritz van Heerden for the global tournament, Canada required David Lougheed and England later added Leon Lloyd to their squad after the withdrawal of the injured David Rees (though Lloyd did not subsequently play). The retirement after 223 appearances of the lock, Matt Poole, with ankle and pelvic injuries, added to the gloomy prospect and, after Gloucester handed out a 34-6 caning, Leicester found themselves tenth in the table.

↑ Matt Poole hung up his boots in his 11th season with the club.

The World Cup came to Welford Road when Tonga and Italy played a wonderfully-contested pool match, won 28-25 by Tonga with a last-minute dropped goal watched by more than 10,000 but England left at the quarter-final stage, beaten by South Africa in Paris. So the drip-drip of returning players became a flood: Lougheed was among the try-scorers when Bristol, contesting top spot in the table with Bath, were beaten 36-19 with the two teenagers, James Grindal and Andy Goode, at half-back. Indeed, this was the season when Pat Howard really began to influence the club's play because of the confidence and trust he offered the likes of Goode and Grindal.

Both youngsters were among the try-scorers in a heavy win over Bedford, when Corry was in the starting XV and Rowntree and Garforth appeared as replacements. When Leicester beat Wasps 28-9 thanks to seven Stimpson penalties, they found themselves in the top three behind Bath and Gloucester. The bubble promptly burst with the much-anticipated return to European competition; Johnson was struggling to overcome an Achilles problem which eventually kept him out of the inaugural six nations championship, Garforth picked up a neck injury and the young half-backs found themselves in at the deep end. Leinster won 27-20 in Dublin and though Leicester beat Stade Français 30-25 at home (22 points for Stimpson), they lost to Glasgow Caledonian Reds 30-17, for whom Tommy Hayes kicked six penalties.

For the return meeting with Glasgow, Leicester chose Healey at fly-half, a move which seemed initially to have backfired. But a half-time chat with Stransky put Healey on the right road and the club on the way to a 34-21 win. They still had a mountain to climb to qualify for the knockout phase and their ambitions were put to rest in Paris, where Stade Français picked Leicester's pack apart and won 38-16. The final pool game, a 32-10 loss to Leinster at Welford Road, ended a two-year, 28-game unbeaten home run and completed a miserable return to Europe.

Still Leicester edged into second place with a 29-20 win at Wasps, inspired by the growing authority of Healey at fly-half. The reverse of the coin was that the fixture schedule forced clubs to play three games in nine days before the start of the six nations and Leicester came violently unstuck in the Tetley's Bitter Cup, crashing 47-7 to London Irish at the Stoop Memorial Ground.

Woodward, whose own future as England coach had been questioned after the World Cup, chose Greenwood for the six nations despite his poor form, with Healey, Garforth, Back and Corry. One notable omission was that of Cockerill who, in the period after the World Cup, had published an autobiography, *'In Your Face,'* containing critical remarks about Woodward's style of management. Coincidence or not, the hooker did not add to his total of 27 caps. Stimpson and Rowntree had to be content with places in the A squad, which also featured Moody and Kay and, in due course, the flanker Paul Gustard.

← Martin Corry was an ever-present for England during the inaugural six nations.

Only Healey and Back started the first international, against Ireland, but both made the most of it, Healey collecting two tries and Back one in the 50-18 win at Twickenham. Corry appeared off the bench in all five England games and Healey scored a treble against Italy, when Back did what very few other forwards ever do and dropped a goal in the 59-12 win in Rome. But another grand slam opportunity passed in the wind and rain of Murrayfield, where Scotland won 19-13; Woodward had the opportunity to restore Johnson to the side, the lock having proved his fitness for his club and by playing against Italy in the A international at L'Aquila, but chose not to do so.

Leicester put their show back on the road by beating Newcastle on the same day that Bristol unseated Northampton, the Premiership leaders. Johnson was back at the helm when Leicester came away from Bedford with the 32-22 win which put them top of the table, helped by a try from Greenwood in one of his increasingly rare appearances. Richards paid a visit to New Zealand on a scouting mission, aware that Stransky would return to South Africa to take up a business opportunity and that two members of the overseas playing contingent, Van Heerden and Lougheed, would be leaving at the end of the season, the South African because of a deteriorating knee condition which forced his retirement, Lougheed to become a wealth advisor in his native Canada.

The Princess Royal was the guest of honour at Welford Road when Gloucester became the latest victim of Leicester's charge towards the title, to accept a £100,000 cheque towards the New Millennium Campaign charity. In sad contrast, Leicester mourned the death of Derek Limmage, not a name writ large in the club's history but their groundsman for more than thirty years who had retired only a few months earlier and whose hard work was visible every weekend.

Victory in the East Midlands derby against Northampton left Leicester leading Bath with a game in hand at the top of the table and the title was secured with a week to spare when Leicester won 30-23 at Bristol. There was no disguising the creative presence of Howard, who appeared in every Premiership game of the season and also seemed a ready-made replacement for Stransky as a player-coach. The trophy was not at the Memorial Ground for presentation but, fittingly perhaps, that was staged at Welford Road on the final weekend of the season when Bath were beaten 43-25, Leicester's highest total against their old rivals which left an eight-point gap between Leicester and the rest.

Healey was named the Allied Dunbar Premiership player of the season as well as Leicester's player of the season and he was one of eight Leicester players named in a 40-strong England squad to tour South Africa in the summer. The others were Johnson, restored as captain, Stimpson, Greenwood, Lloyd, Garforth, Back and Corry. The surprise was the omission of Rowntree but the loose-head prop caught up with the party as an early replacement for the injured Trevor Woodman.

On the eve of departure, and a fortnight after the final league game with Bath, Leicester were thrashed 85-10 by the Barbarians in the Scottish Amicable Trophy match at Twickenham. It was the worst defeat in the club's history, predictable perhaps if not on so great a scale, though Woodward's only concern was that the club's England contingent did not turn up injured. They did not and though England lost the first test with the Springboks by 18-13 in Pretoria, they won the second 27-22 in Bloemfontein, as well as the three midweek games against provincial opposition which gave Greenwood, en route from Leicester to Harlequins, the chance to restore his reputation.

Healey, moreover, made a remarkable contribution in the first test when he was called on to play fly-half less than two hours before the kick-off, following the withdrawal of Jonny Wilkinson with food poisoning. Healey played with his usual elan and his move from the wing allowed Stimpson to play while Lloyd also won his first cap when he replaced Mike Catt late in the game. At the same time, on the other side of the Atlantic Ocean, Murphy was winning his first cap for Ireland, against the United States.

→ Derek Limmage kept the Welford Road pitch in superb condition over a 30-year career.

← Tigers celebrate becoming back-to-back Premiership champions.

Even more satisfactory for Leicester was the announcement of a £56,000 profit, the first declared by any professional club in the country. As Greenwood headed south, Craig Joiner back to Scotland and Stuart Potter retired, Leicester signed another Canada wing, Winston Stanley, and the first of an unlikely Samoan connection in Fereti Tuilagi, the bustling St Helens wing. The club may not have appreciated, at that stage, how big the Tuilagi family was or how well it would settle in the Midlands.

2000/2001

Leicester did not make the best of starts to the new season: Andy Goode, the young fly-half, cracked a leg bone in the opening round of the Premiership, now under the auspices of another insurance company, Zurich, who had replaced Allied Dunbar as main sponsors of the club competition. Moreover Pat Howard gave notice that he would return to Australia at the end of the season to take part in the Super 12 provincial tournament.

The champions did secure a 24-22 win at Wasps after Goode's departure and sneaked a three-point win at Newcastle where they scored four tries to one but could scarcely kick a goal. Some familiar faces were back too: Dusty Hare, the former full-back, took charge of player development and Rory Underwood accepted an invitation to help the coaches with regular analysis of the club's back play.

The satisfaction of a 33-19 win over Northampton, the new European champions, in the Premiership came to an abrupt halt with losses at Saracens and Bristol. Tim Stimpson dominated the early European rounds, with 23 points in each of the straightforward wins over Pau and Glasgow; Goode and Hamilton were back for the game against the French club though Healey missed the first two rounds, suffering a hamstring injury before the first and whiplash in a car accident before the second.

A Friday night in Sardis Road saw a check to progress, Pontypridd winning 18-11. The return match with the Welsh club, though, proved notable for the debut of "Freddie" Tuilagi, his arrival coming a few days after he had helped St Helens win the Super League grand final. The Samoa wing's dreadlocked appearance and the evident joie de vivre with which he played in a 27-19 win saw the Welford Road crowd take him immediately to their hearts.

There was considerable speculation in a season which took Jason Robinson from rugby league with Wigan Warriors to rugby union with Sale that the rival codes might, in the not-so-distant future, merge into year-round operations, indeed Leicester undertook a feasibility study into whether Welford Road might host just such a franchise. At the same time they took a "backward" look by concluding a competition to name Leicester's team of the twentieth century. It read: Ken Scotland; Alastair Smallwood, Clive Woodward, Paul Dodge, Rory Underwood; Les Cusworth, Bernard Gadney; Bob Stirling, Peter Wheeler, Darren Garforth, Martin Johnson (captain), George Beamish, Doug Prentice, Dean Richards, Neil Back.

By melancholy coincidence Gadney, the outstanding scrum-half of the 1930s, died in November, aged 91. What he would have made of the 21st-century shenanigans around England during the autumn, who knows? He would have enjoyed the 22-19 win over Australia in which Healey, who had let the club know he would be quite happy to play fly-half on a regular basis, played on the wing with Johnson (becoming his country's most-capped lock) and Back in the pack. Two days later and five before the next engagement, against Argentina, the players went on strike as a nine-month dispute with the RFU about rates of pay boiled over.

↑ Pat Howard's typical hard running style won him player of the season.

Johnson, as captain, was at the heart of the stand-off in which the players claimed that the remuneration on offer was too dependent upon winning. The margin of victory over Australia, Johnson said, proved how slim was the difference between winning and losing, and players needed greater security. They were offered up to £70,000 a year for the next four years but their representatives argued that a losing run could earn them as little as £25,000. "The players regard [the RFU's approach] as being old-fashioned, patronising and arrogant when it is those very players that pull in the crowds," Johnson said. Over the next 24 hours the issues were resolved, with Peter Wheeler helping to broker a deal between players and union because of his relationship with Johnson, the club captain, and knowledge of the RFU's inner workings. Johnson duly led England out to wins over the Pumas and South Africa before the players reverted to club duties.

In early November, these had centred around the Tetley's Bitter Cup, a couple of promising youngsters appearing in Leicester's side that beat Otley in the shape of Ollie Smith at centre and Louis Deacon at lock. Smith, 18, scored a decisive try in the 25-13 fifth-round win at Gloucester and Leicester drew level on points with Saracens in the Premiership after beating Wasps, Stimpson kicking seven penalties. By the time their England representatives returned, Leicester had opened a six-point gap over Saracens, thanks substantially to Stimpson's eight penalties against Gloucester and a try from Tuilagi which preserved the unbeaten home record with a 31-28 win.

↓ 'Freddie' Tuilagi immediately makes his presence known in Tigers colours.

So Leicester were in good heart for the cup quarter-final with Saracens whose former hooker, George Chuter, they had just signed. The margin of victory was convincing, at 41-24, with four tries complemented by Stimpson's 21 points. But yet again, Johnson was in the news, cited for dropping a knee on Duncan McRae, the Saracens fly-half, and then stamping on him, and punching Julian White, the England prop destined to become a colleague at Welford Road. With five games scheduled in 26 days, a disciplinary hearing for their captain was the last thing Leicester wanted.

Three days after Christmas a RFU panel suspended Johnson for five weeks but by then Leicester had built an 11-point gap between themselves and the nearest challenger, now Northampton. Johnson missed the Tetley's Bitter Cup semi-final at Harlequins, two Heineken Cup pool games and the quarter-final; conveniently for England, he remained available for the start of the six nations. Leicester presented evidence of 21 separate incidents during the Saracens match, after which McRae missed six weeks with two cracked ribs and a sprung rib cartilage. Of longer-term significance was the contribution of this case to an eventual change in judicial proceedings, speeding up the process and introducing an independent citing commissioner.

Leicester were expected to prevail against Harlequins but no-one did them greater damage than their former centre, Will Greenwood, who scored one try and created two more in Harlequins' 22-18 win. Still, Europe and the domestic Premiership offered recompense: Deacon found himself promoted to second row for the trip to Pau where two dropped goals by Goode contributed significantly to a 20-3 win. A week later Leicester made their way into the quarter-finals by beating Glasgow 41-26, both hookers, West and his final-quarter replacement, Cockerill, scoring tries.

In the last eight they showed that they could play with or without Johnson. A week before the England-Wales opening to the six nations, Leicester disposed of Swansea 41-10 at Welford Road. Geordan Murphy scored two tries, two more came from Healey (starting at scrum-half) and Goode, who also dropped a goal, with Stimpson contributing four penalties and three conversions.

But one of the match's form players was West and the hooker, born in Wales, duly made his first start for England at the age of 33 in Cardiff where Wales were crushed 44-15, the start of a championship in which England averaged nearly 54 points. Four more Leicester players, Goode, Lewis Moody, Leon Lloyd and Ben Kay, played in the England A side that drew 19-19 with their Welsh counterparts and Will Johnson, younger brother of the captain, subsequently appeared in the back row for the A side. James Grindal appeared in England's under-21 side and, remarkably, the under-19s included eight Leicester players, among them Ollie Smith, Harry Ellis and James Hamilton.

However English First-Division Rugby now introduced a play-off system for the title among the top eight clubs in the league. "Leicester supporters will find this announcement very difficult to understand," Wheeler, a member of the EFDR board, said. "It is unfortunate they have decided to change the rules more than halfway through the season." The fact that two trophies would be awarded, one to the Premiership winners and one to the Zurich Championship winners, was confusing, even more so when EFDR confirmed initially that the Championship winners would be England's premier club, then reversed it a month later.

Leicester pulled 18 points clear of the pack by beating Northampton 12-9 and when the England cavalry returned, Newcastle were drubbed 51-7, giving the club an unassailable lead as early as mid-March. Bearing in mind what was still to come, Leicester pulled out of the Scottish Amicable match with the Barbarians, knowing that in May they would have commitments elsewhere and their Lions would be unavailable. What amounted to a second XV went down to Gloucester but the Premiership trophy was paraded at Welford Road after the defeat of Harlequins and Leicester ended the season eight points clear of Wasps in second place.

Yet still there were five weeks of high drama to come. They began with a Heineken Cup semi-final in the humdrum surroundings of Vicarage Road, the Saracens ground in Watford, against Gloucester and drew a crowd of little more than 14,000, well short of capacity. Gloucester rose magnificently to the challenge in a match of great passion rather than great skill and Leicester were relieved to hear the final whistle blow on a 19-15 win.

The refereeing decisions of Joel Dumé, from France, created problems, Johnson and Gloucester's Junior Paramore spent time in the sin bin and Leicester's try, the only one of the match, was attended by controversy. Graham Rowntree's knock-on allowed Gloucester the chance to counter-attack but when they kicked the ball on, Stimpson broke clear and sent Lloyd over to score with several Gloucester players waiting for the referee to call a scrum against Rowntree. Stimpson kicked the conversion and four penalties against five by Simon Mannix and Leicester were through to a final against Stade Français.

The Lions confirmed that Johnson would captain the party due to travel to Australia in the summer and that he would have Healey (as a scrum-half) and Back for company, which left the club disappointed that no room had been found for West or Corry. What with speculation that Leicester were in the hunt for two overseas internationals, Josh Kronfeld, the New Zealand flanker, and Rod Kafer, the Australia fly-half, it was almost enough to exclude thoughts of the new Zurich Championship, which gave Leicester a home quarter-final against London Irish.

After disposing of the Exiles 24-11, they came up against Northampton and had to work hard (having rested their three Lions) to produce a 17-13 win in which one of the better moments was the try scored by Steve Booth, the wing who had joined from Huddersfield Giants rugby league club at the start of the season. The prize was a final at Twickenham - the big pay day that the clubs had been seeking - against Bath, and the RFU, with a due sense of mischief, appointed as referee Steve Lander, the object of Back's ire five years earlier after defeat to the same opponents.

There was to be no such outcome this time. If anyone had doubted Leicester's credentials as the domestic champions, those doubts were laid to rest by a 22-10 victory in which they were so far the superior team, they felt able to haul off a clutch of players in the second half to rest them for the Heineken Cup final, only six days later. Leicester's team was: Tim Stimpson; Geordan Murphy, Leon Lloyd (Glenn Gelderbloom, 70), Pat Howard, Winston Stanley; Andy Goode (Healey, 60), Austin Healey (Jamie Hamilton, 50); Graham Rowntree (Perry Freshwater, 48), Dorian West (Richard Cockerill, 70), Darren Garforth (Ricky Nebbett, 70), Martin Johnson, Ben Kay, Martin Corry (Paul Gustard, 69), Will Johnson, Neil Back (Lewis Moody, 69).

The Treble

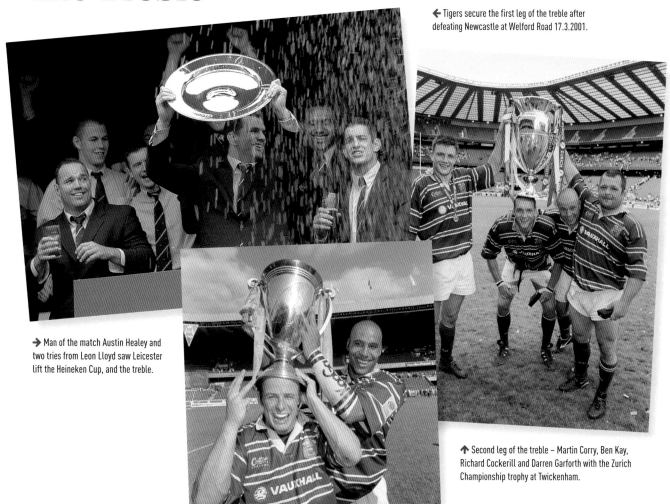

← Tigers secure the first leg of the treble after defeating Newcastle at Welford Road 17.3.2001.

→ Man of the match Austin Healey and two tries from Leon Lloyd saw Leicester lift the Heineken Cup, and the treble.

↑ Second leg of the treble – Martin Corry, Ben Kay, Richard Cockerill and Darren Garforth with the Zurich Championship trophy at Twickenham.

Efficiency was Leicester's aim and though they led only 7-3 at the interval, on a day when the accuracy of the respective kickers, Stimpson and Bath's Matt Perry, deserted them, they dominated where and how the game was played. Johnson crashed over for the first-half try, Healey scored the second and Stanley the third to go with two conversions and a penalty by Stimpson which carried him past Joel Stransky's club record of 459 points in a season (he ended on 486). Bath's try, from Rob Thirlby, came with barely two minutes left. "We are the English rugby champions now, aren't we?" Richards asked. "Somebody tell me we are. We've won it twice, so we must be."

It should have been a time for celebration: the arrival of Kronfeld, after a 54-cap career with the All Blacks, was confirmed and Howard was named Premiership player of the season but the visit to Paris, which drew some 20,000 visitors supporting Leicester, loomed. "I have no doubt that this is the biggest day in the club's history," Wheeler said. "And, whatever happens, we have already had the best season." The teams for the final, described in chapter two, were:

Stade Français: Christophe Dominici; Thomas Lombard, Franck Comba, Cliff Mytton (David Venditti, 76), Arthur Gomes; Diego Dominguez, Morgan Williams; Sylvain Marconnet, Fabrice Landreau (sin bin 6-16), Pieter de Villiers, David Auradou, Mike James, Christophe Moni (Patrick Tabacco, 67), Christophe Juillet (Mathieu Blin, 8-16), Richard Pool-Jones.
Leicester: Tim Stimpson; Geordan Murphy (Glenn Gelderbloom, 76), Leon Lloyd, Pat Howard, Winston Stanley; Andy Goode (Jamie Hamilton, 73), Austin Healey; Graham Rowntree, Dorian West, Darren Garforth, Martin Johnson (sin bin 48-58), Ben Kay, Martin Corry, Will Johnson (Paul Gustard, 37), Neil Back.
Referee: David McHugh (Ireland).

This is the game that will live longest in the memories of those players involved, for many ranking even higher than their international appearances. A week after Leicester's tumultuous 34-30 European triumph, Stimpson, Lloyd, Rowntree, West, Kay and Corry were in England's white at Twickenham, trying to keep pace with a Barbarians side that included Murphy, Howard, Cockerill and the new recruit, Kronfeld. Howard departed for Australia where he popped up against the Lions, playing for ACT Brumbies. In his place came Kafer, capped 12 times by Australia and a similarly creative midfield influence. Stanley departed for Worcester, the Lions for Australia and an England squad, including John Wells as part of the coaching panel, for North America.

Captain Martin Johnson imparts his wisdom during the 2001 Lions Tour.

That took care of much of the summer for Stimpson, Lloyd, Rowntree, West, Kay, Corry, Moody and Ricky Nebbett, though Corry was soon on his way to Australia as a Lions replacement for the injured Scotland No 8, Simon Taylor. So well did he play that Corry became first choice at blind-side flanker for the opening test in Brisbane where the Lions won 29-13. He was later joined by West, when there were concerns that neither Keith Wood nor Robin McBryde would complete the tour because of injuries.

By that time England had returned from North America where seven of Leicester's eight representatives started as first choice against Canada, which meant first caps for Moody and Kay. But the Lions went down to Australia in the remaining two tests, Back and Corry joining Johnson in the pack for the decisive encounter in Sydney where the Wallabies won 29-23; Healey's tour ended in acrimony after a column appeared under his name in a daily newspaper which was highly critical of all things Australian and for which he was subsequently fined £2,000.

LEICESTER FOOTBALL CLUB 1999/2000
Back: Read, Goode, Kay, Zaltzman, Short, Critchley, Becconsall, Ferris.
3rd row: Smith (Extras coach), Hamilton, Ezulike, Freshwater, Balding, Fletcher, W.Johnson, Fourie, Jelley, Murphy, Key (Extras coach).
2nd row: Geeson (Physiotherapist), Shephard (Team secretary), Howard, Potter, Stimpson, Moody, Lloyd, Gustard, West, Joiner, Duggan (Fitness advisor), Richards (Rugby manager).
Front: Stransky (Coach), Lougheed, Greenwood, Healey, Back, M.Johnson (capt), Garforth, Cockerill, Rowntree, Corry, Wells (Forwards coach).

LEICESTER FOOTBALL CLUB 2000/01
Back: Booth, Meenan, Gelderbloom, Smith, Deacon, Lewitt, Buxton, Reeves.
2nd Row: Smith (Extras coach), Grindal, Goode, Balding, Kay, Short, Freshwater, Nebbett, Atkinson (Strength & conditioning coach).
3rd row: Shephard (Team secretary), Hamilton, West, Gustard, Lloyd, Moody, W.Johnson, Murphy, Jelley, Key (Extras coach).
Front: Wells (Forwards coach), Stimpson, Corry, Healey, Howard (Backs coach), M.Johnson (capt), Back, Garforth, Cockerill, Rowntree, Richards (Director of rugby).

1999/00	Home Ground: Welford Road	Trophy Cabinet: Allied Dunbar Premiership(4)	OVERALL RECORD:					T	C	PG	DG	PTS
	Rugby Manager: Dean Richards assisted by Joel Stransky and John Wells		PLD	W	D	L	Tigers scored:	92	63	85	5	856
	Captain: Martin Johnson		31	21	1	9	Opponents scored:	76	59	78	5	747

GM	DATE		VEN	OPPONENTS	RESULT	POS/LGE	TRIES	KICKS	ATT
ALLIED DUNBAR PREMIERSHIP 1 (1ST)						**CHAMPIONS: LEICESTER TIGERS**			
1	Sep	11	a	Northampton Saints	L 24-46	12	Ezulike 9, Goode 40, Joiner 69	Stimpson 3c/p	9512
2		**25**	**H**	**Sale Sharks**	W 18-3	7	-	Stimpson 6p	8721
3	Oct	1f	a	Gloucester	L 6-34	10	-	Stimpson 2p	5338
4		16	a	London Irish	W 31-30	9	Murphy 46, Ezulike 53, Read 65, Gustard 80	Stimpson 4c/p	3705
5		**23**	**H**	**Bristol**	W 36-19	8	Lougheed 15, Kay 31, Ezulike 80	Stimpson 3c/5p	7785
6		**30**	**H**	**Bedford Blues**	W 61-12	4	Goode 19, Corry 25, Grindal 44/65, Gustard 52/69, Penalty 61, Howard 72	Goode d, Stimpson 6c/2p	8308
7	Nov	5f	a	Newcastle Falcons	D 12-12	4	-	Stimpson 4p	2835
8		**13**	**H**	**London Wasps**	W 28-9	3	Back 73	Stimpson c/7p	10043
11	Dec	5s	a	Saracens	L 20-36	5	Stimpson 1, Greenwood 25, Healey 53	Stimpson c/p	8182
14		26s	a	Bath Rugby	W 13-3	3	Murphy 58	Stimpson c/2p	8200
15		**29w**	**H**	**NEC Harlequins**	W 29-17	3	Murphy 15, Lougheed 30, Joiner 36	Murphy p, Stimpson c/2p/d	15499
18	Jan	**22**	**H**	**Saracens**	W 48-20	3	Murphy 3, Lougheed 22/62, Healey 41, Back 72	Stimpson 4c/5p	13910
19		25tu	a	London Wasps	W 29-20	3	West 45, Murphy 76	Stimpson 2c/5p	5168
21	Feb	**12**	**H**	**Newcastle Falcons**	W 34-26	2	West 8, Lougheed 12/25, Kay 36, van Heerden 44/62	Stimpson 2c	13246
22	Mar	11	a	Bedford Blues	W 32-22	1	Back 19/76, Greenwood 26, Howard 58	Murphy 3c/2p	4722
23		**25**	**H**	**London Irish**	W 41-16	1	Grindal 8/46, Moody 15, Stimpson 22, Balding 80	Stimpson 5c/2p	13247
25	Apr	**18tu**	**H**	**Gloucester**	W 24-13	1	-	Stimpson 7p, Healey d	14850
26		22	a	Sale Sharks	W 48-13	1	Murphy 1, Lougheed 13/36, Healey 21, Lloyd 39, Stimpson 40, Greenwood 73	Stimpson 5c/p	3443
27		**29**	**H**	**Northampton Saints**	W 26-21	1	Lloyd 12, Corry 32, Stimpson 40	Stimpson c/3p	16880
28	May	6	a	NEC Harlequins	W 54-5	1	Healey 2, Stimpson 22, Hamilton 31, Lougheed 35/58, Murphy 41, Joiner 65/75	Stimpson 7c	5628
29		14s	a	Bristol	W 30-23	1	Murphy 24, Moody 40, Lloyd 66	Stimpson 3c/3p	7775
30		**21s**	**H**	**Bath Rugby**	W 43-25	1	Murphy 18, Kay 51, Back 58/70/76	Stimpson 3c/4p	17109
HEINEKEN CUP						**EUROPEAN CHAMPIONS: NORTHAMPTON SAINTS**			
9	Nov	19f	a	Leinster	L 20-27	3	Howard 6	Stimpson 5p	6500
10		**27**	**H**	**Stade Francais CASG**	W 30-25	3	Stimpson 30, Lloyd 44	Stimpson c/5p, Goode d	13188
12	Dec	12s	a	Glasgow Caledonians Reds	L 17-30	3	Healey 63, Moody 69, Back 73	Goode c	4000
13		**18**	**H**	**Glasgow Caledonians Reds**	W 34-21	2	Back 19, Lougheed 47, Healey 61	Stimpson 2c/5p	9801
16	Jan	8	a	Stade Francais CASG	L 16-38	3	Lloyd 61	Stimpson c/3p	10000
17		**15**	**H**	**Leinster**	L 10-32	3	Ezulike 28, Lloyd 67	-	12458
RFU CLUB COMPETITION (TETLEY'S BITTER CUP)						**CUP WINNERS: LONDON WASPS**			
20	Jan	29	a	London Irish (5)	L 7-47	P	Joiner 51	Stimpson c	6161
CLUB MATCHES									
24	Apr	**7f**	**H**	**Munster**	W 25-17		Lloyd 5, Rowntree 9, Moody 59	Stimpson 2c/p, Goode d	3308
31	Jun	4s		Barbarians	L 10-85		M.Johnson 2, Lougheed 66	-	52263

Note: *#31 at Twickenham for Scottish Amicable Trophy*

INDIVIDUAL APPEARANCES 1999/00

Name / Game #	1	2	3	4	5	6	7	8	9	10	11	12	13	14	15	16	17	18	19	20	21	22	23	24	25	26	27	28	29	30	31	Apps	T	Pts
SRD (Stuart) Abbott E+	-	>12	<12	-	-	-	-	-	-	-	-	-	-	-	-	-	-	-	-	-	-	-	-	-	-	-	-	-	-	-	-	2	-	-
JF (John) Akurangi	-	-	-	-	-	-	-	-	-	-	-	-	-	>3	3	-	-	r	x	-	r	x	r	r	r	r	r	<r	x	-	-	2+8	-	-
NA (Neil) Back E32 L2	-	-	-	-	-	x	7	7	△7	7	7*	7	7*	7*	7*	-	-	7*	7*	7*	-	7	-	-	7	7	7	7	7	7	8	20	9	45
AL (Adam) Balding	r	x	r	-	8	r	x	r	x	x	x	x	8	r	r	r	r	-	-	r	x	-	r	r	6	6	-	-	-	8	r	5+12	1	5
R (Richard) Cockerill E27	-	-	-	-	-	r	r	r	-	r	-	-	-	r	2	r	2	-	-	r	r	2	r	-	2	r	2	2	2	2	-	8+10	-	-
ME (Martin) Corry E16 L+	-	-	-	-	-	8	8	8	8	8	8	8	4	4	4	4	4*	8	8	8	8	8	8	8	8	8	8	8	8	-	7	25	2	10
NC (Nnamdi) Ezulike	11	11	11	11	14	-	-	-	-	-	-	-	14	14	-	-	11	-	-	14	14	14	-	14	-	-	-	-	-	-	<14	13	4	20
NR (Neil) Fletcher	-	■4	<4	-	x	-	-	-	-	-	-	-	-	-	-	-	-	-	-	-	-	-	-	-	-	-	-	-	-	-	-	2	-	-
KA (Ken) Fourie	>3	r	3	r	r	-	-	-	r	-	x	x	<r	-	-	-	-	-	-	-	-	-	-	-	-	-	-	-	-	-	-	2+5	-	-
PT (Perry) Freshwater E+	r	1	r	1	1	1	-	r	r	r	r	r	1	r	1	1	1	r	r	r	r	r	r	r	-	r	r	r	r	r	r	8+21	-	-
DJ (Darren) Garforth E25	-	-	-	-	-	r	3	3	-	-	-	-	-	-	-	-	-	3	3	3	3	3	3	-	-	-	-	-	-	r	3	9+2	-	-
AJ (Andy) Goode E+	10	r	x	r	10	10	10	10	10	10	x	10	r	-	-	-	10	-	-	-	-	-	-	10	-	-	-	-	-	-	r	10+4	2	21
PJ (Phil) Greenbury	x	-	x	x	x	-	-	-	-	-	-	-	-	-	-	-	<r	-	-	-	-	-	-	-	-	-	-	-	-	-	-	0+1	-	-
WJH (Will) Greenwood E15 L+	-	-	-	-	-	-	13	13	13	13	13	12	x	x	r	r	r	r	r	r	r	13	13	x	r	r	x	r	x	r	<13	9+11	3	15
JS (James) Grindal	-	-	-	>9	9	9	9	9	9	9	-	-	-	-	-	x	x	r	x	x	r	x	r	9	x	r	x	r	x	r	9	9+6	4	20
PSK (Paul) Gustard	6	6	6	6	7	7	6	6	6	6	6	6	r	r	6	6	7	r	r	6	r	r	-	-	-	r	r	r	r	r	6	17+11	3	15
JG (Jamie) Hamilton	9	9	9	x	x	x	x	x	x	-	9	r	9	9	9	9	9	9	9	9	9	9	9	x	9	9	9	9	9	9	-	21+1	1	5
AS (Austin) Healey E30 L2	-	-	-	-	-	-	-	-	-	14	14	9	10	10	10	10	-	10	10	10	10*	10	10	-	10	10	10	10	10	10	10	20	6	33
PW (Pat) Howard A20	12	10	10	10	12	12	12	12	△12	r	10	r	12	12	12	12	12	12	12	12	12	12	12	12	12	12	12	12	12	12	12	29+2	3	15
DA (Derek) Jelley	1	3	1	3	3	3	r	1	1	1	1	1	r	-	r	r	3	-	-	-	-	-	-	r	r	-	-	-	-	r	r	12+8	-	-
MO (Martin) Johnson E53 L5	-	-	-	-	-	-	4*	4*	4*	4*	-	4*	-	-	-	-	-	-	-	-	-	4*	4*	4*	4*	4*	4*	4*	4*	4*	4*	15	1	5
WW (Will) Johnson	8	8	8	8	-	-	-	-	r	-	4	r	-	8	8	8	8	6	6	-	6	6	6	6	-	-	-	-	-	-	-	15+2	-	-
CA (Craig) Joiner S22	13	13	13	-	r	-	r	r	x	-	r	-	r	13	13	13	13	-	-	13	13	r	-	-	-	-	r	r	r	<r	-	9+10	5	25
BJ (Ben) Kay E+ L+	>5	-	-	5	5	5	x	x	x	5	5	5	5	5	5	r	5	5	4	4	4	-	5	r	r	5	r	5	r	5	r	19+6	3	15
BJ (Ben) Lewitt	-	-	-	-	>r	-	-	-	-	-	-	-	-	-	-	-	-	-	-	-	-	-	-	-	-	-	-	-	-	-	-	0+1	-	-
LD (Leon) Lloyd E+	-	-	-	-	-	13	14	-	-	12	12	-	-	-	-	r	14	13	13	-	-	-	r	13	13	13	13	13	13	13	-	14+2	7	35
DC (Dave) Lougheed C32	-	-	-	-	11	11	11	11	11	11	11	11	11	11	11	11	-	11	14	11	11	11	11	11	11	11	11	11	11	11	<11	26	12	60
LW (Lewis) Moody E+ L+	7	7	7	7	-	-	-	-	-	x	x	r	6	6	r	7	△6	x	x	r	7	x	7	7	-	-	6	6	6	6	-	15+3	4	20
GEA (Geordan) Murphy I+ L+	14	14	14	14	x	14	x	14	14	x	r	14	r	r	14	14	15	14	11	-	-	15	14	-	14	14	14	14	14	14	-	21+3	9	60
RJ (Ricky) Nebbett	-	-	-	-	-	-	-	-	-	-	-	-	-	-	-	-	-	-	-	-	-	-	-	>3	3	3	3	3	3	3	r	7+1	-	-
S (Stuart) Potter E1	x	r	-	13	13	x	-	-	-	-	-	13	13	r	<r	-	-	-	-	-	-	-	-	-	-	-	-	-	-	-	-	4+3	-	-
SS (Scott) Read	x	-	x	<12	-	-	-	-	-	-	-	-	-	-	-	-	-	-	-	-	-	-	-	-	-	-	-	-	-	-	-	1	1	5
CG (Graham) Rowntree E26 L+	-	-	-	-	-	r	1	r	3	3	3	3	3	1	-	3	r	1	1	1	1	1	1	1	1	1	1	1	1	1	1	22+3	1	5
PT (Peter) Short	>r	r	-	r	6	6	-	-	-	-	-	-	-	-	-	-	-	4	x	r	-	-	-	-	x	-	-	-	-	-	r	3+5	-	-
TRG (Tim) Stimpson E13 L1	15	15	15	15	15	15	15	15	15	15	15	15	15	15	15	15	r	15	15	15	15	-	15	15	15	15	15	15	15	15	15	29+1	6	397
FJ (Fritz) van Heerden SA14	-	-	-	-	-	-	-	-	-	-	-	-	-	-	r	5	-	r	5	5	5	5	r	5	5	r	5	r	5	-	<5	10+5	2	10
JP (John) Welborn A6	-	-	>5	4	4	4	5	5	5	<r	-	-	-	-	-	-	-	-	-	-	-	-	-	-	-	-	-	-	-	-	-	7+1	-	-
DE (Dorian) West E2	2*	2*	2*	2*	2*	2*	2	2	2	2	2	2	2	2	x	2*	r	2	2	2	2	r	2	2	r	2	-	-	-	-	2	23+3	2	10
DA (Danny) Zaltzman	>4	5	x	<r	-	-	-	-	-	-	-	-	-	-	-	-	-	-	-	-	-	-	-	-	-	-	-	-	-	-	-	2+1	-	-

The key for how to read the stats is on the last page

2000/01

2000/01	
Home Ground: Welford Road	**Trophy Cabinet:** Heineken Cup(1), Zurich Premiership(5), Zurich Championship(1)
Director of Rugby: Dean Richards assisted by Pat Howard and John Wells	
Captain: Martin Johnson	

OVERALL RECORD:					T	C	PG	DG	PTS
PLD	W	D	L	Tigers scored:	114	77	116	6	1090
39	32	1	6	Opponents scored:	50	31	106	3	639

GM	DATE		VEN	OPPONENTS	RESULT	POS/LGE	TRIES	KICKS	ATT
ZURICH PREMIERSHIP (1ST)						**CHAMPIONS: LEICESTER TIGERS**			
2	Aug	19	a	London Wasps	W+ 24-22	5	Healey 9/80, Stanley 27	Stimpson 3c/p	6328
3		27s	a	Newcastle Falcons	W+ 25t-22	2	Murphy 17, Lloyd 28, West 44, Stanley 47	Murphy c, Stimpson p	4298
4	Sep	**2**	**H**	**Northampton Saints**	W 33-19	1	Lloyd 19, Corry 25, Healey 80	Murphy 3c/4p	14088
5		**6w**	**H**	**Rotherham**	W 26t-18	1	Back 12/29, Healey 20, Booth 53	Healey 2c, Murphy c	9801
6		10s	a	Saracens	L 9-17	1	-	Stimpson 3p	13021
7		**16**	**H**	**London Irish**	W 33t-20	1	Back 13, Howard 20, Stanley 57, Newmarch 62	Stimpson 2c/3p	12168
8		23	a	Bristol	L+ 20-24	2	Goode 25, Howard 56, Gustard 68	Goode c, Stimpson p	6200
9		30	a	Sale Sharks	D 17-17	2	Murphy 29	Stimpson 4p	3407
16	Nov	**18**	**H**	**London Wasps**	W 28-13	2	Hamilton 66	Stimpson c/7p	9300
17		24f	a	NEC Harlequins	W+ 16-13	1	Stimpson 75	Stimpson c/3p	4613
18	Dec	**2**	**H**	**Gloucester**	W+ 31-28	1	Tuilagi 80	Stimpson c/8p	11800
20		**16**	**H**	**Bath Rugby**	W 27-19	1	Rowntree 6, Howard 45	Stimpson c/5p	14552
21		23	a	Rotherham	W 27-9	1	Smith 8, Booth 13, M.Johnson 66	Booth 3c/2p	4000
22		26tu	a	Bath Rugby	W+ 17-16	1	Back 43	Stimpson 3p, Goode d	8500
		30	**H**	**Sale Sharks**	PP (frost)	-			
	Jan	**6**	**H**	**Bristol**	PP (cup)	-			
27	Feb	**6tu**	**H**	**Bristol**	W+ 17-10	1	Stanley 64	Stimpson 4p	12332
28		10	a	London Irish	W 28t-9	1	Stimpson 25/78, Back 41, Murphy 52	Stimpson 4c	7531
29		**24**	**H**	**Saracens**	W 56t-15	1	Murphy 16/40/64/74, Garforth 51, Stimpson 62/79	Stimpson 6c/3p	14212
30	Mar	**6tu**	**H**	**Sale Sharks**	W 24-12	1	M.Johnson 11, Balding 68	Stimpson c/4p	9000
31		10	a	Northampton Saints	W+ 12-9	1	-	Stimpson 4p	10000
32		**17**	**H**	**Newcastle Falcons**	W 51t-7	1	Stanley 12, Goode 15, Back 26/47, Stimpson 28/34, Lloyd 38, Booth 63	Stimpson 4c/p	15009
33		31	a	Gloucester	L 13-22	1	Cockerill 11, Stanley 70	Booth p	7614
34	Apr	**14**	**H**	**NEC Harlequins**	W 37t-5	1	Healey 13, Murphy 23, Howard 40, Back 59, Lloyd 74	Stimpson 3c/2p	16006
ZURICH CHAMPIONSHIP						**ZURICH CHAMPIONSHIP WINNERS: LEICESTER TIGERS**			
36	Apr	**28**	**H**	**London Irish (qf)**	W 24-11	-	Stanley 24, Healey 63	Stimpson c/4p	8112
37	May	**5**	**H**	**Northampton Saints (sf)**	W 17-13	-	Howard 16, Booth 38	Stimpson 2c/p	10787
38		13s		Bath Rugby (f)	W 22-10	-	M.Johnson 26, Healey 48, Stanley 65	Stimpson 2c/p	33500
HEINEKEN CUP						**EUROPEAN CHAMPIONS: LEICESTER TIGERS**			
10	Oct	**7**	**H**	**Pau**	W 46-18	1	Hamilton 41, Howard 55, Penalty 67, Back 76	Stimpson 4c/5p, Goode d	12331
11		15s	a	Glasgow Caledonians	W 33-21	1	Lloyd 14, Back 33, Stimpson 70	Stimpson 3c/4p	3500
12		20f	a	Pontypridd	L 11-18	1	Stimpson 18	Stimpson 2p	6500
13		**28**	**H**	**Pontypridd**	W 27-19	2	Penalty 13, Healey 45	Healey d, Stimpson c/4p	13913
24	Jan	13	a	Pau	W 20-3	1	Back 18	Stimpson 3p, Goode 2d	7325
25		**20**	**H**	**Glasgow Caledonians**	W 41-26	1	West 11, Hamilton 33, Smith 55, Cockerill 80	Stimpson 3c/5p	12260
26		**28s**	**H**	**Swansea (qf)**	W 41-10	-	Murphy 24/42, Healey 45, Goode 65	Goode d, Stimpson 3c/4p	13000
35	Apr	21		Gloucester (sf)	W 19-15	-	Lloyd 22	Stimpson c/4p	14010
39	May	19		Stade Francais CASG (f)	W 34-30	-	Lloyd 41/78, Back 60	Stimpson 2c/5p	45000
RFU CLUB COMPETITION (Tetley's Bitter Cup)						**Cup winners: Newcastle Falcons**			
14	Nov	**4**	**H**	**Otley (4)**	W 83-11	N1	Tuilagi 2/17/48, Lloyd 20, Gustard 29, Healey 34, Goode 41, Freshwater 52/60/76, Short 64, W.Johnson 66, O'Reilly 73	Goode 9c	5328
15		11	a	Gloucester (5)	W 25-13	P	Lloyd 22/80, Smith 56	Stimpson 2c/2p	5100
19	Dec	**9**	**H**	**Saracens (qf)**	W 41-24	P	Balding 42, West 57, Healey 69, Back 80	Stimpson 3c/5p	10007
23	Jan	6	a	NEC Harlequins (sf)	L 18-22	P	Murphy 19, Goode 22	Stimpson c/2p	8800
JEWSON CHALLENGE TROPHY									
1	Aug	12	a	Cardiff	L 17-29		Murphy 29, Jelley 71	Stimpson 2c/p	7000

Neutral Venues: *#35 at Vicarage Road - Watford, #38 at Twickenham, # 39 at Parc des Princes - Paris*

INDIVIDUAL APPEARANCES 2000/01

Name / Game #	1	2	3	4	5	6	7	8	9	10	11	12	13	14	15	16	17	18	19	20	21	22	23	24	25	26	27	28	29	30	31	32	33	34	35	36	37	38	39	Apps	T	Pts
NA (Neil) Back E41 L2	H	8	7	7	7	7	7	-	7	7	7	7	7	-	-	-	-	-	7	7	x	7	7*	7*	-	7*	r	7	-	-	-	7	-	7	7	-	7*	7	7	25+1	13	65
AL (Adam) Balding	G	r	x	r	8	r	8	7	r	r	8	x	-	8	r	x	r	r	r	r	r	r	r	r	r	x	-	x	r	6	x	r	r	-	-	8	-	-	-	8+18	2	10
SE (Steve) Booth	x	-	-	x	>r	x	-	-	-	-	-	-	-	-	-	-	-	-	-	-	14	-	-	-	-	-	-	-	-	11	-	r	10	-	-	-	14	-	-	4+2	4	35
GS (George) Chuter E+	-	-	-	-	-	-	-	-	-	-	-	-	-	-	-	-	-	-	-	-	-	-	-	-	-	-	-	-	-	x	-	-	>r	r	-	2	r	-	-	1+3	-	-
R (Richard) Cockerill E27	B	r	x	r	2	x	r	2*	r	r	r	r	2	-	r	2*	2*	2*	r	r	2	x	-	r	r	r	2*	-	r	2	r	r	2*	-	r	r	2	r	x	12+19	2	10
ME (Martin) Corry E21 L+	r	7	8	8	-	8	6	8	8	8	-	8	8	-	-	-	-	-	8	-	8	r	4	8	8	8	8	8	8	8	8	8	5	6	6	5	-	6	6	28+2	1	5
LP (Louis) Deacon E+	>r	-	-	-	5	-	-	x	-	-	-	-	-	4	-	4	4	4	-	-	5	-	x	4	4	4	4	5	-	r	-	-	4	-	-	-	4	-	-	13+2	-	-
PT (Perry) Freshwater E+	-	-	-	-	x	-	-	x	-	-	-	-	-	r	x	x	x	r	-	r	r	x	r	x	1	r	x	r	-	-	-	-	1	-	x	1	r	r	x	3+9	3	15
DJ (Darren) Garforth E25	C	3	3	3	x	3	3	3	3	3	3	3	3	r	3	3	3	3	3	3	x	3	3	3	3	3	-	3	3	3	3	3	-	3	3	r	3	3	3	33+2	1	5
GK (Glenn) Gelderbloom	>r	x	r	x	13	r	-	-	-	-	-	-	-	13	r	r	-	x	r	x	12	r	r	-	r	r	12	r	r	12	r	-	13	r	x	-	x	r	r	6+16	-	-
AJ (Andy) Goode E+	r	10	-	-	-	-	10	10	10	10	10	10	x	15	10	10	r	10	10	10	-	10	10	10	10	10	10	r	10	-	10	10	-	10	10	10	10	10	10	28+3	5	60
JS (James) Grindal	I	r	9	9	x	9	r	9	-	-	r	x	-	9	-	x	-	x	-	-	-	-	-	-	x	-	-	-	-	-	-	-	9	-	-	-	-	-	-	7+3	-	-
PSK (Paul) Gustard	F	6	6	6	6	6	r	6	6	6	6	-	6	6	6	6	6	6	-	6	-	6	6	-	-	-	-	-	r	r	r	r	6	r	r	6	r	r	r	21+10	2	10
JG (Jamie) Hamilton	-	-	-	-	-	-	-	-	r	9	9	9	9	-	9	9	9	9	r	x	9	x	x	r	9	r	9	9	r	9	-	r	-	-	x	9	9	r	r	15+8	3	15
AS (Austin) Healey E38 L2	J	9	10	10	10	10	9	r	9	-	-	-	10	10	14	-	10	-	9	9	10	9	9	9	-	9	-	10	9	10	9	9	r	9	9	r	-	9	9	28+3	11	62
PW (Pat) Howard A20	0	12	12	12	12	12	12	12	12	12	12	12	12	-	12	12	r	12	12	12	x	12	12	12	12	12	r	12	12	r	12	12	12	12	12	12	12	12	12	34+3	6	30
DA (Derek) Jelley	r	1	1	1	-	1	x	r	1	1	r	r	r	1	-	-	x	-	r	r	1	-	-	r	-	-	x	-	r	x	x	r	r	r	-	-	-	-	-	8+12	1	5
MO (Martin) Johnson E62 L5	D*	4*	4*	4*	4*	4*	4*	-	4*	4*	4*	4*	4*	r	4*	-	-	-	4*	4*	4*	4*	-	-	-	-	r	4*	4*	4*	4*	4*	-	4*	4*	4*	r	4*	4*	27+3	3	15
WW (Will) Johnson	-	-	-	-	-	-	-	-	-	-	-	-	-	r	8	8	8	8	6	8	6	8	8	6	6	6	6	6	6	-	6	6	-	8	8	r	8	8	8	22+2	1	5
BJ (Ben) Kay E+ L+	E	5	5	5	-	5	5	5	r	5	5	5	5	5	5	5	5	5	5	5	-	5	5	5	5	5	5	-	5	5	5	5	x	5	5	x	5	5	5	33+1	-	-
BJ (Ben) Lewitt	-	-	-	-	-	-	-	-	-	-	-	-	-	-	-	-	-	x	<r	-	-	-	-	-	-	-	-	-	-	-	-	-	x	-	-	-	-	-	-	0+1	-	-
LD (Leon) Lloyd E2	M	13	13	13	-	13	13	13	13	13	13	13	13	14	11	14	13	13	-	13	r	11	13	13	-	13	-	-	13	r	13	14	-	13	13	13	-	13	13	30+2	11	55
LW (Lewis) Moody E+ L+	-	-	-	-	r	r	-	-	-	-	r	6	r	-	7	7	7	7	-	r	7	-	r	r	7	r	7	r	7	7	7	-	7	r	x	7	-	r	x	13+11	-	-
GEA (Geordan) Murphy I3 L+	N	14	14	15	15	-	-	-	14	14	14	14	14	-	-	-	14	14	14	14	r	14	14	14	14	11	x	11	15	-	15	-	11	15	15	15	-	14	14	28+1	12	82
RJ (Ricky) Nebbett	r	r	x	x	3	r	r	r	r	r	r	-	-	3	x	x	r	x	r	-	3	x	r	-	-	r	3	-	r	x	x	r	3	r	x	3	r	r	x	6+17	-	-
AP (Ali) Newmarch	-	-	>r	14	14	14	14	14	-	-	-	x	x	r	x	x	-	-	-	-	<15	-	-	-	x	-	-	-	-	-	-	-	-	-	-	-	-	-	-	6+2	1	5
JP (John) O'Reilly	-	-	-	-	>9	-	-	-	-	-	-	-	-	r	-	-	-	-	-	-	-	-	-	-	-	-	x	x	-	-	r	-	-	r	-	-	<r	-	-	1+4	1	5
P (Paul) Reeves	x	-	-	-	-	-	-	-	-	-	-	-	-	>r	-	-	-	-	-	-	-	-	-	-	-	-	-	-	-	-	-	-	<15	-	-	-	-	-	-	1+1	-	-
CG (Graham) Rowntree E26 L+	A	r	r	r	1	r	1	1	r	r	1	1	1	-	1	1	1	1	1	1	-	1	1	1	r	1	1	1	1	1	1	1	-	1	1	r	1	1	1	28+8	1	5
PT (Peter) Short	x	x	r	r	r	-	r	4	5	r	r	r	x	7	x	x	-	-	-	-	-	-	-	-	r	-	-	x	-	-	-	-	8	-	-	-	6	-	-	5+8	1	5
OJ (Ollie) Smith E+ L+	-	-	-	-	-	-	>r	x	r	r	r	x	x	12	13	13	12	-	13	-	13	13	-	r	13	-	13	13	-	13	-	13	-	-	-	r	13	-	-	13+6	3	15
WU (Winston) Stanley C45	>K	11	11	11	11	11	11	11	11	11	11	11	-	-	-	11	x	-	-	11	11	-	-	-	11	-	11	-	-	-	11	11	14	11	11	11	11	11	<11	26	8	40
TRG (Tim) Stimpson E14 L1	L	15	15	-	-	15	15	15	15	15	15	15	15	-	15	15	15	15	15	15	-	15	15	15	15	15	15	11	15	14	15	r	14	14	14	15	15	15	15	34+1	9	486
F (Freddie) Tuilagi Sa9	-	-	-	-	-	-	-	-	-	-	-	-	>11	11	-	-	11	11	11	-	-	-	11	11	-	14	14	14	14	14	-	-	-	-	-	-	-	-	-	12	4	20
DE (Dorian) West E7	r	2	2	2	-	2	2	-	2	2	2	2	r	2*	2	-	-	r	2	2	-	2	2	2	2*	2	-	2	2	-	2	2	-	2	2	-	-	2	2	26+3	3	15

The key for how to read the stats is on the last page

CHAPTER 31

Back to Back

2001/2002

For Leicester there were plenty of reasons to be cheerful. Leicester City Council made the club freemen of the city two months after the Heineken Cup triumph and pre-tax profits on the season rose to £346,000. Super League once more visited Welford Road in the shape of Bradford Bulls and London Broncos as Leicester continued their study of the rival code and the new season opened with yet another agreement between the RFU and Premier Rugby Ltd, as the umbrella body for the Premiership clubs was now called.

Among other elements, it established 12 club academies of which Leicester received one of the first licences, it granted the clubs a share of the union's commercial income and limited players to 32 games a season, a total that Leon Lloyd was unlikely to pass since he returned from the England tour with a shoulder injury that took five months to mend. On the credit side, speculation that Lewis Moody might leave because of the arrival of Josh Kronfeld proved wide of the mark; the silver tongue of Dean Richards talked him into learning more about his trade from two of the game's great practitioners, Kronfeld and Neil Back, and Moody's reward was a place in the England training squad preparing for an October encounter with Ireland in Dublin, to complete the 2001 six nations championship after an outbreak of foot-and-mouth disease had forced a postponement from spring.

Martin Johnson, Austin Healey, Dorian West, Martin Corry and Back joined him, as did Ben Kay, but Leicester rested Johnson, Healey and Back from the opening Premiership game of the season. The club felt their leading players needed an extended rest and promptly lost 19-16 at Newcastle where Rod Kafer, at centre, made his debut alongside a promising local youngster, Harry Ellis, at scrum-half. But by the end of the first tranche of Premiership games, Leicester sat happily at the top of the table, eager to begin the defence of their European title. They struggled to beat Llanelli 12-9 despite home advantage; with a hamstrung Geordan Murphy absent, Leicester were curiously anonymous and remained so in the 37-3 win at Calvisano despite scoring five tries.

At least they kept winning, which is more than could be said for England. Against Ireland they were without Johnson, their captain, who broke a bone in his hand in the club game against Northampton (the match in which Kronfeld finally made his competitive debut) and another grand slam went west in a 20-14 defeat despite Healey's late try. Woodward dropped three Lions for the November internationals, Corry among them though the back-row forward had been struggling with a hamstring injury. With Johnson still unavailable, the captaincy went to Back for the tests against Australia and Romania but Johnson was fit to lead against South Africa.

→ Josh Kronfeld became Leicester's first All Black of modern times.

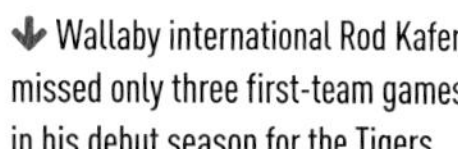

↓ Wallaby international Rod Kafer missed only three first-team games in his debut season for the Tigers.

While England were in Dublin, something amounting to a Leicester second team beat Saracens 36-10 in the Premiership but that was as nothing compared to the visit made to Perpignan when the Heineken Cup resumed. Johnson's absence gave Louis Deacon an opportunity at lock and the match was a magnificent occasion in front of a baying crowd at the Stade Aimé Giral. Thierry Lacroix kicked nine penalties and a dropped goal for the home side but Stimpson replied with seven penalties, Andy Goode dropped a goal, Steve Booth grabbed the only try of the contest, whilst Stimpson's magnificent penalty from the most awkward of angles from just inside the Perpignan half in injury time made the critical difference in a 31-30 Leicester win which equalled Brive's record of nine consecutive European wins.

In the return match, Leicester wiped out the French club 54-15 with six tries. Healey played fly-half and Perry Freshwater, the prop from New Zealand, appeared as a replacement against the club that he subsequently joined. By mid-December they had opened a nine-point gap on the chasing pack in the league, which made it an appropriate moment for the council's renaming of the road leading from Leicester Station towards Welford Road, from Waterloo Way to Tigers Way in acknowledgement of the renown brought to the city by the rugby club. Chalkie White, who had done so much to start that process, received the Dyson Award from the Princess Royal at a reception in London's Café Royal in recognition of his work for the RFU in producing the next generation of coaches.

Eight Leicester players appeared in the elite England squad to prepare for the six nations and four more - Ellis, Deacon, Lloyd and Adam Balding - were in a development squad. Going into the new year, the gap at the head of the Premiership had widened to 17 points but Stimpson fractured a cheekbone against Sale and missed the remaining two pool games in the Heineken Cup, as did Healey, suspended by the club after kicking Anthony Elliott, the Sale wing; a subsequent RFU hearing added a further fortnight to his ban.

Coincidence or not, Leicester were deeply unimpressive in a 29-7 win over Calvisano and lost 24-12 at Llanelli, their first visit to Stradey Park in 28 years where they were beaten at their own game of set-piece dominance. Stephen Jones kicked eight penalties out of eight and Goode could land only four in reply but Leicester were already assured of a quarter-final place and a home tie with Leinster, which may have been on their minds when they lost 22-20 to Harlequins in the quarter-finals of the domestic cup, now sponsored by Powergen.

It was the first time in two years they had lost successive matches but defeat only burnished their ambitions for Europe. With the return from suspension of Healey, they produced moments of magic in a 28-19 win over Leinster. They played adventurous rugby on a saturated pitch and, though the Irish province took a ten-point lead in the first quarter, five home tries within 28 minutes washed Leinster away and earned Leicester a semi-final against....Llanelli.

↓ Neil Back scored two tries against Leinster in the quarter-final of the Heineken Cup.

Healey and Murphy were among the try-scorers and both were named by their respective countries for the start of the six nations. In England's case, this took them to Scotland with Johnson and Kay starting together in the second row for the first time, Rowntree and Back adding support. Goode and Nebbett made the trip north too, to play in the A international where Goode's two penalties earned a 6-6 draw with Scotland, the seniors playing considerably better to come away from Murrayfield with a 29-3 win.

A fortnight later, England played Ireland but in the intervening period Johnson found himself on a disciplinary hook yet again. Leicester's 48-7 over Saracens had all the look of an easy day at the office but the England captain found himself in a wrestling match with Robbie Russell, the opposing hooker, who received an elbow and punch in the face. Both players were sent to the sin bin but Saracens were angry that Johnson had not received a red card and the RFU decided he had a case to answer, convening a hearing in Bristol during the week following the 45-11 win over Ireland.

Even Johnson acknowledged belatedly that that he had overreacted to Russell, who needed six stitches in a cheek wound. Initially he was banned for three weeks by the disciplinary panel after a hearing lasting more than seven and a half hours but then appealed. Leicester, with the support of Premier Rugby Ltd and the Professional Rugby Players' Association, mounted a vigorous defence on technical grounds which queried the jurisdiction of the RFU panel; then Johnson himself failed to sign the appeal paper and, once that technicality had been addressed, Woodward picked him to lead England in Paris.

As luck would have it, England lost and so did Johnson, his appeal failing. Indeed, though Leicester protested that Johnson had been subject to two different forms of discipline, a yellow card on the field and a suspension off it, their arguments were roundly dismissed by David Pannick, the independent QC who heard the appeal. "If the on-field incident deserves a greater punishment than the referee awarded and the charge can be proved to the satisfaction of an independent disciplinary panel, I can see no unfairness in the player suffering an additional sanction," Pannick said.

Johnson missed two Premiership games, against Bath and Gloucester, as well as the international against Wales in which Back took over the captaincy. In his absence, Leicester won both games and made virtually certain of the Premiership title and England won too, posting a half-century. Healey played full-back after injury removed Jason Robinson, Moody made his first start in the championship and Stimpson joined the replacements, subsequently making his first championship appearance for five years and marking it with a try in the 50-10 win.

And even if one Johnson missed the international weekend, the other did not. Will Johnson joined

↑ Lewis Moody, Steve Booth and Adam Balding parade the Zurich Premiership trophy at Welford Road 13.4.2002.

Balding in the back row of the A team that lost 29-21 to Wales in Bristol, Nebbett also played and Steve Booth picked up an appearance from the bench. Before the six nations concluded, Leicester might have wrapped up the Premiership title but they managed to lose 36-34 at low-lying Wasps, a remarkable scoreline which contained ten penalties and two dropped goals for the home club.

So they had to wait until mid-April, by which time Johnson was back in the international fold (though Woodward picked him on the bench against Italy, Back retaining the captaincy; it was the first of only two times in his career that Johnson started an international among the replacements). Leicester made mathematically certain of the Premiership against Newcastle, their fourth title in a row which equalled the record of Bath between 1991-94. With three games still to play their nearest challenger, London Irish, was 19 points adrift, leaving Tigers free to concentrate on becoming the first side to make a successful defence of the Heineken Cup.

"A Tigers shirt was spotted near the North Korean border recently," Wheeler said in a newspaper article. "That is the power of the Heineken Cup. It gives the winner the right to call themselves European champions and it creates interest, not only in your own country, or Europe, but right across the world. It adds value to everything you do. We've had 1,500 new members since winning, many of whom have joined as a result of the European experience."

That experience now extended to the City Ground, headquarters of Nottingham Forest Football Club, which was packed to its 29,500 capacity for the third meeting of the season with Llanelli. Richards opted for youth in his back division, picking the two 19-year-olds, Ollie Smith and Harry Ellis. It demonstrated how and where Leicester wanted to play the game and, given that Ellis scored the only try from a coruscating break through the centre of a ruck, was entirely justified. But Llanelli controlled matters at the breakdown nor did Healey exercise the patient control from fly-half that the occasion required. Instead the issue hung on a penalty awarded against Martyn Madden, the Llanelli prop, in the last minute of proper time when the Welsh club led 12-10 and were encamped close to the Leicester 10-metre line.

Stimpson leapt forward to take the kick. From 58 metres the ball spun to hit first the crossbar, bouncing upwards to hit an upright and then fell the right way to give Leicester their 13-12 win. "When it went over there was relief and elation," the full-back said. It was his only penalty attempt of the second half; he had kicked an early goal, and converted Ellis's second-half try, only to see Stephen Jones land three first-half penalties and a fourth midway through the second half.

Leicester could prepare for the final in Cardiff, against Munster, while completing the league season which, when it ended, showed Leicester 14 points clear of second-placed Sale. A week after the climactic European game, they lost at Bristol, a match in which Balding and Julian White, the then Bristol prop, were sent off for fighting, which earned Balding a fortnight's suspension from the club. The rumour mill linked Cockerill with a move to Montferrand, Goode with a switch to Saracens while Gustard, on loan to London Irish, confirmed a permanent change of club.

A week before the Heineken Cup final, a weakened Leicester side went down to Bristol again, in the Zurich Championship quarter-finals, though this time at home. For the final, against Munster at Cardiff's Millennium Stadium, Leicester were forced to omit Leon Lloyd, the hero of Paris a year earlier, because of a damaged shoulder and Ellis, the try-scorer at Nottingham, gave way to Jamie Hamilton for the match.

Leicester: Tim Stimpson; Geordan Murphy, Ollie Smith (Glenn Gelderbloom, 77), Rod Kafer, Fereti Tuilagi; Austin Healey, Jamie Hamilton (Harry Ellis, 51); Graham Rowntree (Perry Freshwater, 74), Dorian West, Darren Garforth, Martin Johnson, Ben Kay, Lewis Moody, Martin Corry, Neil Back.
Munster: Dominic Crotty (Jeremy Staunton, 66); John O'Neill, Rob Henderson (Mike Mullins, 67), Jason Holland, John Kelly; Ronan O'Gara, Peter Stringer; Peter Clohessy (Marcus Horan, 61), Frankie Sheahan (James Blaney, 17-29), John Hayes, Mick Galwey, Paul O'Connell (Mick O'Driscoll, 61), Alan Quinlan, Anthony Foley (Jim Williams, 53), David Wallace.
Referee: Joel Jutge (France).

It was debatable which upshot was more remarkable, Leicester's 15-9 win over Munster (see chapter two) in front of 74,000 supporters which gave them a place in European history or the furore provoked by Back's sleight of hand as the clock ticked down. "The game wasn't won or lost on that one incident," Back said. "We crossed their line four times and were awarded two tries. They never crossed our line." Many Munstermen might have disagreed but there was no word of complaint from the Irish team: "We don't feel robbed," Mick Galwey,

→ Tim Stimpson launches his monster penalty goal in the Heineken Cup semi-final against Llanelli at the City Ground, Nottingham, 28.4.2002.

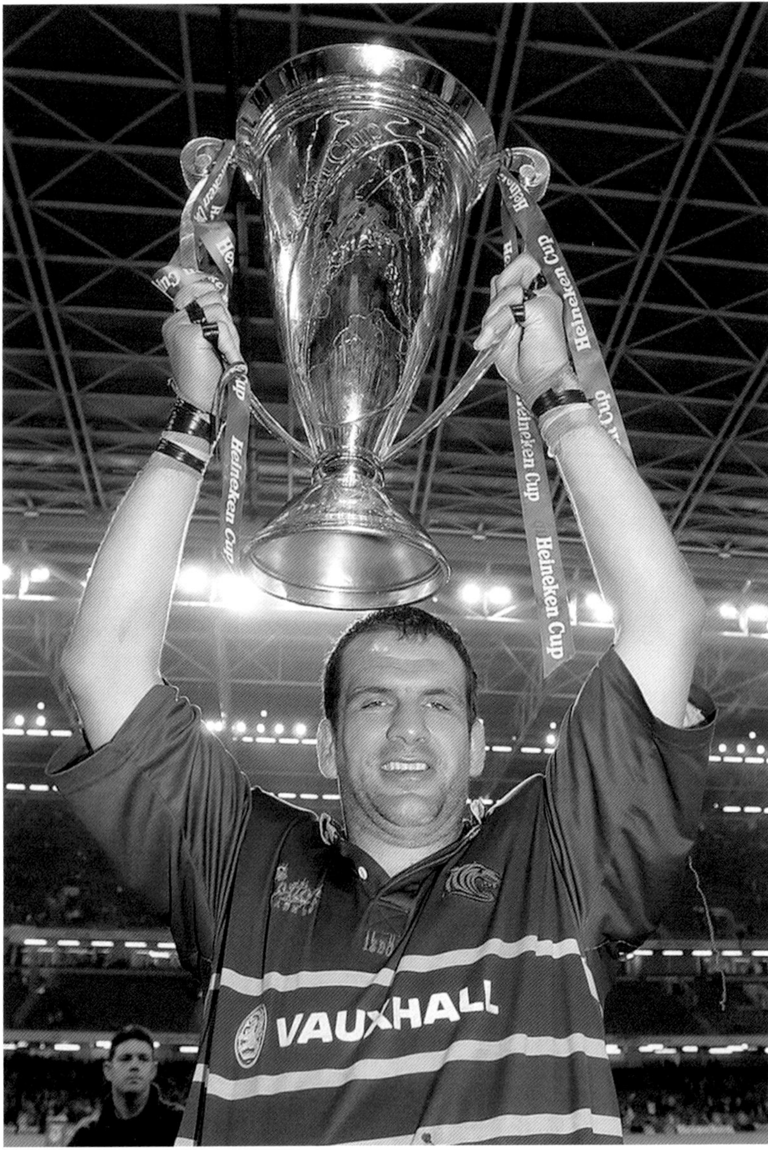

the Munster captain playing his final game, said. "In my book the team that scores the tries deserves to win."

Having secured back-to-back European wins, Leicester promptly contacted Canterbury Crusaders, to see if a challenge match could be arranged between the champions of the two hemispheres. Kronfeld, the New Zealand flanker of whom so much had been expected, found himself playing in the relative sideshow of the Barbarians against an England XV prior to the departure for Argentina of an England side including Stimpson, Kay, Moody and Balding. Many of England's most experienced players were deliberately rested before the build-up to the 2003 World Cup began; Ireland included Murphy in their touring team to New Zealand so he postponed a shoulder operation and missed, as a result, the start of the following season.

Balding found a place in England's midweek XV in Buenos Aires, his three club colleagues all started the international against Argentina and did their long-term prospects no harm at all with a 26-18 win. Stimpson, playing on the wing, kicked a late penalty to go with three earlier ones from Charlie Hodgson, while Kay scored a try. A back row including Moody played well enough to put pressure on the three incumbents, Back, Hill and Dallaglio, leaving England in the best of shape a year out from the World Cup.

↑ Martin Johnson holds the Heineken Cup aloft for the second year in succession.

↓ Sam Vesty broke into the first-team during the Orange Cup success in Biarritz.

2002/2003

In retrospect, it seemed significant that Leicester announced plans in the summer for the £7 million replacement of the Next Stand, the old Members Stand, but were held up because they could not proceed with the purchase of land on the Granby Hall site. Everything should have been set fair to sustain the incredible success of the preceding four years - pre-tax profits of £644,000, a new sponsorship agreement with Bradstone, the garden landscaping products company, worth more than £1 million over a three-year period, and the arrival of the hugely-experienced France prop, Franck Tournaire.

But some old and not-so-old favourites were off: Richard Cockerill to Montferrand, Andy Goode to Saracens and James Grindal to Newcastle. Moreover Peter Wheeler appeared before a RFU disciplinary panel charged with breaching the International Rugby Board's code of conduct as a result of critical comments made in a newspaper column about Steve Lander's refereeing of Leicester's most recent Premiership match with Bristol, and about Dean Ryan, the Bristol head coach. The former, described by the panel as "injudicious", earned him a £3,000 fine but he was found not guilty of insulting Ryan or bringing the game into disrepute.

With Martin Johnson and Neil Back hinting at retirement from international rugby after the World Cup, something of a shadow lingered over the new season which was not entirely dispelled by a 14-13 victory over Biarritz, the French champions, in the Orange Cup clash in August. Danny Hipkiss, 19, scored a crucial try and Sam Vesty (the fourth generation of his family to represent the club) kicked the winning conversion; they showed that a fresh generation was on its way up but a rash of injuries set the stage for the poorest of starts to the Zurich Premiership.

Two defeats and one win in the first three rounds left Leicester ninth in the table. Tim Stimpson, yet again, took it out on his former club by scoring a Premiership record-equalling 32 points in a 52-9 win over Newcastle but another

defeat followed at Bristol even though the West Country club played most of the match with 14 men after the dismissal of Julian White for butting Graham Rowntree. "There's not a great deal wrong...things will start to happen," Dean Richards said, in the knowledge that this season would end with a play-off between the top three clubs for one title, after the demise of the unlamented Zurich Championship. But Austin Healey, now first choice at fly-half after Goode's departure, was struggling with a groin injury and Leicester were no higher than sixth in the Premiership when they broke for the Heineken Cup.

A solo try by Healey helped towards a 16-16 draw against Neath in appalling conditions at The Gnoll and Calvisano received a 63-0 thumping at Welford Road. Heading towards the international window, it seemed that Leicester's ship had steadied with wins at Saracens (where Goode missed his first four kicks against his old club) and Northampton, and at home to Wasps and Gloucester.

This, of course, was without their England players. Clive Woodward named eight from Leicester in his initial training squad though there was no place for Martin Corry, and chose only Martin Johnson and Lewis Moody to start against New Zealand. Neil Back, Ben Kay and Healey appeared off the bench in a nail-biting 31-28 win over the All Blacks, and Kay became a regular alongside Johnson thereafter. But it was the beginning of the end of Healey's international career while Stimpson won his 19th and last cap as a replacement against South Africa.

By the time the internationals were over, Leicester had moved up to fourth in the Premiership. But Back returned to Welford Road with a fractured eye socket after the violence of England's win over South Africa and Moody required a shoulder operation; at the end of the month the cherished home league record of 57 matches without defeat crashed to their East Midlands rivals, Northampton, who scored three tries in a 25-12 win.

There were back-to-back wins in the Heineken Cup over Béziers but the Premiership remained a different kettle of fish as Leicester lost the Christmas clash at Wasps. In the absence of the injured Healey, the fly-half spot rotated between Kafer and Vesty but Leicester secured a place in the knockout stage of the Heineken Cup with straightforward wins over Calvisano and Neath, which gave them three months to contemplate a home quarter-final against Munster, the team they had beaten in the final the previous May.

They also had the domestic cup to consider, having finally managed to force a way past Harlequins in the quarter-finals. There was disappointment that no bigger venue for the semi-final with Gloucester could be found than Northampton and, at the same time, there was the prospect of asking members to return tickets for the Heineken Cup quarter-final so that Leicester could meet the requirements of European Rugby Cup Ltd in terms of the allocation to visiting Irish supporters.

It helped create a fractious air about the club. "The thing that has affected us most is our England players and their involvement elsewhere," John Wells said. "The emphasis Clive Woodward and his

crew put on training and development for England is certainly, bit by bit, chipping away at us. There will be a greater emphasis on England over the next 12 months, leading up to the World Cup, and that's understandable, there isn't an issue there. But there are only so many high-quality games you can get out of our senior players and that they will be highly motivated for."

Emphasising the point, six Leicester players were named in England's new-year training squad, a seventh, Ollie Smith, in the academy squad and Ireland happy to have Murphy's services. Going into the six nations, Leicester stood third in the Premiership and remained involved in both European and domestic cups. Dorian West captained England in the A international against France with Smith and Corry among his troops while Johnson, Kay, Moody, Back and Rowntree were involved in the opening international, against France at Twickenham.

Controversy raged in the Powergen Cup semi-final.

It was the start of a year of unparalleled glory for England with Leicester providing the hardest of hard cores to the team that won a grand slam, beat New Zealand and Australia on their own soil and finished by becoming the first northern-hemisphere country to win the World Cup. Glory was not on Leicester's agenda. They lost their Powergen Cup semi-final 16-11 to Gloucester, unhappy at the controversy that erupted in the final minutes when Gloucester lost a second prop to injury. Steve Lander, Leicester's old refereeing friend, ruled uncontested scrums with Leicester poised for a pushover from a five-metre scrum which, with the conversion, would have won the match. The argument ran that Olivier Azam, the Gloucester hooker, was adept at propping but Lander, quite rightly, could not force such a move on Gloucester.

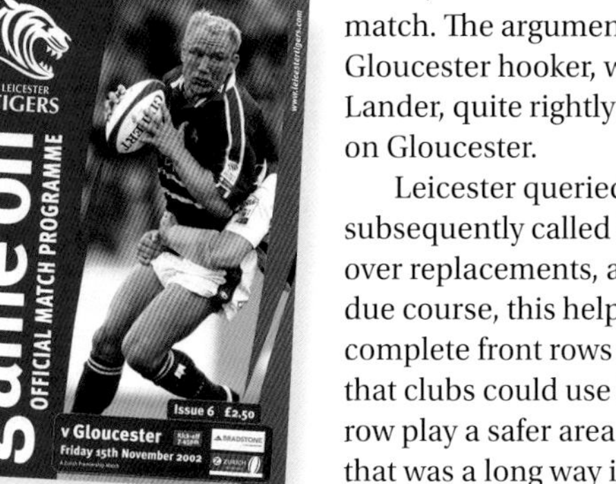

Leicester queried the result with the RFU and subsequently called for a review of the regulations over replacements, across all competitions. In due course, this helped lead to the introduction of complete front rows on the bench after suspicions that clubs could use laws introduced to make front-row play a safer area to their own advantage. But that was a long way in the future.

There was a nod to the past, when the Barbarians lost 21-12 at Welford Road in a testimonial match for Back (Richards playing the final ten minutes), then delight when Smith won his first cap as a replacement against Italy, becoming at 20 the third-youngest Tigers player to be capped, behind Paul Dodge and Ralph Buckingham - also centres. Back returned against Scotland from a calf strain and he, Johnson, Kay and Rowntree, with West perched on the bench, shared in the tumultuous 42-6 win over Ireland (for whom Murphy played) that clinched the first England grand slam since 1995.

At home Leicester opposed a move by Premier Rugby to decrease the size of the salary cap but were unsuccessful. "Leicester will be forced to re-assess the recruitment policy," Richards warned. "There is a disincentive to nurture England-qualified players. In a couple of years we will be on the slide and have a league inundated with pension-trail boys from the southern hemisphere." Richards expressed the view that the salary system should be based on a percentage of a club's annual turnover, knowing well that Leicester's far outweighed that of their rivals but also asking why the club should be penalised for its commercial success.

Not that they looked like champions when Munster came to town. The Irish province was still smarting at the manner in which they had been denied in the previous season's final; Leicester havered over whether to move the quarter-final to Leicester City's Walkers Stadium, capable of accommodating 15,000 more spectators, but decided to stay at Welford Road. Rowntree missed the match having injured a knee against Ireland and though Healey was fit once more to play fly-half, Kafer withdrew after injuring himself during the warm-up, meaning a move into the centre for Freddie Tuilagi.

But Leicester's international lineout was picked apart by Paul O'Connell and Donncha O'Callaghan, Healey tried to play the ambitious game that had not worked for Leicester all season; when injured in a collision with Leon Lloyd, he should have come off but did not until Munster had attacked his channel and scored a try through Ronan O'Gara. With Stimpson having an off-day

↑ Ollie Smith on his England debut against Italy at Twickenham 9.3.2003.

→ Darren Garforth in his 346th and last game for the Tigers, helped the club qualify for the Heineken Cup by beating Saracens in the wildcard final 31.5.2003.

↓ Ronan O'Gara was instrumental in knocking the defending champions out of the Heineken Cup at Welford Road 13.4.2003.

with the boot, Munster won 20-7, a late try by Peter Stringer erasing all hope that Leicester could build anything on Steve Booth's try.

Healey, having spent four months overcoming a groin injury, now required an operation to his knee. When Leicester lost their Premiership match with Harlequins, they were doomed to their first season since 1998 without a trophy (unless you count the Orange Cup, which not many people did). Kafer did not agree the terms of a new contract and moved to Saracens in the summer, Freshwater headed for Perpignan after eight years in the Midlands and Tournaire, who had never settled, returned to France for family reasons.

Garforth, now 37, announced his retirement at the end of the season, after 346 appearances and 25 England caps. But he was still able to help his club ensure a place in the following season's Heineken Cup which, at one stage, seemed in considerable doubt: they ended the Premiership season no higher than sixth and needed to qualify for Europe through the new wildcard tournament, involving the clubs finishing between fifth and eighth in the table. They did so by beating Harlequins over two legs and overcoming Saracens 27-20 at Northampton thanks to an extra-time try by Back when the players from both sides were virtually out on their feet.

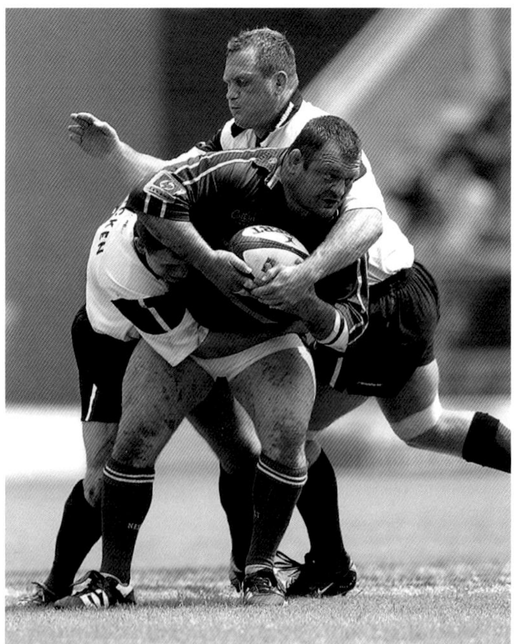

That game was a mere two days before the departure for their southern-hemisphere tour of an England squad including Johnson, Kay, Back, Corry, West and Rowntree, all of whom played against Saracens. It was a gesture of solidarity for their club at a time when it was needed, Leicester having unveiled a new shirt missing the stripes around the body, which offended traditionalists. It was green, with red and white stripes running down the arm, and represented another venture into the commercial world which has now become the norm.

Two Bristol players arrived at Welford Road during the close season, Julian White, the England prop, and Daryl Gibson, the New Zealand centre. They were joined by the Wales and Lions prop, Darren Morris, another fly-half in Ramiro Pez, the Italy player who was with Rotherham, and Henry Tuilagi, younger brother of Fereti, while Dan Lyle, the former Bath and USA No 8, came on a short-term contract to cover the World Cup absentees. Such recruitment added strength to the views Richards had expressed earlier in the year and Kronfeld was invited to lead the side until Back returned from the World Cup, the flanker taking over from Johnson who had been Leicester's captain for six years.

There were, though, still places in Woodward's World Cup squad to be played for. Johnson, Kay, Rowntree and Back all shared in the dramatic 15-13 win over New Zealand in Wellington, when the forwards played so well to deny the All Blacks at a time when Back and Lawrence Dallaglio were both in the sin bin. But Rowntree was replaced by Gloucester's Trevor Woodman for the test against Australia in Melbourne, when the 25-14 win was probably England's best of the year. Ten Leicester players, including Moody, Healey, Smith and the newcomer, White, were in the training squad of 43 named in July as the global tournament that dominated the start of the new season edged ever nearer.

Graham Rowntree and Neil Back were kingpins of the England pack leading up to the World Cup.

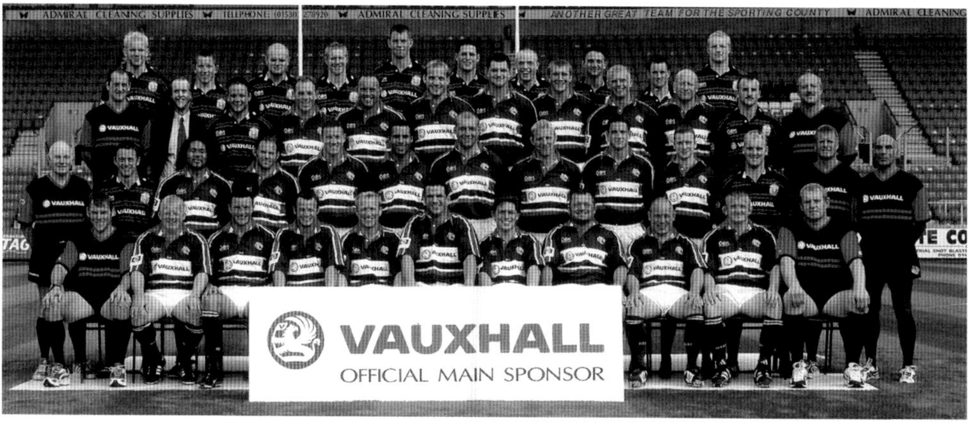

LEICESTER FOOTBALL CLUB 2001/02
Back: Lewitt, Grindal, Naylor, O.Smith, Deacon, Billig, Holford, Ellis, Booth, Wheeler.
2nd row: Atkinson (Strength & conditioning coach), Finlay (Doctor), Nebbett, Gelderbloom, Freshwater, Gustard, Manson-Bishop, Short, Balding, Jelley, Chuter, I.Smith (Extras coach).
3rd row: Shephard (Team secretary), Ja.Hamilton, Tuilagi, Kronfeld, Stimpson, Lloyd, Kay, Moody, W.Johnson, Murphy, Goode, Key (Backs coach), Duggan (Fitness advisor).
Front: Wells (Forwards coach), West, Corry, Healey, Back, M.Johnson (capt), Kafer, Garforth, Cockerill, Rowntree, Richards (Director of rugby).

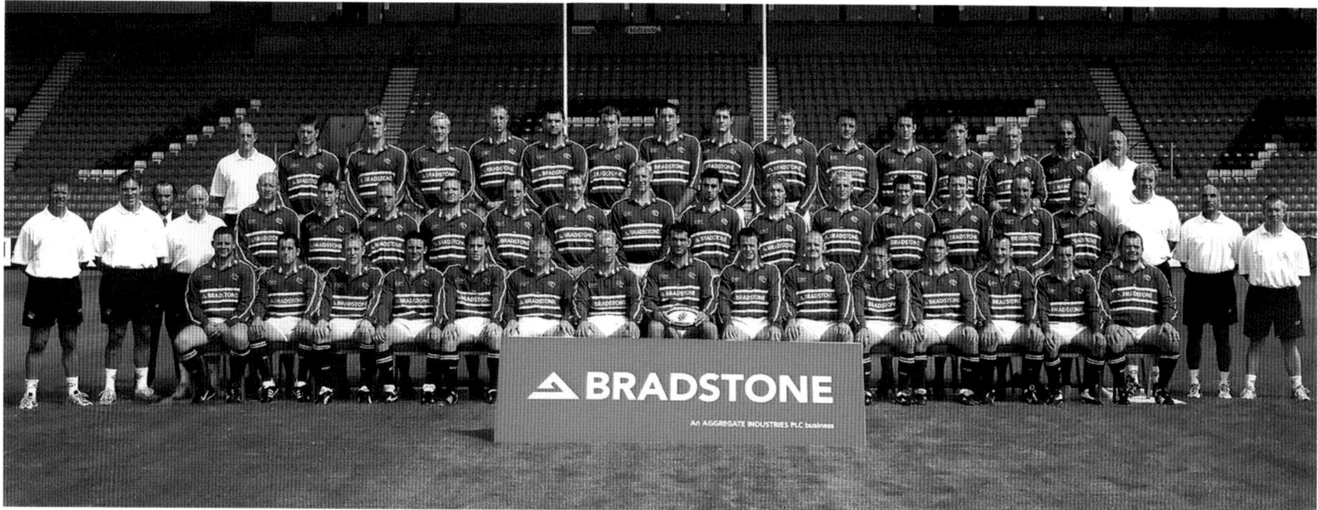

LEICESTER FOOTBALL CLUB 2002/03
Back: Atkinson (Strength & conditioning coach), Holtby, Hayman, Wheeler, Hurrell, Manson-Bishop, B.Deacon, Jim Hamilton, Morley, Short, Corry, W.Johnson, L.Deacon, Balding, Lloyd, I.Smith (Extras coach).
Middle: Key (Backs coach), Wells (Forwards coach), Finlay (Doctor), Shephard (Team secretary), Jelley, Tierney, Holford, Buckland, Gelderbloom, O.Smith, Moody, Abraham, Tournaire, Billig, Hipkiss, Murphy, Freshwater, Kronfeld, Richards (Director of rugby), Duggan (Fitness & conditioning coach), Brookes (Physiotherapist).
Front: Nebbett, Williams, Vesty, Ellis, Skinner, West, Back, M.Johnson (capt), Healey, Rowntree, Jamie Hamilton, Kafer, Chuter, Booth, Garforth.

20 01/02			OVERALL RECORD:					T	C	PG	DG	PTS
Home Ground: Welford Road	**Trophy Cabinet:** Heineken Cup(2), Zurich Premiership(6)		PLD	W	D	L	Tigers scored:	104	71	92	9	965
Director of Rugby: Dean Richards assisted by Pat Howard and John Wells			35	27	0	8	Opponents scored:	30	24	113	6	555
Captain: Martin Johnson												

GM	DATE		VEN	OPPONENTS	RESULT	POS/LGE	TRIES	KICKS	ATT
ZURICH PREMIERSHIP (1ST)						**CHAMPIONS: LEICESTER TIGERS**			
2	Sep	2s	a	Newcastle Falcons	L+ 16-19	7	Goode 17, Tuilagi 26	Goode 2p	7490
3		**8**	**H**	**London Wasps**	W 45t-15	3	Stimpson 25/80, Kay 46, Murphy 69/73, Gelderbloom 77	Stimpson 2p, Goode 3c/d	13837
4		15	a	Gloucester	W 40t-18	2	Moody 46/61, Booth 70, Murphy 80	Stimpson 4c/2p, Goode 2d	9729
5		**22**	**H**	**Bath Rugby**	W 48t-9	1	Healey 14, Goode 32, Moody 34, Booth 70, Stimpson 80	Stimpson 4c/5p	15145
8	Oct	13	a	Northampton Saints	W 21-11	1	Healey 58, Kafer 61	Stimpson c/p, Booth d, Goode d	11700
9		**20**	**H**	**Saracens**	W 36t-10	1	Kafer 12, Booth 28/77, Jelley 48	Stimpson 2c/3p, Goode d	13762
12	Nov	11s	a	Leeds Tykes	L 16-37t	1	Kronfeld 72	Stimpson c/3p	7162
13		17	a	Sale Sharks	W 37t-3	1	Murphy 40/69, Goode 44, Booth 64	Goode 4c/3p	5429
14		**23f**	**H**	**NEC Harlequins**	W+ 23-18	1	Stimpson 30/44	Stimpson 2c/3p	16017
15	Dec	2s	a	London Irish	W 30-15	1	Ja.Hamilton 16, Moody 79, Lloyd 80	Stimpson 3c/3p	11124
16		**8**	**H**	**Bristol Shoguns**	W+ 26-19	1	Moody 54, Booth 71	Stimpson c/3p, Goode c/p	15519
18		22	a	NEC Harlequins	W 38t-21	1	Murphy 1, Healey 44/58, M.Johnson 53/75	Murphy 4c/p, Stimpson c	9000
19		**27th**	**H**	**Sale Sharks**	W 33t-10	1	Lloyd 39, Garforth 41, Murphy 54, Booth 65	Booth d, Murphy c, Goode c/2p	16250
	Jan	**26**	**H**	**Leeds Tykes**	PP (European cup)	-			
24	Feb	9	a	Saracens	W 48t-7	1	Back 10, Goode 40, Smith 48, Kafer 61, Murphy 63, Tuilagi 69, Booth 79	Goode 5c/p	9347
25		**23**	**H**	**Northampton Saints**	W 17-6	1	Freshwater 27	Goode 4p	16251
26	Mar	9	a	Bath Rugby	W 27-9	1	Deacon 33, Smith 80	Stimpson c/5p	8200
27		**16**	**H**	**Gloucester**	W 27-10	1	Back 23, Healey 36, West 73	Stimpson 3c/2p	16250
28		31s	a	London Wasps	L 24-36	1	Tuilagi 2, Booth 76	Stimpson c/4p	9621
29	Apr	**13**	**H**	**Newcastle Falcons**	W 20-12	1	Tuilagi 68	Stimpson 5p	16250
30		**19f**	**H**	**Leeds Tykes**	W 31t-10	1	Back 13/32/42, Smith 21	Stimpson 4c/p	14145
32	May	5s	a	Bristol Shoguns	L 21-38t	1	Murphy 34, Kronfeld 55, Gelderbloom 78	Goode 2p	6500
33		**12s**	**H**	**London Irish**	W 34t-16	1	Lloyd 21/66, Back 46, Corry 50, Penalty 63	Stimpson c/p, Goode 2c	15800
ZURICH CHAMPIONSHIP						**ZURICH CHAMPIONSHIP WINNERS: GLOUCESTER**			
34	May	**18**	**H**	**Bristol Shoguns (qf)**	L 13-27	-	Goode 80	Goode c/2p	4771
HEINEKEN CUP						**EUROPEAN CHAMPIONS: LEICESTER TIGERS**			
6	Sep	**29**	**H**	**Llanelli**	W 12-9	2	-	Stimpson 4p	15170
7	Oct	7s	a	Amatori & Calvisano	W 37-3	1	Tuilagi 13, Ellis 33, Back 47/51, Healey 75	Stimpson 3c/2p	3000
10		27	a	Perpignan	W 31-30	1	Booth 66	Stimpson c/7p, Goode d	12000
11	Nov	**3**	**H**	**Perpignan**	W 54-15	1	Kay 11, Moody 30, Stimpson 40, Booth 63, Murphy 76, Smith 77	Stimpson 6c/4p	15622
20	Jan	**5**	**H**	**Amatori & Calvisano**	W 29-7	1	Murphy 8/52, Booth 11, Smith 20, Corry 80	Murphy c, Goode c	15140
21		12	a	Llanelli	L 12-24	1	-	Goode 4p	10614
23		**27s**	**H**	**Leinster (qf)**	W 29-18	-	Back 23/51, Lloyd 28, Healey 33, Murphy 38	Murphy 2c	16249
31	Apr	28s		Llanelli (sf)	W 13-12	-	Ellis 43	Stimpson c/2p	29849
35	May	25		Munster (f)	W 15-9	-	Murphy 25, Healey 58	Stimpson c/p	74000
RFU CLUB COMPETITION (POWERGEN CUP)						**CUP WINNERS: LONDON IRISH**			
17	Dec	**15**	**H**	**Exeter Chiefs (6)**	W 27-0	N1	Smith 4/16, Lloyd 63, Manson-Bishop 67	Goode 2c/p	5549
22	Jan	19	a	NEC Harlequins (qf)	L 20-22	P	Smith 51, Kafer 71	Goode 2c/2p	8500
ORANGE CUP (English Champions v French Champions)									
1	Aug	25	a	Toulouse	L 15-30		-	Goode 4p/d	15000

Neutral Venues: *#31 at City Ground - Nottingham, #35 at Millennium Stadium - Cardiff*

INDIVIDUAL APPEARANCES 2001/02

Name / Game #	1	2	3	4	5	6	7	8	9	10	11	12	13	14	15	16	17	18	19	20	21	22	23	24	25	26	27	28	29	30	31	32	33	34	35	Apps	T	Pts
NA (Neil) Back E50 L4	-	-	r	r	-	7	7	7	-	r	7*	-	-	-	7	7	x	7	r	r	7	r	7	7	-	r	7	7	r	7	7	-	7	-	7	16+8	10	50
AL (Adam) Balding	r	-	-	-	-	-	-	-	r	-	-	r	8	8	8	8	8	r	r	-	-	8	r	-	-	-	r	r	8	8	r	■8	-	-	-	9+9	-	-
AJ (Adam) Billig	-	-	-	-	-	-	-	-	-	-	-	-	-	-	-	-	-	-	-	-	-	-	-	-	-	-	-	-	-	-	-	-	-	=15	-	1	-	-
SE (Steve) Booth	11	x	r	r	14	14	14	14	14	11	11	14	14	11	11	11	14	r	11	14	14	r	x	14	14	14	14	14	14	x	-	11	-	-	-	24+4	12	66
GS (George) Chuter E+	x	r	r	x	r	x	r	x	2	r	2	2	x	x	-	-	r	-	-	-	-	-	x	r	-	-	-	-	-	-	-	r	-	-	-	3+8	-	-
R (Richard) Cockerill E27	2*	-	-	-	-	-	-	-	x	-	r	r	2	2*	x	r	2*	x	r	2	x	r	2	2	2*	r	r	r	2	r	x	2*	r	r	x	10+11	-	-
ME (Martin) Corry E25 L3	-	-	-	r	-	8	8	-	-	-	-	-	-	-	-	-	r	6	8	8	8	6	8	8	r	8	8	8	6	6	8	-	8	8	8	18+3	2	10
LP (Louis) Deacon E+	4	4	4	4	r	x	5	r	4	4	4	5	5	5	-	-	-	-	-	5	x	4	-	r	4	4	4	-	-	5	x	4	r	4	-	19+4	1	5
HA (Harry) Ellis E+ L+	>9	9	9	9	r	r	9	-	r	-	r	r	r	r	r	r	9	r	9	x	x	r	r	-	9	r	9	-	9	9	9	r	-	-	r	12+15	2	10
PT (Perry) Freshwater E+	-	-	-	-	r	-	-	-	r	x	r	r	1	1	x	r	1	-	-	1	-	-	-	-	1	-	r	r	1	r	x	1	1	r	r	8+10	1	5
DJ (Darren) Garforth E25	3	3	3	3	3	3	3	3	3	3	3	3	3	3	-	-	-	r	3	3	3	r	3	3	3	3	3	3	3	-	3	-	-	-	3	26+2	1	5
GK (Glenn) Gelderbloom	12	x	13	13	13	13	13	13	13	13	13	13	-	x	-	-	12	-	x	r	-	-	-	r	x	r	r	13	r	12	-	12	12	r	r	16+7	2	10
AJ (Andy) Goode E+	15	10	10	10	10	10	10	10	10	10	-	-	10	10	r	r	10	r	10	10	10	10	x	10	10	x	-	r	10	r	x	10	10	10	x	23+5	5	174
JS (James) Grindal	-	-	-	-	-	-	-	-	-	-	-	-	-	-	-	-	r	-	-	-	-	-	-	r	x	-	-	r	-	-	-	9	-	-	-	1+3	-	-
PSK (Paul) Gustard	r	7	6	6	r	-	r	-	r	-	-	-	-	r	-	-	7	-	-	<6	-	x	-	-	-	-	-	-	-	-	-	-	-	-	-	5+5	-	-
JG (Jamie) Hamilton	r	r	-	-	-	-	-	r	9	r	9	9	9	9	9	9	-	9	r	9	9	9	9	9	-	9	r	9	r	r	r	-	r	r	9	16+11	1	5
AS (Austin) Healey E47 L2	-	-	r	r	9	9	r	9	-	9	10	-	-	-	10	10	-	10	14	-	-	-	10	-	15	10	10	10	r	10	10	r	9	9	10	19+5	8	40
JN (John) Holtby	-	-	-	-	-	-	-	-	>r	-	-	-	-	-	-	-	-	-	-	-	-	-	-	-	-	-	-	-	-	-	-	-	-	-	-	0+1	-	-
DA (Derek) Jelley	x	r	r	x	-	-	r	-	1	-	r	1	-	-	-	-	r	-	-	-	-	1	-	-	x	-	-	-	-	-	-	r	r	-	-	3+7	1	5
MO (Martin) Johnson E67 L8	-	-	r	r	4*	4*	4*	4*	-	-	-	-	4*	-	4*	4*	-	4*	4*	4*	4*	r	4*	4*	-	-	-	4*	4*	4*	4*	x	4*	-	4*	19+3	2	10
WW (Will) Johnson	r	8	-	-	6	x	r	6	6	x	8	6	6	6	r	r	6	8	-	-	6	-	-	r	8	x	r	x	-	-	-	6	x	r	x	13+7	-	-
RB (Rod) Kafer A12	>10	12	12	12	12	12	12	12	12*	12	12	10*	12	12	12	12	r	12	12	12	12	12	12	12	12	12	12	12	12	-	12	-	-	12	12	31+1	4	20
BJ (Ben) Kay E10 L+	5	5	5	5	5	5	-	5	5	5	5	-	-	-	5	5	5	5	5	r	5	5	5	5	5	5	5	5	r	r	5	-	5	5	5	27+3	2	10
JA (Josh) Kronfeld NZ54	>6	-	-	-	-	-	-	r	7	7	x	7	7	7	-	-	-	-	7	7	r	7	r	6	7	7	-	6	-	-	-	7	r	7	x	15+4	2	10
LD (Leon) Lloyd E5	-	-	-	-	-	-	-	-	-	-	-	r	13	13	13	13	13	-	13	13	13	13	13	-	-	-	-	r	13	11	r	13	14	14	-	15+3	6	30
G (Guy) Manson-Bishop	x	-	-	-	-	-	-	-	>r	x	-	4	r	4	-	-	<4	-	-	-	-	-	-	-	-	-	-	-	-	-	-	-	-	-	-	3+2	1	5
LW (Lewis) Moody E9 L+	7	6	7	7	7	6	-	r	-	6	6	-	-	-	6	6	-	r	6	r	r	-	6	r	6	6	6	-	7	-	6	r	6	6	6	20+6	6	30
GEA (Geordan) Murphy I8 L+	-	14	14	14	-	-	-	-	-	14	14	-	15	14	14	14	15	14	15	15	15	15	15	15	-	-	-	-	-	14	14	15	r	-	14	21+1	14	89
JR (Jim) Naylor	>r	-	-	-	r	x	-	x	-	-	-	11	-	-	-	-	-	-	-	-	-	-	-	-	-	-	-	-	-	-	-	-	-	<r	-	1+3	-	-
RJ (Ricky) Nebbett	r	-	r	-	r	x	r	r	-	-	-	x	r	x	3	3	3	3	r	-	r	3	x	r	x	x	x	-	-	3	-	3	3	3	-	9+9	-	-
CG (Graham) Rowntree E38 L+	1	1*	1*	1*	1	1	1	1	-	1	1	-	-	-	1	1	-	1	1	r	1	-	1	1	-	1	1	1	r	1	1	-	-	1	1	24+2	-	-
PT (Peter) Short	8	x	8	8	8	-	6	8	8	8	r	8	r	r	x	x	r	-	-	-	-	-	-	-	x	-	-	-	5	r	-	5	-	x	-	11+5	-	-
OJ (Ollie) Smith E+ L+	13	13	-	-	-	r	x	11	11	x	r	12	r	r	x	x	11	13	r	11	r	14	14	13	13	13	13	-	-	13	13	14	13	13	13	20+6	8	40
TRG (Tim) Stimpson E17 L1	-	15	15	15	15	15	15	15	15	15	15	15	r	15	15	15	-	15	-	-	-	-	-	-	-	15	15	15	15	15	15	r	15	-	15	23+2	6	301
TD (Tim) Taylor	>r	-	-	-	-	-	-	-	-	-	-	-	-	-	-	-	-	-	-	-	-	-	-	-	-	-	-	-	-	-	-	-	-	-	-	0+1	-	-
F (Freddie) Tuilagi Sa12	14	11	11	11	11	11	11	-	-	-	-	-	11	-	-	-	-	11	-	-	11	11	11	11	11	11	11	11	11	-	11	-	11	11	11	22	5	25
DE (Dorian) West E16	-	2	2	2	2	2	2	2	-	2*	-	-	-	-	2	2	-	2	2	r	2	2*	-	-	r	2*	2*	2	r	2	2	-	2	2*	2	22+3	1	5

The key for how to read the stats is on the last page

2002/03										
Home Ground: Welford Road	OVERALL RECORD:						T	C	PG	DG	PTS
Director of Rugby: Dean Richards assisted by John Wells	PLD	W	D	L	Tigers scored:	93	61	80	6	845
Captain: Martin Johnson	36	22	1	13	Opponents scored:	47	34	90	7	596

GM	DATE		VEN	OPPONENTS	RESULT	POS/LGE	TRIES	KICKS	ATT
ZURICH PREMIERSHIP (6TH)						**CHAMPIONS: LONDON WASPS**			
2	Aug	31	a	Leeds Tykes	L 13-26	11	Healey 55	Stimpson c/2p	4301
3	Sep	**7**	**H**	**NEC Harlequins**	W 30t-6	6	Back 23, Booth 58, Hamilton 69, Stimpson 80	Stimpson 2c/2p	15387
4		13f	a	Sharks	L 16-29	9	Ellis 56	Stimpson c/2p, Healey d	5678
5		**21**	**H**	**Newcastle Falcons**	W 52t-9	5	Kafer 38, Back 51, Smith 57, Rowntree 74	Stimpson 4c/7p/d	15656
6		29s	a	Bristol Shoguns	L+ 20-25	7	Kafer 29, Ellis 67	Stimpson 2c/2p	6237
7	Oct	**5**	**H**	**Bath Rugby**	W+ 22-20	6	Corry 40, West 60, Back 65	Stimpson 2c/p	16811
10		27s	a	Saracens	W 26-18	5	Booth 41, Murphy 72	Murphy d, Stimpson 2c/3p	10531
11	Nov	**2**	**H**	**London Wasps**	W+ 9-6	3	-	Stimpson 3p	16845
12		9	a	Northampton Saints	W 16-3	3	Kronfeld 70	Murphy c/3p	12600
13		**15f**	**H**	**Gloucester**	W+ 20-15	3	Lloyd 16, Kronfeld 26/37	Vesty c/p	16845
14		24s	a	London Irish	L 7-27	4	Smith 40	Booth c	10605
15		**30**	**H**	**Northampton Saints**	L 12-25	5	-	Stimpson 4p	16875
19	Dec	27f	a	London Wasps	L 13-26	6	Ellis 22	Stimpson c/2p	10000
20	Jan	**4**	**H**	**Saracens**	W+ 23-18	4	Kronfeld 19, Smith 62, Lloyd 69	Murphy c/2p	16845
24	Feb	1	a	Bath Rugby	W+ 15-8	4	Kay 29, Murphy 70	Murphy c, Vesty p	8200
25		**8**	**H**	**Bristol Shoguns**	W 40t-6	3	Murphy 7/38, Kronfeld 47, Smith 73, Kafer 75, Booth 80	Murphy 2c, Stimpson 3c	16875
27	Mar	16s	a	Newcastle Falcons	L+ 22-24	4	Booth 16, West 70/79	Booth c/p, McMullen c	9105
28	Apr	**6s**	**H**	**Sharks**	W 33t-20	4	Healey 9, Murphy 20, Lloyd 37, Tuilagi 47	Stimpson 2c/3p	16815
30		19	a	NEC Harlequins	L 9-17	5	-	Stimpson 3p	7123
31		**26**	**H**	**Leeds Tykes**	W+ 18-17	4	-	Booth 5p, McMullen p	16815
32	May	**3**	**H**	**London Irish**	L+ 19-20	6	Stimpson 2, Holtby 37	Stimpson 2p, Murphy d	16815
33		10	a	Gloucester	L 13-31t	6	Tuilagi 36	Murphy c/2p	11000
ZURICH WILDCARD (HEINEKEN CUP QUALIFICATION)									
34	May	14w	a	NEC Harlequins (sf - 1st leg)	L 23-26	-	Murphy 53, Corry 76	Stimpson 2c/3p	2350
35		**18s**	**H**	**NEC Harlequins (sf - 2nd leg)**	W 28-13	-	Gelderbloom 34, Back 57, Skinner 77	Stimpson 2c/3p	5552
36		31		Saracens (f)	W 27-20 (aet)	-	West 60, Back 96	Stimpson c/4p, McMullen d	8066
***Note:** #34/#35: Leicester Tigers won 51-39 on aggregate*									
HEINEKEN CUP						**EUROPEAN CHAMPIONS: TOULOUSE**			
8	Oct	11f	a	Neath	D 16-16	2	Healey 79	Stimpson c/3p	6834
9		**19**	**H**	**Amatori & Calvisano**	W 63-0	2	Booth 14/60/80, Back 30/44, Freshwater 40, Murphy 40/65, Tierney 43, Corry 72	Murphy c, Stimpson 3c, Healey c/p	14525
16	Dec	8s	a	Bèziers	W 24-12	1	Smith 60, Lloyd 76	Murphy c/3p, Kafer d	8000
17		**14**	**H**	**Bèziers**	W 53-10	1	Tuilagi 19/46/75, Deacon 27, West 32, Kafer 52, Murphy 61, Vesty 80	Murphy 5c/p	15444
21	Jan	11	a	Amatori & Calvisano	W 40-22	1	Chuter 2, Ellis 9/44, Booth 19, Stimpson 30, Tournaire 78	Stimpson 5c	3000
22		**18**	**H**	**Neath**	W 36-11	1	Murphy 2, Hamilton 24, Kronfeld 70, Kay 73	Stimpson 2c/4p	16845
29	Apr	**13s**	**H**	**Munster (qf)**	L 7-20	-	Booth 59	Stimpson c	17500
RFU CLUB COMPETITION (POWERGEN CUP)						**CUP WINNERS: GLOUCESTER**			
18	Dec	**21**	**H**	**Worcester Warriors (6)**	W 36-9	N1	Lloyd 9, Chuter 26, Short 50, Smith 58, Balding 69	Vesty 4c/p	6427
23	Jan	25	a	NEC Harlequins (qf)	W 19-12	P	Stimpson 15, Moody 33	Stimpson 3p	8183
26	Mar	1		Gloucester (sf)	L 11-16	P	Kronfeld 76	Stimpson 2p	8000
ORANGE CUP (ENGLISH CHAMPIONS V FRENCH CHAMPIONS)									
1	Aug	24	a	Biarritz Olympique	W 14-13		Hipkiss 36, Booth 74	Stimpson c, Vesty c	3000
***Neutral Venues:** #1 Stade Jean Dauger - Bayonne, #26 #36 at Franklin's Gardens - Northampton*									

INDIVIDUAL APPEARANCES 2002/03

Name / Game #	1	2	3	4	5	6	7	8	9	10	11	12	13	14	15	16	17	18	19	20	21	22	23	24	25	26	27	28	29	30	31	32	33	34	35	36	Apps	T	Pts
LC (Luke) Abraham	-	-	-	-	-	-	-	-	-	-	-	-	-	-	-	-	-	>r	-	-	-	-	-	-	-	-	-	-	-	-	x	r	-	-	-	-	0+2	-	-
NA (Neil) Back E57 L4	7	7	7	r	7	-	7	7	7*	7	7	-	-	-	-	-	-	-	r	r	7*	7	r	7	r	-	r	7	7	-	-	-	-	-	7	7	16+6	7	35
AL (Adam) Balding	-	-	-	-	-	-	-	-	r	-	x	8	8	8	r	r	7	7	8	8	r	8	x	x	r	8	8	r	r	8	8	8	8	8	r	r	15+9	1	5
SE (Steve) Booth	r	14	14	14	r	r	14	r	11	11	11	11	11	14	r	-	r	15	-	r	11	11	r	r	r	r	15	11	11	r	11	-	-	-	-	-	17+12	10	72
GS (George) Chuter E+	r	x	r	2	r	r	x	x	2	2	r	r	r	r	2	r	r	2	x	2	2	x	x	x	r	x	-	x	r	x	2	2	2	2	-	r	11+13	2	10
PK (Peter) Cook	-	-	-	-	-	-	-	-	-	-	-	-	-	-	-	-	-	-	-	-	-	-	-	-	-	-	-	-	-	>1	x	-	-	-	-	-	1	-	-
ME (Martin) Corry E25 L3	8	8	6	8	8	7	8	8	5	8	8	5	5	5	6	6	6	6*	-	6	8	-	8	8	8	6	6	5	6	6	6	6	-	5	8	8	33	3	15
LP (Louis) Deacon E+	-	-	-	5	-	-	5	-	4	-	-	4	4	4	-	5	5	5	x	5	4	r	-	-	5	-	5	-	-	r	5	5	x	4	5	-	17+2	1	5
HA (Harry) Ellis E+ L+	11	r	9	9	14	14	-	-	-	-	-	9	9	9	9	r	r	-	9	-	9	9	-	-	-	-	-	-	r	9	9	9	11	9	9	9	19+4	5	25
PT (Perry) Freshwater E+	1	r	r	1	-	-	-	r	1	r	1	1	1	1	r	1	-	-	-	-	-	-	r	-	-	r	1	1	1	-	1	1	r	1	x	<r	14+9	1	5
DJ (Darren) Garforth E25	-	-	-	-	3	3	r	3	x	3	3	r	3	3	-	r	r	3	3	r	3	x	r	3	r	3	r	3	3	3	3	3	3	r	r	<3	19+10	-	-
GK (Glenn) Gelderbloom	-	-	-	13	r	r	x	13	r	r	12	x	x	x	-	-	-	12	r	-	12	x	-	x	-	-	r	x	r	r	r	r	x	13	13	13	8+10	1	5
BJA (Ben) Gerry	-	-	-	-	-	-	-	-	-	-	-	x	x	x	=r	-	-	-	-	-	-	-	-	-	-	-	-	-	-	-	-	-	-	-	-	-	0+1	-	-
JG (Jamie) Hamilton	9	9	r	-	-	-	r	r	r	r	9	r	-	-	-	-	-	9	-	9	r	r	9	9	9	9	r	-	-	-	r	x	9	r	x	<r	10+12	2	10
AS (Austin) Healey E50 L2	10	10	10	10	-	-	10	10	14	-	-	-	-	-	10	10	10	-	-	-	-	-	-	-	-	-	-	10	10	-	-	-	-	-	-	-	12	3	23
DJ (Dan) Hipkiss E+	>12	12	x	r	-	-	-	-	-	-	-	-	-	-	-	-	-	-	-	-	-	-	-	-	-	-	-	-	-	-	-	-	-	-	-	-	2+1	1	5
JN (John) Holtby	14	-	-	-	-	-	-	-	-	-	-	-	-	-	-	-	-	r	14	14	-	-	-	-	-	-	-	-	-	-	-	14	14	-	-	14	6+1	1	5
DA (Derek) Jelley	-	-	-	-	-	-	-	-	-	-	-	-	-	-	-	-	-	-	1	1	1	<1	-	-	-	-	-	-	-	-	-	-	-	-	-	-	4	-	-
MO (Martin) Johnson E74 L8	4*	4*	4*	4*	4*	4*	4*	4*	x	4*	4*	-	-	-	4*	4*	4*	r	4*	4*	r	4*	4*	4*	4*	4*	4*	4*	4*	4*	4*	4*	4*	r	4*	4*	29+3	-	-
WW (Will) Johnson	r	r	8	-	-	8	x	x	8	-	x	6	6	-	8	8	8	8	6	-	-	6	-	-	-	x	-	8	8	-	-	-	-	-	-	-	13+2	-	-
RB (Rod) Kafer A12	-	-	-	-	12	12	12	12	12	12	-	12	12	12	12	12	12	x	12	12	10	12	12	12	12	12	12	-	-	<12	x	x	x	-	-	-	22	4	23
BJ (Ben) Kay E19 L+	5	5	5	r	5	5	r	5	-	5	5	-	-	-	5	r	x	-	5	r	5	5	5	5	-	5	r	x	5	5	r	r	5	-	r	5	19+8	2	10
JA (Josh) Kronfeld NZ54	6	6	r	7	r	r	x	x	6	x	6	7	7	7	7	7	-	-	7	7	6	r	7	r	7	7	7	6	r	7	-	-	7	7*	-	-	21+6	7	35
LD (Leon) Lloyd E5	-	-	-	-	-	-	13	14	13	13	13	14	15	15	r	14	14	13	-	11	-	13	11	14	14	11	14	13	13	13	13	13	13	11	11	11	27+1	5	25
CJ (Craig) McMullen	-	-	-	-	-	-	-	-	-	x	>r	10	-	-	-	-	-	-	-	x	-	-	-	-	-	-	10	-	-	-	10	10	10	10	10	<10	8+1	-	8
LW (Lewis) Moody E14 L+	-	-	-	-	6	6	6	6	-	6	-	-	-	-	-	-	-	-	-	-	-	r	6	6	6	-	-	-	-	-	-	-	-	-	-	-	8+1	1	5
GEA (Geordan) Murphy I16 L+	-	-	-	-	-	-	-	-	15	14	14	15	-	-	14	15	15	-	-	15	14	14	14	15	15	14	-	14	14	14	15	11	15	14	14	-	22	10	115
JSP (Joe) Naufahu	-	>r	12	12	r	<r	-	-	-	-	x	-	-	-	-	-	-	-	-	-	-	-	-	-	-	-	-	-	-	-	-	-	-	-	-	-	2+3	-	-
RJ (Ricky) Nebbett	3	-	-	-	-	-	-	-	-	-	-	-	-	-	-	-	-	r	-	-	-	-	-	-	-	-	-	-	-	x	x	x	r	3	3	r	3+3	-	-
G (Gareth) Raynor	-	-	-	-	-	-	-	-	-	-	-	-	x	>r	-	-	-	-	r	-	r	-	-	-	-	-	-	x	-	-	<14	-	-	-	-	-	1+3	-	-
CG (Graham) Rowntree E43 L+	-	1	1	r	1	1	1	1	-	1	-	-	-	-	1	r	1	-	-	-	-	-	1	1	1	1	r	-	-	-	-	r	1	r	1	1	16+5	1	5
PT (Peter) Short	r	x	r	6	r	x	-	-	-	-	x	x	x	6	-	-	r	4	-	-	-	-	-	-	-	-	-	-	-	r	-	-	6	6	6	<6	7+5	1	5
WJ (Will) Skinner	-	-	-	-	-	-	-	-	-	-	-	-	-	-	-	-	-	-	-	-	-	-	-	-	-	x	-	-	-	-	>7	7	r	r	r	r	2+4	1	5
OJ (Ollie) Smith E1 L+	-	13	13	-	13	13	-	-	-	-	-	13	13	13	13	13	13	14	13	13	13	-	13	13	13	13	13	-	-	-	-	-	-	-	-	-	19	6	30
TRG (Tim) Stimpson E19 L1	15	15	15	15	15	15	15	15	r	15	15	-	-	-	15	-	-	-	15	-	15	15	15	-	r	15	-	15	15	15	-	15	-	15	15	15	23+2	4	273
T (Tom) Tierney I8	>r	-	-	r	9	9	9	9	9	9	-	-	r	x	r	9	9	r	r	x	-	-	x	x	x	r	9	9	9	x	-	-	r	-	-	-	11+8	1	5
F (Franck) Tournaire Fr49	>r	3	3	3	r	x	3	r	3	r	r	3	r	r	3	3	3	1	r	3	r	3	3	x	3	-	3	<r	x	-	-	-	-	-	-	-	15+10	1	5
F (Freddie) Tuilagi Sa17	13	11	11	11	11	11	11	11	-	-	-	-	14	11	11	11	11	11	11	-	-	-	-	11	11	x	11	12	12	11	12	12	12	12	12	12	27	5	25
SB (Sam) Vesty E+	>r	r	x	x	10	10	-	-	10	10	10	r	10	10	-	x	r	10	10	10	-	10	10	10	10	10	r	x	r	10	-	-	-	r	x	x	16+7	1	26
DE (Dorian) West E16	2	2	2	r	2	2	2	2	x	x	2	2*	2*	2*	-	2	2	r	2	r	r	2	2	2	2	2	2	2	2	2	-	-	-	r	2	2	25+5	5	25

The key for how to read the stats is on the last page

CHAPTER 32

Changing the Guard

2003/2004

At least in financial terms, Leicester remained in good shape with record season-ticket sales during the summer of more than 11,000 raising nearly £2.5 million. Andy Key, the former full-back who had become the academy coach, was asked to coach the backs after the departure of Rod Kafer, and Martin Johnson extended his contract for a further year. But the pre-season friendly, when a young Leicester team conceded four tries in Perpignan, was overshadowed by Tim Stimpson's agreement to leave Welford Road for the French club.

There was some bickering over a transfer fee but the full-back departed in November, after five and a half years, 141 starts and 1,713 points, placing him third in the club's all-time list of scorers behind Dusty Hare (4,507) and John Liley (2,518). Leicester acquired yet another England captain when Dorian West, at 35 the oldest man to be asked to fill the role for the first time, led the side out against France in Marseilles, the second of the warm-up matches prior to Clive Woodward confirming his party of 30 for the World Cup.

Austin Healey, who had spent time with Bill Knowles, the American knee specialist, trying to find a way back to health, played scrum-half in the same game but neither he nor Graham Rowntree made the final cut. Nor was Geordan Murphy to make it to Australia: the Ireland full-back suffered an horrific-looking broken leg in a warm-up match against Scotland and missed two-thirds of the new season. When the England party was confirmed, Leicester had seven representatives - Johnson, the captain, Neil Back, Ben Kay, Martin Corry, Lewis Moody, Julian White and West.

The seven World Cup winning Tigers pose on Manly beach, Sydney, with the Webb Ellis trophy.

They were guests at a civic reception before departure, leaving behind a club understanding how hard it would be to hoist themselves back up the Zurich Premiership though grateful that Henry Tuilagi had turned down a place in Samoa's squad. Tuilagi promptly scored his first try in the 29-19 win over London Irish with which the league season opened but Leicester had a league point deduced for fielding an unregistered player, Darren Morris, in the drawn game with Saracens.

There was administrative fault on both the club's side and the RFU's but a season remained to make good the error. Ramiro Pez marked his debut with a try against Newcastle and two young locks, James Hamilton and Tom Ryder, took the chance to make their mark in the absence of Johnson and Kay. Any sense of wellbeing was swiftly erased when Sale, for the first time in 37 visits since 1890, won at Welford Road and a swingeing 24-3 loss to Gloucester at Kingsholm left Leicester in eighth place on the same day that England opened their World Cup campaign by scoring 84 points against Georgia. Hamilton was sent off in the first half of the 39-18 loss at Leeds and later banned for eight weeks; after five defeats in a row, Leicester sunk to eleventh in the Premiership.

Victory over Wasps stopped the rot but only temporarily for Sale, having shrugged off the notion that they could not win at Welford Road, did so again in the Powergen Cup by 43-28 and Harry Ellis was cited for butting, an offence for which a disciplinary panel imposed a ten-week suspension (reduced on appeal to seven). It was as well that, a week later, Leicester could join in the national sense of pride induced by England's 20-17 win over Australia in the World Cup final, a side led by Johnson and including Kay, Back and, off the bench in extra time, Moody. Corry and Dorian West watched from the replacements bench as Kay knocked on the pass on Australia's tryline that might have avoided extra-time and the drama surrounding Jonny Wilkinson's winning dropped goal.

Inevitably there were local calls for a knighthood for Johnson, the honour that went in the new year to Woodward, as manager, though Johnson received the CBE and the rest of the squad the MBE. It was suggested, too, when Leicester relaunched in January proposals for the development of the Next Stand, that they should incorporate a statue of Johnson. The club's seven representatives took part in the victory parade in London that drew thousands on to the streets the following month and, in the new year, were greeted by 2,500 people when they attended a city and county councils' civic reception in Town Hall Square. In a wonderful postscript, West put his World Cup final shirt up for auction and raised £500,000 for the Rainbow Trust, the children's charity, thanks to the generosity of Philip Green, the BHS magnate.

Of more immediate concern was the task faced by Richards and his senior players to lift Leicester out of a deep rut. He took the obvious step of asking all his World Cup players to be part of the squad that played Bath in the Premiership, under the captaincy of Rowntree; the move did not work since Bath won 13-12 though Leicester also found the World Cup effect to be so great that they had to ban a ticket tout caught re-selling tickets for the sold-out match.

It was no great surprise when Leicester lost their opening Heineken Cup match to Stade Français in Paris but there was a fresh face at full-back in the starting XV against Newport Gwent Dragons a week later. Jaco van der Westhuyzen, the gifted South Africa playmaker, had arrived just as Josh Kronfeld announced his impending return to New Zealand, making his debut in a 34-3 win and bringing a sense of confidence to a team that badly needed it.

West and White required knee surgery and Moody was struggling with a damaged foot which kept him out for the rest of the season. Moreover the game organised for Twickenham between an England XV and the New Zealand Barbarians removed Corry, Ollie Smith and Daryl Gibson just when Leicester needed them. Johnson spurned the chance to lead an England side one more time and was found, instead, in Leicester's second row losing 14-0 at Northampton along with Kay, Back and White.

Twenty-four hours earlier, Leicester had struck an unusual note by playing India's national side with a team which included Johnny Zhang, the captain of China who was on loan for a month. The contact with Zhang, a popular visitor, helped lead three years later to a club delegation visiting China. Over Christmas, too, a familiar face reappeared in Leicester colours: Andy Goode parted company with Saracens after 18 months and Richards was quick to bring him back to Welford Road.

After losing at home to Gloucester, the debate about Richards's future intensified: "I'm a bit surprised but I suppose it goes with the territory," he said. "We do expect to do well but, at the same time, people have short memories, which is nothing unusual in sport. Unless you are at the top, people are calling for your head." Then came the nadir when a team including 12 internationals was trounced 33-0 by Ulster at Ravenhill in the Heineken Cup. Not even the loss of both centres, Smith and Gibson, in the opening ten minutes was any excuse for Leicester's heaviest defeat in any competition for four years and their worst day in Europe, in which they conceded four tries and could make no use in the second half of the gale-force wind that swept down the pitch.

A week later came the return game, coinciding with Johnson's decision to go public on his plans for the future. That was another element in the growing storm around Richards's head, the suggestion that Johnson could slip into a managerial role just as Richards himself had done six years earlier. Ellis returned from suspension to help Leicester to five tries in a 49-7 riposte, the last of those tries going to Johnson himself who, when the match was over, confirmed his retirement from international rugby.

"I was thinking about it post-World Cup and over the Christmas period," he said. "I gradually realised I wasn't going to change my mind and you have to make the decision. You don't really need to talk to any other people.

↑ Springbok Jaco van der Westhuyzen may have only made 18 appearances for the first-team but he had a huge bearing on Tigers qualifying for Europe.

↓ Martin Johnson led the team out a record 202 times during his Tigers career.

You just know. It's the right time. I have had a great career and been very lucky to play with great teams, successful teams, great players and coaches." The previous ten years had carried Johnson to every conceivable peak in the game, with his club, his country for whom he played 84 times, and the Lions. No wonder his autobiography, largely self-written, achieved sales over 200,000.

That was 17 January 2004. Sixteen days later another icon was making headlines as Richards resigned as director of rugby, ending a 23-year association with Leicester. It was an emotional and angry conclusion, the board certain that Richards should go after meeting with senior players, but anxious not to sack one of their greatest servants. The home defeat by Stade Français had ensured Leicester would not qualify for the knockout phase of the Heineken Cup, their only remaining ambition for the season to ensure qualification for Europe in 2004/05. Richards could point to the fact that, prior to that match, 21 players were unavailable or receiving treatment but it cut no ice.

"Unfortunately there has been a steady decline in the team's performance over the past two seasons," Peter Tom, the chairman, said in a statement. "The board felt that this decline could only be checked by significant changes within the playing structure. Dean did not find these changes acceptable."

Leicester won two European titles and four successive league titles under the guidance of Richards, setting an almost unmatchable standard. Now Wheeler took overall charge of team affairs with a rugby committee of John Wells, Johnson and Back. Another reason for Leicester's plight, of course, was the contribution to England who, in the post-Johnson era, still named eight Leicester players in a training squad. Only one, though - Ben Kay - started the six nations championship against Italy, the club's lowest England representation for ten years. During the championship, in which England slipped to mid-table mediocrity, one more Leicester player, Julian White, made two appearances as a replacement.

Leicester's recovery began slowly, almost imperceptibly some might say, with a 3-3 draw at Sale and a 22-9 win at London Irish in which Goode kicked 17 points while playing full-back. The lack of a reliable goalkicker had cost Leicester dear in the last Heineken Cup outing, against Stade Français, so at least the last signing made by Richards was making up the deficit. Also Geordan Murphy was back to fitness after nearly six months recovering from his broken leg (Ireland wheeled him back in mid-March as soon as they decently could) and contacts were being made with Pat Howard, now enjoying another phase in his varied career as player-coach to Montferrand.

That London Irish match also marked Johnson's 166th as club captain, beating the record established by Percy Lawrie between 1910-23. Johnson had agreed to resume his old role while Back completed his international obligations but the flanker, too, confirmed his retirement from England duty once the six nations was over. As it turned out, the World Cup final was Back's last appearance as well as Johnson's, after 66 caps, since England moved Richard Hill across to the open-side flank and chose not to bring Back off the bench at any stage.

By mid-April, Leicester had clambered to sixth in the Premiership and Wheeler, after touring the world in search of a potential replacement for Richards, found the answer relatively close to home. At the end of the month, Leicester confirmed Wells as head coach and brought back as his assistants Howard and Richard Cockerill, who had helped Montferrand to the final of the European Challenge Cup. Cockerill, the former hooker, was still playing but looking to coach the forwards; given that West had announced his intention to retire at the end of the season, he was a doubly useful acquisition while the return of the innovative Howard was warmly welcomed.

"Whether the club likes it or not, it's going through a transitional period," Wells said. "Good teams don't arrive overnight. So it could be four, five, six years." A week later Leicester scored 75 points against Rotherham, three tries going to George Chuter. Goode scored 30 points in what was the club's biggest Premiership win, surpassing the 72 points scored against West Hartlepool in 1999. When Wasps were beaten 48-17 (another 28 points from Goode), Leicester found themselves fifth in the table with European qualification hanging on the wildcard place. A 43-26 win over Harlequins in the semi-finals, in which Van der Westhuyzen signed off prior to taking up an engagement with NEC in Japan, was followed by a 48-27 win over Sale in the final, thus ensuring a place in the Heineken Cup.

Ellis, the rising star, was one of four uncapped players in England's summer touring party to Australia, with Corry and White alongside. England's squad for the Churchill Cup, the second-tier competition designed to boost rugby in North America, included Chuter and Louis Deacon. Ellis was not given any game time which, given the thumpings handed out by the All Blacks (twice) and Australia, may have been just as well though White played all three tests and Corry came off the bench in the 51-15 loss to Australia in Brisbane, when the World Cup triumph seemed a long way away.

↑ John Wells took over from Dean Richards.

Murphy toured South Africa with Ireland, Darren Morris went to Argentina with Wales while behind them there was a changing of the guard: Ramiro Pez, his defensive frailties always apparent, had already gone, Adam Balding headed for Gloucester, Glenn Gelderbloom to Plymouth Albion and Fereti Tuilagi to Cardiff. In their place came Seru Rabeni, Fiji's wing, from the Otago Highlanders, Ephraim Taukafa, the Tonga hooker playing in Sydney club rugby, Roger Warren, Samoa's fly-half, and Scott Bemand, the Harlequins scrum-half, while rumour had it there were two more Tuilagis, Alesana and Anitele'a, on the horizon.

↓ Try scorers Leon Lloyd and Daryl Gibson get to grips with Sale's Jason Robinson during the wildcard final at Twickenham 29.5.2004.

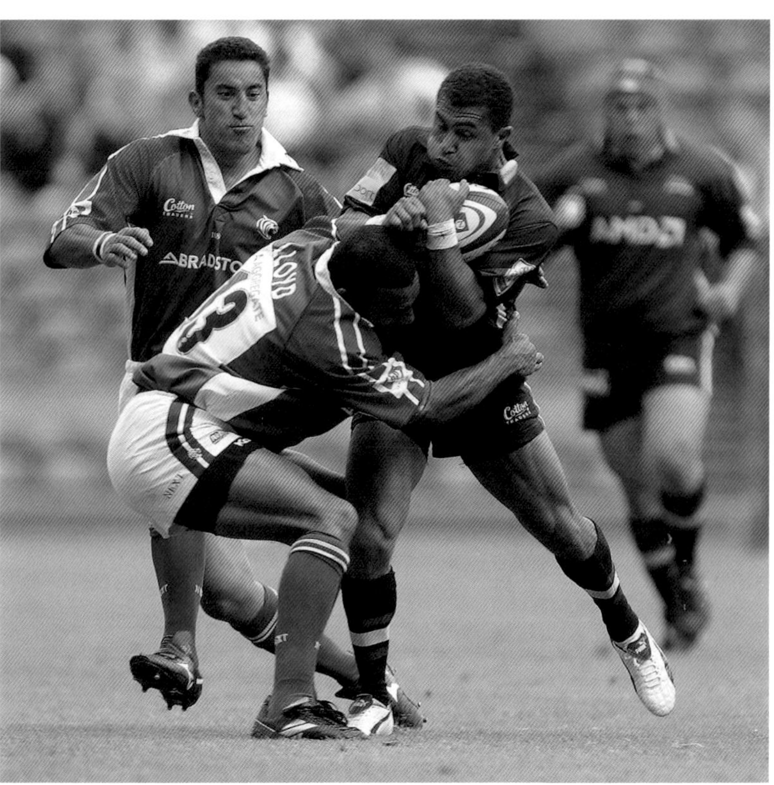

2004/2005

It was an odd start to the new season. During the summer, Sir Clive Woodward named ten Leicester players in his England training squads - George Chuter, Martin Corry, Ben Kay, Lewis Moody, Graham Rowntree and Julian White in the seniors, Louis Deacon, Harry Ellis, Will Skinner and Ollie Smith in the academy. Two months later Woodward resigned as England manager, though he remained deeply involved in rugby since he was to coach the Lions in New Zealand in 2005. The former Leicester centre wanted to see if he could carry his skills into football but he felt strongly that the RFU had not built the progressive structure which would keep England on top of the world. Martin Johnson, well out of it, was awarded a testimonial season by Leicester, his last with the club and his seventh as captain.

Buoyed by pre-tax profits of £783,000 and, at last, an agreement with the city council for the sale of the freehold of Welford Road and part of the adjoining Granby Halls site, Leicester set a cracking pace, the back line in the 44-15 win over Newcastle had an average age of 22 and Moody returned from his longstanding foot injury in October in an A league game at Welford Road against Northampton Wanderers watched by 9,209, a crowd record for the second-team competition and one which many senior sides envied. Moody was in time to claim a place for the opening of the Heineken Cup and press for a spot in England's back row.

Stamping incidents involving Corry and Chuter in the drawn game with Bath earned the two forwards suspensions of two weeks and six weeks respectively. But the playing record allowed Peter Wheeler to stand down as acting director of rugby and concentrate more on his new role as chairman of Euro Rugby, the umbrella body established four years earlier to try to give the leading clubs a louder mouthpiece at International Rugby Board level.

As luck would have it, Leicester had been drawn in the same pool as Wasps who had taken over their European crown in a thrilling final against Toulouse five months earlier. The campaign opened with a workmanlike win over Calvisano and defeat at Biarritz before hearing that Ellis and five forwards had been included in the first squad picked by England's new coach, Andy Robinson. It might have been six forwards but Deacon was nursing a damaged shoulder and missed the Premiership win over Gloucester in which Tom Varndell, 19, made his debut on one wing and Alesana Tuilagi scored two tries on the other.

Shrugging off the loss of five players to England's game with Canada, Leicester returned to the top of the table with a comfortable win over Worcester and then slugged out a 17-17 draw at Wasps, the prelude to their European meetings. Ellis, having recovered from an Achilles tendon problem, won his first cap off the bench against South Africa in a season when he played box and cox with both Andy Gomarsall and Matt Dawson for England.

Leicester chose the week of the England-Australia match to announce proposals for a ground-sharing scheme with Leicester City. Negotiations had been in train for six months as the Tigers found themselves having to put on hold the redevelopment of the Next Stand while capacity at Welford Road was reaching saturation point; in the Walkers Stadium, a couple of minutes down the road, was a facility which the football club, fresh out of administration, were eager to use to its full extent.

There was an agreement in principle to create a new company to own and manage the new stadium, which would also involve Teachers Pension Fund of America, the company whose loan had funded the move from City's old Filbert Street home in 2001. The cost of buying back the stadium from Teachers was put at £12-16 million, compared with the £20 million refurbishment of Welford Road, Leicester's home since 1892, or a move to a new green-field site costing £28 million.

"So we give up the best rugby ground anywhere for a soulless toilet bowl," was the reaction of one Tigers supporter. "No terrace, no character, no history, no thanks," the pithy response of another though in strict commercial terms, the proposal had much to commend it. The point disenchanted fans were making is that sport is not only about the money, it is about the shared experience running through generations, the magic of the moment forever associated with one ground. As a marketing exercise, of course, Leicester's board learned a lot and five months later the plans were put on the back burner.

Ollie Smith and Leon Lloyd returned from injury in the win over Saracens as Leicester prepared for the back-to-back Heineken Cup games with Wasps dubbed (with scant regard for the European context) "the Battle of Britain." Pat Howard set his players a target from the two games of nine points, everyone else merely savoured two outstanding jousts between England's leading clubs, in which Leicester threatened to run away with both games but ended hanging on for grim death.

Chuter returned from suspension in time to play, Smith's fitness was equally valuable since Rabeni - who had been scoring tries for fun from centre in his first season with the club

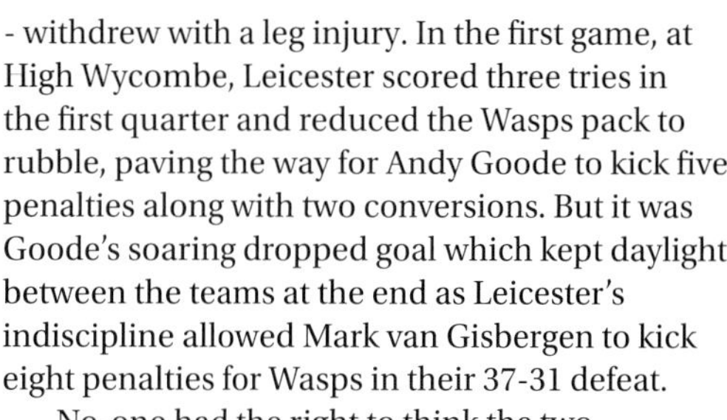

- withdrew with a leg injury. In the first game, at High Wycombe, Leicester scored three tries in the first quarter and reduced the Wasps pack to rubble, paving the way for Andy Goode to kick five penalties along with two conversions. But it was Goode's soaring dropped goal which kept daylight between the teams at the end as Leicester's indiscipline allowed Mark van Gisbergen to kick eight penalties for Wasps in their 37-31 defeat.

No-one had the right to think the two protagonists could produce more of the same a week later, yet they did. With 21 minutes played, Leicester led 19-0, Goode had kicked the first four of six penalties, Ellis had scored a try and played a key role in setting up a second, just on half-time, for Lloyd which stemmed from turnover ball in their own 22. But Wasps came back with three tries and, at the end, Leicester had won 35-27 but remained uncertain whether they would qualify for the quarter-finals.

Man of the match Harry Ellis scores his try in the Heineken Cup pool game against Wasps at Welford Road 12.12.2004.

After such a tumultuous fortnight, it was not entirely surprising that Leicester lost at home to Gloucester in the Powergen Cup. Two weeks later, that result was reversed at Kingsholm in the Premiership, at the cost of a dislocated elbow for Corry which kept him out for six weeks, and European hopes plummeted when Biarritz left Welford Road clutching a 21-17 win. Leicester needed to beat Calvisano by as many points as possible and hope other results would take them through to the knockout phase as one of the best runners-up. The first part of the equation was achieved with ten tries and a 62-10 win in Italy; the second part came with the news on their flight home that Perpignan had lost in Edinburgh, which made Leicester the eighth and final qualifier, their prize a visit to Leinster.

Typically, Johnson waited until the European situation was clarified before confirming what everyone expected, that he would retire from the game at the season's end. The club re-emphasised their hope of finding him a role: "We have to use his expertise, the unique experience he has gained from leading people, motivating them," Wheeler said. "He knows how we operate, he knows the people involved." What with Back becoming the greatest cumulative try-scorer in league rugby with his 74th (against Worcester), surpassing Jeremy Guscott (Bath) and Daren O'Leary (Harlequins and Worcester), the oldies were making their mark but the start of a new year was etched with sadness with the death, after a long illness, of Chalkie White at the age of 76.

England, meanwhile, set off on another frustrating six nations championship. Rowntree reached fifty caps against France (no small achievement given that he played in the same position and at the same time as England's first centurion, Jason Leonard), Ellis was handed the starting jersey for the rest of the season and, against Ireland, Goode was called into the senior squad for the first time. His debut came two weeks later, at Twickenham against Italy, by which time the national captaincy had passed to Corry, the fourth Leicester player to lead England in three years following Johnson, Back and Dorian West. Smith and Goode came off the bench during a 39-7 win over Italy, Goode marking the occasion by kicking the last conversion.

All the while Leicester kept daylight between themselves and Wasps at the head of the Premiership, including an 83-10 defeat of Newcastle in which they scored 11 tries, all of which were converted by Goode. At the end of the six nations, the gap was seven points which, given that the club contributed 16 players to various international teams, was an achievement of which to be proud. But they now prepared for life after Wells who, with one year left on his contract, agreed with the RFU to become a senior academy coach during the summer (where he joined West).

After 23 years at Leicester it was a natural move for Wells, 41, to further his personal ambitions. The club acted swiftly in response: Howard, despite his intention of returning to Australia in 2006, became head coach, Cockerill moved to coach the forwards and Back was appointed technical director with responsibilities for defence, analysis and individual player development.

On the same March day as these promotions were announced started a chapter in the club's history which reflected the worst and best sides of rugby. Matt Hampson, a prop who was one of Leicester's most promising young forwards, damaged his neck while training at Northampton with England for their under-21 international against Scotland. Hampson, 20, learned his rugby at the Oakham and Syston clubs before becoming part of Leicester's academy; at 16st and 6ft, he had yet to play for the senior team but had won England honours at under-19 and under-21 level.

He was taken to Northampton General Hospital and subsequently underwent a four-hour operation at Stoke Mandeville Hospital for a dislocated neck and trapped spinal cord. The accident left him a quadriplegic and requiring 24-hour care; his response to so devastating an injury, and the support of his family, friends and players up and down the country, has provided one of the most inspiring stories sport can offer. He spent 17 months in hospital, receiving a constant stream of visitors, and Leicester helped put in place a trust fund to ensure that he could lead as full a life as possible.

But, confined as he was to a wheelchair, Hampson – 'Hambo' as his many friends know him - did not allow his disability to limit the range of his activities. He continued to follow and support rugby, and achieved the necessary qualifications to coach at schools and junior clubs; he became a fundraiser for the children's charity, Special Effect, developed a sports memorabilia website and began a regular column in the *Leicester Mercury*. Phil, his father, built a specially-adapted home so that Matt could live as normal a life as possible for a man who depends for his existence on a tube running through his neck which pumps oxygen into his body.

"When I was able-bodied, I would look at people in a wheelchair and see through them," he said in an interview in *The Times*. "They did not register as real people. But today I see people for who they are. I look past the wheelchair to the human being within. I do that today with everyone I meet, whatever their circumstances. They are individuals with hopes and fears and dreams. In that sense you could say the accident has made me a better person, a more accepting person. The most rewarding thing I do is to offer hope to others with my example. I am not ill or diseased. I just have a problem with my spinal cord."

↑ Andy Goode has a perfect day with the boot in the record victory over Newcastle Falcons, landing all 13 of his kicks at goal 19.2.2005.

Hampson's accident lent a certain perspective as Leicester girded their loins for the Heineken Cup quarter-final with Leinster. In front of a record quarter-final crowd of 48,000 at Lansdowne Road, Tigers became the first English side to reach the last four from an away tie, winning 29-13. Daryl Gibson, who had just signed a new contract, and Smith scored tries and Goode's boot (two conversions, four penalties and a dropped goal) did the rest, though the platform was set by the Leicester scrum. Leinster's pack included two players, Shane Jennings on the flank and Leo Cullen at lock, who had either agreed terms, or shortly would, to move to Welford Road while an old friend, Eric Miller, was at No 8.

Smith and Back offered convincing arguments for Lions selection and duly became two of the eight Leicester players to be summoned by Woodward for the summer trip to New Zealand: Corry, Murphy, Moody, Kay, White and Rowntree were the others to feature in a far more extended Lions squad than usual with Back, at 36, the oldest ever.

↓ Ollie Smith runs in the opening try of the momentous Heineken cup quarter-final against Leinster at the old Lansdowne Road 2.4.2005.

Between beating Leinster and playing Toulouse in the semi-final, Leicester tripped up against Saracens which cost them the top spot in the Premiership. It also brought Johnson his third yellow card of the season and Corry a red one for elbowing Richard Hill; he received no more than a three-week suspension but it was enough to keep him out of the European semi-final which, the club decided, should be played at the Walkers Stadium. It was an opportunity for supporters to sample the atmosphere though the joint venture with Leicester City was moving only slowly, with primacy of tenure something of an issue.

Still, a crowd just short of 32,000 was twice the capacity of Welford Road and they watched a XV in which Healey resumed operations on the wing while Kay returned after a month out with an ankle injury. They did not enjoy what they saw: Toulouse won 27-19 and Leicester contributed significantly to their own demise. If the French club enjoyed good fortune in that two of their three tries seemed to stem from forward passes, they created far more opportunities. All their tries came from Leicester's failure to find touch and Tom Varndell's late try only put something of a gloss on the scoreline.

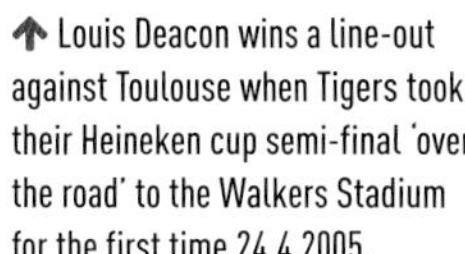

↑ Louis Deacon wins a line-out against Toulouse when Tigers took their Heineken cup semi-final 'over the road' to the Walkers Stadium for the first time 24.4.2005.

At least Johnson was able to see out the final month of his career as scheduled. Twenty-four hours after the disappointment against Toulouse, a disciplinary panel accepted his appeal against the yellow card awarded against Saracens; he led the team to a 45-10 Premiership win over Wasps, and back to the top of the table, though Henry Tuilagi, who had been joined by two brothers, Fereti and Alesana, in the match against the Barbarians in March, suffered a double fracture of the leg. Two weeks later the same two clubs met in the Premiership final at Twickenham, the day on which all Leicestrians hoped that Johnson and Back, and coach Wells, would ride off into the sunset (or to New Zealand, in Back's case) clutching a trophy one more time.

→ Johnson and Back bring the curtain down on their glittering careers at Welford Road 30.4.2005.

At Welford Road, Lawrence Dallaglio had made a typically generous gesture by bringing Wasps back on the field to acknowledge Johnson's last game on his home ground. There was no such generosity now for a Leicester team to which Corry returned after his suspension with Lloyd taking over from Healey, troubled by a sciatic problem, on the wing. The team was: Sam Vesty (Alesana Tuilagi, 69); Geordan Murphy, Ollie Smith, Daryl Gibson, Leon Lloyd (Austin Healey, 51); Andy Goode, Harry Ellis (Scott Bemand, 19); Darren Morris (Graham Rowntree, 41), George Chuter (James Buckland, 75), Julian White, Martin Johnson (captain), Ben Kay (Will Johnson, 74), Louis Deacon (Lewis Moody, 41), Martin Corry, Neil Back.

Wasps had run up 13 points before the first of Goode's three penalties and led 19-6 at the interval. It could have been worse had Back been sent to the sin bin - or worse - for punching Joe Worsley and the Wasps flanker hit back by playing with a brilliance that made a nonsense of his omission from the Lions squad. But the executioner-in-chief during Wasps' 39-14 win was Van Gisbergen, with a try, three conversions and five penalties as Leicester struggled to discover any fluidity. Tom Voyce scored an early try for Wasps, Rob Hoadley a late one, and all Leicester could manage was Bemand's injury-time try in a game which bore no relationship to those two full-blooded Heineken Cup encounters.

"On Monday morning I'll be very disappointed," Johnson said. "Not because I've played my last game but because we didn't do ourselves justice. That's difficult to take." Back was suspended for four weeks for the punch and missed the first three games of the Lions tour and Wells left in philosophical mood: "I have been at Leicester for 23 years and a lot of good has come out of it," he said. "The club is moving into a new era. The guys I played with and coached have all but gone. I wouldn't say the club needs new ideas but it won't do any harm to have a new face and a fresh voice. It won't do me any harm either. There are other challenges."

If there was no silver on the table, the season was a vast improvement on the preceding one and an independent review of the Premiership confirmed Leicester's status as the biggest generator of cash and season tickets in England. Dean Richards was back in the Premiership, now as director of rugby at Harlequins after a year of varying fortunes with Grenoble in France. Not that the rugby was over: Goode, Vesty, Chuter and Deacon played for an England XV against the Barbarians before departing for the Churchill Cup, Johnson led an international team (with a smattering of Leicester players, including Will, his brother, and Pat Howard, his coach) in his testimonial match at Twickenham against a XV led by Jonah Lomu, the legendary New Zealand wing, and the Lions left for New Zealand.

It was not one of the touring team's finest hours. The test series was lost 3-0 and never looked like going any other way: four Leicester players, Back, Kay, White and Corry, started the first international, in Christchurch, with Rowntree on the bench. Corry had enjoyed the privilege of leading the Lions against Taranaki in the provincial programme and was a candidate for tour captain when Brian O'Driscoll's tour ended at Christchurch with a shoulder injury caused by a spear tackle. Corry, in fact, took over on the pitch but was dropped for the second international, the leadership going instead to Gareth Thomas, the Wales back.

White and Moody were retained for the Wellington test with Rowntree and Corry coming off the bench, and the two forwards were joined in the starting XV by Murphy for the final encounter, in Auckland. But adverse scorelines of 48-18 and 38-19 told the story of the difference between the sides. Moody scored the Lions try in Auckland but few of the players looked back on the tour with affection, as opposed to Leicester's representatives in the Churchill Cup squad who won the trophy by beating Argentina A 45-16 in Edmonton. Of the younger generation, Matt Cornwell, the centre, captained England in the under-21 world championships with Varndell and Skinner among his team-mates.

↑ Eight Lions and the shirt! The octet of Tigers named in the British & Irish Lions touring squad to New Zealand.

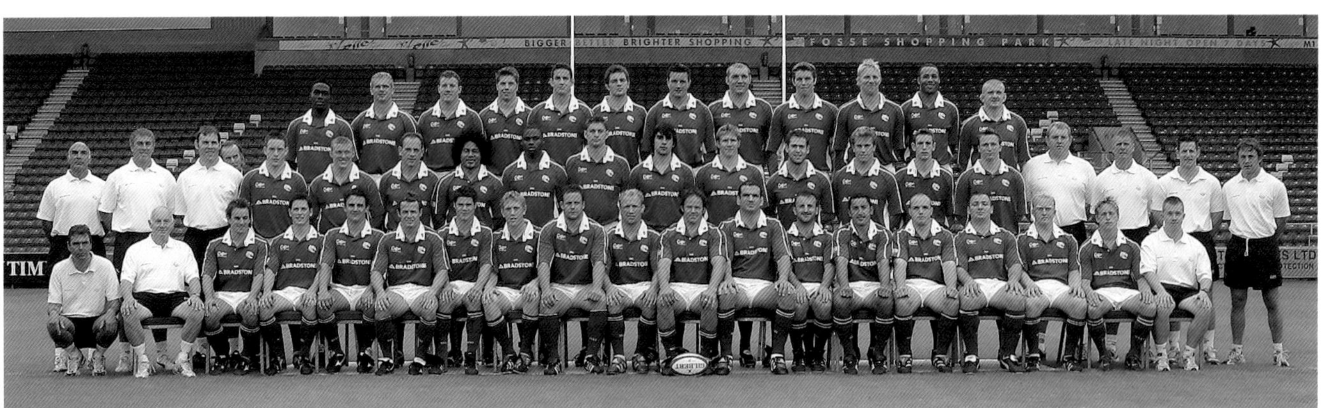

↑ LEICESTER FOOTBALL CLUB 2003/04

Back: Akinyemi, Balding, Stimpson, B.Deacon, W.Johnson, Ryder, Corry, Kay, L.Deacon, Moody, Lloyd, Rowntree.

Middle: Duggan (Fitness & conditioning coach), McGrath (Skills coach), Wells (Forwards coach), Finlay (Doctor), Myring, Friswell, Gelderbloom, F.Tuilagi, Ajuwa, Holtby, Abraham, Smith, Tierney, Skinner, Broadfoot, Glitherow, Richards (Director of rugby), Key (Backs coach), Tombs (Strength & conditioning coach), Hamilton (Video analyst).

Front: Geeson (Physiotherapist), Shephard (Team secretary), Booth, Jones, Ellis, Healey, Hipkiss, Vesty, Nebbett, Back, Kronfeld, M.Johnson (capt), Chuter, Gibson, Holford, Buckland, Cook, Taylor, Brookes (Rehab co-ordinator).

↑ LEICESTER FOOTBALL CLUB 2004/05

Back: Finlay (Doctor), Robertson (Athletic performance coach), Montagu, H.Tuilagi, B.Deacon, W.Johnson, Ryder, Corry, Jim Hamilton, Kay, L.Deacon, Moody, Lloyd, Grewcock (Fitness coach), Shephard (Kit man).

Middle: Jamie Hamilton (Video analyst), Dams (Athletic performance coach), Mack (Director of athletic performance), Holtby, Hipkiss, Thorne, An.Tuilagi, Al. Tuilagi, Murphy, Bemand, Abraham, Smith, Warren, Skinner, Broadfoot, Vesty, Varndell, Hayton (Rehabilitation coach), Brookes (Physiotherapist).

Front: Cockerill (Assistant forwards coach), Wells (Head coach), Hampson, Booth, Wright, Ellis, Healey, Morris, White, Rowntree, M.Johnson (capt), Back, Gibson, Goode, Chuter, Cook, Holford, Buckland, Howard (Backs coach), Key (Assistant backs coach).

20 03/04	
Home Ground: Welford Road	
Director of Rugby: Dean Richards then John Wells (head coach) in February	
Captain: Neil Back then Martin Johnson	

OVERALL RECORD:					T	C	PG	DG	PTS
PLD	W	D	L	Tigers scored:	98	69	80	4	880
33	18	3	12	Opponents scored:	64	43	81	6	596

GM	DATE		VEN	OPPONENTS	RESULT	POS/LGE	TRIES	KICKS	ATT
ZURICH PREMIERSHIP (5TH)						CHAMPIONS: LONDON WASPS			
1	Sep	13	H	**London Irish**	W 29-19	3	Smith 62, H.Tuilagi 76	Stimpson 2c/5p	16029
2		21s	a	Saracens	D 19-19	3	Skinner 80	Stimpson c/4p	7730
3		26f	H	**Newcastle Falcons**	W+ 28-21	4	Pez 40, Holtby 45, Hamilton 58	Stimpson 2c/3p	16815
4	Oct	4	H	**Sale Sharks**	L+ 16-22	5	Vesty 73	Stimpson c/3p	15507
5		11	a	Gloucester	L 3-24	8	-	Stimpson p	11000
6		19s	a	Leeds Tykes	L 18-39t	10	Vesty 20, Skinner 23	Stimpson c/p, Myring p	4073
7		25	H	**Northampton Saints**	L 15-32	10	-	Booth 5p	16815
8	Nov	1	a	Bath Rugby	L 17-31	11	Healey 79	Pez 3p/d	9980
9		8	H	**London Wasps**	W 32-22	10	Richards 12, Baxter 28	Pez 2c/5p, Healey d	15384
11		22	a	Rotherham Titans	W 27-17	9	Pez 40, Lyle 46, Healey 59	Pez 3c/2p	2900
12		29	H	**Bath Rugby**	L+ 12-13	10	-	Pez 4p	16815
15	Dec	20	a	Northampton Saints	L 0-14	10	-	-	12150
16		27	H	**Leeds Tykes**	W 39t-11	9	Healey 30, Rowntree 37, F.Tuilagi 40, Back 44, Baxter 78	Goode 4c/2p	16815
17	Jan	3	H	**Gloucester**	L 18-28	9	Smith 20, Baxter 52	Goode c/2p	16815
22	Feb	6f	a	Sale Sharks	D 3-3	9	-	Goode p	10541
		15s	H	**NEC Harlequins**	PP (6 Nations)	-			
23		21	a	London Irish	W 22-9	9	Gibson 30	Goode c/4p/d	10836
26	Mar	19f	H	**NEC Harlequins**	W 30-21	9	van der Westhuyzen 12/76, Gibson 20	Goode 3c/3p	16815
27		27	a	NEC Harlequins	W+ 23-20	9	Back 27, H.Tuilagi 40, Healey 67	Goode c/2p	7871
28	Apr	4s	a	Newcastle Falcons	D 25-25	9	van der Westhuyzen 30/56, Back 62	Goode 2c/2p	10000
29		16f	H	**Saracens**	W 38t-10	7	Ellis 15, Murphy 40/80, Gibson 80	Goode 3c/4p	16815
30	May	1	H	**Rotherham Titans**	W 75t-13	6	Chuter 2/27/40, Goode 5/21, Back 11, van der Westhuyzen 31, Murphy 39, Corry 48, Gibson 59, Holtby 62	Goode 10c	16815
31		8	a	London Wasps	W 48t-17	5	Smith 29, Healey 34/48, Goode 58/66, Ellis 73	Goode 6c/2p	10000
ZURICH WILDCARD (HEINEKEN CUP QUALIFICATION)									
32	May	15	H	**NEC Harlequins (sf)**	W 43-26	-	van der Westhuyzen 17, Penalty 40, Back 45, Murphy 48, Ellis 52	van der Westhuyzen d, Goode 3c/3p	12004
33		29		Sale Sharks (f)	W 48-27	-	Healey 29, Gibson 40, Lloyd 42/80, Back 50/69	Goode 3c/4p	30000
HEINEKEN CUP						EUROPEAN CHAMPIONS: LONDON WASPS			
13	Dec	6	a	Stade Francais Paris	L 15-26	3	Vesty 39, Pez 55	Pez c/p	11848
14		14s	H	**Newport Gwent Dragons**	W 34t-3	1	Baxter 3, Lloyd 35, Smith 45/75	Pez 4c/2p	15093
18	Jan	11s	a	Ulster	L 0-33t	3	-	-	12300
19		17	H	**Ulster**	W 49t-7	1	Lloyd 25/40, Back 46, van der Westhuyzen 57, M.Johnson 78	Vesty 3c/6p	16815
20		24	a	Newport Gwent Dragons	W+ 26t-20	1	van der Westhuyzen 5/71, H.Tuilagi 26, West 54	Booth 2c, Vesty c	8319
21		30f	H	**Stade Francais Paris**	L 13-26	2	Ellis 12, Smith 25	van der Westhuyzen p	16815
RFU CLUB COMPETITION (POWERGEN CUP)						CUP WINNERS: NEWCASTLE FALCONS			
10	Nov	15	H	**Sale Sharks (6)**	L 28-43 (aet)	P	Baxter 36, Richards 64, Smith 67	Pez c/3p, Booth c	5542
CLUB MATCHES									
24	Mar	3w	H	**Barbarians**	W 69-21		Balding 2, Murphy 6, White 20, Holtby 23/48, van der Westhuyzen 28/70, Goode 32, Gelderbloom 38/57, Wright 74	van der Westhuyzen c, Goode 6c	10022
25		13	a	Northampton Saints	W 18-5		Back 35/56, Holtby 80	Goode p	7500

Neutral Venue: *#33 at Twickenham*

INDIVIDUAL APPEARANCES 2003/04

Name / Game #	1	2	3	4	5	6	7	8	9	10	11	12	13	14	15	16	17	18	19	20	21	22	23	24	25	26	27	28	29	30	31	32	33	Apps	T	Pts
LC (Luke) Abraham	-	-	-	-	-	x	-	-	x	-	-	-	-	-	-	-	-	-	-	-	-	-	-	7	r	-	r	-	-	-	-	-	-	1+2	-	-
NA (Neil) Back E66 L4	-	-	-	-	-	-	-	-	-	-	-	r	7*	7*	7*	7*	7*	7*	7*	7*	7*	7	7	-	7*	7	7	7	7	7	7	7	7	20+1	10	50
AL (Adam) Balding	-	-	8	-	8	-	r	r	8	8	8	8	8	8	8	-	-	-	-	-	-	-	-	8	-	-	-	-	r	r	r	r	<r	10+7	1	5
N (Neil) Baxter	-	-	-	-	-	-	-	>r	14	14	-	-	14	14	14	14	14	14	14	-	-	-	-	r	<r	-	-	-	-	-	-	-	-	9+3	5	25
SE (Steve) Booth	-	-	-	-	-	-	15	15	x	r	-	-	-	-	-	-	-	-	r	14	15	-	-	-	-	r	-	x	-	-	-	-	<r	4+4	-	21
SJ (Stewart) Campbell S17	-	-	-	-	-	-	-	>4	4	4	<4	-	-	-	-	-	-	-	-	-	-	-	-	-	-	-	-	-	-	-	-	-	-	4	-	-
GS (George) Chuter E+	2	2	2	2	2	2	2	2	x	x	x	-	-	-	x	r	r	-	-	-	-	-	-	r	r	r	x	-	2	2	2	2	2	13+5	3	15
PBD (Peter) Clarke	-	-	-	-	-	-	-	-	-	-	-	-	-	-	-	-	-	-	-	-	-	-	-	=r	-	-	-	-	-	-	-	-	-	0+1	-	-
ME (Martin) Corry E29 L3	-	-	-	-	-	-	-	-	-	-	-	6	6	6	-	-	-	-	-	r	r	6	6	4*	4	6	-	6	6	6	6	6	6	14+2	1	5
BR (Brett) Deacon	>4	6	-	6	-	6	4	x	r	-	-	-	-	-	-	-	-	-	-	-	-	-	-	-	-	-	-	-	-	-	-	-	-	5+1	-	-
LP (Louis) Deacon E+	5	5	5	5	5	5	5	5	5	5	5	4	5	r	x	4	r	4	x	5	x	x	5	-	5	5	5	5	r	5	5	5	5	25+3	-	-
HA (Harry) Ellis E+ L+	9	9	9	r	9	9	9	9	9	9	9	-	-	-	-	-	-	-	9	9	9	9	-	-	r	9	9	9	9	9	9	9	9	22+2	4	20
GK (Glenn) Gelderbloom	-	-	-	-	13	-	-	-	-	-	x	r	x	-	12	-	x	r	12	13	13	r	r	13	-	-	r	13	x	-	<r	-	-	7+6	2	10
DPE (Daryl) Gibson NZ19	>12	12	12	12	12	12*	12	12	12	12	12	12	12	12	-	-	-	12	-	-	-	12	12	12	12	12	12	12	12	12	-	12	12	26	5	25
SP (Steven) Glitherow	-	-	-	-	-	-	-	-	-	-	-	-	-	-	-	-	-	-	-	-	-	-	-	=r	-	-	-	-	-	-	-	-	-	0+1	-	-
AJ (Andy) Goode E+	-	-	-	-	-	-	-	-	-	-	-	-	-	-	-	10	10	-	-	-	-	15	15	15	10	15	15	15	15	15	15	15	10	14	5	204
JL (Jim) Hamilton S+	>r	r	4	4	4	■4	-	-	-	-	-	-	-	-	-	-	-	-	-	-	-	-	r	5	r	x	x	-	-	-	-	-	-	5+4	1	5
AS (Austin) Healey E51 L2	r	-	r	9	-	-	10	14	15	15	14	15	9	9	9	9	9	9	11	-	-	-	-	-	11	11	11	r	11	11	11	11	11	22+3	7	38
DJ (Dan) Hipkiss E+	-	-	-	-	r	-	-	x	-	-	-	-	-	-	x	-	-	-	-	-	-	-	14	-	-	-	x	-	-	-	-	-	-	1+1	-	-
MO (Michael) Holford	-	-	x	x	-	>r	-	-	-	-	-	-	-	-	-	-	-	-	-	-	-	-	-	1	-	-	-	-	-	r	x	r	x	1+3	-	-
JN (John) Holtby	11	11	11	11	11	11	11	11	-	-	r	11	11	-	-	-	-	-	-	-	-	-	-	11	14	x	14	11	r	r	-	-	r	14+4	5	25
MO (Martin) Johnson E84 L8	-	-	-	-	-	-	-	-	-	-	-	r	4	4	4	r	4	r	4	4	4	4*	4*	-	-	4*	4*	4*	4*	4*	4*	4*	4*	17+3	1	5
WW (Will) Johnson	6	8	6	8	r	8	8	8	-	-	-	-	-	-	6	6	6	6	6	6	6	r	r	6	6	r	6	r	8	8	8	8	8	22+5	-	-
BJ (Ben) Kay E33 L+	-	-	-	-	-	-	-	-	-	-	-	5	-	5	5	5	5	5	5	-	5	5	-	-	-	-	-	r	5	r	x	r	x	10+3	-	-
JA (Josh) Kronfeld NZ54	7*	7*	7*	7*	7*	-	7*	7*	7*	7*	<7*	-	-	-	-	-	-	-	-	-	-	-	-	-	-	-	-	-	-	-	-	-	-	10	-	-
LD (Leon) Lloyd E5	13	13	13	13	-	14	13	-	-	-	-	-	-	13	13	13	13	11	13	12	12	13	-	-	-	13	13	-	13	13	13	13	13	22	5	25
DJ (Dan) Lyle US45	>8	-	-	-	-	-	-	-	-	6	<6	-	-	-	-	-	-	-	-	-	-	-	-	-	-	-	-	-	-	-	-	-	-	3	1	5
DJ (Dan) Montagu	-	-	-	-	-	-	-	-	-	-	-	-	-	-	-	-	-	-	-	-	-	-	-	>r	-	-	-	-	-	-	-	-	-	0+1	-	-
LW (Lewis) Moody E24 L+	-	-	-	-	-	-	-	-	-	-	-	7	r	-	-	-	-	-	-	-	-	-	-	-	-	-	-	-	-	-	-	-	-	1+1	-	-
DR (Darren) Morris W15 L1	>r	r	1	1	x	-	3	3	3	3	3	r	x	r	x	3	3	3	3	3	3	3	3	-	1	3	3	r	r	1	1	1	1	22+6	-	-
GEA (Geordan) Murphy I22 L+	-	-	-	-	-	-	-	-	-	-	-	-	-	-	-	-	-	-	-	-	-	-	r	14	15	-	-	14	14	14	14	14	15	8+1	5	25
LDS (Luke) Myring	-	-	-	-	>15	15	-	-	-	-	-	-	-	-	-	r	x	r	r	r	<r	-	-	-	-	-	-	-	-	-	-	-	-	2+5	-	3
RJ (Ricky) Nebbett	3	3	3	3	3	3	r	r	x	r	x	-	-	-	-	r	x	r	r	x	x	r	r	r	<r	x	x	-	-	-	-	-	-	6+10	-	-
RE (Ramiro) Pez It16	-	>r	10	10	-	-	-	10	10	10	10	10	10	10	10	-	-	10	x	x	<r	-	-	-	-	-	-	-	-	-	-	-	-	11+2	3	100
AT (Andy) Powell W+	-	-	-	-	-	-	-	-	-	-	-	-	-	-	-	=r	-	-	-	-	-	-	-	-	-	-	-	-	-	-	-	-	-	0+1	-	-
JM (Jimmy) Richards	-	-	x	x	>r	r	r	r	2	2	2	2	2	r	2	2	2	x	r	r	x	r	x	2	-	-	-	r	x	<r	-	-	-	9+10	2	10
CG (Graham) Rowntree E45 L+	1	1	-	-	1	1	1	1	1	1	1	1*	1	1	1	1	1	1	1	1	1	1	1	-	-	1	1	1	1	-	-	-	-	25	1	5
TP (Tom) Ryder S+	-	>4	x	x	r	<r	x	-	-	-	-	-	-	-	-	-	-	-	-	-	-	-	-	-	-	-	-	-	-	-	-	-	-	1+2	-	-
WJ (Will) Skinner	r	r	r	r	r	7	6	6	6	r	r	-	-	r	r	r	r	r	r	x	x	x	-	-	-	-	-	-	-	-	-	-	-	4+13	2	10
OJ (Ollie) Smith E3 L+	14	14	14	14	-	13	14	13	13	13	13	13	13	11	-	12	12	13	-	-	14	14	13	-	13	14	-	-	-	r	12	r	14	23+2	7	35
TRG (Tim) Stimpson E19 L1	15	15	15	15	14	<r	-	-	-	-	-	-	-	-	-	-	-	-	-	-	-	-	-	-	-	-	-	-	-	-	-	-	-	5+1	-	65
TD (Tim) Taylor	-	-	-	-	-	-	-	-	-	-	-	-	-	-	-	-	-	-	-	-	-	-	-	-	<r	-	-	-	-	-	-	-	-	0+1	-	
T (Tom) Tierney I8	-	r	-	-	x	r	-	-	-	r	x	9	x	r	x	-	-	-	-	x	-	x	9	9	9	x	-	-	-	-	-	<r	-	4+5	-	-
F (Freddie) Tuilagi Sa17	-	-	-	-	-	-	r	-	11	11	11	14	r	r	11	11	11	-	-	11	11	11	11	-	-	-	r	x	x	r	r	r	r	11+8	1	5
H (Henry) Tuilagi Sa4	>r	r	r	r	6	r	r	-	r	r	x	x	r	-	r	8	8	8	8	8	8	8	8	-	8	8	8	8	-	-	r	-	-	13+11	3	15
JNB (Jaco) van der Westhuyzen SA9	-	-	-	-	-	-	-	-	-	-	-	-	-	>15	15	15	15	15	10	10	10	10	10	10	-	10	10	10	10	10	10	<10	-	18	11	63
SB (Sam) Vesty E+	10	10	r	r	10	10	x	r	r	r	15	r	15	r	-	r	x	r	15	15	-	-	-	-	-	-	-	-	-	-	-	-	-	8+9	3	41
DE (Dorian) West E21	-	-	-	-	-	-	-	-	-	-	-	r	r	2	-	-	-	2	2	2	2	2	2	-	2	2	2	2	-	-	r	r	<r	11+5	1	5
JM (Julian) White E21 L+	-	-	-	-	-	-	-	-	-	-	-	>3	3	3	3	-	-	-	-	-	-	-	-	3	3	-	-	3	3	3	3	3	3	12	1	5
A (Alex) Wright	-	-	-	-	-	-	-	-	-	-	-	-	-	-	-	-	-	-	-	-	-	-	-	>r	-	-	-	-	-	-	-	-	-	0+1	1	5

The key for how to read the stats is on the last page

20 04 / 05	Home Ground: Welford Road	OVERALL RECORD:					T	C	PG	DG	PTS
	Head Coach: John Wells assisted by Pat Howard and Richard Cockerill	PLD	W	D	L	Tigers scored:	111	78	80	9	978
	Captain: Martin Johnson	33	21	3	9	Opponents scored:	48	35	77	6	559

GM	DATE		VEN	OPPONENTS	RESULT	POS/LGE	TRIES	KICKS	ATT
ZURICH PREMIERSHIP (1ST)						**CHAMPIONS: LONDON WASPS**			
1	Sep	5s	a	Sale Sharks	L+ 19-26	10	Gibson 31	Goode c/2p/2d	6952
2		**11**	**H**	**Leeds Tykes**	W 42t-20	6	M.Johnson 12, Rabeni 40, Ellis 53, Penalty 59, H.Tuilagi 73	Goode 4c/3p	16533
3		19s	a	London Irish	W 39t-22	5	Corry 1, Rabeni 9, B.Deacon 40, Goode 60, Healey 68	Goode 4c/2p	9472
4		**25**	**H**	**Northampton Saints**	W 32t-13	3	Healey 18, Back 40, Ellis 53, Rabeni 67	Broadfoot 3c/2p	16815
5	Oct	2	a	Newcastle Falcons	W 44t-15	2	Murphy 2, Penalty 35, Rabeni 53/78, Back 60, Corry 74	Murphy 2c/p, Broadfoot 2c/p	8609
6		**9**	**H**	**Bath Rugby**	D 16-16	1	Murphy 54, Ellis 80	Murphy p, Broadfoot p	16815
7		16	a	NEC Harlequins	W+ 15-9	1	-	Goode 5p	9954
10	Nov	**6**	**H**	**Gloucester**	W 28-13	2	Rabeni 11, A.Tuilagi 54/74	Goode 2c/3p	16815
11		13	a	Worcester Warriors	W 38t-11	1	Bemand 13, Back 34, Healey 40, Varndell 50/59/63	Goode 4c	8477
12		21s	a	London Wasps	D 17-17	1	Varndell 18, Healey 77	Goode 2c/p	10000
13		**27**	**H**	**Saracens**	W 21-9	1	Varndell 36, Smith 77	Goode c/3p	16815
17	Dec	**27m**	**H**	**Worcester Warriors**	W 50t-7	1	Back 15, Penalty 39, Goode 40, Gibson 40, Murphy 48, Ellis 67, Hipkiss 76	Goode 6c/p	16815
18	Jan	2s	a	Gloucester	W 28-13	1	Lloyd 15, Smith 39, Gibson 50	Goode 2c/2p/d	13000
21		**29**	**H**	**NEC Harlequins**	W 32-17	1	Healey 32, H.Tuilagi 80	Goode 2c/6p	16815
22	Feb	5	a	Bath Rugby	D 6-6	1	-	Goode p, Healey d	10500
23		**19**	**H**	**Newcastle Falcons**	W 83t-10	1	Healey 23, Smith 28/37, Gibson 31, Lloyd 43/76, H.Tuilagi 47, Back 55/68, W.Johnson 63, Murphy 70	Goode 11c/2p	16815
24		26	a	Northampton Saints	L 11-26	1	Lloyd 40	Vesty 2p	12084
25	Mar	**11f**	**H**	**London Irish**	W 15-6	1	A.Tuilagi 38, Abraham 75	Vesty p, Broadfoot c	16815
27		27s	a	Leeds Tykes	L+ 22-23	1	Lloyd 51	Goode c/4p/d	6723
29	Apr	**9**	**H**	**Sale Sharks**	W 45t-15	1	Moody 24, Lloyd 30, Goode 33, M.Johnson 39, A.Tuilagi 50, Varndell 57	Goode 6c/d	16815
30		17s	a	Saracens	L+ 17-19	1	Chuter 22	Goode 4p	16812
32		**30**	**H**	**London Wasps**	W 45t-10	2	Ellis 23, Gibson 32, Murphy 43, Back 59, Hipkiss 67	Goode 4c/3p/d	16815
33	May	14		London Wasps (f)	L 14-39	1	Bemand 77	Goode 3p	60762
HEINEKEN CUP						**EUROPEAN CHAMPIONS: TOULOUSE**			
8	Oct	**23**	**H**	**Ghial Calvisano**	W 37t-6	1	Ellis 13/52, Rabeni 44, Moody 58/62	Goode 3c/2p	16815
9		30	a	Biarritz Olympique	L 8-23	2	Rabeni 48	Goode p	9000
14	Dec	5s	a	London Wasps	W+ 37-31	1	Moody 2, Murphy 12, Corry 18	Goode 2c/5p/d	10000
15		**12s**	**H**	**London Wasps**	W 35-27	3	Ellis 5, Chuter 38, Lloyd 40	Goode c/6p	16815
19	Jan	**9s**	**H**	**Biarritz Olympique**	L+ 17-21	3	A.Tuilagi 75, Ellis 80	Goode 2c/p	16815
20		15	a	Ghial Calvisano	W 62t-10	2	Ellis 13, A.Tuilagi 16/37, Chuter 33/47, Murphy 40/62/68, Goode 70, White 80	Goode 6c	2500
28	Apr	2	a	Leinster (qf)	W 29-13	-	Smith 38, Gibson 58	Goode 2c/4p/d	48500
31		24s		Toulouse (sf)	L 19-27	-	Varndell 80	Goode c/4p	31883
RFU CLUB COMPETITION (POWERGEN CUP)						**CUP WINNERS: LEEDS TYKES**			
16	Dec	**18**	**H**	**Gloucester (6)**	L 13-20	P	Varndell 36	Broadfoot c/p, Vesty p	9902
CLUB MATCH									
26	Mar	**18f**	**H**	**Barbarians**	W 42-19		Howard 4, W.Johnson 58, H.Tuilagi 60, A.Tuilagi 63/79/80, Vesty 79	Warren 2c/p	10198

Neutral Venues: *#31 at Walkers Stadium, #33 at Twickenham*

INDIVIDUAL APPEARANCES 2004/05

Name / Game #	1	2	3	4	5	6	7	8	9	10	11	12	13	14	15	16	17	18	19	20	21	22	23	24	25	26	27	28	29	30	31	32	33	Apps	T	Pts
LC (Luke) Abraham	r	-	x	-	-	-	-	-	-	-	-	-	-	-	-	-	-	-	x	r	x	x	-	r	r	-	-	-	-	-	-	-	-	0+4	1	5
NA (Neil) Back E66 L4	-	7	7	7	7	7	7	x	7	r	7	7	7	7	7	x	7	7	7	r	7	7	7	7	7	-	7	7	x	7	7	7	<7	26+2	7	35
SK (Scott) Bemand	-	>r	r	-	x	x	9	x	x	9	9	9	9	x	r	9	9	x	x	r	x	9	9	9	9	9*	r	r	9	r	r	r	r	13+10	2	10
PR (Ross) Broadfoot	x	>r	-	10	10	10	-	-	-	r	r	x	x	-	-	10	-	-	-	-	-	-	-	-	r	-	-	-	-	x	-	-	-	4+4	-	29
JDH (James) Buckland	x	>r	r	r	x	x	x	2	r	2	2	2	r	-	-	-	r	r	r	r	-	-	r	r	2	r	r	x	r	r	x	r	r	5+17	-	-
GS (George) Chuter E+	2	2	2	2	2	2	2	-	-	-	-	-	-	2	2	2	2	2	2	2	2	2	2	2	r	-	2	2	2	2	2	2	2	25+1	4	20
R (Richard) Cockerill E27	-	-	-	-	-	-	-	r	2	r	r	-	<2	x	x	-	-	-	-	-	-	-	-	-	-	-	-	-	-	-	-	-	-	2+3	-	-
PK (Peter) Cook	-	-	-	x	-	-	-	-	-	-	-	-	-	-	-	-	-	-	-	-	-	-	-	-	-	<r	-	-	-	-	-	-	-	0+1	-	-
MJ (Matt) Cornwell	-	-	-	-	>r	r	r	r	r	-	r	13	-	-	-	-	r	r	-	r	-	-	-	-	-	-	-	-	-	13	-	-	-	2+9	-	-
ME (Martin) Corry E37 L3	8	8	8	-	8	8	6	-	-	8	-	-	-	8	8	-	8	8	-	-	-	-	8	-	-	-	8	8	8	■8	-	-	8	17	3	15
BR (Brett) Deacon	6	6	6	6	6	6	x	6	r	r	6	-	6	-	-	6	r	-	-	-	8	r	-	r	r	6	-	-	-	-	-	r	-	12+7	1	5
LP (Louis) Deacon E+	r	5	5	r	5	x	-	-	-	-	5	5	5	5	x	x	5	x	5	8	4	5	5	-	5	5	5	5	5	5	5	8	6	22+2	-	-
AW (Alex) Dodge	-	-	-	-	-	-	-	-	-	-	-	x	-	-	-	-	-	-	-	-	-	-	-	-	x	>r	-	-	-	-	-	-	-	0+1	-	-
HA (Harry) Ellis E7 L+	9	9	9	9	9	9	r	9	9	-	-	-	-	9	9	-	r	9	9	9	9	-	r	-	-	-	9	9	r	9	9	9	9	20+4	10	50
DPE (Daryl) Gibson NZ19	12	12	12	12	-	-	-	12	12	12	12	12	12	12	12	-	12	12	12	12	r	12	12	12	12	-	12	12	12	12	12	12	12	27+1	6	30
AJ (Andy) Goode E2	10	10	10	-	-	-	10	10	10	10	10	10	10	10	10	-	10	10	10	10	10	10	10	-	-	-	10	10	10	10	10	10	10	26	4	382
JL (Jim) Hamilton S+	-	-	-	-	-	-	-	-	-	-	r	x	x	-	-	4	-	-	-	-	-	-	-	5	x	4	-	-	-	-	-	-	-	3+1	-	-
AS (Austin) Healey E51 L2	11	11	11	11	-	-	-	11	-	-	11	11	11	11	11	-	-	-	11	r	11	11	11	11	10	r	11	r	-	-	11	11	r	19+4	6	33
DJ (Dan) Hipkiss E+	-	-	-	-	-	r	-	-	-	14	-	-	13	-	-	r	r	-	-	-	-	-	-	r	14	13	-	-	-	-	-	r	-	4+5	2	10
MO (Michael) Holford	-	-	-	-	-	-	-	-	-	-	1	1	1	-	-	1	-	x	-	-	-	1	-	1	1	1	r	-	-	-	-	r	-	8+2	-	-
JN (John) Holtby	14	-	-	r	14	14	11	14	14	-	-	-	-	-	-	-	-	-	-	-	14	14	-	<14	-	-	-	-	-	-	-	-	-	9+1	-	-
PW (Pat) Howard A20	-	-	-	-	-	-	-	-	-	-	-	-	-	-	-	-	-	-	-	-	-	-	-	-	-	12	-	-	-	-	-	-	-	1	1	5
MO (Martin) Johnson E84 L8	4*	4*	4*	4*	4*	4*	4*	4*	4*	4*	4*	4*	4*	4*	4*	-	4*	4*	4*	4*	-	4*	4*	4*	4*	r	4*	4*	4*	4*	4*	4*	<4*	30+1	2	10
WW (Will) Johnson	-	-	-	8	r	r	8	8	8	-	r	6	r	x	x	8	6	r	8	6	6	8	r	6	8	8	6	x	6	6	r	r	r	17+9	2	10
BJ (Ben) Kay E40 L+	5	-	r	5	r	5	5	5	5	5	-	-	-	x	5	5*	r	5	r	5	5	-	-	-	-	-	-	-	-	-	r	5	5	14+5	-	-
LD (Leon) Lloyd E5	13	-	-	-	-	-	-	-	-	-	-	-	r	14	14	13	-	13	13	-	13	x	14	13	13	14	14	11	13	-	14	-	11	16+1	7	35
DJ (Dan) Montagu	-	-	-	-	-	-	-	-	-	-	-	r	-	-	-	-	-	-	-	-	-	x	-	-	-	7	-	-	-	-	-	-	-	1+1	-	-
LW (Lewis) Moody E31 L+	-	-	-	-	-	-	x	7	6	7	-	-	-	6	6	7	-	6	6	7	-	-	r	-	-	-	r	6	7	r	6	-	r	12+4	4	20
DR (Darren) Morris W18 L1	3	r	x	-	r	r	1	3	r	1	3	3	3	x	r	3	r	1	1	3	3	3	3	3	3	-	1	3	3	x	r	1	1	21+7	-	-
GEA (Geordan) Murphy I31 L+	15	15	15	15	15	15	15	-	15	-	-	-	-	15	15	-	15	15	15	14	15	-	r	-	-	-	15	14	15	14	15	14	14	22+1	9	55
CG (Colin) Noon	-	-	-	-	-	-	-	-	-	-	=r	-	-	-	-	-	-	-	-	-	-	-	-	-	-	-	-	-	-	-	-	-	-	0+1	-	-
RSR (Seru) Rabeni Fi17 PI3	>r	14	14	14	12	12	12	13	13	13	13	-	-	-	-	-	14	-	-	-	-	-	r	15	-	-	-	-	-	-	-	-	-	12+2	8	40
J (John) Rawson	-	-	-	-	-	-	-	-	-	-	-	-	-	-	-	-	-	-	-	-	-	>r	r	r	x	3	-	x	r	-	-	-	-	1+4	-	-
CG (Graham) Rowntree E52 L+	1	1	1	1	1	1	r	1	1	r	-	-	-	1	1	x	1	-	r	1	1*	-	1	-	-	-	-	1	1	1	1	-	r	18+4	-	-
WJ (Will) Skinner	7	x	-	-	-	-	-	-	-	-	r	x	-	-	-	-	-	-	-	-	-	-	-	-	-	-	-	-	-	-	-	-	-	1+1	-	-
OJ (Ollie) Smith E5 L+	r	13	13	13	13	13	13	-	-	-	-	-	r	13	13	12	13	14	14	13	12	13	13	-	-	-	13	13	r	-	13	13	13	21+3	5	25
E (Ephraim) Taukafa T12	-	-	-	-	-	-	-	-	-	-	-	>r	-	-	-	r	-	-	-	-	x	x	-	-	-	2	-	-	-	-	-	-	-	1+2	-	-
AT (Alesana) Tuilagi Sa3 PI+	-	>r	r	r	r	-	-	r	r	r	-	-	-	r	x	14	-	-	r	11	x	x	-	r	11	11	r	x	11	11	-	r	r	6+13	10	50
F (Freddie) Tuilagi Sa17	-	-	-	-	-	-	-	-	-	-	-	-	-	-	-	-	-	-	-	-	-	-	-	-	-	r	-	-	-	-	-	-	-	0+1	-	-
H (Henry) Tuilagi Sa4	-	r	r	r	-	-	-	r	r	6	8	8	8	-	-	-	-	-	-	-	r	6	6	8	6	r	r	x	r	r	8	6	-	10+10	4	20
TW (Tom) Varndell E+	-	-	-	-	-	-	x	-	-	>11	14	14	14	-	-	11	-	11	-	-	-	-	-	-	-	-	-	-	14	r	r	-	-	7+2	8	40
SB (Sam) Vesty E+	-	-	-	-	11	11	14	15	11	15	15	15	15	x	x	15	11	r	x	15	-	15	15	10	15	10	x	15	r	15	x	15	15	21+2	1	17
R (Roger) Warren Sa2	-	-	-	>r	-	-	-	-	-	-	-	-	-	-	-	r	-	-	-	-	-	-	-	x	-	<15	-	-	-	-	-	-	-	1+2	-	7
JJ (Joe) Wheeler	-	-	-	-	-	-	-	-	-	-	-	-	-	-	-	-	-	-	-	-	-	-	-	-	-	=r	-	-	-	-	-	-	-	0+1	-	-
JM (Julian) White E28 L+	r	3	3	3	3	3	3	r	3	3	-	-	-	3	3	-	3	3	3	r	r	-	-	-	-	-	3	-	-	3	3	3	3	18+4	1	5
A (Alex) Wright	-	-	-	-	-	-	-	-	-	x	-	-	-	-	-	x	-	-	-	-	-	-	-	-	-	r	-	-	-	-	-	-	-	0+1	-	-

The key for how to read the stats is on the last page

CHAPTER 33

Howard's Way

2005/2006

Leicester's fortunes, of course, were not related to those of the Lions. Sales of season tickets soared past 13,000 during the summer until the club had to stop selling to preserve space for visitors during European competition; and that was another reason for supporters to salivate, since Leicester's Heineken Cup pool in the new season included Stade Français, Clermont Auvergne (as a rebranded Montferrand were now known) and the Ospreys, the Welsh regional combination of Swansea and Neath.

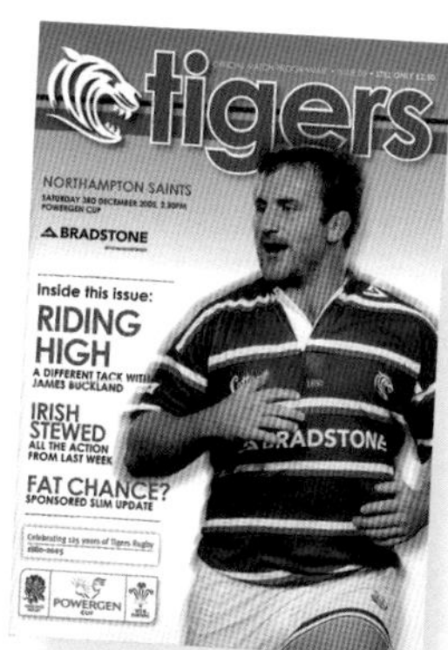

To the satisfaction of many, a £20 million redevelopment plan was agreed for Welford Road and designed to begin in 2006. "We have to make sure that, when we've finished it, we have a 21st-century stadium not a 20th-century stadium," Peter Tom said, the aim being to lift capacity from 16,815 to around 25,000. Further detail, later in the year, confirmed that the Next Stand would be replaced and extra land bought on the old Granby Halls site and in January 2006, Leicester agreed a contract with the city council to buy Welford Road and adjoining land. Councillor Roger Blackmore, the council leader, said: "Having such a high-profile club in the city brings many benefits" but for Tigers, it was wonderful confirmation of the ground move which had been made 114 years earlier.

For the fifth successive season too Tom, who was awarded the CBE in the new year honours, was able to announce a pre-tax profit, this time of £1 million on a turnover of £12.65 million. There was a change to the board later in the season, when David Jones retired, but he was replaced by Sir Digby Jones, director general of the Confederation of British Industry. Nor was that all. The club laid out £360,000 on an all-weather pitch at Oval Park, bringing to more than £2 million the money spent on the training facility.

↓ New head coach, Pat Howard, casts his eye over a training session at Oval Park.

Only Martin Corry of the Lions contingent started the opening match, a 32-0 win over Northampton. Another Lion, Lewis Moody, made his return in an A league game with Leeds and was promptly suspended, by Leicester for four weeks and by an RFU disciplinary panel for six, for punching Jordan Crane, the opposition No 8 (who, nothing daunted, joined Leicester the following summer). Tom Varndell's form was raising interest in England circles: the young wing scored tries against Northampton, Wasps and Bath in the opening sequence of matches, his pace and height posing difficulties for opponents.

Corry was named to lead England into their autumn series against Australia, New Zealand and Samoa and he was joined in the national squad by Moody, Harry Ellis, Andy Goode and Ollie Smith, Louis Deacon being added later. Graham Rowntree made against Newcastle his 200th league start, only the second player after Martin Johnson, to achieve that mark, but it was not an auspicious occasion: Rowntree himself damaged his neck, Julian White and Andy Perry, the Newcastle lock, were sent off for fighting and Leicester were fortunate to take a 16-16 draw since TV re-runs suggested a Goode conversion had gone wide.

As White started an eight-week suspension, Moody returned full of vim and vigour. He was in time for the opening round of the Heineken Cup, when Leicester plastered Clermont Auvergne all over Welford Road, winning 57-23 with six tries, all of them converted by Goode who also kicked five penalties for a match haul of 32 points. A week later, though, came a drab 12-6 defeat in Paris by Stade Français and Moody suffered gouging by an unidentified assailant.

The first weekend of club v country action saw Corry and Moody in the back row of an England side that beat Australia 26-16 while Leicester, despite 16 players being unavailable, beat Gloucester 25-20 with a bright new talent in their back row. Tom Croft's debut came just after his twentieth birthday, the 6ft 5in blind-side flanker, fresh out of Oakham School, winning praise from Richard Cockerill: "We think there's a big future for him," Cockerill said.

A week later, the silver lining had gone when Tigers went down at Sale and England, despite a try by Corry, lost 23-19 to New Zealand. Yet the international window added to the club's laurels when Ireland recalled Leo Cullen to join Geordan Murphy in their squad to play Romania and Varndell, the Premiership's leading try scorer with six, was added to the England squad for the game against Samoa at Twickenham even though he had made only 17 senior starts. England started with four Tigers - Ellis, Deacon, Moody and Corry, and Varndell made his bow as a replacement in the final quarter.

It was an eventful weekend. First came a four-try, 35-3 win over London Irish for the club. Second came Varndell's try-scoring debut for England in a 40-3 win which is better remembered for the red cards shown to two other Tigers, Moody and

Alesana Tuilagi. Samoa had two Tuilagis in their squad, Anitele'a being on the bench, but it was the older of the brothers who tangled with Moody after a mid-air tackle on Mark Cueto, the England wing. Moody steamed in to help his team-mate and the resulting imbroglio earned him another suspension, this time for nine weeks, while Tuilagi was given a six-week ban.

It did not help Leicester's overall disciplinary record, the worst in the Premiership since there had been two red cards and ten yellows. But if the collective confidence needed massaging, wins in the Powergen Cup over Northampton and the Heineken Cup over the Ospreys did so. The 30-12 European win over the Welsh region might have been anticipated at Welford Road, and there were 24 unanswered points in the second half though not before the Ospreys had posed all kinds of problems before the interval.

→ Martin Corry in his first season as Tigers' skipper points the way during the Powergen Cup semi-final against Wasps at the Millennium Stadium 4.3.2006.

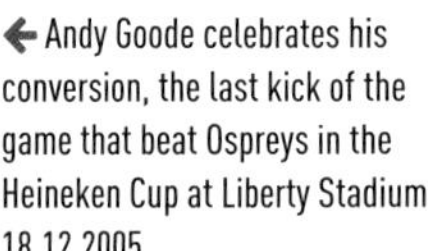

← Andy Goode celebrates his conversion, the last kick of the game that beat Ospreys in the Heineken Cup at Liberty Stadium 18.12.2005.

The return match in Swansea, a week later, was completely different as Leicester pulled off what amounted to a smash-and-grab raid to win 17-15. Trailing by 12 points, they were reduced to 13 men when first Ollie Smith and then Louis Deacon were sent to the sin bin; but the Ospreys could not make a five-metre scrum count, they failed to kick their goals and, in the fifth minute of time added on, Varndell was freed to make a 50-metre run. Support arrived and Dan Hipkiss scored the try which, with Goode's conversion, snatched the result.

The fractious nature of the match was compounded by a touchline argument between Cockerill and Mike Cuddy, the Ospreys managing director, and two Ospreys, Gavin Henson and Ian Evans, were subsequently cited and banned. The Heineken Cup season progressed to the last eight, if not smoothly. Though Ellis recovered from damaged knee ligaments, Leicester started Austin Healey at scrum-half against their old foes, Stade Français. On their own pitch, with ten minutes remaining, Tigers were ten points adrift and Goode, their goalkicker, misfiring which was ironic because, a week earlier against London Irish, he had racked up 23 points and become the fifth player (after Jonny Wilkinson, Tim Stimpson, Paul Grayson and Barry Everitt) to pass 1,000 points in the Premiership.

In those final ten minutes, however, Leicester scored 17 points, the second of two tries going again to Hipkiss and won 29-22 amid feverish excitement. The quarter-final place was secured with a 40-27 win at Clermont Auvergne; Varndell scored four tries with a fifth going to Hipkiss but, on a ground where Clermont had lost only once in two years, the forwards were outstanding.

With matters going so well, on and off the field, Corry was confirmed as England captain for the six nations championship and Moody returned from his second suspension in the 27-27 draw against Sale. It was enough for him to be included in the England squad to meet Wales along with Corry, Ellis, Goode and White, now approaching 33, while four more Tigers, Varndell, Deacon, Smith and Sam Vesty, were in the squad to play Italy in an A international. Varndell duly scored four more tries in a 57-13 win at Colleferro but equally significant news out of Italy was the signing from Calvisano of Martin Castrogiovanni, born in Argentina but already with 29 caps at tight-head prop for Italy under his belt at the age of 24.

Moody was among England's try-scorers in the 47-13 win over Wales and Goode, capped twice as a replacement the previous season, made his first start against Ireland, becoming with Ellis the first all-Leicester half-back combination to play for England since Les Cusworth and Nick Youngs in 1984. Goode also kicked 14 of England's 24 points but Murphy, at full-back on the winning side, was the happier individual.

Leicester's season had become a struggle. When the six nations ended they were nine points behind the Premiership pacemakers, Sale, and had been knocked out of the Powergen Cup, beaten 22-17 by Wasps despite scoring three tries to one. They had already decided to move their Heineken Cup quarter-final with Bath to the Walkers Stadium,

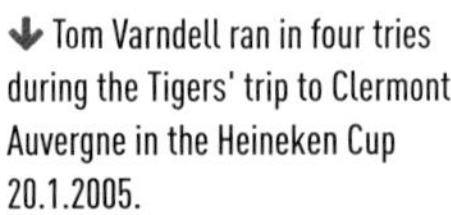

↓ Tom Varndell ran in four tries during the Tigers' trip to Clermont Auvergne in the Heineken Cup 20.1.2005.

and secured a capacity crowd of 32,000. They were fortified by the 19-12 Premiership win at Bath's Recreation Ground a week earlier which left Bath only one place off the bottom of the table but the visitors reached the last four in Europe by beating Tigers 15-12 in a quite awful tactical display from the home side.

Four penalties by Goode were overtaken by five from Chris Malone, the Bath fly-half, on a day when a fluky wind made goalkicking difficult. But in the final ten minutes, Bath lost both their props to the sin bin and still Leicester could not clinch victory; the departure of a second prop, Filisi Taufa'ao following David Flatman to the bin, forced uncontested scrums but had Leicester played wide rather than trying to plough their way through areas where Bath had most defenders, they would surely have won.

↓ Alesana Tuilagi in a typically robust run in the Heineken Cup quarter-final clash with Bath at Walkers Stadium, 1.4.2006.

For all the disappointment, 12,769 spectators watched Leicester secure a second successive A league title against Harlequins, an occasion when Dean Richards, director of rugby at the London club, made his first official appearance at Welford Road since his resignation. Richards made off with Skinner, the Leicester flanker, at the season's end while his old friend and colleague, John Wells, was promoted to coach England's forwards after a wholesale clearout of the England staff. Leicester, meanwhile, had secured the services of Pat Howard as coach for another season after persuading him not to return to Australia.

Success against Saracens clinched a Premiership play-off and a 32-3 win over Bristol ensured home advantage against London Irish, a match that marked the last competitive appearance at Welford Road of Rowntree after 16 years in Leicester colours, though the old warrior was far from finished. He had a Premiership final still to play and, after that, took his place on tour with England alongside Moody, Kay, White, Deacon, Chuter, Varndell, Goode and Scott Bemand, the scrum-half who had broken his leg in pre-season. In addition Geordan Murphy and Leo Cullen toured with Ireland in Australasia and Sam Vesty, the club's player of the year, and James Buckland, the hooker, were included in England's Churchill Cup squad.

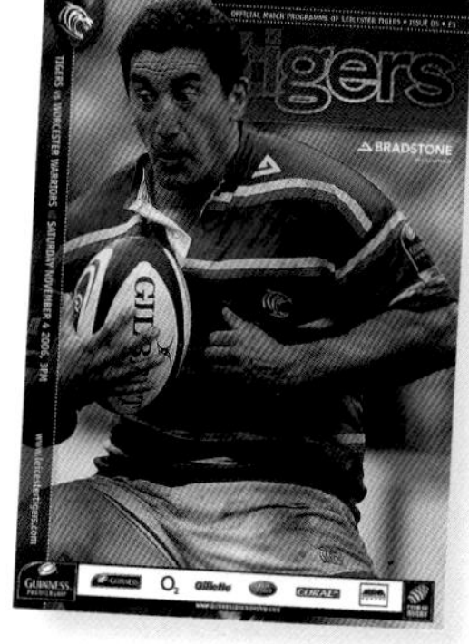

The match with London Irish was a straightforward 40-8 win, made more memorable by the half-time appearance, 14 months after his devastating injury, of Matt Hampson. The young prop had received the Professional Rugby Players' Association 'Blyth Spirit' award a couple of days earlier, testimony to the strength of character which had carried him through so many dark days.

Had Leicester played at Twickenham with the strength and direction they showed in the semi-final, they might have concluded the season with the Premiership title. Instead, having been the only English club in contention for three trophies at the beginning of March, they ended with none. Sale Sharks, driven forward by their half-backs, Charlie Hodgson and Richard Wigglesworth, romped home to a 45-20 win.

Leicester's team was: Geordan Murphy; Alesana Tuilagi (Sam Vesty, 47), Ollie Smith (Leon Lloyd, 67), Daryl Gibson, Tom Varndell; Andy Goode, Harry Ellis (Austin Healey, 52); Graham Rowntree (Michael Holford, 62), George Chuter (James Buckland, 66), Julian White, Leo Cullen (Jim Hamilton, 56), Ben Kay, Lewis Moody, Martin Corry (captain), Shane Jennings (Louis Deacon, 51).

Just like the previous year, two of the club's legends were departing, Rowntree and Healey, the impish scrum-half, fly-half, wing, full-back, call him what you will. "I realised today that the clutch had gone, I could only find third gear," Healey, plagued by a recurrent knee injury, said. Mark Cueto scored Sale's first try and though, Moody responded five minutes later, the ball stayed close to the powerful Sale forwards and Leicester were frozen out.

Before the interval Magnus Lund and Oriol Ripol had scored further Sale tries and, with Hodgson adding a conversion and two penalties, a 13-point gap had opened up. Hodgson kicked three more penalties and a dropped goal before Leicester's second try, by Hamilton, and though Goode added a conversion and penalty to his two successful first-half kicks, Sale grabbed the last try through Chris Mayor when the ball went down between Healey and Vesty. Hodgson ended with 23 points from six penalties, a dropped goal and a conversion with Valentin Courrent adding the final conversion.

2006/2007

The summer was not spent in contemplation. Leicester's leading players toured on the far side of the world and the club's leading administrators headed for the Far East. Martin Johnson and Rory Underwood were called up to accompany Peter Wheeler and Sir Digby Jones on a goodwill mission to China to explore whether Leicester's playing and commercial expertise could help the development of the game and, perhaps, produce a business return from the world's fastest growing economy.

Leicester had been supportive of Japan's bid the previous year to host the 2011 World Cup, the city of Leicester is twinned with Chongqing, the huge metropolis in south-west China, so there was ample reason for the exploratory trip of which the high point was the signing in Beijing of a formal agreement for a strategic partnership with the China Rugby Football Association.

"China is a market for the long-haul game," Jones said and compared Leicester with football's Manchester United as an "exportable" brand. "If we could position Leicester, in ten or fifteen years'

← George Chuter scores his first try for England in his second international against Australia in Melbourne 17.6.2006.

time, where Manchester United are now, that would be fabulous but there are enormous social benefits for the young. We need to take the brand overseas in a socially-inclusive way. Leicester have a great sponsorship following already but it's my job to get more corporations on board who don't know Leicester."

The presence at coaching seminars of Johnson and Underwood, demonstrations of non-contact tag rugby for small children and the ambition of China's rugby administrators left a positive impression at the end of a week which took the delegation from Beijing to Shanghai. "It's a completely different culture but we have talked to guys who have the spirit of the game," Johnson said. "We have tried to find out about the Chinese and what they need. We've tried to tell them that it's not just about international success but it's a good, healthy pastime for children, with other values."

While the missionary work was under way, Leicester's international players were heavily involved elsewhere. Varndell made his first start for England against Australia in Sydney alongside Rowntree, White, Deacon and Moody; in due course they were joined by Goode and, winning his first cap, George Chuter but England lost 34-3. For the second international in Melbourne, England started with the club's entire front row of Rowntree, Chuter and White as well as Varndell, Goode and Kay; there were tries for Varndell and, with a dummying flourish, Chuter, but England lost again by 43-18.

Back home, Welford Road played host for the first time to international tennis when the Lumbers 125 veterans event brought such names as Pat Cash and Ilie Nastase to Leicester to raise funds for the Matt Hampson Trust. Marcos Ayerza, a little-known prop from Argentina who played as an amateur for the Cardinal Newman club in Buenos Aires, arrived and Jordan Crane was signed from Leeds passing, on the way out, another back-row forward in Will Johnson en route to Coventry after 16 years with Leicester.

For all the disappointments of 2005/06, the club could announce pre-tax profits of £1.1 million on a turnover which had increased by nearly 20 per cent. "In the last three years, the company's turnover has increased by 50 per cent and profits have tripled," Peter Tom said. "This is an outstanding performance by a sports club and unparalleled in domestic club rugby in the UK." Acknowledging the contribution of a great player to this situation, Leicester subsequently awarded life membership to Martin Johnson, an honour accorded in more recent times to Jerry Day, John Allen and David Matthews.

Eight players were included in England's elite squad of forty (Corry, Chuter, Deacon, Kay, Moody, White, Ellis and Goode) and two more, Varndell and Crane, in the academy squad. Croft served notice of intent with his contribution to a Leicester VII which reached the final of the Middlesex sevens before losing to Wasps, then promptly damaged an ankle coming off the bench for his Premiership debut against Sale in the re-run of the final with which the new season began.

Castrogiovanni also made his debut in a marvellous match to which the season as a whole did not quite live up. Leicester beat Sale 35-23 but then conceded forty points at Bath and their poor disciplinary record returned to haunt them with yellow cards for Castrogiovanni, Deacon and Hipkiss. There were first starts for Crane and Ayerza in the 27-27 draw with Gloucester and Rowntree - now helping Cockerill coach the forwards - predicted a bright future for the young Argentinian prop.

↓ Martin Castrogiovanni was the Premiership's Player of the Season in his debut year for Tigers.

As the Heineken Cup approached, Leicester consulted their strong Irish contingent, having been drawn in the same European pool as Munster, winners of the cup against Biarritz the previous May. Not only was there Geordan Murphy but his namesakes Johne and Frank, Paul Burke, the much-travelled former Ireland fly-half, Shane Jennings, Leo Cullen, Gavin Hickie, a hooker, and Ian Humphreys, a fly-half loaned to Leeds. Indeed Burke and Frank Murphy had been members of Munster's cup-winning squad.

Memories of the 2002 final informed the build-up and Ronan O'Gara put the final knife into Leicester on a rain-swept afternoon: a penalty try and conversion by Goode, who subsequently added a penalty, had given Leicester a 19-18 lead with six minutes remaining but as the clock ticked down, Jennings was penalised in a tackle on O'Gara. The fly-half admitted afterwards that he had knocked on in the tackle but Jennings

↑ Geordan Murphy grabs the opening score in the momentous victory at Thomond Park 20.1.2007.

complained about the decision and Nigel Owens, the referee, duly marched Leicester back ten metres. Munster, who had scored two first-half tries, were still 51 metres from Leicester's posts but O'Gara, who had played quite beautifully in the conditions, landed the goal and the Irish province won 21-19.

By a twist of fate, a week later Leicester found themselves playing Cardiff Blues at the Millennium Stadium where, four years earlier, Neil Back's illicit handling at a scrum helped deny Munster the Heineken Cup. Now Louis Deacon denied the Blues: with Leicester leading 18-17 Cardiff, reduced to 14 men for the last half-hour after their prop, Gary Powell, was sent off, forced a lineout from which they mauled to within striking distance of the Leicester line. Deacon, lying on the wrong side of the maul, appeared to poke the ball away with his foot, the match officials missed it, Deacon escaped a yellow card and Leicester won 21-17.

Six players were named in England's autumn squad with Corry resuming as captain while Scotland called up Jim Hamilton, the Swindon-born lock who had played for England's under-21 side but whose father came from Glasgow. In making his debut from the bench against Romania, Hamilton became Scotland's 1,000th international. Ayerza was summoned to tour with Argentina whose director of rugby was now the former Leicester fly-half, Les Cusworth.

It was a fateful month for England though an instructive one for Leicester. A former Tiger, Perry Freshwater, the prop now with Perpignan and capped three times as a replacement the previous season, made his first start (against Argentina) while Chuter, White, Kay, Moody and Corry were in the pack that lost the opening international 41-20 to New Zealand. It was England's sixth loss in succession but the seventh - to an Argentina side including Ayerza that recorded a first ever win at Twickenham by 25-18 - cost Andy Robinson his job as England head coach.

The beleaguered Robinson saw his team beat South Africa by two points, ending a run of seven successive defeats, then lose to the Springboks a week later. While the focus was on the autumn internationals, Leicester managed three wins out of four and the young side dispatched to Northampton for an EDF Energy Cup pool match saw debuts for Ollie Dodge (son of Paul) and Tom Youngs (son of Nick). But Henry Tuilagi, the No 8 and the biggest of the brotherhood, broke his arm, having just recovered from a broken leg, and missed the back-to-back Heineken Cup wins against Bourgoin. The second of these, at Welford Road, earned Tigers a 57-3 victory in which Moody scored the first hat-trick of his career, the first try coming after a mere 29 seconds.

Three Premiership games in 11 days saw Leicester return to the top of the table, their victims during the Christmas period including Bristol, the leaders. But looming on the horizon was the closing round of the Heineken Cup, the must-win game at that graveyard for visiting teams, Thomond Park in Limerick, against Munster. Ian Humphreys was retained at fly-half for only his second Heineken game (his older brother, David, had guided Ulster to a famous European Cup crown in 1999) and helped write yet another resounding chapter for the club.

"As a coach, this is the best win I have been involved with," Pat Howard said after watching Leicester win 13-6, Munster's first European loss at the ground in 27 games over a 12-year period. In wet conditions, Leicester executed their game plan brilliantly, Humphreys kicked well out of hand, but above all the pack would not be moved and Ollie Smith, a late inclusion for the injured Daryl Gibson, scored the try that clinched the match. In the first half, Humphreys and O'Gara traded penalties before Leicester put down a scrum on Munster's 22; Ellis ran to a big short side, Castrogiovanni and Moody supported before Geordan Murphy provided the finishing touch.

A two point-advantage at the interval, after O'Gara's second penalty, did not seem enough but Leicester now had the wind at their backs and Munster chose not to give O'Gara a penalty kick at goal which might have given them the lead. Humphreys led the decisive strike: first the fly-half who, when defending, was banished to the wing so that the big Fijian, Seru Rabeni, could defend closer to the set-piece, broke from his own half. Then, from a scrum, he drew Tomas O'Leary off his wing before sending Smith galloping to the line for Leicester's second try.

The win, embellished by the remarkable generosity of Munster fans who raised €11,000 for the Matt Hampson Trust, gave Tigers a home quarter-final against Stade Français. Further forward planning was in evidence with the recruitment from the French club, Albi, of the former England under-21 prop, Boris Stankovich, who had been born in New Zealand; so had the rather better known Aaron Mauger, the All Blacks centre who agreed a two-and-a-half-year contract.

It all left Tigers in good heart as the home unions stripped them of players for the six nations. England's new coach, Brian Ashton, preferred Phil Vickery, the Wasps prop, to Corry as captain but the No 8 remained a vital squad member and, with Ellis, Deacon and Chuter, started against Scotland with Moody and White on the bench. Hamilton was less fortunate; picked to make his first start for Scotland, the lock suffered a shoulder injury and missed the entire championship.

↓ The scoreboard tells the story.

↑ Graham Rowntree skippered the Tigers in his 398th and final game against the touring Argentinians at Welford Road, 11.2.2007.

It was another mixed season for England, three wins and two losses. Back at Welford Road, Rowntree finally confirmed that his playing days were over after his 398th appearance, against an Argentinian XV. Newcomers in view, as well as Mauger and Stankovich, included the Wellington flanker, Ben Herring, Ayoola Erinle, the Wasps centre, and Richard Blaze, Worcester's lock.

A new coach too: knowing that Howard could not be persuaded to stay another year, Leicester reviewed the worldwide situation and came up with Marcelo Loffreda, who did so much to make Argentina the surprise package of the 2007 World Cup. Loffreda, a former Pumas centre, agreed to join Leicester once the World Cup was over, leaving Richard Cockerill in a caretaker role for the opening months of the 2007/08 season.

It was good to settle this business because Leicester were struggling to overcome the absence of their international contingent. It hurt when Northampton won 10-9 at Welford Road, the first home Premiership loss since 2004, and Leicester did well to hang on against Bath in a match when they finished with 12 men on the field; Alesana and Henry Tuilagi were both sent to the sin bin near the end and Scott Bemand was carried off, with every replacement used. But Gibson scored the try that gave Tigers their 29-25 win and, spurred on, Leicester reached the EDF Energy Cup final by beating Sale 29-19.

That left the club well placed in all three competitions as they prepared for the Heineken Cup quarter-final against Stade Français which Leicester won 21-20. On a blustery day, neither team could break clear of the other: Rabeni scored an early try but a try by Juan Martin Hernandez and the goalkicking of David Skrela, the Stade fly-half, made the half-time score 11-11. Turning to play into the wind, Leicester were six points adrift with ten minutes remaining and had to cast caution aside: Alesana Tuilagi rampaged into midfield, Kay and Hipkiss lent a hand and Varndell was set free 30 metres from the line. Crucially the wing was able to score under the posts, leaving Goode to apply the coup de grace.

The only cloud was the three-week suspension awarded to Ayerza for punching Remy Martin, the Stade flanker, which cost the prop a place in the EDF Cup final against the Ospreys and the Heineken Cup semi-final against the Scarlets, a period when Leicester faced four games in 14 days. In between the European quarter- and semi-finals, Leicester ensured a Premiership play-off by beating Sale 26-25, thanks to a last-minute penalty kicked by Vesty and carried off their first trophy for five years by beating the Ospreys at Twickenham.

It was a pressurised period for Howard as he juggled his resources. His starting XV for Twickenham, the Sunday date falling only six days before the Heineken Cup semi-final, was arguably six short of the optimum but of the three competitions, this was the least prestigious. Leicester's side was: Sam Vesty; Tom Varndell, Dan Hipkiss, Daryl Gibson, Alesana Tuilagi; Paul Burke (Andy Goode, 41), Harry Ellis (Frank Murphy, 41-51); Martin Castrogiovanni (Alex Moreno, 73), George Chuter, Julian White, Leo Cullen (Louis Deacon, 65), Ben Kay, Tom Croft (Brett Deacon, 51), Martin Corry (captain), Shane Jennings.

"It doesn't hurt to have the monkey off your back," Howard said after a thrilling 41-35 win. At half-time, indeed, the monkey was strolling in the afternoon sunshine with Leicester leading by 19 points. Two tries by Shane Williams, the diminutive Wales wing, changed the situation completely and brought the Welsh region to within three points, Leicester vainly chasing shadows as Williams and his colleagues threw the ball wide at every opportunity.

The Ospreys took an early lead through two penalties from James Hook but in the space of 17 first-half minutes, Leicester ran in tries through Varndell, Croft, Kay and Tuilagi with Hipkiss demonstrating why, in Howard's view, he was the form centre in England. Burke converted each try before being forced off with a damaged knee at half-time and all the Ospreys could muster in reply was Hook's third penalty. But Nikki Walker, the Scotland wing, created a position from which Lee Byrne scored, Williams added his brace and Hook converted twice and with Goode adding only a penalty, suddenly there were only three points between the teams.

There was no panic in Leicester ranks. Hipkiss broke to give Varndell a second try, Goode converted and added a penalty, and though Walker scored a fourth try for the Ospreys which Hook converted, the Tigers forwards were able to retain possession for long enough to deny the Welsh. It was a huge relief for the club to be able to reward their followers in a crowd of more than 43,000 but it cost them the services of Castrogiovanni, the Italy prop's strained hamstring keeping him out of the European semi-final.

↓ Tigers take the Anglo-Welsh cup for the first time defeating Ospreys at Twickenham, 15.4.2007.

➔ Alesana Tuilagi, Geordan Murphy and Seru Rabeni with the spoils following the Premiership final victory over Gloucester 12.05.2007.

With Ayerza suspended, Leicester fielded a front row of Alex Moreno, George Chuter and Julian White against the Scarlets at the unloved Walkers Stadium. But they were able to bring Lewis Moody and Geordan Murphy back, refreshed, and Goode started at fly-half against the in-form Stephen Jones who, three years earlier, had turned down an offer to join Leicester. This time there were no mistakes: Leicester won handsomely, by 33-17, to reach their fourth Heineken Cup final and Goode scored 23 of those points with the first try, three conversions and four penalties.

It was not all plain sailing. Leicester took a 16-3 lead but tries either side of half-time by Mark Jones and Matthew Rees, both converted by Stephen Jones, gave the Scarlets a 17-16 lead. Goode promptly chipped over a flat defence for Shane Jennings to score and another try, three minutes from time, from Louis Deacon made sure there would be no tomorrow for the Welsh region. Instead, with Wasps beating Northampton 30-13, it set up the first (and so far the only) all-English final for which some Leicester supporters camped out for 13 hours to ensure a ticket.

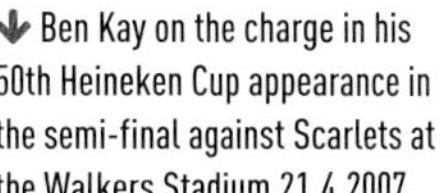

➔ Ben Kay on the charge in his 50th Heineken Cup appearance in the semi-final against Scarlets at the Walkers Stadium 21.4.2007.

In the month before the final, Leicester needed to secure a home tie in the Premiership play-offs but sent what was close to a second XV to Bristol where they lost 30-13. That game did, though, mark the arrival (in the 79th minute) of Ben Youngs when he replaced Frank Murphy at scrum-half. Youngs, aged 17, became the club's youngest Premiership player and, like his older brother, Tom, carved out a sparkling career.

The home semi-final was secured with a 40-26 win over Wasps which left the London club with no rugby before the Heineken Cup final. "Today's result will have no bearing on that match," Howard said with prophetic insight. Bristol were duly dispatched at Welford Road leaving the Premiership final to be played off against another West Country club, Gloucester, but Harry Ellis damaged ligaments in his left knee against Bristol and missed not only the two finals but, ultimately, the World Cup.

With Scott Bemand also out of action, Leicester had minimal resources at scrum-half with Frank Murphy now the senior pro. The younger Youngs, though he was on the bench for the Premiership final, was not registered for Europe but Murphy was given an armchair ride on 12 May at Twickenham by a pack that squeezed the life out of Gloucester. Leicester's side was: Geordan Murphy; Seru Rabeni (Tom Varndell, 62), Dan Hipkiss, Ollie Smith (Sam Vesty, 68), Alesana Tuilagi; Andy Goode, Frank Murphy (Ben Youngs, 67); Marcos Ayerza, George Chuter (James Buckland, 70), Julian White (Alex Moreno, 67), Louis Deacon (Leo Cullen, 56), Ben Kay, Lewis Moody, Martin Corry (captain), Shane Jennings (Brett Deacon, 70).

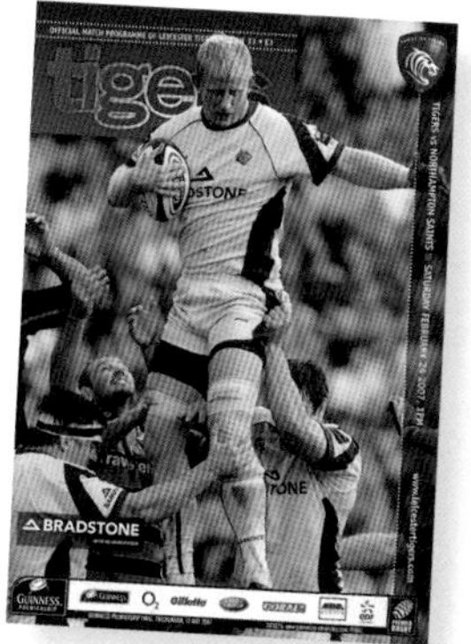

Victory by 44-16 gave Leicester their seventh league title, surpassing Bath's six, and Gloucester could not live with the muscular approach of the Tigers. The two wings, Tuilagi and Rabeni, each weighed in at over 17st and when released into midfield, caused mayhem. There were seven Leicester tries in total and 22 points in each half, against which Gloucester could offer only three penalties from Willie Walker, who also converted an interception try from Ryan Lamb.

Frank Murphy led the try fest, crawling over the line beneath a heap of bodies, and by the interval Tuilagi and Corry had crossed too. So great was Leicester's superiority that, in the second half, they were able to introduce replacements at will, among them Youngs who became the youngest player ever to appear in a Twickenham final. Tuilagi scored a second try, Goode, Jennings and Moody followed and if Goode's goalkicking had been as consistent as normal - he landed only three conversions and a penalty - the Tigers would have passed fifty.

Though they had twice completed doubles (Premiership and Europe) in 2001 and 2002, Leicester had never done the domestic double of league and cup before. If left them chomping at the bit for a treble on 20 May, in the joust with Wasps for the Heineken Cup. They made only one change from the Premiership final, replacing Ollie Smith with Daryl Gibson for the New Zealander's last appearance before he moved to Glasgow. The teams in the final were:

Leicester: Geordan Murphy (Sam Vesty, 77); Seru Rabeni, Dan Hipkiss, Daryl Gibson (Matt Smith, 51), Alesana Tuilagi; Andy Goode (Ian Humphreys, 63), Frank Murphy; Marcos Ayerza (Alejandro Moreno, 74), George Chuter (James Buckland, 78), Julian White, Louis Deacon (Leo Cullen, 46-51), Ben Kay (Cullen, 54), Lewis Moody (Brett Deacon, 78), Martin Corry (captain), Shane Jennings.
London Wasps: Danny Cipriani; Paul Sackey, Fraser Waters (Dominic Waldouck, 77), Josh Lewsey, Tom Voyce; Alex King (Mark van Gisbergen, 74), Eoin Reddan (Mark McMillan, 78); Tom French, Raphael Ibañez (Joe Ward, 77), Phil Vickery (Peter Bracken, 75), Simon Shaw (Dan Leo, 55; Ward, 64-70), Tom Palmer, Joe Worsley, Lawrence Dallaglio (captain; James Haskell, 51), Tom Rees.
Referee: Alun Lewis (Ireland).

A third trophy proved a step too far in front of a world record attendance for a club game of 81,076. Wasps, coached by the wily Ian McGeechan, won 25-9; they had examined every point of Leicester strength and found a way to neutralise it. More, they turned that strength against the Tigers by scoring their two first-half tries direct from line-outs and then punishing every piece of indiscipline as Leicester, growing more frustrated with each second, contributed to their own demise.

The young Wasps loose-head prop, Tom French, who had never played in the Premiership, stood up to Julian White in the scrums. Leicester were turned over very early in the game in what was to be the tale of the match and Alex King, the Wasps fly-half returning after a seven-week absence, kicked the first of five goals for offside. Goode levelled matters before Wasps pulled off a masterstroke, waving their own players infield at a line-out which created a yawning gap at the front for Eoin Reddan to streak through and score.

Goode kicked a second penalty but then Wasps repeated the trick: Raphael Ibañez threw low to Simon Shaw at the front of a line-out and took the instant return to make 15 metres to the corner for a second try. Goode recovered three points with his third penalty just before the interval but, though they dominated territory and possession in the second half, Leicester could not find a way through. Instead King kicked three more penalties and a dropped goal and the Leicester dream evaporated.

Yet it had been a mighty season-long effort and Pat Howard was named the Premiership's director of rugby for 2006/07, with Castrogiovanni the player of the season. "I am immensely proud of the guys for what they have achieved," Howard, who worked wonders in rotating his squad so as to keep his players as fresh as possible, said. "We didn't play well enough, we deserved to lose, that's life. But when I sat down with Craig White [the conditioning coach] 14 months ago, I said the treble was possible and I am proud of how the players had a go at achieving that."

Leicester said farewell to the Australian with sadness: "I'm pretty sure there isn't a job he couldn't do," Peter Wheeler said, not knowing then that Howard would be appointed general manager of the Australian Rugby Union's high-performance unit and subsequently move into cricket. "When Pat agreed to come, one of his promises was that he would leave us in better shape for his successor. I'd say we are in better shape."

↓ As a parting shot Pat Howard picks up the Premiership Director of Rugby of the Season award.

← LEICESTER FOOTBALL CLUB 2005/06
Back: Lloyd, L.Deacon, Nimmo, Jim Hamilton, Cullen, Croft, Kay.
4th row: O.Smith, Dodge, Varndell, Montagu, Johnson, B.Deacon, Moody, Rabeni, Murphy.
3rd row: Shephard (Kit man), Jamie Hamilton (Video analyst), Broadfoot, Buckland, Jennings, Young, Abraham, Moreno, Cornwell, Vesty, Taukafa, Finlay (Doctor), Hollis (First team manager).
2nd row: Stanton (Head physiotherapist), Limna (Academy physiotherapist), Brookes (Senior physiotherapist), Hayton (Rehabilitation coach), Holford, Humphreys, Bemand, Skinner, Hipkiss, Rawson, Dams (Athletic performance coach), Richardson (Athletic performance coach), Mack (Performance & medical director).
Front: Cockerill (Forwards coach), Howard (Head coach), Morris, Chuter, Healey, Rowntree, Corry (capt), Gibson (Vice-capt), White, Goode, Ellis, Key (Assistant backs coach), Back (Technical director).

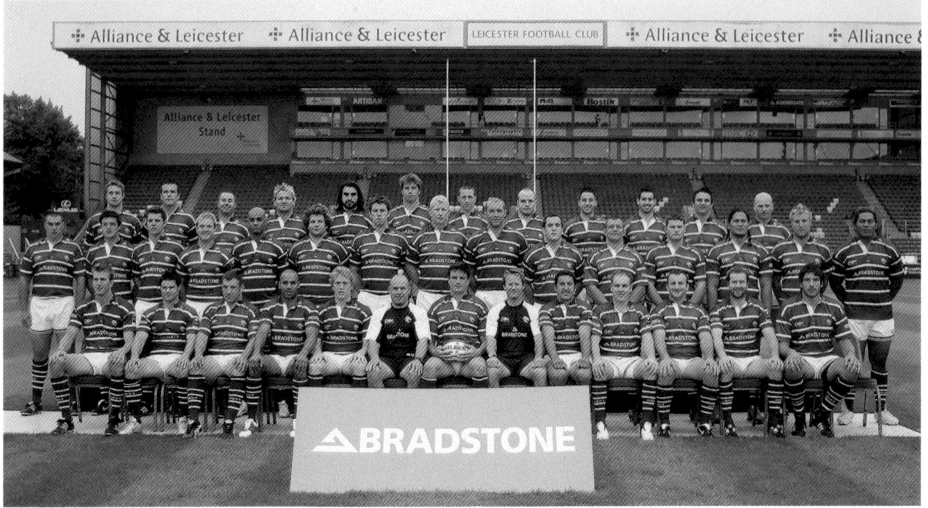

← LEICESTER FOOTBALL CLUB 2006/07
Back: J.Murphy, Jennings, Hickie, Buckland, Abraham, B.Deacon, Bemand, Holford, Humphreys, F.Murphy, Ellis, Burke.
Middle: Parr, M.Smith, Pienaar, Cornwell, Varndell, Castrogiovanni, L.Deacon, Cullen, Kay, Ayerza, Moreno, Young, A.Tuilagi, Crane, H.Tuilagi.
Front: Croft, Hipkiss, White, Lloyd, Vesty, Cockerill (Forwards coach), Corry (capt), Howard (Head coach), Gibson, Goode, Chuter, G.Murphy, Hamilton.

20 05/06	
Home Ground: Welford Road except #30 at Walkers Stadium	
Head Coach: Pat Howard assisted by Neil Back and Richard Cockerill	
Captain: Martin Corry	

OVERALL RECORD:					T	C	PG	DG	PTS
PLD	W	D	L	Tigers scored:	97	69	95	2	914
36	22	3	11	Opponents scored:	53	39	116	11	724

GM	DATE		VEN	OPPONENTS	RESULT	POS/LGE	TRIES	KICKS	ATT
GUINNESS PREMIERSHIP (2ND)						**CHAMPIONS: SALE SHARKS**			
1	Sep	**3**	**H**	**Northampton Saints**	W 32t-0	1	Hamilton 15, Holford 33, Al.Tuilagi 36, Hipkiss 44, Varndell 80	Goode 2c/p	16815
2		10	a	London Wasps	D 29-29	2	Varndell 9, Ellis 36	Goode 2c/5p	8459
3		**17**	**H**	**Bath Rugby**	W 40t-26	1	Varndell 1/63, Murphy 25, Jennings 80	Goode 4c/4p	16815
4		25s	a	Leeds Tykes	W 28-20	1	Lloyd 14, Cornwell 40, L.Deacon 80	Broadfoot 2c/3p	7143
7	Oct	**14f**	**H**	**Newcastle Falcons**	D 16-16	2	Hamilton 49	Goode c/3p	16815
10	Nov	4f	a	Worcester Warriors	L+ 11-15	4	Skinner 16	Broadfoot p, Goode p	9776
11		**12**	**H**	**Gloucester Rugby**	W+ 25-20	3	Holford 8, Varndell 20/46	Goode 2c/2p	16815
12		18f	a	Sale Sharks	L 16-24	4	Cornwell 74	Broadfoot 3p, Goode c	10641
13		**25f**	**H**	**London Irish**	W 35t-3	3	Healey 8, Kay 28, Chuter 49, Holford 79	Goode 3c/3p	16815
17	Dec	27tu	a	Bristol Rugby	L 3-15	4	-	Broadfoot p	11916
18	Jan	**2m**	**H**	**Saracens**	W+ 34-27	3	Penalty 23, Morris 27, Varndell 72	Goode 2c/5p	16815
19		8s	a	London Irish	W+ 28-25	3	Vesty 27	Goode c/7p	11096
22		**28**	**H**	**Sale Sharks**	D 27-27	3	-	Goode 8p/d	16815
23	Feb	10f	a	Gloucester Rugby	L 16-34	4	Johnson 69, Taukafa 78	Humphreys 2p	12500
24		**17f**	**H**	**Worcester Warriors**	W+ 28-22	4	O.Smith 10, Al.Tuilagi 46, Cornwell 58	Goode 2c/3p	16815
25		24f	a	Newcastle Falcons	L 16-24	5	H.Tuilagi 71	Humphreys 3p, Vesty c	10200
27	Mar	**10f**	**H**	**Leeds Tykes**	W+ 26t-23	4	Buckland 8, Vesty 16, O.Smith 23, Skinner 80	Vesty 3c	16815
29		25	a	Bath Rugby	W+ 19-12	3	Lloyd 29	Goode c/4p	10600
	Apr	**8s**	**H**	**London Wasps**	PP (cup)	-			
31		14f	a	Northampton Saints	W+ 24-19	4	Varndell 3/63, Al.Tuilagi 35	Vesty 2c/p, Goode c	13493
32		**22**	**H**	**London Wasps**	W+ 20-19	3	Varndell 2/25/33	Goode c/p	16815
33		28f	a	Saracens	W+ 13-12	2	Varndell 31	Goode c/2p	9828
34	May	**6**	**H**	**Bristol Rugby**	W 32t-3	2	Chuter 28/46, Varndell 33, Al.Tuilagi 51, Holford 59	Murphy p, Goode c, Vesty c	16815
35		**14s**	**H**	**London Irish (sf)**	W 40-8	-	Al.Tuilagi 15, Ellis 32, Lloyd 60/73, Murphy 67	Goode 3c/3p	14069
36		27		Sale Sharks (f)	L 20-45	-	Moody 9, Hamilton 74	Goode 2c/2p	58000
HEINEKEN CUP						**EUROPEAN CHAMPIONS: MUNSTER**			
8	Oct	**22**	**H**	**ASM Clermont Auvergne**	W 57t-23	1	Ellis 23, Lloyd 35, Varndell 44, Goode 50, Chuter 62, Murphy 70	Goode 6c/5p	16815
9		29	a	Stade Francais Paris	L+ 6-12	1	-	Goode 2p	19700
15	Dec	**11s**	**H**	**Ospreys**	W 30t-12	1	B.Deacon 54, Ellis 61, Chuter 72, Healey 80	Goode 2c/2p	16815
16		18s	a	Ospreys	W+ 17-15	1	Lloyd 64, Hipkiss 80	Goode 2c/p	11448
20	Jan	**15s**	**H**	**Stade Francais Paris**	W+ 29-22	1	L.Deacon 74, Hipkiss 79	Goode 2c/5p	16815
21		20f	a	ASM Clermont Auvergne	W 40t-27	1	Varndell 25/33/45/70, Hipkiss 38	Goode 2c/2p/d, Broadfoot c	10000
30	Apr	**1**	**H**	**Bath Rugby (qf)**	L 12-15	-	-	Goode 4p	32500
ANGLO-WELSH CUP (POWERGEN CUP)						**CUP WINNERS: LONDON WASPS**			
5	Sep	30f	a	Newport Gwent Dragons	L 15-24	1	Jennings 29, Lloyd 80	Goode c/p	6327
6	Oct	**8**	**H**	**Worcester Warriors**	W 42t-16	3	Chuter 7, Lloyd 24, Healey 53, Ellis 55, Varndell 73	Humphreys 2c/2p, Goode 2c/p	8642
14	Dec	**3**	**H**	**Northampton Saints**	W 29t-16	1	Lloyd 40/70, Kay 45, Jennings 55	Goode 3c/p	11072
26	Mar	4		London Wasps (sf)	L 17-22	-	Varndell 33, Lloyd 47, Hipkiss 80	Goode c	50811
CLUB MATCH									
28	Mar	**17f**	**H**	**Barbarians**	L 42-52		Al.Tuilagi 11/49, Bemand 22, Wilson 32/65, F.Tuilagi 67	Humphreys 6c	8304

***Neutral Venues:** #26 at Millennium Stadium - Cardiff, #36 at Twickenham*

INDIVIDUAL APPEARANCES 2005/06

Name / Game #	1	2	3	4	5	6	7	8	9	10	11	12	13	14	15	16	17	18	19	20	21	22	23	24	25	26	27	28	29	30	31	32	33	34	35	36	Apps	T	Pts
LC (Luke) Abraham	r	r	-	-	-	-	6	-	-	-	-	-	r	r	r	r	7	r	r	r	7	r	7	-	6	-	6	-	-	r	-	-	-	-	-	-	6+11	-	-
SK (Scott) Bemand	-	-	-	-	-	-	-	-	-	-	-	-	-	-	-	-	r	-	-	-	-	-	r	r	r	-	9	9*	-	-	9	9	-	9	-	-	5+4	1	5
PMJ (Phil) Boulton	-	-	-	-	-	-	-	-	-	-	-	-	-	-	-	-	-	-	-	-	-	-	-	-	-	-	-	=r	-	-	-	-	-	-	-	-	0+1	-	-
PR (Ross) Broadfoot	r	r	x	10	-	-	-	-	x	10	x	10	r	-	r	-	10	x	x	x	r	-	r	-	-	-	x	<15	-	-	-	-	-	-	-	-	5+6	-	30
JDH (James) Buckland	-	-	-	-	-	r	x	r	x	x	x	r	r	r	r	x	2	x	r	x	r	r	2	-	2	x	2	-	2	r	r	2	r	r	r	r	6+15	1	5
GS (George) Chuter E+	2	2	2	r	2	2	2	2	2	2	2	2	2	2	2	2	-	2	2	2	2	2	-	2	-	2	-	-	-	2	2	r	2	2	2	2	28+2	6	30
ND (Neil) Cole	-	-	-	-	-	-	-	-	-	x	>r	x	r	r	-	-	<9	x	-	-	-	-	-	-	-	-	-	-	-	-	-	-	-	-	-	-	1+3	-	-
MJ (Matt) Cornwell	-	r	-	12	15	-	-	-	-	-	-	r	12	12	12	12	-	-	-	-	-	x	-	13	-	x	-	-	r	x	-	r	-	-	-	-	7+4	3	15
ME (Martin) Corry E45 L7	8*	8*	8*	-	-	8*	8*	8*	8*	-	-	-	-	8*	8*	8*	-	8*	8*	8*	8*	-	-	8*	-	6*	-	-	8*	8*	8*	8*	8*	r	8*	8*	23+1	-	-
TR (Tom) Croft E+ L+	-	-	-	-	-	-	-	-	-	x	>6	6	x	-	-	-	-	-	-	-	-	-	-	-	-	-	-	-	-	-	-	-	-	-	-	-	2	-	-
LFM (Leo) Cullen I18	>5	4	-	r	r	5	r	5	5	r	4	4	-	-	x	4	4	r	r	r	r	4*	-	5	r	r	4	-	x	x	4	4	4	5	4	4	18+10	-	-
BR (Brett) Deacon	-	6	-	6	6	r	-	-	-	6	8	8	8	6	6	6	6	-	6	-	6	6	6	-	-	-	-	8	-	-	-	-	-	-	-	-	16+1	1	5
LP (Louis) Deacon E1	-	r	4	4*	4*	r	4	-	-	-	-	-	-	4	4	r	5*	4	4	4	4	r	4	r	4	4	8	-	5	4	6	6	6	8	-	r	21+6	2	10
AW (Alex) Dodge	-	-	-	-	-	-	-	-	-	-	-	-	-	-	-	-	-	-	-	-	-	-	r	x	r	-	x	<11	-	-	-	-	-	-	-	-	1+2	-	-
HA (Harry) Ellis E13 L+	9	9	9	x	9	r	9	9	9	-	-	-	-	9	9	9	-	-	r	r	9	9	-	9	-	r	-	-	9	9	-	-	9	r	9	9	18+5	5	25
DPE (Daryl) Gibson NZ19	12	12	12	-	12	-	-	12	12	-	-	-	-	-	-	-	12	-	-	-	-	-	-	-	-	-	-	-	-	-	r	r	12	12	12	12	11+2	-	-
AJ (Andy) Goode E5	10	10	10	-	10	r	10	10	10	r	10	r	10	10	10	10	-	10	10	10	10	10	-	10	-	10	-	-	10	10	r	15	10	r	10	10	25+5	1	347
JL (Jim) Hamilton S+	4	-	r	5	5	-	5	4	4	4	r	r	4	r	-	-	-	-	-	-	-	-	r	4	-	-	r	4	-	-	r	r	r	4	r	r	11+11	3	15
AS (Austin) Healey E51 L2	r	r	11	9	r	9	r	r	r	9*	9*	9*	9*	-	r	r	-	9	9	9	r	r	9*	-	9*	9	10*	-	r	r	10	10	r	10*	r	<r	17+15	3	15
DJ (Dan) Hipkiss E+	13	-	-	r	-	13	12	-	r	12	12	12	13	r	r	r	14	12	12	12	12	-	-	-	-	12	12	-	12	12	13	-	-	-	-	-	17+5	5	25
MO (Michael) Holford	1	1	r	3	x	r	-	r	x	1	1	r	r	1	r	-	r	-	-	x	-	-	r	1	r	r	3	-	x	x	r	1	r	r	r	r	9+15	4	20
PW (Pat) Howard A20	-	-	-	-	-	-	-	-	-	-	-	-	-	-	-	-	-	-	-	-	-	-	-	-	-	-	-	<12	-	-	-	-	-	-	-	-	1	-	-
IW (Ian) Humphreys	-	-	-	-	>r	10	-	-	-	-	-	-	-	-	-	-	r	-	-	-	-	-	10	x	10	-	-	10	-	-	-	-	-	-	-	-	4+2	-	37
S (Shane) Jennings I+	>7	7	7	r	7	7	7	7	7	-	7	-	7	7	7	7	-	7	7	7	-	-	-	7	7	r	7	-	6	7	r	7	r	6	6	6	25+4	3	15
WW (Will) Johnson	6	-	6	8	8	-	-	r	r	8	r	r	6	-	-	-	8	6	-	6	r	8	8	x	8	-	-	-	-	-	-	-	-	r	<r	-	12+7	1	5
BJ (Ben) Kay E40 L2	r	5	5	-	-	4	-	r	r	5	5	5	5	5	5	5	r	5	5	5	5	5	5	-	5	5	5	r	4	5	5	5	5	-	5	5	26+5	2	10
LD (Leon) Lloyd E5	r	13	13	11	r	14	14	14	-	13	14	14	14	14	14	14	-	14	14	14	-	13	13	-	13	13	14	-	11	14	-	r	r	13	r	r	24+6	11	55
DJ (Dan) Montagu	-	-	-	-	-	-	-	-	-	-	-	-	-	-	-	-	-	-	-	-	-	-	-	-	-	-	-	<5	-	-	-	-	-	-	-	-	1	-	-
LW (Lewis) Moody E39 L3	-	-	-	-	-	-	-	6	6	-	-	-	-	-	-	-	-	-	-	-	-	7	-	6	-	7	-	-	7	6	7	-	7	7	7	7	12	1	5
AC (Alejandro) Moreno Ar/It7	>3	3	1	-	-	-	-	1	1	3	r	1	1	3	1	3	-	-	-	-	-	-	-	-	-	-	-	-	-	-	-	-	-	-	-	-	11+1	-	-
DR (Darren) Morris W18 L1	-	-	-	-	-	-	r	3	3	r	3	3	3	-	3	1	1	r	x	-	r	r	3	r	3	-	r	3	-	-	-	-	1	<3	-	-	13+7	1	5
GEA (Geordan) Murphy I39 L2	-	15	15	15	-	15	15	15	15	-	-	-	-	11	11	15	-	11	11	11	11	-	-	15	-	14	-	-	14	11	15	-	15	15	15	15	23	3	18
RG (Ryan) Owen	-	-	-	-	-	-	-	-	-	-	-	-	-	-	-	-	-	-	-	-	-	-	-	-	-	-	-	=r	-	-	-	-	-	-	-	-	0+1	-	-
BJM (Ben) Pienaar	-	-	-	-	-	-	-	-	-	-	-	-	-	-	-	-	-	-	-	-	-	-	-	-	-	-	-	>r	-	-	-	-	-	-	-	-	0+1	-	-
RSR (Seru) Rabeni Fi17 PI3	-	-	-	-	-	-	-	-	-	-	-	-	r	r	-	-	13	-	-	-	-	14	-	-	-	-	-	-	-	-	-	-	-	-	-	-	2+2	-	-
J (John) Rawson	-	-	-	-	-	-	-	-	-	-	-	-	-	-	-	-	-	-	-	-	-	-	-	-	-	-	-	<1	-	-	-	-	-	-	-	-	1	-	-
CG (Graham) Rowntree E52 L3	-	-	-	1	1	1	1	-	-	-	-	-	-	-	-	r	-	1	1	1	1	1	1	-	1	1	1	-	1	1	1	-	-	1	1	1	19+1	-	-
WJ (Will) Skinner	-	-	x	7	r	6	x	-	-	7	-	7	-	-	-	-	r	-	-	-	-	-	r	-	r	-	r	7	r	-	-	<r	-	-	-	-	5+7	2	10
MW (Matt) Smith	-	-	-	-	-	-	-	-	-	-	-	-	-	-	-	-	-	-	-	-	-	-	-	-	-	-	-	>13	-	-	-	-	-	-	-	-	1	-	-
OJ (Ollie) Smith E5 L1	-	-	r	13	13	-	13	13	13	r	13	13	11	13	13	13	r	13	13	13	13	12	12	12	12	-	13	-	13	13	r	13	13	-	13	13	26+4	2	10
E (Ephraim) Taukafa T16	r	x	r	2	r	-	-	-	-	-	-	-	-	-	-	-	r	-	-	-	-	-	r	r	r	-	x	<2	x	-	-	-	-	-	-	-	2+7	1	5
AT (Alesana) Tuilagi Sa10 PI+	14	14	r	14	14	11	r	r	14	14	-	-	-	-	-	-	-	-	-	-	r	r	14	14	14	x	11	14	x	r	14	14	14	14	14	14	18+6	7	35
AF (Andy) Tuilagi Sa6	-	-	-	-	-	-	-	-	-	-	=r	-	-	-	-	-	-	-	-	-	-	-	-	-	-	-	-	-	-	-	-	-	-	-	-	-	0+1	-	-
F (Freddie) Tuilagi Sa17	-	-	-	-	-	-	-	-	-	-	-	-	-	-	-	-	-	-	-	-	-	-	-	-	-	-	-	<r	-	-	-	-	-	-	-	-	0+1	1	5
H (Henry) Tuilagi Sa4	-	-	-	-	-	-	-	-	-	-	-	-	-	-	-	-	-	-	-	-	-	-	-	-	r	8	r	-	-	-	-	-	-	-	-	-	1+2	1	5
TW (Tom) Varndell E1	11	11	14	r	11	r	11	11	11	11	11	11	-	-	-	11	11	r	r	r	14	11	11	11	11	11	-	-	-	-	11	11	11	11	11	11	24+5	21	105
SB (Sam) Vesty E+	15	-	-	-	-	12	r	r	-	15	15	15	15	15	15	r	15	15	15	15	15	15	15	-	15	15	15	-	15	15	12	12	r	r	r	r	22+7	2	27
JM (Julian) White E33 L4	r	r	3	-	3	3	■3	-	-	-	-	-	-	-	-	-	3	3	3	3	3	3	-	3	-	3	-	-	3	3	3	3	3	-	3	3	19+2	-	-
CJ (Chris) Whitehead	-	-	-	-	-	-	-	-	-	-	-	-	-	-	-	-	-	-	-	-	-	-	-	-	-	-	-	=r	-	-	-	-	-	-	-	-	0+1	-	-
BA (Brent) Wilson	-	-	-	-	-	-	-	-	-	-	-	-	-	-	-	-	-	-	-	-	-	-	-	-	-	-	-	=6	-	-	-	-	-	-	-	-	1	2	10
A (Alex) Wright	-	-	-	-	-	-	-	-	-	-	-	-	-	-	-	-	-	-	-	-	-	-	-	-	-	-	-	<r	-	-	-	-	-	-	-	-	0+1	-	-
DJW (Dave) Young	-	-	-	x	-	-	-	-	-	-	-	-	-	>r	-	-	-	-	-	-	-	-	-	-	-	-	-	-	-	-	-	x	-	-	-	-	0+1	-	-

The key for how to read the stats is on the last page

20 06/07	Home Ground: Welford Road	Trophy Cabinet: Guinness Premiership(7), EDF Energy Cup(6)
	Head Coach: Pat Howard assisted by Neil Back and Richard Cockerill	
	Captain: Martin Corry	

OVERALL RECORD:					T	C	PG	DG	PTS
PLD	W	D	L	Tigers scored:	115	81	100	3	1046
39	27	1	11	Opponents scored:	68	35	106	10	758

GM	DATE		VEN	OPPONENTS	RESULT	POS/LGE	TRIES	KICKS	ATT
GUINNESS PREMIERSHIP (2ND)						**CHAMPIONS: LEICESTER TIGERS**			
1	Sep	**3s**	H	**Sale Sharks**	W 35t-23	2	G.Murphy 10, L.Deacon 17, Corry 43, Penalty 74	Goode 3c/3p	16815
2		9	a	Bath Rugby	L 25-43t	7	Bemand 10	Goode c/5p, Vesty d	10600
3		**16**	H	**Gloucester Rugby**	D 27-27	7	Hipkiss 19, Rabeni 54	Goode c/5p	16815
4		23	a	NEC Harlequins	W+ 21-15	5	Varndell 1, Bemand 55	Burke c/3p	10164
7	Oct	14	a	Northampton Saints	W+ 15-10	5	-	Goode 5p	13564
10	Nov	**4**	H	**Worcester Warriors**	W 40t-21	5	Crane 11, B.Deacon 31, Varndell 33, Castrogiovanni 46, Hipkiss 73, Jennings 79	Burke 2c/2p	16766
11		12s	a	Saracens	L+ 16-22	5	Goode 64	Goode c/p, Burke 2p	8895
12		**18**	H	**London Irish**	W 26-18	4	Varndell 2/44	Humphreys 2c/4p	16815
13		26s	a	London Wasps	W+ 19-13	3	Jennings 25	Humphreys c/4p	9500
17	Dec	**22f**	H	**Bristol Rugby**	W 43t-15	1	Jennings 21, Humphreys 25, Crane 40, Varndell 45, Hipkiss 50, L.Deacon 58	Humphreys 2c/p, Burke 3c	16815
18		26tu	a	London Irish	L+ 25t-26	2	J.Murphy 17, Corry 29, Moody 68, A.Tuilagi 80	Goode c/p	13380
19	Jan	**1m**	H	**Saracens**	W 28t-15	2	A.Tuilagi 24/47, Kay 40, Penalty 62	Humphreys 4c	16815
20		7s	a	Newcastle Falcons	L+ 29-31	2	Goode 26, Lloyd 57	Goode 2c/4p, Vesty p	7565
23		**27**	H	**Newcastle Falcons**	W 39t-5	1	Jennings 28, Crane 39, Ayerza 58, Varndell 71/74	Burke 3c/2p, Humphreys c	16815
25	Feb	17	a	Worcester Warriors	W+ 13-6	1	Rabeni 12	Humphreys c/2p	9623
26		**24**	H	**Northampton Saints**	L+ 9-10	1	-	Humphreys 3p	16815
27	Mar	**3**	H	**NEC Harlequins**	W+ 27-22	1	Rabeni 45, Hipkiss 50	Goode c/5p	16815
28		11s	a	Gloucester Rugby	L+ 24t-28	1	A.Tuilagi 12/40, Varndell 19, G.Murphy 66	Humphreys 2c	12000
29		**17**	H	**Bath Rugby**	W+ 29t-25	1	J.Murphy 20, Lloyd 33, Varndell 36, Gibson 64	Goode 3c/p	16815
32	Apr	6f	a	Sale Sharks	W+ 26-25	1	Croft 30, Abraham 51	Vesty 2c/3p, Humphreys p	10037
35		24tu	a	Bristol Rugby	L 13-30	2	O.Smith 6	Humphreys c/2p	12495
36		**28**	H	**London Wasps**	W 40t-26	2	A.Tuilagi 38, Penalty 47, Hipkiss 50, Moody 68	Goode 3c/4p, Vesty c	17418
37	May	**5**	H	**Bristol Rugby (sf)**	W 26-14	-	Ellis 9, G.Murphy 33	Goode 2c/4p	10675
38		12		Gloucester Rugby (f)	W 44-16	-	F.Murphy 10, A.Tuilagi 32/52, Corry 39, Goode 45, Jennings 64, Moody 79	Goode 3c/p	59400
HEINEKEN CUP						**EUROPEAN CHAMPIONS: LONDON WASPS**			
8	Oct	**22s**	H	**Munster**	L+ 19-21	3	Penalty 72	Goode c/2p, Burke 2p	16000
9		29s	a	Cardiff Blues	W+ 21-17	3	O.Smith 13, Varndell 20	Goode c/2p, Vesty d	26645
15	Dec	8f	a	Bourgoin-Jallieu	W 28-13	2	G.Murphy 16, Varndell 36, Corry 40	Goode 2c/3p	7200
16		**16**	H	**Bourgoin-Jallieu**	W 57t-3	2	Moody 1/59/61, Ellis 7, Jennings 17/77, Gibson 31, Varndell 51	Goode 7c/p	16000
21	Jan	**13**	H	**Cardiff Blues**	W 34t-0	2	A.Tuilagi 3, Hipkiss 4, Gibson 10, Rabeni 31, Moody 64, Corry 72	Humphreys 2c	16000
22		20	a	Munster	W+ 13-6	1	G.Murphy 23, O.Smith 68	Humphreys p	13200
31	Apr	**1s**	H	**Stade Francais Paris (qf)**	W 21-20	-	Rabeni 3, Varndell 73	Goode c/3p	17418
34		21		Llanelli Scarlets (sf)	W 33-17	-	Goode 35, Jennings 52, L.Deacon 77	Goode 3c/4p	30121
39	May	20s		London Wasps (f)	L 9-25	-	-	Goode 3p	81076
ANGLO-WELSH CUP (EDF ENERGY CUP)						**CUP WINNERS: LEICESTER TIGERS**			
5	Sep	**30**	H	**Newport Gwent Dragons**	W 41t-17	1	J.Murphy 18, Penalty 40, Buckland 43, Jennings 65, Humphreys 80	Humphreys 2c, Burke 3c/2p	16057
6	Oct	7	a	Worcester Warriors	W 35t-20	1	J.Murphy 4, Vesty 7, Buckland 61, Gibson 71/80	Burke c/2p, Goode c	6260
14	Dec	2	a	Northampton Saints	L 5-18	1	Abraham 65	-	13058
30	Mar	24		Sale Sharks (sf)	W 29-19	-	A.Tuilagi 38, Hipkiss 67	Goode 2c/2p/d, Burke 2p	27558
33	Apr	15s		Ospreys (f)	W 41-35	-	Varndell 13/63, Croft 15, Kay 26, A.Tuilagi 30	Burke 4c, Goode c/2p	43755
CLUB MATCH									
24	Feb	**11s**	H	**Argentina**	L 21-41		Croft 37, Varndell 75, M.Smith 80	Vesty 3c	11003

Neutral Venues: *#30 at Millennium Stadium - Cardiff, #33 #38 #39 at Twickenham, #34 at Walkers Stadium*

INDIVIDUAL APPEARANCES 2006/07

Name / Game #	1	2	3	4	5	6	7	8	9	10	11	12	13	14	15	16	17	18	19	20	21	22	23	24	25	26	27	28	29	30	31	32	33	34	35	36	37	38	39	Apps	T	Pts
LC (Luke) Abraham	-	7	7	-	-	-	-	-	-	r	r	r	6	7	-	-	7	-	7	-	-	-	-	-	-	x	6	x	r	-	-	7	-	-	7	-	-	-	-	9+4	2	10
MI (Marcos) Ayerza Ar11	-	>r	1	-	1	1	1	1	r	1	-	-	-	-	1	-	1	-	1	-	1	r	1	-	1	1	r	1	1	1	1	1	-	-	-	1	1	1	1	22+4	1	5
SK (Scott) Bemand	9	9	9	r	9	9	9	9	r	r	9	-	r	r	x	r	9	-	9	r	-	-	-	9	-	9	-	r	<r	-	-	-	-	-	-	-	-	-	-	12+9	2	10
JDH (James) Buckland	r	r	x	x	2	2	x	x	x	2	2	r	2	r	x	2	x	2	2	x	r	x	2	r	2	r	2	r	r	-	-	r	-	-	2	r	r	r	<r	12+14	2	10
PA (Paul) Burke I13	-	-	>r	10	10	10	r	10	x	10	10	-	-	-	-	-	r	r	-	-	-	-	10	-	-	10	-	-	r	10	-	-	10	-	x	-	-	-	-	10+5	-	85
ML (Martin) Castrogiovanni It43	>3	1	r	1	3	-	-	3	1	3	-	-	-	-	3	3	r	3	r	3	3	1	r	-	-	-	-	-	-	-	r	3	1	-	-	-	-	-	-	15+5	1	5
GS (George) Chuter E11	2	2	2	2	x	-	2	2	2	-	-	-	-	-	2	x	2	r	-	2	2	2	x	-	-	-	r	-	-	2	2	-	2	2	-	2	2	2	2	20+2	-	-
MJ (Matt) Cornwell	13	12	12	-	-	-	-	-	-	r	r	r	x	12*	r	-	12	-	12	-	-	-	-	13	-	-	-	-	-	-	-	-	-	-	12	-	-	-	-	8+4	-	-
ME (Martin) Corry E54 L7	8*	8*	6*	8*	-	r	8*	8*	8*	-	-	-	-	-	8*	8*	-	8*	r	8*	8*	8*	r	-	-	-	r	-	-	8*	8*	-	8*	8*	-	8*	8*	8*	8*	21+4	5	25
JS (Jordan) Crane E+	-	-	>8	x	8	8	x	x	-	8	8	8	8	6	-	-	8	-	8	-	r	x	8	-	r	8	-	8	8	-	-	r	-	-	8	-	-	-	-	15+3	3	15
TR (Tom) Croft E+ L+	r	-	-	-	-	-	-	-	-	-	x	-	r	-	-	-	r	x	r	-	-	-	r	5	6	r	-	6	4	x	-	6	6	-	6	-	-	-	-	7+6	3	15
LFM (Leo) Cullen I18	-	-	5	4	5*	4*	4	4	-	4*	4*	5	4*	-	4	-	4*	r	4*	4	4	4	-	-	4*	4*	-	4*	-	-	r	5	4	r	4*	-	5	r	<r	23+5	-	-
BR (Brett) Deacon	-	r	x	-	r	-	-	-	x	6	6	6	-	4	r	r	-	6	-	6	-	-	6	8	8	6	8	r	6	r	r	-	r	r	r	r	x	r	r	12+13	1	5
LP (Louis) Deacon E8	6	6	-	6	r	6	6	6	6	5	5	4*	5	r	5	4	5	-	-	-	5	5	-	-	-	-	r	-	-	4	4	r	r	4	x	4	4	4	4	23+5	3	15
OP (Ollie) Dodge	-	-	-	-	-	-	-	-	-	-	-	-	-	>11	-	-	-	-	-	-	-	-	-	-	-	-	-	-	-	-	-	-	-	-	-	-	-	-	-	1	-	-
HA (Harry) Ellis E18 L+	-	-	-	9	-	-	-	r	9	9	r	r	9	-	9	9	-	9	-	9	9	9	r	-	r	-	x	-	-	9	9	-	9	9	-	9	9	-	-	16+5	2	10
DPE (Daryl) Gibson NZ19	12	13	-	-	r	12	-	12	12	12	12	12	12	-	12	12	-	-	-	r	12	-	-	12	r	r	12	12	12	12	12	-	12	12	-	-	-	-	<12	21+4	5	25
G (Greg) Gillanders	-	-	-	-	-	-	-	-	-	-	-	-	-	-	-	-	-	-	-	-	-	-	-	>4	-	-	-	-	-	-	-	-	-	-	-	-	-	-	-	1	-	-
AJ (Andy) Goode E9	10	10	10	-	-	r	10	r	10	-	r	-	-	-	10	10	-	10	r	10	-	-	-	-	-	-	10	-	10	r	10	-	r	10	-	10	10	10	10	17+6	4	286
JL (Jim) Hamilton S7	4	4	4	-	4	-	-	-	4	r	-	r	-	5	r	r	x	4	-	5	-	-	4	-	x	-	4	-	-	-	-	4*	-	-	5	r	-	-	-	12+5	-	-
GD (Gavin) Hickie	-	-	-	-	-	>r	-	-	-	r	x	2	x	2	-	-	-	-	-	-	-	-	-	2	r	2	-	2	2	x	x	2	x	x	<r	-	-	-	-	7+4	-	-
DJ (Dan) Hipkiss E+	r	r	13	13	13	-	12	-	-	13	-	13	13	r	13	13	13	-	13	-	13	13	-	-	12	13	13	13	13	13	13	r	13	13	-	13	13	13	13	26+4	7	35
MO (Michael) Holford	-	-	-	x	-	r	3	-	-	-	3	3	3	1	-	-	-	r	-	-	-	-	3	r	-	r	1	3	r	3	-	-	-	r	3	-	-	-	-	10+6	-	-
IW (Ian) Humphreys	-	-	-	-	r	-	-	-	-	-	-	10	10	10	-	-	10	-	10	-	10	10	r	-	10	r	-	10	-	-	x	10	-	-	10	-	-	-	r	11+4	2	100
S (Shane) Jennings I+	7	-	-	x	6	r	r	r	r	7	7	7	7	-	7	7	6	-	6	r	6	7	7	-	7	7	7	7	7	6	7	-	7	7	-	7	7	7	<7	26+5	9	45
BJ (Ben) Kay E45 L2	5	5	-	5	-	5	5	5	5	-	-	-	-	-	-	5	-	5	5	r	r	x	5*	-	5	5	5*	5	5*	5	5	-	5	5	-	5	r	5	5	23+3	2	10
LD (Leon) Lloyd E5	-	-	-	-	14	r	r	-	-	r	13	14	-	-	-	11	11	-	-	14	-	r	14	11	-	-	-	r	14	-	-	14	-	-	<14	-	-	-	-	11+5	2	10
RA (Rory) McKay	-	-	-	-	-	-	-	-	-	-	-	-	-	-	-	-	-	-	-	-	-	-	-	=r	-	-	-	-	-	-	-	-	-	-	-	-	-	-	-	0+1	-	-
LW (Lewis) Moody E44 L3	-	-	r	7	7	7	7	7	7	-	-	-	-	-	6	6	-	7	-	7	7	6	-	-	-	-	-	-	-	7	6	-	-	6	-	6	6	6	6	19+1	7	35
AC (Alejandro) Moreno Ar/It7	1	-	-	-	-	-	-	-	-	r	1	1	1	r	r	1	-	1	r	1	-	-	-	3	r	3	-	r	3	r	-	r	r	1	1	r	3	r	r	13+12	-	-
F (Frank) Murphy	x	>r	x	-	r	r	x	-	-	-	-	9	-	9	-	-	r	r	r	-	r	x	9	r	9	r	9	9	9	r	x	9	r	x	9	r	r	9	9	11+13	1	5
GEA (Geordan) Murphy I46 L2	14	-	14	15	-	14	14	-	14	-	-	-	x	-	14	14	r	15	15	-	15	15	-	-	x	-	15	r	-	15	15	-	x	15	-	15	15	15	15	20+2	5	25
JE (Johne) Murphy	-	-	-	>14	15	11	11	14	-	14	14	r	14	r	r	r	-	11	-	15	-	-	15	15	-	-	-	-	15	-	-	15	-	-	15	-	-	-	-	15+4	4	20
IA (Ian) Nimmo	-	-	-	-	-	-	-	-	-	-	-	-	-	-	-	-	-	-	-	-	-	-	-	=r	-	-	-	-	-	-	-	-	-	-	-	-	-	-	-	0+1	-	-
BJM (Ben) Pienaar	-	-	-	-	-	-	-	-	-	-	-	-	-	r	-	-	-	-	-	-	-	-	-	6	-	-	-	-	-	-	-	-	-	-	-	-	-	-	-	1+1	-	-
RSR (Seru) Rabeni Fi21 Pl6	r	14	11	-	-	-	-	r	r	-	-	-	-	-	-	-	-	-	r	11	14	14	13	-	11	14	14	-	-	r	14	13	-	r	-	14	14	14	14	15+6	5	25
CG (Graham) Rowntree E54 L3	-	-	-	-	-	-	-	-	-	-	-	-	-	-	-	-	-	-	-	-	-	-	-	<1*	-	-	-	-	-	-	-	-	-	-	-	-	-	-	-	1	-	-
AP (Alex) Shaw	-	-	-	-	-	-	-	-	-	-	-	-	-	-	-	-	-	-	-	-	-	-	-	=7	-	-	-	-	-	-	-	-	-	-	-	-	-	-	-	1	-	-
MW (Matt) Smith	-	r	-	-	-	-	-	-	-	-	-	-	-	15	-	-	-	-	-	-	-	-	-	r	-	-	-	-	-	-	-	-	-	-	-	-	-	-	-	1+2	1	5
OJ (Ollie) Smith E5 L1	-	-	-	r	12	13	13	13	13	-	-	-	-	-	-	-	-	12	-	13	r	12	-	-	13	12	r	-	-	-	-	-	-	-	13	r	r	12	r	12+6	3	15
AT (Alesana) Tuilagi Sa10 Pl1	-	-	-	x	11	-	-	-	-	-	-	-	-	14	-	-	-	14	11	r	11	11	r	-	14	11	11	11	r	11	11	r	11	11	-	11	r	11	11	17+5	11	55
H (Henry) Tuilagi Sa4	r	r	-	-	-	-	-	-	-	-	-	-	x	8	-	-	-	-	-	-	-	-	-	-	-	-	-	-	r	-	-	<8	-	-	-	-	-	-	-	2+3	-	-
TW (Tom) Varndell E3	11	11	r	11	-	-	-	11	11	11	11	11	11	-	11	r	14	-	14	-	-	-	11	14	-	-	-	14	11	14	r	11	14	14	11	r	11	r	-	22+5	16	80
SB (Sam) Vesty E+	15	15	15	12	-	15	15	15	15	15	15	15	15	-	15	15	15	r	-	12	r	r	12	10	15	15	r	15	-	-	-	12	15	r	-	12	12	r	r	25+7	1	35
JM (Julian) White E44 L4	r	3	3	3	r	3	-	r	3	-	-	-	-	-	-	r	3	-	3	r	r	3	-	-	3	-	3	-	-	-	3	-	3	3	-	3	r	3	3	16+7	-	-
DJW (Dave) Young	-	-	-	-	-	-	x	-	-	-	x	r	x	3	-	-	-	-	-	-	-	-	-	-	-	-	-	-	-	-	-	-	-	-	r	-	-	-	-	1+2	-	-
BR (Ben) Youngs E+ L+	-	-	-	-	-	-	-	-	-	-	-	-	-	-	-	-	-	-	-	-	-	-	-	>r	-	-	-	-	-	-	-	x	-	-	r	-	-	r	-	0+3	-	-
TN (Tom) Youngs E+ L+	-	-	-	-	-	-	-	-	-	-	-	-	-	>13	-	-	-	13	-	-	-	-	-	-	-	-	-	-	-	-	-	-	-	-	r	-	-	-	-	2+1	-	-

The key for how to read the stats is on the last page

CHAPTER 34

Coaches Derailed

2007/2008

Even as Tigers secured a double triumph, work had already begun on a revised squad for the new season. At least players could rest for the summer since England decided not to select from any club involved in a European final (Leicester, Wasps and Bath, the Challenge Cup finalists) for their pre-World Cup tour to South Africa, though Geordan Murphy went with Ireland to Argentina, who picked Marcos Ayerza for a 2-0 winning series. Leo Cullen and Shane Jennings returned to Leinster while Leon Lloyd (to Gloucester), James Buckland (Wasps), Henry Tuilagi (Perpignan) and Daryl Gibson (Glasgow) moved on.

The new arrivals included Marco Wentzel, the twice-capped South Africa lock who had been playing for Treviso in Italy, Mefin Davies, the Wales hooker from Gloucester, Ayoola Erinle from Wasps and Benjamin Kayser, the Stade Français hooker who was to be capped by France. The promise of two young players, Tom Croft and Jordan Crane, was confirmed when both played in England's winning Saxons side in the Churchill Cup. Croft's blinding pace was demonstrated in a wonderful long-range try he scored in the cup final against the New Zealand Maori at Twickenham while Frank Murphy's fine season was enhanced with an appearance for Ireland A in the same competition.

Leicester unveiled plans for a 25,000-capacity stadium. Five months later they were able to talk about as many as 30,000 in the longer term, complete with an integrated hotel: the programme included rebuilding both the Crumbie and the Next stands, and redeveloping the clubhouse, all at a cost of £30 million. Their ambition was all the more laudable given rugby's chaotic finances: Leicester's annual meeting heard that the 2006/07 successes had come at an extra cost of £250,000 in travel, accommodation and playing bonuses, as against prize money amounting to less than £100,000. On the other hand, membership had passed 15,000 and the club was at saturation point on many match days; before the season ended, Leicester

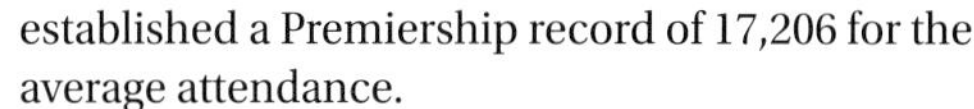

established a Premiership record of 17,206 for the average attendance.

Early in the new year, Leicester City Council granted planning permission, with the proviso that parking and transport problems needed to be resolved. "The most important issue is that we are not putting the club at financial risk," Peter Tom said of a long-term plan for which £60 million had been earmarked. Stage one, for which £15 million was in place, was the development of the Next Stand which would take capacity from 17,500 to 23,500 but Tom was careful to point out that a standing area - regarded as one of the ground's unique features and beloved of many supporters - would be maintained.

Seven Leicester players were called up for England's World Cup training camp in Portugal, among them Dan Hipkiss who celebrated his international debut in the warm-up match against Wales at Twickenham. In due course, Hipkiss was named in Brian Ashton's squad, along with Martin Corry, Lewis Moody, Ben Kay and George Chuter. When the global tournament began, Leicester found themselves shorn of 12 players - five with England, two with Samoa, one each with Ireland, Scotland, Argentina, Fiji and New Zealand.

George Chuter and Ben Kay congratulate each other on England reaching the semi-finals of RWC2007.

In a tournament of troughs and peaks for England, Kay played every minute of all seven games en route to the losing final with South Africa. Corry appeared in all seven games but only as a replacement in the opening pool game with the USA in Lens, though he did take over the captaincy from Phil Vickery in the remaining pool games against South Africa, Samoa and Tonga. Emphasising England's dependence on their Leicester contingent, Moody and Chuter appeared in every game too, Moody as first-choice open-side flanker against Tonga and all through the knockout stage, Chuter largely as back-up to Mark Regan at hooker. Hipkiss came off the bench four times but his last two games included the entire second half of the semi-final with France and the last half-hour of the final, won by the Springboks 15-6.

Before the year was out Corry had announced his retirement from international rugby, aged 34 and with 64 caps to his credit, and planned one more year with his club who had been defending their crown in straitened circumstances. With neither Harry Ellis nor Scott Bemand, who required a cartilage graft, available at scrum-half,

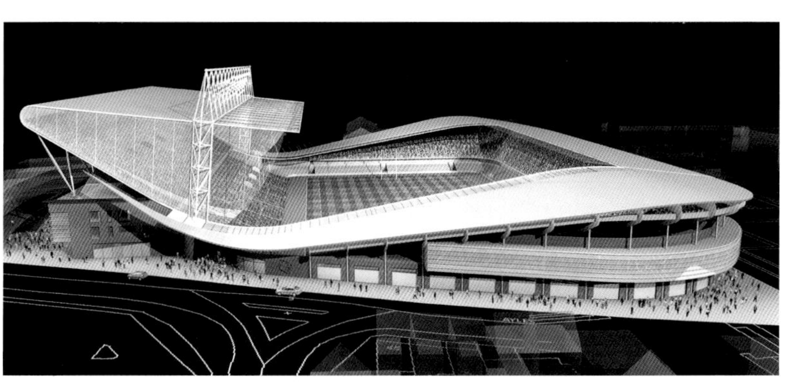

The architect's impression of the proposed Tigers stadium.

Christophe Laussucq, capped three times by France, was signed from Castres as cover. For the first time in seven years Tigers opened with an away Premiership win, at Bath, and beat Wasps (themselves shorn of ten players) at Adams Park in High Wycombe. In the process Andy Goode passed 1,500 points for Leicester, following where Dusty Hare, John Liley and Tim Stimpson had gone.

Change on the playing front was matched in the boardroom: John Allen, Bob Beason and David Matthews, who between them totalled more than 130 years of service to the club, retired and were replaced by Terry Gateley and two easily-recognised former players, Rory Underwood and Sir Clive Woodward.

← Marcelo Loffreda and Richard Cockerill talk tactics.

The defence of the EDF Energy Cup did not begin well at Bath but it did mark the first appearance at loose-head prop of Dan Cole. In early November, Marcelo Loffreda, the new director of rugby, arrived after taking Argentina to third place in the world: "I am very enthusiastic at coming to one of the best teams in Europe," he said. "It will be a new culture, a new way of life for me and my family." He left selection of the team to Richard Cockerill for the opening round of the Heineken Cup and watched Leicester go down 22-9 to a Leinster XV including Cullen and Jennings in Dublin.

At least there was an outbreak of peace between the Premiership clubs and the RFU after years of bickering. The two sides negotiated an eight-year agreement over player-release periods and appropriate levels of compensation for the clubs whose preparation created players for the national side. As if to celebrate the new accord, Tigers Events, the club's commercial arm, received an official licence to operate at Twickenham and Aaron Mauger arrived at Welford Road, one of five New Zealanders joining Premiership clubs.

In Mauger, Leicester had bought one of his country's brightest tactical brains, a second five-eighth who could run a midfield and pass on a vast amount of experience to young English colleagues. "It's a matter of re-assessing what I want out of the game," Mauger said after eight years of playing for Canterbury Crusaders, the leading franchise in Super Rugby. "I'm not here to muck around. I'm here to play rugby and do the best I can."

At the same time, Sam Vesty made the valid point that provincial English clubs should tend their roots. "I remember playing with [Harry Ellis, Matt Smith and Louis Deacon] at under-15 level and to be able to do what we have done together is an awesome feeling," the utility back said on the verge of his 100th start for Leicester. "We have a level of camaraderie that you can only have with people you have played with for that length of time. It will be harder to keep that core of local players as the league gets more competitive and more foreigners come into the game. But it's very important for Leicester to keep that family feel and remain a local club."

Goode passed the club record of 358 Heineken Cup points (established by Tim Stimpson) with a 19-point haul against Edinburgh, Tom Youngs made a good impression at centre against Leeds in the Premiership and an EDF Energy Cup semi-final (against Wasps) was guaranteed with a 32-8 win over Sale. Mauger's debut came against Toulouse in the Heineken Cup which Tigers won 14-9, Ben Youngs enjoying a good second half off the bench. But a week later, Leicester lost the return match 22-11 and, this being their second pool defeat, a place in the last eight was in considerable doubt. In the Premiership they slipped to fifth in the table though they did celebrate the award of life membership to the faithful Tudor Thomas by beating London Irish.

Defeat at Edinburgh ensured Leicester would not repeat their European heroics of the previous year. It was only the third time in the 11 seasons of English involvement that they had failed to reach the knockout phase and, rubbing salt into the wound, White received a five-week suspension for punching Malcolm O'Kelly during the final pool game, a home win over Leinster.

England called up Chuter, Kay, Deacon, Moody (who had captained Tigers against Leeds) and Croft after only 15 starts for Leicester but only one Leicester player, Moody, started England's opening international of the six nations though Kay came on as a replacement. That did not go well either: England lost at Twickenham to Wales and Moody damaged his right Achilles tendon, missing the rest of the season. That Jordan Crane led England Saxons to a 31-13 win over Ireland A at Welford Road with Tom Varndell (two tries) and Ollie Smith in the back division was only limited comfort.

↓ Midfield general Aaron Mauger arrived from New Zealand.

For the first time in 32 years, England started a championship game (against Italy) with no Leicester representation though Kay, as he did throughout the tournament, came off the bench. There was a first cap, as a replacement, for Croft against France in Paris and he retained the number-six shirt against Scotland and Ireland, when Chuter was also involved. But though England finished on a high by beating Ireland 33-10, it was not enough to save Brian Ashton, the head coach, despite the fact that he had taken England to the World Cup final only five months earlier.

In the subsequent reshuffle, Martin Johnson was given a three-and-a-half year contract as England team manager, a job for which he had few credentials save his huge reputation and experience as a player, and his innate rugby sense. Johnson's new coaching team included his old playing

↑ The Leicester trio, Graham Rowntree, John Wells and Martin Johnson, all transferred their skills to the England coaching set-up.

colleagues at Leicester, John Wells and Graham Rowntree, who was now forging ahead as a scrum specialist. In due course they were joined as attack coach by another former Tiger, Brian Smith, the Australian who was director of rugby at London Irish. Johnson took up his job after the England summer tour to New Zealand, on the day that the new eight-year agreement between the RFU and the clubs over player-release came into action, something none of his predecessors had enjoyed.

Back at Welford Road, Seru Rabeni received a three-week ban for an off-the-ball incident against Newcastle and Ollie Smith announced his impending departure for Montpellier. But Julien Dupuy, the Biarritz scrum-half, agreed to come to Welford Road and Dupuy's older compatriot, Laussucq, did well in the 20-13 win which ended Gloucester's 22-game unbeaten home run. Success at Kingsholm narrowed to one point the gap between Leicester in second place in the Premiership and Gloucester at the top.

Hipkiss and Alesana Tuilagi returned after groin injuries that had kept them out for two and three months respectively, and the sight of Harry Ellis stepping out from the replacements against Leeds was encouraging. Ellis had been absent for ten months recovering from the knee damaged the previous spring and when he was picked for his first start, against Worcester, his charge-down led to a first-minute try for Brett Deacon.

But Leicester lacked consistency. Victory over Saracens was offset by a subsequent 14-week suspension for Rabeni after a gouging incident and though Leicester reached the final of the EDF Cup yet again, by virtue of a 34-24 win over Wasps at Cardiff's Millennium Stadium, they promptly lost at home in the Premiership the following weekend to Wasps, whose first win at Welford Road in the professional era it was. Goode outplayed England's Danny Cipriani in the semi-final with Wasps but in the EDF Cup final at Twickenham, he was up against another great talent in James Hook and the Ospreys, the same opponents as in the 2007 final.

Leicester's team for the final was: Johne Murphy; Ollie Smith, Dan Hipkiss, Aaron Mauger, Alesana Tuilagi (Tom Varndell, 77); Andy Goode, Harry Ellis; Boris Stankovich (Julian White, 52), George Chuter, Martin Castrogiovanni (Stankovich, 72; Benjamin Kayser, 75), Louis Deacon, Ben Kay, Martin Corry, Jordan Crane, Ben Herring (Tom Croft, 58).

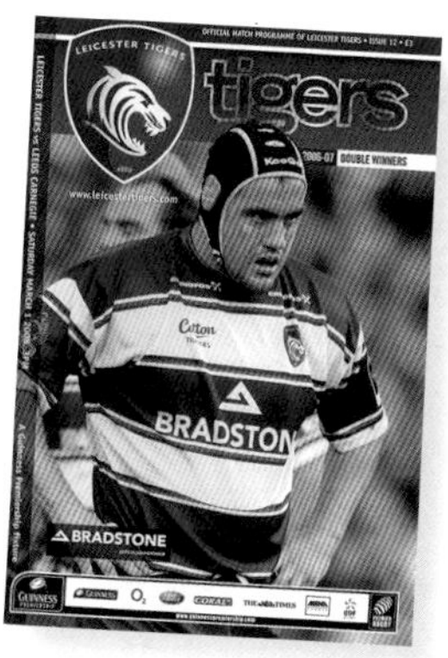

What a difference a year makes. The cup slipped away from Leicester in a 23-6 defeat and it was cold comfort that Lyn Jones, the Ospreys head coach, acknowledged that "we have learned more about rugby playing against Leicester than anyone else." Apart from an initial flurry of activity which brought Goode a penalty and a dropped goal, Leicester were out of sorts and ragged.

In front of more than 65,000, they showed a lack of imagination behind the scrum whereas the Ospreys did the basics well. Before half-time they had claimed the lead when Andrew Bishop cut past two defenders with relative ease and Hook converted the try. There was a second try, for Alun Wyn Jones, after Leicester knocked on and Hook kicked not only the conversion but three penalties to make sure that the Ospreys became the first Welsh side to win the trophy.

Inevitably the questions were asked: will Leicester make it to the Premiership play-offs, will they qualify for Europe by finishing in the top six? The squad was in the process of being trimmed too: Scott Bemand was on his way to Bath, Frank Murphy to Connacht, Ian Humphreys back to Ulster, Luke Abraham to Sale and Jim Hamilton to Edinburgh. The other Hamilton, Jamie, the former scrum-half who had been working as a video analyst for the club, was going even farther away, to join the Canterbury Crusaders in New Zealand.

When Leicester lost at Newcastle, they were sixth in the Premiership and needed to beat Harlequins (with a bonus point) to make the play-offs, while also needing Sale and Wasps to lose their remaining games. They did their part thanks to a late try by Varndell, his second of the match, which gave them a breathless 31-28 win; results elsewhere elevated them to fourth place and an away play-off against Gloucester, who finished the regular season in top spot. There was an ominous tone to Tom's comment: "Leicester is a ruthless club," the chairman said. "It is all about success and, if it is not quite there, you have to try and sort it out. We had a good heart-to-heart with the coaches and senior players. We cleared the air and everybody knows what they need to do. It has been frustrating because, off the pitch, it has been a great year."

News came in from Florida of the death of the former captain, Tom Bleasdale, who had played 340 games for Leicester in the 1950s and 60s. The rumbustious forward would have been pleased to

↓ Front row union, Julian White, Mefin Davies and Boris Stankovich about to engage at Gloucester in the Premiership semi-final. Tigers became the first team ever to win away from home in such a fixture.

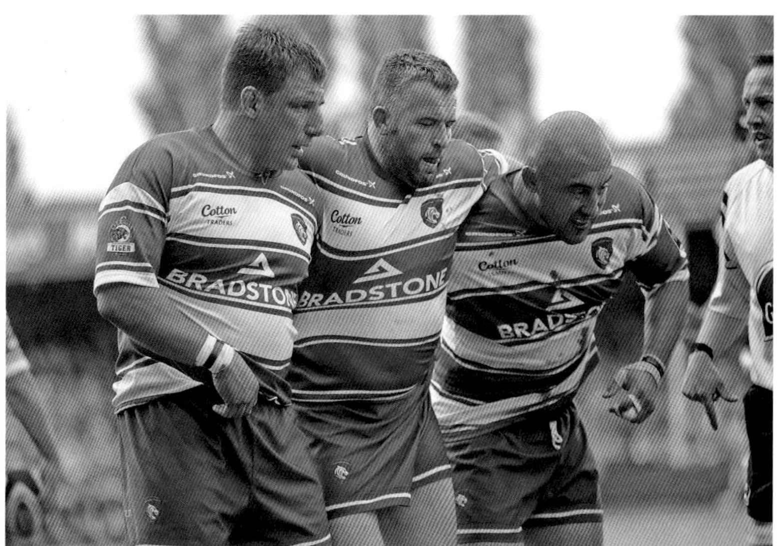

see Tigers fighting to retain their league title. Play-off success at Kingsholm looked less than likely when Gloucester turned round 12-5 ahead and two Leicester players, Ellis and Crane, had spent time in the sin bin; yet tries by Alesana Tuilagi and Mauger and the kicking of Goode brought them back to a tenuous one-point lead with ten minutes remaining. Gloucester nosed ahead with three to go but as the clock ticked past eighty minutes, Goode dropped the goal which gave Leicester a 26-25 win and a place in the final against....Wasps.

➜ Construction giant Caterpillar began their long association as sponsors of the Tigers in May 2008.

It would be Lawrence Dallaglio's last match for the London club, the chance for Leicester to serve him as he and his colleagues had served Johnson and Back three years earlier. At last it seemed as though the fates were looking kindly on the Tigers: Julian White escaped with a week's ban for trampling during the Gloucester game and was available for Twickenham. Hipkiss was called up by England for the summer tour in place of the injured Wasps fly-half, Danny Cipriani, thereby joining Kay, Croft and Toby Flood, the Newcastle fly-half who had agreed to join Leicester. On the eve of the final, Leicester announced a multi-million pound sponsorship agreement with Caterpillar, the construction company with a plant at Desford.

Leicester's team was: Geordan Murphy; Tom Varndell, Dan Hipkiss (Ayoola Erinle, 41), Aaron Mauger (Erinle, 17-26), Alesana Tuilagi; Andy Goode, Harry Ellis (Christophe Laussucq, 80); Boris Stankovich (Marcos Ayerza, 57), Mefin Davies (Benjamin Kayser, 47), Julian White, Marco Wentzel (Richard Blaze, 53), Ben Kay, Martin Corry (captain), Jordan Crane, Ben Herring (Tom Croft, 57).

Once again they were disappointed. Wasps ran up 23 points by half-time and though Tigers won the second half 10-3, the damage had been done and Wasps, 26-16 winners, were champions. Their set-piece, questioned during the season, did not falter and their back row had the upper hand at the breakdowns. Corry and Crane did their best to stem the tide but before the interval, Wasps had scored tries through Tom Rees and Josh Lewsey, both converted by Mark van Gisbergen who had opened the scoring with the first of four penalties. Goode responded with two penalties but this was not a great afternoon for the goalkicker; Wasps led 23-6 at half-time and though Varndell and Ellis clawed back two tries, the final word lay with Van Gisbergen with his sixth successful kick at goal nine minutes from time.

True, Leicester had the upper hand in the second half and the game went to uncontested scrums for the final quarter when Wasps lost their second prop, Tim Payne joining Phil Vickery on the sidelines. This allowed them to introduce the experienced loose forward, Joe Worsley, and Leicester, who lost Hipkiss at half-time after a blow to the face, could not find sufficient rhythm to overtake their old rivals. Hipkiss had fractured an eye socket and missed the England tour to New Zealand; however Paul Sackey, the Wasps wing, also sustained an injury which allowed Varndell to replace him down under.

Six days after the final, Leicester decided to terminate Loffreda's contract after only seven months of a three-year agreement. "We are not happy just to reach finals, we want to win them," Peter Tom said after a wholesale review of the playing and management staff at Welford Road. "Maybe we have been distracted by the redevelopment of the stadium and some of the other things. Perhaps we have not given as much time as we should to helping the playing side." Not everyone was in agreement: David Matthews and Tudor Thomas both considered the Argentinian should have been given more time. "We will be in danger of looking like a football club if we're not careful," Matthews added.

Loffreda's Leicester won 16 of 26 matches and reached two finals. "Our decision has been made with a degree of sadness," a board statement said. "We felt this had to be done now to allow everyone to prepare fully to meet the challenge of the new season." Loffreda himself admitted that "this kind of club needs permanent success. That outlook does not breed tolerance." He placed his affairs in the hands of his solicitor and Leicester, having scoured the world for Loffreda in the first place, began their search all over again.

➜ Harry Ellis spilt blood for the cause but alas it was in vain as Wasps carried off the 2008 Premiership trophy at Twickenham.

← Benjamin Kayser made his debut for France in the summer of 2008, and became the first French international capped from the club.

2008/2009

Richard Cockerill had earned himself consideration as the new director of coaching, Neil Back was known to be ambitious in his coaching aims and both sustained the club's boot-room philosophy. But towards the end of June a South African name appeared on the horizon in the shape of Heyneke Meyer, who had made the Pretoria-based Blue Bulls one of the most successful franchises in Super Rugby, yet had been overlooked as coach of the Springboks.

Meyer duly agreed a three-year contract while two of Leicester's coaching staff, Back and Andy Key, left for Leeds after associations with the club that had lasted 18 and 30 years respectively. Back was appointed head coach and Key director of rugby at the Yorkshire club, who had been relegated from the Premiership at the season's end.

The best that could be said of an unfortunate business was that Leicester had moved swiftly to plug the gap, for which their players involved in summer tours must have been duly relieved. In New Zealand, Ben Kay made two appearances off the bench and Tom Croft one on an England trip beset by off-field problems while Varndell scored a try in the first of two internationals, both lost by 17 and 32 points respectively. Jordan Crane was player of the tournament for the England Saxons who won the Churchill Cup in Chicago and when Martin Johnson came to pick his first elite squad as England team manager, it included eight Leicester players - Crane, Croft, Varndell, Dan Hipkiss, Harry Ellis, Toby Flood, George Chuter and Lewis Moody. Four more, Kay, Andy Goode, Louis Deacon and Richard Blaze, appeared in the Saxons squad.

But Goode had made his last appearance for Leicester. Though a year remained on his contract, he decided to join Brive at a time when the French club were recruiting heavily. "It's an exciting move," Goode, then the Premiership's leading points scorer and whose Leicester record read 1,799 points in 200 appearances, said. "I can look back with no regrets during my time at Tigers. I want to be remembered as a Leicester lad through and through."

Meyer brought with him a replacement fly-half in Derick Hougaard from the Bulls and already capped eight times by South Africa. Cockerill remained as forwards coach and was joined by Matt O'Connor, a centre capped once by Australia but better known for his coaching with the ACT Brumbies in Canberra. Paul Burke, his playing career over, became kicking coach.

The South African began his new job without the injured quartet of Deacon, Moody, Martin Castrogiovanni and Ayoola Erinle and with a shadow over Seru Rabeni. The Fijian was found to have played in a sevens tournament at Bath while under suspension, and was banned for a further nine weeks as well as being fined by Leicester. Still, the season opened with a win over Gloucester at Kingsholm; a second win followed at home, against London Irish, but cost Leicester the services of Alesana Tuilagi for six weeks with a knee injury.

This was also the season of the ELV - experimental law variations inflicted upon an unwilling northern hemisphere by the International Rugby Board - and plenty of clubs found difficulty adjusting to what could or could not be done at scrum and breakdown. In addition there was growing concern over Harry Ellis, who suffered constant swelling on the knee he damaged 18 months earlier. Hougaard made his debut against Bath in the EDF Energy Cup, a 19-15 win at the Recreation Ground which also marked the first appearance in the senior side together of Ben and Tom Youngs, the latter still at centre.

When the Heineken Cup came round, Meyer was eager to show he could triumph in Europe as he had with the Bulls in the Super 14. The Ospreys were beaten 12-6 but Ben Woods, another summer recruit from Newcastle, damaged knee ligaments which left Leicester short of open-side flankers since Moody and Ben Herring were both recovering from injury. Croft played there against Treviso, a 60-16 success in which Johne Murphy scored three of Leicester's nine tries, but there was an urgent need for the arrival of Craig Newby, the Otago flanker capped three times by New Zealand. A fortnight later another New Zealander, Scott Hamilton, a wing capped twice from the Crusaders, joined too.

Johnson's first England selection, against the Pacific Islanders at Twickenham, involved only Croft in the starting XV with the half-backs, Ellis and Flood, among the replacements. Though the islanders were beaten, England lost to Australia, South Africa and New Zealand, Croft lost his place at blind-side flank midway through the series though there were brief appearances as replacements in the last two internationals for Crane - his first cap - and Hipkiss.

Off the field, Leicester had to announce their first loss since 1998/99. It was no more than £202,000

↓ Heyneke Meyer took over from Loffreda for the 2008/09 campaign.

and overall, turnover had increased as the country entered a period of bitter economic recession. Yet the aim of the new stand was to increase turnover beyond £20 million by 2011, including as it would a hospitality suite capable of holding 1,000 people. David Clayton, the managing director, said Leicester hoped for an extended catchment area which took in the West Midlands, Staffordshire and Notts, Lincs and Derby.

"We know we have Tigers supporters in those areas so it's now a question of getting out there and marketing the club," Clayton said. Leicester were invigorated by the return of European competition. Julian White, fit again after a neck injury, proved his old-school worth in a scrum that bullied Perpignan into submission: Flood scored 23 points in a 38-27 win that included four tries, the first by Flood himself. A week later Perpignan won 26-20 but that left Leicester with a losing bonus point and sharing the top of their pool with the Ospreys.

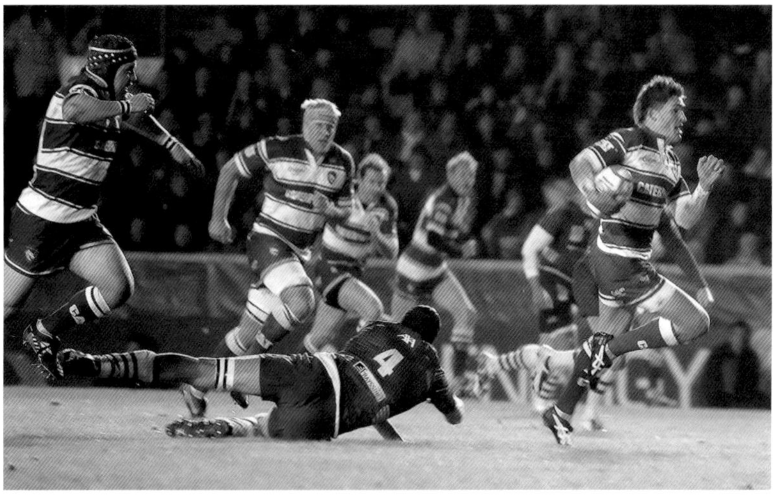

🡻 Toby Flood, a try scorer against Perpignan, went on to become the Tigers' top points scorer in his debut season for the club.

Ellis, though, was cited for a dangerous tackle on Dan Carter, the All Blacks fly-half on a six-month sojourn with Perpignan, and subsequently suspended for six weeks. Moreover there were flickers of concern when Meyer, who was settling in well, had to return to South Africa because of a family illness, leaving coaching in Richard Cockerill's hands. It was not long before Peter Tom warned that Meyer might not be back, owing to the illness of both his in-laws. "We accept that his family is his priority," Tom said, "and it could be some time before he returns."

Before the end of January, Meyer made it clear than his stay at Welford Road was over after only 26 weeks, five weeks fewer than Loffreda. "This has been a very difficult decision for me to make, in difficult circumstances, but I hope everyone can understand my reasons," he said. "Leicester Tigers is a very special rugby club and I accepted the job there because I felt it was equipped to go on to greater success. But I have always said that if a player can't give me 100 per cent effort 100 per cent of the time, then he can't play for me. The same principle counts for me. I could not focus 100 per cent on my coaching there and I needed to make a decision."

🡻 Geordan Murphy poses with the RBS 6 Nations and Triple Crown trophies following Ireland's 2009 grand slam success.

It was a bad blow for the club, exacerbated by the loss of Hipkiss for six weeks through a knee injury but Leicester were well represented in the new-year England elite squad through Chuter, Croft, Ellis, Flood and Moody (who then broke an ankle in training and missed the 2009 six nations). There was added excitement to the international championship since it was a Lions year; Graham Rowntree, promoted to the senior England squad as scrum coach, had already been earmarked for the same role for the Lions tour to South Africa in the summer. Before the six nations, though, Leicester had to attend to the final two Heineken Cup pool games: Ben Youngs made only his fourth start, against Treviso in a routine 52-0 win, and though Tigers lost 15-9 to the Ospreys in Swansea, the losing bonus point secured leadership of the pool and a quarter-final place.

It was another uncomfortable affair, overshadowed by Ospreys allegations of gouging, with the finger pointed at White. Leicester were incensed that one individual had been publicly singled out before the citing procedure had taken place and, in the end, that procedure named Martin Corry. His act in making contact with the eye of Richard Hibbard, the Ospreys hooker, was deemed unintentional but he still received a six-week ban.

Ellis, himself returning from suspension, scored two tries for England Saxons in a 66-0 win over Portugal and found himself promoted to the senior side for England's first game of the 2009 six nations, against Italy. His partner turned out to be Goode who scored one of England's five tries in a 36-11 win while Ellis himself scored another two. Overall, Leicester lost 11 players to the first round of internationals and had to make ground in the Premiership without Hougaard, suffering from appendicitis.

The answer to the problem at fly-half turned out to be that jack-of-all-trades, Sam Vesty, at the start of an ascent that would carry him to an England cap. At Christmas, Vesty's future at the club seemed less than secure: "I'm a professional rugby player who wasn't playing, which made me a professional weightlifter," he said. His appearance against Wasps was only his second start of the season and though Leicester lost 36-29, many considered it to be their most ambitious display of the season. They scored four tries to three by Wasps in a game of three yellow cards and uncontested scrums.

Another five tries came against Worcester while England climbed up to second place in the championship, a long way behind grand slam-winning Ireland for whom Geordan Murphy appeared regularly from the bench and was on the field for the closing stage of the climactic encounter with Wales. Few in Leicester would have denied the popular Murphy his share in Ireland's triumph, even as they watched Tigers climb, all of a sudden, from sixth to second in the Premiership, four points behind Gloucester.

Their upward progress included the first away win for five months, over London Irish; in three games with Vesty at 10, Leicester had scored 98 points and 12 tries: "When you only have 22 men to pick from - which is pretty much what we had last week - it's easy," the stand-in coach, Cockerill, said laconically. Gloucester, the leaders, became another scalp and victory over Bristol briefly gave Tigers top spot in the table.

At a time when there was a sense of movement within the club - Tom Varndell confirmed a move to Wasps, Benjamin Kayser and Julien Dupuy were returning to France, Hougaard's future involvement seemed limited - it was interesting to see the result of a *Leicester Mercury* poll for a Walk of Legends feature to be built into the new stand. Readers of the paper voted for the following all-time team: Dusty Hare; John Duggan, Paul Dodge, Clive Woodward, Rory Underwood; Bleddyn Jones, Austin Healey; Graham Rowntree, Peter Wheeler, Steve Redfern, Martin Johnson, Matt Poole, Graham Willars, Dean Richards, David Matthews.

↑ Fans voted for the players to be included in the Tigers' Walk of Legends.

Leicester announced a freeze on season-ticket prices and new young-adult and full-time student tickets: "We felt the current increase from junior to adult category was too steep," Clayton said. "We have introduced the new category of ticket which recognises that many young supporters in this age range may be in their first jobs and on relatively low incomes." Such moves off the field combined with the fluent approach on it chimed with Peter Tom's view as he took on the chairmanship of Premier Rugby Ltd. "We are all interested in the good of the game and we all need each other," Tom said. "We are in the sport entertainment business and we know we have to produce a good product because we compete with football, shopping centres and the like."

At the beginning of April, Leicester played the final game before work began on the destruction of the old Members Stand. The 37-31 win over Sale, five tries to three, was a decent tribute to a part of the club's history and confirmed Tigers' position at the head of the Premiership, though White received a red card (and subsequent two-week ban) for punching Andrew Sheridan, the Sale prop.

↓ The giant new stand emerges from behind the old.

It cost White a place in the Heineken Cup quarter-final against Bath, which Leicester played at the Walkers Stadium despite the bad memories of the meeting there three years earlier. This time Leicester won 20-15, a nervy affair settled by two players who might be said to have been reserves - Vesty at fly-half and Dupuy at scrum-half. Vesty, playing because of Flood's withdrawal, kicked five penalties and Dupuy, who came off the bench for the final half-hour instead of Ellis, scored the clinching try, shimmying through from a ruck 30 metres from the Bath line.

The down side was yet another suspension, for Alesana Tuilagi for a dangerous tackle and the loss of Louis Deacon with damaged knee ligaments. That down side was mild compared with the shadow the quarter-finals cast over Harlequins, whose game against Leinster led to the notorious "Bloodgate" scandal and cost Dean Richards, Leicester's former captain and manager, his job as director of rugby at Harlequins and a three-year suspension from involvement in the game.

If Leicester's board needed confirmation of the decision to be made on their next head coach, a place in Europe's last four did just that and Cockerill was able to take the 'stand-in' away from his job description. "We have watched his coaching and management style develop since he joined the coaching staff," Tom said. "We are convinced he is the man to push Tigers forward."

Under Cockerill's guidance, individuals such as Vesty, Ben Woods and Ben Pienaar had been given lead roles rather than acting as spear carriers, and had repaid his faith. A penalty by Vesty brought a 16-13 win over Saracens in Watford and guaranteed a Premiership play-off place though, in stark contrast to previous touring parties in the professional era, only one Leicester player was named in the Lions squad to tour South Africa, Harry Ellis. The scrum-half was subsequently joined by Tom Croft after Ireland's Alan Quinlan was suspended for foul play.

Not that the Lions loomed large on Leicester's horizon. Their back-row resources, so weakened by injury for much of the season, were improved by the return of Corry from suspension and Moody from injury. Bristol, on their way out of the Premiership, were washed away on a 73-3 flood the week before Leicester played Cardiff Blues at the Millennium Stadium in the Heineken Cup semi-finals, a game which produced a finale unprecedented in European competition.

Cockerill rewarded Dupuy's form by starting the Frenchman ahead of Ellis and Woods ahead of Moody, while Vesty played at centre rather than Mauger, and Croft in the second row. It was an unusual line-up in a far from usual game: Leicester led by 14 points around the hour mark and ended fighting for their lives as the game ended 26-26. For 18 minutes in the final quarter they played with 14 men and for six minutes only 13, as first Craig Newby then Geordan Murphy were sent to the sin bin, the first for slowing ball at a ruck, the second for a deliberate knock-down. During that period, Jamie Roberts and Tom James scored the tries that brought the Blues back into contention and made Leicester regret three early penalty misses by Dupuy.

Tigers are champions of England for the eighth time after overcoming London Irish in a nail-biting final at Twickenham.

But the scrum-half did kick four penalties and converted tries by Scott Hamilton and Geordan Murphy. With the scores tied at full-time, and no further score in extra-time, a penalty shoot-out was required to decide who would face Leinster in the final. Flood, one of Leicester's best kickers, had already left the field with the ruptured Achilles tendon that cost him six months out of rugby but Leicester were able to get Dupuy back because of an extra-time blood injury to Hipkiss.

Whatever the rights or wrongs of shoot-outs in rugby, it was a nail-biter. The first three Leicester kickers, Dupuy, Vesty and Murphy, all matched their Cardiff counterparts, Ben Blair, Nicky Robinson and Leigh Halfpenny. The first player to blaze wide was Johne Murphy but then Tom James did the same for the Blues and Mauger restored equality at the end of the first stanza of kicks to be taken by five designated individuals. Thereafter came sudden death: Richie Rees, Cardiff's scrum-half, scraped his kick over the bar and Newby, the first forward to aim at the posts, did the same.

Then Martyn Williams, that wonderful Wales flanker but with no kicking record to speak of, pushed his attempt wide of the left upright. Enter Jordan Crane, a player never short of confidence who had played football in West Bromwich Albion's academy, albeit as a goalkeeper. But he had kicked goals for Colston's College in Bristol, he and Newby would amuse themselves after training by joining in kicking practice and now he fired straight between the posts and raised his hands aloft in triumph.

Even the front row can't watch as Jordan Crane takes his history-making kick 3.5.2009.

He had carried Leicester to their fifth European final, which took place a week after the assault on the domestic title. To reach Twickenham, Leicester had first to overcome Bath in the Premiership play-off at the Walkers Stadium and they did so 24-10 though the greatest cheers were for Martin Corry, sent out to accept the applause of the 18,000-crowd after confirming that he would retire at the season's end after 290 appearances for Tigers, 64 England caps and two Lions tours. The No 8, the epitome of a never-say-die attitude, had been a wonderful servant for club and country and was to end with a last hurrah in Barbarians colours.

Cockerill, meanwhile, was voted the Premiership's director of rugby for the season, and settled back for the Premiership final against London Irish. Leicester's team was: Geordan Murphy (captain); Scott Hamilton, Ayoola Erinle, Dan Hipkiss, Johne Murphy (Matt Smith, 21); Sam Vesty, Julien Dupuy; Marcos Ayerza, George Chuter (Benjamin Kayser, 57), Julian White (Dan Cole, 75), Tom Croft, Ben Kay, Craig Newby, Jordan Crane (sin bin 40-50), Ben Woods (Lewis Moody, 59).

More than 81,000 watched the Irish give Leicester the most almighty fright before losing 10-9. The good form of the previous month deserted Tigers, the set-piece struggled and Steffon Armitage, the Irish flanker, had the upper hand at the breakdown. Peter Hewat dropped a goal for Irish in the first minute and the only other score of the first half was Dupuy's penalty which levelled matters. On a day when his side's goalkicking was awry, Delon Armitage added a penalty to nose the Irish in front but they could make nothing of a series of scrums on the Leicester line, even when Crane was sent to the sin bin for a professional foul.

Whatever else failed to work, there was nothing wrong with Leicester's defence and when Hamilton and Hipkiss carried them to within range of the Irish tryline, they struck. Erinle and Smith made ground and forced the ruck from which Crane bounced through a tackle and scored, Dupuy converting. Some 17 minutes remained, in which Delon Armitage kicked another penalty to reduce the gap to one point, but the momentum had switched to Leicester and they rode out the storm.

In between the domestic final and the European final, England named a squad to play against the Barbarians and home and away tests with Argentina that included Vesty, as well as Chuter, White, Kay, Deacon, Moody, Crane and Hipkiss; Cole and Woods were named in the Saxons squad for the Churchill Cup. Cockerill preferred Alesana Tuilagi on the left wing, while Martin Castrogiovanni recovered from the sore neck that kept him out of the Premiership final and displaced White but Mauger's season ended in frustration, the New Zealander missing the last month because of back trouble.

By coincidence, Irishmen led both sides in the Heineken Cup final at Murrayfield on 23 May. Geordan Murphy and Leo Cullen were old friends from their school days and Cullen, of course, had spent two years at Welford Road along with Shane Jennings, Leinster's flanker. "Of all the clubs in the world, that was the one place I wanted to play more than any other," Cullen said of his time with the Tigers. "It is a tight-knit environment that demands success. Everything there is set up for the team to be successful. They do not want individuals to shine, they want the team to shine and that is a philosophy that I would certainly always want to be associated with."

Leicester: Geordan Murphy (captain; Matt Smith, 46); Scott Hamilton, Ayoola Erinle, Dan Hipkiss, Alesana Tuilagi; Sam Vesty, Julien Dupuy (Harry Ellis, 74); Marcos Ayerza, George Chuter (Benjamin Kayser, 53), Martin Castrogiovanni (Julian White, 52), Tom Croft, Ben Kay, Craig Newby, Jordan Crane (Louis Deacon, 29), Ben Woods (Lewis Moody, 60).
Leinster: Isa Nacewa; Shane Horgan, Brian O'Driscoll, Gordon D'Arcy, Luke Fitzgerald (Rob Kearney, 70); Jonathan Sexton, Chris Whitaker; Cian Healy (Ronan McCormack, 60-65), Bernard Jackman (John Fogarty, 55), Stan Wright (sin bin, 32-43), Leo Cullen (captain), Malcolm O'Kelly, Rocky Elsom, Jamie Heaslip, Shane Jennings.
Referee: Nigel Owens (Wales)

Here again there was little enough in it when the dust settled but this time Leicester were on the wrong side of a 19-16 result. Maybe the strain of the high-profile games of the previous month took its toll, maybe the loss in the first half of Crane and just after the interval to a hip injury, Geordan Murphy, was hard to overcome; maybe Leinster were just that much better and possessed, in Rocky Elsom, the Australia flanker, the game's defining figure. When Jonny Sexton kicked his second penalty, ten minutes remained in which the Tigers could have snatched the brand from the fire but it proved beyond them.

Leinster did not make enough of their initial dominance and though Brian O'Driscoll and Sexton dropped goals, they sandwiched a penalty from Dupuy. A second from the Frenchman, against a Sexton penalty, was the prelude to the game's first try, scored while Leinster's prop, Stan Wright, was in the sin bin for an early tackle on

→ Club captain Martin Corry finally hung up his boots after almost 300 appearances for Leicester.

Vesty. Ben Woods was the try scorer and Dupuy's conversion gave Leicester a 13-9 lead at half-time, which Dupuy increased with his third penalty.

But Leinster, in pursuit of their first European title, levelled through Jamie Heaslip's try, converted by Sexton, and the decisive score came when Matt Smith was penalised at a ruck and Sexton kicked the goal from forty metres. "We could not have given any more," Cockerill said. "We should be proud of our season."

← LEICESTER FOOTBALL CLUB 2007/08
Back: Humphreys, F.Murphy, Mauger, Cornwell, M.Smith, Varndell, A.Tuilagi, Stankovich, Young, Abraham, Ayerza, Castrogiovanni, Moreno.
Middle: Back (Skills & defence coach), T.Youngs, Vesty, Herring, Crane, Erinle, Croft, Wentzel, Hamilton, Blaze, Moody, Pienaar, Cole, Dodge, Kayser, B.Deacon, Cockerill (Forwards coach), L.Deacon.
Front: Burke, Chuter, O.Smith, Feijoo, Hipkiss, G.Murphy, Corry (capt), Loffreda (Head coach), Goode, Laussucq, Ellis, Davies, Rabeni.

← LEICESTER FOOTBALL CLUB 2008/09
Back: T.Youngs, Dupuy, Smith, J.Murphy, Pienaar, Tonks, Woods, Herring, Sammons, B.Youngs, Vesty, Hougaard.
Middle: O'Connor (Backs coach), Burke (Kicking coach), Cole, B.Deacon, Erinle, Crane, Varndell, Blaze, Wentzel, L.Deacon, Croft, Rabeni, Ayerza, Gonzalez Bonorino, Castrogiovanni, Stankovich, Cockerill (Forwards coach).
Front: Tuilagi, Davies, Hipkiss, Kay, Ellis, G.Murphy, Corry (capt), Meyer (Head coach), Mauger, Moody, Kayser, Chuter, White, Flood.

20 07/08		OVERALL RECORD:					T	C	PG	DG	PTS
Home Ground: Welford Road											
Head Coach: Marcelo Loffreda (Richard Cockerill during RWC) assisted by Richard Cockerill & Neil Back		PLD	W	D	L	Tigers scored:	90	58	86	7	845
Captain: Martin Corry		36	20	0	16	Opponents scored:	66	44	85	7	694

GM	DATE		VEN	OPPONENTS	RESULT	POS/LGE	TRIES	KICKS	ATT
GUINNESS PREMIERSHIP (4TH)						**CHAMPIONS: LONDON WASPS**			
1	Sep	16s	a	Bristol Rugby	W 26-13	5	Erinle 16, Varndell 59	J.Murphy c/2p, Burke c/p, Vesty d	8125
2		**22**	**H**	**Bath Rugby**	W 26-16	3	J.Murphy 50, M.Smith 80	Goode 2c/3p/d	17059
3		30s	a	London Wasps	W+ 20-17	2	O.Smith 9	Goode 4p, J.Murphy p	7313
4	Oct	**6**	**H**	**Gloucester Rugby**	L 17-30	6	Croft 70, Cornwell 79	Burke 2c, Goode p	17101
5		14s	a	Saracens	L+ 19-26	6	Crane 3, Stankovich 73	Burke 3p	7427
6		**20**	**H**	**Worcester Warriors**	W 28-20	5	Herring 20, O.Smith 35, Kayser 59	Burke 2c/3p	16219
11	Nov	24	a	Leeds Carnegie	W 29-6	4	Varndell 34/80, T.Youngs 48	Goode c/4p	9496
15	Dec	23s	a	Sale Sharks	L+ 14-20	5	J.Murphy 40	Goode 3p	10872
16		**29**	**H**	**London Irish**	W 25t-17	5	Vesty 7, Rabeni 39, Castrogiovanni 56, White 73	Humphreys c/p	17498
17	Jan	6s	a	Harlequins	W 42t-13	3	Varndell 32/54/70, Croft 52/66	Goode 4c/2p, G.Murphy d	12605
20		**26**	**H**	**Newcastle Falcons**	W 41t-14	2	Corry 3, Crane 12, J.Murphy 46, Ayerza 52	Goode 3c/4p/d	17498
21	Feb	9	a	Gloucester Rugby	W+ 20-13	2	O.Smith 34, Erinle 67	Goode 2c/2p	12597
22		17s	a	London Irish	L 13-22	2	Erinle 11	Goode c/2p	10559
23		**23**	**H**	**Sale Sharks**	L+ 11-14	2	Crane 71	Goode 2p	17498
24	Mar	**1**	**H**	**Leeds Carnegie**	W 34t-21	2	Crane 26, Varndell 30, Penalty 47, J.Murphy 53, Humphreys 73	Humphreys 3c/p	17002
25		8	a	Worcester Warriors	L+ 19-23	3	B.Deacon 1	Goode c/4p	10047
26		**15**	**H**	**Saracens**	W 36-23	2	Rabeni 47, A.Tuilagi 57, Varndell 78	Goode 3c/4p/d	17071
		22	a	Gloucester Rugby	PP (cup)	-			
28		**29**	**H**	**London Wasps**	L+ 19-24	4	Rabeni 47	Goode c/4p	17498
30	Apr	15tu	a	Bath Rugby	L 12-26	5	Humphreys 48, F.Murphy 76	Humphreys c	10600
31		**19**	**H**	**Bristol Rugby**	W 32t-14	6	Mauger 6, Herring 23, Varndell 27, Penalty 57, Goode 66	Goode 2c/p	17324
32	May	4s	a	Newcastle Falcons	L+ 25-28	6	Crane 8, Varndell 31/72	Goode c/p, Vesty c/p	9184
33		**10**	**H**	**Harlequins**	W+ 31t-28t	4	Herring 8, Varndell 15/76, J.Murphy 42, Crane 65	Goode 3c	17498
34		18s	a	Gloucester Rugby (sf)	W 26-25	-	A.Tuilagi 52, Mauger 63	Goode 2c/3p/d	16500
36		31		London Wasps (f)	L 16-26	-	Varndell 56, Ellis 62	Goode 2p	81600
HEINEKEN CUP						**EUROPEAN CHAMPIONS: MUNSTER**			
9	Nov	10	a	Leinster	L 9-22	4	-	Goode 3p	18563
10		**17**	**H**	**Edinburgh**	W 39t-0	2	Goode 5, Varndell 16, G.Murphy 40, Penalty 47, Corry 80	Goode 4c/2p	15865
13	Dec	**8**	**H**	**Toulouse**	W+ 14-9	2	O.Smith 12	Goode 3p	17498
14		16s	a	Toulouse	L 11-22	2	Varndell 16	Goode 2p	32500
18	Jan	12	a	Edinburgh	L+ 12-17	3	-	Goode 4p	5850
19		**19**	**H**	**Leinster**	W 25-9	2	B.Deacon 20, Rabeni 23, Herring 75	Goode 2c/2p	17033
ANGLO-WELSH CUP (EDF ENERGY CUP)						**CUP WINNERS: OSPREYS**			
7	Oct	27	a	Bath Rugby	L+ 14-20	3	Vesty 27	Humphreys 3p	10555
8	Nov	**3**	**H**	**Cardiff Blues**	W 42t-20	1	Varndell 44, J.Murphy 50/70, Hipkiss 66, Penalty 76	Goode c/3p, Burke 3c	17118
12		**30f**	**H**	**Sale Sharks**	W 32t-8	1	J.Murphy 3, Hipkiss 49, Varndell 76, Croft 80	Goode 3c/2p	17172
27	Mar	22		London Wasps (sf)	W 34-24	-	Goode 34, Rabeni 44, Hipkiss 56, Castrogiovanni 68	Goode 4c/2p	41018
29	Apr	12		Ospreys (f)	L 6-23	-	-	Goode p/d	65756
CLUB MATCH									
35	May	**25s**	**H**	**Classic All Blacks**	L 26-41		Gillanders 37, Hemingway 65, Hurrell 71, Penalty 78	Twelvetrees 2c, F.Murphy c	8184

Neutral Venues: *#27 at Millennium Stadium - Cardiff, #29 #36 at Twickenham*

INDIVIDUAL APPEARANCES 2007/08

Name / Game #	1	2	3	4	5	6	7	8	9	10	11	12	13	14	15	16	17	18	19	20	21	22	23	24	25	26	27	28	29	30	31	32	33	34	35	36	Apps	T	Pts
LC (Luke) Abraham	7	7	7	7	7	r	7	r	x	r	r	7	7	x	<7	-	-	-	-	-	-	-	-	-	-	-	-	-	-	-	-	-	-	-	-	-	9+4	-	-
MI (Marcos) Ayerza Ar15	-	-	-	-	-	-	r	1	1	1	1	1	1	1	1	-	1	1	r	1	1	-	1	-	r	1	r	1	-	1	r	r	r	r	-	r	16+9	1	5
RW (Rob) Bell	-	-	-	-	-	-	-	-	-	-	-	-	-	-	-	-	-	-	-	-	-	-	-	-	-	-	-	-	-	-	-	-	-	-	=7	-	1	-	-
RJ (Richard) Blaze	>r	r	r	x	-	-	4	-	-	-	r	-	-	x	-	-	-	-	-	-	-	-	-	-	-	-	-	r	x	4	r	r	r	r	-	r	2+10	-	-
AJ (Andy) Brown	-	-	-	-	-	-	-	-	-	-	-	-	-	-	-	-	-	-	-	-	-	-	-	-	-	-	-	-	-	-	-	-	-	-	=r	-	0+1	-	-
PA (Paul) Burke I13	10	x	-	r	10	10	-	r	x	<r	x	-	-	-	-	-	-	-	-	-	-	-	-	-	-	-	-	-	-	-	-	-	-	-	-	-	3+3	-	37
ML (Martin) Castrogiovanni It54	-	-	-	r	3	3	-	r	r	3	-	-	r	3	r	3	3	-	1	3	-	3	-	r	-	-	3	3	3	-	1	1	-	-	-	-	14+6	2	10
GS (George) Chuter E21	-	-	-	-	-	-	-	-	-	-	r	r	r	2	2	-	r	2	r	2	2	r	2	-	-	-	2	2	2	-	-	-	r	r	2	-	10+8	-	-
J (Jack) Cobden	-	-	-	-	-	-	-	-	-	-	-	-	-	-	-	-	-	-	-	-	-	-	-	-	-	-	-	-	-	-	-	-	-	-	=11	-	1	-	-
DR (Dan) Cole E+ L+	-	-	-	-	-	-	>1	-	-	-	-	-	-	-	-	-	-	-	-	-	-	-	-	-	-	-	-	-	-	-	-	-	-	-	3	-	2	-	-
MJ (Matt) Cornwell	r	x	r	12	r	r	12	-	-	-	-	-	-	-	-	-	-	-	-	-	-	-	-	-	x	-	x	-	-	12	-	-	-	-	10	-	4+4	1	5
ME (Martin) Corry E64 L7	-	-	-	-	-	-	-	6*	6*	6*	-	6*	6*	6*	8*	-	8*	8*	-	6*	6*	8*	4*	r	4*	5*	8*	6*	6*	r	4*	6*	6*	6*	-	6*	23+2	2	10
JS (Jordan) Crane E+	-	r	6	8	8	r	8	8	8	8	-	8	8	8	-	8	-	r	8	8	8	r	8	8	8	8	r	8	8	r	8	8	8	8	-	8	25+6	6	30
TR (Tom) Croft E3 L+	x	6	-	r	r	-	6	-	-	-	6	r	x	-	6	7	6	7	-	-	4	6	-	5	-	-	6	7	r	6	6	7	r	r	-	r	15+7	4	20
MD (Mitch) Culpin	-	-	-	-	-	-	-	-	-	-	-	-	-	-	-	-	-	-	-	-	-	-	-	-	-	-	-	-	-	-	-	-	-	-	=15	-	1	-	-
DM (Mefin) Davies W38	x	x	>r	r	2	r	2*	r	r	r	2	-	-	-	x	2	-	-	-	-	-	-	-	2	2	2	-	-	-	r	2	r	2	2	-	2	11+8	-	-
BR (Brett) Deacon	8	8	8	6	6	8	-	-	-	-	8	-	-	-	x	6	r	6	6	x	r	x	6	6	6	6	-	r	-	8	r	x	-	-	8*	-	16+4	2	10
LP (Louis) Deacon E8	4*	4*	4*	4*	4*	5*	-	4	4	4	-	4	4	-	-	4*	4	4	4*	4	-	-	5	4*	5	4	4	4	4	-	-	-	-	-	-	-	23	-	-
OP (Ollie) Dodge	-	-	-	-	-	-	-	-	-	-	-	-	-	-	-	-	-	-	-	-	-	-	-	-	-	-	-	-	-	<11	-	-	-	-	-	-	1	-	-
HA (Harry) Ellis E18 L+	-	-	-	-	-	-	-	-	-	-	-	-	-	-	-	-	-	-	-	-	-	-	-	r	9	9	9	9	9	-	9	9	9	9	-	9	10+1	1	5
AO (Ayoola) Erinle E+	>14	-	-	r	11	-	13	-	-	-	r	x	-	-	-	-	r	-	13	-	13	13	14	-	-	-	-	-	-	13	r	x	r	x	-	r	8+6	3	15
ODA (Owen) Finegan A55	=6	-	-	-	-	-	-	-	-	-	-	-	-	-	-	-	-	-	-	-	-	-	-	-	-	-	-	-	-	-	-	-	-	-	-	-	1	-	-
G (Greg) Gillanders	-	-	-	-	-	-	-	-	-	-	-	-	-	-	-	-	-	-	-	-	x	-	x	-	x	r	-	-	-	-	-	-	-	-	<4	-	1+1	1	5
JJ (Josh) Goldspink	-	-	-	-	-	-	-	-	-	-	-	-	-	-	-	-	-	-	-	-	-	-	-	-	-	-	-	-	-	-	-	-	-	-	>r	-	0+1	-	-
AJ (Andy) Goode E9	-	10	10	10	-	-	-	10	10	10	10	10	10	10	10	-	10	10	10	10	10	10	10	x	10	10	10	10	10	-	10	10	10	10	-	<10	28	3	320
CD (Calum) Green	-	-	-	-	-	-	-	-	-	-	-	-	-	-	-	-	-	-	-	-	-	-	-	-	-	-	-	-	-	-	-	-	-	-	>5	-	1	-	-
JL (Jim) Hamilton S16	-	-	-	-	x	4	r	r	r	r	4	r	r	4	4	-	r	-	-	-	-	<4	-	-	-	-	-	-	-	-	-	-	-	-	-	-	5+7	-	-
DP (Dan) Hemingway	-	-	-	-	-	-	-	-	-	-	-	-	-	-	-	-	-	-	-	-	-	-	-	-	-	-	-	-	-	-	-	-	-	-	>r	-	0+1	1	5
B (Ben) Herring	-	-	>r	-	-	7	x	-	-	-	-	-	-	-	-	x	-	-	7	-	■7	7	7	7	-	-	7	-	7	-	7	-	7	7	-	7	12+1	4	20
DJ (Dan) Hipkiss E6	-	-	-	-	-	-	-	13	-	12	13	12	13	12	r	13	-	r	-	-	-	x	13	13	-	13	12	12	13	-	13	13	13	13	-	13	18+2	3	15
IW (Ian) Humphreys	-	-	-	-	-	-	10	-	-	-	-	-	-	-	-	10	x	x	x	r	x	x	x	10	x	x	-	-	-	10	<r	-	-	-	-	-	4+2	2	35
WH (Will) Hurrell	-	-	-	-	-	-	-	-	-	-	-	-	-	-	-	-	-	-	-	-	-	-	-	-	-	-	-	-	-	-	-	-	-	-	>r	-	0+1	1	5
BJ (Ben) Kay E58 L2	-	-	-	-	-	-	-	5	5	-	5	5	-	5	5	x	5	5	x	5	-	5	-	-	-	-	5	5	5	5*	5	5	5	5	-	5	19	-	-
B (Benjamin) Kayser Fr+	>2	2	2	2	r	2	-	2	2	2	-	2	2	r	-	r	2	r	2	r	r	2	r	r	r	r	r	r	r	2	r	2	-	-	-	r	15+15	1	5
C (Christophe) Laussucq Fr4	x	x	>9	-	r	-	-	r	x	-	-	-	-	-	x	9	9	9	-	-	9	9	r	-	-	x	x	x	x	9	-	x	x	x	-	<r	7+4	-	-
WE (Will) Lawson	-	-	-	-	-	-	-	-	-	-	-	-	-	-	-	-	-	-	-	-	-	-	-	-	-	-	-	-	-	-	-	-	-	-	=12	-	1	-	-
AJD (Aaron) Mauger NZ45	-	-	-	-	-	-	-	-	-	-	-	-	>12	r	12	12	12	12	-	12	12	-	12	-	-	-	-	-	12	r	12	12	12	12	-	12	14+2	2	10
LW (Lewis) Moody E53 L3	-	-	-	-	-	-	-	7	7	7	7*	-	-	7	-	-	7	-	-	7	-	-	-	-	-	-	-	-	-	-	-	-	-	-	-	-	7	-	-
AC (Alejandro) Moreno Ar/It7	-	-	r	1	-	-	r	-	-	-	3	r	-	-	-	-	-	x	-	-	3	x	3	-	x	x	-	-	-	<r	-	-	-	-	-	-	4+4	-	-
F (Frank) Murphy	9	9	-	9	-	r	9	9	9	9	9	9	9	9	9	r	-	r	9	9	x	x	9	9	r	-	-	-	-	r	r	-	-	-	<9	-	17+6	1	7
GEA (Geordan) Murphy I56 L2	-	-	-	15	15	15	-	15	15	15	-	15	-	15	15	-	15	15	15	15	-	15	-	15	-	-	-	-	-	-	15	15	15	15	-	15	20	1	8
JE (Johne) Murphy	15	15	15	14	14	14	14	r	12	r	14	14	x	-	14	14	14	14	14	14	15	11	r	11	-	15	15	15	15	r	-	-	11	-	-	-	24+4	8	51
BJM (Ben) Pienaar	-	-	-	-	-	-	-	-	-	-	-	-	-	-	-	-	-	-	-	-	-	-	x	r	7	7	-	-	-	7	-	-	-	-	6	-	4+1	-	-
RSR (Seru) Rabeni Fi26 Pl6	-	-	-	-	-	11	-	12	14	-	-	-	r	14	-	11	-	-	12	13	-	-	-	-	-	12	13	13	-	-	-	-	-	-	-	-	10+1	5	25
GA (Greg) Sammons	-	-	-	-	-	-	-	-	-	-	-	-	-	-	-	-	-	-	-	-	-	-	-	-	-	-	-	-	-	-	-	-	-	-	=r	-	0+1	-	-
MW (Matt) Smith	r	14	14	-	-	-	-	-	-	-	-	-	-	-	-	-	-	-	-	-	-	-	-	-	-	-	-	-	-	-	-	-	-	-	-	-	2+1	1	5
OJ (Ollie) Smith E5 L1	13	13	13	13	13	13	-	-	13	13	-	13	14	13	13	x	13	13	-	r	11	12	11	12	13	x	-	x	<14	-	-	-	-	-	-	-	20+1	4	20
B (Boris) Stankovich	>1	1	1	-	1	1	-	-	-	-	-	-	-	-	-	1	-	-	-	-	-	1	-	1	1	r	1	-	1	-	-	-	1	1	-	1	14+1	1	5
AT (Alesana) Tuilagi Sa17 Pl1	-	-	-	-	-	-	-	11	11	11	-	-	-	-	-	-	-	-	-	-	-	-	-	r	11	11	11	11	11	-	11	11	-	11	-	11	12+1	2	10
EM (Manusamoa) Tuilagi E+ L+	-	-	-	-	-	-	-	-	-	-	-	-	-	-	-	-	-	-	-	-	-	-	-	-	-	-	-	-	-	-	-	-	-	-	>14	-	1	-	-
SV (Vavae) Tuilagi	-	-	-	-	-	-	-	-	-	-	-	-	-	-	-	-	-	-	-	-	-	-	-	-	-	-	-	-	-	-	-	-	-	-	=r	-	0+1	-	-
WWF (Billy) Twelvetrees E+	-	-	-	-	-	-	-	-	-	-	-	-	-	-	-	-	-	-	-	-	-	-	-	-	-	-	-	-	-	-	-	-	-	-	>13	-	1	-	4
TW (Tom) Varndell E3	11	11	11	11	r	x	11	14	-	14	11	11	11	11	11	r	11	11	11	11	14	14	-	14	14	14	14	14	r	14	14	14	14	14	-	14	29+3	18	90
SB (Sam) Vesty E+	12	12	12	-	12	12	15	-	x	-	15	r	15	x	x	15	-	-	x	-	x	-	15	-	15	-	r	x	x	15	-	r	x	r	-	x	12+4	2	18
MVZ (Marco) Wentzel SA2	>5	5	5	5	5	6	5	-	-	5	-	-	5	-	x	5	-	x	5	r	5	-	-	-	-	-	-	-	-	-	-	4	4	4	-	4	16+1	-	-
JM (Julian) White E44 L4	3	3	-	3	-	-	-	3	3	r	-	3	3	x	3	r	-	3	3	-	-	-	-	3	3	3	r	r	r	3	3	3	3	3	-	3	19+5	1	5
DJW (Dave) Young	x	r	3	-	x	r	3	-	-	-	r	-	-	-	-	-	r	-	r	r	x	-	r	-	-	-	-	-	-	-	-	-	-	-	<1	-	3+7	-	-
BR (Ben) Youngs E+ L+	-	-	r	r	9	9	x	-	-	r	r	x	r	r	-	-	r	-	r	x	-	-	-	-	-	-	-	-	-	-	-	-	-	-	r	-	2+9	-	-
TN (Tom) Youngs E+ L+	-	-	x	-	-	-	r	-	-	-	12	-	-	-	-	-	-	-	-	-	-	-	-	-	12	-	-	-	-	-	-	-	-	-	-	-	2+1	1	5

The key for how to read the stats is on the last page

2008/09

Home Ground: Welford Road except #30 #32 #34 at Walkers Stadium	Trophy Cabinet: Guinness Premiership(8)	OVERALL RECORD:					T	C	PG	DG	PTS
Head Coach: Heyneke Meyer then Richard Cockerill in January		PLD	W	D	L	Tigers scored:	97	77	93	3	927
Captain: Martin Corry		36	24	2	10	Opponents scored:	59	42	75	8	628

GM	DATE		VEN	OPPONENTS	RESULT	POS/LGE	TRIES	KICKS	ATT
GUINNESS PREMIERSHIP (1ST)						**CHAMPIONS: LEICESTER TIGERS**			
1	Sep	7s	a	Gloucester Rugby	W 20-8	3	G.Murphy 68, Flood 79	Flood c/2p, Dupuy c	13109
2		**13**	**H**	**London Irish**	W+ 24-22	2	G.Murphy 10, Croft 56, Herring 66	Flood 3c/p	16553
3		20	a	Worcester Warriors	W+ 19-17	1	Dupuy 68	Dupuy c, Flood 4p	10846
4		**26f**	**H**	**London Wasps**	L 19-28	3	J.Murphy 34	Flood c/4p	17498
5	Oct	**1w**	**H**	**Northampton Saints**	W 29-19	2	J.Murphy 56, Hipkiss 71, Flood 79	Flood c/4p	17498
11	Nov	15	a	Bath Rugby	L+ 21-25	4	J.Murphy 60, Davies 77	Hougaard 3p, G.Murphy c	10600
12		**22**	**H**	**Harlequins**	W 27-14	4	J.Murphy 2, Hougaard 31, Smith 44	Hougaard 3c/2p	17432
13		28f	a	Sale Sharks	L 13-27	6	Mauger 48	Dupuy c/2p	9586
16	Dec	**20**	**H**	**Newcastle Falcons**	W 20-3	4	G.Murphy 33, Mauger 65	Flood 2c/2p	17240
17		27	a	Harlequins	D 26-26	5	J.Murphy 39, Croft 50	Flood 2c/4p	50000
18	Jan	**4s**	**H**	**Bath Rugby**	W+ 24-22	4	Croft 66/77	Hougaard c/3p/d	17498
19		10	a	Northampton Saints	L+ 13-17	5	Flood 61	Flood c/2p	13582
22	Feb	15s	a	London Wasps	L+ 29t-36	6	Hamilton 5, Vesty 36, Crane 67, J.Murphy 80	Vesty c, Dupuy 2c/p	9581
23		**21**	**H**	**Worcester Warriors**	W 38t-5	6	Ayerza 28, Tuilagi 31, B.Youngs 64, Vesty 70, Smith 73	Vesty 3c, Dupuy 2c/p	17081
24	Mar	1s	a	London Irish	W+ 31-28t	5	Ayerza 22, Smith 36/52	Dupuy 2c/4p	12104
25		**7**	**H**	**Gloucester Rugby**	W 24-10	2	-	Dupuy 7p, G.Murphy d	17498
26		13f	a	Bristol Rugby	W+ 23-17	2	Cole 13, Hipkiss 68	Vesty c/3p, Dupuy c	6037
27		**21**	**H**	**Saracens**	W 46t-16	1	L.Deacon 5, Hamilton 35/65, Hipkiss 40, Penalty 77, Varndell 79	Hougaard 2c/p, Dupuy c/p, Vesty 2c	16328
28		27f	a	Newcastle Falcons	L+ 10-14	1	B.Youngs 80	Flood c/p	7614
29	Apr	**4**	**H**	**Sale Sharks**	W+ 37t-31	1	Tuilagi 6, Hamilton 19/60, Hipkiss 53, Vesty 70	Vesty c, Flood 2c/2p	17498
31		19s	a	Saracens	W+ 16-13	1	Hamilton 9, Erinle 56	Vesty 2p	11275
32		**25**	**H**	**Bristol Rugby**	W 73t-3	1	Vesty 7, White 11, Hipkiss 26, Crane 31, G.Murphy 38/55, Flood 44, Varndell 68, Woods 72, J.Murphy 75, Erinle 80	G.Murphy 2c, Vesty 3c, Dupuy 4c	18816
34	May	**9**	**H**	**Bath Rugby (sf)**	W 24-10	-	Hipkiss 17, Vesty 38, Moody 69	Dupuy 3c/p	18850
35		16		London Irish (f)	W 10-9	-	Crane 61	Dupuy c/p	81601
HEINEKEN CUP						**EUROPEAN CHAMPIONS: LEINSTER**			
7	Oct	**12s**	**H**	**Ospreys**	W+ 12-6	2	-	Flood 4p	17498
8		18	a	Benetton Treviso	W 60t-16	1	Flood 16/39, Crane 22/78, J.Murphy 54/79/80, G.Murphy 59, Penalty 64	Flood 3c/p, Hougaard 3c	7000
14	Dec	**6**	**H**	**Perpignan**	W 38t-27	1	Flood 19, Mauger 40, Crane 62, Smith 67	Flood 3c/4p	17371
15		14s	a	Perpignan	L+ 20-26	2	Croft 38, Hamilton 67	Flood 2c/2p	14466
20	Jan	**17**	**H**	**Benetton Treviso**	W 52t-0	1	Hamilton 4/14, Penalty 22, Mauger 26/38, Smith 30, G.Murphy 49, J.Murphy 56	Flood 6c	16746
21		24	a	Ospreys	L+ 9-15	2	-	Hougaard 3p	18205
30	Apr	**11**	**H**	**Bath Rugby (qf)**	W 20-15	-	Dupuy 80	Vesty 5p	26100
33	May	3s		Cardiff Blues (sf)	D 26-26 (aet: 7-6 pens)	-	Hamilton 22, G.Murphy 45	Dupuy 2c/4p	44212
36		23		Leinster (f)	L 16-19	-	Woods 39	Dupuy c/3p	66523
ANGLO-WELSH CUP (EDF ENERGY CUP)						**CUP WINNERS: CARDIFF BLUES**			
6	Oct	4	a	Bath Rugby	W+ 19-15	1	B.Youngs 18	Hougaard c/3p/d	10600
9		25	a	Cardiff Blues	L 9-23	3	-	Hougaard 3p	9815
10		**31f**	**H**	**Sale Sharks**	W 30-20	2	Penalty 19, T.Youngs 57, Crane 80	Hougaard 2c/3p, Newby c	16550

Neutral Venues: *#33 at Millennium Stadium - Cardiff, #35 at Twickenham, #36 at Murrayfield - Edinburgh*

INDIVIDUAL APPEARANCES 2008/09

Name / Game #	1	2	3	4	5	6	7	8	9	10	11	12	13	14	15	16	17	18	19	20	21	22	23	24	25	26	27	28	29	30	31	32	33	34	35	36	Apps	T	Pts
MI (Marcos) Ayerza Ar21	1	1	1	1	r	-	1	1	-	r	-	-	1	1	1	-	-	-	-	-	-	r	1	1	1	1	1	-	1	1	1	-	1	1	1	1	21+3	2	10
RJ (Richard) Blaze	4	4	-	-	-	-	r	r	4	4	4	-	-	-	-	-	-	-	-	-	-	-	-	-	-	-	-	-	-	-	-	-	-	-	-	-	5+2	-	-
ML (Martin) Castrogiovanni It59	-	-	-	-	-	-	-	-	-	-	-	-	-	-	-	r	r	r	r	1	r	-	3	-	r	-	-	3	r	3	3	r	3	3	-	3	8+8	-	-
GS (George) Chuter E21	2	2	r	r	r	r	r	r	2	-	2	2	2	r	r	2	r	r	2	2	r	2	r	r	-	x	2	2	2	2	2	x	2	2	2	2	19+13	-	-
DR (Dan) Cole E+ L+	x	r	r	3	-	3	r	r	r	3	3	3	3	r	r	-	-	-	-	-	-	3	-	3	-	3	3	r	-	x	r	-	-	-	r	-	10+10	1	5
ME (Martin) Corry E64 L7	-	-	4*	4*	4*	-	4*	6*	6*	-	6*	6*	4*	4*	4*	r	4*	4*	r	r	4*	-	-	-	-	-	-	<8*	-	-	-	-	-	-	-	-	15+3	-	-
JS (Jordan) Crane E1	8	8	8	8	8	-	8	8	8	r	8	-	8	8	8	-	8	-	-	8	8	8	8	8	-	-	-	-	-	r	8	8	8	8	8	8	24+2	7	35
TR (Tom) Croft E13 L+	6	6	6	6	6	-	6	7	7	-	-	-	-	6	6	-	6	6	6	6	6	-	r	-	6	-	-	6	6	6	4	4	4	4	4	4	25+1	5	25
DM (Mefin) Davies W38	-	-	-	-	-	2	-	-	r	r	r	r	-	-	-	r	-	-	-	-	-	r	-	2	r	2	r	r	x	x	-	-	-	-	-	-	3+9	1	5
BR (Brett) Deacon	-	-	-	-	-	8	-	r	x	6	r	8	6	r	x	8	-	r	8	r	x	r	r	r	-	-	-	-	-	-	-	-	-	-	-	-	6+8	-	-
LP (Louis) Deacon E8	-	-	-	-	-	-	-	-	-	-	-	-	-	-	-	-	-	-	-	-	-	4	4	4	4	4	4	4	4	4	-	-	-	-	x	r	9+1	1	5
J (Julien) Dupuy Fr+	>r	r	9	9	r	-	x	r	r	9	9	9	9	9	9	9	9	9	9	-	9	9	9	9	9	9	9	-	r	r	-	9	9	9	9	<9	24+7	2	129
HA (Harry) Ellis E27 L+	9	9	-	-	9	-	9	9	9	-	-	-	-	-	r	-	-	-	-	-	-	-	-	-	-	-	-	9	9	9	9	r	r	r	x	r	10+5	-	-
AO (Ayoola) Erinle E+	-	-	r	r	-	13	-	-	r	r	-	-	-	-	-	-	-	-	-	-	-	r	r	r	x	-	-	13	r	12	13	r	-	13	13	<13	7+9	2	10
TGAL (Toby) Flood E26	>10	10	10	10	10	-	10	10	12	-	-	-	-	10	10	10	10	-	10	10	12	-	-	-	-	-	-	10	10	-	-	10	10	-	-	-	19	7	202
JJ (Josh) Goldspink	-	-	-	-	-	<r	-	-	-	-	-	-	-	-	-	-	-	-	-	-	-	-	-	-	-	-	-	-	-	-	-	-	-	-	-	-	0+1	-	-
SH (Santiago) Gonzalez Bonorino Ar15	-	-	-	-	-	>r	-	-	-	-	r	r	r	-	-	-	-	-	-	-	-	-	-	r	-	<r	-	-	-	-	-	-	-	-	-	-	0+6	-	-
CD (Calum) Green	-	-	-	-	-	-	-	-	-	-	-	-	-	-	-	-	-	-	-	-	-	-	-	-	-	-	r	-	x	-	-	-	-	-	-	-	0+1	-	-
SE (Scott) Hamilton NZ2	-	-	-	-	-	-	-	-	-	-	-	>15	r	14	14	14	15	-	r	14	14	15	14	15	14	15	15	14	14	14	14	-	14	14	14	14	21+2	10	50
SJ (Sam) Harrison	-	-	-	-	-	x	-	-	-	-	-	-	-	-	-	-	-	-	-	>r	-	-	-	-	-	-	-	-	-	-	-	-	-	-	-	-	0+1	-	-
DP (Dan) Hemingway	-	-	-	-	-	6	-	-	-	-	-	x	-	-	-	-	-	-	-	-	-	r	-	-	x	x	r	r	r	-	x	-	-	-	-	-	1+4	-	-
B (Ben) Herring	7	7	7	r	7	-	-	-	-	-	-	-	-	-	-	r	r	-	7	-	-	-	-	-	-	r	<7	-	-	-	-	-	-	-	-	-	6+4	1	5
DJ (Dan) Hipkiss E7	12	13	-	-	13	-	13	13	13	-	13	13	-	13	13	-	13	13	-	-	-	-	-	-	-	13	13	-	13	13	12	13	13	12	12	12	22	6	30
DJ (Derick) Hougaard SA8	-	-	-	-	-	>10	r	r	10	10	10	10	10	-	-	-	-	10	-	r	10	-	-	r	x	x	<r	-	-	-	-	-	-	-	-	-	8+5	1	98
BJ (Ben) Kay E60 L2	5*	5	5	r	r	5*	5	5	r	5*	r	5	5	5	5	5*	-	5	5	5	r	5	5	5	5	5	5	5	5	5	5	5	5	5	5	5	30+5	-	-
B (Benjamin) Kayser Fr9	r	r	2	2	2	-	2	2	-	2	-	-	r	2	2	-	2	2	x	r	2	-	2	-	2	-	-	-	-	-	r	2	r	r	r	<r	14+9	-	-
AJD (Aaron) Mauger NZ45	-	12*	12	12	12	-	12	12	-	-	12	12	12	12	12	12	12	12	12*	12*	-	12*	12*	12*	12*	12*	12*	12	-	-	-	-	r	-	-	-	23+1	5	25
LW (Lewis) Moody E53 L3	-	-	-	-	-	-	-	-	-	7	7	7	7	7	7	7	7	7	-	-	-	-	-	-	-	-	-	-	-	-	-	7	r	r	r	r	10+4	1	5
GEA (Geordan) Murphy I63 L2	15	15	15	15	15	-	15	15	-	-	15	-	15	15	15	15	-	15	15	15	15	-	15	-	15	-	-	15	15*	15*	15*	15*	15*	15*	15*	15*	27	8	49
JE (Johne) Murphy	-	r	11	11	14	-	14	14	15	14	14	14	14	r	x	11	14	14	14	r	r	r	r	14	-	-	14	r	x	x	11	11	11	11	11	x	21+7	11	55
CA (Craig) Newby NZ3	-	-	-	-	-	-	-	-	-	>8	r	-	r	-	-	6	r	8	r	-	-	6	6	6	-	-	-	-	-	r	6	6	6	6	6	6	12+5	-	2
S (Seb) Pearson	-	-	-	-	-	=7	-	-	-	-	-	-	-	-	-	-	-	-	-	-	-	-	-	-	-	-	-	-	-	-	-	-	-	-	-	-	1	-	-
BJM (Ben) Pienaar	-	-	-	-	-	-	-	-	-	-	-	-	-	-	-	-	-	-	-	-	-	-	-	-	8	8	8	r	8	8	x	-	-	-	-	-	5+1	-	-
RSR (Seru) Rabeni Fi26 PI9	-	-	-	-	-	-	-	r	14	13	-	-	13	r	r	r	x	r	13	13	13	13	-	-	-	-	-	-	-	x	<r	-	-	-	-	-	7+6	-	-
SI (Sam) Raven	-	-	-	-	-	>4	-	-	-	-	-	-	-	-	-	-	-	-	-	-	-	-	-	-	-	-	-	-	-	-	-	-	-	-	-	-	1	-	-
MW (Matt) Smith	13	11	13	13	11	r	11	11	11	15	11	11	11	11	11	13	11	11	11	11	11	14	13	13	13	14	-	-	-	-	-	14	r	r	r	r	26+5	6	30
B (Boris) Stankovich	-	-	-	-	1	1	-	-	1	1	1	1	-	-	-	1	1	1	1	r	1	1	-	-	-	-	r	1	-	-	-	1	-	-	-	-	14+2	-	-
AT (Alesana) Tuilagi Sa17 PI1	11	-	-	-	-	11	r	-	-	-	-	-	-	-	-	-	-	-	-	-	-	11	11	11	11	11	11	11	11	11	-	-	-	-	-	11	12+1	2	10
TW (Tom) Varndell E4	14	14	14	14	x	14	-	-	r	11	r	r	x	-	-	r	r	r	-	-	-	-	-	-	-	r	r	-	-	-	x	r	-	<r	x	-	6+10	2	10
SB (Sam) Vesty E+	x	x	-	-	-	15	-	-	-	r	-	r	-	-	-	-	-	-	x	-	x	10	10	10	10	10	10	r	12	10	10	12	12	10	10	10	15+3	5	77
MVZ (Marco) Wentzel SA2	r	r	r	5	5	r	r	4	5	r	5	4	r	r	r	4	5	r	4	4	5	-	-	r	r	6	-	-	-	-	-	r	r	<r	-	-	12+15	-	-
JM (Julian) White E49 L4	3	3	3	r	3	-	3	3	3	-	-	-	-	3	3	3	3	3	3	3	3	-	r	-	3	-	-	-	■3	-	-	3	r	r	3	r	19+5	1	5
BN (Ben) Woods	>r	r	r	7	r	-	7	-	-	-	-	-	-	-	-	-	-	-	-	7	7	7	7	7	7	7	6	7	7	7	7	r	7	7	7	7	18+5	2	10
BR (Ben) Youngs E+ L+	-	-	r	r	-	9	-	-	-	r	r	r	x	r	-	r	x	r	r	9	x	r	r	x	x	r	r	r	-	-	r	-	-	-	-	-	2+15	3	15
TN (Tom) Youngs E+ L+	r	-	x	r	x	12	-	-	-	12	-	-	-	-	-	-	-	-	-	-	-	-	-	-	-	-	-	-	-	-	-	-	-	-	-	-	2+2	1	5

The key for how to read the stats is on the last page

CHAPTER 35

Standing Room Only

2009/2010

The recession was beginning to bite. While various Tigers went off to become Lions or play for England, the club set about the difficult task of trimming their squad from 42 to 37. During the 2008/09 season they had used 46 players but they had to recognise that the rising profiles of certain players required appropriate financial recognition and the money available in France (where the value of the euro was similar to that of the pound) had already caused disruption within the English game.

"We can get considerably less for the money we are allowed to spend under the salary cap," Simon Cohen, Leicester's head of operations, said. "We would have loved to keep the numbers the same, and stay within the cap." There was toing and froing with Stade Français over a transfer fee for Julien Dupuy, whose form was recognised when France capped him on tour against New Zealand.

In South Africa, Tom Croft became one of the shining lights of the Lions tour which ended in a 2-1 series loss to the Springboks. The flanker started both the first and second internationals, scoring two tries in the 26-21 loss in Durban and suffering the heartbreak of defeat in Pretoria when Morné Steyn's last-minute penalty earned South Africa a 28-25 win. Croft reverted to the bench for the final international in Johannesburg, but both he and Harry Ellis shared in the glorious finale of a 28-9 win, the highest ever score by the Lions against South Africa.

Louis Deacon, Dan Hipkiss, Julian White and Ben Kay all featured in both of England's matches with Argentina, the first won at Old Trafford (when White celebrated his fiftieth cap), the second lost in Salta. So did the persevering Sam Vesty, capped twice as a replacement centre to round off a remarkable year; in the same series, Jordan Crane and George Chuter added to their laurels against a Pumas side including Marcos Ayerza at prop. Johne Murphy helped Ireland A win the Churchill Cup against a Saxons XV in which Dan Cole and Ben Woods both started while in Japan, Ben Youngs helped England to the final of the under-20 world cup where they lost to New Zealand.

When everyone came home again, nine Leicester players were named in England's elite squad - Chuter, Crane, Croft, Deacon, Ellis, Flood, Hipkiss, Kay and White. Lewis Moody had to be content as one of five Tigers in the Saxons squad where he was joined by Cole, Woods, Vesty and Richard Blaze. All of which was deemed secondary to the preparations for the opening of the new Caterpillar Stand after a summer when, despite everything, more than £3 million was raised in season-ticket sales. The finishing touches to the new stand, capable of seating 10,000, meant that Leicester could not play at home until the third week of the new season but adding to the lustre was the granting of a fixture with South Africa on 6 November to mark opening day.

It was the second-biggest single-tier stand in the country, behind Liverpool Football Club's Kop, and offered a 1,000-seat dining area and space in which the club's artefacts could be brought together. But Leicester needed it in working order as swiftly as possible: they declared a loss on the previous season of £829,000, largely because of the costs involved in the stand. Peter Tom, referring to a "challenging" year, told the annual meeting: "I believe we are in good shape to take advantage of the [financial] recovery, when it comes." Later in the season, Tom's title changed to executive chairman and Peter Wheeler, chief executive for 15 years, became rugby director, moves that recognised the growth of the company off the field, as well as on it.

That same annual meeting also awarded life membership to Matt Hampson: "In the face of personal adversity," the citation read, "Matt has shown tremendous courage and determination, and has been an inspiration to so many people

↙ Harry Ellis forced his way into the decisive Lions team for the third test following some strong performances.

↓ Tom Croft escapes the attentions of François Steyn to score in the first test.

around him, whether they are able-bodied or have suffered traumatic injuries and disability." Apart from his local activities, Hampson had been made Patron of Special Effect, the organisation designed to help disabled youngsters use leisure technology. To top it off, the former prop was a benevolent fund ambassador for the Rugby Professionals' Association and for the RFU's injured players' fund.

On the field, however, it was a difficult start: there were new midfield players in Jeremy Staunton (from Wasps) and Anthony Allen (Gloucester) to embrace, Geordan Murphy recovered from a hernia operation in time to resume the captaincy but Hipkiss, Woods and Moody collected injuries annoyingly early in the season. If there was a certain amount of muddling through, other clubs were in the same state as they came to terms with revised laws after the shelving of most of the experimental laws trialled the previous season.

↑ The new 10,000-seat Caterpillar Stand was first used when Newcastle came to Welford Road 19.9.2009.

There was a sell-out crowd of 24,000 for the meeting with Newcastle Falcons, the first occasion on which the Caterpillar Stand was used and the Walk of Legends was opened. Their reward was a grim 15-6 win for Tigers, who waited until the fourth match of the season (against Worcester) before scoring a try though, against that, they only conceded one in the same period. When the first round of Heineken Cup matches came round, Leicester stood a modest fifth in the Premiership table, having scored 81 points against 64.

Leicester's European pool included their old friends, the Ospreys, who arrived at Welford Road and, with five minutes of the first half remaining, led 26-8. It had been a dire morning for Tigers: Mauger, Ellis, Smith and Hipkiss all withdrew with injuries and a fourth centre, Allen, left during the interval which meant that Craig Newby, a flanker, had to spend the second half in midfield. The starting XV included Lucas Gonzalez Amorosino, the Argentinian wing, James Grindal, who had returned to the club during the summer, at scrum-half and Billy Twelvetrees, a Leicester academy product who had previously been released to play for Bedford.

Twelvetrees proved the hero of the hour. Having become National Division One's leading try-scorer with Bedford, here he not only scored one of four Leicester tries, he kicked his goals nervelessly, his final conversion levelling the scores at 32-32. It was a sensational debut by a young man who knew only ten minutes before the start that he would be playing and was second choice (behind Staunton) as goalkicker. At one point in the first half Tigers were 18 point in arrears, then came the fightback. "It was just a titanic battle, given the situation we were in," Richard Cockerill said. "You can buy sides but you can't buy spirit like that, the attitude to play and not give up."

Unsurprisingly, Twelvetrees started the next match, a 46-11 win in Viadana, but was absent when the Premiership resumed in defeat at London Irish. It was an uncertain prelude to the official opening of the Caterpillar Stand, the meeting with South Africa on 6 November. It was the first time Leicester had played the Springboks and they were without five players required by England against Australia the following day; they did have the services of the experienced Australian wing, Lote Tuqiri, signed earlier in the week on a short-term contract after being released by the Australian Rugby Union after 67 caps and 30 international tries. South Africa, at the start of their European tour, were the holders of the Webb Ellis Cup, the tri-nations champions, victors over the Lions and they had certain expectations of their midweek players. The teams were:

Leicester: Scoll Hamilton; Lucas Amorosino (Lote Tuqiri, 56), Andy Forsyth, Manu Tuilagi, Johne Murphy; Aaron Mauger (captain), Ben Youngs; Boris Stankovich, Mefin Davies (George Chuter, 52), Martin Castrogiovanni (Dan Cole, 65), Calum Green, Dan Hemingway, Geoff Parling, Brett Deacon (Craig Hammond, 13), Ben Pienaar (Tom Armes, 60).
South Africa XV: Earl Rose (Riaan Viljoen, 65); Odwa Ndungane, Juan de Jongh, Wynand Olivier (Meyer Bosman, 64), Jongi Nokwe; Ruan Pienaar, Heini Adams (François Hougaard, 54); Gurthro Steenkamp (Heinke van der Merwe, 43), Chiliboy Ralepelle (captain; Bandise Maku, 20), Jannie du Plessis, Danie Roussouw (Alistair Hargreaves, 60), Andries Bekker, Dewald Potgieter, Ashley Johnson, Davon Raubenheimer (Jean Deysel, 48).
Referee: Stuart Dickinson (Australia).

Leicester's starting XV included five players of 20 or under, including two centres promoted from the academy in Andy Forsyth and Manu Tuilagi. It would have been a particularly prescient pundit who would have foretold that three of them would become Lions in 2013 - Tuilagi, Ben Youngs and Geoff Parling, the lock recruited from Newcastle during the summer. But on a brilliant night for the club, they won 22-17 in front of a capacity crowd who could scarcely believe what they were watching.

The touring side, with nine full internationals, went 8-0 ahead when Ruan Pienaar kicked a penalty and a cross-kick by Earl Rose laid on a try for Jongi Nokwe. But Youngs, who had played fly-half at school and was accustomed to kicking,

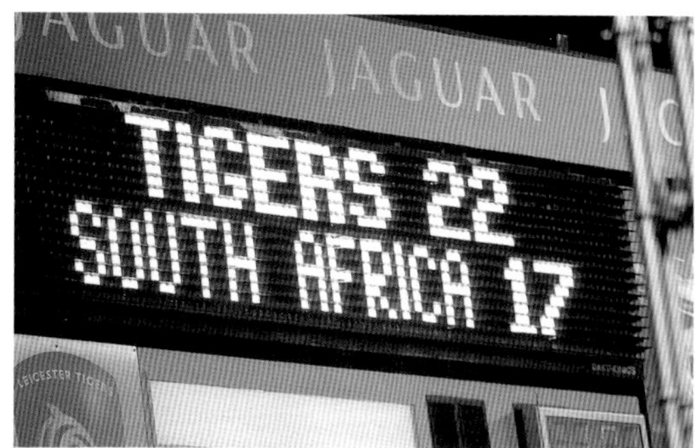

landed the first of five penalties and Johne Murphy started the move that, aided by Tuilagi, gave Lucas Amorosino the space to sprint and swerve 40 metres for a try which, with the conversion by Youngs, gave Leicester the lead.

Two more penalties, against one by Pienaar, made the half-time score 16-11 but the South Africans were thoroughly disconcerted by the first-time tackling of the Leicester midfield and the power of the home scrum. The country which so prides itself on outmuscling most opponents was itself outmuscled and Youngs casually knocked over two more penalties to push Leicester into an 11-point lead. Pienaar added two more goals but, though pinned in their own half for much of the final quarter, Leicester hung on.

"We managed to stay composed under pressure and the young guys kept their heads," Aaron Mauger said. "It was pretty special." It was even more special that Leicester were able to do what England could not: Tigers forced ten turnovers in general play, they turned over one Springbok scrum and took penalties at two more, and stole four Springbok lineouts. While losing 18-11 to Australia at Twickenham, with a side including a complete Leicester back row of Tom Croft, Lewis Moody and Jordan Crane (plus Dan Hipkiss and Louis Deacon), England had none of those basics in place.

↑ 16-year-old George Ford made his first-team debut at Leeds in the LV=Cup on 8.11.2009

The international autumn brought caps for two former Tigers, Andy Goode and Ayoola Erinle, while Leicester, taking youth as their signature, gave George Ford a debut at fly-half in the LV= Cup match against Leeds two days after the Springbok triumph. Ford, son of the England assistant coach, Mike, thereby became the youngest player to represent the club in the professional era, at 16 years and 237 days old, an improvement on the mark set by the youngest of the Tuilagis to represent the club, Manu who was 17 years and seven days old when he played against a Classic All Blacks XV in May 2009.

The second cup match, against Newport Gwent Dragons, was memorable for an entirely different reason: Cockerill was charged with two counts of verbal abuse of match officials and a RFU disciplinary hearing banned him for four weeks and fined him £2,000. Cockerill, upset by the refereeing of the scrum during the match in question, pleaded guilty and so missed match-day involvement with his team for two Premiership and two Heineken Cup games.

The first of those games, against Leeds, marked the first start for six months of Toby Flood, who had recovered from the ruptured Achilles sustained in the Heineken Cup semi-final with Cardiff Blues. Flood scored a try and kicked 12 points in a 39-6 win and the older Tuilagi, Alesana, made his first appearance of the season off the bench. On the down side, Croft tweaked knee ligaments and Richard Blaze, the highly-regarded lock who had been on the fringe of an England cap, would be out for the best part of a year to recover from another operation of a stress fracture in the foot.

Defeat to Wasps in the Premiership presaged the most topsy-turvy of visits to Clermont Auvergne in the Heineken Cup. With 70 minutes on the clock, Leicester were down and out: they trailed 35-9, they had been turned over numerous times and everything they tried turned to dust. But in the final nine minutes they scored three tries, one of them to Flood who also kicked 15 points. The 40-30 defeat left qualification for the knockout phase on a knife's edge.

Cockerill told his players they had to win all three remaining games to avoid such a fate and they started with a 20-15 win at home to Clermont, a game notable for the maturity of Youngs at scrum-half, for Parling's growing authority and Dan Cole's ability to go the distance against the hard-nut front row fielded by the French club. All three retained their places for the Premiership visit of Sale, when Moody captained the club for only the second time.

But it was a gloomy start to 2010: Harry Sibson, former player, first-team secretary and president, died at the age of 90 and Dusty Hare, after an association of 34 years, left to join Northampton in a recruitment and development role. Hare had not only been full-back and leading points scorer for much of the 1970s and 1980s, he had been a constant presence as coach and mentor to the younger players and had acted as chief scout for four years. His departure was like losing some of the family silver.

Still, Leicester buckled to. They removed 24 tonnes of snow from Welford Road before the Wasps game to become the only club in the country to fulfil their Premiership fixture. The 34-8 win took them momentarily to the top of the table and Cole confirmed his growing reputation by outplaying Tim Payne, the England loose-head prop. It also left them in good heart for the resumption of European games, a 47-8 win over Viadana leaving them delicately poised at the top of pool three, one point clear of Ospreys and Clermont.

↓ Had it not been for the ground staff and volunteers shifting 24 tonnes of snow, the game against Wasps would not have gone ahead. It did, and Leicester won 34-8 to go top of the table, 9.1.2010.

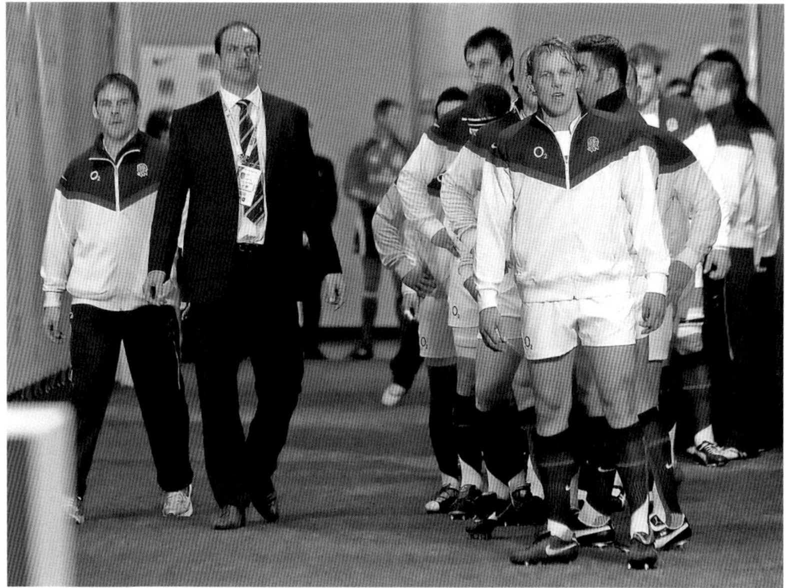

↑ Lewis Moody leads England out for the first time in the six nations game against France in Paris, 20 March 2010, John Wells and Martin Johnson to his right.

But Tigers could not take that final step. They lost 17-12 to the Ospreys at the Liberty Stadium and failed to qualify for the quarter-finals. The game, though, became known as the affair of the sixteenth man. For just under a minute in the second half, the Ospreys had 16 players on the field; Lee Byrne, the Wales full-back, having been replaced by Sonny Parker for a blood injury, went back on without the authority of the referee, Ireland's Alun Lewis.

The upshot was a formal investigation by European Rugby Cup Ltd, responding to an official complaint by Leicester. "ERC and the officials have to face up to their responsibility," Tom said. "It's not an amateur game any more. A serious error has been made." Leicester's hope was that a replay might be ordered or competition points deducted from the Ospreys. In the event, neither happened: Byrne was suspended for a fortnight but appealed successfully and did not miss the Wales-England international. The Ospreys were fined around £30,000 but the investigation decided that neither team nor player had taken premeditated action. It left Leicester unhappy and England with only one qualifier (Northampton) for the knockout phase of the Heineken Cup.

Cockerill had already outlined the difficulties for English clubs: "When any decent players become available, the French market is so hard to compete against," he said. "The price of players is going up...so, if you have a ceiling of £4 million, you're always going to have a smaller squad, if you want to keep the quality. Or you have the same amount of players, but less quality. The money can't go both ways." Simon Cohen called for a 25 per cent increase in the salary cap: "If [the cap] is to maintain a level where all 12 Premiership clubs are competing on a level playing field, then £4 million seems to be the appropriate figure," he said. "If you want one that allows English clubs to compete in Europe, then it needs to be higher."

Meanwhile 13 of Leicester's squad were required for national duty, eight in the elite squad, five in the Saxons. Croft's knee kept him out of the Six Nations but Youngs and Parling confirmed their advance by playing for the Saxons in the 17-13 win over Ireland A. Moody and Flood (at centre) started against Wales, the match in which Cole came off the bench to earn his first cap; a week later, against an Italy front row including Martin Castrogiovanni, Cole was the starting tight-head prop and stayed for the rest of the championship.

↑ Richard Cockerill has been the head man off the field at the Tigers since the summer of 2007.

Moreover he scored a try against an Ireland side with Geordan Murphy recalled at full-back. Murphy it was who finished on the winning side as Ireland won 20-16 and he remained there for the rest of the championship. In another indifferent season for England, Ben Youngs won his first cap in a dull draw against Scotland when he came on as a replacement for Ugo Monye on the left wing and Flood was recalled at fly-half ahead of Jonny Wilkinson for the final international, against France in Paris. That match saw another of the club's players at England's helm: Moody, dropped for the Scotland game, took over from the injured Steve Borthwick as captain against France and became the fifth Leicester player to lead his country in the professional era.

Where he would be playing his club rugby in the future, however, was up in the air. The Leicester management could perceive a situation in which Moody would constantly be away with England, hence their interest in Thomas Waldrom, the Hawke's Bay No 8, and Moody's eventual departure to Bath. Tuqiri signed for Wests Tigers, the Sydney rugby league club, and Johne Murphy headed for Munster.

One other player was making the unusual transition from centre to hooker and would make a unique success of it. During his half-season with Leicester, Heyneke Meyer had suggested that Tom Youngs might consider a career in the front row after seeing him take on opposing front rowers in a scuffle during an A league game. The four-square Youngs, an England under-21 centre, thought about it and decided that, with the requisite hard work, the switch might work and started his first match with number two on his back in an irrelevant LV= Cup game against Northampton. With two knowledgeable minders, Julian White and Boris Stankovich, on either side of him, Youngs lasted fifty minutes and a star was born.

However, Aaron Mauger, the influential New Zealand centre - "a real asset to this club, on and off the field," Cockerill said - was forced by his persistent back injury to retire and as activity in the transfer market increased, Leicester set about defending their position at the head of the Premiership. A 40-22 success against Harlequins secured a home play-off game but the regular season was marred by the 23-32 defeat at Welford Road against Saracens.

It ended a 19-month unbeaten home league record and earned Saracens their first win at Leicester in 33 attempts. Brendan Venter, the visiting director of rugby, became so animated that there were exchanges with members of the crowd; Venter, the former South Africa centre, was already under a suspended four-week ban for making adverse comments about the refereeing of his club's game with Leicester in January and the upshot here was a charge of conduct prejudicial to the interests of the game. To make matters worse for Saracens, Schalk Brits, their hooker, was also charged with making an abusive gesture to the crowd when he was replaced.

At a disciplinary hearing, Brits - who apologised to the crowd at the end of the game - received no more than a reprimand and Venter suffered a ten-week touchline ban for provocative behaviour. That prevented any match-day involvement with his players in the Premiership final - against, as it turned out, Leicester. The Tigers had first to make their way past Bath and did so thanks to five penalties from Flood in a 15-6 win, the match marking Moody's last appearance for the club at Welford Road.

Venter would have noted wryly the warning about future conduct given to Cockerill for his animated attitude during the semi-final. The Leicester head coach was cautioned by the club's board and received a written warning from the RFU after failing to restrain his passionate reactions to on-field decisions made during the Bath game. Leicester's team in their sixth successive final at Twickenham was: Geordan Murphy (captain); Scott Hamilton, Matt Smith (Dan Hipkiss, 68), Anthony Allen, Alesana Tuilagi (Jeremy Staunton, 74); Toby Flood, Ben Youngs; Marcos Ayerza, George Chuter, Martin Castrogiovanni (Dan Cole, 67), Louis Deacon, Geoff Parling, Tom Croft, Jordan Crane, Lewis Moody (Craig Newby, 68).

The game, played out in front of more than 81,000 people, was arguably the best Premiership final in the seven years since the introduction of the play-off format. The lead changed hands seven times in the first half and twice in the second as Saracens, nine points down shortly after the interval, charged back into the fray and, with four minutes remaining, had a one-point advantage thanks to the fifth of Glen Jackson's penalties. But Dan Hipkiss, throughout his Leicester career, made a habit of late interventions and when Scott Hamilton plunged into the opposition from a restart, Hipkiss rode a high tackle and found his way to the line for the third and decisive try which gave Leicester a 33-27 win and the title.

The rancour which existed between the clubs was dismissed by two sides playing to their potential, shrugging off the negativity with which the season began. Young players like Crane, whose season was so badly affected by an ankle injury, Ben Youngs and Parling showed they were coming of age, particularly in the second half when rain returned and both sides tightened their approach. Two penalties by Jackson to one by Flood were the only scores of the first quarter but Leicester claimed the first try when Tuilagi charged into the heart of the defence and Allen and Hamilton set Smith free down the touchline.

↑ Champions again! The Tigers hold on to their Premiership title with a narrow victory over Saracens at Twickenham.

Flood converted but Saracens capitalised on an overthrown Leicester line-out, moving the ball to midfield then going wide where Ernst Joubert, the No 8, lurked on the wing and made his way through Murphy's tackle to the tryline. Two more penalties from Flood and Jackson kept matters bubbling and, just before half-time, backs and forwards combined to give Leicester a ruck 15 metres out, from which Youngs dummied and shot through to score under the posts. Flood converted and kicked a penalty early in the second half but, collecting a high ball from Tigers, Saracens attacked through Jackson and Alex Goode before Andy Saull sent Joubert galloping over for a second try.

Jackson converted and added two more penalties to Flood's one, giving Saracens their 27-26 advantage. But Hipkiss, on his first appearance (as a replacement for Smith) after seven weeks out with a damaged knee, determined the outcome, Flood converted, Parling had time to steal a threatening Saracens line-out and the trophy remained at Welford Road.

↓ Dan Hipkiss bursts through the Saracens defence to score the crucial try.

← LEICESTER FOOTBALL CLUB 2009/10
Back: T.Youngs, Davies, Allen, J.Murphy, M.Smith, Cole, Pienaar, Woods, Staunton, R.Harris, Duffey, Grindal, B.Youngs.
Middle: B.Deacon, Tuqiri, Croft, Hemingway, Twelvetrees, Parling, Blaze, A.Tuilagi, Crane, Green, Stankovich.
Front: Hipkiss, Ayerza, Newby, Moody, Kay, Mauger, G.Murphy (capt), L.Deacon, Hamilton, Flood, Vesty, Chuter, Ellis.

20 09/10	Home Ground: Welford Road	Trophy Cabinet: Guinness Premiership(9)
	Head Coach: Richard Cockerill assisted by Matt O'Connor and Paul Burke	
	Captain: Geordan Murphy	

OVERALL RECORD:					T	C	PG	DG	PTS
PLD	W	D	L	Tigers scored:	83	67	109	2	882
35	23	2	10	Opponents scored:	40	22	103	9	580

GM	DATE		VEN	OPPONENTS	RESULT	POS/LGE	TRIES	KICKS	ATT
GUINNESS PREMIERSHIP (1ST)						**CHAMPIONS: LEICESTER TIGERS**			
1	Sep	4f	a	Sale Sharks	L+ 12-15	9	-	Staunton 4p	8751
2		12	a	Harlequins	W+ 15-9	6	-	Staunton 5p	9805
3		**19**	**H**	**Newcastle Falcons**	W 15-6	5	-	Staunton 5p	24000
4		26	a	Bath Rugby	D 20-20	5	Davies 25, Hipkiss 74	Staunton 2c/2p	11700
5	Oct	**3**	**H**	**Worcester Warriors**	W+ 19-14	5	Moody 32	Staunton c/3p/d	17974
8		24	a	London Irish	L+ 12-18	5	-	Staunton 3p, B.Youngs p	16199
9		**31**	**H**	**Northampton Saints**	W 29-15	4	Amorosino 22, Allen 76	Staunton 2c/5p	23641
13	Nov	20f	a	Gloucester Rugby	L+ 9-12	5	-	Staunton 3p	12521
14		**28**	**H**	**Leeds Carnegie**	W 39t-6	4	Penalty 43, Allen 47, B.Deacon 57, Flood 62, Moody 74	Flood 3c/2p, Staunton c	18408
15	Dec	6s	a	London Wasps	L+ 22-24	4	Crane 80	Flood 5p, Mauger c	10116
18		**27s**	**H**	**Sale Sharks**	W 32t-6	4	J.Murphy 19, Kay 46, Moody 59, Crane 80	Flood 3c/2p	24000
19	Jan	2	a	Saracens	W+ 22-15	4	Hipkiss 51	Flood c/5p	14013
20		**9**	**H**	**London Wasps**	W 34t-8	1	J.Murphy 40, Tuqiri 44/63, Penalty 53	Flood 4c/2p	24000
25	Feb	14s	a	Leeds Carnegie	W+ 14-9	1	Newby 32	Staunton 3p	5265
26		**20**	**H**	**Gloucester Rugby**	W 33-11	1	Tuqiri 35, G.Murphy 43, B.Youngs 78	Flood 3c/4p	22320
27		27	a	Northampton Saints	L 3-19	1	-	Staunton p	13538
28	Mar	**6**	**H**	**London Irish**	W 35t-19	1	A.Tuilagi 5, Hamilton 23, Castrogiovanni 26, Chuter 70	Flood 2c/2p, Staunton p, G.Murphy c	23314
29		27	a	Worcester Warriors	W 39-18	1	Staunton 13, B.Youngs 50, Grindal 80	Flood 3c/6p	11530
30	Apr	**3**	**H**	**Bath Rugby**	W 43t-20	1	A.Tuilagi 1/16, Parling 40, Allen 44, Penalty 75	Flood 3c/4p	22811
31		18s	a	Newcastle Falcons	W 31t-7	1	Moody 19/34, J.Murphy 24, Flood 28	Flood 4c, Staunton p	6825
32		**24**	**H**	**Harlequins**	W 40t-22	1	Flood 3, M.Smith 47, B.Youngs 50, Penalty 72	Flood 4c/4p	22604
33	May	**8**	**H**	**Saracens**	L 23-32	1	A.Tuilagi 10, Ayerza 56	Staunton 2c/3p	24000
34		**16s**	**H**	**Bath Rugby (sf)**	W 15-6	-	-	Flood 5p	21575
35		29		Saracens (f)	W 33-27	-	M.Smith 13, B.Youngs 28, Hipkiss 77	Flood 3c/4p	81600
HEINEKEN CUP						**EUROPEAN CHAMPIONS: TOULOUSE**			
6	Oct	**11s**	**H**	**Ospreys**	D 32t-32	2	J.Murphy 2, Twelvetrees 36, Amorosino 47, Staunton 76	Twelvetrees 3c/p, Staunton p	20029
7		17	a	MPS Viadana	W 46t-11	1	J.Murphy 10, Hamilton 30/60/75, Croft 36, Amorosino 67, Penalty 79	Staunton 2c/p, Twelvetrees 2c	4320
16	Dec	13s	a	ASM Clermont Auvergne	L 30-40t	3	Allen 69, Flood 71, Staunton 77	Flood 3c/3p	14657
17		**19**	**H**	**ASM Clermont Auvergne**	W+ 20-15	3	Allen 29, Hamilton 75	Flood 2c/2p	21286
21	Jan	**16**	**H**	**MPS Viadana**	W 47t-8	1	Hipkiss 6/70, Woods 20, Flood 32, Hamilton 34/39, Mauger 74	Flood 5c, Vesty c	21726
22		23	a	Ospreys	L+ 12-17	3	-	Flood 3p, Staunton d	15626
ANGLO-WELSH CUP (LV= CUP)						**CUP WINNERS: NORTHAMPTON SAINTS**			
11	Nov	8s	a	Leeds Carnegie	L 17-28	3	Armes 51, Hurrell 69	Ford 2c/p	3893
12		**14**	**H**	**Newport Gwent Dragons**	W 29-20	2	Crane 25, Allen 42, Penalty 55	Staunton c/2p, Flood 2p	16297
23	Jan	**29f**	**H**	**Bath Rugby**	W 27t-11	1	Twelvetrees 39/75, Penalty 58, A.Tuilagi 80	Vesty 2c/p	19772
24	Feb	6	a	Northampton Saints	L 11-23	2	Twelvetrees 26	Twelvetrees 2p	13092
CLUB MATCH									
10	Nov	**6f**	**H**	**South Africa**	W 22-17		Amorosino 27	B.Youngs c/5p	24000

Neutral Venue: *#35 at Twickenham*

INDIVIDUAL APPEARANCES 2009/10																																						
Name / Game #	1	2	3	4	5	6	7	8	9	10	11	12	13	14	15	16	17	18	19	20	21	22	23	24	25	26	27	28	29	30	31	32	33	34	35	Apps	T	Pts
AO (Anthony) Allen E2	>12	12	12	13	12	13	13	12	13	-	-	12	13	13	13	13	12	12	12	-	-	-	-	-	r	12	12	12	12	12	12	12	12	12	12	27+1	6	30
TR (Tom) Armes	-	-	-	-	-	-	-	-	>r	r	8	-	-	-	-	-	-	-	-	-	-	-	x	-	-	-	-	-	-	-	-	-	-	-	-	1+2	1	5
MI (Marcos) Ayerza Ar26	1	1	1	1	r	1	r	1	1	-	-	-	-	-	1	r	1	1	r	1	1	1	-	-	1	1	1	1	1	1	1	1	1	1	1	24+4	1	5
RJ (Richard) Blaze	4	4	-	4	-	-	r	<5	-	-	-	-	-	-	-	-	-	-	-	-	-	-	-	-	-	-	-	-	-	-	-	-	-	-	-	4+1	-	-
ML (Martin) Castrogiovanni It67	3	3	3	r	3	r	3	r	3	3	-	-	-	-	-	3	3	-	-	-	-	r	-	-	-	3	-	3	-	3	3	r	3	3	3	16+5	1	5
GS (George) Chuter E22	2	2	-	-	-	2	2	2	-	r	-	2	r	2	r	r	r	r	2	r	2	r	-	-	2	x	r	r	r	r	r	r	2	2	2	13+14	1	5
J (Joe) Cobden	-	-	-	-	-	-	-	-	-	-	>12	-	-	-	-	-	-	-	-	-	-	-	-	-	-	-	-	-	-	-	-	-	-	-	-	1	-	-
DR (Dan) Cole E5 L+	-	-	-	-	-	-	-	-	r	r	3	3	3	3	3	x	r	3	3	3	3	3	-	-	-	-	-	-	3	r	r	3	r	r	r	12+8	-	-
RM (Rob) Conquest	-	-	-	-	-	-	-	-	-	-	=r	-	-	-	-	-	-	-	-	-	-	-	-	x	-	-	-	-	-	-	-	-	-	-	-	0+1	-	-
JS (Jordan) Crane E3	8	8	-	8	8	8	8	8	-	-	-	8	8	8	8	8	8	8	8	8	8	8	-	-	8	8	8	8	8	8	8	-	r	8	8	27+1	3	15
TR (Tom) Croft E16 L3	-	6	6	-	6	6	6	6	-	-	-	-	-	6	-	-	-	-	-	r	6	-	-	-	-	-	-	r	6	6	6	6	6	6	6	15+2	1	5
DM (Mefin) Davies W38	r	r	2	2	r	-	-	-	2	2	-	r	2	-	2	2	2	2	x	2	x	2	-	-	r	2	2	2	2	2	2	<2	-	-	-	18+5	1	5
BR (Brett) Deacon	-	r	8	r	-	x	r	r	8	8	-	-	6	r	6	r	x	-	6	r	-	-	8	8	x	r	r	r	r	-	-	r	-	-	-	8+12	1	5
LP (Louis) Deacon E18	5	5	4	-	4*	4*	4*	4*	-	-	-	-	-	-	4	4*	4*	-	4*	4*	4*	4*	-	-	-	4*	-	-	-	4	4	-	-	4	4	19	-	-
JJ (Joe) Duffey	-	-	x	x	>2	x	r	-	-	-	-	-	-	r	-	-	-	-	-	-	-	-	2	r	-	-	-	-	-	-	-	-	r	x	x	2+4	-	-
HA (Harry) Ellis E27 L1	-	9	9	-	-	-	-	-	-	-	-	-	-	-	-	-	x	r	-	-	-	-	9	<9	-	-	-	-	-	-	-	-	-	-	-	4+1	-	-
ME (Matt) Everard	-	-	-	-	-	-	-	-	-	-	>7	-	-	-	-	-	-	-	-	-	-	-	-	x	-	-	-	-	-	-	-	-	-	-	-	1	-	-
TGAL (Toby) Flood E29	-	-	-	-	-	-	-	-	-	-	-	r	r	10	10	10	10	10	10	10	10	10	-	-	-	10	-	10	10	10	10	10	-	10	10	17+2	5	276
GT (George) Ford E+	-	-	-	-	-	-	-	-	-	-	>10	-	-	-	-	-	-	-	-	-	-	-	-	-	-	-	-	-	-	-	-	-	-	-	-	1	-	7
AR (Andy) Forsyth	-	-	-	-	-	-	-	x	>r	13	r	13	-	-	-	-	-	-	-	-	-	-	x	-	-	-	-	-	r	-	-	-	-	-	-	2+3	-	-
LP (Lucas) Gonzalez Amorosino Ar4	-	-	x	-	>r	11	11	11	14	14	15	-	-	-	-	-	-	-	-	-	-	-	15	15	-	-	-	-	-	-	r	r	-	-	-	8+3	4	20
CD (Calum) Green	-	-	-	-	-	-	-	-	4	4	-	r	x	r	-	-	-	x	-	-	-	-	4	-	r	x	x	4	-	-	-	-	-	-	-	4+3	-	-
JS (James) Grindal	x	-	-	9	9	9	9	9	9	x	9*	r	x	r	x	9	-	-	x	r	r	x	r	r	r	x	r	r	r	r	r	r	r	x	x	8+14	1	5
SE (Scott) Hamilton NZ2	11	14	14	14	15	15	15	15	15	15	-	15	15	15	15	15	15	15	15	15	15	15	-	-	15	14	15	14	14	14	14	14	14	14	14	32	7	35
CJ (Craig) Hammond	-	-	-	-	-	-	-	-	-	>r	<6	-	-	-	-	-	-	-	-	-	-	-	-	-	-	-	-	-	-	-	-	-	-	-	-	1+1	-	-
JC (Jonny) Harris	-	-	-	-	-	-	-	-	-	-	x	x	x	>r	x	-	-	-	-	-	-	-	-	-	-	-	-	-	-	-	-	-	-	-	-	0+1	-	-
RL (Robbie) Harris	-	x	x	-	-	-	-	-	-	-	>1	r	x	r	x	-	-	x	x	r	-	-	x	r	3	x	x	-	-	-	<r	-	-	-	-	2+5	-	-
SJ (Sam) Harrison	-	-	-	-	-	-	-	-	-	-	r	-	-	-	-	-	-	-	-	-	-	-	-	-	-	-	-	-	-	-	-	-	-	-	-	0+1	-	-
DP (Dan) Hemingway	-	-	-	-	-	-	-	-	r	5	r	x	x	-	-	-	-	-	-	-	-	-	x	4	-	-	-	-	-	-	-	-	-	-	-	2+2	-	-
DJ (Dan) Hipkiss E13	13	-	-	r	13	-	-	13	-	-	-	-	-	-	-	-	13	13	13	13	13	13	-	-	13	13	-	-	-	-	-	-	-	-	r	11+2	5	25
WH (Will) Hurrell	-	-	-	-	-	-	-	-	r	-	11	11	-	-	-	-	-	-	-	-	-	-	-	-	-	-	-	-	-	-	-	-	-	-	-	2+1	1	5
BJ (Ben) Kay E62 L2	r	-	5	5	5	5	-	-	5	-	5	5*	5	5	r	r	x	5	x	-	-	x	5	5	5*	-	5	-	5	r	r	5	<5	-	-	17+5	1	5
A (Alex) Lewington	-	-	-	-	-	-	-	-	-	-	>14	-	-	-	-	-	-	-	-	-	-	-	-	-	-	-	-	-	-	-	-	-	-	-	-	1	-	-
AJD (Aaron) Mauger NZ45	-	r	r	12	-	-	-	-	12*	10*	-	-	12*	12*	12*	12	-	-	-	-	r	r	12*	<12*	-	-	-	-	-	-	-	-	-	-	-	9+4	1	7
LW (Lewis) Moody E61 L3	r	-	-	7	7	7	7	7	-	-	-	-	-	7	7	7	7	7*	-	7	r	7	-	-	-	-	-	-	7*	7	7	7	7	7	<7	19+2	5	25
GEA (Geordan) Murphy I66 L2	15*	15*	15*	15*	-	-	-	-	-	-	-	-	-	-	-	-	-	-	-	-	-	-	-	r	r	15	-	15*	-	15*	15*	15*	15*	15*	15*	12+2	1	7
JE (Johne) Murphy	x	11	11	11	11	14	14	14	11	11	-	-	11	-	14	x	r	14	14	14	r	14	r	-	-	-	r	-	-	r	11	11	r	<r	-	17+7	5	25
CA (Craig) Newby NZ3	6	r	7	6	r	r	-	-	-	-	-	6	-	-	r	6	6	6	r	6	r	6	-	-	6	6	6*	6	r	r	r	8	8	r	r	15+11	1	5
GMW (Geoff) Parling E+ L+	-	-	>r	r	r	r	5	r	6	6	-	4	4	4	5	5	5	4	5	5	5	5	-	-	4	5	4	5	4	5	5	4	4	5	5	25+5	1	5
BJM (Ben) Pienaar	-	-	r	-	-	-	-	-	7	7	-	7	7	-	-	-	-	-	-	-	-	-	6	6	-	-	-	-	-	-	-	-	-	-	-	6+1	-	-
SI (Sam) Raven	-	-	-	-	-	-	-	-	-	-	<4	-	-	-	-	-	-	-	-	-	-	-	-	-	-	-	-	-	-	-	-	-	-	-	-	1	-	-
CS (Connor) Smith	-	-	-	-	-	-	-	-	-	-	=r	-	-	-	-	-	-	-	-	-	-	-	-	-	-	-	-	-	-	-	-	-	-	-	-	0+1	-	-
MW (Matt) Smith	14	13	13	r	14	-	r	-	-	-	-	r	x	11	-	-	-	-	-	-	-	-	11	11	-	-	13	r	13	13	13	13	13	13	13	15+4	2	10
B (Boris) Stankovich	-	-	-	r	1	r	1	x	r	1	-	1	1	1	-	1	x	r	1	x	r	r	1	1	r	r	r	r	r	r	-	r	x	x	r	10+14	-	-
JW (Jeremy) Staunton I5	>10	10	10	10	10	10	10	10	10	-	-	10	10	r	x	r	r	-	r	12	-	12	-	r	10	r	10	r	15	r	r	r	10	x	r	17+11	3	172
GA (Greig) Tonks S+	-	-	-	-	-	-	-	-	-	x	=13	-	-	-	-	-	-	-	-	-	-	-	-	-	-	-	-	-	-	-	-	-	-	-	-	1	-	-
AT (Alesana) Tuilagi Sa17 PI1	-	-	-	-	-	-	-	-	-	-	-	-	-	r	r	11	14	r	r	r	14	r	14	14	14	r	14	11	11	11	-	-	11	11	11	13+7	5	25
EM (Manusamoa) Tuilagi E+ L+	-	-	-	-	-	-	-	-	-	12	-	-	-	-	-	-	-	-	-	-	-	-	-	-	-	-	-	-	-	-	-	-	-	-	-	1	-	-
LD (Lote) Tuqiri A67	-	-	-	-	-	-	-	-	-	>r	-	14	14	14	11	14	11	11	11	11	11	11	-	-	11	11	11	<13	-	-	-	-	-	-	-	15+1	3	15
WWF (Billy) Twelvetrees E+	x	x	-	-	x	12	12	x	-	-	-	-	-	-	-	-	-	-	-	-	-	-	13	13	12	-	-	-	r	-	-	-	-	-	-	5+1	4	39
SB (Sam) Vesty E2	-	-	-	-	-	-	-	-	-	-	-	-	-	-	-	-	-	r	-	r	12	-	10	10	-	-	<r	-	-	-	-	-	x	-	-	3+3	-	9
JM (Julian) White E51 L4	r	r	r	3	r	3	r	3	-	-	-	-	-	-	-	-	-	-	-	-	r	-	3	3	-	-	3	r	r	-	-	-	-	-	-	6+8	-	-
BN (Ben) Woods	7	7	-	-	-	-	-	-	-	-	-	-	-	-	-	-	-	r	7	-	7	r	7	7	7	7	7	7	-	-	-	x	r	r	x	10+4	1	5
BR (Ben) Youngs E1 L+	9	r	r	r	r	r	r	r	r	9	-	9	9	9	9	r	9	9	9	9	9	9	-	-	9	9	9	9	9	9	9	9	9	9	9	23+9	4	40
TN (Tom) Youngs E+ L+	-	-	-	-	-	x	x	x	r	-	2	-	-	-	-	-	-	-	-	-	-	-	r	2	-	-	-	-	-	-	-	-	-	-	-	2+2	-	-

The key for how to read the stats is on the last page

CHAPTER 36

Lean and Hungry

Line-out king Ben Kay retired after 281 first-team appearances in his 11-year career.

2010/2011

A generation was passing. Not only did Lewis Moody leave for Bath, so did Sam Vesty whose jack-of-all-trades abilities behind the scrum had been under-used. Another World Cup winner, Ben Kay, retired from the game to become a TV pundit alongside his old colleague, Austin Healey; Kay played 281 games in his 11 years with Leicester, winning 62 England caps, statistics which demonstrate his value to club and country all too well. One of the country's best line-out analysts, he was also the undemonstrative glue in so many dominant Leicester forward displays.

As he left, the star of another lock, Geoff Parling, was in the ascendant. Also an industrious analyst, Parling was named in England's tour party to Australia along with Dan Cole, Tom Croft, Toby Flood, Lewis Moody and Ben Youngs, a sextet to which George Chuter was later added. Moody captained England in the two internationals with the Wallabies, the first of which in Perth should have been won, the second in Sydney was.

The starting XV for the 27-17 loss in Perth included Flood, Croft and Cole while Youngs came off the bench as a replacement at scrum-half for Danny Care, as did Chuter at hooker for Steve Thompson. A week later, Youngs made his first international start and what a start - he scored a fine try through the middle of a line-out and helped England win 21-20.

Matt O'Connor was promoted to head coach.

While Geordan Murphy was with Ireland in New Zealand, Marcos Ayerza found a new Tiger in the Argentina squad that played Scotland: Horacio Agulla, a bouncy wing, had signed from Brive and other newcomers to Welford Road included Thomas Waldrom, who had fallen just short of a cap in his native New Zealand, George Skivington, the Wasps lock who led the Saxons in the summer's Churchill Cup tournament, and Rob Hawkins, the Bath hooker who replaced Mefin Davies, returning home to join the Ospreys in Swansea after passing on so much experience to, among others, Tom Youngs after his change of position.

But an ongoing concern during the summer was retaining the services of Manu Tuilagi. The youngest of the brothers had been to John Cleveland School in Hinckley, having moved to Leicestershire in 2004, but as a professional rugby player he required a work permit having arrived initially on a six-month holiday visa. Threatened with deportation, a campaign began to keep him with Leicester, through the *Leicester Mercury*, petitions on the Tigers website and social networks, all of which led to a Home Office review. Edward Garnier, the Conservative MP for Market Harborough and Solicitor General for England and Wales, offered help and in July, Tuilagi received his work permit. Richard Cockerill confirmed his value: "He will have a significant role in the senior squad," he said and Tuilagi was also named in England's under-20 squad along with George Ford, Ryan Bower, Matt Everard and Johnny Harris.

But Harry Ellis, the livewire scrum-half, was forced to retire on medical advice at the age of 28, after 173 appearances over nine seasons and 27 England caps: "All last summer I was taking a hell of a lot of painkillers and I was constantly having blood and fluid drained from my [left] knee," Ellis said. "The amount of painkillers...was causing my stomach real problems. It took a lot of soul-searching to decide to retire. Any player I know would want to carry on playing for a club like Leicester."

It was an illustration of the toll professional rugby can take. He was joined two months later in retirement by Richard Blaze, aged only 25 but unable to overcome his foot injury which meant that, over three years, the lock started only 11 games for Leicester; he set off down the coaching road. Parling's burgeoning international career had to be put on hold because of surgery to a disc in his neck, which brought the Tongan back-five forward, Sitiveni 'Steve' Mafi, to the club from the Waratahs in Australia. Cockerill changed hats, becoming director of rugby with the head-coach role passing to Matt O'Connor.

In an attempt to find a different audience (and make the most of their enlarged ground), Leicester staged two pop concerts at Welford Road, James Morrison and Will Young treading in the footsteps of Martin Johnson. After a financial loss the previous year of nearly £1 million, the club returned to a £284,000 profit with a turnover

↑ Dan Cole went from strength to strength for both Tigers and England during the season.

of more than £18 million, helped by the enhanced conference and banqueting facilities in the Caterpillar Stand. On the other side of the ground, a three-year deal with Holland and Barrett, the health foods chain, led to the renaming of the Crumbie Stand and you suspect that even Tom Crumbie, wearing his commercial hat, might have approved.

After so much good news, it was almost inevitable that the season would begin poorly, in a 27-19 defeat at Northampton when Flood was helped off with medial ligament damage, and when Jeremy Staunton damaged his Achilles tendon in a 37-30 loss at Wasps, Tigers were in the bottom half of the Premiership table and badly short of fly-halves. As the autumn wore on, 12 senior players (eight of them internationals) were out of action, among them Louis Deacon with a niggling back complaint which made room for a hard-working utility forward, Ed Slater, fresh from playing club rugby in Sydney.

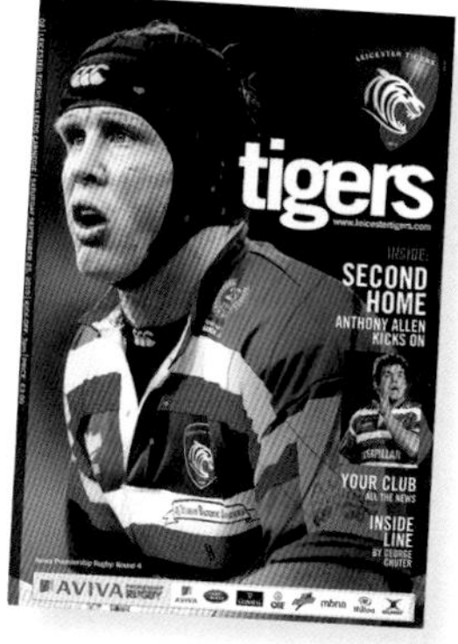

Tigers made a shaky start in Italy to the Heineken Cup, trailing 29-27 to Treviso with 12 minutes remaining but the older Tuilagi came through with a late try to earn a bonus point as well as victory. Flood, returning earlier than expected from his knee injury, agreed a three-year extension to his contract and kicked 16 points in the best display of the season thus far, a 46-10 win over the Scarlets in which Croft scored two of six tries.

The international window came round with Leicester no higher than fifth in the Premiership, Boris Stankovich joining the long casualty list after the prop fractured an eye socket. Flood, Ben Youngs, Cole and Croft started the first of England's internationals, a 26-16 loss to New Zealand, and two more props, Ayerza and Martin Castrogiovanni, were absent with their respective countries. It left Leicester thin on the ground and, in the LV= Cup match with Harlequins, they played what might be called a complementary pair of half-backs - George Ford, at 17 half the age of Jason Spice, the 35-year-old New Zealander on a short-term contract.

But they had another international occasion to grace Welford Road. As English champions, they received Australia for a midweek game prior to the Wallabies playing England though this time they could not emulate the heroics of the game with South Africa a year earlier. The teams were:

Leicester: Geordan Murphy (captain); Scott Hamilton, Matt Smith (Dan Hipkiss, 79), Anthony Allen, Manu Tuilagi; Billy Twelvetrees, James Grindal; Peter Bucknall, George Chuter (Rob Hawkins, 69), Julian White, Ed Slater, George Skivington, Thomas Waldrom (Steve Mafi, 62), Jordan Crane, Craig Newby.
Australia XV: Peter Hynes; Rod Davies, Pat McCabe, Anthony Fainga'a, Lachie Turner (Luke Morahan, 68); Berrick Barnes (captain), Luke Burgess; James Slipper, Huia Edmonds (Saia Fainga'a, 68), Salesi Ma'afu, Van Humphries, Rob Simmons (Dean Mumm, 67), Scott Higginbotham, Richard Brown, Matt Hodgson (Pat McCutcheon, 67).
Referee: Jonathan Kaplan (South Africa).

Australia went out to a 13-0 lead within 25 minutes, Luke Burgess creating a try for Lachie Turner and Berrick Barnes adding a conversion and two penalties. Amid teeming rain, there were numerous off-the-ball incidents, Billy Twelvetrees exacted retribution, four penalties (one from halfway) bringing Leicester to within a point before half-time when an old Welford Road favourite, Pat Howard, travelling with his compatriots, was introduced to the 20,000 crowd.

A fifth penalty by Twelvetrees in the 68th minute gave the club hopes of another famous victory but Australia stirred themselves. Barnes, having missed three attempts at a penalty, found his mark, added a dropped goal for good measure and, when Leicester were turned over on their own 10-metre line, Scott Higginbotham ran in from 35 metres for a try which Barnes converted for a 26-15 win.

The first-choice Leicester half-backs gained some measure of revenge four days later. Youngs distinguished himself in England's 35-18 win over the Wallabies and Flood kicked seven penalties and two conversions for a 25-point tally. Cole and Croft came off the bench in the next international, a 26-13 win over Samoa in which Croft scored a try, but once more England's autumn ended in disappointment, losing to South Africa in a game when Croft damaged a shoulder blade and missed three months while Flood was concussed.

Parling, having recovered from a damaged neck, played for barely a minute off the bench against Harlequins in his comeback before a serious knee injury ruled him out for the rest of the season. The same fate overtook Ben Pienaar, the flanker rupturing an Achilles tendon in training. Since Ben Woods had already broken a wrist, Newby settled in at open-side; indifferent form, as well as unsympathetic television schedules, had

→ Jordan Crane and Billy Twelvetrees take on the Wallabies 9.11.2010.

← Manu Tuilagi, who scored a try on his England Saxons debut at Worcester, was named Tigers, Premiership and RPA Young Player of the Season.

an impact on attendances which were down by 11 per cent. The fact that Leicester appeared in 11 of 12 scheduled broadcasts went unappreciated by the club; they derived no additional income from the broadcaster who also called the tune in changing kick-off times.

In need of some good news, Louis Deacon played his first game of the season against Newcastle after undergoing "dry needling" treatment (similar to acupuncture) for his back. Tigers followed with their first away win of the season, at London Irish, restoring morale before the back-to-back European games with Perpignan in which they became only the third club (after Toulouse and Munster) to make 100 Heineken Cup appearances. As it turned out, it was their scrum that needed lifting after a 24-19 loss at the Stade Aimè Giral. Perpignan forced a goal-line stand of eight reset scrums, during which both hookers, Marius Tincu and George Chuter, were sent to the sin bin. A losing bonus point was something to savour but when Perpignan, with Henry Tuilagi at No 8, forced a 22-22 draw at Welford Road a week later, Leicester's quarter-final prospects looked distinctly slim.

Over the Christmas period they clambered back to the top of the Premiership and Manu Tuilagi began the run which would carry him to the Saxons and then the senior England side. He scored two tries in a trouncing of Sale, retained his place in the Premiership wins over Northampton and Exeter and, significantly, the 32-18 European win over Scarlets at Llanelli, which left Leicester tied with Perpignan at the top of pool five. Scott Hamilton returned from his wedding in New Zealand in time to play full-back against the Welsh region and Deacon, taking over the captaincy, made his 200th appearance in the 62-15 win over Treviso.

Leicester qualified for the last eight as one of the best runners-up from pool play, leaving them with the doubtful privilege of visiting Leinster ten weeks later. They had also lost Geordan Murphy, who broke a bone in his foot in the win over Northampton and missed the rest of the season. Deacon's return to fitness and form earned him a place in England's elite squad and Manu Tuilagi was named with Ryan Bowers, Matt Everard, Jonny Harris and George Ford in the under-20s squad (Ford and Everard were key components in the winning of a junior grand slam).

But 2011 held higher honours for Tuilagi. First he was added to the Saxons squad and then the senior squad instead of the injured Sale back, Mathew Tait. Leicester had an interest in Tait's wellbeing. His talent was obvious, even though he was never able to settle in one position for England for whom he played centre, wing and full-back in the course of winning 38 caps between 2005-10. Tigers thought that, in the long term, he might replace Murphy, meantime they enjoyed the sight of Tuilagi and Twelvetrees making their Saxons debut together in a 45-17 win over Italy A at Worcester.

With the World Cup in New Zealand only seven months away, Flood and Youngs formed England's half-back pairing throughout a six nations that brought England their first championship title since 2003. Cole and Deacon were ever-presents too, Deacon picking up a yellow card during England's first win over Wales in Cardiff for eight years. Tom Croft returned from his shoulder injury and scored a try against Scotland from the bench and three successive wins at Twickenham gave England the chance of a grand slam in Dublin. Ireland closed the door very firmly on that notion, winning 24-8.

Without their internationals, Leicester ploughed on, completing an indifferent LV= Cup season before resuming the Premiership campaign against Leeds. Alesana and Manu Tuilagi scored tries in a mediocre 15-9 win and another narrow victory, over Sale, left Leicester nine points clear at the top of the table. Capturing the moment, the club announced season-ticket price reductions for 80 per cent of their 13,000 ticket holders (including free entry for children under 10 accompanying a ticket holder).

The feel-good atmosphere was dampened somewhat when Saracens completed a season's double by winning 15-14 at Welford Road. However the return of the international contingent helped greatly towards a 37-6 win at Bath, Croft and Flood both scoring two tries in Tigers' biggest win at the Recreation Ground in 96 years. Another away win, over Harlequins at the Twickenham Stoop, was satisfactory but cost Leicester the services of Marcos Ayerza, banned for a fortnight after butting Joe Marler, the Quins prop.

↓ Anthony Allen on his way to the tryline to open Leicester's account in what was to become their biggest win at Bath in almost 100 years.

Ayerza, therefore, missed the Heineken Cup quarter-final against Leinster, European competition having been spiced for Leicester off the field. Peter Wheeler put his name in the frame to become chairman of European Rugby Cup Ltd, a post held by the former France centre, Jean-Pierre Lux. "I have been involved in European rugby for 15 years and have a pretty good idea of what works," Wheeler, who believed he had significant French support, said. But, when push came to shove, the Ligue National de Rugby - the French equivalent to Premier Rugby Ltd - claimed their voting powers had been annexed by their own federation and Lux continued.

Nor did events on the field offer solace, Leinster winning 17-10 at the Aviva Stadium. Leicester lost Deacon midway through the first half, Ed Slater joining Steve Mafi in the second row but suffering at the line-out against the knowledgeable Leo Cullen. Yet Tigers trailed only 9-3 when Alesana Tuilagi put a foot in touch in the act of crossing the try line; minutes later Isa Nacewa made no mistake in scoring Leinster's try and though Rob Hawkins crossed with two minutes remaining, it was the end of Leicester's aspirations.

Not, though, at home. The issue of convertible loan notes and an ordinary share issue raised £4.4 million towards the development of Welford Road and the Tigers got down to the familiar task of ensuring another domestic final. With the departure to NEC Green Rockets in Japan as forwards coach of Ben Herring, the former flanker, Richard Blaze was added to the coaching staff and the club carried off the A league title by beating Sale Jets 35-30 at Heywood Road, Twelvetrees scoring 20 points.

🡅 Alesana Tuilagi grabbed a hat-trick of tries at home to Gloucester and went on to dot down for 17 during the 2010/11 campaign.

Leicester let slip a 14-point lead when a Gloucester side led by Brett Deacon left Welford Road with a 41-41 draw. It was the highest scoring draw in Premiership history and featured a hat-trick by Alesana Tuilagi: "That performance is not acceptable," Cockerill said. "We did enough to win the game and we didn't." Victory at Newcastle secured a home semi-final and Leicester finished top of the table, two points ahead of Saracens.

"Leicester is never a side in transition," Cockerill said. "It's not good enough to say we will be good in two years' time, or three years' time. You don't get that grace in sport. We have been missing 15 or 16 players at times and just had to get on with it." So Tigers did, in a controversial play-off with Northampton (Heineken Cup finalists against Leinster a week later) which saw almost as much action off the field as on it.

🡆 George Chuter and Steve Mafi attempt a charge-down during the 2011 Premiership final against Saracens at Twickenham.

Leicester won 11-3 but Manu Tuilagi was involved in a shoving match with Chris Ashton, the England wing, before the young centre threw three punches. Both players were sent to the sin bin but, inevitably, Tuilagi was cited and banned for five weeks, missing both the Premiership final and the Churchill Cup though he still received the Rugby Players' Association and the Premiership young player of the year awards. Moreover the RFU investigated heated comments made in the stand by Cockerill and Matt O'Connor, apparently directed at Brian Campsall, the highly-regarded referees assessor; happily for Leicester, the investigation found no evidence that the two coaches abused match officials.

Awaiting at Twickenham were Saracens, who had the Indian sign on Leicester over the season. The trend continued in the Premiership final in front of more than 80,000 when Leicester decided to omit the RPA player of the year, Thomas Waldrom, from their back row in favour of the in-form Jordan Crane. The team was: Scott Hamilton; Horacio Agulla (Billy Twelvetrees, 75), Matt Smith, Anthony Allen, Alesana Tuilagi; Toby Flood, Ben Youngs (sin bin 5-15); Marcos Ayerza (Boris Stankovich, 77), George Chuter (Rob Hawkins, 69), Martin Castrogiovanni (Dan Cole, 52), Steve Mafi (Ed Slater, 71), George Skivington, Tom Croft, Jordan Crane (Thomas Waldrom, 49), Craig Newby (captain).

Reluctantly Leicester would acknowledge the bloody-mindedness that gave Saracens their 22-18 win. For the last seven minutes, Tigers camped on the opposing try line, looking for the score in a 32-phase movement that would allow them to retain the title. But the defence held firm until finally Owen Farrell, Saracens' teenaged fly-half, forced a turnover and relieved the siege. "We have had a few seasons with nothing in the cabinet, it happens," Cockerill said. "Is it a disastrous season? No, we have played some good stuff." Indeed Leicester's 67 tries during the Premiership season made them the most effective attacking team in the country but none of those tries came at Twickenham.

Farrell opened the scoring with the first of five penalties. Flood kicked two of his own but Saracens led 16-6 at the interval, thanks to two more penalties by Farrell who also converted a try by James Short, the Saracens wing. Flood kicked four more goals in the second half to two from Farrell but Tigers did not come closer than the four points by which they trailed at the end. Flood also missed with a couple of kicks, nor could Leicester find a way round Schalk Brits, the Saracens hooker whose run created the space for Short and who hauled down Alesana Tuilagi when the wing looked clear.

2011/2012

Even though the seventh World Cup was looming large, Leicester had plenty of business at home to consider. With 10,000 season tickets sold, there was a new look to the playing squad that would be on display to members: after a 14-year association with Tigers, Dan Hipkiss left for Bath, Lucas Amorosino for Montpellier and Dan Hemingway, who had played in that memorable win over South Africa, for Leeds.

The arrivals included Micky Young and Kieran Brookes, a scrum-half and prop, from Newcastle Falcons; Graham Kitchener, the Worcester Warriors lock, Niall Morris, Leinster's wing, and Mathew Tait, once the wunderkind from Newcastle who played for England as a teenager but was now plagued by injury. As an indication of the quality of the newcomers, three of them - Kitchener, Brookes and Young - joined Jordan Crane and Billy Twelvetrees in the England Saxons squad that won the Churchill Cup during the summer. When Crane, as captain, lifted the trophy after beating Canada in the final at Worcester, he little thought that he would miss the entire season because of a damaged knee.

With Craig Newby out for five months following knee surgery, Leicester took the precaution of adding more southern-hemisphere talent to their back row. This time they went for Julian Salvi from the Brumbies, though the Australian flanker knew his way around the Premiership having spent a season with Bath. There was a return, too, for Tom Youngs after two years at Nottingham learning his new trade as a hooker.

Commercially the future looked brighter. The shop at Welford Road was doubled in size to 2,000 square feet, helped by a ten-year commercial deal with the retail specialists, Kitbag, and two months later a report by Deloitte showed Leicester third in a European cash league comparing the turnovers of leading clubs. Toulouse stood at the head on £27.4 million, Clermont Auvergne second on £19.5 million and Tigers next on £18.5 million. "The figures show factually that Tigers are far and away the biggest club in the country and the challenge for us now is to continue to increase our turnover," David Clayton, the club's managing director, said. "If you look at the sponsorship deals Leicester generate, they are in excess of other clubs in this country and that is largely down to the success we have had on the pitch over the years."

Moreover Leicester's average home attendance of 21,096 was nearly 3,000 ahead of Toulouse and later in the year, the club announced an operating profit for 2010/11 of £559,000. That situation was helped by a five per cent increase in ticket sales and significant revenue from Welford Road conferences and events, while Tigers Events Ltd, the body for international hospitality, achieved record sales of £2.1 million, a 28 per cent increase. Clayton stood down after 12 years at the club and changes to the board brought in Simon Cohen as acting chief operating officer; early in the new year Cohen, who had joined the club in 2005 after working as a sports lawyer in Manchester, was appointed chief executive officer.

Eight Leicester players were involved in England's initial 45-strong training squad for the World Cup, one of them being Thomas Waldrom, who had discovered an English grandmother and qualified without the need of residency. Another was Manu Tuilagi though Ben Youngs required surgery to a knee and missed a great swathe of the preparations over July and August. Geordan Murphy was with Ireland, Alesana Tuilagi (who scored the try that helped the island nation beat Australia during the summer) with Samoa, Martin Castrogiovanni with Italy, Marcos Ayerza and Horacio Agulla with Argentina.

↑ Canterbury became the kit supplier with the new strip being unveiled against Bath in May.

↓ Horacio Agulla played for Argentina in RWC2011 and went on to become Tigers' Player of the Season.

In due course England released Waldrom and George Chuter before giving the younger Tuilagi his debut in the warm-up game against Wales at Twickenham, the centre scoring a try in a tight match won 23-19. When England's World Cup squad was confirmed, Leicester had six representatives - Dan Cole, Louis Deacon and Tom Croft in the forwards, Ben Youngs, Toby Flood and Tuilagi in the backs. Five of them, the exception being Youngs, featured in the final warm-up game, a 20-9 win over Ireland in Dublin when Tuilagi scored again and which, in retrospect, may have assumed a greater significance than it merited.

To say it was not a happy World Cup for England would be a considerable understatement. Youngs scored in England's opening pool fixture, against Argentina in Dunedin, but the 13-9 win was not promising and the post-match celebrations started a downward spiral in which every off-field move made by England became the subject of intense media scrutiny. Tuilagi scored a try in the 40-10 win over Georgia and another in the 67-3 win over Romania, as did Youngs and Croft, and the call went out for Waldrom to join England in his native New Zealand as cover.

In the event, Waldrom was not required nor did Ireland find the need to give Murphy game time after his pool game against the USA. England ended their pool games unbeaten but few gave them much chance of progress; Tuilagi was fined £4,800 for wearing a gum shield sponsored by a non-accredited company (Alesana had suffered the same fate a week earlier) and it all ended in tears when France, eventual finalists, won 19-12 in the quarter-finals. Manu Tuilagi's name found its way to the wrong pages of the papers when, after a visit to Waikeke Island, he jumped off a ferry in Auckland Harbour.

Back at home George Ford, having helped England to another world under-20 final in Italy during the summer (which led to his becoming the first English winner of the International Rugby Board's young player of the year award), started his first Premiership match in the opening fixture against Exeter Chiefs. Tait was picked to play on the wing but withdrew with a grumbling groin injury which would destroy his first season at the club. It was not a good start since Exeter won 30-28 and a second defeat followed, by 35-29 at Wasps where Twelvetrees scored all Leicester's points.

Saracens left Welford Road after imposing Leicester's highest defeat of the professional era, by 50-25, and another home defeat, this time to Harlequins, left Leicester languishing in eleventh place. A very young side led by Geoff Parling, fit again after a ten-month absence, crashed 31-3 to

➜ Despite being injured over the summer, Ben Youngs added to his growing reputation during the RWC2011 in New Zealand.

Scarlets in the opening LV= Cup game but nine internationals became available for the cup clash with Gloucester the following week and Leicester won 41-14 with Tom Youngs starting at hooker.

It was only the second win of the season in the third week of October but 16,000 turned out on a Friday night to cheer Tigers on or, in the case of Tuilagi junior, sympathise when the young centre fractured a cheekbone and joined Anthony Allen on the sidelines. Illustrating the dangers of DIY, Allen had severed an artery in his thumb while laying a kitchen floor. A home draw with London Irish did not leave Leicester in the best of shape for Europe. A lacklustre 28-12 win over Aironi in Monza reflected the situation and the mood was not improved by the news in mid-November that Martin Johnson had resigned as England manager. While not unexpected, the decision of one of Leicester's favourite sons caused both sadness and anger.

Leicester, though, had their own reputation for winning rugby matches to think about. The angst around the club was mirrored in the home game with Northampton, when there were red cards for Alesana Tuilagi and Tom Wood, the Northampton and England flanker, after a touchline melee and it took a late try by Agulla and conversion from Flood to win the match 30-25. There was no further punishment for Tuilagi, though Chris Ashton, Northampton's wing, was suspended for four weeks for pulling Tuilagi's hair and both Murphy and Agulla were warned for their parts in the incident.

More cards were flourished when Leicester, after a home win over Ulster, visited Clermont Auvergne in the Heineken Cup. This time the colour was yellow for Manu Tuilagi and Chuter, leaving Tigers playing with 13 men for a brief period of the 30-12 defeat; it was some compensation to beat the French club 23-19 in the return fixture and to confirm an agreement with Clermont to swap selected academy players as an aid to their development. Leicester's first beneficiaries of the scheme were Fraser Balmain, a prop, and lock Tom Price.

Cockerill had further concerns when Louis Deacon ruptured a hamstring against Worcester and was out for the rest of the season. Still, Leicester were clawing their way back up the table and victory over Sale carried them into familiar territory, the top four; after 12 Premiership matches, Tigers averaged 27 points for and 26 against. The middle of the season was becoming a time to take stock: Alesana Tuilagi, now 30, had been offered a move to Japan. "The numbers they talk about would be impossible for us to compete with," Cockerill said and the impending departure lent urgency to talks with Miles Benjamin, the wing who had scored 55 tries in five seasons with Worcester.

Flood damaged knee ligaments, which caused him to miss the start of the 2012 six nations, though Twelvetrees stepped in and scored all 29 points from fly-half in a 29-11 win over Wasps - remarkably, the second time he scored precisely that number against those opponents in one season. A 20st Samoan prop, Logovi'i Mulipola, who had been at the club on trial, came off the bench in the same match and such was the quality of his work that he earned an extended contract.

However Twelvetrees, eager for more game time, was on his way to Gloucester. Leicester's optimum midfield was Flood, Allen and Manu Tuilagi - if they all turned out to be uninjured at the same time. Only Allen, for example, was available for the Heineken Cup visit to Ulster which turned out to be a disaster on a par with the 33-0 loss at Ravenhill in 2004; this time the margin was 41-7, Cole was sin binned and Tigers were virtually out of the quarter-finals.

↑ Billy Twelvetrees scored all Tigers' 58 points in their two meetings against Wasps in 2011/12.

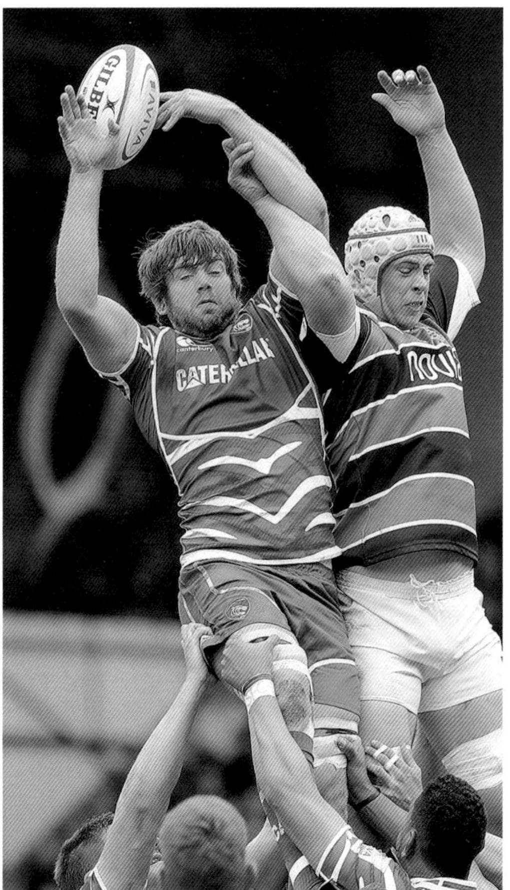

← Geoff Parling won a first England cap off the bench against Scotland in the RBS 6 Nations.

When Ulster lost the following weekend at Clermont, Leicester's 33-6 win over Aironi counted for nothing and, rubbing salt in the wound, Micky Young - starting his first game at scrum-half - was cited and subsequently banned for eight weeks. George Skivington agreed a summer move to London Irish and the cheerful Agulla would not be retained because the expansion of the southern-hemisphere Rugby Championship to include Argentina would take their players away for too long (though Leicester, knowing the value of good props, made an exception for Ayerza).

Good news was required at Welford Road and it came first from the LV= Cup. A young Leicester side beat Harlequins and Newcastle to reach the semi-finals for the first time in five years. At the same time a new-look England under the management of Stuart Lancaster started Ben Youngs, Cole and Croft against Scotland and gave a first cap off the bench to Geoff Parling. The lock occupied the same role against Italy (when Martin Castrogiovanni, in the opposition front row, damaged ribs and missed the next six weeks) and made his first start in the 19-12 loss to Wales at Twickenham. Manu Tuilagi reappeared in England's centre in the same game while Flood and a relegated Youngs were among the replacements.

→ Peter Wheeler presents Geordan Murphy with a memento to mark the Irishman's 300th game for the club against Newcastle 25.2.2012.

When Flood, Manu Tuilagi and Murphy returned, Leicester took great satisfaction from their trip to Watford. There, the latest of dropped goals by Murphy gave them a 20-19 win over Saracens, unbeaten at home for 16 months and who had inflicted such indignities on them at Welford Road nearly five months earlier. "One of the all-time great Leicester players," Cockerill said of Murphy when the Irishman played his 300th game for the club against Newcastle and, when Gloucester conceded 36 points at Welford Road, Leicester were third in the table.

Thoughts now turned to the LV= Cup. It remained an important development tournament as reflected in the team Leicester sent to Bath for the semi-finals. The starting XV included George Ford, Andy Forsyth, Alex Lewington and Calum Green; Ford (against the club he was to join a year later) kicked the penalty that carried Leicester to a 17-16 win and into a final against Northampton at Worcester.

On the same weekend that England trounced Ireland 30-9 with five Tigers in the squad, Leicester won the cup with the following team: Geordan Murphy (captain, sin bin 74); Horacio Agulla, Matt Smith (Andy Forsyth, 72), Billy Twelvetrees, Scott Hamilton; George Ford (Toby Flood, 64), James

↑ Tigers won the Anglo-Welsh Cup for a second time (now under the sponsorship of LV=), beating Northampton in the final at Worcester.

Grindal; Boris Stankovich (Marcos Ayerza, 13), Rob Hawkins (Tom Youngs, 24), Logovi'i Mulipola, George Skivington, Graham Kitchener, Steve Mafi, Thomas Waldrom, Craig Newby (Julian Salvi, 51).

It was the first time the Midland rivals had met in a cup final and Leicester's 26-14 win, with only 14 men for the last six minutes after a yellow card for Murphy, was thoroughly deserved. It was achieved after losing two front-row forwards in the first half-hour, Stankovich with a calf strain and Hawkins with a broken elbow for which Calum Clark, the Northampton flanker, was cited and later suspended for 32 weeks for "an act contrary to good sportsmanship."

Northampton took an early lead through two Stephen Myler penalties but Ford levelled matters with two kicks of his own and the fly-halves made it 9-9 before the first try. Ford's long pass put Murphy into space and Mafi galloped over, Ford adding the conversion. When Hamilton intercepted Myler's floated pass and ran in from eighty metres, the game had gone beyond Northampton.

Ford, who had earlier kicked his fourth penalty, added the conversion to end with 16 points and a much-enhanced reputation for his tactical aplomb. Christian Day scored a late try for the Saints but Leicester's defence held well, even without Murphy, dispatched to the sin bin for a professional foul. The resilience showed by players young and old as Northampton battered away demonstrated the value placed on the competition by such individuals as Waldrom, whose first success in a final it was, and Julian White, the veteran prop heading towards retirement.

The trophy provided impetus on and off the field. Plans were announced for the building of a 140-room hotel on the Granby Halls site, though development was to a degree contingent on Leicester hosting World Cup pool matches in 2015 and here there was to be tremendous disappointment. But the club's vision was hailed by the city's mayor, Sir Peter Soulsby: "There is huge potential to replace [the Granby Halls car park] with something good for the city and good for Tigers," Sir Peter said.

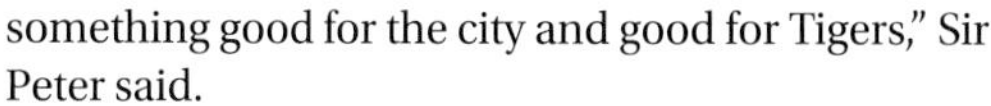

The push for a home semi-final in the Premiership continued with away wins against Northampton and Harlequins but Croft, in tackling Nick Easter, damaged his neck and required surgery; the back-row forward was not to play again for six months. By the end of the regular season, Leicester were second to Harlequins by a single point and had booked a home semi-final against Saracens. They had accumulated 70 tries, 17 more than their nearest challenger, Harlequins, and totalled 647 points, 108 more than Northampton.

It was a remarkable tally for a team that, at one stage, lay only one place off the bottom of the Premiership table and had made do without so many leading players for so long. As if to emphasise Leicester's contribution to the national cause, nine Tigers were named in England's tour party to South Africa - Cole, Parling, Flood, Tuilagi, Kitchener, Allen, Waldrom and both Youngs brothers, Ben and Tom. The older Youngs had made only one start at hooker during the Premiership season, though he came off the bench 14 times. It was a quite remarkable rise to national prominence and a tribute to the player's dedication, as well as the help and advice he received both at Leicester and Nottingham.

But George Chuter wore the number-two shirt against Saracens when a 24-15 win earned yet another final appearance and Ford, playing instead of the injured Flood, registered 14 points. It also featured Alesana Tuilagi's 63rd and last try for Tigers in his 162nd appearance before departing to play for NTT Shining Arcs in Tokyo. Tuilagi had one more game to play in Leicester colours, in front of 81,779 people at Twickenham and against Harlequins which, in the absence of the injured Flood, gave Ford the biggest platform of his burgeoning career in the following team: Geordan Murphy (captain); Horacio Agulla (Scott Hamilton, 73), Manu Tuilagi, Anthony Allen, Alesana Tuilagi; George Ford (Billy Twelvetrees, 73), Ben Youngs; Marcos Ayerza

(Logovi'i Mulipola, 73), George Chuter (Tom Youngs, 61), Dan Cole (Martin Castrogiovanni, 55), George Skivington (Graham Kitchener, 73), Geoff Parling, Steve Mafi, Thomas Waldrom (sin bin 39-49), Julian Salvi.

It was a wonderful climax to the club season, though not for Tigers since Harlequins won 30-23 and deserved to do so. Given the mountain climbed to reach the final, though, Leicester had nothing of which to feel ashamed and if their play was inaccurate and their control of the ball erratic, the old obduracy was there in the rally over the last 15 minutes from 30-13 down to within a converted try of extra-time.

The first of six penalties by Nick Evans put Harlequins on their way and an unconverted try from Tom Williams confirmed their good start. Ford responded with a penalty then another before converting a glorious try by Mafi to give his side the lead but the loss to the sin bin of Waldrom around half-time proved a defining period. Waldrom was shown a yellow card for offside entry to a ruck and, in his absence, Evans kicked three penalties.

Chris Robshaw added a try and Evans converted before adding his sixth penalty to give Harlequins their 17-point cushion but Ben Youngs, with two fine breaks, brought Leicester back into contention. His pass made a try for Allen, Ford added the conversion and a penalty and there was all to play for, had Leicester's discipline been better - a tip tackle by Manu Tuilagi on Danny Care, the Harlequins scrum-half, for which the centre escaped subsequent censure, illustrated the lack of control.

"We had been on such a good run and had worked so hard that I felt hollow," Cockerill said. "We played as poorly as we had for a long time. Our ball retention and control was poor, we forced the game and made stupid decisions when we had no need to." Murphy, who announced his retirement from international rugby during the week before the final, rued the "uncharacteristic" errors that littered Leicester's game and also observed that too many 50-50 decisions went against his team.

As if in mourning, three former stalwarts of the club died over the following five months. Frank Chawner, who played over 300 games between 1949-64, died at the age of 85; Jim Kempin, the Melton Mowbray flanker with 109 appearances between 1974-79, at the early age of 60; and Jerry Day at the age of 88. Day had been secretary of the club between 1966-82 and, in his slightly abrasive way, followed in the fine administrative tradition of Tom Crumbie and Eric Thorneloe over a period of singularly mixed fortunes for Tigers.

↑ Tigers Players' Player of the Season, Steve Mafi, in action during the Premiership final against Harlequins at Twickenham.

← LEICESTER FOOTBALL CLUB 2010/11
Back: Agulla, Allen, M.Tuilagi, Gonzalez Amorosino, Smith, Bucknall, Pienaar, Hurrell, Staunton, Duffey, Grindal, Harrison.
Middle: Cockerill (Director of rugby), Herring (Assistant forwards coach), Robinson, Twelvetrees, Green, Parling, Blaze, Skivington, Woods, Hawkins, Stankovich, Castrogiovanni, Burke (Assistant backs coach), O'Connor (Head coach), Hollis (First-team manager).
Front: Ayerza, Croft, Newby, Hipkiss, Flood, Murphy (capt), Hamilton, A.Tuilagi, Waldrom, Chuter, Youngs, Cole.

← LEICESTER FOOTBALL CLUB 2011/12
Back: Young, Allen, Bucknall, Brookes, Robinson, de Carpentier, Green, Woods, Pienaar, Armes, Agulla, Tait, Grindal, Harrison.
Middle: Burke (Assistant backs coach), Cockerill (Director of rugby), Bower, T.Youngs, Smith, Hawkins, Twelvetrees, Slater, Mafi, Kitchener, Skivington, Parling, Castrogiovanni, Stankovich, Salvi, Staunton, Morris, Harris, Balmain, Blaze (Assistant forwards coach), Stevens, O'Connor (Head coach), Hollis (First-team manager).
Front: Mulipola, Hamilton, Waldrom, A.Tuilagi, Cole, Croft, Crane, Deacon, Murphy (capt), Newby, Flood, Ayerza, Chuter, M.Tuilagi, B.Youngs.

2010/11		OVERALL RECORD:					T	C	PG	DG	PTS
Home Ground: Welford Road		PLD	W	D	L	Tigers scored:	100	69	94	1	923
Director of rugby: Richard Cockerill assisted by Matt O'Connor and Paul Burke		36	21	2	13	Opponents scored:	63	50	98	7	730
Captain: Geordan Murphy											

GM	DATE		VEN	OPPONENTS	RESULT	POS/LGE	TRIES	KICKS	ATT
AVIVA PREMIERSHIP RUGBY (1ST)						**CHAMPIONS: SARACENS**			
1	Sep	5s	a	Northampton Saints	L 19-27	8	A.Tuilagi 26, Hamilton 70/73	Flood c, Staunton c	13498
2		**11**	**H**	**Exeter Chiefs**	W 37t-27	4	Murphy 12, Hamilton 64, Hipkiss 69, Penalty 79	Staunton 4c/3p	17956
3		18	a	London Wasps	L+ 30t-37	7	Smith 19, Youngs 28, Twelvetrees 35, Croft 38	Staunton 2c/2p	8006
4		**25**	**H**	**Leeds Carnegie**	W 48t-6	5	Hamilton 7, Waldrom 21, Croft 31, A.Tuilagi 36/45, Smith 55, Skivington 60, M.Tuilagi 77	Twelvetrees 4c	17063
5	Oct	3s	a	Saracens	L+ 20-26	6	Penalty 37, Amorosino 68	Twelvetrees 2c/2p	7517
8		**23**	**H**	**Bath Rugby**	W+ 21-15	5	-	Flood 6p/d	21194
9		30	a	Gloucester Rugby	L+ 12-19	5	-	Twelvetrees 4p	13970
13	Nov	**19f**	**H**	**Harlequins**	W+ 18-13	5	-	Twelvetrees 6p	17441
14		**27**	**H**	**Newcastle Falcons**	W 44t-19	3	Penalty 31, Crane 41, M.Tuilagi 46/58, Allen 55, Smith 67	Twelvetrees 4c/2p	18738
15	Dec	4	a	London Irish	W 23-14	2	Waldrom 54, Penalty 77	Twelvetrees 2c/3p	11405
18		**27m**	**H**	**Sale Sharks**	W 54t-21	2	Allen 5, A.Tuilagi 7, Hawkins 14, M.Tuilagi 36/49, Hamilton 43/61, Smith 66	Staunton 7c	24000
19	Jan	2s	a	Exeter Chiefs	W+ 22-15	1	A.Tuilagi 3, Crane 32/70	Staunton c/p, Flood c	10495
20		**8**	**H**	**Northampton Saints**	W 27-16	1	Newby 10, Ayerza 63	Flood c/5p	24000
25	Feb	13s	a	Leeds Carnegie	W+ 15-9	1	M.Tuilagi 4, A.Tuilagi 52	Staunton c/p	6762
26		**19**	**H**	**London Wasps**	W 21-12	1	Staunton 11, Mafi 28	Staunton c/3p	21215
27		25f	a	Sale Sharks	W+ 18-16	1	-	Staunton 6p	8115
28	Mar	**5**	**H**	**Saracens**	L+ 14-15	1	M.Tuilagi 29	Staunton 3p	22451
29		26	a	Bath Rugby	W 37t-6	1	Allen 14, Croft 24/63, Flood 39/51	Flood 3c/2p	12200
30	Apr	2	a	Harlequins	W+ 17-13	1	A.Tuilagi 42, Penalty 57	Flood 2c/p	14282
32		**16**	**H**	**Gloucester Rugby**	D 41t-41t	1	Hamilton 8, A.Tuilagi 43/46/57, Twelvetrees 69	Flood 5c/2p	24000
33		22f	a	Newcastle Falcons	W 24-13	1	A.Tuilagi 15, Smith 47, Grindal 73	Staunton 3c/p	6470
34	May	**7**	**H**	**London Irish**	W 32t-23	1	Smith 20, Agulla 69, Allen 74, Croft 76, A.Tuilagi 80	Flood 2c/p	24000
35		**14**	**H**	**Northampton Saints (sf)**	W 11-3	-	A.Tuilagi 71	Flood 2p	20137
36		28		Saracens (f)	L 18-22	-	-	Flood 6p	80016
HEINEKEN CUP						**EUROPEAN CHAMPIONS: LEINSTER**			
6	Oct	9	a	Benetton Treviso	W+ 34t-29	1	Smith 2, Newby 21, Castrogiovanni 46, Youngs 56, A.Tuilagi 78	Twelvetrees 3c/p	5800
7		**17s**	**H**	**Scarlets**	W 46t-10	1	Castrogiovanni 17, Youngs 42, Waldrom 49, Croft 51/62, Smith 74	Flood 5c/2p	19160
16	Dec	11	a	Perpignan	L+ 19-24	1	Murphy 54	Flood c/4p	13705
17		**19s**	**H**	**Perpignan**	D 22-22	2	A.Tuilagi 33	Twelvetrees c/5p	19519
21	Jan	15	a	Scarlets	W 32-18	2	A.Tuilagi 51, Youngs 61, Mafi 78	Flood c/5p	12392
22		**23s**	**H**	**Benetton Treviso**	W 62t-15	2	Crane 18/32/42, Hamilton 26/71, A.Tuilagi 39, Waldrom 48, M.Tuilagi 78, Mafi 80	Flood 7c/p	17601
31	Apr	9	a	Leinster (qf)	L+ 10-17	1	Hawkins 77	Flood c/p	49762
ANGLO-WELSH CUP (LV= CUP)						**CUP WINNERS: GLOUCESTER RUGBY**			
10	Nov	**5f**	**H**	**Harlequins**	L 25-34	2	Penalty 73	Twelvetrees 6p, Ford c	16197
12		12f	a	Ospreys	L 13-46t	4	Armes 28	Ford c/2p	6632
23	Jan	29	a	Exeter Chiefs	L 10-35t	4	Hipkiss 48, Stankovich 79	-	7445
24	Feb	**4f**	**H**	**Bath Rugby**	L 12-26t	4	Amorosino 27, Slater 35	Staunton c	13156
CLUB MATCH									
11	Nov	**9tu**	**H**	**Australia**	L 15-26		-	Twelvetrees 5p	20299

***Neutral Venue:** #36 at Twickenham*

INDIVIDUAL APPEARANCES 2010/11

Name / Game #	1	2	3	4	5	6	7	8	9	10	11	12	13	14	15	16	17	18	19	20	21	22	23	24	25	26	27	28	29	30	31	32	33	34	35	36	Apps	T	Pts
H (Horacio) Agulla Ar28	-	-	>r	r	11	13	-	-	x	14	-	-	-	-	-	-	-	-	r	r	r	r	-	15	14	14	14	14	14	14	14	14	r	r	r	14	13+9	1	5
AO (Anthony) Allen E2	12	12	-	-	-	-	12	12	12	-	L	-	12	12	12	12	12	12	12	12	12	12	-	12*	12	12	12	12	12	12	12	-	12	12	12	12	28	4	20
TR (Tom) Armes	-	-	-	-	-	-	-	-	-	-	-	7	-	-	-	-	-	-	-	-	-	-	-	-	-	-	-	-	-	-	-	-	-	-	-	-	1	1	5
MI (Marcos) Ayerza Ar32	1	r	1	-	-	-	1	r	1	1	-	-	-	-	1	1	1	1	1	1	1	1	-	x	1	r	1	1	1	■1	-	-	1	1	1	1	22+3	1	5
FJ (Fraser) Balmain	-	-	-	-	-	-	-	-	-	-	-	>r	x	-	-	-	-	-	-	-	-	-	-	r	x	-	-	-	-	-	-	-	-	-	-	-	0+2	-	-
RTE (Ryan) Bower	-	-	-	-	-	-	-	-	-	-	-	>3	x	r	-	-	-	-	-	-	-	-	r	-	-	-	-	-	-	-	-	-	-	-	-	-	1+2	-	-
PJ (Peter) Bucknall	-	-	-	>r	-	-	-	-	x	x	A	x	1	1	x	x	-	r	-	-	-	-	3	3	3	x	x	-	-	-	-	-	-	-	-	-	6+2	-	-
ML (Martin) Castrogiovanni It76	3	r	3	-	r	3	3	r	3	r	-	-	-	-	r	r	3	3	r	3	3	r	-	-	-	3	-	r	-	r	r	3	3	3	3	3	15+11	2	10
GS (George) Chuter E24	2	2	2	2	-	2	2	2	2	-	B	-	2	2	2	2	2	-	2	2	2	2	-	-	2	2	2	2	2	2	2	r	2	2	2	2	29+1	-	-
J (Joe) Cobden	-	-	-	-	-	-	-	-	-	-	-	-	-	-	-	-	-	-	-	-	-	-	<15	-	-	-	-	-	-	-	-	-	-	-	-	-	1	-	-
DR (Dan) Cole E16 L+	r	3	r	3	3	r	r	3	-	-	-	-	-	-	3	3	x	-	3	r	r	3	-	-	-	-	-	-	3	3	3	r	r	r	r	r	11+11	-	-
JS (Jordan) Crane E3	-	-	-	-	-	-	-	-	r	8*	G	-	8	8*	8	8	-	-	8	8	8	8	-	-	-	-	-	-	r	8	8	r	-	-	8	8	14+3	6	30
TR (Tom) Croft E24 L3	-	r	6	6	6*	6	6	6	-	-	-	-	-	-	-	-	-	-	-	-	-	-	-	-	-	r	5	6	6	6	6	6*	6	6	6	6	16+2	7	35
LP (Louis) Deacon E23	-	-	-	-	-	-	-	-	-	-	-	-	-	4	4	4	4	4	4	4	4*	4*	-	-	-	-	-	-	-	-	4	-	-	-	-	-	10	-	-
JJ (Joe) Duffey	r	x	-	-	x	-	r	x	-	r	-	x	-	-	-	-	-	r	-	-	-	-	r	<r	x	-	-	-	-	-	-	-	-	-	-	-	0+6	-	-
ME (Matt) Everard	-	-	-	-	-	-	-	-	-	-	-	r	-	-	-	-	-	-	-	-	-	-	<6	-	-	-	-	-	-	-	-	-	-	-	-	-	1+1	-	-
TGAL (Toby) Flood E40	10	-	-	-	-	-	10	10	-	-	-	-	-	-	10	-	-	r	10	10	10	-	-	-	-	-	-	-	10	10	10	10	-	10	10	10	14+1	2	187
GT (George) Ford E+	-	-	-	-	x	-	-	-	x	10	x	10	x	r	-	-	-	-	-	-	-	-	10	-	-	-	-	-	-	-	-	-	-	-	-	-	3+1	-	10
AR (Andy) Forsyth	-	-	-	-	-	-	-	-	-	-	-	12	-	r	-	-	-	-	-	-	-	-	12	r	-	-	-	-	-	-	-	-	-	-	-	-	2+2	-	-
LP (Lucas) Gonzalez Amorosino Ar10	-	-	-	-	15	x	-	-	-	15	-	-	-	-	-	-	-	-	-	-	-	-	-	<11	-	-	-	-	-	-	-	-	-	-	-	-	3	2	10
CD (Calum) Green	4	4	-	-	-	-	-	-	-	4	-	4	-	-	-	-	x	r	x	-	-	-	4	4	r	x	x	x	-	-	-	-	r	-	-	-	6+3	-	-
JS (James) Grindal	r	x	x	r	9	x	r	x	9	x	I	-	9	9	x	x	x	9	x	x	x	r	-	-	9	9	9	9	r	x	x	x	9	r	r	x	11+7	1	5
BA (Ben) Gulliver	-	-	-	-	-	-	-	-	-	>5	-	<5	-	-	-	-	-	-	-	-	-	-	-	-	-	-	-	-	-	-	-	-	-	-	-	-	2	-	-
SE (Scott) Hamilton NZ2	14	14	14	14	14	14	14	14	14	-	N	-	14	15	14	14	14	14	-	-	15	15	-	-	15	15	15	15	15	15	15	15	15	15	15	15	30	9	45
JC (Jonny) Harris	-	-	-	-	-	-	-	-	-	-	-	-	-	r	-	-	-	-	-	-	-	-	-	-	-	-	-	-	-	-	-	-	-	-	-	-	0+1	-	-
SJ (Sam) Harrison	-	-	-	-	x	-	-	-	-	-	-	r	-	-	-	-	-	r	-	-	-	-	9	9	x	x	x	x	-	-	-	-	r	-	-	-	2+3	-	-
RA (Rob) Hawkins	-	-	x	>r	2	r	-	-	r	2	r	2	x	r	x	r	x	2	r	x	r	r	2	■2	-	x	x	x	r	x	r	2	r	r	x	r	7+14	2	10
DP (Dan) Hemingway	-	-	-	-	-	-	-	-	-	-	-	6	-	-	-	-	-	r	-	-	-	-	8	<r	x	-	-	-	-	-	-	-	-	-	-	-	2+2	-	-
DJ (Dan) Hipkiss E13	13	13	-	13	13	-	-	-	-	13	r	13	-	-	-	-	-	-	-	-	-	-	13	13	x	x	x	<r	-	-	-	-	-	-	-	-	8+2	2	10
WH (Will) Hurrell	-	-	-	-	-	-	-	-	-	-	-	<11	-	-	-	-	-	-	-	-	-	-	-	-	-	-	-	-	-	-	-	-	-	-	-	-	1	-	-
A (Alex) Lewington	-	-	-	-	-	-	-	-	-	-	-	15	-	-	-	-	-	-	-	-	-	-	11	-	-	-	-	-	-	-	-	-	-	-	-	-	2	-	-
RWR (Rory) Lynn	-	-	-	-	-	-	-	-	-	-	-	=r	-	-	-	-	-	-	-	-	-	-	x	-	-	-	-	-	-	-	-	-	-	-	-	-	0+1	-	-
SJ (Steve) Macauley	-	-	-	-	-	-	-	-	-	-	-	=r	-	-	-	-	-	-	-	-	-	-	x	-	-	-	-	-	-	-	-	-	-	-	-	-	0+1	-	-
SO (Steve) Mafi T3	-	-	x	>r	r	x	r	x	r	6	r	x	r	r	r	x	6	6	6	x	r	r	-	6	4	4	4	4	4	4	5	4	-	r	4	4	15+11	3	15
DJ (Dave) Markham	-	-	-	-	-	-	-	-	-	-	-	-	-	-	-	-	-	-	-	-	-	-	=r	-	-	-	-	-	-	-	-	-	-	-	-	-	0+1	-	-
GEA (Geordan) Murphy I69 L2	15*	15*	15*	15*	-	15*	15*	15*	15*	x	0*	-	15*	-	15*	15*	15*	15*	15*	15*	-	-	-	-	-	-	-	-	-	-	-	-	-	-	-	-	16	2	10
PA (Pieter) Myburgh	-	-	-	-	-	-	-	-	-	-	-	-	-	-	-	-	-	-	-	-	-	-	>7	<r	-	-	-	-	-	-	-	-	-	-	-	-	1+1	-	-
CA (Craig) Newby NZ3	6	6	-	r	7	7	7	7	6	-	H	-	7	7	7	7	7	7	7	7	7	7	-	-	6*	6*	6*	7*	7*	7*	7*	r	7*	7*	7*	7*	29+2	2	10
CE (Camilo) Parilli-Ocampo	-	-	-	-	-	-	-	-	-	-	-	>1	-	-	-	-	-	-	-	-	-	-	x	<1	-	-	-	-	-	-	-	-	-	-	-	-	2	-	-
GMW (Geoff) Parling E+ L+	-	-	-	-	-	-	-	-	-	-	-	-	r	-	-	-	-	-	-	-	-	-	-	-	-	-	-	-	-	-	-	-	-	-	-	-	0+1	-	-
BJM (Ben) Pienaar	r	-	x	-	8	x	-	-	-	7	x	8*	-	-	-	-	-	-	-	-	-	-	-	-	-	-	-	-	-	-	-	-	-	-	-	-	3+1	-	-
LM (Lee) Robinson	-	-	-	-	>r	x	-	-	-	-	-	14	x	14	-	-	-	-	-	-	-	-	14	<r	-	-	-	-	-	-	-	-	-	-	-	-	3+2	-	-
L (Luix) Roussarie	-	-	-	-	-	-	-	-	-	-	-	-	-	-	-	-	-	-	-	-	-	-	x	=r	-	-	-	-	-	-	-	-	-	-	-	-	0+1	-	-
GA (George) Skivington	>5	5	5	5	5	5	5	5	5	-	E	-	5	5	5	5	5	-	-	5	5	5	-	-	5	5	r	5	-	-	-	5	5	5	5	5	26+1	1	5
EN (Ed) Slater	>r	r	4	4	4	4	4	4	4	x	D	-	4	r	r	x	x	5	5	x	r	r	5	5	-	-	-	-	5	5	r	-	4	4	r	r	17+9	1	5
MW (Matt) Smith	-	-	13	12	12	12	13	13	13	-	M	-	13	13	13	13	13	r	14	14	14	14	-	14	-	-	-	-	r	r	r	r	14	14	14	13	22+5	8	40
JE (Jason) Spice	-	-	-	-	-	-	-	-	x	>9	x	9	x	<r	-	-	-	-	-	-	-	-	-	-	-	-	-	-	-	-	-	-	-	-	-	-	2+1	-	-
B (Boris) Stankovich	r	1	x	1	1	1	r	1	-	-	-	-	-	-	-	-	-	-	-	-	r	r	1*	-	x	1	x	x	r	r	1	1	r	r	x	r	9+9	1	5
JW (Jeremy) Staunton I5	r	10	10	-	-	-	-	-	-	-	-	-	-	-	x	x	x	10	10	x	x	r	-	10	10	10	10	10	r	x	x	r	10	x	x	x	10+4	1	107
AT (Alesana) Tuilagi Sa20 PI1	11	11	11	11	-	11	11	11	11	11	-	-	-	-	11	11	11	11	11	11	11	11	-	-	11	11	11	11	11	11	11	11	11	11	11	11	29	17	85
EM (Manusamoa) Tuilagi E+ L+	r	r	r	r	-	-	r	x	-	r	K	-	11	11	r	x	x	13	13	13	13	13	-	-	13	13	13	13	13	13	13	13	13	13	13	-	19+7	8	40
WWF (Billy) Twelvetrees E+	-	r	12	10	10	10	r	x	10	12	J	-	10	10	10	-	10	r	-	-	-	-	-	-	x	x	x	r	-	-	-	12	r	-	-	r	12+6	2	144
TR (Thomas) Waldrom E+	>8	8	8	8	-	8	8	8	8	x	F	-	6	6	6	6	8	8	r	6	6	6	-	8	8	8	8	8	8	r	r	8	8	8	r	r	27+5	4	20
JM (Julian) White E51 L4	-	-	-	r	x	x	-	-	r	3	C	-	3	3	-	-	x	r	x	x	-	-	-	-	-	-	3	3	r	-	x	x	-	-	-	-	6+4	-	-
BN (Ben) Woods	7	7	7	7	r	-	r	r	7	-	-	-	-	-	-	-	-	-	-	-	-	-	r	7	7	7	7	r	r	x	-	7	r	r	-	-	10+8	-	-
BR (Ben) Youngs E12 L+	9	9	9	9	-	9	9	9	-	-	-	-	-	-	9	9	9	-	9	9	9	9	-	-	-	-	-	-	9	9	9	9	-	9	9	9	21	4	20

The key for how to read the stats is on the last page

20	11/12	Home Ground: Welford Road	Trophy Cabinet: LV= Cup(7)	OVERALL RECORD:					T	C	PG	DG	PTS
		Director of rugby: Richard Cockerill assisted by Matt O'Connor, Paul Burke & Richard Blaze		PLD	W	D	L	Tigers scored:	99	65	105	2	946
		Captain: Geordan Murphy		36	25	1	10	Opponents scored:	65	50	99	4	734

GM	DATE		VEN	OPPONENTS	RESULT	POS/LGE	TRIES	KICKS	ATT
AVIVA PREMIERSHIP RUGBY (2ND)						**CHAMPIONS: HARLEQUINS**			
1	Sep	**3**	**H**	**Exeter Chiefs**	L+ 28-30	7	Waldrom 3, Morris 19/56	Ford d, Twelvetrees 2c/2p	18251
2		11s	a	London Wasps	L+ 29-35t	11	Twelvetrees 16/37	Twelvetrees 2c/5p	5078
3		17	a	Newcastle Falcons	W+ 27-26	8	Slater 18, Salvi 52, Mafi 76	Twelvetrees 4p	4214
4		**24**	**H**	**Saracens**	L 25-50t	9	Morris 37, Salvi 51, Woods 76	Twelvetrees 2c/2p	17557
5	Oct	1	a	Bath Rugby	L+ 25-26	10	Staunton 7	Staunton c/6p	11768
6		**8**	**H**	**Harlequins**	L 18-27	11	Stankovich 2, Hamilton 20	Staunton c/2p	17227
9		28f	a	Sale Sharks	W 34t-13	10	A.Tuilagi 57, Castrogiovanni 60, Flood 64, Ayerza 69	Flood 4c/2p	8673
10	Nov	**5**	**H**	**London Irish**	D 24-24	10	Penalty 22, Agulla 61	Flood c/4p	20479
13		26	a	Gloucester Rugby	W+ 19-14	10	Flood 59, A.Tuilagi 67	Flood 3p	14437
14	Dec	**3**	**H**	**Northampton Saints**	W+ 30t-25	7	Smith 20, Mafi 32, B.Youngs 59, Agulla 75	Flood 2c/2p	24000
17		27tu	a	Worcester Warriors	W 32t-13	5	Smith 2, Flood 21, Deacon 56, Agulla 78	Flood 3c/2p	12024
18	Jan	**1s**	**H**	**Sale Sharks**	W+ 28-23	4	Penalty 5, Murphy 14, A.Tuilagi 54	Flood 2c/3p	23132
19		**7**	**H**	**London Wasps**	W 29-11	4	Twelvetrees 32/72	Twelvetrees 2c/5p	21310
24	Feb	11	a	Exeter Chiefs	L 11-19	4	A.Tuilagi 8	Flood 2p	9025
25		19s	a	Saracens	W+ 20-19	4	Slater 64	Flood 4p, Murphy d	7265
26		**25**	**H**	**Newcastle Falcons**	W 42t-15	4	Salvi 10, Twelvetrees 22, Agulla 34, Waldrom 42/68, Morris 74	Ford 3c/2p	18759
27	Mar	**4s**	**H**	**Gloucester Rugby**	W 36t-3	3	Mulipola 12, Mafi 22, B.Youngs 38, Smith 57, A.Tuilagi 60	Flood 4c/p	21699
30		25s	a	London Irish	W 41t-32	3	Flood 22, Salvi 27, M.Tuilagi 60, Croft 80	Flood 3c/5p	20905
31		**30f**	**H**	**Worcester Warriors**	W 43t-13	3	Hamilton 18, Chuter 28, Croft 36, Castrogiovanni 47, Waldrom 57, T.Youngs 61, Ford 68	Flood 3c, Ford c	21344
32	Apr	14	a	Northampton Saints	W 35t-21	2	Flood 14/43, A.Tuilagi 16, Agulla 53	Flood 3c/3p	13475
33		21	a	Harlequins	W 43t-33	2	Waldrom 6/70, Mafi 37, A.Tuilagi 65	Flood 4c/5p	14282
34	May	**5**	**H**	**Bath Rugby**	W 28-3	2	Allen 54, Penalty 70, Agulla 78	Flood p, Twelvetrees 2c/2p	24000
35		**12**	**H**	**Saracens (sf)**	W 24-15	-	A.Tuilagi 21, Mafi 48	Ford c/4p	20173
36		26		Harlequins (f)	L 23-30	-	Mafi 30, Allen 66	Ford 2c/3p	81779
HEINEKEN CUP						**EUROPEAN CHAMPIONS: LEINSTER**			
11	Nov	12	a	Aironi Rugby	W 28-12	1	Croft 12, A.Tuilagi 22, Morris 80	Flood 2c/3p	8151
12		**19**	**H**	**Ulster**	W 20-9	1	Smith 68	Flood 5p	21473
15	Dec	11s	a	ASM Clermont Auvergne	L 12-30	3	B.Youngs 16, Penalty 70	Flood c	17688
16		**17**	**H**	**ASM Clermont Auvergne**	W+ 23-19	2	M.Tuilagi 16, Salvi 47	Flood 2c/3p	20202
20	Jan	13f	a	Ulster	L 7-41t	3	Murphy 14	Twelvetrees c	11900
21		**21**	**H**	**Aironi Rugby**	W 33t-6	3	Waldrom 42, Woods 47, Murphy 55, Ford 71	Flood c, Twelvetrees c/3p	19652
ANGLO-WELSH CUP (LV= CUP)						**CUP WINNERS: LEICESTER TIGERS**			
7	Oct	15	a	Scarlets	L 3-31t	2	-	Ford p	6314
8		**21f**	**H**	**Gloucester Rugby**	W 40t-14	2	Cole 29, M.Tuilagi 40, T.Youngs 42, Agulla 77	Flood 3c/4p, Ford c	16408
22	Jan	28	a	Harlequins	W 19-9	1	Forsyth 4, Lewington 55, Pienaar 68	Ford 2c	13780
23	Feb	**4**	**H**	**Newcastle Falcons**	W 24-13	1	Waldrom 6, Skivington 48	Staunton c/4p	19767
28	Mar	9f	a	Bath Rugby (sf)	W 17-16	-	Kitchener 20	Ford 4p	10205
29		18s		Northampton Saints (f)	W 26-14	-	Mafi 25, Hamilton 49	Ford 2c/4p	11895

Neutral Venues: *#29 at Sixways - Worcester, #36 at Twickenham*

INDIVIDUAL APPEARANCES 2011/12

Name / Game #	1	2	3	4	5	6	7	8	9	10	11	12	13	14	15	16	17	18	19	20	21	22	23	24	25	26	27	28	29	30	31	32	33	34	35	36	Apps	T	Pts
H (Horacio) Agulla Ar34	-	-	-	-	-	-	-	14	13	13	-	14	14	14	14	14	14	14	14	14	14	-	14	14	14	14	14	14	14	14	-	14	14	14	14	<14	26	7	35
AO (Anthony) Allen E2	12	12	12	12	-	-	-	-	-	-	-	-	-	-	-	-	-	-	12	12	12	-	12	12	12	-	-	-	-	x	12	12	12	12	12	12	16	2	10
TR (Tom) Armes	x	-	-	r	-	-	7	-	-	-	-	-	-	-	-	-	-	-	-	-	-	<7	-	-	-	-	-	-	-	-	-	-	-	-	-	-	2+1	-	-
MI (Marcos) Ayerza Ar34	-	-	-	-	-	-	-	1	1	1	1	1	1	1	1	-	-	-	-	1	1	-	1	1	1	1	1	r	r	1	1	1	1	1	1	1	22+2	1	5
RTE (Ryan) Bower	-	-	-	-	-	-	3	r	-	-	-	-	-	-	-	-	-	-	-	-	-	x	x	x	x	-	-	-	-	-	-	-	-	-	-	-	1+1	-	-
K (Kieran) Brookes E+	>3	3	r	-	-	-	-	-	-	-	-	-	-	-	-	-	-	-	-	-	-	-	-	-	-	-	-	-	-	-	-	-	-	-	-	-	2+1	-	-
PJ (Peter) Bucknall	r	r	-	r	r	x	<r	-	-	-	-	-	-	-	-	-	-	-	-	-	-	-	-	-	-	-	-	-	-	-	-	-	-	-	-	-	0+5	-	-
ML (Martin) Castrogiovanni It85	-	-	-	-	-	-	-	-	r	3	r	r	3	r	3	3	r	1	-	3	3	-	-	-	-	-	-	-	-	r	3	r	r	3	r	r	9+10	2	10
GS (George) Chuter E24	2*	2*	2*	2*	2*	2*	-	r	2	2	2	2	2	2	2	2	2	r	2	r	2	-	2	2	2	2	2	-	-	2	2	2*	2	2	2	2	29+3	1	5
DR (Dan) Cole E28 L+	-	-	-	-	-	-	-	3	3	r	3	3	r	3	r	r	3	3	3	r	r	-	-	-	-	-	-	-	-	3	r	3	3	r	3	3	13+8	1	5
TR (Tom) Croft E36 L3	-	-	-	-	-	-	-	6	6	6	6	6	6	-	6	6	6	r	6	6	6	-	-	-	-	-	-	-	-	r	6	6	6	-	-	-	15+2	3	15
LP (Louis) Deacon E29	-	-	-	-	-	-	-	r	-	4	4	4	4	4	4	4	4*	-	-	-	-	-	-	-	-	-	-	-	-	-	-	-	-	-	-	-	8+1	1	5
RA (Richard) de Carpentier	-	-	-	-	-	-	=r	-	-	-	-	-	-	-	-	-	-	-	-	-	-	-	-	-	-	-	-	-	-	-	-	-	-	-	-	-	0+1	-	-
JP (James) Doyle	-	-	-	-	-	-	-	-	-	-	-	-	-	-	-	-	-	-	-	-	-	=r	-	-	-	-	-	-	-	-	-	-	-	-	-	-	0+1	-	-
TGAL (Toby) Flood E47	-	-	-	-	-	-	-	10	10	10	10	10	10	10	10	10	10	10	-	-	-	-	r	10	10	-	10	-	r	10	10	10	10	10	-	-	19+2	6	260
GT (George) Ford E+	10	10	10	10	x	x	10	r	-	-	-	-	-	-	-	-	-	-	-	-	r	10	-	x	x	10	r	10	10	-	r	-	-	-	10	10	11+4	2	93
AR (Andy) Forsyth	x	r	14	-	14	-	13	-	-	-	12	12	-	-	-	-	-	-	-	-	-	12	r	-	-	-	-	13	r	-	-	-	-	-	-	-	7+3	1	5
CD (Calum) Green	-	-	-	-	-	-	-	-	-	-	-	-	-	-	-	-	-	-	-	-	-	4	-	-	-	-	-	4	x	-	-	-	-	<4	-	-	3	-	-
JS (James) Grindal	9	9	9	9	9	x	r	r	r	r	-	-	-	-	-	-	-	-	-	-	-	r	r	r	9	9	x	9	9	r	9	-	-	<r	-	-	10+9	-	-
SE (Scott) Hamilton NZ2	15	15	15	15	-	r	-	r	14	14	x	-	x	r	r	r	15	r	r	x	r	14	11	-	x	11	r	15	11	11	14	15	x	r	x	r	15+11	3	15
JC (Jonny) Harris	x	x	-	r	x	-	1	r	-	-	-	-	-	-	-	-	-	-	-	-	-	r	-	-	x	-	-	-	-	-	-	-	-	-	-	-	1+3	-	-
SJ (Sam) Harrison	-	-	-	-	x	9	9	9	9	9	9	9	9	r	x	x	-	-	r	r	r	9	9	9	-	-	-	-	-	-	r	r	x	9	x	x	12+6	-	-
RA (Rob) Hawkins	r	x	-	x	-	-	2	-	-	-	-	x	x	x	r	x	x	2	r	2	-	-	r	r	x	r	r	2	2	-	-	-	-	-	-	-	5+7	-	-
MO (Michael) Holford	-	-	r	3	3	r	-	-	-	-	-	-	-	-	-	-	-	-	-	-	-	-	-	-	-	-	-	-	-	-	-	-	-	-	-	-	2+2	-	-
GP (Graham) Kitchener	-	>r	r	5	x	x	4	-	-	-	-	-	-	-	-	-	-	5	-	-	r	5	5	-	x	r	5	5	5	-	5	-	x	-	x	r	9+5	1	5
A (Alex) Lewington	-	-	-	-	-	-	11	-	-	-	-	-	-	-	-	-	-	-	-	-	-	11	-	-	-	-	-	11	-	-	-	-	-	-	-	-	3	1	5
SO (Steve) Mafi T3	6	6	6	6	6	6	-	-	r	-	x	r	r	6	8	x	r	6	4	4	r	-	6	6	6	6	6	6	6	6	r	r	r	6	6	6	22+8	7	35
EDM (Dante) Mama	-	-	-	-	-	-	>r	-	-	-	-	-	-	-	-	-	-	-	-	-	-	<13	-	-	-	-	-	-	-	-	-	-	-	-	-	-	1+1	-	-
NE (Niall) Morris	>11	11	11	11	15	15	15	-	r	x	14	r	-	-	-	-	r	-	-	-	-	15	15	-	-	r	-	-	-	-	-	-	-	-	-	-	10+4	5	25
L (Logovi'i) Mulipola Sa6	-	-	-	-	-	-	-	-	-	-	-	-	-	-	-	-	-	x	>r	-	-	3	r	r	3	3	3	r	3	r	r	r	x	r	x	r	5+9	1	5
GEA (Geordan) Murphy I72 L2	-	-	-	-	-	-	-	15*	15*	15*	15*	15*	15*	15*	15*	15*	-	15*	15*	15*	15*	-	-	15*	15*	15*	15*	-	15*	15*	15*	-	15*	15*	15*	15*	24	3	18
CA (Craig) Newby NZ3	-	-	-	-	-	-	-	-	-	-	-	-	-	-	-	-	-	-	-	-	-	-	r	x	r	r	r	7*	7	x	7	r	-	r	<7	x	4+6	-	-
GMW (Geoff) Parling E5 L+	-	-	-	-	5	5	5*	5	5	5	5	5	-	-	-	-	-	-	5	5	-	-	-	-	-	-	-	-	-	5	-	5	5	5	5	5	16	-	-
BJM (Ben) Pienaar	-	-	-	-	x	x	6	-	-	-	-	-	-	-	-	-	-	-	-	-	-	8	-	-	-	-	r	8	-	-	-	-	-	<r	-	-	3+2	1	5
E (Ed) Rolston HK5	-	-	-	-	-	-	=14	-	-	-	-	-	-	-	-	-	-	-	-	-	-	-	-	-	-	-	-	-	-	-	-	-	-	-	-	-	1	-	-
JM (Julian) Salvi	>7	8	7	8	8	8	-	7	7	7	7	7	-	7	7	7	r	7	7	7	-	-	r	7	7	7	7	r	r	7	x	7	7	7	-	7	26+4	5	25
GA (George) Skivington	5	5	5	-	-	-	r	4	4	r	x	r	5	5	5	5	-	-	-	-	5	-	4	5	5	5	4	-	4	4	-	4	4	-	4	<4	21+3	1	5
EN (Ed) Slater	4	4	4	4	4	4	8	-	r	r	-	-	r	r	r	-	5	4	r	r	4	-	-	4	4	4	-	-	-	-	4	-	-	-	-	-	14+7	2	10
MW (Matt) Smith	14	14	-	14	13	13	-	13	12	12	13	13	13	13	13	13	11	13	13	13	-	r	13	r	11	13	13	r	13	x	r	r	-	-	-	-	23+5	4	20
B (Boris) Stankovich	1	1	1	1	1	1	-	-	r	x	x	r	x	r	r	1	1	r	1	x	r	1	-	-	-	r	r	1	1	-	-	-	-	-	-	-	12+8	1	5
JW (Jeremy) Staunton I5	-	x	x	r	10	10	r	-	r	r	x	x	x	x	-	-	x	x	r	r	10	x	10	-	-	r	-	<r	-	-	-	-	-	-	-	-	4+8	1	47
SK (Scott) Steele	-	-	-	-	-	-	-	-	-	-	-	-	-	-	-	-	-	-	-	-	-	-	-	-	x	>r	-	r	x	-	-	-	-	-	-	-	0+2	-	-
JD (Jimmy) Stevens	-	-	-	-	-	-	-	-	-	-	-	-	-	-	-	-	-	-	-	-	>r	2	-	-	-	-	-	-	-	-	-	-	-	-	-	-	1+1	-	-
AG (Andy) Symons	-	-	-	-	-	-	>12	-	-	-	-	-	-	-	-	-	-	-	-	-	-	-	-	-	-	-	-	-	-	-	-	-	-	-	-	-	1	-	-
MJM (Mathew) Tait E38	-	-	-	>r	11	14	-	-	-	-	-	-	-	-	-	-	-	-	-	-	-	-	-	-	-	-	-	-	-	-	-	-	-	-	-	-	2+1	-	-
AT (Alesana) Tuilagi Sa26 PI1	-	-	-	-	-	11	-	11	11	11	11	11	11	■11	11	11	-	11	11	11	11	-	-	11	-	-	11	-	-	-	11	11	11	11	11	<11	22	9	45
EM (Manusamoa) Tuilagi E10 L+	-	-	-	-	-	-	-	12	-	-	-	-	-	-	12	12	13	-	-	-	-	-	-	13	13	-	-	-	-	13	13	13	13	13	13	13	13	3	15
WWF (Billy) Twelvetrees E+	13	13	13	13	12	12	-	-	-	-	-	-	12	12	r	x	12	12	10	10	13	-	-	-	-	12	12	12	12	12	-	r	x	r	x	<r	18+4	5	118
TR (Thomas) Waldrom E+	8	r	8	-	-	-	-	8	8	8	8	8	8	8	r	8	8	8	8	8	8	-	8	8	8	8	8	r	8	8	8	8	8	8	8	8	28+3	8	40
JM (Julian) White E51 L4	-	-	3	-	-	3	-	-	-	-	-	-	-	-	-	x	x	-	r	-	-	-	3	3	-	r	r	<3	x	-	-	-	-	-	-	-	5+3	-	-
BN (Ben) Woods	r	7	x	7	7	7	-	r	-	-	-	-	7	r	-	x	7	r	r	r	7	6*	<7*	x	-	-	-	-	-	-	-	-	-	-	x	-	9+6	2	10
MLR (Micky) Young	>r	r	r	r	-	-	-	-	-	-	x	-	-	-	-	-	r	r	-	-	9	-	-	-	-	-	-	-	-	-	-	-	-	-	-	-	1+6	-	-
BR (Ben) Youngs E22 L+	-	-	-	-	-	-	-	-	-	-	-	r	r	9	9	9	9	9	9	9	-	-	-	-	-	-	9	-	-	9	-	9	9	-	9	9	13+2	3	15
TN (Tom) Youngs E+ L+	-	-	r	r	r	r	r	2	r	r	r	-	-	-	-	-	-	-	-	-	-	-	-	-	-	-	-	r	r	x	r	r	x	r	x	r	1+14	2	10

The key for how to read the stats is on the last page

CHAPTER 37

Premier Pride

2012/2013

Confirming faith in their director of rugby, Leicester extended Richard Cockerill's contract for a further three years in the wake of their Aviva Premiership final disappointment. At the same time Cockerill's predecessor as club coach, Heyneke Meyer, was preparing for his first examination as coach of South Africa, against an England side chock full of Tigers.

Meyer knew precisely what to expect from the likes of Dan Cole and Ben Youngs, who started the first of three internationals against the Springboks in Durban. Geoff Parling and Manu Tuilagi, who had not enjoyed the best of Premiership finals, were less well known in England's starting XV and Flood joined them from the bench for a 22-17 defeat. Anthony Allen, Graham Kitchener and Thomas Waldrom started the midweek game with the South African Barbarians in Kimberley and were joined from the bench by Tom Youngs, who started against another Barbarians combination in Potchefstroom a week later.

The same Leicester quartet began the second international, in Johannesburg, where Ben Youngs scored two tries in a 36-27 defeat but also damaged his shoulder so badly that he missed the next four months. Flood started at fly-half and ended with the other 17 points from a try, three conversions and two penalties in an English comeback so strong that they believed they could return home with a win, even though the series was gone. As it happened the third test, in Port Elizabeth, was a 14-14 draw in which Waldrom, who had won his first cap off the bench in Johannesburg, started at No 8.

When England's elite squad was announced at the tour's end, it included eight Tigers and Tom Youngs found a place in the Saxons squad. But gone from Leicester's squad were the two wings, Alesana Tuilagi and Horacio Agulla, plus Billy Twelvetrees, Julian White, Jeremy Staunton, James Grindal and Ben Pienaar. Newcomers included a pair of London Irish backs, Dan Bowden and Adam Thompstone; Miles Benjamin, the Worcester wing, Vereniki Goneva, the Fiji wing from French second division club, Tarbes, and a familiar face, Matt Cornwell, the centre who played for the club between 2004-08 and now rejoined from Mogliano. Among the new forwards was a South African with a name familiar to English ears, Rob Andrew, a lock who had been playing with Pau; the returning Brett Deacon and the London Irish flanker, Richard Thorpe.

⬇ Adam Thompstone joined the club from London Irish and by the end of his debut season had become the top individual try scorer.

Also back with appetite revived was Jordan Crane, who had missed the entire 2011/12 season, and he emerged from the bench in the first game of the new season, a 38-13 win over promoted London Welsh in Oxford. But Louis Deacon (shoulder) and Benjamin (toe and then a damaged neck which prevented him playing for the rest of the season) were unavailable and Ben Woods, the flanker, was forced to retire after trying for 23 months to overcome a wrist injury. He was joined in short order by Craig Newby, who gave best to a persistent knee injury.

Scrum-half Micky Young broke an ankle and, with Ben Youngs out of action, Leicester called up Sam Harrison against Worcester with back-up from the Australian Pat Phibbs, signed on a short-term contract. Harrison retained his place for the club's first visit to Wembley, where Saracens were drawing crowds in excess of 40,000 for a handful of selected games; Cockerill had played at football's headquarters, for England in 1999, but neither Tigers nor their supporters would have rushed to return after a flat 9-9 draw.

When Leicester entertained Exeter at the end of September, they were without an entire XV, the casualties including Murphy, Allen, Mafi and Tuilagi. However the forthright Thompstone chose the occasion of his first start to score three tries in a 30-8 win. In the top three Tigers may have been but events beyond their control created great disappointment.

When Rugby World Cup Ltd announced the venues for matches in the 2015 tournament, Welford Road was not among them; to make matters worse, among the 17 potential venues was King Power Stadium (formerly the Walkers), home of Leicester City and one of a great clutch of football stadia named. "That the organisers do not think this is an appropriate venue for its fixtures is disappointing and confusing, both for the professional club game in this country and for its supporters," Peter Tom said.

"Welford Road has hosted many major occasions over the years, including visits from the South Africa, Australia and Argentina national teams in recent seasons. It is home to the best supported and most successful club in the history of the professional game in this country and as such, we believe, is worthy of Rugby World Cup status." Of course, the ground had already enjoyed such status, in both 1991 and 1999, when the organisers had overlooked the reason now given for its omission - that the playing area was too small. The minimum size was given as 95m by 68m whereas Welford Road is no longer than 91m.

The outburst of anger was not confined to Leicestershire but regret was also based on the fact that, outside Twickenham, the only purpose-built rugby grounds in England required were Gloucester and Exeter, even though Kingsholm's capacity (16,500) was more than 7,000 fewer than Leicester. Given that the main consideration for hiring football grounds was their greater capacity for maximising ticket sales, it was - to say the least - an oddity. It was some consolation when, a month later, Welford Road was named rugby venue of the year at the annual Rugby Expo awards evening.

The club announced an operating loss of £1 million, the consequence of reduced attendances during the 2011 global tournament and no income from autumn internationals. "The overall financial good health of the club enables us to absorb the shortfall without damaging our long-term position or prospects," Tom told the annual meeting.

Of more immediate concern was the start of the Heineken Cup from which, the English and French clubs decided, they would withdraw in 2014 if the structure of European competition did not receive a root-and-branch overhaul. There had been grumbling for several years that success was not appropriately rewarded and that the competition was weighted in favour of the Celtic countries. Leicester's first outing, to Toulouse, brought their sixth consecutive loss in France but Tigers bounced back by beating the Ospreys, Louis Deacon returning after a ten-month absence.

Shortly after the club celebrated the elevation to the senior England squad of Tom Youngs, one of eight Tigers chosen for the autumn series, and he became the latest Leicester international when, with Northampton's Dylan Hartley sidelined by injury, he started against Fiji and retained the berth through all four autumn games. Tuilagi, Flood, Cole, Parling and Waldrom were alongside him at the beginning of the series, Ben Youngs having to be content with appearing from the bench. The younger Youngs joined his brother in the starting XV (in a one-point defeat against South Africa) and shared in the thunderous display which consigned New Zealand to a 38-21 defeat and made the entire rugby world sit up and take notice. Tuilagi, scoring his fourth try of the autumn, with Cole and Parling in a pack that out-muscled the All Blacks, completed the club quintet on a memorable day.

Meanwhile at Welford Road another international was poised to complete a prolonged rehabilitation. Leicester had waited 13 months for Mathew Tait to recover from inflammation of the pubic bone and display the qualities that had earned him 38 caps; an A league game in early October was the prelude to an appearance against the New Zealand Maori, the second visit of these particular opponents, the first having come in 1926 when the Maori won 15-13 and as a tribute to history, the following Leicester XV again wore their old lettered jerseys: Mathew Tait; Niall Morris, Matt Smith (Dan Bowden, 42, sin bin 56-66), Anthony Allen, Adam Thompstone (Andy Forsyth, 66); George Ford, Pat Phibbs (Sam Harrison, 59); Boris Stankovich, George Chuter (Jimmy Stevens, 62), Fraser Balmain, Louis Deacon (captain), Graham Kitchener, Ed Slater, Jordan Crane (Richard Thorpe, 74), Julian Salvi.

↑ Mathew Tait tries to find a way through against the New Zealand Maori 13.11.2012.

An attendance of 17,000 was down on the 1926 gate by 3,000 but they saw Leicester win 32-24, with 22 points coming from the boot of Ford. The first of his six penalties gave Leicester an early lead and though the Maori scored a try through Frae Wilson, converted by Willie Ripia, Tigers created tries for Morris and Thompstone. Ford converted both and landed three penalties though before the interval, the Maori had recovered to 26-17 thanks to a try by Tim Bateman, converted by Ripia who also added a penalty.

The gap increased with Ford's fifth penalty but when Bowden departed for the sin bin, the Maori worked Charlie Ngatai into the corner, Ripia converting. A third yellow card, this time to Jarrad Hoetea, the Maori lock, gave Ford his eighth successful kick of the night and Leicester breathing space. "It's nice to prove to those people who don't come to Welford Road regularly that it is a venue capable of hosting a great rugby occasion," Simon Cohen said pointedly.

Tait played a second game at full-back when Leicester beat London Irish despite a red card for Stankovich after a dangerously high tackle. A 17-12 home win over Bath was littered with cards when Tim Wigglesworth, the referee, flourished three reds and two yellows in the final half-hour, Bath bearing the brunt of his wrath.

Flood returned from England with damaged toe ligaments (which had kept him out of the victory over New Zealand) and missed the European games with Treviso, the second of which

↓ Niall Morris comes up just short against Toulouse at a snowy Welford Road 20.1.2013.

was won in Italy by the narrowest of margins. Thompstone scored a wonderful 90-metre try but controversy attended the award by the World Cup final referee, Alain Rolland, of penalty tries to each side. The first went to Treviso even though their forwards were some way from the line when the award was made. The second went to Leicester with three minutes left and gave them a 14-13 win, denying Treviso what would have been the most famous win in their Heineken Cup history.

Scrummaging refused to go away as a talking point. Leicester received two penalty tries in a 31-9 win over London Irish in the Premiership and a 17-12 win over Gloucester was marred by four yellow cards and post-match criticism by Cockerill of the refereeing of the scrum (where Gloucester were penalised ten times). There were two more penalty tries in the win over Worcester, the second in the eightieth minute which brought a 19-14 win after Worcester had gone out to a 14-0 lead. It carried Leicester to the top of the table and saw the welcome return after his neck injury of Tom Croft, who promptly became one of eight Tigers in England's senior squad. The Saxons called up a Leicester quintet including, for the first time, Ed Slater.

Matt Smith joins his father Ian as a member of the Tigers 100 Cap Club 9.2.2013.

Tait received the most severe examination of his old skills in a 15-15 draw with the Ospreys when the Heineken Cup resumed and passed with flying colours. Two late tries, by Ben Youngs and Niall Morris, helped Leicester set up a winner-takes-all game with Toulouse at Welford Road a week later. Snow and frost did their best to make life difficult but a capacity crowd rolled up to see Leicester win 9-5 and deny Toulouse a quarter-final place for only the third time in the competition's history. Flood's three penalties, the third a booming kick from 60 metres through the snowstorm, were the winning of a match which closed with the fly-half in the sin bin. But Toulouse, who missed six attempts at goal, could respond only with a try from Yoann Huget.

By now Ford, eager to start more games, had confirmed a move to Bath where Mike, his father, was coach. "Leicester did everything they could, financially and contractually, to keep him," Cockerill said, recognising both a serious individual talent and the fact that no one player is ever bigger than the club. Another youngster, Tom Price, made his senior debut in the LV= Cup game with Wasps but was carried off in the first half, the lock lasting not much longer than Croft, forced off after only nine minutes with a muscle spasm in the back. That game was won but not the following game with the Scarlets, a 40-19 defeat which marked Leicester's cup exit but not before the young Welsh fly-half, Owen Williams, had put a glint in Cockerill's eye by kicking seven penalties and with his general play.

England started their six nations against Scotland without Tuilagi, still struggling with his ankle though he did make his way back for the remaining four games. That left scope for a Leicester old boy, Billy Twelvetrees, to make his international debut at centre and to score a try in a 38-18 win alongside four Tigers, the Youngs brothers, Cole and Parling. With a Lions tour to Australia on the horizon, international form was critical and England went well to set up a grand-slam opportunity against Wales in Cardiff. Croft started the finale but Wales won 30-3, their record score over the old enemy, and deprived England of the championship and triple crown. Nevertheless, Leicester's eventual representation of six in the Lions party was the greatest for any single club or region, matching that of Leinster: Ben and Tom Youngs became the first brothers chosen since Rory and Tony Underwood in 1993 and they were joined by Cole, Parling, Tuilagi and Croft.

While the internationals were being played, Leicester's Premiership form suffered. Matt Smith's 100th appearance (against London Welsh) created the first father-and-son combination to have each played over 100 games for the club (Ian, his father, played 331 times between 1977-91) and the occasion was marked with the presentation of a cap to Smith junior by Martin Johnson. But losses to Harlequins and Saracens saw Leicester back in third place before girding their loins and producing, under the captaincy of Croft in his 100th start, their best display of the season in a 48-10 win over Sale.

Past team-mates Jonny Wilkinson and Toby Flood are on opposing sides during the Heineken Cup quarter-final in Toulon, 7.4.2013.

The return of the international contingent raised hopes for the Heineken Cup quarter-final in Toulon, with whom Leicester were wrangling for the services of Martin Castrogiovanni. But Tigers lost 21-15 though they might have won had not first Flood and then Cole been sent to the sin bin, both for deliberate knock-downs. Flood kicked five penalties, pushing Leicester out to a 9-0 lead in the first half, but Jonny Wilkinson responded with six penalties and a dropped goal even though the star-studded Toulon pack were outplayed for much of the game. The defeat also cost Marcos Ayerza the rest of the season; he fractured his clavicle when he attempted to tackle Bakkies Botha, the Springbok lock, and joined Louis Deacon and Boris Stankovich on the long-term casualty list.

Toulon went on to win the cup while Leicester were left in the familiar position of concentrating on domestic honours. Victory over Wasps ensured a Premiership play-off but the club had to digest the impending departure of Matt O'Connor, their head coach. After five years, the Australian accepted the same role at Leinster, succeeding Joe Schmidt who had been appointed Ireland coach. Moreover Geordan Murphy, now 35, confirmed his retirement at the season's end. After 322 games and 72 caps for Ireland, it was time to rest the knee that had given him so much trouble and his going was the end of a quite outstanding playing career. Not that Murphy was going far: with O'Connor's departure, the opportunity arose to elevate Paul Burke in the coaching hierarchy and introduce Murphy as backs coach in 2013/14.

The business end of 2012/13 still remained. Tom Youngs was named Premiership player of the year and all six of the new Lions played in the semi-final with Harlequins, who had won the last three meetings of the clubs. Not this time. Leicester won 33-16 to reach their ninth successive final and they did so in style, Tait confirming that he could more than adequately fill the hole left at full-back by Murphy. There was also a cameo for Castrogiovanni, his last home appearance for Leicester after seven years during which time he had not only established a popular restaurant in the city but become a cult figure himself.

The opposition in the final came from Northampton, a match made in heaven for the East Midlands. Leicester fielded the following team: Mathew Tait; Niall Morris, Manu Tuilagi, Anthony Allen, Vereniki Goneva (Matt Smith, 75); Toby Flood (George Ford, 23), Ben Youngs (Sam Harrison, 76); Logovi'i Mulipola (Fraser Balmain, 76), Tom Youngs (Rob Hawkins, 67), Dan Cole (Martin Castrogiovanni, 67), Graham Kitchener (Ed Slater, 55), Geoff Parling, Tom Croft, Jordan Crane (Steve Mafi, 72), Julian Salvi.

Leicester's winning scoreline of 37-17, their tenth league title, suggests a comfortable victory. It was anything but, in a match full of passion and controversy. On the stroke of half-time, Dylan Hartley uttered the words "F***ing cheat" which Wayne Barnes, the referee, felt were directed at him. Hartley said they were made to his opposite number, Tom Youngs, but the Northampton captain was sent off and a hearing banned him for 11 weeks which cost him the Lions tour since both England hookers had been selected.

↑ Tom Youngs's transition to hooker was complete when he was named the Premiership Player of the Season and the Tigers Players' Player of the Year.

Cockerill, out of his seat in the stand and down the steps to remonstrate with the fourth official after Flood was laid out in a tackle, was later disciplined for using foul and abusive language to a match official. That cost him another lengthy touchline ban but in the immediate aftermath he could not contain his pleasure: "We talk about yesteryear and all those great players who have worn the shirt here - and so we should because that is important - but these guys are part of that now," Cockerill said.

The match stood at 10-5 when Leicester lost Flood, their captain. The fly-half went down in a marginally late tackle by Courtney Lawes, Northampton's lock, and as he fell his head struck Cole's knee. Flood, clearly groggy, tried to play on but suffered another tackle from Lawes and gave way in the 23rd minute to Ford, who added two further penalties to Flood's earlier penalty and conversion of a try by Morris, who finished off a lovely flowing move.

→ Julian Salvi is the first to congratulate Vereniki Goneva on his Premiership final game-sealing score.

Northampton responded with a try by Stephen Myler and if the Northampton fly-half had correctly taken a drop-out just before the interval, the ensuing red card might not have happened. But he kicked out on the full, Leicester called for a scrum on the 22 and amid the subsequent disruption, were awarded a penalty which was when Hartley, having been warned about his behaviour a couple of minutes earlier, passed his comment and was dispatched.

But Northampton did not go quietly. Ben Foden, their full-back who had just missed a first-half try, scored one early in the second half and even though Ben Youngs sent Kitchener sprinting through for Leicester's second try, Luther Burrell created a score for Lee Dickson which, with Myler's conversion, left Northampton trailing only 24-17. It took a solo effort by Tuilagi to finally break the Saints and an interception by Mafi which gave Goneva a try added the icing to Leicester's cake, Ford finishing with four penalties.

↓ Tigers celebrate in the Twickenham dressing room following their tenth league title success against Northampton 25.5.2013.

The aftermath was the charge faced by Cockerill of using "obscene, inappropriate and/or unprofessional language and behaviour" to Stuart Terheege, the fourth official. But the summer had drifted on 37 days and into July before the the coach was able to plead not guilty to conduct prejudicial to the interests of the game. After a four-hour hearing in Coventry, the charge was upheld and Cockerill suspended from match-day involvement from 7 September to 2 November, nine matches in the season proper because the incident had taken place at a high-profile occasion.

Cockerill, who had been banned for four weeks in 2009, also paid £500 costs and the RFU judgement deemed that the game's core principles of respect, discipline and sportsmanship appeared to have passed him by. But even then it was not over. "There are elements in the way in which [the RFU] have conducted this case which, in our opinion, call into question the new disciplinary structure and we will be taking this up with the RFU at the earliest opportunity," a Leicester statement said. They appealed against the length of the ban which was amended to include two pre-season games, meaning Cockerill could return to match-day involvement in mid-October, after the first two rounds of the Heineken Cup.

2013/2014

While Leicester and the RFU were exchanging legal pleasantries, their six Lions joined up with the touring party in Australia. Sadly a torn tricep prevented Ed Slater from touring Argentina with England but three academy players, Tom Price, Harry Wells and Henry Purdy, represented England in the under-20 world cup in France which proved hugely successful; for the first time, after being frustrated by New Zealand in successive finals, England won the title by beating Wales in Vannes, Price starting the final in the second row before being replaced by Wells and Purdy coming off the bench to the wing in the closing stages of a 23-15 win.

It was confirmation of the young talent emerging for club and country. Nor were Leicester standing still on the development front: a joint programme with the RFU aimed to fund training centres for 13- to 16-year-olds in a catchment area embracing Nottinghamshire, Derbyshire, Lincolnshire, Norfolk and Staffordshire. "Around 95 per cent of the players who come through this programme will not go into the academy," Neil McCarthy, the academy manager, said. "But even if they get released they will form the basis of the community game for years to come. It's very expensive for us but we are committed to raising the standard in our region and the 95 per cent will do just that."

The established players were also enjoying themselves as part of a Lions squad which, for the first time since 1997, won a series. Arguably the most successful of Leicester's sextet was Geoff Parling, who played from the bench in the first international in Brisbane which the Lions won 23-21, and started the second and third internationals after a broken arm removed the experienced Irish lock, Paul O'Connell, from the tour.

↑ Geoff Parling was a stand-out performer on the Lions tour to Australia in 2013.

Tom Youngs started the first two tests, the second in Melbourne which the Lions lost 15-16. It had been a fabulous year for the hooker, even though he gave way to Wales's Richard Hibbard in the starting XV for the third test in Sydney which the Lions won at a gallop, 41-16. Dan Cole was a replacement in all three internationals, Tom Croft started the first and appeared off the bench in the second, Ben Youngs was a first test replacement and started the second while Manu Tuilagi, whose tour was disrupted by shoulder damage against Queensland Reds in the third match, squeezed in the final ten minutes of the third test.

↑ The Tigers contingent celebrate following the Lions series win against the Wallabies in Sydney.

It was a notable all-round contribution and when England announced revised squads, 13 Leicester players were included, among them in the Saxons the persevering Mathew Tait. The overall representation was the highest from any English club. The most significant departures during the close season were those of Geordan Murphy, George Ford and Martin Castrogiovanni. Micky Young joined Ford at Bath and Kieran Brookes went back to Newcastle Falcons. Brett Deacon retired in December on medical advice because of a blood condition and moved swiftly into the academy staff while newcomers included David Mélé, the Perpignan scrum-half and his propping colleague, Jerome Schuster; Jamie Gibson, the promising London Irish flanker who had toured South Africa with England in 2012, was signed along with Owen Williams

← Owen Williams, signed during the summer from Scarlets, ended the season with 187 points and the Tigers Young Player of the Year accolade.

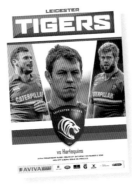

(Scarlets), Neil Briggs (London Welsh), Ryan Lamb (Northampton), Gonzalo Camacho (Exeter Chiefs) and Sebastian de Chaves (Mont-de-Marsan). There was also Blaine Scully, the USA Eagles full-back, who arrived for a trial and did so well that he was offered an extended contract.

Ben Youngs and Tuilagi returned from Australia with shoulder damage and Flood was concussed in a pre-season game with Ulster. With Allen recovering from a knee operation and Matt Smith breaking a thumb in training, Leicester hastily added Terrence Hepetema, the Waratahs centre, to their imports before fielding four Lions in the opening Aviva Premiership fixture against Worcester Warriors. Towards the end of the game, Croft ruptured knee ligaments which ended his season almost before it had begun.

Yet another search for a replacement back-row forward ended with the arrival of Pablo Matera, a 20-year-old who had played for Argentina in the Rugby Championship, a deal coinciding with a changing landscape for the English game. The signing by Premier Rugby Ltd a year earlier of a four-year £152 million agreement with BT Sport, which allowed the new broadcaster unparalleled access to Premiership matches, gave the English clubs unaccustomed muscle. In alliance with the leading French clubs, they announced proposals for a Rugby Champions Cup to replace the Heineken Cup, lending greater urgency to the talks over Europe on which Peter Wheeler was a major cog in PRL's negotiating team.

Leicester, reflecting the bullish mood of English clubs, announced that they had turned a £1 million loss from the previous financial year into a £396,000 profit and increased turnover to more than £19 million. Season-ticket sales peaked at 14,700 and, when it was whispered that Clermont Auvergne wished to approach Cockerill as a potential replacement head coach for the departing Vern Cotter, Leicester promptly tied him into an extended contract.

The injury jinx continued when Tuilagi, outstanding in a 31-6 win over Newcastle, tore pectoral muscles and was out for five months. It had not been the best of weeks for the young centre, whose antics in Auckland Harbour two years earlier had made unwanted headlines. At a Downing Street reception for the 2013 Lions five days before his first game of the season at Newcastle, Tuilagi had made a "bunny ears" gesture behind the head of David Cameron, the Prime Minister, during a photo opportunity which caused both mirth and censure in the rugby world. Cockerill remarked sagely: "He should have known better. We have reminded him of his responsibility."

Vereniki Goneva moved into midfield and proved much more than a stop-gap but it was Slater who came to the rescue in the home game with Northampton, Flood's conversion of his late try forcing a 19-19 draw. Interest in Flood's future was growing; with England looking towards Owen Farrell as their starting fly-half, clubs from France and Japan were trailing powerful financial lures which Flood, having achieved most targets the domestic game could offer, would find hard to resist.

The withdrawal of Allen from the opening Heineken Cup game against Ulster at Ravenhill - the centre was out for three months after surgery for compartment syndrome, bruising to the lower leg similar to that sustained in a car crash but which Allen suffered against Northampton - forced Leicester to focus on the present. Once more they lost but Miles Benjamin, at long last, made his senior debut and a late penalty from Owen Williams earned a losing bonus point in a 22-16 defeat. Another bonus-point game, this time for a four-try win over Treviso, was marred by a calf injury to Goneva which kept him out for the next six weeks.

↓ Puma Marcos Ayerza completed an eighth season as a vital cog in the Leicester pack.

The same game marked the end of Cockerill's match-day ban and Marcos Ayerza returned from international duty with Argentina. But the club slipped to sixth in the table and a casualty tally for the first two months of the season showed that 26 of 41 potential first-team players had suffered short-, medium- or long-term injuries. That situation was exacerbated by the November internationals, when Tom Youngs and Dan Cole started for England against Australia with Ben Youngs and Flood on the bench. Geoff Parling came into the squad for the subsequent games against Argentina (for whom Ayerza and Matera started) and New Zealand but this was not to be an outstanding season for international representation: Tom Youngs slipped behind Northampton's Dylan Hartley in the pecking order, Ben Youngs slipped to number three scrum-half in the new year, Flood's decision to look overseas for future employment pushed him off the England radar altogether and injury accounted for both Cole and Parling as the season wore on. In three of the 2014 six nations games, England's starting XV included no Tigers.

In November Leicester also discovered that Tuilagi would need surgery to his damaged chest muscles, keeping him out until early spring. Another centre, this time of the "former" variety, departed Welford Road when Sir Clive Woodward stepped down from the club board, citing lack of time for the required commitments. Leicester dug deep for Premiership wins over London Irish and Gloucester before the back-to-back Heineken Cup games with Montpellier.

↓ Tom Youngs finally broke the deadlock with the opening score of the return match in Montpellier with his 51st-minute try.

The first of those, at Welford Road, proved a topsy-turvy affair, Leicester taking a 24-3 lead after only 15 minutes and then depending on a late dropped goal from Ryan Lamb to deny the French club (who would lead the Top 14 later in the season) a losing bonus point. Benjamin scored two tries in a 41-32 win and Goneva, returning from his calf injury, registered another; but Goneva's contribution was far more significant a week later. Both clubs played out that rarity, a scoreless first half, but in the dying moments Leicester trailed 14-8, only for Goneva to find a way over the Montpellier line with Lamb adding the angled conversion for a 15-14 win.

The pleasure did not last long. Mathew Tait's first appearance of the season was somewhat marred in the Premiership visit to Allianz Park in Barnet where Saracens administered a 49-10 thrashing, scoring six tries. Flood confirmed his departure at the season's end, though not for another couple of months did Toulouse indicate that the fly-half would be heading in their direction. "He wants to go and do something different, I don't think it's a money thing," Cockerill said. "I think he sees his England potential as limited and he has made that choice." The fly-half was duly omitted in the new year from England's elite playing squad, his place being taken by George Ford.

So it was important that Williams played the best game at fly-half of his short Leicester career in the 30-23 defeat of Sale. He was rewarded with the number-ten shirt against Bath, with Flood playing centre and, though the visitors led by ten points going into the final quarter, a late try from Jamie Gibson forced a 27-27 draw. Gibson, showing many of the qualities found in Tom Croft, grew steadily in influence the longer the season wore on. Another back-five forward of growing stature, Slater, was summoned to train with England who kept the Youngs brothers, Cole, Parling and Tuilagi in the elite group, Allen, Tait and Kitchener maintaining places in the Saxons squad.

A 34-19 win in Treviso ensured a place in the Heineken Cup quarter-finals which was just as well since, in the last round of pool games, Ulster left Welford Road with a 22-19 win to end Leicester's eight-year unbeaten home record in Europe. A try by Niall Morris, who dislocated a thumb and missed the next three months, a conversion and four penalties by Flood gave Tigers a 19-9 lead going into the last half-hour but nothing could keep Ruan Pienaar down; the Springbok scrum-half scored all Ulster's points, from a charge-down try, conversion and five penalties.

Leicester were almost literally blown out of the LV= Cup, losing 20-6 to Harlequins at the Twickenham Stoop where a freak storm blew over scaffolding, ripped up advertising hoardings and caused the abandonment of the game after 70 minutes. A grim January was enlivened only by Adam Thompstone's call-up to the Saxons to play in a 16-16 draw with Scotland A in Glasgow. There was also a well-deserved honour for George Chuter, the veteran hooker, now 37 and in his eighteenth season of first-class rugby; he was admitted into the Aviva Premiership hall of fame, alongside two other club legends, Martin Johnson and Lewis Moody. Three months later, Chuter retired after 290 appearances in all competitions for Leicester to go with the hundred or so he played for Saracens.

↑ Three Leicester legends – Lewis Moody, Martin Johnson and George Chuter – were inducted into the Premiership Rugby Hall of Fame in January.

If there was a slightly premature end-of-season feeling with the announcement that Thomas Waldrom was to leave for Exeter Chiefs in the summer, that Boris Stankovich would join Newport Gwent Dragons, and that Ryan Lamb was off to Worcester only seven months into a two-year contract, it did not show. Upset also by the news that a bulging disc in his neck would keep Cole out of action for three months (the subsequent need for surgery extended that absence into 2014/15), Leicester tightened their collective belt and ground out Premiership wins over Worcester, Gloucester and London Irish, where Slater was awarded the captaincy.

Hopes of a play-off place remained bright, and brighter still when Tuilagi returned against Newcastle - the club against whom he had suffered chest damage in September - and helped in a 41-18 win, England promptly recalling him to the bench for the final six nations game against Italy. For the first time in the season, Tuilagi and Allen played together against Exeter, another high-scoring affair won 45-15 by Tigers and featuring a wonderful try by Logovi'i Mulipola. It also marked Ben Youngs's 100th start and he received a cap from his father, Nick, who also played over 100 games, thus ensuring the Youngs family joined the exclusive club formed by Ian and Matt Smith a year earlier.

At the same time Leicester swooped for two Italy internationals from Treviso, Leonardo Ghiraldini (hooker) and Robert Barbieri (flanker) together with another Treviso player, the Japan centre born in Tonga, Christian Loamanu. The announcement came as an overture to the European quarter-finals but Leicester could not buck a trend: Clermont Auvergne, who could reasonably be regarded as France's mirror-image of Leicester, had not lost at the Stade Marcel Michelin for five years and 74 matches and they did not do so now.

Indeed they went into a 16-point lead after a half-hour yet won by no more than 22-16. In the final minute, Slater was held up metres from the line when a converted try would have snatched victory. Morgan Parra, the home scrum-half, kicked four first-half penalties and converted a try by Wesley Fofana but the first sign of retaliation came when a cross-kick by Williams was collected by Gibson and Blaine Scully's inside pass gave Crane the try. Leicester nibbled away at the lead, Williams kicking three penalties to go with his conversion of Crane's try. But for all the creativity shown by Goneva and Scully, they could not break Clermont's defence a second time. Parra's fifth penalty with 15 minutes remaining proved a sufficient buffer.

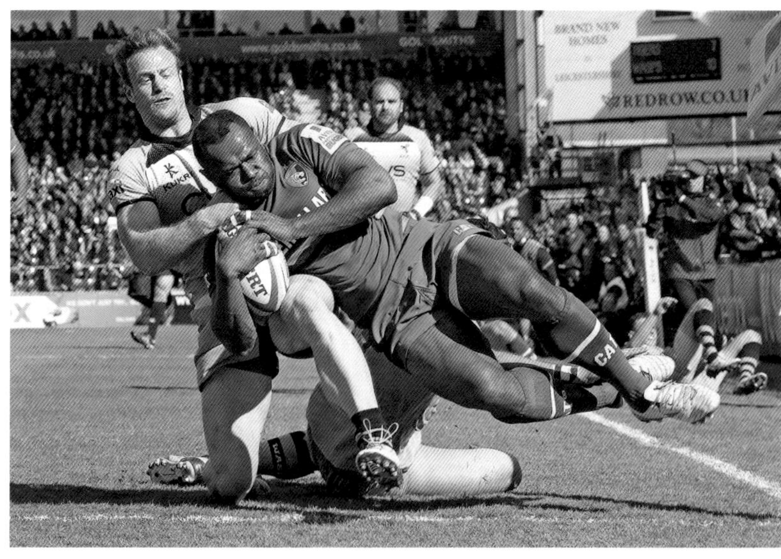

↑ Vereniki Goneva scores against Wasps on 12 April 2014 and went on to tally 14 in the season when he was named Tigers and RPA Player of the Year.

↓ American Eagle Blaine Scully finds a way through the Clermont defence in the Heineken Cup quarter-final 5.4.2014.

From a broader perspective, April brought resolution to the two-year debate over the future of European rugby. A new eight-year deal consigned European Rugby Cup Ltd, organisers of the Heineken Cup since its inception, to history, created a new administration based in Switzerland and a three-tier competition - the European Rugby Champions Cup, the European Rugby Challenge Cup and a qualifying competition. Having been champions of Europe twice and enjoyed some of their best days of the professional era in the Heineken Cup, Leicester had every reason to be relieved that a settlement had been achieved.

Meanwhile in the Premiership, Saracens and Northampton were clear of the pack so Tigers, buoyed by the decision of Goneva to agree a new two-year contract which ended speculation that he was bound for Castres, focused on a play-off place. An unbeaten run of ten league matches ended at Harlequins but the situation was resolved in a 42-22 win at Sale during which Toby Flood, coming off the bench when Anthony Allen hurt a knee, scored two tries. It had been a difficult few months for Flood, club captain but effectively second choice behind Williams since confirming his departure for Toulouse.

"I have understood the predicament the coaching staff are in with the environment and also having one eye on next season," the fly-half said. Flood's maturity was an important ingredient as the season made its way into May, never mind his ability to play centre as well as fly-half as Leicester secured their tenth successive play-off place and Tom Croft, out since the opening weekend of the season, returned for the second half of the last regular-season fixture, against Saracens.

For the first time since 2004, Leicester could take it no further but how they tried. Six internationals returned for the semi-final at Northampton - the Youngs brothers, Ayerza, Crane, Goneva and Mulipola - but when the smoke cleared, Leicester were on the wrong end of a 21-20 verdict. The intensity of both sides was of the highest order and at one stage Tigers led 17-6, having had much the better of the first half and scored smart tries through Tuilagi and Ben Youngs.

But Northampton dominated the second half, most of which Tigers spent in deep defence with Salvi and Crane working exceptionally hard. Goneva and Bowden spent time in the sin bin and there was a bout of fisticuffs between Tom Youngs and Salesi Ma'afu, the Northampton prop, for which Youngs received a yellow card and Ma'afu a red. The penalty count went against Leicester by 22-8 yet only three minutes remained when Tom Wood, England's flanker, finally scored the try that gave Saints their first win over Leicester since September 2010.

"Hopefully we will get everyone fit and we will come back and double our efforts," Cockerill said as he summed up the season. "It was a great game, Northampton played pretty well and so did we. They were celebrating like they had won the whole thing. That is how important beating Leicester is.

If you can win and take the plaudits, you have to put up with this when you lose. Sometimes you get beaten. That's life." As it happened, Northampton did go on to win the whole thing, beating Saracens in the final a fortnight later.

One unwanted aftermath was the citing of Williams for making contact with the eye area of Luther Burrell. The young fly-half had been named in the Possibles squad for Wales's pre-tour trial match but, that being an unscheduled representative fixture prior to Wales's summer tour to South Africa, players with English clubs were not permitted to play. So Williams would have been unavailable, even had he not subsequently suffered a six-week suspension for the offence which ensured he spent the summer resting. Others would do the same. England decided that Croft had not played enough to risk taking him on tour to New Zealand and Tom Youngs was given compassionate leave because Tiffany, his wife, needed treatment for an illness.

On the credit side, Goneva was named not only the supporters' player of the year, he was also the RPA player of the year. Over the season as a whole, Leicester attracted more than 355,000 through the gates of Welford Road, with an average league attendance of 22,850, a remarkable expression of loyalty by supporters throughout a far-from-easy season. Six games were sold out and season-ticket sales for 2013/14 hovered around 15,000, far in excess of any other club.

Graham Kitchener led an England XV in a well-contested defeat to an experienced Barbarians team at Twickenham, alongside Jamie Gibson, while England took Geoff Parling, Ed Slater, Ben Youngs and Manu Tuilagi on the three-test summer tour of New Zealand where Parling recovered his place and Slater led the midweek XV against the Crusaders. Meanwhile Cockerill confirmed further new arrivals for 2014/15 in Freddie Burns, the Gloucester fly-half, Seremaia Bai, the experienced Fijian fly-half/centre who helped Castres to win the Top 14 in 2013, and Rotherham's No 8, Laurence Pearce. A new face was added to the coaching roster in Phil Blake, the former rugby league player whose speciality, defence, had been used by the Western Force in Super rugby and by Australia.

Departures included (as well as Toby Flood, Thomas Waldrom, Boris Stankovich and Rob Hawkins) Scott Steele, Dan Bowden and Jerome Schuster. Another departure, far more fundamental, was that of Peter Wheeler, stepping down after 45 years during which he had occupied virtually every role of significance, as player and administrator, that club rugby could offer. Not that Wheeler was going far: he remained a non-executive director, the breadth of his experience readily available, but his going was illustrative of an oncoming period of change. Throughout their long history, the club has shown an ability to adapt that has kept them at the forefront of the game in England. After twenty years of professional rugby, that ability is even more important but there is no reason to suppose that Leicester, who have set the bar for so long, will not continue to do so.

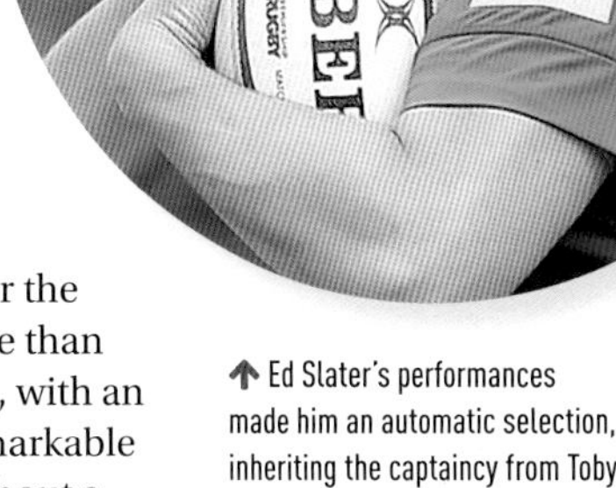

↑ Ed Slater's performances made him an automatic selection, inheriting the captaincy from Toby Flood and winning an England tour place to New Zealand.

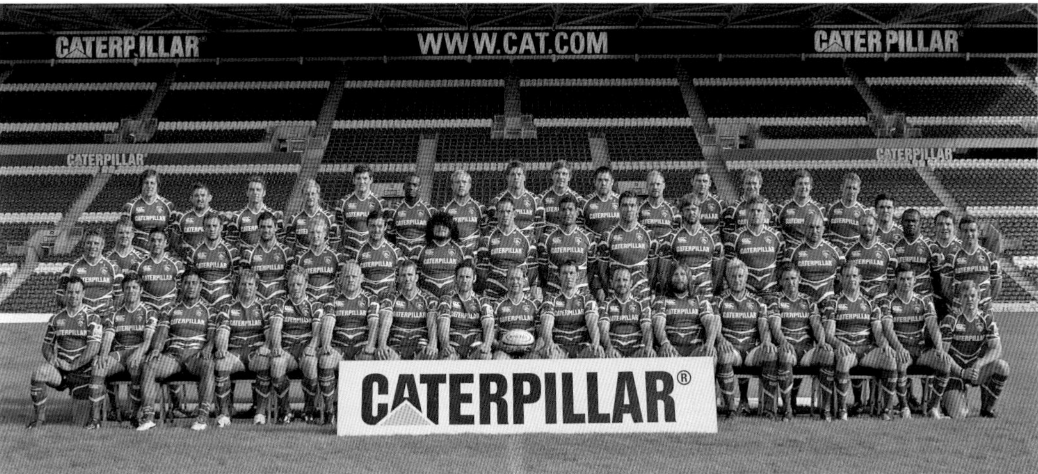

← LEICESTER FOOTBALL CLUB 2012/13
Back: Cain, Stevens, Lewington, Phibbs, Symons, Benjamin, Thorpe, B.Deacon, Wells, Brookes, Cornwell, Thompstone, Tait, Clare, Harrison.
Middle: T.Youngs, Harris, Bowden, Forsyth, Morris, Oliver, Smith, Mulipola, Andrew, Mafi, Kitchener, Parling, Slater, Stankovich, Hawkins, Price, Goneva, Balmain, Ford.
Front: Young, Allen, Tuilagi, Waldrom, Hamilton, Cole, Croft, Newby, Murphy (capt), L.Deacon, Chuter, Castrogiovanni, Crane, Flood, Salvi, B.Youngs, Steele.

← LEICESTER FOOTBALL CLUB 2013/14
Back: Bristow, Harrison, Tait, Morris, Hamilton, Noone, Thompstone, O.Williams, Goneva, Briggs, Lamb, Balmain.
Middle: Cockerill (director of rugby), Blaze (coach), Bowden, Schuster, Hawkins, Mulipola, Mafi, de Chaves, Kitchener, Slater, Crane, Gibson, Smith, Stankovich, Murphy (coach), Burke (coach), Hollis (team manager).
Front: Mele, T.Youngs, Waldrom, Salvi, Croft, Allen, Flood (capt), Deacon, Parling, Cole, Tuilagi, Chuter, B.Youngs.

20	12/13	Home Ground: Welford Road	Trophy Cabinet: Aviva Premiership(10)
		Director of rugby: Richard Cockerill assisted by Matt O'Connor, Paul Burke & Richard Blaze	
		Captain: Geordan Murphy	

OVERALL RECORD:					T	C	PG	DG	PTS
PLD	W	D	L	Tigers scored:	91	62	97	0	870
36	24	2	10	Opponents scored:	55	32	94	2	627

GM	DATE		VEN	OPPONENTS	RESULT	POS/LGE	TRIES	KICKS	ATT
AVIVA PREMIERSHIP RUGBY (2ND)						**CHAMPIONS: LEICESTER TIGERS**			
1	Sep	2s	a	London Welsh	W 38t-13	3	Waldrom 13/23, Parling 41, Salvi 48, Goneva 62	Flood 5c/p	6850
2		**8**	**H**	**Worcester Warriors**	W 34t-26	2	Tuilagi 2/12, Goneva 42, Penalty 66, Kitchener 73	Flood 3c/p	19250
3		15	a	Saracens	D 9-9	3	-	Flood 3p	41063
4		**22**	**H**	**Harlequins**	L 9-22	4	-	Flood 3p	20354
5		**29**	**H**	**Exeter Chiefs**	W 30-8	4	Thompstone 7/46/66	Flood 3c/3p	19292
6	Oct	5f	a	Sale Sharks	W 20-8	3	B.Youngs 46	Ford 5p	8212
9		27	a	Gloucester Rugby	L+ 21-27	5	Hamilton 12, Penalty 60	Flood c/3p	15110
10	Nov	**3**	**H**	**Northampton Saints**	W+ 16-12	3	Smith 42	Ford c/3p	24000
14		25s	a	London Wasps	L+ 12-14	5	-	Ford 4p	7658
15	Dec	**1**	**H**	**Bath Rugby**	W+ 17-12	4	Thompstone 61	Ford 4p	20170
18		22	a	London Irish	W 31t-9	3	Morris 12/79, Penalty 31/72	Flood 4c/p	10958
19		**29**	**H**	**Gloucester Rugby**	W+ 17-12	3	Allen 46	Ford 3p, Murphy p	24000
20	Jan	4f	a	Worcester Warriors	W+ 19-14	3	Hamilton 40, Penalty 55/79	Flood 2c	12024
25	Feb	**9**	**H**	**London Welsh**	W 28-12	1	Thompstone 25, Morris 57, Bowden 80	Ford 2c/3p	20065
26		16	a	Harlequins	L+ 21-25	3	Flood 7, Thompstone 38	Flood c/3p	14800
27		**23**	**H**	**Saracens**	L+ 27-32t	3	Salvi 28, Bowden 32, Penalty 80	Ford 3c/2p	20728
28	Mar	**2**	**H**	**Sale Sharks**	W 48t-10	3	Slater 26/40, Penalty 36, Smith 49/54, Tait 68	Ford 6c/2p	20585
29		23	a	Exeter Chiefs	W+ 12-9	2	-	Flood 4p	10427
30		30	a	Northampton Saints	W 36t-8	2	Tuilagi 42/61, Morris 71, Tait 74	Flood 2c/4p	13479
32	Apr	**14s**	**H**	**London Wasps**	W 35t-16	2	B.Youngs 21/45, Kitchener 25, Hawkins 36 Thompstone 59	Flood 2c/2p	24000
33		20	a	Bath Rugby	L+ 26-27t	2	Croft 14, B.Youngs 24	Flood 2c/4p	12200
34	May	**4**	**H**	**London Irish**	W 32t-20	2	Croft 14, B.Youngs 16, Tait 48, Goneva 61, Flood 67	Flood 2c/p	24000
35		**11**	**H**	**Harlequins (sf)**	W 33-16	-	Goneva 40, Morris 62, Croft 65, Tait 72	Flood 2c/3p	20243
36		25		Northampton Saints (f)	W 37-17	-	Morris 8, Kitchener 48, Tuilagi 66, Goneva 74	Flood c/p, Ford 4p	81703
HEINEKEN CUP						**EUROPEAN CHAMPIONS: TOULON**			
7	Oct	14s	a	Toulouse	L 9-23	4	-	Flood 3p	28002
8		**21s**	**H**	**Ospreys**	W 39t-22	2	Tuilagi 31/79, Flood 70, B.Youngs 75	Flood 2c/5p	20224
16	Dec	**9s**	**H**	**Benetton Treviso**	W 33t-25	2	Penalty 16, Tuilagi 24, Salvi 30/38, Smith 55	Ford 4c	18432
17		15	a	Benetton Treviso	W+ 14-13	1	Thompstone 13, Penalty 78	Ford 2c	3500
21	Jan	13s	a	Ospreys	D 15-15	2	B.Youngs 67, Morris 72	Flood c/p	13126
22		**20s**	**H**	**Toulouse**	W+ 9-5	1	-	Flood 3p	24000
31	Apr	7s	a	Toulon (qf)	L 15-21	-	-	Flood 5p	15263
ANGLO-WELSH CUP (LV= CUP)						**CUP WINNERS:HARLEQUINS**			
11	Nov	9f	a	Saracens	L 21-38t	4	Cain 51, Noone 55, Thacker 80	Cornwell 3c	3168
13		**18s**	**H**	**London Irish**	W+ 22-15	4	Andrew 20	Ford c/5p	17569
23	Jan	**26**	**H**	**London Wasps**	W 34t-8	2	Mulipola 18, Noone 38, Tait 62, Goneva 68/78	Bowden c/p, Cornwell 2c	19757
24	Feb	3s	a	Scarlets	L 19-40	2	Waldrom 11, Penalty 31, Forsyth 40	Cornwell 2c	6496
CLUB MATCH									
12	Nov	**13tu**	**H**	**Maori All Blacks**	W 32-24		Morris 18, Thompstone 30	Ford 2c/6p	17206

Neutral Venue: *#36 at Twickenham*

INDIVIDUAL APPEARANCES 2012/13

Name / Game #	1	2	3	4	5	6	7	8	9	10	11	12	13	14	15	16	17	18	19	20	21	22	23	24	25	26	27	28	29	30	31	32	33	34	35	36	Apps	T	Pts
AO (Anthony) Allen E2	12	12	12	12	r	12	12	12	12	12	-	L	-	-	12	-	12	12	12	r	12	12	-	-	12	12	-	-	12	12	12	12	12	12	12	12	26+2	1	5
RD (Rob) Andrew	>4	r	x	x	-	r	-	-	-	-	4	-	4	-	-	-	-	-	-	-	-	-	4	< 5	-	-	-	-	-	-	-	-	-	-	-	-	5+2	1	5
MI (Marcos) Ayerza Ar40	-	-	-	-	-	-	r	r	r	1	-	-	-	-	1	1	1	1	1	r	1	1	-	-	1	1	1	1	1	1	1	-	-	-	-	-	15+4	-	-
FJ (Fraser) Balmain	-	-	-	-	r	-	-	-	-	x	x	C	3	3	r	-	-	x	-	-	-	-	r	r	r	x	x	r	-	-	-	r	x	r	r	r	3+10	-	-
DR (Dan) Bowden	-	-	-	-	>12	-	-	-	-	x	-	r	12	12	r	12	-	-	x	12	-	-	10	10	r	-	12	12	-	-	-	-	x	-	-	-	9+3	2	15
RTE (Ryan) Bower	-	-	-	-	-	-	-	-	-	-	r	-	-	-	-	-	-	-	-	-	-	-	-	<r	-	-	-	-	-	-	-	-	-	-	-	-	0+2	-	-
K (Kieran) Brookes E+	-	-	-	-	-	-	-	-	-	-	3	x	r	x	-	-	-	-	-	-	-	-	-	-	x	x	x	<r	-	-	-	-	-	-	-	-	1+2	-	-
J (Joe) Cain	-	-	-	-	-	-	-	-	-	-	>5	-	x	-	-	-	-	-	-	-	-	-	-	-	-	-	-	-	-	-	-	-	-	-	-	-	1	1	5
ML (Martin) Castrogiovanni It95	r	3	r	3	r	3	r	r	x	3	-	-	-	-	3	3	r	-	r	3	r	r	-	-	-	-	-	-	r	r	r	r	r	3	r	<r	8+16	-	-
GS (George) Chuter E24	r	-	r	r	-	-	x	x	x	2	-	B	-	2	2	-	x	-	r	x	-	x	r	2	x	x	x	r	-	-	-	r	-	-	-	-	5+7	-	-
DR (Dan) Cole E40 L+	3	r	3	r	3	r	3	3	3	-	-	-	-	-	-	x	3	3	3	r	3	3	-	-	-	-	-	-	3	3	3	3	3	r	3	3	18+5	-	-
MJ (Matt) Cornwell	-	-	-	-	-	-	-	-	-	-	10*	-	-	-	-	-	-	-	-	-	-	-	12	12	-	-	x	<r	-	-	-	-	-	-	-	-	3+1	-	14
JS (Jordan) Crane E3	r	r	r	8*	6*	6*	8*	8*	8	-	-	G	r	6	r	r	r	8	8	-	8	r	-	-	8	r	8	r	8	8	8	8	r	8	8	8	20+11	-	-
TR (Tom) Croft E38 L3	-	-	-	-	-	-	-	-	-	-	-	-	-	-	-	-	-	-	-	6	-	-	6	-	6	-	6	6*	6	6	6	-	6	6	6	6	12	3	15
BR (Brett) Deacon	r	-	-	-	r	r	-	-	-	-	-	-	8*	-	■6	-	6	6	6	-	-	-	8*	6*	r	6	x	r	-	-	-	<r	-	-	-	-	8+6	-	-
LP (Louis) Deacon E29	-	-	-	-	-	-	-	r	4	4	-	D*	-	4*	4*	-	4*	4*	4*	5*	4*	4*	-	-	4*	4*	-	-	-	-	-	-	-	-	-	-	13+1	-	-
TGAL (Toby) Flood E57	10	10	10	10	10	x	10	10	10	-	-	-	-	-	-	-	-	10	-	10	10	10	-	-	-	10	-	-	10*	10*	10*	10*	10*	10	10*	10*	21	3	243
GT (George) Ford E+	r	r	x	x	r	10	x	x	x	10	x	J	10	10	10	10	10	x	10	-	x	r	-	-	10	x	10	10	x	r	x	r	-	r	r	<r	12+9	-	165
AR (Andy) Forsyth	-	-	-	-	-	-	-	-	-	-	13	r	14	x	-	-	-	-	-	-	-	-	13	<13	-	-	-	-	-	-	-	-	-	-	-	-	4+1	1	5
V (Niki) Goneva Fi29	>11	11	11	11	11	11	11	11	11	r	-	-	-	-	-	11	-	-	-	-	-	-	11	11	-	-	-	-	-	-	-	-	-	11	11	11	15+1	7	35
LJV (Lucas) Guillaume	-	-	-	-	-	-	-	-	-	-	= 6	-	-	-	-	-	-	-	-	-	-	-	-	-	-	-	-	-	-	-	-	-	-	-	-	-	1	-	-
SE (Scott) Hamilton NZ2	14	14	14	15	-	-	15	15	14	14	-	-	-	-	-	14	-	-	-	14	-	r	14	14	-	14	14	r	-	-	-	-	-	-	-	-	14+2	2	10
JC (Jonny) Harris	-	-	-	-	-	-	-	-	-	-	1	x	r	1	x	-	-	-	-	-	-	-	<r	-	-	-	-	-	-	-	-	-	-	-	-	-	2+2	-	-
SJ (Sam) Harrison	r	9	9	9	9	r	x	x	9	x	r	r	r	9	-	-	x	x	x	-	x	x	9	r	9	9	9	9	x	r	x	r	x	r	r	r	11+11	-	-
RA (Rob) Hawkins	-	r	-	-	-	-	-	-	-	-	-	-	2	x	r	r	-	r	-	2	r	-	2	r	2	2	2	2	x	r	x	2	r	r	r	r	8+11	1	5
MO (Michael) Holford	-	-	-	-	-	-	-	-	-	-	-	-	-	<r	-	-	-	-	-	-	-	-	-	-	-	-	-	-	-	-	-	-	-	-	-	-	0+1	-	-
MI (Matt) Hubbart	-	-	-	-	-	-	-	-	-	-	-	-	-	-	-	-	-	-	-	-	-	-	-	=r	-	-	-	-	-	-	-	-	-	-	-	-	0+1	-	-
GP (Graham) Kitchener	-	4	4	4	4	5	4	4	x	5	-	E	-	5	5	4	x	5	-	x	-	x	-	-	5	5	5	5	x	r	r	5	-	4	4	4	21+2	3	15
A (Alex) Lewington	-	-	-	-	-	-	-	-	-	-	11	-	<11	-	-	-	-	-	-	-	-	-	-	-	-	-	-	-	-	-	-	-	-	-	-	-	2	-	-
SO (Steve) Mafi T9	6	6	6	6	-	-	6	6	6	6	-	-	-	-	-	-	-	-	r	7	6	6	-	-	-	-	-	-	-	-	-	6	4	r	r	r	13+4	-	-
NE (Niall) Morris	-	-	-	14	15	15	14	14	-	11	15	M	-	14	14	-	14	14	14	r	14	14	-	-	14	-	-	14	14	14	14	14	-	14	14	14	24+1	8	40
L (Logovi'i) Mulipola Sa10	1	r	1	r	1	1	1	1	1	-	-	-	-	-	-	r	r	r	r	1	r	x	3	3	3	3	3	3	r	r	r	1	1	1	1	1	19+10	1	5
GEA (Geordan) Murphy I72 L2	15*	15*	15*	-	-	-	-	-	15*	15*	-	-	-	x	r	x	r	15	15	-	-	-	-	r	r	-	15*	-	-	-	-	-	r	<15*	-	-	9+5	-	3
M (Michael) Noone	-	-	-	-	-	-	-	-	-	x	>8	x	6	-	-	-	-	-	-	-	-	-	r	-	-	-	-	-	-	-	-	-	-	-	-	-	2+1	2	10
GW (George) Oliver	-	-	-	-	-	-	-	-	-	-	>r	-	-	-	-	-	-	-	-	-	-	-	-	<r	-	-	-	-	-	-	-	-	-	-	-	-	0+2	-	-
GMW (Geoff) Parling E17 L+	5	5	5	5	5	-	5	5	5	-	-	-	-	-	-	5*	5	r	5	-	5	5	-	-	-	-	-	-	5	5	5	-	5	5	5	5	20+1	1	5
PK (Patrick) Phibbs	-	>r	x	r	r	-	-	-	x	-	-	I	-	<r	x	-	-	-	-	-	-	-	-	-	-	-	-	-	-	-	-	-	-	-	-	-	1+4	-	-
TR (Tom) Price	-	-	-	-	-	-	-	-	-	-	x	-	-	-	-	-	-	-	-	-	-	-	>5	-	-	-	-	-	-	-	-	-	-	-	-	-	1	-	-
HA (Henry) Purdy	-	-	-	-	-	-	-	-	-	-	>14	-	-	-	-	-	-	-	-	-	-	-	-	-	-	-	-	-	-	-	-	-	-	-	-	-	1	-	-
JM (Julian) Salvi	7	7	7	7	7	-	-	-	-	7	-	H	-	7	7	7	7	7	7	r	7	7	-	-	7	7	7	7	7	7	7	7	7	7	7	7	27+1	4	20
EN (Ed) Slater	-	-	-	-	r	4	r	-	r	r	-	F	5	x	r	6	-	r	x	4	x	-	-	-	r	r	4	4	4	4	4	4	r	-	-	r	11+10	2	10
MW (Matt) Smith	x	r	r	13	13	r	r	r	x	13	-	N	13	13	13	r	x	x	x	13	r	13	-	-	13	r	13	13	x	r	x	r	14	-	r	r	13+12	4	20
B (Boris) Stankovich	r	1	r	1	-	r	-	-	-	x	-	A	■1	-	-	-	-	-	-	-	-	-	1	1	-	-	-	-	-	-	-	-	-	-	-	-	6+3	-	-
JD (Jimmy) Stevens	-	-	-	-	r	r	-	-	-	x	2	<r	x	-	-	-	-	-	-	-	-	-	-	-	-	-	-	-	-	-	-	-	-	-	-	-	1+3	-	-
AG (Andy) Symons	-	-	-	-	-	-	-	-	-	-	12	-	r	-	-	-	-	-	-	-	-	-	r	<r	-	-	-	-	-	-	-	-	-	-	-	-	1+3	-	-
MJM (Mathew) Tait E38	-	-	-	-	-	-	-	-	-	-	r	O	15	15	15	15	15	-	-	15	15	15	15	15	15	15	r	15	15	15	15	15	15	r	15	15	21+3	5	25
HJ (Harry) Thacker	-	-	-	-	-	-	-	-	-	-	>r	-	-	-	-	-	-	-	-	-	-	-	-	-	-	-	-	-	-	-	-	-	-	-	-	-	0+1	1	5
AD (Adam) Thompstone	-	-	-	>r	14	14	-	-	-	-	-	K	-	11	11	-	11	11	11	11	11	11	r	-	11	11	11	11	11	11	11	11	11	-	-	-	20+2	9	45
RJ (Richard) Thorpe	-	-	-	-	-	>7	r	x	-	8	7	r	7	r	-	r	-	-	-	-	-	-	7	<7	-	-	x	-	-	-	-	-	-	-	-	-	6+4	-	-
EM (Manusamoa) Tuilagi E21 L+	13	13	13	-	-	13	13	13	13	-	-	-	-	-	-	13	13	13	13	-	13	-	-	-	-	13	-	-	13	13	13	13	13	13	13	13	21	8	40
TR (Thomas) Waldrom E5	8	8	8	r	8	8	7	7	7	-	-	-	-	8	8	8	8	-	-	8	r	8	-	8	-	8	-	8	x	r	r	r	8	r	r	-	18+7	3	15
HR (Harry) Wells	-	-	-	-	-	-	-	-	-	-	-	-	-	-	-	-	-	-	-	-	-	-	>r	4	-	-	-	-	-	-	-	-	-	-	-	-	1+1	-	-
MLR (Micky) Young	9	-	-	-	-	-	-	-	-	-	9	-	9	-	9	r	-	-	-	x	-	-	r	9	r	x	r	<r	-	-	-	-	-	-	-	-	5+5	-	-
BR (Ben) Youngs E33 L+	-	-	-	-	-	9	9	9	-	9	-	-	-	-	-	9	9	9	9	9	9	9	-	-	-	-	-	-	9	9	9	9	9	9	9	9	19	7	35
TN (Tom) Youngs E9 L+	2	2	2	2	2	2	2	2	2	-	-	-	-	-	-	2	2	2	2	-	2	2	-	-	-	-	-	-	2	2	2	-	2	2	2	2	22	-	-

The key for how to read the stats is on the last page

20 13/14		OVERALL RECORD:					T	C	PG	DG	PTS
	Home Ground: Welford Road	PLD	W	D	L	Tigers scored:	86	60	88	2	820
	Director of rugby: Richard Cockerill assisted by Paul Burke, Geordan Murphy & Richard Blaze	34	21	2	11	Opponents scored:	64	42	87	3	674
	Captain: Toby Flood										

GM	DATE		VEN	OPPONENTS	RESULT	POS/LGE	TRIES	KICKS	ATT
AVIVA PREMIERSHIP RUGBY (3RD)						**CHAMPIONS: NORTHAMPTON SAINTS**			
1	Sep	**8s**	**H**	**Worcester Warriors**	W 32t-15	3	Thompstone 14, Mele 40, Crane 48, Goneva 80	Lamb 2c/2p, O.Williams c	20230
2		14	a	Bath Rugby	L+ 20-27	4	Mafi 47, Slater 60, Goneva 68	Mele c/p	11253
3		**21**	**H**	**Newcastle Falcons**	W 31t-6	2	Crane 7, Kitchener 13, Scully 34, Bowden 53, Waldrom 69	Flood 2c, O.Williams c	19723
4		29s	a	Exeter Chiefs	W 21-9	3	B.Youngs 11, Goneva 39	Flood c/3p	9524
5	Oct	**5**	**H**	**Northampton Saints**	D 19-19	3	Slater 76	Flood c/4p	24000
8		27s	a	London Wasps	L 12-22	5	-	O.Williams 4p	7040
9	Nov	**2**	**H**	**Harlequins**	L+ 16-23	6	Penalty 80	O.Williams c/3p	24000
12		**23**	**H**	**London Irish**	W 20-11	6	Penalty 10/64	Flood 2c/2p	23284
13		29f	a	Gloucester Rugby	W+ 22-17	5	Bowden 32	Flood c/5p	14803
16	Dec	21	a	Saracens	L 10-49t	6	Kitchener 37	Lamb c/p	9999
17		**28**	**H**	**Sale Sharks**	W+ 30-23	5	Slater 3, Thompstone 23, Penalty 74	O.Williams 3c/3p	24000
18	Jan	**5s**	**H**	**Bath Rugby**	D 27-27	5	Benjamin 9, Waldrom 65, Gibson 79	O.Williams 4p	22479
23	Feb	7f	a	Worcester Warriors	W+ 23-22	5	Goneva 4/24	Flood 2c/3p	7516
24		**16s**	**H**	**Gloucester Rugby**	W+ 11-8	5	Tait 68	Flood 2p	22195
25		23s	a	London Irish	W+ 20-15	4	B.Youngs 9, Mulipola 35, Goneva 47	O.Williams c/p	9114
26	Mar	2s	a	Newcastle Falcons	W 41t-18	4	Goneva 38/62, Waldrom 68, Matera 79	O.Williams 2c/5p, Flood c	7073
27		**23s**	**H**	**Exeter Chiefs**	W 45t-15	4	Tuilagi 9, Mulipola 13, Goneva 29, Thompstone 52, Mele 69/79	O.Williams 2c/3p, Flood c	23466
28		29	a	Northampton Saints	W+ 22-16	3	Allen 16	O.Williams c/5p	13459
30	Apr	**12**	**H**	**London Wasps**	W 27t-15	3	Tuilagi 19/48, Goneva 40, Mele 78	O.Williams 2c/p	24000
31		18f	a	Harlequins	L+ 20-24	4	Goneva 4, Gibson 58	Flood 2c/2p	14800
32	May	3	a	Sale Sharks	W 42t-22	3	Goneva 15, Flood 38/54, Morris 45, Penalty 59, Mele 80	O.Williams 6c	10092
33		**10**	**H**	**Saracens**	W+ 31t-27t	3	Penalty 40, Tuilagi 44, Scully 48, Kitchener 57	O.Williams p, Flood 4c	24000
34		16f	a	Northampton Saints (sf)	L 20-21	-	Tuilagi 25, B.Youngs 35	Flood 2c/p, O.Williams p	13491
HEINEKEN CUP						**EUROPEAN CHAMPIONS: TOULON**			
6	Oct	11f	a	Ulster	L+ 16-22	3	Mulipola 7	Flood c/20, O.Williams p	14026
7		**18f**	**H**	**Benetton Treviso**	W 34t-3	2	Waldrom 38, T.Youngs 56, Scully 66, Thompstone 80	Flood 4c/2p	19838
14	Dec	**8s**	**H**	**Montpellier**	W 41t-32t	2	Goneva 4, Benjamin 13/15, Gibson 61	Flood 3c/4p, Lamb d	21404
15		15s	a	Montpellier	W+ 15-14	2	T.Youngs 51, Goneva 80	Lamb c/p	10859
19	Jan	11	a	Benetton Treviso	W 34t-19	2	Salvi 10, Benjamin 44/68, Penalty 64	O.Williams p, Mele c/3p	4425
20		**18**	**H**	**Ulster**	L+ 19-22	2	Morris 50	Flood c/4p	24000
29	Apr	5	a	ASM Clermont Auvergne (qf)	L 16-22	-	Crane 37	O.Williams c/3p	17962
ANGLO-WELSH CUP (LV= CUP)						**CUP WINNERS: EXETER CHIEFS**			
10	Nov	**8f**	**H**	**Ospreys**	W 39t-16	1	Waldrom 28, Harrison 62, Wells 70, Noone 80	O.Williams 2c/5p	18098
11		15f	a	Worcester Warriors	W+ 21-18	1	Noone 45 Penalty 69	O.Williams c/2p/d	9855
21	Jan	25	a	Harlequins	L 6-20 (Abandoned 70')	3	-	Lamb 2p	11444
22		**31f**	**H**	**Bath Rugby**	L 17-35t	4	Matera 9, Scully 23	O.Williams 2c/p	20616

INDIVIDUAL APPEARANCES 2013/14

Name / Game #	1	2	3	4	5	6	7	8	9	10	11	12	13	14	15	16	17	18	19	20	21	22	23	24	25	26	27	28	29	30	31	32	33	34	Apps	T	Pts
AO (Anthony) Allen E2	13	12*	-	12	12	-	-	-	-	-	-	-	-	-	-	-	-	-	r	12	-	-	12	12	-	-	12	12	12	-	12	12	-	-	12+1	1	5
MI (Marcos) Ayerza Ar48	-	-	-	-	-	-	-	1	1	-	-	-	1	1	1	r	1	1	1	1	-	-	1	1	1	1	1	1	1	r	1	1	r	1	19+3	-	-
FJ (Fraser) Balmain	x	x	-	r	x	x	x	x	r	3	3	3	x	r	x	3	x	x	r	x	3	3	r	r	x	r	r	r	x	3	x	r	3	x	8+10	-	-
MD (Miles) Benjamin	-	-	-	-	-	>14	-	x	-	11	11	11	11	14	11	11	-	11	11	-	-	-	-	-	-	-	-	-	-	-	-	-	-	-	10	5	25
DR (Dan) Bowden	12	r	12	x	r	12	12	12	12	-	-	12	12	12	12	-	12	-	-	-	-	-	-	-	12	12	-	-	-	-	-	-	r	< 12	14+3	2	10
NR (Neil) Briggs	>r	r	2	r	x	r	r	2	2	-	r	r	r	r	x	2	x	-	2	-	-	-	-	-	r	x	-	-	-	-	2	r	2	r	7+12	-	-
TA (Tom) Bristow	-	-	>r	-	-	-	-	-	-	r	r	r	-	-	-	-	-	-	-	-	1	1	-	-	-	-	-	-	-	-	-	-	-	x	2+4	-	-
J (Joe) Cain	-	-	-	-	-	-	-	-	-	4	<4	-	-	-	-	-	-	-	-	-	-	-	-	-	-	-	-	-	-	-	-	-	-	-	2	-	-
GJ (George) Catchpole	-	-	-	-	-	-	-	-	-	>13	-	-	-	-	-	-	-	-	-	-	-	11	-	-	-	-	-	-	-	-	-	-	-	-	2	-	-
GS (George) Chuter E24	-	-	-	-	-	-	-	x	r	r	-	-	-	-	-	-	-	-	-	-	r	< r	-	-	-	-	-	-	-	-	-	-	-	-	0+4	-	-
DR (Dan) Cole E45 L3	3	3	r	3	3	3	3	-	-	-	-	r	3	3	3	-	3	3	3	3	-	-	-	-	-	-	-	-	-	-	-	-	-	-	13+2	-	-
JS (Jordan) Crane E3	8	8	8	8	8	8	r	r	8	-	8	8	x	8	r	8*	r	8	r	8	-	-	-	8	8	8	8	8	8	8	8	8	-	8	23+5	3	15
TR (Tom) Croft E38 L5	6	-	-	-	-	-	-	-	-	-	-	-	-	-	-	-	-	-	-	-	-	-	-	-	-	-	-	-	-	-	-	-	r	-	1+1	-	-
LP (Louis) Deacon E29	4*	-	-	4	4	4	r	4*	4*	-	-	4	4	4	4	-	4*	4	4	r	-	-	4	r	4	4	4	4	4	-	-	r	4*	4	21+4	-	-
SJ (Sebastian) de Chaves	-	>5	-	-	x	-	-	x	-	5	5	r	x	-	-	r	x	r	5	-	5	<5	-	-	-	x	-	-	-	-	-	-	-	-	6+3	-	-
PM (Pas) Dunn	x	-	-	-	-	-	-	-	-	-	><r	-	-	-	-	-	-	-	-	-	-	-	-	-	-	-	-	-	-	-	-	-	-	-	0+1	-	-
TGAL (Toby) Flood E60	-	-	10*	10*	10*	10*	10*	-	-	-	-	10*	10*	10*	10*	-	-	12*	12*	10*	-	-	10*	10*	r	r	r	r	r	r	10	r	12	<10	17+7	2	168
JGS (Jamie) Gibson	-	>r	7	r	-	-	-	6	-	7	7	6	6	6	6	6	6	6	6	6	-	-	6	6	6	6	6	6	6	6	6	6	-	6	24+2	3	15
V (Niki) Goneva Fi29	14	13	14	13	13	13	13	-	-	-	-	-	-	13	13	13	13	13	13	11	-	-	11	14	13	11	14	14	11	11	11	11	-	11	25	14	70
SE (Scott) Hamilton NZ2	-	14	-	-	-	-	-	-	14	15	15	15	15	15	15	-	-	x	-	r	15	14	r	-	r	-	15	15	x	-	-	-	-	-	12+3	-	-
SJ (Sam) Harrison	-	x	-	x	-	-	-	x	r	9	-	-	r	-	-	-	-	-	-	-	-	9	-	-	-	-	-	r	-	-	-	-	r	-	2+4	1	5
RA (Rob) Hawkins	-	-	-	-	-	-	-	-	-	-	-	-	-	-	-	-	-	x	r	r	2	2	2	r	2	-	r	r	x	r	r	-	<r	-	4+8	-	-
TRT (Terrence) Hepetema	-	-	-	-	-	>r	r	13	13	-	-	-	-	-	-	r	-	-	-	-	12	12	-	-	-	-	-	-	-	-	-	-	-	-	4+3	-	-
PB (Perry) Humphreys	-	-	-	-	-	-	-	-	-	>r	x	-	-	-	-	-	-	-	-	-	-	-	-	-	-	-	-	-	-	-	-	-	-	-	0+1	-	-
GP (Graham) Kitchener	-	-	5	r	5	r	4	-	5	-	-	5	5	5	5	5	-	-	-	5	-	-	-	5	-	-	r	r	r	5	5	-	r	r	13+7	3	15
R (Ryan) Lamb	>10	10	-	-	-	-	-	-	-	-	-	-	-	r	r	10	r	-	-	-	<10	x	-	-	-	-	-	-	-	-	-	-	-	-	4+3	-	29
SO (Steve) Mafi T9	-	6	-	-	-	-	-	-	r	-	-	-	-	-	-	-	-	-	r	r	4	6	r	-	r	-	-	-	-	-	-	-	6	<r	4+6	1	5
PN (Pablo) Matera Ar11	-	-	-	-	-	-	-	>r	-	-	-	-	-	-	-	7	-	-	-	-	7	7	x	-	-	7	-	x	-	r	r	-	7	-	5+3	2	10
DL (David) Mele	>9	9	r	-	r	r	r	9	9	r	9	x	-	x	x	r	x	r	r	r	9*	-	r	r	r	r	r	-	r	r	r	r	9	x	7+18	5	41
NE (Niall) Morris	15	15	r	15	15	15	15	15	15	-	-	14	-	-	14	14	14	14	14	14	-	-	-	-	-	-	-	-	-	r	r	14	14	14	18+3	2	10
L (Logovi'i) Mulipola Sa14	1	1	3	1	1	1	1	3	3	-	-	-	-	-	-	-	-	-	-	-	-	-	3	3	3	3	3	3	3	r	3	3	-	3	19+1	3	15
M (Michael) Noone	-	-	-	-	-	-	-	-	-	6	6	-	-	-	-	-	-	-	-	-	6	<r	-	-	-	-	-	-	-	-	-	-	-	-	3+1	2	10
GMW (Geoff) Parling E19 L3	5	-	r	5	-	5	5	-	-	-	-	-	-	-	-	-	-	-	-	-	-	-	-	-	-	-	-	-	-	r	r	5	5	-	6+3	-	-
T (Tiziano) Pasquali	-	-	-	-	-	-	-	-	-	>r	-	-	-	-	-	-	-	-	-	-	r	r	-	-	-	-	-	-	-	-	-	-	r	-	0+4	-	-
JKM (Javiah) Pohe	-	-	-	-	-	-	-	-	-	>12	12	-	x	-	-	-	-	-	-	-	-	-	-	-	-	-	-	-	-	-	-	-	-	-	2	-	-
TR (Tom) Price	-	-	-	-	-	-	-	-	-	r	r	-	-	-	-	-	-	-	-	-	-	4	-	-	-	-	-	-	-	-	-	-	-	-	1+2	-	-
HA (Henry) Purdy	-	-	-	-	-	-	-	-	-	r	14	-	-	-	-	-	-	-	-	-	<r	-	-	-	-	-	-	-	-	-	-	-	-	-	1+2	-	-
JM (Julian) Salvi	7	7	x	7	7	7	7	7	7	-	-	7	7	7	7	-	7	7	7	7	-	-	7	7	7	-	7	7	7	7	7	7	-	7	26	1	5
JCH (Jerome) Schuster Fr2	-	-	-	-	-	-	-	-	-	-	>r	-	-	-	-	<r	-	-	-	-	-	-	-	-	-	-	-	-	-	-	-	-	-	-	0+2	-	-
BH (Blaine) Scully US17	-	-	>15	14	14	-	14	14	r	14	-	-	14	r	-	-	-	-	-	-	14	15	14	r	14	14	-	-	14	14	14	r	11	-	16+4	4	20
EN (Ed) Slater	r	4	4	6	6	6	6	5	6	-	-	-	-	r	r	4	5	5	-	4	-	-	5	4	5*	5*	5*	5*	5*	4*	4*	4*	-	5*	23+3	3	15
MW (Matt) Smith	-	-	-	-	-	-	-	-	r	-	13	13	-	-	r	12	r	x	r	13	13	13	13	13	-	-	r	x	-	13	-	-	-	-	9+5	-	-
B (Boris) Stankovich	x	r	1	r	x	x	x	x	r	1*	1*	1	x	x	x	1	x	x	r	x	r	r	x	x	x	r	r	x	r	1	x	r	<1	-	7+10	-	-
SK (Scott) Steele	x	-	-	-	-	-	-	-	-	-	-	-	-	-	-	-	-	-	-	-	<r	x	-	-	-	-	-	-	-	-	-	-	-	-	0+1	-	-
MJM (Mathew) Tait E38	-	-	-	-	-	-	-	-	-	-	-	-	-	-	-	15	15	15	15	15	-	-	15	15	15	15	-	-	15	15	15	15	15	15	15	1	5
HJ (Harry) Thacker	-	-	-	-	-	-	-	-	-	2	2	-	-	-	-	-	-	-	-	-	-	-	r	-	-	-	-	-	-	-	-	-	-	-	2+1	-	-
AD (Adam) Thompstone	11	11	11	11	11	11	11	11	11	-	-	r	13	11	-	r	11	-	-	-	11	-	-	11	11	r	11	11	-	-	-	-	r	r	17+5	4	20
EM (Manusamoa) Tuilagi E22 L1	-	-	13	-	-	-	-	-	-	-	-	-	-	-	-	-	-	-	-	-	-	-	-	-	-	13	13	13	13	12	13	13	13	13	10	5	25
TR (Thomas) Waldrom E5	r	r	6	-	x	x	8	8	r	8	-	r	8	r	8	r	8	r	8	-	8	8*	8	r	r	r	r	-	r	-	-	r	<8	-	12+13	5	25
HR (Harry) Wells	-	-	-	-	-	-	-	-	-	r	r	-	-	-	-	-	-	-	-	-	r	<r	-	-	-	-	-	-	-	-	-	-	-	-	0+4	1	5
OR (Owen) Williams	>r	r	r	x	x	r	x	10	10	10	10	x	x	-	-	-	10	10	10	r	r	10	x	x	10	10	10	10	10	10	r	10	10	r	16+8	-	187
JR (Rhys) Williams	-	-	-	-	-	-	-	-	-	-	-	-	-	-	-	-	-	-	-	-	-	>r	-	-	-	-	-	-	-	-	-	-	-	-	0+1	-	-
BR (Ben) Youngs E35 L2	-	-	9	9	9	9	9	-	-	-	-	9	9	9	9	9	9	9	9	9	-	-	9	9	9	9	9	9	9	9	9	9	-	9	25	3	15
TN (Tom) Youngs E17 L3	2	2	x	2	2	2	2	-	-	-	-	2	2	2	2	r	2	2	-	2	-	-	-	2	-	2	2	2	2	2	-	2	-	2	21+1	2	10

The key for how to read the stats is on the last page

Tigers 100 Cap Club

Trying to provide a profile of all of the 2,204 players who are known to have appeared for the club in a first-team game would elongate this book hugely. An alphabetical index of all players is to be found after this section, but we have chosen to focus on the 209 individuals who have started 100 Tigers matches, recognised these days by the award of a club cap.

Entries are listed in alphabetical order; those of the same surname are listed in order of their initials. After the players' name in brackets is the chronological number of the player joining the club, ie the latest addition, Ben Youngs is number 209.

Where we do not have a precise date of birth or death we have recorded the quarter of registration ie "regd Q2" for the 2nd quarter of the year.

Details are correct up to 1 August 2014, with players still in the Tigers squad for the 2014/15 season denoted with an asterisk, and those still playing first-class rugby for other clubs at the same time denoted with a plus sign.

In this section as well as the later encyclopædia, a coloured marker next to a match date denotes the competition, as per the following key:

- ● Domestic cup (Midland Counties Cup, Knockout Cup or Anglo-Welsh Cup)
- ● League or Premiership match (including play-offs)
- ● Post-season play-off tournaments (Wildcard, Championship)
- ● European Cup
- ● Other Competitions (Floodlit Cup, Merit Tables, International Challenge Cup, Cheltenham & Gloucester Cup, Jewson Challenge Trophy, Orange Cup)
- ● Anglo-Welsh League

GARRY ADEY

ADAMS, Newton (77)

Born: *Leicester, 29.11.1912*
Died: *Pershore, Worcestershire, May 1998*
Educated: *Mill Hill*
Clubs: *Westleigh, Leicester*
Tigers debut: *11.3.1933 v Northampton, lost 3-21*
Last game: *17.12.1938 v Rosslyn Park, won 14-5*

Newton Adams, a back-row forward, played for Leicestershire and for the Possibles in an England trial in 1936. He was a reserve for England against Scotland at Murrayfield in March 1937. He scored three tries in a fixture against Penarth in September 1934. Adams retired from the RAF with the rank of group captain.

Appearances: *126 (W60, D9, L57)*
Scoring: *26 tries, 78 pts*

ADEY, Garry John (128)

Born: *Loughborough, Leicestershire, 13.6.1945*
Educated: *Humphrey Perkins GS (Barrow-upon-Soar), Loughborough Technical College*
Clubs: *Loughborough Town, Leicester*
Tigers debut: *8.3.1967 v Loughborough Colleges, won 14-6*
Last game: *2.5.1981 v Gosforth (at Twickenham), won 22-15* ●
Caps: *England (2) 1976*

Though he was a prop for the county under-15s and a lock for the under-19s and colts, Garry Adey made his name as an industrious No 8, taking over the role when John Quick left the club. A strong upper body - he was a shot putter for the county at school - made him a wonderful mauling forward, the precise opposite to Andy Ripley whom he replaced in the England pack for two games in the 1976 five nations.

He played for Leicestershire and the Midlands against Fiji, New Zealand (twice), Argentina, Australia and Japan, and for the England under-25 XV that played the Fijians in 1970. He toured Canada with the Barbarians in 1976, and played in four successive John Player Cup finals, losing to Gloucester in 1978 but winning against Moseley (1979), London Irish (1980) and Gosforth (1981).

Adey announced his retirement midway through the 1980/81 season after an ankle injury against Cambridge University and increased domestic and work commitments, his place in the back row going to the persevering Angus Collington. But injuries to Collington and Ian Smith later that season persuaded Adey to have a change of heart and his last three games included the cup final win over Gosforth, when Collington occupied the bench.

He became managing director of Adey Holdings, the family steel fabricating and stockholding business. He was elected president of the club for 1997-99 and has been a non-executive director of Leicester FC plc since 1997.

Appearances: *381 (W234, D15, L132)*
Scoring: *57 tries, 215 pts*

AKERS, Arthur (13)

Born: *Leicester, regd Q1 1869*
Died: *Leicester, 8.10.1899*
Club: *Leicester*
Tigers debut: *25.11.1893 at Rugby, won 8-7*
Last game: *15.4.1899 v Gloucester, won 6-4*

ARTHUR AKERS

"Tough" Akers was still at the height of his powers when he died from pneumonia in the autumn of 1899, only a few months after helping Tigers win the Midland Counties Cup. The club's first XV attended his memorial service at Welford Road cemetery and the lesson was read by the Reverend Carey-Elwes, one of the backs.

He picked up his nickname 'Tough un' from his exploits in the boxing ring, before taking up rugby. He contested the English light middleweight title against Glasgow's Lachie Thompson at the Pelican Club in London in 1891, with stake money of £400, and the local press was greatly distressed when he lost.

An outstanding forward, Akers played in the side that won the Midlands cup in 1898 as well as the following year, and was popular with colleagues and spectators. Though physically very strong, he gained a reputation for sporting play (he was also known as 'The Admiral') and for being the life and soul of the party when the club toured.

Appearances: *160 (W102, D18, L40)*
Scoring: *10 tries, 1 conv, 32 pts*

*ALLEN, Anthony Owen (207)

Born: *Southampton, 1.9.1986*
Educated: *Millfield*
Clubs: *Gloucester, Leicester*
Tigers debut: *4.9.2009 at Sale Sharks, lost 12-15* ●
Caps: *England (2) 2006*

Anthony Allen sprang to prominence when he was capped against New Zealand and Argentina two months after his twentieth birthday. He was then a centre in a young and immensely promising Gloucester back division, having made his debut against Bristol in the Anglo-Welsh Cup competition of 2005/06 and played in the Gloucester team that won the Middlesex Sevens in 2005 (scoring two tries in the final against Wasps).

ANTHONY ALLEN

JOHN ALLEN

He made 91 appearances for Gloucester, scoring 22 tries, before moving to Leicester in 2009 and becoming the linchpin of the Tigers back division, despite a tendency to incur unfortunate injuries. His consistency won him a place on England's tour to South Africa in 2012 where he played twice in the midweek XV against South African Barbarians and he was named in the Elite Player Squad later that year, reverting to the Saxons squad after the autumn period.

Allen was the Leicester players' player of the 2010/11 season and won the supporters' try of the year for his solo score at Bath. He has played in four successive Premiership finals, scoring a try in the 2012 loss to Harlequins, and was named man of the match after the 2013 final against Northampton. He required surgery to a knee during the summer of 2013, missing England's tour to Argentina, and missed three months of the 2013/14 season because of an injury which required emergency surgery to his lower leg.

Appearances: *109+4 (W76, D6, L31)*
Scoring: *14 tries, 70 pts*

ALLEN, John Albert (113)

Born: *Leicester, 29.7.1942*
Educated: *Lutterworth GS*
Club: *Leicester*
Tigers debut: *26.1.1961 v Royal Air Force (at the Rec), lost 6-11*
Last game: *13.9.1975 v Bath, won 37-7 (1T, 4 pts)*

Only the fourth player to make over 400 appearances for the club, John Allen played all his 457 games at scrum-half. Particularly adept at linking with his back row at a time when Tigers possessed some notable practitioners, his industry won him England trials in 1969 and 1973 but a senior cap eluded him. He was Leicester's captain in 1970/71.

He played at Lutterworth Grammar School with two others who would join him at Welford Road, Richard and John Cooper, while Trevor, his brother, also spent four years with Tigers between 1957-61. Allen played regularly for Leicestershire, for the Midland Counties (East) against South Africa in 1969 and for the same Midland combination against New Zealand in 1973, when he scored a try. He toured with the Barbarians in Wales in 1974.

A chartered accountant at the Leicester offices of Grant Thornton, Allen brought his financial acumen to bear as club treasurer from 1976 and then as the club secretary from 1982-95, when he stood down because he did not seek to be an administrator in a professional sport. He was appointed a life member in 1997 and, that same year, became a non-executive director of Leicester FC plc, doing much to help the club's conversion from a friendly society to that of a public limited company.

Appearances: 457 (W273, D23, L161)
Scoring: 58 tries, 27 conv, 17 pens, 2 drops, 297 pts

JIMMY ALLEN

ALLEN, Walter James (42=)

Born: *Rugby, regd Q2 1882*
Died: *Warwick, regd Q2 1953*
Clubs: *Rugby, Leicester*
Tigers debut: *20.11.1909 at Newport, lost 3-23*
Last game: *12.4.1921 at Nuneaton, won 19-3*

Jimmy "Jumbo" Allen played in the Rugby pack aged 17 and made 132 appearances, scoring 44 tries, for that club between 1899-1909. He was Rugby's captain in 1909/10 when he was invited to tour Wales with Leicester and promptly joined Tigers.

He played regularly for the Midland Counties and once for the Rest in an England trial in 1911. He played in the Midland Counties Cup-winning sides of 1910, 1912 and 1913 and captained Leicester in 1919/20. His 100th game was played in 1912, his 200th seven years later, after the First World War. He worked as an engineer mechanic, originally on steam engines.

Appearances: *209 (W129, D15, L65)*
Scoring: *37 tries, 25 conv, 3 pens, 170 pts*

ALMEY, Gordon Arthur (106)

Born: *Market Harborough, Leicestershire, 16.8.1936*
Educated: *Welland Park School (Market Harborough)*
Clubs: *Kibworth, Leicester, British Police, Hinckley, Market Bosworth*
Tigers debut: *21.12.1957 at Bristol, lost 6-12*
Last game: *14.3.1964 v British Army, won 14-3 (1T, 3 pts)*

GORDON ALMEY

Gordon Almey, a fiery flanker (and occasional wing), was Leicester's leading try scorer with ten in 1958/59 and played in all 38 fixtures that season. He played cricket and rugby for Leicestershire schools, and rugby for Kibworth before joining Tigers. He worked as a plumber before joining the police, working at Market Harborough, Oadby, Hinckley (where he showed a young PC Dean Richards the ropes) and Burbage.

After leaving Leicester he turned out occasionally for Hinckley and, in 1965, helped form the Market Bosworth club, where he became fixture secretary. He continued to play junior rugby into his mid-forties.

Appearances: *150 (W81, D14, L55)*
Scoring: *31 tries, 93 pts*

KEVIN ANDREWS

ANDREWS, Kevin Paul (125)

Born: *Southampton, Hampshire, 28.4.1939*
Educated: *Downside*
Clubs: *Trojans, Burton, Bath, Leicester*
Tigers debut: *13.2.1965 v Newport, lost 10-30*
Last game: *25.4.1970 v Halifax, won 31-8*

Born in Southampton, where he played for the local Trojans club, Kevin Andrews retained an affection for his Hampshire roots and particularly Southampton Football Club. His father, Clifford, played for Hampshire at cricket and rugby and his uncle, Bill, bowled Don Bradman while playing for Somerset against Australia at Taunton in 1938 (Bradman had scored 202 when his wicket fell).

Andrews played in Bath's second row for six years, leading that club before moving to Marstons Brewery at Burton-on-Trent and joining Leicester. He helped Hampshire to the 1962 county championship final against Warwickshire and led Staffordshire between 1964-67. He represented London Counties and led the Midland Counties to a 17-6 win over the Australians at Coventry in 1967. He captained Leicester during his final two seasons.

For many years Andrews enjoyed the distinction of being the only uncapped Englishman to have led the Barbarians (v Penarth in 1967 and Swansea in 1968). He played for the Possibles in an England trial in 1965 and would have played in the final trial but for injury incurred playing against the Barbarians for Tigers. A hard-working committee man, Andrews was Leicester's president in 1987.

Appearances: *191 (W122, D14, L55)*
Scoring: *12 tries, 36 pts*

ASHURST, Alfred Derek Brian (103)

Born: *Leicester, 19.11.1932*
Educated: *Hinckley GS*
Clubs: *Leicester Thursday, Aylestone Athletic, Leicester, Coventry*
Tigers debut: *27.10.1951 at Northampton, lost 11-13*
Last game: *15.9.1962 v Plymouth Albion, won 11-6*

Over 12 years, Derek Ashurst never played more than twenty games in a season except 1955/56 when he hit a high of 28. But he was a valuable support player, a back-row forward with sufficient skill to play wing once at Gloucester and full-back twice on the 1959 Easter tour.

He was a chicken farmer in the family business near Cosby and emigrated to South Africa in 1962, working with Sunnyside Chicks, one of the most successful processing companies in the republic. He made his home in Durban.

Appearances: *112 (W50, D11, L51)*
Scoring: *14 tries, 3 conv, 3 pens, 57 pts*

DEREK ASHURST

DUDLEY ATKINS

ATKINS, Dudley Beaumont (28)

Born: *Hinckley, Leicestershire, 17.10.1879*
Died: *Abergele, Conwy, Wales, 17.10.1945*
Educated: *Bedford*
Clubs: *Hinckley, Leicester*
Tigers debut: *7.9.1901 v Nuneaton, won 27-3*
Last game: *31.10.1908 v Cardiff, won 7-0*

Dudley Atkins, a powerful forward, was a member of the Leicester teams that won the Midland Counties Cup between 1902-05. The youngest son of John Atkins from The Hall, Hinckley, he served in the Imperial Yeomanry in South Africa and subsequently ran a sheep farm in New Zealand.

He was a founder member of Hinckley RFC (where he was club president between 1919-39) and Hinckley Cricket Club. He was a member of the Hinckley Amateur Operatic Society and a benefactor of the Hinckley and District Hospital.

Appearances: *147 (W88, D12, L47)*
Scoring: *10 tries, 30 pts*

ATKINS, Hugh Percival (25)

Born: *Hinckley, Leicestershire, 13.3.1877*
Died: *Burbage, Leicestershire, 19.4.1958*
Educated: *Bedford*
Clubs: *Hinckley, Leicester, Nuneaton*
Tigers debut: *5.4.1897 v Llanelly, drew 0-0*
Last game: *6.10.1906 v Devonport Albion, lost 0-8*

A versatile player, Atkins began his career as a centre or wing before moving to the pack, though he could also play either half-back position. He made his debut for Nuneaton in 1895/96, leading them the following season. He scored 15 tries in 24 appearances before joining Leicester in 1897 (Shirley, his brother, also played for Tigers).

Percy Atkins played in 15 Midland Counties Cup ties, winning every one including four finals, three with his cousin, Dudley. He scored 42 tries for Leicester and earned an England trial. Between 1893-1914 he was also secretary to Hinckley RFC, having been a founder member of both the local rugby and cricket clubs.

Owner of the Hinckley shoe manufacturers, W Johnson's, he was an expert rifle marksman and represented the Army at tournaments at Bisley. He served with the 5th Battalion the Leicestershire Regiment, and became a captain in 1901. Promoted to major during the First World War, he was appointed a chief instructor in charge of sniping and when the USA entered the war, he instructed American soldiers in the sniper's art. During the Second World War he commanded the Wolvey Home Guard.

PERCY ATKINS

Appearances: *186 (W126, D17, L43)*
Scoring: *42 tries, 126 pts*

*AYERZA, Marcos Ivan (202=)

Born: *Buenos Aires, Argentina, 12.1.1983*
Educated: *Cardinal Newman (Buenos Aires)*
Clubs: *Newman (Argentina), Leicester*
Tigers debut: *9.9.2006 at Bath (replacement), lost 25-43* ●
Caps: *Argentina (48) 2004-13*

Marcos Ayerza became one of the most respected props in Premiership rugby after signing for Leicester from his amateur club in Buenos Aires. A fine exponent of his country's strong scrummaging tradition, he played for the Pumas at tight-head prop as well as his favoured loose-head position, and was a member of the Argentina side that finished third in the 2007 World Cup.

MARCOS AYERZA

He did not take long to make an impression at Welford Road, collecting his first Premiership winners' medal in 2007 and being included in the Sky Sports dream team for 2008/09. His 100th appearance for the club came against Harlequins in April 2010 and his value was confirmed when Argentina joined the southern hemisphere's Rugby Championship in 2012, meaning that their leading players would miss even more of the northern-hemisphere season.

But Leicester were in no doubt that in Ayerza they had a prop of such quality that his contract was extended. He has started for Tigers in six Premiership finals and in two Heineken Cup finals, in 2007 and 2009.

Appearances: *161 starts + 32 reps (W134, D8, L51)*
Scoring: *7 tries, 35 pts*

B

BACK, Neil Antony (177)

Born: *Coventry, 16.12.1969*
Educated: *Woodlands (Coventry)*
Clubs: *Earlsdon, Barkers' Butts, Nottingham, Leicester*
Tigers debut: *1.9.1990 v Bedford, won 57-6 (1T, 4 pts)*
Last game: *14.5.2005 v London Wasps (at Twickenham), lost 14-39* ●
Caps: *England (66) 1994-2003, British & Irish Lions (5) 1997-2005*

The argument about Neil Back's value as an international back-row forward raged for the first seven years of his senior career. At 5ft 10in and 90kg, he was deemed too small despite his obvious skills as an open-side flanker, both in winning the ball on the ground and as a link between forwards and backs. Few internationals have possessed greater all-round ability - many good judges deemed Back's handling skills to be the equal of, or better than, many centres - and he is one of the few forwards to have dropped a goal in international rugby.

He was a member of the illustrious back row, along with Lawrence Dallaglio and Richard Hill, who started 37 games together for England, the last of them the 2003 World Cup final against Australia which brought the Webb Ellis Cup to the northern hemisphere for the only time. He started in six of the seven games of that tournament, scoring two tries,

NEIL BACK

after playing in both the 1995 World Cup in South Africa, where a hamstring injury limited his appearances, and the 1999 tournament hosted by Wales. He captained England to four wins and his dropped goal came against Italy in Rome's Stadio Flaminio in 2000.

Although he did not play for England after the 2003 World Cup, he made his third Lions tour in 2005, becoming the oldest player to have appeared in a Lions test against the All Blacks in Christchurch. Though he was not playing for his country at the time, he went with the 1997 Lions to South Africa. He also toured with the 2001 party to Australia.

Back played mini-rugby for Earlsdon and joined Barkers' Butts at 13. He also played football and represented Coventry and Warwickshire at age-group cricket. He made 38 appearances for Nottingham over two seasons, scoring ten tries, and scored three tries for England in an under-21 international against Romania in Bucharest in 1989. He had already represented England at schools, colts and under-21 levels before joining Leicester in 1990.

His floppy blond hair was as distinctive a trademark as his non-stop support work which earned him first an England A cap and then a full international appearance against Scotland in 1994. But the vogue then was for tall flankers and Back had to wait until Clive Woodward became England's coach in 1997 before securing his place; he had started the 1996/97 season under a cloud, having been suspended for six months by the RFU for pushing Steve Lander, the referee, after the end of the 1996 Pilkington Cup final, which Leicester lost to Bath.

The enforced rest enabled Back to give even more time to his personal fitness level, which contributed towards his remarkable scoring sequence for Tigers. His 125 tries for the club, many of them at the back of a rolling maul, are a record for a forward and place him eighth on the all-time scoring record. He was voted the members' player of the 1997/98 season when he was also the RFU player of the year. In 1999 he was named player of the year by the Professional Rugby Players' Association.

Back played in the Heineken Cup finals of 1997, 2001 and 2002 and in five league championship squads: the Courage League of 1994/95 and the four successive Zurich Premiership wins of 1999, 2000, 2001 and 2002. He won two Pilkington Cup winners' medals, in 1993 and 1997, and played in two further finals. His aggregate of 339 Leicester games puts him 22nd in the overall appearances list.

He captained the club after the 2003 World Cup but relinquished the role when adding coaching responsibilities later in the season. He made his final appearance in the 2005 Zurich Premiership final, against London Wasps at Twickenham, though not on the winning side. He was awarded the MBE in 2004, along with all his World Cup colleagues.

After retiring, Back joined Leicester's coaching staff as defence/forwards coach. In 2008 he coached Leeds, and followed this with spells at Rugby and Edinburgh. He is now an insurance specialist with Adelphi Special Risks Limited.

Appearances: *320 starts + 19 reps (W252, D12, L75)*
Scoring: *125 tries, 615 pts*

BANN, Eric Edward (133)

Born: *Lynmouth, Devon, 17.10.1946*
Educated: *City of LeicesterBoys' GS, Alsager College*
Clubs: *Leicester, St. Mary's College (Dublin), Dolphin (Cork), Stoneygate*
Tigers debut: *27.4.1968 v Manchester, won 13-6*
Last game: *1.11.1975 v Gloucester, lost 12-22*

Few Tigers have played for Leicester at Welford Road and Filbert Street but Eric Bann, an athletic lock, did so. As a youngster his goalkeeping took him to Notts County and Leicester City reserves before he was persuaded by Alan Black, the former Wasps lock, to change from football to rugby at Alsager College of Education.

His all-round talents made him a member of the Leicestershire athletics team. He was a county high jump, triple jump and 110m hurdles champion, a decathlete who played for England's under-21 basketball team, so his line-out performances invariably attracted rave reviews. Since he could also run fast he was, in many ways, the prototype modern, mobile tight forward who, had he wished, might have gained representative honours.

Appearances: *162 (W90, D7, L65)*
Scoring: *26 tries, 18 conv, 18 pens, 188 pts*

ERIC BANN

BOB BARKER

BARKER, Robert George (130)

Born: *Leicester, 23.10.1944*
Educated: *Alderman Newton GS, Scraptoft Training College*
Clubs: *Stoneygate, Leicester*
Tigers debut: *19.10.1968 v Northampton, drew 17-17 (1T, 3 pts)*
Last game: *23.11.1979 at Moseley, lost 6-13*

An elusive wing who started playing as a centre, Bob Barker proved a valuable points-scoring commodity throughout the 1970s. He became the third Tiger (after Harry Wilkinson and Percy Lawrie) to score more than 150 tries and his goalkicking made him the club's leading scorer in two seasons.

Barker captained Leicestershire at under-15 and under-19 level and played for England under-15 against Wales in 1960. At senior level he played for Leicestershire and Midland Counties East and, as a sporting all-rounder, he played cricket for Leicestershire Young Amateurs and became a qualified tennis coach. He also ran in five All-England Athletics Championships, recording a best time of 22.9 seconds for the 220 yards and 9.9 seconds for the 100 yards.

He held both the post-Second World War records for tries and points scored, until overtaken by Barry Evans and Dusty Hare respectively. He was Leicester's leading try scorer in five seasons and reached the 150 mark with a hat-trick against Nottingham in 1977. His 1,000th point for the club was scored with a try at Twickenham, against Harlequins.

When he qualified as a teacher, he specialised in PE and geography but he also gained a diploma of education to teach the physically and mentally handicapped and became head of special needs at Rushey Meads School in Leicester.

Appearances: *318 starts + 2 reps (W192, D15, L113)*
Scoring: *158 tries, 92 conv, 107 pens, 2 drops, 1,117 pts*

BARNWELL, Richard Charles (150)

Born: *Coventry, 31.1.1953*
Educated: *Warwick, Loughborough Colleges*
Clubs: *Loughborough Colleges, Coventry, Leicester*
Tigers debut: *14.9.1977 at Birmingham, won 28-9 (2T, 8 pts)* ●
Last game: *30.4.1983 v Bristol (at Twickenham), lost 22-28* ●

'Tim' Barnwell's playing career ended abruptly during the 1983 John Player Cup final at Twickenham when he was forced to leave the field after a clash of heads against Bristol. Kept under observation at West Middlesex Hospital, he lapsed into a coma and underwent five hours of surgery for the removal of a blood clot on his brain; he spent 24 hours on a life support system but recovered after a lengthy rehabilitation process in London and at Leicester Royal Infirmary.

He played on the wing six times for England's under-19 schools side between 1970-72 and for England's under-23 team in 1974. During his four seasons with Coventry he played in the 1974 national knockout final, scoring a try against London Scottish, and for Warwickshire and the Midlands. He joined Leicester in 1977 and scored four tries in the fixture against the RAF in March 1978.

TIM BARNWELL

Fast and elusive, he was Leicester's leading try scorer in 1978/79 and 1981/82, and played in the three winning John Player finals of 1979-81, as well as the losing final of 1983. His greatest regret was that, despite sitting on the bench for the Barbarians, he never played for the famous invitation club.

After recovering his health, he worked as a cruise operations manager for the Leicester travel company, Page and Moy. He was also a familiar voice on Leicester Sound and Radio Leicester. He took part in fund-raising activities on the twentieth anniversary of his accident, including the London Marathon, to raise money to help buy a new brain scanner for the hospital that saved his life.

Appearances: *188 starts + 1 rep (W136, D4, L49)*
Scoring: *95 tries, 1 conv, 382 pts*

BOBBY BARR

BARR, Robert John (73)

Born: *Blisworth, Northamptonshire, 26.5.1907*
Died: *Great Oxendon, near Market Harborough, Leicestershire, 22.9.1975*
Educated: *Stamford*
Clubs: *Westleigh, Leicestershire Regiment, Leicester*
Tigers debut: *3.11.1928 at Cambridge University, lost 3-20*
Last game: *15.4.1939 v Blackheath, lost 10-23*
Caps: *England (3) 1932*

Bobby Barr, who played 241 games at full-back for Tigers, was one of only two individuals (the other being John Parsons) to have held the three senior positions at Welford Road of captain, secretary and president. That he never scored a try during his long playing career is an indication of the defensive qualities then required of a full-back but he could kick the ball and twice dropped goals from over forty metres, no mean feat given the heavy balls then in use.

He played for Leicestershire and for the combined Leicestershire/East Midlands XV in the famous 30-21 defeat of the 1931 South Africans at Welford Road. On the strength of that game, Barr played for England against Wales, South Africa and Ireland later in the season and in 1935 he played for the Barbarians in the Mobbs Memorial Match at Northampton.

During the Second World War he was a Territorial officer in the Leicestershire searchlights unit and was captured during a rearguard action at Boulogne. He spent five years as a prisoner of war and was one of 24 who escaped from a tunnel dug in a camp at Ulm, only to be recaptured four kilometres from the Swiss border. At one stage he and other senior officers were advised by the camp commandant: "Your men have not made much progress with the tunnel, I find they have only done two yards since yesterday...may I suggest that they might do better if they go westwards, instead of east, as they will strike less water that way."

After the first two years of his captivity, it was decided that more recent arrivals should be helped to escape so he spent the rest of his imprisonment in planning. When he was repatriated, he was awarded the Military Cross. He founded the hosiery brand-label manufacturing firm of Barr, Radcliffe and Co at Sileby and Oadby, and was a member of the Worshipful Company of Framework Knitters. He also played cricket occasionally as a wicketkeeper batsman for Leicestershire's second XI.

After the war he became Leicester's team secretary and, from 1957, secretary until 1962 when he was elected club president for two years. One of his daughters, Judith, married Roger Clark, the rally driver.

Appearances: *241 (W121, D16, L104)*
Scoring: *12 conv, 6 pens, 6 drops, 66 pts*

BATES, Ian (166)

Born: *Earl Shilton, Leicestershire, 16.5.1963*
Educated: *Heathfield HS, Earl Shilton Community College, Hinckley College*
Clubs: *Market Bosworth, Leicester, Manly (Australia)*
Tigers debut: *5.2.1983 at London Scottish, won 18-12*
Last game: *4.11.1995 at Harlequins, won 29-25* ●

Ian Bates, a self-employed carpenter, joined the Leicester youth team from Market Bosworth as a scrum-half but was converted to centre by Graham Willars. In that position he became a dependable player good enough to win selection for England's under-23 squad between 1984-86, despite serving at Welford Road behind Paul Dodge and Clive Woodward.

IAN BATES

He played for Leicestershire and appeared in 13 games for the Midlands, including matches against South Africa and New Zealand. His strong running helped Leicester win the inaugural Courage league title in 1987/88, when he started all ten league games, and he won a Pilkington Cup medal in 1993.

Appearances: *286 starts + 1 rep (W208, D4, L75)*
Scoring: *38 tries, 154 pts*

BAYNES, Christopher James (131=)

Born: *Gillingham, Kent, 24.11.1946*
Educated: *Gillingham GS, Loughborough College*
Clubs: *Loughborough Colleges, Leicester, Nottingham*
Tigers debut: *19.3.1969 v Coventry, won 15-6*
Last game: *24.4.1973 at Wilmslow, lost 10-16*

CHRIS BAYNES

A powerful flanker, Chris Baynes was a consistent presence in Leicester's back row and earned call-ups to the Midland Counties (East) XVs that played Fiji in 1970 and New Zealand in 1973. A schoolteacher at Trent College, he played for Notts, Lincs and Derbys and made his 100th appearance against Nottingham, before joining that club in 1973 and playing for them in 145 games (as top try scorer in 1975/76).

He became a financial consultant for the Royal Bank of Scotland and was chairman of the Midlands under-21s and a member of the RFU's under-21 panel.

Appearances: *116 (W67, D6, L43)*
Scoring: *37 tries, 125 pts*

BEAMISH, George Robert (67)

Born: *Dunmanway, County Cork, Ireland, 29.4.1905*
Died: *Castlerock, County Derry, Ireland, 13.11.1967*
Educated: *Coleraine Academical Institute*
Clubs: *Coleraine (Ireland), Leicester, London Irish*
Tigers debut: *27.12.1924 v Heriotonians, won 22-0*
Last game: *17.4.1933 at Plymouth Albion, won 11-6 (1T, 3 pts)*
Caps: *Ireland (25) 1925-33, Great Britain (5) 1930*

One of the great players of his era and one of four Irish brothers (along with Charles, Cecil and Victor) all of whom appeared in Leicester colours. George Beamish, knighted in 1955, came to the Midlands thanks to his RAF career, which brought him to Cranwell. He won his first cap in Ireland's back row as a 19-year-old and captained Ireland to a share of the championship in 1932.

But his fame in the Midlands hinged on his leadership of the Leicestershire/

East Midlands team that beat South Africa at Welford Road in 1931. Beamish, a powerful No 8 with a magnificent physique, carried the battle to the opposition and was one of his side's four try scorers in a 30-21 win. His rumbustious play, though, was improved by the discipline he always demanded of his teams, whether with Leicester, Ireland or the Lions on tour in Australasia in 1930 when he played in all five internationals and made more appearances (21) than any other player.

During a five-year period from 1928, he missed only one Ireland international and set a record for a No 8 forward which stood for nearly fifty years. Before his international career ended, he played in the same pack as Charles, his younger brother who played prop for Ireland and was also an RAF officer. George played rugby for the RAF and was their golf champion in 1925 and heavyweight boxing champion in 1929; in 1932 he lost the heavyweight final to the Wales prop, Cecil Davies.

Beamish fought in the Battle of Britain during the Second World War and, in 1942, became the first RAF officer to reach the rank of air commodore. That same year he was awarded the CBE and, in 1949, was appointed air officer commanding and commandant of the RAF College, Cranwell, retiring from the service nine years later as an air marshal. In January 1959 he was nominated as Unionist candidate for North Belfast but was defeated by the incumbent MP.

Appearances: *118 (W72, D9, L37)*
Scoring: *24 tries, 1 conv, 74 pts*

BEASON, Robert (117)

Born: *Leicester, 1.9.1938*
Educated: *Dixie GS (Market Bosworth), Nottingham University*
Clubs: *Old Bosworthians, Leicester*
Tigers debut: *3.9.1960 v Bedford, drew 9-9*
Last game: *9.9.1972 v Bath, won 34-4*

BOB BEASON

TOM BERRY

Bob Beason, who converted from lock to prop, played for England against Wales in a schools international in 1954 and led Old Bosworthians for the first three years of that club's existence (his two sons, Richard and Michael, both served in the same capacity). He played more than 200 games for Leicester and also captained Leicestershire.

A chartered engineer, he was an enthusiastic administrator who filled a variety of roles, including youth team manager and coach, fixture secretary, treasurer and chairman. He was president of Leicester from 1985-87 and a non-executive director of Leicester FC plc from 1997-2007.

Appearances: *203 (W128, D9, L66)*
Scoring: *3 tries, 9 pts*

BERRY, Joseph Thomas Wade (75)

Born: *Slawston, Leicestershire, 17.7.1911*
Died: *Market Harborough, Leicestershire, 1.7.1993*
Educated: *Eastbourne College*
Clubs: *Market Harborough, Leicester*
Tigers debut: *5.3.1932 v Harlequins, won 13-11 (1T, 3 pts)*
Last game: *17.4.1948 v Blackheath, won 6-5*
Caps: *England (3) 1939*

Tom Berry, a farmer at Ashley near Market Harborough, was the first Leicestershire representative to be elected president of the RFU, in 1968/69. He was also the manager of the first England side to tour the southern hemisphere, that of 1963 in New Zealand and Australia.

A back-row forward, Berry played for Leicestershire and a full season for England before the outbreak of the Second World War. He played in two war-time internationals against Wales and was available to help put Leicester back on its feet when hostilities ended, becoming captain as he had been before the war. He represented the Barbarians in the 1939 Mobbs Memorial Match and was a keen cricketer who played for the Gentlemen's Cricket Club.

Berry represented Leicestershire on the RFU committee from 1953-68 and was an England selector from 1951-66. He was Leicester president between 1971-74. Mac Hodgson, another Leicester back-row forward, was his brother-in-law and Margaret, his wife, played golf for England. Three sons went on to become Tigers: John (also fixture secretary for twenty years), twins David and Richard, while a fourth son, Michael, played for Leicester Extras.

Appearances: *277 (W136, D17, L124)*
Scoring: *15 tries, 45 pts*

BIRD, David William (111)

Born: *Broughton Astley, Leicestershire, 26.8.1940*
Educated: *Lutterworth GS, Loughborough Colleges*
Clubs: *Hinckley, Leicester*
Tigers debut: *3.9.1960 v Bedford, drew 9-9 (1T, 3 pts)*
Last game: *21.4.1973 at Broughton Park, won 10-9*

A stalwart on the wing throughout the 1960s and (inevitably) known as 'Dickie', Bird was born in the same house as his cousin, Mike (MJK) Smith, the former Warwickshire and England cricketer who played fly-half for England. Bird himself played cricket at Loughborough before beginning his career as a PE teacher and joining Tigers.

He was the club's leading try scorer in 1963/64 and 1967/68 and scored a hat-trick on three occasions, against Bradford (1962), Bristol (1964) and Birkenhead Park (1969). He played for the Midland Counties against New Zealand in 1963 and would have scored a try had the referee allowed advantage; as it was the All Blacks hung on for a tightly-contested 14-6 win, the high point of Bird's playing career.

He later moved to teach in Leamington Spa. Diane, his twin sister, was an England hockey international who coached the Great Britain women's team to a bronze medal in the Barcelona Olympic Games of 1992.

Appearances: *285 (W167, D19, L99)*
Scoring: *86 tries, 258 pts*

DICKIE BIRD

TOM BLEASDALE

BLEASDALE, Tom (91)

Born: *St. Anne's, Lancashire, 9.6.1930*
Died: *Naples, Florida, USA, 8.5.2008*
Educated: *King Edward VII (Lytham), Leicester University*
Clubs: *Fylde, Leicester*
Tigers debut: *5.11.1949 at Gloucester, lost 6-18*
Last game: *4.1.1964 at Bath, lost 0-11*

In a long and distinguished Leicester career, in which he started at a flanker and became a strapping lock, Tom Bleasdale chalked up 340 appearances. He joined Leicester as a student from the university, who made him captain which limited his initial availability for Tigers.

He was given an England trial in 1951, when he also played for the Midland Counties in a 3-0 loss to South Africa. That season he was travelling reserve for the England-Wales match and, in 1955, played in another trial at Gosforth but just missed a full cap. He appeared in the back row of the Midland side that lost 3-0 to New Zealand in 1953 and in the second row of the Leicestershire/East Midlands XV that lost 18-3 to Australia in 1957.

He was Leicester's leading try scorer (13 from thirty games) in 1951/52 and, on a short-service commission, led the RAF and the Combined Services in 1955. Returning to civilian life a year later, Bleasdale worked for United Shoe Machinery and captained Leicester for three seasons.

He emigrated to the USA in 1973 to work as general manager of the USM Division in Beverley, Massachusetts. He sat the Harvard advanced management programme and became a trustee for the Colonial Group of Mutual Funds. He was among the guests at the celebratory 100-cap dinner at the Walkers Stadium in 2003.

Appearances: *340 (W173, D25, L142)*
Scoring: *53 tries, 159 pts*

BOLESWORTH, Arthur Denis (78)

Born: *Hinckley, Leicestershire, 2.9.1916*
Died: *Rock, Cornwall 2.11.1999*
Educated: *Ratcliffe College (Sileby)*
Clubs: *Hinckley, Leicester, Nuneaton*
Tigers debut: *4.11.1936 at Oxford University, won 16-13*
Last game: *12.3.1955 v Coventry, drew 11-11*

During an admirable playing career of nearly twenty years, Denis Bolesworth was nicknamed 'milord' after an Easter tour on which he entered two Grand National sweepstakes, picked the 100-1 shot Russian Hero both times and had a bet on the horse himself. Having won, he was then asked on every occasion the team bus passed a mansion which was for sale, whether 'milord' was going to buy it with his newly-acquired wealth.

A prop forward, Bolesworth joined the RAF during the Second World War (when he played for the Midland Counties against the Barbarians in a fund-raising match and six times for Nuneaton). In 1946 he played for the Barbarians in the Mobbs Memorial Match and played in England trials in 1952/53, as well as captaining Leicester and representing the RAF in the inter-services tournament.

When he retired at the end of the 1953/54 season he was carried off shoulder high in tribute by his colleagues at the end of the Sale match but returned for one more game, against Coventry, in 1955 after the late withdrawal of David Hazell through illness. He became team secretary from 1957-64. He was a hosiery manufacturer and, in retirement, moved to Cornwall.

Appearances: *330 (W159, D16, L155)*
Scoring: *23 tries, 69 pts*

DENIS BOLESWORTH

BRAITHWAITE, John (20)

Born: *Leeds, Yorkshire, 21.4.1873*
Died: *West Humberstone, Leicester, 14.11.1915*
Clubs: *Leeds St Cuthbert's, Holbeck, Vulcan Rovers, Leicester, Nottingham*
Tigers debut: *12.10.1895 at Bedford, lost 3-8*
Last game: *22.12.1906 at Coventry, drew 0-0*
Caps: *England (1) 1905*

Jacky 'Nipper' Braithwaite started playing as a 13-year-old in Leeds club rugby, helping St Cuthbert's to two successive junior league titles. After joining Leicester he helped the A side win the Nuneaton Cup then won promotion to the senior side and the Midland Counties team, all by the age of 22.

A diminutive scrum-half - he was only 5ft 2in and 9st - he was a clever and resourceful player who had played 330 games for Leicester before England awarded him his solitary cap, against New Zealand at Crystal Palace in 1905. Dave Gallaher, the All Blacks captain, paid him the compliment after the game of saying that Braithwaite, "was one of the most determined little men he had ever met".

He was only once on the losing side in 34 Midland Counties Cup ties, including eight successive tournament victories from 1898-1905. He was a member of the most enduring half-back partnership in Leicester history, playing 236 games with Billy Foreman at fly-half, and finished with 359 appearances before a brief fling with Nottingham.

An engineer, a serious work accident threatened the loss of a leg but Braithwaite made a complete recovery. A hardy, unassuming character, it was a shock to family and friends when he died, aged 42, from pneumonia only a week after declaring his intention to enlist to fight in the First World War.

Appearances: *359 (W228, D35, L96)*
Scoring: *67 tries, 45 conv, 2 pens, 15 drops, 1 mark, 361 pts*

JACKY BRAITHWAITE

BILLY BREAM

BREAM, John William (47)

Born: *Blaby, Leicester, regd Q2 1891*
Died: *Quorn, Leicestershire, 21.8.1937*
Clubs: *Aylestone St James, Leicester, Northampton, Bedford*
Tigers debut: *28.1.1911 v Moseley, won 21-5 (1PG, 3 pts)*
Last game: *21.3.1914 at Newbold-on-Avon, won 27-0 (3C, 2PG, 12 pts)* ●

Billy Bream, a full-back good enough to play in an England trial in 1913, won Midland Counties Cup medals in 1912 and 1913 and was Leicester's leading points scorer in his three seasons with the club. His 137 points in 1912/13 set what was then a club record. In the 23-0 win over Llanelly in 1913, he was reported to have "returned to his goal-kicking mood. He converted all [four] tries and landed a penalty goal, several of the kicks being of a difficult character."

He served in the Indian Army, rising to the rank of captain, and received a military OBE while stationed at Quetta. After returning home, Bream played 16 games for Northampton in 1921/22, scoring 38 points, and appeared twice for Bedford the following season. He was manager of Baxter's Leather Company in Leicester and played cricket for Leicester Ivanhoe. He died suddenly, aged 46, playing a North Leicestershire League cricket match for Quorn against Rothley.

Appearances: *101 (W67, D9, L25)*
Scoring: *4 tries, 125 conv, 22 pens, 1 drop, 332 pts*

BROWN, William Arthur (81)

BILL BROWN

Born: *Hinckley, Leicestershire, 5.5.1919*
Died: *Sapcote, Leicestershire, December 1993*
Educated: *Hinckley*
Clubs: *Hinckley, Coventry, Leicester*
Tigers debut: *13.10.1945 v Nuneaton, won 8-3*
Last game: *19.4.1949 at Bath, won 8-3 (1T, 3 pts)*

Bill Brown, a lock who also played for Leicestershire, introduced Dean Richards to the Tigers when he was a scout in Hinckley. Brown scored a try on his sixth appearance (against Bedford in December 1945) but did not score another until his final match, against Bath.

Appearances: *106 (W53, D3, L50)*
Scoring: *2 tries, 6 pts*

RALPH BUCKINGHAM

BUCKINGHAM, Ralph Arthur (60)

Born: *Blaby, Leicester, 15.1.1907*
Died: *Stoneygate, Leicester, 10.4.1988*
Educated: *Rossall*
Clubs: *Stoneygate, Leicester*
Tigers debut: *10.9.1924 at Rugby BTH, won 24-0*
Last game: *23.4.1935 at Exeter, won 42-0 (3C, 6 pts)*
Caps: *England (1) 1927*

An elegant centre who was the mainstay of the back division for more than ten years, Ralph Buckingham played football at school and won colours for boxing and cricket. He was Leicester's top try scorer in three seasons, recording 117 in his 325 appearances though his wings often paid tribute to the service they received from him.

A travelling reserve for England on ten occasions, he only won one cap, against France in 1927, the last international played by two legends, Wavell Wakefield and Len Corbett, Buckingham's midfield partner. He was a key member of the Leicestershire/East Midlands team that beat South Africa in 1931, steady in defence and the creator of one of Charlie Slow's two tries.

He captained Leicester in 1933/34 and, in his final season, became the regular goalkicker and was top points scorer with 101. He played for the Barbarians in the 1935 Mobbs Memorial Match and, when he retired, was elected a Leicester vice-president.

He became the company director of the shoe merchandisers, Sowter and Buckingham. During the 1920s he was a member of the Leicester Rowing Club and Kirby Muxloe Golf Club. During the Second World War he served with the Civil Defence Force and later as a flight lieutenant in the RAF. In 1942 he was awarded the BEM for gallantry.

Appearances: *325 (W192, D25, L108)*
Scoring: *117 tries, 38 conv, 4 pens, 1 drop, 443 pts*

BURDETT, James Charles (41)

Born: *Aylestone, Leicester, regd Q1 1885*
Died: *Market Harborough, Leicestershire, 26.10.1966*
Clubs: *Stoneygate, Leicester*
Tigers debut: *5.12.1903 v Coventry, won 14-5*
Last game: *5.10.1912 v Aberavon, won 18-0*

Jimmy Burdett, a forward, had a curious claim to fame in that he played for the Barbarians against Leicester in 1912 when he was a Leicester player. He also played for the invitation club against Cardiff that year and helped Leicester win two Midland Counties Cup finals, in 1910 and 1912. He captained Leicester nine times in 1911/12 when Percy Lawrie was absent.

The son of the Lloyds Bank manager in Leicester, Burdett was commissioned as a second lieutenant in the 6th Battalion of the Royal Leicestershire Regiment. He was wounded at the Battle of the Somme in 1916 but recovered to win promotion to major and commanded his battalion by April 1917. He was awarded the Military Cross and the Legion d'Honneur. His brother, John, a first-class cricketer for Leicestershire, was a captain in the Leicestershire Regiment and also won the Military Cross.

Appearances: *108 (W65, D11, L32)*
Scoring: *12 tries, 36 pts*

JIMMY BURDETT

TERRY BURWELL

BURWELL, Terrence Raymond (151)

Born: *Northampton, 27.7.1951*
Educated: *Northampton GS, Bournemouth School, Loughborough Colleges*
Clubs: *Loughborough Colleges, Leicester, Northampton*
Tigers debut: *18.1.1975 at Bedford, lost 19-23*
Last game: *26.3.1983 at London Scottish (replacement), won 30-9* ●

Terry Burwell was a reliable centre who went on to become one of the earliest professional directors of rugby and later a key member of the RFU's administrative staff. He helped Leicester to the first of their three successive John Player Cup wins, in 1979.

Burwell played for British Universities in 1971 and at full-back for England Students and English Universities. He represented the East Midlands and considered the high point of his career to be Leicester's win over Randwick in 1980, a match billed in Sydney as the world club championship.

He taught at Northampton Grammar School then later became a building society manager. Burwell coached at Northampton before becoming director of rugby at Newbury with responsibility for player development and commercial management. He took those skills with him to the RFU where he became community and operations director, also driving competitions and governance of the game.

He spent 12 years as a director on the board of European Rugby Cup Ltd and was competitions director when the RFU made sweeping administrative changes in 2011. Since then he has become executive director of the charity R4UK Ltd.

Appearances: *111 starts + 9 reps (W85, D1, L34)*
Scoring: *27 tries, 1 drop, 111 pts*

MALCOLM BUSSEY

BUSSEY, William Malcolm (118=)

Born: *Halifax, Yorkshire, 19.2.1941*
Educated: *Heath GS (Halifax), Downing College (Cambridge)*
Clubs: *Halifax, Cambridge University (Blues 1960-62), Leicester, Irish Wolfhounds.*
Tigers debut: *2.9.1963 at Torquay Athletic, won 18-5*
Last game: *4.10.1967 v Nuneaton, won 17-8*

Malcolm 'King' Bussey won three Blues between 1960-62 while taking a natural science degree at Downing College, Cambridge, playing on the wing outside Mike Wade and, in the pack, Nick Drake-Lee who would be club colleagues at Leicester. All three games were won by Cambridge.

He played for England schools in 1960, having won the All England schools 440-yard title the year before in 50.5 seconds. As a freshman wing in 1960, he played for Cambridge against South Africa and, three years later, toured South Africa with a combined Oxbridge side.

Bussey joined Leicester after taking up a teaching post at Uppingham, where he became a senior master. He played for Yorkshire and Leicestershire and, in 1966, for the East Midlands against Australia.

Appearances: *121 (W74, D6, L41)*
Scoring: *38 tries, 1 drop, 117 pts*

BUTLIN, Alfred Charles (15)

Born: *Rugby, Warwickshire, regd Q4 1872*
Died: *Chelsea, London, regd Q2 1952*
Clubs: *Rugby, Leicester*
Tigers debut: *23.11.1895 at Swinton, lost 0-13*
Last game: *13.12.1902 at Northampton, won 12-6 (1DG, 4 pts)*

Leicester were accused of poaching when Alf Butlin transferred from Rugby in November 1895 and he was suspended until an enquiry (the costs of which were paid by Rugby) permitted the transfer. A resourceful full-back, he made 31 appearances for Rugby and, between 1898-1902, played for Leicester in five successive Midland Counties Cup-winning teams.

He also played for the Midland Counties and scored a hat-trick for Leicester against Bridgwater in the 44-3 win of 1896, passing 200 appearances for the club in 1901. He was an engine cleaner and later a carpenter/joiner.

Appearances: *252 (W172, D19, L61)*
Scoring: *19 tries, 11 conv, 1 pen, 9 drops, 118 pts*

ALF BUTLIN

C

CAMPBELL, Robert Newton (14)

Born: *Carnforth, Lancashire, 21.12.1870*
Died: *Salford, Lancashire, regd Q4 1915*
Clubs: *Morecambe, Leicester*
Tigers debut: *21.9.1895 v Nuneaton, won 24-0 (1T, 3 pts)*
Last game: *21.9.1901 v Bristol, lost 3-6*

BOB CAMPBELL

Bob Campbell, a forward, scored a try against Nuneaton on his debut but only added six more in a further 206 games for Leicester. He also dropped a goal (against Nuneaton) at Welford Road on the opening day of the 1900/01 season.

He played for London and universities against the Rest of the South in a trial game in 1899 but Lancashire only picked him as a reserve when he played with Morecambe. He appeared for Tigers in four successive Midland Counties Cup-winning teams. He ran the Wagon and Horses pub in Belgrave Gate at the beginning of the 20th century.

Appearances: *207 (W149, D20, L38)*
Scoring: *7 tries, 1 drop, 25 pts*

CHANNER, Melville Ramsay (93)

Born: *Uitenhage, Eastern Cape, South Africa, 4.9.1924*
Died: *Mount Croix, Port Elizabeth, South Africa, 18.9.2006*
Educated: *Muir College (South Africa)*
Clubs: *Leicester, Rhodesia, Wanderers (Kroonstad), Orange Free State*
Tigers debut: *16.3.1946 v Bedford, won 10-9 (1T, 3 pts)*
Last game: *27.12.1955 v Barbarians, lost 3-12*

Mel Channer, a fly-half, served with the South African Air Force during the Second World War and was stationed at Market Harborough where he gained Leicester's attention. His grandfather founded a South African regional team, the Swifts, and Channer became a popular figure at Welford Road, though not for his time-keeping after he was moved to RAF Cosford.

He arrived ten minutes late for a game with Oxford University in 1946 and failed to appear for the game with Blackheath later that season. In 1947 he travelled with

MEL CHANNER

Scotland for a five nations game against France but was reported to have fallen foul of the management though eight years later he did play in a Scotland trial at Murrayfield.

He played four matches for Rhodesia in the 1950 Currie Cup, dropping goals against Western and Eastern Transvaal, and played in three matches against the Junior Springboks that year. He played for the RAF, for whom he was also the long-jump champion, and for the Combined Services against Australia in 1947, and kicked a penalty for the Midland Counties against the touring New Zealanders in 1953.

His final match for Leicester, against the Barbarians, was played on the wing before he returned home and made eight appearances for Orange Free State in 1956 and 1957. He possessed an acerbic tongue and became one of South Africa's leading sports journalists, working for overseas publications from Port Elizabeth. He returned to Welford Road in 2000 for the LFC Past Players Association dinner.

Appearances: *127 (W69, D5, L53)*
Scoring: *33 tries, 19 conv, 35 pens, 26 drops, 327 pts*

CHAWNER, Frank (94)

Born: *Leicester, 11.7.1927*
Died: *Leicester, 6.9.2012*
Clubs: *Vipers, Leicester*
Tigers debut: *19.2.1949 v Swansea, won 14-3*
Last game: *18.4.1964 v Saracens, won 9-3*

Frank Chawner made his debut as a lock but moved to prop during the 1951/52 season and proved a durable forward in the course of 331 games for Leicester.

FRANK CHAWNER

Between October 1961 and October 1963, he played in 74 successive games, passing the 300-mark against Bristol on the way before the "big freeze" suspended sport for two months. Len, his cousin, was a hooker and the two played in the same front row on five occasions.

Appearances: *331 (W171, D26, L134)*
Scoring: *23 tries, 69 pts*

CHILTON, Keith (116)

Born: *Ogmore Vale, Glamorgan, Wales, 28.5.1938*
Educated: *Christ's Hospital*
Clubs: *Old Blues, London Welsh, Leicester*
Tigers debut: *2.9.1963 at Torquay Athletic, won 18-5 (3C, 6 pts)*
Last game: *22.4.1967 v Aberavon, won 9-0 (1PG, 3 pts)*

Keith Chilton played initially for his school's old boys side, with whom Leicester had regular fixtures between 1924-58. He was a full-back who switched to centre and won three trials for Wales while playing with London Welsh between 1959-60. While with the Exiles he played on the wing for Midland Counties in the 3-3 draw against South Africa in 1960.

He worked for English Electric at Whetstone and later became managing director of Oakland Elevators in Oadby. He was Leicester's top scorer in successive seasons between 1963-67. Against Old Belvedere in November 1964, he scored in every possible way with a try, conversion, penalty and dropped goal. He was at centre for the East Midlands in the 17-9 loss to Australia in 1966 and passed 500 points for Leicester that season.

Appearances: *144 (W91, D6, L47)*
Scoring: *26 tries, 91 conv, 95 pens, 2 drops, 551 pts*

KEITH CHILTON

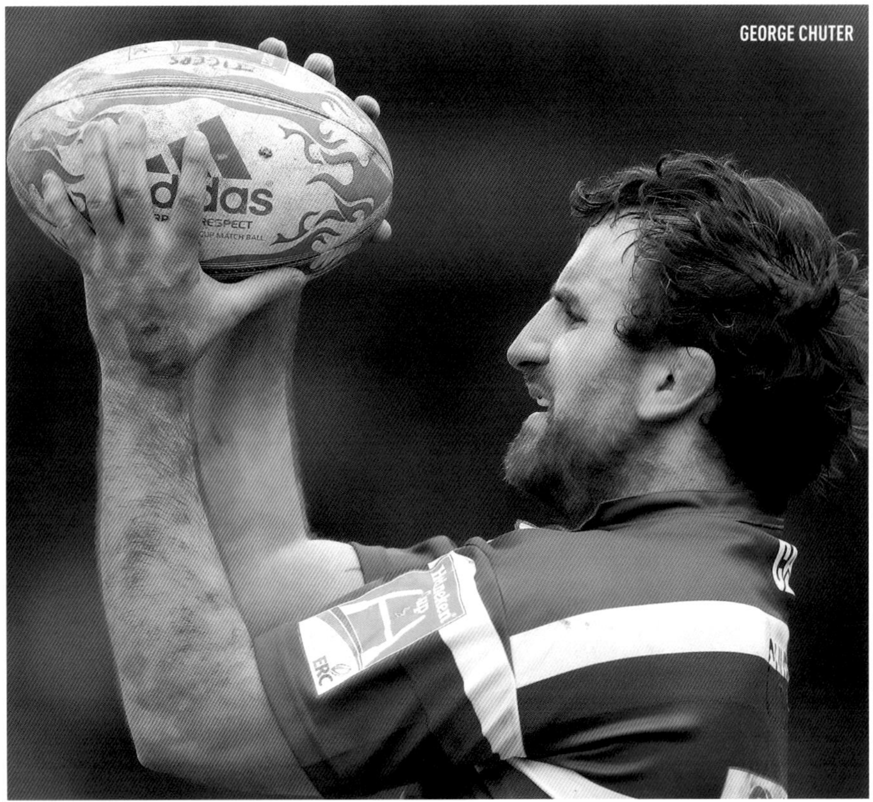
GEORGE CHUTER

CHUTER, George Scala (197)

Born: *Greenwich, London, 9.7.1976*
Educated: *Trinity (Croydon), West London Institute*
Clubs: *Old Mid-Whitgiftians, Saracens, Leicester*
Tigers debut: *31.3.2001 at Gloucester (replacement), lost 13-22* ●
Last game: *31.1.2014 v Bath (replacement), lost 17-35* ●
Caps: *England (24) 2006-10*

George Chuter was a youthful member of the new-look Saracens team whose horizons expanded so greatly in the early years of the professional era. He helped the club win the national cup in 1998 but took a year-long sabbatical from rugby in 2000, travelling in Australia and the United States before returning home and joining Leicester.

He had to bide his time behind two international hookers, Richard Cockerill and Dorian West, but his patience was rewarded when he forced his way into the club's first-choice front row and then, just before his thirtieth birthday, to an England cap in 2006, on tour in Australia. He scored a try in his second international (his first start, also against Australia), started regularly throughout the 2006/07 season and appeared in all seven of England's matches en route to the 2007 World Cup final in France.

He captained England Saxons in 2008 and remained a consistent performer for Tigers in the Premiership, starting the 2009 and 2010 finals as well as the 2009 Heineken Cup final. He reached 200 Premiership appearances against Worcester in 2010 and became the holder of the record for most Premiership appearances in January 2012. He was inducted into the Aviva Premiership Hall of Fame early in 2014 and retired from rugby three months later.

Appearances: *206 starts + 84 reps (W189, D14, L87)*
Scoring: *17 tries, 85 pts*

NORMAN COATES

COATES, Norman (50)

Born: *Bath, Somerset, 25.9.1892*
Died: *Moulsford-on-Thames, Oxfordshire, 22.12.1953*
Educated: *Haileybury, Cambridge University, Edinburgh University*
Clubs: *Bath, Cambridge University, Wallingford, Leicester*
Tigers debut: *8.2.1919 v Gloucester, won 15-0*
Last game: *16.4.1927 at Bristol, lost 6-26*

'Sam' Coates arrived as a fully-fledged centre, having spent four seasons with Bath (one as captain) before the First World War, playing alongside his brother, Vincent, who was capped on England's wing. During the war, he was a dispatch rider with the Royal Engineers and when hostilities ended he established a motor business in Leicester's Market Street.

A fine distributor of the ball and a jovial presence on tour, Coates played both centre and in the pack for Leicester. He played for Leicestershire and for the Barbarians (against Leicester) in 1923 and, after retiring, ran the line for many seasons. He managed Leicester Speedway for three years and founded a New Walk pub before moving to run an hotel in Wallingford-on-Thames.

During the Second World War he served with the RASC and was commanding officer of a corps covering the south of France. He returned to Wallingford after the war, then ran an hotel in Bath before moving, in 1951, to manage the George, the old coaching hotel in Hinckley.

Appearances: *203 (W136, D9, L58)*
Scoring: *62 tries, 4 conv, 194 pts*

COCKERILL, Richard (180)

Born: *Rugby, Warwickshire, 16.12.1970*
Educated: *Harris C of E (Rugby)*
Clubs: *Newbold-upon-Avon, Coventry, Leicester, Montferrand (France)*
Tigers debut: *1.9.1992 at Sheffield, won 27-7*
Last game: *27.11.2004 v Saracens, won 21-9* ●
Caps: *England (27) 1997-99*

The central member of Leicester's famed ABC club (a reference to the amateur era when Tigers front row was identified by the letters A, B and C), Richard Cockerill earned a reputation as an aggressive hooker who would give best to no-one. During his international career, he was remembered for eyeballing Norm Hewitt, his opposite number, as New Zealand ended their haka before playing England at Old Trafford in 1997.

He arrived at Leicester as an antiques restorer from Rugby, having played for Warwickshire Schools and England under-21s. He swiftly formed a close alliance with Graham Rowntree and Darren Garforth, the two props who made up the ABC club, because of the frequency of their appearances and the sustained quality of their play (though they never started together for England, coming together only against Fiji in 1999).

He was a regular during the internationals of 1998 and 1999, when he was a member of England's World Cup squad. His consistency carried him to cup finals for Tigers in 1993 and 1997 and he started the Heineken Cup final against Brive in 1997. He won four league titles and two European Cups before leaving the club in 2002 to play for Montferrand, for whom he appeared in the European Challenge Cup final of 2004 against Harlequins.

He returned to Leicester that year and became the club's forwards coach in 2005 (having been assistant coach, while still a player, to the English National Divisions XV that played Australia at Welford Road in 2001). He was acting head coach before the arrival in 2007 of Marcelo Loffreda and after the departure in 2009 of Heyneke Meyer; he was confirmed as head coach that same year, when Leicester reached both the Heineken Cup final and the Premiership final. Under his direction, Leicester played in five successive domestic finals, winning three of them.

Appearances: *212 starts + 50 reps (W204, D5, L53)*
Scoring: *14 tries, 70 pts*

ERNIE COLEMAN

RICHARD COCKERILL

COLEMAN, Edgar George (61)

Born: *Leicester, regd Q4 1899*
Died: *Evington, Leicester, 30.7.1983*
Clubs: *Westleigh, Leicester, Nuneaton*
Tigers debut: *27.10.1921 at Cambridge University, won 13-11*
Last game: *11.3.1933 v Northampton, lost 3-21*

'Ernie' Coleman played mostly in the front row and was regarded as unfortunate not to win representative honours. He played for Warwickshire and his playing days at Welford Road were split by a three-year period he spent with Nuneaton (1922-25) for whom he made 87 appearances and scored 18 tries.

He worked for the Standard Engineering Company on Evington Valley Road until the outbreak of the Second World War, and thereafter as chief instructor at the Government Training Centre in Humberstone Lane.

Appearances: *260 (W143, D20, L97)*
Scoring: *18 tries, 1 conv, 56 pts*

COLEMAN, James George Sherrard (3)

Born: *Leicester, December quarter 1860*
Died: *Leicester, 29.10.1908*
Club: *Leicester*
Tigers debut: *30.10.1880 v Leicester Victoria, won 10-0*
Last game: *2.1.1892 at Gloucester, lost 0-6*

Sherrard 'Coley' Coleman was a three-quarter who also played in the pack and captained Leicester between 1882-85. He was the leading try-scorer in 1886/87 and appeared in Leicester's first Midland Counties Cup final, the 1894 defeat by Coventry.

He worked as a clerk in the hosiery trade for Riley and Co and was also a keen cricketer, playing as a wicketkeeper for Leicester Ivanhoe and Leicestershire (before they attained first-class status). He played football for Leicester Fosse between 1884-88 and Mill House in 1888/89.

Appearances: *141 (W64, D19, L58)*
Scoring: *31 tries, 7 drops, 52 pts*

SHERRARD COLEMAN

GUS COLLINGTON

COLLINGTON, Andrew Peter (153)

Born: *Leicester, 2.2.1956*
Educated: *Wyggeston GS*
Clubs: *Leicester, Westleigh, Old Bosworthians, Leicester Thursday*
Tigers debut: *19.2.1975 v Moseley, lost 9-27*
Last game: *31.3.1986 at Pontypool, lost 6-39*

Known as Angus at school because his mother was from Aberdeen, 'Gus' Collington was one of the earliest graduates of the Leicester youth team. An industrious No 8, he joined Leicester from school having played for the county at all age levels. He was a replacement for England colts which became something of a theme throughout his career, much of which was played in the shadow of Garry Adey.

He appeared in the closing stages of the 1981 John Player Cup final against Gosforth, having been among the unused replacements in the three previous finals. Collington, a demolition contractor, possessed great physical strength and went on to run his own builders supply company.

A keen cricketer and squash player, he played regularly for the Droglites (the Old Tigers team) in charity matches and became chairman/secretary of the LFC Past Players Association after the death of Graham Willars.

Appearances: *112 starts + 18 reps (W91, D2, L37)*
Scoring: *22 tries, 88 pts*

COOKE, Albert Edward (9)

Born: *Painswick, Gloucestershire, regd Q2 1869*
Died: *Montreal, Canada, 22.2.1913*
Educated: *Painswick GS (Gloucestershire)*
Clubs: *Leicester Nelson, Leicester Swifts, Leicester*
Tigers debut: *28.9.1889 at Stratford-on-Avon, lost 0-7*
Last game: *11.9.1897 v Nuneaton, won 22-8*

TED COOKE

Though brought up in Gloucestershire, Ted Cooke played all his senior rugby in Leicester as a three-quarter and a forward. He helped Leicester Swifts win the Leicestershire Senior Cup in 1890/91 as a back and made his Leicester debut at half-back; his second match was on the wing and thereafter he played in the pack.

He played for the Midland Counties for four seasons and was described as "a sterling forward who does a lot of work in the scrummage and is very quick on the ball when it comes out." Rupert, his brother, also played for Tigers but in 1904 Cooke, a traveller in the flour trade, emigrated to Canada.

Appearances: *158 (W94, D18, L46)*
Scoring: *31 tries, 18 conv, 6 pens, 3 marks, 163 pts*

CORRY, Martin Edward (184)

Born: *Birmingham, 12.10.1973*
Educated: *Tunbridge Wells GS, Newcastle Polytechnic (later Northumbria University)*
Clubs: *Newcastle Gosforth, Bristol, Leicester*
Tigers debut: *30.8.1997 v Gloucester, won 33-16* ●
Last game: *27.3.2009 at Newcastle Falcons, lost 10-14* ●
Caps: *England (64) 1997-2007, British & Irish Lions (7) 2001-05*

It was typical of Martin Corry's career that he produced his most outstanding form as a replacement - on the Lions tour to Australia in 2001. So much of his representative career was spent in the shadow of others, notably the apparently immoveable back-row England trio of Lawrence Dallaglio, Richard Hill and Neil Back. Yet he captained his country 17 times and left a firm imprint on domestic rugby with the physicality of his rugby and the drive he produced from No 8.

Corry started playing in the Tunbridge Wells mini section and, while at Northumbria University, led the students to a winning UAU final and played for Newcastle Gosforth. He represented England's under-18 and student teams and toured Australia and Fiji with England A before joining Bristol, whom he led during the 1996/97 season, winning his first cap on the 1997 England tour to Argentina.

In the same year he joined Leicester as a mobile, ball-handling No 8 also happy to play blind-side flanker and, at need, lock. He swiftly became a regular selection and a key member of the squad that won four successive Premiership titles between 1999-2002, and two Heineken Cup finals. Picked to tour Canada with England in 2001, he was summoned to join the Lions in Australia after a tour-ending injury to Simon Taylor and played so well that he appeared in all three internationals.

He was an equally significant ingredient in the 2005 Lions tour to New Zealand, taking over the captaincy in the first test when Brian O'Driscoll was injured in the opening minutes of the game. Earlier in the year he had succeeded Jason Robinson as England captain, against Italy, and during the 2007 World Cup led England in three games while Phil Vickery served a period of suspension. It was Corry's most successful World Cup; he had played a bit part in the 1999 and 2003 tournaments (when he was named in the 22-man squad for five of the seven matches but appeared only once) but started all except one of England's seven games in 2007, including the final.

He was the Zurich Premiership and Professional Rugby Players' Association player of the season in 2005, having been awarded the MBE the previous year. He retired from international rugby after the 2007 World Cup but played one further season for Leicester. He has since established himself as a motivational and after-dinner speaker, and as a media analyst.

Appearances: *269 starts + 21 reps (W200, D12, L78)*
Scoring: *27 tries, 135 pts*

MARTIN CORRY

COWLING, Robin James (143)

Born: *Ipswich, Suffolk, 24.3.1944*
Educated: *Sidcot (Weston-super-Mare), Royal Agricultural College (Cirencester)*
Clubs: *Gloucester, Leicester*
Tigers debut: *7.9.1974 v Bedford, won 19-12*
Last game: *2.5.1981 v Gosforth (at Twickenham), won 22-15* ●
Caps: *England (8) 1977-79*

ROBIN COWLING

Taken to Gloucestershire as a baby to escape wartime bombing, Robin Cowling found himself in something of an ancestral home. His paternal grandfather had been a Gloucester player and, on his mother's side, an uncle, John G A'Bear, had captained Gloucester for five seasons and toured Argentina with a British side in 1936.

Cowling farmed both at home and, for two years, in Scandinavia and Germany before qualifying at the Royal Agricultural College, Cirencester. He joined Gloucester on the advice of John Pullin, another farmer who played in the front row at the highest level, as a hooker but moved to loose-head prop.

He played for Gloucestershire in five consecutive county finals, twice on the winning side, and for Gloucester in the inaugural national knockout competition final against Moseley in 1972. He appeared for the Western Counties against the 1972/73 New Zealanders before moving to Market Harborough and joining Leicester.

Though on the small side, Cowling was a fine technician and won the first of his caps against Scotland in 1977. He put in an heroic display against France a year later, when he remained on the field with a dislocated shoulder because England had already used their permitted replacements, the injury ending his season.

He played in Leicester's four successive John Player Cup finals between 1978-81, winning three of them. After retiring, his job as a farm manager took him first to Ipswich then to Cornwall where he coached Hayle in his spare time. He became manager of the RFU's south-west England academy, based in Truro, after joining the academy as assistant coach in 2002 and subsequently joined Exeter Chiefs as a member of their management team.

Appearances: *184 (W127, D3, L54)*
Scoring: *8 tries, 32 pts*

*CRANE, Jordan Stephen (201)

Born: *Bromsgrove, Worcestershire, 3.6.1986*
Educated: *South Bromsgrove HS, Colston's*
Clubs: *Leeds Tykes, Leicester*
Tigers debut: *16.9.2006 v Gloucester, drew 27-27 ●*
Caps: *England (3) 2008-09*

As a teenager, Jordan Crane played in goal for West Bromwich Albion youth sides, acquiring football skills that subsequently served him well in rugby. He switched to rugby at 14 and led England under-18 and under-21 sides while a member of the successful Leeds Tykes academy.

A powerful ball carrier from No 8, Crane joined Leicester for the 2006/07 season in which they reached the finals of both domestic competitions and the Heineken Cup. He played for England Saxons in 2007 and 2008, leading them to victory in the Churchill Cup in 2008, and won his first senior cap against South Africa in November that year. His only England start came against Australia a year later but he remained a regular in the Saxons squad, leading them to another Churchill Cup win in 2011.

In the nerve-tingling 2009 Heineken Cup semi-final against Cardiff Blues which went to a penalty shoot-out, Crane kicked the goal that won Leicester a place in the final. He scored a vital try in Leicester's Premiership final win over London Irish in 2009 and was man of the match in the 2010 final, against Saracens, after a season ruined by an ankle injury. A knee injury kept him out of the entire 2011/12 season but he added another Premiership winners' medal to his collection in 2013, against Northampton.

Appearances: *148 starts + 31 reps (W10, L58)*
Scoring: *28 tries, 140 pts*

JORDAN CRANE

TOM CROFT

*CROFT, Thomas Richard (206)

Born: *Basingstoke, Hampshire, 7.11.1985*
Educated: *Park House, Oakham*
Club: *Leicester*
Tigers debut: *12.11.2005 v Gloucester, won 25-20 ●*
Caps: *England (38) 2008-13, British & Irish Lions (5) 2009-13*

A rangy back-row forward with an astonishing turn of pace, Tom Croft made his Leicester debut as a lock a week after his twentieth birthday. He played in the same Oakham School team as his club colleague, Matt Smith, and the England cricketer, Stuart Broad, but announced his appearance on a wider stage when he played in the 2007 EDF Energy Cup final against the Ospreys then scored a wonderful long-range try for England Saxons against the New Zealand Maori, also at Twickenham, the same year.

He established himself in Leicester's team in 2007/08 and made his England debut against France as a replacement, holding the place for the rest of the 2008 six nations. He played as a lock in the 2009 Heineken Cup and Premiership finals and was called into the Lions party to tour South Africa after the suspension of the Ireland flanker, Alan Quinlan.

He fitted admirably into the tactical approach of the Lions, scored a try on his first appearance against the Golden Lions and was a member of the starting XV for the first two internationals. He scored two tries in the first-test defeat and also appeared off the bench for the third international which the Lions won. He toured again with the Lions to Australia in 2013, starting the first test and appearing as a replacement in the second.

Injuries disrupted various seasons, including 2013/14 which was almost completely written off by knee ligament damage, but he toured Australia with England in 2010 and was a member of the 2011 World Cup squad. Croft played in four Premiership finals before missing the 2012 final (against Harlequins) with a neck injury; he played in the 2013 final against Northampton but, needing to complete his rehabilitation, did not tour with England to New Zealand in 2014.

Appearances: *108 starts + 21 reps (W89, D5, L35)*
Scoring: *26 tries, 130 pts*

CROSS, Charles Woodrow (51)

CHARLIE CROSS

Born: *Norwich, Norfolk, 24.11.1886*
Died: *Leicester, 23.4.1957*
Clubs: *Stoneygate, Leicester*
Tigers debut: *9.4.1910 v London Welsh, won 11-3 (1T, 3 pts)*
Last game: *26.12.1923 v Birkenhead Park, won 17-3*

Charlie Cross made a name for himself when, while travelling to play Birkenhead Park in April 1921, a group of players came across a runaway horse and cart near Eastham Ferry. Cross jumped out of his car and, after a short sprint, overtook the runaway and pulled the horse up before much damage was done.

A jovial forward, Cross scored tries in his first two Leicester matches and in his 100th, against Nuneaton in 1922. He was president of Leicester from 1952 until his death and the first president of the Tigers' Supporters Club. He was also president of Leicester Thursday, a vice-president of South Leicester and Oadby, and after his death Stoneygate inaugurated the Charlie W Cross Memorial Trophy, to go to the winner of the annual referees and club secretaries match.

Appearances: *131 (W98, D5, L28)*
Scoring: *19 tries, 57 pts*

CULLEN, George Henry (89)

Born: *Newark, Nottinghamshire, 28.2.1928*
Educated: *Magnus GS (Newark), Loughborough Colleges*
Clubs: *Newark, Nottingham, Loughborough Colleges, Leicester, Bedford*
Tigers debut: *26.12.1949 v Birkenhead Park, lost 0-5*
Last game: *23.4.1957 at Exeter, lost 10-14*

George Cullen's ability as a fly-half was highly regarded by his colleagues and earned him an England trial in 1950. A teacher in Windsor before moving to Bedford Modern, where he taught PE and English until his retirement, Cullen initially played centre and made a couple of appearances for Nottingham in 1945/46.

He was Leicester's leading try scorer in four successive seasons, 1949-53, and again in 1954/55 and 1955/56. He played for Notts, Lincs and Derbys and on the wing for the Midland Counties against New Zealand in 1953. After leaving Leicester he played a season for Bedford. He was appointed to the RFU's English Schools committee and chaired the East Midlands coaching committee.

Appearances: *180 (W100, D6, L74)*
Scoring: *66 tries, 77 conv, 57 pens, 9 drops, 550 pts*

GEORGE CULLEN

LES CUSWORTH

CUSWORTH, Leslie (152)

Born: *Normanton, Yorkshire, 3.7.1954*
Educated: *Normanton GS, West Midlands Teacher Training College (Walsall), Birmingham University*
Clubs: *Wakefield, Moseley, Leicester*
Tigers debut: *28.10.1978 at Swansea, lost 12-21 (1DG, 3 pts)*
Last game: *28.4.1990 at Bath, lost 15-26* ●
Caps: *England (12) 1979-88*

One of the most talented fly-halves of his era, Les Cusworth's forte was attacking rugby, which regularly put him at odds with England selectors of a safety-first nature. His caps were won over a nine-year period, indicative of a failure to trust his instinctive play which was seen to wonderful effect for Leicester and on the international sevens stage.

The son of a miner, Cusworth was influenced at school by Alan Jubb, a former Harlequin and sevens enthusiast. He played for England colts, British Colleges and the UAU and senior county rugby for Yorkshire and the North Midlands. In 1974/75 he established a world record while at Wakefield of 25 dropped goals in a season (surpassing the 22 kicked by Keith James for Newport three years earlier).

He toured Romania with England B in 1978 and won his first cap a year later, against New Zealand just after the All Blacks had been beaten by a North XV with a former Leicester player, Alan Old, at fly-half and playing in a different style. He had to wait three years for his second cap and only once, in 1983/84, played a complete international season.

He was a member (with two other Tigers, Peter Wheeler and Clive Woodward) of the Barbarians team that became the first northern-hemisphere winners of the Hong Kong sevens in 1981 and was player of the tournament in 1984. Nine years later he coached England to success in the inaugural World Cup sevens at Murrayfield.

He played in Leicester's three successive John Player Cup wins in 1979-81 and in the losing finals of 1983 and 1989 and he still holds the Leicester record of four dropped goals in a match, in the Pilkington Cup tie at Liverpool St Helens in 1989. He was a member of the squad that won the inaugural league title in 1988, the year in which he was the *Leicester Mercury's* sports personality, and made 364 starts as Leicester's fly-half.

A schoolmaster who became a sales director for the insurance company, P and G Bland, Cusworth moved naturally towards coaching, first with England A and then, from 1994-97, with England including the grand-slam season of 1995. In 1997 he became director of rugby at Worcester then, in April 2002, was named managing director of Rugby School's business development company.

Cusworth acquired an attachment to Argentinian rugby, organising the first international coaching seminar in Mar del Plata, and he eventually emigrated to Buenos Aires. He helped coach the Pumas in the 2003 and 2007 world cups and took on a development role in that country's domestic rugby.

Appearances: *365 (W278, D4, L83)*
Scoring: *66 tries, 100 conv, 65 pens, 96 drops, 947 pts*

HAROLD DAY

D

DAY, Harold Lindsay Vernon (53)

Born: *Darjeeling, West Bengal, India, 12.8.1898*
Died: *Hadley Wood, Hertfordshire, 15.6.1972*
Educated: *Bedford Modern*
Club: *Leicester*
Tigers debut: *11.1.1919 v New Zealand Services, lost 0-19*
Last game: *26.1.1929 at Richmond, lost 3-12*
Caps: *England (4) 1920-26*

Once characterised as one of the slowest wings ever to play for England, Harold Day's reputation rested solidly on his goal-kicking and his shrewd reading of play. He was Leicester's leading points scorer for 55 years, until his total of 1,151 was overtaken by Dusty Hare.

During the First World War he served as a lieutenant in the Royal Artillery and was severely wounded during fighting in France. When the war ended he was stationed in the Midlands and joined Leicester. When he resigned his commission, he joined the teaching staff at Felsted School and, while there, caused the result of a county championship match to be declared void.

Day captained the Leicestershire side (all of them from Tigers) that won the championship in 1925 but, the following season, played for the county against North Midlands at Moseley. Leicestershire won 6-3 but Day was found ineligible to play, being neither resident in, nor employed in, Leicestershire. The game was replayed and North Midlands won 6-3.

He captained Leicester between 1924-28 and became the first Tiger to pass 1,000 points in his playing career on 26 March 1927, against Old Merchant Taylors. Day was the club's leading points scorer in seven successive seasons between 1921-28 and the leading try scorer in 1923/24 and 1924/25.

He represented the Army in 1920, 1922 and 1923, captaining the side once. He won his first England cap after only six senior games in the first international to be played after the war. He replaced Wilfred Lowry after the team photograph for the 1920 game against Wales had been taken with Lowry in it, the selectors deciding the conditions would better suit Day and he scored England's try and conversion in a 19-5 defeat at Swansea.

He scored another try against Wales two years later and his kicking earned England an 11-11 draw with France that same season. Playing for Leicester against Cambridge University in 1924, Day switched to full-back and ran in a try from his own 22; it was reported as "somewhat unique when a full-back scores a try."

He played cricket for Bedfordshire and then Hampshire, scoring 1,000 runs in his first season. Between 1922-31 he played 78 first-class games. He also became a leading rugby referee, handling the international between Scotland and Wales at Murrayfield in 1934.

He became the rugby correspondent of *The Sunday Chronicle* and, in 1952, published a coaching book titled *Rugby Union Football.* In 1968 *The Cricketer* magazine erroneously carried his obituary, Day hearing about it only when a friend called his wife. "She told him I certainly wasn't dead although I was on the compost heap," Day, who had been working in his garden, said.

Appearances: *212 (W141, D11, L60)*
Scoring: *108 tries, 281 conv, 81 pens, 4 drops, 2 marks, 1,151 pts*

*DEACON, Louis Paul (194)

Born: *Leicester, 7.10.1980*
Educated: *Parkland (South Wigston), Ratcliffe College*
Clubs: *Wigston, Syston, Leicester*
Tigers debut: *12.8.2000 at Cardiff (replacement), lost 17-29* ●
Caps: *England (29) 2005-11*

Louis Deacon, the older (with Brett) of two brothers to have played for Leicester, played local club rugby with Wigston and Syston before joining the Tigers academy in 1997. He played for Leicestershire, Midlands and England at under-16, under-18 and under-21 levels and made his Tigers debut in 2000, learning from such luminaries as Martin Johnson and Ben Kay.

Six years later, against Bourgoin, he chalked up his 150th appearance for the club, indicative of fitness as well as consistency. He played for England A in the Churchill Cups of 2004 (when he was the club's players' player of the year) and 2005, making his senior international debut against Samoa in 2005. Switched from his natural position of lock to the back row the following season, he reclaimed an England place on tour in Australia in 2006 and was a regular in the second row in the 2007 six nations.

Overlooked for that year's World Cup, Deacon started the 2007/08 season as club captain and ended players' player of the season again. He returned to England duty against Argentina in the summer of 2009 and though he missed the 2010 tour to Australia, was a regular presence up to and including the 2011 World Cup.

Deacon was in the squad for all three finals of 2007 in which Leicester played, as well as playing in the 2008 EDF Energy Cup final and appearing in the match squad for both the Premiership and Heineken Cup finals of 2009. Outstanding in the 2010 Premiership final against Saracens, he remains a valued squad member.

Appearances: *243 starts + 31 reps (W191, D13, L70)*
Scoring: *9 tries, 45 pts*

LOUIS DEACON

DODGE, Paul William (141)

Born: *Leicester, 26.2.1958*
Educated: *Roundhill (Syston), Wreake Valley Upper*
Club: *Leicester*
Tigers debut: *6.9.1975 at Bedford, lost 12-24*
Last game: *3.4.1993 at Richmond (replacement), won 29-15*
Caps: *England (32) 1978-85, British Isles (2) 1980*

PAUL DODGE

One of the finest centres to play for Leicester, Paul Dodge's excellence was evident early in his career. He made his debut in 1975 and, by Christmas, had achieved his player's tie (for 20 games) when no more than 17 years and 305 days old. By then he had already appeared for Midland Counties (East) against the touring Australians and he completed 100 games for the club before his 21st birthday.

At 6ft 2in and over 14st, Dodge was powerfully built for his era and possessed good hands and a raking left boot; he was also a more than capable goalkicker. He developed at Roundhill School under the guidance of David Lyons, the former Leicester player who was so influential in producing the club's first youth team in 1972. He played for Leicestershire under-15s and in the county colts side that won the Midlands championship.

Dodge possessed the physical maturity to survive a difficult first season in senior rugby, winning an England colts cap in 1976. Later that year he played for the Midlands and North against Argentina and toured Canada with England's under-23 side in 1977. His first senior cap came in 1978, against Wales, and he toured the Far East with England in 1979, the year in which he also struck up a complementary partnership with Clive Woodward at club level.

He played in the latter half of England's grand slam in 1980 (with Woodward) and joined the Lions tour of South Africa that summer as a replacement, quickly winning a place in the last two internationals. He remained a regular in England's midfield before breaking a leg in a club match at Blackheath in 1983. After recovering fitness he was picked to tour South Africa in 1984 but returned home early with injury.

He was appointed England captain for the 1985 five nations and led the side that toured New Zealand in the summer. He ended his international career with 32 caps, then a record for a centre, but continued to be an influential figure in Leicester's midfield for another eight years, becoming only the fifth player to pass 400 appearances for the club against Pontypridd in 1989.

Dodge played in six John Player and Pilkington cup finals, as captain in 1989, and he was captain of the club when Leicester won the inaugural Courage League in 1988. After retiring, he coached Leicester's under-21 squad then went on to form a successful coaching partnership with Ian Smith, helping Leicester to the 1993 Pilkington Cup (and two other finals) and the 1994/95 league title.

He worked in the family bookbinding business in Leicester and his two sons, Alex and Oliver, both represented Tigers. He was elected club president in 2013.

Appearances: *434 starts + 3 reps (W316, D7, L114)*
Scoring: *93 tries, 33 conv, 40 pens, 3 drops, 567 pts*

DUGGAN, Michael John (135)

Born: *Dublin, Ireland, 5.6.1948*
Educated: *Oakham, Loughborough Colleges*
Clubs: *Oakham Town, Loughborough Colleges, Leicester*
Tigers debut: *3.1.1970 at Bath, lost 9-13*
Last game: *16.8.1980 at Lautoka (Fiji), won 12-6*

A fast and gymnastic wing, John Duggan spent his early years travelling the world since his father was serving in the RAF. The family settled in Oakham, from where he went to Loughborough to study PE and biology and qualified as a teacher.

He possessed both strength and elusive running, with outstanding balance in touchline dashes, and became one of the club's great crowd-pleasers. He played for Leicestershire and Midland Counties (East) against Fiji and New Zealand, and for the Midlands against the All Blacks.

He toured with the Irish Wolfhounds in 1975 and turned down a trial for England on the grounds that he was Irish qualified. But Ireland, at the time, selected from their own provincial sides and Duggan declined an opportunity to play for Dublin Wanderers.

He played more matches on the wing than any other Leicester player and became only the fourth to score 150 tries for the club against Cambridge University in 1979. He was the club's leading try scorer in three seasons (scoring the last three-point try and the first four-point try for Leicester in 1971), and ended with 158, third in the all-time list.

He lectured at Southfields College, specialising in fitness and exercise, and was secretary of the Leicestershire Schools Gymnastic Association, producing international competitors from his school squad. He was Leicester's fitness and conditioning coach between 1997-2004 then joined the Lancaster School staff and, in 2011, received an Aviva/*Daily Telegraph* award for his contribution to school sport, working with young disabled men and women.

Appearances: *302 (W193, D13, L96)*
Scoring: *158 tries, 608 pts*

E

EDMISTON, James Henry Fownes (69=)

Born: *Crosby, Liverpool, 6.6.1905*
Died: *West Wittering, Sussex, 26.8.1962*
Educated: *Haileybury, Brasenose College (Oxford)*
Clubs: *Blackheath, Oxford University (Blues 1926-27), Leicester, Birkenhead Park*
Tigers debut: *20.3.1926 v Old Blues, won 21-5*
Last game: *13.10.1934 at Bridgwater & Albion, drew 0-0*

HARRY EDMISTON

Harry Edmiston, a back-row forward who also played lock and, occasionally, centre, won Blues while at Oxford in 1926 and 1927. John, his younger brother and a scrum-half, made the odd appearance for Tigers while Edmiston also represented Kent and London against New Zealand in 1935/36. He was the director of Grosvenor and Co, a jointing and packaging company.

Appearances: *112 (W67, D4, L41)*
Scoring: *9 tries, 8 conv, 5 pens, 1 drop, 62 pts*

EDWARDS, Peter George (114)

Born: *Birmingham, 15.7.1937*
Educated: *Saltley GS, Sheffield University*
Clubs: *London Welsh, Leicester, Christchurch FC (New Zealand)*
Tigers debut: *16.9.1961 v Plymouth Albion, lost 9-11*
Last game: *20.4.1968 at Llanelli, lost 5-14*

Peter Edwards joined Leicester when his work in chemical engineering brought him to the midlands having previously played for London Welsh, effectively changing places with hooker Arthur Jones who was going in the other direction. Initially the understudy to Mick Walker, Edwards took over in November 1963 when Walker was injured and did not miss a game for the next 21 months (70 games).

Following his Tigers career work commitments took him to New Zealand, where he remained for four years. He is now retired and living in Wales.

Appearances: *145 (W80, D7, L58)*
Scoring: *2 tries, 6 pts*

ELDERS, John (97)

Born: *Middlesbrough, Yorkshire, 18.12.1930*
Educated: *Acklam Hall GS (Middlesbrough), Loughborough Colleges*
Clubs: *Loughborough Colleges, Leicester, Northern*
Tigers debut: *5.9.1953 v Bedford, won 12-6*
Last game: *27.12.1958 v Birkenhead Park, drew 8-8 (1T, 3 pts)*

A talented centre who came close to England honours, John Elders went on to a distinguished coaching career. A mathematics and PE teacher at South Wigston and Alderman Newton's schools, he played for Leicestershire and Northumberland; he appeared for the Midlands against New Zealand in 1953/54 and for the North-East Counties against Australia four years later.

He played in an England trial at Bristol in 1956 and captained Leicester between 1955-57. He moved to teach at RGS Newcastle and became coach to Northumberland, then to England between 1972-74, a period in which England recorded away victories over both South Africa and New Zealand. He became a selector and took over the coaching of England schools from Mike Davis in 1979.

In 1981 Elders emigrated to Australia and became sports master at Toowoomba's Downlands College in Queensland where his charges included Tim Horan, subsequently the leading Australia centre. He returned to England in 1990 and became director of rugby to Northern before returning to teaching.

Appearances: *144 (W75, D13, L56)*
Scoring: *38 tries, 3 pens, 1 drop, 126 pts*

ELLIOTT, John James (127)

Born: *Nottingham, 10.6.1943*
Educated: *High Pavement GS (Nottingham), Loughborough Colleges*
Clubs: *Old Paviors, Loughborough Colleges, Nottingham, Edinburgh Wanderers, Leicester*
Tigers debut: *18.2.1967 v Wasps, won 6-3*
Last game: *19.12.1970 at Bristol, lost 0-10*

One of several Leicester hookers to go close to international honours, John Elliott became a member of the England management team that turned the national side's fortunes round in the late 1980s. Alongside Geoff Cooke and Roger Uttley, he became a selector in 1987 and then assistant team manager as England reached the 1991 World Cup final.

Elliott played for Notts, Lincs and Derbys under-19 team and in the senior county championship. He appeared for the North of England and for the Midlands and in several England trials, being a travelling reserve for England in 1976. He played 272 games for Nottingham in two spells, scoring 36 tries for the club.

He managed England's under-21 side for seven years and remained in the senior team management until the 1995 World Cup. He became head of marketing for the East Midlands Electricity Board until joining the Rugby Football Union full-time in 1995 as national player development manager. He had a second stint managing the under-21s, four years as England sevens manager and in 2004 became national academy development and under-19 manager.

Appearances: *126 (W81, D8, L37)*
Scoring: *20 tries, 60 pts*

ELLIS, Harry Alistair (196)

Born: *Wigston, Leicestershire, 17.5.1982*
Educated: *Leicester GS, De Montfort University*
Clubs: *South Leicester, Wigston, Leicester*
Tigers debut: *25.8.2001 at Toulouse, lost 15-30* ●
Last game: *6.2.2010 at Northampton, lost 11-23* ●
Caps: *England (27) 2004-09, British & Irish Lions (1) 2009*

The Ellis family is imbued with Leicester colours. Harry's father, Bob, played in the club's back row, older brothers Mark and Robert also wore the club shirt, and Harry Ellis joined the youth team in 1997 after spells in local rugby with South Leicester (where he started as a seven-year-old) and Wigston.

His senior debut at scrum-half came in an Orange Cup clash with Toulouse in 2001 and, at the end of that season, he made a significant contribution with a try in the Heineken Cup semi-final win over Llanelli and appeared off the bench in the final against Munster. He was the club's young player of the year for 2001/02 and, having played for England teams from under-16 to under-21 and England A levels, he toured to Australia and New Zealand with the seniors in 2004 and won his first cap against South Africa in November that year.

He and the experienced Matt Dawson jousted for the shirt for the next two years and he was a regular in the 2007 six nations but damaged knee ligaments in a club game against Bristol ruled him out of Premiership and Heineken Cup finals that year, as well as the 2007 World Cup. Ultimately the injury brought about his premature retirement but he battled back to recover an international place in 2008, and a starting place in the 2009 six nations. That earned him a tour to South Africa with the Lions, when he came off the bench during the third international.

But his knee caused so many problems that he retired in 2010 and returned to his studies at Loughborough University while also working his way up through the coaching ranks. He is now teaching at Leicester Grammar School.

Appearances: *131 starts + 42 reps (W116, D8, L49)*
Scoring: *29 tries, 145 pts*

BARRY EVANS

EVANS, Barry John (157)

Born: *Hinckley, Leicestershire, 10.10.1962*
Educated: *John Cleveland College (Hinckley), Derby Lonsdale Teacher Training College*
Clubs: *Hinckley, Leicester, Coventry, Worcester, Market Bosworth*
Tigers debut: *31.10.1981 at Saracens, won 34-14 (1T, 4 pts)*
Last game: *2.9.1995 v Northampton, won 23-17*
Caps: *England (2) 1988*

Possessed of tremendous pace and a powerful swerve, Barry Evans played as a centre in Leicestershire age-group sides and for England under-16s before turning to the wing at under-19 level. He toured with England Schools to Portugal, with England Students to Japan and the under-23s to Spain.

He represented the Midlands at all levels and played in four England B games before winning his caps on tour with England in Australia and Fiji in 1988, after being added to the squad at the eleventh hour. On that tour he scored tries in three games against regional opposition.

He became Leicester's leading post-war try scorer, passing 150 with the first of two tries against Gosforth in 1989 (in one match against the RAF in 1990 he scored five tries). He played in the 1983 John Player Cup final and the 1989 Pilkington Cup final, and was a member of the squad that won the inaugural Courage league title in 1988.

He subsequently joined Coventry and became their club captain. Trained as a teacher of PE and mathematics, Evans became an office systems executive then a global account manager with British Telecom before moving to Dell Computers.

Appearances: *272 starts + 1 rep (W201, D5, L67)*
Scoring: *170 tries, 1 conv, 683 pts*

F

FARNDON, William Ewart (62)

Born: *Market Harborough, Leicestershire, 29.12.1901*
Died: *Bognor Regis, Sussex, 27.4.1982*
Clubs: *London Welsh, Stoneygate, Leicester*
Tigers debut: *18.4.1925 at Birkenhead Park, won 11-5*
Last game: *21.11.1931 at Swansea, lost 0-11*

In his first game at Welford Road, Ewart Farndon was said to have given "a wonderful exhibition of speed and football brains." A wing, he was the club's leading try scorer with thirty in 1929/30 and four times scored a hat-trick, all at home, against Hartlepool Rovers, Bridgwater, the RAF and Percy Park.

He played for Warwickshire but also played cricket and competed in athletics events. A liveryman of the Worshipful

EWART FARNDON

Company of Framework Knitters, Farndon became the managing director of Dorothy Perkins until his retirement in 1967.

Appearances: *183 (W99, D11, L73)*
Scoring: *86 tries, 258 pts*

FLEWITT, Edward Charles Ansell (63)

Born: *Sutton Coldfield, Warwickshire, regd Q4 1907*
Died: *Castle Bromwich, Warwickshire, 12.7.1931*
Educated: *Dunchurch Hall, Brighton College*
Clubs: *Leicester, Moseley*
Tigers debut: *26.12.1925 v Birkenhead Park, won 16-3 (2T, 6 pts)*
Last game: *5.11.1930 at Oxford University, won 16-9*

Ted 'Buller' Flewitt, one of the best wings to play for Leicester between the wars, died aged 23 at Castle Bromwich Aerodrome when his Gypsy Moth crashed shortly after take-off. The aircraft was piloted by Roderick Baker, his companion, and came down near the Chester Road, a main thoroughfare into Birmingham.

Flewitt, a frequent visitor to Leicestershire Aero Club at Desford, had bought the aircraft two years before. He was also an enthusiastic motorist, travelling to away games with Ralph Buckingham while the rest of the team went by train. He represented Warwickshire and played alongside Buckingham in an England trial at Camborne in 1928.

He was Leicester's leading try scorer in 1926/27 and 1928/29 with 22 and 17 tries respectively. Upon his death, Leicester officials described him as "a strong, thrustful player who, on his day, was one of the best wing three-quarters the Tigers have had. His full-hearted dash for the line will not easily be forgotten." Though he had independent means, he represented a Birmingham brewery.

TED FLEWITT

Appearances: *129 (W75, D6, L48)*
Scoring: *73 tries, 1 conv, 221 pts*

+FLOOD, Tobias Gerald Albert Lieven (208)

TOBY FLOOD

Born: *Frimley, Surrey, 8.8.1985*
Educated: *Chantry (Morpeth), King's (Tynemouth), Northumbria University*
Clubs: *Alnwick, Morpeth, Newcastle Falcons, Leicester, Toulouse*
Tigers debut: *7.9.2008 at Gloucester, won 20-8 (1T, 1C, 2P, 13 Pts)* ●
Last game: *16.5.2014 at Northampton, lost 20-21 (2C, 1P)* ●
Caps: *England (60) 2007-13*

Toby Flood comes from an acting family but took a degree in business management at Northumbria and a postgraduate law diploma. He played cricket for Northumberland under-16s and was coached, while at King's, by Jonny Wilkinson whom he subsequently joined at Newcastle Falcons, for whom he made his senior debut in 2005, aged 19.

He won his first England cap less than a year later, having previously played for the under-18s and under-21s. His international debut was against Argentina and, in 2007, he replaced his injured club colleague, Jamie Noon, in the England squad that reached the World Cup final, appearing as a replacement in each of the knockout games.

Flood played inside centre during the 2008 six nations but returned to his favoured fly-half position the following season. At Twickenham in 2010 he scored 25 points against Australia (7pg, 2c), a record for that series, and went into the 2011 World Cup as first-choice fly-half, only to be supplanted by Wilkinson. He remained a member of England's elite squad until his 2014 move to Toulouse was announced; he scored 301 points in his 60 internationals, fourth highest in the all-time England list.

He missed the 2009 Heineken Cup and Premiership finals after sustaining an Achilles tendon injury in the European semi-final against Cardiff Blues. Thereafter he collected three Premiership titles in five seasons and captained Leicester in 2013/14, though once he had decided to join Toulouse, he was replaced for several games by Owen Williams, a delicate situation he handled well.

Flood, an attacking player eager to carry the ball to the line and adept at creating space for his centres, kicked all his side's points (6pg) in the 2011 Premiership final loss to Saracens. He came off the bench during the successful EDF Energy final of 2012 but missed the Premiership final against Harlequins through injury. He led Tigers out in the 2013 final against Northampton but went off with concussion midway through the first half.

Appearances: *107 starts + 12 reps (W84, D8, L27)*
Scoring: *25 tries, 199 conv, 270 pens, 1 drop, 1,336 pts*

BILLY FOREMAN

FOREMAN, William James (11)

Born: *Farnham, Surrey, regd Q3 1869*
Died: *Oadby, Leicester, 15.7.1945*
Clubs: *Woolwich Clarendon, Walthamstow, London Caledonians, Kent Wanderers, Leicester*
Tigers debut: *7.10.1893 v Gloucester, lost 3-8*
Last game: *3.2.1906 at Coventry, lost 3-12*

Billy Foreman scored seven tries as a three-quarter in his first game for Woolwich Clarendon against Roan's School in Greenwich. He moved to half-back and captained London Caledonians before moving to Kent Wanderers, for whom he was playing when Tom Crumbie persuaded him to join Leicester, finding him a job as a mechanic with Gimson and Sons.

In his second season with Tigers he played for Leicestershire against Kent, his former side, which caused some press comment. Standing only 5ft 7in, he was the first Leicester captain to win the Midland Counties Cup since he replaced AO Jones when the latter was taken ill; his pass sent Percy Oscroft over for the try that gave Tigers their 5-3 win in 1898.

He remained in the cup-winning side at fly-half for the next five seasons. "For tricky play around the scrum, Foreman takes some beating," *The Wyvern* said. He was approached several times by Northern Union clubs but preferred to stay at Leicester because of "the good feelings that existed between himself, the committee and the people of the town."

Noted for his fitness and consistency, Foreman became the first player to pass 300 appearances for Leicester in 1902, though he also helped Northampton on three occasions when their fly-half, Billy Patrick, was injured. He became landlord of the Marlborough Head public house in Welford Road.

Before moving to Leicester he had been a member of the Polytechnic Boxing Club. He was a founding member of Glen Gorse Golf Club in Oadby and died on the first hole at the club at the start of a round of golf. His grandson was the Leicester and England scrum-half, Bill Moore.

Appearances: *358 (W243, D23, L92)*
Scoring: *85 tries, 4 conv, 263 pts*

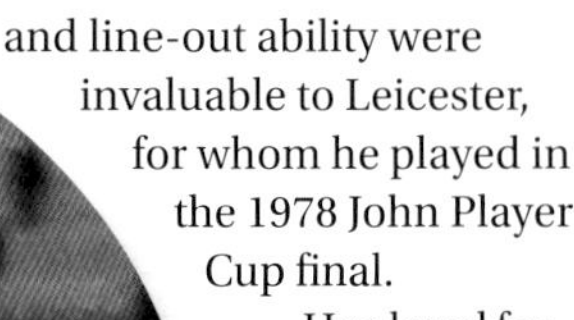
DAVE FORFAR

FORFAR, David John (139)

Born: *Salford, Lancashire, 6.9.1951*
Educated: *Stonehill HS, Longslade College*
Clubs: *Syston, Leicester*
Tigers debut: *13.4.1971 at Manchester, won 17-9*
Last game: *25.11.1981 v Australia, lost 15-18*

The career of Dave Forfar, a flanker who won an England B cap, ended when, during the game against Australia in 1981, his knee was trampled so badly that he could not play again. But during a decade of service, his all-embracing tackling and line-out ability were invaluable to Leicester, for whom he played in the 1978 John Player Cup final.

He played for Leicestershire at under-19 and senior level, for the Midlands and North against Argentina in 1976 and for the Midlands against New Zealand in 1979. He appeared in an England trial in 1977 and played in a B international against France in 1979. He was a salesman then became a partner in an engineering company.

Appearances: *222 starts + 1 rep (W133, D8, L82)*
Scoring: *14 tries, 56 pts*

FOULKES-ARNOLD, Malcolm Victor (158)

Born: *Peterborough, Cambridgeshire, 29.11.1957*
Educated: *Deacon's GS (Peterborough), Leicester Polytechnic*
Clubs: *Peterborough, Harlequins, Leicester, Luctonians*
Tigers debut: *12.9.1979 v Birmingham, won 38-0* ●
Last game: *16.4.1994 at Sale, lost 27-50*

Known as 'Flutter', Malcolm Foulkes-Arnold joined Leicester from Harlequins while a student at the polytechnic. He played for England Students, British Polytechnics and Eastern Counties under-19s, and also played football and hockey for Cambridgeshire.

MALCOLM FOULKES-ARNOLD

A consistent lock, he was a member of the squad that won the inaugural Courage league and appeared in two losing cup finals. He scored 21 tries, some in such diverse places as Zimbabwe, Dubai, Singapore and Denver; after retiring, he helped Dusty Hare with the coaching and management of the Leicester development team and served on the steering committee when Leicester became a limited company.

A chartered architect with his own business, Corporate Architecture Limited, he is treasurer of the Past Players Association team (the Droglites) and is involved with the Wooden Spoon and Lord's Taverners charities.

Appearances: *260 starts + 2 reps (W188, D7, L67)*
Scoring: *21 tries, 84 pts*

FREER, Michael Edmund (100)

Born: *Stoke Albany, near Market Harborough, Leicestershire, 4.2.1935*
Educated: *Welland Park (Market Harborough)*
Clubs: *Kibworth, Leicester*
Tigers debut: *21.1.1956 v Rugby, lost 0-3*
Last game: *11.3.1965 v Loughborough Colleges, lost 11-24*

Mike Freer, one of a group of talented fly-halves at the club in the same period, played for the RAF during his national service with Bomber Command. He became only the eighth player ever to have dropped two goals in a single game for Leicester when he did so against Newport at Rodney Parade in February 1960. His rugby career ended in the game against Loughborough Colleges when he seriously damaged a shoulder. After two years serving as a policeman he went on to run his own fencing contractors business in Caldecote.

Appearances: *203 (W96, D22, L85)*
Scoring: *15 tries, 7 drops, 66 pts*

MIKE FREER

G

GADNEY, Bernard Cecil (71)

Born: *Oxford, 16.7.1909*
Died: *Ipswich, Suffolk, 14.11.2000*
Educated: *Dragon (Oxford), Stowe*
Clubs: *Richmond, Leicester, Headingley*
Tigers debut: *9.11.1929 at Nuneaton, won 4-3*
Last game: *11.4.1939 at Bath, won 28-3 (1T, 3 pts)*
Caps: *England (14) 1932-38*

The outstanding England scrum-half of the 1930s, Bernard Gadney spent much of his international career jousting with Jimmy Giles (Coventry) for the international shirt. A big man for his position - he occasionally played centre - Gadney was noted for his strong running from the scrum and was captain of England when they beat the 1935/36 New Zealanders at Twickenham.

Gadney was appointed to the teaching staff at the Manor House School in Brackley but Leicester secured his services ahead of Northampton. He made an early impression and, in a game against Harlequins, "electrified the crowd, getting away on his own," it was reported. "Three times he was pulled down but each time he got away again and at last, with opponents hanging on to him, he forced his way over the line."

He played for Leicestershire, East Midlands, Oxfordshire and Yorkshire, played for the Barbarians first in 1932 and won his first cap against Ireland that year. He captained England to the triple crown throughout the 1934 season and returned (as captain) in 1935 when England chose a different half-back pairing in every game. His leadership was critical in the 13-0 defeat of New Zealand in 1936 and, later that year, he led the British touring team to Argentina (when the manager was Leicester's Doug Prentice). He played in eight of the ten tour matches.

Both the Hull rugby league clubs made overtures to him but he remained a teacher and became headmaster of Malsis School in Yorkshire until his retirement in 1960. During the Second World War he served in the Royal Naval Volunteer Force. His older brother, Cyril, was an international referee and RFU president in 1962/63.

Appearances: *170 (W104, D13, L53)*
Scoring: *63 tries, 189 pts*

GARFORTH, Darren James (175)

Born: *Coventry, Warwickshire, 9.4.1966*
Educated: *Binley Park (Coventry)*
Clubs: *Coventry Saracens, Nuneaton, Leicester*
Tigers debut: *21.9.1991 at Northampton, lost 17-21*
Last game: *31.5.2003 v Saracens (at Northampton), won 27-20* ●
Caps: *England (25) 1997-2000*

Darren Garforth switched from football to rugby to help out his local club when they were short of numbers and was still playing at the age of 37. He played for Warwickshire at colts and senior level, joining Leicester after making 84 appearances for Nuneaton for whom he scored 21 tries over three seasons.

As tight-head prop, he became the third member of Leicester's ABC club (with Richard Cockerill and Graham Rowntree), with whom he played in 166 games out of an overall tally of 346 Leicester appearances. He was a scaffolder and was famously described as a 'tubular executive' in an international-match programme - and his industry earned him honours for the Midland Division, England's emerging and A sides and, in 1997, a first cap in the final five nations game of that year, against Wales. He held a regular England place up to and including the 1999 World Cup and toured South Africa in 2000.

DARREN GARFORTH

He played in Leicester's league championship side of 1993/94 and subsequently included three Heineken Cup finals and four Pilkington Cup finals in his club career. He was a cornerstone of the side that won four successive Premiership titles between 1999-2002 and twice received Leicester's outstanding service award, in 1999 and 2001. Against Bristol in 2003 he became the first player to record 200 league games in England's top flight and, after leaving Leicester that year, he played a final season with Nuneaton.

He now runs his own business - Garforth Scaffolding.

Appearances: *325 starts + 21 reps (W258, D8, L80)*
Scoring: *19 tries, 90 pts*

GARNER, John William (21)

Born: *Leicester, regd Q2 1869*
Died: *Leicester, 16.5.1927*
Clubs: *Belgrave St. Peter's, Leicester*
Tigers debut: *6.4.1895 v Sale, won 14-0*
Last game: *4.10.1902 v Devonport Albion, won 10-7*

'Josh' Garner, a forward, led Belgrave St Peter's to the final of the Leicestershire Junior Cup in 1891 and, three years later, became the first Belgrave player to win a county cap. He played in 22 Midland Counties Cup ties for Leicester, only once on the losing side, and captained the club in 1901/02. He celebrated his first match as captain with a try against Manchester in 1900. He worked as a shoe clipper in the family business, Garner and Sons.

Appearances: *209 (W140, D15, L54)*
Scoring: *3 tries, 9 conv, 27 pts*

JOSH GARNER

MIKE GAVINS

GAVINS, Michael Neil (108=)

Born: *Leeds, Yorkshire, 14.10.1934*
Educated: *Roundhay, Leeds University, Loughborough Colleges*
Clubs: *Old Roundhegians, Leeds University, Loughborough Colleges, Leicester, Moseley, Middlesbrough*
Tigers debut: *31.1.1957 v Royal Air Force, lost 8-18*
Last game: *28.11.1970 at Moseley, lost 13-16 (2C, 4 pts)*
Caps: *England (1) 1961*

Injuries to two full-backs, Robin Money and Richard Cooper, gave Mike Gavins an unexpected extension to his Tigers career in 1970/71. He came out of retirement at the start of the season, aged 36, and became the club's top points scorer, for the third time, with 115 in 14 games (including a career-best haul of 18 against Harrogate) before retiring once more in November 1970.

It was a reminder of his achievements a decade earlier when he established a post-war club record in 1958/59 and broke it the following season. After captaining Leeds University and British Universities, Gavins represented Leicestershire, Midland Counties and North Midlands. He played for the Midlands against South Africa in 1960/61 and against New Zealand in 1963/64, squeezing in his solitary cap against Wales in 1961.

He was a teacher and became head of economics at Uppingham, as well as coaching the school rugby team. He coached the Midlands against Fiji in 1970 and his son, Dave, played once for Tigers in 1981.

Appearances: *121 (W65, D10, L46)*
Scoring: *5 tries, 107 conv, 119 pens, 2 drops, 592 pts*

GILLINGHAM, Nigel Kenneth (154)

Born: *Guildford, Surrey, 16.1.1953*
Educated: *RGS (Guildford), Loughborough Colleges*
Clubs: *Richmond, Loughborough Colleges, Leicester*
Tigers debut: *2.9.1978 v Bedford, won 37-12* ●
Last game: *23.4.1984 at Pontypool, lost 0-19*

A mobile lock, Nigel Gillingham spent one season with Richmond before going to Loughborough where he captained the students, their achievements including success in the Middlesex sevens in 1976. That same year he played for England under-23 against the touring Japanese.

He played for Midland Counties (East) in the 1975 win over Australia and, after joining the RAF, played for the Combined Services against New Zealand in 1978. He played in the John Player Cup finals of 1980 and 1983. Gillingham became a group captain and head of RAF physical education from 2000-04. For many years he represented the service on the RFU committee and subsequently sat on the union's management board. He was awarded the OBE in 1997.

Appearances: *144 starts + 1 rep (W107, D1, L37)*
Scoring: *12 tries, 48 pts*

NIGEL GILLINGHAM

+GOODE Andrew James (193)

Born: *Coventry, West Midlands, 3.4.1980*
Educated: *King Henry VIII (Coventry), Bromsgrove*
Clubs: *Barkers' Butts, Nuneaton, Coventry, Leicester, Saracens, Brive, Sharks (South Africa), Worcester Warriors, London Wasps*
Tigers debut: *2.10.1998 v Cardiff (replacement), lost 20-35 (1C, 2 pts)*
Last game: *31.5.2008 v London Wasps (at Twickenham), lost 16-26 (2PG, 6 pts)* ●
Caps: *England (17) 2005-09*

ANDY GOODE

Andy Goode was a talented schoolboy cricketer, as well as a rugby player who represented England at under-18, under-21 and A level. However, for several seasons he was the one uncapped player in Leicester's back division, having learned his Premiership trade alongside Pat Howard, the Australian midfield back who subsequently became head coach.

Goode and James Grindal formed a new half-back pairing in 1999, when Leicester's leading lights were at the World Cup. Howard, playing centre, encouraged them to play attacking rugby, Goode backing that up with the accuracy of his goalkicking, which made him one of the leading points scorers in the Premiership.

Goode was the starting fly-half in the 2001 Heineken Cup final, against Stade Français, and in the match squad for the 2002 final, against Munster. He also contributed significantly to the four successive Premiership wins of 1999-2002 though for much of that period, Tim Stimpson was first-choice kicker. He spent the 2002/03 season at Saracens but returned to Leicester to chalk up a litter of records.

He was Leicester's player of the season in 2004/05, when he scored 382 points, and recorded a club league record of 11 conversions in the 83-10 win over Newcastle Falcons. He was capped by England from the bench against Italy and Scotland in 2005. Seven of his first nine international appearances were as a replacement but, after a two-year hiatus, he appeared in all the 2009 six nations matches and scored 107 points during his international career.

He signed for Brive in 2008, having scored 1,799 points for Tigers and was the second highest points scorer in France's Top 14 that season with 235. He went on loan to Natal Sharks in 2010 then joined Worcester Warriors, leaving them to join London Wasps in 2013.

Appearances: *173 starts + 27 reps (W136, D10, L54)*
Scoring: *29 tries, 275 conv, 335 pens, 33 drops, 1,799 pts*

GOODRICH, Alfred (29)

Born: *St Margarets, Leicester, regd Q2 1877*
Died: *Leicester, 11.5.1952*
Clubs: *Aylestone, Leicester, Nottingham*
Tigers debut: *10.11.1900 v Manchester, won 18-3*
Last game: *12.4.1909 at Llanelly, lost 3-11*

ALF GOODRICH

Alf Goodrich appeared in 11 Midland Counties Cup ties and was never on the losing side, including the finals of 1904, 1905 and 1909. A forward, he dropped a goal against London Welsh in 1903. He made one appearance for Nottingham during the 1907/08 season. Goodrich worked in the hosiery trade.

Appearances: *179 (W98, D21, L60)*
Scoring: *9 tries, 1 drop, 31 pts*

GOODRICH, Thomas William (26)

Born: *Leicester, regd Q4 1873*
Died: *Leicester, 5.7.1947*
Clubs: *Old Humberstone, Belgrave, Leicester*
Tigers debut: *25.10.1899 v Bedford School, won 29-3 (1T, 3 pts)*
Last game: *9.3.1910 at Moseley, won 20-0*

Tom Goodrich, a forward like his younger brother, Alf, played in an England trial in 1902 but became as recognised for his work for the club after his playing career ended, as trainer and groundsman.

TOM GOODRICH

He won all twenty of his Midland Counties Cup ties, including five successive finals between 1901-05, and scored six tries in a career spanning more than 200 games. Though a printing packer in the hosiery trade, he helped condition players for forty years and was head groundsman from 1922-45.

Appearances: *205 (W120, D18, L67)*
Scoring: *6 tries, 3 conv, 24 pts*

GREASLEY, George (38)

Born: *Leicester, 3.4.1886*
Died: *Leicester, regd Q3 1972*
Clubs: *Bakers Thursday, Leicester*
Tigers debut: *3.2.1906 at Coventry, lost 3-12*
Last game: *21.4.1919 v British Army, lost 5-8*

A forward good enough to be an England reserve on one occasion, George Greasley played in Leicester's Midland Counties Cup-winning sides of 1909, 1910, 1912 and 1913, scoring tries in the 1912 final against Coventry and the 1913 final against Belgrave Premier Works. He worked in the family bakers' business.

Appearances: *174 (W109, D15, L50)*
Scoring: *28 tries, 84 pts*

GEORGE GREASLEY

GREENLEES, Henry Dickson (64)

Born: *Pollokshields, Glasgow, 31.7.1903*
Died: *Houghton-on-the-Hill, Leicestershire, 23.5.1969*
Educated: *Rossall, Glasgow Academy*
Clubs: *Glasgow Academicals, Stoneygate, Leicester*
Tigers debut: *20.3.1926 v Old Blues, won 21-5*
Last game: *16.4.1932 v Blackheath, lost 3-5*
Caps: *Scotland (6) 1927-30*

The career of Harry Greenlees was blighted by injury yet he won six caps at fly-half for Scotland and would have toured Australasia with the 1930 Lions had he been allowed time off work by his uncles.

He captained Leicester from 1930-32 but, in 1931, broke his collarbone in a Scottish trial and, when he returned, suffered the same injury on tour against Bristol. He was Leicester's leading points scorer in 1931/32 and marked his 100th game for the club with a try against Gloucester in 1930.

He was a director of Easi-Fit Shoes which moved from Glasgow to Leicester in the mid-1920s, then became chairman of Grahame Gardner Ltd, school outfitters, and of the sportswear manufacturers, Gymphlex Ltd of Horncastle, Lincolnshire. He was a scratch golfer and was county champion on several occasions, captaining Leicestershire Golf Club from 1942-44 and becoming club president in 1950. He married the daughter of JG Grahame, who ran the Leicester Supporters' Club and whose other daughters married the Meikle brothers, both England internationals.

Appearances: *153 (W88, D13, L52)*
Scoring: *32 tries, 19 conv, 6 pens, 10 drops, 192 pts*

GREENWOOD, Arthur Henry (65)

Born: *Bedford, September 1903*
Died: *in action, 26.8.1940*
Clubs: *Bedford, Leicester*
Tigers debut: *11.9.1926 v Coventry, lost 9-11*
Last game: *26.11.1932 v Nuneaton, won 12-0*

Henry Greenwood, a forward, was Bedford's leading scorer in 1925/26. He played for the East Midlands in the Mobbs Memorial matches against the Barbarians of 1925 and 1926 and scored two tries for Leicester in the 1931 draw with Waterloo. A lance corporal in the Royal Army Service Corps, Greenwood was killed in action early in the Second World War and is buried in Bedford Cemetery.

Appearances: *157 (W90, D9, L58)*
Scoring: *12 tries, 4 conv, 44 pts*

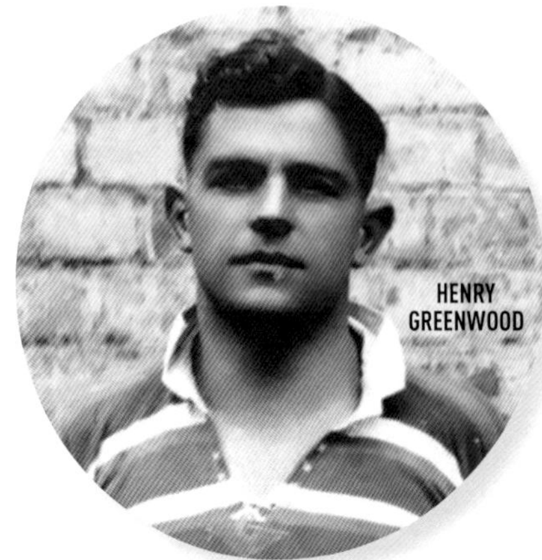
HENRY GREENWOOD

ROGER GROVE

GROVE, Roger Vincent (126)

Born: *Solihull, Warwickshire, 1.2.1940*
Educated: *Bristol College of Technology*
Clubs: *Clevedon, Bristol, Leicester, Moseley*
Tigers debut: *1.10.1966 at Coventry, drew 8-8*
Last game: *25.1.1973 v Royal Navy, won 29-12*

Roger Grove, a prop, reached England trial status in 1963 while with Bristol, whom he helped to the *Daily Telegraph* pennant twice. He played 153 games for Bristol, scoring twenty tries and kicking four conversions; he represented Somerset and played for Western Counties against Australia in 1966. The following year he played for the South of England against New Zealand at Bristol and received another England trial.

His work brought him to Leicester where he spent seven years and captained the club in 1971/72. He scored a try in his 100th match, against Moseley in 1969. Grove worked as an approved-school instructor and as a social worker for Cornwall County Council and, when he retired, became coach and chairman to Roseland, the Truro club.

Appearances: *172 (W107, D12, L53)*
Scoring: *9 tries, 2 conv, 1 pen, 34 pts*

H

HACKNEY, Stephen Thomas (179)

Born: *Stockton-on-Tees, County Durham, 13.6.1968*
Educated: *Stockton VIth Form College, Loughborough University,*
Clubs: *Loughborough University, Nottingham, Leicester, Moseley, Waterloo*
Tigers debut: *14.8.1991 at Edmonton (Canada), won 30-18 (1T, 4 pts)*
Last game: *26.4.1997 v Harlequins, lost 12-13* ●

Steve Hackney, a particularly speedy wing with a good swerve, played for England at schools, colts, student and A level, scoring four tries in an A international against Spain in 1993. He also played for England in the Hong Kong sevens tournament of 1995.

He made his name in student rugby circles and joined Nottingham, for whom he scored 27 tries in 67 games over a three-year period. He moved to Leicester to find greater competition and to learn from the resident England wing, Rory Underwood, whose younger brother, Tony, was also at the club. Hackney was a member of the squad that won the Courage League in 1995, the year in which Tony Underwood moved to Newcastle when the game went open.

STEVE HACKNEY

BRIAN HALL

In the 1995/96 season, Hackney was the club's leading try scorer with 18 in 33 appearances and started the Pilkington Cup final against Bath. The following season he and Darren Garforth played more games than any other player and Hackney was a member of the starting XV that lost to Brive in the 1997 Heineken Cup final. Formerly head of sales and marketing at the insurance brokers, Bland Bankart, he has written books and advises the accountancy industry on marketing strategy.

Appearances: *152 (W118, L34)*
Scoring: *85 tries, 404 pts*

HALL, Brian Philip (137)

Born: *Newark, Nottinghamshire, 30.12.1946*
Educated: *Mundella GS (Nottingham)*
Clubs: *Notts Moderns, Nottingham, Leicester, Dubai Exiles (UAE)*
Tigers debut: *2.9.1970 at Newport, lost 6-16*
Last game: *29.4.1984 at South Gulf Select XV, won 44-3*

Leicester reached their first John Player Cup final, in 1978, under Brian Hall's leadership though injury nearly cost him a place at Twickenham. A hard-tackling centre, he spent three seasons with Nottingham, where he scored 26 tries and 184 points, before moving to Leicester.

He played for Midland Counties (East) against Fiji in 1970 and for the Midland Counties against New Zealand in 1978. Hall represented Notts, Lincs and Derbys, and the East Midlands, in the county championship. He marked his 200th appearance for Tigers with two tries against Bath in 1977 and was 37 when he played his final game.

He was Leicester's president between 2007-09. Hall, a production manager with BSS, became sales manager with Velan Engineering Co Ltd.

Appearances: *308 starts + 4 reps (W179, D10, L123)*
Scoring: *67 tries, 2 conv, 3 drops, 275 pts*

HAMILTON, James Garth (185)

Born: *Guildford, Surrey, 1.7.1970*
Educated: *Stonefield House (Lincoln); Gleanon (Sydney)*
Clubs: *Lincoln, Linwood (New Zealand), London Scottish, Leicester, Nuneaton*
Tigers debut: *29.12.1990 at Nuneaton, won 32-6*
Last game: *31.5.2003 v Saracens (replacement) (at Northampton), won 27-20* ●

Jamie Hamilton had to wait behind Aadel Kardooni for his opportunity at scrum-half and spent time in 1994/95 at the Linwood club in Christchurch, in New Zealand's South Island, as part of a player-development programme. However his first league try was scored from the wing when he was a late call up in a 20-20 draw

JAMIE HAMILTON

at Bath for Tony Underwood who was held up in traffic and did not reach the ground in time.

Hamilton's ability as a sevens player earned him England selection in Hong Kong and later at the 2001 International Rugby Board world sevens. He played in the Tigers squad which won the Middlesex sevens in 1995 and the Madrid sevens in 1997. He spent 1996/97 with London Scottish, from where he was selected for the Scottish Exiles and became a member of Scotland's development squad.

He returned to Leicester in 1997 and garnered five league winners' medals. He came off the bench in the last ten minutes of the 2001 Heineken Cup final against Stade Français and started the 2002 European final against Munster. After retiring he became one of the club's coaching analysts before moving in 2008 to join the Canterbury Crusaders in New Zealand, as video analyst and IT co-ordinator.

Appearances: *127 starts + 57 reps (W133, D5, L46)*
Scoring: *24 tries, 118 pts*

*HAMILTON, Scott Elliot (204)

Born: *Christchurch, New Zealand, 4.3.1980*
Educated: *Christchurch Boys HS*
Clubs: *Canterbury (New Zealand), Crusaders (New Zealand), Leicester*
Tigers debut: *22.11.2008 v Harlequins, won 27-14* ●
Caps: *New Zealand (2) 2006*

Although he failed to make his school first XV Scott Hamilton became a regular wing or full-back with Canterbury and then in Super Rugby with the Crusaders, for whom he scored 21 tries between 2003-08. He scored a vital try in Buenos Aires against Argentina in the second of his two games for the All Blacks and joined Leicester in 2008 as one of Heyneke Meyer's signings.

Hamilton became the newcomer of the year in his first season and the supporters' player of the season for 2009/10. He consistently demonstrated the New Zealander's understanding of support lines and played in successive Premiership finals between 2009-12, as well as the 2009 Heineken Cup final against Leinster. In 2012 he scored a runaway try that helped Leicester win the EDF Energy Cup against Northampton and his ability to fill in at full-back has proved of great value to the club.

Appearances: *124 starts + 18 reps (W93, D8, L41)*
Scoring: *31 tries, 155 pts*

SCOTT HAMILTON

HARE, William Henry (146)

Born: *Newark, Nottinghamshire, 29.11.1952*
Educated: *Magnus GS (Newark)*
Clubs: *Newark, Nottingham, Leicester*
Tigers debut: *20.10.1976 v Oxford University, won 46-8 (5C, 4PG, 22 pts)*
Last game: *29.4.1989 v Bath (at Twickenham), lost 6-10 (2PG, 6 pts)* ●
Caps: *England (25) 1974-84*

The holder of the world record for first-class points scored, 'Dusty' Hare was a vital part of the generation which led Leicester to the top of the English club tree. His goal-kicking won matches for both club and country but he was also a talented attacking footballer, timing runs from full-back with great precision.

Raised on the family farm at South Clifton, he was only 17 when he played for the Midland Counties (East) against Fiji in 1970. Over five years with Nottingham he scored 1,578 points in 166 appearances, represented England under-23 and won his first senior cap, against Wales in 1974.

He scored 22 points on his Leicester debut in 1976 and played in the four successive John Player Cup finals of 1978-81. He would have played in the 1983 final too but withdrew so as to ensure his place on the Lions tour of New Zealand that summer, when he was the second highest points scorer with 88 in six provincial appearances. His last game was the 1989 Pilkington Cup final.

His international career was chequered: England dropped him five times, only to recall him and he became the country's most-capped full-back and record points scorer before both marks were overtaken by Jonathan Webb in the 1990s. His three penalties in the 9-8 win over Wales in 1980 were crucial to England's grand-slam success that year.

Hare toured with England to the Far East in 1979, Argentina (1981), North America (1982) and South Africa (1984). He broke the career points total of 3,651 held by Moseley's Sam Doble on 25 April 1981, at the Reddings, Doble's home ground, and went on to a career aggregate of 7,191, of which 240 were scored for England.

He played tennis for Nottinghamshire juniors and, as a batsman, appeared in ten first-class cricket matches for the county. An autobiography, *Dusty*, was published in 1985. He received an honorary degree from Leicester University in 1989 and was awarded the MBE the same year. He served on the Barbarians committee for three years and, in 1990, became director of rugby to Nottingham.

He returned to Leicester in 1994 as development co-ordinator then moved into coaching, his development squad winning the Zurich A league in 2004/05. He subsequently became the club's chief scout before moving to Northampton in 2010 in a development role.

Appearances: *393 starts + 1 rep (W287, D9, L98)*
Scoring: *87 tries, 779 conv, 820 pens, 47 drops, 4,507 pts*

DUSTY HARE

JAMES HARGRAVE

HARGRAVE, Oswald John (46)

Born: *Paddington, London, September 1891*
Died: *Northampton, 18.6.1969*
Clubs: *Stoneygate, Leicester*
Tigers debut: *17.4.1909 v London Welsh, won 10-0*
Last game: *2.2.1914 at Pontypool, lost 3-24*

'James' Hargrave first appeared as a fly-half but played nearly all his games on the wing, scoring over fifty tries in five years. He played in the side that won the 1912 Midland Counties Cup and in an England trial; in 1911, against Birkenhead Park, he was joined in the side by Leonard, his older brother.

A machine repairer at British United Shoe, Hargrave played cricket for Leicester Ivanhoe and, during the First World War, was a lieutenant in the Royal Flying Corps.

Appearances: *110 (W72, D11, L27)*
Scoring: *53 tries, 1 drop, 163 pts*

HARRIS, Jeremy Charles (170)

Born: *Kettering, Northamptonshire, 22.2.1965*
Educated: *Welland Park HS, Robert Smyth College (Market Harborough)*
Clubs: *Kibworth, Vipers, Leicester, Coventry, Nuneaton*
Tigers debut: *29.9.1984 v Saracens, won 22-15*
Last game: *21.4.1996 v Sanyo World XV (replacement) (at Twickenham) Lost 31-40*

Always known as 'Jez', Harris took up rugby as a ten-year-old with Kibworth under the tutelage of Bleddyn Jones, and played for the county schools at under-14 and under-16 level, going on to represent Leicestershire from colts through to senior level. After appearing a permanent understudy at fly-half to Les Cusworth, Brian Smith and Gerry Ainscough, Harris came into his own in the 1992/93 season which ended with a Pilkington Cup win

JEZ HARRIS

over Harlequins at Twickenham, when he dropped a goal.

He played for the Midlands Division, for an emerging England XV (at the age of 28) and for England A and set a club record for dropped goals (14) in 1993/94, passing Cusworth's mark. Just for good measure he did it again in 1994/95 and played in the Pilkington Cup final of 1996, against Bath. He then joined Coventry, who narrowly missed promotion to the Premiership in his first season, before ending his active career as player-coach at Nuneaton.

Appearances: *213 starts + 12 reps (W170, D3, L52)*
Scoring: *23 tries, 165 conv, 178 pens, 70 drops, 1,171 pts*

HARRISON, Michael John (115)

Born: *Leicester, 23.8.1940*
Educated: *Wyggeston Boys, Loughborough Colleges*
Clubs: *Old Wyggestonians, Loughborough Colleges, Leicester*
Tigers debut: *6.1.1962 at Bath, lost 5-8*
Last game: *3.4.1971 v Birkenhead Park, won 23-11*

A staunch presence at centre throughout the 1960s, Mike Harrison played in five England trials, among them one for the senior side at Twickenham in 1966. His father, Harold, played twice for Tigers and Michael played for Leicestershire schools and English Universities before joining the club. He took over from Mike Wade as captain in 1965/66 and became the club's leading try scorer that season.

He was vice-principal of Wyggeston and Queen Elizabeth I College for 23 years and, when he retired, the school named their sports hall after him. Harrison was Leicester's president between 2009-13; he was also president of the Leicestershire schools RFU and a vice-president of the Leicestershire Tennis Association. He became the part-time academy education officer to Tigers, helping young players with life outside rugby.

Appearances: *210 (W135, D14, L61)*
Scoring: *58 tries, 1 drop, 177 pts*

MIKE HARRISON

TEDDY HASELMERE

HASELMERE (HASSELMEIER), Edward Ernest (49)

Born: *Rugby, Warwickshire, 1.4.1895*
Died: *Rugby, Warwickshire, 8.10.1983*
Educated: *Murray (Rugby)*
Clubs: *Rugby, Leicester, Northampton*
Tigers debut: *26.12.1918 v 4th Bn Leicestershire Regiment, won 6-5*
Last game: *8.9.1923 v Plymouth Albion, won 14-5*

Teddy Haselmere, a prolific wing, first played for Rugby under his birth name of Hasselmeier. Gustav, his father, was German but the family changed their name because of anti-German feeling arising from the First World War.

Haselmere played for Rugby as a fly-half in 1913 but switched to Leicester after the war and, in his first full season, set a record of 59 tries which has never been beaten. His fiftieth try for the club came after only forty games and his 100th after 89 appearances. In 180 games he scored 136 tries and his career tally at Rugby, Leicester and Northampton was a remarkable 310 in 448 games.

He was Leicester's leading points scorer in 1918/19 and 1919/20, his record of 242 in 1920 lasted until 1978 when Dusty Hare overtook it. Haselmere was also a kicker and, against Burton in

1919, scored 31 points from five tries, six conversions and a dropped goal, another individual mark which lasted fifty years. He is one of only two Leicester players (Alfred Hind was the other) to have scored five tries in a match on three occasions, and he scored hat-tricks in 17 matches.

He gained an England trial in 1920 and played for England against the South in 1921. When he returned to Rugby, he established a club record of 32 tries in the 1924/25 season which remained until 1987/88 when it was overtaken by Eddie Saunders. He scored 78 tries in 106 games for Rugby and 96 tries in 162 games for Northampton.

He became a referee after his playing career ended, handling Leicester's 10-23 defeat by Blackheath in 1939. He was Leicestershire sprint champion in 1920 and, in later life, played for Rugby Bowls Club. He was an engineer with British Thomson-Houston of Rugby.

Appearances: *180 (W122, D12, L46)*
Scoring: *136 tries, 35 conv, 6 pens, 8 drops, 528 pts*

HEALEY, Austin Sean (182)

Born: *Wallasey, 26.10.1973*
Educated: *St Anselm's College (Birkenhead), Leeds Polytechnic*
Clubs: *Birkenhead Park, Waterloo, Orrell, Leicester*
Tigers debut: *26.8.1996 v Agen, lost 22-28*
Last game: *27.5.2006 v Sale Sharks (replacement) (at Twickenham), lost 20-45*
Caps: *England (51) 1997-2003, British & Irish Lions (2) 1997*

Austin Healey arrived at Leicester as a scrum-half but his mercurial talents allowed him to play virtually anywhere in the back division. Fly-half, wing, full-back, he played in all those positions at international level, thanks to a breadth of vision given to few and the self-confidence that, wherever he played, he would make a difference.

As a youngster he played football for Wirral District and rugby at Birkenhead Park. He toured Australia in 1993 with England under-21s, playing on the wing, represented England at the Hong Kong sevens between 1995-97 and made his England A debut (at Welford Road) in 1996. He made his international debut as a replacement against Ireland in 1997 and started against Wales, winning a place on the Lions tour to South Africa that summer.

He appeared as a replacement in two of the three tests but, with Matt Dawson and Kyran Bracken the main contenders at scrum-half, most of his subsequent England games were on the wing. He played in the 1999 World Cup, made a notable appearance at fly-half against South Africa on the 2000 tour when Jonny Wilkinson went down with food poisoning and toured Australia with the Lions in 2001. He scored 15 tries in his 51 England internationals, just missing a place in the 2003 World Cup squad though he did make a fleeting visit to Australia to provide cover, if required, at scrum-half.

If his versatility hindered his international career at times, it proved a blessing for Leicester. His speed off the mark, his ability to read a game, created a threat all over the playing field. He scored what was subsequently deemed the try of the season in his first season at Leicester, a 60-metre solo against Llanelli, but his most memorable moments came in the Heineken Cup wins of 2001 and 2002.

His move from scrum-half to fly-half late in the final against Stade Français produced the break that made the clinching try for Leon Lloyd. The following year he started at fly-half against Munster and scored the try that, in the end, proved the difference. He was an integral part of Leicester's successive Premiership wins between 1999-2002 and his last match was the Premiership final against Sale Sharks in 2006.

Since retiring, Healey has carved out a career as a rugby analyst on television and has made numerous appearances on game shows and talent contests. In 2008 he was on the BBC's *Strictly Come Dancing* and in 2013 he injured himself in the diving show, *Splash*. He has also helped in the production of rugby programmes aimed at less fortunate young people.

Appearances: *212 starts + 36 reps (W174, D11, L63)*
Scoring: *61 tries, 3 conv, 1 pen, 6 drops, 332 pts*

HESMONDHALGH, William Robert (10)

Born: *Green, Ambleside, Cumberland, 28.12.1869*
Died: *Leicester, 12.9.1953*
Clubs: *Ambleside, St Helens, Leicester*
Tigers debut: *26.11.1892 v Bedford, won 8-0 (1T, 2 pts)*
Last game: *26.2.1898 at Burton, lost 0-3*

'Clasher' Hesmondhalgh made his debut on a visit to Leicester, when C J Mason withdrew. He was said to have been so pleased with his try-scoring reception that he wanted to move and he became a regular and a popular favourite.

Reports claimed he was the finest centre Leicester had then seen, a good tackler and strong on attack. He was the leading try and points scorer in 1893/94 but placed his name firmly in the annals by turning out against Manchester Free Wanderers on 14 April 1894 only hours after his wedding at St Andrew's Church.

'CLASHER' HESMONDHALGH

He represented Westmorland and Midland Counties and captained Leicester once, against Ashby-de-la-Zouch in March 1893. A printers' cutter, he scored a hat-trick against Stoneygate during the Midland Counties Cup run of 1894.

Appearances: *101 (W64, D7, L30)*
Scoring: *33 tries, 7 conv, 1 pen, 4 drops, 129 pts*

AUSTIN HEALEY

HIND, Alfred Ernest (27)

Born: *Preston, Lancashire, 7.4.1878*
Died: *Oadby, Leicester, 21.3.1947*
Educated: *Uppingham, Trinity Hall (Cambridge)*
Clubs: *Cambridge University (Blue 1900), Leicester, Nottingham*
Tigers debut: *7.10.1899 v Exeter, won 11-0*
Last game: *27.1.1906 at Moseley, won 3-0*
Caps: *England (2) 1905-06*

The high point of Alfred Hind's career came in the 1905/06 season when he played against New Zealand for Leicester, for the Midland Counties and for England. Six weeks later he played his second international, against Wales.

While studying at Trinity Hall he won a Blue for Cambridge in 1900, scoring two tries against Oxford, and won athletics Blues in 1899 and 1901. A wing with a best time for the 100 yards of 9.8 seconds, he also played cricket and appeared in four successive university matches as a lower-order batsman and medium pace bowler.

He toured South Africa with the British team of 1903 but only played in the first three games. He played on the winning side in five consecutive Midland Counties Cup finals, scoring three tries in the 1905 final; he scored six tries against Belgrave in 1903 and five tries on two other occasions, all of them cup games. A solicitor, he was Leicester's leading try and points scorer in 1902/03.

Appearances: *127 (W85, D9, L33)*
Scoring: *81 tries, 1 conv, 4 drops, 261 pts*

HIPKISS, Daniel James (200)

Born: *Ipswich, Suffolk, 4.6.1982*
Educated: *Hartismere HS, Uppingham, Loughborough University*
Clubs: *Diss, Loughborough Students, Leicester, Bath*
Tigers debut: *24.8.2002 v Biarritz Olympique (at Bayonne), won 14-13 (1T, 5 pts)* ●
Last game: *5.3.2011 v Saracens (replacement), lost 14-15* ●
Caps: *England (13) 2007-10*

Dan Hipkiss, whose father, Chris, was an England schools wing and coached the juniors at Diss, was spotted by Dusty Hare, then Leicester's chief scout. Hipkiss went to Uppingham on a Tigers scholarship and studied sports science at Loughborough but, though he made a try-scoring debut in an Orange Cup match against Biarritz, his Premiership experience was limited until he was 23.

By then he had come through a career-threatening injury in 1999 to his left knee and played for England at every age level. A squat centre, Hipkiss possessed swift acceleration and the ability to ride a tackle and find his support. He played for England's sevens team between 2003-07 but made significant strides in 2007, keeping Ollie Smith, a Lions centre, out of the sides that won the EDF Energy Cup and the Premiership.

He also started that year's Heineken Cup final against London Wasps and won his first England cap in the World Cup warm-up game against Wales. He made four appearances in the 2007 World Cup, all from the bench but including the semi-final and final. However injuries constantly interrupted his international career; a fractured cheekbone in the 2008 Premiership final cost him a place on tour in New Zealand and, though he reappeared off the bench against the All Blacks at Twickenham, his best run of games came in 2009, when he started five in succession.

Hipkiss played in the 2009 Heineken Cup final against Leinster and that year's Premiership final against London Irish. He came off the bench a year later to score the try that beat Saracens in the Premiership final but in 2011 moved to Bath where he spent two seasons before being forced into retirement by a shoulder injury.

Appearances: *109 starts + 22 reps (W86, D6, L39)*
Scoring: *31 tries, 155 pts*

HOBBS, Arthur James (35)

Born: *Hardingstone, Northampton, regd Q2 1881*
Died: *Cardiff, Wales, regd Q1 1939*
Clubs: *Northampton, Leicester*
Tigers debut: *8.9.1906 v Hartlepool Rovers, won 8-0*
Last game: *23.11.1912 v Moseley, won 24-0*

Leicester were accused of poaching Arthur Hobbs, a forward, by Northampton's fixture secretary in a letter to *The Birmingham Post*. He played 112 games for Northampton between 1900-06, scoring 18 tries, then became a regular for Leicester with whom he won three Midland Counties Cup finals between 1909 and 1912.

He was part of the combined Midlands and East Midlands Counties team that beat Australia at Welford Road in 1908 and played for the South against the North in an England trial a few months later, at Northampton. He was a warehouseman in the boot and shoe trade.

Appearances: *195 (W113, D16, L66)*
Scoring: *26 tries, 78 pts*

JOHNSON, Martin Osborne (178)

Born: *Solihull, Warwickshire, 9.3.1970*
Educated: *Welland Park College, Robert Smyth (Market Harborough)*
Clubs: *Wigston, Tihoi & College Old Boys (New Zealand), King Country (NZ), Leicester*
Tigers debut: *14.2.1989 v Royal Air Force, won 34-12*
Last game: *14.5.2005 v London Wasps (at Twickenham), lost 14-39* ●
Caps: *England (84) 1993-2003, British & Irish Lions (8) 1993-2001*

In rugby terms, Leicester's most decorated player by a distance. England's captain for the winning of the 2003 World Cup, twice captain of the Lions (in 1997 and 2001), a feat unmatched in the touring side's history, England's fifth most-capped player of all time and only Will Carling has led the country in more than Johnson's 39 internationals.

Yet when all the statistics have been recorded, it was Johnson's presence that made him a truly great player. His physical presence as a lock but also his mental presence, his ability to control the ebb and flow of a game, to intimidate not only opponents but his own players with a look or a word, qualities surely honed during the period he spent playing in New Zealand's King Country where he was chosen in 1990 for the national colts team.

Johnson, a keen follower of Liverpool FC, played football and rugby before joining Wigston and moved through England under-18 and colts between 1987-89. After his stay in New Zealand, he returned to work as a Midland Bank officer in Market Harborough, played for England under-21s in 1992 and for England B against France before being called up, at 24 hours' notice, to replace the injured Wade Dooley in the five nations game with France at Twickenham.

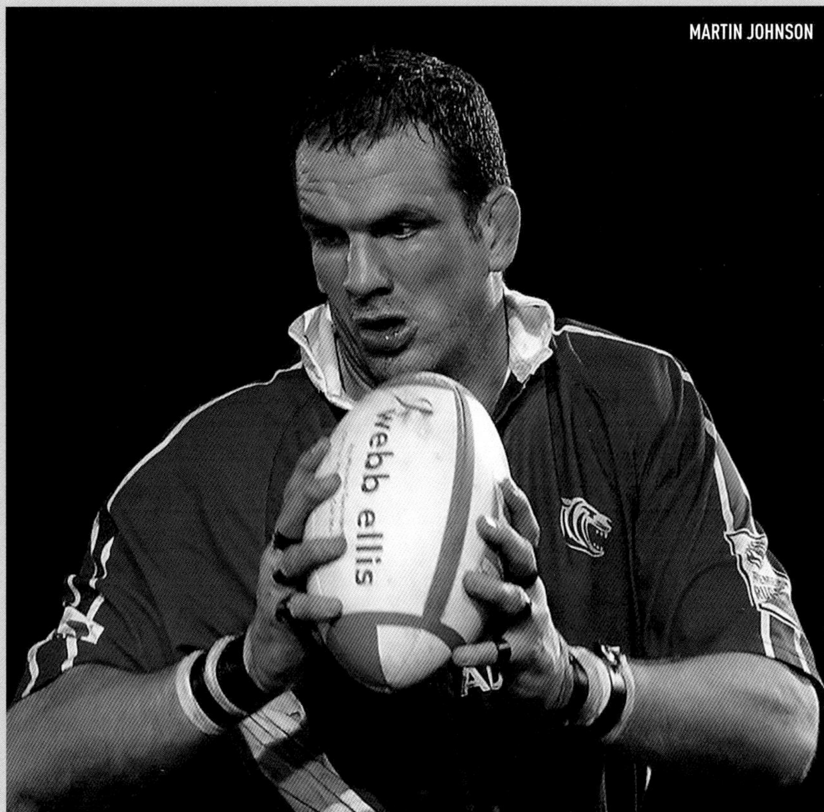

MARTIN JOHNSON

Five months later he was called from the England A tour in Canada to join the Lions in New Zealand after Dooley had to fly home on the death of his father. Johnson played two provincial matches and went straight into the second row for the second and third internationals. Thereafter he was an automatic selection for England, playing in the grand-slam side of 1995, and for the Lions, who asked him to lead the 1997 tour party to South Africa despite his lack of captaincy experience.

The series against the Springboks was won and, despite off-field controversies, that against Australia in 2001 might have been when Johnson was also captain but an injury-racked party lost the deciding third test by six points. By then he had also become England's captain; he played in the 1995 World Cup in South Africa and first led England in two World Cup qualifying games in November 1998. He took over from Lawrence Dallaglio the following year and retained the job, apart from injury absence, until he stood down from international rugby in 2003.

He led England into the 1999 World Cup, missed the 2000 six nations with injury, but returned for the summer tour to South Africa when England's win in Bloemfontein allowed them a share of the series. Three years later he led England to their first grand slam for eight years, to successive away victories over New Zealand and Australia and to the World Cup, becoming the first and, so far, the only northern-hemisphere captain to lift the Webb Ellis Cup, after which he was appointed CBE.

Johnson had become a regular in Leicester's second row by the time they won the 1993 Pilkington Cup (in which he scored a try), lost the 1994 cup final (to Bath) and won the 1995 league title. He was appointed club captain in 1997 and, under his leadership, Leicester won the 1997 Pilkington Cup, four successive Premiership titles between 1999-2002 and back-to-back Heineken Cup wins in 2001 and 2002. He regarded the 2001 European final, against Stade Français in Paris, as one of the greatest days of his playing career.

After ending his England career, Johnson played two further seasons for Tigers, helping them to the 2005 Premiership final, his last competitive game which was lost to London Wasps. He worked as a media analyst (including on American football, one of his great enthusiasms) and speaker until 2008, when he became England manager. His team won the 2011 six nations championship but under-performed at that year's World Cup in New Zealand, after which Johnson stood down. He was inducted into the International Rugby Board's hall of fame in 2011 and the Aviva Premiership hall of fame in 2014.

Appearances: *348 starts + 14 reps (W269, D12, L81)*
Scoring: *18 tries, 90 pts*

JOHNSON, Stephen Robert (148)

Born: *Leicester, 19.12.1949*
Educated: *Spencefield*
Clubs: *Vipers, Leicester*
Tigers debut: *2.10.1976 at Coventry, lost 15-18*
Last game: *30.4.1983 v Bristol (at Twickenham), lost 22-28* ●

Steve Johnson, a back-row forward big enough to play occasionally at lock, went from school to Vipers and played there for four years, as well as for the Leicestershire Police. He represented Leicestershire but did not join Tigers until he was 25, breaking five ribs on his debut at Coventry (the match report suggested he "played quite well but tended to fade in the last twenty minutes").

He represented the British Police and the Midlands, and was the first Leicester player to win an England B cap, against Romania in 1978. He captained the club from 1981-83 and appeared in five John Player Cup finals (winning three), including his last match for the club, against Bristol.

A detective inspector in the Leicestershire Constabulary for much of his career, he was chief superintendent at Charles Street police station when he retired in 1999. For many years he has been a summariser on Tigers matches for Radio Leicester.

Appearances: *207 (W146, D6, L55)*
Scoring: *31 tries, 124 pts*

STEVE JOHNSON

JOHNSON, William Warwick (189)

Born: *Solihull, Warwickshire, 18.3.1974*
Educated: *Robert Smyth (Market Harborough), Birmingham University*
Clubs: *Wigston, Kibworth, Linwood (New Zealand), Leicester, Coventry, Benetton Treviso (Italy), Nice (France)*
Tigers debut: *16.4.1994 at Sale (replacement), lost 27-50*
Last game: *14.5.2006 v London Irish (replacement), won 40-8* ●

Will Johnson, unlike older brother Martin, opted for the back row rather than the second row. Learning his rugby at Kibworth and Wigston, he joined Leicester's youth team before going on an exchange visit to New Zealand where he played for Linwood, in Christchurch.

WILL JOHNSON

He played for England A in 2000/01 and was one of three Leicester players in the A side which played the 2004 Churchill Cup final against New Zealand Maori. He started the 2001 Heineken Cup final against Stade Français and gained four Premiership winners' medals between 1999-2002. He started for Leicester on 75 occasions alongside Martin. After leaving Tigers in 2006 he captained Coventry, Treviso and Nice, where he also coached.

Appearances: *157 starts + 53 reps (W142, D7, L61)*
Scoring: *10 tries, 50 pts*

JONES, Arthur Owen (18)

Born: *Shelton, Nottinghamshire, 16.8.1872*
Died: *Dunstable, Bedfordshire, 21.12.1914*
Educated: *Bedford Modern, Jesus College (Cambridge)*
Clubs: *Bedford, Blackheath, Burton-on-Trent, Leicester*
Tigers debut: *20.4.1895 at Bedford, won 5-3*
Last game: *26.12.1910 v Birkenhead Park, won 25-5*

A wonderful all-round sportsman, Arthur Jones achieved lasting fame as a cricketer, his 12 caps all coming in Ashes tests against Australia. He won a cricket Blue while at Cambridge in 1893 and was one of Wisden's five cricketers of the year in 1900.

A fine batsman, Jones scored nearly 23,000 runs, including 34 centuries. An outstanding slip fielder, he took 497 catches for Nottinghamshire and was said to have invented the position of gully while at school. He led Notts between 1900-14 and they won the county championship in 1907.

In July 1903 he made what was then the highest score by a Notts player, carrying his bat for an unbeaten 296 in 350 minutes against Gloucestershire at Trent Bridge. He led England in two tests on the 1908 MCC tour of Australia.

In the winter he played rugby as a full-back or three-quarter, making 18 appearances for Bedford between 1889-95 before joining Leicester. He led the club between 1896-99 and again between 1902-04 and raised the record for points scored in successive seasons, 1897-99. He became the first player to pass 500 points for the club with nine points against Moseley in 1903.

Jones played in six Midland Counties Cup-winning teams and appeared for the South against the North in an England trial at Dewsbury in 1897. Between 1906-12 he refereed five international matches, including that of 1911 in Paris when France achieved their first test win, over Scotland.

His home was in Market Bosworth and he worked at Oakham School but suffered from poor health. Although he played six championship matches for Nottinghamshire in 1914, he died of tuberculosis six months later, aged only 42.

Appearances: *224 (W161, D19, L44)*
Scoring: *39 tries, 113 conv, 20 pens, 37 drops, 3 marks, 563 pts*

ARTHUR JONES

BLEDDYN JONES

JONES, Bleddyn (131=)

Born: *Brynamman, West Glamorgan, Wales, 7.8.1948*
Educated: *Amman Valley GS, Swansea College of Education*
Clubs: *Brynamman, Swansea TC, Leicester*
Tigers debut: *15.11.1969 v Wilmslow, lost 13-23*
Last game: *23.9.1978 at Harlequins, lost 9-21*

The slim, self-effacing Bleddyn Jones literally stumbled into a Tigers training session on the Recreation Ground in 1969 after moving to teach in Leicester, and joined on the same evening as Peter Wheeler. A fly-half, he had played for his junior club in West Wales but his bravery in the tackle and his willingness to run the ball made him a Tigers regular throughout the 1970s.

He played for Midland Counties (East) against New Zealand in 1973 and passed 300 games for Leicester in October 1977. He played in the club's first John Player Cup final appearance, against Gloucester in 1978, and when he retired the following season the *Leicester Mercury* said "his style on the field and his gentle demeanour off it made him one of the club's most popular players."

Jones taught general subjects at Humberstone Junior School with a particular interest in physical education; with John Duggan and Frank Jones, fellow players, he ran a successful club for aspiring gymnasts in Leicestershire. The same trio were the first organisers of mini-rugby, under the aegis of the Leicestershire RFU. He became headmaster at Little Bowden Primary School until retiring in 2005 and, for many years, has been the voice of Leicester rugby on Radio Leicester.

Appearances: *333 (W200, D13, L120)*
Scoring: *42 tries, 1 conv, 4 drops, 172 pts*

JONES, Francis Horace (22)

Born: *Shelton, Nottinghamshire, 22.2.1874*
Died: *Hemingford Grey, near St Ives, Buckinghamshire, 24.1.1937*
Educated: *Bedford GS, Emmanuel College (Cambridge)*
Clubs: *Cambridge University (Blues 1898-1900), Hinckley, Nuneaton, Leicester*
Tigers debut: *2.11.1895 v Rugby, won 33-0 (1T, 3 pts)*
Last game: *27.12.1905 v United Services, won 25-4*

The youngest of eight sons born to the Reverend Cartwright Jones, Frank followed his brother, Arthur, into Leicester's back division. A wing, he played for and captained Nuneaton between 1893-96 when he joined Leicester.

FRANK JONES

His appearances were interrupted by his time at Emmanuel College, Cambridge, where (unlike Arthur) he won Blues in 1898 and 1900. He played for the South against the North in an England trial in 1900 and in three successive winning Midland Counties Cup sides, scoring three tries in the 1899 final against Nuneaton. He and Arthur played in 83 club games together.

A bank clerk in Hinckley, he was ordained in 1900 and was a curate in Blyth (Northumberland) before becoming a naval chaplain in 1904. He served with the North Sea Fleet during the First World War and was awarded the OBE in 1918.

After the war he became chaplain at the Royal Hospital School, Greenwich, where he met his wife, Edith, the sister-in-charge of the infirmary. He officiated at Leicester's thirtieth annual service in 1926 and, when he retired from the Navy in 1929, became vicar at Ashby-de-la-Zouch church. He retired through ill health in 1931 but became an active member of the St Ives branch of the Royal British Legion.

Appearances: *115 (W83, D12, L20)*
Scoring: *35 tries, 32 conv, 1 pen, 1 drop, 176 pts*

JOYCE, Nicholas James (140)

Born: *Ashby-de-la-Zouch, Leicestershire, 16.1.1953*
Educated: *Ashby Boys GS*
Clubs: *Old Ashbeians, Leicester*
Tigers debut: *12.4.1971 at Fylde, won 22-20*
Last game: *7.12.1985 v Gloucester, lost 9-15*

Known universally as 'Plod,' Nick Joyce joined the police from school after playing in the county under-15 and under-19 sides. He came from a well-known sporting family which was the backbone of cricket in Ashby for four generations and led the Midlands colts to a rare victory over Welsh Youth, and the first England youth side against Wales.

A lock with good handling skills, he played for Midlands under-23, for Leicestershire and for the Midlands against Australia in 1981. He played for Leicester in four successive John Player Cup finals between 1978-81 and made more appearances in the letter D shirt (218) than any other player. After retiring he helped Ian Smith coaching at Oakham School when they reached two *Daily Mail* schools cup finals.

Appearances: *284 starts + 3 reps (W195, D6, L86)*
Scoring: *28 tries, 112 pts*

NICK JOYCE

K

KARDOONI, Aadel (171)

Born: *Tehran, Iran, 17.5.1968*
Educated: *Sherborne, Leicester Polytechnic*
Clubs: *North Dorset, Wasps, Leicester, Bedford, Blackheath, Rugby*
Tigers debut: *15.10.1988 at Swansea, lost 16-35*
Last game: *10.5.1997 v Sale (replacement) (at Twickenham), won 9-3*

One of three brothers who has lived in England since he was eight, Aadel Kardooni blossomed at Sherborne under the guidance of Mike Davis, England's 1980 grand-slam coach. He played for England schools at 16 and 18 group level and subsequently for England Students and England B, with whom he toured New Zealand in 1992.

Kardooni played for the Midland Division against South Africa the same year and in two Pilkington Cup finals, in 1989 and 1993. He was a member of the squad that won the league in 1993/94 and made his 200th appearance for Tigers against Wasps in April 1996. He twice

AADEL KARDOONI

scored three tries in a league match, against West Hartlepool and Sale in 1996, and his Leicester career ended with an appearance in the 1997 Pilkington Cup final, against Sale. Formerly a City broker, Kardooni is self-employed as a property developer.

Appearances: *217 starts + 5 reps (W170, D2, L50)*
Scoring: *67 tries, 302 pts*

KAY, Benedict James (191)

Born: *Liverpool, 14.12.1975*
Educated: *Merchant Taylors' (Crosby), Loughborough University*
Clubs: *Waterloo, Queensland University (Australia), Leicester*
Tigers debut: *11.9.1999 at Northampton, lost 24-46* ●
Last game: *8.5.2010 v Saracens, lost 23-32* ●
Caps: *England (62) 2001-09, British & Irish Lions (2) 2005*

Only three other locks have been capped more times by England, one of them Martin Johnson who was Ben Kay's partner in so many Leicester scrums. A leading line-out analyst for club and country, Kay was also a thoughtful player in the loose, scoring a try in his first six nations campaign.

The son of Lord Justice of Appeal Sir John Kay, he was nicknamed 'M'lud' when he arrived at Leicester, having played for England at under-18, under-19 and under-21 level, and at the student world cup of 1996. Kay took a degree in sports science at Loughborough and settled so swiftly at Welford Road that he was named Tigers members' player of the season for 2001/02, participating in the three Premiership wins of 2000-02.

He played for England A in 2000 and 2001 (as captain) and received his senior cap on tour in Canada in the summer of 2001. A try-scorer against Argentina in Buenos Aires in 2002, the year in which he became England's regular middle-of-the-line jumper, Kay went to the 2003 World Cup and played every minute in six of England's seven games, remaining on the bench for the pool game with Uruguay. In the final against Australia he spilled a try-scoring opportunity but ended on the winning side, subsequently being awarded the MBE.

Kay missed the 2004 tour to Australia but returned with a string of powerful displays to earn a Lions tour to New Zealand in 2005, playing in the first international. He missed the 2006 six nations but returned the following season to secure a place in the England squad for the 2007 World Cup, where he played every minute of every game en route to the final. His last nine internationals were played from the bench.

He played in both Leicester's Heineken Cup wins of 2001 and 2002 and the losing European finals of 2007 and 2009. He also started all five Premiership finals of 2005-09 before bowing out on the last day of the regular Premiership season in 2010. He became a media analyst with satellite television.

Appearances: *237 starts + 44 reps (W186, D10, L85)*
Scoring: *12 tries, 60 pts*

KEMPIN, James Stuart (144)

Born: *Melton Mowbray, Leicestershire, 4.2.1952*
Died: *Melton Mowbray, Leicestershire, 13.10.2012*
Educated: *Melton Upper*
Clubs: *Melton Mowbray, Leicester*
Tigers debut: *23.10.1974 v Oxford University, won 20-13*
Last game: *28.4.1979 at Moseley, lost 8-14*

With his flamboyant sideburns, Jim Kempin was a distinctive presence in the Leicester back row, his voracious tackling earning him the nickname of 'bite your legs'. He played hooker at school and captained Melton in 1973/74 before moving to Leicester, for whom three of his 15 tries came in successive matches in 1976, against Solihull, Bedford and Bath. He was a cousin of Jenny Pitman, the race horse trainer.

Appearances: *107 starts + 2 reps (W73, D1, L35)*
Scoring: *15 tries, 60 pts*

JIM KEMPIN

KENNEY, Stephen (142)

Born: *Edinburgh, Scotland, 24.8.1956*
Educated: *Roundhill HS, Longslade Upper, Charles Keen College, Leicester Polytechnic*
Club: *Leicester*
Tigers debut: *10.9.1975 v Nuneaton, won 46-3 (2T, 8 pts)*
Last game: *10.3.1990 at Bristol, won 13-11* ●

One of the alliterative half-back combination with Les Cusworth, Steve Kenney was a mainstay of the club from scrum-half for 15 years. The first product of the youth team to receive a senior debut in 1975, when he scored two tries against Nuneaton, he won representative honours for England schools (1971) and

STEVE KENNEY

England Colts (1975) and played for England under-23 in 1979.

A fiery player in his youth, Kenney's speed off the mark helped create many tries and became a feature of the club's tap-penalty routines. Alongside Paul Dodge, he was influenced by the thinking of David Lyons while still at school and his positive approach to scrum-half play should have carried him closer to a senior cap.

He scored the winning try in the 1979 John Player Cup final against Moseley and helped retain the cup for two further years. When he and Cusworth played together, opponents seldom knew which player to mark and, even when Leicester preferred other scrum-halves such as Nick Youngs or Aadel Kardooni, they frequently came back to Kenney, who finished with 365 appearances.

A sales account manager with BT, Kenney became a specialist scrum-half coach and also helped Vipers, where his son, Stuart, played. He was a member of the Leicestershire RFU executive committee and of the LFC Past Players Association committee.

Appearances: *361 starts + 4 reps (W257, D8, L100)*
Scoring: *69 tries, 276 pts*

KONIG, Peter Hans (96)

Born: *Vienna, Austria, 16.10.1931*
Educated: *Moat Road*
Clubs: *Moat Old Boys, Leicester, Cranleigh*
Tigers debut: *14.4.1952 at Plymouth Albion, won 19-0*
Last game: *23.4.1960 v Rugby, won 9-6*

Born to Jewish parents, Peter Konig's family left Austria before the Second World War. He won schoolboy trials as a flanker in 1945 and was a wicketkeeper

PETER KONIG

with Leicestershire, playing one first-class cricket match in 1949, against Northamptonshire at Wantage Road.

An industrious back-row forward, he came briefly out of retirement in 1966 when he went to Welford Road to watch Leicester play Blackheath and filled a vacancy in the Leicester University XV that was playing the Extras. He was managing director of ICI Seeds UK Ltd before becoming a business consultant in the UK, Europe and the USA. Martyn, his son, represented Great Britain as a slalom canoeist.

Appearances: *185 (W89, D18, L78)*
Scoring: *32 tries, 96 pts*

L

ERIC LACEY

LACEY, Eric Charles (84)

Born: *Leicester, 14.10.1921*
Died: *Leicester, 11.8.1996*
Educated: *Wyggeston GS*
Clubs: *Old Wyggestonians, Leicester Thursday, Leicester*
Tigers debut: *11.10.1947 at Neath, lost 5-6*
Last game: *21.2.1959 v Wasps, won 22-0*

Eric Lacey, a lock, distinguished himself in his thirteenth appearance for the club in 1948 by dropping a goal against Blackheath, as well as scoring a try in the same match. He played for Leicestershire and East Midlands against South Africa in 1951/52 and, when he retired, became a member of the selection committee. Four years later he made up the numbers for the second half of the game with Wasps when Phil Horrocks-Taylor, best man at a wedding that day, failed to appear.

Lacey played for the Barbarians in three Mobbs Memorial matches between 1951-55. He was Leicester president between 1979-81 and helped organise the early displays of memorabilia in the clubhouse.

Appearances: *175 (W89, D7, L79)*
Scoring: *15 tries, 1 drop, 49 pts*

LAWRENCE, Clifford Gwynne Steele (88)

Born: *Swansea, Wales, 23.6.1927*
Died: *Swansea, Wales, 25.7.1971*
Educated: *Alderman Newton's*
Clubs: *Old Newtonians, Leicester, Swansea*
Tigers debut: *19.3.1949 v Nuneaton, won 9-3*
Last game: *18.4.1953 at Sale, won 24-19 (2T, 6 pts)*

Gwynne Lawrence moved to Leicester with his family as a four-year-old. Originally a centre, he switched to the wing and played there for Leicester and Midland Counties against South Africa in 1951/52. In his final season, 1952/53, he was the club's leading try scorer with 13, two of them coming in his final match against Sale.

He returned to Swansea, his birthplace, but opportunities to play for Swansea were few and he retired in 1956. When Steele and Sons, the family constructional engineering business, was sold he joined Thyssen's mining engineers but became ill and died aged 44.

Appearances: *118 (W58, D5, L55)*
Scoring: *40 tries, 120 pts*

LAWRENCE, Samuel Frank (57)

FRANK LAWRENCE

Born: *Leicester, regd Q4 1898*
Died: *Leicester, 14.3.1968*
Educated: *Moat Road*
Club: *Leicester*
Tigers debut: *1.10.1921 v Headingley, won 14-5*
Last game: *14.4.1928 v Blackheath, lost 8-10 (1T, 3 pts)*

A forward who occasionally played full-back or wing, Frank Lawrence played for England in the schools international in 1913 when Wales were beaten at Welford Road (the first match in which the players were numbered, England from 1-15, Wales from 16-30). He played for Leicester in 1927 against the touring Waratahs, one of the most accomplished sides to emerge from Australia.

Appearances: *135 (W86, D11, L38)*
Scoring: *11 tries, 33 pts*

HARRY LAWRIE

LAWRIE, Harry Stephen Balmer (40)

Born: *Lutterworth, Leicestershire, regd Q3 1886*
Died: *Leicester, 15.2.1952*
Clubs: *Stoneygate, Leicester*
Tigers debut: *30.1.1904 at Swansea, lost 0-17*
Last game: *2.1.1915 v Barbarians, won 21-6 (1C, 2 pts)*

Harry Lawrie is the only player in the club's history to have started matches in every position in the back division, as well as playing in the forwards. He made 124 appearances in the pack, having started as a wing and then moved around the backs. The older brother of Percy, he played for the Midland Counties against South Africa in 1912 and was an England reserve two years later.

He was Leicester's leading points scorer in 1909/10 with 72 and played in two Midland Counties Cup-winning sides. He was at the centre of a controversial incident against Harlequins in 1912 when he was sent off for rough play. Adrian Stoop, the Harlequins captain, told reporters afterwards that Lawrie had not been near the player alleged to have been kicked and that the referee had made a mistake. Stoop asked one of his own players to leave the field so that Leicester should not be disadvantaged.

He made his debut for the Barbarians when the invitation club was short-handed against Leicester in 1914 alongside another Tiger, Steve Farmer, who scored the winning try. He was managing director of a company he founded in 1913, Lawrie and Co Ltd, underwear manufacturers in Birstall Street.

Appearances: *168 (W106, D12, L50)*
Scoring: *29 tries, 60 conv, 11pens, 1 drop, 6 marks, 262 pts*

LAWRIE, Percy William (37)

Born: *Lutterworth, Leicestershire, 26.9.1888*
Died: *Leicester, 27.12.1956*
Educated: *Wyggeston*
Clubs: *Stoneygate, Leicester*
Tigers debut: *16.11.1907 at Devonport Albion, lost 0-5*
Last game: *22.4.1924 at Bath, lost 3-28*
Caps: *England (2) 1910-11*

Percy Lawrie, a wing who changed to centre, became Leicester's leading try scorer with 206 after 318 games, a mark which no other player has come near to passing. Had the First World War not intervened, his achievement would have been significantly greater and he might have made more international appearances.

He was the club's leading try scorer in six successive seasons between 1908-14; in 1910 he became the first (of only four players) to score three tries in the annual match against the Barbarians and he broke the Leicester try record held by Harry Wilkinson on Boxing Day 1918, when he registered his 154th try against the 4th Battalion Leicestershire Regiment. Lawrie's 200th try came against United Services in January 1924.

He captained Leicester between 1911-14 and 1920-23 and only Martin Johnson has led Tigers more times than Lawrie's 165 games. He played on England's wing against Scotland twice, scoring a try in his second international. He played for Leicestershire and the Midlands, and joined Harry, his brother, in the Midland Counties side that played South Africa in 1912.

During the war, he served as a lieutenant in the Royal Artillery and, when his senior career ended in 1924, he rejoined Stoneygate for whom he first played at 17. He served on the Leicester committee from 1925 until 1954 when ill health forced him to retire and he died thirty minutes before the start of the 1956 match against the Barbarians. Gordon, his son, played for Leicester in 1938.

Lawrie was an accountant with strong views about the playing of the game in the 1950s: he believed it was spoiled by three elements - the non-application of football brains, absence of straight running and the destructive habits of wing forwards.

Appearances: *318 (W195, D25, L98)*
Scoring: *206 tries, 23 conv, 9 pens, 9 drops, 727 pts*

PERCY LAWRIE

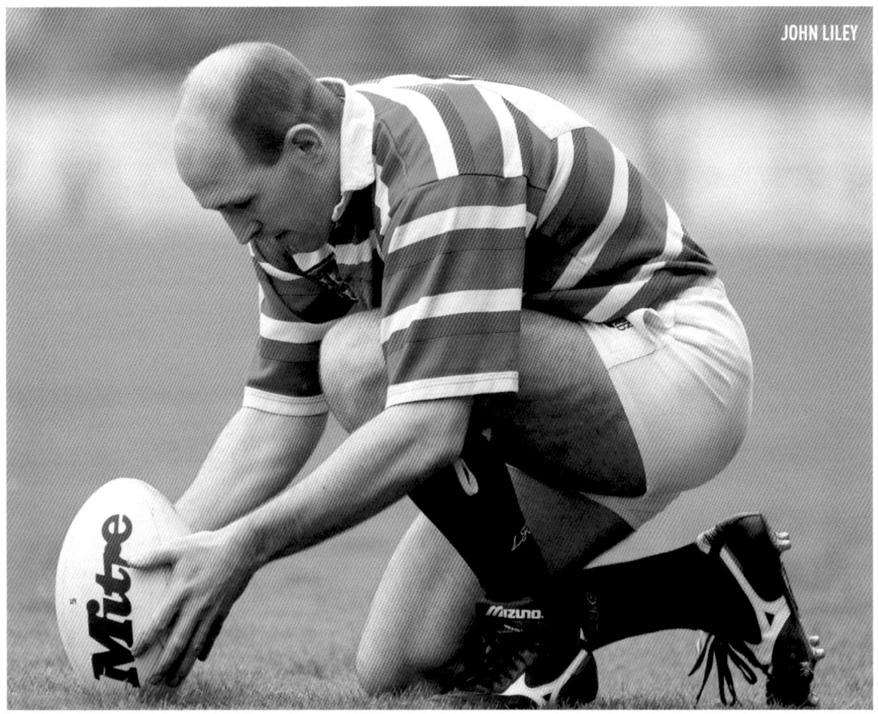

LILEY, John Garin (173)

Born: *Wakefield, Yorkshire, 21.8.1967*
Educated: *Eastmoor HS, Wakefield College, Loughborough University*
Clubs: *Sandal, Wakefield, Leicester, Moseley, Worcester, Doncaster*
Tigers debut: *8.10.1988 v Orrell (replacement), lost 15-27* ●
Last game: *26.4.1997 v Harlequins, lost 12-13 (2PG, 6 pts)* ●

The full-back who stepped into Dusty Hare's boots always faced a difficult task, so crucial had Hare been to Leicester's success in the previous ten years. John Liley cleared the hurdle with aplomb: in the last game of his first season, against Bath, he took his points tally to 439, one better than Hare's club record, and showed a similar ability in attack that earned him 74 tries.

He played volleyball as a youngster and rugby league for English Colleges against their Welsh counterparts in 1986/87. He made his way up the Yorkshire representative ranks and, after moving to Leicester, played for England B against Namibia in 1990 and toured Argentina with the senior squad.

Adept at kicking goals with both feet, he broke the record for points scored in the divisional championship with 51 when the Midlands won the title in 1991/92. In his nine seasons with the Tigers he scored 2,518 points in 230 appearances and was joined, for a season, by his younger brother, Robert. After finishing his playing career, Liley became director of rugby at Ampleforth College.

Appearances: *226 starts + 4 reps (W175, D2, L53)*
Scoring: *74 tries, 417 conv, 449 pens, 2 drops, 2,518 pts*

LINCOLN, William Frederick (23)

Born: *Hawarden, Flintshire, Wales, 6.11.1874*
Died: *Liverpool South, 1.4.1956*
Clubs: *Rugby, Leicester*
Tigers debut: *18.4.1896 at Hartlepool Rovers, drew 6-6*
Last game: *17.4.1900 at Cheltenham, lost 0-3*

William Lincoln, a printer's compositor, was a forward who joined Leicester from Rugby in 1896/97, after guesting for the Tigers on tour the previous season. Lincoln had appeared for Rugby from December 1891 until March 1894 making 22 appearances and scoring three tries, and also skippered their second XV in season 1894/95. He turned out in eleven Midland Counties Cup ties with the Tigers and was never on the losing side. Lincoln's 100th first-team match for Leicester was against Gloucester on 27 January 1900.

Appearances: *110 (W73, D8, L29)*
Scoring: *15 tries, 1 conv, 47 pts*

LLOYD, Leon David (183)

Born: *Coventry, West Midlands, 22.9.1977*
Educated: *Coundon Court (Coventry)*
Clubs: *Barkers' Butts, Leicester, Gloucester*
Tigers debut: *8.1.1996 v Bridgend (replacement), won 60-22 (1T, 5 pts)* ●
Last game: *24.4.2007 at Bristol, lost 13-30* ●
Caps: *England (5) 2000-01*

Leon Lloyd's name is indelibly linked with Leicester's first Heineken Cup success, against Stade Français in 2001. He scored two tries in the final, the second of which (with Tim Stimpson's conversion) put the game beyond the French club's reach. Appropriately, European rugby helped define his career, since he announced his presence as a 19-year-old with a match-winning try in a testing encounter in Pau.

Lloyd was preferred on the wing to Rory Underwood by Bob Dwyer, the Australian coach, after scoring successive hat-tricks in the Leicester development team. He also helped Leicester win the Madrid sevens in 1996 and represented England at colts, under-21 and A level before visiting Australia with the senior squad in 1999 for the pre-World Cup tour.

His international debut came a year later on tour in South Africa, as a replacement in Pretoria and Bloemfontein, and he started all three internationals of the 2001 Canada/USA tour, playing centre in the first two games. He was hampered by injuries for a couple of seasons but played in 27 of a possible 29 matches in 2003/04. He started on the wing in the 2005 Premiership final and was a replacement in the 2006 final. A year later he moved to Gloucester and though injury restricted his appearances to six, he scored five tries.

He retired in 2008 and became foundation director for Oakham School. He was also an ambassador for the Prince's Trust and the Christina Noble Children's Foundation.

Appearances: *233 starts + 27 reps (W181, D11, L68)*
Scoring: *84 tries, 420 pts*

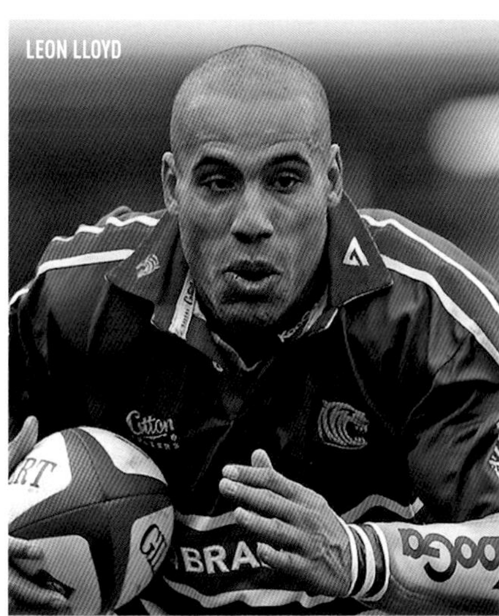

LOVETT, John Thomas (5)

JACK LOVETT

Born: *Barrow-upon-Soar, Leicestershire, 6.1.1859*
Died: *Barrow-upon-Soar, Leicestershire, 28.11.1938*
Clubs: *Loughborough, Leicester*
Tigers debut: *23.10.1880 v Moseley, drew 0-0*
Last game: *15.2.1890 v Manningham, lost 2-5*

Jack Lovett, a forward, was a member of the very first Leicester team which played Moseley in October 1880. He clocked up nine tries in his first 30 matches but none thereafter and made his 100th appearance for the club in the away game at Swinton on 23 November 1889. A schoolmaster at a board school, in 1895 he was one of the founder members of Loughborough RFC.

A useful cricketer, Lovett was opening bowler and middle order batsman for the Gentlemen of Leicestershire.

Appearances: *104 (W52, D13, L39)*
Scoring: *9 tries, 9 pts*

McALPIN, Kenneth (6)

Born: *Leicester, regd Q3 1865*
Died: *Leicester, 16.5.1943*
Educated: *Mill Hill House, Bedford*
Clubs: *Bedford, Leicester*
Tigers debut: *11.10.1884 v Moseley, won 10-0 (2T)*
Last game: *16.11.1892 v Ashby-de-la-Zouch, won 8-0*

Kenneth McAlpin was a member of a famous Leicester footballing family. John, his father, and younger brothers, Colin, Allan, Donald and Jack, were noted association and rugby players. He played football at Mill Hill House School but turned to rugby at Bedford and became a forward who played for the Midland Counties and in two Midland Counties Cup finals (both lost). He scored two tries on his debut and was Leicester's leading try scorer in 1888/89.

McAlpin was the club secretary between 1884-92 and president in 1924-26. He played cricket for Leicester Ivanhoe and, as a partner in the legal firm of McAlpin and Halkyard, was the oldest practising solicitor in Leicester when he died. He was a tenor with the Leicester Philharmonic Society and sang in 100 consecutive concerts; he was a member of the choir at St John's Baptist Church.

Elsa, his daughter, better known as Mrs R E Haylock, was a prominent Leicestershire tennis player who reached the ladies' doubles semi-final at Wimbledon in 1935.

Appearances: *136 (W59, D20, L57)*
Scoring: *13 tries, 13 pts*

KENNETH McALPIN

ARTHUR McKECHNIE

McKECHNIE, Arthur (4)

Born: *New Town, Colne, Lancashire, 26.3.1863*
Died: *St Neots, Cambridgeshire, 19.9.1947*
Educated: *Mellion Street, Elmfield College (York)*
Clubs: *Horbury, Leicester*
Tigers debut: *11.11.1882 at Coventry, drew 0-0*
Last game: *27.1.1894 v Old Leysians, lost 0-3*

The first player to score in the inaugural match at Welford Road in 1892, when he dropped a goal against Leicestershire, 'Mac' McKechnie played football at York under "Sheffield" rules. He moved to Wakefield and played for several junior clubs under local rules, developing into a sound full-back, safe tackler and good kicker.

A scholastic appointment took him to Coalville and he joined Leicester as a three-quarter. He was the leading try scorer in 1889/90 and captained Leicester the following season, becoming a popular figure with players and public.

He became headmaster of Keysoe School in Bedfordshire in 1895 and spent ten years in that post before becoming head of Eaton Socon Council School in St Neots. McKechnie was clerk to the parish council for 26 years and championed various sports: he was chairman of St Neots FC and helped form the local lawn tennis and bowls club. He was interested in politics and, as a forthright speaker and stalwart of the St Neots Liberal Club, helped the Liberals fight elections in Bedfordshire and Huntingdonshire for many years.

Appearances: *217 (W104, D30, L83)*
Scoring: *20 tries, 25 conv, 7 drops, 97 pts*

MANSON, Charles Septimus (69=)

Born: *West Hartlepool, County Durham, 27.1.1905*
Died: *Nottingham, 26.6.1985*
Clubs: *Nottingham, Leicester*
Tigers debut: *1.9.1928 v Bath, won 17-5*
Last game: *28.12.1933 v Waterloo, won 7-6*

The seventh son of a seventh son, hence the name Septimus, Charlie Manson was a full-back who represented Notts, Lincs and Derbys. He moved from the north-east through involvement in the timber-importing business and established his own timber merchants company, Charles Manson and Sons. He played 107 games for Leicester and squeezed in seven appearances for Nottingham between 1928/29 and 1932/33.

Appearances: *107 (W60, D7, L40)*
Scoring: *9 conv, 1 drop, 22 pts*

CHARLIE MANSON

ADEY MARRIOTT

MARRIOTT, Adrian Noel (169)

Born: *Leicester, 9.7.1962*
Educated: *Stonehill HS, Longslade Upper*
Clubs: *Syston, Leicester*
Tigers debut: *3.3.1982 v Royal Navy (replacement), won 17-12*
Last game: *25.4.1992 v Rugby Lions, drew 22-22*

Adey Marriott played football at school but joined Syston as a full-back, playing for Leicestershire under-18s before joining Leicester youth. He changed to flanker, understudying Steve Johnson and taking his back-row place when Johnson retired. Marriott made three appearances in the inaugural Courage league season of 1987/88, when Leicester took the title. A qualified farrier/blacksmith, he ran his own blacksmith's business in Rothley.

Appearances: *114 starts + 16 reps (W93, D3, L34)*
Scoring: *12 tries, 48 pts*

MARTIN, Colin Gerald (102)

Born: *Taihape, New Zealand, 19.1.1933*
Educated: *Tauranga HS, Auckland University*
Clubs: *Auckland University, Auckland (New Zealand), Westleigh, Leicester*
Tigers debut: *29.9.1956 at Newport, lost 3-22 (1PG, 3 pts)*
Last game: *12.4.1966 at Exeter, lost 0-6*

Colin Martin brought a fresh cultural approach to Leicester, the harder edge of the New Zealander and the tactical awareness not always evident in that (or any previous) generation of English players. He also introduced the concept of coaching, relieving the captain of that responsibility and paving the way for the successful era of Chalkie White.

An engineering graduate from Auckland where he won rowing honours at university, he played four matches for the Auckland provincial side and for NZ Universities against their Australian counterparts. He was involved in a fatal car accident while working in the construction of a paper mill; the car in which he was travelling was hit by a train, two friends in it died and Martin was in intensive care for 48 hours.

He was advised that he would not play rugby again but recovered from a back injury so well that he played 272 games for Leicester. He joined the Shell Oil Company and was posted to Holland to learn about oil drilling. That job did not suit him and he moved to England to become a systems engineer with the Nuclear Power Construction Consortium, projects included the Sizewell Nuclear Power Station, working at first at English Electric at Whetstone.

"I had a very clear idea of what the game was about, how to involve the opposition in one place then move your resources to another place very quickly," Martin said. Though a No 8 by inclination, he played mostly at lock initially; he kicked a penalty on his debut against Newport and his goal-kicking made him the club's leading points scorer in his first two seasons.

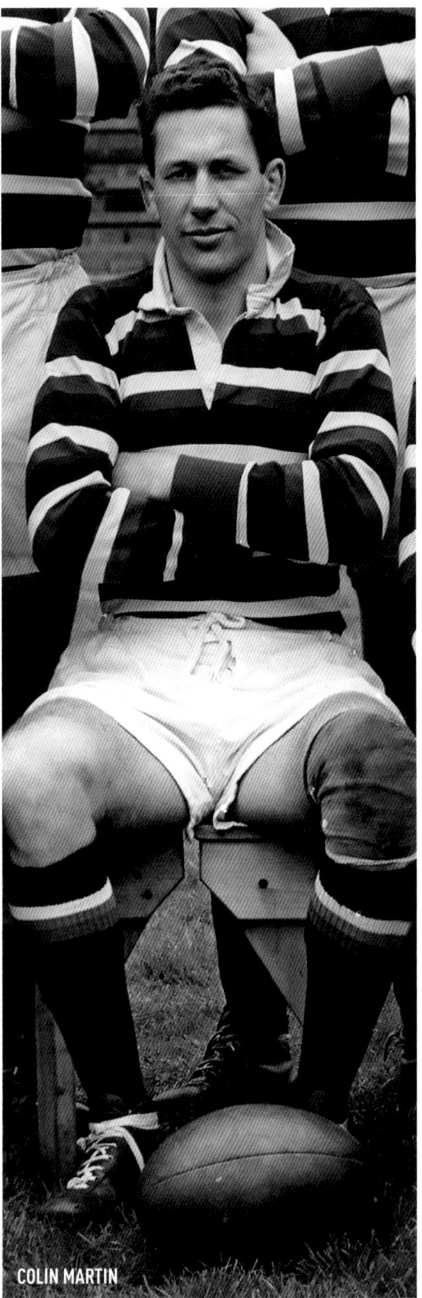

COLIN MARTIN

He was Leicester captain between 1960-63 and played for the Midland Counties against South Africa in 1960 and for Leicestershire and East Midlands against New Zealand in 1963. The 3-3 draw with the Springboks at Welford Road, when he was the captain (and coach), remains Martin's outstanding memory of his time in England; it was the best result any side achieved against the tourists until they lost the final match to the Barbarians 6-0. He also played for the Barbarians in the 1959/60 season.

But his primary influence was the organisation he brought to bear, in training and on match days, and the game awareness he passed on to the likes of David Matthews. "I had trouble with the English system of the day, where the captain of the team was also regarded as the coach, I didn't see how you could make that work," Martin said. "There was some feeling that I was pushing one way, against the system, but in the end the players and Leicester's results benefited.

"Speed to the breakdown, win the ball at the breakdown, that was key to my philosophy, I wanted forwards who could form a loose ruck effectively." During the last two years of his stay, Martin occupied an informal coaching role, working closely with Matthews, the captain, and creating a template for Leicester back rows of the future.

His return home came about after a chance conversation in the bar after Leicester had played Plymouth Albion on an Easter tour. Martin was invited to take a management role in the New Zealand off-shoot of Parkinson Cowan, the Birmingham-based firm of gas appliances; within five years he returned to electronics and became managing director of Thorn EMI Consumer Electronics.

He later became Thorn's Western Pacific director, based in Tokyo, retiring in 1993. He continued to hold various directorships and was also appointed director of the Centre for Advanced Engineering which had been established by Canterbury University. His hectic business life precluded any involvement with rugby, apart from opportunities to attend matches at Auckland's Eden Park when Thorn was an official sponsor. In retirement he lives on Auckland's North Shore, not far from the Albany rugby stadium.

Appearances: *272 (W155, D20, L97)*
Scoring: *13 tries, 126 conv, 88 pens, 555 pts*

MATTHEWS, David Joseph (104)

Born: *Red House, Barrow, Oakham, Rutland, 17.4.1937*
Educated: *Oakham*
Clubs: *Oakham Town, Stoneygate, Leicester*
Tigers debut: *3.9.1955 v Bedford, lost 11-20*
Last game: *9.3.1974 at Coventry, won 36-16*

DAVID MATTHEWS

No player appeared more times for Leicester than David Matthews and no-one ever will. He played 502 games as a back-row forward between 1955 and 1974 and continued to contribute, as coach, president, mentor and board member for the next 35 years, culminating in the award of life membership in 2005.

He came from farming stock, hence his durability (Andy, his younger brother, propped for Leicester). Accustomed to hard work from an early age, he developed great upper-body strength; he played for Oakham Town's first team when only 14 and played his first game for Leicester as an 18-year-old. He became a regular in the back row two years later, when Colin Martin's influence was growing and Matthews learned much from the New Zealander.

His reading of the game helped him towards a career total of 119 tries, at that time more than any other forward in the club's history, and compensated for a lack of natural pace which always made England selectors turn towards his great Bedford rival and lifelong friend, Budge Rogers. Matthews played in three England trials between 1965-67 without clearing the final hurdle, though he did play twice for the Barbarians in 1966 and 1969.

When Leicester won 24 matches in 1960/61, a post-war record, Matthews scored 14 tries, more than any other forward for nearly fifty years. In 1962/63 he was the leading try scorer with 11 and in 1968/69, he scored 21, a record for a forward. A year earlier, adding goal-kicking to his skills, he was the club's leading points scorer with 85.

He played for Midland Counties (East) against Australia in 1966 (in the same back row as Rogers) and against South Africa in 1969. He captained Leicester between 1965-68, the club winning 30 games in his first season and 33 in his second. Martin helped with the coaching and, when he returned to New Zealand, Matthews invited Chalkie White to fill that role.

He reached 100 tries against Bristol at the Memorial Ground in 1969 and made his 500th appearance against Northampton on 23 February 1974, when the opposition formed an honour guard for him. At a dinner in celebration of the achievement, he received a presentation from Rogers.

Matthews coached Leicester from 1988-91 when, for all his lack of formal coaching qualifications, the club's consistency was high and he was at the helm when Tony Russ became the club's first director of rugby, the pair working in harmony. He was a non-executive director of Leicester plc from 1997-2007 and club president between 2001-03.

He was awarded life membership in 2005, "a fitting tribute for someone who has done so much for no financial reward," Peter Tom, Leicester's chairman, said. "He gave his all, as a player and a coach, and he remains a highly influential figure at the club, epitomising all that is so special about the Tigers."

Appearances: *502 (W291, D35, L176)*
Scoring: *119 tries, 15 conv, 20 pens, 451 pts*

SAMMY MATTHEWS

MATTHEWS, Samuel (24)

Born: *Tugby, Leicestershire, 31.1.1878*
Died: *Oadby, Leicestershire, 21.11.1960*
Clubs: *Oadby, Leicester*
Tigers debut: *8.1.1898 at Coventry, won 9-0*
Last game: *20.4.1908 at Cardiff, lost 11-24*

Sammy Matthews, a bustling forward, was a bricklayers' labourer who played more than 300 games in ten years for Tigers. He won England trials in 1900 and 1902 and, during two spells as club captain between 1904-06 and 1907-09, led the club against New Zealand in 1905.

He played for the Midlands against South Africa in 1906 and, in 27 Midland Counties Cup ties, was never on the losing side. That record included seven successive finals between 1899-1905. From April 1902 to December 1905 he played in 127 of a possible 128 games, missing only a match at Swansea.

Appearances: *340 (W199, D34, L107)*
Scoring: *19 tries, 14 conv, 1 pen, 88 pts*

MONEY, Robin Strang (134)

Born: *Falkirk, Scotland, 5.9.1945*
Educated: *Hawick HS, Ardrossan Academy, Harris Academy (Dundee), St Andrews University, Jordanhill College of PE*
Clubs: *Jordanhill, Glasgow, Leicester*
Tigers debut: *8.10.1968 v Rugby, won 12-11*
Last game: *8.4.1978 at Bristol (replacement), lost 0-23*

A diminutive full-back with a flair for attack and the endearing habit of heading bouncing balls into touch, Robin Money represented Scottish Midland schools and Glasgow before taking up a teaching appointment at Wyggeston School. He played for the Anglo-Scots in trial matches between 1974-76.

He was captain of Jordanhill, Leicester (in 1975/76) and Leicestershire. A keen golfer and squash player, he left teaching to join the sportswear firm, Adidas UK Ltd., becoming head of sports marketing.

Appearances: *255 starts + 3 reps (W147, D12, L99)*
Scoring: *23 tries, 12 drops, 123 pts*

ROBIN MONEY

MOODY, Lewis Walton (192)

Born: *Ascot, Berkshire, 12.6.1978*
Educated: *Oakham, De Montfort University*
Clubs: *Bracknell, Oakham, Leicester, Bath*
Tigers debut: *25.8.1996 v Boroughmuir, won 72-33 (2T, 10 pts)* ●
Last game: *29.5.2010 v Saracens (at Twickenham), won 33-27* ●
Caps: *England (71) 2001-11, British & Irish Lions (3) 2005*

A blond flanker known for much of his playing career as 'Mad dog' because of his utter disregard for his own wellbeing in loose play (which led to a career littered with injuries). Moody became the sixth Leicester player in the professional era to captain England and led his country into the 2011 World Cup.

He played mini-rugby at Bracknell and came to Leicester's notice while at Oakham School. He played for England at school, colts, under-18 and under-21 level and toured the southern hemisphere with the England senior side in 1998. The following season he was voted Leicester's young player of the year, having made his league debut at the age of 18 years 94 days - then a club record.

He won his first cap on England's 2001 tour to Canada and the USA, retaining his

LEWIS MOODY

place over the next two seasons before an injury setback removed him from the 2003 six nations. He returned in time to win a place in the World Cup squad and appeared in all seven games, including the final against Australia when his line-out catch sparked the move which led to Jonny Wilkinson's match-winning dropped goal. He was subsequently awarded the MBE.

He returned from Australia with a stress fracture of the foot but recovered his England place in 2004/05, earning selection for the Lions tour to New Zealand where he played in two tests, scoring a try in the last. He settled as first-choice open-side over the next two seasons, despite a red card against Samoa in 2005 for punching Alesana Tuilagi (Samoa's wing and a Leicester colleague), before injury removed him from the 2007 six nations. But he returned for that year's World Cup, again appearing in all seven games on the way to the final.

A succession of injuries to shoulder, Achilles tendon and ankle disrupted the next two seasons but Moody returned in 2009 and took over from the injured Steve Borthwick as England captain for the final 2010 six nations game, against France. A knee injury kept him out of the 2011 six nations but he returned in time for the World Cup in New Zealand, playing in four of England's five games in what proved to be his international swansong.

Both for club and country, Moody had to wait for an open-side berth behind Neil Back and promptly displayed his ability at blind-side flanker. He played No 6 in the Heineken Cup finals of 2002 and 2007, and was a replacement in the 2009 final. He was part of the squad that won four successive Premiership titles between 1999-2002, he started the 2006 and 2007 Premiership finals and was a replacement in 2005 and 2009.

He agreed a three-year deal with Bath in 2010 but was forced by injury to retire in 2012. Moody was diagnosed with an inflammatory bowel disease, ulcerative colitis in 2005, and has raised awareness of the Crohn's and Colitis UK charity since retirement. He was inducted into the Aviva Premiership hall of fame in 2014.

Appearances: *174 starts + 49 reps (W152, D8, L63)*
Scoring: *36 tries, 180 pts*

MOORE, William Kenneth Thomas (82)

Born: *Leicester, 24.2.1921*
Died: *Leicester, 22.8.2002*
Educated: *Wyggeston GS*
Clubs: *Old Wyggestonians, Devonport Services, Leicester*
Tigers debut: *8.9.1945 at Cardiff, lost 6-12*
Last game: *18.4.1953 at Sale, won 24-19*
Caps: *England (7) 1947-50*

Bill Moore was the grandson of the Leicester half-back, Billy Foreman, and served as an electrical artificer on HMS Defiance during the Second World War before becoming a pilot officer in the Royal Navy.

He played scrum-half for England against Scotland in two "Victory" internationals in 1946 and won his first cap against Wales a year later, after only 11 first-team games for Leicester. He played in the five nations championships of 1949 and 1950, represented Cornwall and Leicestershire, and was Leicester's captain between 1950-52.

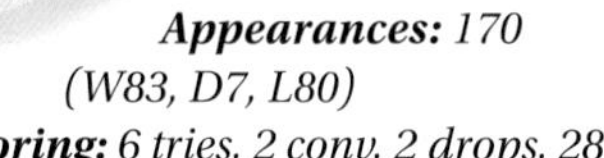
BILL MOORE

A lengthy passer of the ball and an original thinker, Moore became a referee when his playing career ended and took charge of the Leicester v Leicestershire game of 1961. After leaving the Navy he studied boot and shoe manufacture and became a sales manager with British United Shoes.

Appearances: *170 (W83, D7, L80)*
Scoring: *6 tries, 2 conv, 2 drops, 28 pts*

MORTIMER, Michael Richard (138)

Born: *Huddersfield, Yorkshire, 31.10.1943*
Educated: *Teignmouth GS (Devon), St John's College (York)*
Clubs: *St John's College, Stoneygate, Leicester*
Tigers debut: *19.3.1971 v Royal Air Force, won 11-6*
Last game: *13.12.1975 at Blackheath, won 13-8*

Mike Mortimer, a prop tall enough to play the occasional game at lock, represented Devon schools at football, basketball and athletics. He played rugby at St John's and moved to teach in Leicester, playing for South Leicester and Stoneygate before joining Tigers midway through the 1969/70 season.

MIKE MORTIMER

He played for Devon and Leicestershire and was twice a replacement for Midland Counties (East) against representative sides. He became a sales representative for Rank Xerox and was a member of the Leicestershire Society of Referees from 1982. He ran courses on rugby law explained and was the author of books of the same name, aimed at examining finer points of law for the layman.

Appearances: *132 (W76, D6, L50)*
Scoring: *10 tries, 40 pts*

MURPHY, Geordan Edward Andrew (188)

Born: *Dublin, Ireland, 19.4.1978*
Educated: *Newbridge College, Waterford Institute of Technology, De Montfort University*
Clubs: *Naas (Ireland), Auckland GS, Leicester*
Tigers debut: *14.11.1997 v Rotherham, won 60-19* ●
Last game: *4.5.2013 v London Irish, won 32-20* ●
Caps: *Ireland (72) 2000-11, British & Irish Lions (2) 2005*

Geordan Murphy, memorably described by Dean Richards as "the George Best of rugby", arrived at Leicester on trial as a teenager in 1997 and never left. His all-round skills, demonstrated most notably from full-back, allowed him to play wing and, occasionally, fly-half but his sleight of hand with the ball mesmerised opponents (and sometimes colleagues).

GEORDAN MURPHY

Blessed with pace and an eye for the gap, Murphy made a huge contribution over 16 seasons with Leicester, including as an occasional goalkicker. At school he helped Newbridge to the Leinster Senior Cup final and also played Gaelic football; he played in Ireland's under-18, under-21 and A sides before scoring two tries on his senior debut in 2000, against the USA.

He remained a part of Ireland squads over the next 11 years, much of the time as a full-back rival to Girvan Dempsey. He was his country's player of the year in 2003 but a broken leg in a warm-up match against Scotland kept him out of that year's World Cup. His return to form earned him a place on the Lions tour to New Zealand in 2005, when he started the final test.

He went to the World Cups of 2007 and 2011 but had to play second fiddle to Dempsey in France and Rob Kearney in New Zealand. In between he was able to participate in Ireland's second grand-slam season, that of 2009 when he was on the pitch at the moment of triumph against Wales in Cardiff.

His talents seemed appreciated far more at Leicester. He played on the wing in the Heineken Cup finals of 2001 and 2002, scoring a try in the win over Munster, and at full-back in the finals of 2007 and 2009. He was also a try scorer in the pool game of 2006 at Thomond Park, when Leicester's 13-6 win ended Munster's unbeaten home run in Europe.

Murphy contributed towards the four successive Premiership wins of 1999-2002 and was a constant presence at full-back in the Premiership finals of 2005-10. He took over as club captain in 2008, in the absence of Martin Corry, and was confirmed in the role the following season. He led Tigers to the EDF Energy Cup final win of 2012 and the Premiership final that year and when he retired, in 2013 he joined the coaching staff.

Appearances: *298 starts + 24 reps (W233, D11, L78)*
Scoring: *93 tries, 53 conv, 34 pens, 6 drops, 691 pts*

N

NEEDHAM, Raymond Ernest (145)

Born: *Bingley, Yorkshire, 2.11.1949*
Educated: *Bingley GS, St. Luke's College (Exeter)*
Clubs: *Bingley, St. Luke's, Leicester*
Tigers debut: *5.9.1973 v Nottingham, won 12-9*
Last game: *30.4.1982 at Ballymena, won 21-18*

Ray Needham was a valuable deputy at loose-head prop to Robin Cowling and appeared in the club's first John Player Cup final, against Gloucester in 1978. He represented Yorkshire and Leicestershire and was an accomplished cricketer, playing in the competitive Yorkshire Federation after appearing for the county at under-16 and under-18 level.

A teacher specialising in PE and mathematics, Needham became a qualified coach after retiring and took over the running of Leicester's youth team. He became development team secretary and, as a committeeman during the amateur era, sat on selection, playing and ground sub-committees.

Appearances: *123 starts + 3 reps (W84, D2, L40)*
Scoring: *5 tries, 3 conv, 26 pts*

RAY NEEDHAM

NICHOLAS, Walter Kenneth (85)

Born: *Newbridge, Monmouthshire, Wales, 17.8.1926*
Educated: *Newbridge GS, Loughborough Colleges*
Clubs: *Newbridge, Loughborough Colleges, Leicester, Bedford*
Tigers debut: *6.3.1948 v Harlequins, won 32-3*
Last game: *5.12.1953 at Waterloo, lost 9-12 (2T, 6 pts)*

KEN NICHOLAS

A fly-half who could also play centre or wing, Ken Nicholas enjoyed the distinction of coaching and then playing with and against a future England centre in Mike Wade. He served with the Fleet Air Arm during the Second World War and joined Wyggeston School as a geography and PE teacher.

He represented Leicestershire, Surrey, Midland Counties and London Counties and appeared in a Scotland trial in 1954 despite his strong Welsh accent. Wade was a pupil at Wyggeston and played with Nicholas for Leicestershire before Nicholas moved to Bedford, when the two became opponents.

Nicholas scored two tries in his last match for Leicester, against Waterloo, then played 82 games for Bedford between 1954-59, scoring 12 tries and nine dropped goals. He was a master at Whitgift School from 1956-91.

Appearances: *151 (W76, D5, L70)*
Scoring: *24 tries, 1 conv, 3 pens, 4 drops, 95 pts*

NORMAN, Douglas James (52)

Born: *Leicester, 12.6.1897*
Died: *Oadby, Leicester, 27.12.1971*
Educated: *Medway Street*
Clubs: *Medway Athletic, Oadby, Leicester*
Tigers debut: *17.1.1920 v Headingley, won 54-11 (3C, 6 pts)*
Last game: *18.4.1933 at Bath, lost 8-15*
Caps: *England (2) 1932*

Doug Norman, a hooker, won his caps at the ripe age of 34 after appearing in the famous win by Leicestershire and East Midlands over South Africa in 1931. His international career began and ended within a fortnight in January 1932, against the Springboks and Wales, though for much of his career a cap seemed likely to elude him.

He learned his rugby at Medway Street School under the guidance of James Cooper, founder of the English Schools RFU, and led England schools to their first win over Wales in 1911. He was also an athlete, swimmer and cricketer at school before serving in the First World War with the Royal Artillery in Mesopotamia.

Originally a full-back, Norman played his first six seasons as a flanker before changing to hooker in 1927 and making the position his own. He played in several England trials but seemed destined to remain a travelling reserve. After the Midland win over South Africa, he was injured in another trial match but recovered from strained neck muscles to make his international debut.

He was Leicester's vice-captain from 1926-31 and captain in 1932/33, the season when he left the field with a shoulder injury against Old Blues, something he had never done before. He retired in 1933 having played 453 games for the club but continued to play junior rugby.

During the Second World War he served with the Home Guard and organised the Leicestershire Harlequins, a team designed to provide rugby for local players on leave and servicemen passing through the county. The Harlequins proved the nucleus for the reformation of Tigers when hostilities ceased.

Brought up in the printing trade, Norman worked at the College of Art and Technology, and Blackfriars Press Ltd. After the war he edited and produced the Midland Counties handbook. He became Leicester's fixture secretary and president; he was also president of the Leicestershire Schools RFU and of the Oadby club.

Appearances: *453 (W268, D35, L150)*
Scoring: *21 tries, 29 conv, 2 pens, 1 drop, 131 pts*

DOUG NORMAN

P

PARSONS, John (1)

Born: *Leicester, regd Q4 1860*
Died: *Leicester, 12.9.1941*
Educated: *Franklin's*
Clubs: *Leicester, Harlequins, Lansdowne (Ireland)*
Tigers debut: *27.11.1880 v Burton, drew 0-0*
Last game: *23.3.1889 v Moseley (at Coventry), lost 0-6* ●

Jack Parsons was one of only two people to have held every senior post at Leicester: he was secretary and player in 1880/81, captain from 1886-89 and president from 1891-1901. He was also an invaluable utility player, appearing initially as a forward but later starting at half-back, three-quarter and full-back.

He was the first player to appear 100 times, against Rugby on 21 January 1888, indeed he played in 100 of the first 138 games played by the club until a knee injury ended his career. Against Northampton Unity in 1887 he scored three tries, three conversions and a dropped goal in a 17-0 win. He made four appearances for Harlequins in 1883/84 while doing legal training in London.

A solicitor with Parsons, Wykes and Davis, he played cricket for Lansdowne, Leicester Ivanhoe and Leicestershire (before they attained first-class status). He was a member of the Leicestershire side when they first beat Surrey, giants of the county game, at Grace Road in May 1883. He was treasurer of the county for 47 years.

Parsons stood in the St Martin's ward for the city council in 1902 and became an alderman in 1915. He was accorded the honorary freedom of the city in October 1940.

Appearances: *113 (W62, D18, L33)*
Scoring: *15 tries, 48 conv, 13 drops, 150 pts*

JACK PARSONS

SID PENNY

PENNY, Sidney Herbert (17)

Born: *Finchley, London, 7.10.1875*
Died: *Leicester, 23.5.1965*
Educated: *St Peter's*
Clubs: *Granville, Belgrave St Peter's, Leicester*
Tigers debut: *4.1.1896 at Gloucester, lost 12-20*
Last game: *26.12.1910 v Birkenhead Park, won 25-5*
Caps: *England (1) 1909*

A hooker who was 33 when he made his only international appearance, Sid Penny was the first player to pass 400 games for the club and was presented with a testimonial scroll for 500 appearances after the Barbarians match on 28 December 1911. Club records, however, confirm only 491 games, still a remarkable tally and only overtaken by David Matthews in 1974.

At the time of his death, aged 89, Penny was the longest surviving member of the 1898 Midland Counties Cup-winning side. He appeared in a record ten winning finals (eight in succession), and was only once on the losing side in forty cup ties. He played for the Midland Counties and was invited to tour New Zealand with the 1908 Anglo-Welsh party but could not afford time off work (he was a clicker at Rawsons Ltd in the boot and shoe trade).

Penny played for the combined Midlands and East Midlands Counties team that beat Australia in December 1908 and played for England against the tourists in the 3-9 defeat at Blackheath a month later.

He captained Leicester once, against Plymouth on the Easter tour of 1907, his 347th match. He retired from work aged 85 and, when asked if he had any advice for the younger generation, said: "If you can give young people any advice then you're a lucky man, they won't have it."

Appearances: *491 (W309, D45, L137)*
Scoring: *16 tries, 48 pts*

POOLE, Matthew David (174)

Born: *Leicester, 6.2.1969*
Educated: *Roundhill College*
Clubs: *Syston, Leicester*
Tigers debut: *18.10.1988 v Oxford University, won 24-6*
Last game: *7.11.1998 v Bath (replacement), won 36-13* ●

A product of the Leicester youth team, Matt Poole played for England colts and in the inaugural England under-21 team and toured Argentina with England's senior squad in 1990. He also toured South Africa with the seniors in 1994 but a cap eluded him.

However he gave yeoman service in Leicester's second row, packing down with Martin Johnson on 129 occasions (a club record), and played in four Pilkington Cup finals for the club. He scored a try in the 1996 cup final against Bath, played in the squad that won the league title a year earlier and started the 1997 Heineken Cup final against Brive.

He played more matches in the letter E shirt (192) than any other player in the club's history. Since retiring, Poole has remained closely associated with the club's commercial activities and is on the board of Tigers Events Ltd.

Appearances: *215 starts + 8 reps (W172, D3, L48)*
Scoring: *20 tries, 95 pts*

PORTER, William Robert (2)

Born: *Rockingham, Northamptonshire, regd Q4 1858*
Died: *Leicester, 28.3.1936*
Club: *Leicester*
Tigers debut: *23.10.1880 v Moseley, drew 0-0*
Last game: *9.4.1892 at Handsworth, won 12-4 (1T, 2 pts)*

One of the original members of Leicester Football Club, William Porter was a forward whose appearance in the first fixture was the start of a 55-year association with the club. He became captain in the 1889/90 season and was a member of the first Tigers team to contest a Midland Counties Cup final.

He was the first player to pass 150 appearances, as captain against Ashby-de-la-Zouch on 5 March 1890, and though he only scored ten tries in his playing career, four came in his last seven games, including one in each of his last two matches.

He played in 16 games between 1883-88 with his younger brother, Samuel, and five more between 1889-91 with another brother, George.

A stay and corset maker with a business in Highcross Street, Porter took a yarn agency later in life. He joined Leicester's committee and became a vice-president; he was also a longstanding member of Leicestershire County Cricket Club.

Appearances: *170 (W82, D23, L65)*
Scoring: *10 tries, 11 pts*

POTTER, Stuart (181)

Born: *Lichfield, Staffordshire, 11.11.1967*
Educated: *Lichfield Friary Grange*
Clubs: *Lichfield, Nottingham, Leicester, Rugby*
Tigers debut: *1.9.1992 at Sheffield, won 27-7*
Last game: *29.12.1999 v Harlequins (replacement), won 29-17* ●
Caps: *England (1) 1998*

Stuart Potter, who was an insurance broker before rugby turned professional, came to Leicester having twice been named Nottingham's player of the season during a four-year spell at Beeston. A strongly-built centre with a low centre of gravity, he made the first of 15 appearances for England A in 1993 and toured with them to Canada in 1993 and Australia/Fiji in 1995.

He was a member of England's senior touring side to South Africa in 1994 and won his only cap as a replacement against Australia on tour in 1998. He played in four Pilkington Cup finals with Leicester, scoring a try in the 1993 win over Harlequins, and was a member of the squad that won the 1994/95 league title. He received the club's outstanding service award for 1997/98.

Appearances: *166 starts + 3 reps (W129, D4, L36)*
Scoring: *36 tries, 180 pts*

POVOAS, Simon John (172)

Born: *Leicester, 10.6.1966*
Educated: *Kibworth HS, Robert Smyth (Market Harborough)*
Clubs: *Oadby Wyggestonians, Leicester*
Tigers debut: *9.9.1986 at Nuneaton (replacement), won 49-6*
Last game: *2.11.1993 v Cambridge University, won 31-27*

Simon Povoas, a No 8 whose name stems from Portuguese ancestors, spent his entire career as understudy to Dean Richards. Yet he rose to B international status, played for the Barbarians and, in 1989/90, set a club record for a forward of 25 tries in a season, for much of which Richards was absent injured.

He represented Leicestershire, East Midlands and Midlands schools at under-14, under-16 and under-18 level and had England trials at under-16 and under-18 level. He played for Leicester youth and for Leicestershire at senior level and joined the England B squad in Paris in 1990 for the match with France.

At Headingley in September 1991 he became only the fifth forward (and the first since 1938) to score four tries in a match, his hat-trick try being the fiftieth of his career.

He now runs Povoas Packaging Limited, a polythene manufacturing business based near Desborough.

Appearances: *127 starts + 8 reps (W93, D2, L40)*
Scoring: *64 tries, 261 pts*

STAN PRATT

PRATT, Stanley (90)

Born: *Belgrave, Leicester, 26.12.1922*
Died: *Adelaide, Australia, 25.11.2008*
Educated: *Ellis Avenue*
Clubs: *Aylestone Athletic, Leicester*
Tigers debut: *26.2.1949 at Northampton, drew 9-9*
Last game: *24.4.1954 v Sale, won 27-14*

Aylestone Athletic produced several Tigers in the 1950s, among them Stan Pratt, a hooker who worked as an apprentice carpenter for Dried Handicrafts in Thornton Lane. He served during the Second World War in the Royal Navy on convoy duty to Russia, Malta and the Far East.

Initially he was understudy to Ronnie Tudor, becoming a regular in 1950. Two of his four tries for the club came in the home and away fixtures with Blackheath in 1950/51. He moved to South Australia in 1973.

Appearances: *134 (W69, D9, L56)*
Scoring: *4 tries, 12 pts*

PRENTICE, Frank Douglas (58)

Born: *Leicester, regd Q4 1898*
Died: *Paddington, London, 3.10.1962*
Educated: *Wyggeston*
Clubs: *Westleigh, Leicester*
Tigers debut: *26.11.1923 at Neath, lost 6-37 (1T, 3 pts)*
Last game: *18.4.1931 v Blackheath, won 25-5 (3C, 1PG, 9 pts)*
Caps: *England (3) 1928, Great Britain (2) 1930*

Doug Prentice became better known as secretary to the Rugby Football Union for 15 years between 1947-62, but his international career, though brief, included captaincy of the 1930 British Isles team that toured Australasia, the first Leicester player to lead a party which became known as the Lions.

A back-row forward whose 65 appearances for Leicestershire included the side that won the county championship in 1925, Prentice was captain of Leicester between 1928-30. He was also the club's leading points scorer between 1928-31 and played three times in England's grand slam-winning side of 1928.

He was told only at the eleventh hour that he, the oldest player in the squad, would captain the 1930 Lions and did much to pull together a happy squad. However Prentice recognised there were better back-five players in the squad and appeared in only two internationals, the second test against New Zealand and the only game against Australia.

Even so, he was the best goalkicker in the party and registered 49 points, including two conversions against the All Blacks.

His final match, in which he kicked three conversions and a penalty against Blackheath in 1931, was refereed by a former Leicester player, Wavell Wakefield. Prentice managed the British team that toured Argentina in 1936, under the captaincy of Bernard Gadney, and he was an England selector from 1932-47. As RFU secretary he worked in a period when England won a grand slam (1957) until forced by ill health to retire.

During the First World War, when he was badly wounded, he served with the Royal Artillery and when posted to France, joined the ANZACs, whose enthusiasm for rugby converted him from football. In the Second World War, he served as a lieutenant-colonel in the RASC and was taken prisoner.

Appearances: *239 (W140, D14, L85)*
Scoring: *60 tries, 133 conv, 43 pens, 575 pts*

DOUG PRENTICE

PULFREY, Peter Graham Smith (123)

Born: *Grantham, Lincolnshire, 10.9.1938*
Educated: *Magnus GS (Newark)*
Clubs: *Newark, Leicester*
Tigers debut: *15.9.1962 v Plymouth Albion, won 11-6*
Last game: *27.12.1969 v Barbarians, lost 0-35*

GRAHAM PULFREY

Every one of Graham Pulfrey's 173 appearances came at full-back after his move from Newark - the club that also produced Dusty Hare. He gained a regular place when Keith Chilton switched to centre in 1965 and represented Notts, Lincs and Derbys, and Leicestershire.

Pulfrey played for Midland Counties (East) against South Africa in 1969, his final season. A trade director (Ireland) for Scottish and Newcastle Breweries Ltd, his son, Daniel Robert David, played for Scottish Schools in 1987/88.

Appearances: *173 (W109, D11, L53)*
Scoring: *13 tries, 1 conv, 6 pens, 5 drops, 74 pts*

QUICK, John (124)

Born: *Sydney, New South Wales, Australia, 12.11.1940*
Educated: *Sydney Boys HS, Sydney University*
Clubs: *Randwick (Australia), Kibworth, Leicester*
Tigers debut: *12.12.1964 at Headingley, won 21-6 (1T, 3 pts)*
Last game: *20.4.1968 at Llanelli, lost 5-14 (1T, 3 pts)*

John Quick, a dental surgeon, was a powerful and perceptive No 8 who formed an outstanding back row playing alongside David Matthews, Graham Willars and Bob Small. He scored a try on his debut and also in his final club appearance; in between he scored three tries against the 1965 Barbarians and made 15 appearances for Leicestershire.

His 15 tries in 1965/66 made him the leading try scorer that season and he captained Leicester in his last four appearances. After returning home he became a first-grade coach with Randwick, then Sydney's leading club. He was coaching advisor to Japan in 1986 and during their 1987 World Cup campaign; he coached Australia's under-21 side and Sam, his son, appeared for Leicester in 1991/92.

JOHN QUICK

Appearances: *119 (W81, D5, L33)*
Scoring: *41 tries, 123 pts*

R

REDFERN, Stephen Paul (147)

Born: *Leicester, 26.10.1957*
Educated: *Markfield HS, Coalville GS*
Clubs: *Coalville, Leicester, Sheffield Eagles RL, Leicester Cobblers RL*
Tigers debut: *30.10.1976 at Nottingham, won 19-6* ●
Last game: *24.11.1984 v Moseley, lost 19-22* ●
Caps: *England (1) 1984*

Steve 'Granite' Redfern received representative honours early but, in the same year that he made his only senior England appearance (as a replacement for Colin White against Ireland), he switched to rugby league. Injury ensured the move was not a success and he spent considerable time seeking reinstatement before being allowed to coach rugby union once more.

Redfern, a prop, joined Leicester youth from Coalville in 1973 and became a member of the senior squad three years later. He played for England under-23 in 1977, touring Canada, France and Italy. In 1979 he played for the Midland Counties against New Zealand and for England B against France B; two years later he played for Midland Counties in the win over Australia.

Despite a severe neck injury keeping him out of the first half of the 1978/79 season, he played in Leicester's five John Player Cup finals between 1978-83, joined in the last of them (against Bristol) by his younger brother, Stuart, with whom he played 45 times in the Leicester front row. He played more times in the tight-head shirt (letter C) than any other club player (237) and, when he played against Ireland in 1984, brought to the record of seven the number of Leicester players on an international pitch at the same time.

He signed to play rugby league and made his debut for Sheffield Eagles against Doncaster in December 1984 but made only nine appearances before injury forced him to retire.

Appearances: *241 (W177, D7, L57)*
Scoring: *16 tries, 64 pts*

STEVE REDFERN

REDFERN, Stuart Bernard (160)

Born: *Leicester, 16.6.1961*
Educated: *South Charnwood HS, King Edward VII Upper (Coalville)*
Clubs: *Coalville, Leicester*
Tigers debut: *16.3.1982 v Loughborough Students, won 12-9*
Last game: *25.4.1992 v Rugby Lions, drew 22-22* ●

Stuart 'Pebble' Redfern followed a similar path as his older brother, Steve, but played at loose-head prop. He won England colts caps and made two England under-23 appearances; he played for the Midland Division against New Zealand in 1983 but did not become first choice for the Midlands until the divisional championship of 1986/87.

He played for an England XV against the Rest of the World in 1984 and in two losing cup finals for Leicester, in 1983 and 1989. He made more appearances in the letter A shirt (322) than any other player. A former mechanical engineer, he reached the RFU level three coaching award and was a specialist front-row coach for the Leicester academy.

Appearances: *322 starts + 2 reps (W235, D6, L83)*
Scoring: *25 tries, 100 pts*

STUART REDFERN

EDDIE REDMAN

REDMAN, Edward (12)

Born: *Charlestown, Yorkshire, 7.5.1869*
Died: *New Wortley, Yorkshire, 8.7.1924*
Clubs: *Yeadon, Guiseley, Manningham, Leicester, Stoneygate*
Tigers debut: *16.9.1893 v Leicestershire XV, won 26-6 (1T, 3 pts)*
Last game: *5.11.1900 at Llanelly, won 12-6*

Eddie Redman, a forward, played for the clubs near to his home in New Scarborough and, while with Manningham, for Yorkshire against the Rest of England in 1892 and 1893. He played for the North v the South in an 1892 England trial and was selected to play for England against Ireland in Dublin on 4 February 1893.

But he broke a finger playing for Yorkshire against Somerset three weeks before the international and, though he was a reserve for England against Scotland, was never given his international opportunity. When he moved to Leicester he played for the Midland Counties and was regarded as one of the best forwards in the area.

He captained Leicester from 1894-96 and was a member of the club's first Midland Counties Cup-winning team of 1898. He played cricket for the Leicester South End Club and was, for a time, landlord at the Welford Tavern.

Appearances: *143 (W98, D14, L31)*
Scoring: *12 tries, 1 pen, 39 pts*

RICHARDS, Dean (161)

Born: *Nuneaton, Warwickshire, 11.7.1963*
Educated: *St Martin's HS, John Cleveland College (Hinckley)*
Clubs: *Roanne (France), Leicester*
Tigers debut: *10.4.1982 at Neath, won 25-14*
Last game: *30.12.1997 v Newcastle Falcons, lost 19-25* ●
Caps: *England (48) 1986-96, British Isles (6) 1989-93*

Dean Richards, once England's most capped No 8, spent six years as Tigers' director of rugby after 17 seasons with the club as a player spanning both the amateur and professional eras. As iconic a player of his generation, for club and country, as Martin Johnson during his international career, Richards re-invented the role of No 8. There was little of the athlete about him, but everything of the rugby player with an instinctive feel for a game and where the ball would go.

Shirt flapping, socks around his ankles, Richards gave little indication of pace in his game yet was always where he was wanted. Above all he possessed the physical strength which made him a target for colleagues and almost impossible to dispossess in a maul. When cries of 'Deano' echoed around Welford Road, it was an indication that Leicester's forwards had gained the upper hand.

He played for England's 18-group schools side and spent a season, as a teenager, with the junior French club, Roanne. When he returned home he joined the Leicestershire Police and made his Tigers debut at the age of 18; he played for Leicestershire, the Midlands and England under-23 before making his international debut against Ireland in 1986, scoring two tries and becoming the first England player for 57 years to do so.

He played in England's four games of the inaugural World Cup in 1987 and returned to Australia two years later with the Lions, playing a pivotal role in the winning of the series and leading the touring side against Australia B. He missed the 1989/90 season with a shoulder injury but toured Australia/Fiji with England in 1991 and played in that year's World Cup. His omission from the back row during the knockout stages was a major talking point of the tournament, particularly in the final which England lost 12-6 to Australia.

He played in England's grand-slam seasons of 1991, 1992 and 1995 and

in the five nations championship-winning season of 1996. In between he made a second Lions tour, to New Zealand, in 1993, again playing all three internationals and captaining the side that faced Canterbury, and played in a third World Cup, in South Africa in 1995.

Having helped Leicester to the inaugural league title in 1988, he enjoyed two spells as club captain - in 1990/91 and from 1993-97. Leicester won the league in 1995 and reached the Heineken Cup final of 1997, losing to Brive. He also played in the Pilkington Cup final wins of 1993 and 1997 and, when he retired, he had made 314 appearances and become only the second forward (after David Matthews) to have scored over 100 tries for the club. He was awarded the MBE in 1996.

He was appointed director of rugby in February 1998, in succession to Bob Dwyer, and sustained his long playing association with John Wells, who became coach. Under Richards, Leicester enjoyed a period of unsurpassed success, winning four successive Premiership titles between 1999-2002 and two Heineken Cup finals, in 2001 and 2002. But Leicester's failure to reach the knockout phase of Europe in the 2003/04 season cost Richards his job and he spent a not-entirely happy season in France with Grenoble.

He returned to the Premiership with Harlequins in 2005 and played a considerable part in restoring their fortunes after a season of Championship rugby. But he was involved in the Bloodgate scandal after a Heineken Cup quarter-final between Harlequins and Leinster in 2009 which cost him a three-year suspension from involvement with the game. He returned as director of rugby with Newcastle Falcons in 2012 and helped them win promotion from the Championship.

DEAN RICHARDS

Appearances: *306 starts + 8 reps (W233, D6, L75)*
Scoring: *105 tries, 431 pts*

WAYNE RICHARDSON

RICHARDSON, Wayne Philip (165)

Born: *Leicester, 11.3.1961*
Educated: *Soar Valley School and Community College*
Club: *Leicester*
Tigers debut: *28.3.1981 at Sale, lost 6-15*
Last game: *2.11.1993 v Cambridge University, won 31-27*

Wayne Richardson switched to rugby from football at school and joined Leicester at the age of 14. He was advised by Robin Cowling to change from lock to prop and played for Leicestershire, East Midlands and Midland schools at under-14 and under-16 level. He received trials for England schools and went on to play for Midland colts and the senior Midland team.

A replacement for the 1981 and 1983 cup finals, Richardson played in the losing final of 1989. He scored tries in successive matches against Orrell, Sale and an Arabian Gulf XV in 1984 and, of his 220 starts for Tigers, 219 were at tight-head prop, the other at loose-head. After leaving Leicester he coached Syston and Hinckley for whom Lee, his brother, also played. He now runs his own polythene packing business in Leicester, PakPower Ltd.

Appearances: *220 starts + 3 reps (W158, D1, L64)*
Scoring: *8 tries, 32 pts*

ROWELL, Robert Errington (112)

Born: *Corbridge, Northumberland, 29.8.1939*
Educated: *Wymondham College (Norfolk), Hull University, Loughborough Colleges*
Clubs: *Hull University, Loughborough Colleges, Leicester, Fylde, Waterloo*
Tigers debut: *8.3.1962 v Loughborough Colleges, won 16-0 (1T, 3 pts)*
Last game: *29.4.1978 v Northern, won 21-16*
Caps: *England (2) 1964-65*

Bob Rowell, a lock, played a significant role in the restructuring of the club in the mid-1970s and, under his captaincy in 1976/77, the pattern started to emerge which would carry Leicester to four successive cup finals.

He represented the UAU at athletics and became a teacher before moving into the business world. He played for Leicestershire and Lancashire in the county championship and his appearance for the Leicestershire and East Midlands against New Zealand in 1963 helped him towards a first cap against Wales the following year; he played in the England second row against the same opponents a year later.

Rowell scored a try on his Leicester debut and two in the match with Waterloo in 1965. He played for the Barbarians and became a divisional selector; he was Leicester's president in 2003.

Appearances: *355 (W208, D18, L129)*
Scoring: *20 tries, 67 pts*

ROWNTREE, Christopher Graham (176)

Born: *Stockton-on-Tees, County Durham, 18.4.1971*
Educated: *John Cleveland College (Hinckley)*
Clubs: *Nuneaton, Leicester*
Tigers debut: *23.10.1990 v Oxford University, won 23-22*
Last game: *11.2.2007 v Argentina XV, lost 21-41*
Caps: *England (54) 1995-2006, British & Irish Lions (3) 2005*

As loose-head prop, Graham Rowntree was letter A in the ABC front-row club (with Richard Cockerill and Darren Garforth). He spent 18 seasons with Leicester and passed a half-century of

BOB ROWELL

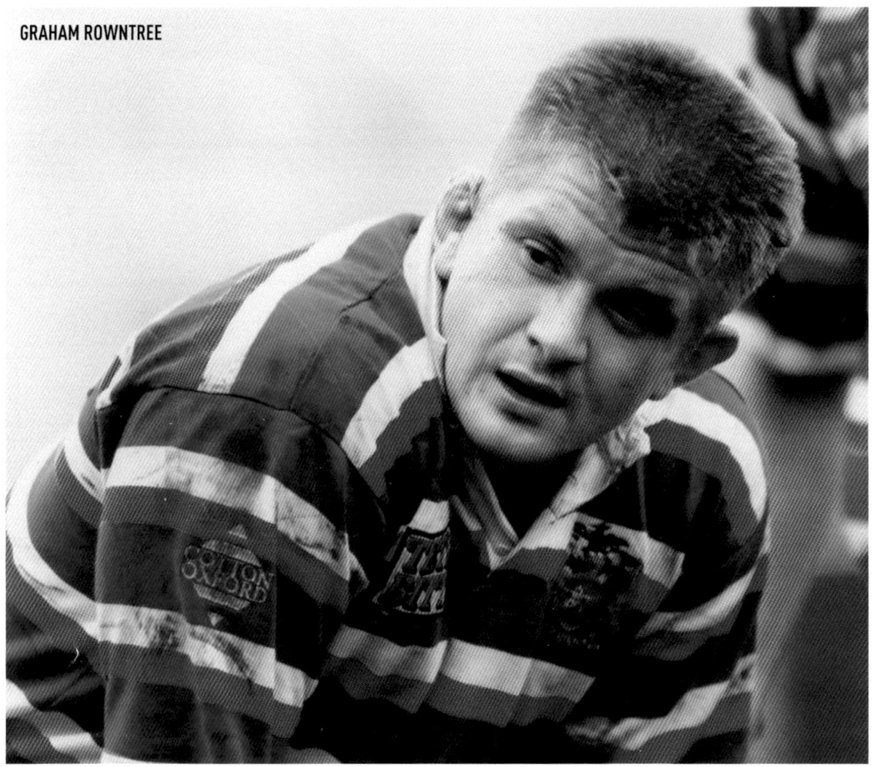
GRAHAM ROWNTREE

caps despite his career coinciding with that of England's most-capped player, Jason Leonard, also a loose-head.

He played for England schools at 16 and 18-group level, then under-21 and A level before winning his first cap during the 1995 five nations. He played in that year's World Cup and was an ever-present over the next two seasons, earning selection for the 1997 Lions party to South Africa. However Scotland's Tom Smith played in the internationals and Rowntree had to wait for eight years and the Lions tour to New Zealand before he played in the test XV.

He remained a valued asset with England, playing in the 1999 World Cup and on the successful summer tour of 2003 to New Zealand and Australia. His omission from that year's World Cup squad was, Clive Woodward, the coach, said, one of the hardest decisions he had ever made. He played throughout England's 2004/05 season and toured Australia in 2006.

Rowntree joined the Leicester youth squad in 1988 and he was a major part of all the club's successes over the following 18 years. An insurance broker before turning professional, he played in the Heineken Cup finals of 1997, 2001 and 2002; the 1995 league success and the Premiership wins of 1999-2002, and four Pilkington Cup finals. In 2004/05 he received the club members' award for outstanding service and when he retired, he had amassed 398 appearances, 166 of them alongside Garforth and Cockerill.

He immediately joined the club coaching staff as scrum specialist and, in 2007, joined England's academy. When Martin Johnson became England manager, he invited Rowntree to join his panel as scrum coach, in which role he went with the Lions to South Africa in 2009 and to Australia in 2013, while continuing to work with England.

Appearances: *362 starts + 36 reps (W282, D13, L103)*
Scoring: *18 tries, 87 pts*

RUSSELL, John Cannan (59)

Born: *Helensburgh, Scotland, 6.3.1896*
Died: *Roehampton, Surrey, 15.8.1956*
Educated: *Fettes*
Clubs: *London Hospitals, Leicester*
Tigers debut: *15.2.1922 v British Army, won 8-3*
Last game: *30.1.1930 v Royal Air Force, won 23-11*

JOHN RUSSELL

John Russell joined the fledgling RAF during the First World War and won swift promotion to squadron leader. He was awarded the DSO in 1919, became station commander in Amman and was made air commodore in 1939.

He was offered a second-team place with London Scottish when he returned home but preferred to play scrum-half for Tigers. He captained the RAF against Leicester in 1923 but, the following season, was unavailable to take up the offer of a Scottish trial.

HLV Day said in his book, *Rugby Union Football*: "[Russell] was the best scrum-half I ever played with. Why he was never asked to play for his country is a complete mystery...he had boundless courage and was a devastating tackler, what more could you ask of any scrum-half?"

Appearances: *141 (W80, D11, L50)*
Scoring: *10 tries, 1 mark, 33 pts*

RUSSELL, Richard Forbes (30)

RICHARD RUSSELL

Born: *Bingham, Nottinghamshire, 5.4.1879*
Died: *Lezayre, Isle of Man, 30.5.1960*
Educated: *St Peter's (York), Cambridge University*
Clubs: *Cambridge University, Leicester, Castleford, Cork (Ireland)*
Tigers debut: *19.9.1903 at Devonport Albion, lost 0-5*
Last game: *6.9.1913 v Bedford, won 17-8*
Caps: *England (1) 1905*

'Tosh' Russell, a forward and nephew of Sir Timothy O'Brien, the Middlesex and England cricketer, played for Yorkshire and won his only cap (against New Zealand) after playing well for Leicester against the touring side. He played for the Midlands against South Africa the following season, when he was Leicester's captain, and his seven Midland Counties Cup ties for the club included the winning finals of 1904 and 1905.

Russell was the club's leading points scorer in 1904/05 with 57 and registered a try in his 100th match, against Percy Park in 1907, when he was also captain. His job as a teacher took him to Fermoy in County Cork. During the First World War he was a special constable on the Isle of Man where he died, aged 81, in retirement.

Appearances: *122 (W68, D16, L38)*
Scoring: *28 tries, 26 conv, 7 pens, 157 pts*

S

CLAUDE SAMBROOK

SAMBROOK, Leonard Claude (54)

Born: *Leicester, 24.11.1895*
Died: *Leicester, 29.8.1957*
Educated: *Moat Road*
Clubs: *Aylestone St James, Leicester*
Tigers debut: *12.9.1921 at Burton, won 22-3*
Last game: *3.3.1928 v Harlequins, drew 18-18*

Claude Sambrook began his Leicester career at centre but switched swiftly to full-back, the position in which he played two England trials in 1923/24. He was an England reserve against Scotland on 15 March 1924 and looked set to play until Bristol's Bev Chantrill announced himself fit for action at the last minute.

Sambrook, who was joined at Leicester by Harold, his brother, played in the Leicestershire side that won the county championship in 1925. He worked in Tom Crumbie's printing business and later became a commercial traveller. He was also employed at the Ministry of Labour. After his playing career ended, Sambrook ran the Welford Road line regularly until the end of the Second World War.

Appearances: *215 (W133, D18, L64)*
Scoring: *24 conv, 6 pens, 1 drop, 1 mark, 73 pts*

SAUNDERS, Stanley Herbert (66)

Born: *Leicester, 1.3.1908*
Died: *Leicester, 13.12.2004*
Educated: *Moat Road, Alderman Newton's*
Clubs: *Aylestone St James, Leicester, Bedford*
Tigers debut: *9.3.1929 at Bridgwater & Albion, lost 5-6*
Last game: *13.1.1934 v Rugby, won 12-0*

Stan 'Tubby' Saunders was the original utility forward, starting in every row of the scrum (including hooker) during his 131 appearances. The majority were either at back row or lock and he was a good enough player to win an England trial in 1928/29, at Northampton, where he collapsed, a year later, when a head wound re-opened during a club match.

The same season he conceded the penalty that gave Harlequins a win though so thick was the fog that neither side was certain a try had been converted. But his last-minute try in 1932 won the home match against Harlequins, his 100th game for Tigers. He made four appearances for Bedford in 1934/35.

Saunders worked as a long-distance lorry driver, making twice-weekly 400-mile round trips between Bradford and Leicester in a heavy six-wheeler with a top speed of 16mph. During the Second World War he trained officers in the RAF and returned to Leicester after the war to run greyhound tracks.

He set up a packaging business, SH Samuel Packaging, where he worked until he was 85. He was the oldest former Tiger to attend the celebratory 100-cap dinner in 2003, where he received a commemorative cap and tie from Martin Johnson.

Appearances: *131 (W77, D10, L44)*
Scoring: *21 tries, 63 pts*

STAN SAUNDERS

SHARRATT, Herbert (55)

Born: *Hinckley, Leicestershire, 28.5.1892*
Died: *Hinckley, Leicestershire, 29.10.1971*
Clubs: *Hinckley, Nuneaton, Leicester*
Tigers debut: *23.2.1921 at Moseley, drew 11-11*
Last game: *28.11.1925 at Cardiff, lost 3-9*

HERB SHARRATT

When Herb Sharratt, a keen boxer and wrestler, played in Leicester's pack against the 1924 New Zealanders, he was described as a forward "who never has an off day." He made 34 appearances for Nuneaton before joining Leicester, against whom he played for the Barbarians in the annual match of 1923.

He played for the Leicestershire team that won the 1925 county championship and, in the same year, was given an England trial. He was the first interlock knitter employed at Atkins Brothers in Hinckley where he was a long-service fireman. Sharratt received the Military Medal for his service in the Coldstream Guards during the First World War.

Appearances: *150 (W97, D13, L40)*
Scoring: *17 tries, 1 drop, 55 pts*

SHEPHARD, Clifford Denis (108=)

Born: *Wigston, Leicester, 21.2.1935*
Died: *Elmesthorpe, Leicestershire, 30.12.2013*
Educated: *South Wigston HS*
Clubs: *Wigston Old Boys, Westleigh, Fylde, Leicester*
Tigers debut: *1.10.1955 v Coventry, lost 8-11*
Last game: *3.10.1964 at Coventry, lost 3-19*

Cliff Shephard was a familiar sight during the professional era, for much of which he was the team's kit man, but he was an elusive wing who scored 36 tries for the club during his playing career. He also appeared at centre and fly-half but had to wait for his 15th game for his first try; he scored a hat-trick against Northern in 1961.

He played for Leicestershire schools and received an England schools trial. He captained the Leicestershire Alliance colts and played for the RAF and Leicestershire. An engineer with English

CLIFF SHEPHARD

Electric, he became a representative in the brewing trade. When his playing days ended, he helped with the organisation of the Swifts (Leicester's third team), became team secretary to the Extras (the second team) and first-team secretary in 1996. He retired as kit man in 2006.

Appearances: *140 (W69, D11, L60)*
Scoring: *36 tries, 1 pen, 111 pts*

SIBSON, Harry William (83)

HARRY SIBSON

Born: *Leicester, 15.7.1919*
Died: *Leicester, 5.1.2010*
Educated: *King Richard's Road Intermediate*
Clubs: *Old Ricadians, Aylestonians, Leicester*
Tigers debut: *19.4.1947 v Blackheath, won 12-9*
Last game: *20.11.1954 v Nuneaton, won 11-3*

Harry Sibson, a flanker, was born in Leicester but spent the first five years of his life in New Zealand. He played for Leicester boys under-14 and was a lock for Aylestonians before the Second World War, when he joined the Leicestershire Regiment. He later joined the Royal Engineers and went to Normandy after the D-Day landings, working as a diver to repair storm damage to the Mulberry Harbour.

He also worked to repair bomb damage at Calais docks and to defuse underwater mines. After the war Sibson returned to work as a monument mason at the Great Central Street yard, where his hand-cut lettering was said to be among the finest in the country.

He was a reserve for an England trial in 1950 and played for Leicestershire and East Midlands against South Africa in 1951. He was first-team secretary from 1969-79 and club president from 1981-83.

Appearances: *183 (W91, D7, L85)*
Scoring: *26 tries, 78 pts*

SKELTON, Rex Patrick (101)

REX SKELTON

Born: *Leicester, 10.7.1931*
Died: *Leicester, 16.4.2010*
Educated: *Wyggeston GS*
Clubs: *Old Wyggestonians, Leicester, Royal Navy*
Tigers debut: *28.1.1956 at Rosslyn Park, lost 0-6*
Last game: *2.5.1970 v New Brighton, won 17-6*

While on national service, Rex Skelton, a tight-head prop, played for Devonport Services and the Royal Navy. He played for Leicestershire and was a reserve for Midland Counties. Between December 1957 and December 1959, he was an ever present in the front row with 75 successive appearances but not managing to score a try in that time. Skelton's 150th game for the first team was in the 11-26 loss to Gloucester at Kingsholm in November 1961. Skelton worked in the shoe component manufacturing industry.

Appearances: *198 (W94, D18, L86)*
Scoring: *5 tries, 15 pts*

SMALL, Brian Thomas Cartner (98)

Born: *Liverpool, 6.1.1932*
Educated: *Kirkham GS (Lancashire), Alderman Newton's, St John's College (Cambridge)*
Clubs: *Westleigh, Leicester Thursday, Cambridge University, Leicester, Rosslyn Park*
Tigers debut: *27.12.1954 v Birkenhead Park, lost 11-13*
Last game: *20.4.1963 v Rugby, lost 3-6*

Most of Brian Small's 158 matches came at full-back, though he also played centre - the position in which he scored his three tries - and once fly-half. He played for the successful Leicestershire side before joining Tigers, one of his earliest games coming against Sale who scored five first-half tries and lost 18-15 to six penalties kicked by George Cullen.

A partner in his own firm of solicitors and older brother of Bob, who also played for Leicester, Small was awarded the MBE in 1977. He played a leading role when Leicester took the city council to appeal at the House of Lords in 1984 over their continued use of the Recreation Ground (later Mandela Park), the council having banned them because of rugby's links with apartheid South Africa. He was Leicester president in 1989-91.

Appearances: *158 (W71, D17, L70)*
Scoring: *3 tries, 8 conv, 3 pens, 2 drops, 40 pts*

BRIAN SMALL

SMALL, Robert Wilford (118=)

Born: *Leicester, 29.3.1938*
Educated: *King Richard III*
Clubs: *Westleigh, Leicester, Rosslyn Park*
Tigers debut: *26.12.1957 v Birkenhead Park, lost 8-15*
Last game: *8.11.1969 at Cambridge University, lost 11-36*

BOB SMALL

Bob Small displayed many of the predatory instincts of his back-row colleague, David Matthews, scoring 22 tries in his 119 appearances. He was a member of a very effective back row throughout the 1960s and was controversially omitted from the Leicestershire and East Midlands side that played New Zealand in 1963. He left England to become an importer of textile machinery in Toronto, returning for the 100-cap dinner in 2003.

Appearances: *119 (W79, D3, L37)*
Scoring: *22 tries, 66 pts*

IAN SMITH

SMITH, Ian Robert (149)

Born: *Leicester, 26.11.1957*
Educated: *Wyggeston GS, Milton Keynes College of Education*
Club: *Leicester*
Tigers debut: *20.9.1977 at Sheffield, won 47-3*
Last game: *26.10.1991 at Sale, lost 9-12 (1T, 4 pts)*

One of a long line of constructive Leicester flankers who missed the highest honours but proved, as players and coaches, of immense value to the club. 'Dosser' Smith (so called because of an alleged tendency to take a snooze during school lessons) was a good ball handler with a wide-legged stance at the breakdown seen so frequently in the modern game.

He joined Leicester youth while at school and was only 19 when he made his senior debut. He played at under-15, under-19 and senior level for Leicestershire, East Midlands and Midlands, he was a member of the England schools under-19 squad in 1976 and represented England under-23.

He played for the Midlands against New Zealand in 1978 and against the Australia tour parties of 1981 and 1984. He played in five John Player Cup finals, winning three of them, and captained the club between 1983-85. Smith retired at the end of the 1989/90 season but returned for one more game in each of the next two seasons; he made 298 appearances at open-side flanker in the letter H shirt, more than any other player.

He also contributed as a committee member and, when he finished playing, formed a fruitful coaching partnership with Paul Dodge for five seasons, during which Leicester won the Pilkington Cup (1993) and the league title (1995). He was responsible for the club's development programme and Leicester's academy side, and coached Loughborough University, England Students and England under-19s.

He taught mathematics and PE at Uppingham School and later moved to take charge of rugby at Oakham School. In 2004/05 he was appointed coach to Newark. Matt, his son, came through the Tigers academy to be a dependable utility back with over 100 appearances, the first father-son combination to achieve that centurion status.

Appearances: *322 starts + 9 reps (W245, D8, L78)*
Scoring: *67 tries, 268 pts*

SMITH, John Willoughby Dixie (33)

Born: *Narborough, Leicester, 11.3.1882*
Died: *Harrow-on-the-Hill, Middlesex, 2.10.1959*
Educated: *Oundle*
Clubs: *Northampton, Leicester, Nuneaton, Nottingham*
Tigers debut: *20.1.1902 at Plymouth, lost 3-5 (1T, 3pts)*
Last game: *2.3.1912 v Headingley, lost 12-14*

Dixie Smith fostered good relations between Northampton and Leicester by turning out for both clubs when either was hit by injuries. He scored 24 tries in 49 appearances for Northampton between 1901-03 and made a single appearance for Nuneaton in 1902/03. He also played for Nottingham in 1911, against Leicester, when both clubs found themselves without a fixture.

He played across the back division and scored a try in his 100th game, against Stratford-on-Avon in 1909. During the First World War he served as a captain in the 8th Battalion of the Royal Leicestershire Regiment. He played as a right-hand batsman for Leicestershire County Cricket Club in two championship matches in May 1921 with a top score of 25 against Gloucestershire.

Appearances: *132 (W69, D17, L46)*
Scoring: *27 tries, 81 pts*

DIXIE SMITH

MATT SMITH

*SMITH, Matthew William (205)

Born: *Leicester, 15.11.1985*
Educated: *Oakham*
Clubs: *Leicester, Nottingham*
Tigers debut: *17.3.2006 v Barbarians, lost 42-51*

Matt Smith followed his father, Ian, in passing 100 games for Leicester during 2011/12, helped by his ability to play virtually anywhere in the back division save scrum-half. His most frequent appearances were at centre or wing and his reliability earned him appearances for England Saxons in 2009.

Smith joined Leicester's academy but had two fruitful seasons in national league one with Nottingham before returning to Welford Road and becoming the supporters' young player of 2008/09. He recovered from an ankle injury to play in both the Heineken Cup final and Premiership final of 2009, also appearing in the Premiership finals of 2010, 2011 and 2013.

Appearances: *112 starts + 39 reps (W99, D8, L44)*
Scoring: *26 tries, 130 pts*

SMITH, Oliver James (195)

Born: *Leicester, 14.8.1982*
Educated: *John Cleveland College (Hinckley), Loughborough University*
Clubs: *Old Bosworthians, Market Bosworth, Leicester, Montpellier (France), Harlequins*
Tigers debut: *16.9.2000 v London Irish (replacement), won 33-20* ●
Last game: *12.4.2008 v Ospreys (at Twickenham), lost 6-23* ●
Caps: *England (5) 2003-05, British & Irish Lions (1) 2005*

Ollie Smith joined Leicester in 1999 and became a shooting star in the centre. He made such rapid progress, with his long, raking stride and swerve, that he started the 2002 Heineken Cup final against Munster before his twentieth birthday and was capped by England as a replacement against Italy in the 2003 six nations after playing at under-19 and under-21 levels.

The club's young player of the season in 2001 and 2002, a long representative career seemed on the horizon. He started a World Cup warm-up match against France and made two further England appearances, from the bench, in 2005 which helped him to a place in the Lions tour party to New Zealand that year, prior to which he scored a try when the Lions played Argentina in Cardiff.

But the premature death of his father in 2005 affected him greatly. He spent the summer of 2006 in Australia, played consistently the following season then took a sabbatical before joining Montpellier. He returned to join Harlequins but played only 11 games before a severe knee injury forced his retirement. He became backs coach, and subsequently head coach, to Esher then moved across London in 2013 to help coach London Welsh.

Appearances: *154 starts + 28 reps (W120, D7, L55)*
Scoring: *38 tries, 190 pts*

OLLIE SMITH

RON SMITH

SMITH, Ronald Hugh (92)

Born: *Leicester, 5.8.1926*
Died: *Oakham, Rutland, 10.6.2013*
Educated: *Wyggeston Boys, Sutton Bonnington Agricultural College*
Clubs: *Westleigh, Leicester, Northampton*
Tigers debut: *26.11.1949 v Middlesex Hospital, won 6-3*
Last game: *12.4.1958 at Birkenhead Park, lost 11-13*

Ron Smith, a lock, played for Westleigh when only 14 and represented Leicestershire before joining Tigers. He played in an England trial in 1954 and helped the county to a championship semi-final against Devon in 1956. He played 34 games for Northampton between 1954-57, scoring eight tries, and toured with Leicestershire Reynards in 1949 and 1951.

A popular and jovial man, Smith farmed in and around Tilton until retiring to Oakham in 2009. When his first-class career ended, he spent several seasons as a mainstay for Leicester's third team, the Swifts.

Appearances: *190 (W86, D13, L91)*
Scoring: *11 tries, 33 pts*

TOM SMITH

SMITH, Thomas (167)

Born: *Leicester, 27.12.1964*
Educated: *Anstey Martin, Longslade College, Southfields College, Trent Polytechnic, Loughborough University*
Clubs: *Anstey, Vipers, Leicester, Bedford*
Tigers debut: *27.4.1984 at Gulf Invitation XV, won 54-3*
Last game: *17.3.1995 at Nottingham, won 29-9*

When Tom Smith gained his player's tie, against the Fiji Barbarians in 1986, the touring side were so impressed by his play they invited him to appear for them against West Hartlepool, but unfortunately injury prevented Smith, a lock, from doing so.

He played for Leicestershire at under-19 and senior level and for Midlands under-23. He appeared in the 1989 Pilkington Cup final and captained the side nine times; though he moved to Bedford for the 1992/93 season, he returned to Leicester for the 1993 tour to South Africa and to be part of the squad that won the 1994/95 league title.

He was a PE teacher at Lancaster School and a rugby development officer for the county. With Paul Dodge he coached the Leicester under-19 and under-21 sides for nine years and scouted for under-16 applicants for Leicester's academy. He became head of mathematics at Maplewell Hall School in Woodhouse Eaves in 2014.

Appearances: *184 starts + 1 rep (W137, D2, L46)*
Scoring: *18 tries, 74 pts*

STIMPSON, Timothy Richard George (187)

Born: *Liverpool, 10.9.1973*
Educated: *Silcoates (Wakefield), Durham University*
Clubs: *Wakefield, West Hartlepool, Newcastle Falcons, Leicester, Perpignan (France), Leeds, Nottingham*
Tigers debut: *5.9.1998 v Harlequins, won 49-15* ●
Last game: *19.10.2003 at Leeds Tykes (replacement), lost 18-39 (1C, 1PG, 5pts)* ●
Caps: *England (19) 1996-2002, British & Irish Lions (1) 1997*

A tall, long-striding full-back, Tim Stimpson spent much of his Leicester career rewriting points-scoring records. He was the first player to pass 1,000 Premiership points (in 2002), he broke Joel Stransky's club record with 486 points in 2000/01 and he is the only player to have won five successive Premiership titles, one with Newcastle Falcons (1998) then four with Leicester (1999-2002).

He played for England at schools, under-21 (while obtaining a degree in anthropology at Durham) and A level before making his senior debut against Italy in 1996. He played throughout the next five nations and was picked for the 1997 Lions tour to South Africa, where he became the party's top points scorer with 111 and appeared in the third international as a replacement for Tony Underwood.

He toured with England to the southern hemisphere in 1998, to South Africa in 2000, and Argentina in 2002. When he moved to Leicester in 1998 he swiftly became an integral part of the squad that dominated the Premiership for the next four years and became the club's top points scorer in four successive seasons. In 2002 he became only the third player (after Dusty Hare and John Liley) to pass 1,500 points for Leicester.

But his most valuable contributions to Tigers came in their two Heineken Cup wins. In 2001, Stimpson kicked five penalties and two conversions in the 34-30 win over Stade Français and in 2002, his 56-metre penalty (off upright and crossbar) gave Leicester their 13-12 semi-final win over Llanelli. In the final, against Munster, he kicked five points in the 15-9 win.

He became Leicester's specialist kicking coach before joining Perpignan for a season. After retiring he established a financial services company, Sporting Partnerships, raising money for charity and grass-roots sport.

Appearances: *141 starts + 10 reps (W106, D4, L41)*
Scoring: *29 tries, 223 conv, 372 pens, 2 drops, 1,713 pts*

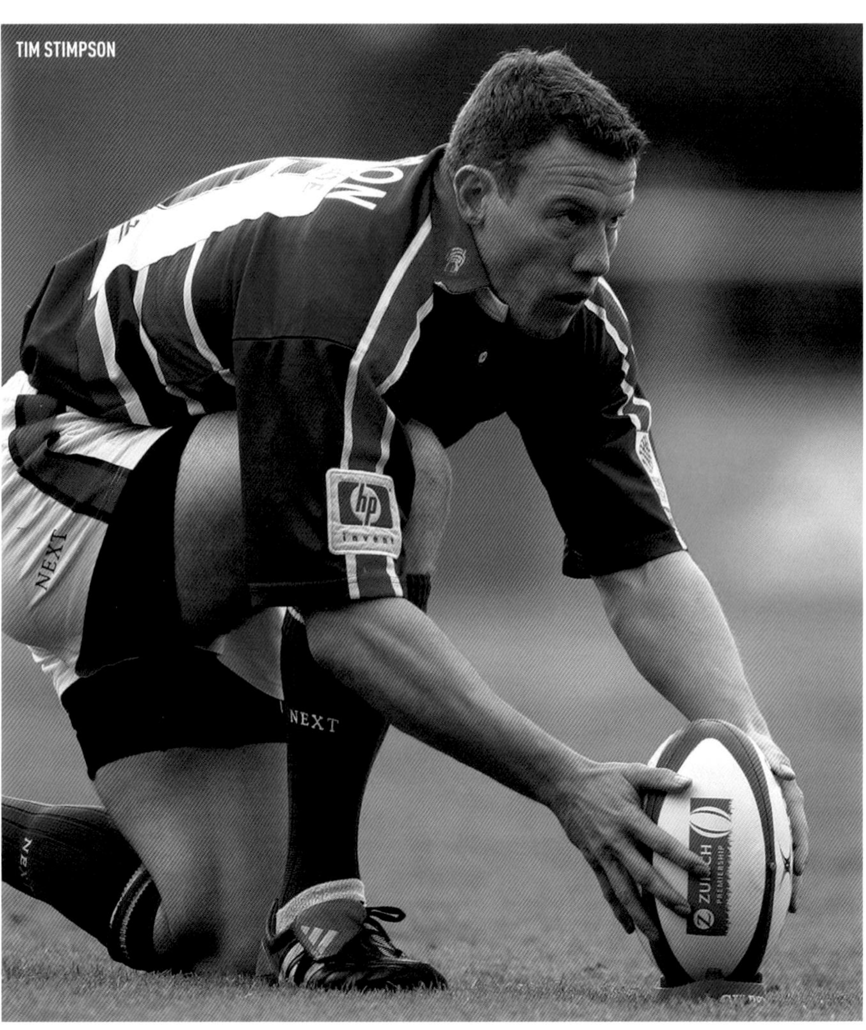

TIM STIMPSON

STURGES, Walter Henry (7)

WALTER STURGES

Born: *Lutterworth, Leicestershire, 5.10.1869*
Died: *Leicester, 11.2.1952*
Educated: *Wyggeston, Mill Hill House*
Clubs: *Mill Hill, Leicester*
Tigers debut: *6.3.1889 v Bedford, won 4-3*
Last game: *29.4.1893 v Cardiff Harlequins, won 11-7*

Walter Sturges played football at Mill Hill and was a contemporary of Jimmy Atter, later of Leicester Fosse. He captained Mill Hill for two years and joined Leicester as a wing in 1888, becoming vice-captain in 1890/91 and captain between 1891-93 for his last 63 games. He played in every Midland Counties Cup tie in 1890/91.

He played cricket for Leicester Ivanhoe and when he sat Law Society examinations in 1891, came second from 280 entrants. He became a solicitor in 1892.

Appearances: *114 (W52, D11, L51)*
Scoring: *22 tries, 32 pts*

T

TAYLOR, Frank (48)

Born: *Leicester, 4.5.1890*
Died: *Leicester, 22.9.1956*
Educated: *Medway Street*
Clubs: *Medway Old Boys, Medway Athletic, Leicester*
Tigers debut: *28.1.1911 v Moseley, won 21-5*
Last game: *26.4.1924 at Bedford, won 5-0*
Caps: *England (2) 1920*

SOS TAYLOR

'Sos' Taylor played mostly at lock or back row and his remarkable career spanned the First World War in which he was badly wounded while serving with the Leicestershire Regiment. He was advised that he would never play rugby again but recovered so well that, shortly before his thirtieth birthday, he played for England against France and Ireland in 1920, both times on the winning side.

He was one of six Leicester boys to play in the first England-Wales schools international in 1904 and went on to represent Leicestershire and the Midland Counties. He was a member of the Leicester side that won the Midland Counties Cup in 1912 and 1913 and HLV Day said of him: "A grand forward who ought to have had more caps. One of the best line-out forwards I have seen anywhere." He was a clerk in a boot factory.

It had long been thought that 'Sos' and 'Tim' Taylor were brothers but census returns show that they were in fact unrelated. They lived in adjacent streets and went to the same school at the same time.

Appearances: *276 (W180, D18, L78)*
Scoring: *36 tries, 108 pts*

TIM TAYLOR

TAYLOR, Frederick Mark (42=)

Born: *Leicester, 18.3.1888*
Died: *Evington, Leicester, 2.3.1966*
Educated: *Medway Street*
Clubs: *Medway Old Boys, Medway Athletic, Leicester*
Tigers debut: *5.10.1907 v Manchester, won 32-6 (1T, 3 pts)*
Last game: *28.4.1923 v Newport, lost 6-7*
Caps: *England (1) 1914*

'Tim' Taylor played fly-half and, occasionally, wing or centre, in 294 games and scored the first of 97 tries in his debut, against Manchester. He played for Leicestershire and the Midland Counties and appeared in three Midland Counties Cup wins.

His one cap came as a replacement for one of England's finest fly-halves, WJA Davies, against Wales in 1914, the start of a grand-slam season for England. He celebrated demobilisation after the war with a try against Bedford in December 1919. Taylor was a clerk with a firm of Leicester solicitors.

Appearances: *294 (W195, D23, L76)*
Scoring: *97 tries, 1 drop, 295 pts*

TEBBUTT, Robert Steven (163)

Born: *Leicester, 14.6.1962*
Educated: *Anstey Martin HS, Longslade Upper, Hinckley College of Further Education*
Clubs: *West Leicester, Leicester, Northampton*
Tigers debut: *16.10.1981 at Northampton, lost 6-22* ●
Last game: *23.3.1991 v Harlequins, lost 12-15* ●

Rob Tebbutt, a flanker, played for Leicestershire schools at under-14 and under-16 level and joined Leicester youth in 1978. He played for the county colts and England colts in 1981, scoring the winning try against Wales. He was also an England under-23 squad member. He helped Leicester win the inaugural Courage League title in 1987/88.

Tebbutt joined Northampton in 1990, returned for a season then in 1992 rejoined Saints for whom he made 29 appearances and scored three tries in the second division. He was a knitting machine mechanic before becoming self-employed in the colour printing business. He became director of coaching at Hinckley Rugby Club.

Appearances: *153 starts + 3 reps (W107, D1, L48)*
Scoring: *28 tries, 112 pts*

ROB TEBBUTT

HAYDN THOMAS

THOMAS, Haydn George (86)

Born: *Dowlais, Merthyr Tydfil, Wales, 7.12.1925*
Educated: *Merthyr County, Loughborough Colleges*
Clubs: *Loughborough Colleges, Leicester, Cardiff, Pontypool, Northampton, Merthyr Tydfil*
Tigers debut: *13.10.1945 v Nuneaton, won 8-3*
Last game: *29.1.1953 v Royal Air Force, lost 11-12*

Haydn Thomas, a centre, was captain of Loughborough Colleges, where he later became Master. He returned to Wales and played a handful of games for Cardiff before taking up a teaching appointment at Humphrey Perkins School in Barrow-on-Soar. He played for Leicestershire, the East Midlands and the Army, and in a Welsh trial in 1949. He became a PE teacher for Glamorgan County Council.

Appearances: *104 starts + 1 rep (W50, D5, L50)*
Scoring: *38 tries, 1 drop, 117 pts*

THOMPSON, John Sidney (99)

Born: *Leicester, 7.8.1930*
Died: *Norwich, Norfolk, 2.7.2004*
Educated: *Moat Road Intermediate*
Clubs: *Aylestone Athletic, Leicester*
Tigers debut: *5.2.1955 at London Scottish, won 11-9*
Last game: *16.9.1961 v Plymouth Albion, lost 9-11*

A durable lock, John Thompson set a post-war record of 104 consecutive appearances (until overtaken by David Matthews) and was presented with a silver tankard by West Humberstone Conservative Club after his 100th game.

JOHN THOMPSON

He played for the Midland Counties against South Africa in 1960 and scored his only two tries both against Northampton in 1956 and 1957.

His older brother, Bill, also played for Leicester, the RAF and Combined Services. His nephew, George Knew, played cricket for Leicestershire and Leicester Nomads. For many years, Thompson was a match-day volunteer at Welford Road and ran the bar in the president's lounge.

Appearances: *166 (W75, D16, L75)*
Scoring: *2 tries, 6 pts*

THORNELOE, Noel Trevor (56)

Born: *Leicester, 13.7.1898*
Died: *Hove, Sussex, 6.7.1968*
Educated: *Mill Hill*
Clubs: *Westleigh, Leicester, Harlequins*
Tigers debut: *1.11.1919 v Royal Navy, won 9-3*
Last game: *21.4.1930 at Plymouth Albion, won 11-9 (1C, 2 pts)*

Trevor Thorneloe was a forward and the youngest of three brothers of whom Eric became the long-serving Leicester secretary. When he left to work in London, Trevor played regularly for Harlequins and appeared for the Barbarians in the 1923 Mobbs Memorial Match at Northampton. He played his 100th Leicester game at Northern in 1926 and appeared in two games for Harlequins later that year.

TREVOR THORNELOE

A lieutenant in the Royal Naval Air Services during the Second World War, Thorneloe won the Air Force Cross and was one of the first pilots to be catapulted off an aircraft carrier. He was a clothing manufacturer.

Appearances: *125 (W75, D10, L40)*
Scoring: *8 tries, 19 conv, 3 pens, 71 pts*

THORNELOE, Peter Bernard Lulham (87)

Born: *Leicester, 21.3.1927*
Educated: *Rugby*
Clubs: *United Services (Portsmouth), Leicester*
Tigers debut: *29.12.1945 v Swansea, drew 6-6*
Last game: *14.12.1957 v Blackheath, lost 6-13*

PETER THORNELOE

A prop and occasional back row, Peter Thorneloe joined the Royal Navy from school and played for United Services Portsmouth, Hampshire and Leicestershire. Nephew of Trevor Thorneloe, he celebrated his 200th game by scoring his eleventh (and final) try against Richmond in 1956.

He was a company director of a Hong Kong-based clothing manufacturing business. His father, Thomas, was secretary of Leicestershire County Cricket Club before the Second World War while another uncle, Eric, was Leicester's secretary and subsequently president.

Appearances: *221 (W99, D11, L111)*
Scoring: *11 tries, 33 pts*

TOM, Peter William Gregory (122)

Born: *St Mellion, Cornwall, 26.7.1940*
Educated: *Hinckley GS*
Clubs: *Hinckley, Leicester*
Tigers debut: *2.9.1963 at Torquay Athletic, won 18-5*
Last game: *3.2.1968 v London Scottish, won 19-11*

A hard-working lock who became as hard-working a chairman of Leicester, Peter Tom moved from Cornwall to Hinckley as a youngster. He played for Leicestershire and the Midlands and he appeared for Midland Counties (East) against Australia in 1966.

He became managing director and then chairman/chief executive of Bardon Hill Quarries Ltd and chairman of the Quarry Product Association. Subsequently he became group chief executive of Aggregate Industries, the holding company of the UK/USA aggregates group.

A member of Leicester's forward planning committee, he became the club's chairman in 1992 and was at the helm when the game went open three years later. He oversaw Leicester's conversion from a friendly society to a public limited company in 1997, becoming the non-executive chairman, and has helped ensure the club's status as market leaders in England throughout the professional period.

He was awarded an honorary doctorate of technology from De Montfort University in 1999 and made CBE in 2006. As well as being executive chairman of Breedon Aggregates, he is the chairman of Channel Islands Property Funds Ltd.

Appearances: *130 (W83, D8, L39)*
Scoring: *7 tries, 21 pts*

PETER TOM

TRESSLER, Christopher James (159)

Born: *Thurmaston, Leicester, 9.1.1961*
Educated: *Stonehill HS, Longslade Upper*
Clubs: *Belgrave, Syston, Leicester*
Tigers debut: *17.9.1980 v Birmingham, won 36-12*
Last game: *25.4.1992 v Rugby Lions, drew 22-22*

A schoolboy centre who converted to hooker, Chris Tressler played for Leicestershire at under-13, under-19 and senior level. He joined Leicester as understudy to Peter Wheeler, then the club captain, and was picked for England's under-23 squad.

He was a replacement for the cup finals of 1981, 1983 and 1989 and a member of the squad that won the

CHRIS TRESSLER

Courage League in 1987/88. He passed 250 appearances in his final season then returned to play for Syston, coaching their juniors. He played cricket for North Leicestershire under-18 and is a keen golfer; he became UK general manager for Metso Lindermann.

Appearances: *262 starts + 2 reps (W173, D7, L84)*
Scoring: *14 tries, 56 pts*

+TUILAGI, Alesana Tiafau (202=)

Born: *Fogapoa, Western Samoa, 24.2.1981*
Educated: *Chanel College (Western Samoa)*
Clubs: *Rugby Parma (Italy), Leicester, NTT Shining Arcs (Japan), Newcastle Falcons*
Tigers debut: *11.9.2004 v Leeds Tykes (replacement), won 42-20*
Last game: *26.5.2012 v Harlequins (at Twickenham), lost 23-30*
Caps: *Samoa (29) 2002-13, Pacfic Islanders (1) 2006*

Alesana Tuilagi followed in the path begun by Fereti, his older brother, and became a stalwart for club and country. A wing of immense power and pace, more than 6ft tall and 18st, he both scored and created tries through his physical presence and, with his distinctive dreadlocks, became a popular figure at Welford Road.

He was first capped by Samoa against Fiji in 2002, alongside his big brother Henry. He scored four tries in the 2005 clash with Tonga but was sent off during Samoa's defeat by England at Twickenham in 2005 (along with Lewis Moody). Alesana, Henry and a third brother, Anitile'a, played in the 2007 World Cup in France and in 2011, Alesana scored a magnificent solo try that helped Samoa to their first win over Australia in Sydney, before going on to play in that year's World Cup.

He started the Heineken Cup finals of 2007 and 2009 and played in all the Premiership finals from 2007-12, except 2009 when he was suspended. He was man of the match in the 2007 win over Gloucester, in which he scored two tries, and in 2012 against Harlequins, played alongside his younger brother, Manu. He was members' player of the year in 2007.

Early in his Leicester career he established an A league record with five tries against Leeds in 2004. He spent two seasons playing club rugby in Japan from 2012-14 but, at the age of 33, agreed a return to the Premiership with Newcastle Falcons for 2014/15.

Appearances: *129 starts + 33 reps (W107, D6, L49)*
Scoring: *63 tries, 315 pts*

ALESANA TUILAGI

U

UNDERWOOD, Rory (168)

Born: *Middlesbrough, Yorkshire, 19.6.1963*
Educated: *Barnard Castle*
Clubs: *Middlesbrough, RAF, Leicester, Bedford*
Tigers debut: *21.9.1983 v Birmingham, won 40-3*
Last game: *3.5.1997 at Sale, drew 20-20* ●
Caps: *England (85) 1984-96, British Isles (6) 1989-93*

Rory Underwood was blessed with the physique and pace of a natural finisher. Early in his career, his all-round athletic ability was compared with that of the Olympic decathlete, Daley Thompson, he seldom suffered injury and his longevity earned him what was then a record number of caps and made him England's record try-scorer with 49.

Born to an English father and Chinese-Malay mother, Underwood spent the first eight years of his life in Malaysia. He discovered rugby (and competitive cricket and swimming) at school in Barnard Castle and played for Yorkshire, Durham and England colts before touring Italy with England's under-23 side in 1982.

That same year he played for the Northern Division and England B and made his international debut against Ireland in 1984. By then he had moved to Leicester, having joined the RAF and begun officer training at Cranwell.

The first of his international tries came against France in the 1984 five nations but RAF duties prevented him touring South Africa that summer and New Zealand in 1985.

Thereafter he was virtually an automatic selection, first on the left wing though later in his career, he played on the right. He possessed both a swerve and a change of pace that baffled many defenders, notably John Kirwan when Underwood scored the try that helped the Lions to a record win over New Zealand in 1993.

He played in the inaugural World Cup of 1987, scored five tries against Fiji at Twickenham in 1989 (equalling the individual record set by 'Dan' Lambert 82 years earlier against France) and played in the 1991 World Cup when England reached the final, becoming the first England player to reach fifty caps in the semi-final against Scotland. He contributed towards England's grand-slam seasons of 1991, 1992 and 1995, despite announcing a short-lived retirement in 1992.

He toured with the Lions to Australia in 1989 and again to New Zealand in 1993, playing in all six tests. He played in his third World Cup in South Africa, in 1995, scoring two tries in the semi-final defeat by New Zealand in Cape Town. Between 1986-96 he appeared in 42 successive five nations championship matches without ever being replaced and in 1992 he was joined by Tony, his younger brother, the first time since 1938 that England fielded two brothers; the pair played together in 19 internationals.

Underwood's Leicester career was disrupted by representative calls and work commitments (he helped the RAF win the 1983 inter-services title) but he played in the side that won the Pilkington Cup in 1993, as did Tony who joined the club while at Cambridge University. Rory played in three other cup finals, those of 1989, 1994 and 1996, and in the league-winning squads of 1987/88 and 1994/95. He also played in the 1997 Heineken Cup final and, when he left Leicester in 1997, he had made 236 appearances and scored 134 tries.

Towards the end of his career he developed other strings to his bow, playing both full-back and centre. In 1992 he was awarded the MBE for services to rugby. After retiring, he returned to Leicester in 2000 as backline advisor and helped Tigers to their first Heineken Cup win. He retained that connection and, in 2007 joined the club's board of directors.

He left the RAF in 1999 as a flight lieutenant and joined an air force colleague, Jon Peters, in establishing UPH Limited, a management consultancy firm. He is also a motivational speaker and developed his own firm, Wingman Ltd.

Appearances: *230 starts + 6 reps (W171, D6, L59)*
Scoring: *134 tries, 580 pts*

V

VALLANCE, George Philip Colles (72)

Born: *Eccles, Manchester, 16.12.1908*
Died: *Widmerpool, Nottinghamshire, 20.2.2008*
Educated: *Willaston (Cheshire)*
Clubs: *Broughton Park, Nottingham, Leicester*
Tigers debut: *1.1.1930 at Manchester, won 9-8*
Last game: *15.4.1939 v Blackheath, lost 10-23*

A swimming and cross country champion at school in Cheshire, George Vallance suffered the disappointment of being picked to play for England (against Wales in 1933) but did not consider himself fit enough to play after a bout of influenza. He was not asked again.

He played 77 games for Nottingham before joining Leicester and playing in the second row. He played for Lancashire and captained Notts, Lincs and Derbys; he appeared in an England trial in 1930 and for the Midland Counties against South Africa in 1931.

He suffered serious illness in 1934 and, after returning from a recuperative visit to Switzerland, found himself travelling by train to Leicester in the company of the England selectors who wanted to see him play. On arrival Vallance was told he had not been picked for Leicester's game.

He played for the Barbarians at Welford Road in 1942 and in a services international for England against Scotland in front of 18,000 people at Welford Road in 1943. He was commissioned into the 8th Battalion the Sherwood Foresters before the Second World War and took part in the failed Norwegian campaign of 1940 as officer commanding the carrier platoon.

Vallance escaped capture but was interned in Sweden for several months before returning to England. He rejoined the 8th Battalion and was posted to Northern Ireland as a major, subsequently taking up staff appointments in North Africa, Italy, Malta and Greece.

He was a wholesale photo finisher for the Rank Organisation and became a master of fox hounds, riding with the Quorn Hunt into his eighties.

Appearances: *200 (W104, D17, L79)*
Scoring: *27 tries, 4 conv, 5 pens, 104 pts*

VESTY, Samuel Brook (198)

Born: *Leicester, 26.11.1981*
Educated: *John Cleveland College (Hinckley), Loughborough University*
Clubs: *Leicester, Nottingham, Bath*
Tigers debut: *24.8.2002 v Biarritz Olympique (replacement) (at Bayonne), won 14-13 (1C, 2 pts)* ●
Last game: *27.2.2010 at Northampton Saints (replacement), lost 3-19* ●
Caps: *England (2) 2009*

Sam Vesty became the fourth generation of his family to play for Leicester but surpassed the marks set by Jack Dickens, his great-grandfather, Bernard Vesty, his grandfather, and Phil, his father. Unlike his father, a prop, Sam played across the back division, but was most accustomed to fly-half and full-back.

He played for England's under-18 and under-21 sides and was Leicester's young player of the year for 2002/03. He also played cricket for Leicestershire's second XI as a right-hand bat and wicketkeeper, catching out India's captain, Mohammad Azharuddin, in a World Cup warm-up match in 1999. But he had to choose between cricket and rugby, opting for the winter sport and, ultimately, winning caps for England as a replacement in 2009.

That was his breakthrough year, after being largely ignored when Marcelo Loffreda and Heyneke Meyer were coaching Tigers. He forced his way into the starting XVs for both the Heineken Cup and Premiership finals before touring Argentina with England in the summer, having played for England Saxons in the 2006 Churchill Cup.

He joined Bath in 2010 and ended his playing career three years later to join Worcester Warriors as academy transition coach.

Appearances: *122 starts + 42 reps (W106, D8, L50)*
Scoring: *15 tries, 38 conv, 30 pens, 3 drops, 250 pts*

SAM VESTY

W

WADE, Michael Richard (110)

Born: *Leicester, 13.9.1937*
Educated: *Wyggeston GS, Emmanuel College (Cambridge)*
Clubs: *Oadby, Old Wyggestonians, Cambridge University (Blues 1958-61), Leicester, Stade Bordelais UC (France)*
Tigers debut: *24.12.1955 at Bedford, drew 0-0*
Last game: *28.2.1967 v Bath, won 11-3*
Caps: *England (3) 1962*

Mike Wade played for Leicester as a schoolboy and within the space of four days over Christmas 1955 he appeared against Bedford (who included his schoolmaster, Ken Nicholas), Birkenhead Park and the Barbarians.

His try-scoring prowess included two in the first of his four university matches, while studying at Emmanuel College, Cambridge; three on his debut for the Barbarians and one in the first minute of England's game with Ireland in 1962, his second cap.

Wade did national service in the RAF, playing for the Combined Services, before university where he played on the wing for his first Blue and subsequently in his normal position of centre, captaining Cambridge to victory in 1961. He played in three internationals that season and went on to captain Leicester in 1963.

He played for Leicestershire and guested for the Irish Wolfhounds and Stade Bordelais University. He represented Leicestershire and East Midlands against Australia in 1957/58 and played for the Midlands against New Zealand in 1963/64.

Pressure of business and cartilage damage precipitated his retirement and in 1970 he moved to the United States as a management consultant in Massachusetts.

Appearances: *166 (W87, D20, L59)*
Scoring: *27 tries, 2 drops, 87 pts*

MIKE WADE

WALKER, Michael Ronald (105)

Born: *Leicester, 16.1.1934*
Educated: *South Wigston, Leicester College of Art*
Clubs: *South Leicester, Nuneaton, Leicester*
Tigers debut: *20.10.1956 at Cheltenham, lost 0-3*
Last game: *3.12.1966 at Waterloo, lost 6-10*

Mick Walker, a builder and joiner, was a hooker and played for Leicestershire and the Leicestershire Alliance. He made four appearances for Nuneaton before joining Leicester, for whom he scored three tries in his 216 games. His 200th game was against Bath at the Recreation Ground on new year's day 1966; he subsequently emigrated to Australia.

MICK WALKER

Appearances: *216 (W121, D18, L77)*
Scoring: *3 tries, 9 pts*

WALTON, Field Laurence Joseph (121)

Born: *Barnstaple, Devon, 17.4.1940*
Educated: *Rugby, Loughborough University*
Clubs: *Stoneygate, Leicester*
Tigers debut: *3.9.1964 v Watcyn Thomas XV, lost 11-12*
Last game: *27.4.1968 v Manchester, won 13-6 (1T, 3 pts)*

While at university, Field Walton propped for the UAU, English Universities and Leicestershire. He played for Midland Counties (East) against John Thornett's Australian tourists in October 1966 and the last of his three tries for Leicester was scored in his final match, against Manchester.

Appearances: *139 (W86, D8, L45)*
Scoring: *3 tries, 9 pts*

FIELD WALTON

GEORGE WARD

WARD, Joseph Alfred George (45)

Born: *Bottesford, Leicester, 19.3.1885*
Died: *Leicester, regd Q3 1962*
Clubs: *Belgrave, Leicester*
Tigers debut: *9.3.1910 at Moseley, won 20-0*
Last game: *4.1.1926 at Northern, lost 6-8*
Caps: *England (6) 1913-14*

George Ward was said to be the best hooker in Britain during his international career in the two seasons immediately prior to the First World War, during which England won successive grand slams.

He played for Leicestershire and Midland Counties, appearing for the latter against South Africa in 1912. He won Midland Counties Cup finals with Leicester in 1912 and 1913 and was vice-captain from 1918-28, deputising regularly for the injured Percy Lawrie during 1922/23.

In 1923 he became only the sixth player to pass 300 appearances. He was described as having "very strong legs, he swung the foot beautifully and could get the ball from anyone when he felt like it." He worked as a boiler riveter for Thorneloe and Clarkson, the clothing manufacturers in Northampton Street.

Appearances: *361 (W220, D30, L111)*
Scoring: *21 tries, 63 pts*

WATKIN, Charles Ernest (79)

Born: *Leicester, 21.11.1914*
Died: *Leicester, 1.4.1980*
Clubs: *Aylestone St James, Leicester*
Tigers debut: *22.1.1938 v Richmond, won 9-3*
Last game: *4.9.1948 v Bedford, lost 3-21*

ERNIE WATKIN

Ernie Watkin's playing career was abbreviated by the Second World War but he played for Leicestershire and East Midlands against the touring New Zealand Services side in 1946 and against Australia the following year, when he kicked a penalty and dropped a goal.

A full-back who played once at centre, he became the only Leicester full-back to score a try in a thirty-year period from 1924-54, playing against the Rest at Welford Road in September 1939. He was the club's leading points scorer in successive seasons, between 1946-48.

He died just before Leicester's second John Player Cup win in 1980 and the following year, when Tigers won the cup outright, Gwyneth, his widow, donated a presentation case to hold the trophy in memory of her husband.

Appearances: *117 (W55, D4, L58)*
Scoring: *2 tries, 64 conv, 34 pens, 236 pts*

WATSON, James Robert (31)

Born: *Foxton, Leicestershire, regd Q1 1884*
Died: *Colchester, Essex, regd Q3 1950*
Clubs: *Stoneygate, Leicester*
Tigers debut: *28.11.1903 at Cambridge University, lost 0-6*
Last game: *3.1.1914 at Gloucester, lost 0-3*

Jamie Watson could play in any midfield position and captained Leicester in the inaugural meeting with the Barbarians in 1909, the second of his three seasons leading the club. He played in the teams that won the Midland Counties Cup in 1909, 1910 and 1913. He also led Leicester on his 200th appearance, against Moseley in 1911, and in his final match at Gloucester. Watson scored hat-tricks against West Hartlepool (1907) and Stoneygate (1909), in a career total of 46 tries. He was a chartered accountant.

Appearances: *229 (W132, D25, L72)*
Scoring: *46 tries, 1 conv, 140 pts*

JAMIE WATSON

WELLS, John Martin (164)

Born: *Driffield, Yorkshire, 12.5.1963*
Educated: *Magnus GS (Newark), Loughborough University*
Clubs: *Newark, Loughborough Students, Leicester*
Tigers debut: *25.9.1982 at Harlequins, won 29-25 (2T, 8 pts)*
Last game: *1.11.1997 v Loughborough Students, won 71-7*

JOHN WELLS

It is hard to disassociate John Wells's career from that of Dean Richards, with whom he played and coached over a 23-year period at Welford Road and subsequently joined at Newcastle Falcons as part of the management team. At one stage they were both members of the Leicestershire police force.

Wells was a contemporary at Loughborough of Andy Robinson, later England coach, and played in the back row of a students side that won the 1984 UAU final. He played for England at under-16, under-18, student, under-23 and B level, touring Spain with England B in 1989; he appeared for an England XV against Italy in Rovigo in 1990 and on the Probables side in a final England trial but a senior cap eluded him.

Yet he was the epitome of industry and the close-quarter work expected of a blind-side flanker, in alliance initially for Leicester with Richards and Ian Smith, later with Neil Back. Altogether he played 367 games for the club, among them five Pilkington Cup finals - he was captain of the side that beat Harlequins in 1993 - and two seasons (1987/88 and 1994/95) when Leicester were league champions. He was also in the starting XV for the 1997 Heineken Cup final against Brive and captained Leicester between 1991-93.

A former partner with his father on a Newark farm, he took a degree in sports science and recreation management and was a police officer in Kegworth. When Richards was appointed director of rugby in 1998, Wells was named forwards coach and his coaching career proved outstanding; under his direction, with Richards removing all the public-duty chores, Leicester won successive Premiership titles between 1999-2002 and the Heineken Cup finals of 2001 and 2002.

When Richards left the club in 2004, Wells continued as head coach and the club did not lose another game that season. In 2004/05, Leicester topped the Premiership table, reached the semi-finals of the Heineken Cup and Wells was named director of rugby of the season. That summer he joined the RFU national academy staff, having coached England A in 2001 and toured with the senior squad to North America.

He joined the England coaching staff as forwards coach (under Robinson) in 2006 and remained under the subsequent managements of Brian Ashton and Martin Johnson. In that role he helped England reach the final of the 2007 World Cup, to the 2011 six nations championship and went to New Zealand with the 2011 World Cup squad. He joined Newcastle on a short-term contract in 2012 and, when Richards took over the Falcons the following season, Wells remained and was appointed head coach for 2014/15.

Appearances: *360 starts + 7 reps (W275, D5, L87)*
Scoring: *50 tries, 208 pts*

WEST, Dorian Edward (186)

Born: *Wrexham, Wales, 5.10.1967*
Educated: *Ashby GS*
Clubs: *Leicester, Nottingham*
Tigers debut: *3.9.1988 v Bedford (replacement), won 40-10 (1T, 4 pts)*
Last game: *29.5.2004 v Sale (replacement) (at Twickenham), won 48-27* ●
Caps: *England (21) 1998-2003*

DORIAN WEST

Dorian West started his first-class playing career as a flanker but found long-term success at hooker, playing in that position for his country and for the Lions. The transition started during a five-year spell at Nottingham and he returned to Leicester to joust for the number-two shirt with Richard Cockerill.

A late developer, West spent his initial two years with Leicester before joining Nottingham where he made 89 appearances and spent one season as captain. He worked as an armed response police officer before becoming a professional player and made his first league appearance for Tigers in 1996.

Having played for the British Police and the Welsh Exiles, England A picked him in 1997 and his first full cap came, at the age of 30, as a replacement against France in 1998. His first England start was against Wales in the 2001 six nations and later that year he toured with England to North America before being called to Australia by the Lions when the Ireland hooker, Keith Wood, was injured. West performed so well he was included in the matchday squad for the second and third internationals.

He toured New Zealand and Australia with England in 2003 and captained England in a World Cup warm-up match against France in Marseilles. He was a member of the victorious World Cup squad that year, appearing against Uruguay and the semi-final against France. He was on the bench for the final against Australia and received the MBE in 2004.

His club honours included two Heineken Cup winners' medals (2001 and 2002), the four Premiership titles from 1999-2002 and the 1997 Pilkington Cup final. When he retired, West joined the RFU national academy coaching staff and was forwards coach to England under-21 and England Saxons before joining Northampton as forwards coach in 2007.

Appearances: *152 starts + 57 reps (W145, D7, L57)*
Scoring: *34 tries, 169 pts*

WHEELER, Peter John (136)

Born: *South Norwood, London, 26.11.1948*
Educated: *John Ruskin GS, Brockley County GS (South London)*
Clubs: *Old Brockleians, Leicester*
Tigers debut: *8.11.1969 at Cambridge University, lost 11-36*
Last game: *23.10.1985 at Oxford University, won 32-7*
Caps: *England (41) 1975-84, British Isles (7) 1977-80*

The only individual in the club's history to have achieved as much off the field as he did on it, Peter Wheeler claimed every playing honour available, captained and coached Tigers, became president and then the first chief executive of the professional era.

As an administrator he became a principal voice for England's leading clubs and executive chairman of Euro Rugby, the pan-European body established by leading clubs in the home unions, France and Italy. Before stepping away from the day-to-day duties in 2014, he completed 45 years of unbroken service to Leicester, a vital component in their dominance of the English game.

He represented Kent after playing for Old Brockleians but moved to Leicester to join Hogg Robinson, the insurance brokers. He was a hooker in the modern mould, comfortable with ball in hand - he scored three tries on his 1973 debut for the Barbarians against the East Midlands - and an adroit passer who also became a goalkicker; his 589 points for the club include 61 conversions and 69 penalties.

He played for Leicestershire between 1970-74, captained Leicester between 1973-75 and again between 1979-81, the years in which Tigers won three successive John Player Cups. He led Midland Counties (East) against New Zealand in 1973, against Australia in 1975 and New Zealand in 1978 and 1979. When Australia opened their 1981 tour, he captained the Midlands side that beat them and again when the Midlands played New Zealand in 1983.

Wheeler toured the Far East with England in 1971 and won his first cap against France in 1975 but a serious neck injury against Wales in his next outing set him back. He recovered to take over from John Pullin as England hooker for, in effect, the next eight years. He toured the Far East again in 1979, played in the grand-slam season of 1980 and toured North America in 1982.

He was picked for the 1977 Lions tour to New Zealand and ousted Bobby Windsor from the test position, playing in the last three internationals with Fran Cotton and Graham Price in a front row widely regarded as one of the best fielded by any Lions party. He played in all four internationals of the Lions tour to South Africa in 1980 and was a leading candidate to captain the 1983 tour to New Zealand, but was overlooked in favour of Ireland's Ciaran Fitzgerald.

He did captain England in his final international season, 1983/84, and led the team to the first home victory over New Zealand since Bernard Gadney captained the winning 1936 side. He also captained the Midlands against the 1984 Australians, when he and the opposing hooker, Mark McBain, were controversially sent off.

He coached the club in the inaugural Courage League season of 1987/88, when Tigers won the title, and became a committee member, being elected president between 1995-97. During that period the game went open and Wheeler, who had been managing director of P and G Bland, the insurance brokers, became the club's chief executive.

He also became a director of Premier Rugby Ltd and represented the clubs on the RFU council and, later, the management board. He spearheaded negotiations between clubs and union over the future of the professional game in England and became executive chairman of Euro Rugby in 2004. He has remained an active presence among the game's politicians in England, giving Leicester a voice when crucial decisions have been made.

Wheeler also found time to complete the Four Peaks challenge in 2002, climbing Ben Nevis, Helvellyn, Snowdon and Carantouhill with Dean Richards to raise money for the Wooden Spoon charity. A former magistrate, he was named deputy lieutenant of Leicestershire in 2000; he is the holder of an honorary MA from Leicester University and an honorary doctorate of business administration from De Montfort University. Two sons, Ben and Joe, have been members of Leicester's first-team squad.

Appearances: *349 (W235, D12, L102)*
Scoring: *66 tries, 61 conv, 69 pens, 589 pts*

PETER WHEELER

WHITE, Herbert Victor (107)

Born: *Carlisle, Cumberland, 16.1.1929*
Died: *Taunton, Somerset, 24.1.2005*
Educated: *Creighton GS (Carlisle), Borough Road College (Isleworth), Carnegie College (Leigh)*
Clubs: *Old Creightonians, Penzance-Newlyn, Camborne, Leicester*
Tigers debut: *19.10.1957 v Cheltenham, drew 3-3*
Last game: *30.11.1963 v Cheltenham, won 9-3*

Generally regarded as the best coach England never had, 'Chalkie' White laid down a playing ethos throughout the 1970s that Leicester have seldom departed from since. He was the most successful club coach in England when the RFU appointed Mike Davis to coach England in 1979 but his sometimes abrasive manner may have cost him friends in the right places.

Born into a farming family in Cumberland, White went into the Royal Navy and then became a teacher at Nottingham High School. He played for Cumberland and Westmorland, Cornwall, and Notts, Lincs and Derbys as a scrum-half, but his playing career ended when he contracted Meniere's disease, which affected his sense of balance.

He turned his analytical mind to coaching, working with Colin Martin and David Matthews during the late 1960s; he moulded the sides that played in four successive John Player Cup finals between 1978-81. Players guided by him include Clive Woodward and Les Cusworth, both of whom became England coaches, Terry Burwell, Robin Cowling and Peter Wheeler, all of whom coached at club level.

He was a member of the advisory panel to the RFU coaching sub-committee from its formation in 1963 and helped bring into operation the union's preliminary and full coaching awards. He coached the Midlands to victories over Australia (1975) and Argentina (1976), became an RFU staff coach and, in 1983, became the RFU divisional administrator for the south-west, based in Taunton.

His contribution to coaching was recognised when he received Sportscoach UK's Geoffrey Dyson award from the Princess Royal, only the third recipient from rugby. In 2000 Leicester made him a life member and, after his death in 2005, a thanksgiving service for his life was held at Leicester Cathedral.

Appearances: *147 (W77, D15, L55)*
Scoring: *6 tries, 18 pts*

CHALKIE WHITE

JULIAN WHITE

WHITE, Julian Martin (199)

Born: *Plymouth, Devon, 14.5.1973*
Educated: *Kingsbridge Community College (Devon)*
Clubs: *Salcombe, Kingsbridge, Okehampton, Plymouth Albion, Dannevirke RSC (New Zealand), Hawke's Bay (New Zealand), Crusaders (NZ), Bridgend, Saracens, Bristol, Leicester*
Tigers debut: *29.11.2003 v Bath, lost 12-13* ●
Last game: *9.3.2012 at Bath, won 17-16* ●
Caps: *England (51) 2000-09, British & Irish Lions (4) 2005*

Possibly the most travelled Leicester player, Julian White learned his rugby in the West Country before moving to New Zealand and he made one appearance in Super Rugby in 1997 for the Crusaders. A driving accident there led to his return to England when he joined Saracens and toured South Africa with England in 2000, winning his first cap.

A specialist tight-head prop, White gained a reputation as one of the strongest scrummagers in the country. Over a nine-year period, England selectors knew precisely what they would get from him and he was a member of the 2003 World Cup squad, receiving the MBE the following year after playing against Samoa and Uruguay.

He appeared in all four internationals played by the Lions in 2005 but, after the 2006/07 season, his international career seemed over. It was revived in 2009 when he was chosen in the six nations squad and visited Argentina with England but he was a reluctant tourist because of the time spent away from his growing farm.

He joined Leicester after a spell with Bristol and started the 2007 Heineken Cup final against Wasps, he also appeared in the 2009 European final against Leinster. He was a member of the squads that won the Premiership titles of 2007, 2009 and 2010. He was 38 when he retired and now runs a farm in Leicestershire.

Appearances: *120 starts + 38 reps (W103, D10, L45)*
Scoring: *4 tries, 20 pts*

MONTY WHITEHEAD

WHITEHEAD, Montague Ernest (16)

Born: *Leicester, regd Q1 1875*
Died: *Blaby, Leicester, 2.6.1948*
Educated: *Cambridge University*
Clubs: *Stoneygate, Leicester*
Tigers debut: *23.2.1895 at Burton, lost 6-8 (1T, 3 pts)*
Last game: *30.11.1901 at Cambridge University, lost 3-21*

'Monty' Whitehead, a forward, became better known in the golfing world after his rugby career ended. He played in the sides that won the Midland Counties Cup in 1898 and 1900 and was involved in 17 successive Leicester wins between November 1896 and March 1897.

He was a leather merchant in the firm of James Whitehead and Co in Duke Street but retired in 1923 and became a legendary golf club secretary. He played off scratch and won the inaugural individual county championship for Leicestershire and Rutland on his home course in Evington Lane in 1910, breaking the course record in the process. The Montague Whitehead Trophy, a solid silver salver, was given as a knockout cup at Evington Lane in 1947 and is still played for annually.

He won a golf Blue at Cambridge and became captain of Luffenham Heath in 1913; he was captain of Leicestershire Golf Club six years later, became president in 1922 and secretary in 1933. He was president of the English Golf Union in 1929.

Appearances: *146 (W95, D15, L36)*
Scoring: *20 tries, 60 pts*

WIENER, Rudolph Alexander Kilgour (68)

Born: *Cape Town, South Africa, 19.2.1901*
Died: *Thurlestone, Devon, 23.2.1991*
Educated: *Rondebosch Boys, University of Cape Town, St Thomas's Hospital*
Clubs: *St Thomas's Hospital, Harlequins, Coventry, Leicester*
Tigers debut: *12.10.1929 at Gloucester, lost 11-20*
Last game: *17.12.1932 v Waterloo, lost 3-13*

Kilgour 'Doc' Wiener, a forward from the Newlands district of Cape Town, played for St Thomas's Hospital and one game for Harlequins before coming to work as a doctor at Leicester Royal Infirmary. Bringing his medical skills to the pitch, in September 1930 he treated the Plymouth player, W Molls, who had been carried off unconscious and taken to hospital after the game ended. Wiener retired to Devon in 1984.

Appearances: *101 (W57, D13, L31)*
Scoring: *3 tries, 9 pts*

KILGOUR WIENER

WILKINSON, Henry (19)

Born: *Leicester, regd Q3 1869*
Died: *Leicester, 15.5.1953*
Educated: *St Matthews*
Clubs: *St Matthews, Leicester*
Tigers debut: *28.9.1895 v Gloucester, won 6-0*
Last game: *25.2.1905 at Newport, lost 5-9*

HARRY WILKINSON

Harry Wilkinson, an extremely fast wing, played in five successive Midland Counties Cup wins from 1898-1902; he only lost one of 24 cup ties in which he played, scoring a record 31 tries. He was the club's leading try scorer for five successive seasons between 1896-1901 and, on 27 December 1899, against Harlequins, became the first Leicester player to reach 100 tries.

Five years later, against Rugby, he scored his 150th, ending with a career total of 153 which stood as a record for twenty years until passed by Percy Lawrie. He was the older brother of another Tiger, Edwin, and helped run the Model, a lodging house in Britannia Street. He also kept the Sultan public house in Belgrave Gate for several years. He served in munitions during the First World War.

Appearances: *233 (W156, D18, L59)*
Scoring: *153 tries, 3 conv, 6 drops, 489 pts*

WILLARS, Graham George (120)

Born: *Leicester, 20.11.1939*
Died: *Leicester, 20.9.1997*
Educated: *Moat Boys*
Clubs: *Moat Old Boys, Birstall, Leicester*
Tigers debut: *17.10.1959 v Cheltenham, won 23-3*
Last game: *4.4.1987 at Waterloo (replacement), won 15-9*

Remarkably for one who played two decades in Leicester's back row, Graham Willars did not play for his school 1st XV. Encouraged by Doug Norman to join Leicester, he had to fight his corner against such notable flankers as David Matthews, Bob Small and John Quick but he impressed so much with his constructive play that he became club captain in 1968/69 and again in 1972/73.

He played for Leicestershire and captained the British Post Office side for seven years. He wanted his sides to play running rugby and, in his second year as captain, failed by only 12 points to achieve his season's target of 1,000 points. His career was extended by numerous comebacks, his final match coming in his 48th year.

He succeeded Chalkie White as coach from 1982-87, taking Leicester to the 1983 John Player Cup final (in a season when Tigers did pass 1,000 points), and became an RFU staff coach. A telecommunications manager for British Telecom, he was club president from 1991-93 and was heavily involved in the Leicester Past Players' Association.

He died after a long illness on the day of Leicester's first Heineken Cup visit to Toulouse and the Droglites (Old Tigers) spent that season raising funds for the St Martha's Ward trust fund who helped care for him during that time.

Appearances: *334 starts + 4 reps (W195, D22, L121)*
Scoring: *38 tries, 129 pts*

WILLIAMS, Alexander Kevin (156)

Born: *Newport, Gwent, Wales, 22.8.1956*
Educated: *St Julian's HS (Newport), Loughborough Colleges*
Clubs: *Newport, Loughborough Colleges, Leicester*
Tigers debut: *12.9.1979 v Birmingham, won 38-0* ●
Last game: *20.3.1987 v Loughborough Students, won 44-16*

KEVIN WILLIAMS

Kevin Williams, a wing and occasional full-back, marked his first game for Newport with a try against Penarth and made five more appearances for the Welsh club before going to Loughborough on a teaching course. He played for Welsh secondary schools and in the Loughborough VII that won the Middlesex sevens in 1976.

He represented the UAU and Leicestershire, and toured South Africa with the Welsh Academicals in 1981. That same year he played against Gosforth in the last of Leicester's three successive John Player Cup wins and was the top try scorer for 1980/81. He won two B caps for Wales in 1981, against France and Australia.

He ran his own insurance broking business, the Williams Partnership in Charles Street, but took early retirement to pursue his interest in athletics. He competed on the masters circuit and represented Great Britain, notably in San Sebastian in 2013 when he won a bronze medal as part of the 4 x 200m relay team.

Appearances: *186 starts + 5 reps (W145, D5, L41)*
Scoring: *64 tries, 256 pts*

GRAHAM WILLARS

PEDLAR WOOD

WOOD, George William (34)

Born: *Leicester, 5.2.1886*
Died: *Leicester, 12.6.1969*
Educated: *Melbourne Road*
Clubs: *Melbourne Road Old Boys, Leicester, Nottingham, Nuneaton*
Tigers debut: *10.11.1906 v Newport, drew 3-3*
Last game: *9.9.1922 v Plymouth Albion, lost 6-11*
Caps: *England (1) 1914*

'Pedlar' Wood won his only England cap in a club half-back pairing with Tim Taylor, against Wales in 1914, the first game of a grand-slam season. Though he played 14 games at fly-half, Wood was a highly-regarded scrum-half and had already played 263 games for Tigers before his international debut.

During his 16 years with Leicester he represented Leicestershire and the Midland Counties, and appeared in four Midland Counties Cup-winning sides. He played a further five seasons with Nuneaton, making 170 appearances and scoring 44 tries, as well as adding two more cup final wins, in 1922 and 1924.

A keen student of the game, he was sent off against Birkenhead Park in 1914 for adopting what the referee decided were incorrect scrum tactics. He scored 102 tries in his 388 games for Leicester, his 100th coming in a rare win at Bristol in 1921. His remarkable longevity earned him the reputation as "the marvel of modern rugby."

When he retired, Nuneaton's Harry Cleaver, later to become RFU president, said: "Mr Wood has served the club as captain and during that period the club has been the most successful in its history. What he achieved on the field with management and tactics will influence future players and playing for many years to come."

Wood made one appearance for Nottingham, in 1907/08, and played for the Barbarians against South African Services in 1915 in a fundraising match to provide comforts for colonial troops. An inspector with the British United Shoe Machinery Company until 1959, he was a keen cricketer and umpired on Victoria Park for many years.

Appearances: *388 (W233, D32, L123)*
Scoring: *102 tries, 15 conv, 336 pts*

KENNETH WOOD

WOOD, Kenneth Berridge (36)

Born: *Leicester, regd Q3 1885*
Died: *South Africa, c 1960*
Clubs: *Stoneygate, Leicester, Nottingham*
Tigers debut: *13.10.1906 v Bristol, drew 0-0*
Last game: *26.4.1919 v Royal Naval Division, lost 4-7*
Caps: *Great Britain (2) 1910*

Kenneth Wood, a centre, toured South Africa with the 1910 British team, appearing in the first and third internationals at Kimberley and Cape Town (both lost) and thus joining the small band of players capped by Britain but who never played for their country. He played in nine tour games, scoring against Natal in two of them.

Wood, whose father, William, played for Leicester Athletic Society before Tigers were founded, played in two Midland Counties Cup-winning sides. He scored a fine try for the Midlands and East Midland Counties in the 16-5 win over Australia in 1908. He played one game for Nottingham in 1907/08. He rose to the rank of major in the Army and emigrated to South Africa where he became a manager at St Michael's Gold Mine in Johannesburg.

Appearances: *121 (W68, D12, L41)*
Scoring: *33 tries, 4 drops, 115 pts*

WOODWARD, Clive Ronald (155)

Born: *Ely, Cambridgeshire, 6.1.1956*
Educated: *HMS Conway, Loughborough Colleges*
Clubs: *Harlequins, Loughborough Colleges, Leicester, Manly (Australia)*
Tigers debut: *1.9.1979 at Bedford, won 34-12 (1T, 4 pts)* ●
Last game: *14.9.1985 v Bath, lost 15-40* ●
Caps: *England (21) 1980-84, British Isles (2) 1980*

One of the most elusive centres to play for England, Clive Woodward gained lasting fame - and a knighthood - for coaching the England side that won the 2003 World Cup in Australia. His vision for the game and ability to think outside the box helped England to become the best side in the world even before the World Cup win, after they beat both New Zealand and Australia on tour in the summer of 2003.

He went on to take his unique approach to football and then to the

CLIVE WOODWARD

British Olympic Association where he spent six years, culminating in the successful 2012 Games in London. Through this period he maintained his Leicester connection as a board member of Leicester plc between 2007-13.

Woodward, born to a service family, enjoyed football and was a reluctant convert to rugby at school in Wales. He was fly-half for England colts in 1975 and played 39 games for Harlequins before taking a sports science degree at Loughborough, where he captained the students and came under the influence of Jim Greenwood, one of the country's most respected coaches.

He played for England under-23 and, after joining Leicester, for England B against France in 1979. He made his senior England debut as a replacement against Ireland in 1980 and retained his place for the remainder of that grand-slam season, delivering what proved to be the outstanding game of his international career against Scotland at Murrayfield.

He toured South Africa with the Lions that summer, playing centre in the second international and wing in the third, ending as the party's second highest points scorer with 53. He toured with England to North America in 1982 and again with the Lions to New Zealand in 1983 but did not appear in the test XV. He was a member of the Barbarians squad that became the first northern-hemisphere side to win the Hong Kong sevens in 1981.

He played in three John Player Cup finals for Leicester, in 1980, 1981 and 1983, forming a complementary midfield partnership with Paul Dodge, and represented Oxfordshire, East Midlands and the Midland Division. He worked for Rank Xerox and moved on that company's behalf to Sydney where he spent four years, played for and captained Manly (whose opponents in 1987 included Leicester).

Returning to England he established his own leasing company and coached Henley, taking them to the national leagues in the 1994/95 season. He moved on to coaching spells with London Irish, Bath and England under-21 before becoming England's first full-time coach in 1997. His England side fell at the quarter-final stage of the 1999 World Cup but, four years later, proved invincible and won the grand slam, beat New Zealand and Australia on tour and carried off the Webb Ellis Cup by beating Australia (again) in Sydney.

In February 2004, he was chosen to coach the 2005 Lions in New Zealand but stood down as England coach six months later, citing differences with the RFU. During his seven years his England record was: played 83, won 59, lost 22, drawn 2. The Lions tour the following year was unsuccessful and Woodward was criticised for his selections.

He moved into football as performance director with Southampton but joined the BOA in 2006 as director of elite performance. He was deputy chef de mission at the 2008 Olympic Games in Beijing and played a significant role in London's successful staging of the Games in 2012.

Appearances: *148 (W114, D4, L30)*
Scoring: *43 tries, 4 conv, 5 drops, 195 pts*

WORMLEIGHTON, John Lawrie (76)

Born: *Leicester, 31.12.1912*
Died: *Leicester, 1.12.1978*
Educated: *Trent College*
Clubs: *Stoneygate, Leicester*
Tigers debut: *8.10.1932 at Bridgwater & Albion, won 11-6*
Last game: *17.4.1937 v Blackheath, won 9-4*

Jack Wormleighton, a prop and hooker, left school at 15 to work in his father's hosiery factory (he later ran Wormleighton and Sons). He was a nephew of Percy Lawrie and registered three tries during his Leicester career, against Guy's Hospital, Blackheath and Old Merchant Taylors. He enjoyed football, cricket and motor cycling and, after his rugby career, took up golf and sailing.

Appearances: *121 (W62, D8, L51)*
Scoring: *3 tries, 9 pts*

YANDLE, Michael John (129)

Born: *Hendy, Carmarthenshire, Wales, 28.3.1945*
Died: *Lima, Peru, 11.3.1995*
Educated: *Llanelli GS, Leeds University*
Clubs: *Hendy, Leicester, Swansea, Headingley*
Tigers debut: *6.9.1969 at Bedford, lost 5-39*
Last game: *28.4.1973 v Hartlepool Rovers, won 15-7*

Mike Yandle was a member of the Llanelli GS squad that dominated the Rosslyn Park sevens in the early 1960s and proved a reliable centre when he moved to Leicester, working as a textile chemist for the Courtaulds Group. He holds the record for the shortest time taken to reach fifty appearances (406 days) and reached 100 in two years and 111 days.

He played for Midland Counties against New Zealand in 1972/73 and was due to captain Leicester in 1973/74 when a business promotion forced him to move away. He joined Swansea and scored the only try of their 9-9 draw with Australia in 1973/74. He subsequently moved to Lima where he died, aged only 49.

Appearances: *155 (W96, D8, L51)*
Scoring: *29 tries, 1 drop, 101 pts*

MIKE YANDLE

NICK YOUNGS

*YOUNGS, Benjamin Ryder (209)

Born: *Cawston, Norfolk, 5.9.1989*
Educated: *Gresham's (Norfolk)*
Clubs: *North Walsham, Leicester*
Tigers debut: *11.2.2007 v Argentina (replacement), lost 21-41*
Caps: *England (38) 2010-14, British & Irish Lions (2) 2013*

Ben, the younger of the two brothers to have played for Leicester since 2007, followed where his father, Nick, went. Both were scrum-halves who played for England but Youngs junior added a Lions tour to his portfolio.

Quick on the break, Youngs played fly-half at school and represented England at under-16 and under-18 level before playing as a scrum-half in the successful under-20 sides of 2008 and 2009. He was only 17 when he became the youngest Leicester player to appear in a league match, against Bristol in April 2007, and he came off the bench against Gloucester in that year's Premiership final.

He attracted great attention for his goal-kicking display for Leicester against South Africa, scoring 17 points in the club's historic win in October 2009, and represented England Saxons against Ireland A in January 2010. Two months later he came off the bench to win his first cap against Scotland as an emergency wing.

At the end of that season he was the players' player of the year, the supporters' young player of the year and the Rugby Players' Association young player of the year. He toured Australia with England in the summer, scoring a vital try in the second test, and was a member of the 2011 World Cup squad, appearing in all five of England's games.

On tour in South Africa in 2012, he scored two tries in the second test before being forced off with a shoulder injury. The following season he earned selection for the 2013 Lions in Australia, alongside Tom, his brother, and was a replacement in the first international before starting the second. He scored a try for Leicester in the 2011 Premiership final against Saracens and started the finals of 2012 and 2013.

Appearances: *105 starts + 38 reps (W100, D7, L36)*
Scoring: *24 tries, 1 conv, 6 pens, 140 pts*

BEN YOUNGS

YOUNGS, Nicholas Gerald (162)

Born: *West Runton, Norfolk, 15.12.1959*
Educated: *Cawston College (Norwich), Gresham's (Norfolk), Shuttleworth Agricultural College*
Clubs: *Bedford, Leicester, Durban HSOB (South Africa)*
Tigers debut: *21.11.1981 v Wasps, won 27-18*
Last game: *8.10.1988 v Orrell, lost 15-27* ●
Caps: *England (6) 1983-84*

A foursquare farm manager and agricultural salesman, Nick Youngs played nine times for England schools (four as captain) and five times for England under-23 while with Bedford. He made 81 appearances for Bedford between 1978-81, scoring 35 tries and 207 points, then moved to Leicester despite the 236-mile round trip for training from his Norfolk home.

He played in the 1983 John Player Cup final and became only the second scrum-half (after Bernard Gadney) to score four tries in a club match, against Birmingham in 1986. He was capped by England against Ireland in 1983 and was one of the six Leicester players who appeared in that year's win over New Zealand at Twickenham, having already played for the Midlands side that beat the All Blacks.

He toured South Africa with England in 1984, having played for a Western Province Invitation XV the previous summer while studying farming methods in the republic. After retiring, he coached North Walsham. His two sons, Tom and Ben, have gone on to play for Leicester, England and the Lions.

Appearances: *145 (W106, D3, L36)*
Scoring: *71 tries, 284 pts*

Pen Portraits

To qualify for this list people must have held the post of Honorary Secretary, General Secretary, Honorary Treasurer or President, or be members of the senior coaching staff, first- team managers, members of the Board, or elected club captains. Also included are players who have won international caps or toured with the British & Irish Lions while at the Tigers, but have not been profiled in the 100 cap section of this book.

Key: Details are correct up to 1 August 2014, with players still in the Tigers squad for the 2014/15 season denoted with an asterisk, and those still playing first-class rugby at the same time denoted with a plus sign. Individuals marked with < have a full biography in 100 cap section of this book.

John David ABELL (Board: 1999-)
b Macclesfield, Cheshire, 15.12.1942.
Executive chairman of Joudain plc. He was previously chairman and chief executive of Suter plc and a director of British Leyland.

<GJ ADEY (Player: 1967-81, President 1997-99, Board: 1997-2014)

+Horacio AGULLA (Player: 2010-12)
b Buenos Aires, Argentina, 22.10.1984.
51 caps for Argentina (2005-). 39+9 games for Tigers, also played for Hindu, Dax, Brive and Bath.

<JA ALLEN (Player: 1971-75, Captain: 1970-71, Treasurer: 1975-82, Hon Secretary: 1982-95, Board: 1997-2007)

<KP ANDREWS (Player: 1965-70, President: 1987-89)

Rodger James ARNEIL (Player: 1969-71)
b Edinburgh, Scotland, 1.5.1944.
22 caps for Scotland (1968-72), 4 caps for Lions (1968), Lions tour (1971). 25 games for Tigers, also played for Edinburgh Academicals, Northampton.

<NA BACK (Player: 1990-2005, Captain: 2003, Coach: 2005-08)

<RJ BARR (Player: 1928-39, Captain: 1936-38, Team Secretary: 1946-57, Hon Secretary: 1957-62, President: 1962-65)

Charles Eric St John BEAMISH (Player: 1926-36)
b Cork, Ireland, 23.6.1908, d Templemore, Ireland, 18.5.1984.
12 caps for Ireland (1933-38), Lions tour (1936). 17 games for Tigers, also played for North of Ireland and Harlequins.

<R BEASON (Player: 1960-72, Treasurer: 1982-85, President: 1985-87, Board: 1997-2007)

Ralph Langford Wing "Rodney" BEDINGFIELD (Treasurer: 1938-59, President: 1959-62)
b Blaby, Leicestershire, 17.12.1901, d Leicester, regd Q2 1971.

<JTW BERRY (Player: 1932-48, Captain: 1938-47, President: 1971-74)

Phil BLAKE (Coach: 2014-)
b London, 24.11.1963.
Joined as defence coach after a glittering career playing rugby league and coaching rugby union in Australia.

Richard James BLAZE (Player: 2007-09, Coach: 2011-)
b Birmingham, 19.4.1985.
11+13 games for Tigers, also played for Moseley and Worcester Warriors. Was on the brink of international recognition with England when a foot injury forced him into retirement at the start of 2010/11 aged 25.

<AD BOLESWORTH (Player: 1936-55, Captain: 1952-53, Team Secretary: 1957-64)

William Newby "Billy" BRADSHAW (Treasurer: 1929-38, President: 1945-52)
b Leicester, regd Q1 1878, d Leicester, regd Q3 1955.

Frederick John BRETT (Treasurer: 1890-95)
b Alford, Lincs, regd Q1 1844, d Leicester, regd Q1 1935.
A chemist's valuer by profession.

Alexander Edward BRICE (Player 1880-86, Captain: 1880-81)
b Kilmersdon, Somerset, regd Q2 1852, d Cape Town, South Africa, 13.1.1903.
21 games for Leicester, he was a schoolmaster who went to South Africa and eventually became the Kimberley inspector of schools.

Paul Anthony BURKE (Player: 2006-07, Coach: 2008-)
b Paddington, London, 1.5.1973.
13 caps and 108 points for Ireland (1995-2003). 13+8 games for Tigers, also played for Cork Constitution, London Irish, Munster, Bristol, Cardiff and Harlequins. Joined coaching staff in 2008.

Edwyn Sherard BURNABY (President: 1881-83)
b Baggrave, Leicestershire, 1830, d Brighton, Sussex, 31.5.1883.
Was conservative MP for North Leicestershire from 1880 until his death in 1883. Major General in the Crimean War.

***Gonzalo Oscar CAMACHO** (Player: 2013-)
b Buenos Aires, Argentina, 28.8.1984.
23 caps for Argentina (2008-). Yet to make his Tigers debut, also played for Buenos Aires C & RC, Harlequins and Exeter Chiefs.

+Martín Leandro CASTROGIOVANNI (Player: 2006-13)
b Paraná, Argentina, 21.10.1981. 105 caps for Italy (2002-). 85+61 games for Tigers, also played for Calvisano and Toulon.

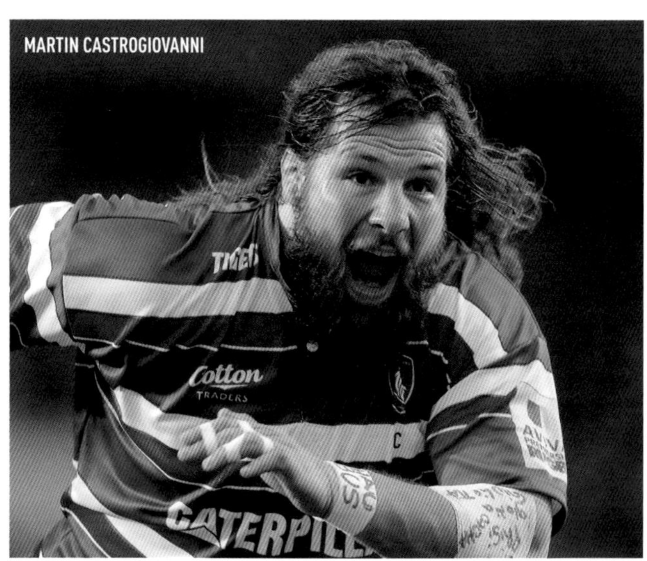

MARTIN CASTROGIOVANNI

Albert Daffurn CHILTON (General Secretary: 1954-65)
b Ladywood, Birmingham, regd Q2 1903, d 17.10.1970.
A Major in the Leicestershire Regiment who was awarded the MBE in 1951. In 1955 he wrote the book *Come on Tigers* – the history of the Regiment up to that point.

David Frederick George CLAYTON (Board: 1999-2011)
b Wolverhampton, Staffordshire, 3.11.1950.
Previously commercial director at Nottingham Forest FC and Wolverhampton Wanderers FC.

<**R COCKERILL** (Player: 1992-2006, Coach: 2004-)

SIMON COHEN

Simon Joshua COHEN (Board: 2011-)
b Macclesfield, Cheshire, 31.10.1956.
Head of Rugby Operations at Tigers from 2005, he joined the board initially as chief operating officer in 2011, and then as chief executive. A former sports lawyer and rugby agent.

***Daniel Richard COLE** (Player: 2007-)
b Leicester, 9.5.1987.
45 caps for England (2010-), 3 caps for Lions 2013. Product of the Tigers Academy. 79+44 games for Tigers, also played for Bedford Blues and Nottingham.

Joseph COLLIER (Player: 1887, President: 1901-12)
b Market Harborough, Leicestershire 26.1.1851, d Leicester, 15.10.1935.
One game for the first-team, also played cricket for Leicestershire when they beat Australia in 1878.

Patrick Bernard "Paddy" COOTE (Player: 1931-33)
b Eton, 7.1.1910, d Trigonon, Greece, 19.4.1941.
1 cap for Ireland (1933). 27 games for Tigers, also played for the RAF. His playing career was cut short when he suffered a severely damaged neck making a tackle against Swansea. He collapsed on the train home before being taken to an RAF hospital. He was not discharged for three months and never played rugby again.

<**CW CROSS** (Player: 1910-23, President: 1952-57)

Morgan Patrick CROWE (Player: 1932-35)
b Dublin, Ireland, 5.3.1907, d Ballsbridge, Dublin, Ireland, 8.4.1993.
13 caps for Ireland (1929-34). 72 games for Tigers, also played for Lansdowne. A doctor at the Royal Infirmary, he was appointed to the City Isolation Hospital in February 1934, but returned to Ireland in 1937 to become deputy medical officer of health for Dublin.

Thomas Henry "Tom" CRUMBIE (Player: 1892-97, Hon Secretary: 1895-1928)
b Leicester 1.2.1868, d Market Harborough, Leicestershire, 13.3.1928.
Appeared in two first-team games for the Tigers on the wing before assuming the role of honorary secretary in 1895 and then playing one more game in the pack in 1897. Was responsible for the development of the ground and making Leicester an invitation club.

Leo Francis Matthew CULLEN (Player: 2005-07)
b Wicklow, Ireland, 9.1.1978.
32 caps for Ireland (2002-11). 41+15 games for Tigers, also played for Blackrock College and Leinster.

Montagu CURZON (President: 1883-90)
b St George Hanover Square, London, 21.9.1846,
d Barrow-upon-Soar, Leicestershire, 1.9.1907.
A Colonel in the Rifle Brigade, he was Conservative MP for North Leicestershire 1883-1885.

John Derrick "Jerry" DAY (Player: 1945-53, Team Secretary: 1965-66, Hon Secretary: 1966-82)
b Leicester, 18.10.1923, d May 2012.
76 games for Tigers, before taking up off-field jobs including 16 years as club secretary.

<**PW DODGE** (Player: 1975-93, Captain: 1987-89, Coach: 1991-96, President: 2013-)

Nicholas Taylor "Nick" DONALD (Board: 1998-99)
b 1961.
HSBC nominated club director when Tigers first became a plc. Director of the corporate finance and advisory division of HSBC.

Nicholas James "Nick" DRAKE-LEE (Player: 1962-68)
b Kettering, Northamptonshire, 7.4.1942.
8 caps for England (1963-65). 73 games for Tigers, also played for Kettering, Cambridge University (Blues 1961-63), Manchester and Waterloo. His son, Bill, played flank forward for the Tigers during the 1990s.

+Julien DUPUY (Player: 2008-09)
b Périgueux, France, 19.12.1983.
8 caps for France (2009-12). 24+7 games for Tigers, also played for Biarritz and Stade Français.

Robert Stuart Francis "Bob" DWYER (Coach: 1996-98)
b Waverley, Australia, 29.11.1940.
Began coaching with Randwick in Sydney in 1977, and then took over with the Wallabies in two spells from 1982-83 and 1988-95 including winning the 1991 Rugby World Cup. Has also coached Racing Club in France, Bristol and NSW Waratahs and in 2011 was inducted into the IRB Hall of Fame.

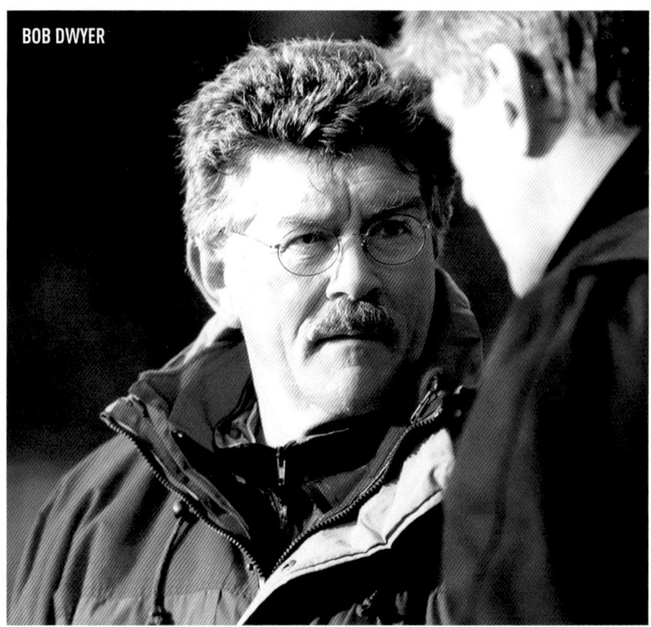

BOB DWYER

Samuel FAIRE (President: 1926-31)
b Derby, 18.10.1849, d Glenfield, Leicester, 18.1.1931.
Chairman of Faire Bros & Co manufacturers. Knighted in 1905 and became High Sheriff of Leicester in 1919.

Richard John FARRANDS (Treasurer: 1985-92)
b Leicester, 22.8.1953

<+TGAL FLOOD (Player: 2008-14, Captain: 2013-14)

Hugh John FORTESCUE (President: 1891-94)
b St Thomas, Devon, 10.8.1844, d Margate, Kent, 6.10.1907.
Rowed for Cambridge in 1866 Boat Race. Ordained as priest in 1869, he was vicar of St George's Leicester 1876-1895.

Allen FOSTER (Coach: 1988-90)
b 1951.

Terence Michael "Terry" GATELEY (Board: 2007-)
b Leeds, Yorkshire, Dec 1953.
A former general partner of KPMG. Since 1999 he has been primarily involved with a variety of private equity backed companies. He is currently also Senior Independent Director of IMI plc.

***Vereniki GONEVA** (Player: 2012-)
b Lautoka, Fiji, 5.4.1984.
29 caps for Fiji (2007-). 40+1 games for Tigers, also played for Western Crusaders, Fiji Barbarians, Rotherham Titans, Colomiers and Tarbes.

Ronald Ernest "Ronnie" GERRARD (Player: 1935-37, Treasurer: 1959-66, Hon Secretary: 1962-66)
b Liverpool, 27.5.1913, d Leicester, March 2002.
35 games for Tigers, also played for Waterloo, Cambridge University and Northampton.

+Lucas Pedro GONZALEZ AMOROSINO (Player: 2009-11)
b Buenos Aires, Argentina, 2.11.1985.
33 caps for Argentina (2007-). 11+3 games for Tigers, also played for Pucara, Montpellier and Oyonnax.

James Gardner GRAHAME (Joint Treasurer: 1936-37)
b Langholm, Scotland, 16.5.1879, d Aldershot, Hants, regd Q2 1959.
A children's and ladies' outfitter by profession, his three daughters all married test rugby players - Harry Greenlees, and the brothers Stephen and Graham Meikle.

William John Heaton GREENWOOD (Player: 1996-2000)
b Blackburn, Lancashire, 20.10.1972.
55 caps for England (1997-2004), Lions tour (1997), 2 caps for Lions (2005). 64+13 games for Tigers, also played for Waterloo, Preston Grasshoppers and Harlequins.
Now a renowned TV pundit at Sky Sports.

<BP HALL (Player: 1970-84, Captain: 1977-78, President: 2007-09)

Duncan Michael HALL (Coach: 1996-98)
b Brisbane, Australia, 16.3.1956.
15 caps for Australia (1980-83). Played for Queensland.
Turned his hand to coaching in 1987, Queensland director of coaching before joining Tigers. Has also been head coach at Worcester Warriors, US Eagles, UAE and Indonesia.

+James Leigh "Jim" HAMILTON (Player: 2001-08)
b Swindon, Wiltshire, 17.11.1982.
56 caps for Scotland (2006-). A product of the Tigers Academy.
36+28 games for Tigers, also played for Barkers' Butts, Nottingham, Edinburgh, Gloucester, Montpellier and Saracens.

<JG HAMILTON (Player: 1990-2003, Video Analyst: 2003-2008)

John Henry HANCOCK (Hon Secretary: 1893)
b Leicester, regd Q4 1840, d Billesdon, Leicestershire, regd Q4 1926

<MJ HARRISON (Player: 1962-71, Captain: 1964-65, President: 2009-13)

Robert John "Bob" HARRISON (Board: 1998-99)
b Rhodesia, 1945
A former director of NEXT Plc.

David St George HAZELL (Player: 1953-56)
b Taunton, Somerset, 23.4.1931, d Taunton, Somerset, 26.5.2007.
4 caps for England (1955). 81 games for Tigers, also played for Loughborough Colleges and Bristol. He appeared for Leicester when teaching in Nottingham.

Peter A H HERBERT (Player: 1946-52, President: 1983-85)
b Leicester, 4.3.1925, d 28.12.2013.
66 games for Tigers, also played for Aylestone St James and the Fleet Air Arm.

Benjamin HERRING (Player: 2007-09, Coach: 2009-11)
b Auckland, New Zealand, 14.3.1980.
18+5 games for Tigers, also played for Southland, Highlanders, Wellington. Is now coaching in Japan with NEC Green Rockets.

John HILL (Player: 1974, Team Secretary: 1993-95)
11 games for Tigers.

Joanne HOLLIS (Team Manager: 1996-)
b Hong Kong, 8.8.1962
A former security manager at Cathay Pacific Airways.

Anthony Edward "Tony" HOPKINS (President: 1999-2001)
b Leicester, 8.5.1941, d Leicester, 1.8.2009.
Played for the Extras and the Swifts, and ran a steel framework design company, Pace Consultants.

John Philip HORROCKS-TAYLOR (Player: 1958-63)
b Halifax, Yorkshire, 27.10.1934.
9 caps for England (1958-62), 1 cap for Lions (1959).
92 games for Tigers, also played for Halifax, Cambridge University (Blues 1956-57), Wasps and Middlesbrough.

Patrick William HOWARD (Player: 1998-2006, Coach: 2000-07)
b Sydney, Australia, 14.11.1973.
20 caps for Australia (1993-97). 91+5 games for Tigers, also played for Brumbies and Montferrand. Initially became backline coach and then head coach. He is now general manager of team performance for the Australia cricket team.

Henry Pierce "Nick" HUGHES (Player: 1945-48, President: 1968-71)
b Wallasey, Cheshire, 5.2.1918, d Loughborough, Leicestershire, November 2001.
43 games for Tigers, also played for Waterloo, RAF and Combined Services, and was the club doctor for many years.

Frederick Stanley JACKSON (Player: 1905-08)
d Auckland, New Zealand, 16.4.1957.
1 cap for Lions (1908). 77 games for Tigers, also played for Plymouth and Auckland RL.
See chapter 7 for a fuller description of this colourful character.

Roy David JACKSON (Board: 1997-2014, President: 2005-07)
b Wrexham, Wales, 13.2.1947.
Was a director of Artisan Press and later chairman of Cavalier Reproductions. He is a vice president of the charity Special Effect and chairman of the Matt Hampson Foundation fundraising committee.

+Shane JENNINGS (Player: 2005-07)
b Dublin, Ireland, 8.7.1981.
13 caps for Ireland (2007-12). 51+9 games for Tigers, also played for St Mary's College and Leinster.

Craig Alexander JOINER (Player: 1996-2000)
b Glasgow, Scotland, 21.4.1974.
25 caps for Scotland (1994-2000). 63+14 games for Tigers, also played for Melrose, Eastern Suburbs (Australia) and Edinburgh.

David Charles JONES (Board: 1997-2005)
b Stourbridge, Worcestershire, regd Q1 1943.
Formerly chairman of NEXT Plc, he was appointed a non-executive director of Aggregate Industries in 2004. Knighted in 2008.

Digby Marritt JONES, Baron Jones of Birmingham (Board: 2005-)
b Birmingham, 28.10.1955
After 20 years in corporate law he served from 2000-06 as Director General of the CBI, moving in 2007 into the House of Lords as Minister of State for Trade & Investment. He is chairman of a number of blue chip companies.

Rodney Bruce KAFER (Player: 2001-03, Coach: 2001-03)
b Newcastle, Australia, 25.6.1971. 12 caps for Australia (1999-2000). 53+1 games for Tigers, also played for ACT Brumbies. Now a TV analyst with Fox Sports in Australia and director of telecommuncations company, Totalcom.

+Benjamin KAYSER (Player: 2007-09)
b Paris, France, 26.7.1984.
24 caps for France (2008-). 29+24 games for Tigers, also played for Stade Français, Castres and Clermont Auvergne.

Douglas Anthony "Joe" KENDREW (Player: 1930-36)
b Barnstaple, Devon, 22.7.1910, d Nottingham, 28.2.1989.
10 caps for England (1930-36), Lions tour (1930). 30 games for Tigers, also played for Woodford, Paignton and Derry.

Alfred Lionel KEWNEY (Player: 1906-13)
b Tynemouth, Northumberland, 13.9.1882, d Howden, Yorkshire, 16.12.1959.
16 caps for England (1906-13). 27 games for Tigers, also played for Rockcliff.

Andrew Michael "Andy" KEY (Player: 1978-92, Coach: 2002-07)
b Market Harborough, 15.1.1959.
60+5 games for Tigers, also played for Bedford and Nottingham. Became the club's general operations manager in 1997 and then had a variety of coaching roles including Academy manager. His father Maurice was full-back at the club in the 1950s.

Kenneth Russell KINDER (President: 1977-79)
b Leicester, regd Q3 1911, d Leicester, regd Q3 1981.

Joshua Adrian KRONFELD (Player: 2001-03, Captain: 2003)
b Hastings, New Zealand, 20.6.1971.
54 caps for New Zealand (1995-2000). 46+10 games for Tigers, also played for Alhambra-Union, Otago and Highlanders. He is now a TV presenter in New Zealand.

<EC LACEY (Player: 1947-59, President: 1979-81)

John Ruthven "Jock" LAWRIE (Player: 1923-26)
b Melrose, Scotland, 11.9.1900, d Folkestone, Kent, 7.7.1981.
11 caps for Scotland (1922-24). 92 games for Tigers, also played for Melrose.

Marcelo Herman LOFFREDA (Coach: 2007-08)
b Buenos Aires, Argentina, 17.5.1959.
46 caps for Argentina (1978-94), 4 caps for South America (1980-82). Argentina head coach from 2000-07, taking them to 3rd place at the 2007 World Cup.

DAVE LOUGHEED

David Cameron "Dave" LOUGHEED (Player: 1998-2000)
b Toronto, Canada, 11.4.1968.
34 caps for Canada (1990-2003). 48+3 games for Tigers, also played for Toronto Welsh, Toronto Balmy Beach, Gloucester and University of British Columbia Ravens.

Allen LOVELL (President: 1939-43)
b Stamford, Lincs, regd Q1 1862, d Oadby, Leicestershire, 16.3.1942.
A yarn merchant and agent by profession.

Daniel Joseph LYLE (Player: 2003)
b San Diego, California, USA, 28.9.1970.
45 caps for United States (1994-2003). 3 games for Tigers, also played for Old Mission Bay AC and Bath.

<K McALPIN (Player: 1884-92, Hon Secretary: 1890-93, President: 1924-26)

Damian P McGRATH (Coach: 2002-04)
b Bradford, Yorkshire, regd Q3 1958.
Played rugby league for Swinton and Batley before moving into coaching. He had various coaching roles at Leeds Rhinos, Huddersfield Giants, England A and sevens and the Spanish national team.

+Sitiveni "Steve" MAFI (Player: 2010-14)
b Fairfield, Australia, 9.12.1989.
10 caps for Tonga (2010-). 54+29 games for Tigers, also played for New South Wales and Greater Sydney Rams.

Niall Gareth MALONE (Player: 1993-98)
b Leeds, England, 30.4.1971.
3 caps for Ireland (1993-94). 60+11 games for Tigers, also played for London Irish, Worcester and Ulster. Is now coaching the Ulster Academy.

<CG MARTIN (Player: 1956-66, Captain: 1960-63, Hon Coach: 1966-67)

Edward John MASSEY (Player: 1923-25)
b West Derby, Lancashire, 2.7.1900, d Woking, Surrey, 30.4.1977.
3 caps for England (1925).
31 games for Tigers, also played for Liverpool.

***Pablo MATERA** (Player: 2013-)
b Buenos Aires, Argentina, 18.7.1993.
11 caps for Argentina (2013). 5+3 games for Tigers, also played for Asociación Alumni and Pampas XV.

<DJ MATTHEWS (Player: 1955-74, Captain: 1965-68, Coach: 1988-91, President: 2001-03, Board: 1997-2007)

Heyneke MEYER (Coach 2008)
b Nelspruit, South Africa, 6.10.1967.
Started coaching at age 20. Head coach of South West District Eagles and then assistant coach at the Stormers and the Bulls. Won the Currie Cup four times with Blue Bulls and went on to win the Super Rugby crown with the Bulls in 2007. He is now head coach of the Springboks.

John Henry "Jack" MILES (Player: 1899-1904)
b Grimsby, Lincolnshire, 14.2.1880,
d Sheffield, Yorkshire, regd Q1 1953.
1 cap for England (1903). 93 games for Tigers, also played for Medway Athletic, Stoneygate and Northampton. He was the first player ever to be capped from the Tigers.

Eric Roger Patrick MILLER (Player: 1995-98)
b Dublin, Ireland, 23.9.1975.
48 caps for Ireland (1997-2005), 1 cap for Lions (1997). 47+5 games for Tigers, also played for Old Wesley, Terenure College, Ulster and Leinster.

Alejandro Cristian MORENO (Player: 2005-08)
b Buenos Aires, Argentina, 21.4.1973.
3 caps for Argentina (1998), 5 caps for Italy (1999-2008). 28+17 games for Tigers, also played for San Fernando, Agen, Gran Parma, Worcester, Perpignan, Brive, Calvisano and Leeds.

Darren Raymond MORRIS (Player: 2003-06)
b Aberdare, Wales, 24.9.1974.
18 caps for Wales (1998-2004), 1 cap for Lions (2001). 56+20 games for Tigers, also played for Neath, Swansea, Worcester Warriors, Cardiff Blues, Northampton, Hartpury College and Doncaster Knights. First player to be capped for Wales whilst at the Tigers.

LOGOVI'I MULIPOLA

***Logovi'i MULIPOLA** (Player: 2012-)
b Manono, Western Samoa, 11.3.1987.
17 caps for Samoa (2009-). 43+20 games for Tigers, also played for Upolu Samoa and Hawke's Bay.

<GEA MURPHY (Player: 1997-2013, Captain: 2009-13, Coach: 2013-)

Edward Sealy "Ernie" NICHOLSON (Player: 1935-36)
b Long Ashton, Somerset, 10.6.1912, d Beccles, Suffolk, 16.3.1992.
5 caps for England (1935-36). 8 games for Tigers, also played for Oxford University (Blues 1931-34), Guy's Hospital and Blackheath.

<DJ NORMAN (Player: 1920-33, President: 1965-68)

Rodney Terry OAKES (Coach: 1979-86)
b Chatham, Kent, regd Q1 1946, d St Lucia, 10.4.2014.
Coached Sherborne as well as the Dorset & Wiltshire county side.

Matthew Gerard O'CONNOR (Coach: 2008-13)
b Canberra, Australia, 29.1.1971.
1 cap for Australia (1994). Played for Paris St Germain in rugby league's Super League. Joined Kubota Spears in Japan as a player then head coach. Assistant coach at ACT Brumbies before joining Leicester. Now head coach at Leinster.

Alan Gerald Bernard OLD (Player: 1972-74)
b Middlesbrough, Yorkshire, 23.9.1945.
16 caps for England (1972-80), Lions tour (1974). 18 games for Tigers, also played for Middlesbrough, Sheffield and Morpeth.

Charles Frederick OLIVER (President: 1931-39)
b Willenhall, Staffs, 1.2.1868, d London, 7.8.1939.
Commanding Officer of the 4th battalion of the Leicestershire Regiment who became a solicitor. Knighted in 1933.

Anthony Joseph Francis Kevin "Tony" O'REILLY (Player: 1958-60)
b Dublin, Ireland, 7.5.1936.
29 caps for Ireland (1955-70), 10 caps for Lions (1955-59). 17 games for Tigers, also played for Old Belvedere and Dolphin.

ST CLAIR PAIN

Frederick St Clair PAIN (Treasurer: 1904-19)
b Bedminster, Somerset, regd Q4 1854, d Leicester, 1.6.1919

***Geoffrey Matthew Walter PARLING** (Player: 2009-)
b Stockton-on-Tees, Durham, 28.10.1983.
21 caps for England (2012-), 3 caps for Lions (2013). 67+10 games for Tigers, also played for Newcastle Falcons.

<J PARSONS (Player: 1880-89, Captain: 1886-89, Hon Secretary: 1880-81, President: 1894-1901)

Thomas Withers "Tom" PETTIFOR (Hon Secretary: 1894-95, Treasurer: 1896-97)
b Leicester, regd Q4 1857, d Leicester, 8.6.1904.
An architect and surveyor by profession.

Ramiro Edouardo PEZ (Player: 2003-04)
b Córdoba, Argentina, 6.12.1978.
40 caps for Italy (2000-07). 11+2 games for Tigers, also played for Roma, Rotherham Titans, Bath, Castres, Perpignan, Venezia and Toulon.

Arthur Thomas PORTER (Player: 1880-89, Captain: 1881-82)
b Leicester, regd Q2 1859, d Leicester, 13.5.1936.
40 games for Leicester. Employed as a leather merchant.

Anthony Patrick "Tony" POWER (Treasurer: 1992-97)
b Leicester, 27.1.1943.

Herbert Leo PRICE (Player: 1922-24)
b Sutton, Surrey, 21.6.1899, d Victoria Park, Manchester, 18.7.1943.
4 caps for England (1922-23). 17 games for Tigers, also played for Oxford University (Blues 1920-21) and Harlequins.

Ratu Seru Raveive RABENI (Player: 2004-09)
b Nabouwalu, Bua, Fiji, 27.12.1978.
30 caps for Fiji (2000-11), 9 caps for Pacific Islanders (2004-08). 46+17 games for Tigers, also played for Otago, Highlanders, Leeds, La Rochelle and Mont-de-Marsan.

<D RICHARDS (Player: 1982-97, Captain: 1989-91 and 1993-97, Coach: 1998-2004)

<RE ROWELL (Player: 1962-78, Captain: 1976-77, President: 2003-05)

Anthony Ollason "Tony" RUSS (Coach: 1990-96)
b Birkenhead, Cheshire, regd Q1 1946.
Coached Eastern Counties and Saracens before joining Tigers as the club's first full-time coach. Later went on to coach at Waterloo, Ulster and the Harlequins academy.

Hedley William SALMON (Player: 1880-87, Hon Secretary: 1881-89, President: 1912-24)
b Nottingham, September 1860, d Leicester, 31.10.1936.
89 games for Tigers. An underwear manufacturer.

Kenneth James Forbes SCOTLAND (Player: 1961-62)
b Warriston, Edinburgh, Scotland, 29.8.1936. 27 caps for Scotland (1957-65), 5 caps for Lions (1959). 40 games for Tigers, also played for Cambridge University (Blues 1958-60), London Scottish, Ballymena, Heriot's FP and Aberdeenshire.

KEN SCOTLAND

Thomas Richard "Tom" SCOTT (Board: 2011-)
b 13.1.1975.
A chartered accountant who, after graduating from the London School of Economics, worked for KPMG in London. Has been a director of several listed companies and is a major investor in the Club.

***Blaine Hansen SCULLY** (Player: 2013-)
b Sacramento, California, USA, 29.2.1988.
20 caps for United States (2011-). 16+4 games for Tigers, also played for UCLA and University of California.

William Alfred SHEFFIELD (Player: 1880-87, Captain: 1885-86)
b Leicester, regd Q1 1863, d Leicester 27.11.1922.
98 games for Leicester. He was a hosiery manufacturer.

<CD SHEPHARD (Player: 1955-64, Team Secretary: 1995-2006)

<HW SIBSON (Player: 1947-54, Team Secretary: 1969-78, President: 1981-83)

Charles Frederick "Charlie" SLOW (Player: 1933-37)
b Northampton, 15.5.1911, d Stony Stratford, Buckinghamshire, 15.4.1939.
1 cap for England (1934). 98 games for Tigers, also played for Northampton and Stony Stratford.

<BTC SMALL (Player: 1954-63, President: 1989-91)

Alastair McNaughton SMALLWOOD (Player: 1920-25)
b Alloa, Scotland, 18.11.1892, d Uppingham, Leicestershire, 9.6.1985.
14 caps for England (1920-25). 64 games for Tigers, also played for Cambridge University (Blue 1919) and Gosforth Nomads.

Brian Anthony SMITH (Player: 1990-91)
b St George, NSW, Australia, 9.9.1966.
6 caps for Australia (1987), 9 caps for Ireland (1989-91).
15 games for Tigers, also played for Wests (Brisbane), Manly (Sydney), Oxford University (Blues 1988-89), Balmain Tigers and Sydney Roosters. Now head coach at London Irish.

<IR SMITH (Player: 1977-91, Captain: 1983-85, Coach: 1991-96)

Philip Michael Forster SMITH (Board: 1997-98)
b Coalville, Leicestershire, regd Q2 1950.
Gained an MBA from Manchester Business School and worked with various financial institutions in London and Sydney.

Thomas William "Tom" SMITH (Player: 1906-08)
b Rearsby, Leicestershire, 15.8.1883,
d Halton Holegate, Lincolnshire, 15.5.1960.
2 caps for Lions (1908). 58 games for Tigers, also played for Aylestonians and Broughton Rangers RL.

Richard Slater "Dickie" SNOWDEN (Player: 1886-93, Captain: 1889)
b Preston, Lancashire, regd Q4 1861, d Leicester, 31.5.1930.
67 games for Tigers, also played for Manningham. A foreman in a hosiery dying business.

Winston Ulysses STANLEY (Player: 2000-01)
b Victoria, BC, Canada, 17.7.1974.
66 caps for Canada (1994-2003). 26 games for Tigers, also played for James Bay AA, UBC Ravens, KATS, Blackheath, Worcester and Leeds.

Robert Victor "Bob" STIRLING (Player: 1948-53)
b Lichfield, Staffordshire, 4.9.1919, d Halton, Cheshire, 15.1.1991.
18 caps for England (1951-54). 75 games for Tigers, also played for Aylestone St James and Wasps.

Joel Theodore STRANSKY (Player: 1997-99, Coach: 1998-2000)
b Pietermaritzburg, South Africa, 16.7.1967.
22 caps and 240 points for South Africa (1993-96). 72+1 games for Tigers, also played for College Rovers, Natal, Villagers, Western Province, L'Aquila, San Donà and Cahors. First Springbok and first Rugby World Cup winner to play for Leicester, now a TV pundit with MNet in South Africa.

Harris Nuttall STROUD (Treasurer: 1897-1904)
b Leicester, regd Q1 1856, d Leicester, 5.3.1932

John Spence "Ian" SWAN (Player: 1957-59, Captain: 1958-59)
b St Andrew's, Scotland, 14.7.1930,
d St Andrew's, Scotland, 18.9.2004.
17 caps for Scotland (1953-58). 51 games for Tigers, also played for Madras College FP, St Andrew's University, London Scottish and Coventry. Would have had a much longer playing career had it not been for a knee injury in a pre-season training accident in 1959.

William Herbert SWINGLER (Treasurer: 1895-96)
b Lambeth, London, regd Q1 1871, d Sevenoaks, Kent, regd Q3 1930.

Francis Nathaniel "Frank" TARR (Player: 1906-13)
b Belper, Derbyshire, 14.8.1887, d Ypres, Belgium, 18.7.1915.
4 caps for England (1909-13). 94 games for Tigers, also played for Oxford University (Blues 1907-09), Headingley and Richmond.

+Ephraim 'Ifalemi TAUKAFA (Player: 2004-06)
b Auckland, New Zealand, 26.6.1976.
33 caps for Tonga (2002-11). 3+9 games for Tigers, also played for Oyonnax, Lyon, Mont-de-Marsan and Châlon-sur-Saône.

John Tudor THOMAS (Team Secretary: 1978-93, President: 1993-95, Hon Secretary: 1995-97)
b Penycae, Wales, 5.11.1928.
Came to Leicester in 1962 teaching at New Parks, became head teacher at Westcotes in 1971. Initially team secretary for the Swifts and then the Extras before moving into the same role with the first-team.

Joseph Eric THORNELOE (Player: 1919, Hon Secretary: 1928-57, President: 1957-59)
b Leicester, 11.11.1896, d Leicester, August 1959.
Played seven first-team games for the Tigers at full-back and wing, but is better known as an official in a 40-year connection with the club.

Arthur Stanley THORPE (Treasurer: 1966-75)
b Leicester, 5.6.1908, d Leicester, January 1988

Thomas THORPE (Treasurer: 1919-29)
b Leicester, regd Q4 1863, d Leicester, 1.9.1934.
Head teacher at an elementary school.

<PWG TOM (Player: 1963-68, Board: 1997-)

Allan Clark TOWELL (Player: 1947-50, Captain: 1949-50)
b Middlesbrough, Yorkshire, 15.5.1925. 2 caps for England (1948-51). 93 games for Tigers, also played for RAF, Middlesbrough and Bedford.

+Anitele'a Faivai "Andy" TUILAGI (Player: 2005)
b Apia, Western Samoa, 5.6.1986.
17 caps for Samoa (2005-). 0+1 game for Tigers, also played for Sharks XV, Leeds, Upolu Samoa, Sale, Newport Gwent Dragons and Newcastle Falcons.

Fereti "Freddie" TUILAGI (Player: 2000-06)
b Apia, Western Samoa, 9.6.1971.
17 caps for Samoa (1992-2002). 72+10 games for Tigers, also played for Marist St Joseph's, Halifax Blue Sox RL, St Helens RL and Cardiff Blues. First of the Tuilagi dynasty to play for the club.

MANU TUILAGI

***Etuale Manusamoa TUILAGI** (Player: 2008-)
b Fatausi-Fogapoa, Western Samoa, 18.5.1991.
25 caps for England (2011-), 1 cap for Lions (2013). A product of the Leicester Academy. 65+7 games for Tigers.

<R UNDERWOOD (Player: 1983-97, Board: 2007-)

Tony UNDERWOOD (Player: 1988-95)
b Ipoh, Malaysia, 17.2.1969.
27 caps for England (1992-99), Lions tour (1993), 1 cap for Lions (1997). 92 games for Tigers, also played for Cambridge University (Blues 1990-91) and Newcastle Falcons.

Jacobus Nicolaas Boshoff VAN DER WESTHUYZEN (Player: 2003-04) b Nelspruit, South Africa, 6.4.1978.
32 caps for South Africa (2000-2006). 18 games for Tigers, also played for Natal Sharks, Mpumalanga Pumas, Blue Bulls, NEC Green Rockets.

Frederick Johannes "Fritz" VAN HEERDEN (Player: 1997-2000)
b Roodepoort, South Africa, 29.6.1970.
14 caps for South Africa (1994-99). 62+5 games for Tigers, also played for Stellenbosch, Northerns and Western Province.

+Thomas William "Tom" VARNDELL (Player: 2004-09)
b Ashford, Kent, 16.9.1985.
4 caps for England (2005-08).
A product of the Leicester Academy. 88+25 games for Tigers, also played for Bedford Blues and London Wasps.

William Wavell WAKEFIELD (Player: 1921-24, Captain: 1923-24)
b Beckenham, Kent, 10.3.1898, d Kendal, Cumbria, 12.8.1983.
31 caps for England (1920-27). 29 games for Tigers, also played for Cambridge University (Blues 1921-22), Furness and Harlequins.

+Thomas Robert WALDROM (Player: 2010-14)
b Lower Hutt, New Zealand, 28.4.1983.
5 caps for England (2012-13). 85+28 games for Tigers, also played for NZ Maori, Wellington Lions, Hurricanes, Crusaders, Hawke's Bay and Exeter Chiefs.

James G WALKER (Treasurer: 1880-81)
b Packington, Leicestershire 1817, d Leicester, regd Q4 1883.
His son George played five games for Leicester at half-back in 1881.

Sidney George "Ranji" WALKER
(Player: 1935-36, General Secretary: 1966-67)
b Nottingham, 30.6.1905, d Southampton, regd Q2 1979.
8 games for Tigers, also played for Nottingham and Old Nottinghamians.

Robert Harry WARNER (Player: 1880-83, Treasurer: 1880-81)
b Cossington, Leicestershire, regd Q2 1859.
10 games for Leicester, his work as a mechanical engineer took him abroad in September 1884.

<JM WELLS (Player: 1982-97, Captain: 1991-93, Coach: 1998-2005)

<PJ WHEELER (Player: 1969-85, Captain: 1973-75 and 1978-81, Coach: 1987-88, President: 1995-97, Board: 1997-)

William Alfred WHEELER (Player: 1880-89, President: 1880-81)
b Smethwick, Staffordshire, 1854, d Leicester, 1.7.1920.
26 games for Leicester, he worked as a hosiers assistant.

<HV WHITE (Player: 1957-63, Coach: 1967-82)

<GG WILLARS (Player: 1959-87, Captain: 1968-69 and 1972-73, Coach: 1983-88, President: 1991-93)

Rodney John WILLCOX (Player: 1935-37, President: 1974-77)
b Fort Brown, South Africa, 1909, d Leicester, July 2002.
41 games for Tigers, also played for Westleigh. An Oakham schoolboy who became a hosiery manufacturer.

<CR WOODWARD (Player: 1979-85, Board: 2007-13)

Thomas WRIGHT (President: 1890-91)
b Northampton, 15.2.1838, d Stoneygate, Leicester, 5.8.1905.
Mayor of Leicester in 1887 and 1891. Knighted in 1893.

Sidney Robert WYKES (Hon Secretary: 1889-90, Player: 1890-92)
b Leicester, 2.7.1866, d Mullion, Cornwall, 7.8.1900.
25 games for Tigers, a solicitor with R & G Toller & Sons in New Street. He was tragically drowned while on holiday in Cornwall aged only 34.

Lawrence YOUNG (Player: 1880-84, Captain: 1882-83)
b Knaresborough, Yorkshire, regd Q3 1855, d Leicester, regd Q1 1894.
37 games for Leicester, an elementary school teacher.

***Thomas Nicholas "Tom" YOUNGS** (Player: 2006-)
b Norwich, Norfolk, 28.1.1987.
17 caps for England (2012-), 3 caps for Lions (2013). A product of the Leicester Academy. 52+21 games for Tigers, also played for Bedford Blues and Nottingham.

TOM YOUNGS

MARTIN JOHNSON 2004

From a painting by Bryan Organ

Martin Johnson became one of the greatest rugby players of the professional era. He captained Leicester Tigers to unprecedented success with four successive Premiership crowns and back-to-back European cups, England to the World Cup title in 2003 and the British and Irish Lions to a series victory in South Africa in 1997. He skippered Leicester in a record 202 matches and made 362 appearances for the first XV between 1989-2005, as well as attaining 84 caps for England and eight tests for the Lions.

Bryan Organ was born in Leicester in 1935 and studied at Loughborough College of Art and the Royal Academy Schools (1952-59). His first solo exhibition was at Leicester City Art Gallery in 1958. Since 1967 he has shown at the Redfern Gallery, London. He currently has 15 portraits in the National Portrait Gallery – including world-famous works of Prince Charles, Prince Phillip, Harold Macmillan and Diana Princess of Wales. He also designed the original artwork for the cover of this book.

PLAYER INDEX

The Complete Tigers' Roll Call

A

NAME	CAREER	APPS	TRIES	PTS
Carl Aarvold	1931	1	-	-
Stuart Abbott	1999	2	-	-
Joseph Abell	1880-87	34	-	-
Luke Abraham	2002-07	25+27	3	15
Myley Abraham	1919	2	-	-
G Ackroyd	1901	1	-	-
Cyril Adams	1922-24	4	-	-
John Adams	1945-46	3	-	-
Newton Adams	1933-38	126	26	78
Tony Adams	1945-48	43	14	42
Albert Adcock	1905	1	-	-
Lewis Adcock	1928-32	8	-	-
Addison	1884	1	-	-
Dave Addison	1997-98	8+1	-	-
Jeff Addison	1959-61	33	-	-
Garry Adey	1967-81	381	57	215
Vendis Afflick	1982-87	26+6	4	16
Horacio Agulla	2010-12	39+9	8	40
Gerry Ainscough	1992	12	4	44
George Aitken	1923	1	-	-
Arthur Akers	1893-99	160	10	32
John Akurangi	1999-00	2+8	-	-
Maxwell Aldred	1898-01	52	2	6
Jason Aldwinckle	1989-98	14+7	1	5
Peter Aldwinckle	1967-70	20	6	18
Paul Alexander	1928	1	-	-
William Alldridge	1934-38	19	-	-
Anthony Allen	2009-14	109+4	14	70
George Allen	1964-67	10	-	-
Jimmy Allen	1909-21	209	37	170
John Allen	1961-75	457	58	297
Trevor Allen	1959-61	31	9	27
WM Allen	1936-37	29	2	6
Allinson	1885	1	-	-
Gordon Almey	1957-64	150	31	93
John Anderson	1935-36	3	-	-
Rob Andrew	2012-13	5+2	1	5
A Andrews	1902-04	23	2	6
Arthur Andrews	1899-03	2	-	-
Kevin Andrews	1965-70	191	12	36
James Ansell	1911	2	2	6
Walter Anson	1883-85	17	1	1
John Anstee	1930	2	-	-
Tony Anthony	1937-39	60	6	18
Fred Apperley	1886-87	14	6	6
Tom Armes	2009-12	4+3	2	10
Arthur Armstrong	1907	1	-	-
Rodger Arneil	1969-71	25	4	12
Willie Arnold	1902	2	-	-
Thomas Arundel	1936	1	-	-
Paul Ash	1946-47	6	1	3
William Ash	1934	1	-	-
Fred Ashley	1947-48	8	3	9
Derek Ashurst	1951-62	112	14	57
Abel Ashworth	1890	2	-	-
Alfred Atkins	1925	2	1	3
Atkins	1887-88	2	-	-
Dudley Atkins	1901-08	147	10	30
Fred Atkins	1913	2	1	3
George Atkins	1912-13	5	-	-
John Atkins	1924	1	-	-
Percy Atkins	1897-06	186	42	126
Shirley Atkins	1895-99	9	-	-
Bert Atkinson	1904-05	2	-	-
Joseph Atterbury	1910-11	4	1	3
Greg Austin	1996-97	8+6	8	43
Dick Auty	1930-38	19	8	24
Steve Avent	1983-84	3+1	-	-
Marcos Ayerza	2006-14	161+32	7	35

B

NAME	CAREER	APPS	TRIES	PTS
T Babington	1929-30	16	5	15
Neil Back	1990-05	320+19	125	615
Norman Bacon	1928-32	2	-	-
Louis Baillon	1933-36	10	1	7
Richard Baillon	1934-35	2	-	-
Bill Bainbridge	1937-38	41	1	27
James Bainbridge	1905-06	51	21	63
George Baines	1915	2	-	-
Seth Baines	1890-92	21	1	1
Alan Baker	1952-54	30	1	9
Ambrose Baker	1923	2	1	3
JL Baker	1899-00	3	-	-
Percy Baker	1912	1	-	-
Peter Baker	1955-57	38	8	27
Adam Balding	1998-04	49+61	5	25
Jack Ball	1934-46	5	-	-
Jesse Ball	1889-99	46	8	19
Ron Ball	1938	1	-	-
Fraser Balmain	2010-14	11+22	-	-
George Banks	1893-98	59	5	17
Eric Bann	1968-75	162	26	188
Charles Barham	1891-92	19	4	8
Bob Barker	1968-79	318+2	158	1117
Clifford Barker	1934	5	1	7
FA Barker	1902	1	-	-
H Barker	1939	2	-	-
John Barker	1934-35	11	-	4
TH Barker	1946	1	-	-
Matt Barkes	1991-92	7	-	-
Morgan Barlow	1926-32	50	22	70
Tim Barlow	1995-98	15+3	7	35
John Barnes	1901	1	-	-
Tim Barnwell	1977-83	188+1	95	382
Bobby Barr	1928-39	241	-	66
Henry Barradell	1887-88	6	-	-
Jack Barradell	1887-93	21	1	7
MD Barratt	1954	1	-	-
Tom Barratt	1947	2	-	-
Alfred Barrett	1920	8	3	9
Charles Barrow	1889	3	-	-
Eric Barrow	1948-53	90	5	45
James Barrow	1909-10	7	3	9
Matt Barrowcliffe	1902-06	3	1	3
William Barth	1894	6	1	3
Ebenezer Barwick	1881-83	4	-	-
Henry Barwick	1880-83	6	-	-
Christopher Bassett	1904	1	-	-
Stanley Bassett	1918-19	4	-	-
Bernard Batchelor	1923	1	-	-
Bateman	1907	1	-	-
Alf Bates	1914-20	61	37	131
Edward Bates	1932-33	36	4	16
Eric Bates	1938-39	6	-	-
G Bates	1956	1	-	-
Ian Bates	1983-95	286+1	38	154
Brian Baxter	1930-32	3	-	-
JG Baxter	1937	1	-	-
JL Baxter	1927	1	-	-
Neil Baxter	2003-04	9+3	5	25
Chris Baynes	1969-73	116	37	125
Cecil Beamish	1938-46	13	-	-
Charles Beamish	1926-36	17	2	6
George Beamish	1924-33	118	24	74
Victor Beamish	1926-29	68	1	3
Edward Beasley	1888-89	11	2	2
Joe Beasley	1919	1	-	-
Bob Beason	1960-72	203	3	9
Simon Beatham	1994-95	3	-	-
Jock Beattie	1933	1	-	-
David Beaty	1963-69	88	-	-
Dick Beaty	1995	1	-	-
Christopher Beaty-Pownall	1930-32	14	2	6
Steven Beaufoy	1997-98	1+2	-	-
Billy Beaver	1921	3	-	-
K Beaver	1952	3	1	3
Leonard Beaver	1905	3	-	-
Niall Beazley	1985	0+1	-	-
Garry Becconsall	1995-99	6+8	2	10
Bev Bedggood	1965-67	59	5	41
Andy Beevers	1976	7	1	4
William Beith	1925-26	4	-	-
David Belasco	1952-54	13	-	3
Dickie Bell	1885-90	43	2	2
Rob Bell	2008	1	-	-
Scott Bemand	2004-07	30+23	5	25
John Bemrose	1923-24	3	1	3
Miles Benjamin	2013-14	10	5	25
AC Bennett	1925	1	-	-
Harold Bennett	1932-36	27	1	3
Leonard Bennett	1903-05	10	-	-
Peter Bennett	1948-54	30	2	9
Barrie Bennetts	1907-10	2	-	-
Benson	1885	2	-	-
Paddy Bernard	1926	1	1	3
David Berry	1964-71	78	6	30
John Berry	1959-68	3	-	-
Richard Berry	1965-69	27	-	-
Tom Berry	1932-48	277	15	45
Steve Betts	1967-69	45	10	30
Tom Betts	1895	1	-	-
Owen Bevan	1935	1	-	-
Spencer Bevan	1932-34	2	-	-
Tom Bevan	1934-36	3	-	-
Eric Bevins	1935-47	44	3	43
Eddie Beynon	1926	1	-	-
Guy Bibby	1995	0+1	-	-
Henry Biggs	1880-81	3	-	-
James Bignal	1934	3	-	-
Adam Billig	2002	1	-	-
Malcolm Billingham	1964	1	-	-
John Billson	1888	1	-	-
William Bingham	1908	8	-	-
Simon Binns	1994-96	5	2	10
Charles Birch	1908	10	-	-
Derek Bircumshaw	1954-57	21	4	12
David Bird	1960-73	285	86	258
WJ Bird	1935	1	-	-
Martin Birkett	1959-63	2	-	-
Tom Birkett	1885-86	4	1	1
Lawrence Bithell	1946	1	-	-
Don Black	1938	1	-	-
Duncan Black	1980-84	49+8	17	68
Gus Black	1953	16	2	9
RB Black	1935	1	-	-
William Blackburn	1903-05	38	1	7
Gordon Blackett	1958-60	12	2	18
Freddie Blakiston	1924	1	-	-
Anthony Blandy	1945	2	-	-
Richard Blaze	2007-09	11+13	-	-
Tom Bleasdale	1949-64	340	53	159
AJ Bloor	1919	1	-	-
William Blower	1919	4	1	3
BC Bloxham	1882	1	-	-
Charles Bloxham	1933	1	-	-
George Blunt	1893	1	-	-
Jon Boden	1999	1	-	3
Bodycote	1882	1	-	-
Jake Boer	1997-98	5	2	10
Denis Bolesworth	1936-55	330	23	69
A Bolus	1931	9	3	9
Edward Bolus	1896-98	5	-	-
Gerald Bolus	1906	1	-	-
George Bond	1907	1	-	-
Frederick Bonner	1886-90	5	1	1
Ernest Booth	1909	5	-	-
Steve Booth	2000-04	49+22	26	194
W Booth	1919	1	-	-
Herbert Bostock	1888	2	-	-
Francis Boston	1924	1	-	-
Norman Boston	1924	2	-	-
John Boswell	1923	3	-	-
Tom Bosworth	1881	1	-	-
Ian Botting	1951-53	38	15	45
W Bottomley	1896	1	-	-
Bill Bottrill	1936-39	70	20	60
Len Boulter	1925	1	-	-
Phil Boulton	2006	0+1	-	-
Charles Bourns	1906-07	15	-	-
Thomas Bovell-Jones	1927	1	-	-
Dan Bowden	2012-14	23+6	4	25
Archibald Bowell	1915	1	-	-
Gareth Bowen	1999	0+1	-	-
Harry Bowen	1947	1	-	2
Norman Bowen	1930	1	-	-
Ryan Bower	2010-13	2+5	-	-
Bernie Bowers	1983-85	7+1	-	-
Sid Bowers	1930-35	6	-	-
Artie Bowman	1901-03	10	-	-
Henry Bown	1892-93	9	-	3
Laurence Boyle	1991-94	51+3	10	53
Ken Bracewell	1974-76	29	8	32
Harold Brackenbury	1898-99	12	1	5
A Bradbury	1922	1	1	3
William Bradford	1895-96	12	-	-
EG Bradley	1932	4	2	6
E Braithwaite	1928-29	8	-	-
Jacky Braithwaite	1895-06	359	67	361
Keith Branston	1952	1	-	-

NAME	CAREER	APPS	TRIES	PTS
Billy Bream	1911-14	101	4	332
John Brennand	1945	3	-	-
Joseph Brewin	1913	1	-	-
Alexander Brice	1880-86	21	2	2
Alfred Brice	1909	2	-	-
Ian Bridgwood	1979	1	-	-
Ben Brier	1991-93	6+3	-	-
Basil Brierley	1945	3	-	-
Harry Briers	1925-29	66	1	3
Neil Briggs	2013-14	7+12	-	-
Tom Bristow	2013-14	2+4	-	-
S Brittain	1908	2	-	-
Harry Britten	1910	1	-	-
Peter Broadbent	1970	1	-	-
Stanley Broadbent	1884-86	16	-	-
Ross Broadfoot	2004-06	9+10	-	59
Jack Broadhurst	1893	1	1	2
Frank Broadley	1911-15	13	8	24
Harry Brockbank	1887-92	84	11	103
Arthur Brodbeck	1924-28	3	-	-
David Brook	1954-56	83	16	48
Kieran Brookes	2011-13	3+3	-	-
Paul Brookes	1986-90	4	-	-
Dave Brookhouse	1954-57	11	-	-
Franklyn Brookman	1950	9	-	28
J Brooks	1938	3	-	-
John Broome	1969	1	-	-
A Brown	1919	5	2	6
Albert Brown	1938-46	34	3	9
Andy Brown	2008	0+1	-	-
Bill Brown	1945-49	106	2	6
Frank Brown	1893-95	37	-	4
Stan Brown	1923-29	4	-	-
Mike Brownhill	1966-69	73	28	84
George Brownless	1901	2	-	-
Monty Brownson	1896	1	1	3
Rab Bruce-Lockhart	1937	3	1	3
Hugh Bryan	1892-97	39	14	104
Oliver Bryson	1922-27	84	25	75
Rankin Buchanan	1922-24	8	2	6
Eliot Buckby	1992-93	2	-	-
Ralph Buckingham	1924-35	325	117	443
James Buckland	2004-07	23+46	3	15
J Buckle	1889-90	3	-	-
Walter Buckler	1913-22	76	5	15
Will Buckler	1921	2	-	-
Peter Bucknall	2010-11	6+7	-	-
Arthur Bull	1918-19	17	2	8
Maurice Bullus	1935-38	6	-	3
Fred Bunney	1928-29	2	-	-
Jackson Burbery	1907	1	-	-
Burbridge	1889	1	-	-
Tom Burch	1966	1	-	-
Jimmy Burdett	1903-12	108	12	36
John Burdett	1919	1	-	-
Arthur Burford	1880-84	46	-	-
AH Burgess	1920	2	-	-
Paul Burke	2006-07	13+8	-	122
Paul Burnell	1986-88	12+1	2	8
Steve Burnhill	1985-88	42+2	15	60
James Burrows	1935	1	-	-
TE Burrows	1926-27	4	-	-
Bramwell Burton	1887-88	5	-	-
CL Burton	1918-24	14	3	9
Hyde Burton	1924	1	-	-
Langley Burton	1925-32	41	8	24
Leo Burton	1911-14	56	5	15
W Burton	1894-97	8	1	3
Terry Burwell	1975-83	111+9	27	111
Malcolm Bussey	1963-67	121	38	117
Edward Butcher	1919	5	-	6
E Butler	1894	1	-	-
ER Butler	1920	1	-	-
Fred Butler	1894-95	9	3	9
Tom Butler	1996	1	-	-
Alf Butlin	1895-02	252	19	118
Tim Buttimore	1985-91	96+2	15	62
Cyril Byrne	1933	1	-	-
Edmund Byrne	1890	2	-	-

C

NAME	CAREER	APPS	TRIES	PTS
Joe Cain	2012-13	3	1	5
John Cambridge	1928	2	-	-
E Cameron	1903	1	-	-
Bob Campbell	1895-01	207	7	25
D Campbell	1908	3	-	-
David Campbell	1937	1	-	-
John Campbell	1946	1	-	-
Stewart Campbell	2003	4	-	-
William Carey	1893-94	28	1	3
Albert Carey-Elwes	1897-99	33	4	12
Bissill Carlisle	1891-93	5	-	-
AW Carr	1911-12	4	-	-
Willy Carr	1988	2	-	-
Alfred Carryer	1882	1	-	-
Rupert Carryer	1930-35	14	1	3
CD Carter	1919	1	-	-
Harry Carter	1922	1	-	-
R Cartwright	1919	1	-	-
J Cass	1890	1	-	-
Roland Castle	1923	1	-	-
Martin Castrogiovanni	2006-13	85+61	8	40
George Catchpole	2013-14	2	-	-
Dick Cattell	1890	2	-	-
George Cattell	1890	2	-	-
Charles Cave	1898	1	2	6
Paul Cave	1983	1+2	1	4
Tony Cavender	1961	9	-	-
EW Chamberlain	1890-92	8	-	-
Mel Channer	1946-55	127	33	327
Arthur Chapman	1961-69	18	5	126
C Chapman	1896	2	-	-
Chapman	1902	1	-	-
John Charles	1935-36	28	17	51
L Charles	1906	1	-	-
Mark Charles	1985-88	34+3	15	60
Frank Charters	1892-93	5	-	-
Frank Chawner	1949-64	331	23	69
Len Chawner	1950-54	29	-	-
Richard Cheffins	1995-96	5+1	-	-
George Cherry	1957-63	66	-	-
Charles Cheshire	1897	1	-	-
A Chettle	1889	14	1	1
Keith Chilton	1963-67	144	26	551
George Chitham	1906	1	-	-
"Mog" Christie	1926-32	61	10	30
RF Church	1951	9	-	-
Mark Churchward	1972	2	1	4
George Chuter	2001-14	206+84	17	85
Nick Clapinson	1995	1	-	-
Raymond Clark	1934-38	27	2	6
C Clarke	1885-96	5	-	-
DC Clarke	1926	1	-	-
Percy Clarke	1930-31	38	3	9
Peter Clarke	2004	0+1	-	-
RA Clarke	1919	6	2	6
Roger Clarke	1961-62	2	-	-
Tom Clarke	1931	1	-	-
WJ Clarke	1952-54	30	1	6
WV Clarke	1946	1	-	-
Leonard Cleaver	1931-33	4	1	3
Mark Cleaver	1985-91	9+3	3	12
Thomas Cleaver	1932	1	-	-
Pete Clements	1968	2	-	-
Lewis Clifford	1984-87	6+4	1	4
Rod Coady	1965-66	27	2	12
Norman Coates	1919-27	203	62	194
TE Coates	1895-96	10	-	-
Jack Cobden	2008	1	-	-
Joe Cobden	2009-11	2	-	-
Richard Cockerill	1992-04	212+50	14	70
AS Cohen	1924	1	-	-
Dan Cole	2007-14	79+44	2	10
Neil Cole	2005	1+3	-	-
Sammy Cole	1945-47	35	2	6
Ernie Coleman	1921-33	260	18	56
Sherrard Coleman	1880-92	141	31	52
F Coles	1906	2	-	5
Roger Coley	1955	1	-	-
Joseph Collier	1887	1	-	-
Angus Collington	1975-86	112+18	22	88
Brian Collins	1962	1	-	-
Gareth Collins	1988	0+1	-	-
Harry Collins	1896	1	-	-
SG Collins	1924	2	-	-
Walter Collis	1896	1	-	-
Dick Collopy	1925	9	-	-
William Collopy	1919	2	-	-
JW Colquhoun	1927	1	-	-
RR Colquhoun	1924	1	-	-
Dennis Colston	1932	2	-	-
Paul Coltman	1987-88	3	-	-
William Coltman	1881-82	7	-	-
William Coltman	1919	1	-	-
William Colver	1881-82	2	-	-
Rob Conquest	2009	0+1	-	-
Harry Constable	1958-59	10	1	3
Hugh Constantine	1930-34	51	9	47
Peter Cook	2003-05	1+1	-	-
TA Cook	1883	1	-	-
Ken Cooke	1936-39	5	3	9
Rupert Cooke	1892-95	41	1	18
Ted Cooke	1889-97	158	31	163
Tim Cooke	1980-81	1+4	2	8
Dick Cooper	1960-72	50	3	143
Paddy Coote	1931-33	27	12	96
David Corby	1880-81	7	-	-
George Cornell	1930	1	-	-
Tim Cornell	1997	0+1	-	-
Matt Cornish	1998	1	-	-
Matt Cornwell	2004-13	24+22	4	34
Martin Corry	1997-09	269+21	27	135
Ralph Cotton	1929-30	11	1	7
WHV Cotton	1932	1	-	-
AJ Coulter	1920	1	-	-
Bill Coutts	1966	3	1	7
Ian Coutts	1953	1	-	-
Edward Coutts-Deacon	1935	1	-	-
W Cowley	1888	1	-	-
Robin Cowling	1974-81	184	8	32
William Cowlishaw	1889	1	-	-
Richard Cowman	1963	2	1	3
HW Cox	1924	5	-	-
Hugh Craigmile	1921-22	8	6	18
Roy Cramb	1945-46	6	-	-
Charlie Cramphorn	1926-27	31	13	39
Frank Cramphorn	1928	1	-	-
John Cramphorn	1926-29	22	8	24
Crane	1882	1	-	-
Jordan Crane	2006-14	148+31	28	140
Mike Crane	1956-57	2	-	-
Thomas Craven	1882	1	1	1
Joshua Cressey	1881-87	62	5	8
Peter Crick	1936-37	16	-	-
Tom Crick	1928	1	-	-
EJ Crisp	1922	3	-	-
Tom Croft	2005-14	108+21	26	130
Alfred Crofts	1882	1	-	-
Charles Cromar	1937	1	-	-
A Crookes	1919-20	8	5	15
Maxwell Crosbie	1935	1	-	-
Viv Crosby	1936-37	2	-	-
Charlie Cross	1910-23	131	19	57
Frederick Cross	1883-84	10	-	-
Morgan Crowe	1932-35	72	18	160
Philip Crowe	1935-36	5	1	3
Frederick Crowhurst	1923	2	-	-
Richard Crowhurst	1938	1	-	-
George Crowson	1901-02	10	1	3
Tom Crumbie	1892-97	3	-	-
Andy Cudmore	1996-97	3	2	10
George Cullen	1949-57	180	66	550
Leo Cullen	2005-07	41+15	-	-
Mitch Culpin	2008	1	-	-
Kenneth Cummings	1935	1	-	-
Cyril Curle	1915	2	-	-
Arthur Currington	1899	1	-	-
A Curry	1926	1	-	-
Les Cusworth	1978-90	365	66	947

D

NAME	CAREER	APPS	TRIES	PTS
Reid Dakin	1901-06	84	23	69
Bill Dalby	1908-14	80	26	78
W Dale	1905-07	10	-	-
Fred Dance	1881	1	-	-
Alfred Daniells	1891	1	1	2
Edward Dann	1893-95	24	1	3
Isaiah Dann	1900-09	25	1	3
Bryan Darlington	1954	7	1	3
Edgar Darnill	1933-35	16	6	18
Maffer Davey	1908	2	-	-
"Tarzan" David	1923	1	-	-
John Davidson	1985-86	30	6	24
WA Davidson	1963	3	-	-
George Davie	1918	1	-	-
AJ Davies	1919	1	-	-
JF Davies	1945-46	18	-	37
Mefin Davies	2007-10	32+22	2	10
Thomas Davies	1933	1	-	-
HS Davis	1922-23	2	-	-
John Davis	1922-26	30	1	3
Terry Davis	1966	1	-	-
William Davis	1895	1	-	-
John Dawson	1969-71	75	3	9
Edward Dawson-Thomas	1889-91	5	1	1
George Day	1893-94	15	-	3
Harold Day	1919-29	212	108	1151
Jerry Day	1945-53	76	2	6
Brett Deacon	2003-13	83+52	6	30
Howard Deacon	1948-51	29	-	-
John Deacon	1981-82	42	1	4
Louis Deacon	2000-14	243+31	9	45
Richard de Carpentier	2011	0+1	-	-
Sebastian de Chaves	2013-14	6+3	-	-
Alan Deere	1938	1	-	-
Phil Delaney	1995-98	17+3	4	20
George Delgado	1935	9	3	9
Chris DeLuca	1978	1	-	-
Jeff Denner	1975-76	3	-	12
Samuel Dennis	1919	4	-	-
Digger Dermott	1945-48	93	5	15
Arthur Derry	1926	1	-	-
Colin Dexter	1982-89	74+8	36	144
Jack Dickens	1909-10	15	8	24
C Dickinson	1883-84	9	-	-
Harry Dickinson	1890	1	-	-
"Thumper" Dingley	1982-83	7	-	-
George Dobbs	1890-91	21	13	13
Denys Dobson	1907	1	-	-

NAME	CAREER	APPS	TRIES	PTS
David Docherty	1997	0+1	-	-
Alex Dodge	2005-06	1+3	-	-
Ollie Dodge	2006-08	2	-	-
Paul Dodge	1975-93	434+3	93	567
C Dodson	1911	1	-	-
Ian Dodson	1981-87	57+5	9	113
Fred Doe	1938-39	46	16	48
Hugh Doherty	1955	4	-	-
Freddy Doore	1954-57	54	3	9
MS Douglas	1937	2	-	-
Sydney Dove	1913-14	12	2	10
Keith Downes	1937-39	15	5	32
Aubrey Dowson	1896	1	-	-
James Doyle	2012	0+1	-	-
Laurie Doyle	1946-52	12	2	10
Bill Drake-Lee	1990-97	75+10	14	68
Nick Drake-Lee	1962-68	73	7	21
A Drew	1919	3	-	-
Fred Drummond	1930-35	30	9	27
Charles Duckering	1880	3	-	-
C Dudley	1923	1	-	-
SM Duff	1953-54	14	-	7
Mark Duffelen	1979-80	26	-	-
Joe Duffey	2009-11	2+10	-	-
William Duffin	1902	1	-	-
John Duggan	1970-80	302	158	608
Dunkley	1909	1	-	-
"Pop" Dunkley	1928-34	32	8	26
John Dunmore	1890	2	-	-
JR Dunn	1945	2	-	-
Pas Dunn	2013	0+1	-	-
Julien Dupuy	2008-09	24+7	2	129
James Duthie	1909	4	-	-
John Dyke	1908	2	3	9
JM Dykes	1926-27	20	6	18
Mike Dymond	1961-63	25	4	12
Ernie Dynes	1924-25	27	1	11

E

NAME	CAREER	APPS	TRIES	PTS
Darren Eagland	1991-92	5	1	5
Grant Eagle	1993	4	2	19
William Earles	1919	1	-	-
HO East	1906	1	-	-
R Eathorne	1908	6	-	-
John Eddison	1912	1	-	-
Richard Edgell	1881-82	2	1	1
Harry Edmiston	1926-34	112	9	62
John Edmiston	1933	2	-	-
John Edmonds	1891-93	51	7	14
Bryn Edwards	1945	3	1	3
Diccon Edwards	1994-95	22	-	-
Francis Edwards	1938-48	62	30	90
Peter Edwards	1961-68	145	2	6
Roland Edwards	1997-98	3+6	3	15
Ted Edwards	1973-74	7	1	4
TL Edwards	1907-08	12	4	12
Tony Edwards	1964	2	-	-
Harold Eking	1929	1	-	-
John Elders	1953-58	144	38	126
Thomas Elkington	1895	13	-	-
John Elliott	1967-70	126	20	60
L Elliott	1904-06	7	-	-
W Elliott	1912-19	5	-	-
Bob Ellis	1964	2	-	-
Harry Ellis	2001-10	131+42	29	145
Mark Ellis	1994	0+1	-	-
Roger Ellis	1946-49	45	16	48
Stanley Ellis	1919	1	-	-
Wilfrid Ellis	1909-10	22	-	-
Gerald Ellis-Danvers	1906	1	-	-
Dan Ellwood	1908-19	53	-	6
English	1895	1	-	-
Ayoola Erinle	2007-09	15+15	5	25
Barry Evans	1981-95	272+1	170	683
Geoff Evans	1962-66	37	2	6
Jason Evans	1992-93	9+1	3	15
Mike Evans	1967-69	48	5	236
R Evans	1923	1	-	-
Walter Evans	1905	1	-	-
Ewan Evans-Evans	1935	1	-	-
Matt Everard	2009-11	2+1	-	-
Denis Evers	1935	1	-	-
W Everson	1895	1	-	-
Bert Ewin	1930	1	-	-
John Ewin	1930	2	3	9
Nnamdi Ezulike	1997-00	29+4	10	50

F

NAME	CAREER	APPS	TRIES	PTS
Guy Falla	1931	1	-	-
Bob Fallowell	1933-35	7	1	3
Ernest Farmer	1890-91	16	-	-
Steve Farmer	1912-19	29	12	36
Ian Farmer-Wright	1948	1	-	-
Ewart Farndon	1925-31	183	86	258
Jimmy Farrell	1931	1	-	-
Charles Fausset	1907	3	1	3
DJ Ferguson	1919-20	34	-	6
Robert Ferguson	1908	1	2	6
J Fernie	1888-89	4	-	-
CD Ferris	1919	1	-	-
James Ferris	1997-99	4+3	1	5
Arthur Fforde	1888	1	-	-
Archie Field	1895-97	71	20	176
Rob Field	1994-97	22+3	1	5
Keith Fielding	1971	1	-	-
Owen Finegan	2007	1	-	-
SH Fisher	1890	1	-	-
Walter Fisher	1910-14	13	2	6
Jim Fisk	1951-53	48	-	21
Tommy Fitchett	1911	4	-	-
J Fitzgerald	1908	1	-	-
Jeff FitzGerald	1925-26	3	-	-
David Fletcher	1957-58	2	-	-
J Fletcher	1949	1	-	-
Neil Fletcher	1996-99	28+14	1	5
T Fletcher	1923	2	-	-
Ted Flewitt	1925-30	129	73	221
Flinn	1886	1	-	-
John Flint	1975	9	1	84
R Flint	1933	1	-	-
Toby Flood	2008-14	107+12	25	1336
Tony Flower	1955-56	2	-	-
Matthias Flude	1909-10	9	2	6
Charles Ford	1887-90	2	-	-
George Ford	2009-13	27+14	2	275
Jim Ford	1954-57	87	2	6
Tom Ford	1947	2	-	-
Billy Foreman	1893-06	358	85	263
Henry Foreman	1880-81	2	-	-
Dave Forfar	1971-81	222+1	14	56
James Forrest	1935	1	-	-
Michael Forrester	1938	1	-	-
Andy Forsyth	2009-13	15+9	2	10
Herbert Foster	1880-85	50	2	13
Malcolm Foulkes-Arnold	1979-94	260+2	21	84
Ken Fourie	1999	2+5	-	-
Eric Fowler	1934-38	27	2	6
F Fox	1894-95	26	15	115
John Fox	1934-39	58	11	49
Arthur Foxon	1901-03	10	3	9
A Francis	1923	1	3	9
Gwyn Francis	1919-22	12	-	-
Robert Francks	1934-36	3	-	-
Herbert Franklin	1927-28	28	-	4
Arthur Freear	1903	7	2	6
Harry Freeman	1895	1	-	-
Bill Freer	1946-49	38	12	36
C Freer	1915-18	2	-	-
Horace Freer	1905-06	6	-	-
John Freer	1907-08	4	-	-
Mike Freer	1956-65	203	15	66
Keith Freeston	1967	1	-	-
Ray French	1973-87	97	7	28
Roy French	1971-76	42	2	8
Perry Freshwater	1996-03	64+73	8	40
G Friend	1885-86	7	1	1
Carl Fripp	1994-97	2+1	-	-
Wally Frisby	1926	3	-	4
Arthur Frith	1898-99	3	-	-
Arthur Frowen	1922	1	-	-
Greg Fry	1996-97	1+2	-	-
Charles Fuller	1885-88	6	-	-
Ken Fyfe	1933	1	-	4

G

NAME	CAREER	APPS	TRIES	PTS
Brian Gabriel	1993-94	9	3	15
Thomas Gabriel	1921-22	2	-	-
Bernard Gadney	1929-39	170	63	189
William Gale	1895-03	41	2	40
John Gall	1891	6	-	-
Leslie Gamble	1924-26	7	-	-
Alan Gardiner	1964-65	5	-	-
Darren Garforth	1991-03	325+21	19	90
Bill Garner	1938	2	-	-
Josh Garner	1895-02	209	3	27
Richard Garratt	1899	1	-	-
JL Gaunt	1947	5	2	10
Dave Gavins	1981	0+1	-	-
Mike Gavins	1957-70	121	5	592
Gordon Gee	1952	11	2	6
Fred Geeson	1882	1	-	-
Glenn Gelderbloom	2000-04	37+39	5	25
Kenneth George	1932	2	-	-
WG George	1906	10	-	-
Claude Gerald	1983-90	37+3	26	104
George German	1890	1	-	-
Guy German	1921-27	66	4	12
Harry German	1889-94	28	5	8
Ronald Gerrard	1933	1	1	3
Ronnie Gerrard	1935-37	35	5	15
Ben Gerry	2002	0+1	-	-
Alfred Gibbons	1880-81	2	-	-
JH Gibbs	1884	1	-	-
WJ Gibbs	1921-24	14	4	12
Daryl Gibson	2003-07	85+7	16	80
Ian Gibson	1961-65	75	14	42
Jamie Gibson	2013-14	24+2	3	15
John Gibson	1882	1	-	-
Norman Giddings	1938	1	-	-
David Gilbert	1898-99	12	-	-
John Gilbert	1880-84	15	-	-
R Gilbert	1896-97	4	-	-
WJ Gilbey	1888-91	52	3	3
Jimmy Giles	1934-36	2	-	2
Greg Gillanders	2007-08	2+1	1	5
Chauncey Gillespie	1903	1	-	-
Nigel Gillingham	1978-84	144+1	12	48
Christopher Gimson	1905-11	72	10	93
G Gimson	1902	1	-	-
Alex Gissing	1987-93	64	16	65
Steven Glitherow	2004	0+1	-	-
DB Glover	1926-38	10	3	9
Jess Glover	1965-68	6	1	3
E Goddard	1896-01	16	4	16
Alfred Godfrey	1919-24	56	10	30
Bernard Golder	1954	4	-	-
Bob Golding	1887-96	5	-	-
J Golding	1970	2	-	-
Josh Goldspink	2008	0+2	-	-
Niki Goneva	2012-14	40+1	21	105
Lucas Gonzalez Amorosino	2009-11	11+3	6	30
Santiago Gonzalez Bonorino	2008-09	0+6	-	-
Ernest Goodall	1907	2	-	-
Andy Goode	1998-08	173+27	29	1799
George Goode	1936	8	-	-
Ernest Goodman	1908-11	6	1	3
Thomas Goodman	1934	7	-	-
Alf Goodrich	1900-09	179	9	31
Tom Goodrich	1899-10	205	6	24
Clark Goodwin	1994	0+1	-	-
John Gordon	1958	1	-	-
Tom Gordon	1885-87	9	-	-
Bill Gornall	1945	1	1	3
Frank Gough	1946	3	-	-
Alistair Graham	1931-32	10	-	-
Alastair Graham-Bryce	1961	1	-	-
Mark Grant	1988-95	50+4	19	76
Paul Grant	1990-97	49+5	9	45
William Graves	1928-29	16	-	-
Brian Gray	1933-34	6	5	15
T Gray	1882	1	-	-
George Greasley	1906-19	174	28	84
Harry Greasley	1934-36	23	2	6
George Greaves	1932-37	87	1	3
Ben Green	1997	0+1	-	-
C Green	1908	1	-	-
Calum Green	2008-12	14+7	-	-
Dan Green	1993	3	-	12
G Green	1901	1	-	-
Phil Greenbury	1999-00	0+2	-	-
Malcolm Greenhow	1961-62	9	4	12
Harry Greenlees	1926-32	153	32	192
H Greenway	1894	1	-	-
Amos Greenwell	1887-88	3	-	-
Henry Greenwood	1926-32	157	12	44
John Greenwood	1892-93	12	2	4
John Greenwood	1920	3	-	26
Sidney Greenwood	1919-21	3	1	3
Will Greenwood	1996-00	64+13	33	165
Darren Grewcock	1985-95	25+15	16	71
WH Grier	1910	1	-	-
Henry Grierson	1922-23	22	2	6
David Grieves	1936	1	-	-
Griffin	1887	1	-	-
Harold Griffin	1933	2	-	-
Daniel Griffiths	1945	1	-	-
HB Griffiths	1959	1	-	-
Niall Griffiths	1993	1	-	-
Charles Grimmett	1890	1	-	-
Andy Grimsdell	1993-94	2+1	1	5
James Grindal	1999-12	46+42	6	30
Joe Grindall	1966-67	2	-	-
Alistair Grocock	1975-78	10	-	-
Norman Grove	1953-54	6	2	6
Roger Grove	1966-73	172	9	34
Dave Guffick	1950-54	5	1	3
Lucas Guillaume	2012	1	-	-
Ben Gulliver	2010	2	-	-
Worthy Gulliver	1907	5	-	-
Gurney	1882	2	-	-
Paul Gustard	1997-02	76+42	14	70
Frederick Gwynne	1919	2	-	-

H

NAME	CAREER	APPS	TRIES	PTS
John Hacker	1947-51	45	3	9
Steve Hackney	1991-97	152	85	404
Edwin Haddon	1936	1	-	-

NAME	CAREER	APPS	TRIES	PTS
Newman Haddon	1880-81	5	-	-
Peter Haddon	1960-61	19	1	3
Bill Hadfield	1889	1	-	-
Bryan Hailes	1957	2	-	-
Dennis Haines	1953-58	43	1	3
N Haines	1968	2	-	-
Joseph Hale	1891	1	-	-
George Halford	1919	1	-	-
AC Hall	1927-32	96	5	15
Brian Hall	1970-84	308+4	67	275
J Hall	1889	2	-	-
T Hall	1905-08	9	2	6
W Hall	1907-08	21	-	-
W Hall	1913-14	15	-	-
Arthur Halliday	1932	1	-	-
L Hamblin	1914-19	3	-	-
Jamie Hamilton	1990-03	127+57	24	118
Jim Hamilton	2001-08	36+28	4	20
Scott Hamilton	2008-14	124+18	31	155
Craig Hammond	2009	1+1	-	-
Arthur Hancock	1891	1	-	-
Dave Hanna	1970	5	-	-
Mick Hanney	1958-60	4	-	-
Rob Harding	1994-96	1+1	-	-
Jeff Hardwicke	1929-34	85	40	120
Fred Hardyman	1905-07	39	11	33
Dusty Hare	1976-89	393+1	87	4507
James Hargrave	1909-14	110	53	163
Leonard Hargrave	1911	1	1	3
Reuben Hargreaves	1892	1	-	-
Arthur Harlow	1894	2	1	3
Septimus Harper-Smith	1894	1	-	-
AW Harris	1921	1	-	-
CS Harris	1933-34	9	1	3
David Harris	1968	6	2	34
Dickie Harris	1945-46	27	4	12
FE Harris	1935	1	-	-
George Harris	1936	1	-	-
GN Harris	1933-34	31	4	12
Ian Harris	1992	2	1	8
Ivor Harris	1956	3	-	-
Jez Harris	1984-96	213+12	23	1171
Jonny Harris	2009-13	3+7	-	-
RA Harris	1932-33	13	-	5
Robbie Harris	2009-10	2+5	-	-
Roderick Harris	1960-61	3	-	-
Steve Harris	1993	0+1	-	-
Cyril Harrison	1935-36	2	-	-
John Harrison	1934	1	-	-
John Harrison	1946-50	16	-	-
Mike Harrison	1962-71	210	58	177
Sam Harrison	2009-14	27+26	1	5
Shirley Harrison	1895-97	4	-	-
Viv Harrison	1947	2	-	-
J Hart	1895	1	-	-
Steve Hart	1996-97	2	-	-
Terry Hart	1983-84	4+1	-	-
Thomas Hart	1931	2	-	4
Tom Hart	1880-81	5	1	1
JR Hart-Davis	1905	1	-	-
Neil Hartley	1977-84	8	2	8
Paddy Harvey	1948-49	21	-	43
R Harvey	1884	1	-	-
RB Harvey	1930	2	-	-
Samuel Harvey	1911	1	-	-
Teddy Haselmere	1918-23	180	136	528
Keith Hassall	1939	1	-	-
Bill Havard	1919	2	-	-
Rob Hawkins	2010-14	24+40	3	15
William Hawley	1901-02	16	1	5
Hayes	1882-83	2	-	-
W Haynes	1894	1	-	-
George Hayward	1906-07	20	-	-
David Hazell	1953-56	81	15	265
Arthur Hazlerigg	1977-81	98	1	4
Austin Healey	1996-06	212+36	61	332
Arthur Heard	1909-10	21	12	36
C Hegarty	1919	7	1	3
Dan Hemingway	2008-11	5+9	1	5
Ralph Hemingway	1905	1	-	-
Mike Hemphrey	1960-63	16	-	-
Chris Hemsley	1976	3	-	-
CD Henderson	1932	2	-	-
Maurice Henderson	1938-45	25	5	15
J Henson	1892	2	-	-
Terrence Hepetema	2013-14	4+3	-	-
Bill Herbert	1947-50	21	-	4
Don Herbert	1930-32	15	-	4
Frank Herbert	1931-39	64	18	130
Geoff Herbert	1935-39	66	3	34
Peter Herbert	1946-52	66	8	24
Ben Herring	2007-09	18+5	5	25
Bob Hesmondhalgh	1892-98	101	33	129
Alan Hett	1922-23	2	1	3
EPA Hewitt	1933-34	21	9	27
George Hicken	1894-96	3	-	-
Gavin Hickie	2006-07	7+4	-	-

NAME	CAREER	APPS	TRIES	PTS
WC Hicks	1919-22	92	11	39
A Higgins	1919	1	-	-
MA Higginson	1964	1	-	-
NL Higginson	1918	1	-	-
DK Hill	1962	1	-	-
Edwin Hill	1881-82	2	-	-
Herbert Hill	1914-20	4	-	-
John Hill	1974	11	1	4
Samuel Hill	1889	1	-	-
Cliff Hilliker	1972-73	2	-	3
Bertie Hills	1897-05	46	13	41
Paul Hilyer	1990-91	6	1	4
Richard Hincks	1891	9	-	-
Alfred Hind	1899-06	127	81	261
Harold Hind	1901-05	88	2	6
Dan Hipkiss	2002-11	109+22	31	155
H Hirst	1915	1	-	-
Hitch	1921	1	-	-
Alfred Hitchcock	1892-95	51	16	45
Richard Hives	1905-07	30	1	21
Arthur Hobbs	1906-12	195	26	78
AE Hodder	1899	1	-	-
Frank Hodder	1932	6	1	3
JD Hodgkinson	1926-27	3	-	-
J Hodgson	1880-81	2	-	-
John Hodgson	1933-36	37	-	52
Anthony Hogarth	1909-11	4	-	-
Thomas Hogarth	1906-14	111+1	7	21
L Holden	1932	2	-	-
Toddy Holden	1923-27	41	14	54
Michael Holford	2003-12	30+29	4	20
Ted Holley	1973-77	39	4	21
Neil Holloway	1978-79	4	-	-
RW Holmes	1922	3	-	-
Chris Holroyd	1964-68	9	-	-
John Holtby	2001-05	29+7	6	30
Holyoak	1882	1	-	-
James Horner	1882-83	2	-	-
Percy Homer	1920	4	-	-
Philip Hope	1919	2	-	-
John Hopkin	1935-36	13	1	3
Alan Hopkins	1959	1	-	-
E Hopkins	1923	2	-	-
Edward Hopkins	1926-31	12	3	9
Gareth Hopkins	1961-63	12	-	2
Gil Hopkins	1908-19	216	14	42
Dave Hopper	1988-93	24+1	3	14
Michael Horak	1997-99	37+7	15	93
John Horn	1955-57	14	1	3
Graham Horner	1971-74	21	7	28
Phil Horrocks-Taylor	1958-63	92	14	48
Henry Horsley	1919	1	-	-
Tom Hoskins	1957	1	-	-
Derick Hougaard	2008-09	8+5	1	98
Percy Hougham	1914	3	-	-
Pat Howard	1998-06	91+5	11	57
Douglas Howson	1932	10	-	-
G Hoyle	1921	4	-	-
Thomas Hoyle	1886-87	10	-	-
J Hubbard	1907-09	21	2	6
Matt Hubbart	2013	0+1	-	-
Edmond Hudson	1880	1	1	1
Francis Hudson	1883	3	-	-
G Hudson	1927	1	-	-
Peter Hudson	1952	2	-	-
Alan Hughes	1931-35	113	3	9
Joe Hughes	1951-52	5	-	-
Nick Hughes	1945-48	43	-	-
Jo Hume	1929	1	-	-
Ian Humphreys	2005-08	19+8	4	172
Perry Humphreys	2013	0+1	-	-
Nick Humphries	1969	1	-	-
Pat Hunt	1955-58	7	1	3
D Hunt-Davies	1923	1	-	-
Ian Hunter	1948	10	4	12
Sam Hunter	1912-19	36	15	60
Noel Huntley	1949-50	6	-	-
Rob Hurrell	1998-99	4+2	-	-
Will Hurrell	2008-10	3+2	2	10
Bernard Hurren	1931	1	-	-
Thomas Huskisson	1936	1	-	-
Robert Hutt	1945	1	-	-
WH Hynd	1919	1	-	-
David Hytch	1954	2	-	-

I

NAME	CAREER	APPS	TRIES	PTS
Abraham Inchley	1894	1	-	-
Arthur Inchley	1921	3	-	-
John Ingleby	1970-74	45	5	354
Angus Innes	1999	1	-	-
R Ireland	1905	3	-	-

J

NAME	CAREER	APPS	TRIES	PTS
Ewen Jack	1935	2	-	-
Dick Jackett	1905-14	59	8	24
John Jackett	1904-11	183	8	108
Arthur Jackson	1890-95	24	-	-
Frank Jackson	1894-04	72	52	176
Fred Jackson	1905-08	77	20	129
Graham Jackson	1967-72	43	16	50
Keith Jackson	1964	1	-	-
Nick Jackson	1978-89	98+7	10	40
Tom Jackson	1904-07	36	7	21
Walter Jackson	1891-98	208	4	14
Wilf Jackson	1932-45	72	16	48
Tom Jacombs	1888-90	15	-	-
Willie Jagger	1896	4	-	-
Henry James	1881	1	-	-
Jamieson	1895	3	-	-
Mark Jasnikowski	1996-98	7+2	2	10
Bill Jeffery	1932	1	-	-
Harold Jeffries	1905	4	-	-
Derek Jelley	1993-03	100+45	21	105
J Jelly	1883	1	-	-
JD Jenkins	1930	1	-	-
Jenkins	1896	1	-	-
John Jenkins	1952-55	112	10	30
Leighton Jenkins	1958-59	32	6	18
Lew Jenkins	1923	2	-	-
Oswald Jenkins	1920	1	-	-
Shane Jennings	2005-07	51+9	12	60
Peter Jerwood	1938-50	135	13	129
Harry Jessop	1957-60	26	5	15
Alan John	1962-67	13	-	2
A Johnson	1890	1	-	-
Ashley Johnson	1991	1	-	-
Chris Johnson	1993-95	19+3	8	40
Ellis Johnson	1892	1	-	-
Martin Johnson	1989-05	348+14	18	90
Steve Johnson	1976-83	207	31	124
Will Johnson	1994-06	157+53	10	50
Craig Joiner	1996-00	63+14	19	95
CK Jolliffe	1938	1	-	-
Alewyn Jones	1902	7	-	-
Arthur Jones	1895-10	224	39	563
Arthur Jones	1958-60	50	2	6
Bleddyn Jones	1969-78	333	42	172
Charles Jones	1922-23	29	1	3
Dai Jones	1928-29	18	3	9
DJ Jones	1912	2	-	-
Eddie Jones	1991-92	1+2	-	-
Frank Jones	1895-05	115	35	176
Frank Jones	1974-75	14	2	8
G Jones	1923	1	2	6
George Jones	1894-96	63	16	48
Ivor Jones	1923	1	-	-
JIT Jones	1932	1	-	-
KB Jones	1964	2	-	-
KD Jones	1952-53	16	2	6
Ken Jones	1948	1	-	-
Matt Jones	1995-97	7+3	-	36
Mike Jones	1961-63	49	2	6
"Pussy" Jones	1903-04	7	2	6
RC Jones	1921	1	-	-
S Jones	1925	2	-	-
Trevor Jones	1947-48	19	1	3
WH Jones	1913-14	3	-	-
WJ Jones	1912	1	-	-
Jimmy Jose	1906	1	-	-
Sam Joy	1999	0+1	-	-
Harry Joyce	1892	11	1	2
Nick Joyce	1971-85	284+3	28	112
Ralph Joyce	1897	1	1	11
William Judd	1883-84	13	-	-

K

NAME	CAREER	APPS	TRIES	PTS
Rod Kafer	2001-03	53+1	8	43
Colin Kail	1950-51	26	4	12
Aadel Kardooni	1988-97	217+5	67	302
Ben Kay	1999-10	237+44	12	60
J Kaye	1934	1	1	3
Benjamin Kayser	2007-09	29+24	1	5
George Keeton	1896-04	45	10	30
GT Kemp	1930	1	-	-
Kemp	1945	1	-	-
Tommy Kemp	1937	1	-	-
Jim Kempin	1974-79	107+2	15	60
Phil Kendall	1985	2	-	4
Joe Kendrew	1930-36	30	3	17
John Kennewell	1951-53	4	-	-
Bill Kenney	1924	15	3	9
John Kenney	1934	1	-	-
Steve Kenney	1975-90	361+4	69	276
Kenny	1883	1	-	-
Harry Kenyon	1935-38	4	-	4
P Kenyon	1896	1	-	-
William Kerby	1930-32	12	2	6
Alf Kewney	1906-13	27	1	3
Andy Key	1978-92	60+5	13	114
Maurice Key	1957-60	29	-	48
Arthur Keywood	1899	1	-	-

NAME	CAREER	APPS	TRIES	PTS
George Kilby	1910	2	1	3
Wayne Kilford	1992-96	62	19	159
A King	1923-25	2	-	-
Arthur King	1912	1	-	-
Jabez King	1892-93	9	2	4
King	1886	2	-	-
Redvers King	1960	2	-	-
Charles Kingston	1890	1	-	-
Tim Kingston	1902	2	-	-
Charles King-Turner	1923	1	-	-
Charles Kinton	1895-99	7	1	3
Danny Kirk	1973-74	10	1	4
Lionel Kirk	1907-08	12	6	31
William Kitchen	1909-10	6	-	-
A Kitchener	1915	1	-	-
Graham Kitchener	2011-14	43+14	7	35
Dave Kitching	1989-90	8	-	-
Ronnie Knapp	1938	5	1	3
Charles Knight	1887-88	2	-	-
Edward Knight	1918-19	4	-	-
"Knott"	1889	1	3	3
Mac Knowles	1980-81	9+2	3	12
Henry Knox	1928	8	-	-
Peter Konig	1952-60	185	32	96
Josh Kronfeld	2001-03	46+10	9	45
Jez Krych	1974-82	28	-	-
Marek Kwisiuk	1998-99	1+1	-	-
Walter Kyle	1936	1	-	-

L

NAME	CAREER	APPS	TRIES	PTS
Eric Lacey	1947-59	175	15	49
John Lacey	1971	1	-	-
RA Laing	1945-46	2	-	-
John Lakin	1880-82	27	6	6
Robert Lakin	1892-94	6	-	-
Ryan Lamb	2013-14	4+3	-	29
Peter Lambert	1938-46	5	2	6
David Lammiman	1950	3	-	-
P Lane	1937	1	-	-
Russell Lane	1986-87	4	2	8
J Lang	1881	1	-	-
John Langdon	1899	2	-	-
James Langham	1881	1	-	-
D Langley	1946	1	-	-
George Lashmore	1928-30	4	1	3
Robert Lauder	1933	1	-	-
Christophe Laussucq	2007-08	7+4	-	-
Frank Lawrence	1921-28	135	11	33
Gwynne Lawrence	1949-53	118	40	120
Thomas Lawrence	1889-90	6	-	-
W Lawrence	1908	1	-	-
Gordon Lawrie	1938	4	-	-
Harry Lawrie	1904-15	168	29	262
Jock Lawrie	1923-26	92	13	39
Percy Lawrie	1907-24	318	206	727
Will Lawson	2008	1	-	-
Hugh Lawson	1882	1	-	-
Tommy Lawton	1924	1	-	3
Tommy Lawton	1982-83	4	-	-
Frank Lea	1888	1	-	-
J Leader	1914	1	-	-
W Leakey	1885-86	6	2	2
Jimmy Leather	1914	3	-	-
Will Leather	1909-10	5	-	-
George Lebens	1939	1	-	-
Geoffrey Lee	1953-55	26	8	24
John Lee	1899	1	1	3
Andrew Leeds	1997-98	6	-	-
Harry Lees	1938	1	-	-
Stan Leete	1957-58	11	-	2
R Leggitt	1910	1	-	-
Hugh le Good	1934	3	-	-
le Manco	1886	1	-	2
Bob Leslie	1952	1	-	-
Oswald Leslie	1919	1	-	-
Alex Lewington	2009-12	8	1	5
Bobby Lewis	1894-95	35	24	122
Brian Lewis	1955-57	15	2	6
Clem Lewis	1912	1	-	-
Cyril Lewis	1932-35	53	1	8
D Lewis	1907	1	-	-
DW Lewis	1934-35	2	-	-
Joseph Lewis	1908-10	7	2	6
RA Lewis	1950-51	17	-	-
Ben Lewitt	1999-00	0+2	-	-
Robert Ley	1888-94	68	5	8
Roy Leyland	1934-36	10	3	9
John Liley	1988-97	226+4	74	2518
Rob Liley	1996-97	24+3	7	167
William Lincoln	1896-00	110	15	47
DA Lindsay	1935	1	-	-
E Line	1885-89	28	-	-
Edward Lines	1901	1	-	-
Samuel Lines	1900-05	21	-	-
Colin Littlewood	1960	3	-	-
S Livingstone	1915	1	-	-
Brian Llewellyn	1968	1	-	-
John Llewelyn	1929-34	39	13	75
I Lloyd	1933-34	10	4	12
Leon Lloyd	1996-07	233+27	84	420
Owen Lloyd-Evans	1898-99	5	-	2
Mike Lockett	1968	2	1	3
Peter Lockman	1904-05	7	-	-
William Lole	1928	1	-	-
Dave Lougheed	1998-00	48+3	23	115
Arthur Loveday	1884	1	-	-
Wortley Lovell	1890	1	-	-
Jack Lovett	1880-90	104	9	9
CL Lowe	1922	3	-	-
Sydney Loxton	1933-36	70	2	6
Mike Lubbock	1955-60	95	7	21
J Lucas	1891-92	5	-	-
William Ludlow	1890	2	-	-
Dan Lyle	2003	3	1	5
Martin Lynch	1946-47	16	2	6
Rory Lynn	2010	0+1	-	-
David Lyons	1966-67	6	1	3
Victor Lyttle	1936	1	-	-

M

NAME	CAREER	APPS	TRIES	PTS
Andy McAdam	1990-96	23+2	7	34
Donal McAlpin	1890	9	-	-
Kenneth McAlpin	1884-92	136	13	13
D McArthur	1929	1	-	-
Kenneth Macauley	1881	4	-	-
Steve Macauley	2010	0+1	-	-
Roy McConnell	1950	1	-	-
John McCormack	1954-57	37	5	15
Bernard McCraith	1900-01	10	-	-
Keith Macdonald	1952	5	-	-
Kevin MacDonald	1985-91	13+6	7	28
MA Macdonald	1922	1	-	-
Dave Macey	1976	3	-	-
N McFarlane	1904-06	40	5	15
Arthur McIntyre	1908-12	46	3	9
RB Mackay	1936-37	12	3	9
Rory McKay	2007	0+1	-	-
Arthur McKechnie	1882-94	217	20	97
JH McKee	1938	1	-	-
Darren Mackenzie	1998	3	-	-
John McLean	1933-38	39	7	42
JN MacLeod	1936	2	1	3
Rod McMichael	1977-78	7	1	4
D MacMillan	1913	5	2	6
Craig McMullen	2002-03	8+1	-	8
Frederick McMurray	1881	1	-	-
William McMurray	1888-90	4	-	-
Ian McNichol	1930-32	6	1	3
Owen McSally	1890-92	21	1	2
John McTigue	1950-51	2	-	-
Thomas Maddocks	1911-12	2	-	-
Steve Mafi	2010-14	54+29	11	55
Dick Mainwaring	1961	6	3	9
Niall Malone	1993-98	60+11	13	170
Dante Mama	2011-12	1+1	-	-
Denis Manley	1932	1	-	-
AO Mann	1937	3	-	-
Arthur Mann	1892	1	-	-
Maurice Mann	1907-08	11	2	6
PJ Mann	1986-88	23	1	4
James Mansell	1888-89	21	2	2
Leigh Mansell	1994-95	6	1	5
Dave Manship	1980-82	9	-	4
Charlie Manson	1928-33	107	-	22
Guy Manson-Bishop	2001	3+2	1	5
Albert Manton	1915-19	5	2	6
Dave Markham	2011	0+1	-	-
AC Marques	1922	1	1	3
Adey Marriott	1982-92	114+16	12	48
John Marriott	1967	1	-	-
Robert Marris	1905	2	-	-
GG Marshall	1919	1	-	-
Mike Marshall	1970-77	31+1	8	31
Rae Marshall	1950-57	87	2	15
Jack Marston	1882	1	-	-
Colin Martin	1956-66	272	13	555
Neil Martin	1992	2	-	-
A Mason	1895	1	-	-
CJ Mason	1892	2	-	-
Henry Mason	1886-91	93	12	12
Mason	1881	1	-	-
Edward Massey	1923-25	31	1	18
William Massey	1882-87	3	-	-
Pablo Matera	2013-14	5+3	2	10
Andy Matthews	1966-73	8	-	16
Austin Matthews	1934	1	-	-
Bob Matthews	1949-56	57	14	42
David Matthews	1955-74	502	119	451
Sammy Matthews	1898-08	340	19	88
George Matts	1946-50	31	-	92
Aaron Mauger	2007-10	46+7	8	42
John Mawbey	1968-69	38	6	24
Norman Mawle	1928	1	-	-
Charles Medhurst	1923-24	17	-	4
Garnet Mee	1900-01	2	2	6
John Meek	1891-97	32	-	-
J Meekin	1884	2	-	-
Mark Meenan	1999	0+1	-	-
Graham Meikle	1933-37	26	14	54
Stephen Meikle	1931-33	6	8	26
Alistair Meldrum	1978	1	-	-
David Mele	2013-14	7+18	5	41
Fred Mellor	1914-21	20	1	7
Joseph Memory	1891-93	9	2	5
Mick Merriman	1979-81	18	3	37
Bill Merry	1902	3	-	-
George Metcalf	1891	2	-	-
Ernie Michie	1957-58	10	-	-
George Middleton	1908-11	29	2	6
Jack Miles	1899-04	93	75	225
Clarence Millar	1931-35	5	-	-
Guy Millar	1965-72	11	3	9
Maurice Millard	1928-29	7	-	-
Eric Miller	1995-98	47+5	6	30
Jock Millican	1975-76	25	4	16
A Mills	1907-09	48	2	6
J Mills	1890	1	-	-
Malcolm Milman	1936	1	-	-
JW Milne	1952	1	-	-
Ken Milne	1956	1	-	-
J Milton	1946	1	-	-
David Moeller	1961	1	-	-
Christopher Moller	1925	2	-	-
Robin Money	1968-78	255+3	23	123
Dan Montagu	2004-06	2+2	-	-
Lewis Moody	1996-10	174+49	36	180
JH Moon	1925	1	-	-
Arthur Moore	1892-93	4	1	2
Bill Moore	1945-53	170	6	28
Charley Moore	1891	1	-	-
George Moore	1887	5	-	-
Jeff Moore	1948	2	-	-
Joseph Moore	1925-26	12	4	12
Peter Moore	1947	1	-	-
RL Moore	1937	1	-	-
Shirley Moore	1927-32	13	5	15
Alejandro Moreno	2005-08	28+17	-	-
Arthur Morgan	1922	1	1	3
Des Morgan	1963	3	-	-
Edgar Morgan	1908	1	-	-
WR Morgan	1935-36	9	2	6
D Morley	1968-72	6	-	-
Joey Morley	1885-92	98	4	4
Darren Morris	2003-06	56+20	1	5
Denis Morris	1930-35	42	10	34
F Morris	1910	1	-	-
J Morris	1915	1	-	-
Jim Morris	1949-52	47	2	128
Niall Morris	2011-14	52+8	15	75
J Morrison	1891-92	6	1	2
Mark Morrison	1898-02	2	-	-
Mike Mortimer	1971-75	132	10	40
Jack Morton	1908	1	-	-
John Morton	1923	1	-	-
Ervine Mosby	1896-01	73	12	111
Mosby	1889	1	-	-
William Moseby	1937-45	18	4	12
Len Moseley	1957-58	11	1	3
Bob Muddimer	1957-58	8	-	-
Logovi'i Mulipola	2012-14	43+20	5	25
Karl Mullen	1954	1	-	-
Roy Murgatroyd	1950-51	5	-	-
William Murmann	1918-19	4	1	3
Frank Murphy	2006-08	28+19	2	12
Geordan Murphy	1997-13	298+24	93	691
John Murphy	1989-95	21+6	5	25
Johne Murphy	2006-10	77+22	28	151
Tom Murphy	1998	1	-	-
A Murray	1927-28	2	-	-
Pieter Myburgh	2011	1+1	-	-
Edward Myers	1919-25	2	-	-
Luke Myring	2003-04	2+5	-	3
Myrtle	1886	1	-	-

N

NAME	CAREER	APPS	TRIES	PTS
Mike Nangreave	1980	0+1	-	-
Joe Naufahu	2002	2+3	-	-
Jim Naylor	2001-02	1+3	-	-
Eddie Neal	1945-48	82	1	3
Oliver Neal	1933-34	2	-	-
AL Neale	1919	2	-	-
Ricky Nebbett	2000-04	31+40	-	-
Ray Needham	1973-82	123+3	5	26
Mike Neil	1958	4	1	3
E Neild	1884-92	16	2	2
Jimmy Nelson	1927	2	1	3
C Nemo	1881	1	-	-
Sydney Neumann	1900-01	29	9	27

NAME	CAREER	APPS	TRIES	PTS
Craig Newby	2008-12	60+24	3	17
Fred Newman	1914	1	-	-
Ali Newmarch	2000	6+2	1	5
Steve Newsome	1977-78	9	-	-
Mick Newton	1976-82	24+2	8	32
Ken Nicholas	1948-53	151	24	95
Peter Nicholls	1971-75	57	24	85
A Nicholson	1891	1	-	-
Charles Nicholson	1895-97	21	3	9
Ernie Nicholson	1935-36	8	-	-
Herbert Nicol	1900	1	-	-
Ian Nimmo	2007	0+1	-	-
Ernest Nixon	1932	3	-	-
David Noble	1961	1	-	-
Reuben Nobleston	1932	1	-	-
Nobren	1890	1	-	-
Rob Nockles	1987-88	2+4	-	3
Colin Noon	2004	0+1	-	-
Frank Noon	1885	2	2	2
Michael Noone	2012-14	5+2	4	20
Doug Norman	1920-33	453	21	131
FJ Norman	1932-33	3	-	-
Fred Norman	1918	2	-	-
Laurie Norman	1946	4	-	-
Roland Norman	1947-48	4	-	5
W Norman	1920	4	-	10
Andy Northen	1975-76	6	-	-
David Norton	1949-50	27	2	6
John Noton	1950-54	12	-	-
Tony Novis	1928-31	3	-	-
Ally Nutt	1880-89	53	12	12
Tommy Nutt	1889-92	39	6	8
"Snooks" Nuttall	1892	1	-	-

O

NAME	CAREER	APPS	TRIES	PTS
Colin Oakes	1934	3	1	3
Keith Oakley	1933	1	-	-
Alexander Obolensky	1934-39	17	12	36
John O'Connor	1955	4	1	3
Tom O'Connor	1954-56	34	4	12
Reginald Odbert	1923-31	13	1	3
JJ Oelofse	1995-98	2+1	-	-
GA Ogden	1889	6	-	-
Alan Old	1972-74	18	3	106
Arthur Oldershaw	1901	1	-	-
William Oldham	1910	1	-	-
Fred Oliver	1923	1	-	-
George Oliver	2012-13	0+2	-	-
Roger Orchard	1933-36	3	-	-
Des O'Regan	1965	4	-	-
John O'Reilly	2000-01	1+4	1	5
Tony O'Reilly	1958-60	17	8	24
T Orme	1899	2	-	-
Herbert Orr	1889	1	-	-
Fred Orton	1891-93	2	-	-
George Orton	1893-95	2	-	-
AJ Osbourne	1915-19	3	-	-
Cecil Oscroft	1919-20	2	-	-
Donald Oscroft	1929-34	20	2	6
Percy Oscroft	1897-01	49	19	106
James Overend	1995-98	30+7	4	20
Chris Owen	1969-71	38	8	25
Ryan Owen	2006	0+1	-	-
"Tuppy" Owen-Smith	1933	1	-	-
Henry Oxlade	1886-89	34	5	14

P

NAME	CAREER	APPS	TRIES	PTS
HE Packer	1932	1	-	-
CA Page	1892-03	16	5	15
H Page	1919	4	-	2
Norman Page	1934	3	-	-
Rowland Page	1894-97	18	-	-
SE Page	1892	4	1	2
Richard Pailthorpe	1890	1	-	-
Ben Pain	1996	1	2	10
Paisley	1923	1	-	-
Arthur Palfreyman	1902-04	18	-	-
Harry Palfreyman	1909-18	4	-	-
Arthur Palmer	1921-25	12	-	-
David Palmer	1948-49	4	-	-
Phil Palmer	1929	3	-	-
RA Palmer	1932-34	2	2	6
Ron Palmer	1923-29	14	2	8
Ted Parfitt	1938-45	3	1	3
Camilo Parilli-Ocampo	2010-11	2	-	-
B Parker	1919-20	13	1	3
Bill Parker	1931-35	30	1	3
George Parker	1925-26	27	-	-
HMG Parker	1924	4	1	3
Malcolm Parker	1924	2	-	-
Albert Parkes	1892-93	13	-	-
Larry Parkes	1976-80	28+6	7	28
Geoff Parling	2009-14	67+10	2	10
James Parry	1881-82	2	-	-
Alfred Parsons	1903-06	44	17	51

NAME	CAREER	APPS	TRIES	PTS
Jack Parsons	1880-89	113	15	150
Jim Parsons	1935-39	60	9	27
Tiziano Pasquali	2013-14	0+4	-	-
John Patchett	1891-94	36	-	-
T Patrick	1898	1	-	-
Pat Pattinson	1931	2	-	-
FW Payne	1905	1	-	-
JF Payne	1932	3	-	3
CJ Pearce	1884	2	-	-
Herbert Pearce	1909-15	13	5	19
SD Pearce	1939	1	-	-
Ernest Peard	1900	1	1	3
Peter Pearse	1928-35	29	2	6
Seb Pearson	2008	1	-	-
E Peddie	1889	2	-	-
JS Peebles	1935	1	-	-
E Pell	1947	1	-	-
Richard Pell	1984-85	18+2	4	33
Herbert Pemberton	1913	1	1	3
Reg Pemberton	1932	1	-	-
Ben Pennington	1998	0+1	-	-
Sid Penny	1896-10	491	16	48
David Perkins	1964-69	21	1	3
David Perry	1960	4	-	-
Dick Peters	1978-79	0+2	-	-
Ramiro Pez	2003-04	11+2	3	100
Heinz Pflugler	1996	1	-	2
Patrick Phibbs	2012	1+4	-	-
Bertie Philbrick	1894	1	-	-
Edgar Phillips	1887-88	12	10	10
W Phillips	1935	2	-	-
G Phillpotts	1928	1	-	-
Gordon Phipps	1946	3	1	3
Ezra Pickard	1895-96	9	6	18
David Pickering	1971-73	20	1	4
Thomas Pickering	1880-81	3	-	-
Ben Pienaar	2006-12	22+8	1	5
ER Pierce	1945	8	-	-
Ernest Pilsbury	1887-88	8	1	1
Harry Pilsbury	1890-91	7	1	1
Javiah Pohe	2013	2	-	-
Jack Pole-Kitson	1894	1	-	-
George Pollard	1935-38	13	-	-
W Pollard	1920-23	6	4	12
Howard Poole	1900	1	-	-
Matt Poole	1988-98	215+8	20	95
Richard Pope	1997	0+1	-	-
Arthur Porter	1880-89	40	5	8
George Porter	1889-90	8	-	-
Samuel Porter	1883-88	21	-	-
Willie Porter	1880-92	170	10	11
Johnny Pott	1929-35	13	3	9
AC Potter	1936	1	-	-
Stuart Potter	1992-99	166+3	36	180
Mike Poulson	1979-83	40+3	7	165
Simon Povoas	1986-93	127+8	64	261
Andy Powell	2003	0+1	-	-
Powell-John	1900	1	-	-
John Powers	1889	6	-	-
Harry Powley	1956	3	-	-
Stan Pratt	1949-54	134	4	12
Doug Prentice	1923-31	239	60	575
Thomas Prentice	1880-82	9	-	-
JR Preston	1936-39	23	8	24
WH Preston	1934	1	-	-
Leo Price	1922-24	17	2	10
Philip Price	1926	1	-	-
Tom Price	2013-14	2+2	-	-
Leonard Price-Stephens	1945	1	-	-
N Pugh	1953	3	-	-
Graham Pulfrey	1962-69	173	13	74
Henry Purdy	2012-14	2+2	-	-
A Purt	1927	1	-	-
Fred Pyart	1906	1	-	-
George Pym	1952-54	14	1	3

Q

NAME	CAREER	APPS	TRIES	PTS
Claude Quarry	1937	1	-	-
John Quick	1964-68	119	41	123
Sam Quick	1991	1	-	-
David Quine	1947-51	27	8	40

R

NAME	CAREER	APPS	TRIES	PTS
Seru Rabeni	2004-09	46+17	18	90
Stephen Radcliffe	1932	1	-	-
Alan Raine	1963-68	63	4	12
S Ramsey	1899	3	-	-
R Randall	1923	1	-	-
Geoffrey Randle	1948-52	5	-	-
WG Rapsey	1903-10	2	1	3
J Rathbone	1890-92	25	13	23
E Raven	1906	1	-	-
John Raven	1925-26	2	-	-
Sam Raven	2008-09	2	-	-
John Rawes	1977	1	-	-

NAME	CAREER	APPS	TRIES	PTS
Dick Rawson	1956-61	63	20	64
John Rawson	2005-06	2+4	-	-
Gareth Raynor	2002-03	1+3	-	-
C Read	1920-21	3	1	3
Frank Read	1912-19	12	-	-
John Read	1881	1	-	-
Mitch Read	1996-99	12	6	30
Scott Read	1998-99	3+1	2	10
R Reading	1880	1	-	-
George Reay	1956	2	-	-
A Redding	1912-14	15	-	-
Steve Redfern	1976-84	241	16	64
Stuart Redfern	1982-92	322+2	25	100
WH Redfern	1950-52	12	-	-
Eddie Redman	1893-00	143	12	39
NF Reed	1934	6	1	3
Steve Reed	1993-94	4	1	5
Alan Rees	1960	1	-	-
Dan Rees	1904	1	-	-
Danny Rees	1947-50	76	32	99
Fred Rees	1912	1	-	-
G Rees	1945-46	4	1	3
Noel Rees	1926	1	-	-
Jim Reeve	1930	1	-	-
John Reeve	1973-77	51	18	72
DJ Reeves	1922	1	-	-
Paul Reeves	2000-01	1+1	-	-
Bill Reichwald	1977-78	18+1	2	11
Mark Reid	1988	13	1	4
JP Reidy	1934	2	-	-
Arthur Rendle	1893-94	32	-	-
Henry Rew	1932	1	-	-
BV Reynolds	1932	1	-	-
Harry Reynolds	1902-03	15	1	7
Tom Reynolds	1992-96	18	4	20
Joseph Rhodes	1880-81	3	-	-
Peter Rhodes	1946-48	33	3	29
E Rice	1919	1	-	-
"Tuffie" Rice	1894-95	25	5	15
Dean Richards	1982-97	306+8	105	431
F Richards	1919	1	-	-
Harry Richards	1936-46	47	-	9
Jimmy Richards	2003-04	9+10	2	10
Ken Richards	1954	6	2	6
Lee Richardson	1985-90	9+3	2	8
Nigel Richardson	1992-94	14+2	6	30
Wayne Richardson	1981-93	220+3	8	32
CB Riddle	1923	1	-	-
George Ridgway	1935-39	95	1	3
Thomas Ridley	1884	1	-	-
Ridsdale	1905	2	-	-
Brian Rigney	1958-60	3	-	-
Peter Riley	1961-71	34	4	12
TA Riley	1938	1	-	-
Brian Ring	1959-60	35	4	15
Paul Ringer	1973-74	56	4	16
Tim Ringer	1974	7	-	-
Robert Ringrose	1914-20	12	5	15
Graham Robb	1984-85	2+1	2	8
ADT Roberts	1924	2	-	-
Harry Roberts	1986-90	54	7	28
HS Roberts	1919	1	2	6
Sydney Roberts	1908	1	1	3
Terry Roberts	1982	5	-	-
WK Roberts	1894	1	-	-
J Robertson	1889	2	-	-
John Robins	1959-62	27	-	115
Basil Robinson	1934	1	-	-
Fred Robinson	1910	1	-	-
Harry Robinson	1910-11	18	-	-
Lee Robinson	2010-11	3+2	-	-
Moggie Robinson	1933-37	96	3	9
R Robinson	1923	1	-	-
Richie Robinson	1993-96	46+1	7	35
Thomas Robinson	1880-90	3	-	-
W Robinson	1901-03	46	1	3
Roy Robson	1992	1	-	-
Nathan Rocyn-Jones	1926	1	-	-
John Roderick	1939	6	1	3
William Roderick	1924-25	17	-	-
Alan Rogers	1935-38	32	3	9
FA Rogers	1890	3	-	-
G Rogers	1945	1	-	-
JG Rogers	1935	1	-	-
Duncan Roke	1997-98	2+3	-	-
Stewart Roke	1994-96	10	2	10
Ed Rolston	2011	1	-	-
Marcus Rose	1975-77	19	9	184
Hugh Rotherham	1886	1	-	-
Calvin Round	1949	4	-	-
Luix Roussarie	2011	0+1	-	-
AJ Rowe	1938-39	2	-	-
Bob Rowell	1962-78	355	20	67
A Rowlands	1919-20	6	4	12
Graham Rowntree	1990-07	362+36	18	87
Andy Roxburgh	1922-23	23	1	3
W Roxburgh	1924	3	1	3

NAME	CAREER	APPS	TRIES	PTS
Steve Roy	1984-85	0+5	1	4
Dick Royce	1972	2	-	-
Alan Royer	1991	0+1	-	-
John Russell	1922-30	141	10	33
Richard Russell	1903-13	122	28	157
Damion Ryan	1991	2	-	-
Mike Ryan	1967	1	-	-
Tom Ryder	2003	1+2	-	-
Bob Ryley	1946-48	33	16	52
Douglas Ryley	1927	16	1	3

S

NAME	CAREER	APPS	TRIES	PTS
Gordon Salmon	1914	3	-	-
Hedley Salmon	1880-87	89	1	1
Percy Salmon	1885-88	3	-	-
Julian Salvi	2011-14	79+5	10	50
Claude Sambrook	1921-28	215	-	73
Harold Sambrook	1924-26	34	3	12
Greg Sammons	2008	0+1	-	-
George Sanderson	1905	1	-	-
Jerry Sanderson	1905	1	-	-
Peter Sandford	1989-93	62+1	35	152
J Sargeant	1938	1	-	-
F Sarson	1897	1	-	-
Eric Saunders	1966	7	-	3
Stan Saunders	1929-34	131	21	63
Malcolm Sayer	1963-68	56	13	39
Ian Scattergood	1965-66	3	1	3
FS Scholes	1918	1	-	-
Jerome Schuster	2013	0+2	-	-
Ken Scotland	1961-62	40	4	240
Algernon Scott	1906-10	11	6	18
FC Scott	1933	1	-	-
H Scott	1919	2	-	-
John Scott	1947-48	5	-	-
MS Scott	1899-11	68	4	20
PG Scott	1924-26	41	9	27
Blaine Scully	2013-14	16+4	4	20
John Seager	1919-23	3	-	-
Seale	1881	1	-	-
Iain Selkirk	1949	4	-	-
John Sellers	1882	1	-	-
David Sellicks	1957-58	3	-	-
David Senior	1959-63	84	58	177
Waisale Serevi	1997-98	16+2	5	53
Arthur Sewell	1892-93	28	2	4
JR Sharp	1937-38	31	-	-
G Sharpe	1911-12	12	-	-
P Sharpe	1933	1	-	-
Herb Sharratt	1921-25	150	17	55
Alex Shaw	2007	1	-	-
Dave Shaw	1970-72	57	2	8
Frank Shaw	1905-07	3	-	-
Ian Shaw	1935-36	2	-	-
Jun Shaw	1995-96	2+3	1	5
Fred Sheen	1880-82	9	1	1
Edward Sheffield	1884-85	5	-	-
William Sheffield	1880-87	98	18	18
Benjamin Shelton	1880	1	-	-
John Shentall	1925	1	-	-
Cliff Shephard	1955-64	140	36	111
John Shepherd	1951	1	-	-
Sheppard	1883	1	-	-
William Sheppard	1933-36	49	25	80
WS Sheppard	1889-90	4	-	-
George Shingler	1907-09	2	-	-
Len Shipton	1926-30	8	1	5
Peter Short	1999-03	26+23	2	10
John Shuttlewood	1952-54	36	9	27
Arthur Sibson	1932-33	2	-	-
Harry Sibson	1947-54	183	26	78
GB Siggins	1958	1	-	-
John Simcoe	1896	1	-	-
Arnold Sime	1932-37	7	1	3
SC Simmonds	1947	1	-	-
A Simpson	1908	2	-	-
Frank Simpson	1904	2	-	-
Fred Simpson	1888-93	7	-	-
Harry Simpson	1891-96	91	9	24
J Simpson	1904	1	2	6
Robert Simpson	1919-24	16	5	15
TM Simpson	1948	1	-	-
FO Sinclair	1925	5	-	-
Rex Skelton	1956-70	198	5	15
Skelton	1897	1	-	-
Sam Skinner	1999	1	-	-
Will Skinner	2003-06	12+25	5	25
Fred Skinner-Jones	1889	1	-	-
George Skivington	2010-12	47+4	2	10
Donald Slack	1921	1	-	-
Ed Slater	2010-14	65+29	8	40
Roy Sleigh	1966-69	71	33	102
Charles Slow	1933-37	98	23	176
Peter Sly	1985	1+1	-	-
Bob Small	1957-69	119	22	66
Brian Small	1954-63	158	3	40

NAME	CAREER	APPS	TRIES	PTS
H Smalley	1901-04	3	-	-
Alastair Smallwood	1920-25	64	47	151
A Smith	1925	1	-	-
AJ Smith	1904-05	2	-	-
Ben Smith	1998-99	2+2	1	5
Bob Smith	1968-69	23	4	12
Brian Smith	1954-60	53	19	60
Brian Smith	1990-91	15	4	49
Connor Smith	2009	0+1	-	-
Darnell Smith	1888	10	-	-
Derek Smith	1952	2	-	-
Dixie Smith	1902-12	132	27	81
Graham Smith	1978-85	3+1	-	-
H Smith	1923	1	-	-
HW Smith	1945	2	-	-
Ian Smith	1977-91	322+9	67	268
J Smith	1886	1	-	-
JB "Smith"	1890	1	-	-
Ken Smith	1962	8	3	9
LA Smith	1932	1	-	-
LW Smith	1948	1	-	-
Matt Smith	2006-14	112+39	26	130
Ollie Smith	2000-08	154+28	38	190
Phil Smith	1979	1	-	-
Ron Smith	1938-49	4	-	-
Ron Smith	1949-58	190	11	33
Stuart Smith	1919-31	80	10	30
Ted Smith	1881	1	-	-
Tom Smith	1906-08	58	4	12
Tom Smith	1984-95	184+1	18	74
W Smith	1905	1	-	-
Walter Smith	1935	4	-	22
WM Smith	1881-88	56	5	5
Percy Smitten	1911-21	16	2	10
Snaith	1923	1	-	-
Dickie Snowden	1886-93	67	10	11
Dennis Sobey	1974	4	-	-
Steve Solomons	1974-80	8+3	-	-
Hugh Somerville	1906	1	-	-
Frederick Souster	1921	13	2	6
Neil Spence	1995	2	-	-
Trevor Spence	1968-69	46	19	57
Jason Spice	2010	2+1	-	-
Ike Spicer	1911-19	15	1	3
Don Sproul	1952	1	-	-
Reginald Squibbs	1937-39	38	9	48
Wilfrid Squirrell	1925-29	8	-	-
Christopher Stafford	1905-07	25	-	-
E Stagg	1924	1	-	-
L Staines	1881-82	5	-	-
Derek Standerwick	1960	1	-	-
Boris Stankovich	2007-14	72+47	3	15
Charles Stanley	1933	6	-	-
Winston Stanley	2000-01	26	8	40
H Stannard	1889	2	-	-
Bert Stanyon	1887	1	-	-
Kenneth Stanyon-Jacques	1932-38	5	2	6
Rodney Stapleford	1946-47	8	2	6
Jim Stapleton	1937-39	32	1	3
NE Starkey	1934	3	-	-
Jeremy Staunton	2009-12	31+23	5	326
Wayne Steedman	1988-89	2+1	-	-
Scott Steele	2012-14	0+3	-	-
John Steinitz	1894	2	1	3
S Stenson	1923	1	-	-
JT Stephens	1923	1	-	-
RJ Stephens	1929	3	1	3
RP Stephens	1927	1	-	-
Kevin Steptoe	1977-86	12+3	2	8
Jimmy Stevens	2012	2+4	-	-
John Stevens	1954-57	66	1	3
LW Stevenson	1936	1	-	-
IGH Stewart	1954	3	-	-
Keith Stewart	1964-65	14	1	3
W Stewart	1891-92	25	1	2
Ken Stimpson	1946	6	3	9
Tim Stimpson	1998-03	141+10	29	1713
Bob Stirling	1948-53	75	1	3
Francis Stocks	1895	1	-	-
Lew Stokes	1945-46	26	-	-
Paul Stone	1979-81	8+1	-	-
Dennis Storer	1957-58	3	-	-
K Storey	1914	1	-	-
Harold Storrs	1922-23	9	5	15
H Straker	1900	4	-	-
Strang	1928	1	-	-
Joel Stransky	1997-99	72+1	23	896
Lindsay Stratton	1985-86	2+2	-	-
Wilfred Streather	1924	8	-	-
Paul Strickland	1978-79	2+1	-	-
Jono Stuart	1998-99	16+10	3	15
Jack Sturges	1889-93	114	22	32
Henry Sturgess	1919	1	-	-
T Sturrock	1905	1	-	-
Gordon Sturtridge	1937	1	1	3
Arthur Sulley	1887-93	6	6	13
William Sully	1881	2	-	-

NAME	CAREER	APPS	TRIES	PTS
J Sutcliffe	1914	4	-	-
Norman Sutton	1903-04	32	10	34
Albert Swain	1903-06	66	2	6
Martinus Swain	1895-04	5	2	6
Paddy Swain	1894-97	97	13	39
Percy Swain	1905-06	2	-	-
Ian Swan	1957-59	51	20	60
Len Swanwick	1954	2	-	-
Eric Sweatman	1926-30	19	3	9
Swift	1892	1	-	-
Bill Sykes	1892	5	-	-
James Symington	1880-84	49	5	8
Kenneth Symington	1928	4	1	3
Andy Symons	2011-13	2+3	-	-
Brian Symons	1954-58	6	3	9

T

NAME	CAREER	APPS	TRIES	PTS
Peter Tahany	1945-48	33	3	12
Mathew Tait	2011-14	38+4	6	30
Chris Tarbuck	1993-96	42+4	17	85
Frank Tarr	1906-13	94	24	72
Charlie Tassell	1975	1	-	-
Cyril Tate	1925-26	7	1	3
Ray Tate	1952	4	-	-
Lyn Tatham	1958-62	89	14	65
Ephraim Taukafa	2004-06	3+9	1	5
GC Taylor	1923	3	1	3
Guy Taylor	1880-82	6	-	-
John Taylor	1954-59	49	12	36
Sandy Taylor	1936-39	37	4	48
"Sos" Taylor	1911-24	276	36	108
Tim Taylor	1907-23	294	97	295
Tim Taylor	2001-04	0+2	-	-
A Tearle	1921	1	-	-
JL Tebbutt	1927	1	-	-
Rob Tebbutt	1981-91	153+3	28	112
Harry Terrington	1947-50	31	2	22
Harry Thacker	2012-14	2+2	1	5
Troy Thacker	1988-93	47	5	20
A Thomas	1897	1	-	-
Alf Thomas	1911-12	6	2	6
David Thomas	1923-24	6	-	-
David Thomas	1982	2	-	-
DW Thomas	1893	1	-	-
Godfrey Thomas	1920-21	19	5	18
Gwyn Thomas	1937	8	3	9
Haydn Thomas	1945-53	104+1	38	117
John Thomas	1909	1	-	-
Mike Thomas	1974	7	2	8
S Thomas	1923	1	-	-
Thomas	1896	1	-	-
Bill Thompson	1946-50	16	1	3
CF Thompson	1893	1	-	-
Charles Thompson	1904	1	-	-
J Thompson	1908	2	-	-
John Thompson	1955-61	166	2	6
WE Thompson	1898-00	17	1	3
William Thompson	1926-32	13	-	-
Adam Thompstone	2012-14	37+7	13	65
Arthur Thomson	1895	1	1	3
James Thomson	1911-12	3	-	-
Eric Thorneloe	1919	7	-	-
Peter Thorneloe	1945-57	221	11	33
Trevor Thorneloe	1919-30	125	8	71
Peter Thornley	1987-88	28	8	32
DL Thornton	1932	1	-	-
John Thornton	1920	2	1	3
Charles Thorpe	1893	1	-	-
Richard Thorpe	2012-13	6+4	-	-
Tom Tierney	2002-04	15+13	1	5
Charles Timlock	1898-03	4	-	-
GE Timms	1913-14	25	10	30
Bob Timson	1949	5	-	-
Timson	1907	1	-	-
NJ Tindall	1932-34	5	3	9
Richard Toach	1929	1	-	-
Daniel Todman	1929	1	-	-
Harry Toews	1998-99	6+1	-	-
Herbert Toft	1935	1	-	-
Peter Tom	1963-68	130	7	21
Ian Tomalin	1977	1	-	-
FM Tomlin	1934	5	-	-
Greig Tonks	2009	1	-	-
A Toone	1955	1	-	-
Freddy Toone	1892-93	22	5	10
Guy Toone	1936	4	-	-
H Toone	1903-04	5	-	-
Harry Topham	1885-86	3	-	-
James Touhey	1893-94	48	7	19
Franck Tournaire	2002-03	15+10	1	5
Allan Towell	1947-50	93	12	52
Stuart Towns	1992	0+1	-	-
JW Townsend	1929-30	3	-	-
Noel Townsend	1934-35	6	1	3
FB Traders	1929	1	-	-
J Trebley	1881	1	-	-

NAME	CAREER	APPS	TRIES	PTS
Glynmor Treharne	1938-39	12	6	18
Chris Tressler	1980-92	262+2	14	56
Dave Truman	1971-73	14	1	4
Geoff Tucker	1949	5	1	3
R Tucker	1966	1	-	-
Ronnie Tudor	1946-50	73	-	-
Alesana Tuilagi	2004-12	129+33	63	315
Andy Tuilagi	2005	0+1	-	-
Freddie Tuilagi	2000-06	72+10	16	80
Henry Tuilagi	2003-07	26+26	8	40
Manusamoa Tuilagi	2008-14	65+7	24	120
Vavae Tuilagi	2008	0+1	-	-
Lote Tuqiri	2009-10	15+1	3	15
F Turnbull	1921	1	-	-
W Turnbull	1928	1	-	-
Arthur Turner	1880-90	25	1	1
Jim Turner	1957	5	-	-
Fleckney Turney	1923-28	3	-	-
Billy Twelvetrees	2008-12	36+11	11	305
John Twigg	1913-14	37	2	6
E Tyler	1882-85	7	-	-
Frank Tyler	1891	1	-	-
Henry Tyler	1928-30	12	2	6

U

NAME	CAREER	APPS	TRIES	PTS
Daniel Underwood	1905-06	21	5	19
Rory Underwood	1983-97	230+6	134	580
Tony Underwood	1988-95	92	57	252
Lynn Ungoed-Thomas	1931	8	2	6
Mark Upex	1990	3	-	-
Bob Usher	1921-24	69	5	15
Herbert Usher	1921-22	10	-	-

V

NAME	CAREER	APPS	TRIES	PTS
George Vallance	1930-39	200	27	104
Jaco van der Westhuyzen	2003-04	18	11	63
Fritz van Heerden	1997-00	62+5	6	30
Tom Varndell	2004-09	88+25	65	325
Harold Varnish	1938	1	-	-
Gordon Vears	1919-21	85	6	18
Percy Venables	1931	7	-	-
Bernard Vesty	1947	1	-	-
Phil Vesty	1972-75	47	-	-
Sam Vesty	2002-10	122+42	15	250
Reg Vine	1936	1	-	-
Edward Vity	1894	32	5	15
William Voakes	1899-02	9	2	6
J Voce	1886	5	1	1
J Voss	1902-06	3	-	-
Marika Vunibaka	1997	1	3	15

W

NAME	CAREER	APPS	TRIES	PTS
EC Wackett	1924	1	-	-
David Waddell	1912-13	11	2	6
Dean Waddingham	1980-85	21+2	-	-
Mike Wade	1955-67	166	27	87
Sidney Wade	1937-38	4	-	-
Charles Wainwright	1881-84	30	1	1
Ken Wait	1938	1	-	-
Wavell Wakefield	1921-24	29	10	30
Charles Waldock	1924-25	7	1	3
Thomas Waldrom	2010-14	85+28	20	100
Arthur Wale	1880-85	68	6	9
H Wale	1907	1	-	-
Charles Wales	1923-25	3	-	-
David Walker	1933	4	-	-
George Walker	1880-81	5	-	-
George Walker	1896	4	1	3
Joseph Walker	1895	1	-	-
Mike Walker	1956-66	216	3	9
"Ranji" Walker	1935-36	8	3	9
Tim Walker	1983-85	4+4	1	4
Billy Wallace	1923-29	10	11	33
Wallace	1890	1	-	2
Tim Walley	1974-79	30	2	8
J Walsh	1889	1	-	-
Field Walton	1964-68	139	3	9
George Walton	1972	1	-	-
Katie Walton	1901	1	-	-
Anthony Ward	1952	2	-	-
E Ward	1906	1	-	-
Ernest Ward	1921	5	-	-
George Ward	1893	1	-	-
George Ward	1902	1	-	-
George Ward	1910-26	361	21	63
Leonard Ward	1889-92	70	15	102
"Puggy" Ward	1929-38	43	1	3
Richard Ward	1929	1	-	-
W Ward	1914-19	2	-	-
D Wardrop	1923	2	1	3
Richard Wareham	1990-92	7+2	-	-
EJ Warner	1945	2	-	-
PA Warner	1934	1	-	-
Robert Warner	1880-83	10	1	1
Roger Warren	2004-05	1+2	-	7
W Warren	1882	1	-	-
Alan Warwood	1988-92	27	4	16
Charles Watchorn	1901-09	65	4	12
W Waterfield	1929	2	-	-
Sidney Waterman	1911	1	-	-
Jack Waters	1933	1	-	-
Ernie Watkin	1938-48	117	2	236
J Watkins	1912	1	-	-
Trevor Watkiss	1960	1	-	-
Henry Watney	1922	1	-	-
Bob Watson	1970-75	70	5	20
Dickie Watson	1900	3	-	-
Jamie Watson	1903-14	229	46	140
W Watson	1912	1	-	-
William Watson	1884	1	-	-
Charlie Watts	1891-96	44	11	33
Jim Watts	1973	2	-	-
L Watts	1928	2	-	-
William Watts	1880-81	6	1	1
William Watts	1914-23	70	29	87
Willie Watts	1890-93	52	11	28
Al Wayte	1924	1	-	-
Dave Webb	1977	1	-	-
Elliot Webb	1998	1+1	-	-
Nick Webb	1997	0+1	-	-
Bob Weighill	1950	8	-	-
Gary Weinberg	1972-73	6	3	12
John Welborn	1999	7+1	-	-
FS Wells	1923-25	13	4	12
Harry Wells	2013-14	1+5	1	5
John Wells	1982-97	360+7	50	208
Jock Wemyss	1926	1	-	-
Marco Wentzel	2007-09	28+16	-	-
Dorian West	1988-04	152+57	34	169
F West	1931	1	-	-
Chris Weston	1947	1	-	-
Tom Weston	1907	1	-	-
Charles Wetherell	1899	1	-	-
Reginald Wetton	1924	2	-	-
Frank Wheeler	1881	1	-	-
Joe Wheeler	2005	0+1	-	-
Peter Wheeler	1969-85	349	66	589
William Wheeler	1880-89	26	-	8
David Whetstone	1896-01	62	5	15
Dave Whibley	1970-73	45	3	379
Martin Whitcombe	1981-86	64+4	8	32
A White	1910-11	2	-	-
Bob White	1988	3	-	-
Chalkie White	1957-63	147	6	18
GA White	1938-39	3	-	6
GR White	1930-31	19	7	21
John White	1959	1	-	-
John White	1962-65	2	-	14
John White	1975-80	73	15	60
Julian White	2003-12	120+38	4	20
Toby White	1993-94	4+2	-	-
White	1888	1	-	-
Alan Whitehall	1968	2	-	-
Arthur Whitehead	1880-85	33	2	2
Chris Whitehead	2006	0+1	-	-
Monty Whitehead	1895-01	146	20	60
John Whitehurst	1892	8	-	-
Herbert Whitley	1926	1	1	3
John Wickson	1920-23	16	3	9
Kilgour Wiener	1929-32	101	3	9
Brian Wigley	1959	14	4	12
Dave Wigley	1991-95	19+2	6	40
Steve Wigley	1990-93	4	2	8
Vic Wigley	1969-71	4	-	-
W Wilby	1892	2	-	-
JH Wilcock	1888-90	5	2	2
Stephen Wilcock	1957	1	-	-
Kelvin Wilford	1979-80	1+4	-	-
Ian Wilkie	1963-65	8	1	3
Gilbert Wilkins	1919-23	4	1	3
WC Wilkins	1921-24	50	20	60
B Wilkinson	1885-90	43	7	7
Edwin Wilkinson	1900-03	12	2	6
Harry Wilkinson	1895-05	233	153	489
Henry Wilkinson	1892-94	37	6	16
J Wilkinson	1909-14	19	1	10
J Wilkinson	1919-22	97	-	169
JS Wilkinson	1886-89	19	1	1
Thomas Wilks	1890	4	-	-
Graham Willars	1959-87	334+4	38	129
J Willcox	1919	1	-	-
Mike Willcox	1963-64	4	-	-
Rodney Willcox	1935-37	41	6	18
William Willey	1888-89	12	3	3
Aneurin Williams	1938	2	-	-
Bob Williams	1973	1	-	-
CH Williams	1929-35	19	3	9
D Williams	1892-93	19	4	8
David Williams	1979-83	13+4	8	32
E Williams	1935-36	3	-	-
Frank Williams	1937	1	-	-
Gareth Williams	1983-84	2	-	-
George Williams	1929-31	7	2	6
GF Williams	1935	1	-	-
Glyn Williams	1958	7	3	9
Ivor Williams	1924	1	-	-
JR Williams	1950	1	-	-
Kevin Williams	1979-87	186+5	64	256
Owen Williams	2013-14	16+8	-	187
Pete Williams	1999	1	-	-
Rhys Williams	2014	0+1	-	-
WA Williamson	1889	5	-	-
Ken Willis	1938-39	3	-	-
Steve Wills	1990-95	19+8	8	93
Brent Wilson	2006	1	2	10
G Wilson	1913-14	25	-	-
Thomas Wilson	1907	5	2	6
Walter Wilson	1909-10	5	1	3
Jim Wingham	1993-97	16+4	4	20
Oscar Wingham	1994-99	29+12	4	20
Sydney Wolfe	1914	10	-	-
Frank Wood	1920-30	69	26	85
GH Wood	1929-30	6	2	6
Jon Wood	1985	1	-	-
Kenneth Wood	1906-19	121	33	115
"Pedlar" Wood	1906-22	388	102	336
Danny Woodford	1903-04	2	-	-
Frederick Woodford	1896	1	-	-
L Woodhead	1920	1	-	-
Ben Woods	2008-12	47+23	5	25
A Woodward	1902	3	-	-
Clive Woodward	1979-85	148	43	195
Archie Woodyatt	1894-99	22	7	27
Jim Woollerton	1909	1	-	-
Gordon Wooller	1936-37	2	-	-
J Woolley	1918-19	6	-	-
John Woolley	1958	5	-	-
Jack Wormleighton	1932-37	121	3	9
Christopher Worsley-Worswick	1905-06	2	1	3
Edward Worthington	1880-86	14	-	-
William Wotherspoon	1889-91	18	-	-
David Wraith	1993	0+1	-	-
Mark Wrench	1961	5	-	-
A Wright	1906	5	-	-
Alex Wright	2004-06	0+3	1	5
David Wright	1990	3	2	8
Frederick Wright	1922-23	38	11	33
George Wright	1923	1	-	-
L Wright	1907-08	3	-	-
"Mamma" Wright	1887-88	5	-	-
RE Wright	1933	1	-	-
Sam Wright	1889-90	3	-	-
Steven Wright	1949	5	-	-
SW Wright	1896	2	-	-
Ben Wyer-Roberts	1997-98	1+2	-	-
Ernest Wykes	1895-04	21	-	-
Sid Wykes	1890-92	25	1	1
Alfred Wyman	1934	1	-	-
Jim Wyness	1967	1	-	-
Charles Wynne	1913-24	7	7	21
Ernest Wynne	1914	7	1	3
Owen Wynne	1890-93	34	-	3

Y

NAME	CAREER	APPS	TRIES	PTS
Mike Yandle	1969-73	155	29	101
Arthur Yarnell	1926-27	2	-	2
George Yeld	1900-08	69	1	52
Samuel Yeomans	1897-98	7	-	-
William Yiend	1895-96	10	2	6
Norman York	1933-38	46	2	109
Jack Yorke	1890-93	70	5	7
AJ Young	1893	1	-	-
Dave Young	2005-08	4+10	-	-
Jeff Young	1972	1	1	4
Lawrence Young	1880-84	37	6	6
Micky Young	2011-13	6+11	-	-
Wilfred Young	1937-39	38	13	47
George Younger	1924	1	-	-
Ben Youngs	2007-14	105+38	24	140
Nick Youngs	1981-88	145	71	284
Tom Youngs	2006-14	52+21	6	30

Z

NAME	CAREER	APPS	TRIES	PTS
Danny Zaltzman	1999	2+1	-	-

Tigers' Encyclopædia

A & B INTERNATIONALS

Listed below are all the Tigers players who have appeared for a country's second team, showing their debut year and number of games whilst playing their rugby for Leicester:

ENGLAND 'B' & 'A' (37)

1978	Steve Johnson
1979	Clive Woodward, Dave Forfar
1985	Barry Evans(4)
1988	John Wells(4), Peter Thornley
1989	Tony Underwood(18)
1990	John Liley(4)
1992	Neil Back(23), Martin Johnson(6), Steve Hackney(9), Aadel Kardooni(6)
1993	Stuart Potter(15), Darren Garforth(15), Dean Richards, Graham Rowntree(5)
1995	Jez Harris(2), Richard Cockerill(6)
1996	Will Greenwood(8), Rob Liley(2), Austin Healey(2)
1997	Dorian West(5), Martin Corry(7)
1999	Leon Lloyd(7), Tim Stimpson(2), Paul Gustard(5)
2000	Ben Kay(6)
2001	Andy Goode(6), Will Johnson(6), Lewis Moody(2), Ricky Nebbett(4)
2002	Adam Balding, Steve Booth(2)
2003	Ollie Smith(8)
2004	George Chuter(6), Louis Deacon(5), Harry Ellis(1)

ENGLAND SAXONS (19)

2006	Tom Varndell(6), Sam Vesty(5), James Buckland(3)
2007	Tom Croft(2), Jordan Crane(14)
2008	Richard Blaze(2),
2009	Matt Smith(2), Ben Woods(3), Dan Cole(3)
2010	Anthony Allen(3), Geoff Parling(2), Ben Youngs
2011	Manu Tuilagi(2), Billy Twelvetrees(7)
2012	Ed Slater(3), Thomas Waldrom
2013	Kieran Brookes(2), George Ford(2), Graham Kitchener(2)
2014	Adam Thompstone

IRELAND 'A' (8)

1995	Niall Malone(3)
1996	Eric Miller(2)
2000	Geordan Murphy(6)
2006	Leo Cullen(3), Shane Jennings(6)
2007	Ian Humphreys
2008	Johne Murphy(9), Frank Murphy(5)

EMERGING IRELAND (1)

2013	Niall Morris (3)

SCOTLAND 'A' (3)

1998	Craig Joiner(8)
2006	Jim Hamilton
2008	Dave Young(3)

WALES 'B' & 'A' (2)

1981	Kevin Williams(2)
1995	Diccon Edwards(2)

ABANDONED

The following nine matches did not reach the final whistle, but in all instances the result stood:

5.11.1881	at Kettering, Leicester left the field 5 minutes early because of a dispute over a try; Draw 0-0
9.2.1884	v Kettering, both teams left the field due to numerous disputes; Won 1G-0
2.4.1887	at Nottingham, Leicester left the field because of a dispute over a try; Lost 1T-1G & 3T
31.10.1896	at Old Edwardians, abandoned after 66 minutes due to bad light; Won 8-3
5.4.1947	at Bristol, abandoned after 64 minutes due to mud and rain; Lost 0-6
18.2.1977	v CASG Paris, abandoned after 69 minutes due to rain; Won 28-4
18.9.1985	at Birmingham, abandoned after 70 minutes due to bad light; Won 33-6
19.1.1996	v Bedford, abandoned after 70 minutes due to floodlight failure, Won 38-13
25.1.2014	at Harlequins, abandoned with 9m 52s left because an advertising hoarding blew off the roof of the stand on to the field of play; Lost 6-20 ●

↑ Steve Johnson, the Tigers' first England B international.

ACADEMY

The Tigers Academy effectively began in 1996 and started by taking over responsibility for the Youth team which had originally been formed in 1971, and the under-21 side formed in 1991. In 1998 the under-17 Academy was introduced, playing their first match as a team against their counterparts from Swansea at St Helens on 8 May 1999, winning 3-0 in appalling conditions. The under-16 Academy began in the summer of 1999 and played their first game at Saracens on 7 May 2000. The under-14 and under-15 Academies were introduced in the summer of 2000.

The Academy has seen the following 20 players go on to become full internationals, although seven of those have been first capped whilst they were at other clubs. The list shows the country and total number of caps:

Jim Hamilton (Scotland 56)
Dan Cole (England 45, Lions 3)
*Chris Wyles (USA 44)
Tom Croft (England 38, Lions 5)
Ben Youngs (England 38, Lions 2)
Louis Deacon, 29
Harry Ellis (England 27, Lions 1)
Manusamoa Tuilagi (England 25, Lions 1)
Tom Youngs (England 17, Lions 3)
Andy Goode, 17
*Billy Twelvetrees (England 14, Lions 0)
Dan Hipkiss, 13
Ollie Smith (England 5, Lions 1)
Tom Varndell, 4
*Phil Christophers, 3
*Tom Ryder (Scotland 2)
*George Ford, 2
Sam Vesty, 2
*Greig Tonks (Scotland 1)
* Kieran Brookes, 2

** capped whilst at other clubs. England unless stated.*
115 Academy members have gone on to play rugby for the Tigers first-team. The Academy is based at Oval Park in Oadby, which was opened in September 1992.

Academy manager Neil McCarthy in his England playing days.

ACADEMY STAFF

Below are all the senior coaching and administration staff, their roles and years in the Academy:

Name	*Role*	*Years*
Tosh Askew	Assistant academy manager	2010-
Neil Back	Head coach	2005-2007
Teresa Carrington	Academy Administrator	1999-
Lewis Clifford	Education & Welfare Officer	2013-
Ruth Cross	Physiotherapist	1995-2005
Brett Deacon	Coach	2013-
Paul Dodge	Backs coach	1998-2005
	Player development coach	2005-2008
Carl Douglas	Elite performance coach	2006-2007
Robin Eager	Sports scientist	2011-
Malcolm Foulkes-Arnold	Second-row coach	1998-2002
Glenn Gelderbloom	Coach	2003-
Ged Glynn	Chief scout	2010-
Dusty Hare	Rugby development co-ordinator	1994-2005
	Assistant academy manager	2005-2006
	Chief scout	2006-2010
Mike Harrison	Education & welfare officer	2005-2013
Andy Key	Head of rugby development	1998-2007
Steve Kenney	Scrum-half coach	1998-2002
John Liley	Coach	1999-2002
Jackie Limna	Physiotherapist	2004-2006
Peter Lowe	Youth team coach	1998
Neil McCarthy	Academy manager	2008-
Kevin MacDonald	Youth team coach	1998-1999
Jim McKay	Assistant academy manager	2009-2010
Alex Martin	Strength & conditioning coach	2006-2007
Patrick Mortimer	Strength & conditioning coach	2004-2007
Mike Penistone	Skills & defence coach	2001-2005
	Player development coach	2005-2006
Stuart Redfern	Forwards coach	1998-2004
Graham Rowntree	Specialist coach	2006-2007
Ian Smith	Coach	1998-2002
Tom Smith	Forwards coach	1998-2005
	Player development coach	2005-2008
Troy Thacker	Coach	1999-
Chris Tombs	Strength & conditioning coach	2003-2004
Matt Williams	Development coach	2013-

AGE

YOUNGEST PLAYERS

Age	*Name*	*Opponent*	*Date*
16y 52d	Martinus Swain	Harlequins	28.12.1895
16y 175d	John Cramphorn	Rugby BTH	15.9.1926
16y 237d	George Ford	Leeds	8.11.2009 ●
16y+	Samuel Yeomans	Old Edwardians	30.10.1897
17y 7d	Manu Tuilagi	Classic All Blacks	25.5.2008
17y+	John Raven	Cardiff	28.11.1925

The youngest points scorer was **George Ford** who kicked two conversions in the above game.

The youngest try scorer is **Charles Wynne,** just a month after his 17th birthday against Birkenhead Park at Welford Road on 26 December 1913, whilst the very next day he became the youngest hat-trick scorer against Jed-Forest.

The youngest try scorer since the war was **Paul Dodge** who was 17y 206d in the game at Mountain Ash on 20 September 1975, whilst the youngest try scorer in the professional era was **Alex Wright** 17y 254d against the Barbarians on 3 March 2004.

The youngest skipper of all time was **Chris Johnson** against Cambridge University on 26 November 1994 aged 21 years 187 days.

YOUNGEST & OLDEST TEAMS

The youngest starting line-up ever was the one selected to face the Classic All Blacks at Welford Road on 25 May 2008 with the starting line-up having an average age of just 21 years 162 days. Seven of the side were teenagers including the entire three-quarter line and full-back, whilst two of these (**Manu Tuilagi** and **Calum Green**) were only 17 years of age. The elder statesman was hooker **George Chuter** who was almost 32, over five years older than the next oldest – skipper **Brett Deacon**.

The oldest team the Tigers ever fielded was the side which lost to London Wasps 24-36 in the Premiership at Loftus Road on 31 March 2002 at an average age of 30 years 251 days. Ten of the side were over 30 with the eldest being **Darren Garforth** just nine days shy of his 36th birthday, the youngest was wing **Steve Booth** at 25y 194d.

TEENAGERS

Just five teenagers have played over 50 games before their 20th birthday, **Paul Dodge** (91), **Ralph Buckingham** (83), **Ted Flewitt** (63), **George Banks** and **Paddy Swain** (56).

The most tries by a player still in his teens is **Ralph Buckingham** (42), **Ted Flewitt** (35) and **Paul Dodge** (21).

The most points scored by a teenager is **George Ford** with 263 in 36 matches, followed by **Paul Dodge** (170), **Marcus Rose** (164), **Ralph Buckingham** (130) **and Ted Flewitt** (107).

Paddy Swain, one of only five Tigers to have played 50 games before his 20th birthday.

OLDEST PLAYERS

Age	*Name*	*Opponent*	*Date*
47y 135d	Graham Willars	Waterloo	4.4.1987
46y+	Jesse Ball	Belgrave St Peters	11.3.1899
40y 291d	George Ward	Northern	4.1.1926
39y 149d	Peter Wheeler	Moseley	23.4.1988
39y+	Jimmy Allen	Nuneaton	12.4.1921
38y 295d	Julian White	Gloucester	4.3.2012
38y 297d	Rex Skelton	New Brighton	2.5.1970
38y 244d	Bob Rowell	Northern	29.4.1978
38y 191d	Denis Bolesworth	Coventry	12.3.1955
38y 132d	Arthur Jones	Birkenhead Park	26.12.1910

The oldest points scorer was **Jesse Ball** with a conversion in the above game, whilst he was also the oldest try scorer aged 42 against Wortley on 4 April 1896. The oldest try scorer since the war was **Bob Rowell** against Wakefield on 22 January 1977 aged 37y 146d. The oldest in the professional era was **Mefin Davies** against Bath on 26 September 2009 aged 37y 24d.

The oldest player on debut is **Alf Brice** who against Headingley on 1 January, 1909 was 37 years 100 days old, whilst the oldest debut in the professional era was **Jason Spice** aged 35y 333d against Harlequins on 5 November 2010.

George Ward was the oldest captain, who was 39 years and 12 days old when the led the Tigers at Nuneaton on 31 March 1924. The oldest on his debut as skipper was **Bob Rowell** at 36 years 113 days against Harlequins on 20 December 1975 on his 295th appearance for the first-team.

OVER 35s

Just two players have appeared in 100 matches AFTER their 35th birthday: **George Ward** (179) and **Bob Rowell** (111).

The most tries scored by anyone aged over 35 is **Neil Back** with 17, followed by **Dusty Hare** (13) and **Jimmy Allen** (11), whilst **Dusty Hare** is the only one to have scored over 500 points after 35, tallying 649 in 50 matches.

AGE GROUP

All players capped for their country at Under-20 or Under-21 level whilst playing at the Tigers, showing the number of appearances.

ENGLAND UNDER-21 (39)

1989	Matt Poole(3)
1990	Graham Rowntree(5)
1991	Laurence Boyle, Martin Johnson, Steve Wills(3)
1993	Chris Johnson(4)
1995	Simon Binns(3), James Overend(2)
1996	Matt Jones
1997	Michael Horak(4), Leon Lloyd(10), Lewis Moody(10)
1998	Adam Balding(14), Elliot Webb
2000	Andy Goode(10), James Grindal(15), Peter Short(5), Mark Meenan
2001	Louis Deacon(3)
2002	Harry Ellis(3), Adam Billig(7), James Buckland(9), Jim Hamilton(4), Michael Holford(17), Ollie Smith(2), Sam Vesty(5)
2003	Peter Cook(5), Dan Hipkiss(5), John Holtby(2), Tim Taylor(3)
2004	Stuart Friswell(9), Luke Myring(3), Will Skinner(8)
2005	Ross Broadfoot(3), Matt Cornwell(18), Matt Hampson(4), Tom Ryder(4), Tom Varndell(10)
2006	Tom Croft(9)

ENGLAND UNDER-20 (21)

2007	Dan Cole(3), Ollie Dodge(4), Alex Shaw(4), Tom Youngs(4)
2008	Greg Gillanders(4), Greig Tonks(9), Ben Youngs(15)
2009	Jack Cobden(4), Sam Harrison(12), Will Hurrell(9)
2010	Andy Forsyth(6), Calum Green(8)
2011	Ryan Bower(4), Matt Everard(10), George Ford(11)
2012	Tom Price(10)
2013	Henry Purdy(18), Harry Wells(6)
2014	Will Owen(2), Harry Rudkin(4), Harry Thacker(4), George Catchpole(2)

IRELAND UNDER-21 (3)

1993	Eric Miller
1999	Geordan Murphy(5)
2001	Neil McMillan(2)

ITALY UNDER-20 (1)

2013	Tiziano Pasquali(4)

SCOTLAND UNDER-21 (3)

2002	James Henry(9)
2005	David Young(13)
2006	Ian Nimmo(18)

SCOTLAND UNDER-20 (1)

2013	Scott Steele(9)

CANADA UNDER-20 (1)

2009	Seb Pearson(5)

SAMOA UNDER-20 (1)

2008	Vavae Tuilagi(5)

↑ David Matthews, the only player to have made 500 appearances for the first-team.

APPEARANCES

350 OR MORE APPEARANCES FOR TIGERS

Pos	*Name*	*Career*	*Apps*	*Starts*	*Rep*
1	David Matthews	1955/56-1973/74	502	502	-
2	Sid Penny	1895/96-1910/11	491	491	-
3	John Allen	1960/61-1975/76	457	457	-
4	Doug Norman	1919/20-1932/33	453	453	-
5	Paul Dodge	1975/76-1992/93	437	434	3
6	Graham Rowntree	1990/91-2006/07	398	362	36
7	Dusty Hare	1976/77-1988/89	394	393	1
8	Pedlar Wood	1906/07-1922/23	388	388	-
9	Garry Adey	1966/67-1980/81	381	381	-
10	John Wells	1982/83-1997/98	367	360	7
11=	Steve Kenney	1975/76-1989/90	365	361	4
	Les Cusworth	1978/79-1989/90	365	365	-
13	Martin Johnson	1988/89-2004/05	362	348	14
14	George Ward	1909/10-1925/26	361	361	-
15	Jacky Braithwaite	1895/96-1906/07	359	359	-
16	Billy Foreman	1893/94-1905/06	358	358	-
17	Bob Rowell	1961/62-1977/78	355	355	-

MOST GAMES FOR TIGERS IN A COMPETITION...

MIDLAND COUNTIES CUP

Sid Penny	40
Billy Foreman	34
Jacky Braithwaite	34
Arthur Jones	33
Alf Butlin	27
Sammy Matthews	27

NATIONAL CUP

Paul Dodge	51
Dusty Hare	49
Dean Richards	48
John Wells	45
Les Cusworth	45
Darren Garforth	41
Peter Wheeler	40

ANGLO-WELSH CUP

George Chuter	19
Boris Stankovich	19
Ben Kay	17
Matt Smith	17
Dan Hipkiss	16
Julian White	16

LEAGUE/PREMIERSHIP

Name	*Lg*	*Prem*	*Total*
Graham Rowntree	84	150	234
Martin Johnson	86	139	225
Neil Back	82	128	210
Darren Garforth	97	109	206
Geordan Murphy	-	205	205
George Chuter	-	194	194
Martin Corry	-	181	181
Ben Kay	-	177	177
Louis Deacon	-	174	174
Austin Healey	18	148	166
Leon Lloyd	9	155	164
Richard Cockerill	76	88	164

Geordan Murphy became the 35th Tiger to play in 300 games, against Newcastle 25.2.2012.

EUROPE

Geordan Murphy	74
Martin Corry	69
Louis Deacon	68
Ben Kay	65
George Chuter	61
Graham Rowntree	59
Lewis Moody	55
Austin Healey	53
Martin Johnson	51
Leon Lloyd	50

PLAYING 300TH GAME

Pos	*Name*	*Opponents*	*Date*	*Age*	
1	Billy Foreman	v Plymouth	27.9.1902	33y 43d	
2	Jacky Braithwaite	v Cardiff	7.1.1905	31y 261d	
3	Sid Penny	v Moseley	11.2.1905	29y 127d	
4	Sammy Matthews	v Coventry	19.1.1907	28y 353d	
5	Pedlar Wood	v Royal Navy	13.9.1919	33y 220d	
6	George Ward	v Nuneaton	27.10.1923	38y 222d	
7	Percy Lawrie	v Birkenhead Park	26.12.1923	35y 91d	
8	Doug Norman	v Bedford	24.11.1928	31y 165d	
9	Ralph Buckingham	at Harlequins	1.12.1934	27y 320d	
10	Denis Bolesworth	v Barbarians	26.12.1952	36y 115d	
11	Tom Bleasdale	v Newport	11.2.1961	30y 247d	
12	Frank Chawner	v Bristol	15.12.1962	35y 157d	
13	David Matthews	at Coventry	12.3.1966	28y 329d	
14	John Allen	at Moseley	17.2.1971	28y 203d	
15	Graham Willars	at Bath	6.1.1973	33y 47d	
16	Bob Rowell	at Rosslyn Park	24.1.1976	36y 148d	
17	Bleddyn Jones	at Richmond	8.10.1977	29y 62d	
18	Garry Adey	v Royal Navy	1.1.1978	32y 233d	
19	Bob Barker	v Rosslyn Park (r2)	25.2.1978	33y 125d	●
20	John Duggan	at Rosslyn Park	29.4.1980	31y 328d	
21	Peter Wheeler	v Barbarians	20.4.1982	33y 145d	
22	Brian Hall	v Newport	12.2.1983	36y 44d	
23	Paul Dodge	v Barbarians	28.12.1985	27y 305d	
24	Dusty Hare	v Oxford University	22.10.1986	33y 327d	
25	Steve Kenney	at London Scottish	7.2.1987	30y 167d	●
26	Les Cusworth	at Ballymena	2.4.1988	33y 273d	
27	Ian Smith	at Moseley	8.4.1989	31y 133d	●
28	Stuart Redfern	at Oxford University	22.10.1991	30y 128d	
29	John Wells	at Harlequins	15.10.1994	31y 156d	●
30	Dean Richards	v Barbarians	25.2.1997	33y 229d	
31	Darren Garforth	v Perpignan	3.11.2001	35y 208d	●
32	Graham Rowntree	v Leinster (qf)	27.1.2002	30y 284d	●
33	Martin Johnson	v Bristol	8.2.2003	32y 336d	●
34	Neil Back	v Stade Français	31.1.2004	35y 14d	●
35	Geordan Murphy	v Newcastle	25.2.2012	33y 312d	●

219 different players have made over one hundred first-team appearances, 89 went on to complete 200 games, and the above 35 made the 300 club.

Most wins tallied by any player in his first 300 games is 233 by **Martin Johnson**, followed by **Les Cusworth** (230), **Darren Garforth** (227), **Dean Richards** (226) **Graham Rowntree** (225) and **Ian Smith** (224).

Pedlar Wood missed just 24 possible matches in reaching the 300 match milestone, whilst **Bleddyn Jones** missed only 35 games, **Sammy Matthews** 37**, Billy Foreman** 41 and **Sid Penny** 48, follow. **Dean Richards** missed 291 possible matches in attaining his personal 300.

The youngest person to make 300 appearances is **Paul Dodge** at 27 years 305 days, beating the 27y 320d age of **Ralph Buckingham** in 1934**.**

The most matches played for the club in the professional era is 322 by **Geordan Murphy**, followed by **Martin Corry** and **George Chuter** with 290 each.

PLAYING 400TH GAME

Pos	*Name*	*Opponents*	*Date*
1	Sid Penny	v Northampton	1.2.1908
2	Doug Norman	v Bath	5.9.1931
3	David Matthews	v Bath	4.1.1969
4	John Allen	at Cambridge University	10.11.1973
5	Paul Dodge	v Pontypridd	2.9.1989

PLAYING 500TH GAME

Pos	*Name*	*Opponents*	*Date*
1	David Matthews	v Northampton	23.2.1974

Note: Sid Penny was given an award for having appeared in 500 first-team games after his final match on Boxing Day 1910, however, subsequent research has revealed this was in fact only his 491st appearance.

BREAKING THE CLUB APPEARANCE RECORD

David Matthews broke **Sid Penny's** all-time club appearance record on 21 April 1973 with his 492nd match for the first-team. Below is a list of all the players who have held the all-time record and where and when they set the new landmark.

Name	*Game*	*Opponent*	*Date*
William Sheffield	16th	v Leamington	26.11.1881
John Parsons	99th	v Nottingham	14.1.1888
William Porter	113th	v Kettering	19.1.1889
Arthur McKechnie	169th	v Handsworth	20.2.1892
Billy Foreman	216th	v Coventry	14.10.1899
Sid Penny	359th	at Northampton	1.12.1906
David Matthews	492nd	at Broughton Park	21.4.1973

SUCCESSIVE APPEARANCES

109	David Matthews	14.1.1961 to 7.12.1963
103	John Thompson	3.4.1956 to 29.11.1958
75	Rex Skelton	27.12.1957 to 5.12.1959
74	Frank Chawner	21.10.1961 to 30.10.1963
70	Doug Norman	11.1.1930 to 28.11.1931
70	Peter Edwards	7.12.1963 to 15.9.1965
68	Alf Butlin	28.12.1897 to 30.9.1899
68	Jacky Braithwaite	3.11.1900 to 11.10.1902

James Bainbridge made his only 41 appearances for the club consecutively from 3 April 1937 to 19 April 1938.

Sammy Matthews played in 127 out of 128 possible games between 19 April 1902 and 9 December 1905, only missing the game at Swansea on 30 January1904, making sequences of 63 and 64 successive games. **Denis Bolesworth** is the only other player with two separate sequences of fifty or more consecutive games in a career.

BETWEEN APPEARANCES

The longest gap between matches is 10 years 218 days by **DB Glover** who made his 3rd appearance away at Cardiff on 26 February 1927 and his 4th at home to Coventry on 2 October 1937. He scored a try in the Cardiff match and then did not add another until crossing against Bath at Welford Road on 19 March 1938 – 11 years and 21 days between tries.

In modern times the greatest gap between first-team games was 7 years 144 days by **James Grindal**, playing his 29th match at Bristol on 5 May 2002 and then his 30th at Bath on 26 September 2009 after he rejoined the club.

LONG CAREERS

Graham Willars has the longest Tigers playing career, 27 years 169 days, during which time the Tigers played 1,154 first-team games, his final three appearances were all as a makeshift replacement. If however, you remove these Graham's career is still the longest at 18 years 194 days, just a week longer than **David Matthews'** career, and in terms of games is 787 against 779.

PLAYING TIME IN THE MOST DIFFERENT SEASONS

Making at least one first-team appearance in the following number of seasons:

20	Graham Willars	1959/60-1986/87
19*	David Matthews	1955/56-1973/74
17*	Peter Wheeler	1969/70-1985/86
17*	Paul Dodge	1975/76-1992/93
17*	Dean Richards	1981/82-1997/98
17*	Graham Rowntree	1990/91-2006/07

** successive seasons*

Three players could have joined the above list had it not been for World Wars; **George Ward** and **Pedlar Wood** played in 14 separate seasons but missed the three complete seasons when the Tigers did not play during the First World War, and **Denis Bolesworth** appeared in 14 seasons and then missed a possible five more during the Second World War.

Scrum-half **Pedlar Wood** had a remarkable career which saw him rack up 388 appearances for Leicester in a 17-year span between 1906-22, he then moved to Nuneaton and played a further 170 first-team games until making his final appearance for the Nuns at Coventry on 18 April 1927 aged 41 – that's almost 600 games over 21 years!

SHORT CAREERS

Sixteen players have appeared for less than ten minutes in a Tigers career, with five players' careers consisting of just one minute of playing time:

Name	*Opponents*	*Date*	*Tournament*
David Wraith	at Swansea	16.10.1993	
Clark Goodwin	at Cambridge University	26.11.1994	
Gareth Bowen	vs Rugby	6.1.1999	C&G Cup
Sam Joy	vs Rugby	6.1.1999	C&G Cup
Rob Conquest	at Leeds	8.11.2009	Anglo-Welsh Cup

ATTENDANCES

Average home attendance for league and Europe since the advent of leagues in 1987/88.

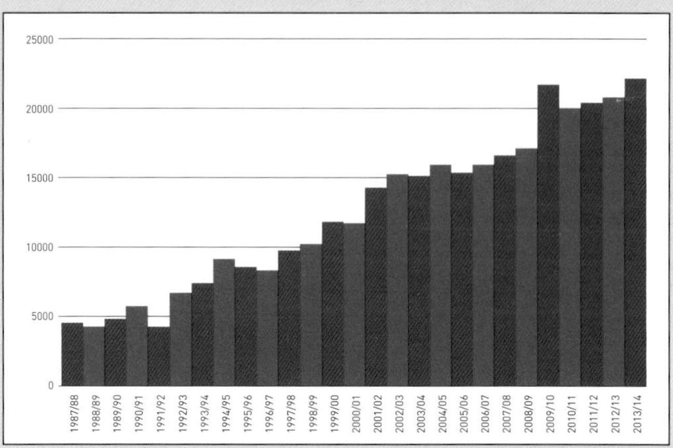

↑ Graham Rowntree made at least one appearance for the club in each of 17 successive seasons.

Chronological Highest Attendance to watch the Tigers

10,000	Old Edwardians	Belgrave Road Ground		21.2.1891	
12,000	Coventry	Welford Road		21.11.1896	
13,000	Northampton	Welford Road		20.11.1897	
15,000	Northampton	Welford Road		5.11.1898	
20,000	New Zealand	Welford Road		30.9.1905	
35,000	New Zealand	Welford Road		4.10.1924	
59,300	Bath	Twickenham	Pilkington Cup final	29.4.1989	●
68,000	Bath	Twickenham	Pilkington Cup final	7.5.1994	●
75,000	Bath	Twickenham	Pilkington Cup final	4.5.1996	●
81,076	London Wasps	Twickenham	Heineken Cup final	20.5.2007	●
81,600	London Wasps	Twickenham	Premiership final	31.5.2008	●
81,601	London Irish	Twickenham	Premiership final	16.5.2009	●
81,779	Harlequins	Twickenham	Premiership final	26.5.2012	●

Lowest Attendances

Leicester began playing in 1880 at the Belgrave Cricket & Cycle Ground and although enclosed and admission was charged it was felt that the ground was too far out of the town centre to attract crowds, so the club decided for forgo gate receipts and move to Victoria Park, the public park in the town in an attempt to build a following. Therefore technically all 59 home games played there between 1881-88 had a paid attendance of zero.

The clubs' official gate receipt books reveal the public's distinct lack of interest in rugby in the late 1960s and early 1970s where gates of less than 500 were commonplace. The low point was reached when Waterloo visited Welford Road on 2 December 1972 and there was a paid attendance (excluding members) of just 47 with a total gate receipt of only £7.60. The gate books reveal that only six turnstiles clicked at any stage with the 30 pence one having nine customers, the 25p one having eight, the 20p one having eight and the 10p turnstile having 22 fans.

The lowest attendance at Welford Road for a league game was 2,177 when Bath were the visitors on 22 April 1989. The smallest at the venue in the Premiership was 7,785 against Bristol on 23 October 1999, whilst in the Heineken Cup just 4,609 attended when the Scottish Borders made their trip on 19 October 1996.

AWARDS

LEAGUE/PREMIERSHIP AWARDS

Player of the Season: 1996/97 – Martin Johnson, 1997/98 – Neil Back, 1998/99 – Martin Johnson, 1999/2000 – Austin Healey, 2000/01 – Pat Howard, 2004/05 – Martin Corry, 2006/07 – Martin Castrogiovanni, 2012/13 - Tom Youngs.
Discovery of the Season: 2001/02 – Lewis Moody, 2004/05 – Ollie Smith, 2005/06 – Tom Varndell, 2009/10 – Ben Youngs, 2010/11 – Manu Tuilagi.
Director of Rugby of the Season: 2000/01 – Dean Richards, 2004/05 – John Wells, 2006/07 – Pat Howard, 2008/09 – Richard Cockerill.
Top Try Scorer: 1991/92 – Rory Underwood, 1998/99 – Neil Back, 2005/06 – Tom Varndell, 2007/08 – Tom Varndell, 2010/11 – Alesana Tuilagi, 2013/14 – Vereniki Goneva.
Golden Boot (Top Points Scorer): 1987/88 – Dusty Hare. 1989/90 – John Liley, 1991/92 – John Liley, 1993/94 – Jez Harris, 1995/96 – John Liley, 2003/04 – Andy Goode, 2004/05 – Andy Goode, 2007/08 – Andy Goode.
Try of the Season: 1996/97 – Austin Healey v Llanelli on 2 November 1996, 2012/13 - Dan Bowden v Saracens on 23 February 2013.
Dream Team Selections: 2000/01 (4) – Martin Johnson, Neil Back, Pat Howard, Geordan Murphy. 2001/02 (3) – Graham Rowntree, Ben Kay, Lewis Moody. 2004/05 (3) – Graham Rowntree, George Chuter, Andy Goode. 2005/06 (2) – Ben Kay, Tom Varndell. 2006/07 (3) – Martin Castrogiovanni, George Chuter, Harry Ellis. 2008/09 (2) – Marcos Ayerza, Ben Kay. 2009/10 (3) – Ben Youngs, Toby Flood, Scott Hamilton. 2010/11 (3) – Thomas Waldrom, Anthony Allen, Manu Tuilagi. 2011/12 (5) – Dan Cole, Geoff Parling, Toby Flood, Horacio Agulla, Alesana Tuilagi. 2012/13 (8) – Tom Youngs, Dan Cole, Ed Slater, Geoff Parling, Julian Salvi, Ben Youngs, Toby Flood, Manu Tuilagi. 2013/14 (2) – Vereniki Goneva, Logovi'i Mulipola
Hall of Fame Inductees: 2012/13 - Martin Castrogiovanni, Richard Cockerill, Martin Corry, Austin Healey, Pat Howard, Dean Richards, John Wells, 2013/14 - Martin Johnson, Lewis Moody, George Chuter.

Neil Back won the Rugby Players' Association award for Players' Player of the Season in 1998/99.

RUGBY PLAYERS' ASSOCIATION AWARDS

Players' Player of the Season: 1998/99 – Neil Back, 2004/05 – Martin Corry, 2010/11 – Thomas Waldrom, 2013/14 – Vereniki Goneva.
Young Player of the Season: 2004/05 – Harry Ellis, 2005/06 – Tom Varndell, 2009/10 – Ben Youngs, 2010/11 – Manu Tuilagi.
Try of the Season: 2006/07 – Tom Varndell v London Irish on 18 November 2006. 2012/13 – Ben Youngs v Bath on 21 April 2013.
Special Merit Award: 2003/04 – Martin Johnson, 2012/13 – Geordan Murphy.
Hall of Fame Inductees: 2002 – Dean Richards, 2003 – Peter Wheeler, 2007 – Martin Johnson.

IRB AWARDS

Junior Player of the Year: 2011 – George Ford.
Coach of the Year: 2003 – Clive Woodward (England).
Hall of Fame Inductees: 2009 – Tony O'Reilly, 2011 – Bob Dwyer, Martin Johnson, Clive Woodward. 2013 – Waisale Serevi.

RUGBY UNION WRITERS' CLUB AWARDS

Pat Marshall Memorial Award: 2001/02 – Martin Johnson.
Rupert Cherry Prize: 1981 – Chalkie White, 1982 – Chalkie White.
RUWC Special Award: 2003/04 – Clive Woodward.

➔ Charles Beamish became a Barbarian in 1934.

BARBARIANS

The official minute books of the Barbarians confirm precisely that the club was formed "at 2am on 9 April 1890 at the Alexandra Hotel in Bradford, by the members of a scratch team captained by **WP Carpmael**."

The following 92 players have appeared for the Barbarians whilst with the Tigers:

1890 William Carey(2)
1896 Percy Oscroft(3)
1910 Chris Gimson(2)
1912 Jimmy Burdett(3)
1914 Steve Farmer, Harry Lawrie(2), Gil Hopkins
1915 GW Hunt, Pedlar Wood
1923 John Davis, Trevor Thorneloe, Norman Coates(2), Herb Sharratt
1924 Percy Lawrie(2)
1927 Doug Norman(4), Doug Prentice(4)
1928 George Beamish(2), Herbert Franklin
1930 Joe Kendrew(6)
1933 Bernard Gadney(7)
1934 Charles Beamish(8)
1935 Bobby Barr, Ralph Buckingham
1939 Tom Berry, Francis Edwards(2)
1942 George Vallance
1946 Cecil Beamish, Denis Bolesworth
1948 Peter Jerwood
1949 Bill Moore
1951 Eric Lacey(3), Bob Stirling(2)
1955 David Hazell
1958 Tom Bleasdale
1959 Tony O'Reilly, Phil Horrocks-Taylor(2), Mike Wade(4)
1960 Colin Martin
1962 Ken Scotland(4)
1966 David Matthews(2)
1967 Kevin Andrews(5)
1970 Rodger Arneil(4)
1972 Alan Old(3)
1974 Peter Wheeler(17), John Allen(2)
1976 Garry Adey(7)
1977 Robin Cowling(3), Bob Rowell, Dusty Hare(6)
1978 Paul Dodge(9)
1979 Clive Woodward(4)
1981 Les Cusworth(9), Brian Hall(2)
1982 Barry Evans(5)
1983 Dean Richards(5)
1984 Rory Underwood(9)
1987 John Wells(3)
1988 Steve Kenney
1989 Tony Underwood(7)
1990 Simon Povoas, Ian Smith(2), Neil Back(14), Brian Smith
1992 Martin Johnson
1993 Stuart Potter, Graham Rowntree(5)
1994 Matt Poole(2), Richard Cockerill(10), Darren Garforth(6), Steve Hackney(3)
1996 Jez Harris, Niall Malone(2)
1997 Perry Freshwater(2), Rob Liley, Leon Lloyd(4), Bill Drake-Lee
1998 Martin Corry(5), Dorian West(3)
1999 Craig Joiner, Ben Kay(2)
2001 Josh Kronfeld(6), Geordan Murphy(3), Pat Howard(4)
2002 Ollie Smith
2003 Franck Tournaire(3)
2004 Ricky Nebbett
2005 Darren Morris
2006 Ian Humphreys, Jim Hamilton(2), Will Skinner
2007 Matt Cornwell(3)
2009 Tom Youngs
2010 Julian White(2)

Note: Total Barbarians appearances whilst at Leicester, if more than one, shown in brackets.

The Barbarians have appeared seven times at Welford Road against opponents other than the Tigers, all between 1940-44 and all to raise funds for various Service Charities. In 1940 they beat the Midland Counties 34-18, in 1941 and 1942 they beat J.E.Thorneloe's Midlands XV 8-3 and 24-11, and from 1942-44 they beat J.E Thorneloe's XV four times.

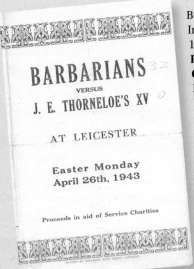

BARBARIANS 32
VERSUS
J. E. THORNELOE'S XV 0
AT LEICESTER
Easter Monday
April 26th, 1943
Proceeds in aid of Service Charities

There was a record five Tigers in the Barbarians team which played against Ireland at Lansdowne Road on 18 May 1996: **Rory Underwood**, **Graham Rowntree**, **Richard Cockerill**, **Darren Garforth**, and **Dean Richards**, whilst **Francis Edwards**, **Mike Wade**, **Peter Wheeler** and **Tony Underwood** have all scored try hat-tricks for the Baa-baas when playing for Leicester, Underwood junior also adding a fourth try against Cardiff at the Arms Park in March 1991. **Rory Underwood** scored a total of eleven tries and a record 46 points in nine Barbarians appearances as a Tiger.

The annual Christmas match between the Tigers and the Barbarians was played at Welford Road, weather permitting, each year between 1909-98. **Peter Wheeler** played in a record 14 such encounters including 13 in succession which ties the record with **Dusty Hare**.

The Tigers have also met other Barbarians national offshoots at Welford Road on a few occasions, playing against Fiji Barbarians on 4 November 1986 (won 39-14), New Zealand Barbarians on 18 March 1987 (lost 3-33) and South African Barbarians on 21 October 1993 (lost 18-24).

BOARD ROOM

The club converted to a public limited company on 8 December 1997 with the first board of directors being: **Peter Tom** (chairman), **Peter Wheeler** (chief executive), **Philip Smith** (finance director), **Garry Adey**, **John Allen**, **Bob Beason**, **Roy Jackson**, **David Jones** and **David Matthews**. Of those only Tom, and Wheeler still remain on the board for the 2014/15 season.

BOARD MEMBERS

Name	*Title*	*Timespan*
JD (David) Abell	Non-executive director	14.7.1999-
GJ (Garry) Adey	Non-executive director	8.12.1997-5.9.2014
JA (John) Allen	Non-executive director	8.12.1997-31.10.2007
R (Bob) Beason	Non-executive director	8.12.1997-31.10.2007
DFG (David) Clayton	Operations director	22.12.1999-2000
	Managing director	2000-30.9.2011
SJ (Simon) Cohen	Chief operating officer	1.10.2011-6.2.2012
	Chief executive officer	6.2.2012-
NT (Nick) Donald	Non-executive director	3.2.1998-14.7.1999
TM (Terry) Gateley	Non-executive director	1.11.2007-
RJ (Bob) Harrison	Operations director	25.11.1998-26.11.1999
RD (Roy) Jackson	Non-executive director	8.12.1997-5.9.2014
DC (David) Jones	Non-executive director	8.12.1997-7.10.2005
Lord DM (Digby) Jones	Non-executive director	8.10.2005-
DJ (David) Matthews	Non-executive director	8.12.1997-31.10.2007
TR (Tom) Scott	Non-executive director	1.10.2011-
PMF (Philip) Smith	Finance director	8.12.1997-25.11.1998
PWG (Peter) Tom	Executive chairman	8.12.1997-
R (Rory) Underwood	Non-executive director	1.11.2007-
PJ (Peter) Wheeler	Chief executive	8.12.1997-31.1.2010
	Executive director	1.2.2010-
Sir CR (Clive) Woodward	Non-executive director	31.10.2007-27.11.2013

↑ Lord Digby Jones joined the Tigers board in 2005.

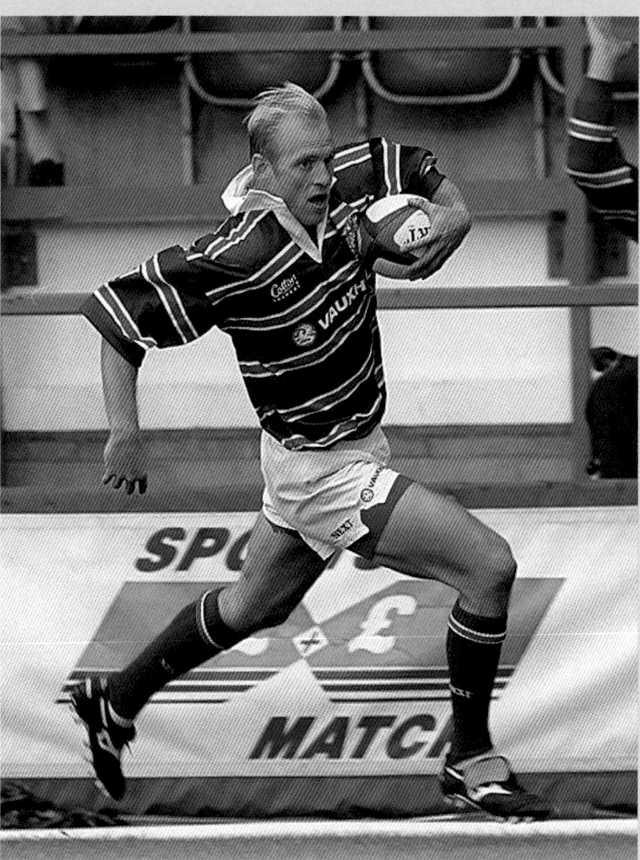

↑ Canadian international wing Winston Stanley grabbed Tigers' first ever try bonus point against Newcastle, 27.8.2000.

BONUS POINTS

The first Tigers game to be played after the introduction of bonus points was against Wasps at Loftus Road in the Premiership on 19 August 2000. Tigers won 24-22 but it was Wasps who got a losing bonus point. Tigers' first try bonus came the following week at Newcastle in a 25-22 victory with **Winston Stanley** grabbing the fourth try after 47 minutes.

Tigers have only four times gained a try bonus but lost the game, all in the Premiership and also grabbing a losing bonus point in each instance:

at London Irish	L 25-26	26.12.2006
at Gloucester	L 24-28	11.3.2007
at Wasps	L 29-36	15.2.2009
at Wasps	L 30-37	18.9.2010

Twice Tigers have drawn a match but gained a try bonus point:

vs Ospreys	D 32-32	11.10.2009
vs Gloucester	D 41-41	16.4.2011

Leicester have on three occasions won a game but allowed their opponents to come away with a try bonus point:

vs Harlequins	W 31-28	10.5.2008
at London Irish	W 31-28	1.3.2009
vs Saracens	W 31-27	10.5.2014

In the London Irish game Tigers failed to get a try bonus themselves, whilst the Harlequins and Saracens encounters were both maximum seven-point matches with Leicester gaining five league points and their opponents two.

When **Andy Goode** scored a 21st minute try against Rotherham at Welford Road on 1 May 2004 it gave Leicester their quickest bonus point ever. In sixteen other games they have registered a try bonus begore the half-time break. The crucial fourth try has been scored on nine occasions by "Mr penalty try", followed by **Alesana Tuilagi** with seven and **Tom Croft** with six. The fastest try bonus conceded by Leicester was claimed by **Ashley Beck** in just 24 minutes, for Ospreys in the Anglo-Welsh Cup at Bridgend on 12 November 2010.

Leicester scored three tries in the first 18 minutes against Wasps at Adams Park in the European Cup on 5 December 2004 but did not score any more tries and failed to register a bonus point, they did at least win the match 37-31.

Tigers scored a try bonus point in six successive games in the Premiership between 25 February 2012 and 21 April 2012.

Leicester scored a bonus point in eight consecutive matches between 16 April 2004 to 2 October 2004, but went 16 games without a try bonus between 19 April 2003 and 6 December 2003.

Tigers won five successive close games where their opponents each gained a losing bonus point between 10 March 2006 and 28 April 2006.

The club gained at least one league point from 27 successive matches between 6 December 2008 and 31 October 2009, but allowed their opponents to tally no league points at all in nine successive matches between 25 February 2012 and 8 September 2012.

BROADCASTING

The first BBC Radio broadcast of a Leicester game was on 11 October 1930 at home to Gloucester.

The first game shown on TV in highlights form was the Tigers visit to London Scottish on 3 February 1951.

The first LIVE broadcast of a complete Tigers match was for the visit of Northampton in the semi-final of the Pilkington Cup on 10 April 1993 when the BBC recorded a 38-6 victory for Leicester.

The first subscription TV broadcast was when Sky Sports covered Leicester's visit to Orrell in the Courage League on 17 September 1994 and won 6-0.

The Tigers first truly "global" live broadcast was for the semi-final of the Heineken Cup against Toulouse at Welford Road on 4 January 1997, which was shown live on BBC Grandstand and also live in France on FR2 and Welsh language channel S4C, as well as live radio commentary from BBC Radio Leicester and Sud Radio.

The armchair audience was in excess of the 8 million mark with Grandstand reporting an average audience of 4.1 million with a peak of 5.8 million. The FR2 figure was around 3.8 million. The final that year against Brive in Cardiff was shown in 86 countries with a worldwide television audience of over 35 million, 18 of those countries showed the match live including BBC, FR2, S4C, RTE in Ireland and MNET in South Africa.

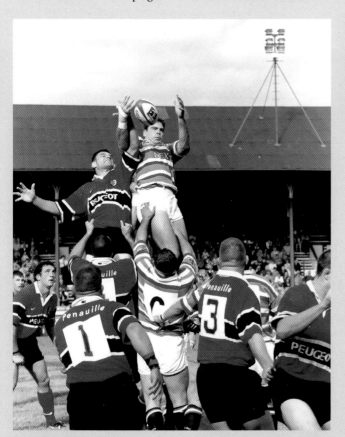

↑ Leicester's victory over Toulouse in the semi-final of the Heineken Cup on 4 January 1997 was the first truly global broadcast of a Tigers game.

CALENDAR MONTH

Only two Leicester players have ever scored 100 points in a calendar month: in March 1973 **John Ingleby** tallied 106 points in seven matches, and in January 2006 **Andy Goode** kicked 101 points.

Alfred Hind had an amazing purple patch for try scoring in March 1903, running in a staggering 17 tries in just four games, which were all cup ties in the Midland Counties Cup. He scored five tries in the 1st round against Stratford, six tries in the 2nd round against Belgrave, five more tries in the semi-final versus Nuneaton and another two in the final victory over Rugby at Coventry.

Seven players have appeared in nine matches in a calendar month: **Alf Butlin**, **Jacky Braithwaite**, **John Garner** and **Sammy Matthews** in December 1900, and **Bob Barker, John Allen** and **David Matthews** in April 1969.

CALENDAR YEAR

These records pertain to matches played between 1 January and 31 December in a particular year as distinct from a rugby season.

TEAM RECORDS

Most wins - 37 in 1980 and 1983
Most draws - 8 in 1888
Most losses - 23 in 1937 and 1956
Fewest wins (full year) - 6 in 1888
Fewest losses - 4 in 1883 and 1995
Best success percentage - 88.9% (W32, L4) in 1995
Worst success percentage - 36.25% (W12, D5, L23) in 1956
Most points scored - 1,497 in 42 matches in 1996
Most points conceded - 847 in 39 matches in 1998
Most tries scored - 194 in 40 matches in 1920
Most tries conceded - 117 in 46 matches in 1969

PLAYER RECORDS

Most points in a calendar year - **Tim Stimpson** 451 in 2001, 447 by **Joel Stransky** in 1997, 443 by **Tim Stimpson** in 2000
Most appearances - 45 by **Graham Pulfrey** (1966), **Robin Money** (1973) and **Tim Barnwell** (1982)
Most tries - 46 by **Teddy Haselmere** in 1920, 43 also by **Teddy Haselmere** in 1919

CAPPED PLAYERS

The first player ever to play for his country from the Leicester club was **John Henry 'Jack' Miles**, a prolific try scoring wing, who gained his only England cap against Wales at St Helens, Swansea on 10 January 1903 during a 5-21 defeat. He had come to the notice of the selectors after scoring 43 tries in just 52 appearances for the Tigers up to that point, making his Leicester debut, aged just 19 against Handsworth at Welford Road in September 1899 and scoring a hat-trick of tries. In his career he went on to play in 93 first-team games for the club, scoring 75 tries.

In all 266 future or past capped players have turned out for the Tigers first-team, with an incredible 128 of those being capped for their country whilst a playing member of Leicester, and 82 playing their first test match when a Tiger. The "No" column denotes the chronological sequence, whilst the cap totals at the right are the number won for their country when at Leicester with any in brackets for the Lions or the Pacific Islanders.

Key:
< number of caps gained whilst at Leicester but before Tigers debut
> number of caps gained whilst at Leicester but after last Tigers appearance.

ENGLAND (82)

No.	Name	Date (Venue)	Caps
52	Garry Adey	6.3.1976 (Twickenham)	2
67	>1 Neil Back	5.2.1994 (Murrayfield)	66 (5)
27=	Bobby Barr	2.1.1932 (Twickenham)	3
36	Tom Berry	21.1.1939 (Twickenham)	3
2=	Jacky Braithwaite	2.12.1905 (Crystal Palace)	1
23	Ralph Buckingham	2.1.1927 (Stade Colombes)	1
102	George Chuter	11.6.2006 (Sydney)	24
73	Richard Cockerill	rep-31.5.1997 (Buenos Aires)	27
115	Dan Cole	6.2.2010 (Twickenham)	45 (3)
79	Martin Corry (3rd cap)	14.11.1998 (Huddersfield)	62 (7)
53	Robin Cowling	15.1.1977 (Twickenham)	8
112	Jordan Crane	22.11.2008 (Twickenham)	3
108	Tom Croft	23.2.2008 (Paris)	38 (5)
56	Les Cusworth	24.11.1979 (Twickenham)	12
16	Harold Day	17.1.1920 (Swansea)	4
100	Louis Deacon	26.11.2005 (Twickenham)	29
55	Paul Dodge	4.2.1978 (Twickenham)	32 (2)
47	Nick Drake-Lee (5th cap)	4.1.1964 (Twickenham)	4
94	Harry Ellis	20.11.2004 (Twickenham)	27 (1)
62	Barry Evans	12.6.1988 (Sydney)	2
111	Toby Flood (19th cap)	rep-8.11.2008 (Twickenham)	42
29	Bernard Gadney	13.2.1932 (Dublin)	13
72	Darren Garforth	rep-15.3.1997 (Cardiff)	25
44	Mike Gavins	21.1.1961 (Cardiff)	1
95	Andy Goode	12.3.2005 (Twickenham)	9
74	Will Greenwood	15.11.1997 (Twickenham)	15
54	Dusty Hare (2nd cap)	21.1.1978 (Parc des Princes)	24
40	David Hazell	22.1.1955 (Cardiff)	4
71	Austin Healey	rep-15.2.1997 (Dublin)	51 (2)
2=	Alfred Hind	2.12.1905 (Crystal Palace)	2
107	Dan Hipkiss	4.8.2007 (Twickenham)	13
42	Phil Horrocks-Taylor (Lions)	29.8.1959 (Christchurch)	5 (1)
2=	John Jackett	2.12.1905 (Crystal Palace)	13 (3)
65	Martin Johnson	16.1.1993 (Twickenham)	84 (5)
85=	Ben Kay	2.6.2001 (Toronto)	62 (2)
30	Douglas Kendrew (3rd cap)	11.2.1933 (Twickenham)	8
8=	>1 Alf Kewney (5th cap)	9.1.1909 (Blackheath)	12
10	Percy Lawrie	19.3.1910 (Inverleith)	2
82	Leon Lloyd	rep-17.6.2000 (Pretoria)	5
22	>1 Edward Massey	17.1.1925 (Twickenham)	3
1	Jack Miles	10.1.1903 (Swansea)	1
85=	>2 Lewis Moody	2.6.2001 (Toronto)	63 (3)
37	Bill Moore	18.1.1947 (Cardiff)	7
35	>1 Ernie Nicholson (4th cap)	4.1.1936 (Twickenham)	2
27=	Doug Norman	2.1.1932 (Twickenham)	2
50	Alan Old (6th cap)	15.9.1973 (Auckland)	6
120	Geoff Parling	4.2.2012 (Murrayfield)	21 (3)
8=	Sid Penny	9.1.1909 (Blackheath)	1
77	Stuart Potter	rep-6.6.1998 (Brisbane)	1
26	Doug Prentice	11.2.1928 (Dublin)	3 (2)
19	Leo Price (3rd cap)	20.1.1923 (Twickenham)	2
60	Steve Redfern	18.2.1984 (Twickenham)	1
61	Dean Richards	1.3.1986 (Twickenham)	48 (6)
48	Bob Rowell	18.1.1964 (Twickenham)	2
68	Graham Rowntree	rep-18.3.1995 (Twickenham)	54 (3)
2=	Richard Russell	2.12.1905 (Crystal Palace)	1
34	Cyril Slow	17.3.1934 (Twickenham)	1
18	Alistair Smallwood (3rd cap)	15.1.1921 (Twickenham)	12
87	Ollie Smith	rep-9.3.2003 (Twickenham)	5 (1)
76	<4 Tim Stimpson (8th cap)	6.6.1998 (Brisbane)	12
39	Bob Stirling	20.1.1951 (Swansea)	13
13	Frank Tarr (4th cap)	15.3.1913 (Twickenham)	1
17	Sos Taylor	31.1.1920 (Twickenham)	2
14=	Tim Taylor	17.1.1914 (Twickenham)	1
38	Allan Towell	29.3.1948 (Stade Colombes)	1
119	Manu Tuilagi	6.8.2011 (Twickenham)	25 (1)
59	Rory Underwood	18.2.1984 (Twickenham)	85 (6)
64	>4 Tony Underwood	17.10.1992 (Wembley)	20
101	Tom Varndell	26.11.2005 (Twickenham)	4
113	Sam Vesty	6.6.2009 (Manchester)	2
46	Mike Wade	20.1.1962 (Twickenham)	3
20	Wavell Wakefield (17th cap)	19.1.1924 (Swansea)	4
123	Thomas Waldrom	16.6.2012 (Johannesburg)	5
12	George Ward	18.1.1913 (Cardiff)	6
75	Dorian West	rep-7.2.1998 (Stade de France)	21
51	Peter Wheeler	1.2.1975 (Twickenham)	41 (7)
89	<5 Julian White (15th cap)	23.8.2003 (Cardiff)	37 (4)
14=	Pedlar Wood	17.1.1914 (Twickenham)	1
57	Clive Woodward	19.1.1980 (Twickenham)	21 (2)
116	Ben Youngs	13.3.2010 (Murrayfield)	38 (2)
58	Nick Youngs	19.3.1983 (Dublin)	6
124=	Tom Youngs	10.11.2012 (Twickenham)	17 (3)

↑ Austin Healey was capped 51 times by England.

Ireland's Leo Cullen became the 99th player capped from the Leicester club in November 2005.

LIONS UNCAPPED FOR THEIR COUNTRY (3)

6	>1 Fred Jackson (Anglo-Welsh)	6.6.1908 (Dunedin)	0 (1)
7	>2 Tom Smith (Anglo-Welsh)	27.6.1908 (Wellington)	0 (2)
11	Kenneth Wood (Great Britain)	6.8.1910 (Johannesburg)	0 (2)

SCOTLAND (7)

49	Rodger Arneil (8th cap)	6.12.1969 (Murrayfield)	11
24	Harry Greenlees	17.1.1927 (Murrayfield)	6
105	>1 Jim Hamilton	11.11.2006 (Murrayfield)	16
69	<1 >2 Craig Joiner (17th cap)	15.6.1996 (Dunedin)	8
21	Jock Lawrie (9th cap)	2.2.1924 (Inverleith)	3
45	Ken Scotland (19th cap)	13.1.1962 (Murrayfield)	4
41	Ian Swan (17th cap)	11.1.1958 (Murrayfield)	1

IRELAND (11)

33	Charles Beamish (3rd cap)	24.2.1934 (Murrayfield)	6
25	George Beamish (4th cap)	28.1.1928 (Belfast)	22
32	Paddy Coote	1.4.1933 (Dublin)	1
31	Morgan Crowe (11th cap)	11.3.1933 (Belfast)	3
99	Leo Cullen (18th cap)	26.11.2005 (Dublin)	1
106	>1 Shane Jennings	2.6.2007 (Buenos Aires)	1
66	Niall Malone (3rd cap)	5.11.1994 (Dublin)	1
70	Eric Miller	4.1.1997 (Dublin)	8 (1)
81	Geordan Murphy	10.6.2000 (Manchester, USA)	72 (2)
43	Tony O'Reilly (21st cap)	18.4.1959 (Dublin)	2
63	>1 Brian Smith (5th cap)	27.10.1990 (Dublin)	5

CANADA (2)

78	<2 Dave Lougheed (24th cap)	18.8.1998 (Buenos Aires)	9
83	>2 Winston Stanley (45th cap)	11.11.2000 (Rovigo)	3

SOUTH AFRICA (2)

91	>8 Jaco van der Westhuyzen (10th cap)	12.6.2004 (Bloemfontein)	8
80	Fritz van Heerden (14th cap)	10.10.1999 (Murrayfield)	1

SAMOA (4)

121=	Logovi'i Mulipola (7th cap)	5.6.2012 (Nagoya)	11
96	Alesana Tuilagi (4th cap)	11.6.2005 (Sydney)	23 (1)
98	<4 >3 Anitele'a Tuilagi	2.7.2005 (Apia)	6
84	Freddie Tuilagi (5th cap)	11.11.2000 (Cardiff)	10

ITALY (3)

103	>3 Martin Castrogiovanni (36th cap)	7.10.2006 (L'Aquila)	63
110	>1 Alejandro Moreno (5th cap)	rep-28.6.2008 (Cordoba)	1
88	<3 Ramiro Pez (15th cap)	23.8.2003 (Murrayfield)	2

UNITED STATES (2)

90	Dan Lyle (42nd cap)	15.10.2003 (Brisbane)	4
127	<2 Blaine Scully (12th cap)	17.8.2013 (Chicago)	9

WALES (1)

92	Darren Morris (16th cap)	rep-12.6.2004 (Tucuman)	3

FIJI (2)

124=	Vereniki Goneva (27th cap)	10.11.2012 (Twickenham)	3
93	<3 >1 Seru Rabeni (Pacific Islanders)	rep-3.7.2004 (Adelaide)	10 (9)

TONGA (2)

121=	Steve Mafi (4th cap)	5.6.2012 (Nagoya)	7
97	Ephraim Taukafa (12th cap)	25.6.2005 (Suva)	4

ARGENTINA (5)

118	Horacio Agulla (28th cap)	28.11.2010 (Dublin)	7
104	Marcos Ayerza (9th cap)	11.11.2006 (Twickenham)	40
126	<3 Gonzalo Camacho (21st cap)	17.8.2013 (Johannesburg)	3
117	Lucas Gonzalez Amorosino (5th cap)	12.6.2010 (Tucuman)	6
128	Pablo Matera (9th cap)	9.11.2013 (Twickenham)	3

FRANCE (2)

114	>2 Julien Dupuy	13.6.2009 (Dunedin)	3
109	Benjamin Kayser	rep-28.6.2008 (Sydney)	9

Freddie Tuilagi was capped ten times by Samoa when playing for the Tigers.

← Jim Parsons played in wartime internationals for England but never gained a full cap.

Francis Edwards played in both of the uncapped Red Cross wartime internationals for England against Wales in 1939/40. **Jim Parsons** appeared in seven uncapped services internationals for England between 1943-45, three of those encounters with Scotland being played at Welford Road. **George Vallance** played for England in their 24-19 victory over Scotland in a services international at Welford Road on 10 April 1943. None of these three players ever gained a full England cap.

Pablo Feijoo was part of the first-team squad in season 2007/08 but was never selected in a matchday squad. He did however appear in six games in the A League and gained one cap for Spain during this time, against the Czech Republic in Madrid.

In addition the following players played during overseas tours with their country, appeared in a non-capped international or were an unused bench replacement in a test match but never went on to gain a full international cap:

1972	Dave Whibley
1984	Stuart Redfern
1988	Tim Buttimore
1990	John Wells, John Liley, Matt Poole
1993	Steve Hackney
2001	Ricky Nebbett
2002	Adam Balding
2006	Scott Bemand
2008	Frank Murphy (Ireland)
2010	*Johne Murphy (Ireland)
2012	*Graham Kitchener
2014	*Fraser Balmain, *Jamie Gibson, *Ed Slater

** Still playing in 2014/15.*

CAPPED AFTER FEWEST TIGERS GAMES

Games	*Name*	*Club Debut*	*Test debut*	*Previous clubs*
6	Harold Day	11.1.1919	17.1.1920	-
11	Bill Moore	8.9.1945	18.1.1947	-
14	Rory Underwood	21.9.1983	18.2.1984	Middlesbrough
16	Frank Tarr	13.1.1906	9.1.1909	-
17	Nick Drake-Lee	6.1.1962	19.1.1963	Kettering
18	Eric Miller	17.11.1995	4.1.1997	Old Wesley
20	Clive Woodward	1.9.1979	24.11.1979	(79 for Harlequins)
20	Austin Healey	26.8.1996	15.2.1997	Waterloo/Orrell
22	Paddy Coote	10.10.1931	1.4.1933	-
22 (18+4)	Tom Varndell	6.11.2004	26.11.2005	-

CAPPED AFTER MOST TIGERS GAMES

Games	*Name*	*Club Debut*	*Test debut*	*Years*
433	Sid Penny	4.1.1896	9.1.1909	13
413	Doug Norman	17.1.1920	2.1.1932	12
330	Jacky Braithwaite	12.10.1895	2.12.1905	10
263	Pedlar Wood	10.11.1906	17.1.1914	8
245	Garry Adey	8.3.1967	6.3.1976	9
215	Steve Redfern	30.10.1976	18.1.1984	8
205	Tom Berry	5.3.1932	21.1.1939	7
204	Barry Evans	30.10.1981	12.6.1988	7

MOST CAPPED PLAYERS IN A TIGERS STARTING LINE-UP

On two occasions the Tigers have taken to the field with a side which contained 14 capped internationals, at Neath on 11 October 2002 in the European Cup when centre **Glenn Gelderbloom** was the uncapped player, and against Saracens on 28 April 2006 when future international **Geroge Chuter** was then uncapped.

Chronological List of the Most Test Players in a Tigers Team:

1	19.10.1895	v Guy's Hospital
2	14.4.1903	at Bristol
4	23.1.1905	v Coventry
5	14.4.1906	at Newport
6	24.4.1909	v Northampton
7	2.10.1920	v Headingley
8	11.12.1920	v Blackheath
10	2.4.1997	v Wasps
11	30.8.1997	v Gloucester
12	20.12.1997	v Harlequins
13	6.2.1999	at Harlequins
14	11.10.2002	at Neath
14	28.4.2006	at Saracens

FIRST INTERNATIONALS

The first international player ever to appear in a Tigers line-up was 34-year-old forward **William Yiend**, who made his Leicester debut in a 19-0 victory against Guy's Hospital at Welford Road on 19 October 1895, after moving into the area when finding work in Peterborough. Yiend had been born at Winchcombe in the Cotswolds in 1861, he gained six caps for England between 1889 and 1893 whilst he was a Hartlepool Rovers player and went on to make ten appearances for the Tigers first-team, the last of which was against his old club at Welford Road in April 1896.

The first future international to play for the club was 27-year-old centre **Abel Ashworth,** a guest player from Oldham who went on the 1890 tour to Wales appearing against both Cardiff and Newport, and went on to gain his only England cap less than two years later, against Ireland at Manchester.

The list that follows show the first players, by nation, who were already capped for their country when they made their Tigers debut:

Country	*Name*	*Tigers Debut*	*Caps*
England	William Yiend	19.10.1895 v Guy's Hospital	6 caps
Ireland	William Davis	26.12.1895 v Salford	9 caps
Scotland	Mark Morrison	31.12.1898 v Cardiff	10 caps
Wales	'Pussy' Jones	26.12.1903 v Treherbert	2 caps
New Zealand	Ernest Booth	4.2.1909 v Richmond	3 caps
Australia	Tommy Lawton	20.12.1924 v Bristol	14 caps
Canada	Nick Clapinson	25.11.1995 v Rugby	1 cap

In August 1997, Waisale Serevi became the first Fijian to appear for Leicester.

South Africa	Joel Stransky	11.1.1997 at Northampton	22 caps	●
Fiji	Waisale Serevi	30.8.1997 v Gloucester	13 caps	●
Samoa	Freddie Tuilagi	28.10.2000 v Pontypridd	9 caps	●
France	Franck Tournaire	24.8.2002 at Biarritz	49 caps	●
Italy	Ramiro Pez	21.9.2003 at Saracens	16 caps	●
USA	Dan Lyle	13.9.2003 v London Irish	45 caps	●
Tonga	Ephraim Taukafa	21.11.2004 at Wasps	12 caps	●
Argentina	Alejandro Moreno	3.9.2005 v Northampton	7 caps	●
Hong Kong	Ed Rolston	15.10.2011 at Scarlets	5 caps	●

Only four League or Premiership games have ever been played with no internationals in the Tigers team:

22.4.1989	vs Bath	Won 15-12	●
29.2.1992	at Orrell	Lost 9-21	●
28.3.1992	at Harlequins	Lost 13-20	●
7.4.1992	vs Northampton	Lost 19-22	●

CAPPED FOR THE FIRST TIME AFTER LEAVING LEICESTER

One-time regular first-team squad members for the Tigers who went on to gain their first test caps after leaving the club:

Name	*Club*	*Country*	*Caps*	*Years*	*Tigers Games*
George Keeton	Richmond	England	3 caps	1904	41
Pop Dunkley	Harlequins	England	2 caps	1931	30
Paul Ringer	Ebbw Vale	Wales	8 caps	1978-80	56
Marcus Rose	Cambridge University	England	10 caps	1981-87	19
Paul Burnell	London Scottish	Scotland	52 caps	1989-99	13
Michael Horak	London Irish	England	1 cap	2002	44
Perry Freshwater	Perpignan	England	10 caps	2005-07	137
Ayoola Erinle	Biarritz	England	2 caps	2009	30
Billy Twelvetrees	Gloucester	England	14 caps	2013-14	47
George Ford	Bath	England	2 caps	2014	41

CAPTAINS

Named below are all the players who have been elected captain of Leicester Football Club in chronological order. Separate spells as skipper are numbered in brackets.

1880-1881	AE (Alexander) Brice Resigned due to severe illness in September 1881
1881-1882	AT (Arthur) Porter
1882-1883	L (Lawrence) Young
1883-1885	JGS (Sherrard) Coleman
1885-1886	WA (William) Sheffield
1886-1888	J (Jack) Parsons resigned at Christmas 1888
1888-1889	RS (Dickie) Snowden
1889-1890	WR (Willie) Porter
1890-1891	A (Arthur) McKechnie McKechnie was appointed for 1891/92 but resigned when he received a teaching appointment at Coalville
1891-1893	WH (Jack) Sturges
1893-1894	AE (Ted) Cooke
1894-1896	E (Eddie) Redman
1896-1899	AO (Arthur) Jones (1)
1899-1901	WJ (Billy) Foreman
1901-1902	JW (Josh) Garner Arthur Jones was originally appointed but resigned
1902-1904	AO (Arthur) Jones (2)
1904-1906	S (Sammy) Matthews (1)

Eddie Redman was captain of Leicester Football Club between 1894-96.

1906-1908	RF (Richard) Russell
1907-1909	S (Sammy) Matthews (2) Matthews did not play in season 1908/09 and so vice-captain Jamie Watson led the club in matches
1909-1911	JR (Jamie) Watson
1911-1919	PW (Percy) Lawrie (1)
1919-1920	WJ (Jimmy) Allen
1920-1923	PW (Percy) Lawrie (2)
1923-1924	WW (Wavell) Wakefield
1924-1928	HLV (Harold) Day
1928-1930	FD (Doug) Prentice
1930-1932	HD (Harry) Greenlees
1932-1933	DJ (Doug) Norman
1933-1934	RA (Ralph) Buckingham
1934-1936	BC (Bernard) Gadney
1936-1938	RJ (Bobby) Barr
1938-1947	JTW (Tom) Berry
1947-1949	HP (Peter) Jerwood
1949-1950	AC (Allan) Towell
1950-1952	WKT (Bill) Moore
1952-1953	AD (Denis) Bolesworth
1953-1955	JM (John) Jenkins
1955-1956	J (John) Elders
1956-1958	T (Tom) Bleasdale (1)
1958-1959	JS (Ian) Swan
1959-1960	T (Tom) Bleasdale (2) (John Jenkins was originally appointed)
1960-1963	CG (Colin) Martin
1963-1964	MR (Mike) Wade (Injury forced his resignation in November 1964)
1964-1965	MJ (Mike) Harrison
1965-1968	DJ (David) Matthews
1968-1969	GG (Graham) Willars (1)
1969-1970	KP (Kevin) Andrews
1970-1971	JA (John) Allen
1971-1972	RV (Roger) Grove
1972-1973	GG (Graham) Willars (2)
1973-1975	PJ (Peter) Wheeler (1) (Mike Yandle was originally appointed)
1975-1976	RS (Robin) Money
1976-1977	RE (Bob) Rowell
1977-1978	BP (Brian) Hall
1978-1981	PJ (Peter) Wheeler (2)
1981-1983	SR (Steve) Johnson
1983-1985	IR (Ian) Smith
1985-1987	L (Les) Cusworth (1)
1987-1989	PW (Paul) Dodge
1989	D (Dean) Richards (1) (injury forced his replacement in September 1989)
1989-1990	L (Les) Cusworth (2)
1990-1991	D (Dean) Richards (2)
1991-1993	JM (John) Wells
1993-1997	D (Dean) Richards (3)
1997-2005	MO (Martin) Johnson
2003	NA (Neil) Back (Josh Kronfeld during World Cup) later Martin Johnson
2005-2009	ME (Martin) Corry
2009-2013	GEA (Geordan) Murphy
2013-2014	TGAL (Toby) Flood

MOST MATCHES AS CAPTAIN

	Record as Captain					*Matches Started Under Other Captains*					
						Not					*%of starts*
Captain	***Capt***	***W***	***D***	***L***	***Win%***	***Capt***	***W***	***D***	***L***	***Win%***	***as Capt***
Martin Johnson	202	146	11	45	72.3%	146	113	1	32	77.4%	58.0%
Percy Lawrie	165	107	10	48	64.8%	153	88	15	50	57.5%	51.9%
Peter Wheeler	131	90	5	36	68.7%	218	145	7	66	66.5%	37.5%
Arthur Jones	131	99	8	24	75.6%	93	62	11	20	66.7%	58.5%
Les Cusworth	130	101	0	29	77.7%	235	177	4	54	75.3%	35.6%
Sammy Matthews	125	60	17	48	48.0%	215	139	17	59	64.7%	36.8%
Colin Martin	123	76	7	40	61.8%	149	79	13	57	53.0%	45.2%
David Matthews	119	79	8	32	66.4%	383	212	27	144	55.4%	23.7%
Tom Bleasdale	115	55	15	45	47.8%	225	118	10	97	52.4%	33.8%
Dean Richards	113	86	1	26	76.1%	193	141	4	48	73.1%	36.9%
Billy Foreman	109	68	8	33	62.4%	249	175	15	59	70.3%	30.4%
Harold Day	104	69	6	29	66.3%	108	72	5	31	66.7%	49.1%
Jamie Watson	101	64	11	26	63.4%	128	68	14	46	53.1%	44.1%

157 different players have led the first-team in a match.

Chris Tarbuck skippered the Tigers seven times from 1995 to 1996 – all the games were won.

Wavell Wakefield was captain in 96.6% of the 29 matches he started, the only game for which he was not skipper was his debut against London at Welford Road on 23 April 1921, when **Percy Lawrie** led the side.

Arguably the player who performed better when skipper than when he was not captain was **Arthur McKechnie** (1882-94) – Tigers won 72% of his 25 matches in charge, but won only 44.8% of the 192 matches he played under other captains. The reverse is true for **Willie Porter** (1880-92) with Leicester winning 22.9% of his 35 games as captain and 54.8% of the other 135 games he played under different skippers.

Tigers played in 61 successive matches with **Colin Martin** as skipper between 28 January 1961 and 8 September 1962, winning 38, drawing 2 and losing 21.

The best individual performance as captain was 25 points in a game by **Joel Stransky** against Rotherham on 14 November 1997, whilst **AO Jones** scored five tries when he led Leicester against Leicestershire on 27 December 1895.

Percy Lawrie scored 116 of his 206 tries whilst skipper, whilst **Josh Garner's** only three tries in 209 appearances all came during the 36 games in which he was captain, and **Harold Day** scored 558 of his 1,151 points when he led the club.

All **Toby Flood's** 25 tries were scored during his 98 appearances playing under other captains. He scored none in the 21 games in which he led the team.

Geordan Murphy, at 79%, has the best winning percentage of any captain in Premiership history, with 38 wins from 50 matches as skipper in the tournament, beating **Martin Johnson** with 76.13% into second place.

INEXPERIENCED CAPTAINS

Only two players have ever been captain on their first-team debut; **Alexander Brice** in the very first game of the club in 1880, and ex-England captain **Bob Weighill** against Bath on 9 September 1950.

In recent years **Mefin Davies** skippered Leicester on his 5th Tigers first-team game against Bath on 27 October 2007, **Daryl Gibson** on his 6th, and **Rod Kafer** on his 9th appearance. Of those, only Kafer had not captained a major side before.

At the other end of the scale **Sid Penny** captained the club for the only time on his 374th appearance against Plymouth on 8 April 1907.

OVERSEAS BORN SKIPPERS

India: **Harold Day** (104 matches, 1924-28)
South Africa: **Mel Channer** (8, 1953-55), **Joel Stransky** (9, 1997-99), **Fritz van Heerden** (2, 1998), **Ben Pienaar** (1, 2010)
New Zealand: **Colin Martin** (123, 1959-65), **Josh Kronfeld** (11, 2003), **Daryl Gibson** (1, 2003), **Aaron Mauger** (16, 2008-10), **Craig Newby** (13, 2010-12), **Boris Stankovich** (3, 2011-13), **Thomas Waldrom** (1, 2014)
Australia: **John Quick** (4, 1968), **Rod Kafer** (2, 2001)
Iran: **Aadel Kardooni** (3, 1990-94)
France: **David Mélé** (1, 2014)

INTERNATIONAL CAPTAINS...

Test match appearances as captain shown in brackets.

BRITISH & IRISH LIONS (2)

1930 Doug Prentice (2)
1997 Martin Johnson (6)

ENGLAND (10)

1924 Wavell Wakefield (4)
1934 Bernard Gadney (8)
1935 Douglas Kendrew (2)
1983 Peter Wheeler (5)
1985 Paul Dodge (7)
1998 Martin Johnson (39)
2001 Neil Back (4)
2003 Dorian West (1)
2005 Martin Corry (17)
2010 Lewis Moody(3)

IRELAND (1)

1932 George Beamish (4)

ITALY (1)

2012 Martin Castrogiovanni (3)

CHRISTMAS & NEW YEAR

The Tigers' first Christmas fixture was scheduled to be the visit of Narborough to Victoria Park on Christmas Eve 1881 but the match was never played. In 1890 the Belgrave Cricket & Cycle Ground was scheduled to host two Christmas fixtures against Old Denstonians and Rugby but the cold snap stopped rugby for a complete month.

Finally in 1892 Leicester began the first Christmas at the new Welford Road ground with a festival, meeting Coventry on Christmas Eve and Swinton on Boxing Day. Thereafter the venue hosted two, three and even four Christmas games, weather and wars permitting, right up until 1960.

Welford Road has only seen play on Christmas Eve on ten occasions and none since Bridgwater & Albion were the visitors in 1927, whilst Birkenhead Park were the usual foe on Boxing Day, virtually every season between 1905-1965. The usual day for the Barbarians match was the 27th December, except when that date fell on a Sunday, the Baa-baas appeared on Boxing Day itself on only eight occasions.

The Tigers' first match over New Year was in their very first season when they made the trip to Rugby Rovers on the 1 January 1881 and drew. The first time Leicester met Irish opposition came on New Year's Day 1894 when Dubliners, Bective Rangers, played at Welford Road. New Year tours were undertaken in the early 1900s initially to Devon but later to Tyneside.

CLUB CAP

In modern times the awarding of a club cap was reintroduced at the "100 Cap Dinner" at the Great Hall, Walkers Stadium on 25 February 2003, when 87 caps were handed out to virtually all the players still alive who had started 100 first-team games for the Tigers during their careers. Since then 22 more players have been presented with their caps on the pitch at Welford Road after their 100th start.

FAMILY CONNECTIONS IN THE 100 CAP CLUB...

FATHER & SON

Ian & Matt Smith
Nick & Ben Youngs

BROTHERS

Alf & Tom Goodrich
Martin & Will Johnson
Arthur & Frank Jones
Harry & Percy Lawrie
Steve & Stuart Redfern
Bob & Brian Small

COUSINS

Dudley & Percy Atkins

UNCLE & NEPHEW

Trevor & Peter Thorneloe

YOUNGEST AND OLDEST

The youngest player to appear in 100 Tigers matches is **Paul Dodge**, who was just 20 years 191 days when he did so against Nuneaton in 1978, followed by **Ralph Buckingham** 20y 266d against Old Blues in 1927, and **Barry Evans** 22y 3d versus Richmond in 1984. The youngest in the professional era was **Ollie Smith** aged 22y 126d against Gloucester in 2004.
The oldest was **Charlie Cross** who was over 35 against Nuneaton in 1922, followed by **Julian White** 34y 361d against Harlequins in 2008.

NEAR MISSES

The unluckiest player not to be awarded a 100-game cap simply has to be prop **Ray French**. On the World Tour in 1987 Ray made what was thought to be his 100th and final Tigers appearance in

↑ Nick Jackson concluded his Tigers career with 98 starts and therefore unluckily missed his club cap by just two appearances.

the match against Queensland at Ballymore, he was even given the honour of leading the side out with the stadium announcer congratulating him on attaining 100 matches. However, an administrative error years before had resulted in a miscount, giving Ray three more appearances than he should have tallied. His official appearance total therefore remains stuck at 97.

The following ten players have made over 100 first-team appearances but have not made 100 starts:

Name	*Starts*	*Reps*	*Total*
Nick Jackson	98	7	105
Tom Varndell	88	25	113
Martin Castrogiovanni	85	61	146
Thomas Waldrom	85	28	113
Brett Deacon	83	52	135
* Dan Cole	79	44	123
Paul Gustard	76	42	118
Boris Stankovich	72	47	119
Perry Freshwater	64	73	137
Adam Balding	49	61	110

** still playing in 2014/15*

Charles Slow (1933-37), **Arthur Hazelrigg** (1977-81), **Nick Jackson** (1978-89), **Joey Morley** (1885-92) and **William Sheffield** (1880-87) all finished their careers just two games shy of 100 starts.

In earlier times club caps had been awarded by a variety of different qualifications, for instance in July 1897 for the first time it was decided in committee that "jackets and caps would be presented to any player appearing in six games for the first-team in any one season."

CLUB AWARDS

MEMBERS' SEASONAL AWARDS

	Player of the Season	*Young Player*	*Outstanding Contribution*
1996/97	Martin Johnson	Eric Miller	John Wells
1997/98	Neil Back	Michael Horak	Stuart Potter
1998/99	Martin Corry	Lewis Moody	Darren Garforth
1999/00	Austin Healey	Adam Balding	Graham Rowntree
2000/01	Pat Howard	Ollie Smith	Darren Garforth
2001/02	Ben Kay	Ollie Smith	Richard Cockerill
2002/03	Geordan Murphy	Sam Vesty	Neil Back
2003/04	J. v.d. Westhuyzen	Will Skinner	Martin Johnson
2004/05	Andy Goode	Tom Varndell	Graham Rowntree
2005/06	Sam Vesty	Matt Cornwell	Austin Healey
2006/07	Alesana Tuilagi	Jordan Crane	Martin Corry
2007/08	Johne Murphy	Tom Croft	Geordan Murphy
2008/09	Aaron Mauger	Matt Smith	Ben Kay
2009/10	Scott Hamilton	Ben Youngs	Lewis Moody
2010/11	Thomas Waldrom	Manu Tuilagi	Julian White
2011/12	Horacio Agulla	Steve Mafi	George Chuter
2012/13	Julian Salvi	Manu Tuilagi	M. Castrogiovanni
2013/14	Veneniki Goneva	Owen Williams	Marcos Ayerza

SPONSORS' SEASONAL AWARDS

	Players' Player	*Young Player*	*Newcomer*
2001/02	Ben Kay	Harry Ellis	-
2002/03	Josh Kronfeld	Sam Vesty	-
2003/04	Louis Deacon	Will Skinner	-
2004/05	Andy Goode	Tom Varndell	-
2005/06	Shane Jennings	Tom Varndell	-
2006/07	Dan Hipkiss	Jordan Crane	M. Castrogiovanni
2007/08	Louis Deacon	Tom Croft	Ben Herring
2008/09	Sam Vesty	Ben Youngs	Scott Hamilton
2009/10	Ben Youngs	Dan Cole	Geoff Parling
2010/11	Anthony Allen	Manu Tuilagi	Thomas Waldrom
2011/12	Steve Mafi	George Ford	Julian Salvi
2012/13	Tom Youngs	Fraser Balmain	Adam Thompstone
2013/14	Veneniki Goneva	Owen Williams	Jamie Gibson

CLUB COLOURS

The original club colours of all black were decided at a meeting at the George Hotel on 3 August 1880.

By 1884 these had changed into chocolate & orange hoops, which were worn until 29 September 1888 when the *Leicester Mercury* wrote "The Tiger can cast his coat, we had evidence of this last season, when the Leicester "man eaters" shod their brimstone and treacle like covering for one of a lighter hue". The fixture card for 1888/89 confirms that the colours were now chocolate & French Grey.

By 1889 this had evolved into claret & French grey, before finally the famous green, scarlet and white colours were adopted at a meeting on 11 August 1891. Initially the colours were in the form of vertical stripes but by season 1895/96 they had become hoops. For a brief three-season hiatus between 1906-08 the club switched to white jerseys and blue shorts, but soon reverted back to green, scarlet and white hoops.

Until 1998/99 it was always the home team that changed shirts if there was a colour clash, but tournament rules were amended that year to make the visiting side change. All known kits are shown in detail on the following pages.

However on 2 December 2001 at Madejski Stadium against London Irish, referee Chris White deemed there was a colour clash and as neither side had brought a change shirt Leicester were forced to play the game with their shirts turned insideout!

1880-84

1884-87

1887-89

1889-91

1891-95

1895-96

1896-1900

1900-06

1906-08

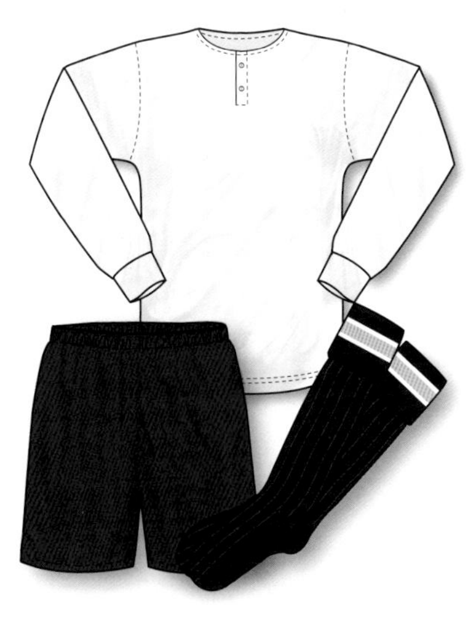

1908-09

1909-47

1947-51 & 1954-56

1951-54

1956-58

1958-75

1975-88

1981-85 CHANGE

1985-91 CHANGE

1988-91

1991-92

1991-93 CHANGE

1992-93

1993-95

1993-95 CHANGE

1995-96

1995-96 CHANGE

1996-97

1996-97 CHANGE

1997-99

1997-99 CHANGE

1999-2001 HOME

1999-2000 AWAY

2001-02 HOME

2000-02 AWAY

2002-03 HOME

2002-04 AWAY

2003-05 HOME

2004-05 AWAY

2004-05 EUROPE

2005-07 HOME

2005-06 AWAY

2006-08 AWAY

2007-08 HOME

2008-09 HOME

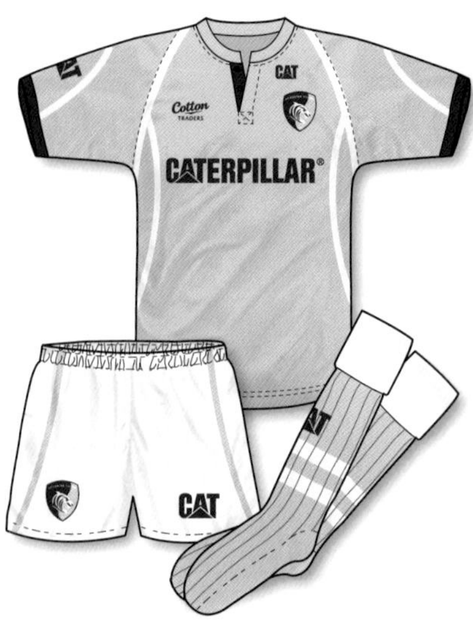

2008-10 AWAY

2009-11 HOME

2010-12 AWAY

2011-12 HOME

2011-12 EUROPE

2012-13 HOME

2012-13 AWAY

2012-14 EUROPE

2013-14 HOME

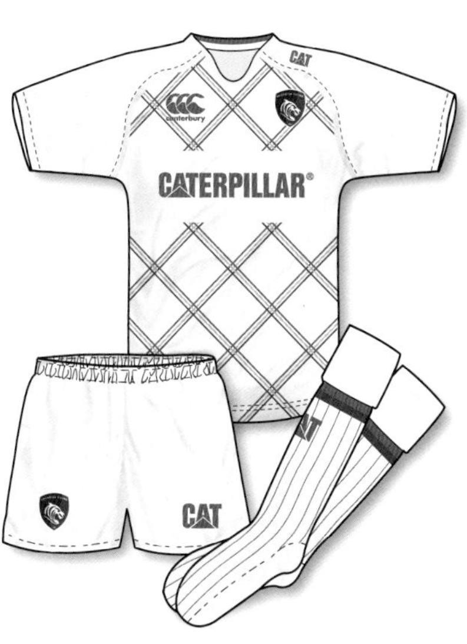

2013-14 AWAY

CLUB CRESTS & LOGOS

1880 A simple outline crest based around the town coat of arms featuring a wyvern and a tudor rose with the town inscription "Semper Eadem" "never changing" underneath. and usually picked out in red

1905 A slightly more elaborate crest again based on the town coat of arms but this time surrounded by much extra foliage, this time usually shown in green

1952 New club playing crest introduced in full colour again based around the city coat of arms – Leicester had become a city in 1919 and were now allowed to introduce two lions holding up the crest. The inscription now says "Leicester FC".

1997 New Tiger head logo commissioned for merchandise and non-playing use. It was designed by Leicester agency Cunnold, Lallo, Minski

2006 The Tiger head insignia is updated to now appear on a shield with background colours of green and red with "Leicester Tigers" stated at the top.

↑ David Whetstone's first 20 games for the club ended in 19 wins and a draw.

CLUB TIE

Since the tradition of awarding a tie for appearing in 20 first-team games began in the 1951/52 season the longest anyone has taken to obtain one is **Jason Aldwinckle** who took eight years 187 days to play his 20th First XV game against Wasps at Loftus Road on 29 April 1998. If the qualification had been in force in the 1920's **Charlie Cross** would have taken just three days short of a decade to obtain his.

Peter Aldwinckle should have won his tie on 30th March 1970, but due to an administrative oversight was not presented with his tie until April 1994 (24 years late), when the *Tigers' Tale* uncovered the error.

The quickest to win a tie is wing **Peter Nicholls** with only 84 days in 1971. In the professional era **Rod Kafer** gained his in just 133 days, followed by **Fritz van Heerden** (134), **Franck Tournaire** (140) and **Geoff Parling** (148).

Paul Dodge is the youngest to receive his tie at only 17 years 304 days against the Barbarians in 1975, he is followed by **George Banks**, **Ralph Buckingham** and **Ted Flewitt**. In the professional era the accolade goes to **Ollie Smith** who attained his tie when just 11 days past his 18th birthday.

The oldest recipient was **Jesse Ball** at 38 years of age in 1891 although **Mefin Davies** ran him close in 2008 at age 36y 32d.

Rob Field (1994-97) uniquely won all his first 20 games and **David Whetstone** between 1896-1900 secured 19 wins and a draw in his first 20 games. English international wing **Alastair Smallwood** won 19 and lost one between 1920-22. Hooker **John Elliott** (1966/67), winger **Kevin Williams** (1979/80), hooker **Troy Thacker** (1988/89), hooker **Chris Johnson** (1993-95) and fly-half **Niall Malone** (1993-95) all won 18 games and lost two of their first 20 Tigers appearances.

The 14 players listed below gained 20-game ties by appearing in their first 20 games in succession, showing in brackets number of matches played in succession until missing one:

1893 – Rupert Cooke (21)
1894 – Arthur Rendle (20)
1895 – Tuffie Rice (all 25)
1905 – James Bainbridge (28)
1907 – Kenneth Wood (41)
1930 – Kilgour Wiener (32)
1937 – Bill Bainbridge (all 41)
1938 – Peter Jerwood (29)
1952 – Jim Fisk (20)
1964 – Keith Chilton (32)
1971 – Peter Nicholls (20)
1975 – Paul Dodge (24)
1982 – Barry Evans (22)
2002 – Rod Kafer (29)

Three players have tallied 18 tries in their first 20 games: **Jack Miles**, **Teddy Haselmere** and **Harold Day**, followed by **Alf Bates** and **Tom Varndell** with 16 apiece.

The scorer of the most points in his first 20 games is **Joel Stransky** (259) followed by **Toby Flood** (208), **John Liley** (188), **Dusty Hare** and **Billy Twelvetress** (182).

COACHING STAFF

Members of the first-team coaching staff who have been involved in rugby skills rather than fitness, from the Tigers' first non-playing coach, **Colin Martin**, who took over coaching the team in conjunction with skipper **David Matthews** who assumed the role of honorary trainer after he retired from playing in the summer of 1965.

Name	*Job Title*	*Timespan*
Neil Back	Coach	June 2004-July 2007
	Technical director	July 2007-30 June 2008
Phil Blake	Defence coach	Sep 2014-
Richard Blaze	Assistant forwards coach	Apr 2011-
Paul Burke	Kicking coach	6 June 2008-July 2010
	Assistant backs coach	July 2010-May 2013
	Backs coach	May 2013
Richard Cockerill	Assistant forwards coach	June 2004-Jul 2007
	Forwards coach	July 2007-Dec 2008
	Interim head coach	June 2007-4 Nov 2007
	Head coach	Jan 2009-July 2010
	Director of rugby	July 2010-
Paul Dodge	Assistant coach	Aug 1991-Mar 1996
	Joint Head coach	Mar-May 1996
Bob Dwyer	Director of coaching	30 May 1996-17 Feb 1998
Allen Foster	Coach	Aug 1988-May 1990
Duncan Hall	Director of coaching dev.	June 1996-17 Feb 1998
Jamie Hamilton	Scrum-half coach	June 2007-June 2008

Irish international Paul Burke finished his playing career at the Tigers and has been part of the coaching set-up ever since.

Ben Herring	Assistant forwards coach	Jan 2009-May 2011
Pat Howard	Backs coach	2000-2002, June 2004-June 2005
	Head coach	June 2005-May 2007
Rod Kafer	Coach	2001-2003
Andy Key	Backs coach	2002-June 2004
	Assistant backs coach	June 2004-2007
Marcelo Loffreda	Head coach	25 Apr 2007-6 June 2008
Damian McGrath	Skills coach	July 2002-May 2004
Colin Martin	Honorary coach	Aug 1965-Feb 1967
David Matthews	Coach	Aug 1988-May 1990
	Assistant coach	Aug 1990-May 1991
Geordan Murphy	Assistant Backs coach	May 2013-
Heyneke Meyer	Head coach	6 June 2008-Dec 2008
Rod Oakes	Assistant coach	Dec 1979-Sep 1986
Matt O'Connor	Backs coach	13 Aug 2008-July 2010
	Head coach	July 2010-May 2013
Dean Richards	Rugby Manager	17 Feb 1998-2000
	Director of rugby	2000-1 Feb 2004
Tony Russ	Head coach	June 1990-1994
	Director of rugby	1994-Mar 1996
Ian Smith	Assistant coach	1991/92-Mar 1996
	Joint head coach	Mar-May 1996
Tim Stimpson	Specialist kicking coach	2003/04
Joel Stransky	Backs coach	Feb 1998-2000
John Wells	Forwards coach	Feb 1998-1 Feb 2004
	Head coach	1 Feb 2004-June 2005
Peter Wheeler	Coach	1987/88
Chalkie White	Coach	Sep 1967-Dec 1982
Graham Willars	Coach	Jan 1983-May 1988

Just three head coaches have picked themselves in a team lineup:
Colin Martin in the second-row in an Easter tour game at Exeter on 12 April 1966.
Graham Willars selected himself three times on the bench v Coventry on 1 October 1983, Cambridge University on 10 November 1984 and Waterloo on 4 April 1987, making late appearances in the last two.
Pat Howard at starting centre against the Barbarians on 17 March 2006 on his 96th and last playing appearance for the first-team.

INTERNATIONAL COACHES

Clive Woodward is probably the most famous international coach to have played for Leicester, however at the 2003 RWC final his opposite number for the Wallabies was **Eddie Jones** – Jones himself made three appearances at hooker for Leicester in 1991/92.
In addition **Dennis Storer** played three first-team games on the wing in the 1957/58 season and later went on to coach the USA Eagles national team in 1976. **John Elders** and **Martin Johnson** both went on to become England head coach.

FITNESS & CONDITIONING COACHES AND SUPPORT STAFF

John Ford was really the club's first physiotherapist. He was appointed in a honorary role in 1971 and remained in place for over 20 years as well as accompanying the team on their tours to Oceania in 1980 and Zimbabwe in 1982. Ex-player **Tom Goodrich** undertook some team fitness work duties just before the Second World War but this was on a very informal basis.
Listed are all those who have had major roles in various conditioning, strength, performance, physiotherapy, fitness and rehabilitation roles, plus senior first-team support staff:

Name	*Job Title*	*Timespan*
Pete Atkinson	Strength & conditioning coach	Aug 1998-June 2003
Chris Brookes	Physiotherapist	Nov 2001-2004
	Senior physiotherapist	2004-06
Ruth Cross	Physiotherapist	1996/97
John Dams	Athletic performance coach	2004-Jan 2008
Martin Dowson	Fitness advisor	1992-1996
John Duggan	Fitness coach	1996-1998
	Fitness advisor	1998-2002
	Fitness & conditioning coach	2002-2004
Andrew Fife	Fitness advisor	1998/99
John Ford	Honorary physiotherapist	1971-1992
Mark Geeson	Physiotherapist	1993-2004
Will Gowtage	Rehabilitation coach	Jan 2010-
Darren Grewcock	Fitness coach	1992-1995
	Athletic performance coach	Jan 2004-2005
Julie Hayton	Rehabilitation coach	2001-2003
	Head of rehabilitation services	May 2003-
Jo Hollis	First-team manager	1996-
Becky Judkins	Medical administrator	2005-
Phil Mack	Director of athletic performance	2004/05
	Performance & medical director	2005/06
Alex Martin	Strength & conditioning coach	2006-2008
	Head of strength & conditioning	2008-
Bill Michelmore	Trainer	1982
Dave Orton	Senior physiotherapist	2010-
Dave Redding	Fitness coach	1996/97
Ollie Richardson	Athletic performance coach	Sep 2004-Oct 2011
Gordon Robertson	Athletic performance coach	Mar 2004-Sep 2005
Bobby Sourbuts	Head physiotherapist	2008-
Paul Stanton	Physiotherapist	2004/05
	Head physiotherapist	2005/06
Charles Timlock	Trainer	1903-1912
Chris Tombs	Strength & conditioning coach	2002-2004
Craig White	Head conditioning coach	April 2006-Sep 2007

COMEBACKS & CAPITULATIONS

In the game against London Irish at The Stoop in the Premiership on 16 October 1999 Tigers trailed 20-3 after 46 minutes and still went on to win the match 31-30. It represents the biggest comeback in the history of the club, surpassing the 12-point deficit at half-time against both Wasps at Sudbury on 15 November 1980 (won 18-12, in a match where all scoring was from kicks and all at one end because of a howling gale blowing down the pitch) and against Bath at Welford Road on 10 September 1983 (won 18-15).

Conversely, on 22 December 1984 at Old Deer Park, Tigers built up a half-time lead of 17-0 against London Welsh but went on to lose 17-25. At Welford Road the biggest half-time lead Leicester have ever surrendered was 13-0, leading Gloucester on 5 November 1938 – they in fact held this score until eight minutes into the second half, only to eventually lose 13-17. If modern scoring values had been adopted this lead would have been 17-0 and they would have lost 17-22. However, against Saracens on 23 February 2013 at Welford Road, Leicester had shot out to a 17-3 lead after 35 minutes only to concede 22 unanswered points and go on to lose the game 27-32. At Twickenham on 21 April 1996 Leicester led the Sanyo World XV 31-12 after 52 minutes but managed to surrender the 19-point lead to lose 31-40.

CONVERSIONS

100 OR MORE CAREER CONVERSIONS

Pos	*Name*	*Career*	*Apps*	*Con*
1	Dusty Hare	1976/77-1988/89	393+1	779
2	John Liley	1988/89-1996/97	226+4	417
3	Harold Day	1918/19-1928/29	212	281
4	Andy Goode	1998/99-2007/08	173+27	275
5	Tim Stimpson	1998/99-2003/04	141+10	223
6	Toby Flood	2008/09-2013/14	107+12	199
7	Jez Harris	1984/85-1995/96	213+12	165
8	Joel Stransky	1996/97-1998/99	72+1	146
9	Doug Prentice	1923/24-1930/31	239	133
10	Colin Martin	1956/57-1965/66	272	126
11	Billy Bream	1910/11-1913/14	101	125
12	Arthur Jones	1894/95-1910/11	224	113
13	Mike Gavins	1956/57-1970/71	121	107
14	Les Cusworth	1978/79-1989/90	365	100

MOST CONVERSIONS IN A SEASON

89	John Liley	1989/90
82	Joel Stransky	1997/98
79	Dusty Hare	1985/86
78	Andy Goode	2005/06

MOST CONVERSIONS IN A GAME BY A PLAYER

For Tigers:

13	Dusty Hare	v Birmingham	17.9.1986
11	Dusty Hare	at Birmingham	16.9.1981
11	Gerry Ainscough	v Liverpool St Helens	11.4.1992
11	Andy Goode	v Newcastle Falcons	19.2.2005
10	John Greenwood	v Richmond	21.2.1920
10	Les Cusworth	at Bedford	3.9.1983
10	Joel Stransky	v Glasgow & District (po)	1.11.1997
10	Andy Goode	v Rotherham Titans	1.5.2004

Against Tigers:

9	Siua Taumalolo	v Barbarians	17.3.1998
9	Neil Jenkins	v Barbarians	4.6.2000

The only forward to have kicked a conversion since **Ray Needham** did so against Bath in 1978 was **Craig Newby** against Sale in the Anglo-Welsh Cup on 31 October 2008.

MOST CONVERSIONS IN A GAME BY A TEAM

For Tigers:

13	v Birmingham	95-6	17.9.1986
12	v Liverpool St Helens	100-0	11.4.1992
11	at Birmingham	78-8	16.9.1981
11	v Newcastle Falcons	83-10	19.2.2005

All nine Tigers tries at Bedford on 19 January 1990 were successfully converted.

Against Tigers:

10	v Barbarians	10-85	4.6.2000
9	v Barbarians	19-73	17.3.1998
7	at Cardiff	5-50	15.11.1947

MISSED CONVERSIONS

For Tigers:

12	v Bedford XV	71-0	15.2.1919

On 27 December 1904 at home to Rugby only one try in eleven was converted.

Against Tigers:

9	at Neath	6-37	26.11.1923

All eight conversions attempted at Pontypool on 2 February 1914 were missed.

John Liley holds the Tigers record for the most conversions kicked in a season, with 89 in 1989/90.

COSMOPOLITAN

When London Irish visited Welford Road for a Premiership encounter on 29 December 2009 the Tigers fielded their most cosmopolitan line-up of all time with nine different nationalities by birth respresented in the starting XV:

Ireland (**Johne Murphy**), New Zealand (**Aaron Mauger/ Boris Stankovich**), Fiji (**Seru Rabeni**), Northern Ireland (**Ian Humphreys**), France (**Christophe Laussucq**), Wales (**Mefin Davies**), Argentina (**Martin Castrogiovanni**), South Africa (**Marco Wentzel**) and the rest were born in England.

COUNTRIES VISITED

FIRST GAME IN A COUNTRY

Nation	*Date*	*Venue*	*Opponent*	*Result*	*Total in Country*
England	23.10.1880	Belgrave Cricket & Cycle Ground, Leicester	v Moseley	D 0-0	4,217
Wales	7.4.1890	Cardiff Arms Park	v Cardiff	L 0-2	247
France	13.2.1923	Stade Colombes, Paris	v Racing Club	L 9-19	29
Scotland	2.1.1926	Arboretum Road, Inverleith	v Heriotonians	L 5-8	5
Ireland	17.11.1956	Lansdowne Road, Dublin	v Lansdowne	L 16-17	15
Australia	6.8.1980	Ballymore, Brisbane	v Queensland	L 12-22	7
Fiji	16.8.1980	Churchill Park, Lautoka	v Lautoka	W 12-6	3
N Ireland	30.4.1982	Eaton Park, Ballymena	v Ballymena	W 21-18	6
Zimbabwe	24.7.1982	Police Grounds, Harare	v Mashonaland	L 23-28	5
Dubai	27.4.1984	Dubai Exiles Rugby Club	v Arabian Gulf XV	W 54-3	2
N Zealand	12.8.1987	Ponsonby Rugby Club, Auckland	v Ponsonby	W 27-16	1
Singapore	18.8.1987	Singapore Cricket Club	v Singapore CC	W 68-0	1
USA	13.8.1989	Vail Rugby Club	v Vail	W 48-0	3
Canada	14.8.1991	Ellerslie Rugby Park, Edmonton	v Edmonton	W 30-18	2
S Africa	7.8.1993	Silvermine, Cape Town	v WP Defence XV	W 75-3	5
Italy	12.10.1997	Stade San Michele, Calvisano	v Amatori Milano	W 37-29	10

Non First-Class:

Spain	5.5.1986	San Sebastian	v Basque XV	W 96-0
Switzerland	9.8.2013	Stade de la Praille, Geneva	v Montpellier	L 15-52

Tigers have won just 32 games in 247 previous visits to Wales for a poor 13% winning rate.

CRICKET CONNECTIONS

The Tigers have played many rugby games at cricket grounds over the years, as often, especially in the late 19th century, the rugby and cricket clubs shared the same venues. Leicester's first game at such a venue was when they played at the iconic Edgbaston Cricket Ground against Edgbaston Crusaders in the first round of the Midland Counties Cup on 22 October 1881. Strictly speaking this was a full five years before Edgbaston staged its first ever cricket match, but the Tigers became regular visitors there playing against Old Edwardians until 1895.

Leicester have played at three other venues which have staged One Day International cricket: 59 matches at St Helen's in Swansea between 1896-1993; the Racecourse - Derbyshire's county cricket ground, in November 1884 and the Padang in Singapore, where the Tigers took on Singapore Cricket Club at rugby in August 1987.

The following 51 Tigers also played First-Class cricket at some time in their careers: **JN Beasley, RB Bruce-Lockhart, JW Burdett, HLV Day, KD Downes, ED Dynes, RDM Evers, HWF Franklin, F Geeson, H German, RA Gerrard, C Gimson, WH Hare, RE Hemingway, AE Hind, FS Hodder, PP Hope, AO Jones, R Joyce, J King, HE Kingston, CJ King-Turner, L Kirk, PH Konig, AS McIntyre, D Moeller, J Morton, FCW Newman, AGB Old, HR Orr, DS Oscroft, PW Oscroft, HG Owen-Smith, GA Palmer, J Powers, HL Price, STA Radcliffe, H Rotherham, GH Salmon, KJF Scotland, G Shingler, WA Sime, JWD Smith, WA Smith, FW Stocks, JAS Taylor, JAC Thornton, HG Topham, DF Walker, LF Ward**, and **SR Wright**. In fact 17 played first-class cricket for Leicestershire, the last of which was **Peter Konig** in 1949, although **Sam Vesty** did play three games for the Leicestershire second team in 2000. In addition **J Collier, RH Hincks** and **AE Wright** appeared for Leicestershire before the County attained First-Class status in 1894.

AO Jones was capped 12 times for the England cricket team during the time that he was playing rugby for the Tigers.

Two of those listed above are test cricketers; **Arthur Jones** made all his 12 test appearances for England during his 224-match Tigers career and also played in 472 first-class cricket matches between 1892-1914; and **Tuppy Owen-Smith**, who gained five Springbok cricket caps in 1929, four years before his only Tigers appearance against Waterloo at Welford Road. Scottish rugby international **Ken Scotland** played cricket for his country against Ireland at Alloway in July 1958 but was unfortunately stumped for a duck on his only first-class appearance.

Freddy Toone played 22 games for the Tigers at half-back between 1892-93 but then went on to become a renowned cricket administrator, first with Leicestershire and latterly the MCC as manager on three successive tours to Australia in the 1920s before becoming only the second man ever to be knighted for cricket-related activities in "promoting good relations between the Commonwealth and the Mother Country".

There were an unprecedented four Tigers players in the Leicestershire team which lost to Yorkshire at Scarborough on 13-15 August 1896. **John Powers** and **Harry German** opened the batting, **Fred Geeson** took ten wickets, whilst **Ralph Joyce**, who played his one and only Tigers game a year later, scored 17 not out and 0 and took two catches.

↑ Fiji international Marika Vunibaka scored three tries on his only first-team appearance in 1997.

JW Dixie Smith played first class cricket and rugby on the same ground! One of his only two first-class cricket matches was for Leicestershire against Glamorgan at St Helen's, Swansea on 28-31 May 1921, scoring 0 and 2, after having played at the same venue six times for the Tigers between 1904 and 1910.

The Tigers took to the field with three future first-class cricketers in the team in the Midland Counties Cup semi-final tie against Stratford at Welford Road on 27 March 1909. **George Shingler** was wing, **Dixie Smith** centre and **Chris Gimson** in the pack. All played for Leicestershire over a decade later.

DAYS OF THE WEEK

The first time that Tigers ever scheduled a match for a day other than a Saturday was on Tuesday 28 December 1886 when Rushden were due to visit Victoria Park, but the match was postponed due to frost. The two clubs tried again two years later and this time the first non-Saturday encounter on Wednesday 26 December 1888 at the Belgrave Cricket & Cycle Ground ended in a 10-0 win for Leicester.

The first time the Tigers ever played a game on a Sunday was at Anglesea Road in Dublin on 18 November 1956 where they went down 3-23 to Old Belvedere. Leicester's first ever "modern" cup tie was also played on a Sunday, against Nottingham at Ireland Avenue, Beeston on 21 November 1971 in the 1st round of the RFU Club Competition, losing 3-10.

Welford Road's first Sunday match involving the Tigers did not come until 16 January 1972 when Bedford played a club fixture, the visitors winning 19-10.

DEBUTS

ONE GAME WONDERS

Scored a hat-trick of tries on only appearance:

"Knott"	v Bedford	6.3.1889
A Francis	at Headingley	1.1.1923
Marika Vunibaka	v Loughborough Students	14.11.1997

Very little is known about the player known as **"Knott"**. The *Leicester Post* said that "his disguise will readily be penetrated. It's a jolly shame that I can't credit him with his own name, for the style in which he got his tries was a real treat. He achieved a very remarkable feat indeed in thrice getting over his opponent's line with the leather in possession."

Six players scored two tries on their only appearance: **Charles Cave** (1898), **J Simpson** (1904), **Robert Ferguson** (1908), **HS Roberts** (1919), **G Jones** (1923), and **Ben Pain** (1996).

TRY ON DEBUT

214 players have scored a try on their first appearance for the Tigers, a hat-trick of tries on debut has been achieved on the following four further occasions in addition to the "one game wonders" above:

Jack Miles	v Handsworth	9.9.1899
John Ewin	at Manchester	1.1.1930
Graham Meikle	v Barbarians	27.12.1933
Ranji Walker	at Exeter	23.4.1935

Seven tries were scored by players making their debut in Leicester's victory over Boroughmuir at Welford Road on 25 August 1996; two each from **Ben Pain**, **Lewis Moody** and **Rob Liley** and a solo strike by **Craig Joiner**.

TRIES IN FIRST THREE STARTS

Nine players have achieved this:
Ezra Pickard (1895), **Charles Wynne** (1913), **Alastair Smallwood** (1930), **Wavell Wakefield** (1921-23), **Pop Dunkley** (1928), **Stephen Meikle** (1931-32), **Leighton Jenkins** (1958), **Steve Hackney** (1991) and **Seru Rabeni** (2004).

Of the above only **Meikle** went on to score a try in his very next start as well.

Nigel Richardson scored tries in his first three league games against London Irish, Gloucester and Harlequins in season 1992/93.

Nnamdi Ezulike holds the Premiership record with tries on his first four games in the competition: for Leicester against Harlequins, London Scottish, Northampton and Bedford in September 1998.

Winston Stanley, **Steve Booth** and **Vereniki Goneva** all scored tries on their first two Premiership appearances for the club.

MOST POINTS ON DEBUT

27 (2t,7c,p)	Rob Liley	v Boroughmuir	25.8.1996*	
22 (5c,4p)	Dusty Hare	v Oxford University	20.10.1976	
15 (3t)	Marika Vunibaka	v Loughborough Students	14.11.1997	
14 (c,3pg,1d)	Derick Hougaard	at Bath	4.10.2008	●
13 (3t,d)	Graham Meikle	v Barbarians	27.12.1933	
13 (t,c,2p)	Toby Flood	at Gloucester	7.9.2008	●

* in this match debut players combined to score 52 of the Tigers' 72 points.

MOST DEBUTS

Ignoring the club's first ever match on 23 October 1880 when of course all 15 players were making their debuts, the most players handed a Leicester debut on the same day was 13, seven in the starting line-up and six more off the bench, against the Classic All Blacks at Welford Road on 25 May 2008.

TRY ON TIGERS DEBUT IN COMPETITIONS

Colin Dexter scored Leicester's first ever league try after 20 minutes in the Tigers' opening league game against Bath on 12 September 1987. The Tigers' first try in the Premiership was scored by **Michael Horak** against Gloucester in August 1997. **Les Cusworth** and **Jez Harris** followed up with tries in that first league game, since then 23 others have repeated the feat on their first league or Premiership appearance for Leicester, although **Ayoola Erinle** in 2007 and Toby Flood in 2008 had both played before in the Premiership for other clubs. In recent years it has been achieved by **Niall Morris**, **Vereniki Goneva**, **David Mélé** and **Blaine Scully**, whilst **Peter Sandford** (against Rosslyn Park in 1989) and **Niall Morris** (versus Exeter in 2011) are the only ones to have scored a brace on their league or Premiership debut.

Rory Underwood scored four tries on his cup debut for the Tigers against Bristol in 1985, **Freddie Tuilagi** got a hat-trick and **Nick Youngs** and **Aadel Kardooni** scored two on their cup debuts.

Eleven players have scored tries on their Anglo-Welsh Cup debut with only **Billy Twelvetrees** scoring two.

Graham Rowntree scored Leicester's first ever European Cup try just before the half-time break against Leinster at Lansdowne Road on 16 October 1996, **Aadel Kardooni** and **John Wells** also scored in this first game. Since then 16 players have scored a try on their Heineken Cup debut for Leicester, with **Ben Herring** doing so on his only appearance in the competition against Leinster in 2008.

↑ Niall Morris, the only Tiger to have two tries on his Premiership debut for the club.

YELLOW CARD ON DEBUT

The only player ever to have picked up a yellow card on his debut was **Lucas Guillaume** after just 8 minutes of the Anglo-Welsh Cup tie against Saracens at Bedford on 9 November 2012 - it was his only appearance for the first-team.

DOMESTIC CUPS

THE ENGLISH KNOCKOUT CUP

On 22 January 1971, just four days short of its one hundredth birthday, the RFU announced a pilot scheme for a new national club knockout competition, the new tournament was known as the RFU Club Competition. Nearly seventy years earlier the RFU Committee had rejected the notion of a national cup competition to be contested by the champions of each county.

Over the years the format changed as the competition expanded - in 1980/81 the Tigers were exempt until the 3rd round based on their form in the previous season's Merit Tables. After National Leagues were first introduced in 1987/88 the following year first division sides were exempt until round three, and in other seasons exempt until the 4th, 5th and even the 6th round in season 2001/02.

Season	*Furthest Reached*	*Match*	*Result*

RFU CLUB COMPETITION

1971/72	1st round	at Nottingham	Lost 3-10
1972/73	Quarter-final	at Sale	Lost 0-7
1973/74	1st round	at Northampton	Lost 6-22
1974/75	Did Not Qualify		

JOHN PLAYER CUP

1975/76	1st round	at Liverpool	Lost 7-10
1976/77	2nd round	at Moseley	Lost 9-23
1977/78	Final	v Gloucester (at Twickenham)	Lost 3-6
1978/79	**Final**	**v Moseley (at Twickenham)**	**Won 15-12**
1979/80	**Final**	**v London Irish (at Twickenham)**	**Won 21-9**
1980/81	**Final**	**v Gosforth (at Twickenham)**	**Won 22-15**
1981/82	Semi-final	at Moseley	Lost 4-12
1982/83	Final	v Bristol (at Twickenham)	Lost 22-28

JOHN PLAYER SPECIAL CUP

1983/84	3rd round	at Coventry	Lost 9-13
1984/85	Quarter-final	at Coventry	Draw 10-10
1985/86	Semi-final	v Bath	Lost 6-10
1986/87	Semi-final	at Wasps	Lost 6-13
1987/88	4th round	v Bath	Lost 6-13

PILKINGTON CUP

1988/89	Final	v Bath (at Twickenham)	Lost 6-10
1989/90	Quarter-final	at Northampton	Lost 7-23
1990/91	4th round	v Wasps	Lost 13-15
1991/92	Semi-final	at Harlequins	Lost 9-15
1992/93	**Final**	**v Harlequins (at Twickenham)**	**Won 23-16**
1993/94	Final	v Bath (at Twickenham)	Lost 9-21
1994/95	Semi-final	v Wasps	Lost 22-25
1995/96	Final	v Bath (at Twickenham)	Lost 15-16
1996/97	**Final**	**v Sale (at Twickenham)**	**Won 9-3**

TETLEY'S BITTER CUP

1997/98	5th round	at Saracens	Lost 13-14
1998/99	Quarter-final	at Richmond	Lost 13-15
1999/00	4th round	at London Irish	Lost 7-47
2000/01	Semi-final	at Harlequins	Lost 18-22

POWERGEN CUP

2001/02	Quarter-final	at Harlequins	Lost 20-22
2002/03	Semi-final	v Gloucester (at Northampton)	Lost 11-16
2003/04	6th round	v Sale Sharks	Lost 13-21 AET
2004/05	6th round	v Gloucester	Lost 13-20

ANGLO-WELSH CUP

There had long been a wish for formal competition between Welsh and English clubs with an ill-fated inaugural Anglo-Welsh League never completed in season 1996/97. After the WRU introduced regional rugby in 2003 it gave the opportunity for the four remaining regions in 2005 to join the twelve Premiership sides in the first Anglo-Welsh Powergen Cup of 2005/06. The teams were divided into four pools of four teams with each side playing the others in its pool once, with the pool winners progressing through to the knockout semi-finals. In 2009/10 when LV= came on board as a sponsor the pool format was changed to introduce cross-pool matches, so that each side now had four games in the first phase, two at home and two away.

POWERGEN CUP

	Pool Stage Record						*Attack*		*Defence*			*Knockout*
Season	***Pos***	***P***	***W***	***D***	***L***	***Pts***	***T***	***For***	***T***	***Agst***	***Rank***	***Stage***
2005/06	1st	3	2	-	1	10	11	86	5	56	3/16	Lost SF

EDF ENERGY CUP

2006/07	**1st**	**3**	**2**	**-**	**1**	**10**	**11**	**81**	**7**	**55**	**3/16**	**Won Final**
2007/08	1st	3	2	-	1	11	10	88	5	48	3/16	Lost Final
2008/09	2nd	3	2	-	1	8	4	58	6	58	9/16	-

LV= CUP

2009/10	2nd	4	2	-	2	9	10	84	9	82	10/16	-
2010/11	4th	4	-	-	4	-	6	60	20	141	16/16	-
2011/12	**1st**	**4**	**3**	**-**	**1**	**13**	**9**	**86**	**8**	**67**	**4/16**	**Won Final**
2012/13	2nd	4	2	-	2	9	12	96	10	101	7/16	-
2013/14	4th	4	2	-	2	9	8	83	11	89	8/16	-

OTHER CUPS & COMPETITIONS...

ANGLO-WELSH LEAGUE

This hastily arranged tournament was only played in season 1996/97. The 24 teams in the English and Welsh top divisions were split into four pools of six with each team playing the other country's three teams in their pool home and away to qualify for a semi-final round. Leicester were drawn in pool 1A with Bristol, Wasps, Neath, Bridgend and Pontypridd. The tournament began on 10 September with the Tigers' first game a day later away at Pontypridd, which Leicester won 48-10. Tigers completed just three of their six games as all teams started to postpone matches. The last match actually played was on 4 December, but there was no wish to continue with the venture and the competition was cancelled mid-season.

LEICESTER V NORTHAMPTON

Over the years various cups and trophies have been played for involving matches between the Tigers and the Saints.

On 22 February 1936 the Northampton Town Boot Manufacturers Association put up an Indian Club as the trophy, which Northampton won 6-0.

On 9 January 1993 a new trophy was put up by sponsors Carlsberg-Tetley for the winner of matches between Leicester and Northampton. The Tigers won this Courage league game at Franklin's Gardens 13-12, and the trophy was up for grabs until 1997/98 when it fell by the wayside.

Leicester met Northampton for the East Midlands Challenge in a friendly at Franklin's Gardens on 13 March 2004, Tigers won 18-5.

CHELTENHAM & GLOUCESTER CUP

This cup was played for only twice, beginning in 1997/98 and set up at short notice with a prize of £20,000 to the winners. Cambridge University joined 19 clubs from Allied Dunbar Premiership 1 and 2 to form four groups of five teams playing each other once during weekends when England were in action. Leicester got through the pool phase with four wins out of four and then disposed of London Irish in the quarter-final before being easily beaten by eventual winners Gloucester at Welford Road in the semi-final.

The following year the format changed to a knockout cup over two legs. The Tigers drew Rugby Lions and were beaten by them in both legs.

INTERNATIONAL CHALLENGE CUP

A one-off tournament played at Welford Road over the August Bank holiday, 25th and 26th August 1996. The four teams involved played two semi-finals on the Sunday, with Leicester beating Boroughmuir 72-33, and Agen accounting for Cardiff, and then the two finals being played on the Monday. Cardiff beat Boroughmuir 48-29 to claim 3rd place and then Agen defeated the Tigers 28-22 to carry off the main prize.

JEWSON CHALLENGE TROPHY

Only played for once, between the Welsh champions and the English champions. Cardiff entertained Leicester at the Arms Park on 12 August 2000, the Welshmen winning 29-17.

MIDLAND COUNTIES CHALLENGE CUP

The Midland Counties Union had been formed in September 1879 through the efforts of EH Richards of Derby Wanderers. The Union comprised the counties of Derby, Worcester, Warwick, Stafford, Northampton and Leicester.

In 1881/82 they introduced a knockout cup competition called the Midland Counties Senior Challenge Cup.

By the First World War there was talk of the demise of the Midland Counties Union, and by 1920/21 this was almost achieved when separate county sides and not the team called "Midland Counties" contested the annual County Championship

Les Cusworth, scored a record 96 drop goals for Leicester.

competition. The cup continued until 1925/26, largely contested by junior clubs, when Newbold-on-Avon became the last ever winners. Seven Midland Counties Cup finals not featuring the Tigers were played at Welford Road: from Coventry beating Moseley in 1892 to the 1914 final which was a bizarre event with Coventry beating Moseley 13-0, only to be disqualified for fielding two ineligible players. Then Moseley themselves were also excluded for not issuing a proper squad list, so the match was declared null and void with no winner.

Season	*Furthest Reached*	*Opponents*	*Result*
1881/82	1st round	at Edgbaston Crusaders	Lost 0-5
1882/83	2nd round	at Moseley	Lost 0-7
1883/84	2nd round	at Rushden	Drew 0-0
1884/85	1st round	at Moseley	Lost 0-8
1885/86	2nd round	at Coventry	Lost 0-6
1886/87	Semi-final	at Rugby	Lost 0-3
1887/88	Semi-final	v Burton	Drew 0-0
1888/89	Final	v Moseley (at Coventry)	Lost 0-6
1889/90	1st round	at Stratford-upon-Avon	Lost 0-13
1890/91	Final	v Coventry (at Rugby)	Lost 0-8
1891/92	3rd round	at Old Edwardians	Lost 0-21
1892/93	2nd round	v Coventry	Lost 0-12
1893/94	Final	v Coventry (at Rugby)	Lost 0-11
1894/95	Semi-final	at Moseley	Lost 0-11
1895/96	3rd round	at Moseley	Lost 0-3
1896/97	Semi-final	v Old Edwardians	Lost 0-3
1897/98	**Final**	**v Moseley (at Coventry)**	**Won 5-3**
1898/99	**Final**	**v Nuneaton (at Coventry)**	**Won 20-3**
1899/00	**Final**	**v Moseley (at Coventry)**	**Won 13-4**
1900/01	**Final**	**v Moseley (at Rugby)**	**Won 8-3**
1901/02	**Final**	**v Moseley (at Coventry)**	**Won 5-0**
1902/03	**Final**	**v Rugby (at Coventry)**	**Won 18-0**
1903/04	**Final**	**v Moseley (at Burton)**	**Won 13-3**
1904/05	**Final**	**v Nottingham (at Coventry)**	**Won 31-0**
1905/06 to 1907/08		Did Not Compete	
1908/09	**Final**	**v Coventry (at Nottingham)**	**Won 8-3**
1909/10	**Final**	**v Coventry (at Nuneaton)**	**Won 8-6**
1910/11	4th round	at Coventry	Lost 6-21
1911/12	**Final**	**v Coventry (at Rugby)**	**Won 16-0**
1912/13	**Final**	**v Belgrave Premier Works**	**Won 39-8**
1913/14	Semi-final	v Coventry	Lost 0-8

ORANGE CUP/ZURICH CHALLENGE

The Orange Cup match between the English and French champions at the start of a new season was played for twice; in 2001 and 2002, with Leicester losing to Toulouse and then beating Biarritz. Zurich then assumed the sponsorship for the next three seasons, where the winners were Wasps twice and Sale.

SANYO CUP

Played for at the end of three seasons only, between 1996-98, where the English champions were invited to Twickenham to take on the might of a Sanyo World XV along the lines of a Barbarians line-up. Leicester lost the 1996 contest 31-40, Wasps lost the following year and Newcastle won in 1998.

SCOTTISH AMICABLE TROPHY

Following on from the Sanyo Cup, the Scottish Amicable Trophy pitted together the English champions and the Barbarians in a season finale at Twickenham. On both occasions it was played, in 1999 and 2000, Leicester were beaten.

DOUBLES & TREBLES

The only English side ever to have achieved a treble of major trophies in a single season was Leicester in 2000/01 when they took the Zurich Premiership title after beating Newcastle Falcons at Kingston Park on 17 March with two games to spare, won the Zurich Championship final at Twickenham, beating Bath 22-10 on 13 May, and topped this with a first Heineken Cup crown against Stade Français in Paris six days later.

Tigers followed this with another league and European Cup double a year later, and remain the only team ever to have achieved two such doubles, let alone in successive years.

Leicester's other double was in 2006/07, winning the EDF Energy Cup and the Premiership title.

DROP GOALS

10 OR MORE CAREER DROP GOALS

Pos	*Name*	*Career*	*Apps*	*DG*
1	Les Cusworth	1978/79-1989/90	365	96
2	Jez Harris	1984/85-1995/96	213+12	70
3	Dusty Hare	1976/77-1988/89	393+1	47
4	Arthur Jones	1894/95-1910/11	224	37
5	Andy Goode	1998/99-2007/08	173+27	33
6	Mel Channer	1945/46-1955/56	127	26
7	Charles Slow	1932/33-1936/37	98	24
8	Jacky Braithwaite	1895/96-1906/07	359	15
9	Jack Parsons	1880/81-1888/89	113	13
10	Robin Money	1968/69-1977/78	255+3	12
11	Mike Poulson	1979/80-1983/84	40+3	11
12	Harry Greenlees	1925/26-1931/32	153	10

MOST DROP GOALS IN A SEASON

14	Jez Harris	1993/94
14	Jez Harris	1994/95
13	Les Cusworth	1979/80

MOST DROP GOALS IN A GAME BY A PLAYER

For Tigers:

4	Les Cusworth	at Liverpool St Helens (r3)	28.1.1989	●
3	Mel Channer	v Bath	13.9.1947	
3	Les Cusworth	at Bristol	9.4.1988	
3	Jez Harris	v Wasps	23.11.1991	●
3	Jez Harris	v Bath	15.4.1995	●

Against Tigers:

3	Gelu Ignat	v Romania	4.9.1990	
3	Rob Andrew	v Wasps (sf)	1.4.1995	●
3	Brock James	v Clermont Auvergne	19.12.2009	●

The Tigers' first ever drop goal was kicked by **Sherrard Coleman** against Nuneaton on 19 February 1881.

DROP GOALS BY POSITION

Since 1925 only three forwards have dropped goals:
Back-row: **Harry Edmiston** v Barbarians on 27 December 1932.
Lock: **Eric Lacey** v Blackheath on 31 January 1948.
Prop: **David Hazell** v Newport on 11 February 1956.
Only two replacements have dropped goals:
Mike Poulson v Oxford University on 19 October 1983
Andy Goode v Sale in the semi-final of the Anglo-Welsh Cup at Millennium Stadium on 24 March 2007.
Since 1974 just one scrum-half has dropped a goal – **Austin Healey** against Leinster in the Heineken Cup on 27 September 1997.
Jez Harris dropped a goal after just 12 seconds against Northampton in the league on 8 January 1994.

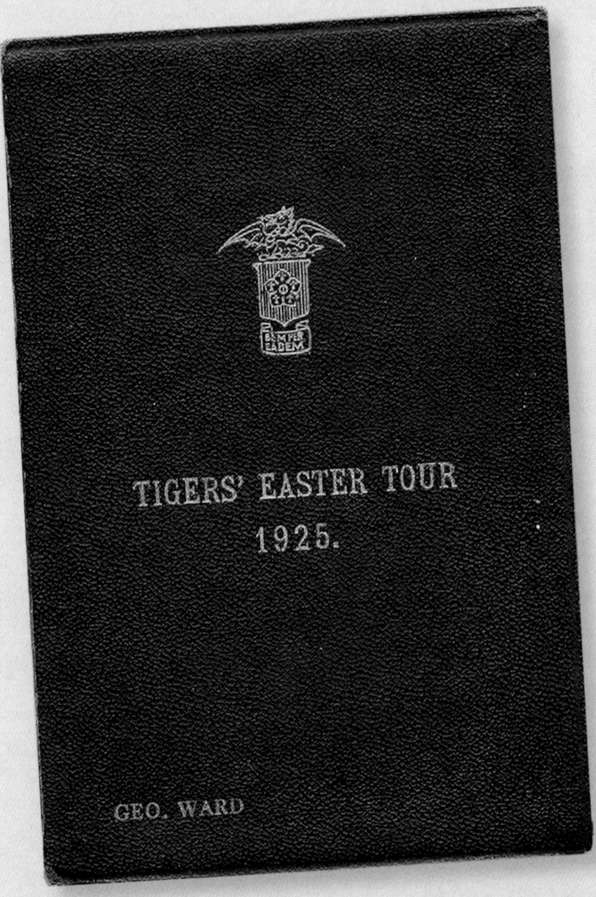

↑ George Ward's leather-bound Easter Tour card from 1925.

MOST DROP GOALS IN A GAME BY A TEAM

For Tigers:

4	at Liverpool St Helens (r3)	37-6	28.1.1989	●

Against Tigers:

3	at Bath	13-17	30.3.1937	
3	v Bedford	11-20	3.9.1955	
3	v Romania	15-12	4.9.1990	
3	v Wasps (sf)	22-25	1.4.1995	●
3	v Clermont Auvergne	20-15	19.12.2009	●

EARLY & LATE STARTS

The earliest kick-off for a Tigers game is 11am which has happened on numerous occasions, the last of which was against London Scottish (won 19-10) at Richmond on 2 February 1985. The latest is 8.30pm local time for two of Leicester's away trips in the Heineken Cup in 2006: at Clermont Auvergne (won 40-27) on 20 January and at Bourgoin (won 28-13) on 8 December.

The most recent 11am kick-off at Welford Road was for the visit of the RAF (won 27-3) on 21 March 1964, whilst the latest kick-off at the venue was 8.05pm when Tigers hosted London Wasps (lost 19-28) in the Premiership on 26 September 2008.

EASTER RUGBY

The first time Tigers ever played a game at Easter was on Easter Saturday, 31 March 1888, when they made the trip to Northampton and lost 0-4 at the St James's End ground.

Tigers have played on Easter Sunday only twice, losing at Wasps 24-36 in the Premiership in 2002 and going down 22-23 at Leeds in the Premiership three years later.

The game at Bristol on Easter Saturday, 5 April 1947, was abandoned after 64 minutes because of rain and mud.

The Tigers' inaugural Easter tour was undertaken on their first ever trip to Wales for Easter Monday and Tuesday in 1890, playing against Cardiff and Newport. The following year they entertained Mossley, Kirkstall and Penygraig at Welford Road. Their first game on Good Friday was on 15 April 1892 away at Dukinfield on a three-game Easter tour to Lancashire, also playing St Helens and Walkden. Leicester have played just four other games on Good Friday, all in the Premiership: in 2005, winning 24-19 at Northampton, beating Sale 26-25 at Edgeley Park a year later, in 2011 travelling to Newcastle and winning 24-13, and in 2014 visiting Harlequins but losing 20-24.

Between 1900 and 1969, excepting the war years, Leicester undertook three-game Easter tours every year, initially to Wales and the West Country, but latterly including Devon. Bristol became part of the Easter tour in 1900, the trip to Memorial Stadium initially being on Easter Tuesday, but between 1920 and 1969 the game was always played on Easter Saturday. Plymouth Albion were the Easter Monday opponents in the same period all bar three seasons, whilst the Easter Tuesday encounter was against Bath, then Bridgwater, Exeter and latterly Stroud.

In 1971, 1973, 1974 and 1976 Tigers undertook a three-game tour to the north with various combinations of opponents featuring Liverpool, Fylde, Manchester, Broughton Park, Wilmslow, Gosforth, Harrogate and Middlesbrough.

Every alternate year between 1978 and 1986 the final two-match Easter tours were undertaken, all to Wales, playing against Neath on Easter Saturday and Pontypool on the Monday. The same adversaries were faced at Welford Road for the years in between. The last game on an Easter Monday was when Wasps visited Welford Road on 12 April 1993 (won 14-13).

EUROPEAN CUP

The European Cup was first played for in season 1995/96 with Toulouse the inaugural winners, although English sides did not compete until the following season when Leicester reached the final at their first attempt but fell at that stage to Brive. In 1996/97 only there were four pools of five teams with each side playing the others in its pool once before the pool winners and runners-up progressed to the knockout quarter-finals. The following season the format was tweaked with five pools of four teams – the pool winners qualifying for the quarter-finals and the pool runners-up plus the best 3rd place team having to negotiate a play-off round. Since 1999/2000 the format has been consistent with six pools of four with the six pool winners and best two runners-up going through to the last eight. From 2009/10 the three next best runners-up qualified to drop down to the quarter-finals of the Amlin Challenge Cup.

TIGERS RECORD IN THE HEINEKEN CUP

	Pool Stage Record						*Attack*		*Defence*			*Knockout*
Season	***Pos***	***P***	***W***	***D***	***L***	***Pts***	***T***	***For***	***T***	***Agst***	***Rank***	***Stage***
1996/97	1st	4	4	-	-	8	14	114	3	43	1/20	Lost Final
1997/98	2nd	6	4	-	2	8	16	163	14	117	7/20	Lost QF
1998/99	Did not compete											
1999/00	3rd	6	2	-	4	4	12	127	11	173	9/24	-
2000/01	**1st**	**6**	**5**	**-**	**1**	**10**	**15**	**178**	**9**	**105**	**2/24**	**Won Final**
2001/02	**1st**	**6**	**5**	**-**	**1**	**10**	**17**	**175**	**3**	**88**	**4/24**	**Won Final**
2002/03	1st	6	5	1	-	11	31	232	6	71	2/24	Lost QF
2003/04	2nd	6	3	-	3	15	17	137	10	115	10/24	-
2004/05	2nd	6	4	-	2	19	24	196	9	118	8/24	Lost SF
2005/06	1st	6	5	-	1	24	19	179	10	111	3/24	Lost QF
2006/07	1st	6	5	-	1	23	22	172	6	60	4/24	Lost Final
2007/08	2nd	6	3	-	3	14	10	110	5	79	14/24	-
2008/09	1st	6	4	-	2	21	23	191	6	90	4/24	Lost Final
2009/10	3rd	6	3	1	2	18	23	187	10	123	10/24	-
2010/11	2nd	6	4	1	1	22	25	215	10	118	7/24	Lost QF
2011/12	3rd	6	4	-	2	17	13	123	8	117	11/24	-
2012/13	1st	6	4	1	1	20	13	119	9	103	6/24	Lost QF
2013/14	2nd	6	4	-	2	21	16	159	9	112	7/24	Lost QF

EUROPEAN RUGBY CHAMPIONS CUP

On 10 April 2014 a new eight-year accord was signed to replace the Heineken Cup with a new merit-based competition called the European Rugby Champions Cup. Initially a 20-team tournament with five pools of four, with the five pool winners and three best runners-up progressing to the quarter-finals.

EVER PRESENTS

The 39 instances by 32 different players who have appeared in all possible matches in a Tigers season:

Season	*Name*	*Matches*
1883/84	William Sheffield (1)	21
1885/86	William Sheffield (2) & Jack Lovett	14
1887/88	John Parsons	21
1890/91	Arthur McKechnie	25
1893/94	James Touhey	37
1898/99	Alf Butlin (1) & William Lincoln	44
1900/01	Alf Butlin (2) & Josh Garner	37
1901/02	Jacky Braithwaite & Sid Penny	35
1902/03	Sammy Matthews (1)	36
1904/05	Sammy Matthews (2)	37
1908/09	Pedlar Wood	41
1922/23	Teddy Haselmere	45
1929/30	Ernie Coleman	39
1930/31	Doug Norman	39
1937/38	Bill Bainbridge	38
1948/49	Denis Bolesworth (1)	37
1950/51	Denis Bolesworth (2) & Harry Sibson	38
1951/52	Gwynne Lawrence & Bill Moore	35
1954/55	John Jenkins	40
1956/57	John Thompson (1)	43
1957/58	John Thompson (2)	39
1958/59	Rex Skelton, Tom Bleasdale & Gordon Almey	38
1961/62	Colin Martin & David Matthews (1)	41
1962/63	Frank Chawner & David Matthews (2)	31
1964/65	Peter Edwards	41
1968/69	John Allen & David Matthews (3)	43
1974/75	Bleddyn Jones	40
1999/00	Pat Howard	29 starts + 2 replacements

Pat Howard played in all 31 possible matches of the 1999/2000 season.

David Matthews is the only player to have played all the games of a season on three occasions, **Sheffield**, **Butlin, Sammy Matthews**, **Bolesworth**, **Thompson** did so twice.

EVOLUTION OF THE LAWS

According to tradition rugby football was first played at Rugby School in 1823. A commemorative plaque on the garden wall of School House on the Close at Rugby School states: "This stone commemorates the exploits of William Webb Ellis who with a fine disregard for the rules of football as played in his time, first took the ball in his arms and ran with it, thus originating the distinctive feature of the rugby game". The origins prior to this could well have dated as far back as the Romans, who had a war game called "Harpastum", (derived from the Greek word

Where the game began. Rugby School as seen from the Close.

meaning to "seize') where two opposing teams tried to carry a ball up to lines marked at each end of a playing area, and then throw it over these lines to register a score. Mauling and driving play certainly formed part of this game.

After Webb Ellis's exploits the handling code of football evolved, and was known to have been played at Cambridge University by 1839, having been introduced there by Old Rugbeians.

On 28 August 1845 the Sixth Form sanctioned 37 Laws of Football played at Rugby School, extracts of this follow:

20. All matches are drawn after five days, but after three if no goal has been kicked.

25. No strangers, in any match, may have a place kick at goal.

26. No hacking with the heel, or above the knee, is fair.

("Hacking" was considered a very good thing, although officially forbidden. "It promoted running scrummages which were the beauty of the game" and "developed the passive virtues by teaching those who play to keep their tempers sometimes under trying circumstances", according to Dr Frederick Temple, the headmaster of the school.)

28. No player may wear projecting nails or iron plates on the heels or soles of his shoes or boots.

29. No player may take the ball out of the Close.

In those early days the playing pitch was 200 yards long by 100 yards wide and the in-goal area was limitless. Players were known to dodge in and out amongst the spectators in an attempt to ground the ball. Some of the original terms that are still in use today are offside, knock-on, touch and goal line. The word "try" also originated here when a touch-down allowed you a try (or attempt) at goal. Goals were the only method of scoring, therefore if the kick failed no score was registered, not even for the try.

On 26 January 1871, 32 representatives from 20 clubs met at Pall Mall Restaurant in central London and formed the Rugby Football Union. The founder members were Blackheath, Richmond, Wellington College, Guy's Hospital, Harlequins, King's College, St Paul's School, Civil Service, Marlborough Nomads, Queen's House, West Kent, Wimbledon Hornets, Gipsies, Clapham Rovers, Law, Flamingoes, Lausanne, Addison, Mohicans and Belsize Park. The Wasps should have been there but did not turn up!

In June of that year the RFU approved 59 rules of rugby football, which was the foundation of the game as we know it today. Matches were to be decided on a majority of goals, that is any successful kick except a punt, either directly from the field of play, or after obtaining a "try at goal". Up until as recently as 1957 the conversion had to be taken with the aid of a "placer", another member of the team who lay on the ground and held or "placed" the ball for the goalkicker to take the kick.

The refereeing of games was done initially by the playing captains of each team, and later by a non-playing umpire from each team. A referee was first seen in 1885/86, in addition to the umpires, who eventually became touch judges. The Rugby Union's *"Regulations for the guidance of Umpires and Referees"* was adopted in October 1886 when referees were provided with whistles and umpires with sticks, later to become flags.

EXPERIENCE

The most experienced Tigers starting line-up of all time is the one which beat Headingley 53-7 at Welford Road on 7 January 1989, it was as follows;

Dusty Hare (380); **Barry Evans** (217), **Paul Dodge** (382), **Ian Bates** (137), **Tony Underwood** (6); **Les Cusworth** (316), **Steve Kenney** (344); **Stuart Redfern** (213), **Chris Tressler** (190), **Wayne Richardson** (149), **Malcolm Foulkes-Arnold** (234), **Tom Smith** (80), **John Wells** (144), **Mark Grant** (6), **Ian Smith** (286), with a grand total of 3,084 games between them.

If you exclude the first few seasons in the history of the club, and the first seasons after the World Wars, then the least experienced team was fielded in the defeat against Saracens at Bedford in the Anglo-Welsh Cup on 9 November 2012, with the Tigers starting line-up having just 115 first-team appearances between them:

Niall Morris (20); **Henry Purdy**, **Andy Forsyth** (19), **Andy Symons** (1), **Alex Lewington** (6); **Matt Cornwell** (42), **Micky Young** (8); **Jonny Harris** (6), **Jimmy Stevens** (4), **Kieran Brookes** (3); **Rob Andrew** (3), **Joe Cain**; **Lucas Guillaume**, **Richard Thorpe** (3), **Michael Noone**. Three players scored a try on debut.

Matt Cornwell was the senior player in Tigers' most inexperienced team, against Saracens on 9.11.2012.

EXTRA-TIME

Eight Tigers games have required extra-time to be played to decide a winner, in each instance 10 minutes each way was played:

12.3.1887	at Rugby, 0-0 at full-time in semi-final of Midland Counties Cup; Lost 0-3.
21.3.1891	v Old Edwardians, 4-4 at full-time in the semi-final of the Midland Counties Cup; Won 7-4
20.3.1897	at Coventry, 3-3 at full-time in the 2nd round of the Midland Counties Cup; Won 6-3
30.3.1901	v Moseley, 3-3 at full-time in the final of the Midland Counties Cup at Rugby; Won 8-3
4.4.1981	at London Scottish, 12-12 at full-time in the semi-final of the John Player Cup; Won 18-12
31.5.2003	v Saracens, 20-20 at full-time in the Zurich Wildcard final at Northampton; Won 27-20
15.11.2003	v Sale Sharks, 28-28 at full-time in 6th round of Powergen Cup; Lost 28-43
3.5.2009	v Cardiff Blues, 26-26 at full-time finished 26-26 after extra-time in the semi-final of the Heineken Cup at Millennium Stadium. Tigers won the penalty shoot-out 7-6.

FAMILY

BROTHERS

The father of the Tuilagi dynasty is **Tuilagi Vavae**, a retired politician and a deputy speaker of the Samoan government, who lives with his wife, Aliitasi, in the village of Fatausi-Fogapoa on the north coast of Savai'i island in Samoa. They had seven children in all - six of them rugby players who all went on to play for Leicester. Fereti, known as Freddie, was the first to play for the Tigers, making his debut against Pontypridd in the European Cup on 28 October 2000. Two of his own sons: Brian and Frederick junior have also played for the Tigers Academy.

Two of the six Tuilagi brothers to have played for the club, Alesana and Manu, celebrate.

Three Tuilagi brothers were in the matchday squad for the Barbarians game on 18 March 2005 – Alesana started on the left wing and scored three tries, whilst Henry and Freddie came off the bench with Henry scoring a try. They were all on the pitch together for the last 16 minutes.

On 27 December 2010 at Welford Road three Tuilagi brothers lined up against each other, Manu and Alesana starting for Tigers whilst Anitele'a was number 12 for Sale Sharks.

SIX BROTHERS (1)

TUILAGI - Freddie, Henry, Alesana, Anitele'a, Vavae & Manu [Freddie & Henry (6), Alesana & Henry (2), Alesana & Manu (26)]

FOUR BROTHERS (1)

BEAMISH - Charles, Cecil, Victor & George [Victor & George (31)]

THREE BROTHERS (5)

PORTER – Willie, Samuel & George [Samuel & Willie (16), Willie & George (5)]
SWAIN - Paddy, Martinus & Albert [Paddy & Martinus (1), Martinus & Albert (2)]
CRAMPHORN - Charlie, Frank & John [Charlie & John (1), Frank & John (1)]
PALMER - Phil, Arthur & Ron [Arthur & Ron (4)]
BERRY - David, John & Richard [David & Richard (5), John & Richard (1)]

TWO BROTHERS (65)

BARWICK - Ebenezer & Henry (1)
WHEELER - William & Frank (1)
HUDSON - Edmond & Francis
SHEFFIELD - Edward & William (5)
NUTT - Tommy & Ally (4)
CATTELL - George & Dick (2)
McALPIN - Kenneth & Donal (8)
PILSBURY - Harry & Ernest
WATTS - Willie & Charlie (4)
COOKE - Ted & Rupert (41)
MOORE - Arthur & Charley
JONES - Arthur & Frank (83)
WALKER - George & Joseph
ATKINS - Percy & Shirley (4)
GOODRICH - Alf & Tom (74)
WILKINSON - Harry & Edwin (9)
LINES – Samuel & Edward (1)
JACKETT - John & Dick (32)
LAWRIE - Percy & Harry (129)
HOGARTH – Anthony & Thomas
HARGRAVE - James & Leonard (1)
ATKINS – George & Fred (2)
LEATHER - Jimmy & Will
WYNNE - Charles & Ernest (3)
THORNELOE - Eric & Trevor (1)
WOOD - Pedlar & Frank (9)
BUCKLER - Will & Walter (1)
WRIGHT - Frederick & George (1)
BOSTON - Norman & Francis (1)
SAMBROOK - Claude & Harold (30)
OSCROFT - Cecil & Donald
EWIN - John & Bert (1)
CLARKE - Percy & Tom
EDMISTON - Harry & John (2)
MEIKLE - Stephen & Graham (1)
BAILLON - Louis & Richard
BARKER - Clifford & John (3)
BEVAN - Spencer & Tom

CROWE - Morgan & Phil (2)
HERBERT - Geoff & Frank (42)
CRICK - Tom & Peter
BALL - Jack & Ron
MOORE - Bill & Jeff
THOMPSON - John & Bill
SMALL - Brian & Bob (14)
ALLEN - Trevor & John (1)
MATTHEWS - David & Andy (5)
WALTON - Field & George
FRENCH - Roy & Ray (23)
RINGER - Paul & Tim (7)
REDFERN - Steve & Stuart (45)
RICHARDSON- Wayne & Lee (4)
UNDERWOOD - Rory & Tony (48)
GRANT - Mark & Paul (6)
WIGLEY - Dave & Steve (1)
WINGHAM - Jim & Oscar (9)
JOHNSON - Martin & Will (77)
LILEY - John & Rob (19)
ROKE - Stewart & Duncan
READ - Mitch & Scott (1)
ELLIS - Mark & Harry
DEACON - Louis & Brett (44)
DODGE - Alex & Ollie
YOUNGS - Ben & Tom (36)
COBDEN - Jack & Joe

Note: The list is in chronological order, with the figures in brackets showing how many times they appeared together in the starting line-up.

The only twins to have appeared for the first-team are Richard and David Berry, whilst their older brother John also played for the first-team, in addition another brother, Michael, appeared for the Extras.

↑ Tony and Rory Underwood, played in the same Leicester team on 48 occasions, and both scored tries on the same day 15 times.

BROTHERS AS PARTNERS

Instances where siblings partnered each other in the team, such as both centres, wings, half-backs or props.

Position	*Names*	*Opponents*	*Date*	
Three-quarters	Henry & Ebenezer Barwick	Northampton	13.1.1883	
Centres	Charlie & Willie Watts	Gloucester	7.10.1893	
Centres	Charlie & Willie Watts	Bedford	23.12.1893	
Half-backs	Paddy & Martinus Swain	Harlequins	28.12.1895	
Centres	Frank & Arthur Jones	21 games	1897-1900	
Wings	Edwin & Harry Wilkinson	3 games	1901	
Wings	Percy & Harry Lawrie	11 games	1908-1909	
Wings	James & Leonard Hargrave	Birkenhead Park	11.11.1911	
Half-backs	George & Fred Atkins	2 games	March 1913	
Wings	Graham & Stephen Meikle	Barbarians	27.12.1933	
Centres	Morgan & Philip Crowe	Bristol	20.4.1935	
Centres	Morgan & Philip Crowe	Plymouth	22.4.1935	
Props	Steve & Stuart Redfern	45 games	1982-1984	
Wings	Rory & Tony Underwood	44 games	1989-1995	
Locks	Mark & Paul Grant	Nottingham	16.3.1994	
Locks	Brett & Louis Deacon	London Irish	13.9.2003	●
Locks	Brett & Louis Deacon	Northampton	25.10.2003	●

TWO SETS OF BROTHERS IN THE SAME TEAM

Two separate sets of brothers starting in the same team has happened 34 times to the end of the 2013/14 season, but the only instances since 1 December 1928, when the Cramphorn and Beamish brothers played against the Harlequins are:
The Lileys and the Johnsons on four occasions in season 1996/97
The Johnsons and the Tuilagis - four times from 2004-05
The Deacons and the Youngs - three games in 2012/13

BROTHERS SCORING A TRY ON SAME DAY

Twelve different sets of brothers have produce 44 instances of brothers both scoring tries on the same day for the Tigers, the most prolific pair being **Rory** and **Tony Underwood**, who did so on 15 separate occasions between 1989-1994.

Names	*Instances*	*Date(s)*
Frank & Arthur Jones	5	1895-1898
Harry & Edwin Wilkinson	2	1901
Percy & Harry Lawrie	11	1908-1914
James (2) & Leonard Hargrave	1	1.11.1911
Frank & Geoff Herbert	1	19.4.1938
Rory & Tony Underwood	15	1989-1994
Steve & Dave Wigley	1	14.8.1991
Jim & Oscar Wingham	1	17.11.1995
John & Rob Liley	1	30.11.1996
Alesana & Henry Tuilagi	1	18.3.2005
Alesana & Freddie Tuilagi	1	17.3.2006
Alesana & Manu Tuilagi	4	2010-2011

BROTHERS AS CAPTAIN IN SUCCESSIVE GAMES

Percy and Harry Lawrie in 1911 (Birkenhead Park, Glasgow University, Barbarians)
Percy and Harry Lawrie in 1913 (London, Bedford)
Percy and Harry Lawrie in 1913 (Devonport Albion, Headingley)
Percy and Harry Lawrie in 1914 (Newbold, Coventry, Bath)
Louis and Brett Deacon in 2012 (NZ Maori, London Irish, London Wasps)
Louis and Brett Deacon in 2012-13 (Toulouse, London Wasps)
Louis and Brett Deacon in 2013 (Scarlets, London Welsh)

FATHER & SON(S)

Below are listed the 23 occurrences in Tigers history of fathers and son(s) both appearing for the first-team:

FATHER & THREE SONS (1)

Tom BERRY and sons David, John and Richard

FATHER & TWO SONS (5)

Percy OSCROFT and sons Cecil & Donald
Bob ELLIS and sons Mark & Harry
Brian WIGLEY and sons Dave & Steve
Paul DODGE and sons Alex & Ollie
Nick YOUNGS and sons Ben & Tom

FATHER & SON (17)

William T COLTMAN and son William G
George GERMAN and son Guy
Alfred CARRYER and son Rupert
Alf BATES and son Edward
James BAINBRIDGE and son Bill
Percy LAWRIE and son Gordon
Cyril HARRISON and son Mike
Bernard VESTY and son Phil
Maurice KEY and son Andy
Mike GAVINS and son Dave
Nick DRAKE-LEE and son Bill
John QUICK and son Sam
David BEATY and son Dick
Phil VESTY and son Sam
Peter WHEELER and son Joe (Ben was also a bench replacement in one game)
Ian SMITH and son Matt
Troy THACKER and son Harry

↑ Sam Vesty became a fourth generation Tiger in 2002, following his father, grandfather and great-grandfather.

The shortest gap between a father's last game for Tigers and his son's debut was just eleven years by **Alf** and **Edward Bates**; Alf playing his final game at home to Headingley on 2 October 1920 and signing off with a hat-trick of tries. Edward's debut came at centre in the game against Harlequins at Welford Road on 5 March 1932.

KEEPING IT IN THE FAMILY

The Vesty family is unique in Tigers history because it has produced four separate generations of Tigers players; Jack **Dickens** was the father-in-law of **Bernard Vesty**, who in turn is father of **Phil Vesty** and grandfather of Phil's son **Sam**.

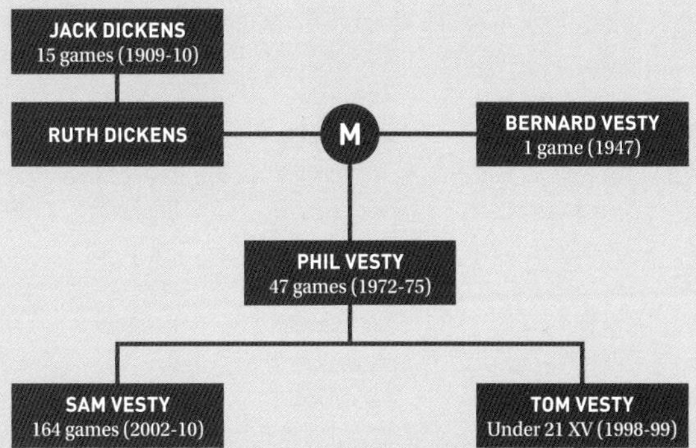

FAST SCORING

For Tigers:

12s	DG	Jez Harris	Northampton	Welford Road	8.1.1994	●
14s	Try	John Duggan	Moseley	Welford Road	22.4.1978	
22s	Try	Brett Deacon	Worcester	Sixways	8.3.2008	●
24s	Try	Martin Corry	London Irish	Madejski Stadium	19.9.2004	●
26s	Try	Geordan Murphy	Harlequins	Stoop	22.12.2001	●
28s	Try	Tom Varndell	Bath	Welford Road	17.9.2005	●
29s	Try	Lewis Moody	Bourgoin	Welford Road	16.12.2006	●

Against Tigers:

19s	DG	Peter Hewat	London Irish	Twickenham (final)	16.5.2009	●
26s	Try	Sireli Naqelevuki	Exeter	Welford Road	3.9.2011	●
30s	Try	WG Pugsley	Bridgwater & A	Welford Road	14.10.1933	
30s	Try	Vince Turner	Bedford	Goldington Road	15.1.1993	
31s	DG	Kris Burton	Treviso	Welford Road	23.1.2011	●
33s	Try	Mathieu Bourret	Northampton	Franklin's Gardens	2.12.2006	●
38s	Try	Farid Sid	Perpignan	Welford Road	3.11.2001	●
39s	Try	Adedayo Adebayo	Bath	Welford Road	6.1.1996	●

FIRST TRY SCORER

For Tigers:
Neil Back grabbed Leicester's first try in a game on an incredible 40 separate occasions, and **Geordan Murphy** did so 35 times, penalty tries are next with 30, followed by **Rory Underwood** and **Leon Lloyd** with 25, and **Steve Hackney** and **Alesana Tuilagi** with 24.
Tom Varndell scored Tigers' opening try in three successive matches in April 2006 against Northampton, Wasps and Saracens.

Against Tigers:
Adedayo Adebayo scored Bath's opening try in seven matches and **Mark Cueto** six for Sale.

FINALS

Listed here are all the major finals, and their outcomes, in Tigers history:

Date	Tournament	Venue	Opponents	Result
23.3.1889	Midland Counties Cup	The Butts, Coventry	Moseley	L 0-6
4.4.1891	Midland Counties Cup	Rugby Cricket Club	Coventry	L 0-8
31.3.1894	Midland Counties Cup	Rugby Cricket Club	Coventry	L 0-11
w6.4.1898	**Midland Counties Cup**	**The Butts, Coventry**	**Moseley**	**W 5-3**
1.4.1899	**Midland Counties Cup**	**The Butts, Coventry**	**Nuneaton**	**W 20-3**
31.3.1900	**Midland Counties Cup**	**The Butts, Coventry**	**Moseley**	**W 13-4**
30.3.1901	**Midland Counties Cup**	**Rugby Cricket Club**	**Moseley**	**W 8-3***
29.3.1902	**Midland Counties Cup**	**The Butts, Coventry**	**Moseley**	**W 5-0**
4.4.1903	**Midland Counties Cup**	**The Butts, Coventry**	**Rugby**	**W 18-0**
2.4.1904	**Midland Counties Cup**	**Burton-on-Trent**	**Moseley**	**W 13-3**
1.4.1905	**Midland Counties Cup**	**The Butts, Coventry**	**Nottingham**	**W 31-0**
3.4.1909	**Midland Counties Cup**	**Nottingham**	**Coventry**	**W 8-3**
2.4.1910	**Midland Counties Cup**	**Nuneaton**	**Coventry**	**W 8-6**
30.3.1912	**Midland Counties Cup**	**Rugby Cricket Club**	**Coventry**	**W 16-0**
5.4.1913	**Midland Counties Cup**	**Welford Road**	**Belgrave PW**	**W 39-8**
15.4.1978	John Player Cup	Twickenham	Gloucester	L 3-6
21.4.1979	**John Player Cup**	**Twickenham**	**Moseley**	**W 15-12**
19.4.1980	**John Player Cup**	**Twickenham**	**London Irish**	**W 21-9**
2.5.1981	**John Player Cup**	**Twickenham**	**Gosforth**	**W 22-15**
30.4.1983	John Player Cup	Twickenham	Bristol	L 22-28
29.4.1989	Pilkington Cup	Twickenham	Bath	L 6-10
1.5.1993	**Pilkington Cup**	**Twickenham**	**Harlequins**	**W 23-16**
7.5.1994	Pilkington Cup	Twickenham	Bath	L 9-21
4.5.1996	Pilkington Cup	Twickenham	Bath	L 15-16
25.1.1997	Heineken Cup	National Stadium, Cardiff	Brive	L 9-28
10.5.1997	**Pilkington Cup**	**Twickenham**	**Sale**	**W 9-3**
s13.5.2001	**Zurich Championship**	**Twickenham**	**Bath**	**W 22-10**
19.5.2001	**Heineken Cup**	**Parc des Princes, Paris**	**Stade Français**	**W 34-30**
25.5.2002	**Heineken Cup**	**Millennium Stadium**	**Munster**	**W 15-9**
14.5.2005	Zurich Premiership	Twickenham	London Wasps	L 14-39
27.5.2006	Guinness Premiership	Twickenham	Sale Sharks	L 20-45
s15.4.2007	**EDF Energy Cup**	**Twickenham**	**Ospreys**	**W 41-35**
12.5.2007	**Guinness Premiership**	**Twickenham**	**Gloucester**	**W 44-16**
s20.5.2007	Heineken Cup	Twickenham	London Wasps	L 9-25
12.4.2008	EDF Energy Cup	Twickenham	Ospreys	L 6-23
31.5.2008	Guinness Premiership	Twickenham	London Wasps	L 16-26
16.5.2009	**Guinness Premiership**	**Twickenham**	**London Irish**	**W 10-9**
23.5.2009	Heineken Cup	Murrayfield	Leinster	L 16-19
29.5.2010	**Guinness Premiership**	**Twickenham**	**Saracens**	**W 33-27**
28.5.2011	Aviva Premiership	Twickenham	Saracens	L 18-22
s18.3.2012	**LV= Cup**	**Sixways, Worcester**	**Northampton**	**W 26-14**
26.5.2012	Aviva Premiership	Twickenham	Harlequins	L 23-30
25.5.2013	**Aviva Premiership**	**Twickenham**	**Northampton**	**W 37-17**

All games played on Saturdays except, w=Wednesday and s=Sunday.
* After extra-time.

MOST APPEARENCES IN A MAJOR FINAL

Finals	Name	W	L
13	Geordan Murphy	7	6
12	Ben Kay	6	6
11	George Chuter	4	7
11	Alesana Tuilagi	3	8
10	Martin Corry	5	5
10	Sid Penny	10	0
10	Graham Rowntree	5	5
9	Neil Back	5	4
9	Martin Johnson	5	4
9	Andy Goode	4	5
9	Marcos Ayerza	4	5
9	Julian White	3	6
9	Lewis Moody	5	4

TIGERS WINNING SILVERWARE

England's champion club has been decided since 2003 by winning the Premiership final at Twickenham. Prior to this it had been just a straight league campaign with the side at the top of the pile at the end of the season being crowned champions. Leicester won the title this way on six occasions, as follows:

Date	Tournament	Venue	Opponents	Result
m4.4.1988	Courage League	Welford Road	Waterloo	W 39-15
Took title with 1 game to spare				
29.4.1995	Courage League	Welford Road	Bristol	W 17-3
Took title by 4 points				
s2.5.1999	Allied Dunbar Premiership	Kingston Park	Newcastle	W 21-12
Took title with 1 game to spare				
s14.5.2000	Allied Dunbar Premiership	Memorial Ground	Bristol	W 30-23
Took title with 1 game to spare				
17.3.2001	Zurich Premiership	Won title when Bath beat Wasps		
Took title with 2 games to spare				
13.4.2002	Zurich Premiership	Welford Road	Newcastle	W 20-12
Took title with 3 games to spare				

All games played on Saturdays except, m=Monday and s=Sunday.

FIXTURE LIST

Clubs from the Midlands were the only opponents for Tigers until Swinton visited the Belgrave Cricket & Cycle Ground on 6 October 1888 (lost 1-11). A first away game outside of the region preceded this, playing at Valley Parade in Bradford against Manningham on 10 March 1888, going down 4-10 to the crack Yorkshire outfit.

Cardiff Harlequins became the first Welsh visitors to Leicester on 30 March 1889 (lost 0-5), whilst Tigers first trip outside England followed at Easter 1890, playing at Cardiff and Newport on successive days but losing both games 0-2 and 1-9.

The West Country was included in 1891/92 with a home and away fixture against Gloucester (lost 0-15 and 0-6), and there was also a first ever trip to London to take on Blackheath on 13 February 1892 (lost 0-37). The first London club to visit Welford Road were Guy's Hospital on 21 January 1893, then in the next month they were followed by three others: St Thomas' Hospital, Old Merchant Taylors and St Bartholomew's Hospital.

↑ Geordan Murphy played in a record 13 major finals for Leicester.

Leicester made their first visit to a top division football ground on 22 September 1996, when they faced Wasps at Loftus Road.

The first trip over the Channel took place in February 1923 when the Tigers played Racing Club de France at the Stade Colombes in Paris after travelling via train and boat, the same opponents being the first Gallic visitors to Welford Road to play against Leicester just six weeks earlier.

Leicester first flew as a team to a game when they visited Ireland in November 1956, flying by Aer Lingus to Dublin on a Dakota. They played against Lansdowne and Old Belvedere in successive days, although Bective Rangers, also from Dublin, had made the reverse trip to Leicester over 60 years earlier.

FLOODLIGHTS

The first game the Tigers ever played under floodlights was at Rodney Parade, Newport, on Saturday, 13 February 1960, kicking off at 6.30pm, which Leicester lost 9-19.

In the summer of 1964 floodlights were erected at Welford Road and were first used in the game against a Midlands XV on Thursday, 8 October.

The floodlights failed for almost half an hour on 23 December 1995 during the Pilkington Cup 4th round tie at the County Ground in Exeter, but the teams carried on in almost total darkness with both sides indistinguishable due to the muddy pitch, ruined by recent inclement weather. Eventually the lights were restored with BBC Radio Leicester's Bleddyn Jones completing an impressive "live" commentary without actually being able to identify any of the players!

FOOTBALL CONNECTIONS

When the Tigers were formed in 1880 it was a golden era for the formation of many football clubs, indeed the title of the Tigers remains Leicester Football Club. Most clubs at this time began fielding teams at both rugby and association football. This was also true of the Tigers, who for the first two seasons had an association team. Leicester Fosse, who evolved into Leicester City, were not originally formed until 1884, so it could be said that it was the Tigers who were actually the pioneers of BOTH codes in the city.

The Tigers actually played Derby County at rugby union on 1 November 1884, six years before Leicester City (nee Fosse) played them at football. Derby won by two tries to one in a match played at Derby's cricket ground – the Racecourse! Previously it had been thought that the Tigers had played Derbyshire on that day, but the researcher mistook the newspaper account referring to "Derby County" as "Derbyshire".

Leicester also played a famous Yorkshire side called Manningham six times between 1888-93 (and lost all six), before they in turn evolved to become Bradford City FC in 1903. Two of the games were played at Valley Parade, the famous football ground.

Before professionalism in 1995 games at out and out football grounds were almost unheard of, the closest Leicester came to appearing at such a venue probably being when they played Harlequins at the White City on 25 September 1954, almost 12 years before the venue became a 1966 Football World Cup stadium. Now ground shares with football clubs are commonplace with Leicester's first ever match at a specialist football ground being their trip to Saracens on the opening day of the 1996/97 league season which was played at the 8,500 capacity Southbury Road Stadium, the home of Isthmian League club Enfield FC. Just over three weeks later was a first visit to a top flight football ground, playing Wasps at Loftus Road, the home of Football League first division side Queens Park Rangers.

Leicester took six games "over the road" to Walkers (now King Power) Stadium, the home of Leicester City, between 2005-09, the first of which was the Heineken Cup semi-final against Toulouse on 24 April 2005.

FOOTBALLERS FOR LEICESTER FOSSE/CITY

Sherrard Coleman, who made 141 appearances for the Tigers first-team at rugby between 1880-92 also played for the Tigers' association team from 1880-82 before going on to play for Leicester Fosse during their first four seasons from 1884-89.

Ernest 'Snooks' Nuttall was the captain of Leicester Fosse and indeed scored their first ever goal in the FA Cup, against Small Heath in October 1891. He made his only appearance for the Tigers against Ashby on 2 March 1892 and is shown in the press under the nom de plume "**EA Phipps**". *The Wyvern* newspaper stated: "The debut of the Fosse skipper as a full blown Rugbyite caused considerable merriment, as he evinced some particularity to taking the man and leaving the ball, probably sound Association but scarcely Rugby, a result he found when penalised by a free!!" He then scored for Fosse three days later in a 2-2 home draw with Kettering.

Alfred Barrett made his only appearance for Leicester Fosse at outside-left at Lincoln City on 2 April 1915. Almost five years later he played in eight games for the Tigers on the wing, scoring three tries.

Frank Broadley made 13 appearances on the wing for the Tigers between 1911-15 and scored eight tries. He played at outside-right for Fosse against Rotherham County in October 1916, and was excused his unremarkable performance by the *Daily Post* reporter on the rather unlikely grounds that he was "playing his first Association game!"

Wally Frisby played football five times for Southampton and twice for Brentford during the First World War while serving with the RAF, and signed for Leicester City as an amateur right-back in August 1919, but failed to make much impact with the round ball. He changed codes after his Filbert Street stint, and by the mid-20s was a noted rugby player with Westleigh before playing in three first-team games for the Tigers at full-back in 1926, scoring a drop goal against United Services.

Andrew Roxburgh made 19 appearances for Leicester City at inside-forward between 1920-22 scoring two goals, before switching to rugby and playing in 23 games for the Tigers first-team at centre and half-back between 1922-23.

The local press noted on 23 December 1922 on the occasion of his Tigers debut at Coventry "that a trial was given to the ex-Leicester City amateur in the three-quarter line; he made a promising first appearance showing plenty of dash".

Richard Pell and **Eric Bann** were both more than useful footballers in the junior ranks at Leicester City before switching to rugby with the Tigers, whilst **Malcom Sayer** who played 56 games in the centre for the Tigers between 1963-68 had already won his Blue for soccer at Cambridge University.

CITY AND TIGERS, SAME CITY, SAME DAY

In earlier years there have been some notable dates where Leicester City and the Tigers have both had fixtures on the same day against clubs from the same city – the first of which was in 1897 when Leicester City visited Manchester City and Tigers took on Manchester just across town. There have been seven instances of Welford Road and Filbert Street hosting teams named after the same city on the same day, featuring Burton/Burton Swifts in 1898, Bristol/Bristol City in 1905, Manchester/Manchester United at Christmas 1928, Cardiff/Cardiff City in 1950, Birmingham/Birmingham City in 1973, Coventry/Coventry City in 1977 and the most recent of which was on 11 December 1993 when City beat Bristol City 3-0 and Tigers defeated Bristol 21-9.

Since the King Power (Walkers) Stadium was opened in 2002 there have been just 21 dates where the City and the Tigers were at home on the same day, all on a Saturday except for New Year's Day 2007 which was a Monday. However, since the end of the 2008/09 season the Safety Advisory Group have insisted that the teams do not play at home on the same day, and hence there have been just two Saturdays when this has occurred: on 7 May 2011 when Ipswich Town visited Leicester City kicking off at 12:45 and the Tigers followed on at 3pm hosting London Irish, and on 1 December 2012 when Tigers entertained Bath kicking off at 12:30 and City then taking on Derby County at 5:20pm.

FORTRESS WELFORD ROAD

The Tigers went an incredible 57 home Premiership games and almost five years at Welford Road without defeat between 1998 and 2002, a run which also included an amazing sequence of 52 straight victories in the competition. Leicester had been beaten 19-25 by champions elect Newcastle Falcons at the famous venue on Tuesday, 30 December 1997 but did not lose there again in the tournament until Northampton were the visitors on 30 November 2002. For the first two games of the sequence the Tigers head coach was **Bob Dwyer**, thereafter it was continued by **Dean Richards** who coincidentally had made his 314th and final appearance as a player in the Falcons defeat.

FULL HOUSES

Players scoring a "full house" of a try, conversion, penalty goal and a drop goal in the same game.

Date	*Opponents*	*Name*	
For Tigers:			
23.3.1901	v Nuneaton (sf)	Arthur Jones	●
15.4.1950	v Nuneaton	George Cullen	
1.11.1964	at Old Belvedere	Keith Chilton	
15.9.1969	v Irish Wolfhounds	Arthur Chapman	
13.11.1976	v Cambridge University	Dusty Hare(1)	
15.11.1977	v Nottingham	Dusty Hare(2)	●
9.2.1980	at Newport	Les Cusworth(1)	
1.3.1980	v Harlequins	Les Cusworth(2)	
5.12.1981	v Waterloo	Dusty Hare(3)	
12.1.1985	v Gloucester	Dusty Hare(4)	
2.3.1985	v Harlequins	Dusty Hare(5)	
12.12.1987	at Blackheath	Jez Harris(1)	
28.12.1993	v Barbarians	Jez Harris(2)	
21.10.1995	at Wasps	John Liley	●
18.4.1998	at Harlequins	Joel Stransky	●
Against Tigers:			
23.3.1974	Sale	Chris Toone	
16.1.1976	Bedford	Neil Bennett	
16.10.1981	Northampton	AN Griffiths	●
23.3.1991	Harlequins	David Pears	●
30.8.1997	Gloucester	Mark Mapletoft	●
8.1.2000	Stade Français	Diego Dominguez	●
24.11.2002	London Irish	Barry Everitt	●
26.2.2005	Northampton Saints	Shane Drahm	●
30.9.2005	Newport Gwent Dragons	Craig Warlow	●

Joel Stansky was the last Tigers' player to score a try, conversion, penalty goal and drop goal in the same game, doing so against Harlequins on 18.4.1998.

GAME WINNING SCORES

Tigers have won three pieces of silverware with late scores snatching the prize from their opponents – the first was **Steve Kenney's** 75th minute try at Twickenham to give Leicester their first John Player Cup win against Moseley in 1979, a score which took Leicester 13-12 ahead.

Leicester repeated the feat with their first Heineken Cup win against Stade Français in Paris in 2001 this time when **Leon Lloyd's** try took them to a 32-30 lead with just two minutes left. **Tim Stimpson's** remarkable conversion meant the gap significantly widened to larger than a penalty or drop goal.

At Twickenham in 2010 Leicester took the Premiership crown with a **Dan Hipkiss** try in the 77th minute wrestling the title from the grasp of Saracens.

There have been two further instances in semi-finals where this time the boot has been the deciding factor – in 2002 against Llanelli in the Heineken Cup at the City Ground, Nottingham, where **Tim Stimpson's** "monster" penalty goal from well inside his own half with just a minute left broke the Welshmen's hearts. Stimpson had also got Leicester out of the pools earlier that season with another huge strike in the last minute to beat Perpignan 31-30 on their own park.

The other semi-final victory was in the Premiership at Gloucester in 2008 with **Andy Goode's** 78th minute drop goal beating the Cherry & Whites 26-25.

Scores in the last ten minutes of major competitions which won the game for Leicester when trailing at the time:

Date	*Opponent*	*Venue*	*Min*	*Name*	*Type*	*Result*	*Rd*
21.4.1979	Moseley	Twickenham	75	Steve Kenney	Try	13-12	F
11.3.1989	Bristol	Welford Road	79	Les Cusworth	Drop	13-12	
10.3.1990	Bristol	Memorial Stadium	83	John Liley	Pen	13-11	
9.1.1993	Northampton	Franklin's Gardens	80	John Liley	Conv	13-12	
12.2.1994	Wasps	Sudbury	81	Jez Harris	Drop	15-13	
25.2.1995	Sale	Heywood Road	80	John Liley	Pen	14-12	
16.9.1995	Sale	Heywood Road	87	Stuart Potter	Try	14-12	
7.9.1996	Bath	Welford Road	81	Penalty Try	Try	26-25	
26.12.1997	Saracens	Vicarage Road	80	Joel Stransky	Drop	22-21	
16.10.1999	London Irish	Stoop	81	Tim Stimpson	Conv	31-30	
19.8.2000	Wasps	Loftus Road	82	Tim Stimpson	Conv	24-22	
24.11.2000	Harlequins	Stoop	75	Tim Stimpson	Try	14-13	
2.12.2000	Gloucester	Welford Road	84	Freddie Tuilagi	Try	29-28	
19.5.2001	Stade Français	Parc des Princes	78	Leon Lloyd	Try	32-30	F
27.10.2001	Perpignan	Aime-Giral	79	Tim Stimpson	Pen	31-30	
28.4.2002	Llanelli	City Ground	79	Tim Stimpson	Pen	13-12	SF
18.12.2005	Ospreys	Liberty Stadium	85	Andy Goode	Conv	17-15	
10.3.2006	Leeds	Welford Road	80	Will Skinner	Try	24-23	
1.4.2007	Stade Français	Welford Road	73	Andy Goode	Conv	21-20	QF
6.4.2007	Sale	Edgeley Park	80	Sam Vesty	Pen	26-25	
10.5.2008	Harlequins	Welford Road	76	Tom Varndell	Try	29-28	
18.5.2008	Gloucester	Kingsholm	78	Andy Goode	Drop	26-25	SF
4.1.2009	Bath	Welford Road	77	Derick Hougaard	Conv	24-22	
29.5.2010	Saracens	Twickenham	77	Dan Hipkiss	Try	31-27	F
9.10.2010	Treviso	Stadio Monigo	78	Alesana Tuilagi	Try	32-29	
17.9.2011	Newcastle	Kingston Park	76	Steve Mafi	Try	27-26	
19.2.2012	Saracens	Vicarage Road	84	Geordan Murphy	Drop	20-19	
15.12.2012	Treviso	Stadio Monigo	77	George Ford	Conv	14-13	
15.12.2013	Montpellier	Yves-du-Manoir	80	Ryan Lamb	Conv	15-14	

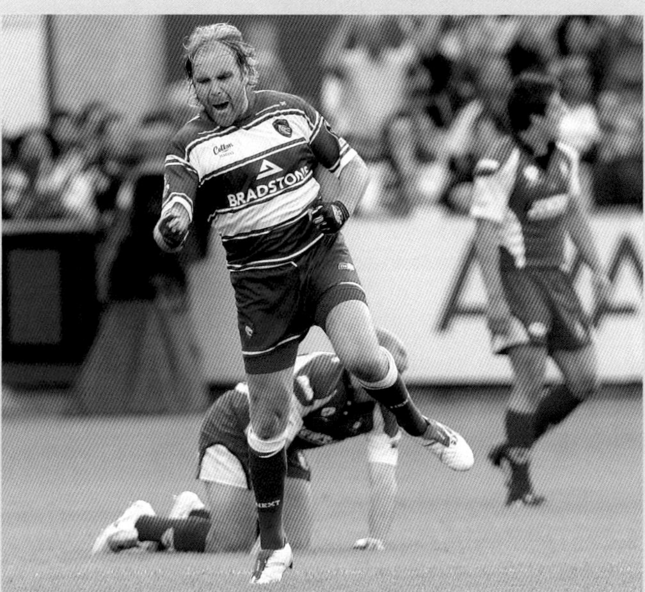

Andy Goode's 78th minute drop goal at Kingsholm in the Premiership semi-final on 18 May 2008 won the game for the Tigers, and broke Gloucester's hearts.

Conversely the Tigers have lost one final in which they were leading with minutes left: against Bath at Twickenham in 1996 (15-16) with **Jon Callard** kicking the winning conversion of a penalty try awarded by referee **Steve Lander**, and lost two more in which they were drawing nearing the end: against Bath at Twickenham in 1989 with a **Stuart Barnes** try (6-10) and in the Heineken Cup final against Leinster at Murrayfield in 2009 with a **Jonathan Sexton** penalty goal (16-19).

Since 1989 an incredible 11 matches against Bath have been decided in the last ten minutes and involved a lead change, in addition five other encounters between the two during this period have ended in a draw.

GOALS FROM A MARK

The Goal From a Mark was a legitimate way of scoring until the laws prohibited it in 1977/78. Up until then a player could make a "fair catch" anywhere on the pitch and not just inside his own 22. On infrequent occasions the Mark was made within goalkicking range, and hence points could be gleaned by kicking a "Goal From a Mark".

MOST GOALS FROM A MARK IN A CAREER

Pos	*Name*	*Career*	*Apps*	*Marks*
1	Harry Lawrie	1903/04-1914/15	168	6
2=	Ted Cooke	1889/90-1897/98	158	3
	Arthur Jones	1894/95-1910/11	224	3
4	Harold Day	1918/19-1928/29	212	2

Twelve other players have kicked one goal from a mark for the club.

The first goal from a mark for Tigers was scored by **Leonard Ward** against Bedford Grammar School on 1 November 1890. The last was kicked by **Norman York** at Bristol on 11 April 1936, coincidentally he is the only prop to have done so.

The first one conceded was to **AC Hill,** the Coventry full-back, in the 2nd round of the Midland Counties Cup on 20 March 1886, and the last was by **Tony Pargetter** for Moseley at Welford Road on 25 November 1961.

GROUND SWAPS

Fourteen games in the history of the Tigers which were scheduled to be played away from home were switched to Welford Road for a variety of reasons, usually to have the chance of a larger attendance. The first such encounter was in the first round of the Midland Counties Cup on 4 March 1893 when Coventry Excelsior were drawn at home but switched the tie to Leicester. The most recent instance was when Barking were drawn at home in the 4th round of the 1998/99 Tetley's Bitter Cup but moved the tie to Leicester to improve their share of a bigger gate. 4,884 attended, far more than could watch at Barking's Goresbrook ground.

GROUNDSMEN

Welford Road had its first full-time groundsman when **Walter Wilby** was appointed in August 1895 at a salary of 25/-. Here are all the subsequent head groundsmen we know of:

Aug 1895	Walter Wilby
Jan 1900	J Tomlinson
1922-1945	Tom Goodrich
1945-1946	Albert Goodrich
1948-Oct 1965	Bill Nash
Oct 1965-1974	Fred Cox
1974-1999	Derek Limmage
1999-2002	Dave Stonebridge
2002-	Steve Packwood

GUEST PLAYERS

The Tigers' first out and out "guest" player was probably Scotland international forward **Mark Coxon Morrison** who made his Leicester debut at home to Cardiff on New Year's Eve 1898 having already been capped seven times by Scotland in the previous three years. He then gained another 11 caps before making his second and final appearance for the Tigers against Bective Rangers at Welford Road on 27 December 1902.

Prior to this Leicester had included a number of guest players in their line-ups, usually when travelling away from home and finding themselves a man short and so resorting to borrowing players from the home club.

The Tigers' first ever visit to Wales was a two-game "tour" in April 1890 to play Cardiff and Newport on Easter Monday and Tuesday for the last two games of the 1889/90 season. Some players could not get time off work for the trip so four guest players were included, who all made their only two appearances for the club: **Abel Ashworth** from Oldham who eventually was capped by England in the pack in 1892 played centre, brothers **George & Dick Cattell** from Moseley, Dick going on to win seven England caps at fly-half between 1895-1900, and **William Ludlow** a forward from the Old Edwardians club in Birmingham.

Another interesting instance of the use of a guest player came against Headingley at Welford Road on Christmas Eve 1910 when Leicester stalwart **Sid Penny** was "loaned" to the Yorkshiremen for the afternoon to play against his own club. It's a good job he wasn't injured because two days later amidst great publicity Penny made his announced 500th and last appearance for the club against Birkenhead Park. Subsequent research has revealed that Penny in fact only played in 491 first-team games for Leicester.

The last out and out guest player fielded by the Tigers was Northampton lock **John Lacey** at Franklin's Gardens on 16 October 1971. **Eric Bann** had travel problems and didn't show up, Leicester started with 14 men, **Garry Adey** playing at lock in a seven man pack. After 23 minutes Lacey entered the fray as a guest player for the Tigers – he went on to play 131 games for the Saints between 1970-74.

HALF-TIME & HALVES

Traditionally in rugby the teams never left the field at half-time, having their oranges on the pitch and then just turning around for the second half. The first Tigers game in which the coach was allowed on to the pitch at half-time was when Bob Dwyer did so against Boroughmuir on 25 August 1996, whilst the first time they actually left the field was against Sale in the Premiership at Welford Road on 13 December 1997.

Up until the 1960s the majority of Tigers matches were played over 35 minutes each way. It was only international games for which 40 minutes each half had to be played, for all other games the playing time was mutually agreed between the two teams. Indeed it wasn't until the 1956/57 season that all home games were played to the 80 minute total duration for the first time.

MOST POINTS IN A HALF

The most points scored in a first half was 62 when Leicester were leading Rotherham 54-8 at Welford Road in the Premiership on 1 May 2004. The Tigers record in the first half is 58 points on 11 April 1992 against Liverpool St Helens in the club's record score. The only time Tigers have conceded over 30 in the first half was when they were trailing the Barbarians 14-31 at Twickenham in the Scottish Amicable Trophy on 23 May 1999.

Most points in a second half was 70 when Leicester led Birmingham 31-0 at half-time and won 95-6 on 17 September 1986 at Welford Road. The 64 second-half points tallied by Tigers also being the most they have ever scored after half-time in a game. The most points Leicester have conceded after half-time was 59 during their 10-85 defeat to the Barbarians at Twickenham on 4 June 2000. **Rory Underwood** scored four second-half tries against London Scottish in a friendly at Welford Road on 7 April 1990.

LEAST POINTS IN A HALF

Leicester's trip to Montpellier on 15 December 2013 saw a pointless first half – the first time this had happened in a Tigers match since they visited Sale in the quarter-finals of the Pilkington Cup on 25 February 1995. The stalemate was finally broken by **Tom Youngs'** 51st minute try, with Leicester going on to win 15-14.

No points in a second half has happened on numerous occasions, the last of which was at Bath in the Premiership on 5 February 2005, where the half-time score was 6-6 and that's how it finished. The most recent instance of a scoreless second half at Welford Road came on 2 November 2002 against Wasps in the Premiership with the half-time and final result being 9-6 to Leicester.

HAT-TRICKS AND BETTER

Dorian West became the first Tigers starting front-row forward to score three tries in the same game when he did so against Loughborough Students on 22 November 1996, although **Chris Johnson** scored three as a replacement hooker for **Richard Cockerill** against Western Province Defence at Cape Town in 1993. West's was the 300th instance of a Leicester player scoring three or more tries in the same match. 145 players have accomplished the feat, with **Teddy Haselmere** a winger in the 1920's achieving an impressive 17 hat-tricks in his Tigers career.

A second-row has only achieved the feat once, which was **Bob Watson** against Liverpool on 21 September 1973.

Alastair Smallwood v Old Blues on 22 March 1924, **Brian Smith** v Harlequins on 22 September 1956 and **John Quick** against Cambridge University on 11 November 1967 are the only players to have scored a hat-trick and still been on the losing side.

Chris Johnson scored a hat-trick of tries as a replacement hooker on tour in South Africa in 1993.

↑ Leon Lloyd scored a first-half hat-trick against Barking on 9 January 1999, in the fourth-round of the Tetley's Bitter Cup.

PERFECT HAT-TRICKS

Three successive tries in a game for the Tigers

Name	*Date*	*Opponent*	*Minutes*
Dusty Hare	7.1.1989	v Headingley	6/12/33m (3 in 27')
Simon Povoas	27.1.1990	at London Welsh (r3)	11/17/24m (3 in 13') ●
Barry Evans	13.2.1990	v RAF	29/42/45m (3 in 16')
Peter Sandford	20.2.1993	at Nuneaton	65/67/73m (3 in 8')
Neil Back	21.5.2000	v Bath	58/70/76m (3 in 18') ●
Tom Varndell	13.11.2004	at Worcester	50/59/63m (3 in 13') ●
Tom Varndell	22.4.2006	v Wasps	2/25/33m (3 in 31') ●
Alesana Tuilagi	16.4.2011	v Gloucester	43/46/57m (3 in 14') ●
Adam Thompstone	29.9.2012	v Exeter	6/45/67m (3 in 61') ●

Peter Sandford recorded the fastest ever hat-trick in just eight minutes between the 65th and 73rd minute against Nuneaton at the Harry Cleaver Ground on 20 February 1993.
Steve Hackney (v London Irish in 1992), **George Chuter** (v Rotherham in 2004) and **Tom Varndell** (v Wasps in 2006) are the only ones to have scored first half hat-tricks in the league/Premiership, whilst **Simon Povoas** (v London Welsh in 1990) and **Leon Lloyd** (v Barking in 1999) have done so in the cup. Three players have scored second half hat-tricks for Tigers in the Premiership – **Neil Back**, **Tom Varndell** and **Alesana Tuilagi**, whilst **Rory Underwood** and **Perry Freshwater** have done so in the cup. **Johne Murphy** is the only Leicester player to have scored three tries after the break in the European Cup, doing so at Treviso on 18 October 2008.

Most successive tries with no other player scoring a try for the club during the sequence:

5	Ian Swan	2 v Coventry on 5.10.1957, 2 at Gloucester 2.11.1957, 1 at Cambridge University 9.11.1957
5	Tom Varndell	1 at Northampton 14.4.2006 ●, 3 v Wasps 22.4.2006 ● and 1 at Saracens 28.4.2006 ●
4	John Cramphorn	2 v Manchester 29.12.1928,1 at Gloucester on 12.1.1929 and 1 v London Welsh on 19.1.1929
4	Neil Back	2 at Sale on 24.4.1999 ● and 2 v West Hartlepool on 16.5.1999 ●
4	Tom Varndell	3 at Worcester 13.11.2004 ● and 1 at Wasps on 21.11.2004 ●

HIGH SCORING

HIGHEST TOTALS IN A GAME

100-0	v Liverpool St Helens	11.4.1992	
95-6	v Birmingham	17.9.1986	
90-19	v Glasgow & District (po)	1.11.1997	●
84-6	v Loughborough Students	22.11.1996	
84-5	v Cambridge University	30.11.1996	
83-11	v Otley (r4)	4.11.2000	●
83-10	v Newcastle Falcons	19.2.2005	●
78-8	at Birmingham	16.9.1981	●
76-0	v Exeter (qf)	27.2.1993	●

MOST POINTS CONCEDED IN A GAME

10-85	v Barbarians (at Twickenham)	4.6.2000	
19-73	v Barbarians	17.3.1998	
33-55	v Barbarians (at Twickenham)	23.5.1999	
15-53	v Gloucester	21.3.1998	
42-52	v Barbarians	17.3.2006	
5-50	at Cardiff	15.11.1947	
27-50	at Sale	16.4.1994	
25-50	v Saracens	24.9.2011	●

COMBINED RECORDS (BOTH SIDES)

Points:	109	Leicester 72, West Hartlepool 37	16.5.1999	●
	109	Leicester 90, Glasgow & District 19 (po)	1.11.1997	●
Tries:	19	Leicester 19, Liverpool St Helens 0	11.4.1992	
	19	Leicester 19, Bedford XV 0	15.2.1919	
Conversions:	14	Leicester 13, Birmingham 1	17.9.1986	
Pen Goals:	16	Perpignan 9, Leicester 7	27.10.2001	●
	14	Stade Français 9, Leicester 5 (f)	19.5.2001	●
	14	London Wasps 10, Leicester 4	31.3.2002	●
Drop Goals:	5	Leicester 3, Bath 2	13.9.1947	
	5	Leicester 3, Plymouth Albion 2	16.9.1950	

HOME GROUNDS

BELGRAVE CRICKET & CYCLE GROUND

The ground, situated a mile north of the town on Belgrave Road and not far from the Great Northern Station, was opened on 15 May 1880 by the MP for Leicestershire North, Colonel **Edwyn Sherard Burnaby** (who became president of the club in 1881). It was a first class general sports arena, oval in shape, covering ten acres with a running and cycle track encircling it, and outside that a trotting track 25 feet wide with three laps to the mile. There was a grandstand on the left hand side looking from Belgrave Road, and a refreshment room placed centrally on the main road frontage. As it was surrounded by a high brick wall admission charges could be made to all games (2d in 1880/81).

Leicester played there in three separate spells; in 1880/81 it was their first ground, but as it was so far from the centre of Leicester that the team could not readily be associated with the town, so the club decided to move after only half a season. They returned in 1882/83 for one season, but as gate receipts had fallen from £5 to £2 the club decided to move again. Their final spell was between 1888/89 and 1891/92, when a dispute over the lease soured relations between the Belgrave Road Ground Company and the club.

The ground was used by many sporting clubs, Leicester Fosse played association football games there in 1887/88, and in June 1881 Leicestershire took on an All England XI at cricket. However the ground only had a short life, in 1901 houses, shops and part of the British United Shoe Machinery were built on the site. Now the area is bordered by Roberts Road, Buller Road and Macdonald Road.

Leicester's record:
Played 84, Won 48, Drew 10, lost 26, Tries for 187, Tries agst 95.

VICTORIA PARK

Victoria Park was originally the town's racecourse between 1809 to 1873 until the track moved to Oadby, hence the park was often referred to by locals as the Racecourse ground. In 1866 the Park was thrown open to the public and an area in the centre of the racecourse was levelled making it suitable for sports, primarily cricket. A large ornamental Victorian pavilion had been built about 1860, with a viewing balcony on the second floor, which served the players and privileged spectators. Situated on the edge of the present car park, slightly to the right of the entrance from Granville Road, the pavilion was partly destroyed by a German land-mine in November 1940, and was later demolished.

Leicester used the ground in two spells; the first from January 1881 ended after one and a half seasons because, as the ground was not enclosed, charges could not be made for admission. During their second spell at Victoria Park between 1883/84 and 1887/88 Leicester developed a large following which moved with them back to the Belgrave Road ground in 1888.

Leicester's record:
Played 59, Won 42, Drew 5, lost 12, Tries for 109, Tries agst 33.

↑ Welford Road, as it was in the early 1970s.

WELFORD ROAD

In December 1891 Leicester Football Club accepted the offer from Leicester Corporation for a ten-year lease on an acre of land between Welford Road and Aylestone Road, which in those days was just outside the boundary of the town.

The *Leicester Guardian* said at the time "it is rather an unkind sneer on the part of non footballers to say that the new ground is in the right place, handy both for the Infirmary and the Cemetery!"

In March 1892 the lease was signed and work began immediately; £1,100 was spent preparing an entirely new playing area, and permission was given to transfer the stand erected on the Tigers' old Belgrave Cricket & Cycle Ground to the new site. The new Aylestone Road ground, as it was called for the first few weeks, was officially opened on 10 September 1892 with a game against the Leicestershire Rugby Union.

South Side Development

1893: 600 seat stand erected
1895: Press Box built
1899: Old Members' Stand relocated from the North side and enlarged to 3,120 seats
2 Oct 1920: New stand (4,500 seat, 4,000 terrace)
1928: Renamed Crumbie Stand
1978: Reroofed
1985: Changing rooms built
1994: Press Box incorporated into stand
2010: Renamed Holland & Barrett Stand

North Side Development

1892: 3,000 seat pavilion moved from Belgrave Cricket & Cycle Ground
1893: Extended for an extra 400-500 people
1899: New stand 304 feet long and 40 feet wide giving a seating capacity of 2,020.
1913: New Members' Stand (4,000 seats) officially opened in December 1918
1999: Renamed Next Stand
2008: Renamed Caterpillar Stand
2009: Rebuilt 10,500 seater £14m Caterpillar Stand constructed by Galliford Try – extra bars, hospitality and new reception
2013: Renamed GNC Stand

East Side (Aylestone Road End)

1909: Clubhouse built
1947: Nissen hut erected to provide additional facilities
1970: Restructuring of clubhouse: including new function facilities upstairs, with an extra changing room and office downstairs, removal of cinder terrace
1975: Leicestershire Room extension
1978: New annexe, toilets, secretarial room on ground floor, new President's Room upstairs
1985: New members' bar and lounge. Scoreboard moved from Welford Road end
1988: Nissen hut removed
1993: New 18' x 45' electronic scoreboard installed
1995: Office and Shop extension and extensive refurbishment to bars
2002: Additional permanent seating in front of clubhouse
2007: Further extension of seating and changes to European lounge
2014: New 9m x 5m TV replay screen sponsored by GE first partially used against Bath in the LV= Cup on 31 January, and fully operational for the visit of Exeter on 23 March

West Side (Welford Road End)

1894: Scoreboard erected
1977: New scoreboard donated by Adey Construction
1986: Banking levelled to make car park
1995: 3,200 seat £2.3m Alliance & Leicester Stand and 26 hospitality boxes
2009: Renamed Santander Stand
2010: Renamed Goldsmiths Stand

WELFORD ROAD RECORDS TO 2013/14

Leicester's record:
Played 2,403, Won 1,771, Drew 130, Lost 502, Tries for 7,625, Tries agst 3,257.

Individual records:
Sid Penny is the only man to have played over 300 games for the Tigers at Welford Road, finishing his career with 301. **David Matthews** 282, **Doug Norman** 265, **John Allen** 252, **Billy Foreman** 233, **Pedlar Wood** 227, **Paul Dodge** 225, **Jacky Braithwaite** 217, **George Ward** 212, **Dusty Hare** 208 and **Sammy Matthews** 205 follow him.

John Allen gets the ball away during one of his 252 Tigers appearances at Welford Road during his career.

Most Wins:	Sid Penny 231 of 301
Most Draws:	Sid Penny 45 of 301
Most Defeats:	Denis Bolesworth 72 of 185

Larry Parkes won all of his 17 Tigers games at Welford Road, and Owen Wynne never won in seven outings.

John Greenwood made just 12 career appearances for the club between 1892/93 with every one of them being played at Welford Road. Each of **Fred Jackson's** 20 tries for Leicester between 1906-08 were scored during 48 games at Welford Road – he never scored a try in 29 other matches played away from home. All 44 career points **Gerry Ainscough** scored for the first-team were tallied in four appearances at Welford Road in 1992.

British Lion **Billy Wallace** appeared in ten games and scored ten tries for the Tigers between 1923-29 with all games being played away from home.

Top points scorers at Welford Road:

Name	*Gms*	*T*	*Con*	*PG*	*DG*	*GM*	*Pts*
Dusty Hare	208	41	487	493	25	-	2,692
John Liley	110+2	43	231	256	1	-	1,423
Tim Stimpson	67+5	18	130	209	2	-	983
Andy Goode	86+12	14	175	160	13	-	939
Harold Day	136	77	193	59	3	2	812
Bob Barker	174	104	71	73	1	-	763
Jez Harris	113+8	14	110	103	36	-	695
Toby Flood	51+4	7	116	131	1	-	663
Percy Lawrie	183	148	12	6	5	-	506

Most tries: **Percy Lawrie** 148 in 183 games, **Harry Wilkinson** 117 in 145 games, **Bob Barker** 104 in 174 games are the only ones to have scored over 100 tries for Tigers at the ground.

Most Drop Goals: **Les Cusworth** dropped 37 goals in 188 games at Welford Road for the Tigers.

WELFORD ROAD RECREATION GROUND

Six games have been played at Welford Road Rec, later known as Nelson Mandela Park.

vs Rosslyn Park on 24 January 1959 - frost at Welford Road - Won 8-6

vs RAF on 26 January 1961 - frost at Welford Road - Lost 6-11

vs London Irish on 23 December 1967 - straw at Welford Road in preparation for the visit of the Barbarians - Won 17-0

vs Manchester on 27 April 1968 - Welford Road seeded for following season - Won 13-6

vs Wasps on 17 February 1973 - frost at Welford Road - Lost 4-10

vs Richmond on 9 October 1976 - North Midlands vs Argentina same day at Welford Road - Won 24-12

Leicester's record:

Played 6, Won 4, Lost 2, Tries for 12, Tries agst 8.

COVERT LANE, SCRAPTOFT

One Tigers home game has been played at Stoneygate RFC, Covert Lane because Welford Road was being used for the Midlands Counties game against the touring New Zealanders the same day.
vs Cheltenham on 28 October 1967 - Lost 8-11

WALKERS STADIUM

Leicester City's 32,000 seater home was opened in 2002 and is now known as King Power Stadium.
Tigers have played six games there:

vs Toulouse 24.4.2005 – Heineken Cup semi-final – Lost 19-27* ●

vs Bath 1.4.2006 – Heineken Cup quarter-final – Lost 12-15 ●

vs Scarlets 21.4.2007 – Heineken Cup semi-final – Won 33-17* ●

vs Bath 11.4.2009 – Heineken Cup quarter-final – Won 20-15 ●

vs Bristol 25.4.2009 – Premiership – Won 73-3 ●

vs Bath 9.5.2009 – Premiership semi-final – Won 24-10 ●

* under European Cup rules these two games are technically classed as matches played at a neutral venue!

Leicester's record:
Played 6, Won 4, Lost 2, Tries for 19, Tries agst 9.

INDOORS

The Tigers have played under a closed roof on three occasions, all at Cardiff's Millennium Stadium:

25.5.2002	Munster	Heineken Cup final	Won 15-9	●
4.3.2006	London Wasps	Powergen Cup semi-final	Lost 17-22	●
29.10.2006	Cardiff Blues	Heineken Cup	Won 21-17	●

KICKING ACCURACY

Place kicking success rates have only been kept since the start of the 1995/96 season, detailed here are the rates of all kickers who have attempted over 20 place kicks at goal since then.

Name	*Good*	*Att*	*%*
Derick Hougaard	33	43	76.7%
Julien Dupuy	47	63	74.6%
Toby Flood	469	629	74.6%
Paul Burke	49	67	73.1%
Joel Stransky	303	420	72.1%
Andy Goode	610	859	71.0%
Jeremy Staunton	110	156	70.5%
Ramiro Pez	31	44	70.5%
Owen Williams	70	100	70.0%
Billy Twelvetrees	95	136	69.9%
Tim Stimpson	595	867	68.6%
George Ford	100	146	68.5%
John Liley	250	368	67.9%
Steve Booth	22	33	66.7%
Ian Humphreys	61	95	64.2%
Geordan Murphy	87	136	64.0%
Matt Jones	14	22	63.6%
Niall Malone	19	30	63.3%
Sam Vesty	68	109	62.4%
Ross Broadfoot	23	39	59.0%
Rob Liley	56	97	57.7%
Jez Harris	29	52	55.8%

↑ Ian Humphreys, during his hot-shot sequence of 19 successful kicks in a row during 2006.

Ian Humphreys landed 19 place kicks in a row in a "purple patch" from the Barbarians match on 17 March 2006 until he missed a penalty shot at Northampton in the Cup on 2 December 2006.

Andy Goode had a perfect day at Welford Road on 19 February 2005 landing 13 successful kicks from 13 attempts against Newcastle Falcons in the Premiership.

Rob Liley missed seven kicks from 14 attempts (all conversions) against Cambridge University at Welford Road on 30 November 1996.

Leicester had a nightmare kicking day against Northampton at Welford Road on 22 October 1960, going down 9-0, but missing eight penalty kicks at goal. First **Mike Gavins** tried his hand and missed four in the first half and another after the break, thereafter skipper **Colin Martin** assumed kicking responsibility but fared little better in missing three of his own. In addition centre **Lyn Tatham** also missed a drop goal!

LANDMARKS

QUICKEST

The quickest player to achieve 50 first-team appearances is **Mike Yandle** in only 406 days; in terms of games played **J Wilkinson** the full-back from 1919-1922 missed one Leicester game in his first 58. Yandle also holds the record for the fastest to make 100 appearances with 2 years 151 days; **Pedlar Wood** only missed five games during his first 100. **Bleddyn Jones** is the quickest to 200 games with 5 years 54 days, whilst **Alf Butlin** missed just 13 Leicester games in attaining 200 personal appearances. **Bleddyn Jones** was also the quickest to 300 games in 7 years 327 days, with **Pedlar Wood** missing only 24 Tigers games in his 300.

SLOWEST

Andy Key took 12 years 118 days and 509 Tigers games to play in 50 games himself. **Charlie Cross** took 12 years 167 days to play in 100 games, **Dorian West** took 15 years 149 days to make 200 appearances, and **Denis Bolesworth** 16 years 52 days to play in 300 games.

During the time it took **Rory Underwood** to make 200 appearances Tigers actually played 493 games, this beats **Bob Beason** for the slowest to 200 first-team games; 483 Tigers matches between 1960 and 1971.

FEWEST GAMES TO RECORD 50 TRIES

The record for the least number of first-team games played to record 50 tries for the club is held by **Teddy Haselmere** with just 40 games between 1918-1920.

Games	*Name*	*Date*	*Opponent*	
40	Teddy Haselmere	24.4.1920	at Northampton	
58	Jack Miles	28.3.1903	v Nuneaton (sf)	●
64	Frank Jackson	18.3.1899	v Five Ways Old Edwardians (r3)	●
66	David Senior	5.4.1962	v Nuneaton	
72	Alfred Hind	21.3.1903	v Belgrave (r2)	●
72	Barry Evans	5.11.1983	v Cardiff	
74	Harold Day	17.11.1923	v Northampton	
74	John Duggan	20.9.1972	at Nottingham	
74	Steve Hackney	17.12.1994	v Blackheath (r4)	●
74	Tom Varndell	24.11.2007	at Leeds	●

LEAD CHANGING HANDS

The lead changed hands an astonishing ten times in the first 62 minutes when Tigers visited Bath in the Premiership on 9 September 2006, before Leicester eventually lost 25-43. However, arguably the most exciting Tigers match of all-time was a trip to Watford to face Saracens on 19 February 2012. The lead had see-sawed seven times between the two clubs with Saracens leading 19-17 until Geordan Murphy's game-winning drop goal in the fifth minute of added time snatched the win.

LEAGUES

MERIT TABLES

The RFU's first attempt at formalised leagues was with the introduction of regional Merit tables in season 1976/77 – the nine top level clubs in the Midlands being grouped together to play each other once during the season to count towards the merit table, with the league placing decided on winning percentage. This nine-team format with the same nine clubs – Bedford, Birmingham, Coventry, Leicester, Moseley, Northampton, Nottingham, Nuneaton and Rugby - was retained until superseded eventually by the National Merit Tables in 1984/85. Tigers topped the Midlands Merit Table for five successive seasons between 1979/80 to 1983/84.

Season	*Clubs*	*Pos*	*P*	*W*	*D*	*L*	*%*
MIDLANDS MERIT TABLE							
1976/77	9	2nd	8	6	-	2	75%
1977/78	9	5th	8	5	-	3	62.5%
1978/79	9	2nd	7	6	-	1	85.7%
1979/80	**9**	**1st**	**7**	**6**	**-**	**1**	**85.7%**
1980/81	**9**	**1st**	**7**	**6**	**1**	**-**	**92.9%**
1981/82	**9**	**1st**	**7**	**6**	**-**	**1**	**85.7%**
1982/83	**9**	**1st**	**7**	**7**	**-**	**-**	**100%**
1983/84	**9**	**1st**	**5**	**5**	**-**	**-**	**100%**
1984/85	9	3rd	7	6	-	1	85.7%
NATIONAL MERIT TABLE A							
1984/85	12	6th	7	3	-	4	42.9%
1985/86	12	4th	10	7	-	3	70%
1986/87	12	2nd	10	7	1	2	75%

COURAGE LEAGUE DIVISION ONE

Leagues in rugby union first began in England in 1987/88 although not on set weekends. The top division had 12 teams in 1987/88, expanding to 13 in 1990/91. It was not until season 1993/94 that home and away games against each opponent was introduced and the league reduced to ten sides. The final season saw 12 teams playing each other home and away.

			Record				Attack		Defence		
Season	*Clubs*	*Pos*	*P*	*W*	*D*	*L*	*Pts*	*T*	*For*	*T*	*Agst*
1987/88	**12**	**1st**	**10**	**9**	**-**	**1**	**37**	**21**	**225**	**14**	**133**
1988/89	12	6th	11	6	1	4	13	19	189	25	199
1989/90	12	5th	11	6	-	5	12	36	248	24	184
1990/91	13	4th	12	8	-	4	16	29	244	12	140
1991/92	13	6th	12	6	1	5	13	33	262	26	216
1992/93	13	3rd	12	9	-	3	18	21	220	13	116
1993/94	10	2nd	18	14	-	4	28	41	425	18	210
1994/95	**10**	**1st**	**18**	**15**	**1**	**2**	**31**	**27**	**400**	**15**	**239**
1995/96	10	2nd	18	15	-	3	30	42	476	16	242
1996/97	12	4th	22	14	1	7	29	60	600	38	395

PREMIERSHIP

The Premiership began in 1997/98 with 12 teams in the top level of the tournament except for season 1998/99 when there were 14 sides for just one season. Until 2001/02 the Premiership was won by the top team in the league, since then it has been decided by the winners of the Premiership final at Twickenham, initially with the top side progressing directly to the final and the 2nd and 3rd placed teams contesting one semi-final. Since 2005/06 the top four teams have qualified for the play-offs with the top two teams playing at home.

For 2000/01 and 2001/02 the top eight sides qualified for an extra knockout tournament, known as the Zurich Championship with its final being played at Twickenham – Leicester winning this competition at the first attempt.

In 2002/03 to 2004/05 the remaining English qualifier for Europe was the winner of an extra event called the Zurich Wildcard – Leicester winning it twice.

			Record				Attack		Defence		Playoffs
Season	*Pos*	*P*	*W*	*D*	*L*	*Pts*	*T*	*For*	*T*	*Agst*	

ALLIED DUNBAR PREMIERSHIP 1

Season	Pos	P	W	D	L	Pts	T	For	T	Agst	Playoffs
1997/98	4th	22	12	2	8	26	64	569	45	449	
1998/99	**1st**	**26**	**22**	**-**	**4**	**44**	**86**	**771**	**34**	**423**	
1999/00	**1st**	**22**	**18**	**1**	**3**	**51**	**74**	**687**	**45**	**425**	

ZURICH PREMIERSHIP

Season	Pos	P	W	D	L	Pts	T	For	T	Agst	Playoffs
2000/01	**1st**	**22**	**18**	**1**	**3**	**82**	**60**	**571**	**25**	**346**	**Won Championship**
2001/02	**1st**	**22**	**18**	**-**	**4**	**83**	**72**	**658**	**19**	**349**	Lost QF Championship
2002/03	6th	22	12	-	10	55	44	448	32	396	Won Wildcard
2003/04	5th	22	11	3	8	55	53	537	37	430	Won Wildcard
2004/05	1st	22	15	3	4	78	75	665	27	323	Lost Final

GUINNESS PREMIERSHIP

Season	Pos	P	W	D	L	Pts	T	For	T	Agst	Playoffs
2005/06	2nd	22	14	3	5	68	51	518	24	415	Lost Final
2006/07	**2nd***	**22**	**14**	**1**	**7**	**71**	**58**	**569**	**37**	**456**	**Won Final**
2007/08	4th	22	13	-	9	64	58	539	40	428	Lost Final
2008/09	**1st***	**22**	**15**	**1**	**6**	**71**	**62**	**582**	**40**	**401**	**Won Final**
2009/10	**1st***	**22**	**15**	**1**	**6**	**73**	**46**	**541**	**18**	**325**	**Won Final**

AVIVA PREMIERSHIP RUGBY

Season	Pos	P	W	D	L	Pts	T	For	T	Agst	Playoffs
2010/11	1st	22	16	1	5	78	67	594	29	403	Lost Final
2011/12	2nd	22	15	1	6	74	70	647	45	475	Lost Final
2012/13	**2nd***	**22**	**15**	**1**	**6**	**74**	**56**	**538**	**29**	**345**	**Won Final**
2013/14	3rd	22	15	2	5	74	59	542	41	430	Lost SF

* Champions by winning Premiership final

LEICESTERSHIRE REGIMENT

The following 43 individuals so far have been identified as playing first-team rugby for Leicester and also serving in the Leicestershire Regiment (Tigers) and can therefore rightly be dubbed "Tiger Tigers". Research is still revealing more names.

Name	*Battalion*	*Name*	*Battalion*
Maj. HP Atkins	5th	2Lt. RM Muddimer	4th
Cpt. RJ Barr		Lt-Col. AL Novis	1st
Cpl. EE Bates	7th	Maj. FE Oliver	4th
Lt. CC Beaty-Pownall	2nd	H Page	4th
2Lt. AGE Bowell	9th	GE Pollard	
Lt-Col. JC Burdett	6th	HW Sibson	
Sgt. WA Dalby	1st	Lt. MS Scott	
Cpt. FC Drummond		Lt. JWD Smith	8th
Cpt. WR Evans	3rd	Sgt.Maj. P Smitten	2nd
Lt. S Farmer	4th	Cpt. WE Squirrell	4th
Pvte. MW Fisher	2nd	Lt-Col. KW Symington	5th
C/Sgt. AH Foxon		Lt. FN Tarr	4th
Lt-Col. GJ German	5th	Cpl. F Taylor	4th
Lt. OJ Hargrave		Sgt. JA Thomas	1st
Cpl. PJ Hougham	2nd	Lt. AC Thomson	
Maj. HJF Jeffries	1st 5th	Sgt. J Twigg	2nd
Maj-Gen. DA Kendrew	2nd/7th	Lt-Col. REH Ward	5th
Pvte. WH Kitchen	1st	Lt-Col. WC Wilson	1st
L/Cpl. J Lewis		Lt. CFA Worsley-Worswick	
Pvte. JT Lovett	1st	Cpt. EE Wynne	1st 5th
Maj. AS McIntyre	3rd 2nd	Col. AL Yarnell	4th
Maj. PJDA Moore	5th		

In addition Lt-Col **Frederick Oliver** was president of the club between 1931-39, and Major **Albert Chilton** was general secretary of the club between 1954-65.

↑ Lieutenant MS Scott played 68 games for the Tigers between 1899-1911, and was also a Tiger in the Leicestershire Regiment.

LETTERS AND NUMBERS

The numbering of players in international matches was first adopted on a regular basis in 1920/21, the Leicester forwards first regularly wore letters in the 1926/27 season. A report in *The Birmingham Post* on the 6 October 1926 of the match against Bath, stated that "Leicester's forwards were picked out easily as their jerseys were decorated with large bold letters - A to G." The reporter continued, "it struck me that the use of the numerals for the men in the rear would have completed a capital scheme which one would thoroughly commend to other clubs, the lettering, in particular, being of great service to all those who wanted to appreciate who was who in the tight and loose." That season the Tigers played in a formation comprising only seven forwards and hence letters A to G and not including H.

On 12 September 1931 against Old Blues the lettering was extended to cover the whole team, however the policy for other clubs changed, some which had originally worn letters now favoured numbers, and this became the standard means of identification.

The tradition at Leicester remained until the late 1990s when tournament rules prohibited the wearing of letters, Leicester exchanging numbers for letters throughout with one strange exception, the number-eight forward always wore "G", and the usual number seven wore "H"!

The Tigers first wore numbers on their backs for the visit of Harlequins to Welford Road on 5 September 1998.

The club have reverted to letters for three matches since the end of the 1998/99 season: at Cardiff on 12 August 2000, against Australia on 9 November 2010, and versus New Zealand Maori on 13 November 2012.

Small letters are now displayed above the badge on first-team shirts, whilst the Academy still wear letters whenever they play.

LIONS & ISLANDERS

The idea behind a touring team from the home nations came from **Alfred Shaw** and **Arthur Shrewsbury** in 1888. The two had already been involved in an England cricket tour to Australia, and they put together a hastily arranged 35-match rugby tour of Australasia lasting over five months. Future tours took on many guises, but it wasn't until 1938 that players were selected from all four home unions. The team were not christened "Lions" until 1924 when they adopted a lion motif on their ties, whilst their modern kit of red shirts, white shorts and blue socks with green top was worn for the first time in 1950. The team was officially known as the British Isles until the 2001 tour of Australia when they were called the British & Irish Lions for the first time.

D. A. KENDREW

The Tigers' first "Lions" were **John Jackett**, **Fred Jackson** and **Tom Smith**, who toured New Zealand, Australia & Canada in 1908 with an Anglo-Welsh side. **Jackett** appeared in 18 games on tour including all three tests, Jackson in six games and one test, and **Smith** 21 of the 26 games including two of the tests.

Listed here are the 40 individuals who have been Lions tourists whilst playing for Leicester, showing the number of test caps gained on that particular tour in brackets:

LIONS TOURISTS...

ANGLO WELSH

1908	New Zealand	John Jackett(3), Fred Jackson(1), Tom Smith(2)

GREAT BRITAIN

1910	South Africa	Kenneth Wood(2)
1930	New Zealand & Australia	Doug Prentice (capt,2), George Beamish, Douglas Kendrew
1936	Argentina	Bernard Gadney (capt)

BRITISH ISLES

1959	Australia & New Zealand	Phil Horrocks-Taylor(1), Tony O'Reilly(6)
1971	Australia & New Zealand	Rodger Arneil
1974	South Africa	Alan Old
1977	New Zealand	Peter Wheeler(3)
1980	South Africa	Peter Wheeler(4), Clive Woodward(2). Replacement: Paul Dodge(2)
1983	New Zealand	Dusty Hare, Clive Woodward
1989	Australia	Dean Richards(3), Rory Underwood(3)
1993	New Zealand	Dean Richards(3), Rory Underwood(3), Tony Underwood. Replacement: Martin Johnson(2)
1997	South Africa	Martin Johnson (capt,3), Graham Rowntree, Neil Back(2), Will Greenwood, Austin Healey(2), Eric Miller(1)

BRITISH & IRISH LIONS

2001	Australia	Martin Johnson (capt,3), Neil Back(2), Austin Healey. Replacements: Martin Corry(3), Dorian West
2005	New Zealand	Neil Back(1), Martin Corry(4), Ben Kay(2), Lewis Moody(3), Geordan Murphy(2), Graham Rowntree(3), Ollie Smith(1), Julian White(4)
2009	South Africa	Tom Croft(3). Replacement: Harry Ellis(1)
2013	Australia	Dan Cole(3), Tom Croft(2), Geoff Parling(3), Manu Tuilagi(1), Ben Youngs(2), Tom Youngs(3)

PACIFIC ISLANDERS

The concept for a Pacific Islanders team combining the resources of Fiji, Samoa and Tonga along the lines of the British & Irish Lions came to fruition in 2004 when the side played a test against each of the Tri-Nations countries. In 2006 and 2008 three-match tours of Europe were undertaken, unfortunately the only one of the nine tests they won was against Italy in November 2008.

2004	Australia, NZ & SA	Seru Rabeni(3)
2006	Wales, Scotland & Ireland	Seru Rabeni(3), Alesana Tuilagi(1)
2008	England, France & Italy	Seru Rabeni(3)

* Test match appearances shown in brackets

MOST TIGERS TO START IN A LIONS TEST TEAM

Five	Argentina	Cardiff	23.5.2005
Four	New Zealand	Christchurch	25.6.2005
Three	South Africa	Port Elizabeth	28.6.1980
	New Zealand	Wellington	26.6.1993
	New Zealand	Auckland	3.7.1993
	New Zealand	Auckland	9.7.2005
	Australia	Melbourne	29.6.2013

On a further eight occasions there have been three Leicester players who have appeared in the same Lions touring team, the first of which was on 3 June 1908 against Southland at Rugby Park, Invercargill in a 14-8 win where **Jackett, Jackson** and **Tom Smith** all played.

MOST TIGERS TO APPEAR IN A LIONS TEST TEAM

Seven	5 start + 2 reps	Argentina	Cardiff	23.5.2005
Five	3 start + 2 reps	New Zealand	Auckland	9.7.2005
	2 start + 3 reps	Australia	Brisbane	22.6.2013
	3 start + 2 reps	Australia	Melbourne	29.6.2013

Tom Croft is the only Leicester player who has scored two tries in a Lions test match, doing so against South Africa in Durban on 20 June 2009, whilst the only Tiger to have scored a hat-trick of tries in a Lions tour game was **Bernard Gadney** against Argentina B in Buenos Aires on 26 July 1936.

The record number of points scored in one Lions game by a Leicester player is 37 by **Alan Old** on 29 May 1974 against South West Districts at the Van Riebeeck Stadium, Mossel Bay in South Africa with a try, 15 conversions and a penalty goal - this is also by some considerable margin the all-time Lions record for all players and a record for the most points in a game by any tourist in South Africa.

LOW SCORING

Nil-nil draws were commonplace and frequent up until the 1940s, in fact 77 of Leicester's matches have finished this way. Since the 2nd World War there have been just seven nil-nil draws and just two of those at Welford Road. Only one instance has occurred since 1965 and that was when the Royal Navy visited Welford Road on 1 February 1978 and nobody managed a score of any description, in a match played in appallingly muddy conditions - in fact the game four days later against London Scottish at the same venue was postponed due to a waterlogged pitch!

There has not been a single-score game - where there was just one scoring action by either side - since Sale visited Welford Road on 24 April 1971 and a first half penalty goal by **Peter Wheeler** was all that separated the teams at the end.

Incredibly Sale also figure twice in the total of just five competition matches in which there were only two scoring actions (ignoring conversions):

Date	*Opponent*	*Venue*	*Competition*	*Result*
10.3.1973	Sale	Heywood Road	RFU Kncokout Cup (qf)	L 0-7 ●
15.4.1978	Gloucester	Twickenham	John Player Special Cup (f)	L 3-6 ●
22.2.1992	Newcastle	Kingston Park	Pilkington Cup (qf)	W 10-0 ●
17.9.1994	Orrell	Edgehall Road	Division 1	W 6-0 ●
6.2.2004	Sale	Heywood Road	Zurich Premiership	D 3-3 ●

MAN OF THE MATCH

Man of the Match awards were first handed out in the Heineken Cup in season 2000/01, the first Leicester player claiming the accolade being **Pat Howard** against Pau on 7 October 2000. Tigers players since have been named Man of the Match on 63 occasions: 7 - **Geordan Murphy**, 6 - **Lewis Moody**, 5 - **Austin Healey, Thomas Waldrom**, 4 - **Tom Croft**, 3 - **Jordan Crane, Louis Deacon, Harry Ellis, Ben Youngs**, 2 - **Neil Back, Martin Corry, Toby Flood, Andy Goode, Tim Stimpson**, 1 - **Martin Castrogiovanni, Daryl Gibson, Scott Hamilton, Pat Howard, Shane Jennings, Martin Johnson, Graham Kitchener, Seru Rabeni, Julian Salvi, Billy Twelvetrees, Jaco van der Westhuyzen, Tom Varndell, Sam Vesty, Julian White.**

↑ Peter Wheeler presents Pat Howard with his memento after becoming Tigers' first recipient of a Heineken Cup Man of the Match award.

Five awards have been given to Tigers players in quarter-finals, three in semi-finals and **Austin Healey** gained one in the two successive finals of 2001 and 2002.

The Peter Deakin Medal is awarded to the Man of the Match in the Premiership Final, and has been given to a Leicester player four times: **Alesana Tuilagi** in 2007, **Geordan Murphy** in 2009, **Jordan Crane** in 2010 and **Anthony Allen** in 2013.

The Man of the Match in the LV= Cup final at Worcester in 2012 was **Steve Mafi**.

MATCH PROGRAMME

The first regular home match programme started in season 1935/36. **Bryan R Baxter**, chairman of the club's Publicity Committee, in his programme notes for the opening game of that season against Bedford, wrote: "We are pleased to welcome you today with the production of No 1 of the new type of programme. It has long been felt that the old team pamphlet was not worthy of the club and its great reputation. Last season a suggestion was made that the Publicity Committee should attempt to produce a real programme, and you will doubtless recall our experiment in the form of a souvenir for the Christmas matches."

This first programme, printed by Willsons in King Street, cost 1d and quickly became a collector's item in selling out shortly after kick-off. In an effort to keep costs low the cover was mass printed at the start of the season and the teamsheets and notes merely stapled into it. Hence until 1949 the date and opponents' name never even appeared on the cover.

Renowned Leicester born artist PC Priestly produced artwork for the cover as well as caricatures of the players reproduced inside. **Philip Collingwood 'Bob' Priestley** (b Leicester, 26.6.1901, d Maidenhead, regd Q3 1973). Studied at Leicester College of Arts & Crafts 1915-1920, whilst there is still an annual award at De Montfort University named after him.

Aldridge & Co in Friar Lane took over as printers in 1935, and Hodgkins, Millar & Co of 111 Church Gate two years later. Aldridge resumed in 1938.

1945/46 saw a return to the pamphlet style for one season due to paper shortages following the war, until proper programme production resumed in 1946/47.

JJ Townsend & Son of 36-38 Colton Street became printers in 1959 and carried on the task until 1982/83.

For the start of the 1983/84 season Impress Ltd, once of Morris Road, became the printers, introducing colour for the first time. From season 2003/04 Ignition Publications took over as designers of the publication.

MEDALLISTS

In rugby union there is no set rule as to who receives winners' medals at the end of a successful campaign. If it is at the conclusion of a final then usually the winning squad will be formally presented with a medal, even if bench replacements never actually took part in the match itself. For instance **Scott Steele** was presented with an LV= Cup winner's medal after the final in 2011/12 despite being an unused replacement in the final and only playing for one minute during the six-match winning campaign. **Aaron Mauger** started every Premiership game between rounds 2 and 19 in season 2008/09 and then missed the rest of the Premiership season including the triumphant final. **John Duggan** played in all four rounds of the 1979/80 John Player Cup but was unfit for the final itself – which the Tigers won 21-9.

Looking at any squad member who played any part in a silverware-winning campaign we find that the most decorated Tiger is **Geordan Murphy**, who was involved in 13 separate triumphs between 1998/99 and 2011/12, gaining eight Premiership crowns, two Heineken Cups, two Anglo-Welsh Cups and a Zurich Championship along the way. **Lewis Moody** and **Louis Deacon** follow him with 11 titles.

MONOPOLISING THE SCORING

The 2009/10 season began with a trip to Sale in the Premiership on 4 September with new recruit **Jeremy Staunton** kicking four from six penalty goals in Tigers' 12-15 loss. Staunton then added five more penalties against both Harlequins and Newcastle, and opened the scoring with two more penalty strikes at Bath on 26 September, until allowing someone else to score a point – a **Mefin Davies** try. That meant that one man scored Leicester's first 48 points of the new season – the longest monopoly of scoring in the club's history, breaking **Tim Stimpson's** previous mark of 45 unbroken solo points between November-December 2000.

↑ Jeremy Staunton scored all Leicester's first 48 points of the 2009/10 season.

HIGHEST MATCH TOTALS WHEN ONE MAN SCORED ALL THE POINTS

29	Billy Twelvetrees at Wasps (11.9.2011) Lost 29-35	●
29	Billy Twelvetrees v Wasps (7.1.2012) Won 29-11	●
27	Andy Goode v Sale (28.1.2006) Drew 27-27	●
25	Jeremy Staunton at Bath (1.10.2011) Lost 25-26	●
23	Tim Stimpson v Harlequins (23.11.2001) Won 23-18	●
21	Toby Flood v Bath (23.10.2010) Won 21-15	●
21	Tim Stimpson at Newcastle (2.5.1999) Won 21-12	●
21	Jez Harris v Bristol (11.12.1993) Won 21-9	●
19	Bob Barker v Bristol (17.12.1977) Won 19-14	

MOST TIMES SCORING ALL TIGERS POINTS IN A GAME:

41	Dusty Hare
23	Harold Day
21	Colin Martin
19	Percy Lawrie
16	John Liley

MOST AND LEAST

There have been 30 occasions that Leicester have played a complete game a player short, six times there have been two players short, and once on 31 March 1888 at Northampton they were three players short, but on 9 December 1882 they played away to Stamford with only 11 men (and they still won easily by 5 goals and 2 tries to a try). Most of these occasions were in the early days, the last time was 2 September 1939 just as war was to break out, playing a 13-a-side game against a team of trial and guest players called "The Rest", prior to this it was 21 February 1920 at home to Richmond, but still winning 62-3.

Conversely though on 27 December 1884 at home to Bedford Swifts, **John Gilbert** scored a try and **Jack Parsons** a drop goal, before it was realised Leicester had been playing with 16 men! Accordingly the game was halted, the extra man dismissed, and all previous Leicester scores were struck from the record. Leicester later went on to win the game by one goal to nil.

The Tigers have played against more than 15 players twice before: on the opening day of the 1886/87 season they played against the 20 of Town & District and still won 11-0, whilst in the final match of the 1888/89 season they took on the 18 of Town & District but this time lost 0-2.

At Ospreys on 23 January 2010 **Lee Byrne** appeared on the pitch as a 16th man for a crucial 50-second period during the 17-12 win by the Welshmen which knocked Tigers out of the Heineken Cup. Byrne had gone off suffering from a dislocated and bloodied toe and was replaced by centre Sonny Parker, but was sent back on three minutes later after treatment without any of his team-mates going off.

A Tigers player pointed out the Ospreys' numerical advantage to referee Alan Lewis, who then berated an Ospreys touchline official for not informing the match fourth official that Byrne had returned.

Fly-half **Dan Biggar** eventually departed as the Ospreys returned to 15 men to hold on during a torrid finale of constant Leicester pressure.

Ospreys were fined €25,000 and Lee Byrne suspended for two weeks.

NAMES

Players names on the back of their shirts to aid identification for TV purposes first appeared at the start of 2000/01 season when Tigers visited Loftus Road on 19 August to take on London Wasps in the Zurich Premiership, winning 24-22.

NEARLY MEN

Forty-three different players have sat on Leicester's replacements bench but never managed any playing time for the first-team, of those three sat on the bench for four complete games but never appeared for the first-team: **Geoff Grist** (1987-88), **Mike Attfield** (1988) and **Chris Conroy** (1993-94).

Nick Booth was part of a virtually full strength Tigers team led by club captain **Paul Dodge** which toured France and Spain in May 1986 and scored four tries in their victory over a Basque XV in San Sebastian. At the time these games were decreed not to count in first-team records, and therefore Nick never actually made an official appearance for the first-team.

On 27 December 1932 **Alan Key** of Old Cranleighans should have played for the Tigers against the Barbarians but transferred over to the Barbarians when **Ross Logan** couldn't turn out. Key never made a first-team appearance for the club.

NEUTRAL VENUE

Welford Road has been used as a neutral venue or hosted international rugby on many occasions, here follows a list of all major instances.

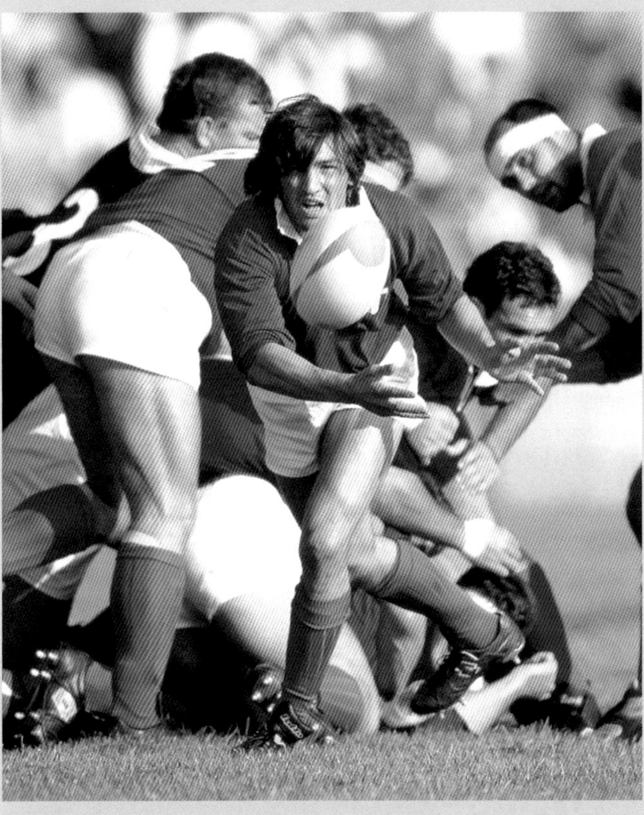

↑ Welford Road hosted its first test match for 58 years when Italy took on New Zealand during the 1991 World Cup.

TEST MATCHES AT WELFORD ROAD

Date	*Team*	*Opponent*	*Result*
8.2.1902	England	v Ireland	6-3
9.1.1904	England	v Wales	14-14
10.2.1906	England	v Ireland	6-16
30.1.1909	England	v France	22-0
10.2.1923	England	v Ireland	23-5
13.10.1991	New Zealand	v Italy	31-21 (RWC)
10.10.1999	Italy	v Tonga	25-28 (RWC)

Interestingly in 1906 Leicester player **John Jackett** played for England on his home ground, as he did again (kicking two conversions) along with **Alf Kewney** in 1909, and **Alastair Smallwood** and **Leo Price** in 1923 (each scoring a try).

SERVICES INTERNATIONALS

10.4.1943	England	v Scotland	24-19
18.3.1944	England	v Scotland	27-15
24.2.1945	England	v Scotland	11-18

'B' INTERNATIONALS

4.3.1988	England B	v Italy B	35-9
3.3.1989	England B	v France B	16-35
2.11.1990	England B	v Namibia	31-16

'A' INTERNATIONALS

15.1.1993	England A	v France A	29-17
3.2.1995	England A	v France A	29-9
31.1.1996	England A	v New South Wales	24-22
28.2.1997	England A	v France A	25-34
2.12.1997	England A	v New Zealand	19-30
20.2.1998	England A	v Wales A	22-41

OTHER INTERNATIONALS

17.3.1995	England Students	v Italy Students	56-18
4.2.1996	England Women	v Wales Women	56-3
28.10.2001	English National Divisions	v Australia	22-34

AGE GROUP INTERNATIONALS

4.3.1905	England Schools	v Wales Schools	0-6
16.3.1907	England Schools	v Wales Schools	5-6
10.4.1909	England Schools	v Wales Schools	0-3
4.3.1911	England Schools	v Wales Schools	4-3
1.3.1913	England Schools	v Wales Boys	18-14
19.3.1921	England Schools	v Wales Schools	0-17
28.3.1925	England Schools	v Wales Schools	6-3
22.3.1947	England Schools	v Wales Schools	0-8
8.4.1950	England Schools	v Wales Schools	6-15
3.4.1954	England Schools	v Wales Schools	3-8
4.4.1959	England Schools	v Wales Schools	5-18
1.4.1961	England Schools	v France Schools	0-19
21.4.1962	England Schools	v Wales Schools	6-12
5.4.1967	England Schools	v France Schools	9-0
28.4.1976	England U23	v England Students	13-15
30.3.1977	England U23	v England Students	18-7
11.4.1981	England U23	v Netherlands	51-3
3.4.1987	England Colts	v Welsh Youth	17-9
5.9.1992	England U21	v Italy U21	37-12
1.2.1995	England Schools	v NZ Schools	12-22
28.2.1997	England U21	v France U21	13-20

ENGLAND TRIALS

24.2.1900	North	v South	9-22
18.12.1920	North	v South	31-8
3.12.1927	Whites	v Colours	15-9
1.12.1951	Probables	v Possibles	11-9
3.12.1966	Probables	v Possibles	9-3
6.12.1975	North & Midlands	v England XV	18-10

INTERNATIONAL TOURING TEAMS

28.10.1905	Midland Counties	v New Zealand	5-21
29.9.1906	Midland Counties	v South Africa	0-29
2.12.1908	East Midlands	v Australia	16-5
9.11.1912	Midland Counties	v South Africa	3-25
29.10.1927	Leicestershire	v Waratahs	8-20
14.11.1931	Leics & East Midlands	v South Africa	30-21
16.11.1935	Leics & East Midlands	v New Zealand	3-16
15.11.1947	Leics & East Midlands	v Australia	11-17
29.12.1951	Midlands	v South Africa	0-3

5.12.1953	Midlands	v New Zealand	0-3
21.12.1957	Leics & East Midlands	v Australia	3-18
5.12.1960	Midlands	v South Africa	3-3
28.12.1963	Midlands	v New Zealand	6-14
22.10.1966	Midlands (East)	v Australia	9-17
28.10.1967	Midlands, London & Home	v New Zealand	3-15
8.11.1969	Midlands (East)	v South Africa	9-11
7.11.1970	Midlands (East)	v Fiji	14-24
13.1.1973	Midlands (East)	v New Zealand	12-43
9.10.1973	Midlands (East)	v Japan	10-6
12.11.1975	Midlands (East)	v Australia	11-8
9.10.1976	North & Midlands	v Argentina	24-9
6.3.1977	Leicestershire Barbarians	v Netherlands	14-18
18.11.1978	Midlands	v New Zealand	15-20
3.11.1979	Midlands	v New Zealand	7-33
17.10.1981	Midlands	v Australia	16-10
6.10.1982	Midlands	v Fiji	25-16
8.11.1983	Midlands	v New Zealand	19-13
6.11.1984	Midlands	v Australia	18-21
1.10.1986	Leicestershire	v Japan	33-22
29.10.1988	Midlands	v Australia	18-25
4.11.1992	Midlands	v South Africa	9-32
26.10.1993	Midlands	v New Zealand	6-12
2.12.1995	Midlands	v Western Samoa	40-19
4.12.1996	Tigers-Saints Select XV	v Western Samoa	20-28

MIDLAND COUNTIES CUP FINALS

2.4.1892	Coventry	v Moseley	13-0*
1.4.1893	Coventry	v Burton	11-0
31.3.1906	Nottingham	v Moseley	14-0
30.3.1907	Coventry	v Stratford-upon-Avon	19-3
4.4.1908	Stratford-upon-Avon	v Nuneaton	0-0
1.4.1911	Coventry	v Moseley	24-0
18.4.1914	Coventry	v Moseley	13-0 match declared void

* Match played at Belgrave Cricket & Cycle Ground

COUNTY CHAMPIONSHIP FINAL

28.3.1914	Midland Counties	v Durham	22-5

INTERNATIONAL CHALLENGE CUP

25.8.1996	Agen	v Cardiff	64-14 (semi-final)
26.8.1996	Cardiff	v Boroughmuir	48-29 (3rd place match)

RFU CHAMPIONSHIP

7.11.2009	Nottingham	v Exeter Chiefs	11-42

RUGBY LEAGUE – SUPER LEAGUE

28.7.1999	London Broncos	v Bradford Bulls	15-19
16.6.2001	London Broncos	v Bradford Bulls	0-42
20.6.2004	London Broncos	v Hull FC	26-42

NOT FIRST CLASS

The following games were played by the first-team, but have not been accorded first-class status. This is for a variety of reasons such as the use of rolling substitutions, not playing for 80 minutes, the quality of the opposition or the fact that they were pre-season trial games.

4.9.1967	v Philadelphia	Won 42-3
14.9.1976	v Caribbean XV	Won 29-22
1.4.1980	v International XV	Lost 20-22
1.5.1986	at Bayonne	Won 35-12
5.5.1986	at Basque XV (San Sebastian)	Won 96-0
2.8.1997	v Llanelli	Won 47-33
16.8.1997	v Caledonia Reds	Won 31-29
23.8.1997	at Bedford	Won 34-17
8.8.1998	at Bourgoin-Jallieu	Lost 21-31
23.8.1998	v Rotherham (at Sheffield Uni)	Won 5-0
7.8.1999	at Llanelli	Lost 3-38
21.8.1999	v Rotherham (Oval Park)	Won 20-13
29.8.1999	at Leeds Tykes	Won 32-16
5.8.2000	at Ulster (at Omagh)	Lost 12-31*
11.8.2001	at Perpignan	Lost 20-29
10.8.2002	v Agen (at La Teste)	Lost 30-34
7.3.2003	v Barbarians	Won 21-12
16.8.2003	at Perpignan	Lost 6-34
22.8.2003	at Cardiff Blues	Won 23-22
29.8.2003	at Sale Sharks	Won 17-16
21.8.2004	at Edinburgh (at Goldenacre)	Won 36-0
28.8.2004	v Cardiff Blues	Won 31-13
19.8.2005	at Connacht	Lost 17-22
26.8.2005	at Munster	Won 50-19
3.8.2006	v Castres Olympique (at Millau)	Won 29-28
5.8.2006	v Stade Français (at Camares)	Lost 18-19
18.8.2006	v Toulon	Won 39-19
25.8.2006	at Munster (Musgrave Park)	Won 26-18
28.8.2006	at Nottingham (Meadow Lane)	Lost 13-26
4.8.2007	at Cornish Pirates	Won 57-28
11.8.2007	at Bedford	Won 61-14
18.8.2007	v Nottingham	Won 59-5
1.9.2007	at Bayonne	Won 10-3
8.9.2007	v Montauban	Won 32-10
15.8.2008	at Biarritz	Lost 35-37
23.8.2008	at Ospreys	Won 30-17
30.8.2008	v Western Force	Won 48-7
5.8.2009	v Montpellier (at Saint-Affrique)	Lost 19-24
8.8.2009	v Castres (at Camares)	Lost 14-24
15.8.2009	at Nottingham (Meadow Lane)	Won 47-5
21.8.2009	at Cardiff Blues (City Stadium)	Won 15-4
28.8.2009	v Munster	Won 34-28
6.8.2010	at Brive	Lost 17-29
13.8.2010	at Nottingham (Meadow Lane)	Won 54-7
20.8.2010	at Munster (Musgrave Park)	Won 17-13
27.8.2010	v Leinster	Won 37-14
8.8.2011	v Montpellier (at Saint-Affrique)	Lost 24-50
20.8.2011	v Lyon OU	Won 38-3
26.8.2011	at Nottingham (Meadow Lane)	Won 32-10
11.8.2012	at Jersey	Won 34-21
18.8.2012	at Ulster	Drew 14-14
25.8.2012	v Nottingham	Won 64-7
9.8.2013	v Montpellier (at Geneva)	Lost 15-52
24.8.2013	at Jersey	Won 69-7
31.8.2013	v Ulster	Won 30-10

* game played over three 40-minute periods

OLYMPICS

Rugby has been played at the Olympics on four previous occasions, at Paris in 1900, London in 1908, Brussels in 1920 and Paris in 1924, the gold medals being won by France, Australia, and USA (twice) respectively.

Five Tigers, **John Jackett**. **Jimmy Jose**, **Maffer Davey**, **Dick Jackett**, and **Herbert Nicol** all won silver medals when they played in the Great Britain (Cornwall) team that were defeated 32-3 by Australia in the Olympic final at White City, London, on 26 October 1908.

Sprinter **Jack Morton** played his only match for Leicester against Headingley at Welford Road on 26 September 1908 predictably on the wing, just two months after competing for Great Britain in the Olympics. He had been the British 100 yard record holder for the previous four years but never made it beyond the semi-finals at White City, a venue where the Tigers met Harlequins on 25 September 1954, losing 16-28.

Tigers played Racing Club at the Stade Colombes in Paris on 13 February 1923, just over 12 months before it was used as the main athletics venue for the 1924 Olympics and the scene for **Eric Liddell's** famous "*Chariots of Fire*" 400m victory - Liddell had already gained seven rugby caps for Scotland between 1922-23.

John Cooper played rugby for the Tigers Extras before going on to win two silver medals for Great Britain at the 1964 Tokyo Olympics in the 400m hurdles and the 4x400m relay. He was unfortunately killed aged 33 in the 1974 Paris air disaster returning home following the five nations match the day before.

OPPONENTS

Tigers have faced eleven different opponents on over 100 occasions each:

Club	*P*	*W*	*D*	*L*	*Win %*
Northampton	231	128	20	83	55.4%
Gloucester	212	99	8	105	46.7%
Coventry	206	100	19	87	48.5%
Harlequins	194	108	9	77	55.7%
Bath	184	109	13	62	59.2%
Bristol	179	92	9	78	51.4%
Moseley	160	93	9	58	58.1%
Bedford	145	93	9	43	64.1%
Newport	121	24	8	89	19.8%
Swansea	119	27	16	76	22.7%
Birkenhead Park	101	64	9	28	63.4%

Leicester have a perfect played 12, won 12 record against Birmingham, whilst of opponents met on more than 20 occasions the best record is against Loughborough Colleges with 33 wins in 36 matches. The poorest record is against Swinton with just one win in 11 encounters, whilst Tigers secured only 24 wins in 121 games against Newport for a disappointing 19.8 winning percentage.

Notes: Bedford Swifts and Bedford Rovers merged to form Bedford (Blues) in 1886/87: Devonport Albion and Plymouth merged to become Plymouth Albion by 1919/20: Gosforth became Newcastle-Gosforth in 1990/91 and then Newcastle Falcons in 1996: Liverpool became Liverpool St Helens in 1986/87. Headingley and Roundhay merged to become Leeds (Tykes then Carnegie and now Yorkshire Carnegie) in 1992/93. The Leeds club in 1895 was the one which evolved to become Leeds Rhinos RL.

Sale became Manchester Sale in 1998/99 and then Sale Sharks in 1999/2000. Wasps became London Wasps from 1999-2014.

TOTAL RECORD	*P*	*W*	*D*	*L*	*F*	*A*	*Tries*	*T Agst*	*Win%*
Home games	2,557	1,868	145	544	45,932	21,844	7,949	3,405	73.1%
Away games	2,005	884	141	980	25,206	24,372	3,994	3,998	44.1%
At Neutral venues	57	33	1	23	1,047	1,028	121	107	57.9%
All games	**4,619**	**2,785**	**287**	**1,547**	**72,185**	**47,244**	**12,064**	**4,556**	**60.3%**

RECORDS AGAINST ONE OPPONENT

The most games played by a Tiger against any one opponent is the 31 made by **Sid Penny** against Coventry between 1896-1910, **David Matthews** is next with 28 appearances, also against Coventry.

The most tries scored against one opponent is the massive 21 grabbed by **Barry Evans** in 15 games versus Bedford, he is a clear five tries ahead of **Percy Lawrie** who ran in 16 against Birkenhead Park in 13 appearances.

Billy Foreman played for Leicester against 81 different teams during his Tigers career.

The most points scored against a single opponent is 248 by **Dusty Hare** in 16 games again facing Bedford. **Dusty Hare** in fact has the top dozen points totals against individual opponents, and is also the only kicker to land over 50 penalty goals against one club with his 51 against Moseley in 24 career appearances.

In drop goals the record is nine in nine games by **Les Cusworth** versus London Scottish.

Billy Foreman and **John Wells** have the honour of playing against the most different opponents, both making an appearance against 81 different foes during their illustrious Tigers careers.

Percy Lawrie and **Bob Barker** are the only players to have scored tries against over 50 different opponents, both crossing the whitewash against 52 separate adversaries.

Dusty Hare recorded points against an impressive 65 different opponents, whilst **Les Cusworth** dropped a goal against each of 37 different clubs.

George Chuter became the first player from any club to appear in a match against all 20 possible Premiership opponents when he came on as a rcplacement against London Welsh at Kassam Stadium on 2 September 2012.

MOST FREQUENT OPPONENT AGAINST TIGERS

Simon Shaw played an incredible 38 matches against the Tigers (all starts) for Bristol, Wasps and the Barbarians between 1993-2010, winning a record 15 of those encounters but losing 21 and drawing two. **Charlie Hodgson** has the most points scored against Leicester with 216 in 24 games for Sale and Saracens between 2001-14. On the try scoring stakes it is **Gordon Wood** who scored 13 tries between 1974-83 for Harlequins, Cambridge University and London Scottish, while **Tony Swift** scored 12 for Swansea and Bath between 1982-95.

Andy Gomarsall played for seven different teams against the Tigers from 1994-2010: Wasps, Barbarians, Bedford, Gloucester, Worcester, Harlequins and Leeds.

OTHER SPORTS

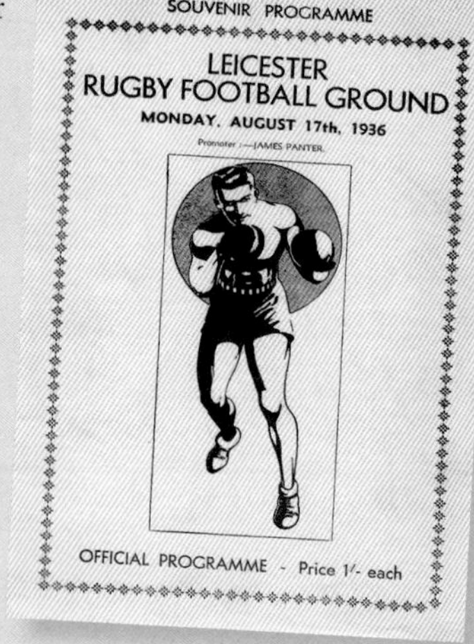

Welford Road has hosted sports other than rugby over the years, with the Harlem Globetrotters playing basketball there on both 3 June 1958 and again on 4 June 1959.

The venue has frequently played host to boxing meetings, the main pitch being used for seven multi-bout bills in the 1930s: On 13 June 1931 Larry Gains won the British Empire heavyweight title there and on 17 August 1936 Jack Petersen took the same title as well as the British Board of Control heavyweight crown.

On 5 June 2010 Welford Road hosted boxing for the first time in over 70 years with a three-bout card and on 13 November 2010 two more bouts were fought there.

Welford Road played host to grass court tennis when **Pat Cash** and **Ilie Nastase** played a doubles match with **Peter Fleming** and **Andrew Castle** on 24 June 2006 for the Lumbers 125 International Tennis Challenge, on a court cut into the Welford Road pitch.

OTHER TEAMS

The Tigers ran a second side, known as the A team between 1884/85 and 1905/06, which was resurrected between 1946/47 and 1954/55. The second team then evolved into the "Extra Firsts" in 1957/58 and played until 2002/03 even going on tour to Florida in 1981. In 1998/99 Tigers Extras won the ERP 2nd XV Challenge Trophy, a midweek league which existed for only one season, beating Sale 27-11 at Welford Road in the final.

The Tigers ran a 3rd side (B team) in 1895/96 only and then not again until the Swifts played between 1958/59 and 1990/91.

Leicester's first age group side was the Youth XV which made its bow in 1971/72 and played until the Academy really kicked-in in 2003/04.

The under-21 side played between 1991/92 and 2002/03, the Development team was fielded between 1993/94 and 1996/97, and has played in the Premiership A League since 2003/04 winning the crown on four occasions.

The Premiership Academy under-18 regional league was introduced in 2012/13 with Leicester winning the Northern Conference with a perfect played six, won six record.

Tigers won the ERP 2nd XV Challenge Trophy in 1998/99.

Season	*Pos*	*Pool*	*P*	*W*	*D*	*L*
PREMIERSHIP UNDER-19 LEAGUE						
2002/03	2nd	-	14	7	-	7
PREMIERSHIP UNDER-21 LEAGUE						
2002/03	**1st**	-	**22**	**20**	-	**2**
PREMIERSHIP UNDER-18 LEAGUE						
2012/13	1st	North	6	6	-	-
2013/14	2nd	North	6	5	-	1
Beat Harlequins 27-7 in 3rd place playoff						
PREMIERSHIP A LEAGUE						
2003/04	2nd	North	10	6	-	4
2004/05	**1st**	**North**	**10**	**7**	**1**	**2**
Beat Wasps in final 74-41 on aggregate (35-19, 29-22)						
2005/06	**1st**	**North**	**10**	**8**	**1**	**1**
Beat Harlequins 58-51 on aggregate (32-34, 26-17)						
2006/07	1st	North	10	8	-	2
Lost to Wasps 49-64 on aggregate (27-34, 22-30)						
2007/08	5th	North	10	4	-	6
2008/09	4th	Group 1	6	2	-	4
2009/10	**1st**	**North**	**10**	**7**	-	**3**
Beat Harlequins 29-27 in final						
2010/11	**2nd**	**North**	**10**	**8**	-	**2**
Beat Sale Jets 35-30 in final						
2011/12	2nd	North	5	4	-	1
Lost semi-final to Exeter Braves 31-36						
2012/13	3rd	North	5	3	-	2
2013/14	3rd	North	5	2	-	3

TIGERS A LEAGUE RECORDS:

Top try scorer: 13 - Alesana Tuilagi and Andy Forsyth, 12 – Ian Humphreys. 10 - Dan Hipkiss, Ben Pienaar.
Top points scorer: 278 – Ian Humphreys, 203 – George Ford, 167 – Ross Broadfoot.
Most appearances: 41 – Ben Pienaar, 40 – Dave Young, 31 – Matt Smith, Matt Cornwell.

Leicester ran an association football team in 1880/81 and 1881/82 playing a total of 25 games, winning 16, drawing two and losing just seven.

In 2014 the Leicester Tigers Wheelchair rugby team were crowned division two champions in their debut season.

OVERSEAS PLAYERS

The first players who were not born in England to appear for the first-team both made their debuts in the same game at Moseley on 8 October 1881: in the three-quarter line was 22-year-old **William Sully** who was born in Guelph, Ontario, Canada, whilst in the pack was **James Parry** who was born 21 years earlier in the East Indies.

The first overseas international ever to have played for the club was All Black **Ernest 'General' Booth**, who had gained three caps for New Zealand between 1906-07. He then relocated to Sydney and accompanied the Australians on their 1908/09 tour to England and Wales as a newspaper reporter. When the Wallabies continued their tour in North America Booth stayed on in England and turned out five times for the Tigers at centre and wing in February and March 1909.

PARTNERSHIPS

HALF-BACK PARTNERSHIPS

Billy Foreman & **Jacky Braithwaite** partnered each other at half-back 236 times for Leicester between 1896-1906. The next most experienced partnerships are **Les Cusworth** & **Steve Kenney** with 193, **Tim Taylor** & **Pedlar Wood** with 188, **Bleddyn Jones** & **John Allen** 186, whilst **Les Cusworth** & **Nick Youngs** with 111, complete the only pairings with over 100 games. **Cusworth** & **Mick Merriman** won 12 and drew one in their 13 combined games, and **Freddy Toone** & **Owen Wynne** lost all six in 1892/93.

FRONT ROW PARTNERS

166 games	Graham Rowntree, Richard Cockerill, Darren Garforth (1992-2002)
100 games	Stuart Redfern, Chris Tressler, Wayne Richardson (1983-92)
57 games	Frank Chawner, Mick Walker, Rex Skelton (1956-63)
54 games	Denis Bolesworth, Eddie Neal, Digger Dermott (1946-48)

Troy Thacker, Stuart Redfern and **Dave Hopper** started ten games together and won the lot.

The "ABC club" of Darren Garforth, Richard Cockerill and Graham Rowntree were Leicester's front-row combination in a record 166 matches between 1992-2002.

OTHER PARTNERSHIPS

Partnership	*Starts*	*Players*	*Years*
Prop	238	Graham Rowntree & Darren Garforth	1991-2003
2nd Row	129	Martin Johnson and Matt Poole	1991-98
Back-row	72	John Wells, Dean Richards, Neil Back	1990-97
Flankers	141	Ian Smith and Steve Johnson	1977-83
Entire Pack	37	Rowntree, Cockerill, Garforth, Johnson, Poole, Wells, Richards, Back	1992-97
Spine	143	John Allen, Bleddyn Jones & Garry Adey	1969-75
Centres	108	Paul Dodge and Clive Woodward	1981-85
Three-quarter line	40	John Duggan, Paul Dodge, Brian Hall and Bob Barker	1975-79
Wing	163	John Duggan and Bob Barker	1970-79
Back-three	88	Robin Money, John Duggan & Bob Barker	1970-78
All backs	22	Hare, Williams, Woodward, Dodge, Barnwell, Cusworth, Kenney	1981-83
Entire team	8	Hare, Williams, Woodward, Dodge, Barnwell, Cusworth, Kenney, Cowling, Wheeler, Steve Redfern, Joyce, Jackson, Johnson, Collington, Smith	1981-82

The back-row trinity of **Neil Back, Lewis Moody** and **Martin Corry** lost just three of the 33 games they started together. The Tigers won 52 of the 62 games (85.5%) in which the spine (number 8, scrum-half and fly-half) were Messrs **Dean Richards, Aadel Kardooni** and **Jez Harris.**

PENALTY GOALS

100 OR MORE CAREER PENALTY GOALS

Pos	*Name*	*Career*	*Apps*	*Pen*
1	Dusty Hare	1976/77-1988/89	393+1	820
2	John Liley	1988/89-1996/97	226+4	449
3	Tim Stimpson	1998/99-2003/04	141+10	372
4	Andy Goode	1998/99-2007/08	173+27	335
5	Toby Flood	2008/09-2013/14	107+12	270
6	Jez Harris	1984/85-1995/96	213+12	178
7	Joel Stransky	1996/97-1998/99	72+1	157
8	Mike Gavins	1956/57-1970/71	121	119
9	Bob Barker	1968/69-1979/80	318+2	107

MOST PENALTY GOALS IN A SEASON

109	Tim Stimpson	2000/01
91	John Liley	1995/96
89	Dusty Hare	1988/89

MOST PENALTY GOALS IN A GAME BY A PLAYER

For Tigers:

8	John Liley	v Bristol	28.10.1995	●
8	Tim Stimpson	v Gloucester	2.12.2000	●
8	Andy Goode	v Sale Sharks	28.1.2006	●

Against Tigers:

9	Diego Dominguez	v Stade Français (f)	19.5.2001	●
9	Thierry Lacroix	at Perpignan	27.10.2001	●
8	Stephen Jones	at Llanelli	12.1.2002	●
8	Mark van Gisbergen	at London Wasps	5.12.2004	●

The first Tiger to kick a penalty goal was **Harry Brockbank** against Kettering at the Belgrave Road Ground on 19 January 1889.

The last forward to kick a penalty goal for the Tigers in a match, rather than a penalty shoot-out, was **Peter Wheeler** when he landed three kicks against Middlesbrough on 26 April 1975.

MOST PENALTY GOALS IN A GAME BY A TEAM

For Tigers:

8	v Bristol	43-6	28.10.1995	●
8	v Gloucester	31-28	2.12.2000	●
8	v Sale Sharks	27-27	28.1.2006	●

Against Tigers:

10	at London Wasps	24-36	31.3.2002	●
9	v Stade Français (f)	34-30	19.5.2001	●
9	at Perpignan	31-30	27.10.2001	●
8	at Llanelli	12-24	12.1.2002	●
8	at London Wasps	37-31	5.12.2004	●

PENALTY SHOOT-OUT

On 3 May 2009 in the semi-final of the Heineken Cup Leicester faced Cardiff Blues at Millennium Stadium. The game finished 26-26 at full-time, and there was no further scoring after ten minutes each way of extra-time.

A penalty shoot-out ensued, which was tied at 4-4 after the first round of five mandatory kicks each side. Tigers penalties were scored by **Julien Dupuy**, **Sam Vesty, Geordan Murphy** and **Scott Hamilton**, the fourth kick by **Johne Murphy** was missed. It then went to sudden death. **Tom Shanklin** scored for the Blues, **Aaron Mauger** made it 5-5. **Richie Rees** and **Craig Newby** were both successful (6-6). **Martyn Williams** then missed his kick, and back-rower **Jordan Crane** became an unlikely hero to land his shot and give Tigers a 7-6 win.

PENALTY TRIES

121 penalty tries have been awarded to the Tigers, the first of which was in September 1919 against Bath by Welsh referee **CR Stephens**. The following eight have been awarded to an individual, as he was the person who was impeded in "The act of scoring" as the law states. These eight have been included as tries in individual career records, however since 1990 this practice has ceased universally, with penalty tries no longer being awarded to players who might have scored.

Date	*Opponents*	*Player*	*Referee*
6.9.1919	v Bath	Teddy Haselmere	CR Stephens
4.12.1954	v Waterloo	George Cullen	L Graham
27.9.1958	at Harlequins	Harry Jessop	L Boundy
4.4.1970	at Birkenhead Park	Mike Yandle	H Smith
15.4.1972	v Nottingham	Peter Wheeler	D Thomas
28.10.1972	at Swansea	John Duggan	N Davies
1.10.1983	v Coventry	Nick Youngs	K Mott
6.11.1990	at Cambridge University	Paul Dodge	S Bradford

Only 30 penalty tries have been given against Leicester, the first of which was by Sale at Welford Road on Christmas Eve 1898, the *Manchester Guardian* stating that Sale were awarded "a try for a foul". Gloucester have been awarded five of those with referee **Ashley Rowden** responsible for awarding three penalty tries against Leicester.

In four games Leicester have been awarded two penalty tries:

10.2.1996	v Saracens	Brian Campsall
22.12.2012	at London Irish	Luke Pearce
4.1.2013	at Worcester	JP Doyle
23.11.2013	v London Irish	Martin Fox

JP Doyle has awarded Tigers a total of six penalty tries, whilst London Irish and Saracens have both conceded nine each.

Referee JP Doyle has awarded Leicester a record six penalty tries.

"Penalty Tries" were the top try scorer for the club in season 2012/13 with 11, the next best individual was **Adam Thompstone** with nine. They were also joint top try scorer in 2009/10 with seven along with **Scott Hamilton**.

PLASTIC PITCH

Leicester's first game on an artificial pitch was against Saracens at Allianz Park in Barnet on 21 December 2013 in the Aviva Premiership. Tigers had a day to forget, going down to their worst ever league defeat, 49-10.

Leicester have played on unusual surfaces before, in fact Welford Road pitch itself was entirely constructed of sand between 1893-1898, the club preferring this so that rugby could still be played during frosty weather. However, they were forced to revert back to turf when the Midland Counties Union ruled that no cup ties could be played at the venue with sand in use, hence the pitch was turfed ready for the start of the 1898/99 season.

More recently Tigers also played in sand in 1995 when they participated at the Dubai Sevens for the only time.

PLAY-OFFS

The concept of play-offs following the league campaign was first introduced in season 2000/01 where a completely different tournament for a separate piece of silverware was contested. Tigers had already won the Zurich Premiership title, the top eight sides in the table then progressed to a knockout tournament known as the Zurich Championship. Leicester beat London Irish in the quarter-finals and Northampton Saints in the last four before carrying off the crown by overcoming Bath 22-10 in the final at Twickenham.

The following season the same format was retained, with Leicester once more winning the Premiership title, but this time going out of the Championship at the first hurdle, losing out to Bristol.

In 2002/03 it was decided that the title of England's champion club would for the first time be awarded not to the side that had topped the league, but to the club who won the Premiership final at Twickenham. The top three finishers in the league would have a chance to claim the prize; the 2nd and 3rd place teams, Wasps and Northampton, playing a solitary semi-final with the winners meeting the 1st place finishers, Gloucester, in the final. The next four highest finishers in the league, who had not already qualified for the Heineken Cup, would then contest another tournament, known as the Zurich Wildcard, to decide which team would attain the one remaining place in the following season's European Cup. That season the Tigers finished 4th and beat Harlequins in a two-legged semi-final to set up a showdown with Saracens at Northampton which Leicester narrowly won 27-20 after extra time.

In 2003/04 the top seven format was repeated with Leicester this time finishing 5th and once more beating Harlequins, although in a one-off match at Welford Road, to progress to the wildcard final at Twickenham where they beat Sale Sharks 48-27 to grab the one remaining Heineken Cup spot.

In 2004/05 Leicester did not have to go through the wildcard route because they finished first in the league, but the week off did them no favours as a London Wasps side who had accounted for Sale in the semi-final easily beat the Tigers 39-14 in the final.

The format was then altered in 2005/06 to the one still in use today, with the top four sides playing semi-finals, 1v4 and 2v3, and the winners meeting in the final at Twickenham.

Dusty Hare scored an unsurpassed 4,507 points for the club during a 13-year career.

POINTLESS

The Tigers being held pointless is a rare occurrence, with just four instances since 1984. There have been only four matches in tournaments in which Leicester have failed to score a point:

Result	*Opponent*	*Venue*	*Competition*	*Date*	
0-7	Sale	Heywood Road	RFU Knockout Cup (qf)	10.3.1973	●
0-28	Gloucester	Kingsholm	Division 1	14.1.1989	●
0-14	Northampton	Franklin's Gardens	Zurich Premiership	20.12.2003	●
0-33	Ulster	Ravenhill	Heineken Cup	11.1.2004	●

The only time that Tigers have been held scoreless at Welford Road since 1966 was in the Barbarians game on 27 December 1969, when the illustrious visitors ran in nine tries without reply to win 35-0.

Leicester have held their opponents scoreless on over 500 occasions. In competitions the list of games is as follows:

Result	*Opponent*	*Venue*	*Competition*	*Date*	
0-22	London Scottish	Welford Road	John Player Cup (qf)	8.3.1980	●
0-15	Rosslyn Park	Priory Lane	John Player Special Cup (r3)	23.1.1988	●
0-12	Bath	Recreation Ground	Pilkington Cup (r3)	24.11.1990	●
0-10	Newcastle Falcons	Kingston Park	Pilkington Cup (qf)	22.2.1992	●
0-9	Orrell	Welford Road	Division 1	13.2.1993	●
0-76	Exeter	Welford Road	Pilkington Cup (qf)	27.2.1993	●
0-23	Harlequins	Welford Road	Division 1	27.3.1993	●
0-18	Orrell	Edgehall Road	Division 1	15.1.1994	●
0-6	Orrell	Edgehall Road	Division 1	17.9.1994	●
0-27	Exeter	County Ground	Pilkington Cup (r4)	23.12.1995	●
0-27	Richmond	Welford Road	Allied Dunbar Premiership	24.10.1998	●
0-26	Bedford	Welford Road	Allied Dunbar Premiership	26.12.1998	●
0-49	Leeds	Welford Road	Tetley's Bitter Cup (r5)	30.1.1999	●
0-27	Exeter	Welford Road	Powergen Cup (r6)	15.12.2001	●
0-63	Calvisano	Welford Road	Heineken Cup	19.10.2002	●
0-32	Northampton	Welford Road	Guinness Premiership	3.9.2005	●
0-34	Cardiff Blues	Welford Road	Heineken Cup	13.1.2007	●
0-39	Edinburgh	Welford Road	Heineken Cup	17.11.2007	●
0-52	Benetton Treviso	Welford Road	Heineken Cup	17.1.2009	●

POINTS SCORING

750 OR MORE CAREER POINTS

Pos	*Name*	*Career*	*Apps*	*Try*	*Con*	*Pen*	*DG*	*Mk*	*Pts*
1	Dusty Hare	1976/77-1988/89	393+1	87	779	820	47	-	4507
2	John Liley	1988/89-1996/97	226+4	74	417	449	2	-	2518
3	Andy Goode	1998/99-2007/08	173+27	29	275	335	33	-	1799
4	Tim Stimpson	1998/99-2003/04	141+10	29	223	372	2	-	1713
5	Toby Flood	2008/09-2013/14	107+12	25	199	270	1	-	1336
6	Jez Harris	1984/85-1995/96	213+12	23	165	178	70	-	1171
7	Harold Day	1918/19-1928/29	212	108	281	81	4	2	1151
8	Bob Barker	1968/69-1979/80	318+2	158	92	107	2	-	1117
9	Les Cusworth	1978/79-1989/90	365	66	100	65	96	-	947
10	Joel Stransky	1996/97-1998/99	72+1	23	146	157	6	-	896

In all 68 players have amassed over 200 points each.
Quickest to 500 points: **Joel Stransky** 35 matches, **John Liley** 43, **Dusty Hare** 53, **Tim Stimpson** 54.
1,000th Point: **Stimpson** 88 games, **Liley** 92, **Hare** 93, **Day** 181, **Harris** 194, **Barker** 280.

BREAKING THE CAREER POINTS SCORING RECORD

Dusty Hare has been the club's all-time top points scorer since he took the record from **Harold Day** during the John Player Cup final against London Irish on 19 April 1980, a mark that Day had held for the previous 55 years. Listed are all the individuals to have held the record and when they first attained it:

Name	*Points*	*Opponent*	*Date*	
John Parsons	10	at Rushden	18.3.1882	
Ted Cooke	151	v Leicestershire XV	27.12.1895	
Archie Field	158	at Bedford Grammar School	17.2.1897	
Arthur Jones	177	v Burton (r2)	12.3.1898	●
Harry Wilkinson	360	v Portsmouth	8.9.1900	
Arthur Jones	475	v Belgrave (r2)	21.3.1903	●
Percy Lawrie	564	v Bristol	16.10.1920	
Harold Day	728	at Bristol	11.4.1925	
Dusty Hare	1,152	v London Irish (f)	19.4.1980	●

MOST POINTS FOR TIGERS IN A COMPETITION...

MIDLAND COUNTIES CUP

Arthur Jones	130
Harry Wilkinson	99
Jacky Braithwaite	84
Alfred Hind	77
Frank Jackson	60
Percy Lawrie	56
Jack Miles	51

NATIONAL CUP

Dusty Hare	531
John Liley	269
Les Cusworth	135
Joel Stransky	115
Jez Harris	108

ANGLO-WELSH CUP

Andy Goode	94
George Ford	71
Paul Burke	40
Billy Twelvetrees	39
Owen Williams	37
Derick Hougaard	36

LEAGUE/PREMIERSHIP

Name	*Lg*	*Prem*	*Total*
Tim Stimpson	-	1180	1180
Andy Goode	-	1165	1165
John Liley	1070	-	1070
Toby Flood	-	954	954
Joel Stransky	101	455	556
Jez Harris	461	-	461
Geordan Murphy	-	428	428
Neil Back	79	295	374

EUROPE

Andy Goode	406
Tim Stimpson	358
Toby Flood	358
Geordan Murphy	157
Joel Stransky	106

1000TH CAREER POINT

Pos	*Name*	*Opponents*	*Date*	*Game*	*Age*
1	Harold Day	v Old Merchant Taylors	26.3.1927	181	28y 226d
2	Bob Barker	at Harlequins	24.9.1977	280	32y 336d
3	Dusty Hare	at Cambridge University	10.11.1979	93	26y 346d
4	John Liley	at Orrell	29.2.1992	92	24y 192d
5	Jez Harris	v Blackheath (r4)	17.12.1994	194	29y 298d
6	Tim Stimpson	v Newcastle Falcons	17.3.2001	88	27y 188d
7	Andy Goode	v Ospreys	11.12.2005	133	25y 252d
8	Toby Flood	v Ospreys	21.10.2012	81	27y 74d

2000TH CAREER POINT

Pos	*Name*	*Opponents*	*Date*	*Game*	*Age*
1	Dusty Hare	v Oxford University	20.10.1982	182	29y 325d
2	John Liley	at Exeter (r4)	23.12.1995	179	28y 124d

3000TH CAREER POINT

Pos	*Name*	*Opponents*	*Date*	*Game*	*Age*
1	Dusty Hare	v Coventry	5.10.1985	263	32y 310d

4000TH CAREER POINT

Pos	*Name*	*Opponents*	*Date*	*Game*	*Age*
1	Dusty Hare	v RAF	8.3.1988	357	35y 100d

MOST POINTS IN A SEASON

486 (9t,57c,109p)	Tim Stimpson	2000/01
459 (11t,82c,77p,3d)	Joel Stransky	1997/98
446 (8t,65c,91p,1d)	John Liley	1995/96
439 (18t,89c,63p)	John Liley	1989/90
438 (12t,60c,89p,1d)	Dusty Hare	1988/89

31 different players have scored 100 points or more in a season, with **Dusty Hare** achieving the mark in each of his 13 seasons with the club. Indeed he accumulated in excess of 200 points in all but his first season (finishing with 199 after missing the first nine games before moving over from Nottingham). **Harold Day** achieved the hundred on seven occasions (all successive), and **Bob Barker** six times.

MOST POINTS IN A GAME BY A PLAYER

For Tigers:

43	Dusty Hare	v Birmingham	17.9.1986
35	Joel Stransky	v Glasgow & District (po)	1.11.1997
34	Dusty Hare	at Birmingham	16.9.1981
32	Tim Stimpson	v Newcastle Falcons	21.9.2002
32	Andy Goode	v Clermont Auvergne	22.10.2005
31	Teddy Haselmere	v Burton-on-Trent	4.10.1919
31	John Liley	v Rosslyn Park	21.3.1992
31	Geordan Murphy	v Loughborough Students	21.11.1997
31	Tim Stimpson	v Saracens	24.2.2001

Against Tigers:

33	Siua Taumalolo	v Barbarians	17.3.1998
30	Diego Dominguez	v Stade Français (f)	19.5.2001
30	Thierry Lacroix	at Perpignan	27.10.2001
27	Mark Mapletoft	at Gloucester	1.2.1998
27	Mark McHugh	at Leinster	19.11.1999
27	Alex King	at London Wasps	31.3.2002

MOST SUCCESSIVE POINTS SCORING GAMES

Dusty Hare scored points in 183 successive games for which he was selected in the starting line-up between 17 December 1983 and the end of his career at Twickenham on 29 April 1989. He did however come on as a replacement for **Paul Dodge** in Australia on 4 August 1987, and did not score any points, therefore strictly speaking the above record is actually broken into two separate runs of 118 and 65 games. **Marcus Rose** (1975-77) scored points in each of his 19 first-team games, whilst **David Beaty** (1963-69) has played in the most games (88) without ever scoring a single point.

FASTEST TO THE 100-POINT MILESTONE

Joel Stransky scored his 100th point in only his eighth appearance, v West Hartlepool at Welford Road in the Courage League on 8 March 1997. This was in fact only his seventh start - his debut was as a 27th minute replacement wing, and he did not kick at goal in that game.

Toby Flood and **Jeremy Staunton** both reached the 100-point target on only their ninth appearance, whilst **Ramiro Pez** got there in 10 games, with **Marcus Rose** and **Dusty Hare** both scoring their 100th point in just 11 games.

↑ Ramiro Pez was one of the quickest to score a century of points for Tigers, doing so in only ten games.

FASTEST 100 POINTS IN A SEASON

6 games - **John Liley** in 1989/90.
7 games - **Dusty Hare** in 1981/82, 1985/86, 1986/87, 1988/89, **John Liley** in 1990/91, **Jez Harris** in 1994/95, **Andy Goode** in 2005/06, **Toby Flood** in 2011/12.
Evolution of the record: 25 matches - **F.Fox** in 1894/95; 21 matches – **Arthur Jones** in 1897/98; 20 matches – **Billy Bream** in 1912/13; 12 matches - **Teddy Haselmere** in 1919/20; 11 matches - **Arthur Chapman** in 1969/70; 9 matches - **Dave Whibley** in 1972/73; 8 matches - **Dusty Hare** in 1977/78; 7 matches - **Dusty Hare** in 1981/82; 6 matches - **John Liley** in 1989/90.

FASTEST 200 POINTS IN A SEASON

13 games - **Dusty Hare** in 1899/89, **John Liley** in 1995/96, **Joel Stransky** in 1997/98.
14 games – **Tim Stimpson** in 2001/02, **Andy Goode** in 2003/04.

FASTEST 300 POINTS IN A SEASON

20 games - **John Liley** in 1995/96, **Joel Stransky** in 1997/98.
21 games - **Dusty Hare** in 1988/89, **Andy Goode** in 2004/05.

FASTEST 400 POINTS IN A SEASON

25 games - **John Liley** in 1995/96.

POSITIONS

MOST MATCHES STARTED BY POSITION

Full-back	392	Dusty Hare	1976/77 to 1988/89
Wing	302	John Duggan	1969/70 to 1980
Centre	423	Paul Dodge	1975/76 to 1992/93
Fly-half	364	Les Cusworth	1978/79 to 1989/90
Scrum-half	457	John Allen	1960/61 to 1975/76
Prop	362	Graham Rowntree	1990/91 to 2006/07
Hooker	347	Peter Wheeler	1969/70 to 1985/86
Lock	355	Bob Rowell	1961/62 to 1977/78
Flanker	428	David Matthews	1955/56 to 1973/74
Number 8	336	Garry Adey	1966/67 to 1980/81
Replacement	84	George Chuter	2000/01 to 2013/14

Notes: Hare also made one other appearance as a replacement full-back and started another game at fly-half.

Dodge was a replacement centre in two other games, and also started six games at fly-half and another five matches at full-back.

Cusworth also started one game at full-back, whilst Wheeler also started one game at prop and another at flanker.

Rowntree made a further 36 appearances off the bench as a replacement prop.

If you include replacement appearances Martin Johnson's lock total is 348 starts plus 14 off the bench, thereby surpassing Rowell.

Matthews started 73 addition games at number 8 and another one at centre.

Adey started 41 other matches in the second-row and a further four at flanker.

PRESIDENTS

Up to the end of the 2013/14 season 39 individuals have held the post of president of Leicester Football Club. Only Alderman **Thomas Wright** has had two separate spells in the job, in seasons 1890/91 and 1892/93, whilst the only one to be president and player at the same time was the inaugural office bearer, **William Wheeler** in 1880/81.

Eric Thorneloe played for Leicester in 1919, was honorary secretary between 1928-57, and then was president from 1957-59.

1880-1881	WA (William) Wheeler
1881-1883	Hon. ES (Edwyn) Burnaby
1883-1890	Hon. M (Montagu) Curzon
1890-1891	Ald. T (Thomas) Wright
1891-1892	Rev. HJ (Hugh) Fortescue
1892-1893	Ald. T (Thomas) Wright
1893-1901	J (Jack) Parsons
1901-1912	J (Joseph) Collier
1912-1924	HW (Hedley) Salmon
1924-1926	K (Kenneth) McAlpin
1926-1931*	Sir S (Samuel) Faire
1931-1939	Sir CF (Frederick) Oliver
1939-1942*	A (Allen) Lovell
1945-1952	WN (Billy) Bradshaw
1952-1957*	CW (Charlie) Cross
1957-1959	JE (Eric) Thorneloe
1959-1962	RL (Rodney) Beddingfield
1962-1965	RJ (Bobby) Barr
1965-1968	DJ (Doug) Norman
1968-1971	HP (Nick) Hughes
1971-1974	JTW (Tom) Berry
1974-1977	RJ (Rodney) Willcox
1977-1979	KR (Ken) Kinder
1979-1981	EC (Eric) Lacey
1981-1983	HW (Harry) Sibson
1983-1985	PAH (Peter) Herbert
1985-1987	R (Bob) Beason
1987-1989	KP (Kevin) Andrews
1989-1991	BTC (Brian) Small
1991-1993	GG (Graham) Willars
1993-1995	JT (Tudor) Thomas
1995-1997	PJ (Peter) Wheeler
1997-1999	GJ (Garry) Adey
1999-2001	AE (Tony) Hopkins
2001-2003	DJ (David) Matthews
2003-2005	RE (Bob) Rowell
2005-2007	RD (Roy) Jackson
2007-2009	BP (Brian) Hall
2009-2013	MJ (Mike) Harrison
2013-	PW (Paul) Dodge

* died in office

PROFESSIONALISM

In 1995 the amateur ethos of rugby union was under severe pressure, especially from the southern hemisphere nations, and if the threats from media moguls like **Kerry Packer** and **Rupert Murdoch** to hijack it were not to materialise there had to be a revolution; it was too late for gradualism.

On Sunday, 27 August 1995, at the Concord Hotel in Paris, **Vernon Pugh** QC, the chairman of the IRB, announced that the game of rugby union would go "open".

This was just six days before Tigers were to begin the 1995/96 season by facing Northampton in a friendly at Welford Road.

The RFU declared a moratorium on professionalism for the 1995/96 season and professionalism per se is deemed to have begun in England at the start of the 1996/97 season with Tigers' first professional match effectively being when they took on Boroughmuir on Sunday, 25 August 1996 at Welford Road in the four-team International Challenge Cup which also saw Agen and Cardiff invited to take part.

The honour of becoming the Tigers' first solely professional players by making their first-class debuts in this game, go to back-row partners **Lewis Moody** and **Ben Pain**, who both scored a brace of tries apiece.

PROFESSIONS

Between 1883 and 1908 thirteen different vicars played for the Tigers, but the only one since was **Edwin Haddon** in 1935/36. Six different reverends – **Charles Barham, Ernest Farmer, Robert Ley, Leonard Ward, John Whitehurst** and **Owen Wynne** - turned out in season 1891/92, whilst in three matches between October 1891 and February 1892 there were five separate members of the clergy in the Leicester XV.

The first ex-policeman in Tigers ranks was **John Jackett** who had served in the Cape Mounted Police in South Africa before making his Tigers debut in 1904. The first serving PC was **William Bingham** in 1908, whilst at least another 18 players have also at one time been policemen: **Gordon Almey, Eric Fowler, Mike Freer, Keith Hassall, John Hopkin, Steve Johnson, Nick Joyce, Derek Bircumshaw, Dean Richards, J Sargeant, JR Sharp, Len Shipton, Graham Smith, Len Swanwick, Ranji Walker, John Wells, Dorian West** and **John White.**

Over 20 medical doctors have played for the club, the last of which was **David Lammiman** in 1951, an ex-Wyggeston schoolboy who went on to become surgeon rear-admiral and Medical Director General of the Navy from 1990-93. In addition **John Quick, Kenneth Stanyon-Jacques** and **Walter Smith** were dentists.

Across all eras teachers have always featured prominently in the Tigers ranks, a third of the club's XV for its very first game in 1880 were school teachers. Well over 50 players have earned their living teaching the latest of which is **Harry Ellis** who now teaches at Leicester Grammar School after having his professional rugby career curtailed early due to injury.

There have been at least 13 solicitors or barristers who have played for the club – **Percy Atkins, Shirley Atkins, Keith Oakley, Herbert Foster, Geoff Herbert, Alfred Hind, Kenneth McAlpin, Jack Parsons, Brian Rigney, Arnold Sime, Brian Small, Walter Sturges** and **Tim Taylor.**

Another 20 or so Tigers players come from farming stock, amongst them **Robin Cowling, David Matthews, Tom Berry, Nick Youngs, Dusty Hare** and **Julian White**. **Derek Ashurst** (1951-62) and **Frank Noon** (1885) were both poultry farmers, whilst front-rower **Jim Stapleton** was born in Market Bosworth but then took up farming in Kenya before returning to his roots and making his Tigers debut aged 26 in 1937.

Uppingham schoolboy **Norman Baker** born and died in Grimsby and perhaps predictably was a fish merchant when he made his two appearances for Leicester in 1928 and 1932.

Australia-born England international **David Campbell,** who hooked in one game for Leicester in 1937 whilst studying at Cambridge University, had a distinguished military career before returning to his native Australia and becoming a renowned poet.

Frederick Ernest Oliver made one first-team appearance at scrum-half in 1923 and 27 years later went on to become Lord Mayor of the City of Leicester.

REFEREES

A number of ex-Tigers have gone on to referee Leicester games, amongst these are **Alexander Brice, Joseph Collier, Harold Day, Dan Ellwood, Bert Ewin, Teddy Haselmere, Arthur Jones, Stephen Meikle, Jack Miles, Bill Moore, Percy Oscroft, Peter Tahany, Sandy Taylor, Gordon Vears,** and **Wavell Wakefield**. In addition **Cyril Gadney** refereed 16 Tigers games, but none when his brother Bernard was playing for Leicester.

Four Tigers players went on to become international referees: **Harold Day, Jack Miles, AO Jones** and **Sandy Taylor**.

Test match referee and ex-England international **Edgar Holmes** of Moseley has refereed the most Tigers games with 75 between 1884-1904, followed by another Moseley man **Gil Evans** with 64 (1900-25), and **Albert Freethy** the Welsh international referee with 62 (1912-36). The only other referee to have taken charge of over 50 Leicester games is Cheltenham's **Chris White** with 55 (1993-2010).

The Tigers won all ten games under the control of **GC Cromwell** of Gloucestershire from 1978-87, and lost only one of 20 games when Welshman **CR Stephens** was in charge between 1912-26. Leicester also only lost one of **E Browning's** 31 games in charge before the First World War.

Albert Freethy refereed the Tigers in 62 matches between 1912-36.

REPLACEMENTS

Substitutions for injured players were first allowed in the 1976/77 season but only on the recommendation of a doctor, although the first instance came at Manchester on 2 January 1911 when centre **Frank Tarr** was carried off after just two minutes with a twisted ankle. The *Manchester Guardian* records "the crowd recognised the sporting instinct of the Manchester captain, who allowed another player to take his place." England international **Thomas Hogarth** came in to join his elder brother **Anthony** in the pack, with **Chris Gimson** moving from the forwards into the three-quarter line.

The first replacement to score a try came in similar circumstances at Blackheath on 14 December 1946, **John Campbell** being replaced by a late arriving **Haydn Thomas** a few minutes after the start - Thomas redeemed himself by scoring a try in a 10-6 victory.

In 1993/94 three replacements were allowed to sit on the bench if required, and in November 1995 this was extended to four replacements. Six had always been allowed in cup finals and the European Cup, and this was extended in March 1997 to cover all league games as well. In season 1998/99 this was further extended to seven replacements, and finally in 2009/10 eight.

Chris Johnson and **Perry Freshwater** are the only players to have scored a hat-trick of tries as replacements, both coming on at hooker, against Western Province Defence at Silvermines, Cape Town on 7 August 1993 and against Otley at Welford Road on 4 November 2000 respectively.

The most penalty goals kicked in a game by a replacement is four by **George Ford** in the 2013 Premiership final against Northampton at Twickenham, whilst only three substitute players have dropped goals: **Mike Poulson** at Oxford University in 1983, **Andy Goode** against Sale in 2007 and **Ryan Lamb** at home to Montpellier on 8 December 2013.

Nine players have made at least 50 appearances as a replacement with **George Chuter** claiming the most with 84, in addition he also spent another 39 complete matches as an unused substitute. Scrum-half **Jamie Hamilton** has warmed the bench the most times without getting on to the pitch with 66 instances between 1991-2003.

Dorian West holds the record for the most appearances off the bench in a season with 24 in 1998/99 when he started just eight matches. He also holds the distinction of having been an unused bench replacement a record 22 times during the 1996/97 season. The most replacement appearances in a season without making any starts is six by **Santiago Gonzalez Bonorino** in 2008/09 and equalled by **Joe Duffey** in 2010/11.

Tom Varndell scored a record seven tries during 25 appearances off the bench for Leicester between 2005-2009. **Henry Tuilagi** scored five tries in 26 appearances as a replacement and only another three from his 26 starts, whilst four of **David Mélé's** five tries have all been scored as a replacement.

The most replaced player in Leicester history is **George Chuter** who left the field 124 times in 292 appearances.

Temporary or "blood" replacements were first introduced in season 1993/94 and Leicester's first such replacement was **Chris Tarbuck** who temporarily took over from **Neil Back** at Newcastle-Gosforth in the Courage League on 9 October 1993.

Tactical substitutions were first allowed in November 1996 with the Tigers' first such instance involving **Leon Lloyd** who was replaced by **Rory Underwood** in the 63rd minute of the European Cup quarter-final at Welford Road against Harlequins on 16 November 1996.

Replacements for concussion checks appeared in 2013 with Leicester's first instance being **Rob Hawkins** going off for assessment and being replaced by **Tom Youngs** at Northampton on 30 March 2013 – he did not return.

The fastest replacement from the start of a match was after just 21 seconds when **Blaine Scully** went off for a concussion check against Northampton at Welford Road on 5 October 2013. He returned after eight minutes on the sidelines.

↑ Boris Stankovich was injured and replaced by Marcos Ayerza after only 51 seconds of Saracens' visit to Welford Road on 10.5.2014.

The fastest permanent replacement due to injury was **Boris Stankovich**, who left the field after just 51 seconds against Saracens at Welford Road on 10 May 2014.

TRIES BY TEMPORARY REPLACEMENTS

26.1.1999	Derek Jelley	Richmond (A)	for Rowntree 71-79'	●
30.4.2005	Dan Hipkiss	Wasps (H)	for Gibson 63-69'	●
2.1.2006	Darren Morris	Saracens (H)	for Rowntree 27-34'	●

REPLAYS AND VOID GAMES

Leicester have been involved in only three cup ties which have required a replay to decide the victors – all these being in the Midland Counties Cup during the 19th century. Uniquely the first instance, against Rushden in 1883/84, required a 2nd replay following two drawn encounters. Against Rugby in 1888/89 the Tigers won 6-5 but it was then discovered that they had fielded an ineligible player (**A Chettle** at full-back) and so were forced to replay the tie four days later, but again triumphed 4-3.

Season	*Round*	*Opponent*	*Result*	*Replay*	*2nd replay*
1883/84	2nd	Rushden (A)	D 0-0	D 1t-1t	W 1t-0
1888/89	2nd	Rugby (A)	W 6-5	W 4-3	
1898/99	semi-final	Moseley (H)	D 0-0	W 8-3	

In the first season of the Courage League, 1987/88, the Leicester v Gloucester match was never actually played. This was because there were no fixed dates on which matches had to be arranged in the fledgling league format, games were played at mutually convenient times for the two clubs concerned for the most part in place of already scheduled club fixtures between the teams.

Leicester and Gloucester already had two club fixtures arranged for that season, to be played at Welford Road on 5 December and Kingsholm on 9 January. However as the first clashed with the Divisional Championship with both clubs missing players to the Midlands and South-West teams, and the second with England call-ups due to the impending five nations, both the clashes were "demerited" and another game was never agreed upon.

Leicester have twice been docked one league point for breaches of eligibility regulations:

On 13 September 2003 **Darren Morris** played against London Irish but was technically unregistered although there were mitigating circumstances, and on 18 and 26 November 2006 **Ian Humphreys** played for the Tigers while he was registered as being on-loan to Leeds Tykes and therefore ineligible under Premiership Regulations.

RUGBY LEAGUE CONNECTIONS

On 29 August 1895 in Huddersfield the Northern Union was formed, an organisation which was eventually to become the Rugby Football League in 1922. Initially matches were played under rugby union laws with the first major rules change abolishing line-outs in 1897, it wasn't until 1906 that teams were reduced from 15 to 13 players a side.

Prior to the split the Tigers had forged fixtures with six founder members of the Northern Union: Broughton Rangers (1893 and 1894), Halifax (1894), Huddersfield (1894-95), Leeds (1895), Oldham (1889) and St Helens (1892). They also played against three teams that would later join the new union: Swinton (1888-95), Keighley (1899) and Salford (1892-95). In addition Leicester were scheduled to play Bradford at Park Avenue in March 1889, and even accepted a challenge from Wigan in November 1891 but rejected one from Rochdale Hornets.

The Northern Union wrote to the club in November 1907 asking if a game with the Kiwis touring team could be played at Welford Road, but this was refused by the committee.

After the formation of the Northern Union there followed almost exactly 100 years of division until the game of rugby union itself went open in August 1995.

The first steps towards reconciliation saw Leicester play a Courage League game against Orrell at the rugby league citadel of Central Park in Wigan on 30 March 1996. Tigers then faced Wigan Warriors in the 1996 Middlesex sevens and Emerging London Broncos in 1998 Middlesex sevens.

On 26 January 1961 on Welford Road Rec the RAF were allowed to pick rugby league players who were on national service in their XV. One such candidate was St Helens superstar **Alex Murphy**, who already had 15 caps for the Great Britain Lions RL team, he in fact played again for the side against France at his beloved Knowsley Road just two days later. Murphy went on to tally 27 caps for the GB Lions as well as winning the Rugby League Challenge Cup at Wembley in 1961, 1966 for St Helens, in 1971 for Leigh and in 1974 for Warrington.

Across all eras 41 players have played for Tigers and also played professional rugby league at some time in their careers, with the following ten Tigers being capped at rugby league: **Ervine Mosby** (England 1905), **FS Jackson** (New Zealand 1910), **Ambrose Baker** (Wales 1925-28), **Viv Harrison** (Wales 1951), **Keith Fielding** (Great Britain 1974-77, England 1975), **Paul Ringer** (Wales 1981-82), **Jason Critchley** (England 1992, Wales 1996-2001), **Diccon Edwards** (Wales 1996), **Lote Tuqiri** (Fiji 2000, Australia 2001-10), **Gareth Raynor** (Great Britain 2005-07).

Three have played in Rugby League World Cups: **Fielding** in 1975 and 1977, **Critchley and Tuqiri** in 2000.

Six have played in Rugby League's Challenge Cup final: **Harry Topham** (Oldham 1907, Leeds 1910), **John Jackett** (Dewsbury 1912), **Alf Bates** (Oldham 1922 and 1924), **Ambrose Baker** (Oldham 1924 and 1926), **Arthur Frowen** (Warrington 1928), **Gareth Raynor** (Hull FC 2005). **Alf Bates** and **Ambrose Baker** appeared together in Oldham's 4-21 loss to Wigan at Rochdale on 12 April 1924.

↑ Lote Tuqiri, on the way to the try-line for Brisbane Broncos, during their NRL grand final victory over Sydney Roosters, 27.8.2000.

Lote Tuqiri won the Australian NRL title with Brisbane Broncos in 2000.

Three Super League matches have been played at Welford Road:

28.7.1999	London Broncos 15, Bradford Bulls 19
16.6.2001	London Broncos 0, Bradford Bulls 42
20.6.2004	London Broncos 26, Hull FC 42

SCORING VALUES

Until 1886 the results of matches were decided by a majority of goals and tries, and in some games by a complicated affair known as "minors". (Minors being rather like "near misses" such as touch in goal, dead balls, missed drop goals etc.) Scoring by points was not introduced until 1886/87, a try being worth one point, a conversion two and a dropped goal three.
Since their introduction in 1886/87 the scoring values have evolved as follows:

	Try (T)	*Conv (C)*	*Drop Goal (DG)*	*Pen Goal (PG)*	*Mark (GM)*
1886/87 to 1888/89	1	2	3	Void	3
1889/90 to 1890/91	1	2	3	2	3
1891/92 to 1892/93	2	3	4	3	4
1893/94 to 1904/05	3	2	4	3	4
1905/06 to 1947/48	3	2	4	3	3
1948/49 to 1970/71	3	2	3	3	3
1971/72 to 1976/77	4	2	3	3	3
1977/78 to 1991/92	4	2	3	3	Void
1992/93 to date	5	2	3	3	Void

The penalty goal was not introduced until 1889, initially just as a "free kick" for offside, and even then you could drop kick the ball between the posts to register the points. A player was allowed to call for a "fair catch" or "mark" virtually anywhere on the field. Hence, if you were within range anyone from your team could then take a place kick to attempt to score "a goal from a mark". This scoring method however, ceased to exist when the Free Kick clause was introduced in 1977/78. Another early method of scoring was a Field Goal, which was achieved by fly kicking a rolling or stationary ball from the ground between the posts, this was abolished in 1905.

Milestone scores:

1 point try	**First:** WM Smith v Town & District XX 9.10.1886
	Last: William Porter v Penygraig 31.3.1891
2 point try	**First:** John Edmonds v Wolverton 3.10.1891
	Last: v Cardiff Harlequins 29.4.1893
3 point try	**First:** v Leicestershire 16.9.1893
	Last: John Duggan v New Brighton 1.5.1971
4 point try	**First:** John Duggan v Bedford 4.9.1971
	Last: Tony Underwood v Rugby Lions 25.4.1992
5 point try	**First:** Matt Poole v Sheffield 1.9.1992
2 point conversion	**First:** Arthur McKechnie v Town & District 9.10.1886
3 point conversion	**First:** Leonard Ward v Wolverton 3.10.1891
	Last: Ted Cooke v Cardiff Harlequins 29.4.1893
2 point penalty goal	**First:** Harry Brockbank v Old Edwardians 5.10.1889
	Last: Leonard Ward v Handsworth 14.3.1891
3 point penalty goal	**First:** Ted Cooke v S Northamptonshire 24.9.1892
3 point drop goal	**First:** Jack Parsons v Town & District 9.10.1886
4 point drop goal	**First:** Arthur McKechnie v Leicestershire 10.9.1892
	Last: Mel Channer v Plymouth Albion 29.3.1948
3 point goal from a mark	**First:** Leonard Ward v Bedford GS 1.11.1890
	Last: Norman York v Bristol 11.4. 1936
4 point goal from a mark	**First:** Ted Cooke v Cardiff Harlequins 29.4.1893
	Last: Arthur Jones v Keighley 11.11.1899

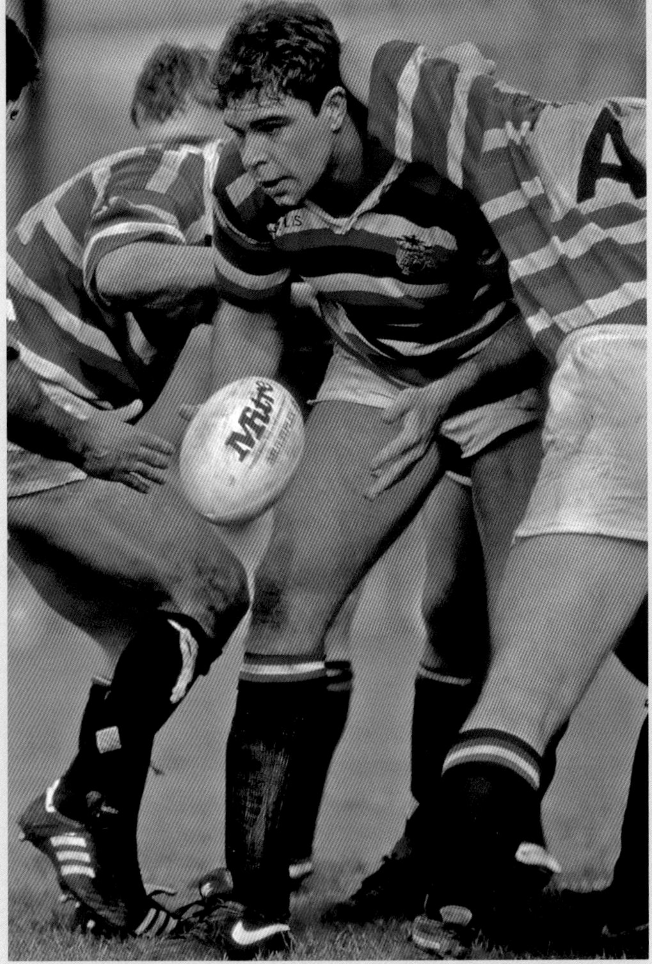

Matt Poole scored the Tigers' first-ever five-point try, when they visited Sheffield on 1.9.1992.

SEASONAL RECORDS

CLUB RECORDS

All records relate to a season of 30 games or more.

MOST:

	All games		*At Home*		*Away*	
Games Played:	46	1923/4	29	1892/3	24	1996/7
	46	1966/7	29	1893/4		
	46	1972/3	29	1968/9		
	46	1996/7				
Wins:	35	1996/7	25	1966/7	16	1979/0
			25	1996/7	16	1996/7
Defeats:	23	1936/7	11	1892/3	16	1970/1
	23	1949/0	11	1949/0		
Draws:	7	1888/9	5	1931/2	4	4 times
Points scored:	1480	1996/7	841	1996/7	639	1996/7
Points conceded:	881	1997/8	453	1997/8	446	1996/7
Tries scored:	192	1919/0	135	1919/0	70	1996/7
Tries conceded:	106	1923/4	58	1968/9	68	1923/4
Conversions scored:	112	1996/7	78	1987/8	47	1996/7
Conversions conceded:	68	1997/8	41	1997/8	32	1969/0
					32	1972/3
Penalty Goals scored:	124	1996/7	69	2000/1	62	1996/7
Penalty Goals conceded:	118	2001/2	42	1995/6	74	2001/2
Drop Goals scored:	23	1979/0	12	1898/9	13	1979/0
Drop Goals conceded:	16	1980/1	9	1955/6	10	1980/1
Goals from a Mark scored:	3	1908/9				
Goals from a Mark conceded:	2	1894/5				

LEAST:

	All games		*At Home*		*Away*	
Wins:	11	1888/9	9	1952/3	1	1888/9
Defeats:	3	1994/5	0	2000/1	3	1893/4
					3	1987/8
					3	1995/6
Draws:	0	16 times				
Points scored:	94	1888/9	82	1888/9	12	1888/9
Points conceded:	95	1894/5	25	1896/7	37	1894/5
Tries scored:	47	1949/0	25	1949/50	7	1888/9
Tries conceded:	20	1894/5	7	1896/7	6	1894/5
			7	1897/8		
Conversions scored:	13	1888/9	9	1945/6	0	1892/3
			9	1952/3		
Conversions conceded:	6	1895/6	1	1895/6	2	1894/5
Penalty Goals scored:	0	1891/2				
Penalty Goals conceded:	0	2 times				
Drop Goals scored:	0	4 times				
Drop Goals conceded:	1	5 times				

Earliest start to a season:	12.8.2000	v Cardiff	Arms Park
Earliest Premiership start:	19.8.2000	v London Wasps	Loftus Road
Latest Finish to a season:	4.6.2000	v Barbarians	Twickenham
Shortest season:	140 days	1882/83	
Longest season:	280 days	2000/01 and 2002/03	

LONGEST HOME RUN

All 19 matches in the 1918/19 season when rugby resumed following the First World War were played at Welford Road, in addition the first nine matches of the following season were also at home, as well as the only two games in 1914/15. That made a run of 30 successive home games between the Tigers trip to Birkenhead Park on 18 April 1914 until they next played an away game, at Swansea on 8 November 1919. The run saw Tigers win 19, draw one, and lose 10 of their encounters.

↑ In 2008/09, Julien Dupuy played 31 games in his only season for the club.

SUCCESSIVE AWAY GAMES

Excluding overseas tours Leicester have twice played sequences of seven successive away matches. The first was in 1948 between the home game against Harlequins on 6 March until the last game of the season at home to Blackheath on 17 April, Tigers secured four wins and three losses from their trips. Leicester finished the 1964/65 season with six successive away games with an even won three, lost three record, and then began the 1965/66 campaign with defeat at Bedford.

BEST & WORST STARTS

The Tigers began the 1983/84 season in the best possible way, reeling off 16 successive victories until finally being beaten at home to Wasps on 19 November.
Conversely the worst start was for their second ever season in 1881/82, when they had to wait until their sixth game against Coventry to record their first victory, following a run of four losses and a draw.

MOST & LEAST PLAYERS IN A SEASON

84 players were used in the 46 games of the 1923/24 season, and this was matched in 1935/36 when only 38 games were played. 79 players were used in the 44-game season of 1934/35.
Only 27 players were used in the 1883/84 season of 21 games, 29 were used in the 17 game 1886/87 season, and 34 players were used in both the 1950/51 and 1951/52 seasons with 38 and 35 games respectively.

MOST APPEARANCES IN A SEASON

45 by **Teddy Haselmere** in 1922/23, followed by **Alf Butlin** and **William Lincoln** in 1898/99, **John Allen** in 1970/71 and **Bob Barker** in 1972/73 all with 44.

MOST TRIES IN DEBUT SEASON

24	Bobby Lewis	1894/95
23	David Senior	1959/60
15	F Fox	1894/95
15	Clive Woodward	1979/80

MOST POINTS IN DEBUT SEASON

202	Toby Flood	2008/09
199	Dusty Hare	1976/77
195	Joel Stransky	1996/97
191	Tim Stimpson	1998/99
187	Owen Williams	2013/14

ONE SEASON WONDERS

Five players have played only one season for the club, but during their brief Tigers careers managed to cram in over 30 appearances for the first-team:

Name	*Season*	*Games*
Arthur Rendle	1893/94	32
Bobby Lewis	1894/95	35
Frederick Wright	1922/23	38
GN Harris	1933/34	31
Julien Dupuy	2008/09	24+7

SECRETARIES

The role of honorary secretary in amateur rugby union was arguably the key post in any club. Leicester have been blessed with some incredible administrators in the position until the role became redundant with the advent of professionalism. The Tigers had just six honorary secretaries in a 100-year period between 1895-1995.

Three of the first four honorary secretaries combined the role with playing for the club, whilst uniquely the other – **Sid Wykes** – went on to become a player after he had been honorary secretary.

1880-1881	J (Jack) Parsons
1881-1889	HW (Hedley) Salmon
1889-1890	SR (Sid) Wykes
1890-1893	K (Kenneth) McAlpin
1893	JH (John) Hancock
1894	HW (Hedley) Salmon
1894-1895	TW (Tom) Pettifor
1895-1928*	TH (Tom) Crumbie
1928-1957	JE (Eric) Thorneloe
1957-1962	RJ (Bobby) Barr
1962-1966	RE (Ronnie) Gerrard
1966-1982	JD (Jerry) Day
1982-1995	JA (John) Allen
1995-1997	JT (Tudor) Thomas

* died in office

GENERAL SECRETARY

Leicester appointed a paid general secretary for a 13-year spell between 1954-1967 to run alongside the honorary role, but it was disbanded following 'Ranji' Walker's resignation after leaving the area.

1954-1965	Major AD (Albert) Chilton
1966-1967	Air Commodore SG (Ranji) Walker

COMPANY SECRETARY

Since the club became a plc on 1997 there have been four company secretaries.

1997-1998	PMF (Philip) Smith
1998-1999	JA (John) Jones
1999	RJ (Bob) Harrison
1999-	M (Mary) Ford

SEMI-FINALS

All the semi-finals in major competitions that Tigers have ever played, and their outcomes:

Date	*Tournament*	*Venue*	*Opponents*	*Result*
12.3.1887	Midland Counties Cup	Rugby Cricket Club	Rugby	L 0-3 (aet)
24.3.1888	Midland Counties Cup	Victoria Park	Burton	D 0-0
16.3.1889	Midland Counties Cup	Belgrave C&C Ground	Stratford	W 4-3
21.3.1891	Midland Counties Cup	Belgrave C&C Ground	Old Edwardians	W 7-4 (aet)
24.3.1894	Midland Counties Cup	Rugby Cricket Club	Rugby	W 6-5
23.3.1895	Midland Counties Cup	The Reddings	Moseley	L 0-11
27.3.1897	Midland Counties Cup	Welford Road	Old Edwardians	L 0-3
19.3.1898	Midland Counties Cup	The Butts	Coventry	W 12-5
25.3.1899	Midland Counties Cup	Welford Road	Moseley	D 0-0
w29.3.1899	Midland Counties Cup	The Reddings	Moseley	W 8-3 (r)
24.3.1900	Midland Counties Cup	Welford Road	Rugby	W 19-0
23.3.1901	Midland Counties Cup	Welford Road	Nuneaton	W 30-9
22.3.1902	Midland Counties Cup	Welford Road	Burton	W 18-3
28.3.1903	Midland Counties Cup	Welford Road	Nuneaton	W 49-11
26.3.1904	Midland Counties Cup	Welford Road	Nuneaton	W 25-0
25.3.1905	Midland Counties Cup	Welford Road	Rugby	W 23-0
27.3.1909	Midland Counties Cup	Welford Road	Stratford	W 17-8
26.3.1910	Midland Counties Cup	Burton-on-Trent	Burton	W 34-8
23.3.1912	Midland Counties Cup	Welford Road	Newbold	W 65-0
29.3.1913	Midland Counties Cup	London Road	Coventry	W 9-0
4.4.1914	Midland Counties Cup	Welford Road	Coventry	L 0-8
1.4.1978	John Player Cup	Welford Road	Coventry	W 25-16
7.4.1979	John Player Cup	Sudbury	Wasps	W 43-7
29.3.1980	John Player Cup	Twickenham	Harlequins	W 16-9
4.4.1981	John Player Cup	Athletic Ground	London Scottish	W 18-12 (aet)
3.4.1982	John Player Cup	The Reddings	Moseley	L 4-12
26.3.1983	John Player Cup	Athletic Ground	London Scottish	W 30-9
5.4.1986	JPS Cup	Welford Road	Bath	L 6-10
28.3.1987	JPS Cup	Sudbury	Wasps	L 6-13
25.3.1989	Pilkington Cup	Stoop	Harlequins	W 16-7
4.4.1992	Pilkington Cup	Stoop Memorial Ground	Harlequins	L 9-15
10.4.1993	Pilkington Cup	Welford Road	Northampton	W 28-6
2.4.1994	Pilkington Cup	Edgehall Road	Orrell	W 31-18
1.4.1995	Pilkington Cup	Welford Road	Wasps	L 22-25
23.3.1996	Pilkington Cup	The Avenue	London Irish	W 46-21
4.1.1997	Heineken Cup	Welford Road	Toulouse	W 37-11
29.3.1997	Pilkington Cup	Kingsholm	Gloucester	W 26-13
21.3.1998	C&G Cup	Welford Road	Gloucester	L 15-53
6.1.2001	Tetley's Bitter Cup	Stoop Memorial Ground	Harlequins	L 18-22
21.4.2001	Heineken Cup	Vicarage Road*	Gloucester	W 19-15
5.5.2001	Zurich Championship	Welford Road	Northampton	W 17-13
s28.4.2002	Heineken Cup	City Ground, Notts*	Llanelli	W 13-12
1.3.2003	Powergen Cup	Franklin's Gardens*	Gloucester	L 11-16
s24.4.2005	Heineken Cup	Walkers Stadium	Toulouse	L 19-27
4.3.2006	Powergen Cup	Millennium Stadium*	London Wasps	L 17-22
s14.5.2006	Guinness Premiership	Welford Road	London Irish	W 40-8
24.3.2007	EDF Energy Cup	Millennium Stadium*	Sale Sharks	W 29-19
21.4.2007	Heineken Cup	Walkers Stadium	Llanelli Scarlets	W 33-17
5.5.2007	Guinness Premiership	Welford Road	Bristol	W 26-14
22.3.2008	EDF Energy Cup	Millennium Stadium*	London Wasps	W 34-24
s18.5.2008	Guinness Premiership	Kingsholm	Gloucester	W 26-25
s3.5.2009	Heineken Cup	Millennium Stadium*	Cardiff Blues	D 26-26 (aet)+
9.5.2009	Guinness Premiership	Walkers Stadium	Bath	W 24-10
s16.5.2010	Guinness Premiership	Welford Road	Bath	W 15-6
14.5.2011	Aviva Premiership	Welford Road	Northampton	W 11-3
f9.3.2012	LV= Cup	The Rec	Bath	W 17-16
12.5.2012	Aviva Premiership	Welford Road	Saracens	W 24-15
11.5.2013	Aviva Premiership	Welford Road	Harlequins	W 33-16
f16.5.2014	Aviva Premiership	Franklin's Gardens	Northampton	L 20-21

+ Tigers progressed to final 7-6 on penalties

** Games played at neutral venues*

All games played on Saturdays except, w=Wednesday, f=Friday and s=Sunday.

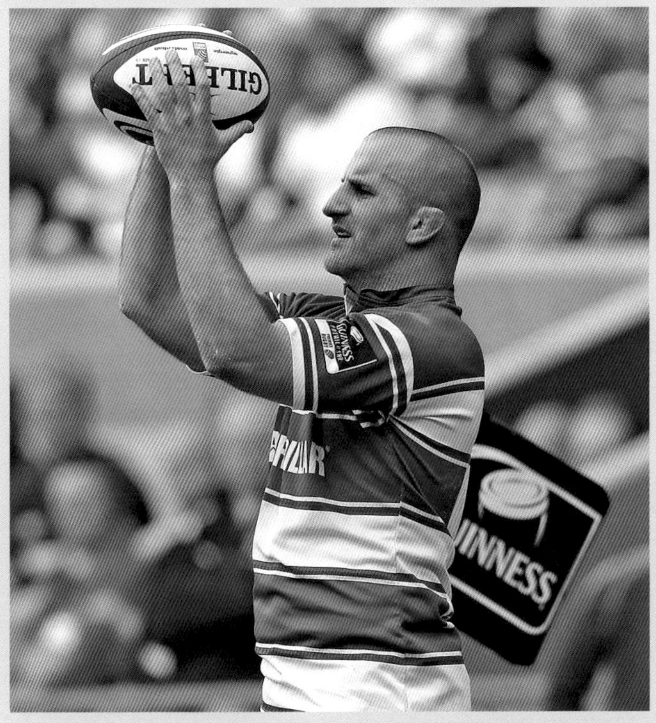

George Chuter was on the winning side in a record eleven major semi-final encounters for Tigers.

MOST SEMI-FINAL APPEARANCES

Semis	*Name*	*W*	*D*	*L*
16	Geordan Murphy	10	1	5
15	Ben Kay	10	1	4
14	Graham Rowntree	9	0	5
14	George Chuter	11	1	2
12	Darren Garforth	8	0	4
12	Sid Penny	10	1	1
12	Martin Johnson	8	0	4
11	Neil Back	7	0	4
11	Martin Corry	8	0	3
11	Andy Goode	8	0	3
11	Harry Ellis	8	1	2
11	Lewis Moody	7	1	3
11	Marcos Ayerza	9	1	1

SENT OFF

Players dismissed during a Tigers game:

TIGERS (27)

Player	*Opponents*	*Date*	*Referee*	*Result*
Monty Whitehead	v Keighley	11.11.1899	Mr Yiend	W 12-9
Harry Lawrie	at Harlequins	9.3.1912	HA Taylor	L 6-18
Pedlar Wood	at Birkenhead Park	18.4.1914	Bim Baxter	L 0-23
Charlie Cross	at Swansea	14.1.1922	J Thomas	W 13-9
Gordon Almey	at Llanelli	21.11.1959	F Croster	W 8-3
Bob Rowell(1)	at Llanelli	18.4.1970	DM Davies	L 11-43
John Dawson	v Harlequins	6.3.1971	M Walker	W 11-6
Paul Ringer	at Northampton	20.10.1973	D Howard	L 7-26
Nick Joyce	at Northampton	22.2.1975	Roger Quittenton	L 6-20
Robin Cowling	at Fylde	19.4.1975	Alan Welsby	W 21-19
Bob Rowell(2)	at Fylde	19.4.1975		
Steve Redfern	v London Welsh	29.1.1977	K Lockerbie	W 19-10
Nick Jackson	v Bath	1.1.1983	Ron Mayo	W 21-9
Martin Corry (1)	v Northampton	7.3.1998	Ed Morrison	D 15-15
Will Greenwood*	at Newcastle	4.5.1998	Ed Morrison	L 10-27
Neil Fletcher*	v Sale Sharks	25.9.1999	Stewart Piercy	W 18-3
Adam Balding	at Bristol	5.5.2002	Steve Lander	L 21-38
James Hamilton	at Leeds Tykes	19.10.2003	Dave Pearson	L 18-39

Martin Corry (2)	at Saracens	17.4.2005	Chris White	L 17-19
Julian White (1)	v Newcastle	14.10.2005	Tony Spreadbury	D 16-16
Ben Herring	at Gloucester	9.2.2008	Tony Spreadbury	W 20-13
Julian White (2)	v Sale Sharks	4.4.2009	Wayne Barnes	W 37-31
Rob Hawkins	at Bath	4.2.2011	James Jones	L 12-26
Marcos Ayerza	at Harlequins	2.4.2011	Wayne Barnes	W 17-13
Alesana Tuilagi	v Northampton	3.12.2011	Wayne Barnes	W 30-25
Boris Stankovich	v London Irish	18.11.2012	Ian Davies	W 22-15
Brett Deacon	v Bath	1.12.2012	Tim Wigglesworth	W 17-12

OPPONENTS (41)

Player	*Opponents*	*Date*	*Referee*	*Result*
WD Muriel	at Rugby	22.12.1888	Edgar Holmes	L 1-4
J Jacques	v Keighley	11.11.1899	Mr Yiend	W 12-9
Dick Hellings	v Llwynypia	26.12.1901	Gil Evans	W 8-0
AC Bell	v Newport	14.2.1914	E Browning	W 13-8
R Allison	v Cardiff	29.11.1919	AJ Trollope	L 0-3
Llewellyn Jones	v Swansea	5.11.1921	J Welshman	L 3-5
SC Craven	v Cardiff	10.11.1928	E Browning	W 8-5
D McArthur	v Cardiff	10.11.1928		
Ron Richards	v Swansea	5.1.1935	RI Scorer	L 3-5
EJF Stephens	v Gloucester	11.1.1969	M Walker	W 12-8
Bruce Wilson	v Harlequins	6.3.1971	M Walker	W 11-6
B Holt	at Coventry	5.10.1974	Norman Sanson	L 3-13
Chris Howcroft	v London Welsh	29.1.1977	K Lockerbie	W 19-10
Alex Keay	at Bedford	1.9.1979	Laurie Prideaux	W 34-12
Micky Skinner	v Blackheath	13.12.1980	Fred Howard	W 43-9
Jim Sydall	at Waterloo	4.12.1982	David Matthews	W 10-9
John Goodwin	at Moseley	23.4.1983	Fred Howard	W 29-10
Nigel Fox	at Northampton	15.10.1983	Ron Mayo	W 25-0
Jock Ross	at London Welsh	31.12.1983	Ron Mayo	W 16-14
Nigel Bezani	v Pontypridd	2.9.1989	Tony Sparks	W 41-18
Steve Binnington	v Bedford	23.9.1989	Ken McCartney	W 60-3
Paul Ashmead	v Gloucester	26.9.1992	David Matthews	W 22-21
Paul Guttridge	at Bristol	13.3.1993	Colin High	L 10-15
Fabio Gomez	v Milan	4.9.1993	Fred Howard	W 53-7
Charles Cusani	at Orrell (sf)	2.4.1994	Tony Spreadbury	W 31-18
Martin Scott	v Orrell	14.1.1995	Tony Spreadbury	W 29-19
Pierre Triep-Capdevielle	v Pau	7.10.2000	Rob Dickson	W 46-18
John Mallett	v Bath	22.9.2001	Brian Campsall	W 48-9
Julian White(1)	at Bristol	5.5.2002	Steve Lander	L 21-38
Julian White(2)	at Bristol	29.9.2002	Chris White	L 20-25
Martyn Wood	v Bath	29.11.2003	Roy Maybank	L 12-13
Andy Perry	v Newcastle	14.10.2005	Tony Spreadbury	D 16-16
Gary Powell	at Cardiff Blues	29.10.2006	Alan Lewis	W 21-17
Joe Marler	at Harlequins	2.4.2011	Wayne Barnes	W 17-13
Tom Wood	v Northampton	3.12.2011	Wayne Barnes	W 30-25
Andy Goode	v Worcester	30.3.2012	Wayne Barnes	W 43-13
Francois Louw	v Bath	1.12.2012	Tim Wigglesworth	W 17-12
Matt Banahan	v Bath	1.12.2012		
Dylan Hartley	v Northampton	25.5.2013	Wayne Barnes	W 37-17
Justin Melck*	v Saracens	10.5.2014	Greg Garner	W 31-27
Salesi Ma'afu	at Northampton	16.5.2014	JP Doyle	L 20-21

* Later recinded

Actual red cards have only been used since the start of the 1994/95 season, prior to this just a point by the referee in the direction of the dressing room was all that was required. The first red card ever handed out in the top flight was to Orrell's **Martin Scott** in the 63rd minute against Leicester at Welford Road on 14 January 1995, for putting his knees into the back of an opposing player. The first given to a Tigers player was to **Martin Corry** for punching in the 24th minute at home to Northampton on 7 March 1998.

No replacement has picked up a red card but the fastest from the start of a game was **Jim Hamilton's** in the 16th minute of Tigers trip to Leeds on 19 October 2003. **Julian White**, then a Bristol player, was sent off after just three minutes against Leicester on 29 September 2002.

SEQUENCES

	BEST WINNING RUN	*WORST LOSING RUN*
At Home	**42** – (22.1.2000 to 12.5.2002)	**6** – (28.1.1937 to 6.3.1937)
Away	**9** – (3.9.1983 to 26.11.1983)	**13** – (27.10.1926 to 16.4.1927)
	9 – (7.9.1985 to 12.11.1985)	**13** – (3.10.1970 to 10.4.1971)
Overall	**22** – (17.11.1995 to 17.4.1996)	**9** – (27.9.1947 to 15.11.1947)

	LONGEST UNBEATEN RUN	*LONGEST WINLESS RUN*
At Home	**42** – (22.1.2000 to 12.5.2002)	**7** – (24.12.1892 to 11.2.1893)
Away	**9** – (3.9.1983 to 26.11.1983)	**15** – (14.1.1928 to 8.12.1928)
	9 – (7.9.1985 to 12.11.1985)	
Overall	**22** – (17.11.1995 to 17.4.1996)	**13** – (6.10.1888 to 22.12.1888)

Leicester went 39 Midland Counties Cup ties in a row without defeat in a 15-year period between March 1897 and March 1912, a run which included 32 successive wins.

The Tigers won 18 consecutive matches in the John Player Cup between January 1979 and March 1982.

Leicester held the record for the most successive European Cup wins with 11 between 2000-02 until that mark was surpassed by Munster in 2007.

The Tigers easily hold the record for the most wins in succession in the history of the Premiership – securing 17 consecutive victories between December 1999 and September 2000, five wins clear of the next best run.

↑ Duncan Roke, Oscar Wingham and Niall Malone collect the runners-up prize at the Middlesex Sevens at Twickenham, 16.5.1998.

SEVENS RUGBY

MIDDLESEX SEVENS

Leicester won the Middlesex sevens and took the Russell Cargill Trophy for the only time at Twickenham on 13 May 1995, beating South African invitational side Ithuba 38-19 in the final (captain John Liley contributing 13 points with a try and four conversions), after overcoming West Sussex Institute 40-12, Selkirk 31-7, then Blackheath 21-5 in the semi-final.

The winning team was: **John Liley (capt), Jamie Hamilton, Chris Johnson, Andy McAdam, Niall Malone, Tom Reynolds, Nigel Richardson, Richie Robinson, Chris Tarbuck, Oscar Wingham.**

It was only the seventh time Tigers had entered the competition, and the first time they had ever got past the quarter- final. In 2006 and 2007 only the first round was played in four pools of three.

Date	*Furthest Reached*	*Opponent*	*Result*
28.4.1951	6th round	Harlequins II	Lost 5-8
25.4.1959	Quarter-final	Wasps	Lost 3-6
30.4.1960	Quarter-final	St Luke's	Lost 10-13 (aet)

30.4.1977	Quarter-final	Richmond	Lost 0-34
9.5.1981	Quarter-final	Saracens	Lost 10-16
9.5.1992	6th round	London Scottish	Lost 10-34
13.5.1995	**Final**	**Ithuba**	**Won 38-19**
11.5.1996	Semi-final	Wigan Warriors RL	Lost 12-35
17.5.1997	Plate semi-final	Wasps	Lost 21-24
16.5.1998	Final	Barbarians	Lost 28-38
29.5.1999	Quarter-final	San Isidro	Lost 12-22
12.8.2000	Quarter-final	Newcastle Falcons	Lost 0-35
18.8.2001	Quarter-final	Newcastle Falcons	Lost 7-31
17.8.2002	1st round	London Wasps	Lost 7-24
16.8.2003	1st round	London Welsh	Lost 12-26
14.8.2004	Quarter-final	British Army	Lost 19-36
13.8.2005	Semi-final	London Wasps	Lost 12-22
12.8.2006	Final	London Wasps	Lost 10-29
18.8.2007	Quarter-final	Newcastle Falcons	Lost 17-22
16.8.2008	Quarter-final	British Army	Lost 7-31
15.8.2009	Plate quarter-final	Sale Sharks	Lost 19-24 (golden point)
14.8.2010	Plate quarter-final	HFW Wailers	Lost 7-43

NATIONAL SEVENS

The National Sevens ran for only four years, the first three as a straight knockout between 16 invited English teams, sponsored initially by Wang then by Courage and in the final two years by Worthington. In 1992 the 12-team event was contested in four pools of three, followed by semi-finals and final.

Date	*Furthest Reached*	*Opponent*	*Result*
23.4.1989	1st Round	Blackheath	Lost 12-28 (at Richmond)
29.4.1990	Quarter-final	Orrell	Lost 10-12 (at Richmond)
28.4.1991	Final	Bath	Lost 10-24 (at Bath)
26.4.1992	Final	London Scottish	Lost 0-38 (at Bath)

DUBAI SEVENS

The prestigious Dubai Sevens tournament began in 1970 and has now been part of the IRB World Sevens Series since that began in 1999. Leicester competed just once – in 1995 – when the tournament was still played on sand at the Dubai Exiles rugby club. Led by **John Liley** they lost two pool games to Hawke's Bay from New Zealand and the Korean national team, and beat American invitation side Atlantis to qualify for the Plate competition. They disposed of Crawshay's in the quarter-final before losing out to Canada's University of British Colombia Old Boys in the last four.

Date	*Furthest Reached*	*Opponent*	*Result*
23/24.11.1995	Plate semi-final	UBC OB	Lost 12-15

PREMIERSHIP RUGBY SEVENS

Premiership Rugby began their own sevens tournament after relinquishing their interest in the Middlesex Sevens in 2010. The twelve Premiership sides are split into three regional pools of four teams each with a Premiership ground hosting each pool with the top two teams progressing to a grand final tournament. Welford Road hosted a pool in 2010 but unfortunately Tigers failed to win a single game for the first three years. In 2013 they fared much better beating Sale and hosts Northampton in the qualifying pool, and then accounting for Worcester and Harlequins at The Rec before losing the final itself to Gloucester.

Date	*Stage*	*Pos*	*Venue*	*Opponent*	*Result*
23.7.2010	Pools	3rd	Welford Road		
29.7.2011	Pools	4th	Edgeley Park		
20.7.2012	Pools	4th	Edgeley Park		
2.8.2013	Pools	2nd	Franklin's Gardens		
9.8.2013	Finals	Final	Bath Rec	Gloucester Rugby	Lost 17-24

Tigers' victorious sevens team from the Madrid Sevens in 1996, with the players posing in the jerseys of the France national team, whom they beat 26-14 in the final.
Back: Robinson, Freshwater, Beatham, Becconsall, Overend, Wolstenholme (coach).
Front: Key (coach), Hamilton, Liley (captain), Lloyd, Wyer-Roberts, O.Wingham.

MADRID SEVENS

Tigers entered the Madrid Sevens at the Campo Universitaria on five occasions in the 1990s, winning the title itself three times, beating Bath, the French national seven and Portuguese outfit Cascais in the three finals. Going for a fourth successive title in 1998 they were beaten in the final by local Madrid side Real Canoe. **John Liley** led the side in 1994 and 1996 with **Oscar Wingham** taking over the reins in 1997 and 1998.

Date	*Furthest Reached*	*Opponent*	*Result*
29.5.1993	Quarter-final	Richmond	Lost 7-28
28.5.1994	**Final**	**Bath**	**Won 42-7**
27.5.1996	**Final**	**France VII**	**Won 26-14**
30.5.1997	**Final**	**Cascais**	**Won 33-19**
6.6.1998	Final	Real Canoe	Lost 21-27

TIGERS INTERNATIONAL SEVENS PLAYERS

Showing year of debut plus number of tournaments played in whilst with the Tigers.

ENGLAND (21)

1995	Steve Hackney
1996	Neil Back (2)
1997	Austin Healey
1998	Rory Underwood
1999	Tim Stimpson
2000	Paul Gustard (2)
2001	Steve Booth, Jamie Hamilton, Mark Meenan(2), Toby Bainbridge-Kay
2002	Adam Balding, Harry Ellis, Leon Lloyd
2003	Will Skinner(2), Dan Hipkiss(11)
2004	Neil Baxter(3)
2005	Tom Varndell(7)
2006	Tom Croft(2)
2008	Ayoola Erinle, Ben Youngs(2), Tom Youngs(4)

IRELAND (2)

1997	Eric Miller(2), Niall Malone

BARBARIANS AT HONG KONG SEVENS (6)

1981	Les Cusworth, Peter Wheeler, Clive Woodward
1990	Barry Evans, Tony Underwood
1991	Neil Back

IRISH WOLFHOUNDS AT HONG KONG SEVENS (3)

1984 Les Cusworth
1985 Barry Evans
1989 Tony Underwood

FIJI (1)

2013 Vereniki Goneva

SHIRTS

Most matches started wearing particular shirts

In Letters

A Stuart Redfern (322)
B Peter Wheeler (347)
C Steve Redfern (237)
D Nick Joyce (218)
E Matt Poole (192)
F John Wells (346)
G Garry Adey (336)
H Ian Smith (298)
I John Allen (457)
J Les Cusworth (364)
K Bob Barker (225)
L Brian Hall (186)
M Paul Dodge (290)
N John Duggan (290)
O Dusty Hare (392)

In Numbers

1 Marcos Ayerza (161)
2 George Chuter (204)
3 Julian White (119)
4 Martin Johnson (163)
5 Ben Kay (231)
6 Tom Croft (91)
7 Neil Back (143)
8 Martin Corry (156)
9 Harry Ellis (127)
10 Andy Goode (160)
11 Alesana Tuilagi (103)
12 Anthony Allen (98)
13 Ollie Smith (110)
14 Geordan Murphy (79)
15 Geordan Murphy (188)

Most successive appearances in particular shirts

In Letters

A Denis Bolesworth (41)
B Peter Edwards (70)
C Mike Mortimer (34)
D Nick Joyce (23)
E John Thompson (36)
F Graham Willars (38)
G Tom Bleasdale (31)
H David Matthews (28)
I John Allen (57)
J Bleddyn Jones (43)
K Bob Barker (39)
L Paul Dodge (24)
M Brian Hall (18)
N David Bird (38)
O Graham Pulfrey (63)

In Numbers

1 Graham Rowntree (19)
2 Dorian West (14)
3 Darren Garforth (17)
4 Martin Johnson (23)
5 Ben Kay (15)
6 Lewis Moody (10)
7 Julian Salvi (14)
8 Martin Corry (12)
9 Ben Youngs (15)
10 Joel Stransky & Toby Flood (11)
11 Dave Lougheed (twice) & Alesana Tuilagi (12)
12 Pat Howard (31)
13 Craig Joiner & Manu Tuilagi (11)
14 Scott Hamilton (17)
15 Tim Stimpson & Scott Hamilton (16)

Neil Back scored an incredible 73 tries wearing shirt number 7, whilst the only other player to rack up 50 tries in one shirt number was **Alesana Tuilagi** with 51 tries in shirt 11.

SILVERWARE

Across all eras Tigers have won 26% of all the major tournaments they have ever entered – equating to 32 pieces of major silverware from 121 tournaments.

Leicester won the Midland Counties Cup (the only piece of silverware on offer at the time) 12 times out of 30 attempts between 1881-1914.

Tigers have taken the Domestic Cup, now known as the LV= Cup, seven times in 43 attempts from 1972, and have won 10 league titles from the 27 seasons of league rugby. Tigers have also taken two Heineken Cups in 17 attempts, and one Zurich Championship from the two times they contested it.

If you look at the professional era alone (1996/97 onwards in England) Tigers have still won 14 cups and trophies for a 25% success rate of all the tournaments they have entered: 8 Premierships, 2 Heineken Cups, 1 Championship and 3 cup titles.

SMOKE ON THE WATER

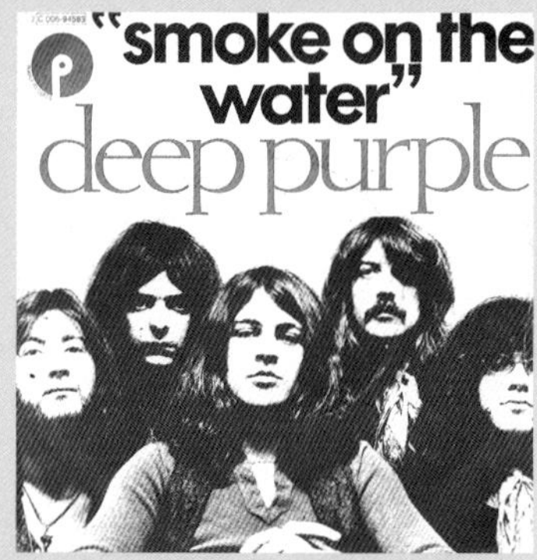

During the 2000/01 season the players thought that the Tigers needed a tune to run out to after listening to opponent's offerings, especially Richard Wagner's "Ride of the Valkyries" for Wasps at Loftus Road.

"Smoke on the Water" was first introduced by **Ian Walker** (aka Doctor Soul) who was at the time in charge of the music on a matchday. He just thought that it was a "good tune" after trying out **Robbie Williams'** "Let Me Entertain You" a few times and deciding against it.

There is a Leicester connection with Deep Purple as well as keyboardist **Jon Lord** was born in Leicester on 9 June 1941, went to Wyggeston School and lived in Humberstone until he moved to London in his late teens!

SPONSORSHIP

The Tigers' first sponsored match was against Australia on 25 November 1981, when Harrogate based Modern Maintenance Products (MMP) supported the club.
The first shirt sponsors were Ansells in 1988, since then six brand names have appeared on the front of players' shirts:

1988/89	Ansells
1994/95	Tetley Bitter
1995/96	Goldstar
1997/98	Next
1999/2000	Vauxhall
2002/03	Bradstone
2008/09	Caterpillar

SUCCESSIVE DAYS

The first time that Tigers played on successive days was on Easter Monday and Tuesday 1890 when they visited Cardiff and Newport, losing both games 0-2 and 1-9.

The first time they played matches on three successive days was at Welford Road at Christmas in 1895: drawing 0-0 with Salford on Boxing Day, beating Leicestershire 40-3 the following day, and losing 0-6 to Harlequins on the 28th.

Uniquely, in 1934 Leicester played on four successive days at Welford Road, staring on Boxing Day with an 8-12 loss to Birkenhead Park and following with a 5-6 loss to Barbarians, a 3-0 victory over Manchester and a 27-0 win against Gloucester. **Ralph Buckingham, John McLean** and **George Vallance** played in all four games.

The most recent time Tigers played matches on successive days was on Sunday and Monday, 25 and 26 August 1996 (August Bank Holiday) when the opening two games of the season were in a four-team tournament for the International Challenge Cup at Welford Road involving Agen, Boroughmuir and Cardiff, with semi-finals on one day and the finals the following day.

TEAM FORMATIONS

15 players a-side was first standardised for rugby union games in 1875. By 1880, two full-backs, two three-quarters, two half-backs, and nine forwards was the usual formation, and the initial one which Leicester adopted. From 1881/82 one of the full-backs moved into the three-quarter line and this formation remained for two seasons, when following the lead of Cardiff, Leicester adopted a fourth three-quarter. This configuration was first used against South Warwickshire Rovers in December 1883, and became the norm by the end of the 1889/90 season.

Up until the turn of the century the half-backs had a dual role; sharing the scrum-half and outside or fly-half duties, and were sometimes known as left or right halves.

In the late 1890s the New Zealanders introduced another back formation which they still use today, comprising of three three-quarters with an extra man permanently stationed between the centre three-quarter and the fly-half. This extra man became known as the five-eighth, or later the second five-eighth (with the fly-half being labelled as the first five-eighth). Leicester experimented with this formation for the first six games of the 1906/07 season, twelve months after testing out a variation of this theme by having just one five-eighth replace the fly-half, this line-up also included a wing-forward or "rover".

Initially Leicester employed nine forwards, and on three occasions ten, but more usually it was eight, a combination they have used since 1893/94. However, between December 1919 and April 1927 only seven forwards were used, when the 2-3-2 diamond scrum was adopted. The extra man was first utilised as an additional centre three-quarter, and from 1924/25 as one of a pair of five-eighths. From 1927/28 team line-ups reverted back to eight forwards and have remained so ever since.

In 1922 the scrummaging laws were changed to outlaw the "rover" or wing forward, and prescribe that front rows had to contain no more than three players, subsequently this became the forerunner of the modern 3-4-1 scrum pattern (always favoured in South Africa). The front-row forward evolved into the hooker or prop; the back or side-row forwards ultimately became flankers; number 8's and second-row men became, much more precisely, lock-forwards.

Specialisation has not always existed therefore it is only since the last war that the prop/hooker/prop/lock/lock/flanker/number-eight/flanker formation so familiar today became popular. Before then scrummages were carried out on a "first-up, first-down" free-for-all basis.

TEAM OF THE CENTURY

The following Team of the Century was unveiled at a Dinner at the Grand Hotel on 1 November 1999 to celebrate the turn of the millennium. A selection panel comprising **Jerry Day, Bleddyn Jones, Bob Rowell, Brian Small** and **Tudor Thomas** came up with the following line-up:

Full-back	Ken Scotland	1961-62
Right wing	Alastair Smallwood	1920-25
Right centre	Clive Woodward	1979-85
Left centre	Paul Dodge	1975-93
Left wing	Rory Underwood	1983-97
Fly-half	Les Cusworth	1978-90
Scrum-half	Bernard Gadney	1929-39
Loosehead prop	Bob Stirling	1948-53
Hooker	Peter Wheeler	1969-85
Tighthead prop	Darren Garforth	* 1991-
Lock and captain	Martin Johnson	* 1989-
Lock	George Beamish	1924-33
Blind-side flanker	Doug Prentice	1923-31
Open-side flanker	Neil Back	* 1990-
No. 8	Dean Richards	1982-97
Coach	Chalkie White	

** still playing in 1999*

Martin Johnson was selected as the captain of the Tigers' Team of the Century on 1.11.1999.

TEST MATCH REPRESENTATION

MOST PLAYERS CAPPED IN ONE TEST MATCH

On 28 August 1999 an incredible ten Tigers were all capped during the same test match, when Canada visited Twickenham for a World Cup warm-up match. **Will Greenwood, Austin Healey, Graham Rowntree, Martin Johnson** (captain) and **Neil Back** started for England and **Winston Stanley** was in the Canada line-up. Later in the game **Martin Corry, Richard Cockerill, Darren Garforth** and **Tim Stimpson** all made appearances from the bench.

MOST PLAYERS TO START A TEST MATCH

The most Tigers players to be named in a starting England line-up is seven, which has occurred on three occasions. The first two instances were in the World Cup qualifying matches against Netherlands and Italy at Huddersfield on 14 and 22 November 1998, when **Austin Healey, Will Greenwood, Richard Cockerill, Darren Garforth, Martin Johnson** (captain), **Neil Back** and **Martin Corry** started both games. Then, against France in Marseille during a World Cup warm-up match on 30 August 2003, the England XV contained **Ollie Smith, Austin Healey, Graham Rowntree, Dorian West (captain), Julian White, Martin Corry** and **Lewis Moody**.

TOURING TEAMS

The Tigers have played national teams both on tour themselves and when touring teams have visited the UK, it is a rare privilege accorded to club side.

Date	*Opponent*	*Result*
30.9.1905	v New Zealand	L 0-28
4.10.1924	v New Zealand	L 0-27
8.9.1956	v Romania	D 6-6
11.9.1973	v Fiji	W 22-17
22.10.1980	v Romania	L 7-39
25.11.1981	v Australia	L 15-18
31.7.1982	v Zimbabwe (in Bulawayo)	W 22-18
7.8.1982	v Zimbabwe (in Harare)	D 15-15
14.9.1983	v Zimbabwe	W 29-12
27.4.1984	v Arabian Gulf XV	W 54-3
20.8.1989	v USA (in Colorado Springs)	L 12-24
4.9.1990	v Romania	W 15-12
5.9.1992	v England XV	L 11-18
4.12.1996	v Samoa	Cancelled
3.12.1998	v Fiji	L 16-22
11.2.2007	v Argentina	L 21-41
6.11.2009	v South Africa	W 22-17
9.11.2010	v Australia	L 15-26

In sevens rugby Tigers have also played Korea (L 5-14) at the 1995 Dubai Sevens, and Morocco (W 35-21) and France (W 26-14) at the 1996 Madrid Sevens.

TOURS

See "Easter" for details of Easter tours.

The first tour undertaken during a season which was not over a public holiday came in 1896 when the club visited Swansea, Llanelly and Mountain Ash on 24, 26 and 27 October, losing all three games. They then undertook a November two-game tour of Wales for the next few seasons. This was replaced in 1903 with a September three-game trip to the South West playing Devonport Albion, Plymouth and Exeter.

In 1923 there came a ground breaking three-match tour to "Paris and South of England". The team departed the Great Central station in Leicester on Sunday, 11 February and met Racing Club de France on the Tuesday (lost 9-19) for a first ever game on the Continent, before returning to England to face the United Services at Portsmouth (drew 3-3) on the Thursday then rounding off the trip with an encounter with Plymouth Albion in Devon on the Saturday (lost 5-15).

Thereafter, the only non-Easter tours were carried out in the off-season and all involved international travel:

Year	*Location*	*Dates*	*P*	*W*	*D*	*L*
1980	Australia & Fiji	6-23 August	6	5	-	1
1982	Zimbabwe	24 July-7 August	5	3	1	1
1984	Bahrain & Dubai	27-29 April	2	2	-	-
1985	South & East France	10-12 May	2	2	-	-
1987	Australia, NZ & Singapore	2-18 August	6	4	-	2
1989	Colorado, United States	13-20 August	3	2	-	1
1991	Western Canada	14-23 August	4	3	-	1
1993	South Africa	7-20 August	5	5	-	-

There was a non-first class two-game tour to South-West France and Spain in May 1986 beating both Bayonne (35-12) and a Basque XV (96-0), whilst the Extras & Swifts undertook a tour to Florida in the summer of 1981.

↑ The team departs for what was to be the last overseas tour, to South Africa in August 1993.

TREASURERS

In conjunction with the secretary, the treasurer had an important role in keeping finances in check at the club until professionalism made the post redundant when the club converted into a plc in 1997.

The two roles of secretary and treasurer were combined between 1884 and 1890, whilst **Billy Bradshaw** and **James Grahame** were joint honorary treasurers in 1936/37.

1880-1881	JG (James) Walker
1881-1884	RH (Robert) Warner
1884-1889	HW (Hedley) Salmon
1889-1890	SR (Sid) Wykes
1890-1895	FJ (Frederick) Brett
1895-1896	WH (William) Swingler
1896-1897	TW (Tom) Pettifor
1897-1904	HN (Harris) Stroud
1904-1919*	F (Frederick) St Clair Pain
1919-1929	T (Thomas) Thorpe
1929-1938	WN (Billy) Bradshaw
1936-1937	JG (James) Grahame – joint honorary treasurer with Billy Bradshaw
1938-1959	RL (Rodney) Bedingfield
1959-1966	RE (Ronnie) Gerrard

Tom Pettifor was the club's treasurer in 1896/97 after previously being secretary in 1894/95.

1966-1975 AS (Stan) Thorpe
1975-1982 JA (John) Allen
1982-1985 R (Bob) Beason
1985-1992 RJ (Richard) Farrands
1992-1997 AP (Tony) Power
* died in office.

TRY SCORING

100 OR MORE CAREER TRIES

Pos	Name	Career	Apps	Tries
1	Percy Lawrie	1907/08-1923/24	318	206
2	Barry Evans	1981/82-1995/96	272+1	170
3=	Bob Barker	1968/69-1979/80	318+2	158
	John Duggan	1969/70-1980	302	158
5	Harry Wilkinson	1895/96-1904/05	233	153
6	Teddy Haselmere	1918/19-1923/24	180	136
7	Rory Underwood	1983/84-1996/97	230+6	134
8	Neil Back	1990/91-2004/05	320+19	125
9	David Matthews	1955/56-1973/74	502	119
10	Ralph Buckingham	1924/25-1934/35	325	117
11	Harold Day	1918/19-1928/29	212	108
12	Dean Richards	1981/82-1997/98	306+8	105
13	Pedlar Wood	1906/07-1922/23	388	102

43 different players have scored over fifty tries each.
Quickest to 50 tries: **Teddy Haselmere** 40 games, **Jack Miles** 58, **Frank Jackson** 64, **David Senior** 66, **Barry Evans/Alfred Hind** 72, **Harold Day/John Duggan/Steve Hackney/Tom Varndell** 74, **Tony Underwood** 77, **Percy Lawrie** 78, **Ted Flewitt** 79.
Youngest to 50 tries: **Ralph Buckingham** 20y 294d, **Barry Evans** 21y 26d, **Ted Flewitt** 21y 37d, **Percy Lawrie** 21y 153d.
Quickest to 100 tries: **Teddy Haselmere** 89 games, **Harry Wilkinson** 139, **Percy Lawrie** 140, **Barry Evans** 153, **John Duggan** 175, **Rory Underwood** 177, **Harold Day** 192
Youngest to 100 tries: **Percy Lawrie** 23y 137d, **Barry Evans** 23y 191d, **Harry Wilkinson** 23y 226d.

BREAKING THE CAREER TRY SCORING RECORD

Percy Lawrie has been the club's all-time top try scorer since Boxing Day 1918, when he surpassed **Harry Wilkinson's** previous record of 153 career tries for Leicester. Listed are all the individuals to have previously held the record and when they achieved the landmark:

Name	Tries	Opponent	Date
William Sheffield	10	v Derby Wanderers	8.12.1883
Sherrard Coleman	20	v Bedford Grammar School	29.10.1887
Bob Hesmondhalgh	32	at Burton	26.10.1895
Billy Foreman	34	at Bedford Grammar School	17.2.1897
Harry Wilkinson	50	v Handsworth	17.9.1898
Percy Lawrie	154	v 4th Leicestershire Regt	26.12.1918

MOST TRIES FOR TIGERS IN A COMPETITION...

MIDLAND COUNTIES CUP

Harry Wilkinson	31
Alfred Hind	25
Percy Lawrie	18
Jack Miles	17
Frank Jackson	16
Jacky Braithwaite	15

NATIONAL CUP

Barry Evans	14
Rory Underwood	14
Dean Richards	13
Neil Back	12
Tim Barnwell	12
Leon Lloyd	11
Les Cusworth	10

ANGLO-WELSH CUP

Tom Varndell	6
Dan Hipkiss	6
Leon Lloyd	5
Johne Murphy	5
Michael Noone	4

LEAGUE/PREMIERSHIP

Name	Lg	Prem	Total
Neil Back	16	59	75
Geordan Murphy	-	57	57
Alesana Tuilagi	-	46	46
Tom Varndell	-	45	45
Rory Underwood	43	-	43
Austin Healey	2	38	40
Leon Lloyd	1	37	38
Steve Hackney	25	-	25
John Liley	25	-	25
Tony Underwood	24	-	24
Ollie Smith	-	21	21
Tim Stimpson	-	21	21
Lewis Moody	0	20	20

EUROPE

Geordan Murphy	25
Leon Lloyd	19
Neil Back	16
Austin Healey	13
Harry Ellis	13
Tom Varndell	12
Scott Hamilton	12
Ollie Smith	11

100TH CAREER TRY

Pos	Name	Opponents	Date	Game	Age
1	Harry Wilkinson	v Harlequins	27.12.1899	139	23y 226d
2	Percy Lawrie	at Swansea	10.2.1912	140	23y 137d
3	Pedlar Wood	at Bristol	26.3.1921	370	35y 49d
4	Teddy Haselmere	at Bath	29.3.1921	89	25y 363d
5	Harold Day	v Old Blues	8.10.1927	192	29y 57d
6	Ralph Buckingham	v London Welsh	25.3.1933	254	26y 69d
7	David Matthews	at Bristol	5.4.1969	413	31y 353d
8	Bob Barker	at Fylde	19.4.1975	209	30y 178d
9	John Duggan	at Waterloo	6.12.1975	175	27y 184d
10	Barry Evans	v Gosforth	19.4.1986	153	23y 191d
11	Dean Richards	v Barbarians	27.12.1994	249	31y 169d
12	Rory Underwood	v Wasps	4.3.1995	177	31y 258d
13	Neil Back	v Leeds Tykes	19.4.2002	265	33y 93d

200TH CAREER TRY

Pos	Name	Opponents	Date	Game	Age
1	Percy Lawrie	v United Services	5.1.1924	304	35y 101d

MOST TRIES IN A SEASON

59	Teddy Haselmere	1919/20
37	Harry Wilkinson	1898/99
37	Alfred Hind	1902/03

21 players have scored over twenty tries in a season, **Percy Lawrie** did so six times (five in succession), **Harry Wilkinson** five (all consecutive), and **Bob Barker** four times. In season 1993/94 Tigers had an incredible 35 different try scorers.

MOST TRIES IN A GAME BY A PLAYER

For Tigers:

7	Alastair Smallwood	v Manchester	30.12.1922
6	Bobby Lewis	v Worcester (r1)	2.3.1895
6	Frank Jackson	v St Bartholomew's H	20.1.1896
6	Alfred Hind	v Belgrave (r2)	21.3.1903
6	Tony Underwood	v Liverpool St Helens	11.4.1992

Against Tigers:

5	Peter Thompson	v Barbarians	27.12.1956
5	David Duckham	v Barbarians	27.12.1969
4	Florica Murariu	v Romania	22.10.1980
4	Mike Carrington	at Cardiff	3.11.1984

Five tries in a game have been recorded by **Teddy Haselmere** (three times); **Alfred Hind** (twice); and **Ally Nutt**, **Arthur Jones**, **Barry Evans, Rory Underwood and Will Greenwood** (once each). Four tries in a game were scored by 29 players; **Haselmere** and **Harry Wilkinson** topping the list with five instances, followed with **Rory Underwood** on four occasions.

FOUR TRIES IN A GAME BY A FORWARD

George Dobbs	v Bromsgrove (r1)	7.3.1891
D Williams	v Ashby-de-la-Zouch	16.11.1892
JM Dykes	v Moseley	23.10.1926
Fred Doe	v Blackheath	9.4.1938
Simon Povoas	at Headingley	28.9.1991

MOST DIFFERENT TRY SCORERS IN A GAME

The Tigers had 11 different try scorers during their 17-try 71-0 victory over Burfield Rangers at Welford Road on 8 September 1894, with **Bobby Lewis** and **George Jones** both grabbing hat tricks, whilst in modern times ten different players ran in tries for Leicester during their 73-3 win against Bristol in the Premiership at Welford Road on on 25 April 2009.

The Cambridge University game at Welford Road on 30 November 1996 marked the only occasion in Tigers history that all seven backs in the starting lineup have each scored tries – **Will Greenwood** got five, **Rory Underwood** two, and there was one each for **John Liley, Steve Hackney, Mark Jasnikowski, Rob Liley** and **Austin Healey**. There was also a penalty try and another for number 8 **Dean Richards** in an 84-5 victory.

MOST TRIES IN A GAME BY A TEAM

For Tigers:

19	v Bedford XV	71-0	15.2.1919
19	v Liverpool St Helens	100-0	11.4.1992
17	v Burfield Rangers	71-0	8.9.1894
17	v Newbold-on-Avon (sf)	65-0	23.3.1912

Against Tigers:

13	v Barbarians	10-85	4.6.2000
11	at Blackheath	0-37	13.2.1892
11	at Neath	6-37	26.11.1923
11	at Cardiff	5-50	15.11.1947
11	v Barbarians	19-73	17.3.1998
10	at Cambridge University	11-36	8.11.1969

MOST SUCCESSIVE GAMES SCORING A TRY

8	Percy Lawrie (12 tries)	19.11.1911 to 28.12.1911
7	Ted Flewitt (10 tries)	28.12.1929 to 1.2.1930
7	Percy Lawrie (9 tries)	17.9.1921 to 27.10.1921

Tries in six successive games have been recorded by **John Charles, Frank Jackson, Percy Lawrie** (twice), **John Liley, Jack Miles, Alexander Obolensky** and **David Senior**.

Alesana Tuilagi scored tries in five successive Premiership matches in April and May 2011, against Harlequins, Gloucester(3), Newcastle, London Irish and the semi-final against Northampton. This feat was also repeated by **Vereniki Goneva** in 2013, versus London Irish on 4 May, followed by Harlequins in the semi-final and Northampton in the final, and then beginning the new season by crossing against Worcester and Bath.

George Jones was one of 11 different try-scorers when Tigers beat Burfield Rangers 71-0 at Welford Road on 8.9.1894.

➔ Bobby Barr failed to score a try in his entire Tigers career of 241 matches.

MOST GAMES WITHOUT A TRY

241	Bobby Barr	3.11.1928 to 15.4.1939	His complete career
215	Claude Sambrook	12.9.1921 to 3.3.1928	His complete career
150	Mick Walker	20.9.1958 to 3.12.1966	His last 150 games
149	Sid Penny	23.11.1901 to 17.3.1906	
147	Josh Garner	6.4.1895 to 5.11.1900	His first 147 games

Will Johnson played in 97 Premiership matches without scoring a try, between 13 December 1997 and 5 February 2005.

MOST SUCCESSIVE GAMES TIGERS SCORED A TRY

The best sequence of successive first-team matches in which Tigers scored at least one try began when Leicester were beaten 6-25 by Northampton at Franklin's Gardens in the Premiership on 18 October 1997 until Leicester failed to score a try at Newcastle in the Premiership on 2 May 1999 – an incredible run of 66 consecutive try scoring fixtures.

66	25.10.1997 to 24.4.1999
48	15.11.1975 to 20.11.1976
35	16.11.1929 to 11.10.1930
35	30.10.1926 to 24.9.1927
33	13.4.1996 to 18.1.1997

MOST SUCCESSIVE GAMES TIGERS CONCEDED A TRY

33	17.9.1949 to 8.4.1950
24	1.3.2003 to 6.12.2003
23	26.1.2008 to 4.10.2008
23	24.2.2007 to 10.11.2007
23	2.3.1991 to 22.10.1991
23	27.3.1920 to 11.12.1920

LONGEST SPELL WITHOUT TIGERS SCORING A TRY

The longest sequence of matches where the Tigers have failed to score a try is eight between when Jack Lovett scored at Kettering on 26 February 1881 until **John Lakin** crossed at home to Coventry on 12 November 1881, a run of eight consecutive tryless matches, during which time Leicester only achieved one score of any description, **Jack Parsons'** drop goal against Rugby Rovers on 5 March 1881.

In more modern times the most has been three complete games from when **Ben Woods** scored in the Heineken Cup final at Murrayfield on 23 May 2009 until **Mefin Davies** crossed at the Rec in the Premiership on 26 September 2009, some 306 minutes later.

LONGEST SPELL WITHOUT TIGERS CONCEDING A TRY

Leicester conceded a try to Bridgwater at Welford Road on 18 January 1896 and the defence was not breached again until Northampton scored at Franklin's Gardens on 28 March 1896 for a tryless sequence of 11 complete games.

In recent times the best run is five complete games from when Newcastle's **Dave Walder** scored at Kingston Park in the Premiership on the first game of the 2001/02 season on 2 September 2001 until **John Leslie** scored Northampton's try at Franklin's Gardens in the Premiership on 13 October 2001 – a spell of 444 minutes with the Tigers try line intact.

TWO LEGGED CUP-TIES

The Tigers have only ever appeared in two cup ties decided by aggregate scores played over two legs, they faced Rugby Lions home and away in the 1st round of Cheltenham & Gloucester Cup in season 1998/99 and lost 5-8 and 23-11. Then four seasons later Leicester met Harlequins in the semi-final of the Zurich Wildcard this time losing the first leg at The Stoop 23-26 but winning the return 28-13 to progress to the final 51-39 on aggregate.

UNCONTESTED SCRUMS

During the period when matchday squads were 22 players and just one replacement had to be a prop, there were ten instances of front-row injury or yellow or red cards resulting in uncontested scrums during a Leicester match. Since the start of the 2009/10 season an eight-man bench was introduced including two props and a hooker, and this has virtually stamped out uncontested scrums.

Date	*Opponent*
1.3.2003	v Gloucester at Northampton Two Gloucester props were injured – uncontested after 80'.
1.4.2006	v Bath at Walkers Stadium Two Bath props in the sin bin - uncontested from 71-79'.
22.9.2007	v Bath **Boris Stankovich** and **Julian White** injured – unconstested after 49'.
20.10.2007	at Worcester **Boris Stankovich** and **Martin Castrogiovanni** injured – uncontested after 38'.
31.5.2008	v Wasps at Twickenham Two Wasps props injured – uncontested after 61'.
26.9.2008	v Wasps Two Wasps props injured – uncontested after 61'.
4.1.2009	v Bath **Boris Stankovich** and **Martin Castrogiovanni** injured – uncontested after 67'.
17.1.2009	v Treviso Two Treviso props injured – uncontested after 54'.
4.4.2009	v Sale **Julian White** sent off and **Marcos Ayerza** injured – uncontested after 69'.
16.5.2009	v London Irish at Twickenham Two London Irish props injured – uncontested after 73'.

Frank Jones gained three rugby Blues at Cambridge University between 1898-1900.

UNIVERSITY BLUES

89 Tigers have attained rugby Blues for Oxford or Cambridge Universities, Listed below are the 21 of those who played for Leicester both before AND after winning their Blues in the annual Varsity Match at Twickenham.

Frank Jones, Alfred Hind, George Keeton, Frank Tarr, Norman Coates, Gwyn Francis, Wavell Wakefield, Guy Herman, Harry Edmiston, Eric Sweatman, Alexander Obolensky, Peter Jerwood, Jim Parsons, Keith Downes, Peter Tahany, Mike Wade, Nick Drake-Lee, Chris Holroyd, Tony Underwood, Laurence Boyle, Nigel Richardson.

UTILITY

Just four players in the history of the club have started a match in all five backs positions - **Arthur Jones** (1895-1910), **Dixie Smith** (1902-12), **John Jackett** (1904-11), and **Harry Lawrie** (1904-15).

In addition **Lawrie** also started a further 124 matches as a forward, making him the most versatile Tiger of all time.

Post war just eight players have started games in four of the five backs positions - **Mel Channer** (1946-55), **Mike Freer** (1956-65), **Keith Chilton** (1963-67), **John Ingleby** (1970-74), **Andy Key** (1978-92), **Jez Harris** (1984-96), **Dave Wigley** (1991-95), and **Austin Healey** (1996-2005).

Forty-nine players have started games in their careers at both fly-half and scrum-half, whilst the only players to have appeared in over ten matches in each position are **Austin Healey** (56 at fly-half and 108 at scrum-half), **Pedlar Wood** (14+374), **Harry Greenlees** (129+14) and **Edward Massey** (11+20).

Since the war ten players have started games as both backs and forwards: **Lew Stokes** (1945-46, 1 as a back +25 as a forward), **Allan Towell** (1947-50, 76+17), **Derek Ashurst** (1951-62, 3+109), **Peter Konig** (1952-60, 4+181), **David Matthews** (1955-74, 1+501), **Bob Small** (1957-69, 2+117), **Gordon Almey** (1957-64, 4+146), **Mike Hemphrey** (1960-63, 1+15), **Steve Solomons** (1974-80, 6+2), and **Tom Youngs** (2006-14, 6+46).

The introduction of replacements means that modern players are more versatile – one of the world's most famous fly-halves, Joel Stransky, made his Tigers debut as a replacement wing!

VENUES

The most frequent opposition venue visited by Leicester is Franklin's Gardens, Northampton, winning almost 41% of their 113 previous visits. Of venues visited more than 50 times the Tigers "graveyard" grounds have been Rodney Parade, Newport, with just six wins in 66 matches, and St Helen's, Swansea producing only seven wins in 59.

Venue	*Town*	*P*	*W*	*D*	*L*	*Win %*
Franklin's Gardens	Northampton	113	46	6	61	40.7%
Kingsholm	Gloucester	103	27	4	72	26.2%
Memorial Stadium	Bristol	93	30	5	58	32.3%
Recreation Ground	Bath	89	33	10	46	37.1%
Goldington Road	Bedford	86	46	6	34	53.5%
Twickenham	London	83	37	4	42	44.6%
The Reddings	Moseley	77	39	3	35	50.6%

Leicester won on all six visits they made to the Newdigate Ground in Nuneaton between 1881-1910, and of grounds visited more than 15 times the best record is at Ireland Avenue, Nottingham with 15 wins and a draw in 18 separate trips.

VIDEO REFEREE

The first Tigers game to utilise a television match official came in the Zurich Championship final at Twickenham against Bath on 13 May 2001. In the 26th minute the new protocol was called into action when **Martin Johnson** ploughed over for a try which referee **Steve Lander** awarded with assistance from video official **Brian Campsall**, who ruled that Johnson grounded the ball despite a combined tackle by **Matt Perry** and prop **John Mallett**.

WAR HEROES

The following 46 known Leicester first-team players died in conflicts whilst on military service. The number is unfortunately increasing all the time as family history projects and further research reveal more names of those who made the supreme sacrifice.

NIGER CONFLICT (1)

Name	*Died*	*Place*	*Age*	*Regiment*
Lt. AC Thomson	26.1.1897	Bida, West Africa	27	Leicestershire Regt

FIRST WORLD WAR (19)

Name	*Died*	*Place*	*Age*	*Regiment*
Sgt. J Twigg	13.3.1915	Le Touret, France	25	Leicestershire Regt
2nd Lt. CR Fausset	2.5.1915	Ypres, Belgium	36	Royal Irish Regt
Sgt. LS Burton	13.5.1915	Ypres, Belgium	26	Leics Yeomanry
Lt. C Bourns	25.5.1915	Ypres, Belgium	34	Rifle Brigade
Lt. FN Tarr	18.7.1915	Ypres, Belgium	27	Leicestershire Regt
Maj. HJF Jeffries	26.9.1915	Lijssenthoek, Belgium	29	Leicestershire Regt
2nd Lt. RE Hemingway	15.10.1915	Loos, France	37	Sherwood Foresters
Cpl. PJ Hougham	8.1.1916	Basra, Iraq	26	Leicestershire Regt
2nd Lt. AGE Bowell	14.7.1916	Somme, France	27	Leicestershire Regt
2nd Lt. SE Dove	16.8.1916	Guillemont, France	27	Queen's Own Regt
Sgt. WA Dalby	15.9.1916	Loos, France	27	Leicestershire Regt
Pvte. J Brewin	25.9.1916	Somme, France	24	Durham Lt.Infantry

L/Cpl. HR Somerville	21.11.1916	Varennes, France	31	Royal Fusiliers
Cpt. WR Evans	15.12.1916	Cardiff Wales	28	Leicestershire Regt
Lt. DA Waddell	6.4.1917	Arras, France	27	Gordon Highlanders
Cpt. EE Wynne	8.6.1917	Bully Grenay, France	21	Leicestershire Regt
Lt. SG Wolfe	22.10.1917	Zonnebeke, Belgium	27	Lancashire Fusiliers
Cpl. RJC Ferguson	9.1.1919	Poona, India	38	Oxford & Bucks Lt.Inf.
Maj. B McCraith	26.1.1919	Sangatte, France	38	Royal Engineers

SECOND WORLD WAR (26)

Name	*Died*	*Place*	*Age*	*Regiment*
Fg.Off. TI Davies	18.9.1939	Pembroke, Wales	23	RAF
Plt Off. A Obolensky	29.3.1940	Martlesham Heath	24	RAF
Sgt. NFF Giddings	6.5.1940	Sarthe, France	26	RAF
Wg/Cdr. JG LLewelyn	23.5.1940	Beuvry, France	31	RAF
Cpt. FC Drummond	11.7.1940	Nairobi, Kenya	32	Kings African Rifles
L/Cpl. AH Greenwood	26.8.1940	Bedford	36	RASC
Wg Cdr. PB Coote	13.4.1941	Trigonon, Greece	31	RAF
2nd Lt. WG Young	20.5.1941	Suda Bay, Crete	23	Leicestershire Regt
Sgt. G Wooller	17.6.1941	El Alamein, Egypt	23	RAF Volunteer
Flt Lt. DF Walker	7.2.1942	over Trondheim, Norway	28	RAF Volunteer
LAC. H Lees	7.3.1942	-	30	RAF Volunteer
Fg.Off. FV Beamish	28.3.1942	Europe	38	RAF
Plt.Off. JD Anderson	30.5.1942	Yvelines, France	31	RAF Volunteer
Maj. AP Hughes	4.9.1942	El Alamein, Egypt	30	Royal Tank Regt
Sgt. KA Wait	6.9.1942	-	27	RAF Volunteer
AB.Sea. GA Harris	2.10.1942	England	25	Royal Navy
Cpt. PC Crick	29.10.1942	El Alamein, Egypt	32	Royal Horse Artillery
Maj. RA Gerrard	22.1.1943	Nr Tripoli, Libya	30	Royal Engineers
Driver A Williams	20.6.1943	Kaqnchanaburi, Thailand	28	Royal Corps of Signals
Gp Cpt. RVM Odbert	18.7.1943	Scunthorpe	39	RAF
Gp.Cpt. BV Robinson	24.8.1943	Berlin, Germany	31	RAF
Gp Cpt. FS Hodder	6.9.1943	Rhein, Germany	37	RAF
Cpl. EE Bates	12.6.1944	Gauhati, India	31	Leicestershire Regt
Cpt. I Shaw	13.7.1944	St Manvieu, France	-	Royal Artillery
Lt-Col. GM Wilkins	17.8.1944	Bayeux, France	43	North Staffs Regt
Sqn Ldr. RA Squibbs	12.9.1944	Durnbach, Germany	35	RAF Volunteer

On Valentine's Day, 1914, almost 10,000 fans paid to see Newport and Leicester play. How would Tigers skipper **Percy Lawrie** have felt if he'd known that five of his team mates that day, including half the pack, would not come home from the impending war? Fellow back **Ernest Wynne**, along with four members of the pack - **Bill Dalby, John Twigg, Leo Burton,** and **Syd Wolfe;** Twigg was the first Tiger to fall just over a year later in France.

↑ Lieutenant AC Thomson of the Leicestershire Regiment was the first Tigers' player to be killed in military conflict, in Niger in 1897.

Leicester were hit hard losing 19 men at the current count who had worn the Tigers shirt, but this is put into context when you consider the sacrifice of the Rosslyn Park club, who lost 87 men.

At a Members' meeting in January 1915 it was revealed by honorary secretary **Tom Crumbie** that 32 of the 38 regular players in the previous season had joined His Majesty's Forces, and the remainder were connected with the territorial forces or engaged on Government work. At the outbreak of war the clubhouse and ground was given over to the military authorities. A junior training corps had also been formed under the auspices of the club with 2,000 youths having been enrolled.

It was a worldwide conflict with 131 test players losing their lives – men from Australia, New Zealand, South Africa and France as well as the home countries.

WEATHER

In recent times the ability of the Welford Road pitch to stand up to adverse weather has been exemplary with only one Premiership game ever falling foul of the weather at the venue – when frost claimed the match against Sale on 30 December 2000. Prior to that just two league games had been postponed there: the Orrell game on 9 February 1991 due to snow and Sale once more because of frost on 30 December 1995.

There have been a couple of "close calls" in the Heineken Cup, both against Toulouse, the semi-final on 4 January 1997 only taking place after a heated "balloon" was inflated over the pitch, and the pool game on 20 January 2013 which was played amidst constant snow flurries and freezing temperatures. The Premiership encounter with Wasps on 9 January 2010 was only played after groundstaff and volunteers managed to clear 35 tonnes of snow from the pitch and terraces. Tigers won 34-8 in what turned out to be the only game of rugby played in England that weekend.

There have been a few big freezes, notably in December-January 1890 when seven successive first-team fixtures were lost. In the 1906/07 season two separate icy blasts saw seven more games postponed. In January-February 1947 eight consecutive matches were unplayed and the next in Cardiff was contested over just 25 minutes each way due to frost, but in 1963 no rugby was played virtually anywhere in the country between mid-December and early March, claiming a dozen Tigers games in a row.

Since then, February 1978 was blank because of frost, whilst the same affliction claimed ten games in four separate spells the following season. The only game played for six weeks in 1981/82 was at Bath on 2 January and the last protracted spell of cold weather to claim multiple games before modern pitch covering methods were adopted came in February and March 1986.

Four further fixtures in Tigers' history were started after agreeing to play just 25 minutes each way because of the weather:

18 November 1893 v Rugby, because of snow
4 December 1909 v Stratford-upon-Avon, snow
22 December 1934 v London Welsh, due to fog
15 March 1947 at Cardiff, snow

In addition, on 3 January 1895 when Dublin's Bective Rangers visited Welford Road they were greeted by a frosty pitch which precluded proper rugby. Accordingly the two sides played an exhibition game of touch rugby, with the only point scored being a dropped goal by Tigers' **Bobby Lewis**, however officially the result goes down as a draw in Leicester's records as the two clubs had previously agreed that the result would be a tie!

On 7 November 1903 for the visit of London Welsh the newspaper headlines read "Farcical Football - Fun in the Fog".

For most of the time play was in progress the players were virtually lost in the fog and for minutes at a time the spectators could see nothing of what was going on. The whole thing was an unqualified farce.

Conversely, when Gloucester visited Welford Road on 28 September 1895 it was under a cloudless sky, very little breeze and a temperature of 112 degrees in the sun.

Indirectly the weather conditions contributed to Richmond failing to turn up for a fixture at Welford Road on 28 January 1928. It had been pouring with rain all day but there was a rumour in London that heavy snow had struck the Midlands. Whilst the Richmond team were waiting at St Pancras for the 11:45 train to Leicester a telegram was handed to the acting captain **ML Maley** saying that the match had been scratched due to weather and hence the team never made the journey. Meanwhile at Welford Road the ground was filling up nicely and at the appointed kick-off time there were 10,000 in attendance when at 3:30pm **Sos Taylor** had to announce that the game was cancelled owing to Richmond not showing up. In fact there had been a mix-up with the telegram – the one given to **Maley** on the platform was in fact intended for the St Bart's Hospital skipper called **Malley** cancelling a minor match. Another irony was that one player who did catch the 11:45 from St Pancras that day was none other than the Leicester full-back **HLV Day**!

WINS AND LOSSES

BIGGEST WINS

(100) 100-0	v Liverpool St Helens	11.4.1992	
(89) 95-6	v Birmingham	17.9.1986	
(79) 84-5	v Cambridge University	30.11.1996	
(78) 84-6	v Loughborough Students	22.11.1996	
(76) 76-0	v Exeter (qf)	27.2.1993	●
(73) 83-10	v Newcastle Falcons	19.2.2005	●
(72) 75-3	at Western Province Defence	7.8.1993	
(72) 83-11	v Otley (r4)	4.11.2000	●

WORST DEFEATS

(75) 10-85	v Barbarians	4.6.2000	
(54) 19-73	v Barbarians	17.3.1998	
(45) 5-50	at Cardiff	15.11.1947	
(42) 0-42	at Bath	6.1.1973	
(40) 7-47	at London Irish (r5)	29.1.2000	●

GOOD LUCK CHARMS & JINXES

Of players that have made a minimum of 50 appearances, the best winning record goes to **Wayne Kilford** (1992-96) who was on the winning side in 55 of his 62 Tigers appearances for a success rate of 88.7%. The best for anyone that has played over 100 matches is **Richard Cockerill** with 204 wins from 262 appearances – a 77.9% winning percentage.

Phil Delaney (1995-98) won all 20 of the games he played for Tigers.

The most wins were gained by **Paul Dodge** with 316 in 437 games, the most draws were obtained by **Sid Penny** with 45 in 491 appearances.

On the other hand, the player with the worst winning percentage of those who have played 50 times is **Dick Jackett** (1905-14) with just 19 wins from 59 appearances for a 32.2% winning rate. The poorest rate of those who have played in 100 games is **Kenneth McAlpin** (1884-92) with just 59 wins from 136 matches (43.4%).

WS Sheppard (1889-90), **J Sutcliffe** (1914), **David Walker** (1933) and **Ben Smith** (1998-99) all lost each of their four Tigers games, and **Paul Ash** (1946-47) was never on the winning side in his six games.

The most losses as a Tiger is attributed to **David Matthews** with 176 in his 502 games, but that is still only a 35% losing rate.

MOST SUCCESSIVE VICTORIES

31	Martin Johnson	28.10.2000 to 5.1.2002	
23	Laurence Boyle	30.1.1993 to 2.4.1994	
22	Jez Harris	8.4.1995 to 17.4.1996	
22	Neil Back	13.1.2001 to 5.1.2002	
21	Derek Jelley	19.11.1994 to 15.3.1996	
21	Rob Field	29.10.1994 to 14.2.1997	First 21 games
21	Oscar Wingham	15.10.1994 to 14.3.1997	
20	Angus Collington	24.2.1979 to 5.4.1980	
20	Alan Warwood	3.12.1988 to 18.4.1992	
20	Darren Grewcock	28.12.1992 to 28.10.1995	Last 20 matches
20	Wayne Kilford	3.9.1994 to 6.1.1996	Last 20 matches

MOST SUCCESSIVE DEFEATS

13	Rab Bruce-Lockhart	27.3.1937 to 2.9.1950	First 13 matches
11	Kenneth McAlpin	23.3.1889 to 23.11.1889	
10	Enoch Bell	23.3.1889 to 23.11.1889	
10	Owen Wynne	12.12.1891 to 19.11.1892	
10	Peter Crick	28.1.1937 to 3.4.1937	

WORLD CUP

TIGERS IN WORLD CUP SQUADS

Players who have participated in the final stages of World Cup competitions whilst playing members of Leicester.

RUGBY WORLD CUP

Year	*Venue*	*Players*
1987	New Zealand & Australia (2)	Dean Richards, Rory Underwood
1991	England (2)	Dean Richards, Rory Underwood
1995	South Africa (6)	Neil Back, Martin Johnson, Dean Richards, Graham Rowntree, Rory Underwood, Tony Underwood
1999	England (11)	Neil Back, Richard Cockerill, Martin Corry, Darren Garforth, Will Greenwood, Austin Healey, Martin Johnson (capt), Leon Lloyd, Graham Rowntree (England), Dave Lougheed (Canada), Fritz van Heerden (South Africa)
2003	Australia (8)	Martin Johnson (capt), Neil Back, Martin Corry, Ben Kay,

↑ Laurence Boyle was in the winning team in 23 consecutive Leicester matches in 1993/94.

Lewis Moody was one of seven Tigers in England's victorious 2003 World Cup squad.

Year	Venue	Players
		Lewis Moody, Dorian West, Julian White (England), Dan Lyle (USA)
2007	France (12)	George Chuter, Martin Corry, Dan Hipkiss, Ben Kay, Lewis Moody (England), Marcos Ayerza (Argentina), Seru Rabeni (Fiji), Geordan Murphy (Ireland), Martin Castrogiovanni (Italy), Aaron Mauger (NZ), Alesana Tuilagi (Samoa), James Hamilton (Scotland)
2011	New Zealand (12)	Dan Cole, Tom Croft, Louis Deacon, Toby Flood, Manu Tuilagi, Ben Youngs, Thomas Waldrom (rep) (England), Horacio Agulla, Marcos Ayerza (Argentina), Martin Castrogiovanni (Italy), Geordan Murphy (Ireland), Alesana Tuilagi (Samoa)

UNDER-21 JUNIOR WORLD CHAMPIONSHIP

Year	*Venue*	*Players*
2002	South Africa (3)	Adam Billig, Michael Holford, Sam Vesty
2003	England (4)	Harry Ellis, Dan Hipkiss, Michael Holford (England), Jim Henry (Scotland)
2004	Scotland (2)	Stuart Friswell, Luke Myring
2005	Argentina (3)	Matt Cornwell (capt), Will Skinner, Tom Varndell
2006	France (4)	Matt Cornwell (capt), Tom Croft (England), Ian Nimmo, David Young (Scotland)

UNDER-19 JUNIOR WORLD CHAMPIONSHIP

Year	*Venue*	*Players*
1999	Wales (4)	Phil Christophers, Andy Goode, James Grindal (England), Mark Meenan (Ireland)
2000	France (2)	Alex Alesbrook, Richard List
2001	Chile (7)	Brett Deacon, Harry Ellis, James Hamilton, Michael Holford, John Holtby, Lee Morley, Ollie Smith
2002	Italy (2)	Luke Abraham, Stuart Friswell
2003	France (4)	Matt Hampson, Nathan Jones, Tom Ryder, Will Skinner
2004	South Africa (4)	Tom Ryder (capt), Ross Broadfoot, Tom Gregory, (rep) Ben Pienaar
2005	South Africa (4)	Kevin Davis, Marc Howgate, Alex Wright, Tom Youngs
2006	Dubai (4)	Dan Cole, Oliver Dodge, Alex Shaw, Tom Youngs
2007	Belfast (1)	Greg Gillanders

UNDER-20 JUNIOR WORLD CHAMPIONSHIP

Year	*Venue*	*Players*
2008	Wales (3)	Greg Gillanders, Ben Youngs (England), Vavae Tuilagi (Samoa)
2009	Tokyo (5)	Jack Cobden, Will Hurrell, Greig Tonks, Ben Youngs (England), Seb Pearson (Canada)
2010	Argentina (3)	Andy Forsyth, Calum Green, Sam Harrison
2011	Italy (4)	Ryan Bower, Matt Everard, George Ford (England), Hamish Watson (Scotland)
2013	France (4)	Tom Price, Henry Purdy, Harry Wells (England), Scott Steele (Scotland)
2013	Chile (JWRT) (2)	Tiziano Pasquali (Italy), Djustice Sears-Duru (Canada)
2014	New Zealand	George Catchpole, Henry Purdy, Harry Rudkin

RUGBY WORLD CUP SEVENS

Year	*Venue*	*Players*
1997	Hong Kong (4)	Neil Back, Austin Healey (England), Eric Miller, Niall Malone (Ireland)
2009	Dubai (1)	Tom Varndell
2013	Moscow (1)	Vereniki Goneva (Fiji)

YELLOW CARDS

Yellow cards were first introduced into English domestic rugby on 7 January 1995, but in those days the card denoted a warning and did not carry any ten-minute sin bin penalty. The first recipient in England's first division was Orrell's long-serving back-row forward **David Cleary** in their match against West Hartlepool. Leicester's first came a week later against Orrell at Welford Road when **Graham Rowntree** was "warned" by referee Tony Spreadbury after 30 minutes for illegal use of the boot.

The quickest cautionary yellow card was handed out after just one minute to **Richard Cockerill** against Bath at Welford Road on 25 October 1997 by French referee **Patrick Thomas**.

Dean Richards was the only Tiger to have picked up warning yellow cards in successive matches - against Bath and Gloucester in September 1995 - landing himself a 14-day suspension at a disciplinary hearing on 13 October for his pains.

Pat Howard is shown the white triangle against Northampton on 13 March 1999, in those days this denoted a ten-minute cooling-off period in the sin bin.

SIN BINS

On 1 November 1997 a white triangle card was introduced, which denoted a ten-minute "cooling off period" in the "sin bin". **Dean Ryan** became the first recipient of one for a taking a man out in the air at a restart for Newcastle at London Irish on the first day. The Tigers first sin binning was handed to **Richard Cockerill** by referee **Ashley Rowden** who decided that Cockerill had persistently failed to retreat 10 metres, against Harlequins on 5 September 1998. In all 255 have now been handed out to 86 different Tigers players, and 278 to their opponents.

In 1999/2000 the white triangle changed into a yellow card for English domestic rugby, but still carrying the ten-minute sin bin penalty. However, for the European Cup competition the sin bin was not allowed and the yellow card was used just for cautionary purposes. Finally in 2000/01 the sin bin was introduced for European matches.

In five games the Tigers have had three different players sent to the sin bin, but only one of these matches was at Welford Road:

Match	*Date*	*Yellow Cards*	*Referee*
at Bath	9.9.2006	Castrogiovanni 23', Deacon 48', Hipkiss 73'	Dave Pearson
at Bourgoin	8.12.2006	Corry 72', B. Deacon 77', Goode 80'	Donal Courtney
v Bath	17.3.2007	Varndell 58', H. Tuilagi 79', Alesana Tuilagi 80'	Wayne Barnes
at Newcastle	2.3.2014	B. Youngs 56', M. Tuilagi 70', Flood 80'	Greg Garner
at Northampton (sf)	16.5.2014	Goneva 29', Bowden 45', T. Youngs 57'	JP Doyle

Four Saracens players were given yellow cards by **David Rose** against the Tigers at Welford Road on 16 April 2004, whilst Benetton Treviso have twice been given three on visits to Leicester in the European Cup in 23 January 2011 and 18 October 2013.

Most sin bins by an individual:

Name	*Sin bins*	*Games played after sin bins were introduced*
Martin Johnson	16	175
Lewis Moody	14	195
Martin Corry	9	257
Darren Garforth	9	131
Graham Rowntree	9	197
Jordan Crane	8	179
Louis Deacon	8	274

The most by a back is seven recorded in 162 games by **Alesana Tuilagi**.

Three players have been sent to the sin bin on three separate occasions by one particular referee: **Martin Corry** by **Ashley Rowden**, **Lewis Moody** by **Chris White** and **Martin Johnson** by **David McHugh**.

Four players have appeared in over 100 Leicester games without ever being sent to the sin bin: **Marcos Ayerza** (193), **Sam Vesty** (164), **Jamie Hamilton** and **Anthony Allen** (113).

Five opponents have each recorded three sin binnings against Leicester: **Richard Arnold** (Newcastle), **Danny Grewcock** (Saracens & Bath), **Robbie Russell** (Saracens & London Irish), **Chris Jones** (Sale & Worcester) and **Will Skinner** (Harlequins).

Yellow cards in successive matches:
Ben Kay was sent to the sin bin in three successive matches against Clermont Auvergne and Stade Français in the Heineken Cup and Worcester in the Premiership in October-November 2005.

Fastest yellow cards:
The fastest yellow card was handed out to **Ed Slater** at Saracens on 19 February 2012 in the first minute of the match, whilst **Graham Rowntree** picked one up after just two minutes at Northampton on 13 October 2001. **Alesana Tuilagi** was handed one within a minute of coming on as a replacement against Northampton on 25 September 2004.

12 players on the pitch:
Three Tigers matches have seen one side or the other reduced to just 12 players for a time because of disciplinary cards.

Leicester at Bourgoin on 8 December 2006: Yellow cards to **Martin Corry** (72'), **Brett Deacon** (77') and **Andy Goode** (80').

Harlequins at the Stoop on 2 April 2011: **Joe Marler** sent off (64'), yellow cards to **Will Skinner** (55') and **Mark Lambert** (56').

Bath at Welford Road on 1 December 2012: **François Louw** (60') and **Matt Banahan** (65') sent off, yellow card to **Stephen Donald** (66').

Ed Slater was the recipient of Leicester's fastest ever yellow card, in the opening minute of the Tigers' trip to Saracens on 19.2.2012.

Sponsors

Out of the Ordinary™

Wealth & Investment

www.investecwin.co.uk

DELIVERED EXACTLY™

www.thedx.co.uk

www.falcon-hotel.co.uk

CHRONOLOGICAL LIST

Subscribers

1. Michael & Lynne Bylina
2. Sophie Bylina
3. Maxwell Bylina
4. Chris Rose
5. Christopher Lewis
6. Jeff Wright
7. Andy Weaver
8. Georgina Newcombe
9. Rob Verrion
10. Iain Jones
11. Michael Statham
12. Ian Caldwell
13. Andrew Baum
14. Daniel Baum
15. Valerie & David Howitt
16. David Rouch
17. Gordon L Millward
18. Lindsay & Lynda Berry
19. Bill Woodward
20. John Hudson
21. David Horwood
22. Michael Devlin
23. Mark Oldbury
24. Andrew Hudson
25. Stuart Aitken
26. Terry Smith
27. Mike Winson
28. Rick Taylor
29. Dean James
30. Aaron James
31. Ellie Robinson
32. Stephen L Brown
33. Gregory Broder
34. Julian Broughton
35. Lindsey Todd
36. Gordon Hall
37. Carl Matthews
38. Peter Haggis Harris
39. Phil Harvey
40. Richard J Groom
41. Paul Winson
42. Maria Crowfoot
43. Colin & Jan Barrett-Treen
44. David Mason
45. Wayne Gadsby
46. Anthony Thomas
47. Andrew Sortwell
48. Carol Barbara Reed
49. Andy "Coops" Cooper
50. Alan & Lynda Burdett
51. Geoff Marsland
52. Colin Wolverson
53. Stuart Fraser
54. Ian Brown
55. Symon Vegro
56. Martyn Smith
57. Dale Miller
58. Stuart Vickers
59. Hollie Vickers
60. Chris Partridge
61. Coll Macdonald
62. Janine Shaw
63. Michael Kaill
64. Simon Martin
65. Ray Martin
66. Malcolm J White
67. John & Valerie Griffin
68. Arthur Grey Hazlerigg
69. Graham Riddleston
70. Dietmar Morley
71. Michael Beck
72. Eddie & Wendy Burke
73. Julia Stone
74. Chris Day
75. Peter Harrison
76. David Milner
77. Roger Taylor
78. Stuart Turpin
79. Joe Elliott
80. Rick Elliott
81. Chris & Karen Whatsize
82. Nathan Hart
83. Matthew
84. Robert J Ross
85. David Jacobs
86. Jonny Hall
87. Marion Szyndler
88. Stuart Bird
89. John Grew
90. David Grew
91. Stephen Henry Peberdy
92. Richard Morrison
93. Kevin Moore
94. Lewis Paffard
95. Ian & Jenny Craven
96. Dave Stone
97. David P W Cooper
98. Alan Briggs
99. Jane Boyer
100. Nigel & Pip Ostell
101. Tom Maitland
102. Steve Kirkman
103. John Robert Lee
104. John Robert Daniel Lee
105. Lawrence Smith
106. Mark John Hall
107. Brian John Hall
108. Jon Kitto
109. Graham Kitto
110. Ian Johnson
111. David, Harry, Ethan & Melanie Mott
112. Glynis Maitland
113. Garry Clarke
114. Stephen Page
115. Professor Peter Swallow
116. Patrick FJ Turner
117. Dayle Jones
118. David Garratt
119. Sheila P Brown
120. Clem MacTaggart
121. Jon Matthews
122. Alec Moore
123. Philippa Stannard
124. Clifford Oakes
125. David & Mandy Hextall
126. Paul David Launders
127. Craig Fitches
128. Richard Wall
129. Steven Bramford
130. Mary Davis
131. Richard Owen
132. Roger Davis
133. Graham Blackwell
134. Rachel Bradley
135. Jo Botterill
136. Richard Botterill
137. Gerald Botterill
138. John Scott
139. Nick Gordon
140. Geoff Reader
141. Brian Thomas Stephens
142. Tim Castleman
143. Simon & Ben Cole
144. Mike Pepperman
145. David Chettle
146. Robert Blakemore
147. John Grant
148. Ross Grant
149. Scott Grant
150. Garry Mason
151. Dean Arthur Woodhouse
152. Brenda Meade
153. Adrian Purvey
154. Lawrence & Sandra Hopwood
155. James Douglas Tyers
156. Ian Cockerill
157. Brian Walker
158. Alan J Williamson
159. Nick Kidd
160. Rosanne Sarratt
161. Alex Carter
162. Jason K Price
163. Robert Ellis
164. Darrel Edwards
165. Roger Baynham
166. Paul Mousley
167. Tony Parkinson
168. Alec Brotherton
169. Jon Smith
170. John Stack
171. Robert Guest
172. Paul Daniels
173. Graham Waring
174. Brian Waring
175. Nigel Ball
176. Michael Phelps
177. Keith Kruge
178. Paul Whitling
179. Keith Whitesides
180. Duncan Chambers
181. David Vanham
182. Ray Reims
183. Chris & Graham Copsey
184. Chris Parkes